CRIMINAL PROCEDURE

Fourth Edition

By

Wayne R. LaFave
*David C. Baum Professor of Law Emeritus and
Center for Advanced Study Professor Emeritus,
University of Illinois*

Jerold H. Israel
*Ed Root Eminent Scholar in Trial Advocacy and Procedure,
University of Florida College of Law
and
Alene and Allan F. Smith Professor of Law Emeritus,
University of Michigan*

and

Nancy J. King
*Lee S. & Charles A. Speir Professor of Law,
Vanderbilt University*

*This book is an updated abridgement of LaFave, Israel and King's six volume,
second edition "Criminal Procedure" in West's Criminal Practice Series.*

HORNBOOK SERIES®

THOMSON

WEST

Mat #40234211

This is an abridgement of LaFave, Israel and King's multi-volume *Criminal Procedure*, Criminal Practice Series, West Group, second edition 1999.

Hornbook Series, *Westlaw*, and West Group are trademarks registered in the U.S. Patent and Trademark Office.

COPYRIGHT © 1985   LaFAVE & ISRAEL

COPYRIGHT © 1992 By WEST PUBLISHING CO.

COPYRIGHT © 2000 By WEST GROUP

© 2004 West, a Thomson business
        610 Opperman Drive
        P.O. Box 64526
        St. Paul, MN 55164–0526
        1–800–328–9352

ISBN 0–314–15211–3

TEXT IS PRINTED ON 10% POST CONSUMER RECYCLED PAPER

Preface

This text is intended primarily for use by law students during their study of criminal procedure. There is, to be sure, no substitute for careful examination of the basic sources—the appellate opinions, statutes, and critical commentary which are to be found in the modern casebooks dealing with this subject. It is neither intended nor expected that this Hornbook on criminal procedure will be of particular use to the student who has not grappled with those materials. Rather, this book has been prepared on the assumption that the diligent student may find a textual treatment of the subject useful as he or she [1] undertakes the necessary process of reviewing and synthesizing the regularly assigned materials.

We have sought to analyze the law governing all of the major steps in the criminal justice process, starting with investigation and ending with post-appeal collateral attacks. Of course, a complete review of all the fine points relating to each and every step in the process would require more than one volume. Accordingly, we have varied the depth of our coverage, taking into consideration both the significance of the particular procedure and the attention typically given to it in a law school criminal procedure course. For every step in the process, however, we have covered, at a minimum, the major themes underlying the governing legal standards and those basic issues that the case law and literature suggest to be the most pressing. We have also sought to go beyond describing "the law" as it currently stands, exploring as well its historical roots and underlying policies. We believe this approach will prove useful to law students.

This book is an updated abridgement of our second edition six-volume Criminal Procedure treatise. We have retained most of the analysis from that larger work, but not much of the supporting documentation. Our supposition in this regard is that a law student who uses a collateral text in connection with course preparation or review is primarily interested in explanation rather than citations to authority. In general, descriptions of lower court rulings and statutory provisions are not followed by illustrative citations, although a specific case or statute noted in the text often will be cited. Supporting citations for descriptions of positions taken by commentators are treated in largely the same manner. So too, brief quotations that are largely illustrative of a line of cases usually are not footnoted. In all instances, readers desiring the full documentation can turn to the treatise, which is readily available on Westlaw as database CRIMPROC. [2]

We have treated the opinions of the Supreme Court of the United States somewhat differently, both because of their special significance

---

1. To make our sentence structure as short and direct as possible, we generally have not used the phrases "he or she" or "his and her." Consistent with traditional rules of construction in statutes and legal texts, masculine pronouns (which is what we usually use) should be read to refer to both male and female actors unless the context clearly indicates otherwise.

2. By using key phrases in the Hornbook text to locate comparable material in CRIMPROC (which in most but not all in-

and because these are the opinions most frequently included in assigned course materials. We have always made reference to the leading Supreme Court opinions which deal with the topic at hand, although we have not included string-citations of Supreme Court rulings on settled points. While our cut-off date for Supreme Court opinions was before the end of the October 2003 term (i.e., June 2004), a pocket part is being published simultaneously with this book updating the Hornbook through the end of that term. (After each successive term, an updated pocket part will be published.).

The authors come away from this project impressed, as always, with the richness of literature in the field. We remain indebted not only to the authors of the articles cited both in the Hornbook and the treatise, but also to many others whose work we could not include without overloading the footnotes. A project of this type also necessarily builds on past endeavors and necessarily reflects the assistance of those who have worked with us on those endeavors. We are especially indebted in this regard to Yale Kamisar, our co-author on *Modern Criminal Procedure, Basic Criminal Procedure* and *Advanced Criminal Procedure*

Over the years, on this project and others, we have received the benefit of the excellent work of many student research assistants. Their number has grown far too long to mention them all, but the size of the group makes us no less appreciative of the individual contribution of each of these students. We also are deeply indebted to our secretaries, Natasha Barton, Carol Haley, Joyce Kenney, and Carolyn Lloyd who have seen this project through from start to finish.

While we stand responsible for the work as a whole, Wayne LaFave had the initial responsibility for chapters 3–7, 9–10, 12–13, 17–18 and 21–22; Jerold Israel for chapters 1, 2, 8, 11, 14–16, 19–20, and 23; and Nancy King for chapters 24–28. Each of us would appreciate hearing from readers who have criticisms or suggestions relating to the chapters for which we have initial responsibility

We would also like to recognize the support of our families. Labor of love though it may be, preparation of a text such as this can be terribly demanding, and we appreciate greatly the patience of our families in this regard.

WAYNE R. LAFAVE
JEROLD H. ISRAEL
NANCY J. KING

May, 2004

stances will have the same section number, subsection letter, and title) the reader should have no difficulty in finding in the treatise footnote references to supporting cases, commentary, and statutes. The documentation in the second edition of the treatise is extensive. For example, over twelve thousand appellate cases are cited.

WESTLAW® Overview

Criminal Procedure offers a detailed and comprehensive treatment of the basic rules, principles and issues relating to the law of criminal procedure. To supplement the information contained in this book, you can access Westlaw, West's computer-assisted legal research service. Westlaw contains a broad array of legal resources, including case law, statutes, expert commentary, current developments and various other types of information.

Learning how to use these materials effectively will enhance your legal research abilities. To help you coordinate the information in the book with your Westlaw research, this volume contains an appendix listing Westlaw databases, search techniques, and sample problems.

The instructions and features described in this Westlaw overview are based on accessing Westlaw via westlaw.com® at **www.westlaw.com**.

THE PUBLISHER

*

Summary of Contents

———

Table of Contents

———————

PART TWO. DETECTION AND INVESTIGATION OF CRIME

PART THREE.   THE COMMENCEMENT OF FORMAL PROCEEDINGS

*

CRIMINAL PROCEDURE

Fourth Edition

*

Part One

INTRODUCTION AND OVERVIEW

Chapter 1

AN OVERVIEW OF THE CRIMINAL JUSTICE PROCESS

Table of Sections

---

§ 1.1 The Subject Under Inquiry

(a) Coverage. The subject of this hornbook is the law of criminal procedure—i.e., the law governing that series of procedures through which the substantive criminal law is enforced. Our focus is on the law as it is set forth in official texts—primarily statutes, appellate cases, and court rules. We recognize, of course, that the everyday administration of the process is shaped by far more than the formal, written law. In large part, however, we leave to others the examination of administrative practice.

(b) Organization. Part One of the hornbook, consisting of the first two chapters, introduces some general features of the criminal justice process and the law governing that process. Our goal here is to provide a general backdrop for the examination in Parts Two to Five of the legal standards governing specific steps in the process. The coverage there largely follows the chronological sequence of the process: the detection and investigation of crime; the institution of formal charges against accused persons; pre-adjudication procedures; the adjudication of the charges; the sentencing of the convicted defendant; and, finally, the appellate and collateral review of judicial decisions rendered throughout the process. The one major step not considered is the administration of those restraints imposed upon the convicted defendant pursuant to his sentence (i.e. the law of corrections).

Because Parts Two to Five largely follow the chronological order of the process, a doctrine or right that contributes to the regulation of more than one stage in the process will be discussed in more than one chapter. For example, the privilege against compelled self-incrimination is discussed in connection with topics relating to investigative procedures (primarily police interrogation, identification procedures, and grand jury investigations), to pretrial preparation for adjudication (discovery), to adjudication (both guilty pleas and the trial), and to sentencing. At each point, the discussion touches upon a different aspect of the self-incrimination privilege, although Chapter Eight also presents an overview of the privilege. Readers interested in pulling together our discussion of the various strands of such pervasive limitations as the self-incrimination privilege, or of such pervasive concepts as "waiver," can find a quick reference to all relevant discussions in the Index.

§ 1.2 Describing the Fifty–Two Separate Criminal Justice Processes

(a) State and Federal Authority. Under the American version of federalism, the federal (i.e., national) government and each of the fifty states has independent authority to enact criminal codes applicable within the territorial reach of its legislative powers. Each also has the authority to enforce those criminal laws through its own criminal justice process—that is, through its own criminal justice agencies and its own laws of criminal procedure. Thus, we have, in many respects, fifty-one different criminal justice processes in this country, one for each of the states and one for the federal government. A fifty-second jurisdiction is provided by Congress' decision to treat separately the District of Columbia, creating for it a separate criminal code and a separate criminal justice process that stands apart from the federal criminal law and process applied in the federal district courts spread throughout the states.

We have sought in this hornbook to provide coverage of sufficient depth to be helpful in the analysis of the laws applicable in each of these fifty-two jurisdictions. This section explores the complications presented in fashioning a description which achieves that objective and explains the pattern of description we have adopted in responding to those complications.

(b) A Federal System That is "One Among Many". In many fields in which both federal and state governments have the authority to regulate, the federal enforcement system has come to dominate. Federal law is the primary source of regulation and the vast majority of all enforcement actions are brought within the federal adjudicatory structure (administrative or judicial). A similar dominance is not found in the field of criminal law. Utilizing any of the traditional standards for measuring its portion of the nation's criminal justice workload, the federal criminal justice system is no more than one among many. Indeed, the federal system is responsible each year for less than 2% of the total number of criminal prosecutions brought in the United States and less than 4% of all felony prosecutions.

(c) The Limits of Mandated Uniformity. The presence of fifty-two separate criminal justice processes would be much less significant if those processes all were subject to a single law that mandated an exclusive, comprehensive regulation for all fifty-two jurisdictions. Contrary to the impression sometimes conveyed by constitutional scholars, the Constitution of the United States is not such a law. This is not to dispute the characterization of federal constitutional law, as interpreted by

the Supreme Court, as "our most important source of criminal procedure law." It is the only source of substantial legal regulation that is applicable to all fifty-two jurisdictions. It locks those fifty-two jurisdictions into a basic procedural structure that guarantees a commonality in most of the overarching principles reflected in the fifty-two different processes. The federal constitution, for many aspects of the process, also is the source of specific standards (sometimes quite detailed) that implement those basic principles. Nonetheless, as discussed in § 1.5(b), the regulation imposed by the federal constitution is not sufficiently comprehensive nor exclusive to relegate the law of the individual jurisdiction to a relatively insignificant role in the regulation of its criminal justice process. For many aspects of the process, the law of the individual jurisdiction provides far more of the governing standards than does the federal constitution, and even where the federal constitution is dominant, the law of the individual jurisdiction often still plays a significant role.

Another possible source of mandated uniform standards of criminal procedure, applicable in all fifty-two jurisdictions, is congressional legislation. Exactly how far Congress may go in adopting criminal procedure rules applicable to the states is uncertain, for Congress has used its legislative authority sparingly, concentrating on police activities that have an obvious impact upon interstate commerce (e.g., wiretapping). As a result, standards mandated by federal legislation play a very limited role in shaping the criminal justice processes of the fifty states.

(d) The Tendency to Individualize. In many fields where federal law does not mandate a uniform standard, and each state is free to adopt its own laws, there nonetheless is a fair degree of uniformity in the laws of the fifty states, as all or almost all of the states have adopted a "model" or "uniform" law proposed by a group such as the National Conference of Commissioners on Uniform State Laws. For several reasons such uniformity has not been achieved in the field of criminal procedure.

Initially, criminal procedure is not a subject as to which there is a natural pressure to achieve uniformity. Unlike areas such as commercial law, the lack of uniformity here is not likely to be a deterrent to the free flow of goods, services, or persons between states or to restrain the full economic or social development of the individuals within the particular state. So too, as to all but a few aspects of criminal procedure, there is little need to provide reciprocity of process between states. Secondly, individuality in each state's criminal procedure law is encouraged by the diversity from state to state of the administrative environment in which the law is applied. Various elements contribute to that environment, including the demography of the population, the resources available to the process, and the structure of the institutions responsible for the administration of the process (particularly police, prosecutor, and judiciary), and as to each, there is considerable variation from state to state. That variation is reflected, in turn, in the criminal justice processes of the states, for that process must be designed to accommodate in its application the state's particular administrative environment.

Arguably, an even more significant obstacle to gaining substantial uniformity in the law of criminal procedure is the character of the decisions that must be made in fashioning a law of criminal procedure. There are few areas, if any, of legislative choice in which the role of symbolic politics is more pervasive than criminal justice reform, and that factor can readily lead lawmakers in different jurisdictions to take different approaches in addressing the same basic issue (as well as produce frequent shifts in basic philosophy even in the same jurisdiction).

Still another important factor is the integrated nature of the overall criminal justice process. The process is composed of a series of interlocking parts, with each stage building upon what was done at earlier stages and those earlier stages shaped in part by anticipation of what will occur at later stages. The different components complement and compensate for each other in producing the character of the process as a whole. Thus, in con-sidering whether to adopt a proposed reform that will change the governing standard at one stage of the process, a state lawmaker must consider the relationship of that standard to the operation of other aspects of the process. As a result, lawmakers in two different states, though sharing the same basic philosophy, may reach different conclusions on a proposed reform in light of differences in other aspects of their state's process.

(e) The Tendency to Emulate. If the factors cited above were the only factors bearing upon lawmaking in the criminal justice field, one might expect the laws of the different states to be so diverse that no description would have value unless it separately and in detail examined the law of each individual state. There are, however, countervailing factors that encourage the lawmakers of the different states to look to common sources in shaping the criminal procedure of their individual state. These include: the common heritage of the English common law; the tradition in some states to look to particular jurisdictions (most often, the federal system) for potential models for law reform; and a sense of caution and concern that encourages adoption of procedures that have proven successful in other jurisdictions and that are accompanied by a substantial body of interpretation as a result of their use in those other jurisdictions.

In general, the interests supporting emulation have had sufficient impact to allow us to characterize the law governing a particular procedure in the vast majority of states as following one of no more than a few distinctive patterns (at least when that law is judged by reference to its general features). The emulated models that provide those patterns come from a variety of different sources. For some aspects of the process, the primary groupings are built around the traditional post-revolution American version of English common law on the one hand, and on the other, a prominent state statute of the late nineteenth century (often associated with the Field Code), or the early twentieth century (often associated with the Progressive movement) that either abolished or substantially modified that common law standard. For most parts of the process, however, more recent "models" have been the primary sources of emulation in the shaping of state statutes and court rules governing the process. The most significant model, without question, has been the federal law of criminal procedure. The ABA Standards of Criminal Justice also have served as a significant model. Each is discussed below.

(f) The Federal Model. As to almost every procedural element within the criminal justice process, a grouping of states, ranging from a handful to a majority, have adopted the basic features of the nonconstitutional law of the federal system. Undoubtedly, the Federal Rules of Criminal Procedure provide the most prominent illustration of the influence of this "federal model." Roughly half of the states have court rules of criminal procedure or statutory codes of criminal procedure that borrow heavily from the Federal Rules. As a result of a substantial stylistic revision of the Federal Rules in 2003, no state has an exact replica of the Federal Rules, but a small group largely replicate the substance of the Federal Rules. Most of the states in the Federal Rules grouping have a criminal procedure law more loosely modeled on the Federal Rules. They typically start with a set of provisions covering basically the same general subjects as the Federal Rules, utilize the specific standards of the Federal Rules for a majority of those subjects, adopt modifications for a fair number, and then completely depart for a few others.

While no other federal law has been as widely emulated as the Federal Rules, several federal statutes have served as models for somewhat smaller groupings of states. These include the federal statutory remedy for attacking convictions collaterally (the motion to vacate sentence), the Federal Bail Reform Act of 1966, the Federal Speedy Trial Act of 1974, and the Jury Selection Act of 1968. In several instances, emulation has occasionally taken the form of an almost verbatim replication, but more often the states deviate from various particulars of the federal law, while incorporating its basic features.

(g) The ABA Standards. The American Bar Association in 1973 completed its original version of the ABA's Standards for Criminal Justice, which was converted to a legislative format in the Pattern Rules of Court and Code Provisions. The ABA subsequently adopted, in 1978–79, a revised second edition of its Standards, and started in the 1990s the still ongoing issuance of third editions for individual titles.

The Standards have been cited thousands of times by appellate courts, and have been used as well in formulating court rules and statutes. Unlike the Federal Rules, the ABA Standards have been incorporated into state law on a piecemeal basis. Appellate court opinions have focused on the possible incorporation of a particular standard or a grouping of related standards dealing with the specific issue before the court. Many of the ABA Standards receiving broad support largely duplicate the federal law, as set forth in the Federal Rules, a prominent federal statute, or federal case law. Where the Standards and the law of the federal system take conflicting positions, the influence of the Standards tends to be less significant, although there are several such areas in which the Standards clearly dominate.

§ 1.3   The Steps in the Process

(a) Overview Objectives. This section presents an overview of the procedural steps that carry a case from start to finish within the process. The basic objectives of the overview are to position each step within the typical progression of the process, to introduce the relevant terminology, and to briefly describe what occurs at each step. This information should provide a useful backdrop for the discussion in later chapters of the legal standards that govern the various steps in process. That discussion concentrates on those steps that commonly are the focus of litigation. This overview, in contrast, also takes note of many steps that are rarely, if ever, seen as raising legal difficulties. Their operation, however, contributes to the overall structure of the process, and often plays a role in shaping the law that governs these steps which frequently are a source of litigation.

(b) The Character of the Overview. The overview presented in this section follows the sequence of the procedure in a "typical" felony case. This approach ignores a host of variations. Initially, variations exist, from one jurisdiction to another, in the legal structure of the procedures which will be utilized at the different stages of the process. The overview takes account only of those differences that are both fundamental and characteristic of a substantial number of our fifty-two basic jurisdictions (i.e., the fifty states, the District of Columbia, and the federal system). Secondly, the administration (and sometimes the legal structure) of the process often varies with the level and of the offense. In particular, substantial variations exist between the processing of misdemeanor and felony cases.[1] Since our focus is on the typical felony case, we take note of only the most basic differences in the procedures applied to misdemeanors.

Third, the overview does not consider all possible variations in chronology. The overview describes the chronology that is followed in the vast majority of all felony cases, but special situations can produce a different chronology. Fourth, the overview's division of the process into separate steps fails to account for the ongoing nature of certain steps. While some steps have definite starting and ending points, others are continuing and overlap later steps. Investigatory procedures, for example, do not always stop with the filing of charges, but may continue through to the initiation (and sometimes the end) of the trial. So too, the decision on pretrial release, though it comes initially at the first appearance, is subject to possible reconsideration as the case progresses.

Finally, the overview does not draw distinctions among different actors performing the same basic role in the administration of the process. Thus, the term "police" encompasses all government employees assigned to the task of enforcing the criminal law and given the

authority (e.g., to carry weapons and to make arrests) that accompanies that responsibility. This includes officers employed by a wide variety of agencies (including for example, the country sheriff, the city police department, the state highway patrol and a park security force). Similarly "prosecutor" encompasses all government officials charged with presenting prosecutions on behalf of the state (officials typically known as "district attorneys," "state's attorneys," or "prosecuting attorneys"). The term "magistrate court" refers to the court (or branch of a court) which has jurisdiction over the preliminary stages in felony cases and both the preliminary stages and trial of misdemeanor cases (courts commonly known in the state systems as "municipal courts," "county courts," "justice of the peace courts," or "district courts"). The term "general trial court" refers to the courts which have trial jurisdiction in felony cases (commonly carrying the titles in state systems of "circuit courts," "superior courts," or "district courts," where that title is not assigned to the magistrate court).

(c) Step 1: Prearrest Investigation. Various distinctions are used in grouping prearrest investigatory procedures. Lawyer tend to group procedures according to the governing legal standards. In this overview, however, we follow the lead of criminal justice analysts, stressing two dividing lines: (1) the agency involved (distinguishing primarily between the investigative activities of the police and the prosecutor) and (2) the focus of the procedure (distinguishing primarily between activities aimed at solving past reported crimes and activities aimed at unknown but anticipated crimes). Those distinctions create three basic groups of prearrest investigative procedures: (1) police procedures that are aimed at solving specific past crimes known to the police (commonly described as "reactive" procedures), (2)

---

§ 1.3

1. American jurisdictions commonly use one of two different standards in distinguishing between felonies and misdemeanors. Some classify as felonies all offenses punishable by a maximum term of imprisonment of more than one year; offenses punishable by imprisonment for one year or less are then misdemeanors. Others look to the location of the possible imprisonment. If the offense is

punishable by imprisonment in a penitentiary, it is a felony; if punishable only by a jail term, it is a misdemeanor. This line in practice also tends to produce a one-year dividing line since state correction codes commonly provide for imprisonment in the penitentiary if a sentence exceeds one year and for imprisonment in jail if the sentence is for one year or less.

police procedures that are aimed at unknown but anticipated ongoing and future criminal activity (commonly described as "proactive" procedures), and (3) prosecutorial and other non-police investigations conducted primarily through the use of subpoena authority. Each of these groups is discussed below, but initially we take note of the large number of cases in which arrests are made by police with little or no prearrest investigation.

"On–Scene" Arrests. A substantial percentage of arrests for a wide variety of crimes are of the "on-scene" variety. These are arrests made during the course of the crime or immediately thereafter either at the place where the crime occurred or in its immediate vicinity. Ordinarily, on-scene arrests will be based on the officer's own observation (leading to the alternative description of such arrests as "on-view"), although they will sometimes be based on the directive of a witness who has just viewed the crime. For some offenses, on-scene arrests typically are the product of proactive prearrest investigative activities designed to place the police in a position where they will be able to view the crime as it is committed. That usually is the case, for example, with so-called "victimless" crimes (i.e., crimes which do not involve an interaction with another person, such as possession of a weapon, and crimes which ordinarily involve willing participants, such as vice crimes or narcotics-transfer offenses). For many other offenses, most on-scene arrests occur, with basically no investigative activity, when a police officer on patrol responds to an event that calls the crime to his attention (e.g., a victim's call for assistance, a burglar alarm, or an observation). Thus, one study concluded that 42% of all arrests for nonviolent property crimes (basically theft and burglary) were such on-scene arrests, made within 5 minutes of the commission of the offense.

Reactive Investigations. General purpose police agencies (e.g., local police departments), who employ over 85% of all police officers in the country, traditionally have devoted the vast majority of their investigative efforts to reactive investigations. This is an "incident driven" or "complaint-responsive" style of policing, flowing from various aspects of local policing, including the neighborhood patrol and the 911 emergency telephone link. The police received a citizen report of a crime (typically from the victim or an eyewitness), or they discover physical evidence indicating that a crime has been committed, and they then proceed to initiate an investigation responsive to that "known crime."[2] This involves (1) determining whether there actually was a crime committed, (2) if so, determining who committed the crime, (3) collecting evidence of that person's guilt, and (4) locating the offender so that he can be taken into custody. A wide variety of investigative activities may be utilized to achieve these objective. Those activities include: (1) the interviewing of victims; (2) the interviewing of witnesses at the crime scene; (3) canvassing the neighborhood for (and interviewing) other witnesses; (4) the interviewing of suspects, which may require a physical stopping of the suspect on the street and a frisking of the suspect (i.e., pat-down of the outer clothing) for possible weapons; (5) the examination of the crime scene and the collection of physical evidence found there; (6) checking departmental records and computer files; (7) seeking information from informants; (8) searching for physical evidence of the crime (e.g., stolen property or weapons) in places accessible to the suspect (e.g., his home or automobile) and seizing any evidence found there; (9) surveillance of a suspect (including electronic surveillance) aimed at obtaining leads to evidence or accomplices; and (10) using undercover operatives to gain information from the suspect.

A variety of factors will determine which of the investigative practices noted above will be used in a particular investigation. One key factor is the investigative direction suggested by those "traces" of the crime that are imme-

---

2. Official reports also include in the "known crime" category (sometimes described as "reported crimes") those crimes witnessed by the police which result in an on-scene arrest. The F.B.I. directives for the Uniform Crime Re-

ports direct police departments not to include in their "known crime" statistics crimes reported by citizens that are later determined to be falsely reported.

diately available to the police. In some instances, the limitations of available traces foreclose the use of a particular investigative practice. Any attempt to interview suspects depends upon the presence of some trace (e.g., a witness who can describe the criminal or a unique modus operandi) that allows for the designation of a manageable group of persons who might be considered possible suspects. A search for physical evidence only makes sense if the traces indicate that the criminal activity was of a type which might produce such evidence. In other instances, though the available traces will not absolutely rule out the use of a particular investigative practice, they suggest that the likelihood of gaining useful information will be so remote that the time, energy, and financial costs involved simply do not make use of that practice worthwhile. There is almost always some possibility, for example, that canvassing the neighborhood will produce a witness who saw the offender, but police frequently will not canvass for witnesses unless there is a fairly substantial likelihood that such a witness might be found.

In general, the strength and nature of the available leads will determine the scope of the investigation, but other factors may alter that natural correlation. A more serious offense may lead police to utilize a technique that would be rejected as to a less serious crime because it is not sufficiently likely to be successful. A technique less likely to be successful may be chosen over one more likely to be successful because the latter simply is not available under the law without stronger leads (as in the case of a search requiring probable cause). In such a situation, the second-choice procedure hopefully will produce additional information that will enable the police legally to use their first choice, but that strategy may not be successful and the investigation may end without the police ever using the preferred procedure. In some instances, a second-choice may be forced on the police by leads that are not useable in court. Where, for example, a witness insists on anonymity, the police may be forced to attempt to build their case through other means that rely upon that infor-

mation, but mask its source (e.g., a wiretap or an undercover agent "plant").

Where the traces of the crime are very weak and the offense is not especially serious, the police are likely to terminate their investigation after having done little more than interview the victim in connection with his reporting of the crime. Police are aware that, for most crimes, the odds of arresting the offender are slim unless witnesses or physical evidence at the scene provide information that either specifically identifies the offender or makes that identification readily determinable. While the absence of such information will not necessarily lead to an immediate termination of the investigation, it will certainly work against a substantial extension of the investigation. The end result is that for a great many crimes, including even offenses as serious as burglary, very little is done besides interviewing the person reporting the crime.

While the variation among investigations is far too great to characterize any single combination of investigative procedures as "average," even for a particular type of offense, it is clear that prearrest investigations rarely take on the characteristics of popular depictions of the crime solving process. In general, investigations do not involve the use of scientific methods of investigation, confrontations with crafty criminals, or reliance upon informants. A study of robbery and burglary investigations found, for example, that the interviewing of the victim and the examination of the crime scene were by far the most common steps in the investigative process. Aside from the canvassing for and the interviewing of additional witnesses, no other procedure was used in as many as a third of all cases. The frequency of interviews of suspects varied considerably, but even as to robberies (where victims were more likely to identify a specific suspect), such interviews occurred in less than 25% of all cases. Interviews of informants occurred in less than 5% of all investigations. Other procedures were even less frequent.

Proactive Investigations. Although general purpose police agencies traditionally have concentrated their investigative efforts on the solving of known crimes, those agencies also have regularly used, in a limited fashion, proactive investigations. Indeed, in recent years, many local police departments in large communities have sharply increased their utilization of proactive investigative procedures. Also, many special-function police agencies (such as the federal Drug Enforcement Administration) traditionally have devoted a much more substantial portion of their resources to proactive investigations.

Proactive investigations are aimed at uncovering criminal activity that is not specifically known to the police. The investigation may be aimed at placing the police in a position where they can observe ongoing criminal activity that otherwise would both be hidden from public view and not reported (as typically is the case with offenses that prohibit the possession of contraband or proscribe transactions between willing participants). It may be aimed at inducing persons who have committed crimes of a certain type, including many unknown to the police, to reveal themselves (as in a "fencing sting"). Proactive investigations also often are aimed at anticipating future criminality and placing police in a position to intercept when the crime is attempted. Here, the investigative technique may be designed simply to gain information that will permit the police to predict when and where a crime is likely to be committed, or it may be designed to "induce" the criminal attempt at a particular time and place by creating a setting likely to spur into action those prone to criminality.

A variety of different procedures may be used in a proactive investigation, with the choice of procedure largely tied to the specific objective of the investigation. Deception is a common element of many proactive procedures. In traditional undercover operations, the police assume a false identity and present themselves as willing to participate in criminal activities (as where undercover agents "set up" fencing operations or narcotics transactions). So too, deception is the key to a "decoy tactic" of providing what appears to be an easy target for victimization (e.g., a drunk with an exposed wallet or a business of the type that is readily subject to extortion). Deception commonly also is critical to the effective use of

informants. Where police utilize as informants persons whose activities expose them to a criminal milieu, they are counting on the criminals associating with those persons being deceived by a belief that those persons will not take what they have learned to the police (usually because the persons are themselves engaged in criminal activity, gain their livelihood in part from criminals, or have social ties to the criminals). Surveillance through stake-outs, covert patrols, and electronic monitoring also rests on deception by hiding the surveillance.

Other proactive techniques rely on intrusive confrontations designed to place police in a position where they can observe what otherwise would be hidden or to elicit nervous or unthinking incriminatory responses that will provide a legal grounding for taking further investigative action (e.g., an arrest or stop). Thus, police following an aggressive motorized patrol strategy will fully utilize traffic laws to maximize stops of motorists, thereby gaining greater opportunity to peer into car windows, to ask questions, and to request consent to a search of the vehicle. Similarly, under a practice of heavy field interrogation, police will frequently approach pedestrians and initiate questioning to determine who they are and what they are doing. Such intrusive confrontations are most often used on a selective basis, with police concentrating their efforts on those characteristics of the social environment that suggest to them possible criminality (e.g., high-crime neighborhood, suspicious class of persons, unusual behavior).

In general, proactive investigative procedures are more resource intensive, more intrusive, arguably more likely to foster community opposition, and clearly pose more legal problems than typical reactive investigative procedures. As a result, although commentators have suggested that their expanded use might increase police effectiveness, proactive procedures remain, for the vast majority of agencies, simply a supplement to the basic complaint-reactive strategy that dominates the use of investigative resources.

Prosecutorial Investigations. Not all prearrest investigations are conducted by police. For certain types of crimes, the best investigatory tool is the subpoena—a court order directing a person to appear in a particular proceeding for the purpose of testifying and presenting specified physical evidence (e.g., documents) within his possession. The subpoena authority generally is available for the investigation of crime only through the grand jury, although other agencies may be able to use it to investigate specific types of crimes in particular jurisdictions. The grand jury, although it tends to be known more for its screening function in reviewing the prosecution's decision to charge, also has authority to conduct investigations into the possible commission of crimes within the judicial district in which it sits. In carrying out this function, the grand jurors, being a group of laypersons with no special expertise in investigation, quite naturally rely heavily on the direction provided by their legal advisor, who is the prosecutor. Thus, grand jury investigations become, for all practical purposes, investigations by the prosecutor.

Grand Jury investigations tend to be used (1) where witnesses will not cooperate with the police (they can be compelled by subpoena to testify before the grand jury and given immunity to replace their self-incrimination privilege should they refuse to testify on that ground); (2) where the critical evidence of the crime is likely to be a "paper trail" buried in voluminous records of business dealings (as the subpoena can be used to require production of such records where the police lack the necessary probable cause predicate for obtaining those documents through a search); and (3) where the area of investigation is especially sensitive, reflecting a strong need to keep the ongoing investigation from the public gaze (an objective facilitated by grand jury secrecy requirements) or to ensure public confidence in the integrity of the investigation (an objective facilitated by the participation of the lay grand jurors). Criminal investigations imposing such special needs are likely to deal with crimes of public corruption (e.g., bribery), misuse of economic power (e.g., price-fixing), and widespread distribution of illegal services or goods (e.g., organized crime operations). The investigation of such offenses through the grand jury often has both reactive and proactive qualities. It starts with some specific information known to the prosecutor (usually through the police) that suggests a specific offense but then will extend beyond that offense to determine whether there exist similar or related criminal activity that is unknown to the prosecutor or police (a portion of the investigation often characterized as a "fishing expedition").

(d) Step 2: Arrest. Once a police officer has obtained sufficient information to justify arresting a suspect (i.e., probable cause to believe the person has committed a crime), the arrest ordinarily becomes the next step in the criminal justice process. The term "arrest" is defined differently for different purposes. We refer here only to the act of taking a person into custody for the purpose of charging him with a crime (the standard commonly used in the reporting of arrest statistics). This involves the detention of the suspect (by force if necessary) for the purpose of first transporting him to a police facility and then requesting that charges be filed against him. As an alternative to such a "full custody" arrest, many jurisdictions authorize the officer in some situations to briefly detain the suspect and then release him upon issuance of an official document (commonly titled a "citation," "summons" or "appearance ticket") which directs the suspect to appear in court on a set date to respond to the charge specified in the document. This release-on-citation alternative commonly is utilized, however, only for minor offenses.

Where there is no immediate need to arrest a suspect, an officer may seek to obtain an arrest warrant (a court order authorizing the arrest) prior to taking the person into custody.[3] Arrest warrants in most jurisdictions are

---

3. Arresting without first obtaining a warrant is the predominant practice in all localities. In a large percentage of all arrests (including, for example, "on scene" arrests), the police officer will make the arrest immediately after obtaining probable cause for believing the person committed a crime. However, even where the investigating officer, after establishing probable cause, expects a lapse of a day or more before making an arrest, the common practice in most jurisdictions is not to use that opportunity to obtain an arrest warrant. Officers here will obtain a warrant, rather than rely on a warrantless arrest, only where the special setting makes a warrant legally necessary or other-

issued by magistrates. To obtain a warrant, the police must establish, to the satisfaction of the magistrate, that there exists probable cause to believe that the prospective arrestee committed the crime for which he will be arrested. The showing of probable cause may be made by affidavits or live testimony of either the investigating officer or a witness (usually the victim). Where a warrant is issued, it ordinarily will authorize the arrest to be made by any police officer in the state, not simply the officer seeking the warrant.

(e) Step 3: Booking. Immediately after making an arrest, the arresting officer usually will search the arrestee's person and remove any weapons, contraband, or evidence relating to a crime. If the arrested person was driving a vehicle, the officer may also search the passenger compartment of the vehicle for the same items. The arrestee will then be taken, either by the arresting officer or other officers called to the scene, to the police station, a centrally located jail, or some similar "holding" facility. It is at this facility that the arrestee will be taken through a process known as "booking." Initially, the arrestee's name, the time of his arrival, and the offense for which he was arrested are noted in the police "blotter" or "log." This is strictly a clerical procedure, and it does not control whether the arrestee will be charged or what charge might be brought. As part of the booking process, the arrestee also will be photographed and fingerprinted.

Once the booking process is completed, the arrestee ordinarily will be allowed to make at least one telephone call. In many jurisdictions, an arrestee booked on a minor charge will be given the opportunity to obtain his immediate release by posting what is described as "stationhouse bail." This involves posting a specified amount of cash, as prescribed for the particular offense in a judicially approved bail

schedule, and agreeing to appear in court on a specified date. Persons arrested for more serious offenses and those eligible to post stationhouse bail but lacking the resources will remain at the holding facility until presented before a magistrate (see step 8). Ordinarily they will be placed in a "lockup," which usually is some kind of cell. Before entering the lockup, they will be subjected to another search, more thorough than that conducted at the point of arrest. This search is designed primarily to inventory the arrestee's personal belongs and to prevent the introduction of contraband into the lockup.

(f) Step 4: Post–Arrest Investigation. The initial post-arrest investigation by the police consists of the search of the person (and possibly the interior of the automobile) as discussed above. The extent of any further post-arrest investigation will vary with the fact situation. In some cases, such as where the arrestee was caught "red-handed," there will be little left to be done. In others, police will utilize many of the same kinds of investigative procedures as are used before arrest (e.g., interviewing witnesses, searching the suspect's home, and viewing the scene of the crime). Post-arrest investigation does offer one important investigative source, however, that ordinarily is not available prior to the arrest—the person of the arrestee. Thus, the police may seek to obtain an eyewitness identification of the arrestee by placing him in a lineup, having the witness view him individually (a "show-up"), or taking his picture and showing it to the witness (usually with the photographs of several other persons in a "photographic lineup"). They may also require the arrestee to provide handwriting or hair samples that can be compared with evidence the police have found at the scene of the crime. The arrest similarly facilitates questioning the arrestee at length about either the crime for which he was

wise advantageous. The most common of those settings are: (1) cases in which the offender is located in another jurisdiction (as a warrant is needed to utilize procedures for having the person arrested by officers of another state and later extradited); (2) cases in which the person cannot be found and the police want to utilize the listing in the computerized state or local law enforcement information network of persons subject to an arrest on the basis of an outstanding warrant; (3) cases in which there will proba-

bly be a need to enter into a dwelling without consent in order to make the arrest (a situation that requires a warrant); (4) cases in which the offense was a misdemeanor not committed in the officer's presence (a situation requiring a warrant in some states); and (5) cases in which the police have sought the advice of the prosecutor before deciding to proceed (where the prosecutor responds affirmatively, a complaint typically will be filed immediately, with a warrant then obtained prior to the arrest).

arrested or other crimes thought to be related (although warnings must be given prior to the custodial interrogation).

(g) Step 5: The Decision to Charge. The initial decision to charge a suspect with the commission of a crime ordinarily comes with the decision of a police officer to arrest the suspect. That decision will subsequently be reviewed, first by the police and then by the prosecutor. As discussed in subsection (j), the arrestee must be brought before a magistrate within a relatively short period (typically 24 or 48 hours), and prior to that point, the charges against the arrestee must be filed with the magistrate. It is during this period that the police will review the arresting officer's initial decision to charge. The prosecutor's review of the decision to charge often occurs during this same period, but prosecutorial review is, in any event, an ongoing process. Whether or not the prosecutor reviewed (and approved) the charges before they were filed with the magistrate, the filed charges remain subject to continuous reevaluation by the prosecutor up to and through the trial.

The decision to charge a person with a crime thus may be seen as having four components: (1) the decision of the investigating officer to arrest and charge; (2) the police review of that decision prior to filing charges; (3) prosecutorial review prior to filing; and (4) ongoing prosecutorial review after the filing. The first component has already been noted in step (2) (the arrest), and we consider here the remaining three. The third component, prosecutorial post-filing screening, is treated here, rather than at the later points in the process where it occurs chronologically, because of its close relationship to the pre-filing screening of the prosecutor.

Pre–Filing Police Screening. Sometime between the booking of the arrestee and the point at which the arrestee is to be taken before the magistrate, there will be an internal police review of a warrant less arrest. Ordinarily that occurs shortly after the booking, when the arresting officer prepares an arrest report to be given to his or her supervisor. The supervisor may approve the bringing of charges at the level recommended in the police report, raise or reduce the level of the recommended charges, or decide against bringing charges. A decision not to bring charges ordinarily will be based on the supervisor's conclusion either that the evidence is insufficient to charge or that the offense can more appropriately be handled by a "stationhouse adjustment" (e.g., in the case of a fight among acquaintances, a warning and lecture may be deemed sufficient). If the supervising officer decides against prosecution, the arrestee will be released from the lockup at the officer's direction (with some departments following the practice of seeking prosecutor approval before releasing felony arrestees). Studies that track the ultimate disposition of arrestees typically have been limited to felony arrests. They report police decisions to release arrestees and forego prosecution in the range of 4% to 10%.

Pre–Filing Prosecutor Screening. Prosecutors' offices vary substantially in their approach to pre-filing review of the decision to charge. In many jurisdictions, all arrests, both for misdemeanors and felonies, will be screened, and no charges will be filed except upon approval of the prosecutor. In many others, however, particularly in urban districts, police often file charges on their own initiative for at least some types of offenses. Typically, prosecutors here will screen the vast majority of the felony charges, but there will be districts in which prosecutors review only the most serious felony charges before they are filed. In those districts, the initial prosecutorial screening of most felony charges occurs sometime between the first appearance and the preliminary hearing or grand jury review (see steps 8 and 9 infra). Prosecutors are more likely to permit police to file misdemeanor charges without advance prosecutorial screening. When that occurs, prosecutors may not review a misdemeanor charge until it is scheduled for trial (and thus may never screen those charges that result in a guilty plea at the first appearance).

A screening prosecutor may accept the charge recommended by the police, raise or reduce that charge, request that the police obtain further evidence (which may require releasing the arrestee at this point and then rearresting him when and if that evidence is obtained), decide against prosecution if the arrestee will participate in a diversion program,[4] or simply decide against prosecution without condition. A prosecutorial decision not to proceed commonly is described as a "rejection," "declination" or "no-paper" decision. That decision most often is based on anticipated difficulties of proof (e.g., the evidence is insufficient, the victim is reluctance to testify, or key evidence was obtained illegally and therefore will not be admissible). However, the prosecutor may decide against proceeding, even though the evidence clearly is sufficient, because other alternatives (e.g., diversion, probation revocation, or prosecution in another jurisdiction) are preferable, or special circumstances render prosecution not "in the interest of justice." As might be expected from the differences among prosecutors' offices in the proportion of arrests reviewed pre-filing, and the subjective nature of many of the grounds for declining prosecution, studies reveal considerable variation from one community to another in the impact of pre-filing prosecutorial screening. Thus, a study of 13 urban prosecutorial districts found that the percentage of felony arrests that did not result in charges ranged from a low of 0% (in a jurisdiction which apparently did no pre-filing screening) to a high of 38%.

Assuming the prosecutor decides to charge, pre-filing screening presents another important prosecutorial decision—setting the level of the charge. Although an arrest was made on a felony charge, the prosecutor may decide to go forward on a lesser charge. As might be expected, substantial variations are found among prosecutorial districts on the rate of reductions, particularly the reductions to a misdemeanor charge. In one district, all felony arrests that result in charges may be filed as felony charges while in another district as many as 50% may be reduced prior to filing to misdemeanor charges. Prosecutors most often reduce the recommended charge because they believe that the evidence only supports a lower charge, but reductions also may be based on the prosecutor's determination that the penalty for the higher charge is too severe for the nature of the crime or that the additional process costs involved in proceeding on a felony (rather than a misdemeanor) are not justified. In some offices, certain felony offenses are viewed as so clearly overgraded legislatively as to necessitate almost automatic reductions on arrests for that offense (e.g., where shoplifting is a felony and all first offender cases are reduced to petty larceny charges).[5]

Post–Filing Prosecutorial Screening. Post-filing prosecutorial review of the charging decision is inherent in the many post-filing procedures (e.g., the preliminary hearing) that require the prosecutor to review the facts of the case. If the prosecutor should determine that the charge is not justified, a dismissal will be obtained through a *nolle prosequi* motion (noting the prosecutor's desire to relinquish prosecution), which ordinarily will be granted in a perfunctory fashion by the court. Similarly, if the prosecutor considers the charge to be too high, a motion can be entered to reduce the

---

4. A diversion program offers the arrestee the opportunity to avoid conviction if he or she is willing to perform prescribed "rehabilitative steps" (e.g., making restitution to the victim, undertaking a treatment program). The diversion agreement operates, in effect, to place the arrestee on a probationary status without conviction. In many jurisdictions, this is achieved by the prosecutor promising not to file charges if the arrestee complies with the prescribed conditions. In others, charges initially are filed with the court, then held in abeyance for the period during which the arrestee is to meet the prescribed conditions, and dismissed with prejudice once the arrestee meets those conditions. If the arrestee fails to meet the prescribed conditions, the prosecution against the arrestee proceeds (with the charges filed, if that had not been done previously). Diversion tends to be used primarily with non-violent misdemeanor arrestees.

5. In some instances, there may be a potential for charging multiple separate offenses (as where the arrested person allegedly committed several separate crimes in a single criminal transaction or engaged in more than one criminal transaction). Here the prosecutor must determine whether the charging instrument should allege all offenses or simply some of the offenses (e.g., only the most serious, or only those easiest to prove). Where the prosecutor chooses to proceed on more than one charge, the law may give to the prosecutor another choice—whether to bring the charges in a single prosecution or in multiple separate prosecutions. A similar choice must be made where several people have been arrested for their participation in the same crime, as each can be proceeded against separately or they can be prosecuted jointly through a single charging instrument naming multiple defendants.

charges. In deciding whether to make such motions, the prosecutor will look to basically the same grounds that might justify a pre-filing rejection or reduction of the charge. Even where a charge was carefully screened and approved prior to filing, post-filing review can readily lead to a contrary conclusion as circumstances change (e.g., evidence becomes unavailable) or the prosecutor learns more about the facts of the case. Of course, where the charge was not previously screened or was screened only on a skimpy arrest report, post-filing review is even more likely to lead to a decision to drop or reduce the charges.

What is the end product of the combined pre-filing screening by police and prosecutor and post-filing screening by the prosecutor? The best source on that question is a series of studies on the attrition of felony arrests. One leading study, using a dozen urban prosecutorial districts, found that those districts screened out of the criminal justice system from 31% to 46% of all felony arrests, with a jurisdictional mean of 39%. A later study, drawing information from 11 states, indicated that screening terminations (including diversions) fell in the range of 31–36% for those states as a group.

(h) Step 6: Filing the Complaint. Assuming that the pre-charge screening results in a decision to prosecute, the next step is the filing of charges with the magistrate court. Typically, the initial charging instrument will be called a "complaint." In misdemeanor cases, which are triable before the magistrate court, the complaint will serve as the charging instrument throughout the proceedings. In felony cases, on the other hand, the complaint serves to set forth the charges only before the magistrate court; an information or indictment will replace the complaint as the charging instrument when the case reaches the general trial court.

For most offenses, the complaint will be a fairly brief document. Its basic function is to set forth concisely the allegation that the accused, at a particular time and place, committed specified acts constituting a violation of a particular criminal statute. The complaint will be signed by a "complainant," a person who swears under oath that he or she believes the factual allegations of the complaint to be true. The complainant usually will be either the victim or the investigating officer. When an officer-complainant did not observe the offense being committed, but relied on information received from the victim or other witnesses, the officer ordinarily will note that the allegations in the complaint are based on "information and belief."

With the filing of the complaint, the person accused in the complaint will have become a "defendant" in a criminal proceeding. The formal charge initiates a judicial record keeping procedure that puts his case on the docket and follows it through to its termination. Ordinarily that termination will come in a dismissal, a conviction, or an acquittal. However, some cases will either be transferred to an "inactive" docket, or dismissed with the prosecution specifically given authority to later reinstate the charge. These are the cases in which the defendant is "unavailable"—usually because he has absconded, but occasionally because he is incarcerated elsewhere or is outside the jurisdiction. The portion of the docket handled in this fashion depends in part on how long a state is willing to wait for the apprehension of a defendant before the charge against him will be "written off" as a disposition. In some jurisdictions, this portion will exceed 10%, while in others, it may not even amount to 1%.

(i) Step 7: Magistrate Review of the Arrest. Following the filing of the complaint and prior to or at the start of the first appearance (see step 8), the magistrate must undertake what is often described as the *"Gerstein* review." As prescribed by the Supreme Court's decision in *Gerstein v. Pugh* [see § 3.5(a)], if the accused was arrested without a warrant and remains in custody, the magistrate must determine that there exists probable cause for the continued detention of the arrestee for the offense charged in the complaint. This ordinarily is an *ex parte* determination, similar to that made in the issuance of an arrest warrant and relying on the same sources of information. If the magistrate finds that probable cause has not been established, she will direct the prosecution to promptly produce more information or release the arrested person. Such instances are exceedingly rare, however. Since a judicial probable cause determination already has been made where an arrest warrant was issued, a *Gerstein* review is not required in such cases (or in cases in which the arrestee was indicted by a grand jury prior to his arrest).

(j) Step 8: The First Appearance. Once the complaint is filed, the case is before the magistrate court, and the accused must appear before the court within a specified period. This appearance of the accused is usually described as the "first appearance," although the terminology varies, with jurisdictions also using "preliminary appearance," "initial presentment," "preliminary arraignment," "arraignment on the warrant," and "arraignment on the complaint." The timing of the first appearance varies with the custodial status of the accused. Where the accused was not taken into custody, but was released on issuance of a citation, there is likely to be a gap of at least several days between the issuance of the citation and the first appearance date as specified in the citation. The same is often true also of the first appearance set for the arrestee who gained his release by posting stationhouse bail.

Almost all felony arrestees and many misdemeanor arrestees will have been held in custody following their arrest, however, and here the time span between the arrest and the first appearance is much shorter. All jurisdictions require that an arrestee held in custody be brought before the magistrate court in a fairly prompt fashion. Ordinarily, the time consumed in booking, transportation, limited post-arrest investigation, reviewing the decision to charge, and preparing and filing the

complaint makes it unlikely that the arrestee will be presented before the magistrate until at least several hours after his arrest. Thus, if the magistrate court does not have an evening session, a person arrested in the afternoon or evening will not be presented before the magistrate until the next day. Many jurisdictions do not allow much longer detention than this, as they impose a 24 hour limit on pre-appearance detention, requiring both the filing of the complaint and the presentation of the detained arrestee within that period. Others, desiring to limit weekend sessions of the court, allow up to 48 hours of pre-appearance detention.

The first appearance often is a quite brief proceeding. Initially, the magistrate will make certain that the person before him is the person named in the complaint. The magistrate then will inform the defendant of the charge in the complaint and will note various rights that the defendant may have in further proceedings. The range of rights mentioned will vary from one jurisdiction to another. Commonly, the magistrate will inform the defendant of his right to remain silent and warn him that anything he says in court or to the police may be used against him at trial. Further advice as to rights may depend upon whether the defendant is charged with a felony or misdemeanor. In felony cases, the magistrate will advise the defendant of the next step in the process, the preliminary hearing, and will set a date for that hearing unless the defendant desires to waive it. If the defendant is charged with a misdemeanor, he will not be entitled to a preliminary hearing or a subsequent grand jury review (see steps 9, and 10).[6]

At least where the defendant is not represented by counsel at the first appearance, the magistrate will inform the defendant of his

---

6. Since a misdemeanor charge will be triable to the magistrate court, the magistrate, at the first appearance, will ask the misdemeanor defendant to enter a plea to the charge contained in the complaint. Indeed, at one time, it was the common practice to dispose of almost all misdemeanor cases at the first appearance, in a fashion similar to that still prevailing in traffic courts. The arresting officer and any witnesses would attend the first appearance, and if the defendant entered a not guilty plea, the trial would be held immediately. With the general recognition of the misdemeanor defendant's right to the assistance of counsel at trial, that practice has largely been

discarded. If the defendant enters a plea of not guilty, the trial ordinarily will be set for at least several days thereafter, allowing for the retaining (or appointment) of counsel and preparation by both the defense and the prosecution. Moreover, where the defendant is not accompanied by counsel at the first appearance and wants to speak with counsel before deciding whether to plead guilty, the magistrate typically will either enter a not guilty plea (which always can be changed) or postpone the entry of a plea for a reasonable period during which counsel can be retained (or appointed if the defendant is indigent).

right to be represented by retained counsel, and, if indigent, his right to court appointed counsel. The scope of the right to appointed counsel may vary with the level of the offense. In some jurisdictions, appointed counsel will not be available for defendants who are charged with low-level misdemeanors if they will not be sentenced to incarceration if convicted. Where there is a right to appointed counsel, which will be the case in all jurisdictions for indigent defendants charged with felonies and serious misdemeanors, the magistrate usually will have the responsibility for at least initiating the appointment process. This involves first determining that the defendant is indigent and that he desires the assistance of counsel. The magistrate then will either directly appoint counsel or notify a judge in charge of appointments that an appointment should be made.

Appointed counsel will be required for a substantial percentage of all felony defendants. A sampling of felony defendants in the nation's 75 largest counties indicated that approximately 80% received court appointed counsel. Three basic systems are used to provide counsel for indigent defendants. In counties containing roughly 70% of the country's population, counsel is provided primarily through a state or county public defender service. In counties containing roughly 25% of the population, reliance is placed primarily upon an assigned counsel system. Here appointed attorneys are selected from a list of available private attorneys, either on an *ad hoc* basis (with individual judges choosing attorneys as they please) or through a coordinated selection system (with selection by a single administrator according to established guidelines). A smaller group of counties, containing less than 10% of the population, rely primarily upon contract systems under which a private law firm, a group of private practitioners, or a nonprofit organization (such as a bar association) contracts to provide representation for the bulk of the indigent defendants for an extended period of time.

One of the most important first-appearance functions of the magistrate is to set bail (i.e., the conditions under which the defendant can obtain his release from custody pending the final disposition of the charges against him). In many misdemeanor cases, there will be no need to set bail. The defendant will already have been released on the police issuance of a citation or on the posting of stationhouse bail or the defendant will enter a guilty plea at the first appearance and be promptly sentenced. However, a bail determination ordinarily must be made in all felony and serious misdemeanor cases and in a substantial portion of the lesser misdemeanor cases.

At one time, bail was limited almost entirely to the posting of cash or a secured bond purchased from a professional bondsman. Today, those are only two of several alternatives available to the magistrate. Others are: (1) release upon a promise to appear (release on "personal recognizance"); (2) release on making a personal promise to forfeit a specified dollar amount upon a failure to appear (an "unsecured" personal bond); (3) release upon the imposition of one or more nonfinancial conditions (e.g., restrictions on defendant's associations or travel); and (4) the posting with the court of a percentage of the bail forfeiture amount (commonly 10%), which will be returned to the defendant if he appears as scheduled. In a few states, the 10% alternative has basically replaced the secured bond, resulting in the elimination of professional bondsmen.

In misdemeanor cases, magistrates most commonly utilize release on personal recognizance or personal bonds, and even where a secured bond is required, the amount is sufficiently low so that only a small percentage of defendants fail to gain their release. As a result, studies that cover both misdemeanor and felony arrestees report overall release rates of 85% or higher, with the vast majority of defendants released on nonfinancial conditions. However, when felony defendants alone are considered, the picture changes dramatically, especially for the more serious felony offenses. Thus, a study of the nation's 75 largest counties found that 37% of all felony defendants were detained until the final disposition of their charges, and that percentage rose to 50% or above for those charged with rape and robbery. As for the defendants who were released, more were released on non-financial conditions than on financial conditions. The group released did not necessarily remain free on bail pending trial; a non-appearance rate of 25% and a rearrest rate of 14% for new offenses led to revocation of bail for a significant number. Also, at the end of a year, 8% of those released were unapprehended fugitives.

(k) Step 9: Preliminary Hearing. Following the first appearance, the next scheduled step in a felony case ordinarily is the preliminary hearing (sometimes called a preliminary "examination"). All but a few of our fifty-two jurisdictions grant the felony defendant a right to a preliminary hearing, to be held within a specified period (typically, within a week or two if the defendant does not gain pretrial release and within a few weeks if released). This hardly means, however, that the preliminary hearing will be held in almost all or even most cases. Initially, the critical stage for post-arrest prosecutorial screening of charges (see step 5) is in the period prior to the scheduled preliminary hearing, and a prosecution can readily dismiss 15–30% of the felony cases before the scheduled hearing (the higher percentage coming in those jurisdictions in which there is little or no pre-filing screening). Where the charges are not dismissed, two additional decisions—one by the prosecutor and one by the defense—can sharply reduce the number of preliminary hearings.

First, in almost all jurisdictions, if the prosecutor obtains a grand jury indictment prior to the scheduled preliminary hearing, the preliminary hearing will not be held, as the grand jury's finding of probable cause has rendered irrelevant any contrary finding that the magistrate might make at the preliminary hearing. Prosecutorial bypassing of the preliminary hearing by immediately obtaining a grand jury indictment occurs with great frequency in many prosecutorial districts, particularly those that regularly prosecute by grand jury indictment (see step 10 infra). Second, even where the preliminary hearing is made available to the defendant, there nonetheless may not be a preliminary hearing because the defendant prefers to waive the hearing and move directly to the trial court. That is often the strategy employed where the defendant intends to plead guilty.

Where the preliminary hearing is held, it will provide, like grand jury review, a screening of the decision to charge by a neutral body. In the preliminary hearing, that neutral body is the magistrate, who must determine whether, on the evidence presented, there is probable cause to believe that defendant committed the crime charged. Ordinarily, the magistrate will already have determined that probable cause exists as part of the *ex parte* screening of the complaint (see step 7). The preliminary hearing, however, provides screening in an adversary proceeding in which both sides are represented by counsel. Jurisdictions vary in the evidentiary rules applicable to the preliminary hearing, but most require that the parties rely primarily on live witnesses rather than affidavits. Typically, the prosecution will present its key witnesses and the defense will limit its response to the cross-examination of those witnesses. The defendant has the right to present his own evidence at the hearing, but traditional defense strategy advises against subjecting defense witnesses to prosecution cross-examination in any pretrial proceeding.

If the magistrate concludes that the evidence presented establishes probable cause, she will "bind the case over" to the next stage in the proceedings. In an indictment jurisdiction (see step 10), the case is bound over to the grand jury, and in a jurisdiction that permits the direct filing of an information (see step 11), the case is bound over directly to the general trial court. If the magistrate finds that the probable cause supports only a misdemeanor charge, she will reject the felony charge and allow the prosecutor to substitute the lower charge, which will then be set for trial in the magistrate court. If the magistrate finds that the prosecution's evidence does not support any charge, she will order that the defendant be released. The rate of dismissals at the preliminary hearing quite naturally varies with the degree of previous screening exercised by the prosecutor. In a jurisdiction with fairly extensive screening, the percentage of dismissals is likely to fall in the range of 5–

10% of the cases heard. However, other jurisdictions (usually those in which hearings are more sparingly utilized) report a much higher dismissal rate. In either type of jurisdiction, the preliminary hearing dismissal is likely to account for the disposition of less than 5% of all felony complaints.

(*l*) **Step 10: Grand Jury Review.** Although almost all American jurisdictions still have provisions authorizing grand jury screening of felony charges, such screening is mandatory only in those jurisdictions requiring felony prosecutions to be instituted by an indictment, a charging instrument issued by the grand jury. In a majority of the states, the prosecution is now allowed to proceed either by grand jury indictment or by information at its option. Because prosecutors in these states most often choose to prosecute by information, the states providing this option commonly are referred to as "information" states. Eighteen states, the federal system, and the District of Columbia currently require grand jury indictments for all felony prosecutions. These jurisdictions commonly are described as "indictment" jurisdictions. Four additional states are "limited indictment" jurisdictions, requiring prosecution by indictment only for their most severely punished offenses (capital, life imprisonment, or both). Apart possibly from capital offenses, the defendant may waive the right to be proceeded against by indictment, thereby allowing the prosecution to proceed by information. Waiver rates vary from one jurisdiction to another but waivers are likely to be made by at least 10% of all felony defendants.

The grand jury is composed of a group of private citizens who are selected to review cases presented over a term that may range from one to eighteen months. Traditionally the grand jury consisted of 23 persons with the favorable vote of a majority needed to indict. Today, many states use a somewhat smaller grand jury (e.g., 12) and some require more than a simple majority to indict. As in the case of the magistrate at the preliminary hearing, the primary function of the grand jury is to determine whether there is sufficient evidence to justify a trial on the charge sought by the

prosecution. The grand jury, however, participates in a screening process quite different from the preliminary hearing. It meets in a closed session and hears only the evidence presented by the prosecution. The defendant has no right to offer his own evidence or to be present during grand jury proceedings. If there was a prior preliminary hearing, the grand jury is in no way bound by the ruling on probable cause at that hearing. The grand jury may indict even though the magistrate dismissed the charge at the preliminary hearing, and may refuse to indict even though the magistrate bound over to the grand jury.

If a majority of the grand jurors conclude that the prosecution's evidence is sufficient, the grand jury will issue the indictment requested by the prosecutor. The indictment will set forth a brief description of the offense charged, and the grand jury's approval of that charge will be indicated by its designation of the indictment as a "true bill." If the grand jury majority refuses to approve a proposed indictment, the charges against the defendant will be dismissed. Indictment jurisdictions vary in the percentage of cases in which grand jurors do not indict, although typically that percentage is quite low (e.g., 2–5%).

(m) Step 11: The Filing of the Indictment or Information. If an indictment is issued, it will be filed with the general trial court and will replace the complaint as the accusatory instrument in the case. Where grand jury review either is not required or has been waived, an information will be filed with the trial court. Like the indictment, the information is a charging instrument which replaces the complaint, but it is issued by the prosecutor rather than the grand jury. In most information states, the charge in the information must be supported by a preliminary hearing bindover (unless the preliminary hearing was waived).

(n) Step 12: Arraignment on the Information or Indictment. After the indictment or information has been filed, the defendant is arraigned—i.e., he is brought before the trial court, informed of the charges against him, and asked to enter a plea of guilty, not guilty, or, as is permitted under some circumstances, *nolo contendere*. In the end, most of those felony defendants whose cases reach the trial court will plead guilty. At the arraignment, however, they are likely to enter a plea of not guilty. Where there has not been a preliminary hearing, defense counsel probably will not be fully apprized of the strength of the prosecution's case at this point in the proceedings. Also, in most jurisdictions, guilty pleas in felony cases are the product of plea negotiations with the prosecution, and in many places, that process does not start until after the arraignment. When the defendant enters a plea of not guilty at the arraignment, the judge will set a trial date, but the expectation generally is that the trial will not be held.

Between the arraignment and the scheduled trial date, three possible dispositions can result in the termination of the case without trial. Although there will have been extensive prosecutorial screening by this point, changed circumstances and new information typically will lead to dismissals on a prosecutor's *nolle prosequi* motion in roughly 5–15% of the cases. A smaller percentage of the information or indictments will be dismissed on motion of the defense, as discussed in step 13. The vast majority of the dispositions without trial will be the product of guilty pleas. General trial courts (particularly in urban judicial districts) regularly report a guilty plea rate within the range of 60–85% for felony defendants.

Guilty pleas in felony cases commonly will be entered in response to a plea agreement under which the prosecution offers certain concessions in return for the defendant's entry of the plea. Those concessions may take the form of a reduction of the charges (sometimes to a misdemeanor and sometimes to a lesser felony charge), a dismissal of related charges where the defendant faces multiple charges, a recommendation on sentence, or a specific sentence (when agreed to by the trial court). Prosecutors' offices vary in the concessions they offer and their willingness to bargain over concessions (as opposed to presenting a take-it-or-leave-it offer). Prosecutors also vary as to the types of cases in which they will offer concessions, with some generally refusing to do so on the most serious charges. Indeed, there are jurisdictions in which prosecutors will not plea bargain, although defendants here may still find an inducement to plead guilty in a general policy of trial judges to give favorable weight in sentencing to the defendant's willingness to plead guilty.

(*o*) Step 13: Pretrial Motions. In most jurisdictions, a broad range of objections must be raised by a pretrial motion. Those motions commonly present challenges to the institution of the prosecution (e.g., claims regarding the grand jury indictment process), attacks upon the sufficiency of the charging instrument, challenges to the scope, location, and timing of the prosecution (claiming improper joinder of charges or parties, improper venue, or violation of speedy trial requirements), requests for discovery when there is a dispute over what is discoverable (discovery disclosures otherwise typically are provided without a court order), and requests for the suppression of evidence allegedly obtained through a constitutional violation. While some pretrial motions tend to be made only by defendants who intend to go to trial, other motions (e.g., for discovery) may benefit as well defendants who expect in the end to plead guilty. Nevertheless, pretrial motions are likely to be made in only a small portion of the felony cases that reach the trial court. Their use does vary considerably, however, with the nature of the case. In narcotics cases, for example, motions to suppress are quite common. In the typical forgery case, on the other, pretrial motions of any type are quite rare. As a group, pretrial motions are highly unlikely to produce the dismissal of more than 5% of the cases before the general trial court, and commonly will not even reach a 2% dismissal rate.

(*p*) Step 14: The Trial. Assuming that there has not been a dismissal and the defendant has not entered a guilty plea (or a *nolo contendere* plea), the next step in the criminal process is the trial. In most respects, the criminal trial resembles the civil trial. There are, however, several distinguishing features that are either unique to criminal trials or of special importance in such trials. These include (1) the presumption of defendant's innocence,

(2) the requirement of proof beyond a reasonable doubt, (3) the right of the defendant not to take the stand, (4) the exclusion of evidence obtained by the state in an illegal manner, and (5) the more frequent use of incriminating statements of defendants. In most jurisdictions, the misdemeanor trial will be almost indistinguishable from a felony trial. In some jurisdictions, however, misdemeanor trials tend to be less formal, with rules of evidence applied in a rather loose fashion.

As noted previously, most felony and misdemeanor cases are likely to be disposed of either by a guilty plea or by a dismissal. Typically, no more than 15% of the felony prosecutions reaching the general trial court will be resolved by a trial—although there are some exceptional jurisdictions in which the percentage is over 30%. Setting aside dismissals, and looking only to guilty pleas and trials, the ratio of guilty pleas to trials in the general trial court typically will exceed ten to one. For misdemeanor cases resolved at the magistrate level (including both cases originally filed as misdemeanors and felony complaints reduced to misdemeanors) the percentage of trials is likely to fall in the range of 3% to 7% on a statewide basis. However, individual judicial districts, particularly in urban areas, not uncommonly have trials in less than 1% of their misdemeanor dispositions.

The median time frame from the arrest of the defendant to the start of the felony trial can exceed a year in judicial districts with slow moving dockets, but for most judicial districts, it is likely to fall within the range of 5–8 months. The median will be influenced, in particular, by the mix of jury and bench trials, as the time frame tends to be considerably longer for jury trials. While most jurisdictions have speedy trial requirements that impose time limits of 6 months or less, there are various excludable time periods (for factors such as witness unavailability and the processing of motions) which commonly extend the time limit by at least a few months.

The trial itself tends to be relatively short. Misdemeanor trials typically last less than a day. Felony jury trials are somewhat longer, but in state courts, most will be completed within 2–3 days. A key variable will be the type of case, as certain types of offense (e.g., white collar offenses and capital homicide cases) produce trials substantially longer than the typical felony. This explains in part why trials in the federal courts (commonly involving greater complexity) often are much longer. In general, trials to the bench are considerably shorter, and in state courts, unlikely to last more than a day.

In all fifty-two jurisdictions, the defendant will have a right to a jury trial for all felony offenses and for misdemeanors punishable by more than 6 months imprisonment. Most states also provide a jury trial for lesser misdemeanors (although that right may exist only through the opportunity to seek a trial *de novo* in the general trial court after an initial bench trial before the magistrate court). Juries traditionally were composed of 12 persons, but most states now utilize 6 person juries in misdemeanor cases and several use the smaller juries in non-capital felony cases as well. Of course, the right to a jury trial can be waived, and in most jurisdictions, a significant number of defendants will waive the jury in favor of a bench trial. Over the country as a whole, roughly 70% of all felony trials are tried to a jury, but in various individual judicial districts, as well as several states, bench trials actually outnumber jury trials. In misdemeanor cases, in contrast, bench trials, typically predominate (often accounting for 95% or more of all trials), even in jurisdictions that extend the defendant's jury trial right to all misdemeanors. In all but a few jurisdictions, the jury verdict in both misdemeanor and felony cases, whether for acquittal or conviction, must be unanimous. Where the jurors cannot agree, no verdict is entered and the case may be retried. For most communities, such "hung juries" occur in only a very small percentage of all jury trials (e.g., 3–6%), but there are large urban districts in which juries cannot reach a verdict in as many as 10–15% of all jury trials.

Whether a criminal case is tried to the bench or the jury, the odds favor conviction over acquittal. A fairly typical ratio for felony charges will be 3 convictions for every acquittal. That ratio may vary significantly, however, with the nature of the offense. In some jurisdictions, the rate of conviction at trial tends to be substantially lower (though still well above 50%) for some crimes (e.g., rape) than for others (e.g., drug trafficking).

With the end of the trial stage, the criminal justice process will have produced a disposition as to all persons who originally entered the process through an arrest or the issuance of citation. As for those who were arrested on felony charges, only one out of a hundred will have had the case against him carried through to a trial that resulted in an acquittal. A much larger portion of the felony arrestees, anywhere from 30–50%, also will not have been convicted, but the dispositions in their favor will have come before the filing of the complaint, through pre-charge police and prosecutor screening, or before the trial, either through *nolle prosequi* motions or judicial and grand jury screening procedures. Of the 50–70% of the felony arrestees who will have been convicted, many will not have been convicted of felonies. Depending upon the plea negotiation practices followed in the particular jurisdiction, anywhere from 10–30% of those felony arrestees convicted are likely to be convicted of misdemeanors.

(q) Step 15: Sentencing. Following conviction, the next step in the process is the determination of the sentence. In all but a few jurisdictions (which allow for jury sentencing, even apart from capital punishment), the sentence determination is the function of the court. Basically three different types of sentences may be used: financial sanctions (e.g., fines, restitution orders); some form of release into the community (e.g., probation, unsupervised release, house arrest); and incarceration in a jail (for lesser sentences) or prison (for longer sentences). The process applied in determining the sentence is shaped in considerable part by the sentencing options made available to the court by the legislature. For a particular offense, the court may have no choice. The legislature may have prescribed that conviction automatically carries with it a certain sentence and there is nothing left for the court to do except impose that sentence.

Most frequently, however, legislative narrowing of options on a particular offense does not go beyond eliminating the community release option (by requiring incarceration) and setting maximums (and sometimes mandatory minimums) for incarceration and fines. However, states vary considerably in shaping the court's authority to choose within available options, particularly as to the length of incarceration. Their approaches include: allowing the sentencing judge considerable discretion within a broad range set by the legislature; narrowing the range and the discretion by imposing certain mandated minimums based on specified factual findings; setting a presumptive sentence range which is raised or lowered on a finding of specified aggravating or mitigating circumstances; and channeling discretion through the use of sentencing guidelines that also require factual determinations.

The process utilized in felony sentencing varies to some extent according to whether judicial discretion is broad or is channeled or limited by guideline or legislative reference to specific sentencing circumstances. In all jurisdictions, the process is designed to obtain for the court information beyond that which will have come to its attention in the course of trial or in the acceptance of a guilty plea. The primary vehicle here is the presentence report prepared by the probation department, although the prosecution and defense commonly will be allowed to present additional information and to challenge the information contained in the presentence report. The presentation of this information is not subject to the rules governing the presentation of information at trial. The rules of evidence do not apply, and neither the prosecution nor the defense has a right to call witnesses or to cross-examine the sources of adverse information presented in the presentence report or in any additional documentation presented by the opposing side. However, where the sentencing authority of the judge is restricted by the reference to specific factors in sentencing guidelines, legislatively set presumptive sentences, or mandated minimum sentences, a judge commonly is required to make findings of fact as to those factors. Here, if relevant facts are in dispute, the court commonly will find it necessary to hold an evidentiary hearing and to utilize trial-type procedures to resolve that dispute.[7]

(r) Step 16: Appeals. For criminal cases disposed of in the general trial court, the initial appeal is to the intermediate appellate court. If the state has no intermediate appellate court, then the initial and final appeal within the state system is to the state's court of last resort. Initial appeals in cases disposed of by the magistrate court will be to the general trial court. In some states, the appeal procedure from a conviction in the magistrate court is a trial *de novo* before the general trial court, rather than that court exercising appellate review of the lower court record.

Although all convicted defendants are entitled to appeal their convictions, appeals are taken predominantly by convicted defendants who were sentenced to imprisonment on a felony conviction. Imprisoned defendants convicted pursuant to a guilty plea are included in this group, but their portion of all appeals depends in large part on the jurisdiction's sentencing law. Though the trial court's acceptance of a guilty plea may be challenged on appeal, the grounds for such challenges are limited, so that appeals by guilty plea defendants tend to be sentencing challenges. Those challenges are readily available only in jurisdictions that use sentencing guidelines or legislatively mandated presumptive sentences. In such jurisdictions, challenges to the sentence alone can constitute a substantial portion (e.g., 15–30%) of all felony appeals, and many of those are by guilty plea defendants.

Appeals challenging the conviction itself come primarily from imprisoned defendants who are seeking review of a trial conviction. Indeed, in some jurisdictions, as many as 90% of the defendants who were convicted after trial and sentenced to prison will appeal their convictions. Even with almost automatic appeal by this group, however, because of the heavy rate of guilty pleas, the total number of appeals to the intermediate appeals court may readily amount to less than 10% of all felony convictions. State intermediate appellate courts commonly have a reversal rate on defense appeals of right in the 5–10% range, although those rates will be somewhat higher when reversals in part are included. Courts of last resort, with discretionary jurisdiction, tend to have a substantially higher rate of reversals than the intermediate appellate courts, as they grant review in cases presenting close questions.

(s) Step 17: Postconviction Remedies. After the appellate process is exhausted, imprisoned defendants may be able to use postconviction remedies to challenge their convictions on limited grounds. In particular, federal postconviction remedies are available to state as well as federal prisoners to challenge their convictions in the federal courts on most constitutional grounds. In the year 2000, the federal district courts received roughly 21,000 state-prisoner postconviction applications. Relief is granted on less than 3 percent of these petitions, however, and the relief often is limited to requiring a further hearing. In the state system, annual postconviction challenges typically fall below 5% of the annual felony filings.

§ 1.4   The Cornerstone Objectives of the Process

As noted in § 1.2, considerable variation exists from one jurisdiction to another in the laws governing the criminal justice process. Nonetheless, several common objectives are reflected in the laws of all fifty-two jurisdictions. This group of "cornerstone" objectives shape the basic structure of the process and the most fundamental of its governing legal principles. Many of these cornerstone objectives are mandated by the federal constitution, but their

---

7. Sentencing procedure for misdemeanor cases is much less complex. The sentencing magistrate will have been given discretion to impose any sentence within the legislatively prescribed maximum, and that discretion will not be channeled by guidelines or restricted by legislature standards tied to specific factors. The sentencing judge often will follow a rough schedule (as to both fines and a possible jail sentence) that looks only to character of the offense and the offender's prior record. Accordingly, the court will have no need for a presentence report, except for the most significant misdemeanors. As a result, the magistrate commonly sets the sentence immediately following the entry of a conviction.

widespread acceptance was not dependent upon that constitutional command. Almost all of the cornerstone objectives were well established in the state systems long before the states were subjected *via* the post civil war adoption of the Fourteenth Amendment (and its subsequent judicial interpretation) to significant regulation by the Federal Constitution.

The subsections that follow provide a brief overview of these cornerstone objectives. While some might question designation of a particular objective as within the "cornerstone" category, the grouping as a whole is fairly noncontroversial. On the other hand, considerable disagreement exists both as to the precise scope of the objectives and as to how (or whether) the objectives should be balanced against each other. Those disagreement often explain, in part, the different approaches taken by different states in their implementation of the same cornerstone objective or in striking a balance between two conflicting objectives. Similar disagreements are reflected in many of the divisions among Supreme Court justices in their interpretations of constitutional provisions shaped by one or more of these cornerstone objectives. Specific disagreements will be discussed in later chapters in the course of describing particular legal standards. Our purpose here merely is to identify the general character of these criminal justice cornerstones, and to identify some of the major structural elements and process requirements that reflect their implementation.

(a) Implementing the Enforcement of the Substantive Law. "Legal procedure," Roscoe Pound long ago noted, "is a means, not an end; it must be made subsidiary to the substantive law as a means of making that law effective in action." While a procedure also may promote values that are independent of the aims of the substantive law, Pound was certainly correct in characterizing the *raison d'etre* of any procedural system as the practical implementation of the substantive law. As applied to the criminal justice process, this universal starting point mandates a process that promotes effective enforcement of the substantive criminal law—that is, a process through

which the government can detect, apprehend, prosecute, convict, and impose punishment upon those who have violated the prohibitions of the substantive criminal law. However, as illustrated by the variety of criminal justice systems that exist throughout the world, processes may be shaped in many different ways to achieve this universal objective. What distinguishes one system from another basically are the choices made in determining what best reaches that objective and what other values should be promoted, at a possible sacrifice to that objective.

The first type of choice requires selection among alternative procedural structures based on furthering effective enforcement of the substantive criminal law. Very often, the debate here centers on whether one structure or another provides the more effective enforcement when the resources allocated to that task are restricted in one fashion or another. The second type of choice asks whether other values are so important that they should be implemented even though they very often operate to make effective enforcement more difficult to achieve. Those other values commonly are said to be aimed at achieving "fairness" in the process. The subsections that follow discuss the choices that have been made in the American criminal justice process to achieve both effective enforcement and fairness. Those choices are reflected in ten cornerstone objectives that have shaped that process: (1) achieving reliable factfinding (i.e., discovery of the "truth"); (2) utilizing an adversary process of adjudication; (3) utilizing an accusatorial system of proof; (4) minimizing erroneous convictions; (5) minimizing the burdens of accusation and litigation; (6) providing for lay participation; (7) respecting the dignity of the individual; (8) maintaining the appearance of fairness; (9) achieving equality in administration; and (10) addressing the concerns of the victim of the crime.

Bearing upon the implementation of these objectives is an ongoing debate concerning the relationship of the objectives to effective law enforcement. Is a particular cornerstone objective fully consistent with effective enforcement (even though it also may be seen as promoting fairness) or does it promote fairness at a sacrifice in enforcement efficiency? Where a particular objective hinders effective enforcement, but was accepted nonetheless because the values it promotes were deemed more important, the extension of its implementation will commonly be viewed as resting on a balancing analysis. In particular, if the extension at issue is deemed less than essential in achieving the goal of the cornerstone objective, a lawmaker considering the adoption of that extension will seek to balance the benefit of that additional implementation in promoting the cornerstone objective against the cost of the implementation in lessening effective enforcement. Of course, a balance was struck in initially accepting that cornerstone objective as an element shaping the criminal justice process, but that does not preclude the lawmaker (particularly the legislator) from reexamining the balance with each extension of the objective. On the other hand, no such balancing is needed if the implementation of the cornerstone objective is viewed as entirely consistent with achieving effective enforcement. The implementation may challenged because it is too costly in terms of the resources it demands, but not because it is directly at odds with effective law enforcement.

Three distinct positions have been advanced on the question of whether the ten cornerstone objectives noted above are consistent with the overall objective of facilitating effective law enforcement. One position maintains that all ten of these cornerstone objectives, at least as they are traditionally implemented, detract from achieving effective enforcement of the substantive criminal law. Under this view, the historical acceptance of all of these objectives depended on a balancing analysis that favored these objectives notwithstanding a loss in the effective enforcement of the substantive criminal law.

This first position starts from the premise that the primary function of law enforcement is to repress criminal conduct through a combination of deterrence and incapacitation. This "crime control" model of enforcement, looking to the classical utilitarian justification of criminal punishment, focuses on preventing future criminal behavior with the maximum efficiency, given the limited resources available to law enforcement. It therefore seeks a sufficiently high rate of apprehension and conviction to deter future wrongdoers. The cornerstone objectives are viewed as inconsistent with this goal both because they shift resources from enforcement to their implementation, and because they hold open to offenders the potential for evading apprehension (as in the case of the dignity objective, which eliminates certain effective police practices) or evading conviction (as in the case of the accusatorial objective, which makes more difficult the prosecution's proof of guilt). Indeed, the crime control model suggests that a strict utilitarian approach to enforcement would allow for some form of administrative finding of guilt that dispenses with almost all of the components of our current adjudicative process, which is largely shaped by the cornerstone objectives. The model finds inconsistent even the current process emphasis on avoiding conviction of the innocent, since an occasional error in this regard would not detract from the deterrence function of enforcement.

A second position, taking a different view of the purpose of criminal punishment, sees effective law enforcement as incorporating some, but not all of the cornerstone objectives. Viewing the function of criminal punishment, and therefore the function of effective law enforcement, as ensuring that offenders receive their "just deserts," this position requires of effective enforcement not only the apprehension and conviction of the guilty, but also the avoidance of the conviction of the innocent. The objective of factfinding accuracy is not simply consistent with effective enforcement, but actually an essential element of that enforcement. Similarly, insofar as the other cornerstone objectives (e.g., an adversary process of adjudication) create a structure that best serves the end of discovery of the truth, those objective also promotes effective law enforcement. However, insofar as an objective serve other ends, particularly where those ends are truth-deflecting, it interferes with ideal enforcement (which convicts as many guilty persons as possible, without also convicting the innocent). Accordingly, under this position, there is a need to engage in a balancing analysis that weighs the loss to effective enforcement only when the cornerstone objective at issue is non-truth-seeking.

A third position, resting on a long range instrumentalist view of the criminal law, contends that all of the cornerstone objectives—including those that are truth-deflecting—promote the ends of the criminal law and therefore are consistent with the effective enforcement of that law. This position stresses that the element of moral education is inherent in the criminal law and therefore a necessary aspect of its enforcement. The criminal law, the position contends, can only be an effective deterrent if it persuades and educates the public as to the values that underlie the substantive criminal law, including respect for the dignity and autonomy of the individual. This moral force is undermined, however, if the process of enforcement fails to recognize those same values. Like the criminal law itself, the criminal process must convey the basic lesson that the "ends do not justify the means." The process must convince the public of the legitimacy of the results of enforcement, and that can be achieved, so the argument goes, only through an enforcement process that convinces the public of its "fairness" by promoting all of the cornerstone objectives.

Of the three positions, the second arguably has gained the most support among lawmakers. In considering the adoption of a new procedure designed to implement a cornerstone objective unrelated to the discovery of the truth, legislators (very often) and judges (with somewhat less frequency) refer to the need for a balancing process. They look to the likely negative impact of the proposed procedural requirement upon effective law enforcement, and will reject the proposal where they conclude that it therefore is not in the public interest: Where courts require a new procedure implementing such an objective without weighing the impact on law enforcement, they often note that balancing by the court is not needed because the legislation or constitutional provision being interpreted has already struck a balance (in favor of the cornerstone

objection). In contrast, where the new procedure is viewed as implementing a truth-seeking cornerstone objective, lawmakers rarely suggest a need for a balancing analysis, but tend to focus instead on administrative feasibility and the effectiveness of the procedure in implementing the cornerstone objective.

(b) Discovery of the Truth. As applied in the criminal justice process, truth-finding has two elements (1) the uncovering of crimes and (2) the determination as to who did, and who did not, commit the crime. The Supreme Court has described the discovery of the truth as a "fundamental goal" of the criminal justice system and the "central purpose of a criminal trial," and lower courts regularly have echoed such characterizations.

Various elements of the criminal justice process are directed to promoting discovery of the truth. Initially the process aims at providing an investigatory capacity sufficient to uncover the crime and identity the offender. It seeks to provide police and prosecutor with the authority needed to identify readily possible sources of information and evidence and to obtain information and evidence from these sources even when they are not cooperative. Thus, the police are allowed, subject to certain limitations, to question possible witnesses and suspects, to search persons and property, to require suspects to participate in identification procedures, and to utilize informers and undercover agents. The prosecutor is granted investigative authority that is even broader in some respects through the use of the investigative grand jury.

Discovery of the truth also requires an adjudication process that is reliable in both convicting the guilty defendant and exonerating the defendant who is erroneously accused. The quest for such reliability underlies many elements of the trial, including its adversary structure, prohibitions against certain potentially deceptive actions of the adversaries, evidentiary rules promoting the production of reliable evidence, disqualification standards aimed at eliminating jurors and judges who are likely to be biased (either in favor of the state or the defendant), and restrictions on the scope of a single trial (designed to preclude a mixing of issues that could confuse a factfinder). Various pretrial procedures, such as providing pretrial discovery of the opponent's case, are aimed at supplementing the capacity of the trial procedures to produce a reliable verdict. Legal restrictions imposed upon adjudication through a guilty plea similarly serve, in part, to ensure the reliability of convictions produced by that process.

Notwithstanding its importance, the truthfinding objective will, in certain respects, be sacrificed for the benefit of other values. As one court put it: "[T]ruth, like all other good things, may be loved unwisely—may be pursued too keenly—may cost too much." Consequently, there comes a point at which factfinding accuracy must give way to other values that are truth deflecting. There is considerable disagreement as to how truth-deflecting values should be weighed against the truthfinding objective, but all agree that the commitment to other values will sometimes prevail.

Most of the values prevailing over truthfinding relate to substantive norms of "fairness," such as preserving human dignity and personal autonomy. Some of the legal standards implementing those substantive norms operate to prevent the discovery of reliable, relevant evidence (or to bar the use of such evidence when discovered through violation of those norms). Thus, the privilege against self-incrimination prohibits the state from compelling the defendant to give incriminating testimony and the Fourth Amendment both bars unreasonable searches and seizures to obtain evidence and prohibits the state's use in its case-in-chief of evidence obtained through an unreasonable search and seizure. Standards implementing other fairness norms bar conviction notwithstanding ample evidence of guilt that has been properly obtained. Thus, the Fifth Amendment's double jeopardy prohibition and Sixth Amendment's speedy trial requirement, though they sometimes operate as a safeguard against potentially unreliable factfinding, also bar conviction even where the retrial or delay casts no doubt upon the accuracy of the conviction.

Although truth-deflecting values commonly operate to benefit the defendant, that is not always the case. Respect for such values also may operate to keep the defendant from obtaining testimony or other evidence that would be exculpatory. This often occurs, for example, where a witness potentially helpful to the defense is excused from testifying on the exercise of an evidentiary privilege.

Still another factor sometimes balanced against the truthseeking objective, although not usually with such open recognition, is the limitation of available administrative resources. In most communities, the criminal justice process operates under the pressures of heavy caseloads. In part those pressures are accommodated by broad grants of discretion that allow law enforcement agencies to allocate their efforts according to the significance of the offense and the likelihood of a successful investigation and prosecution. The end result, however, is the sacrifice of the full detection of the guilty. So too, limited resources may preclude a complete investigation, by prosecution and defense, in cases that are prosecuted. Neither side may have the manpower needed to explore problematic avenues of investigation that could conceivably produce relevant evidence. Some commentators suggest that even basic truthfinding safeguards in the adjudication process have been weakened due to caseload pressures. Those pressures have played a significant role in shaping the law governing such subjects as plea bargaining, the joint trial of offenders, and the availability of appointed counsel for indigent misdemeanor defendants—arguably at some cost to the reliability of adjudications.

(c) Adversary Adjudication. The American criminal justice process also is structured to adjudicate guilt through a process that is basically adversary in character. Although the goal of adversary adjudication relates primarily to the trial and related pretrial proceedings, it is so central to the overall character of the American criminal justice process that the process is characterized generally as an "adversarial system of justice." What exactly is an adversary system of adjudication? Although courts sometimes attribute to it the characteristics of an accusatorial system as well, the key to an adversary system is the division of responsibilities between the decisionmaker and the parties.

An adversary system of adjudication vests decisionmaking authority, both as to law and fact, in a neutral decisionmaker who is to render a decision in light of the materials presented by the adversary parties. In an adversary criminal proceeding, there often will be two such neutral decisionmakers, the jury (as to factual issues) and the judge (as to legal issues); the adversary parties are the prosecution (not the victim) and the defense. The decisionmaker in a pure adversary system operates as "a generally silent referee, determining the case as it is presented, and leaving it very much to the parties to choose the battleground." The adversary model gives to the parties the responsibility of investigating the facts, interviewing possible witnesses, consulting possible experts, and determining what will or will not be told. Each party is expected to present the facts and interpret the law in a light most favorable to its side, and through a searching counter-argument and cross-examination, to challenge the soundness of the presentations made by the other side. The judge and jury are then to adjudicate impartially the issues presented by the opposing presentations.

The American criminal justice process actually seeks a "modified" or "regulated" adversary system as opposed to the "pure" adversary model described above. It does not provide for a totally silent or inactive judge; it seeks to prohibit "excesses" in adversary presentations; and it will in certain respects impose a duty on each party to assist the other in gathering information. Even with these controls, however, the American criminal justice process remains sufficiently adversarial in its overall character to stand in sharp contrast to the "inquisitorial" or "non-adversary" system that prevails in continental Europe. Under that system, the primary responsibility for the initial development of relevant facts lies with a judicial officer or a prosecutor, who is required to collect all relevant evidence (both incriminating and exculpatory) in a comprehensive dossier and to bring charges if that evidence establishes a likelihood of guilt. Once the accusation is filed, the trial court assumes responsibility for the further development of the case and the presentation of evidence, including a dominant role in questioning witnesses. Although the prosecutor and defense counsel have an opportunity to contribute, their role is far more limited than the role of counsel in the American trial.

The adversary system is so well established in this country that the debate as to whether the adversary or inquisitorial system better serves truthfinding is largely rendered moot. However, there remains an open question as to whether the adversary system requires further modification to more effectively obtain truthfinding.

Some critics argue that the adversary system is in need of additional regulation placing a primary emphasis on truthfinding. As they see it, the adversarial ethos, especially defense counsel's overriding obligation to his or her client, naturally fosters an incentive "to win at all costs," and combatting that inclination, so as to make truth "paramount," requires substantially more than the limited and loosely formulated restraints currently imposed upon deception and obfuscation. There has been considerable resistance, however, to changing the traditional structure. Though there is universal acceptance of the proposition that the prosecution's responsibility in an adversary system is to "do justice" rather than "gain victory," considerable disagreement exists as to the types of restraints that should be placed upon the prosecutor to ensure adherence to that responsibility. So too, while there is widespread agreement that defense counsel should be subject to certain restraints in advancing the client's cause, that agreement frequently breaks down when specifics are considered. For example, a requirement that operates to preclude misleading the decisionmaker, but also arguably operates to undercut client confidence in the defense attorney, will be opposed by some who maintain that the truthseeking function will suffer in the long run by chilling client willingness to confide in the attorney.

Disagreements also exist as to whether certain obligations imposed upon both sides (e.g., providing pretrial discovery to the opponent) detract from or add to the effectiveness of the adversary system in seeking the truth. Finally, rules of the adversary system seen by some as facilitating adversary excesses are seen by others as serving independent "fairness" values that override the search for the truth.

A second group of critics challenge the adversary system's truthfinding capacity because of what they characterize as a serious imbalance in the resources available to the two sides. They note, in particular, that the "State has in the police an agency for the discovery of evidence superior to anything which even the wealthiest defendant could employ." What is needed, they argue, are compensatory measures that offset this and other resource advantages of the government. They see many of the truth-deflecting constitutional rights of the accused as serving this purpose by giving added procedural protection to the "weaker party." The need to compensate for the defense's lesser position is also cited as justification for imposing other procedural obligations upon the prosecution, such as pleading requirements that narrowly frame the state's case, and a prosecutorial duty to assist the defense in gaining access to key information.

The "compensatory justification" rationale for imposing special restraints and obligations upon the prosecution has been challenged by other commentators who argue that it misuses the adversary system. That rationale, they argue, ignores the underlying truthseeking function of the adversary system and promotes, instead, what Roscoe Pound described as the "sporting theory" of adversary adjudication—i.e., adversary adjudication structured as a sporting battle between two contestants, each given an equal chance of winning as they take the field, with victory rewarded to the side that displays superior skills. As Pound and others have argued, that is not the objective of the adversary trial, and that should not be the perspective from which the criminal justice process is judged. The defense should be given adequate resources to develop the facts favorable to the defendant, but the prosecution should not be subject to special burdens because of its capacity to uncover and present incriminating facts.

While courts tend to view the adversary process solely as a structure designed to produce accurate verdicts, commentators often stress other values of adversarial adjudication. One such alternative justification values the adversary system for what it says about the status of the defendant as an individual. Consistent with the premise that the individual is the source of the government's sovereignty, the adversary system treats the defendant as an equal to the prosecution. The adversary system also respects individual autonomy in its commitment to the individual's self-control over the basic mode of his participation in the adjudicatory process. The defendant may play an active role in his own defense. Indeed, if he so desires, he may decide to forego his defense and plead guilty. The adversary system recognizes, as the Supreme Court has noted, the "inestimable worth of free choices." This, in turn, is said to increase the defendant's level of confidence in the process and acceptance of even adverse results.

(d) Accusatorial Burdens. The American criminal justice process is designed to be accusatorial as well as adversarial. The concepts of adversarial adjudication and accusatorial procedure complement each other, but are not virtual equivalents. The adversarial element assigns to the participants the responsibility for developing the legal and factual issues of the case, while the accusatorial element allocates burdens as between the parties with respect to the adjudication of guilt. An accusatorial procedure requires the government to bear the burden of establishing the guilt of the accused, as opposed to requiring the accused to bear the burden of establishing his innocence. As the Supreme Court has noted, an accusatorial system requires the "government in its contest with the individual to shoulder the entire load." The prosecution must produce sufficient evidence to convince the trier of fact of the accused's guilt, and it must do so "by evidence independently and freely secured," without compelling the accused to assist in this prosecution responsibility.

England's adoption of an accusatorial system probably grew out of the early English view of the criminal prosecution as a means of providing personal redress, with the person claiming to be the victim of a crime having personally to establish his right to redress. The accusatorial system is justified today, however, on grounds consistent with the subsequent recognition of crimes as public wrongs, with prosecutions brought by the state on behalf of the community as a whole. Foremost among these grounds is the position that criminal sanctions are so severe that extra care must be taken to ensure they are not imposed upon innocent persons. Also involved is a distrust of governmental authority, based on a recognition that public officials may seek to invoke the criminal justice machinery to serve their own ends, rather than to protect the public. Some argue that the accusatorial process also seeks to respond to a governmental capacity to gather and preserve evidence that far exceeds the capacity of the defense.

The accusatorial character of the criminal justice process is reflected in various elements of the process. The most significant of those elements are the placement upon the government of the ultimate burden of persuasion, the placement upon the government of the burden of going forward with the introduction of evidence, the presumption of innocence, and the defendant's privilege against self-incrimination. However, as with other basic themes reflected in the criminal justice process, the accusatorial mode of shifting burdens to the state is subject to limitations. Thus, American jurisdictions commonly impose upon the defense, rather than the prosecution, the burden of initially introducing evidence of "affirmative defenses" (basically defenses that will relieve the defendant of liability even though the basic elements of the crime are established). Many jurisdictions go further and also place on the defendant the ultimate burden of persuasion as to such defenses. Similarly, the defendant may bear the burden of establishing that he is incompetent to stand trial or that evidence was obtained in an illegal manner and therefore is inadmissible.

Although an important element of an accusatorial process, the principle that the state establish its case independently, without requiring the accused to assist it, is confined largely to the historical prohibition against the state's use of coercion to prove its charge against an accused "out of his own mouth," (a prohibition reflected, in part, in the privilege against compelled self-incrimination). The accusatorial process does not prevent the state from offering the accused an opportunity to relieve the state of its burden by entering a guilty plea, from offering concessions in return for such a plea, and even from using certain types of deception or encouragement to obtain a confession that will be its primary evidence of guilt. Nor does it bar using the accused's person in obtaining identification evidence or taking evidence from the possession of the accused by search and seizure. Although all of these investigative procedures involve, to some extent, the assistance of the accused, they have been accepted as consistent with the basic tenets of an accusatorial process.

(e) Minimizing Erroneous Convictions. While the accusatory and adversary elements of the criminal justice process are designed in part to minimize the likelihood of erroneous convictions, protection of the innocent accused against an erroneous conviction is an important independent goal of the process. Indeed, many argue that it is the goal given the highest priority. Where a conflict exists between protecting the innocent and other cornerstone objectives, it is the protection of the innocent that almost always prevails.

Although the goal of minimizing erroneous convictions is closely tied to the truthfinding function of the process, it extends substantially beyond that function. Reliable factfinding, as a goal in itself, would seek to ensure equally the accuracy of both guilty verdicts and acquittals. Protection of the innocent, however, gives priority to the accuracy of the guilty verdict. It reflects a desire to minimize the chance of convicting an innocent person even at the price of increasing the chance that a guilty person may escape conviction. Accordingly, while the Supreme Court has stated that "the basic purpose of the trial is the determination of the truth," it also has noted that impairment of the trial's "truthfinding function" is of primary concern where "serious questions [are raised] about the accuracy of guilty verdicts." For, as the Court also has observed, it is "a fundamental value determination of our system * * * that it is far worse to convict an innocent person than let a guilty man go free."

The goal of minimizing the risk of erroneous conviction is served by two somewhat different types of legal standards. Initially, it is advanced by the various rules designed to ensure factfinding accuracy. Most of these rules apply in an even-handed fashion. Thus, rules excluding certain types of evidence because they are unreliable or likely to be given too much weight by the jury commonly apply to both prosecution and defense. So too, both sides can challenge prejudiced jurors or judges. Other standards relating to factfinding accuracy, however, are aimed specifically at protecting the innocent accused. Thus, the adversarial system is modified to impose an obligation upon the prosecution to disclose material exculpatory evidence that is within its possession or control. Similarly, the defendant's right to a face-to-face confrontation with opposing witnesses rests, in part, on the premise that such a confrontation will "reduc[e] the risk that a witness will wrongfully implicate an innocent person." Protection of innocence also underlies special rules that give the defendant greater protection in testifying than is given to other witnesses.

Protection against erroneous convictions also is provided by legal standards that accord to the defendant the benefit of doubt as to his guilt. The most substantial protection of this type is provided by the requirement that the state establish guilt by proof beyond a reasonable doubt. The Supreme Court has described the reasonable doubt standard as the "prime instrument [in the "American scheme of criminal procedure"] for reducing risk of convictions resting on factual error" and has characterized its "stringency" as operating to "impose almost the entire risk of error" upon the state. The defendant is given the benefit of doubt in a somewhat less direct fashion by other legal standards. Thus, the double jeopardy bar gives absolute finality to an acquittal even where it appears to be based on error.

Like other cornerstone goals of the criminal justice process, protecting against the possible erroneous conviction of an innocent accused has its limits. The prosecution's burden of persuasion is set at proof beyond a reasonable doubt, not at a higher standard that requires absolute certainty in the mind of the jurors. Moreover, that burden, in many jurisdictions, will not apply to some defenses or mitigating factors that do not directly contradict the elements of the offense. Similarly, while eyewitness identification poses a recognized risk of mistake, convictions based upon such identifications are acceptable, subject to limited restraints. So too, though recognizing that confessions can be the product of false self-condemnation, the process permits evidentiary use of confessions, subject to constitutional safeguards.

(f) Minimizing the Burdens of Accusation and Litigation. Even if eventually acquitted, an innocent person charged with a crime suffers substantial burdens. The accusation casts a doubt on the person's reputation that is not easily erased. Moreover, even should an acquittal be accepted by the public as fully vindicating the accused, that does not respond to other burdens borne by a defendant in the course of gaining that acquittal. Unless the defendant is indigent, one such burden will be the financing of his defense, as an acquitted defendant is not thereby entitled to reimbursement of his expenses. Perhaps more significant are costs that cannot quite so readily be measured in dollars. Once accused, a defendant must await trial, and this waiting period brings with it a certain degree of anxiety and insecurity that disrupts the daily flow of life. That disruption is even greater, of course, if the accused is incarcerated pending trial. When the trial finally comes, the ordeal of litigation takes a further emotional toll.

In light of these substantial burdens, a criminal justice process concerned with the protection of the innocent cannot limit itself to ensuring against erroneous convictions. It must seek also to reduce to an acceptable level the risk that accusations will be brought against innocent persons. Because the burdens of an erroneous accusation are not as great as the burdens of an erroneous conviction, the acceptable degree of risk here can be somewhat greater. It is not necessary to limit accusations to cases thought likely beyond a reasonable doubt to produce a conviction, as that would cause the state to forego accusations in many cases in which valid convictions might eventually be obtained. Adequate protection against erroneous accusations does require, however, that accusations at least be supported by sufficient evidence to produce a substantial likelihood of conviction.

Of course, in limiting the number of erroneous accusations, the system does not solve the problem of the accused who is appropriately charged, based on substantial evidence, but is eventually acquitted at trial (and therefore must be viewed as quite possibly innocent). Some defendants inevitably will fall in this category. No matter how careful the screening, predicting the outcome of litigation is too uncertain to avoid mistakes. While the system cannot avoid imposing some substantial litigation burdens on properly accused defendants who will eventually be acquitted, it can seek to minimize their burdens, insofar as that can be achieved while preserving a practicable system of adjudication. Since, however, the defendants who will fall in this category cannot be identified at the outset, to minimize their burdens, the system must minimize litigation burdens for all defendants, including the many who will eventually be found guilty.

The goal of minimizing the risk of erroneous accusations is advanced primarily through the various screening procedures of the criminal justice process. Initially, the police officer is prohibited from taking a person into custody for the purpose of charging him with a crime (i.e., arresting the person) without probable cause to believe he is guilty. Moreover, the officer's probable cause determination is subject to ex parte screening by a magistrate, either in the issuance of a warrant prior to arrest or in the subsequent review of a warrantless arrest. In most jurisdictions, felony charges are subject to further review by the

magistrate at a preliminary hearing, an adversary screening procedure. In many jurisdictions, as an alternative or additional felony screening procedure, the grand jury will review the prosecution's evidence to determine whether it is sufficient to justify the proposed indictment.

The complementary goal of eliminating unnecessary litigation burdens is reflected in various other rights of the accused. Provisions for pretrial release on bail seek to avoid pretrial incarceration where there is an alternative means of reasonably assuring defendant's presence at trial. The defendant's right to a speedy trial is designed, in part, to limit the length of pretrial incarceration (where bail is not available) and to "minimize the anxiety and concern" of the accused pending trial. Venue requirements seek, in part, to ensure that the defendant will be tried in a convenient forum. The double jeopardy prohibition, supplemented by joinder requirements, also seeks to reduce the burdens of litigation by restricting the use of multiple trials for closely related charges.

(g) Providing Lay Participation. Another cornerstone of the American criminal justice process is the use of lay persons as decisionmakers. Traditionally, lay participation was provided through the trial jury, the grand jury, and the use of lay magistrates. Today, the trial jury stands alone as the only universally available source of lay participation. While a majority of the states continue to have some lay magistrates in their judiciaries, the vast bulk of the criminal cases in those states come before those magistrates who are lawyers. As for the grand jury, only 18 states continue to require grand jury participation (through a defense right to prosecution by indictment) for all felony cases.

Of course, the trial jury, in fact, also is not used in most criminal cases. Dismissals and guilty pleas account for far more dispositions than trials, and even as to trials, a fair number are bench trials upon election of the defendant. The defendant does have a *right* to a jury trial, however, in all jurisdictions on felony and serious misdemeanor charges, and in most states, the prosecution has an independent right also to insist upon a jury trial. Since many of the safeguards provided by lay juror participation are aimed at the exceptional case, the very availability of the jury at the election of the defendant, rather than the frequency of its use, is the critical feature in meeting most of the objectives of lay participation.

Lay juror participation in the criminal justice process is designed to serve several distinct functions, but those functions all reflect, to some extent, a single underlying value judgment—that the administration of the criminal justice process is too important to be left exclusively in the hands of government officials. Initially, lay jurors have an independence from the government bureaucracy not found in judges or prosecutors. Secondly, jurors offer advantages that stem from their representation of the community. Their position as community representatives lends a special sense of legitimacy to the criminal justice process, making unpopular decisions more readily acceptable to the public. Their reflection of the community viewpoint permits the process to "bring to bear local conceptions of justice" and to adjust the "crude substantive criminal law to the circumstances of individual cases." Indeed, jurors may refuse to convict (or charge, in the case of the grand jury) where they conclude that, notwithstanding a proven violation, enforcement of the letter of the law would result in a miscarriage of justice.

Finally, the vesting of decisionmaking authority in lay jurors, is viewed as strengthening the factfinding capacity of the process. The jurors' "very inexperience is an asset because it secures a fresh perception of each trial, avoiding the stereotypes said to infect the judicial eye." Their selection from a cross-section of the community is said to give them greater expertise in evaluating testimony, as they are likely to be closer to the varied experiences of those testifying. That same diversity also enhances their ability to bring to their task the "common sense judgments" of everyday citizens.

(h) Respecting the Dignity of the Individual. Perhaps the most sweeping cornerstone objective, as measured by the range of its ramifications, is the object of ensuring that criminal justice administration is consistent with respect for the dignity of the individual. The concept of human dignity, as used in this context, is far from precise, but it may be described roughly as encompassing the basic needs of the human personality, including privacy, autonomy, and freedom from humiliation and abuse.

Requiring that criminal justice practices respect human dignity is justified on several grounds. First, it is argued that all persons, including criminals, are entitled to governmental respect for their dignity as an inherent element of the social compact which provides the foundation for a democratic society. Second, in light of the combination of the "severity of the sanctions administered by the criminal law," the "status-degrading potency of criminal proceedings," and the "community outrage" that tempts officials to solve crime at all costs, the preservation of human dignity in the administration of the criminal law is characterized as the *sine qua non* for maintaining a society that respects individual liberty. Finally, ensuring respect for individual dignity is viewed as essential in obtaining public acceptance of the process and in promoting respect for the law it enforces.

The insistence upon respect for individual dignity is reflected in numerous elements of the criminal justice process. Many of the legal standards that implement other goals serve this objective as well. Thus, requirements promoting an adversary system of adjudication also take cognizance of individual dignity by giving the defendant an element of control over his own defense. Similarly, the privilege against self-incrimination, while an essential element of an accusatorial system, has also been described by the Supreme Court as based on "our respect for the inviolability of the human personality."

Still other legal requirements focus entirely on ensuring respect for human dignity. The prohibition against cruel and unusual punishment bars punishments which lower the honor and dignity of the individual. Insofar as the double jeopardy prohibition looks to granting the convicted defendant a sense of repose (and not simply to protecting the possibly innocent accused), as when it gives finality to a conviction (at the defendant's option), that prohibition also focuses on the limits of the oppression to which the guilty can be subjected. The Fourth Amendment prohibition against unreasonable searches and seizures guarantees respect for another aspect of human dignity, the privacy of the individual, although it does permit government officials to invade that privacy upon a demonstration of sufficient need and grounding. Numerous common law standards, such as that bestowing privileged status upon marital communications, also recognize the essential needs of the human personality.

Legal restrictions aimed at ensuring respect for individual dignity, perhaps more so than standards serving any of the other cornerstone objectives, tend to be truth-deflecting. Typically, such restrictions prevent the prosecution from obtaining probative evidence that could point toward guilt. The consequence of that loss is often unclear. Since the evidence is not obtained, one cannot be certain what would have been discovered and whether that discovery would have led to the conviction of a guilty person who otherwise escaped conviction, In some instances, however, the loss of a conviction as it relates to a specific guilty individual is crystallized; a dignity-promoting legal restriction is violated, incriminating evidence is discovered, and the courts deny its use, resulting in the prosecution's inability to convict a person whose guilt is clearly established by the excluded evidence. In disallowing the use of such incriminating evidence, the criminal justice process is treating the criminal prosecution itself as the appropriate forum for enforcing prohibitions respecting individual dignity. Exclusion of the evidentiary fruits of the violation of the prohibitions is employed as a means of remedying the past violation or deterring future violations.

(i) Maintaining the Appearance of Fairness. The criminal justice process seeks not only to provide fair procedures, but also to maintain the appearance of fairness in the application of those procedures. As the Supreme Court has noted, "justice must satisfy the appearance of justice." That the criminal justice procedures are fair, in fact, is not sufficient; the procedures also must be perceived as fair (and as fairly administered) by both the public and the participants.

The appearance of fairness is deemed essential to the effectiveness of process. Initially, it is vital to maintain public confidence in the process. Because three of the primary administrators of the process—judge, prosecutor, and defense counsel—are all members of the same profession, those outside the profession may tend to view the process with some suspicion. Such suspicion can be offset by ensuring that the application of the process is open to public view and that the groundings for its decisions are part of the public record. These same factors also may be helpful in reconciling the losing defendant to his fate. Even though he may disagree with the result, he knows who made the decision and how it was achieved. Finally, the appearance of fairness, as it relates particularly to the trial stage, is necessary to fulfill what commentators have characterized as the "symbolic function" of the trial.

Legal requirements aimed primarily at maintaining a positive perception of the criminal justice process include a variety of laws guaranteeing the openness of the process. They also include various laws prohibiting practices that suggest possible bias. Here, legal standards rely on the mere possibility of prejudice (rather than proof of actual prejudice) to grant relief. One such standard, for example, requires automatic reversal of a conviction where a judge had a possible financial or personal interest in his rulings, without inquiry as to whether that interest actually produced a biased decision. At times, the process' interest in ensuring an appearance of fairness will prevail even over the defendant's desire to forego a particular procedural right. Thus, some jurisdictions insist that the defendant be present at trial even though he would prefer to be tried in absentia, with only his lawyer present.

(j) Achieving Equality in the Application of the Process. In a society dedicated to achieving "equal justice under law," it is only natural that another goal of the criminal justice process is to achieve equality in the administration of the process. The primary concern here is that each jurisdiction be even-handed in its treatment of persons subjected to the process. This does not mean that procedures must be applied in the same way to all persons with the same criminal justice status (e.g., all suspects, all arrestees, or all defendants), but simply that like persons must be treated alike. In other words, distinctions drawn between persons with the same status must be based on grounds that are properly related to the functions of the process.

What constitutes a proper basis for disparate treatment of persons will vary with what is being decided. In determining whether to press charges, for example, a prosecutor could rationally draw distinctions based on a variety of factors (such as differences in the past criminal records of otherwise similar arrestees) that would have no rational bearing on a determination as to which defendants will receive six-person rather than twelve-person juries. Because the function of the particular procedural step plays such an important role in determining what is relevant, the process grants far more room for disparity in some procedures than in others. Where the function renders relevant a broad range of factors, making highly likely variation from one case to another, the process tends to allow the decisionmaker extensive discretion. On the other hand, where the narrow function of the procedural step presumably should result in fairly uniform treatment for all, the decisionmaker's authority to draw distinctions tends to be narrowly prescribed.

(k) Addressing the Concerns of the Victim. The shaping of the criminal justice process to address the concerns of the victim of the crime is a comparatively recent development. Yet system changes instituted with this objective in mind have been so widespread and have impacted so many different aspects of the process that addressing the concerns of victims can readily be characterized today as a cornerstone objective of the process. The federal criminal justice system and almost every state system is governed by some form of "victims' rights" legislation, and over half of the states have adopted victims' rights amendments to their constitutions. These provisions clearly do not respond to all concerns victims are likely to have. As with other cornerstone objectives, conflicting objectives will sometimes prevail. The victims' rights provisions do reflect, however, a widespread recognition that the interests of the victim may stand apart from the interests of the community (as represented by the prosecution) and that these separate interests should at least be addressed in shaping the process.

The victim is now recognized to be not simply a source of evidence, but an interested third party whose concerns must be considered (though not necessarily vindicated) by police, prosecutor, and judge. Almost every jurisdiction now has a body of at least several different laws aimed at ensuring that the jurisdiction's criminal justice process addresses the concerns of the victims of crime. These laws are far too diverse to be neatly categorized, but most of them can be characterized as seeking to achieve one or more of six objectives: (1) making the victim whole economically, (2) developing administrative sensitivity to the plight of the victim, (3) respecting the victim's privacy, (4) providing protection against potential defendant intimidation of the victim, (5) reducing the burdens borne by victims who are willing to assist in the prosecution, and (6) giving victims a participatory role in various enforcement decisions (typically, as in the case of victim impact statements at sentencing, by providing for a victim input, which is not binding on the decisionmaker).

§ 1.5 The Laws Regulating the Process

(a) Varied Sources. In each jurisdiction, the law governing the criminal justice process will come from several different sources. For cases in the federal system, those sources are: (1) the United States Constitution; (2) federal statutes; (3) the Federal Rules of Criminal Procedure; (4) local district court rules; (5) rulings of federal courts based on their common law decisional authority or their supervisory authority over the administration of criminal justice in the federal courts (as contrasted to rulings interpreting the Constitution, statutes, or court rules); and (6) the internal regulations of the Department of Justice and other agencies involved in the administration of the federal criminal justice process. At the state level, an even larger group of sources come into play. The legal standards applicable to the process in a state typically will come from nine different sources: (1) the United States Constitution; (2) federal statutes; (3) the state's constitution; (4) the state's statutes; (5) the state's general court rules; (6) local court rules; (7) rulings of the state's courts based on their common law authority or their supervisory authority; (8) the internal administrative standards of those state and local agencies involved in the administration of the process; and (9) local ordinances. The subsections that follow discuss the general character of each of the different sources, using the larger group of sources applicable to a state system.

(b) The Federal Constitution. The natural starting point in examining the law governing a particular procedure is the federal constitution. Under Article VI, the mandates of the federal constitution are the "Supreme Law of the Land." Thus, those mandates prevail over conflicting federal law from other sources (e.g., federal statutes), and where the constitutional mandates apply to the state system, they prevail over conflicting state law as well. For some steps in the process, such as the preliminary hearing, the Constitution, as interpreted by the Supreme Court, says very little, and legal regulation comes primarily from other sources. Even where the Constitution regulates extensively, however, as in the area of searches and seizures, other sources usually will play some role in regulating the subject. Constitutional regulation rarely is so comprehensive as not to leave some gaps to be filled by other laws. Also, other sources may play a primary role even where the Constitution regulates comprehensively, if those sources impose a more rigorous requirement than is constitutionally mandated. While Article VI prohibits a jurisdiction from authorizing a practice prohibited by the federal constitution, the jurisdiction remains free to add its own prerequisites or prohibitions above and beyond those mandated by the Constitution.

(c) Federal Statutes. In general, federal statutes regulating criminal procedure apply only to the federal system, and serve the role of local statutory regulation discussed in subsection (e) below. However, a limited body of federal legislation (e.g., the federal wiretap statute) applies to both the state and federal criminal justice systems. Prohibitions and restrictions contained in those statutes prevail over contrary state provisions, and they therefore must be applied by state courts in state prosecutions even though the practices prohibited or restricted would pose no difficulty under state law alone.

(d) State Constitutions. Every state has a series of constitutional provisions that guarantee certain rights of the defendant and limit governmental authority in the administration of the criminal justice process. In large part, these state constitutional provisions cover the same ground as the criminal procedure guarantees in the Bill of Rights of the federal constitution. However, a state court may read its state's constitutional guarantee as imposing a more stringent limitation upon the state government than the corresponding federal guarantee. Also some state guarantees are distinct from any of the guarantees in the federal constitution (e.g., a state constitutional guarantee of a defense right to appeal).

(e) State Statutes. The federal system, the District of Columbia, and each of the states has an extensive group of statutory provisions regulating the criminal justice process. Initially, each jurisdiction has a series of sequentially presented provisions that typically are described as the jurisdiction's "code of criminal procedure." In only about a third of the jurisdictions, however, are these true codifications of the law of criminal procedure. Here, the "code" does set forth the basic governing standards, often accompanied by considerable procedural detail, in a conceptually integrated, comprehensive pattern of regulation. Its coverage reaches almost every step in the process, typically with separate chapters on over twenty separate topics. In contrast, in as many as ten states, the criminal procedure "codes" are little more than a loose conglomeration of criminal procedure statutes, providing spotty coverage on less than half of the subjects typically treated in complete codification. In the remaining jurisdictions, the basic grouping of statutory provisions falls somewhere between the true codes and the loose conglomerations.

(f) General Court Rules. In the federal system, the Federal Rules of Criminal Procedure play a very significant role in the regulation of the criminal process. The provisions of the Federal Rules apply to the process largely from the point of the filing of a complaint through to the final disposition of the case in the district court, and for many of the steps covered, these provisions are the primary governing law. In some instances, the Rules incorporate or build upon constitutional or statutory standards, but in many areas—such as pleading, grand jury secrecy, and motion practice—the Rules deal with subjects largely untouched by constitutional or statutory requirements.

In the District of Columbia and roughly two-thirds of the states, general court rules are similar in their breadth of coverage to the Federal Rules. Indeed, in some of those states, court rules govern subjects, such as speedy trial and bail, as to which legislation dominates in the federal system. In the remaining one-third of the states, the role of court rules is limited, but not necessarily inconsequential. In some, court rules do not apply in any significant way to criminal procedure. In others, however, while the rules relating to criminal procedure fall far short in coverage of the Federal Rules, they still play a significant role in regulating at least a few steps in the process.

Jurisdictions vary considerably in the jurisdictional grounding of their court rules, which may control the relationship of the court rules to conflicting statutes. In the federal system, Supreme Court rulemaking is based on statutory authorization. All federal rules are subject to congressional control, and the rules covering the bulk of the process must be reported to Congress and do not take effect until a specified time period has passed, thereby giving Congress the opportunity to modify or veto prospective rules before they become law. Just under twenty states similarly ground their criminal procedures rules on a delegation of authority from the legislature to the judiciary. In another twenty or so states, however judicial rulemaking has a constitutional grounding, and in many of these states, rules within the scope of constitutional provision (typically covering "practice and procedure"), supersede preexisting inconsistent legislation and cannot be overridden by subsequent legislation.

(g) Local Court Rules. In most jurisdictions, local court rules, adopted by the individual trial court for that court alone, play a limited but sometimes significant role in the governance of criminal procedure. In the federal system, by statute and by Federal Rule 57, federal district courts may adopt local rules that fit within a limited framework. Those rules must fall within the realm of practice and procedure and may not be inconsistent with the provisions regulating the same subject matter in the Federal Rules and in federal statutory law. Moreover, federal courts have stated that, even as to subjects not regulated by statute or Federal Rule, local rules should not undertake to resolve basic issues "relating to important matters [that] require deliberation and factfinding." Even with these limitations, federal local rules manage to impose for various procedures regulations that clearly go beyond the details of administration, such as rules setting the standards for the location of trial within different divisions of the district court, or restrictions on permissible public statements by prosecutor and defense counsel relating to a pending prosecution. Many states utilize local rules in a similar fashion, although others limit such rules to largely "housekeeping" matters.

(h) Common Law Rulings. For over a century, common law rulings were the primary source of the law governing the criminal justice process in the states. However, the introduction of comprehensive codes of criminal procedure, followed by the adoption in many states of extensive court rules, and then by the constitutionalization of the law of criminal procedure, combined to sharply reduce the role of such rulings. Today, for all but a few states, the legal standards governing most aspects of the criminal justice process come from a combination of the federal constitution, the state's own constitution, state statutes, and state court rules (all subject, of course, to judicial interpretation). Nonetheless, the common law and common law rulings remain important, as several key aspects of the process are only lightly governed by constitution, statutes, or court rules. Thus, the law governing such matters as the permissible content of closing statements, and the scope of voir dire, is largely set by common law rulings in most jurisdictions. Moreover as to many subjects typically governed by court rule or statute, a small group of states will still rely heavily on common law decisions of the courts.

Federal courts, unlike their state counterparts, are courts of limited jurisdiction that have not been vested with "open-ended lawmaking powers," and they therefore lack authority to fashion a "general" federal common law covering the total range of substantive common law subjects. Federal courts did recognize from the outset, however, an authority to fashion common law rules of procedure where Congress had not otherwise provided. Still, over the years, they have made less frequent use of that authority in shaping the criminal process than did state courts utilizing their common law authority. In part this came about because the federal courts, for many years, assumed that the lack of federal legislation establishing an independent federal standard indicated a congressional intent that the federal courts conform to the law of the state in which they sat as that law existed when that state was first admitted to statehood. Gradually, Congress turned to framing more federal process standards, giving federal criminal procedure a distinctive character, and the federal courts came to look to federal common law, rather than state law, where no statutory standards were specified. Two major developments, however, subsequently served to reduce sharply federal court references to the common law in their criminal process rulings. In

1946, the Federal Rules of Criminal Procedure came into effect and regulated many areas formerly governed by federal criminal law. At roughly the same time, the Supreme Court recognized a concept of supervisory authority over federal criminal justice which could provide a grounding for judicially imposed procedural requirements fashioned apart from the interpretation of the constitution, statute, or court rule. As discussed below, federal courts have commonly cited this supervisory power in fashioning decisional rules which would be described as common law standards in other jurisdictions.

(i) Supervisory Authority Rulings. In 1943, the Supreme Court, in *McNabb v. United States*[1], first announced its authority to establish decisional rules of criminal procedure in the exercise of "its supervisory authority over the administration of criminal justice in the federal courts." At issue in *McNabb* was the admission of confessions obtained from defendants who allegedly had been detained and interrogated by government agents for two days before being taken before a federal magistrate. The Court viewed the detention as a "flagrant disregard" of a federal statutory requirement that an arrested person promptly be brought before the nearest judicial officer. The Court acknowledged that this federal statute did not itself require exclusion of statements obtained during a detention that violated the statutory command. However, the Court had an obligation, stemming from the obligations of "judicial supervision of the administration of criminal justice in the federal courts," to maintain "civilized standards of procedure and evidence in those courts." That duty mandated exclusion of the confessions, for to allow their use as the grounding of a conviction "would stultify the policy" underlying the prompt presentment statute and make "the courts themselves accomplices in willful disobedience of law." The Court clearly did not base this ruling on the common law development of the rules of evidence. That would have required it to square its ruling with common law precedent, which had focused on the po-

§ 1.5
1. 318 U.S. 332, 63 S.Ct. 608, 87 L.Ed. 819 (1943).

tential untrustworthiness of the individual confession and the possible invasion of some common law privilege of the accused.

The scope of the supervisory authority of the Supreme Court was not clearly defined by *McNabb*. The Court did stress that it was "not concerned with law enforcement practices except insofar as courts themselves became instruments of enforcement." Where the judicial process did become involved, however, *McNabb*'s broad description of the Court's supervisory authority suggested that the Court could shape its own standards of fairness, even apart from situations presenting a statutory violation. That came to pass in a series of later Supreme Court rulings relating to the role of trial courts in regulating the litigation process. The supervisory power was relied upon to establish general procedural standards for such matters as contempt proceedings, jury selection and disqualification, discovery and disclosure, and the permissible scope of cross-examination. The Supreme Court also looked to the supervisory power for *ad hoc* rulings. Without establishing general procedural standards, it ordered new trials under its supervisory power where the circumstances of the particular case indicated that such relief was justified "in the interests of justice."

In many of the Court's supervisory power decisions, the Court's reasoning clearly had constitutional overtones, suggesting that the procedure being required might well be constitutionally mandated. Reliance upon the supervisory power was preferred, however, as it avoided the consequences that would flow from a constitutional ruling. The Court could establish a procedural standard for federal courts without considering the ramifications of a constitutional ruling, which would thereby make that standard applicable also in the more varied settings of state criminal justice processes. Additionally, the non-constitutional grounding left the door open for congressional reshaping or rejection of the standard announced by the Court. Some commentators have suggested that these "strategic advantages" of rulings based on supervisory authori-

ty may have diverted attention from the legitimacy of the grounding for the various uses of the supervisory authority.

United States v. Hasting[2] characterized "the purposes underlying the use of the supervisory powers * * * [as] threefold: to implement a remedy for violation of recognized rights * * *; to preserve judicial integrity by ensuring that a conviction rests on appropriate considerations validly before the jury * * *; and finally, as a remedy designed to deter illegal conduct." Questions have been raised, in particular, as to whether the second of these purposes—the protection of judicial integrity by excluding the influence of "inappropriate" governmental actions—constitutes a legitimate independent grounding for the judicial creation of procedural rights. Reliance upon such a grounding has been challenged as opening the door to the Court's exercise of a "chancellor's foot veto" over the activities of the other branches of government whenever those activities relate to actions taken within the federal judicial system. The Court majority, however, has consistently refused to extend the integrity rationale to that point. Its supervisory ruling have responded only to executive branch actions that either directly violated or substantially undermined principles well established in the law.

Lower courts have extended the judicial integrity grounding to dismiss indictments or exclude evidence based on an action of the prosecutor or police, taken apart from the judicial proceeding, that is viewed as misconduct although not prohibited by statute, court rule, or constitutional provision. In 1992, the Supreme Court, in *United States v. Williams*,[3] rejected one line of such rulings and cast doubt upon the validity in general of using the supervisory authority to create standards for executive branch action occurring outside of the litigation process. At issue in *Williams* was the dismissal of an indictment based upon a prosecutor's failure to present exculpatory evidence before the grand jury. The Court not only rejected use of the supervisory power in this

---

2. 461 U.S. 499, 103 S.Ct. 1974, 76 L.Ed.2d 96 (1983).

3. 504 U.S. 36, 112 S.Ct. 1735, 118 L.Ed.2d 352 (1992), also discussed in § 15.6(b).

fashion, but seemingly limited dismissals of indictments based on prosecutorial presentations before the grand jury to instances of prejudicial violations of independently established legal requirements.

The *Williams* Court initially noted that this was not a case where the supervisory authority was being used "as a means of enforcing or vindicating legally compelled standards of prosecutorial misconduct." There was neither statute, court rule, nor constitutional provision requiring prosecutors to present exculpatory evidence before the grand jury. Here the supervisory power was being used "as a means of prescribing * * * standards of prosecutorial conduct in the first instance." Moreover, it was being used "as a means of establishing standards of prosecutorial conduct" not "before the courts themselves" but before the grand jury. These two characteristics combined basically to tie the hands of the lower court. As the Court put it: "Because the grand jury is an institution separate from the courts over whose functioning the courts do not preside, we think it clear that, as a general matter at least, no such 'supervisory' judicial authority [to prescribe standards] exists."

The precise reach of the *Williams* limitation on supervisory authority remains to be seen. On the one side, the Court's language did not go so far as to bar absolutely all supervisory authority to prescribe misconduct standards even with respect to the grand jury. It initially noted only that, "as a general matter," such authority did not exist. On the other side, the

rationale of the *Williams* opinion could certainly be taken beyond the grand jury setting. It could readily be extended to bar, as a general matter, the judicial creation of misconduct standards for all portions of the process in which the judiciary is not itself directly involved. The same element of institutional independence that characterized the grand jury process would apply as well to other prelitigation elements of the process. It could just as readily serve, for example, to prohibit judicial exercise of the supervisory power to reach activities of the executive branch relating to such matters as investigation and the decision to charge. Here too, a court which prescribes misconduct standards on its own initiative can be said to be dealing with something other than "conduct before the courts themselves," even though it has before it the fruits of that investigative activity or charging decision. So far, the lower federal courts have not read *Williams* so broadly. They see it as largely dealing with the exercise of the supervisory power in relation to grand juries.

Two of the three uses of supervisory authority noted in *Hasting* relate to the fashioning of remedies for violations of recognized rights. A line of Supreme Court rulings have imposed significant limitations on that use of supervisory authority. Two cases, *United States v. Payner*[4] and *Hasting* itself,[5] warned lower courts that, in fashioning supervisory authority remedies for constitutional violations, "they are not free to disregard the limitations the

---

4. 447 U.S. 727, 100 S.Ct. 2439, 65 L.Ed.2d 468 (1980), also discussed in § 9.2 at note 9. *Payner* involved the admissibility of evidence obtained through a violation of the Fourth Amendment rights of a third party, rather than the defendant. Although the Supreme Court had consistently held in its constitutional rulings that the exclusionary rule remedy was not available to the defendant unless his own Fourth Amendment rights were violated, the district court concluded that the deliberate violation taking advantage of that limitation justified exclusion in the exercise of its supervisory power. The Supreme Court, in reversing, responded that "the values assigned to the competing interests [shaping the exclusionary remedy] do not change because a court has elected to analyze the question under the supervisory power instead of the Fourth Amendment." Since the Court's Fourth Amendment rulings had concluded that the "interest in deterring illegal searches does not justify the exclusion of tainted evidence at the instance of a party who was

not the victim of the challenged practice," the lower court's use of the supervisory power "amount[ed] to a substitution of individual judgment for controlling decisions of this Court."

5. United States v. Hasting, supra note 2. In *Hasting*, the court of appeals had utilized its supervisory authority to impose a remedy of automatic reversal in response to continuing prosecutorial disregard of that court's repeated admonitions regarding impermissible prosecutorial comments on the failure of defendants to testify. Earlier Supreme Court rulings had held that the constitutional violation involved in such comments did not constitute per se reversible error, but was subject to a harmless error analysis. The *Hasting* Court held the lower court could not, through the use of the supervisory power, "so lightly and casually ignor[e]" the balance struck in those earlier Supreme Court rulings simply "in order to chastise what the [lower] court viewed as prosecutorial overreaching."

Supreme Court has deliberately placed on constitutional remedies." A third case, *Bank of Nova Scotia v. United States*,[6] held that a federal court may not invoke its supervisory role to craft a remedy inconsistent with limits imposed by a statute or a Federal Rule of Criminal Procedure.

(j) Internal Administrative Standards. All of the major participants in the administration of the criminal process are subject to regulation by what are commonly characterized as "internal administrative standards." These largely are standards of performance imposed by government agencies upon their employees or imposed by licensing bodies upon those acting in a licensed capacity. Thus, prosecutors, police officers, and probation officers are subject to performance standards imposed by the governmental agencies that employ them, and prosecuting attorneys and defense counsel, as lawyers, are subject to the standards of professional responsibility that govern those licensed to practice law. The focus of such standards is not on regulating the criminal justice process as such, but in setting internal standards of performance for the actors.

Without doubt, the most extensive and most prominent set of prosecutorial guidelines are those found in the United States Attorneys' Manual of the Department of Justice. The Manual includes statements of general policy and legal positions, guidelines that enumerate specific factors that should be considered in making a particular decision, and directives mandating that certain procedural steps be taken in certain situations. It covers the whole range of proceedings in which the prosecutor will be involved, including grand jury proceedings, extradition, witness protection, charging under specific statutes, pretrial diversion, plea negotiations, and sentencing. The Manual also specifically notes that the standards set forth there provide "only internal Department of

Justice guidance" and "[do] not create any rights, substantive or procedural, enforceable at law by any party in any manner civil or criminal." A long line of cases have repeatedly upheld this position, and a similar view has been taken in the few state cases to deal with similar internal regulations of local police departments.

Prior to the Supreme Court's ruling in *United States v. Caceres*,[7] some federal lower courts, relying upon their supervisory power, had excluded evidence obtained by the government where the prosecutor or investigative agent had violated an agency policy. The *Caceres* Court ruled against exclusion in an opinion that extended well beyond the facts of the particular violation of agency regulations presented there (a violation of IRS regulations requiring the advance authorization of a Justice Department official, prior to electronic recording by an undercover agent of conversations with a suspected criminal). The Court noted that "regulations governing the conduct of criminal investigations are generally considered desirable," and the courts should not discourage use of such regulations by the rigid application of an exclusionary rule to every regulatory violation. "In the long run", the Court noted, "it is far better to have rules like those contained in the IRS Manual, and to tolerate occasional erroneous administration of the kind displayed by this record, than either to have no rules except those mandated by statute, or to have them framed in a mere precatory form." The *Caceres* opinion did not rule out the possibility that judicial relief might be available where a breach of regulations presented an exceptionally compelling case. Neither did it have before it one of those situations in which the government's failure to comply with its own regulations furnished a grounding for a constitutional violation, either

---

6. 487 U.S. 250, 108 S.Ct. 2369, 101 L.Ed.2d 228 (1988), also discussed in § 15.6(e). The trial court had dismissed the indictment based on prosecutorial misconduct without examining the issue of prejudice, noting that it was using its supervisory authority to "declare [through the dismissal] with unmistakable intention that such conduct * * * will not be tolerated." The Supreme Court held, however, that supervisory authority standards must

be consistent with federal statutes and the Rules of Criminal Procedure. To allow dismissal without considering whether the prosecutorial misconduct could have had a prejudicial impact was "to circumvent the harmless error inquiry prescribed by Federal Rule 52(b)," which directs courts to disregard errors "not affect[ing] substantial rights."

7. 440 U.S. 741, 99 S.Ct. 1465, 59 L.Ed.2d 733 (1979).

because the constitutionality of the governmental action was dependent on adherence to a standard policy or "the individual * * * reasonably relied on agency regulations promulgated for his guidance or benefit and has suffered substantially because of their violation by the agency."

All states have regulations governing the professional responsibility of attorneys, with the vast majority having ethics codes based on the American Bar Association's Model Rules of Professional Responsibility. These ethical regulations are a type of internal regulation. However, unlike the typical guidelines of police agencies or prosecutors' offices, the ethics codes clearly have the status of "law", as they are adopted through court rule as the legal standard for determining when a lawyer will be subject to professional discipline. In large part, courts view disciplinary sanctions as the primary remedy available under that law. Hence, a court that discovers an ethics violation after the fact will not thereby grant relief to a defendant victimized by that violation. Thus, a defendant whose counsel violated the code in a manner adverse to the defendant's interest is not automatically entitled to a new trial, for a code violation does not constitute per se ineffective assistance of counsel. On the other hand, courts do see themselves as having a responsibility to prevent code violations, and will take action during the criminal proceedings to ensure that a violation does not occur. Thus, an attorney will be disqualified if the court finds that the intended representation is prohibited by a code provision on attorney conflicts of interest. So too, courts will issue orders prohibiting prosecutors and defense counsel from making public statements pending trials that would constitute code violations.

(k) Local Ordinances. Local ordinances play a comparatively minor role in the law regulating the criminal justice process. In general, municipal authority bearing upon the process is limited to the regulation of the local police. Even here, the municipality can only regulate in conformity with state law. By and large, ordinances will deal with such administrative matters as the keeping and disclosure of records, the impoundment of vehicles, and the return or other disposition of seized property. Some ordinances, however, may relate directly to investigative practices and enhance police authority. Thus, an ordinance may require that a person stopped under appropriate circumstances bear the responsibility of identifying himself. On the other side, an ordinance may direct local police to avoid utilizing certain authority (e.g., certain investigative practices) except under specified circumstances.

Chapter 2

THE CONSTITUTIONALIZATION
OF CRIMINAL PROCEDURE

Table of Sections

§ 2.1   The Elements of Constitutionalization

During the 1960s, when the Warren Court was rapidly extending the reach of the criminal procedure guarantees of the Bill of Rights,[1] some critics predicted that constitutional regulation of the process eventually would become so extensive as to produce, in effect, a "constitutional code of criminal procedure." That prediction has not materialized, and from today's perspective, it seems most unlikely to materialize in the future. The development of a body of constitutional standards as comprehensive in its coverage and as detailed in its requirements as the typical statutory code of criminal procedure would require substantial modification of current constitutional doctrine. For while many steps in the process have indeed become subject to constitutional standards so extensive and intricate that they rival even the Internal Revenue Code, many other steps are barely touched by constitutional controls. Here, the law of the particular jurisdiction (federal or state) provides such regulation (sometimes extensive and sometimes quite sparse) as is applicable.

The failure of constitutional regulation to completely dominate the criminal justice process should not lead one to depreciate the significance and uniqueness of that regulation. Looking to the totality of the process, constitutional standards combine to constitute what is surely the single most important body of law regulating the process. It also is undisputed that in no other nation has so large and intricate a corpus of law relating to criminal justice emerged from constitutional interpretation.

One need only survey the various provisions of the Constitution to recognize the potential significance of constitutional law in the regulation of the criminal justice process. That was not true, however, of the Constitution as originally adopted. Unlike the constitutions of the original states, the federal constitution did not include a declaration of the rights of the individual. For various reasons, the Federalists considered inclusion of a Bill of Rights to be unnecessary and unwise. Thus, the only restrictions directed specifically to the criminal sanction were those imposed in the course of defining the scope of legislative and judicial authority. Article I, Section 9, included as limitations of congressional power prohibitions against suspending the writ of habeas corpus (with limited exceptions) and against adoption of bills of attainder or ex post facto laws (paralleling the prohibition against state passage of bills of attainder and ex post facto laws in Article I, § 10). Article III, the federal judiciary article, included requirements that the trial of federal crimes be by jury and be held in the state where the crime was committed, and it also specified proof requirements for treason and limitations on the punishment for that offense.

Once the process of obtaining state ratification produced a commitment to add amendments in the nature of a Bill of Rights, it was apparent that the criminal justice process would receive considerable attention in the Constitution as amended. A combination of several factors—including this country's English heritage, misuse of the criminal process against colonial dissidents, and the focus of post-revolutionary political theory upon restraining the growing authority of government where it was the antagonist of the individual—had led to a heavy emphasis upon criminal process rights in bills of rights of state constitutions. The proposed federal Bill of Rights quite naturally drew from those state provisions.

The first ten amendments, although described as a Bill of Rights, are concerned with more than protecting the rights of the individual. They also include provisions that are designed to provide structural safeguards of the retained authority of the state government and the local community. The Ninth and Tenth Amendments clearly reflect that function. Several provisions in the first eight

§ 2.1

1.   See § 2.8(b).

amendments probably fall in the same category (e.g., the Second Amendment), although each might also be characterized as having at least some elements safeguarding individual liberty. However, even if one characterizes all of the guarantees in the first eight amendments as protecting individual rights, it is still the case that a substantial majority of all of the individual rights provisions deal with the criminal justice process. The first eight amendments refer to 27 separate guarantees. Sixteen of those guarantees deal specifically with the criminal justice process. In addition, the due process clause of the Fifth Amendment, though it also has a somewhat broader reach, clearly encompasses the application of criminal sanctions.

Between them, the Fourth, Fifth, Sixth, and Eighth Amendments impose the following broad array of constitutional restrictions:

Fourth Amendment: (1) guarantees the right of the people to be secure against unreasonable searches and seizures and (2) prohibits the issuance of warrants without probable cause and a particular description of the place to be searched and the person or thing to be seized.

Fifth Amendment: (1) prosecution for a capital or otherwise infamous offense shall be upon a presentment or indictment of a grand jury (except for certain military prosecutions); (2) no person shall be twice put in jeopardy for the same offense; (3) no person shall be compelled in a criminal case to be a witness against himself; and (4) no person shall be denied life (capital punishment), liberty (incarceration), or property (fine) without due process of law.

Sixth Amendment: "In all criminal prosecutions" the "accused" is guaranteed: (1) the right to a speedy trial; (2) the right to a public trial; (3) the right to trial by an impartial jury; (4) the right to have that jury be "of the state and district wherein the crime shall have been committed," with that district having been "previously ascertained by law"; (5) the right to be informed of the nature and cause of the accusation against him; (6) the right to be confronted with the witnesses against him; (7) the right to have

compulsory process for obtaining witnesses in his favor; and (8) the right to have the assistance of counsel for his defense.

Eighth Amendment: (1) excessive bail shall not be required; (2) excessive fines shall not be imposed; and (3) cruel and unusual punishment shall not be inflicted.

The inclusion of the above guarantees in the Bill of Rights created a potential for extensive constitutional regulation of the nation's criminal justice processes, but two important doctrinal developments were required before that potential could be realized. First, those guarantees had to be made applicable in large part to state proceedings and not simply to federal criminal proceedings. Roughly 98% of all criminal prosecutions are brought in the state systems. For the Constitution to have a major impact, its major provisions had to be held applicable to the state criminal justice systems. This occurred through the Court's rulings under the Fourteenth Amendment—although it was not until the 1960s, almost 100 years after that Amendment's adoption, that the Court finally concluded that the Amendment made applicable to the states most of those Bill of Rights guarantees relating to criminal procedure.

Extensive constitutional regulation of the criminal justice process was also dependent upon the Supreme Court's adoption of expansive interpretations of the individual guarantees. The Bill of Rights guarantees are not, of course, self-defining. Their impact depends in large part upon choices that must be made in determining their reach. Interpreted narrowly, the guarantees would have a minimal effect on the process; they would govern only a small portion of the total process and impose restrictions of limited significance even as to those areas. Interpreted broadly, and supplemented by requirements designed to secure their implementation, the guarantees could have a significant impact on almost every aspect of the process.

Consider, for example, the Fifth Amendment prohibition which states that "no person * * * shall be compelled in any criminal case to be a witness against himself." Narrowly construed, it would simply bar the prosecution from forcing a defendant to appear as a witness and give incriminating testimony at his own trial. On the other hand, if that prohibition were given an expansive interpretation, it would also have a significant bearing upon the prosecution's use of the defendant to obtain incriminating evidence through such varied aspects of the process as police interrogation, pretrial discovery by the prosecution, and grand jury subpoenas, and upon jury instructions relating to the defendant's refusal to speak at trial or to respond to inquiries in those other parts of the process. That, in fact, is how the Amendment has been interpreted, and its treatment has not been unique among the Bill of Rights criminal procedure guarantees. Over the years, the Supreme Court has tended to favor expansive interpretations of all of those guarantees. This is not to say that its interpretations have necessarily adopted the broadest conceivable readings of individual guarantees, but the readings clearly have been sufficiently broad to give a significant scope to those guarantees.

In this chapter, we will examine in some depth these two crucial developments in the constitutionalization of criminal procedure— the extension of the constitutional guarantees to state proceedings and the adoption of a preference for expansive interpretations of individual guarantees. The first development, discussed in §§ 2.2–2.7, is fairly well completed, but the echoes of the battles that led to its adoption are still heard in disagreements over the role that the "interests of federalism" should play in the formulation of constitutional standards. The second development, discussed in §§ 2.8–2.9, remains the subject of an ongoing debate among the justices, at least as to the relationship of the presumption favoring expansive interpretations to certain guideposts for constitutional interpretation.

§ 2.2 The Fourteenth Amendment and the Extension of the Bill of Rights Guarantees to the States

Prior to adoption of the Fourteenth Amendment in 1868, *Barron v. Baltimore*[1] had firmly established that the Bill of Rights was intend-

ed to constrain only the newly established federal government. Only a few of the provisions in the first eight amendments referred explicitly to actions of the federal government (as in the First Amendment, which states that "Congress shall make no law"). Thus, it was not surprising that some would contend that the rights specified in those provisions lacking such a reference were guaranteed against invasion by both state and federal governments. The petitioner in *Barron* relied on that position, arguing that the Fifth Amendment prohibition against the taking of property without just compensation applied to action of the state that altered his property rights. Rejecting that contention, Chief Justice Marshall noted that the Constitution had been established by the people of the United States "for their own government, and not for the government of the individual State. Each State established a constitution for itself, and in that constitution, provided such limitations and restrictions in the powers of its particular government, as its judgment dictated." In the few instances in which federal constitutional intervention in a state's treatment of its citizens was thought to be necessary, the Constitution had clearly indicated that purpose by explicitly stating that the particular provision applied to the states. Thus, Article I, Section 10 provided that "[n]o State shall * * * pass any Bill of Attainder, ex post facto law, or law impairing the Obligation of Contracts." Marshall reasoned: "Had Congress [which proposed the Amendments] engaged in the extraordinary occupation of improving the constitutions of the several states by affording the people additional protection from the exercise of power by their own governments in matters which concerned themselves alone, they would have declared this purpose in plain and intelligible language."

The framers of the Fourteenth Amendment, the 39th Congress, clearly sought to engage in that "extraordinary occupation" described by Marshall in *Barron*. As in Article I, Section 10, the language of the Amendment clearly evidenced a goal of "affording the people addi-

§ 2.2

1. 32 U.S. (7 Pet.) 243, 8 L.Ed. 672 (1833).

tional protection from the exercise of power by their own governments." What was not so clear was exactly how far Congress intended to go in this regard, particularly in Section One of the Amendment. That section provided:

> All persons born or naturalized in the United States, and subject to the jurisdiction thereof, are citizens of the United States and of the State wherein they reside. No State shall make or enforce any law which shall abridge the privileges or immunities of citizens of the United States; nor shall any State deprive any person of life, liberty, or property, without due process of law; nor deny to any person within its jurisdiction the equal protection of the laws.

The first sentence of Section One obviously was designed to override the ruling in *Dred Scott v. Sanford*.[2] That infamous decision had held that a Negro, because his "ancestors were imported into this country, and sold as slaves," could not become a "citizen" within the meaning of the Constitution. In granting both national and state citizenship to all persons born in the United States, the first sentence of Section One nullified *Dred Scott* and ensured that both the recently freed and previously freed blacks would thereafter be "citizens" under the Constitution.

Once Section One moved beyond the granting of citizenship, its precise objectives became less clear. The second sentence evidenced a purpose of protecting the freed blacks—and others as well—from abuses of state power; but the limitations it sought to impose upon state action were couched in terms—such as "equal protection" and "due process"—that were open to varying interpretations. In the years since the adoption of the Fourteenth Amendment, a substantial part of the Supreme Court's workload has been devoted to defining and redefining those terms. One of the more difficult issues considered in that process has been whether and to what extent the prohibitions of Section One encompass (and therefore make applicable to the states) the guarantees found in the Bill of Rights. Over the years, essentially three different po-

sitions have been advanced within the Court on this issue: (1) the "total incorporation" position, advanced in numerous dissents, but never adopted by the Court majority; (2) the "fundamental fairness" position, consistently supported by a majority prior to the 1960s; and (3) the selective incorporation doctrine that has prevailed as the majority view since the mid–1960s. Not all of the justices supporting each of these positions have agreed as to the precise scope of the particular position, leading some commentators to suggest that as many as five different positions actually have been advanced. For our purposes, however, it is best to focus on the basic division in approach between the three major positions, with the less substantial divisions treated as variants of those positions.

Since the selective incorporation doctrine has clearly won the day, one might ask why we devote two full sections to the "defeated" positions of total incorporation and fundamental fairness. Initially, an understanding of each is needed to fully appreciate the selective incorporation position. The judicial debate between the supporters of the total incorporation and fundamental fairness positions undoubtedly had substantial influence on the much later articulation and eventual adoption of the selective incorporation doctrine. But more significantly, strains of that debate have current vitality. The concerns that were expressed by the judicial proponents of the fundamental fairness position are advanced today, in only slightly altered form, in discussions relating to the need to give consideration to the system variations that exist among different states in fashioning a national standard under a Bill of Rights guarantee that is now incorporated and applicable to the states. So too, as discussed in § 2.6(e), the criticism of the totality-of-the-circumstances approach of the fundamental fairness doctrine reappears today in discussions of the standards to be fashioned under the incorporated guarantees. Also, as will be seen in § 2.7, a basic strand of the fundamental fairness concept remains a viable and frequently used measure for regu-

---

2. 60 U.S. (19 How.) 393, 15 L.Ed. 691 (1857).

lating constitutionally both state and federal criminal procedure under the content of due process that strands apart from the incorporated guarantees.

§ 2.3 Total Incorporation

The total incorporation doctrine maintains that the Fourteenth Amendment incorporates all of the Bill of Rights guarantees, and thereby applies those guarantees to the states with the same content they are given in their application to the federal government. While Justice Douglas once counted ten justices who supported the total incorporation doctrine, others view the correct number as six or seven. The important count, in any event, is the number of justices sitting at one time who supported the position, and that count never rose above four. As a result, total incorporation has always been a minority position. It was an exceptionally influential minority position, however, particularly in its contributions to the Court's eventual adoption of the selective incorporation doctrine.

(a) The Rationale of Total Incorporation. Justices favoring a total incorporation position have offered two different textual groundings for the position. First, they have argued that the privileges and immunities clause of the Fourteenth Amendment (prohibiting any state from making or enforcing a law "which shall abridge the privileges and immunities of citizens of the United States") incorporates and applies to the states the protections of the Bill Rights. Their reasoning is that the Bill of Rights itself establishes these protections as "privileges" of United States citizenship, and the Fourteenth Amendment requires that the states respect those privileges just as the Bill of Rights requires that the federal government respect those privileges. They explain that the generic reference to the "privileges and immunities" was used in the

Fourteenth Amendment, rather than a specific reference to incorporating the Bill of Rights' guarantees, because "privileges and immunities" also encompasses such other rights of federal citizenship as are established by the Constitution or federal legislation. This grounding faces several counter-arguments, including: (1) a literal reading of the "privileges and immunities of citizens of the United States" suggests only such rights as are derived from the citizen's relationship to the federal government, with the privileges and immunities clause simply prohibiting interference with these rights (a position adopted by the Supreme Court[1]); (2) an historical reading of the clause would look to the analogue of Article IV's comity clause (prohibiting states from denying citizens of other states the "privileges and immunities" granted it own citizens), and view the clause's objective as guaranteeing to the newly created citizens of the United States (the former slaves) only those fundamental rights that had been protected by the comity clause, as recognized by Congress in its Civil Rights Act of 1866, which guaranteed such rights, but did not refer to rights of the type noted in the Bill of Rights;[2] (3) if the privileges and immunities encompassed all of the rights recognized in the Bill of Rights, which would include a due process requirement, why was a "due process" clause added to the Fourteenth Amendment; and (4) the privileges and immunities clause, if treated as incorporating the Bill of Rights guarantees, would make such rights available only to citizens, although in the application of the Bill of Rights to the federal government, those guarantees had also been held to protect aliens.

A second textual grounding offered for the total incorporation position is the due process clause of the Fourteenth Amendment. This grounding relies on the assumption that the liberties protected by the due process clause include the freedoms secured by the Bill of

---

§ 2.3

1. See the text at note 6 infra.

2. A major objective of the Fourteenth Amendment arguably was to provide a constitutional grounding for the Civil Rights Act of 1866. That Act declared all persons born in the United States to be citizens and provided that all such citizens, without regard to race, would have "the

same right in every state to contract, sue, and hold and inherit property, and to enjoy the full and equal benefits of all laws and proceedings for the security of person and property" as were enjoyed by "white citizens," Corfield v. Coryell, discussed at note 7 infra, provided the leading pre-Fourteenth Amendment interpretation of privileges and immunities in the context of the comity clause.

Rights and the deprivation of those liberties under circumstances which would be prohibited as to the federal government under the Bill of Rights would also constitute a denial of due process under the Fourteenth Amendment. Some support for this reading of due process is found in a pre-Fourteenth Amendment ruling, *Murray's Lesee v. Hoboken Land & Improvement Co.*,[3] which spoke of first looking to "the Constitution itself" in determining whether a process enacted by Congress is "consistent with due process."[4] However, if it is assumed that the due process clause of the Fourteenth Amendment has the same meaning as the due process clause of the Fifth Amendment, then a total-incorporation interpretation faces two basic difficulties. First, at the time of the adoption of the Fifth Amendment, due process was viewed as a provision governing only procedure, and not substantive rights, while many of the rights include in the Bill of Rights are substantive rather than procedural rights. Second, if due process encompasses all of the rights of the Bill of Rights, why were those rights listed in the Bill of Rights in addition to the Fifth Amendment's due process clause? Similarly, if the drafters of the Fourteenth Amendment desired to make applicable to the states all of the provisions of the Bill of Rights, why did they do so in such an indirect fashion, by making reference to a single provision of the Bill of Rights, even though it might be the most elastic of these provisions?

Justice Black, a strong supporter of the total incorporation position, argued that the position rested on the Fourteenth Amendment "as a whole", with the key being the intent of the framers of the Amendment to overrule *Barron v. Baltimore* and make the Bill of Rights applicable to the states. The appendix to his concurring opinion in *Adamson v. California*[5] reprinted various statements made during the Congressional debates, primarily by Representa-

tative Bingham, a key draftsman, and Senator Howard, who presented the proposed amendment before the Senate, which indicated that the Amendment would render the Bill of Rights applicable to the states. That reading of the Framers' intent was rejected in *Adamson* and later cases, in part because the justices who first rejected a total incorporation reading knew that legislative history as a contemporary event and could put in proper perspective the relative significance of the comments of Bingham and Howard.

(b) Rejection by the Court. Although the total incorporation doctrine was not squarely considered by the Supreme Court until the 1890s, it had already been foredoomed by the earlier ruling in *The Slaughter–House Cases*,[6] the Court's first decision interpreting the Fourteenth Amendment. *Slaughter–House* involved a challenge by a group of butchers to a Louisiana statute granting monopoly rights to a New Orleans slaughterhouse. The butchers argued that the statute violated their right to carry on a trade, recognized in *Corfield v. Coryell*[7] as a privilege and immunity of state citizenship, and therefore was contrary to the privileges and immunities clause of the recently enacted Fourteenth Amendment. In a 5–4 decision, the Court rejected that claim. The majority relied substantially on the phrasing of the Fourteenth Amendment's two references to citizenship. In the first sentence, it was noted, the Amendment refers to both national and state citizenship in the provision granting citizenship to "all persons born or naturalized in the United States, and subject to the jurisdiction thereof." The second sentence, on the other hand, prohibiting state abridgment, speaks only to abridgment of the privileges and immunities of United States citizenship. This indicated that the privileges and immunities of state citizenship, as identified in *Corfield*, were intended to remain

---

3. 59 U.S. (18 How) 272, 15 L.Ed. 372 (1855).

4. See § 2.4 at note 3. That reference however, also may be read as simply applying the "law of the land" mandate of due process, see § 2.4(b), which requires the government to adhere in each case to the previously established law of the jurisdiction. In the federal system, that law clearly would include the Bill of Rights prohibitions.

5. 332 U.S. 46, 67 S.Ct. 1672, 91 L.Ed. 1903 (1947).

6. 83 U.S. (6 Wall.) 36, 21 L.Ed. 394 (1873).

7. 6 Fed. Cas. (No. 3230) 546 (C.C.E.D.Pa.1823) (opinion by Justice Bushrod Washington of the Supreme Court), applying Article IV's comity clause. See note 2 supra.

"with[in] the constitutional and legislative power of the States," subject only to the Article IV's comity requirements. The second sentence of the Fourteenth Amendment sought to protect only the distinct group of privileges and immunities that came out of national citizenship, ensuring that states did not interfere with those rights.

Once the *Slaughter–House* majority limited the protected privileges to those of national citizenship, it followed that the Fourteenth Amendment would not be construed to require the states to recognize the guarantees found in the Bill of Rights. The privileges and immunities of national citizenship were confined, the Court noted, to that class of rights which "owe their existence to the federal government, its National character, its Constitution, or its laws." While the privileges of national citizenship encompassed rights created by the Constitution, those rights, including the rights found in the first eight Amendments, applied only to the citizen's dealings with the federal government. A state's refusal to provide similar rights in its own proceedings had no bearing upon national citizenship since it did not interfere with the citizen's relationship to the federal government. It was only when the state interfered with that relationship that it violated the privileges and immunities clause.

During the early 1890s, three cases involving claims that the state had imposed cruel and unusual punishment squarely presented the total incorporation doctrine. Relying on *Slaughter–House*, the Court reasoned that the privileges and immunities of national citizenship arose out of "the nature and essential character of the national government," and therefore did not encompass an immunity from state imposition of a punishment alleged to be cruel and unusual. In one of the cases, however, three justices dissented, advancing a total incorporation rationale. Although the

cruel and unusual punishment cases might have been thought to have settled the issue, total incorporation was debated again in two cases decided in the early 1900s. Over the dissents of the first Justice Harlan, the Court again reaffirmed the *Slaughter–House* view of the privileges of national citizenship and held that the Fourteenth Amendment did not require state adherence to the Bill of Rights guarantees. In one of those cases, the Court noted that the total incorporation "was undoubtedly entertained by some of those who framed the Amendment" but it was "not profitable to examine the weighty arguments in its favor, for the question is no longer open in this court."

The question was reopened, however, by the dissenting opinions in the 1947 case of *Adamson v. California*.[8] Four dissenters there argued for a total incorporation position, although they divided as to whether the Fourteenth Amendment's due process clause had additional content beyond incorporating the other Bill of Rights guarantees.[9] Thus, almost eighty years after the adoption of the Fourteenth Amendment, the total incorporation position came within one vote of adoption.

The majority opinion in *Adamson* gave only brief attention to the total incorporation doctrine, noting that it was inconsistent with a long line of cases that had prevailed since *Slaughter–House*. However, Justice Frankfurter, in a separate concurring opinion, offered a more extensive response to Justice Black. Although much of Justice Frankfurter's opinion focused on the lack of support for total incorporation in the language and history of the due process clause, he also stressed the practical consequences of total incorporation. Those "sensitive to the relation of the states to the central government as well as the relation of some of the Bill of Rights to the process of justice," could hardly insist upon state compli-

---

8. 332 U.S. 46, 67 S.Ct. 1672, 91 L.Ed. 1903.

9. Justice Black rejected any "fundamental fairness" interpretation of due process which could recognize rights beyond those specified in the Bill of Rights. Aside from incorporating the first eight amendments of the Bill of Rights, the only other content of due process, as he saw it, was to ensure adherence to the "law of the land." See § 2.4(c) The other dissenters accepted the fundamental

fairness interpretation of due process insofar as it encompassed additional rights. They rejected the fundamental fairness position (see § 2.4) only insofar as it refused to view rights identified in the Bill of Rights as per se included within due process. Their position was described by some commentators as "incorporation plus" or "ultra incorporation."

ance with every aspect of the procedure constitutionally imposed upon the federal government. Some of the Bill of Rights requirements, he noted, "are enduring reflections of experience with human nature," but others simply "express the restricted views of Eighteenth Century England regarding the best methods for ascertainment of facts." Surely, he argued, "[t]o suggest that it is inconsistent with a truly free society to begin prosecution without an indictment, to try petty civil cases without the paraphernalia of a common law jury, to take into consideration that one who has full opportunity to make a defense remains silent, is, in de Tocqueville's phrase, to confound the familiar with the necessary."

Without doubt, Justice Frankfurter's illumination of the practical consequences of total incorporation—particularly the imposition of requirements that states prosecute by indictment and provide jury trials in civil cases involving claims above twenty dollars—raised problems for the supporters of total incorporation. Although Justice Black pointed to the ability of the federal justice system to operate under the Bill of Rights, the setting presented by the states arguably was different. For example, the federal government had avoided granting jury trials in minor civil cases by limiting the jurisdiction of federal courts to cases involving substantial monetary claims, but the states could not realistically follow the same approach. To provide jury trials in all cases involving more than twenty dollars might impose an intolerable strain on the already overburdened state courts. When the Court moved to selective incorporation in the 1960s, commentators immediately noted that the selective incorporation doctrine would enable the Court to impose upon the states most of the Bill of Rights guarantees without also including the troublesome grand jury and civil jury trial requirements.

§ 2.4   Fundamental Fairness

Unlike the total incorporation doctrine, the fundamental fairness doctrine rests solely on the due process clause. As applied to criminal procedure, the doctrine has basically two prongs. First, it reads the due process clause as prohibiting state action that violates those rights of the individual that are deemed to be "fundamental." Over the years, the Court variously described the standard for determining whether a right is fundamental. Due process was said to require adherence to those rights that are "implicit in the concept of ordered liberty," that are "so rooted in the traditions and conscience of our people as to be ranked fundamental," and that "lie at the base of all our civil and political institutions." Due process also was described as prohibiting those state actions that "offend those canons of decency and fairness which express the notions of justice of English-speaking peoples even toward those charged with the most heinous offenses," that are "repugnant to the conscience of mankind," or that deprive the defendant of "that fundamental fairness essential to the very concept of justice." Although these different descriptions arguably suggest some subtle variations in content, they generally were viewed as expressing a single standard, frequently described in shorthand form as the "ordered liberty" or "fundamental rights" standard.

The second prong of the fundamental fairness doctrine concerns the relationship between the ordered liberty standard and the guarantees found in the Bill of Rights. Simply put, it maintains that there is no necessary correlation between the protection afforded by the Bill of Rights and due process protection of fundamental rights. The concept of due process has "an independent potency" which exists apart from the Bill of Rights, although in a particular case it may afford protection that parallels a Bill of Rights guarantee. It was this second element of the fundamental fairness doctrine that was eventually rejected by the Court in the 1960s. At that time, after constituting the majority position for almost one hundred years, the second prong of the doctrine was discarded in favor of the selective incorporation position, discussed in §§ 2.5–2.6.

(a) The Rationale of Fundamental Fairness. The fundamental fairness doctrine proceeds from the premise that the Fourteenth Amendment's due process clause was designed to make applicable to the states the same basic limitation that had been imposed upon the federal government under the Fifth Amendment's due process clause. That limitation, however, is viewed as broader in range and more flexible in content than other Bill of Rights limitations. It seeks a very broad objective—to achieve "respect enforced by law for that feeling of just treatment which has evolved through centuries of Anglo–American constitutional history and civilization." Moreover, it pursues that objective by looking to the essence of fairness rather than the historical familiarity of form. Proceeding from a natural law background, it identifies those values, substantive as well as procedural, that can be characterized as "fundamental" under the ordered liberty standard, and then assesses their demands in light of the changing circumstances and goals of modern society.[1]

Viewing due process as a flexible standard that takes account of societal change, the second prong of the fundamental fairness positions finds no necessary correlation between the requirements of due process and the mandates of other Bill of Rights guarantees. As a "standard for judgment in the progressive evolution of the institutions of a free society," due process must have its own independent content. That content may in some instances be parallel to the core of a guarantee found in another Bill of Rights provision, or even encompass the whole of such a guarantee, but fundamental fairness may sometimes be met without adherence to any aspect to a guarantee found in a particular Bill of Rights provision. So too, due process may impose limits beyond those imposed under any of the other Bill of Rights guarantees. Even though a particular practice was historically accepted as consistent with a particular Bill of Rights guarantee, changes in technology or "refinement[s] in our sense of justice" may render it contrary to the ordered liberty standard in its

current setting, and thus a violation of due process.

As discussed in § 2.5, the second prong of the fundamental fairness doctrine was eventually rejected for its failure to encompass a greater portion of the Bill of Rights guarantees. It faced an initial challenge, however, from the other side—in assuming due process could overlap in any respect with those guarantees. Due process was a concept already recognized in the Bill of Rights, but there it stood alongside those other guarantees. If the concept of due process overlapped with those other guarantees, why did the Bill of Rights include those guarantees as well as the due process? In its first consideration of this argument, the Court appeared to find it persuasive. It reasoned that reading the due process clause, whether in the Fourteenth Amendment or the Fifth Amendment, as encompassing rights protected by other Bill of Rights guarantees would be contrary to the "recognized cannon of interpretation" that one of several interrelated provisions should not be read to render the other provisions "superfluous". Subsequently, however, the Court concluded that this cannon was simply "an aid to construction", which had to yield to the historical understanding of due process as encompassing all truly fundamental rights. Because due process was a vague and fluid guarantee, the framers of the Bill of Rights could well have thought it desirable to add the more specific provisions of the other guarantees, even though these guarantees, or some aspects of these guarantees, might also be protected by the Fifth Amendment's due process clause.

The first prong of the fundamental rights doctrine also faced a significant challenge. The concept of "due process" dates back to the "law of the land" clause in Chapter 29 of the Magna Charta, as Lord Coke had declared the two concepts to be one and the same. One reading of Coke suggested that the law of the

---

§ 2.4

1. Although our focus here is on the fundamental fairness standard as it relates to procedure, it must be remembered that the standard also imposes substantive limits upon government. Fundamental fairness is not satisfied simply because a deprivation of life, liberty, or property, no matter how unjust, is achieved through a fair

procedure. The substantive grounding of the deprivation also must be consistent with the ordered liberty standard. This substantive aspect of the fundamental fairness doctrine has most frequently been applied in the contexts of economic regulation and restrictions imposed upon the "rights of personhood and privacy," but it also has had a bearing upon the criminal justice process. See § 2.7(d).

land clause did no more than prohibit the Crown from imposing sanctions upon an individual except by jury verdict or in accord with alternative procedures clearly established in the standing law. The requirement of adherence to the law of the land, under this view, left to the legislature the task of prescribing procedures it deemed appropriate; it only prohibited the government from departing from those procedures once established. Another reading, however, suggested that certain procedures recognized at common law were so fundamental that they could not be altered by the legislature. Neither reading directly supported a fluid concept of due process that could deem fundamental rights not known at common law, but the second reading did suggest a natural law foundation for due process that arguably had led Coke to insist that core common law procedures were not subject to legislative modification.

Prior to the adoption of the Fourteenth Amendment, in *Murray's Lessee v. Hoboken Land and Improvement Co.*,[2] the Court clearly adopted a reading of due process that went beyond the requirement of adherence to the standing law. "It is manifest," the opinion noted, that under the due process clause, "it was not left to the legislative power to enact any process that might be advised." Although the government in the case before it had clearly adhered to a procedure prescribed in preexisting law, that was not sufficient to meet the standard of due process. The procedure utilized also had to be consistent with the key principles of a fair procedure as recognized in the common law. Adherence to the standing law was one element of due process, but that clause also made other demands of process, both civil and criminal.[3]

(b) The Establishment and Initial Application of the Fundamental Fairness Doctrine: From Reconstruction to the 1930s. It was not until the Fourteenth Amendment was adopted, and the due process clause became applicable to the states, that the Court announced the fundamental fairness interpretation of due process. The Court's subsequent applications of that standard in the field of criminal procedure shifted substantially over the years. As a result, the time span during which the doctrine dominated—from its inception at the end of the Reconstruction era to the "replacement" of its second prong by the selective incorporation doctrine in the early 1960s—is often divided into two periods. During the first period, running from the 1880s to the mid–1930s, the Supreme Court's due process rulings were prominent primarily for their imposition of substantive limits on economic regulation. The Court reviewed comparatively few criminal cases, and in most of them, ruled against the defendant's due process claim. Moreover, where that due process claim alleged that the state procedure was inconsistent with a particular aspect of a procedural guarantee found in one of the other provisions of the Bill of Rights, the Court's rejection of the defendant's claim often was not limited to the specific procedure that was at issue. There was a tendency to speak broadly, and to suggest that fundamental fairness did not mandate for the states any aspect of the procedural requisites imposed on the federal system under the particular Bill of Rights guarantee.

The 1884 decision of *Hurtado v. California*[4] was the first major Fourteenth Amendment ruling dealing with the criminal justice process. The petitioner Hurtado had been tried and convicted of murder following the initiation of charges on a prosecutor's information and a determination of probable cause by a magistrate at a preliminary hearing. Hurtado claimed that Fourteenth Amendment due process had been violated by the state's failure to initiate prosecution through an indictment or presentment of a grand jury. He argued that the content of due process looked to the Mag-

---

2. 59 U.S. (18 How.) 272, 15 L.Ed. 372 (1855).

3. Although *Murray's Lessee* also suggested that this additional content was historically frozen by procedures accepted at the common law, that suggestion was rejected in post-Fourteenth Amendment cases. See § 2.4 following notes 4 and 11; § 2.7 at notes 25–28. This opened the door

to the adoption of a flexible fundamental fairness standard.

4. 110 U.S. 516, 4 S.Ct. 111, 28 L.Ed. 232 (1884), also discussed in § 2.3 at note 1.

na Charta's Chapter 29, which had long been viewed as requiring prosecution by indictment or presentment for all felony cases. The net effect of his position would be to impose upon the states under the Fourteenth Amendment's due process clause the same requirement that the Fifth Amendment's indictment clause imposed upon the federal government.

With only Justice Harlan dissenting, the Court flatly rejected Hurtado's claim. Justice Matthews' opinion for the Court initially rejected the contention that due process inherited from the law of the land concept a specific content that was to be found in historic practice. Justice Matthews concluded that neither the writings of Coke nor the ruling in *Murray's Lessee* established such a position. While Coke had referred to various specific procedures, including prosecution by indictment, these were mentioned not as procedures "essential to the idea of due process" but as "illustration[s] of due process of law as it actually existed in cases in which it was customarily used" at the time. So too, *Murray's Lessee* had recognized that historical sanction establishes that a practice is consistent with due process, but it did not hold that such a sanction was essential to comply with due process. The due process clause, Justice Matthews noted, did not lock into the Constitution the particular practices of a particular time. The "Constitution * * * was ordained, it is true, by decedents of Englishmen, who inherited the traditions of English law and history, but it was made for an undefined and expanding future." Accordingly, due process must be read to encompass only those "fundamental principles of liberty and justice which lie at the base of all our civil and political institutions," and judicial determination of its content should look to "the very substance of individual rights" rather than "particular forms of procedure." Like the common law itself, which "dr[ew] its inspiration from every fountain of justice," due process should allow the legislature to take account of "the new and various experiences of our own situation," and looking

to "the best ideas of all systems and ages," to mold basic principles of justice into "new * * * forms."

Justice Matthews noted that determining what specifics met the above principles was best left to " 'the gradual process of judicial inclusion and exclusion, as the cases presented for decision shall require.' " The particular process utilized to prosecute Hurtado clearly imposed no significant difficulties. At issue here was "merely a preliminary proceeding," that "[could] result in no final judgment," except as the "consequence of a regular judicial trial, conducted precisely as in the case of indictments." Moreover, the California procedure, like the indictment process, "carefully considers and guards the substantial interest of the accused." Prosecution by information was allowed only "after examination and commitment by a magistrate, certifying to the probable guilt of the defendant, with the right on his part to the aid of counsel, and to the cross-examination of the witnesses produced for the prosecution"—safeguards not present in the indictment process.

Though the *Hurtado* opinion rejected defendant's grand jury claim, it offered a fundamental fairness analysis that could readily be held to mandate at least some aspect of other Bill of Rights guarantees. The *Chicago Railroad Case,* decided in 1897,[5] did exactly that in holding that due process encompassed a prohibition also found in the Fifth Amendment—the prohibition against the government taking property without providing just compensation. Following *Chicago Railroad,* Supreme Court opinions considered various due process claims based upon procedural safeguards found in specific guarantees of the Bill of Rights. While the Court rejected these claims in all of the pre–1930 cases, it did so solely on the ground that the particular safeguards were not sufficiently fundamental. The two leading decisions in this group were *Maxwell v. Dow*[6] and *Twining v. New Jersey.*[7] In *Maxwell,* the Court, relying on the *Hurtado* analysis, held that due process was not violated by a state's use of an

5. Chicago, Burlington, & Quincy R.R. v. Chicago, 166 U.S. 226, 17 S.Ct. 581, 41 L.Ed. 979 (1897).

6. 176 U.S. 581, 20 S.Ct. 448, 44 L.Ed. 597 (1900).

7. 211 U.S. 78, 29 S.Ct. 14, 53 L.Ed. 97 (1908).

eight person jury, and suggested that due process did not guarantee a jury trial in any form. In *Twining*, the Court held that due process was not violated by a jury instruction allowing an adverse inference to be drawn from the defendant's failure to testify, as the Court concluded that the privilege against self-incrimination was "not an unchangeable principle of universal justice" and therefore was not required by due process.

Although the pre–1930s rulings consistently rejected procedural due process claims tied to safeguards specified in the Bill of Rights, the Court did recognize a few due process claims based upon other types of procedural defects. In each instance the defense stressed the basic unfairness of the state practice rather than any parallel protection in the Bill of Rights. Thus, in *Moore v. Dempsey*,[8] a case involving alleged mob domination of a trial, the Court reasoned that due process was not met where the "whole proceeding is a mask—[where] * * * counsel, jury and judge were swept to the fatal end by an irresistible wave of public passion, and * * * the state courts failed to correct the wrong." The emphasis in *Moore* was on the totality of the circumstances rather than the deprivation of specific safeguards such as an impartial jury or effective assistance of counsel. In *Tumey v. Ohio*,[9] the Court held that due process was violated where the trial judge was compensated by fees received only when the defendant was found guilty. The Court had no difficulty in concluding that a disinterested judge was an essential element of due process, though that safeguard was not mentioned in any of the specific guarantees of the Bill of Rights. These decisions proved to have the greatest long run significance as they established a "free standing" content for due process (i.e., content apart from safeguards specified in other Bill of Rights provisions) that gave the clause continued independent significance (as discussed in § 2.7) even after the Court in the 1960s moved to a selective incorporation doctrine that rendered almost all of those specific Bill of Rights guarantees applicable to the states.

(c) Application of Fundamental Fairness: From the Mid–1930s to the Early 1960s. During the second period in the dominance of the fundamental fairness doctrine, the Court continued, as it had in *Tumey* and *Moore,* to recognize due process claims based on procedural interests that stood apart from the specifics of the Bill of Rights guarantees. In large part, those rulings struck down practices that directly threatened the accuracy of the fact-finding process, such as a prosecutor's knowing reliance on perjured testimony. The major shift in approach during this period was in the Court's treatment of due process claims that looked to procedural rights included in the specifics of the Bill of Rights. Here, the Court was far more willing to find that due process encompassed certain aspects of those Bill of Rights guarantees. The Court moved away from judging the fundamental character of a particular procedure in the abstract, but looked instead to its application in the factual setting of the individual case. Where a defendant contended that a state had denied him due process by failing to recognize a right that would have been protected by the Bill of Rights as to the federal government, the focus was not on the general character of that right, but the particular aspect involved in this case and its impact upon the case.

Apply this circumstance-oriented analysis, due process was held to include many of the same basic principles as the Bill of Rights guarantees, although the due process limitations flowing from those principles generally were also assumed to be narrower in scope that those imposed upon the Federal government under the Bill of Rights guarantees. Thus, as discussed in § 11.1(a), the Court during this period held that due process required that the state provide the indigent defendant with the assistance of court appointed counsel, but only where such assistance was necessary to provide a fair hearing. Unlike the Sixth Amendment, fundamental fairness did not require appointment in all felony cases, but it did require appointment in all capital cases and in those non-capital cases

---

8. 261 U.S. 86, 43 S.Ct. 265, 67 L.Ed. 543 (1923).

9. 273 U.S. 510, 47 S.Ct. 437, 71 L.Ed. 749 (1927).

where the circumstances of the case indicated the defendant could not adequately represent himself. The Court similarly suggested that due process generally prohibited searches that would be deemed unreasonable under the Fourth Amendment, but it would require exclusion of evidence obtained from that violation only in the most exceptional cases. So too, in holding that due process did not bar a practice that would have been prohibited by a Bill of Rights provision, the Court often left open the possibility that other practices violating more essential elements of that Bill of Rights provision would violate due process and be prohibited in state as well as federal criminal proceedings.[10]

By the late 1950s the Court had indicated, either by holding, dictum, or implication, that due process included elements of most of the criminal process guarantees found in the Bill of Rights. The ordered liberty standard could be said to encompass at least one aspect of each of the following guarantees: the Fourth Amendment prohibition against unreasonable searches, the Fifth Amendment double jeopardy bar, the Fifth Amendment privilege against self-incrimination, the Sixth Amendment right to a public trial, the Sixth Amendment right to notice, the Sixth Amendment right to confrontation of opposing witnesses, the Sixth Amendment right to the assistance of counsel, and the Eighth Amendment prohibition against cruel and unusual punishment. The Court had also held, however, that ordered liberty did not encompass various other aspects of these same guarantees, and it did not require prosecution by indictment, as mandated by the Fifth Amendment, under any circumstances. Although the Court's "partly-in and partly-out" treatment of most of the criminal procedure guarantees followed logically from traditional

fundamental fairness analysis, other Bill of Rights guarantees found to be fundamental were treated differently. In holding that due process afforded protection against both the taking of property without just compensation and the abridgment of the freedoms of speech, press, and religion, the Court had indicated that these protections were equal in scope to their counterparts in the Fifth and First Amendments.

The second period in the dominance of the fundamental fairness doctrine was also marked by another shift in approach, less sweeping than the movement to encompass parts of Bill of Rights guarantees, but still of analytical significance. Though viewing *Murray's* reference to historical acceptance as not meant to lock historical practice into the requirements of due process, *Hurtado* appeared to accept the proposition that a practice sanctioned by historical practice was thereby necessarily consistent with due process. However, during the second period of fundamental fairness' dominance, the Court placed greater emphasis on what it considered to be the logical implications of basic principles of fairness, discounting historical acceptance when it was contrary to that logical deduction. Thus, *Powell v. Alabama*[11] held that due process required appointment of counsel at the state's expense as necessary to provide a fair hearing though English and colonial practice did not impose such an obligation on the state. So too, other rulings found due process violations based on the application of general principles of justice without ever turning to the possibility of historical sanction of the practice in question. Historical pedigree clearly was no longer an automatic answer to a due process challenge, and the flexibility of due process now accommodated both the acceptance of a procedure

---

10. Palko v. Connecticut, 302 U.S. 319, 58 S.Ct. 149, 82 L.Ed. 288 (1937), is illustrative. In that case, defendant challenged a Connecticut statute which permitted the state to appeal defendant's initial acquittal, gain reversal on the basis of a trial court error, and then retry the defendant on the same charge. The Court assumed that a similar federal practice would violate the double jeopardy prohibition of the Fifth Amendment. It noted, however, that the decisive issue under the due process clause was more narrowly framed. The question to be asked was: "Is that kind of double jeopardy to which the statute has

subjected * * * [defendant] a hardship so acute and shocking that our policy will not endure it?" The answer here was "No," but the Court added that the answer might be otherwise "if the state were permitted after a trial free from error to try the accused over again." The state here, it noted, was not "attempting to wear the accused out by a multitude of cases with accumulated trials," but simply seeking to obtain a single trial "free from the corrosion of substantial legal error."

11. See § 11.1 at note 1.

that departed from historical tradition (as in *Hurtado*) and the rejection of a procedure that found a counterpart in that tradition (as in *Powell*). A fundamental fairness standard long criticized as unduly vague had become even more uncertain in its application.

(d) Subjectivity and Fundamental Fairness. In *Adamson v. California*,[12] Justice Black, in the course of urging adoption of total incorporation, launched a vigorous attack against the alleged subjectivity of the fundamental fairness doctrine. Although Justice Black could not convince a majority of the Court to adopt his position on total incorporation, his criticism of the fundamental fairness doctrine contributed substantially to the development and eventual adoption of the selective incorporation position. Justice Black contended that the fundamental fairness doctrine permitted the Court to "substitut[e] its own concepts of decency and fundamental justice for the language of the Bill of Rights." Application of the fundamental fairness concept, he noted, "depended entirely on the particular judge's idea of ethics and morals" rather than upon "boundaries fixed by the written words of the Constitution." Although Justice Black thought that many fundamental fairness rulings reflected this basically idiosyncratic approach to adjudication, perhaps his prime examples were the decisions in *Rochin v. California*,[13] and *Irvine v. California*.[14]

In *Rochin,* the police, having "some information" that defendant was selling narcotics, entered his home without a warrant and forced open the door to his bedroom. When the surprised defendant immediately shoved into his mouth two capsules believed to be narcotics, the police grabbed him and attempted to extract the capsules, which defendant then swallowed. The police then took the protesting defendant to a doctor, who forced an emetic solution into defendant's stomach, causing him to vomit up the capsules. Describing the total course of police action as "conduct that shocks the conscience," the Court held that due process no more permitted the use of the capsules in evidence than it would a coerced confession. "Due process," the Court added, was a principle that "precludes defining * * * more precisely than to say that convictions cannot be brought about by methods that 'offend a sense of justice.' "

In *Irvine,* the plurality described the police action as flagrant and deliberate misconduct, but held that it was not so offensive as to violate due process. The police in *Irvine* had made repeated illegal entries into defendant's home for the purpose of installing secret microphones, including one in his bedroom, from which they listened to his conversations for over a month. The plurality distinguished *Rochin* as a case involving "coercion, violence * * * [and] brutality to the person" rather than, as here, a "trespass to property, plus eavesdropping." However, Justice Frankfurter, who had written for the Court in *Rochin,* concluded that the two cases were not distinguishable. Though "there was lacking [in *Irvine*] physical violence, even to the restricted extent employed in *Rochin,*" the police had engaged in "a more powerful and offensive control over Irvine's life than a single limited physical trespass." The division of the Court in *Irvine,* Justice Black later noted, revealed that the "ad hoc approach" of the Court in *Rochin* and *Irvine* consisted of no more than determining whether "five justices are sufficiently revolted by local police action" to "shock [the victim of that action] into the protective arms of the Constitution."

In both *Rochin* and *Irvine,* Justice Frankfurter took sharp exception to Justice Black's characterization of the Court's fundamental fairness analysis as basically subjective. Admittedly, the case-by-case application of the "ordered liberty" standard required the exercise of judicial judgment in an "empiric process" for which there was no "mechanical yardstick." That did not mean, however, that judges were "at large" to draw upon their "merely personal and private notions" of justice. In each case, the Court was required to undertake a "disinterested inquiry pursued in

---

12. 332 U.S. 46, 67 S.Ct. 1672, 91 L.Ed. 1903 (1947), also discussed in § 2.3 at note 9.

13. 342 U.S. 165, 72 S.Ct. 205, 96 L.Ed. 183 (1952).
14. 347 U.S. 128, 74 S.Ct. 381, 98 L.Ed. 561 (1954).

the spirit of science.'' It looked not to personal preferences, but to external evidence of permanent and pervasive notions of fairness, such as the positions taken in the federal constitution and early state constitutions, the standards currently applied in the various states, and viewpoints of other countries with similar jurisprudential traditions.

Justice Black's criticism of the fundamental fairness doctrine also rested in part on his assumption that the alternative of relying upon the "clearly marked boundaries" of specific Bill of Rights guarantees offered far less room for subjective judgments. This assumption also was challenged by justices favoring the fundamental fairness doctrine. Justice Harlan, for example, argued that Justice Black's formula for achieving judicial restraint was "more hollow than real." He suggested that the specific provisions of the Bill of Rights often were no less amenable to a subjective interpretation than the fundamental fairness standard of due process. Under Justice Black's position, the focus of judicial inquiry would be shifted from the flexible concept of "ordered liberty" to equally flexible terms found in most of the Amendments. Terms like "probable cause," "unreasonable search," and "speedy and public trial" it was noted, are hardly self-defining. Justice Harlan acknowledged that reliance upon the specifics of the Bill of Rights might produce different results, but the analysis involved would be no less subjective.

In support of Justice Harlan's response on subjectivity, Justice Black's own position in *Rochin* is commonly cited. Justice Black agreed that there had been a constitutional violation in *Rochin,* but he based that conclusion on the Fifth Amendment privilege against self-incrimination rather than any "evanescent" standard of fundamental fairness. To find that the privilege had been violated, however, Justice Black arguably had to make value judgments very much like those considered under a fundamental fairness analysis. To treat the stomach pumping as compulsory self-incrimination, Justice Black had to conclude

that the privilege extended to the obtaining of nontestimonial evidence (as well as testimonial evidence) and prohibited physical compulsion (as well as the compulsion of a court order). The highly debatable nature of the first proposition, in particular, is evinced by later cases in which a divided Court held that the Fifth Amendment did not extend so far.[15]

§ 2.5 Selective Incorporation

(a) Fundamental Fairness and Selective Incorporation: Similarities and Differences. During the 1960s, the prevailing due process position shifted from the fundamental fairness doctrine to the selective incorporation doctrine. In several respects, the two doctrines are much alike. Both read the due process clause as encompassing only those rights deemed fundamental under an ordered liberty standard. Both recognize that the ordered liberty standard includes substantive as well as procedural rights, and that it is an expansive concept, not limited to rights established by historical usage at the time of the Constitution's adoption. Both agree also that the ordered liberty standard may encompass protections found in the specific Bill of Rights guarantees, and that it may also require safeguards not found in those guarantees. There is crucial disagreement, however, as to how the ordered liberty standard should be used in identifying fundamental rights as they relate to guarantees in the Bill of Rights.

Initially, the two doctrines differ in the scope of the right that is to be assessed under the ordered liberty standard when that right is found in a Bill of Rights guarantee. The fundamental fairness doctrine focuses on that aspect of the Bill of Rights guarantee that was denied by the state in the particular case. Moreover, it often assesses the significance of that element of the guarantee in light of the special circumstances of the individual case. The selective incorporation doctrine, on the other hand, focuses on the total guarantee rather than on the particular aspect presented in an individual case. It assesses the fundamental nature of the guarantee as a whole, rather than the

---

15. See § 8.12(d).

fundamental nature of any one aspect of the guarantee.

Consider, for example, the situation presented in *Palko v. Connecticut*.[1] Applying the fundamental fairness doctrine, the Court there asked whether the ordered liberty standard required protection against "that kind of double jeopardy" which had been imposed on the defendant in this case. Thus, it asked whether fundamental fairness was violated by a retrial following an appellate reversal of an initial acquittal, where that acquittal was based upon legal error. It concluded that other aspects of the double jeopardy prohibition might be fundamental, but not the prohibition against retrials following an acquittal as it related to these circumstances. Applying the selective incorporation doctrine, the Court instead would have asked whether the ordered liberty standard encompasses the basic concept underlying the Fifth Amendment's overall prohibition against double jeopardy. The *Palko* Court appeared to acknowledge that was so, and thus, if it had applied selective incorporation analysis, it would have reached a different result. Since the double jeopardy prohibition, in its general conception, was fundamental, and since a retrial following an acquittal violated one aspect of the double jeopardy prohibition, that retrial would have been held to violate due process.

The difference in the scope of the right assessed produces a dramatic difference in the scope of the ruling under selective incorporation as opposed to the traditional fundamental fairness analysis. A fundamental fairness ruling finding a due process violation goes no farther than to establish due process protection parallel to the one aspect of the Bill of Rights guarantee presented in the particular case. Selective incorporation, however, judging the guarantee as a whole, produces a ruling that encompasses the full scope of the guarantee. When a guarantee is found to be fundamental, due process, in effect, "incorporates" that guarantee, and thereby carries over to the states precisely the same prohibitions as apply to the federal government under that guaran-

tee. Under selective incorporation, a ruling that a particular guarantee is within the "ordered liberty" concept makes applicable to the states "the entire accompanying doctrine" previously developed in applying that guarantee to federal criminal prosecutions.

The selective incorporation doctrine also departs from the fundamental fairness doctrine in its analysis of the ordered liberty concept. Whereas the fundamental fairness cases often asked whether a "fair and enlightened system of justice" would be "impossible" without a particular safeguard, selective incorporation "proceed[s] upon the * * * assumption that state criminal processes are not imaginary and theoretical schemes but actual systems bearing virtually every characteristic of the common law system that has been developing contemporaneously in England and in this country." Accordingly, it directs a court to test the fundamental nature of a right within the context of that common law system of justice, rather than against some hypothesized "civilized system" or some foreign system growing out of different traditions. The question to be asked, the Court has noted, is whether a procedure "is necessary to an Anglo–American regime of ordered liberty." Consistent with this approach, considerable weight is given to the very presence of a right within the Bill of Rights, since that presence in itself establishes that historically a substantial body of opinion viewed that right as essential to the fairness of the common law system.

(b) The Rationale of Selective Incorporation. There are those who argue that the selective incorporation doctrine has no coherent constitutional rationale. They contend that it constitutes no more than a result-oriented modification of the total incorporation theory—a doctrine devised to achieve total incorporation, minus the pragmatically troubling civil jury trial and grand jury guarantees. The Court wanted to expand Fourteenth Amendment protection to encompass all but those few guarantees that would cause the greatest disruption if applied to the states, and selective incorporation was created and

1. See note 10 of § 2.3.

accepted because it could eventually lead to exactly that result. Selective incorporation, these critics argue, is a doctrine that lacks the textual and historical support of either total incorporation or fundamental fairness, a doctrine justified only by its end product. Though the Supreme Court majority never responded to such criticism, individual justices have done so in separate opinions justifying the shift from fundamental fairness to selective incorporation. Together, they offer four reasons, discussed below in subsections (c)–(f), as to why selective incorporation provides a truer application of the ordered liberty standard than the fundamental fairness doctrine.

(c) Prior Precedent and the "Absorption" of Individual Guarantees. The earlier due process cases presented two lines of precedent, one applying the classic case-by-case analysis of fundamental fairness (the approach followed in the criminal procedure cases), and the other fully absorbing a few selected guarantees (all unrelated to criminal procedure). Justices favoring selective incorporation pointed to the latter line of Fourteenth Amendment cases particularly, those that appeared to "absorb," whole and intact, the various First Amendment guarantees. If the due process clause could, in effect, "incorporate" the First Amendment, did that not provide adequate precedent for selectively incorporating other guarantees as well? Admittedly, *Palko, Powell* and other fundamental fairness rulings had adopted a quite different approach, but what was to distinguish one line of cases from the other? There was, of course, the suggestion that the First Amendment freedoms occupied a "preferred position," that the freedom of speech, in particular, occupied a unique role as "the matrix, the indispensable condition, of nearly every other form of freedom." However, that did not explain the just compensation cases, which also appeared to be completely incorporated, although the departure from a traditional fundamental fairness analysis in those cases was clouded.

(d) Selective Incorporation as a Means of Avoiding Subjectivity. Taking a page from Justice Black's argument favoring total incorporation, justices supporting selective incorporation maintained that utilizing selective incorporation would avoid much of the subjectivity inherent in the application of the fundamental fairness doctrine. They noted initially that the selective incorporation doctrine, in contrast to the fundamental fairness doctrine, does not look to the "totality of the circumstances" in a particular case in determining whether a right is necessary to "ordered liberty." To permit evaluation of a right in light of "the factual circumstances surrounding each individual case" led, in their view, to judgments that were "extremely subjective and excessively discretionary." Selective incorporation was also said to reduce subjectivity by focusing on the fundamental nature of the Bill of Rights guarantee as a whole, rather than on a particular aspect of the guarantee. "[O]nly impermissible subjective judgments," it was argued, "can explain stopping short of the full sweep of the specific guarantee being absorbed." Under selective incorporation, once a guarantee is held to be fundamental, discretion is reduced because the Court's analysis thereafter rests on the language and history of the guarantee. There is no need for reference, in case after case, to the standard of "ordered liberty." This was deemed significant even if one assumed, as Justice Frankfurter argued, that the determination of fundamental fairness is guided by objective evidence of pervasive notions of justice. Selective incorporation, once applied, would offer the advantage of "avoid[ing] the impression of personal, ad hoc adjudication by every Court which attempts to apply the vague contents and contours of 'ordered liberty' to every different case that comes before it."

(e) Facilitating State Enforcement of Due Process Standards. The shift from fundamental fairness to selective incorporation was also justified as necessary to ensure effective state court enforcement of due process limitations. Critics of the traditional fundamental fairness doctrine had argued that its end result was due process standards too uncertain to be applied consistently by state courts. Supreme Court decisions tied to the totality of the circumstances of the individual case had failed to provide a "substantial yardstick for the states." It was suggested, for example, that the "case-by-case approach" of the Supreme Court rulings on confessions had left the state courts free to "find authority for affirming or rejecting almost any type of confession." The end product of the fundamental fairness approach, Justice Goldberg suggested, was to "require * * * [the] Supreme Court to intervene in the state judicial process with a considerable lack of predictability and with a consequent likelihood of considerable friction." Moreover, at a time when the criminal side of the Court's docket was growing more and more active, it was doubtful that the Court had the capacity to develop both a general body of principles interpreting specific guarantees for federal criminal cases and a second-level, "shadow" group of principles for all of the issues posed in state cases. Compared to the fundamental fairness doctrine, the "practical utility" of selective incorporation was "undeniable." Once a particular guarantee was held to be fundamental, state courts were directed to the specific language of that guarantee and to the various decisions interpreting that language in the context of federal prosecutions.

(f) The Legitimate Interests of Federalism. The opinions of the Court during the fundamental fairness era rarely failed to note the need to respect the "sovereign character of the several states" by giving the states the widest latitude consistent with assuring fundamental fairness. While those opinions did not explain what values underlying the Constitution's conception of federalism called for restraint in expanding constitutional limits applicable to the states, Justices Frankfurter and Harlan did so in a series of separate opinions. They focused on basically four such values—(1) the protection that diffusion of power provides against the development of a centralized national police authority (such a force presenting a great danger because of the impact of its potential misuse); (2) the preservation of local control in a field where such control was especially beneficial; (3) taking account of major differences between the state and federal criminal justice systems; and (4) providing ample room for the diversity and the experimentation

that could eventually lead to a criminal justice system that was improved both in efficiency and fairness. Opinions supporting selective incorporation took note of the claimed adverse impact of that doctrine upon all four of those values, but either viewed the federal regulation produced by selective incorporation as having no bearing upon a particular value or downgraded the importance of the potential adverse impact upon that value. The "legitimate interests of federalism" were both narrower and less weighty for the justices supporting selective incorporation than they were for the justices supporting the traditional fundamental fairness doctrine.

As for federalism standing as a bulwark against the development of a large centralized police force, justices favoring selective incorporation saw no threat to that value in imposing upon the states many of the procedural limits found in the Bill of Rights. These limitations would hardly place such severe restrictions on state authority as to lead to what Justice Harlan had envisioned, a "shift of responsibility to the Federal government, with its vastly greater resources, * * * bringing us closer to the monolithic society which our federalism rejects." What was occurring here was quite different from the usual transfer of state authority to the federal government. The Court's rulings did not take enforcement responsibility from local police agencies and place it in the hands of a national police agency. Nor did the rulings take the responsibility for defining crime from local legislatures and place it in the hands of Congress. The Court was acting only to protect the individual, and the justices saw in that purpose a crucial distinction.

Justices supporting selective incorporation also did not quarrel with the recognition in previous cases of the desirability, in general, of local control in the shaping of the criminal justice process. In large part, the impact of the criminal law and its enforcement is felt within the local community, leading to a longstanding tradition of relying upon a combination of local units of administration and substantial administrative discretion. That tradition appropriately allows for an administration of the process that is responsive to local conditions and the local electorate. However, these justices argued, the procedural safeguards found in the Bill of Rights are simply too important to give way to the values served by local control of the criminal justice process. In applying the First Amendment in full effect to the states, the Court had subordinated the values of local control in such traditional areas of state or local regulation as education, the licensing of professionals, door-to-door handbill distributions, and the use of public parks for assemblies. The interests protected by the First Amendment were too important to the nation as a whole to give deference to the values of local control. The same was true of the enforcement of what were seen as essential rights of the accused. "The quality of a nation's civilization," it was noted, "can be largely measured by the methods it uses in the enforcement of its criminal law." Supporters of selective incorporation further suggested that local control had largely failed to curb misuses of authority by local officials in criminal justice administration, thereby forcing the Court to impose broader and more clearly defined constitutional limits through the application of various procedural guarantees found in the Bill of Rights.

Justice Harlan (in opposing the selective incorporation doctrine) and Justices Fortas and Powell (in urging its modification) argued that the different problems faced by the state criminal justice systems required constitutional standards more flexible than those applied to the federal system. The differences between the federal and state systems included: (1) different police enforcement responsibilities, with local police departments enforcing a "far wider spectrum of laws" than federal agencies, and having additional responsibilities, such as order maintenance and traffic control, which produced a different allocation of resources and different policing techniques (e.g., street patrols); (2) different caseloads, with many state prosecutors and judges having far heavier caseloads than their federal counterparts; and (3) differences in personnel pools and selection process, with the state and local governments generally accepting lesser qualifications for appointive positions and using the

electoral process to select prosecutors, judges, and some police officials (e.g., sheriffs). In sum, the argument went, the states had to do more with less and hence needed more leeway in their implementation of the basic principles underlying the Bill of Rights guarantees than did the federal government. A "jot-for-jot" application of standards developed in the context of federal proceedings could put "the States, with their differing law enforcement problem * * * in a constitutional straight jacket," yet the traditional selective incorporation doctrine required exactly such a "jot-for-jot" application.

Supporters of selective incorporation offered two responses to this line of reasoning. First, the differences between the federal and state systems were less substantial than suggested by the proponents of separate standards. The federal system encompassed a variety of different settings, including some (e.g., the District of Columbia) that were quite similar to the settings faced by the state systems. Since the standards prescribed under the Bill of Rights had not been a constitutional straight jacket for the federal system, there was no reason to assume they would impose a greater burden on the states. Secondly, where the circumstances faced by the states were substantially different, the various guarantees were sufficiently flexible to give consideration to those differences, even if that required reexamining past precedent. Justice Harlan responded that, to "avoid unduly fettering the states," the Court would frequently be forced to relax the constitutional standards that would now be applied to both the federal and state governments. The end result, he argued, would be a "watering down [of] protections against the Federal government," thereby "discarding * * * the possibility of federal leadership by example." The supporters of selective incorporation apparently assumed, however, that the need for more flexible standards to accommodate special problems of the states would be rare, and that those standards would be carefully tied to the particular setting so as to limit their applicability.

In *New State Ice Co. v. Liebmann*,[2] Justice Brandeis admonished the Court against undue interference with state experimentation:

> To stay experimentation in things social and economic is a grave responsibility. Denial of the right to experiment may be fraught with serious consequences to the Nation. It is one of the happy incidents of the federal system that a single courageous State may, if its citizens choose, serve as a laboratory; and try novel social and economic experiments without risk to the rest of the country.

One of the major justifications advanced for the fundamental fairness doctrine was that it attended to Justice Brandeis' admonition by providing ample room for diversity (and thus experimentation) in state procedure. Indeed, the importance of allowing leeway for experimentation was noted in the first of the fundamental fairness opinions. *Hurtado v. California* stressed that due process ought not to preclude a state, if it so desires, from looking beyond the common law and basing its process on "the best of all systems and of every age," letting the "new and various experiences of our own situation * * * [shape] new and not less useful forms."

When the Court shifted to selective incorporation, justices critical of the new doctrine argued that the majority had failed to heed Justice Brandeis' admonition, as selective incorporation gave no weight whatsoever to the value of experimentation. Justice Goldberg responded that the Brandeis admonition had relevance only to judicial restraint in applying the now discredited doctrine of substantive due process. Recognition of the state's capacity to experiment, Justice Goldberg noted, did not extend to "experiment[s] with the fundamental liberties of citizens safeguarded by the Bill of Rights." A similar response was also offered by Justice Black. However, as discussed in § 2.6(d), the Court later retreated from this suggestion of giving absolutely no weight to the value of state experimentation.

§ 2.6   Application of the Selective Incorporation Doctrine

(a) The Decisions of the Sixties. The shift from fundamental fairness to selective incorporation occurred during the 1960s. It began with a series of cases in which the majority opinions were sufficiently ambiguous so that it could not be said with certainty that the Court had adopted selective incorporation. Those cases appeared to make fully applicable to the states the Fourth Amendment prohibition against unreasonable searches, the Eighth Amendment prohibition against cruel and unusual punishment, and the Sixth Amendment right to counsel, but they failed to clearly base their rulings on a selective incorporation analysis. However, in *Malloy v. Hogan*,[1] decided in 1964, the Court undisputably established that selective incorporation had become the majority view. *Malloy* held that the privilege against self-incrimination was a fundamental right and therefore safeguarded against state action under the "applicable federal standard of the Fifth Amendment." Rejecting the prosecution's contention that the due process protection might be "less stringent" than that provided by the Fifth Amendment itself, the Court noted that its decisions of the 1960s had "rejected the notion that the Fourteenth Amendment applies to the States only a 'watered-down,' subjective version of the individual guarantees of the Bill of Rights." Once the Court had determined, upon analysis of the whole of a guarantee, that the guarantee protected a fundamental right, that guarantee "would be enforced against the States under the Fourteenth Amendment according to the same standards that * * * [apply] against federal encroachment."

A series of cases decided during the remainder of the decade reaffirmed the position taken in *Malloy*. Those cases held applicable to the states, under the same standards applied to the federal government, the Sixth Amendment rights to a speedy trial, to a trial by jury, to confront opposing witnesses, and to compulsory process for obtaining witnesses, and the

---

2. 285 U.S. 262, 52 S.Ct. 371, 76 L.Ed. 747 (1932) (dissenting opinion).

§ 2.6
1. 378 U.S. 1, 84 S.Ct. 1489, 12 L.Ed.2d 653 (1964).

Fifth Amendment prohibition against double jeopardy. In each case, the Court majority relied squarely upon a selective incorporation analysis. At the same time, the Court interpreted past precedent as having held to be "fundamental" the Sixth Amendment rights of the accused to a public trial and to be informed of the nature and cause of the accusation, which thereby rendered those rights selectively incorporated in the Fourteenth Amendment and fully applicable to the states.

The rulings of the 1960s incorporated both guarantees that fundamental fairness rulings had recognized as having some aspects that were essential to ordered liberty and guarantees as to which no aspect had ever been characterized as fundamental. As to the former, the Court treated the guarantee as having been held fundamental in past rulings, and it simply applied the selective incorporation doctrine to make it applicable to the states in all of its aspects. As to the latter, the Court initially had to consider whether the guarantee should now be deemed, considered as a whole, to be fundamental. An affirmative ruling on that issue was facilitated by a doctrinal reshaping of the ordered liberty concept itself. In *Duncan v. Louisiana*,[2] the Court noted that it had narrowed the focus of the inquiry under the "ordered liberty" standard; the crucial issue was not whether a particular guarantee was fundamental to every "fair and equitable" criminal system "that might be imagined," but whether it was fundamental "in the context of the criminal processes maintained by the American states." The *Duncan* Court recognized further that this approach, along with selective incorporation's focus on the nature of the right as a whole, would be far more likely to produce a finding that a particular guarantee was implicit in the concept of "ordered liberty." It cited as an example the Sixth Amendment right to a jury trial. While "a criminal process which was fair and equitable but used no juries is easy to imagine," analysis of the jury trial guarantee in light of the structure of the "Anglo–American regime of ordered liberty" produced a

"quite different" view of the significance of the Sixth Amendment guarantee. One did not find in that Anglo–American structure "alternative guarantees and protections that would serve the purposes that the jury serves in the English and American system," but rather a "supporting framework and * * * subsidiary procedures * * * of the sort that naturally complement jury trial and have developed in connection with and in reliance upon jury trial." This reflected a "deep commitment * * * to the right to jury trial in serious criminal cases" that put that right at the core of the criminal justice process and qualified it "for protection under the Due Process Clause of the Fourteenth Amendment."

(b) Guarantees Not Yet Incorporated. By the end of the 1960s, the Supreme Court had, in Justice Brennan's words, changed the "face of the law." As Justice Harlan noted in 1970, the decisions of the just completed decade, through holding and dictum, had "incorporated * * * almost all of the criminal protections found within the first eight Amendments to the Constitution, and made them 'jot-for-jot' and case-for-case applicable to the states." During the same period, the Court had indicated as to only one criminal procedure safeguard of the Bill of Rights—the Fifth Amendment right to prosecution by indictment—that it was not fundamental and would not be applied to the states. Of all the fundamental fairness cases refusing to apply via Fourteenth Amendment due process criminal procedure protections found in the Bill of Rights, only *Hurtado* survived.[3]

There remained, however, three criminal process safeguards in the Bill of Rights about which the Court simply had not spoken—the Eighth Amendment prohibition against excessive bail, the Eighth Amendment prohibition against excessive fines, and the vicinage requirement of the Sixth Amendment. Indeed, the Court still has not ruled definitively on the application of those guarantees to the states. However, the reasoning of the Court's major selective incorporation opinions of the 1960s, supplemented by comments in later cases, pro-

---

2. 391 U.S. 145, 88 S.Ct. 1444, 20 L.Ed.2d 491 (1968).

3. See § 2.4 at note 4 and § 15.1 (c).

vides a strong indication that at least the two Eighth Amendment guarantees will be selectively incorporated when the issue is appropriately presented.

In one of those later cases, *Schilb v. Kuebel*[4], the Court found it unnecessary to rule on the incorporation of the bail clause of the Eighth Amendment, but did note: "Bail * * * is basic to our system of law * * * and the Eighth Amendment's proscription of excessive bail has been assumed to have application to the states through the Fourteenth Amendment." Subsequent lower court rulings, drawing upon the implicit message of *Schilb*'s characterization of the bail clause as "basic to our system," have unhesitantly viewed that clause as applicable to state proceedings through the Fourteenth Amendment.

The Court did not speak to the possible incorporation of the Eighth Amendment's prohibition against excessive fines until its 1989 ruling in *Browning–Ferris Industries v. Kelco Disposal, Inc.*[5] The majority there found no need to "decide whether the Eighth Amendment's prohibition against excessive fines applies to the several states through the Fourteenth Amendment." However, Justice O'Connor did reach that issue, stating that she saw "no reason to distinguish one Eighth Amendment Clause from another for purposes of incorporation, and would hold that the Excessive Fines Clause also applies to the states." In a subsequent case, the Court considered the possible application of the clause to a state forfeiture proceeding without noting the incorporation issue.[6]

While *Duncan v. Louisiana*[7] is frequently described as having incorporated the Sixth Amendment's jury clause, what it actually incorporated was the right to jury trial, which is only a part of that clause. The *Duncan* holding was that "the Fourteenth Amendment guarantees a right of jury trial in all criminal cases which—were they to be tried in a federal court—would come within the Sixth Amend-

ment guarantee." The jury clause of the Sixth Amendment not only guarantees a right to a trial "by an impartial jury" in "all criminal prosecutions," but it further requires that the jury be "of the State and district wherein the crime shall have been committed, which district shall have been previously ascertained by law." These additional requirements are commonly described as the Sixth Amendment's "vicinage" requirements, although they hardly reflect the common law vicinage requirement of a jury selected from the community in which the crime was committed.[8]

Neither *Duncan* nor subsequent Supreme Court cases applying the jury trial right to the states have spoken to the incorporation of the Sixth Amendment's vicinage provisions. The possibility of applying the Sixth Amendment's vicinage provision to the states via the Fourteenth Amendment has been presented to the lower courts in connection with two quite distinct defense claims, producing strikingly different patterns in the lower court responses. State defendants, claiming that their alleged crime was committed outside of the state, have argued that their convictions were therefore precluded by the Sixth Amendment since the juries that convicted them were not from the state in which the crime was committed. Lower courts ruling on such claims have almost uniformly accepted the contention that the Sixth Amendment's jurors-of-the-state requirement applies to state proceedings. However, they typically have done so without any significant discussion of the incorporation question, moving directly to the question of whether the crime involved was committed, at least in part, in the state of conviction. Moreover, the role of the Sixth Amendment in such cases has not been critical since the states, by their own laws, limit their jurisdiction to crimes that were "committed" within the state, as measured by conduct or consequences occurring within the state. Thus a finding of a

---

4. 404 U.S. 357, 92 S.Ct. 479, 30 L.Ed.2d 502 (1971).

5. 492 U.S. 257, 109 S.Ct. 2909, 106 L.Ed.2d 219 (1989).

6. See Bennis v. Michigan, 516 U.S. 442, 116 S.Ct. 994, 134 L.Ed.2d 68 (1996).

7. See note 2 supra.

8. See § 16.1 (b).

Sixth Amendment violation only backed up a finding of a violation of state law.

Sixth Amendment claims also have been raised by state defendants who were tried in judicial districts other than that in which the crime was committed (with the jury selected from the district of the trial court) or were tried in a division of a judicial district other than that in which the crime was committed (with the jury selected exclusively from that division). In this context, the lower courts have divided on the applicability to the states of the Sixth Amendment requirement that the jurors be of the "district wherein the crime shall have been committed, which district shall have been previously ascertained by law." Several have concluded that this requirement is made applicable to the states by the Fourteenth Amendment. They cite Supreme Court decisions stressing the need for a representative jury as indicative that the Sixth Amendment's vicinage provisions are essential elements of the jury trial guarantee made applicable to the states. Still other courts have assumed arguendo the Fourteenth Amendment's incorporation of the district-of-the-offense provision in the course of concluding that the selection of the jury in the case before it complied with that provision.

On the other side, several courts have flatly rejected the contention that the Fourteenth Amendment incorporates the Sixth Amendment's requirement that jurors be from the district of the offense, with the boundaries of the district previously established by law. They see that requirement as a compromise on vicinage developed for the unique geographical scope of the federal system and expressing no enduring principle of a type that would justify its application to the states under the "ordered liberty" standard of due process. The Sixth Amendment's vicinage provisions were designed to ensure that the jury was selected from a geographical area no larger than the state, as the "previously ascertained" federal districts, to be drawn by Congress, could be as large as the state (as evidenced by the original federal districts). Such a principle, it argued,

would be meaningless as applied to state proceedings, as the states have no power to go beyond their boundaries in drawing jurors.

(c) Acceptance of Selection Incorporation in the Post–1960s. Selective incorporation was a creation of the Warren Court, but it was never subjected to the continuous challenges and efforts to narrow that members of both the Burger and Rehnquist Courts directed at other Warren Court innovations. There was, however, one brief but significant challenge to the doctrine, presented in a series of cases decided during the 1970s. The rationale of that challenge was first articulated in a concurring opinion by Justice Fortas in *Duncan v. Louisiana*[9], one of the landmark incorporation cases of the 1960s. While accepting selective incorporation as the general rule, Justice Fortas argued that a modification of that doctrine was required for guarantees which were like the Sixth Amendment right to jury trial, the guarantee at issue in *Duncan*. With this type of guarantee, he noted, the Court was concerned with "more than a principle of justice applicable to individual cases." The Sixth Amendment, as interpreted in cases involving federal jury trials, also imposed a "system of administration"; it prescribed, for example, the size of the jury (twelve) and the form of their verdict (unanimous). Such requirements, he suggested, might very well not be fundamental, and therefore should not be applied to the states (although they would remain constitutionally binding in federal cases). It was not necessary to adhere so "slavishly" to selective incorporation as to impose upon the states the total Sixth Amendment guarantee, including "all its bag and baggage, however securely or insecurely affixed they may be by law or precedent." The Court had no need to decide in *Duncan* itself whether absolute parallelism (disparagingly characterized by Justice Harlan as "jot for jot" and "case-by-case" incorporation) would be mandated for every aspect of the jury trial guarantee. Nonetheless, Justice White's opinion for the Court strongly indicated that, contrary to Justice Fortas' suggestion, such parallelism would be required. At the same time, however,

---

9. See note 7 supra.

Justice White acknowledged that previous interpretations of the Sixth Amendment, relating to such matters as jury size, may have been influenced by the fact that the requirements there imposed would apply only in the "limited environment" of the federal courts where "uniformity is a more obvious and immediate consideration." But those decisions, he added, were "always subject to reconsideration."

The "reconsideration route" suggested by Justice White was adopted by the Court in *Williams v. Florida,*[10] where the state sought to utilize a six-person jury in a non-capital felony case. Although a long line of Supreme Court precedent had assumed that the Sixth Amendment demanded a twelve-person jury, the Court majority sustained the Florida procedure. *Duncan* was characterized as granting to state defendants a right to precisely the same type of jury trial as the Sixth Amendment would demand "were [defendants] tried in federal courts." However, upon examination of the history and purpose of the jury trial guarantee, the Court concluded that the earlier cases had erred in assuming that a twelve-person jury was a "*sine qua non* of the jury trial guarantee." The twelve-person jury was simply an incidental feature of common law practice and not constitutionally required as to either federal or state cases.

Two years later, in a similar situation, all but one justice agreed that complete parallelism was required, but the one justice rejecting that position determined the outcome of the case. *Apodaca v. Oregon*[11] presented the question of whether a state could allow a less than unanimous jury verdict. Eight justices agreed that the critical issue was whether earlier Supreme Court opinions in cases involving federal juries had been correct in assuming that unanimity was a mandate of the Sixth Amendment. The eight split evenly on that issue, with four reasoning that unanimity was essential to the function of the jury and four reasoning that it was not. Relying on Justice Fortas' reasoning in his *Duncan* concurrence, the re-

maining member of the *Apodaca* Court, Justice Powell, concluded that on this type of issue the Fourteenth Amendment and the Sixth Amendment could produce different results. He would therefore uphold the state's right to utilize a non-unanimous jury verdict, although he would rule otherwise as to a federal jury, where the Sixth Amendment would directly apply. Because Justice Powell contributed the deciding vote, the Court in *Apodaca* reached a result that was anomalous in light of the majority's commitment to parallelism—the state's use of non-unanimous verdicts was upheld, though the same Court would have reached a different constitutional result in a federal case.

Justice Powell gained the support of two other justices in arguing for a separate constitutional standard for state proceedings in *Crist v. Bretz,*[12] but the Court majority again rejected that view. The majority there held that the starting point for the attachment of jeopardy under the double jeopardy clause was the impanelment of the jury as established in federal double jeopardy cases. It rejected the state's contention that due process on such a technical matter should be more flexible and allow the state to continue to adhere to its traditional starting point of the first witness being sworn (a standard utilized in federal cases only for bench trials). Once again, as in *Williams* and *Apodaca,* the majority noted that the proper approach was to reexamine the validity of the assumption made in earlier cases. Here, however, the Court concluded that the earlier cases had not adopted some "arbitrarily chosen rule of convenience" based on traditional federal practice (as the state argued), but a standard tied to a major function of the double jeopardy bar and therefore constitutionally mandated.

In the years since *Crist,* the Court has considered various other constitutional claims that Justices Fortas or Powell might have characterized as dealing primarily with a "system of administration." No member of the Court has suggested, however, that the partic-

---

10. 399 U.S. 78, 90 S.Ct. 1893, 26 L.Ed.2d 446 (1970).

11. 406 U.S. 404, 92 S.Ct. 1628, 32 L.Ed.2d 184 (1972).

12. 437 U.S. 28, 98 S.Ct. 2156, 57 L.Ed.2d 24 (1978).

ular requirement might not be constitutionally demanded for state proceedings while constitutionally mandated in federal proceedings. Thus, absolute parallelism seems to be a settled principle. Indeed, the selective incorporation doctrine has become so firmly embedded in Fourteenth Amendment jurisprudence that its operation has become also invisible, as the Court often speaks of applying a Bill of Rights guarantee to a state proceeding without even mentioning that the application comes about through the Fourteenth Amendment.

(d) Selective Incorporation and the Concerns of Federalism. Although the "pendulum of federalism" in the Supreme Court has swung back from the Warren era to far greater "sensitivity to the prerogatives of the states," that shift in position has not undermined majority support for selective incorporation (as it has for some other doctrinal innovations of the 1960s). In part, the continued strength of selective incorporation may be explained by its continuing administrative advantage in providing more extensive guidelines for state courts. Perhaps more significant, however, has been the Court's ability to find room within the framework of selective incorporation to give special consideration to important interests commonly associated with respect for federalism.

When the selective incorporation doctrine was first adopted, some commentators argued that it would bar consideration of the diverse settings in which state criminal justice systems operated. Application of a single constitutional standard supposedly would undercut important local administrative adjustments, particularly those relating to judicial proceedings. Post-incorporation rulings established, however, that the Court, in many areas, was willing

to adopt a single standard sufficiently flexible to allow the states to justify many local variations based on different administrative needs. In *North v. Russell*,[13] for example, a two-tier system for the trial of misdemeanors, with non-lawyer magistrates the sole decision maker at the first level, was sustained as an appropriate balance of the limited resources of rural communities and the procedural rights of defendants. Similarly, in *Shadwick v. Tampa*,[14] recognizing the "stiff and unrelenting caseloads" borne by many municipal courts, the Court held that the Fourth Amendment was not violated by the issuance of arrest warrants for municipal ordinance violations by non-lawyer clerks of municipal courts. Justice Powell's opinion for a unanimous Court initially noted that the issuance of warrants by judges or lawyers was to be preferred, but "our federal system warns of converting desirable practice into constitutional commandment. It recognizes in plural and diverse state activities one key to national innovation and vitality."

North, Shadwick, and various search and seizure opinions which take account of the special problems of local law enforcement, evidence a substantial potential for accommodation to community diversity within a framework of selective incorporation. Admittedly, not all claims for accommodation have been successful. Also, selective incorporation clearly provides less room for accommodation than would be available under a fundamental fairness analysis. Nevertheless, there apparently remains sufficient opportunity for recognition of local variations to convince those justices who have stressed federalism concerns in other aspects of constitutional law that there is no need to seek to overturn the selective incorporation doctrine.[15]

---

13. 427 U.S. 328, 96 S.Ct. 2709, 49 L.Ed.2d 534 (1976).

14. 407 U.S. 345, 92 S.Ct. 2119, 32 L.Ed.2d 783 (1972).

15. One aspect of allowing for local variations, the Court has noted, is to limit its rulings to the rejection of a particular practice without prescribing precisely what must be done to cure the constitutional defect. See e.g., Smith v. Robbins, 528 U.S. 259, 120 S.Ct. 746, 145 L.Ed.2d 756 (2000), where the Court applied an earlier ruling holding unconstitutional a state practice permitting appointed counsel to withdraw from an appeal that counsel deemed frivolous. *Smith* noted that, while that earlier

ruling had set forth a procedure that would permit a constitutionally acceptable withdrawal in such cases, to convert that "suggestion into a straightjacket would contravene our established practice, rooted in federalism, of allowing the State wide discretion" in fashioning a procedure that would meet the basic prerequisites of the applicable constitutional guarantee (here the Sixth Amendment). In keeping with its "status as a court in the federal system," the Court would "avoid imposing a single solution on the states from top down," recognizing that there were various ways of avoiding the difficulties that had

Critics of selective incorporation also argued that the doctrine would preclude innovative experiments that might otherwise improve the criminal justice process. Grounding decisions on specific guarantees, rather than on a fundamental fairness analysis, would "retard development in the field of criminal procedure by stifling flexibility." Here again, however, the adverse impact has not been nearly as substantial as the critics suggested. Not all innovations presented to the Court have been upheld, but the justices have had no difficulty in giving weight to the value of experimentation. In *Chandler v. Florida*,[16] for example, the Court looked to that value in holding that, subject to certain safeguards, a state could permit the televising of a trial over defendant's objection. The Court noted that Florida had adopted its guidelines for televising trials only after a carefully reviewed pilot program had proven successful, that eighteen other states had experimented with such guidelines, and that the issue was under study in yet another dozen states. This strong display of state interest, supported by their generally careful and cautious approach, worked in Florida's favor. The Court concluded that where, as here, it could not say that the state activity automatically violated due process, it would be guided by Justice Brandeis' admonition in *New State Ice Co. v. Liebmann*[17] to respect state experimentation. In restoring the relevance of Justice Brandeis' admonition, *Chandler* may have put to rest the concerns created by the earlier rejection of that admonition by Justices Goldberg and Black in their support of the selective incorporation doctrine.

(e) The Retention of Due Process Methodology. The traditional due process analysis of the fundamental fairness doctrine focused upon the totality of the circumstances of the individual case. Consideration was given to a variety of factors relating to a challenged state

practice, including administrative justifications, the extent to which the practice might be inconsistent with a fundamental premise of the criminal justice process, and the prejudicial impact of the practice upon the outcome of the particular case. The end result was a methodology that Justice Black characterized as inherently subjective but Justice Frankfurter viewed as both inherent in the concept of due process and a necessary attribute of constitutional adjudication of complex issues. Not all practices, Justice Frankfurter noted, could be readily categorized constitutionally as clearly prohibited or permitted; in many instances, reference had to be made to how they were used and what impact they had in the setting of the particular case. Some proponents of the fundamental fairness position apparently assumed that the Court's ability to continue to use this traditional methodology would be sharply restricted by adoption of an incorporationist position. Reliance upon the specific guarantees, rather than the more flexible concept of due process, would lead to constitutional standards that were more categorical in nature. Admittedly, clauses like the "reasonableness" clause of the Fourth Amendment would still allow a circumstance-specific analysis, but other guarantees, using less flexible terms, would not.

Undoubtedly, the constitutional standards applied to the states in the post-incorporationist era do tend to be less circumstance-specific than the standards applied under the fundamental fairness doctrine. But many rulings under a variety of incorporated guarantees have taken a form very similar to that traditionally applied under due process. The announced standards have incorporated a balancing process, an element of prejudicial impact, or a consideration of governmental motive, each of which necessarily requires examination of the particular circumstances of the individual case. Among the standards that can be so characterized are the *Strickland v. Washington* test for determining

produced the finding of unconstitutionally in the earlier case.

16. 449 U.S. 560, 101 S.Ct. 802, 66 L.Ed.2d 740 (1981).

17. See § 2.5 at note 2.

when counsel's performance was so inadequate as to deny the defendant the effective assistance of counsel guaranteed by the Sixth Amendment,[18] the *Wheat v. United States* standard for determining when a disqualification of defense counsel resulted in a denial of defendant's Sixth Amendment right to counsel of choice,[19] the *Barker v. Wingo* balancing test for determining when defendant has been denied his Sixth Amendment right to a speedy trial,[20] the standard applied in determining the constitutionality of denying public and media access to pretrial proceedings,[21] and the "manifest necessity" test applied in determining when a mistrial ordered without a defense request can produce a double jeopardy violation.[22]

§ 2.7   The Independent Content of Due Process

(a) Procedural Due Process After Selective Incorporation. The selective incorporation doctrine did not challenge the traditional view that due process included a content independent of the Bill of Rights' specific guarantees. Prior to the adoption of the selective incorporation doctrine, the fundamental fairness doctrine had given the Fourteenth Amendment's due process clause a content that overlapped in part with some of the prohibitions contained in the specific guarantees of the Bill of Rights, and also included prohibitions that were not to be found in those guarantees. The selective incorporation doctrine challenged only the standard adopted by the earlier decisions in determining when and to what extent the Fourteenth Amendment's due process clause subjected the state criminal justice systems to restrictions identical to those imposed upon the federal system under the Bill of Rights' specific guarantees. It did not question the conception of due process as also reaching aspects of the process not regulated by those guarantees and imposing additional restrictions as demanded by the concept of "fundamental fairness." Indeed, over the same

decade during which it was selectively incorporating all but a few of the Bill of Rights guarantees governing the criminal process, the Warren Court was relying upon the independent content of due process to impose limitations upon the state criminal justice systems that stood apart from the selectively incorporated guarantees. Because they stood apart from the incorporated guarantees, these ruling were sometimes described as resting on "free-standing due process."

It was not until after the adoption of selective incorporation that the Supreme Court found it necessary to address the distinct roles of the specific guarantees and the independent content of due process in the constitutional regulation of the state criminal justice systems. The primary source of regulation, the Court noted in *Dowling v. United States*,[1] comes from those specific guarantees that have been selectively incorporated and thereby made applicable to the states. "Beyond the specific guarantees enumerated in the Bill of Rights, the Due Process Clause has limited operation." That is so because "[t]he Bill of Rights speaks in explicit terms to many aspects of criminal procedure, and the expansion of those constitutional guarantees under the open-ended rubric of the Due Process Clause invites undue interference with both considered legislative judgments and the careful balance that the Constitution strikes between liberty and order." In the "field of criminal law," the Court stated, "we 'have defined the category of infractions that violate "fundamental fairness" very narrowly,' " recognizing that the due process clause does not "establish this Court as a rule-making organ for the promulgation of state rules of criminal procedure."

The Court's characterization of free-standing due process as a limited supplement to specific guarantees might suggest a sparing use of that grounding,[2] but as noted below in

---

18.   See § 11.10(a).

19.   See § 11.9(d).

20.   See § 18.2(a).

21.   See § 23.1(e).

22.   See § 25.2(c).

§ 2.7

1.   493 U.S. 342, 110 S.Ct. 668, 107 L.Ed.2d 708 (1990).

2.   That characterization also might suggest that the Court would follow the practice of looking to free-standing due process as a possible grounding for a proposed restraint only after first determining that a possibly relevant specific guarantee does not apply. While such a position

subsection (b), that hardly has been the case. A wide array of constitutional regulations of the criminal process are based on the independent content of due process. However, in certain respects, free-standing due process does tend to produce rulings which, in general, are narrower than the typical rulings under the specific guarantees. Most of the free-standing due process rulings make a defense showing of prejudice an element of the constitutional violation, while rulings based on the specific guarantees typically describe constitutional violations without regard to their prejudicial impact in the individual case (although those violations may then be subject to harmless error analysis). So too, free-standing due process rulings tend more frequently to focus on the totality of the circumstances of the case, although, as discussed in § 2.6(e), that approach is also to be found in some rulings under specific guarantees. Similarly, several free-standing due process doctrines tie unconstitutionality to an improper or pernicious purpose on the part of the government actor, a factor less frequently emphasized in rulings under specific guarantees. Finally, free-standing due process rulings tend to be driven by concern for adjudicatory fairness (looking primarily to protection against conviction of the innocent), in contrast to the broader range of values reflected in some of the specific guarantees.

(b) Range of Independent–Content Rulings. The Court has extended constitutional regulation through the independent content of due process to every phase of the criminal justice process. Indeed, as to some phases (such as sentencing), due process constitutes the primary source of constitutional regulation. At the investigatory stage, due process restricts the state's utilization of lineups, showups, and other identification procedures insofar as they present a "substantial likelihood of irreparable misidentification,"[3] prohibits police practices that are so "outrageous" as to "shock the conscience,"[4] and mandates against the intentional destruction or failure to preserve evidence recognized to be exculpatory and governmental action directed at making it more difficult for the defendant to locate potentially favorable witnesses.[5] At the charging stage, due process prohibits unjustified extensive delay in bringing charges where it results in prejudice to the defense and charging decisions that are the product of prosecutorial vindictiveness.[6] At the pretrial stage, due process governs procedural elements of the motion to suppress, ensures that the defense receives reciprocal discovery when it is required to provide discovery to the prosecution, provides the indigent defendant with access to experts as needed to evaluate and present a contention resting on scientific expertise (e.g., insanity), imposes on the prosecution a duty to disclose to the defense or court material excul-

has been adopted as to substantive due process (§ 2.7(d) at note 45), the Court's post-incorporation procedural due process rulings reflect considerable unevenness in this regard. In some areas, the Court has made a point of turning to due process only after first concluding that a particular specific guarantee does not extend so far as to reach the procedure in question. See e.g. United States v. Marion, discussed in § 18.1(c) and 18.5(a) (delay in initiating prosecution considered under due process clause after first concluding that the Sixth Amendment's speedy trial guarantee does not apply to such delay). On the other hand, the Court in other rulings noted its preference for resting its finding of unconstitutionality on due process grounds and thereby avoiding the need to determine whether the state's procedure also violated a specific guarantee. Thus, in Pennsylvania v. Ritchie [discussed in § 24.3(f)], involving the extent of the state's obligation to provide the defense with subpoena access to possibly favorable agency records, the Court noted that, "because the applicability of the Sixth Amendment [compulsory process clause] to this type of case is unsettled," it preferred to turn to a "due process analysis," where "precedents ad-

dressing the fundamental fairness of trials established a clear framework for review." In still other areas, the Court's post-incorporation rulings initially relied on due process and subsequently turned to a specific guarantee as an alternative grounding for imposing basically the same constitutional limitations. Thus, governmental action discouraging a defense witness from testifying was held to violate due process in an early post-incorporation ruling, but a later case looked to both due process and the compulsory process clause of the Sixth Amendment in reviewing government action that denied the defendant access to a potential witness. See Webb v. Texas, and United States v. Valenzuela–Bernal, both discussed in § 24.3(h).

3.   See § 7.4.

4.   Rochin v. California, discussed in § 2.4 at note 14; County of Sacramento v. Lewis, discussed at note 44 infra.

5.   See § 24.3(e), (g).

6.   See § 18.5; § 13.7(c).

patory evidence that is within its possession or control, and prohibits state timing requirements for motions that are so stringent as to deny the defendant a reasonable opportunity to raise a constitutional objection.[7]

Of course, most prosecutions are disposed of without a trial, with a substantial portion resolved by guilty plea. Here, the due process clause is the dominant source of constitutional regulation. Due process establishes the minimum amount of information that must be given to the defendant prior to accepting his plea, requires that the record provide a factual basis for the plea under certain circumstances, restricts the pressures that can be imposed upon a defendant without rendering his plea involuntary, and determines at what point there exists a constitutionally cognizable plea agreement which requires relief when breached by the prosecutor or court.[8]

Notwithstanding the number of specific guarantees in the Fifth and Sixth Amendment applicable to the trial, a wide variety of due process limitations add considerably to the constitutional regulation of the trial. Initially, due process governs many of the structural components of the trial. Due process imposes the requirement of an unbiased judge, and contributes to the constitutionally mandated procedures designed to ensure that the jury is not tainted by prejudicial pretrial publicity.[9] Due process also contributes in part to the defendant's right to be present at various stages of the trial, prohibits forcing upon defendant an unnecessary physical setting that conveys a prejudicial message to the jury, and limits the trial court's authority to exclude the defendant from the courtroom because of his misbehavior and to try him in absentia when he has failed to appear for trial.[10] The constitutional right of the defendant to testify on his own behalf is also grounded in part on due process.[11] Constitutional standards governing defendant's competence to stand trial, including the test for competency, the necessity for a competency hearing, and applicable standard of proof on that issue, also are a product of due process.[12] The state's authority to televise trials over the objection of the defendant is also subject to the constitutional regulation of due process.[13] The state's obligation to establish guilt by proof "beyond a reasonable doubt" is still another due process requirement.[14] This leads, in turn, to due process regulation of the use of presumptions, the shifting of the burden of proof to the defense on particular issues, the utilization of alternatives in the proof of the means or mental state of a single crime, and the explanation given to the jury of the reasonable doubt standard.[15]

Due process also contributes to the constitutional regulation of trial presentations. Due process is violated, for example, where the prosecution introduces material testimony known to be false, fails to bring to the attention of the court or defendant evidence within its possession or control that contradicts its

---

7. As to suppression motions, see §§ 10.4 (discussing Lego v. Twomey); § 10.5(a) (discussing Jackson v. Denno); § 10.5(e) (discussing McCray v. Illinois). As to reciprocal discovery, see § 20.4(a) (discussing Wardius v. Oregon). As to exculpatory evidence, see § 11.2(g); § 24.3(a) and (f) (discussing Pennsylvania v. Ritchie); § 24.3(b). As to timing requirements, see § 15.4(b) (discussing Reece v. Georgia).

8. See §§ 21.2(e); 21.2(f) (discussing North Carolina v. Alford); § 21.2(a), (b); § 21.2(f) (discussing Mabry v. Johnson); § 21.2(e) (discussing Santobello v. New York).

9. As to the unbiased judge, see § 22.4(a). As to pretrial publicity and jury selection, see § 23.2(d) (discussing Murphy v. Florida), and § 23.2(a) (discussing Groppi v. Wisconsin).

10. As to presence and conditions of presence, see § 24.2(a) (discussing United States v. Gagnon); § 24.2(e). As to exclusion and trial in absentia, see § 24.2(c) (discussing Illinois v. Allen); § 24.2(d) (discussing Taylor v. United States).

11. See § 24.3(g) (discussing Rock v. Arkansas, holding that the right of defendant to testify at trial is a product of the confluence of due process, Sixth Amendment right to compulsory process, and Fifth Amendment's guarantee against compulsory self-incrimination).

12. See Drope v. Missouri, 420 U.S. 162, 95 S.Ct. 896, 43 L.Ed.2d 103 (1975); Medina v. California, 505 U.S. 437, 112 S.Ct. 2572, 120 L.Ed.2d 353 (1992); Cooper v. Oklahoma, 517 U.S. 348, 116 S.Ct. 1373, 134 L.Ed.2d 498 (1996).

13. See § 23.3(b).

14. See In re Winship, 397 U.S. 358, 90 S.Ct. 1068, 25 L.Ed.2d 368 (1970).

15. See Sandstrom v. Montana, 442 U.S. 510, 99 S.Ct. 2450, 61 L.Ed.2d 39 (1979); Mullaney v. Wilbur, 421 U.S. 684, 95 S.Ct. 1881, 44 L.Ed.2d 508 (1975); § 24.10(c) (discussing Schad v. Arizona); Cage v. Louisiana, 498 U.S. 39, 111 S.Ct. 328, 112 L.Ed.2d 339 (1990).

key evidence or undercuts the credibility of its key witnesses, or presents a closing argument "so infected with unfairness" as to undermine confidence in the jury's verdict.[16] The trial judge may violate due process by excluding evidence critical to the defendant's presentation of a defense, taking unnecessary actions that "effectively dr[ive] a [defense] witness off the stand," or tolerating courtroom behavior that produces a "carnival atmosphere" prejudicial to the defense.[17]

When the process moves to the sentencing stage, most trial-type rights (e.g., confrontation) do not apply and due process becomes the primary source of constitutional regulation. Due process governs the range of conduct that may be considered by the sentencing judge, the need for notifying the defendant of the information that the judge will consider in making the sentencing decision, the need to ensure that information relied upon is accurate, and the need to provide the defendant with an opportunity to be heard and to offer his own evidence.[18] Due process also sets the minimum burden of proof the government must bear where the sentencing statute calls for a sentence enhancement based on a judge or jury finding of a particular aggravating circumstance as well as the minimum procedural rights that must be granted to the defense where the sentencing statute imposes an extended or alternative term upon a finding of dangerousness or recidivism.[19] Many of the special procedural guarantees attaching to capital sentencing also are prescribed by due process.[20]

Once the process moves beyond the conviction and sentence, due process constitutes the almost exclusive source of constitutionally mandated procedural rights. The rights of an indigent defendant to appointed counsel on a first appeal as of right and at a probation revocation proceeding are the product of due process.[21] The independent content of due process also establishes the prohibition against the vindictive exercise of judicial or prosecutorial discretion directed at defendants who exercise their right to appeal.[22] The Supreme Court also looked to due process in requiring that the state procedure for probation or parole revocation include a prompt preliminary hearing, a final revocation hearing within a reasonable time, a neutral and detached hearing body, advanced written notice of the charges, disclosure of the evidence on which the decision maker relies, a limited right of confrontation and cross-examination, and a right to appear and present evidence on his own behalf.[23] The decision on parole release can under some circumstances also be subject to certain procedural due process rights.[24]

(c) Due Process Analysis. In determining what procedure is mandated by the independent content of due process, the Supreme Court of the post-incorporation era has looked primarily to guideposts that also were used in the Court's earlier applications of due process under the fundamental fairness doctrine. The most significant of these guideposts have been: (1) the acceptance or rejection of the challenged procedural practice under the English common law as it was adapted to the conditions of this country; (2) the current American consensus on the validity of the challenged practice, as reflected in the judicial decisions and statutes of the various states; and (3) whether the challenged practice is consistent with, or contrary to, the logical application of the over-arching structural elements of the American criminal justice process (particular-

---

16.　See § 24.3(d); § 24.3(b); 24.7(h).

17.　See Chambers v. Mississippi, 410 U.S. 284, 93 S.Ct. 1038, 35 L.Ed.2d 297 (1973); § 24.3(h) (discussing Webb v. Texas); § 23.3(a) (discussing Sheppard v. Maxwell).

18.　See § 26.4(c); § 26.4(d); § 26.4(f); § 26.4(g).

19.　See § 26.4(h); 26.4(i).

20.　See e.g., Beck v. Alabama, 447 U.S. 625, 100 S.Ct. 2382, 65 L.Ed.2d 392 (1980) (due process requirement for lesser-included offense instruction); Simmons v. South Carolina, 512 U.S. 154, 114 S.Ct. 2187, 129 L.Ed.2d 133

(1994) (due process instruction as to alternative sentence and impact upon release).

21.　See §§ 11.1(b) and 11.2(b) (discussing Eritts v. Lucey and Gagnon v. Scarpelli).

22.　See § 13.7 (discussing Blackledge v. Perry); § 26.4(c) (discussing North Carolina v. Perace).

23.　See § 26.10(b)–(d) (discussing Morrissey v. Brewer and Gagnon v. Scarpelli).

24.　See § 26.2(c) (discussing Greenholtz v. Inmates of Nebraska Penal and Correctional Complex).

ly, its adherence to an adversary system of adjudication). In light of these guideposts, the Court has concluded that it should not apply to the criminal justice process the utilitarian balancing approach commonly used in determining the independent content of due process as applied to administrative proceedings. This section considers the character and significance of the three key guideposts noted above and the Court's rejection of the utilitarian balancing approach. It should be kept in mind that, while these are the major elements of the Court's due process analysis, other elements also play a role in determining what procedure is mandated by free-standing due process. For example, here, as in other areas of constitutional law, the Court's rulings will build on past precedent and will be influenced by the personal perspectives of the members of the Court.

History. In the Supreme Court's first major ruling on the procedural content of due process, *Murray's Lessee v. Hoboken Land and Improvement Co.,*[25] the Court asked the question: "To what principles * * * are we to resort to ascertain whether * * * [a] process, enacted by Congress, is due process?" Its answer was "to look to those settled usages and modes of proceeding existing in the common law and statute law of England, before the immigration of our ancestors, and which are shown not to have been unsuited to their civil and political condition by having been acted on by them after settlement of this country." Since the procedure at issue (a summary distress warrant) was fully in accord with English common law and with "the laws of many of the States at the time of the adoption of * * * [the Fifth] Amendment," it could not "be denied to be due process." This reasoning suggested a due process clause that was "frozen-in-history." If the challenged procedure had been accepted at the common law as it existed at the time of the adoption of the Constitution, it was *per se* consistent with the mandate of due process. If the challenged procedure had been rejected at common law (either by a direct ruling or by being in conflict with what

was required at common law), it was a *per se* violation of due process. Where the practice was not known at common law, and was not inconsistent with the procedure employed at common law, it presumably was constitutionally acceptable under this reading of *Murray's Lessee* because it did not contradict the "law of the land" mandated by due process.

In *Hurtado v. California,*[26] the Court's first major interpretation of due process under the Fourteenth Amendment, the Court majority rejected such a strict, "frozen-in-history" reading of *Murray's Lessee.* The *Hurtado* Court stated that *Murray's Lessee* had not treated historical pedigree as an "indispensable test of what constitutes 'due process of law.'" Rather, it had established only that "a process of law, which is not otherwise forbidden, must be taken to be due process, if it can show the sanction of settled usage both in England and this country." However exceptional, and however inconsistent with "principles of ordinary procedure," a process that "in substance, has been immemorially the actual law * * * therefore is due process of law." But that did not mean that a process "which is not thus sanctioned by usage, or which supersedes and displaces one that is, cannot be regarded as due process of law." For "to hold that such a characteristic is essential to due process of law, would be to deny every quality of law but its age, and to render it incapable of progress or improvement." Procedures that were inconsistent with the common law, even those that had been specifically rejected at common law, were compatible with due process, provided they adhered to those "fundamental principles of liberty and justice which lie at the base of all our civil and historical institutions." The due process clause focused on the "substance of individual rights," rather than the "particular forms of procedure" developed at common law. It therefore allowed the states the flexibility to "look to the best ideas of all systems and ages" in reshaping their procedures in response to the "new and various experiences of our own situation."

---

25. 59 U.S. (18 How.) 272, 15 L.Ed. 372 (1856), discussed in § 2.4 at note 2.

26. 110 U.S. 516, 4 S.Ct. 111, 28 L.Ed. 232 (1884), discussed in § 2.4 at note 4.

After *Hurtado,* the endorsement of "settled usage" still insulated a procedure from a due process challenge, but an historical rejection did not necessarily mean that the procedure denied due process. A standard that tested procedures against those "immutable principles of justice" which are "implicit in the concept of ordered liberty" could readily lead to discounting the common law's rejection of a particular procedure as reflecting no more than "the restricted views of Eighteenth Century England regarding the best methods for ascertainment of facts." Thus, *Hurtado* found consistent with due process the filing of felony charges by information even though the common law traditionally required that such charges be presented by a grand jury's indictment.

The *Hurtado* conception of due process as open to the lessons of new experiences and the teachings of a new age's "sense of fair play and decency" proved difficult to reconcile with *Hurtado*'s acceptance of the principle that a procedure sanctioned by its acceptance at common law was thereby automatically consistent with due process. Eventually, the Court came to reject that principle. A growth in the understanding of what was needed to produce basic fairness, or a basic change in operative conditions, could lead to the conclusion that an historically accepted practice was no longer consistent with due process. Thus, while the common law accepted the practice of forcing to pro se representation a felony defendant who lacked the resources to retain a lawyer, *Powell v. Alabama* and *Betts v. Brady* held that, under some circumstances, due process required the state to offer to the indigent defendant the services of a court-appointed defense counsel.[27] Similarly, due process was held to render invalid the practice, long accepted in American common law, that allowed the trial judge to give to the jury the determination of whether a confession was obtained by methods so oppressive that it should not be considered admissible evidence.[28]

Although a strong historical pedigree no longer insulated a procedure from a due process challenge, it clearly remained a relevant factor in determining whether a challenged procedure violated the standard of fundamental fairness. However, in some respects, the sanction of common law acceptance was less significant in determining the content of due process than the content of other procedural guarantees. *Gore v. United States,*[29] for example, spoke of the double jeopardy clause as "rooted in history," in contrast to an "evolving concept like due process." Because due process was an "evolving concept," it rendered "old principles * * * subject to re-evaluation in light of later experience" and the "evolving gloss of civilized standards."

Prior to the adoption of selective incorporation, most of the criminal procedure cases stressing that due process analysis was not "frozen-in-history" involved procedures that would have been governed by specific guarantees of the Bill of Rights if those guarantees had been deemed applicable to the states. Once selective incorporation took hold in the 1960s, and almost all of the procedural guarantees relating to criminal procedure were incorporated and made applicable to the states, the due process analysis of the past might have been viewed as ripe for reexamination. However, a reexamination did not occur in either the 1970s or 1980s. Over that period the Court added substantially to the stream of criminal process rulings under procedural due process that stood apart from the application of the incorporated guarantees. In doing so, it relied upon the same "evolving concept" of due process that had dominated due process analysis in the past, which lead it in several instances to condemn practices never thought to raise significant difficulties at common law.[30]

A reexamination of due process analysis did occur, however, in the 1990s. In *Pacific Mutu-*

---

27. See § 11.1(a), and § 2.4(e).

28. See Jackson v. Denno, discussed in § 10.5(a).

29. 357 U.S. 386, 78 S.Ct. 1280, 2 L.Ed.2d 1405 (1958).

30. See e.g. § 18.5(b) (delay in prosecution); § 11.1(c) (failure to appoint counsel on appeal as of right); § 24.5(d) (refusing to allow defendant to testify); § 11.2(e) (failure to appoint expert to assist the defense).

al Life Insurance Co. v. Haslip,[31] a civil case presenting a due process challenge to a state's common law method of assessing punitive damages, Justice Scalia urged that due process analysis return to the lesson of *Murray's Lessee*: if a procedure has a strong common law pedigree, that necessarily makes it the law of the land and consistent with due process. Justice Scalia acknowledged that, over the years, the "concept of 'fundamental fairness' under the Fourteenth Amendment * * * [had become] increasingly decoupled from the traditional historical approach." He attributed that development to the Court carrying over to the states through selective incorporation prior interpretations of incorporated guarantees (as applied in federal cases) that "had departed from their common law meaning." That application, he argued, was distinguishable from determining the independent content of due process. In the latter context, he argued, "no procedure firmly rooted in the practices of our people can be so 'fundamentally unfair' as to deny due process of law."

Justice Scalia stood alone in *Pacific Mutual*. For the majority, Justice Blackmun concluded that even though the common law method for assessing punitive damages was "well established before the Fourteenth Amendment was enacted," that did not preclude an inquiry to determine whether that method as applied violated due process. In light of the longstanding acceptance of the common law method, it would be inappropriate to declare that method "so inherently unfair as to deny due process and be per se unconstitutional," but "[i]t would be just as inappropriate to say that, because punitive damages have been recognized for so long, their imposition is never unconstitutional." Justice Blackmun quoted in this connection, *Williams v. Illinois*,[32] a criminal case, where the Court had noted: " '[N]either the antiquity of a practice nor the fact of steadfast legislative and judicial adherence to it through the centuries insulates it from constitutional attack.' " Justice O'Connor also re-

lied upon *Williams v. Illinois* in her more extensive rebuttal of Justice Scalia's position. Justice Kennedy, in another separate opinion, noted that he agreed with Justice Scalia that "the judgment of history should govern the outcome in the current case," but could not "say with the confidence maintained by Justice Scalia * * * that widespread adherence to a historical practice always forecloses further inquiry when a party challenges an ancient institution or procedure as violative of due process."

Although refusing to go as far as Justice Scalia urged, the Supreme Court since the late 1980s certainly has given great weight to the approval of history in determining the independent content of due process as applied to state criminal systems. The Court has described historical acceptance as providing a "strong indication" that the practice in question does not offend a fundamental principle of justice.[33] Where a procedure has deep common law roots, those roots have helped to sustain it even though all but a few states have now departed from that common law tradition. So too, when the sanction of history supported a procedure, the Court has not spoken of due process as an "evolving concept."

This strong emphasis upon historical acceptance appears to be tied directly to the current Court's view that, "[b]eyond the specific guarantees enumerated in the Bill of Rights the Due Process Clause has limited operation."[34] The Court has warned that carrying procedural rights beyond the specifics of the incorporated guarantees through "the open-ended rubric of the Due Process Clause invites undue interference with both considered legislative judgment and the careful balance that the Constitution strikes between liberty and order." Giving great weight to historical acceptance of a practice restricts the potential of that "open ended rubric" and tends to ensure that the "category of infraction that violate

---

31. 499 U.S. 1, 111 S.Ct. 1032, 113 L.Ed.2d 1 (1991).

32. 399 U.S. 235, 90 S.Ct. 2018, 26 L.Ed.2d 586 (1970).

33. Schad v. Arizona, 501 U.S. 624, 111 S.Ct. 2491, 115 L.Ed.2d 555 (1991). See also Martin v. Ohio, 480 U.S. 228,

107 S.Ct. 1098, 94 L.Ed.2d 267 (1987); Medina v. California, 505 U.S. 437, 112 S.Ct. 2572, 120 L.Ed.2d 353 (1992).

34. See the text following note 1 infra.

fundamental fairness" is "defined * * * very narrowly."

Contemporary consensus. Prior to the adoption of the selective incorporation doctrine, the current consensus among the states was a key guidepost in determining whether a state procedure violated due process. Quite often, the challenged state procedure would have been prohibited by a specific guarantee of the Bill of Rights if that guarantee had been applicable to the states, and the issue for the Court was whether that particular aspect of the Bill of Rights guarantee (typically endorsed by the common law) reflected one of those "immutable principles of justice which inhere in the very idea of free government." Taking account of the evolving character of due process, the Court would find in the widespread current acceptance of a procedure strong evidence that the common law's prohibition of that procedure did not reflect "a fundamental principle," but simply the common law's preference for one form among several that might achieve basic justice. On the other hand, the widespread prohibition of a procedure based upon state counterparts to a federal Bill of Rights guarantee was taken as evidence that this application of the guarantee did reflect a fundamental principle of justice.

Following the adoption of selective incorporation, though the focus of due process analysis shifted to determining the independent content of due process, the articulation of the standard of fundamental fairness remained the same, and it continued to call for consideration of the contemporary consensus. The "relevant inquiry," the Court has repeatedly noted, is whether the challenged state procedure "offends some principle of justice so rooted in the traditions and conscience of our people as to be ranked as fundamental." Where a challenged procedure is widely accepted among the states, that contemporary consensus strongly suggests that the practice is not contrary to the "conscience of our people." Widespread rejection, though less telling in itself, may contribute to the conclusion that the practice does offend one of those " 'fundamental conceptions of justice' * * * which define the 'community's sense of fair play and decency.' " Not surprisingly, therefore, the Court has characterized "widely shared practice" as a "significant indication" of what "fundamental fairness and rationality require" under free-standing due process.[35]

While the Court has taken note of a consensus in state practice in a variety of contexts, those cases clearly indicate that the contribution of a contemporary consensus in determining the independent content of due process varies with the nature of the consensus and its relationship to historical traditions. The contemporary consensus appears to be given the greatest weight where it reflects continued widespread acceptance of a practice that also has deep roots in our common law heritage. This combination is not conclusive, but as the Court has noted: "If a thing has been practiced for two hundred years by common consent, it will need a strong case for the Fourteenth Amendment to affect it." Similarly, where a very strong contemporary consensus rejects a procedure (i.e., where all but a few states reject it), and that rejection follows a position well established at common law, that consensus will contribute significantly to the case against the procedure.[36]

Where the common law and the contemporary consensus point in different directions, the significance of the contemporary consensus is likely to differ according to whether it supports or rejects the challenged practice. In *Medina v. California*,[37] the Court characterized "contemporary practice" as being "of limited relevance to the due process inquiry" and cited in support *Martin v. Ohio* and *Patterson v. New York*. In both cases, the challenged state

---

35. Schad v. Arizona, 501 U.S. 624, 111 S.Ct. 2491, 115 L.Ed.2d 555 (1991).

36. See e.g., Cooper v. Oklahoma, 517 U.S. 348, 116 S.Ct. 1373, 134 L.Ed.2d 498 (1996) (Oklahoma requirement that defendant prove his competency to stand trial by clear and convincing evidence was contrary to "late 18th century" precedents, which suggested use of a stan-

dard more favorable to the defendant , and was contrary to "contemporary practice," with only 4 of 50 states imposing such a heavy burden).

37. 505 U.S. 437, 112 S.Ct. 2572, 120 L.Ed.2d 353 (1992), (due process not violated by placing on the defense the burden of establishing incompetency to stand trial). See also in the text following note 42 infra.

procedure (involving the allocation of the burden of proof) was consistent with the traditional common law position, which prevailed when both the Constitution and the Fourteenth Amendment were adopted, but it subsequently had been rejected by the vast majority of states (all but two in *Martin*). In both cases, the Court sustained the state practice, noting that the abandonment of the common law view by a majority of states did not render that position inconsistent with due process, which "require[s] that only the most basic procedural safeguards be observed." The question of constitutionality, the Court noted, "is not answered by cataloging the practices of * * * [the] states."

On the other hand, where a state practice is widely accepted, but contrary to a now largely discarded common law standard, that acceptance is likely to have far more than "limited relevance." The Court has repeatedly noted, starting with *Hurtado,* that due process does not lock the states into common law forms, which may well have been the product of the conditions and times in which they were developed rather than a fundamental principle of justice. So too, for those portions of the process that were added in more recent times, and therefore lack strong historical traditions, widespread acceptance of a particular practice speaks strongly in favor of its constitutionality. That may be overcome, however, by an analysis which shows that the states in dealing with this relatively new area have lost sight of basic principles of justice that were established in our common law heritage and continue to shape the process as a whole.

Structural prerequisites. In determining whether a procedural practice has the endorsement of history or the sanction of a contemporary consensus, the Court has looked primarily to whether the practice has explicit acceptance in the relevant case law and statutes (historical or current). A practice will not be characterized as part of our common law heritage, or as approved by a contemporary consensus, simply because there is little or no precedent specifically prohibiting the practice. Thus, when the Court had before it such practices as a prosecutor failing to disclose known exculpatory evidence to the defense, a judge failing to inform a defendant convicted of murder that the judge was considering a death sentence even though the prosecutor had recommended life imprisonment, and a police officer using an unnecessarily suggestive procedure in obtaining an eyewitness identification later used at trial, no reference was made to common law traditions or a possible contemporary consensus. Instead, the Court determined whether those practices violated the independent content of due process by testing them against the basic structural prerequisites of the American criminal justice process. The questions asked were whether the challenged practices were in conflict with such prerequisites, and if so, whether the conflict was so sharp and significant as to establish a deprivation of "fundamental fairness." The same questions often are asked as well even where history or a contemporary consensus (or both) speak to the challenged practice.

The structural prerequisites applied by the Court are derived primarily from the structure of the adversarial, accusatorial system of adjudication established under the common law, but also are derived from other cornerstones of the common law system as adopted in this country. Thus, the prerequisites include: (1) providing the defendant with notice of the case against him (including the open presentation of that case); (2) providing the defendant with a "meaningful opportunity to present a complete defense"; (3) providing an unbiased decision maker; (4) "satisfy[ing] the appearance of justice"; (5) respecting the dignity of the individual; and (6) imposing on the state an obligation that does not allow it simply to advocate its case, but requires it to be concerned as well that its advocacy does not lead to the conviction of the innocent.

As the Court has noted, these basic prerequisites of fairness hardly provide a "yardstick" which can be used in a "mechanical" fashion to test the validity of a challenged procedure. Rather, their application requires " 'a delicate process of adjustment inescapably involving the exercise of judgment by those whom the Constitution entrusted with the unfolding of the process.' " Sensitive to the criticism that this task allows for the insertion of personal values and is dependent upon subjective judgments, the Court has emphasized that " 'judges are not free, in "defining due process" to impose * * * their personal and private notions of fairness,' " but are limited by various standards that guide their determination of whether a fundamental conception of justice has been violated. These include, as previously discussed, the weight given to history and to the consensus of contemporary practice, reliance on "the past course of decisions," and the requirement that the application of the basic fairness prerequisites to a particular practice be supported by "reason."

The Court's sensitivity to criticism of the subjective quality of due process analysis dates back to the pre-incorporation days, when that analysis was directed more to the possible overlap with safeguards contained in the specifics of the Bill of Rights than to determining what additional safeguards were to be found in due process. With the adoption of selective incorporation, concerns regarding subjectivity in due process analysis came to focus on the independent content of due process. Closely related was a new concern—the potential for dramatically expanding constitutional regulation of state criminal procedure beyond the incorporated guarantees through a broad reading of the independent content of due process. In *Dowling v. United States*,[38] the Supreme Court noted that "beyond the specific guarantees enumerated in the Bill of Rights, the Due Process Clause has limited operation." In *Medina v. California*,[39] the Court explained the need for "very narrowly" defining the independent content of due process: "The Bill of Rights speaks in explicit terms to many aspects of criminal procedure, and the expansion of those constitutional guarantees under the open-ended rubric of the Due Process Clause invites undue interference with both considered legislative judgments and the careful balance that the Constitution strikes between liberty and order." Of course, the vehicle most likely to produce that expansion is a due process analysis grounded in the application of

the structural prerequisites of fairness. In its evaluation of history and the contemporary consensus, the Court gives greatest weight to the historical endorsement of a procedure and its current widespread acceptance, both of which operate to sustain the constitutionality of the practice.

Reflecting the concern expressed in *Dowling* and *Medina*, the Court has stated that its determinations of the independent content of due process should be guided by deference, caution, and a focus on extreme cases. The Court has noted that, " 'because the States have considered expertise in matters of criminal procedure and the criminal process is grounded in centuries of common-law tradition,' " it will " 'exercise substantial deference to legislative judgments in this area.' " Recognizing that reasonable minds may differ on what process is needed to meet those structural prerequisites that constitute the essence of fundamental fairness, the Court has stressed that it will not "engage in a finely tuned review of the wisdom" of state procedures. It has noted that "[a] state procedure 'does not run foul of the Fourteenth Amendment because another method may seem to our thinking to be fairer or wiser or give a surer promise of protection' " to the defendant, and that "[d]ue process does not require that 'every conceivable step be taken, at whatever cost, to eliminate the possibility of convicting an innocent person.' " The Court also has stressed in various contexts that the focus must be on the operation of the practice in the individual case, and a state practice therefore should not be deemed to violate due process unless it conflicts with a structural prerequisite of fairness in a manner that actually causes substantial prejudice to the particular defendant.

Notwithstanding such guidelines, the independent content of due process has come to play an important role in the constitutional regulation of criminal procedure. As noted in subsection (b), it is the source of constitutional requirements that extend to every stage of the process and that dominate at some stages.

---

38. 493 U.S. 342, 110 S.Ct. 668, 107 L.Ed.2d 708 (1990). See also note 1 supra.

39. 505 U.S. 437, 112 S.Ct. 2572, 120 L.Ed.2d 353 (1992).

Moreover, most of those requirements were imposed in the post-incorporation era. The concern expressed in cases such as *Dowling* and *Medina* has not halted the continuous growth in due process regulation, and has not prevented the Court from imposing due process requirements invalidating practices that had been followed for many years in many states.

Utilitarian balancing. Though the Supreme Court's concern that the due process clause not be overused in criminal justice cases has hardly confined due process to the limited role attributed to it in *Medina* and *Dowling,* that concern did lead the Court in *Medina* to reject for criminal cases application of a utilitarian balancing standard that had guided procedural due process determinations in various other contexts.[40] In *Mathews v. Eldridge,*[41] a case involving an administrative proceeding, the Court announced a three-factor balancing standard, which it later characterized as "a general approach for testing challenged state procedures under a due process claim." Under *Mathews,* once a court determines that a litigant has at stake an interest protected by due process, its task is then to analyze and balance three factors: "First, the private interest that will be affected by the official action; second, the risk of an erroneous deprivation of such interest through the procedures used, and the probable value, if any, of additional or substitute procedural safeguards; and finally, the Government's interest, including the function involved and the fiscal and administrative burdens that the additional or substitute procedural requirement would entail."

Although the Supreme Court considered numerous due process challenges to state criminal procedures in the fifteen year period between *Mathews* and *Medina v. California,* it utilized the *Mathews* balancing test in only one of those cases, and its use there was not debated. In *Medina,* the applicability of the *Mathews* standard was viewed as a central issue in resolving a due process challenge to a state law that allocated to the defense the burden of establishing that the defendant was

incompetent to stand trial. The *Medina* majority rejected the contention that such a law should be judged under the *Mathews* balancing test. *Mathews'* analysis, the Court concluded, was inappropriate for this case and criminal cases in general. In criminal cases, the specific guarantees of the Bill of Rights set the basic constitutional balance "between liberty and order," with the due process clause having only "limited operation" beyond its incorporation of those guarantees. Accordingly, the appropriate standard for judging the independent content of due process in criminal cases was the "narrower inquiry" of the traditional fundamental fairness standard, as set forth in *Patterson v. New York*[42] (also involving a due process challenge on a burden-of-proof issue). *Patterson* had pointed out that appropriate deference to state primacy required that a state decision on the allocation of burden of proof " 'not [be] subject to proscription under the Due Process Clause unless it offends some principle of justice so rooted in the traditions and conscience of our people to be ranked as fundamental.' " Applying this standard, the *Medina* majority looked to both the historical treatment of the burden of proof as to incompetency and the logical implications of the prohibition against the trial of an incompetent defendant ("a recognized principle of 'fundamental fairness' "), and it concluded that neither provided a basis for holding that the state's allocation of the burden of proof to the defendant violated due process.

The *Medina* majority's decision not to apply the *Mathews* standard to criminal justice cases obviously rested, in part, on the failure of the *Mathews* standard to acknowledge the role of history and tradition in the definition of due process. However, the *Mathews* analysis still might have been deemed acceptable, as playing a role alongside history and tradition, as evidenced by the Court's application of the *Mathews* analysis to aspects of civil process that also have deep roots in our common law heritage. The more critical concern for the *Medina* Court apparently was the use of balancing in

---

40. See also § 26.4(d) following note 21.

41. 424 U.S. 319, 96 S.Ct. 893, 47 L.Ed.2d 18 (1976).

42. 432 U.S. 197, 97 S.Ct. 2319, 53 L.Ed.2d 281 (1977). See also the text at note 37 supra.

the *Mathews* analysis. In applying the fundamental fairness standard, the *Medina* majority looked not only to historical practice, but also to what was essential to adhere to a basic structural principle of fairness (the prohibition against forcing to trial an incompetent defendant). This required it to explore the extent to which allocating the burden to the defendant posed a risk to the implementation of that principle. Such an assessment would also be required under the *Mathews* standard, but there the Court would also evaluate the potential for reducing that risk by shifting the burden to the prosecution and the cost to the state of doing so. The *Medina* majority, in contrast, stressed that the question before it was not whether the state could do more to implement the prohibition against trying the incompetent, but simply whether the state's procedure substantially undercut that prohibition. If it did not, deference to the state's legislative judgment required its constitutional acceptance no matter how much more might have been achieved at little or no cost to the state.

(d) Substantive Due Process. Some commentators view procedural rights as basically substantive rights where the rights are designed to protect interests that are not tied to the basic functions of adjudication (as illustrated by an evidentiary privilege designed to protect a privacy interest). However, the Court has treated all due process challenges to the procedures utilized in the adjudicatory process as procedural due process claims, rather than substantive due process claims. Substantive

due process issues are raised primarily by challenges to the definition of criminality and to the use and severity of sanctions. However, substantive due process claims occasionally will be presented in connection with process issues. Thus, in *Riggins v. Nevada*[43], substantive due process was held to forbid forcing a defendant to continue to take antipsychotic drugs during his trial in the absence of a showing that the medication was medically appropriate, and essential for defendant's safety or the safety of others. So too, due process claims relating to the state's power to exercise custodial control over an accused, to utilize physical force against a suspect, and to subject a suspect to coercive interrogation, all have been treated as raising substantive due process issues.[44]

The first obstacle facing a substantive due process claim is the "more-specific provision" rule of *Graham v. Connor*,[45] which has a foundation similar to the *Dowling/Medina* standard for procedural due process. Under the *Graham* rule, where one of the specific constitutional guarantees "provides an external textual source of constitutional protection" against a particular type of government behavior, "that Amendment, not the more generalized notion of 'substantive due process,' must be the guide for analyzing those claims." This position reflects the Court's traditional "reluctan[ce] to expand the concept of substantive due process because the guideposts for responsible decision making in this chartered area are scarce and open-ended."

---

43. 504 U.S. 127, 112 S.Ct. 1810, 118 L.Ed.2d 479 (1992).

44. See United States v. Salerno, discussed in § 12.3(c) (custody control); Rochin v. California, described in § 2.4(f) and County of Sacramento v. Lewis, described at note 44 infra (physical force); and Chavez v. Martinez, 538 U.S. 760, 123 S.Ct. 1994, 155 L.Ed.2d 984 (2003) (coercive interrogation). At issue in *Chavez* was a claim alleging a due process violation in the interrogation itself, rather than the more common coerced confession claim which focuses on the trial use of an involuntary statement. See § 6.2 at note 17, and § 6.5 at note 6. The prohibition against state use of a coerced confession has not clearly been identified as a substantive due process claim, perhaps because of its incorporation of a self-incrimination analysis. That prohibition was recognized long before the self-incrimination clause was held applicable to the states

under the selective incorporation doctrine. The Court subsequently has described the prohibition against trial use of coerced confession as having "two constitutional bases * * *: The Fifth Amendment right against self-incrimination and the Due Process Clause." Dickerson v. United States, 530 U.S. 428, 120 S.Ct. 2326, 147 L.Ed.2d 405 (2000). See also § 6.2.

45. 490 U.S. 386, 109 S.Ct. 1865, 104 L.Ed.2d 443, (1989). See also Albright v. Oliver, 510 U.S. 266, 114 S.Ct. 807, 127 L.Ed.2d 114 (1994) (where petitioner claimed that initiation of a criminal prosecution based on clearly unreliable evidence violated his personal liberty, majority agreed that claim was cognizable under substantive due process only if that liberty interest was distinctive from the pretrial deprivation of liberty that is the focus of the Fourth Amendment requirement that an arrest be supported by probable cause).

A second obstacle facing a substantive due process claim is the Court's general reluctance to turn to that clause absent the most compelling case. Thus, in *County of Sacramento v. Lewis*,[46] the Court majority concluded that acts of a government official would be deemed to violate substantive due process only where so egregiously abusive as to "shock the conscience." The Court there concluded that police recklessness in a high speed chase that resulted in the death of a passenger in the pursued vehicle fell short of that standard as the police were acting on an "instant judgment" and without "harmful purpose." The conscience shocking standard requires egregiousness of the character of the forced stomach pumping which was held to violate that standard in *Rochin v. California*.[47] Moreover, the governmental action also must deprive the individual of a liberty interest that history and tradition establish as entitled to due process protection.

In *Chavez v. Martinez*,[48] the plurality, concurring, and dissenting opinions all recognized that "shock the conscience" was not the only substantive due process test. A substantive due process violation could also be grounded on the state having violated some "fundamental liberty interest", recognized by history and tradition as "implicit in the concept of ordered liberty." However, the Court has also indicated that this requires a strong historical taboo, such as that against torture by government officials. Thus, in *Albright v. Oliver*,[49] the majority concluded that a false criminal accusation by a governmental official did not violate such an interest, once the impact of the accusation was separated from the individual's subsequent custodial restraint as a result of an arrest.[50]

§ 2.8   The Preference for Expansive Interpretations

(a) The Nature of the Preference. As noted in § 2.1, the constitutionalization of

criminal procedure has been a product of Supreme Court decisions that have both extended the application of various Bill of Rights guarantees to the states and adopted expansive interpretations of those guarantees. Of course, what constitutes an expansive interpretation depends upon one's perspective. Some see as expansive any interpretation that goes beyond the narrowest reading that could be derived from the language or history of the particular guarantee. From this perspective, almost all of the Supreme Court's interpretations have been expansive. For example, the Fifth Amendment's self-incrimination prohibition has been held to go beyond merely protecting the defendant from being compelled to give incriminating testimony at his own trial. Similarly, the Sixth Amendment right to assistance of counsel has not been limited to guaranteeing assistance at trial or to guaranteeing only the right of a defendant to retain trial counsel at his own expense. The prohibition against double jeopardy, as another example, has been extended beyond merely barring a retrial on the same offense following an acquittal.

Others would view an interpretation as truly expansive only if it gives a guarantee the broadest reading that could conceivably be developed from any of several guideposts, including language, history, underlying policy, and, for some, a sense that the defense should be entitled to all procedural protections needed to offset the resource advantages of the state. From this perspective, very few of the Court's interpretations of criminal procedure guarantees are likely to be characterized as expansive. The right to jury trial, for example, does not extend to all proceedings that might be deemed "criminal" in their character. The confrontation clause does not limit the prosecution's evidence to the testimony of persons who take the stand at trial. The self-incrimina-

46. 523 U.S. 833, 118 S.Ct. 1708, 140 L.Ed.2d 1043 (1998).

47. 342 U.S. 165, 72 S.Ct. 205, 96 L.Ed. 183 (1952), discussed in § 2.4 at note 13.

48. 538 U.S. 760, 123 S.Ct. 1994, 155 L.Ed.2d 984 (2003), also discussed in note 44 supra.

49. See note 45 supra.

50. The *Albright* Court noted its general reluctance to extend substantive due process beyond its modern home of "matters relating to marriage, family, procreation, and the right to bodily integrity."

tion clause does not prohibit forcing a person to reveal physical evidence that might be incriminating. The double jeopardy prohibition does not bar all retrials of defendants based upon the same criminal conduct.

Most observers agree, however, that for an interpretation to be characterized as "expansive," it is not enough that it simply exceeds the narrowest possible reading, but neither must it necessarily adopt the broadest conceivable reading. The emphasis is as much upon how the Court approaches the provision as upon the scope of its interpretation. Expansive interpretations start from a presumption of liberal construction. They treat a constitutional guarantee not as narrow and technical, but as reflecting an important policy that must be safeguarded against circumvention and even minor encroachments. An expansive approach reflects, in particular, a willingness to expand the scope of the guarantee to meet changed conditions, especially growth in governmental authority. Judged by this standard, the Supreme Court's construction of the criminal procedure guarantees over the last several decades, in general, has reflected a preference for expansive interpretations. The Court's treatment of those guarantees stands in sharp contrast, for example, to its treatment of the constitutional prohibition against state impairment of the obligation of contracts. The much closer analogy is its approach to the First Amendment, where the Court speaks of applying "more exacting judicial scrutiny" in judging the constitutionality of governmental action.

To say that the overall trend of the Court's constitutional criminal procedure rulings has favored expansive interpretation does not, of course, suggest that the Court has uniformly favored that position throughout its history. The degree of support for expansive interpretation has varied from one period in the Court's history to another. Moreover, the preference has always existed as no more than a principle that guides interpretation in a general fashion. Perhaps no period in the Court's history was marked by a more rapid expansion of the constitutional rights of defendants and suspects than the decade of the 1960s, when the Warren Court's rulings produced what is commonly characterized as the "criminal procedure revolution." Yet, even during that period, there were several major rulings that could be described as refusing to adopt an expansive interpretation of a criminal procedure safeguard. In the end, even a strong preference for expansive interpretations may be offset by the special setting of the individual case which pulls the Court in a different direction.

(b) The Reasons for the Preference. The Court has only infrequently commented upon the premises that underlie its adoption of a preference for expansive interpretations of criminal procedure guarantees. Moreover, those comments have explained only in very general fashion why the Court believes it can justifiably play a more "activist" role in interpreting these guarantees than in interpreting other constitutional provisions. Commentators, in contrast, have offered a series of well developed rationales for adoption of especially expansive interpretations of criminal procedure guarantees. One can only speculate as to whether the justices actually have had those rationales in mind as they shaped their criminal procedure rulings. However, several of the rationales cited by the commentators do find support in occasional comments of the justices. Those rationales look primarily to three factors, each discussed below: (1) the relationship of criminal procedure to the general protection of civil liberties; (2) the relationship of criminal procedure to the protection of minorities; and (3) the presence of various structural elements that enhance the Court's authority in exercising constitutional review of the criminal process. It seems likely that all three of these factors have contributed to some extent in the development of the preference for expansionist interpretations, with the contribution of each varying with the individual justice and the particular period in the Court's history.

The civil liberties concern. At least since the late 1930s, the Court has made the protection of civil liberties one of its primary concerns. It has shifted its focus from the protection of property rights to the protection of liberties deemed more fundamental to the preservation of individual freedom. The Court has left no doubt that it considers the procedural rights of the accused to be among those more fundamental freedoms. It has accepted the premise that procedural fairness and regularity in the enforcement of the criminal law are essential to a free society. "In the end," it has explained, "life and liberty can be as much endangered from illegal methods used to convict those thought to be criminals as from actual criminals themselves." Indeed, it has added, the " 'quality of a nation's civilization can be largely measured by the methods it uses in the enforcement of its criminal law.' "

The Court's heightened sensitivity to the role of the constitutional criminal procedure guarantees as a "bulwark against oppression" is said to date back to the 1930s, when two developments may have especially influenced the Court's thinking. It was during the 1930s that the famed Wickersham Commission Report called the nation's attention to widespread "lawlessness" in law enforcement. It also was during the 1930s that the actions of totalitarian regimes recently formed in Western Europe produced stark illustrations of the potential for using the criminal justice process to eliminate political opposition.

Protecting minorities. The decade of 1930s was also marked by the Court's tentative suggestion in the *Carolene Products* case that one of its major functions is to protect against discrimination those "discrete and insular minorities" who cannot count on the protection of the political process.[1] In later years that suggestion took on substantial force, particularly in the Court's application of the Fourteenth Amendment to instances of racial discrimination by government. Safeguarding the rights of the accused has been viewed as relating to the Court's role of protecting minorities in two respects. First, accused persons are themselves viewed as a highly unpopular minority. As Justice Frankfurter noted, it is precisely because appeals based on criminal process guarantees are so often made by "dubious characters" that infringement of those guarantees calls for "alert and strenuous resistance";

other constitutional protections, such as the First Amendment guarantees, "easily summon powerful support against encroachment," but criminal process guarantees are "normally invoked by those accused of crime, and criminals have few friends." In particular, the legislature is unlikely to be sympathetic to the procedural rights of the accused as "an overwhelming preponderance of political incentives favor unrestricted enforcement of the criminal law."

Second, the criminal process is seen as having a special bearing upon various disadvantaged minority groups. Speaking of the Warren Court, former Solicitor General Archibald Cox suggested that "[m]any purely procedural questions * * * were influenced by the realization that in another case they might affect the posture of a Negro in a hostile southern court." So too, it has been noted, once the Court had accepted "the challenge of guaranteeing the rights of Negroes and other disadvantaged groups to equality before the law," it was only natural for it to seek to "ameliorate the invidious discrimination between rich and poor which existed in the criminal process" and to seek to deter unlawful police activities that so often impacted minorities.

"Judicial review" justifications. The Court's preference for expansive interpretations also is attributed to several factors that supposedly make its exercise of judicial review more readily supportable in the criminal justice area than in many other areas of constitutional adjudication. Initially, the structure of many of the applicable guarantees—in particular, the specificity of most of the Fourth, Fifth and Sixth Amendment guarantees—is said to permit criminal procedure rulings to be more firmly rooted in the text and history of the applicable constitutional provisions. Of course, some provisions, such as the due process clause, are open-ended, but at least they present no ambiguity as to their applicability to the criminal process.

Adding to this supposedly firmer foundation for judicial review in the criminal procedure

---

§ 2.8

1. United States v. Carolene Products Co., 304 U.S. 144, 152 n. 4, 58 S.Ct. 778, 783 n. 4, 82 L.Ed. 1234 (1938).

area is the fact that the Court only infrequently is required to overturn legislative decision-making. Rulings on police investigative methods generally deal with practices that have been instituted by the police without formal legislative authorization. Rulings relating to trial and pretrial procedures similarly tend to deal with practices adopted by courts on their own initiative. Criminal procedure rulings, it is argued, largely bypass the concerns raised by the anti-majoritarian character of judicial overturning of legislation.

Another factor cited as contributing to the Court's willingness to act boldly in the area of criminal procedure is its presumed expertise in dealing with at least those procedural issues that relate to the process of adjudication. The Supreme Court has not described its competence in this area in quite the same way as commentators, who claim that lawyers (and judges) have unique expertise in deciding "what procedures are needed fairly to make what decisions." Yet, the Court has clearly indicated that it views itself as exercising a special responsibility in reviewing procedures of adjudication. Those procedures, it has noted, relate directly to the integrity of the judicial process. Moreover, while the Court's rulings on adjudicatory procedure undoubtedly have a bearing on the achievement of substantive policies, they do not prohibit the legislature from setting substantive standards, but merely require that proof of violation of these standards be established in a certain way. Accordingly, as Justice Jackson noted, the determination of "procedural fairness" is treated as "a specialized responsibility within the competence of the judiciary on which they do not bend before political branches of Government, as they should on matters of policy which comprise substantive law."

Finally, the Court is said to feel at home in the area of constitutional criminal procedure because its rulings here are thought to be more effective in achieving their intended reforms than its rulings in many other areas. This greater effectiveness of procedural rulings is supported under two contrasting views of the impact of Supreme Court decisions. Under one view, procedural rulings are less likely than other rulings to be subverted and evaded. Unlike rulings in other areas, the Supreme Court's criminal procedure rulings are not seeking to institute broad social change. Even more significantly, they deal with a process that must work its way through the courts, an institution committed to adhere to the rule of law.

The second view acknowledges that effective enforcement of the Supreme Court's procedural rulings faces serious obstacles. These include: a tradition of police disregarding and evading judicial standards that they view as unrealistic; resource limitations that restrict the defense's capacity to uncover and present in court various types of constitutional violations; the prosecution's use of plea bargaining to avoid litigation on possible constitutional violations; constitutional standards that are sufficiently ambiguous to allow lower courts ample opportunity to sharply confine the impact of the Supreme Court rulings without directly disowning those rulings; and various constitutional violations arising in situations that do not result in a criminal prosecution and therefore reach the courts only if victims pursue civil actions. Taken together, these obstacles may largely offset the natural advantage (noted above) of criminal procedural rulings in gaining implementation. Commentators strongly supportive of the Warren Court argue, however, that even where that natural advantage was largely lost, Supreme Court rulings of the type issued by the Warren Court offered another strength in gaining eventual reform of the criminal justice process. The natural audience for Supreme Court rulings (lawyers and judges) coincides with the actors responsible for a good part of the administration of the process and a large part of its lawmaking. By boldly stating the basic goals of the criminal process as recognized in the Constitution, the Warren Court's opinions are said to have shaped the views of those actors and to have influenced their actions, not simply in their adherence to Supreme Court rulings, but in their general acceptance of those goals in reforming the law and practice of the criminal justice process.

(c) Retroactivity. The doctrine of retroactivity arguably has had a substantial bearing upon the Supreme Court's implementation of its preference for expansive interpretations of the Constitution's criminal procedure guarantees. Prior to the 1960s, each newly announced constitutional standard, no matter how greatly it expanded defendant's rights, was given full retroactive application. This meant that the new ruling would be applied not only to the case before the Court and all subsequent prosecutions, but also to: (1) previously initiated prosecutions that had not yet been tried or that had resulted in a trial conviction that was still subject to appellate review; and (2) previous convictions that had became "final" (i.e., direct appellate review had been exhausted), but were subject to challenge through the collateral remedy of federal habeas corpus.

The application of new rulings to federal habeas petitions was especially significant because the federal writ remained available to challenge a state or federal conviction on constitutional grounds so long as the convicted person remained "in custody" (which included persons on probation or parole as well as those actually imprisoned). Thus, a person receiving a long sentence could overturn his conviction many years after his trial on the basis of a new ruling that rendered unconstitutional a procedure that had been well accepted as constitutional at the time of that trial. While that newly established constitutional error typically would not bar a reprosecution, the time lapse between the offense and the habeas overturning of the conviction often would make a retrial impracticable. As the Supreme Court itself noted, this combination of retroactivity and the broad availability of the writ of habeas corpus raised the specter that a dramatically expansionist new constitutional ruling might "open * * * wide the prison doors of the land." Thus, when the Warren Court in the early 1960s announced a series of new rulings that could affect the convictions of a substantial portion of the prison populace in various states, it was not surprising that the Court shortly thereafter found occasion to reexamine the previous practice of complete retroactive application of new rulings. That reexamination came in *Linkletter v. Walker*,[2] a habeas case, in which the Court refused to apply retroactively a new ruling holding applicable to the states the Fourth Amendment's exclusionary rule.

In rejecting the concept of automatic retroactivity, *Linkletter* characterized that concept as resting on an outmoded Blackstonian view of the judicial process which treated new rulings as merely setting forth the law as it always existed. The principles governing retroactivity, it noted, should recognize that earlier precedent was an "existing fact until overruled," and that where a new ruling went beyond that earlier precedent, retroactive application often imposed a hardship upon a criminal justice administration that had relied upon the earlier precedent. Accordingly, *Linkletter* and its progeny concluded that retroactivity should be evaluated ruling by ruling, taking into consideration that hardship factor as well as the values served by the new ruling. Where that weighing process led to the conclusion that retroactive application was inappropriate, the new ruling would not be applied at a subsequent trial, appeal, or habeas challenge to the operative event that was the subject of the ruling if that event had occurred before the date of the ruling. Thus, a new ruling on Fourth Amendment searches would apply only to searches undertaken after the date of the ruling (with the single exception of the search in the very case in which the new ruling was announced).

The Court later withdrew from the full implications of the *Linkletter* ruling. It concluded that all new rulings would be available to defendants challenging convictions not yet "final" (i.e. convictions still subject to direct appellate review). However, for the many defendants who sought to take advantage of the new rulings on a habeas challenge, a quite different approach was taken. As discussed in § 28.6, the Court here held that only a very limited class of new rulings would be available to the habeas litigant. In general, the habeas petitioner was limited to challenging his conviction on the basis of "the law prevailing at

2.   381 U.S. 618, 85 S.Ct. 1731, 14 L.Ed.2d 601 (1965).

the time [his] conviction became final." Thus, as a practical matter, the Court rarely need be concerned that a new expansive ruling might be used to overturn convictions in cases that cannot readily be retried as a consequence of the time lapse since the original trial.

§ 2.9 Guideposts for Interpretation

As noted in § 2.8(a), the Court's acceptance of a general preference for the liberal construction of criminal procedure guarantees does not invariably produce expansive interpretations of those guarantees. Numerous other guideposts also contribute to the Court's rulings, and these may at times point to a narrower interpretation. Among the most significant of these guideposts are: (1) past precedent; (2) the historical acceptance of the practice being challenged; (3) the relationship of a proposed expansive interpretation to the truth-finding objective of the process; (4) the desirability of fashioning per se and prophylactic standards encompassing more than what would be prohibited under an analysis focusing upon the particular facts of the individual case; and (5) the impact of a proposed ruling on the efficient enforcement of the criminal law. Each of these factors has been viewed by at least some justices as having a substantial bearing on how far the Court should carry its preference for expansive interpretations. The Court's determination of the weight to be given to one or another of these factors often has been crucial in the adoption or rejection of a particular expansive interpretation. That weight has varied, however, with the composition of the Court, as the justices have persistently been divided as to the appropriate treatment of each of these factors.

(a) Stare Decisis. The Supreme Court has long recognized that the doctrine of *stare decisis* ("stand by the thing decided") has only "a limited application in the field of constitutional law." This is so, the Court has explained, because unlike erroneous decisions grounded on other sources of law, erroneous constitu-

tional decisions cannot be corrected by statute, but require a constitutional amendment, thereby rendering "correction through legislative action * * * practically impossible."

In *Payne v. Tennessee*,[1] the Court added that, as among the various fields of constitutional litigation, "[c]onsiderations in favor of *stare decisis* are at their acme in cases involving property and contract rights, where reliance interests are involved, * * * [with the] opposite * * * true in cases such as the present one involving procedural and evidentiary rules." *Payne* involved a criminal prosecution in which the precedent overruled by the Court had operated to exclude evidence (a victim-impact statement sought to be admitted in a capital sentencing hearing). A criminal defendant obviously would not have shaped his conduct in reliance upon such an evidentiary prohibition. But the Court spoke of evidentiary and procedural rulings in general, and not just those that dealt with the exclusion of evidence to the benefit of the defendant. Its reasoning suggested that neither would a reliance interest be recognized where the issue was overruling a precedent that benefitted the state and the prosecution had shaped its prosecution around that precedent (possibly with no prospect for salvaging that prosecution after the overruling). The Court had weighed the state's "reliance interest" in shaping the law governing the retroactive application of rulings establishing new standards favorable to the defense, including rulings that overruled prior precedent[2]. The state's "reliance interest" accordingly would not be given additional weight in determining whether or not to overrule a criminal procedure precedent favoring the prosecution that otherwise is an appropriate candidate for overruling.

While *Payne* concluded that the case for *stare decisis* was at its low point in criminal process cases, that does not render stare decisis irrelevant. *Stare decisis* remains a significant contributor to constitutional decision-making in criminal procedure, as it does in

§ 2.9

1. 501 U.S. 808, 111 S.Ct. 2597, 115 L.Ed.2d 720 (1991).

2. As to the limited retroactive application of such rulings, largely restricted to cases not yet reaching the point of a finalized conviction, see § 2.8(c).

other areas in which adherence to past precedent is not bolstered by substantial reliance interests. Overrulings remain fairly rare. Even during the Warren Court era, the Court averaged less than two constitutional overrulings per term. With the frequent changes in the composition of the Court and the accompanying dramatic shifts in the prevailing judicial philosophy from one decade to the next, the infrequency of overrulings can hardly be attributed to consistent acceptance over the years of the correctness of all the constitutional decisions that have not been overruled. The Court obviously has been accepting and applying past precedent with which its current members would not have agreed had the issue been considered *res nova*.

Commentators suggest that *stare decisis* acts in at least three distinctive ways in preserving constitutional precedent not necessarily viewed as correctly decided by the current Court majority. First, it may operate to make the correctness of the past precedent a non-issue. Many constitutional rulings are so well settled that they simply are not open to reconsideration. The justices simply accept and apply them without asking whether they reflect a correct interpretation of the Constitution. Second, institutional considerations supporting stare decisis lead the Court in many instances to choose the path of simply confining rather than overruling a precedent which the current majority views as erroneous. Supreme Court opinions being what they are, the Court almost invariably has the option of reading a precedent so as not to extend it, or even to shrink it, sometimes to the point of practical nullification. Finally, on occasion, the values underlying *stare decisis* appear to have led a Court majority to not only refuse to overrule a precedent with which it disagrees, but to have begrudgingly accepted the need to extend the reach of that decision in some settings. This occurred, for example, in the Court's treatment of *Miranda*, a decision often restricted in its impact and scope in later decisions, but which nonetheless was extended where the Court felt that was needed to preserve the basic message of the precedent.[3] Of course,

justices who disagree with a decision but are willing to retain it in the interest of the institutional values underlying *stare decisis* are not naturally inclined to conclude that preserving its baseline standard actually requires its extension. Yet instances arise when at least some of the justices in that group will reach that conclusion and combine with supporters of the precedent to extend it. It is in this application in particular that the operation of *stare decisis* is most appropriately described as "operat[ing] with randomness of a lightening bolt."

(b) The Significance of Historical Acceptance. The basic strands of academic questioning of "originalism" in constitutional interpretation have failed to persuade the Supreme Court, at least in its criminal procedure jurisprudence. As evidenced by its inquiries into the historical background and legislative history of each of the Constitution's criminal process guarantees, the Court clearly has acknowledged its obligation to render decisions that are in accord with the guarantee's original design. By accepting the general direction provided by that historical background and legislative history, even when its content is not entirely consistent, the Court has rejected the contention that originalism is rarely helpful because history is almost always far too ambiguous to provide helpful answers on specific interpretive issues. By treating "the intent of the Framers" and the "original understanding" as virtually synonymous interpretive guides, the Court has rendered insignificant the distinctions between determining the common understanding of the language of the guarantee at the time of its adoption and determining the subjective intent (or expectations) as to content held by the drafters (or ratifiers) of the guarantee.

The one aspect of originalism that has troubled the Supreme Court is the choice of the appropriate level of generality at which the guarantee's original design should be understood. That choice has been a significant issue primarily in dealing with challenges to procedures that were known to the Framers and obviously viewed as not prohibited by the con-

---

3. See e.g., the discussion of § 6.9(g) of Edwards v. Arizona, Arizona v. Roberson, and Minnick v. Mississippi.

stitutional guarantee in question. Where a challenged procedure was unknown at the common law and has no close parallel in any common law practice, testing it against the original design of a guarantee necessarily requires reference to the overarching principles reflected by that design. If the Court could not look to those principles in that setting, a guarantee would operate to prohibit only "the specific abuses that give it birth," and thereby fail to fulfill the Framers' objective of enacting a fundamental legal framework for the future as well as the present. On the other hand, where a practice was widely known and considered acceptable at the time of the adoption of the Bill of Rights, or was subsequently developed and became widely known and accepted at the time of the adoption of the Fourteenth Amendment, the Court also has before it strong evidence of the apparent expectation of the Framers that the practice would not be prohibited by the guarantee they were adopting. Where that expectation appears to be inconsistent with the logical application of an overarching principle reflected in the guarantee's general design, the Court must ask whether the two can be reconciled, and if not, which conception of the Framers' design—the specific expectation or the general objective—shall prevail. The Court's response to that question has been guided by lines of analysis that are readily manipulated, leading to answers that often appear to be inconsistent.

Over the years, historical acceptance has sustained a variety of procedures that might be viewed as inconsistent with a basic function of a particular guarantee. Thus, the Court has looked to historical acceptance in holding that: the right to jury trial does not apply to prosecutions for petty offenses notwithstanding that they obviously are criminal prosecutions; the Fourth Amendment does not prohibit warrantless arrests in public places even where the arresting officer had ample time to obtain a warrant; the double jeopardy prohibition of successive prosecutions for the "same offence" does not apply to successive prosecutions for the same basic criminal conduct under two statutes that use different elements in defining the prohibited offense; and due process does not prohibit the forfeiture of the property of an innocent owner which had been used by others as an instrumentality of crime.[4] In support of such rulings, the Court has noted that where a guarantee has "deep historical roots," it must be interpreted in light of its "common-law understanding." Although the general premise of the guarantee might, as a matter of logic, lead to a contrary result, there are guarantees as to which "a page of history is worth a volume of logic," and instances in which "logic * * * must defer * * * to history and experience."

On the other side, the Court has also developed a variety of countervailing rationales in holding unconstitutional a variety of procedures with equally strong historical pedigrees which indicated that the procedures were viewed by the Framers as constitutionally acceptable. In some instances, the Court has reasoned that changed circumstances have deprived that historical acceptance of much of its weight. Thus, in *Tennessee v. Garner*,[5] the Court noted that the common law rule allowing the use of deadly force to prevent the escape of any suspected felon, without regard to the suspect's dangerousness, originally had been deemed reasonable under the Fourth Amendment, but its acceptance came at a time when "virtually all felonies were punishable by death," and when the officer's use of deadly force typically came in hand-to-hand combat that posed a danger to the officer. Today's setting was quite different, with almost all crimes formerly punishable by death no longer subject to that penalty, with many crimes formerly deemed misdemeanors now lifted to the felony level, and with hand guns allowing officers to use deadly force in settings where the escaping suspect poses no threat to the officer. Of course, changes of the type cited in *Garner* are not unique. With so many new developments in the criminal justice process and its administration since the adoption of the Bill of

---

4. See § 22.1(b); § 3.5(a); § 17.4(b); Bennis v. Michigan, 516 U.S. 442, 116 S.Ct. 994, 134 L.Ed.2d 68 (1996) (forfeiture).

5. 471 U.S. 1, 105 S.Ct. 1694, 85 L.Ed.2d 1 (1985).

Rights (or the Fourteenth Amendment), there is almost always some change that casts upon a procedure a somewhat different light than existed at common law. Thus, the critical issue is whether the change truly alters the character of the procedure in such a way as to eliminate the characteristic that led the Framers to view the procedure as consistent with the applicable Bill of Rights guarantee. The Court has offered no clear guidelines on that issue, as evidenced by frequent disagreement over the significance of such changes.

In other instances, the Court has discounted historical acceptance of a particular procedure on the ground that the guarantee in question was designed as an "open ended provision," intended to be "molded to the views of contemporary society." Thus, the due process clause has been described as "the least frozen concept of our law—the least confined to history and the most absorptive of powerful social standards of a progressive society," and it has been applied to condemn various practices never thought to raise significant constitutional difficulties at common law. So too, the "reasonableness clause" of the Fourth Amendment has been characterized as open to interpretation "in light of contemporary norms and conditions" (leading to decisions that "ha[ve] not simply frozen into constitutional law those law enforcement practices that existed at the time of the Fourth Amendment's passage"); the prohibition against cruel and unusual punishments has been described as "draw[ing] its meaning from the evolving standards of decency that marks the progress of a maturing society"; and the equal protection clause has been held to impose a general command that requires the Court "to be open to reassessment of ancient practices." However, the extent to which a particular guarantee incorporates such an "evolving concept" is often unclear. As discussed in § 2.7(b), in recent years, the due process clause, in its independent procedural content,

has hardly been viewed as the guarantee "least confined to history"; rather, the Court has spoken of giving great deference to historical pedigree where due process challenges would impose restrictions upon the criminal process extending beyond the specific guarantees of the Bill of Rights. The "reasonableness clause" of the Fourth Amendment has been viewed in several instances as largely controlled by historical practice, even to the point of accepting practices that appear inconsistent with general Fourth Amendment principles.[6] So too, the Court similarly has struggled at times with the potential for carrying the evolving concept of cruel and unusual punishment beyond its obvious historical purpose of outlawing certain forms of punishment for criminal violations.[7]

Finally, under clauses not characterized as "open-ended," historically accepted practices have also been rejected on the ground that the practice conflicts with a more fully developed understanding of the general principles underlying a particular guarantee. Thus, the practice of not providing court appointed counsel for indigent felony defendants was held to violate the Sixth Amendment in light of experience establishing the "obvious truth that the average defendant does not have the professional legal skill" to ensure that he receives a fair trial.[8] So too, the right to jury trial was held to extend to criminal contempt proceedings, notwithstanding a well established common law practice of allowing judges to try contempt cases without juries, because "experience teaches that convictions for criminal contempts * * * are indistinguishable from those obtained under ordinary criminal laws," and procedures developed over the years to minimize "the malfunctioning of the jury system" ensured that jury participation would not undermine the judicial interest in vindicating its authority through contempt sanctions.[9] The analysis applied in such cases is reconciled

---

6. See e.g. United States v. Watson, discussed in § 3.5 (a) at note 3.

7. See e.g. Harmelin v. Michigan, 501 U.S. 957, 111 S.Ct. 2680, 115 L.Ed.2d 836 (1991) (sharp division as to whether provision imposes some type of proportionality limit on sentences).

8. See §§ 11.1 (a), 11.2.

9. See Bloom v. Illinois, 391 U.S. 194, 88 S.Ct. 1477, 20 L.Ed.2d 522 (1968).

with originalism on the assumption that the Framers would not have wanted a constitutional framework designed for the future as well as the present to lock-in their specific, immediate expectations on the application of a guarantee without regard to what might be learned through subsequent experience in applying that guarantee to a variety of different settings. When such experience reveals that a practice originally thought to be consistent with the guarantee's core purpose is, in fact, in conflict with that purpose, requiring a choice between the Framers' specific expectation and their overall objective, they presumably would have expected coherence in effectuating that overall objective to prevail.

The concepts of changed circumstances, open-ended guarantees that absorb the "evolving gloss of civilized standards," and re-examination in light of the deeper, experienced-based understanding of a guarantee's core purpose, provide ample leeway for holding unconstitutional any historically sanctioned practice viewed by today's Court as inconsistent with the general thrust of its current interpretation of a particular guarantee. Whether that will occur depends in large part on that point within the spectrum of approaches to constitutional interpretation at which a Court majority can be formed. Over the years, individual justices have varied considerably in their general philosophy of constitutional interpretation, particularly as it bears on their analysis of "the original understanding," resulting in sometimes substantial and sometimes subtle shifts in the perspective commanding a Court majority.

(c) Priority for Truth–Finding. Over the last few decades, commentators have debated at length the questions of: (1) should the Court give a priority to the truth-finding function of the criminal justice process in its interpretation of constitutional guarantees; and (2) to what extent has the Court actually granted such a priority in its rulings? The truth-finding function in this context commonly is seen as going beyond simply ensuring reliability in fact-finding and as also encompassing safe-guards that allocate the burden of fact-finding error so as to favor avoidance of the conviction of the innocent. Fully implemented, an interpretive guideline that gives priority to truth-finding would produce substantially more expansive interpretations of truth-finding rights than truth-impairing rights (i.e., rights which withhold from the factfinder reliable relevant evidence, such as the Fourth Amendment restrictions on searches). The priority presumably also would favor truth-finding rights over truth-neutral rights (i.e., rights which neither promote nor hinder an accurate determination of guilt or innocence, but limit the prosecution in its ability to proceed against the defendant irrespective of guilt, such as the equal protection bar against discriminatory prosecution). A truth-finding priority would further insist that the remedies allowed for violations of truth-impairing and truth-neutral guarantees be fashioned to keep to a minimum their adverse impact upon achieving a result based upon truth-finding.

Of course, the specifics of the application of such a truth-finding priority is not always clear. Various constitutional guarantees serve multiple objectives, and the characterization of a particular component of such a guarantee as truth-furthering, truth-impairing, or truth-neutral may be open to debate. Also, comparing the expansiveness of interpretations of different guarantees necessarily involves some degree of subjectivity. Thus, it is not surprising that commentators have disagreed in their assessment of whether and to what extent the Supreme Court has applied in its rulings an interpretative guideline that gives priority to truth-finding.

Although the Supreme Court has frequently spoken of truth-finding as the "central purpose" of the trial, and has emphasized the need to interpret various trial rights in light of their objective of promoting truth-finding, it has discussed in only a handful of settings the need to differentiate among rights according to their impact upon truth-finding. Perhaps the most extensive of these discussions are found in a string of decisions interpreting the federal habeas corpus statute.[10] That analysis of the hierarchy of claims for habeas purposes has led the Court majority to hold that: (1) a Fourth Amendment search and seizure claim generally will not be cognizable on habeas review since the deterrence objective of the prophylactic exclusionary rule remedy for Fourth Amendment violations is adequately served without extending the exclusionary rule's truth-impairing impact to the habeas forum; (2) because the ultimate aim of the habeas safety net is to provide relief from a "fundamentally unjust incarceration," claims that would otherwise be barred by an abuse of writ in a prior habeas proceeding, or by a default in a state proceeding, will nonetheless be cognizable where based on a truth-furthering constitutional right and presented in a case in which the denial of that right might have resulted in the conviction of an "actually innocent defendant"; and (3) an exception will be drawn from the usual review standard confining the habeas petitioner to the law prevailing at the time his conviction became final to permit reliance on subsequent favorable rulings that either establish that the defendant was convicted of a crime that the state constitutionally had no power to create (thereby rendering the defendant "innocent" as a matter of law), or "mandate procedures central to the accurate determination of guilt or innocence."[11] The Court has refused, however, to limit habeas review as a general matter to only truth-furthering guarantees.

The Court has more often differentiated among rights by restricting remedies that operate to deflect the truth. Thus, the relationship of the remedy to truth-finding also has shaped much of the law governing the right to exclude evidence obtained in violation of the Fourth Amendment and the *Miranda v. Arizona* standards governing custodial interrogation. In determining the scope of the "judicially created" exclusionary rule remedy for Fourth Amendment violations, the Court has announced a policy of restricting that remedy to the minimum needed to serve its deterrence function in order to keep also to a minimum the truth-impairment that attends exclusion of reliable evidence.[12] A similar analysis has limited the exclusion of secondary evidence obtained through a violation of the *Miranda* standards and even the use of the incriminating statement itself.[13]

However, though such Fourth Amendment and *Miranda* rulings have stressed the truth-impairment that attends exclusion, they also have repeatedly noted that the exclusionary rule remedy for Fourth Amendment violations is no more than a "judicially created" prophylactic remedy, and that the *Miranda* standards are not themselves constitutionally prescribed but simply judicially created prophylactic standards designed to preclude self-incrimination violations. In light of the special prophylactic grounding of those rulings, the Court has not viewed their limitation as logically leading to similarly restrictive interpretations of remedies for those truth-impairing rights that flow

10. As for another, consider the "special weight" accorded to an acquittal under double jeopardy law. While the double jeopardy protection against the burdens of repeated proceedings also places limits upon reprosecution following a mistrial or a conviction, it affords an "absolute finality" to an acquittal "on the ground that however mistaken the individual acquittal may have been," there would be "an unacceptably high risk" to the innocent in allowing the government to override that acquittal and begin again. See § 25.3 (a).

11. See §§ 28, 3(c); 28.4(f); 28.6(e).

12. This cost-benefit analysis had led the Court to conclude that the exclusionary rule should not apply in grand jury proceedings [§ 3.1(f)], should only rarely apply where the police conducted their search based upon a search warrant or explicit legislative authorization [§ 3.1(c)], should not be available to the defendant who seeks to vindicate the privacy rights of another [§ 9.1], should not extend to evidence which would inevitably have

been discovered even without the illegal search [§ 9.3 (e)], and should not serve as bar to use of illegally seized evidence to impeach the defendant should he testify at his trial [§ 9.6 (a)].

13. The Court has held that a statement obtained from a defendant in violation of *Miranda*, if in fact voluntary, may be used to impeach the defendant because "there is sufficient deterrence when the evidence in question is made unavailable at trial," and *Miranda* should not "be perverted to a license to testify, inconsistently or even perjuriously, free from risk of confrontation with prior inconsistent statements." Oregon v. Haas, discussed in § 9.6(a). So too, where a statement obtained in violation of *Miranda* assists the police in obtaining further evidence, that secondary evidence may be admissible even though it might never have been obtained without the *Miranda* violation. See § 9.5 (a).

directly from the Constitution. The Court has refused, for example, to extend the cases allowing impeachment use of statements obtained in violation of *Miranda* to impeachment use of statements compelled through a grant of immunity[14]. Prohibiting use of the immunized testimony is equally truth-impairing (unlike coerced confessions, immunized testimony is not of questionable reliability), but that testimony clearly has been "compelled" for Fifth Amendment purposes and its use is therefore barred by the Amendment itself. So too, in contrast to the rulings governing secondary evidence obtained through *Miranda* violations, the Court has stated that secondary evidence derived from a statement deemed compelled under the Fifth Amendment must be excluded from evidence.[15]

Similarly, the Court also has not sought to distinguish between truth-impairing and truth-furthering constitutional rights in assessing whether a constitutional violation that bears upon the determination of guilt or innocence can be deemed harmless error on appellate review. Indeed, the Court has applied the same harmless error standard to the trial court's erroneous admission of evidence obtained in violation of *Miranda* or the Fourth Amendment as to the erroneous admission of a potentially unreliable coerced confession or an out-of-court witness statement barred by defendant's Sixth Amendment right of confrontation.

(d) The Appropriateness of Administratively Based Per Se Rules. In many settings the Supreme Court has viewed the constitutional question at issue as naturally calling for what might be described as a "categorical" or "definitional" standard—i.e., a standard that looks to a single characteristic or event and does not adjust to the uniqueness of each case. Such standards are imposed, for example, in determining when jeopardy attaches and what constitutes the minimum acceptable size for a jury. In other settings, the Court has viewed the constitutional question at issue as calling for a standard requiring a fact sensitive judgment geared to a variety of circumstances that

differ with each case. Such standards are applied, for example, in determining whether police had the probable cause needed to obtain a search warrant or whether a defense lawyer's performance was so deficient as to deny defendant the effective assistance of counsel. In still other settings, the Court has concluded that, while the question at issue generally calls for a case-by-case balancing of a variety of circumstances, administrative concerns justify imposing a "per se" or "bright-line" test which finds a particular action to be constitutional or unconstitutional based on a single event or characteristic. Such a standard is similar in formulation to the usual categorical standard, but its grounding is different. The Court is not saying that the function of the applicable constitutional guarantee necessarily requires such a bright-line rule. Indeed, the Court is acknowledging that its per se standard is either over-inclusive or under-inclusive as compared to the application of that function to all relevant circumstances on a case-by-case basis. Nonetheless, practical considerations relevant to administration of the Court's ruling have convinced the Court of the need to adopt a shorthand generalization in the form of a per se rule even though the function of the guarantee might point to the ad hoc application of a totality-of-the-circumstances analysis.

Supreme Court decisions imposing categorical standards often suggest alternative lines of reasoning which leave unclear whether that standard is required logically by the function of the guarantee or has been adopted because the alternative of applying that function to the totality-of-the-circumstances would present unacceptable administrative difficulties. Nonetheless, a variety of rulings imposing categorical standards clearly indicate that the Court there carved out a bright-line rule, even though it might include more or less than the logic of the guarantee would require, because of the difficulties that would be presented in applying that logic via a standard calling for

14. See § 9.6(a).

15. See § 8.11(b).

an ad hoc, multi-circumstance analysis.[16] On the other hand, the Court also has ruled in a variety of settings that administrative concerns did not justify adopting a bright-line rule, and a fair number of those settings involved issues analogous to the issues presented in cases that did adopt administratively based bright-line standards.[17] As might be surmised from the divergence in its rulings, the Supreme Court has not issued a bright-line rule as to when administrative concerns can appropriately lead to the choice of a categorical standard over a standard emphasizing the special circumstance of the individual case.

There is general agreement on the use of a per se standard where it provides an almost perfect fit with the result that would be reached by applying the logic of the guarantee on a case-by-case basis to the circumstances of each case. "Conclusive presumptions," the Court has noted, are "designed to avoid the costs of excessive inquiry where a per se rule will achieve the correct result in almost all cases." The key is to be able to say that, though " 'cases that do not fit the generalization may arise,' " they are " 'not sufficiently common * * * [to] justify the time and expense necessary to identify them.' " Some justices have suggested that unless the bright-line rule meets this standard by producing very little overinclusion or underinclusion (as compared to a case-by-case analysis), it bears the seeds of its own demise. Nonetheless, the Court's rulings suggest that at least three

somewhat distinct administrative concerns may lead to the adoption of bright-lines that fall considerably short of an almost "perfect fit." Where these considerations apply, the Court has shown a willingness, at times, to adopt a bright-line standard which produces for the vast majority of cases the same result as the logical application of the function of the guarantee to the distinctive circumstances of the case, but which produces as well a substantial body of applications that result in condemning more or less than that function would otherwise require.

One setting that may lead to such an administratively based bright-line prohibition is that in which establishing a constitutional violation otherwise requires a difficult factual determination, such as assessing whether an actor was motivated by bad faith or bias. Concern that such a determination can be made accurately only by a potentially pernicious judicial inquiry can lead the Court to prefer a per se prohibition that avoids the necessity of making that factual determination. A per se prohibition also may be justified on the ground that the potential for error in such a determination poses too great a risk that the constitutional violation will go undetected, and as a result, an innocent person will suffer severe consequences.

Another setting is that in which the administrator lacks the capacity, expertise, or opportunity to apply a finely tuned standard. Thus, over the past few decades, the Supreme Court

---

16. These rulings include: New York v. Belton, discussed in § 3.7(a) (allowing police to search the entire passenger compartment of an automobile, contemporaneously with the arrest of the occupant, without seeking to determine whether, in the particular physical setting, that entire area is within the "immediate control" of the arrestee); Cuyler v. Sullivan, discussed in § 11.9(d) (incompetency of counsel established per se where an actual conflict of interest adversely affected counsel's performance, as court will conclusively presume prejudicial impact rather than require usual case-specific inquiry into prejudice); and Turner v. Murray, discussed in § 22.3(a) at note 9 ("because risk of racial prejudice infecting a capital sentencing proceeding is especially serious in light of the complete finality of the death penalty," a capital defendant accused of an interracial crime is entitled automatically to voir dire questioning on racial bias without the usual prerequisite of showing that racial issues are "inextricably bound up with the conduct of the trial").

17. Such rulings include: United States v. Dunn, discussed in § 3.2(c) at note 40 (refusing to adopt a "bright-line rule" that the Fourth Amendment protected area of a dwelling's "curtilage" would "extend no farther than the nearest fence surrounding a fenced house," and instead allowing for consideration of indicia of privacy that could on occasion encompass structures lying outside the fenced area); United States v. Cronic, discussed in § 11.7(d) (rejecting a lower court ruling adopting a per se standard of ineffective assistance of counsel based upon factors such as the tardy appointment of counsel, and requiring, instead, an examination of the actual performance of counsel under the circumstances of the individual case); *Ristaino v. Ross*, discussed in § 22.3(a) at note 6 (rejecting as to noncapital cases an automatic entitlement to voir dire questioning on racial bias where the crime is interracial, as determining the presence of a "constitutionally significant likelihood" of juror bias absent voir dire questioning requires an evaluation of "all of the circumstance" presented by the case).

frequently has extolled the virtues of bright-line standards in the constitutional regulation of police activities. The Court has noted that "a single familiar standard is essential to guide police officers, who have only limited time and expertise to reflect on and balance the social and individual interests in the specific circumstances they confront." Where possible, the lawfulness of a police officer's actions should not depend on "a highly sophisticated set of rules, qualified by all sorts of ifs, ands, and buts and requiring the drawing of subtle nuances and hairline distinctions," but on a "straight forward rule, easily applied and predictably enforced." The Court has cited this need for bright-line rules in adopting both standards over-inclusive and under-inclusive of what a case-by-case analysis of multiple circumstances would produce. Thus, bright-line standards governing police interrogation clearly operate to bar some confessions that would be deemed, upon evaluation of all the circumstances, to be obtained without violation of the Fifth Amendment's self-incrimination clause or the Sixth Amendment's right-to-counsel clause. On the other side, bright-line standards will sustain automatically a particular type of search notwithstanding that, on a case-by-case analysis, there might be some situations in which that search could be deemed unreasonable because excessive in scope or lacking a sufficient foundation.

Although administratively based bright-line standards are commonplace in the constitutional regulation of police investigative practices, the Court at least as frequently has rejected proposed bright-line rules for police regulation. In some instances, the Court has concluded that the character of the constitutional question (e.g., what constitutes probable cause) simply does not lend itself to a bright-line standard. In others, the proposed bright-line standard has been viewed as not needed to provide police with sufficient guidance on the legality of their conduct. Most often, the Court has concluded that costs of the over-inclusive or under-inclusive coverage of a bright-line simply outweigh the benefits of the administrative simplicity it would provide.

A third administrative justification for the use of bright-line rules is limited to per se prohibitions and has been discussed primarily by commentators rather than the Supreme Court. The commentators contend that the Warren Court, in particular, adopted obviously over-inclusive per se prohibitions in recognition that prohibitions in that form were needed to gain successful implementation of the Court's rulings. Having extended the Bill of Rights guarantees to the states, and having made fairness in criminal procedure a central component of the Court's responsibility in protecting civil rights, the Warren Court, it is argued, was compelled to make much heavier use of per se rules than its predecessors by virtue of the "exigencies of its efforts to provide supervision of state and federal systems of criminal justice through the use of judicial power." This was so, it was argued, because: (1) the Court's extremely limited docket restricted its opportunity to formulate comprehensive regulations through rulings tied to the facts of the individual case; and (2) the institutional units asked to administer the Court's rulings (police, prosecutors, and state courts) were highly fragmented, burdened by heavy caseloads, and "unlikely to respond automatically and with enthusiasm," leading to a need for the issuance of high visibility benchmarks that captured the attention of both those administrators and the public.

(e) The Appropriateness of Prophylactic Rules. The Supreme Court also has not formulated a bright-line standard as to when it is appropriate to utilize "prophylactic rules." Indeed, the Court has not yet settled on a standard definition of what constitutes a "prophylactic rule." The key apparently is the rationale underlying the rule rather than the form of the rule. In discussing decisions characterized as establishing prophylactic rules, the Court has emphasized two features of those rules—their function and their grounding.

Initially, as suggested by the term "prophylactic," the rules are characterized as preventive measures. Their purpose is to safeguard against a potential constitutional violation, rather than to identify what constitutes a constitutional violation. Prevention may be achieved by imposing procedural safeguards that provide a protective shield for the underlying constitutional right, by utilizing an evidentiary exclusionary remedy to take away the primary incentive for constitutional violations by law enforcement officers seeking to acquire evidence, or by prohibiting a law enforcement practice that readily might be misused and manipulated to deprive a suspect of a constitutional right. Secondly, the prophylactic rule is grounded not on the conclusion that a violation of the rule invariably produces a violation of the core guarantee, but on the Court's exercise of its authority to craft remedies and procedures that facilitate its adjudication responsibilities.

The Court has emphasized two important consequences that follow from the special function and grounding of prophylactic rules. Because prophylactic rules may be violated without denying a constitutional right, those violations may be given remedial consequences which are narrower or which do not apply in as broad a range of proceedings as the remedies attaching to the actual violation of the constitutional right that the prophylactic rule is designed to prevent. So too, the non-constitutional grounding of prophylactic rules leaves the door open for Congress to replace those rules with other safeguards that serve the same preventive function.[18]

Where the prophylactic rule takes the form of a remedial sanction, designed to deter future violations, its operation ordinarily will be tied to the presence of a constitutional violation. This is the case, for example, of the rule requiring trial exclusion of evidence obtained through Fourth Amendment violations, perhaps the most prominent prophylactic remedial measure. As illustrated in *Maine v. Moulton*,[19] however, a prophylactic remedial measure can also be used in situations in which a violation has not necessarily occurred, but the adjudicatory process would face significant obstacles in determining

whether it had occurred. *Moulton* dealt with the use of an undercover agent or informant to elicit information from an indicted defendant. The Sixth Amendment prohibits the deliberate elicitation of information regarding the offense on which the defendant has been charged, but does not prohibit the elicitation of information relating to other possible criminal activities, as the defendant has not been placed in the status of an "accused" as to those uncharged offenses and the Sixth Amendment therefore does not attach. Because of concerns that law enforcement officials might mask Sixth Amendment violations, by claiming that their agents were only seeking to elicit information relating to uncharged offenses when the defendant serendipitously offered information relating to the charged offense, the Court imposed a general prohibition against prosecution use in evidence of any statements made to the undercover agent or informant relating to the charged offense. The function of the prohibition was to deter Sixth Amendment violations by removing any incentive to elicit information relating to the charged offense. To achieve this prophylactic objective, the prohibition would apply automatically, without attempting to determine whether the excluded statement was responsive to an elicitation that violated the Sixth Amendment by focusing on the charged offense or an elicitation that was acceptable under the Sixth Amendment because directed at uncharged offenses. Thus, the prophylactic remedial measure applied even though there may not have been a violation of the Sixth Amendment.

Prophylactic rules that formulate procedural prerequisites for particular police, prosecutorial, or judicial actions similarly do not declare that such actions would have produced a violation of the core guarantee without those prerequisites being followed. Rather, the prerequisites are described as necessary to combat what would otherwise be a substantial potential for constitutional violations in those ac-

---

18. The *Miranda* Court specifically noted the potential for congressional safeguards replacing the *Miranda* rules, see § 6.5(b), and a similar suggestion was contained in United States v. Wade, discussed in § 7.3(a). The exact

role of Congress in this regard remains uncertain. See note 24 infra.

19. 474 U.S. 159, 106 S.Ct. 477, 88 L.Ed.2d 481 (1985), discussed in § 6.4(g).

tions. Such prerequisites were imposed in two Supreme Court rulings that have come to be viewed as paradigmatic of prophylactic procedural prerequisites—*Miranda v. Arizona*[20] and *North Carolina v. Pearce*.[21] *Miranda* required the police to give various warnings to an interrogated suspect in order to ensure that custodial interrogation did not result in compulsion that would violate the suspect's privilege against self-incrimination. Absent such warnings, a statement obtained through custodial interrogation was automatically excluded from the prosecution's case-in-chief, without regard to what other circumstances might suggest as to whether the statement was compelled in violation of the Fifth Amendment. *Pearce* concluded that there is a significant likelihood that a judge who imposes a higher sentence on a defendant following that defendant's successful appeal (and subsequent retrial and conviction) is doing so vindictively, and thereby violating due process. Because it would be most difficult for the defendant to establish actual vindictiveness, the Court required, as a prophylactic safeguard, that the judge set forth the reasons for the higher sentence and rely upon "objective information concerning identifiable conduct on the part of the defendant." In the absence of such an acceptable statement of reasons, supported by factual data, the higher sentence cannot be accepted, without regard to whether it was or was not in fact a product of vindictiveness.

Edwards v. Arizona[22] illustrates how a prophylactic ruling may shield a constitutional right by simply forbidding an activity which presents a substantial potential for invading that right. *Edwards* holds that when a suspect responds to *Miranda* warnings by requesting the assistance of counsel, police may not thereafter reinitiate interrogation (even with appropriate *Miranda* warnings) while the suspect remains in custody. This prohibition applies even when the interrogation is renewed only after the passage of a significant period of time and relates to a different crime. Any statement obtained from the suspect in response to police initiation of interrogation in violation of *Edwards* is rendered inadmissible in the prosecution case-in-chief. Under *Michigan v. Jackson*,[23] a similar prophylactic rule is applied to an accused person who requests the assistance of counsel and subsequently provides a statement in response to interrogation initiated by the police. Although it is entirely possible that a person, after requesting counsel, might change his mind and respond to subsequent police questioning with a voluntary, knowing, and intelligent waiver of the Fifth Amendment right protected by *Miranda* or the Sixth Amendment right to counsel, *Edwards* and *Jackson* impose a prophylactic prohibition against police initiated questioning after such a request because such questioning is far more likely to produce a waiver that is not voluntary, knowing, and intelligent.

Edwards and *Jackson* also illustrate the close relationship between many prophylactic rules and the administratively based, over-inclusive per se prohibition previously discussed in subsection (d). Although the Court repeatedly characterizes the *Edwards/Jackson* rules as "prophylactic" and extending beyond actual constitutional violations, it also has characterized those rules as adopting a per se approach which provides police with a bright-line standard. Consistent with the latter characterization, *Edwards/Jackson* has been described as creating a conclusive presumption that "after a defendant requests assistance of counsel, any waiver * * * given in a discussion initiated by police" is not "voluntary, knowing, and intelligent." Other prophylactic rules can similarly be cast as resting on a conclusive presumption, which is a common structure for imposing an administratively based, over inclusive per se prohibition. *Miranda*, for example, could be cast as establishing a conclusive presumption that a statement produced by custodial interrogation is "compelled" in violation of the suspect's privilege against self-incrimination unless the suspect was given the

---

20. 384 U.S. 436, 86 S.Ct. 1602, 16 L.Ed.2d 694 (1966), discussed in § 6.5.

21. 395 U.S. 711, 89 S.Ct. 2072, 23 L.Ed.2d 656, discussed in § 26.8(a).

22. 451 U.S. 477, 101 S.Ct. 1880, 68 L.Ed.2d 378 (1981), discussed in § 6.9(g) at note 20.

23. 475 U.S. 625, 106 S.Ct. 1404, 89 L.Ed.2d 631 (1986), discussed in § 6.4(f) at note 51.

Miranda warnings and voluntarily waived the rights noted in those warnings. *Pearce* similarly could be characterized as creating a conclusive presumption that a higher sentence on reconviction was a product of vindictiveness unless the record affirmatively shows that the sentence was based on factors which could not readily be used to mask vindictiveness.

The Supreme Court has not explained why such rulings were established and declared to be prophylactic rules, rather than per se rules that rested on an over-inclusive interpretation of a constitutional guarantee in order to avoid the substantial administrative difficulties that would attend an ad hoc, case-by-case analysis of multiple circumstances. Presumably the latter formulation was not utilized because the generalization that would be at the heart of the per se prohibition would too often be incorrect as an empirical matter. Per se prohibitions need not always provide a close to perfect fit with the results that would be reached on a case-by-case analysis, but they should produce the same result as the case-by-case analysis in a very substantial majority of the instances that would be encompassed by the per se rule. When it becomes obvious that many (if not most) of the instances that fall within a possible conclusive presumption would not actually violate the constitutional right to be safeguarded by that presumption, the Court has presented the safeguard as a prophylactic ruling that operates apart from the violation of that constitutional right.

Although the Courts descriptions of the exact character of prophylactic rulings had been less than precise prior to its ruling in *Dickerson v. United States*,[24] that ruling managed to almost completely cloud that issue. In *Dickerson*, Justice Scalia, in a dissenting opinion joined by Justice Thomas, sharply challenged the legitimacy of the Supreme Court's prophylactic rulings. One issue presented in *Dickerson* was whether Congress could override *Miranda*. In arguing that it could, Justice Scalia rejected the defense contention that the *Miranda* was within the Court's constitutional decisionmaking authority (and therefore immune from a constitutional override) because

that decisionmaking authority extended to "adopting prophylactic rules to buttress constitutional rights." Justice Scalia described that position as allowing the Court to mandate whatever procedural protections it deemed "desirable" without regard to "what the Constitutional actually requires." Contending that the Court lacked the authority to mandate extra protections as a needed prophylactic measure, Justice Scalia characterized as "fundamental[ly] flaw[ed]" the occasional cases resting on the assumed existence of such authority (citing *Miranda* and *North Carolina v. Pearce* as the prime examples).

The *Dickerson* majority held that *Miranda* was a decision "interpreting and applying the Constitution," and Congress therefore lacked "the constitutional authority to supersede *Miranda*." However, as Justice Scalia noted in his dissent, the majority opinion, in explaining the constitutional grounding of *Miranda*, did not refer to the prophylactic rulemaking authority cited by the defendant. The majority acknowledged that *Miranda's* required warnings had been described as "prophylactic" and "not themselves rights protected by the Constitution," but disagreed with the lower court's conclusion that this description established that the "protections announced in *Miranda* are not constitutionally acquired." In explaining the constitutional grounding of the *Miranda* "guidelines," the *Dickerson* majority offered an analysis similar to that traditionally offered in sustaining per se standards. The Court acknowledged that the *Miranda* ruling was overinclusive in the sense that "statements which may be by no means involuntarily made by a defendant who is aware of his rights may nonetheless be excluded" because the *Miranda* warnings had not provided by the police. However, these warnings nonetheless had been required because reliance on an ad-hoc totality-of-the-circumstances analysis to identify involuntariness (the approach of the pre-*Miranda* voluntariness test) had presented an "unacceptably great" risk of "overlooking involuntary confessions."

24. 530 U.S. 428, 120 S.Ct. 2326, 147 L.Ed.2d 405 (2000), also discussed in § 6.5(e).

The *Dickerson* majority, also acknowledged, however, that *Miranda* contained a feature previously associated only with prophylactic rulings. The *Miranda* Court, it noted, "had concluded that something more than the totality test was necessary" to adequately protect against self-incrimination violations through the admission of compelled confessions, but the solution imposed in *Miranda* was not exclusive. As *Miranda* had noted, a legislative solution that differed from *Miranda* could be constitutionally acceptable, but only if it was "at least as effective" in serving the ends of the *Miranda* requirement (an issue not presented in *Dickerson*, as the Congressional legislation there merely sought to substitute the old totality test).

Dickerson put to rest any question as to the constitutional legitimacy of prophylactic rulings, and at the same time, continued to recognize a distinction between these rulings and other constitutional rulings. It provided, however, no clear answers as to how such rulings were distinguishable from other constitutional rulings, (particularly per se rulings) and why their special character produced unique rules as to their implementation (including possible congressional substitution of alternative measures). Commentators speculated that the failure of the *Dickerson* opinion to more completely address these issues stemmed from a division within the Court beyond that reflected by the Scalia dissent. Three years later, the several opinions in *Chavez v. Martinez*[25] provided strong support for that speculation. There, the eight justices speaking to the issue agreed that a *Miranda* violation was quite distinct from a classic Fifth Amendment violation. They were sharply divided, however in their characterization of *Miranda's* distinctive character, and in their assessment of other Fifth Amendment rulings that might fit in that category. They did agree that *Miranda's* distinctive grounding meant that there should

be no civil damage remedy for a *Miranda* violation, but they divided as to the proper rationale for that conclusion.

In *Chavez*, Justice Thomas (joined by Chief Justice Rehnquist and Justices O'Connor and Scalia) described *Miranda* as having established a "prophylactic rule." Moreover, contrary to the *Dickerson* dissent, Justice Thomas spoke of prophylactic rules as having a long history in Supreme Court jurisprudence. He described as "prophylactic," in addition to *Miranda*, several long-standing rulings dealing with self-incrimination. These included rulings allowing witnesses to assert the privilege in civil and administrative proceedings, rulings prohibiting the imposition of administrative penalties on persons who exercise the privilege, and the requirement that the government, to replace the privilege, must grant immunity before compelling the witness to testify.[26] Along with the *Miranda* warnings, these rulings established "prophylactic rules designed to safeguard the core constitutional right protected by the Self–Incrimination Clause." These rulings, he added, "do not extend the scope of the constitutional right itself, just a violations of judicially crafted prophylactic rules do not violate the constitutional rights of any person." Thus, a violation of *Miranda* did not give rise to an action in damages under a statute creating a civil remedy for violations of a "constitutional right".

Another opinion in *Chavez*, by Justice Souter (joined Justice Breyer) described somewhat differently the rulings that Justice Thomas had characterized as prophylactic. Justice Souter described these rulings (including *Miranda*) as establishing "law * * * outside the Fifth Amendment's core, with each case expressing a judgment that the core guarantee, or the judicial capacity to protect it, would be placed at some risk in the absence of some

---

25. 538 U.S. 760, 123 S.Ct. 1994, 155 L.Ed.2d 984 (2003), also discussed in § 8.10 at note 2 and § 6.5 at note 6.

26. See §§ 8.10(a), 8.10(f), and 8.11. The prophylactic nature of these rulings stems from Justice Thomas' view that the Fifth Amendment is not itself violated until the defendant's compelled statement is used against him in a

criminal case (as evidenced by the reference in the Fifth Amendment to compelling a "person * * * in a criminal case to be a witness against himself"). To ensure against such a future violation, protection against compelling a witness' statement is recognized in non-criminal proceedings, absent an advance grant of immunity to protect against such use.

complementary protection." The special character of these "complementary-protection" rulings means that their further expansion (here creating a damage remedy) would require "a 'powerful showing,' subject to a realistic assessment of costs and risks" that the expansion was "necessary to aid the basic guarantee." No such showing had been made as to a damage remedy for a *Miranda* violation. Justice Souter's analysis arguably gives these "complementary protections" a higher status than Justice Thomas' "prophylactic rules"; yet Justice Souter also saw their violation as something less than a violation of the basic prohibition provided by the core guarantee.

In still another Chavez opinion, Justice Kennedy (joined by Justice Stevens and Ginsburg) offered a strikingly different characterization of the rulings protecting a witness in a noncriminal proceeding against being compelled to provide an incriminating statement. They were neither "prophylactic" nor "complimentary," but reflected the basic function of the privilege. However, Justice Kennedy (here joined only by Justice Stevens) took a different view of *Miranda*. The *Miranda* ruling, Justice Kennedy noted, is a "constitutional requirement," but one "adopted to reduce the risk of a coerced confession and to implement the self-incrimination clause." This special character produced a different analysis of needed remedies. Exclusion of a statement obtained in violation of *Miranda* was a "complete and sufficient remedy" (and, indeed, a remedy sometimes subject to exceptions); a civil damage was not available for a *Miranda* violation standing alone, although it was available where the police employed coercive interrogation tactics (a basic Fifth Amendment violation).

All of the opinions in *Chavez* accepted the position that violations of certain constitutional rulings did not constitute violations of the core guarantee. The Court was divided as to what rulings fell in that category, although eight justices agreed that *Miranda* did so. Four were willing to describe such rulings as "judicially created prophylactic rules," but the remaining four avoided that description (as did the majority opinion in *Dickerson*, which they had joined). While the Souter and Kennedy opinions offered arguably similar alternative descriptions ("complementary protections" and requirements adopted "to reduce the risk of coerce confessions and to implement the Self–Incrimination Clause"), they adopted somewhat different perspectives in determining how that special character impacted the issue of a damage remedy (although reaching the same result on that issue). Thus, apart from their constitutional status, the Court appears to be sharply divided as to both the nature and consequences of rulings sometimes (but not always) described as "prophylactic".

How these divisions impact the creation of prophylactic rules in the future (or the interpretation of past prophylactic rulings) remains to be seen. While prophylactic rulings were viewed as a key element of the criminal law revolution of the Warren Court in the 1960s, the Court in subsequent years has not shown any strong inclination to regulate through rulings described as prophylactic. It has only sparingly adopted new prophylactic rulings or extended old prophylactic rulings. Much more frequently, it has rejected the extension of old prophylactic rulings and refused to adopt proposed new prophylactic rulings.

(f) Weighing the Impact Upon Efficiency. A new constitutional regulation often will impose a substantial burden upon the administration of the criminal justice process. That burden can take various forms, including increased expenses for an already underfunded system, additional hearings for already congested court dockets, and perhaps even insurmountable obstacles to the solution of some crimes. The extent to which such "practical costs" should be considered by the Court has been a matter of continuing debate among the justices. In general, the Court tends to discuss the practical impact of a ruling when it views itself as having more flexibility in fashioning its ruling. Thus, discussions of practical impact are more commonly found in decisions interpreting open-ended clauses, decisions applying the more specific clauses to new settings or settings that have been altered by changed circumstances, and decisions setting forth or applying prophylactic rules. On the other side, where the Court views the text or history of a particular provision as setting forth a "constitutional command that * * * is unequivocal," the practical costs incurred in applying that command are said to be irrelevant. The command itself strikes a balance between the rights of the accused and society's need for effective enforcement of the criminal law, and the Court is bound to accept that balance.

Where the applicability of a guarantee is acknowledged to be less than clear, the justices' views on weighing practical costs ordinarily fall within the outer boundaries marked by two distinctive positions. On the one side, there is the view that, if the burden imposed would be great, the Court should hesitate to extend the guarantee unless its extension is essential to fulfilling the function of the guarantee. On the other side, there is the view that practical costs should be a decidedly subordinate concern. They should be given weight only where the burden is substantial and clear, relates to an important state interest, and cannot be offset by other measures; and even then, they need not be controlling. This difference in perspective often extends beyond the issue of what weight (if any) should be given to the practical costs of a particular interpretation. It also appears to be reflected in the justices' evaluation of the likely extent of those costs. Thus, in *Miranda v. Arizona*[27], though looking at the same data, the majority concluded that its decision would "not in any way preclude police from carrying out their traditional investigatory role" and thus "should not constitute an undue interference with a proper system of law enforcement," while one dissent found that the Court was taking "a real risk with society's welfare" and another concluded that the Court's ruling would "measurably weaken" the enforcement of the criminal law and result in an inability to prosecute successfully a "good many criminal defendants."[28]

As a result of these differences in viewpoint, the treatment of practical costs in majority opinions tends to be inconsistent. Many opinions discuss practical costs as a factor to be given serious consideration, and several refer to such costs as a primary reason for not extending a particular doctrine. Other opinions mention such costs, but promptly dismiss them, while still others fail to even acknowledge what are obviously significant administrative burdens imposed by a new ruling.

27. See note 20 supra.

28. See § 6.5.

*

Part Two

DETECTION AND INVESTIGATION OF CRIME

Chapter 3

ARREST, SEARCH AND SEIZURE

Table of Sections

§ 3.1 The Exclusionary Rule and Other Remedies

(a) Origins of the Exclusionary Rule. The Fourth Amendment remained largely unexplored until 1886, when, in *Boyd v. United States*,[1] the Court held that the forced disclosure of papers amounting to evidence of crime violated the Fourth Amendment *and* that such items therefore were not admissible in the proceedings against Boyd. Though the Fourth Amendment unlike the Fifth contains no express exclusionary rule, the Court reached this result by linking the two amendments together, noting it had "been unable to perceive that the seizure of a man's private books and papers to be used in evidence against him is substantially different from compelling him to be a witness against himself." Yet in *Adams v. New York*[2] the Court declared that "the weight of authority as well as reason" supported the common-law rule that courts will not inquire into the means by which evidence otherwise admissible was acquired.

In 1914 the Court decided *Weeks v. United States*,[3] where the defendant questioned the use in a federal trial of evidence seized from his home by local police and later by federal officers. The Court held that to admit evidence illegally seized by federal officers would, in effect, put a stamp of approval on their unconstitutional conduct: "To sustain [unlawful invasion of the sanctity of his home by officers of the law] would be to affirm by judicial decision a manifest neglect, if not an open defiance, of the prohibitions of the Constitution, intended for the protection of the people against such unauthorized action." But while that evidence thus had to be excluded, the Court went on to say that the same result was not required as to the fruits of the first search, "as the 4th Amendment is not directed to individual misconduct of such officials." (In two 1927 cases, the Supreme Court concluded otherwise as to state searches with either federal participation[4] or a federal purpose.[5])

Because the Bill of Rights was designed as a limitation on the federal government only, it was settled very early that the Fourth Amendment "has no application to state process."[6] With the adoption of the Fourteenth Amendment, however, forbidding the states to "deprive any person of life, liberty, or property, without due process of law," there arose the question of the relation of that limitation upon the states to the limitations upon federal action in the first eight Amendments. Over the years, many of those guarantees were "incorporated" into the Fourteenth Amendment and applied to the states, and thus the stage was set for consideration of the issue that reached the Court in *Wolf v. Colorado*:[7] whether a state court conviction violates due process because based upon evidence that, in federal court, would have been excluded on Fourth Amendment grounds. The Court in *Wolf,* while not hesitating to say that the "security of one's privacy against arbitrary intrusion * * * which is at the core of the Fourth Amendment * * * is * * * enforceable against the States," concluded the *Weeks* exclusionary rule was another matter. Because it was "not derived from the explicit requirements of the Fourth Amendment," was not followed in "most of the English-speaking world," and had been expressly rejected in 30 states, the Court concluded it was not "a departure from basic standards" to leave the victims of illegal state

---

§ 3.1

1. 116 U.S. 616, 6 S.Ct. 524, 29 L.Ed. 746 (1886).

2. 192 U.S. 585, 24 S.Ct. 372, 48 L.Ed. 575 (1904).

3. 232 U.S. 383, 34 S.Ct. 341, 58 L.Ed. 652 (1914).

4. Byars v. United States, 273 U.S. 28, 47 S.Ct. 248, 71 L.Ed. 520 (1927) (evidence admissible in federal court because "the search in substance and effect was a joint operation of the local and federal officers").

5. Gambino v. United States, 275 U.S. 310, 48 S.Ct. 137, 72 L.Ed. 293 (1927).

6. Smith v. Maryland, 59 U.S. (18 How.) 71, 15 L.Ed. 269 (1855).

7. 338 U.S. 25, 69 S.Ct. 1359, 93 L.Ed. 1782 (1949).

searches "to the remedies of private action and such protection as the internal discipline of the police, under the eyes of an alert public opinion, may afford."

Any thought that *Wolf* meant state courts were permitted to admit all unconstitutional evidence was dispelled three years later in *Rochin v. California*,[8] where police engaged in a series of unlawful acts that culminated in the defendant being given an emetic by force to retrieve drugs he had swallowed. The Court held that the Fourteenth Amendment required exclusion of evidence obtained by "conduct that shocks the conscience." But it soon became apparent that *Rochin* did not require exclusion with respect to all serious Fourth Amendment violations, for it was held not to apply to illegal month-long electronic eavesdropping[9] or to extraction of blood from an unconscious person.[10] Another post-*Wolf* development of significance was the demise of the "silver platter" doctrine, whereby illegally obtained evidence was admitted in federal courts when obtained by state officers. In rejecting that doctrine in *Elkins v. United States*,[11] the Court emphasized that the determination in *Wolf* that Fourteenth Amendment due process prohibited illegal searches and seizures by state officers marked the "removal of the doctrinal underpinning" for the admissibility of state-seized evidence in federal prosecutions. (As for somewhat the reverse of *Elkins,* the Court had earlier held that a federal official could be enjoined from turning over such evidence and from giving testimony concerning the evidence in a state prosecution.[12])

In *Mapp v. Ohio*,[13] overruling *Wolf* and holding "that all evidence obtained by searches and seizures in violation of the Constitution is, by that same authority, inadmissible in a state court," the Court reasoned:

> Since the Fourth Amendment's right of privacy has been declared enforceable against the States through the Due Process Clause of the Fourteenth, it is enforceable against them by the same sanction of exclusion as is used against the Federal Government. Were it otherwise then just as without the *Weeks* rule the assurance against unreasonable federal searches and seizures would be "a form of words," valueless and undeserving of mention in a perpetual charter of inestimable human liberties, so too, without that rule the freedom from state invasions of privacy would be so ephemeral and so neatly severed from its conceptual nexus with the freedom from all brutish means of coercing evidence as not to merit this Court's high regard as a freedom "implicit in the concept of ordered liberty."

Wolf was pushed aside as "bottomed on factual considerations" lacking "current validity," in that during the intervening years more and more states had opted for the exclusionary rule, and experience had shown that the other remedies alluded to in *Wolf* were "worthless and futile." In an oft-quoted passage the Court in *Mapp* went on to say:

> Moreover, our holding * * * is not only the logical dictate of prior cases but it also makes very good sense. There is no war between the Constitution and common sense. Presently, a federal prosecutor may make no use of evidence illegally seized, but a State's attorney across the street may, although he supposedly is operating under the enforceable prohibitions of the same Amendment. Thus the State, by admitting evidence unlawfully seized, serves to encourage disobedience to the Federal Constitution which it is bound to uphold.

(b) Purposes of the Exclusionary Rule.
The deterrence of unreasonable searches and seizures is a major purpose of the exclusionary

---

8. 342 U.S. 165, 72 S.Ct. 205, 96 L.Ed. 183 (1952).

9. Irvine v. California, 347 U.S. 128, 74 S.Ct. 381, 98 L.Ed. 561 (1954).

10. Breithaupt v. Abram, 352 U.S. 432, 77 S.Ct. 408, 1 L.Ed.2d 448 (1957).

11. 364 U.S. 206, 80 S.Ct. 1437, 4 L.Ed.2d 1669 (1960).

12. Rea v. United States, 350 U.S. 214, 76 S.Ct. 292, 100 L.Ed. 233 (1956), where the Court stressed it was "not asked to enjoin state officials nor in any way to interfere with state agencies in enforcement of state law," and that the case raised "not a constitutional question but one concerning our supervisory powers over federal law enforcement agencies."

13. 367 U.S. 643, 81 S.Ct. 1684, 6 L.Ed.2d 1081 (1961).

rule. This was acknowledged by the Court in *Wolf*, *Elkins* and *Mapp*, and later in *Linkletter v. Walker*[14] and *Terry v. Ohio*.[15] But the rule serves other purposes as well. There is, for example, what the *Elkins* Court referred to as "the imperative of judicial integrity," namely, that the courts not become "accomplices in the willful disobedience of a Constitution they are sworn to uphold," language later relied upon in *Mapp* and *Terry*. A third purpose, as stated most clearly by some members of the Court, is that "of assuring the people—all potential victims of unlawful government conduct—that the government would not profit from its lawless behavior, thus minimizing the risk of seriously undermining popular trust in government."[16] This is not merely another statement of the deterrence objective, for the emphasis is on the effect of exclusion upon the public rather than the police.

The purposes of the exclusionary rule are of more than academic concern, for the Court's perception of them determines the scope and, ultimately, the fate of the exclusionary rule. The Court has never deemed the latter two purposes to be so important that the rule must be unqualified, as is illustrated by the fact that the government may "profit" from wrongdoing and the court may be an "accomplice" thereto whenever the defendant lacks standing.[17] Yet the reach of the exclusionary rule is affected by its perceived purposes, as is illustrated by *United States v. Calandra*.[18] The

majority took into account only the deterrence function in holding that a grand jury witness may not refuse to answer questions on the ground they are based upon illegally seized evidence, reasoning that any "incremental deterrent effect which might be achieved by extending the rule to grand jury proceedings is uncertain at best." The dissenters, in reaching the contrary conclusion, stressed the other two functions and relegated deterrence to "at best only a hoped for effect of the exclusionary rule." What might be called the *Calandra* approach has been used by the Court in many other cases.[19]

That case is noteworthy in another respect. While in *Mapp* the exclusionary rule was said to be "part and parcel of the Fourth Amendment's limitation upon [governmental] encroachment of individual privacy," the *Calandra* majority characterized the rule as "a judicially-created remedy designed to safeguard Fourth Amendment rights generally through its deterrent effect, rather than a personal constitutional right of the party aggrieved." That language has been viewed with dismay as a "signal" that the Court may "reopen the door still further and abandon altogether the exclusionary rule."[20]

(c) The Exclusionary Rule Under Attack. The validity and efficacy of this exclusionary rule have been vigorously debated over

---

14. 381 U.S. 618, 85 S.Ct. 1731, 14 L.Ed.2d 601 (1965).

15. 392 U.S. 1, 88 S.Ct. 1868, 20 L.Ed.2d 889 (1968).

16. United States v. Calandra, 414 U.S. 338, 94 S.Ct. 613, 38 L.Ed.2d 561 (1974) (dissent).

17. See §§ 9.1, 9.2.

18. 414 U.S. 338, 94 S.Ct. 613, 38 L.Ed.2d 561 (1974).

19. Pennsylvania Board of Probation v. Scott, 524 U.S. 357, 118 S.Ct. 2014, 141 L.Ed.2d 344 (1998) (exclusionary rule not applicable in parole revocation proceedings, as it "would provide only minimal deterrent benefits in this context"); Arizona v. Evans, 514 U.S. 1, 115 S.Ct. 1185, 131 L.Ed.2d 34 (1995) (exclusionary rule not applicable where illegal arrest attributable to error by court clerk, as "threat of exclusion of evidence could not be expected to deter such individuals"); Illinois v. Krull, 480 U.S. 340, 107 S.Ct. 1160, 94 L.Ed.2d 364 (1987) (exclusionary rule not applicable where police searched in reasonable reliance upon statutory authorization, as there "nothing to indicate that applying the exclusionary rule * * * will act as a significant, additional deterrent"); I.N.S. v. Lopez–Mendo-

za, 468 U.S. 1032, 104 S.Ct. 3479, 82 L.Ed.2d 778 (1984) (exclusionary rule not applicable in deportation proceedings, as several factors "significantly reduce the likely deterrent value of the exclusionary rule" in that setting); United States v. Leon, 468 U.S. 897, 104 S.Ct. 3405, 82 L.Ed.2d 677 (1984) ("good faith" exception applicable to exclusionary rule in with-warrant cases, as there "no basis * * * for believing that exclusion of evidence" would "have a significant deterrent effect" in such circumstances); Stone v. Powell, 428 U.S. 465, 96 S.Ct. 3037, 49 L.Ed.2d 1067 (1976) (deterrence said to be the "primary justification" for exclusionary rule, which led to holding that state prisoner cannot ordinarily obtain federal habeas corpus relief because the "additional incremental deterrent effect" of exclusion at that stage would be minimal); United States v. Janis, 428 U.S. 433, 96 S.Ct. 3021, 49 L.Ed.2d 1046 (1976), (because "the 'prime purpose' of the rule, if not the sole one, 'is to deter future unlawful police conduct,' " exclusion from federal civil tax proceedings of evidence obtained by state police officer not required because it would not serve that purpose).

20. Brennan, J., dissenting in *Calandra*.

the years. Much of this debate is more remarkable for its volume than its cogency. There is, for example, the oft-heard complaint that the exclusionary rule "handcuffs" the police, which is nonsense because the objection goes not to this particular remedy but to the Fourth Amendment restrictions upon police authority. That argument was rejected when the Fourth Amendment was adopted. The objection that Fourth Amendment standards are often lacking in clarity is of the same order. The concern is legitimate, but to suggest that it would vanish if the exclusionary rule were abandoned is to concede the warning in *Weeks* that without the suppression doctrine the Fourth Amendment would be no more than "a form of words." As for the complaint that the rule only comes to the aid of the guilty, it also rests upon a gross misperception. The exclusionary rule, as noted in *Elkins v. United States*,[21] "is calculated to prevent, not to repair"; suppression in a particular case is intended to influence police conduct in the future, and thus the innocent and society are the principal beneficiaries.

In *Bivens v. Six Unknown Named Agents*,[22] Chief Justice Burger asserted in dissent that the hope the Fourth Amendment could be enforced "by the exclusion of reliable evidence from criminal trials was hardly more than a wistful dream," and that "there is no empirical evidence to support the claim that the rule actually deters illegal conduct of law enforcement officials." A more accurate characterization is that the available data fall short of an empirical substantiation *or* refutation of the deterrent effect of the exclusionary rule, and thus the Chief Justice's allocation of the burden of proof is merely a way of announcing a predetermined conclusion. The exclusionary rule is like capital punishment in that it is easy to see when the deterrent effect has failed but not when it has succeeded. That the suppression doctrine has had a deterrent effect is nonetheless suggested by various post-exclusionary rule events, such as the dramatic increase in use of search warrants where nearly none were used before, stepped up efforts to educate police on Fourth Amendment law where such training had before been virtually nonexistent, and creation and development of working relationships between police and prosecutors. A majority of the Supreme Court has indicated its willingness to assume "that the immediate effect of exclusion will be to discourage law enforcement officials from violating the Fourth Amendment by removing the incentive to disregard it."[23]

In *Bivens* the Chief Justice suggested the exclusionary rule should be "replaced" by a statute permitting victims of Fourth Amendment violations to go before a special tribunal and collect damages from the government. But it is to be doubted that this would be a suitable substitute for a number of reasons: (1) most such victims lack the aura of respectability needed to collect enough damages to make the action worth the effort; (2) for that reason and others these victims will have difficulty securing effective legal representation; (3) requiring government payment of damages will not deter the police, in that the compartmentalization of government will prevent the taxing authorities from putting effective pressure on the police; (4) the violate now and pay latter character of the remedy makes it ineffective both as a deterrent and a means of giving credibility to Fourth Amendment rights; and (5) shunting the issues off to a special tribunal would withdraw from the Supreme Court and other appellate courts the important function of spelling out police authority under the Fourth Amendment.

Various suggestions have been made for limiting the exclusionary rule in one way or another. For example, Justice White, dissenting in *Stone v. Powell*,[24] expressed the view that the exclusionary rule "should be substantially modified so as to prevent its application in those many circumstances where the evidence at issue was seized by an officer acting in the

---

21. 364 U.S. 206, 80 S.Ct. 1437, 4 L.Ed.2d 1669 (1960).

22. 403 U.S. 388, 91 S.Ct. 1999, 29 L.Ed.2d 619 (1971).

23. Stone v. Powell, 428 U.S. 465, 96 S.Ct. 3037, 49 L.Ed.2d 1067 (1976).

24. 428 U.S. 465, 96 S.Ct. 3037, 49 L.Ed.2d 1067 (1976).

good-faith belief that his conduct comported with existing law and having reasonable grounds for this belief," for the simple reason that in such circumstances "the exclusion can have no deterrent effect." This proposal has been questioned on the grounds that because of the difficulty of determining what is a reasonable mistake of law it would put a premium on the ignorance of the police officer and on the department that trains him and would unduly complicate the factfinding process in that evidence of the officer's state of mind would be generally difficult to come by apart from his self-serving testimony. Moreover, it could stop dead in its tracks judicial development of Fourth Amendment rights, as suppression would always be denied absent a clear precedent declaring the search unconstitutional.

In *United States v. Leon*,[25] the Supreme Court, 6–3, adopted part of the "good faith" exception, holding that "the Fourth Amendment exclusionary rule should be modified so as not to bar the use in the prosecution's case-in-chief of evidence obtained by officers acting in reasonable reliance on a search warrant issued by a detached and neutral magistrate but ultimately found to be unsupported by probable cause." The majority reasoned: (i) that the exclusionary rule is "a judicially created remedy designed to safeguard Fourth Amendment rights generally through its deterrent effect," the applicability of which "must be resolved by weighing the costs and benefits of preventing the use" in evidence of illegally seized evidence; (ii) exclusion to deter magistrates is inappropriate, as "the exclusionary rule is designed to deter police misconduct rather than to punish the errors of judges," "there exists no evidence suggesting that judges and magistrates are inclined to ignore or subvert the Fourth Amendment," and there is no basis "for believing that exclusion of evidence seized pursuant to a warrant will have a significant deterrent effect on the issuing judge or magistrate"; (iii) in a with-warrant case, exclusion to deter the policeman is ordinarily inappropriate, for usually "there is no police illegality" because the officer justifi-

ably relied upon the prior judgment of the magistrate; and thus (iv) "the marginal or nonexistent benefits produced by suppressing evidence obtained in objectively reasonable reliance on a subsequently invalidated search warrant cannot justify the substantial costs of exclusion."

The soundness of *Leon* is certainly open to question. The dissenters seriously questioned whether the exclusionary rule is merely a "judicially created remedy" for Fourth Amendment violations, subject to being narrowed "through guesswork about deterrence," rather than (as indicated in *Weeks*) "a right grounded in that Amendment to prevent the government from subsequently making use of any evidence so obtained." As for the majority's concern about the "costs" of the exclusionary rule, the dissenters noted that available statistics indicate "that federal and state prosecutors very rarely drop cases because of potential search and seizure problems," and that to the extent there is a cost "it is not the exclusionary rule, but the Amendment itself that has imposed this cost" by preferring freedom and privacy over more efficient law enforcement processes. As for the "benefits" of the exclusionary rule in deterrence terms, the dissenters observed that the goal of institutional deterrence is served by exclusion even when the actors in a particular case did not know they were acting illegally. Under *Leon,* by comparison, magistrates know "that they need not take much care in reviewing warrant applications, since their mistakes will from now on have virtually no consequence," and police will know "that if a warrant has simply been signed, it is reasonable, without more, to rely on it."

Whether *Leon* is a stepping-stone to adoption of a more general "good faith" exception remains to be seen. Certainly much of the majority's reasoning—especially that in with-warrant cases there is no need to deter the magistrate and usually no need to discourage the officer from relying upon the magistrate's judgment and actions—does not carry over to the without-warrant situation, where there would also exist more difficult (if not impon-

25. 468 U.S. 897, 104 S.Ct. 3405, 82 L.Ed.2d 677 (1984).

derable) issues of what kinds and degrees of ignorance of Fourth Amendment law are objectively reasonable. But some of the majority's language in *Leon,* particularly the assertion that the exclusionary rule "cannot be expected, and should not be applied, to deter objectively reasonable law enforcement activity," will doubtless be relied upon by those seeking an expansion of the *Leon* holding.

Expansion in a different direction occurred in *Illinois v. Krull,*[26] holding 5–4 that "a similar exception to the exclusionary rule should be recognized when officers act in objectively reasonable reliance upon a *statute* authorizing [the search in question], but where the statute is ultimately found to violate the Fourth Amendment." Despite many pre-*Leon* decisions by the Court to the contrary, the *Krull* majority concluded "[t]he approach used in *Leon* is equally applicable to the present case" because (i) application of the exclusionary rule when the police reasonably relied on a statute would "have as little deterrent effect on the officers' actions" as in the *Leon* situation, and (ii) "legislators, like judicial officers, are not the focus of the rule," as there "is nothing to indicate that applying the exclusionary rule to evidence seized pursuant to the statute prior to the declaration of its invalidity will act as a significant, additional deterrent" to the occasional enactment of a statute later determined to confer unconstitutional search authority. The dissenters, though conceding the good faith of the police who relied on the statute, stressed that statutes "authorizing unreasonable searches were the core concern of the Framers of the Fourth Amendment," and rightly so, as a "judicial officer's unreasonable authorization of a search affects one person at a time; a legislature's unreasonable authorization of searches may affect thousands or millions." Moreover, they persuasively noted, "[l]egislators by virtue of their political role are more often subjected to the political pressures that may threaten Fourth Amendment values than are judicial officers." (*Krull* has

also been deemed applicable when the officer's reliance was instead upon a judicial precedent subsequently overturned.)

It is important to understand that *Leon* does not hold that the exclusionary rule is totally inapplicable whenever a warrant had been obtained. *Leon* has to do with a presumptively invalid warrant, such as one issued on less than probable cause (assumed to be so in *Leon*) or one issued with an insufficient particularity in description (assumed to be so in the companion case of *Massachusetts v. Sheppard*[27]). Fourth Amendment violations relating to execution of the warrant are untouched by *Leon,* as is reflected by the majority's caution that its discussion "assumes, of course, that the officers properly executed the warrant and searched only those places for those objects that it was reasonable to believe were covered by the warrant." So too, *Leon* would not seem to apply where an unconstitutional warrantless search by police produced information that was then used to obtain a search warrant and the subsequent search under that warrant is challenged as the fruit of the initial warrantless search.

The *Leon* Court also emphasized that it was not suggesting "that exclusion is always inappropriate in cases where an officer has obtained a warrant and abided by its terms," and that exclusion is still required if the officer lacked "reasonable grounds for believing that the warrant was properly issued." This, the Court added, encompasses at least four situations: (1) where, under the *Franks* doctrine,[28] a facially sufficient warrant is based upon knowingly or recklessly made falsehoods in the affidavit; (2) where the officer knows that the magistrate has "wholly abandoned his judicial role," as where the magistrate "allowed himself to become a member, if not the leader of the search party,"[29] and presumably also the situation earlier referred to in *Leon,* where the magistrate serves "merely as a rubber stamp for the police"; (3) where "a warrant [is] so

26. 480 U.S. 340, 107 S.Ct. 1160, 94 L.Ed.2d 364 (1987).

27. 468 U.S. 981, 104 S.Ct. 3424, 82 L.Ed.2d 737 (1984).

28. See § 3.4(d).

29. Lo–Ji Sales, Inc. v. New York, 442 U.S. 319, 99 S.Ct. 2319, 60 L.Ed.2d 920 (1979).

facially deficient—i.e., in failing to particularize the place to be searched or the things to be seized—that the executing officers cannot reasonably presume it to be valid," which raises the question of how far off the mark of extant particular description requirements[30] a description must be before an officer should know it is deficient[31]; and (4) where the affidavit was "so lacking in indicia of probable cause as to render official belief in its existence entirely unreasonable."

It is on this latter language that most of the post-*Leon* suppression motions in with-warrant cases have focused. Because the Court had adopted a relaxed standard of assessing probable cause just a year earlier in *Illinois v. Gates*,[32] whereunder it suffices if a reviewing court finds the magistrate had a "substantial basis" for concluding there was a "fair probability" evidence would be found, how if at all has *Leon*, in light of this limitation, departed from existing requirements?[33] A partial answer may be that *Gates* and *Leon* can produce different results because of their different focus: the former is concerned with the *magistrate*'s decision, to be given deference in all "doubtful or marginal cases," while the latter involves the decision to seek and execute a warrant by the *police*, who ordinarily are entitled to assume the magistrate is acting properly. This important difference is highlighted in the assertion in *Leon* that the question to be resolved is "whether a reasonably well-trained officer would have known that the search was illegal despite the magistrate's authorization." But this seemingly hindsight perspective was thereafter rejected by the Court in another context where, purporting to follow "the same

standard" as *Leon*, it was concluded that the fact that the magistrate acted favorably on the warrant request was irrelevant. This is because, the Court explained, the question "is whether a reasonably well-trained officer * * * would have known that his affidavit failed to establish probable cause and that he should not have applied for the warrant."[34]

As for the suggestion that the exclusionary rule not apply in the most serious cases, where there is a substantial disproportion between the magnitude of the policeman's constitutional violation and the defendant's crime, such a limitation would withdraw the exclusionary rule from those cases in which it is most effective and other restraints are least effective, and would likely result in the police concluding that the Fourth Amendment could be ignored in such cases. As for the broader "comparative reprehensibility" approach, under which a defendant could invoke the exclusionary rule only where the illegality committed against him was more grave than the crime he committed, it is grounded in the false assumption that a weighing of the relative seriousness of the defendant's crime and the police transgression of his rights somehow captures the relevant concerns regarding the proper boundaries of the exclusionary rule. And the proposal that the exclusionary rule be limited to institutional failures by permitting the police to make a showing of the police department's regulations, training programs, and disciplinary history as to the practice at issue, though directed at the desirable objective of prompting law enforcement agencies to engage in meaningful rule-making, also would

30. See § 3.4(e), (f).

31. In this regard, it should be noted that in *Sheppard* the search warrant authorized search for "controlled substances" and related paraphernalia, though the affidavit in support showed probable cause to search for certain specified evidence of a homicide. In holding this came within the *Leon* rule, the Court stressed that the detective who directed the search apparently never noticed the discrepancy, that he was also the affiant and thus "knew what items were listed in the affidavit presented to the judge," and that "he had good reason to believe that the warrant authorized the seizure of those items." The Court cautioned it was not deciding what the result would be as to "an officer who is less familiar with the warrant application."

32. 462 U.S. 213, 103 S.Ct. 2317, 76 L.Ed.2d 527 (1983), discussed in § 3.3(c).

33. As the *Leon* dissenters put it, is it not "virtually inconceivable that a reviewing court, when faced with a defendant's motion to suppress, could first find that a warrant was invalid under the new *Gates* standard, but then, at the same time, find that a police officer's reliance on such an invalid warrant was nevertheless 'objectively reasonable' under the test announced today"?

34. Malley v. Briggs, 475 U.S. 335, 106 S.Ct. 1092, 89 L.Ed.2d 271 (1986), thus concluding that a rule of absolute immunity would be inappropriate in a § 1983 action against an officer based on his conduct in *applying for* a warrant.

add another especially subjective factual determination to suppression hearings.

(d) The Significance of Underlying Motivation; More on the Deterrence Objective and Inquiry Into Subjective Matters. The question of whether a "bad" intent or motivation by the searching police officer is to be taken into account in deciding whether evidence should be suppressed was presented in *Scott v. United States*,[35] where federal agents operating a judicially authorized wiretap failed to attempt any compliance with the Fourth Amendment requirement of minimization of interception. In rejecting the petitioners' claim that this "lack of good faith efforts" required suppression even if no minimization would have been feasible in this case, the Court elected to evaluate the Fourth Amendment claim by "an objective assessment of an officer's actions in light of the facts and circumstances then known to him" and "without regard to the underlying intent or motivation of the officers involved." Generally, this is a sound rule and is fully consistent with the purposes of the Fourth Amendment and its exclusionary rule,[36] as may be seen by examination of some of the situations in which problems of this kind arise.

One kind of case is that in which the police, though lacking the grounds required by the Fourth Amendment, decide to make an arrest or search, but before they can so act upon that decision they are confronted with additional facts supplying the requisite grounds. Most courts refuse to suppress the evidence in such circumstances, and rightly so. "We might wish that policemen would not act with impure plots in mind," but that is hardly "a sufficient basis for excluding, in the supposed service of the Fourth Amendment, probative evidence obtained by actions—if not thoughts—entirely in accord with the Fourth Amendment," especially since a contrary rule would require courts to undertake "an expedition into the minds of police officers."[37] In other words, the deterrence objective would not be served by exclusion in such circumstances.

What if the officer *does* act on his "bad" state of mind in the sense that he engages in Fourth Amendment activity despite a *mistaken* belief he lacks the grounds for such action? Though it might be argued that in such a case the deterrence objective calls for exclusion so as to impress upon the officer that he should not arrest when he believes probable is lacking (in which case often it will in fact be lacking), the prevailing view is that an officer is no more the judge of the insufficiency of his facts than of their sufficiency. On balance, that is a correct result; here again, the evidence was "obtained by actions—if not thoughts—entirely in accord with the Fourth Amendment," and thus what is to be communicated to the officer is that the information he had *did* amount to probable cause, a message that hardly would be conveyed by suppression of evidence.

Then there are cases in which it might be said that the officer's "underlying intent or motivation" reflects that he was operating under the wrong legal theory, such as where an officer arrested a robbery suspect for vagrancy, but the facts at hand constituted grounds to arrest for robbery but not for vagrancy. The prevailing view is to uphold the arrest, which is correct. Exclusion in the interest of deterrence is unjustified here, especially because such situations are often attributable to complicated legal distinctions between offenses or an officer's failure to record all the bases or the strongest basis upon which the arrest was made. Sometimes the gap between the relied upon but unavailing theory and the availing but unrelied upon theory is greater, as where a warrantless search of a vehicle was undertaken as an inventory of an impounded car, not justified on the facts, but in actuality the car was subject to warrantless search on probable

---

35. 436 U.S. 128, 98 S.Ct. 1717, 56 L.Ed.2d 168 (1978).

36. And thus has been relied upon by the Court in other circumstances. See, e.g., Horton v. California, 496 U.S. 128, 110 S.Ct. 2301, 110 L.Ed.2d 112 (1990) (rejecting inadvertent discovery limitation on plain view doctrine because "evenhanded law enforcement is best achieved by the application of objective standards of conduct, rather than standards that depend upon the subjective state of mind of the officer").

37. White, J., dissenting from dismissal of writ as improvidently granted in Massachusetts v. Painten, 389 U.S. 560, 88 S.Ct. 660, 19 L.Ed.2d 770 (1968).

cause. It has been held that upholding the police action on a court-devised theory of justification would be improper because it would not deter future unconstitutional impoundments or inventories, but the prevailing view is again to the contrary. The *Scott* rule produces the better result even here. Suppression for police reliance upon the wrong theory even when there exists a valid theory would deter unconstitutional searches only if, absent such extension of the exclusionary rule, it may be assumed police will conduct searches on grounds they know or suspect to be insufficient in the hope that their actions will later be upheld on some other grounds of which they are presently unaware. That assumption seems fanciful.

Scott has been objected to on the ground that it undermines the long established rule that an arrest may not be used as a pretext to search, which prompts consideration of *Abel v. United States.*[38] There immigration agents, acting pursuant to an administrative warrant for deportation, arrested Russian spy Colonel Abel, but he later claimed this was an illegal subterfuge because those agents were working hand-in-glove with FBI agents whose underlying objective was to acquire evidence of Abel's espionage. The Supreme Court held that a "finding of bad faith" could not be made on the record, which, as stated by the district court, was that the immigration agents' conduct "differed in no respect from what would have been done in the case of an individual concerning whom no such information was known to exist." Thus, the "underlying intent or motivation of the officers involved" (to use the *Scott* phrase again) does not require suppression where, even assuming that intent or motivation was the dominant one in the particular case, the Fourth Amendment activity undertaken is precisely the same as would have occurred had that intent or motivation been absent. This is a correct result; because the action would have been taken in any event, there is no *conduct* that ought to have been deterred and thus no reason to bring the Fourth Amendment exclusionary rule into play.

That highlights the remaining situation in which the Fourth Amendment activity would not have been undertaken *but for* the "underlying intent or motivation" that, standing alone, could not supply a lawful basis for the police conduct. Illustrative is a case in which the driver of an automobile suspected of unlawful drug activity is subjected to a traffic stop leading to discovery of drugs, though the stop was not one that would have been made by an officer on routine patrol against any citizen driving in the same manner. Such situations, so the argument goes, involve what the Supreme Court in *Abel* characterized as "serious conduct by law-enforcing officers," and consequently evidence obtained by such pretextual seizures should be suppressed. But many lower courts applied the *Scott* rule in these circumstances as well and resisted all efforts by defendants affected by these practices to find a way around *Scott*. Some other lower courts, however, felt *Scott* simply could not extend this far and thus, in ordering the evidence suppressed, emphasized the underlying "bad" motive of the officers involved. Still other courts also suppressed the fruits of such subterfuge activity, but by use of a test deemed to be objective and thus not within the *Scott* prohibition. They would ask whether, assuming no ulterior motive, a reasonable officer "would" (not merely "could") have made such an intrusion.

So matters stood when the Supreme Court decided *Whren v. United States,*[39] a case similar to the illustration set out above. (Vice squad officers patrolling a "high drug area" became suspicious of the occupants of a truck and then stopped the truck for minor traffic violations, resulting in the observation of cocaine in the vehicle.) The petitioners argued that probable cause the traffic code was being violated should not suffice for a traffic stop because "the use of automobiles is so heavily and minutely regulated that total compliance with traffic and safety rules is nearly impossible." Otherwise "a police officer will almost

38.   362 U.S. 217, 80 S.Ct. 683, 4 L.Ed.2d 668 (1960).

39.   517 U.S. 806, 116 S.Ct. 1769, 135 L.Ed.2d 89 (1996).

invariably be able to catch any given motorist in a technical violation," a situation that "creates the temptation to use traffic stops as a means of investigating other law violations, as to which no probable cause or even articulable suspicion exists." A *unanimous* Court rejected that proposition. Viewed as a claim that pretextual seizures violate the Fourth Amendment, it was deemed contrary to the Court's prior cases (especially *Scott*) treating the officers' subjective intent as irrelevant on the constitutional issue. Cases in which the Court had previously expressed concern about pretextual action[40] were distinguishable, said the Court in *Whren*, because those decisions—unlike the instant case—involved police searches "conducted in the absence of probable cause" and exempt from that requirement only when made for a special purpose. The petitioners claimed their test did not violate the *Scott* rule because it was an objective one, "whether the officer's conduct deviated materially from usual police practices," shown in the instant case, they claimed, because the stop was in violation of police regulations generally barring traffic stops by plainclothes officers in unmarked cars. The Court answered that this was merely another attempt to get at the pretextual stop, which is not "unreasonable" under the Fourth Amendment because the existence of probable cause settles the issue of reasonableness. True,

some of the Court's prior cases ascertained reasonableness by resort to a balancing analysis, but, the *Whren* Court explained, this was done as to Fourth Amendment activity "unusually harmful to an individual's privacy or even physical interests."[41] Violation of the police regulation in the instant case was not "such an extreme practice, and so is governed by the usual rule that probable cause to believe the law has been broken 'outbalances' private interest in avoiding police contact."[42]

(e) Constitutional vs. Other Violations. *Mapp v. Ohio*[43] declared that state and federal officers were obligated to respect "the same fundamental criteria," and in *Ker v. California*[44] the Court held that "the standard of reasonableness is the same under the Fourth and Fourteenth Amendments." This means that close attention must be paid to the basis of Supreme Court decisions dealing with searches and seizures by federal officers, as a declared standard based upon the Fourth Amendment would be equally applicable to the states, but this would not be so as to a standard based only upon the Court's supervisory power over federal courts.

When a state court finds that a certain arrest or search passes muster under the Fourth Amendment but that it violates the comparable provision of the state constitution, there appears to be no dissent from the conclusion

---

40. Florida v. Wells, 495 U.S. 1, 110 S.Ct. 1632, 109 L.Ed.2d 1 (1990); Colorado v. Bertine, 479 U.S. 367, 107 S.Ct. 738, 93 L.Ed.2d 739 (1987) (both having to do with inventory of impounded vehicles); and New York v. Burger, 482 U.S. 691, 107 S.Ct. 2636, 96 L.Ed.2d 601 (1987) (dealing with administrative inspection of business premises).

Whren thus seemed to leave open the interesting question of whether, in seeking to suppress evidence obtained in such a vehicle inventory, the defendant was limited to claiming pretext only as to the post-arrest decision to inventory, or whether he could claim pretext as to the arrest that provided the basis for impoundment and then inventory. A state case taking the latter view was summarily reversed by the Supreme Court, but only on the limited ground that the state court had asserted a nonexistent power to construe the U.S. Constitution more broadly than the Supreme Court. Arkansas v. Sullivan, 532 U.S. 769, 121 S.Ct. 1876, 149 L.Ed.2d 994 (2001). However, four concurring Justices declared that the state court "was moved by a concern rooted in the Fourth Amendment" when it expressed unwillingness "to sanction conduct where a police officer can trail a targeted vehicle with a driver merely suspected of criminal activity, wait for the

driver to exceed the speed limit by one mile per hour, arrest the driver for speeding, and conduct a full-blown inventory search of the vehicle with impunity," but the concurring Justices then added that "such exercises of official discretion are unlimited by the Fourth Amendment" in light of *Whren*.

41. For example, the *Whren* Court noted, seizure by means of deadly force, Tennessee v. Garner, 471 U.S. 1, 105 S.Ct. 1694, 85 L.Ed.2d 1 (1985); unannounced home entry, Wilson v. Arkansas, 514 U.S. 927, 115 S.Ct. 1914, 131 L.Ed.2d 976 (1995); entry of a home without a warrant, Welsh v. Wisconsin, 466 U.S. 740, 104 S.Ct. 2091, 80 L.Ed.2d 732 (1984); or physical penetration of the body, Winston v. Lee, 470 U.S. 753, 105 S.Ct. 1611, 84 L.Ed.2d 662 (1985).

42. Although *Whren* involved a traffic stop rather than a custodial arrest, its reasoning appeared equally applicable to the latter form of seizure as well, as the Court later confirmed in Arkansas v. Sullivan, 532 U.S. 769, 121 S.Ct. 1876, 149 L.Ed.2d 994 (2001).

43. 367 U.S. 643, 81 S.Ct. 1684, 6 L.Ed.2d 1081 (1961).

44. 374 U.S. 23, 83 S.Ct. 1623, 10 L.Ed.2d 726 (1963).

that the fruits thereof must be suppressed in proceedings in the courts of that state. Where, however, the police conduct is merely in violation of a statutory provision, a rule of court, or an administrative regulation, the same result does not inevitably follow. If the provision in question actually says that the sanction is exclusion of evidence, as is true of some federal and state statutory provisions, then that settles the matter. Absent such a declaration, courts are more likely to utilize the exclusionary rule when the provision in question confers a substantial right, especially if it is one that can be said to relate rather closely to Fourth Amendment protections. In the search warrant area, for example, courts are not inclined to require exclusion of evidence for failure to follow statutes dealing with such matters as prompt return of the warrant to the court, but are likely to rule otherwise as to statutes requiring very prompt execution. Somewhat the same approach is generally taken as to administrative regulations, though there is greater reluctance to utilize an exclusionary rule in this setting and possibly influence the administrative agency involved to reduce its efforts at self-regulation.[45]

In *Elkins v. United States*,[46] the Court abolished the so-called "silver platter" doctrine under which federal courts could receive the fruits of unconstitutional searches by state officers. Thus, it is now clear that if the Fourth Amendment has been violated the evidence must be suppressed: (i) when offered in federal court, though the search was by state officers; (ii) when offered in state court, though the search was by federal officers; and (iii) when offered in one state, though the search was by officers of another state. What then is the result when the violation in question is not of Fourth Amendment dimensions, as in *Burge v. State*,[47] where evidence offered in a Texas court was constitutionally obtained

in Oklahoma but yet was acquired in violation of the Oklahoma rule that a wife cannot give a consent to search effective against her husband? Courts do not utilize the exclusionary rule in such circumstances, and rightly so; the prospect of deterrence is remote, as is the judicial taint from acceptance of the evidence, and there has been no profit from wrongdoing attributable to the prosecuting jurisdiction. Sometimes that result is explained upon the conflict-of-laws principle that the law of the forum governs on the lawfulness-of-the-search issue, but that surely is not the reason. If the situation in *Burge* had been reversed, so that consent-by-spouse was illegal in Texas (the prosecuting state) but not in Oklahoma (the state where the search occurred), it would be ridiculous to suppress the evidence.

(f) Application of Exclusionary Rule in Criminal Proceedings. Questions sometimes arise as to the applicability of the exclusionary rule at stages of the criminal process other than the trial, as illustrated by *United States v. Calandra*.[48] A grand jury witness objected that he should not have to answer questions based upon information acquired by an earlier illegal search of his premises, but the Supreme Court disagreed. The Court reasoned that such "extension of the exclusionary rule would seriously impede the grand jury" by requiring suppression hearings on "issues only tangentially related to the grand jury's primary objective," damage that would not be offset by substantial benefits in terms of "incremental deterrent effect." This is because illegally seized evidence is already excludable at trial, and thus additional exclusion at the grand jury stage, the Court explained, "would deter only police investigation consciously directed toward the discovery of evidence solely for use in a grand jury investigation." This overlooks the fact that the prior search had been directed at witness Calandra and that thus under the law

---

45. In United States v. Caceres, 440 U.S. 741, 99 S.Ct. 1465, 59 L.Ed.2d 733 (1979), the Court declined to utilize the exclusionary sanction as to evidence obtained in violation of IRS regulations prohibiting "consensual electronic surveillance" between taxpayers and IRS agents unless certain prior authorization is obtained, reasoning: "In the long run, it is far better to have rules like those contained in the IRS Manual, and to tolerate occasional erroneous

administration of the kind displayed by this record, than either to have no rules except those mandated by statute, or to have them framed in a mere precatory form."

46. 364 U.S. 206, 80 S.Ct. 1437, 4 L.Ed.2d 1669 (1960).

47. 443 S.W.2d 720 (Tex.Cr.App.1969).

48. 414 U.S. 338, 94 S.Ct. 613, 38 L.Ed.2d 561 (1974).

of standing only Calandra and not the person later indicted could call the police to task for their conduct.

In *Costello v. United States*[49] the Court concluded that "neither the Fifth Amendment nor any other constitutional provision prescribes the kind of evidence upon which grand juries must act," and in that case and subsequent decisions[50] the Court rejected self-incrimination challenges to grand jury indictments. Relying upon those cases, federal courts and most state courts have refused to permit defendants to attack indictments on the ground that evidence before the grand jury was obtained in violation of the Fourth Amendment, which is a sound result. Because the objection would be made by the same person who could object at trial, the standing problem noted above does not exist here. Moreover, there is no feasible way to determine these issues in an adversary setting *before* the evidence is received by the grand jury, and post-indictment challenges on Fourth Amendment grounds would necessitate an elaborate assessment of all the evidence tendered to the grand jury in that case, a burden that is hardly worth whatever deterrent effect would be achieved by nullifying indictments grounded in illegally acquired evidence. That reasoning obviously does not carry over to the issue of whether the exclusionary rule should be applied to the probable cause determination at a preliminary hearing, but there as well the rule in the federal system[51] and most but not all states is that suppression of evidence is not possible at the preliminary hearing. That result is typically explained on the ground that it thus avoids the necessity for multiple determinations of admissibility and for lesser judicial officers to pass upon complex constitutional issues. If those reasons are convincing, they would also support the conclusion that a Fourth Amendment suppression motion may not be utilized to keep evidence out of a pretrial bail hearing, an issue that has seldom reached the courts.

If a defendant manages to have certain evidence suppressed from his trial on Fourth Amendment grounds but is convicted nonetheless, may the excluded evidence be taken into account at his sentencing hearing? Utilizing a *Calandra*-style balancing approach, it has been held that the answer is yes, as there is a need for unfettered access to information by the sentencing judge, and no appreciable increment in deterrence would result from excluding a second time at sentencing. But this is not inevitably true, and thus it is necessary to recognize two exceptions: (1) where the police are assembling a dossier to be offered to a sentencing judge should the subject ever be convicted of an offense, and (2) where police have accumulated sufficient evidence to convict and then seize additional evidence unlawfully solely to affect the sentence.

By a somewhat similar balancing process, the prevailing view in the lower courts for many years has been that the exclusionary rule generally need not be applied in proceedings to revoke a suspended sentence, probation or parole. Some courts held (and many others suggested in dictum) that the result would be different if the search was conducted by an official aware of the conditional release status of the individual. But in *Pennsylvania Board of Probation and Parole v. Scott*,[52] involving a parole officer's illegal search of the residence of a known parolee, the Court opted for *total* inapplicability of the exclusionary rule in parole board hearings. The majority declared that the cost of the exclusionary rule, altering "the traditionally flexible, administrative nature of parole revocation proceedings," was not worth the "minimal" deterrence that would result. The latter characterization was correct even in instances in which the parolee's status was known, the *Scott* majority reasoned, because even then a searching official would be deterred by the risk of evidence exclusion at a criminal trial and, if a policeman, would be unaffected by what might happen at a parole hearing, which "falls outside

---

49. 350 U.S. 359, 76 S.Ct. 406, 100 L.Ed. 397 (1956).

50. Lawn v. United States, 355 U.S. 339, 78 S.Ct. 311, 2 L.Ed.2d 321 (1958); United States v. Blue, 384 U.S. 251, 86 S.Ct. 1416, 16 L.Ed.2d 510 (1966).

51. Giordenello v. United States, 357 U.S. 480, 78 S.Ct. 1245, 2 L.Ed.2d 1503 (1958); Fed.R.Crim.P. 5.1.

52. 524 U.S. 357, 118 S.Ct. 2014, 141 L.Ed.2d 344 (1998).

the offending officer's zone of primary interest," and, if a parole officer, because he is "not engaged in the competitive enterprise of ferreting out crime," could be sufficiently deterred by "departmental training and discipline and the threat of damages actions." The four dissenters in *Scott* cogently noted that because police typically know of a parolee's status, the criminal trial exclusionary rule is less likely to deter than a parole hearing exclusionary rule, for it is generally understood (as the Supreme Court had itself noted on an earlier occasion[53]) that parole revocation "is often preferred to a new prosecution because of the procedural ease of recommitting the individual on the basis of a lesser showing by the State." As for parole officers, the dissenters added, they "are considered police officers with respect to the offenders under their jurisdiction" and thus can no more than other police be thought to be adequately deterred by the risk of departmental discipline or the threat of damages actions.

(g) Application of Exclusionary Rule in Non-criminal Proceedings. In *One 1958 Plymouth Sedan v. Pennsylvania*,[54] the Court held that in proceedings for the forfeiture of an automobile to the state on the ground that it had been used in the illegal transportation of liquor, that use could not be proved by admission of the liquor taken from that car in an unconstitutional search. As for earlier cases holding that the government was not required to return unlawfully seized narcotics[55] or an unregistered still, alcohol and mash,[56] the Court noted that they "concerned objects the possession of which, without more, constitutes a crime," so that repossession would have subjected the owners to criminal penalties and "would clearly have frustrated the express public policy against the possession of such objects." By comparison, in the instant case there "is nothing even remotely criminal in possessing an automobile," and return of it "to the owner would not subject him to any possible criminal penalties for possession or frustrate any public policy concerning automobiles, as automobiles." The Court added that it would be "anomalous" to apply the exclusionary rule in a criminal proceeding for the crime in question, for which a $500 fine could be imposed, but not in proceedings intended to penalize the criminal by depriving him of a $1,000 automobile. Under the *Plymouth Sedan* analysis, the exclusionary rule does not apply in proceedings to forfeit such per se contraband as gambling devices and obscene literature. When the object is the fruits of crime, such as gambling profits, the application of *Plymouth Sedan* is unclear; it could be argued, on the one hand, that permitting the criminal to keep his ill-gotten gains frustrates public policy, and on the other that absent exclusion police will be encouraged to make lawless searches for the very purpose of depriving criminals of their profits. The latter concern is legitimate, and explains why most courts do apply the exclusionary rule in that type of forfeiture action. Somewhat similar analysis supports the conclusion that police should not be free of Fourth Amendment restraints when dealing with juveniles or drug addicts, so that the exclusionary rule applies in juvenile delinquency proceedings and addict commitment proceedings.

In *United States v. Janis*,[57] a city police officer seized certain records and funds in a gambling raid and then turned them over to the Internal Revenue Service, where they served as the basis of an IRS assessment satisfied in part by levying upon the seized funds. Janis then sued in federal court for return of the money, and the government counterclaimed for the unpaid balance. The Supreme Court held that the exclusionary rule did not apply in those proceedings in such circumstances, reasoning that no appreciable gain in terms of deterrence would be realized by suppression in a proceeding "to enforce only the civil law of the other sovereign," as it "falls

---

53. Morrissey v. Brewer, 408 U.S. 471, 92 S.Ct. 2593, 33 L.Ed.2d 484 (1972).

54. 380 U.S. 693, 85 S.Ct. 1246, 14 L.Ed.2d 170 (1965).

55. United States v. Jeffers, 342 U.S. 48, 72 S.Ct. 93, 96 L.Ed. 59 (1951).

56. Trupiano v. United States, 334 U.S. 699, 68 S.Ct. 1229, 92 L.Ed. 1663 (1948).

57. 428 U.S. 433, 96 S.Ct. 3021, 49 L.Ed.2d 1046 (1976).

outside the offending officer's zone of primary interest." The trouble with *Janis* is that the facts of the case do not support the result, for it was shown that there was an established pattern of cooperation whereby that officer routinely notified the IRS whenever he uncovered a gambling operation involving a substantial amount of cash. Thus, as the *Janis* dissenters noted, "the deterrent purpose of the exclusionary rule is wholly frustrated" by the decision. Absent the special facts relied upon in *Janis,* the exclusionary rule is applied in civil tax proceedings, a conclusion supported by the *Plymouth Sedan* case in that here as well the penalties can far exceed those from criminal prosecution.

Courts have held or assumed that the exclusionary rule applies in a wide range of administrative proceedings, all the way from FTC hearings to uncover discriminatory pricing practices to hearings to suspend or expel a student from school. Many of these decisions are supported by the *Plymouth Sedan* reasoning that the exclusionary rule applies to proceedings that are "quasi-criminal in character," in that their object "is to penalize for the commission of an offense against the law" and could "result in even greater punishment than the criminal prosecution." Under the *Calandra* balancing approach, it may be said that the exclusion-for-deterrence point is quite strong when the search was undertaken for the specific purpose of obtaining information to offer in such administrative proceedings and relatively weak when the search was not directed at a person known to be amenable to such proceedings. As for the cost side of the *Calandra* equation, it may vary from situation to situation. Similar analysis is called for as to the seldom-litigated question of whether the exclusionary rule applies to legislative hearings.

An extreme and fundamentally unsound cost-benefit analysis was utilized by the majority in *Immigration and Naturalization Service v. Lopez–Mendoza,*[58] where the Court held 5–4 that the exclusionary rule is inapplicable in a civil deportation hearing. The deterrent value of the exclusionary rule in this context was deemed to be reduced because (i) "deportation will still be possible when evidence not derived directly from the arrest is sufficient to support deportation," (ii) INS agents know "that it is highly unlikely that any particular arrestee will end up challenging the lawfulness of his arrest," (iii) "the INS has its own comprehensive scheme for deterring Fourth Amendment violations" by training and discipline, and (iv) "alternative remedies" including the "possibility of declaratory relief" are available for institutional practices violating the Fourth Amendment. On the cost side, the Court continued, are these factors: (i) that application of the exclusionary rule "in proceedings that are intended not to punish past transgressions but to prevent their continuance or renewal would require courts to close their eyes to ongoing violations of the law," (ii) that invocation of the exclusionary rule at deportation hearings, where "neither the hearing officers nor the attorneys * * * are likely to be well versed in the intricacies of Fourth Amendment law," "might significantly change and complicate the character of these proceedings," and (iii) that because many INS arrests "occur in crowded and confused circumstances," application of the exclusionary rule "might well result in the suppression of large amounts of information that had been obtained entirely lawfully." White, J., dissenting, correctly noted that "unlike the situation in *Janis,* the conduct challenged here falls within 'the offending officer's zone of primary interest,'" and that "the costs and benefits of applying the exclusionary rule in civil deportation proceedings do not differ in any significant way from the costs and benefits of applying the rule in ordinary criminal proceedings."

Finally, it must be asked whether the Fourth Amendment exclusionary rule applies in purely private litigation, that is, a civil action in which a governmental unit or representative is not a party. Some authority is to be found to the effect that the fruits of an illegal police search may not be used in a private lawsuit, but it is to be doubted that this conclusion is compelled under the *Calan-*

58.　468 U.S. 1032, 104 S.Ct. 3479, 82 L.Ed.2d 778 (1984).

dra approach. The *Janis* reasoning that there is no gain in deterrence when the proceeding in which the evidence is offered "falls outside the offending officer's zone of primary interest" is more persuasive here than in *Janis*.

(h) The Exclusionary Rule and "Private" or Nonpolice Searches. In *Burdeau v. McDowell*,[59] the Court concluded that because the Fourth Amendment's "origin and history clearly show that it was intended as a restraint upon the activities of sovereign authority and was not intended to be a limitation upon other than governmental agencies," it did not call for exclusion in the instant case, where "no official of the federal government had anything to do with the wrongful seizure * * * or any knowledge thereof until several months after the property had been taken." The *Burdeau* rule squares with the modern emphasis upon the deterrence function of the exclusionary rule, as the private searcher is often motivated by reasons independent of a desire to secure a criminal conviction and seldom engages in searches upon a sufficiently regular basis to be affected by the exclusionary sanction.

It should not be assumed that a search is private whenever the physical act is done by a private person. This quite clearly is not the case when the search has been ordered or requested by a government official, when it is a joint endeavor of a private person and government official, or when the government official was standing by giving tacit approval. It is otherwise if the private person acted in direct contravention of police instructions. One recurring situation is that in which a private person examines an object and then turns it over to the police for further examination, where close attention is needed to exactly what was done on both occasions. In *Walter v. United States*,[60] for example, private persons to whom a shipment of boxes were misdelivered opened them and found packages of film with suggestive drawings and explicit descriptions of the contents on the outsides, so they turned the boxes over to FBI agents who screened the films and determined they were obscene. The Court held the screening was a governmental search because it exceeded the scope of the prior private search, and distinguished the case from one in which "the results of the private search are in plain view when materials are turned over to the Government," in which case mere observation of what remained exposed by the private search would not amount to a governmental search. (The Court later held, in *United States v. Jacobsen*,[61] that "field testing" of a white powder first uncovered by a private search did not itself constitute a search because the test would only reveal whether or not the powder was an illegal substance and thus would not "compromise any legitimate interest in privacy."[62]) This leaves the hardest case, namely, where a private party opens a package and finds something incriminating and then repackages it and delivers it to the police, who examine the contents of the package in no greater detail than did the private party. *Walter* does not resolve this situation, but in *Jacobsen* the Court held that so long as the police conduct enabled them "to learn nothing that had not previously been learned during the private search" it "infringed no legitimate expectation of privacy and hence was not a 'search' within the meaning of the Fourth Amendment."

Courts have not hesitated to admit into evidence under the *Burdeau* rule the fruits of searches conducted by persons who, while not employed by the government, have as their responsibility the prevention and detection of criminal conduct, such as store detectives and insurance investigators. Some have argued for the contrary result, contending that the reasoning of *Marsh v. Alabama*,[63] holding that when a private company owned and operated a town it was performing a "public function"

---

59.   256 U.S. 465, 41 S.Ct. 574, 65 L.Ed. 1048 (1921).

60.   447 U.S. 649, 100 S.Ct. 2395, 65 L.Ed.2d 410 (1980).

61.   466 U.S. 109, 104 S.Ct. 1652, 80 L.Ed.2d 85 (1984).

62.   The Court applied the reasoning from United States v. Place, 462 U.S. 696, 103 S.Ct. 2637, 77 L.Ed.2d

110 (1983), holding that the sniffing of a suitcase by a narcotics detection dog was no search because it "discloses only the presence or absence of narcotics, a contraband item."

63.   326 U.S. 501, 66 S.Ct. 276, 90 L.Ed. 265 (1946).

and thus was subject to constitutional restraints in the same fashion as any other town, applies here. The *Marsh* analogy is especially appealing where private police actually supplant the public police or deal regularly with the general public, particularly if it may be said they are not disinterested in criminal convictions as an aid to the private objectives of their employer, for in such instances there is both a need for and an opportunity for deterrence by application of the Fourth Amendment exclusionary rule.

Somewhat the reverse of the above situation is that in which the search was by a public employee not assigned to law enforcement responsibilities. Because *Burdeau* says the Fourth Amendment "applies to governmental actions" and is a "restraint upon the activities of sovereign authority," it follows (as the Court held in *New Jersey v. T.L.O,*[64] involving search of a student by a high school administrator) that "the Fourth Amendment [is] applicable to the activities of civil as well as criminal authorities." But in *Arizona v. Evans,*[65] the Court concluded that some government searches covered by the Fourth Amendment are nonetheless inappropriate occasions for use of the exclusionary rule, considering the kind of government official who was at fault. In *Evans,* where the defendant was arrested on the basis of an erroneous computer indication of an outstanding warrant, attributable to a court clerk's failure to advise the police that the warrant had been quashed, the Court used *Leon*-style[66] reasoning to conclude the exclusionary rule should not apply: the arresting officer acted reasonably in relying on the computer record and thus was not in need of deterrence; and exclusion would not deter such errors by court clerks, who "have no stake in the outcome of particular criminal prosecutions." *Evans* will doubtless be deemed applicable to at least some searches actually conducted by nonpolice government officials, especially those whose responsibilities would only rarely uncover evidence of criminal activity.

A court has occasionally relied upon a "ratified intent" theory, reasoning that if a private person made a search for the purpose of aiding the government and the government then uses that evidence later, the taint of the illegal action is thereby transferred to the government so as to make the use unlawful. The theory is in error because it wrongly assumes that the Government has some control over the taker's intent, and has been rejected by other courts. One step beyond that theory is the position that the action of the judicial branch in receiving the fruits of the search into evidence is standing alone sufficient government involvement to bring the Fourth Amendment into play. But, while some have suggested that position is supported by *Shelley v. Kraemer,*[67] holding that judicial enforcement of private restrictive covenants constitutes "state action" subject to constitutional restraints, this is not the case. In *Shelley* the lower court was asked to compel a private citizen to do an act that would be unconstitutional for the state to perform, not merely to give evidentiary status to illegally seized information. Moreover, in *Shelley* the challenged racial discrimination could not have occurred unless the court enforced the discriminatory restrictive covenant, while in the case of a search by a private party the invasion of privacy has taken place before the court is called on to admit the evidence.

(i) The Exclusionary Rule and Searches by Foreign Police. If the police of a foreign country, acting to enforce their own law and without any instigation by American officials, conduct a search that would not meet the requirements of the Fourth Amendment if conducted in this country, and the fruits are later offered into evidence here, the evidence is not subject to suppression on constitutional grounds. The Fourth Amendment is not directed at foreign police, and no purpose would be served by applying the exclusionary rule in such a case, as it would not alter the search and seizure policies of the foreign nation. If the foreign official acted with the purpose, at

---

64.   469 U.S. 325, 105 S.Ct. 733, 83 L.Ed.2d 720 (1985).

65.   514 U.S. 1, 115 S.Ct. 1185, 131 L.Ed.2d 34 (1995).

66.   See § 3.1(c).

67.   334 U.S. 1, 68 S.Ct. 836, 92 L.Ed. 1161 (1948).

least in part, of finding evidence that could be turned over to American authorities, the result is no different. There is no reason why the foreign official in such circumstances should be expected to discover and apply a rather complicated body of law from another country. This is so even if the foreign official may have been prompted to so act because information was supplied to him about the suspect by American authorities.

If the American authorities have actually requested or participated in the foreign search, it has been suggested that the case should be dealt with just as were state police searches in response to a federal request in the silver platter era, which means that the exclusionary rule would be applicable because of such request or participation.[68] But this is not the law, and rightly so, as the dynamics here are quite different. The state-federal silver platter problem was one of preventing federal authorities from circumventing the Fourth Amendment by getting state officials to do what they would otherwise do themselves, while the foreign-American relationship is legitimate because investigations extending to other countries naturally depend on cooperation from the local authorities. Thus, it may generally be said that noncompliance with Fourth Amendment standards by the foreign police does not require exclusion in this situation either, as there is no reason why foreign officers need to be or could be expected to be deterred from their failure to know and follow the law of another country. There doubtless are a few special situations in which it may fairly be concluded that the exclusionary rule should apply because the circumstances indicate the American authorities are rather directly accountable for the excesses that have occurred.

Even if there has been direct U.S. involvement in the foreign search, the Fourth Amendment may be inapplicable for yet another reason. In *United States v. Verdugo–Urquidez*,[69] the Court apparently ruled that the phrase "the people" in the Fourth Amendment (and the First, Second, Ninth and Tenth Amendments) "refers to a class of persons who are part of a national community or who have otherwise developed sufficient connection with this community to be considered part of that community." The defendant in the instant case was deemed not to be such a person; he was a Mexican citizen and resident who, to be sure, just two days before the search had been turned over to U.S. authorities by Mexican police, but "this sort of presence—lawful but involuntary—is not the sort to indicate any substantial connection with our country."[70] But, because the three dissenters agreed that the Fourth Amendment applies whenever "a foreign national is held accountable for purported violations of the U.S. criminal laws," while two concurring Justices placed great emphasis upon the inapplicability of the Fourth Amendment's warrant clause to the search in the instant case,[71] the application of *Verdugo–Urquidez* to a foreign search of an alien's property made even without probable cause is less than clear.

(j) Challenge of Jurisdiction. In *Ker v. Illinois*,[72] the Court indicated that the mere fact the defendant had been arrested in violation of the Fourth Amendment did not affect the jurisdiction or power of the court to subject that individual to trial. The result is the same even when the illegality amounted to total avoidance of established extradition procedures in acquiring the presence of the defendant from another country[73] or another state.[74]

---

68. See Lustig v. United States, 338 U.S. 74, 69 S.Ct. 1372, 93 L.Ed. 1819 (1949), a leading case on the state-federal silver platter.

69. 494 U.S. 259, 110 S.Ct. 1056, 108 L.Ed.2d 222 (1990).

70. The Court added it was an open question whether even the illegal aliens seized in the United States in I.N.S. v. Lopez–Mendoza, 468 U.S. 1032, 104 S.Ct. 3479, 82 L.Ed.2d 778 (1984), were such persons, though their situation was different from the defendant's here because they "were in the United States voluntarily and presumably had accepted some societal obligations."

71. Kennedy, J., stressed this was not a case in which "the full protections of the Fourth Amendment would apply" because of the "absence of local judges or magistrates available to issue warrants"; Stevens, J., emphasized that "American magistrates have no power to authorize such searches."

72. 119 U.S. 436, 7 S.Ct. 225, 30 L.Ed. 421 (1886).

73. United States v. Alvarez–Machain, 504 U.S. 655, 112 S.Ct. 2188, 119 L.Ed.2d 441 (1992); Ker v. Illinois, 119 U.S. 436, 7 S.Ct. 225, 30 L.Ed. 421 (1886).

74. Frisbie v. Collins, 342 U.S. 519, 72 S.Ct. 509, 96 L.Ed. 541 (1952).

As the Court explained in *Frisbie v. Collins*[75]: "There is nothing in the Constitution that requires a court to permit a guilty person rightfully convicted to escape justice because he was brought to trial against his will." That now appears to be somewhat of an overstatement, for there is developing the view that if defendant's presence is acquired by government conduct of a most shocking and outrageous character, then due process would bar conviction.[76]

A somewhat different question is whether, when extradition processes are utilized to acquire the presence of the defendant, he is entitled to a determination in the asylum state of probable cause. In *Michigan v. Doran*,[77] where the state court had refused extradition because papers submitted by the demanding state were in conclusory form and did not set out facts showing probable cause, the Supreme Court reversed. Because the Extradition Clause[78] contemplates "a summary and mandatory executive proceeding," said the Court, "once the governor had granted extradition,[79] a court considering release on habeas corpus can do no more then decide (a) whether the extradition documents on their face are in order; (b) whether the petitioner has been charged with a crime in the demanding state; (c) whether the petitioner is the person named in the request for extradition; and (d) whether

the petitioner is a fugitive."[80] This means that "once the governor of the asylum state has acted on a requisition for extradition based on the demanding state's judicial determination that probable cause existed, no further judicial inquiry may be had on that issue in the asylum state." The Michigan court had thus taken a step not open to it under the Extradition Clause in finding the arrest warrant asserting a probable cause finding deficient merely because the factual basis of that finding was not revealed.

The concurring opinion in *Doran* correctly noted that the majority had ignored the "presence and significance of the Fourth Amendment in the extradition context," and went on to conclude that *Gerstein v. Pugh*[81] means "that, even in the extradition context, where the demanding State's 'charge' rests upon something less than an indictment, there must be a determination of probable cause by a detached and neutral magistrate, and that the asylum State need not grant extradition unless that determination has been made." Nothing said by the *Doran* majority refutes this, and thus it may be said that at a minimum a person facing extradition is protected by the Fourth Amendment from the "significant restraint on liberty" inevitably involved in forced interstate transportation, when the papers sent to the asylum state by the demand-

---

75. 342 U.S. 519, 72 S.Ct. 509, 96 L.Ed. 541 (1952).

76. It would be, in the language of United States v. Russell, 411 U.S. 423, 93 S.Ct. 1637, 36 L.Ed.2d 366 (1973), "conduct * * * so outrageous that due process principles would absolutely bar the government from invoking judicial processes to obtain a conviction."

77. 439 U.S. 282, 99 S.Ct. 530, 58 L.Ed.2d 521 (1978).

78. U.S. Const. Art. IV, § 2: "A Person charged in any State with Treason, Felony, or other Crime, who shall flee from Justice, and be found in another State, shall on Demand of the executive Authority of the State from which he fled, be delivered up, to be removed to the State having Jurisdiction of the Crime."

79. In Puerto Rico v. Branstad, 483 U.S. 219, 107 S.Ct. 2802, 97 L.Ed.2d 187 (1987), the Court stated and then examined the two propositions of Kentucky v. Dennison, 65 U.S. (24 How.) 66, 16 L.Ed. 717 (1861): "first, that the Extradition Clause creates a mandatory duty to deliver up fugitives upon proper demand; and second, that the federal courts have no authority under the Constitution to compel performance of this ministerial duty of delivery."

The Court reaffirmed the first, concluding that the Extradition Clause "afford[s] no discretion to the executive officers or courts of the asylum State." But the Court rejected the second because "there is no justification for distinguishing the duty to deliver fugitives from the many other species of constitutional duty enforceable in the federal courts."

80. Relying on this language, the Court held in California v. Superior Court, 482 U.S. 400, 107 S.Ct. 2433, 96 L.Ed.2d 332 (1987), that when Smolin was charged with kidnapping under a Louisiana statute covering taking one's own child from a person to whom custody had been granted, the California court erred in barring extradition upon the basis of an earlier California custody decree awarding Smolin sole custody of his children. Because the Louisiana information and related documents "set forth the facts that clearly satisfy each element of the crime of kidnapping as it is defined" by statute, the court in the asylum state may not even inquire into whether the charge would withstand a motion to dismiss in the demanding state.

81. 420 U.S. 103, 95 S.Ct. 854, 43 L.Ed.2d 54 (1975).

ing state include neither a copy of an indictment nor a copy of an arrest warrant that asserts a judicial finding of probable cause has occurred. The major weakness in the *Doran* majority opinion is the willingness to assume that such a self-serving declaration in the warrant is inevitably correct, which empirical studies have shown is not the case. Perhaps *Doran* does not foreclose all forms of attack upon such a warrant; the concurring opinion, noting the majority says the governor's grant of extradition "is prima facie evidence that the constitutional and statutory requirements have been met," construes this as "a suggestion that the governor's review and determination effects only a rebuttable presumption that there has been a judicial determination in the demanding State." But the Supreme Court's language in one post-*Doran* case, albeit on another point, is not particularly encouraging; the Court asserted that "claims related to what actually happened in the demanding State [and] the law of the demanding State * * * are issues that must be tried in the courts of that State, and not in those of the asylum State."[82] In any event, it should be noted that the *Doran* reasoning has no application with respect to international extradition, where the Fourth Amendment protects all persons from arbitrary arrest, including persons arrested pursuant to treaties.

(k) The "Constitutional Tort." 42 U.S.C.A. § 1983 provides: "Every person who,

under color of any statute, ordinance, regulation, custom, or usage, of any State or Territory, subjects, or causes to be subjected, any citizen of the United States or other person within the jurisdiction thereof to the deprivation of any rights, privileges, or immunities secured by the Constitution and laws, shall be liable to the party injured in an action at law, suit in equity, or other proper proceeding for redress." Pursuant to this statute, an action for damages may be brought in a federal court against municipal and state officers[83] by a plaintiff alleging a violation of his Fourth Amendment rights. It is a defense that a reasonable person in the officer's position would have a good faith belief that his conduct was lawful.[84]

In *Monell v. New York City Department of Social Services*,[85] the Court overturned its earlier ruling that governments were "wholly immune" from such suits, concluding that Congress had intended municipalities to be included "among the persons to whom § 1983 applies."[86] The municipality may not be held liable on a respondeat superior theory, that is, simply because it employed the offending officer. "Instead," the Court said in *Monell*, "it is when execution of a government's policy or custom, whether made by its lawmakers or by those whose edicts or acts may fairly be said to represent official policy,[87] inflicts the injury that the government as an entity is responsible under § 1983."[88] Thus, when the

82. New Mexico ex rel. Ortiz v. Reed, 524 U.S. 151, 118 S.Ct. 1860, 141 L.Ed.2d 131 (1998).

83. Virtually all § 1983 actions involving a Fourth Amendment claim are brought against police officers and not prosecutors, who generally enjoy absolute immunity from such suit. But see Kalina v. Fletcher, 522 U.S. 118, 118 S.Ct. 502, 139 L.Ed.2d 471 (1997) (prosecutor protected "when performing the traditional functions of an advocate" but not when, as here, performing "the function of a complaining witness" by swearing to the truth of allegations set out in a document intended to support issuance of an arrest warrant).

84. Harlow v. Fitzgerald, 457 U.S. 800, 102 S.Ct. 2727, 73 L.Ed.2d 396 (1982). This is so even when the action is brought against the officer for his conduct in applying for a warrant. The argument that absolute immunity should be the rule here, given the fact that a magistrate found the officer's request proper and issued the warrant, was rejected in Malley v. Briggs, 475 U.S. 335, 106 S.Ct. 1092, 89 L.Ed.2d 271 (1986), reasoning that the proper question in such circumstances "is whether a reasonably well-

trained officer * * * would have known that his affidavit failed to establish probable cause."

85. 436 U.S. 658, 98 S.Ct. 2018, 56 L.Ed.2d 611 (1978).

86. But, the Court later held, "a State is not a person within the meaning of § 1983." Will v. Michigan Dep't of State Police, 491 U.S. 58, 109 S.Ct. 2304, 105 L.Ed.2d 45 (1989).

87. Whether an official acts for the state or for the local government must be answered with respect to a particular issue or subject matter area (e.g., law enforcement) rather than as an "all or nothing" proposition, and such inquiry is dependent upon state law. McMillian v. Monroe County, 520 U.S. 781, 117 S.Ct. 1734, 138 L.Ed.2d 1 (1997) (sheriffs in Ala. represent the state rather than the county, though role of sheriffs and importance of county government may produce different result in many other states).

88. Where "action is directed by those who establish government policy, the municipality is equally responsible whether the action is to be taken only once or to be taken

question arises as to whether a Fourth Amendment violation by an officer may be said to amount to "execution of a government's policy or custom," it may be necessary for a court to resolve such questions as whether a directive in a police manual can be said to be "official policy," whether a poor hiring decision[89] or inadequate training[90] of police can constitute the requisite "official policy," and whether a "custom" may be established by a pattern of nondiscipline for certain Fourth Amendment violations. A municipality has no immunity from liability under § 1983 flowing from its constitutional violations and may not assert the good faith of its officers as a defense to such liability.[91]

Though § 1983 is not applicable to federal officials, the gap was filled, at least with respect to Fourth Amendment violations, in *Bivens v. Six Unknown Named Agents*,[92] where plaintiff's complaint seeking damages for an alleged illegal arrest and search by federal officers was held to state "a cause of action under the Fourth Amendment," so that he was "entitled to recover money damages for any injuries he has suffered as a result of the agents' violation of the Amendment." If the officer invokes his qualified immunity, the "relevant question . . . is the objective (albeit fact-specific) question whether a reasonable officer could have believed" the action taken "to be lawful, in light of clearly established law and the information [the officer] possessed."[93] Though *Bivens* was not read as also imposing liability upon the employer-government,[94] in 1974 Congress amended the Federal Tort Claims Act to permit recovery against the government, "with regard to acts or omissions of investigative or law enforcement officers of the United States Government," for any claim arising "out of assault, battery, false imprisonment, false arrest, abuse of process, or mali-

---

repeatedly," so dismissal of the county was improper where the prosecutor directed deputies on one occasion forcibly to enter a clinic to serve capiases on employees there. Pembaur v. Cincinnati, 475 U.S. 469, 106 S.Ct. 1292, 89 L.Ed.2d 452 (1986).

89. In Board of County Commissioners v. Brown, 520 U.S. 397, 117 S.Ct. 1382, 137 L.Ed.2d 626 (1997), where plaintiff alleged a county police officer used excessive force in arresting her and that the county was liable because the sheriff had hired that officer without adequately checking into his background, the Court ruled that the plaintiff could not prevail because she had failed to show that the sheriff's decision "reflected a conscious disregard for a high risk that [the arresting officer] would use excessive force in violation of respondent's federally protected right."

90. In City of Canton, Ohio v. Harris, 489 U.S. 378, 109 S.Ct. 1197, 103 L.Ed.2d 412 (1989), the Court held "that the inadequacy of police training may serve as the basis for § 1983 liability only where the failure to train amounts to deliberate indifference to the rights of persons with whom the police come into contact. This rule is most consistent with our admonition in *Monell* * * * that a municipality can be liable under § 1983 only where its policies are the 'moving force [behind] the constitutional violation.' "

91. Owen v. City of Independence, 445 U.S. 622, 100 S.Ct. 1398, 63 L.Ed.2d 673 (1980). But where the officer asserted no such defense and the jury verdict was in his favor, this finding removes any basis for liability against the city, and this is so even if department regulations might have authorized the kind of unconstitutional action alleged to have occurred. City of Los Angeles v. Heller, 475 U.S. 796, 106 S.Ct. 1571, 89 L.Ed.2d 806 (1986).

92. 403 U.S. 388, 91 S.Ct. 1999, 29 L.Ed.2d 619 (1971).

93. Anderson v. Creighton, 483 U.S. 635, 107 S.Ct. 3034, 97 L.Ed.2d 523 (1987). The Court went on to reject the Creightons' contentions that such qualified immunity was inappropriate as to any warrantless searches or to any search in violation of the Fourth Amendment (because, they claimed, it "is not possible * * * to say that one 'reasonably' acted unreasonably"), explaining: "Law enforcement officers whose judgments in making these difficult determinations are objectively legally reasonable should no more be held personally liable in damages than should officials making analogous determinations in other areas of law."

As noted in Saucier v. Katz, 533 U.S. 194, 121 S.Ct. 2151, 150 L.Ed.2d 272 (2001), *Anderson* thus "rejected the argument that there is no distinction between the reasonableness standard for warrantless searches and the qualified immunity inquiry." But in *Saucier*, the Court was confronted with the contention that the same could not be said of claims of excessive force in violation of the Fourth Amendment because the excessive force test in Graham v. Connor, 490 U.S. 386, 109 S.Ct. 1865, 104 L.Ed.2d 443 (1989), already afforded sufficient latitude for mistaken beliefs as to the amount of force necessary. The Court disagreed, explaining that the excessive force test takes into account reasonable mistakes of fact as to the circumstances, such as where "an officer reasonably, but mistakenly, believed that a suspect was likely to fight back," while the "qualified immunity inquiry * * * has a further dimension"; the "concern of the immunity inquiry is to acknowledge that reasonable mistakes can be made as to the legal constraints on particular police conduct" because it "is sometimes difficult for an officer to determine how the relevant legal doctrine * * * will be applied to the factual situation the officer confronts."

94. F.D.I.C. v. Meyer, 510 U.S. 471, 114 S.Ct. 996, 127 L.Ed.2d 308 (1994) (*Bivens* cause of action cannot be brought against federal agency).

cious prosecution."[95] In such an FTCA action, the government may assert the same good faith-reasonable belief defense that is available to individual officers. This FTCA amendment was not intended by Congress to provide an exclusive remedy, and thus a *Bivens* action against the offending officer is still permissible.[96]

(l) Criminal Prosecution; Disciplinary Proceedings. 18 U.S.C.A. § 242 provides: "Whoever, under color of any law, statute, ordinance, regulation, or custom, willfully subjects any inhabitant of any State, Territory, or District to the deprivation of any rights, privileges, or immunities secured or protected by the Constitution or laws of the United States, * * * shall be fined not more than $1,000 or imprisoned not more than one year, or both; and if death results shall be subject to imprisonment for any term of years or for life." One who "acts under 'color' of law" within the meaning of that statute "may be a federal officer or a state officer,"[97] and it makes no difference that state or federal law does not affirmatively authorize the deprivation that has occurred.[98] The "willfully" requirement has been construed by the Supreme Court to avoid vagueness objections, and as interpreted means "a purpose to deprive a person of a specific constitutional right."[99]

In light of the concern that has been expressed about the sufficiency of existing machinery for disciplining police who have violated the constitutional rights of citizens, it is appropriate to ask to what extent federal courts may remedy such deficiencies. In *Rizzo*

v. Goode,[100] where the district court had directed police administrators in Philadelphia to revise police manuals so as to spell out for police their powers and also to upgrade the disciplinary system, the Supreme Court reversed. The Court concluded that equitable relief against the administrators was not available where they "had played no affirmative part" in the constitutional violations objected to, and that "principles of federalism" did not permit the federal district court to inject itself "by injunctive decree into the internal disciplinary affairs of this state agency."[101]

(m) Expungement of Arrest Records. Though some legislatures have adopted statutes dealing with the use, dissemination and expungement of arrest records, the question here is whether there is a constitutional right to such expungement when the arrest violated the Fourth Amendment. Some cases have held that there is as part of the constitutional right to privacy, but the more recent cases have ruled otherwise on the strength of *Paul v. Davis*,[102] holding that this penumbral right has to do only with "matters relating to marriage, procreation, contraception, family relationships, and child rearing and education." Some authority is to be found to the effect that the expungement remedy can be grounded on the Fourth Amendment, but while dictum in some cases would suggest that an arrest without probable cause is per se a basis for expungement, the decisions do not support that proposition. Typically, expungement has occurred or been recognized as potential relief where there

---

95. 28 U.S.C.A. § 2680(h).

96. Carlson v. Green, 446 U.S. 14, 100 S.Ct. 1468, 64 L.Ed.2d 15 (1980).

In Correctional Services Corp. v. Malesko, 534 U.S. 61, 122 S.Ct. 515, 151 L.Ed.2d 456 (2001), the Court held that there was no implied private right of action, pursuant to *Bivens*, for damages against private entities that engaged in alleged constitutional deprivations while acting under color of federal law, as a contrary result would constitute "a marked extension of *Bivens* to contexts that would not advance *Bivens'* core purpose of deterring individual officers from engaging in unconstitutional wrongdoing." The four dissenters deemed the majority's position inconsistent with *Carlson* because the majority argued the instant case was distinguished from those encompassed within *Bivens* because the respondent enjoyed alternative remedies against the corporate agent.

97. Screws v. United States, 325 U.S. 91, 65 S.Ct. 1031, 89 L.Ed. 1495 (1945).

98. United States v. Classic, 313 U.S. 299, 61 S.Ct. 1031, 85 L.Ed. 1368 (1941).

99. Screws v. United States, 325 U.S. 91, 65 S.Ct. 1031, 89 L.Ed. 1495 (1945).

100. 423 U.S. 362, 96 S.Ct. 598, 46 L.Ed.2d 561 (1976).

101. Because the Court at another point asserted that such relief should not be given "except in the most extraordinary circumstances," it may be that upon a more extreme set of facts the kind of relief ordered by the district judge would be proper.

102. 424 U.S. 693, 96 S.Ct. 1155, 47 L.Ed.2d 405 (1976).

was a Fourth Amendment violation of an egregious nature. In any event, a balancing process is called for, which suggests that total expungement (as contrasted to limits on use) will be inappropriate when some legitimate future use could be made of the record.

(n) Injunction. The longstanding principle that equity will not grant relief to a petitioner who has an adequate remedy at law has proved to be no barrier to plaintiffs seeking to enjoin repeated or continuing Fourth Amendment violations, for in such circumstances neither the exclusionary rule nor an action for money damages will suffice. Another requirement is that there be a threat of imminent harm, which means injunctive relief will not be available absent a clear pattern or stated policy of continuing police action of the kind challenged. In *Rizzo v. Goode*,[103] the Court ruled that repeated unconstitutional conduct by only a few officers would justify injunctive relief only against them, not against the department at large or the officers in charge of the department. This is unfortunate, for the approach utilized by the district court in *Rizzo*, directing those in charge of the department to revise police manuals and complaint procedures, avoided the major practical limitations upon federal injunctive relief: the virtual impossibility of formulating an injunction against police violations that clearly expressed what was prohibited and what was permitted, and the impracticality of involving the court in the day-to-day operations of the police department.

(o) Self–Help. The common law right to resist an unlawful arrest[104] has given way in many jurisdictions to the modern view that the use of force is not justifiable to resist an arrest that the actor knows is being made by a peace officer, although the arrest is unlawful. It has sometimes been asserted that this view cannot be squared with the Fourth Amendment, but as a general proposition this is not so. The state in removing the right to resist has merely withdrawn a remedy that not infrequently causes far graver consequences for both the officer and the suspect than does the unlawful arrest itself, and has required the arrestee to submit peacefully to the inevitable and to pursue his available remedies through the orderly judicial process. But if an arrest was so flagrant an intrusion on a citizen's rights that his resistance would be virtually inevitable, it well may be that conviction for the resistance would violate due process.

The same reasoning applies to other forms of self-help undertaken in active resistance to a Fourth Amendment violation, such as forcible opposition to the execution of an invalid search warrant. But it does not follow that criminal punishment may be imposed for a mere failure to surrender rights under the Amendment. For example, one may not be convicted for assisting a federal offender to avoid apprehension where the charge was based upon a passive refusal to submit to an illegal search.

§ 3.2 Protected Areas and Interests

(a) The *Katz* Expectation of Privacy Test. For some years the Court was of the view that for there to be a Fourth Amendment search there must have been a physical intrusion into "a constitutionally protected area."[1] These areas were those enumerated in the Fourth Amendment itself: "persons," including the bodies[2] and attire[3] of individuals; "houses," including apartments,[4] hotel rooms,[5] garages,[6] business offices,[7] stores,[8] and ware-

---

103. 423 U.S. 362, 96 S.Ct. 598, 46 L.Ed.2d 561 (1976).

104. John Bad Elk v. United States, 177 U.S. 529, 20 S.Ct. 729, 44 L.Ed. 874 (1900).

§ 3.2

1. Silverman v. United States, 365 U.S. 505, 81 S.Ct. 679, 5 L.Ed.2d 734 (1961).

2. Schmerber v. California, 384 U.S. 757, 86 S.Ct. 1826, 16 L.Ed.2d 908 (1966).

3. Beck v. Ohio, 379 U.S. 89, 85 S.Ct. 223, 13 L.Ed.2d 142 (1964).

4. Clinton v. Virginia, 377 U.S. 158, 84 S.Ct. 1186, 12 L.Ed.2d 213 (1964).

5. Stoner v. California, 376 U.S. 483, 84 S.Ct. 889, 11 L.Ed.2d 856 (1964).

6. Taylor v. United States, 286 U.S. 1, 52 S.Ct. 466, 76 L.Ed. 951 (1932).

7. United States v. Lefkowitz, 285 U.S. 452, 52 S.Ct. 420, 76 L.Ed. 877 (1932).

8. Amos v. United States, 255 U.S. 313, 41 S.Ct. 266, 65 L.Ed. 654 (1921).

houses;[9] "papers," such as letters;[10] and "effects," such as automobiles.[11] Then came *Katz v. United States*,[12] where FBI agents overheard defendant's end of telephone conversations by attaching an electronic listening and recording device to the exterior of the public telephone booth from which he was calling. The Court rejected a characterization of the issue as whether a public telephone booth is a constitutionally protected area within which a person has a right of privacy. Though the Fourth Amendment "protects individual privacy against certain kinds of governmental intrusion, * * * its protections go further, and often have nothing to do with privacy at all," while other aspects of privacy are protected by other provisions of the Constitution or left to state law. As for determining whether a particular area is "constitutionally protected," it "deflects attention" from the problem: "For the Fourth Amendment protects people, not places. What a person knowingly exposes to the public, even in his own home or office, is not a subject of Fourth Amendment protection. * * * But what he seeks to preserve as private, even in an area accessible to the public, may be constitutionally protected." It was thus deemed "clear that the reach of that Amendment cannot turn upon the presence or absence of a physical intrusion into any given enclosure," and that instead the critical point, justifying the conclusion that this activity amounted to a search, was that "a person in a telephone booth * * * who occupies it, shuts the door behind him, and pays the toll that permits him to place a call is surely entitled to assume that the words he utters into the mouthpiece will not be broadcast to the world."

Justice Harlan, concurring, elaborated the point in language that has often been relied upon by lower courts in interpreting and applying *Katz:*

As the Court's opinion states, "the Fourth Amendment protects people, not places." The question, however, is what protection it affords to those people. Generally, as here, the answer to that question requires reference to a "place." My understanding of the rule that has emerged from prior decisions is that there is a twofold requirement, first that a person have exhibited an actual (subjective) expectation of privacy and, second, that the expectation be one that society is prepared to recognize as "reasonable." Thus, a man's home is, for most purposes, a place where he expects privacy, but objects, activities, or statements that he exposes to the "plain view" of outsiders are not "protected" because no intention to keep them to himself has been exhibited. On the other hand, conversations in the open would not be protected against being overheard, for the expectation of privacy under the circumstances would be unreasonable.

Katz is an extremely important case even outside of electronic eavesdropping settings because it marks a movement toward a redefinition of the scope of the Fourth Amendment. This is not to say that it produced clarity where before there had been uncertainty, as the Court substituted for a workable tool that often proved unjust a new test that was difficult to apply. But this was perhaps inevitable and in some respects desirable. The full potential of the *Katz* approach (which certainly has not in all respects been realized) can thus be seen only by consideration of various police investigative practices in light of *Katz,* as is done herein. But a few general observations are called for first.

Justice Harlan said that the defendant must "have exhibited an actual (subjective) expectation of privacy," while the majority in *Katz* likewise introduced a subjective element by saying that the government's conduct directed at Katz "violated the privacy upon which he

9. See v. City of Seattle, 387 U.S. 541, 87 S.Ct. 1737, 18 L.Ed.2d 943 (1967).

10. Ex parte Jackson, 96 U.S. (6 Otto) 727, 24 L.Ed. 877 (1878).

11. Preston v. United States, 376 U.S. 364, 84 S.Ct. 881, 11 L.Ed.2d 777 (1964).

12. 389 U.S. 347, 88 S.Ct. 507, 19 L.Ed.2d 576 (1967).

justifiably relied." But while it is often rather easy to say that the police made no search because the defendant surely did not actually expect privacy, as where a person openly engaged in criminal conduct in Times Square at high noon, a subjective expectation does not add to, nor can its absence detract from, an individual's claim to Fourth Amendment protection, for otherwise the government could diminish that protection by announcing in advance an intention to do so. Justice Harlan later came around to this position, counseling that analysis under *Katz* "must * * * transcend the search for subjective expectations," for "our expectations, and the risks we assume, are in large part reflections of laws that translate into rules the customs and values of the past and present."[13]

Consider next Justice Harlan's second requirement, that the expectation be one "that society is prepared to recognize as 'reasonable,'" which was apparently intended to give content to the word "justifiably" in the majority statement that the eavesdropping "violated the privacy upon which he justifiably relied while using the telephone booth." Though the Court has since, at least on occasion, referred to this as the "reasonable 'expectation of privacy' test,"[14] suggesting that a justified expectation is one a reasonable man would have, based upon the statistical probability of being discovered in the circumstances, this is not really what *Katz* is all about.[15] If two narcotics peddlers were to rely on the privacy of a desolate corner of Central Park in the middle of the night to carry out an illegal transaction, this would be a reasonable expectation of privacy; there would be virtually no risk of discovery. Yet if by extraordinary good luck a patrolman were to illuminate the desolate spot with his flashlight, the criminals would be unable to suppress the officer's testimony as a violation of their rights under the fourth amendment.[16] Thus, for an expectation to be considered justified it is not sufficient that it be merely reasonable; something in addition is required. As for what this something is, Justice Harlan later suggested it must "be answered by assessing the nature of a particular practice and the likely extent of its impact on the individual's sense of security balanced against the utility of the conduct as a technique of law enforcement."[17] That is, the ultimate question under *Katz* "is a value judgment," namely, "whether, if the particular form of surveillance practiced by the police is permitted to go unregulated by constitutional restraints, the amount of privacy and freedom remaining to citizens would be diminished to a compass inconsistent with the aims of a free and open society."[18]

The Fourth Amendment proscription on unreasonable "searches and seizures" extends not only to cases (such as *Katz*) deemed to involve both a search and a seizure, but also to those in which either a search or a seizure has occurred alone.[19] Illustrative of the former is *United States v. Place*,[20] holding that detention of a traveler's luggage for 90 minutes was an unreasonable deprivation of the defendant's "possessory interest in his luggage" and his "liberty interest in proceeding with his itinerary."[21]

---

13. United States v. White, 401 U.S. 745, 91 S.Ct. 1122, 28 L.Ed.2d 453 (1971) (dissent).

14. Terry v. Ohio, 392 U.S. 1, 88 S.Ct. 1868, 20 L.Ed.2d 889 (1968).

15. Probability is occasionally important in making a judgment as to whether the place of police surveillance was a "public vantage point," but a place that is on other grounds clearly such a point does not have to be frequently used. Thus in Florida v. Riley, 488 U.S. 445, 109 S.Ct. 693, 102 L.Ed.2d 835 (1989), all members of the Court agreed that whether aerial surveillance at 400 ft. was a search depended upon whether such use of helicopters was sufficiently "rare," but several Justices emphasized that as for any surveillance of defendant's residence from an adjacent public road, it would make no difference how often travelers used the road.

16. Note, 43 N.Y.U.L.Rev. 968, 983 (1968) . .

17. United States v. White, 401 U.S. 745, 91 S.Ct. 1122, 28 L.Ed.2d 453 (1971) (dissent).

18. Amsterdam, Perspectives on the Fourth Amendment, 58 Minn.L.Rev. 349, 403 (1974).

19. Soldal v. Cook County, 506 U.S. 56, 113 S.Ct. 538, 121 L.Ed.2d 450 (1992).

20. 462 U.S. 696, 103 S.Ct. 2637, 77 L.Ed.2d 110 (1983).

21. The Fourth Amendment only comes into play, however, where the "governmental termination of freedom of movement [is] *through means intentionally applied*," as it does not address "the accidental effects of otherwise lawful government conduct." Brower v. County of Inyo, 489 U.S. 593, 109 S.Ct. 1378, 103 L.Ed.2d 628 (1989).

(b) Plain View, Smell and Hearing and Touch; Aiding the Senses. In *Coolidge v. New Hampshire*[22] the Court discussed at some length the notion that "under certain circumstances the police may seize evidence in plain view without a warrant." The fact there has been a plain view in the *Coolidge* sense does not mean there has been no search; indeed, the Court's discussion was of cases of searches by warrant, during hot pursuit, incident to arrest, and the like in which objects other than those that justified the search were discovered. That is, the concern in *Coolidge* was with when a *seizure* of those objects would be permissible, as to which the requirements of (i) a valid prior intrusion; (ii) inadvertent discovery of the objects;[23] and (iii) it being immediately apparent the objects are evidence, were discussed. By comparison, the concern here is with plain view in the sense of there being no Fourth Amendment *search* at all, as where an officer without making any intrusion sees an object on the person of an individual, in premises, or in a vehicle, in which case the three *Coolidge* requirements are simply irrelevant.

It is equally important to understand that while the characterization of an observation as a nonsearch plain view situation settles the lawfulness of the observation itself, it does not inevitably follow that a warrantless seizure of the observed object would be lawful. As the Supreme Court has explained, the plain view doctrine "authorizes seizure of illegal or evidentiary items visible to a police officer" only if the officer's "access to the object" itself has a "Fourth Amendment justification."[24] If an officer standing on the public way is able to look through the window of a private residence and see contraband, he must except in extraordinary circumstances obtain a warrant before entering those premises to seize the contraband.[25] If he had been looking into a vehicle, the warrant issue must again be resolved, though in most instances a warrant is not required in such circumstances.[26] If the object had been seen on an individual, it is still necessary that the seizure of that object occur pursuant to a warrant, incident to arrest, or without warrant but under exigent circumstances.[27] But if the object is in plain view within an accessible container[28] then there is apparently no constitutional barrier to the seizure and opening of that container.[29] Because in at least some other circumstances a search warrant is needed to open even an accessible container,[30] this means that what can be properly characterized as a plain view situation in such circumstances—a matter that has caused the Court considerable difficulty[31]—is especially important.

---

22. 403 U.S. 443, 91 S.Ct. 2022, 29 L.Ed.2d 564 (1971).

23. This dictum in *Coolidge* was later rejected in Horton v. California, 496 U.S. 128, 110 S.Ct. 2301, 110 L.Ed.2d 112 (1990). See § 3.4(k).

24. Illinois v. Andreas, 463 U.S. 765, 103 S.Ct. 3319, 77 L.Ed.2d 1003 (1983). See also Horton v. California, 496 U.S. 128, 110 S.Ct. 2301, 110 L.Ed.2d 112 (1990) ("not only must the officer be lawfully located in a place from which the object can be plainly seen, but he or she must also have a lawful right of access to the object itself").

25. Compare Taylor v. United States, 286 U.S. 1, 52 S.Ct. 466, 76 L.Ed. 951 (1932) (though police, standing where they had a right to be, saw contraband in open view in a garage by looking through a small opening, their warrantless entry to seize the contraband was unconstitutional); with Steele v. United States, 267 U.S. 498, 45 S.Ct. 414, 69 L.Ed. 757 (1925) (police, standing where they had a right to be, looked into garage and saw contraband in open view through doorway; this furnished probable cause for obtaining warrant by which they lawfully entered and seized the contraband).

26. See § 3.7(b).

27. See, e.g., Cupp v. Murphy, 412 U.S. 291, 93 S.Ct. 2000, 36 L.Ed.2d 900 (1973), finding exigent circumstances to be present.

28. That is, one not within a protected place, or one within a place (e.g., an automobile) that may ordinarily be searched on probable cause without a warrant.

29. Cf. Illinois v. Andreas, 463 U.S. 765, 103 S.Ct. 3319, 77 L.Ed.2d 1003 (1983), relying upon the plain view doctrine in concluding that a container may be opened without a warrant if the contents were previously lawfully exposed to police view and were then determined to be illegal or evidentiary items and the surveillance of the container in the interim, while not perfect, did not give rise to "a substantial likelihood that the contents have been changed."

30. See, e.g., United States v. Chadwick, 433 U.S. 1, 97 S.Ct. 2476, 53 L.Ed.2d 538 (1977).

31. In Texas v. Brown, 460 U.S. 730, 103 S.Ct. 1535, 75 L.Ed.2d 502 (1983), the plurality took the position that when an officer saw in a car a tied balloon with a powdery substance within it, the warrantless seizure and search of that container was justified under the plain view doctrine. Two concurring Justices said that reasoning accorded "less significance to the Warrant Clause of the Fourth Amendment than is justified," while three other concurring Justices said that under the *Ross* rule (see § 3.7(c)) the container could be seized without a warrant but could

Just as what an officer sees where he is lawfully present is a nonsearch plain view, what he learns by reliance upon his other senses while so located is likewise no search. Thus, when surveilling officers in one motel room are able to hear with the naked ear conversations occurring in the adjoining room, this is not a search because there has been no intrusion upon a justified expectation of privacy. By like reasoning it has been held that it is no search for a lawfully positioned officer "with inquisitive nostrils" to detect incriminating odors. Even a so-called "plain touch" could amount to no search under some circumstances.[32] However, it must be remembered that "[p]hysically invasive inspection is simply more intrusive than purely visual inspection," a point the Supreme Court emphasized in holding that the squeezing of a bus passenger's luggage in the overhead rack, resulting in discovery of a brick-shaped object within, was an illegal search because a bus passenger justifiably expects other passengers or bus employees to "move" or "handle" his bag but does not expect that they "will, as a matter of course, feel the bag in an exploratory manner."[33]

Over seventy-five years ago, in *United States v. Lee*,[34] the Supreme Court held that use of a Coast Guard cutter searchlight at night to see aboard a schooner was no search. *Lee* was cited with approval in *Katz* for the proposition that "what a person knowingly exposes to the public * * * is not a subject of Fourth Amendment protection," and that reference has been stressed in post-*Katz* cases holding that use of

artificial illumination by a lawfully positioned officer does not constitute a search. *Lee* likened the use of the searchlight "to the use of a marine glass or a field glass," and thus it is not surprising that the cases after *Katz* agree that the use of binoculars does not, per se, constitute a search. But, while it is certainly sensible to conclude that ordinary use of such common devices for aiding the senses does not intrude upon any justified expectation of privacy (as compared to use of a magnetometer or X-ray machine or radiographic scanner to see inside an object, a gas chromatograph to identify organic compounds in an object, or use of electronic eavesdropping or wiretapping equipment[35] to overhear conversations, all of which are Fourth Amendment searches), there may be particular situations in which the nature of the equipment or the manner of its use dictates a contrary conclusion. Illustrative would be use of a very high-powered telescope to observe from a considerable distance what was occurring inside premises (including the contents of documents being read), where those premises were so situated that it was impossible to see inside from any closer vantage point. By like reasoning, the better view is that if a flashlight is used not simply to illuminate at night what would be readily visible in the daytime, but rather to see what is inside a secured building through a minute opening, this constitutes a search.

Many uses of photo surveillance, though they enhance the naked-eye perception, do not constitute a search. This is true where a tele-

---

not be searched without a warrant unless there was probable cause as to the vehicle generally or there was "virtual certainty" as to the contents of the balloon.

See also United States v. Jacobsen, 466 U.S. 109, 104 S.Ct. 1652, 80 L.Ed.2d 85 (1984), utilizing a sort of plain-view-once-removed doctrine in holding that where a private person had searched a package and then partially closed it, a federal agent at the invitation of such person could expose to view what had previously been seen by the private person without this constituting a search.

32. This would be the case if the police were to feel a specific object, say a gun, inside a soft-sided container that the defendant had dealt with in such a way so as to lack a justified expectation vis-a-vis tactile examination of it. In Minnesota v. Dickerson, 508 U.S. 366, 113 S.Ct. 2130, 124 L.Ed.2d 334 (1993), the Court used a plain view-plain touch analogy for a different purpose: to emphasize that the touching there (of defendant's pockets), which most

decidedly *was* a search, went beyond the purpose that authorized it (determining whether a detained suspect was armed) and thus was illegal.

33. Bond v. United States, 529 U.S. 334, 120 S.Ct. 1462, 146 L.Ed.2d 365 (2000). The language quoted above, plus the Court's emphasis upon the fact that "travelers are particularly concerned about their carry-on luggage," which they use "to transport personal items that, for whatever reason, they prefer to keep close at hand," suggests *Bond* is not unquestionably applicable to checked baggage of passengers on any form of public conveyance, or to the security-checked carry-on luggage of airline passengers.

34. 274 U.S. 559, 47 S.Ct. 746, 71 L.Ed. 1202 (1927).

35. Katz v. United States, 389 U.S. 347, 88 S.Ct. 507, 19 L.Ed.2d 576 (1967).

scopic lens of a type generally in use is employed and where pictures taken with standard equipment are then enlarged in the development process, but not necessarily where more sophisticated equipment is used. In *Dow Chemical Co. v. United States*,[36] the majority held it was no search to engage in aerial photography of the outdoor areas of a large industrial complex even though as a result it was possible to detect pipes as small as half an inch in diameter. But *Dow* was limited in several ways: (1) the Court grounded the decision in the character of the place being surveilled, and intimated the result would be different as to "an area immediately adjacent to a private home, where privacy expectations are most heightened"; (2) the Court also deemed significant what was revealed, noting that "no objects as small as ½-inch diameter such as a class ring, for example, are recognizable, nor are there any identifiable human faces or secret documents captured in such a fashion as to implicate more serious privacy concerns"; and (3) the Court indicated that, in any event, the result might be different if the surveillance involved "highly sophisticated surveillance not generally available to the public, such as satellite technology." (The four dissenters in *Dow* objected that "satellite photography hardly could have been more informative" than the $22,000 camera used here, which members of the public are not "likely to purchase.")

Still another type of equipment is an infrared thermal detection device (thermal imager), which without sending rays or beams into premises determines the amount of heat emanating therefrom by measuring differences in surface temperatures of targeted objects. Although most appellate courts that had considered the issue had ruled that use of the imager is not a search, the Supreme Court decided otherwise in the 5–4 decision in *Kyllo v. United States*.[37] The majority restated the *Katz* expectation-of-privacy test in less abstract terms as to one important genre of cases, stating "that obtaining by sense-enhancing technology any information regarding the inte-

rior of the home that could not otherwise have been obtained without physical 'intrusion into a constitutionally protected area' constitutes a search where (as here) the technology in question is not in general public use." Significantly, the majority (i) refused to accept the dissenters' "off-the-wall"—"through the wall" distinction, noting that in *Katz* the device only measured vibrations on the outside surface of the phone booth; (ii) recognized a need to take a stand *now* against the increasing intrusiveness of modern technology, instead of waiting as would the dissenters until the equipment became more sophisticated and the intrusions more severe; and (iii) was unwilling to impose added burdens on those unwilling to suffer this kind of privacy intrusion, as compared to the dissenters' conclusion that such people should "make sure the surrounding area is well insulated." The most telling criticism of the dissenters concerned the majority's "not in general public use" qualification, which they condemned as "somewhat perverse because it seems likely that the threat to privacy will grow, rather than recede, as the use of intrusive equipment becomes more readily available."

In recent years police have made extensive use of specially trained dogs to detect the presence of explosives or, more commonly, narcotics. Such reliance upon the trained canine nose to detect that which the officer could not discover by his own sense of smell does not constitute a search, the Court held in *United States v. Place*.[38] The Court emphasized that "the canine sniff is *sui generis*" because unlike any other investigative procedure, it "discloses only the presence or absence of * * * a contraband item" and "does not expose noncontraband items that otherwise would remain hidden from public view." The Court's analysis apparently means that the conduct there, exposure of luggage in a public place to a trained canine, is constitutionally permissible even if done without any suspicion or in a wholesale or at random fashion. Arguably the same is

36. 476 U.S. 227, 106 S.Ct. 1819, 90 L.Ed.2d 226 (1986).

37. 533 U.S. 27, 121 S.Ct. 2038, 150 L.Ed.2d 94 (2001).

38. 462 U.S. 696, 103 S.Ct. 2637, 77 L.Ed.2d 110 (1983).

not true as to use of these dogs against people, even if this can be accomplished without first detaining the person. Use of such dogs to ascertain what is inside a dwelling has been held to be a search.

(c) Residential Premises. If a person has abandoned the place where he formerly resided, this terminates any justified expectation of privacy that he had with respect to those premises. The question of abandonment for Fourth Amendment purposes does not turn on strict property concepts, and thus it is possible for there to be abandonment even if a tenant retained the lawful right to possession. The question in such circumstances is whether the defendant abandoned the premises in the sense of having no apparent intention to return and make further use of them. If the tenant has not left but the rental period has expired, this does not inevitably terminate the justified privacy expectation, for it may generally be said that the tenant would be justified in expecting the landlord to resort to the eviction procedures required by law rather than self-help. Because of the transitory nature of most motel and hotel rental arrangements, a guest would not be justified in assuming that the manager, at the termination of the rental period, would not immediately clear the room for occupation by another guest.

An unconsented police entry into a residential unit, be it a house, apartment, or hotel or motel room, constitutes a search under *Katz*. The mere presence of a hallway in the interior of a single family dwelling, without more, is not in itself an invitation to the public to enter, so that entry of even such a place is a search, but there is no invasion of privacy when a policeman without force enters the common hallway of a multiple-family house in the furtherance of an investigation. The result is otherwise when the apartment building hallway is accessible only by key or a buzzer system, for such safeguards give rise to a justi-

fied privacy expectation in the hallway. As for merely looking into the residence, it may generally be said that it is no search for an officer to obtain such a view from the public way, a neighbor's property, or that part of the curtilage constituting the normal means of access to and egress from the house, while on the other hand it *is* a search for an officer to stray from that path to engage in window-peeping. But it would not be consistent with *Katz* to say there is *never* a search when the observation is from outside the building and curtilage, for there certainly is a justified expectation of privacy in not being seen or heard from vantage points not ordinarily utilized by the public or other residents. By like reasoning, the better view is that even when the officer is lawfully present in a place used by the public (e.g., the hallway of an apartment building), it is a search to engage in conduct offensive in its intrusiveness in the sense that it uncovers that which the resident may fairly be said to have sufficiently protected from scrutiny. Certainly *Katz* should not be read as permitting unrestrained peeping through keyholes and transoms.[39]

Under the traditional pre-*Katz* view, the protections of the Fourth Amendment also extend to other structures within the curtilage, that is, all buildings in close proximity to a dwelling and used in connection therewith. On this basis, it has been held that police entry of such buildings as a garage or barn is a search, which is also the result under *Katz*. By contrast, the other aspect of the pre-*Katz* rule, which was that a garage or barn outside the curtilage was not protected by the Fourth Amendment has no current vitality; it is now necessary to inquire whether the nature of the structure and other circumstances are indicative of a justified privacy expectation. Thus, in *United States v. Dunn*[40] the Court assumed without deciding that a barn *outside* the curti-

---

39. In the pre-*Katz* decision of McDonald v. United States, 335 U.S. 451, 69 S.Ct. 191, 93 L.Ed. 153 (1948), where an officer climbed through a window into a rooming house and then stood on a chair so as to look through the transom into defendant's room, the government argued that the entry of the house only trespassed on the landlady's rights and that looking through the transom was no

search, so that the viewing of gambling paraphernalia was lawfully obtained. The Court did not "stop to examine that syllogism for flaws," but merely proceeded to "reject the result."

40. 480 U.S. 294, 107 S.Ct. 1134, 94 L.Ed.2d 326 (1987).

lage "enjoyed Fourth Amendment protection and could not be entered and its contents seized without a warrant," but yet held that merely peering into the barn's open front from an open fields vantage point was no search.

Lands adjoining the dwelling also fell within the pre-*Katz* curtilage concept and are clearly protected by *Katz* under some circumstances. In expectation of privacy terms, quite clearly it is not objectionable that an officer has come upon the land in the same way that any member of the public could be expected to do, as by taking the normal route of access along a walkway or driveway or onto a porch. The nature of the premises must be taken into account, for as a general matter lands adjacent to a multiple-occupancy dwelling are more likely to be viewed as public areas. Consideration must also be given to the degree of scrutiny involved; casual observation of what any visitor could have seen may be no search, while a detailed examination even in an area frequently used by the public may well constitute a search under *Katz*. Looking into protected adjoining lands from other locations is governed by considerations like those previously discussed. It is no search to observe on that land what a neighbor could readily see, but resort to extraordinary efforts to overcome the defendant's reasonable attempts to maintain the privacy of his curtilage is a search.

As for viewing by overflight, the Supreme Court took a permissive stance in *California v. Ciraolo*,[41] where police flew over defendant's fenced curtilage and saw marijuana plants growing there. Because the observations "took place within public navigable airspace" and were of "plants readily discernible to the naked eye as marijuana," the majority reasoned this was no search because "any member of the public flying in this airspace who glanced down could have seen everything that these officers observed." The four dissenters cogently reasoned that "the actual risk to privacy from commercial or pleasure aircraft is virtually nonexistent," as persons in them "normally obtain at most a fleeting, anonymous, and nondiscriminatory glimpse of the landscape and buildings over which they pass." (*Ciraolo,* involving surveillance from a fixed-wing aircraft at 1,000 feet, was relied upon in *Florida v. Riley*,[42] holding surveillance from a helicopter at 400 feet was likewise no search but denying "that an inspection of the curtilage of a house from an aircraft will always pass muster under the Fourth Amendment simply because the plane is within the navigable airspace specified by law."[43]) *Ciraolo* does not settle what the result would be if the police in the aircraft had used some sense-enhancing equipment; in the companion case of *Dow Chemical Co. v. United States*,[44] holding use of rather sophisticated camera equipment from an airplane was no search, the decision was grounded in the nature of the premises surveilled, a large industrial plant, and the Court cautioned that the result might be different if the surveillance had been of "an area immediately adjacent to a private home, where privacy expectations are most heightened."[45]

(d) "Open Fields." In *Hester v. United States*,[46] where agents retrieved evidence that had been thrown into a field, the Court held that "the special protection accorded by the Fourth Amendment * * * is not extended to the open fields." Courts applied *Hester* to virtually any land not within the curtilage, even

41. 476 U.S. 207, 106 S.Ct. 1809, 90 L.Ed.2d 210 (1986).

42. 488 U.S. 445, 109 S.Ct. 693, 102 L.Ed.2d 835 (1989).

43. Somewhat curiously, the *Riley* plurality noted there was no "intimation here that the helicopter interfered with respondent's normal use of the greenhouse or of other parts of the curtilage. As far as this record reveals, no intimate details connected with the use of the home or curtilage were observed, and there was no undue noise, no wind, dust, or threat of injury." All members of the *Riley* Court seemed to agree that flights at some particular altitude would be sufficiently "rare" to make a

householder's expectation of privacy reasonable, but there is not agreement on just what degree of rarity is required or on who has to prove what on the degree-of-rarity issue.

44. 476 U.S. 227, 106 S.Ct. 1819, 90 L.Ed.2d 226 (1986).

45. The Court also asserted "that surveillance of private property by using highly sophisticated surveillance equipment not generally available to the public, such as satellite technology, might be constitutionally proscribed absent a warrant."

46. 265 U.S. 57, 44 S.Ct. 445, 68 L.Ed. 898 (1924).

if fenced or posted with no trespassing signs, such as wooded areas, desert, vacant lots in urban areas, open beaches, reservoirs, and open waters. Although the vitality of this *Hester* "open fields" rule was uncertain after *Katz*, it was ultimately reaffirmed in *Oliver v. United States*.[47] One reason for this result given by the *Oliver* majority, that the "persons, houses, papers, and effects" language of the Fourth Amendment means its protections cannot be extended to open fields, constitutes a literal-minded interpretation totally inconsistent with the Court's prior decisions such as *Katz*. A second reason given in *Oliver*, "that an individual may not legitimately demand privacy for activities conducted out of doors in fields, except in the area immediately surrounding the home," makes sense only if there is some good reason to proceed upon the basis of such a generalization in lieu of assessing the facts of the particular case (e.g., in *Oliver*, that the police had bypassed a locked gate and a "No Trespassing" sign in order to get to the so-called "open fields"[48]). The *Oliver* majority concluded there was: an ad hoc approach would make it too "difficult for the policeman to discern the scope of his authority" in a particular instance. But the dissenters argued with some force that it would not be an unfair imposition upon the police to expect them to make precisely the same kinds of judgments that the rest of us must make to avoid violating the criminal trespass laws.[49]

But somewhat similar case-by-case assessments are sometimes necessary to ascertain where the curtilage ends and "open fields" begins. In *United States v. Dunn*,[50] the Court asserted "that curtilage questions should be resolved with particular reference to four fac-

tors: the proximity of the area claimed to be curtilage to the home, whether the area is included within an enclosure surrounding the home, the nature of the uses to which the area is put, and the steps taken by the resident to protect the area from observation by people passing by." Thus the Court in that case concluded that a barn and immediately adjoining lands were outside the curtilage, as they were (i) 60 yards from the house, (ii) outside a fence surrounding the house, (iii) "not being used for intimate activities of the home," and (iv) not protected from observation from nearby open fields.

(e) Business and Commercial Premises. Offices and stores and other business and commercial premises are also entitled to protection against unreasonable searches and seizures,[51] though the nature of these premises is such that much police investigative activity directed at them will not constitute a search. Law enforcement officials may enter commercial premises at the times they are open to the public and may explore those portions of the premises to which the public has ready access, including the examination of articles available for inspection by potential customers. On the other hand, it is a search for police to enter without consent premises to which the public at large does not have access, such as the work area of a factory or a private club open only to members. Surveillance from outside business premises is governed by the same considerations discussed earlier concerning looking into dwellings. As for surveillance of the outdoor areas of businesses, such as the space between buildings within a large, fenced-in industrial complex, the Supreme Court in *Dow*

---

47. 466 U.S. 170, 184, 104 S.Ct. 1735, 80 L.Ed.2d 214 (1984).

48. The Court apparently accepted the traditional, broad view of what comes within the "open fields" rule, stating it was clear "that the term 'open fields' may include any unoccupied or undeveloped area outside of the curtilage," including an area "neither 'open' nor a 'field' as those terms are used in common speech."

49. Marshall, J., joined by Brennan and Stevens, JJ., dissenting, thus concluded: "A clear, easily administrable rule emerges * * * : Private land marked in a fashion sufficient to render entry thereon a criminal trespass under the law of the state in which the land lies is

protected by the Fourth Amendment's proscription of unreasonable searches and seizures."

50. 480 U.S. 294, 107 S.Ct. 1134, 94 L.Ed.2d 326 (1987).

51. Mancusi v. DeForte, 392 U.S. 364, 88 S.Ct. 2120, 20 L.Ed.2d 1154 (1968). In United States v. Dunn, 480 U.S. 294, 107 S.Ct. 1134, 94 L.Ed.2d 326 (1987), the Court assumed without deciding that a barn outside the curtilage would be protected against physical entry; respondent argued "that he possessed an expectation of privacy, independent from his home's curtilage, in the barn and its contents, because the barn is an essential part of his business."

Chemical Co. v. United States[52] declared that such places "can perhaps be seen as falling somewhere between 'open fields' and curtilage, but lacking some of the critical characteristics of both." The Court intimated that with regard to physical entry of such lands the curtilage analogy would prevail, but then held that as to aerial surveillance the place was "more comparable to an open field," meaning such surveillance was no search. The four dissenters in *Dow* understandably complained about the majority's failure to "explain how its result squares with *Katz* and its progeny."

Police sometimes engage in clandestine surveillance of public rest rooms in an attempt to detect criminal activity—typically use of drugs or homosexual conduct—occurring therein. When this is done by looking through a hole or vent into a closed stall, it is clear that under *Katz* this amounts to a search. It has been held that such surveillance into a stall without doors is no search, on the theory that there is no justified expectation of given this design. But some cases recognize that even in such circumstances there is still a justified expectation of privacy against being observed from hidden vantage points. On the other hand, if police merely enter a rest room and see conduct occurring within a stall that is readily visible to anyone who so enters, this is not a search. By like reasoning, it has correctly been held that surveillance into fitting rooms in clothing stores to detect shoplifting is a search.

(f) Vehicles. There is no justified expectation of privacy in an abandoned vehicle. Abandonment in this context is not a question of whether someone had a proprietary or possessory interest in the automobile under common law property concepts, but rather whether the defendant was entitled to have a reasonable expectation that the automobile would be free from governmental intrusion. Thus, abandonment may occur not only by intending to relinquish any claim to the vehicle but by dealing with it in such a way that privacy could hardly be justifiably expected, as where a car is left behind in escaping from pursuit by the police or is left unclaimed for some time on another's property. When a car is parked by the side of the road, it is necessary to consider such factors as the condition of the vehicle, its location, and the length of time it has remained there.

Assuming lawful presence of the officer by the vehicle, generally it is no search for the officer to see or smell what is inside the car without physical intrusion into it, or for him to photograph or examine the exterior of the vehicle or perhaps even to do some "testing" of the exterior.[53] There will occasionally be instances, however, in which the scrutiny is so intense, resulting in discovery of what had been concealed by reasonable means, that under the *Katz* rationale the police conduct must be designated a search. As for examination of vehicle identification numbers, obviously no search is involved when the number can be seen through the window of the vehicle.[54] The cases holding that it is no search to intrude physically into the car in order to ascertain a hidden number are short on analysis and conflict with *Katz,* as the Supreme Court later concluded in *New York v. Class.*[55] More appealing is the contention that because these numbers are quasi-public information, a search of that part of the car displaying the number is but a minimal invasion of a person's privacy that may be undertaken without a warrant upon reasonable suspicion. But in *Class* the Court accepted a somewhat different proposition, namely, that inspection of the VIN "is within the scope of police authority pursuant to a traffic stop" prompted by an observed traffic violation, and that "concern for the officer's safety" justifies the officer's entry of

---

52. 476 U.S. 227, 106 S.Ct. 1819, 90 L.Ed.2d 226 (1986).

53. In Cardwell v. Lewis, 417 U.S. 583, 94 S.Ct. 2464, 41 L.Ed.2d 325 (1974), where the police conduct was the taking of paint scrapings from the exterior of the car and the matching of the tread of a tire with a cast of a tire impression left at the crime scene, the plurality said it failed "to comprehend what expectation of privacy was

infringed. Stated simply, the invasion of privacy, 'if it can be said to exist, is abstract and theoretical.'" The four dissenters deemed it unnecessary to reach that issue, as they concluded the car had earlier been illegally seized.

54. New York v. Class, 475 U.S. 106, 106 S.Ct. 960, 89 L.Ed.2d 81 (1986).

55. 475 U.S. 106, 106 S.Ct. 960, 89 L.Ed.2d 81 (1986).

the car to uncover the VIN on the door jamb or dashboard instead of having the driver reenter to do so.

(g) Personal Characteristics. In *United States v. Dionisio*,[56] the Court held that requiring the person to give voice exemplars is no search because "the physical characteristics of a person's voice, its tone and manner, as opposed to the content of a specific conversation, are constantly exposed to the public," so that "no person can have a reasonable expectation that others will not know the sound of his voice." By the same reasoning the Court ruled in the companion case of *United States v. Mara*[57] that it is no search to require a person to give handwriting exemplars. *Dionisio* likened the sound of a person's voice to his "facial characteristics," and thus it is clear that it is not a search simply to observe those characteristics or to photograph them. The Court has also referred to fingerprinting as nothing more than obtaining "physical characteristics * * * constantly exposed to the public."[58] At the other extreme, seizing evidence from within the body by taking a blood or urine sample quite clearly is a search.[59] Hard situations exist in between, such as the taking of a sample of hair. It may be said that hair is also a characteristic "constantly exposed to public view" and that consequently the taking of it is no search, but *Cupp v. Murphy*[60] (holding it was a search to scrape visible dried blood from defendant's finger and subject it to microscopic analysis) suggests that in such cases it may make a difference whether the hair is being kept merely to preserve a readily observable characteristic or to enable much closer scrutiny than "public view" allows.

(h) Abandoned Effects. The Supreme Court has upheld the examination of certain effects on the ground that they had been abandoned, such as glass containers thrown into a field[61] and objects put into a hotel room waste basket before checking out.[62] Abandonment in this context may be based upon an intent to relinquish all claim to the object, as in those cases, or by simply relinquishing control of the object to such an extent and in such circumstances that examination of it by others would not be unlikely.[63] Property is not considered abandoned when a person throws away incriminating articles due to the unlawful activities of police officers, as where the disposal was prompted by police efforts to make an illegal arrest or search. Mere denial of ownership is not proof of an intent to abandon, but at least in some circumstances courts are inclined to hold that the denial deprived the person disclaiming ownership of any justified expectation in the object.

Even inspection of one's garbage left for collection outside the curtilage of a home is no search, the Supreme Court held in *California v. Greenwood*.[64] In that case, police obtained evidence of the defendants' narcotics use by having the trash collector pick up the plastic garbage bags the defendants had left on the curb in front of their house, and then give the bags to the police without first mixing the contents with refuse from other houses. The Court reasoned this was no search because the defendants had no "subjective expectation of privacy in their garbage that society accepts as objectively reasonable," as "plastic garbage bags left on or at the side of a public street are readily accessible to animals, children, scavengers, snoops, and other members of the public. * * * Moreover, respondents placed their refuse at the curb for the express purpose of conveying it to a third party, the trash collector, who might himself have sorted through respondents' trash or permitted others, such

---

56. 410 U.S. 1, 93 S.Ct. 764, 35 L.Ed.2d 67 (1973).

57. 410 U.S. 19, 93 S.Ct. 774, 35 L.Ed.2d 99 (1973).

58. Cupp v. Murphy, 412 U.S. 291, 93 S.Ct. 2000, 36 L.Ed.2d 900 (1973).

59. Skinner v. Railway Labor Executives' Ass'n, 489 U.S. 602, 109 S.Ct. 1402, 103 L.Ed.2d 639 (1989).

60. 412 U.S. 291, 93 S.Ct. 2000, 36 L.Ed.2d 900 (1973).

61. Hester v. United States, 265 U.S. 57, 44 S.Ct. 445, 68 L.Ed. 898 (1924).

62. Abel v. United States, 362 U.S. 217, 80 S.Ct. 683, 4 L.Ed.2d 668 (1960).

63. Under this approach, a person "clearly has not abandoned that property" when, in response to a police inquiry, he tossed the grocery bag he was carrying onto the hood of his car and then attempted to protect it from inspection by the officer. Smith v. Ohio, 494 U.S. 541, 110 S.Ct. 1288, 108 L.Ed.2d 464 (1990).

64. 486 U.S. 35, 108 S.Ct. 1625, 100 L.Ed.2d 30 (1988).

as the police, to do so." This is, as the two dissenters pointed out,[65] an unduly narrow interpretation of the kind of police activity that is subject to Fourth Amendment limitations under the *Katz* test. Because *Greenwood* is limited to "trash left for collection in an area accessible to the public," it should not be construed as permitting police to enter the curtilage and seize garbage kept there. It is unclear what the result should be if the police have the garbage collector make his usual pickup from within the curtilage but then turn the refuse over to them unmixed with neighbors' garbage, for that part of the *Greenwood* reasoning about defendant "conveying * * * to a third party" is seemingly applicable even there.

(i) "Mere Evidence" in General and Private Papers in Particular. In *Gouled v. United States*[66] the Court held that a search warrant could not always be utilized "to secure evidence to be used against [a person] in a criminal or penal proceeding" because such action is permissible only "when a primary right to such search and seizure may be found in the interest which the public or the complainant may have in the property to be seized, or in the right to the possession of it." This "mere evidence" rule, whereby items were subject to lawful seizure only if they were the fruits or instrumentalities of crime, was later extended by the Court to warrantless searches as well,[67] but was finally abandoned by the Court in *Warden v. Hayden*.[68] The Court reasoned that

> nothing in the nature of property seized as evidence renders it more private than property seized, for example, as an instrumentality; quite the opposite may be true. Indeed, the distinction is wholly irrational, since, depending on the circumstances, the same "papers and effects" may be "mere evidence" in one case and "instrumentalities" in another. * * *

* * * The requirement that the Government assert in addition some property interest in material it seizes has long been a fiction, obscuring the reality that government has an interest in solving crime.

Hayden did not mark the end of uncertainty as to whether certain effects were immune from seizure, for the Court cautioned that "the items of clothing involved in this case are not 'testimonial' or 'communicative' in nature, and their introduction therefore did not compel respondent to become a witness against himself in violation of the Fifth Amendment." The Court finally addressed the Fifth Amendment issue squarely in *Andresen v. Maryland*,[69] involving seizure pursuant to warrant of specified documents relating to a fraudulent sale of land. Noting that the "historic function" of the privilege against self-incrimination has been to protect a "natural individual from compulsory incrimination through his own testimony or personal records," the Court concluded there had been no Fifth Amendment violation in this case because there was no compulsion, that is, the "petitioner was not asked to say or to do anything." In particular, the Court stressed that (i) the creation of the documents by petitioner had been voluntary; (ii) he was not required to play a part in handing them over to the police; and (iii) he was not required to authenticate them at trial. This situation, then, is quite different from that in which the means of acquiring the evidence is a subpoena, where "the Fifth Amendment may protect an individual * * * because the very act of production may constitute a compulsory authentication of incriminating information."

Though the Court in *Andresen* repeatedly stressed that the papers seized were "business records," it seems clear that the Court's Fifth Amendment analysis would compel the very same result were the documents much more

---

65. They emphasized that the defendants had only exposed to the public the exterior of opaque containers, that the "mere *possibility* that unwelcome meddlers *might* open and rummage through containers does not negate the expectation of privacy," and that the defendants placed their refuse at the curb only because a county ordinance commanded them to do so.

66. 255 U.S. 298, 41 S.Ct. 261, 65 L.Ed. 647 (1920).

67. United States v. Lefkowitz, 285 U.S. 452, 52 S.Ct. 420, 76 L.Ed. 877 (1932).

68. 387 U.S. 294, 87 S.Ct. 1642, 18 L.Ed.2d 782 (1967).

69. 427 U.S. 463, 96 S.Ct. 2737, 49 L.Ed.2d 627 (1976).

private in nature, such as a diary. This leaves the question that was neither raised nor resolved in *Andresen,* whether, because diaries and personal letters that record only their author's personal thoughts lie at the heart of our sense of privacy, such private papers are entitled to special Fourth Amendment protection. It has sometimes been argued that the Fourth Amendment should be read as barring seizure of such very private papers, or that, even if not constitutionally required, it is sound policy to bar seizure of such papers unless they have served or are serving a substantial purpose in furtherance of a criminal enterprise.

(j) Surveillance of Relationships and Movements. One way in which law enforcement agents obtain information concerning a person's associations and activities is by examination of the detailed records kept by those agencies with which that person has had occasion to do business. Such activity is unlikely to be characterized as a search after *United States v. Miller,*[70] involving subpoenas directed at two banks for all records concerning defendant and his company in their hands. Defendant's contention that the subpoenas were defective was brushed aside because the Court concluded "that there was no intrusion into any area of which respondent had a protected Fourth Amendment interest." In support, the Court reasoned that (1) because the records in question were "the business records of the banks," respondent "can assert neither ownership nor possession"; (2) there was no "legitimate expectation of privacy concerning the information kept in bank records," as "the documents obtained, including financial statements and deposit slips, contain only information voluntarily conveyed to the banks and exposed to their employees in the ordinary course of business"; and (3) a "depositor takes the risk, in revealing his affairs to another, that the information will be conveyed by that person to the government."

The *Miller* result and reasoning are highly questionable. Certainly the assertion that there is no protected Fourth Amendment interest when there is "neither ownership nor possession" is contrary to *Katz,* which teaches that such property concepts cannot "serve as a talismanic solution to every Fourth Amendment problem." As for the Court's expectation of privacy point, the fact of the matter is that the customer of a bank expects that the documents, such as checks, which he transmits to the bank in the course of his business operations will remain private, and rightly so given banks' legal obligation to maintain the secrecy of their depositors' transactions. Finally, the Court in *Miller* is in error in saying that its result is supported by the "false friend" cases of *United States v. White,*[71] *Hoffa v. United States,*[72] and *Lopez v. United States.*[73] The proposition (as it was put in *Hoffa*) that the Fourth Amendment will not come to the rescue of one who "voluntarily confides his wrongdoing" to another is not applicable here, as for all practical purposes, the disclosure of one's financial affairs to a bank is not entirely volitional, since it is impossible to participate in the economic life of contemporary society without a bank account. Moreover, in cases like *Hoffa* the police obtained nothing more than was known by the intermediary, which is not true in a *Miller* type of case because the authorities are able to piece together all of the banking records so as to obtain a virtual current biography of the individual, while the bank and its employees see the customer's checks briefly and individually and thus have no direct, significant contact with the underlying transactional information that would reveal conclusions about the customer's lifestyle.

Miller was relied upon in *Smith v. Maryland,*[74] holding that it is no search for the police to utilize a "pen register," a device that records all telephone numbers dialed from a particular phone. The Court concluded Smith could claim no legitimate expectation of privacy because when he used his phone he "voluntarily conveyed numerical information to the

---

70. 425 U.S. 435, 96 S.Ct. 1619, 48 L.Ed.2d 71 (1976).

71. 401 U.S. 745, 91 S.Ct. 1122, 28 L.Ed.2d 453 (1971).

72. 385 U.S. 293, 87 S.Ct. 408, 17 L.Ed.2d 374 (1966).

73. 373 U.S. 427, 83 S.Ct. 1381, 10 L.Ed.2d 462 (1963).

74. 442 U.S. 735, 99 S.Ct. 2577, 61 L.Ed.2d 220 (1979).

telephone company and 'exposed' that information to its equipment in the ordinary course of business." and thereby "assumed the risk that the company would reveal to police the numbers he dialed." This reasoning is just as unsound as that in *Miller*. Even if it may be said that subscribers know phone companies monitor calls for internal reasons, it hardly follows that they expect this information to be made available to the general public or the government. By like reasoning, a mail cover (a form of surveillance in which law enforcement authorities have postal authorities record all external markings, including return addresses, on all mail to a particular addressee) should be considered a search, but the contrary result has been reached by resort to the all-or-nothing approach to privacy reflected in *Miller* and *Smith*. *Smith* may also support the conclusion that use of Carnivore/DCS 1000 electronic surveillance software in "pen mode" to obtain addressing information in e-mails is no search, though some argue otherwise on the grounds that it is unlike the traditional pen register in the amount and revealing nature of the information collected. But interception of the contents of communications sent by regular mail or e-mail *is* a search.

Another increasingly common surveillance technique involves the use of an electronic tracking device, as where a beacon or "beeper" is attached to a car, airplane or container and the movements of that object are then tracked by picking up the signals emitted periodically. Some courts have focused upon the act whereby the beeper was attached to the underbody of a vehicle parked in a public place or was attached to a vehicle or inserted into a container before delivery of same to the suspect, with varying results. But the Supreme Court in *United States v. Karo*[75] concluded that the mere installation of a beeper or transfer to another of a beeper-laden object is no "search," because that act alone "infringed no privacy interest" in that it "conveyed no information at all," and is no "seizure" because "it cannot be said that anyone's possessory interest was interfered with in a meaningful way."

It is thus necessary to consider the more significant event of the beeper's subsequent monitoring.

In *United States v. Knotts*,[76] the Supreme Court was confronted with a situation in which police first arranged with the seller of chloroform to place a beeper inside a chloroform container thereafter sold to a suspect and then traced the chloroform by beeper monitoring alone to a secluded cabin, resulting in the issuance and execution of a warrant to search that cabin for an illegal drug laboratory. In response to a challenge of the monitoring of the beeper, the Court held that no Fourth Amendment search had occurred. The Court reasoned that the surveillance objected to "amounted principally to the following of an automobile on public streets and highways," which if accomplished merely by visual surveillance would be no search because one "travelling in an automobile on public thoroughfares has no reasonable expectation of privacy in his movements from one place to another," and that "scientific enhancement of this sort raises no constitutional issues which visual surveillance would not also raise."

But the practice of beeper monitoring cannot be dismissed on the notion that it merely permits the police to learn what they could otherwise have discovered by direct observation, as the value of the device lies in its ability to convey information not otherwise available to the government. Nor is it correct to say, as the Court assumed in *Knotts*, that use of a beeper is essentially the same as use of binoculars. It involves something more than magnification of the observer's senses, for it transforms the vehicle into a messenger in the service of those watching it and thus conveys information as useful as any obtained from a wiretap. Precisely because the unrestrained utilization of electronic tracking devices to monitor the movements of anyone who travels from one place to another would be intolerable, the practice should be characterized as a search under the *Katz* formula and subjected

75. 468 U.S. 705, 104 S.Ct. 3296, 82 L.Ed.2d 530 (1984).

76. 460 U.S. 276, 103 S.Ct. 1081, 75 L.Ed.2d 55 (1983).

to at least some Fourth Amendment restraints.

In *Karo* the Court answered in the affirmative the question reserved in *Knotts,* "whether monitoring of a beeper falls within the ambit of the Fourth Amendment when it reveals information that could not have been obtained through visual surveillance." Noting first that unquestionably it would be an unreasonable search to surreptitiously enter a residence without a warrant to verify that the container was there, the Court reasoned that "the result is the same where, without a warrant, the Government surreptitiously employs an electronic device to obtain information that it could not have obtained by observation from outside the curtilage of the home. * * * Even if visual surveillance has revealed that the article to which the beeper is attached has entered the house, the later monitoring not only verifies the officers' observations but also establishes that the article remains on the premises." The Court next concluded that absent "truly exigent circumstances" such use of the beeper was governed by "the general rule that a search of a house should be conducted pursuant to a warrant."[77] Such monitoring was characterized by the Court as "less intrusive than a full-scale search," but the Court did not have occasion to decide whether as a consequence such a warrant could issue upon reasonable suspicion rather than probable cause.

§ 3.3 Probable Cause

(a) General Considerations. Because the warrant clause of the Fourth Amendment provides that "no Warrants shall issue, but upon

probable cause," it is apparent that a valid arrest warrant[1] or a valid search warrant[2] may issue only upon a showing of probable cause to the issuing authority. In the many instances in which police arrest and search without first obtaining a warrant,[3] their conduct is governed by the other half of the Fourth Amendment, which declares the right of the people to be secure "against unreasonable searches and seizures." But it is clear that such an arrest[4] or search[5] is unreasonable if not based upon probable cause; as the Supreme Court explained in *Wong Sun v. United States,*[6] were the requirements less stringent than when a warrant is obtained, then "a principal incentive now existing for the procurement of * * * warrants would be destroyed."

It is generally assumed that the same quantum of evidence is required whether one is concerned with probable cause to arrest or probable cause to search. But each requires a showing of probabilities as to somewhat different facts and circumstances, and thus one can exist without the other. In search cases, two conclusions must be supported by substantial evidence: that the items sought are in fact seizable by virtue of being connected with criminal activity, and that the items will be found in the place to be searched. It is *not* also necessary that a particular person be implicated in the crime under investigation. By comparison, in arrest cases there must be probable cause that a crime has been committed and that the person to be arrested committed it, which of course can exist without any showing that evidence of the crime will be found at premises under that person's control.

The Supreme Court has long expressed a strong preference for the use of arrest war-

---

77. In response to the government's claim that a warrant should not be required because of the difficulty in satisfying the particularity requirement of the Fourth Amendment, in that it is usually not known in advance to what place the container with the beeper in it will be taken, the Court concluded that it would suffice if the warrant were "to describe the object into which the beeper is to be placed, the circumstances that led agents to wish to install the beeper, and the length of time for which beeper surveillance is requested."

§ 3.3

1. Henry v. United States, 361 U.S. 98, 80 S.Ct. 168, 4 L.Ed.2d 134 (1959).

2. United States v. Harris, 403 U.S. 573, 91 S.Ct. 2075, 29 L.Ed.2d 723 (1971).

3. See §§ 3.5, 3.6, 3.7.

4. Henry v. United States, 361 U.S. 98, 80 S.Ct. 168, 4 L.Ed.2d 134 (1959).

5. Chambers v. Maroney, 399 U.S. 42, 90 S.Ct. 1975, 26 L.Ed.2d 419 (1970).

6. 371 U.S. 471, 83 S.Ct. 407, 9 L.Ed.2d 441 (1963).

rants and search warrants. Resort to the warrant process, the Court has declared, is preferred because it "interposes an orderly procedure"[7] involving "judicial impartiality"[8] whereby "a neutral and detached magistrate"[9] can make "informed and deliberate determinations"[10] on the issue of probable cause. To leave such decisions to the police would allow "hurried actions"[11] by those "engaged in the often competitive enterprise of ferreting out crime."[12] This preference has resulted in a subtle difference between the probable cause required when there is no warrant and that required when there is. As the Court put it in *United States v. Ventresca*,[13] "in a doubtful or marginal case a search under a warrant may be sustainable where without one it would fail." This "deference to the decision of the magistrate to issue a warrant" means that a reviewing court is not to conduct "a de novo probable cause determination" but instead is merely to decide "whether the evidence viewed as a whole provided a 'substantial basis' for the magistrate's finding of probable cause."[14]

When the police make an arrest or search without a warrant, they initially make the probable cause decision themselves. The "on-the-scene assessment of probable cause provides a legal justification for arresting a person suspected of crime, and for a brief period of detention to take the administrative steps incident to arrest," but an ex parte "judicial determination of probable cause [is] a prerequisite to extended restraint on liberty following arrest."[15] This means that judicial review of probable cause for the arrest need occur only if the arrestee fails to obtain his prompt release unaccompanied "by burdensome conditions

that effect a significant restraint on liberty."[16] Otherwise, a subsequent judicial determination of whether there was probable cause for the warrantless police action will ordinarily occur only if initiated by the defendant upon a motion to suppress evidence claimed to be a fruit of an illegal arrest or search.

When the police arrest or search with a warrant, the probable cause determination is made by a magistrate in the first instance. Under the traditional approach, his decision was not final; it was still open to the defendant upon a motion to suppress to argue that evidence obtained by execution of the warrant should be suppressed because the warrant was not in fact issued upon probable cause. However, in *United States v. Leon*[17] the Supreme Court adopted a "good faith" exception to the exclusionary rule in with-warrant cases. This means that upon the motion to suppress evidence obtained pursuant to a warrant, the evidence will be admissible (without regard to whether there was in fact probable cause) if the officer could have reasonably believed that warrant was valid.[18]

(b) Nature of Probable Cause. In *Brinegar v. United States*,[19] the Court characterized the probable cause requirement as "the best compromise that has been found for accommodating" the often opposing interests of privacy and effective law enforcement. This raises the question of whether this "compromise" must always be struck in precisely the same way, or whether instead probable cause may require a greater or a lesser quantum of evidence, depending upon the facts and circumstances of the individual case.

It is now clear that certain unique investigative techniques are governed by a special, less

---

7. United States v. Jeffers, 342 U.S. 48, 72 S.Ct. 93, 96 L.Ed. 59 (1951).

8. Ibid.

9. Johnson v. United States, 333 U.S. 10, 68 S.Ct. 367, 92 L.Ed. 436 (1948).

10. Aguilar v. Texas, 378 U.S. 108, 84 S.Ct. 1509, 12 L.Ed.2d 723 (1964).

11. Ibid.

12. Johnson v. United States, 333 U.S. 10, 68 S.Ct. 367, 92 L.Ed. 436 (1948).

13. 380 U.S. 102, 85 S.Ct. 741, 13 L.Ed.2d 684 (1965).

14. Massachusetts v. Upton, 466 U.S. 727, 104 S.Ct. 2085, 80 L.Ed.2d 721 (1984), applying the holding in Illinois v. Gates, 462 U.S. 213, 103 S.Ct. 2317, 76 L.Ed.2d 527 (1983).

15. Gerstein v. Pugh, 420 U.S. 103, 95 S.Ct. 854, 43 L.Ed.2d 54 (1975).

16. Ibid. For more on this, see § 3.5(a).

17. 468 U.S. 897, 104 S.Ct. 3405, 82 L.Ed.2d 677 (1984).

18. See § 3.1(c).

19. 338 U.S. 160, 69 S.Ct. 1302, 93 L.Ed. 1879 (1949).

demanding probable cause test. In *Camara v. Municipal Court*,[20] for example, the Court engaged in a "balancing" of "the need to search against the invasion which the search entails" in approving such a probable cause test for housing inspection warrants; thus " 'probable cause' to issue a warrant to inspect must exist if reasonable legislative or administrative standards for conducting an area inspection are satisfied with respect to a particular building." This *Camara* balancing approach was thereafter employed in upholding other kinds of so-called administrative or regulatory searches,[21] and was later used by the Court in *Terry v. Ohio*[22] to support the conclusion that a brief stopping for investigation and a frisk incident thereto are permissible upon grounds falling short of probable cause to make a full-fledged arrest and a full search of the person incident thereto. In both instances, the Court deemed it most significant that the practices at issue were clearly distinguishable from the typical arrest or search in that they involved a significantly lesser intrusion into freedom and privacy.

Some have argued for a more extended use of this balancing process, whereby in each case the probable cause for the investigative technique used would be determined by weighing the degree of intrusion and the law enforcement need in that particular case. But the Supreme Court has declined the invitation to adopt a proposed "multifactor balancing test" along these lines. As the Court put it in *Dunaway v. New York*,[23]

the protections intended by the Framers could all too easily disappear in the consideration and balancing of the multifarious circumstances presented by different cases, especially when that balancing may be done in the first instance by police officers engaged in the "often competitive enterprise of ferreting out crime." * * * A single, familiar standard is essential to guide police officers, who have only limited time and expertise to reflect on and balance the social and individual interests involved in the specific circumstances they confront.

Notwithstanding this language, it might still be argued that there are a few search practices (such as eavesdropping and wiretapping,[24] search of a private home during the nighttime,[25] or intrusions into the human body[26]) that, because of their unusual degree of intrusiveness, require more than the usual quantum of probable cause.[27]

Probable cause may not be established simply by showing that the officer who made the challenged arrest or search subjectively believed he had grounds for his action. As emphasized in *Beck v. Ohio*[28]: "If subjective good faith alone were the test, the protections of the Fourth Amendment would evaporate, and the people would be 'secure in their persons, houses, papers, and effects,' only in the discretion of the police." The probable cause test, then, is an objective one; for there to be probable cause, the facts must be such as would warrant a belief by a reasonable man. (If the

20.　387 U.S. 523, 87 S.Ct. 1727, 18 L.Ed.2d 930 (1967).

21.　See § 3.9.

22.　392 U.S. 1, 88 S.Ct. 1868, 20 L.Ed.2d 889 (1968), discussed in § 3.8.

23.　442 U.S. 200, 99 S.Ct. 2248, 60 L.Ed.2d 824 (1979), discussed in § 3.8(g).

24.　See Berger v. New York, 388 U.S. 41, 87 S.Ct. 1873, 18 L.Ed.2d 1040 (1967), where Stewart, J., concurring, observed that "electronic eavesdropping for a 60–day period * * * involves a broad invasion of a constitutionally protected area. Only a most precise and rigorous standard of probable cause should justify an intrusion of this sort."

25.　See Gooding v. United States, 416 U.S. 430, 94 S.Ct. 1780, 40 L.Ed.2d 250 (1974), where three members of the Court argued that such searches "involve a greater intrusion than ordinary searches and therefore require a greater justification."

26.　See Schmerber v. California, 384 U.S. 757, 86 S.Ct. 1826, 16 L.Ed.2d 908 (1966), stressing that "intrusions into the human body" are particularly offensive and thus may be undertaken only upon "a clear indication that in fact such evidence will be found," seemingly a higher test than that usually required to show probable cause. See also Winston v. Lee, 470 U.S. 753, 105 S.Ct. 1611, 84 L.Ed.2d 662 (1985), discussed in § 3.4 at note 9.

27.　However, the Supreme Court has rejected the notion that a higher probable cause standard should apply "when First Amendment interests would be endangered by the search," as when search warrants for allegedly obscene materials are involved. New York v. P.J. Video, Inc., 475 U.S. 868, 106 S.Ct. 1610, 89 L.Ed.2d 871 (1986). The Court reasoned that "the longstanding special protections" of other kinds that apply in such cases, see, e.g., § 3.4(a), (f), were sufficient.

28.　379 U.S. 89, 85 S.Ct. 223, 13 L.Ed.2d 142 (1964).

objective probable cause test is met, it is not also necessary to establish that the particular officer making the arrest or search subjectively believed probable cause was present.) Notwithstanding this objective test, the Supreme Court has made it clear that the expertise[29] and experience[30] of the officer are to be taken into account, which is as it should be. This usually means that a trained and experienced officer will have probable cause in circumstances when the layman would not, as when an officer is able to identify an illegal substance by smell, feel, or sight because of his training and experience. But sometimes an experienced officer will be held *not* to have had probable cause if a man with his special skills, though perhaps not a layman, should have recognized that no criminal conduct was involved.

Though the Supreme Court once held that a "search warrant may issue only upon evidence which would be competent in the trial of an offense before a jury,"[31] this is no longer the law. In *Brinegar v. United States*,[32] the Court noted:

> For a variety of reasons relating not only to probative value and trustworthiness, but also to possible prejudicial effect upon a trial jury and the absence of opportunity for cross-examination, the generally accepted rules of evidence throw many exclusionary protections about one who is charged with standing trial for crime. Much evidence of real and substantial probative value goes out on considerations irrelevant to its probative weight but relevant to possible misunderstanding or misuse by the jury. * * *

In dealing with probable cause, however, as the very name implies, we deal with probabilities. These are not technical; they are the factual and practical considerations of everyday life on which reasonable and prudent men, not legal technicians, act. The standard of proof is accordingly correlative to what must be proved.

Information that would be inadmissible at trial on hearsay grounds may be used to show probable cause,[33] as may a person's criminal record.[34] But in *Spinelli v. United States*[35] the Court characterized a general assertion of criminal reputation (i.e., that defendant was "known" as a gambler) as "a bald and unilluminating assertion of suspicion that is entitled to no weight" in determining probable cause. That conclusion is solidly grounded in the fundamental Fourth Amendment principle that probable cause must be shown on the basis of facts rather than mere conclusions,[36] which means that *facts* that would contribute to a bad reputation may be taken into account.[37]

The Court in *Brinegar* declared that "in dealing with probable cause, * * * as the very name implies, we deal with probabilities," but did not identify the degree of probability needed other than to say that "more than bare suspicion" and "less than evidence which would justify * * * conviction" was required. Some of the Supreme Court's decisions may be read as adopting a more-probable-than-not test, so that, for example, there would not be grounds to arrest unless the information at hand provided a basis for singling out but one person.[38] But the lower court cases generally

---

29. United States v. Ortiz, 422 U.S. 891, 95 S.Ct. 2585, 45 L.Ed.2d 623 (1975) ("officers are entitled to draw reasonable inferences from these facts in light of their knowledge of the area and their prior experience with aliens and smugglers").

30. Johnson v. United States, 333 U.S. 10, 68 S.Ct. 367, 92 L.Ed. 436 (1948) (probable cause may be based upon a distinctive odor where the officer is "qualified to know the odor").

31. Grau v. United States, 287 U.S. 124, 53 S.Ct. 38, 77 L.Ed. 212 (1932).

32. 338 U.S. 160, 69 S.Ct. 1302, 93 L.Ed. 1879 (1949).

33. Draper v. United States, 358 U.S. 307, 79 S.Ct. 329, 3 L.Ed.2d 327 (1959).

34. Brinegar v. United States, 338 U.S. 160, 69 S.Ct. 1302, 93 L.Ed. 1879 (1949).

35. 393 U.S. 410, 89 S.Ct. 584, 21 L.Ed.2d 637 (1969).

36. Aguilar v. Texas, 378 U.S. 108, 84 S.Ct. 1509, 12 L.Ed.2d 723 (1964).

37. E.g., Jones v. United States, 362 U.S. 257, 80 S.Ct. 725, 4 L.Ed.2d 697 (1960) (relevant that suspects "are familiar to the undersigned and other members of the Narcotics Squad" and "had admitted to the use of narcotic drugs and display needle marks as evidence of same").

38. Wong Sun v. United States, 371 U.S. 471, 83 S.Ct. 407, 9 L.Ed.2d 441 (1963) (where informant said Toy, operator of laundry on certain street, had heroin, but several laundries on that street operated by persons named Toy, probable cause lacking because there was no showing the officers "had some information of some kind which had narrowed the scope of their search to this

do not go this far, and instead merely require that the facts permit a fairly narrow focus, so that descriptions fitting large numbers of people or a large segment of the community will not suffice. This latter position has been defended on the ground that it strikes a fair balance between the interests of privacy and effective law enforcement, in that arrests for investigative purposes sometimes must be permitted upon somewhat general descriptions provided by crime victims and witnesses. If that is so, then it may be necessary to distinguish those cases in which the uncertainty goes not to who the perpetrator of the crime is but rather to whether any crime has occurred, as when the police observe a person engaging in suspicious activity. As to this latter situation, it is commonly said that an arrest and search based on events as consistent with innocent as with criminal activity are unlawful, so that if the observed pattern of events occurs just as frequently or even more than frequently in innocent transactions, then it is too equivocal to constitute probable cause. Utilizing the more-probable-than-not test here but not in the first situation is defensible on two grounds: (1) permitting arrests for equivocal conduct would result in more frequent interference with innocent persons than would permitting arrests upon a just-received somewhat general description from a crime victim or witness, as the latter is anchored in a time-space sense to known criminal activity; and (2) the law enforcement need is greater in the victim/witness description situation, as these cases often involve much more serious criminal activity as to which experience has shown that the likelihood of apprehending the offender is slight unless he is promptly arrested in the vicinity of the crime.

Probable cause is not defeated by an after-the-fact showing that the relevant provision in the substantive criminal law is unconstitutional. In reaching that conclusion in *Michigan v. DeFillippo*,[39] the Court reasoned:

> Police are charged to enforce laws until and unless they are declared unconstitutional. The enactment of a law forecloses speculation by enforcement officers concerning its constitutionality—with the possible exception of a law so grossly and flagrantly unconstitutional that any person of reasonable prudence would be bound to see its flaws. Society would be ill served if its police officers took it upon themselves to determine which laws are and which are not constitutionally entitled to enforcement.[40]

(c) Information From an Informant. The term "informant" is used here to describe an individual who learns of criminal conduct by being a part of the criminal milieu; it does not refer to the average citizen who by happenstance finds himself in the position of a victim of or a witness to a crime. The Supreme Court and other courts have with considerable frequency confronted the question of when probable cause may be said to exist exclusively or primarily upon the basis of information from such a person.

At issue in *Aguilar v. Texas*[41] was a search warrant affidavit that stated: "Affiants have received reliable information from a credible person and do believe that heroin, marijuana, barbiturates, and other narcotics and narcotic paraphernalia are being kept at the above described premises for the purpose of sale and use contrary to the provisions of the law." The

particular Toy"); Mallory v. United States, 354 U.S. 449, 77 S.Ct. 1356, 1 L.Ed.2d 1479 (1957) (arrest of three blacks with access to basement where rape by masked black man occurred was illegal; police may not "arrest, as it were, at large * * in order to determine whom they should charge before a committing magistrate on 'probable cause'"); Johnson v. United States, 333 U.S. 10, 68 S.Ct. 367, 92 L.Ed. 436 (1948) (where officers smelled burning opium outside hotel room, entry could not be justified as a step toward a lawful arrest because "the arresting officer did not have probable cause to arrest petitioner until he had entered her room and found her to be the sole occupant").

39.   443 U.S. 31, 99 S.Ct. 2627, 61 L.Ed.2d 343 (1979).

40.   Though the Court in *DeFillippo* distinguished the instant case from those in which exclusion of evidence was required because the unconstitutional provisions, "by their own terms, authorized searches under circumstances which did not satisfy the traditional warrant and probable cause requirements of the Fourth Amendment," this substantive-procedural line was later obliterated entirely in *Illinois v. Krull*, 480 U.S. 340, 107 S.Ct. 1160, 94 L.Ed.2d 364 (1987), discussed in § 3.1 at note 26.

41.   378 U.S. 108, 84 S.Ct. 1509, 12 L.Ed.2d 723 (1964).

Court concluded this affidavit did not meet the requirements of the Fourth Amendment:

Although an affidavit may be based on hearsay information and need not reflect the direct personal observations of the affiant, * * * the magistrate must be informed of some of the underlying circumstances from which the informant concluded that the narcotics were where he claimed they were, and some of the underlying circumstances from which the officer concluded that the informant, whose identity need not be disclosed, * * * was "credible" or his information "reliable." Otherwise, "the inferences from the facts which lead to the complaint" will be drawn not "by a neutral and detached magistrate," as the Constitution requires, but instead, by a police officer "engaged in the often competitive enterprise of ferreting out crime," * * * or, as in this case, by an unidentified informant.

This two-pronged approach was also applied by the Court to police claims of probable cause to make an arrest or search without a warrant.[42] Under the first or "basis of knowledge" prong, facts had to be revealed that permitted the judicial officer making the probable cause determination to reach a judgment as to whether the informant had a basis for his allegations that a certain person had been, was or would be involved in criminal conduct or that evidence of crime would be found at a certain place. By contrast, under the second or "veracity" prong of *Aguilar,* sufficient facts had to be brought before the judicial officer so that he could determine either the inherent credibility of the informant or the reliability of his information on this particular occasion. But in *Illinois v. Gates,*[43] the Supreme Court, though casting not the slightest doubt upon the correctness of the result in *Aguilar,* decided

to abandon the "two-pronged test" established by our decisions in *Aguilar* and *Spinelli.*[44] In its place we reaffirm the totality of the circumstances analysis that traditionally has informed probable cause determinations. * * * The task of the issuing magistrate is simply to make a practical, common-sense decision whether, given all the circumstances set forth in the affidavit before him, including the "veracity" and "basis of knowledge" of persons supplying hearsay information, there is a fair probability that contraband or evidence of a crime will be found in a particular place. And the duty of a reviewing court is simply to ensure that the magistrate had a "substantial basis for * * * conclud[ing]" that probable cause existed. * * * We are convinced that this flexible, easily applied standard will better achieve the accommodation of public and private interests that the Fourth Amendment requires than does the approach that has developed from *Aguilar* and *Spinelli.*

The majority in *Gates* felt that the two-pronged test was too rigid and that it improperly accorded "these two elements * * * independent status," when in fact "a deficiency in one may be compensated for * * * by a strong showing as to the other."

This abandonment of the *Aguilar* test in *Gates* is most unfortunate. As Justice White (concurring because he found probable cause to exist by applying the *Aguilar* factors) wisely noted, "the question whether a particular anonymous tip provides the basis for issuance of a warrant will often be a difficult one." This being the case, he continued, the Supreme Court should "attempt to provide more precise guidance by clarifying *Aguilar–Spinelli,*" instead of opting for the direct opposite course by which "it appears that the question whether the probable cause standard is to be diluted is left to the common-sense judgments of issuing magistrates" without meaningful review. Moreover, as Justice White also cogently noted, the *Gates* majority's claim that a deficiency as to one of the *Aguilar* prongs can be compensated for by a strong showing as to the other cannot be taken literally. Were it so interpret-

---

42. McCray v. Illinois, 386 U.S. 300, 87 S.Ct. 1056, 18 L.Ed.2d 62 (1967).

43. 462 U.S. 213, 103 S.Ct. 2317, 76 L.Ed.2d 527 (1983).

44. The reference is to Spinelli v. United States, 393 U.S. 410, 89 S.Ct. 584, 21 L.Ed.2d 637 (1969), an oft-cited case applying the *Aguilar* formula and elaborating upon it.

ed, it would lead to the bizarre result, repeatedly rejected by the Court in the past[45] in cases reaffirmed by the *Gates* majority, that the unsupported assertion or belief of an honest person satisfies the probable cause requirement.

Although *Gates* constitutes some "watering-down" of the probable cause standard as it had developed under the *Aguilar* two-pronged formula, this does *not* mean that lower courts are writing on a completely clean slate when they now confront the question of when an informant's information amounts to probable cause. Even the *Gates* majority agreed "that an informant's 'veracity,' 'reliability' and 'basis of knowledge' are all highly relevant in determining the value of his report." Because this is so, courts continue to rely upon the elaboration of these factors in earlier cases decided under the now-discarded *Aguilar* formula. (But it must be remembered, as the Court later emphasized,[46] that *Gates* "did not merely refine or qualify the 'two-pronged test'" but instead abandoned it in favor of a "totality of the circumstances analysis.") Thus, while the discussion that follows relies in part upon several decisions predating *Gates*, it is nonetheless relevant on the question of what constitutes probable cause in the post-*Gates* era.

Police often attempt to establish the credibility of the informant on the basis of his past performance, as in *McCray v. Illinois*.[47] There, the officer testified the informant had given him information about narcotics activities 15 or 16 times in the past, resulting in numerous arrests and convictions, and on cross-examination even named some of the persons convicted. Because this testimony "informed the court * * * of the underlying circumstances from which the officer concluded that the informant * * * was 'credible,'" the Supreme Court unhesitantly concluded there was "no doubt * * * that there was probable cause to sustain the arrest and incidental search in this case."

Lower courts have consistently held that a declaration that the informant's past information led to convictions is a sufficient showing of the informer's credibility, even when information on a single past occasion produced a single conviction and even without any specific identification of the prior convictions. It will also suffice that on a prior occasion the informant said a certain object, such as narcotics, would be found at a certain place and that this information was verified by a search uncovering the object. It has frequently been held sufficient that the informant's prior information led to arrests, but the better view is that such an allegation is inadequate, as a mere statement the police decided to arrest on the prior occasion indicates nothing about the lawfulness of that arrest or whether anything learned incident to or following the arrest verified what the informant had said. And while cases may be found approving of assertions merely saying the informant's prior information proved to be "correct," "true and correct," "reliable" "reliable and accurate," or "valid," other decisions view such characterizations as conclusory and thus insufficient. Although *Gates* has occasionally been interpreted as approving such general assertions, that is incorrect. To view such allegations as alone establishing veracity would violate a cardinal principle reaffirmed by the *Gates* majority: "Sufficient information must be presented to the magistrate to allow *that official* to determine probable cause; his action cannot be a mere ratification of the bare conclusions of others."[48] In any event, past performance relates only to the matter of veracity; as Justice White put it in *Spinelli v. United States*[49]: "The past reliability of the informant can no more furnish probable cause for believing his current report than can previous experience with the officer himself."

45. E.g., Whiteley v. Warden, 401 U.S. 560, 91 S.Ct. 1031, 28 L.Ed.2d 306 (1971); Jones v. United States, 362 U.S. 257, 80 S.Ct. 725, 4 L.Ed.2d 697 (1960); Nathanson v. United States, 290 U.S. 41, 54 S.Ct. 11, 78 L.Ed. 159 (1933).

46. Massachusetts v. Upton, 466 U.S. 727, 104 S.Ct. 2085, 80 L.Ed.2d 721 (1984).

47. 386 U.S. 300, 87 S.Ct. 1056, 18 L.Ed.2d 62 (1967).

48. Emphasis added.

49. 393 U.S. 410, 89 S.Ct. 584, 21 L.Ed.2d 637 (1969).

If no showing is made as to the informant's credibility, then it is necessary to consider whether it has been shown that the informant's information is reliable on this particular occasion. One means of showing this was recognized in *United States v. Harris*,[50] where the search warrant affidavit recited that the informant said he had purchased illicit whiskey from a named person for two years, most recently in the past two weeks, in the course of which he saw that person obtain the whiskey from a specified building. What appeared to be a majority of the Court concluded that the information given was shown to be reliable because it "was plainly a declaration against interest since it could readily warrant a prosecution and could sustain a conviction against the informant himself." The Court reasoned:

Common sense in the important daily affairs of life would induce a prudent and disinterested observer to credit these statements. People do not lightly admit a crime and place critical evidence in the hands of the police in the form of their own admissions. Admissions of crime, like admissions against proprietary interests, carry their own indicia of credibility—sufficient at least to support finding of probable cause to search. That the informant may be paid or promised a "break" does not eliminate the residual risk and opprobrium of having admitted criminal conduct. Concededly admissions of crime do not always lend credibility to contemporaneous or later accusations of another. But here the informant's admission that over a long period and currently he had been buying illicit liquor on a certain premises, itself and without more, implicated that property and furnished probable cause to search.

The four dissenters in *Harris* objected that "where the declarant is also a police informant it seems at least as plausible to assume, without further enlightenment either as to the Government's general practice or as to the particular facts of this case, that the declarant-confidant at least believed he would receive absolution from prosecution for his confessed crime in return for his statement." That criticism does not compel the conclusion that the admission-against-interest approach should never be used, but rather that it should be used with caution; as the Supreme Court said in a related context, a person's statement "against his penal interest" carries with it an "indicia of reliability" if it may also be said that the statement was made "under circumstances when he would have no reason to lie."[51] Certainly the admission-against-interest rationale is inappropriate when not even the police know the identity of the informant, for if the informant is not known to the police he stands no real risk of prosecution. It does not follow, as the *Harris* dissenters argued, that this is also the case if the informant's identity is known to the police but not disclosed to others. But such a case does call for particular caution, for if the informant's name is not disclosed then it is more likely (at least as a general proposition) that he is a person whose indiscretions are tolerated by the police on a continuing basis in exchange for information and who thus will perceive little risk in admitting such indiscretions. By comparison, there is much more reason to conclude that veracity is shown when the informant comes forward as an affiant or when his identity is disclosed in the affidavit or upon the motion to suppress.

For a declaration against penal interest to establish reliability, the declaration must have a sufficient nexus to the information critical to the probable cause determination. To take an obvious and unlikely case, if a person were to walk into a police station and give a full confession to a robbery and then announce that a named person was guilty of an unrelated rape, the admission with respect to the robbery could hardly be taken as showing that the information about the rape was reliable. What is needed is a showing that the informant's statements against his own penal interest were closely related to the criminal activity for which probable cause to arrest or search is being established; it is *not* necessary that the

---

50. 403 U.S. 573, 91 S.Ct. 2075, 29 L.Ed.2d 723 (1971).

51. Dutton v. Evans, 400 U.S. 74, 91 S.Ct. 210, 27 L.Ed.2d 213 (1970).

admissions incriminate the informant in the *same* crimes as the ones then under investigation. Moreover, for the rationale of *Harris* to apply the admission must be unequivocal; it will not suffice that the informant admits to being present during another's crime or describes the crime in such detail as to suggest his possible involvement in it.

Just how important it remains after *Gates* to show veracity in one of these ways is not entirely clear. The *Gates* majority says that the informant's veracity is still "highly relevant," but then asserts that a deficiency in that respect could be compensated for by a "strong showing" of basis of knowledge. Thus, "even if we entertain some doubt as to an informant's motives, his explicit and detailed description of alleged wrongdoing, along with a statement that the event was observed first-hand, entitles his tip to greater weight than might otherwise be the case." But surely the mere act of reciting a detailed account does not show veracity, nor does an informant's claim of first-hand knowledge. To conclude otherwise would be to put informants on the same footing as police and the victims of and witnesses to crime[52] when, as Justice Brennan noted in his *Gates* dissent, "there certainly is no basis for treating anonymous informants as presumptively reliable."

The other prong of the now-abandoned *Aguilar* test concerned "basis of knowledge," which *Gates* teaches also remains a "highly relevant" consideration in determining the value of an informant's report. The most obvious and direct way of showing such a basis is by setting out for the benefit of the judicial officer who must make the probable cause decision an explanation as to exactly how the informant claims to have come by the information he gave to the officer. As Justice White explained in his very helpful concurring opinion in *Spinelli v. United States*[53]:

If the affidavit rests on hearsay—an informant's report—what is necessary under *Aguilar* is one of two things: the informant must declare either (1) that he has himself seen or perceived the fact or facts asserted; or (2) that his information is hearsay, but there is good reason for believing it—perhaps one of the usual grounds for crediting hearsay information. * * * [I]f, for example, the informer's hearsay comes from one of the actors in the crime in the nature of admission against interest, the affidavit giving this information should be held sufficient.

But this does not mean that a basis of knowledge may be shown only in such a direct fashion. If there is not such a direct showing, said the Court in *Spinelli*, it may nonetheless be possible to assume a sufficient basis of knowledge from the wealth of detail that has been provided:

The detail provided by the informant in *Draper v. United States*[54] * * * provides a suitable benchmark. While Hereford, the Government's informer in that case, did not state the way in which he obtained his information, he reported that Draper had gone to Chicago the day before by train and that he would return to Denver by train with three ounces of heroin on one of two specified mornings. Moreover, Hereford went on to describe, with minute particularity, the clothes that Draper would be wearing upon his arrival at the Denver station. A magistrate, when confronted with such detail, could reasonably infer that the informant had gained his information in a reliable way. Such an inference cannot be made in the present case. Here, the only facts supplied were that Spinelli was using two specified telephones and that these phones were being used in gambling operations. This meager report could easily have been obtained from an offhand remark heard at a neighborhood bar.

If self-verifying detail can establish a basis of knowledge (clearly, it cannot show the informant's veracity), then exactly what kind of detail will suffice? What is needed, to put the proposition in the language of the *Gates* case, are details about matters sufficiently related to

---

52. See § 3.3(d).

53. 393 U.S. 410, 89 S.Ct. 584, 21 L.Ed.2d 637 (1969).

54. 358 U.S. 307, 79 S.Ct. 329, 3 L.Ed.2d 327 (1959).

the criminal activity reported that it may be fairly concluded the informant "had access to reliable information of the * * * illegal activities." Such was the case in *Draper* because, as Justice White later explained in his *Gates* concurring opinion, the fact the informer could predict two days in advance what clothing Draper would be wearing suggested Draper "had planned in advance to wear these specific clothes so that an accomplice could identify him," and this gave rise to a "clear inference * * * that the informant was either involved in the criminal scheme himself or that he otherwise had access to reliable, inside information." By contrast, if in the *Aguilar* case the informant had been able to describe the furnishings inside the house (instead of, say, a particular furnishing in which it was indicated the drugs were stored), that would not give rise to such a "clear inference." It would only show that the informant or someone with whom he communicated had been in that house, and a direct assertion to that effect would not suffice to show basis of knowledge re the presence of drugs there.

Just how important it remains after *Gates* to show a basis of knowledge in one of these ways is not entirely clear. Though it is at least arguable that a basis of knowledge was established in that case, some of the majority's comments on this point are none too reassuring. As noted earlier, in abandoning the *Aguilar* two-pronged test the Court in *Gates* said that "a deficiency in one may be compensated for * * * by a strong showing as to the other." By way of example, the Court then declared that if "a particular informant is known for the unusual reliability of his predictions of certain types of criminal activities in a locality, his failure, in a particular case, to thoroughly set forth the basis of his knowledge surely should not serve as an absolute bar to a finding of probable cause based on his tip." But this assertion does not deserve to be taken too seriously. For one thing, the case cited in support of this proposition, *United States v. Sellers*,[55] is in fact a very striking example of the self-verifying-detail principle. For another,

as Justice White noted in his concurrence regarding that statement by the majority:

> If this is so, then it must follow *a fortiori* that "the affidavit of an officer, known by the magistrate to be honest and experienced, stating that [contraband] is located in a certain building" must be acceptable. * * * It would be "quixotic" if a similar statement from an honest informant, but not one from an honest officer, could furnish probable cause. * * * But we have repeatedly held that the unsupported assertion or belief of an officer does not satisfy the probable cause requirement, and the majority "expressly reaffirms" these holdings.

Although the *Spinelli* Court utilized the earlier *Draper* case to illustrate the self-verifying detail situation, *Draper* was not decided upon such a basis. Rather, *Draper* was based upon yet another device for rehabilitating what would otherwise be an insufficient or incomplete report of an informant: partial corroboration. Federal narcotics agent March had been told by an informant who had given him reliable information in the past that Draper would return from Chicago by train on one of two specified days; in addition, the informer gave a detailed physical description of Draper and of the clothing he would be wearing, and said that he would be carrying a tan zipper bag and that he habitually walked real fast. These details were not put before a magistrate. Rather, the agent maintained a surveillance at the train station and when the described person appeared as predicted he was arrested, resulting in the discovery of the heroin. In upholding the arrest and search, the majority in *Draper* emphasized that

> Marsh had personally verified every facet of the information given him by Hereford except whether petitioner had accomplished his mission and had the three ounces of heroin on his person or in his bag. And surely, with every other bit of Hereford's information being thus personally verified, Marsh had "reasonable grounds" to believe that the remaining unverified bit of Here-

---

55. 483 F.2d 37 (5th Cir.1973).

ford's information—that Draper would have the heroin with him—was likewise true.

Corroboration of part of the informant's tale is another way in which the concern with veracity may be met, as the informant's present good performance shows him to be probably credible just as surely as does past good performance. But in *Draper* the informant's credibility was otherwise established, and thus the corroboration of which the Court spoke was apparently deemed relevant on the matter of basis of knowledge. Courts have commonly used corroboration in this way. Any lingering doubts about the propriety of utilizing corroboration for this latter purpose[56] have been dispelled by *Gates*. There the majority found probable cause because of the partial corroboration even though, as Justice Stevens lamented in his dissent, *neither* veracity *nor* basis of knowledge was otherwise established.

As for what kind or amount of corroboration is needed, *Gates* rejects the notion that corroboration of innocent activity will not suffice. "In making a determination of probable cause the relevant inquiry is not whether particular conduct is 'innocent' or 'guilty,' but the degree of suspicion that attaches to particular types of non-criminal acts." In that case, an anonymous letter said that a named couple made their living selling drugs, that the wife drives the car to Florida and flies back, after which the husband flies to Florida and drives back with a car full of drugs, and that another such trip was about to occur. A few days later the police determined that the husband had flown to Florida, and surveillance of him there established that upon arrival he took a taxi to a motel where his wife had rented a room and that the next day they left in his car and drove

north on an interstate highway. On those facts a warrant to search the car and their residence was obtained. In concluding this amounted to probable cause, the *Gates* majority none too convincingly reasoned as follows: (1) the facts obtained by independent investigation were alone quite suspicious, as "Florida is well-known as a source of narcotics and other illegal drugs," and Gates' observed conduct "is as suggestive of a pre-arranged drug run, as it is of an ordinary vacation trip"; (2) the anonymous letter was then deserving of some weight, as the "corroboration of the letter's predictions that the Gates' car would be in Florida, that Lance Gates would fly to Florida in the next day or so, and that he would drive the car north toward Bloomingdale all indicated, albeit not with certainty, that the informant's other assertions also were true"; and (3) the details in the letter concerned "future actions of third parties ordinarily not easily predicted," thus suggesting the writer of the letter "also had access to reliable information of the Gates' alleged illegal activities." But, as the Stevens dissent quite properly notes, the corroboration in this case actually counts for very little. For one thing, the limited investigation established neither when the wife had gone to Florida nor whether the husband was making an immediate return trip to Illinois, and thus there was nothing inherently suspicious in what had been observed. For another, both the husband and wife had been seen together in Florida, thus disproving the assertion in the letter that they were never gone at the same time, a rather critical allegation because it squared with the further assertion that they already had "over $100,000 worth of drugs in their basement."

---

56. Justice White, concurring in *Spinelli,* was often taken to mean that corroboration relates only to the veracity prong of *Aguilar,* as he said that "the proposition is not that the tenth fact may be logically inferred from the other nine or that the tenth fact is usually found in conjunction with the other nine. No one would suggest that just anyone getting off the 10:30 train dressed as Draper was, with a brisk walk and carrying a zipper bag, should be arrested for carrying narcotics. The thrust of *Draper* is not that the verified facts have independent significance with respect to proof of the tenth. The argument instead relates to the reliability of the source: because an informant is right about some things, he is more

probably right about other facts, usually the critical, unverified facts." But in *Gates* he explained: "I did not say that corroboration could *never* satisfy the basis of knowledge prong. My concern was, and still is, that the prong might be deemed satisfied on the basis of corroboration of information that does not in any way suggest that the informant had an adequate basis of knowledge for his report. If, however, as in *Draper,* the police corroborate information from which it can be inferred that the informant's tip was grounded on inside information, this corroboration is sufficient to satisfy the basis of knowledge prong."

Upon a motion to suppress in a case where the prosecution claims information from an informant supplies probable cause, the defendant may seek the identity of the informant in an effort to learn whether the informant actually exists, whether he actually gave fruitful information in the past, and whether the informant actually gave the information alleged in this instance. Counsel will usually be thwarted in these efforts because of what is commonly referred to as the informer's privilege. In *McCray v. Illinois*,[57] the Court rejected the claim that defendants are *always* entitled upon demand to learn of the informant's name, and instead concluded "that it should rest entirely with the judge who hears the motion to suppress to decide whether he needs such disclosure as to the informant in order to decide whether the officer is a believable witness." This means that disclosure should be required on occasion, as when some aspect of the police conduct appears inexplicable if an informant actually reported what it is claimed he said. But, because it is difficult if not impossible to articulate a standard that sufficiently honors the informer's privilege and yet sufficiently guards against undetectable police perjury, a growing number of courts are utilizing the device of an in camera hearing, whereby the informant is produced privately for examination by the judge only.

(d) Information From a Victim or Witness. The Supreme Court has seldom had occasion to speak to the matter of victim-witness veracity. However, in *Jaben v. United States*,[58] involving a complaint filed by an IRS agent that was based in part upon interviews with persons who had knowledge of the defendant's financial condition, the Court made it clear that these persons were not to be viewed in the same light as the typical police informant:

> [U]nlike narcotics informants, for example, whose credibility may often be suspect, the sources in this tax evasion case are much less likely to produce false or untrustworthy

information. Thus, whereas some supporting information concerning the credibility of informants in narcotics cases or other common garden varieties of crime may be required, such information is not so necessary in the context of the case before us.

The Court has since proceeded as if veracity may be assumed when information comes from the victim of or a witness to criminal activity,[59] a position rather consistently taken by lower courts. But circumstances may make that presumption inoperative in a particular case; the cases holding veracity was properly presumed frequently emphasized that the police were unaware of any apparent motive to falsify. If the person who purports to have witnessed criminal activity is unwilling to identify himself to the police, then it would ordinarily be improper to presume reliability.

As for "basis of knowledge," one prong of the since-abandoned *Aguilar* test but now a "highly relevant" consideration under the *Illinois v. Gates*[60] "totality of the circumstances" formula, it is generally not a major problem as to the so-called citizen-informer. Eyewitnesses by definition are not passing along idle rumor, for they have been the victims of the crime or have otherwise seen some portion of it. Great detail as to why the person was in a position to observe what was reported is not required, though some explanation regarding the basis of knowledge of the victim or witness is clearly called for when it appears the purported knowledge could have been obtained only by the utilization of some expertise beyond that of the typical layman. As for the somewhat unusual case in which the victim or witness also conveys to the police information from others, this hearsay-upon-hearsay may also be considered if it is specially shown or fairly inferable from the circumstances that both the veracity and basis of knowledge requirements are met by the source of the information related.

57. 386 U.S. 300, 87 S.Ct. 1056, 18 L.Ed.2d 62 (1967).

58. 381 U.S. 214, 85 S.Ct. 1365, 14 L.Ed.2d 345 (1965).

59. Chambers v. Maroney, 399 U.S. 42, 90 S.Ct. 1975, 26 L.Ed.2d 419 (1970).

60. 462 U.S. 213, 103 S.Ct. 2317, 76 L.Ed.2d 527 (1983).

In a victim-witness type of case there is seldom any serious problem presented concerning either veracity or basis of knowledge; rather, the major difficulty usually encountered is whether the information obtained from direct observation by a presumptively reliable person is complete and specific enough to constitute probable cause to search a particular place or (as is much more frequently in issue) to arrest a particular person. Sometimes the victim or witness can identify the perpetrator by name or by identifying his picture in police files, but more typically the police must act quickly on the basis of a description of the perpetrator. Even assuming that the Fourth Amendment probable cause test does not mean more-probable-than-not in this context,[61] the description will not suffice if it was equally applicable to a great many individuals in the area. In determining what kind of description by a victim or witness together with what kind of attendant circumstances adds up to probable cause, the courts have considered these factors:

(1) Particularity of description. A victim or witness will typically describe the perpetrator in terms of some of the following characteristics: race, sex, age, height, weight, build, complexion, hair, and clothing. Generally, the more of these identifying characteristics that are available, the more likely it is there will be grounds to arrest a person found with most or all of those characteristics. But there is more to it than counting the number of points of comparison; consideration must be given to the uniqueness of the points of identification—the extent to which they aid in singling out a person from the general public.

(2) Size of the area. The time that has elapsed between the crime and the arrest is an important consideration, for it shows what distance the perpetrator of the crime could have traveled—the radius of the area within which the perpetrator might then be. If the elapsed time is short, such as five or ten minutes, then this area is fairly small, and a matching up of a person in the area with a rather general

description that might not otherwise suffice will be adequate for probable cause.

(3) Number of persons in the area. The fewer persons about, the less chance there is that a description of a given particularity would fit persons other than the individual at hand. Thus, rather general descriptions have been found sufficient in the early morning hours when few persons were on the street.

(4) Direction of flight. Courts frequently take note of the fact that the police had been advised of the direction in which the offender was fleeing on foot or by vehicle. This is appropriate, for it shows that of the total relevant area (measured by a radius the length of possible flight since the time of the crime), a particular slice is more likely than the rest to contain the individual or vehicle sought.

(5) Actions by or condition of person arrested. Illustrative of such additional facts are that the suspect was running in a direction away from the crime scene, that he was furtively looking back, or that upon a lawful stopping for investigation he gave an implausible explanation for his presence.

(6) Knowledge that the person or vehicle was involved in other similar criminality on a prior occasion. Thus the arrest of the occupants of a car for bank robbery was supported by the fact that the car was recognized as having been used to transport the fruits of an earlier robbery and one of the occupants was recognized as a person involved in that prior robbery.

(e) Information From or Held by Other Police. In *United States v. Ventresca*,[62] involving a search warrant affidavit reciting that certain events had been observed by the affiant's fellow officers, the Court in upholding the warrant stated: "Observations of fellow officers of the Government engaged in a common investigation are plainly a reliable basis for a warrant applied for by one of their number." Following the lead of *Ventresca*, lower courts have consistently held that another law enforcement officer is a reliable source and that consequently no special showing of relia-

---

61. See § 3.3(b).

62. 380 U.S. 102, 85 S.Ct. 741, 13 L.Ed.2d 684 (1965).

bility need be made as a part of the probable cause determination.

In *Ventresca,* the other officers passed on to the affiant the facts they had uncovered in their investigation, and thus that case is unlike the common situation in which a directive or request for action is circulated within or between law enforcement agencies unaccompanied by any recitation of the underlying facts and circumstances, resulting in an arrest being made by an officer who has never been told of the facts deemed to amount to probable cause. Such was the case in *Whiteley v. Warden,*[63] where a policeman arrested two men in response to a bulletin stating an arrest warrant for them had issued in another part of the state. After concluding the warrant was invalid because issued upon a conclusory complaint, the Court turned to the contention that the arrest was lawful because the policeman was entitled to assume that whoever authorized the bulletin had probable cause:

> We do not, of course, question that the Laramie police were entitled to act on the strength of the radio bulletin. Certainly police officers called upon to aid other officers in executing arrest warrants are entitled to assume that the officers requesting aid offered the magistrate the information requisite to support an independent judicial assessment of probable cause. Where, however, the contrary turns out to be true, an otherwise illegal arrest cannot be insulated from challenge by the decision of the instigating officer to rely on fellow officers to make the arrest.

Thus, under the *Whiteley* rule police are in a limited sense "entitled to act" upon a communication through official channels. Although the Court did not elaborate upon that observation, it apparently means that the arresting officer is himself not at fault and thus should not be held personally responsible in a civil action or disciplinary proceedings if it turns out that there was no probable cause at the source. But when the question arises in the context of an effort to exclude evidence obtained as a consequence of action taken pursu-

ant to the communication, then the question legitimately is whether the law enforcement system as a whole has complied with the requirements of the Fourth Amendment. This means that the evidence must be excluded if facts adding up to probable cause were not in the hands of the officer or agency that gave the order or made the request, for were it otherwise an officer or agency possessed of facts insufficient to establish probable cause could circumvent the Fourth Amendment by the simple device of directing or asking some other officer or agency to make the arrest and search.

Whiteley must in turn be distinguished from the case in which there has been no directive or request but the arresting or searching officer attempts to justify his action on the ground that other officers were at that time in possession of the necessary underlying facts. In such circumstances, the knowledge of other police cannot ordinarily be imputed to the arresting or searching officer, for to hold otherwise would encourage police officers to search on the hope that the total knowledge of all those officers involved in a case will later be found to constitute probable cause if the search is challenged. A contrary result has been reached when there was a close working relationship between the officer who acted and the officer who had the requisite information and in addition the circumstances indicate that had not the former officer acted the latter most certainly would have conducted the arrest or search himself.

When police come into contact with an individual for some reason, it is not uncommon for them to run a radio check on him and his vehicle to see if either is wanted, and a lawful arrest may result if the requirements of *Whiteley* are met. Problems arise when the records do not accurately reflect the current situation, as where a person is arrested for driving a car listed in police files as stolen notwithstanding its earlier recovery by the police. This arrest is illegal, for the police may not rely upon incorrect or incomplete information when they are

---

63.   401 U.S. 560, 91 S.Ct. 1031, 28 L.Ed.2d 306 (1971).

at fault in permitting the records to remain uncorrected.

(f) First–Hand Information. Although the kinds of suspicious events and circumstances that police on patrol confront are virtually infinite in their variety, there are a few recurring situations worth noting, such as where a person is arrested because of his association with a known offender, as in *United States v. Di Re.*[64] There, an OPA investigator was told by one Reed that he was to buy counterfeit ration coupons from one Buttitta at a certain place, so the investigator and a detective trailed Buttitta's car to the designated place. There they found Reed in the rear seat holding counterfeit coupons, and upon being asked he said he received them from Buttitta, the driver. Di Re, a passenger in the front seat, was also arrested on the theory that his presence indicated he was implicated in a conspiracy to knowingly possess counterfeit coupons, but the Supreme Court concluded that probable cause for his arrest was lacking:

> The argument that one who "accompanies a criminal to a crime rendezvous" cannot be assumed to be a bystander, forceful enough in some circumstances, is farfetched when the meeting is not secretive or in a suspicious hide-out but in broad daylight, in plain sight of passers-by, in a public street of a large city, and where the alleged substantive crime is one which does not necessarily involve any act visibly criminal. If Di Re had witnessed the passing of papers from hand to hand, it would not follow that he knew they were ration coupons, and if he saw that they were ration coupons, it would not follow that he would know them to be counterfeit. Indeed it appeared at the trial to require an expert to establish that fact. Presumptions of guilt are not lightly to be indulged from mere meetings.

Di Re intimates that when the offense *does* involve an "act visibly criminal," then the chances are substantially greater that a companion is more than a mere bystander. As a general matter this is so, and thus the likelihood of there being probable cause as to the companion is greater in such a situation, but yet it cannot be said that probable cause is always present upon those facts. If, for example, *A* and *B* are standing on a corner and *C* walks up to *B* and makes a purchase of narcotics from *B,* it is by no means apparent that *A* is an accomplice in this transaction.[65] When as in *Di Re* the ongoing criminal activity is not evident to the associate, it is then clearly necessary to give careful consideration to those aspects of the nature and extent of the association that may indicate that the associate is also an accomplice.

Observation of furtive gestures is a factor that may properly be taken into account in determining whether probable cause exists. As the Supreme Court concluded in *Peters v. New York*,[66] "deliberately furtive actions * * * at the approach of strangers or law officers are strong indicia of mens rea, and when coupled with specific knowledge on the part of the officer relating the suspect to the evidence of crime, they are proper factors to be considered in the decision to make an arrest." Thus, if the police see a person in possession of a highly suspicious object and then observe that person make an apparent attempt to conceal that object from police view, probable cause is then present. But when no such object is seen and the officer merely observes a movement that could be an attempt to hide something, this does not amount to probable cause.

Flight of a person from the presence of police does not alone amount to probable cause. But, as the Supreme Court recognized in *Peters,* flight is a "strong indicia of mens rea." Thus, a person's flight upon the approach[67] of the police may be taken into ac-

---

64. 332 U.S. 581, 68 S.Ct. 222, 92 L.Ed. 210 (1948).

65. By comparison, it does seem clear that there is probable cause to arrest a person who on a continuing basis is present at a place where criminal activity is openly and repeatedly conducted. Ker v. California, 374 U.S. 23, 83 S.Ct. 1623, 10 L.Ed.2d 726 (1963).

66. 392 U.S. 40, 88 S.Ct. 1889, 20 L.Ed.2d 917 (1968).

67. The approach itself is no Fourth Amendment seizure, and thus even if no reasonable suspicion then exists, the flight cannot be characterized as a fruit of the illegal seizure. See discussion of California v. Hodari D., 499 U.S. 621, 111 S.Ct. 1547, 113 L.Ed.2d 690 (1991), in § 3.8 at note 25.

count and may well elevate the pre-existing suspicion up to probable cause. But in some circumstances the flight will be so ambiguous that it cannot be considered even to that limited extent.[68]

Officers on patrol frequently utilize interrogation as a means to obtain more information about suspicious persons and circumstances, and the suspect's response to the interrogation may again elevate the prior suspicions up to the level of probable cause. Responses known to be false, or that are incriminating, implausible, conflicting, evasive or unresponsive may well constitute probable cause when considered together with the prior suspicions. Justice White, concurring in *Terry v. Ohio*,[69] asserted that "refusal to answer furnishes no basis for arrest," which may well be correct if construed to mean that such refusal does not alone constitute grounds for arrest.[70] But, though it has occasionally been held that no adverse inference may be drawn from a refusal to respond, the better view is that refusal to answer is one of "the factual and practical considerations of everyday life"[71] that an officer may consider, together with the evidence that gave rise to his prior suspicion, in determining whether there are grounds for an arrest. When there is no questioning, however, mere silence or failure to protest or claim innocence may not be viewed as an indication of guilt.[72]

(g) Special Problems in Search Cases. Probable cause in arrest cases usually involves historical facts (i.e., is it probable that a certain person did at some *prior* time commit an offense), while in search cases the concern is always with facts relating to a current situation (i.e., is it probable that evidence of crime is *presently* to be found in a certain place). This is why search cases often present the unique problem of whether the information relied upon to establish probable cause has grown "stale." Illustrative is *Sgro v. United States*,[73] holding that there was not probable cause to search a hotel for illegal intoxicants where the affidavit alleged a purchase of beer there over three weeks earlier.

Probable cause is not determined by merely counting the number of days between the time of the facts relied upon and the warrant's issuance, and thus, as stated in *Sgro*, the matter "must be determined by the circumstances of each case." One important factor is the character of the criminal activity under investigation. When the affidavit recites an isolated violation, probable cause ordinarily dwindles rather quickly with the passage of time, but when it recites facts indicating activity of a protracted and continuous nature the passage of time becomes less significant. Especially when the crime under investigation is not a continuing one, the nature of the property sought is an important factor. Illustrative is *United States v. Steeves*,[74] involving a warrant to search for various items relating to a bank robbery that had occurred three months earlier, where the court concluded there was no longer probable cause that the robber still had at his residence the "highly incriminating" money bag taken from the bank, though there was probable cause he still had the clothing he had worn during the robbery. Yet another factor is the opportunity those involved in the crime would have had to remove or destroy the items sought during the time that has elapsed. Some cases assert it is relevant that the police

---

68. Wong Sun v. United States, 371 U.S. 471, 83 S.Ct. 407, 9 L.Ed.2d 441 (1963) (where federal agent knocked on door of laundry at 6 a.m. and used ruse that he seeking his laundry and then said he an agent when suspect was closing door, suspect's flight into the house was ambiguous, as "the officer never adequately dispelled the misimpression engendered by his own ruse").

69. 392 U.S. 1, 88 S.Ct. 1868, 20 L.Ed.2d 889 (1968).

70. But in Brown v. Texas, 443 U.S. 47, 99 S.Ct. 2637, 61 L.Ed.2d 357 (1979), the Court noted it did not have to decide "whether an individual may be punished for refusing to identify himself in the context of a lawful investigatory stop which satisfies Fourth Amendment requirements." And in Kolender v. Lawson, 461 U.S. 352, 103

S.Ct. 1855, 75 L.Ed.2d 903 (1983), the Court held unconstitutional on void for vagueness grounds a statute making it a crime for a person lawfully stopped under *Terry* not to provide "credible and reliable" identification, but did not have occasion to decide whether a more certain substantive offense of this type would be constitutional.

71. Brinegar v. United States, 338 U.S. 160, 69 S.Ct. 1302, 93 L.Ed. 1879 (1949).

72. United States v. Di Re, 332 U.S. 581, 68 S.Ct. 222, 92 L.Ed. 210 (1948).

73. 287 U.S. 206, 53 S.Ct. 138, 77 L.Ed. 260 (1932).

74. 525 F.2d 33 (8th Cir.1975).

acted with dispatch as soon as the facts were made known to them, but this obviously has *no* bearing on the probable cause issue.

Because the time the facts relied upon occurred is critical in determining whether there is probable cause to search, failure to state when the alleged facts occurred is fatally defective. But where undated information is factually interrelated with other, dated information in the affidavit, then the inference that the events took place in close proximity to the dates actually given may be permissible. Similarly, when the affidavit says that the events occurred "within" a specified period of time, it must be tested by considering whether the information would be stale if the events occurred at the earliest possible time in that period. Use of the word "recently" is permissible when the reported facts clearly show a continuing course of conduct that would support a finding of present probable cause even if those facts had occurred a few months ago, but under the better view is insufficient when the fact in question is a one-time purchase or viewing of drugs.

Some cases present the converse issue of whether the officer's information was too fresh. This issue most often arises when the police have obtained an "anticipatory search warrant," one based upon an affidavit showing probable cause that at some future time (but not presently) certain evidence of crime will be located at a specific place. Despite some contrary authority, the better and prevailing view is that such warrants are constitutional and indeed are to be preferred over forcing the police to go to the scene without a warrant and there make a decision at the risk of being second-guessed by the judiciary if they are successful in recovering evidence. Moreover, the cases condemning reliance upon stale information in no sense cast doubt upon the propriety of anticipatory warrants; indeed, the typical anticipatory warrant is more likely to establish that probable cause will exist at the time of the search than the typical warrant based solely upon the known prior location of the items to be seized. It is important, of course, that the issuing judge should be satisfied that there is no likelihood that the war-rant will be executed before the events critical to the ripening of probable cause.

The more complicated probable cause determination that must be made in search cases may be said to include four ingredients: time; crime; objects; and place. Assuming no problem with respect to time (as discussed above), it is still necessary that there be established a sufficient nexus between (1) criminal activity, (2) the things to be seized, and (3) the place to be searched. Difficulties concerning whether the necessary relationships have been established can arise in an infinite variety of ways, but only a few illustrations will be given here. Even if the connection between things and places is clear beyond question, probable cause may still be lacking because it is not also shown to be probable that those items constitute the fruits, instrumentalities, or evidence of crime. Thus, an affidavit stating a truckload of lumber had been unloaded at defendant's residence at night makes it sufficiently probable that the lumber would be found there, but yet is defective because it fails to connect the lumber with any criminal offense. A second type of situation is that in which it is clear that certain identifiable items are connected with criminal activity, but the difficult question is whether it is probable that those items are to be found at the specified place. For example, if a warrant to search a person's apartment for drugs was based upon an affidavit disclosing that he had made an isolated street sale of drugs at a distant location, it might be doubted whether there had been a sufficient showing that he probably keeps a stash of drugs at the apartment.

§ 3.4   Search Warrants

(a) When Warrant May Be Utilized. Later sections of this Chapter define the various situations—such as search incident to arrest, search in response to exigent circumstances, and search by consent—in which the police may conduct a search without first obtaining a search warrant. By examination of the boundaries of those warrantless search categories, it may be determined when a search warrant *must* be obtained in order to conduct a lawful search under the Fourth Amendment. By comparison, the concern here is with whether there are some situations in which, because of what is sought, from whom it is sought, or how it would be obtained, not even the usual protections of the search warrant process will permit the search to be made.

At one time, under what came to be known as the "mere evidence" rule, search warrants could only be used to find property that constituted an instrumentality or fruit of crime or contraband.[1] But this rule was rejected in *Warden v. Hayden*;[2] the Court noted that nothing in the Fourth Amendment supported such a rule and that nothing in the nature of the property seized as evidence renders it more private than other property, particularly since the same object could be "mere evidence" in one case and an instrumentality in another. The evidence seized in *Hayden* was items of clothing, and the Court cautioned that they "are not 'testimonial' or 'communicative' in nature, and their introduction therefore did not compel respondent to become a witness against himself in violation of the Fifth Amendment." The self-incrimination issue was finally resolved in *Andresen v. Maryland*,[3] upholding the seizure of business records pursuant to a search warrant. Though the records were incriminating and some contained statements made by the petitioner, the Court concluded that when a search warrant rather than a subpoena is used there is no Fifth Amendment violation because "the individual against whom the search is directed is not required to aid in the discovery, production, or authentication of incriminating evidence."

Whenever the seizure of large quantities of books or films or similar materials is contemplated for the purpose of bringing about their destruction as contraband, the protections afforded by the search warrant process will not suffice. Rather, under such circumstances

there must be a prior judicial determination of obscenity in an *adversary* proceeding in order to avoid "danger of abridgement of the right of the public in a free society to unobstructed circulation of nonobscene books."[4] That rule does not bar use of the usual search warrant procedures in order to obtain a limited number of copies of an allegedly obscene publication for evidentiary purposes. The usual warrant procedures will also suffice for seizure of a single copy of an allegedly obscene film, provided (i) that "a prompt judicial determination of the obscenity issue in an adversary proceeding is available at the request of any interested party," and (ii) that copying of the film is permitted "on a showing to the trial court that other copies of the film are not available" to the exhibitor pending that determination.[5]

Some intrusions into the body are so extreme that they cannot be permitted at all, and some require more than the usual search warrant safeguards. In *Rochin v. California*,[6] the Court was confronted with a case in which the police made a forcible entry into Rochin's room and, upon observing him put two capsules in his mouth, unsuccessfully attempted to extract them by force, after which they took him to a hospital where a doctor forced an emetic solution through a tube into Rochin's stomach, resulting in vomiting by which the two capsules were retrieved. Characterizing this series of events as "conduct that shocks the conscience," the Court concluded the evidence had to be suppressed because the police actions violated Fourteenth Amendment due process.[7] But in *Schmerber v. California*,[8] where a physician took a blood sample at police direction from an injured arrestee over his objection, the majority ruled that the extraction of blood violated neither the due process clause nor the Fourth Amendment. The Court identified three factors that were critical

---

§ 3.4

1. Gouled v. United States, 255 U.S. 298, 41 S.Ct. 261, 65 L.Ed. 647 (1921).

2. 387 U.S. 294, 87 S.Ct. 1642, 18 L.Ed.2d 782 (1967).

3. 427 U.S. 463, 96 S.Ct. 2737, 49 L.Ed.2d 627 (1976).

4. A Quantity of Copies of Books v. Kansas, 378 U.S. 205, 84 S.Ct. 1723, 12 L.Ed.2d 809 (1964).

5. Heller v. New York, 413 U.S. 483, 93 S.Ct. 2789, 37 L.Ed.2d 745 (1973).

6. 342 U.S. 165, 72 S.Ct. 205, 96 L.Ed. 183 (1952).

7. The police conduct was not assessed in Fourth Amendment terms, for at that time the Fourth Amendment exclusionary rule had not yet been held applicable to the states.

8. 384 U.S. 757, 86 S.Ct. 1826, 16 L.Ed.2d 908 (1966).

to that holding: (i) there had been a "clear indication" that the extraction would produce evidence of crime, i.e, that defendant was intoxicated while driving; (ii) the test was "a reasonable one" in the sense that such tests are "commonplace" and involve "virtually no risk, trauma, or pain"; and (iii) the test "was performed in a reasonable manner," in that the blood was "taken by a physician in a hospital environment according to accepted medical practices."

Similarly, court-ordered surgery has been allowed where (1) the evidence sought was relevant, could have been obtained in no other way, and there was probable cause to believe that the operation would produce it; (2) the operation was minor, was performed by a skilled surgeon, and every possible precaution was taken to guard against any surgical complications, so that the risk of permanent injury was minimal; (3) before the operation was performed the court held an adversary hearing at which the defendant appeared with counsel; and (4) thereafter and before the operation was performed the defendant was afforded an opportunity for appellate review. In *Winston v. Lee*,[9] the Supreme Court applied the *Schmerber* balancing test to the surgery issue by focusing "on the extent of the intrusion on respondent's privacy interests and on the State's need for the evidence," and concluded that in the case before it the lower court had properly declined to authorize surgery to remove a bullet. The Court placed particular emphasis upon two facts: (i) "the proposed surgery, which for purely medical reasons required the use of a general anesthetic, would be an 'extensive' intrusion on respondent's personal privacy and bodily integrity"; and (ii) the state's need for the bullet to establish that defendant was the robber shot by the victim was not high, as the state had "substantial additional evidence" that defendant was the robber.

Zurcher v. Stanford Daily[10] concerned execution of a warrant at a newspaper's offices for photographs of demonstrators who had injured several policemen. The lower court had reasoned that the much less intrusive subpoena duces tecum should ordinarily be utilized against nonsuspects, and concluded "that unless the Magistrate has before him a sworn affidavit establishing proper cause to believe that the materials in question will be destroyed, or that a subpoena duces tecum is otherwise 'impractical,' a search of a third party for materials in his possession is unreasonable *per se*, and therefore violative of the Fourth Amendment." The Supreme Court disagreed, observing that there was nothing in the language or history of the Fourth Amendment to support such a distinction, and that the Amendment "has itself struck the balance between privacy and public need" by permitting issuance of warrants to search property in *all* cases upon a showing of probable cause. Dissenting Justice Stevens cogently responded that this history should not be controlling because the risk to third parties alluded to by the lower court was virtually nonexistent prior to the recent abandonment of the "mere evidence" rule. But he provided no answer to the other point made by the majority: "that search warrants are often employed early in an investigation, perhaps before the identity of any likely criminal and certainly before all the perpetrators are or could be known," so that as a practical matter it would seldom be possible for the police to show which seemingly blameless third parties were in fact involved in the criminal activity or sufficiently sympathetic to those who were involved to destroy or remove evidence implicating them.

The Court in *Zurcher* went on to reject the contention that the First Amendment ordinarily bars execution of a search warrant on the premises of a newsgathering organization, but did stress the need for courts to "apply the warrant requirements with particular exactitude when First Amendment interests would be endangered by the search." So too, courts have held that the Sixth Amendment does not preclude the issuance of warrants to search law offices, but that certain precautions may be needed, both in setting the scope of the search and in its mode of execution, because of

9.   470 U.S. 753, 105 S.Ct. 1611, 84 L.Ed.2d 662 (1985).

10.   436 U.S. 547, 98 S.Ct. 1970, 56 L.Ed.2d 525 (1978).

the potential for undermining the attorney-client privilege and the work product doctrine, thereby chilling communication between lawyer and client and hampering trial preparation.

(b) The "Neutral and Detached Magistrate" Requirement. The search warrant process is preferred because it involves a "neutral and detached magistrate" in the critical decision of whether to permit the search, and thus it is necessary to ask what kinds of persons under what circumstances may be allowed to issue warrants under the Fourth Amendment. In *Coolidge v. New Hampshire*,[11] for example, the warrant was issued by the state attorney general, acting as a justice of the peace, although he had personally taken charge of the murder investigation to which the warrant related and was later to serve as chief prosecutor at trial. To the state's argument that the attorney general had in fact acted as a "neutral and detached magistrate," the majority responded "that there could hardly be a more appropriate setting than this for a *per se* rule of disqualification rather than a case-by-case evaluation of all the circumstances," as "prosecutors and policemen simply cannot be asked to maintain the requisite neutrality with regard to their own investigations." The courts are not in agreement as to whether this *per se* rule also applies when the person issuing the warrant had law enforcement responsibilities that did not or could not extend to the case for which the warrant was sought, but there is much to be said for the proposition that any effort to assess the neutrality of a law enforcement official in such instances on a case-by-case basis would involve the lower courts in a complicated fact-finding process better avoided by a prophylactic rule.

At issue in *Connally v. Georgia*,[12] was a warrant issued by an unsalaried justice of the peace who received five dollars for each warrant issued but nothing for reviewing and denying a warrant application. A unanimous Court held that a warrant issued under such circumstances violated the protections of the Fourth Amendment:

> His financial welfare * * * is enhanced by positive action and is not enhanced by a negative action. The situation, again, is one which offers "a possible temptation to the average man as a judge * * * or it might lead him not to hold the balance nice, clear and true between the State and the accused." It is, in other words, another situation where the defendant is subjected to what surely is judicial action by an officer of a court who "has a direct, personal, substantial, pecuniary interest" in his conclusion to issue or deny the warrant.

The Court held in *Shadwick v. City of Tampa*[13] that municipal court clerks could constitutionally issue *arrest* warrants for breach of municipal ordinances. A unanimous Court concluded that a "magistrate," in the Fourth Amendment sense, need not necessarily be a lawyer or judge, but "must meet two tests. He must be neutral and detached, and he must be capable of determining whether probable cause exists for the requested arrest or search." These tests were found to be met because the clerk worked within the judicial branch and, by virtue of his position, would be able to determine if there was probable cause as to "common offenses covered by a municipal code." *Shadwick* has been relied upon in holding that *search* warrants may be issued by nonlawyer commissioners or judges, but there is something to be said for the conclusion that search warrant cases are different because the probable cause issues are much more complex and likely to be beyond the ken of a layman.

The conduct of the magistrate in a particular case may show that he was not then "neutral and detached," as is illustrated by *Lo–Ji Sales, Inc. v. New York*,[14] where a town justice issued an open-ended search warrant for obscene materials and then accompanied the police during its execution and made probable cause determinations at that time as to particular articles. In rejecting the claim that the on-the-scene determinations saved the war-

---

11. 403 U.S. 443, 91 S.Ct. 2022, 29 L.Ed.2d 564 (1971).

12. 429 U.S. 245, 97 S.Ct. 546, 50 L.Ed.2d 444 (1977).

13. 407 U.S. 345, 92 S.Ct. 2119, 32 L.Ed.2d 783 (1972).

14. 442 U.S. 319, 99 S.Ct. 2319, 60 L.Ed.2d 920 (1979).

rant, the Court stated that there had been "an erosion of whatever neutral and detached posture existed at the outset" because the justice "allowed himself to become a member, if not the leader of the search party which was essentially a police operation."

(c) Oath or Affirmation; Record. The Fourth Amendment command that "no Warrants shall issue but upon probable cause, supported by Oath or affirmation," has prompted litigation concerning what information, transmitted in what fashion and under what circumstances, may be taken into account later in deciding whether a warrant was issued on probable cause. In *Whiteley v. Warden*[15] the Court ruled that "an otherwise insufficient affidavit cannot be rehabilitated by testimony concerning information possessed by the affiant when he sought the warrant but not disclosed to the issuing magistrate," reasoning that a contrary rule would "render the warrant requirement of the Fourth Amendment meaningless." Where by statute or court rule a search warrant may issue only upon affidavit, a defective affidavit may not be saved by oral statements to the magistrate, even if they were given under oath. Such reliance on oral testimony does not violate the Fourth Amendment, and while it has been held that this is so even when no contemporaneous record was made, it has been persuasively argued that reliance upon oral testimony should not be allowed in such a case because there is too much leeway for after-the-fact rehabilitation of insufficient testimony. Such utilization of oral testimony must be distinguished from the so-called oral or telephonic search warrant procedure authorized in some jurisdictions, whereby the affiant gives his sworn statement to the magistrate via telephone or other means of communication, after which if the magistrate approves issuance of the warrant he causes an original warrant to be prepared and orally authorizes the officer to prepare a duplicate warrant for use in execution. It has been held that this procedure complies with the "Oath or affirmation" requirement and is not otherwise constitutionally defective.

Whether the information is transmitted orally or in writing, the "Oath or affirmation" requirement means the information must be sworn to. No particular ceremony is necessary to constitute the act of swearing; it is only necessary that something be done that is understood by both the magistrate and the affiant to constitute the act of swearing. The true test is whether the procedures followed were such that perjury could be charged therein if any material allegation contained therein is false. There is a split of authority as to whether a false-name affidavit, utilized to conceal the identity of an informer-affiant, meets that test.

(d) Probable Cause: The Facially–Sufficient Affidavit. Until *Franks v. Delaware*,[16] courts were split on whether a defendant could ever introduce additional evidence at a suppression hearing for the purpose of proving that some of the allegations in a facially-sufficient search warrant affidavit were false. The Supreme Court in *Franks,* rejecting the lower court's absolute ban upon such evidence, stressed several "pressing considerations": (i) "a flat ban on impeachment of veracity could denude the probable cause requirement of all meaning," as an officer could resort to false allegations and "remain confident that the ploy was worthwhile"; (ii) the hearing before the magistrate, because "necessarily ex parte" and "frequently * * * marked by haste," "not always will suffice to discourage lawless or reckless misconduct"; (iii) *Mapp* rejected the claim that alternative sanctions are likely "to fill the gap"; (iv) given the fact the magistrate's determination of the sufficiency of the evidence is now open to challenge at the suppression hearing, also allowing veracity challenges "would not diminish the importance and solemnity of the warrant-issuing process"; (v) probable cause is already at issue at the suppression hearing, and thus the claim this added challenge "will confuse the issue of the defendant's guilt with the issue of the State's possible misbehavior is footless"; and (vi) allowing a veracity challenge does not extend

---

15. 401 U.S. 560, 91 S.Ct. 1031, 28 L.Ed.2d 306 (1971).

16. 438 U.S. 154, 98 S.Ct. 2674, 57 L.Ed.2d 667 (1978).

the exclusionary rule to a new area, as there is "no principled basis for distinguishing between the question of the sufficiency of an affidavit, which also is subject to a post-search re-examination, and the question of its integrity."

As for what inaccuracies jeopardize the warrant, the Court in *Franks* held it must be established "that a false statement knowingly and intentionally, or with reckless disregard for the truth, was included by the affiant in the warrant affidavit." This means, as the Court emphasized, that "allegations of negligence or innocent mistake are insufficient." Some have argued that even innocent mistakes should be covered, but surely this is not so, as the Fourth Amendment only requires that the affiant act reasonably. But because that is the case, one might logically argue that negligent (i.e., unreasonable) mistakes should be covered. The Court in *Franks* did not explain its failure to draw the line in that way, but may have been influenced by doubts as to whether negligent misrepresentations could be effectively deterred and by the difficulty in determining whether an officer was negligent or completely innocent in not checking his facts further.

Franks emphasizes that the deliberate falsity or reckless disregard must be "that of the affiant, not of any nongovernmental informant." This means that if a private informer gives information to an officer who then is the affiant, reporting what he was told and why he has reason to consider the informer reliable (e.g., past experience with him), the defendant could challenge the accuracy of the officer's recitation of what he was told or why he believed the informer reliable, but may not raise the issue of whether in fact the informer was lying to the officer. This is as it should be, for the Fourth Amendment "probable cause" test requires not absolute certainty but only that the government have good reason for believing in the existence of the necessary facts. *Franks* strongly intimates that the result would be otherwise if the officer-affiant received his information from another policeman, as the Court took note of its declaration on a prior occasion "that police could not

insulate one officer's deliberate misstatement merely by relaying it through an officer-affiant personally ignorant of its falsity." As for the unusual situation in which a private person is himself the affiant and makes a deliberately or recklessly false statement, there has been no government wrongdoing in such a case, and thus it would seem that the warrant should be upheld if the cooperating police and the magistrate had reasonable grounds to believe the affiant.

Franks leaves no doubt as to what consequences are to follow from the requisite inaccuracies. No hearing is needed unless "the alleged false statement is necessary to the finding of probable cause," and suppression is to occur only if the defendant proves perjury or reckless disregard *and* it then appears that "with the affidavit's false material set to one side, the affidavit's remaining content is insufficient to establish probable cause." This is a sound result in the case of reckless misrepresentation, but the Court in *Franks* never explained why it rejected the position that a number of other courts had previously adopted, namely, that intentional falsehoods always render the warrant invalid because the fullest deterrent sanctions of the exclusionary rule should be applied to such serious and deliberate wrongdoing.

To obtain a *Franks* hearing, the defendant must "point out specifically the portion of the warrant affidavit that is claimed to be false" and give "a statement of supporting reasons. Affidavits or sworn or otherwise reliable statements of witnesses should be furnished, or their absence satisfactorily explained." If that threshold showing is made, then a hearing is held at which the defendant has the burden to prove "by a preponderance of the evidence" that the challenged statements are false and that their inclusion in the affidavit amounted to perjury or reckless disregard for the truth. The *Franks* allocation of the burden is unjust; it should suffice that the defendant proves the statements false, after which the affiant should have to show that the false statement was not intentionally or deliberately made, for he alone is in a position to justify his errors. Indeed, without access to the informant it may be impossible for the defendant even to prove that the affiant (rather than the informant) lied, and thus it is to be doubted that this burden may constitutionally be imposed on defendant if at the same time the informer privilege is used to deny defendant the identity of the informant.[17]

(e) Particular Description of Place to Be Searched. The Fourth Amendment provides that no warrants shall issue except those "particularly describing the place to be searched." Absolute perfection in description is not required; it "is enough if the description is such that the officer with a search warrant can, with reasonable effort, ascertain and identify the place intended."[18] As for urban premises, the common practice is to identify the place by street address. This is sufficient, but a street address is not essential when other descriptive facts identify the premises to be searched. Rural property is often described by giving the owner's name and general directions for reaching it, which will suffice.

Problems arise when a facially-sufficient description is determined to be less precise than was assumed, as where the warrant refers to apartment 3 in a certain building but there are apartments with that number on each floor, or where identifying numbers and other descriptive facts do not all fit the same premises. In these circumstances, courts are inclined to permit officers to resolve the matter on the basis of other facts (e.g., owner's name) not in the warrant description but known to them from the affidavit or otherwise, or by making common-sense judgments as to which of the several descriptive facts was most likely mistaken.

A search warrant for an apartment house or hotel or other multiple-occupancy building will usually be held invalid if it fails to describe the particular subunit to be searched with sufficient definiteness to preclude a search of one or more subunits indiscriminately. This is because the basic requirement of the Fourth Amendment is that the officers who are commanded to search be able from the particular description of the search warrant to identify the specific place for which there is probable cause. This means that, in the absence of a probable cause showing as to all the living units so as to justify a search of them all, a search warrant directed at a multiple-occupancy structure will ordinarily be held invalid if it describes the premises only by street number or other identification common to all the subunits located within the structure. A significant exception to that rule is: if the building in question from its outward appearance would be taken to be a single-occupancy structure and neither the affiant nor other investigating officers nor the executing officers knew or had reason to know of the structure's actual multiple-occupancy character until execution of the warrant was under way, then the warrant is not defective for failure to specify a subunit within the named building. This exception is sensible if narrowly construed so as to apply only when: (i) the multiple-occupancy character of the building was not known and could not have been discovered by reasonable investigation; (ii) the discovery of the multiple occupancy occurred only after the police had proceeded so far that withdrawal would jeopardize the search; and (iii) upon discovery of the multiple-occupancy, reasonable efforts were made to determine which subunit is most likely connected with the criminality under investigation and to confine the search accordingly.

A similar situation was involved in *Maryland v. Garrison*,[19] where police obtained and executed a search warrant for "the premises known as 2036 Park Avenue third floor apartment," only to discover thereafter that the third floor was divided into two apartments and that the contraband they had discovered was in the apartment of a person not theretofore suspected. The Court held the warrant itself was valid, though "we now know that the description of that place was broader than appropriate"; such a warrant is invalid, the Court explained, only if when obtained "the

---

17. Cf. Lego v. Twomey, 404 U.S. 477, 92 S.Ct. 619, 30 L.Ed.2d 618 (1972), declaring that suppression hearing procedures must be such as to allow "a reliable and clearcut determination" of the defendant's claim.

18. Steele v. United States, 267 U.S. 498, 45 S.Ct. 414, 69 L.Ed. 757 (1925).

19. 480 U.S. 79, 107 S.Ct. 1013, 94 L.Ed.2d 72 (1987).

officers had known, or even if they should have known, that there were two separate dwelling units on the third floor." Similarly, the execution of the warrant was lawful as well, as "the officers' failure to realize the overbreadth of the warrant was objectively understandable and reasonable."[20]

A search pursuant to a warrant into certain premises may be upheld notwithstanding the absence of *any* description whatsoever of those premises. Such a possibility is contemplated by the federal electronic eavesdropping/wiretapping law, for while there is a general requirement that there be "a particular description of the nature and location of the facilities from which or the place where the communication is to be intercepted,"[21] such description is unnecessary as to interception of an oral communication if "such specification is not practical" and as to wire or electronic communication if there is "a purpose [by the person whose communications are to be intercepted] to thwart interception by changing facilities."[22] Rather, in either of those circumstances it will suffice if "the person committing the offense and whose communications are to be intercepted" is identified.[23] The courts have concluded that this latter provision satisfies the Fourth Amendment's particularly requirement, often noting in the process that the Supreme Court has in another context ruled that advance identification in the warrant of the place to be searched is unnecessary.[24]

As for a warrant to search a vehicle, there are many descriptive facts that can be given: owner's or operator's name, make, model, year, color, license number, location, etc. A few of these, such as make-plus-license or make-plus-operator, are sufficient to meet the Fourth Amendment particularity requirement. Assuming an otherwise sufficient description, it is not necessary that the warrant indicate the location of the car or the name of the owner. When a warrant is issued for search of certain premises and "all automobiles thereon," it is likely to be vulnerable to attack because of insufficiency of description and lack of probable cause extending also to such vehicles. As for a facially-sufficient vehicle description that turns out to be partially erroneous because not all of the facts fit, the rule is the same as noted above as to premises: the warrant will still be upheld if other facts known by the executing officer or reasonable inferences by him as to where the mistake lies make it possible to identify a particular vehicle.

As for the infrequent cases in which a warrant is obtained to *search* a person,[25] the individual must be described with such particularity that he may be identified with reasonable certainty. The person's name will suffice, but a name is not essential if certain other facts, such as location and physical description, are given. Sometimes a search warrant will authorize the search of a specified premises or vehicle and in addition "any and all persons found therein"; such a warrant is not lacking particularity in the sense that the officer will be unable to ascertain to whom the warrant applies, but may well be defective because the probable cause showing is insufficient in that it does not establish that anyone present at the time of warrant execution probably is in-

---

20. Alluding to the line of lower court authority summarized in the preceding paragraph, the three dissenters in *Garrison* distinguished the instant case, where the building *was* known to be of a multiple-occupancy character, as one that imposed an obligation on the police to "make an investigation adequate to draw the warrant with sufficient specificity." They reasoned that neither the warrant nor its execution were valid, as the police should have known when obtaining the warrant and did know when executing it that there were seven units in the 3-story building, and thus "should have been aware that further investigation was necessary to eliminate the possibility of more than one unit's being located on the third floor."

21. 18 U.S.C.A. § 2518(1)(b).

22. 18 U.S.C.A. § 2518(11).

23. 18 U.S.C.A. § 2518(11).

24. United States v. Karo, 468 U.S. 705, 104 S.Ct. 3296, 82 L.Ed.2d 530 (1984). This aspect of *Karo* is discussed in § 3.2 at note 75.

25. See, e.g., Conn v. Gabbert, 526 U.S. 286, 119 S.Ct. 1292, 143 L.Ed.2d 399 (1999), where a search warrant for an attorney's person was served while his client was a witness before a grand jury. The Court in *Conn* held "that the Fourteenth Amendment right to practice one's calling is not violated by the execution of a search warrant, whether calculated to annoy or even to prevent consultation with a grand jury witness."

volved in the criminal activity in such a way as to have evidence thereof on his person.

(f) Particular Description of Things to Be Seized. Another specific command of the Fourth Amendment is that no warrants shall issue except those "particularly describing the * * * things to be seized." Speaking of that limitation, the Supreme Court said in *Marron v. United States:*[26] "The requirement that warrants shall particularly describe the things to be seized makes general searches under them impossible and prevents the seizure of one thing under a warrant describing another." A particular description of the objects to be seized does aid in preventing general searches, as that description determines the permissible intensity and length of the search that may be undertaken in executing the warrant. As for the second objective of preventing the seizure of objects on the mistaken assumption that they fall within the magistrate's authorization, *Marron* goes on to say that "nothing is left to the discretion of the officer executing the warrant," but few warrants could pass such a strict test, and thus it is more accurate to say that the warrant must be sufficiently definite so that the officer executing it can identify the property sought with reasonable certainty. A third purpose underlying the particularity requirement, not mentioned in *Marron,* is to prevent "the issuance of warrants on loose, vague or doubtful bases of fact."[27] That is, the requirement of particularity is closely tied to the requirement of probable cause to search, under which it must be probable (i) that the described items are connected with criminal activity, and (ii) that they are to be found in the place searched. The less precise the description of the things to be seized, the more likely it will be that either or both of those probabilities has not been established. (By the same token, a clear statement of the objects to be seized will be defective if it is broader than can be justified by the probable cause showing.)

Consistent with these three purposes are certain general principles that may be distilled from the decided cases in this area. They are: (1) A greater degree of ambiguity will be tolerated when the police have done the best that could be expected under the circumstances, by acquiring all the descriptive facts reasonable investigation of this type of crime could be expected to uncover and by ensuring that all of those facts were included in the warrant. (2) A more general type of description will be sufficient when the nature of the objects to be seized are such that they could not be expected to have more specific characteristics. (3) A less precise description is required of property that is, because of its particular character, contraband. (4) Failure to provide all of the available descriptive facts is not a basis for questioning the adequacy of the description when the omitted facts could not have been expected to be of assistance to the executing officer. (5) An error in the statement of certain descriptive facts is not a basis for questioning the adequacy of the description if the executing officer was nonetheless able to determine, from the other facts provided, that the object seized was that intended by the description. (6) Greater care in description is ordinarily called for when the type of property sought is generally in lawful use in substantial quantities. (7) A more particular description than otherwise might be necessary is required when other objects of the same general classification are likely to be found at the particular place to be searched. (8) The greatest care in description is required when the consequences of a seizure of innocent articles by mistake is most substantial, as when the objects to be seized are books or films[28] or the papers of a newsgathering organization.[29] (9) The mere fact that some items were admittedly improperly seized in execution of the warrant does not mean that the warrant was not sufficiently particular. (10) The Fourth Amendment's particularity requirement does not require particularity with respect to the criminal activity suspected. (11)

26. 275 U.S. 192, 48 S.Ct. 74, 72 L.Ed. 231 (1927).

27. Go–Bart Importing Co. v. United States, 282 U.S. 344, 51 S.Ct. 153, 75 L.Ed. 374 (1931).

28. Stanford v. Texas, 379 U.S. 476, 85 S.Ct. 506, 13 L.Ed.2d 431 (1965).

29. Zurcher v. Stanford Daily, 436 U.S. 547, 98 S.Ct. 1970, 56 L.Ed.2d 525 (1978).

Some leeway will be tolerated where it appears additional time could have resulted in a more particularized description, where there was some urgency to conduct a search before the defendant had the opportunity to remove or destroy the evidence.

A defective description in the warrant sometimes may be saved by an adequate description in the affidavit. At a minimum it must appear that the executing officer also had the affidavit with him and made reference to it (or, some courts say, that the executing officer was the affiant), but some courts require that the two documents be physically connected and that the warrant expressly refer to the affidavit. However, a warrant with an insufficient description may not be rehabilitated by showing that the executing officer was aware of other facts that enabled him to know exactly what things were intended to be covered, or that the officer for that reason or by luck only seized the items an adequate description would have covered.

If a search warrant is issued to search a place for several items, but it is later determined that not all of those items are described with sufficient particularity or that probable cause does not exist as to all of the items described, it is often possible to sever the tainted portion of the warrant from the valid portion so that evidence found in execution of the latter will be admissible. Assume, for example, a warrant for a gun used in and money taken in a bank robbery, and assume also that there is probable cause to search for the gun and that it is particularly described but that there is either no probable cause or no adequate description of the money. If the police, while looking in a desk drawer for the gun, were to find money that by its wrappings clearly came from that robbery, the money would be admissible because found in plain view in execution of the valid part of the warrant. But if the money was found after the gun was located or by looking where the gun could not be (e.g., an envelope), the money would not be admissible.

(g) Time of Execution. Some jurisdictions provide by statute or court rule that a search warrant must be executed within a certain time after issuance, such as ten days, in which case execution after the specified time will result in exclusion of the evidence. Sometimes a delay in execution will amount to a Fourth Amendment violation, for such delay is constitutionally permissible only where the probable cause recited in the affidavit continues until the time of execution. It is possible, therefore, that an unconstitutional delay may have occurred notwithstanding execution within the time set by rule or statute, and, of course, notwithstanding the fact that the jurisdiction has set no fixed time within which warrants must be executed.

About half of the states restrict the execution of search warrants to daytime hours absent some special showing and authorization. One common restriction is that the affidavit must be "positive" the property sought is on the premises, which has not been read literally but has been construed to require a much stronger probability showing than otherwise would be necessary. A second, more sensible approach is to require a special showing of a need to execute the warrant in the nighttime. Relatively little attention has been given to the question of whether special limitations upon nighttime searches flow from the Fourth Amendment, but in *Gooding v. United States*[30] three members of the Court took the view that a special showing of need for such a search was constitutionally required under the Fourth Amendment principle "that increasingly severe standards of probable cause are necessary to justify increasingly intrusive searches."

No special showing is needed to execute a search warrant for premises in the absence of the occupant, as such execution is not significantly different from that which would otherwise occur. An inventory is required in any event; the occupant if present could not necessarily detect or prevent a broader search; and the fact that such execution will likely require forcible entry is not a sufficient detriment to

---

30. 416 U.S. 430, 94 S.Ct. 1780, 40 L.Ed.2d 250 (1974).

make a search unreasonable where a warrant based on probable cause has been obtained. As for when the execution of the warrant is deliberately timed to occur without being known to those living at or using the premises (e.g., entry to install wiretapping devices), which appeared to concern the Supreme Court in *Berger v. New York*,[31] the cases upholding the federal wiretapping law have stressed that normal investigative procedures were tried and failed or appeared unlikely to succeed. It has been intimated that some such showing might also be necessary for a so-called "surreptitious entry" warrant, authorizing police to enter and merely scrutinize an ongoing criminal operation (e.g., an illegal drug lab) within, permitted in some circumstances by federal legislation.[32]

(h) Entry Without Notice. It is generally required, often by statute, that police give notice of their authority and purpose prior to making entry in the execution of a search warrant. This requirement, grounded in the Fourth Amendment,[33] serves several worthwhile purposes: (i) it decreases the potential for violence, as an unannounced breaking and entering into a home could quite easily lead an individual to believe that his safety was in peril and cause him to take defensive measures; (ii) it protects privacy by minimizing the chance of entry of the wrong premises and even when there is no mistake, allows those within a brief time to prepare for the police entry; and (iii) it prevents the physical destruction of property by giving the occupant the opportunity to admit the officer.

Such notice is ordinarily required as a prerequisite to entry[34] by force, by use of a pass key, or by merely opening a closed door. Whether passage through an open door is the kind of entry that ordinarily requires prior announcement is a matter that continues to divide the courts, though it would appear that the need for notice in such a case may depend upon other circumstances. Notice is not required when there is entry by ruse, as when an undercover agent gains access to premises, for in such circumstances the concerns underlying the notice requirement are not present. To comply with the notice requirement, police must identify themselves as police and indicate that they are present for the purpose of executing a search warrant, after which they may enter when admitted by an occupant or upon

---

31. 388 U.S. 41, 87 S.Ct. 1873, 18 L.Ed.2d 1040 (1967), noting the invalidated state wiretap law "permits uncontested entry without any showing of exigent circumstances."

32. The applicable statute, 18 U.S.C.A. § 1303a, says, with respect to issuance of a warrant or court order to search for and seize any property or any evidence of a federal offense, that any notice otherwise required may be delayed if three conditions are all met. These conditions are: (1) that "the court finds reasonable cause to believe that providing immediate notification of the execution of the warrant may have an adverse result" (cross-referencing a definition of that phrase in 18 U.S.C.A. § 2705 as: "(A) endangering the life or physical safety of an individual; (B) flight from prosecution; (C) destruction of or tampering with evidence; (D) intimidation of potential witnesses; or (E) otherwise seriously jeopardizing an investigation or unduly delaying a trial"); (2) that "the warrant prohibits the seizure of any tangible property, any wire or electronic communication * * *, or * * * any stored wire or electronic information, except where the court finds reasonable necessity for the seizure"; and (3) that "the warrant provides for the giving of such notice within a reasonable period of its execution, which period may thereafter be extended by the court for good cause shown."

33. In Wilson v. Arkansas, 514 U.S. 927, 115 S.Ct. 1914, 131 L.Ed.2d 976 (1995), a unanimous Court held "that the common-law principle of announcement * * * is an element of the reasonableness inquiry under the Fourth Amendment." The Court cautioned that this common-law principle "was never stated as an inflexible rule requiring announcement under all circumstances," and remanded for a determination whether announcement was unnecessary in this case because it would have produced an unreasonable risk of evidence destruction or harm to the executing officers.

Analysis under the federal knock-and-announce statute and under the Fourth Amendment was in a sense brought together in United States v. Ramirez, 523 U.S. 65, 118 S.Ct. 992, 140 L.Ed.2d 191 (1998), where the Court reasoned that because the statute "codifies the common law in this area," while "the common law in turn informs the Fourth Amendment," it follows that the Supreme Court's decision on the extent of the Fourth Amendment's protections in this area "serve as guideposts in construing the statute."

34. The typical case involves a full physical entry by a police officer, but apparently the Fourth Amendment has broader application, or at least the Supreme Court so assumed in United States v. Ramirez, 523 U.S. 65, 118 S.Ct. 992, 140 L.Ed.2d 191 (1998), where it characterized as an "entry" police action in breaking a garage window to deter the occupants from seeking a weapon in the garage, and where the occupants thereafter left the premises and were arrested outside, obviating any need for a full entry by the police.

being refused admittance (which includes both affirmative refusal and failure to respond to the announcement).

As for the failure-to-respond situation, the often litigated issue of how long the police must wait after announcement before entering was never directly addressed by the Supreme Court until *United States v. Banks,*[35] where the Court initially declared that the requirement is one of "reasonable execution," to be "fleshed out * * * case by case, largely avoiding categories and protocols for searches." In a case where there is "no reason to suspect an immediate risk of frustration or futility in waiting at all," *Banks* teaches, it is important "to give a person inside the chance to save his door," meaning "the reasonable wait time may well be longer when police make a forced entry, since they ought to be more certain the occupant has had time to answer the door." But *Banks* was not such a case, for the warrant was for cocaine being sold by defendant, so that "what matters is the opportunity to get rid of cocaine, which a prudent dealer will keep near a commode or kitchen sink," meaning there is thus "no reason * * * to peg the travel time to the location of the door."[36] Rather, given "the arrival of the police during the day, when anyone inside would probably have been up and around,"[37] the question is whether the elapsed time would suffice for "getting to the bathroom or the kitchen to start flushing cocaine down the drain." A unanimous Court, though conceding that the "call is a close one," concluded the 15–20 second wait by

the police before using a battering ram on the door was sufficient.[38]

Police are excused from the usual notice requirement in some instances. For a time, some courts applied a so-called "blanket rule" regarding when notice was excused; for example, in some states felony drug cases were assumed to *always* carry a risk of evidence destruction and physical harm to the police sufficient to justify entry without notice. But in *Richards v. Wisconsin,*[39] the Court rejected that approach because of "two serious concerns": (i) such an exception "contains considerable overgeneralization," as "not every drug investigation will pose these risks to a substantial degree" (as illustrated by the situation in which "the only individuals present in a residence have no connection with the drug activity"); and (ii) "the reasons for creating an exception in one category can, relatively easily, be applied to others," so that a felony drug exception could lead to an armed bank robbers exception, and so on. And thus, the *Richards* Court ruled, the police are excused only when they "have a reasonable suspicion[40] that knocking and announcing their presence, under the particular circumstances, would be dangerous or futile,[41] or that it would inhibit the effective investigation of the crime by, for example, allowing the destruction of evidence." The Court then concluded the entry without notice in *Richards* was nonetheless lawful because, as the state trial judge had properly concluded, the facts of the particular

---

35. ___ U.S. ___, 124 S.Ct. 521, 157 L.Ed.2d 343 (2003).

36. Meaning there is "no reliable basis for giving the proprietor of a mansion a longer wait than the resident of a bungalow, or an apartment like Banks's."

37. As for Banks' objection that he was in the shower at the time and did not hear the announcement, the Court responded that "the facts known to the police are what count in judging reasonable waiting time."

38. In such circumstances, the Court emphasized, the same "reasonable suspicion of exigent circumstances" suffices without regard to whether damage to the premises is necessary to gain entry.

As in *Ramirez,* note 33 supra, the Court then reached the same result under the federal knock-and-announce statute.

39. 520 U.S. 385, 117 S.Ct. 1416, 137 L.Ed.2d 615 (1997).

40. In United States v. Ramirez, 523 U.S. 65, 118 S.Ct. 992, 140 L.Ed.2d 191 (1998), the Court resolved a question not explicitly addressed in *Richards,* holding that "[w]hether such a 'reasonable suspicion' exists depends in no way on whether police must destroy property in order to enter."

41. Use of the word "futile" here may be intended to encompass what lower courts have commonly called the "useless gesture" exception to the notice requirement, which simply means that notice is not required when it is evident from the circumstances that the authority and purpose of the police is already known to those within the premises. The *Richards* case itself is arguably such a situation, though the Court instead dealt with it as one in which risk of evidence destruction was shown by awareness the police were knocking on the door.

case showed a sufficient risk of evidence destruction.[42] Similarly, in *United States v. Ramirez*,[43] a case involving intended execution of a search warrant to enter and seize a wanted person, the Court upheld the challenged entry without notice because the police "had a 'reasonable suspicion' that knocking and announcing their presence might be dangerous to themselves or to others."[44]

A small number of jurisdictions have adopted legislation permitting magistrates to issue search warrants specifically authorizing entry without prior notice upon a sufficient showing to the magistrate of a need to thereby prevent destruction of evidence or harm to the executing officers. It has sometimes been held that these so-called no-knock search warrants are unconstitutional because the existence of the requisite emergency can be judged only in light of circumstances of which the officer is aware at the moment of execution, but this is somewhat of an overstatement.[45] As for whether the Fourth Amendment *requires* the magistrate to pass on the no-knock issue if the facts are then available, the answer would appear to be no, as the Court in another context has rejected the contention that "search warrants also must include a specification of the precise manner in which they are to be executed."[46]

(i) Detention and Search of Persons. Police executing a search warrant sometimes search individuals found in the described place

at the commencement of the warrant execution or who arrive there during the course of the search of that place. On occasion this occurs because the warrant describes certain premises and also a certain person. There is no inherent defect in a single warrant that authorizes search of a place and a person, and thus the search in such a case will be a valid execution of the warrant, subject of course to the possibility that upon a subsequent motion to suppress it will be found that the information supporting the warrant did not show probable cause as to the named person. A second kind of situation is that in which a person at the scene is arrested and then searched. This will constitute a valid search incident to arrest *if* the arrest was lawful, but it must be remembered that mere presence at a place for which the police have a search warrant does not alone constitute grounds to arrest.[47]

If the person is not named in the warrant and cannot be lawfully arrested, the police may still desire to search him for the objects named in the search warrant. In *Ybarra v. Illinois*,[48] the state claimed that in such a situation the police should be entitled to search if there was only a reasonable suspicion, under the *Terry v. Ohio*[49] standard, that this person had the named objects on his person. But the Court, following the "governing

42. A police officer knocked on the door of Richard's hotel room and stated he was the maintenance man; Richards opened the door slightly, saw a uniformed officer outside, and then slammed the door, which the police then kicked in. "These actual circumstances—petitioner's apparent recognition of the officers combined with the easily disposable nature of the drugs—," the Court concluded, "justified the officer' ultimate decision to enter without first announcing their presence and authority."

43. 523 U.S. 65, 118 S.Ct. 992, 140 L.Ed.2d 191 (1998).

44. In elaborating upon the circumstances that there added up to the requisite suspicion, the Court mentioned (i) that a "reliable confidential informant" had notified police that the wanted person might be inside; (ii) that the police "had confirmed this possibility"; (iii) that the wanted person "was a prison escapee with a violent past"; (iv) that he "reportedly had access to a large supply of weapons"; and (v) that he "had vowed that he would 'not do federal time.' "

45. On occasion those circumstances will be known in advance. A risk of evidence destruction may be based upon

an informer's revelation that gambling records are on flash paper, or a risk of harm to the officer may be established upon information that the defendant regularly answers the door with a weapon at the ready.

But, if a no-knock warrant is sought but refused by the magistrate, this hardly means that the officers at the scene will inevitably lack grounds to enter without notice. As the Court stressed in *Richards*, supra note 39, "a magistrate's decision not to authorize a no-knock entry should not be interpreted to remove the officers' authority to exercise independent judgment concerning the wisdom of a no-knock entry at the time the warrant is being executed."

46. Dalia v. United States, 441 U.S. 238, 99 S.Ct. 1682, 60 L.Ed.2d 177 (1979) (court order authorizing interception of conversations need not specify covert entry as the manner of execution).

47. See § 3.3(f).

48. 444 U.S. 85, 100 S.Ct. 338, 62 L.Ed.2d 238 (1979).

49. 392 U.S. 1, 88 S.Ct. 1868, 20 L.Ed.2d 889 (1968).

principle" of *United States v. Di Re*,[50] concluded that the interest in productive warrant execution was not so strong as to justify a departure from the usual probable cause standard, and thus the police may lawfully search the person on the premises only upon probable cause that he has the named objects on his person. That probable cause was not present in *Ybarra,* where the person searched was merely a customer in a bar being searched for drugs.

Yet another possibility is that the police will want to search persons present for their own protection, that is, to ensure they will not be attacked with weapons while they proceed with execution of the warrant. The Court in *Ybarra* also spoke to this issue, and concluded that the *Terry* frisk standard was applicable in this context, so that an officer may conduct such a limited search of persons present "to find weapons that he reasonably believes or suspects are then in the possession of the person he has accosted."

As for whether a person on the premises where a search warrant is being executed sometimes may be detained incident to execution of the warrant absent grounds for arrest, the Court answered in the affirmative in *Michigan v. Summers*.[51] Using the balancing test of the *Terry* case,[52] the Court reasoned that such a detention was "substantially less intrusive" than a full-fledged arrest and served three important government interests: (i) "the legitimate law enforcement interest in preventing flight in the event that incriminating evidence is found"; (ii) "minimizing the risk of harm to the officers"; and (iii) "the orderly completion of the search," which "may be facilitated if the occupants of the premises are present." Although the *Summers* Court thus concluded that such a detention was permissible absent full probable cause, it is important to note that the Court did not merely extend *Terry* to this situation and require a case-by-case determination of whether there was reasonable suspicion sufficient to justify the detention. Rather, the Court opted to relieve police and lower courts of the necessity to engage in case-by-case balancing by announcing a general rule: detention of persons at the scene of a search warrant execution is permissible incident to that execution if (1) those persons are "occupants" (apparently meaning "residents," another term used by the Court), and (2) the warrant authorizes a "search for contraband" rather than a "search for evidence." This is a sensible rule, for it is in such circumstances that all three of the government interests mentioned above are likely to come into play.

(j) Scope and Intensity of the Search. A search made under authority of a search warrant may extend to the entire area covered by the warrant's description. For example, if the warrant authorizes a search of "premises" at a certain described geographical location, buildings standing on that land may be searched. If the place is identified by street number, the search may extend to those buildings within the curtilage and the yard within the curtilage. If the warrant specifies only a certain portion of a building, such as the first floor, only that portion may be searched, but if the warrant also refers to the curtilage the search may extend to such areas as courtyards, driveways and parking areas. Police may pass through areas adjacent to the described premises (so that what they see while doing so is a lawful "plain view") when such action is necessary to gain access to the described area.

In order to search containers in the described premises that might contain the items named in the warrant, it is not necessary that the warrant also describe those containers. But where the container is a personal item, caution is required, for the warrant will not inevitably extend to that item. In *United States v. Micheli*,[53] on the one hand, upholding

---

50. 332 U.S. 581, 68 S.Ct. 222, 92 L.Ed. 210 (1948) (holding that an occupant of a vehicle may not be subjected to a search merely because there are grounds to search the car).

51. 452 U.S. 692, 101 S.Ct. 2587, 69 L.Ed.2d 340 (1981).

52. Over the objection of the three dissenters, who argued that a departure from the probable cause standard was justified only in very limited circumstances, not including the present case, where there was "some governmental interest independent of the ordinary interest in investigating crime and apprehending suspects."

53. 487 F.2d 429 (1st Cir.1973).

search of a briefcase found in an office and known to belong to a co-owner of the business, the court reasoned that because he thus "had a special relation to the place, which meant that it could reasonably be expected that some of his personal belongings would be there," it was reasonable for the police to conclude that the warrant "comprehended within its scope those personal articles, such as his briefcase, which might be lying about the office." But in *Commonwealth v. Platou*,[54] concerning search of suitcases known to belong to the tenant's overnight guest, the court concluded the warrant authority did not extend to those containers because the probable cause showing did not cover them. Had there been some reason to believe that the tenant could have concealed the objects named in the warrant in his guest's suitcases, the result in *Platou* would have been different. (*Platou* was later overruled on the ground that "it would be ineffective and unworkable to require police officers to make the distinction between which articles of clothing and personal property belong to the resident and which belong to the visitor before beginning to search."[55] While similar "practical realities" were an important consideration in the Supreme Court's later holding in *Wyoming v. Houghton*[56] that probable cause to search a vehicle permits search of packages belonging to passengers, the *Houghton* holding does not itself encompass the present situation, as that holding was reached by a balancing of those realities against the "reduced expectation of privacy" that passengers have as to effects transported in vehicles.)

A single search warrant may be issued for certain premises and also for a described vehicle, in which case search of both will be lawful if the supporting affidavit establishes probable cause as to both. It has often been held that a warrant describing only premises authorizes search of vehicles found on those premises, a dubious proposition in any event, but certainly

not applicable as a matter of course to vehicles known to belong to a visitor.

The permissible intensity of the search within the described premises is determined by the description of the things to be seized. As the Supreme Court has put it, "the same meticulous investigation which would be appropriate in a search for two small canceled checks could not be considered reasonable where agents are seeking a stolen automobile or an illegal still."[57] This means the police may move objects to one side in the course of the search only if this will facilitate search into an area where the described items might be found. This means as well that in executing a warrant for certain documents, "some innocuous documents will be examined, at least cursorily, in order to determine whether they are, in fact, among those papers authorized to be seized."[58] And this also means that a search into closets, desks, boxes and other containers will exceed the authority of the warrant unless at least one of the items described in the warrant as an object of the search could be concealed therein. When the purposes of the warrant have been carried out, the authority to search is at an end. Thus, if the warrant describes only a particular package and it is found, any evidence discovered in a continuation of the search of the premises beyond that time must be suppressed. But under some circumstances, such as where the warrant authorizes search for "an unknown quantity of narcotics," the police apparently have a free hand—notwithstanding the quantity of the described item already found—to continue with the search until the entire described place has been covered. Police executing a search warrant are properly accompanied by others, even nonpolice, when "the presence of the third parties directly aided in the execution of the warrant," as when the owner of sought stolen property was along to make identification, but

---

54.　455 Pa. 258, 312 A.2d 29 (1973).

55.　Commonwealth v. Reese, 520 Pa. 29, 549 A.2d 909 (1988).

56.　526 U.S. 295, 119 S.Ct. 1297, 143 L.Ed.2d 408 (1999).

57.　Harris v. United States, 331 U.S. 145, 67 S.Ct. 1098, 91 L.Ed. 1399 (1947), dealing with the analogous

situation of search of premises incident to arrest at a time when it was deemed permissible to search defendant's premises if he was arrested there.

58.　Andresen v. Maryland, 427 U.S. 463, 96 S.Ct. 2737, 49 L.Ed.2d 627 (1976).

it is a violation of the Fourth Amendment for the police to bring along persons whose presence is "not in aid of the execution of the warrant."[59]

(k) What May Be Seized. At one time it was the rule, per *Marron v. United States*,[60] that the "requirement that warrants shall particularly describe the things to be seized * * * prevents the seizure of one thing under a warrant describing another." But in *Coolidge v. New Hampshire*[61] the Court held that unnamed objects "of incriminating character" could be seized under the "plain view" doctrine:

> As against the minor peril to Fourth Amendment protections, there is a major gain in effective law enforcement. Where, once an otherwise lawful search is in progress, the police inadvertently come upon a piece of evidence, it would often be a needless inconvenience, and sometimes dangerous—to the evidence or to the police themselves—to require them to ignore it until they have obtained a warrant particularly describing it.

Though the Court in *Coolidge* did not elaborate upon the proposition that the object found in plain view may be seized only if it is an "article of incriminating character," it has been properly interpreted to mean that there must exist probable cause that the object is a fruit, instrumentality or evidence of a crime.[62] In determining whether there is probable cause, it is necessary to consider what the executing officers knew concerning the nature of the crime under investigation, its elements, and possible means of proving those elements, as is illustrated by *Andresen v. Maryland*.[63]

There, the warrant was for documents relating to defendant's crime of false pretenses in the sale and conveyance of a certain Lot 13T, but the executing officers also seized documents pertaining to another lot in the same subdivision. In upholding the seizure, the Court stressed the perceived relevance of those documents in proving the intent-to-defraud element of the Lot 13T charge because the defendant had dealt with this other lot in essentially the same way and thus could not claim "his failure to deliver title to Lot 13T free of all encumbrances was mere inadvertence."

The Court in *Coolidge* cautioned that a seizure based upon the plain view doctrine "is legitimate only where it is immediately apparent to the police that they have evidence before them; the 'plain view' doctrine may not be used to extend a general exploratory search from one object to another until something incriminating at last emerges."[64] The Court referred to the concurring opinion in *Stanley v. Georgia*,[65] where police executing a warrant for gambling paraphernalia found reels of film that they viewed with a projector found in another room and then seized as obscene. The concurring opinion in *Stanley*, endorsed in *Coolidge*, said it was "not a case where agents in the course of a lawful search came upon contraband, criminal activity, or criminal evidence in plain view" because "the contents of the films could not be determined by mere inspection." If interpreted literally, the "immediately apparent" requirement might be viewed as barring any examination at all of an article beyond that necessary to determine it is not one of the items named in the warrant. For many years, most courts were not that

---

59. Wilson v. Layne, 526 U.S. 603, 119 S.Ct. 1692, 143 L.Ed.2d 818 (1999), which involved execution of an *arrest* warrant. For more on *Wilson*, including its significance in an exclusionary rule context, see § 3.6 at note 11.

60. 275 U.S. 192, 48 S.Ct. 74, 72 L.Ed. 231 (1927).

61. 403 U.S. 443, 91 S.Ct. 2022, 29 L.Ed.2d 564 (1971).

62. In Texas v. Brown, 460 U.S. 730, 103 S.Ct. 1535, 75 L.Ed.2d 502 (1983), the plurality opinion asserted that "the phrase 'immediate apparent' [in *Coolidge*] was very likely an unhappy choice of words, since it can be taken to imply that an unduly high degree of certainty as to the incriminating character of evidence is necessary for an application of the 'plain view' doctrine," and then concluded it was intended to be merely a "statement of the rule

* * * requiring probable cause for seizure in the ordinary case."

63. 427 U.S. 463, 96 S.Ct. 2737, 49 L.Ed.2d 627 (1976).

64. Later, in construing *Coolidge*, the Court stated that the incriminating character must *itself* be in plain view. In Horton v. California, 496 U.S. 128, 110 S.Ct. 2301, 110 L.Ed.2d 112 (1990), the Court gave, as one reason the seizure of vehicles *as* evidence in *Coolidge* did not meet the requirements for a plain view warrantless seizure, the failure to meet the "immediately apparent" requirement: "the cars were obviously in plain view, but their probative value remained uncertain until after the interiors were swept and examined microscopically."

65. 394 U.S. 557, 89 S.Ct. 1243, 22 L.Ed.2d 542 (1969).

strict; a limited inspection of an object, such as picking it up to note a brand name or serial number, was permitted as to objects not named in the warrant *provided* there was a pre-existing reasonable suspicion that the inspected items were the fruits, evidence or instrumentalities of crime. But that approach was rejected in *Arizona v. Hicks*,[66] holding full probable cause was needed to pick up an item of stereo equipment to ascertain its serial number (which revealed it was stolen property). The majority deemed it unwise "to send police and judges into a new thicket of Fourth Amendment law" by recognizing a third category of police conduct between "a plain-view inspection" requiring no suspicion and "a 'full-blown search'" requiring probable cause.

The most controversial aspect of the exploration of the plain view doctrine in *Coolidge* is the conclusion that "the discovery of evidence in plain view must be inadvertent" because, while "the inconvenience of procuring a warrant to cover an inadvertent discovery is great," "the situation is altogether different" when "the police know in advance the location of the evidence," for in such a case they could have easily had the object in question included in their warrant authorization. Though less than a majority of the Court subscribed to this limitation,[67] most lower courts embraced the inadvertence requirement, usually interpreted to mean that a discovery of objects not named in the warrant is *always* inadvertent, without regard to the personal hopes or expectations of the executing officers, if there were not sufficient grounds to justify the issuance of a warrant that also named those objects as among the things to be seized. Even so interpreted, the "inadvertent discovery" limitation is unsound, for it does nothing to prevent illegal

entries or to limit the scope of searches under a warrant, but only protects the possessory interest of a defendant in his effects, an interest hardly worth protecting by a difficult-to-administer rule whereunder the police turn out to have greater power if it is *not* shown at the suppression hearing that they had probable cause. Such considerations doubtless influenced the Court to hold in *Horton v. California*[68] that inadvertence "is not a necessary condition" to a plain view seizure. In *Horton,* the Court explained that adherence to the Fourth Amendment's particularity-of-description requirements "serves the interest in limiting the area and duration of the search that the inadvertence requirement inadequately protects."[69]

(*l*) Miscellaneous Requirements. By statute or court rule, many jurisdictions have imposed requirements upon the execution of search warrants that go beyond those already discussed. One common provision is that an officer executing a warrant must exhibit or deliver a copy of the warrant at the place searched, so that the aggrieved party will know there is color of authority for the search. Another is that the officer must provide a receipt for the things seized in execution of the warrant. Yet another is that a prompt return of an executed warrant, accompanied by an inventory of the things seized, be made to the issuing authority. Under the prevailing view, these provisions are deemed to be ministerial only, so that failure to comply with them does not void an otherwise valid search.

When a failure to leave an inventory serves to conceal from the absent occupant the fact that a search warrant execution occurred there, then the problem is more serious. In striking down a state wiretapping law, the

---

66. 480 U.S. 321, 107 S.Ct. 1149, 94 L.Ed.2d 347 (1987).

67. Four members of the Court vociferously dissented from any such qualification of the plain view doctrine, while Justice Harlan concurred in a part of the Stewart opinion other than that in which the "inadvertent discovery" limitation is set out.

68. 496 U.S. 128, 110 S.Ct. 2301, 110 L.Ed.2d 112 (1990).

69. The now-abandoned inadvertence requirement must be distinguished from the requirement, recognized

by some courts, that the search warrant execution must be made in "good faith," as would not be the case, for example, if officers with enforcement interests and responsibilities unrelated to the crime for which the warrant was issued participated in the execution of the search warrant. But *Horton* has been read as also extinguishing this doctrine, and even if that were not the case it would appear not to survive after Whren v. United States, 517 U.S. 806, 116 S.Ct. 1769, 135 L.Ed.2d 89 (1996), discussed in § 3.1 at note 39.

Supreme Court in *Berger v. New York*[70] object-ed it "has no requirement for notice as do conventional warrants, nor does it overcome this defect by requiring some showing of special facts." (The problem is solved in the federal wiretapping law by the provision that an inventory must be served within 90 days.[71]) The issue has recently arisen as to the so-called "surreptitious entry" warrant authorizing police to enter and look around during the occupant's absence, as to which the warrant must provide explicitly for notice "within a reasonable period of its execution."[72]

In the context of a civil action to recover seized tangible property, the Supreme Court in *City of West Covina v. Perkins*[73] concluded that a notice requirement exists as a matter of Fourteenth Amendment due process. The Court declared "that when law enforcement agents seize property pursuant to warrant, due process requires them to take reasonable steps to give notice that the property has been taken so the owner can pursue available remedies for its return." In the instant case the police had left at the premises where a search warrant was executed a notice of the warrant execution and an inventory of the property seized, so the Court did not have to "decide how detailed the notice of the seizure must be or when the notice must be given." But the Court did go on to hold that there is no constitutional requirement of "individualized notice of state-law remedies which, like those at issue here, are established by published, generally available statute and case law." Because of the context of the *Perkins* case, the Court had no occasion to consider whether violation of the due process notice requirement recognized there could serve as a basis for suppression of the seized evidence in a criminal prosecution.

§ 3.5 Seizure and Search of Persons and Personal Effects

(a) Arrest. "To deprive a person of his liberty by legal authority" is the traditional definition of arrest, and for many years courts tended to accept such a definition, so that a mere stopping of a vehicle constituted an illegal arrest if probable cause could be established only by consideration of facts obtained subsequent to the stopping. But this is no longer true in light of *Terry v. Ohio*,[1] which established (i) that a seizure need not be called an arrest in order to subject it to the requirements of the Fourth Amendment; and (ii) that a seizure limited in its intrusiveness may be reasonable under the Fourth Amendment even in the absence of the probable cause traditionally required for arrest.

If a person is stopped upon less than probable cause, after which the officer sees incriminating evidence, it must be determined whether this amounts to an illegal arrest at the moment of stopping, as the defendant will claim, or a lawful arrest after observation of the evidence, as the prosecution will contend. Though the fact the officer did not make a formal announcement of arrest is not controlling, it is sometimes said that for police restraint to be an arrest it must have been performed with the intent to effect an arrest and must have been so understood by the party arrested. But, while the prosecution can hardly deny the existence of an arrest in the face of both of these elements, this is not to say that the absence of one or the other always necessitates the conclusion there was yet no arrest. Because making the issue turn upon either the subjective intent of the police officer or the subjective perception of the suspect would mean that the matter would be decided by swearing contests, courts are now inclined to use an objective test. The question is said to be what a reasonable man, innocent of any crime, would have thought had he been in the defendant's shoes. Essentially the same approach is taken when the issue is not whether there was an arrest or some lesser seizure, but instead whether there was an arrest or merely

---

70. 388 U.S. 41, 87 S.Ct. 1873, 18 L.Ed.2d 1040 (1967).

71. 18 U.S.C.A. § 2518(8)(d).

72. See the applicable statute at note 32 supra..

73. 525 U.S. 234, 119 S.Ct. 678, 142 L.Ed.2d 636 (1999).

§ 3.5

1. 392 U.S. 1, 88 S.Ct. 1868, 20 L.Ed.2d 889 (1968).

a nonseizure voluntary presence by the defendant.

The question of when an arrest occurred cannot be answered in the abstract, that is, without consideration of why the question is being asked. Courts properly take a somewhat different approach when the prosecution is contending that an arrest was made at a particular time so as to justify a search as incident to that arrest. In this context, "the prosecution must be able to date the arrest as *early* as it chooses following the obtaining of probable cause,"[2] for given grounds for arrest and some degree of seizure that ripened into an arrest thereafter, the search should not be brought into question by speculation about the precise point at which the arrest occurred.

At common law, a peace officer was authorized to arrest a person for a felony without first obtaining an arrest warrant whenever he had "reasonable grounds to believe" that a felony had been committed and that the person to be arrested had committed it (i.e., what now constitutes Fourth Amendment probable cause). Under this approach, followed today by most jurisdictions, an arrest warrant is not required in a felony case even when it was feasible to obtain one. But it was not until *United States v. Watson*,[3] "the first square holding that the Fourth Amendment permits a duly authorized law enforcement officer to make a warrantless arrest in a public place[4] even though he had adequate opportunity to procure a warrant after developing probable cause for arrest,"[5] that the constitutionality of this rule was settled. The Court in *Watson* commenced with the proposition that a "strong presumption of constitutionality" was due the statute under which the arrest was made, and then concluded the presumption was not overcome in light of the fact that the statute was consistent with "the Court's prior cases," "the ancient common-law rule," and "the prevailing rule under state constitutions and statutes." The Court declined to trans-

form its oft-stated preference for arrest warrants "into a constitutional rule" and thereby "encumber litigation with respect to the existence of exigent circumstances, whether it was practicable to get a warrant, whether the suspect was about to flee, and the like." The *Watson* majority failed to examine the issue stated by the dissenters, "whether the privacy of our citizens will be better protected by ordinarily requiring a warrant to be issued before they may be arrested." Had they done so, they could have responded that a greatly expanded warrant system might well turn the warrant process into a mechanical routine without meaningful protection.

The common law rule with respect to misdemeanors was quite different: a warrant was required except when the offense occurred in the presence of the arresting officer, and some cases and commentators added a second requirement that the offense in question constitute a "breach of the peace." But because of the "divergent conclusions" reached on the latter point prior to adoption of the Fourth Amendment, as well as the fact that the post-Amendment history "is of two centuries of uninterrupted (and largely unchallenged) state and federal practice permitting warrantless arrests for misdemeanors not amounting to or involving breach of the peace," the Supreme Court has rejected the claim that this breach-of-the-peace limitation is a part of the Fourth Amendment's reasonableness requirement.[6] Most jurisdictions now follow a broader rule, usually that arrest without warrant is proper for *any* misdemeanor occurring in the officer's presence, sometimes that the felony arrest rule applies also to misdemeanors, and sometimes the middle position that warrantless misdemeanor arrests are permitted on probable cause if certain exigent circumstances are believed to be present. It appears that the Fourth Amendment presents no barrier to abolition of the felony-misdemeanor distinction

---

2. Peters v. New York, 392 U.S. 40, 88 S.Ct. 1889, 20 L.Ed.2d 917 (1968) (Harlan, J., concurring).

3. 423 U.S. 411, 96 S.Ct. 820, 46 L.Ed.2d 598 (1976).

4. A warrant is ordinarily required to enter private premises to arrest; see § 3.6(a).

5. As correctly characterized by Powell, J., concurring.

6. Atwater v. City of Lago Vista, 532 U.S. 318, 121 S.Ct. 1536, 149 L.Ed.2d 549 (2001).

so as to permit warrantless arrests on probable cause in all cases.[7]

As for the meaning of the "in presence" test, it certainly includes those instances in which the officer views the offense, even when done with binoculars or when instruments (e.g., a radar speed measuring device) must be utilized to make a judgment about what has been seen. An officer may utilize all of his senses in determining whether a misdemeanor is occurring, and thus, for example, there are situations in which the officer will detect the misdemeanor by hearing, smell or touch. But it is not enough that the officer relied only upon his own senses in determining that the misdemeanor occurred; the offense must occur in the officer's presence. Thus, an in presence arrest may not be made for the misdemeanor of driving under the influence when a policeman comes upon the scene of an accident and is told by an obviously intoxicated person that he had been driving the vehicle. (This illustration indicates why the "in presence" requirement is an unsatisfactory limitation upon the power of the police to make warrantless arrests.) Though the "in presence" rule might be construed as requiring that the misdemeanor *in fact* have occurred in the officer's presence, the modern view is that the officer may arrest if he has probable cause to believe the offense is being committed in his presence. This is sound, for it provides a workable standard (based on how the situation is reasonably perceived at the time, rather than how it turned out) for judging police conduct, and makes it apparent that the officer's senses need not directly detect the misdemeanor so long as they reveal facts providing the reasonable belief that the offense is *now* occurring. The "in presence" standard also imposes limits concerning the necessary timing of the arrest; such a warrantless arrest must be made promptly, that is, at the time of the offense or as soon thereafter as circumstances permit, meaning that some delay is tolerable when fairly attributable to pursuit of the offender or summoning assistance.

On the question of whether the lawfulness of a warrantless arrest is affected by the way in which the arrest is characterized by the police at the time of arrest or subsequent booking, it has sometimes been held that an arrest "for investigation" or "on suspicion" of a certain crime is unlawful. Those cases are in error; especially because such designations are often utilized to indicate that the situation requires special attention, such as evaluation by detectives or by the prosecutor's office, the lawfulness of the arrests should be determined upon the basis of the facts at hand when they were made and not because of the characterization employed. What then if the arrest was made for one offense but the prosecution later, conceding grounds to arrest for that crime were lacking, tries to justify the arrest as being for another offense? Because there is some justification for concern about post hoc manipulation of the facts by the police in order to give what was in fact an unlawful arrest the appearance of legality, it might be contended that the arrest should be judged exclusively in terms of the offense entered at the time of booking. That view has not prevailed. Some courts take the position that the booking entry is irrelevant to the determination of the lawfulness of the arrest, some take the more cautious approach that booking for another offense will not invalidate the arrest if there was no bad faith on the part of the arresting officer, while some others attempt to provide leeway for reasonable mistakes in the booking process by requiring that there be a nexus between the crime specified at booking and the offense now relied upon to uphold the arrest.

Though under *Watson* an officer may arrest without first obtaining a warrant, the Court in *Gerstein v. Pugh*[8] decided that the officer's probable cause assessment justified only the arrest and "a brief period of detention to take the administrative steps incident to arrest." At that point, "the reasons that justify dispensing with the magistrate's neutral judgment evaporate," as there is "no longer any danger that

---

7. This has generally been the view of the lower courts. In *Atwater,* note 6 supra, the Court cautioned: "We need not, and thus do not, speculate whether the Fourth

Amendment entails an 'in the presence' requirement for purposes of misdemeanor arrests."

8. 420 U.S. 103, 95 S.Ct. 854, 43 L.Ed.2d 54 (1975).

the suspect will escape or commit further crimes while the police submit their evidence to a magistrate." Consequently, the Court held in *Gerstein* "that the Fourth Amendment requires a judicial determination of probable cause as a prerequisite to extended restraint on liberty following arrest." This post-arrest probable cause showing, the Court added, may be made "without an adversary hearing" because the standard "is the same as that for arrest," which "traditionally has been decided by a magistrate in a nonadversary proceeding on hearsay and written testimony." This means the required procedure here is essentially like that utilized to obtain an arrest warrant; the magistrate must be given the underlying facts rather than mere conclusions, and a complaint merely reciting the charge in the language of the statute will not suffice. *Gerstein* says the determination is to be made "promptly after arrest," but left the states with the "flexibility" to incorporate the requisite post-arrest probable cause determination into other pretrial procedures (e.g., defendant's first appearance in court). Taking both interests into account, the Court later concluded in *County of Riverside v. McLaughlin*:[9] (1) that a probable cause determination within 48 hours of arrest is presumptively reasonable, though a particular defendant may show such a delay was unreasonable because "for the purpose of gathering additional evidence to justify the arrest, a delay motivated by ill will against the arrested individual, or delay for delay's sake"; and (2) that a later probable cause determination is presumptively unreasonable, meaning "the burden shifts to the government to demonstrate the existence of a bona fide emergency or other extraordinary circumstance" (i.e., something more than an

intervening weekend or a desire to consolidate the probable cause determination with other pretrial proceedings).[10] As for which defendants arrested without a warrant are entitled to a post-arrest probable cause determination, *Gerstein* clearly applies to a defendant who is unable to obtain his release on bail and consequently is held in jail pending trial. The Court stressed that "pretrial release may be accompanied by burdensome conditions that effect a significant restraint on liberty," citing statutory provisions permitting imposition of restrictions on travel and place of abode and release only during the daytime, justifying the conclusion that a probable cause determination is required when release is accompanied by restraints of that magnitude. The Court did not refer to other bail provisions concerning release on financial conditions, and thus it appears the protections of *Gerstein* do not extend to a defendant who has been able to gain release by posting bail. But it would often seem unfair and impractical to defer the probable cause determination until after it is learned whether the defendant was able to "pay his way" out of jail.[11]

The requirement of the Fourth Amendment that no warrant shall issue, but upon probable cause, supported by oath or affirmation and particularly describing the person or things to be seized, applies to arrest warrants as well as search warrants, and thus much of what has been said earlier with respect to the issuance of search warrants[12] applies also to the obtaining of arrest warrants. For one thing, the warrant must be issued by a "neutral and detached magistrate."[13] This is not to say that the authority to issue arrest warrants must "reside exclusively in a lawyer or judge," for a

---

9. 500 U.S. 44, 111 S.Ct. 1661, 114 L.Ed.2d 49 (1991).

10. In Powell v. Nevada, 511 U.S. 79, 114 S.Ct. 1280, 128 L.Ed.2d 1 (1994), where an untimely probable cause determination was made four days after defendant's arrest, shortly after he gave the police an incriminating statement, the Court declared that "whether a suppression remedy applies in that setting remains an unresolved question," and thus remanded the case for decision of that issue.

11. Indeed, such a scheme could be deemed unreasonable under the analysis of County of Riverside v. McLaughlin, supra note 9, even when the determination is made within 48 hours. Although the Court there rejected

the contention that *Gerstein* required a probable cause determination made immediately upon completing the administrative steps incident to an arrest, a delay for this purpose would not appear to be comparable to the factors that the Court cited as justifying a presumption of reasonable delay within a 48 hour period (e.g., magistrate unavailability, obtaining the presence of an arresting officer, and other "practical realities").

12. See § 3.4.

13. Giordenello v. United States, 357 U.S. 480, 78 S.Ct. 1245, 2 L.Ed.2d 1503 (1958).

court clerk may constitutionally be given that power if he works within the judicial branch under the supervision of a judge and, though not law-trained, is capable of making the kinds of probable cause judgments needed in the category of cases that may come before him.[14] For another, the warrant may issue only upon probable cause, and this requires a sworn complaint or testimony setting out the underlying facts and circumstances.[15] A conclusory information sworn by the prosecutor will not suffice,[16] but an indictment "fair on its face" returned by a "properly constituted grand jury" conclusively determines the existence of probable cause and requires issuance of an arrest warrant without further inquiry.[17] Also, to meet the Fourth Amendment particularity requirement an arrest warrant must name the person to be arrested or give other facts that permit his identification with reasonable certainty. An arrest made pursuant to a previously issued warrant is not inevitably valid. As the Supreme Court has explained, while an officer is "entitled to assume" that the warrant was issued upon "the information requisite to support an independent judicial assessment of probable cause," if it turns out that this was not the case or that the arrest warrant was invalid in some other respect, the arrest cannot be upheld on the basis of the warrant.[18] Arrest of the wrong person under the warrant does not render the arrest unlawful if the officer acted in good faith and had reasonable, articulable grounds to believe that the suspect was the intended arrestee.

A warrant to arrest a person as the perpetrator of a crime requires a showing of probable cause the named individual has committed that crime, but (as with warrantless arrests, as discussed below) does not in addition require any showing of a need to take custody. To be

distinguished from the traditional arrest warrant in that respect is an arrest warrant for a material witness. It has been held that the power to arrest and detain a person as a material witness is "fairly inferable" from the applicable statute,[19] but that under the Fourth Amendment such arrest is permissible only upon a need-for-custody showing. Hence the conclusion that a material witness arrest warrant must be based upon probable cause, which must be tested by two criteria: (a) that the testimony of a person is material, and (2) that it may become impracticable to secure his presence by subpoena. The view that the first of these could be met by "a mere statement by a responsible official, such as the United States Attorney," when later subjected to a Fourth Amendment challenge, has been upheld on the ground that such an approach "strikes a proper and adequate balance between protecting the secrecy of the grand jury's investigation and subjecting an individual to an unjustified arrest." The authority to arrest and detain a person as a material grand jury witness has been increasingly relied upon especially since the 9/11/01 terrorist attack; an appellate court has rejected a district court's conclusion "that the federal material witness statute, 18 U.S.C. § 3144, does not authorize the detention of material witnesses for a grand jury investigation." The district court had concluded that the term "criminal proceeding" in § 3144 does not encompass grand jury proceedings because, inter alia, in such a context the judge would be unable to make a materiality determination because of grand jury secrecy.[20]

Over the years, the prevailing assumption in most jurisdictions has been that, except for minor traffic violations, arrest is the normal way by which to invoke the criminal process.

---

14. Shadwick v. City of Tampa, 407 U.S. 345, 92 S.Ct. 2119, 32 L.Ed.2d 783 (1972).

15. Whiteley v. Warden, 401 U.S. 560, 91 S.Ct. 1031, 28 L.Ed.2d 306 (1971).

16. Albrecht v. United States, 273 U.S. 1, 47 S.Ct. 250, 71 L.Ed. 505 (1926). See also Kalina v. Fletcher, 522 U.S. 118, 118 S.Ct. 502, 139 L.Ed.2d 471 (1997).

17. Ex parte United States, 287 U.S. 241, 53 S.Ct. 129, 77 L.Ed. 283 (1932), which the Court in *Gerstein* empha-

sized was still valid. See also Kalina v. Fletcher, 522 U.S. 118, 118 S.Ct. 502, 139 L.Ed.2d 471 (1997).

18. Whiteley v. Warden, 401 U.S. 560, 91 S.Ct. 1031, 28 L.Ed.2d 306 (1971).

However, an officer's belief in the validity of the warrant will ordinarily suffice under the *Leon* "good faith" exception to the exclusionary rule, discussed in § 3.1(c).

19. 18 U.S.C. § 3144.

20. On grand jury secrecy, see § 8.5.

This state of affairs has rightly been criticized, and various recent law reform efforts have stressed the need for broader use of the citation alternative. As for the notion that the Fourth Amendment's reasonableness requirement is met only when probable cause is present *and* an actual need for custody exists, a bare majority of the Supreme Court has found such a claim less than persuasive. The case is *Atwater v. City of Lago Vista*,[21] a § 1983 action brought by a woman who had been subjected to a custodial arrest, for misdemeanor seat belt violations punishable only by a $50 fine, pursuant to a statute allowing the officer total discretion to opt for either custodial arrest or issuance of a citation. The plaintiff's argument was that the Fourth Amendment reasonableness requirement mandated "a modern arrest rule * * * forbidding custodial arrest, even upon probable cause, when conviction could not ultimately carry any jail time and when the government shows no compelling need for immediate detention." But the *Atwater* majority, although conceding that any balancing of the interests in this particular case would certainly favor the plaintiff, concluded that the general rule required for her to prevail would lack "the values of clarity and simplicity" needed for any rule intended to govern a police decision made "on the spur (and in the heat) of the moment." In particular, police would be confounded by the necessity of making case-by-case judgments as to whether the offense in question was of the "jailable" or "fine-only"

variety, and as to whether there was present some special circumstance justifying a taking of custody. Placing that burden upon the police, the majority opined, was not worth the candle, considering the substantial doubts "whether warrantless misdemeanor arrests need constitutional attention" absent a showing of "anything like an epidemic of unnecessary minor-offense arrests."[22]

But *Watson*, the Court cautioned in *Tennessee v. Garner*,[23] should not be read as meaning that if the probable cause "requirement is satisfied the Fourth Amendment has nothing to say about *how* that seizure is made." Thus, the Court in *Garner* held that "use of deadly force to prevent the escape of all felony suspects, whatever the circumstances, is constitutionally unreasonable," and then explained:

> Where the officer has probable cause to believe that the suspect poses a threat of serious physical harm, either to the officer or to others, it is not constitutionally unreasonable to prevent escape by using deadly force. Thus, if the suspect threatens the officer with a weapon or there is probable cause to believe that he has committed a crime involving the infliction or threatened infliction of serious physical harm, deadly force may be used if necessary to prevent escape, and if, where feasible, some warning has been given.[24]

The Fourth Amendment reasonableness standard,[25] the Court later elaborated, (1) ap-

21.   532 U.S. 318, 121 S.Ct. 1536, 149 L.Ed.2d 549 (2001).

22.   The four dissenters, on the other hand, stressing that "a full custodial arrest is such a severe intrusion on an individual's liberty," concluded that "giving police officers constitutional carte blanche to effect an arrest whenever there is probable cause to believe a fine-only misdemeanor has been committed is irreconcilable with the Fourth Amendment's command that seizures be reasonable." They thus "would require that when there is probable cause to believe that a fine-only offense has been committed the police officer should issue a citation unless the officer is 'able to point to specific and articulable facts which, taken together with rational inferences from those facts, reasonably warrant [the additional] intrusion' of a full custodial arrest." When, just a month later, the Court received a case involving a custodial arrest for speeding, the *Atwater* dissenters noted in a concurring opinion that if this marked the beginning of the epidemic then the time might come when the Court would have to reconsider

Atwater. Arkansas v. Sullivan, 532 U.S. 769, 121 S.Ct. 1876, 149 L.Ed.2d 994 (2001).

23.   471 U.S. 1, 105 S.Ct. 1694, 85 L.Ed.2d 1 (1985).

24.   The three dissenters objected: "A proper balancing of the interests involved suggests that use of deadly force as a last resort to apprehend a criminal suspect fleeing from the scene of a nighttime burglary is not unreasonable within the meaning of the Fourth Amendment."

25.   This standard applies *only* to Fourth Amendment activity, not other police conduct causing death or physical injury, which is instead governed by the Fourteenth Amendment's due process shocks-the-conscience standard. In *County of Sacramento v. Lewis*, 523 U.S. 833, 118 S.Ct. 1708, 140 L.Ed.2d 1043 (1998), the Court ruled that "when unforeseen circumstances demand an officer's instant judgment, even precipitate recklessness fails to inch close enough to harmful purpose to spark the shock that implicates 'the large concerns of the governors and the governed.' * * * Accordingly, we hold that high-speed

plies to "*all* claims that law enforcement officers have used excessive force—deadly or not—in the course of an arrest, investigatory stop, or other 'seizure' of a free citizen"; (2) "requires careful attention to the facts and circumstances of each particular case, including the severity of the crime at issue, whether the suspect poses an immediate threat to the safety of the officers or others, and whether he is actively resisting arrest or attempting to evade arrest by flight"; (3) "must embody allowance for the fact that police officers are often forced to make split-second judgments—in circumstances that are tense, uncertain, and rapidly evolving—about the amount of force that is necessary in a particular situation"; and (4) asks "whether the officers' actions are 'objectively reasonable' in light of the facts and circumstances confronting them, without regard to their underlying intent or motivation."[26]

(b) Search of the Person at Scene of Prior Arrest. In *Chimel v. California*,[27] the Court declared that when an arrest is made "it is reasonable for the arresting officer to search the person arrested in order to remove any weapons that the latter might seek to use in order to resist arrest or effect his escape" and also "to search for and seize any evidence on the arrestee's person in order to prevent its concealment or destruction." This language highlighted a very significant issue that the Court did not have to resolve on that occasion: whether, on the one hand, the right to make such searches of the person flows automatically from the fact a lawful arrest was made, or whether, on the other, such searches may be undertaken only when the facts of the individual case indicate some likelihood that either evidence or weapons will be found. Lower courts were divided on the issue until the Supreme Court, in *United States v. Robinson*[28] and the companion case of *Gustafson v. Florida*,[29] held that the broader view was consistent with the protections of the Fourth Amend-

ment. In *Robinson,* where heroin had been found in a cigarette package in defendant's pocket following his arrest for driving after revocation of his license, the court of appeals held the search to be unreasonable because there was no evidence to search for, given the nature of the offense, and because the officer's interest in self-protection could have been met by only a frisk of the arrestee. But the Supreme Court, noting its "fundamental disagreement" with the court of appeals' "suggestion that there must be litigated in each case the issue of whether or not there was present one of the reasons supporting the authority for a search of the person incident to a lawful arrest," concluded:

A police officer's determination as to how and where to search the person of a suspect whom he has arrested is necessarily a quick ad hoc judgment which the Fourth Amendment does not require to be broken down in each instance into an analysis of each step in the search. The authority to search the person incident to a lawful custodial arrest, while based upon the need to disarm and to discover evidence, does not depend on what a court may later decide was the probability in a particular arrest situation that weapons or evidence would in fact be found upon the person of the suspect. A custodial arrest of a suspect based on probable cause is a reasonable intrusion under the Fourth Amendment; that intrusion being lawful, a search incident to the arrest requires no additional justification. It is the fact of the lawful arrest which establishes the authority to search, and we hold that in the case of a lawful custodial arrest a full search of the person is not only an exception to the warrant requirement of the Fourth Amendment, but is also a "reasonable" search under that Amendment.

The majority in *Robinson* justified this result by claiming that the prior decisions of the Court and also the "original understanding"

chases with no intent to harm suspects physically or to worsen their legal plight do not give rise to liability under the Fourteenth Amendment."

26. Graham v. Connor, 490 U.S. 386, 109 S.Ct. 1865, 104 L.Ed.2d 443 (1989).

27. 395 U.S. 752, 89 S.Ct. 2034, 23 L.Ed.2d 685 (1969).

28. 414 U.S. 218, 94 S.Ct. 467, 38 L.Ed.2d 427 (1973).

29. 414 U.S. 260, 94 S.Ct. 488, 38 L.Ed.2d 456 (1973).

of the Fourth Amendment established that the "general authority" to search a person incident to arrest is "unqualified." Though a close examination of those sources justifies the conclusion that they are hardly unequivocal in this respect, there is much to be said for the *Robinson* holding. Standardized procedures to be applied in all cases regardless of particular factual variations are sometimes to be preferred over a case-by-case-determination approach, especially as to those forms of police action that involve relatively minor intrusions into privacy, occur with great frequency, and virtually defy on-the-spot rationalization on the basis of the unique facts of the individual case. Search of an arrested person is precisely that kind of police activity, for: (1) search incident to arrest is the most common variety of police search practice and occurs under an infinite variety of circumstances; (2) though the police would have already determined there was probable cause to arrest, it does not necessarily follow that there is also probable cause the arrestee *presently* has evidence of that crime with him or *presently* is armed, and the latter are much more complex and difficult determinations; (3) the decision to search an arrestee's person cannot be made with the degree of forethought and reflection possible for most other search decisions, as the circumstances arise from the arrest itself, which is often unanticipated, and the fact of arrest produces an immediate need to search if the self-protective and evidence-saving functions are to be realized; (4) search of a person is a relatively minor intrusion upon a person who, by hypothesis, has already been subjected to the more serious step of arrest. Finally, the frisk alternative put forward by the court of appeals would not suffice to accomplish the self-protection objective. It is sufficient in a *Terry v. Ohio*[30] type of situation in which there is a brief on-the-street face-to-face encounter in which the officer can observe the suspect's every move, but would not be certain to uncover more carefully concealed weapons to which the arrestee would have access during his subsequent transportation to the station and further detention thereafter.

Yet, there is reason for concern about the application of this "general authority" to search in cases involving traffic violations. "There is," as the *Robinson* dissenters put it, "always the possibility that a police officer, lacking probable cause to obtain a search warrant, will use a traffic arrest as a pretext to conduct a search." What avenues are open to deal with the pretext arrest problem, which the *Robinson* majority preferred to "leave for another day"? The most obvious is to meet it head on by excluding evidence obtained in a search incident to a traffic arrest upon a showing that the arrest was nothing more than a pretext to search for evidence. But this result has been virtually foreclosed as a result of the Supreme Court's unanimous decision in *Whren v. United States*[31] that when a purportedly pretextual traffic stop has been made on sufficient evidence of the traffic violation, no Fourth Amendment challenge may be undertaken on the grounds that "the actual motivations of individual officers" was to stop in order to investigate some other offense or that "the officer's conduct deviated materially from usual police practices." Another way of dealing with the problem might be to remove the temptation to engage in pretext arrests by broadening the exclusionary rule so as to exclude from evidence anything but a weapon found in a search incident to an arrest for a crime, such as a traffic violation, for which there existed no justification to search for anything but a weapon. However, the Supreme Court has not indicated it is receptive to such an extension of the exclusionary rule.[32] Yet another possibility, inasmuch as *Robinson* declares what may be done incident to a "custodial arrest," (i.e., a seizure of the person with the intention of thereafter having him transported to the police station or other place to be

---

30. 392 U.S. 1, 88 S.Ct. 1868, 20 L.Ed.2d 889 (1968).

31. 517 U.S. 806, 116 S.Ct. 1769, 135 L.Ed.2d 89 (1996), discussed in § 3.1 at note 39.

32. In Terry v. Ohio, 392 U.S. 1, 88 S.Ct. 1868, 20 L.Ed.2d 889 (1968), the Court asserted that the exclusionary rule "cannot properly be invoked to exclude the products of legitimate police investigative techniques on the ground that much conduct which is closely similar involves unwarranted intrusions upon constitutional protections."

dealt with according to law), would be to require that there be established by legislation or police regulation some rational scheme for determining when a noncustodial alternative (i.e., a citation) should be utilized as the means for invoking the criminal process.[33] But when the Supreme Court nearly thirty years later finally confronted that issue head on, a bare majority of the Court rejected the proposition that such a requirement could be derived from the Fourth Amendment's reasonableness requirement.[34]

The other issue considered by the court of appeals in *Robinson*, what the officer could do in the absence of a "custodial arrest," was not reached by the Supreme Court in that case but was later resolved in part in *Knowles v. Iowa*.[35] An officer stopped Knowles for speeding and then, pursuant to a statute authorizing but not requiring him to issue a citation in lieu of arrest for most bailable offenses, issued a citation. The officer then made a full search of Knowles' car and found a bag of marijuana. That search was upheld by the state courts on the ground that because a state statute declared that issuance of a citation in lieu of arrest "does not affect the officer's authority to conduct an otherwise lawful search," it sufficed that the officer had probable cause to make a custodial arrest. A unanimous Supreme Court reversed on the ground that the two search-incident-arrest rationales discussed in *Robinson* did not justify the search in the instant case. The "threat to officers safety from issuing a traffic citation * * * is a good deal less than in the case of a custodial arrest," where (as it was put in *Robinson*) there is "the extended exposure which follows the taking of a suspect into custody and transporting him to the police station." And thus the "concern for officer safety" incident to a traf-

fic stop is sufficiently met by the officer's authority under existing decisions of the Court: he could order the driver and passengers out of the car,[36] "perform a 'patdown' of a driver and any passengers upon a reasonable suspicion they may be armed and dangerous,"[37] and conduct a patdown "of the passenger compartment of a vehicle upon reasonable suspicion that an occupant is dangerous and may gain immediate control of a weapon."[38] As for the "need to discover and preserve evidence," the Court continued, there was no such need in the instant case, as "no further evidence of excessive speed was going to be found on the person of the offender or in the passenger compartment of the car." Thus left unresolved in *Knowles* was the question of whether, incident to citation for an offense for which there *could be* evidence on the person or in the vehicle, the officer would have the search authority he would have if he instead had opted for custodial arrest, or whether instead any search would have to be justified on the ground that there existed probable cause to *search* (a question distinct from whether there is probable cause to arrest).[39]

Police sometimes find it necessary to employ force in conducting a search of a person at the arrest scene. Such force cannot be used as a matter of course as a part of the previously discussed "standardized procedures," and thus it is necessary at the outset that the officer act on probable cause to believe that specific evidence is being disposed of. If that is the case, then the police may use reasonable force to prevent loss of the evidence. The problem usually arises when the arrestee attempts to swallow evidence, as to which the police may properly respond by forcing open his mouth or choking him to the extent necessary to prevent swallowing of the evidence.

---

33. For more on whether the Fourth Amendment reasonableness requirement should be interpreted to require attention to the need-for-custody issue, see § 12.5.

34. Atwater v. City of Lago Vista, 532 U.S. 318, 121 S.Ct. 1536, 149 L.Ed.2d 549 (2001), discussed in § 3.5 at note 21.

35. 525 U.S. 113, 119 S.Ct. 484, 142 L.Ed.2d 492 (1998).

36. As authorized in Maryland v. Wilson, 519 U.S. 408, 117 S.Ct. 882, 137 L.Ed.2d 41 (1997) (passengers); Penn-

sylvania v. Mimms, 434 U.S. 106, 98 S.Ct. 330, 54 L.Ed.2d 331 (1977) (driver). See § 3.8(e).

37. As authorized by Terry v. Ohio, 392 U.S. 1, 88 S.Ct. 1868, 20 L.Ed.2d 889 (1968). See § 3.8

38. As authorized by Michigan v. Long, 463 U.S. 1032, 103 S.Ct. 3469, 77 L.Ed.2d 1201 (1983). See § 3.8(e).

39. For further discussion of the impact of *Knowles*, see § 12.5(b).

Finally, it is important to distinguish a *search* of the person from *seizure* of the objects found. Even though under *Robinson* the search may be undertaken following a lawful custodial arrest as a matter of routine and without particular grounds, what is found may be seized and retained by the police only if they have probable cause that the object is a fruit, instrumentality or evidence of crime. If the rule were otherwise, an officer who desired to inculpate an arrested person in another crime, could seize everything in such person's immediate possession and control upon the prospect that on further investigation some of it might prove to have been stolen or to be contraband.

(c) Search of the Person During Post–Arrest Detention. When an arrested person has been delivered to the place of his forthcoming detention, he may be subjected to a rather complete search of his person. One ground upon which such searches are commonly upheld is as a search incident to arrest; in *United States v. Edwards*[40] the Court held "that searches and seizures that could be made on the spot at the time of arrest may legally be conducted later when the accused arrives at the place of detention." As already noted, no advance probable cause is needed to justify such a search except that which establishes grounds for the preceding arrest.

A second theoretical justification for search of an arrestee's person upon his arrival at the station is that of inventory incident to his booking into jail. This inventory, which is a search for Fourth Amendment purposes,[41] has been rather consistently upheld by the courts as meeting these legitimate objectives: (1) protecting the arrestee's property while he is in jail; (2) protecting the police from groundless

claims that they have not adequately safeguarded the defendant's property; (3) safeguarding the detention facility by preventing introduction therein of weapons or contraband; and (4) ascertaining or verifying the identity of the person arrested. That view has been taken by the Supreme Court where "standardized inventory procedures" have been followed, even if the contents of containers such as a purse are examined in the process.[42] In those few jurisdictions that have adopted a search-incident-to-arrest rule narrower than *Robinson*, the extent of legitimate inventory activity is likely to be litigated and on occasion results in a decision imposing limits grounded in state law upon that conduct, such as that the inventory may not extend to closed containers.

Assuming a lawful search upon defendant's arrival at the station, there remains the question of what may be seized. There is authority that here as with search at the arrest scene, objects may be seized only upon probable cause that they constitute evidence, instrumentalities or fruits of crime, while another view is that after a person has been deprived of the possession of his property upon being incarcerated, he may not thereafter complain if police have his property examined. The latter position makes sense only if an arrestee has no privacy interest in the effects being held for him, an issue that is raised more directly by consideration of whether the arrestee and his effects remain legitimate targets of search during the entire period of custody.

An issue of that kind reached the Supreme Court in *United States v. Edwards*,[43] where defendant was arrested and jailed for attempting to break into a post office and then, a day

---

40. 415 U.S. 800, 94 S.Ct. 1234, 39 L.Ed.2d 771 (1974).

41. Harris v. United States, 390 U.S. 234, 88 S.Ct. 992, 19 L.Ed.2d 1067 (1968).

42. Illinois v. Lafayette, 462 U.S. 640, 103 S.Ct. 2605, 77 L.Ed.2d 65 (1983), where a unanimous Court rejected the claim that the interests stated above could be sufficiently served by merely sealing the purse within a bag or box and putting it in a secured locker. The Court declared it was "hardly in a position to second-guess police departments as to what practical administrative method will best deter theft by and false claims against its employees and preserve the security of the stationhouse. It is evident that

a stationhouse search of every item carried on or by a person who has lawfully been taken into custody by the police will amply serve the important and legitimate governmental interests involved.

"Even if less intrusive means existed of protecting some particular types of property, it would be unreasonable to expect police officers in the everyday course of business to make fine and subtle distinctions in deciding which containers or items may be searched and which must be sealed as a unit."

43. 415 U.S. 800, 94 S.Ct. 1234, 39 L.Ed.2d 771 (1974).

later, his clothing was taken from him to determine whether it contained paint chips from the window the burglar had tried to pry open. The Court upheld this warrantless search, reasoning "that Edwards was no more imposed upon than he could have been at the time and place of the arrest or immediately upon arrival at the place of detention," and that "it is difficult to perceive what is unreasonable about the police examining and holding as evidence those personal effects of the accused that they already have in their lawful custody as the result of a lawful arrest." In trying to identify the scope of the *Edwards* holding, it is useful to note at the outset that the broad issue of whether an arrestee's person and effects remain "fair game" for search during his incarceration can be broken down into two inquiries: whether a warrant is required; and whether probable cause the search will produce evidence is required.[44] In *Edwards* the Court focused on the warrant issue and concluded no warrant was needed, hardly a surprising result because, though there were no exigent circumstances, the clothing was clearly evidence of the crime and was in plain view at the time of seizure. But the Court says that the result would be the same had the police seized evidence then "held under the defendant's name in the 'property room' of the jail," and thus it may fairly be concluded that *Edwards* means at least that no warrant is needed when (i) an object lawfully came into police view at the time of a search upon the arrestee's arrival at the place of detention, (ii) later investigation established that this item is of evidentiary value, and (iii) the item remains in police custody as a part of the arrestee's inventoried property.[45]

In contrast to that situation, which might be characterized as a second look-probable cause type of case, is that in which what is involved is a search into the arrestee's effects to discover that which was not found in the booking inventory. Illustrative is *Brett v. United States*,[46] where three days after booking, defendant's clothes, then stored in the property room of the police department, were searched and found to contain packets of heroin. The court concluded this was an illegal search because even if there was probable cause there was no basis for proceeding without a warrant; this was not a "plain view" case, there was "ample opportunity" to get a warrant, and the fact "the police have custody of a prisoner's property for the purpose of protecting it while he is incarcerated does not alone constitute a basis for an exception to the requirement of a search warrant." The contrary and prevailing view is that no warrant is required in such a case because the warrant process is intended to determine whether probable cause exists, and thus is unnecessary because these searches may be made without probable cause. In the language of the *Edwards* majority, the police may do during the entire period of incarceration what "they were entitled to do incident to the usual custodial arrest and incarceration." It is not correct to say, however, that *Edwards* has settled this point, for the Court there cautioned that such warrantless searches must still be reasonable and that in the instant case "probable cause existed for the search and seizure of respondent's clothing." Thus, it may still be argued that a "second look," especially for evidence unrelated to the crime for which the arrest was made, which involves a greater degree of scrutiny than was undertaken at the time of arrest or booking, should be permitted only upon probable cause, for to allow police the unlimited authority to scrutinize an arrestee's effects to see if he can be linked with some offense bestows upon the police an undeserved windfall and provides them with a temptation to make subterfuge arrests.

Whatever *Robinson* and *Edwards* mean in other contexts, they have no effect upon the limits imposed by the Court in *Schmerber v.*

---

44. They are in a sense related, for there would be little point in requiring a warrant if the magistrate was not expected to pass upon the existence of probable cause. But one could logically conclude that a warrant is not required but that probable cause is.

45. Cases involving this type of fact situation have held such a warrantless seizure is lawful.

46.   412 F.2d 401 (5th Cir.1969).

California[47] upon the taking of a blood sample or a comparable intrusion into the body. A warrantless search of that kind will be upheld only if (i) the process is "a reasonable one" "performed in a reasonable manner," such as that the "blood was taken by a physician in a hospital environment according to accepted medical practices"; (ii) there was in advance "a clear indication that in fact [the evidence sought] will be found"; and (iii) there were exigent circumstances, such as "a need to take the test before the percentage of alcohol in the blood diminishes." Also, some authority is to be found to the effect that so-called "routine" strip searches may not be employed against all classes of arrestees, as such an extreme intrusion on one's personal dignity occasioned by such searches requires that some justifiable basis exists.

In assessing any search occurring during post-arrest detention, it is essential to determine not only that the initial arrest was lawful, but also that the custody at the very time of the search was lawful. One possibility is that the evidence found must be suppressed because the custody at that time was unlawful in that, in the interim since the lawful arrest, the police have come upon additional facts now indicating that there is *not* probable cause the defendant has committed an offense. Another possibility is that suppression will be ordered because, though the original probable cause persists, the police failed to afford the this defendant the usual opportunities for stationhouse release.

(d) Other Search of the Person. Sometimes the police will conduct a warrantless search of a person and find evidence of crime and then place that individual under arrest. Although a search may not both precede an arrest and serve as part of its justification, sometimes a broader rule is asserted, namely, that a search of the person without a search warrant is unlawful when it is made prior to an arrest. But that is not the case; as the Supreme Court concluded in *Rawlings v. Kentucky*,[48] "where the formal arrest followed

quickly on the heels of the challenged search of petitioner's person, we do not believe it particularly important that the search preceded the arrest rather than vice versa," so long as the fruits of the search were "not necessary to support probable cause to arrest."

As for searching a person for evidence without any arrest at all, the Court confronted this issue in *Cupp v. Murphy*,[49] where defendant voluntarily appeared at the station in connection with the strangulation murder of his wife, police asked him to submit scrapings from under his fingernails when they saw what appeared to be dried blood on his finger, and when he refused the police proceeded to take the scrapings without a warrant. The Court, though stressing it was not holding "that a full *Chimel* search would have been justified in this case," concluded that in light of the circumstances (including that Murphy began rubbing his fingers together when he ascertained the police believed there was evidence on them), the police were justified "in subjecting him to the very limited search necessary to preserve the highly evanescent evidence they found under his fingernails." At a minimum, therefore, *Cupp* establishes that (i) if there is probable cause for arrest but no arrest, and (ii) if the suspect is reasonably believed to be in the actual process of destroying "highly evanescent evidence," then (iii) that evidence may be preserved if this can be accomplished by a search "very limited" as compared to a full search of the person. Many lower court cases, however, support a broader but sound rule: a warrantless search is proper if the officer had probable cause to believe that a crime had been committed and probable cause to believe that evidence of the crime in question would be found and that an immediate, warrantless search was necessary in order to prevent the destruction or loss of evidence. This means, for example, that when a person reasonably believed to have been driving under the influence is taken to a hospital for treatment instead of arrested, a warrantless taking of a blood sam-

47. 384 U.S. 757, 86 S.Ct. 1826, 16 L.Ed.2d 908 (1966). On the Fifth Amendment aspect of *Schmerber*, see § 8.12(d).

48. 448 U.S. 98, 100 S.Ct. 2556, 65 L.Ed.2d 633 (1980).

49. 412 U.S. 291, 93 S.Ct. 2000, 36 L.Ed.2d 900 (1973).

ple to determine alcohol content would be proper in the same way as if that person had been arrested.

(e) Seizure and Search of Containers and Other Personal Effects. If the police lawfully arrest a person, may they then[50] search containers and other personal effects belonging to that individual on the ground that this is a legitimate search incident to arrest? The teaching of *Chimel v. California*[51] is that, at a minimum, the arrestee's effects may be examined on a search-incident-to-arrest theory only if they can be said to be " 'within his immediate control'—construing that phrase to mean the area from within which he might gain possession of a weapon or destructible evidence." At least until recently, courts were inclined to uphold searches of effects as searches incident to arrest without close attention to whether in the particular case the police restraints upon the arrestee or the nature of the fastening devices on the container were such that there was no realistic opportunity for the arrestee to gain access to the *interior* of that container, which would seem to be the issue posed by *Chimel*. It was as if the carried container was an extension of the person and thus subject to search under *United States v. Robinson*[52] without any showing of justification based upon the facts of the individual case, and likewise subject to search under *United States v. Edwards*[53] even after it had been taken from the arrestee.

But the Court's later decision in *United States v. Chadwick*[54] indicated the search-incident-to-arrest theory was much more limited than customarily assumed. There, the defendants were arrested while standing next to an open auto trunk into which they had just placed a double-locked footlocker the agents

believed contained marijuana; the defendants, the car and the footlocker were all taken to the federal building, where the agents unlocked and searched the locker without a warrant. The Court held this was not a lawful search incident to arrest, as "once law enforcement officers have reduced luggage or other personal property not immediately associated with the person of the arrestee to their exclusive control, and there is no longer any danger that the arrestee might gain access to the property to seize a weapon or destroy evidence, a search of that property is no longer an incident of the arrest." Though the reach of *Chadwick* was somewhat unclear because the Court did not say whether the result would be different had the police *immediately* searched the footlocker,[55] the case appeared to have this effect: (i) the right to routinely search incident to arrest without showing any need in the particular case, recognized as to search of the person in *United States v. Robinson*,[56] also extends to containers on the person such as a wallet and containers such as a purse that are "immediately associated" with the person; (ii) in all other instances probable cause and (absent true exigent circumstances) a search warrant is needed whenever the police have—or, could have—taken exclusive control of the container, even if the container was in the arrestee's control at the moment of arrest.

But the vitality of the second half of that equation is to be doubted in light of the Court's more recent analysis in *New York v. Belton*.[57] The Court there adopted the general rule that incident to the arrest of an occupant of a car the passenger compartment of the vehicle (including containers found therein) may be searched as a matter of routine. Be-

---

50. A search of a container cannot be justified as incident to arrest if the probable cause for the contemporaneous arrest was provided by the fruits of that search. Smith v. Ohio, 494 U.S. 541, 110 S.Ct. 1288, 108 L.Ed.2d 464 (1990).

51.   395 U.S. 752, 89 S.Ct. 2034, 23 L.Ed.2d 685 (1969).

52.   414 U.S. 218, 94 S.Ct. 467, 38 L.Ed.2d 427 (1973).

53.   415 U.S. 800, 94 S.Ct. 1234, 39 L.Ed.2d 771 (1974).

54.   433 U.S. 1, 97 S.Ct. 2476, 53 L.Ed.2d 538 (1977).

55.   The two *Chadwick* dissenters thought it clear that "the agents could have made a search of the footlocker at

the time and place of the arrests" because it then "was within the area of [the defendant's] 'immediate control.' " Brennan, J., concurring, thought otherwise, noting the *contents* were not then within defendant's "immediate control." The majority, by emphasizing there is no valid search incident to arrest if it "is remote in time or place from the arrest," went out of its way to avoid accepting the Brennan reasoning.

56.   414 U.S. 218, 94 S.Ct. 467, 38 L.Ed.2d 427 (1973).

57.   453 U.S. 454, 101 S.Ct. 2860, 69 L.Ed.2d 768 (1981).

cause the Court had earlier held that the Fourth Amendment protection of a container is the same whether it is within or without a vehicle,[58] and because the assertion in *Belton* of a need for a "bright line" on what constitutes "immediate control" seems equally applicable to containers not found in cars, the likely consequence of *Belton* is a comparably broad search-of-container-incident-to-arrest rule. This would mean that a container in the arrestee's possession may be searched incident to arrest if the search is contemporaneous with the arrest, without regard to any of the following: (i) whether on the facts of the particular case there was a likelihood the arrestee could get into the container; (ii) whether the police had already subjected the container to their exclusive control; or (iii) whether there was a likelihood that a weapon or evidence of the crime for which the arrest was made would be found. The criticisms that may be directed to the *Belton* rule[59] are equally applicable to the above rule.

A second possible basis upon which to justify a search into containers possessed by an arrestee is the need to inventory them incident to the arrestee's booking and post-arrest detention. There is authority that whenever the defendant's suitcase or some similar container was properly impounded by the police at the time of his arrest (or otherwise lawfully came into the custody of the police), an item-by-item inventory of its contents at the station is permissible both to preserve the property of the accused and to forestall the possibility that the accused may later claim that some item has not been returned to him. That view was adopted by the Supreme Court unanimously in *Illinois v. Lafayette*,[60] permitting "a stationhouse search of every item carried on or by a person who has lawfully been taken into custo-

dy by the police," if done pursuant to "standardized inventory procedures,"[61] because it "will amply serve the important and legitimate governmental interests involved." As for the position theretofore taken by a minority of courts that it would suffice if the container was merely sealed and secured without examination of the contents, the Court rejected this as a Fourth Amendment limitation on the grounds that it could not "second-guess police departments as to what practical administrative method will best deter theft by and false claims against its employees and preserve the security of the stationhouse," and that "it would be unreasonable to expect police officers in the everyday course of business to make fine and subtle distinctions in deciding which containers or items may be searched and which must be sealed as a unit."

Another potential basis for upholding a warrantless search of personal effects is that the search in question was made (i) upon probable cause to believe that the effects contained evidence of crime and (ii) when it would not have been practicable to obtain a search warrant first because of certain exigent circumstances. The significant issue here is precisely what constitutes exigent circumstances in this context. At one time, courts were inclined to permit warrantless searches of containers by analogy to the rules governing vehicle searches,[62] especially the ruling in *Chambers v. Maroney*[63] that "for constitutional purposes" there was no difference between seizing the item to be searched and holding it while a warrant is obtained, and simply proceeding to make an immediate warrantless search. This meant that if the circumstances were sufficiently exigent as to justify a warrantless seizure of a container, it somehow

---

58. Arkansas v. Sanders, 442 U.S. 753, 99 S.Ct. 2586, 61 L.Ed.2d 235 (1979).

59. See § 3.7(a).

60. 462 U.S. 640, 103 S.Ct. 2605, 77 L.Ed.2d 65 (1983).

61. The requirement of standardized procedures was also set out in the later vehicle inventory case of Colorado v. Bertine, 479 U.S. 367, 107 S.Ct. 738, 93 L.Ed.2d 739 (1987), where the Court also emphasized that "there was no showing that the police * * * acted in bad faith or for the sole purpose of investigation." That qualification, which would seem equally applicable in the present con-

text, was later recognized by the Supreme Court as a proper exception to the prevailing Fourth Amendment doctrine that police conduct is not made invalid by alleged pretexts because subjective intent is irrelevant in determining what is reasonable under the Amendment. Whren v. United States, 517 U.S. 806, 116 S.Ct. 1769, 135 L.Ed.2d 89 (1996).

62. See § 3.7(b).

63. 399 U.S. 42, 90 S.Ct. 1975, 26 L.Ed.2d 419 (1970).

followed that an immediate warrantless search was also permissible. But that conclusion was rejected by the Supreme Court in the previously described *Chadwick* case, where it was reasoned that because "a person's expectations of privacy in personal luggage are substantially greater than in an automobile," the rule for automobiles could not be extended to such containers; rather, when the circumstances are sufficiently exigent to allow the police to make a warrantless seizure of the luggage, this does not permit the "far greater intrusion" of examining the contents thereof but only the continued possession of the container while a warrant is sought. Any thought that these "substantially greater" expectations derived from the special steps taken by the defendant in *Chadwick,* who was transporting a double-locked footlocker, was dissipated by *Arkansas v. Sanders,*[64] holding that *Chadwick* also applied to a "small, unlocked suitcase" because "respondent's failure to lock his suitcase [did not] alter its fundamental character as a repository for personal, private effects." This means a search warrant is needed to search containers absent true exigent circumstances, such as that the object contained evidence which would lose its value unless the container were opened at once or that immediate search would facilitate the apprehension of confederates or the termination of continuing criminal activity. To this must be added the following caveat from *Sanders:*

> Not all containers and packages found by police * * * will deserve the full protection of the Fourth Amendment. Thus, some containers (for example a kit of burglar tools or a gun case) by their very nature cannot support any reasonable expectation of privacy because their contents can be inferred

from their outward appearance. Similarly, in some cases the contents of a package will be open to "plain view," thereby obviating the need for a warrant.[65]

The holding in *Sanders*, that a search warrant is needed even when the container is located within a vehicle, was later overruled in *California v. Acevedo.*[66] But because *Acevedo* is grounded primarily in a perceived need for "one clear-cut rule to govern automobile searches," whether the requisite probable cause extends to the automobile generally or only to a specific container therein, that decision does not appear to eliminate the warrant requirement for search of containers *not* found in vehicles. However, it will doubtless be argued by some that *Acevedo* should be extended to the latter situation as well, for (as the concurring opinion in that case put it) "it is anomalous for a briefcase to be protected by the 'general requirement' of a prior warrant when it is being carried along the street, but for that same briefcase to become unprotected as soon as it is carried into an automobile."

A variation of sorts on the plain view situation referred to in *Sanders* is the so-called "controlled delivery." When police lawfully see the contents of a container in transit (most likely because it was lawfully opened by a customs official upon its entry into the country or by the suspicious agents of a private domestic courier), they often arrange for it to be delivered under surveillance, after which the recipient is arrested and the container seized and opened. No warrant is needed to justify the opening of the container, the Supreme Court explained in *Illinois v. Andreas,*[67] because this does not amount to a Fourth Amendment search. "No protected privacy interest remains in contraband in a container

---

64. 442 U.S. 753, 99 S.Ct. 2586, 61 L.Ed.2d 235 (1979).

65. In Texas v. Brown, 460 U.S. 730, 103 S.Ct. 1535, 75 L.Ed.2d 502 (1983), involving the warrantless seizure and search of a tied-up balloon seen in a car under circumstances strongly suggesting it contained drugs, three concurring Justices said the warrantless search of the balloon might well be justified on the ground that its contents could be so inferred: "Whereas a suitcase or a paper bag may contain an almost infinite variety of items, a balloon of this kind might be used only to transport drugs. Viewing it where he did could have given the officer a degree of certainty that is equivalent to the plain view of

the heroin itself." They later said, as to this exception to *Ross,* that " 'virtual certainty' is a more meaningful indicator than visibility," as one "might actually see a white powder without realizing that it is heroin, but be virtually certain a balloon contains such a substance in a particular context."

66. 500 U.S. 565, 111 S.Ct. 1982, 114 L.Ed.2d 619 (1991), discussed in § 3.7 at note 26.

67. 463 U.S. 765, 103 S.Ct. 3319, 77 L.Ed.2d 1003 (1983).

once government officers lawfully have opened that container and identified its contents as illegal. The simple act of resealing the container to enable the police to make a controlled delivery does not operate to revive or restore the lawfully invaded privacy rights."[68] In *Andreas,* the container (a metal container with a wooden table inside, within which a customs inspector found marijuana) had been out of police view inside defendant's apartment 30 to 45 minutes before he reemerged with it, but the Court concluded that did not require a different result absent "a substantial likelihood that the contents of the container had been changed during the gap in surveillance." Because of the "unusual size of the container, its specialized purpose, and the relatively short break in surveillance," the Court deemed it "substantially unlikely that the respondent removed the table or placed new items inside the container while it was in his apartment."

§ 3.6   Entry and Search of Premises

(a) Basis for Entry to Arrest. *Payton v. New York*[1] holds "that the Fourth Amendment * * * prohibits the police from making a warrantless and nonconsensual entry into a suspect's home in order to make a routine felony arrest." The Court first noted it was "a 'basic principle of Fourth Amendment law' that searches and seizures inside a home without a warrant are presumptively unreasonable," while "objects * * * found in a public place may be seized by the police without a warrant." The *Payton* majority then concluded that "this distinction has equal force when the seizure of a person is involved" because "an entry to arrest and an entry to search for and to seize property implicate the same interest in preserving the privacy and the sanctity of the

home, and justify the same level of constitutional protection." The Court reasoned that

any differences in the intrusiveness of entries to search and entries to arrest are merely ones of degree rather than kind. The two intrusions share this fundamental characteristic: the breach of the entrance to an individual's home. The Fourth Amendment protects the individual's privacy in a variety of settings. In none is the zone of privacy more clearly defined than when bounded by the unambiguous physical dimensions of an individual's home—a zone that finds its roots in clear and specific constitutional terms: "The right of the people to be secure in their * * * houses * * * shall not be violated." * * * In terms that apply equally to seizures of property and to seizures of persons, the Fourth Amendment has drawn a firm line at the entrance to the house. Absent exigent circumstances,[2] that threshold may not reasonably be crossed without a warrant.

In response to the contention that "only a search warrant based on probable cause to believe the suspect is at home at a given time can adequately protect the privacy interests at stake," the Court in *Payton* declared:

It is true that an arrest warrant requirement may afford less protection than a search warrant requirement, but it will suffice to interpose the magistrate's determination of probable cause between the zealous officer and the citizen. If there is sufficient evidence of a citizen's participation in a felony to persuade a judicial officer that his arrest is justified, it is constitutionally responsible to require him to open his doors to the officers of the law. Thus, for Fourth Amendment purposes, an arrest warrant founded on probable cause implicitly carries

---

68. This language was relied upon in United States v. Jacobsen, 466 U.S. 109, 104 S.Ct. 1652, 80 L.Ed.2d 85 (1984), where employees of a shipping company opened a suspicious package and found a white powder and then summoned a federal drug agent, who upon arrival was invited to reopen the then unsealed package and examine the powder. The Court deemed that limited reopening, because it "enabled the agent to learn nothing that had not previously been learned during the private search" and thus "infringed no legitimate expectation of privacy," to constitute no search at all.

§ 3.6

1. 445 U.S. 573, 100 S.Ct. 1371, 63 L.Ed.2d 639 (1980).

2. In Kirk v. Louisiana, 536 U.S. 635, 122 S.Ct. 2458, 153 L.Ed.2d 599 (2002), the Court, per curiam, summarily reversed a lower court holding that a warrantless entry, arrest and search of the arrestee were lawful, even absent any showing of exigent circumstances, because there was probable cause to arrest. That holding, the Court noted, "plainly violates our holding in *Payton.*"

with it the limited authority to enter a dwelling in which the suspect lives when there is reason to believe the suspect is within.

This makes sense if there is some reason why it is unnecessary to have a judicial determination of "probable cause to believe the suspect is at home," which would seem to be the case. Though it appears that such probable cause is needed, this requirement would often be an insurmountable barrier if it could be met only by specific facts in the individual case instead of by inference. Because rudimentary police procedure dictates that a suspect's residence be eliminated as a possible hiding place before a search is conducted elsewhere, it is permissible for the police to infer that the defendant is home except when they have "special knowledge" indicating otherwise. That being so, the Court in *Payton* was quite correct in concluding there was no need to involve the magistrate in simply applying that inference.

When the police wish to enter the premises of a third party to make an arrest, it is clear that they must have probable cause to believe that the named suspect is present within at the time. Quite obviously this probable cause can be established only by facts of the particular case rather than by inference, and quite obviously as well this probable cause determination is central to protection of the privacy rights of the third party. This explains why the Supreme Court in *Steagald v. United States*[3] held that a search warrant, based upon a magistrate's determination that it is probable the person to be arrested is now in those premises, is the kind of warrant needed in those circumstances.

In *Payton,* the Court noted it had "no occasion to consider the sort of emergency or dan-

gerous situation, described in our cases as 'exigent circumstances,' that would justify a warrantless entry into a home" to make an arrest. The Court's prior cases have only declared that any possible warrant requirement was obviated when the police were in "hot pursuit" of the offender.[4] Many lower courts utilize the list of "considerations" set out in *Dorman v. United States*[5]: (1) whether "a grave offense is involved"; (2) whether "the suspect is reasonably believed to be armed"; (3) whether there is "a clear showing of probable cause" of the person's guilt; (4) whether there is "strong reason to believe that the suspect is in the premises"; (5) whether there is a "likelihood that the suspect will escape if not swiftly apprehended"; (6) whether the entry is "made peaceably"; and (7) whether the entry is "made at night," which on the one hand is more intrusive and on the other may show the impracticality of getting a warrant.[6] It is to be doubted, however, that an on-the-spot balancing of these factors makes for a workable test, and thus it may be that warrants should be required for "planned" arrests but not for those in which the occasion for arrest arose while the police were in the field investigating the conduct providing the basis for the arrest.

Though declining to express approval of "all of the factors included in" the *Dorman* standard, the Court in *Welsh v. Wisconsin*[7] placed great emphasis (too much, it would seem) on the first of these factors in concluding that "it is difficult to conceive of a warrantless home arrest that would not be unreasonable under the Fourth Amendment when the underlying offense is extremely minor." In *Welsh* police had entered defendant's home without a warrant to arrest him for the offense of driving while intoxicated, in which he had been en-

3. 451 U.S. 204, 101 S.Ct. 1642, 68 L.Ed.2d 38 (1981).

4. United States v. Santana, 427 U.S. 38, 96 S.Ct. 2406, 49 L.Ed.2d 300 (1976); Warden v. Hayden, 387 U.S. 294, 87 S.Ct. 1642, 18 L.Ed.2d 782 (1967). But in Welsh v. Wisconsin, 466 U.S. 740, 104 S.Ct. 2091, 80 L.Ed.2d 732 (1984), the Court declined to uphold the police entry on a hot pursuit theory, as the police entered on the basis of a witness' information of defendant's nearby activity of driving while intoxicated minutes earlier, and thus "there was no immediate or continuous pursuit of the petitioner from the scene of a crime."

5. 435 F.2d 385 (D.C.Cir.1970).

6. In Minnesota v. Olson, 495 U.S. 91, 110 S.Ct. 1684, 109 L.Ed.2d 85 (1990), where the grave crime of murder was involved but the murder weapon had been recovered, and 3 or 4 police squads had the house surrounded, the Court did "not disturb the state court's judgment that these facts do not add up to exigent circumstances."

7. 466 U.S. 740, 104 S.Ct. 2091, 80 L.Ed.2d 732 (1984).

gaged in the immediate vicinity just minutes before. The state claimed exigent circumstances, namely, a need to obtain evidence of the defendant's blood alcohol level, which the Supreme Court had previously found compelling in other circumstances.[8] But the Court concluded "the best indication of the state's interest in precipitating an arrest" was the fact that the state had "chosen to classify the first offense for driving while intoxicated as a noncriminal, civil forfeiture offense for which no imprisonment is possible," and thus held that in such circumstances "a warrantless home arrest cannot be upheld simply because evidence of the petitioner's blood-alcohol level might have dissipated while the police obtained a warrant." As the two dissenters correctly observed, the statutory scheme was doubtless adopted "to increase the ease of conviction and the overall deterrent effect of the enforcement effort" and thus hardly manifested an expression that the defendant's conduct was so insignificant as to be undeserving of effective enforcement.[9]

The *Payton–Steagald* warrant requirement is inapplicable when the police are otherwise lawfully present within the premises, such as to execute a search warrant or by virtue of consent. There is likewise no need for a warrant, the Court concluded in *United States v. Santana*,[10] if the arrested defendant was standing directly in the doorway, but *Payton* teaches it is not enough that the door is open and the person to be arrested is clearly visible within. The lower courts are not in agreement as to whether *Santana* may be extended to cases in which the defendant was "at" but not "in" the door, but the better view is that such de minimis physical intrusions as reaching in to seize the person do not invoke the warrant

requirement. Such a warrantless arrest is not rendered illegal by the fact that the police summoned the defendant to the door without revealing their intention to arrest him or by resort to noncoercive subterfuge, but the result is otherwise when the police utilize coercion or a false claim of authority to gain the defendant's presence at (or even outside) the door.

Assuming now a situation in which the *Payton–Steagald* warrant requirement *is* applicable and in which the police are armed with the requisite warrant, the Fourth Amendment requires "that police actions in execution of a warrant be related to the objectives of the authorized intrusion." This means, for one thing, that police entering the premises to execute the warrant may not be accompanied by others whose presence therein "was not related to the objectives of the authorized intrusion." Such was the holding in *Wilson v. Layne*,[11] concluding that the Fourth Amendment was thus violated when police entering a private dwelling to execute an arrest warrant allowed members of the news media to accompany them. Violation of the rule in *Wilson* (which was a § 1983 action) would appear to have significance in an exclusionary rule context, if at all, only if the persons improperly present discovered evidence now to be introduced at defendant's trial.[12]

(b) Entry Without Notice to Arrest. The proposition that police must ordinarily give notice of their authority and purpose prior to making an entry of premises to arrest a person therein, which has common law credentials and is often found expressed by statute, seems to have been viewed by the Supreme Court in *Ker v. California*[13] as a Fourth Amendment

8. Schmerber v. California, 384 U.S. 757, 86 S.Ct. 1826, 16 L.Ed.2d 908 (1966) (warrantless extraction of blood).

9. They also correctly observed that "the Court's approach will necessitate a case-by-case evaluation of the seriousness of particular crimes, a difficult task for which officers and courts are poorly equipped."

10. 427 U.S. 38, 96 S.Ct. 2406, 49 L.Ed.2d 300 (1976).

11. 526 U.S. 603, 119 S.Ct. 1692, 143 L.Ed.2d 818 (1999).

12. The Court in *Wilson* emphasized in a footnote that though media presence "might violate the Fourth Amend-

ment if the police are lawfully present, the violation of the Fourth Amendment is the presence of the media and not the presence of the police in the home. We have no occasion here to decide whether the exclusionary rule would apply to any evidence discovered or developed by the media representatives."

13. 374 U.S. 23, 83 S.Ct. 1623, 10 L.Ed.2d 726 (1963). *Ker* is a less than definitive treatment of the issue, however, for Justice Harlan concurred on the limited ground that state searches should only be judged by "concepts of fundamental fairness," four members of the Court con-

requirement,[14] just as the Court later held regarding entry to execute a search warrant.[15] It reduces the potential for violence to both the police officers and the occupants of the house into which entry is sought, guards against the needless destruction of private property, and symbolizes the respect for individual privacy summarized in the adage that a man's house is his castle. The requirement applies to entry by force, by use of a pass key, by merely opening an unlocked door, and at least in some circumstances to passage through an already open door, but it does not extend to entry by ruse because such activity does not intrude upon the aforementioned interests.

What is required is that a police officer, upon identifying himself as such an officer, demand that he be admitted to such premises for the purpose of making the arrest. He may then enter upon submission by the occupant or if his demand is not promptly complied with, which means he must give the occupant a reasonable opportunity to come to the door. Entry without such notice is permissible in an emergency, that is, when the officer acts on a reasonable and good faith belief that compliance would increase his peril, frustrate an arrest, or permit the destruction of evidence. Some jurisdictions followed the so-called "blanket rule" under which an emergency can be grounded upon the general category of the case involved, but the Supreme Court's recent rejection of that approach re search warrant execution[16] would seem equally applicable here. Thus, it is not enough that the person to be arrested is known to own a weapon or is involved in criminal activity typically necessi-

tating use of easily disposable evidence. What is necessary is that the police "had a 'reasonable suspicion' that knocking and announcing their presence might be dangerous to themselves or to others."[17] (A few jurisdictions authorize the issuance of so-called no-knock warrants, whereunder the magistrate would authorize entry without prior notice because of a sufficient showing to him of a need to do so.) Announcement is also unnecessary when it would be a "useless gesture," that is, when the authority and purpose of the police is already known to those inside.

(c) Search Before and Incident to Arrest. In *Warden v. Hayden*,[18] the Supreme Court made clear the unquestioned authority of police lawfully within premises for the purpose of making an arrest to search those premises to the extent necessary to find the individual to be arrested. Such a search is ordinarily limited to examining places where a fugitive could conceal himself, but *Hayden* also establishes that sometimes the police may do more. There one officer found weapons in a bathroom flush tank and another found clothing of the type described by the victim in the washing machine, and the Court upheld the search into those places because it was necessary for the police to ensure that they "had control of all weapons which could be used against them or to effect an escape." Because the Court stressed that these searches occurred "as part of an effort to find a suspected felon, armed, within the house into which he had run only minutes before," it is to be doubted that a weapons search is permissible as a matter of course in every case in which the police enter to arrest.

cluded there were grounds to enter without notice, and the four dissenters concluded otherwise.

14. Analysis in this area is likely to come out the same way under the Fourth Amendment and under the federal knock-and-announce statute, as both involve consideration of common law principles. See United States v. Ramirez, 523 U.S. 65, 118 S.Ct. 992, 140 L.Ed.2d 191 (1998).

15. Wilson v. Arkansas, 514 U.S. 927, 115 S.Ct. 1914, 131 L.Ed.2d 976 (1995), holding "that the common-law principle of announcement * * * is an element of the reasonableness inquiry under the Fourth Amendment."

16. Richards v. Wisconsin, 520 U.S. 385, 117 S.Ct. 1416, 137 L.Ed.2d 615 (1997), discussed in § 3.4 at note 39.

17. United States v. Ramirez, 523 U.S. 65, 118 S.Ct. 992, 140 L.Ed.2d 191 (1998). In elaborating the circumstances that allowed the police to forego notice when executing a search warrant to search for a wanted person (in a real sense a form of entry for the purpose of arrest, which is the focus here), the Court in *Ramirez* emphasized that a "reliable confidential informant" had notified police that the wanted person might be inside; that the police "had confirmed this possibility"; that the wanted person "was a prison escapee with a violent past"; that he "reportedly had access to a large supply of weapons": and that he "had vowed that he would 'not do federal time.'"

18. 387 U.S. 294, 87 S.Ct. 1642, 18 L.Ed.2d 782 (1967).

The longstanding rule that if the defendant was arrested in his own premises this automatically justified a warrantless search of the entire premises incident to that arrest was rejected in *Chimel v. California.*[19] After noting that it is reasonable to search the *person* of the arrestee to prevent him from concealing or destroying evidence and to prevent resistance or escape, the Court continued:

> And the area into which an arrestee might reach in order to grab a weapon or evidentiary items must, of course, be governed by a like rule. A gun on a table or in a drawer in front of one who is arrested can be as dangerous to the arresting officer as one concealed in the clothing of the person arrested. There is ample justification, therefore, for a search of the arrestee's person and the area "within his immediate control"—construing that phrase to mean the area from within which he might gain possession of a weapon or destructible evidence.
>
> There is no comparable justification, however, for routinely searching any room other than that in which an arrest occurs—or, for that matter, for searching through all the desk drawers or other closed or concealed areas in that room itself. Such searches, in the absence of well-recognized exceptions, may be made only under the authority of a search warrant. The "adherence to judicial processes" mandated by the Fourth Amendment requires no less.

The Court thus wisely limited the authority to search without warrant incident to arrest by circumscribing that authority in terms of the rationale for making such a search.

Especially in the years that immediately followed *Chimel,* courts applied the rule loosely by finding unhesitantly that the arrestee had a substantial area "within his immediate control" notwithstanding his arrest. The correct approach is to inquire what places it would be *possible* for the arrestee presently to reach, which necessitates consideration of such factors as (1) whether the arrestee was placed in some form of restraints, such as handcuffs; (2) the position of the officer vis-a-vis the defendant in relation to the place searched; (3) the ease or difficulty of gaining access within the container or enclosure searched; and (4) the number of officers present in relation to the number of arrestees or other persons. (More recently, in *New York v. Belton,*[20] the Court adopted a more generous search-incident-arrest rule for search of vehicles after arrest of passengers,[21] but gave no indication that *Chimel* itself was being expanded.) Courts generally have not considered whether *Chimel* obligates the police to take measures to narrow the range of the arrestee's control, but when the police rely upon their purported knowledge of the arrestee's dangerous propensities in support of a search somewhat broader than might otherwise be permissible, their claim may be rejected because of their failure to take appropriate steps to restrain the arrestee.

(d) Search and Exploration After Arrest. If the defendant is arrested at a particular place in the premises, even at the front door, the circumstances may be such that he will be allowed to move about the premises prior to departure, as where it is necessary for him to change his clothes or put on additional clothing. In such a situation, it is proper for the police in the interest of self-protection to accompany the defendant to the other part of the residence where the clothes are to be obtained and inspect the interior of a closet or drawer where the defendant says he wants to obtain clothing.

After a defendant is arrested within premises, the police sometimes make a cursory inspection of other parts of those premises for the purpose of determining whether there are possible accomplices present. Such a search has been upheld when the police had *some* reason to anticipate finding accomplices, but is not justified if police enter to arrest defendant for a past offense it is known he committed alone or for which all confederates are known to have been apprehended. But at least when

---

19. 395 U.S. 752, 89 S.Ct. 2034, 23 L.Ed.2d 685 (1969).

20. 453 U.S. 454, 101 S.Ct. 2860, 69 L.Ed.2d 768 (1981).

21. See § 3.7(a).

the criminal activity is rather serious, exploration for potential accomplices is reasonable even absent concrete information indicating the accomplices are now present.

Yet another reason why police sometimes make a cursory inspection of the balance of the premises is to ensure their own safety while departing with the arrestee. The question of when such a "protective sweep"[22] is permissible reached the Supreme Court in *Maryland v. Buie*,[23] where the state court had required full probable cause of a dangerous situation. By analogy to *Terry v. Ohio*[24] and *Michigan v. Long*,[25] the Court opted for a less demanding reasonable suspicion test. The state had argued for a "bright-line rule" to the effect that "police should be permitted to conduct a protective sweep whenever they make an in-home arrest for a violent crime"; the Court responded that individualized suspicion is required under *Terry*, but then without explanation adopted a two-part sweep rule that included another kind of bright line. Specifically, the Court in *Buie* held (1) "that as an incident to the arrest the officers could, as a precautionary matter and without probable cause or reasonable suspicion, look in closets and other spaces immediately adjoining the place of arrest from which an attack could be immediately launched"; and (2) that for a more extensive sweep "there must be articulable facts which, taken together with the rational inferences from those facts, would warrant a reasonably prudent officer in believing that the area to be swept harbors an individual posing a danger to those on the arrest scene." No effort was made to define either the "immediately adjoining" category or the factors bearing on this variety of reasonable suspicion. As to the latter, earlier lower court decisions have said this is a matter that requires consideration of the seriousness of the offense, the

likelihood that the crime for which the arrest was made involved confederates, the likelihood that other persons are now present in the premises, and the extent to which the circumstances and surroundings make difficult a safe withdrawal from the premises with the arrestee.

As for whether the police may accompany the defendant into the home following his arrest outside so that the defendant may obtain identification, get his effects, or change clothes, the Supreme Court answered in the affirmative in *Washington v. Chrisman*.[26] Such action was deemed permissible without regard to the likelihood that the arrestee would attempt to escape; as the Court put it in *Chrisman*, "it is not 'unreasonable' under the Fourth Amendment for a police officer, as a matter of routine, to monitor the movements of an arrested person, as his judgment dictates, following the arrest."

(e) Warrantless Entry and Search for Evidence. In earlier days, the Supreme Court sometimes intimated that a warrantless search of premises for evidence could *never* be justified under the Fourth Amendment,[27] and sometimes alluded to the possibility that such a search would be upheld upon a showing of genuine exigent circumstances.[28] No case concerning this issue reached the Court in the pre-*Chimel* era, for then the police could usually avoid the issue by the simple expedient of arresting the defendant there and then searching the entire premises incident to that arrest. But after *Chimel* a case seemingly raising this issue, *Vale v. Louisiana*,[29] reached the Court. Police set up a surveillance of a house in which Vale was thought to be residing, as they had a warrant to arrest him because of a bond increase on his previous narcotics charge. They saw him come out of the house and apparently

---

22. Defined by the Court in *Buie*, infra, as "a quick and limited search of a premises, incident to an arrest and conducted to protect the safety of police officers or others," which "is narrowly confined to a cursory visual inspection of those places in which a person might be hiding."

23. 494 U.S. 325, 110 S.Ct. 1093, 108 L.Ed.2d 276 (1990).

24. 392 U.S. 1, 88 S.Ct. 1868, 20 L.Ed.2d 889 (1968).

25. 463 U.S. 1032, 103 S.Ct. 3469, 77 L.Ed.2d 1201 (1983).

26. 455 U.S. 1, 102 S.Ct. 812, 70 L.Ed.2d 778 (1982).

27. Agnello v. United States, 269 U.S. 20, 46 S.Ct. 4, 70 L.Ed. 145 (1925).

28. Johnson v. United States, 333 U.S. 10, 68 S.Ct. 367, 92 L.Ed. 436 (1948).

29. 399 U.S. 30, 90 S.Ct. 1969, 26 L.Ed.2d 409 (1970).

make a drug sale to a person who drove up and sounded his horn, so the police moved in and arrested Vale just as he was about to reenter the house. The police then took him inside and made a cursory inspection of the house, during which time Vale's brother and mother entered the premises, and the officers then proceeded to search the house and discovered Vale's stash of narcotics. Though the state claimed that the search was lawful because made on probable cause narcotics would be found and in response to a risk the narcotics would be disposed of if the police were to delay for a search warrant, the Court in *Vale* disagreed.

One response by the Court was that the state's rationale "could not apply to the present case, since by their own account the arresting officers satisfied themselves that no one else was in the house when they first entered the premises." This observation does not square with the facts, which again were that when the detailed search uncovering the drugs was undertaken two close relatives of the defendant were on the premises. Equally baffling is the assertion that because the officers "were able to procure two warrants for the appellant's arrest" and "had information that he was residing at the address where they found him," there was "no reason * * * to suppose that it was impracticable for them to obtain a search warrant as well." The facts support precisely the opposite conclusion; a search warrant for drugs could hardly have issued merely because Vale's bond was being raised, as the probable cause for the warrant came into being only minutes before the search was conducted. But putting those two points aside, *Vale* is significant because it appears to recognize that a warrantless search of a dwelling for evidence may be undertaken in "an exceptional situation," and also because it seemingly asserts that the risk-of-evidence-loss "emergency" is to be very narrowly circumscribed. In concluding no such emergency existed in the instant case, the Court emphasized that the "goods ultimately seized were not in the process of destruction" nor "about to be removed from the jurisdiction."

Although some courts have resisted a broader formulation on the ground that the police can too easily conjure up reasons why evidence within premises might be subject to future destruction or disposal, most lower courts have not accepted the *Vale* formulation as controlling. They have been inclined to state the exception in broader terms, covering instances in which the police reasonably conclude that the evidence would be destroyed or removed before they could secure a search warrant. The most careful treatment of this point appears in *United States v. Rubin*,[30] where the court, after noting the broader dictum in other Supreme Court cases,[31] concluded the *Vale* language should not be taken too seriously in light of the Court's assumption that not even a threat of destruction was present. The court in *Rubin* then formulated this test:

> When Government agents, however, have probable cause to believe contraband is present and, in addition, based on the surrounding circumstances of the information at hand, they reasonably conclude that the evidence will be destroyed or removed before they can secure a search warrant, a warrantless search is justified. The emergency circumstances will vary from case to case, and the inherent necessities of the situation at the time must be scrutinized. Circumstances which have seemed relevant to courts include (1) the degree of urgency involved and the amount of time necessary to obtain a warrant * * *; (2) reasonable belief that the contraband is about to be removed * * *; (3) the possibility of danger to police officers guarding the site of the contraband while a search warrant is sought * * *; (4) information indicating the possessors of the contraband are aware that the police are on their

---

30. 474 F.2d 262 (3d Cir.1973).

31. United States v. Jeffers, 342 U.S. 48, 72 S.Ct. 93, 96 L.Ed. 59 (1951) (warrant needed as "no question of * * * imminent destruction, removal, or concealment of the property"); McDonald v. United States, 335 U.S. 451, 69 S.Ct. 191, 93 L.Ed. 153 (1948) (warrant needed, as no

"property in the process of destruction" or "likely to be destroyed"); Johnson v. United States, 333 U.S. 10, 68 S.Ct. 367, 92 L.Ed. 436 (1948) (warrant needed as "no evidence or contraband was threatened with removal or destruction").

trail * * *; and (5) the ready destructibility of the contraband and the knowledge "that efforts to dispose of narcotics and to escape are characteristic behavior of persons engaged in the narcotics traffic."

What one thinks of the *Rubin* formulation is likely to depend upon one's assumptions as to whether the police could resolve their dilemma by some less intrusive alternative, which naturally leads to the so-called impoundment alternative. It has sometimes been suggested that it would be preferable for officers to impound the dwelling until they can obtain a search warrant, during which time those occupants who could not lawfully be arrested would be forced to leave the building or else remain under police surveillance. In recent years more and more courts have expressed their approval of the impoundment alternative. For impoundment to be reasonable, these decisions indicate, the persons present when the police enter should be permitted to leave if they choose that option, and in any event the period of impoundment should be relatively short.

The Supreme Court addressed this important practice, albeit in a somewhat obscure manner, in *Segura v. United States*.[32] There police made a warrantless entry of an apartment, arrested all the occupants (who were promptly removed from the scene), and then remained within 19 hours until a search warrant was obtained and executed. The Court held, 5–4, "that where officers, having probable cause, enter premises, and with probable cause, arrest the occupants who have legitimate possessory interests in its contents and take them into custody and, for no more than the period here involved, secure the premises from within to preserve the status quo while others, in good faith, are in the process of

obtaining a warrant, they do not violate the Fourth Amendment's proscription against unreasonable seizures." The Court went on to hold that in any event any illegality in the initial entry would not require suppression of the evidence first discovered in the later execution of the search warrant.

Curiously, the first holding in *Segura* was elaborated and explained in a part of the opinion joined in by only two members of the Court. It was there noted that the Court had in other contexts approved warrantless seizures in circumstances where a warrantless search would have been impermissible,[33] and the two could see "no reason * * * why the same principle should not apply when a dwelling is involved." Those two Justices next concluded that the entry could be disregarded; absent exigent circumstances, the entry might constitute an illegal *search* (as the lower court had held), but it had nothing to do with the *seizure* because the interference with possessory interests was no greater than had the officers guarded the premises without entry. This would make the 19 hours of occupation irrelevant, but presumably only because those persons with a possessory interest in the premises were in custody during that time.[34]

A somewhat different tactic was at issue in *Illinois v. McArthur*,[35] where two police officers stood by outside to keep the peace while defendant's wife removed her effects from the family residence, a trailer. Upon exiting, she told the officers her husband had hidden marijuana under the couch, so the officers sought his permission to search the premises. When he refused, one officer left to obtain a search warrant, while another officer remained on the porch with defendant, who was told he could

---

32. 468 U.S. 796, 104 S.Ct. 3380, 82 L.Ed.2d 599 (1984).

33. E.g., Arkansas v. Sanders, 442 U.S. 753, 99 S.Ct. 2586, 61 L.Ed.2d 235 (1979); United States v. Chadwick, 433 U.S. 1, 97 S.Ct. 2476, 53 L.Ed.2d 538 (1977), discussed in § 3.7(c).

34. The two Justices emphasized that those persons "were under arrest and in the custody of the police throughout the entire period the agents occupied the apartment," so that the "actual interference with their possessory interests in the apartment and its contents was, thus, virtually nonexistent." The dissenters argued

that the occupation was an unreasonable search, infringing upon a reasonable expectation of privacy, and an unreasonable seizure, involving exercise of "complete dominion and control over the apartment and its contents"; that the Fourth Amendment protects possessory interests in a residence even when the occupants are in custody; and declared that "what is even more strange about the Chief Justice's conclusion is that it permits the authorities to benefit from the fact that they had unlawfully arrested" an occupant of the apartment.

35. 531 U.S. 326, 121 S.Ct. 946, 148 L.Ed.2d 838 (2001).

not reenter unless he was accompanied by the officer. A warrant was obtained and executed two hours later, but in the interim defendant entered the trailer two or three times, and on each occasion the officer stood just inside the door and observe his actions. The Court held "that the restriction at issue was reasonable, and hence lawful, in light of" four enumerated circumstances: (i) "the police had probable cause to believe that McArthur's trailer home contained evidence of a crime and contraband, namely, unlawful drugs";[36] (ii) "the police had good reason to fear that, unless restrained, McArthur would destroy the drugs before they could return with a warrant," as they reasonably concluded that even before the requested consent to search he realized his angry wife had informed the police about the drugs; (iii) "the police made reasonable efforts to reconcile their law enforcement needs with the demands of personal privacy" by imposing "a significantly less strict restraint" than a warrantless search of the premises; and (iv) "the police imposed the restraint for a limited period of time, namely, two hours."[37]

Some courts for years recognized an exception to the general rule that a search warrant is needed to search premises for evidence, namely, that police could enter without a warrant to conduct an investigation at the scene of a possible homicide. But in *Mincey v. Arizona*,[38] after noting that no "emergency threat-ening life or limb" had been established, the Court "decline[d] to hold that the seriousness of the offense under investigation itself creates exigent circumstances of the kind that under the Fourth Amendment justify a warrantless search," and thus concluded "that the 'murder scene exception' created by the Arizona Supreme Court is inconsistent with the Fourth and Fourteenth Amendments." *Mincey* lacks *all* of the characteristics that lower courts traditionally relied upon in recognizing such an exception: this was not an investigation into a then unknown cause of death, as the police knew it was murder and knew who the perpetrator was; this was not a case in which an occupant of the premises had summoned police and tacitly approved of the investigation;[39] and this was not an investigation kept within narrow temporal and spatial dimensions. This makes it more understandable why the Court failed to permit some degree of warrantless investigation as it had done just a few weeks before in the analogous case of *Michigan v. Tyler*,[40] concerning investigation within premises of the cause of a fire.[41] But in the more recent case of *Thompson v. Louisiana*,[42] lacking the various extreme circumstances present in *Mincey*, the Court again declined to recognize a murder scene exception to the warrant requirement. Absent a warrant, the Court declared, evidence would be admissible only if discovered in plain view while police

36. As for defendant's reliance upon *Welsh v. Wisconsin*, note 7 supra, the *McArthur* majority distinguished *Welsh* because (a) the offense involved here was punishable by up to 30 days in jail, and (b) "the restriction at issue here is less serious." (Only Justice Stevens concluded otherwise as to the *Welsh* doctrine.)

37. Souter, J., concurring, in *McArthur*, reasoned that the "probability of destruction" of the marijuana that "would have justified the police in entering McArthur's trailer promptly to make a lawful, warrantless search" had he remained inside "abated and so did the reasonableness of entry by the police" once he came outside, but that then it was reasonable for the police to keep him from reentering, not because "the law officiously insists on safeguarding a suspect's privacy from search," but rather because of "the law's strong preference for warrants, which underlies the rule that a search with a warrant has a stronger claim to justification on later, judicial review than a search without one. * * * The law can hardly raise incentives to obtain a warrant without giving the police a fair chance to take their probable cause to a magistrate and get one."

38. 437 U.S. 385, 98 S.Ct. 2408, 57 L.Ed.2d 290 (1978).

39. Whether this makes a difference remains to be determined by the Supreme Court. In Flippo v. West Virginia, 528 U.S. 11, 120 S.Ct. 7, 145 L.Ed.2d 16 (1999), after defendant's 911 call that he and his wife had been attacked at a cabin in a state park, police arrived at the scene and found defendant outside wounded and his wife inside dead. The contents of a briefcase near the body, found upon a warrantless police reentry and search several hours later, were held admissible by the trial judge because found "within the crime scene area," a position the Court unanimously concluded "squarely conflicts with *Mincey*." As for the state's contention "that the trial court's ruling is supportable on the theory that petitioner's direction of the police to the scene of the attack implied consent to search as they did," the Court expressed no opinion because this "factual" issue had not been raised below.

40. 436 U.S. 499, 98 S.Ct. 1942, 56 L.Ed.2d 486 (1978).

41. See § 3.9(e).

42. 469 U.S. 17, 105 S.Ct. 409, 83 L.Ed.2d 246 (1984).

were assisting the injured party or were checking the premises for other victims or the killer. Yet another consequence of *Mincey* is that courts are inclined to uphold search warrants issued in such situations even though they are not at all specific as to what is being sought, the reason being that *Mincey* has deprived the police of an opportunity to make sufficient observations to enable the officers to identify the specific instruments or other evidence of the crimes to which a warrant would be directed.

(f) Warrantless Entry and Search for Other Purposes. Police may enter a dwelling without a warrant to render emergency aid and assistance to a person they reasonably believe to be in distress and in need of that assistance. If they entered because of a purported emergency and find evidence of crime, that evidence will be admissible only if the state shows that the warrantless entry fell within the exception, using and an objective standard as to the reasonableness of the officer's belief. But that standard is to be applied by reference to the circumstances then confronting the officer, including the need for a prompt assessment of sometimes ambiguous information concerning potentially serious consequences. The question is whether the officers would have been derelict in their duty had they acted otherwise.

Police may also enter private property for the purpose of protecting the property of the owner or occupant or some other person. The most common case is that in which the police have reason to believe that the premises in question have been burglarized or vandalized. If the police are lawfully on the premises for this purpose, they may look to see if the burglar or vandal is still present, and may also take necessary steps to identify the occupant so that he may be notified.

The other reasons for which police or other public officials might enter private premises are so varied that generalization is virtually impossible, though it is useful to ask in all such cases whether there was a "compelling urgency" for the action taken. Thus in *G.M. Leasing Corp. v. United States*,[43] where IRS agents made a warrantless entry of corporate offices to levy on property subject to seizure, the Court rejected the government's contention "that the warrant protections of the Fourth Amendment do not apply to invasion of privacy in furtherance of tax collection," and thus held the agents' entry unreasonable because there had been no showing of exigent circumstances.

(g) What May Be Seized. Assuming now a lawful warrantless entry or search of private premises on one of the bases heretofore discussed, there remains the separate question of what may be seized. The Court in *Coolidge v. New Hampshire*[44] indicated "plain view" seizures would often be proper in such circumstances, and then referred to *Warden v. Hayden*,[45] which teaches that to justify such a seizure there must be "a nexus—automatically provided in the case of fruits, instrumentalities or contraband—between the item to be seized and criminal behavior," that is, probable cause "to believe that the evidence sought will aid in a particular apprehension or conviction."

Except when there is some established justification for more closely examining an object (e.g., where it is within the "immediate control" of the arrestee for *Chimel* purposes), this probable cause, the Court also said in *Coolidge,* must be "immediately apparent," as "the 'plain view' doctrine may not be used to extend a general exploratory search from one object to another until something incriminating at last emerges."[46] For a time, many lower courts held it was nonetheless proper for police to pick up an item and take closer note of

---

43. 429 U.S. 338, 97 S.Ct. 619, 50 L.Ed.2d 530 (1977).

44. 403 U.S. 443, 91 S.Ct. 2022, 29 L.Ed.2d 564 (1971).

45. 387 U.S. 294, 87 S.Ct. 1642, 18 L.Ed.2d 782 (1967).

46. Later, in construing *Coolidge,* the Court stated that the incriminating character must *itself* be in plain view. In Horton v. California, 496 U.S. 128, 110 S.Ct. 2301, 110 L.Ed.2d 112 (1990), the Court gave, as one

reason the seizure of vehicles *as* evidence in *Coolidge* did not meet the requirements for a plain view warrantless seizure, the failure to meet the "immediately apparent" requirement: "the cars were obviously in plain view, but their probative value remained uncertain until after the interiors were swept and examined microscopically."

its character and identifying characteristics, *provided* there was a pre-existing reasonable suspicion the object was subject to seizure. But that approach was rejected in *Arizona v. Hicks*,[47] holding full probable cause was needed to pick up an item of stereo equipment to ascertain its serial number (which revealed it was stolen property). The majority deemed it unwise "to send police and judges into a new thicket of Fourth Amendment law" by recognizing a third category of police conduct between "a plain-view inspection" requiring no suspicion and "a 'full-blown search'" requiring probable cause.

Yet another requirement set out in *Coolidge* is "that the discovery of evidence in plain view must be inadvertent." This requirement, though not endorsed by a majority of the Court,[48] was readily accepted by most lower courts. However, the doctrine is by no means sound,[49] and was ultimately rejected by the Court in *Horton v. California*.[50] In *Horton,* the Court indicated its disapproval of Fourth Amendment "standards that depend upon the subjective state of mind of the officer," and added that adherence to the Fourth Amendment's particularity-of-description requirements "serves the interest in limiting the area and duration of the search that the inadvertence requirement inadequately protects."

Somewhat different than the "inadvertent discovery" doctrine is the notion that evidence found within premises will be suppressed if the entry was a subterfuge, as where the police passed up a prior opportunity to arrest defendant on the street and followed him home and then entered the premises to arrest, though there was absolutely no reason for foregoing the earlier arrest opportunity. The cases adopting this position appear to have been deprived of their vitality by the subsequent Supreme Court decisions in *Scott v. United States*[51] and *Whren v. United States*,[52] which foreclose pretext-type claims grounded in either the officer's subjective motivation or material deviation from usual practice.

Finally, it is important to note that whatever rules may exist with respect to the seizure of other objects in plain view within premises, they do not automatically carry over to instances in which the seizure is of allegedly obscene materials. As pointed out in *Roaden v. Kentucky*,[53] involving the warrantless seizure of a film from a projection booth incident to arrest of the theatre owner there, the First Amendment is also involved in such a situation, necessitating examination of "what is 'unreasonable' in the light of the values of freedom of expression." This being so, a warrantless seizure is permissible in that kind of case only where "there are exigent circumstances in which police action literally must be 'now or never' to preserve the evidence of the crime."

§ 3.7   Search and Seizure of Vehicles

(a) Search Incident to Arrest. Back when courts generally permitted a full warrantless search of the defendant's premises merely because of his arrest there, a comparable unrestrained search was permitted of vehicles in the possession or general control of the arrestee at the time of his arrest. But then came *Chimel v. California*,[1] in which the Court held that because the rationale underlying search incident to arrest is the need to prevent the arrestee from obtaining a weapon or destroying evidence, such a search could extend only to "the arrestee's person and the area 'within his immediate control'—construing that phrase to mean the area from within which he might gain possession of a weapon or destructible evidence." Though it was sometimes held that the *Chimel* rule did not carry

---

47. 480 U.S. 321, 107 S.Ct. 1149, 94 L.Ed.2d 347 (1987).

48. Four members of the Court dissented, and Harlan, J., concurred in a part of the opinion other than that in which the inadvertent discovery limitation is stated.

49. See § 3.4(k).

50. 496 U.S. 128, 110 S.Ct. 2301, 110 L.Ed.2d 112 (1990).

51. 436 U.S. 128, 98 S.Ct. 1717, 56 L.Ed.2d 168 (1978).

52. 517 U.S. 806, 116 S.Ct. 1769, 135 L.Ed.2d 89 (1996).

53. 413 U.S. 496, 93 S.Ct. 2796, 37 L.Ed.2d 757 (1973).

§ 3.7

1. 395 U.S. 752, 89 S.Ct. 2034, 23 L.Ed.2d 685 (1969).

over to vehicles, the prevailing view was otherwise. Courts thus deemed the proper inquiry to be whether and to what extent it was *possible* for the arrestee to reach the particular place in the car notwithstanding his arrest, necessitating consideration of such factors as whether the arrestee had been handcuffed, the position of the defendant and the arresting officer in relation to the vehicle, and the ease or difficulty of gaining entry to the vehicle or to a particular container or enclosure therein.

The need for such a case-by-case assessment was largely obviated by *New York v. Belton*.[2] In that 5–4 decision, the majority reasoned: (1) Fourth Amendment protections "can only be realized if the police are acting under a set of rules which, in most instances, make it possible to reach a correct determination beforehand as to whether an invasion of privacy is justified in the interest of law enforcement"; (2) "no straight-forward rule has emerged from the litigated cases respecting the question involved here"; (3) this has caused the courts "difficulty" and has put the appellate cases into "disarray"; (4) the cases suggest "the generalization that articles inside the relatively narrow compass of the passenger compartment of an automobile are in fact generally, even if not inevitably, within 'the area into which an arrestee might reach in order to grab a weapon or evidentiary item'"; and thus (5) "the workable rule this category of cases requires" is best achieved by holding "that when a policeman has made a lawful custodial arrest of the occupant[3] of an automobile, he may, as a contemporaneous incident of that arrest, search the passenger compartment of that automobile," inclusive of "the contents of any containers found within the passenger compartment."

Despite the fact that it is often advantageous to both privacy interests and law enforcement interests if rules of police conduct are stated in terms of easily understood standardized procedures that may be routinely followed, the wisdom of the *Belton* rule is open to question. The Court is unconvincing in its claim that a case-by-case application of the *Chimel* principle in vehicle cases has proved unworkable. Moreover, the results produced under the *Belton* "bright line" well exceed those that usually would be reached by a case-by-case application of *Chimel*. This is particularly troubling when it is considered that *Belton* permits broad searches of vehicles without any probable cause that evidence will be found therein, provided only that there is probable cause to arrest an occupant. This is no less than an invitation to subterfuge, for police wishing to search a car but lacking grounds to do so need only await the commission of some minor offense by the driver or other occupant and then arrest before the search.[4]

Belton applies only when there has been a "custodial arrest," and therefore such search of an automobile incident to arrest is not permissible when the person merely receives a citation at the scene, even though he will be allowed to reenter his car and go his way.[5] *Belton* requires that the arrest and search be "contemporaneous," and thus it appears that the search of the vehicle must occur at the place of arrest and not later at the station. There is disagreement as to whether *Belton* also means the search must be made before the arrestee is taken from the scene, but clearly it is unnecessary that he have continuing access to the car. Thus, a search of a vehicle under *Belton* is permissible even after the defendant has been removed from the car, handcuffed and placed in a squad car, and even if he is in the custody of several officers. The

---

2. 453 U.S. 454, 101 S.Ct. 2860, 69 L.Ed.2d 768 (1981).

3. Lower courts are not in agreement as to what "occupant" means in this context, but the matter remains unresolved by the Supreme Court. The Court granted certiorari to review a ruling that "*Belton*'s bright-line rule is limited to situations where the law enforcement officer initiates contact with the defendant" while defendant remains in the car, but then decided it lacked jurisdiction because after so holding the state court had remanded for further factfinding and a determination of the outcome

under *Chimel*. Florida v. Thomas, 532 U.S. 774, 121 S.Ct. 1905, 150 L.Ed.2d 1 (2001).

4. Such a pretext may not be challenged because of "the actual motivations of individual officers" or because "the officer's conduct deviated materially from usual police practice." Wren v. United States, 517 U.S. 806, 116 S.Ct. 1769, 135 L.Ed.2d 89 (1996).

5. Knowles v. Iowa, 525 U.S. 113, 119 S.Ct. 484, 142 L.Ed.2d 492 (1998), discussed in § 3.5 at note 35.

term "passenger compartment" in *Belton* has been construed to mean all areas reachable without exiting the vehicle, without regard to the likelihood that such reaching actually occurred in the particular case. It would seem, notwithstanding the fears of the *Belton* dissenters of a contrary interpretation, that the *Belton* "bright line" rule does not permit the dismantling of the vehicle to get inside door panels, the opening of sealed containers, or other searches into particular places to which the arrestee unquestionably had no access immediately preceding his apprehension.

(b) Search and Seizure to Search for Evidence. The Supreme Court considered the question of whether a warrantless automobile search for evidence was lawful in the prohibition-era case of *Carroll v. United States.*[6] Federal agents stopped a car they had probable cause to believe contained illegal liquor and immediately subjected it to a warrantless search. In upholding that action, the Court recognized "a necessary difference between a search of a store, dwelling house, or other structure in respect of which a proper official warrant readily may be obtained and a search of a ship, motor boat, wagon, or automobile for contraband goods, where it is not practicable to secure a warrant, because the vehicle can be quickly moved out of the locality or jurisdiction in which the warrant must be sought." On the facts of *Carroll,* the point was well taken, for the officers lacked a basis for "in presence" misdemeanor arrests of the occupants and thus could not have prevented them from moving the vehicle while a warrant was being sought.

Some courts concluded *Carroll* could not be extended to cases in which the vehicle occupants were arrested for the simple reason that exigencies do not exist when the vehicle and the suspect are both in police custody. But the Supreme Court, in *Chambers v. Maroney,*[7] did not agree. In upholding the warrantless search at the police station of a station wagon seized upon arrest of the occupants for a just-committed armed robbery, the Court stated:

Neither *Carroll,* nor other cases in this Court require or suggest that in every conceivable circumstance the search of an auto even with probable cause may be made without the extra protection for privacy that a warrant affords. But the circumstances that furnish probable cause to search a particular auto for particular articles are most often unforeseeable; moreover, the opportunity to search is fleeting since a car is readily movable. Where this is true, as in *Carroll* and the case before us now, if an effective search is to be made at any time, either the search must be made immediately without a warrant or the car itself must be seized and held without a warrant for whatever period is necessary to obtain a warrant for the search.
* * *

Arguably, because of the preference for a magistrate's judgment, only the immobilization of the car should be permitted until a search warrant is obtained; arguably, only the "lesser" intrusion is permissible until the magistrate authorizes the "greater." But which is the "greater" and which the "lesser" intrusion is itself a debatable question and the answer may depend on a variety of circumstances. For constitutional purposes, we see no difference between on the one hand seizing and holding a car before presenting the probable cause issue to a magistrate and on the other hand carrying out an immediate search without a warrant. Given probable cause to search, either course is reasonable under the Fourth Amendment.

On the facts before us, the blue station wagon could have been searched on the spot when it was stopped since there was probable cause to search and it was a fleeting target for a search. The probable-cause factor still obtained at the station house and so did the mobility of the car unless the Fourth Amendment permits a warrantless seizure of the car and the denial of its use to anyone until a warrant is secured. In that event there is little to choose in terms of practical consequences between an immediate search

---

6. 267 U.S. 132, 45 S.Ct. 280, 69 L.Ed. 543 (1925).

7. 399 U.S. 42, 90 S.Ct. 1975, 26 L.Ed.2d 419 (1970).

without a warrant and the car's immobilization until a warrant is obtained.[8]

This passage from *Chambers* is truly remarkable. There is no explanation as to why it is a "debatable question" whether the seizure of a car is a lesser intrusion than a search of its interior, when the Court just months before had found not at all debatable a similar issue.[9] Secondly, the choices are characterized as "immediate search" and "holding a car before presenting the probable cause issue to a magistrate," thus ignoring the fact that the case involved neither of these but instead a holding of the car followed by a warrantless search. Thirdly, the Court jumped to the conclusion that "the mobility of the car" "still obtained at the station house," though the owner of the car was among those arrested for a serious crime; he clearly would be in no position to claim the car in the interval needed to get a warrant, and there is no indication that the owner asked that the car be turned over to some third party. That is, resort to the warrant process in order to protect the owner's privacy interest would not have involved any greater intrusion upon the owner's possessory interest in the car. Because *Chambers* cannot be rationalized in terms of the oft-stated principle that a search warrant is required except in exigent circumstances, it was perhaps inevitable that members of the Court would later disagree frequently as to its application.

In *Coolidge v. New Hampshire*,[10] the police, after months of investigation, arrested defendant for murder and contemporaneously seized his car from his driveway and later searched it because it was believed to have been used in commission of the crime. Though the car was seized pursuant to a warrant, the warrant was invalid, and thus an effort was made to justify it as a lawful warrantless seizure and search. Four members of the Court noted that "the police had known for some time of the probable role of the Pontiac car in the crime" and that the defendant "had already ample opportunity to destroy any evidence he thought incriminating," which might well distinguish *Coolidge* from *Chambers* and *Carroll* if the notion were that a warrant is necessary when there is neither a need for an immediate search nor a need for an immediate seizure. But in concluding the warrantless seizure and search were unlawful, they emphasized other purported distinguishing characteristics: that the objects sought "were neither stolen or contraband nor dangerous"; that this was not a car "stopped on the open highway" but "an unoccupied vehicle, on private property"; and that the police had taken steps so that neither Coolidge nor his wife could gain access to the car. But, as other members of the Court correctly noted,[11] none of those three facts distinguishes the case from *Chambers*. *Coolidge* was limited to its facts in a series of subsequent decisions all upholding warrantless search of vehicles.[12] Though in some of these

8. The warrantless search need not occur immediately upon arrival of the vehicle at the place where it is to be held. As the Court noted in United States v. Johns, 469 U.S. 478, 105 S.Ct. 881, 83 L.Ed.2d 890 (1985), there "is no requirement that the warrantless search of a vehicle occur contemporaneously with its lawful seizure." But the Court cautioned that police could not "indefinitely retain possession of a vehicle and its contents before they complete a vehicle search," for in some circumstances "the owner of a vehicle or its contents might attempt to prove that delay in the completion of a vehicle search was unreasonable because it adversely affected a privacy or possessory interest."

9. United States v. Van Leeuwen, 397 U.S. 249, 90 S.Ct. 1029, 25 L.Ed.2d 282 (1970) (holding that the proper course of action, given probable cause to search packages placed in the mails, was to withhold routing and delivery of the packages for the period necessary to obtain a search warrant).

10. 403 U.S. 443, 91 S.Ct. 2022, 29 L.Ed.2d 564 (1971).

11. To suggest that the nature of the objects sought is relevant, Justice White observed, "is reminiscent of the confusing and unworkable approach that I thought *Warden v. Hayden* had firmly put aside," a reference to the abandonment of the "mere evidence" rule, see § 3.4(a). He also pointed out that it made no sense to limit the warrantless-search-of-vehicles rule to those in motion when seized, for in *Chambers* the Court "approved the search of a vehicle that was no longer moving and, with the occupants in custody, no more likely to move than the unattended movable vehicle parked on the street or in the driveway of a person's house." As for the police action to secure the car, Justice Black correctly noted that the *Chambers* vehicle was no more amenable to tampering once it had been seized by the police.

12. Florida v. Meyers, 466 U.S. 380, 104 S.Ct. 1852, 80 L.Ed.2d 381 (1984) (holding on authority of *Thomas*, below, that lower court erred in concluding warrantless search of car improper where, as here, car had been impounded 8 hours earlier and was presently stored in a secure area); Michigan v. Thomas, 458 U.S. 259, 102 S.Ct.

cases the Court pretended that exigent circumstances were necessary, it became apparent (as the Court finally acknowledged in *United States v. Chadwick*[13]) that warrantless vehicle searches were being permitted "in cases in which the possibilities of the vehicle's being removed or evidence in it destroyed were remote, if not non-existent." On what basis? Because, as the majority said in *Chadwick*: "One has a lesser expectation of privacy in a motor vehicle because its function is transportation and it seldom serves as one's residence or as the repository of personal effects * * *. It travels public thoroughfares where both its occupants and its contents are in plain view." Putting aside the fact that this characterization is certainly not beyond dispute, it would appear to provide the only possible basis for explaining *Chambers* and the post-*Coolidge* cases. Consequently, as the Court later made unmistakably clear, the so-called automobile exception to the Fourth Amendment's warrant requirement "does not have a separate exigency requirement,"[14] which means there is no necessity whatsoever to show circumstances in the particular case that prevented or even made more difficult the procurement of a search warrant.[15]

In *California v. Carney*,[16] the *Chambers* vehicle exception was held applicable to a motor home that "is being used on the highways, or if it is readily capable of such use and is found stationary in a place not regularly used for residential purposes."[17] The majority emphasized both justifications for the vehicle exception, noting that a motor home in such circumstances is "readily mobile" and has "a reduced expectation of privacy stemming from its use as a licensed motor vehicle subject to a range of police regulation inapplicable to a fixed dwelling." The three dissenters objected that the Court's prior cases (especially the container-in-a-vehicle cases discussed in the next subsection) "teach us that inherent mobility is not a sufficient justification for the fashioning of an exception to the warrant requirement * * * in the face of heightened expectations of privacy in the location searched," and that motor homes, "by their common use and construction, afford their owners a substantial and legitimate expectation of privacy when they dwell within."[18]

3079, 73 L.Ed.2d 750 (1982) (stressing that "the justification to conduct such a warrantless search does not vanish once the car has been immobilized; nor does it depend upon a reviewing court's assessment of the likelihood in each particular case that the car would have been driven away, or that its contents would have been tampered with, during the period required for the police to obtain a warrant"); Colorado v. Bannister, 449 U.S. 1, 101 S.Ct. 42, 66 L.Ed.2d 1 (1980) (unanimous Court concludes that where probable cause to search developed after car stopped for traffic violation, "it would be especially unreasonable to require a detour to a magistrate before the unanticipated evidence could be lawfully seized"); Texas v. White, 423 U.S. 67, 96 S.Ct. 304, 46 L.Ed.2d 209 (1975) (defendant arrested while attempting to pass fraudulent checks at bank, car later searched without warrant at the station; search lawful under *Chambers* rule that "police officers with probable cause to search an automobile on the scene where it was stopped could constitutionally do so later at the station house without first obtaining a warrant"); Cardwell v. Lewis, 417 U.S. 583, 94 S.Ct. 2464, 41 L.Ed.2d 325 (1974) (after defendant's arrest, his car towed from nearby public lot and examined; four Justices distinguished *Coolidge* because the seizure here was from a public place, and purported to be requiring exigent circumstances but said such circumstances were present even though "the police might have obtained a warrant earlier").

13.   433 U.S. 1, 97 S.Ct. 2476, 53 L.Ed.2d 538 (1977).

14.   Maryland v. Dyson, 527 U.S. 465, 119 S.Ct. 2013, 144 L.Ed.2d 442 (1999).

15.   And thus the Court summarily reversed two state cases holding that the Fourth Amendment "requires police to obtain a warrant before searching an automobile unless exigent circumstances are present," noting that those "holdings rest on an incorrect reading of the automobile exception to the Fourth Amendment's warrant requirement." Pennsylvania v. Labron, 518 U.S. 938, 116 S.Ct. 2485, 135 L.Ed.2d 1031 (1996). (There were two dissenters in *Labron*, but on the ground that the two state decisions "rested upon the Pennsylvania court's independent consideration of its own Constitution.")

16.   471 U.S. 386, 105 S.Ct. 2066, 85 L.Ed.2d 406 (1985).

17.   The Court declined to "pass on the application of the vehicle exception to a motor home that is situated in a way or place that objectively indicates that it is being used as a residence," but suggested: "Among the factors that might be relevant in determining whether a warrant would be required in such a circumstance is its location, whether the vehicle is readily mobile or instead, for instance, elevated on blocks, whether the vehicle is licensed, whether it is connected to utilities, and whether it has convenient access to a public road."

18.   The dissenters then concluded a warrantless search would be permissible only "when the motor home is traveling on the public streets or highways, or when exigent circumstances otherwise require an immediate search without the expenditure of time necessary to obtain a warrant."

(c) Search of Containers and Persons Within. In *United States v. Chadwick*,[19] three persons were arrested for transportation of marijuana, following which the police seized and later searched without a warrant a double-locked footlocker that had just been put into the open trunk of a car belonging to one of the defendants. The Court declined to uphold the search by analogy to the previously-discussed vehicle cases, reasoning that vehicles have a "diminished expectation of privacy" but that the footlocker did not because it was "not open to public view" or "subject to regular inspections and official scrutiny on a continuing basis" and because it "is intended as a repository of personal effects." But because "the Government does not contend that the footlocker's brief contact with Chadwick's car makes this an automobile search," *Chadwick* did not settle the questions of whether containers in a vehicle may be searched without a warrant in an otherwise lawful warrantless search of the vehicle.

That issue was first considered by the Court in the subsequently-overruled[20] case of *Arkansas v. Sanders*,[21] involving a warrantless search of an unlocked suitcase found in the trunk of a cab in which the arrestee had been riding at the time of his arrest. Thus confronted with "the task of determining whether the warrantless search of respondent's suitcase falls on the *Chadwick* or the *Chambers/Carroll* side of the Fourth Amendment line," the Court ruled "that the warrant requirement of the Fourth Amendment applies to personal luggage taken from an automobile to the same degree it applies to such luggage in other locations." This is because the container's location within a vehicle affected neither the defendant's expectation of privacy as to the contain-

er's contents nor the true exigencies of the situation; the use of a suitcase "as a repository for personal items" is especially evident in such circumstances, and once the police have taken the case from the car its mobility is no longer affected by its prior location. Thus, said the Court in *Sanders,* the police should have seized the suitcase and then held it while a search warrant was sought, as there were no truly exigent circumstances mandating an immediate search.

Sanders was later limited to the special situation present in that case, where there was probable cause to search a particular container but not probable cause to search the vehicle generally. When the latter, broader form of probable cause exists, the Court held in *United States v. Ross*,[22] "the scope of the warrantless search authorized by [the automobile] exception is no broader and no narrower than a magistrate could legitimately authorize by warrant," so that if "probable cause justifies the search of a lawfully stopped vehicle, it justifies the search of every part of the vehicle and its contents that may conceal the object of the search." Thus in *Ross,* where (unlike *Chadwick* and *Sanders*) there was probable cause to search the entire vehicle for drugs, the police lawfully searched a brown paper bag and a zippered pouch found in the trunk. The *Ross* Court explained that this conclusion was consistent with its earlier application of the *Carroll* rule on search of vehicles,[23] and that it was justified by the practical consideration that "prohibiting police from opening immediately a container in which the object of the search is most likely to be found and instead forcing them first to comb the entire vehicle would actually exacerbate the intrusion on privacy interests."[24] *Ross* was correctly decided

---

19. 433 U.S. 1, 97 S.Ct. 2476, 53 L.Ed.2d 538 (1977).

20. See text at note 26 infra.

21. 442 U.S. 753, 99 S.Ct. 2586, 61 L.Ed.2d 235 (1979).

22. 456 U.S. 798, 102 S.Ct. 2157, 72 L.Ed.2d 572 (1982).

23. In *Carroll* the Court had upheld the tearing open of upholstery to find illegal liquor; in *Chambers* the lawful warrantless search had extended to a compartment under the dashboard; in Scher v. United States, 305 U.S. 251, 59 S.Ct. 174, 83 L.Ed. 151 (1938), the Court upheld a search of "packages wrapped in brown paper, and tied with

twine," found in the car trunk; and in Husty v. United States, 282 U.S. 694, 51 S.Ct. 240, 75 L.Ed. 629 (1931), the permitted search was of "whiskey bags" found in the car.

24. This is not to suggest that the search of the package must occur immediately. In United States v. Johns, 469 U.S. 478, 105 S.Ct. 881, 83 L.Ed.2d 890 (1985), two pickup trucks smelling of marijuana and containing many packages wrapped in the manner marijuana was commonly packaged were seized by agents. The packages were placed in a warehouse and opened without a warrant three days later. Applying *Ross*, the Court declined to hold "that searches of containers discovered in the course of a

within the framework of existing Fourth Amendment law, as it is more akin to *Chambers* than to *Chadwick,* but is for that reason subject to the same criticisms that have been directed at *Chambers*.[25]

The distinction drawn in *Ross* is now irrelevant, however, for in *California v. Acevedo*,[26] involving search of a paper bag in a car on probable cause limited to the bag, the Court concluded "that it is better to adopt one clear-cut rule to govern automobile searches and eliminate the warrant requirement for closed containers set forth in *Sanders*." The Court could see "no principled distinction in terms of either the privacy expectation or the exigent circumstances between the paper bag found by the police in *Ross* and the paper bag found by the police here," for in each case the container was "equally easy for the police to store and for the suspect to hide or destroy." Also, the Court reasoned, the distinction drawn in *Ross* (i) "provided only minimal protection for privacy," given the search-incident-to-arrest rule of *Belton* and the inducement that *Ross* offers for police stretching probable cause to include the entire vehicle, and (ii) "impeded effective law enforcement" because police had experienced difficulty in determining whether *Ross* or *Sanders* was applicable in particular cases.

Assuming a lawful warrantless search of a vehicle, may it automatically extend to the person of an occupant? No, the Supreme Court held in *United States v. Di Re*,[27] for the need to do so is no greater than the necessity "for searching guests of a house for which a search warrant had issued," which the government conceded would not be lawful.[28] However, it has been argued that if the objects sought are not found in the car and they are of a size that they could be concealed on the person, then the occupants of the vehicle should be subject to search if the officer has reason to suspect one of them has the objects concealed on his person. In support, it is said that the *Di Re* analogy is unsound and that it is absurd to say that the occupants can take the narcotics out of the glove compartment and stuff them in their pockets, and drive happily away after the vehicle has been fruitlessly searched.

However, *Di Re* was not overturned but only distinguished when the Court later confronted the related question of when a passenger's effects may be searched. In *Wyoming v. Houghton*,[29] the state court had held that while an officer with probable cause to search a vehicle may search all containers that might conceal the object of the search, if the officer knows or should know that a container belongs to a passenger who is not suspected of criminal activity, then that container is outside the scope of the search unless someone had the opportunity to conceal contraband within it to avoid detection. But the Supreme Court instead decided that "when there is probable cause to search for contraband in a car, it is reasonable for police officers * * * to examine packages and containers without a showing of individualized probable cause for each one," meaning that the search may extend to "a passenger's personal belongings, just like the driver's belongings or containers attached to the car like a glove compartment." And this is so, the Court added, even without any information suggesting either involvement by that passenger in the criminality under investigation or placement of contraband into the passenger's effects by the driver. Such a rule, the Court explained, was justified by "the balancing of the relative interests" involved: (i) "passengers, no less than drivers, possess a reduced expectation of privacy with regard to the property that they transport in cars," as distinguished from the "heightened protec-

vehicle search are subject to temporal restrictions not applicable to the vehicle search itself." Thus the packages—as with the vehicle in which they were found—could be searched well after seizure of the vehicles, provided only that the delay was not "unreasonable because it adversely affected a privacy and possessory interest." There was no unreasonable delay here, as a warrantless search of the packages would have been lawful earlier, and in the interim the defendants had not sought return of the property.

25. See § 3.7(b).

26. 500 U.S. 565, 111 S.Ct. 1982, 114 L.Ed.2d 619 (1991).

27. 332 U.S. 581, 68 S.Ct. 222, 92 L.Ed. 210 (1948).

28. Quite correctly. See § 3.4(i).

29. 526 U.S. 295, 119 S.Ct. 1297, 143 L.Ed.2d 408 (1999).

tion" re search of the person recognized in *Di Re*;[30] and (ii) the "practical realities" are that "a car passenger * * * will often be engaged in a common enterprise with the driver" or else the criminal "might be able to hide contraband in a passenger's belongings as readily as other containers in the car * * * without the passenger's knowledge or permission," thus justifying a bright-line rule here because of the difficulty that would be involved in sorting out, on a case-by-case basis, such questions as whether the passenger's claim of ownership is valid, whether the passenger was a confederate, or whether the driver might have introduced the contraband into the package even without the passenger's knowledge. Such a conclusion, the three dissenters in *Houghton* objected, could not be squared with the teaching of *Ross* that the scope of a search "is defined by the object of the search and the places in which there is probable cause to believe that it may be found."

(d) Seizure for Other Purposes. If a vehicle is itself evidence of crime, may it be seized without a warrant as evidence in plain view? Not necessarily, concluded at least four members of the Court in *Coolidge v. New Hampshire*,[31] as a warrantless seizure on a plain view theory is permissible only upon "inadvertent discovery" of the item seized, because the "requirement of a warrant to seize imposes no inconvenience whatever" when "the police know in advance the location of the evidence and intend to seize it." But in *Cardwell v. Lewis*,[32] involving the warrantless seizure of defendant's car from a public parking lot some time following his arrest elsewhere, four members of the Court deemed this lawful; no mention was made of the "inadvertent discovery" limitation, though it was claimed the instant case differed from *Coolidge* "in the circumstances of the seizure," apparently a reference to the possibility that

the defendant's wife might have gained access to the car had it not been immediately seized. In *Horton v. California*,[33] the Court rejected the *Coolidge* "inadvertent discovery" requirement but then seemingly endorsed the *result* in *Coolidge* as grounded in noncompliance with two other conditions of a plain view warrantless seizure: (i) the seized objects' incriminating character "must also be 'immediately apparent,'" which was not the case in *Coolidge* because "the cars were obviously in plain view, but their probative value remained uncertain until after the interiors were swept and examined microscopically"; and (ii) "not only must the officer be lawfully located in a place from which the object can be plainly seen, but he or she must also have a lawful right of access to the object itself," which was not the case in *Coolidge* because "the seizure of the cars was accomplished by means of a warrantless trespass on the defendant's property."

Coolidge and *Cardwell* predate the broad rule in *California v. Carney*[34] allowing warrantless search of vehicles for evidence absent any genuine exigent circumstances, and thus it might be argued that the *Carney* rule also applies in this context to permit a warrantless seizure of a car seized *as* evidence. But, *Carney* focuses upon the low privacy interest in the vehicle, while seizure of a vehicle as evidence is also likely to amount to a major intrusion upon a possessory interest, for the vehicle itself will probably be held a substantial period of time, much longer than necessary to facilitate the typical *Carney* search. This being the case, it might be concluded that the initial seizure of a vehicle as evidence is permissible without a warrant (by analogy to *Carney*), but that a substantial continuation of that dispossession would require a warrant.

It is common at both the federal and state level to find statutes authorizing the seizure

---

30. Given this property/person distinction, there will doubtless arise cases where it is difficult to decide which privacy expectation is applicable. Breyer, J., concurring in *Houghton*, noted "that the container here at issue, a woman's purse, was found at a considerable distance from its owner," and intimated that the result should be different "if a woman's purse, like a man's billfold, were attached to her person."

31. 403 U.S. 443, 91 S.Ct. 2022, 29 L.Ed.2d 564 (1971).

32. 417 U.S. 583, 94 S.Ct. 2464, 41 L.Ed.2d 325 (1974).

33. 496 U.S. 128, 110 S.Ct. 2301, 110 L.Ed.2d 112 (1990).

34. 471 U.S. 386, 105 S.Ct. 2066, 85 L.Ed.2d 406 (1985).

and subsequent forfeiture of a vehicle because it was used in certain criminal activity. The courts were once in disagreement as to whether such seizures could be made without a warrant, but over time more and more lower courts upheld the warrantless seizure of automobiles for forfeiture, usually by analogy to the *Chambers–Carney* line of cases. The matter was finally settled when the Supreme Court, in *Florida v. White*,[35] upheld the warrantless seizure of a vehicle from a public place on probable cause that it constituted forfeitable contraband under a state forfeiture statute. Taking note of "the special considerations recognized in the context of movable items" in the above-mentioned line of cases, the Court concluded the need was "equally weighty when the *automobile*, as opposed to its contents, is the contraband that the police seek to secure."[36] Next noting that "our Fourth Amendment jurisprudence has consistently accorded law enforcement officials greater latitude in exercising their duties in public places," the Court in *White* deemed the instant case "nearly indistinguishable" from *G.M. Leasing Corp. v. United States*,[37] involving a warrantless seizure of automobiles from public streets and lots as part of a levy on a corporation's assets for tax deficiencies. A unanimous Court in *G.M. Leasing* upheld the seizures with the brief comment that the seizures "did not involve any invasion of privacy," but went on to hold that the rule was otherwise as to warrantless searches, and thus unanimously held the agents had violated the Fourth Amendment when they entered the premises of the corporation and seized its books. The Court explained this was because under the *Camara* principle[38] the where-to-

search issue could not be left to the discretion of an agent in the field, which highlights the fact that the Court never satisfactorily explained why the what-to-seize issue (i.e., was the corporation the alter ego of the taxpayer, subjecting its cars to levy) should be left to the agents in the field.

Police impound vehicles for a variety of reasons. This occurs when a vehicle is found abandoned, illegally parked or in unsafe mechanical condition, and, most frequently, when the owner or operator of the vehicle has been arrested in or near the car. Generally, courts are of the view that when a person is arrested away from home, the police may impound the personal effects that are with him at the time to ensure the safety of those effects. But the better view, consistent with *Dyke v. Taylor Implement Manufacturing Co.*,[39] is that immediate impoundment of a car after the driver has been arrested for a minor traffic violation is improper because the police are obligated to give the defendant a reasonable opportunity to post his bail and obtain his prompt release. Moreover, if the driver is not afforded the usual opportunity to post bond, as provided by statute, rule of court or perhaps even police custom, then his improper continued detention contaminates the impoundment of the vehicle resulting therefrom, so that whatever is found in the course of an inventory during impoundment must be suppressed.

A broader question, relevant whatever the cause of the vehicle operator's arrest, is whether impoundment should be considered the only feasible disposition of the car or whether, instead, the police should consider other possible alternatives or even consult the arrestee concerning them. Some courts took

---

35. 526 U.S. 559, 119 S.Ct. 1555, 143 L.Ed.2d 748 (1999).

36. Two concurring Justices cautioned the decision should not be read as allowing a warrantless seizure of "anything a State chooses to call 'contraband,'" while the two dissenters objected (i) that an exigent circumstances rationale had no application "when the seizure is based upon a belief that the automobile may have been used at some time in the past to assist in illegal activity and the owner is already in custody," and (ii) that a warrant requirement "is bolstered by the inherent risks of hindsight at post-seizure hearings and law enforcement agencies' pecuniary interest in the seizure of such property."

37. 429 U.S. 338, 97 S.Ct. 619, 50 L.Ed.2d 530 (1977).

38. See § 3.9(a).

39. 391 U.S. 216, 88 S.Ct. 1472, 20 L.Ed.2d 538 (1968), where the driver, arrested for reckless driving, was at the courthouse to make bail at the time of the search, and the Court noted that the search of the vehicle could not be deemed incident to impoundment because "the police seem to have parked the car near the courthouse merely as a convenience to the owner, and to have been willing for some friend or relative to McKinney (or McKinney himself if he were soon released from custody) to drive it away."

the latter positions, but in *Colorado v. Bertine*,[40] the Court rejected, as a Fourth Amendment matter, the argument that the impoundment of the car was improper because the arrested driver was not "offered the opportunity to make other arrangements." Rejecting an "alternative 'less intrusive' means" approach,[41] the Court concluded impoundment was lawful "even though courts might as a matter of hindsight be able to devise equally reasonable rules requiring a different procedure." But the Court cautioned that the individual officer's impound-or-lock-and-leave decision must be made "according to standard criteria," which was deemed to be met in the instant case because a police "directive establishes several conditions that must be met before an officer may pursue the park and lock alternative." This latter conclusion seems erroneous, for the applicable police regulation placed *no* restrictions upon resort to the impoundment alternative.

(e) Search for Other Purposes. It is common practice for the police to conduct an inventory of the contents of vehicles they have taken into their custody in order to protect the vehicle and the property in it, and to safeguard the police or other officers from claims of lost possessions. This practice received little attention from the Supreme Court[42] until *South Dakota v. Opperman*,[43] in which defendant's illegally parked car was towed to the city impound lot where an officer, observing articles of personal property in the car, proceeded to inventory it, finding a bag of marijuana in the unlocked glove compartment. The Court concluded:

> The Vermillion police were indisputably engaged in a caretaking search of a lawfully impounded automobile. * * * The inventory

was conducted only after the car had been impounded for multiple parking violations. The owner, having left his car illegally parked for an extended period, and thus subject to impoundment, was not present to make other arrangements for the safekeeping of his belongings. The inventory itself was prompted by the presence in plain view of a number of valuables inside the car. * * * [T]here is no suggestion whatever that this standard procedure, essentially like that followed throughout the country, was a pretext concealing an investigatory police motive.

> On this record, we conclude that in following standard police procedures, prevailing throughout the country and approved by the overwhelming majority of courts, the conduct of the police was not "unreasonable" under the Fourth Amendment.

Although some jurisdictions have as a matter of local law taken a narrower view, such as that noninvestigative police inventory searches of automobiles without a warrant must be restricted to safeguarding those articles that are within plain view of the officer's vision, most courts are likely to follow what they perceive to be the implications of the *Opperman* holding.

The Court in *Opperman* was unwilling to impose upon the police, in the case where they have impounded a car without contemporaneous contact with the owner or possessor, the burden of complying with the procedure proposed by the four dissenters: "reasonable efforts under the circumstances to identify and reach the owner of the property in order to facilitate alternative means of security or to obtain his consent to the search." What then of the more common situation in which the car

---

40. 479 U.S. 367, 107 S.Ct. 738, 93 L.Ed.2d 739 (1987).

41. Relying upon the earlier rejection as to an arrestee's carried effects in Illinois v. Lafayette, 462 U.S. 640, 103 S.Ct. 2605, 77 L.Ed.2d 65 (1983).

42. The practice in its most common form failed to reach the Court. See Cady v. Dombrowski, 413 U.S. 433, 93 S.Ct. 2523, 37 L.Ed.2d 706 (1973) (atypical in that police had probable cause car contained gun, search upheld as part of "community caretaking functions"); Dyke v. Taylor Implement Manufacturing Co., 391 U.S. 216, 88 S.Ct. 1472, 20 L.Ed.2d 538 (1968) (inventory improper

because car parked temporarily while driver arranging for bail); Harris v. United States, 390 U.S. 234, 88 S.Ct. 992, 19 L.Ed.2d 1067 (1968) (evidence lawfully found while officer doing no more than securing the doors and windows); Cooper v. California, 386 U.S. 58, 87 S.Ct. 788, 17 L.Ed.2d 730 (1967) (car being held for forfeiture action several months away, inventory proper where police to have "car in their custody for such a length of time").

43. 428 U.S. 364, 96 S.Ct. 3092, 49 L.Ed.2d 1000 (1976).

was impounded incident to arrest of the operator? The four *Opperman* dissenters concluded that in such a case "his consent to the inventory is prerequisite to an inventory search." But in *Colorado v. Bertine*,[44] the Court rejected the notion that resort to such "alternative 'less intrusive' means"[45] is ever necessary. (However, the Court indicated that if such alternatives are sometimes utilized, then this must occur pursuant to "standardized criteria" set out in police regulations.)

In *Opperman* the vehicle was kept at "the old county highway yard," only partially fenced and a situs of past vandalism. The Court was unwilling to impose the burden of providing secure impoundment facilities as an alternative to inventory. There remained the claim, however, that if a particular jurisdiction does have secure facilities, then it has no need for inventory. But in *Bertine* the Court rejected such a claim, reasoning that "the security of the storage facility does not completely eliminate the need for inventorying; the police may still wish to protect themselves or the owners of the lot against false claims of theft or dangerous instrumentalities." Yet another issue is whether some special need vis-a-vis the particular car is necessary to trigger the authority to inventory. Because the Court's opinion in *Opperman* notes that the "inventory was prompted by the presence in plain view of a number of valuables inside the car," the case may be read as permitting inventory only upon such an observation. But that would be an unsound limitation; whatever right of inventory otherwise exists need not be "triggered" by the observation of such articles, for their absence does not reduce the likelihood of personal effects being present elsewhere in the car. To put the matter another way, the right to inventory is not limited by a probable cause requirement in the sense that there must be a case-by-case determination of the likelihood of valuables being in the vehicle.[46] Rather, it is sufficient that a particular inventory is not arbitrary, that is (as it was put in *Opperman*), that it "was carried out in accordance with *standard procedures* in the local police department."[47]

Finally, assuming that a particular inventory is otherwise lawful, *Opperman* does not foreclose challenge regarding the permissible scope of a vehicle inventory. The Court approved of examination within the unlocked glove compartment, "since it is a customary place for documents of ownership and registration, * * * as well as a place for the temporary storage of valuables." This would indicate that inventories may routinely extend to unlocked glove compartments, and also supports the conclusion that there is *no* right to "inventory" those parts of a vehicle in which one would not expect to find valuables stored. The inventory in *Opperman* did not extend to the locked trunk, and thus the case (as the dissenters noted) does not settle "whether the police might search a locked trunk or other compartment." But *Colorado v. Bertine*,[48] although not involving inventory into a trunk, rather clearly indicates such an inventory would be approved by the Court, as the Court upheld inventory within a vehicle kept in a secure storage facility on the ground the police are entitled "to protect themselves * * * against false claims of theft or dangerous instrumentalities."

The *Opperman* inventory did not involve an opening of containers in the vehicle, and the dissenters were thus prompted to stress that "the Court's opinion does not authorize the inspection of suitcases, boxes, or other containers which might themselves be sealed, removed and secured without further intrusion." However, the Supreme Court more recently held "that it is not 'unreasonable' for police,

---

44.　479 U.S. 367, 107 S.Ct. 738, 93 L.Ed.2d 739 (1987).

45.　Relying upon the earlier rejection as to an arrestee's carried effects in Illinois v. Lafayette, 462 U.S. 640, 103 S.Ct. 2605, 77 L.Ed.2d 65 (1983).

46.　In *Bertine*, the Court rejected the notion that the inventorying police must weigh the defendant's privacy interest against "the possibility" in the individual case that "dangerous or valuable items" would be found during an inventory.

47.　In *Bertine*, the Court reemphasized that "[o]ur decisions have always adhered to the requirement that inventories be conducted according to standardized criteria," and in *Florida v. Wells*, 495 U.S. 1, 110 S.Ct. 1632, 109 L.Ed.2d 1 (1990), the Court held the inventory there to be unconstitutional because the local police department did not have a standardized procedure for such searches.

48.　479 U.S. 367, 107 S.Ct. 738, 93 L.Ed.2d 739 (1987).

as part of the routine procedure incident to incarcerating an arrested person, to search any container or article in his possession, in accordance with established inventory procedures."[49] Relying on that case, the Court in *Colorado v. Bertine*[50] upheld an inventory extended to a backpack within the vehicle, and held that extending a vehicle inventory to containers therein did not depend upon the likelihood "that the containers might serve as a repository for dangerous or valuable items."

Bertine indicated a majority of the Court would deem it "permissible for police officers to open closed containers in an inventory search only if they are following standard police procedures that mandate the opening of such containers in every impounded vehicle."[51] However, the Court's later decision in *Florida v. Wells*[52] suggests that something short of this will likely suffice. The holding in *Wells,* agreed to by the entire Court, is only that the inventory there was unlawful because the police agency "had no policy whatever with respect to the opening of closed containers encountered during an inventory search." But dictum in *Wells,* justifiably objected to by four members of the Court,[53] goes on to say that "a police officer may be allowed sufficient latitude to determine whether a particular container should or should not be opened in light of the nature of the search and characteristics of the container itself."

In *Opperman,* the police, when they looked in the glove compartment, also found "miscellaneous papers" (a checkbook, an installment loan book, and a social security status card), which, so far as the record indicates, they removed without examination. *Opperman* thus should not be read as authorizing examination

of such documents. Justice Powell, in his separate opinion, emphasized that approval of the inventory in the instant case "provides no general license for the police to examine all the contents of such automobiles," and correctly noted in this connection that "the police may discover materials such as letters or checkbooks that 'touch upon intimate areas of an individual's personal affairs,' and 'reveal much about a person's activities, associations and beliefs.' "

Courts have also upheld warrantless searches into vehicles for a variety of other purposes. If an arrestee's car is not impounded but is to be left at the scene of the arrest, some limited police activity to secure the car and its contents is reasonable. If a person's car, because of an accident or other circumstances, is to remain in a location where it is vulnerable to intrusion by vandals, then the police, if they have probable cause that the vehicle contains a weapon or similar device that would constitute a danger if it fell into the wrong hands, may conduct a warrantless search for that item.[54] A limited search of an automobile in an effort to ascertain ownership is permissible in some circumstances, such as where the car has apparently been abandoned or where the arrested driver is possibly not the owner and does not otherwise establish the matter of ownership. Also, if "an officer has probable cause to believe that a vehicle has been the subject of burglary, tampering, or theft, he may make a limited entry and investigation, without a search warrant, of those areas he reasonably believes might contain evidence of ownership." And if the police find a person unconscious or disoriented and incoherent in a vehicle, it is reasonable for them to enter the vehicle for

---

49. Illinois v. Lafayette, 462 U.S. 640, 103 S.Ct. 2605, 77 L.Ed.2d 65 (1983).

50. 479 U.S. 367, 107 S.Ct. 738, 93 L.Ed.2d 739 (1987).

51. This language is from the opinion of three concurring Justices. The four-Justice plurality opinion seems less demanding, requiring only that the opening of closed containers be "according to standardized criteria." The two dissenters would not permit a vehicle inventory to extend to closed containers within the car.

52. 495 U.S. 1, 110 S.Ct. 1632, 109 L.Ed.2d 1 (1990).

53. Brennan and Marshall, JJ., interpreted *Bertine* as "premised on the city's inventory policy that left no dis-

cretion to individual officers as to the opening of containers"; Blackmun and Stevens, JJ., opined a state "probably could adopt a policy which requires the opening of all containers that are not locked, or a policy which requires the opening of all containers over or under a certain size, even though these policies do not call for the opening of all or no containers," but objected to the "entirely different" proposition of the majority "that an individual policeman may be afforded discretion in conducting an inventory search."

54. Cady v. Dombrowski, 413 U.S. 433, 93 S.Ct. 2523, 37 L.Ed.2d 706 (1973).

the purpose of giving aid to the person in distress and of finding information bearing upon the cause of his condition.

(f) Plain View, Subterfuge and Related Matters. Police may ordinarily seize evidence in plain view without a warrant, provided the initial intrusion that brings the police within plain view of such an article is itself lawful,[55] and thus when police seize evidence from a vehicle pursuant to any of the activities heretofore discussed, it is necessary at the outset to ascertain the lawfulness of the activity by which the police obtained the car and entered it. An object may not be seized from a car merely because the police plain view of it was lawfully acquired; there must be probable cause that the object is a fruit, instrumentality or evidence of crime.[56] And under the "immediately apparent" requirement of *Coolidge v. New Hampshire*,[57] this probable cause must be determined without examination of the object other than is justified by the purpose underlying police entry of the vehicle.[58]

Somewhat related is the question of under what circumstances the police may conduct an examination of some object (a car or personalty found therein) subsequent to the time they have taken custody of it. If the basis of the initial seizure of the item is that it constitutes evidence, it is plainly within the realm of police investigation to subject such an object to scientific testing and examination for the purpose of determining its evidentiary value. If a vehicle is seized because it is reasonably believed to contain evidence, we have seen in *Chambers v. Maroney*[59] that the search may be undertaken later at the station instead of at

the scene, and this is so even though it was feasible to conduct the search at the scene.[60] It would seem, however, that *Chambers* "contemplated some expedition in completing the searches so that automobiles could be released and returned to their owners."[61] In *United States v. Johns*,[62] where packages in a truck were opened three days after the vehicle was seized on probable cause the packages contained marijuana, the Court in upholding the search cautioned that possession of the vehicle "indefinitely" was not being approved and noted that in the instant case the defendants "never sought return of the property." A third situation is that in which a vehicle is in police custody for some other reason (e.g., an impoundment), and there then develops for the first time probable cause to search the car. Warrantless searches have been upheld in such circumstances, a result which might be defended on the ground that the vehicle was no less mobile than the vehicle in *Chambers* at the time of the search. Finally, it must be asked whether a lawfully impounded vehicle or items removed therefrom for safekeeping may later be searched or examined without probable cause that evidence will be discovered. *United States v. Edwards*,[63] discussed earlier,[64] seems to permit doing later what could have been done earlier, and thus may support the argument that when items have been exposed to police view under unobjectionable circumstances, then no reasonable expectation of privacy is breached by an officer taking a second look at such items. But *Edwards* cannot be extended to permit either (1) observation of items that need not be observed in the first

---

55. Coolidge v. New Hampshire, 403 U.S. 443, 91 S.Ct. 2022, 29 L.Ed.2d 564 (1971).

56. In Soldal v. Cook County, 506 U.S. 56, 113 S.Ct. 538, 121 L.Ed.2d 450 (1992), in rejecting the Court of Appeals' argument that the Fourth Amendment is not applicable to seizure unaccompanied by a search the Court notes that even as to the seizure of objects lawfully discovered and accessed, "in the absence of consent or a warrant permitting the seizure of the items in question, such seizures can be justified only if they meet the probable cause standard."

57. 403 U.S. 443, 91 S.Ct. 2022, 29 L.Ed.2d 564 (1971).

58. Moreover, the fact the car is itself in plain view and is *itself* of apparent evidentiary value as a probable cause matter does not provide a basis for a plain view

seizure of the vehicle. Horton v. California, 496 U.S. 128, 110 S.Ct. 2301, 110 L.Ed.2d 112 (1990) (construing *Coolidge* as not plain view because "the cars were obviously in plain view, but their probative value remained uncertain until after the interiors were swept and examined microscopically").

59. 399 U.S. 42, 90 S.Ct. 1975, 26 L.Ed.2d 419 (1970).

60. Texas v. White, 423 U.S. 67, 96 S.Ct. 304, 46 L.Ed.2d 209 (1975).

61. White, J., dissenting in *Coolidge*.

62. 469 U.S. 478, 105 S.Ct. 881, 83 L.Ed.2d 890 (1985).

63. 415 U.S. 800, 94 S.Ct. 1234, 39 L.Ed.2d 771 (1974).

64. See § 3.5(c).

instance for purposes of safekeeping, or (2) reexamination of items earlier inventoried to a significantly greater extent than was first necessary for purposes of completing the inventory.

The assertion by some members of the Court in *Coolidge* that a seizure on a plain view theory is permissible only upon "inadvertent discovery" of that object was later repudiated by a majority of the Court in *Horton v. California*.[65] This is an especially desirable turn of events in this context, for the previously stated criticisms[66] of the "inadvertent discovery" limitation are particularly compelling as to vehicle inventories. Though it has occasionally been held that evidence found in such an inventory must be suppressed if the police had suspected they might find such an item, this makes no sense whatsoever. What makes an inventory search reasonable under the requirements of the Fourth Amendment is not that the subjective motives of the police were simplistically pure, but rather that the facts of the situation indicate that an inventory search was reasonable under the circumstances, i.e., that per *Opperman* and *Bertine* it was conducted pursuant to "standard police procedures." Moreover, in light of *Whren v. United States*,[67] a pretext objection to a vehicle search will only rarely be possible. *Whren* involved a pretextual traffic stop, and as to it the Court applied this rule: when certain police conduct is permitted upon probable cause, the existence of that probable cause establishes the reasonableness of the police conduct, and thus neither the officer's ulterior motives nor his departure from ordinary practice or governing police regulations makes that conduct unreasonable under the Fourth Amendment. The Court in *Whren* then distinguished the expression of concern about "pretext" in *Bertine* by explaining that in an inventory context, where a search is being allowed without probable cause because of the special purpose being served, the exemption from the usual probable cause

requirement would not obtain if the search was not made for that purpose.

§ 3.8 Stop and Frisk and Similar Lesser Intrusions

(a) Stop and Frisk: Fourth Amendment Theory. The issue of whether the police have the right to stop and question a suspect, without his consent, in the absence of grounds for an arrest was confronted by the Supreme Court in *Terry v. Ohio*.[1] A Cleveland police officer, after seeing three men repeatedly look into a store as if they were "casing" it for a stickup, approached the men and asked them to identify themselves and, when they only mumbled something, patted them down and found weapons on two of them. After stating the issue in the narrowest possible terms, "whether it is always unreasonable for a policeman to seize a person and subject him to a limited search for weapons unless there is probable cause for an arrest," the Court concluded:

> Each case of this sort will, of course, have to be decided on its own facts. We merely hold today that where a police officer observes unusual conduct which leads him reasonably to conclude in light of his experience that criminal activity may be afoot and that the persons with whom he is dealing may be armed and dangerous, where in the course of investigating this behavior he identifies himself as a policeman and makes reasonable inquiries, and nothing in the initial stages of the encounter serves to dispel his reasonable fear for his own or others' safety, he is entitled for the protection of himself and others in the area to conduct a carefully limited search of the outer clothing of such persons in an attempt to discover weapons which might be used to assault him.

Such a search is a reasonable search under the Fourth Amendment, and any weapons seized may properly be introduced in

---

65. 496 U.S. 128, 110 S.Ct. 2301, 110 L.Ed.2d 112 (1990).

66. See § 3.4(k).

67. 517 U.S. 806, 116 S.Ct. 1769, 135 L.Ed.2d 89 (1996).

§ 3.8

1. 392 U.S. 1, 88 S.Ct. 1868, 20 L.Ed.2d 889 (1968).

evidence against the person from whom they were taken.

It soon became clear that *Terry* was not limited to cases based upon direct observations by the investigating officer, as in *Adams v. Williams*[2] the Court concluded that "reasonable cause for a stop and frisk" had been provided when an informant who had given reliable information in the past said a man seated in a nearby car was carrying narcotics and had a gun at his waist.

One important contribution of the *Terry* case to Fourth Amendment theory was the Court's conclusion that restraining a person on the street is a "seizure" and an exploration of the outer surfaces of his clothing is a "search," without regard to the labels police or others choose to put on those activities. Another was the Court's further development of its recently-adopted balancing test as a means for judging the constitutionality of unique practices. Just the year before, in *Camara v. Municipal Court*,[3] the Court, by "balancing the need to search against the invasion which the search entails," held that warrants for housing inspections could be issued without the traditional quantum of case-by-case probable cause if appropriate legislative or administrative standards for area or periodic inspections were met. The *Camara* balancing test was quoted and relied upon in *Terry*, but it was now applied in a slightly different way: the police conduct had to be justified upon the facts of the individual case, but a lesser quantum of evidence was required.

Some have suggested that use of the balancing test in the manner contemplated by *Terry*, necessitating application on a case-by-case basis of some sort of probability standard different in some degree from the traditional probable cause standard, involves such subtle considerations that police would have great difficulty applying the test and courts would be most reluctant to second-guess the police. This would be a legitimate concern if the *Terry* balancing test somehow required striking

the balance anew in each and every case, instead of merely calling for somewhat different treatment of street encounters generally and custodial arrests generally. That *Terry* involves only the latter was made clear in *Dunaway v. New York*,[4] where the Court rejected a proposed "multifactor balancing test of 'reasonable police conduct under the circumstances' to cover all seizures that do not amount to technical arrests" because it would provide insufficient guidance to police.

A third contribution to Fourth Amendment theory in *Terry* lies in the Court's response to the argument that a police power to stop and frisk should not receive express recognition because police have often utilized such street encounters for improper purposes, such as the wholesale harassment of minority groups. To this, the Court noted that the exclusionary rule "is powerless to deter invasions of constitutionally guaranteed rights where the police either have no interest in prosecuting or are willing to forego successful prosecution in the interest of serving some other goal." That language has been criticized in some quarters as saying that the police can set the limits of the exclusionary rule by ignoring it under some circumstances. But it must be read with another comment by the Court, namely, that the "exclusionary rule * * * cannot properly be invoked to exclude the products of legitimate police investigative techniques on the ground that much conduct which is closely similar involves unwarranted intrusions upon constitutional protections." Thus, the Court's quite valid point is really this: If exclusion of the fruits of *all* street encounters by declaring them all to be in violation of the Fourth Amendment would somehow put a stop to those engaged in for harassment and other improper purposes, it could at least be argued that the benefits derived would be worth the cost, but no such argument can be made here because the illegal encounters are usually motivated by objectives other than conviction and thus cannot be influenced by the exclusionary rule.

---

2.   407 U.S. 143, 92 S.Ct. 1921, 32 L.Ed.2d 612 (1972).

3.   387 U.S. 523, 87 S.Ct. 1727, 18 L.Ed.2d 930 (1967), discussed further in § 3.9(a), (b).

4.   442 U.S. 200, 99 S.Ct. 2248, 60 L.Ed.2d 824 (1979).

(b) Dimensions of a Permissible "Stop." If, as *Terry* teaches, there is a certain kind of police conduct, typically called a "stop," which may be undertaken upon less evidence than is needed for arrest because it is a lesser intrusion than an arrest, then it is obviously important to know just what kind of a seizure, undertaken for what purpose and made in what manner, can qualify as that lesser intrusion. For example, because in *Terry* the officer acted in the interest of crime *prevention*, which was stressed by the Court, and because all members of the Court agreed some added power was necessary for that purpose, it might be asked if *Terry* stops may also be made for the purpose of crime *detection*. The proper answer is yes. When immediately after the perpetration of a crime the police may have no more than a vague description of the possible perpetrator, it would be irrational to deprive the officer of the opportunity to "freeze" the situation for a short time, so that he may make inquiry and arrive at a considered judgment about further action to be taken.

This conclusion is supported by *United States v. Hensley*,[5] where the Court concluded that a *Terry* stop on less than full probable cause would sometimes be permissible for the purpose of investigating criminal activity that had occurred on some prior occasion. But the Court cautioned that the "factors in the balance may be somewhat different" in such a case,[6] so that the reasons for permitting a seizure merely upon reasonable suspicion might not always be compelling. Thus, the Court cautiously limited its holding, expressly authorizing the stopping of "a person suspected of involvement in a past crime" only as to "felonies or crimes involving a threat to public safety," where "it is in the public interest that the crime be solved and the suspect detained as promptly as possible." Similar reasoning supports the conclusion that a *Terry* stop may

be made of a nonsuspect who might be able to supply information, though it may well be that the Fourth Amendment does not permit the stopping of potential witnesses to the same extent as those suspected of crime.

As for whether a *Terry* stop may be made for investigation of all types of crimes or only those of a relatively serious nature, the *Adams* decision is sufficiently ambiguous that this may fairly be said to be an open question outside the *Henley* type of situation. Though admittedly articulation of offense-category limits as a matter of Fourth Amendment interpretation (as opposed to a policy reflected in a statute) would be most difficult, in support of such limits it may be said (i) that the need factor of the *Camara* balancing test cannot be sufficiently assessed without consideration of the seriousness of the crime under investigation, (ii) that meaningful review of police action is most difficult as to minor offenses such as loitering or disorderly conduct because these crimes are so diverse and diffuse, and (iii) that permitting stops for such minor crimes as marijuana possession presents the most obvious temptation to abuse the frisk as an occasion for searching for contraband.

Another important issue is whether the police conduct may still qualify as a lesser intrusion and thus a *Terry* stop if it includes force or a threat of force. Though it has occasionally been held that such action as surrounding the suspect or drawing weapons converts the police conduct into an arrest because the restriction of liberty of movement was complete, this is in error, for a stopping differs from an arrest not in the incompleteness of the seizure but in the brevity of it. The better view, therefore, is that surrounding the suspect will sometimes be an appropriate way of making the stop and maintaining the status quo, just as the drawing of weapons will sometimes be a reasonable precaution for the protection of of-

---

5. 469 U.S. 221, 105 S.Ct. 675, 83 L.Ed.2d 604 (1985).

6. As the Court explained: "A stop to investigate an already completed crime does not necessarily promote the interest of crime prevention as directly as a stop to investigate suspected ongoing criminal activity. Similarly, the exigent circumstances which require a police officer to step in before a crime is committed or completed are not

necessarily as pressing long afterwards. Public safety may be less threatened by a suspect in a past crime who now appears to be going about his lawful business than it is by a suspect who is currently in the process of violating the law. Finally, officers making a stop to investigate past crimes may have a wider range of opportunity to choose the time and circumstances of the stop."

ficers and bystanders.[7] Handcuffing ordinarily is improper, but may be resorted to when necessary to thwart the suspect's attempt to frustrate further inquiry. Although as a general matter it is not proper to place the detainee in a police car, such a step is permissible when dictated by special circumstances (e.g., inclement weather). There may occasionally be instances in which the use of physical force to make the stop will be justified, and also instances in which entry of private premises will be necessary to seize a fleeing suspect.

The police conduct should be judged in terms of what was done rather than what the officer involved may have called it at the time. If an officer tells the suspect he is under arrest but then conducts only a frisk and finds a weapon, a later determination that grounds for arrest were lacking should not render inadmissible the discovered weapon if there were in fact grounds for a stop and the frisk. Obviously the result would be otherwise if the search exceeded that permissible under *Terry*. In *Peters v. New York*[8] the Court approved the reverse of the above proposition, so that if an officer perceives his conduct as a stop only but he makes a full search of the person rather than a mere frisk, the evidence found is admissible if in fact the officer had grounds to arrest.

Though the Court in *Terry* had little to say about the stopping part of the stop-and-frisk phenomenon, it did stress that an arrest "is a wholly different kind of intrusion upon individual freedom * * * inevitably accompanied by future interference with the individual's freedom of movement," thus intimating that there were time and place limits upon a lawful stop. The permissible length depends upon the circumstances of the particular case. The re-

sults of the initial stop may arouse further suspicion or may dispel the questions in the officer's mind. If the latter is the case, the stop may go no further and the detained individual must be free to go. If, on the contrary, the officer's suspicions are confirmed or are further aroused, the stop may be prolonged and the scope enlarged as required by the circumstances. This is not to say that the detention may continue as long as the reasonable suspicion persists; rather, it must be asked whether the police are diligently pursuing a means of investigation likely to resolve the matter one way or another very soon[9] and whether there is a reason for continuing the suspect's presence during that interval.

In pre-*Terry* days courts were inclined to hold that any movement of the suspect, even to a police call box a block away, converted the detention into an arrest for which full probable cause was required, but today courts are inclined to permit some movement of the suspect in the immediate area of the stop. It has been held that it is improper to transport the suspect to the crime scene, even if it is relatively close, for possible identification by the victim or witnesses when there exist less intrusive and more reasonable alternatives, such as bringing the victim and witnesses to the detention scene or arranging for such a confrontation on some future occasion. The prevailing view is to the contrary, and rightly so; usually the matter can be resolved most expeditiously by transporting the suspect, and if the identification is delayed the risks of error are substantially increased. However, a taking of the suspect to the police station in lieu of conducting the investigation at the scene will ordinarily take the police conduct outside the *Terry* rule.[10]

---

7. As the Supreme Court recognized in United States v. Hensley, 469 U.S. 221, 105 S.Ct. 675, 83 L.Ed.2d 604 (1985). Responding to a flyer that the driver of a car was wanted for investigation of robbery and that the suspect should be considered armed and dangerous, the officer approached the car "with his service revolver drawn and pointed in the air." The Court declared that this "conduct was well within the permissible range in the context of suspects who are reported to be armed and dangerous."

8. 392 U.S. 40, 88 S.Ct. 1889, 20 L.Ed.2d 917 (1968).

9. This approach was taken by the Court in United States v. Sharpe, 470 U.S. 675, 105 S.Ct. 1568, 84 L.Ed.2d

605 (1985), rejecting the court of appeals' approach because it "would effectively establish a *per se* rule that a 20–minute detention is too long to be justified under the *Terry* doctrine."

10. Dunaway v. New York, 442 U.S. 200, 99 S.Ct. 2248, 60 L.Ed.2d 824 (1979), discussed further in § 3.8(g).

As the Court reiterated in Hayes v. Florida, 470 U.S. 811, 105 S.Ct. 1643, 84 L.Ed.2d 705 (1985), "our view continues to be that the line is crossed when the police, without probable cause or a warrant, forcibly remove a person from his home or other place in which he is

Florida v. Royer[11] illustrates that a wrong choice of investigative techniques by the police can escalate a valid *Terry* stop into an illegal arrest. There a suspected drug courier was lawfully questioned in an airport concourse and then required to accompany the police about 40 feet to a small police office, where the suspect consented to a search of his suitcases after they were obtained from the airline and also brought to the room. Although the total elapsed time was 15 minutes, the four-Justice plurality in *Royer* concluded that the consent was the fruit of an illegal arrest. Some of the plurality's language suggests these Justices viewed the situation as equivalent to a taking to a police station, for it was stressed that Royer was held in "a police interrogation room." But they placed greater emphasis upon the asserted requirements that a *Terry* stop "last no longer than is necessary to effectuate the purpose of the stop" and that "the investigative methods employed should be the least intrusive means reasonably available to verify or dispel the officer's suspicion in a short period of time." These requirements were not met here, the plurality reasoned, as "the primary interest of the officers was * * * in the contents of his luggage," and thus the officers could have more expeditiously sought consent on the spot or could have used a narcotics detection dog, available at the airport, to check out the suitcases. Justice Brennan, concurring, though not "certain that the use of trained narcotics dogs constitutes a less intrusive means," asserted that a *Terry* stop "must be so strictly limited that it is difficult to conceive of a less intrusive means that would be effective to accomplish the purpose of the stop." The four dissenting Justices in *Royer,* though prepared to require that the police act reasonably in investigating a *Terry* detainee, rejected the more demanding "least intrusive means" principle, for which they found no support in prior cases. More recently, the Court has cautioned against "unrealistic second-guessing," and has declared that the "question is not simply whether some other alternative was available, but whether the police acted unreasonably in failing to recognize or to pursue it."[12]

What *Terry* and *Royer* make clear, the Court later noted, is that whether a *Terry* stop has been kept within lawful bounds depends upon whether the circumstances "justified the length and intrusiveness of the stop and detention that actually occurred."[13] The temporal limitation means, e.g., that any consent to search be obtained before the time has run out, while the intrusiveness limitation means, e.g., that any interrogation even before expiration of the time must concern an offense for which there was then reasonable suspicion. But when it comes to those stops made for a traffic infraction (what courts call "routine traffic stops," although in fact such stops are frequently made on a hunch that the vehicle contains drugs), the *Terry* limitations are honored more often in the breach than in the observance. For one thing, the temporal limits are loosely observed, and courts even go so far as to state that such limits may be even extended briefly in the interest permitting procedures only relevant to drug law enforcement. For another, the intensity limitation is treated as if it did not exist at all, so that nonsearch investigative procedures undertaken to uncover drugs are deemed permissible so long as they actually or approximately occurred within whatever temporal limits are being observed.

A leading case for these latter positions, *United States v. Childs,*[14] argues in support of watered-down temporal limits upon traffic stops as follows: while a person stopped for a traffic violation "typically is given a citation (a

entitled to be and transport him to the police station, where he is detained, although briefly, for investigative purposes." But the Court went on to intimate that the investigative procedure used in *Hayes,* fingerprinting, would have been permissible without a warrant and on reasonable suspicion were it achieved by "a brief detention in the field."

11. 460 U.S. 491, 103 S.Ct. 1319, 75 L.Ed.2d 229 (1983).

12. United States v. Sharpe, 470 U.S. 675, 105 S.Ct. 1568, 84 L.Ed.2d 605 (1985).

13. United States v. Hensley, 469 U.S. 221, 105 S.Ct. 675, 83 L.Ed.2d 604 (1985).

14. 277 F.3d 947 (7th Cir.2002).

'ticket') and released," *Atwater v. Lago Vista*[15] "holds that the Constitution allows the police to place the person in custody and take him to be booked" when there is probable cause (usually the case as to a traffic stop), meaning that "although traffic stops usually proceed like *Terry* stops, the Constitution does not require this equation." Though denied by the *Childs* court, this is nothing more than a determination of the lawfulness of a seizure because of what the police might have done, rather than what they actually did, and hence *Childs* cannot be squared with *Knowles v. Iowa*,[16] holding that where an officer engages in a traffic stop/citation for speeding, a full search of the car cannot be undertaken incident to that stop even though the officer could have made such a search had he opted to make a full custodial arrest. The correct view, therefore, is that the *Terry* temporal limits do apply to traffic stops, meaning that the appropriate time limits are those necessary to serve the traffic enforcement purposes justifying the stop in the first place.

As for the intensity limitation of *Terry*, *Childs* denies that it means a traffic stop is limited to investigation of the traffic offense because, e.g., since the Supreme Court has held that "mere police questioning does not constitute a seizure,"[17] it follows that "because questions are neither searches nor seizures, police need not demonstrate justification for each inquiry" and thus may question about drugs incident to a traffic stop. But the fatal flaw in this analysis is the assumption that unless certain conduct is itself a search or seizure, it cannot be taken into account in judging the intrusiveness of a stop under the *Terry* limitations. As another opinion in *Childs* put it, "the majority conveniently ignores the fact that detention involves official coercion

and therefore concerns quite a different relationship of the police officer to the person questioned" than when there is no custody at all. And thus the correct view is that incident to a traffic stop when there does not also exist reasonable suspicion of drug possession, the officer may not question the vehicle occupants about drugs, may not quiz them about the details of their past and pending travels, may not seek a consent to search the vehicle for drugs, and may not lead a drug-sniffing dog around the stopped vehicle.[18]

(c) **Action Short of a Stop.** Not all police-citizen contacts constitute Fourth Amendment "seizures" that must be justified by showing grounds for the detention. "Only when the officer, by means of physical force or show of authority, has in some way restrained the liberty of a citizen," said the Court in *Terry*, "may we conclude that a 'seizure' has occurred." The Court then proceeded to "assume" that no seizure had occurred in that case until the frisk because it was unnecessary to pinpoint the precise earlier time at which the seizure commenced. The issue of what constitutes an encounter short of a *Terry* stop appeared to be presented more directly in *United States v. Mendenhall*,[19] where federal drug agents approached the defendant as she was walking through an airport concourse, identified themselves and asked to see her identification and airline ticket, which she produced for their inspection. Justice Stewart, in a part of his opinion joined by only one other member of the Court, concluded there had been no seizure, explaining:

> We conclude that a person has been "seized" within the meaning of the Fourth Amendment only if, in view of all of the circumstances surrounding the incident, a

---

15. 532 U.S. 318, 121 S.Ct. 1536, 149 L.Ed.2d 549 (2001), holding police have full discretion to decide to resort to custodial arrest for a minor traffic violation.

16. 525 U.S. 113, 119 S.Ct. 484, 142 L.Ed.2d 492 (1998)

17. Florida v. Bostick, 501 U.S. 429, 111 S.Ct. 2382, 115 L.Ed.2d 389 (1991).

18. Whether questioning about the presence of a weapon in the vehicle should be allowed is a harder question. In favor of allowing such an inquiry is the notion that ensuring the safety of the police and bystanders is a more

compelling interest than acquiring information of criminality and thus justifies a variety of minimal intrusions in service of that particular interest. The contrary position is that precisely because there are many other means available for ensuring officer safety, including requiring the traffic violator to exist his vehicle and remain outside during the entire period of the detention, such questioning is unnecessary.

19. 446 U.S. 544, 100 S.Ct. 1870, 64 L.Ed.2d 497 (1980).

reasonable person would have believed that he was not free to leave. Examples of circumstances that might indicate a seizure, even where the person did not attempt to leave, would be the threatening presence of several officers, the display of a weapon by an officer, some physical touching of the person of the citizen, or the use of language or tone of voice indicating that compliance with the officer's request might be compelled. * * * In the absence of some such evidence, other inoffensive contact between a member of the public and the police cannot, as a matter of law, amount to a seizure of that person.

On the facts of this case, no "seizure" of the respondent occurred. The events took place in the public concourse. The agents wore no uniforms and displayed no weapons. They did not summon the respondent to their presence, but instead approached her and identified themselves as federal agents. They requested, but did not demand to see the respondent's identification and ticket. Such conduct, without more, did not amount to an intrusion upon any constitutionally protected interest. The respondent was not seized simply by reason of the fact that the agents approached her, asked her if she would show them her ticket and identification, and posed to her a few questions. Nor was it enough to establish a seizure that the person asking the questions was a law enforcement official.

By way of footnote, it was added that "the subjective intentions of the DEA agent in this case to detain the respondent, had she attempted to leave, is irrelevant except insofar as they may have been conveyed to the respondent."[20] More recently, a majority of the

Supreme Court has endorsed the Stewart "reasonable person" standard.[21] However, in *Florida v. Bostick*,[22] the Court recognized that literal application of the "free to leave" test would be inappropriate in some circumstances (e.g., the present case, where defendant was questioned on a bus he did not want to leave in any event), and thus said that in such circumstances "the appropriate inquiry is whether a reasonable person would feel free to decline the officers'' requests or otherwise terminate the encounter.

The Court applied the *Bostick* standard in *United States v. Drayton*,[23] where during a scheduled stop the bus driver left the bus in the hands of three police officers; one stood guard at the front of the bus and another at the rear while the third questioned the passengers individually without informing them of their right not to cooperate. In holding there had been no seizure, the *Drayton* majority emphasized that the questioning officer did not brandish a weapon or make any intimidating movements, left the aisle free, spoke in a polite and quiet voice, and said nothing to indicate the person was barred from leaving the bus or otherwise terminating the encounter. Noting that "had this encounter occurred on the street, it would be constitutional," the majority concluded that the "fact that an encounter takes place on a bus does not on its own transform standard police questioning of citizens into an illegal seizure" and that, indeed, "because many fellow passengers are present to witness officers' conduct, a reasonable person may feel even more secure in his or her decision not to cooperate with police on a bus than in other circumstances."[24]

---

20. That must be distinguished from the quite different point made in Brower v. County of Inyo, 489 U.S. 593, 109 S.Ct. 1378, 103 L.Ed.2d 628 (1989), namely, that for a seizure to have occurred there must have been "a governmental termination of freedom of movement *through means intentionally applied*," as the Fourth Amendment does not address "the accidental effects of otherwise lawful government conduct."

21. Florida v. Royer, 460 U.S. 491, 103 S.Ct. 1319, 75 L.Ed.2d 229 (1983) (4–Justice plurality and Blackmun, J., dissenting, apply that standard; no express rejection of that standard by other members of the Court).

22. 501 U.S. 429 111 S.Ct. 2382, 115 L.Ed.2d 389 (1991).

23. 536 U.S. 194, 122 S.Ct. 2105, 153 L.Ed.2d 242 (2002).

24. The three dissenters, stressing the close quarters, the presence of the other two officers, the fact that the driver had "yielded his control of the bus" to them, and that "no [other] passenger had refused the cooperation requested," cogently concluded that "there was no reason for any passenger to believe that the driver would return and the trip resume until the police were satisfied."

The lower court cases tend to find that it is not a seizure to approach a stationary pedestrian and ask him a question, or even to overtake a walking pedestrian and ask him to halt or to summon him to where the officer is, but that more dramatic steps, such as stopping a vehicle, do bring the Fourth Amendment into play. Though the proposition is seldom articulated in precisely this form, the lower court decisions for the most part can be reconciled by this proposition: there is no Fourth Amendment seizure when the policeman, although perhaps making inquiries that a private citizen would not be expected to make, has otherwise conducted himself in a manner consistent with what would be viewed as a nonoffensive contact if it occurred between two ordinary citizens.

In *California v. Hodari D.*,[25] after a group of youths fled upon approach of a police car, one officer pursued Hodari on foot, prompting Hodari to throw to the ground what upon inspection proved to be cocaine. The state court concluded that Hodari had been "seized" when he saw the officer pursuing him, and that consequently the cocaine was the fruit of that illegal (because without reasonable suspicion) seizure, but the Supreme Court disagreed. The word "seizure" in the Fourth Amendment, the Court declared, means "a laying on of hands or application of physical force to restrain movement, even when it is ultimately unsuccessful,"[26] and also a "*submission* to the assertion of authority," but it did not encompass a "show of authority" as to which "the subject does not yield." As for Hodari's reliance on the *Mendenhall* test, the Court responded that the requirement "a rea-

sonable person would have believed that he was not free to leave" "states a necessary, but not a *sufficient* condition for seizure * * * effected through a 'show of authority.' "[27]

(d) Grounds for a Permissible "Stop." Although the Court in *Terry* claimed it was "decid[ing] nothing today concerning the constitutional propriety of an investigative 'seizure' upon less than probable cause," a lesser standard was suggested when the Court related the holding to a situation "where a police officer observes unusual conduct which leads him reasonably to conclude in light of his experience that criminal activity may be afoot." The Court later indicated in *Adams v. Williams*[28] that a stopping for investigation could be made even when "there is no probable cause to make an arrest," but made no effort to articulate exactly what the standard was. More recently, in *United States v. Cortez*,[29] the Court noted that the various phrases used by the lower courts, such as "founded suspicion," were "not self-defining" but that the essence of the standard was that "the detaining officers must have a particularized and objective basis for suspecting the particular person stopped of criminal activity." Because a " 'totality of the circumstances' principle * * * governs the existence *vel non* of 'reasonable suspicion,' " the various factors relied upon to establish such suspicion are not to be independently assessed one-by-one and rejected if susceptible to an innocent explanation.[30] Assuming a sufficient degree of suspicion, it is *not* also necessary that there be unavailable a less intrusive investigative technique.[31]

25. 499 U.S. 621, 111 S.Ct. 1547, 113 L.Ed.2d 690 (1991).

26. But, the majority went on to say that if the application of physical force was unsuccessful the seizure would terminate, for it is incorrect "to say that for Fourth Amendment purposes there is a *continuing* arrest during the period of fugitivity." This means, the Court added, that if the officer had grabbed Hodari "but Hodari had broken away and had then cast away the cocaine, it would hardly be realistic to say that the disclosure had been made during the course of an arrest."

27. The two dissenters argued that "the character of the citizen's response should not govern the constitutionality of the officer's conduct," and noted that the majority's holding could well "encourage unlawful displays of

force that will frighten countless innocent citizens into surrendering whatever privacy rights they may still have."

28. 407 U.S. 143, 92 S.Ct. 1921, 32 L.Ed.2d 612 (1972).

29. 449 U.S. 411, 101 S.Ct. 690, 66 L.Ed.2d 621 (1981).

30. United States v. Arvizu, 534 U.S. 266, 122 S.Ct. 744, 151 L.Ed.2d 740 (2002), adding that such "divide-and-conquer analysis" was precluded by *Terry*, where a series of acts each "perhaps innocent in itself" was deemed to add up to reasonable suspicion.

31. United States v. Sokolow, 490 U.S. 1, 109 S.Ct. 1581, 104 L.Ed.2d 1 (1989) (concluding "such a rule would unduly hamper the police's ability to make sufficient on-the-spot decisions" and "would require courts to 'indulge in "unrealistic second-guessing" ' ").

But the precise words used are less important than an understanding of the manner in which the standard differs from that for arrest. The *Terry* reference to when "criminal activity *may be* afoot" strongly suggests that though the arrest standard may sometimes require that guilt be more probable than not, this is never the case as to a stopping for investigation,[32] where the very purpose is to clarify an ambiguous situation. Thus, if police saw men moving from one residence to another via car several boxes seen to contain large commercial-type electric typewriters, this would not be grounds for arrest, but these actions, though consistent with innocent activity, are suspicious enough to justify a temporary detention for the purpose of inquiry. Sometimes it is certain that a crime has occurred but quite uncertain as to who the perpetrator is, in which case again a stop may be permissible though an arrest would not be. *Luckett v. State*,[33] where a police officer stopped a green car with a license prefix 82J on the basis of a radio broadcast that such a car had been used by persons fleeing from a recent burglary, provides an excellent illustration of this point. The court quite properly concluded that while the officer "did not have probable cause to stop every green automobile with an 82J license prefix and formally arrest its occupants," there was a basis for a *Terry* stop.

The most common type of investigative stop situation occurs when, as in *Terry,* a patrolman observes suspicious conduct. The protean variety of observed circumstances that might lead to a stop makes generalization about this situation virtually impossible, but a few comments are in order: (1) Most such stops are for investigation of property crimes, and thus often are based upon the fact that the suspect is carrying some object in suspicious circumstances or is in a suspicious relationship to a car or building. (2) Because "deliberate furtive actions and flight at the approach of strangers or law officers are strong indicia of *mens rea*,"[34] efforts to avoid the police or avoid being seen by them can contribute to grounds for a stop. Although it has occasionally been held that if the means of avoidance are sufficiently extreme they alone may justify the stop, that conclusion may be in some doubt as a result of *Illinois v. Wardlow*.[35] In that 5–4 decision, the majority held there were grounds for a *Terry* stop where the defendant engaged in "[h]eadlong flight," "unprovoked flight upon noticing the police," where there was the additional factor of defendant's "presence in an area of heavy narcotics trafficking." The other four Justices, concurring in part and dissenting in part, (i) made much of the majority's failure to endorse the state's proposed *per se* rule regarding the sufficiency of "unprovoked flight upon seeing a clearly identifiable police officer"; (ii) appeared to admit that flight under the proper circumstances would justify a police inference of wrongdoing;[36] but (iii) then cogently found the majority's ultimate conclusion unsound "because many factors providing innocent motivations for unprovoked flight are concentrated in high crime areas."[37] (3) It is proper to consider the surrounding circumstances and the suspect's relationship to them, such as whether he "fits" the area in which he is found, whether it is a high crime area, whether he is about at a time of day when the suspected criminality is most likely to occur,

---

32. As the Supreme Court has more recently put it, the requisite "level of suspicion is considerably less than proof of wrongdoing by a preponderance of the evidence." United States v. Sokolow, 490 U.S. 1, 109 S.Ct. 1581, 104 L.Ed.2d 1 (1989).

33. 259 Ind. 174, 284 N.E.2d 738 (1972).

34. Peters v. New York, 392 U.S. 40, 88 S.Ct. 1889, 20 L.Ed.2d 917 (1968).

35. 528 U.S. 119, 120 S.Ct. 673, 145 L.Ed.2d 570 (2000).

36. They stated: "The inference we can reasonably draw about the motivation for a person's flight, rather, will depend on a number of different circumstances. Fac-

tors such as the time of day, the number of people in the area, the character of the neighborhood, whether the officer was in uniform, the way the runner was dressed, the direction and speed of the flight, and whether the person's behavior was otherwise unusual might be relevant in specific cases."

37. As they elaborated in another part of the opinion: "Among some citizens, particularly minorities and those residing in high crime areas, there is also the possibility that the fleeing person is entirely innocent, but, with or without justification, believes that contact with the police can itself be dangerous, apart from any criminal activity associated with the officer's sudden presence."

and whether he is in the company of one who can be arrested for a present or recent crime. (4) It is proper to take account of the suspect's past criminal record, though such a record standing alone is never a basis for a stop. (5) The officer, based upon his training and experience, is allowed to make "inferences and deductions that might well elude an untrained person," but if his actions are later challenged he must be able to explain those inferences and deductions so as to show that there was "a particularized and objective basis" for the stop.[38] (6) If during an earlier nonseizure contact the person made contradictory or otherwise suspicious remarks, those comments may be taken into account.[39]

Another common situation is that in which a stop is made because a person is found near the scene of a recent crime and the police wish to determine if that person was the perpetrator. Though a "dragnet approach" is impermissible, detentions greater in number than the number of known perpetrators are proper if selective investigative procedures are utilized that provide a reasonable possibility that any person stopped is a perpetrator. In making that judgment, officers may properly consider: (1) the particularity of the description of the offender or the vehicle in which he fled; (2) the size of the area in which the offender might be found, as indicated by such facts as the elapsed time since the crime occurred; (3) the number of persons about in that area; (4) the known or probable direction of the offender's flight; (5) observed activity by the particular person stopped; and (6) knowledge or suspicion that the person or vehicle stopped has been involved in other criminality of the type presently under investigation.

A third kind of situation, that in which the stopping is made on the basis of information received from an informant, occurs with much less frequency, but reached the Supreme Court in *Adams v. Williams*,[40] where an informant told the officer a man in a nearby car was carrying narcotics and had a gun at his waist.

The Court concluded this "information carried enough indicia of reliability to justify the officer's forcible stop of Williams," as the "informant was known to him personally and had provided him with information in the past," the "informant here came forward personally to give information that was immediately verifiable at the scene," and under state law the informant was "subject to immediate arrest for making a false complaint had Sgt. Connolly's investigation proven the tip incorrect." The question raised by *Adams* is to what extent there is a lesser standard here than when a full arrest or search is made on an informant's tale, in which case probable cause is usually lacking unless (i) the underlying circumstances show reason to believe that the informant is a credible person, and (ii) the underlying circumstances show the basis of the conclusions reached by the informant. As to the first or credibility aspect, the points relied upon in *Adams* are extremely weak; merely saying the informant had given information in the past without even indicating whether it proved to be accurate does not show credibility, and in the absence of any suggestion that the informer was aware of the seldom-used false complaint statute it cannot be said that credibility has been shown by the fact the informer was in the area and could have been arrested if his story proved to be false. As for the second or basis-of-knowledge prong, the Court in *Adams* offers nothing; the informer never said how she knew what she claimed to know, and certainly she did not give so many details as to permit an inference that she had a reliable source. Because of this failure of the Court in *Adams* to explain what departure from the then extant *Aguilar v. Texas*[41] formula, if any, was permissible, the post-*Adams* lower court cases were in disarray and not infrequently permitted stops based upon an informant's story though there was *absolutely no indication* of that informant's credibility or basis of knowledge.

---

38. United States v. Cortez, 449 U.S. 411, 101 S.Ct. 690, 66 L.Ed.2d 621 (1981).

39. Florida v. Rodriguez, 469 U.S. 1, 105 S.Ct. 308, 83 L.Ed.2d 165 (1984).

40. 407 U.S. 143, 92 S.Ct. 1921, 32 L.Ed.2d 612 (1972).

41. 378 U.S. 108, 84 S.Ct. 1509, 12 L.Ed.2d 723 (1964).

There is much to be said for the proposition that just as strong a showing of both credibility and basis of knowledge should be required here as for arrest, though here the facts would not need to show as high a probability of criminal conduct. But when the Court revisited this area in *Alabama v. White*,[42] it decided otherwise: "Reasonable suspicion is a less demanding standard than probable cause not only in the sense that reasonable suspicion can be established with information that is different in quantity or content than that required to establish probable cause, but also in the sense that reasonable suspicion can arise from information that is less reliable than that required to show probable cause." In *White*, police received an anonymous call that the defendant, Ms. White, would leave a certain apartment in a certain vehicle, would be going to a certain motel, and would be in possession of an ounce of cocaine inside a brown attache case. A woman was then seen to leave the building where that apartment was, get in the described vehicle and drive in the direction of the motel, at which point she was stopped. The Court declared: (i) that it was not prepared to say that an anonymous call by itself "could never provide the reasonable suspicion necessary for a *Terry* stop"; (ii) that nonetheless the call in this case was standing alone insufficient, for like the letter in *Illinois v. Gates*[43] it gave absolutely no indication of reliability or basis of knowledge; (iii) that some corroboration of the anonymous informant's story is clearly insufficient, such as the discovery of the described vehicle outside the specified apartment, for "anyone could have 'predicted' that fact because it was a condition presumably existing at the time of the call"; and (iv) that the total corroboration in the instant "close case" was sufficient, as "the caller's ability to predict respondent's *future behavior,* because it demonstrated inside information—a

special familiarity with respondent's affairs," meant it was "reasonable for police to believe that a person with access to such information is likely to also have access to reliable information about that individual's illegal activities." But that is a questionable conclusion; as the three dissenters in *White* noted, "anybody with enough knowledge about a given person to make her the target of a prank, or to harbor a grudge against her, will certainly be able to formulate a tip about her like the one predicting Vanessa White's excursion."

In *Florida v. J. L.*,[44] where police, acting solely on an anonymous telephone tip that a described person at a certain bus stop had a gun, frisked that person and found a gun, the Court held the tip "lacked the moderate indicia of reliability present in *White*," for mere confirmation of the suspect's present location and appearance "does not show that the tipster has knowledge of concealed criminal activity." As for the so-called "firearms exception" to *White* theretofore adopted by several lower courts, the Court responded it "would rove too far," as it "would enable any person seeking to harass another to set in motion an intrusive, embarrassing police search of the targeted person simply by placing an anonymous call falsely reporting the target's unlawful carriage of a gun." The Court in *J. L.* declined "to speculate about the circumstances under which the danger alleged in an anonymous tip might be so great as to justify a search even without a showing of reliability," as with "a report of a person carrying a bomb," and also left open what result would obtain regarding places such as schools where "the reasonable expectation of Fourth Amendment privacy is diminished." Two concurring Justices in *J. L.* helpfully noted that, unlike the instant case, there might be circumstances other than that identified in *White* where an anonymous tip might be deemed sufficient.[45]

---

42. 496 U.S. 325, 110 S.Ct. 2412, 110 L.Ed.2d 301 (1990).

43. 462 U.S. 213, 103 S.Ct. 2317, 76 L.Ed.2d 527 (1983).

44. 529 U.S. 266, 120 S.Ct. 1375, 146 L.Ed.2d 254 (2000).

45. They gave these illustrations: (1) where an anonymous caller with a distinctive voice had previously given

information that turned out to be true; (2) where the anonymous tip was received face-to-face, as where an unknown driver stops momentary to provide police with information; and (3) where a telephone caller identification device and/or recording of calls make it possible to locate anonymous callers, especially significant where giving false information to police is a crime.

As for stops made on the basis of information received via police channels, a useful illustration is provided by *United States v. Hernandez*.[46] There, an officer stopped a van on the basis of a radio message that it contained several illegal aliens, and *after* the stop observed circumstances providing grounds for an arrest that when made resulted in the discovery of certain evidence. The defendant relied upon *Whiteley v. Warden*,[47] holding that an arrest made in response to a police bulletin may be upheld only upon a subsequent showing of probable cause at the source (which had not been done here), but the court responded that no such showing was needed to support an investigatory stop instead of an arrest. Such a conclusion is in error and has been properly rejected by other courts, for to accept all police bulletins at face value is to abandon any requirement of an "indicia of reliability" (to use the *Adams* language). By the same token, there is no reason to be more demanding than *Whiteley* in this context, and thus (as the Supreme Court held in *United States v. Hensley*[48]) a stopping in reliance upon a conclusory flyer issued by another department indicating the person is wanted for investigation of a felony is lawful, *provided* the flyer "has been issued on the basis of articulable facts supporting a reasonable suspicion." In other words, with a *Terry* stop as with a full-fledged arrest, it suffices that the facts justifying the seizure were then in the hands of the directing or requesting agency.

In *Brown v. Texas*,[49] in the course of holding that police did not have grounds to stop a man who was seen walking away from another man in an alley in an area with a high incidence of drug traffic, a unanimous Court emphasized that under the Fourth Amendment a seizure must either "be based on specific, objective facts" or "be carried out pursuant to a plan embodying explicit, neutral limitations on the conduct of individual officers." In support of

the latter part of this statement, the Court cited *Delaware v. Prouse*[50] and *United States v. Martinez–Fuerte*,[51] which state that stopping of all cars at a checkpoint to examine drivers' licenses or to question occupants about their alienage would be lawful because the intrusion is not "subject to the discretion of the official in the field." This raises the question of whether this standardized procedures approach, which originated in *Camara v. Municipal Court*[52] and has been utilized generally in assessing so-called inspections or administrative searches,[53] has any application to stop-and-frisk cases. That is, if in *Brown* it had been established that the officers stopped the defendant pursuant to a police department "plan" to question all pedestrians found in the "high drug problem area," would the outcome have been different? Though certainly there is a good reason to favor such law enforcement planning by police agencies, it is rather doubtful that resort to that kind of plan, in lieu of continued reliance upon an individualized suspicion approach, would be permitted. This is because, as the Supreme Court has intimated, the neutral plan approach is for use in those situations "in which the balance of interests precludes insistence upon 'some quantum of individualized suspicion.' "[54] If a plan dealing generally with a certain constant law enforcement concern, such as drug trafficking, could somehow be more carefully and tightly formulated than suggested above, it is of course possible that it would be deemed to pass muster under *Camara*. More likely, however, is the possibility that a plan addressing a "special" problem existing at a certain time and place would be upheld.

(e) "Frisk" for Weapons. In determining the lawfulness of a frisk, two matters are to be considered: (i) whether the officer was rightly in the presence of the party frisked so as to be endangered if that person was armed; and (ii)

---

46. 486 F.2d 614 (7th Cir.1973).

47. 401 U.S. 560, 91 S.Ct. 1031, 28 L.Ed.2d 306 (1971).

48. 469 U.S. 221, 105 S.Ct. 675, 83 L.Ed.2d 604 (1985).

49. 443 U.S. 47, 99 S.Ct. 2637, 61 L.Ed.2d 357 (1979).

50. 440 U.S. 648, 99 S.Ct. 1391, 59 L.Ed.2d 660 (1979).

51. 428 U.S. 543, 96 S.Ct. 3074, 49 L.Ed.2d 1116 (1976).

52. 387 U.S. 523, 87 S.Ct. 1727, 18 L.Ed.2d 930 (1967).

53. See § 3.9.

54. United States v. Martinez–Fuerte, 428 U.S. 543, 96 S.Ct. 3074, 49 L.Ed.2d 1116 (1976).

whether the officer had a sufficient degree of suspicion that the party frisked was armed and dangerous. As to the first, Justice Harlan helpfully commented in his separate *Terry* opinion that if "a policeman has a right * * * to disarm a person for his own protection, he must first have a right not to avoid him but to be in his presence." Thus a mere bulge in a pedestrian's pocket, insufficient to justify a stopping for investigation, would not be a basis for a frisk by a passing officer, though quite clearly the same bulge would entitle the officer to frisk a person he had already lawfully stopped for investigation. And while some language in *Terry* could be read as saying a frisk would be in order incident to a lawful stop only if a preliminary inquiry were made and did not clear up the matter, such a limitation would be unsound and has not been followed by the Supreme Court[55] or the lower courts.

As for the second factor, *Terry* says that what is required is that the officer's observations lead him "reasonably to conclude * * * that the persons with whom he is dealing may be armed and presently dangerous." The use of the phrase "may be" makes it apparent that it will suffice that there is a substantial possibility the person is armed,[56] and that there need not be the quantum of evidence that would justify an arrest for the crime of carrying a concealed weapon. Sometimes this possibility may be said to exist merely because of the nature of the crime under investigation, while on other occasions something in addition will be required, such as a bulge in the suspect's clothing, a sudden movement by the suspect toward a pocket or other place where a weapon could be hidden, or awareness that the suspect was armed on a previous occasion. The

test is an objective one, and thus the officer need not later demonstrate that he was in actual fear. If the *Terry* test for a frisk cannot be met, this does not mean that the officer is powerless to do anything in the interest of self-protection. The teaching of *Pennsylvania v. Mimms*[57] is that without any showing the particular suspect may be armed, an officer may require a person lawfully stopped to alight from his car in order to diminish "the possibility, otherwise substantial, that the driver can make unobserved movements." The *Mimms* rule is equally applicable to passengers; though there has been no reason to detain the passenger, as a practical matter the passenger is detained whenever the vehicle is stopped, and so again a minimal added intrusion is justified in the interest of the officer's safety.[58]

The Court in *Terry* emphasized that what is here referred to as a "frisk" must "be confined in scope to an intrusion reasonably designed to discover guns, knives, clubs, or other hidden instruments for the assault of the police officer," and found the officer had so limited his actions by patting down the clothing first and reaching inside only upon feeling a weapon. In the companion case of *Sibron v. New York*,[59] the officer was deemed to have exceeded the permissible scope of such a search in that he made "no attempt at an initial limited exploration for arms" but instead "thrust his hand into Sibron's pocket." Though this means that usually a frisk must commence with a pat-down, *Adams v. Williams*[60] indicates there are exceptions, for there the officer's conduct was upheld though he immediately reached into the suspect's clothing. Because the informant in that case had indicated the exact location of the weapon,

55. In Adams v. Williams, 407 U.S. 143, 92 S.Ct. 1921, 32 L.Ed.2d 612 (1972) the protective search was upheld though the officer asked no questions of the suspect.

56. Some lower courts have indicated that the requisite possibility the suspect is armed is lower than the possibility of criminal activity necessary to make the stop in the first place. Similarly, the Supreme Court appears to have suggested a difference between stops and frisks as to the requisite reliability of the information, for in Florida v. J. L., 529 U.S. 266, 120 S.Ct. 1375, 146 L.Ed.2d 254 (2000), discussed in text at note 44 supra, the Court concluded by cautioning that "the requirement that an anonymous tip bear standard indicia of reliability in order

to justify a stop in no way diminishes a police officer's prerogative, in accord with *Terry*, to conduct a protective search of a person who has already been legitimately stopped. We speak in today's decision only of cases in which the officer's authority to make the initial stop at issue."

57. 434 U.S. 106, 98 S.Ct. 330, 54 L.Ed.2d 331 (1977).

58. Maryland v. Wilson, 519 U.S. 408, 117 S.Ct. 882, 137 L.Ed.2d 41 (1997).

59. 392 U.S. 40, 88 S.Ct. 1889, 20 L.Ed.2d 917 (1968).

60. 407 U.S. 143, 92 S.Ct. 1921, 32 L.Ed.2d 612 (1972).

some courts have taken that to be the basis of the *Adams* exception, but a more reasonable interpretation is that the immediate search was upheld because the suspect's failure to comply with the officer's request that he get out of the car made the possible weapon, as the Court put it, "an even greater threat." As for the permissible extent of the pat-down, the Court in *Terry* unfortunately quoted a rather distressing description,[61] in fact intended to describe what may be done after arrest and before transportation to the station. The need is only to find implements that could be reached by the suspect during the brief face-to-face encounter, not to uncover items cleverly concealed and to which access could be gained only with considerable delay and difficulty, and thus the pat-down should be limited accordingly. In any event, once the officer is satisfied that an object in the suspect's pocket is *not* a weapon, then the officer may not continue the tactile examination of it in an effort to ascertain whether it is otherwise incriminating.[62]

In *Terry,* the Court stressed that the officer "did not place his hands in [the suspects'] pockets or under the outer surface of their garments until he had felt weapons." But the officer need not be absolutely certain that the individual is armed, and thus the question is whether there was anything in the officer's perception to indicate it was not a weapon either because of its size or density. This would, for example, bar a search when only a soft object was felt in the pat-down. Assuming grounds for a search because of the pat-down, that search must be limited to retrieving and inspecting the suspect object; as the Court stressed in *Terry,* the officer there, once he felt what appeared to be weapons, "merely reached for and removed the guns."

As for whether such a protective search may ever extend beyond the person of the suspect, one way in which this question arises is when an officer searches within a vehicle in which the stopped suspect was riding. In *Michigan v. Long,*[63] the Supreme Court held "that the search of the passenger compartment of an automobile, limited to those areas in which a weapon may be placed or hidden, is permissible if the police officer possesses a reasonable belief based on 'specific and articulable facts that, taken together with the rational inferences from those facts, reasonably warrant' the officers in believing that the suspect is dangerous and the suspect may gain immediate control of weapons." In *Long,* an officer actually saw a knife in the car before the search and the person under investigation for erratic driving was being allowed to reenter the car to get the vehicle registration. But the Court unfortunately took an expansive view of what constitutes danger in the context of a *Terry* stop of a person in an automobile, understandably prompting the dissenters to declare that "the implications of the Court's decision are frightening." For one thing, the Court in *Long* asserted that if the investigation did not result in an arrest, then the suspect "will be permitted to reenter his automobile, and he will then have access to any weapons inside." Just why the suspect would want to attack the officer who had told him he was free to go was not explained. For another, the Court stressed the risk that a *Terry* suspect might "break away from police control and retrieve a weapon from his automobile." One might think that in any case where such a danger was perceived by the officer, who is entitled to order the suspect out of the car,[64] he would move him a sufficient distance away or take other steps to overcome the danger. But the Court in *Long* declared that officers are not required to "adopt alternate means to insure their safety in order to avoid the intrusion involved in a *Terry* encounter."

---

61. "[T]he officer must feel with sensitive fingers every portion of the prisoner's body. A thorough search must be made of the prisoner's arms and armpits, waistline and back, the groin and the area about the testicles, and entire surface of the legs down to the feet."

62. Minnesota v. Dickerson, 508 U.S. 366, 113 S.Ct. 2130, 124 L.Ed.2d 334 (1993) (by such action "the police

officer in this case overstepped the bounds of the 'strictly circumscribed' search for weapons allowed under *Terry*").

63. 463 U.S. 1032 103 S.Ct. 3469, 77 L.Ed.2d 1201 (1983).

64. Pennsylvania v. Mimms, 434 U.S. 106, 98 S.Ct. 330, 54 L.Ed.2d 331 (1977).

Another circumstance in which the question arises whether a protective search may extend beyond the person of the suspect is when the officer examines the contents of items carried by the suspect, such as a purse, shopping bag, or briefcase. Though case authority upholding such conduct is to be found, there is much to be said for the notion that the officer should simply put the object out of the suspect's reach for the duration of the encounter. But given the Supreme Court's approach in *Long,* it may be argued that even this alternative means can be disregarded.

Because a frisk, unlike a search incident to an arrest, has the single purpose of finding weapons that could be used to harm the officer, it has sometimes been suggested that the best way to ensure that officers act for that purpose alone and do not use the frisk as a pretext to search for evidence is by adopting a special exclusionary rule for frisk situations to the effect that *only* weapons are admissible. The Supreme Court has declined to adopt such a rule,[65] and lower courts readily admit other objects deemed to have been lawfully uncovered by the frisk. The objection to the proposal is that it would introduce difficult fact issues (e.g., if a gun was found, was it found before the narcotics were found so that the narcotics may be said to have been found incident to an arrest rather than incident to a stop only) and would often confront the officer with the "repellent" obligation to turn loose an obviously guilty person.

(f) Roadblocks. The use of checkpoints to uncover violations of a certain type by persons passing by is one kind of regulatory search discussed later.[66] By contrast, the concern here is with utilization of a roadblock for much the same purpose as in many stop-and-frisk situations: discovery and apprehension of a person who recently has committed a particular crime

in the area. Illustrative would be a case in which, following a bank robbery and information the robber had left town in a vehicle via a certain road, all cars travelling that road were stopped at a checkpoint so that each of them could be checked for the robber. It has been suggested that if an officer has reasonable cause to believe that a felony has been committed and stopping all or most vehicles moving in a particular direction or directions is reasonably necessary to permit a search for the perpetrator or victim of such felony in view of the seriousness and special circumstances of such felony, then he may order the drivers of such vehicles to stop, and may search such vehicles to the extent necessary to accomplish such purpose.

The Supreme Court has never dealt with the issue,[67] and the lower court cases are not particularly helpful, for in the main they merely assume the legality of the roadblock in the course of holding admissible items seen in plain view when a car stopped or thrown from the car as it was being required to stop, or in holding there were grounds to arrest by matching an occupant in the stopped car with a description of the wanted person. It would seem, however, that the Fourth Amendment limits on use of roadblocks should be somewhat different than those upon an ordinary *Terry* stop: (1) a roadblock should be permitted only upon a reliable report of a crime, and not upon suspicion of criminal conduct; (2) a roadblock should be permitted only for a rather serious crime carrying with it a strong public interest in prompt apprehension of the perpetrator; (3) a roadblock should be permitted only if reasonably located, that is, there must be some reasonable relation between the commission of the crime and the establishment and location of the roadblock, which necessi-

---

65. In Michigan v. Long, 463 U.S. 1032, 103 S.Ct. 3469, 77 L.Ed.2d 1201 (1983), the Court concluded: "If, while conducting a legitimate *Terry* search * * * the officer should, as here, discover contraband other than weapons, he clearly cannot be required to ignore the contraband, and the Fourth Amendment does not require its suppression in such circumstances."

66. See § 3.9(f), (g). The cases discussed there, and also the statement in Brown v. Texas, 443 U.S. 47, 99 S.Ct. 2637, 61 L.Ed.2d 357 (1979), that a seizure must be

upon reasonable, individualized suspicion *or* "must be carried out pursuant to a plan embodying explicit, neutral limitations on the conduct of individual officers," suggest that a roadblock conducted in conformance with such a plan might pass Fourth Amendment muster even when not directed at the apprehension of the perpetrator of a specific recent and most serious crime.

67. But see note 42 in § 3.9.

tates consideration of police knowledge concerning the number of alternative paths of escape or the particular direction in which the perpetrator is reasonably believed to be headed.

(g) Detention at the Police Station for Investigation. In *Davis v. Mississippi*,[68] petitioner and 24 other black youths were detained for questioning and fingerprinting in connection with a rape for which the only leads were a general description and a set of fingerprints. The Court held that petitioner's prints should have been excluded as the fruits of a seizure in violation of the Fourth Amendment, but intimated that a detention at the station might sometimes be permissible on evidence insufficient for arrest:

> Detentions for the sole purpose of obtaining fingerprints are no less subject to the constraints of the Fourth Amendment. It is arguable, however, that because of the unique nature of the fingerprinting process, such detentions might, under narrowly defined circumstances, be found to comply with the Fourth Amendment even though there is no probable cause in the traditional sense. * * * Detention for fingerprinting may constitute a much less serious intrusion upon personal security than other types of police searches and detentions. Fingerprinting involves none of the probing into an individual's private life and thoughts that marks an interrogation or search. Nor can fingerprint detention be employed repeatedly to harass any individual, since the police need only one set of each person's prints. Furthermore, fingerprinting is an inherently more reliable and effective crime-solving tool than eyewitness identifications or confessions and is not subject to such abuses as the improper lineup and the "third degree." Finally, because there is no danger of destruction of fingerprints, the limited detention need not come unexpectedly or at an inconvenient time. For this same reason, the general requirement that the authorization of a judicial officer be obtained in advance of detention would seem not to admit of any exception in the fingerprinting context.

The *Davis* dictum has had considerable impact. Statutes or court rules authorizing brief detention at the station by court order on less than the grounds needed for arrest, where the purpose of the detention is to conduct various identification procedures, were adopted in several jurisdictions. These provisions have been upheld by the courts, and other cases have upheld such procedures even in the absence of a specific statute or rule.

The matter was cast into doubt by the Supreme Court's later decision in *Dunaway v. New York*,[69] where defendant confessed after being picked up and brought to the station for a brief period of questioning. Though he had not been told that he was under arrest and had not been booked, the Court rejected the state's claim that such a seizure did not require probable cause for arrest but only a lesser quantum of evidence under the *Terry* balancing test. The Court reasoned that "the detention of petitioner was in important respects indistinguishable from a traditional arrest," as he "was not questioned briefly where he was found" but instead was "transported to a police station" and "would have been physically restrained if he had refused to accompany the officers or had tried to escape their custody." Though this language might be viewed as a repudiation of the *Davis* dictum, a more careful assessment of *Dunaway* shows that it is fully compatible with *Davis*.[70]

This conclusion is supported by the following: (1) The issue in *Dunaway* is narrowly stated as concerning only "the legality of custodial questioning on less than probable cause for a full-fledged arrest." (2) The holding is likewise limited to seizure "for interrogation." (3) The only reference back to *Davis* by the

---

68. 394 U.S. 721, 89 S.Ct. 1394, 22 L.Ed.2d 676 (1969).

69. 442 U.S. 200, 99 S.Ct. 2248, 60 L.Ed.2d 824 (1979).

70. This conclusion is not brought into question by Kaupp v. Texas, 538 U.S. 626, 123 S.Ct. 1843, 155 L.Ed.2d 814 (2003), where a unanimous Court found that the "evidence points to arrest even more starkly than the facts in *Dunaway*," but then, quoting *Hayes*, note 71 infra, declared: "Such involuntary transport to a police station for questioning is 'sufficiently like arres[t] to invoke the traditional rule that arrests may constitutionally be made only on probable cause.' "

Court was to show that the detention there did not come within the dictum because the suspect was "also subjected to interrogation." (4) The *Davis* dictum contemplated a limited detention that "need not come unexpectedly or at an inconvenient time," while in *Dunaway* the Court was dealing with defendant's abrupt seizure from a neighbor's home. (5) The *Davis* dictum also contemplated that without exception "the authorization of a judicial officer be obtained in advance of detention," while in *Dunaway* the Court was confronted with a warrantless seizure under circumstances unquestionably not exigent. (6) A major concern voiced in *Dunaway,* that a separate balancing test for stationhouse detentions could cause Fourth Amendment protections to "all too easily disappear * * * when that balancing may be done in the first instance by police officers," is inapplicable to the warrant procedure contemplated by *Davis.* (7) Especially because both decisions were authored by Justice Brennan, one would expect any repudiation of the *Davis* dictum to be stated forthrightly. (8) The *Dunaway* Court makes absolutely no mention of the statutes, court rules or appellate decisions that have *Davis* as their foundation. It is thus not at all surprising that the Court has more recently opined again that "the Fourth Amendment might permit the judiciary to authorize the seizure of a person on less than probable cause and his removal to the police station for the purpose of fingerprinting," and has taken specific note of the adoption of procedures in several states in reliance upon the *Davis* dictum.[71]

(h) Brief Seizure of Objects. A detention for investigation of a somewhat different kind, involving objects rather than a person, was involved in *United States v. Van Leeuwen.*[72] A postal clerk advised a policeman that he was suspicious of two packages of coins just mailed, and the packages were then held at that post office while an investigation was conducted that culminated in the issuance of a warrant and search of the packages there 29 hours after they were mailed. Citing *Terry,* a unanimous Court declared that the suspicious circumstances "certainly justified detention, without a warrant, while an investigation was made." But the Court then disposed of the case with a broader pronouncement:

> No interest protected by the Fourth Amendment was invaded by forwarding the packages the following day rather than the day when they were deposited. The significant Fourth Amendment interest was in the privacy of this first class mail; and that privacy was not disturbed or invaded until the approval of the magistrate was obtained.

Van Leeuwen was an easy case for the Court because the defendant was unable to show that the invasion intruded upon either a privacy interest in the contents of the packages or a possessory interest in the packages themselves. It thus did not resolve the constitutionality of the practice of detaining the luggage possessed by suspected drug couriers at airports while further investigation (typically, exposure of the suitcases to a drug-detection dog) was conducted, later confronted by the Court in *United States v. Place.*[73] Using the *Terry* balancing of interests approach, the Court there concluded that "the governmental interest in seizing the luggage briefly to pursue further investigation is substantial," and that because "seizures of property can vary in intrusiveness, some brief detentions of personal effects may be so minimally intrusive of Fourth Amendment interests that strong countervailing governmental interests will justify a seizure based only on specific articulable facts that the property contains contraband or evidence of a crime." But the Court then cautioned that "in the case of detention of luggage within the traveler's immediate possession, the police conduct intrudes on both the suspect's possessory interest in his luggage as well as his liberty interest in proceeding with his itinerary," in that "such a seizure can effectively restrain the person since he is subjected to the possible disruption of his travel plans in order to remain with his luggage or to

---

71. Hayes v. Florida, 470 U.S. 811, 105 S.Ct. 1643, 84 L.Ed.2d 705 (1985).

72. 397 U.S. 249, 90 S.Ct. 1029, 25 L.Ed.2d 282 (1970).

73. 462 U.S. 696, 103 S.Ct. 2637, 77 L.Ed.2d 110 (1983).

arrange for its return." For this reason, said the Court in *Place,* "the limitations applicable to investigative detentions of the person * * * define the permissible scope of an investigative detention of the person's luggage on less than probable cause." This would appear to mean that in such circumstances the container may be detained without full probable cause only so long as could the suspect from whose possession it was taken, so that the suspect at his option may also remain at the place of the seizure for that length of time and then reclaim the container unless in the interim the suspicion has grown into probable cause.

§ 3.9 Inspections and Regulatory Searches

(a) General Considerations. In the discussion that follows, the concern is with a variety of rather special search practices commonly described either as "inspections" or as "regulatory searches." These practices are directed toward certain unique problems unlike those ordinarily confronted by police officers in their day-to-day investigative and enforcement activities. Some of the practices, such as the examination of the effects of persons entering the country from abroad, have been followed for many years and have rather strong historical credentials, while others, such as the airport hijacker detection screening process, are rather recent innovations undertaken in an effort to respond to new problems. However, they all have this in common: it is generally assumed that the problems to which they are addressed could not be adequately dealt with under the usual Fourth Amendment restraints and that consequently the practices must be judged by somewhat different standards.

A theoretical basis for doing precisely this did not clearly emerge until the Supreme Court's decision in *Camara v. Municipal Court*[1] in 1967. In the course of holding that unconsented safety inspections of housing could be conducted pursuant to a warrant issued upon less than the usual quantum of probable cause, the Court declared that "there can be no ready test for determining reasonableness other than by balancing the need to search against the invasion which the search entails." Under this balancing theory, the Court continued, it is necessary to consider (i) whether the practice at issue has "a long history of judicial and public acceptance," (ii) whether the practice is essential to achieve "acceptable results," and (iii) whether the practice involves "a relatively limited invasion of * * * privacy." Assessing those factors, the Court in *Camara* held that inspection warrants could issue pursuant to "reasonable legislative or administrative standards" even without case-by-case probable cause. That is, searches of the kind at issue could occur so long as procedures were followed to ensure against the arbitrary selection of those to be subjected to them. The *Camara* balancing test was later used in *Terry v. Ohio*[2] to permit brief seizures for investigation on the street upon evidence less than that required for a full-fledged arrest. There a case-by-case determination was required, but the special circumstances justified the practice on what one might call a "watered-down" version of probable cause. Use of the *Camara–Terry* balancing test in assessing the various practices discussed herein has frequently resulted in the conclusion that these practices may constitutionally be undertaken on one or both of the bases just described, that is, upon a showing in the individual case of reasonable suspicion short of traditional probable cause, or upon a showing that the individual case arose by application of standardized procedures involving neutral criteria.

It must be emphasized, however, that (in contrast to *Terry*) the situations discussed in this section are typically justified in terms of what it is that necessitates deviation from the usual Fourth Amendment requirements, usually described in terms of some "special need" distinct from ordinary law enforcement.[3] That

---

§ 3.9

1. 387 U.S. 523, 87 S.Ct. 1727, 18 L.Ed.2d 930 (1967).

2. 392 U.S. 1, 88 S.Ct. 1868, 20 L.Ed.2d 889 (1968).

3. E.g., Griffin v. Wisconsin, 483 U.S. 868, 107 S.Ct. 3164, 97 L.Ed.2d 709 (1987); Vernonia School District 47J v. Acton, 515 U.S. 646, 115 S.Ct. 2386, 132 L.Ed.2d 564 (1995).

being the case, the special need must itself be something other than an ordinary law enforcement goal,[4] and, indeed, must in any event be sufficiently divorced from ordinary law enforcement.[5] But, as is illustrated by *United States v. Knights*,[6] when the Court is able to justify one of the special search rules discussed herein on the basis of general Fourth Amendment theory instead of by reliance upon the "special needs" doctrine, then the aforementioned limitation apparently disappears.

(b) Inspection of Housing. In *Camara v. Municipal Court*,[7] concerning the constitutionality of the San Francisco housing inspection scheme whereunder "routine" inspections for violations of the city housing code could be made without a warrant, the Court had occasion to resolve two important issues: (i) whether such inspections must be conducted pursuant to a warrant; and (ii) what grounds are needed to undertake such inspections. On the warrant issue, the majority reasoned that because no showing had been made "that fire, health, and housing code inspection programs could not achieve their goals within the confines of a reasonable search warrant requirement," and because also the searches at issue "are significant intrusions" that "when authorized and conducted without a warrant procedure lack the traditional safeguards which the Fourth Amendment guarantees," unconsented housing inspections could ordinarily be conducted only pursuant to a search warrant. But then, utilizing the balancing test described above, the Court rejected appellant's claim that such a warrant requires "probable cause to believe that a particular dwelling contains violations of the minimum standards prescribed by the code being enforced," and instead held that reasonable standards based upon such factors as the passage of time, the nature of the building, or the condition of the entire area would suffice:

First, such programs have a long history of judicial and public acceptance. * * * Second, the public interest demands that all dangerous conditions be prevented or abated, yet it is doubtful that any other canvassing technique would achieve acceptable results. Many such conditions—faulty wiring is an obvious example—are not observable from outside the building and indeed may not be apparent to the inexpert occupant himself. Finally, because the inspections are neither personal in nature nor aimed at the discovery of evidence of crime, they involve a relatively limited invasion of the urban citizen's privacy.

This branch of *Camara* is exceedingly important because of the fact that the Court gave express recognition to the balancing theory, which permitted the Court on that and later occasions to view the Fourth Amendment as something other than a rigid standard, requiring exactly the same quantum of evidence in all cases. But precisely because this balancing approach is so important, it is unfortunate that the Court in *Camara* did not apply it with more precision and care. For one thing, the Court's reliance upon a "long history of judicial and public acceptance" is vulnerable from the point of view of both accuracy and cogency. As to the longstanding judicial acceptance, the fact is that housing inspection cases reached the courts only in recent years and in small numbers, and that these cases typically focused upon the warrant issue rather than the question of what grounds were needed to conduct an inspection. As for the longstanding public acceptance, the continued operation of these inspection programs may show only a "history of acquiescence."[8] Because that is so and also because similar or greater evidence of judicial and public acceptance of long-used pro-

---

4. City of Indianapolis v. Edmond, 531 U.S. 32, 121 S.Ct. 447, 148 L.Ed.2d 333 (2000) (drug interdiction checkpoint contravenes Fourth Amendment, as—unlike checkpoints previously approved by the Court—its "primary purpose was to detect evidence of ordinary criminal wrongdoing").

5. Ferguson v. City of Charleston, 532 U.S. 67, 121 S.Ct. 1281, 149 L.Ed.2d 205 (2001) (drug testing of pregnant women contravenes Fourth Amendment, even if ulti-

mate purpose is "a beneficent one," as "threat of law enforcement" was the means to that end).

6. 534 U.S. 112, 122 S.Ct. 587, 151 L.Ed.2d 497 (2001), discussed in text infra at note 63.

7. 387 U.S. 523, 87 S.Ct. 1727, 18 L.Ed.2d 930 (1967).

8. Frank v. Maryland, 359 U.S. 360, 79 S.Ct. 804, 3 L.Ed.2d 877 (1959).

cedures has not deterred the Court from finding those procedures constitutionally defective, as in the other branch of *Camara* in which the *Frank* no-warrant rule was overturned, the first factor listed in *Camara* as an ingredient of the balancing test is in fact deserving of little if any weight.

As for the second factor, the Court unfortunately begins with the assertion that "the public interest demands that all dangerous conditions be prevented or abated," which ties in with the Court's earlier emphasis upon the need for "universal compliance" with housing code standards. But one might just as logically contend that there is a need for universal compliance with the criminal law and that the public interest demands that all dangerous offenders be convicted and punished, so that *Camara*-style warrants would also be permissible for that purpose as well. The fact of the matter is, as four members of the *Camara* majority had earlier stated: "Health inspections are important. But they are hardly more important than the search for narcotics peddlers, rapists, kidnappers, murderers, and other criminal elements."[9] Thus, the Court should have instead elaborated upon its statement that "acceptable results" cannot be achieved under the traditional probable cause requirement. The essential point is that criminal law enforcement typically is directed toward aggressive conduct, most often occurring in public places, which usually leaves a trail of discernible facts, so that the traditional probable cause test has not prevented an acceptable level of criminal law enforcement. By comparison, most housing code violations occur within private premises and cannot be detected from the outside and are not often the subject of a complaint that could serve as the basis for a warrant if the traditional probable cause requirement were applicable.

In describing the third factor, the Court in *Camara* says the invasion of privacy from these inspections is "limited" because they are "neither personal in nature nor aimed at the discovery of evidence of crime." This language is unfortunate, for it lends itself to the interpretation that a lesser quantum of evidence is required when the object of the search is not criminal prosecution. That interpretation would be unsound; the Fourth Amendment is intended to protect personal privacy rather than to prevent the conviction of criminals. The meaningful distinction here is that these inspections involve a lesser intrusion than that which ordinarily occurs in the course of a criminal investigation. Inspection for the accumulation of debris and of plumbing, heating, ventilation, gas and electrical systems takes less time than the usual search for evidence of crime and does not involve rummaging through private papers and effects. A police search for evidence brings with it damage to reputation resulting from an overt manifestation of official suspicion of crime, while a routine inspection as part of a periodic or area inspection plan does not single out any one individual. A search in a criminal investigation is made by armed officers, whose presence may lead to violence, it may be conducted at any time of the day or night, and must usually be conducted by surprise. By contrast, the housing inspection is conducted by an inspector whose presence is perceived by the public as less offensive, is performed during regular business hours, and need not involve inspection without advance notice.

The overstated necessity of 100 per cent code enforcement, the reliance upon assumed judicial and public acceptance of current enforcement programs, and the failure to be more precise about the significance of the fact that evidence of crime was not sought, all make *Camara* an imperfect model of this new Fourth Amendment calculus. The result would have carried more force had the Court set forth with more precision and detail the two factors that support it: (1) the inability to accomplish an acceptable level of code enforcement under the traditional probable cause test; and (2) the relatively minor invasion of personal privacy and dignity that attends periodic and area inspection programs. That is, after all, what the balancing process should be all about.

9. Frank v. Maryland, 359 U.S. 360, 79 S.Ct. 804, 3 L.Ed.2d 877 (1959) (dissent).

As for the extent of the *Camara* warrant requirement, the Court stressed its holding was not "intended to foreclose prompt inspections, even without a warrant, that the law has traditionally upheld in emergency situations." Such an emergency is unlikely to arise in this context. Most housing code violations cannot readily be concealed without being corrected; to the extent that householders take advantage of notice to correct deficiencies, the purposes of the housing code are advanced rather than thwarted. Warrantless entry is permissible in the face of an imminent and substantial threat to life, health, or property, but such a danger is unlikely as to an inspection that is merely part of an area or periodic inspection plan. *Camara* also indicates that "warrants should normally be sought only after entry is refused," and thus the consent alternative has been given preferred status.

(c) Inspection of Businesses. In *See v. City of Seattle*,[10] concerning defendant's conviction for not permitting a warrantless fire inspection of his locked commercial warehouse, the Court concluded that a "businessman, like the occupant of a residence, has a constitutional right to go about his business free from unreasonable official entries upon his private commercial property" and that consequently the *Camara* holding extended to the instant case. But the Court cautioned it was not implying "that business premises may not reasonably be inspected in many more situations than private homes, nor do we question such accepted regulatory techniques as licensing programs which require inspections prior to operating a business or marketing a product." A few years later, in *Colonnade Catering Corp. v. United States*,[11] the Court ruled the *See* warrant requirement was inapplicable to inspection of the business premises of a liquor licensee. This conclusion was based upon "the long history of the regulation of the liquor industry during pre-Fourth Amendment days" rather than any close analysis of the benefits or burdens of requiring a warrant in

this context. Then came *United States v. Biswell*,[12] upholding a warrantless inspection pursuant to a statute authorizing such inspections during business hours of the premises of any firearms or ammunition dealer for the purpose of examining required records and the firearms or ammunition stored there. The Court reasoned that (1) such inspections are a "crucial part of the regulatory scheme" for controlling the firearms traffic; (2) that the negligible protections of a warrant were offset by the fact that a warrant requirement "could easily frustrate inspection" here, as under this inspection scheme (unlike that in *Camara*) "unannounced, even frequent, inspections are essential," and the "necessary flexibility as to time, scope and frequency is to be preserved"; and (3) that these inspections "pose only limited threats to the dealer's justifiable expectations of privacy," as when he "chooses to engage in this pervasively regulated business and to accept a federal license, he does so with the knowledge that his business records, firearms and ammunition will be subject to effective inspection."

Colonnade and *Biswell* were distinguished in *Marshall v. Barlow's, Inc.*,[13] because each concerned a "closely regulated industry," while the statutory provision held unconstitutional in the instant case permitted warrantless OSHA inspections of "any factory, plant, establishment, construction site, or other area, workplace or environment where work is performed by an employee." Though it was acknowledged that the act in question "regulates a myriad of safety details that may be amenable to speedy alteration or disguise," the Court in *Barlow's* deemed this an insufficient reason to permit warrantless inspections, for "the great majority of businessmen can be expected in normal course to consent to inspection without a warrant." *Barlow's* was in turn distinguished in *Donovan v. Dewey*,[14] upholding a statute authorizing warrantless inspections of underground and surface mines. While in *Barlow's* the statutory scheme was so loose as to

10.   387 U.S. 541, 87 S.Ct. 1737, 18 L.Ed.2d 943 (1967).

11.   397 U.S. 72, 90 S.Ct. 774, 25 L.Ed.2d 60 (1970).

12.   406 U.S. 311, 92 S.Ct. 1593, 32 L.Ed.2d 87 (1972).

13.   436 U.S. 307, 98 S.Ct. 1816, 56 L.Ed.2d 305 (1978).

14.   452 U.S. 594, 101 S.Ct. 2534, 69 L.Ed.2d 262 (1981).

leave matters in the "unbridled discretion" of administrative officers, that was not true in the instant case because "the statute's inspection program * * * provides a constitutionally adequate substitute for a warrant." The *Dewey* Court stressed that (1) "the Act requires inspection of *all* mines and specifically defines the frequency of inspection;" (2) a mine operator could know the inspector's purpose and the limits of the inspection because "the standards with which a mine operator is required to comply are all specifically set forth" in the statute and published administrative regulations; and (3) "the Act provides a specific mechanism for accommodating any special privacy concerns that a specific mine operator might have," as if entry is refused the government may only seek to enjoin future refusals, a proceeding which "provides an adequate forum for the mine owner to show that a specific search is outside the federal regulatory authority, or to seek from the District Court an order accommodating any unusual privacy interests that the mine owner might have."

Similarly, in *New York v. Burger*,[15] upholding a warrantless inspection of an auto junkyard, the Court stressed the presence of these factors: (1) the business was "closely regulated," considering the duration and extensive nature of the regulatory scheme; (2) "a 'substantial' government interest," combatting auto theft, supported the regulatory scheme; (3) warrantless inspections are "necessary to further [the] regulatory scheme," as frequent and unannounced inspections are necessary to detect stolen cars and parts; (4) the statutory inspection scheme "provides a 'constitutionally adequate substitute for a warrant'" by informing the businessman that inspections will occur regularly, of their permissible scope, and who may conduct them; and (5) the permitted inspection is "carefully limited in time, place, and scope" (business hours only, auto dismantling business only, and of records, cars and parts only).

Generally, it may be said that courts have tended not to give close scrutiny to business inspection schemes, largely because of two erroneous assumptions. One, to be found in the earlier Supreme Court case of *Zap v. United States*[16] and still occasionally relied upon by lower courts, is that certain privileges, such as doing business with the government or obtaining a license from the government, may be conditioned upon the surrender of Fourth Amendment rights. But the Supreme Court has more recently rejected that kind of theory,[17] and has done so in cases where the so-called privilege was a license issued by the state[18] or a contractual relationship with the state.[19] The second assumption is that the decision to enter into a business subject to regulation by the government, including inspection, amounts to "implied consent" to such inspections. Though utilized in *Barlow's* to support the conclusion that the businessmen in *Colonnade* and *Biswell* had "in effect" consented by engaging in a "closely regulated industry," the theory is unsound; as the *Barlow's* dissenters correctly note, the "consent is fictional" and thus is no substitute for analysis of the particular regulatory scheme under the *Camara* balancing test (during which another form of "implied consent," that businessmen consent to entry by the general public to public parts of their business during regular business hours, is properly taken into account). This latter view was accepted by the Court in *Dewey*.

Precisely when a warrantless business inspection scheme is constitutional remains unclear. For one thing, the Court seems to have adopted the dubious assumption that if the inspection is of a "closely regulated industry," then (at least if, as the Court put it in *Biswell*, the inspection is in "the context of a regulatory inspection system of business premises which is carefully limited in time, place, and scope") this alone is enough to justify proceeding without a warrant, and there is no need to

---

15. 482 U.S. 691, 107 S.Ct. 2636, 96 L.Ed.2d 601 (1987)

16. 328 U.S. 624, 66 S.Ct. 1277, 90 L.Ed. 1477 (1946).

17. Sherbert v. Verner, 374 U.S. 398, 83 S.Ct. 1790, 10 L.Ed.2d 965 (1963).

18. Spevack v. Klein, 385 U.S. 511, 87 S.Ct. 625, 17 L.Ed.2d 574 (1967).

19. Slochower v. Board of Higher Education, 350 U.S. 551, 76 S.Ct. 637, 100 L.Ed. 692 (1956).

show that a warrant system would actually be impracticable in that context. But *Burger* may mark a departure from that unwise assumption, for the Court there listed as a separate important consideration the need for frequent and unannounced inspections that would make the warrant requirement impractical. For another, by saying that warrants for OSHA inspections would not impose a "serious burden" because "the great majority of businessmen can be expected in normal course to consent to inspection," the *Barlow's* majority appears to have overlooked the fact that there is no way to tell in advance which businessmen will not consent. Thus, it is either necessary for the inspector to be armed with a warrant in advance in every case or else to get a warrant after being turned away, thereby making possible the "speedy alteration or disguise" of safety violations the Court acknowledged could readily occur. The former is certainly undesirable, and the latter practice makes sense only if it may be said that correction of violations before the inspector reappears with a warrant is not objectionable, which appears to be what the majority assumed in *Barlow's*. But in any event, *Dewey* suggests that a warrantless inspection scheme is most likely to pass muster if the businessman is free to turn the inspector away and then is afforded an opportunity to challenge the authority to inspect in an adversary setting (there, an action by the government to enjoin further refusal), a procedure that would seem to afford even greater protection than the administrative warrant process.

As for the grounds needed to conduct a business inspection, the Court in *Barlow's* followed the *Camara* standard, stating:

A warrant showing that a specific business has been chosen for an OSHA search on the basis of a general administrative plan for the enforcement of the Act derived from neutral sources such as, for example, dispersion of employees in various types of industries across a given area, and the desired frequency of searches in any of the lesser divisions

of the area, would protect an employer's Fourth Amendment rights.

Thus, the magistrate is to determine that there are reasonable legislative or administrative standards in existence and that the proposed inspection would conform to those standards, especially in terms of selection of the place to be inspected. As for the grounds needed when no warrant is required, the lower court cases are silent on the question, and the Supreme Court has not been particularly helpful. The Court's observations in *Biswell* concerning the need for "unannounced, even frequent, inspections" and "flexibility as to time, scope, and frequency" might be read as meaning the authorities never need show why they selected a particular business in a no-warrant situation, or as meaning only that the standards in such a case are somewhat different (e.g., re-inspection permitted with greater frequency).

In *Burger,* the Court asserted that "the warrant and probable-cause requirements * * * have lessened application" to a closely regulated business, but then gave no indication that any grounds were required to justify a particular warrantless inspection. This understandably prompted the three dissenters to object that "the State could not explain why Burger's operation was selected for inspection," highlighting that the inspection here had the same defect as in *Barlow's:* failure "to provide any standards to guide inspectors either in their selection of establishments to be searched or in the exercise of their authority to search." The essential point is that even a "closely regulated" businessman should not be singled out for more intensive attention than is the norm for those in that business.

(d) Welfare Inspections. The question in *Wyman v. James*[20] was whether a recipient of welfare benefits may be required to submit to a warrantless home visit by a caseworker as a condition to the continued receipt of those benefits. The Court answered in the affirmative, but relied primarily upon two erroneous notions (that a home visit is not a "search * * * in the Fourth Amendment meaning of

20.   400 U.S. 309, 91 S.Ct. 381, 27 L.Ed.2d 408 (1971).

that term"; and that the Fourth Amendment limits of *Camara* have no application when criminal prosecution is not threatened) making it unnecessary to confront directly the basic questions of whether either the warrant requirement or the usual probable cause requirement should apply in such circumstances.

As for the grounds needed to justify such an inspection, the *Camara* reasoning would seem to be equally applicable here, for the primary concern in this context is that the search be related to a coherent policy followed by the agency and not merely an excuse for harassing a particular unpopular welfare recipient. Thus it would suffice that a particular home visit was in accordance with an established schedule to make such visits at designated intervals or was undertaken upon a "watered-down" probable cause showing that the child's welfare was in danger. As for the warrant requirement, no reason is apparent why it would be impractical in this context, provided of course it is recognized that warrantless action may be undertaken upon a suspicion the child is in some immediate jeopardy.

(e) Inspections at Fire Scenes. As the Supreme Court put it in *Michigan v. Tyler*,[21] a "burning building clearly presents an exigency of sufficient proportions to render a warrantless entry 'reasonable'," as "it would defy reason to suppose that firemen must secure a warrant or consent before entering a burning structure to put out the blaze." But the question here is whether, when the occupant's justified expectation of privacy remains notwithstanding the fire,[22] it is permissible for the authorities to conduct an inspection of those premises for the purpose of determining the cause of the fire. *Camara* suggests an affirma-

tive answer; applying the balancing test to this situation, it may be reasoned that the "need to search" is in part a need to ascertain if the cause is one that could result in a renewal of the fire, hardly a matter that can be determined by external observation of the premises, and that there is here as in *Camara* a "limited invasion" because once again the inspection does not require rummaging through personal effects but instead is directed toward such facilities as the heating, ventilation, gas and electrical systems and the possible accumulation of combustibles. The Court in *Tyler* did not engage in such an assessment, but reached a result consistent with it, namely, that the mere fact a fire has occurred on the premises justifies officials "to remain in a building for a reasonable time to investigate the cause of a blaze after it has been extinguished," and that if later entries "detached from the initial exigency and warrantless entry"[23] are made, then a warrant is required.

It is to be doubted that requiring a warrant here after the "initial exigency" has passed makes sense, provided that the authorities give "fair notice of an inspection."[24] So the argument goes, a warrant is unnecessary to prevent arbitrariness in this context, for the places subject to such an inspection are limited and determined by a prior event that is beyond dispute—that the fire department recently extinguished a fire there. The majority in *Tyler* felt a warrant was nonetheless useful as a means of reassuring the property owner of the legality of the entry and "preventing harassment by keeping that invasion to a minimum," but more recently a majority of the Court would not require a warrant for a with-notice post-fire inspection into the cause of the fire.[25]

---

21.   436 U.S. 499, 98 S.Ct. 1942, 56 L.Ed.2d 486 (1978).

22.   In Michigan v. Clifford, 464 U.S. 287, 104 S.Ct. 641, 78 L.Ed.2d 477 (1984), the plurality stated: "Some fires may be so devastating that no reasonable privacy interests remain in the ash and ruins, regardless of the owner's subjective expectations." However, in that case, where defendant's home was rendered uninhabitable by the fire but personal belongings remained therein and defendant had arranged to have the house secured against intrusion in their absence, they concluded he "retained reasonable privacy interests" in the premises.

23.   In Michigan v. Clifford, 464 U.S. 287, 104 S.Ct. 641, 78 L.Ed.2d 477 (1984), the plurality asserted that

"where a homeowner has made a reasonable effort to secure his fire-damaged home after the blaze has been extinguished and the fire and police units have left the scene, * * * a subsequent post-fire search must be conducted pursuant to a warrant, consent, or the identification of some new exigency."

24.   As Justice Stevens, concurring, proposed.

25.   In Michigan v. Clifford, 464 U.S. 287, 104 S.Ct. 641, 78 L.Ed.2d 477 (1984), four members of the Court followed the *Tyler* rule. Stevens, J., concurring, "would require the fire investigator to obtain a traditional criminal search warrant in order to make an unannounced

Unaffected by this development is the other *Tyler* holding, namely, that "if the investigating officials find probable cause to believe that arson has occurred and require further access to gather evidence for a possible prosecution, they may obtain a warrant only upon a traditional showing of probable cause applicable to searches for evidence of crime." Such a warrant can confer greater search authority than an administrative warrant obtained to ascertain the cause of the fire.[26]

(f) Border Searches and Related Activities. In *United States v. Ramsey*,[27] the Court declared that "searches made at the border, pursuant to the long-standing right of the sovereign to protect itself by stopping and examining persons and property crossing into this country, are reasonable simply by virtue of the fact that they occur at the border." Thus, routine searches of persons and things may be made upon their entry into the country without first obtaining a search warrant and without establishing probable cause or any suspicion at all in the individual case. *Ramsey* held that the same was true of incoming international mail, at least if that mail is of a nature to contain more than correspondence and the inspection does not include the reading of correspondence. These routine border searches may be made at the border when entry is by land from Canada or Mexico, at a place where a ship finally docks after coming from foreign waters, or a place where aircraft land at the end of an international flight, and there is also authority that they may be conducted inland at a functional equivalent of the border or if there has been virtual constant surveillance since the time of the border crossing, thus ensuring that whatever is found in the search can be said to be an object that crossed the border. In the main, these routine searches

can be justified by resort to the *Camara* balancing analysis, as there is a vital national interest in preventing illegal entry and smuggling and the searches are a limited invasion in the sense that they are directed at a morally neutral class of persons who have it within their power to determine the time and place of the search.

Certain kinds of border searches are deemed to be more than routine and to require some kind of case-by-case justification. Thus a strip search, where the person is forced to disrobe to a state that would be offensive to the average person, may be undertaken only upon a "real suspicion" supported by objective, articulable facts that would reasonably lead an experienced, prudent customs official to suspect that the individual is concealing something on his person contrary to law. This standard lies somewhere in the nebulous region between mere suspicion and probable cause. As for a border search involving examination of the rectum, examination of the vagina, or the use of laxatives or emetics to determine what is in the stomach, it may be conducted only upon a "clear indication" of smuggling, which is also a standard that falls below the usual probable cause requirement. No search warrant is required even as to these non-routine and highly intrusive searches, a state of affairs that has frequently been questioned. But intrusions into the body are unreasonable if not done by medical personnel in medical surroundings utilizing customary medical techniques

Because of the increasing utilization of alimentary canal smuggling, customs agents sometimes detain suspects at the border to await the "call of nature." The Court addressed this practice in *United States v. Montoya de Hernandez*,[28] holding: (i) "that the detention of a traveler at the border, beyond the

---

entry, but would characterize a warrantless entry as reasonable whenever the inspector had either given the owner sufficient advance notice to enable him or an agent to be present or had made a reasonable effort to do so." The four dissenters argued that "the utility of requiring a magistrate to evaluate the grounds for a search following a fire is so limited that the incidental protection of an individual's privacy interests simply does not justify imposing a warrant requirement."

26. In Michigan v. Clifford, 464 U.S. 287, 104 S.Ct. 641, 78 L.Ed.2d 477 (1984), the plurality emphasized that

the scope of an administrative search "is limited to that reasonably necessary to determine the cause and origin of a fire and to ensure against rekindling," and thus concluded the officers were not authorized to go from the basement area where the fire originated to upper rooms in the house to seek evidence incriminating the owners.

27. 431 U.S. 606, 97 S.Ct. 1972, 52 L.Ed.2d 617 (1977).

28. 473 U.S. 531, 105 S.Ct. 3304, 87 L.Ed.2d 381 (1985).

scope of a routine customs search and inspection, is justified at its inception if customs agents, considering all the facts surrounding the traveler and her trip, reasonably suspect that the traveler is smuggling contraband in her alimentary canal"; and (ii) that such a detention is "reasonably related in scope to the circumstances which justified it initially" if the suspect is held so long as is "necessary to either verify or dispel the suspicion." This means that if, as in *de Hernandez*, the suspect declines to submit to an x-ray, then the detention on reasonable suspicion may continue until a bowel movement occurs.

To be distinguished from these border searches are a variety of activities conducted in the interior in an effort to identify and apprehend illegal aliens. One, the use of roving patrols to stop and search vehicles on the highways for illegal aliens, came before the Supreme Court in *Almeida–Sanchez v. United States*.[29] The Court held that such a search, made without a warrant and without probable cause, violated the Fourth Amendment; it could not be upheld under the *Carroll–Chambers* rule[30] because that rule applies only when there is probable cause, and it could not be upheld as a *Camara* administrative search because that case condemned searches "at the discretion of the official in the field." Two years later, in *United States v. Brignoni–Ponce*,[31] the Court was confronted with the related question of "whether a roving patrol may stop a vehicle in an area near the border and question its occupants when the only ground for suspicion is that the occupants appear to be of Mexican ancestry," and again answered in the negative. Because the "broad and unlimited discretion" claimed by the government could result in the stopping of many innocent people, this practice likewise could

not be brought within the reasoning of *Camara*. Rather, the stop-and-frisk rule of *Terry v. Ohio*[32] was deemed to strike the proper balance in this context, which means that roving patrols may stop vehicles for the purpose of questioning only upon facts "that reasonably warrant suspicion that the vehicles contain aliens who may be illegally in the country." Factors that may be taken into account, the Court helpfully added in *Brignoni*, include: (i) the "characteristics of the area," including its "proximity to the border, the usual patterns of traffic on the particular road, and previous experience with alien traffic"; (ii) "information about recent illegal border crossings in the area"; (iii) the "driver's behavior," such as "erratic driving or obvious attempts to evade officers"; (iv) the type of vehicle, such as a station wagon with large compartments, which "are frequently used for transporting concealed aliens"; (v) that the vehicle seems "heavily loaded" or has "an extraordinary number of passengers"; (vi) that persons are observed "trying to hide"; (vii) "the characteristic appearance of persons who live in Mexico, relying on such factors as the mode of dress and haircut"; and (viii) such other facts as are meaningful to the officer "in light of his experience detecting illegal entry and smuggling."[33]

Two other decisions of the Court are concerned with the use of fixed checkpoints to discover illegal aliens. In *United States v. Ortiz*,[34] involving use of a checkpoint at which all cars travelling on a certain road were required to stop for investigation and were sometimes searched as a part of that investigation, the government claimed that use of the checkpoint sufficiently limited the officers' discretion and made the circumstances of the search less intrusive. The Court disagreed on both counts. For one thing, the record indicated that only a

---

29.   413 U.S. 266, 93 S.Ct. 2535, 37 L.Ed.2d 596 (1973).

30.   See § 3.7(b).

31.   422 U.S. 873, 95 S.Ct. 2574, 45 L.Ed.2d 607 (1975).

32.   392 U.S. 1, 88 S.Ct. 1868, 20 L.Ed.2d 889 (1968).

33.   But when a court of appeals in a later case, concerned that such fact-specific weighing of circumstances introduced "a troubling degree of uncertainty and unpredictability" into Fourth Amendment analysis, sought "to describe and clearly delimit the extent to which certain factors may be considered" by examining the factors relied

upon by the officer one-by-one and dismissing some as entitled to "no weight" because individually susceptible to an innocent explanation, a unanimous Supreme Court reversed, explaining that such an approach would "seriously undercut the 'totality of the circumstances' principle which governs the existence *vel non* of 'reasonable suspicion.'" United States v. Arvizu, 534 U.S. 266, 122 S.Ct. 744, 151 L.Ed.2d 740 (2002).

34.   422 U.S. 891, 95 S.Ct. 2585, 45 L.Ed.2d 623 (1975).

small percentage of the vehicles passing the checkpoint were stopped to the extent that questioning or search was undertaken, making it apparent that "checkpoint officers exercise a substantial degree of discretion in deciding which cars to search." For another, the "greater regularity attending the stop does not mitigate the invasion of privacy that a search entails," especially when "only a few are singled out for a search." The Court in *Ortiz* thus held "that at traffic checkpoints removed from the border and its functional equivalents, officers may not search private vehicles without consent or probable cause."

This then leaves the possibility of utilizing a fixed checkpoint merely to stop vehicles and question the occupants, as to which the government prevailed in *United States v. Martinez–Fuerte*.[35] The *Camara* balancing test produced a different result here than in the three other cases, the Court reasoned, as "the potential interference with legitimate traffic is minimal," and the "checkpoint operations both appear to and actually involve less discretionary enforcement activity." Though it is true that the practices at issue in *Martinez–Fuerte* are certainly less intrusive than those held unconstitutional in the three earlier cases, this is not to say that the reasoning or result in *Martinez–Fuerte* is unassailable. One major weakness in the Court's analysis is the conclusion it need not consider the "less-restrictive-alternative arguments" of the defendants, that is, the defendants' contention that the government could check the flow of illegal aliens by other means which did not so intrude upon Fourth Amendment values. This seems inconsistent with *Camara,* where one critical factor was that "acceptable results" could not be achieved in any other way. The second weakness concerns the Court's conclusion that "no particularized reason need exist to justify" the selective referral of some motorists to a secondary inspection area. Given the opportunity for arbitrariness in this screening process, it may be argued (as did the *Martinez–Fuerte* dissenters) that these referrals should be tested by the *Terry* reasonable suspicion standard.

(g) Vehicle Use Regulation. Although the practice of stopping vehicles at random to check drivers' licenses and vehicle registrations and determine that the vehicles are in proper mechanical condition had been upheld by the lower courts, the Supreme Court decided otherwise in *Delaware v. Prouse*[36] "by balancing its intrusion on the individual's Fourth Amendment interests against its promotion of legitimate governmental interests." On the need side of the scales, the Court agreed "that the States have a vital interest in ensuring that only those qualified to do so are permitted to operate motor vehicles, that these vehicles are fit for safe operation, and hence that licensing, registration, and vehicle inspection requirements are being observed." But the Court then pointed out that discretionary spot checks would not greatly advance those interests. On the matter of drivers' licenses, "the percentage of all drivers on the road who are driving without a license is very small and * * * the number of licensed drivers who will be stopped in order to find one unlicensed operator will be large indeed," while by comparison checking those drivers who have committed a traffic violation is "much more likely" to uncover an unlicensed driver. As for vehicle registration, this can be determined by simply noting "license plates indicating current registration," which does not require stopping of the vehicle. Likewise, random stopping of vehicles for safety inspections would make little "incremental contribution to highway safety," as many violations of safety requirements "are observable" without stopping the car, and others can be detected by an "annual safety inspection" scheme. On the intrusion side of the scale, the Court in *Prouse* correctly concluded that such a random stop is not "of any less moment than that occasioned by a stop by border agents on roving patrol" in terms of creating anxiety, interfering with freedom of movement, causing inconvenience, and consuming time. The Court thus held

that except in those situations in which there is at least articulable and reasonable

35. 428 U.S. 543, 96 S.Ct. 3074, 49 L.Ed.2d 1116 (1976).

36. 440 U.S. 648, 99 S.Ct. 1391, 59 L.Ed.2d 660 (1979).

suspicion that a motorist is unlicensed or that an automobile is not registered, or that either the vehicle or an occupant is otherwise subject to seizure for violation of law,[37] stopping an automobile and detaining the driver in order to check his driver's license and the registration of the automobile are unreasonable under the Fourth Amendment. This holding does not preclude the State of Delaware or other States from developing methods for spot checks that involve less intrusion or that do not involve the unconstrained exercise of discretion. Questioning of all oncoming traffic at roadblock-type stops is one possible alternative.

It thus appears that the Court would uphold the use of a checkpoint, as have the lower courts, when used to check drivers' licenses and vehicle registrations or to conduct safety inspections of vehicles. And while the *Prouse* majority describes the practice in terms of dealing with "all oncoming traffic," it would seem that Justice Blackmun is correct in saying in his concurring opinion "that the Court's reservation also includes other not purely random stops (such as every 10th car to pass a given point) that equate with, but are less intrusive than, a 100% roadblock stop." It is not necessary for a checkpoint to stop every car in order to be systematic but only for officers to be following some pattern that will minimize their discretion in choosing whether to stop a particular auto. Also, it should be noted that the Court in *Prouse* explained its ruling was not intended to "cast doubt on the permissibility of roadblock truck weigh stations and inspection checkpoints, at which some vehicles may be subject to further detention for safety and regulatory inspection than are others," another procedure that has been upheld by the lower courts.

Yet another practice that is being more frequently relied upon by the police is the sobriety checkpoint, at which traffic is stopped at a temporary location so that each driver may be observed to see if he is under the influence and, if signs of intoxication are detected, may be directed out of the traffic flow for further scrutiny and perhaps sobriety tests. In *Michigan Dept. of State Police v. Sitz*,[38] an injunctive action in which only the initial stopping was at issue, the Court upheld the use of such checkpoints. Utilizing a balancing test similar to that employed in *Prouse*, the majority in *Sitz* stressed these factors: (1) the states' strong interest in eradicating the serious drunken driving problem; (2) the slight "intrusion on motorists subjected to a brief stop at a highway checkpoint," where (as in the instant case) "checkpoints are selected pursuant to [established] guidelines, and uniformed police officers stop every approaching vehicle"; and (3) that it is for "politically accountable officials" to decide "as to which among reasonable alternative law enforcement techniques should be employed," and that this checkpoint was such an alternative because it produced results superior to those in *Martinez–Fuerte*.[39] Lower courts, in upholding the operation of such checkpoints when proper procedures have been followed, typically stress the necessity (i) that the decision of where and when the roadblock is to be operated not be left to officers in the field; (ii) that the checkpoint be conducted in a regularized manner so as not to alarm those approaching and stopping at it; (iii) that all vehicles be stopped at the roadblock or at least that those stopped be selected by neutral criteria; (iv) that selective referral for continued investigation (and thus more than momentary detention) of some of those stopped be pursuant to the *Terry* reasonable suspicion test; and (v) that advance publicity be given to the forthcoming use of this enforcement technique.

The Coast Guard is authorized by statute[40] to stop vessels upon the high seas and waters of the United States to conduct inspections.

---

37. In New York v. Class, 475 U.S. 106, 106 S.Ct. 960, 89 L.Ed.2d 81 (1986), the Court concluded "that a demand to inspect the VIN, like a demand to see license and registration papers, is within the scope of police authority pursuant to a traffic stop" prompted by an observed traffic violation.

38. 496 U.S. 444, 110 S.Ct. 2481, 110 L.Ed.2d 412 (1990).

39. In *Sitz*, 1.5% of the drivers passing the checkpoint were arrested for being under the influence; in *Martinez–Fuerte* illegal aliens were found in 0.12% of the vehicles.

40. 14 U.S.C.A. § 89(a).

These special inspection powers do not extend to search into private books, papers or personal belongings, but it is permissible to examine safety equipment, inspect documentation papers, check the identification number on the beam or frame to ensure it matches the number in those papers, and otherwise identify the ship when no documentation is supplied. The *Prouse* decision does not bar or limit exercise of that statutory authority. As explained in *United States v. Villamonte–Marquez*[41]:

> The nature of waterborne commerce in waters providing ready access to the open sea is sufficiently different from the nature of vehicular traffic on highways as to make possible alternatives to the sort of "stop" made in this case less likely to accomplish the obviously essential governmental purposes involved. The system of prescribed outward markings used by States for vehicle registration is also significantly different than the system of external markings on vessels, and the extent and type of documentation required by federal law is a good deal more variable and more complex than are the state vehicle registration laws. The nature of the governmental interest in assuring compliance with documentation requirements, particularly in waters where the need to deter or apprehend smugglers is great, are substantial; the type of intrusion made in this case, while not minimal, is limited.

Whenever departure from the usual warrant and/or probable cause requirements is claimed to be justified on the basis of some "special need," as is ordinarily the case with respect to a vehicle checkpoint,[42] it is necessary that this need be something other than the state's general law enforcement interest, as is illustrated by *City of Indianapolis v. Edmond*.[43] The Court there held that city-operated vehicle checkpoints, complete with drug dogs, under-

taken to interdict unlawful drugs, contravened the Fourth Amendment. As for the city's reliance on *Martinez–Fuerte*, *Prouse* and *Sitz*, the *Edmond* majority distinguished those cases because in none of them "did we indicate approval of a checkpoint program whose primary purpose was to detect evidence of ordinary criminal wrongdoing." As for the city's response that securing the border and apprehending drunk drivers "are * * * law enforcement activities, and law enforcement officers employ arrests and criminal prosecutions in pursuit of these goals," the Court responded that analysis at that "high level of generality" would mean there "would be little check on the ability of the authorities to construct roadblocks for almost any conceivable law enforcement purpose."[44]

(h) Airport Searches. When airplane hijacking became a major problem in the late 1960's, the government first attempted to deal with it by establishing procedures for identifying a relatively select group of air passengers who should be subjected to close preboarding screening. When a passenger checked in for a flight, the agent would apply a behavioral profile, based upon a detailed study of all then known hijackers, to determine if he was a potential hijacker. In the boarding area, a person so identified would have to pass through a magnetometer set to detect the amount of metal in a small handgun. A person who both fit the profile and triggered the magnetometer would be interviewed, and if he failed to supply adequate identification he would be frisked and his carry-on luggage searched. Consequently, these more intrusive actions were undertaken against a very small percentage of passengers. Utilizing the balancing test, courts upheld these searches on the ground that they were based upon the reasonable suspicion re-

---

41. 462 U.S. 579, 103 S.Ct. 2573, 77 L.Ed.2d 22 (1983).

42. In *Edmond*, discussed in the text following, the Court did make the following qualification: "Of, course, there are circumstances that may justify a law enforcement checkpoint where the primary purpose would otherwise, but for some emergency, relate to ordinary crime control. For example, * * * the Fourth Amendment would almost certainly permit an appropriately tailored roadblock set up to thwart an imminent terrorist attack or to

catch a dangerous criminal who is likely to flee by way of a particular route."

43. 531 U.S. 32, 121 S.Ct. 447, 148 L.Ed.2d 333 (2000).

44. The three dissenters argued that the checkpoints at issue shared the critical characteristics of those previously approved by the Court: they "effectively serve the State's legitimate interests; they are executed in a regularized and neutral manner, and they only minimally intrude upon the privacy of the motorists."

quired by *Terry v. Ohio*.[45] On the need side of the equation there was the fact that air piracy presented extreme dangers to the traveling public and could be effectively dealt with only if the potential hijacker was intercepted on the ground. On the intrusion side, it was relevant that the searches were of a morally neutral class who must voluntarily come to and enter the search area and were under the supervision of airlines who have a substantial interest in assuring that their passengers are not unnecessarily harassed. Those considerations made it reasonable to conduct the searches upon the degree of suspicion provided by the profile-plus-magnetometer-plus-questioning selection process, which experience had shown produced a person carrying a weapon six per cent of the time.

In 1973, efforts to utilize this selective process were abandoned in favor of a program whereunder *all* passengers were checked before boarding. Every passenger was required to pass through the magnetometer, and his carry-on luggage was inspected either by hand or by passing it through an X-ray device. If the magnetometer sounded, the passenger had to remove items from his person until he was able to pass through the device without triggering it, and if the X-ray detected a suspicious object the passenger was not allowed to proceed unless he permitted an examination of the contents of the luggage. Especially because use of the magnetometer and X-ray both qualify as searches, the question arose as to whether subjecting all passengers to these searches was constitutionally permissible. Employing the balancing test once again, the courts decided this procedure also passed Fourth Amendment muster, not because there was a reasonable suspicion of those searched, but rather because (as in *Camara*) it involved a general regulatory scheme without the potential for arbitrariness. But, because an administrative screening search must be as limited in its intrusiveness as is consistent with satisfaction of the administrative need that justifies it, it is critical that each person be able to avoid search by electing not to board the aircraft. The point is not that one has consented or

impliedly consented to the search by virtue of deciding to be an airline passenger; rather, it is a matter of narrowing the search to the need, plus the notion that advance notice of the risks and how to avoid them is an ingredient that may make an inspection system reasonable. Even under the new system, *Terry* reasonable suspicion will sometimes come into play, as where a person has "passed" the inspection in the literal sense but it has produced facts of a highly suspicious nature.

As a consequence of the tragic events of 9/11/01, Congress enacted the Aviation and Transportation Security Act of 2001, which placed all airport screening in the hands of a new agency, the Transportation Security Administration. The screening procedures required under the Act are considerably more intrusive and intensive than those earlier mandated by the FAA, and now include examination of checked luggage for explosives by a variety of methods–bomb-scan machines, dog sniffs, and manual searches. But, while the screening of passengers and their luggage has generally become more intense than in the past, it has often proved impossible to give the "full treatment" to each and every traveler, and hence some degree of selectivity has proved necessary. Whether a selective process tending to focus upon Arab Muslim men is justified has been a matter of vigorous debate. A new computerized screening system, claimed "not to use race or ethnicity as criteria," is being made operational, but because it would involve gathering much background information about travelers it is a matter of concern on that basis.

Analysis similar to that used in the airport screening cases has been used to uphold other inspection schemes contemplating examination of all persons who wish to enter a particular place where there are special security needs. Illustrative are checkpoint inspections of visitors to a penal institution, to a military installation, or to government buildings that have been the targets of violence or threats of violence.

45.   392 U.S. 1, 88 S.Ct. 1868, 20 L.Ed.2d 889 (1968).

(i) Searches Directed at Prisoners. In keeping with the Supreme Court's declaration that "a prisoner is not wholly stripped of constitutional protections when he is imprisoned for crime,"[46] many courts held that prisoners have a Fourth Amendment expectation of privacy of a diminished scope. Under that approach, a "shakedown" search of the cell and personal effects of prisoners, undertaken either pursuant to an established routine of making such searches periodically or in response to an incident at the prison or jail, is constitutionally permissible under the *Camara* standardized procedures principle, and even a search directed at only one or a few prisoners is proper if undertaken upon reasonable suspicion. But that approach was rejected by the Supreme Court in the 5–4 decision of *Hudson v. Palmer*,[47] involving a section 1983 action brought by a state prison inmate who alleged a prison guard had conducted a "shakedown" search of his cell and had destroyed his noncontraband property for purposes of harassment. In holding "that the Fourth Amendment has no applicability to a prison cell," the majority reasoned:

> The two interests here are the interest of society in the security of its penal institutions and the interest of the prisoner in privacy within his cell. The latter interest, of course, is already limited by the exigencies of the circumstances: A prison "shares none of the attributes of privacy of a home, an automobile, an office, or a hotel room." * * * We strike the balance in favor of institutional security, which we have noted is

"central to all other correctional goals" * * *. A right of privacy in traditional Fourth Amendment terms is fundamentally incompatible with the close and continual surveillance of inmates and their cells required to ensure institutional security and internal order. We are satisfied that society would insist that the prisoner's expectation of privacy always yield to what must be considered the paramount interest in institutional security. We believe that it is accepted by our society that "[l]oss of freedom of choice and privacy are inherent incidents of confinement."

The Court added that for "the same reasons" the seizure and destruction of a prisoner's effects did not fall within the protections of the Fourth Amendment.[48] (The four dissenters in *Hudson* seriously questioned this latter conclusion[49] and also disputed whether it was inevitably the case that a prisoner had no privacy expectation in his effects.[50]) *Hudson* is not unquestionably applicable to pretrial detention facilities.[51]

As for search of the person of a prisoner, a particular prisoner may be searched upon reasonable suspicion that he is in possession of the fruits, instrumentalities or evidence of either criminal behavior or conduct in violation of prison regulations. A search of the person also may be lawfully undertaken as part of a general routine inspection without any showing of individualized suspicion. The general routine theory also covers the standardized practice of searching prisoners whenever they

46. Wolff v. McDonnell, 418 U.S. 539, 94 S.Ct. 2963, 41 L.Ed.2d 935 (1974).

47. 468 U.S. 517, 104 S.Ct. 3194, 82 L.Ed.2d 393 (1984).

48. But the Court did indicate that if a prisoner was subjected to "calculated harassment unrelated to prison needs," then this would violate the Eighth Amendment proscription upon cruel and unusual punishment.

49. They reasoned (i) that the majority's assumption that a prisoner was without any legal possessory interests whatsoever to which the Fourth Amendment's unreasonable seizures prohibition could attach did not "comport with any civilized standard of decency"; (ii) that the majority's claim society would not recognize any such expectation as reasonable was wrong, as reflected by the contrary view reflected with virtual unanimity in the recent commentary and federal decisions; and (iii) that the seizure here, assuming plaintiff's allegations to be true,

was most certainly "unreasonable" under the Fourth Amendment because undertaken without any "penological justification."

50. "I cannot see any justification for applying this rule to minimum security facilities in which inmates who pose no realistic threat to security are housed. I also see no justification for reading the mail of a prisoner once it has cleared whatever censorship mechanism is employed by the prison and has been received by the prisoner."

51. The Court's holding is stated in terms of "a prison cell," and much (but certainly not all) of the Court's analysis concerns circumstances existing in facilities housing those convicted of crime. But O'Connor, J., concurring, stated the broader proposition that the "fact of arrest and incarceration abates all legitimate Fourth Amendment privacy and possessory interests in personal effects."

have come into contact with others, such as visitors, who could have passed them contraband. Even strip searches are allowed in such circumstances; in *Bell v. Wolfish*,[52] the Supreme Court used the balancing test to uphold a practice whereby pretrial detainees were required to expose their body cavities for visual inspection as a part of a strip search conducted after every visit with a person from outside the institution, but the Court's assertion that there was a security risk that could be met in no other way is not particularly convincing. (The status of those limitations is, at best, uncertain after *Hudson*, as it is unclear whether that decision has application to searches and seizures of the person of a prisoner.[53])

The Supreme Court in *Procunier v. Martinez*,[54] concerning censorship of prison mail, declared that an "obvious example of justifiable censorship of prisoner mail would be refusal to send or deliver letters concerning escape plans or containing other information concerning proposed criminal activity, whether within or without the prison," and lower courts have reasoned that by implication this permits the inspection of all mail for such contents. The same reasoning has been used to justify eavesdropping upon conversations of prisoners and visitors. It has been questioned, however, whether the risk of escape or further criminal conduct is sufficiently great as to *all* types of detainees to justify those practices across the board. In one post-*Hudson* decision, the Supreme Court concluded that when prison regulations affect outgoing mail, as opposed to incoming mail, there must be a "closer fit between the regulation and the purpose it serves," but yet concluded that in neither case must the regulation satisfy a "least restrictive means" test.[55] It is thus not surprising that more recent lower court decisions have upheld the review of prison inmates' outgoing general correspondence.

(j) Searches Directed at Probationers and Parolees. Although there is some authority to the effect that the Fourth Amendment rights of probationers and parolees are of precisely the same scope and dimension as those of the public at large, the weight of authority is to the contrary. As to parolees, it has often been held that their residences may be searched without a warrant or even without probable cause, that their vehicles may be searched without either a warrant or a probable cause showing, and that they may be arrested without probable cause. And while there is some disagreement as to whether a probationer's Fourth Amendment rights are diminished to the same extent and degree as those of a parolee, there is considerable authority supporting the proposition that probationers may also be lawfully subjected to searches that, absent their probation status, would be deemed unlawful because of the absence of probable cause or a search warrant or both.

A variety of theories have been articulated by the courts in purported justification for these holdings. With respect to parolees, a notion commonly relied upon is that such persons are in the "constructive custody" of the government while on parole and thus are in essentially the same position, in terms of their Fourth Amendment rights, as persons who are still serving time in prison. But this is more of a conclusion than a theory, resting upon a fiction that tends to divert attention from the underlying issues, and has been rejected by the Supreme Court in other contexts.[56] Some courts instead stress that parole or probation is an "act of grace," from which it is concluded that such beneficence may be attended by whatever restrictions upon privacy the government may deem appropriate. Other courts have wisely rejected that notion, and the Supreme Court has declared in a related context

52. 441 U.S. 520, 99 S.Ct. 1861, 60 L.Ed.2d 447 (1979).

53. The *Hudson* dissenters observed that the majority "appears to limit its holding to a prisoner's 'papers and effects' located in his cell" and apparently "believes that at least a prisoner's 'person' is secure from unreasonable search and seizure." The *Hudson* majority did, however, refer to the necessity for "close and continual surveillance of inmates and their cells."

54. 416 U.S. 396, 94 S.Ct. 1800, 40 L.Ed.2d 224 (1974).

55. Thornburgh v. Abbott, 490 U.S. 401, 109 S.Ct. 1874, 104 L.Ed.2d 459 (1989).

56. Morrissey v. Brewer, 408 U.S. 471, 92 S.Ct. 2593, 33 L.Ed.2d 484 (1972).

that it "is hardly useful any longer to try to deal with this problem in terms of whether the parolee's liberty is valuable and must be seen as within the protection of the Fourteenth Amendment."[57] A third theory, most likely to be relied upon when such a "waiver" is expressly set out and agreed to by the probationer or parolee at the time of his conditional release, is that searches of such persons are proper because consented to as part of the "contract" of release. But this simply is not so under the *Schneckloth v. Bustamonte*[58] voluntariness test for consent searches; the probationer who purportedly waives his rights by accepting such a condition has little genuine option to refuse, and the waiver cannot be said to be voluntary in any generally-accepted sense of the term.[59]

There is yet another theory that *does* make sense, which is that some "special" Fourth Amendment rules apply in this area by application of the *Camara* balancing test. On the need side of the equation, the basic point is that the very existence of these forms of conditional release for convicted criminals reflects a legislative judgment that these men can achieve effective rehabilitation only with the aid of supervision and guidance from governmental officials, and that in certain types of cases, at least, close surveillance tends to reduce the rate of recidivism. Such was the approach taken in *Griffin v. Wisconsin*,[60] upholding search of a probationer's home without a warrant or full probable cause because of the "special needs" of the probation system. The warrant requirement was deemed inappropriate for probation officers, who "have in mind the welfare of the probationer" and must "respond quickly to evidence of misconduct." The usual probable cause standard was

deemed inapplicable because it "would reduce the deterrent effect of the supervisory arrangement" and because "the probation agency must be able to act based upon a lesser degree of certainty than the Fourth Amendment would otherwise require in order to intervene before a probationer does damage to himself or society."

Because the degree of risk is not the same as to all probationers and parolees, it would seem that under the *Camara* approach the special restrictions upon each parolee and probationer should not be imposed routinely by the use of identical "boilerplate" language inserted in every probation or parole agreement. Rather, they should result from a case-by-case assessment at the time of release of what degree of surveillance is necessary in the particular case. But *Griffin* is to the contrary. As for that part of the *Camara* balancing test requiring that the special search authority be limited to the unique problem giving rise to the need for it, it may fairly be concluded that the rehabilitation objective is best served by giving the special authority only to parole and probation officers and not to the police. It follows that if a probation or parole officer used his special power as nothing more than the agent of the police, then the search would be unlawful.

Those conclusions, supported by the reasoning in *Griffin*, seemed even more solid as a result of the Court's later *Edmond*[61] and *Ferguson*[62] decisions. But the Supreme Court then found it possible to avoid any such limitations in the probationer search area by developing a different supporting theory in *United States v. Knights*.[63] After Knights' state conviction for a drug offense, he was placed on probation subject to the condition that he "[s]ubmit his . . .

57. Morrissey v. Brewer, 408 U.S. 471, 92 S.Ct. 2593, 33 L.Ed.2d 484 (1972).

58. 412 U.S. 218, 93 S.Ct. 2041, 36 L.Ed.2d 854 (1973).

59. In the *Knights* case, discussed in text at note 63 infra, Knights signed the probation order containing the search condition and a declaration he agreed "to abide by same." "The Government, advocating the approach of the Supreme Court of California, * * * contends that the search satisfied the Fourth Amendment under the 'consent' rationale of * * * * *Schneckloth* * * *. In the Government's view, Knights's acceptance of the search condition was voluntary because he had the option of rejecting probation and going to prison instead, which the Govern-

ment argues is analogous to the voluntary decision defendants often make to waive their right to a trial and accept a plea bargain." The Court found it unnecessary to decide the consent issue.

60. 483 U.S. 868, 107 S.Ct. 3164, 97 L.Ed.2d 709 (1987).

61. See text at note 43 supra.

62. See text at note 74 infra.

63. 534 U.S. 112, 122 S.Ct. 587, 151 L.Ed.2d 497 (2001).

person, property, place of residence, vehicle, personal effects, to search at any time, with or without a search warrant, warrant of arrest or reasonable cause by any probation officer or law enforcement officer." Three days later, a sheriff's detective, without the knowledge or participation of probation officials, made a warrantless search of Knights' residence on reasonable suspicion he was involved in vandalism, resulting in federal charges. The district court granted his motion to suppress the evidence found in his home on the ground that the search had been "investigatory" rather than "probationary," and the court of appeals affirmed.

In response to the contention that such a limitation followed from *Griffin*, a unanimous Supreme Court, per the Chief Justice, noted that *Griffin* expressly declared that its "special needs" holding made it "unnecessary to consider whether" warrantless searches of probationers were otherwise reasonable within the meaning of the Fourth Amendment. The Court in *Knights* then proceeded to answer the reserved question in the affirmative, declaring that the search in the instant case passed muster "under our general Fourth Amendment approach of 'examining the totality of the circumstances'" and then determining reasonableness "by assessing, on the one hand, the degree to which it intrudes upon an individual's privacy and, on the other, the degree to which it is needed for the promotion of legitimate government interests." Proceeding with the balancing of interests, the Court concluded (a) that the "probation order clearly expressed the search condition and Knights was unambiguously informed of it," meaning the "probation condition thus significantly diminished Knights's reasonable expectation of privacy"; (b) that because a probationer "will be more likely to engage in criminal conduct than an ordinary member of the community," the State's "interest in apprehending violators of the criminal law * * * may therefore justifiably focus on probationers in a way that it

does not on the ordinary citizen"; and (c) that "the balance of these considerations requires no more than reasonable suspicion to conduct a search of this probationer's house"[64] and "render[s] a warrant requirement unnecessary." Distinguishing *Edmond*, the Court then concluded: "Because our holding rests on ordinary Fourth Amendment analysis that considers all the circumstances of a search, there is no basis for examining official purpose."

(k) Searches Directed at Students. Searches directed at the persons or effects of students while on the premises of an educational institution have on occasion been upheld even when they could not pass the Fourth Amendment requirements applicable in the typical criminal investigation. This is sometimes done under the doctrine of *in loco parentis* (literally, in place of a parent). But that doctrine can hardly be applied at the college level, where the overwhelming majority of the students have reached adulthood, and at the high school and grade school levels is so often used merely as a slogan that it is much more forthright simply to assess all such searches under the *Camara* balancing test. Likewise, exaggerated doctrines of consent and implied consent have no place here either.

At the pre-college level, the lower court cases indicate that the person and locker of a student may be searched upon reasonable suspicion of a violation of the criminal law or reasonable regulation of the educational institution. Part of the *Camara*-type reasoning used to justify such a rule is that schools are confronted with serious discipline problems, especially concerning the use of drugs, and have a unique responsibility to deal with those problems effectively. The state, so the argument goes, having compelled students to attend school and thus associate with the immature and unwise closely and daily, thereby owes those students a safe and secure environment. It is less apparent, however, that "acceptable results" (to use the *Camara* terminology) can be achieved only by watered-down

---

64. In a footnote the Court added: "We do not decide whether the probation condition so diminished, or completely eliminated, Knights's reasonable expectation of privacy * * * that a search by a law enforcement officer

without any individualized suspicion would have satisfied the reasonableness requirement of the Fourth Amendment."

Fourth Amendment standards, as many of the appellate cases indicate that the search was undertaken on the basis of information from another student sufficient to meet the traditional probable cause test. As far as the "limited intrusion" factor of *Camara* goes, again it is very difficult to make a judgment on that factor in this context, but it is noteworthy that most of the reported cases that have approved searches of the student's person have involved relatively mild intrusions. As for locker searches, it is certainly relevant whether the school has made it clear that possession of the locker is nonexclusive as against the school, not because this shows consent, but rather because it is a factor bearing upon the reasonableness of the inspection system. The point is that such advance notice provides the student with an opportunity to limit the effect of the intrusion by not keeping highly personal materials in the locker provided by the school.

The Supreme Court dealt with this general problem in *New Jersey v. T.L.O.*,[65] involving search of a high school student's purse. The Court held that "the Fourth Amendment applies to searches conducted by school authorities," but that under the *Camara* balancing test such a search could be conducted without a warrant and without full probable cause. What is required is that the search of the student be justified at its inception (i.e., that there be "reasonable grounds for suspecting that the search will turn up evidence that the student has violated or is violating either the law or the rules of the school") and that it be reasonable in scope (i.e., that "the measures adopted are reasonably related to the objectives of the search and not excessively intrusive in light of the age and sex of the student and the nature of the infraction"). The Court also cautioned that there were several issues regarding searches directed at students that it had not resolved, such as "whether individualized suspicion is an essential element of the reasonableness standard," "whether a schoolchild has a legitimate expectation of privacy in lockers, desks, or other school property provid-

ed for storage of school supplies," and whether a higher standard would be needed in "assessing the legality of searches conducted by school officials in conjunction with or at the behest of law enforcement agencies."

Later, in *Vernonia School District 47J v. Acton*,[66] the Court held on the facts presented that there was one type of search which did *not* require individualized suspicion: drug testing of student athletes. The Court deemed the privacy expectations intruded upon to be somewhat limited, as per *T.L.O.* all school children are subject to considerable supervision and control, and student athletes' expectations "are even less" because they voluntarily chose to subject themselves to greater regulation, "somewhat like adults who choose to participate in a 'closely regulated industry.'" Also, the intrusion upon privacy complained of was limited, as the tests were taken under conditions "nearly identical to those typically encountered in public restrooms," and the test results "are disclosed only to a limited class of school personnel who have a need to know." That intrusion, the Court concluded, was outweighed by the legitimate government interests advanced: deterring drug use by school children and, in the case of student athletes, preventing physical harm to drug users and other players. The less intrusive alternative of testing only upon individualized suspicion was dismissed by the *Acton* majority as "probably impracticable."

Acton was applied so as to uphold drug testing of students in much less compelling circumstances in the 5–4 decision in *Board of Education of Independent School District No. 92 of Pottawatomie County v. Earls*,[67] where the random testing policy was applicable to middle and high school students participating in *any* extracurricular activity. The quite different views of *Acton* by the *Earls* majority and dissenting Justices highlights the difference between the two cases. As for the *Acton* emphasis upon the especially low privacy expectations of student-athletes, the *Earls* ma-

65. 469 U.S. 325, 105 S.Ct. 733, 83 L.Ed.2d 720 (1985).
66. 515 U.S. 646, 115 S.Ct. 2386, 132 L.Ed.2d 564 (1995).
67. 536 U.S. 822, 122 S.Ct. 2559, 153 L.Ed.2d 735 (2002).

jority says that this factor "was not essential to our decision" in the earlier case and that, "in any event," all students who "voluntarily subject themselves" to additional regulations by opting for extracurricular activities have as a consequence "a limited expectation of privacy." The *Earls* dissenters, on the other hand, object that extracurricular activities other than athletics do not involve any significant reduction in privacy, and that opting out of such activities is not a realistic alternative in light of the fact that they are "a key component of school life, essential in reality for students applying to college." As for the "nature and immediacy of the government's concern," the *Earls* majority says that it suffices that "the nationwide epidemic makes the war against drugs a pressing concern in every school" and that, in addition, there was "specific evidence of drug use" at the schools. The *Earls* dissenters contend the instant case, where school officials repeatedly reported no "major problems" with drugs, is a far cry from *Acton*, where there was a drug-induced "state of rebellion," and in addition assert that *Acton*, because of the focus on athletes, squares with other drug testing decisions of the Court permitting testing to "avoid enormous risks to the lives and limbs of others," while the instant case tests students "engaged in activities that are not safety sensitive to an unusual degree." As for the efficacy of the policy in meeting the government's concerns, the *Earls* majority says the policy in question "is a reasonably effective means of * * * preventing, deterring, and detecting drug use," and asserts that the fact that in *Acton* the athletes were at the heart of the drug problem there "was not essential to the holding" in that case, which "did not require the school to test the group of students most likely to use drugs." The *Earls* dissenters, citing findings that "students who participate in extracurricular activities are significantly less likely to develop substance abuse problems than are their less-involved peers," conclude that the policy "invades the privacy of students who need deterrence the least, and risks steering students at greatest risk for substance abuse away from extracur-

ricular involvement that potentially may palliate drug problems."

At the college level, the cases in the main have concerned searches of rooms in dormitories maintained by the educational institution and rented to students matriculating there. One view is that here as well the reasonable suspicion test applies, and the emphasis once again is upon the special need to maintain a proper educational atmosphere. The contrary view is that traditional Fourth Amendment standards apply to such searches, a conclusion that is supported by the fact that application of the *Camara* balancing test here does not produce a convincing showing that broader authority is needed. For one thing, the searches at issue cannot be characterized as a limited intrusion; a student's dormitory room is his house and home for all practical purposes, and he has the same interest in the privacy of his room as any adult has in the privacy of his home, dwelling, or lodging. Nor is the need as strong as at the high school level. College students are more mature and less in need of general supervision, their presence is not compelled by attendance laws, they are not in day-long close contact with one another in a single location, and their dorm rooms are not concerned with the academic affairs of the university community.

As for drug testing of athletes at public institutions of higher education, there is authority that random, suspicionless urinalysis-drug-testing of students violates the Fourth Amendment. The status of such cases after *Acton* is uncertain at best. Some of the *Acton* analysis (e.g., the reduced privacy expectation of student athletes, and their voluntary choice to engage in athletics) would seem to carry over to the college level. But other *Acton* points (especially the foundational proposition that the student body generally has a lesser expectation of privacy) cannot in the same way be transferred to the college setting.

(l) Searches Directed at Public Employees. *O'Connor v. Ortega*,[68] a § 1983 action challenging search by a doctor's supervisors of his desk and filing cabinets at the state hospi-

68. 480 U.S. 709, 107 S.Ct. 1492, 94 L.Ed.2d 714 (1987).

tal where he was employed, focused attention upon the somewhat limited Fourth Amendment rights of public employees. Though the Court was firmly of the view that "[s]earches and seizures by government employers or supervisors of the private property of their employees * * * are subject to the restraints of the Fourth Amendment," the protections of the Amendment were deemed to be somewhat different in this context. Even assuming that the facts of the particular case show that the employee had a justified expectation of privacy in the particular area searched,[69] it is necessary in this context to "balance the invasion of the employee's legitimate expectations of privacy against the government's need for supervision, control and the efficient operation of the workplace." One consequence of this balancing is that no search warrant is needed for intrusions "for legitimate work-related reasons wholly unrelated to illegal conduct." Moreover, intrusions "for noninvestigatory, work-related purposes, as well as for investigation of work-related misconduct, should be judged by the standard of reasonableness under all the circumstances" rather than the traditional quantum of probable cause.[70]

Drug testing of government employees (or, of private employees pursuant to government regulation) has been addressed by several courts recently. Upon a weighing of the competing public and private interests, most lower courts have concluded that such testing is constitutional at least in those instances in which there was reasonable individualized suspicion. These cases reflect the judgment that the individualized suspicion test fairly accommodates the legitimate interest in employee privacy without unduly restricting the employer's opportunity to monitor and control drug use by employees. Whether random or more generalized testing is also permissible upon some special showing is a more difficult question, though the Supreme Court has upheld two such inspection schemes where testing was triggered by a specific event and where, in addition, it was concluded a special need existed for testing in such circumstances. In *Skinner v. Railway Labor Executives' Ass'n*,[71] concerning blood and urine tests required of railroad employees following major train accidents or incidents and breath and urine samples authorized to be taken from railroad employees who violate certain safety rules, the Court stressed the need "to prevent or deter that hazardous conduct" by "those engaged in safety-sensitive tasks" and also the "limited discretion exercised" by the testing employers. In *National Treasury Employees Union v. Von Raab*,[72] concerning urinalysis tests required of Customs Service employees upon their transfer or promotion to positions having a direct involvement in drug interdiction or requiring the carrying of firearms, the Court emphasized the "Government's compelling interests in preventing the promotion of drug users to positions where they might endanger the integrity of our Nation's borders or the life of the citizenry."[73]

---

69. Though finding the record in the instant case inconclusive on the point, the four-Justice plurality opinion asserted that "some government offices may be so open to fellow employees or the public that no expectation of privacy is reasonable." That conclusion was rejected by a majority of the Court—the four dissenters, and also Scalia, J., concurring, who would accept as a governing general rule that "the offices of government employees * * * are covered by Fourth Amendment protections." Even the plurality opinion accepted the conclusion that the doctor had a justified expectation of privacy as to the interior of the desk and filing cabinets in his office, as he "did not share his desk or filing cabinets with any other employees," he kept personal effects therein, and the hospital had no regulation or policy discouraging such practice.

70. The four dissenters objected that the warrant and probable cause requirements had been abandoned in favor of a more lenient balancing approach by assertion of a "special need" that was never demonstrated. "There was

no special practical need that might have justified dispensing with the warrant and probable-cause requirements. Without sacrificing their ultimate goal of maintaining an effective institution devoted to training and healing, to which the disciplining of Hospital employees contributed, petitioners could have taken any evidence of Dr. Ortega's alleged improprieties to a magistrate in order to obtain a warrant."

71. 489 U.S. 602, 109 S.Ct. 1402, 103 L.Ed.2d 639 (1989).

72. 489 U.S. 656, 109 S.Ct. 1384, 103 L.Ed.2d 685 (1989).

73. Two Justices dissented in both cases, reiterating their opposition to any "special needs" exception to the probable cause requirement, protesting widening of that exception to include search of the person without even reasonable suspicion, and questioning the majority's weighing of the factors in the balancing-of-interests process. Two other Justices dissented in *Von Raab*, contend-

The two drug testing cases just mentioned, as well as the testing-of-students cases (*Acton; Earls*), must be distinguished from *Ferguson v. City of Charleston*,[74] where a task force made up of representatives of the Charleston public hospital, police and other public officials developed a policy for identifying and testing pregnant patients suspected of drug use and then turning the results over to law enforcement agents without the knowledge or consent of the patients. This policy, which also contained procedures for arresting patients and for prosecuting them for drug offenses and/or child neglect, was challenged by a group of obstetrical patients at that hospital who had been arrested after testing positive for cocaine. The Court answered in the negative the question of "whether the interest in using the threat of criminal sanctions to deter pregnant women from using cocaine can justify a departure from the general rule that an official nonconsensual search is unconstitutional if not authorized by a valid warrant." The instant case, the majority reasoned, was different from the Court's prior drug testing cases in two material respects: (1) in the previous cases "there was no misunderstanding about the purpose of the test or the potential use of the test results, and there were protections against the dissemination of the results to third parties"; and (2)

the "critical difference" between the earlier cases and the instant one "lies in the nature of the 'special need' asserted as justification for the warrantless searches," for in all the earlier cases the "special need" advanced was "one divorced from the State's general interest in law enforcement," while here "the central and indispensable feature of the policy from its inception was the use of law enforcement to coerce the patients into substance abuse treatment." As for the respondents' argument that their ultimate purpose of protecting both the mother and child was "a beneficent one," the majority responded that the policy itself "plainly reveals" that the purpose actually served "is ultimately indistinguishable from the general interest in crime control," for "an initial and continuing focus of the policy was on the arrest and prosecution of drug-abusing mothers," and local "prosecutors and police were extensively involved in the day-to-day administration of the policy."[75]

§ 3.10   Consent Searches

(a) **Nature of Consent.** Consent searches are sometimes relied upon by police when probable cause is present but they feel either that they do not have time to get a warrant or that they would simply like to avoid that time-

---

ing that while the result in *Skinner* was supported by "the demonstrated frequency of drug and alcohol use by the targeted class of employees, and the demonstrated connection between such use and grave harm," in *Von Raab* the government had not cited a single instance "in which the cause of bribe-taking, or of poor aim, or of unsympathetic law enforcement, or of compromise of classified information, was drug use."

Compare Chandler v. Miller, 520 U.S. 305, 117 S.Ct. 1295, 137 L.Ed.2d 513 (1997), invalidating a Georgia statute requiring each candidate for public office to submit to drug testing, where the Court stated: "Georgia asserts no evidence of a drug problem among the State's elected officials, those officials typically do not perform high-risk, safety-sensitive tasks, and the required certification immediately aids no interdiction effort. The need revealed, in short, is symbolic, not 'special,' as that term draws meaning from our case law." As for the state's reliance on *Von Raab*, where there was likewise no showing of a drug problem, the Court noted that there the affected employees and their work product were not amenable to "day-to-day scrutiny," and then concluded: "Candidates for public office, in contrast, are subject to relentless scrutiny—by their peers, the public, and the press." Their day-to-day conduct attracts attention notable beyond the norm in ordinary work environments.

74. 532 U.S. 67, 121 S.Ct. 1281, 149 L.Ed.2d 205 (2001).

75. The Court added that it made no difference that the "threat of law enforcement" may have been "a means to an end," for if that did make a difference then "virtually any nonconsensual suspicionless search could be immunized under the special needs doctrine by defining the search solely in terms of its ultimate, rather than immediate purpose." A concurring Justice questioned the latter point and would have rested the decision solely on the fact that none of the Court's "special needs precedents has sanctioned the routine inclusion of law enforcement, both in the design of the policy and in using arrests, either threatened or real, to implement the system designed for the special needs objectives."

The three dissenters objected that it was not so that "the addition of a law-enforcement related purpose to a legitimate medical purpose destroys applicability of the 'special-needs' doctrine," "since the special-needs doctrine was developed, and is ordinarily employed, precisely to enable searched by law enforcement officials who, of course, ordinarily have a law enforcement objective," as illustrated by Griffin v. Wisconsin, text at note 60 supra.

consuming process, but more often an effort is made to obtain consent where probable cause is lacking and no warrant could be obtained. The practice of making searches based on consent is by no means a disfavored one.[1] The issue of whether a consent search is simply a matter of the consenting party having acted voluntarily or whether instead the waiver of a constitutional right is involved, so as to bring into play the need to show "an intentional relinquishment or abandonment of a known right," was finally resolved in *Schneckloth v. Bustamonte*.[2] The Court there upheld a consent to search a car given during a street encounter in which no Fourth Amendment warnings were given. Noting that the voluntariness standard was the traditional means for balancing the interests in the police interrogation area, the Court observed that in the consent search area there are also "two competing concerns [which] must be accommodated * * *—the legitimate need for such searches and the equally important requirement of assuring the absence of coercion." A "fair accommodation" of those competing interests, the majority concluded in *Schneckloth*, lies in "the traditional definition of 'voluntariness,' " as a need to show the consenting party was aware of his rights would "create serious doubt whether consent searches could continue to be conducted" in light of the prosecution's difficulty in proving such awareness.

As for the suggestion that this would not be so if the police advised a person of his rights before eliciting his consent, the Court responded:

[I]t would be thoroughly impractical to impose on the normal consent search the detailed requirements of an effective warning. Consent searches are part of the standard investigatory techniques of law enforcement agencies. They normally occur on the highway, or in a person's home or office, and under informal and unstructured conditions.

The circumstances that prompt the initial request to search may develop quickly or be a logical extension of investigative police questioning. The police may seek to investigate further suspicious circumstances or to follow up leads developed in questioning persons at the scene of a crime. These situations are a far cry from the structured atmosphere of a trial where, assisted by counsel if he chooses, a defendant is informed of his trial rights. * * * And, while surely a closer question, these situations are still immeasurably, far removed from "custodial interrogation" where, in *Miranda v. Arizona*, we found that the Constitution required certain now familiar warnings as a prerequisite to police interrogation.

Thus, while a "strict standard of waiver" applies "to those rights guaranteed to a criminal defendant to insure * * * a fair criminal trial," it need not extend to the "protections of the Fourth Amendment," which "are of a wholly different order, and have nothing whatever to do with promoting the fair ascertainment of truth at a criminal trial."

The most common criticisms of *Schneckloth* are: (1) the Court at the very outset asserted that the "precise question in this case * * * is what must the state prove to demonstrate that a consent was 'voluntarily' given," thus overlooking the critical fact that *coercion* (did the police use undue pressure) and *unknowing surrender* (did defendant know he had a right not to surrender his privacy) are two quite different matters; (2) the Court assumed without question that "guidance" on the issue at hand could be gleaned from the decisions on the voluntariness of confessions, when in fact the nature of the competing interests in the two areas is quite different, as police can obtain information verbally from a suspect only if he chooses to give it, while much physical evidence can be acquired without the cooperation of the suspect; and (3) the Court never

---

§ 3.10

1. As the Court put it in United States v. Drayton, 536 U.S. 194, 122 S.Ct. 2105, 153 L.Ed.2d 242 (2002): "In a society based on law, the concept of agreement and consent should be given a weight and dignity of its own. Police officers act in full accord with the law when they ask citizens for consent. It reinforces the rule of law for

the citizen to advise the police of his or her wishes and for the police to act in reliance on that understanding. When this exchange takes place, it dispels inferences of coercion."

2. 412 U.S. 218, 93 S.Ct. 2041, 36 L.Ed.2d 854 (1973).

satisfactorily explained why the intentional-relinquishment-of-a-known-right waiver concept should apply to trial rights but not to the right to privacy, and overlooked its prior teaching that "no system of criminal justice can, or should, survive if it comes to depend for its continued effectiveness on the citizens' abdication through unawareness of their constitutional rights."[3]

A somewhat different issue concerning the meaning of consent in this context is illustrated by *United States v. Elrod*,[4] where Wright consented to a search of a room occupied by him and Elrod, revealing the fruits of a bank robbery, but that evidence was suppressed because of later-acquired information showing "that Wright was mentally incompetent at the time that he signed the consent form." As for the government's claim the matter should not be controlled by that evidence, the court said of that objection:

> Presumably it is a lamentation that to the burdens which now almost make a constitution seer out of a policeman on the beat will be added the esoteric function of an amateur psychiatrist. No matter how genuine the belief of the officers is that the consenter is apparently of sound mind and deliberately acting, the search depending on his consent fails if it is judicially determined that he lacked mental capacity. It is not that the actions of the officers were imprudent or unfounded. It is that the key to validity—consent—is lacking for want of mental capacity, no matter how much concealed.

Some courts, however, have articulated the consent search standard in a way that would produce a different result on the *Elrod* facts; the issue is said to be whether the officers, as reasonable men, could conclude that defendant's consent was given.

When *Schneckloth* was decided, the Court's "voluntariness" test from the confession cases would have supported the *Elrod* result, for it was then accepted that a confession could be "coerced" by innocent conduct of the police when a condition of the suspect was unknown to them.[5] But the rule is now otherwise as to confessions,[6] and presumably this means that the *Schneckloth* rule will not produce the result reached in *Elrod*. Other aspects of *Schneckloth* also lend support to that conclusion. The Court emphasized both the value of searches made by consent and the fact that the Fourth Amendment is unique because it does not protect against police action undertaken upon "reasonably though mistakenly believed" facts. Both of these considerations underlie the appealing notion that because the Fourth Amendment is only concerned with discouraging unreasonable activity on the part of law enforcement officers, it is not violated when a search is conducted upon a reasonable (albeit mistaken) belief that voluntary consent has been granted.

(b) Factors Bearing on Validity of Consent. The Court held in *Schneckloth* that "the question whether a consent to a search was in fact 'voluntary' or was the product of duress or coercion, express or implied, is a question of fact to be determined from the totality of the circumstances." One factor likely to produce a finding of no consent under this test is a claim by the police that they can make the search in any event. Thus, if the police claim that they have a search warrant and the person then submits to a search because of that claim, but it later turns out that the police actually had no warrant[7] or the prosecution later declines to rely upon the warrant as the basis for the search,[8] the evidence must be suppressed because it was obtained by a submission to a claim of lawful authority. The same is true when the police have incorrectly asserted that they have a right to make a warrantless search under the then existing circumstances or have intimated as much by

---

3. Escobedo v. Illinois, 378 U.S. 478, 84 S.Ct. 1758, 12 L.Ed.2d 977 (1964).

4. 441 F.2d 353 (5th Cir.1971).

5. Blackburn v. Alabama, 361 U.S. 199, 80 S.Ct. 274, 4 L.Ed.2d 242 (1960).

6. See Colorado v. Connelly, 479 U.S. 157, 107 S.Ct. 515, 93 L.Ed.2d 473 (1986), discussed in § 6.2(b), (c).

7. Go–Bart Importing Co. v. United States, 282 U.S. 344, 51 S.Ct. 153, 75 L.Ed. 374 (1931).

8. Bumper v. North Carolina, 391 U.S. 543, 88 S.Ct. 1788, 20 L.Ed.2d 797 (1968).

merely declaring that they have come to search or are going to search. A threat by the police to *obtain* a search warrant is not materially different from a claim that a warrant has already issued, and thus such a threat is likely to invalidate a subsequent consent if there were not then grounds upon which a warrant could issue. But if there were grounds for issuance of a search warrant, then the advice of a law enforcement agent that, absent a consent to search, a warrant can be obtained does not constitute coercion, as in such a case the person has been correctly advised of his legal situation. In the eyes of some courts, a police threat to *seek* a search warrant is not coercive because the officer was merely telling the defendant what he had a legal right to do. But it is to be doubted whether the ordinary person, when confronted with a request by an officer to consent to a search, would discriminate between the statement that otherwise the officer would *get* a search warrant, as compared with a statement that otherwise he would *apply for* a warrant. Absent such claims, consideration must be given to whether the circumstances were coercive, which necessitates attention to whether the person was confronted with many officers or a display of weapons, whether he was in custody and if so whether the circumstances of the custody were coercive, and whether the alleged consent was obtained in the course of stationhouse interrogation. Of course, if the prior police restraint was itself illegal, the consent may also be challenged as the fruit of the poisonous tree.[9]

In *Schneckloth*, the majority, in responding to the argument that the failure to require the prosecution to establish knowledge as prerequisite to a valid consent would relegate the Fourth Amendment to the special province of "the sophisticated, the knowledgeable, and the privileged," observed that the "traditional definition of voluntariness we accept today has always taken into account evidence of minimal schooling [and] low intelligence." Consistent with this position, courts deter-

mining the voluntariness of a consent must assess whether the individual was immature and impressionable or experienced and well-educated, and whether that person was in an excited emotional state, mentally incompetent, or under the influence of drugs or alcohol at the time the purported consent was given. (But, by virtue of the significant change in the "voluntariness" test that has occurred in the law on confessions as a result of *Colorado v. Connelly*,[10] involuntariness cannot be grounded solely in the defendant's mental condition, for "the crucial element of police overreaching"—that is, "coercive" police conduct, such as exploiting defendant's deficient mental condition—must be present.) A consent is suspect if given by one who earlier refused to consent, unless some reason appears to explain the change in position. By like reasoning, if the consent is preceded by a valid confession or by cooperation in the investigation generally, this enhances the chances that the consent was voluntary, and the same may be said of cooperation in the search itself. What then if the consent was by a person suspected of the crime under investigation but who denied his guilt? One view, taken in *Higgins v. United States*,[11] is that if such a denial preceded an alleged consent which led to the discovery of incriminating evidence, then the consent must be held invalid, as "no sane man who denies his guilt would actually be willing that policemen search his room for contraband which is certain to be discovered." But *Higgins* has not received general acceptance. Sometimes it is simply distinguished away, which is certainly correct in cases where it appears the defendant thought the incriminating evidence had been removed or was cleverly concealed and thus not likely to be discovered, or where the objects found were not obviously incriminating in character. On other occasions the *Higgins* test has been rejected as an unworkable test based upon hindsight that, in any event, is grounded in the erroneous assumption that the pressure exerted on a criminal by the realization that the "jig is up"

9. See § 9.4(b).

10. 479 U.S. 157, 107 S.Ct. 515, 93 L.Ed.2d 473 (1986), discussed in § 6.2(b),(c).

11. 209 F.2d 819 (D.C.Cir.1954).

amounts to coercion. The Supreme Court has summarily rejected a *Higgins*-type argument by asserting the question is what a reasonable innocent person would have done.[12]

The Supreme Court in *Schneckloth,* as a consequence of adopting the voluntariness test for consent searches, concluded that "while the subject's knowledge of a right to refuse is a factor to be taken into account, the prosecution is not required to demonstrate such knowledge as a prerequisite to establishing a voluntary consent." That is, consent may be established without a showing that the police warned the consenting party of his Fourth Amendment rights or that he was otherwise aware of those rights. Indeed, as the Court emphasized in a later case, it is *not* the case that "a presumption of invalidity attaches if a citizen consented without explicit notification that he or she was free to refuse to cooperate."[13] (Relying on *Schneckloth,* the Court later held that if a person has been lawfully seized, for example, because of commission of a traffic violation, and following the point at which the detainee would be free to go he consents to a search, that consent is not made involuntary by virtue of the officer's failure to specifically advise the detainee that he was free to go.[14]) Though the Court in *Schneckloth* emphasized that the decision was "a narrow one," extending only to the situation in which "the subject of the search is not in custody," a few years later the Court extended the *Schneckloth* rule to a case in which the consent was obtained from a person in police custody. In that case, *United States v. Watson,*[15] it was stressed that the "consent was given while on a public street, not in the confines of the police station," but lower courts have in the main utilized the "totality of the circumstances" approach without regard to the nature of the custody. Such an extension of *Schneckloth,* it may be argued, ignores the teaching of *Miranda v. Arizona*[16]

that there is "compulsion inherent in custodial surroundings" and overlooks the fact that the concern in *Schneckloth* about warnings being "impractical" under the "informal and unstructured conditions" of a roadside search does not extend to situations in which the person has been taken into custody. In any event, proof by the prosecution that the consenting party was warned of his rights or that he was aware of his rights is often a significant factor leading to a finding of voluntary consent, and sometimes will be essential if prior coercion is to be overcome.

Some courts have held that a consent to search given during custodial interrogation must be preceded by *Miranda* warnings because the request to search is a request that defendant be a witness against himself he is privileged to refuse under the Fifth Amendment. But the prevailing and better view is to the contrary, for a consent to search, as such, is neither testimonial nor communicative in the Fifth Amendment sense. Although the giving of *Miranda* warnings may contribute to a finding of voluntariness, these warnings are not equivalent to Fourth Amendment warnings in terms of overcoming prior coercion, for a defendant might well not understand that the "silence" referred to covers not allowing a search. There may be circumstances in which a consent to search will be invalidated because made without counsel or waiver of the right to counsel. The Supreme Court has held that "a person's Sixth and Fourteenth Amendment right to counsel attaches only at or after the time that adversary judicial proceedings have been initiated against him,"[17] and then only as to a "critical stage," which means when "the accused required aid in coping with legal problems or assistance in meeting his adversary."[18] A post-charge solicitation of the defendant to consent to a search would appear to be such a situation. And in any event, a pre-consent

12. Florida v. Bostick, 501 U.S. 429, 111 S.Ct. 2382, 115 L.Ed.2d 389 (1991).

13. United States v. Drayton, 536 U.S. 194, 122 S.Ct. 2105, 153 L.Ed.2d 242 (2002).

14. Ohio v. Robinette, 519 U.S. 33, 117 S.Ct. 417, 136 L.Ed.2d 347 (1996).

15. 423 U.S. 411, 96 S.Ct. 820, 46 L.Ed.2d 598 (1976).

16. 384 U.S. 436, 86 S.Ct. 1602, 16 L.Ed.2d 694 (1966).

17. Kirby v. Illinois, 406 U.S. 682, 92 S.Ct. 1877, 32 L.Ed.2d 411 (1972).

18. United States v. Ash, 413 U.S. 300, 93 S.Ct. 2568, 37 L.Ed.2d 619 (1973).

refusal of a person's request to consult counsel would weigh heavily against finding that consent to be voluntary.

(c) Consent by Deception. A rather special type of consent case, involving considerations different from those discussed above, is that in which the police have obtained consent to intrude into a certain private area by resort to deceit. One situation, which the Supreme Court has confronted with some frequency, is that in which the person conceals the fact that he is a policeman or that he has already agreed to act on behalf of the police. In *On Lee v. United States*,[19] where an informant wired for sound entered defendant's laundry and engaged him in incriminating conversations, the Court rather summarily concluded that "Chin Poy entered a place of business with the consent, if not by the implied invitation, of the petitioner," and that "the claim that Chin Poy's entrance was a trespass because consent to his entry was obtained by fraud must be rejected." Similarly, in *Hoffa v. United States*,[20] where an old friend of the defendant gave incriminating testimony based upon his visits to defendant's hotel room as an agent of the government, the Court characterized the situation as one of "misplaced confidence" and concluded that it was *not* true that "the Fourth Amendment protects a wrongdoer's misplaced belief that a person to whom he voluntarily confides his wrongdoing will not reveal it." *Lewis v. United States*,[21] decided the same day, involved a situation in which a federal drug agent gained access to defendant's home by misrepresenting his identity and expressing a willingness to purchase narcotics. Stressing that "the petitioner invited the undercover agent to his home for the specific purpose of executing a felonious sale of narcotics," the Court concluded that

> when, as here, the home is converted into a commercial center to which outsiders are invited for purposes of transacting unlawful business, that business is entitled to no greater sanctity than if it were carried on in a store, a garage, a car, or on the street. A

government agent, in the same manner as a private person, may accept an invitation to do business and may enter upon the premises for the very purposes contemplated by the occupant.

These decisions, then, appear to support the following proposition: when an individual gives consent to another to intrude into an area or activity otherwise protected by the Fourth Amendment, aware that he will thereby reveal to this other person either criminal conduct or evidence of such conduct, the consent is not vitiated merely because it would not have been given but for the nondisclosure or affirmative misrepresentation that made the consenting party unaware of the other person's identity as a police officer or police agent.

Though some consider even *Lewis* as objectionable on the ground that deliberate deception about an obviously material fact should be regarded as inconsistent with voluntariness, a more appropriate concern is that of keeping the above-stated principle within reasonable bounds. One attractive proposal is that permissible deception by a stranger *must* include a stated intention on his part to join the consenting party in criminal activity, for in that way innocent persons will be spared from intrusions upon their privacy by deception. But lower courts in the main have not recognized such a limitation, and have instead relied upon the broader proposition that the Fourth Amendment affords no protection to the person who voluntarily reveals incriminating evidence to another in the mistaken belief that the latter will not disclose it. Even that formulation should often bar some of the more extreme forms of deception, such as police entry of a private home in the guise of an employee of the gas company.

A somewhat different kind of case is that in which the consenting party knows he is dealing with a law enforcement officer or agent, but there is some deception as to the latter's objective or purpose. Certainly it is not objectionable that the agent has manifested a will-

---

19.   343 U.S. 747, 72 S.Ct. 967, 96 L.Ed. 1270 (1952).

20.   385 U.S. 293, 87 S.Ct. 408, 17 L.Ed.2d 374 (1966).

21.   385 U.S. 206, 87 S.Ct. 424, 17 L.Ed.2d 312 (1966).

ingness to be bribed.[22] But what of a misrepresentation as to the reason a consent to search was being sought, as in *Alexander v. United States*,[23] where officers seeking stolen marked money obtained consent to search by claiming they were looking for stolen jewelry? Though the court there concluded the "fraudulent warning" deprived the consent of its validity, it is by no means clear that this is so. The fact remains that the police did not "see * * * anything that was not contemplated," an important factor in *Lewis;* that such deception has been tolerated in the voluntariness-of-confession cases; and that this kind of deception does not pose a risk to innocent persons because it will likely produce a consent that would otherwise have been withheld only from a person guilty of the undisclosed crime. By comparison, when the police misrepresentation of purpose is so extreme that it deprives the individual of the ability to make a fair assessment of the need to surrender his privacy, as in *People v. Jefferson*,[24] where police gained entry to defendant's apartment on the false claim they were investigating a gas leak, the consent should not be considered valid.

(d) Third Party Consent: General Considerations. Although in *Schneckloth* it was noted that under some circumstances a person's privacy may be lawfully invaded by virtue of consent obtained by police from a third party, the Court has experienced some difficulty in identifying just what it takes to give a certain third party this power. In *Stoner v. California*,[25] holding a hotel clerk could not consent to search of a guest's room, the Court reasoned that the guest could surrender his rights only "directly or through an agent" and found no evidence that the "clerk had been authorized by the petitioner" to permit the police to enter his room. In *Bumper v. North Carolina*,[26] holding the consent by defendant's grandmother had been coerced, the Court left little doubt that but for the coercion the evidence would have been admitted because she

"owned both the house and the rifle," that is, the place searched and the thing seized. Then, in *Frazier v. Cupp*,[27] holding defendant's cousin could consent to a search of a duffel bag that he held and in which both he and his cousin kept some of their personal effects, the Court appeared to abandon the agency and property theories in favor of an "assumption of risk" formulation: "Petitioner, in allowing [his cousin] Rawls to use the bag and in leaving it in his house, must be taken to have assumed the risk that Rawls would allow someone else to look inside."

Then came *United States v. Matlock*,[28] where, following defendant's arrest in the yard of the house in which he lived, a Mrs. Graff consented to search of the bedroom she shared with defendant. The Court deemed it clear that the prosecution "may show that permission to search was obtained from a third party who possessed common authority over or other sufficient relationship to the premises or effects sought to be inspected." The Court then dropped this explanatory footnote:

> Common authority is, of course, not to be implied from the mere property interest a third party has in the property. The authority which justifies the third-party consent does not rest upon the law of property, with its attendant historical and legal refinements, * * * but rests rather on mutual use of the property by persons generally having joint access or control for most purposes, so that it is reasonable to recognize that any of the co-inhabitants has the right to permit the inspection in his own right and that the others have assumed the risk that one of their number might permit the common area to be searched.

The Court thus identified two bases for its "common authority" rule: (i) that the consenting party could permit the search "in his own right"; and (ii) that the defendant had "assumed the risk" a co-occupant might permit a search. It is important to keep both of them in

---

22. Lopez v. United States, 373 U.S. 427, 83 S.Ct. 1381, 10 L.Ed.2d 462 (1963).

23. 390 F.2d 101 (5th Cir.1968).

24. 43 A.D.2d 112, 350 N.Y.S.2d 3 (1973).

25. 376 U.S. 483, 84 S.Ct. 889, 11 L.Ed.2d 856 (1964).

26. 391 U.S. 543, 88 S.Ct. 1788, 20 L.Ed.2d 797 (1968).

27. 394 U.S. 731, 89 S.Ct. 1420, 22 L.Ed.2d 684 (1969).

28. 415 U.S. 164, 94 S.Ct. 988, 39 L.Ed.2d 242 (1974).

mind in assessing the issues that commonly arise about the circumstances which will validate or invalidate a search by third party consent:

(1) Does the validity of third party consent depend upon the existence of amicable relations between that party and the defendant? In *Kelley v. State*,[29] where defendant's wife summoned police to their home to have him arrested on a charge of beating her and then showed them where he kept his supply of illegal liquor, the court answered in the affirmative, suppressing the evidence because "her actions were hostile to her husband and obviously to his interests." But the prevailing and better view is to the contrary, for the antagonism does not bear upon the two considerations stressed in *Matlock*. By remaining in the marital household the wife has maintained her "equal authority" over those premises, and the defendant's expectations of privacy are, if anything, diminished as a consequence of his assault upon another occupant of those premises.

(2) Can a third party give effective consent after being instructed by defendant not to do so? In *People v. Fry*,[30] police obtained the consent of defendant's wife to search the family home, but the evidence obtained thereby was suppressed because the police "knew her husband had instructed her not to consent and, under these circumstances, were not entitled to rely upon her consent as justification for their conduct." If the *Stoner* agency theory were the sole basis upon which a third party consent could be upheld, there would be little reason to question the *Fry* result. But it cannot be squared with the two *Matlock* bases. In light of the third party's ability to permit the search "in his own right," it may be said that defendant's instructions cannot invalidate consent that did not depend on his authority in the first place. As for the "assumption of risk" aspect, certainly there is a risk, stronger in some cases than in others, that the other occupant will not comply with such a request.

(3) Is a third party's consent invalidated by the defendant's prior or contemporaneous refusal to consent to such a search? Yes, it has sometimes been held, because constitutional rights may not be defeated by the expedient of soliciting several persons successively until the sought-after consent is obtained. But the cases holding to the contrary may be more readily squared with *Matlock*, for here again the other occupant retains his "own right" to allow a search and the defendant has participated in a living situation in which there inheres the risk that in defendant's absence another occupant might admit the police. What then if defendant was *present* and objecting at the time? *Matlock* cautiously puts this situation to one side, for the Court there said that "the consent of one who possesses common authority over premises or effects is valid as against the *absent*, nonconsenting person with whom that authority is shared."[31] One view is that even here *Matlock* permits the third party to act in his own or the public interest, while the contrary position is that the consent of both is required when both are present because persons with equal rights in a place would ordinarily accommodate each other by not admitting persons over another's objection while he was present. So the argument would proceed, using *Matlock* terminology, a person's authority to consent in his "own right" does not go so far as to outweigh an equal privacy claim by another occupant who is actually present asserting his right, and the defendant by his joint occupancy or use has only "assumed the risk" as to what will happen when he is not present to protect his own interests. Even if this is so, there will be cases in which some other circumstance justifies giving one of these "equal" rights greater recognition than the other, and of course there are also cases in which the rights of the two occupants are not equal and the matter can thus be resolved by giving recognition to the superior interest.

(4) Is a third party's consent ineffective when the police bypassed an opportunity to seek consent from the defendant? The cases answer no, and they appear to be supported by

---

29. 184 Tenn. 143, 197 S.W.2d 545 (1946).

30. 271 Cal.App.2d 350, 76 Cal.Rptr. 718 (1969).

31. Emphasis added.

both the facts and the rationale of *Matlock*. This is generally a sound result, perhaps even when the bypassed opportunity was at the time of the defendant's arrest while present at the place later searched. But when the positions of the two persons are not equal, so that it may be said the police passed up an obvious opportunity to seek consent from a defendant with a clearly superior interest in the place, this has been held to invalidate the consent obtained from the third party with a lesser interest.

(5) Is a third party's consent affected by the fact that the defendant maintained exclusive control as to certain areas or effects? *Matlock* is rather ambiguous on this point, for the Court said the question was whether Ms. Graff had "common authority" over the premises, which was deemed to rest on "mutual use of the property" by one "having joint access or control for most purposes." Perhaps it is of no significance that the Court failed to allude specifically to the principle, recognized in prior lower court decisions, that persons sharing premises may nonetheless retain areas of exclusive control. But it is well to remember that the Court has taken a firm stand against extreme or strained applications of the exclusive control concept. In *Frazier v. Cupp*,[32] in response to defendant's argument that his cousin (who possessed and consented to search of defendant's duffel bag) only had permission to use one compartment in the bag, the Court declined to "engage in such metaphysical subtleties in judging the efficacy of Rawls' consent" and concluded defendant had assumed the risk by allowing Rawls to use the bag and in leaving it in his house. Thus, while it has sometimes been suggested that under *Matlock* police are obligated to ascertain the possibly unique pattern of living arrangements between defendant and the third party so as to determine the extent of the "common authority," courts generally are not inclined to be that demanding.

(6) May a third party consent be upheld when the police had a reasonable but mistaken belief that the third party had authority over the place searched? In *Stoner v. California*,[33] in response to the argument that the police "had a reasonable basis for the belief that the [hotel] clerk had authority to consent to the search" of a guest's room, the Court properly asserted that "the rights protected by the Fourth Amendment are not to be eroded * * * by unrealistic doctrines of 'apparent authority.' " The police in *Stoner* were fully aware of the relevant facts (i.e., that the person consenting was a clerk and that defendant was currently renting the room in question), and thus the mistake was as to the clerk's *legal* authority, which if it were to prevail would in effect allow the police to expand the law of third party consent by their misperceptions of what the Fourth Amendment allows. But what if the error was as to a *factual* matter and the reasonably assumed fact, if true, would put the consenting party in a position to give a valid consent; that is, what if in *Stoner* the police had acted upon the clerk's consent in the reasonable but mistaken belief that no one was renting the room in question? In such a case, the Supreme Court concluded in *Illinois v. Rodriguez*,[34] the search is lawful, for what the defendant "is assured by the Fourth Amendment itself * * * is not that no government search * * * will occur unless he consents; but that no such search will occur that is 'unreasonable.' " In this and many other Fourth Amendment contexts, a police officer's actions can be reasonable even when grounded in factual assumptions which turn out to be incorrect. But the Court in *Rodriguez* cautioned it was *not* suggesting "that law enforcement officers may always accept a person's invitation to enter premises. Even when the invitation is accompanied by an explicit assertion that the person lives there, the surrounding circumstances could conceivably be such that a reasonable person would doubt its truth and not act upon it without further inquiry," in which case "warrantless entry without further inquiry is unlawful unless authority actually exists."

---

32. 394 U.S. 731, 89 S.Ct. 1420, 22 L.Ed.2d 684 (1969).
33. 376 U.S. 483, 84 S.Ct. 889, 11 L.Ed.2d 856 (1964).

34. 497 U.S. 177, 110 S.Ct. 2793, 111 L.Ed.2d 148 (1990).

(7) May a third party consent be upheld when the defendant had a reasonable but mistaken belief as to the extent of the risk involved? This interesting question is prompted by *Commonwealth v. Latshaw*,[35] where defendant *A* stored containers of marijuana in a barn with the consent of *B*, who *A* was led to believe had exclusive possession and control of that barn, but in fact the barn belonged to and was under the control of *C*, who consented to a police search of the barn. In upholding the consent, the court in *Latshaw* concluded that *C*'s "independent right * * * to authorize the search of her property" could not be affected by *B*'s conduct in misleading *A*. In other words, when the two bases of the *Matlock* "common authority" rule come into conflict, the consenting person's authority to permit the search "in his own right" is to prevail over a showing that the defendant had not "assumed the risk" of consent by the person who gave it. This is a sound result, as (a) it is still important in such circumstances to recognize the owner's "legitimate interest in exculpating himself or herself from possible criminal involvement with the suspected contraband," as the court put it in *Latshaw;* (b) *A* was ignorant as to the true identity of the person in possession, but in a more general sense "assumed the risk" that whoever was in possession might for some reason admit others; and (c) permitting the police to proceed on the situation as it appears to the person who summoned them and consented to the search is to be preferred over a rule that nullifies the search by an after-the-fact assessment of defendant's reasonably mistaken impressions of the situation.

(e) Common Relationships in Third Party Consent. It may generally be said that one spouse may give consent to a search of the family residence that will be effective against the other spouse. At one time there was a tendency to view consent by the wife with greater suspicion on the ground that the husband is the head of the household, but the modern view is that the wife has no less authority than the husband because she normally exercises as much control over the property

in the home as the husband. It is possible in a particular case that the consent will be held ineffective because the area searched was within the "exclusive control" of the defendant, but this is much less likely in husband-wife cases than in other shared occupancy situations. There is somewhat greater reluctance to uphold a wife's consent to search of her husband's car, but it is not inconsistent with *Matlock* to suggest that the wife's consent should suffice if the vehicle is the family car, without regard to whether the wife is a registered co-owner or uses it as a driver instead of only as a passenger.

If a son or daughter, whether or not still a minor, is residing in the home of the parents, generally it is within the authority of the father or mother to consent to a police search of that home that will be effective against the offspring. This is unquestionably so as to areas of common usage, and is also true of the bedroom of the son or daughter when a parent has ready access for purposes of cleaning it or when because of the minority of the offspring the parent is still exercising parental authority. Because in the latter circumstances the parent's rights are superior to the rights of children who live in the house, a parent's consent would prevail even if the child were present and objecting and even if the child had taken special measures in an effort to ensure he had exclusive use of the area searched. When the tables are turned and it is the offspring who has consented and a parent is the defendant, the effectiveness of the consent depends upon: (1) the age of the child, because as children grow older they gradually acquire discretion to admit whom they will on their own authority; and (2) the scope of the consent given, in that a teenager could admit police to look about generally but a child of eight could merely admit police to that part of the house any caller would be allowed to enter.

Turning to property relationships, it may generally be said that a lessor who has granted the lessee exclusive possession over a certain area may not, during the period of the tenancy, give an effective consent to a police search

---

35.   481 Pa. 298, 392 A.2d 1301 (1978).

of that area. This is so whether the arrangement involves the rental of a house, an apartment, a room in a rooming house, hotel or motel, or even a locker. The rule is not otherwise merely because the lessor has by express agreement or by implication reserved the right to enter for some special and limited purpose. The landlord may consent to search of common areas, such as a hallway in an apartment building. It logically follows that the tenant may consent to a search of the area he has leased, but not a portion of the premises the landlord has retained as his own. Where two or more persons occupy a dwelling place jointly, the general rule is that a joint tenant can consent to police entry and search of the entire house or apartment, even though they occupy separate bedrooms. This is certainly true of common areas such as a kitchen or bathroom, but not as to places under the "exclusive control" of another tenant, a matter the police are obligated to make some inquiry about in ambiguous situations. Similarly, while a host can consent to a search of his premises occupied by a guest, this does not inevitably extend to a suitcase or like object in which a person has a high expectation of privacy even when a guest in another's home. Generally, a guest cannot give consent to a search of the premises that will be effective against his host. In bailment cases, the bailee may give effective consent if the nature of the bailment is such, as it was in *Frazier v. Cupp*,[36] where defendant left his duffel bag with his cousin, that defendant has "assumed the risk" the bailee would do so. The bailor does not have authority to consent to an intrusion into the bailee's possessory interest, but in some circumstances may have the power to terminate the bailment for violation of its terms by the bailee and to then allow the search.

In employment relationships, where the question arises whether an employee's consent was effective, courts are inclined to assess the responsibilities of the particular employee, which makes sense from both an agency and an assumption of risk point of view. Thus, a caretaker left in charge of a farm for a few weeks has greater authority to consent to a search there than a farm hand working at a particular location on the farm while his employer is occupied elsewhere on the property. Courts are understandably influenced by the "status" of the employee (e.g., officer manager vs. clerk) and the character of the place searched (e.g., warehouse vs. private office). When the consent is by the employer and the objecting defendant is an employee, courts consider (1) the extent to which the particular area searched had been set aside for the personal use of the employee, and (2) the extent to which the search was prompted by a unique or special need of the employer to maintain close scrutiny of employees. Finally, there are the third party consent cases involving what might be called the educational relationship, in which a student objects to a search allowed by a school official. Generally, it may be said that the courts have upheld such searches when made of lockers in a high school, but not when made of a college dorm room. These cases reflect both that such consent is more likely to be upheld in order to maintain discipline over young students and that it is less likely to be upheld when the place in question is a residential area having only a tangential relationship to the educational enterprise.

(f) Scope of Consent. Even if it is determined that the consent of the defendant or another authorized person was "voluntary" within the meaning of *Schneckloth,* it does not inevitably follow that evidence found in the ensuing search will be admissible. This is because it is also necessary to take account of any express or implied limitations on the consent that mark the permissible scope of the search in terms of its time, duration, area or intensity. The matter of scope, the Supreme Court has decided, is to be determined by neither the subjective intentions of the consenting party or the subjective interpretation of the searching officer; rather, the standard is "that of 'objective' reasonableness—what would the typical reasonable person have understood by the exchange between the officer

---

36.   394 U.S. 731, 89 S.Ct. 1420, 22 L.Ed.2d 684 (1969).

and the suspect?"[37] Police customarily ask for consent not in the abstract but in terms of a particular place, such as a certain residence or vehicle, and if the person responds with a consent that is general and unqualified, then ordinarily the police may conduct a general search of that place. This means that when the object the police indicated they are looking for could be concealed therein,[38] they may even search unlocked containers found in that place, but not that they may break into locked containers or otherwise do physical damage in carrying out the search.[39] The scope of the search must be more narrowly confined when expressly stated to cover only a portion of a certain place, when the thing the police say they are looking for quite obviously necessitates looking only in a particular place, or when the person giving the consent makes it apparent that he does not expect that the police can gain access to a certain part of the designated place. The most common limitation on the scope of a search by consent is that upon the intensity of the police activity permitted. This limitation is not ordinarily expressly stated by the consenting party, but arises from the fact that the police have indicated that the consent is being sought for a particular purpose. Illustrative is *United States v. Dichiarinte*,[40] where defendant consented to a search of his home in response to a police inquiry whether he had any narcotics, but the police opened and read incriminating

documents. The court quite correctly concluded that this conduct extended beyond that authorized by the defendant, and asserted: "Government agents may not obtain consent to search on the representation that they intend to look only for certain specified items and subsequently use that consent as a license to conduct a general exploratory search." But if the police search only where the items they purport to be looking for could be concealed, under the "plain view" doctrine they may seize other items if they have probable cause they are the fruits, instrumentalities or evidence of some crime.

As a general rule, it would seem that a consent to search may be said to have been given on the understanding that the search will be conducted forthwith and that only a single search will be made. Though there is some authority that consent once given may not be withdrawn, the better view is that though a consent to search is not terminated merely by a worsening of the consenting party's position, a consent may be withdrawn or limited at any time prior to the completion of the search. A revocation of consent does not operate retroactively to render unreasonable a search conducted prior to the time of revocation, any more than the giving of consent may be said to retroactively validate a search conducted prior to the time the consent was given.

37. Florida v. Jimeno, 500 U.S. 248, 111 S.Ct. 1801, 114 L.Ed.2d 297 (1991).

38. In Florida v. Jimeno, 500 U.S. 248, 111 S.Ct. 1801, 114 L.Ed.2d 297 (1991), the Court noted that "the scope of a search is generally defined by its expressed object," meaning that when the officer told defendant "that he would be looking for narcotics in the car," it was "objectively reasonable for the police to conclude that the general consent to search respondent's car included consent to search containers within that car which might bear drugs."

39. "It is very likely unreasonable to think that a suspect, by consenting to the search of his trunk, has agreed to the breaking open of a locked briefcase within the trunk, but it is otherwise with respect to a closed paper bag." Florida v. Jimeno, 500 U.S. 248, 111 S.Ct. 1801, 114 L.Ed.2d 297 (1991).

40. 445 F.2d 126 (7th Cir.1971).

Chapter 4

WIRETAPPING AND ELECTRONIC SURVEILLANCE

Table of Sections

§ 4.1 Historical Background

(a) The *Olmstead* Case. The first wiretapping case to reach the United States Supreme Court was *Olmstead v. United States*,[1] involving the interception by federal agents of messages passing over telephone wires. In a 5–4 decision, the Court held that such activity did not amount to a Fourth Amendment search or seizure because (1) the agents obtained access to the telephone wires without any "entry of the houses or offices of the defendants," meaning that no "place" had been searched within the meaning of the Amendment; and (2) the agents obtained the content of the conversations that passed over the wires but did not acquire any physical objects, and thus no "things" had been seized within the meaning of the Amendment. It made no difference that the conduct was in violation of a state law making it a misdemeanor to "intercept" telegraphic or telephonic messages, as that statute did not declare evidence so obtained was inadmissible and, in any event, a state statute "can not affect the rules of evidence applicable in courts of the United States."

As discussed later, both reasons given in *Olmstead* for holding the Fourth Amendment inapplicable have since been rejected by the Supreme Court. It is not surprising, therefore, that in recent years the forceful dissents in *Olmstead* have received the greatest attention. In an exhaustive dissenting opinion, Justice Brandeis argued that "every unjustifiable intrusion by the Government upon the privacy of the individual, whatever the means employed, must be deemed a violation of the Fourth Amendment." In addition, he contended that the government, as "the omnipresent teacher," should not be upheld in its admitted violation of a state wiretapping law. Justice Holmes, in a brief separate dissent on the latter ground only, characterized wiretapping in violation of state law as "dirty business" that a judge should not "allow * * * to suc-

ceed." In an oft-quoted passage, Holmes reasoned that it is "a less evil that some criminals should escape than that the Government should play an ignoble part."

(b) Section 605. The majority in *Olmstead* noted that "Congress may of course protect the secrecy of telephone messages by making them, when intercepted, inadmissible in evidence in federal criminal trials." The Federal Communications Act of 1934 was later enacted, and it provided in part in § 605 that "no person not being authorized by the sender shall intercept any communication and divulge or publish the existence, contents, substance, purport, effect, or meaning of such intercepted communication to any person."[2] Though this legislation did not contain an express declaration of an exclusionary rule as apparently contemplated by *Olmstead,* it was interpreted to have this effect. In *Nardone v. United States*,[3] the Supreme Court held that under § 605 a federal officer could not testify in federal court concerning the contents of wiretapped conversations because to "recite the contents of the message in testimony before a court is to divulge the message." This case reached the Court a second time after the defendants were retried on evidence discovered as a result of information acquired by the wiretapping, and this time it was held that this exclusionary rule extended to derivative evidence as well.[4] In other cases also having to do only with the admissibility of the fruits of wiretapping in federal courts, the Court held that the prohibitions of § 605 extended to intrastate communications[5] and to actions of state officers.[6]

The protections of § 605 were not absolute. For one thing, traditional notions of standing were applied to this exclusionary rule, meaning that one who was not a party to the tapped conversation could not object to the use against him of evidence obtained by wiretapping.[7] For another, § 605 did not cover tapping by consent. "Each party to a telephone conversation takes the risk that the other party

§ 4.1

1. 277 U.S. 438, 48 S.Ct. 564, 72 L.Ed. 944 (1928).

2. Former 47 U.S.C.A. § 605.

3. 302 U.S. 379, 58 S.Ct. 275, 82 L.Ed. 314 (1937).

4. Nardone v. United States, 308 U.S. 338, 60 S.Ct. 266, 84 L.Ed. 307 (1939).

5. Weiss v. United States, 308 U.S. 321, 60 S.Ct. 269, 84 L.Ed. 298 (1939).

6. Benanti v. United States, 355 U.S. 96, 78 S.Ct. 155, 2 L.Ed.2d 126 (1957).

7. Goldstein v. United States, 316 U.S. 114, 62 S.Ct. 1000, 86 L.Ed. 1312 (1942).

* * * may allow another to overhear the conversation."[8] Moreover, federal investigative agencies continued to engage in a considerable amount of wiretapping notwithstanding the prohibitions of § 605. Some occurred pursuant to the generally accepted notion that the statute did not entirely prohibit foreign intelligence wiretapping undertaken in the interest of national security. Much more was attributable to the fact that the Department of Justice and the FBI took the position that § 605 did not prohibit wiretapping alone, but only tapping followed by "divulgence," and that it was not "divulgence" when one member of the government communicated to another, but only when he communicated outside the government (e.g., by seeking to introduce the wiretap information in court).

Since it involved the use of state-gathered wiretap evidence in a prosecution in a state court, the case of *Schwartz v. Texas*[9] posed the wiretapping counterpart of *Wolf v. Colorado*.[10] Relying upon *Wolf,* the Court held the evidence admissible. Though it was recognized that "[t]he problem under § 605 is somewhat different [than *Wolf*] because the introduction of the intercepted communication would itself be a violation of the statute," i.e., a prohibited "divulgence," the Court nonetheless concluded that "in the absence of an expression by Congress, this is simply an additional factor for a state to consider in formulating a rule of evidence for use in its own courts." But in *Benanti v. United States*[11] the Court ignored the search and seizure precedents (later overruled in *Elkins v. United States*[12]) and proceeded to exclude state-gathered wiretap evidence proffered in a federal prosecution, reasoning that the statute "contains an express, absolute prohibition against the divulgence of intercepted communications."

This last observation, especially when coupled with the later overruling of *Wolf* by *Mapp*

v. Ohio,[13] made it apparent that *Schwartz* could not survive. But it was not actually overruled until *Lee v. Florida*,[14] decided just two days before the electronic surveillance provisions of the Crime Control Act of 1968[15] were signed into law. The Court in *Lee* emphasized that its ruling was "counseled by experience," especially that "[r]esearch has failed to uncover a single reported prosecution of a law enforcement officer for violation of § 605 since the statute was enacted." Thus the Court concluded that here as in *Mapp* "nothing short of mandatory exclusion of the illegal evidence will compel respect for the federal law 'in the only effectively available way—by removing the incentive to disregard it.' " *Lee* was held to be nonretroactive,[16] and thus it had a limited impact because later wiretapping was covered by Title III of the 1968 Act.

(c) Non-telephonic Electronic Eavesdropping. As time passed it became apparent that the fears expressed by Justice Brandeis in *Olmstead*—that the "progress of science in furnishing the Government with means of espionage is not likely to stop with wire-tapping"—were justified. Highly sophisticated means of electronic eavesdropping were developed and put into use. They were largely uncontrolled by the law. They were not within the prohibitions of § 605, for it applied only when telephone, telegraph or radiotelegraph conversations were overheard. Moreover, the protections of the Fourth Amendment applied only if there was a physical invasion or "trespass" into a constitutionally protected area. No such trespass was deemed to exist in *Olmstead,* where the taps from house lines were made in the streets near the house; in *Goldman v. United States*,[17] where federal officers merely placed a detectaphone against the wall of an adjoining office where they were lawfully

---

8. Rathbun v. United States, 355 U.S. 107, 78 S.Ct. 161, 2 L.Ed.2d 134 (1957).

9. 344 U.S. 199, 73 S.Ct. 232, 97 L.Ed. 231 (1952).

10. 338 U.S. 25, 69 S.Ct. 1359, 93 L.Ed. 1782 (1949).

11. 355 U.S. 96, 78 S.Ct. 155, 2 L.Ed.2d 126 (1957).

12. 364 U.S. 206, 80 S.Ct. 1437, 4 L.Ed.2d 1669 (1960).

13. 367 U.S. 643, 81 S.Ct. 1684, 6 L.Ed.2d 1081 (1961).

14. 392 U.S. 378, 88 S.Ct. 2096, 20 L.Ed.2d 1166 (1968).

15. 18 U.S.C.A. §§ 2510–2520.

16. Fuller v. Alaska, 393 U.S. 80, 89 S.Ct. 61, 21 L.Ed.2d 212 (1968).

17. 316 U.S. 129, 62 S.Ct. 993, 86 L.Ed. 1322 (1942).

present; or in *On Lee v. United States*,[18] where incriminating statements were picked up via a "wired for sound" former acquaintance of petitioner who entered his premises with consent.

That the Constitution furnished some protection against the electronic seizure of conversations was finally established in *Silverman v. United States*.[19] There, a unanimous Court held that listening to incriminating conversations within a house by inserting an electronic device (a so-called "spike mike") into a party wall and making contact with a heating duct serving the house occupied by petitioners, "thus converting their entire heating system into a conductor of sound," amounted to an illegal search and seizure. The Court declared that in such circumstances "we need not pause to consider whether or not there was a technical trespass under the local property law relating to party walls," thus suggesting that *Silverman* established not only that conversations can be seized within the meaning of the Fourth Amendment but also that a Fourth Amendment search for them might occur without a trespass. This seemed even more certain when a few years later the Court, in *Clinton v. Virginia*,[20] summarily rejected the state court's holding that *Silverman* did not apply where the spike mike "was not driven into the wall but was 'stuck in' it."[21]

Any lingering doubts were dispelled by *Katz v. United States*.[22] The issue in *Katz* was whether recordings of defendant's end of telephone conversations, obtained by attaching an electronic listening and recording device to the outside of a public telephone booth, had been obtained in violation of the Fourth Amendment. Expressly rejecting the "trespass" doctrine of *Olmstead* and *Goldman,* the court held that the government action constituted a

search and seizure within the meaning of the Fourth Amendment. This was because that conduct "violated the privacy upon which [the defendant] justifiably relied while using the telephone booth." *Katz* thus made it clear that, with the possible exception of the case in which a conversation is overheard or recorded with the consent of a party to the conversation, wiretapping and electronic eavesdropping are subject to the limitations of the Fourth Amendment.

§ 4.2 Title III and the Fourth Amendment

(a) **Summary of Title III.** About a year after the Supreme Court in *Berger v. New York*[1] held that a certain state eavesdropping statute violated the Fourth Amendment, the Congress adopted comprehensive legislation on the subject of wiretapping and electronic surveillance. This legislation is commonly referred to simply as Title III (as it will be hereinafter), as it makes up that part of the Omnibus Crime Control and Safe Streets Act of 1968.[2] Title III was adopted because there was common agreement that its predecessor, § 605, was the worst of all possible solutions. Private citizens and public officials could ignore the prohibition against wiretapping without fear of prosecution, while law enforcement officers could not use electronic surveillance to investigate and prosecute even the most serious crimes.

Under Title III, the Attorney General, Deputy Attorney General, Associate Attorney General, or any Assistant Attorney General, any acting Assistant Attorney General, or any Deputy Assistant Attorney General in the Criminal Division specially designated by the Attorney General may authorize application to a federal judge for an order permitting inter-

---

18. 343 U.S. 747, 72 S.Ct. 967, 96 L.Ed. 1270 (1952).

19. 365 U.S. 505, 81 S.Ct. 679, 5 L.Ed.2d 734 (1961).

20. 377 U.S. 158, 84 S.Ct. 1186, 12 L.Ed.2d 213 (1964).

21. Clinton v. Commonwealth, 204 Va. 275, 130 S.E.2d 437 (1963).

22. 389 U.S. 347, 88 S.Ct. 507, 19 L.Ed.2d 576 (1967).

§ 4.2

1. 388 U.S. 41, 87 S.Ct. 1873, 18 L.Ed.2d 1040 (1967).

2. 18 U.S.C.A. §§ 2510–20. In 1986 there was added 18 U.S.C.A. §§ 2701–2710, having to do with stored wire and electronic communications and transactional records access, including the requirements for government access. But, per § 2708 there is no statutory exclusionary rule for violation of these provisions, and thus they are not discussed extensively herein.

ception of wire or oral communications (i.e., wiretapping or electronic eavesdropping) by a federal agency having responsibility for investigation of the offense as to which application is made, when such interception may provide evidence of certain enumerated federal crimes.[3] A comparable provision permits, when authorized by state law, application by a state or county prosecutor to a state judge when the interception may provide evidence of "murder, kidnapping, gambling, robbery, bribery, extortion, or dealing in narcotic drugs, marijuana or other dangerous drugs, or other crime dangerous to life, limb, or property, and punishable by imprisonment for more than one year."[4] The judge may only grant an interception order as provided in § 2518 of the Act, and evidence obtained in the lawful execution of such order is admissible in court.

An interception order may be issued only if the judge determines on the basis of facts submitted that there is probable cause for belief that an individual is committing, has committed, or is about to commit one of the enumerated offenses; probable cause for belief that particular communications concerning that offense will be obtained through such interception; that normal investigative procedures have been tried and have failed or reasonably appear to be unlikely to succeed if tried or to be too dangerous; and probable cause for belief that the facilities from which, or the place where, the communications are to be intercepted are being used, or are about to be used, in connection with the commission of such offense, or are leased to, listed in the name of, or commonly used by such person. Each interception order must specify the identity of the person, if known, whose communications are to be intercepted; the nature and location of the communications facilities as to which, or the place where, authority to intercept is granted; a particular description of the type of communication sought to be intercepted, and a statement of the particular offense to which it relates; the identity of the agency authorized to intercept the communications and of the person authorizing the application;

and the period of time during which such interception is authorized, including a statement as to whether or not the interception shall automatically terminate when the described communication has been first obtained. No order may permit interception "for any period longer than is necessary to achieve the objective of the authorization, nor in any event longer than thirty days." Extensions of an order may be granted for like periods, but only by resort to the procedures required in obtaining the initial order.

Interception without prior judicial authorization is permitted whenever a specifically designated enforcement officer reasonably determines that "(a) an emergency situation exists that involves (i) immediate danger of death or serious physical injury to any person, (ii) conspiratorial activities threatening the national security interest, or (iii) conspiratorial activities characteristic of organized crime, that requires a wire, oral electronic[5] communication to be intercepted before an order authorizing such interception can with due diligence be obtained, and (b) there are grounds upon which an order could be entered." In such a case, application for an order must be made within 48 hours after the interception commences, and, in the absence of an order, the interception must terminate when the communication sought is obtained or when the application for the order is denied, whichever is earlier. Title III does not limit the constitutional power of the President to act for various purposes such as to obtain foreign intelligence information deemed essential to the security of the United States.

Within a reasonable time but not later than 90 days after the filing of an application that is denied or the termination of an authorized period of interception, the judge must cause to be served on the persons named in the order or application and other parties to the intercepted communications, an inventory that shall include notice of (1) the fact of the entry of the order or application; (2) the date of the entry and the period of authorized intercep-

---

3.   18 U.S.C.A. § 2516(1).

4.   18 U.S.C.A. § 2516(2).

5.   Defined in § 4.3(a).

tion, or the denial of the application; and (3) the fact that during the period communications were or were not intercepted. A similar inventory is required as to interceptions terminated without an order having been issued.

Where the disclosure would be in violation of Title III, "no part of the contents of [an intercepted wire or oral] communication and no evidence derived therefrom may be received in evidence in any trial, hearing, or other proceeding in or before any court, grand jury, department, officer, agency, regulatory body, legislative committee, or other authority of the United States, a State, or a political subdivision thereof." Any intentional interception or disclosure of any wire, oral or electronic communication without the prior consent of a party thereto, except as authorized under Title III, is a criminal offense punishable by a fine, imprisonment for not more than five years, or both. Any person whose wire, oral or electronic communications are intercepted, disclosed or used may bring a civil action against the offending party and may recover the actual damages suffered or statutory damages (the greater of $10,000 or $100 a day for each day of violation); plus punitive damages and a reasonable attorney's fee and other reasonable litigation costs. A good faith reliance on a court order or legislative authorization constitutes a complete defense to any civil or criminal action brought. Willful violations are also a basis for a civil action against the United States[6] and administrative discipline of the offending officer or employee.[7]

(b) Continued Surveillance. The most obvious difference between a search for tangible items and the search for wire, oral or electronic communications allowed under Title III is the time dimension of the latter kind of search. A search warrant for some physical object permits a single entry and prompt search of the described premises,[8] while Title III permits continuing surveillance up to 30 days, with extensions possible. During the authorized time, all conversations over the tapped line or within the bugged room may be overheard and recorded without regard to their relevance.

As reflected in *Berger v. New York*,[9] this striking difference accounts for the major constitutional obstacle to legalized electronic surveillance. In holding a New York law unconstitutional, the Court emphasized that it (1) permitted installation and operation of surveillance equipment for 60 days, "the equivalent of a series of intrusions, searches, and seizures pursuant to a single showing of probable cause"; (2) permitted renewal of the order "without a showing of present probable cause for the continuance of the eavesdrop"; and (3) placed "no termination date on the eavesdrop once the conversation sought is seized." While Title III permits extensions only upon a new showing of probable cause and requires that interception cease once "the objective of the authorization" is achieved, it does permit continued surveillance for up to 30 days upon a single showing of probable cause, and thus goes well beyond the kind of with-warrant electronic surveillance the Supreme Court has approved or indicated would be permitted.

As was emphasized in *Berger,* the bugging of a secret agent earlier upheld by the Court in *Osborn v. United States*[10] was pursuant to an order that "authorized one limited intrusion rather than a series or a continuous surveillance. And, we note that a new order was issued when the officer sought to resume the search and probable cause was shown for the succeeding one. Moreover, the order was executed by the officer with dispatch, not over a prolonged and extended period." Similarly, in *Katz v. United States*[11] the Court noted that the "surveillance was so narrowly circumscribed that a duly authorized magistrate * * * clearly apprised of the precise intrusion * * * could constitutionally have authorized * * * the very limited search and seizure that the Government asserts in fact took place."

---

6.   18 U.S.C.A. § 2712(a).

7.   18 U.S.C.A. § 2520(f).

8.   See § 3.4(j).

9.   388 U.S. 41, 87 S.Ct. 1873, 18 L.Ed.2d 1040 (1967).

10.   385 U.S. 323, 87 S.Ct. 429, 17 L.Ed.2d 394 (1966).

11.   389 U.S. 347, 88 S.Ct. 507, 19 L.Ed.2d 576 (1967).

The surveillance in *Katz* was limited in that the agents had probable cause to believe defendant was using certain public telephones for gambling purposes about the same time almost every day and thus activated the surveillance equipment attached to the outside of the phone booth only when defendant entered the booth.

Decisions holding that continued surveillance may also be squared with the Fourth Amendment rely upon the analysis of Justices Harlan and White, who dissented in *Berger*. Their contention was that an electronic surveillance that is continued over a span of time is no more a general search than the typical execution of a search warrant over a described area. As Justice White argued:

> Petitioner suggests that the search is inherently overbroad because the eavesdropper will overhear conversations which do not relate to criminal activity. But the same is true of almost all searches of private property which the Fourth Amendment permits. In searching for seizable matters, the police must necessarily see or hear, and comprehend, items which do not relate to the purpose of the search. That this occurs, however, does not render the search invalid, so long as it is authorized by a suitable search warrant and so long as the police, in executing that warrant, limit themselves to searching for items which may constitutionally be seized. Thus, while I would agree with petitioner that individual searches of private property through surreptitious eavesdropping with a warrant must be carefully circumscribed to avoid excessive invasion of privacy and security, I cannot agree that all such intrusions are constitutionally impermissible general searches.

This analogy by Justice White is less than perfect unless it may be concluded that the overhearing or recording of a series of conversations is merely a search, from which certain particularly described conversations will thereafter be seized. This was the position of Justice Harlan, who contended: "Just as some exercise of dominion, beyond mere perception,

is necessary for the seizure of tangibles, so some use of the conversation beyond the initial listening process is required for the seizure of the spoken word." A majority of the Supreme Court has never spoken clearly on this particular point, although language in the opinions seemingly contrary to Justice Harlan's theory is to be found. In *Katz*, for example, there is language characterizing "electronically listening to and recording" of defendant's words as a "search and seizure." But this has not deterred the lower courts from consistently holding that Title III is not rendered unconstitutional solely because it authorizes wiretaps which may last several days and encompass multiple conversations. So too, lower courts have held that the Fourth Amendment permits issuance of a search warrant that authorizes a silent ongoing video surveillance through the installation of hidden video camera in places believed to be used in criminal activities. Indeed, they have looked to the non-technical requirements of Title III (e.g., the inappropriateness of alternative, "normal investigative procedures") as prerequisites for compliance with the Fourth Amendment in issuing such warrants.

(c) Lack of Notice. The Supreme Court in *Berger v. New York*[12] also found the New York eavesdropping law "offensive" because it "has no requirement for notice, as do conventional warrants, nor does it overcome this defect by requiring some showing of special facts. On the contrary, it permits uncontested entry without any showing of exigent circumstances. Such a showing of exigency, in order to avoid notice would appear more important in eavesdropping, with its inherent dangers, than that required when conventional procedures of search and seizure are utilized." This criticism, it is important to note, goes to the very heart of all eavesdropping practices because, as the Court observed, success inevitably depends upon secrecy.

The *Berger* Court did not explore this matter in greater detail, and thus it is not entirely clear whether Title III is somewhat vulnerable on this basis. However, the lower courts have

---

12.　388 U.S. 41, 87 S.Ct. 1873, 18 L.Ed.2d 1040 (1967).

consistently rejected constitutional challenges to the legislation on such grounds with the following arguments: (1) One reason for advance notice, as emphasized by four members of the Court in *Ker v. California*,[13] is to guard the entering officer from attack on the mistaken belief he is making a criminal entry, and this danger is generally not present in eavesdropping cases. Either the eavesdropping is accomplished without any trespass or else a covert entry to plant an eavesdropping device is made at a time when it is known no one is present within. (2) Another reason for notice is so that the individual will be aware that a search was conducted, but in the more typical search case this notice may come only after the event by discovery of the warrant and a receipt at the place searched. That notice is comparable to the Title III requirement of service of an inventory within 90 days. (3) In executing search warrants for physical evidence, prior notice is not required when there is reason to believe such notice would result in the destruction or removal of the evidence sought.[14] Though the Court in *Berger* was unwilling to uphold all eavesdropping without notice on this ground, this "exigency" does exist in some circumstances. One of these circumstances, so the argument goes, is that which must exist under Title III by virtue of the requirement of a showing that "normal investigative procedures have been tried and have failed or reasonably appear to be unlikely to succeed if tried or to be too dangerous."[15]

The Supreme Court apparently finds these arguments compelling, for in *Katz v. United States*,[16] after noting that it had previously upheld a court-ordered use of a concealed device to record particular conversations in *Osborn v. United States*,[17] the Court stated:

Although the protections afforded the petitioner in *Osborn* were "*similar * * * to those * * * of conventional warrants*," they were not identical. A conventional warrant ordinarily serves to notify the suspect of an intended search. But if Osborn had been told in advance that federal officers intended to record his conversations, the point of making such recordings would obviously have been lost; the evidence in question could not have been obtained. In omitting any requirement of advance notice, the federal court that authorized electronic surveillance in *Osborn* simply recognized, as has this Court, that officers need not announce their purpose before conducting an otherwise authorized search if such an announcement would provoke the escape of the suspect or the destruction of critical evidence.

(d) Probable Cause. One aspect of the more general Fourth Amendment issue of whether the "probable cause" requirement is a fixed or a variable test,[18] is the question of whether the probable cause needed to conduct a Title III surveillance is in some respects greater than the probable cause ordinarily required to obtain a search warrant. Justice Stewart spoke to this question in his concurring opinion in *Berger v. New York*[19]:

I would hold that the affidavits on which the judicial order issued in this case did not constitute a showing of probable cause adequate to justify the authorizing order. The need for particularity and evidence of reliability in the showing required when judicial authorization is sought for the kind of electric eavesdropping involved in this case is especially great. The standard of reasonableness embodied in the Fourth Amendment demands that the showing of justification match the degree of intrusion. By its very nature electronic eavesdropping for a 60–day period, even of a specified office, involves a broad invasion of a constitutionally protected area. Only the most precise and rigorous standard of probable cause should justify an intrusion of this sort.

Justice Stewart thus concluded that though the evidence in the instant case "might be enough to satisfy the standards of the Fourth

---

13. 374 U.S. 23, 83 S.Ct. 1623, 10 L.Ed.2d 726 (1963).

14. See § 3.4(h).

15. 18 U.S.C.A. § 2518(3).

16. 389 U.S. 347, 88 S.Ct. 507, 19 L.Ed.2d 576 (1967).

17. 385 U.S. 323, 87 S.Ct. 429, 17 L.Ed.2d 394 (1966).

18. See § 3.3(b).

19. 388 U.S. 41, 87 S.Ct. 1873, 18 L.Ed.2d 1040 (1967).

Amendment for a conventional search or arrest," it "was constitutionally insufficient to constitute probable cause to justify an intrusion of the scope and duration that was permitted in this case." However, defendants who have made this type of argument to the lower courts have not prevailed.

(e) Particular Description. The eavesdropping statute struck down in *Berger* required very little by way of particularizing the conversations to be seized; it merely required the naming of "the person or persons whose communications * * * are to be overheard or recorded." The Court held this did not meet the Fourth Amendment requirement that the things to be seized be particularly described, and declared that the "need for particularity * * * is especially great in the case of eavesdropping [because it] involves an intrusion on privacy that is broad in scope." Yet, as Justice Harlan noted in his dissent, the cases on search for tangible items make it clear that the particularity requirement of the Amendment is a flexible one, depending upon the nature of the described things and whether the description readily permits identification by the executing officer.

Title III requires a particular description of the "type of communication sought to be intercepted, and a statement of the particular offense to which it relates."[20] Just what was intended by this language is unclear, as the legislative history fails to define the phrase "type of communication." These are among the most important words in the entire statute because the particularization requirement serves two very important functions here as in other contexts: it helps indicate to the officers where they are to look for the evidence sought; and it tells the officers when the search must cease because the described items have been found. It is now generally accepted that this particularization requirement can be fulfilled by indicating the offense under investigation, without further details about the anticipated conversations. Despite that development, the lower courts have rather consistently held that the statutory formula in Title III is sufficient

to meet the Fourth Amendment particularity requirement as explicated in *Berger*. The reasoning underlying these decisions is not unlike that in the Harlan dissent in the *Berger* case; it is said that it would be virtually impossible to predict in advance the exact language of a conversation that has not yet occurred, and that to demand more would render Title III totally ineffective.

(f) Covert Entry. In *Dalia v. United States*,[21] FBI agents entered an office to install a bug and reentered to remove it, all pursuant to a court order that allowed the interception of all oral communications at that office concerning a certain conspiracy but that did not explicitly authorize entry of those premises. In upholding the surveillance, the Court first concluded that the "Fourth Amendment does not prohibit *per se* a covert entry performed for the purpose of installing otherwise legal electronic bugging equipment." This naturally led to the question whether Congress had intended to authorize such an entry pursuant to the Title III procedures, which the Court answered in the affirmative. In light of the legislative history of Title III, "one simply cannot assume that Congress, aware that most bugging requires covert entry, nonetheless wished to except surveillance requiring such entries from the broad authorization of Title III, and that it resolved to do so by remaining silent on the subject."

The most controversial part of *Dalia*, however, involves the third branch of the decision, where the majority rejected the contention that because the authorizing court did not explicitly set forth its approval of the covert entries, the entry violated petitioner's Fourth Amendment privacy rights. Noting that the Warrant Clause of the Fourth Amendment imposes requirements that warrants issue on "probable cause" by "neutral, disinterested magistrates" and that they "particularly describe" the place to be searched and things to be seized, the Court found nothing in the Amendment or prior decisions under it suggesting that "search warrants also must in-

---

20. 18 U.S.C.A. § 2518(4).

21. 441 U.S. 238, 99 S.Ct. 1682, 60 L.Ed.2d 177 (1979).

clude a specification of the precise manner in which they are to be executed. On the contrary, it is generally left to the discretion of the executing officers to determine the details of how best to proceed with the performance of a search authorized by warrant—subject of course to the general Fourth Amendment protection 'against unreasonable searches and seizures.'" The Court in *Dalia* added that it "would promote empty formalism * * * to require magistrates to make explicit what unquestionably is implicit in bugging authorizations: that a covert entry, with its attendant interference with Fourth Amendment interests, may be necessary for the installation of the surveillance equipment." Three of the four dissenters in *Dalia* disagreed with the majority's interpretation of Title III, while two said that interpretation could not be squared with the Fourth Amendment because covert entry "entails an invasion of privacy of constitutional significance distinct from that which attends nontrespassory surveillance; indeed, it is tantamount to an independent search and seizure."

(g) Emergency Interception Without a Warrant. There has been virtually no use of the provision in Title III that permits interception without prior judicial approval when there are grounds for an interception order but an emergency exists involving "(i) immediate danger of death or serious physical injury to any person, (ii) conspiratorial activities threatening the national security interest, or (iii) conspiratorial activities characteristic of organized crime, that requires a wire, oral, or electronic communication to be intercepted before an order authorizing such interception can with due diligence be obtained."[22] As a consequence the courts have not been called upon to assess its constitutionality.

In *Katz v. United States*[23] the Supreme Court condemned the warrantless eavesdropping challenged in that case, but the facts made it perfectly clear that there was ample time to secure a warrant. *Katz* therefore can-

not be read as prohibiting all warrantless electronic surveillance. The Fourth Amendment doubtless would permit such surveillance under at least some circumstances, but it is unclear whether that may be said of all of the situations that might be fit within the statutory language just quoted. This is attributable in part to the fact that the relevant statutory terms are ambiguous and are not clarified by legislative history, and in part to the uncertainty that generally exists as to when a warrantless search is permissible to prevent the destruction or loss of evidence. It does seem, however, that the case in which the strongest showing of need could be made falls within the more recently enacted item (i) of the statutory exception.

(h) Use of Secret Agents. Because Title III declares interception to be lawful where "one of the parties to the communication has given prior consent to such interception,"[24] it does not forbid the use of eavesdropping equipment to record or transmit what a suspect says to a secret agent. Whether this practice can be squared with the Fourth Amendment is an issue the Supreme Court has had before it on several occasions. In *On Lee v. United States*,[25] an undercover agent "wired for sound" entered defendant's laundry and engaged him in an incriminating conversation, which an agent outside the laundry was able to hear on a receiving set. In a 5–4 decision, the Court rejected the claim that the undercover agent had committed a trespass because consent to his entry was obtained by fraud, and dismissed as "verging on the frivolous" the further contention that the agent outside "was a trespasser because by these aids he overheard what went on inside." Similarly, in *Lopez v. United States*,[26] where the secret agent had a recording device concealed on his person, the majority, relying upon *On Lee*, concluded that

> this case involves no "eavesdropping" whatever in any proper sense of that term. The Government did not use an electronic device

---

22. 18 U.S.C.A. § 2518(7).

23. 389 U.S. 347, 88 S.Ct. 507, 19 L.Ed.2d 576 (1967).

24. 18 U.S.C.A. § 2511(2)(c).

25. 343 U.S. 747, 72 S.Ct. 967, 96 L.Ed. 1270 (1952).

26. 373 U.S. 427, 83 S.Ct. 1381, 10 L.Ed.2d 462 (1963).

to listen in on conversations it could not otherwise have heard. Instead, the device was used only to obtain the most reliable evidence possible of a conversation in which the Government's own agent was a participant and which that agent was fully entitled to disclose. And the device was not planted by means of an unlawful physical invasion of petitioner's premises under circumstances which would violate the Fourth Amendment. It was carried in and out by an agent who was there with petitioner's assent, and it neither saw nor heard more than the agent himself.[27]

When the Court in *Katz v. United States*[28] rejected the "constitutionally protected area" approach in a favor of justified expectation of privacy analysis of the what-is-a-search issue, the continuing vitality of *On Lee* and *Lopez* was in doubt. Then came *United States v. White*,[29] where a government informer engaged defendant in conversations in a restaurant, defendant's home, and the informer's car while the informer was carrying a concealed radio transmitter. The court of appeals held that this electronic eavesdropping constituted a search, but the Supreme Court did not agree. Asserting that *Katz* "left undisturbed" the notion "that however strongly a defendant may trust an apparent colleague, his expectations in this respect are not protected by the Fourth Amendment when it turns out that the colleague is a government agent regularly communicating with the authorities," the Court concluded:

If the law gives no protection to the wrongdoer whose trusted accomplice is or becomes a police agent, neither should it protect him when that same agent has recorded or transmitted the conversations which are later offered in evidence to prove the State's case.

Inescapably, one contemplating illegal activities must realize and risk that his companions may be reporting to the police. If he sufficiently doubts their trustworthiness, the association will very probably end or never materialize. But if he has no doubts, or allays them, or risks what doubt he has, the risk is his. In terms of what his course will be, what he will or will not do or say, we are unpersuaded that he would distinguish between probable informers on the one hand and probable informers with transmitters on the other. Given the possibility or probability that one of his colleagues is cooperating with the police, it is only speculation to assert that the defendant's utterances would be substantially different or his sense of security any less if he also thought it possible that the suspected colleague is wired for sound. At least there is no persuasive evidence that the difference in this respect between the electronically equipped and the unequipped agent is substantial enough to require discrete constitutional recognition, particularly under the Fourth Amendment which is ruled by fluid concepts of "reasonableness."

The Court added that this result was bolstered by the fact that a recording will often produce a "more reliable rendition of what a defendant has said than will the unaided memory of a police agent," and that "with the recording in existence it is less likely that the informant will change his mind, and there is 'less chance that threat or injury will suppress unfavorable evidence and less chance that cross-examination will confound the testimony.'"

Although the way in which the Court split in *White*[30] has prompted some dispute as to whether there were five votes for the above position, the lower courts have consistently read *White* to mean that there is no Fourth

---

27. Three members of the Court, dissenting, found the instant case indistinguishable from *On Lee* and maintained that the evidence should have been excluded in both cases. Warren, C.J., concurring, agreed that *On Lee* was wrongly decided, but found the instant case "quite dissimilar constitutionally" because in *On Lee* the use of the transmitter was not to corroborate the testimony of the secret agent but rather "to obviate the need to put him on the stand."

28. 389 U.S. 347, 88 S.Ct. 507, 19 L.Ed.2d 576 (1967).

29. 401 U.S. 745, 91 S.Ct. 1122, 28 L.Ed.2d 453 (1971).

30. Four members of the Court joined in the opinion quoted above. Brennan, J., concurred in the result on the ground that *Katz* was not retroactive, but opined that both *On Lee* and *Lopez* were "no longer sound law." Black, J., concurred with the result for the reasons stated in his *Katz* dissent.

Amendment barrier to participant monitoring of conversations.[31] But there is much to be said for the position taken in Justice Harlan's forceful dissent in *White:*

> Authority is hardly required to support the proposition that words would be measured a good deal more carefully and communication inhibited if one suspected his conversations were being transmitted and transcribed. Were third-party bugging a prevalent practice, it might well smother that spontaneity—reflected in frivolous, impetuous, sacrilegious, and defiant discourse—that liberates daily life. Much offhand exchange is easily forgotten and one may count on the obscurity of his remarks, protected by the very fact of a limited audience, and the likelihood that the listener will either overlook or forget what is said, as well as the listener's inability to reformulate a conversation without having to contend with a documented record. All of these values are sacrificed by a rule of law that permits official monitoring of private discourse limited only by the need to locate a willing assistant.

He thus concluded a contrary result was needed "to protect * * * the expectation of the ordinary citizen, who has never engaged in illegal conduct in his life, that he may carry on his private discourse freely, openly, and spontaneously without measuring his every word against the connotations it might carry when instantaneously heard by others unknown to him and unfamiliar with his situation or analyzed in a cold, formal record played days, months, or years after the conversation."

§ 4.3 Title III: What Surveillance Covered

(a) Meaning of "Interception." Title III prohibits, except as provided therein, any "interception" of communications. As amended in 1986,[1] Title III defines "intercept" as meaning "the aural or other acquisition of the contents of any wire, electronic or oral communication through the use of any electronic, mechanical, or other device."[2] To determine the precise scope of this definition, three questions must be answered: (1) what communications are protected—that is, what is included within the categories of "wire communication," "electronic communication," and "oral communication"? (2) What means of interception are covered—that is, what is "any electronic, mechanical, or other device"? (3) What kind of activity is covered—that is, what are the "contents" of a communication and what constitutes their "aural or other acquisition"? Each of these questions is considered below.

Wire communication: Section 2510(1) defines a "wire communication" as

> any aural transfer made in whole or in part through the use of facilities for the transmission of communications by the aid of wire, cable, or other like connection between the point of origin and the point of reception (including the use of such connection in a switching station) furnished or operated by any person engaged in providing or operating such facilities for the transmission of interstate or foreign communications or communications affecting interstate or foreign commerce and such term includes any electronic storage of such communication.

This extensive definition establishes several prerequisites that combine to classify an intercepted communication as a "wire communication."

Because wire communications are limited to "aural transfer[s]," defined in § 2510(8) as "transfer[s] containing the human voice," communications through wire that transfer only printed or electronic data are not protected under this provision (although they are likely to fall within the definition of "electronic communications," discussed later). The transfer only need contain the human voice at some point between and including the point of

---

31. Holmes v. Burr, 486 F.2d 55 (9th Cir.1973).

§ 4.3

1. Those amendments were a part of the Electronic Communications Privacy Act of 1986, P.L. 99–508, 100 Stat. 1848, which became effective on January 20, 1987.

2. 28 U.S.C.A. § 2510(4).

origin and the point of reception, and thus a communication remains a wire communication even though a voice signal is converted to digital form in the course of transmission.

An aural transfer is a wire communication only if it is transmitted, at least in part, through the "aid of wire, cable, or other like connection between the points of origin and reception (including the use of such connection in a switching station)." This language carries the definition of "wire communication" beyond the standard "land line" telephone communication to also cover telephone transmissions carried by fiber optic cable and the cellular telephone. The reference to a "switching station" connection makes it clear that cellular transmissions are included even when made between telephones that are both cellular.

Since the aural transfer need be made only "in part" by "wire, cable, or other like connection," a transfer of the human voice does not lose its characterization as a wire communication simply because other means are also used in carrying the voice between the points of origin and reception. That is the situation as to cellular technology utilizing radio signals in the initial stage of its transmission, voice communication made by telephone and then transmitted by radio to a person carrying a pager, and telephone calls carried in part by wire (or by fiber optic cable) and in part by microwave (commonplace in long distance telephone calls). The cordless phone exception to the

above rule on "hybrids," recognized by a 1986 amendment to the § 2510(1) definition quoted above, was deleted by Congress in 1994, apparently because technological advances had made cordless communications more private.

The 1986 amendment of § 2510(1) specifically included in the definition the "electronic storage" of an aural transfer made in whole or in part through wire, cable, or other like connection so as to encompass the voice mail communication. However, the core Title III protection extends only to the "interception" of the aural transfer, which occurs as the voice mail transfer is made and placed in storage. To gain access to completed voice mail messages already held in storage,[3] law enforcement officers only need comply with Chapter 121 of title 18 of the U.S. Code,[4] which is not enforced by an exclusionary remedy.[5] By a 2001 amendment of § 2501(1), the term "electronic storage" was removed from the definition of an aural transfer, which with other changes made it clear that it is lawful—rather than unlawful but not a basis for exclusion—to obtain unopened voice mail messages (just as with e-mail messages) by a regular search warrant instead of a Title III warrant.

The definition of wire communication also was amended in 1986 to delete the requirement that the intercepted communication be transmitted via the facilities of a common carrier. The statute now extends to all facilities furnished or operated to transmit communications "affecting interstate or foreign com-

---

3. 18 U.S.C.A. § 2510(17) defines electronic storage as including "any temporary, intermediate storage of a wire or electronic communication incidental to the electronic transmission thereof," as well as "any storage of such communication by an electronic communication service for purposes of backup protection."

4. This chapter is found at 18 U.S.C.A. § 2701–2711. It is titled "Stored Wire and Electronic Communication and Transactional Records Access." Section 2701 prohibits intentionally accessing without authorization a facility providing an electronic communication service and thereby obtaining a wire or electronic communication while in storage in such system. It authorizes accessing as provides in §§ 2703, 2704, and 2518. The latter section contains the provisions on court authorized interception by law enforcement, as discussed in § 4.4 infra, and includes wire and electronic communications. Section 2703 provides for the authorization of government access to the contents of electronic communications held in storage. It requires a

search warrant if the communication is held in storage by an electronic communication service provider for less than 180 days, but allows for accessing by administrative or grand jury subpoena or court order (issued upon a showing of relevance) if the communication has been held in storage over 180 days by the provider of an electronics communication service or if the communication is being held in storage in a remote computing service. Section 2703 further provides for government access to transactional records, which also is allowed through a subpoena or court order. Section 2704 provides for subpoena or court order requiring the making of a backup copy of the content of the electronic communication by the service provider.

5. Section 2708 includes the exclusive remedies and sanctions for statutory violations in accessing stored material, and does not include suppression in that list. It operates in the same fashion as § 2518(10)(c) with respect to interception of electronic communications.

merce," which encompasses a private telephone system established by a company whose activities affected interstate commerce.

Conversations transmitted entirely by radio are not "wire communications" under the § 2510(1) definition as amended; the presence of wires within the radio transmitting equipment does not make the transmission one conducted by the aid of wire. However, the 1986 amendments added the new category of electronic communications, and radio transmissions may be protected under that classification. Similarly, when the conversation was not intended to be transmitted through a wire, but inadvertently was so transmitted, the proper analysis is under the protection of oral communications rather than wire communications. Thus, the wire communication category does not apply to background conversations in a room that happened to be overheard in the interception of telephone conversation, or to a conversation overheard when a wiretapped phone was left off of the hook.

Electronic communication. The category of "electronic communication," added to the statute in the 1986 amendment, was not placed on same plane as the "wire communication" and "oral communication" categories. Although unauthorized interception of protected electronic communications is prohibited, authorization requirements are not as stringent, and violation of the prohibition is not grounds for suppression of the evidence obtained. Section 2510(12), defining this new category of protected communication, states that an electronic communication

means any transfer of signs, signals, writings, images, sounds, data, or intelligence of any nature transmitted in whole or in part by a wire, radio, electromagnetic, photoelectronic or photooptical system that affects interstate or foreign commerce, but does not include—(A) any wire or oral communication; (B) any communication made through a tone-only paging device; (C) any communication from a tracking device (as defined in section 3117 of this title); or (D) electronic funds transfer information stored by a financial institution in a communications system used for the electronic storage and transfer of funds.

The initial portion of this definition is so broad that it would completely envelop all wire communications and might include as well certain interceptions of oral communications, but this potential overlap is eliminated by the exception (A), which excludes any "wire or oral communication." Thus, an electronic communication is a transmission that fits the general description of § 2510(12) but also does not fit the definitions of wire and oral communications.

The critical distinction between wire and electronic communications is that the former is limited to aural transfers and only the aural transfers by specific electronic means (in whole or in part by wire, cable or other like connection). When a communication is transferred by those specified means, it will constitute a wire communication insofar as it contains the human voice, but it will be an electronic communication if it is a non-aural transfer. Thus, electronic mail, which typically consists of typewritten messages transferred over telephone lines, falls within the electronic communications category. Where the technology of transmission does not meet the requirements for wire communications (e.g., it is a radio transmission), the transmitted communication will be an electronic communication even if it does contain the human voice (as in a microwave transmission of a closed circuit video teleconference). If the technology is being used not to transfer a voice communication from one device to another, but simply to pick up the sound waves transmitted as a person speaks in the presence of another, then the communication is an oral communication, and it will not constitute an electronic communication even though it arguably involves a transfer transmitted "in part" through the electronic device used to pick up those sound waves.

The definition of electronic communications also specifies exceptions that exclude (i) the tone-only paging device communication, (ii) the tracking device communication, and (iii) electronic funds transfer information stored by a financial institution in a communications system used for electronic storage and transfer of funds. An additional exception, not contained in the definition of electronic communication, but incorporated by its reference to transmissions by radio, comes from § 2511(2)(g). That section provides that it shall not be unlawful under Title III to intercept an electronic communication that "is configured so that such electronic communication is readily accessible to the general public." Under § 2510(16) a radio communication is deemed "readily accessible to the general public" if it does not fall within specified modes, such as being "scrambled or encrypted" or being transmitted through "modulation techniques whose essential parameters have been withheld from the public with the intention of preserving the privacy of such communications." The combined effect of § 2511(2)(g) and § 2510(16) is to remove from the protection of the electronic communications category those radio communications that lack the attributes of privacy characteristic of the non-radio electronic communications that fall within that category.

Oral communication. The category of oral communications is defined in § 2510(2) as meaning "any oral communication uttered by a person exhibiting an expectation that such communication is not subject to interception under circumstances justifying such expectation, but such term does not include any electronic communication." The mode of communication here is sound waves as opposed to an electronic medium, which ordinarily means that the speaker is communicating to a listener who is within normal hearing distance.[6] The critical element of the § 2510(2) definition is its limitation to persons having a justifiable expectation that their conversations would not be intercepted. This limitation, intended to reflect existing law, follows the Fourth Amend-

ment "reasonable expectation of privacy standard" as set forth in *Katz v. United States*.[7] This being so, it would seem that the Supreme Court's decisions interpreting that Fourth Amendment standard[8] should be the touchstone for applying the "justifiable expectation" component of the oral communication definition. If there is any doubt about this, it is because some of the legislative history goes into more detail and thus arguably deprives the statute of some of the opportunity for the "growth" that *Katz* has experienced on the Fourth Amendment level.[9]

"Electronic, mechanical, or other device." Title III applies only to interception through the use of any "electronic, mechanical, or other device." Section 2510(5) defines such a device as "any device or apparatus which can be used to intercept a wire, oral, or electronic communication" other than two exempted groups of devices. The first exempted group is "any telephone or telegraph instrument, equipment or facility or any component thereof (i) furnished to the subscriber or user by a provider of wire or electronic communication service in the ordinary course of its business and being used by the subscriber or user in the ordinary course of its business or furnished by such subscriber or user for connection to the facilities of such service and used in the ordinary course of its business; or (ii) being used by a communications common carrier in the ordinary course of its business or by an investigative or law enforcement officer in the ordinary course of his duties." The second exempted group consists of "a hearing aid or similar device being used to correct subnormal hearing to not better than normal."

The major form of interception occurring without the use of a "device or apparatus" is

---

6. That, however, is not always the case. If an eavesdropper uses a mechanical device to pick up one end of a telephone conversation from the place at which the speaker is talking, that still is an interception of an oral communication rather than a wire communication. The same would be true of the use of such a device to overhear what a speaker was saying to himself.

7. See § 3.2(a).

8. See § 3.2.

9. Of particular note is that part of the legislative history declaring that an expectation of privacy "would clearly be unjustified in certain areas; for example, a jail cell * * * or an open field." As to jails, however, lower courts generally have held that the electronic monitoring of conversations between inmates and between inmates and visitors or police does not constitute an interception of a protected "oral conversation" because there is lacking a justifiable expectation that such conversations would not be subject to interceptions by jail authorities.

the overhearing with the naked ear. Of course, a conversation that can be overheard by the naked ear ordinarily would not constitute a protected "oral communication" under § 2510(2) because there would be no justifiable expectation that the communication would not be intercepted. It is partly for that reason that conversations overheard with the naked ear can also be tape recorded surreptitiously without violating Title III. However, even if a person were hidden in such a way that there would be a reasonable expectation that the conversation could not be overheard, thus presenting a protected oral communication, there would be no Title III interception if the communication was overheard without an artificial aid.

The first of the two exceptions noted in the § 2510(5) definition, that for devices used in ordinary business activities, has been the subject of considerable litigation. Courts have held that this exception exempts nonconsensual listening to conversation over an extension phone by other members of the same household, employer use of extension phones and other elements of the employer's phone system to monitor calls by employees under some circumstances, and the police officer who answers a telephone while lawfully on the premises (including that in which the caller is misled as to the identity of the answerer). The exemption's provisions on use in the ordinary course of business by a communications service provider has been held to apply to the listening in by a telephone operator who sought to verify that the call was connected and by a telephone lineman who broke into a line to check out a complaint of excessive noise. The ordinary course of duties exemption for police use has been held applicable primarily to police monitoring of calls from and to prisoners at jail and the routine monitoring and recording of all calls at police stations.

"Aural or other acquisitions." Section 2510 applies to "aural or other acquisitions" of the contents of wire, electronic, or oral communications. The Act does not define the phrase "aural acquisition," but that lack of definition has not created difficulties in the application of Title III. Courts are in agreement that replaying a recording of an intercepted conversation does not constitute a new "aural acquisition," which would make necessary an additional authorization. So too, where an individual hears a conversation without an auditory device, his surreptitiously recording of that conversation uniformly has been held not to violate Title III.[10] At one time, there was some disagreement as to whether a recording constituted an aural acquisition when nobody was listening to the recording at the time, but unmonitored recording is presently viewed as covered by the statute. To treat an unattended recording as not constituting a aural transfer and then to allow disclosure of the recording on the ground that there had never been an interception would clearly be contrary to the purpose of the statute. The 1986 amendment, as noted previously, gave protection to electronic communications, which includes non-voice communications such as electronic mail. In keeping with this change, that amendment expanded the reference to "aural acquisition" in the definition of "intercept" to read "aural or other acquisition." This has been held, however, to apply only to acquiring the contents of the communication as it takes place, not to gaining subsequent access to stored non-voice communications.

"Contents." Interception applies only to the "contents" of the wire, oral, or electronic communication, defined in § 2510(8) as "including any information concerning the substance, purport, or meaning of the communication." In *United States v. New York Telephone Co.*,[11] the Supreme Court held that "the language of the statute and its legislative history establish

---

10. The courts have not always been in agreement as to whether that is because there has been no further "aural transfer" by the recording, as other grounds may also remove the recording from the proscriptions of Title III. Many of these cases involve recording by a party to the conversation, and the recording there can be upheld under the consent exemption. So too, where the eavesdropper's

location obviously permits him to overhear the conversation, his location will take the recorded conversation out of the protected "oral communication" category due to the absence of a justifiable expectation of non-interception.

11. 434 U.S. 159, 98 S.Ct. 364, 54 L.Ed.2d 376 (1977).

beyond any doubt that pen registers," devices that do not record phone conversations but merely make a record of the numbers dialed from a given phone and the time of dialing "are not governed by Title III." The Court reasoned:

> Pen registers do not "intercept" because they do not acquire the "contents" of communications, as that term is defined by 18 U.S.C. § 2510(8). Indeed, a law enforcement official could not even determine from the use of a pen register whether a communication existed. These devices do not hear sound [and thus] do not accomplish the "aural acquisition" of anything. They decode outgoing numbers by responding to changes in electrical voltage caused by the turning of the telephone dial (or the pressing of buttons on push button telephones) and present the information in a form to be interpreted by sight rather than by hearing.[12]

At the time that *New York Telephone* was decided, the § 2510(8) definition of contents referred to information concerning "the identity of the parties" to the communication or the "existence" of the communication. To both codify *New York Telephone* and to ensure that devices similar to the pen register would be given similar treatment, the 1986 amendment deleted that language. Thus, it is now clear that "transactional information"—i.e., information that only reveals that a communication occurred (and between what parties or devices), without revealing what was said or communicated—are not within the protection of Title III. This is what is described by statute as a "trap and trace device"—"a device which captures the incoming electronic or other impulses which identify the originating number of an instrument or device from which a wire or electronic communication was transmitted."[13] So too, Title III does not regulate silent video surveillance.

In 1986, Congress also adopted a special chapter[14] in Title 18 prohibiting use of pen registers and trap and trace devices without proper authorization. Law enforcement use is allowed upon judicial order, in emergency situations without court order, and pursuant to the Foreign Intelligence Surveillance Act. To obtain a court order, an attorney for the government must certify that the information sought is relevant to an ongoing investigation and identify the possibly relevant offenses, but judicial review is limited only to the completeness of the application. The court does not make its own determination as to relevancy on the basis of the investigation.

(b) Phone Company Activities. By virtue of the limitations upon the meaning of "interception" in the context of Title III, discussed above, it is clear that certain activities engaged in by telephone companies are not at all proscribed by the Act. This includes the making and keeping of toll records, the use of pen registers or other call-tracing devices to see if a particular person is making harassing phone calls or is otherwise misusing the telephone service, and the use of a diode trap whereby annoying phone calls can be traced by preventing disconnection when a call is made to a phone to which the device is attached. But sometimes investigations conducted by telephone companies go beyond this. Especially when the company is investigating the fraudulent use of company lines by the use of a "blue box" or other equipment permitting the bypassing of long distance automatic billing mechanisms, investigators will actually monitor and record calls to determine the speakers' identities and the extent of illegal use.

Because such activity *does* fall within the statutory definition of what constitutes an interception, it must be assessed under a special provision declaring that it is not unlawful "for an operator of a switchboard, or an officer, employee, or agent of a provider of wire or electronic communication services, whose facilities are used in the transmission of a wire or electronic communication, to intercept, dis-

---

12. Later, in Smith v. Maryland, 442 U.S. 735, 99 S.Ct. 2577, 61 L.Ed.2d 220 (1979), the Court held that use of a pen register is not governed by the Fourth Amendment. See § 3.2(j).

13. 18 U.S.C.A. § 3127.

14. Chapter 206 at 18 U.S.C.A. §§ 3121–3127.

close, or use that communication in the normal course of his employment while engaged in any activity which is a necessary incident to the rendition of his service or to the protection of the rights or property of the provider of that service."[15] (This statute goes on to say that these providers may "not utilize service observing or random monitoring except for mechanical or service quality control checks.") Monitoring by the company to obtain evidence for a wire fraud prosecution falls within the "protection of the rights of property" part of the statute. Such monitoring has been upheld where it continued for several weeks, where it continued after the identity of one perpetrator was learned but it was known unidentified others were involved, and even where entire conversations were recorded. As for the "rendition of his service" part of the statute, it has been held to permit, for example, a long distance operator to remain on the line to verify that the call has been connected, and a telephone lineman to intercept a conversation while checking the noise level on a line.

(c) Consent. An important exception to the usual Title III requirement that an interception occur only pursuant to a court order is that which has to do with interceptions made by prior consent. The Act specifically provides that it "shall not be unlawful under this chapter for a person acting under color of law to intercept a wire, oral or electronic communication, where such person is a party to the communication or one of the parties to the communication has given prior consent to such interception."[16] A similar provision covers persons not acting under color of law.[17] The legislative history indicates that the consent exception was intended to reflect existing law in such cases as *Lopez v. United States*[18] and *On Lee v. United States*,[19] which has since been followed by the Court in *United States v. White*.[20] It is thus clear that law enforcement authorities are free to make consensual interceptions in a variety of ways: (1) by having the consenting party wear or carry a tape recorder with which he records his face-to-face conversations with another; (2) by having the consenting party wear a transmitter that broadcasts his conversations to agents equipped with a receiver; or (3) by having the consenting party to a telephone conversation record it or permit another to listen in on an extension.

The legislative history sheds some light upon the scope of this consent exception. For one thing, the "prior consent" language of the statute means that retroactive authorization would not be possible. Secondly, the requisite consent "may be express or implied. Surveillance devices in banks or apartment houses for institutional or personal protection would be impliedly consented to." And finally, "party" would mean the person actually participating in the communication, so that interception by impersonation is permissible under the consent provision. For example, if police officers executing a search warrant for gambling paraphernalia answer the phone while there, impersonate the gambler and record the ensuing conversation, this is lawful under Title III. Another consent provision allows the victim of a "hacker" under some circumstances to consent to interception of the hacker's messages transmitted to, through or from the victim's computer.[21]

(d) National Security Surveillance. When Title III was enacted, there was included in it an express declaration that nothing therein "shall limit the constitutional power of the President to take such measures as he deems necessary to protect the Nation against actual or potential attack or other hostile acts of a foreign power, to obtain foreign intelligence information deemed essential

---

15. 18 U.S.C.A. § 2511(2)(a)(i).

16. 18 U.S.C.A. § 2511(2)(c).

17. 18 U.S.C.A. § 2511(2)(d), which is, however, qualified so as to not cover the situation in which "such communication is intercepted for the purpose of committing any criminal or tortious act in violation of the Constitution or laws of the United States or of any State or for the purpose of committing any other injurious act."

18. 373 U.S. 427, 83 S.Ct. 1381, 10 L.Ed.2d 462 (1963) (bribe offer recorded by use of concealed recorder).

19. 343 U.S. 747, 72 S.Ct. 967, 96 L.Ed. 1270 (1952) (incriminating remarks made to undercover agent wired for sound).

20. 401 U.S. 745, 91 S.Ct. 1122, 28 L.Ed.2d 453 (1971).

21. 18 U.S.C.A. § 2511(2)(i).

to the security of the United States, or to protect national security information against foreign intelligence activities," or "to protect the United States against the overthrow of the Government by force or other unlawful means, or against any other clear and present danger to the structure or existence of the Government."[22] Since at least 1940, there had been presidential sanction for warrantless electronic surveillance in furtherance of national security, and the apparent purpose of the above language was not to disturb whatever powers in this regard the President actually has under the Constitution.

The scope of those powers was at issue in *United States v. United States District Court*,[23] where the government claimed that its warrantless surveillance of a purely domestic radical group engaged in a conspiracy to destroy federal government property was authorized under that statutory provision. But the Court without dissent concluded "that the Government's concerns do not justify departure in this case from the customary Fourth Amendment requirement of judicial approval prior to initiation of a search or surveillance." That conclusion was rested upon the following four considerations: (1) Though in a case such as this the investigative duty of the executive may be stronger, it is equally true that "Fourth Amendment protections become the more necessary when the targets of official surveillance may be those suspected of unorthodoxy in their political beliefs." (2) Executive officers of government do not qualify under the Fourth Amendment as neutral magistrates, as "unreviewed executive discretion may yield too readily to pressures to obtain incriminating evidence and overlook potential invasions of privacy and protected speech." (3) It is not true "that internal security matters are too subtle and complex for judicial evaluation." (4) Prior judicial approval will not "fracture the secrecy essential to official intelligence gathering," as judges "may be counted upon to be especially conscious of security requirements in national se-

curity cases." The Court added that it recognized "that domestic security surveillance may involve different policy and practical considerations from the surveillance of 'ordinary crime,'" and that consequently "Congress may wish to consider protective standards for [domestic security surveillance] which differ from those already prescribed for specified crimes in Title III."

In the *United States District Court* case, the Supreme Court emphasized that it was dealing with a situation in which the warrantless surveillance had been directed at a "domestic organization," said "to mean a group or organization (whether formally or informally constituted) composed of citizens of the United States and which has no significant connection with a foreign power, its agents or agencies." Though this certainly implied that a case arising under the foreign affairs part of the statute might come out differently, the Court did not have occasion to pursue that point or to elaborate just what kind of connection with a foreign government would be necessary to put a case into that category. The question seldom reached the lower courts, though *Zweibon v. Mitchell*[24] deserves mention. Damages were sought by members of the Jewish Defense League from the Attorney General and several FBI agents because of warrantless wiretapping purportedly undertaken to obtain foreign intelligence information. The theory was that JDL activities were putting a severe strain on Soviet–American relations and had created the threat of retaliation by Soviet citizens against American Embassy personnel in Moscow. Relying individually upon either the Fourth Amendment or the language in Title III, the eight members of the court concluded that the mere fact the actions of the domestic organization might provoke action abroad harmful to the United States was not enough to put the case into the foreign affairs category. It was thus concluded "that a warrant must be obtained before a wiretap is installed on a domestic organization that is neither the agent

---

22. Former 18 U.S.C.A. § 2511(3), repealed upon enactment of the Foreign Intelligence Surveillance Act of 1978, discussed herein.

23. 407 U.S. 297, 92 S.Ct. 2125, 32 L.Ed.2d 752 (1972).

24. 516 F.2d 594 (D.C.Cir.1975).

of nor acting in collaboration with a foreign power."

The matter is now dealt with by another statute, the Foreign Intelligence Surveillance Act of 1978.[25] This Act provides that the Chief Justice of the United States is to publicly designate 11 district judges from seven of the federal judicial circuits "who shall constitute a court which shall have jurisdiction to hear applications for and grant orders approving electronic surveillance anywhere within the United States under the procedures set forth in this Act," and that he is also to publicly designate three judges from the federal district courts or courts of appeals who shall "comprise a court of review which shall have jurisdiction to review the denial of any application made under this Act." Upon a proper application, a judge of this court is to enter an ex parte order approving electronic surveillance for 90 days or until its purpose is achieved, whichever is less, if he finds, inter alia, that "there is probable cause to believe" that "the target of the electronic surveillance is a foreign power[26] or an agent of a foreign power" and that "each of the facilities or places at which the electronic surveillance is directed is being used, or is about to be used, by a foreign power or an agent of a foreign power." But, it is further provided that "no United States person[27] may be considered a foreign power or an agent of a foreign power solely upon the basis of activities protected by the first amendment to the Constitution of the United States."

The FISA also deals with warrantless surveillance. It provides that "the President, through the Attorney General, may authorize electronic surveillance without a court order under this title to acquire foreign intelligence information for periods of up to one year" if, inter alia, the Attorney General certifies in writing under oath (with a copy of that certification transmitted under seal to the special court) that the surveillance is "solely directed at" the acquisition of the contents of communications "transmitted by means of communications used exclusively between or among foreign powers" and that "there is no substantial likelihood that the surveillance will acquire the contents of any communication to which a United States person is a party."

Evidence acquired in noncompliance with FISA is subject to suppression by "an aggrieved person" in "any trial, hearing, or other proceeding in or before any court, department, officer, agency, regulatory body, or other authority of the United States, a State or a political subdivision thereof." However, "if the Attorney General files an affidavit under oath that disclosure or an adversary hearing would harm the national security of the United States," then the appropriate federal district court must "review in camera and ex parte the application, order and such other materials relating to the surveillance as may be necessary to determine whether the surveillance of the aggrieved person was lawfully authorized and conducted. In making the determination, the court may disclose to the aggrieved person, under appropriate security procedures and protective orders, portions of the application, order, or other materials relating to the surveillance only where such disclosure is necessary to make an accurate determination of the legality of the surveillance."

§ 4.4 Title III: Application for and Issuance of Court Order

(a) Application Procedure. In contrast to the situation that generally obtains as to conventional search warrants, which may be

---

25. 50 U.S.C.A. §§ 1801–1811,

26. Defined as meaning "a foreign government or any component thereof," "a faction of a foreign nation or nations, not substantially composed of United States persons," "an entity that is openly acknowledged by a foreign government or governments to be directed and controlled by such foreign government or governments," "a group engaged international terrorism or activities in preparation therefor," "a foreign-based political organization not substantially composed of United States persons," or "an

entity that is directed and controlled by a foreign government or governments."

27. Defined as meaning "a citizen of the United States, an alien lawfully admitted for permanent residence * * *, an unincorporated association a substantial number of members of which are citizens of the United States or aliens lawfully admitted for permanent residence, or a corporation which is incorporated in the United States, but does not include a corporation or an association which is a foreign power."

sought by any law enforcement officer, application for a Title III order must be authorized by a high-level official. In the federal system, only the "Attorney General, Deputy Attorney General, Associate Attorney General, or any Assistant Attorney General, any acting Assistant Attorney General, or any Deputy Assistant Attorney General or Acting Assistant Attorney General in the Criminal Division specially designated by the Attorney General, may authorize an application."[1] This provision is intended to centralize in a publicly responsible official subject to the political process the formulation of law enforcement policy on the use of electronic surveillance techniques.

In *United States v. Giordano*,[2] the Court was confronted with a violation of this authorization requirement, for the Attorney General's executive assistant, not an official designated by the statute, had in fact been the person who placed the Attorney General's initials on an authorizing memo that the Attorney General had not seen. The Court held "that the provision for pre-application control was intended to play a central role in the statutory scheme and that suppression must follow when it is shown that this statutory requirement has been ignored." Similarly, if at the state level the authorization is by a person other than enumerated in Title III, the "principal prosecuting attorney of any State, or the principal prosecuting attorney of any political subdivision thereof, if such attorney is authorized by a statute of that State to make application,"[3] then once again the application is invalid and the evidence must be suppressed. But the authority at the state level may be delegated.

In *Giordano,* the Court noted that under the statute "the mature judgment of a particular, responsible Department of Justice official is interposed as a critical precondition to any judicial order." Though this might suggest that an authorization could be brought into question because of the limited extent of the review by the authorizing official, that is not the case. While it has been held that the authorizing official's personal judgment is necessary, courts have not been inclined to permit any challenge of the quality of the review undertaken by him. That view has sometimes been criticized on the ground that the authorization requirement is meaningless if some semblance of meaningful review is not required.

In adding protection for electronic communications in 1986, Congress departed from the requirements of high level authorization within the Justice Department. Section 2516(3) provides that "any attorney for the Government (as defined in the Federal Rules of Criminal Procedure)" may apply for court authorization of an interception of an electronic communication. Under Federal Rule 54, the phrase "attorney for the government" includes a United States Attorney and "an authorized assistant of a United States attorney." Section 2516(3) also allows for broader use of interception of electronic communications by allowing application to be made in connection with the investigation of "any federal felony," rather than the limited group of felonies specified in § 2516(1) as to the interception of wire or oral communications. In other respects, however, the application process is the same, including the limitation as to the judges before whom the application must be brought.

Under Title III, applications for surveillance orders in both the federal and state systems may be made only to a "judge of competent jurisdiction."[4] In the federal system, this means only "a judge of a United States district court or a United States court of appeals."[5] On the state level it means "a judge of any court of general criminal jurisdiction of a State who is authorized by a statute of that State to enter orders authorizing interceptions of wire, oral, or electronic communications."[6]

§ 4.4

1. 18 U.S.C.A. § 2516(1).
2. 416 U.S. 505, 94 S.Ct. 1820, 40 L.Ed.2d 341 (1974).
3. 18 U.S.C.A. § 2516(2).

4. 18 U.S.C.A. § 2516(1) & (2).
5. 18 U.S.C.A. § 2510(9)(a).
6. 18 U.S.C.A. § 2510(9)(b).

(b) Contents of Application. Each Title III application must "be made in writing upon oath or affirmation" and must include a considerable amount of information specified in the statute. It must "state the applicant's authority to make such application," which presumably can be met merely by identifying that person as holding the office specified in the statute, and it must also disclose "the identity of the investigative or law enforcement officer making the application, and the officer authorizing the application." In *United States v. Chavez,*[7] the Supreme Court was confronted with a situation in which the latter requirement was not met in that the application erroneously asserted that a certain assistant Attorney General was the authorizing official when in fact the Attorney General had authorized the application. Noting that the application would have been in order if the Attorney General had been identified, the Court concluded this identification requirement was not so central to the protections of Title III as to require suppression of the evidence obtained as a consequence of that application.

Next, the statute requires that the application set out "a full and complete statement of the facts and circumstances relied upon by the applicant to justify his belief that an order should be issued." Certain particulars are then specified in the statute, beginning with "details as to the particular offense that has been, is being, or is about to be committed," which has been interpreted to require only an indication of the general nature of the criminal conduct under investigation rather than a specification of a particular statute. Another requisite particular is "a particular description of the nature and location of the facilities from which or the place where the communication is to be intercepted," which in the case of a wiretap can be met by giving the particular phone number or (if the probable cause showing permits) by referring to all phones at a certain address. Under the so-called "roving tap" provision added in 1986, specification of the facilities or place may be excused upon a particularized showing of need.[8] Still another particular is "a particular description of the type of communications sought to be intercepted," which courts have generally read as requiring no more than an indication of the offense under investigation. In justification, it is said that the actual content need not and cannot be stated since the conversations have not yet taken place at the time the application is made and it is virtually impossible for an applicant to predict exactly what will be said.

The fourth particular, "the identity of the person, if known, committing the offense and whose communications are to be intercepted," has proved a source of difficulty and has twice been considered by the Supreme Court. One question, dealt with in *United States v. Kahn,*[9] concerns just what the obligation of the government is to discover and name the persons to be heard. *Kahn* involved a wiretap to intercept bookmaking-related conversations "of Irving Kahn and others as yet unknown," pursuant to which agents heard calls by Kahn from Arizona to his wife at his Chicago home in which he discussed his gambling wins and

---

7. 416 U.S. 562, 94 S.Ct. 1849, 40 L.Ed.2d 380 (1974).

8. 18 U.S.C.A. § 2518(11) says noncompliance is permitted in the case of oral communications when there is in the application "a full and complete statement as to why such specification is not practical and identifies the person committing the offense and whose communications are to be intercepted" and when also the judge "finds that such specification is not practical." As for wire communications, this provision originally required an adequate showing of a purpose by the person whose communications were to be intercepted "to thwart interception by changing facilities," but by virtue of amendment in 1998 the showing now must be "that there is probable cause to believe that the persons's actions could have the effect of thwarting interception from a specified facility." (This amendment also added a requirement that "the order authorizing or approving the interception is limited to interception only

for such time as it is reasonable to presume that the person identified in the application is or was reasonably proximate to the instrument through which such communication will be or was transmitted.") Illustrative of an oral communication would be a case in which the suspect moves from room to room in a hotel; illustrative of a wire communication would be where a terrorist went from phone booth to phone booth numerous times to avoid interception. Only a limited number of federal officials are authorized to seek this special kind of order. 18 U.S.C.A. § 2518(12) says that if such an order is issued interception is not to begin "until the facilities from which, or the place where, the communication is to be intercepted is ascertained by the person implementing the interception order."

9. 415 U.S. 143, 94 S.Ct. 977, 39 L.Ed.2d 225 (1974).

losses, and calls by his wife to another gambler in which she discussed betting information. The court of appeals held that all of these conversations had to be suppressed—those by the wife because Irving Kahn was not a party, and those by him because the government should have discovered his wife's involvement (meaning she was not an "other, as yet unknown"). The Supreme Court reversed. After concluding that conversations not involving Irving Kahn were covered by the order because it authorized interceptions of conversations "of" (not "between") him "and others," the Court turned to the question of what persons must be identified in the application. Rejecting the lower court's "known or discoverable" test, the Court held "that Title III requires the naming of a person in the application or interception order only when the law enforcement authorities have probable cause to believe that that individual is 'committing the offense' for which the wiretap is sought." Nothing in the statute, the Court concluded, supports "an additional requirement that the Government investigate all persons who may be using the subject telephone in order to determine their possible complicity." The probable cause referred to in *Kahn* goes to the person's name, his involvement in the criminal activity under investigation, and also his use of the phones or facilities to be tapped or bugged. *Kahn* has been read as meaning the authorities need not make even a minimal effort to learn the identity of a person as to whom probable cause regarding complicity and use already exists. Some have criticized *Kahn,* arguing that a better approach would be to impose a standard of reasonable diligence in the attempt to learn each of the elements necessary to the naming of an individual in an application.

The question in *United States v. Donovan*[10] was what the consequences of noncompliance with this part of the statute, as construed in

Kahn, must be. There, government agents lawfully executing a wiretap learned the named individuals were discussing gambling with several other persons, but in obtaining an extension they failed to name these other persons. Though there was probable cause as to these others, so that this was a violation of the statute, the Court held that suppression was nonetheless not required. This was because the "naming" requirement was deemed not to play a "substantive role" in the regulatory scheme, in that even with the omissions "the application provided sufficient information to enable the issuing judge to determine that the statutory preconditions were satisfied." The reasoning was brought into serious question by the three *Donovan* dissenters.[11]

The statute also requires that the application contain "a full and complete statement as to whether or not other investigative procedures have been tried and failed or why they reasonably appear to be unlikely to succeed if tried or to be too dangerous." This is an important part of the legislative scheme. As the Supreme Court has explained, it is designed to assure that that electronic eavesdropping is not "routinely employed as the initial step in criminal investigation"[12] or "resorted to in situations where traditional investigative techniques would suffice to expose the crime."[13] Yet, the requisite showing is not great and is to be tested in a practical and commonsense fashion, and in practice the standard has been watered down to one of investigatory utility, rather than necessity. The showing can be made in any one of three ways. One is by showing the failure of other methods, which need not go so far as to indicate that every conceivable investigatory alternative has been unsuccessfully attempted. The second is by showing other methods are unlikely to succeed, which can be accomplished, for example, by indicating the difficulty in

---

10.   429 U.S. 413, 97 S.Ct. 658, 50 L.Ed.2d 652 (1977).

11.   They noted that "what is at issue here is more than a simple list of names," in that there is another requirement in the statute that the government disclose the history of all prior applications as to the named persons, which "would at the least cause a judge to consider whether the application before him was an at-

tempt to circumvent the restrictive rulings of another judge or to continue an unjustified invasion of privacy."

12.   United States v. Giordano, 416 U.S. 505, 94 S.Ct. 1820, 40 L.Ed.2d 341 (1974).

13.   United States v. Kahn, 415 U.S. 143, 94 S.Ct. 977, 39 L.Ed.2d 225 (1974).

penetrating a particular conspiracy or by asserting that a conventional search warrant would not likely produce incriminating evidence. The third alternative is showing other methods would be too dangerous, either in terms of disclosing the investigation or placing an officer or informant in physical danger.

Title III also requires that the application contain "a statement of the period of time for which the interception is required to be maintained." Moreover, if "the nature of the investigation is such that the authorization for interception should not automatically terminate when the described type of communication has been first obtained," then "a particular description of facts establishing probable cause to believe that additional communications of the same type will occur thereafter" is also required. When the objective is to intercept a particular conversation, it is usually not difficult to state the time period,[14] but most cases are not of that kind. The statute contemplates that where a course of conduct embracing multiple parties and extending over a period of time is involved, the order may properly authorize proportionally longer surveillance. In such circumstances, making the requisite showing has not proved difficult; where there is probable cause of a continuing offense, almost inevitably there is probable cause to believe that there will be more than one relevant conversation.

The application must also include "a full and complete statement of the facts concerning all previous applications known to the individual authorizing and making the application, made to any judge for authorization to intercept, or for approval of interceptions of, wire, oral, or electronic communications involving any of the same persons, facilities or places specified in the application, and the action taken by the judge on each such application." This provision serves to prevent "judge shopping" and also provides the judge with a basis upon which to assess the statements of proba-

ble cause and investigative necessity in the application. If the earlier request was granted, the judge is alerted to inquire why there is a need for further surveillance; if it was denied, the judge is alerted to determine whether its deficiencies carry over to the present application. The "previous applications" provision is central to the statutory scheme, so that a deliberate omission of that information requires suppression of evidence obtained by a warrant issued pursuant to the defective application. It must be emphasized, however, that the provision only requires disclosure of what is "known" by the person authorizing and making the application, and also that it does not cover prior interceptions of the same person pursuant to an application in which that person was not named or required to be named.

The final requirement, applicable only "where the application is for the extension of an order,"[15] is that the application contain "a statement setting forth the results thus far obtained from the interception, or a reasonable explanation of the failure to obtain such results." It is designed to provide the issuing judge with an opportunity to evaluate the actual investigative need for continued electronic surveillance at the time the extension application is presented.

(c) Review of Application. In reviewing a Title III application, the judge "may require the applicant to furnish additional testimony or documentary evidence in support of the application."[16] Though such inquiry is discretionary, resort to it may sometimes be critical, for it provides an informal and expeditious means of curing minor, technical defects, or supplying even a major element omitted by oversight, such as an informant's "track record." Use of the word "testimony" highlights the fact that information in support of any search warrant must be given under oath. A suitable record should be made of it, and the

---

14. See Osborn v. United States, 385 U.S. 323, 87 S.Ct. 429, 17 L.Ed.2d 394 (1966), a pre-Title III case that nonetheless illustrates the point very well.

15. Under 18 U.S.C.A. § 2518(5), extensions may be granted, but only upon an application that meets all the

usual requirements under § 2518(1) and only if the judge makes all the usual findings under § 2518(3).

16. 18 U.S.C.A. § 2518(2).

best practice in this regard is to use a court reporter.

Before a Title III eavesdropping order may be entered by the judge, he must determine on the basis of the facts submitted that

(a) there is probable cause for belief that an individual is committing, has committed, or is about to commit a particular offense enumerated in section 2516 of this chapter;

(b) there is probable cause for belief that particular communications concerning that offense will be obtained through such interception;

(c) normal investigative procedures have been tried and have failed or reasonably appear to be unlikely to succeed if tried or to be too dangerous;

(d) except as provided in subsection (11),[17] there is probable cause for belief that the facilities from which, or the place where, the wire or oral communications are to be intercepted are being used, or are about to be used, in connection with the commission of such offense, or are leased to, listed in the name of, or commonly used by such person.[18]

There is nothing in the statute that requires particular words be used in the requisite finding or indeed that the finding be actually expressed in words rather than by the act of the judge.

Absent a finding of each of the four matters listed in the statute, the judge may not issue the order. But by the statute's use of the word "may," it would appear that the judge has discretion not to issue the order even if such findings can be made. There is not complete agreement, however, as to whether this is so. In any event, denial of an application is appealable[19] but should only be overturned on appeal if it is clearly erroneous.

(d) Contents of Order. A Title III interception order must specify certain matters that go to satisfying the particularity of description requirement of the Fourth Amendment. These are: "(a) the identity of the person, if known, whose communications are to be intercepted; (b) the nature and location of the communications facilities as to which, or the place where, authority to intercept is granted; (c) a particular description of the type of communications sought to be intercepted, and a statement of the particular offense to which it relates."[20] These requirements are comparable to those that exist as to the application, and what was said about them in that context earlier[21] is equally applicable here. The order must also identify the person authorizing the application, as to which the same may be said, and in addition must identify the agency authorized to intercept the communications.[22]

The order must also contain several directives concerning its execution, most of which go to the time of the permitted surveillance. There must be "a provision that the authorization to intercept shall be executed as soon as practicable,"[23] which reflects not only the need for prompt execution before the probable cause information becomes stale[24] but also the fact that eavesdropping devices often cannot be installed as promptly as a conventional warrant may be executed. The order must also specify "the period of time during which such interception is authorized,"[25] which may not be "for any period longer than is necessary to achieve the objective of the authorization, nor in any event longer than thirty days."[26] That specification must include "a statement as to whether or not the interception shall automatically terminate when the described communication has been first obtained."[27] In addition, the order must contain a provision that it "must terminate upon attainment of the authorized objective, or in any event in thirty

---

17. This is a reference to the "roving tap" provision discussed in note 8 supra.

18. 18 U.S.C.A. § 2518(3).

19. 18 U.S.C.A. § 2518(10)(b).

20. 18 U.S.C.A. § 2518(4).

21. See § 4.4(b).

22. 18 U.S.C.A. § 2518(4)(d).

23. 18 U.S.C.A. § 2518(5).

24. See § 3.3(g).

25. 18 U.S.C.A. § 2518(4)(e).

26. 18 U.S.C.A. § 2518(5).

27. 18 U.S.C.A. § 2518(4)(e).

days."[28] Apart from these time limits, the order must also contain a directive that the interception "be conducted in such a way as to minimize the interception of communications not otherwise subject to interception,"[29] and, at the discretion of the court, "may require reports to be made to the judge who issued the order showing what progress has been made toward achievement of the authorized objective and the need for continued interception."[30] These reports constitute an extremely important safeguard when the authorized surveillance is lengthy.

Finally, in a case in which the applicant has so requested, the order is to "direct that a provider of wire or electronic communication service, landlord, custodian, or other person shall furnish the applicant forthwith all information, facilities, and technical assistance necessary to accomplish the interception unobtrusively and with a minimum of interference with the services that such service provider, landlord, custodian, or person is according the person whose communications are to be intercepted."[31] This language was added in 1970 in response to a decision holding that in the absence of such a provision the phone company could not be compelled to cooperate. Similar provisions have been adopted in several states. The Communications Assistance for Law Enforcement Act,[32] adopted in 1994, defines more precisely the assistance that telecommunications carriers are required to provide in connection with court orders for wire and electronic interceptions.

§ 4.5   Title III: Executing the Order

(a) Recording. Execution of a Title III order has no functional or theoretical equivalent in traditional search warrant law. The traditional warrant typically is served very promptly, is executed in a brief period of time, results in the seizure of a few objects, and by its observed execution or receipt of an inventory assures that the subject of the search is promptly made aware of the search and what was seized. By contrast, a Title III order often cannot be executed very promptly, is likely to be executed over a considerable span of time, usually results in the interception of many communications, and is executed secretly and thus without the subject of the search being aware of it or of what had been seized. For this reason, certain special requirements have understandably been imposed by statute with respect to execution of Title III orders.

One such requirement is that the contents of any intercepted communication "shall, if possible, be recorded on tape or wire or other comparable device * * * in such way as will protect the recording from editing or other alterations."[1] The purpose of this requirement is to ensure that an accurate record of the conversation is made in the first instance and not altered in the interim before its use. This means that monitoring agents should record everything overheard by them, whether or not it is deemed pertinent.

(b) Minimization. One very important provision in Title III requires that an interception order be executed "in such a way as to minimize the interception of communications not otherwise subject to interception under this chapter."[2] This minimization duty implements a constitutional prerequisite to the va-

---

28. 18 U.S.C.A. § 2518(5).

By 1986 amendment to this provision, the 30 days "begins on the earlier of the day on which the investigator or law enforcement officer first begins to conduct an interception under the order or ten days after the order is entered."

29. 18 U.S.C.A. § 2518(5).

30. 18 U.S.C.A. § 2518(6), also stating these reports "shall be made at such intervals as the judge may require."

31. 18 U.S.C.A. § 2518(4), also providing: "Any provider of wire or electronic communication service, landlord, custodian or other person furnishing such facilities or technical assistance shall be compensated therefor by the applicant at the prevailing rates."

32. 47 U.S.C.A. §§ 1001–1110; 18 U.S.C.A. § 2522.

§ 4.5

1. 18 U.S.C.A. § 2518(8)(a).

2. 18 U.S.C.A. § 2518(5).

A 1986 amendment to this section adds: "In the event the intercepted communication is in a code or foreign language, and an expert in that foreign language or code is not reasonably available during the interception period, minimization may be accomplished as soon as practicable after such interception. An interception under this chapter may be conducted in whole or part by Government person-

lidity of all court-ordered electronic surveillance, for the Supreme Court, in striking down the New York eavesdropping statute in *Berger v. New York*,[3] deemed that statute to permit unconstitutional general searches because it allowed seizure of "the conversations of any and all persons coming into the area covered by the device * * * indiscriminately and without regard to their connection to the crime under investigation."

What is to be minimized is the interpretation of "communications not otherwise subject to interception" under Title III, which appears to mean communications other than those "concerning" the offense that was the basis of the order.[4] This suggests that a communication is pertinent and thus not subject to the minimization limitation if it in some respect provides information helpful to the investigation, without regard to whether it includes an incriminating remark directly implicating the speaker in criminal activity. As for the other, nonpertinent communications, it must be emphasized that the statute does not forbid their interception, but merely requires that measures be adopted to reduce the extent of such interception to a practical minimum.

In determining whether the surveying agents sufficiently complied with the minimization requirement, it is necessary to assess the facts of the particular case. The Supreme Court has had one occasion to make such an assessment, in *Scott v. United States*.[5] There, government agents intercepted for a one-month period virtually all conversations over a particular telephone suspected of being used in furtherance of a conspiracy to import and distribute narcotics, though only forty percent of those conversations were shown to be narcotics related. In the course of concluding that the minimization requirement had not been violated, the Court enumerated a number of factors that are to be taken into account in deciding the minimization issue:

[B]lind reliance on the percentage of nonpertinent calls intercepted is not a sure guide to the correct answer. Such percentages may provide assistance, but there are surely cases, such as the one at bar, where the percentage of nonpertinent calls is relatively high and yet their interception was still reasonable. The reasons for this may be many. Many of the nonpertinent calls may have been very short. Others may have been one-time only calls. Still other calls may have been ambiguous in nature or apparently involved guarded or coded language. In all these circumstances agents can hardly be expected to know that the calls are not pertinent prior to their termination.

In determining whether the agents properly minimized, it is also important to consider the circumstances of the wiretap. For example, when the investigation is focusing on what is thought to be a widespread conspiracy more extensive surveillance may be justified in an attempt to determine the precise scope of the enterprise. And it is possible that many more of the conversations will be permissibly interceptable because they will involve one or more of the co-conspirators. The type of use to which the telephone is normally put may also have some bearing on the extent of minimization required. For example, if the agents are permitted to tap a public telephone because one individual is thought to be placing bets over the phone, substantial doubts as to minimization may arise if the agents listen to every call which goes out over that phone regardless of who places the call. On the other hand, if the phone is located in the residence of a person who is thought to be the head of a major drug ring, a contrary conclusion may be indicated.

Other factors may also play a significant part in a particular case. For example, it

nel, or by an individual operating under a contract with the Government, acting under the supervision of an investigative or law enforcement officer authorized to conduct the interception." Under the first sentence, says the legislative history, the translator or decoder will listen to tapes and make available to investigators the minimized portions and preserve the rest for possible court perusal later.

The last sentence added is intended to free FBI agents from the routine activity of monitoring.

3.   388 U.S. 41, 87 S.Ct. 1873, 18 L.Ed.2d 1040 (1967).

4.   That is the nature of the probable cause determination under 18 U.S.C.A. § 2518(3)(b).

5.   436 U.S. 128, 98 S.Ct. 1717, 56 L.Ed.2d 168 (1978).

may be important to determine at exactly what point during the authorized period the interception was made. During the early stages of surveillance the agents may be forced to intercept all calls to establish categories of nonpertinent calls which will not be intercepted thereafter. Interception of those same types of calls might be unreasonable later on, however, once the nonpertinent categories have been established and it is clear that this particular conversation is of that type. Other situations may arise where patterns of nonpertinent calls do not appear. In these circumstances it may not be unreasonable to intercept almost every short conversation because the determination of relevancy cannot be made before the call is completed.

In the instant case, the Court reasoned, most of the 60% of the calls that turned out not to be material to the narcotics investigation were either "very short," "ambiguous in nature," or "one-time conversations" that fit into no previously established category, and thus there had been no minimization violation.

A more controversial aspect of the *Scott* case concerns the fact that the district court had found the surveilling agents "made no attempt to comply" with a minimization requirement and had concluded that this standing alone was a basis for suppression. The Supreme Court rejected that position in favor of the notion that "[s]ubjective intent alone * * * does not make otherwise lawful conduct illegal or unconstitutional," meaning that the officers' presumed failure to make even a good-faith effort to comply with the minimization requirement was not itself a reason for excluding the evidence obtained. The Court asserted this was sound Fourth Amendment doctrine and also good Title III law.

(c) Amendment and Extension. It is necessary to distinguish the Title III procedures for extension of an eavesdropping order from those dealing with what amounts to a retro-

spective amendment of a prior order. As for extension, this is possible only upon an application that meets the usual requirements and only after the court makes the findings usually required before an interception order may issue.[6] "The period of extension shall be no longer than the authorizing judge deems necessary to achieve the purposes for which it was granted and in no event for longer than thirty days,"[7] but there is no prohibition on obtaining successive extensions of the same original order. The statute does not require by its own terms a fresh showing of probable cause in the extension application, but it has been suggested that such a showing is essential in light of the *Berger v. New York*[8] prohibition upon protracted electronic searches upon a single showing of probable cause.

When officers are conducting a court-ordered surveillance under Title III with respect to one particular crime, they will sometimes intercept conversations that refer to or are evidence of some other type of crime. The contents of such communications are for some purposes treated just like the contents of communications of the type named in the order[9]; that is, an officer with authorized knowledge of them may use them "to the extent such use is appropriate to the proper performance of his official duties"[10] and also "may disclose such contents to another investigative or law enforcement officer to the extent that such disclosure is appropriate to the proper performance of the official duties of the officer making or receiving the disclosure."[11] But, the contents of these communications concerning other crimes may be testified to in a federal or state proceeding only if a judge finds upon subsequent application, "made as soon as practicable," that "the contents were otherwise intercepted in accordance with the provisions of this chapter."[12] This latter situation does not include instances in which these contents are merely set out and sworn to in an

6.   18 U.S.C.A. § 2518(5).

7.   Ibid.

8.   388 U.S. 41, 87 S.Ct. 1873, 18 L.Ed.2d 1040 (1967).

9.   18 U.S.C.A. § 2517(5).

10.   18 U.S.C.A. § 2517(2).

11.   18 U.S.C.A. § 2517(1).

12.   18 U.S.C.A. § 2517(5).

application for another Title III order or in a complaint for an arrest warrant.

Though the statute does not state what is to appear in the amendment application, the legislative history indicates it should include a showing that the original order was lawfully obtained, that it was sought in good faith and not as subterfuge search, and that the communication was in fact incidentally intercepted during the course of a lawfully executed order. The courts have not been very demanding with respect to the "as soon as practicable" timing limitation on an amendment application, but these cases have been criticized on the ground they disregard the principle of ongoing judicial supervision embodied in that part of the Act.

(d) Post–Surveillance Notice. Title III also provides that certain persons are to receive post-surveillance notice that the surveillance occurred. The judge is required to serve this notice "[w]ithin a reasonable time but not later than ninety days after the filing of an application for an order of approval * * * which is denied or the termination of the period of an order or extensions thereof," except that upon "an ex parte showing of good cause to a judge of competent jurisdiction the serving of the inventory required by this subsection may be postponed."[13] The "reasonable time" requirement has been broadly construed. As for the "good cause" for postponement, it has been held to include such reasons as protecting the integrity of an ongoing investigation or ensuring that persons would not flee to avoid arrest.

By statute, this notice is to include "(1) the fact of the entry of the order or the application; (2) the date of the entry and the period of authorized, approved or disapproved interception, or the denial of the application; and (3) the fact that during the period wire, oral, or electronic communications were or were not intercepted."[14] The notice is to be served "on the persons named in the order or the application, and such other parties to intercepted communications as the judge may determine

in his discretion that is in the interest of justice."[15] This in no event covers a person who is merely identified in the communications of another, and as to parties to communications not named in the order or application appellate courts have been disinclined to question the discretion exercised by the judge in deciding which of them should receive notice. Because "a judge is likely to require information and assistance beyond that contained in the application papers and the recordings of intercepted conversations made available by law enforcement authorities" in order to exercise his discretion intelligently, the Supreme Court concluded in *United States v. Donovan*[16] that those authorities have a "routine duty to supply the judge with relevant information." Specifically,

> the judicial officer must have, at a minimum, knowledge of the particular categories into which fall all the individuals whose conversations have been intercepted. Thus, while precise identification of each party to an intercepted conversation is not required, a description of the general class, or classes, which they comprise is essential to enable the judge to determine whether additional information is necessary for a proper evaluation of the interests of the various parties. Furthermore, although the judicial officer has the duty to cause the filing of the inventory [notice], it is abundantly clear that the prosecution has greater access to and familiarity with the intercepted communications. Therefore we feel justified in imposing upon the latter the duty to classify all those whose conversations have been intercepted, and to transmit this information to the judge. Should the judge desire more information regarding these classes in order to exercise his [statutory] * * * discretion, * * * the government is [also] required to furnish such information as is available to it.

In *Donovan,* where two names had been omitted from the list and those individuals thus did not receive notice until they were

---

13.   18 U.S.C.A. § 2518(8)(d).

14.   18 U.S.C.A. § 2518(8)(d).

15.   18 U.S.C.A. § 2518(8)(d).

16.   429 U.S. 413, 97 S.Ct. 658, 50 L.Ed.2d 652 (1977).

indicted eight months later,[17] the Court held this did not require suppression because Congress did not mean for "post intercept notice * * * to serve as an independent restraint on resort to the wiretap procedure." The *Donovan* Court emphasized that the omission was inadvertent and had not prejudiced the defendants, which has been taken to mean that suppression is required if names are deliberately withheld or if prejudice resulted from lack of timely notice. Courts are generally disinclined to find that a defendant has established prejudice, but it would seem prejudice exists when the conversation is not inherently incriminating but is subject to explanation and interpretation and the delay in notice has diminished the speaker's opportunity to marshal his explanations.

(e) Sealing. Title III also requires that "the contents of any wire, oral, or electronic communication intercepted by any means authorized by this chapter shall, if possible, be recorded on tape or wire or other comparable device" and that such recording "be done in such way as will protect the recording from editing or other alterations."[18] It further provides that "immediately upon the expiration of the period of the order, or extension thereof, such recordings shall be made available to the judge issuing such order and sealed under his direction."[19] This sealing requirement, the Supreme Court has noted, "is to ensure the reliability and integrity of evidence obtained by means of electronic surveillance"; "the seal is a means of ensuring that subsequent to its placement on tape, the Government has no opportunity to tamper with, alter, or edit the conversations that have been recorded."[20]

The Title III sealing requirement has an explicit exclusionary remedy for noncompliance. It provides that "the presence of the seal provided for by this subsection, or a satisfacto-

ry explanation for the absence thereof, shall be a prerequisite for the use or disclosure of the contents of any wire, oral, or electronic communication or evidence derived therefrom."[21] This provision was construed in *United States v. Ojeda Rios*,[22] where the Court held: (1) that the requirement is not that of "just any seal but a seal that has been obtained *immediately* upon expiration of the underlying surveillance order"; (2) that consequently the "absence" the Government must explain "encompasses not only the total absence of a seal but also the absence of a timely applied seal"; (3) that the required "satisfactory explanation" requires "that the Government explain not only why such a delay occurred but also why it is excusable"; and (4) that the Government may establish a reasonable excuse for delay by showing reliance upon an erroneous interpretation of Title III that "was objectively reasonable at the time."

§ 4.6   Title III: Remedies

(a) Violations Requiring Exclusion. If a particular instance of electronic eavesdropping does not meet the requirements of the Fourth Amendment, then of course the judicially-created exclusionary rule for that Amendment comes into play,[1] in which case what is said elsewhere herein about the dimensions of that rule is applicable. Of concern here, by contrast, is the statutory exclusionary rule of Title III. The statute at one point declares that no information derived from eavesdropping "may be received in evidence in any trial, hearing, or other proceeding * * * if the disclosure of that information would be in violation of this chapter."[2] This language is somewhat misleading, and it has been properly suggested that it should be read as requiring the exclusion of evidence the *seizure* of which was in violation of the chapter. In any event, more attention

---

17. Notice was then given to them as a party to the forthcoming trial, as provided in 18 U.S.C.A. § 2518(9).

18. 18 U.S.C.A. § 2518(8)(a).

19. 18 U.S.C.A. § 2518(8)(a).

20. United States v. Ojeda Rios, 495 U.S. 257, 110 S.Ct. 1845, 109 L.Ed.2d 224 (1990).

21. 18 U.S.C.A. § 2518(8)(a).

22. 495 U.S. 257, 110 S.Ct. 1845, 109 L.Ed.2d 224 (1990).

§ 4.6

1. Berger v. New York, 388 U.S. 41, 87 S.Ct. 1873, 18 L.Ed.2d 1040 (1967).

2. 18 U.S.C.A. § 2515. Such seemingly absolute language has not been deemed to bar admission of such information for impeachment purposes.

has been focused upon the wording of another provision to the effect that a suppression motion may be made "on the grounds that (i) the communication was unlawfully intercepted; (ii) the order of authorization or approval under which it was intercepted is insufficient on its face; or (iii) the interception was not made in conformity with the order of authorization or approval."[3]

Because the Fourth Amendment exclusionary rule "was intended as a restraint upon the activities of sovereign authority and was not intended to be a limitation upon other than governmental agencies,"[4] it has no application to purely private searches.[5] Some courts have reasoned that the same should be true when the conduct objected to is eavesdropping or wiretapping, and thus have held that the Title III exclusionary rule likewise applies only to governmental searches. But the Title III exclusionary rule expresses no such limitation, and thus several other courts have held it is also applicable to private searches otherwise covered by that legislation.

In 1986, Title III was substantially amended so as to also cover the interception of any "electronic communication," defined as "any transfer of signs, signals, writing, images, sounds, data, or intelligence of any nature transmitted in whole or in part by a wire, radio, electromagnetic, photoelectronic or photooptical system that affects interstate or foreign commerce."[6] However, neither of the two exclusionary rule provisions quoted above was amended, so that both continue to be limited only to violations having to do with wire or oral communications.[7] This was no oversight. A new provision states that the "remedies and sanctions described in this chapter with respect to the interception of electronic communications are the only judicial remedies and sanctions for nonconstitutional violations of this chapter involving such communications."[8] The legislative history expressly declares that the Title III statutory exclusionary rule has no application to the interception of electronic communications, but no rationale for this curious distinction is given.

In *United States v. Giordano*,[9] the government argued that the phrase "unlawfully intercepted" in that provision meant only an interception obtained in violation of the Constitution. The Supreme Court rejected that contention and concluded from the legislative history that "Congress intended to require suppression where there is failure to satisfy any of those statutory requirements that directly and substantially implement the congressional intention to limit the use of intercept procedures to those situations clearly calling for the employment of this extraordinary investigative device." As the Court put it later in *Giordano,* suppression under this statutory exclusionary rule is required whenever the particular statutory provision violated "was intended to play a central role in the statutory scheme." This obviously means, as the Court noted in the companion case of *United States v. Chavez*,[10] "that paragraph (i) was not intended to reach every failure to follow statutory procedures."

Giordano supplies a useful illustration of how the "central role" test is to be applied. At issue there was a failure to comply with the statutory requirement that the "Attorney General, or any Assistant Attorney General specifically designated by the Attorney General" must authorize application for a federal surveillance order.[11] That requirement, the Court concluded, did play a "central role" because the statute reflected a Congressional intent to limit eavesdropping not merely by a

3. 18 U.S.C.A. § 2518(10)(a).
4. Burdeau v. McDowell, 256 U.S. 465, 41 S.Ct. 574, 65 L.Ed. 1048 (1921).
5. See § 3.1(h).
6. 18 U.S.C.A. § 2510(12).
7. For definition of these terms, see § 4.3(a).
8. 18 U.S.C.A. § 2518(10)(c).
9. 416 U.S. 505, 94 S.Ct. 1820, 40 L.Ed.2d 341 (1974).
10. 416 U.S. 562, 94 S.Ct. 1849, 40 L.Ed.2d 380 (1974).

11. 18 U.S.C.A. § 2516(1). This provision was amended in 1984 to also include the Deputy Attorney General; in 1986 to also include any Assistant Attorney General and any acting Assistant Attorney General, plus any Deputy Assistant Attorney General in the Criminal Division designated by the Attorney General; and in 1994 to also include any Acting Deputy Assistant Attorney General in the Criminal Division designated by the Attorney General.

probable cause requirement and a nature-of-offense limitation but also by having "a senior official in the Department of Justice" decide that the situation was one warranting resort to such surveillance. But it was "reasonable to believe that such a precondition would inevitably foreclose resort to wiretapping in various situations where investigative personnel would otherwise seek intercept authority from the court and the court would very likely authorize its use," this precondition was unquestionably central to the statutory scheme.

By comparison, in *Chavez* the Court concluded that the misidentification of the authorizing official in the application and order "did not affect the fulfillment of any of the reviewing or approval functions required by Congress" because the statutory provisions thereby violated do "not establish a substantive role to be played in the regulatory system." (Four members of the Court, dissenting in *Chavez*, persuasively argued that these identification requirements were central to the intention of Congress to attach "personal responsibility and political accountability" to the person actually giving the approval.) And in *United States v. Donovan*,[12] where the violation was the failure to include in the application the names of all persons as to whom there was probable cause and who were likely to be overheard, the Court concluded *Chavez* rather than *Giordano* was controlling. This was because the missing information would not "have precluded judicial authorization of the intercept," and even without that information "the application provided sufficient information to enable the issuing judge to determine that the statutory preconditions were satisfied." (There were three dissenters in *Donovan*, who cogently noted that the requirement of naming all such persons was very important in the statutory scheme and could affect whether the judge issued the warrant, for the government would also have to disclose the history of prior applications as to the named persons, which would "at the least cause a judge to consider whether the application before him was an attempt to circumvent the restrictive rulings

of another judge or to continue an unjustified invasion of privacy.")

As for the "insufficient on its face" test of paragraph (ii), it was also addressed in *Chavez*. The Court concluded, in effect, that it applies only when the order can be determined to be insufficient without resort to other facts. Thus, because in that case the order did identify a person as having authorized the application who had the authority to give such authorization, the fact it was subsequently shown he actually did not give the requisite approval "does not detract from the facial sufficiency of the order." By like reasoning, it was concluded in *Donovan* that the failure to have a complete list of persons in the order did not make the order "insufficient on its face," for again this was not apparent from the order itself. As for the paragraph (iii) "not made in conformity" test, the Court in *Giordano* observed it concerns only "the manner of conducting the court-approved interceptions" and thus was not in issue there.

One final problem, addressed in another branch of the *Donovan* case, needs to be specially noted. The government in that case also failed to inform the judge of all identifiable persons whose conversations were intercepted, thus making it impossible for the judge to exercise fully his discretionary authority to decide what parties should receive notice. In concluding that violation did not require suppression, the Court reasoned:

> Nothing in the structure of the Act or this legislative history suggests that incriminating conversations are "unlawfully intercepted" whenever parties to those conversations do not receive discretionary inventory notice as a result of the Government's failure to inform the District Court of their identities. At the time inventory notice was served on the other identifiable persons, the intercept had been completed and the conversations had been "seized" under a valid intercept order. The fact that discretionary notice reached 39 rather than 41 identifiable persons does not in itself mean that the conversations were unlawfully intercepted.

12. 429 U.S. 413, 97 S.Ct. 658, 50 L.Ed.2d 652 (1977).

One way to read that paragraph is as just another illustration of the "central role" test being used to admit evidence notwithstanding the statutory violation. But another plausible reading, especially in light of the Court's recognition that there remained open the question whether "suppression might be required if the agents knew before the interception that no inventory would be served," is that any noncompliance subsequent to a lawful interception, no matter how serious, cannot operate to retroactively invalidate the prior interception. This would mean, for example, that if the government *deliberately* withheld names from the judge or if the withholding actually prejudiced a person who thereby was deprived of timely notice, there would still be no suppression under the statute. Though this result is arguably supported by a literal reading of the statute, it is well to note that the legislation does not even cover the post-interception violation that *is* prejudicial. It thus may be that courts are empowered to exclude evidence, even beyond what is provided for in the Title III exclusionary rule, when they do so for the purpose of overcoming prejudice. Whether it follows that courts may also do so for the purpose of deterring deliberate statutory violations is another matter. The Court in *Donovan* appears to have left these issues open by carefully noting that the defendants made no claim of prejudice and also that the violation was unintentional, so that it was "not called upon to decide whether suppression would be an available remedy if the Government knowingly sought to prevent the District Court from serving inventory notice on particular parties."

(b) Who May Exclude When. The subject of Fourth Amendment standing, including the ruling in *Alderman v. United States*[13] that in an eavesdropping case the parties to the conversation and the persons with a possessory interest in the place where the conversation occurs all have standing, is discussed elsewhere herein.[14] Of concern here is Title III standing. The statute says that any "aggrieved

person" may move for suppression,[15] and that term is defined as meaning "a person who was a party to any intercepted wire, oral, or electronic communication or a person against whom the interception was directed."[16] Read literally, this definition would seem to be narrower in some respects and broader in some respects than Fourth Amendment standing; it seems to leave out the person with the possessory interest in the place surveilled and to include the target of the surveillance who was neither that person nor one of the speakers. But, as the Court noted in *Alderman,* the legislative history shows this definition was intended "to reflect existing law," and thus the Court there concluded Congress had not extended the exclusionary rule. Thus, courts are inclined to define Title III standing as being exactly the same as Fourth Amendment standing, and even take into account developments in the Fourth Amendment area that have occurred after enactment of Title III. This is not to suggest that the Title III exclusionary rule has the same dimensions as the Fourth Amendment exclusionary rule; for example, its exclusionary rule also extends to evidence falling into the government's hands after a private search.

There is another way, however, in which the Fourth Amendment exclusionary rule and the Title III exclusionary rule are unquestionably different. The former, as a creature of the Supreme Court, can be applied in such circumstance as the Court believes will further its objectives.[17] Thus, while it applies at a criminal trial, it does not inevitably apply in other proceedings, as is best illustrated by *United States v. Calandra*.[18] There, the Court refused to allow a grand jury witness to invoke the exclusionary rule, reasoning that a contrary result "would achieve a speculative and undoubtedly minimal advance in the deterrence of police misconduct at the expense of substantially impeding the role of the grand jury." But the Title III exclusionary rule, by virtue of the statute, applies "in any trial, hearing, or pro-

---

13. 394 U.S. 165, 89 S.Ct. 961, 22 L.Ed.2d 176 (1969).

14. See § 9.1(b).

15. 18 U.S.C.A. § 2518(10)(a).

16. 18 U.S.C.A. § 2510(11).

17. See § 3.2(f), (g).

18. 414 U.S. 338, 94 S.Ct. 613, 38 L.Ed.2d 561 (1974).

ceeding in or before any court, department, officer, agency, regulatory body, or other authority of the United States, a State, or a political subdivision thereof."[19] This means, for example, that the Title III exclusionary rule may be invoked by a party in a bail hearing, a parole revocation proceeding, or a police department disciplinary proceeding.

The legislative·history of the language quoted above unequivocally states that "[b]ecause no person is a party as such to a grand jury proceeding, the provision does not envision the making of a motion to suppress in the context of such a proceeding itself," but only that if a motion to suppress is granted in another context "its scope may include use in a future grand jury proceeding."[20] This means, for example, that a prospective defendant cannot merely by virtue of that status invoke the Title III exclusionary rule before the grand jury considering his case. But in *Gelbard v. United States*,[21] the Court held that a grand jury witness may refuse to testify where his testimony is sought on the basis of illegal electronic surveillance. This is because, the Court explained, that testimony would constitute "evidence derived" from violation of Title III, and another part of the Act expressly provides that such evidence may not "be received in evidence in any trial, hearing, or other proceeding in or before any court, *grand jury,* department, officer, agency, regulatory body, legislative committee, or other authority of the United States, a State, or a political subdivision thereof."[22] The Court reasoned that if that prohibition was "not available as a defense to the contempt charge, disclosure through compelled testimony makes the witness the victim, once again, of a federal crime."

It is important to note that *Gelbard* was a 5–4 decision and that a majority was achieved only with the concurring opinion of Justice White. He agreed that "at least where the United States has intercepted communications without a warrant in circumstances where court approval was required, it is appropriate

* * * not to require the grand jury witness to answer and hence further the plain policy of the wiretap statute." But he suggested a different result would obtain "where the Government produces a court order for the interception" but "the witness nevertheless demands a full-blown suppression hearing to determine the legality of the order":

> Suppression hearings in these circumstances would result in protracted interruption of grand jury proceedings. At the same time prosecutors and other officers who have been granted and relied on a court order for the interception would be subject to no liability under the statute, whether the order is valid or not; and, in any event, the deterrent value of excluding the evidence will be marginal at best.

(c) Disclosure of Illegal Electronic Surveillance. After enacting Title III, Congress recognized that victims of illegal wiretapping might have grounds to suspect, but yet have difficulty proving, that wiretapping had occurred. It thus enacted a provision[23] that in "any trial, hearing, or other proceeding in or before any court, grand jury, department, officer, agency, regulatory body, or other authority of the United States," upon a claim by "a party aggrieved" that the evidence is inadmissible as the fruit of an "unlawful act," "the opponent of the claim shall affirm or deny the occurrence of the alleged unlawful act."

In order to put the government to the task of responding, the aggrieved party must articulate a colorable basis for his claim of surveillance. Once that burden has been met, the government must make a factual, unambiguous, and unequivocal response. Something more than a purely conclusory denial of surveillance is required, but precisely what will suffice may vary from case to case. This is because the more specific the defendant's claim of surveillance, the more detailed and extensive must be the government's response.

19.   18 U.S.C.A. § 2518(10)(a).

20.   S.Rep. No. 1097, 90th Cong., 2d Sess. 106 (1968).

21.   408 U.S. 41, 92 S.Ct. 2357, 33 L.Ed.2d 179 (1972).

22.   18 U.S.C.A. § 2515 (emphasis added).

23.   18 U.S.C.A. § 3504(a)(1).

The response by the government must normally be in the form of sworn testimony or an affidavit. This response, which ordinarily will come from the prosecutor, must indicate the results of his inquiry of all appropriate investigative agencies to determine if any of them have conducted surveillance of the complaining party. The cases require that the prosecutor or the primary investigating agency submit an affidavit, but impose no affidavit requirement upon the various agencies responding to a request to check their records. The assumption is that responses to such requests, signed by responsible officials with obvious awareness that their replies are to be submitted in court proceedings, suffice to permit the court to determine compliance with the statute.

(d) Disclosure of Electronic Surveillance Records. Under Title III, suppression is provided for not only as to the contents of an illegally intercepted wire or oral communication, but also as to "evidence derived therefrom."[24] This naturally raises the question of what procedures are required to facilitate a determination whether other evidence is the fruit of such a surveillance. The statute merely provides that if a suppression motion is made, then the judge "may in his discretion make available to the aggrieved person or his counsel for inspection such portions of the intercepted communication or evidence derived therefrom as the judge determines to be in the interests of justice."

The issue reached the Supreme Court in 1969 in a series of cases not involving Title III: *Alderman v. United States, Ivanov v. United States,* and *Butenko v. United States.*[25] *Alderman* concerned convictions for conspiring to transmit murderous threats in interstate commerce, while the other cases involved convictions for transmitting national defense information to the Soviet Union. The defendants sought disclosure of all surveillance records so that they might show that some of the evidence admitted against them grew out of illegally overheard conversations. The government urged that in order to protect innocent third parties participating or referred to in irrelevant conversations overheard by the government, surveillance records should first be subjected to in camera inspection by the trial judge. He would then turn over to defendants and their counsel only those materials "arguably relevant" to defendants' convictions, in the sense that the overheard conversations arguably underlay some items of evidence offered at trial.

The Court, in a 5–3 decision, held that a defendant should receive *all* surveillance records as to which he has standing. The government's proposal was rejected on the ground that the trial judge often would not be in a position to determine what conversations were relevant:

> An apparently innocent phrase, a chance remark, a reference to what appears to be a neutral person or event, the identity of a caller or the individual on the other end of a telephone, or even the manner of speaking or using words may have special significance to one who knows the more intimate facts of an accused's life. And yet that information may be wholly colorless and devoid of meaning to one less well acquainted with all relevant circumstances. Unavoidably, this is a matter of judgment, but in our view the task is too complex, and the margin for error too great, to rely wholly on the *in camera* judgment of the trial court to identify those records which might have contributed to the Government's case.

To protect innocent third parties, the Court added, the trial court could place defendants and counsel under enforceable orders against unwarranted disclosure of the materials they would be entitled to inspect.

Justice Fortas, dissenting in part in *Alderman,* argued that the in camera screening procedure should be followed when the trial judge makes written and sealed findings "that disclosure would substantially injure national security interests." In his dissent, Justice Harlan subscribed to a narrower view that such screening would be appropriate whenever the defendant is charged with spying for a foreign

24. 18 U.S.C.A. § 2518(10)(a).

25. 394 U.S. 165, 89 S.Ct. 961, 22 L.Ed.2d 176 (1969).

power, in which case protective orders would not deter disclosure to others and the location of listening devices crucial to espionage work would otherwise be needlessly disclosed. In an unsuccessful petition for rehearing, the Attorney General argued against disclosure of records of surveillance activities to gather "foreign intelligence information" on the ground that such activity was practiced by all nations and thus not unreasonable.

Giordano v. United States[26] emphasized that disclosure under *Alderman* was available only to one who "has standing to assert the illegality of the surveillance" and that "a finding by the District Court that the surveillance was lawful would make disclosure and further proceedings unnecessary." And in *Taglianetti v. United States*,[27] the Court rejected defendant's contention that he was entitled to examine additional surveillance records to establish that he might be a party to some other conversations. Distinguishing *Alderman,* the Court concluded that the trial judge could be expected to identify defendant's voice without the defendant's assistance.

By statute, Congress has attempted to limit the impact of *Alderman* in the federal courts. For one thing, records of an unlawful surveillance that occurred prior to the enactment of Title III need not be disclosed "unless such information may be relevant to a pending claim of * * * inadmissibility,"[28] which presumably is to be determined by the judge in camera. For another, on the legislative finding that "there is virtually no likelihood" that evidence offered to prove an event would have been obtained by exploitation of an unlawful surveillance occurring more than five years prior to that event, no such claim is to be considered.[29] The constitutionality of these provisions is open to some doubt, as the *Alderman* decision was cast in terms of "the scrutiny which the Fourth Amendment exclusionary rule demands."

(e) Civil Remedies. Title III expressly provides that "any person whose wire, oral, or electronic communication is intercepted, disclosed,[30] or intentionally used in violation of this chapter may in a civil action recover from the person or entity that engaged in that violation" appropriate relief, including: appropriate equitable or declaratory relief; damages and punitive damages in appropriate cases; and a reasonable attorney's fee and other reasonable litigation costs.[31] The damages may be the greater of the sum of the plaintiff's actual damages and the violator's resulting profits, or statutory damages of the greater of $100 a day or $10,000. Good faith reliance on a court warrant or order, grand jury subpoena, legislative authorization, or request of a law enforcement officer is a defense. Any willful violation of the provisions on interception and disclosure of wire, oral or electronic communications or on access to stored communications provides the basis for a civil action against the United States to collect money damages of $10,000 or actual damages, whichever is greater, plus reasonable litigation costs.[32] Where there are "serious questions" about whether an officer or employee of the U.S. acted willfully or intentionally in that regard, an investigation must promptly be initiated to determine whether disciplinary action is warranted.[33]

(f) Criminal Penalties. Title III makes it a crime for a person, except as permitted by the statute, to "intentionally" intercept, endeavor to intercept, or procure another to intercept or endeavor to intercept a communication; to "intentionally" disclose or endeavor to disclose to another the contents of a communication "knowing or having reason to know"

---

26. 394 U.S. 310, 89 S.Ct. 1163, 22 L.Ed.2d 297 (1969).

27. 394 U.S. 316, 89 S.Ct. 1099, 22 L.Ed.2d 302 (1969).

28. 18 U.S.C.A. § 3504.

29. Ibid.

30. In Bartnicki v. Vopper, 532 U.S. 514, 121 S.Ct. 1753, 149 L.Ed.2d 787 (2001), a civil damage action for violation of Title III, the Court held that the prohibition on disclosure constitutes a regulation of speech protected by the First Amendment under the presumed facts of this case, where a radio commentator played a tape of conversation he had reason to know were unlawfully intercepted, where he played no part in the illegal interception, his access to the information was obtained lawfully, and the conversations dealt with a matter of public concern.

31. 18 U.S.C.A. § 2520.

32. 18 U.S.C.A. § 2712(a).

33. 18 U.S.C.A. § 2520(f).

that it was obtained by an illegal interception; or to "intentionally" use or endeavor to use the contents of a communication "knowing or having reason to know" that it was obtained by an illegal interception.[34] The "intentionally" mental state was substituted for "willfully" in 1986 to emphasize that inadvertent interception is not criminal. Under this provision, a person acts intentionally if his conduct or the result thereof was his conscious objective. The previously mentioned "good faith reliance" defense[35] is also available in a criminal prosecution. With limited exceptions, a person convicted of this offense may be fined, imprisoned not more than five years, or both.[36] Another provision with like penalties makes it a crime to possess, manufacture, distribute, advertise or mail "any electronic, mechanical, or other device, knowing or having reason to know that the design of such device renders it primarily useful for the purpose of the surreptitious interception of wire, oral, or electronic communication."[37] Exceptions are provided for law enforcement agents and their suppliers and for providers of wire or electronic communication service and their agents.[38]

34. 18 U.S.C.A. § 2511(1).
35. 18 U.S.C.A. § 2518(10)(a).
36. 18 U.S.C.A. § 2511(4)(a).

37. 18 U.S.C.A. § 2512(1).
38. 18 U.S.C.A. § 2512(2).

Chapter 5

POLICE "ENCOURAGEMENT" AND THE ENTRAPMENT DEFENSE

Table of Sections

§ 5.1 Encouragement of Crime and the Defense of Entrapment

(a) Encouragement of Criminal Activity. Certain criminal offenses present the police with unique and difficult detection problems because they are committed privately between individuals who are willing participants. Consequently, in addition to employing search and seizure techniques, routine and electronic surveillance, and informants to expose such consensual crime, law enforcement officers actually encourage commission of these offenses. At the heart of the encouragement practice is the need to simulate reality. An environment is created in which the suspect is presented with an opportunity to commit a crime. The simulation of reality must be accurate enough to induce the criminal activity at the point in time when the agents are in a position to gather evidence of the crime.

The tactics used vary from case to case. Some solicitations are innocuous, but since persons engaged in criminal activity are generally suspicious of strangers, government agents typically do more than simply approach a target and request the commission of a crime. Multiple requests or the formation of personal relationships with a subject may be necessary to overcome that suspicion. In addition, appeals to personal considerations, representations of benefits to be derived from the offense, and actual assistance in obtaining contraband or planning the details of the crime are frequently employed.

(b) Entrapment Defense as a Limit. The more extreme forms of encouragement activity

298

are a matter of legitimate concern for a variety of reasons. Of central concern is the possibility that the encouragement might induce a person who otherwise would be law-abiding to engage in criminal conduct. Yet, as a historical matter, the traditional response of the law was that there were no limits upon the degree of temptation to which law enforcement officers and their agents could subject those under investigation. Even today, neither courts nor legislatures have affirmatively developed detailed guidelines for police and their agents to follow when engaging in encouragement activity. However there did ultimately develop, originally in the state courts, a defense called "entrapment" that may be interposed in a criminal prosecution. Beginning with the decision in *Sorrells v. United States*[1] in 1932, the development of the law of entrapment became largely an activity of the federal courts, with the states then adopting the doctrine thereby created. The classic definition of entrapment is that articulated by Justice Roberts in *Sorrells:* "Entrapment is the conception and planning of an offense by an officer, and his procurement of its commission by one who would not have perpetrated it except for the trickery, persuasion, or fraud of the officer."

(c) Scope of the Defense. The defense of entrapment has been asserted in the context of a wide variety of criminal activity, including prostitution, alcohol offenses, counterfeiting, price controlling, and, probably most spectacularly, bribery of public officials. However, the great majority of the cases in which an entrapment defense is interposed involve a charge of some drug offense. There is a dearth of case authority on the question of whether the entrapment defense is available no matter what the nature of the charge brought against the defendant. But in *Sorrells* there appears a caution that the defense might be unavailable where the defendant is charged with a "hei-

nous" or "revolting" crime, and the Model Penal Code formulation of the defense expressly makes it "unavailable when causing or threatening bodily injury is an element of the offense charged and the prosecution is based on conduct causing or threatening such injury to a person other than the person perpetrating the entrapment."[2] This latter limitation has been explained on the ground that one "who can be persuaded to cause such injury presents a danger that the public cannot safely disregard, and that the impropriety of the inducement will likely be dealt with by punishment of the conniving or cooperating officers."

The defense of entrapment does not extend to *all* inducements, and thus another important issue concerning the scope of the defense is that of whose inducements may result in entrapment. As the Supreme Court cases themselves illustrate,[3] entrapment can occur through an undercover agent, a confidential informant or a private citizen knowingly acting under the direction of government agents. This is not to suggest, however, that any sort of relationship between the police and a private citizen will suffice; for example, it is not enough that the police had earlier made an informal request for potential future information to the person who made the inducements. But on the other hand, a sufficient agency relationship can exist even when the police did not expressly request the particular inducement techniques later challenged via an entrapment defense. As it was put in *Sherman v. United States,*[4] the government "cannot make such use of an informer and then claim disassociation through ignorance."

As for the troublesome question of whether entrapment can occur through a third party who is not knowingly furthering a government scheme, it is necessary to distinguish between

§ 5.1

1. 287 U.S. 435, 53 S.Ct. 210, 77 L.Ed. 413 (1932).

2. ALI Model Penal Code § 2.13 (1962). Only a few states have adopted such a limitation.

3. Jacobson v. United States, 503 U.S. 540, 112 S.Ct. 1535, 118 L.Ed.2d 174 (1992) (undercover agent); Mathews v. United States, 485 U.S. 58, 108 S.Ct. 883, 99 L.Ed.2d 54 (1988) (private citizen acting under direction of

agents); Hampton v. United States, 425 U.S. 484, 96 S.Ct. 1646, 48 L.Ed.2d 113 (1976) (same); United States v. Russell, 411 U.S. 423, 93 S.Ct. 1637, 36 L.Ed.2d 366 (1973) (undercover agent); Sherman v. United States, 356 U.S. 369, 78 S.Ct. 819, 2 L.Ed.2d 848 (1958) (confidential informant); Sorrells v. United States, 287 U.S. 435, 53 S.Ct. 210, 77 L.Ed. 413 (1932) (undercover agent).

4. 356 U.S. 369, 78 S.Ct. 819, 2 L.Ed.2d 848 (1958).

three different situations, beginning with what might be called "private entrapment" in the purest sense, an instance in which a private individual, of his own will and without any official involvement, induces another person to commit a crime. The entrapment defense does not extend to such inducements. If the entrapment defense was conceived of as being based upon the notion that a person is not culpable whenever he engages in what would otherwise be criminal conduct because of the strong inducement of another person, this limitation would be open to serious question. What this limitation reflects, then, is that the purpose of the defense is to deter misconduct in enforcing the law.

The two other situations are "vicarious entrapment" and "derivative entrapment." In the case of vicarious entrapment, a private individual, who himself has been induced by an undercover law enforcement officer or agent, now in turn induces someone else to join in the scheme. The views of some courts is that even when the government has no reason to expect that a target of an investigation will induce a nonessential collaborator to join in criminal activity, the third party should still be able to plead entrapment if it is found that the initial target was himself entrapped, as in such a case the third party is another victim of the same misconduct. But other courts deem it inappropriate to confer an entrapment defense upon individuals never targeted by the government in the first place. Consistent with the latter view but going further are those decisions that assert, in effect, that the entrapment defense is *never* available to a defendant who was not directly induced by a law enforcement officer or an agent knowingly acting on the officer's behalf. Such a broad rule would, of course, extend even to the third situation, "derivative entrapment," by which is meant the case in which the undercover government officer or agent uses the unsuspecting middleman as a means of passing on an inducement to a distant target. Some other federal and state courts, however, have taken the view that the entrapment defense should be available to the distant target under these circumstances. The notion is that it should make no difference that the intermediary is unwitting, for the purpose behind allowing such a defense is to prevent the government from circumventing rules against entrapment merely by deploying intermediaries, only one degree removed from the officials themselves, who carry out the government's instructions to persuade a particular individual to commit a particular crime using a particular type of inducement.

Though the defense of entrapment is ordinarily interposed in the context of a criminal prosecution, a number of states have recognized entrapment as a defense to an administrative proceeding involving revocation or suspension of a license to practice a profession, trade, or business. Few courts have considered the issue, and the cases in which the matter is alluded to at all usually reflect nothing but the tacit assumption that the defense is available in administrative proceedings but inapplicable to the case at bar. Nevertheless, extension of the entrapment defense to administrative disciplinary proceedings seems to be warranted by the policies underlying its application in criminal cases.

§ 5.2 Subjective Versus Objective Test for Entrapment

(a) The Subjective Approach. There are currently two major approaches to the defense of entrapment, each involving a distinct test and rationale and each with somewhat different procedural consequences. This division is reflected in the Supreme Court's decisions dealing directly with the subject of entrapment.[1] The majority view is usually referred to as the "subjective approach," although it is also called the federal approach or the *Sherman–Sorrells* doctrine, a reference to the fact that this test was adopted by a majority of the

§ 5.2

1. See Jacobson v. United States, 503 U.S. 540, 112 S.Ct. 1535, 118 L.Ed.2d 174 (1992); United States v. Russell, 411 U.S. 423, 93 S.Ct. 1637, 36 L.Ed.2d 366 (1973); Masciale v. United States, 356 U.S. 386, 78 S.Ct. 827, 2 L.Ed.2d 859 (1958); Sherman v. United States, 356 U.S. 369, 78 S.Ct. 819, 2 L.Ed.2d 848 (1958); Sorrells v. United States, 287 U.S. 435, 53 S.Ct. 210, 77 L.Ed. 413 (1932).

Supreme Court in the cases of *Sherman v. United States*[2] and *Sorrells v. United States*.[3] This subjective approach is still followed in the federal courts, and has also been adopted in about two-thirds of the states as well.

A two-step test is used under the subjective approach: the first inquiry is whether or not the offense was induced by a government agent; and the second is whether or not the defendant was predisposed to commit the type of offense charged. A defendant is considered to have been predisposed if he was ready and willing to commit the crimes charged whenever an opportunity was afforded. If the accused is found to be predisposed, the defense of entrapment may not prevail. The predisposition test reflects an attempt to draw a line between "a trap for the unwary innocent and the trap for the unwary criminal."[4] The emphasis under the subjective approach is clearly upon the defendant's propensity to commit the offense rather than on the officer's misconduct.

In *Jacobson v. United States*,[5] where the defendant ordered sexually explicit photos of children through the mail after the government, over two and a half years, made repeated efforts through five fictitious organizations and a bogus pen pal to explore his willingness to do so, the Court held the government had failed to establish defendant's predisposition. In so concluding, the Court emphasized that it was not enough the defendant was "ready and willing" by the time he was specifically asked to engage in the proscribed conduct; the government needed and failed to prove "that this predisposition was independent and not the product of the attention" the government had directed at him over that previous time span. The defendant's purchase of a similar publication before any government contact *and* before the conduct was made illegal did not establish predisposition, "for, there is a common understanding that most people obey the law

even when they disapprove of it." Moreover, the defendant's later communication with the government's fictitious organizations, while "indicative of * * * a predisposition to view photographs of preteen sex," could "hardly support an inference that he would commit the crime of receiving child pornography through the mails."

The underlying rationale of the subjective approach is grounded in the substantive criminal law. The defense is explained in terms of the defendant's conduct not being criminal because the legislature intended acts instigated by the government to be excepted from the purview of the general statutory prohibition. As stated by the majority in *Sorrells*: "We are unable to conclude that it was the intention of the Congress in enacting this statute that its processes of detection and enforcement be abused by the instigation by government officials of an act on the part of persons otherwise innocent in order to lure them to its commission and to punish them."

(b) The Objective Approach. There is growing support for the objective approach, variously described as the "hypothetical person" approach or the Roberts–Frankfurter approach (after the writers of the concurring opinions in *Sorrells* and *Sherman*). The objective approach is favored by a majority of the commentators, is reflected in the formulation of the entrapment defense appearing in the American Law Institute's Model Penal Code, and has been adopted by about one-third of the states.

The objective approach focuses upon the inducements used by the government agents. This means that entrapment has been established if the offense was induced or encouraged by "employing methods of persuasion or inducement which create a substantial risk that such an offense will be committed by persons other than those who are ready to commit it."[6] In applying this test, it is necessary to consider

---

2. 356 U.S. 369, 78 S.Ct. 819, 2 L.Ed.2d 848 (1958).

3. 287 U.S. 435, 53 S.Ct. 210, 77 L.Ed. 413 (1932).

4. Sherman v. United States, 356 U.S. 369, 78 S.Ct. 819, 2 L.Ed.2d 848 (1958).

5. 503 U.S. 540, 112 S.Ct. 1535, 118 L.Ed.2d 174 (1992). Because *Jacobson* is a refinement of federal entrapment doctrine, state courts need not follow it, and some have declined to do so,

6. ALI Model Penal Code § 2.13 (1962).

the surrounding circumstances, such as evidence of the manner in which the particular criminal business is usually carried on. Though such practices as appeals to sympathy or friendship, offers of inordinate gain, or persistent offers to overcome hesitancy are suspect, courts in jurisdictions using the objective test have been reluctant to lay down absolutes. Though such temptations may be impermissible in some instances, each case must be judged on its own facts. Thus, it would seem that this "objective" focus upon the propriety of the police conduct leaves as much room for value judgments to be made as does the "subjective" focus upon the defendant's state of mind.

The rationale behind the objective approach is grounded in public policy considerations. Proponents of this approach reject the legislative intent argument. They believe that courts must refuse to convict an entrapped defendant not because his conduct falls outside the proscription of the statute, but rather because, even if his guilt has been established, the methods employed on behalf of the government to bring about the crime "cannot be countenanced."[7] To some extent, this reflects the notion that the courts should not become tainted by condoning law enforcement improprieties. If government agents have instigated the commission of a crime, then the courts

should not in effect approve that "abhorrent transaction"[8] by permitting the induced individual to be convicted. But the primary consideration is that an affirmative duty resides in the courts to control police excesses in inducing criminal behavior, and that this duty should not be limited to instances in which the defendant is otherwise "innocent."[9] So viewed, the entrapment defense appears to be a procedural device (somewhat like the Fourth Amendment and *Miranda* exclusionary rules) for deterring undesirable governmental intrusions into the lives of citizens.

As currently applied, the two approaches differ more than merely at the theoretical level. True, in *Sorrells* and *Sherman* the majority (subjective approach) and minority (objective approach) opinions agreed as to the result on the facts there presented.[10] But the concurring justices in *Sherman* were the dissenters in *Masciale v. United States*,[11] decided the same day. And in *United States v. Russell*,[12] the result would certainly have been different had the objective test been utilized. However, neither of the two approaches is uniformly more favorable to defendants, as is reflected by this brief comparison:

Under the [subjective approach], if A, an informer, makes overreaching appeals to compassion and friendship and thus moves

---

7. Sherman v. United States, 356 U.S. 369, 78 S.Ct. 819, 2 L.Ed.2d 848 (1958) (Frankfurter, J., concurring).

8. Sorrells v. United States, 287 U.S. 435, 53 S.Ct. 210, 77 L.Ed. 413 (1932) (Roberts, J., concurring).

9. ALI Model Penal Code 20 (Tent.Draft No. 9, 1959).

10. In *Sherman*, a government informer met defendant at a doctor's office where he was being treated to cure his narcotics addiction, and the informer induced defendant to sell him drugs after making repeated requests and saying that he was not responding to treatment and was suffering as a consequence. The majority, applying the subjective approach, concluded that a 9-year-old sale of narcotics conviction and a 5-year-old possession conviction did not show predisposition, "particularly when we must assume from the record he was trying to overcome the narcotics habit at the time." The four concurring Justices concluded that such appeals to sympathy "can no more be tolerated when directed against a past offender than against an ordinary law-abiding citizen."

In *Sorrells*, the majority held the lower court had erred in ruling as a matter of law that there could be no entrapment, where it was shown "that the act for which defendant was prosecuted was instigated by the prohibition agent, that it was the creature of his purpose, that

defendant had no previous disposition to commit it but was an industrious, law-abiding citizen, and that the agent lured defendant, otherwise innocent, to its commission by repeated and persistent solicitation in which he succeeded by taking advantage of the sentiment aroused by reminiscences of their experiences as companions in arms in the World War." Three members of the Court concurred, but relied upon the objective approach.

11. 356 U.S. 386, 78 S.Ct. 827, 2 L.Ed.2d 859 (1958). The majority, using the subjective approach, concluded the "trial court properly submitted the case to the jury"; the four dissenters, using the objective approach, concluded that the lower court "should itself have ruled on the issue of entrapment and not left it to determination by the jury."

12. 411 U.S. 423, 93 S.Ct. 1637, 36 L.Ed.2d 366 (1973). There, an undercover agent supplied an essential but difficult to obtain ingredient for defendant's operation of a "speed" laboratory. The majority ruled that "the jury finding as to predisposition was supported by the evidence" and was "fatal to his claim of entrapment." Three dissenters urged adoption of the objective test.

D to sell narcotics, D has no defense if he is predisposed to narcotics peddling. Under the [objective approach] a defense would be established because the police conduct, not D's predisposition, determines the issue. Under the [subjective approach], A's mere offer to purchase narcotics from D may give rise to the defense provided D is not predisposed to sell. A contrary result is reached under the [objective approach]. A mere offer to buy hardly creates a serious risk of offending by the innocent.[13]

(c) Objections to the Subjective Approach. Proponents of the objective approach raise three main arguments against the subjective approach. First of all, the "legislative intent" theory is attacked as sheer fiction. It is argued that the Congress or state legislature intended to proscribe precisely the conduct in which the defendant engaged, as is reflected by the fact that the conduct is unquestionably criminal if the tempter was a private person rather than a government agent. Because the prior innocence of the defendant will not sustain the defense of entrapment, then, so the argument proceeds, the public policies of deterring unlawful police conduct and preserving the purity of the courts must be controlling. Those policies, it is concluded, are not effectuated by looking to the defendant's predisposition.

A second criticism of the subjective approach is that it creates, in effect, an "anything goes" rule for use against persons who can be shown by their prior convictions or otherwise to have been predisposed to engage in criminal behavior. This is because if the trier of fact determines that a defendant was predisposed to commit the type of crime charged, then no level of police deceit, badgering or other unsavory practices will be deemed impermissible. Such a result is unsound, it is argued, because it ignores "the possibility that no matter what his past crimes and general disposition the defendant might not have committed the particular crime unless confronted with inordi-

nate inducements."[14] Moreover, so this reasoning proceeds, this notion that the permissible police conduct may vary according to the particular defendant is inconsistent with the objective of equality under the law.

Yet a third objection to the subjective approach is that delving into the defendant's character and predisposition not only "has often obscured the important task of judging the quality of police behavior,"[15] but also has prejudiced the defendant more generally. This is because once the entrapment defense is raised, certain usual evidentiary rules are discarded, and the defendant will be subjected to an "appropriate and searching inquiry into his own conduct and predisposition as bearing upon that issue."[16] This means a prosecutor may admit evidence of a prior criminal record, reputation evidence, acts of prior misconduct, and other information generally barred as hearsay or as being more prejudicial than probative.

(d) Objections to the Objective Approach. Proponents of the subjective approach have likewise raised various criticisms concerning the objective approach. One of them is that defendant's predisposition, at least if known by the police when the investigation in question was conducted, has an important bearing upon the question of whether the conduct of the police and their agents was proper. For example, if it is known that a particular suspect has sold drugs in the past, then it is proper to subject that person to more persuasive inducements than would be permissible as to an individual about whose predisposition the authorities knew nothing. By like token, knowledge that a target has a weakness for a vice crime but is currently abstaining is also a fact that merits consideration when assessing an agent's conduct. Thus, the objective approach is said to be inherently defective because it eliminates entirely the need for considering a particular defendant's criminal predisposition.

---

13. ALI Model Penal Code 19 (Tent.Draft No. 9, 1959).

14. Sherman v. United States, 356 U.S. 369, 78 S.Ct. 819, 2 L.Ed.2d 848 (1958) (Frankfurter, J., concurring).

15. ALI Model Penal Code 20 (Tent.Draft No. 9, 1959).

16. Sorrells v. United States, 287 U.S. 435, 53 S.Ct. 210, 77 L.Ed. 413 (1932).

A second major criticism of the objective approach is that the "wrong" people end up in jail if a dangerous, chronic offender may only be offered those inducements that might have tempted a hypothetical, law-abiding person. This is because, for example, the fact that the defendant in a particular case has been a shrewd, active member of a narcotics ring prior to and continuing through the incident in question is irrelevant under the objective test to a determination of the propriety of the inducements used. So the argument continues, to avoid this acquittal of wary criminals, courts are likely to allow agents substantial leeway in determining the limits of permissible inducement, with the result that this same freedom will allow the police to lead astray the "unwary innocent".

Still another criticism directed at the objective approach to entrapment is that it will foster inaccuracy in the factfinding process. It is argued that the nature of the inducement offered in secret is a factual issue less susceptible to reliable proof than the issue of predisposition. This is because if a defendant claims that an inducement was improper, the agent can take the stand and rebut the allegations, resulting in a swearing match. Especially because the defense of entrapment ordinarily assumes an admission of guilt (unless inconsistent defenses are permitted), this means the factfinder will often have to make the "imponderable choice" between the testimony of an informer, often with a criminal record, and that of a defendant who has admittedly committed the criminal act.

A fourth objection relates to the public policy justifications of the objective approach. It is questioned whether the "purity" of the courts is itself a sufficient justification, and whether the objective approach can be expected to serve the deterrence objective in a meaningful way. Because courts are disinclined to adopt per se rules regarding what are impermissible police inducements, it is doubted whether there will actually result significant restrictions upon the types of inducements that police are entitled to utilize. Moreover, so the

argument continues, even if such limitations are developed the police will still be left with the discretion to decide upon the context or target of encouragement activity. To this are added the familiar arguments against other attempts to deter the police, such as that they can be thwarted by police perjury or that they will be totally ineffective when the police are acting for objectives other than conviction. For all these reasons, this line of argument concludes, the deterrence objective should be dismissed in favor of an effort to do justice to the individual defendant in the particular case.

§ 5.3 Procedural Considerations

(a) Admissibility of Evidence of Defendant's Past Conduct. Entrapment has sometimes been characterized as a dangerous defense that should only be used in a few cases with ideal fact situations or in desperate circumstances where no other defense is possible. This perceived danger is largely attributable to various procedural consequences that attend interposition of an entrapment defense where the majority, subjective approach is followed. And of the procedures that are relevant in this respect, certainly of primary importance is the readiness with which evidence of defendant's past conduct is received as bearing upon defendant's predisposition.

As the Supreme Court put it in *Sherman v. United States*,[1] under the subjective approach the prosecution may engage in a " 'searching inquiry into [defendant's] own conduct and predisposition' as bearing on his claim of innocence." In most jurisdictions this means that once entrapment has been raised as a defense, the usual evidentiary rules are no longer followed. For the purported purpose of allowing the factfinder access to all information bearing upon the "predisposition" issue, courts have allowed the receipt into evidence of defendant's prior convictions, prior arrests, and information about his "reputation" and even concerning "suspicious conduct" on his part. The result is that otherwise inadmissible hearsay, suspicion and rumor are brought into the

§ 5.3
1. 356 U.S. 369, 78 S.Ct. 819, 2 L.Ed.2d 848 (1958).

case and the defendant, in effect, is put on trial for his past offenses and character.

This indiscriminate attitude toward predisposition evidence is by no means a necessary feature of the subjective test. This is because less prejudicial means of determining the readiness and willingness of a defendant to engage in the criminal conduct will often be available. The most promising alternative is testimony about the defendant's actions during the negotiations leading to the charged offense, such as his ready acquiescence, his expert knowledge about such criminal activity, his admissions of past deeds or future plans, and his ready access to the contraband. Another possibility is evidence obtained in a subsequent search or otherwise showing the defendant was involved in a course of ongoing criminal activity.

(b) Triable by Court or Jury. Traditionally, the entrapment defense has been regarded as a matter for the jury rather than for determination by the judge. (Even where this is unquestionably the case, the judge may rule on the sufficiency of the proof to raise the issue in the first place, and where uncontradicted evidence supports the conclusion that the defendant was entrapped the issue may of course be decided as a matter of law by the court.) Under the majority, subjective approach to entrapment, grounded upon the implied exception theory, it is apparent that "the issue of whether a defendant has been entrapped is for the jury as part of its function of determining the guilt or innocence of the accused."[2] In support of this state of affairs, it has been argued that determining matters of credibility and assessing the subjective response to the stimulus of police encouragement are peculiarly within the ken of the jury. Also, it has been observed that if the matter is placed in the hands of the jury there is an opportunity for jury nullification, meaning that the jury, if it wishes, can acquit because of the moral revulsion that the police conduct evokes in them, notwithstanding any amount of convincing evidence of the defendant's predisposition. On the other hand, the argument

has been made that the case for putting the matter in the hands of the court is especially strong under the subjective approach. This is because where the rules of evidence on proving predisposition are very loose, which is usually the case, the defense can be raised only at a great price to the defendant if that evidence becomes known to the jury.

Under the objective approach to entrapment, the judge-versus-jury issue is more evenly balanced. In favor of having the matter decided by the judge is the notion that it is the function of the court to preserve the purity of the court. Similarly, it may be said that to the extent the objective approach rests upon a deterrence-of-police rationale this function also is the proper responsibility of the court, just as it is when the court rules on suppression motions. And there is the added point made by Justice Frankfurter in *Sherman,* namely,

> that a jury verdict, although it may settle the issue of entrapment in the particular case, cannot give significant guidance for official conduct for the future. Only the court, through the gradual evolution of explicit standards in accumulated precedents, can do this with the degree of certainty that the wise administration of criminal justice demands.

Also, there is a sense in which trial of the issue before the judge would be to the state's advantage; the defendant would not be able to divert the jury's attention from his crime by attacking the police.[3]

However, not all of the states that have adopted the objective approach submit the issue to the judge instead of the jury. In light of the above considerations, it is not entirely clear why this is so. Perhaps the explanation is that issue is deemed an appropriate one for the jury because the jury has particular competence on the question of what temptations would be too great for an ordinary law-abiding citizen.

2. Sherman v. United States, 356 U.S. 369, 78 S.Ct. 819, 2 L.Ed.2d 848 (1958).

3. ALI Model Penal Code 22 (Tent.Draft No. 9, 1959).

(c) Inconsistent Defenses. The traditional view has been that the defense of entrapment is not available to one who denies commission of the criminal act with which he is charged, for the reason that the denial is inconsistent with the assertion of such a defense. However, a trend in the opposite direction appears to be developing, and there is much to be said in favor of this latter position. For one thing, it avoids serious constitutional questions concerning whether a defendant may be required, in effect, to surrender his presumption of innocence and his privilege against self-incrimination in order to plead entrapment. Also, it would seem that the adversary process is itself a sufficient restraint upon resort to positions that are truly inconsistent. In a case where two positions are unquestionably logically inconsistent, a defendant who pursued both positions would certainly be found to be lacking credibility.

The matter was settled in the federal courts by *Mathews v. United States*,[4] where the Supreme Court held that even if a defendant denies one or more elements of the crime, he is entitled to an entrapment instruction whenever there is sufficient evidence from which a reasonable jury could find entrapment. Such a result, the Court noted, squares with the fact that federal defendants are allowed to raise inconsistent defenses in other contexts. The Court found unpersuasive the government's claims "that allowing a defendant to rely on inconsistent defenses will encourage perjury, lead to jury confusion, and subvert the truth-finding function of the trial."

Even in jurisdictions where the traditional view persists, the defendant must be allowed to raise the defense of entrapment without admitting the crime whenever the circumstances are such that there is no inherent inconsistency between claiming entrapment and yet not admitting commission of the criminal acts. Thus, the inconsistency rule does not apply when the government in its own case in chief has interjected the issue of entrapment into the case. And if a defendant testifies that a government agent encouraged him to commit a crime that he had never contemplated before that time and that he resisted the temptation nonetheless, there is nothing internally inconsistent in thereby claiming entrapment and that the crime did not occur. Asserting the entrapment defense is not necessarily inconsistent with denial of the crime even when it is admitted that the requisite acts occurred, for the defendant might nonetheless claim that he lacked the requisite bad state of mind.

(d) Burden of Proof. In those jurisdictions following the majority, subjective approach to entrapment, it is generally accepted that the defendant has the burden of establishing the fact of inducement by a government agent. The extent of this burden is less than clear. Some courts require a defendant to sustain a burden of persuasion by proving government inducement by a preponderance of the evidence. Many courts, however, indicate that the defendant only has the burden of production, which can be met by coming forward with "some evidence" of government conduct that created a risk of persuading a nondisposed person to commit a crime. In any event, once the defendant's threshold responsibility is satisfied, the burden is then on the government to negate the defense by showing beyond a reasonable doubt defendant's predisposition or an absence of inducement.

In states where the objective approach is followed, the entire burden of production and persuasion is on the defendant, who must establish the impropriety of the police conduct by a preponderance of the evidence. This is a consequence of the entrapment defense under this approach being an "affirmative defense" rather than something that negatives the existence of an element of the crime charged. Such an allocation of the burden of proof might be questioned on the ground that as a general matter the government is in a much better position than the defendant to obtain and preserve evidence on the question of what kinds of government inducements were utilized in the particular case. This has led to the suggestion that perhaps the real basis for placing the burden of persuasion on the defendant is that

4. 485 U.S. 58, 108 S.Ct. 883, 99 L.Ed.2d 54 (1988).

entrapment is a disfavored defense, so that factual doubts should be resolved against it.

§ 5.4 Other Challenges to Encouragement Practices

(a) Contingent Fee Arrangements. From time to time the courts have given consideration to whether additional restraints upon encouragement practices by police and their agents are needed. The restraints considered in some respects resemble the entrapment defense, for they are also concerned with situations in which a government agent has induced a crime. But they are clearly different than the majority, subjective approach to entrapment, for these other restraints (if imposed) would protect even those defendants predisposed to commit the crime charged. They are also different in some respects from the objective approach to entrapment, though they share with it the purpose of deterring the police from improper practices.

One practice occasionally a cause of concern is that of entering into a contingent fee arrangement with a person acting on behalf of the police to bring about commission of a crime by some other person. The compensation may be monetary, but frequently it takes the form of offers of leniency regarding charges pending against the informant. Depending upon the particular arrangement, contingent fee arrangements may provide the informant with an incentive to engage in unfair tactics and then misrepresent the nature of those tactics subsequently. If the contingency only involves providing a controlled opportunity to another person to engage in criminal conduct, then the incentive to employ unfair tactics may not be great. But if the compensation is contingent upon the subject's commission of a controlled offense, the informer's testimony about that commission in court, or the conviction of the subject for commission of that offense, then the risks of misrepresentation and unfair tactics substantially increase.

The landmark case on this subject is *Williamson v. United States*,[1] where federal agents told one Moye that they would give him $200 and $100, respectively, for legally admissible evidence that two specified persons were engaged in illicit liquor dealings. Moye made a purchase from one of them and produced evidence against both, for which he was paid the promised amount. Exercising its supervisory power over the administration of criminal justice in the federal courts, the court of appeals reversed the resulting conviction. The court explained:

> Without some * * * justification or explanation, we cannot sanction a contingent fee agreement to produce evidence against particular named defendants as to crimes not yet committed. Such an arrangement might tend to a "frame up," or to cause an informer to induce or persuade innocent persons to commit crimes which they had no previous intent or purpose to commit. The opportunities for abuse are too obvious to require elaboration.

While *Williamson* had broad potential, the case has actually had relatively little impact. Courts confronted with a *Williamson* claim have almost invariably been able to distinguish that case in some way. *Williamson* itself contains language supporting one such distinction, for it was indicated therein that a contingent fee would be permissible if the informant was carefully instructed about the distinction between permissible encouragement opportunities and impermissible entrapment. Moreover, *Williamson* has been deemed not controlling where there existed a special need for contingent fees due to the difficulty of the investigation or where the informant was directed to a person as to whom the police already had a reasonable suspicion.

Williamson was, in effect, disapproved in *United States v. Grimes*.[2] The court there reasoned that a contingent fee informer is "no more likely to [lie and manufacture crimes]

---

§ 5.4

1. 311 F.2d 441 (5th Cir.1962).

2. 438 F.2d 391 (6th Cir.1971).

In United States v. Cervantes–Pacheco, 826 F.2d 310 (5th Cir.1987), the court rejected *Williamson*, cited decisions of other Circuits also rejecting *Williamson*, and summarized how the *Williamson* doctrine has been narrowed otherwise.

than witnesses acting for other, more common reasons," such as a codefendant hoping for leniency or an informant who feels that his future employment may depend upon his success on this occasion. Thus it was held in *Grimes* that in all such circumstances the better rule is one leaving "the entire matter to the jury to consider in weighing the credibility of the witness-informant." It may be questioned, however, whether that is a sufficient response to cases where the contingencies are likely to provide a strong incentive for overreaching and falsification, as where the fee is paid only upon conviction of the target of the investigation. But *Grimes* finds support in the Supreme Court's expressed unwillingness in *United States v. Russell*[3] to establish "fixed rules" of due process in the entrapment area or to give the federal judiciary "a 'chancellor's foot' veto" over law enforcement practices of which it disapproves.

(b) Inducements to Those Not Reasonably Suspected. It has sometimes been suggested that a government agent should not be permitted to solicit an offense absent at least "reasonable suspicion" that his target is engaged in such criminal activity. Thus, one commentator argues:

> To hold that government agents need no reasonable basis for selecting an individual as a target for inducement to commit a crime would be intolerable. The effect would be to give police officers untrammelled discretion to test the criminal propensities of any citizen.

An imperfect analogy may be drawn to the Supreme Court's recent decision[4] that discretionary spot stops to check motorists' licenses and automobile registrations violate the fourth amendment unless the police officer has an articulable and reasonable suspicion that the law is being violated.[5] Such a requirement would to some degree lend support to the entrapment doctrine's objective of ensuring that the police detect but not create crime. Its main thrust, however, would be to protect the interests of privacy and freedom from unreasonable intrusions.

Some authority is to be found that reasonable suspicion is an encouragement prerequisite, but most of the decisions on this issue have rejected this theory. *Russell* seems to have sapped it of any remaining vitality by indicating that the entrapment defense is intended to protect nondisposed defendants rather than to control police conduct.[6]

(c) Government "Overinvolvement" in a Criminal Enterprise. In *Sorrells v. United States*[7] and *Sherman v. United States*,[8] the entrapment doctrine was explained in terms of the presumed intention of Congress rather than as a matter of constitutional law. This means, of course, that Congress may depart from the *Sorrells–Sherman* test if it wishes, and that state courts and legislatures may do likewise. In short, the law of entrapment is not itself of constitutional dimension. But there remains for consideration the question of whether certain kinds of government involvement in a criminal enterprise would warrant the conclusion that the due process rights of the person induced had been violated.[9]

---

3. 411 U.S. 423, 93 S.Ct. 1637, 36 L.Ed.2d 366 (1973).

4. The reference is to Delaware v. Prouse, 440 U.S. 648, 99 S.Ct. 1391, 59 L.Ed.2d 660 (1979).

5. Note, 67 Geo.L.J. 1455, 1471 (1979).

6. In Jacobson v. United States, discussed in § 5.2 at note 5, the dissenters claimed that the majority "introduces a new requirement that government sting operations have a reasonable suspicion of illegal activity before contacting a suspect." However, the majority's position, even as to defendant's predisposition prior to the government's initial contact, does not necessarily limit the government to evidence of predisposition of which it was aware at the time of the conduct (which would be the case under a reasonable suspicion standard). Moreover, the majority's standard of predisposition independent of the government's pre-solicitation contacts does not preclude

looking to separate events occurring during the period between the first contact and the actual solicitation.

7. 287 U.S. 435, 53 S.Ct. 210, 77 L.Ed. 413 (1932).

8. 356 U.S. 369, 78 S.Ct. 819, 2 L.Ed.2d 848 (1958).

9. The matter under consideration here must be distinguished from a quite different variety of defense that also has due process underpinnings and that is sometimes labeled as if it were a variety of entrapment, e.g., "entrapment by estoppel." It applies where the defendant establishes by a preponderance of the evidence that a government official told the defendant that certain criminal conduct was legal, the defendant actually relied on the government official's statement, and the defendant's reliance was in good faith and reasonable in light of the identity of the government official, the point of law represented, and the substance of the official's statement.

In *United States v. Russell*,[10] an undercover agent supplied the defendant and his associates with 100 grams of propanone, an essential but difficult to obtain ingredient in the manufacture of methamphetamine ("speed"); they used it to produce two batches of "speed," which pursuant to agreement the agent received half of in return. The defendant, convicted of unlawfully manufacturing and selling the substance, conceded on appeal that the jury could have found him predisposed, but claimed that the agent's involvement in the enterprise was so substantial that the prosecution violated due process. In particular, he contended that prosecution should be precluded when it is shown that the criminal conduct would not have been possible had not the agent "supplied an indispensable means to the commission of the crime that could not have been obtained otherwise, through legal or illegal channels." The Court in *Russell* found it unnecessary to pass on that contention because the record showed that propanone "was by no means impossible" to obtain by other sources. Though acknowledging that "we may some day be presented with a situation in which the conduct of law enforcement agents is so outrageous that due process principles would absolutely bar the government from invoking judicial processes to obtain a conviction," the majority concluded "the instant case is distinctly not of that breed" because the agent had simply supplied a legal and harmless substance to a person who had theretofore been "an active participant in an illegal drug manufacturing enterprise." Three dissenters urged adoption of the objective approach to entrapment and asserted that if propanone "had been wholly unobtainable from other sources" the agent's actions would be "conduct that constitutes entrapment under any definition."[11]

Then came *Hampton v. United States*,[12] where petitioner, convicted of distributing heroin, objected to the denial of his requested jury instruction that he must be acquitted if the narcotics he sold to government agents had earlier been supplied to him by a government informant. Three members of the Court concluded that the difference between the instant case and *Russell* was "one of degree, not of kind," for here the government supplied an illegal substance that was the corpus delicti of petitioner's crime and thus "played a more significant role" in enabling the crime to occur. But such conduct as to a predisposed defendant was deemed not to violate due process. Significantly, two concurring Justices, while agreeing that "this case is controlled completely by *Russell*," expressed their unwillingness "to join the plurality in concluding that, no matter what the circumstances, neither due process principles nor our supervisory power could support a bar to conviction in any case where the Government is able to prove disposition." The three dissenters[13] in *Hampton* urged that conviction be "barred as a matter of law where the subject of the criminal charge is the sale of contraband provided to the defendant by a Government agent." The instant case, they contended, was different from *Russell* because (i) here the supplied substance was contraband, and (ii) here the "beginning and end of this crime" coincided with the government's involvement. "The Government," they protested, "is doing nothing less than buying contraband from itself through an intermediary and jailing the intermediary."

Russell and *Hampton,* then, indicate that a majority of the Court accepts the notion that there may well be *some* circumstances in which a due process defense would be available even to a defendant found to be predisposed. However, those two cases do not provide clear guidance as to how the police conduct is to be assessed in making this judgment, though they do justify the conclusion that instances of government conduct outrageous enough to violate

---

10.   411 U.S. 423, 93 S.Ct. 1637, 36 L.Ed.2d 366 (1973).

11.   One of those dissenters also joined in another dissent by another member of the Court in which it was argued that whether the ingredient could be obtained from other sources was "quite irrelevant" and concluding: "Federal agents play a debased role when they become the instigators of the crime, or partners in its commission, or the creative brain behind the illegal scheme."

12.   425 U.S. 484, 96 S.Ct. 1646, 48 L.Ed.2d 113 (1976).

13.   The ninth member of the Court, Stevens, J., took no part in the case.

due process will be exceedingly rare. Among the possibilities are (1) an instance in which government agents induce others to engage in violence or threat of violence against innocent parties; (2) where concern for overreaching government inducement overlaps with concern for first amendment freedoms, as where the government sends provocateurs into political organizations to suggest the commission of crimes; (3) where the government initiated or exploited a sexual relationship to bring about the crime; (4) where the government offered such extraordinarily large financial inducements as to bring about a coercive situation; and (5) the situation put by the *Russell* dissenters, supplying contraband "wholly unobtainable from other sources" so as to "make possible the commission of an otherwise totally impossible crime."

Special note must be taken of *United States v. Twigg*,[14] apparently the first post-*Hampton* case in which a defendant prevailed on a due process defense. Neville and Twigg were convicted of conspiracy to manufacture "speed." A government informer proposed to Neville that the laboratory be established, and Neville assumed responsibility for raising the capital and arranging for distribution, while the informer supplied the equipment, raw materials and laboratory site and was in complete charge of the lab because he alone had the expertise to manufacture the drug. Distinguishing *Russell* as a case in which the defendant was an active participant before the government agent appeared on the scene, and *Hampton* as concerned with "a much more fleeting and elusive crime to detect," the majority in *Twigg* concluded that the government involvement had reached "a demonstrable level of outrageousness." In reaching that conclusion, the court stressed (i) that "the illicit plan did not originate with the criminal defendants"; (ii) that the informer's expertise was "an indispensable requisite to this criminal enterprise"; and (iii) that, "as far as the record reveals, [Neville] was lawfully and peaceably minding his own affairs" until approached by the informant.

Twigg thus suggests that the previously discussed "reasonable suspicion" prerequisite may on occasion emerge as an aspect of the due process limits upon encouragement activity. The point seems to be that overinvolvement by the government to the extent reflected in *Twigg* is permissible, if at all, only against a person who is reasonably suspected of criminal conduct or design. The other important principle recognized in *Twigg* is that "the practicalities of combating" a certain type of criminal activity must be taken into account in determining whether "more extreme methods of investigation" are constitutionally permissible. However, there is reason to question the application of that sound principle in the *Twigg* case to conclude that more extreme methods are needed to detect drug distribution than drug manufacture.

14.   588 F.2d 373 (3d Cir.1978).

Chapter 6

INTERROGATION AND CONFESSIONS

Table of Sections

§ 6.1   Introduction and Overview

(a) The Need for Confessions. No area of constitutional criminal procedure has provoked more debate over the years than that dealing with police interrogation. In large measure, the debate has centered upon two fundamental questions: (1) how important are confessions in the process of solving crimes and convicting the perpetrators? and (2) what is the extent and nature of police abuse in seeking to obtain confessions from those suspected of crimes? Conclusive evidence on these two points is lacking, and thus it is not surprising that this debate continues.

An oft-quoted statement supporting the proposition that confessions are necessary in criminal investigation and prosecution is that of Justice Frankfurter in *Culombe v. Connecticut:*[1]

Despite modern advances in the technology of crime detection, offenses frequently occur about which things cannot be made to speak. And where there cannot be found innocent human witnesses to such offenses, nothing remains—if police investigation is not to be balked before it has fairly begun— but to seek out possibly guilty witnesses and ask them questions, witnesses, that is, who

are suspected of knowing something about the offense precisely because they are suspected of implication in it.

In elaboration of this position, a leading proponent of police interrogation as an investigative technique has presented forceful argument in support of these three points:

1. Many criminal cases, even when investigated by the best qualified police departments, are capable of solution only by means of an admission or confession from the guilty individual or upon the basis of information obtained from the questioning of other criminal suspects. * * *

2. Criminal offenders, except, of course, those caught in the commission of their crimes, ordinarily will not admit their guilt unless questioned under conditions of privacy, and for a period of perhaps several hours. * * *

3. In dealing with criminal offenders, and consequently also with criminal suspects who may actually be innocent, the interrogator must of necessity employ less refined methods than are considered appropriate for the transaction of ordinary, everyday affairs by and between law-abiding citizens.[2]

§ 6.1

1. 367 U.S. 568, 81 S.Ct. 1860, 6 L.Ed.2d 1037 (1961).

2. Inbau, Police Interrogation—A Practical Necessity, 52 J.Crim.L.C. & P.S. 16, 17, 19 (1961).

The major difficulty, however, is that of trying to quantify the first of these propositions. Statistics have occasionally been offered on one side of the argument or the other, but they are inconclusive. Those tending to show that confessions are offered into evidence in only a small fraction of criminal prosecutions for serious crimes hardly demonstrate that confessions are unimportant, for they do not show how many of the considerable number of cases disposed of by guilty plea were not contested precisely because the defendant had given a confession. As for statistics offered to show that confessions are frequently relied upon in criminal prosecutions, they are also prove something other than the matter at issue; the fact a confession was obtained in a particular case and was tendered by the prosecutor at trial does not, standing alone, establish there existed a need in that instance to resort to interrogation. But even if we could fairly assess the availability of alternatives, there remains the question of whether interrogation is necessarily the most undesirable of the lot. Justice Goldberg answered this in the affirmative in *Escobedo v. Illinois*[3] when he declared "that a system of criminal law enforcement which comes to depend on the 'confession' will, in the long run, be less reliable and more subject to abuses than a system which depends on extrinsic evidence independently secured through skillful investigation." But this is not a proposition that is beyond dispute. Some forms of "extrinsic evidence," such as eyewitness identification, are also attended by serious risks of unreliability.

(b) The Extent of Police Abuse. As the Supreme Court noted in *Miranda v. Arizona,*[4] police interrogation "still takes place in privacy," which "results in secrecy and this in turn results in a gap in our knowledge as to what in fact goes on in the interrogation rooms." Because of this secrecy (for some a sufficient indication in itself of abuse), there is lacking sufficient empirical evidence to assert with confidence what always, usually, or often occurs in the course of police interrogation. This being so, attention has often turned to cele-

brated cases of confessions later proved false or to judicial opinions (including many Supreme Court decisions) revealing outrageous police tactics. Those favoring restrictions upon interrogation rely heavily upon these cases, while their opponents claim such incidents are extraordinary, having no relation to the ordinary day-to-day operations of the police.

Because complete factual data is lacking, it is not surprising that the participants in the confessions controversy have different perceptions of what occurs in interrogation rooms. But, there does seem to be general agreement that the forms of illegality have become less extreme, in that the use of overt physical violence has largely given way to the employment of more subtle kinds of pressure. But to say, as was conceded in *Miranda,* that "the modern practice of in-custody interrogation is psychologically rather than physically oriented," is not to conclude that police abuse is nonexistent. It does complicate the assessment, however, because it thus becomes somewhat more difficult to determine exactly what ought to be encompassed within the term "abuse."

(c) The Supreme Court's Response. From 1936 to nearly thirty years later, the Supreme Court dealt with confessions admitted in state criminal proceedings in terms of the fundamental fairness required by the Fourteenth Amendment due process clause. A so-called "voluntariness" test, which depended upon the "totality of the circumstances," was used to determine whether the Constitution required exclusion of a confession. The dimensions of this test changed over the years as the Supreme Court's concerns about the interrogation process broadened. At first, the question was simply one of whether the methods used had produced a confession that was unreliable; then the Court undertook to deter unfair police interrogation practices even if they produced reliable statements; and still later the Court's decisions reflected concern with whether the interrogated defendant had been substantially deprived of the choice whether or

---

3. 378 U.S. 478, 84 S.Ct. 1758, 12 L.Ed.2d 977 (1964).

4. 384 U.S. 436, 86 S.Ct. 1602, 16 L.Ed.2d 694 (1966).

not to talk to the police. As the years passed, it became increasingly apparent that this test was most difficult to administer because it required a finding and appraisal of all relevant facts surrounding each challenged confession.

Essentially the same approach was used by the Supreme Court during this period on the infrequent occasions when confessions admitted in federal prosecutions were reviewed. In such instances, it might logically be thought that the Court was then relying upon the due process clause of the Fifth Amendment. However, the tendency was to refer to earlier holdings in which the basis of exclusion was the Fifth Amendment privilege against self-incrimination or a common law rule of evidence. Beginning in 1943, a confession obtained by federal officers and offered in a federal prosecution could also be excluded on the ground that it was received during a period of "unnecessary delay" in taking the arrested person before a judicial officer. Although these decisions were grounded upon the Court's supervisory power over the federal courts, most commentators viewed them as attempts by the Court to avoid the tremendous problems inherent in the due process voluntariness test, and there was some expectation that this so-called *McNabb–Mallory* rule would ultimately be rested upon a constitutional foundation and applied to the states. This did not come to pass; indeed, Congress enacted legislation that appears to have repealed this rule even on the federal level.

Perhaps the reason this did not come to pass was because subsequent decisions holding that there was a constitutional right to counsel at certain pretrial "critical stages" provided a better stepping stone. The anticipated move away from sole reliance upon the voluntariness test occurred in *Escobedo v. Illinois*,[5] suppressing the defendant's confession because it was obtained in violation of his right to counsel at the time of interrogation. *Escobedo* was a cautious step, for the holding was carefully limited to the unique facts of the case. It was generally assumed, however, that this newly established right to counsel in the police station would thereafter be expanded on a case-by-case basis. That did not occur, for in the now famous case of *Miranda v. Arizona*[6] the Court moved off in a different direction by relying instead upon the Fifth Amendment privilege against self-incrimination. But thereafter the Court returned to the right-to-counsel theory as a means of deciding certain cases not amenable to easy resolution under *Miranda*.

In *Miranda,* the Court held that a person "deprived of his freedom of action in any significant way" could not be questioned unless he waived his rights after being advised (i) "that he has the right to remain silent"; (ii) "that anything said can and will be used against the individual in court"; (iii) "that he has the right to consult with a lawyer and to have the lawyer with him during interrogation"; and (iv) "that if he is indigent a lawyer will be appointed to represent him." Today *Miranda* is most often invoked in confession suppression hearings, and thus the emphasis in this Chapter is upon the basis and meaning of that decision.[7]

This is not to suggest, however, that today the admissibility of an incriminating statement is determined only by application of the *Miranda* rules, for this most certainly is not the case. For one thing, there will be times when *Miranda* will not even be applicable, either because the defendant was not in custody or otherwise "deprived of his freedom of action in any significant way" or because the police did not engage in interrogation or its "functional equivalent." As for the right to counsel, it will be applicable only to those cases in which the statement was obtained after that right has attached, but in such cases it may be extremely important because, for example, police conduct can violate that right even if it does not constitute interrogation under *Miranda*. As for the "voluntariness" due process test, it is always worthy of consideration; it is possible that there has been an effective waiver of *Miranda* rights followed by

---

5. 378 U.S. 478, 84 S.Ct. 1758, 12 L.Ed.2d 977 (1964).

6. 384 U.S. 436, 86 S.Ct. 1602, 16 L.Ed.2d 694 (1966).

7. The *Miranda* rules are discussed in further detail in §§ 6.5–6.10.

police conduct that made the subsequent confession involuntary.

§ 6.2   The "Voluntariness" Test

(a) The Common Law Rule. Under the early common law, confessions were admissible at trial without any restrictions whatsoever, so that even an incriminating statement obtained by torture was not excluded. But some time prior to the middle of the eighteenth century, English trial judges began placing restrictions on the admissibility of confessions. Sometimes the question was put in terms of whether the defendant's confession had been induced by a promise of benefit or threat of harm,[1] while on other occasions the inquiry was more directly put in terms of whether the circumstances under which the defendant had spoken impaired the reliability of the confession.[2] But it became more common for the courts simply to ask whether the confession had been made "voluntarily," that is, without certain improper inducements. These included actual or threatened physical harm, a promise not to prosecute, a promise to provide lenient treatment upon conviction, and deceptive practices so extreme that they might have produced a false confession (not merely using a fellow prisoner as an undercover agent or misleading the defendant as to the strength of the case against him). There was no attempt to assess the effect of an inducement on a particular suspect.

The Supreme Court's early decisions on the admissibility of confessions in federal courts relied upon the common law rule. The rule was stated by the Court in terms of whether there had been such an inducement that "the presumption upon which weight is given to

such evidence, namely, that one who is innocent will not imperil his safety or prejudice his interests by an untrue statement, ceases."[3] In the 1897 case of *Bram v. United States*,[4] the Court appeared to base exclusion upon violation of the Fifth Amendment privilege against self-incrimination, but the Court later pulled back from that position.[5] Nonetheless, *Bram* influenced the Court to state the rule of exclusion more broadly, so that it was not merely a matter of whether the confession was reliable or whether a forbidden inducement had been used, but rather whether the confession "was, in fact, voluntarily made."[6] So expanded, the common law standard seems merged into the definition of due process voluntariness developed in the state court cases subsequently decided by the Court.

(b) Due Process and the "Complex of Values". It was not until *Brown v. Mississippi*[7] that the Court barred the use of a confession in the state courts. It could not, of course, dispose of the state confession on the same grounds as were resorted to in the earlier cases. Under our federal system, the Supreme Court may not proscribe mere rules of evidence for the states, and the Fifth Amendment privilege was then not deemed applicable to the states.[8] Thus the confessions in *Brown*, obtained by brutally beating the suspects, were struck down on the notion that interrogation is part of the process by which a state procures a conviction and thus is subject to the requirements of the Fourteenth Amendment due process clause. Though *Brown* declared that due process was violated when a conviction was rested "solely" upon a confession so obtained, later cases made it clear that the

---

§ 6.2

1. Regina v. Moore, 169 Eng.Rep. 608, 2 Den.C.C. 522 (Ct.Crim.App.1852).

2. People v. Fox, 319 Ill. 606, 150 N.E. 347 (1925).

3. Hopt v. Utah, 110 U.S. 574, 4 S.Ct. 202, 28 L.Ed. 262 (1884).

4. 168 U.S. 532, 18 S.Ct. 183, 42 L.Ed. 568 (1897).

5. Thus in United States v. Carignan, 342 U.S. 36, 72 S.Ct. 97, 96 L.Ed. 48 (1951), the Court expressed doubt about "[w]hether involuntary confessions are excluded from federal criminal trials on the ground of a violation of

the Fifth Amendment's protection against self-incrimination, or from a rule that forced confessions are untrustworthy."

6. Ziang Sung Wan v. United States, 266 U.S. 1, 45 S.Ct. 1, 69 L.Ed. 131 (1924).

7. 297 U.S. 278, 56 S.Ct. 461, 80 L.Ed. 682 (1936).

8. Twining v. New Jersey, 211 U.S. 78, 29 S.Ct. 14, 53 L.Ed. 97 (1908), overruled by Malloy v. Hogan, 378 U.S. 1, 84 S.Ct. 1489, 12 L.Ed.2d 653 (1964).

mere use at trial of such a confession was unconstitutional.[9]

This due process test is customarily referred to as the "voluntariness" requirement, the term used by the Court in enunciating the due process requisites for admissibility.[10] But that term is not at all helpful in determining the policies underlying this particular constitutional limitation. As the Court candidly put it in *Blackburn v. Alabama,*[11] "a complex of values underlies the stricture against use by the state of confessions which, by way of convenient shorthand, this Court terms involuntary." A closer examination of the Court's decisions in this area over the years reflects three important values deserving specific mention here.

In *Brown,* the confessions clearly were of doubtful reliability, and thus that case might be read as announcing a due process test for excluding confessions obtained under circumstances presenting a fair risk that the statements are false. Concern with this risk was emphasized in several subsequent cases, and this led many state courts to the conclusion that unfairness in violation of due process exists when a confession is obtained under circumstances affecting its testimonial trustworthiness. But while ensuring the reliability of confessions is *a* goal under the due process voluntariness standard, it is incorrect to define the standard in terms of that one objective. In *Rogers v. Richmond,*[12] defendant's confession was obtained after the police pretended to order his ailing wife arrested for questioning, and the state court had ruled that the statement need not be excluded "if the artifice or deception was not calculated to procure an untrue statement." The Supreme Court disagreed, emphasizing that convictions based upon coerced confessions must be overturned "not because such confessions are unlikely to be true but because the methods used to extract them offend an underlying principle in the enforcement of our criminal law: that ours

is an accusatorial and not an inquisitorial system." *Rogers* thus made certain what had been strongly intimated in several earlier cases, namely, that the due process exclusionary rule for confessions (in much the same way as the Fourth Amendment exclusionary rule for physical evidence) is also intended to deter improper police conduct.

In *Townsend v. Sain,*[13] the ailing defendant had been given a drug with the properties of a truth serum, after which he gave a confession in response to questioning by police who were unaware of the drug's effect. Although the confession was not obtained by conscious police wrongdoing and apparently was reliable, the Court nonetheless held its use impermissible: "Any questioning by police officers which *in fact* produces a confession which is not the product of free intellect renders that confession inadmissible." *Townsend* thus highlights another theme running through many of the earlier cases: the confession must be a product of the defendant's "free and rational choice." This phrase, however, was not used in an absolute sense, but rather in conjunction with a recognized need to exert some pressure to obtain confessions. As the Court seems to have acknowledged in *Miranda v. Arizona,*[14] the question of whether a confession was "voluntary" had theretofore been determined by a lesser standard than, say, the question of whether a testator's will was his voluntary act.

Viewing the voluntariness test in terms of its underlying values, then, it might be said that the objective of the test is to bar admission of those confessions (i) of doubtful reliability because of the practices used to obtain them; (ii) obtained by offensive police practices even if reliability is not in question (for example, where there is strong corroborating evidence); or (iii) obtained under circumstances in which the defendant's free choice was significantly impaired, even if the police did not resort to offensive practices.

---

9. Payne v. Arkansas, 356 U.S. 560, 78 S.Ct. 844, 2 L.Ed.2d 975 (1958). On whether admission of such a confession can ever qualify as harmless error, see § 27.6(d).

10. E.g., Watts v. Indiana, 338 U.S. 49, 69 S.Ct. 1347, 93 L.Ed. 1801 (1949).

11. 361 U.S. 199, 80 S.Ct. 274, 4 L.Ed.2d 242 (1960).

12. 365 U.S. 534, 81 S.Ct. 735, 5 L.Ed.2d 760 (1961).

13. 372 U.S. 293, 83 S.Ct. 745, 9 L.Ed.2d 770 (1963).

14. 384 U.S. 436, 86 S.Ct. 1602, 16 L.Ed.2d 694 (1966).

But in *Colorado v. Connelly*,[15] the Court in effect denied the existence of the third category listed above, holding that the state court had erred in excluding a confession volunteered to police by a defendant who suffered from a psychosis that interfered with his ability to make free and rational choices. Absent "the crucial element of police overreaching," the Court reasoned, "there is simply no basis for concluding that any state actor has deprived a criminal defendant of due process." *Townsend* was distinguished as a case involving "police wrongdoing" in questioning a person who had been given a truth serum, though in fact the Supreme Court in that earlier case proceeded on the assumption that neither the police doctor who administered the drug nor the police who did the questioning were aware of the drug's truth serum character. *Connelly* is grounded in the notion that "state action" beyond merely receiving defendant's confession into evidence is necessary, that at a minimum there must be "police conduct causally related to the confession," and that this conduct must be "coercive" (such as exploiting defendant's deficient mental condition).

Connelly also emphasized the narrow reading that must be given to the first category listed above. The Court conceded that a "statement rendered by one in the condition of respondent might be proved to be quite unreliable," but then declared that "this is a matter to be governed by the evidentiary laws of the forum * * * and not by the Due Process Clause of the Fourteenth Amendment." This is so, the Court explained, because the aim of the due process requirement "is not to exclude presumptively false evidence, but to prevent fundamental fairness in the use of evidence, whether true or false." Moreover, because the Fourteenth Amendment only covers state action, the "most outrageous behavior by a private party," even if it produces an unreliable confession, "does not make that evidence inadmissible under the Due Process Clause."[16]

In *Chavez v. Martinez*,[17] where a majority agreed that a § 1983 plaintiff had no Fifth Amendment claim regarding persistent police interrogation of him over his objection and while he was suffering from serious injuries because the confession obtained was never admitted against him in a criminal case,[18] another majority held: "Whether Martinez may pursue a claim of liability for a substantive due process violation is * * * an issue that should be addressed on remand, along with the scope and merits of any such action that may be found open to him." Some members of the Court, however, had no doubt what the outcome should be, and in the process expressed quite different views on what constituted due process in that context. Three Justices[19] declared that the "shocks the conscience" test would apply but would not be met on these facts, and that the due process protection of any "fundamental liberty interest" test would not either because there is nothing in the Court's jurisprudence supporting the position "that freedom from unwanted police questioning is a right so fundamental that it cannot be abridged absent a compelling state interest." Three others,[20] however, citing *Brown*, asserted that the due process requirement of a voluntary confession makes it "a simple enough matter to say that use of torture or its equivalent in an attempt to induce a statement violates an individual's fundamental right to liberty of the person."

(c) Relevant Factors in the "Totality of Circumstances." The Fourteenth Amendment due process voluntariness test requires examination of the "totality of circumstances"[21] surrounding each confession. As a general matter, this means that it is necessary to assess carefully the conduct of the police in obtaining the confession. Indeed, it has long been the case that if the conduct of the police

---

15. 479 U.S. 157, 107 S.Ct. 515, 93 L.Ed.2d 473 (1986).

16. For more on the involvement of private persons in obtaining confessions, see § 6.10(b).

17. 538 U.S. 760, 123 S.Ct. 1994, 155 L.Ed.2d 984 (2003).

18. On this branch of the case, see § 6.5(a).

19. Thomas, J., joined by the Chief Justice and Scalia, J.

20. Kennedy, J., joined by Stevens and Ginsburg, JJ.

21. Haynes v. Washington, 373 U.S. 503, 83 S.Ct. 1336, 10 L.Ed.2d 513 (1963).

was "inherently coercive,"[22] then suppression in the interest of deterring such conduct in future cases is appropriate without first making any judgment about the impact of that conduct upon the particular defendant. In the pre-*Connelly* era, when the question came down to whether *this* defendant's free choice was substantially impaired, any facts that tended to show that he was more or less susceptible to pressures than the average person were particularly relevant. Since *Connelly*, as will be discussed further herein, it is less clear just what relevance the characteristics and status of the person who gave the confession has in determining whether the requisite element of "police overreaching" is present.

A significant number of the confession cases that have reached the Supreme Court have involved actual or threatened physical brutality or deprivation, such as whipping or slapping the suspect, depriving him of food or water or sleep, keeping him in a naked state or in a small cell, holding a gun to his head or threatening him with mob violence. As the Court noted in *Stein v. New York*,[23] when such outrageous conduct is present "there is no need to weigh or measure its effects on the will of the individual victim." However, this *per se* approach is subject to limitations even as to the use or threatened use of violence.

The *Stein* approach was not applied by either the majority or the dissent in a much more recent coerced confession case involving a threat of force, *Arizona v. Fulminante*.[24] That case involved a defendant who confessed to a fellow prison inmate (who was actually a government agent) after that inmate stated that he had heard that Fulminante was "starting to get some tough treatment" from the other inmates and suggested that he might be able to protect Fulminante, but only if he was told the truth. The Court majority found *both* that the circumstances presented "a credible threat of physical violence unless Fulminante confessed" *and* that, as a result, "Fulminante's will was overborne in such a way as to

render his confession the product of coercion." The four dissenters found no grounding in the record for the majority's conclusion that the defendant (described by the dissent as "an experienced habitué of prisons and able to fend for himself") had "his capacity for self-determination critically impaired" by a perceived need for protection against possible physical recriminations by his fellow inmates. Neither the *Fulminante* majority nor the dissenters sought to distinguish the per se approach of *Stein*. However, the Court did cite as analogous *Payne v. Arkansas*,[25] a case where the police interrogator offered protection from mob violence, and it noted that *Payne* also was a case in which it had found that there was a credible threat of violence that had in fact operated on the particular defendant to overbear his will. The assumption seems to be that where the threat of physical violence stems not from the interrogator who holds the defendant in custody, but from third persons, the cogency of the threat is less apparent, making inappropriate a conclusive presumption that it operated to overbear the free will of the defendant. Even where force was actually applied by the police, lower courts have held that *Stein's per se* approach is limited to those confessions made substantially concurrently with physical violence, so that those sufficiently attenuated from such misconduct are subject to the more lenient totality of the circumstances test.

Another very important "totality of the circumstances" factor is whether the defendant was subjected to extended periods of incommunicado interrogation. Of particular significance in this regard is whether the suspect was subjected to lengthy and uninterrupted interrogation, whether he was kept in confinement an extended period of time even though subjected only to intermittent questioning, whether he was moved from place to place and questioned by different persons so as to be disoriented, whether he was questioned in solitary confinement or at some isolated place away from the jail, and whether he was held

22. Ashcraft v. Tennessee, 322 U.S. 143, 64 S.Ct. 921, 88 L.Ed. 1192 (1944).

23. 346 U.S. 156, 73 S.Ct. 1077, 97 L.Ed. 1522 (1953).

24. 499 U.S. 279, 111 S.Ct. 1246, 113 L.Ed.2d 302 (1991).

25. 356 U.S. 560, 78 S.Ct. 844, 2 L.Ed.2d 975 (1958).

incommunicado up until the time of the confession (especially if family, friends or counsel were turned away). Under the more extreme of these circumstances, such as where there have been a couple of weeks of uninterrupted detention or virtual nonstop interrogation for 36 hours,[26] the situation is "inherently coercive" and suppression of the confession is mandated. But in less extreme circumstances the confession has typically been excluded only upon a showing that the defendant was especially susceptible to coercion.

In *Bram v. United States*,[27] the Court declared that a confession "obtained by any direct or implied promises, however slight," is not voluntary. Read literally, this passage suggests a standard holding automatically involuntary any confession that was a "but for" product of a promise that might benefit the defendant. But *Arizona v. Fulminante*[28] noted that such a reading of the *Bram* passage "under current precedent does not state the standard for determining the voluntariness of a confession." The role of the promise must be evaluated in light of the totality of the circumstances, and the promise must have been sufficiently compelling to overbear the suspect's will in light of those circumstances. Supreme Court opinions suggest, however, that certain promises, by their very nature, can be presumed to have that impact absent special circumstances pointing in the opposite direction. Illustrative are *Rogers v. Richmond*,[29] holding defendant's confession was coerced where it was obtained in response to a police threat to take defendant's wife into custody, and *Lynumn v. Illinois*,[30] deciding that the confession was coerced where defendant was told she could lose her welfare payments and the custody of her children but that if she cooperated the police would help her and recommend leniency.

Similarly, lower courts have often held that a confession is involuntary if made in response to a promise that the result will be nonprose-

cution, the dropping of some charges, medical treatment, or a certain reduction in the punishment defendant may receive (although in recent years there has been a movement away from treating such promises of leniency as *per se* producing involuntariness, especially in light of *Fulminante's* reading of *Bram*). Merely promising to bring defendant's cooperation to the attention of the prosecutor is not objectionable, nor is a promise that if defendant confesses the prosecutor would *discuss* leniency. Also, more generalized assurances that assistance will be sought or that certain facilities are available are not inherently coercive. But the cases go both ways on the question of what the result should be when a confession has been obtained in response to a police assertion that cooperation would facilitate prompt release on bail or would mean that the defendant would fare better in subsequent proceedings. In the latter situation, the difficulty is in attempting to reconcile the voluntariness requirement with the plea bargaining process and especially the role of the police in that practice.

The Court in *Bram* also stated that a confession was involuntary if obtained by any other "improper influence," but the courts have not had an easy time in trying to resolve what other police conduct deserves to be so characterized. This is particularly true with respect to police trickery and deception. Although dictum in *Miranda v. Arizona*[31] was highly critical of such activity, as a general matter it may be said that the courts have not deemed such conduct sufficient by itself to make a confession involuntary. One type of trickery involves misrepresenting to the suspect the strength of the existing case against him, as in *Frazier v. Cupp*.[32] During the interrogation of Frazier concerning a homicide, the police told him that his cousin Rawls, with whom he had been on the evening in question, had been brought in and had already confessed. The Court concluded that the "fact that the police misrepresen-

26. Ashcraft v. Tennessee, 322 U.S. 143, 64 S.Ct. 921, 88 L.Ed. 1192 (1944).

27. 168 U.S. 532, 18 S.Ct. 183, 42 L.Ed. 568 (1897).

28. See note 24 supra.

29. 365 U.S. 534, 81 S.Ct. 735, 5 L.Ed.2d 760 (1961).

30. 372 U.S. 528, 83 S.Ct. 917, 9 L.Ed.2d 922 (1963).

31. 384 U.S. 436, 86 S.Ct. 1602, 16 L.Ed.2d 694 (1966).

32. 394 U.S. 731, 89 S.Ct. 1420, 22 L.Ed.2d 684 (1969).

ted the statements that Rawls made is, while relevant, insufficient in our view to make this otherwise voluntary confession inadmissible." Similarly, lower courts have held confessions admissible when they were prompted by such misrepresentations as that the murder victim was still alive, that the police only sought defendant's statement as a witness, that non-existent witnesses have been found, that the murder weapon had been uncovered, that defendant's prints were found at the crime scene, that an accomplice had confessed and implicated the defendant, or that the results of defendant's polygraph exam showed that he had lied. Courts are much less likely to tolerate misrepresentations of law, such as that defendant's confession could not be used against him at trial or that the previously obtained confession of an accomplice could be so used.

Another type of deceit is the so-called "false friend" technique, whereby the interrogator represents that he is a friend acting in the suspect's best interest. Extreme versions of this technique have been condemned by the Supreme Court. In *Leyra v. Denno*[33] a confession was held involuntary where obtained by a police psychiatrist who was represented as a general practitioner brought in to relieve his acutely painful sinus attack, and in *Spano v. New York*[34] a confession was ruled involuntary where obtained by a policeman who was a close friend of the defendant and who told defendant he would be in trouble unless defendant confessed. Dictum in the *Miranda* case was critical of the "Mutt and Jeff" routine, whereby the defendant is questioned by a hostile interrogator and then a supposedly sympathetic one. But the courts have not generally disapproved of the police giving "friendly" advice to the defendant or expressing sympathy for him. A quite different kind of "false friend" situation, that in which by deception the defendant is made unaware that the person with whom he is conversing is a police officer or police agent, clearly does not make the defendant's statement involuntary even though he acted in the mistaken impression

that this person could be trusted not to reveal it. Police appeals to the defendant's sympathies, such as by the now-famous "Christian burial speech" ploy, do not automatically render a confession involuntary, and the same is true of exhortations to tell the truth or assertions that the suspect had been lying.

Under *Miranda*, certain warnings must precede custodial interrogation, and this means a failure to give those warnings will result in exclusion of the confession under that decision. Nonetheless, on occasion the question may arise as to the relevance of the absence of such warnings to the voluntariness issue. This can occur when the confession at issue (i) was obtained prior to the *Miranda* decision, (ii) was obtained from a suspect not in custody and thus not covered by *Miranda,* or (iii) is admissible for a special purpose if voluntary notwithstanding the *Miranda* violation. As the Court put it in *Procunier v. Atchley,*[35] failure to give the warnings is not inherently coercive, but is "relevant only in establishing a setting in which actual coercion might have been exerted." On the other hand, the fact the warnings were given is an important factor tending in the direction of a voluntariness finding. This fact is important in two respects. It bears on the coerciveness of the circumstances, for it reveals that the police were aware of the suspect's rights and presumably prepared to honor them. And, as with the factors discussed below, it bears upon the defendant's susceptibility, for it shows that the defendant was aware he had a right not to talk to the police. Where, however, the police give the warnings but then suggest that the exercise of the right to consult with a lawyer would be prejudicial, denying the defendant all opportunities for leniency, that action not only will render involuntary the waiver of *Miranda* rights but also add a coercive element to the interrogation that could render the statement itself involuntary. (This additional consequence may become important because limitations upon the prosecution's use of involuntary statements extend beyond the limitation upon the use of

---

33. 347 U.S. 556, 74 S.Ct. 716, 98 L.Ed. 948 (1954).

34. 360 U.S. 315, 79 S.Ct. 1202, 3 L.Ed.2d 1265 (1959).

35. 400 U.S. 446, 91 S.Ct. 485, 27 L.Ed.2d 524 (1971).

statements that are voluntary but obtained in violation of *Miranda*.[36])

Especially in an otherwise close case, it is appropriate also to take account of the particular characteristics of the person who was subjected to interrogation, in order to judge the extent of his ability to resist the external pressures brought to bear upon him. The Supreme Court has taken into consideration the suspect's age, sex, and race whenever those factors have tended to indicate less than average ability to resist. Likewise relevant is the fact that the defendant might have been more willing to confess because he was suffering from a physical injury, physical illness, physical fatigue, mental illness, mental deficiency, emotional distress, or an abnormality caused by drugs or alcohol. Courts have also taken into account the suspect's education level, and his prior experience with the police. But *Connelly*, discussed above, makes it clear that such characteristics of the defendant, in isolation, cannot alone "ever dispose of the inquiry into constitutional 'voluntariness.'" Thus, as the Court in *Connelly* elaborated, "while mental condition is surely relevant to an individual's susceptibility to police coercion, mere examination of the confessant's state of mind can never conclude the due process inquiry."

Connelly says there must also exist "the crucial element of police overreaching," which was not present in that case because the police merely received the confession of a person who approached them and volunteered it. *Connelly* thus leaves uncertain how the "overreaching" judgment is to be made in the more typical interrogation situation. There is a split of authority as to whether the very act of interrogating one known to be under a substantial mental disability supplies the requisite coercion. It would seem, however, that the propriety of the investigative and interrogation techniques used must be judged in light of what the police knew or should have known about defendant's ability to comprehend the events and circumstances.

Connelly also highlights the fact that coercive tactics utilized by private persons cannot alone produce a confession that is involuntary in the constitutional sense. (Under the law of some states, however, such private coercion may be a basis for suppression on some other grounds.) However, the "police overreaching" language of *Connelly* should not be taken literally, for a government employee need not be a law enforcement official for his questioning to implicate the strictures of the Fifth Amendment.

(d) Critique of the "Voluntariness" Test. One major defect in the due process "voluntariness" test is that it leaves the police without needed guidance. This is in part attributable to the fact that the term itself is imprecise. Virtually all incriminating statements—even those made under brutal treatment—are "voluntary" in the sense of representing a choice of alternatives, yet very few are "voluntary" in the sense that they would have been given even absent official pressure of some kind. Moreover, a standard that varies from case to case depending upon how dull or alert or how soft or tough the particular suspect happened to be was not likely to have had much of an impact upon the police.

Secondly, the due process standard impaired the effectiveness and the legitimacy of judicial review. Because of the aforementioned ambiguity, even conscientious trial judges were left without guidance for resolving confession claims. Moreover, the nature of the voluntariness test virtually invited judges to give weight to their subjective preferences. The "totality of circumstances" approach of the Supreme Court both facilitated pro-police rulings at suppression hearings and diminished the chances that the defendant would obtain relief at the appellate level. And the Supreme Court, which took only about one confession case a year during the heyday of the voluntariness test, was able to deal only with the tip of the iceberg. Perhaps the strongest evidence of the ineffectiveness and the unworkability of the voluntariness test is the case of *Davis v. North Carolina*.[37] No one other than the police had

---

36. See § 9.5(a) (use of fruits of illegally obtained confession); § 9.6(a) (impeachment).

37. 384 U.S. 737, 86 S.Ct. 1761, 16 L.Ed.2d 895 (1966).

spoken to the defendant during the sixteen days of detention and interrogation that preceded his confessions, and in holding the confessions involuntary the Court noted it had "never sustained the use of a confession obtained after such a lengthy period of detention and interrogation as was involved in this case." Yet two state courts and two federal courts had previously held that these confessions were lawfully admitted into evidence against Davis.

Davis was an unusual confession case in that the relevant facts clearly appeared on the record and were uncontested. The more typical case is one in which there is a "swearing contest" over what happened behind closed doors, and thus a third major defect in the due process voluntariness test is that its application is fatally dependent upon resolution of that swearing contest. In the usual case, it is impossible to determine whether the "facts" asserted by the police or those put forward by the defendant more closely corresponded to the events that actually occurred in the interrogation room.

These circumstances explain why the Supreme Court undertook the search, discussed in the balance of this Chapter, for alternative means to deal with the confessions problem.

§ 6.3 The Prompt Appearance Requirement

(a) The *McNabb–Mallory* Rule. The previously discussed voluntariness test was, of course, equally applicable to confessions utilized in federal prosecutions, for any confession that was inadmissible because obtained in violation of the due process clause of the Fourteenth Amendment would likewise be subject to suppression under the Fifth Amendment due process clause. Beginning in 1943, however, the Supreme Court developed another line of authority, not expressly grounded in the Constitution, which was frequently utilized in federal criminal prosecutions. Under what became known as the *McNabb–Mallory* rule, the Court required the suppression of any confession obtained during custody that was illegal

by virtue of a failure to honor a defendant's right to be brought promptly before a judicial officer following his arrest. This rule provided a basis for suppressing many confessions that, upon closer examination of the circumstances, might have been found to be excludable as a matter of due process, but it clearly extended to other confessions unquestionably voluntary.

The rule had an uncertain beginning in *McNabb v. United States,*[1] a case involving the murder of a federal revenue agent during a raid on an illegal still. Several uneducated mountaineers were arrested late at night and were subjected intermittently to prolonged questioning over the next several days, resulting in confessions by three of them. The confessions were admitted as voluntary and the defendants were convicted. But the Supreme Court found it "unnecessary to reach the Constitutional issue pressed upon us" because the case could be resolved by the Court's "exercise of its supervisory authority over the administration of criminal justice in the federal courts." Specifically, because the record did not show that the confessing defendants had been taken before a judicial officer in a timely fashion as required by federal law, the Court concluded the convictions

> cannot be allowed to stand without making the courts themselves accomplices in wilful disobedience of law. Congress has not explicitly forbidden the use of evidence so procured. But to permit such evidence to be made the basis of a conviction in the federal courts would stultify the policy which Congress has enacted into law.

Because the Court in *McNabb* repeatedly stressed the "circumstances disclosed here," such as that the defendants were uneducated, and at another point asserted that a conviction could not stand when based on evidence obtained in "flagrant disregard of the procedure which Congress has commanded," it was by no means clear that the decision required suppression of any confession obtained in violation of a prompt appearance statute. But in

1. 318 U.S. 332, 63 S.Ct. 608, 87 L.Ed. 819 (1943).

the later case of *Upshaw v. United States*[2] the Court flatly stated that "a confession is inadmissible if made during illegal detention due to failure promptly to carry a prisoner before a committing magistrate." Then, finally, came *Mallory v. United States*,[3] in which a unanimous Court held that a confession was inadmissible because procured in violation of a provision in the federal rules[4] (not extant when *McNabb* was decided) to the effect that an arrested person must be taken before a committing magistrate "without unnecessary delay."

Mallory is also important because it contains a detailed discussion of what constitutes "unnecessary delay":

> The police may not arrest upon mere suspicion but only on "probable cause." The next step in the proceeding is to arraign the arrested person before a judicial officer as quickly as possible so that he may be advised of his rights and so that the issue of probable cause may be promptly determined. The arrested person may, of course, be "booked" by the police. But he is not to be taken to police headquarters in order to carry out a process of inquiry that lends itself, even if not so designed, to eliciting damaging statements to support the arrest and ultimately his guilt.

> The duty enjoined upon arresting officers to arraign "without unnecessary delay" indicates that the command does not call for mechanical or automatic obedience. Circumstances may justify a brief delay between arrest and arraignment, as for instance, where the story volunteered by the accused is susceptible of quick verification through third parties. But the delay must not be of a nature to give opportunity for the extraction of a confession. * * *

In every case where the police resort to interrogation of an arrested person and secure a confession, they may well claim, and

quite sincerely, that they were merely trying to check on the information given by him.

Lower courts ordinarily treated the *McNabb–Mallory* rule as less than an absolute prohibition upon pre-appearance interrogation or upon delays in bringing an arrestee before a magistrate. Questioning has been allowed in "threshold" situations (i.e., shortly after arrest at the arrest scene, in the squad car, or at the station), in circumstances where it was intended to clarify or verify a story given earlier by the defendant, and even in other circumstances in which the interrogation was characterized as "investigatory." Delays in taking the defendant before a magistrate have been deemed not "unnecessary" where attributable to the unavailability of a magistrate outside of normal hours, the booking process, efforts to apprehend defendant's confederates, efforts to confirm information through independent sources, cooperation of the defendant with the police, or efforts by the police to reduce an oral confession to written form.

Early Supreme Court decisions marked other important limits upon this particular exclusionary rule, namely: a confession obtained during a period of lawful detention is not subject to suppression merely because of a subsequent failure promptly to take the confessing defendant before a magistrate;[5] at least absent a showing that a subterfuge was involved, a confession for one crime is not subject to suppression where it was obtained upon remand of defendant to the police following his prompt appearance before a magistrate on a different (even lesser) charge;[6] and a confession obtained by federal agents from a defendant in state custody is not subject to suppression even where exclusion would have been required if the custody had been federal, unless it appears there was a "working arrangement" between state and federal officials.[7] And in the post-*Mallory* case of *Cleary v. Bolger*[8]

---

2.   335 U.S. 410, 69 S.Ct. 170, 93 L.Ed. 100 (1948).

3.   354 U.S. 449, 77 S.Ct. 1356, 1 L.Ed.2d 1479 (1957).

4.   Fed.R.Crim.P. 5(a).

5.   United States v. Mitchell, 322 U.S. 65, 64 S.Ct. 896, 88 L.Ed. 1140 (1944).

6.   United States v. Carignan, 342 U.S. 36, 72 S.Ct. 97, 96 L.Ed. 48 (1951).

7.   Anderson v. United States, 318 U.S. 350, 63 S.Ct. 599, 87 L.Ed. 829 (1943).

8.   371 U.S. 392, 83 S.Ct. 385, 9 L.Ed.2d 390 (1963).

the Court, stressing the traditional reluctance of federal courts to interfere with state proceedings, held it was improper for a federal court to enjoin a state official from testifying at a state criminal trial about his witnessing of a confession that would have been inadmissible in federal court under *McNabb–Mallory*.

(b) Reactions to the Rule. Reactions to the *McNabb–Mallory* rule over the years have been mixed. On the one hand, some see the prompt appearance requirement coupled with an exclusionary sanction as serving several worthwhile functions: it prevents wholesale or dragnet arrests on suspicion, gives force to the notion that an arrest (even on probable cause) is not properly a vehicle for the investigation of crime, and ensures that the substance of the accusatorial system of criminal justice is preserved. But of greatest significance here is the notion that this rule is intimately related to the problem of eliminating the third degree, in that use of coercion to obtain confessions most frequently occurs while the accused is being held in violation the prompt appearance requirement. The *McNabb–Mallory* rule was thus seen as an outgrowth of the Court's awareness of the tremendous problems of proof raised by the "coerced confession" issue, which meant to some that there was a need for something like it to govern state confession cases.

Those generally opposed to the exclusion of evidence as a means of deterring the police saw *McNabb–Mallory* as another instance of an unsound judicial policy that turns known criminals loose as a means of punishing the police. Others objected to the rule on the ground that it unwisely tended to "collapse" the arrest and charging decisions and to prevent even fair questioning intended to determine whether a person lawfully arrested should be charged. Such views prompted repeated efforts to have Congress either repeal

or revise the *McNabb–Mallory* rule. This was finally accomplished as a part of the Omnibus Crime Control and Safe Streets Act of 1968. One provision states that a voluntary confession "shall not be inadmissible solely because of delay" in bringing the person before a magistrate "if such confession was made or given by such person within six hours immediately following his arrest or other detention," to which there is added the proviso that this time limitation "shall not apply in any case in which the delay in bringing such person before such magistrate or other officer beyond such six-hour period is found by the trial judge to be reasonable considering the means of transportation and the distance to be traveled to the nearest available such magistrate or other officer."[9] Though that language would seem to restrict the *McNabb–Mallory* rule to confessions obtained after the six-hour period and reasonable extensions thereof, other provisions declare that any confession shall be admissible in a federal prosecution "if it is voluntarily given"[10] and that delay in appearance before a magistrate is but one of several factors "to be taken into consideration by the judge" but which "need not be conclusive on the issue of voluntariness."[11]

This confusing combination of provisions in § 3501 has produced disagreement among lower courts as to what is left of the *McNabb–Mallory* rule. One view is that exclusion based solely on impermissible delay is no longer allowed, and that impermissible delay is merely a factor to be considered in judging voluntariness. A contrary position holds that *McNabb–Mallory* survives § 3501, but is now applicable only to a delay occurring prior to the confession that extended beyond the six hour period and that was unreasonable as measured by the logistical concerns noted in § 3501(c). A middle position holds that the per se exclusion formerly mandated by *McNabb–Mallory* is no longer appropriate, but that a federal court

9. 18 U.S.C.A. § 3501(c).

This provision does not apply if the suspect is arrested and in custody of state or local authorities only on state or local charges at the time of the confession (regardless of whether those authorities have reason to believe the suspect also may have violated federal law), as no delay in presentment can occur absent an obligation to present the

suspect before a federal judicial officer, which cannot arise until the suspect is arrested or detained for a federal crime. United States v. Alvarez–Sanchez, 511 U.S. 350, 114 S.Ct. 1599, 128 L.Ed.2d 319 (1994).

10. 18 U.S.C.A. § 3501(a).

11. 18 U.S.C.A. § 3501(b).

retains discretion to employ an exclusionary remedy as a response to unreasonable delay beyond the six hour period. In *United States v. Alvarez–Sanchez*,[12] which unanimously held that § 3501(c) "does not apply to statements made by a person who is being held solely on state charges,"[13] the Supreme Court took note of the aforementioned division among the lower courts but found no need to resolve it.

(c) Prompt Appearance in the States. Early on in the development of the *McNabb–Mallory* rule, the Supreme Court held that it was not constitutionally mandated and that consequently it was not applicable to trials in the state courts.[14] Although, as noted above, some have praised the rule as a means of dealing with an issue of constitutional magnitude—the coerced confession problem, it does not now seem at all likely that the Court will impose such a rule upon the states. But prompt appearance is a common if not universal requirement under state law, and thus there remains the possibility that a state might adopt an exclusionary rule as a means of enforcing such a law.

The vast majority of state courts passing on the question have rejected the *McNabb–Mallory* approach outright, opting instead for a traditional due process voluntariness test. But there are now several states that follow the *McNabb–Mallory* approach in some respect. Some utilize a per se rule of exclusion, while others require a showing of a causal connection between the illegal delay and the challenged confession. The wisdom of this development at the state level is a matter of dispute, and involves much the same considerations noted above regarding the *McNabb–Mallory* debate. It has been argued, however, that the case for this approach is now less substantial

than it once was because the Supreme Court has in the interim provided other effective means for safeguarding the vital Fourth and Fifth Amendment interests that the *McNabb–Mallory* rule was intended to protect.

§ 6.4   The Right to Counsel

(a) Pre–*Massiah* Developments. Under the "totality of circumstances" approach to the due process voluntariness test, the Court began making special note of the fact that the confessing defendant had been denied access to counsel,[1] and thus this deprivation together with other circumstances could justify the conclusion that the defendant's confession was not voluntary. By the late 1950's, however, a minority of the Court was actually asserting that a suspect had a constitutional right to have counsel present during police interrogation.

In *Crooker v. California*,[2] the petitioner claimed his voluntary confession should be suppressed because obtained after the police denied his specific request to contact his lawyer. The majority rejected this contention, asserting that such a rule "would effectively preclude police questioning—*fair as well as unfair*—until the accused was afforded opportunity to call his attorney," and found support in the *Betts v. Brady*[3] rule that due process did not impose a flat requirement of appointed counsel in all serious state trials. But the four dissenters declared that as a matter of due process "the accused who wants a counsel should have one at any time after the moment of arrest."

A year later came *Spano v. New York*,[4] where, after an indicted defendant surrendered with his retained attorney, police ques-

---

12. 511 U.S. 350, 114 S.Ct. 1599, 128 L.Ed.2d 319 (1994).

13. The Court noted it did not have before it a case in which "state or local authorities, acting in collusion with federal officers arrest[ed] and detain[ed] someone in order to allow all the federal agents to interrogate him in violation of his right to prompt presentment." Pre–§ 3501 precedent had mandated suppression of confession that was a product of such collusion, but there was no need here "to address § 3501's effect, if any, on [that precedent]."

14. Gallegos v. Nebraska, 342 U.S. 55, 72 S.Ct. 141, 96 L.Ed. 86 (1951).

§ 6.4

1. Harris v. South Carolina, 338 U.S. 68, 69 S.Ct. 1354, 93 L.Ed. 1815 (1949); Haley v. Ohio, 332 U.S. 596, 68 S.Ct. 302, 92 L.Ed. 224 (1948); Malinski v. New York, 324 U.S. 401, 65 S.Ct. 781, 89 L.Ed. 1029 (1945).

2. 357 U.S. 433, 78 S.Ct. 1287, 2 L.Ed.2d 1448 (1958).

3. 316 U.S. 455, 62 S.Ct. 1252, 86 L.Ed. 1595 (1942).

4. 360 U.S. 315, 79 S.Ct. 1202, 3 L.Ed.2d 1265 (1959).

tioned him and obtained a confession. The opinion of the Court by the Chief Justice concluding the confession was not voluntary emphasized numerous factors, including that the police "ignored his reasonable requests to contact the local attorney whom he had already retained." However, four concurring Justices accepted the defendant's contention that his absolute right to counsel (defendant had been indicted on a capital charge and thus did not fall under the *Betts* rule) had attached prior to his interrogation, as he had already been indicted for murder and the police had thus not been involved in the questioning of a suspect in the course of investigating an unsolved crime. Because a year earlier the Chief Justice, dissenting in *Crooker*, had taken the position that the right to counsel should begin even earlier, it appeared that the position taken by the *Spano* concurring Justices commanded a majority of the Court.

Several cases decided in 1963 strengthened the assumption that there was now a right to counsel at post-indictment interrogation. One was *White v. Maryland*,[5] holding that the absolute right to counsel in a capital case was applicable at defendant's preliminary arraignment where he entered a guilty plea that, though subsequently withdrawn, was later introduced into evidence against him. Because *White* concerned the evidentiary use of White's uncounseled plea of guilty, a problem not greatly different from the use of an uncounseled confession, and because it recognized a pretrial right to a lawyer who would have helped only to avoid making incriminating evidence available, the decision seemed quite relevant. *White* took on even greater significance when *Betts* was overruled in *Gideon v. Wainwright*,[6] holding that the absolute right to counsel for indigent state defendants extended to all serious cases. Also noteworthy was *Haynes v. Washington*,[7] which appeared to recognize a closer relationship than had theretofore been acknowledged between the due process voluntariness requirement and a suspect's

right to contact his attorney during the interrogation process.

(b) The *Massiah* Case. The argument that the right to counsel attaches when the defendant is indicted and his status thereby changes from "suspect" to "accused" was finally accepted by the Court in a case that did not even involve custodial interrogation. In *Massiah v. United States*,[8] Massiah, indicted for federal narcotics violations, retained counsel, pled not guilty and was released on bail. Codefendant Colson, who unknown to Massiah was cooperating with the authorities and had a radio transmitter in his car, invited Massiah to discuss the pending case, and during their conversations in that car Massiah's damaging admissions were overheard by a federal agent, who testified as to them at Massiah's trial. Perhaps to avoid a difficult eavesdropping issue, the Supreme Court decided *Massiah* on Sixth Amendment grounds, holding

> that the petitioner was denied the basic protections of that guarantee when there was used against him at his trial evidence of his own incriminating words, which federal agents had deliberately elicited from him after he had been indicted and in the absence of his counsel. It is true that in the *Spano* case the defendant was interrogated in a police station, while here the damaging testimony was elicited from the defendant without his knowledge while he was free on bail. But, as Judge Hays pointed out in his dissent in the Court of Appeals, "if such a rule is to have any efficacy it must apply to indirect and surreptitious interrogations as well as those conducted in the jailhouse. In this case, Massiah was more seriously imposed upon * * * because he did not even know that he was under interrogation by a government agent."

The three dissenters objected that in the instant case there was neither any "inherent danger of police coercion justifying the prophylactic effect of another exclusionary rule," nor any "unconstitutional interference with Massiah's right to counsel" in the sense of prevent-

---

5. 373 U.S. 59, 83 S.Ct. 1050, 10 L.Ed.2d 193 (1963).

6. 372 U.S. 335, 83 S.Ct. 792, 9 L.Ed.2d 799 (1963).

7. 373 U.S. 503, 83 S.Ct. 1336, 10 L.Ed.2d 513 (1963).

8. 377 U.S. 201, 84 S.Ct. 1199, 12 L.Ed.2d 246 (1964).

ing or spying upon his consultations with counsel.

Although *Massiah* was also applied in state proceedings,[9] it had a rather limited impact until finally, in 1977, it was revitalized and expanded in *Brewer v. Williams*.[10] In the confessions area, it was overshadowed by *Escobedo v. Illinois*,[11] decided just a few weeks later, and by *Miranda v. Arizona*,[12] which came two years later. Lower courts were inclined to give *Massiah* as narrow an interpretation as possible.

(c) The *Escobedo* Case. Just five weeks after *Massiah,* the Court decided the case of *Escobedo v. Illinois*.[13] Escobedo was taken into custody and questioned concerning the fatal shooting of his brother-in-law, but his retained counsel obtained his release. About ten days later one DiGerlando told police that Escobedo had fired the fatal shots, so Escobedo was again arrested and then told of that allegation. He repeatedly asked to see his retained attorney, who came to the police station but was barred from seeing his client. After the police arranged a confrontation between DiGerlando and Escobedo, Escobedo incriminated himself in the killing, and this enabled an assistant prosecutor to obtain a more elaborate written confession, which was admitted at Escobedo's trial. He was convicted of murder.

The Supreme Court, in a 5–4 decision, reversed the conviction. The majority opinion was highly critical of reliance upon confessions in general and interrogation of those without counsel in particular, asserting "that a system of criminal law enforcement which comes to depend on the 'confession' will, in the long run, be less reliable and more subject to abuses than a system which depends on extrinsic evidence independently secured through skillful investigation." It seemed that the Court was about to announce a broad right-to-counsel-at-the station rule, for it was said that preindictment interrogation was just as much

a "critical stage" as the preliminary hearing in *White v. Maryland,*[14] and that *Massiah* was apposite because "no meaningful distinction can be drawn between interrogation of an accused before and after formal indictment." But the *Escobedo* holding was cautiously limited to the facts of the case:

> We hold, therefore, that where, as here, [1] the investigation is no longer a general inquiry into an unsolved crime but has begun to focus on a particular suspect, [2] the suspect has been taken into police custody, [3] the police carry out a process of interrogations that lends itself to eliciting incriminating statements, [4] the suspect has requested and been denied an opportunity to consult with his lawyer, and [5] the police have not effectively warned him of his absolute constitutional right to remain silent, the accused has been denied "the Assistance of Counsel" in violation of the Sixth Amendment to the Constitution as "made obligatory upon the States by the Fourteenth Amendment," * * * and that no statement elicited by the police during the interrogation may be used against him at a criminal trial.

The combination of sweeping language at some points and the above limited holding engendered conflicting views about the implications of the case. But *Escobedo* appeared to be a landmark decision that could only expand as the Court further considered the Sixth Amendment's application at the police station. This did not happen because just two years later the Court instead, in *Miranda v. Arizona,*[15] adopted a much broader rule based upon the Fifth Amendment privilege against self-incrimination. But in the interim, and thereafter as to trials that predated *Miranda* and thus were not governed by that decision,[16] the lower courts had occasion to determine the meaning of *Escobedo*. Most attributed significance to each of the five "elements" in the

---

9. McLeod v. Ohio, 381 U.S. 356, 85 S.Ct. 1556, 14 L.Ed.2d 682 (1965).

10. 430 U.S. 387, 97 S.Ct. 1232, 51 L.Ed.2d 424 (1977).

11. 378 U.S. 478, 84 S.Ct. 1758, 12 L.Ed.2d 977 (1964).

12. 384 U.S. 436, 86 S.Ct. 1602, 16 L.Ed.2d 694 (1966).

13. 378 U.S. 478, 84 S.Ct. 1758, 12 L.Ed.2d 977 (1964).

14. 373 U.S. 59, 83 S.Ct. 1050, 10 L.Ed.2d 193 (1963).

15. 384 U.S. 436, 86 S.Ct. 1602, 16 L.Ed.2d 694 (1966).

16. Johnson v. New Jersey, 384 U.S. 719, 86 S.Ct. 1772, 16 L.Ed.2d 882 (1966).

Escobedo holding: (1) While the Court later and rather unconvincingly said in *Miranda* that the focus requirement of *Escobedo* was intended to mean deprivation of freedom in a significant way, this requirement was utilized to find *Escobedo* inapplicable where the suspect was in custody on another charge and the interrogation was undertaken while the case was in the investigatory rather than accusatory stage. (2) *Escobedo* was deemed not to apply when the suspect was not in police custody, though it was acknowledged that custody could exist without there being a formal arrest. (3) *Escobedo* was read as not governing volunteered statements, or even interrogation undertaken primarily for another purpose, such as to locate a kidnapping victim. (4) *Escobedo* was considered not to require a warning of the right to counsel, and to be applicable only if the suspect made a clear and unambiguous request for counsel. (5) *Escobedo* was held not to apply if the police had warned the suspect of his right to remain silent.

Indeed, the Supreme Court itself ultimately came to treat *Escobedo* as nothing more than a "false start" toward the new approach to the confessions problem undertaken later in *Miranda.* In *Kirby v. Illinois,*[17] the Court held that the Sixth Amendment right to counsel at a police lineup attached "only at or after the time that adversary judicial proceedings had been initiated." Noting that *Escobedo* was the "only seeming deviation" from a long line of cases accepting that starting point, the Court in retrospect concluded that the " 'prime purpose' of *Escobedo* was not to vindicate the constitutional right to counsel as such, but, like *Miranda,* 'to guarantee full effectuation of the privilege against self incrimination.' " Moreover, added the *Kirby* Court, *Escobedo* is now limited in its "holding * * * to its own facts."

(d) The *Williams* Case. When in 1966 the Supreme Court decided *Miranda v. Arizona,*[18] grounded in the Fifth Amendment privilege against self-incrimination, it remained unclear at best whether the "pure" Sixth Amendment right to counsel approach[19] continued to have any vitality or significance in the confession area. It seemed clear that *Miranda* had displaced *Escobedo,* but just what it had done to the *Massiah* rule was quite uncertain—*Massiah* was not even mentioned in *Miranda.* So matters stood until 1977, when in *Brewer v. Williams*[20] the Supreme Court breathed new life into *Massiah.*

Williams was arraigned in Davenport, Iowa on an outstanding arrest warrant prior to his transportation to Des Moines on a murder charge. Though the police had assured Williams' lawyer that he would not be interrogated during the trip, a detective made a "Christian burial speech," to the effect that because of the worsening weather it would be necessary to find the body now to ensure the victim a Christian burial. Williams then directed the police to the body. On Williams' motion to suppress all evidence relating to or resulting from the statements he made to the police, the trial judge found that "an agreement was made between defense counsel and the police officials to the effect that the Defendant was not to be questioned on the return trip to Des Moines" and that the evidence had been elicited from Williams during "a critical stage in the proceedings requiring the presence of counsel on his request," but ruled that Williams had "waived his right to have an attorney present during the giving of such information." There was no mention of *Massiah* by either the bare majority or the dissenters when the state supreme court affirmed. On federal habeas corpus, the district court concluded that Williams had not waived any of his constitutional protections, and ruled for him on three alternative and independent grounds: (1) that he had been denied his constitutional right to the assistance of counsel; (2) that he had been denied his rights under *Escobedo* and *Miranda;* and (3) that in any event his self-incriminatory statement had

---

17.   406 U.S. 682, 92 S.Ct. 1877, 32 L.Ed.2d 411 (1972).

18.   384 U.S. 436, 86 S.Ct. 1602, 16 L.Ed.2d 694 (1966).

19.   To be contrasted with the "right" to counsel under the *Miranda* case, which is not derived directly from the Sixth Amendment but which the Court deemed a neces-

sary safeguard of the Fifth Amendment privilege against self-incrimination.

20.   430 U.S. 387, 97 S.Ct. 1232, 51 L.Ed.2d 424 (1977).

been involuntarily made. The federal court of appeals affirmed on the first two grounds.

The Supreme Court, in yet another 5–4 decision, affirmed the judgment of the court of appeals. The majority concluded there was "no need" either to assay the district court's ruling the statements were involuntary or the district and appellate courts' application of the *Miranda* rule to these facts, because "it is clear that the judgment before us must in any event be affirmed upon the ground that Williams was deprived of a different constitutional right—the right to the assistance of counsel." One theory as to why the Court opted for the long-dormant *Massiah* rule is that the Court thereby avoided for the moment the question of whether *Miranda* claims, like Fourth Amendment claims under *Stone v. Powell*,[21] could not be raised by state prisoners on federal habeas corpus. Another is that *Massiah* afforded an easier route to reversal than *Miranda* because it was unnecessary under the former decision to determine whether the Christian burial speech was "interrogation," and because a waiver of *Massiah* rights is not as readily found as a waiver of *Miranda* rights. But the *Williams* majority made no mention of any of these points.

Rather, the Court proceeded immediately to the conclusion that "[t]he circumstances of this case are * * * constitutionally indistinguishable from those presented in *Massiah*." Though *Massiah* was a post-indictment case, it was now clear under *Kirby v. Illinois*[22] that the right to counsel arises "at or after the time that judicial proceedings have been initiated," which was the case here because Williams had been arraigned on the warrant in Davenport. It was also clear that the detective had "designedly set out to elicit information from Williams." Moreover, the fact that

> the incriminating statements were elicited surreptitiously in [*Massiah*], and otherwise here, is constitutionally irrelevant. Rather, the clear rule of *Massiah* is that once adversary proceedings had commenced against an

individual, he has a right to legal representation when the government interrogates him. It thus requires no wooden or technical application of the *Massiah* doctrine to conclude that Williams was entitled to the assistance of counsel guaranteed to him by the Sixth and Fourteenth Amendments.

The *Williams* majority then rejected the state court's conclusion that waiver had occurred here merely because during the trip Williams did not assert that right or a desire not to talk in the absence of counsel. The four dissenters, on the other hand, contended that Williams had "relinquished his right not to talk to the police about his crime," and also claimed that the instant case was unlike *Massiah* because the police had not deliberately sought to isolate Williams from his counsel, had not acted solely for the purpose of obtaining incriminating evidence, and had not engaged in conduct that was "tantamount to interrogation."

(e) When the Right to Counsel Begins. Although the *Massiah* right to counsel had generally been interpreted as arising only upon indictment, in *Brewer v. Williams*[23] the Court declared that "the right to counsel granted by the Sixth and Fourteenth Amendments means at least that a person is entitled to the help of a lawyer at or after the time that judicial proceedings have been initiated against him—'whether by way of formal charge, preliminary hearing, indictment, information, or arraignment.'"[24] Noting that a warrant had been issued for Williams' arrest and that he had been arraigned on that warrant before a judge and that he had been committed by the court to confinement in jail, the Court concluded there "can be no doubt in the present case that judicial proceedings had been initiated."

Clearly this test is not met merely because the defendant had been arrested without a warrant, nor is it met merely because the investigation has focused upon the defendant. Though "focus" was one of the several ele-

---

21. 428 U.S. 465, 96 S.Ct. 3037, 49 L.Ed.2d 1067 (1976), also discussed in § 28.3 at note 60.

22. 406 U.S. 682, 92 S.Ct. 1877, 32 L.Ed.2d 411 (1972).

23. 430 U.S. 387, 97 S.Ct. 1232, 51 L.Ed.2d 424 (1977).

24. Quoting Kirby v. Illinois, 406 U.S. 682, 92 S.Ct. 1877, 32 L.Ed.2d 411 (1972).

ments in *Escobedo,* that case has been limited to its own facts,[25] and the Supreme Court later held in *Hoffa v. United States*[26] that focus alone did not ripen the Sixth Amendment right to counsel. Even against the contention that indictment was delayed for the specific purpose of allowing the government to "beef up" its case with admissions to be obtained by stealth and trickery, it has been held that the government is under no obligation to cease an ongoing investigation when probable cause to obtain an indictment comes into existence.

There is an apparent split of authority on the question of whether the filing of a complaint is alone enough to give rise to a Sixth Amendment right to counsel, though the difference probably is explainable by the fact that this document is used for multiple purposes. Cases holding that filing the complaint constitutes the initiation of judicial proceedings for Sixth Amendment purposes under *Williams* typically stress express recognition in that jurisdiction of the complaint as one type of charging document. On the other hand, decisions holding that filing the complaint (or, indeed, filing the complaint and issuance of an arrest warrant thereon) does not have this effect emphasize use of the complaint simply as a means of obtaining a warrant. In support of the latter position, it is noteworthy that the *Williams* test quoted above was taken from *Kirby v. Illinois,*[27] where the Supreme Court explained that a person is entitled to counsel once the government has "committed itself to prosecute, and * * * the adverse positions of government and defendant have solidified." Thus, so the argument proceeds, the mere fact the police obtained an arrest warrant for some purpose, such as to comply with *Payton v. New York,*[28] should hardly be determinative. But

this issue, which the Supreme Court seems to have recognized remains open for decision by that Court,[29] is complicated by the fact that in many jurisdictions a complaint might be utilized for either of the two purposes mentioned above. At no point in *Williams* does the Court discuss the circumstances behind the issuance of the complaint and warrant, that is, whether the government really had "committed itself to prosecute." Perhaps the assumption is that whatever the reasons underlying the complaint-warrant process, at least from the time defendant is brought into court and arraigned on the warrant (at which point it or the complaint underlying it becomes a tentative charging document) the Sixth Amendment right to counsel applies. The Court later declared in *Michigan v. Jackson*[30] that "arraignment [in the sense of the defendant's initial appearance] signals the initiation of adversary judicial proceedings," without regard to whether it has the particular characteristics that would make "the arraignment itself * * * a critical stage requiring the presence of counsel."

Assuming that "judicial proceedings have been initiated," is it in addition essential to recognition of the Sixth Amendment right that counsel actually have been retained by or appointed for the defendant? While in both *Massiah* and *Williams* the defendant was already represented by an attorney at the time in question, this is not necessary. As the Court has noted, "in *McLeod v. Ohio*[31] * * * we summarily affirmed a decision that the police could not elicit information after indictment even though counsel had not yet been appointed."[32] What then if such judicial proceedings have not been initiated but the defendant in fact has counsel appointed for or (more likely)

---

25. Kirby v. Illinois, 406 U.S. 682, 92 S.Ct. 1877, 32 L.Ed.2d 411 (1972).

26. 385 U.S. 293, 87 S.Ct. 408, 17 L.Ed.2d 374 (1966).

27. 406 U.S. 682, 92 S.Ct. 1877, 32 L.Ed.2d 411 (1972).

28. 445 U.S. 573, 100 S.Ct. 1371, 63 L.Ed.2d 639 (1980), holding that a warrant is ordinarily needed to enter defendant's premises to arrest him.

29. In Edwards v. Arizona, 451 U.S. 477, 101 S.Ct. 1880, 68 L.Ed.2d 378 (1981), the Court decided the case on *Miranda* grounds and thus found it unnecessary to respond to the state's argument that *Massiah–Williams* was not applicable where only a criminal complaint had been

filed, which under the state constitution was not a sufficient charging document.

30. 475 U.S. 625, 106 S.Ct. 1404, 89 L.Ed.2d 631 (1986).

31. 381 U.S. 356, 85 S.Ct. 1556, 14 L.Ed.2d 682 (1965).

32. Edwards v. Arizona, 451 U.S. 477, 101 S.Ct. 1880, 68 L.Ed.2d 378 (1981). Consider also that in United States v. Henry, 447 U.S. 264, 100 S.Ct. 2183, 65 L.Ed.2d 115 (1980), the Court applied *Massiah–Williams* to use of an undercover agent on dates where the use was arranged for on Nov. 21 but counsel was not appointed until Nov. 27.

retained by him? In *Miranda v. Arizona,*[33] the Court dropped a footnote commenting that in *Escobedo* the police also prevented his attorney from seeing him and that this action by itself "constitutes a violation of the Sixth Amendment right to the assistance of counsel and excludes any statement obtained in its wake." But when the Court later discredited *Escobedo* to the extent that it purported to mark the beginnings of the Sixth Amendment right to counsel,[34] it was apparent this footnote did not settle the matter. In *Moran v. Burbine,*[35] the Court concluded that "it makes little sense to say that the Sixth Amendment right to counsel attaches at different times depending on the fortuity of whether the suspect or his family happens to have retained counsel," especially since the Sixth Amendment, "by its very terms, * * * becomes applicable only when the government's role shifts from investigation to accusation."[36]

If judicial proceedings have been initiated and the *Massiah–Williams* right to counsel has thus attached, does it attach for all purposes or only with respect to matters related to those proceedings? This issue reached the Supreme Court in *Maine v. Moulton,*[37] where, after Colton and Moulton were indicted for theft, Colton told police of Moulton's suggestion a state witness be killed and agreed to record later conversations with Moulton, and the recorded statements thereafter obtained in which Moulton discussed the thefts were admitted in his trial on those and other charges. The Court in *Moulton* agreed that the fact a defendant had been charged with one offense was no reason to give him special protection in

the investigation of other, uncharged crimes, and thus concluded that "to exclude evidence pertaining to charges as to which the Sixth Amendment right to counsel had not attached at the time the evidence was obtained, simply because other charges were pending at that time, would unnecessarily frustrate the public's interest in the investigation of criminal activities." From this, the four dissenters reasoned there was no basis for exclusion in the instant case, as the simple fact was that the *Massiah–Brewer* Sixth Amendment right did not apply where, as here, "the police undertook an investigation of separate crimes." Though there is some logic to that position, the *Moulton* majority rejected it on essentially pragmatic grounds in favor of the conclusion that any statements obtained in such circumstances are admissible at trial of the uncharged crime but not at trial of crimes theretofore charged. The majority saw this as "a sensible solution to a difficult problem" because the dissenters' approach "invites abuse by law enforcement personnel in the form of fabricated investigations."

The *Moulton* decision did not settle that the right to counsel attached to the charged offense and nothing else; indeed, the fact the Supreme Court in that case vacated defendant's theft conviction *and* burglary conviction led some lower court's to conclude, even after the Court later characterized the Sixth Amendment right as "offense-specific,"[38] that it carried over to closely related but uncharged crimes. One such case, where the right to counsel that attached upon defendant being charged with burglary was held to apply as

---

33. 384 U.S. 436, 86 S.Ct. 1602, 16 L.Ed.2d 694 (1966).

34. Kirby v. Illinois, 406 U.S. 682, 92 S.Ct. 1877, 32 L.Ed.2d 411 (1972).

35. 475 U.S. 412, 106 S.Ct. 1135, 89 L.Ed.2d 410 (1986).

36. A situation could arise, however, where judicial proceedings had not yet commenced and where in addition defendant was presently without retained or appointed counsel, but yet the conduct of government agents might be viewed as intruding upon the Sixth Amendment right of counsel, especially if those agents were dealing with the defendant outside the normal sequence of events, as with pre-charge plea bargaining with the defendant.

Moreover, where a prosecutor or his agent has obtained information from the defendant, the defendant might seek

suppression by relying on ABA Model Rules of Professional Conduct rule, 4.2, which prohibits a lawyer from communicating with a party he knows to be represented by counsel regarding the subject matter of that representation. The prevailing view in the federal courts is that this provision does not preclude undercover investigations of unindicted suspects merely because they have retained counsel. However, by virtue of 28 U.S.C. § 530B(a), federal prosecutors are now subject to such state provisions, which sometimes have been given a broader interpretation.

37. 474 U.S. 159, 106 S.Ct. 477, 88 L.Ed.2d 481 (1985).

38. McNeil v. Wisconsin, 501 U.S. 171, 111 S.Ct. 2204, 115 L.Ed.2d 158 (1991).

well to the murders of the occupants of the premises burglarized, reached the Supreme Court in *Texas v. Cobb*.[39] The 5–4 majority, in reversing the state court, rejected the claim that a truly offense-specific limitation would permit the police almost total license to conduct unwanted and uncounseled interrogations, responding (1) that defendants still have the protections of *Miranda*; and (2) that the Constitution does not negate society's interest in the ability of the police to talk to those witnesses and suspects charged with other offenses.[40] But, the *Cobb* majority added, the definition of "offense" under the Sixth Amendment is not limited to the four corners of the charging document; it has the same meaning as in the double jeopardy clause, and thus "the test to be applied to determine whether there are two offenses or only one, is whether each provision requires proof of a fact which the other does not."[41]

(f) Waiver of Counsel. The Court in *Brewer v. Williams*[42] acknowledged that the right to counsel there recognized could be waived, and that such waiver would not inevitably necessitate the participation of the defendant's lawyer. The majority declared it was *not* holding "that under the circumstances of this case," namely, where an attorney had actually advised defendant not to talk to the police and had extracted an agreement from the police not to question defendant, "Williams *could not,* without notice to counsel, have waived his rights under the Sixth and Fourteenth Amendments." *Williams* is thus consistent with prior authority that the Sixth Amendment right to counsel is the right of the client rather than the attorney, so that it may

be waived by the client without counsel's participation.

Seemingly inconsistent with this conclusion is the previously quoted statement in *Miranda* about *Escobedo,* namely, that the conduct of the police in turning away the lawyer was by itself "a violation of the Sixth Amendment." If, as noted above, the right is that of the defendant, then it might be asked why there is any violation here if the defendant on his own waives the right. As to such tactics, perhaps the point is that they bear upon the effectiveness of any waiver of the right to counsel by the defendant. If, as in *Escobedo,* the defendant was aware that his lawyer was being prevented from seeing him, this certainly should cast doubt upon any waiver of counsel subsequently obtained from the defendant, for defendant's realization may well have underscored the police dominance of the situation. Even absent such awareness, it has sometimes been held that if police failed to admit counsel to a person in custody or to inform the person of the attorney's efforts to reach him, then they cannot thereafter rely on defendant's "waiver" of counsel because, having been denied facts critical to his decision, he cannot be said to have made a knowing choice. The Supreme Court rejected this latter conclusion in a *Miranda* context,[43] but has thereafter asserted that "in the Sixth Amendment context, this waiver would not be valid."[44]

The Court in *Williams* emphasized in various ways that courts should be reluctant to find a waiver of the right to counsel. It was noted that the burden of showing waiver is on the prosecution, that what must be shown is "an intentional relinquishment or abandonment of a known right,"[45] that the right is not

---

39. 532 U.S. 162, 121 S.Ct. 1335, 149 L.Ed.2d 321 (2001).

40. The four dissenters in *Cobb* deemed the majority's rule to constitute an "unnecessarily technical definition" that "has proved extraordinarily difficult to administer in practice" and was "inconsistent with any common understanding of the scope of counsel's representation." In agreement with "virtually every lower court in the United States to consider the issue," they would define "offense" for purposes of the Sixth Amendment to include those "criminal acts that are 'closely related to' or 'inextricably intertwined with' the particular crime set forth in the charging instrument."

41. Blockburger v. United States, 284 U.S. 299, 52 S.Ct. 180, 76 L.Ed. 306 (1932), further discussed in § 17.4(b).

42. 430 U.S. 387, 97 S.Ct. 1232, 51 L.Ed.2d 424 (1977).

43. Moran v. Burbine, 475 U.S. 412, 106 S.Ct. 1135, 89 L.Ed.2d 410 (1986), discussed in § 6.9(c).

44. Patterson v. Illinois, 487 U.S. 285, 108 S.Ct. 2389, 101 L.Ed.2d 261 (1988).

45. Johnson v. Zerbst, 304 U.S. 458, 58 S.Ct. 1019, 82 L.Ed. 1461 (1938).

lost merely by a lack of request by the defendant, that "every reasonable presumption" must be indulged against waiver, and that a "strict standard" equal to that concerning waiver of counsel at trial applies. Whether this means that waiver of the "pure" right to counsel under *Williams* calls for something more than the waiver of counsel under *Miranda* is a matter on which lower courts were divided until the issue was resolved by the 5–4 decision in *Patterson v. Illinois.*[46] Taking the "pragmatic approach" that the warnings and waiver procedure required depend largely upon "the scope of the Sixth Amendment right to counsel" at the particular stage of the criminal process at issue, the *Patterson* majority concluded the requirements of *Miranda* would suffice because the "State's decision to take an additional step and commence formal adversarial proceedings against the accused does not substantially increase the value of counsel to the accused at questioning, or expand the limited purpose that an attorney serves when the accused is questioned by authorities." That is, "because the role of counsel at questioning is relatively simple and limited," as compared to counsel's responsibilities at trial, there is "no problem in having a waiver procedure at that stage which is likewise simple and limited," as compared to the more complicated waiver procedures that obtain with respect to counsel at trial.[47] However, the Court in *Patterson* noted that the defendant had not yet retained or accepted appointment of counsel to represent him, and stated that "once an accused has a lawyer, a distinct set of constitutional safeguards aimed at preserving the sanctity of the attorney-client relationship take effect." Based on that language, it has been held that when defendant *is* represented by counsel a response to police questioning after *Miranda* warnings is not a sufficient waiver of the Sixth Amendment right.

The Court did not have occasion in *Patterson* to decide whether a valid waiver of Sixth Amendment rights is possible if the defendant was unaware of the event (typically, a formal charge) that caused those rights to attach. As noted in *Patterson,* it has occasionally been suggested that "an accused should be informed that he has been indicted before a postindictment waiver is sought." However, there is post-*Patterson* authority that it suffices if the defendant is otherwise apprised of the nature of the crime for which he was being arrested and the gravity of his situation.

In *Williams* the Supreme Court stressed that "waiver requires not merely comprehension but relinquishment." Thus, while it there appeared that defendant "had been informed of and appeared to understand his right to counsel," any claim of relinquishment was refuted by his "consistent reliance upon the advice of counsel in dealing with the authorities," his statements "that he desired the presence of an attorney before any interrogation took place," his awareness of the agreement between the police and his counsel "that no interrogation was to occur during the journey," and that the police "made no effort at all to ascertain whether Williams wished to relinquish that right." Lower courts take into account such factors as whether there was a police agreement with counsel not to interrogate, whether defendant asserted his right to counsel, whether the police tried to talk defendant out of consulting with counsel, and whether defendant's statement was volunteered.

Waiver is a possibility only when the defendant makes a statement to one known to be in a position adverse to him, such as a police officer, police agent, or examining psychiatrist.[48] As the Supreme Court ruled in *United*

---

46. 487 U.S. 285, 108 S.Ct. 2389, 101 L.Ed.2d 261 (1988).

47. The dissenters contended that a formal charge "substantially alters the relationship between the state and the accused," so that from that time forward "warnings offered by an opposing party, whether detailed or cursory, simply cannot satisfy this high standard."

48. See Estelle v. Smith, 451 U.S. 454, 101 S.Ct. 1866, 68 L.Ed.2d 359 (1981) (*Massiah–Williams* covers examina-

tion by psychiatrist to determine defendant's competency to stand trial, and thus fruits thereof may not be used at penalty phase of capital case).

Compare Buchanan v. Kentucky, 483 U.S. 402, 107 S.Ct. 2906, 97 L.Ed.2d 336 (1987) (because defendant's counsel himself requested the examination and presumably discussed it with his client, and *Smith* put counsel on notice that if he invoked an extreme emotional disturbance defense the report of examination might be used by the

States v. Henry,[49] "the concept of a knowing and voluntary waiver of Sixth Amendment rights does not apply in the context of communications with an undisclosed undercover informant acting for the government." This is because in such an instance the defendant, being unaware the other person "was a government agent expressly commissioned to secure evidence, cannot be held to have waived his right to the assistance of counsel" by freely communicating with him.

The special waiver-after-assertion-of-rights rules that govern in the *Miranda* area as to a case in which the defendant, upon receiving the *Miranda* warnings from police, invoked his right to counsel,[50] also apply to the Sixth Amendment right. Thus the Court held in *Michigan v. Jackson*[51] that when the Sixth Amendment right has attached, "if police initiate interrogation after a defendant's assertion, at an arraignment or similar proceeding, of his right to counsel, any waiver of the defendant's right to counsel for that police-initiated interrogation is invalid." The Court in *Jackson* explained (i) that "the reasons for prohibiting the interrogation of an uncounseled prisoner who has asked for the help of a lawyer are even stronger after he has been formally charged"; (ii) that even though the request for counsel at arraignment is not specifically tied to the matter of police questioning, it is proper to "presume that the defendant requests the lawyer's service at every critical stage of the prosecution"; and (iii) that police ignorance of that at-arraignment invocation of the right is irrelevant, for "one set of state actors (the police) may not claim ignorance of defendant's unequivocal request for counsel to another state actor (the court)." "Preserving the integrity of an accused's choice to communicate with police only through counsel is the es-

sence" of *Jackson*, and thus the bar on any police-initiated interrogation does not arise automatically with the filing of the charging instrument but requires as well the accused's invocation of this right to the assistance of counsel.[52] And in any event, because the Sixth Amendment right is "offense-specific" and "cannot be invoked once for all future prosecutions," it follows that "its *Michigan v. Jackson* effect of invalidating subsequent waivers in police-initiated interviews is offense-specific."[53] This means, for example, that if a defendant exercises his Sixth Amendment right when brought into court on an armed robbery charge, that is no bar to subsequent police-initiated questioning about an unrelated murder.[54]

(g) Infringement of the Right. Assuming now a situation in which judicial proceedings have been initiated and consequently the Sixth Amendment right to counsel has attached, and assuming also that this right has not been waived by the defendant, there remains the question of what activity constitutes an infringement of that right so as to require suppression of any statement obtained thereby. In *Massiah v. United States,*[55] the police arranged for a codefendant to discuss their pending trial with the defendant while they were in the codefendant's car, which had a radio transmitter concealed in it. The Court declared that defendant's right to counsel was violated "when there was used against him at his trial evidence of his own incriminating words, which federal agents had deliberately elicited from him." And in *Brewer v. Williams,*[56] where the activity objected to was the "Christian burial speech" on the ride from Davenport to Des Moines, the Court deemed *Massiah* applicable because the detective "deliberately and

---

prosecution in rebuttal, such use did not infringe upon defendant's right to counsel).

49. 447 U.S. 264, 100 S.Ct. 2183, 65 L.Ed.2d 115 (1980).

50. See § 6.9(g).

51. 475 U.S. 625, 106 S.Ct. 1404, 89 L.Ed.2d 631 (1986). The wisdom and vitality of the *Jackson* case is vigorously debated by the three concurring and four dissenting justices in Texas v. Cobb, 532 U.S. 162, 121 S.Ct. 1335, 149 L.Ed.2d 321 (2001).

52. Patterson v. Illinois, 487 U.S. 285, 108 S.Ct. 2389, 101 L.Ed.2d 261 (1988).

53. McNeil v. Wisconsin, 501 U.S. 171, 111 S.Ct. 2204, 115 L.Ed.2d 158 (1991).

54. McNeil v. Wisconsin, 501 U.S. 171, 111 S.Ct. 2204, 115 L.Ed.2d 158 (1991). Just what it means to say the Sixth Amendment is "offense-specific" was later resolved by the Court in Texas v. Cobb, text at note 39 supra.

55. 377 U.S. 201, 84 S.Ct. 1199, 12 L.Ed.2d 246 (1964).

56. 430 U.S. 387, 97 S.Ct. 1232, 51 L.Ed.2d 424 (1977).

designedly set out to elicit information from Williams just as surely as—and perhaps more effectively than—if he had formally interrogated him." Both *Massiah* and *Williams* at some point refer to the police conduct as "interrogation," but the facts of those cases make it clear that this does not mean interrogation in the narrow sense of the word.

The claim that the "decisive fact in *Massiah* * * * was that the police set up the confrontation between the accused and a police agent" was rejected in *Maine v. Moulton*,[57] finding an infringement of the right to counsel even when it was the defendant who initiated the meeting with his codefendant, who by the time of the meeting was a police agent. As the Court explained, while "the Sixth Amendment is not violated whenever—by luck or happenstance—the State obtains incriminating statements from the accused," a "knowing exploitation by the State of an opportunity to confront the accused without counsel being present is as much a breach of the State's obligation not to circumvent the right to assistance of counsel as is the intentional creation of such an opportunity."

Though the language used in the *Massiah* and *Brewer* cases would seem to require "action undertaken with the specific intent to evoke an inculpatory disclosure,"[58] whether that is still the case remains somewhat unclear because of the confusing case of *United States v. Henry*.[59] *Henry* is a "jail plant" case; government agents contacted a federal informant serving a term in a city jail and "told him to be alert to any statements made by the federal prisoners, but not to initiate any conversation with or question Henry regarding the bank robbery." The informant later reported "that he and Henry had engaged in conversation and that Henry had told him about the robbery of the Janaf bank," and he so testified at Henry's trial. Though the government argued before the Supreme Court that the incriminating statements were "not the result of any affirmative conduct on the part of government agents to elicit evidence," the 6–3 majority in

Henry held that the incriminating statements had been "deliberately elicited." This was so, the Court stated later on in the opinion, by virtue of the government "intentionally creating a situation likely to induce Henry to make incriminating statements." That language was understandably criticized by the dissenters, who noted that it removed the word "deliberately" from the *Massiah–Williams* test and "would cover even a 'negligent' triggering of events resulting in reception of disclosures." But despite the unfortunate "likely to induce" phrase, *Henry* appears to be viewed by the majority as a genuine "deliberately elicited" type of case. Though the majority's analysis lacks precision, the Court seems to conclude that the government's instructions not to question Henry about the robbery (i) are not to be taken too seriously given the fact that the government was using an informer who would be paid only if he produced incriminating information, (ii) did not bar all affirmative action by the informer, who admittedly had "some conversations" with Henry on the topic of the robbery, and (iii) consequently disproved neither that the government intended to obtain incriminating statements nor that the government contemplated some affirmative action by its agent to achieve that result. In other words, after *Henry* it is still true that *Massiah* turns solely on the underlying intent of the government's agents. This means there is no *Massiah–Williams* violation if the person acting with the intention of eliciting an incriminating statement is not a government agent, or if the government agent who elicits an incriminating response does so exclusively for some other legitimate purpose.

A slightly different question that may be asked about *Henry* is whether it extends *Massiah* so as to include both "active" and "passive" efforts to obtain incriminating evidence from a defendant. For the reasons stated above, the majority did not believe it was dealing with a "passive" type of case. Moreover, the majority cautioned it was not "called

---

57. 474 U.S. 159, 106 S.Ct. 477, 88 L.Ed.2d 481 (1985).

58. United States v. Henry, 447 U.S. 264, 100 S.Ct. 2183, 65 L.Ed.2d 115 (1980) Blackmun, J., (dissenting).

59. 447 U.S. 264, 100 S.Ct. 2183, 65 L.Ed.2d 115 (1980).

upon to pass on the situation where an informant is placed in close proximity but makes no effort to stimulate conversations about the crime charged." Later, in *Kuhlmann v. Wilson*,[60] the Court ruled that because "the primary concern of the *Massiah* line of decisions is secret interrogation by investigatory techniques that are the equivalent of direct police interrogation," "a defendant does not make out a violation of that right simply by showing that an informant, either through prior arrangement or voluntarily, reported his incriminating statements to the police." *Kuhlmann* illustrates, however, the difficulty in drawing the line between "active" and "passive" efforts. Defendant first gave his cellmate the same story of noninvolvement he had earlier given the police, to which the cellmate, placed there by police with instructions not to question defendant but to listen for information, responded that the explanation "didn't sound too good." The defendant did not alter his story until a few days later, after his brother visited him and expressed the family's concern with his apparent involvement in a murder. The majority concluded this meant defendant's confession had not been "deliberately elicited" by his cellmate, but three dissenting Justices thought otherwise because, though "the *coup de grace* was delivered by respondent's brother," the "informant, while avoiding direct questions, nonetheless developed a relationship of cellmate camaraderie with respondent and encouraged him to talk about his crime."

To be distinguished from the "jail plant" cases, the *Henry* majority noted, is the "situation where the 'listening post' is an inanimate electronic device, for 'such a device has no capability of leading the conversation into any particular subject or prompting any particular replies.'" Especially after *Kuhlmann*, it seems clear mere use of the device does not infringe upon the right to counsel, for it cannot be said that the bugging in any sense increases the defendant's predisposition toward making an incriminating response. Thus, the existing authority, noted in *Henry*, to the effect that the mere use of an electronic device to record a prisoner's conversations with a visitor does not violate the Sixth Amendment, is correct.

(h) Critique of the Right to Counsel Approach. Whether the *Massiah* rule, as elaborated and extended in such cases as *Williams* and *Henry,* is a sensible and desirable doctrine is a matter on which opinions differ. In criticism, it is asserted that the *Massiah* rule is unnecessary because *Miranda* protects against the coercive pressures of custodial interrogations while the due process voluntariness test affords sufficient protection in noncustodial situations. In much the same vein, it is objected that if *Massiah* is perceived of as providing some sort of protection against improper police practices, then it is fundamentally unsound because those practices do not somehow become improper only upon the initiation of judicial proceedings. On the other hand, some do find offensive certain police practices likely to be reached only by the *Massiah* rule, such as use of an undercover agent to elicit incriminating remarks, and for them the problem with the rule is that it is too narrow because not extended to similar conduct that occurs after formal arrest.

In answer to such criticisms, it might be observed that *Massiah,* after all, is grounded in the Sixth Amendment right to counsel and thus should be assessed in terms of its protection of that right instead of as some sort of alternative to or extension of either *Miranda* or the voluntariness test. But there is disagreement even when *Massiah* is so viewed. One position, as reflected by Justice Rehnquist's dissent in *Henry,* is that the *Massiah* rule cannot be explained even on this basis because it does not protect legitimate Sixth Amendment interests: "the confidentiality of communications between the accused and his attorney," and the "role of counsel * * * to offer advice and assistance in the preparation of a defense and to serve as a spokesman for the accused in technical legal proceedings." In response, it is contended that this overlooks the fact that from at least the time of *White v.*

60. 477 U.S. 436, 106 S.Ct. 2616, 91 L.Ed.2d 364 (1986).

Maryland[61] the Sixth Amendment has also functioned as a shield, enabling the defendant to frustrate the state's efforts to obtain evidence directly from him.

Even assuming the latter position is correct, so that there properly comes a point after which the Sixth Amendment right to counsel protects against all self-incrimination, compelled or not, there is room for dispute as to whether that point has been correctly defined in the *Massiah* line of cases. One question is whether the right to counsel rule turns on distinctions that are unresponsive to the government's need for evidence. It thus might be asked whether *Massiah,* which erected a Sixth Amendment shield around a defendant who had been arrested and indicted many months earlier, is more understandable than *Williams,* where such a shield was erected around a defendant shortly after his arrest and apparently before even the magnitude of the crime had been ascertained by the proper prosecuting authority. A second question is whether these distinctions are objectionable because often, albeit not in *Williams,* they are conducive to manipulation by the police.

(i) The "Repeal" of the *Massiah* Rule. In the Crime Control Act of 1968, Congress purported to "repeal" the *Massiah* rule for federal prosecutions. This was done by providing that in the federal courts a confession "shall be admissible in evidence if it is voluntarily given,"[62] and that various, enumerated factors to be taken into account on the voluntariness issue, including "whether or not such defendant was without the assistance of counsel when questioned and when giving such confession," "need not be conclusive on the issue of voluntariness."[63] This legislation has been largely ignored, and properly so, for to the extent it purports to nullify the Sixth Amendment right to counsel as recognized in

Massiah and subsequent Supreme Court decisions it is most certainly unconstitutional.

§ 6.5 The Privilege Against Self–Incrimination; *Miranda*

(a) The Privilege in the Police Station. The Fifth Amendment of the United States Constitution provides that no person "shall be compelled in any criminal case to be a witness against himself." A literal reading of that language certainly suggests that the privilege against self-incrimination has no application to unsworn statements obtained by station-house interrogation, and for a good many years this was the common assumption. The notion was that compulsion to testify meant *legal* compulsion, which is not present in the police questioning context because the interrogated suspect is threatened neither with perjury for testifying falsely nor with contempt for refusing to testify at all. However, the Supreme Court in *Bram v. United States*[1] seemed quite clearly to conclude otherwise, for it was there asserted that "[i]n criminal trials, in the courts of the United States, wherever a question arises whether a confession is incompetent because not voluntary, the issue is controlled by that portion of the fifth amendment * * * commanding that no person 'shall be compelled in any criminal case to be a witness against himself.' " But this assertion was not relied upon by the Court in subsequent confession cases, and the Court later expressed doubt that the privilege was relevant in confession cases.[2] Then came *Malloy v. Hogan,*[3] which did not involve a confession but nonetheless was important in two significant respects to the ultimate acceptance of the privilege against self-incrimination as a constitutional restraint upon police interrogation practices. *Malloy* held that the privilege was applicable to the states, and then supported that conclusion by declaring that "today the admissibility of a confession in a state criminal prosecution is

---

61. 373 U.S. 59, 83 S.Ct. 1050, 10 L.Ed.2d 193 (1963), holding on Sixth Amendment grounds that defendant's withdrawn guilty plea, obtained at a hearing at which he was not represented by counsel, could not be admitted against him.

62. 18 U.S.C.A. § 3501(a).

63. 18 U.S.C.A. § 3501(b).

§ 6.5

1. 168 U.S. 532, 18 S.Ct. 183, 42 L.Ed. 568 (1897).

2. United States v. Carignan, 342 U.S. 36, 72 S.Ct. 97, 96 L.Ed. 48 (1951).

3. 378 U.S. 1, 84 S.Ct. 1489, 12 L.Ed.2d 653 (1964).

tested by the same standard applied in federal prosecution since 1897" in the *Bram* decision. This made it appear that the privilege was the established basis for assaying federal confessions. Promptly thereafter came *Escobedo v. Illinois,*[4] which, while grounded upon the Sixth Amendment right to counsel, spoke unhesitantly of "the right of the accused to be advised by his lawyer of his privilege against self-incrimination." Any lingering doubts were dispelled two years later by *Miranda v. Arizona,*[5] holding that the privilege "is fully applicable during a period of custodial interrogation." Although, for the reasons already noted, the apparent assumption of the *Miranda* majority that this proposition was "settled" in the precedents is open to question, this of course does not necessarily mean that the *Miranda* holding was in error. Even the dissenters in *Miranda* conceded that the Fifth Amendment privilege "embodies basic principles always capable of expansion," although they forcefully argued that those principles would not be served by extending the privilege to the police station. Moreover, any "expansion" that occurred in *Miranda* was in important respects comparable to the earlier growth of the privilege against self-incrimination.

The applicability of the privilege at the police station, in a quite different sense, was much later the central issue in *Chavez v. Martinez,*[6] which, although a civil case, is worthy of consideration here. Martinez was interrogated by police officer Chavez under circumstances that would have made his resulting confession inadmissible under *Miranda* in a criminal case, but Martinez was not thereafter even charged with a crime. In a § 1983 action for damages, Martinez relied in part upon the Fifth Amendment,[7] and was upheld in that respect by the district court and court of appeals, but a splintered Supreme Court reversed. Four members of the Court,[8] relying upon the literal language of the Fifth Amend-

ment, concluded: "Martinez was never made to be a 'witness' against himself in violation of the Fifth Amendment's Self–Incrimination Clause because his statements were never admitted as testimony against him in a criminal case." Two other Justices,[9] while also rejecting the self-incrimination claim, did so in less absolute terms, noting that on occasion the Court had previously applied the privilege in other circumstances, always "expressing a judgment that the core guarantee, or the judicial capacity to protect it, would be placed at some risk in the absence of such complementary protection." But, they added, Martinez had not made the requisite "powerful showing" needed to come within that line of cases, especially since he "offers no limiting principle or reason to foresee a stopping place short of liability in all * * * cases" where *Miranda* was violated. The remaining members of the Court,[10] dissenting on this point, asserted that the self-incrimination clause "provides both assurance that a person will not be compelled to testify against himself in a criminal proceeding and a continuing right against government conduct intended to bring about self-incrimination. * * * The principle extends to forbid policies which exert official compulsion that might induce a person into forfeiting his rights under the Clause." "The conclusion that the Self–Incrimination Clause is not violated until the government seeks to use a statement in some later criminal proceeding," they lamented, "strips the Clause of an essential part of its force and meaning."

(b) The *Miranda* Rules. In *Miranda,* yet another 5–4 decision, the majority began by examining "various police manuals and texts," a "valuable source of information about present police practices." From the several psychological ploys and stratagems outlined therein, the Court concluded that even without resort to brutality "the very fact of custodial interrogation exacts a heavy toll on individual liberty

---

4. 378 U.S. 478, 84 S.Ct. 1758, 12 L.Ed.2d 977 (1964).

5. 384 U.S. 436, 86 S.Ct. 1602, 16 L.Ed.2d 694 (1966).

6. 538 U.S. 760, 123 S.Ct. 1994, 155 L.Ed.2d 984 (2003).

7. He also relied on the due process clause. On this branch of the case, see § 6.2(b).

8. Thomas, J., joined by the Chief Justice and by O'Connor and Scalia, JJ.

9. Souter, J., joined by Breyer, J.

10. Kennedy, J., joined by Stevens and Ginsburg, JJ.

and trades on the weaknesses of individuals." Next examining the facts of the four cases under collective consideration, the Court concluded that even though it "might not find the defendants' statements to have been involuntary in traditional terms," those statements were obtained under circumstances in which the "potentiality for compulsion is forcefully apparent." In each case the defendant was interrogated by police who had custody of him and who did not advise him that he could remain silent or otherwise "insure that the statements were truly the product of free choice." The Court thus concluded that "[u]nless adequate protective devices are employed to dispel the compulsion inherent in custodial surroundings, no statement obtained from the defendant can truly be the product of his free choice."

The necessary "protective devices" were then described in some detail in what the *Miranda* dissenters disparagingly called a "constitutional code of rules for confessions." *Miranda* thus represents a striking contrast to both *Escobedo v. Illinois*,[11] decided two years earlier, and the Court's usual "totality of circumstances" approach to the due process voluntariness issue. While the holding in *Escobedo* had been cautiously limited to the facts of the particular case before the Court, the *Miranda* holding most certainly was not, for it contained a set of rules to be followed by police in all future custodial interrogations. And while "totality of circumstances" holdings were not easily applied to other cases with somewhat different pressures or defendants of somewhat different susceptibilities, the nature of the *Miranda* rules was such that this was not true of this landmark decision. These rules, discussed further in the remaining sections of this Chapter, may be summarized as follows:

(1) These rules are required to safeguard the privilege against self-incrimination, and thus must be followed in the absence of "other procedures which are at least as effective in apprising accused persons of their right of silence and in assuring a continuous opportunity to exercise it."

(2) These rules apply "when the individual is first subjected to police interrogation while in custody at the station or otherwise deprived of his freedom of action in any significant way," and not to "[g]eneral on-the-scene questioning as to facts surrounding a crime or other general questioning of citizens in the fact-finding process" or to "[v]olunteered statements of any kind."

(3) Without regard to his prior awareness of his rights, if a person in custody is to be subjected to questioning, "he must first be informed in clear and unequivocal terms that he has the right to remain silent," so that the ignorant may learn of this right and so that the pressures of the interrogation atmosphere will be overcome for those previously aware of the right.

(4) The above warning "must be accompanied by the explanation that anything said can and will be used against the individual in court," so as to ensure that the suspect fully understands the consequences of foregoing the privilege.

(5) Because this is indispensable to protection of the privilege, the individual also "must be clearly informed that he has the right to consult with a lawyer and to have the lawyer with him during interrogation," without regard to whether it appears that he is already aware of this right.

(6) The individual must also be warned "that if he is indigent a lawyer will be appointed to represent him," for otherwise the above warning would be understood as meaning only that an individual may consult a lawyer if he has the funds to obtain one.

(7) The individual is always free to exercise the privilege, and thus if he "indicates in any manner, at anytime prior to or during questioning, that he wishes to remain silent, the interrogation must cease"; and likewise, if he "states that he wants an attorney, the interrogation must cease until an attorney is present."

11.   378 U.S. 478, 84 S.Ct. 1758, 12 L.Ed.2d 977 (1964).

(8) If a statement is obtained without the presence of an attorney, "a heavy burden rests on the Government to demonstrate that the defendant knowingly and intelligently waived his privilege against self-incrimination and his right to retained or appointed counsel," and such waiver may not be presumed from the individual's silence after warnings or from the fact that a confession was eventually obtained.

(9) Any statement obtained in violation of these rules may not be admitted into evidence, without regard to whether it is a confession or only an admission of part of an offense or whether it is inculpatory or allegedly exculpatory.

(10) Likewise, exercise of the privilege may not be penalized, and thus the prosecution may not "use at trial the fact that [the defendant] stood mute or claimed his privilege in the face of accusation."

Although these rules sound inflexible and unbending, neither the Supreme Court nor the lower courts have generally taken a rigid approach in the application of *Miranda*. Indeed, the Supreme Court asserted in *Michigan v. Tucker*[12] that the *Miranda* decision

> recognized that these procedural safeguards were not themselves rights protected by the Constitution but were instead measures to insure that the right against compulsory self-incrimination was protected. * * * The suggested safeguards were not intended to "create a constitutional straitjacket," * * * but rather to provide practical reinforcement for the right against compulsory self-incrimination.

This curious characterization of *Miranda*, which ignores much of the language in that case, seems to have deprived *Miranda* of its constitutional basis without explaining that other basis it might have. But it is most likely explainable by the fact that in *Tucker* the Court was trying to avoid exclusion of a pre-*Miranda* confession obtained by a policeman

who failed to foresee the necessity to give all of the warnings outlined in *Miranda*.[13]

(c) The Experience Under *Miranda*. Various surveys and empirical studies have been undertaken in an effort to gauge the impact of the *Miranda* decision upon police interrogation practices. As for police compliance with the *Miranda* requirements, in the months immediately following that decision it was determined that the police did not regularly or completely give the warnings before interrogation. This was largely attributable to delays in police training about the new requirements, and later studies found that police were regularly advising suspects of their rights before attempting to question them. However, this implementation of *Miranda* has been on a limited, formalistic basis. The practice is to read the suspect the warnings printed on "*Miranda* cards" carried by the police, often intoned in a manner designed to minimize or negate their importance and effectiveness.

Although the early verdict on *Miranda* was that it had little impact, the extent to which this is still true today, now that *Miranda* has become a part of our culture and presumably the rights declared therein are more widely perceived by the public at large, is not entirely clear. The conflicting assessments are doubtless attributable to the fact that we lack sufficient reliable empirical data on *Miranda*'s impact and that, consequently, existing evidence is amenable to differing interpretations. This is so both as to the ultimate question of the "cost" of *Miranda* in terms of lost convictions, and with respect to the basic question of how the post-*Miranda* confession rate compares with that which existed prior to the *Miranda* decision.

(d) Critique of the *Miranda* Approach. There exists a considerable difference of opinion concerning the extent to which *Miranda* has "solved" pre-existing problems concerning police interrogation practices in this country. Nonetheless, it is possible to identify some of the strengths and weaknesses of *Miranda*. On

---

12. 417 U.S. 433, 94 S.Ct. 2357, 41 L.Ed.2d 182 (1974).

13. A consequence of the fact that the Court held in Johnson v. New Jersey, 384 U.S. 719, 86 S.Ct. 1772, 16 L.Ed.2d 882 (1966), that *Miranda* was not retroactive but

that nonetheless it would apply to trials begun after the date of that decision even though the interrogation predated *Miranda*.

the plus side, it may be said that *Miranda* serves important symbolic functions, such as correcting the appearance that the poor and the unsophisticated were particularly vulnerable to police exploitation. *Miranda* has also served an educational purpose of ensuring that police are frequently reminded of the rights of the people with whom they deal.

Moreover, *Miranda* provided much needed guidance for the police by prescribing a series of set procedures to be followed in every instance of custodial interrogation. It was thus not difficult for the well-intentioned police officer to perceive exactly what was expected of him—a distinct improvement over the ambiguous due process voluntariness test. *Miranda* also simplified to some extent judicial review of police interrogation practices.

Yet there appears to be a very fundamental inconsistency in the *Miranda* majority's analysis. The Court places heavy emphasis on the notion that the decision of one in custody whether or not to incriminate himself cannot be truly voluntary but yet concludes that the choice to dispense with counsel can be voluntary in the same circumstances. This inconsistency has been noted both by those who believe that *Miranda* did not go far enough— that the Court should have insisted on the presence of an attorney during interrogation, required initial consultation with an attorney or friend, or even by mandating that warnings and waivers occur before a neutral magistrate—and by those, such as the dissenters in *Miranda,* who believe the Court went too far.

A cogent criticism of the old "voluntariness" test namely, that because the critical events occur in secrecy the admissibility of the confession will be determined by the outcome of a "swearing contest" in court, applies to *Miranda* as well. This is because the heralded warnings need not be given by a disinterested person, and the defendant's decision to waive his rights need not be made before a disinterested party or recorded in any fashion. The warnings and waivers may and often do occur while the suspect is isolated in the privacy of the interrogation room, with only the police as observers, and this raises doubts not only about the validity of the waiver, but about the propriety of post-waiver actions as well.

(e) The "Repeal" of *Miranda.* In the Crime Control Act of 1968, Congress purported to "repeal" the *Miranda* decision in federal prosecutions. This was done by providing that in the federal courts a confession "shall be admissible in evidence if it is voluntarily given,"[14] and that various enumerated factors taken into account on the voluntariness issue, such as "whether or not such defendant was advised or knew that he was not required to make any statement and that any such statement could be used against him," "whether or not such defendant had been advised prior to questioning of his right to the assistance of counsel," and "whether or not such defendant was without the assistance of counsel when questioned and when giving such confession," "need not be conclusive on the issue of voluntariness."[15]

In *Dickerson v. United States,*[16] the Court determined that "Congress intended by its enactment to overrule *Miranda,*" and thus found it necessary to address the critical question of "whether Congress has constitutional authority" to do so. Because Congress "retains the ultimate authority to modify or set aside any judicially created rules of evidence and procedure that are not required by the Constitution" but "may not legislatively supersede our decisions interpreting and applying the Constitution," the case consequently turned "on whether the *Miranda* Court announced a constitutional rule or merely exercised its supervisory authority to regulate evidence in the absence of congressional direction." In deciding it was the former, the majority in *Dickerson* emphasized: (i) "that both *Miranda* and two of its companion cases," as well as many cases in which the Court later interpreted and applied *Miranda,* involved "prosecutions arising in state courts," as to which the Supreme Court's authority "is limited to enforcing the com-

---

14. 18 U.S.C.A. § 3501(a).
15. 18 U.S.C.A. § 3501(b).

16. 530 U.S. 428, 120 S.Ct. 2326, 147 L.Ed.2d 405 (2000), also discussed in § 2.9(e) at note 24.

mands of the United States Constitution"; (ii) that the *Miranda* majority opinion "is replete with statements indicating that the majority thought it was announcing a constitutional rule"; and (iii) that the contrary is not shown by the Court's later decision's narrowing *Miranda*, for those decisions (as well as others broadening the application of *Miranda*) "illustrate the principle—not that *Miranda* is not a constitutional rule—but that no constitutional rule is immutable."[17]

The Court in *Dickerson* then turned to a critical passage in *Miranda* reading as follows:

> It is impossible for us to foresee the potential alternatives for protecting the privilege which might be devised by Congress or the States in the exercise of their creative rule-making capacities. Therefore we cannot say that the Constitution necessarily requires adherence to any particular solution for the inherent compulsions of the interrogation process as it is presently conducted. Our decision in no way creates a constitutional straitjacket which will handicap sound efforts at reform nor is it intended to have this effect. We encourage Congress and the States to continue their laudable search for increasingly effective ways of protecting the rights of the individual while promoting efficient enforcement of our criminal laws. However, unless we are shown other procedures which are at least as effective in apprising accused persons of their right of silence and in assuring a continuous opportunity to exercise it, the following safeguards must be observed.

Despite this "invitation for legislative action" in *Miranda*, the *Dickerson* Court concluded that § 3501 could not be upheld in light of that invitation's clearly-expressed "requirement that a legislative alternative to *Miranda* be equally as effective in preventing coerced confessions." This is because the statute merely "reinstates the totality test as sufficient,"

while the *Miranda* Court "concluded that something more than the totality test was necessary." And even taking into account the fact "that there are more remedies available for abusive police conduct than there were at the time *Miranda* was decided," those remedies plus § 3501 are not together "an adequate substitute for the warnings required by *Miranda*."[18]

Having thus concluded that the statutory provision "cannot be sustained if *Miranda* is to remain the law," the Court in *Dickerson* next declared it would *not* strike down *Miranda*. Longstanding "principles of *stare decisis* weigh heavily against overruling it now," the Court explained, for its "doctrinal underpinnings" have not been undermined, and it "has become embedded in routine police practice to the point where the warnings have become part of our national culture." And while under *Miranda* it may sometimes be the case that "a guilty defendant go[es] free," the Court deemed that a lesser disadvantage than trying to operate exclusively under a totality-of-the-circumstances test, which "is more difficult than *Miranda* for law enforcement officers to conform to, and for courts to apply in a consistent manner."

§ 6.6 *Miranda*: When Interrogation Is "Custodial"

(a) "Custody" vs. "Focus." Because these *Miranda* safeguards were deemed necessary to counteract the combined effects of interrogation and custody, the meaning of the Court's "custodial interrogation" phrase is a matter of considerable importance. By way of explanation, the Court said this meant "questioning initiated by law enforcement officers after a person has been taken into custody or otherwise deprived of his freedom of action in any significant way."

---

17. As to the special character of *Miranda*'s constitutional grounding, see the discussion in § 2.9(e) following note 24.

18. There were two dissenters in *Dickerson*. The majority, noting that the "dissent argued that it is judicial overreaching for this Court to hold § 3501 unconstitution-

al unless we hold that the *Miranda* warnings are required by the Constitution, in the sense that nothing else will suffice to satisfy constitutional requirements," responded that it "need not go farther than *Miranda* to decide this case." In other words, *Dickerson* did not cancel out the "invitation for legislative action" found in *Miranda*, but merely adhered to the terms of that invitation.

Some of the difficulty that arose concerning the exact meaning of that language was prompted by a footnote appended thereto: "This is what we meant in *Escobedo* when we spoke of an investigation which had focused on an accused." This made it appear that custody and focus were alternative grounds for requiring the warnings, though there was certainly reason to question such a conclusion. For one thing, *Escobedo v. Illinois*[1] had held that the Sixth Amendment right to counsel attached when a series of events coincided, but "focus" was one of the events and "custody" was another, thus making it quite plain that the Court had *not* then viewed the two terms as synonymous. Moreover, any notion that this footnote meant *Miranda* rights commenced upon arrest *or* the accumulation of facts justifying arrest appeared to be dispelled shortly thereafter in *Hoffa v. United States*.[2] There the Court emphatically declared, albeit not in a *Miranda* context, that there "is no constitutional right to be arrested" and that police "are under no constitutional duty to call a halt to a criminal investigation the moment they have the minimum evidence to establish probable cause."

The "focus" approach was expressly rejected in *Beckwith v. United States*.[3] There the petitioner claimed that he was entitled to the full *Miranda* warnings when he was interviewed at home by agents of the Intelligence Division of the IRS, because he was at that time the focus of a criminal investigation. The Court responded:

> An interview with government agents in a situation such as [this one] simply does not present the elements which the *Miranda* Court found so inherently coercive as to require its holding. Although the "focus" of an investigation may indeed have been on [petitioner] at the time of the interview in the sense that it was his tax liability which was under scrutiny, he hardly found himself in the custodial situation described by the *Miranda* Court as the basis for its holding. *Miranda* implicitly defined "focus," for its purposes, as "questioning initiated by law enforcement officers *after* a person has been taken into custody or otherwise deprived of his freedom of action in any significant way."

On like reasoning, a plurality of the Court in *United States v. Mandujano*[4] rejected the argument that a "putative" or "virtual" defendant called before a grand jury is entitled to the *Miranda* warnings, which "were aimed at the evils seen by the Court as endemic to police interrogation of a person in custody."[5]

(b) Purpose of Custody. *Mathis v. United States*[6] posed the question of whether *Miranda* applies when the purpose of the custody is unrelated to the purpose of the interrogation. There an IRS agent failed to give petitioner

---

§ 6.6

1. 378 U.S. 478, 84 S.Ct. 1758, 12 L.Ed.2d 977 (1964).

2. 385 U.S. 293, 87 S.Ct. 408, 17 L.Ed.2d 374 (1966).

3. 425 U.S. 341, 96 S.Ct. 1612, 48 L.Ed.2d 1 (1976).

Beckwith was relied upon in Minnesota v. Murphy, 465 U.S. 420, 104 S.Ct. 1136, 79 L.Ed.2d 409 (1984), holding that noncustodial questioning of a probationer by his probation officer at the latter's office was not governed by *Miranda* notwithstanding "the probation officer's knowledge and intent" as a result of having previously learned the probationer had admitted to a counselor he had committed a rape and murder.

So too, in Stansbury v. California, 511 U.S. 318, 114 S.Ct. 1526, 128 L.Ed.2d 293 (1994) (per curiam), the Court held, "not for the first time, that an officer's subjective and undisclosed view concerning whether the person being interrogated is a suspect is irrelevant to the assessment whether the person is in custody." In that case, Stansbury, one of two suspects in the possible murder of a young girl, agreed to answer some questions and accompa-

nied an officer to the stationhouse. There he was questioned without being given *Miranda* warnings. The trial court concluded that the officer's "mind" was on the other suspect until Stansbury revealed certain information, and therefore statements Stansbury made before that time should be admitted into evidence. The state supreme court affirmed, viewing "whether the investigation has focused on the subject" one of the important considerations "in deciding the custody issue." In reversing and remanding for reconsideration of the custody issue, the Supreme Court emphasized that "[s]ave as they are communicated or otherwise manifested to the person being questioned, an officer's evolving but unarticulated suspicions do not affect the objective circumstances of an interrogation or interview, and thus cannot affect the *Miranda* custody inquiry."

4. 425 U.S. 564, 96 S.Ct. 1768, 48 L.Ed.2d 212 (1976).

5. Brennan and Marshall, JJ., concurring, cited *Miranda* as putting in doubt earlier dictum that there is no right to counsel for a grand jury witness.

6. 391 U.S. 1, 88 S.Ct. 1503, 20 L.Ed.2d 381 (1968).

the *Miranda* warnings when questioning him about his prior income tax returns while petitioner was incarcerated in a state jail serving a state sentence. The government argued that *Miranda* was inapplicable because the petitioner had not been jailed by the interrogating federal officers but was there for an entirely different offense, but the Court rejected that distinction as "too minor and shadowy to justify a departure from the well-considered conclusion of *Miranda* with reference to warnings to be given to a person held in custody." The significance of *Mathis* is best highlighted by setting out the position of the three dissenters, rejected by the majority: "*Miranda* rested not on the mere fact of physical restriction but on a conclusion that coercion—pressure to answer questions—usually flows from a certain type of custody, police station interrogation of someone charged with or suspected of a crime. Although petitioner was confined, he was at the time of interrogation in familiar surroundings. * * * The rationale of *Miranda* has no relevance to inquiries conducted outside the allegedly hostile and forbidding atmosphere surrounding police station interrogation of a criminal suspect." Thus, it is now clear that *Miranda* applies to interrogation of one in custody for another purpose or with respect to another offense. Nonetheless, in various settings, the interrogation of jail and prison inmates has been held not to be subject to *Miranda*.

(c) Subjective vs. Objective Approach.
A most fundamental question concerning the *Miranda* "custody" element is whether it is to be determined by some subjective factor, either that the suspect in fact believed he was in custody or that the police officer intended to take custody, or whether instead an objective test of the "reasonable man" type governs. Under the first subjective approach, which focuses upon the state of mind of the suspect, a defendant would be in custody for *Miranda* purposes if he believed he was in custody. In defense of this approach, it may be said that it relates directly to the "potentiality for compulsion" with which the Court was concerned in

Miranda: if the combination of custody and questioning is sufficiently coercive to call for warnings, then certainly the situation is no less coercive as to the defendant who actually but erroneously believes he is in custody. The trouble with this approach, however, is that it would place upon the police the burden of anticipating the frailties or idiosyncracies of every person they question.

The second subjective approach would make the outcome depend upon the intentions of the police officer, without regard to whether they were communicated to the suspect. This test, once followed by some courts and rejected by others, was at one time utilized by the Supreme Court. This first occurred in the case of *Orozco v. Texas*,[7] where four policemen entered defendant's bedroom at 4 a.m. and questioned him without the *Miranda* warnings. The Court held that *Miranda* applied, not on the plausible ground that these unique facts established a "potentiality for compulsion" equivalent to stationhouse interrogation, but rather on the narrower point that one of the officers later testified as to his uncommunicated intentions, namely, that "petitioner was under arrest and not free to leave when he was questioned in his bedroom in the early hours of the morning." In the later case of *Oregon v. Mathiason*,[8] a majority of the Court appears to have persisted in this approach. Defendant, a parolee, was "invited" to the police station for an interview, and when he arrived he was questioned about a burglary after the officer told him falsely that his fingerprints had been found at the crime scene. In holding this was a "noncustodial situation," the *Mathiason* Court declared that the officer's false statement had "nothing to do with whether respondent was in custody for purposes of the *Miranda* rule." Such an assertion would be absurd if either a subjective understanding-of-the-suspect test or an objective test were used, and thus seems to indicate adherence to the *Orozco* intent-of-the-officer approach. Unlike the other subjective test, this approach is easy for the officer to understand, but it hardly makes sense in terms of the

7. 394 U.S. 324, 89 S.Ct. 1095, 22 L.Ed.2d 311 (1969).

8. 429 U.S. 492, 97 S.Ct. 711, 50 L.Ed.2d 714 (1977).

"potentiality for compulsion," as the uncommunicated intentions of the officer do not change the situation from the suspect's point of view.

Both of these subjective approaches have a common defect, which is that the governing test would involve matters exceedingly difficult for courts to determine after the fact. As the point was put in *United States v. Hall*,[9] it makes no sense to have the *Miranda* "custody" factor "decided by swearing contests in which officers would regularly maintain their lack of intention to assert power over a suspect save when the circumstances would make such a claim absurd, and defendants would assert with equal regularity that they considered themselves to be significantly deprived of their liberty the minute officers began to inquire of them." Doubtless this is why a majority of the lower courts came to adopt an objective standard. The Supreme Court expressly adopted this position in *Berkemer v. McCarty*,[10] involving roadside interrogation of a motorist stopped for a traffic violation. The Court, after holding *Miranda* is inapplicable in that context,[11] confronted the fact that apparently the trooper who made the stop "decided as soon as respondent stepped out of his car that respondent would be taken into custody and charged with a traffic offense," though he "never communicated his intention to respondent." This did not require a different result, the Court concluded without dissent, for a "policeman's unarticulated plan has no bearing on the question whether a suspect was 'in custody' at a particular time; the only relevant inquiry is how a reasonable man in the suspect's position would have understood his situation."[12] Under *Berkemer,* the question is *not* whether a reasonable person would believe he was not free to leave, but rather whether such a person

would believe he was in police custody of the degree associated with formal arrest.

This objective approach will often require a careful examination of all the circumstances of the particular case. Account must be taken of those facts intrinsic to the interrogation: when and where it occurred, how long it lasted, how many police were present, what the officers and the defendant said and did, the presence of physical restraint or the equivalent (e.g., drawn weapons, guard stationed at the door), and whether the defendant was being questioned as a suspect or as a witness. Events before the interrogation are also relevant, especially how the defendant got to the place of questioning—whether he came completely on his own, in response to a police request, or escorted by police officers. The Supreme Court[13] and the lower courts have also looked to what happened after the interrogation, relying upon the fact that the suspect was allowed to leave following the interrogation as strong evidence that the interrogation was not custodial. But as a matter of logic it is unsound to say that what happens later has some bearing on how a reasonable person would have perceived the situation at some earlier time. The same objection may be made as to the reliance by some courts on whether there was "focus." As a matter of logic, neither "focus" nor its absence (when not communicated to the suspect) has any direct bearing upon how a reasonable man would perceive the situation. Perhaps these cases reflect only the fact that courts are more willing to accept police representations of a noncustodial environment when it appears they lacked a basis for arrest and even after the questioning elected not to arrest.

(d) Presence at Station. One situation given specific mention in *Miranda* as being custodial is where the individual is "in custody

---

9. 421 F.2d 540 (2d Cir.1969).

10. 468 U.S. 420, 104 S.Ct. 3138, 82 L.Ed.2d 317 (1984).

11. See § 6.6(e).

12. In Stansbury v. California, 511 U.S. 318, 114 S.Ct. 1526, 128 L.Ed.2d 293 (1994), the Court reaffirmed "that the initial determination of custody depends on the objective circumstances of the interrogation, not the subjective views harbored by either the interrogating officers or the

person being questioned," though an "officer's knowledge or beliefs may bear upon the custody issue if they are conveyed, by word or deed, to the individual being questioned."

13. Oregon v. Mathiason, 429 U.S. 492, 97 S.Ct. 711, 50 L.Ed.2d 714 (1977), stressing that after the questioning defendant departed "the police station without hindrance."

at the station." This is obviously so when, as in the four cases involved in *Miranda,* the defendant is being held at the police station following his arrest. It does not follow, however, that all presence at the station is custodial in nature. To take the most obvious case, there is no custody if the person came to the station on his own initiative.

It has also been held that there is no custody when the person is present at the station in response to an "invitation" from the police, although in such cases a close look at all the surrounding circumstances is necessary. In *Oregon v. Mathiason,*[14] a police officer left a note at the apartment of defendant, a parolee, stating he wanted "to discuss something with you," so defendant called the officer and arranged to meet him at the state patrol office a few blocks from the apartment. When defendant appeared, he was told he was not under arrest and that the officer wanted to talk to him about a burglary. Later the officer falsely told defendant that his fingerprints had been found at the burglary scene, and defendant then confessed, after which he left the station. The Supreme Court's conclusion that defendant "came voluntarily to the police station" and thus was not initially in custody is unobjectionable. However, the Court's added conclusion that the circumstances never became custodial is open to serious question. It is true, as the Court put it in *Mathiason,* that the requirement of warnings is not imposed "simply because the questioning takes place in the station house, or because the questioned person is one whom the police suspect." But it is rather difficult to accept the conclusion that a parolee who is told his fingerprints had been found at a burglary scene would believe he was still free to leave.

If the so-called "invitation" involves the person going to the station in the company of the police, then a finding of custody is much more likely. *Dunaway v. New York,*[15] though not involving a *Miranda* issue, is illustrative. Acting on instructions to "pick up" petitioner and "bring him in," officers found him at a

friend's house and drove him to the station. He was not told he was under arrest, no weapons were displayed, no handcuffs or any touching of petitioner was resorted to, and he was not booked, but he was then subjected to interrogation and was not told that he was free to go. The Court concluded there was "little doubt that petitioner was 'seized' in the Fourth Amendment sense when he was taken involuntarily to the police station," as "the detention of petitioner was in important respects indistinguishable from a traditional arrest." On the facts of *Dunaway,* it would seem that it also could be concluded that the situation was "custodial" for *Miranda* purposes. The result would be different if the suspect had been clearly and unequivocally advised that he was not under arrest and was free to leave at any time, or if it was made to appear that the person's presence was sought only as a witness.

(e) Presence Elsewhere. The *Miranda* Court stated that interrogation is custodial if it occurs while the individual is "in custody at the station or otherwise deprived of his freedom of action in any significant way." One reason for the latter part of this disjunctive definition is obvious: if *Miranda* governed only station-house interrogations, the police could easily circumvent the warning requirements by conducting interrogations in such places as hotel rooms or squad cars. Thus, it has been held that *Miranda* applies where, for example, a person has been apprehended and is in a police car at the time of his interrogation.

On the other hand, courts are much less likely to find the circumstances custodial when the interrogation occurs in familiar or at least neutral surroundings. Thus the Supreme Court in *Beckwith v. United States*[16] held, as have many lower court decisions, that interrogation in the suspect's home was noncustodial. Generally, the notion is that the suspect was in familiar surroundings and thus did not face the same pressures as in the police-dominated atmosphere of the station house. But the circumstances of each case must be carefully

---

14.   429 U.S. 492, 97 S.Ct. 711, 50 L.Ed.2d 714 (1977).

15.   442 U.S. 200, 99 S.Ct. 2248, 60 L.Ed.2d 824 (1979).

16.   425 U.S. 341, 96 S.Ct. 1612, 48 L.Ed.2d 1 (1976).

examined. The view that at-home questioning is noncustodial is strengthened when the suspect's friends or family members were present at the time. By contrast, in *Orozco v. Texas*[17] the Supreme Court concluded *Miranda* applied where four police officers entered defendant's bedroom at 4 a.m. to question him about a shooting, a proper result in that the circumstances produced a "potentiality for compulsion" equivalent to station house interrogation. Similarly, questioning has been held to be noncustodial where it occurred at the home of a friend or relative, a place of employment, a place of public accommodation, or a hospital. Once again, however, it must be emphasized that the circumstances of the particular case need to be carefully assessed. Thus, the situation might well be different as to an employee who was marched off to a security office of his employer, or as to a hospital patient who was taken to the hospital by the police or who was put into a police-dominated situation. But a person is not in custody for *Miranda* purposes merely because of his compelled appearance at a judicial proceeding to give testimony.

In *Minnesota v. Murphy*,[18] a probationer met with his probation officer at her office pursuant to her order and admitted in response to her questioning that he had committed a rape and murder some years ago. The Court held *Miranda* was inapplicable because there was not custody:

Custodial arrest is said to convey to the suspect a message that he has no choice but to submit to the officers' will and to confess. * * * It is unlikely that a probation interview, arranged by appointment at a mutually convenient time, would give rise to a similar impression. * * * Many of the psychological ploys discussed in *Miranda* capitalize on the suspect's unfamiliarity with the officers and the environment. Murphy's regular meetings with his probation officer should have served to familiarize him with her and her office and to insulate him from psychological intimidation that might overbear his desire to claim the privilege. Finally, the coercion inherent in custodial interrogation derives in large measure from an interrogator's insinuations that the interrogation will continue until a confession is obtained. * * * Since Murphy was not physically restrained and could have left the office, any compulsion he might have felt from the possibility that terminating the meeting would have led to revocation of probation was not comparable to the pressure on a suspect who is painfully aware that he literally cannot escape a persistent custodial interrogator.

Though the language of *Murphy* might suggest otherwise, and though the Supreme Court on an earlier occasion assumed that a person serving a prison sentence is "in custody" for *Miranda* purposes,[19] lower courts have often found questioning of those serving prison sentences to be not custodial. The notion is that the coercive effects that *Miranda* found to be associated with custodial interrogation arise in the prison context only if an inmate's liberty is limited beyond the usual conditions of his confinement.

In *Miranda,* the Court declared: "General on-the-scene questioning as to facts surrounding a crime or other general questioning of citizens in the factfinding process is not affected by our holding. * * * In such situations the compelling atmosphere inherent in the process of in-custody interrogation is not necessarily present." This is not to suggest, however, that all "on-the-scene" questioning falls outside *Miranda,* even if the person questioned is under arrest. As stated in *New York v. Quarles,*[20] "the ultimate inquiry is simply whether there is a 'formal arrest or restraint on freedom of movement' of the degree associated with a formal arrest." Such was the case in *Quarles,* where the questioning occurred in a supermarket minutes after defendant's ar-

17.   394 U.S. 324, 89 S.Ct. 1095, 22 L.Ed.2d 311 (1969).

18.   465 U.S. 420, 104 S.Ct. 1136, 79 L.Ed.2d 409 (1984).

19.   Mathis v. United States, 391 U.S. 1, 88 S.Ct. 1503, 20 L.Ed.2d 381 (1968) (government only argued *Miranda* not applicable except to "one who is 'in custody' in con-

nection with the very case under investigation," which Court summarily rejected).

20.   467 U.S. 649, 104 S.Ct. 2626, 81 L.Ed.2d 550 (1984).

rest by four police officers with guns drawn and after defendant had been handcuffed. By contrast, the Court in *Berkemer v. McCarty*[21] concluded without dissent that *Miranda* warnings are not required in the circumstances present there, where defendant was subjected to roadside questioning during a routine traffic stop. The Court acknowledged that the defendant had been "seized" for Fourth Amendment purposes, but noted the seizure was a limited one, much like a *Terry* stop for investigation, and then concluded as to both that the "comparatively nonthreatening character" of the detentions justified the holding "that persons temporarily detained pursuant to such stops are not 'in custody' for the purposes of *Miranda*." Specifically, the Court deemed it significant that such detentions are "presumptively temporary and brief" and are so perceived by the detainees, and that the circumstances of the stops are not such that a detainee "feels completely at the mercy of the police," as the stops occur in public and involve only one or two officers. Applying *Berkemer*, lower courts have held that *Miranda* does not apply in various settings judged to involve no more than a *Terry* stop, but the circumstances of some *Terry* stops have been deemed coercive so as to constitute "custody" for *Miranda* purposes even if they are not full-fledged arrests in a Fourth Amendment sense.

(f) Other Considerations. While the place of the interrogation is a very significant factor, it must be considered together with the other surrounding circumstances. In ascertaining, as called for by *Miranda,* whether the deprivation of freedom of action was "significant," it is particularly important whether some indicia of arrest are present. A court is not likely to find custody for *Miranda* purposes if the police were not even in a position to physically seize the suspect, but is likely to find custody if there was physical restraint such as handcuffing, drawing a gun, holding by the arm, or placing into a police car. Merely having the suspect move a short distance to facilitate conversion does not itself constitute custody. Also

relevant are whether or not the suspect was told that he was free to leave and, if the events occur at the station, whether or not booking procedures were employed.

Because the Court in *Miranda* expressed concern with the coerciveness of situations in which the suspect was "cut off from the outside world" and "surrounded by antagonistic forces" in a "police dominated atmosphere" and interrogated "without relent," circumstances relating to those kinds of concerns are also relevant on the custody issue. Thus, custody is less likely to be deemed present when the questioning occurred in the presence of the suspect's friends or other third parties, and more likely to be found when the police have removed the suspect from such individuals. A court is more likely to find the situation custodial when the suspect was confronted by several officers instead of just one, when the demeanor of the officer was antagonistic rather than friendly, and when the questioning was lengthy rather than brief and routine. And surely a reasonable person would conclude he was in custody if the interrogation is close and persistent, involving leading questions and the discounting of the suspect's denials of involvement. The argument that the giving of some of the *Miranda* warnings itself establishes that the situation was custodial has been rightly rejected, for it would be bizarre if such solicitude for a suspect not actually in custody were deemed to make the suspect's statement subject to suppression under *Miranda*.

§ 6.7 *Miranda*: "Interrogation"

(a) The "Functional Equivalent" Test. Just what is encompassed within the "interrogation" part of *Miranda's* "custodial interrogation" term has caused the courts considerable difficulty. One view often taken, which finds support in the *Miranda* Court's explanation that "we mean questioning initiated by law enforcement officers," was that nothing but the asking of questions will bring a case within the constraints of *Miranda*. Another view, consistent with the observation in *Mi-*

---

21. 468 U.S. 420, 104 S.Ct. 3138, 82 L.Ed.2d 317 (1984), first holding there is no general traffic violation

exception to *Miranda* even when there is custody. See § 6.10(a).

randa that it is the placing of an individual "into police custody" and then subjecting him "to techniques of persuasion" which together produce the "compulsion to speak," was that the word "interrogation" should not be given a narrow or literal interpretation. So matters stood until the Supreme Court finally resolved this fundamental dispute in *Rhode Island v. Innis.*[1]

In *Innis,* defendant was arrested for robbery with a sawed-off shotgun and promptly given his *Miranda* warnings, at which he said he wished to speak with a lawyer. The arresting officers then began their journey to the station with the prisoner, and during this time the officers conversed among themselves about the desirability of finding the shotgun because there was a school for handicapped children in the vicinity. At this, defendant said he would show the officers where the gun was located, which he did. His murder conviction was overturned by the state supreme court, as the gun and testimony about its discovery was held to have been improperly admitted because defendant had been subjected to "subtle coercion" equivalent to *Miranda* "interrogation," A majority of the Supreme Court, though ultimately concluding that "respondent was not 'interrogated' within the meaning of *Miranda,*" nonetheless opted for a rather broad definition of what constitutes "interrogation."

The *Innis* majority first rejected the two extreme positions. The notion "that the *Miranda* rules were to apply only to those police interrogation practices that involve express questioning" was found to be inconsistent with the *Miranda* Court's discussion of the use of various "psychological ploys" that, "no less than express questioning, were thought, in a custodial setting, to amount to interrogation." But this did not mean "that all statements obtained by the police after a person has been taken into custody are to be considered the product of interrogation," for interrogation, "as conceptualized in the *Miranda* opinion, must reflect a measure of compulsion above

and beyond that inherent in custody itself." The *Innis* Court then concluded

> that the *Miranda* safeguards come into play whenever a person in custody is subjected to either express questioning or its functional equivalent. That is to say, the term "interrogation" under *Miranda* refers not only to express questioning, but also to any words or actions on the part of the police (other than those normally attendant to arrest and custody) that the police should know are reasonably likely to elicit an incriminating response from the suspect. The latter portion of this definition focuses primarily upon the perceptions of the suspect, rather than the intent of the police. This focus reflects the fact that the *Miranda* safeguards were designed to vest a suspect in custody with an added measure of protection against coercive police practices, without regard to objective proof of the underlying intent of the police. A practice that the police should know is reasonably likely to evoke an incriminating response from a suspect thus amounts to interrogation. But, since the police surely cannot be held accountable for the unforeseeable results of their words or actions, the definition of interrogation can extend only to words or actions on the part of police officers that they *should have known* were reasonably likely to elicit an incriminating response.

The *Innis* definition of "interrogation" was expressly noted to be "not necessarily interchangeable" with the *Brewer v. Williams*[2] and *Massiah v. United States*[3] definition of what constitutes a violation of the Sixth Amendment right to counsel once that right has attached. For one thing, the *Williams–Massiah* "deliberately elicited" test focuses upon the intent of the police, while the *Innis* test does not. Only Justice Stevens, dissenting in *Innis,* felt that " 'interrogation' must include any police statement or conduct that has the same purpose or effect as a direct question," that is, both those "that appear to call for a response from the suspect" and "those that are de-

---

§ 6.7

1. 446 U.S. 291, 100 S.Ct. 1682, 64 L.Ed.2d 297 (1980).

2. 430 U.S. 387, 97 S.Ct. 1232, 51 L.Ed.2d 424 (1977).

3. 377 U.S. 201, 84 S.Ct. 1199, 12 L.Ed.2d 246 (1964).

signed to do so." But one of the ambiguities of *Innis* is just how far apart these two positions actually are. In an apparent attempt to bridge the gap, the majority dropped a footnote saying that the intent of the police is not irrelevant, "for it may well have a bearing on whether the police should have known that their words or actions were reasonably likely to evoke an incriminating response." This footnote goes on to say that "where a police practice is designed to elicit an incriminating response from the accused, it is unlikely that the practice will not also be one which the police should have known was reasonably likely to have that effect," which drew the following footnote rejoinder by Justice Stevens: "This factual assumption is extremely dubious. I would assume that police often interrogate suspects without any reason to believe that their efforts are likely to be successful in the hope that a statement will nevertheless be forthcoming."

This exchange is indicative of more fundamental problems with both the majority opinion and the Stevens dissent. To take the latter first of all, it surely does not make sense to conclude that under *Miranda* the existence of "interrogation" (any more than the existence of "custody"[4]) depends upon the undisclosed intentions of the officer. *Miranda* is grounded in the notion that custody plus interrogation produces a coercive atmosphere, which makes sense only when the suspect is aware of both the custody and the interrogation. The court noted in *Innis* that it would not constitute "interrogation" for the police merely to drive past the site of the concealed weapon while taking the most direct route to the police station, and surely the result should not be different even if the police admitted their "purpose" in driving by was to elicit an incriminating response. To take a phrase from *Miranda,* the "potentiality for compulsion" would be no different in the latter situation than in the former.

Justice Stevens was apparently attracted to his intention-of-the-officer alternative because it would largely overcome what he saw as a

glaring weakness in the majority's approach in *Innis.* His reading of the majority's (perhaps unfortunate) "reasonably likely to elicit" language is that it necessitates a determination of the apparent probability that police speech or conduct will elicit an incriminating response. This interpretation cannot be dismissed out of hand; for one thing, it would explain the otherwise questionable *Innis* result. But so interpreted the *Innis* test would not provide adequate guidance to police and lower courts. However, that does not appear to be what the *Innis* majority really meant, for such a view of the case is inconsistent with the majority's professed aim of defining "interrogation" in a manner consistent with *Miranda*'s underlying policy of prohibiting all speech or conduct that is the "functional equivalent" of direct questioning.

Just what *Innis* does mean is a matter of some uncertainty, although it would seem to turn upon the *objective* purpose *manifested* by the police. Thus, an officer "should know" that his speech or conduct will be "reasonably likely to elicit an incriminating response" when he should realize that the speech or conduct will probably be viewed by the suspect as designed to achieve this purpose. To ensure that the inquiry is entirely *objective*, the proposed test could be framed as follows: If an objective observer (with the same knowledge of the suspect as the police officer) would, on the sole basis of hearing the officer's remarks, infer that the remarks were designed to elicit an incriminating response, then the remarks should constitute "interrogation." This interpretation is consistent with the result reached in *Innis,* would not be difficult to apply because it is an objective test not requiring a determination of the actual perception of the suspect, but yet is fully responsive to the concerns in *Miranda* because it identifies the situation in which the suspect will experience the "functional equivalent" of direct questioning by concluding that the police are trying to get him to make an incriminating response. Moreover, it has the added advantage that it would put to rest a concern expressed by one member of the Court in *Innis:* that the police were

---

4. See § 6.6(c).

expected to "evaluate the suggestibility and susceptibility of an accused."[5]

Consistent in some respects with the preceding interpretation is *Arizona v. Mauro*,[6] where, after defendant invoked his right to counsel, the police acceded to a request of his wife, also a suspect in the investigation of their son's death, to speak with defendant, but had a police officer and tape recorder conspicuously present at the meeting. The Court, in a 5–4 decision, held this did not constitute "interrogation" under the *Innis* formulation. *Mauro* apparently reflects an unwillingness of a majority of the Court to ground the "interrogation" determination in the subjective intentions of the police. The state supreme court had concluded that the proper focus was upon the intent of the police and that this intent was "so clear" that it was unnecessary to "address appellant's perceptions," and this approach was accepted by the four dissenters in *Mauro*. The *Mauro* majority, on the other hand, asserted that there was no such intent shown and added, even more unconvincingly, that the police were not even aware of "a sufficient likelihood of incrimination" under the legal standard articulated in *Innis*.

But what seems to lie at the heart of the majority position in *Mauro* is that neither the subjective intentions of the police nor their perception of a significant likelihood that a certain scenario will prompt incriminating statements by the defendant is determinative. This is reflected in the majority's statement that "the weakness of Mauro's claim that he was interrogated is underscored by examining the situation from his perspective. * * * We doubt that a suspect, told by officers that his wife will be allowed to speak to him, would feel that he was being coerced to incriminate himself in any way." That is, the bottom line in *Mauro*, as the majority sees it, is that "Mauro was not subjected to compelling influences, psychological ploys, or direct questioning."

There is much to be said for the proposition, which *seems* to underlie the majority's position in *Mauro* notwithstanding all the disclaimers, that neither the officers' intentions nor their strong expectations should be decisive. Rather, as suggested earlier, it makes more sense to consider the objective purpose manifested by the police—that is, what an objective observer with the same knowledge as the suspect would conclude the police were up to. *If* that is the proper approach,[7] then it is by no means clear that the majority in *Mauro* reached the correct result. When the defendant was suddenly confronted with what must have appeared to him as a police-arranged meeting with his wife at which the police maintained a presence with a tape recorder operating, it would seem that he was subjected to the "functional equivalent" of interrogation. This is because Mauro had learned that those having custody of him had produced a scenario that (in the language of Justice Stevens in *Innis*) "appear[ed] to call for a response."

(b) Questioning. The Court in *Innis* set out to determine what "words or actions on the part of the police" other than "express questioning" constitute "interrogation" within the meaning of *Miranda*. Putting the matter this way would certainly suggest that *any* time a person in custody is asked a question, surely the *Miranda* requirements apply. But no such absolute rule had been recognized by the lower courts prior to *Innis*, and it does not seem that all of those decisions are cast in doubt by the *Innis* decision. If other "words or actions" fall within *Miranda* only if "the police should know [they] are likely to elicit an incriminating response," then it is not fanciful to suggest that certain types of questioning also do not come within *Miranda* because they are unlikely to produce that kind of response. Or if, as suggested above, the unfortunate "likely to elicit" language is ignored in favor of an inquiry whether an objective observer

---

5. Burger, C.J., concurring but responding to a footnote by the majority asserting the relevance of "[a]ny knowledge the police may have had concerning the unusual susceptibility of a defendant to a particular form of persuasion."

6. 481 U.S. 520, 107 S.Ct. 1931, 95 L.Ed.2d 458 (1987).

7. In Pennsylvania v. Muniz, 496 U.S. 582, 110 S.Ct. 2638, 110 L.Ed.2d 528 (1990), certain words were deemed not to constitute interrogation because they "were not likely to be perceived as calling for any incriminating response." Significantly, the Court did *not* say "perceived by the suspect."

would infer that the remarks were designed to elicit an incriminating response, it still does not follow that *all* questioning of those in custody is governed by *Miranda*.

Miranda requirements are inapplicable to questioning producing an incriminating response not "testimonial" in nature. Illustrative is *Pennsylvania v. Muniz*,[8] where the defendant, under arrest for driving under the influence, was asked a series of questions about his name, address, birthday, age, etc. The Court concluded that though defendant's videotaped responses incriminated him because his slurred speech manifested his drunkenness, the lack of *Miranda* warnings did not require suppression. Relying upon the established distinction between "testimonial" and "real or physical evidence" for purposes of the privilege against self-incrimination,[9] the Court concluded

> that any slurring of speech and other evidence of lack of muscular coordination revealed by Muniz's responses to [the officer's] direct questions constitute nontestimonial components of those responses. Requiring a suspect to reveal the physical manner in which he articulates words, like requiring him to reveal the physical properties of the sound produced by his voice,[10] * * * does not, without more, compel him to provide a "testimonial" response for purposes of the privilege.

The *content* of one of the defendant's answers in *Muniz,* that he did not know the date of his sixth birthday, was incriminating because it would allow the inference that his mental state was confused. Four members of the Court believed this also fell into the "real or physical evidence" category,[11] but the majority disagreed. They explained that even if

the matter inferred had to do with physical condition, the critical issue "is whether the inference is drawn from a testimonial act or from physical evidence.[12] * * * Whenever a suspect is asked for a response requiring him to communicate an express or implied assertion of fact or belief, the suspect confronts the 'trilemma' of truth, falsity, or silence and hence the response (whether based on truth or falsity) contains a testimonial component." Under this test, the sixth birthday question "required a testimonial response": the coercive environment precluded the option of remaining silent, and the truth (that he did not know the date) was incriminating, as would have been a false statement (an incorrect guess).

Both prior to and following *Muniz,* lower courts—usually relying upon the *Innis* assertion that "interrogation" does not include those words and actions "normally attendant to arrest and custody" have held that routine inquiries during the booking process are lawful even absent *Miranda* warnings. *Muniz,* in holding admissible the answers given to a series of booking questions, supports this conclusion. Four members of the Court concluded the answers were admissible "because the questions fall within a 'routine booking question' exception which exempts from *Miranda's* coverage questions to secure the 'biographical data necessary to complete booking or pretrial services.' "[13] Four others deemed it "unnecessary to determine whether the questions fall within the 'routine booking question' exception to *Miranda*" because they believed the defendant's responses "were not testimonial."

A related but more difficult issue concerns questions asked for purposes of identification

---

8. 496 U.S. 582, 110 S.Ct. 2638, 110 L.Ed.2d 528 (1990).

9. Schmerber v. California, 384 U.S. 757, 86 S.Ct. 1826, 16 L.Ed.2d 908 (1966), discussed in § 7.2(a).

10. See United States v. Wade, 388 U.S. 218, 87 S.Ct. 1926, 18 L.Ed.2d 1149 (1967), discussed in § 7.2(b).

11. They stated: "If the police may require Muniz to use his body in order to demonstrate the level of his physical coordination, there is no reason why they should not be able to require him to speak or write in order to determine his mental coordination."

12. They explained that therefore, while drawing a blood sample to prove intoxication was "outside of the Fifth Amendment's protection," the same would not be true "had the police instead asked the suspect directly whether his blood contained a high concentration of alcohol."

13. They also concluded that because *Innis* focuses primarily upon "the perspective of the suspect," the booking questions could not be placed outside the *Innis* definition "merely because the questions were not intended to elicit information for investigative purposes."

(e.g., "what is your name?", "where do you live?") other than as part of the booking process. For example, in the unlikely event that an on-the-street interrogation were deemed custodial, may the police make inquiries limited to the purpose of identifying a person found under suspicious circumstances or near the scene of a recent crime? An affirmative answer is suggested by *California v. Byers,*[14] holding that a statute requiring the driver of a car involved in an accident to stop and give the driver of the other car his name and address does not violate the privilege against self-incrimination, even without a restriction on the use of the required disclosures. The *Byers* Court, indicating that the required conduct was not "testimonial" in the Fifth Amendment sense and did not entail a "substantial risk of self-incrimination," noted:

A name, linked with a motor vehicle, is no more incriminating than the tax return, linked with the disclosure of income * * *. It identifies but does not by itself implicate anyone in criminal conduct.

Although identity, when made known, may lead to inquiry that in turn leads to arrest and charge, those developments depend on different factors and independent evidence. Here the compelled disclosure of identity could have led to a charge that might not have been made had the driver fled the scene; but this is true only in the same sense that a taxpayer can be charged on the basis of the contents of a tax return or failure to file an income tax return. There is no constitutional right to refuse to file an income tax return or to flee the scene of an accident in order to avoid the possibility of legal involvement.

Application of *Byers* to the situation here under discussion (which finds support in the many holdings that the privilege presents no bar to various other identification techniques[15]) would not seem inconsistent with the *Innis* definition of "interrogation." Yet in various other settings supposed identification questions that would otherwise be innocuous will constitute interrogation under *Innis* because the circumstances of the particular case gave the officer reason to know that the suspect's answer would likely incriminate him.

An innocuous question resulting in an incriminating response does not fall within *Miranda*; as the Court put it in *Innis,* "the police surely cannot be held accountable for the unforeseeable results of their words or actions." As for questions not quite so innocuous but not accusatory either (e.g., "what happened?", "what's going on here?") the issue has been infrequently litigated because those situations usually arise in the context of a brief noncustodial encounter between an officer and citizen. However, there is authority that such situations are likewise not covered by *Miranda*. This is often explained by reliance upon the *Miranda* Court's statement that "[g]eneral on-the-scene questioning as to facts surrounding a crime or other general questioning of citizens in the fact-finding process is not affected by our holding," though sometimes that language has been deemed inapplicable whenever the situation has become custodial. In any event, it would seem that at least some such inquiries are not interrogation under the suggested interpretation of *Innis*: whether an objective observer would infer the remarks were designed to elicit an incriminating response. Such an inference might well not be drawn when the question is very general in nature, not directed at one particular person, obviously asked before it is known that any criminal conduct has occurred or before there has been any sorting of suspects from witnesses, apparently asked about a seemingly innocuous matter not directly related to the police intervention, obviously spontaneous in nature, or seemingly a natural question anyone would ask given defendant's condition or other unusual circumstances.

Still another type of case is that in which the authorities claim that they were questioning for the purpose of protecting themselves or others from weapons by asking the defendant whether he had a gun or where a gun was

14.   402 U.S. 424, 91 S.Ct. 1535, 29 L.Ed.2d 9 (1971).

15.   See § 7.2(b).

located. Illustrative is *New York v. Quarles*,[16] where police chased a rape suspect, who was reportedly armed, inside a supermarket and then arrested him there; a frisk uncovered an empty shoulder holster, so one officer asked him "Where is the gun?"; the suspect gestured toward a stack of soap cartons and said, "The gun is over there," and police then found a revolver behind the cartons. A majority of the Supreme Court concluded that "on these facts there is a 'public safety' exception to the requirement that *Miranda* warnings be given."[17] The Court characterized *Miranda* as representing a willingness by the Court to impose procedural safeguards "when the primary social cost of those added protections is the possibility of fewer convictions," to be distinguished from the instant situation in which the cost would be an inability "to insure that further danger to the public did not result from the concealment of the gun." It was thus concluded that the need for answers to questions in a situation posing a threat to the public safety outweighs the need for the prophylactic rule protecting the Fifth Amendment's privilege against self-incrimination. Otherwise, the *Quarles* majority recognized, police would be "in the untenable position of having to consider, often in a matter of seconds, whether it best serves society for them to ask the necessary questions without the *Miranda* warnings and render whatever probative evidence they uncover inadmissible, or for them to give the warnings in order to preserve the admissibility of evidence they might uncover but possibly damage or destroy their ability to obtain that evidence and neutralize the volatile situation confronting them." (Somewhat similar is the so-called "rescue doctrine," under which it has been held that *Miranda* warnings are unnecessary before custodial questioning undertaken to save life (e.g., in an effort to locate a kidnap victim).)

The four dissenters in *Quarles* understandably objected that the majority's "public-safety exception destroys forever the clarity of *Miranda* for both law enforcement officers and members of the judiciary," and also that the majority's cost-benefit analysis was irrelevant under the reasoning in *Miranda* and in any event failed to take account of the fact that police could lawfully question for public safety purposes provided the defendant's statements and the fruits thereof were not later used against him. But perhaps the most troublesome aspect of *Quarles* is the apparent breadth of the exception that has been created. Though the record below did not indicate that the police questioning was prompted by an actual concern for public safety, the majority disposed of that problem by declaring that the public safety exception "does not depend upon the motivation of the individual officers involved." That is, the notion put forward by the majority is that the facts of the case, objectively viewed, show that the police,

> in the very act of apprehending a suspect, were confronted with the immediate necessity of ascertaining the whereabouts of a gun which they had every reason to believe the suspect had just removed from his empty holster and discarded in the supermarket. So long as the gun was concealed somewhere in the supermarket, with its actual whereabouts unknown, it obviously posed more than one danger to the public safety; an accomplice might make use of it, a customer or employee might later come upon it.

But the facts in *Quarles* shows no such thing. At the time of the questioning, Quarles was handcuffed and in the custody of four armed officers, and thus there was no danger whatsoever that he could get at the gun. Nor was there the slightest suggestion that he had been aided by an accomplice in the rape. As for the possibility that some other person might

---

16. 467 U.S. 649, 104 S.Ct. 2626, 81 L.Ed.2d 550 (1984).

17. Although the matter was put this way in *Quarles*, the principle of that case is equally applicable when the defendant is given the *Miranda* warnings and invokes his rights, for the danger does not abate with *Miranda* warnings and assertions.

It does not necessarily follow, however, that *Quarles* applies outside the *Miranda* area; the Court noted in *Quarles* that "we have before us no claim that respondent's statements were actually compelled by police conduct which overcame his will to resist." But even if the coerced statement is suppressed, it is not necessarily the case that the weapon will also be suppressed.

come onto the gun before the police could locate it, this seems equally fanciful in light of the facts that the events occurred after midnight when the store was apparently deserted and that the police knew the gun had been discarded in the immediate vicinity. But at least we know that the *Quarles* exception is not broad enough to encompass any questioning about the location of a weapon. The majority asserted *Quarles* was not inconsistent with *Orozco v. Texas,*[18] where police entered the sleeping defendant's room and then questioned him about a gun used in a murder at a restaurant several hours earlier, as there "the questions about the gun were clearly investigatory" because "they did not in any way relate to an objectively reasonable need to protect the police or the public from any immediate danger associated with the weapon."

One other special purpose type of questioning deserves mention, especially because it has been specifically considered by the Supreme Court. In *Estelle v. Smith,*[19] defendant was indicted for murder and the state announced its intention to seek the death penalty. Though defense counsel had not interposed an insanity defense or questioned his client's competency to stand trial, defendant was subjected to a psychiatric examination and the psychiatrist testified at the penalty phase of the trial concerning defendant's "future dangerousness," after which defendant was sentenced to death. The state claimed that a psychiatric examination did not infringe upon Fifth Amendment interests because an inquiry into defendant's state of mind was like obtaining a blood sample or voice and handwriting exemplars, but the Court rejected this contention. Because the doctor's testimony "was not based simply on his observation of respondent" but came "largely from respondent's account of the crime during their interview," the "Fifth Amendment privilege * * * is directly involved here because the State used as evidence against respondent the substance of his disclosures during the pretrial psychiatric

examination." The Court added that the result would have been otherwise had the doctor testified at a hearing on defendant's competency to stand trial, for "no Fifth Amendment issue would have arisen" in that context. The Court also emphasized that the instant case was not analogous

> to a sanity examination occasioned by a defendant's plea of not guilty by reason of insanity at the time of his offense. When a defendant asserts the insanity defense and introduces supporting psychiatric testimony, his silence may deprive the State of the only effective means it has of controverting his proof on an issue that he interjected into the case. Accordingly, several courts of appeals have held that, under such circumstances, a defendant can be required to submit to a sanity examination conducted by the prosecution's psychiatrist.

The Court did not have occasion to rule on such a situation in *Smith*, and in the later case of *Buchanan v. Kentucky*[20] found it necessary only to hold that "if a defendant requests [a psychiatric] evaluation or presents psychiatric evidence, then, at the very least, the prosecution may rebut this presentation with evidence from the reports of the examination that the defendant requested."

(c) Other "Words or Actions." The major impact of *Innis* is with respect to conduct other than express questioning. Prior to that decision there was a split of authority as to what the outcome should be when the police engaged in such tactics as confronting the defendant with physical evidence, with an accusing accomplice, or with the confession of an accomplice. One explanation given for admitting incriminating statements obtained in these ways was that questioning does not exist absent verbal conduct by the police, a notion *Innis* clearly repudiates. Indeed, under *Innis* such tactics will usually be characterized as "interrogation." This may seem less likely af-

---

18. 394 U.S. 324, 89 S.Ct. 1095, 22 L.Ed.2d 311 (1969).

19. 451 U.S. 454, 101 S.Ct. 1866, 68 L.Ed.2d 359 (1981).

20. 483 U.S. 402, 107 S.Ct. 2906, 97 L.Ed.2d 336 (1987), involving not an insanity defense but rather a mental state defense of extreme emotional disturbance.

ter *Mauro,* discussed earlier,[21] rejecting the conclusion of the four dissenters "that a police decision to place two suspects in the same room and then to listen to or record their conversation may constitute a form of interrogation even if no questions are asked by any police officers." Perhaps that is so, though the majority distinguished the situation before it from those in which the police resorted to " 'psychological ploys, such as to "posi[t]" "the guilt of the subject" * * *.' "

Another line of reasoning in the pre-*Innis* cases is that it is not unfair to communicate to the defendant information about the strength of the case against him, for such information is relevant to an intelligent decision by him as to whether he should cooperate or remain silent. To the extent that this view persists, there will doubtless be pressure not to apply *Innis* to every instance in which such information has been made available to a defendant. And in any event, *Innis* is not so broad; as noted earlier, it is best interpreted as covering those instances in which the officer's words or actions would be viewed by an objective observer as designed to elicit an incriminating response, which is preferable to asking (to take some of the language in *Innis*) whether the police should have known the activity was "reasonably likely to elicit an incriminating response." This point is best illustrated by two situations that have been viewed as not within *Miranda's* constraints and as to which *Innis* is not likely to produce a different result: where the defendant made a confession after being identified in a lineup or after witnessing police discovery of physical evidence. In terms of the probability of a defendant making an incriminating remark, these two situations probably are not significantly different from many of the others described above. But the important fact about these two situations is that the police were engaged in activity calculated to produce evidence against the defendant by other means, and thus objectively viewed they would not appear to be designed to get an incriminating response from the defendant.

Another kind of case that requires closer analysis after *Innis* is where the police within the hearing of defendant engage in comments or conversation short of questions put to the defendant. *Innis* itself was this kind of case, as it involved a conversation among the officers about the desirability of finding the shotgun so that it would not fall into the hands of a handicapped child. The majority concluded this was not *Miranda* interrogation because the comments were just "a few off-hand remarks" rather than a "lengthy harangue," were not made to one the police knew "was peculiarly 'evocative,' " and were not made to one the police knew "was peculiarly susceptible to an appeal to his conscience concerning the safety of handicapped children." Though *Innis* is a close case, surely there are other instances in which the comments or conversations of the police will be deemed interrogation. Illustrative is the "Christian burial" speech in *Brewer v. Williams.*[22] Though the Court decided that case on other grounds, prompting concern that it was not prepared to extend the concept of interrogation as it later did in *Innis,* certainly the conduct of the police in *Williams,* where the remarks were directed at the defendant by police who knew of and were taking advantage of the fact he was deeply religious, amounts to interrogation.

But there are other instances in which the police activity will not amount to "interrogation" or a functional equivalent, though it is clear beyond dispute that an officer directed words to the suspect. Illustrative is *Pennsylvania v. Muniz,*[23] where the defendant, arrested for driving under the influence, made incriminating remarks when asked by officers to perform physical sobriety tests and to submit to a breathalyzer examination. The Court concluded there was no "interrogation within the meaning of *Miranda*" because the "limited and focused inquiries were necessarily 'attendant to' the legitimate police procedure * * * and were not likely to be perceived as calling for any incriminating response." The Court earlier reached the same conclusion as to a

---

21. See text at note 6 supra.

22. 430 U.S. 387, 97 S.Ct. 1232, 51 L.Ed.2d 424 (1977).

23. 496 U.S. 582, 110 S.Ct. 2638, 110 L.Ed.2d 528 (1990).

police request that a suspect take a blood alcohol test,[24] while lower courts have so ruled as to police statements to the suspect by way of warning him of his rights or explaining why he was arrested.

Finally, it must be asked what the significance of *Innis* is in the so-called "jail plant" case, where an undercover agent is placed with the defendant while he is in custody and listens to defendant's remarks or even encourages the defendant to make remarks about the crime. In *Hoffa v. United States*,[25] involving a "plant" of a government agent with an unincarcerated defendant, the Court summarily dismissed the claim that Hoffa's incriminating statement had been obtained in violation of the Fifth Amendment. The Court there noted that "a necessary element of compulsory self-incrimination is some kind of compulsion," and that Hoffa's choice to make incriminating remarks in the agent's presence was "wholly voluntary" and not "the product of any sort of coercion, legal or factual." It has sometimes been questioned, however, whether the same result should obtain when the defendant is in jail. So the argument goes, the confinement increases a suspect's anxiety and makes him more likely to seek discourse with others to relieve this anxiety, meaning he will be more susceptible to an undercover investigator seeking information. Moreover, though *Hoffa* was fooled he at least had the choice of his companions, but when the suspect's ability to select people with whom he can confide is completely within police control, they have a unique opportunity to exploit the suspect's vulnerability.

While the Supreme Court has applied the *Massiah* rule (available only after the right to counsel has attached) to the "jail plant" situation, at least when the plant has taken some affirmative steps to bring about the defendant's statements,[26] the Court more recently held in *Illinois v. Perkins*[27] "that an undercover law enforcement officer posing as a fellow inmate need not give *Miranda* warnings to an

incarcerated suspect before asking questions that may elicit an incriminating response." The Court in *Perkins* reasoned:

> Conversations between suspects and undercover agents do not implicate the concerns underlying *Miranda*. The essential ingredients of a "police-dominated atmosphere" and compulsion are not present when an incarcerated person speaks freely to someone that he believes to be a fellow inmate. Coercion is determined from the perspective of the suspect. * * * When a suspect considers himself in the company of cellmates and not officers, the coercive atmosphere is lacking. * * *

> It is the premise of *Miranda* that the danger of coercion results from the interaction of custody and official interrogation. We reject the argument that *Miranda* warnings are required whenever a suspect is in custody in a technical sense and converses with someone who happens to be a government agent. Questioning by captors, who appear to control the suspect's fate, may create mutually reinforcing pressures that the Court has assumed will weaken the suspect's will, but where a suspect does not know that he is conversing with a government agent, these pressures do not exist.

(d) "Volunteered" Statements and Follow–Up Questioning. The *Miranda* Court emphasized that "there is no requirement that police stop a person who enters a police station and states that he wishes to confess to a crime, or a person who calls the police to offer a confession or any other statement he desires to make. Volunteered statements of any kind are not barred by the Fifth Amendment and their admissibility is not affected by our holding today." It is thus clear that a statement not preceded by the *Miranda* warnings will be admissible when, for example, the defendant walks into a police station and confesses or blurts out an admission when approached by

---

24. South Dakota v. Neville, 459 U.S. 553, 103 S.Ct. 916, 74 L.Ed.2d 748 (1983).

25. 385 U.S. 293, 87 S.Ct. 408, 17 L.Ed.2d 374 (1966).

26. United States v. Henry, 447 U.S. 264, 100 S.Ct. 2183, 65 L.Ed.2d 115 (1980), discussed in § 6.4(g).

27. 496 U.S. 292, 110 S.Ct. 2394, 110 L.Ed.2d 243 (1990).

an officer near a crime scene. More important, because *Miranda* found only custody-plus-interrogation coercive, a statement may qualify as "volunteered" even though made by one in custody, one who had previously asserted his right to silence, or one who had previously requested counsel. Indeed, a statement following a police officer's question may qualify as at least the equivalent of being volunteered when it is unresponsive, as when an officer's question is met by a bribery attempt.

Assuming a truly volunteered statement, may the police follow up that statement with some questions? *Miranda* is not entirely clear on this issue; at one point custodial interrogation is defined as "questioning initiated by law enforcement officers," suggesting that police questioning designed to clarify or amplify a volunteered statement is permissible, but elsewhere it is said that the suspect must be warned "prior to any questioning." Except in extreme circumstances, courts have generally been quite willing to admit the answers to follow-up questions on the ground that these answers are a continuation of the volunteered statement. The better view, however, is that the part of defendant's statement given after the follow-up questions is volunteered only if the questions are neutral efforts to clarify what has already been said rather than apparent attempts to expand the scope of the statement previously made. This means a question that would clarify a prior ambiguous statement (e.g., "did what?" in response to "I did it") would not constitute *Miranda* interrogation but a question that would enhance the defendant's guilt or raise the offense to a higher degree would.

Innis should not be read as a prohibition upon all follow-up questions. While the Court there made an unqualified reference to "express questioning" as falling within *Miranda,* it was not confronted with a follow-up questioning situation. The underlying rationale of *Innis* is that *Miranda* covers only police conduct likely to be coercive when coupled with defendant's custody, which cannot be said of a

question that does nothing more than seek clarification of what the defendant has already volunteered. Here again, however, the *Innis* Court's unfortunate "likely to elicit an incriminating response" language may prove a source of difficulty. If applied literally, it would seem to foreclose even a clarifying question.

§ 6.8 *Miranda:* Required Warnings

(a) Content. The Supreme Court in *Miranda* held that before a person in custody[1] may be subjected to interrogation[2] he "must be adequately and effectively apprised of his rights." In particular,

> he must first be informed in clear and unequivocal terms that he has the right to remain silent. * * *

> The warning of the right to remain silent must be accompanied by the explanation that anything said can and will be used against the individual in court.

> * * * [A]n individual held for interrogation must be clearly informed that he has the right to consult with a lawyer and to have the lawyer with him during interrogation * * *.

> [I]t is necessary to warn him not only that he has the right to consult with an attorney, but also that if he is indigent a lawyer will be appointed to represent him.

Whether the warnings must be given in precisely that language reached the Court in *California v. Prysock,*[3] on review of a lower court decision grounded in the proposition that the "rigidity of the *Miranda* rules and the way in which they are to be applied was conceived of and continues to be recognized as the decision's greatest strength." The Supreme Court noted that it "has never indicated that the 'rigidity' of *Miranda* extends to the precise formulation of the warnings given" and that, "[q]uite the contrary, *Miranda* itself indicates that no talismanic incantation was required to satisfy its strictures." The Court in *Prysock* thus concluded that what is required is not "a

---

§ 6.8

1. See § 6.6.

2. See § 6.7.

3. 453 U.S. 355, 101 S.Ct. 2806, 69 L.Ed.2d 696 (1981).

verbatim recital of the words of the *Miranda* opinion" but rather words that in substance will have "fully conveyed to [defendant] his rights as required by *Miranda*." Just when that has been accomplished, of course, is sometimes a difficult question.

The warning "that he has the right to remain silent" has been the source of little difficulty, as police apparently do not often deviate from this language. One variation that has surfaced, telling the suspect that he "need not make any statement," has usually been held acceptable. As for the second warning, concerning possible use of anything said by the suspect, in the excerpt quoted above the Court employed the overstatement "can and will be used."[4] But at an earlier point the Court described the warning as being that what is said "may be used," and this alternative has been consistently approved by the lower courts. The courts have also upheld other formulations, including use of "can" alone, of "might," and of "could." The part of the second warning cautioning about use of the statement "against" the suspect has sometimes been changed so that he is told what he says may be used "for or against you." Some courts have disapproved of this variation, while others have criticized it but yet held it not an impermissible deviation from the *Miranda* formula. The former is the better view, for such a variation is not only misleading but is likely to undercut the effect of the warning by offering an inducement to speak.

Under *Miranda*, it is necessary that these warnings cover the right to appointed counsel and the immediacy of the right in the sense that it exists both before and during interrogation. This has given rise to the question of whether the statement about appointment of counsel must particularize that appointment will precede questioning. No such language appears in the warnings quoted above, but at another point the *Miranda* Court said the defendant must be warned "that if he cannot afford an attorney one will be appointed for him prior to any questioning if he so desires."

However, in *California v. Prysock*[5] the Court held that where defendant "was told of his right to have a lawyer present prior to and during interrogation" and also of "his right to have a lawyer appointed at no cost if he could not afford one," these warnings collectively "conveyed to respondent his right to have a lawyer appointed if he could not afford one prior to and during interrogation." The three *Prysock* dissenters objected rather convincingly that under the circumstances the juvenile defendant might have understood the right to "appointed" counsel to refer only to the trial and that his right to counsel at the police station was dependent upon his or his parents' ability to hire one.

Somewhat different from *Prysock* is the case in which the police warnings convey the message that appointed counsel cannot be made available until some future time. Such a case reached the Court in *Duckworth v. Eagan*,[6] where the defendant was given the full *Miranda* warnings (including: "You have a right to talk to a lawyer for advice before we ask you any questions, and to have him with you during questioning"), but was also told: "We have no way of giving you a lawyer, but one will be appointed for you, if you wish, if and when you go to court." In holding these warnings sufficient, the majority stressed that the "if and when" statement "accurately described the procedure for the appointment of counsel in Indiana" and squared with *Miranda*, which "does not require that attorneys be producible on call. * * * If the police cannot provide appointed counsel, *Miranda* requires only that the police not question a suspect unless he waives his right to counsel." The four dissenters cogently objected that the "if and when" qualification "leads the suspect to believe that a lawyer will not be provided until some indeterminate time in the future *after questioning.*"

Assuming incomplete or inadequate *Miranda* warnings are given, may the prosecution overcome this by showing the suspect was

---

4. Lower courts have held that this "can and will" version is not objectionable.

5. 453 U.S. 355, 101 S.Ct. 2806, 69 L.Ed.2d 696 (1981).

6. 492 U.S. 195, 109 S.Ct. 2875, 106 L.Ed.2d 166 (1989).

in fact knowledgeable concerning the rights the warnings did not cover? The *Miranda* Court answered no, explaining that

> we will not pause to inquire in individual cases whether the defendant was aware of his rights without a warning being given. Assessments of the knowledge the defendant possessed, based on information as to his age, education, intelligence, or prior contact with authorities, can never be more than speculation; a warning is a clearcut fact. More important, whatever the background of the person interrogated, a warning at the time of the interrogation is indispensable to overcome its pressures and to insure that the individual knows he is free to exercise the privilege at that point in time.

As the Court put it at another point, giving warnings to the knowledgeable suspect "will show the individual that his interrogators are prepared to recognize his privilege should he choose to exercise it." Most courts have thus properly concluded that the warnings must be given even to lawyers and other suspects knowledgeable as to their *Miranda* rights.

A somewhat similar issue is whether omission of that part of the *Miranda* warnings concerning appointment of counsel can later be excused by a showing that the defendant was not indigent and thus would not have qualified for appointed counsel. The *Miranda* Court recognized some leeway was permissible here by the following footnote:

> While a warning that the indigent may have counsel appointed need not be given to the person who is known to have an attorney or is known to have ample funds to secure one, the expedient of giving a warning is too simple and the rights involved too important to engage in ex post facto inquiries into financial ability when there is any doubt at all on that score.

Some courts have read this as meaning that it must be shown the police were actually aware of defendant's ability to retain counsel, while others have deemed it sufficient if the prosecution later established that the defendant did have that ability at the time of the interrogation. The latter view is unobjectionable, but

the same cannot be said of those decisions holding that a defendant has the burden of showing he was indigent and thus entitled to warnings about appointment of counsel.

The characteristics of the particular suspect are relevant when the issue is whether the police did enough in giving the warnings in the language set out in *Miranda*. To take the most obvious case, if the suspect does not comprehend English then the warnings must be given in a language he understands. If the suspect is illiterate or of low intelligence, then great care must be taken to ensure that he understands his rights.

Sometimes the police have commenced giving the *Miranda* warnings only to be interrupted by the suspect, in which circumstances the courts are somewhat more sympathetic to the prosecution's position. When the interruption in effect stated what the police omitted (e.g., "I know I don't have to make a statement"), courts are inclined to conclude that *Miranda* has been complied with. Some courts reach the same result when the interruption is a more general declaration, such as "I know my rights," though the better view is that such an ambiguous assertion does not foreclose the need for specification of those rights by the police. But even when there is the latter type of interruption or one that includes no reference to *Miranda* rights, the subsequent statement will be admissible in any event if it was volunteered.

If the defendant is actually represented by counsel at the time of his interrogation, this may have some bearing on the need for *Miranda* warnings. It is generally accepted that if the attorney was actually present during the interrogation, then this obviates the need for the warnings. As for those instances in which the attorney was not present but had arranged for the contact, there is a split of authority. One view is that it may not be assumed the defendant knew of his rights because, for example, he came to the station with his lawyer; the other is that such an assumption is justified in such circumstances. In these cases, it may make some difference whether the defendant merely surrendered himself to police custody on advice of counsel or whether he and his counsel actually arranged for an interrogation session to occur.

(b) Time and Frequency. With respect to the timing of the *Miranda* warnings, one question that arises is whether the warnings were given soon enough. Though it has been held, with respect to post-warnings statements, that the warnings need not have preceded any and all questioning, a careful assessment of the events preceding the warnings is necessary. It is one thing if the warnings followed mere casual conversation or limited and brief inquiries. But the warnings come too late if they were preceded by extended interrogation or conversations regarding waiver of rights. Assuming the warnings were given in a timely fashion, the question then may be whether they became "stale" after the passage of time. It is generally accepted that fresh warnings are not required after the passage of just a few hours. Authority is also to be found to the effect that this is also true even after the passage of several days where the custody has been continuous, but the contrary view has much to commend it. Clearly the passage of weeks or months is too long.

Even when the passage of time has been fairly brief, consideration must be given to changes in the circumstances in the interim. However, the courts have generally taken the position that new warnings are not required just because there has been a change in the locale of the interrogation, in the officers doing the questioning, or in the subject matter of the investigation. Even a combination of these circumstances is not deemed to call for new warnings. The rationale of these cases appears to be that to require repetition of the warnings would merely add a perfunctory ritual which would not afford meaningful additional protection to the defendant. But that is a questionable conclusion in many circumstances and is not in keeping with the *Miranda* Court's teachings that a defendant's "opportunity to exercise these rights must be afforded to him throughout the interrogation" and that the warnings when given to one already aware of his rights serve to "show the individual that his interrogators are prepared to recognize his privilege should he choose to exercise it." In any event, repetition of the *Miranda* warnings will be necessary if the authorities are to "undo" the effects of coercive conduct following the initial warnings. Similar analysis is required when the defendant claims his *Miranda* warnings came too soon.

(c) Manner; Proof. In *Miranda*, the Court declared that "[s]ince the State is responsible for establishing the isolated circumstances under which the interrogation takes place and has the only means of making available corroborated evidence of warnings given during incommunicado interrogation, the burden is rightly on its shoulders." Though this would suggest that it is desirable to tape record the warnings or have them stenographically reported, most courts have not imposed such a requirement. Indeed, the uncorroborated testimony of a police officer that the warnings were given (if sufficiently detailed) will suffice even in the face of contradictory testimony by the defendant.

The warnings may be given either orally or in writing, though it has been noted that the better practice is to do both. Though giving the warnings in writing alone will suffice, it must be shown that the defendant could and did read the warnings and that he acknowledged an understanding of them. More commonly the warnings are given orally by the officer reciting the provisions from a "*Miranda* card." This alone is sufficient, provided of course that the reading is not done in a hurried or mechanical fashion.

If both oral and written warnings were given but one version was defective or incomplete, courts have held it suffices that the one set of warnings was complete and correct. This may be a sensible result when the difference between the two sets of warnings is merely that something was omitted from one of them, but a contrary result is necessary if the conflict between the two is such that the suspect would be confused by the discrepancy. Two sets of warnings, *each* of which is deficient, may not be read together to create one valid set of warnings.

(d) Additional Admonitions. Defendants have sometimes contended that warnings other than those set out earlier are generally or in particular circumstances required by *Miranda*. For example, because the Court in *Miranda* noted that many suspects will assume that "silence in the face of accusation is itself damning and will bode ill when presented to a jury," it might well be argued that suspects are entitled to be explicitly warned of another important part of the *Miranda* holding—that the "prosecution may not * * * use at trial the fact that he stood mute or claimed his privilege in the face of accusation." But, neither the Supreme Court nor the lower courts have mandated the giving of such a warning. Similarly, while the *Miranda* Court recognized that a defendant has a right to stop answering questions at any time, this right was not included within the mandated warnings and thus lower courts have concluded that such a warning is not necessary.

Defendants have also claimed that under *Miranda* they are entitled to be told of the nature of the crime about which the police wish to interrogate them. The lower courts have rather consistently held that such advice is not required. The Supreme Court concluded in *Colorado v. Spring*[7] that there is no affirmative obligation on the police to advise the defendant about the crime concerning which they wish to interrogate—even when the circumstances rather strongly suggest the desired questioning will be about a matter quite different from that later encompassed by the interrogation. Although in *Spring* the arrest had been by federal ATF agents but the post-arrest questioning after a *Miranda* waiver was about an unreported homicide in another state, defendant's statements were held to be admissible even absent any pre-waiver warning that questions about the homicide would be asked. The Court reasoned that since the defendant had been told he had a right to remain silent and that *anything* he said could be used against him, he had all the information necessary for a knowing and intelligent waiver of his Fifth Amendment rights; "the additional

information could affect only the wisdom of a *Miranda* waiver, not its essentially voluntary and knowing nature." As for the statement in *Miranda* that "any evidence that the accused was threatened, tricked, or cajoled into a waiver will * * * show that the defendant did not voluntarily waive his privilege," the Court responded that mere "official silence" about the desire to question concerning the murder did not constitute trickery, and cautiously left unresolved whether a waiver of *Miranda* rights would be valid had there been "an affirmative misrepresentation by law enforcement officials as to the scope of the interrogation."

When a foreign national has sought suppression of his confession because police failed to advise him of his right under a treaty to contact a consular official, the courts have responded that violation of rights created by treaty is not a constitutional error and thus does not require use of the exclusionary rule.

§ 6.9 *Miranda:* Waiver of Rights

(a) **Express or Implied.** Although the Court in *Miranda* ruled that interrogation when accompanied by custody is so likely to be coercive that the defendant must be warned of his right not to talk to the police and to have the assistance of counsel before and during any questioning, this does not mean the police are free to interrogate whenever they have given the requisite warnings. The Court in *Miranda* went on to hold that if thereafter the defendant is interrogated and a statement is obtained, it will be admissible only if the government meets its "heavy burden"[1] of demonstrating "that the defendant knowingly and intelligently waived his privilege against self-incrimination and his right to retained or appointed counsel." Moreover, if "the individual indicates in any manner, at any time prior to or during questioning, that he wishes to remain silent, the interrogation must cease," for

---

7.   479 U.S. 564, 107 S.Ct. 851, 93 L.Ed.2d 954 (1987).

§ 6.9

1.   On what this means in burden-of-proof terms, see § 10.3(c).

he has thus "shown that he intends to exercise his Fifth Amendment privilege."

The tone and language of the majority opinion in *Miranda* seemed to indicate that the Court would be receptive to nothing short of an express waiver of the rights involved. The Court declared:

> An express statement that the individual is willing to make a statement and does not want an attorney followed closely by a statement could constitute a waiver. But a valid waiver will not be presumed simply from the silence of the accused after warnings are given or simply from the fact that a confession was in fact eventually obtained. A statement we made in *Carnley v. Cochran*[2] * * * is applicable here:
>
>> "Presuming waiver from a silent record is impermissible. The record must show, or there must be an allegation and evidence which show, that an accused was offered counsel but intelligently and understandably rejected the offer. Anything less is not waiver."
>
> * * * Moreover, where in-custody interrogation is involved, there is no room for the contention that the privilege is waived if the individual answers some questions or gives some information on his own prior to invoking his right to remain silent when interrogated.

Most lower courts nonetheless took the position that the *Miranda* waiver of rights did not have to be express, and this view was ultimately adopted by the Supreme Court in *North Carolina v. Butler*.[3] There defendant was given his *Miranda* rights orally at the time of arrest and later at the FBI office he read an "Advice of Rights" form which he said he understood, after which he said he would talk to the agents but would not sign the waiver on the form. The state supreme court excluded defendant's incriminating statement on the ground that a waiver of *Miranda* rights "will not be recognized unless such waiver is 'specifically made' after the *Miranda* warnings have been given,"

but the Supreme Court, in a 5–3 decision, disagreed:

> An express written or oral statement of waiver of the right to remain silent or of the right to counsel is usually strong proof of the validity of that waiver, but is not inevitably either necessary or sufficient to establish waiver. The question is not one of form, but rather whether the defendant in fact knowingly and voluntarily waived the rights delineated in the *Miranda* case. As was unequivocally said in *Miranda,* mere silence is not enough. That does not mean that the defendant's silence, coupled with an understanding of his rights and a course of conduct indicating waiver, may never support a conclusion that a defendant has waived his rights. The courts must presume that a defendant did not waive his rights; the prosecution's burden is great; but in at least some cases waiver can be clearly inferred from the actions and words of the person interrogated.

The *Butler* dissenters objected that by not adopting the "simple prophylactic rule requiring the police to obtain an express waiver of the right to counsel before proceeding with interrogation," the Court had resurrected the problems that had haunted it under the pre-*Miranda* voluntariness approach.

(b) Competence of the Defendant. The Court in *Butler* indicated that the question of whether there has been a waiver of *Miranda* rights must be ascertained on "the particular facts and circumstances surrounding that case, including the background, experience, and conduct of the accused." This highlights the fact that whether the defendant has (as the *Miranda* Court put it) "knowingly and intelligently waived" his rights depends in part upon the competency of the defendant—that is, upon his ability to understand and act upon the warnings *Miranda* requires the defendant have received. *Tague v. Louisiana*[4] stresses that this showing of competency was part of the "heavy burden" to be carried by the government. The arresting officer there "could

---

2.   369 U.S. 506, 82 S.Ct. 884, 8 L.Ed.2d 70 (1962).

3.   441 U.S. 369, 99 S.Ct. 1755, 60 L.Ed.2d 286 (1979).

4.   444 U.S. 469, 100 S.Ct. 652, 62 L.Ed.2d 622 (1980).

not recall whether he asked petitioner whether he understood the rights as read to him, and * * * 'couldn't say yes or no' whether he rendered any tests to determine whether petitioner was literate or otherwise capable of understanding his rights," but the state court held that "it can be presumed that a person has capacity to understand, and the burden is on the one claiming a lack of capacity to show that lack." The Supreme Court summarily reversed, noting that the lower's court's position was clearly contrary to the previously quoted language from *Miranda* and *Butler*.

In assessing the personal characteristics of the defendant, one factor that obviously must be considered is his youthfulness. Especially when a youth has had no prior experience with the police or has a low IQ, his waiver may be found ineffective. This is not to suggest, however, that a valid waiver cannot be given by an underage defendant, for courts have frequently found waivers by juveniles to be valid. In *Fare v. Michael C.*[5] the Supreme Court held that the "totality of the circumstances approach is adequate to determine whether there has been a waiver even where interrogation of juveniles is involved." Thus, the Court continued, what is mandated is an "evaluation of the juvenile's age, experience, education, background, and intelligence, and into whether he has the capacity to understand the warnings given him, the nature of his Fifth Amendment rights, and the consequences of waiving those rights." Most states follow this "totality of the circumstances" approach, while the others have opted for the so-called "interested adult" rule, under which a juvenile's waiver is not effective unless he was allowed to consult and have with him an adult interested in his welfare.

If the defendant is seriously mentally retarded, this reduces the chances that his waiver will be found valid. Either limited schooling or a low IQ can contribute to a finding of an ineffective waiver, but waivers have not infrequently been upheld notwithstanding such circumstances A waiver can be effective even though the defendant was emotionally upset at having been apprehended or by other circumstances, though again this condition can contribute to a contrary determination. Obviously, the fact a defendant is well-educated and mature enhances the likelihood of a finding that his waiver was effective. If at the time of the alleged waiver the defendant was in considerable pain from a serious injury, this can contribute to a finding that the waiver was not effective. But defendants have generally been unsuccessful in claiming that their *Miranda* waivers should be held invalid because they were either intoxicated or under the influence of drugs or medication at that time.

It must be emphasized, however, that such personal characteristics of the defendant existing at the time of the purported waiver are often relevant only as they relate to police overreaching. Such is the teaching of *Colorado v. Connelly,*[6] rejecting a state court ruling that a defendant's *Miranda* waiver was not voluntary because he suffered from a psychosis that interfered with his ability to make free and rational choices. Noting that the "voluntariness of a waiver * * * has always depended on the absence of police overreaching, not on 'free choice' in any broader sense of the word," the Court in *Connelly* concluded that "*Miranda* protects defendants against government coercion" but "goes no further than that." The Court's later teaching in *Colorado v. Spring*[7]— that a *Miranda* waiver must be *both* (i) "voluntary in the sense that it was the product of a free and deliberate choice" and (ii) "made with full awareness both of the nature of the right being abandoned and the consequences of the decision to abandon it"—serves to mark *Connelly*'s limits: it has to do only with the first of these two requirements.

A great many defendants who give *Miranda* waivers are not "competent" to do so in a certain sense, for the tactical error of that decision was not perceived by them. But this is no bar to an effective waiver for *Miranda* purposes, for a waiver need not be wise to be "intelligent" within the meaning of that case.

5. 442 U.S. 707, 99 S.Ct. 2560, 61 L.Ed.2d 197 (1979).

6. 479 U.S. 157, 107 S.Ct. 515, 93 L.Ed.2d 473 (1986).

7. 479 U.S. 564, 107 S.Ct. 851, 93 L.Ed.2d 954 (1987).

This result is consistent with *Miranda's* emphasis upon the need to overcome the coerciveness of in-custody interrogation, and also may be explained in part by the impracticability of inquiring into defendant's awareness of all possible tactical considerations.

(c) Conduct of the Police. *Miranda* also says it must be shown that the defendant did "voluntarily waive his privilege," and as to this the conduct of the police will be particularly relevant. In *Fare v. Michael C.*,[8] the Court declared that the "totality of the circumstances approach is adequate to determine whether there has been a waiver," which indicates that the two categories of inducement that were considered sufficiently compelling to render a resulting confession inadmissible under longstanding and traditional confessions law—promises and threats—have a like adverse effect upon *Miranda* waivers. Lower courts have held waivers involuntary where obtained by a promise of some benefit or a threat of some adverse consequence.

The Court in *Miranda* indicated that even absent such threats or promises a waiver would not be upheld if obtained under coercive circumstances:

> Whatever the testimony of the authorities as to waiver of rights by an accused, the fact of lengthy interrogation or incommunicado incarceration before a statement is made is strong evidence that the accused did not validly waive his rights. In these circumstances the fact that the individual eventually made a statement is consistent with the conclusion that the compelling influence of the interrogation finally forced him to do so. It is inconsistent with any notion of a voluntary relinquishment of the privilege.

Lower courts have held waivers invalid where the defendant had been held in custody an extended period of time before being given the warnings, or where the defendant had first been subjected to persistent questioning.

The *Miranda* Court also asserted that "any evidence that the accused was threatened, tricked, or cajoled into a waiver will, of course, show that the defendant did not voluntarily waive his privilege." This condemnation of the use of trickery suggests that using interrogation techniques creating either false confidence or resignation in a defendant will per se make the defendant's subsequent waiver ineffective. As we have seen, trickery has no such per se effect under the voluntariness approach to confessions, and thus the language from *Miranda* just quoted would suggest that a waiver-of-rights analysis is, at least in this respect, more demanding than the old voluntariness inquiry. But the lower courts have not reached this conclusion; rather, they have taken an approach that, if anything, is strengthened by the Supreme Court's more recent use of "totality of the circumstances" language in this context, namely, that trickery bears on the waiver issue in essentially the same way that it does on the due process voluntariness-of-confession issue. Under this approach, *Miranda* waivers have been upheld even when obtained after the police had misrepresented the strength of the case against the defendant or the seriousness of the matter under investigation. Even assuming that these cases can be squared with *Miranda* because the trickery concerned only the wisdom of exercising the rights of which the defendant had been warned, it still follows that there is an absolute prohibition upon any trickery that misleads the suspect as to the existence or dimensions of any of the applicable rights or as to whether the waiver really is a waiver of those rights.

Though some lower courts had held that a defendant's waiver of counsel is not sufficiently "knowing and intelligent" if police withheld from him information that an attorney had sought to consult him, the Supreme Court ruled otherwise in *Moran v. Burbine*.[9] The Court reasoned that under the *Johnson v. Zerbst*[10] waiver standard "events occurring outside of the presence of the suspect and entirely unknown to him," as compared to defendant's knowledge an attorney had been barred access, "can have no bearing on the

---

8.   442 U.S. 707, 99 S.Ct. 2560, 61 L.Ed.2d 197 (1979).

9.   475 U.S. 412, 106 S.Ct. 1135, 89 L.Ed.2d 410 (1986).

10.   304 U.S. 458, 58 S.Ct. 1019, 82 L.Ed. 1461 (1938).

capacity to comprehend and knowingly relinquish a constitutional right." This is so even if the withheld information "might have affected his decision to confess," as a valid waiver only requires that the defendant "understand the nature of his rights and the consequences of abandoning them." As for the defendant's other argument, that such deception should be constitutionally proscribed because it was "inimical to the Fifth Amendment values *Miranda* seeks to protect," the Court declined to disturb *Miranda's* clarity by introducing new questions about just what events would require the police to give a defendant additional information. The three dissenters in *Burbine* agreed with the majority's statement of the waiver standard, but concluded information about the ready availability of a particular attorney had a direct bearing on the waiver. As to the dissenters' fears that the doors had been opened to all sorts of deception by the police, the majority responded that on unspecified "facts more egregious that those presented here police deception might rise to a level of a due process violation." *Burbine* stresses that the privilege against self-incrimination is personal to the defendant, from which it also follows that a defendant's *Miranda* rights cannot be invoked by a third party.

(d) Implied Waiver. While inquiry into the defendant's competency may indicate whether he *could* knowingly and intelligently waive his rights, and assessment of the police conduct may show whether such a waiver *would* be voluntary, it is still necessary to scrutinize the defendant's words and actions to see if he did *in fact* waive his *Miranda* rights. Assuming the other two inquiries present no bar to finding a waiver, the relatively easy cases are those in which the defendant makes an "express written or oral statement of waiver" constituting "strong proof of the validity of that waiver,"[11] or in which at the other extreme the defendant explicitly asserts his right to remain silent or his right to counsel. But courts are frequently confronted with

fact situations lying at neither of these extremes.

As noted earlier, the Supreme Court in *North Carolina v. Butler*[12] held that "an explicit statement of waiver is not invariably necessary to support a finding that the defendant waived the right to remain silent or the right to counsel guaranteed by the *Miranda* case." But if this is so, then even in cases not complicated by conduct of the defendant arguably constituting a feeble attempt to assert his rights, there remains the difficult question of what facts will justify a finding of waiver by implication. On this issue, *Butler* instructs that "mere silence is not enough" but that this "does not mean that the defendant's silence, coupled with an understanding of his rights and a course of conduct indicating waiver, may never support a conclusion that a defendant has waived his rights." This certainly means, as the lower courts and the Supreme Court itself[13] have held, that a waiver is not established merely by showing that a defendant was given the complete *Miranda* warnings and thereafter gave an incriminating statement.

But what if the defendant expresses an understanding of the *Miranda* warnings he has received and thereafter an incriminating statement is obtained from him? In the language of *Butler,* does this amount to a showing of "an understanding of his rights and a course of conduct indicating waiver"? Several courts have answered this question in the affirmative. There is, however, authority to the contrary, and it has been argued with some force that his acknowledgement of understanding adds nothing more to the circumstances beyond mere silence. The point, quite simply, is that an understanding of rights and an intention to waive them are two different things, and the latter should not be inferred merely because the former is now clearly established. That is true, yet when it is clear the defendant does understand his rights it is somewhat easier to make some judgments about the significance of his subsequent conduct in terms of

---

11. North Carolina v. Butler, 441 U.S. 369, 99 S.Ct. 1755, 60 L.Ed.2d 286 (1979).

12. 441 U.S. 369, 99 S.Ct. 1755, 60 L.Ed.2d 286 (1979).

13. Tague v. Louisiana, 444 U.S. 469, 100 S.Ct. 652, 62 L.Ed.2d 622 (1980).

whether or not those rights are being invoked. Thus, while an acknowledgment of understanding should not inevitably carry the day, it is especially significant when defendant's incriminating statement follows immediately thereafter. On the matter of waiver by implication, courts have also taken into account the fact the defendant initiated the conversation that occurred after the warnings were given and that the defendant's contact with the police was attributable to his cooperation. Moreover, a finding of waiver is likely when the defendant has engaged in certain conduct falling a bit short of an express waiver, such as a declaration of a cooperative attitude or even a nod or a shrug.

(e) "Qualified" or Limited Waiver. A second group of cases in which the focus is primarily upon the conduct of the defendant presents an added complication, as there is conduct which in isolation seems to amount to a waiver, but it is accompanied by other conduct that can be interpreted as a refusal to waive or even as an assertion of rights. Illustrative are the facts of *North Carolina v. Butler*,[14] where the defendant read a written "Advice of Rights" form, stated he understood his rights, and then refused to sign the form but nonetheless indicated he would talk. (The Court in *Butler* did not hold that this constituted a waiver, but only rejected the state court's view that nothing short of an express waiver would suffice under *Miranda*.) Another illustration would be where the suspect indicates he is willing to talk but is unwilling to have his remarks reduced to writing, as in *United States v. Frazier*.[15]

The court in *Frazier* held that the waiver was effective notwithstanding the defendant's unwillingness to permit note taking, and some other courts have similarly ruled that a waiver is effective notwithstanding the defendant's refusal to permit taping of his oral confession or to sign a copy of his confession, and that an oral waiver is effective in the face of defendant's refusal to sign a written waiver. As the court put it in *Frazier,* since the suspect there

had the capacity to comprehend the warnings, the police officer questioning him was not required to "place a legal interpretation on the language of *Miranda* warnings he was directed to give." But this approach conflicts with *Miranda's* policy of trying to place the accused on a more equal footing with the police at the interrogation stage and gives the accused minimal protection against a misunderstanding of the warnings. It overlooks the fundamental point noted by the *Frazier* dissenters: "capacity to understand the warnings does not by any means guarantee that they will actually be understood."

An objective view of the facts of the *Frazier* case strongly suggests that the defendant acted as he did because of a mistaken impression that an oral confession not contemporaneously recorded could not be used against him. Similarly, the *Butler* facts certainly suggest the defendant misperceived the effect of a waiver that was oral rather than written. Under such circumstances, there is much to be said for the view that the police are under an obligation to clear up misunderstandings of this nature which are apparent to any reasonable observer. Short of this, it certainly makes sense in such cases to conclude that the defendant's conduct should significantly increase the prosecution's burden to overcome the presumption against waiver of *Miranda* rights.

Somewhat similar to *Frazier* is *Connecticut v. Barrett*,[16] where after receiving his *Miranda* warnings the defendant repeatedly asserted his willingness to talk about the incident and his unwillingness to give a written statement unless his attorney was present. Though the state court had ruled this amounted to an invocation of the right to counsel for all purposes, the Supreme Court concluded otherwise: "Barrett's limited requests for counsel * * * were accompanied by affirmative announcements of his willingness to speak with the authorities. The fact that officials took the opportunity provided by Barrett to obtain an oral confession is quite consistent with the Fifth Amendment. *Miranda* gives the defen-

---

14.   441 U.S. 369, 99 S.Ct. 1755, 60 L.Ed.2d 286 (1979).

15.   476 F.2d 891 (D.C.Cir.1973).

16.   479 U.S. 523, 107 S.Ct. 828, 93 L.Ed.2d 920 (1987).

dant a right to choose between speech and silence, and Barrett chose to speak." Significantly, the Court in *Barrett* emphasized that the defendant's distinction between oral and written statements might have been "illogical," but that this alone would not make the waiver ineffective. But the Court also emphasized the defendant had testified to a full understanding of his *Miranda* warnings, and thus *Barrett* was not a case in which the partial or limited character of the waiver demonstrated an insufficient understanding by the defendant of the warnings he had received.

In other instances the question is the scope of the waiver, as is illustrated by *Wyrick v. Fields.*[17] Fields, charged with rape, after release on bail and consultation with privately retained counsel, agreed to a polygraph examination. Prior to the examination, he executed a waiver of *Miranda* rights, both in writing and orally. At the conclusion of the examination, an agent told him there had been some deceit and asked him if he would explain why his answers were bothering him. Fields then admitted the intercourse but claimed it was with consent, and that statement was admitted against him at trial. A federal court held this waiver covered only the polygraph examination and that a new set of warnings was required once the polygraph examination had been discontinued and Fields was asked if he could explain the test's unfavorable results. The Supreme Court disagreed, stressing that discontinuing the polygraph "effectuated no significant change in the character of the interrogation" and that neither Fields nor his attorney could have reasonably assumed "that Fields would not be informed of the polygraph readings and asked to explain any unfavorable result."

(f) Waiver After Assertion of Rights. The discussion up to this point has been concerned with the question of what the prosecution must do in order to carry its "heavy burden" of showing a waiver of *Miranda* rights. A somewhat special problem, reserved to this point, is whether the situation is different once the defendant has actually asserted

his rights. Are the police then foreclosed from thereafter seeking a waiver from that defendant? If not, is the burden in such circumstances even heavier?

The significance of the defendant's invocation of the right to remain silent reached the Supreme Court in *Michigan v. Mosley.*[18] There, defendant was arrested for several robberies and at the station was given his *Miranda* warnings; he declined to discuss the robberies and no effort was made to have him reconsider his position. Two hours later another detective in another part of the building sought to question defendant about an unrelated murder; he was given the *Miranda* warnings again and thereafter gave an incriminating statement. The *Mosley* Court concluded that the propriety of this action depended upon the interpretation to be given the following passage in *Miranda:*

> Once warnings have been given, the subsequent procedure is clear. If the individual indicates in any manner, at any time prior to or during questioning, that he wishes to remain silent, the interrogation must cease. At this point he has shown that he intends to exercise his Fifth Amendment privilege; any statement taken after the person invokes his privilege cannot be other than the product of compulsion, subtle or otherwise. Without the right to cut off questioning, the setting of in-custody interrogation operates on the individual to overcome free choice in producing a statement after the privilege has been once invoked.

After rejecting two "possible literal interpretations" of this language, that it permits "the continuation of custodial interrogation after a momentary cessation," or at the other extreme, that it constitutes "a blanket prohibition against the taking of voluntary statements or a permanent immunity from further interrogation, regardless of the circumstances," the *Mosley* Court continued:

> The critical safeguard identified in the passage at issue is a person's "right to cut off questioning." Through the exercise of his

---

17.   459 U.S. 42, 103 S.Ct. 394, 74 L.Ed.2d 214 (1982).

18.   423 U.S. 96, 96 S.Ct. 321, 46 L.Ed.2d 313 (1975).

option to terminate questioning he can control the time at which questioning occurs, the subjects discussed, and the duration of the interrogation. The requirement that law enforcement authorities must respect a person's exercise of that option counteracts the coercive pressures of the custodial setting. We therefore conclude that the admissibility of statements obtained after the person in custody has decided to remain silent depends under *Miranda* on whether his "right to cut off questioning" was "scrupulously honored."

As for application of the *Mosley* "scrupulously honored" test, the majority concluded it was met on the facts of that case because "the police here immediately ceased the interrogation, resumed questioning only after the passage of a significant period of time and the provision of a fresh set of warnings, and restricted the second interrogation to a crime that had not been a subject of the earlier interrogation." Some courts have viewed the latter fact an essential one to a finding that defendant's rights were "scrupulously honored," and there is much to be said for this position. Other courts have not deemed a change in the subject matter of the inquiry to be essential. Perhaps that is unobjectionable when it is the defendant who initiated the subsequent conversation, but in other circumstances it is a highly questionable position. In any event, the "scrupulously honored" test is not met where the police did not honor the original in-custody assertion of the right to remain silent, ignored that assertion and expressed sympathy for defendant's plight, resumed questioning after a short interval, or made repeated attempts to obtain a waiver.

Justice White, concurring in *Mosley,* expressed the view that it is proper for the police to reapproach a defendant who has invoked his right to remain silent when they have new information bearing upon that decision. He put illustrations where the police undertake to

tell a defendant "that his ability to explain a particular incriminating fact or to supply an alibi for a particular time period would result in his immediate release" or where on the other hand they would tell him that "the case against him was unusually strong and * * * that his immediate cooperation with the authorities in the apprehension and conviction of others or in the recovery of property would redound to his benefit in the form of a reduced charge." It is open to question whether this plea-bargaining-at-the-police-station scenario is consistent with the concerns expressed in *Miranda* and *Mosley,* though it has sometimes been held that it is proper to present the defendant with an objective, undistorted presentation of the extensive evidence against him. However, it is well to note that at least under some circumstances the confrontation of the defendant with incriminating evidence will itself constitute "interrogation" within the meaning of *Miranda,*[19] clearly prohibited as to one who has asserted and not yet waived his rights.

The defendant in *Mosley* had not invoked his *Miranda* right to counsel, and Justice White suggested that had he done so the result might well be different. He later made the point for a majority of the Court in *Edwards v. Arizona,*[20] which held "that an accused, * * * having expressed his desire to deal with the police only through counsel, is not subject to further interrogation by the authorities until counsel has been made available to him, unless the accused himself initiates further communication, exchanges or conversations with the police." This result, the Court noted, is consistent with the language in *Miranda* that "[i]f the individual states that he wants an attorney, the interrogation must cease until an attorney is present." (Consequently, the Court clarified in a later case,[21] the "available to him" language in *Edwards* means "that when counsel is requested, interrogation must cease, and officials may not reinitiate interrogation

---

19. See § 6.7(c).

20. 451 U.S. 477, 101 S.Ct. 1880, 68 L.Ed.2d 378 (1981).

The Court held in Solem v. Stumes, 465 U.S. 638, 104 S.Ct. 1338, 79 L.Ed.2d 579 (1984), that "*Edwards* should

not be applied retroactively" and thus "is not to be applied in collateral review of final convictions."

21. Minnick v. Mississippi, 498 U.S. 146, 111 S.Ct. 486, 112 L.Ed.2d 489 (990).

without counsel present, whether or not the accused has consulted with his attorney."[22]) Thus the defendant's confession in *Edwards* was inadmissible, for the police had visited the defendant in his cell and obtaining a waiver of *Miranda* rights the morning after defendant had declared he wanted an attorney.

Edwards, best viewed as a *per se* rule proscribing any interrogation of a person held in custody who has invoked his right counsel[23] absent the individual's subsequent initiation of conversation, thus limits the application of *Mosely's* "scrupulously honored" test to those cases where only the right to silence was invoked. This is evidenced by *Arizona v. Roberson*,[24] holding that *Edwards* rather than *Mosely* governs even when the later interrogation concerns a wholly unrelated crime. The *Roberson* majority emphasized the desirability of maintaining *Edwards* as a "bright line rule," without qualifications or exceptions, where there has been an unlimited invocation of the *"Miranda"* right to counsel,[25] and noted that a defendant's manifestation "that he did not feel sufficiently comfortable with the pressures of custodial interrogation to answer questions without an attorney" should no more be limited to a particular offense than is a waiver of *Miranda* rights.[26]

In *Oregon v. Bradshaw*,[27] eight members of the Court agreed that the admissibility of a confession given by a defendant who earlier invoked his *Miranda* right to counsel is to be determined by a two-step analysis. It first must be asked whether defendant "initiated" further conversation. This means that the impetus must come from the accused, not from the officers. However, if there has been some kind of police conduct preceding and allegedly contributing to the defendant's supposed "initiation," the question then becomes how that conduct is to be judged in determining where the "impetus" lies. One view, certainly subject to dispute, is that the prior police conduct is not relevant unless it actually amounted to interrogation or its functional equivalent under *Innis*. Another finds police initiation also in certain conduct not falling within the *Innis* formulation, though even under this approach certain police contacts that are insignificant, regarding unrelated matters, or made for other legitimate purposes concerning the case do not constitute such initiation. *Bradshaw* goes on to say that if it is found the defendant "initiated" further conversation, it must then be inquired whether defendant waived his right to counsel and to silence, "that is, whether the purported waiver was knowing and intelligent * * * under the totality of the circumstances, including the necessary fact

---

22. In rejecting the state court's conclusion that the special protections of *Edwards* ceased once the defendant had consulted with an attorney, the Court in *Minnick* noted: "A single consultation with an attorney does not remove the suspect from persistent attempts by officials to persuade him to waive his rights, or from the coercive pressures that accompany custody and that may increase as custody is prolonged."

23. *Edwards* involved the invocation of the *Miranda* right to counsel, but Michigan v. Jackson, 475 U.S. 625, 106 S.Ct. 1404, 89 L.Ed.2d 631 (1986), held that the *Edwards* limitation applied when defendant invoked his Sixth Amendment right to counsel at his first appearance. See § 6.4(f).

24. 486 U.S. 675, 108 S.Ct. 2093, 100 L.Ed.2d 704 (1988).

25. Thus, *Roberson* does *not* mean that if defendant's Sixth Amendment right had attached as to one offense, this fact alone brings the *Edwards* rule into play as to the *Miranda* right to counsel vis-a-vis some other, uncharged offense. McNeil v. Wisconsin, 501 U.S. 171, 111 S.Ct. 2204, 115 L.Ed.2d 158 (1991) (while *Edwards* rule per *Roberson* is "*not* offense-specific," Sixth Amendment right to counsel "is offense-specific" and does not focus exclusively upon custodial interrogation, so invocation of Sixth

Amendment right is not also invocation of *Miranda*, which is broader "because it relates to interrogation regarding *any* suspected crime and attaches whether or not the 'adversarial relationship' produced by a pending prosecution has yet arisen").

26. Referring to Colorado v. Spring, discussed in § 6.8(d), upholding a *Miranda* waiver notwithstanding defendant's ignorance at that time of the subject matter of the subsequent questioning.

The two dissenters in *Roberson* objected the majority's rule "will bar law enforcement officials, even those from some other city or other jurisdiction, from questioning a suspect about an unrelated matter if he is in custody and has requested counsel to assist in answering questions put to him about the crime for which he was arrested," and asserted a "more realistic view of human nature suggests that a suspect will want the opportunity, when he learns of the separate investigations, to decide whether he wishes to speak to the authorities in a particular investigation with or without representation."

27. 462 U.S. 1039, 103 S.Ct. 2830, 77 L.Ed.2d 405 (1983).

that the accused, not the police, reopened the dialogue with the authorities."

As for what constitutes "initiation," those eight Justices in *Bradshaw* could not agree. The four-Justice plurality concluded that "inquiries or statements * * * relating to routine incidents of the custodial relationship" would not suffice but that questions "evinc[ing] a willingness and a desire for a generalized discussion about the investigation" would. The four dissenters defined "initiation" more narrowly as "communication or dialogue *about the subject matter of the criminal investigation.*" As for the defendant's statement in *Bradshaw*, "Well, what is going to happen to me now?", the plurality concluded this was initiation under their test, while the dissenters asserted it was not under theirs. But an objective assessment of the circumstances in that case would seem to justify only one conclusion—as the dissenters put it, the defendant was merely trying "to find out where the police were going to take him." That would not amount to "initiation" under either of the tests, and is quite different from the conduct lower courts have quite properly found sufficient to establish that the defendant had reopened the dialogue about the criminal investigation. Uncertainty about the applicable test persists after *Bradshaw*, as the other member of the Court, Justice Powell, rejected the two-step approach and deemed the confession admissible merely because there had later occurred a knowing and intelligent waiver by defendant of his rights.

In *Smith v. Illinois*,[28] the Supreme Court characterized the *Edwards* holding as a "bright-line rule" prohibiting all police overreaching, be it "deliberate or unintentional." This suggests, as the lower courts have rather consistently held, that police conduct can violate the *Edwards* prohibition even when the particular officer who makes contact was unaware of the defendant's prior invocation of his right to counsel. Sometimes this interpretation of *Edwards* is stated in terms of others within the same investigatory authority, and sometimes it is stated more broadly as extending to all law enforcement officers who subse-

quently deal with the suspect. On the other hand, some lower courts have recognized another type of limitation on *Edwards*: a break in custody concludes the special hands-off status a defendant has by virtue of having invoked his right to counsel. This is because the release of the defendant, after the defendant has invoked his right to counsel while in police custody, ends the need for the *Edwards* rule because the defendant is no longer under the inherently compelling pressures of continuous custody. But absent such a break, the mere passage of time between the time defendant invoked his right to counsel and the next interrogation does *not* make *Edwards* inapplicable.

(g) Ambiguous, Equivocal, Limited and Untimely Assertions of Rights. The Court in *Miranda* emphatically declared that if "the individual indicates in any manner at any time prior to or during questioning, that he wishes to remain silent, the interrogation must cease" and that if he "states that he wants an attorney, the interrogation must cease until an attorney is present." Whether there has been such an assertion of rights is of considerable importance; as we have seen, under the *Mosley* and *Edwards* doctrines the assertion puts the defendant into a somewhat "special" situation in terms of the subsequent dealings of the police with him.

As for assertion of the right to remain silent, any declaration of a desire to terminate the contact or inquiry (e.g., "Don't bother me") should suffice. The same is true of silence in the face of repeated questioning, or an effort to end the contact with the interrogator. On the other hand, a statement that is much more limited by expressing an unwillingness to respond to a particular interrogator (e.g., "I don't want to talk to you guys"), an unwillingness to discuss the matter at a particular time (e.g., not "right now"), or an unwillingness or inability to respond to a particular inquiry (e.g., "You've done asked me a question I can't answer") is not a general claim of the privilege. Depending upon the surrounding circumstances, even a statement that itself appears to

28.   469 U.S. 91, 105 S.Ct. 490, 83 L.Ed.2d 488 (1984).

amount to an assertion of the right to remain silent (e.g., "I ain't saying nothing") may be held not to have that effect. Some courts have concluded that in the event of an "equivocal" invocation of the right to silence, the only permissible course of action for the police is to attempt to clarify the defendant's intentions, which would be a dubious position in a post-waiver setting given the Court's treatment in *Davis v. United States* of an ambiguous or equivocal reference in that setting to speaking with counsel.[29]

As for assertion of the right to counsel, here as well some courts have concluded that something short of a formal or direct request will suffice, such as an unsuccessful attempt to reach an attorney or an inquiry whether the police officer could recommend an attorney. The Supreme Court has held that defendant's statement that "maybe I should talk to a lawyer" does not qualify as invocation of the right to counsel, and many lower court cases have found similarly equivocal or ambiguous assertions to be likewise insufficient. An indication by the defendant that he will only want counsel at some future time or for some other purpose is not an assertion of the right to counsel for *Miranda* purposes, just as a current reference by defendant on the later occasion to the fact that he had actually spoken to an attorney on a prior occasion is not a present invocation of the right to counsel.

In *Fare v. Michael C.,*[30] the Supreme Court confronted the question of whether a request for someone other than an attorney constitutes an invocation of *Miranda* rights. There, a juvenile in custody on suspicion of murder was given his warnings and he then asked to have his probation officer present; this request was denied, a waiver of rights was obtained, and the juvenile then made incriminating statements. The Court held, 5–4, that the request to see the probation officer was not a per se invocation of *Miranda* rights (that is, not

the equivalent of asking for a lawyer), but rather was merely a factor to be considered in the "totality of circumstances" determination of the voluntariness of the subsequent waiver. The majority explained that the per se aspect of *Miranda* was

> based on the unique role the lawyer plays in the adversary system of criminal justice in this country. Whether it is a minor or an adult who stands accused, the lawyer is the one person to whom society as a whole looks as the protector of the legal rights of that person in his dealing with the police and the courts. For this reason the Court fashioned in *Miranda* the rigid rule that an accused's request for an attorney is *per se* an invocation of his Fifth Amendment rights, requiring that all interrogation cease.

A probation officer, on the other hand, the Court continued, "is not trained in the law, and so is not in a position to advise the accused as to his legal rights," and is actually an adversary of the juvenile because "the probation officer is duty bound to report wrongdoing by the juvenile when it comes to his attention, even if by communication from the juvenile himself."

Three of the dissenters in *Fare*[31] questioned that characterization of the probation officer's responsibilities[32] and persuasively argued that *Miranda* requires that interrogation cease whenever a juvenile requests an adult who is obligated to represent his interests because such a request "constitutes both an attempt to obtain advice and a general invocation of the right to silence." This reasoning would appear to be especially compelling when the juvenile requests the presence of a parent, but the *Fare* rule has sometimes been applied even to such facts. But certainly a different result is called for if the juvenile manifests a desire to see his parent in order to obtain an attorney.

---

29. See text at note 34 infra.

30. 442 U.S. 707, 99 S.Ct. 2560, 61 L.Ed.2d 197 (1979).

31. The fourth, Powell, J., agreed with the majority that the state court's interpretation of *Miranda* was in error, but concluded the confession was not voluntary under the teaching of In re Gault, 387 U.S. 1, 87 S.Ct. 1428, 18 L.Ed.2d 527 (1967), that "the greatest care"

must be taken to assure that a confession of a juvenile is voluntary.

32. Noting it "ignores the California Supreme Court's express determination that the officer's responsibility to initiate juvenile proceedings did not negate his function as personal adviser to his wards."

If the defendant's conduct suffices to constitute an invocation of one of his *Miranda* rights, then there is no need for the police to seek clarification, and thus the Court held in *Smith v. Illinois*[33] that a defendant's "*post-request* responses to further interrogation may not be used to cast retrospective doubt on the clarity of the initial request itself." This is as it should be, for otherwise police could disregard a defendant's invocation of his rights in the hope that subsequent interrogation would cast retrospective doubt upon it. The other side of the coin, it would seem, is that if the defendant's initial assertion *was* equivocal or ambiguous and thus not alone sufficient to constitute invocation of the defendant's *Miranda* rights, then it is permissible for the police to seek clarification. A significant body of lower court authority to this effect is to be found with respect to both the right to silence and the right to counsel.

But in *Davis v. United States*,[34] the Court held that in a post-waiver setting[35] the rule of *Edwards v. Arizona*[36] would not be extended so as to "require law enforcement officers to cease questioning immediately upon the making of an ambiguous or equivocal reference to an attorney."[37] The Court recognized that its holding "might disadvantage some suspects who—because of fear, intimidation, lack of linguistic skills, or a variety of other reasons—will not clearly articulate their right to counsel although they actually want to have a lawyer present," but deemed that consideration to be outweighed by the fact that the "clarity and ease of application" of the bright-line *Edwards* rule "would be lost" if "we were to require questioning to cease if a suspect makes a statement that might be a request for an attorney." But the *Davis* majority then went on to assert

without further explanation that the cautious approach of the officers in the instant case, who obtained clarification of the ambiguous statement from the suspect and proceeded with the interrogation only when he said he did not want an attorney, was "good police practice" yet not a requirement under the *Miranda–Edwards* line of cases. Four members of the Court, concurring only in the judgment,[38] cogently noted that the "bright line" argument was not compelling on this branch of the case, for under the rejected rule the police would not have to guess at their peril in ambiguous circumstances but would only have to seek clarification from the suspect, "the party most competent to resolve the ambiguity." (The *Davis* rule has been deemed equally applicable to post-waiver ambiguous references to the right to remain silent.)

It is possible that the defendant's invocation of his right to counsel will be limited in some way, in which case application of the *Edwards* rule is limited to the same extent, as the Supreme Court concluded in *Connecticut v. Barrett*.[39] The record there reflected a clear understanding by defendant of his *Miranda* warnings, and thus his assertion of a desire to have counsel present before making a written statement meant only that "[h]ad the police obtained such a statement without meeting the waiver standards of *Edwards*, it would clearly be inadmissible"; defendant's oral statements were not likewise barred by *Edwards*.

In *Michigan v. Jackson*,[40] the Court held that when the Sixth Amendment right to counsel has attached, "if the police initiate interrogation after a defendant's assertion, at an arraignment or similar proceeding, of the right to counsel, any waiver of the defendant's

---

33. 469 U.S. 91, 105 S.Ct. 490, 83 L.Ed.2d 488 (1984).

34. 512 U.S. 452, 114 S.Ct. 2350, 129 L.Ed.2d 362 (1994).

35. *Davis* is so limited; the Court's ruling was that "after a knowing and voluntary waiver of the *Miranda* rights, law enforcement officers may continue questioning until and unless the suspect clearly requests an attorney."

36. 451 U.S. 477, 101 S.Ct. 1880, 68 L.Ed.2d 378 (1981), discussed further in § 6.9(f).

37. The defendant's statement in the instant case, "Maybe I should talk to a lawyer," was deemed to be such

an ambiguous statement rather than an actual request for counsel triggering the *Edwards* prohibition on further questioning.

38. Because under their view the defendant still would not have prevailed, as the police below did clarify the ambiguity as they would require.

39. 479 U.S. 523, 107 S.Ct. 828, 93 L.Ed.2d 920 (1987).

40. 475 U.S. 625, 106 S.Ct. 1404, 89 L.Ed.2d 631 (1986).

right to counsel for that police-initiated interrogation is invalid." Does it follow that such an assertion is an invocation of the *Miranda* right to counsel as to any uncharged offense? No, the Court later held in *McNeil v. Wisconsin*,[41] reasoning that invocation of the Sixth Amendment interest does not also constitute invocation of *Miranda* as to other, uncharged offenses, for a defendant "might be quite willing to speak to the police without counsel present concerning many matters, but not the matter under prosecution." Moreover, the Court noted, a contrary rule would not be wise policy, for it would mean that "most persons in pretrial custody for serious offenses would be *unapproachable* by police officers suspecting them of involvement in other crimes, *even though they have never expressed any unwillingness to be questioned.*"

But the *McNeil* case would appear to have even broader significance, as is reflected in *Alston v. Redman*.[42] The defendant was arrested for two robberies, waived his *Miranda* rights and admitted the crimes, and then was remanded to prison for pretrial detention. Three days later defendant filed with the warden a letter saying he did not wish to speak to police without the public defender present, and a few days after that defendant was taken to the police station for interrogation about other crimes, after which he waived his rights and gave a confession. The defendant claimed the latter interrogation violated *Edwards* in light of his prior invocation of his right to counsel, but the court responded that the invocation on which defendant relied was ineffective because it was premature. That conclusion was grounded in several of the Supreme Court's observations in *McNeil*: that the Court had "never held that a person can invoke his *Miranda* rights anticipatorily, in a context other than 'custodial interrogation' "; that "[m]ost rights must be asserted when the government seeks to take the action they protect against"; and that the Court's conclusion a *Miranda* assertion of a right to counsel remains in effect "does not necessarily mean that we will

allow it to be asserted initially outside the context of custodial interrogation, with similar future effect." Other cases likewise take the position that for there to be a valid assertion of *Miranda* rights, the authorities must be conducting custodial interrogation, or such interrogation must be imminent.

§ 6.10 *Miranda:* Nature of Offense, Interrogator, and Proceedings

(a) Questioning About Minor Offense. Although the Supreme Court in *Miranda* gave no indication that its holding regarding warning and waiver of rights prior to custodial interrogation was somehow limited to serious cases, a number of lower courts concluded that such a limitation existed. Several jurisdictions held that *Miranda* has no application to misdemeanors or at least to traffic offenses. In support of this result general references were often made to the large number of these minor offenses, the lack of a need for the full panoply of constitutional protections regarding such offenses, and the "practical" and "historical" differences between minor offenses and more serious crimes.

The issue reached the Supreme Court in *Berkemer v. McCarty*,[1] where a unanimous Court rejected any such exception to *Miranda*. The Court first noted that the exception for misdemeanor traffic offenses proposed there "would substantially undermine" a "crucial advantage" of the *Miranda* doctrine—its clarity. Police would often be uncertain in a particular instance what the magnitude of the crime was and consequently whether warnings were required, and courts would become involved in "doctrinal complexities" concerning, for example, when a misdemeanor investigation escalates into or is a pretext for a felony investigation. The Court then concluded that the purposes of *Miranda*—relieving the inherent compelling pressure of custodial interrogation, and freeing courts from the necessity of making frequent case-by-case volun-

---

41. 501 U.S. 171, 111 S.Ct. 2204, 115 L.Ed.2d 158 (1991).

42. 34 F.3d 1237 (3d Cir.1994).

§ 6.10

1. 468 U.S. 420, 104 S.Ct. 3138, 82 L.Ed.2d 317 (1984).

tariness determinations—are also served in the context of police interrogation related to minor traffic offenses.

(b) Questioning by Private Citizen. In the *Miranda* case the Court defined interrogation as "questioning initiated by law enforcement officers." Because of this and also because of the general doctrine that state action is a prerequisite to application of constitutional protections, it is clear that *Miranda* does not govern interrogation by private citizens acting on their own. This covers such instances as where the defendant was questioned by the victim, an arresting private citizen, a friend, a relative, or a newspaper reporter. Even if the private citizen falsely held himself out to the defendant as a police officer, so that it may be said the defendant was under just as much pressure as if his interrogator had been an actual officer, *Miranda* still does not apply because of the absence of state action.

That situation must be distinguished from one in which the defendant is questioned by a person who is not a government employee but who has employment responsibilities of a law enforcement nature, such as a department store security guard. In such circumstances, it might be argued that the protections of *Miranda* would be appropriate, for such security personnel also utilize detention, privacy, the appearance of authority, and psychologically coercive methods to facilitate fruitful interrogation. Moreover, it could well be contended that in such cases the "state action" hurdle may be overcome by a public function analysis, i.e., that persons performing functions essentially like those ordinarily left to governmental agencies are also subject to constitutional restraints. However, the courts have rather consistently held that such persons as security officers, store detectives, railroad detectives, insurance investigators, and private investigators are not required to comply with the *Miranda* procedures. A contrary result has sometimes been reached if the interrogator, though then serving private security functions, has been given police powers by a governmental unit.

Some courts have concluded that the private person exception does not apply when the person is at the time acting as an agent of the police. Thus, *Miranda* has been held to govern where such persons as the victim, a private security officer, the defendant's parents, the defendant's friend, or the victim's attorney questioned the defendant at the behest of the police. But, more compelling is the view that unless a person realizes he is dealing with a police agent, their efforts to elicit incriminating statements from him do not constitute "police interrogation" within the meaning of *Miranda*. It is the impact on the suspect's mind of the interplay between police interrogation and police that creates "custodial interrogation" within the meaning of *Miranda*. This, of course, is precisely the theory that was adopted by the Supreme Court in *Illinois v. Perkins*[2] regarding the very similar "jail plant" situation.

(c) Questioning by Non-police Official. In cases where the interrogator is a public employee and thus not outside the "state action" requirement, but yet is someone other than a police officer, the *Miranda* definition of interrogation as "questioning initiated by law enforcement officers" takes on added significance. Though the extent to which the decisions rest upon this particular point is often clouded by uncertainty as to whether the defendant was even in a "custodial" situation, the courts have generally held that government agents not primarily charged with enforcement of the criminal law are under no obligation to comply with *Miranda*. Thus, at least where the official has not been given police powers, *Miranda* has been held inapplicable to questioning by school officials, welfare investigators, medical personnel, prison counselors, and parole or probation officers.

The notion that *Miranda* does not inevitably apply whenever questions are asked in a custodial setting by a government employee is an appealing one, for not all such interrogations would seem to have a coercive impact comparable to the police questioning that concerned the Court in *Miranda*. This is not to say,

2. 496 U.S. 292, 110 S.Ct. 2394, 110 L.Ed.2d 243 (1990) discussed in text, § 6.7 at note 27.

however, that the decisions referred to above are beyond dispute, for the Supreme Court in *Mathis v. United States*[3] seems to have rejected the notion that *Miranda* applies only to criminal law enforcers. *Mathis* is a case not clouded by uncertainties about custody, for the interrogation at issue occurred while the defendant was serving a jail sentence on an unrelated matter. The questioning was by an IRS agent and—more importantly for present purposes—one who was a "civil investigator * * * required, whenever and as soon as he finds 'definite indications of fraud or criminal potential,' to refer a case to the Intelligence Division for investigation by a different agent who works regularly on criminal matters." Such a referral occurred eight days *after* the questioning in issue, and there was no suggestion that it was improperly delayed, but yet the Court held that *Miranda* applied. The *Mathis* majority acknowledged that "tax investigations differ from investigations of murder, robbery, and other crimes" because they "may be initiated for the purpose of a civil action rather than criminal prosecution," but then concluded this was not a controlling difference because, "as the investigating revenue agent was compelled to admit, there was always the possibility during his investigation that his work would end up in a criminal prosecution." Additional proof that the Court does not view *Miranda* as limited to interrogation by police officers is provided by *Estelle v. Smith*,[4] holding *Miranda* applicable to a psychiatric examination. The Court declared: "That respondent was questioned by a psychiatrist designated by the trial court to conduct a neutral competency examination, rather than by a police officer, government informant, or prosecuting attorney is immaterial."

Viewed in terms of the theory underlying *Miranda*, neither *Mathis* nor *Smith* is particularly objectionable. Mathis was doubtless under just as much pressure to talk to the "civil investigator" who visited him in jail as the criminal investigator who called on him later, and certainly Smith would feel compelled to converse with a psychiatrist appointed by the

court to examine him. Because that is so and because the Court in these two cases did not explore the issue in greater depth, those decisions cannot be read as settling that *all* public-official interrogation of those in custody is governed by *Miranda*. They do, however, lend support to the conclusion some courts have reached that custodial interrogation (other than routine interviews) by a probation or parole officer is governed by *Miranda* because the probationer or parolee is under heavy psychological pressure to cooperate with one who can recommend his imprisonment. They also support the conclusion that questioning by any government employee comes within *Miranda* whenever prosecution of the defendant being questioned is among the purposes, definite or contingent, for which the information is elicited, as will often be manifested by the fact the questioner's duties include the investigation or reporting of crimes.

(d) Questioning by Foreign Police. Foreign police, even when investigating an American citizen, can hardly be expected to know and follow all of the procedures that would be required if that individual were under investigation in his own country. Thus, even if (as commonly assumed) a defendant may be entitled to keep out of a prosecution in this country a confession by him involuntarily given to a foreign policeman, he may not obtain the suppression of a confession obtained by such an official merely because the *Miranda* warnings were not given. This result is ordinarily explained on the same grounds customarily given for not suppressing evidence obtained in a foreign search: the exclusion would have little if any deterrent effect upon foreign officials.

This is not to say that *Miranda* has no extraterritorial effect. Law enforcement officers of this country are bound by *Miranda* even when interrogating on foreign soil. Moreover, it has been recognized that foreign police are governed by *Miranda* when they are acting as the agents of United States law enforcement authorities. But in this context it will take a bit more to establish the requisite agen-

---

3.   391 U.S. 1, 88 S.Ct. 1503, 20 L.Ed.2d 381 (1968).

4.   451 U.S. 454, 101 S.Ct. 1866, 68 L.Ed.2d 359 (1981).

cy than when police obtain the assistance of private citizens in this country. This is because cooperative efforts among police agencies of different countries is a natural and desirable arrangement, and thus should not be inherently suspect as a likely effort to accomplish indirectly that which could not be done directly. At least where the foreign police were also serving law enforcement interests of their own country, it is not enough that American officers have played a substantial role in events leading up to the arrest or that the cooperation has the character of a joint venture.

(e) Proceedings at Which Confession Offered. Finally, there is the question of the kinds of proceedings at which a person may object to receipt of his incriminating statements because they were obtained in violation of the *Miranda* procedures. Because *Miranda* is grounded in the Fifth Amendment privilege against self-incrimination, this presents a question of exactly what constitutes incrimination within the meaning of the Amendment. As a general matter, this constitutional provision itself supplies the answer, for it declares that no person "shall be compelled in any criminal case to be a witness against himself." This most certainly means, as occurred in *Miranda,* that an improperly obtained confession is subject to suppression when offered in a criminal trial as evidence of defendant's guilt of the crime charged.[5] Some of the cases discussed earlier holding *Miranda* inapplicable to certain minor offenses, though ordinarily explained in terms of the subject matter of the interrogation, might be read as meaning *Miranda* rights cannot be invoked in a criminal

trial of a minor offense. If so viewed, they are even more clearly in error.

What if the confession is tendered only at the sentencing stage of the trial? This issue confronted the Court in *Estelle v. Smith,*[6] for there defendant's statements to an examining psychiatrist were received at the penalty phase of a capital case on the crucial issue of his future dangerousness. The state argued that this raised no Fifth Amendment issue because "incrimination is complete once guilt has been adjudicated," but the Court did not agree:

> Just as the Fifth Amendment prevents a criminal defendant from being made " 'the deluded instrument of his own conviction,' " * * * it protects him as well from being made the "deluded instrument" of his own execution.
>
> We can discern no basis to distinguish between the guilt and penalty phases of respondent's capital murder trial so far as the protection of the Fifth Amendment privilege is concerned. * * * Any effort by the State to compel respondent to testify against his will at the sentencing hearing clearly would contravene the Fifth Amendment. Yet the State's attempt to establish respondent's future dangerousness by relying on the unwarned statements he made to Dr. Grigson similarly infringes Fifth Amendment values.[7]

This latter point, that defendant may invoke *Miranda* at this proceeding because he could not be compelled to testify first-hand at such a proceeding, is fully consistent with the Court's analysis in *Miranda.* And it indicates that

5. However, it is suggested in Estelle v. Smith, 451 U.S. 454, 101 S.Ct. 1866, 68 L.Ed.2d 359 (1981), that under some circumstances a defendant may be required to waive his Fifth Amendment protections as a condition to submitting his own evidence on a certain issue. In particular, the Court noted: "When a defendant asserts the insanity defense and introduces supporting psychiatric testimony, his silence may deprive the State of the only effective means it has of controverting his proof on an issue that he interjected into the case. Accordingly, several courts of appeals have held that, under such circumstances, a defendant can be required to submit to a sanity examination conducted by the prosecution's psychiatrist."

In the later case of Buchanan v. Kentucky, 483 U.S. 402, 107 S.Ct. 2906, 97 L.Ed.2d 336 (1987), the Court held that "if a defendant requests [a psychiatric] evaluation or

presents psychiatric evidence, then, at the very least, the prosecution may rebut this presentation with evidence from the report of the examination that the defendant requested." See also § 6.7 at note 20.

6. 451 U.S. 454, 101 S.Ct. 1866, 68 L.Ed.2d 359 (1981).

7. In Penry v. Johnson, 532 U.S. 782, 121 S.Ct. 1910, 150 L.Ed.2d 9 (2001), where on habeas corpus the issue is not whether the state court's decision was erroneous, but only whether it was an "unreasonable application" of a Supreme Court precedent, the Court held it was not unreasonable for the state court to distinguish Smith from the instant case because in the latter case the psychiatric evidence obtained in violation of the Fifth Amendment was introduced at a death penalty hearing at which the defense has also introduced psychiatric testimony.

Smith is not limited to capital case penalty phase hearings, for it is more generally true that the privilege protects against use of compelled testimony in setting the sentence.

Smith also teaches that *Miranda* cannot be invoked at every proceeding somehow connected to a criminal case. The state attempted to exempt the case from the reach of *Miranda* by pointing out that the psychiatrist's examination of defendant had been undertaken in the first instance for the beneficial purpose of determining if defendant was competent to stand trial. The Court quite properly responded that this made no difference given the use actually made of defendant's statements. But the Court then added that "if the application of Dr. Grigson's findings had been confined to serving" the function of "ensuring that respondent understood the charges against him and was capable of assisting in his defense," then "no Fifth Amendment issue would have arisen." In other words, *Miranda* could not be invoked at a competency-to-stand-trial hearing. Similarly, it appears that *Miranda* has no application at a parole or probation revocation proceeding, though by virtue of *Smith* the result would be otherwise at a probation revocation proceeding involving deferred sentencing. And in *Baxter v. Palmigiano*,[8] holding that "prison disciplinary hearings are not criminal proceedings" for Fifth Amendment purposes, the Court asserted in passing that *Miranda* had no relevance in that context.

On the other hand, the *Smith* approach would appear to make it certain that *Miranda* applies in juvenile delinquency proceedings. This is because the Supreme Court earlier held in *In re Gault*[9] that the Fifth Amendment privilege is otherwise applicable in juvenile court proceedings. The Court explained this result in *Gault* by saying that

> juvenile proceedings to determine "delinquency," which may lead to commitment to a state institution, must be regarded as "criminal" for purposes of the privilege against self incrimination. To hold otherwise would be to disregard substance because of

the feeble enticement of the "civil" label-of-convenience which has been attached to juvenile proceedings. * * * [O]ur Constitution guarantees that no person shall be "compelled" to be a witness against himself when he is threatened with a deprivation of his liberty.

Though this last statement might be read as saying the Fifth Amendment privilege (and thus *Miranda*) is applicable in any proceeding that could result in a deprivation of liberty, *Gault* does not go this far. Hence, neither the Fifth Amendment privilege generally nor *Miranda* in particular has been deemed applicable in a civil commitment proceeding, a deportation hearing, a driver's license revocation hearing, or on trial of a civil offense.

In *Allen v. Illinois*,[10] the 5–4 majority characterized "*Gault's* sweeping statement" as "plainly not good law," and went on to hold that admissions obtained in violation of *Miranda* requirements were thus properly received in a sexually dangerous persons proceeding against the petitioner. This conclusion was grounded in the fact that the applicable statute had a "civil label" and in addition was not "punitive either in purpose or effect" because "the State has disavowed any interest in punishment, provided for the treatment of those it commits, and established a system under which committed persons may be released after the briefest time in confinement. The Act thus does not appear to promote either of 'the traditional aims of punishment—retribution and deterrence.' Neither the fact that the statute applied only to those charged with crime nor the fact that it required many of the safeguards applicable to criminal trials made such proceedings 'criminal' within the meaning of the Fifth Amendment." The dissenters, on the other hand, believed the proceedings *were* criminal because they required proof of a crime beyond a reasonable doubt, were initiated by a prosecutor, and resulted in incarceration in the state's prison system. As to the latter point, the *Allen* majority cau-

8. 425 U.S. 308, 96 S.Ct. 1551, 47 L.Ed.2d 810 (1976).

9. 387 U.S. 1, 87 S.Ct. 1428, 18 L.Ed.2d 527 (1967).

10. 478 U.S. 364, 106 S.Ct. 2988, 92 L.Ed.2d 296 (1986).

tioned: "Had petitioner shown, for example, that the confinement of such persons imposes on them a regimen which is essentially identical to that imposed upon felons with no need for psychiatric care, this might well be a different case."

Chapter 7

IDENTIFICATION PROCEDURES

Table of Sections

---

§ 7.1 Introduction

(a) The Problem of Misidentification. Eyewitness identification can be a powerful piece of evidence in a criminal prosecution. It is frequently an essential piece of evidence as well, as more scientific forms of identification evidence, such as fingerprint and handwriting analyses, are not always available. Yet it is well known that eyewitness evidence is inher-ently suspect and that suggestive procedures may prejudicially affect the ultimate identifica-tion. A pretrial identification proceeding may increase the risk of mistaken identification, as it occurs outside the courtroom and therefore is beyond the immediate supervision of the court.

A dramatic example of the dangers inherent in accepting the identification testimony even of several eyewitnesses in the absence of corroborative evidence is the case of Adolph Beck. Mistakenly identified by twenty-two witnesses, Beck served seven years in prison for crimes he did not commit. Subsequently, a committee formed to investigate the case concluded that "evidence as to identity based on personal impressions, however *bona fide,* is perhaps of all classes of evidence the least to be relied upon, and therefore, unless supported by other facts, an unsafe basis for the verdict of a jury."[1] More recently, seven eyewitnesses swore that Bernard T. Pagano was the man who politely pointed a small, chrome-plated pistol at them and demanded their money. Fortunately, midway through the trial of the Roman Catholic priest, Ronald Clouser admitted that he, not Father Pagano, had committed the six armed robberies.[2] These and many other examples recorded in the "annals of criminal law"[3] indicate that the identification problem is a serious one and has long existed.

(b) The Causes of Misidentification. Identification testimony has at least three components. First, witnessing a crime, whether as a victim or a bystander, involves perception of an event actually occurring. Second, the witness must memorize details of the event. Third, the witness must be able to recall and communicate accurately. Dangers of unreliability in eyewitness testimony arise at each of these three stages of the identification process, for whenever people attempt to acquire, retain and retrieve information accurately they are limited by normal human fallibilities and suggestive influences. Some of these potential limitations can be regulated by law, but others are unavoidable.

At one time, it was assumed by some psychological theorists that the brain operates more or less as a mechanical recording device: a person sees everything in front of himself and simultaneously records the information on a memory tape. Later, when the person wants to describe the event, he simply selects the appropriate tape and plays it back, producing a

faithful account of the original event. Psychological research has clearly demonstrated, however, that this "videotape recorder" analogy is misleading. In the first place, perception is not a mere passive recording of an event but instead is a constructive process by which people consciously or unconsciously use decisional strategies to attend selectively to only a minimal number of environmental stimuli. Selective perceptual processes result in a failure to observe the details of an event, especially those that are first unimportant but later assume great significance. People have difficulty perceiving time accurately, either the duration of an event or the interval between successive events. In addition to perceptual inaccuracies caused by the brain's inherent limitations, many identification errors are due to circumstances of the observation such as a brief observation period, poor lighting conditions or a stress-inducing situation. Psychological research has demonstrated that anxiety and fear produce significant perceptual distortion. Furthermore, personal expectations, needs and biases may distort perception. Evidence indicates that people are poorer at identifying members of another race than of their own. Perception is both incomplete and inaccurate.

Furthermore, memories are not indelibly preserved on tape. The representation of an event stored in memory undergoes constant change. Some details may be altered to resolve the cognitive dissonance that arises when new information about the event differs from the original memory representation. Other details are simply forgotten. Considerable memory loss occurs during the many days—and often months—that typically elapse between the offense and an eyewitness identification of the suspect. Memory is a constructive process to which details may be added that were not present in the initial representation or in the event itself. The mere wording of a question put to an eyewitness during a deposition, interview or trial may affect not only the imme-

§ 7.1

1. E. Watson, The Trial of Adolph Beck 250 (1924).

2. See Winer, Pagano Case Points Finger at Lineups, Nat'l L.J., Sept. 10, 1979, at 1, col. 4.

3. "The vagaries of eyewitness identification are well-known; the annals of criminal law are rife with instances of mistaken identification." United States v. Wade, 388 U.S. 218, 87 S.Ct. 1926, 18 L.Ed.2d 1149 (1967).

diate answer, but also the witness' memory of the original event and thus any answers to subsequent questions about the event. Interestingly, a witness's feeling of confidence in the details of memory generally does not validly measure the accuracy of that recollection. Witnesses, in fact, frequently become more confident of the correctness of their memory over time while the actual memory trace is probably decaying. Furthermore, individual witnesses may vary in reliability and completeness of memory. Factors such as age, sex or intelligence seem to correlate significantly with reliability of memory.

Another source of errors in identification is the process by which information is retrieved from memory for purposes of making an identification. The recall process suffers from the inadequacy of the eyewitness's vocabulary. Verbal recall—a narrative description unprompted by questions—results in incomplete information retrieval. On the other hand, as the questions become more structured in order to achieve completeness, the resulting responses become more inaccurate because the witness may feel compelled to complete answers in spite of incomplete knowledge. Lineups and photo arrays are structured recognition tests. Witnesses are likely to perceive them as multiple-choice tests that lack a "none of the above" option. Thus, the witness may view the task as one of identifying the individual who best matches the witness' recollection of the culprit, even if that match is not perfect. The reliability of a lineup identification, therefore, depends upon the similarity between the suspect and the other members of the lineup. Various social psychological factors increase the danger of suggestibility and exertion of suggestive influences by authority figures, such as policemen, therefore tends to magnify these other social psychological pressures.

(c) The Supreme Court's Response. Traditionally, eyewitness identification testimony has been readily accepted in American criminal trials. The witness will be asked if he sees in the courtroom the person who committed the crime, and will almost invariably answer in the affirmative and identify the defendant. Moreover, it is now generally accepted that the hearsay doctrine does not bar receipt as substantive evidence of the fact that this witness on a prior occasion, such as at a police lineup, identified the defendant as the perpetrator of the crime charged. Indeed, this earlier identification is likely to be the most important of the two.

Except in the unusual case in which the identification testimony would be the fruit of an illegal arrest of the person identified,[4] there was for many years no solid constitutional basis upon which an objection to the receipt of eyewitness identification testimony could be grounded. In contrast to the situation that obtains as to the defendant's confession, the Fifth Amendment privilege against self-incrimination does not afford a criminal suspect a right of nonparticipation in identification procedures. But in 1967 the Supreme Court recognized two constitutional grounds upon which such testimony could sometimes be successfully challenged. In *United States v. Wade*,[5] the absence of counsel at a post-indictment lineup was held to make inadmissible at trial testimony about the lineup identification and also identification testimony at trial that was the fruit of the earlier identification. But the Court has since given *Wade* a narrow reading, and consequently it has had a limited impact. In *Stovall v. Denno*,[6] the Court held that identification testimony must be suppressed if the confrontation "was so unnecessarily suggestive and conducive to irreparable mistaken identification" as to constitute a denial of due process of law. *Stovall* has likewise been given a limited application, and consequently some commentators believe that a need exists for additional safeguards regarding potentially unreliable eyewitness testimony.

---

4. See § 9.4(d).

5. 388 U.S. 218, 87 S.Ct. 1926, 18 L.Ed.2d 1149 (1967).

6. 388 U.S. 293, 87 S.Ct. 1967, 18 L.Ed.2d 1199 (1967).

§ 7.2　The Privilege Against Self–Incrimination

(a) The *Schmerber* Rule. In the case of *Schmerber v. California*,[1] the Supreme Court upheld the taking of a blood sample by a physician at police direction from the defendant over his objection after his arrest for drunken driving. Among the grounds upon which the defendant challenged the admission of the blood sample into evidence against him was that it violated his Fifth Amendment privilege not to be "compelled in any criminal case to be a witness against himself." The Court, in a 5–4 decision, rejected this contention, holding that "the privilege protects an accused only from being compelled to testify against himself, or otherwise provide the State with evidence of a testimonial or communicative nature, and that the withdrawal of blood and use of the analysis in question in this case did not involve compulsion to these ends."

In the earlier decision in *Miranda v. Arizona*,[2] the Court had described the policies underlying the privilege, there said to include such notions as that the government must "respect the inviolability of the human personality" and that the government must produce evidence against a defendant "by its own independent labors." To some extent, the taking of the blood sample had infringed those two interests, but this alone was not deemed sufficient to bring the Fifth Amendment into play. As the Court put it in *Schmerber*, "the privilege has never been given the full scope which the values it helps to protect suggest," but instead is limited to those situations in which the state seeks to submerge those values by obtaining evidence from the defendant "by the cruel, simple expedient of compelling it from his own mouth." In reaching that conclusion, the Court noted that many identification procedures were not protected by the Fifth Amendment; *Holt v. United States*,[3] holding that a defendant could be compelled to model a blouse, was cited as the "leading case."

The majority in *Schmerber* then declared:

It is clear that the protection of the privilege reaches an accused's communications, whatever form they might take, and the compulsion of responses which are also communications, for example, compliance with a subpoena to produce one's papers. * * * On the other hand, both federal and state courts have usually held that it offers no protection against compulsion to submit to fingerprinting, photographing, or measurements, to write or speak for identification, to appear in court, to stand, to assume a stance, to walk, or to make a particular gesture. The distinction which has emerged, often expressed in different ways, is that the privilege is a bar against compelling "communications" or "testimony," but that compulsion which makes a suspect or accused the source of "real or physical evidence" does not violate it.[4]

The dissenting Justices in *Schmerber* took a less restrictive view of the Fifth Amendment's privilege. Justice Black observed that the purpose of the extraction was to obtain "testimony" from some person that the defendant was intoxicated. Furthermore, he argued, the blood sample was "communicative" in the sense of supplying information to enable a witness to communicate to the court and jury about the defendant's guilt.[5] But it is the *Schmerber* majority position that has prevailed[6] and that

§ 7.2

1. 384 U.S. 757, 86 S.Ct. 1826, 16 L.Ed.2d 908 (1966), also discussed in § 8.12(d).

2. 384 U.S. 436, 86 S.Ct. 1602, 16 L.Ed.2d 694 (1966).

3. 218 U.S. 245, 31 S.Ct. 2, 54 L.Ed. 1021 (1910).

4. But the Court then cautioned: "Although we agree that this distinction is a helpful framework for analysis, we are not to be understood to agree with past applications in all instances. There will be many cases in which such a distinction is not readily drawn. Some tests seemingly directed to obtain 'physical evidence,' for example, lie detector tests measuring changes in body function during interrogation, may actually be directed to eliciting responses which are essentially testimonial. To compel a person to submit to testing in which an effort will be made

to determine his guilt or innocence on the basis of physiological responses, whether willed or not, is to evoke the spirit and history of the Fifth Amendment."

5. Dissenting Justice Fortas agreed that the defendant's privilege against self-incrimination was applicable, and then added a due process objection: "As prosecutor, the State has no right to commit any kind of violence upon the person, or to utilize the results of such a tort, and the extractions of blood, over protest, is an act of violence."

6. *Schmerber* was relied upon in South Dakota v. Neville, 459 U.S. 553, 103 S.Ct. 916, 74 L.Ed.2d 748 (1983), holding that the admission into evidence of a defendant's refusal to submit to a blood-alcohol test does not offend his Fifth Amendment privilege against self-incrimination. The Court reasoned that because "the state could legiti-

has subsequently been relied upon in holding a great variety of identification practices are not in conflict with the privilege.

(b) Application to Identification Procedures. Once again splitting 5–4 on this issue, the Supreme Court held in *United States v. Wade*[7] that requiring a defendant to appear in a lineup and to say "put the money in the bag" did not violate his privilege against self-incrimination. The *Wade* majority reasoned:

> We have no doubt that compelling the accused merely to exhibit his person for observation by a prosecution witness prior to trial involves no compulsion of the accused to give evidence having testimonial significance. * * * Similarly, compelling Wade to speak within hearing distance of the witnesses, even to utter words purportedly uttered by the robber, was not compulsion to utter statements of a "testimonial" nature; he was required to use his voice as an identifying physical characteristic, not to speak his guilt.

On like reasoning the Court held in the companion case of *Gilbert v. California*[8] that the taking of handwriting exemplars did not violate the defendant's rights.

The dissenters in *Wade* and *Gilbert* argued that *Schmerber* was wrongly decided, in that the privilege was designed to bar the government from forcing a person to supply proof of his own crime. Alternatively, assuming *Schmerber* was controlling, the dissenters claimed the instant cases were distinguishable in that in each of them the defendant had been compelled "actively to cooperate—to accuse himself by a volitional act." But the majority's conclusion that the privilege does not necessarily apply even when the defendant is put into an active rather than a passive posture still prevails, as is indicated by the fact that the Supreme Court has since reaffirmed that there is no Fifth Amendment privilege not to give handwriting exemplars[9] or voice exemplars.[10] The lower courts have followed the *Schmerber–Wade–Gilbert* view and have thus held the Fifth Amendment privilege inapplicable to a great variety of identification procedures. Included are fingerprinting, physical examination, examination of the defendant by X-rays or ultraviolet light, taking casts of defendant's teeth or requiring him to show his teeth, requiring the defendant to remove his glasses or to put on a hat, shoe, jacket, mask or wig and beard, or requiring him to display a limp or a tattoo.

(c) Refusal to Cooperate. What happens if a defendant refuses to cooperate in an identification procedure requiring his active participation? One possibility is that the prosecutor may be permitted to comment on the refusal to cooperate. If the identification procedure in which the defendant has refused to participate or cooperate, such as a lineup or taking of exemplars, is not protected by the Fifth Amendment, then of course there is no right to refuse and thus the act of refusal is not itself a compelled communication.[11] Rather, that refusal is considered circumstantial evidence of consciousness of guilt just as is escape from custody, a false alibi, or flight. But if the refusal to speak follows the giving of the *Miranda* right-to-silence warning to the defendant, and that warning did not clearly distin-

---

mately compel the suspect, against his will, to accede to the test," the action of the state "becomes no *less* legitimate when the State offers a second option of refusing the test, with the attendant penalties, for making that choice."

7. 388 U.S. 218, 87 S.Ct. 1926, 18 L.Ed.2d 1149 (1967).

8. 388 U.S. 263, 87 S.Ct. 1951, 18 L.Ed.2d 1178 (1967).

9. United States v. Euge, 444 U.S. 707, 100 S.Ct. 874, 63 L.Ed.2d 141 (1980); United States v. Mara, 410 U.S. 19, 93 S.Ct. 774, 35 L.Ed.2d 99 (1973).

10. United States v. Dionisio, 410 U.S. 1, 93 S.Ct. 764, 35 L.Ed.2d 67 (1973).

11. Cf. South Dakota v. Neville, 459 U.S. 553, 103 S.Ct. 916, 74 L.Ed.2d 748 (1983) (refusal to give blood sample admissible at criminal trial, as refusal "is not an act coerced by the officer," and it makes no difference that the state did not warn the defendant of this possible consequence, as "such a failure to warn was not the sort of implicit promise to forego use of evidence that would unfairly 'trick' [him] if the evidence were later offered against him at trial"). However, in Schmerber v. California, 384 U.S. 757, 86 S.Ct. 1826, 16 L.Ed.2d 908 (1966), the Court cautioned that in some cases the administration of tests might result in "testimonial products" proscribed by the privilege. For example, the fear of pain or danger resulting from a particular test may provide a coercive device to elicit incriminating statements. Such compelled testimonial product would, of course, be inadmissible.

guish between speech in terms of communications and speech for voice identification, then the "silence is insolubly ambiguous"[12] and thus cannot be treated as some evidence of defendant's guilt.

Another possible consequence of a failure to cooperate in identification procedures is imprisonment. On occasion, courts have utilized civil contempt and criminal contempt as a means to coerce or punish the suspect who failed to comply with a court order to participate in some identification proceeding. Some, however, have objected to the use of such a sanction where the defendant has done no more than refuse to participate in a procedure that might identify him as the perpetrator of a crime.

Yet another possibility is that the police will proceed to conduct the identification procedure over the defendant's objection. It has been suggested, however, that the use of force to compel the accused to mount the stage and remain there would make the proceeding unduly suggestive and thus a violation of due process under *Stovall v. Denno*.[13] But since the *Stovall* rule extends only to identifications that are "unnecessarily suggestive," it may be argued in response that the suggestiveness has been made necessary by the defendant's resistance. Indeed, it has been reasoned that a refusal to participate in a lineup would justify the use by the police of a showup procedure in which defendant is alone viewed by the witness and, if *United States v. Wade*[14] applies, in which substitute counsel is provided. Although it has also been suggested that the use of force by the police in carrying out the identification procedure may be sufficiently shocking to the conscience of the Court to require exclusion of the real evidence so obtained under the due process rule of *Rochin v. California*,[15] it is not objectionable that the authorities have used only so much force as is necessary to overcome the defendant's resistance.

(d) Change in Appearance. A related question is what may be done in response to a suspect's drastic alteration of his appearance between the time of arrest (or the occurrence of the crime) and his appearance in a lineup. One possibility is that this alteration will be brought to the attention of the jury for consideration as some evidence of defendant's guilt. Courts have concluded that evidence of defendant's alteration in appearance may be received, and even that it is appropriate to give an instruction to the jury that the evidence may be considered an indication of consciousness of guilt.

A second possibility is that the identification procedure will be conducted in such a way as to simulate the defendant's prior appearance. Illustrative is *People v. Cwikla*,[16] where defendant appeared at a pretrial identification hearing with his head and face newly shaved, allegedly for medical reasons. On application of the prosecutor, the defendant was required to don a wig and false beard for purposes of the identification hearing. Though the defendant claimed this violated his privilege against self-incrimination, the court ruled "it was not error to compel defendant to conform his appearance at the lineup to his appearance at the time of the crime." On like reasoning, other courts have held it lawful to require the defendant to dye his hair, to wear a wig, to wear an artificial goatee, and even to submit to extensive work by makeup experts who changed his appearance to conform to an earlier photograph of him.

In *United States v. Lamb*[17] the court upheld, against a Fifth Amendment challenge, a court order requiring defendant to shave his beard "where testimony indicated that Lamb had been clean-shaven at the time of the robbery, and that, therefore, Lamb's beard was an at-

---

12. As the Supreme Court put it in the somewhat analogous situation in Doyle v. Ohio, 426 U.S. 610, 96 S.Ct. 2240, 49 L.Ed.2d 91 (1976).

13. 388 U.S. 293, 87 S.Ct. 1967, 18 L.Ed.2d 1199 (1967).

14. 388 U.S. 218, 87 S.Ct. 1926, 18 L.Ed.2d 1149 (1967).

15. 342 U.S. 165, 72 S.Ct. 205, 96 L.Ed. 183 (1952).

16. 46 N.Y.2d 434, 414 N.Y.S.2d 102, 386 N.E.2d 1070 (1979).

17. 575 F.2d 1310 (10th Cir.1978).

tempt to disguise his appearance to prevent trial identification." But, forcing a person to change his appearance in this way is obviously a more serious matter than simply requiring a suspect to don a wig or false beard, and thus due process considerations come into play. As concluded in *People v. Vega*,[18] when "dealing with a procedure which would deprive the defendant of his constitutionally protected right to determine his personal appearance," the state "bears the burden of establishing substantive justification for any action it may impose which limits that right." That burden was not met, the court concluded in *Vega*, where the prosecutor had not even established probable cause that the suspect had committed the crime for which the identification procedure was sought.

Finally, it is well to note that there exists a difficult question concerning whether it is ethical for a defense attorney to encourage his client to change his appearance, such as by shaving his beard, prior to a lineup or prior to a trial at which identification testimony is to be received. It has been suggested that such conduct raises serious ethical questions which ought to be addressed by improvement in the definition of standards for lawyers' conduct and more effective discipline. Such conduct does not obviously fall within existing disciplinary rules.

§ 7.3 The Right to Counsel and to Confrontation

(a) Procedures Required. In *United States v. Wade*,[1] the Supreme Court confronted the question of "whether courtroom identifications of an accused at trial are to be excluded from evidence because the accused was exhibited to the witnesses before trial at a post-indictment lineup conducted for identification purposes without notice to and in the absence of the accused's appointed counsel." The defendant had been placed in a lineup made up of himself and five or six other prisoners, and each person had been required to wear strips of tape on each side of his face and to say "put the money in the bag," the words used by the perpetrator of a recent bank robbery. This lineup was conducted over a month after defendant had been indicted for the robbery and fifteen days after defense counsel had been appointed, but counsel was not notified of and was not present at the identification proceeding. At defendant's trial, two bank employees identified defendant as the robber and testified that they had earlier identified him in the lineup. In a 6–3 decision, the Court ruled that those procedures had been constitutionally inadequate, and thus concluded

> that for Wade the post-indictment lineup was a critical stage of the prosecution at which he was "as much entitled to such aid [of counsel] * * * as at the trial itself." * * * Thus both Wade and his counsel should have been notified of the impending lineup, and counsel's presence should have been a requisite to conduct of the lineup, absent an "intelligent waiver."

Earlier, in *Schmerber v. California*,[2] the Court had rejected the claim that there was a right to counsel at the taking of a blood sample because "[n]o issue of counsel's ability to assist petitioner in respect of any rights he did possess is presented." The government in *Wade* argued this was equally true of a lineup, also characterized "as a mere preparatory step in the gathering of the prosecution's evidence," but the Court did not agree. Unlike scientific techniques, such as the taking and assessment of a blood sample, "the confrontation compelled by the State between the accused and the victim or witnesses to a crime to elicit identification evidence is peculiarly riddled with innumerable dangers and variable factors which might seriously, even crucially, derogate from a fair trial." The Court in *Wade* explained that under past lineup practices, the defense was often unable "meaningfully to attack the credibility of the witness' courtroom identification" because of several factors that militate against developing fully the circum-

---

18. 51 A.D.2d 33, 379 N.Y.S.2d 419 (1976).

§ 7.3

1. 388 U.S. 218, 87 S.Ct. 1926, 18 L.Ed.2d 1149 (1967).

2. 384 U.S. 757, 86 S.Ct. 1826, 16 L.Ed.2d 908 (1966).

stances of a prior lineup identification by that witness. In particular: (1) other participants in the lineup are often police officers, or, if not, their names are rarely recorded or divulged at trial; (2) neither witnesses nor lineup participants are apt to be alert for or schooled in the detection of prejudicial conditions; (3) the suspect (often staring into bright lights) may not be in a position to observe prejudicial conditions, and, in any event, might not detect them because of his emotional tension; (4) even if the suspect observes abuse, he may nonetheless be reluctant to take the stand and open up the admission of prior convictions; and (5) even if he takes the stand, his version of what transpired at the lineup is unlikely to be accepted if it conflicts with police testimony. Moreover, the Court pointed out, the need to learn what occurred at the lineup is great; the risk of improper suggestion is substantial, and once the witness has picked out the accused in a lineup, he is unlikely to go back on his word in court.

The intended constitutional foundation of the *Wade* decision was not entirely clear from the Court's decision. The Court talked about the lineup being "a critical stage" at which defendant was as much entitled to counsel as at trial, which would seem to indicate that *Wade* is grounded in the Sixth Amendment right to counsel. But in explaining why this was so, the *Wade* majority referred to the fact that "presence of counsel itself can often * * * assure a meaningful confrontation at trial." Indeed, the Court repeatedly referred to the Sixth Amendment right to confrontation and cross-examination in *Wade*, suggesting that the decision was grounded in the Sixth Amendment right of confrontation and cross-examination, with counsel being required simply to give sufficient protection to that other right. But when the choice between these two theories later became important in determining the scope of *Wade,* the Supreme Court opted for the narrower right to counsel theory.[3]

The *Wade* majority emphasized that lineups as they were customarily conducted constituted a "critical stage" for right to counsel purposes, but that it might be otherwise if appropriate reforms were adopted:

Legislative or other regulations, such as those of local police departments, which eliminate the risks of abuse and unintentional suggestion at lineup proceedings and the impediments to meaningful confrontation at trial may also remove the basis for regarding the stage as "critical." But neither Congress nor the federal authorities have seen fit to provide a solution. What we hold today "in no way creates a constitutional straitjacket which will handicap sound efforts at reform, nor is it intended to have this effect."

Just what substitute procedures would suffice, so that the lineup could be constitutionally conducted without counsel, is not entirely clear. The answer may depend to some extent upon precisely what the function of counsel at the lineup is thought to be, about which there is less than complete agreement.[4] But in any event it seems clear that an adequate substitute must at least provide for a means whereby the defendant can have an opportunity at trial effectively to reconstruct the procedure by which he was identified in a pretrial lineup.

(b) Time of Identification. Because both *Wade* and the companion case of *Gilbert v. California*[5] involved lineups held after indictment and appointment of counsel, lower courts were in disagreement as to whether counsel was required at any pre-indictment identifications. The issue was finally resolved by the Supreme Court in the case of *Kirby v. Illinois,*[6] which involved a police station identification of the defendant shortly after his warrantless arrest and before he had been formally charged in any way. The Court held that the *Wade–Gilbert* rule applies only to identifications occurring "at or after the initiation of adversary judicial criminal proceedings— whether by way of formal charge, preliminary hearing, indictment, information, or arraign-

---

3. See § 7.3(b).

4. See § 7.3(e).

5. 388 U.S. 263, 87 S.Ct. 1951, 18 L.Ed.2d 1178 (1967).

6. 406 U.S. 682, 92 S.Ct. 1877, 32 L.Ed.2d 411 (1972).

ment." The rationale was that the constitutional right to counsel has traditionally been so limited, and with good reason, in that only after such initiation is a defendant "faced with the prosecutorial forces of organized society, and immersed in the intricacies of substantive and procedural criminal law."[7]

In the main, the commentators have been critical of the *Kirby* decision and have sided with the four dissenters, who pointed out that the decision did not square with the rationale of *Wade*. As one commentator put it:

> The plurality's justification for refusing to apply—or, in its words, "extend"—*Wade* and *Gilbert* is not persuasive. Although both cases involved postindictment lineups, *Wade*'s rationale leaves little doubt that the postindictment language was merely descriptive. Pointing to the vagaries of eyewitness identification and to the suggestion inherent in identification procedures, *Wade* found lineups in the absence of counsel to be a serious threat to the fairness of the subsequent trial. *Wade* also concluded that such lineups undermine the right of confrontation at trial since they are difficult to reconstruct either with direct evidence or on cross-examination. The first reason has nothing to do with the defendant's immersion in legal intricacies. From the defendant's viewpoint, the lineup is virtually devoid of legal issues; at the police officer's discretion, the defendant can be required to participate, walk, talk, and wear certain clothing. Of course, the proceeding must be fairly conducted, but this has little to do with the accused since his opinion or advice is rarely solicited or heeded. Even if the fairness requirement did confront the accused with legal intricacies, those intricacies are obviously the same whenever the lineup is conducted.
>
> *Wade*'s second reason for requiring counsel—to protect the right of confrontation—

does relate to the intricacies of procedural criminal law, at least to some extent. Acute perception of all lineup conditions, including the reaction of witnesses, is necessary for effective cross-examination at trial. Yet, the Court recognized in *Wade* that the perception of lineup conditions by most defendants is adversely affected by lack of training and emotional tension. These difficulties are not at all dependent upon the lineup's sequential location in the criminal process. The defendant's inability to protect his constitutional right of confrontation remains constant throughout the proceedings against him.[8]

In short, the Court in *Kirby* managed to limit *Wade* by treating it as a "pure" right to counsel case, necessitating a determination of when that right begins, instead of, as it seemed to be, a case grounded in the Sixth Amendment right to confrontation at trial, which is threatened no matter when the pretrial identification occurs. As a result, so the argument goes, the right to counsel is afforded the defendant where he least needs it, namely, for post-arraignment lineups typically conducted to refresh uncertain identifications previously made.

On the other hand, if one accepts the *Kirby* right to counsel characterization, then the ruling there is certainly an understandable one. Even accepting the premise that the need for counsel is often equivalent in the post-indictment and pre-indictment lineup, it does not necessarily follow that appointment of counsel is constitutionally required in both situations, for the Sixth Amendment does not provide for counsel at every stage in which counsel's assistance is helpful. Moreover, that characterization of *Wade* perhaps can best be explained on the ground that the Court deemed it impractical to impose a counsel requirement on *all* police-conducted identification proceedings, especially on-the-scene confrontations occurring

---

7. This language in *Kirby* was relied upon in United States v. Gouveia, 467 U.S. 180, 104 S.Ct. 2292, 81 L.Ed.2d 146 (1984), holding that the Sixth Amendment does not require the appointment of counsel prior to the initiation of adversary judicial proceedings against indigent inmates who are confined in administrative detention

for lengthy periods while being investigated for crimes committed in prison.

8. Grano, *Kirby, Biggers* and *Ash*: Do Any Constitutional Safeguards Remain Against the Danger of Convicting the Innocent?, 72 Mich.L.Rev. 717, 726 (1974).

just after the commission of the crime. By treating the issue solely in right to counsel terms, it was possible to exclude the earlier stages of the criminal process from the strictures of the *Wade* procedures, a limitation that would be much more difficult to rationalize under the right of confrontation theory. To some, this limitation is advantageous because police are encouraged and enabled to conduct identification proceedings more expeditiously, at a time when the recall of witnesses will be fresher and thus the identifications will generally be more reliable.

Except for the language quoted earlier, the Court in *Kirby* did not explore exactly what it takes to "initiate" adversary judicial criminal proceedings and thus bring the *Wade–Gilbert* rule into play. But that language was later relied upon by the Court in *Moore v. Illinois*,[9] where it was held that an identification at a preliminary hearing was governed by *Wade*. The Court in *Moore* emphasized that it was "plain that 'the government ha[d] committed itself to prosecute' " by that time and that defendant "faced counsel for the State" at that time. By this reasoning, it seems clear that the *Wade* right to counsel comes into existence even before the preliminary hearing. Certainly

> a convincing argument can be made that a criminal prosecution commences at least with the preliminary arraignment when a formal complaint is filed in court against the accused. * * * Professor Miller, supporting his exhaustive analysis of the charging function with extensive field study data, has called the decision to file a complaint 'the heart of the charging process.'[10] * * * It would defy common sense to say that a criminal prosecution has not commenced against a defendant who, perhaps incarcerated and unable to afford judicially imposed bail, awaits preliminary examination on the authority of a charging document filed by the prosecutor, less typically by the police, and approved by a court of law.[11]

On the other hand, it seems clear under the *Kirby–Moore* test that the *Wade* right to counsel does not ripen merely because the defendant has first been subjected to a warrantless custodial arrest. This means that a person so arrested may be viewed in a lineup without the presence of counsel if that occurs prior to the time of his appearance before a magistrate, except in those jurisdictions providing as a matter of state law for a broader right to counsel at identification proceedings. And if a person is summoned to appear before a grand jury for purposes of being identified, there is again no *Wade–Gilbert* right to counsel, as the government was still in the process of investigation. There is a split of authority on the question of whether the issuance of an arrest warrant marks the initiation of adversary judicial proceedings within the meaning of *Kirby*. This may be attributable in part to the fact that a document called a "complaint" is sometimes used as a basis for issuance of an arrest warrant and on other occasions is utilized to manifest the prosecutor's preindictment charging decision. But where the complaint simply serves to provide the probable cause to issue an arrest warrant, which may be needed for reasons having nothing to do with charging,[12] it makes no sense under the *Kirby–Moore* formula to view either the issuance of the warrant or the arrest of the defendant pursuant to the warrant as marking the commencement of the *Wade* right to counsel. Moreover, if the right to counsel has not otherwise attached, it does not attach merely because the defendant is represented by counsel.

(c) Nature of Identification Procedure. Regardless of when they occur, certain types of identification procedures will not trigger the right to counsel. For example, as held in *United States v. Ash*,[13] there is no right to have counsel present when the police show photographs of the defendant and others to witnesses, and this is so even if the defendant has already been indicted. Throughout the expansion of the constitutional right to counsel to

---

9. 434 U.S. 220, 98 S.Ct. 458, 54 L.Ed.2d 424 (1977).

10. F. Miller, Prosecution 14 (1969).

11. Grano, supra note 8, at 788–79.

12. See § 3.6(a).

13. 413 U.S. 300, 93 S.Ct. 2568, 37 L.Ed.2d 619 (1973).

certain pretrial proceedings, said the majority in *Ash*, "the function of the lawyer has remained essentially the same as his function at trial," which is to give the accused "aid in coping with legal problems or assistance in meeting his adversary." This being so, the Court reasoned that there is no such right at photo-identification, as unlike a lineup there is no "trial-like confrontation" involving the "presence of the accused." Although the defendant in *Wade* had not been confronted with legal questions, the lineup offered opportunities for the authorities to take advantage of the accused, a problem that the Court in *Ash* concluded did not exist with respect to identification by use of a photo display. Moreover, the *Ash* majority emphasized that absence of counsel from the photo-identification would not impair effective cross-examination at trial as would absence from a lineup, for photographic identifications are relatively easy to reconstruct. Justice Stewart, concurring in *Ash*, objected to the majority's distinction of *Wade* as a situation in which the lawyer is giving advice or assistance to the defendant at the lineup. He construed the lawyer's role to be that of "an observer," but then concluded that such a role need not be performed with respect to photo-identification, as in that context "there are few possibilities for unfair suggestiveness."

To the extent that *Ash* is grounded in the notion that the function of counsel in a pretrial setting is "the same as his function at trial," it cannot be squared with *Wade*.

> In post-indictment line-ups, it is not readily apparent what immediate assistance an attorney can provide. He cannot stop the line-up or see that it be conducted in a certain manner. He can give no legal advice, proffer no defenses, advance no arguments. The defendant is not in need of legal advice and the lawyer is not in a position to provide on the spot assistance against the skills of the prosecutor. In fact, his own recognized function is as a trained observer.[14]

The critical question in *Ash*, therefore, was really whether such a "trained observer" was needed at identifications made by examination of photographs. Justice Stewart did perceive this as the issue but, as noted, answered in the negative; the three dissenters, however, presented a most forceful argument to the contrary. They noted that the risk of impermissible suggestiveness is equally present in photo-identifications as it is in lineups, and that in the former situation there is even less likelihood any irregularities will ever come to light because even the accused is not present to observe them. Moreover, photographic identifications lack scientific precision and are difficult to fully reconstruct at trial.

The majority in *Ash* also argued that even if a broader view were taken of the right to counsel, it need not extend "to a portion of the prosecutor's trial-preparation interviews with witnesses," especially in light of "the equal ability of defense counsel to seek and interview witnesses himself." The implication is that granting a right to counsel at photographic displays might lead to the extension of the right to counsel to all pretrial interviews of prospective witnesses. But this is not so.

> The fact that photographic identifications were found to be "critical" would not necessarily lead to a finding that other interviews between the prosecutor and his witnesses were "critical." * * * The basis for extending the right to counsel to the identification context was that identifications by eyewitnesses—like confessions—are such damning evidence that they may completely decide the guilt or innocence of the accused. Photographic identifications can be just as critical to the future outcome of a trial as can corporeal identifications. Routine interviews between the prosecutor and his witnesses, on the other hand, do not have the potential for such damaging results, at least assuming good faith on the part of the prosecutor.[15]

One unfortunate consequence of the *Ash* case is that police are encouraged to resort to photo-identification in lieu of lineups in order to obviate the necessity to have defense counsel present at the identification. This is a most unfortunate development, as a photographic

---

14. Note, 64 J.Crim.L.C. & P.S. 428, 433 (1973).

15. Note, 26 Stan.L.Rev. 399, 417 (1974).

identification, even when properly obtained, is clearly inferior to a properly obtained corporeal identification. Some state courts have appreciated this problem and thus, as a matter of local law, have gone beyond *Ash* in some way. One view is that photo-identification is an improper identification procedure when the suspect is in custody and could be placed in a lineup, while another is that in such circumstances a photo-identification must be conducted in the presence of defense counsel.

Whether the lawyer is viewed as an advisor and advocate or as merely a trained observer, it is clear that the right to counsel does not attach to more scientific identification procedures, such as the taking of a blood sample. As the Court explained in *United States v. Wade*[16]:

> Knowledge of the techniques of science and technology is sufficiently available, and the variables in techniques few enough, that the accused has the opportunity for a meaningful confrontation of the Government's case at trial through the ordinary processes of cross-examination of the Government's expert witnesses and the presentation of the evidence of his own experts.

The procedures for taking and analyzing blood samples, fingerprints, clothing, hair and the like are distinguishable from lineups and photographic arrays in that they do not depend for their reliability on the recollection of a witness. Rather, their reliability depends on the scientific validity of the techniques and the skill and precision with which they are administered. The risk of suggestiveness present in eyewitness identification simply does not extend to such procedures.

On similar reasoning, the Supreme Court by a 5–4 majority held in *Gilbert v. California*[17] that the taking of handwriting exemplars is not a critical stage entitling the defendant to the assistance of counsel. The majority explained that

there is minimal risk that the absence of counsel might derogate from his right to a fair trial. * * * If, for some reason, an unrepresentative exemplar is taken, this can be brought out and corrected through the adversary process at trial since the accused can make an unlimited number of additional exemplars for analysis and comparison by government and defense handwriting experts.

Thus, while the suspect might benefit from counsel's advice as to whether to give the exemplars or refuse and suffer the consequences, this does not involve a constitutional right to which the right to counsel might be linked.[18]

Although the *Wade* holding is stated in terms of a right to counsel at a "lineup," unquestionably it extends beyond that. In *Moore v. Illinois*,[19] the holding in *Wade* was more expansively stated as being "that a corporeal identification is a critical stage of a criminal prosecution for Sixth Amendment purposes," and thus the Court concluded that there was a right to counsel at a one-on-one showup. Indeed, as the Court observed, such a procedure is so highly suggestive that the need for counsel is especially great. The identification in *Moore* occurred at a preliminary hearing when the prosecutor asked a rape victim to point out her assailant in the courtroom, but the Court rejected the contention that there is no right to counsel at an identification procedure conducted in the course of a judicial proceeding. Though the more formal proceeding involved in *Moore* may have reduced substantially the chances of undetectable suggestiveness as compared with the typical police lineup, this was offset in the eyes of the Court by the fact that in the judicial setting the lawyer could more readily have caused something to be done to avoid the suggestiveness.

---

16. 388 U.S. 218, 87 S.Ct. 1926, 18 L.Ed.2d 1149 (1967).

17. 388 U.S. 263, 87 S.Ct. 1951, 18 L.Ed.2d 1178 (1967).

18. Black, J., one of the four dissenters in *Gilbert*, objected: "But just as nothing said in our previous opinions 'links the right to counsel only to protection of Fifth Amendment rights,' * * * nothing has been said which

justifies linking the right to counsel only to the protection of other Sixth Amendment rights. And there is nothing in the Constitution to justify considering the right to counsel as a second-class, subsidiary right which attaches only when the Court deems other specific rights in jeopardy."

19. 434 U.S. 220, 98 S.Ct. 458, 54 L.Ed.2d 424 (1977).

Finally, in the case of corporeal identification there is the question of whether the *Wade* right to counsel applies only to the time of the viewing of the defendant by the witness or whether it extends as well to the time at which the witness communicates to the police the fact of identification. There is much to be said for the broader view, which some courts have adopted, as otherwise the defendant has no way of knowing whether the witness was improperly led, whether the witness was hesitant or unsure in his identification. There is, however, authority to the contrary, and it seems more consistent with the approach taken by the Supreme Court in *Ash*.

(d) Waiver or Substitution of Counsel. In *United States v. Wade*,[20] the Supreme Court indicated that there could be an "intelligent waiver" of counsel, in which case presence of an attorney at the identification procedures would not be required. Although this may seem consistent with the waiver permitted in *Miranda v. Arizona*,[21] it might be questioned whether the right to counsel at an identification should be subject to waiver. The argument is that while waiver of counsel under *Miranda* serves the legitimate objective of permitting the suspect to bear witness to the truth, no comparable value is served by waiver under *Wade*. However, the lower courts have consistently held that the right to counsel at identification procedures can be waived, provided of course the waiver is both intelligent and voluntary. Waiver of counsel for another purpose will not suffice, and thus a waiver following receipt of the *Miranda* warnings does not carry over to the lineup.

The *Wade* opinion does not dwell upon the question of what is required to show an effective waiver, although it seems likely that an approach similar to that dictated by *Miranda* is to be followed here. This means that a "heavy burden" rests upon the government to

show an express waiver following the requisite warnings, which at least must include notice to the defendant that he has a right to counsel for this particular purpose and that counsel will be provided for him if he is indigent. The better practice is also to advise the defendant that the lineup will be delayed for a reasonable time after the lawyer is notified, in order to allow the lawyer to appear. Because the privilege against self-incrimination does not extend to identification procedures, surely there is no need to tell the defendant that he has a right not to participate or that any identification will be used against him at trial.

While there is language in *Wade* that, if read literally, would seem to support the view that waiver of counsel must occur in the presence of counsel,[22] it is fully consistent with other waiver of counsel developments[23] to conclude that the right is that of the defendant rather than the lawyer and that consequently it may be waived by the defendant alone. Indeed, there is a sense in which a broader variety of waiver must be recognized here than in the confession context. The police have no right to require a suspect to converse with them, but surely there is a police-prosecution-public interest in a prompt lineup of a person who has been lawfully arrested. This being so, a defendant who is not indigent and thus could hire a lawyer but unreasonably delays in doing so may be deemed to have waived his right to counsel at the identification proceeding.[24]

The Court in *Wade*, in response to the argument that a counsel requirement would "forestall prompt identifications," deliberately opted to "leave open the question whether the presence of substitute counsel might not suffice where notification and presence of the suspect's own counsel would result in prejudicial delay." Given the state's interest in a prompt lineup, it would seem that substitute

---

20. 388 U.S. 218, 87 S.Ct. 1926, 18 L.Ed.2d 1149 (1967).

21. 384 U.S. 436, 86 S.Ct. 1602, 16 L.Ed.2d 694 (1966).

22. "Thus both Wade *and his counsel should have been notified* of the impending lineup, and counsel's presence should have been a requisite to conduct of the lineup, absent an 'intelligent waiver.' " (Emphasis added.).

23. See §§ 6.4(f), 6.9.

24. By similar reasoning it has been held that if defense counsel has been properly notified but he fails to attend the lineup, then the identification may be made in his absence. However, there is some authority that if the defendant's own attorney is not available, then the defendant must be advised that substitute counsel may be arranged.

counsel would suffice where he was sufficiently apprised of the circumstances so as to be able effectively to represent the defendant. On the other hand, it is not sufficient that there was a lawyer present at the lineup for some other purpose, such as to represent another individual, for that attorney could not be expected to be alert to any problems that existed as to the defendant. Moreover, police claims that they had somehow provided substitute counsel are not likely to be favorably received by the courts where it appears the police had taken their good time in arranging the lineup, so that no prejudicial delay could have resulted from permitting defendant to engage his own attorney.

(e) Role of Counsel. *Wade* stresses the need to protect the defendant's "right meaningfully to cross-examine the witnesses against him and to have effective assistance of counsel at the trial itself," while in *Ash* the *Wade* rule was explained on the basis that "[c]ounsel was seen by the Court as being more sensitive to, and aware of, suggestive influences than the accused himself, and better able to reconstruct the events at trial." This indicates that the lawyer is to be only an observer at the lineup so that, at the trial, he would then be in a position to decide on the basis of his earlier observations whether it is tactically wise to bring out the lineup identification in order to cast doubt upon an in-court identification. And, if he decides to do so, he will better know what questions to ask the witness about the circumstances of the lineup.

If the lawyer is to serve as an observer because, as the Court indicated in *Wade* and *Ash,* he is better able than the defendant and others present to recognize suggestive influences, then this would suggest that it may well be necessary for him to take the stand himself to testify as to what went on at the lineup. This places the defense attorney in a dilemma. Under the Model Rules of Professional Conduct, if a lawyer learns he will be required to be a witness at trial for his client, except as to an uncontested issue, he should withdraw

from the case unless doing so "would work substantial hardship on the client."[25] At least some courts have taken even a stronger stance. In *State v. Caldwell,*[26] holding that defense counsel may not testify regarding events at the lineup unless he withdraws from the case, the court explained: "An advocate who becomes a witness is in the unseemly and ineffective position of arguing his own credibility. The roles of an advocate and of a witness are inconsistent; the function of an advocate is to advance or argue the cause of another, while that of a witness is to state facts objectively."

A second position with respect to defense counsel's function is that the identification procedure is to be a fully adversary proceeding in which the counsel for the suspect may make objections and proposals, which if they are proper or even reasonable must be respected. Support for this position can be found in the Supreme Court cases. *Wade* says that "presence of counsel itself can often avert prejudice" and assist law enforcement "by preventing the infiltration of taint in the prosecution's identification evidence," and this prompted the dissenters to find in *Wade* "an implicit invitation to counsel to suggest rules for the lineup and to manage and produce it as best he can." Similarly, in *Ash* the Court asserts that "[c]ounsel present at lineup would be able to remove disabilities of the accused."

If the defense lawyer is to have an active role then, as a matter of tactics, he will have to decide in each case whether to try to prevent and remedy the suggestive aspects of the identification process or whether instead simply to allow them to occur so that he can bring them out at trial to the possible advantage of his client. But, it is by no means clear that he would or ought to have these choices. As one court put it, if defense counsel is allowed to take an active role in setting up the lineup, then "it might well be that, absent plain error or circumstances unknown to counsel at the time of the lineup, no challenges to the physical staging of the lineup could successfully be raised beyond objections raised at the time of

---

25. ABA Model Rules of Professional Conduct, rule 3.7(a).

26. 117 Ariz. 464, 573 P.2d 864 (1977).

the lineup."[27] Such a waiver rule seems undesirable, and this suggests that the notion of defense counsel playing an active role at the identification proceeding is unsound if this is to be the consequence. If the possibility of such waiver exists, then defense counsel would be obligated to raise every conceivable objection unless there was a sound tactical reason for not doing so, a hard choice for an attorney at a very early stage of his contact with the case. Moreover, it would result in courts frequently being confronted with incompetency of counsel claims because of the defense attorney's inaction at the identification proceeding.

The situation is quite different when the identification procedure in question occurs in court rather than at the police station. With respect to an in-court identification, made on the record and in the presence of a judicial officer and other observers, it is difficult to make a convincing argument that presence of a lawyer is essential to reveal otherwise undiscoverable suggestiveness. Yet the Court in *Moore v. Illinois*[28] unhesitatingly extended the *Wade* rule to in-court identifications, and in doing so emphasized that the identification in that case had been done in a "suggestive manner" and that "[h]ad petitioner been represented by counsel, some or all of this suggestiveness could have been avoided." In this context, then, in contrast to the police station identification, the defense attorney is properly considered to have an active role to play. The reasons militating against that role at the police station do not obtain here; defense counsel's proposals as to how the identification should be conducted can be countered by the prosecutor and ruled on by the judge, and the case is now sufficiently far along that it is not unfair to expect defense counsel to make binding tactical choices.

(f) Consequences of Violation. If the procedures mandated by the *Wade* case are not followed and consequently a pretrial identification occurs without counsel, what are the consequences of this violation of defendant's Sixth Amendment rights? One is that testimony as to the fact of that pretrial identification is inadmissible at trial. As the Court explained in *Gilbert v. California*,[29] such testimony

> is the direct result of the illegal lineup "come at by exploitation of [the primary] illegality." * * * The State is therefore not entitled to an opportunity to show that that testimony had an independent source. Only a *per se* exclusionary rule as to such testimony can be an effective sanction to assure that law enforcement authorities will respect the accused's constitutional right to the presence of his counsel at the critical lineup. * * * That conclusion is buttressed by the consideration that the witness' testimony of his lineup identification will enhance the impact of his in-court identification on the jury and seriously aggravate whatever derogation exists of the accused's right to a fair trial.

Under this *per se* exclusionary rule, the Court explained in *Gilbert,* if evidence of the pretrial identification was received at trial, then any resulting conviction must be reversed unless the appellate court is "able to declare a belief that it was harmless beyond a reasonable doubt." Three Justices objected that such a severe sanction was unnecessary and inappropriate.[30]

What then of a subsequent in-court identification by a witness who earlier identified the defendant at an improperly conducted pretrial identification proceeding? This, the Court declared in *Wade,* presents a "fruit of the poisonous tree" problem that, consistent with the approach generally taken as to that kind of issue,[31] necessitates a determination of "[w]hether, granting establishment of the primary illegality, the evidence to which instant

---

27. United States v. Allen, 408 F.2d 1287 (D.C.Cir. 1969).

28. 434 U.S. 220, 98 S.Ct. 458, 54 L.Ed.2d 424 (1977).

29. 388 U.S. 263, 87 S.Ct. 1951, 18 L.Ed.2d 1178 (1967).

30. They objected in *Wade* that under the harsh per se rule it "matters not how well the witness knows the

suspect, whether the witness is the suspect's mother, brother, or long-time associate, and no matter how long or well the witness observed the perpetrator at the scene of the crime."

31. See § 9.3.

objection is made has been come at by exploitation of that illegality or instead by means sufficiently distinguishable to be purged of the primary taint." And this means, the Court added, that the prosecution must "establish by clear and convincing evidence that the in-court identifications were based upon observations of the suspect other than the lineup identification." The relevant factors, the Court explained in *Wade,* include

> the prior opportunity to observe the alleged criminal act, the existence of any discrepancy between any pre-lineup description and the defendant's actual description, any identification prior to lineup of another person, the identification by picture of the defendant prior to the lineup, failure to identify the defendant on a prior occasion, and the lapse of time between the alleged act and the lineup identification. It is also relevant to consider those facts which, despite the absence of counsel, are disclosed concerning the conduct of the lineup.

The lower court cases reflect reliance upon these and related factors. In favor of a determination that the in-court identification was not tainted, it is emphasized that the witness had a clear or lengthy opportunity to observe the perpetrator of the crime, that the witness was previously acquainted with the defendant, or that the witness gave an accurate and specific description prior to the identification. Some courts also take into account certain external factors, such as defendant's possession of the fruits of the crime, which is improper because such factors have nothing to do with whether the in-court identification is independent of the earlier improperly conducted identification. As for factors tending to show that the taint is not dissipated, the lower courts consider the witness's limited opportunity for observation, any discrepancy in the description given, and any failure of the witness to identify the defendant on an earlier occasion.

The taint approach of the Court in *Wade* does not accord with psychological theory concerning identification, discussed earlier.[32] It is none too surprising, therefore, that when confronted with illegal pretrial identifications the lower courts have easily found an "independent source" for an in-court identification and have readily avoided reversing convictions by stretching, often beyond reason and logic, the doctrines of independent source and harmless error. As a practical matter, the burden is on the defense to show the presence of taint. This being so, it may well be asked whether it would be preferable, as Justice Black contended in *Wade,* that all in-court identifications be admissible so long as not supplemented or corroborated by admission of the earlier illegal identification, or whether instead the per se exclusionary rule should be extended to in-court identifications by witnesses who participated in earlier illegal identifications.

(g) The "Repeal" of the Right. In the Omnibus Crime Control and Safe Streets Act of 1968, the Congress purported to "repeal" the *Wade–Gilbert* rule in federal prosecutions. The Act provides: "The testimony of a witness that he saw the accused commit or participate in the commission of the crime for which the accused is being tried shall be admissible in evidence in a criminal prosecution in any trial court ordained and established under article III of the Constitution of the United States."[33] Though the Court in *Wade* said that the need for counsel could be removed by "[l]egislative * * * regulations * * * which eliminate the risks of abuse and unintentional suggestion at lineup proceedings and the impediments to meaningful confrontation at trial," this statute hardly does that and thus cannot be treated as having nullified the *Wade* decision.

§ 7.4 Due Process: "The Totality of the Circumstances"

(a) Generally. A companion case to *United States v. Wade*[1] and *Gilbert v. California,*[2] both recognizing a right to counsel at postin-

---

32. See § 7.1(b).

33. 18 U.S.C. § 3502.

§ 7.4

1. 388 U.S. 218, 87 S.Ct. 1926, 18 L.Ed.2d 1149 (1967).

2. 388 U.S. 263, 87 S.Ct. 1951, 18 L.Ed.2d 1178 (1967).

dictment lineups, was *Stovall v. Denno*.[3] There, a victim of a stabbing was hospitalized for major surgery, and defendant, arrested for the offense, was brought to the victim's hospital room for a confrontation. The defendant was handcuffed to one of the seven law enforcement officials who brought him to the hospital room, and he was the only black person in the room. After being asked by an officer whether the defendant "was the man," the victim identified him. At his trial, both the victim and the police who were present in the hospital room testified to that identification.

Although the defendant in *Stovall* had not been accompanied by counsel, the Court declined to decide the case under the *Wade–Gilbert* rule, holding instead that the principles in those cases would not be applied retroactively but would affect only those identification procedures conducted after the date those decisions were handed down.[4] But the Court then went on to recognize another basis upon which identification testimony could be challenged on constitutional grounds. It must be determined, said the Court in *Stovall*, by a consideration of "the totality of the circumstances," whether the confrontation "was so unnecessarily suggestive and conducive to irreparable mistaken identification" that the defendant was denied due process of law. As the Court later explained, when the issue is whether a witness at the earlier identification may now identify the defendant at trial, then it must be determined whether the identification procedure "was so impermissibly suggestive as to give rise to a very substantial likelihood of irreparable misidentification."[5] "While the phrase was coined as a standard for determining whether an in-court identification would be admissible in the wake of a suggestive out-of-court identification, with the deletion of 'irreparable' it serves equally well as a standard for the admissibility of testimony concerning the out-of-court identification itself."[6]

(b) The "Unnecessarily Suggestive" Element.

Under the two-pronged *Stovall* due process test, the first question to be asked is whether the initial identification procedure was "unnecessarily" or "impermissibly" suggestive. (The burden is on the defendant to prove by a preponderance of the evidence that the identification was unnecessarily suggestive.) This first inquiry can in turn be broken down into two constituent parts: that concerning the suggestiveness of the identification, and that concerning whether there was some good reason for the failure to resort to less suggestive procedures. As for what is sufficiently suggestive to prompt a *Stovall* inquiry, the Court in that case found itself confronted with one such situation, noting that the "practice of showing suspects singly to persons for the purpose of identification, and not as part of a lineup has been widely condemned." This should not be taken to mean that resort to a lineup procedure inevitably means there is an absence of suggestiveness. As the Court later concluded in *Foster v. California*,[7] the manner in which a particular lineup is conducted may make it suggestive in the *Stovall* sense. Similarly, as the Court concluded in *Simmons v. United States*,[8] in some circumstances a photographic array may be suggestive.

Assuming suggestive circumstances, the question then is whether they were impermissible or unnecessary. The Court gave a negative answer in *Stovall*, quoting the following language from the lower court's decision in support of the conclusion that "an immediate hospital confrontation was imperative":

> Here was the only person in the world who could possibly exonerate Stovall. Her words, and only her words, "He is not the man" could have resulted in freedom for Stovall. The hospital was not far distant from the courthouse and jail. No one knew how long Mrs. Behrendt might live. Faced with the responsibility of identifying the attacker, with the need for immediate action

---

3. 388 U.S. 293, 87 S.Ct. 1967, 18 L.Ed.2d 1199 (1967).

4. On retroactivity, see § 2.10.

5. Simmons v. United States, 390 U.S. 377, 88 S.Ct. 967, 19 L.Ed.2d 1247 (1968).

6. Neil v. Biggers, 409 U.S. 188, 93 S.Ct. 375, 34 L.Ed.2d 401 (1972).

7. 394 U.S. 440, 89 S.Ct. 1127, 22 L.Ed.2d 402 (1969).

8. 390 U.S. 377, 88 S.Ct. 967, 19 L.Ed.2d 1247 (1968).

and with the knowledge that Mrs. Behrendt could not visit the jail, the police followed the only feasible procedure and took Stovall to the hospital room. Under these circumstances, the usual police station line-up, which Stovall now argues he should have had, was out of the question.

Although the *Stovall* Court's conclusion that the law enforcement authorities in that case were confronted with an emergency is open to question,[9] as is the Court's assumption that less suggestive identification procedures could not have been resorted to at the hospital, the lower courts have usually applied the *Stovall* necessity analysis broadly. Many cases have upheld hospital room showups where there has been a serious injury to the victim or witness or to the defendant; even when it appears that the hospitalized person will recover, such a procedure has been justified merely because a period of extended hospitalization lies ahead. Some courts, however, have been more demanding and thus find hospital showups unnecessary if no immediate danger of death to the suspect or witness exists.

A somewhat different kind of emergency was recognized by the Court in the *Simmons* case. The court noted that

> it is not suggested that it was unnecessary for the FBI to resort to photographic identification in this instance. A serious felony had been committed. The perpetrators were still at large. The inconclusive clues which law enforcement officials possessed led to Andrews and Simmons. It was essential for the FBI agents swiftly to determine whether they were on the right track, so that they could properly deploy their forces in Chicago and, if necessary, alert officials in other cities. The justification for this method of procedure was hardly less compelling than that

which we found to justify the "one-man lineup" in *Stovall v. Denno.*

The *Simmons* notion that suggestive procedures may be necessary when there is a need for law enforcement officials "to determine whether they were on the right track" has most often been applied by lower courts to justify identification procedures conducted within several hours of the crime. Perhaps because the Supreme Court in *Simmons* went on to discuss the fact that in the circumstances there present the chances of misidentification were slight, these lower court cases typically emphasize the reliability of the identification as well. These cases often give the impression, though the point is not articulated, that the finding of a need for immediate identification is balanced against the unreliability factor, in the sense that a higher risk of error will be tolerated when there was a strong need to conduct the identification procedure at that time.

Another type of case involves the so-called "accidental" showup, not planned by the police, as where a witness just happens to see the defendant in custody in the corridors of the courthouse or at the police station. Some courts seem to take the view that no due process issue exists in such circumstances, apparently because the confrontation was not due to the fault of the police or prosecutor. But this appears to be an unwarranted broadening of the *Stovall–Simmons* exception, for the mere fact that the confrontation was not deliberate does not mean that it was necessary. Perhaps because of doubts about the legitimacy of this extension, the courts frequently proceed to the next step of assessing these "accidental" showups in terms of their unreliability.

In *Neil v. Biggers,*[10] the Court found it unnecessary to decide "whether, as intimated by

---

9. As the dissenters in the court of appeals decision, 355 F.2d 731 (2d Cir.1966), noted, the argument that law enforcement officials were confronted with an emergency "ignores the huge amount of circumstantial identification the excellent police investigation had produced; moreover, if the state officials were motivated [by] solicitude [for Stovall], the natural course would have been to ask Stovall whether he wanted to go. The emergency argument fails both on the facts and on the law. * * * If Mrs. Behrendt's condition had been as serious as my brothers suppose,

nothing prevented the prosecutor from informing the state district judge at the preliminary hearing that Stovall had to be taken immediately before her, and suggesting that counsel be assigned forthwith for the limited purpose of advising him in that regard—rather than standing silent when Stovall told the judge of his desire to have counsel and then carting him off to a confrontation by the victim which counsel might have done something to mitigate."

10. 409 U.S. 188, 93 S.Ct. 375, 34 L.Ed.2d 401 (1972)

the District Court, unnecessary suggestiveness alone requires the exclusion of evidence." But the Court recognized that such a result might be explained on grounds similar to the Fourth Amendment and *Miranda* exclusionary rules, namely, to induce the police to follow proper procedures in the future. Such a per se rule was later rejected in *Manson v. Brathwaite*[11] in favor of a "more lenient" test based on the "totality of the circumstances":

> The *per se* rule * * * goes too far [in furnishing protection against the use of unreliable eyewitness testimony] since its application automatically and peremptorily, and without consideration of alleviating factors, keeps evidence from the jury that is reliable and relevant.
>
> * * * Although the *per se* approach has the more significant deterrent effect, the totality approach also has an influence on police behavior. The police will guard against unnecessarily suggestive procedures under the totality rule, as well as the *per se* one, for fear that their actions will lead to the exclusion of identifications as unreliable.
>
> The third factor is the effect on the administration of justice. Here the *per se* approach suffers serious drawbacks. [I]n those cases in which the admission of identification evidence is error under the *per se* approach but not under the totality approach—cases in which the identification is reliable despite an unnecessarily suggestive identification procedure—reversal is a Draconian sanction. Certainly, inflexible rules of exclusion, that may frustrate rather than promote justice, have not been viewed recently by this Court with unlimited enthusiasm.

The two dissenters in *Manson* objected that there were "two significant distinctions" between the per se rule being advocated and other exclusionary rules: (1) the evidence suppressed is not "forever lost," as "when a prosecuting attorney learns that there has been a suggestive confrontation, he can easily arrange another lineup conducted under scrupulously fair conditions"; and (2) the exclusion is not of "relevant and usually reliable evidence," as exclusion "both protects the integrity of the truth-seeking function of the trial and discourages police use of needlessly inaccurate and ineffective investigatory methods." This reasoning takes on added appeal when it is considered, as noted below, that lower courts have applied the risk of misidentification element of the *Stovall* rule in such a way that due process violations are seldom found to exist.

(c) The Risk of Misidentification Element. If, as the Court has made clear, unnecessary suggestiveness "without more does not violate due process,"[12] then it might be thought that the unreliability of the pretrial identification or the trial identification, whichever is being challenged, must be established by the defendant as part of his burden to show that his constitutional rights have been violated. However, the courts, though seldom speaking to the issue, have been inclined to allocate the burden of showing reliability to the prosecution. As one court explained: "Having utilized an unfair means to establish the defendant's guilt, the State must show that the defendant was not harmed by its own transgression."[13]

When the question is the reliability of the in-court identification, the issue is phrased in terms of whether the earlier suggestive procedure created "a very substantial likelihood of irreparable misidentification."[14] When, on the other hand, the question is the reliability of the earlier identification occurring in the context of the unnecessarily suggestive procedure, the standard is quite similar; the same language, "with the deletion of 'irreparable,' "[15] is utilized. It is unlikely but theoretically possible that there could be a risk of misidentification which was substantial but not irreparable, meaning that in a particular case applying the *Stovall* rule the pretrial identification would

---

11. 432 U.S. 98, 97 S.Ct. 2243, 53 L.Ed.2d 140 (1977).

12. Neil v. Biggers, 409 U.S. 188, 93 S.Ct. 375, 34 L.Ed.2d 401 (1972).

13. State v. Cefalo, 396 A.2d 233 (Me.1979).

14. Simmons v. United States, 390 U.S. 377, 88 S.Ct. 967, 19 L.Ed.2d 1247 (1968).

15. Neil v. Biggers, 409 U.S. 188, 93 S.Ct. 375, 34 L.Ed.2d 401 (1972).

be suppressed but not the at-trial identification by the same person. Both issues necessitate evaluation of "the totality of the circumstances," and the factors to be considered, the Court explained in *Manson,*

> include the opportunity of the witness to view the criminal at the time of the crime, the witness' degree of attention, the accuracy of his prior description of the criminal, the level of certainty demonstrated at the confrontation, and the time between the crime and the confrontation. Against these factors is to be weighed the corrupting effects of the suggestive evidence itself.

These and similar factors have been utilized by the lower courts. Tending to support a finding of reliability is the fact that the witness had a clear or extended opportunity to view the perpetrator of the crime, that the witness had prior knowledge of the perpetrator's identity, that the witness had previously given an accurate description, that the identification was made promptly after the crime, that the circumstances prompted a high degree of attention by the witness at the time of the crime, or that the witness was certain in his identification. On the other hand, a finding of unreliability is somewhat more likely if the witness had a limited opportunity for observation, gave an earlier conflicting description, failed to identify the defendant on a prior occasion, or was under such stress at the time of the crime as to have his perceptions distorted. Generally, however, these lower court cases show that a *Stovall* due process violation will not be found except in outrageous situations and that a variety of very suggestive lineup procedures are being upheld. This is particularly worrisome when it is considered that the *Manson* reliability test is not very demanding in the first place and is not in all respects in accord with established psychological knowledge[16] of the phenomenon of eyewitness identification. The "level of certainty demonstrated at the confrontation" by the witness, for example, is not a valid indicator of the accuracy of the recollection. Unrelated evidence corroborating defendant's guilt has no bearing on an

identification's reliability (but can be considered in determining whether identification resulting from unnecessarily suggestive procedures was harmless error).

(d) Lineups. It may generally be said that lineups are the most useful and least questionable witness identification procedure. They are obviously less suggestive than one-man show-ups, and are also more reliable than photographic identifications. Yet not every lineup is free from the danger of suggestive procedures. An apt illustration of a due process violation in a lineup identification is provided by *Foster v. California.*[17] In that case, the defendant was convicted of robbing a Western Union office. The manager viewed a police station lineup in which the defendant was placed with two other men who were half a foot shorter and was the only one wearing a leather jacket similar to that worn by the robber. When this did not lead to positive identification, the police permitted a one-on-one confrontation, but the witness's identification was still tentative. Ten days later another lineup was arranged at which defendant was the only person who had also appeared in the first lineup, and at last the manager was "convinced" that defendant was the man. The Supreme Court quite properly concluded that "the suggestive elements in this identification procedure made it all but inevitable" that the suspect would be identified "whether or not he was in fact 'the man.'" In effect, the police repeatedly said to the witness, '*This* is the man.'"

Unfortunately, most courts have not applied the due process test this vigorously and thus have often held suggestive lineups not violative of due process under the ambiguous "totality of the circumstances" approach. For example, while commentators agree that lineups should contain about six similar participants, lower courts have upheld lineups of as few as three people. And while it seems obvious that similarity of race, physical features, size, age and dress of lineup participants is a prerequisite to avoidance of suggestion, courts have been reluctant to find due process violations

---

16. See § 7.1(b).

17. 394 U.S. 440, 89 S.Ct. 1127, 22 L.Ed.2d 402 (1969).

even where there were significant dissimilarities of appearance or dress. Suggestive police statements, photographic displays or confrontations with the suspect occurring before the actual lineup can cast serious doubt upon the reliability of the witness' subsequent identification. When a lineup has failed to result in a successful identification, a flagrant form of police suggestion, as in *Foster,* has been the viewing of another lineup in which the suspect reappears. Courts have held, however, that multiple confrontations do not necessarily violate due process. When a suspect has an unusual physical characteristic or defect that was included in the witness's earlier description, it is desirable that the noticeable abnormality be either concealed or duplicated by other members of the lineup, but identification procedures in which the abnormality was apparent have often been upheld.

(e) Use of Pictures. Several factors bear upon the suggestiveness of photographic identification procedures. Certainly a photographic array should "so far as practicable include a reasonable number of persons similar to any person then suspected whose likeness is included in the array." As the number of photographs displayed decreases the suggestivity increases, and obviously displaying a single photograph to a witness is very suggestive. Still, courts have been reluctant to hold that display of a single photograph violates due process, frequently relying on the witness's prior opportunity to view the defendant. Though certainly the array should not be arranged so that a particular individual stands out, courts have generally not found violations of due process simply because the contents of an array point to a particular suspect. Even if the size, color, or repetitious nature of photographs of suspects are not suggestive by themselves, the manner of presentation by the police may indicate to the witness exactly which person is suspected by the police. Yet an improper remark by a police officer will not necessarily be viewed as a due process violation, nor will the use of successive photo arrays in which only the defendant's picture reappears. In short, while

photographic identifications are generally less reliable than lineup identifications and thus deserving of greater precautions to ensure maximum reliability, the courts have generally been unsympathetic to defendants attacking the suggestiveness of photographic identification procedures.

(f) One–Man Showups. As the Supreme Court acknowledged in *Stovall,* "[t]he practice of showing suspects singly to persons for the purpose of identification, and not as part of a lineup, has been widely condemned." This would suggest that showups should be deemed to violate due process absent the most imperative circumstances, but courts generally are not this demanding. Showups are commonly permitted when they occur within several hours of the crime; the two justifications given are the need for quick solution of the crime and the desirability of fresh, accurate identification by eyewitnesses. This may be convincing in the case of an on-the-scene identification, but courts have been inclined also to uphold the showup procedure when it does not take place at the scene of the crime and when it occurs many hours after the occurrence of the crime. Similarly, courts have been reluctant to hold that a showup violates due process when the confrontation is accidental, when some sort of emergency exists, when the suspect is unknown or at large, or when external factors "prove" the accuracy of the identification. Here as well, therefore, courts have relied upon the vagueness of the "totality of the circumstances" test to brush over substantial due process claims.

(g) In–Court Identifications. If a one-on-one confrontation at the police station is highly suggestive, then surely such a confrontation in court is the most suggestive situation of all, for the witness is given an even stronger impression that the authorities are already satisfied that they have the right man. As the Supreme Court declared in *Moore v. Illinois,*[18] where after defendant was led to the bench for his preliminary hearing the rape victim was called upon to make her first corporeal identi-

18.   434 U.S. 220, 98 S.Ct. 458, 54 L.Ed.2d 424 (1977).

fication of him, it "is difficult to imagine a more suggestive manner in which to present a suspect to a witness for their critical first confrontation than was employed in this case." The due process issue was not before the Court in *Moore,* and thus the Court declined to state exactly what must be done to avoid such a situation.

The Court did, however, mention some ways in which the suggestiveness might have been prevented had defendant been represented by counsel. "For example, counsel could have requested that the hearing be postponed until a lineup could be arranged at which the victim would view petitioner in a less suggestive setting." A leading case on this point is *Evans v. Superior Court,*[19] where the court held that due process requires the prosecution to honor a defense request for a lineup where "eyewitness identification is shown to be a material issue and there exists a reasonable likelihood of a mistaken identification which a lineup would tend to resolve." The court in *Evans* reasoned that "[b]ecause the People are in a position to compel a lineup and utilize what favorable evidence is derived therefrom, fairness requires that the accused be given a reciprocal right to discover and utilize contrary evidence." Other decisions are also to be found holding that a defense request for a lineup should have been granted, although generally courts are inclined to say merely that whether such relief is called for is left to the trial court's discretion.

The Court in *Moore* also noted that "counsel could have asked that the victim be excused from the courtroom while the charges were read and the evidence against petitioner was recited, and that petitioner be seated with other people in the audience when the victim attempted an identification." Here as well, the prevailing view is to leave the matter largely within the trial judge's discretion. This is surprising, as an identification more unreliable than the witness's familiar selection of the conspicuous defendant is difficult to imagine.

Perhaps because of the fact that it is within the judge's discretion whether to grant such requests, defense counsel have on occasion resorted to self-help, sometimes with unfortunate consequences. In a case in which the defense attorney used a decoy without the trial judge's knowledge or approval, the decoy was convicted and temporarily jailed. Defense counsel's act of substituting another person for the defendant at counsel table without the court's permission or knowledge has been viewed as a violation of ethical standards and an obstruction of justice punishable by criminal contempt.

(h) The "Repeal" of the Right. As a part of the Omnibus Crime Control and Safe Streets Act of 1968, Congress in its wisdom adopted this provision: "The testimony of a witness that he saw the accused commit or participate in the commission of the crime for which the accused is being tried shall be admissible in evidence in a criminal prosecution in any trial court ordained and established under article III of the Constitution of the United States."[20] Just as Congress cannot by such an act destroy the constitutional right to counsel under the *Wade–Gilbert* rule,[21] it surely cannot do away with a defendant's right under *Stovall* not to be convicted on the basis of an identification so unreliable as to violate due process.

§ 7.5   Additional Possible Safeguards

(a) Jury Instructions. Because the *Wade* and *Stovall* rules have not resulted in the substantial elimination of the danger of unrealistic eyewitness identification, it is appropriate to consider other possible safeguards such as jury instructions. Instructions cannot make the identifications any more reliable, but hopefully they can alert the jury to the necessity for a most careful assessment of identification evidence. In *United States v. Telfaire,*[1] the court set out an instruction for use in future identification cases. It states in part:

19.   11 Cal.3d 617, 114 Cal.Rptr. 121, 522 P.2d 681 (1974).

20.   18 U.S.C.A. § 3501.

21.   See § 7.3(g).

§ 7.5

1.   469 F.2d 552 (D.C.Cir.1972).

Identification testimony is an expression of belief or impression by the witness. Its value depends on the opportunity the witness had to observe the offender at the time of the offense and to make a reliable identification later.

In appraising the identification testimony of a witness, you should consider the following:

(1) Are you convinced that the witness had the capacity and an adequate opportunity to observe the offender?

Whether the witness had an adequate opportunity to observe the offender at the time of the offense will be affected by such matters as how long or short a time was available, how far or close the witness was, how good were lighting conditions, whether the witness had had occasion to see or know the person in the past. * * *

(2) Are you satisfied that the identification made by the witness subsequent to the offense was the product of his own recollection? You may take into account both the strength of the identification, and the circumstances under which the identification was made.

If the identification by the witness may have been influenced by the circumstances under which the defendant was presented to him for identification, you should scrutinize the identification with great care. You may also consider the length of time that lapsed between the occurrence of the crime and the next opportunity of the witness to see defendant, as a factor bearing on the reliability of the identification. * * *

(3) You may take into account any occasions in which the witness failed to make an identification of defendant, or made an identification that was inconsistent with his identification at trial.

(4) Finally, you must consider the credibility of each identification witness in the same way as any other witness, consider whether he is truthful, and consider whether he had the capacity and opportunity to make a reliable observation on the matter covered in his testimony.

I again emphasize that the burden of proof on the prosecutor extends to every element of the crime charged, and this specifically includes the burden of proving beyond a reasonable doubt the identity of the defendant as the perpetrator of the crime with which he stands charged. If after examining the testimony, you have a reasonable doubt as to the accuracy of the identification, you must find the defendant not guilty.

A few other federal circuits have likewise strongly recommended that such an instruction be given when identification is a key issue in the case, while others have recommended such a special instruction in those circumstances but leave the trial judge with considerable discretion in deciding whether to use the instruction. Some state courts also utilize an instruction like that in *Telfaire,* while some others take the view that such an instruction is inappropriate because the matter is best left to final argument by the parties. Also, there is some authority that an instruction regarding the risks of cross-racial identification should be given.

(b) Expert Testimony. Some have argued that in a case in which eyewitness testimony is of central importance, the defendant should be entitled to have a psychologist testify in his behalf on such circumstances as may be present in the particular case (e.g., presence of stress or passage of time, cross-racial or cross-ethnic identification) that psychological research has shown may cast doubt upon an eyewitness identification. But the appellate cases typically say that whether to receive such expert testimony lies within the sound discretion of the trial court. In holding that the trial judge acted within the scope of his discretion in not permitting such testimony, these cases make such assertions as that work in the field is not sufficiently developed, that the testimony would invade the province of the jury or have undue influence upon the jury, that the undue consumption of time would substantially outweigh its probative value, and that what the expert has to offer can be effectively communicated to the jury by probing questioning of the identification witnesses. In recent years, however, there has been some-what greater willingness by trial courts to receive such evidence.

(c) Improved Police Procedures. *Wade* and *Stovall* mark only the constitutional mini-mum of what must be done rather than the maximum of what should be done to enhance the reliability of eyewitness identifications. As some police agencies have discovered, this is an area in which the existence of clear regula-tions, in the formulation of which law enforce-ment agencies have themselves participated, are especially beneficial. Setting clear and rea-sonable standards for each type of identifica-tion procedure can be of great benefit to those suspected of crime and also those charged with the responsibility of enforcing the law. "There are, thus, real benefits to be realized by the prosecution, and the public it represents, in presenting evidence of a pretrial identification made under conditions which vouch for its fairness, and hence, its probable accuracy."[2] Beyond this, improvements in police investiga-tive activities directed toward uncovering evi-dence corroborating eyewitness identifications are especially desirable.

As the body of scientific knowledge in this area has grown over recent decades, the gap between the procedures used by most police forces and procedures demonstrated by the eyewitness research to produce superior eye-witness evidence became increasingly obvious. Consequently, psychologists have intensified their efforts to influence police identification procedures, culminating in the publication of various proposed "guidelines" for law enforce-ment. The recommendations most often made are: (1) The witness should be instructed that the actual perpetrator may or may not be in the lineup or photo array, and that conse-quently they should not feel that they have to make an identification. (2) The lineup or photo array should be composed in such a way that the suspect does not unduly stand out. (3) A clear statement should be taken from the wit-ness at the time of identification, and prior to any feedback, indicating the degree of confi-dence by the witness that the person identified is the perpetrator. (4) The person conducting the lineup or photo array should not know the identity of the suspect. (5) Mock witnesses should be used to test the neutrality of the lineup or photo array. (6) Sequential rather than simultaneous identification procedures should be used.

---

2. McGowan, Constitutional Interpretation and Crimi-nal Identification, 12 Wm. & Mary L.Rev. 235, 241 (1970).

Chapter 8

GRAND JURY INVESTIGATION

Table of Sections

§ 8.1 Dual Functions of the Grand Jury

(a) The Traditional Grand Jury. The common law grand jury is said to constitute both "the shield and the sword" of the American criminal justice process. It is likened to a shield in its performance as a screening agency interposed between the government and the individual. In deciding whether to issue an indictment, the grand jury reviews the government's evidence and, in effect, screens the prosecutor's decision to charge. By refusing to indict when the evidence is insufficient or the prosecution otherwise appears unjust, the grand jury is said to "function as a shield, standing between the accuser and the accused, protecting the individual citizen against oppressive and unfounded government prosecution." The grand jury is likened to a sword in its performance as an investigative body. Here the grand jury is not reviewing cases that the prosecutor believes to be ready for prosecution, but rather examining situations that are still at the inquiry stage. Utilizing its investigative authority, the grand jury uncovers evidence not previously available to the prosecution, and thereby provides the sword that enables the government to secure convictions that might otherwise not be obtained.

In the federal system and all but two states, statutes authorize the impanelment of grand juries with the authority to perform the dual functions of the traditional grand jury. However, that authority is not necessarily utilized. As discussed in § 15.1(g), twenty-eight states allow all felony prosecutions to be brought by prosecutor's information, and in these states, the regular use of the grand jury to screen felony charges (and issue indictments) largely has been discarded. In most of these "information states," as well as all states still requiring prosecution by indictment, the grand jury continues to be used as an investigatory tool. In a small group of information states (and in individual counties in many other information states), the discarding of grand jury screening has led to the demise of investigations by grand juries as well; grand juries have not been impaneled for any purpose for at least a few decades. In the federal system, the character of the crimes being investigated naturally leads to frequent use of the grand jury for investigative purposes. Even here, however, as is true of indictment jurisdictions generally, grand juries are more frequently used simply to screen cases fully investigated by the prosecution, than to first investigate possible criminality and then decide whether to indict.

This chapter will focus on the law governing the investigative authority of the traditional grand jury; the law governing the screening function of that grand jury is considered in Chapter 15. It should be kept in mind that the two roles of the grand jury often combine in shaping the law governing grand jury practices. Considered in this chapter are the aspects of grand jury structure and authority that bear particularly on the investigative function of the grand jury, but quite often these features are designed also to promote the grand jury's screening role. Grand jury secrecy, for example, strengthens the investigative function by safeguarding witnesses against possible reprisals from those against whom they testify, but it also is designed to serve the screening function by protecting the innocent suspect whom the grand jury refuses to charge.

(b) Special Grand Juries. Many jurisdictions have special grand juries, authorized primarily for use in investigations. In most instances, these special grand juries operate under the same legal standards as regular grand juries, but have certain structural features that enhance their capacity to conduct investigations. Thus, the special grand jury may have a longer term (as is the case of federal grand juries impaneled under the Organized Crime Control Act rather than Federal Rule 6), or may have broader jurisdiction (as in the case of statewide grand juries impaneled on request of the State Attorney General). In some states, the special grand juries are impaneled only on a special showing of investigatory need with respect to an identified crime or class of crimes. In general, special grand juries have the authority to indict as to offenses investigated, but in a few states they are limited to issuing what amounts to complaints, subject to the same screening as other complaints (e.g., preliminary hearings) before being converted to charging instruments.

(c) Alternative Procedures. The primary investigative tool of the grand jury investigation is the subpoena. Many jurisdictions authorize the prosecutor, the court, or one or more governmental agencies to utilize subpoena authority to conduct criminal investigations. While such investigations lack many of the key characteristics (particularly lay participation and secrecy) that shape the law of grand jury investigations, their use of the subpoena power renders relevant several aspects of that law. Thus, the discussion in §§ 8.10–8.14 of the application of the privilege against self-incrimination largely applies as well to self-incrimination objections to an investigatory subpoena issued as part of a judicial inquest, a prosecutor's investigation, or an agency investigation. So too the Fourth Amendment prohibition of an overly broad subpoenas duces tecum (see § 8.7) applies as well to subpoenas duces tecum issued in those investigations.

§ 8.2 Historical Development

The law governing the grand jury has been strongly influenced by the historical development of that institution initially in England and later in this country. What follows is a brief summary of the highlights of that history as they relate to the dual functions of the grand jury. These highlights have contributed substantially to the image of the grand jury as an independent body that reflects the concerns of the community both in precluding prosecutions the community views as unjust and in uncovering crimes suspected by the community but unsuccessfully investigated by the police. This perception of the grand jury as the "people's panel" has provided, in turn, the foundation for much of the grand jury's common law authority. So too, legislative and judicial efforts to limit that authority largely have been fueled by challenges to that image, which

often offer a different view of these same historical highlights.

(a) English Origins. The grand jury commonly is traced back to the Assize of Clarendon, issued in 1166. The Assize provided for "an inquiry" to be made in each community by twelve of its "good and lawful" men. Those jurors were to be put under oath and questioned by the itinerant justices of the peace or the sheriff. It was the obligation of the jurors to accuse all they suspected, and those accused were then to be subjected to trial by ordeal. The Assize clearly was designed not to provide protection for those suspected of crime, but rather to lend assistance to government officials in the apprehension of criminals. The jurors were familiar with the local scene and could present charges that otherwise might not be known by the Crown's representatives. Any hesitancy the jurors might have in bringing accusations against their neighbors would be overcome by the substantial fines the jurors faced for failing to bring forward any known offense.

By the end of the fourteenth century the English had turned to trial by jury rather than by ordeal and the original jury had been divided into two separate juries. The trial of guilt was before a twelve-person petit jury, and the accusatory jury was expanded to twenty-four persons, chosen from the entire county (eventually reduced to twenty-three, to avoid the problem of ties in voting). At this point, the accusatory jury (which came to be known as the "grand jury") remained a body essentially designed to assist the Crown in ferreting out criminals. Accusations issued by the grand jury were initiated either by the jurors themselves, acting on the basis of their own knowledge, by private complainants, or by a representative of the Crown, typically a justice of the peace, who produced witnesses to testify before the grand jury in support of a particular charge. When the accusation was initiated by the jury itself, the formal charge filed with the court was described as a "presentment." When the accusation stemmed from a case placed before the jury by the Crown's representative, the grand jury's charging document was described as an "indictment." The Crown's representative ordinarily would place a proposed indictment before the grand jury, and if the grand jury found the Crown's evidence sufficient to proceed, it issued the indictment, declaring it to be a "true bill." If the jury concluded that the evidence was insufficient, it returned a finding of *ignoramus* ("we ignore it"), or, in later years, "no bill."

Over the next few centuries, the grand jury began to assume a significant degree of independence. Grand juries developed the custom of hearing witnesses privately in their chambers and the courts no longer required the grand jurors to explain their reasons for refusing to indict. The secrecy of the hearings and deliberation was said to provide both jurors and witnesses protection against retribution from displeased royal officials. In the late seventeenth century, a period of great upheaval in Britain, the grand jury's newly found independence was put to its severest test. The Crown brought considerable pressure upon grand juries to indict noted supporters of the Protestant cause. Grand juries resisted that pressure in several cases, including two that attracted widespread public attention. Grand juries refused to indict Stephen Colledge and the Earl of Shaftesbury, both accused of high treason, notwithstanding the Crown's insistence that its evidence be presented in open court in contravention of the established custom. Although, the Crown later obtained an indictment against College from a different grand jury, the *Shaftesbury* and *Colledge* cases led to the grand jury being widely celebrated as a "bulwark against the oppression and despotism of the Crown." During the same period, grand juries also achieved some prominence in fighting governmental corruption, as they issued presentments based upon their inquiries into the misconduct of minor officials in matters of local administration. Thus, by the end of the century, the English grand jury had emerged, as one article put it, as "a virtual Janus who, one moment acted as the vigilant prosecutor and the next as the defender of those who were unjustly accused."

(b) Developments in the United States. Along with other elements of the English law, the grand jury was adopted as part of the criminal justice process in the American colonies. The grand jury soon developed, however, into an important vehicle of colonial government that extended beyond the enforcement of the criminal law. The English grand jury had occasionally used its power of presentment to criticize action or inaction of government officials that fell short of criminal misconduct. The American grand juries made extensive use of that authority, and their presentment reports became the primary vehicle for the expression of the complaints of the citizenry on a wide range of matters. As community dissatisfaction with England's colonial policies grew stronger, these reports were most frequently critical of the Crown's officials in America. At the same time, colonial grand juries were more frequently at odds with royal officials as to appropriate cases for criminal prosecution. Thus, the infamous prosecution of John Peter Zenger for seditious libel was brought by prosecutor's information because colonial grand juries twice refused to issue requested indictments. On the other side, grand juries issued criminal presentments against various royal officials, including British soldiers, on which the Crown frequently refused to proceed. The British sought to eliminate their grand jury difficulties by packing the grand juries with citizens sympathetic to their position, but this tactic proved difficult as jurors generally were appointed at town meetings controlled by community leaders.

As a result of its opposition to the British, the grand jury emerged from the American Revolution with increased prestige. The constitutions of almost all of the original states required that felony prosecutions be brought by grand jury indictment or presentment, and once it was decided to add a Bill of Rights to the federal constitution, the inclusion of such a requirement in the Fifth Amendment was accepted without controversy. In the post-revolutionary period, there were several notable instances in which grand juries rejected highly partisan indictments (as in the initial attempts to prosecute Aaron Burr), although there were others in which grand juries readily supported such indictments (as in various Sedition Act prosecutions brought against Republican publishers). At the same time grand juries also continued to pursue on their own initiative a "public watchdog" function, especially in the western territories. Grand juries actively reviewed a wide range of grievances presented by citizens, and often conducted "searching investigations into corruption in government or widespread evasion of the laws."

During the 1820s, Jeremy Bentham vigorously criticized the English grand jury, claiming that it was both unrepresentative and inefficient. The latter criticism caught hold in the United States, particularly in the sparsely populated states. The requirement that all felony prosecutions be instituted by indictment was criticized as cumbersome, costly, and unnecessary to protect the innocent. In 1859, Michigan became the first state to grant prosecutors the option of proceeding either by grand jury indictment or by a prosecutor's information. Several states followed Michigan's lead, and in 1884, the constitutionality of this shift from indictment to information was upheld by the Supreme Court. There followed a gradual movement of the majority of the states to prosecution by information, so that today only eighteen states continue to grant the defendant a right to grand jury screening in all felony cases (although four others still require an indictment for capital and/or life-imprisonment offenses). No state, however, has gone as far as England, which finally heeded Bentham's advice and abolished the grand jury. Among those states which allow prosecution by information, all but two still authorize the optional use of the grand jury indictment, and all states provide for the continued use of the investigative grand jury (although, as discussed in § 8.1(a), not all make use of that authority).

During the same period in which a majority of the states moved to prosecution by information, grand juries were active in both information and indictment states in the investigation of corruption in local government. In several instances, the resulting indictments were so widespread as to unseat entire municipal administrations. As might be expected, local prosecutors were sometimes less than enthusiastic in cooperating with such investigations.

Grand juries responded by seeking outside help (usually through court appointment of a special prosecutor) or by simply pushing forward against the wishes of a reluctant prosecutor. The most famous of these "runaway" grand jury investigations was the mid–1930s New York investigation of "racketeering" offenses, which led to the appointment of special prosecutor Thomas E. Dewey. The exploits of Dewey and his "racket busters" inspired a series of runaway grand jury investigations throughout the country and established the reputation of the grand jury as the nation's number one "instrument of discovery against organized crime." In later years, federal grand jury investigations of a variety of white collar crimes helped the grand jury establish a similar reputation in that field and investigations of government corruption at every level further enhanced its image as the community's "watchdog over government." At the same time, the grand jury's reputation was sullied by investigations that suggested partisan political use of the grand jury's investigative authority—such as highly publicized investigations of public figures that led to damaging accusations that could not be supported at trial and the 1960s investigations of various "radical" groups, which often seemed to be directed more toward harassment than producing supportable indictments. This led in various states to the adoption of reform legislation that enhanced the rights of grand jury witnesses. More expansive regulation was proposed for the federal system, but failed to gain legislative support (although the Justice Department did adopt as internal policy several requirements protective of witnesses and targets).

(c) Relevance of History. As might be expected, the critics and supporters of the investigative grand jury are divided over the lessons to be drawn from the history of that institution. They disagree in particular on two issues: (1) whether that history establishes an accommodation, particularly at the time of the adoption of the federal constitution, between the broad investigatory authority of the grand jury and the accusatory framework of American criminal procedure, and (2) whether that broad investigatory authority, if granted to the early American grand juries, was tied to a capacity for its independent exercise that has been lost with the expansion of the role of police and prosecutor in criminal investigations.

The grand jury investigation is frequently described as introducing an "inquisitorial element" into a criminal justice system that is basically accusatorial. Critics argue that the grand jury's investigative authority should therefore be viewed as an anomaly and kept within narrow confines by close judicial supervision. They recognize that this position faces difficulties if history reveals that the grand jury inquest was accepted from the outset as an institution that coexisted with the accusatorial elements of the Anglo–American criminal justice process. The critics argue, however, that a careful reading of the history of the grand jury reveals no such accommodation. First, they note, the early grand juries did not frequently exercise the basic element of its modern investigative authority—its power to compel testimony—but instead relied primarily upon information known to the jurors or the voluntary testimony of aggrieved persons. Secondly, they argue, the investigative role of the grand jury was not critical to its initial acceptance in this country. It was the shielding role of the grand jury that earned it a place in the Bill of Rights and the early state constitutions. The grand jury's investigatory role was then viewed as entirely secondary and not necessarily distinct from its screening role. Today, it is argued, the significance of the two roles has been reversed.

Supporters of the grand jury respond that the early history of the grand jury clearly establishes the legitimacy of its extensive investigative authority. The power of the grand jury to compel testimony was recognized well before the adoption of the Constitution and was used in some of the most notable grand jury inquests. At the time of the Constitution's adoption, the grand jury was a revered institution not simply because it served as a buffer between the state and the individual, but equally for its service as a watchdog against public corruption and its capacity to ferret out criminal activity that local officials either chose to ignore or were unable to investigate. The importance of this investigative authority was implicitly recognized, it is argued, in constitutional and statutory provisions authorizing the institution of prosecution by presentment as well as indictment.

With few exceptions, American courts have accepted the position that the history of the grand jury provides a solid foundation for its broad investigative authority. The Supreme Court's discussion of that authority in *Blair v. United States*[1] is typical. The Court there noted that the grand jury's authority to resort to compulsory process had been recognized in England as early as 1612, and the inquisitorial function of the grand jury was well established at the time of the Constitution's adoption. Both the Fifth Amendment and the earliest federal statutes recognized an investigative authority of the grand jury that included the "same powers that pertained to its British prototype." The Supreme Court would not view that authority with suspicion and subject it to new limitations. The grand jury, the Court concluded, "is a grand inquest, a body with powers of investigation and inquisition, the scope of whose inquiries is not to be limited narrowly by questions of propriety or forecasts of the probable result of the investigation."

Critics of the grand jury contend that, even if a broad investigative authority is sanctioned by history, the same historical sources also indicate that such authority was tied to an assumption of substantial grand jury independence. That assumption, they continue, is contrary to current practice, and the eighteenth century prototype of the grand jury therefore is no longer relevant. Today, the critics argue, the sweeping powers of the grand jury are exercised in reality by the prosecutor alone. Working with the police, the prosecutor determines what witnesses will be called and when they will appear. The prosecutor examines the witnesses and advises the grand jury on the

§ 8.2

1. 250 U.S. 273, 39 S.Ct. 468, 63 L.Ed. 979 (1919).

validity of any legal objections the witnesses might present. If a witness refuses to comply with a subpoena, it is the prosecutor who seeks a contempt citation. If a witness refuses to testify on grounds of self-incrimination, it is the prosecutor who determines whether an immunity grant will be obtained. The grand jury, it is argued, must almost invariably look to the prosecutor's leadership, as the prosecutor has the expertise, and the supplementary resources, needed for success in their venture.

The critics argue that this change in the nature of the investigative grand jury, which has converted it into the "prosecutor's puppet," requires a corresponding change in judicial attitudes. The courts should not, they argue, feel bound by precedent that was developed during an era when grand juries were independent bodies. Instead, they should "pull back the veil of history" and subject the power of the grand jury to the same kinds of limitations as are imposed upon other investigative weapons in the government's arsenal (typically exercised by the police).

Supporters of the grand jury readily acknowledge that the prosecutor plays a substantial role in directing today's grand jury investigations. They suggest that this is a beneficial development that makes the investigatory authority more effective and helps to ensure that it is not misused. Moreover, it is noted, this development dates back over one hundred years, preceding many of the decisions that speak most eloquently of the necessary breadth of the grand jury's investigative authority. The key to the historical grant of that authority, they argue, was a legal structure that rendered the government's use of the grand jury's investigative powers subject to the veto of the jurors, who sat as community representatives. That structure has not been substantially altered, and its very presence, the argument continues, serves to hold the prosecutor in check and to distinguish grand jury investigations from investigatory tools granted directly to the prosecutor or the police. The fact that the grand jury only occa-

sionally exercises its power to override the prosecutor does not detract from the significance of that power. The prosecutor must respect the existence of that power and act in a way that he knows, from past experience, will be acceptable to the jurors.

In recent years, courts have been divided as to whether the larger role played by prosecutors in the typical grand jury investigation requires a reexamination of the historical precedents establishing the grand jury's broad investigative authority. The Supreme Court, over some dissents, has continued to accept those precedents. In *United States v. Williams*,[2] its latest major ruling on federal court review of grand jury procedures, the Supreme Court made clear that any major alteration of common law grand jury procedure, as reflected in the "history of the grand jury institution," must come from the legislature, not the judiciary. Other courts have argued that a lesser degree of grand jury independence requires a greater degree of judicial supervision. These courts have urged that the grand jury be treated as being "for all practical purposes" no more than "an investigative and procedural arm of the executive branch of government." Most such statements, however, came from lower federal courts prior to the *Williams* ruling.

§ 8.3   Investigative Advantages

Compared to police investigations, grand jury investigations are expensive, time consuming, and logistically cumbersome. However, the grand jury also offers certain investigative advantages over the police. Those advantages stem mainly from five elements in the grand jury process—(1) subpoena authority backed up by potential contempt sanctions, (2) lay participation, (3) closed proceedings, (4) immunity grants, and (5) grand jury secrecy requirements. For the investigation of most crimes, these aspects of the grand jury process are superfluous. Police investigations work as well and do so at far less cost. There are certain types of cases, however, in which prosecutors are likely to view the grand jury's

---

2. 504 U.S. 36, 112 S.Ct. 1735, 118 L.Ed.2d 352 (1992).

investigatory assistance as either essential or highly desirable, and therefore worth the extra costs of the grand jury process. These are primarily cases in which investigators face one or more of the following tasks: unraveling a complex criminal structure, dealing with victims or other witnesses reluctant to cooperate, obtaining information contained in extensive business records, keeping a continuing investigative effort from the public gaze, or counteracting public suspicion of political manipulation of the investigation. Criminal activities likely to present such investigative problems include governmental corruption (e.g., bribery), misuse of economic power (e.g., price-fixing), and widespread distribution of illegal services (e.g., gambling, money laundering, and loan-sharking).

(a) Subpoena Authority and the Contempt Sanction. The basic investigative advantage of the grand jury stems from its ability to use the subpoena authority of the court that impaneled it. The grand jury may utilize the subpoena duces tecum to obtain tangible evidence and the subpoena ad testificandum to obtain testimony. Both subpoenas are supported by the court's authority to hold in contempt any person who willfully refuses, without legal justification, to comply with a subpoena's directive. That authority encompasses both civil and criminal contempt, although use of the former is far more common than use of the latter.[1] In rare cases, a recalcitrant witness may be subject to both forms of contempt.

(b) Subpoena Ad Testificandum. The grand jury is especially useful in obtaining statements from persons who will not voluntarily furnish information to the police. While an individual has the right to refuse to cooperate with the police, his refusal to comply with a subpoena ad testificandum (commanding him to appear and testify before the grand jury) subjects him to a possible jail sentence for contempt. Faced with that threat, a recalcitrant witness often will have a change of heart and will give the grand jury information that he or she has refused to give to the police. Of course, the recalcitrant witnesses called before the grand jury may rely upon the standard privileges that would also be available at trial. Thus, if the information sought could be incriminating, the recalcitrant witness (unless granted immunity) may still refuse to cooperate by relying on his privilege against self-incrimination. Many persons, however, are unwilling to furnish information to the police, yet will provide that information before the grand jury, without regard to the availability of the privilege, because they feel more comfortable providing information in that setting. Thus, an employee may wish to avoid the appearance of voluntarily assisting police investigating his employer, yet testify freely under the compulsion of a subpoena.

The grand jury subpoena ad testificandum also has the advantage of requiring witnesses to give information under oath. If a witness fails to tell the truth, he may be prosecuted for perjury. Apart from the federal system, a person who gives false information to a police officer ordinarily will not have committed a crime. Accordingly, where a witness might be willing to talk to the police, but also is likely to "shade his story," requiring him to testify before a grand jury may produce more complete and truthful statements. Even where a witness is willing to give an entirely truthful statement to the police, there may be value in requiring him to testify before the grand jury. Once a person has testified under oath, he is likely to think twice about changing his testimony at trial and thereby providing the grounds for a perjury prosecution based on inconsistent sworn statements.

---

§ 8.3

1. Civil contempt is used to coerce the recalcitrant witness into complying with the subpoena. The witness is sentenced to imprisonment or to a fine (which may increase daily), but he may purge himself by complying with the subpoena. It is said that he "carries the keys of the prison in his own pockets." The civil contemnor who refuses to purge himself will remain under sentence until the grand jury completes its term and is discharged. Moreover, if the information that the contemnor possesses is still needed, he may be subpoenaed by a successor grand jury and again held in contempt if he continues to refuse to supply that information.

(c) Subpoena Duces Tecum. The grand jury subpoena duces tecum offers several advantages over the primary device available to the police for obtaining records and physical evidence—the search pursuant to a warrant. Unlike the search warrant, the subpoena duces tecum can issue without a showing of probable cause. Moreover, even where probable cause could be established, there are times when the subpoena will have administrative advantages. For example, there may be a need to seize so many records from various locations that a search would be impractical. With a subpoena duces tecum, the party served may be required to undertake the extensive task of bringing together records from several different locations and sorting through them to collect those covered by the subpoena. At other times, there may be a need to obtain records from uninvolved third parties (e.g., a bank), and a subpoena will be preferred because it will be far less disruptive to the third party's business operations. The subpoena duces tecum also facilitates keeping from the target the grounding of the investigation, as the subpoena may simply identify the documents to be produced, without stating why they are sought. A search warrant, in contrast, requires an affidavit setting forth the probable cause on which the search is based, and preventing its disclosure requires a not readily-available court order sealing the affidavit. Finally, the remedy for a search that turns out to be unconstitutional often is suppression of the evidence seized. Where a subpoena duces tecum is impermissible in scope or issuance, the challenge must be raised prior to the response and the consequence is the quashing of the subpoena. This allows the government to refashion the subpoena to meet the sustained objections, and there is no loss of evidence that could have been obtained through a curable illegality.

(d) Psychological Pressure. The psychological pressure exerted by the grand jury setting also is cited as a factor that frequently enables the grand jury to obtain information from witnesses unwilling to cooperate with the police. Proponents of grand jury investigations claim that this pressure stems from the moral force exerted by the lay group of jurors. Critics, however, claim the psychological pressure stems from what they describe as the "star chamber setting" of grand jury interrogation. "In all of the United States legal system," they note, "no person stands more alone than a witness before a grand jury; in a secret hearing he faces an often hostile prosecutor and 23 strangers with no judge present to guard his rights, no lawyer present to counsel him and sometimes no indication of why he is being questioned."[2]

(e) Immunity Grants. An immunity grant is a court order granting a witness sufficient immunity from future prosecution to supplant the witness' self-incrimination privilege. Once the witness has been granted immunity, he may no longer rely upon the privilege. Since immunity grants are tied initially to the exercise of the privilege by a person under a legal obligation to testify, they are not available to persons who simply refuse to give a statement to the police. At the investigatory stage, almost the only way the prosecution can make use of an immunity grant is in conjunction with a subpoena directing the uncooperative witness to testify before the grand jury. The immunity grant may be used to gain information from various types of recalcitrant witnesses. For example, immunity quite frequently is given to a lower-level participant in organized crime in order to obtain testimony against higher-level participants. It also often is used to force testimony from witnesses who are not themselves involved in criminal activities, but desire not to give testimony that may hurt others. Although the privilege is not available simply to protect others, witnesses who do not actually fear personal incrimination have been known to claim that they do so in order to avoid testifying against their friends. Since such

---

2. As discussed in § 8.15, a fair number of jurisdictions have substantially altered this setting by allowing the witness to be accompanied by counsel, and others permit the witness to leave the grand jury room in the midst of testifying to consult with retained counsel located in the anteroom. In these jurisdictions, the most significant psychological pressure may stem from the fact that the prosecutor may ask questions, potentially embarrassing, almost without limit as to subject matter, and the witness must respond under oath.

claims are difficult to dispute, the prosecutor may simply prefer to grant the witness immunity.

(f) Secrecy. Grand jury secrecy requirements are commonly cited as another investigative advantage of the grand jury. Initially, those requirements are said to facilitate keeping the target of the investigation "in the dark" as to the nature of the inquiry. A person may be investigated without even knowing that he is the subject of an investigation or, if he is aware of his "target" status, without knowing which of his activities are being examined or who is providing information on those activities. Keeping these matters from the target may be essential where there is a likelihood that he might flee to avoid possible indictment or might attempt to destroy evidence or tamper with possible grand jury witnesses.

Secondly, grand jury secrecy requirements are said to have the independent value of keeping the investigation from coming to the attention of the public. When the target of a possible investigation occupies a position of prominence, public disclosure of the investigation may cause irreparable harm to his reputation even though the investigation eventually reveals no basis for prosecution. Accordingly, where investigations are likely to become public, the prosecutor might hesitate to initiate an investigation unless fairly well convinced that it will lead to a prosecution. On the other hand, with the grand jury process keeping the investigation secret, the prosecutor might be willing to undertake an investigation on the basis of suspicions that have far less grounding. If the suspicions prove erroneous, the suspect's reputation will not have been harmed; but if the suspicions prove well founded, the prosecution will have the basis for a prosecution that otherwise might never have been brought.

Where grand jury secrecy requirements succeed in keeping targets "in the dark" and in keeping investigations from the public gaze, they clearly do offer a significant investigative advantage for certain types of cases. In practice, however, those objectives are difficult to achieve. The legal requirements as to grand jury secrecy are discussed at length in § 8.5. As noted there, those requirements are far from absolute even during the pendency of an investigation. In most jurisdictions, the grand jurors, prosecutors, and grand jury personnel are sworn to secrecy, but witnesses testifying before the grand jury may disclose what they want to whomever they want. A witness friendly to the target may discuss his appearance with the target, and by reporting the prosecutor's questions, give the target a fairly complete picture of the scope of the investigation. A witness not so friendly to the target may disclose the nature of the investigation, including the specific accusations suggested by the prosecutor's questions, to those who will give that information wide circulation within the community. Thus, for an investigation to be kept secret, all of the witnesses must want to keep it secret and all must avoid confidants who might disclose their secret. There also must be no leaks from governmental personnel or jurors and no open judicial hearings that disclose the subject under inquiry.

Grand Jury secrecy is more likely to be successful in keeping from the target, at least until the target is prosecuted, the names of those grand jury witnesses who do not want the target to know that they have testified. Indeed, even where the witness is known to the target, and is in a position where he cannot readily refuse to discuss his testimony with the target (e.g., the witness is an employee of the target), grand jury secrecy permits the witness to describe his testimony as he pleases, as all the other persons present when he testified were sworn to secrecy [although, in many jurisdictions, the witness must keep in mind that the target, once indicted, will be entitled to a transcript of the grand jury testimony of those persons who will be prosecution witnesses at trial, see § 8.5(a)].

(g) Maintaining Public Confidence. Assuming that the investigation will become known to the public sooner or later, grand jury participation often helps in maintaining community confidence in the integrity of the investigatory process, a particularly valuable asset when the person under investigation is a public official. The community tends to be suspicious of partisan influences in such investigations, especially where the investigation results in a decision not to prosecute. As one court noted: "Where corruption is charged, it is desirable to have someone outside the administration [i.e., the grand jury] act, so that the image, as well as the fact of impartiality in the investigation can be preserved and allegations of cover-up or white-wash can be avoided." The prosecutor may also look to the grand jury to help allay other public concerns, as in cases in which investigated parties are almost certain to claim police and prosecutor harassment.

(h) Grand Jury Reports. Another investigative advantage of the grand jury is its ability to issue reports in those situations in which an investigation reveals activities that are of questionable propriety, though not criminal, and of public concern. Such reports have been issued, for example, where grand jury investigations revealed conflicts of interest that violated only civil prohibitions and clearly fraudulent business schemes that escaped criminal liability because of the inadequate coverage of state law. Though of less significance to the prosecutor than those grand jury powers that facilitate development of a successful prosecution, grand jury reports may be helpful in maintaining the image of the prosecutor's office as an effective "public watchdog," unearthing misconduct that requires an expansion of the criminal code. The grand jury report also may deflect public criticism of the prosecutor's failure to prosecute investigated activity of public notoriety by explaining why it was not criminal.

Both state and federal courts have divided as to whether the grand jury has a "common law authority" to issue reports in the absence of specific legislative authorization. However, jurisdictions today authorizing such reports typically do so through detailed statutes. Roughly half of the states now have such statutes. Several of these provisions deal only with specific areas of public administration, and either explicitly limit the grand jury to those reports or are so read by courts. Thus, no more than a fourth of the states today recog-

nize a broad reporting authority that includes reports critical of individuals (with some apparently limiting such reports to public officials). These jurisdictions typically impose procedural safeguards designed to ensure the "fair treatment" of persons criticized in such reports. Those safeguards are likely to include judicial review of the record to ensure that the report has evidentiary support, and the right of individuals criticized in the report to attach a reply.

§ 8.4   The Legal Structure of the Investigative Grand Jury

The legal structure of the grand jury plays a significant role in shaping the law that governs the use of the grand jury's investigative authority. Thus, grand jury secrecy, discussed in the next section, is often mentioned in judicial discussions of challenges to grand jury subpoenas. Two other elements of the grand jury's structure—the lay composition of the grand jury and the relationship between the grand jury and the court—have been noted in discussions of almost every aspect of the grand jury's investigative authority. This section considers some major features of those two structural elements as they relate particularly to grand jury investigations. A more complete description of the grand jury's legal structure is provided in § 15.2. While the additional features discussed there are examined from the perspective of grand jury screening, many of those features also bear upon the exercise of the grand jury's investigative authority and are sometimes noted in judicial discussions of that authority. Most judicial discussions of the investigative authority however, concentrate on the features discussed here, particularly those noted in subsections (b) and (c), and various aspects of grand jury secrecy.

(a) The Representativeness of the Grand Jurors. When the grand jury first became a body separate and distinct from the trial jury, there was a tendency to select as grand jurors persons of "a higher social class" than their trial jury counterparts because "the grand jurors' jurisdiction was broader and their potential power was greater." That tradition was carried over to the United States. The investigative authority of the grand jury, in particular, was thought to call for jurors who occupied positions of responsibility and leadership in the community. For many years, that could readily be achieved through selection procedures sufficiently flexible to impanel what were known as "blue ribbon" grand juries. Starting in the 1960s, as petit jury selection procedures were altered to provide more representative trial juries, that objective was carried over to grand juries as well. Legislative reform measures imposed cross-section requirements upon grand juries, and various judicial decisions suggested that was a constitutional requirement as well. The end result was the elimination of the blue ribbon grand jury.

Today, in all but a handful of jurisdictions, the grand jury array is drawn from the same constituency, and selected in the same manner, as the array for the petit jury. Nonetheless, the grand jurors actually seated often will be less representative than the typical petit jury. Because grand jurors sit for much longer terms (particularly where assigned investigations), there often is a tendency to be more lenient in excusing persons who claim that jury service will impose a severe hardship. As a result, in many jurisdictions, the grand jury is likely to have a heavier concentration of homemakers, retirees, and persons whose employers will continue their compensation during jury service.

(b) Independent Investigative Authority. It is undisputed that the typical grand jury investigation is dominated by the prosecutor, but courts generally consider that dominance less significant if it is attributable to the grand jury's voluntary deference, rather than to the prosecutor's legal authority over the proceedings. At one time, the prosecutor's dominance was dependant entirely upon the prosecutor's ability to persuade the grand jurors to accept his leadership, as the prosecutor appeared before the grand jury largely at its sufferance. To some extent that situation has changed. In most jurisdictions, the prosecutor has obtained by statute the right to make various presentations before the grand jury. In the end, however, for most jurisdictions, the grand jury still

retains the ultimate authority to control the direction of the investigation if it so chooses.

Most jurisdictions today give to the prosecutor the authority to obtain the issuance of a subpoena duces tecum or a subpoena ad testificandum, directing appearance before the grand jury, without prior consultation with the grand jury. However, the grand jury retains its independent authority to go beyond the evidence produced by the prosecutor. Initially, the jurors have a right to ask their own questions, although the prosecutor may request that he be allowed to screen the questions to ensure that they are proper as to form and content. As discussed in § 15.2, the grand jury also has the authority to require the production of additional witnesses or other evidence relevant to the proposed charges being presented by the prosecutor. Where the subpoena provision allows for issuance of a subpoena on request of the grand jury, the grand jury can gain production of that evidence without seeking the assistance of the prosecutor (although here too, prosecutors, may ask that such requests first be presented to them, so they can speak to the need for such witnesses). Where statutes provide only for subpoenas being issued by the prosecutor, they commonly refer to calling both witnesses designated by the prosecutor and such other witnesses as the grand jury may direct.

The common law grand jury, in what commonly is described as its "inquisitorial function," had authority to seek evidence as to events in the community that may not have been called to its attention by the prosecutor. This independent investigatory power flowed, in part, from two obligations of the grand jury, both related to the issuance of presentments. The first, dating back to the origins of the English grand jury, was the obligation of the individual grand jurors to inform their fellow jurors of criminal activity known to them. The grand jurors "knowledge" for this purpose was not limited to criminal activity that they personally observed, but included as well what they had learned from their neighbors and others. Thus, the common law grand jury was said to have the authority to initiate investigations based upon "rumors" and "suspicions" that were about in the community. Second, the common law grand jury had the authority to hear from private complainants who desired the grand jury to press charges. To gain information relevant to accusations reported by individual grand jurors or private complainants, the grand jurors were given the right to send for witnesses and have them sworn to give evidence. Still another justification for that authority was the grand jury's obligation in many states to issue reports on non-indictable misfeasance in public administration.

When the grand jury system was challenged during the middle portion of the nineteenth century, the proposed reforms included not only eliminating the requirement of prosecution by indictment, but also restricting the inquisitorial and reporting powers of the grand jury to matters presented by the prosecutor. At a time when private prosecution without prosecutorial permission was being eliminated, grand jury authority to issue presentments based on information gathered from private complainants was criticized as an evasion of that reform. Reliance upon its own knowledge also was seen as potentially pernicious in light of the grand jury's lack of expertise and the possible political motivations of blue ribbon grand juries. These concerns led to a call to limit the grand jury to screening and investigating cases put before it by the prosecution. Some courts adopted that limitation and others adopted somewhat less restrictive limitations (such as permitting grand jurors to proceed in their "own knowledge", but only when that knowledge was based on personal observation, rather than the statements of others). Still other courts refused to alter the common law authority of grand juries to proceed on their own initiative with no judicial questioning of the grounding of their action.

In *Hale v. Henkel*,[1] the Supreme Court supported the latter position in holding that the grand jury's right to subpoena witnesses was not limited to situations in which a "specific 'charge' [was] pending before the grand jury against any particular person." The Court noted that the traditional grand jury oath directed

the jurors to "diligently inquire" not only as to matters "given to you in charge," but also as to matters "as shall come to your own knowledge touching this present service." That "oath of the grand juryman," as Justice Wilson had noted, "assigns no limits except those marked by diligence itself to the course of [the jury's] inquiries." The Court also cited with approval Justice Catron's comment regarding the grand jury's authority to "send for witnesses" on its own initiative, and noted the well established principle that a presentment could be based on information obtained from the grand jury's examination of witness called upon a juror's "personal knowledge." The Court acknowledged that some state court cases had taken a contrary view, but those cases had involved "abuses of the system, [such] as the indiscriminate summoning of witnesses with no definite object in view and in a spirit of meddlesome inquiry." Such abuses could be "called to the attention of the trial court," which "would doubtless be alert to repress them." They therefore did not justify imposing new limitations upon the traditional powers of the grand jury.

Another key attribute of the grand jury's inquisitorial authority at common law was the right of a private citizen to "freely bring before the grand jury the fact that a crime has been committed, request an investigation, and furnish such information as he has in aid of the prosecutor." Roughly a dozen states clearly continue to recognize such a right, at least to the extent of allowing the private citizen to directly contact the grand jury (usually through a letter to the foreperson), explain what the citizen desires to report, and request the opportunity to testify. Some of these states recognize such a right by statute, while others have judicial precedent stating that the common law right continues to apply. On the other side, a somewhat smaller group of jurisdictions clearly reject such a right. In some, statutes hold that a request to testify must be presented to the court, which will then determine, in its discretion, whether the grand jury will be asked (or required) to hear the individual's testimony. In others, judicial decisions

§ 8.4

1. 201 U.S. 43, 26 S.Ct. 370, 50 L.Ed. 652 (1906).

have concluded that a private citizen conveying information to the grand jury for the purpose of initiating an investigation is simply another form of unauthorized interference with the grand jury process, not to be distinguished from the obviously impermissible contact by a target to convince the grand jury not to indict.

Of course, a grand jury desiring to pursue an investigation opposed by the prosecutor faces a major obstacle in its lack of independent authority over resources other than the subpoena. In some jurisdictions, that obstacle can be overcome by obtaining the appointment of special investigators, usually with the permission of the court. Ordinarily, however, the grand jury will need to take the more drastic and complete step of requesting appointment of a special prosecutor. Although such appointments are rarely made, most states have statutory provisions authorizing appointment of a special prosecutor when the grand jury investigation relates to the operation of the prosecutor's office, and several states have provisions permitting appointment for any investigation upon a showing that the prosecutor has not furnished the grand jury with sufficient legal or investigative assistance. Moreover, some state courts have indicated that they have inherent authority to make such appointments when necessary to preserve "the integrity of the grand jury function." In the federal system, which has no general statutory provision for disqualification, the appointment of a special prosecutor to advise a grand jury in a particular investigation rests with the Attorney General and not the court.

(c) Judicial Supervision. Although opinions occasionally describe the grand jury as an "independent body" that draws its authority from the "people themselves," it is more frequently characterized as "an arm of the court by which it is appointed." As the Supreme Court noted in *Brown v. United States*:[2] "A grand jury is clothed with great independence in many areas, but it remains an appendage of the court, powerless to perform its investigative function without the court's aid, because

powerless itself to compel the testimony of witnesses." However, as the Supreme Court later noted in *United States v. Williams*[3]: "Although the grand jury normally operates * * * under judicial auspices, its institutional relationship with the judicial branch has traditionally been, so to speak, at arm's length."

At one time, the grand jury's reliance upon the authority of the court was thought to give the court supervisory power over all aspects of the grand jury's basic structure. Over the years, however, judicial control over various structural elements of the grand jury has been limited by statute or court rule. For example, while the decision to impanel an investigatory grand jury traditionally rested within the discretion of the court, many jurisdictions now require automatic impanelment upon request of the prosecutor. Similarly, while it was formerly said that a court could discharge a grand jury "at any time, for any reason or no reason," many jurisdictions now permit an early discharge only where justified by "cause."

The scope of the court's supervisory authority over the operations of the grand jury is most often discussed in connection with challenges to indictments, where the primary focus is upon judicial prescription of standards designed to ensure "fairness" in grand jury screening. However, courts are also called upon to exercise their supervisory authority over grand jury investigations, usually upon a motion of a witness challenging a grand jury subpoena or a proposed contempt sanction, but sometimes upon a motion of the target of the investigation or the grand jury itself. Decisions supporting extensive use of the supervisory authority in that context include: a ruling insisting that the prosecutor either present certain information to the grand jury on a particular manner or allow the private complainant to present the matter; a ruling suspending the continued investigation of a state official, which had been marked by extensive leaks, until after the forthcoming election; rulings requiring that the grand jury itself partic-

---

2.   359 U.S. 41, 79 S.Ct. 539, 3 L.Ed.2d 609 (1959).

3.   504 U.S. 36, 112 S.Ct. 1735, 118 L.Ed.2d 352 (1992).

ipate in demands for evidence or applications for judicial imposition of contempt sanctions; rulings requiring a preliminary government showing of legitimacy as a prerequisite for enforcement of a subpoena; rulings requiring a preliminary government showing of need as a prerequisite for enforcement of a subpoena that might chill the target's relationship with counsel; and rulings imposing transcription or disclosure requirements beyond what is required by grand jury statutes.

The above rulings reflect a perspective that places the court's supervisory authority over grand jury proceedings on much the same plane as the court's supervisory authority over courtroom and related pretrial proceedings. Grand jury proceedings are seen as an out-of-court appendage of the judicial process, no less subject to judicial supervision and regulation than, for example, pretrial discovery. Other courts reject this view, stressing both the independence of the grand jurors and the prerogatives of the prosecutor that come with the responsibility of the executive branch for investigation and prosecution. They adhere to a standard of limited intervention, as suggested in the following, widely-quoted formulation: "[T]here should be no curtailment of the inquisitorial power of the grand jury except in the clearest case of abuse, and mere inconvenience not amounting to harassment does not justify judicial interference with the functions of the grand jury." For the federal courts, the Supreme Court's majority opinion in *United States v. Williams*[4] clearly favors the latter position, if not an even more tightly confined supervisory power.

Williams, discussed more fully in § 15.6(b), presented the question of whether a district court could dismiss an indictment based upon the prosecutor's failure to comply with a court-created standard requiring the presentation of known exculpatory evidence before the grand jury. In holding that a court could not impose such a standard (and therefore could not dismiss an indictment based upon a failure to comply with the standard), the *Williams* Court distinguished between a federal court's use of supervisory power "as a means of enforcing or

vindicating legally compelled standards of prosecutorial conduct before the grand jury" that are set forth in a Federal Rule of Criminal Procedure or in a statute, and a federal court's use of supervisory power "as a means of prescribing those standards of prosecutorial conduct in the first instance." The former use is appropriate, as the federal courts here are merely assuring adherence to "those few clear rules which were carefully drafted and approved by this Court and by Congress to ensure the integrity of the grand jury's functions." The prescription of standards, on the other hand, assumes a federal court authority to create a "common law" of grand jury practice, which is inconsistent with the "grand jury's functional independence from the judicial branch." The *Williams* Court concluded as to such use of superintending control: "Because the grand jury is an institution separate from the courts, over whose functioning the courts do not preside, we think it clear that, as a general matter at least, no such 'supervisory' authority exists."

Though the *Williams* Court dealt with the prescription of standards relating to the grand jury's decision to indict, the Court's analysis of the supervisory power clearly extends as well to the regulation of the investigatory process. The *Williams* majority opinion stressed the federal courts' traditional recognition of the "grand jury's functional independence from the judicial branch," particularly with respect to the grand jury's "power to investigate criminal wrongdoing." The Court noted that the "grand jury is mentioned in Bill of Rights [i.e., the Fifth Amendment], but not in the body of the Constitution," thereby establishing it as an actor "that has not been textually assigned * * * to any of the branches described in the first three articles" but is " 'a constitutional fixture in its own right.' " Thus, "the Fifth Amendment's constitutional guarantee presupposes an investigative body 'acting independently of either prosecuting attorney or judge.' " This "tradition of independence," *Williams* noted, has led the Court to "insist * * * that the grand jury remain 'free to pur-

---

4. See note 3 supra. This opinion also is discussed in § 1.5(i) at note 3 and § 15.6(b).

sue its investigations unhindered by external influence or supervision so long as it does not breach upon the legitimate rights of any witnesses called before it.' "

Post–*Williams* federal lower court rulings, not surprisingly, have concluded that the *Williams* standards on supervisory authority apply to challenges to the grand jury's investigative procedures as well as to challenges to indictments. Those rulings suggest that federal courts in the post-*Williams* era must reexamine earlier supervisory authority rulings to determine whether they can now be explained as enforcing standards prescribed by statute, court rule or Constitution. If they cannot, then those rulings must be discarded.

§ 8.5   Grand Jury Secrecy

(a) Underlying Considerations. Following the *Colledge* and *Shaftesbury* cases,[1] the secrecy of grand jury proceedings came to be recognized as an essential element of the grand jury process. However, grand jury secrecy requirements, at least as to the evidence received by the grand jury, were never absolute. Grand jurors were always allowed, for example, to disclose the grand jury testimony of a witness for the purpose of charging that witness with perjury. The courts recognized at a very early point that grand jury secrecy was not an end in itself. It was to be imposed only insofar as it might contribute to the grand jury's effectiveness in performing its investigative and screening functions.

Courts today see grand jury secrecy as contributing in several ways to the grand jury's dual roles. The most frequently quoted list of secrecy objectives is that set forth by the United States Supreme Court in *United States v. Procter & Gamble Company*.[2] The Court there cited five different objectives of secrecy requirements:

(1) to prevent the escape of those whose indictment may be contemplated; (2) to in-

sure the utmost freedom to the grand jury in its deliberations, and to prevent persons subject to indictment or their friends from importuning the grand jurors; (3) to prevent subornation of perjury or tampering with the witnesses who may testify before grand jury and later appear at the trial of those indicted by it; (4) to encourage free and untrammeled disclosures by persons who have information with respect to the commission of crimes; (5) to protect the innocent accused who is exonerated from disclosure of the fact that he has been under investigation, and from the expense of standing trial where there was no probability of guilt.

Notwithstanding the breadth of this statement of objectives, which some see as going beyond the original purpose of grand jury secrecy, courts and legislatures clearly have been moving in the direction of relaxing the rules of secrecy. This development may be attributed to several factors. The widespread availability of transcripts of grand jury proceedings permits disclosure without imposing a substantial burden on the grand jurors. The widespread criticism of blanket secrecy standards has led courts to adopt a more finely tuned approach, analyzing the particular disclosure in light of the purposes underlying grand jury secrecy and the function served by disclosure. Finally, courts and legislatures very often have simply struck a new balance in weighing the justifications for grand jury secrecy against the various interests served by disclosure. They have given greater weight, in particular, to the criminal defendant's interest in having available all information that will be helpful in challenging the prosecution's case.

(b) Statutory Structure. Grand jury secrecy requirements are imposed in almost every jurisdiction by statute or court rule.[3] Secrecy provisions typically state that the grand jurors and specified persons appearing before the grand jury (usually prosecuting attorneys,

---

§ 8.5

1. See § 8.2(a).

2. 356 U.S. 677, 78 S.Ct. 983, 2 L.Ed.2d 1077 (1958).

3. Some jurisdictions recognize the possibility of courts ordering disclosure, in the exercise of their "inherent

authority" over grand jury secrecy, where the court concludes that disclosure would not undercut the groundings of grand jury secrecy and would be in the "interest of justice," even though no statutory provision or court rule specifically authorizes disclosure.

clerks, and stenographers) are bound not to disclose any matter occurring before the grand jury except in accordance with an authorized judicial order or other stated exception. It is disclosure by these specified persons only that is subject to punishment as contempt or as a special criminal offense.

Undoubtedly the most complex secrecy provision is Federal Rule 6(e).[4] It includes: (1) a general rule of secrecy; (2) a list of several specified exceptions, some requiring court authorization and others allowing disclosure without prior judicial approval; (3) procedural provisions governing applications for court approved disclosure; (4) a provision authorizing the sealing of indictments until the defendant has been taken into custody or released pending trial; (5) a requirement of a closed judicial hearing, where necessary to avoid disclosure of grand jury matter, subject to "any right to an open hearing in a contempt proceedings"; (6) a provision for keeping various records under seal as a security measure; and (7) a provision making a "knowing violation of Rule 6 * * * punish[able] as contempt of court".

While Rule 6(e), like other provisions in the Federal Rules, serves as a model for many state secrecy provisions, most state provisions are not nearly as complex. Some simply specify as authorized exceptions (i) disclosures without a court order by specified officials (e.g., prosecutors) in the discharge of their lawful duties and (ii) disclosure upon order of the court that impaneled the grand jury. Still others refer only to a court ordering disclosure of grand jury testimony at trial. In general, courts interpreting such provisions will look to the general classes of disclosure allowed under the federal rule, and adopt the standards utilized by the federal courts unless those standards are tied to the idiosyncrasies of the language of Rule 6(e).

A critical administrative element in preserving grand jury secrecy is the closure of hearings that would reveal grand jury matter. A variety of motions made by witnesses, targets, and others will require consideration of grand jury materials and if those hearings are not held in camera, they can result in the disclosure of grand jury testimony or other information relating to the grand jury's investigation. Jurisdictions with provisions modeled on Federal Rule 6(e)(5) direct that all such hearings be closed, subject to a constitutional right of a defendant in a contempt proceeding to an open proceeding. In other jurisdictions, closing the hearing is left to the discretion of the court hearing the motion.

(c) Protected Information. The information protected by grand jury secrecy provisions varies with the jurisdiction. The most extensive body of precedent on what is and is not protected by grand jury secrecy is found in the federal system. The federal cases raise a variety of questions common to most secrecy provisions. Federal Rule 6(e)'s secrecy provision applies to "a matter occurring before the grand jury." State provisions, whether Rule 6(e)-type provisions or more simple provisions, contain similar language. Moreover, the federal courts have applied a functional analysis of the information within the protection of the federal secrecy provision, which can readily be adopted by state courts notwithstanding differences in statutory language.

The first lesson of the federal precedent is that the phrase "matter occurring before the grand jury" is a term of art, not to be construed literally as encompassing only events that have taken place before the grand jury. Thus, the caselaw has established the following basic principles as guides to determining what constitutes grand jury matter: (1) the protection of grand jury secrecy extends to what will come before the grand jury as well as

---

4. Notwithstanding its length and complexity, Rule 6(e) does not provide the totality the federal law regulating grand jury secrecy. Other provisions in the Federal Rules also relate to grand jury secrecy. See Fed.R.Crim. P.16 (provisions on pretrial disclosure of prior recorded statements of defendants and prospective witness include recorded testimony before grand jury); Fed.R.Crim. P.26.2 (similar coverage of provision governing disclosure at trial of witness' prior recorded statements). Also statutes governing investigative subpoenas, including grand jury subpoenas, directed to certain types of institutions (in particular, financial institutions and providers of electronic communications services) have provisions relating to the institution's disclosure of such subpoenas. See note 6 infra.

what already has come before it; (2) that protection extends beyond testimony to encompass all substantive aspects of the proceedings; and (3) events that occurred outside the grand jury room (in particular, events within the prosecutor's office) may fall within that protection where the events have a sufficiently close connection to the grand jury process and the disclosure of information relating to those events is likely to reveal what has occurred or will occur in the grand jury room.

The application of the third principle cited above undoubtedly has caused the courts the greatest difficulty. Certain events occurring outside the grand jury are readily viewed as creating "grand jury matter." Thus, courts uniformly hold that grand jury secrecy covers the fact that a grand jury subpoena has been served a particular person. Memorandums and records that describe or analyze information presented to the grand jury will constitute grand jury matter even though prepared by the prosecution and not part of the official record of the grand jury. Courts have divided, however, as to whether Rule 6(e) governs prosecutorial disclosure of the contents of statements made to the police by persons who will later testify before the grand jury. Although the subsequent grand jury testimony might differ from the interview record, disclosure of the interview is likely to reveal the substance ôf that witness' testimony, and for some courts that is enough to constitute disclosure of "grand jury matter." Other courts suggest that as long as the interview statement was not itself presented to the grand jury, the fact that it might suggest the content of witness' subsequent testimony is irrelevant, as it was not part of "what transpired in the grand jury room." Relying on a similar analysis, one court held that where prosecutor's office revealed publicly that it was considering the possibility of bringing certain charges, that statement did not reveal grand jury matter as it did not state that "an indictment has been sought or will be sought," or that the consideration of the charges related to any evidence presented to a grand jury (as opposed to evidence simply collected by investigators).

Where prosecutors obtain physical evidence by means other than grand jury subpoena and subsequently present that evidence before the grand jury, the courts almost uniformly look to whether the evidence was obtained in an independent parallel investigation. If so, that renders the prosecution free to disclose that evidence as it pleases, even though it is apparent that the evidence was presented to the grand jury in connection with a particular investigation. Thus, a prosecutor who desires to avoid the restrictions of grand jury secrecy may look to a search warrant or an administrative agency's subpoena as the preferred route for obtaining a document initially, with the document then being presented to the grand jury. However, at least one court has suggested that a document obtained initially by search warrant could be grand jury matter where the investigator obtaining the warrant is a grand jury agent.

Even where documents were obtained by grand jury subpoena and were presented to the grand jury, they may not be treated as grand jury matter in all possible disclosure situations. Consider, for example, the situation in which the document in question was preexisting (i.e., it was not prepared for the purpose of complying with the subpoena), the prosecutor did not return the document to the subpoenaed party after presenting it to the grand jury, a civil litigant or government agency was aware of the document and sought to obtain it from the subpoenaed party, that party then responded that the document had been subpoenaed by the grand jury and was currently in the possession of the prosecutor, and the civil litigant or government agency then sought to obtain the document from the prosecutor. A handful of federal court decisions have adopted a standard that would require the third party in such a situation to seek court ordered disclosure under Rule 6(e)(3) (requiring a showing of particularized need), as they viewed the government's disclosure to a third party of any document presented to the grand jury as an otherwise prohibited disclosure of "matter occurring before the grand jury." However, most federal courts have adopted standards that would hold disclosure in this type of situation not to fall within Rule 6(e), under at least some circumstances. The least restrictive of those standards asks whether the third party seeks the document for its own sake (i.e., for its "intrinsic value" as a source of data) rather than to learn what occurred before the grand jury. Under this standard, so long as the third party's request does not describe the documents sought by reference to their presentation before the grand jury and suggests an apparently legitimate purpose for seeking the documents (e.g., an agency investigation or a civil litigation), disclosure will be deemed not to be governed by Rule 6(e). A second test, adopted by several circuits, looks to the effect of the disclosure of the requested documents. The disclosure is held to fall under Rule 6(e) only if it would "reveal the inner workings of the grand jury," pointing to such matters as "the strategy or the direction of the [grand jury] investigation." Where the disclosure reveals little more than what the requesting party already knows (i.e., that the particular document was subpoenaed), disclosure does not fall within Rule 6(e). Still another standard presumes that the document is grand jury matter, but allows that presumption to be rebutted by showing that "disclosure would be otherwise available by civil discovery and would not reveal the nature, scope, or direction of the grand jury inquiry."

(d) Disclosure by a Witness. Roughly a dozen states impose an obligation of secrecy on the grand jury witness, subject to the exemption of the witness' discussion of his testimony with counsel. In *Butterworth v. Smith*,[5] the Supreme Court sustained a First Amendment challenge to a state statute that imposed a secrecy obligation upon a grand jury witness— so broad as to prohibit disclosure of the "content, gist, or import" of the witness' testimony—insofar as that secrecy obligation extended beyond the point of discharge of the grand jury. The Court reasoned that several of the traditional functions of grand jury secrecy were no longer served by a witness-secrecy requirement once the grand jury's investigation ended, and those functions that remained

were "not sufficient to overcome [the witness'] First Amendment right to make a truthful statement of information he acquired on his own." *Butterworth* does not necessarily preclude a permanent disclosure prohibition (at least with exemption possible upon a showing of compelling justification to a court) where that prohibition is limited to a discussion of the specific content of the testimony itself, as opposed to the broader prohibition presented in *Butterworth*, which would have prevented the witness from describing his personal knowledge of the events that he described in his testimony. Such a limited prohibition could be viewed as analogous to the secrecy obligation imposed upon the grand jurors and prosecutors.

In the vast majority of jurisdictions, the witness is not bound by secrecy. In Federal Rule 6(e) and many similar state provisions, the secrecy provision initially sets forth a list of persons subject to the secrecy obligation (e.g., jurors, prosecutors, and investigative staff)—a list that does not include witnesses. The provision then adds that "no obligation of secrecy may be imposed on any person" except in accordance with that provision. What the absence of a secrecy obligation means is that witnesses, if they so choose, can freely disclose publicly or privately both their own testimony and whatever information was revealed to them by the grand jurors or prosecutor in the course of giving that testimony. Although this exception has been criticized as creating a gigantic loophole in grand jury secrecy, it has been justified on grounds of practical necessity and the need to prevent grand jury abuses. Imposition of a witness secrecy requirement has been characterized as "impractical and unreal—a partner, an employee, a relative, a friend called on to testify will come back and tell the person concerning whom he testified, and it should be so." The key to encouraging "free and untrammeled disclosures" by witnesses, it is argued, is to assure the witness who desires secrecy that others will not disclose his testimony, not to require secrecy from those who feel duty bound to disclose.

---

5. 494 U.S. 624, 110 S.Ct. 1376, 108 L.Ed.2d 572 (1990).

Some commentators add that the ability of a witness to "go public" stands as a deterrent against grand jury harassment of witnesses.

Even though the jurisdiction does not hold witnesses to secrecy, the prosecution may ask them not to make disclosures or to at least inform the prosecutor of any disclosures. In the federal system, notwithstanding the Rule 6(e) prohibition against imposing a secrecy obligation except in accord with that provision, several courts have suggested that the court's inherent authority over grand jury proceedings permits it to issue a protective order prohibiting witness disclosures during an ongoing investigation upon a government showing of "compelling necessity" (i.e., that the investigation will be undermined without continuing secrecy). Other courts, however, view such orders as beyond the court's authority in light of Rule 6(e)'s specific prohibition against imposing additional secrecy requirements.[6]

(e) Disclosure to Further Criminal Law Enforcement. Since no more than one or two prosecutors will ordinarily appear before the grand jury, provision must be made, as a matter of practical necessity, for disclosure by those attorneys to other members of the prosecutor's staff (including nonattorney support personnel) and police officers assisting in the investigation. Almost all jurisdictions will allow disclosure to such persons without court order. Not surprisingly, the Federal Rule 6(e) provisions on such disclosures are the most detailed.[7] Unlike many state provisions, they set forth explicit limitations aimed at ensuring that the disclosure are used only for criminal law enforcement.

Initially Rule 6(e) authorizes disclosure without a court order to an "attorney for the government," which includes both attorneys on the staff of the United States Attorney and any other Department of Justice Attorney authorized to "conduct proceedings * * * as a prosecutor" (which includes attorneys within several different D.O.J. divisions, such as Antitrust). Rule 6(e) further provides, however, that the disclosure may be made to an attorney for the government only to assist that attorney in the performance of a "duty to enforce federal criminal law." Thus, if an AUSA (Assistant United States Attorney) or D.O.J. attorney first participates in a grand jury investigation, and then joins a government legal team pursuing a civil action relating to the same subject matter, that attorney cannot disclose the grand jury matter to those other attorneys.[8] Such a disclosure requires a

6. Several federal statutes, regulating investigative subpoenas directed to certain third party service providers (e.g., financial institutions), include provisions under which the third party may be precluded from informing its customer that records of the customer's transactions have been subpoenaed by the grand jury. The Supreme Court has held that a customer lacks standing to object on Fourth Amendment grounds to a subpoena directing a third-party provider to disclose its records of the customer's transactions. See United States v. Miller, discussed in § 9.1(c). However, these statutes allow the customer to raise certain other challenges to the subpoena. In that connection, the regulatory statute typically will require that the customer be given notice of the subpoena. Creating an exception to this ordinary process of notification, the statutes also provide for a court order delaying notification for a specified period of time. The order is issued on a showing of "reason to believe" that notification will result in destruction of evidence or other action "seriously obstructing an investigation." One statute, relating to investigations of bank fraud, includes a permanent prohibition against notifying the customer.

7. Apart from the provisions on disclosures to government attorneys and assisting personnel which are discussed below, Rule 6(e) also has several other provisions that authorize disclosures to further criminal law enforcement. Thus, it authorizes disclosure without a court order to another grand jury and disclosure with a court order to

state enforcement officials of grand jury matter that may disclose a violation of state criminal law, to Indian tribal enforcement officials of grand jury matter that may disclose a violation of Indian tribal criminal law, and to military enforcement officials of grand jury matter that may disclose a violation of military criminal law.

Still other authorized disclosures relate to criminal law enforcement, but are not strictly limited to that use. Rule 6(e) authorizes disclosure without a court order to officials of financial institutions and to government attorneys for use in enforcing the Financial Institutions Reform, Recovery, and Enforcement Act. Rule 6(e) also authorizes disclosure without a court order to specified intelligence officials of grand jury matter that relates to "foreign intelligence or counterintelligence."

8. In United States v. John Doe, Inc. I, 481 U.S. 102, 107 S.Ct. 1656, 95 L.Ed.2d 94 (1987), the Court held that Rule 6(e) did not bar an antitrust division attorney, who had been a member of the prosecution team, from reviewing grand jury materials (after the completion of the grand jury investigation), without court authorization, for the purpose of preparing a civil action. Rule 6(e) applies only to the "disclosure" of grand jury materials, and the Court concluded that what was involved here, "a solitary reexamination of grand jury materials in the privacy of an attorney's office," did not constitute a "disclosure." The Court noted, however, that the civil complaint eventually

court order under the Rule 6(e) provision governing third party disclosures [discussed in subsection (h) infra]. The related Rule 6(e) provision on disclosure to investigative personnel working with the prosecutor imposes a similar prohibition against disclosure for use outside criminal law enforcement.[9] Thus, if the grand jury investigation is conducted with staff borrowed from an administrative agency (e.g., the S.E.C.), that staff cannot then share its information with its home agency. Here again, a court approved disclosure would be needed.

In the course of a grand jury investigation and a subsequent prosecution, the prosecutor or assisting personnel may have need to reveal grand jury matter to third parties in a variety of settings relating to the resolution of the investigation and prosecution. These include asking a possible witness about grand jury matter in determining whether that person should be subpoenaed, asking a possible recipient of an immunity grant about grand jury matter, asking a grand jury witness or a trial witness about grand jury matter not provided by that witness, revealing grand jury matter to the defendant or defense counsel in the course of plea negotiations or providing informal discovery, and revealing grand jury matter to a court in connection with a judicial hearing on such matters as sentencing or the issuance of a search warrant. While secrecy provisions authorizing disclosures on court approval typically would cover such disclosures, prosecutors commonly take the position that such disclosures can be made without court approval as they fall within the prosecutor's authority to make disclosure in the performance of his duty to enforce the criminal law. Here, however, unlike disclosures made under that principle to the prosecutor's staff or investigative personnel, the disclosure is to persons who would not constitute agents of the prosecutor and

would not be subject to the prosecutor's obligation of secrecy.

Although such disclosures must be quite common, the caselaw is quite sparse, with the courts reaching mixed results. Moreover, much of that caselaw comes from the federal system, where the presence of the special provision on disclosures to government personnel arguably suggests a special concern that even disclosures for law enforcement purposes be made only to persons who are under an obligation of continued secrecy. Of course, even if it assumed that Rule 6(e) so limits disclosures for law enforcement purposes to assisting government personnel, disclosures to others may be acceptable if the information disclosed is not identified as coming from the grand jury. Several cases have suggested that secrecy provisions are not violated when prosecutors or investigators refer to grand jury matter in interviewing a prospective witness without identifying the matter as coming from the grand jury. Also, in some settings (e.g., disclosures to a court in a sentencing hearing), the prosecutor will have ample opportunity to obtain in advance a court order authorizing the disclosure.

(f) Disclosure Pursuant to a Challenge to Grand Jury Proceedings. As discussed in § 15.2(i), most jurisdictions have provisions, like Federal Rule 6(e)(3), authorizing court ordered disclosure in connection with a motion "to dismiss the indictment because of a matter that occurred before the grand jury." However, as also noted there, the preliminary showing required to gain disclosure incident to a grand jury challenge tends to be quite rigorous. In part, this reflects concern that defendants will bring challenges for the very purpose of learning more about the grand jury's investigation. Thus courts appear somewhat less reluctant to respond to such chal-

---

filed in the case did not in any way refer to grand jury materials and the case therefore did not present the "very different matter of an attorney's disclosing grand jury information to others, inadvertently or purposefully, in the course of a civil proceeding."

9. To implement this prohibition, the provision on assisting personnel requires that the prosecutor (1) conclude that the particular personnel is "necessary to assist

in performing that attorney's duty to enforce federal criminal law," (2) promptly provide the court with the "names of all personnel to whom disclosure has been made", and (3) certify that the personnel have "been advised of their obligation of secrecy under this rule," including their "use of information disclosed only to assist the attorney for the government in performing that attorney's duty to enforce federal criminal law."

lenges by undertaking their own in camera review of the grand jury transcript to determine if it supports the challenge. In any event, such disclosure, since it comes after indictment, is unlikely to disrupt an ongoing investigation, although it will give the defense more disclosure than is ordinarily provided under discovery provisions.

(g) Disclosure to Defendant Pursuant to Discovery Rules. As noted in § 15.2(i), approximately a dozen states grant defendant a complete transcript of the grand jury proceedings that produced his indictment. Apart from those provisions, grand jury matter tends to be treated no differently than other material of the same character. Thus, documents and physical evidence subpoenaed by the grand jury are treated in the same fashion as documents and physical evidence otherwise obtained by the prosecution. They are discoverable insofar as they meet the traditional standards for discovery of such material—that it was obtained from the defendant, will be introduced by the prosecutor, or will be material to the defendant's preparation of a defense.

Similarly, recorded grand jury testimony (apart from those states requiring disclosure of the complete transcript) tends to be treated no differently than other prior recorded statements (e.g., statements obtained by the police). Indeed, in defining what constitutes a witness' "recorded statement," statutes and judicial decisions tend to utilize the Jencks Act definition, which specifically includes a transcript of testimony given before the grand jury.[10] Thus, in the substantial number of states which provide pretrial discovery of the prior recorded statements of prosecution witnesses, the defendant can obtain pretrial the grand jury testimony of those witnesses. A witness testifying before a grand jury in such states must recognize that his testimony will eventually be disclosed if the grand jury issues an indictment and the government then lists him as a possible trial witness. In the federal system and the many states that do not permit pretrial discovery of a witness' prior recorded statement, but grant a right to such statements at trial for use in impeachment, the same standards apply to the trial witness' grand jury testimony. Here, the grand jury witness stands a better chance of not having his testimony disclosed, because even if an indictment is issued and the grand jury witness is likely to be needed as a trial witness, the defendant will only be able to demand disclosure if the trial occurs, and most cases are resolved by a guilty plea.

The most widely adopted pretrial discovery provision relating to grand jury testimony grants to the defendant a copy of his own testimony before the grand jury. Such provisions simply place the defendant's grand jury testimony in the same category as other previously recorded statements of the defendant that are in the possession of the prosecution. Thus, when the defendant is a corporation or other entity, it will be entitled to the grand jury testimony of its employees under the same conditions as recorded statements of employees given to investigators.

Several states appear to still recognize a secrecy interest in grand jury material that restricts defense discovery of a witness' recorded grand jury testimony as compared to his other prior recorded statements. In large part, however, grand jury secrecy no longer plays a significant role in itself in limiting pretrial and trial discovery of grand jury material by defendants. Two changes in perspective have contributed to this development. First, courts have come to view the "traditional reasons for grand jury secrecy" as "largely inapplicable" to post-indictment disclosure of a trial witness' grand jury testimony, particularly where disclosure is delayed until the witness testifies at trial. Second, the interest of the defendant and the judicial system in ensuring that "a criminal conviction not be based on the testimony of untruthful or inaccurate witnesses" is generally recognized as having substantially higher priority than the interests supporting grand jury secrecy.

(h) Disclosure to Third Parties. No aspect of grand jury secrecy has caused more difficulty than determining the permissible

10.   See § 20.3(b).

scope of disclosure of grand jury matter to third parties (i.e., persons other than prosecution personnel or defendants) for use in other proceedings. The most common third party recipients are litigants in a civil suit, administrative agencies, and government personnel outside of the law enforcement field. In jurisdictions with provisions similar to Federal Rule 6(e), disclosures to such persons are governed by Rule 6(e)(3), which authorizes court ordered disclosure "preliminary to or in connection with a judicial proceeding." In jurisdictions with less detailed provisions, third party disclosures may be authorized under a general exception for disclosure "upon written order of the court." In all jurisdictions, third party disclosures for purposes other than criminal law enforcement must be authorized by the court, typically by the judge exercising supervisory authority over the grand jury. The court ordinarily rules on a proposed disclosure after hearing from both the prosecutor and the proposed recipient, but in many instances, other interested persons (e.g., the targets of the grand jury investigation) also are heard.

The traditional standard applicable to court ordered disclosures to third parties is that set forth by the Supreme Court in *Douglas Oil Co. of California v. Petrol Stops Northwest*:[11]

Parties seeking grand jury transcripts under Rule 6(e) must show that the material they seek is needed to avoid a possible injustice in another judicial proceeding, that the need for disclosure is greater than the need for continued secrecy, and that their request is structured to cover only material so needed. Such a showing must be made even when the grand jury whose transcripts are sought has concluded its operations. * * * [T]he interests in grand jury secrecy, although reduced, are not eliminated because the grand jury has ended its activities. It is clear from [past precedent] that disclosure is appropriate only in those cases where the need for it outweighs the public interest in secrecy, and that the burden of demonstrating this balance rests upon the private party seeking disclosure. It is equally clear that as the

considerations justifying secrecy become less relevant, a party asserting a need for grand jury transcripts will have a lesser burden in showing justification. * * * In sum, as so often is the situation in our jurisprudence, the court's duty in a case of this kind is to weigh carefully the competing interests in light of the relevant circumstances and the standards announced by this Court.

The *Douglas Oil* standard is commonly known as the "particularized need" standard. Although a showing of need that is particularized is a part of the standard, it is only one component of the balancing process prescribed by *Douglas*. Supreme Court and lower federal court decisions point to a variety of factors that should be weighed in the balancing process prescribed by *Douglas Oil*. As to most, little more can be said than that they are factors to be considered though not conclusive in themselves.

Initially, the court will look to the status of the investigation that produced the requested grand jury material. The need for secrecy clearly is greatest while the jury is still gathering evidence and considering whether to indict. As a result, third party disclosure during the pendency of an investigation rarely will be granted. Particularized need for such disclosure presumably would require a combination of a pressing need that could not await the end of the investigation (e.g., a regulatory agency's need to obtain immediate termination of a harmful practice) and a disclosure that either could be subjected to conditions that would preclude conveyance to the target of the investigation or would reveal no more about the workings of the grand jury than is already known. Where courts treat subpoenaed preexisting business documents as "grand jury matter," such documents may be an appropriate candidate for disclosure prior to the end of the investigation. Courts frequently note that the secrecy interest here is substantially reduced because disclosure of such documents tends to reveal little about the workings of the grand jury not already known.

11. 441 U.S. 211, 99 S.Ct. 1667, 60 L.Ed.2d 156 (1979).

On the other hand, once the grand jury is finished with the matter, the need for secrecy declines and the petitioner's burden in establishing a particularized need declines. However, as the Supreme Court noted in *Douglas Oil*, the value of grand jury secrecy is only "reduced," not "eliminated," by the termination of the investigation: "[I]n considering the effects of disclosure on grand jury proceedings, the courts must consider not only the immediate effects upon a particular grand jury, but also the possible effect upon the function of future grand juries. Persons called upon to testify will consider the likelihood that their testimony may one day be disclosed to outside parties."

In general, the broader the disclosure requested, the greater the burden in establishing particularized need. As the Supreme Court noted in *Douglas Oil*, the "typical showing of particularized need arises when a litigant seeks to use the grand jury transcript at the trial to impeach a witness, to refresh his recollection, to test his credibility and the like." The disclosure there "can be limited to those portions of a particular witness' testimony that bear upon his * * * direct testimony at trial." Moreover, such requests are less likely to be based on a speculative judgment as to need, while the use involved serves the important interest of ensuring that the factfinder is not misled. The movant must establish, however, that the testimony is likely to serve that need by showing an actual failure of the witness' recollection on a particular point or an indication of inconsistency between the witness' anticipated current testimony and grand jury testimony. Courts tend to be much more wary of requests of private litigants grounded on the possibility that the grand jury testimony will lead the litigant to evidence it otherwise could not find, as such requests are deemed more speculative and not as susceptible to disclosure that is "discrete and limited."

In assessing the petitioner's showing of need, even as to a fairly limited disclosure, the court also may take into consideration alternative means (such as civil discovery) that might produce the same information. Some courts have suggested that the availability of a discovery alternative should preclude disclosure. Under this standard, disclosure of a document may require a showing that it is available only from the grand jury, and disclosure of grand jury testimony may require a showing either that the grand jury witnesses cannot be deposed in the civil proceeding or that their deposition testimony suggests a possible inconsistency with the grand jury testimony. Other courts suggest, however, that the availability of discovery will not close the door to ordering disclosure, and the saving of time and expense is a legitimate consideration as to private litigants although not sufficient justification in itself.

In *United States v. Sells Engineering, Inc.*,[12] the Supreme Court rejected the contention that a government agency can justify disclosure simply by showing the relevancy of the requested grand jury material to the agency's function. The government would receive no "special dispensation," relieving it from establishing particularized need. However, *Sells* also noted that the balancing process of particularized need may be somewhat different for disclosure to government bodies as compared to private litigants. Three factors, in particular, point to imposing a less rigorous standard on disclosure to a government agency. Initially, where the prosecution is seeking to disclose information to another government unit, it obviously will have taken into consideration the impact of disclosure upon the enforcement of the criminal law. Thus, the Court noted in *Sells*, such requests typically are made "after the criminal aspect of the matter is closed." Second, at least in some contexts, disclosure to the government "poses less risk of further leakage or improper use than would disclosure to private parties or the general public."

A third factor is the element of public interest in the government's intended use of the grand jury material. Thus, where the contemplated disclosure was to civil attorneys within the government for the purpose of deciding whether to file a civil action, the district court could properly take into account the likelihood

---

12. 463 U.S. 418, 103 S.Ct. 3133, 77 L.Ed.2d 743 (1983).

that the disclosure would "sav[e] the Government, the potential defendants, and witnesses, the pains of costly and time consuming depositions and interrogatories which might later have turned out to be wasted if the Government decided not to file a civil action after all." Where the benefit is exclusively to the government, and involves the application of regulatory functions, the public interest also would appear to be high. Where, however, the government interest relates simply to a contractual matter, it arguably should be treated no differently than a private litigant.

Another factor of special importance in government cases is the alternative discovery tools available to the government. Unlike private litigants, government agencies often have investigatory subpoena or summons authority. *Sells* noted that the availability of that authority weighs against the government's statement of need, but as the Court later noted in *United States v. John Doe, Inc. I.*,[13] that alternative route does not constitute a per se bar to ordering disclosure. Consideration could be given also to avoiding the costs and delays involved in duplicating the grand jury's investigation and thereby hindering the efficient and effective enforcement of regulatory policy by the government.

Also, the availability of alternative procedures tends to negate another concern raised in *Doe*—that the disclosure not pose a threat to the "integrity of the grand jury" by tempting the government's grand jury lawyers to "manipulate the grand jury's powerful investigative tools to root out additional evidence useful in the [government's] civil suit." That concern is particularly pertinent where a government agency lacks the subpoena authority needed to itself obtain the additional evidence, as the incentive to utilize the grand jury to aid the agency is strongest in that setting. Of course, on the other side, the unavailability of the evidence apart from grand jury disclosure makes for a stronger agency showing of need. To rely on that need, however, the prosecutor seeking to gain approval of disclosure to the agency may be required to point to factors

indicating that there has been no misuse of the grand jury's subpoena authority to develop evidence for the agency.

Under Federal Rule 6(e)(3) and similar state provisions, the requirement that the disclosure be "preliminary to or in connection with a judicial proceeding," poses a significant obstacle to disclosure to government agencies for various purposes. As the Supreme Court noted in *United States v. Baggot*,[14] this requirement "reflects a judgment that not every beneficial purpose, or even every valid government purpose, is an appropriate reason for breaching grand jury secrecy." The Rule "contemplates only uses related fairly directly to some identifiable litigation, pending or anticipated," as measured by the "primary purpose of the disclosure." *Baggot* held that disclosure for use in an IRS audit of civil tax liability did not meet this prerequisite since the agency's determination of tax liability and its collection of any amount determined to be due did not require judicial intervention. The mere possibility that the taxpayer might challenge the agency's non-judicial means of enforcing its determination would not make the agency proceeding "preliminary to a judicial proceeding."

(i) Remedies. What relief is available when there has been an unauthorized governmental disclosure of grand jury matter? Federal Courts have divided as to whether Rule 6(e) creates a private cause of action for a breach of its secrecy requirements. Where there is no cause of action, an interested party (e.g., a witness whose testimony was disclosed or the subject of the disclosed testimony, typically the target of the investigation) may call the unauthorized disclosure to the attention of the supervisory court, but it then rests in the court's discretion as to what further action is taken. While the court has a duty to protect the integrity of the grand jury proceedings, it may conclude that the most appropriate procedure is initially to submit the matter to the Department of Justice for its internal investigation and application of internal sanctions.

13.　481 U.S. 102, 107 S.Ct. 1656, 95 L.Ed.2d 94 (1987).

14.　463 U.S. 476, 103 S.Ct. 3164, 77 L.Ed.2d 785 (1983).

Courts holding that a governmental breach of grand jury secrecy creates a private cause of action have cited various different types of relief that may be sought by a person potentially prejudiced by the breach. These include injunctive relief to preclude further disclosure, civil contempt sanctions where the information was purposefully leaked, a prohibition against use by a litigant to whom grand jury testimony was improperly disclosed, and providing disclosure to litigation opponents to offset the benefit obtained by the party who was the recipient of an unauthorized disclosure. Since the grand jury's decision to indict is not likely to have been influenced by the unauthorized disclosure of information brought before it, disclosure violations ordinarily will not provide an adequate grounding for a defense challenge to the indictment. To some extent, the nature of the disclosure will determine the range of remedies to be considered. Thus, where the disclosure was made openly in the belief (now found to be incorrect) that the disclosure was allowed by the secrecy provision, contempt would be inappropriate and there ordinarily would be no need for injunctive relief. So too, an exclusionary remedy is unlikely where the violation occurs because disclosure was made without a court order, but a court order authorizing disclosure would have been granted had it been requested.

In cases in which the disclosure was not made openly, but involves a leak by government personnel to the press, contempt sanctions would be appropriate, but courts rarely reach that issue because of the almost insurmountable hurdle that the complaining party (usually the target of the investigation) faces in establishing that there was such a leak. Initially, to establish the grounding even for an evidentiary hearing, the complaining party must make a prima facie showing both that the information disclosed constituted grand jury matter as defined by Rule 6(e) and that the sources of the information were government personnel. Although this burden has been described as "relatively light," meeting it depends largely on the willingness of reporters to suggest in their published reports that their sources where within the government. If the

reports fail to identify the source as government personnel and the grand jury information reported is not of a type known almost exclusively by government personnel, the showing will fail because the information could very well have been furnished by a witness or someone with whom a witness shared information.

Should a prima facie case be established, the government will be required to respond at an evidentiary hearing. While the supervisory court has discretion in determining the scope of that hearing, appellate courts have prohibited giving the complaining party either significant access to the material presented by the government in response or the opportunity to "conduct direct or cross-examination of government personnel." The "norm" they note, should be an ex parte presentation by the government, reviewed in camera. Since journalists will not reveal their sources, the court's determination often will rest on accepting or rejecting affidavits by relevant government personnel denying disclosure on their part. As a result, it will be a rare case where the complaining party is able to make the showing needed to impose sanctions (as opposed to the impositions of safeguards to preclude further leaks), but the publicity accompanying the challenge process itself may benefit the target in a high-profile case.

§ 8.6 The Right to Every Man's Evidence

(a) The Public's Right and the Grand Jury. The grand jury's investigative authority is commonly said to rest largely on "the long standing principle that 'the public has a right to every man's evidence.' " Indeed, no aspect of grand jury power is more frequently extolled by the courts, particularly in cases rejecting challenges to subpoenas, than its right to compel the testimony of any person, subject only to "constitutional, common law or statutory privilege." The Supreme Court has described the grand jury's authority to compel testimony as "[a]mong the necessary and most important of the powers * * * [that] assure the effective functioning of government in an ordered society." While the Court has never stated precisely why it views this authority as so essential to the "welfare of society," its opinions appear to support the conventional explanation that effective law enforcement requires the cooperation of the public, and that there are many instances in which such cooperation would not be forthcoming if it could not be compelled.

The modern tradition has been to relieve citizens of any legal responsibility to assist the police or prosecutor in the investigation of crime. Misprision is no longer a crime in most jurisdictions, and the individual has no obligation (even when there is absolutely no possibility of personal incrimination) to respond to police inquiries. At the same time, increased urbanization may have produced a setting in which fewer people feel a responsibility to the community and hence a responsibility to assist law enforcement officials. The grand jury's authority to compel testimony therefore takes on added importance. That authority is accepted, the Court has noted, not simply because it is "historically grounded," but because the "obligation of every person to appear and give testimony" is "indispensable to the administration of justice." Without that authority, criminal activity could be hidden behind a "wall of silence" that finds no justification in legal privilege, but is based simply on an individual's desire not to get "involved," fear of retaliation, dislike for the substantive law, or private code against "snitching."

Assuming that the authority to compel cooperation must of necessity be lodged somewhere, the courts find wisdom in the traditional delegation of that authority to the grand jury—an independent body, composed of laymen and having a membership that shifts from one term to the next. The structure of the grand jury provides assurance that investigations will be carried out free from political pressures. The capacity of a grand jury to take an investigation wherever it may lead serves to counteract suspicions of corruption and partisanship in criminal law enforcement. The grand jury therefore has the capacity not only to ferret out hidden crimes, but to relieve public concern generated by false rumors. The courts stress, however, that to serve its purpose, the grand jury must be free to carry forward wide ranging investigations.

Two points in particular have been stressed with respect to the necessary breadth of grand jury investigations. First, the grand jury must be "free from any restraint comparable to * * * [a] specific charge and showing of probable cause." It must be able to investigate "merely on suspicion that the law is being violated, or even just because it wants assurance that it is not." The jurors must be able to "act on tips, rumors, evidence offered by the prosecutor, or their own personal knowledge." They must have the capacity to "run down every available clue" and to examine "all witnesses * * * in every proper way." It is recognized, in this connection, that "if the investigation is to be meaningful, some exploration or fishing necessarily is inherent and entitled to exist."

Second, courts frequently note that the grand jury must be free of technical rules that would cause grand jury proceedings to be punctuated by litigation and delay. Judicial rulings must not provide the recalcitrant witness with a long list of challenges that can be used "to tie the grand jury into knots—to drag out the proceedings with technicalities instead of matters of substance." In determining whether a particular objection should be recognized, a court must consider whether its holding "would saddle a grand jury with minitrials and preliminary showings [that] would assuredly impede its investigation and frustrate the public's interest in the fair and expeditious administration of the criminal laws." The grand jury must be left "free to pursue its investigations unhindered by external influence or supervision so long as it does not trench upon the legitimate rights of a witness called before it."

The Supreme Court has acknowledged that the obligation of the citizen to appear and testify before the grand jury is not without its burdens. Appearance may be "onerous at times" and required answers "may prove embarrassing or result in an unwelcome disclosure of * * * personal affairs"; but such personal sacrifices, the Supreme Court has noted, are "part of the necessary contribution of the individual to the welfare of the public." In this regard, the duty to testify before the grand jury is sometimes compared to the duty to testify at trial, which is imposed simply upon a determination of one of the parties that a particular person should be subpoenaed. There are, of course, certain distinctions in the two situations. The witness summoned to testify at trial knows the subject to be considered, and is not himself the target of inquiry. In the grand jury setting, the subject under inquiry may not be revealed, and the person summoned may well be a prospective defendant. The witness at trial testifies in public while the witness before the grand jury testifies in a closed proceeding. Justice Thurgood Marshall suggested that a grand jury appearance may carry with it a substantial stigma, not attached to a trial appearance, since "the public often treats an appearance before a grand jury as tantamount to a visit to the stationhouse." Courts have recognized that these distinctions may require somewhat different treatment of the grand jury witness in a few situations, but they also have concluded that the protection afforded the grand jury witness is sufficient to impose a general duty to appear similar to that imposed upon the trial witness. That protection is said to stem from four sources. First, the grand jury witness retains the same constitutional, statutory and common law privileges as the trial witness. Second, the secrecy of the grand jury proceeding affords the witness protection against damage to his reputation and mitigates any element of embarrassment in his testimony. Third, the witness has the protection afforded by the presence of the grand jurors. Justice Black, in particular, gave considerable weight to this factor:

> They [the grand jurors] have no axes to grind and are not charged personally with the administration of the law. No one of them is a prosecuting attorney or law-enforcement officer ferreting out crime. It would be very difficult for officers of the

state seriously to abuse or deceive a witness in the presence of the grand jury.[1]

Finally, grand juries remain subject to judicial supervision. Thus, the Supreme Court noted in one of its earliest opinions recognizing broad grand jury investigative authority: "Doubtless abuses of this power may be imagined * * * but were such abuses called to the attention of the court, it would doubtless be alert to repress them."

Over the past few decades, the sufficiency of such protections has been continuously questioned. Commentators, legislators, and lawyer associations have called for reform. Some have argued for strengthening the position of witnesses and targets by allowing for challenges to the inadequate grounding for an investigation and the inadequate need for subpoenaing the particular witness. Some argue that the grand jurors must be more directly involved in the process. They have proposed that no subpoena, grant of immunity, or contempt citation be issued except upon approval of the jurors. Others would prohibit various prosecutorial practices thought to be abusive in the presentation of evidence before the grand jury. A few of these reforms have been rather warmly received. A substantial number of states, for example, now allow the witness to be accompanied by a lawyer. However, in general, those proposals that might lead to substantial delay in grand jury proceedings have gained little, if any, legislative support.

(b) Privileges and Other Protections. As discussed in § 15.2(d), the one common denominator to the various positions on the application of the rules of evidence to grand jury proceedings is the applicability of testimonial privileges. Thus, in every jurisdiction, a subpoenaed person may challenge the subpoena itself or a question put by the grand jury if compliance would violate a testimonial privilege recognized in that jurisdiction. With one exception, the privilege against self-incrimination, we leave the discussion of the testimonial privileges to the evidence treatises. That privi-

§ 8.6

1. In re Groban, 352 U.S. 330, 77 S.Ct. 510, 1 L.Ed.2d 376 (1957) (dissenting opinion).

lege is considered at length (§§ 8.10–8.14) because of its central role in grand jury investigations.

Statutes and constitutional provisions may impose still other limits upon the type of evidence that can be obtained by grand jury subpoena. Thus, § 8.9(b) discusses the limitation imposed by the federal statute on electronic surveillance, and § 8.8(d) considers special prerequisites that may be imposed where the requested disclosure could have a chilling impact upon the exercise of First Amendment rights or the Sixth Amendment right of counsel in criminal cases.

§ 8.7   Fourth Amendment Challenges to Subpoenas

(a) Applicability of the Fourth Amendment to Subpoenas for Documents. The application of the Fourth Amendment to court orders requiring production of documentary evidence began with *Boyd v. United States*,[1] a widely celebrated case that in most respects has little current vitality. *Boyd* involved a customs forfeiture proceeding in which the government sought to utilize an 1847 statutory provision allowing it to gain documentary evidence from the importer of the property to be forfeited. The provision authorized the trial judge, on motion of the government describing a particular document and indicating what it might prove, to issue a notice directing the importer to produce that document. The petitioners in *Boyd* challenged a notice that directed them to produce the invoice for thirty-five cases of plate glass allegedly imported without payment of customs duties. The Supreme Court sustained their challenge, holding that the notice and the statute authorizing it violated both the Fourth Amendment and the self-incrimination clause of the Fifth Amendment.

Speaking to the Fourth Amendment, the *Boyd* Court acknowledged that the notice procedure "lacked certain aggravating incidents of actual search and seizure, such as forcible entry into a man's house and searching among his papers," but stressed that it nonetheless "accomplish[ed] the substantial object of those

acts in forcing from a party evidence against himself." Accordingly, a "compulsory production of a man's private papers" would be treated as "within the scope of the Fourth Amendment to the Constitution, in all cases in which a search and seizure would be." Having found the Fourth Amendment applicable, the *Boyd* opinion turned to the question as to whether this particular "search and seizure, or what is equivalent thereto," was unreasonable within the meaning of that Amendment. It concluded that the compelled production of a private document was per se unreasonable.

Boyd cited several factors in concluding that the Fourth Amendment simply did not allow a search, or its equivalent, as to private papers. The Court initially noted that the searches for contraband or instrumentalities of crime allowed in past cases involved "totally different things from a search for and seizure of a man's private books and papers for the purpose of obtaining information therein contained or of using them as evidence against him." The former involved situations in which "the government is entitled to the possession of the property," but that was not true of the latter. The Court then turned to the landmark English ruling in *Entick v. Carrington & Three Other King's Messengers*, which had found a trespass in government officials entering the plaintiff's home and breaking open his boxes and examining his papers. This decision, which undoubtedly influenced "those who framed the Fourth Amendment," had spoken of the individual's papers as his "dearest property," and it was the invasion of the individual's indefeasible right in that property, rather than the "breaking of his doors and the rummaging of his drawers" that was the "essence" of the violation of individual liberty in that case. Finally, the "compulsory extortion" of private papers to be used as evidence to convict the individual was parallel to compelling testimony for the same purpose, and here, "the Fourth and Fifth Amendments run into each other." What "is condemned in the Fifth Amendment throws light on * * * what is an 'unreasonable search and seizure'" and ren-

1. 116 U.S. 616, 6 S.Ct. 524, 29 L.Ed. 746 (1886).

ders per se unreasonable a search which is not "substantially different from compelling [a person] * * * to be a witness against himself."

The *Boyd* position on per se unreasonableness was short-lived. In *Hale v. Henkel*,[2] decided twenty years later, the Supreme Court rejected that position, but reaffirmed the applicability of the Fourth Amendment to a "compulsory production of a man's private papers." The *Hale* majority initially noted that *Boyd* had erred in reading together the Fourth and Fifth Amendment protections. Any absolute prohibition against compelled production of documentary items lay in the self-incrimination clause alone, and that clause had no application in the case before it; the challenged grand jury subpoena was directed to corporate documents and corporations did not have the benefit of the privilege. However, the Court continued, the corporation was entitled to the protection of the Fourth Amendment, and "an order for the production of books and papers" could still constitute "an unreasonable search and seizure." While it was true that "a search ordinarily implies a quest of an officer of the law, and a seizure contemplates a forcible dispossession of property, still, as was held in *Boyd,* the substance of the offense is * * * [unreasonable] compulsory production, whether under a search warrant or a subpoena duces tecum." Here, Fourth Amendment protection was violated by a subpoena duces tecum "far too sweeping in its terms to be regarded as reasonable." The subpoena had required production of corporate papers relating to transactions with various different companies, and such a broad request was capable of preventing the corporation from carrying on its business. Reasonableness for a subpoena, like reasonableness for a search warrant, required "particularity" in the description of the documents to be produced. While the government might have need for many of these documents, it would have to make some showing of "materiality" before it could "justify an order for the production of such a mass of papers."

Justice McKenna, concurring separately in *Hale*, argued that the Fourth Amendment should not apply in any respect to a subpoena to compel the production of documents. The majority had acknowledged that the subpoena did not involve a "quest" by the officer or a "forcible dispossession of the owner." Did not that distinction in itself establish the inapplicability of the Fourth Amendment? The service of the subpoena involved "no element of trespass or force," nor was it "secret and intrusive." The subpoena could not be "finally enforced except after challenge, and a judgment of the court upon the challenge." These safeguards and limitations, from Justice McKenna's perspective, clearly distinguished the subpoena from the search. Justice McKenna also considered the possibility that the majority was saying that a subpoena did not involve a search except where it was "too sweeping," but he could not understand how that quality alone, improper though it may be, could transform the subpoena into a search.

The *Hale* majority failed to respond to Justice McKenna's criticism, apart from its reference to *Boyd*'s analysis, and failed also to explain why the subpoena, though governed by the Fourth Amendment, was not subject to the usual Fourth Amendment requirement of probable cause, but only its requirement of particularity. Neither did it explain why that requirement here went beyond specificity of identification and prohibited overbreadth in the documents specified. Commentators and lower courts have sought to provide answers where *Hale* failed to do so. Explaining *Hale* as a Fourth Amendment case, they have offered two somewhat different explanations for the positions taken there.

One explanation rests in large part on Fourth Amendment concepts that had not been articulated at the time of the *Hale* ruling. Those concepts are: (1) the Fourth Amendment's reach must be determined by reference to its primary function of protecting expectations of privacy; and (2) the Fourth Amendment imposes different standards of reasonableness depending upon the character of the

2. 201 U.S. 43, 26 S.Ct. 370, 50 L.Ed. 652 (1906).

search involved. In light of the obvious expectation of privacy in private papers, the state is said to engage in activity within the reach of the Fourth Amendment when it examines papers not voluntarily exposed. The examination invades privacy without regard to whether there is an additional invasion of privacy in placing the state agent in the location where that examination is possible. However, the search conducted through the use of the subpoena is less invasive because the agent looks only at the papers subpoenaed (not the premises in which they were kept) and the subpoena provides an opportunity for a prior judicial challenge. Taking these factors into consideration, along with the long history of grand jury subpoenas issued without probable cause, *Hale* is seen as the forerunner of a series of later Supreme Court cases that sustained regulatory searches under the Fourth Amendment without probable cause.[3] In this context, Fourth Amendment reasonableness required no more than a showing of need that restricted the subpoena to documents material to the investigation.

An analysis that focuses on the special privacy interest in non-public documents fails to explain, however, a Fourth Amendment standard that does not appear to distinguish between documents based on the extent to which they have been treated as highly confidential. Such an analysis would suggest, for example, different standards for the subpoena of a diary and the subpoena of a typical business document, and it arguably would require for the former something more than a mere showing of possible relevancy to the subject of investigation. Also, such an analysis does not lead to a protection conditioned on the subpoena compelling production of a substantial body of documents (as *Hale's* overbreadth analysis seemed to suggest) and would not test overbreadth by reference to the economic burden imposed upon the individual or entity by being forced to relinquish those documents (as *Hale* clearly did). Finally, a Fourth Amendment theory that focuses upon the individual's privacy interest in the content of the documents he is

being compelled to produce, rather than upon the physical attributes of a search, would be difficult to limit to the subpoena of documents. What is revealed by a subpoena compelling the production of a document typically is no more private than what may be revealed by a subpoena compelling testimony, but the Court has never suggested that the Fourth Amendment places limits on the disclosure compelled by a subpoena ad testificandum.

A second explanation of *Hale* builds upon Justice McKenna's suggestion that the *Hale* majority found the Fourth Amendment applicable only when the subpoena was overly-broad. The theory here is that the subpoena which is too sweeping, which calls for a mass of documents without regard to what is relevant, necessarily requires a sifting through of the documents to obtain those that are needed. Whether that sifting takes place on the premises of the owner or in the offices of the prosecutor assisting the grand jury, it constitutes a search. Thus, *Hale* and other courts have compared the overbroad subpoena to a "general warrant." The issue was not with the particularity of the description. In *Hale*, for example, a subpoena for all of the documents located in the corporation's office would not have presented difficulties in identifying the documents. The problem of particularity arose in failing to identify the specific documents in which the government had an interest, but instead compelling production of what was known to include both relevant and irrelevant, and then identifying the relevant through what would amount to a physical search. While this explanation arguably fits the fact situation in *Hale*, it fails to explain the various lower court rulings that have applied *Hale's* condemnation of subpoena overbreadth to subpoenas that did not require a large volume of documents.

Forty years after *Hale*, in *Oklahoma Press Publishing Co. v. Walling*,[4] the Supreme Court suggested still a third explanation—that the Fourth Amendment had no direct application to subpoenas, but was looked to only by analogy to protect against a different form of "offi-

---

3. See § 3.9(b).

4. 327 U.S. 186, 66 S.Ct. 494, 90 L.Ed. 614 (1946).

cious intermeddling by government officials." In that case, which involved an administrative agency subpoena duces tecum, the Court acknowledged that certain misconceptions had arisen due to the failure of lower courts to distinguish between "so-called 'figurative' or 'constructive'" searches by subpoena and "cases of actual search and seizure." The Court noted that "only in * * * [an] analogical sense can any question related to search and seizure be thought to arise" in subpoena cases. It stressed that the Fourth Amendment, "if applicable," did no more than "guard against abuse only by way of too much indefiniteness or breadth" in the subpoena. The interests to be protected were "not identical with those protected against invasion by actual search and seizure" but arose out of the right of persons to be free from "officious examination [that] can be expensive, so much so that it eats up men's substance," and thereby "become[s] persecution when carried beyond reason."

The *Oklahoma Press* explanation focuses not on privacy interests, but on property rights and the burden that comes with being required to gather and then relinquish large quantities of documents. Part of that burden (the costs of gathering the documents) is not even present when the government conducts a search. Because Fourth Amendment requirements tied to the protection of privacy are not relevant, there is no reason to require probable cause or some similar grounding for investigation. The primary concern is simply that compliance with subpoena does not produce an unnecessary burden because the subpoena requires numerous documents bearing no potential relevancy to the subject of the inquiry.

In its post-*Oklahoma Press* rulings the Supreme Court has returned to referring to the prohibition against "overbreadth" in the subpoena of documents as a Fourth Amendment requirement. It has not, however, retreated from *Oklahoma Press's* explanation of the function of the overbreadth limitation. Thus, lower courts applying that limitation to grand jury subpoenas have looked in large part to the avoidance of undue burdens upon the subpoenaed party. In some instances, however, those rulings have appeared to take into consider-

ation as well the especially private nature of the papers involved. A survey of those lower court rulings is set forth in subsection (b) below. Because a very similar limitation is found in provisions like Federal Rule 17(c), which provides protection against subpoenas duces tecum that are "unreasonable or oppressive," the decisions applying such provisions, discussed primarily in § 8.8(b) and (c), must also be considered in assessing the potential for successful objections based upon the "too sweeping" reach of a subpoena.

(b) The Prohibition Against Overbreadth in Documentary Subpoenas. Courts applying the constitutional prohibition against overlybroad subpoenas duces tecum frequently start out by noting that the stated standard, proscribing breadth "far too sweeping * * * to be regarded as reasonable," necessarily requires a fact-specific judgment, with each ruling tied to the circumstances of the individual case. At the same time, the courts have sought, with limited success, to develop some general criteria to guide that judgment. Initially, the question arises as to whether the party challenging the subpoena must establish sufficient breadth to suggest that compliance will be burdensome. While there is language in Supreme Court opinions suggesting that is a prerequisite and most successful challenges have involved such subpoenas, a small group of rulings have struck down subpoenas that would have presented no significant burdens in collecting and relinquishing the records. Those cases involved subpoenas that either suggested on their face that no effort had been made to limit the subpoena to what was needed or that dealt with sensitive information.

Assuming some potential for overbreadth, courts then will turn to the three "components" of reasonableness initially developed by the lower federal courts: (1) the subpoena may command only the production of things relevant to the investigation being pursued; (2) specification of things to be produced must be made with reasonable particularity; and (3) production of records covering only a reasonable period of time may be required.

The second element of the above formulation is commonly described as having "two prongs": first, "particularity of description" so that the subpoenaed party "know[s] what he is being asked to produce"; and second, "particularity of breadth" so that the subpoenaed party "is not harassed or oppressed to the point that he experiences an unreasonable business detriment." The requirement of adequate notice rarely poses significant difficulty, although ambiguities may arise where documents are described by their relationship to a particular event. Accordingly, courts looking to the second component tend to focus on the second factor, the degree of burden imposed by production.

While many courts have treated the elements of relevancy, sufficient particularity to avoid an undue burden of production, and reasonableness of time period as separate requirements of reasonableness, so that deficiency as to any one element can invalidate the subpoena, it is clear that the three elements are interrelated. Greater particularity, by narrowing the range of documents to be produced, will extend the time period into which the subpoena may reach. On the other hand, as a subpoena reaches farther into the past, a court is more likely to require a stronger showing of relevancy. So too, the significance of the burden of production will be weighed against the strength of the showing as to relevancy and the reasonableness of the time period. Thus, courts have noted that a subpoena that clearly meets the relevancy and time-period requirements will be rejected on the basis of a substantial burden of production only in the most extreme cases.

While the subpoenaed party bears the ultimate burden of establishing that a challenged subpoena is unreasonable, many courts insist that the government make an initial showing of relevancy since it alone knows the precise nature of the grand jury inquiry. Ordinarily, this showing requires no more than a general description of the relationship of the material sought to the subject matter of the investigation. A critical factor here will be the character of that subject matter. Some activities (e.g., crimes involving the illicit use of funds) will render relevant all financial records, as total income and receipts must be traced. The possibility of unknown conspirators similarly opens up the range of documents relating to other parties. Similarly, antitrust investigations demand a broad range of documents since the violation may be reflected in many different aspects of a company's business.

Courts generally give grand juries considerable leeway in judging relevancy. They recognize that "some exploration or fishing necessarily is inherent" since the grand jury will not ordinarily have a "catalog of what books and papers exist" nor "any basis for knowing what their character or contents immediately are." Similarly, the grand jury cannot be expected to anticipate the full range of criminal activity that might be connected with a possible criminal enterprise. Where the time period clearly is reasonable and the burden of production is limited, courts have accepted as sufficient showings of "some possible relationship, however indirect." This produces a relevancy standard very similar to the standard announced by the Supreme Court in *R. Enterprises*, in applying Rule 17(c)'s reasonableness requirement.[5]

The government's showing on relevancy also provides a foundation for determining the reasonableness of the time span covered by the subpoena. That period must bear "some relation to the subject of the investigation," which readily can go beyond the statute of limitations. Even in antitrust investigations, where the greatest leeway exists, a period beyond ten years is ordinarily suspect. However, where courts have held such a substantial time period to be unreasonable, they generally also have left open the possibility of reconsideration in light of a request for a narrower range of documents or a stronger showing of relevancy based on subsequently received information.

Objections to a subpoena duces tecum based solely upon the burden and expense of assembling a large quantity of records are almost

---

5.   See § 8.8 at note 5.

always doomed to failure. With the advent of photocopying and the easy reproduction of computerized records, the possibility that the subpoenaed party will be unable to carry on its business without the relinquished records—a major concern in *Hale*—is largely mooted. Courts commonly have viewed the expense of assembling and duplicating the materials as simply another cost of doing business, particularly where the subpoenaed party is a large corporation. Moreover, in cases where that expense imposes a true financial hardship, the government may respond by offering reimbursement of all costs. The end result is that the burden of production is given weight primarily where the court has substantial doubts as to the relevancy of the documents or the reasonableness of the time span. Without such concerns, subpoenas have been upheld which required production of as much as fifty tons of documents.

(c) Application of the Fourth Amendment to Other Subpoenas: Dionisio and Mara. In *United States v. Dionisio*[6] and *United States v. Mara*,[7] the Court left no doubt that the Fourth Amendment ordinarily does not apply to subpoenas apart from the "too sweeping" limitation upon subpoenas for documents. *Dionisio* and *Mara* were companion cases arising from separate grand jury investigations. In *Dionisio,* the grand jury had subpoenaed approximately 20 persons, including Dionisio, to give voice exemplars for comparison with recorded conversations that had been received in evidence. In *Mara,* the witness was directed to produce handwriting exemplars for the purpose of determining whether he was the author of certain writings. Both witnesses claimed that the subpoenas constituted unreasonable searches and seizures because they had not been supported by any showing of reasonableness. The Court of Appeals agreed. It compared the dragnet effect of the subpoena in *Dionisio* to the mass police roundup of possible suspects for fingerprinting that was condemned in *Davis v. Mississippi.*[8] The *Davis* opinion had suggested that a court order de-

taining a suspect for the purpose of obtaining identification evidence might be possible on a showing of less than probable cause (i.e., a reasonable suspicion), but the subpoena here had not been supported by anything other than a prosecutor's claim that the exemplars were "essential and necessary." The "interposition of the grand jury between the witnesses and the government" would not be allowed to "eliminate the Fourth Amendment protection that would [otherwise] bar the government's obtaining the evidence." *Mara* did not involve the same "dragnet procedure," but the Court of Appeals held that here too a showing of reasonableness was necessary. It was incumbent upon the government to establish that it was not engaged in a "general fishing expedition under grand jury sponsorship."

The Supreme Court rejected the lower court rulings in both *Dionisio* and *Mara*. The majority opinion noted that the Fourth Amendment did prohibit the "sweeping subpoena duces tecum," as noted in *Hale,* but there was no such extreme breadth of production required in either subpoena here. The Court of Appeals had erred in analogizing the subpoena in *Dionisio* to the action of police in detaining or arresting a person for the purpose of obtaining identification exemplars. "It is clear," the Court noted, "that a subpoena to appear before a grand jury is not a 'seizure' in the Fourth Amendment sense." As a different Court of Appeals had recently explained, there was a dramatic difference in the "compulsion exerted" by a subpoena as opposed to an "arrest or even an investigative stop":

> The latter is abrupt, is effected with force or the threat of it and often in demeaning circumstances, and, in the case of arrest, results in a record involving social stigma. A subpoena is served in the same manner as other legal process; it involves no stigma whatever; if the time for appearance is inconvenient, this can generally be altered; and it remains at all times under the control and supervision of a court.

---

6. 410 U.S. 1, 93 S.Ct. 764, 35 L.Ed.2d 67 (1973).

7. 410 U.S. 19, 93 S.Ct. 774, 35 L.Ed.2d 99 (1973).

8. 394 U.S. 721, 89 S.Ct. 1394, 22 L.Ed.2d 676 (1969) (discussed in § 3.8(g)).

The majority acknowledged that a grand jury subpoena, though differing from the arrest or investigative stop, could be both "inconvenient" and "burdensome." Any "personal sacrifices" required, however, were merely incidental to the "historically grounded obligation of every person to appear and give his evidence before the grand jury." The addition here of directives to give identification evidence did not alter the nature of the burden imposed. Neither the voice exemplar nor the handwriting sample invaded a privacy interest protected under the Fourth Amendment. Both related to physical characteristics "constantly exposed to the public" and were to be distinguished, for example, from the taking of a blood sample.

Having found that the Fourth Amendment had no application to either the summons to appear nor the directive to provide identification exemplars, the Court concluded that there was "no justification for requiring the grand jury to satisfy even the minimal requirement of 'reasonableness' imposed by the Court of Appeals." The grand jury "could exercise its 'broad investigative powers' on the basis of 'tips, rumors, evidence offered by the prosecutor, or [the jurors] own personal knowledge,'" and it should not be required to explain the basis for each of its subpoenas. To "saddle a grand jury with minitrials and preliminary showings would assuredly impede its investigation and frustrate the public's interest in the fair and expeditious administration of the criminal laws."

(d) Subpoenas For Identification Evidence. The *Dionisio* opinion clearly did not go so far as to hold the Fourth Amendment inapplicable to subpoenas compelling the production of any and all types of identification evidence. Indeed, in noting that a subpoena directive to produce a voice sample was "immeasurably further removed" from Fourth Amendment protection than the taking of a blood sample, the Court intimated that a grand jury subpoena requiring a witness to furnish such a sample might well be subject to Fourth Amendment limitations. Not surprisingly, several lower court cases subsequently held that the Fourth Amendment does apply

to a blood-sample subpoena. Whereas *Dionisio* and *Mara* involved the production of physical characteristics exposed to the public, which had previously been held in other contexts not to involve a reasonable expectation of privacy, the taking of blood constitutes a penetration of the skin and production of internal fluid, which had long been held to constitute a search when performed under the direction of the police. Courts have noted the possibility that the taking of other identification evidence (the hair root, though not a hair clipping, and saliva) also may be subject to Fourth Amendment limitations.

The issue that has troubled the courts where the Fourth Amendment applies to the taking of identification evidence is whether the presence of a grand jury subpoena makes the search reasonable on less than the probable cause that presumably would be necessary for the taking of that evidence at the direction of the police. Some courts have concluded that the grand jury subpoena makes no difference, and probable cause is required. Indeed, one court held that the grand jury must obtain a search warrant to compel production of a blood sample. Other courts reject that conclusion. They note that there is no arrest involved, that the grand jury cannot be expected to show probable cause that the blood will constitute evidence of a crime where its very purpose is to determine whether there is probable cause to charge a person with a crime, and that the subpoena affords the opportunity for challenge prior to the taking of the blood. One court has viewed the lesser Fourth Amendment standard of "reasonable suspicion" to be appropriate, while another has described the appropriate standard as a "reasonable basis for believing * * * that a blood sample will provide test results that will significantly aid * * * the grand jury in their investigation of circumstances in which there is good reason to believe a crime ha[s] been committed."

§ 8.8 Challenges to Misuse of the Subpoena Authority

(a) Improper Subject of Investigation. It generally is conceded that "a subpoenaed [grand jury] witness has no right to know the subject matter of the inquiry or the person[s] against whom the investigation is directed." Ordinarily, however, the witness will become aware of at least the general area of inquiry through a designation of the subject matter in the subpoena, the questions asked, or the documents requested. In rare instances, this information may suggest that the grand jury is investigating an activity for which it cannot indict. Although such an investigation would ordinarily be beyond the grand jury's investigative authority, a witness' objection on that ground generally will be unavailing. *Blair v. United States*,[1] though it involved a rather convoluted subject matter objection, is generally viewed as barring all witness challenges to the grand jury's "jurisdiction" to investigate.

In *Blair,* the witness claimed that the transaction under investigation was beyond the grand jury's investigative authority because the applicable federal criminal statute was unconstitutional. The Supreme Court initially noted that consideration of the constitutionality of the statute at this point, prior to any indictment, would be contrary to the long-established practice of "refrain[ing] from passing upon the constitutionality of an act of Congress unless obliged to do so." It then proceeded, however, to speak in quite general terms of a witness' lack of capacity to challenge the "authority * * * of the grand jury," provided the jury had "de facto existence and organization." The Court treated the position of the grand jury witness as analogous to that of the trial witness. Neither could raise objections of "incompetency or irrelevancy," for those matters were of "no concern" to a witness, as opposed to a party. For the same reasons, witnesses also should not be allowed "to take exception to the jurisdiction of the grand jury or the court over the particular subject matter that is under investigation." The grand jury operates as a "grand inquest," which requires broad investigative powers. It must have authority, in particular, "to investigate the facts in order to determine the question of whether the facts show a case within [its] jurisdiction." The witness could not be

allowed "to set limits to the investigation that the grand jury may conduct."

Relying upon *Blair,* federal courts have refused to recognize witness challenges alleging that the grand jury inquiry concerned offenses as to which prosecution would be barred by the statute of limitations, offenses that occurred outside the grand jury's judicial district, or offenses immunized from prosecution. A few federal decisions have suggested openness to subpoena challenges alleging that the grand jury is investigating offenses that occurred outside the jurisdiction, but they also note that leeway must be given to the grand jury in evaluating such challenges. Given the broad expanse of federal venue provisions, the court must recognize the possibility that a grand jury investigation of an offense seemingly committed elsewhere may disclose some event that places venue in the grand jury's district, and also the possibility that information relating to crimes committed elsewhere may be relevant to the investigation of related or similar crimes, involving the same or different actors, that occurred in the grand jury's district.

(b) Relevancy Objections. In commenting upon the objections of a witness, either at trial or before the grand jury, *Blair* noted that "[h]e is not entitled to urge objections of incompetency or irrelevancy, such as a party might raise, for this is no concern of his." This statement was commonly viewed by federal courts as barring all witness objections to the relevancy of information sought by a grand jury. Although relevancy was properly considered in determining whether a subpoena duces tecum was "too sweeping to be reasonable," a subpoena duces tecum limited in scope presumably could not be challenged solely on the ground that it was seeking information not material to the inquiry. Similarly, a witness could not object to questions put to him on the ground that they had no bearing upon that inquiry.

The absence of a relevancy objection in federal courts appeared to be reaffirmed in *Unit-*

§ 8.8
1. 250 U.S. 273, 39 S.Ct. 468, 63 L.Ed. 979 (1919).

ed States v. Mara, a companion case to United States v. Dionisio.[2] The lower court there had held that a subpoena duces tecum requiring production of a handwriting exemplar would not be enforced without an initial showing that the grand jury was investigating a matter within its jurisdiction and that the information sought by subpoena was relevant to its inquiry. The prosecution had made such a showing by affidavit filed in camera, but the Court of Appeals ruled that the affidavit had to be disclosed in open court so as to permit challenge by the witness. The Supreme Court reversed. The Court held, as discussed in § 8.7(c), that the Fourth Amendment does not apply to a subpoena duces tecum, absent a Hale claim of overbreadth. It then added that, with the Fourth Amendment inapplicable, no preliminary showing of relevancy was required.

Shortly after Mara was decided, the Court of Appeals for the Third Circuit fashioned for its circuit a preliminary showing requirement not substantially different from that rejected in Mara. The Court of Appeals viewed the Dionisio and Mara rulings as concerned only with the demands of the Fourth Amendment. In the course of enforcing administrative agency subpoenas, federal courts traditionally had required a preliminary governmental showing that the information sought was relevant to an appropriate subject of investigation. A similar showing was needed in enforcing grand jury subpoenas, to ensure that the grand jury's subpoena power was not being misused by the prosecutor. That showing would be required in the exercise of the court's supervisory powers over both the use of the grand jury subpoena and the use of the court's contempt power. To obtain contempt enforcement of a subpoena duces tecum against a recalcitrant witness, the "government [would] be required to make some preliminary showing by affidavit that each item [sought] is at least relevant to an investigation being conducted by the grand jury and properly within its jurisdiction, and is not sought primarily for another purpose." The Court of Appeals left open the possibility

that in "extraordinary circumstances," that affidavit might be presented in camera, but noted that the affidavit ordinarily should be disclosed to the witness so that he could challenge the government's showing. The Third Circuit's preliminary showing requirement also applied to witness refusals to testify, but here a showing of relevancy was needed only as to the general subject matter covered in the total grouping of questions, rather than as to the information sought in specific questions.

While the Third Circuit's preliminary showing requirement has received support from several state and federal courts, it has been rejected by most of the courts that have considered the issue. They note that such a requirement flies in the face of Dionisio's warning against saddling a grand jury with preliminary requirements "that would assuredly impede its investigation and frustrate the public's interest in the fair and expeditious administration of the criminal laws." Also, they find inapposite the Third Circuit's analogy to the enforcement of the administrative agency subpoena. The grand jury, because of the nature of its task, has a far greater need for secrecy. It cannot establish relevancy by simply pointing to prior testimony which is already a matter of public record. Moreover, the nature of the criminal activity it seeks to investigate often requires consideration of a substantial amount of information that will prove in the end to be irrelevant.

In 1991, the Supreme Court addressed the relevancy issue in United States v. R. Enterprises, Inc..[3] Though Justice O'Connor's opinion for the Court did not comment directly upon either the Third Circuit's position or the lower court decisions rejecting that position, it did speak at length to the issues raised in those rulings. At issue in R. Enterprises was the interpretation of the Rule 17(c) provision that authorizes a federal district court to quash or modify a subpoena duces tecum "if compliance would be unreasonable or oppressive." In United States v. Nixon,[4] which dealt with a subpoena duces tecum directing produc-

---

2. See § 8.7 (c).

3. 498 U.S. 292, 111 S.Ct. 722, 112 L.Ed.2d 795 (1991).

4. 418 U.S. 683, 94 S.Ct. 3090, 41 L.Ed.2d 1039 (1974).

tion of items for use at trial, the Supreme Court had held that the party seeking the subpoena must show that the documents to be subpoenaed are relevant, admissible in evidence, and adequately specified. The lower court in *R. Enterprises* had held that these three requirements also applied to a subpoena duces tecum in a grand jury proceeding. There was no issue here as to specificity, but the government had failed to make a showing as to relevancy and admissibility. The Supreme Court unanimously ruled that the lower court had erred, as the *Nixon* standard clearly did not apply in the grand jury context.

Justice O'Connor's opinion cited several reasons for refusing to extend the *Nixon* standard to grand jury proceedings. Insofar as that standard looked to the evidentiary admissibility of the items subpoenaed, it contradicted a line of earlier Supreme Court rulings holding that the grand jury could consider, and issue an indictment based upon, evidence that would be inadmissible at trial. The "teaching of the Court's decision[s]," Justice O'Connor noted, "is clear: A grand jury 'may compel the production of evidence or the testimony of witnesses as it considers appropriate, and its operation generally is unrestrained by the technical procedural and evidentiary rules governing the conduct of criminal trials.'" Applying the *Nixon* standard to grand juries also would present unacceptable administrative difficulties. It "would invite procedural delays and detours while courts evaluate the relevancy and admissibility of documents sought by a particular subpoena." In *Dionisio*, the Court had "expressly stated that grand jury proceedings should be free of such delays." So too, insisting that the government make a preliminary showing of relevancy would be inconsistent with the "strict secrecy requirements" of grand jury proceedings. "Requiring the Government to explain in too much detail the particular reasons underlying a subpoena" would "compromise 'the indispensable secrecy of grand jury proceedings,'" and it would "afford the targets of the investigation far more information about the grand jury's internal workings * * * than the Federal Rules of Criminal Procedure appear to contemplate."

Having rejected the application of the *Nixon* standard, Justice O'Connor then turned to the more difficult task of "fashion[ing] an appropriate standard of reasonableness" in the application of Rule 17. It was well established that "the investigatory powers of the grand jury are * * * not unlimited." The grand jury could not, for example, "engage in arbitrary fishing expeditions" or "select targets of investigation out of malice or an intent to harass." Applying such limits, however, required consideration of conflicting elements in the grand jury process. On the one hand, the decision as to the appropriate charge "is routinely not made until after the grand jury has concluded its investigation," and "one simply cannot know in advance whether information sought during the investigation will be relevant and admissible in the prosecution for a particular offense." On the other hand, the party to whom the subpoena is directed "faces a difficult situation" in challenging the improper use of a subpoena. Grand juries ordinarily "do not announce publicly the subjects of their investigations," and the subpoenaed party therefore "may have no conception of the Government's purpose in seeking production of the requested information." Thus, what was needed was a standard of reasonableness that "gives due weight to the difficult position of subpoena recipients but does not impair the strong governmental interests in affording grand juries wide latitude, avoiding minitrials on peripheral matters, and preserving a necessary level of secrecy."

Turning to the specific guidelines that would give substance to such a standard, Justice O'Connor noted initially that "the law presumes, absent a strong showing to the contrary, that a grand jury acts within the legitimate scope of its authority." Consequently, "a grand jury subpoena issued through normal channels is presumed to be reasonable, and the burden of showing unreasonableness must be on the recipient who seeks to avoid compliance." In this case, that party "did not challenge the subpoena as being too indefinite, nor did [it] claim that compliance would be overly burdensome." The challenge was strictly on relevancy grounds and for such a challenge, the presumption of regularity produced the following standard: "[T]he motion to quash must be denied unless the district court determines that there is no reasonable possibility that the category of materials the Government seeks will produce information relevant to the general subject of the grand jury's investigation."[5]

Recognizing that the above standard imposed an "unenviable task" upon the party raising a relevancy challenge, Justice O'Connor suggested that the district court had authority to ease that task through appropriate procedures. Her opinion noted in this regard:

In cases where the recipient of the subpoena does not know the nature of the investigation, we are confident that district courts will be able to craft appropriate procedures that balance the interests of the subpoena recipient against the strong governmental interests in maintaining secrecy, preserving investigatory flexibility, and avoiding procedural delays. For example, to ensure that subpoenas are not routinely challenged as a form of discovery, a district court may require that the Government reveal the subject of the investigation to the trial court *in camera*, so that the court may determine whether the motion to quash has a reasonable prospect for success before it discloses the subject matter to the challenging party.

While this language opens the door to requiring the government to make a preliminary showing under special circumstances, it falls short of authorizing the automatic preliminary showing prerequisite adopted by the Third Circuit (or its standard of ordinarily making such showing available to the witness). Also, since the *R. Enterprise* opinion relies on Rule 17(c), which speaks only of challenges to subpoenas duces tecum, it apparently does not undercut the statement in *Blair* indicating that a witness testifying before the grand jury cannot object to the relevancy of the questions asked.

Although the Court in *R. Enterprises* was unanimous in rejecting application of the *Nixon* standard, there was division as to the specific guidelines advanced in Justice O'Connor's opinion. Justice Scalia did not join the paragraph discussing the district court's possible authority to require the prosecution to set forth the general subject of the investigation. Three justices, in a separate opinion by Justice Stevens, argued that the burden imposed upon the challenging party will vary with the nature of the subpoena. They noted, in particular, that a less rigorous showing of lack of relevancy should be sufficient where other significant interests are involved (e.g., where the subpoena "would intrude significantly on * * * privacy interests or call for disclosure of trade secrets or other confidential material"). Admittedly, Justice O'Connor's opinion did not propose a standard for such special circumstances, but Justice Stevens expressed concern that the Court's opinion "not be read to suggest that the deferential relevance standard the Court has formulated will govern decision in every case, no matter how intrusive or burdensome the request."

(c) Oppressiveness Objections. Federal Rule 17(c) and similar state provisions authorizing quashing subpoenas where compliance would be "unreasonable or oppressive." In setting forth oppressiveness as an alternative ground, Rule 17(c) implicitly recognizes that a demand may be reasonable as measured by the *R. Enterprises* standard of relevancy, yet nonetheless be oppressive. Typically claims of oppressiveness rest on the costs and disruption associated with collecting and relinquishing large quantities of documents, with the subpoenaed party arguing that the prosecution should be required to narrow the subpoena by reference to time or category of documents.

5. The Court concluded that the lower court had appropriately denied the motion to quash under this standard. The grand jury, setting in the Eastern District of Virginia, was investigating the shipment of sexually explicit materials into that district. Such a shipment clearly had been made by one of three companies owned by the same person, and the two other companies were objecting to their subpoenas. With all three companies engaged in the distribution of sexually oriented materials and all three owned by the same person, "there was a reasonable possibility that the business records of [the two objecting companies] would produce information relevant to the grand jury's investigation into the interstate transportation of obscene materials," notwithstanding the two companies' "self-serving assertions" that they had no connection to Virginia.

These claims are analyzed in much the same fashion as the largely identical claims brought under the Fourth Amendment overbreadth doctrine, discussed in § 8.7(b). Another fairly common type of oppressiveness claim rests on the alleged chilling impact of compliance on the exercise of some right. These claims are discussed in subsection (d) below.

(d) "Chilling Effect" Objections. Grand jury witnesses in several contexts have argued that even where the testimony or documents demanded of them clearly would be relevant, the grand jury should be required to show a "compelling need" for that information where the impact of its inquiry would be to chill the exercise of a constitutionally protected right. Those challenges commonly are grounded on the court's authority to protect the constitutional right said to be chilled. They also may be framed as Rule 17(c) challenges to the oppressiveness of the subpoena. The two claims of this character receiving the most attention involve the alleged chilling impact of grand jury subpoenas upon the exercise of First Amendment rights and upon the lawyer-client relationship.

First Amendment claims. "Chilling impact" claims based upon the First Amendment stand apart from any testimonial privileges that may bear upon the exercise of rights of free speech, freedom of association, and the free exercise of religion. Where the information sought falls within a statutory or common law privilege recognized in the particular jurisdiction (e.g., a clergy or journalist privilege), that privilege will afford protection. First Amendment claims look to the First Amendment itself to restrict grand jury access to information on the theory that its disclosure will chill the exercise of a First Amendment right. Such claims have been raised by a variety of persons with respect to a variety of activities, including: reporters contending that being forced to reveal their sources, to produce their notes, or simply to be required to appear before the grand jury would chill their capacity to gather and report news; reporters contending that being forced to furnish information about the internal oper-

ations of a newspaper would chill the newspaper's capacity to print controversial articles; sellers of sexually explicit materials contending that their First Amendment right to convey non-pornographic materials would be chilled by subpoenas that require them to disclose copies of the materials distributed or business records that reveal the identity of their customers; a religious organization contending that a grand jury demand for its financial records would injure its standing in the community and chill its capacity to attract new members; organizations engaged largely or partly in political advocacy contending that being required to furnish documents that identify their members would chill the participation of those members and restrict their capacity to attract new members; a private association of a controversial character (Hells Angels Motorcycle Club) contending that a grand jury demand for information relating to its membership, funding, and organizational structure would chill the members' freedom of association; a public official contending that his right of association was chilled by a grand jury demand that he produce his calendar and schedule for past years; and the author of a book who contended that a subpoena requiring him to produce records of alleged interviews cited in the book would chill future publications. With few exceptions, such challenges have not succeeded in obtaining the quashing of the grand jury directive. However, the courts have been far less consistent in their analysis of the legal standards applicable to these "chilling-impact" claims than in their disposition of the claims.

The one Supreme Court decision directly addressing such a challenge is *Branzburg v. Hayes*,[6] involving the First Amendment claims of reporters who had been subpoenaed to testify before state and federal grand juries. In each instance, newspaper articles written by the reporters indicated that they had knowledge of specific criminal activities, based upon either personal observations or interviews of the alleged participants. The reporters contended that they should not be compelled to testify in breach of their promises of confiden-

---

6. 408 U.S. 665, 92 S.Ct. 2646, 33 L.Ed.2d 626 (1972).

tiality to their sources absent a special showing by the grand jury of a "compelling need" for the information the reporters might provide. Justice White's opinion for a closely divided Court majority rejected that contention. Justice White acknowledged that requiring the reporters to testify might deter future confidential sources, but noted that the extent of that deterrence was "unclear." Moreover, even if there would be some negative impact upon news gathering, that impact did not outweigh the interest of the public in the grand jury's investigation of crime.

Justice White's opinion noted that the Court was not leaving "newsgathering" without any "First Amendment protections." Judicial control of the grand jury process always was available to provide an appropriate remedy if the grand jury process was misused to harass the press. Justice Powell (who provided the majority's fifth vote and joined Justice White's opinion) offered as an illustration of what might be deemed harassment in his separate concurring opinion: He noted: "If the newsman is called upon to give information bearing only a remote and tenuous relationship to the subject of the investigation, or if he has some other reason to believe that his testimony implicates confidential source relationships without a legitimate need of law enforcement, he will have access to the court on a motion to quash and an appropriate protective order may be entered."

Reading *Branzburg* narrowly (as a case dealing with something less than an established chilling impact on a First Amendment right), some lower courts view *Branzburg* as not inconsistent with their requiring the government to bear a special burden of justification for a subpoena clearly having a chilling impact on the exercise of a basic First Amendment right. The Ninth Circuit once held that the government in such a case must show a "compelling need," which included establishing an "immediate, substantial, and subordinating" governmental interest in the particular investigation, a "substantial connection" of the information sought to that investigation, and that this subpoena was a means for obtaining

that information "not more drastic than necessary." However, the other courts requiring a special showing for First Amendment cases impose a considerably less demanding standard. Initially, these courts insist that the objecting witness make a prima facie showing that compliance with the subpoena will chill the future exercise of First Amendment protected activity, notwithstanding the secrecy that attaches to grand jury testimony. Once this prima facie case is established, the government is required to justify that impact by showing that the information sought by the subpoena is "substantially related" to a "compelling government interest." *Branzburg*, however, is viewed as having established that a government interest in investigating crime is per se a "compelling interest." Thus, absent a showing by the objecting witness strongly suggesting that the grand jury investigation was initiated in bad faith, the critical issue is whether the information sought is "substantially related" to the investigation of crime. This government burden typically requires no more than an explanation as to why the information sought clearly is relevant to the grand jury's investigation. The explanation must establish a linkage somewhat more substantial than the *R. Enterprises* standard of a "reasonable possibility" of relevancy, but that showing may fall far short of the critical need required by the Ninth Circuit's original standard.

Still other courts, relying on *Branzburg*, have rejected entirely the contention that the government must make a special showing to sustain a subpoena that may chill the exercise of First Amendment rights. The Fourth Circuit adopted that position upon remand in the *R. Enterprises* case,[7] considering a First Amendment challenge that had not been presented to the Supreme Court. The Fourth Circuit concluded that adoption of a substantial relationship prerequisite was contrary to the reasoning of *Branzburg*. It found particularly influential the concurring opinion in *Branzburg* of Justice Powell, who provided the majority's fifth vote. Justice Powell had stated that the majority's recognition of district court

---

7. In re Grand Jury 87–3 Subpoena Duces Tecum, 955 F.2d 229 (4th Cir.1992).

capacity to respond to a "bad faith exercise of grand jury powers" would allow for "striking * * * a proper balance between freedom of the press and the obligation of all citizens to give relevant testimony with respect to criminal conduct," but that balance would be struck on a case-by-case analysis of the facts, not through a threshold imposition of "constitutional preconditions." This indicated that the Supreme Court did not believe it necessary to impose any special burden on the government, as would be imposed under a "substantial relationship test," in order to protect adequately First Amendment interests. It was sufficient that the district court apply, "with special sensitivity where values of expression are potentially implicated," the standards of *R. Enterprises*, keeping in mind the "traditional rule," as set forth in *R. Enterprises* that " 'grand juries are not licensed to engage in arbitrary fishing expeditions, nor may they select targets out of malice or an intent to harass.' "

Attorney-client relationships. Chilling impact objections have also been raised in connection with grand jury subpoenas requiring attorneys to testify in connection with the investigation of past or current clients. Of course, insofar as questions posed to the attorney/witness seek information protected by the attorney-client privilege, that privilege can be relied upon to refuse to furnish that information. However, certain essential facts that are likely to be sought by the grand jury (e.g., client identity and fee information) commonly are not protected by the privilege. Here, attorneys have argued that, because of the chilling impact that such disclosure would have upon the attorney-client relationship, the grand jury should not be allowed to force disclosure from the attorney in the absence of an initial showing of special need and relevance. This position has been consistently rejected, however, by both federal and state appellate courts.

In refusing to require that government make a showing of need to compel an attor-

ney to provide non-privileged information relating to the representation of a client, the courts have noted that: (1) the attorney-client privilege and work product doctrine provide adequate protection of the attorney-client relationship; (2) even where the subpoenaed attorney currently is representing the client, it typically is at a point where the client is simply a target of the investigation and therefore has no Sixth Amendment right to representation; (3) neither is the subpoena likely to interfere with the target/client's future Sixth Amendment right to counsel (assuming a subsequent indictment) because the possibility that the attorney's grand jury testimony will lead to the attorney's disqualification at trial tends to be no more than an "abstract possibility," hinging upon the happenstance of a variety of speculative occurrences; and (4) the attorney/witness is asking for exactly the kind of preliminary showing that the Supreme Court warned against in *Dionisio* and *Branzburg* as causing indeterminate delays in grand jury investigations. The Second Circuit has suggested that the first and fourth factors are sufficient in themselves to reject a "compelling need standard," as it has refused to require such a showing even where the information sought relates to a currently represented criminal defendant and could conceivably lead to counsel's disqualification in the ongoing criminal case. The appellate courts note, however, that the supervisory court has sufficient discretionary authority under provisions like Rule 17(c) (prohibiting "oppressive" subpoenas) to quash or delay enforcement of a subpoena to an attorney where requiring immediate compliance would interfere with counsel's representation of the defendant in a currently pending trial. In such situations, the supervisory court may insist that the government make some showing of a need to obtain the information sought prior to that trial, at least where counsel shows that compliance with the subpoena will disrupt preparation for the trial.[8]

---

8. In 1991, the ABA added to Rule 3.8 of the Model Rules of Professional Conduct a provision applicable to prosecutors who seek to subpoena lawyers in grand jury or other criminal proceedings for the purpose of obtaining

from the lawyer information "about a past or present client." Rule 3.8 held prosecutorial use of such a subpoena to constitute unprofessional conduct unless (1) the "evidence sought is essential to the successful completion of

(e) Use for Civil Discovery. In *United States v. Procter & Gamble*,[9] the lower court granted broad disclosure of grand jury testimony to defendants in a civil antitrust action, with its ruling apparently influenced by the belief that the government had used the grand jury process "to elicit evidence" that it could later introduce in its civil action. The Supreme Court rejected the disclosure order as not supported by a showing of particularized need, but it also acknowledged that the alleged government subversion of the criminal process could constitute "good cause" warranting such extensive disclosure to the opposing party in the civil suit. There had been no finding, however, that the grand jury proceeding had in fact "been used as a short cut to [civil discovery] goals otherwise barred or more difficult to reach." If the grand jury had been employed in that fashion, the Court noted, the government clearly would have been guilty of "flouting the policy of the law," both as to the grand jury's proper function and the prescribed procedures for civil discovery. On the other hand, if the grand jury investigation were legitimate, there was no need to deny the government the incidental benefit of civil use of properly acquired evidence.

Lower courts applying the civil misuse standard of *Procter & Gamble* agree that whether or not an abuse exists depends upon the government's purpose in using the grand jury process, rather than the relevancy of the requested information to possible civil litigation. They recognize that a proper criminal investigation may readily encompass elements that also relate to civil cases, and that in some areas of the law (e.g., antitrust), the overlap

between the criminal and civil investigation will be substantial. Some disagreement appears to exist, however, as to exactly how "pure" the government's purpose must be. Several courts have suggested that the *Procter & Gamble* standard is violated only when the investigation was aimed "primarily" at civil discovery. The issue, as they see it, is whether the grand jury proceedings were a "cover" or "subterfuge" for a civil investigation. Other courts suggest that the grand jury can be used only to conduct investigations that are in their inception "exclusively criminal." This standard arguably would bar an investigation that is initiated with "a completely open mind as to what the appropriate remedy should be, criminal, civil, or both." If so, it probably goes beyond what the Supreme Court had in mind in *Procter & Gamble*.

To establish an improper purpose, the party claiming misuse (whether the target of the investigation or the witness called to testify) must overcome the traditional "presumption of regularity," in the grand jury process. That burden clearly is the heaviest when the objection is made during an ongoing investigation by a motion to quash a subpoena or terminate the investigation. Courts hesitate to project the purpose of an investigation while it is still ongoing. Even where the surrounding circumstances strongly suggest misuse (e.g., where the grand jury investigation was instituted shortly after the target's legal challenges stymied a civil investigation), courts have been willing on a motion to quash or terminate to accept a prosecution affidavit of good faith as a sufficient response. A more appropriate assessment, it is argued, can be made after the

---

an ongoing investigation or prosecution"; (2) "there is no other feasible alternative to obtain the information"; and (3) "the prosecutor obtains prior judicial approval after an opportunity for an adversarial proceeding." The requirement of prior judicial approval for issuance of an attorney subpoena was deleted in 1995, but several states adopted the original version. When federal district courts incorporated those state provisions in local rules binding upon United State's attorneys, the reviewing circuit courts split on whether the district courts had exceeded their authority. However, in 1998, Congress adopted the Citizen's Protection Act (CPA), which subjects an "attorney for the [federal] government" (including United States Attorneys) to the "state laws * * * governing attorneys in such State where such [federal] attorney engages in that attorney's

duties, to the same extent and in the same manner as other attorneys in that State." Lower courts have held, however, that CPA does not operate to provide a grounding for quashing a grand jury subpoena allegedly issued in violation of a state ethics rule similar to Rule 3.8. They have reasoned that: (1) Rule 3.8 is more than an "ethical standard" insofar as it imposes a "novel procedural step" of pre-issuance court approval, contrary to Fed.R.Crim. P.17; and (2) the remedy for violating a standard of professional responsibility cannot be extended beyond a disciplinary sanction, to also include the exclusion of evidence obtained through the violation, as that would override the Federal Rules of Evidence.

9. 356 U.S. 677, 78 S.Ct. 983, 2 L.Ed.2d 1077 (1958).

investigation is ended, with adequate relief still available to the target. If the grand jury should return an indictment, that act will constitute strong evidence "that there has been no perversion of grand jury processes." If an indictment has not been returned, the target retains the opportunity to challenge the proceeding when and if a civil agency requests disclosure for use in connection with a civil suit. At that point, a more detailed government affidavit may be required, or the court may hold an evidentiary hearing. Exactly how much explanation will be demanded from the government will vary with the strength of the suggestion of possible misuse in the surrounding circumstances. As one court noted, in the end, the judge's ruling on a misuse objection must seek to strike an equitable balance between "(1) the need of the [prospective civil] defendants to ascertain whether there has been an abuse of the grand jury process, and (2) the policies of grand jury secrecy and freedom in government decisionmaking."

(f) Use for Post–Indictment Criminal Discovery. The grand jury is given its broad investigative powers to determine whether a crime has been committed and an indictment should issue, not to gather evidence for use in cases in which indictments have already issued. Accordingly, both state and federal courts hold that it is an abuse of the grand jury process to use grand jury subpoenas "for the sole or dominating purpose of preparing an already pending indictment for trial." Those courts also hold, however, that where the primary purpose of the investigation is to determine whether others not indicted were involved in the same criminal activity, or whether the indicted party committed still other crimes, the government may go forward with the inquiry even though one result may be the production of evidence that could then be used at the trial of the pending indictment. They note also that, prior to indictment, nothing prevents the prosecution from bringing before the grand jury evidence that will fully explore the case, beyond what is needed for probable cause, although one consequence is to better prepare the prosecution for trial on

the indictment it hopes the grand jury will issue.

A claim of a dominant purpose of post-indictment discovery may be raised in various procedural settings, including a witness' motion to quash a subpoena, an indicted target's motion for a protective order restricting the scope of an investigation, and a defense objection at trial to the admission of evidence arguably derived from such grand jury misuse. In evaluating such claims, the general approach of the courts has paralleled that applied to claims of the misuse of a grand jury to obtain civil discovery. Here too, courts start with the principle that a "presumption of regularity" attaches to the grand jury proceeding and that the objecting party bears the burden of overcoming that presumption. Courts also have noted their reluctance to interfere with an ongoing investigation, suggesting that the true purpose of the investigation can best be assessed after it is completed. Where the objecting party can point to surrounding circumstances highly suggestive of improper use, the court may require a governmental affidavit explaining the purpose of the post-indictment investigation or it may examine the grand jury transcript in camera to determine that purpose.

(g) Prosecution or Police Usurpation of the Subpoena Power. The subpoena power of the grand jury is designed for its own use, not to further independent investigations of the prosecutor or police. In most jurisdictions, the prosecutor may have subpoenas issued without advance authorization of the grand jury, but the purpose of the subpoena must be to produce evidence for use by the grand jury. This does not bar the prosecutor from screening the requested information before it is formally presented to the grand jury. Documents produced pursuant to a grand jury subpoena duces tecum commonly are first viewed and summarized by the prosecution staff, and in some instances, only the summaries are actually presented to the jurors. Similarly, it is not uncommon for prosecutors to use the occasion of the witness' grand jury appearance to conduct a preliminary interview. The prosecutor may not, however, have the grand jury subpoena issued "as a ploy to secure the attendance of a witness at the prosecutor's office." Nor may the prosecutor use the subpoena authority to force a witness to submit to an office interview. Similarly, while the prosecutor may utilize the grand jury subpoena to compel testimony from a witness after he has first refused to provide information to the police, this may be done only if the information sought truly is needed for the grand jury inquiry. Thus, when a person refuses to give the police any information that may assist in locating a fugitive, the prosecutor may not then seek to compel that testimony through a grand jury subpoena, absent a situation in which the grand jury has a legitimate interest in obtaining the testimony of the fugitive or in determining whether the fugitive has been assisted in his flight.

Courts have divided as to whether special safeguards are needed to ensure that subpoenas for identification exemplars are really directed at a grand jury inquiry rather than at assisting an independent police investigation. Some courts have treated such subpoenas no differently than any other subpoena duces tecum. Other courts have concluded, however, that the potential for misuse requires special prerequisites where a subpoena demands production of identification exemplars. They have held, for example, that such subpoenas should not issue unless first approved by the grand jurors, thereby ensuring that the grand jury has an interest in the evidence sought. One court, concerned that the grand jury not be used to bypass the showing required under local law for the police to place a non-arrestee in a lineup, imposed the requirement that "a prosecutor seeking judicial enforcement of a grand jury directive to appear in a lineup * * * make a minimal factual showing sufficient to permit the judge to conclude that there is a reason for the lineup which is consistent with the legitimate function of the grand jury."

(h) Harassment. In the course of upholding broad investigatory powers of the grand jury, courts frequently note that, of course, use of those powers for the purpose of "harassment" is always subject to judicial remedy. Precisely what a court has in mind by this reference to "harassment" is often left open, but it apparently refers to something more than simply using the grand jury process for some unauthorized purpose, such as civil discovery. Courts that have offered illustrations of harassment tend to stress a vindictive element in the use of the grand jury, usually a use designed to intimidate the witness. Thus, illustrations are offered of "bad faith harassment of a political dissident" by imposing the burdens (political and otherwise) of a grand jury appearance with "no expectation that any testimony concerning a crime would be forthcoming." Similarly, repeated subpoenas to appear before one grand jury after another may reflect harassment. So too, subpoenas utilized to provide leaks to the press would constitute harassment. It has also been argued that calling a witness before the grand jury solely to trap him into committing perjury constitutes a form of harassment.

(i) Structural Objections. May a grand jury witness refuse to comply with a subpoena because the grand jury is not lawfully constituted? A grand jury has no authority to take action after its term has expired, and an indictment issued by such a grand jury is viewed as a jurisdictional nullity, subject to challenge even after conviction. Although *Blair*[10] stated that a grand jury witness lacked standing to challenge the "authority of the court or of the grand jury, provided they have a de facto existence and organization," that limitation has never been viewed as precluding a witness challenge to the territorial reach of the subpoena authority of the issuing court. Arguably, the legal existence of the grand jury falls in the same category. The same presumably would not be said of the unconstitutional composition of the grand jury, but the Second Circuit once suggested that a witness could raise such an objection. However, later cases have rejected that conclusion as inconsistent with *Blair*, and the Second Circuit later indicated its suggestion rested upon the grand jury

---

10. See note 1 supra.

in that case having elected to hold the witness in criminal contempt.

§ 8.9 Grand Jury Inquiries Based on Illegally Obtained Evidence

(a) The Calandra Rule. In *United States v. Calandra*,[1] grand jury witness Calandra was asked questions about certain records that had been seized previously in a search of his office. He then requested and received a postponement of the grand jury proceedings so that he could present a pre-charge motion for return and suppression of the seized records under then Federal Rule 41(e). The district court granted the motion, holding that the search had been unconstitutional, and further ordered that "Calandra need not answer any of the grand jury's questions based on the suppressed evidence." A divided Supreme Court (6–3) reversed, holding that the exclusionary rule could not be invoked by a grand jury witness to bar questions based on unconstitutionally seized evidence.

Viewing the exclusionary rule as basically a prophylactic remedy, the *Calandra* majority concluded that its applicability in the grand jury setting should be determined by weighing "the potential injury [in the rule's application] to the historic role and functions of the grand jury" against the potential for increased deterrence of illegal searches. On the one side, "it [was] evident that this extension of the exclusionary rule would seriously impede the grand jury": "permitting witnesses to invoke the exclusionary rule and would delay and disrupt grand jury proceedings," and the resulting "suppression hearings would halt the orderly progress of an investigation and necessitate extended litigation of issues only tangentially related to the grand jury's primary objective." On the other side, the incremental deterrent effect that might be achieved by applying the exclusionary rule in grand jury proceedings was "uncertain at best." That application would provide additional deterrence, beyond that provided by application at trial, only in the unlikely case in which a police investiga-

tion was directed "toward the discovery of evidence solely for use in a grand jury investigation." Any "incentive to disregard the requirements of the Fourth Amendment" as to grand juries, the Court noted, "is substantially negated by the inadmissibility of the illegally-seized evidence in a subsequent criminal prosecution of the search victim." On balance, the Court would not "embrace a view that would achieve a speculative and undoubtedly minimal advance in the deterrence of police misconduct at the expense of substantially impeding the role of the grand jury."

Lower courts have viewed the balance struck in *Calandra* as going beyond Fourth Amendment violations. They have also rejected witness objections to grand jury use of evidence obtained illegally through violations of other constitutional provisions and statutory prohibitions. This is consistent with *Calandra's* concern that witnesses not be allowed to "delay and disrupt" the grand jury proceedings by raising challenges to the source of that Grand jury's inquiry. It also is consistent with *Calandra's* reliance upon Supreme Court precedent holding that an indicted defendant cannot challenge a grand jury's reliance upon unconstitutionally obtained evidence in its decision to indict—a precedent that has been applied to a variety of illegalities in the acquisition of evidence.[2]

Courts have recognized, however, two exceptions to *Calandra*. The broader exception relating to illegal electronic surveillance, is discussed in subsection (b) below. The second and narrower exception relates to *Silverthorne Lumber Co. v. United States*.[3] *Calandra* distinguished in a footnote the *Silverthorne* case, which had upheld the right of indicted defendants to refuse to respond to a grand jury subpoena duces tecum which would have required them to produce the same documents that had been returned to them following their successful Fourth Amendment challenge to the police seizure of those documents. *Silverthorne* reasoned that the subpoena was the fruit of

§ 8.9

1. 414 U.S. 338, 94 S.Ct. 613, 38 L.Ed.2d 561 (1974).

2. See § 15.5(a).

3. 251 U.S. 385, 40 S.Ct. 182, 64 L.Ed. 319 (1920).

the poisonous tree, as knowledge of the documents came from the illegal search, and that knowledge was thereby rendered permanently inaccessible to the government. The *Calandra* footnote cited three distinguishing characteristics of *Silverthorne*: (1) "there, plaintiffs in error had previously been indicted * * * and thus could invoke the exclusionary rule on the basis of their status as criminal defendants"; (2) the "government's interest in recapturing the original documents was founded on a belief they might be useful in the criminal prosecution already authorized by the grand jury," rather than a "need to perform its investigatory or accusatorial functions"; and (3) "prior to the issuance of the grand jury subpoenas, there had been a judicial determination that the search and seizure were illegal" (in contrast to a claim of an illegal search "raised for the first time on a pre-indictment motion to suppress requiring interruption of grand jury proceedings"). Lower court opinions examining the "*Silverthorne* exception" suggest that all three distinguishing factors must be present to challenge a grand jury subpoena as derived from an illegal search.

(b) Illegal Electronic Surveillance. In *Gelbard v. United States*,[4] grand jury witnesses refused to answer questions put to them by the prosecutor, asserting that the questions were derived from electronic surveillance that violated Title III of the Omnibus Crime Control and Safe Streets Act. The issue before the Supreme Court was whether, assuming that the witnesses assertions were correct, such use of illegally intercepted communications constituted "just cause" for a refusal to answer (and therefore relieved the witnesses of contempt liability). The Court in a 5–4 decision held that: (1) § 2515 of Title III prohibited interrogation of grand jury witnesses based on illegally intercepted communications, and (2) the witness could advance this prohibition as "just cause" for refusing to testify. The Court had little difficulty on the first point since § 2515 specifically refers to grand jury proceedings as among those proceedings in which "no evidence derived [from an illegal interception] may be received." On the second point, some

difficulty was presented by § 2518(10)'s failure to include grand jury proceedings among the specified proceedings in which a motion to suppress might be brought. This omission was viewed as not inconsistent with simply allowing a grand jury witness to refuse to respond to questions based on illegal interceptions. The Court noted, however, that it reserved the issue as to whether a witness could refuse to answer if the interceptions had been made pursuant to a court order issued under Title III. Speaking to that situation, Justice White, the crucial fifth vote for the *Gelbard* majority, noted that the presence of a court order for the interception required a "different accommodation between the dual functioning of the grand jury system and the federal wiretap statute." Allowance of a suppression hearing would result in "protracted interruption" of the grand jury proceedings. Moreover, the deterrent value of excluding the evidence where the prosecutor had relied in good faith on a court order would be "marginal at best."

Lower courts applying *Gelbard* have accepted Justice White's suggestion that a witness objecting to grand jury use of a court ordered interception should not be entitled to a full-blown suppression hearing, but have also sought to provide reasonable assurance that a witness is not required to respond to questions based upon an invalid court order. One line of cases has held that the proper accommodation requires no more than an in camera inspection of the surveillance documents to ensure that the court order is in compliance with the statute. Another line of decisions provides for witness access to the key documents unless the government can show that grand jury secrecy requires in camera review. The witness is still limited, however, to challenging defects found on the face of those documents.

Gelbard left to the lower courts the task of establishing procedures for determining whether grand jury questions were in fact based upon an electronic surveillance. Frequent *Gelbard* objections have produced a substantial number of lower courts opinions dealing in particular with two issues relating to

4. 408 U.S. 41, 92 S.Ct. 2357, 33 L.Ed.2d 179 (1972).

those procedures: (1) the nature of the allegation that must be made by the witness to trigger a government obligation to make inquiry and respond as to the existence of wiretaps; and (2) the nature of the showing that must be made by the government in support of its response denying the existence of wiretaps. In determining the sufficiency of the witness' claim, courts recognize that the presence of wiretapping often is difficult to detect, and imposing a substantial burden on the witness would result in rewarding the use of more sophisticated equipment that leaves fewer traces of interception. On the other hand, many courts also believe that recalcitrant grand jury witnesses, seeking delay, will not be reluctant to raise totally unfounded *Gelbard* objections. Balancing these concerns, some courts have concluded that the "mere assertion" of wiretapping is sufficient to require a response, but the prosecutor need not make an extensive investigation in responding to such a general claim. Other courts, however, have held that the prosecutor has no obligation to inquire and respond unless the witness makes some minimal showing, supported by specific factual averments. That showing may be based on the subject matter of the questions, the fact that the witness was required to furnish a voice exemplar, or unique telephone difficulties.

In determining whether a government denial of wiretapping is supported by sufficient investigation, the Court will consider the strength of the witness' showing that there may have been a wiretap, the likelihood that a particular unchecked source may have contributed to the investigation, and the range of the questions asked of the witness. The fact that law enforcement agents working directly on the case are unaware of a wiretap does not necessarily mean that one did not exist; the agents may be relying on information obtained from other agencies (perhaps more than once removed) that did come from a wiretap. However, prosecutors rarely are required to check with all seven of the federal agencies that customarily conduct electronic surveillance. Indeed, unless the witness' claim is supported by substantial indication of a probable wiretap, the courts are likely to permit a response that does not go beyond checking with the single agent in charge of the investigation.

§ 8.10 Grand Jury Testimony and the Privilege Against Self-Incrimination

(a) The Availability of the Privilege. *Counselman v. Hitchcock*,[1] decided in 1892, put to rest any doubts as to whether the Fifth Amendment privilege against self-incrimination was available to a grand jury witness. The grand jury witness testifies pursuant to a subpoena so the requisite element of "compulsion" clearly is present. However, the Amendment states only that a person shall not be compelled to be a witness against himself "in a criminal case." The *Counselman* Court reasoned that the grand jury inquiry into criminal liability was itself a "criminal case," but that characterization was not, in any event, a prerequisite to the availability of the privilege. The Fifth Amendment's "criminal case" requirement, it noted, refers to the eventual use of the testimony, not the nature of the proceeding in which it is compelled. Accordingly, the Fifth Amendment applies to a witness "in any proceeding" who is being compelled to give testimony that might incriminate him in a subsequent criminal case.

Counselman's analysis of the function of the "criminal case" phrasing in the Fifth Amendment had significance far beyond the grand jury. It led to a long line of cases holding the self-incrimination privilege available to witnesses in various non-criminal proceedings, including civil cases and administrative agency hearings. These rulings traditionally were viewed, consistent with *Counselman's* analysis, as reflecting the command of the Fifth Amendment itself; but that position seemingly was rejected by a majority of the Court in the 2003 ruling in *Chavez v. Martinez*.[2] Although

---

§ 8.10

1. 142 U.S. 547, 12 S.Ct. 195, 35 L.Ed. 1110 (1892).

2. 538 U.S. 760, 123 S.Ct. 1994, 155 L.Ed.2d 984 (2003), also discussed in § 2.9 at note 25 § 6.2 at note 17, and § 6.5 at note 6.

Chavez did not involve the exercise of the privilege by a witness in a non-criminal proceeding, the Court considered the non-criminal cases relevant to the question before it: whether the Fifth Amendment was violated by coercive interrogation of a suspect that compelled a statement which was never used against the suspect in a criminal case.[3] The non-criminal cases were deemed relevant because the privilege was being made available to witnesses in those proceedings notwithstanding that there was no assurance that the statement being compelled would later be used in a criminal case. Six justices discounted the non-criminal cases by explaining that the availability of the privilege there rested not on the language of the Amendment as read in *Counselman*, but on the authority of the Court to craft protective procedures to implement the basic constitutional right.

Four Justices, in an opinion by Justice Thomas, concluded that the prohibition of the Fifth Amendment is tied to the actual admission of a compelled statement in a criminal case because only that makes the person "a witness against himself" in "a criminal case". While the Court had recognized "an evidentiary privilege that protects witnesses from being forced to give incriminatory testimony, even in noncriminal cases," that privilege was established as a "prophylactic rule". It was "necessary to allow the assertion of the privilege prior to the commencement of a 'criminal case' to safeguard the core Fifth Amendment trial right." Allowing the assertion of the privilege at that point, and then insisting on a grant of immunity before compelling any subsequent testimony, served to "memorialize the fact that the testimony had indeed been compelled" and thereby enabled courts in subsequent criminal proceedings to distinguish between compelled statements and statements deemed "voluntary" (a consequence of the witness "failure to assert the privilege.")

Justice Souter (joined by Justice Kennedy), in a concurring opinion in *Chavez*, offered a somewhat similar (but also distinct) characterization of the cases recognizing a witness' assertion of the privilege in non-criminal cases.

Those cases, the opinion noted, establish "law * * * outside the Fifth Amendment's core." That "core" was "focus[ed] on the courtroom use of a criminal defendant's compelled self-incriminating testimony." However, allowing the assertion of the right in non-criminal proceedings appropriately reflected "a judgment that the core guarantee, or the judicial capacity to protect it" required some "complementary protection." Thus, the rulings upholding privilege claims in non-criminal/proceedings were "extensions of the bare guarantee" to ensure the "efficiency of the core."

Both the Souter and Thomas opinions treat the non-criminal-case *Counselman* progeny (if not *Counselman* itself) as establishing court-created safeguards that are not part of the "core" of the privilege—a core violated only when a person is compelled to furnish incriminatory testimony in his own "criminal case" or when the prosecution uses against a person in a criminal case an incriminatory statement compelled in a proceeding not part of that case. The characterization of the *Counselman* progeny as resting on a lesser constitutional grounding may have little impact, apart from the absence of a damage remedy for violation of such a non-core safeguard (as suggested in Justice Souter's opinion). In determining whether an assertion of the privilege is justified by a potential of incrimination, the Court has long held that the same general standard of potential incrimination (described below) applies to assertions of the privilege in both criminal and non-criminal cases.

(b) The Standard of Potential Incrimination. Under the standard construction of the Fifth Amendment privilege, a broad range of information can be classified as potentially incriminating and therefore protected by the privilege. However, the concept of potential incrimination is not without limits. The threat posed by the information is limited only to possible criminal liability, and that liability must relate to the witness himself, not others. The threat must be "real and appreciable," not "imaginary and unsubstantial." Moreover, a witness' assertion of the privilege is not

---

3. See § 6.5 at note 6 (discussing the Court's rejection of this claim).

conclusive. "It is for the court to say whether his silence is justified, and to require him to answer 'if it clearly appears to the court that he is mistaken.'" The Supreme Court has indicated, however, that courts are to give the witness every benefit of the doubt in reviewing his assertion of the privilege. *Hoffman v. United States*[4] sets forth the applicable standard.

> This provision of the [Fifth] Amendment must be accorded liberal construction in favor of the right it was intended to secure. The privilege afforded not only extends to answers that would in themselves support a conviction * * * but likewise embraces those which would furnish a link in the chain of evidence needed to prosecute the claimant for a federal crime. * * * [T]his protection must be confined to instances where the witness has reasonable cause to apprehend danger from a direct answer. * * * However, if the witness, upon interposing his claim, were required to prove the hazard in the sense in which a claim is usually required to be established in court, he would be compelled to surrender the very protection which the privilege is designed to guarantee. To sustain the privilege, it need only be evident from the implications of the question, in the setting in which it is asked, that a responsive answer to the question or an explanation of why it cannot be answered might be dangerous because injurious disclosure could result.

Applying this standard, it will be a rare case in which a claim of the privilege, made in the grand jury context, will be rejected by a court. The leading Supreme Court application of the *Hoffman* standard is illustrative. In *Malloy v. Hogan*,[5] the lower court was held to have erred in rejecting a self-incrimination claim by a witness who had pled guilty to a gambling charge and was now being asked about the circumstances surrounding his arrest and plea.

The questions were obviously designed to determine the identity of his employer, and "if this person were still engaged in unlawful activity, disclosure of his identity might furnish a link in a chain of evidence sufficient to connect the [witness] with a more recent crime for which he still might be prosecuted." If the questions in *Malloy* had related to a past offense of conviction that did not have a distinct potential for ongoing criminality and the information sought appeared to have no bearing beyond that offense, the rejection of the claim of privilege could very well have been sustained. "The ordinary rule," the Court has stated, is that once a person "is convicted of a crime, he no longer has the privilege against self-incrimination as he can no longer be incriminated by his testimony about the crime."[6] Even in this situation, however, the circumstances often preclude a judge from reaching the conclusion that *Hoffman* described as needed for rejecting a witness' claim—that it is "perfectly clear, from a careful consideration of all the circumstances in the case, that the witness is mistaken and the answer cannot possibly have such tendency to incriminate." First, the finality of the conviction must be considered; many jurisdictions do not view a conviction as eliminating potential incrimination for the crime of conviction if the opportunity for appellate review (and therefore for a possible reversal and new trial) remains open. Second, in light of the capacity of both state and federal governments to prosecute for the same criminal activity, the possibility often remains of incrimination under the laws of the other jurisdiction.

(c) Incrimination Under the Laws of Another Sovereign. For many years, American courts took the position that the privilege protected only against incrimination under the laws of the sovereign which was attempting to

---

4. 341 U.S. 479, 71 S.Ct. 814, 95 L.Ed. 1118 (1951).

5. 378 U.S. 1, 84 S.Ct. 1489, 12 L.Ed.2d 653 (1964).

6. The same is true of an acquittal, since here too double jeopardy precludes a second prosecution for the same offense. On the other hand, as the Supreme Court noted in *Ohio v. Reiner*, 532 U.S. 17, 121 S.Ct. 1252, 149 L.Ed.2d 158 (2001), a person who claims under oath to be innocent is not thereby precluded from exercising the

privilege in the same testimony. "Truthful responses of an innocent witness, as well as those of a wrongdoer, may provide the government with incriminating evidence from the speakers own mouth." In *Reiner*, while the witness claimed to be innocent, she also acknowledged (in subsequently immunized testimony), that she "was with [the deceased infant] within the potential timeframe of [his] fatal trauma."

compel the incriminating testimony. In applying this rule, which was said to be derived from the English common law, the individual states and the federal system were treated as separate sovereigns. Thus, if a witness appearing before a federal grand jury was granted immunity against federal prosecution, he could not refuse to testify on the ground that his answers might be incriminating under the laws of a state. In *Murphy v. Waterfront Commission*,[7] the Supreme Court rejected this "separate sovereign" doctrine as applied to state and federal prosecutions. Noting that a contrary position would allow a witness to be "whipsawed into incriminating himself under both state and federal law," the Court concluded that the "policies and purposes" of the Fifth Amendment required that the privilege protect "a state witness against incrimination under federal immunity as well as state law and a federal witness against incrimination under state as well as federal law." This meant that the immunity granted to replace the privilege had to extend to both state and federal prosecutions. Neither a state nor the federal government could compel testimony by granting immunity as to that testimony only within its own jurisdiction and thereby make that testimony available to be used by other jurisdictions (the "whipsaw" that would follow from application of the separate sovereign limitation).

The *Murphy* opinion contains language suggesting that the separate sovereign limitation was flawed even in its consideration of other nations, and the privilege therefore should be available where the witness realistically feared that his responses could lead to prosecution in a foreign country. However, the Court noted shortly afterwards that *Murphy's* rejection of the separate sovereign limitation related only to American jurisdictions and the issue remained open as to incrimination under the laws of foreign countries. In *United States v. Balsys*,[8] that issue was squarely presented by a case in which a resident alien, subpoenaed to testify at a deposition concerning his possible participation in Nazi persecutions during World War III, sought to claim the privilege because of a "real and substantial" danger that his answers could lead to criminal prosecution in either Lithuania or Israel. A divided Court concluded that the incrimination under the laws of foreign country was beyond the protection afforded by the self-incrimination privilege.

The *Balsys* majority rejected the contention that the phrase "any criminal case" in the self-incrimination clause literally encompasses all prosecutions, no matter where they might occur. That phrase, the Court noted, must be read in the context of a Fifth Amendment which encompasses various other guarantees (grand jury indictment, double jeopardy, due process, and just compensation), which are only implicated "by action of the government that it binds." The *Murphy* reading of the privilege as applicable to incrimination under both federal and state law was consistent with this reading because it was the product of the application of the self-incrimination privilege to the states via the Fourteenth Amendment. Once the states become bound by the Fifth Amendment guarantee, the self-incrimination clause "could no longer be seen as framed for one jurisdiction [i.e., state or federal government] alone, each jurisdiction having instead become subject to the same claim of privilege flowing from the one limitation." This concept of a single guarantee, applicable to both state and federal governments, was consistent with a "feature unique to the [self-incrimination] guarantee," the "option to exchange the privilege for an immunity to prosecutorial use of any compelled testimony," as both state and federal immunity grants can readily be extended to bar use in a prosecution by the other government [see § 8.11(a)]. In contrast, neither state nor federal government could grant immunity that would extend to a prosecution by a foreign nation.

(d) Compelling the Target to Appear. The self-incrimination privilege has long been held to prohibit the prosecution from forcing a defendant to appear as a witness at his own

7. 378 U.S. 52, 84 S.Ct. 1594, 12 L.Ed.2d 678 (1964).

8. 524 U.S. 666, 118 S.Ct. 2218, 141 L.Ed.2d 575 (1998).

trial. Should the prosecutor similarly be prohibited from forcing the target of an investigation to appear before the grand jury, or is the Fifth Amendment satisfied by simply allowing the target-witness, like any other witness, to refuse to respond to individual questions where his answer might be incriminating? Several state courts have argued that the target of an investigation is, in effect, a "putative" or "de facto" defendant, and he therefore should be allowed to exercise his privilege in much the same manner as a "de jure defendant" at trial. In some of these jurisdictions, the target/witness must claim the privilege before the grand jury, which then excuses him from further testifying. In others, the privilege is viewed as a bar to the subpoena itself, so the target/witness cannot be called to testify unless first formally waiving his right not to appear. This position can result in subsequently prohibiting the prosecution's use of a witness' testimony against the witness where the prosecution treated the witness as a non-target (and did not seek a waiver) but the court subsequently determines that the witness was actually a target. Such a mistake is most likely to occur where "target" is defined by a strictly objective test (whether evidence known to the government established probable cause) as opposed to a subject test (whether the prosecutor believed it likely that the person would be indicted).

The federal courts and majority of state courts treat the target no differently than other witnesses as to being subpoenaed and exercising the privilege. As with grand jury witnesses generally, the self-incrimination privilege is said to present only "an option of refusal and not a prohibition of inquiry." The witness intending to exercise the privilege must appear in response to the subpoena and assert the privilege as to individual questions that would require an incriminating answer. In subjecting even target-witnesses to this requirement, courts stress that the grand jury is part of the investigatory stage of the process, which distinguishes the status of the target from that of the defendant at trial. The defendant's right of silence at trial grew out of the

early common law rule on the incompetency of parties to testify, which had bearing only at trial. It also rested in part on the fear that a defendant "forced in open court to refuse to answer questions" might be viewed by the jury as having something to hide. This concern has less significance in the grand jury setting; since that body looks only to the issue of probable cause, its proceedings need not be conducted "with the assiduous regard for the preservation of procedural safeguards which normally attends the ultimate trial of the issues."

Courts have further argued that the right to subpoena targets is inherent in the grand jury's combined investigative and shielding roles. Having an obligation to "run down every available clue," the jury cannot ignore the possibility that any one participant in a criminal enterprise may be willing to identify others. Having an obligation to "shield against arbitrary accusations," it has a right to be certain that the target's own testimony might not explain away the evidence against him. Another concern is that the establishment of a right not to appear based upon whether the prosecutor knew or should have known someone was a "target" would create a new source of tangential disputation.

Notwithstanding the authority to subpoena targets, subpoenas ad testificandum directed at targets are unusual. Indeed, the internal guidelines of the Department of Justice suggest that because of the possible "appearance of unfairness," where the target's testimony might be helpful, an effort should first be made to secure the voluntary appearance of the target.[9] However, the grand jury and U.S. Attorney may jointly agree to subpoena the target in exceptional cases. In making that determination, the grand jury and U.S. Attorney are directed to give "careful attention" to the importance of the testimony sought from the target, whether the substance of that testimony could be provided by other witnesses, and whether the "questions the prosecutor and the grand jurors intend to ask * * * would be protected by a valid claim of the privilege."

---

9. As for the guidelines definition of "target," see note 13 infra.

Should the subpoenaed "target and his or her attorney state in writing, signed by both, that the 'target' will refuse to testify in Fifth Amendment grounds, the witness ordinarily should be excused." However, the guidelines add that here too, the "grand jury and United States Attorney [may] agree to insist on appearance" based on the considerations "which justified the subpoena in the first place."

(e) **Advice as to Rights.** It generally is agreed that the Fifth Amendment does not demand that a non-target witness be advised of his privilege against self-incrimination. Courts are divided, however, as to whether such advice must be given to a target, with the more recent rulings leaning in the direction of holding that self-incrimination warnings are constitutionally required. In *United States v. Mandujano*,[10] the Supreme Court left that issue open for future consideration. *Mandujano* held that even if warnings were required, the failure to give the warnings could not constitute a defense to a perjury charge based on the witness' false grand jury testimony. Six justices, however, went on to speak to the need for warnings, with four suggesting that they were not required.

Although the witness in *Mandujano* had been informed of both his privilege against self-incrimination and his right to consult with counsel, the district court had held that that warning was insufficient. Since the witness was a "putative defendant," the district court reasoned, he should have been given full *Miranda* warnings, including notification of a right to appointed counsel. Chief Justice Burger's plurality opinion, speaking for four members of the Court, rejected the district court's reasoning. *Miranda,* he noted, applied only to "custodial interrogation," which clearly did not include questioning before the grand jury. The position of the subpoenaed witness could hardly be compared to that of the arrestee subjected to interrogation in the "hostile" and "isolated" setting of the police station. The appropriate analogy was to the questioning of a witness in an administrative or judicial hear-

ing. As noted by Justice Frankfurter in *United States v. Monia*,[11] a witness in that setting, "if * * * he desires the protection of the privilege, * * * must claim it or he will not be considered to have been 'compelled' within the meaning of the Amendment."

Chief Justice Burger added that, since Mandujano had been given self-incrimination warnings, there was no need to rule on whether such warnings were constitutionally required. Nevertheless the Chief Justice's reliance on *Monia* suggested that, in his view, grand jury witnesses, whether targets or nontargets, are not entitled to any special notification of rights. Rather, they would seem to bear the obligation, like witnesses generally, to assert the privilege on their own initiative. Justice Brennan, joined by Justice Marshall, viewed the Chief Justice's reference to *Monia* in this way, and responded that the plurality had read the privilege too narrowly. The *Monia* principle, he argued, rests on the assumption that the government ordinarily has no grounds for assuming that its compulsory processes are eliciting incriminating information. However, where the prosecutor is questioning a target witness, he is "acutely aware of the potentially incriminating nature of the disclosures sought." This knowledge, Justice Brennan reasoned, carried with it an obligation to advise the witness of his rights so as to ensure that any waiver of the privilege was "intelligent and intentional."

Minnesota v. Murphy[12] also casts light on the constitutional necessity for providing warnings. The issue before the Supreme Court in *Murphy* was the constitutional necessity of giving *Miranda*-type warnings to a probationer being questioned by a probation officer at his office. In holding that the warnings were not required, the Court drew an analogy to the grand jury setting. The interview setting in *Murphy*, the Court noted, subjected the probationer to "less intimidating pressure than is imposed upon a grand jury witness," and the Court has "never held that [warnings] must be given to the grand jury witness." This

10.   425 U.S. 564, 96 S.Ct. 1768, 48 L.Ed.2d 212 (1976).

11.   317 U.S. 424, 63 S.Ct. 409, 87 L.Ed. 376 (1943)

12.   465 U.S. 420, 104 S.Ct. 1136, 79 L.Ed.2d 409 (1984).

"expansive dictum," along with the reasoning of the plurality opinion in *Mandujano*, has led the Seventh Circuit to conclude that "the Supreme Court would be reluctant to extend a warning requirement to grand jury proceedings." Several state courts, however, have concluded that the special status of a person viewed by the prosecutor as a target carries with it constitutional obligation to inform that person of his right to refuse to answer on self-incrimination ground. Most federal and state courts have found it unnecessary to reach the issue as a result of regular notification pursuant to statutory requirements or practice guidelines.[13]

Justice Brennan's concurring opinion in *Mandujano* argued that target warnings had to go beyond simply explaining the availability of the self-incrimination privilege. In his view, the Fifth Amendment also required the prosecution to inform the target-witness that "he was currently subject to possible criminal prosecution for the commission of a stated crime." In *United States v. Washington*,[14] the Court rejected (over Justice Brennan's dissent) any suggestion that the Fifth Amendment required some form of "target" warning. The witness there had been given full *Miranda*-type warnings, but had not been told that he might be indicted in connection with his possession of a stolen motorcycle. The Court initially noted that previous discussions with the police and prosecutor had given the witness ample notice that he was a suspect in the motorcycle theft, but it then added that such awareness was, in any event, "largely irrelevant." A failure to give a potential defendant a target warning simply did not put the witness at a "constitutional disadvantage." His status as a target "neither enlarg[ed] nor diminish[ed]" the

scope of his constitutional protection. He "knew better than anyone else" whether his answers would be incriminating, and he also knew that anything he did say, after failing to exercise the privilege, could be used against him. The "constitutional guarantee," the Court noted, ensures "only that the witness be not *compelled* to give self-incriminating testimony."

As a matter of internal Justice Department policy, federal prosecutors are advised to inform witnesses who are "known 'targets'" that "their conduct is being investigated for possible violation of federal criminal law." Several state take the further step of imposing a statutory obligation upon prosecutors to inform targets of their target status prior to testifying. Because of the ambiguities presented in applying the various definitions of a "target," a cautious approach here will lead prosecutors to give notice whenever the witness presents even a remote potential of possible prosecution. If a witness should later be prosecuted and a court should conclude that the witness was a target and the prosecutor failed to give the statutorily required target warnings, the consequence may be exclusion of the witness' grand jury testimony or even dismissal of the indictment where the grand jury relied heavily on that testimony in indicting.

(f) Waiver. Assuming the witness receives those warnings, if any, that are constitutionally required, the privilege may be relinquished by the witness without an express statement of waiver. When the witness answers the question, his waiver is automatically assumed as to the content of that answer. Moreover, by providing in that answer certain incriminating information, the witness may relinquish his right to raise the privilege with respect to

13. Almost a dozen states now impose statutory requirements that the prosecutor inform a witness of the privilege against self-incrimination prior to testifying. While some of these requirements apply to all witnesses, others are limited to witnesses who are "targets" or "subjects" of the investigation. Even where the statutes are limited, prosecutors often will prefer to avoid subsequent judicial reexamination of the status of the witness by simply providing a notification of rights to all witnesses. In the federal system, prosecutors have followed the practice of providing notification to all subpoenaed witnesses as a matter of internal policy. Justice Depart-

ment guidelines require that all witnesses in the "target" and "subject" categories be advised of their right to exercise the self-incrimination privilege. ("Targets" are persons against whom "substantial evidence" exists, and who, in "the judgment of the prosecutor is a putative defendant"; "subjects" are persons "whose conduct is within the scope of the grand jury inquiry"). Also, a notification of the witness' privilege is included in the D.O.J.'s "advice of rights" form, which commonly is attached to all subpoenas.

14. 431 U.S. 181, 97 S.Ct. 1814, 52 L.Ed.2d 238 (1977).

further incriminating information. *Rogers v. United States*[15] is the leading case on such "testimonial waiver." The witness there testified before a grand jury that, as treasurer of the Communist Party of Denver, she had been in possession of party records, but had subsequently delivered those records to another person. She refused, however, to identify the recipient of the records, asserting that would be incriminating. A divided Supreme Court affirmed her contempt conviction, holding the privilege inapplicable. The Court noted that Rogers had already incriminated herself by admitting her party membership and past possession of the records; disclosure of her "acquaintanceship with her successor present[ed] no more than a 'mere imaginary possibility' of increasing the danger of prosecution." A witness would not be allowed to disclose a basic incriminating fact and then claim the privilege as to "details." To uphold such a claim of the privilege would "open the way to distortion of facts by permitting a witness to select any stopping point in her testimony."

Although *Rogers* often is described as posing great danger for the witness who answers even seemingly "innocuous questions," the decision actually is fairly limited. Courts have held, for example, that where a witness' initial admission related to only one element of an offense, that did not constitute a waiver as to questions that might require him to admit other elements of the offense. The fact that the second question asks for further detail as to the same event does not in itself establish that the privilege is not available. Indeed, most of the reported cases finding waiver have involved, as did *Rogers,* a refusal to "name others" in a setting in which it appears likely that the witness is concerned about incriminating those persons rather than himself.

As with other constitutional rights, a waiver is acceptable only if voluntary. In the grand jury setting, as contrasted to in-custody police interrogation, the setting itself does not inherently exert pressures that might render the waiver involuntary. However, the waiver still may be rendered involuntary by unconstitutional burdens placed on the exercise of the privilege. Thus, in *Garrity v. New Jersey*,[16] where police officers were warned that they would be removed from office if they did not waive their privilege and testify as to the fixing of traffic tickets, the Court held that their waivers were coerced and their testimony could not be used against them in subsequent criminal proceedings. If the grand jury witness should voluntarily waive the privilege, the generally accepted rule is that he may still exercise the privilege as an accused in a subsequent criminal prosecution. Waiver of the privilege applies only to the particular proceeding, and the dominant view is that the grand jury investigation and the criminal prosecution are separate proceedings.

(g) Adverse consequences. A witness who exercises the privilege before the grand jury is fully shielded against adverse legal consequences. The prohibition against drawing an adverse inference from a defendant's exercise of the privilege in a criminal trial has been held to apply as well to the grand jury's determination as to whether to indict a witness who exercised the privilege before the grand jury. The Supreme Court has held that a defendant who testifies at trial cannot be impeached by reference to his having asserted the privilege when questioned about the same events before the grand jury. The Court also has held that the state may not impose an administrative sanction (such as an employee discharge or a disqualification from government contracts) based upon an individual's exercise of the privilege before the grand jury. A state "may not impose substantial penalties because a witness elects to exercise his Fifth Amendment right not to give incriminating testimony against himself."[17]

---

15. 340 U.S. 367, 71 S.Ct. 438, 95 L.Ed. 344 (1951).

16. 385 U.S. 493, 87 S.Ct. 616, 17 L.Ed.2d 562 (1967).

17. The Court similarly had held the state may not impose an administrative sanction as punishment for the exercise of the privilege in an administrative investigation. See Spevack v. Klein, 385 U.S. 511, 87 S.Ct. 625, 17

L.Ed.2d 574 (1967) (state could not automatically disbar attorney because he had exercised the privilege in a disciplinary inquiry). However, in other respects, the shield against adverse consequences is not as complete for the person who exercises the privilege in a non-criminal proceeding. In particular, the finder of fact may draw an adverse inference as to the information not provided by a

§ 8.11 Immunity and Compelled Testimony

(a) Constitutionality. The use of immunity grants to preclude reliance upon the self-incrimination privilege predates the adoption of the constitution. The English adopted an immunity procedure, known as providing "indemnity" against prosecution, "soon after the privilege against compulsory self-incrimination became firmly established," and a similar practice was followed first in the colonies and then in the states. The first federal immunity act was not adopted until 1857, however, and the first Supreme Court ruling upholding immunity grants did not come until 1896, when *Brown v. Walker*[1] was decided. In that case, a sharply divided Court (5–4) concluded that the immunity procedure was consistent with the history and purpose of the Fifth Amendment privilege. The majority stressed that the Fifth Amendment could not be "construed literally as authorizing the witness to refuse to disclose any fact which might tend to incriminate, disgrace, or expose him to unfavorable comments." The history of the Amendment clearly indicated that its object was only to "secure the witness against criminal prosecution." Thus, the self-incrimination privilege had been held inapplicable where the witness' compelled testimony would relate only to an offense as to which he had been pardoned or as to which the statute of limitations had run. So too, the privilege had been held not to apply where the witness' response might tend to "disgrace him or bring him into disrepute" but would furnish no information relating to a criminal offense. Such rulings implicitly sustained the constitutionality of the immunity procedure. Since the immunity grant removed the only danger against which the privilege protected the wit-

ness, the witness could no longer claim that he was being compelled to incriminate himself.

In *Counselman v. Hitchcock*,[2] decided prior to *Brown,* the Court struck down a federal immunity statute that granted the witness protection only against the admission of his immunized testimony in evidence in a subsequent prosecution. The Court stressed that the statute failed to provide protection against derivative use of the witness' testimony, including "the use of his testimony to search out other testimony to be used in evidence against him." At the conclusion of its opinion, the Court spoke in terms of even broader protection, which would, "afford absolute immunity against future prosecution for the offense to which the question relates." This statement was taken as indicating that a valid immunity grant must absolutely bar prosecution for any transaction noted in the witness' testimony. Accordingly, Congress adopted a new immunity statute providing for such "transactional immunity." That statute provided that a witness directed to testify or produce documentary evidence pursuant to an immunity order could not be prosecuted "for or on account of any transaction, matter, or thing concerning which he may testify or produce evidence." The constitutionality of this provision was upheld in *Brown v. Walker,* and subsequent state and federal immunity statutes were largely patterned upon the *Brown* statute.

Later decisions—and the language of the later statutes—recognized two limitations in transactional immunity. The witness may still be prosecuted for perjury committed in his immunized testimony. Similarly, the immunity does not extend to a transaction noted in an answer totally unresponsive to the question asked. Thus, the witness cannot gain immunity from prosecution for all previous criminal acts by simply including a reference to those

---

person claiming the privilege. See Baxter v. Palmigiano, 425 U.S. 308, 96 S.Ct. 1551, 47 L.Ed.2d 810 (1976) (where a prison inmate summoned before a disciplinary board was told that the charge against him also involved a potential criminal violation, he could exercise the privilege, but the disciplinary board could draw an adverse inference from that silence as to the disciplinary charge; in criminal cases, "where the stakes are higher and the State's sole interest is to convict," allowing the factfinder to draw an adverse inference imposes too great a burden on the exercise of the

privilege [see § 24.5(b)], but the context of a civil or administrative proceeding changes the balance, and here the failure to respond to the other side's evidence, for whatever reason, may be given such evidentiary value as is "warranted by the facts surrounding the case").

§ 8.11

1. 161 U.S. 591, 16 S.Ct. 644, 40 L.Ed. 819 (1896).

2. 142 U.S. 547, 12 S.Ct. 195, 35 L.Ed. 1110 (1892).

acts in his testimony without regard to the subject on which he was asked to testify.

In *Murphy v. Waterfront Commission*,[3] the Court first upheld immunity that was not as broad in scope as the traditional transactional immunity. *Murphy,* as previously discussed, held that the self-incrimination privilege extends to possible incrimination under both federal and state law. Accordingly, to be constitutionally acceptable, the immunity granted to a witness had to provide adequate protection against both federal and state prosecutions. If that protection had to encompass transactional immunity, the state immunity provisions would necessarily fail. Congress could use its legislative authority to preempt state prosecutions, but the states lacked authority to prohibit federal prosecutions. The Court held, however, that the immunity grant need not absolutely bar prosecution in the other jurisdiction. It was sufficient that the witness was guaranteed that neither his testimony nor any fruits derived from that testimony would be used against him in any criminal prosecution. The Court, to accommodate "the interests of State and Federal Governments in investigating and prosecuting crime," would exercise its supervisory power to prohibit the federal government from using in federal courts state immunized testimony or the fruits thereof.

Following *Murphy,* Congress adopted a new immunity provision for federal witnesses, replacing transactional immunity with a prohibition against use and derivative use as to both federal and state prosecutions. The statute provided that "no testimony or other information compelled under the [immunity] order (or any information directly or indirectly derived from such testimony or other information) may be used against the witness in any criminal case, except a prosecution for perjury, giving a false statement, or otherwise failing to comply with the order." In *Kastigar v. United States*,[4] a divided Court upheld the new federal provision. The "broad language in *Counselman,*" which suggested the need for transactional immunity, was discounted as inconsistent with the "conceptual basis" of the

Counselman ruling. The crucial question, as *Counselman* noted, was whether the immunity granted was "coextensive with the scope of the privilege against self-incrimination." Both the immunity upheld in *Murphy* and the traditional Fifth Amendment remedy of excluding compelled statements and their fruits (as, for example, in the coerced confession cases) indicated that the privilege did not require an absolute bar against prosecution. A prohibition against use and derivative use satisfied the privilege by placing the witness "in substantially the same position as if * * * [he] had claimed his privilege."

The *Kastigar* majority rejected the argument, relied upon by the dissenters, that the bar against derivative use could not be enforced so effectively as to ensure that the witness really was placed in the same position as if he had not testified. The statute's "total prohibition on use," it noted, "provides a comprehensive safeguard, barring the use of compelled testimony as an 'investigatory lead,' and also barring the use of any evidence obtained by focusing investigation on a witness as a result of his compelled disclosures." Appropriate procedures for "taint hearings" could ensure that this prohibition was made effective. Those procedures, the Court noted, would be identical to the procedures prescribed in *Murphy.* Once the defendant demonstrates that he testified under a grant of immunity, the prosecution would "have the burden of showing that their evidence is not tainted by establishing that they had an independent, legitimate source for the disputed evidence." This was deemed to constitute "very substantial protection, commensurate with that resulting from invoking the privilege itself."

(b) Transactional vs. Use/Derivative–Use Immunity. In a companion case to *Kastigar,* the Supreme Court upheld a state immunity statute providing for use/derivative-use immunity. More than twenty states eventually moved from transactional to use/derivative-use immunity in their general immunity statutes. However, various groups, including the Ameri-

---

3. 378 U.S. 52, 84 S.Ct. 1594, 12 L.Ed.2d 678 (1964), discussed in § 8.10(b).

4. 406 U.S. 441, 92 S.Ct. 1653, 32 L.Ed.2d 212 (1972).

can Bar Association and the Commissioners on Uniform State Laws, have urged retention of transactional immunity, and almost as many states continue to provide the broader immunity. The remaining states have immunity statutes limited to testimony regarding certain offenses (e.g., gambling), which often provide transactional immunity as to those offenses.

Several state high courts have rejected the reasoning of *Kastigar* and held that their state constitutions require transactional immunity. In most states, however, the choice between transaction and use/derivative-use immunity is seen as an issue to be resolved by the legislature. That choice has lead to an extensive debate among commentators and various interest groups within the bar. The debate has tended to focus on three issues—the adequacy of taint hearings in preventing derivative use of immunized testimony, the comparative effectiveness of the two types of immunity in achieving witness cooperation, and the practical significance of the prosecutor's ability to bring a subsequent prosecution under use/derivative-use immunity.

With respect to taint hearings, proponents of transactional immunity contend that such hearings will not effectuate the goal of granting to the immunized witness the same protection against criminal prosecution that he would have had if allowed to refuse to testify on the basis of his self-incrimination privilege. They argue that the procedural safeguards required under *Kastigar* will fail to preclude all prosecutorial advantages gained through the immunized testimony both because of difficulties in detecting all derivative evidentiary uses and the failure of the derivative use prohibition to reach all prosecutorial decisions that might be influenced by awareness of the immunized testimony. Proponents of use/derivative-use immunity respond that the prosecutor's burden in establishing a truly independent source provides an adequate safeguard against derivative evidentiary use, and means are available to insulate all subsequent prosecutorial decisions from knowledge of the content of the immunized testimony.

With respect to the effectiveness of the immunity in gaining truthful and complete testimony from a recalcitrant witness, each side claims that the other will lead witnesses to give shallow and incomplete testimony. Proponents of transactional immunity claim that witnesses given use/derivative-use immunity will respond in that manner because they fear subsequent prosecution. Proponents of use/derivative-use immunity argue that, to the contrary, such immunity will encourage the witness to give more complete testimony because that makes it more difficult for the government to establish that no use was made of that testimony in any subsequent prosecution. Under transactional immunity, they argue, the witness is encouraged to say no more than he has to since a single admission gains him full immunity from prosecution. Finally, supporters of use/derivative-use immunity contend that the absence of an absolute protection against prosecution makes the immunized witness' testimony more credible to the jury.

As for the significance of the subsequent prosecutions that may be lost by granting transactional rather than use/derivative-use immunity, proponents of transactional immunity point to "the small number of actual successful prosecutions of immunized witnesses with 'use' immunity." Proponents of use/derivative-use immunity respond that the interests of justice would suffer if the witnesses involved, though small in number, were given the "gratuity of absolute immunity." There is no reason, they note, to run the "risk that a witness, who is subsequently and independently found to be more deserving of prosecution than originally thought, will be absolutely immune from a prosecution despite the existence of such independent evidence." Subsequent prosecution is especially important, they argue, in two situations where the prosecutor can most readily establish that the immunized testimony was not used in the prosecution. The first is the case where the defendant has been convicted, but retains the self-incrimination privilege pending final disposition of his appeal. If the prosecutor compels his testimony under transactional immunity, but the appellate court reverses and requires a new trial, the reprosecution would be barred by that immunity. A related situation is that in which the prosecutor has sufficient evidence to convict, but needs the compelled testimony now, and cannot wait to convict and then grant immunity. Under a use/derivative-use procedure, the prosecutor can make a record of the evidence available prior to the grant of immunity (called "canning" the testimony) and then use only that evidence in the subsequent prosecution; but under a transactional scheme, a prosecutor has no such option.

(c) Applying the Use/Derivative–Use Prohibition. Federal case law developments since *Kastigar* have cast considerable light on one of the central points of the debate over use/derivative-use immunity—the protections afforded by *Kastigar* in a subsequent prosecution of an immunized witness (and their impact upon the feasibility of bringing such prosecutions). Initially, the lower courts have held that the prosecution's burden of establishing that its evidence was derived from an independent source and not from the defendant's immunized testimony is subject to a preponderance of the evidence standard (rather than a higher burden of persuasion). Typically this burden must be carried at an evidentiary hearing (commonly described as a "taint hearing" or a "*Kastigar* hearing"), although in exceptional cases (e.g., where the government relies upon evidence produced in a prior trial), affidavits alone may be sufficient. Many courts insist that the hearing be held prior to trial, which incidentally gives the defense far broader pretrial discovery than it would ordinarily obtain, but others will allow the government to make its showing after the trial is completed and all of its evidence has been seen. As *Kastigar* noted, the government burden at the hearing is not limited to "negation of taint," but must include a showing that it has "an independent legitimate source for the disputed evidence." Typically, "to establish a 'wholly independent source', the government must demonstrate that each step of the investigative chain through which the evidence was obtained is untainted."

Federal caselaw applying *Kastigar* suggests that the prosecution is most likely to meet its burden of showing an independent source

when the investigation of the defendant was completed or substantially completed before the defendant was compelled to give immunized testimony. The preferred practice in such cases is for the prosecutor to make a record of all of the evidence collected prior to the grant of immunity, to file that record with the court, and then at the taint hearing, note its intent to utilize only the previously acquired evidence and further evidence directly derived from that evidence. That procedure, however, is hardly foolproof. Thus, where trial witnesses gave grand jury testimony prior to the grant of immunity, but then became aware of the immunized testimony (usually because it was given in a public forum), their subsequent trial testimony is likely to be viewed as influenced by that immunized testimony (and therefore excludable) unless it provides a perfect match to their earlier grand jury testimony. So too, even if the government case is based entirely on documentary evidence obtained prior to the immunized testimony, if the prosecutors were aware of that immunized testimony, it may have impacted their strategic decisions in using that documentary evidence.

Although the *Kastigar* opinion spoke primarily of the protection afforded by barring introduction of the compelled testimony and evidence derived from that testimony, it also used language suggesting a more sweeping prohibition. The Court noted, for example, that the federal immunity statute (which refers to prohibiting use of "information" derived from immunized testimony) "prohibits the prosecutorial authorities from using the compelled testimony in *any* respect." Accordingly, several lower courts have held that the *Kastigar* prohibition extends to "tactical" or "nonevidentiary use" of the compelled testimony. Strategic decisions may include deciding to initiate prosecution, refusing to plea bargain, and any cross-examination strategy that stands apart from forcing disclosure of particular information. Under this view, where the prosecutor was familiar with the immunized testimony, the government, to meet its *Kastigar* burden, will have to go beyond simply showing that all of its evidence was derived from an independent source.

Other federal circuit courts have either rejected or seriously questioned the proposition that *Kastigar* bars all nonevidentiary uses of immunized testimony by the prosecution. They note that *Kastigar* described the requisite scope of the immunity as placing the individual in "substantially the same position" as if he had claimed the privilege, and that nonevidentiary uses are often so tangential to the presentation of the prosecution as to hardly alter the strength of a case against the defendant that is based exclusively upon independently derived evidence. Most of these rulings do not flatly reject the possibility that a nonevidentiary use can violate *Kastigar*, but they certainly would insist at least upon a defense showing that a specific trial strategy was formed by reference to the immunized testimony and had a measurable bearing upon the strength of the case presented by the prosecution. Although this standard reduces the burden faced by the government where its prosecutor is familiar with immunized testimony, the assignment of the prosecution to prosecutors and investigators who have no knowledge of the content of the immunized testimony is deemed advisable even by courts taking this narrower view of what *Kastigar* prohibits.

(d) Immunity Procedures. Several states authorize the prosecutor to grant immunity without a court order, and in a few, grand jury witnesses receive automatic immunity simply by testifying before the grand jury (absent their waiver of that immunity). In the vast majority, however, an immunity order issued by a court is required before a witness will be compelled to testify over an exercise of the privilege.

In the federal system and numerous states, the court has a quite limited role in issuing the order. Typically, the court is required to issue the immunity order upon a showing that the witness would not testify without immunity and that the prosecutor has concluded that granting immunity as to the specified inquiry is in the public interest. The court here may not refuse to grant the order on the ground that the prosecutor erred in arriving at that

conclusion. Other jurisdictions, however, subject the prosecutor's decision to limited judicial review. The immunity statute will provide, for example, that the prosecutor's application not be approved if granting immunity (typically transactional immunity) would be "clearly contrary to the public interest." Courts in these jurisdictions typically start from the assumption that the weighing of the cost of immunity against the value of the anticipated testimony is largely the task of the prosecutor and the court should guard only against the clearly improvident grant of immunity.

Once the immunity order is granted, the witness must either testify or face contempt sanctions, unless the witness has some legal justification (e.g., the attorney-client privilege) for refusing to respond. The witness may not refuse to testify because his answers will subject him to substantial civil liability. Neither may he refuse to testify because he is fearful of physical or economic retaliation by associates or others. Some courts have suggested a duress defense could be available where the witness reasonably feared a sufficiently immediate threat of death or serious bodily harm, but the government can then respond by making available its witness protection program. Of course, even where available, such programs are not without costs, leading certain types of witness to very often choose a contempt sentence over testifying. This opens the possibility of prosecutorial use of the immunity grant as the easiest route for gaining the incarceration, at least for a limited period, of members of a criminal organization where the evidence is insufficient to prosecute, but the prosecutor knows that such persons will stand in contempt (or lie and be subjected to perjury charges) rather than testify truthfully. Recognizing this potential, an earlier version of the Justice Department's internal guidelines specifically prohibited the use of immunity grants "solely to make possible the securing of a perjury or contempt conviction against the witness."

(e) Informal Grants of Immunity. Where the witness is willing to testify under a grant of immunity, the prosecutor may prefer to provide immunity through an agreement whereby the witness agrees to testify in exchange for a promise of non-prosecution or non-use. For the prosecutor, non-statutory immunity offers primarily two advantages. First, it bypasses the statutory procedure for obtaining an immunity order which may be cumbersome or pose a risk to grand jury secrecy. Second, it permits the prosecutor to tailor the scope of the immunity to the needs of the case. Thus, a prosecutor in a jurisdiction with a use/derivative-use statute may believe that an informal grant of transactional immunity will be more effective in gaining witness cooperation. In other situations, the immunity provided by statute may be more than the witness requires or the prosecutor is willing to give; an informal grant may be limited to barring prosecution only as to certain aspects of the transaction, or it may provide only use and not derivative-use immunity. Finally, the prosecution can condition the immunity on full cooperation, allowing for use of information initially provided should the defendant fail to be as forthcoming in subsequent testimony. For the witness, informal immunity has an advantage primarily where it will permit him to obtain broader protection than would otherwise be available.

Several state courts have held that the prosecutor lacks authority to grant informal immunity, particularly where the informal grant bypasses limitations applicable to statutorily authorized immunity. Most courts, however, view informal immunity agreements as within the exercise of the prosecutor's traditional discretion over the decision to prosecute. Thus, where the witness has performed as agreed, enforcement is available under standard contract principles. The courts will not, however, compel a recalcitrant witness to testify on the basis of such a promise. They note that the arrangement with the witness must be viewed simply as a lawful "promise not to prosecute," not as a form of "hip pocket immunity" that either replaces or bypasses statutory immunity.

§ 8.12 Self–Incrimination and the Compulsory Production of Documents

(a) The Boyd "Principle." Although a subpoena duces tecum may be used to compel production of various types of physical evidence, it is most frequently used, at least in the grand jury setting, to require the production of documents. *Boyd v. United States*,[1] decided in 1886, was the first Supreme Court case to consider the applicability of the self-incrimination privilege to court ordered production of documents. Although *Boyd* involved a different form of court order, the reasoning of the Court clearly encompassed the subpoena duces tecum. Under the analysis adopted in *Boyd*, a subpoena requiring the production of a document was subject to challenge under both the Fourth Amendment and self-incrimination clause of the Fifth Amendment. As noted in § 8.7(a), *Boyd's* Fourth Amendment analysis was soon thereafter modified so as to limit the Fourth Amendment challenge to subpoenas that were overly broad in the documents requested. *Boyd's* Fifth Amendment analysis survived for a considerably longer period and provided a far more significant barrier to the compelled production of documents.

Under current precedent, very little, if anything, remains of *Boyd's* Fifth Amendment analysis. Yet the *Boyd* analysis remains a universally accepted starting point for understanding the many strands of current Fifth Amendment doctrine applicable to the subpoena duces tecum. For much of the current doctrine was developed in the process of first limiting and then replacing the *Boyd* analysis. Moreover, there still remains a question, at least for some jurisdictions, as to whether some elements of the *Boyd* analysis might not have current vitality in limited situations.

Boyd upheld a self-incrimination challenge to a court order requiring an importing firm organized as a partnership to produce the invoice it had received for items allegedly imported illegally. Quoting from Lord Camden's opinion in *Entick v. Carrington,* the *Boyd* opinion noted that papers are an owner's

§ 8.12

1. 116 U.S. 616, 6 S.Ct. 524, 29 L.Ed. 746 (1886).

"dearest property," respected by a well established common law prohibition against forcing such evidence "out of the owner's custody by process." Allowing the state to compel production of private books and papers, even where necessary to convict for the most serious crime, would be "abhorrent to the instincts" of an American or Englishman and "contrary to the principles of a free government." Just as the Fifth Amendment prohibited "compulsory discovery by extorting the party's oath," it also prohibited discovery by "compelling the production of his private books and papers." The documentary production order was simply another form of "forcible and compulsory extortion of a man's own testimony."

Boyd relied on what has been described as a "property oriented" view of the Fourth and Fifth Amendments, built upon the owner's right of privacy in the control of his lawfully held possessions. It recognized a special Fifth Amendment interest in the privacy of documents, viewing the forced production of their contents as equivalent to requiring a subpoenaed party to reveal that content through his testimony. Although the Court spoke of "private books and papers," it obviously was not referring only to confidential documents relating to personal or private matters. The document at issue in *Boyd* was a business record that had not been prepared by the partners themselves but by the shipper of the item alleged to have been illegally imported.

Insofar as it relied upon the self-incrimination privilege, the *Boyd* ruling might well be read as limited to documents. As documents contain words, the compelled disclosure of their content could be seen as more closely analogous to the compelling of testimonial utterances than the compelled disclosure of other forms of property possessed by the subpoenaed party. Yet, the key to the Court's analysis appeared to be the invasion through forced production of the individual's privacy interest in his possession of property in which the public had no entitlement (such

entitlement existing, the Court noted, only where a third-party had a superior right, as with stolen property, or the state had a superior interest, as with records required to be kept by law). Although the invasion might be more serious as to the individual's "dearest property" (i.e., his papers), the same principle would appear to forbid the forced production of any form of personally held property where there was no such public entitlement and the property could be used as incriminating evidence. Thus, the Supreme Court later spoke of the self-incrimination privilege as protecting the individual "from any disclosure, in the form of oral testimony, documents, or *chattels*, sought by legal process against him as a witness."

Starting with *Hale v. Henkel*,[2] decided only two decades after *Boyd*, the Court gradually developed a series of doctrines that chipped away at the broad implications of *Boyd's* property-rights/privacy analysis of Fifth Amendment protection. Finally, in *Fisher v. United States*,[3] decided close to a century after *Boyd*, the Court majority was forced to conclude that all that remained of *Boyd* was a "prohibition against forcing the production of private papers" that had "long been a rule searching for a rationale." The subsections that follow discuss the most significant of the doctrinal developments that restricted the privacy analysis of *Boyd*, and the quite different act-of-production analysis that was adopted in *Fisher*. Taken together, the rulings in those cases provided the basic legal principles currently governing the application of the privilege against self-incrimination to a subpoena duces tecum and clearly reject the *Boyd* ruling on its facts. The possibility that some remnant of the *Boyd* analysis remains is discussed in the last subsection. Because of its special significance and complexity, the act-of-production doctrine is given further attention in § 8.13, which discusses a variety of issues raised in applying that doctrine.

(b) The Entity Exception. *Hale v. Henkel*[4] not only reconstructed *Boyd's* Fourth

---

2. 201 U.S. 43, 26 S.Ct. 370, 50 L.Ed. 652 (1906), discussed in subsection (b) infra.

3. 425 U.S. 391, 96 S.Ct. 1569, 48 L.Ed.2d 39 (1976), discussed in subsection (f) infra.

4. 201 U.S. 43, 26 S.Ct. 370, 50 L.Ed. 652 (1906).

Amendment analysis, but also added a major exception to its Fifth Amendment rationale. *Hale* held that the self-incrimination privilege was not available to a corporation and therefore *Boyd* did not bar a grand jury subpoena duces tecum requiring production of corporate records. The Court's refusal to allow a corporation to utilize the privilege rested basically on two grounds. First, the self-incrimination privilege is designed in large part to protect interests unique to the individual. Thus, in a later case, the privilege was described as designed to prevent "inhumane" methods of compulsion, to ensure "respect for the inviolability of the human personality," and to maintain the "right of each individual to a private enclave where he may lead a private life." A corporation, as a fictional entity, needs no such protection. Second, *Hale* spoke of the state's greater regulatory power over corporations, which were merely "creature[s] of the state." The individual, it noted, "owes no duty to the State * * * to divulge his business, or to open his doors to an investigation, so far as it may tend to incriminate him." The corporation, in contrast, "is a creature of the State," and exercises it franchise subject to the "reserved right" of the State to compel its assistance in ensuring that it has not "exceeded its powers."

The Court in *Hale* took special note of the enforcement needs of the government in compelling the production of corporate records; if such production were precluded by a self-incrimination claim, "it would result in a failure of a large number of cases where the illegal combination was determinable only upon such papers." In light of this concern, it was not surprising that, in *Wilson v. United States*,[5]

the Court subsequently rejected the claim of a corporate officer possessing subpoenaed corporate records that he could refuse to produce those records because they would personally incriminate him. The State's "reserved power of visitation," the Court noted, "would seriously be embarrassed, if not wholly defeated in its effective exercise, if guilty officers could refuse inspection of the records and papers of the corporation." As the records were those of the corporation, not personal records, and were held "subject to the corporate duty," the official could "assert no personal right * * * against any demand of the government which the corporation was bound to recognize."

In *United States v. White*,[6] the Court extended the *Hale* exception to other entities. *White* held that the president of an unincorporated labor union could not invoke his personal privilege to a subpoena demanding union records. Characterizing the Court's previous reliance on the State's visitorial power as "merely a convenient vehicle for justification of governmental investigation of corporate books and records," the *White* Court concluded that the exception recognized in *Hale* was derived from the inappropriateness of affording the privilege to an impersonal collective entity, whether or not that entity took the corporate form.[7]

The *White* opinion characterized the labor union as an organization with "a character so impersonal in the scope of its membership and activities that it cannot be said to embody or represent the purely private or personal interests of its constituents, but rather to embody their common or group interests only." In *Bellis v. United States*,[8] however, the Court concluded that the entity exception remained

---

5. 221 U.S. 361, 31 S.Ct. 538, 55 L.Ed. 771 (1911).

6. 322 U.S. 694, 64 S.Ct. 1248, 88 L.Ed. 1542 (1944).

7. Just as *Hale* and *Wilson* noted how application of the privilege to corporate records would seriously undermine the State's exercise of its visitorial powers, the Court in *White* spoke to regulatory considerations "underlying the restriction of this constitutional privilege to natural individuals acting in their own private capacity." Justice Murphy's opinion noted: "The scope and nature of the economic activities of incorporated and unincorporated organizations and their representatives demand that the constitutional power of the federal and state governments to regulate those activities be correspondingly effective. The greater portion of evidence of wrongdoing by an

organization or its representatives is usually to be found in the official records and documents of that organization. Were the cloak of the privilege to be thrown around these impersonal records and documents, effective enforcement of many federal and state laws would be impossible. The framers of the constitutional guarantee against compulsory self-disclosure, who were interested primarily in protecting individual civil liberties, cannot be said to have intended the privilege to be available to protect economic or other interests of such organizations so as to nullify appropriate governmental regulations."

8. 417 U.S. 85, 94 S.Ct. 2179, 40 L.Ed.2d 678 (1974).

applicable even though the entity embodied personal as well as group interests. The functional key was that the organization "be recognized as an independent entity apart from its individual members." Thus, a small law firm, organized as a partnership, was an entity for this purpose even though it "embodie[d] little more than the personal legal practice of the individual partners." The partnership was not an "informal association or a temporary arrangement for the undertaking of a few projects of short-lived duration," but a "formal institutional arrangement organized for the continuing conduct of the firm's legal practice." State law, through the Uniform Partnership Act, imposed a "certain organizational structure"; the firm maintained a bank account in the partnership name; it had employees who worked for the firm as such; and, the firm "held itself out to third parties as an entity with an independent institutional identity."

Bellis left open the possibility that a "small family partnership" might be treated differently, as might a temporary arrangement for undertaking a short-lived project, or an association based on some "pre-existing relationship of confidentiality among the partners." Lower courts view any such exceptions as quite narrow. Indeed, even when there is no formal partnership, a structured organization operating as a joint entity will be held to fall within the entity exception. Also, a corporation, even a one-person corporation or a closely held family corporation, will be viewed as an entity no matter how closely it would otherwise resemble the possible "small-family-partnership" exception noted in *Bellis*.

(c) The Required Records Exception. Building upon dictum in *Wilson* to the effect that the privilege did not extend to corporate records because they were required by law to be kept for the public benefit, *Shapiro v. United States*[9] held that the same principle could apply to the records of individuals engaged in regulated businesses. *Shapiro* upheld against a self-incrimination objection a subpoena direct-

ing production of records of commodity sales that the petitioner, a wholesale fresh produce dealer, was required to keep, and to make available for inspection by federal regulators, under the wartime Emergency Price Control Act. The Court acknowledged that "there are limits which the Government cannot constitutionally exceed in requiring the keeping of records which may be inspected by an administrative agency and may be used in prosecuting statutory violations committed by the recordkeeper himself," but it concluded that there was no need in this case to define precisely where those limits might lie. For, the Court noted, "no serious misgivings that those bounds were overstepped would appear to be evoked where there is a sufficient relation between the activity sought to be regulated and the public concern so that the Government can constitutionally regulate or forbid the basic activity concerned." This broad description of the acceptable nexus between the records and regulating authority offered the possibility of a far reaching required records doctrine. However, in the 1968 companion cases of *Marchetti v. United States*[10] and *Grosso v. United States*,[11] the Court later made clear that the required records doctrine could not be carried to that extreme.

Marchetti and *Grosso* presented self-incrimination challenges to federal wagering tax statutes that required gamblers to identify themselves by registering with the government and by paying an occupational tax. The government contended that the disclosure requirements, though raising a "real and appreciable" hazard of self-incrimination, were nonetheless constitutional because they fit within the rationale of the required records doctrine. In rejecting that contention, the Court noted that it was unnecessary here to "pursue in detail the question left open in *Shapiro* of what limits the Government cannot constitutionally exceed in requiring the keeping of records." It was "enough that there [were] significant points of difference between the situations here and in *Shapiro*." There were "three principle elements" of the

---

9.　335 U.S. 1, 68 S.Ct. 1375, 92 L.Ed. 1787 (1948).

10.　390 U.S. 39, 88 S.Ct. 697, 19 L.Ed.2d 889 (1968).

11.　390 U.S. 62, 88 S.Ct. 709, 19 L.Ed.2d 906 (1968).

required records doctrine, as it was "described in *Shapiro*," which did not apply to the wagering registration requirements. Those three elements, which furnished the "premises of the [required records] doctrine," were: "[F]irst, the purpose of the United States' inquiry must be essentially regulatory; second, information is to be obtained by requiring the preservation of records of a kind which the regulated party has customarily kept; and third, the records themselves must have assumed 'public aspects' which render them at least analogous to public documents."

Although decided in 1968, *Marchetti* and *Grosso* continue to provide the Supreme Court's leading discussions of the required records doctrine. A later case, *California v. Byers*,[12] although not relying directly on the required records doctrine, also helps to put that doctrine in perspective. In *Byers*, the Court upheld a "hit and run" statute which required a driver involved in an accident to stop at the scene and leave his name and address. The plurality noted that in judging the constitutionality of regulatory schemes requiring disclosures that might conceivably lead to criminal prosecutions, the Court had to "balanc[e] the public need on the one hand, and the individual claim to constitutional protections on the other." That balancing approach presumably was at the core of the required records doctrine as well. Under such an approach, the critical factors in defining the limits of the required records doctrine, assuming a truly regulatory scheme, would be the significance of the government's regulatory interest, and the importance of the disclosure to making that interest effective. Such factors may readily be considered in determining whether the records can be characterized as having "public aspects." However, the importance of the second *Shapiro* element—that records be of a type customarily kept—is problematic under such a balancing analysis. Arguably, the presence of that element may support the government's claim that its interest is truly regulatory, but there certainly may be

instances, as suggested by *Byers*, in which a regulatory interest requires the keeping of records of activities that would not otherwise be recorded in the normal course of business. Of course, the first element is an absolute prerequisite; the government's interest truly must be "regulatory," reflecting some interest other than facilitating the prosecution of crime.

Lower court rulings assessing the scope of the required records doctrine largely have been consistent with above analysis. A regulation that required automobile dealers to report altered serial numbers was held to extend beyond the limits of the doctrine; the regulation had no statutory purpose independent of a desire to "ferret out criminal activities." So too, check and deposit slips required by regulation to be kept as substantiation for a tax return were held not to have sufficient public aspects to constitute required records because the keeping of such records was not an ongoing condition of operating the taxpayer's business under a comprehensive regulatory scheme. On the other hand, found to be required records were records of a custom-house brokerage service kept pursuant to customs regulations, records relating to cattle purchases that licensed cattlemen were required to keep as part of a government program for controlling communicable diseases in domestic animals, and medical records as to patient treatment required for the purpose of reviewing professional competency. The thrust of these decisions is that a person who fears incrimination has no special exemption from record keeping duties imposed generally upon a regulated class that is not by its nature suspected of criminal activity.

(d) The Schmerber Rule. Though it did not restrict the *Boyd* ruling as such, the limitation of the Fifth Amendment to "testimonial" compulsion, as held in *Schmerber v. California*,[13] did raise questions as to the scope of the *Boyd* analysis. As discussed in § 7.2(a), *Schmerber* held that the privilege did not prohibit the compelled extraction of a blood sample from an accused and the subsequent admission of that sample as incriminatory ev-

---

12.   402 U.S. 424, 91 S.Ct. 1535, 29 L.Ed.2d 9 (1971).

13.   384 U.S. 757, 86 S.Ct. 1826, 16 L.Ed.2d 908 (1966).

idence at his trial. The Court reasoned that the history of the privilege limited its application to compelled production of an accused's "communications" or "testimony." While this protection extended beyond words compelled from "a person's own lips" and extended to "communications * * * in whatever form they may take," it did not encompass "compulsion which makes a suspect or accused the source of 'real or physical' evidence." Citing *Boyd*, the *Schmerber* opinion distinguished the "compulsion of responses which are also communications, for example, compliance with a subpoena to produce one's papers." It did not explain, however, how such compliance could constitute a communication through the forced disclosure of contents of the subpoenaed document, which was what *Boyd* had suggested. Arguably, a document authored by the individual might be seen as "speaking" for him, as it contains his words. In *Boyd*, however, the required production was of a document written by another, an invoice sent to the *Boyd* partnership by a supplier.

Schmerber limited any "private inner sanctum" protected by the privilege to that of contents of the mind, which a compelled communication forces the individual to reveal. This limitation was later made evident in *Doe v. United States (Doe II).*[14] The Court there held that a court order requiring an individual to sign a form directing any foreign bank to release the records of any account he might have at that bank did not compel "testimony." This was so since the government did not seek to use the consent form itself as a factual assertion of the individual, expressing the "contents of his mind." While the government did intend to use the contents of the document, if any, released by the bank, that document constituted statements not of the defendant, but of a third party. The same analysis arguably would apply to *Boyd* insofar as petitioner claimed that the content of the invoice

to be produced there constituted an incriminating communication.

(e) Third–Party Production. *Couch v. United States*[15] and *Fisher v. United States*[16] both involved situations in which an individual had transferred records to an independent professional who was then served with an IRS summons requiring production of those records. In *Couch*, the sole proprietress of a restaurant had delivered various financial records to her accountant for the purpose of preparing her income tax returns. In *Fisher*, sole owners of separate businesses had delivered to their attorneys various workpapers that had been prepared by their accountants in the course of filing income tax returns. In both cases, the taxpayers relied upon *Boyd*, arguing that the government was seeking to obtain disclosure of papers of an even more confidential nature than the invoice subpoenaed in *Boyd*. The taxpayers acknowledged that the IRS summonses required their agents rather than the taxpayers themselves to produce the documents, but contended that factor was irrelevant since they had maintained a reasonable expectation of privacy in the documents even after delivered to the agents.

The Supreme Court rejected the taxpayers' position in both cases, noting incidentally that *Boyd* lent them no support. The Fifth Amendment applied only to personal compulsion and there was none here. Unlike the importers in *Boyd*, the taxpayers here were not themselves required "to do anything." The Court was not persuaded by the contention that its focus on personal compulsion was too formalistic to serve adequately the goals of the privilege. Responding in *Fisher*, it noted: "We cannot cut the Fifth Amendment completely loose from the moorings of its language and make it serve as a general protector of privacy—a word not mentioned in its text and a concept directly addressed in the Fourth Amendment." The Fifth Amendment, it continued, "protects against 'compelling testimony, not the disclosure of private information.'"

14. 487 U.S. 201, 108 S.Ct. 2341, 101 L.Ed.2d 184 (1988) (commonly known as *Doe II*, to distinguish United States v. Doe, infra note 19), further discussed in § 8.13 at note 2.

15. 409 U.S. 322, 93 S.Ct. 611, 34 L.Ed.2d 548 (1973).

16. 425 U.S. 391, 96 S.Ct. 1569, 48 L.Ed.2d 39 (1976).

Both *Fisher* and *Couch* acknowledged that "situations might exist where constructive possession is so clear or the relinquishment of possession is so temporary and insignificant as to leave the personal compulsions upon the accused substantially intact." Lower courts have suggested, however, that where documents have been delivered to an independent third party, this "constructive-possession exception" will be available only if the third party received the records strictly for custodial safekeeping and the owner retained ready access to the records. Constructive possession is more likely to be found where a sole proprietor seeks to raise the privilege in response to a subpoena directing an employee to produce company records kept by that employee. Even here, however, a constructive possession argument may be denied, and the employer barred from raising the privilege, where, for example, the employer was an absentee proprietor who had delegated exclusive responsibility for the records to the subpoenaed employee. Indeed, the argument has been rejected even where the employer shared the offices in which the records were kept, and directly supervised the employee who kept the records, but delegated to the employee considerable control over the preparation and distribution of the records.

(f) Testimonial Aspects of Production. Because the documents in *Fisher* had been transferred to an attorney, the Court found it necessary to decide whether the taxpayer there would have had a valid self-incrimination claim if he had been compelled himself to produce the documents. Under the attorney-client privilege, the attorney could refuse to produce documents that "would have been privileged in the hands of the client by reason of the Fifth Amendment." The taxpayer argued that the documents here would have been privileged against self-production under the "*Boyd* rule" that "a person may not be forced to produce his private papers." However, Justice White's opinion for the Court in *Fisher* took a quite different view of *Boyd*.

Justice White initially noted that *Boyd* had relied on a combined Fourth and Fifth Amendment theory that had "not stood the test of time." Much of *Boyd*'s Fourth Amendment

analysis had been flatly rejected and the rulings in cases like *Schmerber* and *Bellis* had adopted a different view of the Fifth Amendment. What was left was a "prohibition against forcing the production of private papers [that] has long been a rule searching for a rationale consistent with the proscriptions of the Fifth Amendment against compelling a person to give 'testimony' that incriminates him." In light of *Schmerber*, that prohibition could not rest on the incriminating content of the subpoenaed records. The court order of production of preexisting records does not require the subpoenaed party to author those records. Where the preparation of subpoenaed records was voluntary, those records "cannot be said to contain compelled testimonial evidence." The records may contain incriminating writing, but whether the writing of the subpoenaed party or another, that writing was not a communication compelled by the subpoena. Accordingly, the prosecution's acquisition of that writing by subpoena is no more compelling testimony than its acquisition of physical evidence with similar incriminating content.

Having found that application of the privilege could not rest on the declarations contained in the writings, Justice White then turned to what the Court majority viewed as a more appropriate explanation of the *Boyd* rule. The act of producing subpoenaed documents, Justice White noted, "has communicative aspects of its own, wholly aside from the contents of the papers produced." Compliance with a subpoena "tacitly concedes the existence of the papers demanded and their possession or control by the [subpoenaed party]." It also would indicate that party's "belief that the papers are those described in the subpoena," and in some instances this could constitute authentication of the papers. Indeed, post-*Boyd* decisions suggest that such "implicit authentication" is the "prevailing justification for the Fifth Amendment's application to documentary subpoenas." These three elements of production—acknowledgment of existence, acknowledgment of possession or control, and potential authentication by identification—are clearly compelled, but whether they also are "testimonial" and "incriminating" would depend upon the "facts and circumstances of particular cases or classes thereof." The resolution of that question, Justice White reasoned, should determine whether a particular documentary production is subject to a Fifth Amendment challenge.[17]

Upon examining the implications of the act of production in the case before it, the *Fisher* Court, for reasons explored in § 8.13, concluded that the taxpayer did not have a valid self-incrimination claim. "In light of the records now before us," Justice White noted, "however incriminating the contents of the accountant's workpapers might be, the act of producing them—the only thing which the taxpayer is compelled to do—would not itself involve testimonial self-incrimination." Justice White also added, however, a comment that could be taken to significantly limit the Court's ruling. He noted: "Whether the Fifth Amendment would shield the taxpayer from producing his own tax records in his possession is a question not involved here; for the papers demanded here are not 'private papers,' see *Boyd v. United States.*"

Following *Fisher*, some lower courts saw the act-of-production doctrine and *Boyd*'s content-based analysis as alternative grounds for sustaining a self-incrimination challenge to the compelled production of the business records of a sole proprietor. This position was taken notwithstanding that the *Fisher* majority had rejected the privacy-based analysis of *Boyd*

that been offered in the *Fisher* concurring opinions by Justices Brennan and Marshall.[18] In *United States v. Doe (Doe I)*,[19] the Court reaffirmed that the *Fisher* analysis had rejected the view that the self-incrimination privilege is available whenever a person is ordered to disclose the content of personal records.

Doe I involved a subpoena directing a sole proprietor to produce for grand jury use a broad range of records, including billings, ledgers, canceled checks, telephone records, contracts, and paid bills. The district court sustained the proprietor's claim of privilege. It concluded that compliance with the subpoena would require the proprietor to "admit that the records exist, that they are in his possession, and that they are authentic" and that each of these testimonial elements of production was potentially incriminatory. The Third Circuit agreed with this reasoning, but also added that the privilege applied because compelled disclosure of the contents of the documents violated the Fifth Amendment. Relying upon the privacy analysis of *Boyd*, it reasoned that the contents of personal records were privileged under the Fifth Amendment and that "business records of a sole proprietorship are no different from the individual's personal records."

Justice Powell's opinion for the Court in *Doe I* affirmed the rulings below insofar as they relied on the act-of-production doctrine. *Fisher* had recognized that the act of production

---

17. In United States v. Hubbell, 530 U.S. 27, 120 S.Ct. 2037, 147 L.Ed.2d 24 (2000), Justice Thomas, in a concurring opinion joined by Justice Scalia, suggested that the Court should reexamine *Fisher* and other rulings which assume that the self-incrimination privilege applies only when a subpoena compels a production with "testimonial content." Justice Thomas noted that "[a] substantial body of evidence suggests that the Fifth Amendment privilege [was intended to] protect against the compelled production not just of incriminating testimony, but of any incriminating evidence." The holding in *Boyd*, he added, was in accord with this broader reading of the privilege, though *Boyd* admittedly did not refer to the concept that a person is being a "witness" against himself when compelled to "furnish incriminating physical evidence." Restoring *Boyd* in this fashion would have the advantage, he noted, of rendering irrelevant "the difficult parsing of the act of responding to a subpoena duces tecum" as required by *Fisher.*

18. In separate concerning opinions, Justices Marshall and Brennan argued that the Fifth Amendment protects a

privacy interest that "extends not just to the individual's immediate declarations, oral or written, but also to his testimonial materials in the form of books and papers." The "zone of privacy protected by the Amendment" did not go so far as to reach papers widely shared with others (such as the accountants' work papers subpoenaed in *Fisher*), but it did encompass business records that were personal, "such as canceled checks or tax records." The majority, as noted in subsection (e), noted that the Fifth Amendment privilege was not a "general protector of privacy," as it focused on "compelling testimony, not the disclosure of private information." This point was made as well in its act-of-production analysis. However, it did hold open the possible different treatment of a person's personal writings in its reference to the taxpayer's "own tax records." See also subsection (g) infra.

19. 465 U.S. 605, 104 S.Ct. 1237, 79 L.Ed.2d 552 (1984) (commonly referred to as *Doe I*, to distinguish Doe v. United States, supra note 14).

could be testimonial and incriminatory under the facts of a particular case, and here two lower courts had so found. That finding would be accepted in accordance with the Court's traditional "reluctan[ce] to disturb findings of fact in which two courts below concurred." Three concurring Justices argued that, in light of the acceptance of this finding, there was no reason to speak to the alternative grounding of the Third Circuit's opinion, but the Court majority concluded that it was desirable to resolve the "apparent conflict" between that grounding and "the reasoning underlying this Court's holding in *Fisher*." That resolution resulted in the majority's flat rejection of the Third Circuit's conclusion that the contents of the subpoenaed documents were protected by the privilege.

Justice Powell initially acknowledged that the Court in *Fisher* had "declined to reach the question whether the Fifth Amendment privilege protects the contents of an individual's tax records in his possession." The "rationale" underlying *Fisher's* holding, however, was equally persuasive here. *Fisher* had emphasized that "the Fifth Amendment protects the person asserting the privilege only from *compelled* self-incrimination." That a record was prepared by a subpoenaed party and is in his possession is "irrelevant to the determination of whether its creation * * * was compelled." The business records here, like the accountant's workpapers in *Fisher*, had been prepared voluntarily, and therefore only their production, and not their creation, was compelled. The contention that the Fifth Amendment created a "zone of privacy" that protected the content of such papers had been rejected in *Fisher*. The respondent could not avoid compliance with a subpoena "merely by asserting that the item of evidence which he is required to produce contains incriminating writing, whether his own or that of someone else."

(g) The Remnants of Boyd. Although *Doe I* flatly rejected the Third Circuit's "zone of privacy" analysis, the Court had before it only a subpoena to compel the production of business records. Arguably, the most private records of an individual could be treated differently. Justice White had noted at one point in *Fisher* that that case did not raise "the special problems of privacy which might be presented by subpoena of a personal diary." However, the *Doe I* majority opinion did not suggest any opening for separate treatment of personal recollections in confidential documents. It emphasized that the key to the application of the self-incrimination clause was the testimonial and incriminating aspects of the act of production, not the content of the voluntarily prepared document. Based upon that analysis, if intimate personal papers were to receive greater production, it was only because the confidential nature of those papers made it more likely that their production would have those attributes that made the production of the document "testimonial." This reading of *Doe I* was made explicit in Justice O'Connor's concurring opinion in that case, which led to a responding concurring opinion by Justice Marshall, who argued for a much narrower reading of the majority's position.

Justice O'Connor, in her concurring opinion, suggested that the *Doe–Fisher* rationale rejected a content based analysis as to all types of documents. She noted that the Court's analysis in *Doe I* and *Fisher* made clear "that the Fifth Amendment provides absolutely no protection for the contents of private papers of any kind. The notion that the Fifth Amendment protects the privacy of papers originated in *Boyd v. United States,* but our decision in *Fisher v. United States* sounded the death-knell for *Boyd*." Responding to Justice O'Connor, Justice Marshall noted that the case before the Court, "presented nothing remotely close to the question that Justice O'Connor eagerly poses and answers." The documents in question here were business records, "which implicate a lesser degree of concern for privacy interests than, for example, personal diaries." It accordingly could not be said that the Court had "reconsidered the question of whether the Fifth Amendment provides protection for the content of 'private papers of any kind.'"

In the years since *Doe I*, lower courts usually have found it unnecessary to decide whether anything remains of *Boyd*. "If the contents of papers are protected at all," they note, "it is only in rare situations, where compelled disclosure would break the heart of our sense of privacy." That might be the case as to subpoena compelling production of "intimate papers such as private diaries and drafts of letters or essays," but it certainly would not cover the business and other financial records that typically are in issue. A growing number of courts have considered the issue, however, and have concluded that the rationale of *Doe* and *Fisher* precludes self-incrimination protection of the contents of a voluntarily prepared document, no matter how personal the document. Thus, courts have held that the act-of-production doctrine provides the only protection for such personal records as diaries and pocket calendars.

§ 8.13   Application of the Act-of-Production Doctrine

(a) Testimonial Character and the Foregone Conclusion Standard. As discussed in § 8.12(f), *Fisher v. United States*[1] concluded that the act of producing subpoenaed documents could have "communicative aspects of its own, wholly aside from the contents of the papers produced." Compliance with a subpoena "tacitly concedes the existence of the papers demanded and their possession or control by the [subpoenaed party]." It also indicates that party's "belief that the papers are those described in the subpoena," and in some instances this could constitute authentication of the papers. These three elements of production—acknowledgment of existence, acknowledgment of possession or control, and potential authentication by identification—are clearly compelled, but whether they are "testimonial" and "incriminating," *Fisher* noted, would depend upon the "facts and circumstances of particular cases or classes thereof." This subsection considers the analysis applied in determining whether the "facts and circumstances" establish that the particular act-of-production has a "testimonial" component. The next subsection considers the analysis applied in determining whether that testimonial component presents the potential of "incrimination." Of

course, both elements must be present to sustain a self-incrimination claim.

The *Fisher* opinion itself provided the basic analytical structure for determining whether the elements of the act of production are testimonial in character in the particular case. The Court there concluded that there was no basis for holding "testimonial" the implicit admissions as to existence and possession that would be made in that case with the taxpayer's production of his accountant's workpapers. Relying upon what came to be known as the "foregone conclusion" standard, the *Fisher* Court reasoned:

> It is doubtful that implicitly admitting the existence and possession of the papers rises to the level of testimony within the protection of the Fifth Amendment. The papers belong to the accountant, were prepared by him, and are the kind usually prepared by an accountant working on the tax returns of his client. Surely the Government is in no way relying on the "truthtelling" of the taxpayer to prove the existence of or his access to the documents. The existence and location of the papers are a foregone conclusion and the taxpayer adds little or nothing to the sum total of the Government's information by conceding that he in fact has the papers. Under these circumstances by enforcement of the summons "no constitutional rights are touched. The question is not of testimony but of surrender."

Justice Brennan, in his concurring opinion, criticized the Court's "foregone conclusion" rationale as relying upon "the untenable proposition" that an admission as to existence and possession is not testimonial "merely because the Government could otherwise have proved [those facts]." Undoubtedly, as Justice Brennan noted, in assessing whether compelled testimony falls within the privilege, courts have never deemed it significant that the government could otherwise establish the incriminating information that might be disclosed in the witness' testimony; the critical question is simply whether the witness' testimony would be usable against him. However, the *Fisher* Court

1.   425 U.S. 391, 96 S.Ct. 1569, 48 L.Ed.2d 39 (1976).

was not dealing with a traditional form of testimony, but with what it viewed as a quite different issue—whether the incidental communicative aspects of a physical act (production) were "testimonial." The Court cited by analogy its rulings holding the Fifth Amendment inapplicable to a court order requiring an accused to submit a handwriting sample. Incidental to the performance of that act, the Court noted, the accused necessarily "admits his ability to write and impliedly asserts that the exemplar is his writing." But the government obviously is not seeking this information—the "first would be a near truism and the latter self-evident"—and therefore "nothing he has said or done is deemed to be sufficiently testimonial for purposes of the privilege." Where the existence and possession of the documents to be produced are a "foregone conclusion," the act of production similarly "adds little or nothing to the sum total of the government's information" and therefore is no more testimonial than other compelled physical acts. The government in such a case obviously is not seeking the assertions of the subpoenaed party as to the facts of existence and possession, and his incidental communication as to those facts, inherent in the physical act that the government had the authority to compel, therefore does not rise to the level of compelled "testimony."

The explanation in *Fisher* of the relationship of the foregone conclusion standard to the lack of "testimonial" compulsion was brief and perhaps somewhat obfuscated by a second analogy drawn by the Court—that of the required production of entity records through an entity. However, in a later case, *Doe v. United States (Doe II)*,[2] the Court made quite clear that the communicative element of an act, even the act of making a statement, rises to the level of testimony only where the government's objective is to seek to have the actor, through that act itself, "relate a factual assertion or disclose information." *Doe II* held that a court order requiring an individual to sign a form directing any foreign bank to release the records of any account he might have at that bank did not compel "testimony" for Fifth Amendment purposes. This was so since the government did not seek to use the signed form itself as a factual assertion of the individual (although it would use the documents that might be produced by the bank in response to the signed directive). Indeed, the form was carefully drafted so that the signing party noted that he was acting under court order and did not acknowledge the existence of any account in any particular bank. The form did not indicate whether the requested documents existed, and offered no assistance to the government in later establishing the authenticity of any records produced by the bank. Thus, while the signed form did constitute a communication, it did not constitute "testimony." The government was not relying on the "truth-telling" of the directive, but simply requiring the petitioner to engage in the act of producing that directive.

Similarly, where the communicative elements of the act of producing a preexisting document merely established what is already a foregone conclusion, that factor suggests that the government is compelling the act for what it will produce (the voluntarily prepared documents, with a content not itself compelled) rather than the communication inherent in the act. To allow the privilege to be claimed simply because the required act incidentally provided information, even though the government did not seek that information, would be to make every compelled act a testimonial communication, contrary to the *Schmerber* rule.

The *Fisher* Court concluded that the existence and location of the accountant's workpapers were a foregone conclusion, but the Court never explained why that was so—apart from noting that the papers were of the kind usually prepared by an accountant. In *United States v. Doe (Doe I)*,[3] in contrast to *Fisher*, the Court held the privilege applicable to an act of production, and noted that there the government had failed to "rebu[t] the respondent's claim" as it had not shown "that possession, exis-

2. 487 U.S. 201, 108 S.Ct. 2341, 101 L.Ed.2d 184 (1988), discussed in § 8.12 at note 14.

3. 465 U.S. 605, 104 S.Ct. 1237, 79 L.Ed.2d 552 (1984), also discussed in § 8.12 at note 19.

tence, and authentication were a foregone conclusion." Unfortunately, because of its procedural setting, *Doe I* may be only slightly more helpful than *Fisher* in explaining the application of the foregone conclusion standard. In distinguishing *Fisher*, the *Doe I* Court relied basically on the presence there of the "explicit finding of the District Court that the act of producing the [subpoenaed] documents would involve testimonial self-incrimination." That finding rested essentially "on the determination of factual issues" and it had been affirmed by the Third Circuit. The Supreme Court had "traditionally been reluctant to disturb findings of fact in which two courts below have concurred" and there was no reason to do so here.

Notwithstanding the Court's reliance in *Doe I* on its limited role in reviewing factual findings, *Doe I* seemed to reject the assumption, made by some lower courts in light of *Fisher*, that the foregone conclusion standard was automatically met by the commonplace nature of the records subpoenaed. The *Doe I* subpoena had sought a variety of standard business records, including cancelled checks, telephone records, and paid bills. Also, both lower courts had stressed that the government made no specific showing that the records existed or that the subpoenaed party was "even * * * somehow connected" to the businesses for which the records were supposedly kept. At least such showings presumably would be needed to establish a foregone conclusion as to existence and possession.

In *United States v. Hubbell*,[4] the Court again spoke only briefly about the foregone conclusion doctrine, but provided substantially more content than *Fisher or Doe I*. The subpoena in *Hubbell* called for 11 categories of documents, which were broadly stated (e.g., calling for "any and all materials * * * relating to any direct or indirect sources of money or other things of value" received over a three year period). The Court reasoned that, "given the breadth of the 11 categories, * * * the collection and production of the materials demanded was tantamount to answering a series of interrogatories asking a witness to disclose the exis-

tence and location of particular documents fitting broad descriptions." Thus, there obviously was a "communicative aspect" in the act-of-production, as "it was unquestionably necessary for respondent to make extensive use of the 'contents of his own mind' in identifying the hundreds of documents responsive to the subpoena." The government argued, however, that this "communicative aspect" of production was not sufficiently testimonial "because the existence and possession of such records by any businessman is a foregone conclusion." Rejecting that contention, the Court reasoned:

> Whatever the scope of this "foregone conclusion" rationale, the facts of this case plainly fall outside of it. While in *Fisher* the Government already knew that the documents were in the attorneys' possession and could independently confirm their existence and authenticity through the accountants who created them, here the Government has not shown that it had any prior knowledge of either the existence or the whereabouts of the 13,120 pages of documents ultimately produced by respondent. The Government cannot cure this deficiency through the overbroad argument that a businessman such as respondent will always possess general business and tax records that fall within the broad categories described in this subpoena. The *Doe* subpoenas also sought several broad categories of general business records, yet we upheld the District Court's finding that the act of producing those records would involve testimonial self-incrimination.

Hubbell puts to rest the notion that the commonplace character of the document in itself establishes existence and possession as a foregone conclusion. It also precludes limiting *Doe I* to a situation on which the government could not tie the individual to the business activities reflected in the records; most of the records sought in the *Hubbell* subpoena were defined by reference to Hubbell's own activities (e.g., "tickets for transportation"), but the government still had to do more to establish their existence and Hubbell's possession. In describing why the showing was sufficient in

---

4. 530 U.S. 27, 120 S.Ct. 2037, 147 L.Ed.2d 24 (2000), also discussed at note 6 infra.

Fisher, the Court noted the existence of an outside source (the accountants) who could "independently confirm * * * existence and authenticity," and while *Hubbell* did not declare that route to be exclusive, it is a common feature of many lower court rulings finding that the government had met the foregone conclusion standard. Still other rulings have relied on similar extrinsic evidence, such as the subpoenaed party have acknowledged existence and possession in another context, or similar documents in the government's possession indicating that the subpoenaed documents also exist and are in the subpoenaed person's possession. Similarly, as to authentication, courts have held that the foregone conclusion standard is met where the government can point to another person who can authenticate, or where authentication can be achieved by other means (e.g., comparison with other documents independently authenticated or matching the handwriting with that of the subpoenaed party).

Hubbell's description of the satisfactory showing in *Fisher* includes one element that ordinarily will be difficult to match. *Hubbell* noted that in *Fisher* the "government already knew the documents were in the attorneys' possession." That was the case since the Fifth Amendment issue was a part of a claim of lawyer-client privilege, which required the attorneys to acknowledge their current possession (as well as receipt from the client). In an ordinary case, an independent source will not be able to similarly establish that the documents once in the subpoenaed party's possession still exist and are still there. However, lower courts have often sustained government foregone-conclusion showings without such positive evidence of current existence and possession.

(b) Potential Incrimination. To raise a successful self-incrimination claim based on the act of production doctrine, the subpoenaed party must establish not only that the communicative aspects of production rise to the level of testimony, but also that such testimony

would meet the traditional standard of potential incrimination. Thus, in *Fisher*, after indicating that the act of production there would not be testimonial, the Court went on to conclude that the Fifth Amendment claim failed in any event because there had been no showing that the communicative aspects of production posed a "realistic threat of incrimination to the taxpayer." The Court there examined separately the potential incrimination stemming from implicit authentication and implicit acknowledgment of existence and possession. As to authentication, it noted that production would not provide the government with evidence that could be used to authenticate the subpoenaed workpapers since production by the taxpayer would "express nothing more than the taxpayer's belief that the papers are those described in the subpoena" and the taxpayer could not thereby establish their authenticity as he "did not prepare the papers and could not vouch for their accuracy."[5] As to existence and possession, "surely it was not illegal to seek accounting help in connection with one's tax returns or for the accountant to prepare workpapers and deliver them to the taxpayer." Accordingly, "at this juncture," the Court was "quite unprepared to hold that either the fact of the existence of the papers or their possession by the taxpayer" posed a sufficient threat to raise a legitimate self-incrimination claim.

Fisher's discussion of the incrimination possibilities was both brief and suggestive of a quite narrow application of the potential incrimination standard as applied to the act of production. In its discussion of authentication, *Fisher* could be read as suggesting that the subpoenaed party's inability to establish the "accuracy" of papers he did not author rendered any testimonial communication on this issue so insignificant as not to be incriminatory. As to existence and possession, *Fisher's* reference to the innocuous nature of accountant's workpapers on their face might be read to suggest that no weight should be given to the possibility that the documents might have

---

5. The Court thus appeared to distinguish between two aspects of what might be described as "authentication"—testifying that the person responding believes that the documents are those specified in the subpoena, and testifying that the documents are genuine (i.e. what they profess to be).

an incriminating content. Such a position would be contrary to the traditional application of the potential incrimination standard to testimony, but arguably supported by the *Fisher* conclusion that the contents of the documents are not protected by the privilege.

In *Doe I*, the Court returned to the issue of incrimination in a footnote that appeared to reject both of the narrowing features arguably suggested in *Fisher*. In that footnote, the *Doe I* Court responded to the government's contention that even if the act of production there were viewed as having sufficient "testimonial aspects," any incrimination would be "so trivial" that the Fifth Amendment would not be implicated. The Court agreed that the Fifth Amendment would only be implicated if the risk of incrimination were "substantial and real," not merely "trifling or imaginary." It rejected, however, the government's claim that the risk of incrimination here clearly did not meet that standard. Respondent Doe had never conceded that the records subpoenaed actually existed or were within his possession. As respondent also noted, "even if the government could obtain the documents from another source, by producing the documents, respondent would relieve the government of the need for authentication." The potential prosecution uses of respondent's production, the Court noted, "were sufficient to establish a valid claim of the privilege."

Doe I's comment on the incriminatory potential of production through authentication certainly put to rest any suggestion that such potential would not exist where the records were authored by another. Although the Court did not comment on the fact, many of the records subpoenaed (which included telephone records and paid bills) obviously had not been authored by respondent Doe. Read in light of *Doe I*, the distinguishing feature in *Fisher* may have been the obvious availability there of the accountants as the most likely source of authentication testimony (although the availability of that independent source of authentication would more appropriately seem to relate to establishing authentication as a foregone conclusion, rather than to establishing the absence of sufficient incriminatory potential in

the possible use of the act of production in authentication).

Doe I's discussion of the incrimination element also made clear that the acknowledgment of the existence and possession of standard business records could have a sufficient incriminatory potential based on the content of those records. The records described in the *Doe I* subpoena were as innocuous in their general character as the accountant's workpapers subpoenaed in *Fisher*. The potential for incrimination existed in tying the subpoenaed party to the contents of those records through his acknowledgment that he was aware of their existence and possessed them—factors that were significant to the government's case as the respondent had never conceded that the records existed or were in his control. What distinguished this case from *Fisher*, the *Doe I* Court noted, was the finding of the District Court, affirmed by Court of Appeals, that the potential for incrimination through the testimonial aspects of production was "substantial and real." The Court stated that this conclusion was based on a "determination of factual issues" which it would not revisit, but its descriptions of the lower court proceedings suggested at least a few of the factors that contributed to the lower court's determination. The subpoena was issued by a grand jury investigating corruption in the awarding of government contracts; the government had "conceded [before the District Court] that the materials sought in the subpoena were or might be incriminating"; and the government was seeking through the act of production to establish a connection between Doe and several businesses under investigation (a link it apparently otherwise could not establish).

In *Fisher* in contrast to *Doe I*, the materials were subpoenaed in a standard IRS investigation, with no criminal overtones, a proceeding in which lower courts have commonly required the contesting party to make some showing of potential incrimination. The taxpayer had raised, however, no more than a blanket claim of the privilege as to the records as group. In stating that it was unprepared "at this juncture" to find a realistic threat of incrimination, the Court may have been leaving the door open for the taxpayer to make a more particularized showing of possible incrimination. Thus, a valid self-incrimination claim arguably could have been presented in *Fisher* if the taxpayer had pointed to particular records that posed a real and appreciable threat of containing incriminatory information and had indicated that the government was seeking to link the taxpayer to those potentially incriminatory records through his act of production.

Lower court cases, analyzing the self-incrimination issue in light of *Doe I* and *Fisher*, have rejected "blanket claims" of self-incrimination based on the testimonial aspects of the act of production. Where the documents to be produced are innocuous on their face, the witness has been asked to make a "contextual" showing indicating how the linkage to the documents established by the act of production (or further evidence derived from that linkage) "would, in any sense, create a hazard of prosecution against him or a link in a chain of evidence establishing guilt." The lower courts have allowed that showing to be made *in camera*, have permitted the showing to be made by reference to different categories of documents (rather than as to production of each individual document), and have been willing to take account of the possible contents of the document. The standard of potential incrimination is the same as that applied to testimony, but in requiring a contextual showing, even where the documents have been subpoenaed by a grand jury, these rulings demand more of the witness than would ordinarily be demanded as to testimony.

(c) Act-of-Production Immunity. *Doe I* also considered the possibility that the government could obtain and make use of documents, even where the self-incrimination protection applied to the act of production, by granting act-of-production immunity. The Court there rejected the contention that the courts could fashion an immunity procedure apart from the immunity statute. It recognized, however, that the government "could have compelled respondent to produce the documents" by utilizing the federal immunity statute providing for use/derivative-use immunity. Moreover, that immunity need not have covered the contents of the documents, but could have been limited to the act of production since "immunity need be only as broad as the privilege against self-incrimination."

The critical aspect of this part of the *Doe I* ruling was the Court's acknowledgment that the necessary immunity need go only to the act of production itself, and not to the contents of the subpoenaed records. That such limited immunity was acceptable clearly followed from the mainspring of *Fisher's* reassessment of the "*Boyd* rule." A significant question remained, however, as to what uses of the documents and their content would be precluded as derived from the testimonial aspects of the act of production. In particular, does the document itself become the fruit of information garnered from the immunized act of production, or does the act convey only information as to when, where, and how the records were produced in response to the subpoena, leaving the government with the same access to the records as it would have had if the records mysteriously appeared on the prosecutor's desk?

Concurring in *Fisher*, Justice Marshall suggested that production immunity commonly would "effectively shield" the contents of the documents, as the contents would be a "direct fruit" of the "immunized testimony" contained in the act of production. Justice Marshall's assumption was that the testimonial component of the act of production would usually include an implicit admission of existence and possession, and the document itself would be the fruit of those admissions. Accordingly, if those implicit admissions were immunized, then the document itself would be immunized and the prosecution could not use either its contents or evidence derived from its contents. The situation would be different, however, where the act of production was testimonial only because of its implicit authentication of the document (i.e., where existence and possession were foregone conclusions, but authentication was not a foregone conclusion). Here, the immunity would not bar use of the document, as its existence would be independently established. The government would be precluded from using the act of production to authenticate, but if it found through the document's contents another means of authenticating (e.g., a reference to a third person who could authenticate or a handwritten entry that could be matched against the producer's handwriting sample), then it could use the document. Moreover, even if the government did not discover a means of authentication independent of the act of production, if authentication was the sole testimonial component of the immunized act, the government could still use the document as a source of leads to other evidence.

In contrast to Justice Marshall, the United States Department of Justice took the position that act-of-production immunity has no bearing on the use of the contents, irrespective of the range of the testimonial components in the particular act-of-production. It reasoned that, since the contents of the record are not privileged, the immunity is fully satisfied if the government is prohibited from in any way (investigative or evidentiary) looking to the act of production itself. The documents must be viewed as if they "magically appear[ed] before the grand jury" from an unknown source. At this point, the documents speak for themselves in establishing their existence. The government can use them and their contents, provided that use is not guided by the knowledge that they were produced by a particular person. If the contents of the documents (or the contents combined with information possessed prior to production) lead to a means of authentication, the documents can be used in evidence against the producer even if their existence had been uncertain prior to the immunized production. If use in evidence is precluded by a lack of authentication, the documents will always be available as a source of investigatory leads.

In *United States v. Hubbell*,[6] the Supreme Court rejected the Department of Justice's position. The prosecution there argued that its grant of act-of-production immunity (resulting in the production of documents totaling 13,120 pages) did not impact the evidence to be used in its subsequent prosecution of the respondent. It was not using the documents produced by respondent under the immunity order, but other evidence discovered through an examination of the produced documents, and there was no need "to advert to respondent's act of production in order to prove the existence, authenticity or custody" of the documents that the government would introduce at trial. The Court rejected this explanation as inadequate since the government did not show (and could not show) that it had not made derivative use of the "testimonial aspects" of the respondent's act of production. The contention that the produced documents should be useable as if they "magically appeared in the prosecutor's office, like manna from heaven," was not persuasive; in fact those documents "arrived there only after respondent asserted his constitutional privilege, received a grant of immunity, and * * * took the mental and physical steps necessary to provide the prosecutor with an accurate inventory of the many sources of potentially incriminating evidence sought by the subpoena." "It was only through respondent's truthful reply to the subpoena that the Government received the incriminating documents of which it made 'substantial use . . . in the investigation'."

The reasoning of *Hubbell* would appear to support Justice Marshall's position on the consequences of act-of-production immunity. The Court notes that without the witness' immunized truthtelling in producing the documents, the government would never have received them, as it could not establish existence and possession as a foregone conclusion. It would seem to follow that every bit of evidence derived from the receipt of the documents (which obviously includes evidence derived from the content of the documents) is immunized. However, the Court also took note of special circumstances in *Hubbell* that tied the government's evidence to the act of production apart from providing the documents themselves. In particular, in responding to the broadly stated subpoena, the witness made critical distinctions that provided the government with crucial information as to the use of particular documents and their relationship to particular transactions. Indeed, the act of production was

---

6.   530 U.S. 27, 120 S.Ct. 2037, 147 L.Ed.2d 24 (2000), also discussed at note 4 supra.

compared in this regard to answering a series of interrogatories about the documents. This roadmap clearly had assisted the government in building its case. In sum, while language in *Hubbell* would appear to preclude use of the content of the document even when the government obtains through act-of-production immunity a specifically described document (e.g., a communication identified by date and source), that clearly was not the situation before the Court.

(d) Claims By Entity Agents. In many instances, the person subpoenaed to produce entity records may himself be incriminated by what is to be found in those records. However, as noted in § 8.12(b), the Supreme Court has held that the entity agent may not rely upon his personal privilege to refuse to produce the records. The individual who holds the entity records (whether or not a formally designated custodian) does so in a representative rather than individual capacity. By voluntarily accepting the custodianship of the records, he assumes the entity's responsibility for making the records available to a government agency (including a grand jury) entitled to see them. If the rule were otherwise, the Court has noted, the entity exception would be meaningless.

The Supreme Court rulings establishing these principles were decided prior to *Fisher's* adoption of the act-of-production rationale as the basic grounding for a self-incrimination objection to a subpoena requiring the production of documents. In *Braswell v. United States*,[7] the petitioner, a corporate president and sole shareholder who had been subpoenaed to produce various corporate records, argued that the act-of-production doctrine provided a new grounding for recognizing a corporate custodian's exercise of the privilege, which had been ignored in the Court's earlier entity rulings. Petitioner claimed that the Court's earlier rulings had assumed that the availability of the privilege flowed from the "privacy rationale" of *Boyd* and protected the contents of "personal books and records" (therefore excluding entity records), but had not considered the personal testimonial in-

crimination of the custodian that attends his act of producing those entity records. A closely divided Supreme Court rejected that contention and reaffirmed the unavailability of the privilege to a custodian of entity records.

The *Braswell* majority concluded that the earlier rulings had not ignored the testimonial aspects of the act of production, but rather had considered any testimonial elements of that act to be properly attributed to the entity rather to the agent acting on its behalf. Even where the subpoena was directed to the custodian by name, rather than simply to the entity, the custodian was not performing "a personal act, but rather an act of the [entity]." *Fisher* itself had accepted this distinction in the course of analyzing the act-of-production rationale. Thus, the majority noted, "whether one concludes—as did the Court [in *Fisher*]— that a custodian's production of corporate records is deemed not to constitute testimonial self-incrimination or instead that a custodian waives the right to exercise the privilege, the lesson of *Fisher* is clear: A custodian may not resist a subpoena for corporate records on Fifth Amendment grounds."

Braswell, however, added an evidentiary limitation not mentioned in the earlier cases that had rejected self-incrimination claims by entity agents. Since the agent's act of production is an act of the entity and not the individual, the government "may make no evidentiary use of the 'individual act' against the individual." Illustrating this point, the Court noted that, "in a criminal prosecution against the custodian, the Government may not introduce into evidence before the jury the fact that the subpoena was served upon, and the corporation's documents were delivered by, one particular individual, the custodian." The government would be limited to showing that the entity had produced the document and to using that act of the entity in establishing that the records were authentic entity records that the entity had possessed and had produced. If the defendant's position in the entity were such that it could be assumed that he had possession or knowledge of the docu-

---

7. 487 U.S. 99, 108 S.Ct. 2284, 101 L.Ed.2d 98 (1988).

ments, the jury could make that assumption; it would not be doing so because of defendant's act of production but would be relying on reasonable inferences applicable without regard to who produced the documents.

In its discussion of the limited use the government might make of the act of production in a subsequent prosecution of the custodian, the Court, in a footnote, added what may be a very important caveat: it was "leav[ing] open the question [of] whether the agency rationale supports compelling a custodian to produce corporate records when the custodian is able to establish, by showing for example that he is the sole employee and officer of the corporation, that the jury would inevitably conclude that he produced the records." The petitioner in *Braswell* might himself have fit that description, but no showing directed at the inevitability of such a jury conclusion was made there. Where such a showing is made, one judicial response might be to require the custodian to produce the documents, but preclude the prosecution from making reference even to the corporation's act of production. This would put the burden on the government to authenticate and to establish entity possession through other means, but would still fall short of placing on the government the burden it would bear as to the lack of taint in other evidence if it had been required to grant act-of-production immunity (as the *Braswell* dissenters suggested). Still another possibility would be to direct the subpoena to the corporation itself, and require it to make production through some third-party custodian (e.g., counsel or an unaffiliated agent) who would not be incriminated by the act of production. This obligation presumably would require that the corporation, through the sole-participant/custodian, assist the third-party custodian in locating and identifying the subpoenaed records, but the government would then have to note that production was by the third-party agent, and refrain from referring to the assistance of the sole-participant/custodian in presenting the documents in evidence.

The responsibility of the custodian to produce the records ordinarily will encompass a duty to testify for the limited purpose of identifying the material produced. In *Curcio v. United States*,[8] the Supreme Court distinguished between such testimony and what was required there. In that case, defendant Curcio, a secretary-treasurer of a union, had informed the grand jury that he could not produce the subpoenaed records because they were not in his possession. Without challenging the truth of his statement, the prosecution sought to compel him to testify as to the whereabouts of the documents. Although Curcio exercised his privilege against self-incrimination at this point, the government argued that the custodial duty that required the production of the documents also carried with it a relinquishment of the privilege as to "auxiliary testimony" that would permit the government to locate the documents. The Supreme Court rejected that argument, noting that an entity agent did not "waive his constitutional privilege as to oral testimony by assuming the duties of his office."

Curcio did suggest, however, that where the documents are produced, the custodian has an obligation to provide basic authentication testimony—i.e., to testify as to "the location of the documents produced and that the produced records are those called for in the subpoena." In *Braswell*, the Court characterized *Curcio* as having drawn a line between the duty to produce the documents, and the giving of oral testimony, thereby suggesting that the authenticating testimony could be compelled not because the custodian had a duty to provide it as part of the act of production, but because it simply did not add to the incriminating testimony provided by the act of production. However, that may not always be the case, as the additional specifics provided by testimony as to matters such as the prior location of the documents may provide additional information incriminating to the custodian. *Braswell* also indicates that whatever authentication testimony may be compelled, that testimony may not be admitted against the custodian should he be prosecuted.

8.   354 U.S. 118, 77 S.Ct. 1145, 1 L.Ed.2d 1225 (1957).

An employee subpoenaed to produce what are supposedly entity records can assert the privilege if those records are actually his personal documents. Thus, a substantial body of lower court opinions consider the question of whether, under the circumstances of the case, such documents as employee desk and pocket calendars are personal rather than corporate records. The burden is on the subpoenaed employee to show that the records are personal rather than entity records. In making that determination, courts commonly examine the documents *in camera* to determine their content. A multi-factored analysis is employed, with the court seeking to determine the "essential nature" of the document by looking at such criteria as: "who prepared the document; the nature of its contents; its purpose or use; who possessed it; who had access to it; whether the corporation required its preparation; and whether its existence was necessary to or in furtherance of corporate business." The clearest case of a personal document is a diary containing an employee's end-of-the-day reflections on social and business experiences, not used in conducting office affairs and not shared with others, though kept in the employee's office.

(e) Non–Documentary Subpoenas. The act-of-production doctrine is not limited in its potential application to documentary subpoenas. A subpoena requiring production of some item of physical evidence also can be challenged if the acknowledgment of existence and possession through the act of production is "testimonial" and "incriminating." The act-of-production doctrine's potential range in this regard, and its relationship to other self-incrimination doctrines in this context, are strikingly illustrated by *Baltimore City Department of Social Services v. Bouknight*.[9] In that case, the Supreme Court rejected a self-incrimination objection to a subpoena directing respondent Bouknight to produce her infant son, who was a ward of the court. The Court noted that the respondent could not claim the privilege based upon "anything an examination of the [child] might reveal," as that would be a claim based upon "the contents or nature of the

thing demanded." However, the mother could conceivably claim the privilege because "the act of production would amount to testimony regarding her control over and possession of [the child]." While the state could "readily introduce [other] evidence of Bouknight's continuing control over the child" (including the court order giving her limited custody and her previous statements), her "implicit communication of control over [the child] at the moment of production might aid the state in prosecuting Bouknight [for child abuse]." The Court had no need to decide, however, whether "this limited testimonial assertion is sufficiently incriminating and sufficiently testimonial for purposes of the privilege." In receiving conditional custody from the juvenile court, the mother had "assumed custodial duties related to production" (analogous to that of an entity agent) and had done so as part of a noncriminal regulatory scheme which included a production component (analogous to regulations sustained under the required records doctrine). The Court added that it had no need in the case before it "to define the precise limitations that may exist upon the State's ability to use the testimonial aspects of Bouknight's act of production in subsequent criminal proceedings," but the "imposition of such limitations," as done in *Braswell*, was not "foreclosed."

§ 8.14   Judicial Decisions and the History and Policies of the Self–Incrimination Privilege

(a) Range of Self–Incrimination Issues. The Supreme Court has considered self-incrimination issues in a variety of different contexts, including police interrogation of suspects, compelled arrestee participation in identification procedures, grand jury subpoenas, suppression procedures, court-ordered defense discovery to the prosecution, the defendant's exercise of the privilege (through silence) at his trial, sentencing procedures, claims in civil proceedings, claims in legislative investigations, and regulatory schemes requiring disclo-

---

9.   493 U.S. 549, 110 S.Ct. 900, 107 L.Ed.2d 992 (1990).

sures.[1] It has considered issues such as who is protected,[2] what constitutes "compulsion,"[3] what constitutes "incrimination,"[4] what kinds of compelled and incriminatory evidence may not be used against defendant,[5] how far does that prohibition against use extend,[6] what governmentally imposed burdens so impair the exercise of the privilege as to be unconstitutional,[7] and what should be required for waiver of the privilege.[8] The end result has been a variety of different doctrinal standards, each shaped to fit both the particular issue and the particular context in which it is presented. Those standards are discussed at various points in the text as they arise in the chronological sequence of the criminal justice process. Treated here are two common threads that run through the Supreme Court opinions dealing with self-incrimination issues—the frequent reference to the history of the privilege and to the basic policies that underlie the privilege. While those common thread extends beyond the Supreme Court cases discussed in §§ 8.10–8.13, their consideration at this point is especially appropriate, as many of the most prominent discussions of the history and policies of the Fifth Amendment privilege are found in cases involving grand jury subpoenas.

(b) History of the Privilege. The pre–1791 historical development of the privilege in England is clear in its major features but sometimes clouded in its grounding. In its initial formulation, the privilege reflected a rejection of the oath procedure used by the ecclesiastical Court of High Commission and the Privy Council's Court of Star Chamber. Both of those prerogative tribunals were active in the persecution of religious and political dissidents, and both used an oath procedure to engage in roving inquiries. A person could be brought before the tribunal without any private accusation or charges files against him, and there required to take an oath—the oath *ex officio*—to answer truthfully all questions that might be put to him. Refusal to take the oath could result in serious consequences, typically imprisonment for contempt or a fine. Indeed, in the case of the Star Chamber, corporal punishment (though not torture) also was used on occasion. Nonetheless, there were those who refused to take the oath, citing the maxim *nemo tenetur seipsum prodere* (no man is bound to produce himself). This maximum was in fact narrower than the quoted phrase. In full it stated that no man is bound to "produce himself" (i.e., accuse himself), but when accused by common repute, he would be held "to show, if he can, his innocence and purge himself." Accordingly, when Parliament in 1641 abolished the courts of High Commission and Star Chamber and prohibited the administration by any ecclesiastical court of an *ex officio* oath requiring an answer to "things penal," the question remained as to whether a defendant could properly be put to oath after a proper presentment had been made against him. This issue would not arise at trial because the common law disqualified the defendant from testifying under oath. However, the legality of placing the defendant under oath was questioned in connection with the magistrate's examination of the accused in the pretrial committal procedure (the "preliminary examination").

---

§ 8.14

1. As for self-incrimination issues that arise in the course of the criminal justice process, see §§ 3.2(i), 3.4(a) (searches for documents); §§ 6.5–6.10 (police interrogation); § 7.2 (identification procedures); § 8.10 (grand jury testimony); § 8.11 (immunity grants); §§ 8.12–8.13 (documentary production); § 9.2 (suppression hearing testimony); §§ 9.5–9.6 (evidentiary uses of illegally obtained confessions); § 12.1(e) (bail hearing testimony); § 15.4 (indictments based on information obtained in violation of the privilege); § 20.4 (prosecution discovery); § 24.5 (defendant's right of silence at trial); and § 26.4(c) (sentencing procedures).

2. See § 8.12(b) (entity exception).

3. See § 6.5 (*Miranda*); § 9.2 (*Simmons*); § 8.12(e) (third-party compulsion).

4. See § 8.10(a) (potential incrimination standard); § 8.10(b) (incrimination under laws of another sovereign); § 8.11 (immunity).

5. See §§ 7.2(a), 8.12(d) (*Schmerber* rule); § 8.12(c) (required records); §§ 8.12(f), 8.13 (act-of-production doctrine).

6. See § 8.11 (scope of immunity); § 9.5 (derivative use); § 9.6 (impeachment use).

7. See § 8.1(f) (various adverse consequences; § 24.5(b)) (comment and instruction on defendant's silence).

8. See § 6.9 (*Miranda* waiver standards); § 8.10(d) (grand jury witness waiver); § 23.4 (waiver by accused).

Although some magistrates at first concluded that they had authority to use the oath, the general arguments advanced against the oath *ex officio* prevailed, and a consensus developed that the accused could not be sworn before being interrogated. Still another significant development in the common law courts was granting to witnesses in both civil and criminal cases the right to refuse to respond to a question when the answer would be incriminating. As a result of these rulings, the common law was viewed as having established by the early eighteenth century a general privilege against self-incrimination. Since a person could not be required under oath to provide an incriminating answer, even if the disqualification of the defendant as a witness at trial were to be eliminated, the nemo tenetur maxim— now converted into an absolute prohibition— would have precluded a common law court from compelling the defendant to testify under oath and forcing him to answer incriminating questions.

Exactly why the English courts extended the privilege beyond the original meaning of the *nemo tenetur* principle, creating an absolute privilege, rather than one conditioned on the absence of a proper accusation, is far from clear. The narrowest view is that this development simply reflected the desire of the common law courts to avoid any form of procedure that remotely resembled that of the hated courts of High Commission and Star Chamber. In this regard, the privilege has been praised by the Supreme Court as a protector against what are now seen as the twin evils of these courts—investigative fishing expeditions and the use of torture. It is difficult, however, to square such a broad privilege with those limited objectives. The *nemo tenetur* maxim in its original version served as a safeguard against fishing expeditions, at least if read to require a proper presentment before the defendant could be compelled to answer; that objective did not require its further extension. The English had managed to abolish torture at least several decades before the privilege was established, and torture had not been used in either the High Commission or the Star Chamber. Allowance of the privilege to witnesses in civil cases also does not fit neatly with such limited objectives.

A much broader reading of the common law's expansion of the *nemo tenetur* maxim views it as a critical step in acceptance of an accusatorial system of justice. It placed the burden on the prosecution to establish its case through evidence independently secured, without requiring the defendant to explain his actions. However, this view of the privilege's original purpose is difficult to reconcile with the retention of the practice of magistrate interrogation of the accused (not under oath) at the preliminary examination, with the accused's statement or failure to respond duly noted by the magistrate in his testimony at trial. So too, while the accused at trial could not testify, since he was without the assistance of a lawyer and restricted in the witnesses he could present, he had almost no choice but to take advantage of his right to make an unsworn presentation of his side of the case (which, in turn, meant responding to any questions of judge or jury). It was not until well into the nineteenth century—when magistrate interrogation had ceased, the assistance of counsel was more commonly utilized, the defense had broader rights in presenting its own witnesses, and the burden of proof was clearly established as beyond a reasonable doubt— that the law realistically gave to the defendant a right to put the state to making its case without personally responding. Viewing the establishing of the privilege as part of a criminal law's shaping of a truly accusatorial system (again arguably a reaction to the High Commission and Star Chamber) also fails to explain the availability of the privilege to witnesses in civil and criminal cases.

Still another explanation for the extension of the *nemo tenetur* maxim centers upon the special role of the oath. Opponents of the Star Chamber and High Commission had compared the coercive power of the oath to that of torture. Questioning under oath did not simply pose the choice between self-accusation, perjury (for lying), or contempt (for refusing to testify); it placed an individual under an obligation to God to tell the truth even where the threat of criminal liability posed great temptation to at least shade the truth. This explanation of the privilege, as resting on the spiritual coercion of the oath, finds support in the willingness of the common law to have the magistrate question the unsworn accused, pushing hard for his explanation of events, while prohibiting the magistrate from placing the accused under oath. It is consistent also with a system that placed great pressure on the accused to make an unsworn statement at trial, but prohibited the court or prosecution from placing the accused under oath, with an obligation to testify. So too, it explains the extension of the self-incrimination privilege to witnesses, including witnesses in civil and criminal actions. On the other hand, it rests on a premise and a distinction (between sworn and unsworn statements) that obviously has lost considerable force (at least as to threat of supernatural sanctions) in today's world.

The privilege as developed in the English common law courts was carried over to the American colonies and it was included in the constitutions of eight states prior to the adoption of the Fifth Amendment. Most of those state provisions were limited to criminal cases, providing that in such cases "no man" could be "compelled to give evidence." Two granted such a right applicable to all judicial proceedings. The phrasing of the privilege in the Fifth Amendment—as a prohibition against a person "being compelled in any criminal case to be a witness against himself"—was therefore quite distinctive, but its uniqueness at the time attracted no attention. Indeed, the privilege itself attracted little attention in the adoption of the Bill of Rights. There had been only a handful of references to the privilege in the earlier ratifying conventions that urged adoption of a federal bill of rights, and those were accompanied by no explanation of the privilege's scope apart from its general role as protection against employment of inquisitional practices. Subsequently, in presenting the privilege as part of the proposed Bill of Rights, Madison offered nothing except the language of the proposal.

What is to be made of this history? Initially, the Court has noted that the Fifth Amendment itself provides "no helpful legislative history." As a result, the Court looks to the common law history of the privilege on the assumption that the framers adopted the privilege as it then existed at common law. As to the significance of that history, the treatment has varied with the setting. Justice Frankfurter once described the privilege as "a specific provision of which it is particularly true that 'a page of history is worth a volume of logic.'" That statement was made, however, in a case presenting a self-incrimination issue on which the historical practice was quite clear—the use of immunity grants to displace the witness' right to claim the privilege. But changed circumstances make rare such a square fit.

Most often, the Court has noted that it is looking to the general "lessons of history" as they point to the need for a "liberal construction" of the privilege. Those lessons, in turn, repeatedly bring the Court back to the evils of "ecclesiastical inquisitions and Star Chamber proceedings" and the need to avoid a system that "creates a temptation on the part of the State to resort to the expedient of compelling incriminating evidence from one's own mouth." Very often, however, as the Court has noted, that historical experience "sheds no light whatever on the subject [before the Court], unless indeed that which is adverse, resulting from the contrast between the dilemma of which petitioner complains and the historical excesses which gave rise to the privilege."

When the common law appears to accept a practice as consistent with the original understanding of the privilege, that does not always end the matter. Where the historical confines of the privilege seem not to fit its general lessons of history, the Court has not hesitated to note, as it did in *Miranda*, that "a noble principle often transcends its origins." Although the practice of magistrate questioning of the accused (not under oath) had continued for several decades following the adoption of the Constitution, the *Miranda* Court concluded that the privilege could extend beyond the use of judicial process to compel testimony under oath where, as in the case of the "informal compulsion" of in-custody police interrogation, the policies underlying the privilege, as reflected by the basic themes of its "historical development," supported its application.

(c) Policies of the Privilege. While the Supreme Court's opinions have referred frequently to the history of the privilege, they even more commonly have cited the policy foundations of the privilege. That is to be expected, for where the history is entangled and the current context substantially changed, a broader, functional analysis is commonly seen as the more appropriate source for determining the modern day scope of a constitutional right.

The classic listing of the "policies and purposes" underlying the privilege is that provided by Justice Goldberg in his opinion for the Court in *Murphy v. Waterfront Commission.*[9]

[The privilege] reflects many of our fundamental values and most noble aspirations: [1] our unwillingness to subject those suspected of crime to the cruel trilemma of self-accusation, perjury or contempt; [2] our preferences for an accusatorial rather than an inquisitorial system of criminal justice; [3] our fear that self-incriminating statements will be elicited by inhumane treatment and abuses; [4] our sense of fair play which dictates "a fair state-individual balance by requiring the government to leave the individual alone until good cause is shown for disturbing him and by requiring the government in its contest with the individual to shoulder the entire load"; [5] our respect for the inviolability of the human personality and of the right of each individual "to a private enclave where he may lead a private life"; [6] our distrust of self-deprecatory statements; [7] and our realization that the privilege, while sometimes "a shelter to the guilty", is often "a protection to the innocent."

Murphy viewed the policy foundations of the privilege quite broadly, arguably including not only the primary objectives of the privilege but also a variety of values which those objectives incidentally serve. The end result was a collection of values so extensive that, if each were followed to its logical end in defining the privi-

lege, the practical consequences would not be tolerable—at least from the perspective of a Court majority. Consequently, the Court, on several occasions, has stressed the limits of a values analysis. It has been forced to note that, while it has said that the privilege should be construed "as broad[ly] as the mischief against which it seeks to guard," it also is true that "the privilege has never been given the full scope which the values it helps to protect suggests." Indeed, the Court has restricted the privilege through doctrinal limitations which, though they find support in certain values of the privilege, are acknowledged to leave the privilege short of fulfilling the full "complex of values" noted in *Murphy*. Nonetheless, *Murphy's* "underlying values" continue to be cited both by the Supreme Court and lower courts, and they have provided the starting point for analysis of the scope of the privilege in hundreds of state and federal cases.

The policies cited by Justice Goldberg can usefully be divided, for analytical purposes, into two categories. First, there are those values that provide a "systemic rationale" for the privilege, viewing it as an instrumentalist guarantee designed to further procedural objectives that exist independent of the privilege. This category includes the second, fourth, sixth and seventh values listed by Justice Goldberg. Second, there are the values that recognize the privilege as an end in itself, serving to recognize human dignity and individuality. The first, third, and fifth values in the *Murphy* listing fall in this category. The two subsections that follow consider the values within each of the two categories as they relate to Supreme Court rulings setting the scope of the privilege.

(d) Systemic Rationales. Justice Goldberg's sixth listed value sees the privilege as based in part on "our distrust of self-deprecatory statements." The basic assumption here is that such statements, at least where compelled, are less reliable as a class than other types of admissible evidence. While that assumption has been vigorously challenged by commentators, it arguably finds some support

---

9. 378 U.S. 52, 55, 84 S.Ct. 1594, 12 L.Ed.2d 678 (1964).

in the common law prohibition against basing a conviction upon a confession that is not corroborated by other evidence. Assuming the validity of the assumption, the question naturally arises as to why there is a need for the privilege in addition to the common law corroboration requirement. The usual response is the "lazy prosecutor" rationale for the privilege. This rationale sees the privilege as designed to serve a prophylactic function. Because it is much easier for the prosecution to build its case by forcing confessions from the suspect, the privilege bars the use of such statements and thereby forces the prosecution to establish its case through more reliable evidence. While the "lazy prosecutor" rationale is often seen as directed primarily against the compulsion of incriminatory statements in the investigative process, Wigmore saw it as justifying as well the application of the privilege to the accused at trial. Prosecutors anticipating a capacity to bolster their case by forcing the accused to testify at trial would lose the incentive to thoroughly investigate and would thereby risk the possibility both of missing exculpatory evidence that would prevent the conviction of the innocent accused and of failing to establish as conclusively as possible the guilt of the person rightfully convicted.

Accepting Wigmore's addendum to the lazy prosecutor argument, that argument would explain the application of the privilege in many contexts, but not all. The distinction drawn in *Schmerber*[10] can be justified, for example, as recognizing the government's interest in acquiring evidence (e.g., blood samples) far more likely to be reliable than "self-deprecatory statements." On the other hand, this distinction would seem to extend as well to other areas in which the privilege is deemed applicable. Focusing on reliability, why should the privilege bar prosecutorial use of reliable physical evidence that is uncovered through the content of a compelled statement of the accused? Why too should the privilege be applicable to the act of producing documents or other physical evidence (and if some question as to reliability is seen in this context, why should the privilege be unavailable to a corporation—

as surely the accuracy of verdicts is important in the prosecution of corporations as well as individuals)? Since the "lazy prosecutor" rationale is directed to the efforts of the government in gathering evidence, the availability of the privilege to a witness in a civil case not involving the government also may be questioned. So too, it does not explain the availability of the privilege to witnesses that the defendant would call on the premise that their self-incriminatory answers to defense counsel's questions would be helpful to the defense. Perhaps in part because of such questions, the Supreme Court often (but not always) has refused to characterize the privilege as a constitutional right aimed at discouraging the use of potentially unreliable evidence. The "privilege against self-incrimination," the Court has noted, "is not designed to enhance the reliability of the fact-finding determination: it stands in the Constitution for entirely independent reasons."

Murphy's seventh value—protecting the innocent—is based in large part on the concern reflected in the sixth value as to the reliability of self-deprecatory statements. Commentators have suggested, however, that the privilege may also protect the innocent in another way. In some situations, an innocent accused, if forced to testify, would be likely to leave the jury with a false impression as to his guilt, even though he truthfully testified as to his innocence, because of his poor demeanor on the stand or an extensive criminal record used to impeach his credibility. The Supreme Court has also taken note of that possibility. But this grounding, even if thought to raise a situation of sufficient seriousness to justify a constitutional right, would explain only the defendant's right to refuse to testify. Neither it nor any other "innocence" rationale would justify many other aspects of the privilege (e.g., its availability to the witness and its application to the act of production). Moreover, here too, the Supreme Court has seemingly rejected such a rationale for the privilege. Although occasionally describing the trial portion of the privilege as protecting the innocent, in those

10. See §§ 7.2(a), 8.12(d).

areas where the Court has been called upon to distinguish between constitutional rights designed to protect the innocent and other constitutional rights, the Court has placed the privilege at trial in the latter category.

Murphy's fourth value—achieving a "fair state-individual balance" in the criminal justice process—actually has two components. The first, insisting that the government "leave the individual alone until good cause is shown," affords protection against investigative "fishing expeditions." The second, requiring the government "to shoulder the entire load" in its "contest with the individual," reflects the basic character of an accusatorial process. It thus coincides with *Murphy's* second value—"our preference for an accusatorial rather than an inquisitorial system of justice." In an accusatorial system, the state must bear the responsibility for establishing guilt, as contrasted to a system in which the defendant is expected to come forward and establish his innocence.

That the privilege should be seen as designed to protect the individual from being compelled to respond to a prosecutorial fishing expedition is hardly surprising. The opposition to the oath *ex officio* procedure used in the courts of High Commission and Star Chamber was directed at precisely such compulsion. However, the objective of providing such protection not only fails to justify the full breadth of the privilege, but also raises questions as to limits placed upon the privilege by the *Schmerber* rule. The protection against prosecutorial fishing expeditions explains the availability of the privilege in the investigative process (and arguably in congressional investigations that often constitute a different form of roving inquiry), but not its availability at trial (the state by then having shown "good cause" for questioning the accused by virtue of its properly supported charge). Nor does it explain the availability of the privilege in a civil proceeding that is in no way connected with the investigative process. Moreover, if the individual truly has a broad right to be "let alone" absent a prosecutorial

showing of "good cause," the privilege arguably should extend to compelled participation in identification procedures, especially where the state has no greater grounding than a grand jury subpoena (which may issue without any showing of cause whatsoever). The restriction of the privilege to testimonial compulsion obviously looks to other values that are narrower than that right to be let alone.

Although more frequently cited by the Court than perhaps any other justification for the privilege, the requirement that the state "bear the full responsibility for establishing guilt" also fails to fully explain the self-incrimination doctrine. It fails to explain, for example, the availability of the privilege in contexts in which the government is not seeking evidence, such as civil suits brought by private parties. Yet even where the government is seeking to establish its criminal case, the accusatorial structure of the process falls short of justifying distinctions drawn in applying the privilege. While the accusatorial structure commonly is described as mandating that the prosecution establish its case through its "own independent labors," the Fourth Amendment makes clear that this does not preclude the use of defendant as a source of evidence. The questions therefore arise as to why compelling the defendant to disclose evidence is distinguished from "taking evidence" from the accused (through a search), and why that direct compulsion prohibition is limited to testimonial evidence and thereby fails to encompass all compelled acts of the defendant that produce evidence for the prosecution (e.g., the acts compelled in *Doe II* and in identification procedures[11]). The answers apparently lie in the special qualities of testimonial compulsion, but what gives those qualities particular significance is not the procedural structure produced by a preference for an accusatorial over an inquisitorial process, but values that exist independent of that structure. This was recognized in *Schmerber*, where the Court acknowledged that "the compulsion [through forced participation in an identification procedure] violates at least one meaning of the requirement that the State procure the evidence

11. See § 8.12(d).

against an accused 'by its own independent labors.' " The *Schmerber* Court concluded, however, that the "independent-labors" concept, taken in light of other privilege values, was basically limited to precluding the state from producing evidence through "the cruel, simple expedient of compelling it through [defendant's] own mouth." So too, the entity cases implicitly recognize that the privilege rests on values that go beyond implementing an accusatorial process, since a corporation no less than an individual is entitled to the safeguards traditionally found in an accusatory process (e.g., the presumption of innocence).

(e) Dignity Rationales. The third value cited in *Murphy*—the "fear that self-incriminating statements will be elicited by inhumane treatment and abuses"—reflects a concern for human dignity that finds support in the earliest commentary on the privilege. While doubt exists as to whether the preclusion of physical torture played a significant role in gaining common law recognition of the privilege in the early eighteenth century, the *ex officio* oath procedure clearly was viewed by its opponents as an inhumane procedure. Indeed, it was characterized by some as a species of torture. Other abusive practices, such as the third degree and just plain browbeating or bullying, might be viewed as a similar mischief against which the privilege was to guard. This would explain holding the privilege applicable to custodial interrogation or even grand jury questioning, but it would not explain its availability at trial, where the judge is available to prevent such tactics, or its application to the simple act of producing documents. Just as the privilege grew historically to bar more than the *ex officio* oath, so the rationale of the privilege must extend beyond precluding torture or similar abuses.

Just as the "torture rationale" is too narrow to explain the privilege, the "privacy rationale" suggested in *Murphy's* fifth value is too broad. As the Court noted in *Fisher v. United States*: "Within the limits imposed by the language of the Fifth Amendment, which we necessarily observe, the privilege truly serves pri-

vacy interests; but the Court has never on any ground, personal privacy included, applied the Fifth Amendment to prevent the otherwise proper acquisition or use of evidence which, in the Court's view, did not involve compelled testimonial self-incrimination of some sort." The end result of limiting the privilege to "compelled testimonial self-incrimination" is a very restricted sphere of protected privacy. The testimony requirement narrows the focus to the disclosure "of the contents of the mind," as the state must be seeking to secure a "communication * * * upon which reliance is to be placed as involving the accused's consciousness of the facts and the operation of his mind in expressing it." Moreover, the privilege does not preclude all efforts to obtain such information, but only that in which the individual is "compelled" to make the disclosure. Thus, as *Fisher* also noted, *Katz v. United States*[12] and its progeny clearly accept the government's authority to electronically record and later use in evidence the private incriminating statements of the accused, though such statements also reflect the contents of the mind. Finally, as *Fisher* further noted, even where the individual is compelled to reveal the contents of his mind, the privilege is not violated unless the content poses a real and appreciable danger of incrimination. Thus, where immunity is granted consistent with *Kastigar*, compelled disclosure does not violate the privilege no matter how personal and private the subject of the testimony.

With the elements of testimony, compulsion, and incrimination restricting the privacy protection of the privilege to a quite specific and narrow band of privacy, some explanation as to the special quality of that privacy is needed if the privilege is to be defined by reference to a privacy rationale. One suggestion, finding possible support in *Murphy's* reference to the "inviolability of the human personality," is the special privacy of the individual's "conscience." Compelling a person to condemn himself out of his own mouth—and thereby to acknowledge his guilt—is said to deprive that person of his moral autonomy to come to grips with his conscience on his own terms. This

---

12. See § 3.2(a).

view, however, fails to explain the application of the privilege to various instances of incriminating testimony, including that found in the act of production, which clearly fall far short of self-condemnation. Measured by reference to the preservation of moral autonomy, many of these forced disclosures are not readily distinguishable from being forced to provide an incriminating blood sample. Also, from this perspective, self-condemnation should hardly be tied to the traditional self-incrimination standard of providing a "link in a chain of evidence." So too, moral autonomy would appear to be equally invaded when the individual is forced to confess by a grant of immunity.

The cruel trilemma cited in *Murphy's* first listed value arguably receives the strongest historical support as a grounding for the privilege. Although some commentators quarrel with the underlying moral judgment, almost all acknowledge that the privilege arose from a belief that it was uniquely cruel and inhumane to subject a person to the trilemma of "self-accusation, perjury, or contempt." However, the true "cruelty" here arose in large part from underlying religious convictions relating to the oath, arguably lost today where, for most citizens, the consequences of lying under oath do not go beyond the state's sanction of perjury.

Accepting the continuing validity of the trilemma justification, it does explain why the privilege was carried beyond the criminal defendant and made available to witnesses in all types of judicial proceedings. It also explains why the grant of immunity displaced the privilege, as the individual could then testify truthfully without fearing incrimination. The testimonial distinction, as drawn in *Schmerber*, also finds support in this rationale. For a critical element of the trilemma is the pressure imposed upon the individual to violate his oath by committing perjury. Where the individual is not being required to communicate the content of his mind, as in his forced participation in identification procedures, he is not given the opportunity to lie under oath. The act of production, in contrast, does present a perjury

potential through the false disclaimer that the subpoenaed item does not exist or is not in the possession of the subpoenaed party. Of course, the same potential is present where one is required to produce "required records" or entity records, but here the special responsibility that the individual assumed for the records may be seen as a distinguishing factor.

The cruel trilemma does not, of course, explain the extension of the privilege to custodial interrogation.[13] In that setting, the individual faces no threat of perjury. Nonetheless, the Court in *Miranda* concluded that "all the principles embodied in the privilege apply to informal compulsion exerted by law-enforcement officers during in-custody questioning." The policies cited in *Murphy*, the Court noted, "point to one overriding thought"—that the government must respect "the dignity and integrity of its citizens." That respect was missing where the compulsion of custodial interrogation, which "may well be greater" than that imposed by judicial process, is used to force the individual to furnish incriminatory evidence "from his own mouth." Thus, the Court looked beyond the element of the oath, and focused on the need to respect the individual's instinct for self-preservation as it related to controlling whether he would reveal the contents of his mind.

As evidenced by *Miranda*, the "complex of values" that underlie the privilege offer more than a little leeway in defining the "mischief against which the privilege seeks to guard." Those values do not necessarily explain in themselves why the privilege has the scope that it currently possesses. The Court has looked to a mixture of considerations—of which the values are only one—in setting the scope of the privilege. It has looked to the strength of historical patterns as they suggest the core elements of the privilege, whether a particular interpretation flows logically from a value underlying that privilege, the priority of the particular value where the values do not all combine to point in a particular direction (as is usually the case), and the potential bear-

13. See § 6.5.

ing of a particular interpretation upon the effectiveness of law enforcement.

§ 8.15 The Witness' Right to Counsel

(a) **Constitutional Requirements.** Although the Supreme Court has not ruled directly on whether a grand jury witness has a constitutional right to the assistance of counsel, the justices have made major statements on that issue in two cases, *In re Groban,*[1] and *United States v. Mandujano.*[2] *Groban,* did not involve a grand jury proceeding, but rather a special investigative proceeding of a state fire marshall at which the witness was not allowed to be accompanied by counsel. In finding that the exclusion of counsel from that proceeding did not violate due process, the Court majority drew an analogy to the grand jury proceeding. There, it noted, the law was clear that "a witness cannot insist, as a matter of constitutional right, on being represented by counsel." Justice Black, in dissent, agreed that there was no constitutional right to counsel in the grand jury proceeding, but viewed the fire marshall's proceeding as not truly analogous. The witness before the grand jury had the protection of "the presence of jurors," which offered a "substantial safeguard" against abuse.

In *Mandujano,* a grand jury witness was told that "he could have a lawyer outside the room with whom he could consult," but he was not offered the assistance of an appointed attorney, although claiming to be indigent. The lower courts held that, as a "putative" or "virtual" defendant, he was in a position akin to an arrestee and should have been given complete *Miranda* warnings, including advice as to appointed counsel. As noted in § 8.10(d), the Court upheld Mandujano's perjury conviction without reaching the lower court's ruling on the *Miranda* warnings. Six members of the Court, however, did speak to that ruling.

Four justices, through Chief Justice Burger's plurality opinion, concluded that the advice given Mandujano as to the availability of

counsel was fully consistent with any constitutional requirements. Since "no criminal proceedings had been instituted," the "Sixth Amendment right to counsel had not come into play." The prerequisite of an "initiation of adversary judicial proceedings," as set forth in *Kirby v. Illinois,*[3] rendered the Sixth Amendment inapplicable. The *Miranda* right to counsel, "fashioned to secure the suspect's Fifth Amendment privilege," also did not apply. It was premised upon an "inherently coercive" interrogation setting, clearly distinguishable from grand jury questioning. Under "settled principles," as reflected in *Groban,* "the witness may not insist upon the presence of his attorney in the grand jury room."

Justice Brennan, joined by Justice Marshall, took a quite different view of the witness' right to counsel. Reliance upon cases like *Kirby* was inappropriate, he argued, because the questioning of a putative defendant "inextricably involve[s]" the privilege against self-incrimination, as well as the Sixth Amendment. "Given the inherent danger of subversion of the adversary system in the case of a putative defendant called to testify * * *, and the peculiarly critical role of the Fifth Amendment as the bulwark against such abuse, it is plainly obvious that some guidance by counsel is required." The dictum in *Groban,* Justice Brennan argued, was subject to reexamination in light of more recent decisions like *Miranda* and *Escobedo.*

Prior to *Mandujano,* the lower courts, relying on *Groban,* had uniformly held that the grand jury witness had no constitutional right to counsel, and that position has largely been reaffirmed in light of the *Mandujano* plurality opinion. A line of lower court cases, both state and federal, have held that there is no Sixth Amendment right to counsel in grand jury proceedings. In some, the claim rejected was limited to a right to have counsel appear with the witness before the grand jury, but most recognized a general principle that a Sixth Amendment right simply has not "come into play" at the point of a grand jury inquiry. A

---

§ 8.15

1. 352 U.S. 330, 77 S.Ct. 510, 1 L.Ed.2d 376 (1957).

2. 425 U.S. 564, 96 S.Ct. 1768, 48 L.Ed.2d 212 (1976).

3. See § 7.3 (b)

few courts have suggested, however, that where a witness has counsel present in the anteroom, the privilege against self-incrimination carries with it a right to leave the grand jury room and consult with counsel should the witness be uncertain as to the availability of the privilege.[4]

(b) Counsel Within the Grand Jury Room. In one of the major developments in grand jury reform, roughly twenty states today have statutes permitting at least certain witnesses to be assisted by counsel located within the grand jury room. About half of these provisions apply to all witnesses, but several are limited to either targets, witnesses who have not been granted immunity, or witnesses who have waived immunity. Some, but not all of these provisions, require the appointment of counsel when the qualified witness is indigent.

The statutes commonly contain provisions limiting the role of counsel while before the grand jury. Several state that the lawyer may "advise the witness," but "may not otherwise take any part in the proceeding." One jurisdiction also allows counsel to "interpose objections on behalf of the witness." Another provides for such participation upon agreement of the prosecutor and the foreperson. To ensure that the witness does not use the statutory right to delay his or her appearance, two provisions state that counsel's unavailability does not excuse the witness' failure to appear. Others impose time restraints on the witness' obtaining counsel of choice.

Almost all of the above statutes were adopted over the last few decades. Over the same time period, many other jurisdictions rejected similar proposals. Opponents of counsel legislation argue that the better practice is that followed in the absence of such legislation—allowing witness to be accompanied by counsel retained at their own expense, who will remain in the anteroom for consultation there. They acknowledge that the need to leave the grand jury room poses certain difficulties for the witness, but argue that those difficulties are not so great as to undermine the witness' ability to exercise his rights, particularly as to the privilege against self-incrimination. They see any additional protection of witness rights as clearly outweighed by the damaging effects that counsel's presence would have upon the grand jury's capacity to conduct effective investigations. They argue that, notwithstanding statutory prohibitions, counsel accompanying witnesses will find techniques, such as stage whispers and objections presented through the witness, for challenging the prosecutor's questions or conveying arguments to the jurors. They argue further that, with counsel at the witness' side, more witnesses will reply to questions by merely parroting responses formulated by counsel—responses that too often give away as little information as possible or are purposely ambiguous so as to avoid potential perjury charges. The critics draw an analogy to the trial, where the defendant, once taking the stand, is not allowed to interrupt his testimony for further discussions with counsel. Finally, it is noted that, in some instances, the witness may not be entirely trustful of counsel and therefore prefer not to have

---

4. Some support for this position may be found in Maness v. Meyers, 419 U.S. 449, 95 S.Ct. 584, 42 L.Ed.2d 574 (1975). In that case, the Supreme Court held that the Fifth Amendment precluded holding a lawyer in contempt "for advising his client, during the trial of a civil case, to refuse to produce material demanded by a subpoena duces tecum when the lawyer believed in good faith the material might tend to incriminate his client." Noting the layman's need for legal advice in determining the "nuances and boundaries" of the Fifth Amendment privilege, the Court reasoned that the privilege would be "drained of its meaning if counsel, being lawfully present, * * * could be penalized for advising his client." The Court noted, however, that it was not carrying its ruling as far as suggested by the concurring opinion of Justice Stewart, who argued that due process granted the witness in a civil case a general right to be advised by retained counsel. The due

process right to counsel noted by Justice Stewart would constitute an extension of the Court's suggestion in *Powell v. Alabama*, 287 U.S. 45, 53 S.Ct. 55, 77 L.Ed. 158 (1932), that due process would be denied, even in a civil case, if the court "were arbitrarily to refuse to hear a party by counsel, employed by and appearing for him."

In Conn v. Gabbert, 526 U.S. 286, 119 S.Ct. 1292, 143 L.Ed.2d 399 (1999), the Court noted: "A grand jury witness has no constitutional right to have counsel present during the grand jury proceeding, United States v. Mandujano, and no decision of this Court has held that a grand jury witness has a right to have her attorney present outside the courtroom. We need not decide today whether such a right exists, because Gabbert clearly had no standing * * *."

counsel present. The witness may be forced to accept counsel provided by others (e.g., his employer) and fear retaliation if the full scope of his testimony is carried back to such persons. Once the law permits counsel to be present, the witness will be under pressure to allow counsel to accompany him, and will lose the capacity to be selective in the disclosure of his testimony to counsel.

(c) Counsel in the Anteroom. In those jurisdictions in which the witness must leave the grand jury room to consult with counsel, different approaches are taken as to the frequency of such consultations. Lawyers sometimes urge witnesses to consult after each question, which allows the lawyer to construct a complete record of the questions asked. Many federal courts permit such a practice, while others go almost that far, limiting witnesses to departures after every few questions. Other jurisdictions are more stringent. They note, for example, that the grand jury may properly refuse a witness' request to leave where the witness obviously is seeking "strategic advice" rather than counseling as to the exercise of any legal rights.

(d) Multiple Representation. In recent years, many state and federal prosecutors have adopted a policy of seeking disqualification of counsel who are simultaneously representing more than one witness or target (or combination thereof) in a particular grand jury investigation. Those motions have been based on two grounds. First, it is argued that the courts have an obligation to preclude joint representation of clients with conflicting interests. This obligation stems from judicial authority to protect the interests of the client and to safeguard the integrity of the administration of justice. Second, the government maintains, often as a supplementary ground, that courts may bar multiple representation where it has been used to undermine "the right of the public to an effectively functioning grand jury investigation." As between the two grounds, the courts generally have been far more receptive to the former. Indeed, it has been argued that almost all of the cases granting disqualification mo-

tions find support in the conflicting-interests justification alone.

Challenges to multiple representation based on the need to preclude a conflict of interest are viewed as presenting issues roughly analogous to those faced by a trial court when it is suggested that a potential conflict may exist between jointly represented co-defendants. There are, however, certain differences in the two settings that may lead a court to adopt a somewhat different approach for each. Initially, the criminal defendant's claim to the assistance of counsel rests squarely on the Sixth Amendment whereas the grand jury witness' constitutional right (if any) rests on a more flexible due process right to seek legal advice. Secondly, the advantages to a witness of multiple representation at the grand jury stage may well be greater than the advantages to a defendant of multiple representation at post-indictment stages. For example, representation by a single lawyer may give a group of witnesses far greater discovery as to the nature of the grand jury proceeding than they would obtain through separate representation; at the trial stage, joint representation is less likely to give co-defendants any substantial advantage in discovering the government's case. Finally, grand jury secrecy may preclude a full development of all the facts that may have a bearing on the existence of a conflict. Very often, the presence of a conflict depends upon the government's view of the status of the jointly represented individuals (e.g., whether one is a target and another a prime candidate for immunity); however, disclosure of such information to those persons as a group would lose for the government a major advantage it hopes to gain through grand jury secrecy.

Prior to the Supreme Court's ruling in *Wheat v. United States*,[5] some lower courts held that disqualification could only be ordered where the attorney was in an "actual" rather than a "potential" conflict situation. However, *Wheat* held that disqualification at trial could be ordered where there was a "serious potential for conflict," and it generally is assumed that the authority to disqualify in the grand

5. See § 11.9 (c).

jury setting is at least as broad as in the trial setting. So too, since *Wheat* concluded that disqualification could be ordered at trial even though the jointly represented defendants were willing to waive their rights to conflict-free counsel, a willingness of persons jointly represented in a grand jury proceeding to waive their right to conflict-free counsel should not limit the court's authority to disqualify. Indeed, waiver at this stage is even more suspect as individuals are less likely to know what their eventual legal status will be in relation to others represented by the same counsel.

Prosecutors have sometimes argued that the right of the public to an effectively functioning grand jury is a sufficient ground in itself for precluding joint representation of witnesses. Their argument is that, even if the court would otherwise view a waiver as a satisfactory solution to a possible conflict in the interests of jointly represented witnesses, the court should disqualify a lawyer who is not treating each client-witness separately but simply advising them all to exercise the self-incrimination privilege. The utilization of such a "stonewalling strategy," in preference to seeking for each client the best possible accommodation (e.g., immunity), is viewed as inappropriate even though all the clients are in a similar position with respect to the investigation. Disqualification motions have been granted in such "stonewalling" cases, but each also involved additional elements of possible conflict. Those courts have suggested, however, that the disruption of the grand jury process is a factor entitled to significant weight. Other courts, in denying disqualifications in "stonewalling" cases, have suggested that consideration should be given to "preserving the effectiveness of the grand jury investigation" only where the government also shows that the various witnesses in fact have directly conflicting interests. They note that "discomfort to the grand jury process, without more, is not sufficient to vitiate an individual's important right to counsel of his own choosing."

Chapter 9

SCOPE OF THE EXCLUSIONARY RULES

Table of Sections

§ 9.1 Standing: The "Personal Rights" Approach

(a) "Personal Rights" as to Searches, Confessions and Identifications. When a motion to suppress evidence is made in a criminal case on the ground that the evidence was obtained in violation of the Constitution, there may be put in issue the question of whether the movant is a proper party to assert the claim of illegality and seek the remedy of exclusion. This question is ordinarily characterized as one of whether the party has "standing" to raise the contention.

496

One aspect of standing is that the party seeking relief must have an adversary interest in the outcome. As the Supreme Court explained in *Baker v. Carr*,[1] requiring that this party establish "a personal stake in the outcome of the controversy" is intended "to assure that concrete adverseness which sharpens the presentation of issues upon which the court so largely depends for illumination of difficult constitutional questions." On this score, any defendant in a criminal case against whom evidence alleged to have been illegally seized is being offered surely qualifies. In most areas of constitutional law, however, it is also necessary that the adverse interest be based upon a violation of the rights of the individual raising the claim rather than the violation of the rights of some third party. This is generally true with respect to the various constitutional issues that might arise in the context of a suppression hearing.

For example, when a Fourth Amendment claim is involved it is not sufficient that the defendant "claims prejudice only through the use of evidence gathered as a consequence of a search or seizure directed at someone else"; rather, he "must have been a victim of a search or seizure."[2] "This standing rule," the Court explained on another occasion, "is premised on a recognition that the need for deterrence and hence the rationale for excluding the evidence are strongest where the Government's unlawful conduct would result in imposition of a criminal sanction on the victim of the search."[3] Just who should be deemed a "victim of the search" under this line of reasoning has proved over the years to be a difficult and provocative question. The current view of the Supreme Court, however, is that the fundamental inquiry to be made in ascertaining whether the defendant has Fourth Amendment standing is whether the conduct that the defendant wants to put in issue involved an intrusion into *his* reasonable expectation of privacy.[4]

Because expectation-of-privacy analysis is also used in deciding whether any Fourth Amendment search has occurred, it has been concluded that there no longer exists a concept of standing "distinct from the merits"[5] of a Fourth Amendment claim. But this notion that the search and standing "inquiries merge into one"[6] is best avoided; the question traditionally labelled as standing (did the police intrude upon *this defendant's* justified expectation of privacy?) is not identical to the question of whether any Fourth Amendment search occurred (did the police intrude upon *anyone's* justified expectation of privacy?), and thus the former inquiry deserves separate attention no matter what label is put upon it.

Questions of standing seldom arise as to confessions because established evidentiary rules normally permit a confession to be admitted as substantive evidence only against the maker. But the issue comes to the fore when, for example, the confession reveals the location of physical evidence that is recovered and then offered as evidence in the trial of another person. Such was the situation in *People v. Varnum*,[7] where the confession had admittedly been obtained in violation of the *Escobedo–Miranda* rules and where the situation was further complicated by a well-established state rule that constitutional rights could be vicariously asserted. In holding the physical evidence admissible, the court reasoned no constitutional violation had occurred in that "the Fifth and Sixth Amendment rights protected by *Escobedo* * * * and *Miranda* are violated only when evidence obtained without the required warnings and waiver is introduced against the person whose questioning produced the evidence." Although this reason-

§ 9.1

1. 369 U.S. 186, 82 S.Ct. 691, 7 L.Ed.2d 663 (1962).

2. Jones v. United States, 362 U.S. 257, 80 S.Ct. 725, 4 L.Ed.2d 697 (1960).

3. United States v. Calandra, 414 U.S. 338, 94 S.Ct. 613, 38 L.Ed.2d 561 (1974).

4. Rawlings v. Kentucky, 448 U.S. 98, 100 S.Ct. 2556, 65 L.Ed.2d 633 (1980); Rakas v. Illinois, 439 U.S. 128, 99 S.Ct. 421, 58 L.Ed.2d 387 (1978); Mancusi v. DeForte, 392 U.S. 364, 88 S.Ct. 2120, 20 L.Ed.2d 1154 (1968).

5. Rakas v. Illinois, 439 U.S. 128, 99 S.Ct. 421, 58 L.Ed.2d 387 (1978).

6. Rawlings v. Kentucky, 448 U.S. 98, 100 S.Ct. 2556, 65 L.Ed.2d 633 (1980).

7. 66 Cal.2d 808, 59 Cal.Rptr. 108, 427 P.2d 772 (1967).

ing has been questioned, the *Varnum* result would certainly be correct under a "personal rights" analysis, for any constitutional violation that occurred intruded only upon the rights of the person who made the confession. Thus, even if the defendant was himself subjected to an arrest or search based upon a confession obtained from another in violation of *Miranda,* he would lack standing to claim that what was obtained by the arrest or search should be suppressed as the fruits of the *Miranda* violation.

While the court in *Varnum* carefully distinguished the case from one in which the police obtained the confession by using "physically and psychologically coercive tactics condemned by due process," under the "personal rights" approach there would be no standing even as to such a confession. Thus, if the police beat *A* until he confesses his role as an accomplice in a murder and says that his gun (used by *B*) is in his house and the police then retrieve the gun from *A's* house, defendant *B* is not entitled to have the gun suppressed as a fruit of *A's* coerced confession. If *A* had said the gun was in *B's* house and the police on that basis obtained a warrant to search *B's* house and found the gun there, *B* would still lack standing to claim this was a fruit of the confession but would have standing to raise his own Fourth Amendment claim that the warrant was invalid because based upon information known to be unreliable. More problematical would be a case in which a coerced confession is itself offered, as might happen if *A* testifies at *B's* trial on *B's* behalf and the prosecution then wants to impeach that testimony with a confession coerced from *A.* Though *B* could not be impeached by a coerced or involuntary statement obtained from him,[8] it is unclear whether it follows from this that he would have standing as to *A's* confession. It may well be that *B* is entitled to an assurance that "the trustworthiness of the evidence satisfies legal

standards,"[9] but this is a narrower proposition, for *A's* confession could be coerced or involuntary in a due process sense but yet be trustworthy.

Standing issues also arise infrequently with respect to unconstitutional identification procedures. But they can occur, as where in an accomplice's trial identification evidence is offered to show that his principal committed the crime charged. Where the nature of the constitutional violation was denial of the right to counsel at a lineup provided under *United States v. Wade,*[10] it has been held by analogy to Fourth Amendment standing rules that the defendant lacks standing to raise the other person's Sixth Amendment rights. Doubtless the cases noted above disallowing standing as to another's denial of counsel under *Miranda* might also be thought relevant here. But it may be seriously questioned whether either of these analogies is sound. *Wade,* after all, is grounded on the proposition that if a defendant's conviction rests on "a suspect pretrial identification which the accused is helpless to subject to effective scrutiny at trial, the accused is deprived of that right of cross-examination which is an essential safeguard to his right to confront the witnesses against him." In other words, the constitutional right at issue belongs to the person on trial rather than the person identified, and thus the defendant has standing, for otherwise there would be present a serious risk that the issue of his guilt or innocence might not be reliably determined. Whatever the result in such circumstances, surely a defendant has standing to object to an identification procedure conducted in violation of *Stovall v. Denno,*[11] for such a due process violation exists only when the procedure has been such as to create "a very substantial likelihood of irreparable misidentification."[12] Such evidence is just as unreliable when it is directed toward the identity of a

---

8. Mincey v. Arizona, 437 U.S. 385, 98 S.Ct. 2408, 57 L.Ed.2d 290 (1978).

9. Harris v. New York, 401 U.S. 222, 91 S.Ct. 643, 28 L.Ed.2d 1 (1971).

10. 388 U.S. 218, 87 S.Ct. 1926, 18 L.Ed.2d 1149 (1967).

11. 388 U.S. 293, 87 S.Ct. 1967, 18 L.Ed.2d 1199 (1967).

12. Simmons v. United States, 390 U.S. 377, 88 S.Ct. 967, 19 L.Ed.2d 1247 (1968).

coparticipant in a crime as when it relates to the identity of the defendant on trial.

A final word of caution concerning the "personal rights" approach: in determining in any particular case whether a defendant has standing, it is critical that the police conduct being objected to be properly identified, for this may turn out to be determinative on the standing issue. A very useful illustration of this point is provided by *Wong Sun v. United States*.[13] Federal narcotics agents made an illegal entry into the premises of Toy and then illegally arrested him, after which Toy in response to questioning said he had no narcotics but that Yee did. The agents then went to and entered Yee's premises and obtained narcotics from him, which Yee said he had obtained from Toy and Wong Sun. The narcotics were later admitted against both Toy and Wong Sun. The Court concluded that Wong Sun had no standing to seek their suppression, for their seizure "invaded no right of privacy of person or premises which would entitle Wong Sun to object." This would mean that Toy would likewise lack standing if he were also objecting merely to the agents' conduct at the Yee premises. However, Toy was held to have standing because he was objecting to the actions of the agents at his own premises that led to Yee and thus made the narcotics obtained from Yee the "fruit of the poisonous tree" of the violation of his own Fourth Amendment rights.

(b) Residential Premises. It has long been true[14] and is still so under the modern expectation-of-privacy test[15] that an individual with a present possessory interest in the premises searched has standing to challenge that search even though he was not present when the search was made. This includes those who are tenants or other continuing lawful occupants of a house or apartment or who are renting a room in a hotel, motel or rooming house, and also includes an owner-occupant but of course not an owner who has by lease given the full possessory right to another. Family members regularly residing upon the premises, such as a spouse or offspring, have standing of essentially the same dimensions. In *Bumper v. North Carolina*,[16] for example, the Supreme Court summarily concluded that there could "be no question of the petitioner's standing" to challenge a search of his grandmother's home during his absence in light of the fact that he regularly resided there as well. (However, an absent occupant or owner would lack standing as to violation of any Fourth Amendment requirement intended only for the benefit of those present—e.g., violation of the knock-and-announce rule without damage to the premises, violation of the rule on serving a copy of the warrant on a present party.)

Establishing such an interest in the premises searched itself suffices to establish standing, and thus the defendant need not also show an interest in the particular items seized by the police. As the Supreme Court explained in *Alderman v. United States*:[17]

If the police make an unwarranted search of a house and seize tangible property belonging to third parties * * * the home owner may object to its use against him, not because he had any interest in the seized items as "effects" protected by the Fourth Amendment, but because they were the fruits of an unauthorized search of his house, which is itself expressly protected by the Fourth Amendment.[18]

---

13.   371 U.S. 471, 83 S.Ct. 407, 9 L.Ed.2d 441 (1963).

14.   See Alderman v. United States, 394 U.S. 165, 89 S.Ct. 961, 22 L.Ed.2d 176 (1969), noting this to be the long-accepted rule.

15.   In Rakas v. Illinois, 439 U.S. 128, 99 S.Ct. 421, 58 L.Ed.2d 387 (1978), the Court stated: "One of the main rights attaching to property is the right to exclude others, * * * and one who owns or lawfully possesses or controls property will in all likelihood have a legitimate expectation of privacy by virtue of this right to exclude."

16.   391 U.S. 543, 88 S.Ct. 1788, 20 L.Ed.2d 797 (1968).

17.   394 U.S. 165, 89 S.Ct. 961, 22 L.Ed.2d 176 (1969).

18.   This approach was reaffirmed in United States v. Karo, 468 U.S. 705, 104 S.Ct. 3296, 82 L.Ed.2d 530 (1984), having to do with the monitoring of a "beeper" inside a container that revealed that this container was presently within a certain residence. The majority concluded that the tenants of this residence, who would have standing to object to a physical intrusion therein, also had standing regarding this nontrespassory search by beeper. But two members of the Court argued that the occupants of the house lacked standing regarding this activity, merely revealing the location of the container, "unless it is *their* container or under *their* dominion and control." The position of these two Justices is incorrect, given the fact that

The majority in *Alderman* thus concluded that a person should have standing to object to illegal electronic eavesdropping that "overheard conversations of * * * himself or conversations occurring on his premises, whether or not he was present or participated in those conversations." A vigorous dissent contended this should not be so when the eavesdropping occurred without physical penetration of the premises, for then the householder's property interest has not been intruded upon, and he can claim no privacy interest in conversations that he neither participated in nor heard.

If a defendant claims standing derived from his interest in the premises searched, he will not prevail if it appears that he had abandoned the premises prior to the time the search being objected to occurred.[19] But under the modern expectation-of-privacy approach the abandonment question must be examined in terms of reasonable expectations flowing from conduct rather than in a technical, property sense. In any event, abandonment must be distinguished from a mere disclaimer of a property interest made to the police prior to the search, which under the better view does not defeat standing.

It is sometimes important to ascertain the physical dimensions of defendant's property interest in the premises, as is reflected by the cases holding a lessee has no standing as to a portion of the premises not leased to him. But under the expectation-of-privacy approach it could be argued that at least sometimes one's justified expectations are somewhat broader than the area of exclusive possession. Consider *McDonald v. United States,*[20] where police illegally entered the house of defendant's landlady and then, by standing on a chair in a second-floor hallway, looked through the transom and saw illegal activity in defendant's room. Though a majority of the Court never responded specifically to the government's argument that McDonald could not complain of

the police intrusion into his landlady's portion of the premises, Justice Jackson helpfully commented: "But it seems to me that each tenant of a building, while he has no right to exclude from the common hallways those who enter lawfully, does have a personal and constitutionally protected interest in the integrity and security of the entire building against unlawful breaking and entry." This is a very sensible approach, but one cannot state with assurance it would be followed by the Supreme Court today, for the Court has sometimes (but not always[21]) taken the unduly narrow position that one cannot have a legitimate expectation of privacy for standing purposes without having a "right to exclude other persons from access to" the place in question.[22] But surely any family member residing there should be deemed to have standing to object to an illegal entry of the family residential unit, though if that entry is lawful it may well be that search into certain areas therein will only intrude on the privacy of a particular resident, in which case the other family members would lack standing as that search.

Yet another way by which one could acquire standing as to residential premises was recognized in *Jones v. United States,*[23] where defendant was present in the apartment of another at the time of the search and he testified that the apartment belonged to a friend who had given him the use of it and a key with which he had admitted himself. The Court, after declaring that "[d]istinctions such as those between 'lessee,' 'licensee,' 'invitee' and 'guest,' often only of gossamer strength, ought not to be determinative in fashioning procedures ultimately referable to constitutional safeguards," held that "anyone legitimately on premises" at the time of the search had standing. Under *Jones,* courts held that a guest present at the search had standing, but that standing did not extend to a guest then absent or to one who was present but unlawfully so.

the beeper monitoring was, in effect, a search of the premises.

19. Abel v. United States, 362 U.S. 217, 80 S.Ct. 683, 4 L.Ed.2d 668 (1960).

20. 335 U.S. 451, 69 S.Ct. 191, 93 L.Ed. 153 (1948).

21. See Minnesota v. Olson, discussed in text following note 25, infra.

22. Rawlings v. Kentucky, 448 U.S. 98, 100 S.Ct. 2556, 65 L.Ed.2d 633 (1980).

23. 362 U.S. 257, 80 S.Ct. 725, 4 L.Ed.2d 697 (1960).

But in *Rakas v. Illinois*[24] the Court rejected the "legitimately on premises" formulation on the view that "the holding in *Jones* can best be explained by the fact that Jones had a legitimate expectation of privacy in the premises he was using and therefore could claim the protection of the Fourth Amendment with respect to a governmental invasion of those premises, even though his 'interest' in those premises might not have been a recognized property interest at common law."

Rakas, it must be emphasized, did not question the *result* in *Jones;* the Court noted that Jones had been given a key and left alone in the apartment by the owner, so that, except with respect to the owner, "Jones had complete dominion and control over the apartment and could exclude others from it." But, the Court later held in *Minnesota v. Olson,*[25] this does not mark the outer limits of guest standing; "an overnight guest has a legitimate expectation of privacy in his host's home," even when the guest lacks such "complete dominion and control," as it is generally true "that hosts will more likely than not respect the privacy interests of their guests." Lower courts were split as to whether the logic of *Olson* extended as well to those visitors present for a shorter term, but in *Minnesota v. Carter*[26] a majority of the Justices embraced the position that a *social* guest would not have to be an overnight guest in order to have standing in the premises of another.[27] But the respondents in *Carter* were observed by an illegal search while they were in an apartment engaged with the tenant in bagging cocaine, and a different majority held that they lacked standing given "the purely commercial nature of the transaction engaged in here, the relatively short period of time on the premises, and the lack of any previous connection between respondents and the householder."[28]

Assuming now a guest who *does* have standing, there remains the question of exactly what kinds of Fourth Amendment violations are encompassed within that guest's standing. It seems clear that such a guest has standing to object to an illegal warrantless entry that leads to his own arrest in the host's premises, for that was the situation in *Olson.*[29] It would also seem that such a guest has standing with respect to an illegal search of the guest's effects there. *Olson* describes the guest's privacy expectation in terms of "a place where he and his possessions will not be disturbed by anyone but his host and those his host allows inside," and in *Rakas* the Court emphasized it was *not* suggesting "that such visitors could not contest the lawfulness of the seizure of evidence or the search if their own property were seized during the search."

24. 439 U.S. 128, 99 S.Ct. 421, 58 L.Ed.2d 387 (1978).

25. 495 U.S. 91, 110 S.Ct. 1684, 109 L.Ed.2d 85 (1990).

26. 525 U.S. 83, 119 S.Ct. 469, 142 L.Ed.2d 373 (1998).

27. The three dissenters concluded that "the logic of [*Olson*] extends to shorter term guests as well"; another Justice, while concurring in the Court's judgment on the ground no search had occurred, agreed with the dissenters' standing analysis; and still another concurring Justice asserted acceptance of the "view that almost all social guests have a legitimate expectation of privacy * * * in the host's home."

On the other side re the social guest were the two remaining concurring Justices, who argued that the Fourth Amendment confers a right of privacy only in one's own home, so that *Olson* was "the absolute limit" because only an overnight guest could plausibly be viewed as being at "his 'temporary' residence." The other two Justices were less absolute regarding *Olson*, though they viewed the guest in that case "as typifying those who may claim the protection of the Fourth Amendment in the home of another."

28. This language is from the opinion of the Court, joined in by a total of five Justices. One of the five wrote a concurring opinion similarly stressing that the record indicated that "respondents used Thompson's house simply as a convenient processing station, their purpose involving nothing more than the mechanical act of chopping and packing a substance for distribution," and two other of the five Justices joined in a concurring opinion asserting that the Fourth Amendment protects people only in their own houses, and that one who uses an apartment only to package cocaine cannot be said to be within "his 'temporary' residence."

29. This is so even if the guest's activities are of an illegal nature. In *Carter*, discussed in the text above, the majority purported to be relying not upon the illegal nature of the respondents' activity, but rather upon its commercial nature, but the three dissenters in *Carter* appeared to believe that the majority had actually taken into account the illegality of the respondents' conduct, prompting the dissenters to assert: "If the illegality of the activity made constitutional an otherwise unconstitutional search, such Fourth Amendment protection, reserved for the innocent only, would have little force in regulating police behavior toward either the innocent or the guilty."

Does a guest have standing in other circumstances—that is, when the police illegality does not involve or culminate in either arrest of the guest or seizure of his effects? *Rakas* suggests the answer is no. By way of supporting the holding there that passengers in cars do not have standing simply by virtue of their lawful presence, the Court indicated by analogy that it would not "permit a casual visitor who has never seen, or been permitted to visit the basement of another's house to object to a search of the basement if the visitor happened to be in the kitchen of the house at the time of the search." But such a result is not inevitable under *Rakas,* for the four dissenters and two concurring justices all noted that the Fourth Amendment also protects security of the person and that this aspect of the Amendment was not at issue because the defendants there had not challenged the constitutionality of the police action in stopping the vehicle initially. In a premises context, this means that if the police, without required notice or without probable cause or without a required search warrant, burst into *B*'s home and disrupt a dinner party at which *A* is present as a guest, then certainly *A* should be deemed to have standing to object; he has had *his* freedom, privacy and solitude intruded upon by the police, and thus he has standing to object to that encroachment upon *his* rights, even if it led to the discovery of evidence in *B*'s basement, a place *A* "has never seen, or been permitted to visit." On the other hand, it is fully consistent with the *Rakas* reasoning and result to say that if the intrusion itself was lawful, then *A*'s lawful presence would not alone give him standing as to any subsequent illegalities that did not increase appreciably the interference with *A*'s personal freedom.

Unfortunately, lower courts frequently have not recognized this critical distinction.

Still another type of case is that in which the defendant claims standing with respect to search of *his* personal property at a place that is not his and at a time when he was not present there. Standing has frequently been recognized in such circumstances, often by reliance upon *United States v. Jeffers.*[30] There, police entered defendant's two aunts' hotel room, for which he had a key and their permission to enter at will, and found his stash of drugs; the Supreme Court concluded with little by way of explanation that the government was in error in claiming "the search did not invade respondent's privacy." The Court expressly rejected the contention that defendant's interest in the seized property must be disregarded because it was illegal to possess such property,[31] but did not make it clear whether that interest alone conferred standing or whether his continuing access to the place was essential to the outcome. It has sometimes been held that absent such access there is not the expectation of privacy needed for standing, but it has been forcefully argued that a bailment arrangement without continued access confers standing because the bailor has sought to maintain the security and privacy of his possessions in a place he regarded as safe.

That analysis and even the *Jeffers* result have been put into doubt as a result of *Rawlings v. Kentucky,*[32] where police searched the purse of defendant's female companion and found therein the drugs she was carrying for him. The Supreme Court ruled that defendant had no standing to object to that search because he had no reasonable expectation of pri-

---

30.　342 U.S. 48, 72 S.Ct. 93, 96 L.Ed. 59 (1951).

31.　The Court stated: "We are of the opinion that Congress, in abrogating property rights in such goods, merely intended to aid in their forfeiture and thereby prevent the spread of the traffic in drugs rather than to abolish the exclusionary rule formulated by the courts in furtherance of the high purposes of the Fourth Amendment."

As for whether standing can be established under the *Jeffers* rule when the items in question are stolen property is unclear. Compare Combs v. United States, 408 U.S. 224, 92 S.Ct. 2284, 33 L.Ed.2d 308 (1972) (Court in remanding for standing determination as to stolen goods intimates

one could have a privacy interest in stolen goods); with Brown v. United States, 411 U.S. 223, 93 S.Ct. 1565, 36 L.Ed.2d 208 (1973) (Court holds defendants without standing where they had sold the stolen goods to another, but then adds in footnote that in any event "their 'property interest' in the merchandise was totally illegitimate"). In expectation of privacy terms, it is difficult to see how it can be concluded that if *A* is permitted to leave certain effects on *B*'s property, his reasonable expectations as to the security of that place from police intrusion are somehow affected by the nature of those effects.

32.　448 U.S. 98, 100 S.Ct. 2556, 65 L.Ed.2d 633 (1980).

vacy as to the purse, but the several reasons given by the Court for this conclusion are less than convincing. Of particular interest here is the Court's assertion in *Rawlings* that it was extremely important the defendant did not "have any right to exclude other persons from access to Cox's purse." But while a "right to exclude" may be an easy way to establish the requisite legitimate expectation of privacy, it hardly follows that it is the only way; as the *Rawlings* dissenters note, "such a harsh threshold requirement was not imposed even in the heyday of a property rights oriented Fourth Amendment." A bailor's right to exclude others is important in Fourth Amendment law, but for another purpose: deciding the lawfulness of a search consented to by the bailee.[33] To now utilize the same approach for standing would produce the incredible result that whenever the police could conduct a lawful search with the bailee's consent, they may instead proceed to make that search without the bailee's consent because the bailor will lack standing. This is not only wrong, but is inconsistent with the Court's prior[34] and subsequent[35] pronouncements on the law of standing.

As did *Rawlings* itself, lower courts applying *Rawlings* have looked to the totality of the circumstances in determining whether a person who stores property on the premises (or in the container) of another has sufficient indicia of security to establish the expectation of privacy needed for standing. Thus defendants have been held to have standing as to the search of their own closed containers stored on the premises of others with the permission of those persons. On the other hand, even before *Rawlings* several lower courts had held that storage of possessions on the person of another

did not provide standing to object to the search of that person, and *Rawlings* has been viewed as reaffirming that position.

(c) Business Premises. Analysis similar to that in the preceding subsection is appropriate when the question concerns standing to challenge a search of business premises. In *Mancusi v. DeForte*,[36] for example, where state officials conducted a search and seized records belonging to a Teamsters Union local from an office defendant shared with several other union officials, the Court characterized the "crucial issue" as being "whether the area was one in which there was a reasonable expectation of freedom from governmental intrusion." The Court answered in the affirmative, reasoning that defendant would certainly have had standing if the search were of his private office and that the "situation was not fundamentally changed because DeForte shared an office with other union officers," for he "still could reasonably have expected that only those persons and their personal or business guests would enter the office, and that records would not be touched except with their permission or that of union higher-ups."[37]

Consistent with *Mancusi,* courts have held that a corporate or individual defendant in possession of the business premises searched has standing, and that an officer or employee of the business enterprise has standing if there was a demonstrated nexus between the area searched and the work space of the defendant. Exclusive use would seem clearly to establish standing, but (as *Mancusi* teaches) there can be a justified expectation of privacy even absent exclusivity. As noted earlier, the "legitimately on the premises" basis of standing has

---

33. See § 3.10(e).

34. In Mancusi v. DeForte, 392 U.S. 364, 88 S.Ct. 2120, 20 L.Ed.2d 1154 (1968), for example, where the Court held an office worker had standing as to a search of records in an office used by him and his co-workers, it was properly said to be "irrelevant" that his employer and fellow employees "might validly have consented to a search of the area where the records were kept."

35. In Minnesota v. Olson, 495 U.S. 91, 110 S.Ct. 1684, 109 L.Ed.2d 85 (1990), the Court recognized that a guest has standing re his host's premises, a place where he expects that "he and his possessions will not be disturbed by anyone but his host and those his host allows inside,"

and expressly declared that the fact "the guest has a host who has ultimate control of the house is not inconsistent with the guest having a legitimate expectation of privacy."

36. 392 U.S. 364, 88 S.Ct. 2120, 20 L.Ed.2d 1154 (1968).

37. Defendants in a business setting did not fare as well in Minnesota v. Carter, discussed at note 26 supra, for there the respondents, visitors at an apartment of another to package drugs, were deemed to lack a sufficient connection with that place to have standing there, as they "were essentially present for a business transaction."

now been rejected by the Supreme Court;[38] it was never a meaningful basis for analysis as to business premises of some size.

Sometimes the question is whether a person who was not present and who in addition was not related to the business premises, in the sense of being a participant in the business enterprise, might ever have standing as to those premises. If, as suggested above, standing may be based upon an expectation of privacy as to certain effects temporarily put into the custody of another (a matter put in doubt by *Rawlings v. Kentucky*[39]), the answer would be yes. Thus, if *A* leaves his jacket at *B's* dry cleaning establishment to be cleaned and the police thereafter enter that establishment and search or seize that jacket, *A* would by virtue of his privacy interest in that item have standing to bring that police action into question. But if the customer does not have effects of his own on the premises, he is apparently out of luck. This is the thrust of *United States v. Miller*,[40] holding that the customer of a bank lacks standing to challenge subpoenas directed at the bank for records of his transactions that were "the business records of the banks." As the Court put it, "[t]he depositor takes the risk, in revealing his affairs to another, that the information will be conveyed by that person to the government," and consequently has no standing to challenge the subpoenas (or, as the Court concluded in a later case, to challenge acquisition of such records by burglary![41]).The reasoning and result in *Miller* are open to serious question. To resolve the standing issue on the basis that the person had assumed the risk of disclosure by someone else makes no sense, and simply cannot be squared with the Court's earlier standing decisions.[42]

(d) Vehicles. The holding in *Jones v. United States*[43] that standing could be founded upon being "legitimately on premises where a search occurs" prompted other courts to rule that a person driving a car with the owner's consent and a passenger who is present in the vehicle by permission have standing to object to a search of that vehicle. But then came *Rakas v. Illinois*,[44] where police stopped what they believed to be a robbery getaway car, ordered the occupants out of the car, and then searched the vehicle and found a rifle under the seat and shells in the glove compartment. The Court concluded that the passengers, who claimed no ownership of the seized objects, lacked standing because

> they made no showing that they had any legitimate expectation of privacy in the glove compartment or area under the seat of the car in which they were merely passengers. Like the trunk of an automobile, these are areas in which a passenger *qua* passenger simply would not normally have a legitimate expectation of privacy.

This should not be taken to mean that persons who are "merely passengers" will never have standing. It is important to note, as the *Rakas* concurring opinion emphasized, that the "petitioners do not challenge the constitutionality of the police action in stopping the automobile in which they were riding; nor do they complain of being made to get out of the vehicle," so that the question before the Court was "a narrow one: Did the search of their friend's automobile after they had left it violate any Fourth Amendment right of the petitioners?" This would indicate, as two-thirds of the Court recognized,[45] that a passenger *does* have standing to object to police conduct intruding upon his Fourth Amendment protection against unreasonable seizure of his person. If either the stopping of the car or the passenger's removal from it are unreasonable in a Fourth Amendment sense, then surely the passenger has standing to object to those con-

---

38. Rakas v. Illinois, 439 U.S. 128, 99 S.Ct. 421, 58 L.Ed.2d 387 (1978).

39. 448 U.S. 98, 100 S.Ct. 2556, 65 L.Ed.2d 633 (1980).

40. 425 U.S. 435, 96 S.Ct. 1619, 48 L.Ed.2d 71 (1976).

41. United States v. Payner, 447 U.S. 727, 100 S.Ct. 2439, 65 L.Ed.2d 468 (1980).

42. Such risks existed, for example, in Mancusi v. DeForte, 392 U.S. 364, 88 S.Ct. 2120, 20 L.Ed.2d 1154

(1968); Bumper v. North Carolina, 391 U.S. 543, 88 S.Ct. 1788, 20 L.Ed.2d 797 (1968); Jones v. United States, 362 U.S. 257, 80 S.Ct. 725, 4 L.Ed.2d 697 (1960).

43. 362 U.S. 257, 80 S.Ct. 725, 4 L.Ed.2d 697 (1960).

44. 439 U.S. 128, 99 S.Ct. 421, 58 L.Ed.2d 387 (1978).

45. Two concurring justices and four dissenters.

stitutional violations and to have suppressed any evidence found in the car that is their fruit.

It is very significant that the passengers in *Rakas* disclaimed ownership of the gun and shells. Even when there has been nothing unlawful about either the stopping of the vehicle or removal of the passengers from it, certainly a passenger has standing as to any search into *his* effects in the car. The Court's crabbed interpretation in *Rawlings v. Kentucky*[46] of what constitutes a justified expectation of privacy does not go so far as to bar such standing, though it may put in doubt whether standing can be gained by a nonpassenger whose effects in the car are searched.

Rakas deals only with passengers and thus does not place into question the notion that some persons with a stronger interest in the vehicle will have standing even as to vehicle searches in their absence. This is unquestionably so as to the owner of the car if he has not abandoned it or made a substantial bailment of it, the bailee of the vehicle, family members who share in the use of the car, and others who share use of the vehicle with the owner on a regular and recurring basis. This is not to suggest that such persons will have standing as to every kind of Fourth Amendment violation occurring in the vehicle; consistent with the earlier analysis, the owner-driver could not object if following the lawful stopping of his car a passenger's purse was opened.

The "wrongful presence" exception to the standing rule of the *Jones* case has its counterpart in the vehicle search cases: most courts agree that an occupant of a vehicle cannot be said to have standing by virtue of his presence if he is in possession of a stolen or otherwise illegally possessed or controlled vehicle. It has been argued that this should be so only if the police know they are dealing with a stolen car, but this is unsound, for a person's reasonable expectation of privacy hardly depends upon what someone else knows. While a thief driving a stolen car thus cannot gain standing as

to the car by his wrongful possession of it, that possession does not deprive him of standing he otherwise has. This means that a thief is still entitled to challenge unlawful interferences with his person, and consequently it would be open to him to question a search of the car that was a fruit of his illegal arrest.

§ 9.2 Standing: Other Possible Bases

(a) "Automatic" Standing. In *Jones v. United States*,[1] the defendant charged with narcotics offenses was found by the court below to lack standing to object to the search of the apartment where the narcotics were found and where he was present as an invitee at the time of the search. The Supreme Court concluded otherwise and held that the "same element in this prosecution which has caused a dilemma, i.e., that possession both convicted and confers standing, eliminates any necessity for a preliminary showing of an interest in the premises searched or the property seized, which ordinarily is required when standing is challenged." The Court in *Jones* indicated it would be improper "to permit the Government to have the advantage of contradictory positions as a basis for conviction."

Some years later the Court took another look at the problem of a defendant who is confronted with the dilemma of having to give incriminating testimony to establish standing and came up with a different type of solution applicable to a broader range of cases. In *Simmons v. United States*,[2] defendant Garrett moved to suppress a suitcase and incriminating evidence found therein that the police had seized from another person. In an unsuccessful effort to establish standing, he testified that the suitcase was similar to one he had owned and that clothing therein was his, and this testimony was later admitted against him at trial. Noting that he could not benefit from the *Jones* rule because he was charged with bank robbery, a nonpossessory offense, and that testimony as to ownership was "the most natural

---

46.   448 U.S. 98, 100 S.Ct. 2556, 65 L.Ed.2d 633 (1980).

§ 9.2

1.   362 U.S. 257, 80 S.Ct. 725, 4 L.Ed.2d 697 (1960).

2.   390 U.S. 377, 88 S.Ct. 967, 19 L.Ed.2d 1247 (1968).

way in which he could found standing," the Court reversed. As for the argument that such testimony was voluntary and thus not obtained in violation of the Fifth Amendment self-incrimination clause, the Court responded:

> However, the assumption which underlies this reasoning is that the defendant has a choice: he may refuse to testify and give up the benefit. When this assumption is applied to a situation in which the "benefit" to be gained is that afforded by another provision of the Bill of Rights, an undeniable tension is created. Thus, in this case Garrett was obliged either to give up what he believed, with advice of counsel, to be a valid Fourth Amendment claim or, in legal effect, to waive his Fifth Amendment privilege against self-incrimination. In these circumstances, we find it intolerable that one constitutional right should have to be surrendered in order to assert another. We therefore hold that when a defendant testifies in support of a motion to suppress evidence on Fourth Amendment grounds, his testimony may not thereafter be admitted against him at trial on the issue of guilt unless he makes no objection.

Simmons gave rise to the question of whether the *Jones* automatic standing rule had lost its vitality, which the Court finally answered affirmatively in *United States v. Salvucci*.[3] *Simmons*, the Court declared, provides protection "broader than that of *Jones*" because it "not only extends protection against this risk of self-incrimination in all of the cases covered by *Jones,* but also grants a form of 'use immunity' to those defendants charged with nonpossessory crimes." As for the vice of prosecutorial contradiction, the Court stated it need not decide if that "could alone support a rule countenancing the exclusion of probative evidence on the grounds that someone other than the defendant was denied a Fourth Amendment right," for at least after *Rakas v. Illinois*[4] it is clear "that a prosecutor

may simultaneously maintain that a defendant criminally possessed the seized good, but was not subject to a Fourth Amendment deprivation, without legal contradiction," for a "person in legal possession of a good seized during an illegal search has not necessarily been subject to a Fourth Amendment deprivation."

The defendants in *Salvucci* claimed that there were reasons for the automatic standing rule "not articulated by the Court in *Jones,*" most significantly that *Simmons* "did not eliminate other risks to the defendant which attach to giving testimony on a motion to suppress," primarily that "the prosecutor may still be permitted to use the defendant's testimony to impeach him at trial." But the *Salvucci* majority chose to sidestep that argument with the curious and unconvincing comment that this issue "need not be and is not resolved here, for it is an issue which more aptly relates to the proper breadth of the *Simmons* privilege, and not to the need for retaining automatic standing." Moreover, the Court erroneously asserted that the "Court has held that 'the protective shield of *Simmons* is not to be converted into a license for false representations,' "[5] thus hinting how the issue would be resolved. But it is to be doubted that this would be a correct resolution. The best analogy here is not those cases holding that illegally obtained evidence can be admitted at trial for the limited purpose of impeachment,[6] but rather *New Jersey v. Portash*,[7] holding that testimony given before a grand jury following a grant of use immunity could not be used for impeachment purposes at the subsequent criminal trial. In *Portash* the Court reasoned that statements made after an immunity grant and thus under threat of contempt involved "the constitutional privilege against compulsory self-incrimination in its most pristine form," so that there was no occasion to balance the privilege against the interest in pre-

---

3.   448 U.S. 83, 100 S.Ct. 2547, 65 L.Ed.2d 619 (1980).

4.   439 U.S. 128, 99 S.Ct. 421, 58 L.Ed.2d 387 (1978).

5.   Quoting from United States v. Kahan, 415 U.S. 239, 94 S.Ct. 1179, 39 L.Ed.2d 297 (1974). But *Kahan* involved use for impeachment purposes of false testimony given at a pretrial hearing to establish defendant's eligibility for

appointed counsel, and the holding is somewhat different than is suggested by that selective quotation.

6.   See § 9.6(a).

7.   440 U.S. 450, 99 S.Ct. 1292, 59 L.Ed.2d 501 (1979).

venting perjury. It would seem that defendant's testimony at a suppression hearing is likewise "compelled" in the *Portash* sense, for, as *Simmons* teaches, the defendant is confronted with the choice "either to give up what he believed, with advice of counsel, to be a valid Fourth Amendment claim or, in legal effect, to waive his Fifth Amendment privilege against self-incrimination."

(b) "Target" Standing. Assume that *X* is arrested for armed robbery and that some time thereafter, acting with the specific intention of finding additional evidence incriminating *X* with respect to that crime, the police conduct a fruitful illegal search of *X's* wife. Or, assume that the police are seeking robber *Y,* who was known to have taken refuge in a certain apartment building, and that they then conduct an apartment-by-apartment search until they find *Y* in the last apartment, as to which probable cause existed because of the other illegal searches. By virtue of their being the "target" of the searches, do *X* and *Y* have standing to object to those illegal searches? The Supreme Court finally confronted the issue directly in *Rakas v. Illinois*[8] and concluded that

> since the exclusionary rule is an attempt to effectuate the guaranties of the Fourth Amendment, * * * it is proper to permit only defendants whose Fourth Amendment rights have been violated to benefit from the rule's protections. * * * There is no reason to think that a party whose rights have been infringed will not, if evidence is used against him, have ample motivation to move to suppress it. * * * Even if such a person is not a defendant in the action, he may be able to recover damages for the violation of his Fourth Amendment rights * * * or seek redress under state law for invasion of privacy or trespass. * * *

Conferring standing to raise vicarious Fourth Amendment claims would necessarily mean a more widespread invocation of the exclusionary rule during criminal trials. * * * Each time the exclusionary rule is applied it exacts a substantial social cost for the vindication of Fourth Amendment rights. Relevant and reliable evidence is kept from the trier of fact and the search for truth at trial is deflected. * * * Since our cases generally have held that one whose Fourth Amendment rights are violated may successfully suppress evidence obtained in the course of an illegal search and seizure, misgivings as to the benefit of enlarging the class of persons who may invoke that rule are properly considered when deciding whether to expand standing to assert Fourth Amendment violations.

A very forceful argument in favor of the concept of target standing can be put by merely reciting the facts of the remarkable case of *United States v. Payner*.[9] In 1965, the IRS launched an investigation into the financial activities of American citizens in the Bahamas. An IRS special agent, knowing that the vice president of a Bahamian bank would be in Miami, agreed to and participated in a scheme whereby that person's locked briefcase was stolen for a short period of time while the case was opened and 400 bank records photographed. This led to other information establishing that Payner had a bank account in that bank and that he had falsified his federal income tax return in that connection. This "briefcase caper," in fact a calculated and deliberate extreme violation of the banker's Fourth Amendment rights and also a criminal act, was undertaken with full understanding by the IRS agent that a person such as Payner—precisely the kind of violator they were seeking—would not have Fourth Amendment standing to object. It would seem that if ever a fact situation cried out for recognition of target standing, *Payner* was it. Nonetheless, the Supreme Court reaffirmed that there is no Fourth Amendment target standing, and even overturned the lower court's conferral of standing under the inherent supervisory power of the federal courts. As the *Payner* dissenters put it, that holding "effectively turns the standing rules created by this Court for assertion of Fourth Amendment violations into a sword to be used by the Government to permit

8. 439 U.S. 128, 99 S.Ct. 421, 58 L.Ed.2d 387 (1978).

9. 447 U.S. 727, 100 S.Ct. 2439, 65 L.Ed.2d 468 (1980).

it deliberately to invade one person's Fourth Amendment rights in order to obtain evidence against another person."

(c) "Derivative" Standing. In *McDonald v. United States*,[10] McDonald and Washington were together convicted of operating a lottery after McDonald's motion to suppress gambling paraphernalia was denied. The Supreme Court reversed and then, though assuming Washington was without personal standing, held he was also entitled to a new trial at which the seized items would not be admitted against him. The Court explained that denial of McDonald's motion "was error that was prejudicial to Washington as well" because if "the property had been returned to McDonald, it would not have been available for use at trial." But in *Wong Sun v. United States*,[11] the Court, without any mention of *McDonald,* held that defendant Wong Sun was not entitled to suppression of narcotics that were excluded as to codefendant Toy, as the "seizure of this heroin invaded no right of privacy of person or premises which would entitle Wong Sun to object to its use at his trial." And in *Alderman v. United States*[12] the Court adhered to "the general rule that Fourth Amendment rights are personal rights" and thus concluded there was "no necessity to exclude evidence against one defendant in order to protect the rights of another."

McDonald might be thought to have survived *Wong Sun* and *Alderman* if it is viewed not as a rule of standing but rather as a rule to the effect that a person should not have admitted against him evidence that ought to have been returned to another person as a consequence of this other person's motion to suppress. But such a rule would make little sense. It ignores the fact that courts are empowered to retain suppressed evidence if it is of evidentiary value, and would make the outcome turn on the happenstance of whether the defendant without standing was tried after or contemporaneously with instead of before the

defendant with standing. And the argument that *McDonald* produces necessary equality in results between codefendants or co-conspirators is not convincing.

Derivative standing must be distinguished from a line of Ninth Circuit cases adopting the so-called "coconspirator exception," under which a coconspirator was deemed to have obtained a legitimate expectation of privacy for Fourth Amendment purposes if he had either a supervisory role in the conspiracy or joint control over the place or property involved in the search or seizure. In *United States v. Padilla*,[13] a unanimous Supreme Court rejected that view. Noting that it is privacy expectations and property interests which govern as to standing issues, the Court declared: "Participants in a criminal conspiracy may have such expectations or interests, but the conspiracy itself neither adds nor detracts from them."

(d) Abolition of Standing. The California supreme court adopted a search and seizure exclusionary rule well before it was required to do so by *Mapp v. Ohio*,[14] and shortly thereafter held that a defendant would be recognized as having standing in all circumstances in that jurisdiction. This conclusion, the court reasoned in *People v. Martin*,[15] was a logical result of the fact that the exclusionary rule was based

> on the ground that "other remedies have completely failed to secure compliance with the constitutional provisions on the part of police officers with the attendant result that the courts under the old rule have been constantly required to participate in, and in effect condone, the lawless activity of law enforcement officers." * * * This result occurs whenever the government is allowed to profit by its own wrong by basing a conviction on illegally obtained evidence, and if law enforcement officers are allowed to evade the exclusionary rule by obtaining evidence in violation of the rights of third parties, its deterrent effect is to that extent

10.   335 U.S. 451, 69 S.Ct. 191, 93 L.Ed. 153 (1948).

11.   371 U.S. 471, 83 S.Ct. 407, 9 L.Ed.2d 441 (1963).

12.   394 U.S. 165, 89 S.Ct. 961, 22 L.Ed.2d 176 (1969).

13.   508 U.S. 77, 113 S.Ct. 1936, 123 L.Ed.2d 635 (1993).

14.   367 U.S. 643, 81 S.Ct. 1684, 6 L.Ed.2d 1081 (1961).

15.   45 Cal.2d 755, 290 P.2d 855 (1955).

nullified. Moreover, such a limitation virtually invites law enforcement officers to violate the rights of third parties and to trade the escape of a criminal whose rights are violated for the conviction of others by use of the evidence illegally obtained against them.

Though the analysis in *Mapp* as to the underpinnings of the exclusionary rule was very similar, the Supreme Court in *Alderman v. United States*[16] declined to adopt the *Martin* approach. Despite the fact that "the deterrent aim of the rule" might be advanced by abolition of the standing requirement, the Court was "not convinced that the additional benefits of extending the exclusionary rule to other defendants would justify further encroachment upon the public interest in prosecuting those accused of crime and having them acquitted or convicted on the basis of all the evidence which exposes the truth."[17]

Some argue that the *Alderman* approach to standing actually invites police illegality by telling them that they can direct a search at one person and use the evidence against another. But that problem, it has been countered, could be dealt with by recognition of "target" standing, which may be correct unless it is thought that defendants would be unable to establish their target status when it existed. In any event, total abolition of standing would seem to push the exclusionary rule on occasion to ridiculous results, such as that a criminal must go free because his crime was detected by conduct that only infringed the Fourth Amendment rights of that criminal's victim.

§ 9.3   "Fruit of the Poisonous Tree" Theories

(a) Generally. In the simplest of exclusionary rule cases, the challenged evidence is quite clearly "direct" or "primary" in its relationship to the prior arrest, search, interrogation, lineup or other identification procedure. Such is the case when that evidence is an identification occurring at the confrontation between suspect and victim or witness, a confession or admission made in response to questioning, or physical evidence obtained by search or arrest. Not infrequently, however, challenged evidence is "secondary" or "derivative" in character. This occurs when, for example, a confession is obtained after an illegal arrest, physical evidence is located after an illegally obtained confession, or an in-court identification is made following an illegally conducted pretrial identification. In these situations, it is necessary to determine whether the derivative evidence is "tainted" by the prior constitutional or other violation. To use the phrase coined by Justice Frankfurter, it must be decided whether that evidence is the "fruit of the poisonous tree."[1] As is apparent from the examples just given, the "poisonous tree" can be an illegal arrest or search, illegal interrogation procedures or illegal identification practices.[2]

The genesis of the "taint" doctrine was in *Silverthorne Lumber Co. v. United States*,[3] where federal officers unlawfully seized certain documents from the Silverthornes, and after a district court ordered those documents returned the prosecutor caused the grand jury to issue subpoenas to the defendants to produce the very same documents. In holding that the subpoenas were invalid, the Court declared:

> The essence of a provision forbidding the acquisition of evidence in a certain way is that not merely evidence so acquired shall not be used before the Court but that it shall not be used at all. Of course this does not mean that the facts thus obtained be-

---

16. 394 U.S. 165, 89 S.Ct. 961, 22 L.Ed.2d 176 (1969).

17. *Martin*'s acceptance of "vicarious standing" was later held to be abrogated by California's adoption of a constitutional amendment requiring the admission of all relevant evidence except where suppression is required by the federal constitution.

§ 9.3

1. Nardone v. United States, 308 U.S. 338, 60 S.Ct. 266, 84 L.Ed. 307 (1939).

2. Because the fruits issues in this context are more closely connected with the development of doctrine concerning what identification practices are illegal, they are not discussed herein but are instead considered in Chapter 7.

3. 251 U.S. 385, 40 S.Ct. 182, 64 L.Ed. 319 (1920).

come sacred and inaccessible. If knowledge of them is gained from an independent source they may be proved like any others, but the knowledge gained by the Government's own wrong cannot be used by it in the way proposed.

In *Nardone v. United States*,[4] the Court refused to permit the prosecution to avoid an inquiry into its use of information gained by illegal wiretaps, observing that "[t]o forbid the direct use of methods * * * but to put no curb on their full indirect use would only invite the very methods deemed 'inconsistent with ethical standards and destructive of personal liberty.' " This case established the doctrine of "attenuation" by authoritatively recognizing that the challenged evidence might sometimes be admissible even if it did not have an "independent source" because the "causal connection * * * may have become so attenuated as to dissipate the taint." Thus, in the later case of *Wong Sun v. United States*,[5] it was said that the question to be answered as to derivative evidence is "whether, granting establishment of the primary illegality, the evidence to which instant objection is made has been come at by exploitation of that illegality or instead by means sufficiently distinguishable to be purged of the primary taint." In more recent cases the Court has been concerned with what factors bear upon the determination of whether or not there has been attenuation.

(b) "But for" Rejected. In *Wong Sun,* the Court declined to "hold that all evidence is 'fruit of the poisonous tree' simply because it would not have come to light but for the illegal actions of the police." Thus the Court ruled that Wong Sun's confession was untainted by his illegal arrest because it was given after he had obtained his release and voluntarily returned to the station later, although there seemed to be no doubt that he would never have come in and confessed but for the prior arrest. But, it might quite appropriately be asked: Why not suppress the confession, for it was quite clearly caused by the arrest, and

thus admission of the confession permits the government to profit from the Fourth Amendment violation?

Complete exclusion of fruits would be excessive in light of the obvious competing considerations: that exclusion of evidence thwarts society's interest in convicting the guilty. The Court's rejection of the "but for" test, therefore, as Justice Powell once pointed out, "recognizes that in some circumstances strict adherence to the Fourth Amendment exclusionary rule imposes greater cost on the legitimate demands of law enforcement than can be justified by the rule's deterrent purposes."[6]

(c) "Attenuated Connection". In neither *Nardone* nor *Wong Sun* did the Court elaborate upon the "attenuated connection" test, thus leaving it rather uncertain exactly what lower courts were expected to look for, to say nothing of what facts would be relevant to an "attenuation" determination. But here as well it is useful to view the question from the perspective of the exclusionary rule's deterrence function. The notion of the "dissipation of the taint" attempts to mark the point at which the detrimental consequences of illegal police action become so attenuated that the deterrent effect of the exclusionary rule no longer justifies its cost. In short, the underlying purpose of the "attenuated connection" test is to mark the point of diminishing returns of the deterrence principle. When courts lose sight of that point the results can be most unfortunate, as is illustrated by the not uncommon holding prior to *Brown v. Illinois*[7] that the *Miranda* warnings alone supply the requisite attenuation between an illegal arrest and a confession. That is not attenuation in the deterrence function sense, for it is clear that "the effect of the exclusionary rule would be substantially diluted"[8] under such an approach.

Of course, an appellate court's judgment as to that point at which admission of the evi-

---

4. 308 U.S. 338, 60 S.Ct. 266, 84 L.Ed. 307 (1939).

5. 371 U.S. 471, 83 S.Ct. 407, 9 L.Ed.2d 441 (1963).

6. Concurring in Brown v. Illinois, 422 U.S. 590, 95 S.Ct. 2254, 45 L.Ed.2d 416 (1975).

7. 422 U.S. 590, 95 S.Ct. 2254, 45 L.Ed.2d 416 (1975).

8. Brown v. Illinois, 422 U.S. 590, 95 S.Ct. 2254, 45 L.Ed.2d 416 (1975).

dence will significantly dilute deterrence will be informed by the court's views on a variety of subsidiary questions, such as whether police are likely to view the court's ruling as providing a significant "incentive" to engage in illegal searches and whether judges ruling on suppression motions can and will readily identify those situations in which police act with the specific objective of exploiting the limitations of the fruits doctrine.[9] As evidenced by the majority, concurring, and dissenting opinions in many of the leading Supreme Court opinions on the fruits doctrine, judges may bring widely different perspectives to these issues. However, at times courts have appeared to be influenced as much by a desire to limit the scope of the exclusionary rule as by any judgment that a finding of attenuation would, indeed, not undermine the deterrence function of that rule.[10]

The "question of attenuation inevitably is largely a matter of degree,"[11] and thus application of the test is dependent upon the particular facts of each case. But while there may never be any litmus-paper test for determining when there is only an "attenuated connection" between a violation and certain derivative evidence, it is possible to point toward some relevant criteria. One thoughtful commentator has suggested these three:

(1) "Where the chain between the challenged evidence and the primary illegality is long or the linkage can be shown only by 'sophisticated argument,' exclusion would seem inappropriate. In such a case it is highly unlikely that the police officers foresaw the challenged evidence as a probable product of their illegality; thus it could not have been a motivating force behind it. It follows that the threat of exclusion could not possibly operate as a deterrent in that situation."[12]

(2) The same may be said where evidence "is used for some relatively insignificant or highly unusual purpose. Under these circumstances it is not likely that, at the time the primary illegality was contemplated, the police foresaw or were motivated by the potential use of the evidence and the threat of exclusion would, therefore, effect no deterrence."[13]

(3) "Since the purpose of the exclusionary rule is to deter undesirable police conduct, where that conduct is particularly offensive the deterrence ought to be greater and, therefore, the scope of exclusion broader."[14]

(d) "Independent Source". The Court in *Wong Sun* quoted from *Silverthorne* the proposition that "the exclusionary rule has no application" when "the Government learned of the evidence 'from an independent source.'" As ordinarily applied, this means that if not even the "but for" test can be met, then clearly the evidence is not a fruit of the prior violation. So stated, the "independent source" limitation upon the taint doctrine is unquestionably sound. It is one thing to say that officers shall gain no advantage from violating the individual's rights; it is quite another to declare that such a violation shall put him beyond the law's reach even if his guilt can be proved by evidence that has been obtained lawfully.

A useful illustration is provided by *State v. O'Bremski*,[15] where a 14-year-old girl was found in an illegal search of defendant's apartment. The girl's testimony that defendant had carnal knowledge with her was held to be untainted because it had an independent source that even predated the search of the apartment. This was because in advance of the search the girl's parents had reported her missing and a police informant had already located her in defendant's apartment. *O'Bremski* is not a difficult case in light of this se-

---

9. This is true as well in determining the scope of the "independent source" and "inevitable discovery" doctrines that also limit the scope of the fruits doctrine. See, e.g., the discussions infra of Murray v. United States and Nix v. Williams.

10. See the discussion of the *Segura* case in § 9.4 at note 20.

11. Powell, J., concurring in Brown v. Illinois, 422 U.S. 590, 95 S.Ct. 2254, 45 L.Ed.2d 416 (1975).

12. Comment, 115 U.Pa.L.Rev. 1136, 1148–49 (1967).

13. Id. at 1149.

14. Id. at 1150–51.

15. 70 Wash.2d 425, 423 P.2d 530 (1967).

quence of events. But when the independent source is found to exist or comes into existence after the initial illegality, then the situation must be much more carefully examined.

The problem, of course, is that there is no way to get the cat back into the bag, so that once illegally obtained evidence incriminating the defendant has been found it can always be asserted with some plausibility that any information acquired thereafter is attributable to the authorities being spurred on and their investigation focused by the earlier discovery. Thus the question is whether the "independent source" test sometimes can be met even though it may well be that "but for" the earlier violation the investigation which uncovered the tendered evidence would never have been commenced. An affirmative answer was given in *United States v. Bacall*,[16] where, after U.S. customs agents illegally seized inventory from the defendant, they contacted French officials and asked them to investigate a matter relating to him. In their investigation the French agents seized certain letters and checks implicating defendant in certain crimes. In holding that evidence admissible the court declared:

> [W]e reiterate our assumption that illegal seizure *was* a "but for" cause of the foreign investigation. [But the] question to be answered is * * * whether anything seized or any leads gained from the seizure tended significantly to direct the foreign investigation toward those specific letters and checks—whether the Customs officers had after [the illegal] seizure a substantially greater reason to seek those specific items than they had before the seizure. We conclude that they did not and that the letter and checks were not tainted * * *.

This approach has been applauded on the ground that where unconstitutional action only leads the police to "focus" their investigation on a particular individual, this should not, in effect, grant him immunity from prosecution. Others object to the *Bacall* view, reasoning that if the police know that their initial

illegality can be covered up later by legal police work, then there is nothing to stop them from committing the initial illegality. This objection is especially compelling under certain circumstances, as where the prior illegality has caused the authorities to "focus" upon the defendant as a likely tax violator.

Another troublesome independent source problem is presented where the police (i) have probable cause to obtain a search warrant, (ii) subsequently enter the premises without a warrant and discover that the contraband is indeed there, and (iii) then leave the premises, obtain a warrant based on the previously obtained probable cause (without any reference to the information obtained during the unlawful entry), and return with the warrant and seize the contraband in the execution of the warrant. In *Murray v. United States*,[17] the Court of Appeals assumed that it had such a situation before it and held that the independent source doctrine applied. The Supreme Court remanded the case for further findings of fact, but agreed that the independent source doctrine would apply if the agents' decision to seek the warrant had not been "prompted" by what had been seen during the earlier unlawful entry (i.e., if the lower court found that the agents "would have sought a warrant [even] if they had not earlier entered the [premises]"). The dissenters argued that this ruling would encourage police officers to enter premises illegally for the purpose of making certain that the contraband is actually there before they undertake the "inconvenient and time-consuming task" of obtaining a warrant. The majority responded:

> We see the incentives differently. An officer with probable cause sufficient to obtain a search warrant would be foolish to enter the premises first in an unlawful manner. By doing so, he would risk suppression of all evidence on the premises, both seen and unseen, since his action would add to the normal burden of convincing a magistrate that there is probable cause the much more onerous burden of convincing a trial court

---

16.   443 F.2d 1050 (9th Cir.1971).

17.   487 U.S. 533, 108 S.Ct. 2529, 101 L.Ed.2d 472 (1988).

that no information gained from the illegal entry affected either the law enforcement officers' decision to seek a warrant or the magistrate's decision to grant it.[18]

(e) "Inevitable Discovery". Yet another theory that has been utilized by many courts in dealing with "fruit of the poisonous tree" issues is the so-called "inevitable discovery" rule. This rule, which has now been accepted by the Supreme Court,[19] is in a sense a variation upon the "independent source" theory. But it differs in that the question is not whether the police did in fact acquire certain evidence by reliance upon an untainted source but instead whether evidence found because of an earlier violation would inevitably have been discovered lawfully. A useful illustration is provided by *Somer v. United States*.[20] There, federal agents made an illegal search of defendant's apartment and found a still in operation, and while there questioned his wife as to his whereabouts and learned from her that he was out delivering the "stuff" and "would be back shortly." The agents waited out on the street, and when defendant drove up about twenty minutes later he was arrested and when the odor of alcohol was then detected his car was searched and illicit liquor was found. On defendant's appeal, the court noted that the agents may well have had probable cause to search the car even before they searched the apartment, but added that

> even though the search might have been lawful if made upon that information alone, it was not so made. Somer's whereabouts was unknown to the officers; they might have waited his return in the apartment; they might have sought him elsewhere; or they might have gone to the street, and arrested him where in fact they did. If they

had not done the last, they would not have caught him red-handed, or seized the evidence now in question.

Thus, the court concluded, the evidence must be suppressed *unless* on remand "further inquiry will show that, quite independently of what Somer's wife told them, the officers would have gone to the street, have waited for Somer and have arrested him, exactly as they did."

Some have objected that the inevitable discovery rule is based on conjecture and can only encourage police shortcuts whenever evidence may be more readily obtained by illegal than by legal means. These concerns, though unquestionably legitimate, are directed not so much to the rule itself as to its application in a loose and unthinking fashion. Courts must not lose sight of the fact that a mechanical application of the inevitable discovery objective will encourage unconstitutional shortcuts. Because one purpose of the exclusionary rule is to deter such shortcuts, it has been suggested that the inevitable discovery exception should be applied only when it is clear that the police did not act in bad faith to accelerate the discovery of the evidence in question. Such a limitation has been deemed necessary, in particular, to prevent a bypassing of the Fourth Amendment's warrant requirement, as is illustrated by *United States v. Griffin*.[21] There, after one agent had been dispatched to get a search warrant, others entered and made the search without a warrant, following which their colleague appeared on the scene with the warrant. Acceptance of the government's "inevitable discovery" argument in such circumstances, the court concluded, "would tend in actual practice to emasculate the search warrant requirement of the Fourth Amendment."

---

18. In light of its view of the incentives, and its requirement that the district court "be satisfied that the warrant would have been sought without the illegal entry," the majority saw no adequate justification for adopting a "prophylactic rule" (as urged by the dissent) that would mandate per se inadmissibility absent a police demonstration by some "historically verifiable fact" (e.g., a prior initiation of the warrant process) that the "subsequent search pursuant to a warrant was wholly unaffected by the prior illegal search." The present case itself "provided no basis" for suggesting "a 'search first, warrant later' [police] mentality." The district court had found

that the agents had entered the premises in an effort to "apprehend any participants * * * and guard against the destruction of possibly critical evidence" rather than "merely to see if there was anything worth getting a warrant for."

19. Nix v. Williams, 467 U.S. 431, 104 S.Ct. 2501, 81 L.Ed.2d 377 (1984).

20. 138 F.2d 790 (2d Cir.1943).

21. 502 F.2d 959 (6th Cir.1974).

But in *Nix v. Williams*,[22] the Supreme Court rejected a lower court holding that the prosecution, to utilize the inevitable discovery doctrine, must prove the absence of bad faith. The Court explained that such a condition "would place courts in the position of withholding from juries relevant and undoubted truth that would have been available to police absent any unlawful police activity" and "would put the police in a *worse* position than they would have been in if no unlawful conduct had transpired." The Court in *Nix,* which incidentally involved an unwitting violation of the subsequently-expanded *Massiah* doctrine,[23] went on to say that when the officer contemplates inevitable discovery, "there will be little to gain from taking any dubious 'shortcuts' to obtain the evidence."

Lower courts have had the least difficulty in applying the inevitable discovery doctrine where that discovery would have come about through a routine procedure invariably applied under the particular circumstances, as commonly is the case where the government argues that the evidence discovered through an illegal warrantless search would have been uncovered in an inventory search. But these courts often find more troubling a situation, such as *Griffin*, in which the government claims as its source of inevitable discovery an investigatory procedure that is not routine, but dependent upon a police determination that the procedure's potential value would outweigh its costs. Here, there is greater uncertainty as to whether the procedure would have been performed and often greater incentive for police to take shortcuts. In the *Griffin* situation, for example, the police might well view a warrantless search as a worthwhile shortcut because it would tell them whether it would be worth the bother of obtaining and executing the warrant. However, the same type of argument could have been made in *Nix v. Williams*, where the discovery of the corpse through the *Massiah* violation allowed the police to cut short by several hours a systematic

search of the highway that was utilizing the efforts of 200 volunteers. In light of the Court's willingness to apply the inevitable discovery doctrine in that situation, lower courts have applied the doctrine to various non-routine investigatory procedures where the government can establish that the investigative procedure, as in *Nix*, had already been initiated prior to the actual discovery through a constitutional violation. Thus, in the *Griffin*-type situation, the doctrine is readily applied where the government can show that police had taken steps to obtain a warrant prior to the illegal warrantless search, that they would have been able to obtain the warrant, and that the warrant would have been executed successfully.

More difficult proof problems are presented where the government can show only that, at the time of the actual discovery through an illegal procedure, the police had not yet started to pursue a non-routine procedure that would have uncovered the evidence. Illustrative is a *Griffin*-type situation in which the police claim that at the time of the illegal warrantless search, a separate evaluation of the case had been initiated and it would have led to obtaining and successfully executing a warrant, but that determination had not yet been made. If the inevitable discovery doctrine is to be treated as analytically similar to the independent source doctrine, then the government should not be precluded from establishing inevitable discovery in such a situation, but should be required to make a showing similar to that demanded in *Murray v. United States*.[24] In that case, the illegal entry and discovery of the evidence was trumped by the independent source of a subsequently-obtained warrant (based upon previously obtained probable cause) under which the police later seized the evidence. The Court insisted upon a showing that the decision to obtain the warrant was not influenced by the illegal entry (which confirmed that the evidence was actually on the premises), but did not impose an additional

---

22. 467 U.S. 431, 104 S.Ct. 2501, 81 L.Ed.2d 377 (1984).

23. Brewer v. Williams, 430 U.S. 387, 97 S.Ct. 1232, 51 L.Ed.2d 424 (1977), discussed in § 6.4(d).

24. See text at note 18 supra.

requirement that the police had to have initiated the warrant application process, or even have finalized the decision to seek a warrant prior to the illegal entry.

Of course, to gain application of the inevitable discovery doctrine, the government must establish not only that its employment of an independent, lawful investigative procedure was inevitable, but also that that procedure inevitably would have led to the discovery of the same evidence actually found through the Constitutional violation. "Inevitably," for this purpose means that the discovery definitely would have occurred, not that it "might" or "could" have occurred. However, *Nix* held that the Constitution is satisfied if the government establishes inevitability by a preponderance of the evidence; a higher burden of proof (e.g., clear and convincing evidence) is not constitutionally required. Typically, lower courts insist that the government introduce specific evidence (ordinarily, testimony by a police officer) establishing that another investigative procedure would have been employed and would have been successful. In some instances, however, the successful employment of that other procedure appears to the court to be so obvious that it will hold inevitably discovery applicable as a matter of judicial notice.

§ 9.4 Fruits of Illegal Arrests and Searches

(a) Confessions. The question of whether a confession, otherwise admissible, must be suppressed as the fruit of an antecedent illegal arrest was first dealt with by the Supreme Court in *Wong Sun v. United States*.[1] Federal agents broke into Toy's laundry and pursued him into his living quarters, where his wife and child were sleeping, and there held him at gunpoint and handcuffed him, after which Toy made incriminating statements also implicating one Yee. The agents then recovered drugs from Yee, who said he had obtained them from Toy and Wong Sun, both of whom were thereafter arrested and then released on their own recognizance after being charged. Later Wong Sun, on being questioned by an agent who advised him of his right to withhold incriminating information and that he was entitled to advice of counsel, made a confession. The Court concluded that Toy's admissions were the fruits of his unlawful arrest in his premises, and in response to the government's claim that the admissions resulted from "an intervening independent act of free will" the Court took note of the above facts and said that in "such circumstances it is unreasonable to infer that Toy's response was sufficiently an act of free will to purge the primary taint of the unlawful invasion." By contrast, the connection between Wong Sun's confession and his earlier arrest had "become so attenuated as to dissipate the taint" because of his release from custody and voluntary return to make a statement days later.

The more typical case was assayed in *Brown v. Illinois*,[2] where following his illegal arrest defendant was taken to the station and given the *Miranda* warnings, after which he gave incriminating statements within two hours of the arrest. The Supreme Court first rejected the per se rule of the Illinois court whereunder the *Miranda* warnings were deemed to break the causal chain between the arrest and confession. The Court explained that the mere fact a statement was voluntary under *Miranda* did not make it untainted, for if

> *Miranda* warnings, by themselves, were held to attenuate the taint of an unconstitutional arrest, regardless of how wanton and purposeful the Fourth Amendment violation, the effect of the exclusionary rule would be substantially diluted. * * * Any incentive to avoid Fourth Amendment violations would be eviscerated by making the warnings, in effect, a "cure-all," and the constitutional guarantee against unlawful searches and seizures could be said to be reduced to "a form of words."

The Court in *Brown* then declined to adopt a per se rule running the other direction, and instead concluded that such taint issues "must be answered on the facts of each case." It was

§ 9.4
1. 371 U.S. 471, 83 S.Ct. 407, 9 L.Ed.2d 441 (1963).

2. 422 U.S. 590, 95 S.Ct. 2254, 45 L.Ed.2d 416 (1975).

explained that the "voluntariness of the statement is a threshold requirement"; this is obviously so, for absent voluntariness the statement could be suppressed without resort to any fruits analysis. Assuming voluntariness, various factors must be considered: (1) whether the *Miranda* warnings were given (though again, if they were not this would be a basis for suppression without reaching the fruits issue); (2) the "temporal proximity of the arrest and the confession"; (3) "the presence of intervening circumstances"; and (4) "the purpose and flagrancy of the official misconduct." This meant the confession in the instant case was poisoned fruit, for it was obtained just two hours after the arrest without any intervening event of significance, and the arrest was obviously illegal and was undertaken "in the hope that something might turn up."[3]

The Court's assumption in *Brown* that the mere passage of time between the arrest and the confession increases the likelihood of the confession being untainted is not sound, for illegal custody becomes more oppressive as it continues uninterrupted. It is fair to conclude, therefore, as the lower court cases indicate, that temporal proximity is the least important factor involved in the *Brown* formula. Though the short time lapse between arrest and confession is often relied upon in support of a holding that the confession is tainted, a lapse of time in itself cannot make a confession independent of an illegal arrest. Indeed, the passage of time without an appearance in court can bring about yet another Fourth Amendment violation under the rule of *Gerstein v. Pugh*[4] and this will make the confession the fruit of yet another poisonous tree.

The "purpose and flagrancy" factor of *Brown* is certainly a legitimate consideration, for to maximize the policy of deterrence, the Fourth Amendment exclusionary rule should be most strictly applied in cases where flagrantly unlawful police activity has occurred. But, especially in light of the inherent difficulties in establishing improper motive, this does not mean that an otherwise inadmissible confession should be admitted into evidence simply because a flagrant and purposeful Fourth Amendment violation has not been established. Lower courts have been especially willing to find taint if the arrest was made without any apparent justification, as part of a dragnet operation or upon a pretext, or where it appeared that the illegal arrest was for the purpose of obtaining a confession or was exploited for that purpose. On the other hand, suppression is less likely where the illegality is an arrest slightly short of probable cause after a lawful stopping for investigation or an arrest on evidence that would be sufficient but for its acquisition during a stopping for investigation on grounds barely insufficient.[5]

The Court in *Brown* did not elaborate on what would qualify as an intervening circumstance, but significantly referred to *Johnson v. Louisiana*,[6] holding that a lineup identification need not be excluded as the fruit of a prior Fourth Amendment violation where the detention at the time of the lineup was under the authority of the magistrate's commitment. The, same would seem to be true where a confession is obtained after such commitment.[7] Termination of the illegal custody, as in *Wong Sun*, also qualifies as an intervening circum-

---

3. Subsequently, in Kaupp v. Texas, 538 U.S. 626, 123 S.Ct. 1843, 155 L.Ed.2d 814 (2003), the Court applied the *Brown* factors and found the defendant's confession to be the fruit of his prior illegal arrest, stressing: (i) there was "no indication * * * that any substantial time passed between Kaupp's removal from his home in handcuffs and his confession after only 10 or 15 minutes of interrogation"; (ii) at least some of the six officers involved in taking defendant into custody "were conscious that they lacked probable cause to arrest"; and (iii) "the state has not even alleged 'any meaningful intervening event' between the illegal arrest and Kaupp's confession."

4. 420 U.S. 103, 95 S.Ct. 854, 43 L.Ed.2d 54 (1975), holding that the Fourth Amendment requires a judicial determination of probable cause as a prerequisite to an

extended restraint on liberty following arrest without a warrant.

5. Similarly, in *Rawlings v. Kentucky*, 448 U.S. 98, 100 S.Ct. 2556, 65 L.Ed.2d 633 (1980), the Court, in the course of holding defendant's statements were not the fruit of his possibly illegal detention at a residence while a search warrant was sought, emphasized that it was "an open question" whether detention for such purposes was lawful.

6. 406 U.S. 356, 92 S.Ct. 1620, 32 L.Ed.2d 152 (1972).

7. But *Johnson* does not mean that the mere issuance of an arrest warrant, an ex parte procedure which does not deliver defendant into the hands of the judiciary, is a significant intervening event. Taylor v. Alabama, 457 U.S. 687, 102 S.Ct. 2664, 73 L.Ed.2d 314 (1982).

stance, as does consultation with counsel. Some courts have treated a volunteered statement, not made in response to police interrogation, as a significant intervening circumstance. That view is unobjectionable, but the same cannot be said for the conclusion that a statement given in response to interrogation following an illegal arrest is untainted because of the sense of remorse felt by the defendant or because the defendant was then confronted with his accomplice, who successfully urged him to confess. But such results may be more likely after *Rawlings v. Kentucky*,[8] where Rawlings and Ms. Cox were detained at a house while a search warrant was sought and when the warrant arrived Ms. Cox was compelled to empty her purse, after which she called upon Rawlings to claim what was his and he claimed the revealed controlled substances because he "wasn't going to try to pin that on her." The majority had "little doubt that this factor weighs heavily in favor of a finding that petitioner acted 'of free will unaffected by the initial illegality.' " The dissenters properly objected that Rawlings' statement was in response to Cox's demand, which was a product of the illegal search of her purse, which in turn was made possible by the illegal detention of the people at the house.

Given the nonutility of the "temporal proximity" factor, what ordinarily is required is a balancing of the last two *Brown* factors. The "clearest indication of attenuation," such as release from custody, is called for where the "official conduct was flagrantly abusive of Fourth Amendment rights."[9] Mere confrontation of defendant with untainted evidence, for example, clearly would not suffice. But when the police conduct is not flagrant, some lesser intervening circumstances (but more than mere *Miranda* warnings[10]) will suffice.

The *Brown* approach, applied in that and other cases to situations in which the alleged poisonous tree was an arrest made without probable cause, was deemed inapplicable in *New York v. Harris*,[11] where the poisonous tree was an in-premises arrest on probable cause but without an arrest warrant as required by *Payton v. New York*.[12] The Court in *Harris* instead adopted, 5–4, a per se rule: "where the police have probable cause to arrest a suspect, the exclusionary rule does not bar the State's use of a statement made by the defendant outside of his home, even though the statement is taken after an arrest made in the home in violation of *Payton*." The majority reasoned (i) that once Harris had been removed from his home his continued custody was lawful, so that his statement given at the police station was not the product of unlawful custody; and (ii) that the statement was likewise not a fruit of the arrest occurring in the home instead of somewhere else, as the *Payton* warrant requirement "is imposed to protect the home" and thus is vindicated by suppression of "anything incriminating the police gathered from arresting Harris in his home, rather than elsewhere." The dissenters effectively challenged both points[13] and, in addition, cast serious doubt upon the majority's assumption that *Harris* would not create an incentive for police to violate the *Payton* rule for the express purpose of obtaining an incriminating statement.

Cases in which it is contended that a confession was the fruit of a prior illegal search are usually easier to resolve. In the typical case in which the defendant was present when incriminating evidence was found in an illegal search or in which the defendant was confronted by the police with evidence they had illegally

---

8. 448 U.S. 98, 100 S.Ct. 2556, 65 L.Ed.2d 633 (1980).

9. Powell, J., concurring in *Brown*.

10. Three concurring Justices in *Brown* believed the *Miranda* warnings would alone break the causal chain in such circumstances, but this view was not accepted by a majority of the Court.

11. 495 U.S. 14, 110 S.Ct. 1640, 109 L.Ed.2d 13 (1990).

12. 445 U.S. 573, 100 S.Ct. 1371, 63 L.Ed.2d 639 (1980), discussed in § 3.6(a).

13. They responded (i) that *Brown* and the Court's other poisonous tree cases had never before required that the constitutional violation have been continuing at the very moment the challenged evidence was obtained; and (ii) that "violations of privacy in the home are especially invasive" and produce effects which "extend far beyond the moment the physical occupation of the home ends," meaning the *Brown* factors should be applied to determine "the point at which those effects are sufficiently dissipated that deterrence is not meaningfully advanced by suppression."

seized, it is apparent that there has been an "exploitation of that illegality"[14] when the police subsequently question the defendant about that evidence or the crime to which it relates. Because the realization that the cat is out of the bag plays a significant role in encouraging the suspect to speak, the more fine-tuned assessment used in *Brown* for determining when a confession is the fruit of an illegal *arrest* is ordinarily unnecessary when the "poisonous tree" is an illegal search.

Giving the *Miranda* warnings in such a case clearly will not break the causal chain, for these warnings do not advise the defendant whether the evidence he is confronted with is unlawfully obtained or whether it will be admissible at trial. If a magistrate or counsel did unequivocally and clearly advise the defendant that the evidence had been illegally seized and neither it nor its fruits could be used against him, it would seem that this would dissipate the taint of the illegal search. Here again those cases that attribute defendant's confession to remorse or some similar feeling in holding that it is not a fruit of the earlier police illegality are unsound. More plausible, at least in some circumstances, is the claim that a confession was not the product of a prior illegal search because the defendant was equally influenced by other, lawfully obtained evidence already in the hands of the police.

(b) Searches. In the typical case in which an illegal arrest is followed by a search, no "fruits" problem of any magnitude is presented. Where the search of the person or the surrounding area has its only justification as being "incident to" the arrest under *Chimel v. California*,[15] then unquestionably the evidence found in the search must be suppressed if the antecedent arrest was unlawful. This is direct rather than derivative evidence, and there is no occasion to be concerned about the limits of the fruit of the poisonous tree doctrine.

On occasion, however, fruits issues do arise when the connection between the arrest and

search is not that direct. One type of case is that in which there was an antecedent illegal arrest and the justification for the later search is that it is incident to arrest, but it is claimed a valid arrest intervened. Illustrative is *United States v. Walker*,[16] where defendant was illegally detained by officer Davis after which officer Shaull came to the scene and discovered evidence upon which to arrest defendant and did arrest him, after which evidence was found on defendant's person. Though the court held that "even assuming *arguendo* that Davis's arrest of Walker was illegal, it is obvious that the evidence seized by Shaull was not discovered through any exploitation of that initial arrest," this is at best a questionable result. It would seem to encourage the seizure of suspects on insufficient evidence while an investigation is conducted for the purpose of establishing probable cause.

A second type of situation is that in which the search is based upon a consent theory rather than a search-incident-to-arrest theory, as in *State v. Fortier*.[17] There, an officer made an illegal stop of a vehicle and then obtained defendant's consent to an opening of the trunk, and the court held the evidence thereby discovered admissible on the ground it was obtained by "an intervening act of free will" by defendant. But, the mere fact a consent to a search is "voluntary" within the meaning of *Schneckloth v. Bustamonte*[18] does not mean it is untainted. As noted earlier, in *Brown v. Illinois*[19] the Court rejected the notion that a confession is untainted merely because it is voluntary, and thus it follows that the voluntariness of a consent does not alone remove the taint. Rather, the factors from *Brown* discussed earlier should be applied to this situation.

Yet another situation is that in which the search is undertaken pursuant to a search warrant based upon lawfully acquired probable cause, but the police attempted to ensure that the warrant could be successfully executed by

14. Wong Sun v. United States, 371 U.S. 471, 83 S.Ct. 407, 9 L.Ed.2d 441 (1963).

15. 395 U.S. 752, 89 S.Ct. 2034, 23 L.Ed.2d 685 (1969).

16. 535 F.2d 896 (5th Cir.1976).

17. 113 Ariz. 332, 553 P.2d 1206 (1976).

18. 412 U.S. 218, 93 S.Ct. 2041, 36 L.Ed.2d 854 (1973).

19. 422 U.S. 590, 95 S.Ct. 2254, 45 L.Ed.2d 416 (1975).

illegally holding the defendant until the warrant was obtained and served. On such facts, it has been held that the evidence obtained in execution of the warrant is a fruit of the illegal detention. This is a sound result, for to hold the evidence was not a fruit of a detention undertaken for the precise purpose of ensuring the later availability of that evidence, would unquestionably run contrary to the deterrence objective of the exclusionary rule. (This is not to suggest, however, that in any case in which execution of a search warrant has been preceded by an illegal arrest of the person who lives at the place searched, the evidence must be suppressed simply because that person, "but for" the arrest, might have disposed of the evidence. Certainly if the arrest was in no sense related to the pending application and execution of a warrant, then exclusion in the name of deterrence is not necessary.)

Somewhat related to the first situation discussed in the preceding paragraph, and perhaps dictating a different result even there, is *Segura v. United States*,[20] where police entered premises without a warrant and arrested the occupants and then remained on the scene several hours until a search warrant was obtained and executed there. The claimed "poisonous tree" was "the initial illegal entry and occupation of the premises," which the Court held did not require suppression of the evidence later obtained in execution of the search warrant. This was because the warrant affidavit was based only on information acquired prior to the illegal entry, and because the possibility that absent the illegal entry the

evidence would have been removed or destroyed "was pure speculation." "Even more important," the *Segura* majority added, "we decline to extend the exclusionary rule, which already exacts an enormous price from society and our system of justice, to further 'protect' criminal activity, as the dissent would have us do." The four dissenters forcefully argued that such a conclusion "provides an affirmative incentive for warrantless and plainly unreasonable and unnecessary intrusions into the home" because police now know that if they illegally impound premises for the very purpose of facilitating a later successful warrant execution, that illegality will have no effect upon the evidence first discovered during the warrant execution. Whether this is so remains unclear, however, because of the limited scope of the *Segura* ruling, particularly the Court's rejection there of any link between the illegal entry/impoundment and the effectiveness of the later execution of the warrant.[21]

Sometimes upon a motion to suppress evidence obtained in execution of a search warrant, a showing is made that some of the information in the affidavit presented to the magistrate was acquired in a prior illegal search. The question then becomes how this affects the status of the search warrant, which most courts have answered by saying that the warrant is nonetheless valid if it could have issued upon the untainted information in the affidavit. Illustrative is *James v. United States*,[22] where an officer lawfully looked through an open garage door and saw a par-

20. 468 U.S. 796, 104 S.Ct. 3380, 82 L.Ed.2d 599 (1984).

21. In *Segura,* the "only issue" was said to be whether items "not observed during the initial entry and first discovered by the agents the day after the entry, under an admittedly valid search warrant, should have been suppressed," and the Chief Justice argued that illegal entries would be deterred by the officers' realization "that whatever evidence they discover as a direct result of the entry may be suppressed." However, a requirement of absolute suppression of evidence observed during the first entry later was rejected in Murray v. United States, discussed in § 9.3 at note 24. The Court concluded that the independent source doctrine could apply to evidence first seen during an initial illegal entry but subsequently seized under a warrant based on previously acquired probable cause. However, the questioned relationship in *Murray* concerned the possible contribution of the initial discovery

to the subsequent obtaining of the warrant, with the court holding that the seizure under the warrant would constitute an independent source only if the initial discovery has not prompted the police to expend the effort to obtain the warrant. Since the police in *Murray* had left the premises after the illegal entry (although continuing to keep the premises under surveillance), the Court did not have before it the contention that the initially illegal entry had facilitated the subsequent seizure under the warrant by ensuring that contraband was not removed from the premises. In *Segura* too, although the actual entry into the premises was illegal, the Court stressed that the "seizure" of the premises was not illegal—i.e., the police could lawfully have ensured against the removal by securing the premises from the outside and the entry did not further contribute to that capacity.

22. 418 F.2d 1150 (D.C.Cir.1969).

tially stripped down car and then a few days later made the same lawful observation and saw that the car was entirely stripped down, after which he illegally entered the garage and examined the license tag and owner's manual. He then determined that the car was listed as stolen, and on the basis of all these facts obtained a search warrant. Defendant argued that "any taint in the police conduct nullified the entire investigatory process so that no warrant can issue," but the court rejected this position as going "beyond the sound limits of the deterrence philosophy" and ruled: "If the lawfully obtained information amounts to probable cause and would have justified issuance of the warrant, apart from the tainted information, the evidence seized pursuant to the warrant is admitted."

The current status of the *James* rule is somewhat uncertain in light of the Supreme Court's decision in *United States v. Giordano.*[23] There the court first held that evidence obtained by certain court-ordered wiretaps had to be suppressed, and then ruled that evidence obtained under two pen register extension orders and a wiretap extension order were derivatively tainted by the initial invalid interception. The Court explained that "the illegally monitored conversations should be considered a critical element in extending the pen register authority." Four members of the Court dissented; applying *James,* they concluded the pen register extension orders were valid because sufficiently supported by untainted information. Some have read *Giordano* as rejecting the *James* rule in favor of a "critical element" test, meaning an impressive or important element in relation to the totality of material put before the court, even though the rest independently establishes probable cause. Others have reasoned that the Court clearly meant the extension order could not have been granted absent the illegal evidence and thus was merely applying the *James* rule.

Some courts have been a bit more demanding than *James,* and rightly so. If illegally-obtained information is merely stricken and

the balance of the affidavit assessed as if the tainted information had never been included, then police are tempted to make illegal searches to bolster what would otherwise be borderline affidavits. If the illegality is never uncovered, then they have a warrant solidly based on probable cause where otherwise their warrant application might have been rejected. If, on the other hand, the illegality comes to light, then the police are no worse off than if they had not made the illegal search. At a minimum, a warrant should be held invalid where the tainted information was used to bolster what would otherwise have been a doubtful showing of probable cause. This involves nothing more than depriving such warrants of the special treatment they would otherwise receive under *United States v. Ventresca,*[24] where the Court declared that "in a doubtful or marginal case a search under a warrant may be sustainable where without one it would fall."

Sometimes a second search is undertaken to acquire precisely the same information that the authorities obtained under an earlier, illegal search. *Silverthorne Lumber Co. v. United States*[25] was such a case, for there federal officers unlawfully seized certain documents belonging to the Silverthornes and then, after a court ordered them returned, subpoenaed the same documents. The Court held the subpoenas invalid because based on knowledge obtained from illegally seized evidence, but cautioned that "this does not mean that the facts thus obtained become sacred and inaccessible. If knowledge of them is gained from an independent source they may be proved like any others." An independent source determination can be relatively easy where the information constituting the other source was obtained by officers who did not communicate with those who were engaged in the initial illegality. But, as noted earlier[26] that determination can raise troublesome questions of possible connection where there was such communication, especially where the alleged independent source came

23. 416 U.S. 505, 94 S.Ct. 1820, 40 L.Ed.2d 341 (1974).

24. 380 U.S. 102, 85 S.Ct. 741, 13 L.Ed.2d 684 (1965).

25. 251 U.S. 385, 40 S.Ct. 182, 64 L.Ed. 319 (1920).

26. See § 9.3(d).

into existence after the initial illegality. However, as the discussion there of *Murray v. United States*[27] makes clear, an earlier illegal search can taint a later search warrant even if *no* information from the earlier search was included in the search warrant affidavit, for the taint can also arise from the fact that the illegal search otherwise "prompted" the seeking of a search warrant.

(c) Arrests. If police by an illegal search discover evidence providing probable cause that a particular person has committed a crime, an arrest of that person based upon this information is unquestionably tainted, provided of course the arrestee had standing to object regarding the antecedent search. But the mere existence of such a prior illegal search does not inevitably taint a subsequent arrest, for it may be that the arrest will be found to have a sufficient factual basis apart from the illegal search. The reasoning of the cases in the preceding subsection is applicable here as well, and thus for example, an officer possessing legally obtained information constituting probable cause for arrest is not barred from making the arrest solely because he also has information that was unlawfully obtained. However if the lawfully acquired evidence established probable cause but illegally obtained information influenced the making of the arrest at a particular time or place, which had a bearing on what was uncovered in the search incident to arrest, this would be yet another basis for concluding that the arrest was the fruit of the prior illegality.

(d) Identification of Person. Yet another issue is whether identification evidence (e.g., fingerprints, photographs, face-to-face confrontation) acquired following an illegal arrest is a tainted fruit of the arrest. Assume, for example, that defendant is illegally arrested on suspicion of armed robbery, after which he is placed in a lineup and identified by a victim of the robbery as the perpetrator of the crime. If the victim is later called to testify at trial, may he give evidence of his stationhouse identification or now identify the defendant in court?

As for the stationhouse identification, some decisions are to be found taking the position that this kind of evidence is not to be deemed the fruit of the prior illegal arrest. This result is explained upon reasons that will not withstand analysis, such as that somehow there would inevitably have been a confrontation between victim and defendant on some later occasion, that it was within the realm of possibility that defendant could have been identified without first being taken into custody, or that the arrest is not causally connected with the identification because the witness was merely applying his recollections from the time of the crime. But the correct view under ordinary circumstances is that because a stationhouse lineup is the direct result of the illegal arrest, that identification is unlawful fruit of the poisonous tree. This is not inevitably the case, however, for what is required here is analysis essentially like that used in *Brown v. Illinois*[28] in assaying the connection between an illegal arrest and a confession.

Brown enumerated three factors: "temporal proximity," "the presence of intervening circumstances," and "the purpose and flagrancy of the official misconduct." The "temporal proximity" factor is relatively unimportant, and thus it does not make much difference whether the identification occurs immediately after arrest or later. As for "purpose and flagrancy," the absence of a flagrantly illegal arrest for the purpose of obtaining an identification does not alone dissipate the taint, but merely means it will take something less than would otherwise be the case to constitute intervening circumstances. As for what intervening circumstances will dissipate the taint, such events as appearance before a magistrate[29] and a truly voluntary election by defendant to participate in a lineup will suffice in some circumstances at least.

Assuming now a case in which it may be concluded that the pretrial identification was a fruit of a prior illegal arrest and thus must be

27. 487 U.S. 533, 108 S.Ct. 2529, 101 L.Ed.2d 472 (1988).

28. 422 U.S. 590, 95 S.Ct. 2254, 45 L.Ed.2d 416 (1975).

29. Johnson v. Louisiana, 406 U.S. 356, 92 S.Ct. 1620, 32 L.Ed.2d 152 (1972).

suppressed, what then of an at-trial identification by the same witness? The Supreme Court dealt with an analogous problem in *United States v. Wade*,[30] where the question was the admissibility of an in-court identification preceded by an at-the-station identification that was illegal for denial of counsel, and it was concluded the answer depended upon whether the in-court identification

> " 'has been come at by exploitation of that illegality or instead by means sufficiently distinguishable to be purged of the primary taint.' * * * " Application of this test in the present context requires consideration of various factors; for example, the prior opportunity to observe the alleged criminal act, the existence of any discrepancy between any pre-lineup description and the defendant's actual description, any identification prior to lineup of another person, the identification by picture of the defendant prior to the lineup, failure to identify the defendant on a prior occasion, and the lapse of time between the alleged act and the lineup identification. It is also relevant to consider those facts which, despite the absence of counsel, are disclosed concerning the conduct of the lineup.

Lower courts have used this same approach in determining whether an in-court identification is the fruit of a prior identification that was tainted because it occurred while defendant was being held in violation of the Fourth Amendment. The correctness of this position was confirmed by the Supreme Court in *United States v. Crews*,[31] where the Court helpfully noted that a victim's in-court identification has "three distinct elements": (1) the victim is present at trial, (2) the victim possesses knowledge of and the ability to reconstruct the crime and to identify the defendant from observations at the time of the crime; and (3) the defendant is physically present. In then concluding that "none of these three elements 'has been come at by exploitation' of the violation of the defendant's Fourth Amendment rights," the Court readily determined, as to the first element, that the victim's identity

and cooperation were not the product of any police misconduct; and, as to the third element, that because an "illegal arrest, without more, has never been viewed as a bar to subsequent prosecution, nor as a defense to a valid conviction," the defendant was "not himself a suppressible 'fruit.' " With respect to the second element, the Court declared:

> Nor did the illegal arrest infect the victim's ability to give accurate identification testimony. Based upon her observations at the time of the robbery, the victim constructed a mental image of her assailant. At trial, she retrieved this mnemonic representation, compared it to the figure of the defendant, and positively identified him as the robber. No part of this process was affected by respondent's illegal arrest. In the language of the "time-worn metaphor" of the poisonous tree, * * * the toxin in this case was injected only after the evidentiary bud had blossomed; the fruit served at trial was not poisoned.

In support of this conclusion, the Court in *Crews* applied several of the factors in the *Wade* "independent origins" test: "the victim viewed her assailant at close range for a period of 5–10 minutes under excellent lighting conditions and with no distractions * * *; respondent closely matched the description given by the victim immediately after the robbery * * *; the victim failed to identify anyone other than respondent * * *, but twice selected respondent without hesitation in nonsuggestive pretrial identification procedures * * *; and only a week had passed between the victim's initial observation of respondent and her first identification of him * * *."

It might well be argued, however, that facts which would suffice in a *Wade* context to show an in-court identification was reliable do not inevitably also show it was not obtained in exploitation of a prior Fourth Amendment violation, any more than showing a confession to be voluntary per se dissipates the taint. This reasoning appears to have been accepted by the Court in *Crews*. In a part of the opinion

---

30. 388 U.S. 218, 87 S.Ct. 1926, 18 L.Ed.2d 1149 (1967).

31. 445 U.S. 463, 100 S.Ct. 1244, 63 L.Ed.2d 537 (1980).

joined by all participating members of the Court, note was taken of defendant's contention that the *Wade* test "seeks only to determine whether the in-court identification is sufficiently reliable to satisfy due process, and is thus inapplicable in the context of this Fourth Amendment violation." The Court then agreed "that a satisfactory resolution of the reliability issue does not provide a complete answer to the considerations underlying *Wong Sun,*" but concluded "that in the present case both concerns are met."

It is far from clear exactly what the Court meant by this. In particular, it is uncertain whether a majority of the Court would agree with the conclusion of the court below,[32] which was that the "extreme sanction" of suppressing the in-court identification would have been necessary had there been "egregious misconduct" such as was present in *United States v. Edmons.*[33] In that case pretextual dragnet arrests were made on information falling far short of probable cause for the precise purpose of identifying persons who shortly before had interfered with the execution of an arrest warrant. The court concluded that "where flagrantly illegal arrests were made for the precise purpose of securing identifications that would not otherwise have been obtained, nothing less than barring any use of them can adequately serve the deterrent purpose of the exclusionary rule."

Only three members of the Court in *Crews* distinguished away an *Edmons*-type case by asserting it was unnecessary to "decide whether respondent's person should be considered evidence, and therefore a possible 'fruit' of police misconduct," because in the instant case "the record plainly discloses that prior to his illegal arrest, the police both knew respondent's identity and had some basis to suspect his involvement in the very crimes with which he was charged." Two members of the Court stated they "would reject explicitly * * * the claim that a defendant's face can be a suppressible fruit of an illegal arrest," while three others made essentially the same assertion and concluded with the "note that a majority of the Court agrees that the rationale of *Frisbie*[34] forecloses the claim that respondent's face can be suppressible as a fruit of the unlawful arrest." But that language should not be read as closing the door to an *Edmonds* kind of argument, for the question is *not* (as those concurring opinions seem to assume) whether the Court should retreat from the *Frisbie* rule that an illegal arrest does not alone bar prosecution or conviction. Rather, what is involved is an application of the Court's own teaching in *Brown v. Illinois*[35] that sound fruit-of-the-poisonous-tree analysis necessitates very close attention to "the purpose and flagrancy of the official misconduct."

Turning now to the identification practice of viewing a photograph, one kind of case is that in which the illegal arrest and photographing was for the purpose of getting a picture that could be used in making such an identification, in which case the situation is indistinguishable from the face-to-face confrontation cases already discussed, and must be resolved in the same way. But, because photographs are typically taken as a matter of routine in the course of booking and then become a permanent part of the police files, it sometimes happens that a photograph routinely taken after an illegal arrest will on some future occasion serve to connect that person with some other crime totally unrelated to the reasons why the pre-photographing illegal arrest was made. In these circumstances, courts are understandably inclined to find attenuation, although a contrary result is called for if the original arrest was so far lacking probable cause as to justify the conclusion that it was made solely to acquire data regarding the defendant.

As for fingerprint identification, the Supreme Court dealt with it in *Davis v. Mississippi,*[36] where defendant's fingerprints, acquired when he was illegally arrested as part

---

32. Crews v. United States, 369 A.2d 1063 (D.C.App. 1977), on rehearing 389 A.2d 277.

33. 432 F.2d 577 (2d Cir.1970).

34. The reference is to Frisbie v. Collins, 342 U.S. 519, 72 S.Ct. 509, 96 L.Ed. 541 (1952), discussed in § 3.1(j).

35. 422 U.S. 590, 95 S.Ct. 2254, 45 L.Ed.2d 416 (1975).

36. 394 U.S. 721, 89 S.Ct. 1394, 22 L.Ed.2d 676 (1969).

of a dragnet roundup conducted as part of a rape investigation, were matched with the prints at the crime scene. In holding the prints were the suppressible fruits of an illegal arrest, the Court rejected the state's claim that the taint concept should not be extended to fingerprints because of their inherent trustworthiness. (By like reasoning, it has been held that other trustworthy identification evidence, such as handwriting exemplars, may likewise be the fruit of an illegal arrest.) *Davis* must be distinguished from a case where the prints were taken as a matter of routine following an arrest that was illegal but not made for the express purpose of having the prints on file for later use, and then were used on a later occasion to connect the defendant with some crime totally unrelated to the reasons underlying the illegal arrest. On such facts, a finding of attenuation is likely.

(e) Testimony of Witness. In *United States v. Ceccolini,*[37] an officer in a flower shop on a social visit illegally picked up an envelope and found it to contain money and policy slips, and then learned from his friend, an employee there who did not notice his discovery, that the envelope belonged to defendant, who owned the shop. The information reached the FBI, and four months later an agent questioned the employee about defendant's activities without specific mention of the illegally discovered policy slips. She was most cooperative and later served as a witness against defendant at his trial for perjury based upon his grand jury testimony that he had not taken policy bets at the shop. The Court declined to accept the government's *"per se* rule that the testimony of a live witness should not be excluded at trial no matter how close and proximate the connection between it and a violation of the Fourth Amendment," but did renounce its earlier declaration in *Wong Sun v. United States,*[38] that "the policies underlying the exclusionary rule [do not] invite any logical distinction between physical and verbal evidence." The Court reasoned:

> [W]e are first impelled to conclude that the degree of free will exercised by the witness is

not irrelevant in determining the extent to which the basic purpose of the exclusionary rule will be advanced by its application. This is certainly true when the challenged statements are made by a putative defendant after arrest, * * * and *a fortiori* is true of testimony given by nondefendants.

The greater the willingness of the witness to freely testify, the greater the likelihood that he or she will be discovered by legal means and, concomitantly, the smaller the incentive to conduct an illegal search to discover the witness. Witnesses are not like guns or documents which remain hidden from view until one turns over a sofa or opens a filing cabinet. Witnesses can, and often do, come forward and offer evidence entirely of their own volition. And evaluated properly, the degree of free will necessary to dissipate the taint will very likely be found more often in the case of live-witness testimony than other kinds of evidence. The time, place and manner of the initial questioning of the witness may be such that any statements are truly the product of detached reflection and a desire to be cooperative on the part of the witness. And the illegality which led to the discovery of the witness very often will not play any meaningful part in the witness's willingness to testify. * * *

Another factor which is not only relevant in determining the usefulness of the exclusionary rule in a particular context, but also seems to us to differentiate the testimony of all live witnesses—even putative defendants—from the exclusion of the typical documentary evidence, is that such exclusion would perpetually disable a witness from testifying about relevant and material facts, regardless of how unrelated such testimony might be to the purpose of the originally illegal search or the evidence discovered thereby. * * * In short, since the cost of excluding live-witness testimony often will be greater, a closer, more direct link between the illegality and that kind of testimony is required.

---

37.   435 U.S. 268, 98 S.Ct. 1054, 55 L.Ed.2d 268 (1978).

38.   371 U.S. 471, 83 S.Ct. 407, 9 L.Ed.2d 441 (1963).

This is not to say, of course, that live-witness testimony is always or even usually more reliable or dependable than inanimate evidence. Indeed, just the opposite may be true. But a determination that the discovery of certain evidence is sufficiently unrelated to or independent of the constitutional violation to permit its introduction at trial is not a determination which rests on the comparative reliability of that evidence. Attenuation analysis, appropriately concerned with the differences between live-witness testimony and inanimate evidence, can consistently focus on the factors enumerated above with respect to the former, but on different factors with respect to the latter.

The two dissenters in *Ceccolini* quite correctly pointed out that the majority's approach involved "judicial 'double counting'" because it allowed a court to consider whether the witness in the particular case so came forward and then, if defendant did not prevail, to consider the fact that generally (but not in this case) witnesses come forward. The dissenters made two other telling criticisms of the majority's logic: (1) the claim that the "greater the willingness of the witness to freely testify, * * * the smaller the incentive to conduct an illegal search to discover the witness" actually "reverses the normal sequence of events," for it is unlikely that "a witness' willingness to testify is known before he or she is discovered"; (2) the claim that exclusion would "perpetually disable" the witness ignores the fact that "at least as often the exclusion of physical evidence * * * will be as costly to the same societal interest."

The majority in *Ceccolini,* having concluded "that the exclusionary rule should be invoked with much greater reluctance where the claim is based on a causal relationship between a constitutional violation and the discovery of a live witness than when a similar claim is advanced to support suppression of an inanimate object," found that the taint had been dissipated in the instant case. The Court stressed the following factors, which have been utilized by lower courts in dealing with witness-as-a-fruit situations: (1) "the testimony given by the witness was an act of her own free will in no way coerced or even induced by official authority as a result of [the] discovery of the policy slips"; (2) the slips were not used in questioning the witness; (3) substantial time passed between the search and contact with the witness and between the contact and the testimony; (4) even before the search, "both the identity of [the witness] and her relationship with the respondent was well known to those investigating the case"; (5) there was "not the slightest evidence" that the officer made the search "with the intent of finding a willing and knowledgeable witness to testify against" defendant.

(f) New Crime. On occasion, when the police conduct an illegal arrest or an illegal search, this will prompt the person arrested or subjected to the search to react by committing some criminal offense. He might attack the officer, attempt to bribe him, or make some criminal misrepresentation in an effort to bring the incident to a close. In the bribery cases, the courts have consistently held that the evidence of the attempted bribe is admissible notwithstanding the prior illegal search of arrest. The most common explanation for this, that bribery attempts are sufficiently acts of free will to purge the taint, is not particularly satisfying, for it might be asked why the bribe offer is any more an act of free will than an incriminating admission or attempt to dispose of the evidence, neither of which is per se untainted. The answer may lie in the underlying deterrent purpose of the exclusionary rule, which is a prime consideration in marking the limits on fruit-of-the-poisonous-tree doctrine. Incriminating admissions and attempts to dispose of incriminating objects are common and predictable consequences of illegal arrests and searches, and thus to admit such evidence would encourage such Fourth Amendment violations in future cases. Bribery attempts, by comparison, are so infrequent and unpredictable that admission of evidence of such criminal activity in a particular case is not likely to encourage future illegal arrest and searches in order to accomplish the same result.

In cases where the response has been a physical attack upon the officer making the illegal arrest or search, courts have again held that the evidence of this new crime is admissible. Here as well the common explanation is that the attack was a free and independent action, but once more the better basis of distinction is that the rationale of the exclusionary rule does not justify its extension to this extreme. Of course, it is possible that the nature of a particular Fourth Amendment violation could be such that defensive action by the victim can fairly be characterized as having been brought about by exploitation, in which case a different result would be appropriate.

§ 9.5 Fruits of Illegally Obtained Confessions

(a) **The Confession as a "Poisonous Tree".** Under the early common law, the inadmissibility of a confession obtained from the defendant had no effect upon the admissibility of other evidence that was acquired as a consequence of that confession. The rationale of this position was that the defendant's statement was suppressed solely because of its untrustworthiness, and thus there was no reason to extend the exclusion to other evidence that itself did not suffer from that defect.

The early Supreme Court cases suppressing confessions on due process grounds also focused upon their purported unreliability, and thus the reliable fruits of such constitutional violations were deemed admissible no matter how close the connection. But as this due process theory expanded to encompass other concerns, that rule was put into question. Some courts nonetheless adhered to the old view, but the better reasoned decisions reached a contrary conclusion on the ground that even indirect products of police misconduct violating our sense of fair play and decency must be suppressed. Although the Supreme Court has never had occasion expressly to adopt that position, it is unquestionably correct. This does not mean that an involuntary confession causes the rejection of all evidence which follows it, but merely requires application of the previously-discussed fruit-of-the-poisonous-tree doctrine to such confessions.

As for a confession merely obtained in violation of *Miranda,* the prophylactic exclusionary rule adopted in that case to ensure that the police follow certain interrogation procedures is in many respects like the Fourth Amendment exclusionary rule, and thus it would seem that the fruit-of-the-poisonous-tree doctrine (which developed in search and seizure cases) would also be applicable. But there has not been complete agreement on this score. One view is that if *Miranda* is read as meaning the Fifth Amendment violation occurs when defendant's statement is used against him in court rather than when it is obtained in violation of the *Miranda* procedures, then physical evidence discovered by the confession would be admissible. At the opposite extreme is the view that the need to suppress the byproduct of a *Miranda*-tainted confession exists totally apart from the fruits doctrine, in that the Fifth Amendment's built-in exclusionary rule has long been interpreted to protect against such use of compelled testimony.

The Supreme Court did not speak fully to this issue until almost two decades after *Miranda* was decided. The *Miranda* case itself states that unless the prosecution shows at trial that defendant waived his rights, "no evidence obtained as a result of interrogation can be used against him." But this would seem to be obiter dictum, for none of the several cases considered in *Miranda* involved the admissibility of evidence other than the confessions themselves. Equally puzzling is the decision in *Michigan v. Tucker,*[1] dealing with the admissibility of the testimony of a witness whose identity had been learned by questioning a defendant who was not given the full *Miranda* warnings. In holding the testimony was admissible even though defendant's confession was not, the Court viewed the *Miranda* warnings as "not themselves rights protected by the Constitution" but only "prophylactic standards" designed to "safeguard" or to "provide practical reinforcement" for the privilege against self-incrimination. Noting that the deviation from *Miranda* was slight because the police had merely failed to tell defendant

§ 9.5
1. 417 U.S. 433, 94 S.Ct. 2357, 41 L.Ed.2d 182 (1974).

that if he could not afford a lawyer one would be provided for him, the Court said this meant that "the police conduct here did not deprive respondent of his privilege against compulsory self-incrimination as such, but rather failed to make available to him the full measure of procedural safeguards associated with that right since *Miranda*." Thus the *Wong Sun* fruits doctrine was dismissed, in effect, with the observation that there had been no constitutional violation, no "poisonous tree" for which the testimony of the witness could be a "fruit." Though *Tucker* thus might have been read as supporting the proposition that a confession obtained by violating *Miranda* cannot be a "poisonous tree," other aspects of the case made that a highly questionable interpretation. For one thing, though *Miranda* was technically applicable in *Tucker*,[2] the interrogation occurred prior to *Miranda* and thus at a time when the police could not have been aware of a responsibility to give the omitted warning. Suppression of the fruits in such circumstances would have been especially harsh. Secondly, the alleged fruit in *Tucker* was testimony of a witness, which the Supreme Court has since treated in a special way favoring admissibility even in a Fourth Amendment context.[3]

Nonetheless, in *Oregon v. Elstad*[4] the Court rejected such a narrow reading of *Tucker* and held that *Tucker's* reasoning applied with "equal force when the alleged 'fruit' of a non-coercive *Miranda* violation is neither a witness nor an article of evidence but the accused's own voluntary testimony." In *Elstad*, two officers initially questioned defendant at his home without first giving him *Miranda* warnings. When they expressed their belief that he had been involved in a burglary, he responded, "Yes, I was there." That this statement was excludable under *Miranda* was not contested.

However, the defendant was questioned again at the stationhouse; there, after being given the *Miranda* warnings, and after waiving his rights, he made an extensive statement explaining his exact involvement in the burglary. Defendant argued that this statement should be excluded as the fruit of the poisonous tree, but the *Elstad* majority held the fruits doctrine was inapplicable.

The Court noted that the fruits doctrine had been developed in the context of the Fourth Amendment exclusionary rule, where the objective was to deter unreasonable searches no matter how probative their fruits. The objective of the Fifth Amendment, on the other hand, was to bar use of compelled statements. Moreover, the *Miranda* ruling, upon which petitioner relied, had adopted an exclusionary rule that "sweeps more broadly" than the Fifth itself by establishing an irrebuttable presumption that unwarned statements obtained through custodial interrogation are compelled. This prophylactic element of *Miranda* would not be carried, however, beyond prohibiting the state's use of the unwarned statement in its case in chief. Just as *Miranda* had been held not to bar use of an unwarned statement, if in fact voluntary, for impeachment use,[5] so too it should not bar use of a subsequently obtained statement where there was compliance with *Miranda* in obtaining that statement and the earlier unwarned statement was voluntary. Violation of *Miranda's* prophylactic safeguards does not in itself create a coercive atmosphere that renders involuntary any subsequent, properly warned, statement. The relevant inquiry should be "whether, in fact, the second statement was also voluntarily made," considering the "surrounding circumstances and the entire course of police conduct with respect to the suspect."[6]

---

2. Because it was held applicable in all trials beginning after the *Miranda* decision. Johnson v. New Jersey, 384 U.S. 719, 86 S.Ct. 1772, 16 L.Ed.2d 882 (1966).

3. United States v. Ceccolini, 435 U.S. 268, 98 S.Ct. 1054, 55 L.Ed.2d 268 (1978).

4. 470 U.S. 298, 105 S.Ct. 1285, 84 L.Ed.2d 222 (1985).

5. See Harris v. New York, discussed in § 9.6(a).

6. Justice Brennan's dissent (joined by Justice Marshall) argued that "the correct approach * * * is to pre-

sume that an admission or confession obtained in violation of *Miranda* taints a subsequent confession unless the prosecution can show that the taint is so attenuated as to justify the admission of the subsequent confession." In making that attenuation determination, courts were to be guided by the standard announced in Wong Sun v. United States, see § 9.3(b), and to give consideration to the various factors cited in Brown v. Illinois, see § 9.4(a).

Because *Elstad* purported to be dealing only with a "simple failure to administer the warnings, unaccompanied by any actual coercion or other circumstances *calculated* to undermine the suspect's ability to exercise his free will,"[7] some courts have concluded that *Elstad* is inapplicable (even assuming voluntariness of the confession) if the police failed to honor the defendant's invocation of his right to silence or right to counsel. But because the *Elstad* majority's reasoning suggested a more sweeping rejection of the fruit of the poisonous tree doctrine as applied to *Miranda* violations, most lower court rulings have taken *Elstad* in that direction and thus advance the position that an admission or confession obtained in violation of *Miranda* should not be treated as a poisonous tree. This position distinguishes confessions obtained in violation of *Miranda* not only from confessions obtained in violation of due process (i.e., coerced confessions), but also from confessions held inadmissible under other doctrines similarly treated as creating a poisonous tree.

One such illegally obtained confession is one obtained in violation of the *Massiah* right to counsel. In that situation, it is clear that the constitutional violation occurs at the time of the deprivation of counsel, and thus it may be concluded that the confession can constitute a "poisonous tree" for purposes of fruits analysis. The Supreme Court acknowledged as much when it indicated in *Brewer v. Williams*[8] that on retrial it would be necessary to determine whether evidence of the body's location and condition was a fruit of defendant's confession, obtained in violation of his right to counsel, revealing where the body could be located.

(b) Searches. Where the confession was involuntary lower courts have held suppressible under the fruits doctrine physical evidence acquired through that illegally obtained confession, provided the connection between the confession and the acquisition of the physical evidence was rather close and direct. Such is the case when the confession supplies the probable cause for an evidence-producing arrest or search, when the defendant's statement indicates that the physical evidence is at a certain location and the police find it there as a consequence, or when the physical evidence was given to the police as part of the suspect's direct response to the illegal interrogation.

As for *Miranda* violations, both *Tucker* and *Elstad* could be distinguished from the "physical evidence" cases described above, for both involved situations in which the *Miranda* violation led to the claimed evidentiary fruit only through the decision of an individual to voluntarily provide the police with that evidence (the decision of the witness to testify in *Tucker,* and the decision of the defendant to make a second incriminating statement in *Elstad*). Thus, Justice Brennan in his *Elstad* dissent argued that a closer nexus exists between the *Miranda* violation and the typical discovery of physical evidence and that this should lead to the continued applicability of the fruits doctrine in determining the admissibility of such evidence. Nonetheless, there is much in the *Elstad* majority opinion suggesting that such distinctions would be irrelevant to the *Elstad* majority. Pointing in that direction are the *Elstad* opinion's broad reading of *Tucker*, its characterization of the fruits doctrine as standing apart from the basic objective of the Fifth Amendment (to bar use of compelled statements), its characterization of *Miranda* as imposing safeguards that extend beyond the compulsion that violates the self-incrimination clause, and its analysis of the appropriate limits of the prophylactic sanction of *Miranda*. Not surprisingly, most lower courts view *Elstad* as allowing admission of physical evidence discovered through a statement obtained in violation of *Miranda*, even where the link between the discovery and the statement is direct and immediate.

In *Nix v. Williams*,[9] the Supreme Court applied the inevitable discovery doctrine in the context of a Sixth Amendment violation that

---

7. Emphasis added.

8. 430 U.S. 387, 97 S.Ct. 1232, 51 L.Ed.2d 424 (1977). See also the discussion of Nix v. Williams at note 9 infra.

9. 467 U.S. 431, 104 S.Ct. 2501, 81 L.Ed.2d 377 (1984), discussed in § 9.3(e).

produced a statement which led police to physical evidence. The logical implication of *Nix* is that the fruits doctrine does apply to physical evidence discovered through a statement inadmissible under the Sixth Amendment, unless that discovery falls within one of those limitations (e.g., inevitable discovery) that makes that doctrine inapplicable.

(c) Confessions. As for the admissibility of a confession obtained subsequent to an earlier one illegally obtained from the same party, one approach is reflected in *Lyons v. Oklahoma*.[10] There a confession was coerced from defendant, but 12 hours later in the presence of different persons and after having been transferred from a jail to a prison, defendant gave a second confession. The Court in *Lyons* first declared that the "admissibility of the later confession depends upon the same test—is it voluntary," and then ruled that while sometimes the "effect of earlier abuse may be so clear as to forbid any other inference than that it dominated the mind of the accused to such an extent that the later confession is involuntary," this was not such a case. The fruit-of-the-poisonous-tree doctrine was never mentioned and quite obviously was not being applied. The issue, as the Court saw it, was whether the events at the time of the first confession—not the confession itself—brought about the second confession, and the focus was not on the impact of the first confession on the second but on the continuing effect of *prior coercive practices*. On other facts, the Court has held a second confession involuntary because the coercive circumstances of the first carried over to the second.[11]

In *United States v. Bayer*,[12] the lower court applied the fruit-of-the-poisonous-tree doctrine to exclude a second confession that, while preceded by a warning that it might be used against the defendant, was made after defendant had reread the first confession without being told it could not be used against him. But the Supreme Court reversed. The majority in *Bayer* first noted that though "after an accused has once let the cat out of the bag by confessing * * * [h]e can never get the cat back in the bag," this does not mean "that making a confession under circumstances which preclude its use, perpetually disables the confessor from making a usable one after those conditions have been removed." That conclusion is unobjectionable, but some questioned whether the same could be said for the Court's next statement that the lower court improperly used a fruits theory here because the Supreme Court's earlier cases in that line "did not deal with confessions but with evidence of a quite different category and do not control this question."

Although some lower courts read *Bayer* narrowly and continued to apply the fruits doctrine to successive confessions, that interpretation was open to serious question even before *Elstad*. In a series of post-*Bayer* decisions involving an initial confession that had been involuntary, the Court had asked the question posed in *Lyons*—whether the second confession was itself involuntary—rather than whether the second confession was a fruit of the first. The critical issue was whether there was a "break in the stream of events" sufficient to "insulate" the later confession from the coercive practices that had rendered the first involuntary. Although this approach looked to many of the same factors as a fruits analysis, such as temporal attenuation, intervening circumstances, and the "flagrancy" of the coercive practices that rendered the initial confession involuntary, it apparently placed less emphasis on the impact of the initial confession on the willingness of the individual to make a second statement.

The difference between the two approaches was brought home in *Elstad*, where the Court explicitly rejected application of the fruits doctrine to determine the admissibility of a second confession that followed a first obtained in violation of *Miranda*. The crucial issue, the Court noted, was whether the second confes-

---

10. 322 U.S. 596, 64 S.Ct. 1208, 88 L.Ed. 1481 (1944).

11. Leyra v. Denno, 347 U.S. 556, 74 S.Ct. 716, 98 L.Ed. 948 (1954).

12. 331 U.S. 532, 67 S.Ct. 1394, 91 L.Ed. 1654 (1947).

sion was voluntary, not whether it could be tied to the first under a fruits doctrine developed for determining the Fourth Amendment's exclusionary rule. The Court noted in this regard that it previously had refused to automatically exclude all second confessions under a "cat-out-of-the-bag" theory, and it was certainly not about to do so when the original confession was excludable only because of a *Miranda* violation. Any psychological compulsion that flowed from an unwarned but entirely voluntary statement was too speculative and attenuated, as it relates to official coercion, to justify exclusion of a second statement itself obtained after the administration of *Miranda* warnings. While it was true that the defendant had not been told prior to his second statement that the first statement was excludable, the Court "has never embraced the theory that the defendant's ignorance of the full consequences of his decisions vitiates their voluntariness." The officers here had not attempted to "exploit the [earlier] unwarned admission to pressure [the suspect] into waiving his right to remain silent," and they should not be expected to give the suspect legal advice as to the inadmissibility of his earlier statement.

(d) Testimony of Witness. *Harrison v. United States*[13] involved these facts: after three confessions allegedly made by defendant were introduced at his trial, he took the stand and testified to his own version of the events, making damaging admissions in the process; his conviction was later reversed on the ground that the confessions had been obtained in violation of the *McNabb–Mallory* rule; upon retrial the prosecution introduced defendant's testimony at the first trial, and he was convicted once again. A 6–3 majority of the Court reversed, explaining:

> In his opening statement to the jury [at the first trial], defense counsel announced that the petitioner would not testify in his own behalf. Only after his confessions had been admitted in evidence did he take the stand. It thus appears that, but for the use

of his confessions, the petitioner might not have testified at all. But even if the petitioner would have decided to testify whether or not his confessions had been used, it does not follow that he would have admitted being at the scene of the crime and holding the gun when the fatal shot was fired. On the contrary, the more natural inference is that no testimonial admission so damaging would have been made if the prosecutor had not already spread the petitioner's confession before the jury. That is an inference the Government has not dispelled.

> It has not been demonstrated, therefore, that the petitioner's testimony was obtained "by means sufficiently distinguishable" from the underlying illegality "to be purged of the primary taint."

The Court in *Harrison* cautioned that it was reserving for future decision the question of whether testimony by some other person could be a fruit. This question was later raised in *Michigan v. Tucker*,[14] where after incomplete *Miranda* warnings defendant gave a statement that identified a person the prosecution used as a witness at trial. The Court declined to treat that testimony as a suppressible fruit, but, for the reasons earlier stated[15] it is impossible to draw any general conclusions from *Tucker*. However, some courts have concluded, even as to a post-*Miranda* interrogation, that the testimony of persons discovered thereby is not a fruit of the noncompliance with *Miranda,* but that a fruits inquiry is appropriate if the confession is either involuntary or obtained in violation of the Sixth Amendment right to counsel. Even as to the latter situations, however, it is well to remember the Supreme Court's "special" approach to claims that testimony is an inadmissible fruit, designed to limit the circumstances in which such evidence would be suppressed,[16] for doubtless it is applicable in this context as well. And in any event, the testimony of the discovered witness will be held admissible under the "inevitable discovery" rule if it ap-

---

13. 392 U.S. 219, 88 S.Ct. 2008, 20 L.Ed.2d 1047 (1968).

14. 417 U.S. 433, 94 S.Ct. 2357, 41 L.Ed.2d 182 (1974).

15. See § 6.5(b).

16. United States v. Ceccolini, 435 U.S. 268, 98 S.Ct. 1054, 55 L.Ed.2d 268 (1978), discussed in § 9.4(e).

pears to the court that sooner or later his identity would have been independently revealed by standard investigation procedures.

§ 9.6 Permissible Use of Illegally Obtained Evidence at Trial

(a) Impeachment. Under the various exclusionary rules, if a constitutional violation has occurred then upon a timely objection by a defendant with standing the fruits of that illegality must be suppressed and consequently may not be introduced into evidence at the criminal trial of that defendant. There exist, however, a few exceptions to that statement, one of which concerns the use of that evidence for impeachment purposes. The dimensions of that particular exception have broadened over the years, which can best be seen by a brief chronological look at the Supreme Court's leading decisions in this area.

First in the series was *Agnello v. United States*.[1] Defendant, charged with conspiracy to sell cocaine, testified on direct examination that he received certain packages without knowing they contained cocaine, and on cross-examination said he had never seen narcotics, at which point the government was permitted to introduce in rebuttal a can of cocaine that had been illegally seized from his room and suppressed from the government's case in chief. A unanimous Court reversed, relying upon its earlier statement that the "essence of a provision forbidding the acquisition of evidence in a certain way is not merely that evidence so acquired shall not be used before the court but that it shall not be used at all."[2] About thirty years passed before a somewhat similar case, *Walder v. United States*,[3] reached the Court; there, defendant testified on direct and cross-examination that he had never purchased, sold or possessed any narcotics, which the government was allowed to impeach by questioning defendant concerning heroin illegally seized from his home two years earlier. The Court upheld this procedure, reasoning

that the defendant could not use the exclusionary rule to "provide himself with a shield against contradiction of his untruths" where, as in *Walder,* he had been "free to deny all the elements of the case against him" without the impeached "sweeping claim that he had never dealt in or possessed any narcotics." *Walder* thus appeared to say that where a defendant (i) on direct examination (ii) did not merely deny the elements of the case against him but instead made sweeping claims putting his character in issue, then the government could introduce illegally obtained evidence (iii) for the limited purpose of impeachment (iv) if the evidence was obtained as a consequence of police misconduct unrelated to the instant case. So viewed, *Walder* seemed to strike a reasonable balance between the competing interests involved.

The third case is *Harris v. New York*,[4] where, after the defendant upon direct examination denied having made the charged sale of narcotics, the prosecutor was allowed to impeach the defendant's credibility by resort to a statement made by him to the police under circumstances that concededly made that statement inadmissible under *Miranda*. In a 5–4 decision, the Supreme Court affirmed, reasoning that though in *Walder* defendant "was impeached as to collateral matters" while here he "was impeached as to testimony bearing more directly on the crimes charged," this did not amount to a "difference in principle" between the two cases:

> The impeachment process here undoubtedly provided valuable aid to the jury in assessing petitioner's credibility, and the benefits of this process should not be lost, in our view, because of the speculative possibility that impermissible police conduct will be encouraged thereby. Assuming that the exclusionary rule has a deterrent effect on proscribed police conduct, sufficient deterrence flows when the evidence in question is made unavailable to the prosecution in its case in chief.

§ 9.6

1. 269 U.S. 20, 46 S.Ct. 4, 70 L.Ed. 145 (1925).
2. Quoting Silverthorne Lumber Co. v. United States, 251 U.S. 385, 40 S.Ct. 182, 64 L.Ed. 319 (1920).

3. 347 U.S. 62, 74 S.Ct. 354, 98 L.Ed. 503 (1954).
4. 401 U.S. 222, 91 S.Ct. 643, 28 L.Ed.2d 1 (1971).

Every criminal defendant is privileged to testify in his own defense, or to refuse to do so. But that privilege cannot be construed to include the right to commit perjury. * * * Having voluntarily taken the stand, petitioner was under an obligation to speak truthfully and accurately, and the prosecution here did no more than utilize the traditional truth-testing devices of the adversary process.

Harris was rightly criticized because it selectively quoted from *Walder,* carefully excising any reference to the broader principle that the defendant "must be free to deny all the elements of the case against him without thereby giving leave to the Government to introduce by way of rebuttal evidence illegally secured by it," and also because it claimed to be extending a general rule laid down in *Walder* when in truth *Walder* was a limited exception to the general rule established in *Agnello,* which thus was overruled without even being cited.

Next in the series was *United States v. Havens,*[5] where on direct examination defendant denied being involved with his codefendant in the transportation of cocaine, and on cross-examination denied being involved in sewing a pocket (in which drugs were found) into his codefendant's clothing or having in his own suitcase cloth from which the swatch was cut to make the pocket. That testimony was impeached by admitting the illegally seized cloth, but the appellate court reversed because the impeached testimony was not given on direct examination. But the Supreme Court, again in a 5–4 decision, ruled otherwise:

In terms of impeaching a defendant's seemingly false statements with his prior inconsistent utterances or with other reliable evidence available to the government, we see no difference of constitutional magnitude between the defendant's statements on direct examination and his answers to questions put to him on cross-examination that are plainly within the scope of the defendant's direct examination.

What started out in *Walder* as a narrow and reasonable exception has thus taken on awesome proportions. Under *Havens,* statements elicited on cross-examination now may be impeached. This violates the waiver doctrine of *Walder,* and actually encourages constitutional violations for purposes of "boxing in" the defendant, for now "even the moderately talented prosecutor [can] 'work in * * * evidence on cross-examination * * * [as it would] in its case in chief * * *,' " and "a defendant will be compelled to forego testifying on his own behalf" to avoid this consequence.[6] Secondly, *Harris* (as the Court later put it in *Havens*) "made clear that the permitted impeachment by otherwise inadmissible evidence is not limited to collateral matters," but may relate directly to commission of the offense itself. Of course, the defendant's testimony must open the door to such impeachment, but neither *Harris* nor *Havens* indicated precisely how far the defendant had to go in his testimony relating to an element of the offense to permit impeachment as to that element. As a consequence, some courts allow impeachment when the defendant does no more than deny the elements of the crime, though many courts refuse to read *Harris* as bringing about such an unfair result. Thirdly, as *Havens* makes plain, a defendant may now be impeached by evidence bearing directly upon the crime charged. This departure from *Walder* is also most unfortunate, for the discarded limitation minimized the danger that a jury might view unconstitutionally obtained impeaching evidence as establishing guilt, even if instructed to consider it only for credibility purposes.

Yet another question that must be asked about the impeachment exception concerns what kinds of constitutional or other violations are encompassed within the exception. *Walder* and *Havens* make it clear that Fourth Amendment violations qualify. What then if instead the evidence was obtained in violation of Title III of the Omnibus Crime Control Act of 1968, which imposes limitations upon resort to eavesdropping and wiretapping? Though this legislation expressly provides that "no part" of

---

5.   446 U.S. 620, 100 S.Ct. 1912, 64 L.Ed.2d 559 (1980).

6.   As noted by the *Havens* dissenters.

the contents of an invalid interception and "no evidence derived therefrom may be received in evidence in any trial,"[7] the legislative history indicates that this and related provisions were not intended to press the scope of the suppression rule beyond present search and seizure law, and thus the result in such cases is no different.

The reasons justifying some sort of impeachment exception as to Fourth Amendment violations might well be thought not to carry over to violations of the Fifth Amendment privilege against self-incrimination. For one thing, illegally seized tangible evidence is inherently reliable, but the same cannot necessarily be said where there has been a *Miranda* violation. Moreover, the Fourth Amendment exclusionary rule is a court-created device intended to deter the police, and thus arguably ought not be applied when the objective of deterrence is outweighed by other considerations, while by contrast the Fifth Amendment on its face prohibits the government from using "compelled" statements "against" a defendant. But in *Harris,* where the defendant was not given the complete *Miranda* warnings and it was asserted he made "no claim that the statements made to the police were coerced or involuntary," the Court unhesitantly extended the impeachment exception to *Miranda* violations. The same result was reached in *Oregon v. Hass,*[8] although there the suspect was advised of his rights and then asked for counsel but was questioned without his request being honored. The majority saw the case as indistinguishable from *Harris* because "inadmissibility would pervert the constitutional right into a right to falsify," while the two dissenters argued that *Hass* was far worse because it provided police with an incentive for dishonoring such requests—they had nothing to lose and something significant to gain, "a statement which can be used for impeachment if the accused has the temerity to testify in his own defense."

In *New Jersey v. Portash,*[9] the Court emphasized that "central to the decisions" in *Harris* and *Hass* was the fact that the defendant made no claim the statements were coerced or involuntary. That served to distinguish the statements obtained in the instant case, defendant's testimony before a grand jury given in response to a grant of use immunity, which was "the essence of coerced testimony." Confronted with "the constitutional privilege against compulsory self-incrimination in its most pristine form," the Court concluded that the balancing of interests undertaken in *Harris* and *Hass* was "impermissible" in the present context. And in *Mincey v. Arizona*[10] the Court again distinguished *Harris* and *Hass* and declared that use of an "involuntary statement" even for impeachment purposes would constitute "a denial of due process of law." The Court did not comment on the fact that in a particular case a statement could be involuntary but yet very truthworthy.

In *Michigan v. Harvey,*[11] the Supreme Court overturned a state court ruling that because defendant's statement after arraignment and appointment of counsel was taken "in violation of defendant's Sixth Amendment right to counsel" it could not be used for impeachment purposes. The majority focused upon the state court's reliance upon *Michigan v. Jackson,*[12] which held that after a defendant requests assistance of counsel, any waiver of Sixth Amendment rights given in a discussion initiated by police is presumed invalid. Because it "simply superimposed the Fifth Amendment analysis" of *Edwards v. Arizona*[13] onto the Sixth Amendment right, the majority reasoned, *Jackson* did not mark the exact boundary of the Sixth Amendment right itself but rather constituted a "prophylactic rule * * * designed to ensure voluntary, knowing, and

---

7. 18 U.S.C.A. § 2515.

8. 420 U.S. 714, 95 S.Ct. 1215, 43 L.Ed.2d 570 (1975).

9. 440 U.S. 450, 99 S.Ct. 1292, 59 L.Ed.2d 501 (1979). For the argument that *Portash* may bar impeachment by use of defendant's testimony given at a suppression hearing, see § 10.5(c).

10. 437 U.S. 385, 98 S.Ct. 2408, 57 L.Ed.2d 290 (1978).

11. 494 U.S. 344, 110 S.Ct. 1176, 108 L.Ed.2d 293 (1990).

12. 475 U.S. 625, 106 S.Ct. 1404, 89 L.Ed.2d 631 (1986).

13. 451 U.S. 477, 101 S.Ct. 1880, 68 L.Ed.2d 378 (1981).

intelligent waivers of the Sixth Amendment right to counsel." From this, it was deemed to follow that the reasoning of such cases as *Hass* and *Havens* carried over to the instant case: once again, "the 'search for truth in a criminal case' outweighs the 'speculative possibility' that exclusion of evidence might deter future violations of rules not compelled directly by the Constitution in the first place."

It is important to note that the *Harvey* majority did *not* hold that the fruits of a violation of the Sixth Amendment right to counsel may be used for purposes of impeachment. Having characterized the case as it did, the Court did not have to "consider the admissibility for impeachment purposes of a voluntary statement obtained in the absence of a knowing and voluntary waiver of the right to counsel," that is, in a situation in which the prosecution even apart from the *Jackson* presumption could not carry its burden of proving such a waiver. (The four dissenters cogently argued (1) that the Sixth Amendment right, unlike *Miranda,* extends "to all efforts to elicit information from the defendant whether for use as impeachment or rebuttal at trial or simply to formulate trial strategy"; (2) that "exclusion of statements made by a represented and indicted defendant outside the presence of counsel follows not as a remedy for a violation that has preceded trial but as a necessary incident of the constitutional right itself"; and (3) that under the majority's rule the police after formal charge "have everything to gain and nothing to lose by repeatedly visiting with defendant and seeking to elicit as many comments as possible about the pending trial.")

Sometimes the question is whether defendant's silence may be utilized for impeachment purposes. In *Doyle v. Ohio*,[14] the Court held that impeachment by defendant's post-arrest silence after he had received the *Miranda* warnings was impermissible.[15] Not only is "every post-arrest silence * * * insolubly ambiguous" because it "may be nothing more than the arrestee's exercise of [his] *Miranda* rights," but use of the silence to impeach "would be fundamentally unfair" given the fact that the warnings carry the implicit "assurance that silence will carry no penalty."[16] *Doyle* has been distinguished in three later cases. In *Anderson v. Charles*,[17] impeachment by prior inconsistent statements given after *Miranda* warnings was permitted because "a defendant who voluntarily speaks after receiving *Miranda* warnings has not been induced to remain silent." In *Jenkins v. Anderson*,[18] where at his murder trial defendant claimed self defense, the Court ruled it was permissible to impeach that story by defendant's prearrest silence in not reporting the stabbing to the authorities for at least two weeks. This was not compelled self-incrimination, for, as the Court had concluded many years earlier,[19] the possibility of impeachment by prior silence is

14. 426 U.S. 610, 96 S.Ct. 2240, 49 L.Ed.2d 91 (1976).

15. In Greer v. Miller, 483 U.S. 756, 107 S.Ct. 3102, 97 L.Ed.2d 618 (1987), the Supreme Court held that a *Doyle* violation exists only where the post-arrest and post-warnings silence is actually used by the prosecution for impeachment purposes. The prosecution there asked the defendant on cross-examination why he hadn't "told this story to anybody when you got arrested," but the defense counsel immediately objected, the objection was sustained, and the jury was told to "disregard questions ... to which objections were sustained." The Court held that, under these facts, there was no *Doyle* violation. The prosecutor had not been " 'allowed to undertake impeachment on' or 'permit[ted] to call attention to' [defendant's] silence" and the fact of that silence "was not submitted to the jury as evidence from which it was allowed to draw any permissible inference."

16. *Doyle* was distinguished in South Dakota v. Neville, 459 U.S. 553, 103 S.Ct. 916, 74 L.Ed.2d 748 (1983), upholding a statute that permits a person suspected of driving while intoxicated to refuse to submit to a blood-

alcohol test, but authorizing revocation of the driver's license of a person so refusing the test and permitting such refusal to be used against him at trial. Though the defendant in *Neville* had not been told of the latter possibility, he was warned he could lose his license by refusing, which "made it clear that refusing the test was not a 'safe harbor' free of adverse consequences." Moreover, the failure to warn "was not the sort of implicit promise to forego use of evidence that would unfairly 'trick' [the defendant] if the evidence were later offered against him at trial." The Court in *Doyle* recognized a further exception that has been applied in numerous cases: the silence of a Mirandized defendant can be "used by the prosecution to contradict a defendant who testifies to an exculpatory version of events and claims to have told the police the same version upon arrest."

17. 447 U.S. 404, 100 S.Ct. 2180, 65 L.Ed.2d 222 (1980).

18. 447 U.S. 231, 100 S.Ct. 2124, 65 L.Ed.2d 86 (1980).

19. Raffel v. United States, 271 U.S. 494, 46 S.Ct. 566, 70 L.Ed. 1054 (1926).

not an impermissible burden upon the exercise of Fifth Amendment rights. Nor was it a denial of fundamental fairness, for unlike *Doyle* "no government action induced petitioner to remain silent before arrest." The claim has been made that the silence in *Jenkins* was just as equivocal as that in *Doyle,* for an individual's reluctance to hand himself over to the police and admit a stabbing, in self-defense or otherwise, is not probative of guilt. But in *Fletcher v. Weir*[20] the Court followed *Jenkins* and distinguished *Doyle* in allowing impeachment by post-arrest silence not preceded by *Miranda* warnings, explaining that this was not "a case where the government had induced silence by implicitly assuring the defendant that his silence would not be used against him." So too, *Brecht v. Abrahamson*[21] held that where defendant did not receive *Miranda* warnings until his arraignment, the prosecution did not violate due process insofar as it impeached him by reference to his post-arrest silence up to that point. The Supreme Court has not passed on use of such silence as substantive evidence of guilt in the prosecution's case-in-chief, a matter on which lower courts are divided.

An effort to extend the impeachment exception from the defendant's own testimony to the testimony of all defense witnesses was rejected in *James v. Illinois.*[22] The Court, 5–4, concluded that such an expansion of *Walder* "would not promote the truth-seeking function to the same extent as did creation of the original exception, and yet it would significantly undermine the deterrent effect of the general exclusionary rule," thus serving to "frustrate rather than further the purposes underlying the exclusionary rule." The same beneficial effects would not be present, the Court reasoned, because (1) the threat of subsequent criminal prosecution is alone more likely to deter a defense witness than a defen-

dant, already facing conviction for the underlying offense; and (2) such expansion "likely would chill some defendants from presenting their best defense—and sometimes any defense at all—through the testimony of others," as a variety of factors make it problematical whether a defense witness will testify as expected and thus avoid such impeachment. Moreover, there would be present under such expansion greater threat to "the exclusionary rule's deterrent effect on police misconduct"; the expansion would "vastly increase the number of occasions on which such evidence could be used" and would serve to deter not only perjury but also the calling of defense witnesses in the first place, from which "police officers and their superiors would recognize that obtaining evidence through illegal means stacks the deck heavily in the prosecutions's favor." In an earlier, more limited ruling, relying upon *Doyle,* the Supreme Court held that the prosecution's use of defendant's post-arrest, post-*Miranda*-warnings silence as evidence of his sanity violates due process.[23]

(b) Defense Tactics That "Open the Door". In the impeachment case of *Walder v. United States,*[24] the Court emphasized that it was the defendant who "opened the door" to the admissibility of the illegally seized evidence by his sweeping assertions upon direct examination. On rare occasion, defense tactics that likewise seek to gain extraordinary advantage from the fact of suppression of certain evidence may also be deemed to have "opened the door" to at least limited receipt of that evidence. As shown by *Commonwealth v. Wright,*[25] defense tactics are more likely to be found to have opened the door if they involved a calculated effort to create a high degree of confusion based upon knowledge that any adequate explanation would require some reference to evidence previously suppressed. In

20. 455 U.S. 603, 102 S.Ct. 1309, 71 L.Ed.2d 490 (1982).

21. 507 U.S. 619, 113 S.Ct. 1710, 123 L.Ed.2d 353 (1993).

22. 493 U.S. 307, 110 S.Ct. 648, 107 L.Ed.2d 676 (1990).

23. Wainwright v. Greenfield, 474 U.S. 284, 106 S.Ct. 634, 88 L.Ed.2d 623 (1986). The *Greenfield* Court found it

unnecessary, in light of the applicability of *Doyle,* to rule on the prosecution's contention that "an insanity defense should be viewed as an 'affirmative defense,' and that the use of silence to overcome an insanity defense should thus be viewed as impeachment."

24. 347 U.S. 62, 74 S.Ct. 354, 98 L.Ed. 503 (1954).

25. 234 Pa.Super. 83, 339 A.2d 103 (1975).

Wright, one packet of heroin taken from defendant was held admissible under the plain view doctrine, but nine others were suppressed. A chemist testified that the material turned over to him by the officer had been analyzed and found to be heroin, and he carefully avoided any reference to the number of packets involved so as to prevent the claim he had testified as to suppressed evidence. But defense counsel then conducted a cross-examination of the chemist which created considerable confusion about whether the packet received in evidence had been so analyzed, precisely because the witness could never make specific reference to the other packets. The court ruled that in these circumstances it was permissible to allow the chemist to state explicitly that he had examined all ten packets and found them all to contain heroin. "The references made to the nine bundles were clearly the result of the defendant's trial strategy. He cannot now complain of testimony which he produced."

This does not mean, however, that merely because the defendant intrudes an issue into the trial as to which illegally obtained evidence would be relevant, the door has thereby been opened to receipt of that evidence on the issue. In *United States v. Hinckley,*[26] the government asserted "that because insanity is an affirmative defense, and proof of sanity is therefore not part of the prosecution's case-in-chief," evidence obtained in violation of *Miranda* and the Fourth Amendment "can be used generally to rebut an insanity defense without jeopardizing constitutional principles." The court responded that such a drastic curtailment of the exclusionary rules "would provide little or no deterrence of constitutional violations against defendants whose sanity is the principal issue in the case."

(c) Prosecution for Perjury or Other "New" Offense. In *Walder v. United States*[27] the Court saw no "justification for letting the defendant affirmatively resort to perjurious testimony in reliance on the Government's disability to challenge his credibility," and, as we have seen, this same view has been taken

in the later impeachment cases. From this, it might be argued that illegally obtained evidence should be admissible in the prosecution's case in chief on a charge of perjury. This argument was accepted in *United States v. Raftery,*[28] where hashish was found in defendant's house but was suppressed in defendant's prosecution for possession of it because the warrant was improperly executed. Several months later defendant was summoned before a federal grand jury, given use immunity and questioned about his participation in marijuana smuggling and distribution activities. He was thereafter indicted for perjury as a result of his negative answer to the question of whether he had ever been on premises where hashish oil was manufactured, and the appellate court ruled that in the perjury prosecution the suppressed evidence would be admissible, stating: "The purpose of the rule would not be served by forbidding the Government from using the evidence to prove the entirely separate offense of perjury before a grand jury occurring after the illegal search and seizure and suppression of the evidence in the state court."

As stated in *United States v. Turk,*[29] such a result should be reached only when it is clear that "no significant additional deterrent effect could be realized" by suppression and that the benefits to be derived from admission are substantial. For one thing, this means the search must have preceded the perjured testimony, for otherwise there would be incentive to conduct such searches against individuals suspected of perjury. Likewise, actual awareness of the search by the defendant at the time his testimony was given is essential, as if that were not so there would be incentive to make undisclosed illegal searches and then subpoena the search victim. By contrast, certain other special facts noted in *Raftery*—that the search was by officers in a different jurisdiction, that the violation was a minor one, and that the perjury occurred after a grant of immunity—are less likely requirements. Finally, there is

---

26.   672 F.2d 115 (D.C.Cir.1982).

27.   347 U.S. 62, 74 S.Ct. 354, 98 L.Ed. 503 (1954).

28.   534 F.2d 854 (9th Cir.1976).

29.   526 F.2d 654 (5th Cir.1976).

the question of whether the *Raftery* rule needs to be limited to perjury prosecutions. *Turk* suggests the answer is no, for it is said there that "no significant additional deterrent effect could be realized by suppressing the evidence at a trial of the search victim for a crime committed after the illegal search and with the knowledge that the illegal search occurred," and that to suppress "would in effect give the victim of an illegal search a license to commit any new crimes he cares to, free from the concern that the illegally seized evidence might be used against him in prosecution for these subsequent crimes." Some courts have so held.

Chapter 10

ADMINISTRATION OF THE EXCLUSIONARY RULES

Table of Sections

---

§ 10.1   The Pretrial Motion to Suppress

(a) Contemporaneous Objection or Pretrial Motion. Some states continue to follow the "contemporaneous objection rule," which only requires that an objection be made at trial at the time the prosecution seeks to introduce the illegally obtained evidence. However, the great majority of jurisdictions have abandoned the contemporaneous objection rule in favor of a requirement that objections be raised before trial by way of a pretrial motion to suppress. This requirement usually applies to exclusion based on all grounds relating to the illegal acquisition of the evidence.

The minority of jurisdictions following the contemporaneous objection rule view it as a more efficient procedure. However, there are many valid reasons underlying the prevailing practice of requiring pretrial motions. The pretrial motion requirement eliminates from the trial disputes over police conduct not immediately relevant to the question of guilt, and avoids interruptions of a trial in progress with such auxiliary inquiries. It also prevents having to declare a mistrial because the jury has been exposed to unconstitutional evidence. Moreover, it is to the advantage of both the prosecution and defense to know in advance of the time set for trial whether certain items will or will not be admitted into evidence. If the pretrial motion is granted, this could result in abandonment of the prosecution, thus avoiding the waste of prosecutorial and judicial resources occasioned by preparation of a trial, or in the prosecution changing the theory of its case or developing untainted evidence. If the pretrial motion is denied, then the defendant is in a position at that time either to plead guilty and gain whatever concessions might be obtained by so pleading without causing the commencement of a trial, or to go to trial with a somewhat different defense strategy. Finally, in those jurisdictions where interlocutory appeal by the prosecution is permitted, the requirement of a pretrial motion to suppress protects that right of immediate appeal.

(b) Form of the Motion. The pretrial motion to suppress, which in many jurisdictions must be in writing, must identify the evidence the defendant seeks to suppress and specify with particularity the grounds upon which the motion is based. This requirement is one of specificity in the statement of defendant's legal theory, which may be met, for example, by alleging that the evidence in question was obtained from the defendant incident to an arrest that was not made upon probable cause.

Many jurisdictions require a defendant making a pretrial suppression motion also to set out facts in support of the motion, and it may even be necessary that defendant's motion be accompanied by an affidavit or affidavits on behalf of the defendant setting forth all facts within his knowledge upon which he intends to rely in support of the motion. This requirement has been held constitutional, which perhaps it is so long as the holding in *Simmons v. United States*[1]—that testimony given by the defendant at the hearing on his motion is not admissible against him at trial on the question of guilt or innocence—is extended to such affidavits.

(c) Pre-charge Motions Distinguished. The pretrial motion to suppress, made in the context of criminal proceedings, must be distinguished from the action that may be taken in many jurisdictions prior to the filing of criminal charges, in order to challenge continued government possession of objects acquired in an earlier search. Though this precharge motion is sometimes referred to as a motion to suppress, it is more correct to call it a motion for return of property or a motion to quash a search warrant, for even if the movant is successful it does not necessarily follow that this evidence will be suppressed if a criminal prosecution is later undertaken.

Such anomalous jurisdiction in the federal system is exercised with caution and restraint and subject to equitable principles. A foremost consideration is whether there is a clear and definite showing that constitutional rights have been violated. A second consideration is whether the plaintiff has an individual interest in and need for the material whose return he seeks, as where those goods are necessary to conduct a legitimate business. Yet a third consideration is whether the plaintiff would be irreparably injured by denial of the return of the property or instead has an adequate remedy at law. But courts are disinclined to grant relief when a criminal prosecution is anticipated, for they usually take the view that in such

§ 10.1

1. 390 U.S. 377, 88 S.Ct. 967, 19 L.Ed.2d 1247 (1968), discussed in § 10.5(c).

circumstances intervention would impede prosecuting officers and interfere with the grand jury.

Pre-charge proceedings to quash search warrants or for the return of items seized in searches are also available in many states. They are commonly authorized by statutes governing the issuance of warrants, but in some jurisdictions are permitted by courts of equity without express statutory authority. Where such proceedings rest exclusively upon statute, they may be limited to searches made pursuant to a warrant or even to warrants for certain types of property (e.g., obscene materials).[2]

§ 10.2 Waiver or Forfeiture of Objection

(a) Failure to Make Timely Objection. In those jurisdictions requiring a contemporaneous objection to the introduction of illegally obtained evidence, failure to make such an objection ordinarily bars consideration of any subsequent objection at trial or on appeal. Similarly, in states requiring that a pretrial motion to suppress be made by a specified time, a motion that is not made until trial or even until some later pretrial stage is not timely and thus ordinarily will not receive consideration. Noncompliance with these requirements is commonly characterized as a "waiver" of the constitutional objection, but because such a failure does not ordinarily involve an intentional relinquishment of a constitutional right it is better to view it as a "forfeiture."

In many jurisdictions a court may in its discretion entertain a suppression motion even when the motion could be barred as untimely.

If the court entertains the motion and receives evidence going to the merits, under the prevailing view it may still decline to suppress on the ground that the motion was not timely. The minority position is that once the hearing has been held the timeliness of the motion becomes moot and can no longer be a proper ground for denial. In any event, if an untimely motion is denied on the merits, this denial may be appealed after conviction.

All jurisdictions grant relief from pretrial motion requirements when it is shown that the defendant lacked a reasonable opportunity to raise the objection by the required time. Statutes and court rules articulating this exception vary somewhat in their phrasing, and this may influence to some degree how courts construe its breadth. It is fair to say, however, that there is a general disinclination to find such lack of opportunity except under the most compelling circumstances. Ignorance of the legal grounds for having the evidence suppressed will not suffice, but ignorance by the defendant that the item in question had been seized will. If the defendant was personally aware of the police action that led to their acquisition of the evidence, he is responsible for informing counsel of those facts.[1]

In *Henry v. Mississippi*,[2] the Supreme Court, applying the "proposition that a litigant's procedural defaults in state proceedings do not prevent vindication of his federal rights unless the State's insistence on compliance with its procedural rule serves a legitimate state interest," concluded that the less demanding contemporaneous objection rule did serve such an interest. But the Court went on to say that the purpose of this rule was substantially served

---

2. All federal and state laws governing execution of search warrants and procedures for return of seized property are cited in an appendix in City of West Covina v. Perkins, 525 U.S. 234, 119 S.Ct. 678, 142 L.Ed.2d 636 (1999), where the Court concluded "that where law enforcement agents seize property pursuant to warrant, due process requires them to take reasonable steps to give notice that the property has been taken so the owner can pursue available remedies for its return," but that there is no constitutional requirement of "individualized notice of state-law remedies which, like those at issue here, are established by published, generally available statute and case law."

1. To avoid difficulties presented by defendant's unawareness of the need for a suppression motion, some states have mandatory disclosure provisions as to evidence subject to a suppression motion challenge. Some others have permissive provisions (as in Fed.R.Crim.P. 12(b)(4)) allowing the prosecutor to preclude a claim of cause for an untimely suppression motion by making disclosure. Still other states have broad discovery provisions that allow the defense to determine through discovery whether the prosecution intends to use evidence in a manner that raises a possibility of a motion to suppress. See § 20.3.

2. 379 U.S. 443, 85 S.Ct. 564, 13 L.Ed.2d 408 (1965).

by the motion defendant had made at the close of the state's evidence, and thus suggested that noncompliance with the rule could not be deemed an independent state ground supporting defendant's conviction. A few states have read *Henry* as placing constitutional limits upon their power to treat failure to comply with a timely objection rule as a waiver of the constitutional objection. In the main, however, the courts have not read *Henry* as barring enforcement of either the contemporary objection rule or the pretrial motion rule, though *Henry* may have influenced some jurisdictions to be somewhat more ready to find the existence of good cause for failure to comply.

The Court in *Henry* found it unnecessary to resolve the independent state ground issue because the record suggested defendant's counsel had deliberately bypassed the opportunity to make a timely objection, which the Court concluded would constitute a forfeiture of the constitutional claim even "without prior consultation with an accused" by counsel. This branch of *Henry* has been relied upon by courts in holding that noncompliance with a timely objection rule, prompted by counsel's deliberate and strategic choice not to attempt to have the evidence in question suppressed, is binding upon the defendant even if that choice was made without the defendant's knowledge or participation.

(b) Failure to Renew Objection. In most jurisdictions a defendant will have preserved the suppression issue for appeal simply by having made the requisite pretrial motion that was denied. But some states require that the defendant renew his objection at the time the evidence is offered at trial. In support, it is argued that such a requirement ensures that the trial judge (as opposed to some lesser judicial officer) will have passed on the issue, serves to bar appeal where defendant later concludes as a matter of trial strategy that he would prefer to have the evidence admitted, also bars appeal where defense counsel later concludes the motion was without merit, and ensures reconsideration upon the added facts developed at trial. But requiring renewal robs the pretrial motion of its greatest benefit: the

saving of much time during and immediately prior to trial.

Even where renewal of the motion is not generally required, special circumstances may make renewal essential. Such is the case where it appears at the pretrial hearing that the facts cannot be fully developed at that point, so that the judge defers ruling on the motion until trial or denies the motion "without prejudice" to renewal at trial. Even absent such circumstances, renewal is the safer course in a jurisdiction in which the pretrial order is not binding on the trial judge. If the motion is renewed and reconsidered by the trial court, then it is customary for the appellate court on review to consider all the evidence available to the trial judge up to that point.

Defense counsel must be alert to other traps for the unwary. For example, in some jurisdictions it is the law that even if the defendant made a timely pretrial motion to suppress and (if required) a contemporaneous objection at the time the evidence was offered against him, the issue is *still* not preserved for appellate review unless the objection is made yet another time in a motion for a new trial.

(c) Testimony by Defendant. A small number of jurisdictions adhere to the position that a defendant may not complain on appeal about the admission of illegally obtained evidence, notwithstanding timely objection at or before trial, if the defendant gave testimony at trial admitting possession of that evidence. A variety of reasons have been given for this result: that defendant's admission is a "waiver" of the constitutional objection; that it amounts to a judicial confession; and that it makes admission of the evidence harmless error. The rule has been applied when defendant's testimony was equivocal, remote in its relationship to the evidence, or given to explain away the evidence and make possession of it appear innocent. The rule serves no legitimate state interest, and places the defendant in the dilemma where he must either ignore the damaging evidence introduced against him or waive his right to appeal its erroneous introduction, and thus it is encouraging that some states have abandoned the rule.

Some courts have concluded that the rule is unconstitutional in light of *Harrison v. United States*.[3] In *Harrison*, after three confessions were introduced at defendant's trial he took the stand and testified as to his version of the events, making damaging admissions in the process; his conviction was reversed on the ground the confessions were illegally obtained, but on retrial defendant's testimony from the first trial was introduced and another conviction resulted. The Supreme Court reversed on the ground that the former testimony was a "fruit" of the illegally obtained confessions, as the "natural inference is that no testimonial admission so damaging would have been made if the prosecutor had not already spread the petitioner's confessions before the jury." Significantly, a dissent in *Harrison* objected that the majority, contrary to earlier "fruits" decisions,[4] had used a "broad 'but for' sense of causality" and had failed to consider whether such an extension of the exclusionary rule would serve its deterrence objective. Because the Supreme Court's more recent "fruits" cases have focused upon the issue of "exploitation" and upon the notion of deterrence, it is by no means clear that the minority rule under discussion here is unconstitutional.

(d) Plea of Guilty or Nolo Contendere. A plea of guilty is an admission of guilt and a waiver of all non-jurisdictional defects. It "represents a break in the chain of events which has preceded it in the criminal process,"[5] and thus once a valid plea is received defendant may not appeal on the ground that his earlier suppression motion was erroneously denied. The same is true of a valid nolo contendere plea. As for a *Harrison*-type argument that the plea was a fruit of the prior illegality, this is "at most a claim that the admissibility of his confession was mistakenly assessed and that since he was erroneously advised * * * his plea was an unintelligent and voidable act."[6] And, the Supreme Court added in *McMann v. Richardson*,[7] this is not a claim that will prevail if the attorney's advice "was within the range of competence demanded of attorneys in criminal cases."

Some jurisdictions have by statute or court rule created an exception to the general rule, so that a "conditional" guilty plea may be made reserving the right to appeal an earlier denial of the suppression motion. Such pleas are discussed elsewhere herein.[8]

§ 10.3 Burden of Proof

(a) Generally. At a hearing on a motion to suppress, who has the burden of proof with respect to the matters at issue? To understand the full significance of this inquiry, it is first necessary to recall that the term "burden of proof" actually encompasses two separate burdens. One burden is that of producing evidence, sometimes called the "burden of evidence" or the "burden of going forward." If the party who has the burden of producing evidence does not meet that burden, the consequence is an adverse ruling on the matter at issue. The other burden is the burden of persuasion, which becomes crucial only if the parties have sustained their respective burdens of producing evidence and only when all the evidence has been introduced. It becomes significant if the trier of fact is in doubt; if he is, then the matter must be resolved against the party with the burden of persuasion.

It is not inevitably true that the burden of production and the burden of persuasion must both fall upon the same party, but the prevailing practice is to allocate the two burdens jointly to one party or another. Sometimes courts expressly state that this is what they are about, but more commonly it results as a consequence of a general ruling that the "burden of proof" on the motion to suppress rests upon either the defendant or the state.

Various principles are often advanced in the course of discussions of where, as a matter of sound policy, the burden of proof should lie in

---

3. 392 U.S. 219, 88 S.Ct. 2008, 20 L.Ed.2d 1047 (1968).

4. See § 9.3(b).

5. Tollett v. Henderson, 411 U.S. 258, 93 S.Ct. 1602, 36 L.Ed.2d 235 (1973).

6. McMann v. Richardson, 397 U.S. 759, 90 S.Ct. 1441, 25 L.Ed.2d 763 (1970).

7. 397 U.S. 759, 90 S.Ct. 1441, 25 L.Ed.2d 763 (1970).

8. See § 21.6(b).

various circumstances. In summary, they are: (1) that the burdens should be placed on the party who has the best access to the relevant facts; (2) that the burdens should be placed on the party desiring change; (3) that the burdens should be allocated so as to avoid providing an incentive for use of the objection primarily to gain general discovery of the other side's case, particularly where discovery is otherwise quite limited; (4) that the burdens should be allocated so as to have one party proving a limited ground rather than the other party disproving many grounds; (5) that the burdens should be allocated in accordance with the best judicial estimate of the probabilities of the particular event having occurred; and (6) that the burdens should be used to "handicap" disfavored contentions. These principles will sometimes be helpful in working out burden of proof issues, but they do not inevitably all point in the same direction and thus will not always show where as a matter of policy the burden would best be placed.

The practical significance of the allocation of the ultimate burden of proof at suppression hearings is a matter on which opinions differ, as is illustrated by *People v. Berrios*.[1] There the prosecutor joined the defendant in urging that the burden of persuasion be placed on the state in so-called "dropsy" cases—that is, where the police claim that a suspect dropped the seized item and thus created a situation in which a permissible plain view seizure could occur. The court declined to do so, and stated that such "a change in the burden of proof would be ineffective to combat the alleged evil" because the judge "would still be faced with the same credibility question" of whether the defendant or the officer was lying. But this is not so; the burden of persuasion is significant in those cases in which the trier of fact is actually in doubt. Thus, as stated in the *Berr-*

ios dissent, if the burden was placed on the state the judge would "be permitted to suppress evidence in cases where, for instance, he finds the testimony of each side evenly balanced on the scales of credibility and is unable to make up his mind as to who is telling the truth."

But allocation of the burden of going forward may be of greater significance. A basic tactical objective of the defense is to avoid first disclosing its factual theories, lest the police conform their testimony to evade those theories. But if the defendant has the burden of going forward he must often take the stand first and tell his side of the story. Even if the officers, as prospective witnesses, may be excluded from the courtroom while that testimony is received, the defendant is still not in as good a position to rebut their testimony as he would be if he testified last. If the defense tries to satisfy its burden without defendant's testimony by calling the police officers as its own witnesses, this tactic may backfire; the court may be unwilling to treat the officers as "adverse" witnesses subject to impeachment.

(b) Search and Seizure. With respect to the issue that is usually central in a Fourth Amendment suppression hearing—the reasonableness of the challenged search or seizure— most states follow the rule utilized in the federal courts: if the search or seizure was pursuant to a warrant, the defendant has the burden of proof; but if the police acted without a warrant the burden of proof is on the prosecution. The warrant-no warrant dichotomy is typically explained on the ground that when the police have acted with a warrant an independent determination on the issue of probable cause has already been made by a magistrate, thereby giving rise to a presumption of legality,[2] while when they have acted without a

---

§ 10.3

1. 28 N.Y.2d 361, 321 N.Y.S.2d 884, 270 N.E.2d 709 (1971).

2. When evidence obtained pursuant to a warrant is challenged on a motion to suppress by a claim that probable cause was lacking, the suppression hearing judge is to give "great deference" to the issuing magistrate's decision, United States v. Ventresca, 380 U.S. 102, 85 S.Ct. 741, 13 L.Ed.2d 684 (1965), but the same is *not* true in any situation where information is excised or redacted from a

search warrant application after the fact, regardless of the reason why the redaction occurred, for in such circumstances the suppression hearing judge would not in effect consider the same search warrant application as the magistrate did when determining the sufficiency of probable cause.

warrant the evidence comprising probable cause is particularly within the knowledge and control of the arresting agencies.

Some jurisdictions, however, do not draw a distinction between warrant and no-warrant cases in allocating the burden of proof. A few uniformly place the burden of proof upon the prosecution on the ground that the state is the party seeking to use the evidence and thus ought to bear the burden of establishing that it was lawfully come by. Some states place the burden of proof uniformly upon the defendant. By way of explanation, it is commonly stated that the burden is so placed because (a) the burden should be upon the moving party, (b) there is a presumption of regularity attending the actions of law enforcement officials, (c) relevant evidence is generally admissible and thus exceptions must be justified by those claiming the exception, and (d) it will deter spurious allegations wasteful of court time.

Placing the burden upon the defendant even in the no warrant situation would seem to place him in a most disadvantageous position. It would be impossible, for example, for a defendant to prove a lack of probable cause in the abstract, as he cannot be expected to prove such a lack until he knows on what the government bases its claim of its existence. However, the situation is not necessarily this bad in jurisdictions purporting to place the burden of proof upon the defendant, for they may in fact permit the defendant to shift the burden to the prosecution with a minimum of effort.

There are certain types of Fourth Amendment issues that customarily receive special treatment with respect to burden of proof. One of these is that of whether a so-called consent search occurred. In *Bumper v. North Carolina*,[3] the Supreme Court held: "When a prosecutor seeks to rely upon consent to justify the lawfulness of a search, he has the burden of proving that the consent was, in fact, freely and voluntarily given. This burden cannot be discharged by showing no more than acquiescence to a claim of lawful authority." *Bumper* so places the burden as a matter of constitu-

tional law, meaning states may not adopt a contrary rule.

Another issue ordinarily singled out for special treatment is that of whether the defendant has standing. In *Jones v. United States*,[4] the Court emphasized that the Fourth Amendment exclusionary rule keeps out evidence "otherwise competent" as "a means for making effective the protection of privacy," and thus concluded that it was "entirely proper to require of one who seeks to challenge the legality of a search as the basis for suppressing relevant evidence that he alleged, and if the allegation be disputed that he establish, that he himself was the victim of an invasion of privacy." Most lower courts follow *Jones* and place the burden on the defendant to establish standing, though a few have gone the other way.

Yet another issue usually receiving special burden-of-proof treatment is that of whether any "search" in the Fourth Amendment sense has actually occurred. Thus, in *Nardone v. United States*,[5] where the defendant contended that the case against him was based upon evidence acquired as a consequence of an illegal wiretap, the Court ruled that the burden was on him to show that such a wiretap had occurred. The Court in *Nardone* expressed concern that if the rule were otherwise the defendant would obtain full pretrial discovery of the prosecution's case, but doubtless was influenced by the fact that unless the burden were on the defendant there would likely be a flood of frivolous claims of wiretapping. The lower courts have generally placed the burden on the defendant to prove the existence of a wiretap. Some courts also apply the *Nardone* rule to other occurrence-of-search issues, such as whether or not the object seized was in plain view, though some place the burden on the prosecution in such circumstances on the ground that plain view is a justification for not having a warrant and as such ought to be established by the party claiming the exception. (The Supreme Court is divided on the question of whether the was-there-a-search

---

3. 391 U.S. 543, 88 S.Ct. 1788, 20 L.Ed.2d 797 (1968).

4. 362 U.S. 257, 80 S.Ct. 725, 4 L.Ed.2d 697 (1960).

5. 308 U.S. 338, 60 S.Ct. 266, 84 L.Ed. 307 (1939).

burden should always fall on the defendant.[6]) The defendant also has the burden of proof as to whether there was sufficient government involvement in seemingly private conduct and whether a seizure occurred.

Nardone is also relevant with respect to yet another special situation, namely, that in which the issue is whether certain evidence is the fruit[7] of some prior Fourth Amendment violation. The Court said that once wiretapping was established the defendant would have an opportunity "to prove that a substantial portion of the case against him was a fruit of the poisonous tree," after which the government would have an opportunity "to convince the trial court that its proof had an independent origin." This language was cited with approval in *Alderman v. United States*,[8] holding that in such a situation the defendant "must go forward with specific evidence demonstrating taint," upon which the government "has the ultimate burden of persuasion to show that its evidence is untainted." This would mean, for example, that the government could prevail by showing an independent source for its evidence or that the evidence would inevitably have been discovered by lawful means.[9] In the main, the lower courts have followed the *Nardone–Alderman* allocation of burdens in fruit-of-the-poisonous-tree situations.

The extent to which the states remain free to allocate the burden of proof in Fourth Amendment cases is a matter of considerable uncertainty. It appears clear the Court has held, albeit without any extended discussion of the issue, that the burden of proof *must* be on the prosecution when it is claimed the evidence was obtained in a search by consent.[10] However, the Court has not spoken in such direct terms about the allocation of the burden in other situations. True, the Court has frequently spoken of the burden being on those who claim an exemption from the Fourth Amendment warrant requirement,[11] but these assertions are subject to varying interpretations. They may be read as referring only to the state's burden in appellate argument of justifying any request that the Court recognize any new or expanded exception to the warrant requirement. Or, as some courts have concluded, they may be interpreted as signaling a requirement that the burden of proof be placed upon the state whenever the police have acted without a warrant. The latter interpretation seems closer to the mark. At least, it is most unlikely the Court would find it constitutionally permissible for a state to impose burdens of proof upon defendants to such a degree and extent as to foreclose "a reliable and clearcut determination"[12] of Fourth Amendment claims, as would be the case, for example, if a defendant had to bear the burden of production and persuasion on the issue of whether the police lacked probable cause for a warrantless arrest.[13]

(c) Confessions. When the issue at a suppression hearing is whether a confession ob-

---

6. Florida v. Riley, 488 U.S. 445, 109 S.Ct. 693, 102 L.Ed.2d 835 (1989) (5 Justices say burden on defendant to show use of helicopters at 400 feet so rare as to produce reasonable expectation of privacy; 4 say burden on state to show nonrarity).

7. On the "fruit of the poisonous tree" doctrine, see § 9.3.

8. 394 U.S. 165, 89 S.Ct. 961, 22 L.Ed.2d 176 (1969).

9. See Nix v. Williams, 467 U.S. 431, 104 S.Ct. 2501, 81 L.Ed.2d 377 (1984), accepting the inevitable discovery doctrine (in a confessions context) but as a constitutional matter placing the burden of proof on the prosecution to show that inevitability by a preponderance of the evidence.

10. Bumper v. North Carolina, 391 U.S. 543, 88 S.Ct. 1788, 20 L.Ed.2d 797 (1968).

11. E.g., Coolidge v. New Hampshire, 403 U.S. 443, 91 S.Ct. 2022, 29 L.Ed.2d 564 (1971); United States v. Jeffers, 342 U.S. 48, 72 S.Ct. 93, 96 L.Ed. 59 (1951).

12. See Lego v. Twomey, 404 U.S. 477, 92 S.Ct. 619, 30 L.Ed.2d 618 (1972), reiterating that such a determination is constitutionally required as to the voluntariness of a confession, and seeming to make no distinction between Fourth and Fifth Amendment suppression hearings.

13. In Beck v. Ohio, 379 U.S. 89, 85 S.Ct. 223, 13 L.Ed.2d 142 (1964), where the Court ruled that the officer's testimony as to his knowledge of the defendant's physical appearance and criminal record and as to having received information about the defendant did not establish probable cause, it was said that "it was incumbent upon the prosecution to show with considerably more specificity than was shown in this case what the informer actually said, and why the officer thought the information was credible." It is virtually beyond belief that the Court would have reached a contrary conclusion if the state ruling had been expressly grounded upon the proposition that the burden was on the defendant to prove the absence of probable cause.

tained from the defendant was voluntary, most jurisdictions place the burdens of production and persuasion upon the prosecution. A few states, however place the burden of proving involuntariness on the defendant. The Supreme Court's decision in *Lego v. Twomey*[14] raises serious doubts as to the constitutionality of the latter position. Though the Court was concerned primarily with the applicable standard of proof, *Lego* indicated that it was the constitutional obligation of the prosecution to meet that standard of proof. The Court declared that "the prosecution must prove at least by a preponderance of the evidence that the confession was voluntary."

As for compliance with the requirements of the *Miranda* case, it is clear that as a constitutional matter the burden is on the prosecution. The Court in that case stated:

> If the interrogation continues without the presence of an attorney and a statement is taken, a heavy burden rests on the Government to demonstrate that the defendant knowingly and intelligently waived his privilege against self-incrimination and his right to retained or appointed counsel. This Court has always set high standards of proof for the waiver of constitutional rights, * * * and we re-assert these standards, as applied to in-custody interrogation. Since the State is responsible for establishing the isolated circumstances under which the interrogation takes place and has the only means of making available corroborated evidence of warnings given during incommunicado interrogation, the burden is rightly on its shoulders.[15]

When a "fruits" issue arises with respect to a confession, either that the confession is the fruit of some earlier illegality or that some later-acquired evidence is the fruit of an illegal confession, it is customary to use the *Nardone* approach. This means that once the defendant has established a relationship between the unlawful police activity and the evidence to which objection is made, the burden is on the prosecution to show that the unlawful taint has been dissipated.[16] So too, where the defendant gave immunized testimony, the prosecution bears the burden in any subsequent prosecution of establishing that its evidence is not tainted.

(d) Identification. If a lineup or other identification procedure is conducted at a time and in a manner so that it is a "critical stage" for right to counsel purposes, then resort to such procedure without counsel imposes upon the prosecution the burden of establishing that defendant intelligently waived his right to counsel.[17] If such a showing is not made, a per se rule of exclusion applies as to testimony about that identification,[18] while an at-trial identification by the witness who made the earlier identification is barred only if it is the fruit of the previous constitutional violation.[19] In *United States v. Wade*,[20] the Court held as a constitutional matter that the burden must be on the government to show "that the in-court identifications were based upon observations of the suspect other than the lineup identification."

An identification procedure may also be challenged on the ground that it was so unnecessarily suggestive as to violate due process. In such circumstances many courts have assumed, typically without extensive discussion, that the defendant has the burden of proving the due process violation because he is the moving party. But the prosecution should bear the burdens of production and persuasion whenever the identification procedure was conducted out of the presence of defendant's attorney, for in such a situation the defendant

---

14.   404 U.S. 477, 92 S.Ct. 619, 30 L.Ed.2d 618 (1972).

15.   Miranda v. Arizona, 384 U.S. 436, 86 S.Ct. 1602, 16 L.Ed.2d 694 (1966).

16.   See also Nix v. Williams, 467 U.S. 431, 104 S.Ct. 2501, 81 L.Ed.2d 377 (1984), holding the burden of proof is on the prosecution to show that the fruits of an illegally obtained confession would inevitably have been discovered by lawful means.

17.   United States v. Wade, 388 U.S. 218, 87 S.Ct. 1926, 18 L.Ed.2d 1149 (1967).

18.   Gilbert v. California, 388 U.S. 263, 87 S.Ct. 1951, 18 L.Ed.2d 1178 (1967).

19.   United States v. Wade, 388 U.S. 218, 87 S.Ct. 1926, 18 L.Ed.2d 1149 (1967).

20.   388 U.S. 218, 87 S.Ct. 1926, 18 L.Ed.2d 1149 (1967).

may not even be aware that witnesses were seeking to identify him (e.g., where a "show-up" was conducted through a one-way mirror), and even if aware, he still may be unable to know what facts existed that might make the procedure unnecessarily suggestive. Some jurisdictions have divided the burden of proof between the defense and the prosecution; the defense carries the burden of showing that the identification procedure was unnecessarily suggestive, and the burden then shifts to the prosecution to show that the identification nevertheless was sufficiently reliable to be accepted under due process.

Under the due process approach, a later, at-trial identification must be excluded if there was an earlier identification "unnecessarily suggestive"[21] to the degree that there was "a very substantial likelihood of irreparable misidentification."[22] In making the latter calculation, the factors to be considered[23] are essentially the same as those utilized in determining whether an at-trial identification is the fruit of a lineup held in violation of defendant's right to counsel. This being the case, it is not surprising that some courts have concluded that here as well the burden must be on the government to show that the in-court identification is not so tainted. However, in the due process cases the question whether the at-trial identification is unreliable in light of what occurred earlier is not a "fruits" issue at all, but is part and parcel of the basic question of whether any violation of the constitution has occurred. Because this is so (and assuming that establishment of the due process violation is otherwise a burden that may be placed on the defendant), it may well be permissible to put on the defendant the that of showing the unreliability of the at-trial identification.

§ 10.4   Standard of Proof

(a) Generally. Various standards of proof are used in the law. In the trial of criminal

cases, as the Supreme Court held in *In re Winship*,[1] it is a requirement of due process that the defendant be proved guilty beyond a reasonable doubt. In civil cases, by contrast, the standard usually is a preponderance of evidence, commonly defined as proof that leads the jury to find that the existence of the contested fact is more probable than its nonexistence. But in certain circumstances a standard somewhere between these two is utilized; it is usually called the clear and convincing evidence standard, and means that the factfinder must be persuaded that the truth of the contention is highly probable.

Depending upon the jurisdiction and the matter at issue, any one of these three standards of proof may be used in the context of a suppression hearing. In large measure, the choice of the standard is a matter of local law, but at least in some circumstances the Constitution may compel use of something beyond the preponderance standard.

(b) Confessions. In *Lego v. Twomey*,[2] the Court rejected the contention that the voluntariness of a confession must be established beyond a reasonable doubt. The Court first concluded that *Winship* was not controlling:

Since the purpose that a voluntariness hearing is designed to serve has nothing whatever to do with improving the reliability of jury verdicts, we cannot accept the charge that judging the admissibility of a confession by a preponderance of the evidence undermines the mandate of *In re Winship*. * * * A high standard of proof is necessary, we said, to ensure against unjust convictions by giving substance to the presumption of innocence. A guilty verdict is not rendered any less reliable or less consonant with *Winship* simply because the admissibility of a confession is determined by a less stringent standard.

21. Stovall v. Denno, 388 U.S. 293, 87 S.Ct. 1967, 18 L.Ed.2d 1199 (1967).

22. Neil v. Biggers, 409 U.S. 188, 93 S.Ct. 375, 34 L.Ed.2d 401 (1972).

23. See Manson v. Brathwaite, 432 U.S. 98, 97 S.Ct. 2243, 53 L.Ed.2d 140 (1977).

§ 10.4

1. 397 U.S. 358, 90 S.Ct. 1068, 25 L.Ed.2d 368 (1970).

2. 404 U.S. 477, 92 S.Ct. 619, 30 L.Ed.2d 618 (1972).

Lego also rejected the contention that application of a reasonable doubt standard was necessary "to give adequate protection to those values that the exclusionary rules are designed to serve." The Court responded that it was

unconvinced that merely emphasizing the importance of the values served by exclusionary rules is itself sufficient demonstration that the Constitution also requires admissibility to be proved beyond a reasonable doubt. Evidence obtained in violation of the Fourth Amendment has been excluded from federal criminal trials for many years. The same is true of coerced confessions offered in either federal or state trials. But, from our experience over this period of time no substantial evidence has accumulated that federal rights have suffered from determining admissibility by a preponderance of the evidence. * * * Sound reason for moving further in this direction has not been offered here nor do we discern any at the present time. This is particularly true since the exclusionary rules are very much aimed at deterring lawless conduct by police and prosecution and it is very doubtful that escalating the prosecution's burden of proof in Fourth and Fifth Amendment suppression hearings would be sufficiently productive in this respect to outweigh the public interest in placing probative evidence before juries for the purpose of arriving at truthful decisions about guilt or innocence.[3]

The three *Lego* dissenters[4] argued that while the preponderance standard was satisfactory in civil cases, where an error in favor of one party was no more serious than an error in favor of the other, its use on the voluntariness issue reflected acceptance of the mistaken view "that it is no more serious in general to admit involuntary confessions than it is to exclude voluntary confessions." It has been argued

that a reasonable doubt standard was called for in *Lego* because the test of involuntariness (as opposed to other exclusionary rule standards) is designed to exclude unreliable evidence that, if admitted, would be given great weight by the jury.

Though the Supreme Court in *Lego* concluded that due process was satisfied by application of the preponderance standard and was not even persuaded "to impose the stricter standard of proof as an exercise of supervisory power" over federal courts, note was taken that the states were always "free, pursuant to their own law, to adopt a higher standard." Prior to *Lego*, several jurisdictions had utilized a reasonable doubt standard; some have shifted to a preponderance standard in light of *Lego*, while others have retained the reasonable doubt standard as a matter of local law. In addition, a few new states have joined the reasonable doubt grouping, but a substantial majority now follow the preponderance standard.

As for confessions challenged on *Miranda* grounds, the Supreme Court in that case declared that "a heavy burden rests on the Government to demonstrate that the defendant knowingly and intelligently waived his privilege against self-incrimination and his right to retained or appointed counsel."[5] But in *Colorado v. Connelly*,[6] the Court reaffirmed *Lego* and applied it in this context as well: "If, as we held in *Lego v. Twomey*, the voluntariness of a confession need be established only by a preponderance of the evidence, then a waiver of the auxiliary protections established in *Miranda* should require no higher burden of proof." Although the federal courts and many states utilize the preponderance standard, other states continue to apply, as a matter of state law, either the reasonable doubt or the clear and convincing standard.

---

3. Relying upon this analysis in *Lego*, the Court in Nix v. Williams, 467 U.S. 431, 104 S.Ct. 2501, 81 L.Ed.2d 377 (1984), held that the preponderance standard would suffice on the issue of whether certain fruits of an illegally obtained confession would have been inevitably discovered by lawful means.

4. Brennan, J., joined by Douglas and Marshall, JJ. Powell and Rehnquist, JJ., did not participate in the

decision. The dissenters also argued that the majority's position was inconsistent with "the rule that automatically reverses a conviction when an involuntary confession was admitted at trial."

5. Miranda v. Arizona, 384 U.S. 436, 86 S.Ct. 1602, 16 L.Ed.2d 694 (1966).

6. 479 U.S. 157, 107 S.Ct. 515, 93 L.Ed.2d 473 (1986).

(c) Search and Seizure. That part of *Lego* rejecting the claim that *Winship* governs at the suppression stage of a criminal case is equally applicable or perhaps even more applicable to Fourth Amendment suppression hearings. And the other branch of *Lego,* focusing upon the purpose of exclusionary rules, expressly encompasses Fourth Amendment suppression cases as well. Thus it is as a general matter constitutional to conclude, as the Supreme Court later put it in *United States v. Matlock,*[7] that "the controlling burden of proof at suppression hearings should impose no greater burden than proof by a preponderance of the evidence." Again, states are free to impose a higher standard, but state courts have generally held that the preponderance standard applies at a hearing where a search or seizure is challenged. Significantly, this position has been taken even in jurisdictions that apply a reasonable doubt standard when the voluntariness of a confession is at issue. This can be explained by the fact that an involuntary confession may be unreliable while illegally seized evidence is always reliable, and by the added fact that the police have a greater capacity to keep records and otherwise to prepare to meet a higher standard of proof in establishing the events surrounding a custodial interrogation as opposed to a typical warrantless search.

Some authority is to be found seeming to require more than a preponderance of evidence under certain circumstances. In particular, at least some courts have found the higher clear and convincing evidence standard appropriate when the prosecution's claim is that the search was consented to or that the evidence was obtained after a voluntary abandonment of it by the defendant, or that the illegally obtained evidence would inevitably have been lawfully discovered. The policy judgment underlying these cases—that a higher standard is called for in situations where it would be particularly easy for the police to manipulate events or fabricate an interpretation of events that could not be effectively challenged by the defendant—does not conflict with the reasons given above as to why the preponderance standard should ordinarily suffice.

This is not to suggest that the states are constitutionally required to use this higher standard in those circumstances. True, the Supreme Court instructed in *Schneckloth v. Bustamonte*[8] that "[t]o approach [consent] searches without the most careful scrutiny would sanction the possibility of official coercion." But *Schneckloth* also teaches that the test to be applied in determining the validity of a consent is "voluntariness," the meaning of which "has been developed in those cases in which the Court has had to determine the 'voluntariness' of a defendant's confession." Because the Court in *Lego* was not prepared to require more than the preponderance standard where the question to be resolved was the voluntariness of a confession, there is no reason to believe that a higher standard will be imposed when the question is the voluntariness of a consent to a search.

(d) Identification. In *United States v. Wade,*[9] establishing a right to counsel at certain pretrial identification proceedings, the Court expressly stated that the burden was on the government "to establish by clear and convincing evidence that the in-court identifications were based upon observations of the suspect other than the lineup identification."[10] It is thus clear that the states are constitutionally compelled to utilize a standard at least this demanding. Some states have carried this concept over to in-court identifications allegedly tainted by a out-of-court identification procedure that violated due process. Once the court concludes that the initial, out-of-court

---

7.　415 U.S. 164, 94 S.Ct. 988, 39 L.Ed.2d 242 (1974).

8.　412 U.S. 218, 93 S.Ct. 2041, 36 L.Ed.2d 854 (1973).

9.　388 U.S. 218, 87 S.Ct. 1926, 18 L.Ed.2d 1149 (1967).

10.　*Wade* was distinguished in Nix v. Williams, 467 U.S. 431, 104 S.Ct. 2501, 81 L.Ed.2d 377 (1984), holding the preponderance standard sufficient on the issue of whether the fruits of defendant's illegally obtained confession would inevitably have been discovered by lawful

means. The Court stressed that while in a *Wade* situation there exists "the difficulty of determining whether an in-court identification was based on independent recollection unaided by the lineup identification," by contrast "inevitable discovery involves no speculative elements but focuses on demonstrated historical facts capable of ready verification or impeachment and does not require a departure from the usual burden of proof at suppression hearings."

identification procedure violated due process, the state assumes the burden of establishing by clear and convincing evidence the independent reliability of the in-court identification. As to the due process violation in the original identification procedure, here the burden is usually placed on the defendant (at least in part), and the defendant's burden typically is limited to a preponderance of the evidence standard.

§ 10.5   The Suppression Hearing

(a) The Trier of Fact. Prior to the Supreme Court's decision in *Jackson v. Denno*,[1] at least three different factfinding allocations were used in determining whether a confession was voluntary. In states following the "orthodox rule," voluntariness was determined solely and finally by the judge. If the judge found the confession voluntary, it was admissible without any separate determination by the jury. Evidence relating to police methods in obtaining the confession might well be admitted to assist the jury in its assessment of the credibility of the confession, but the jury was not called upon to consider the voluntariness of the confession. By comparison, under the "Massachusetts rule" a determination that a confession was voluntary had to be made twice. Once again the trial court initially ruled on the admissibility of the confession, and if the judge concluded the confession was involuntary his ruling excluding it was final. But if the judge found the confession voluntary, it was then admitted at trial subject to the jury's independent determination of voluntariness. The jury received evidence of the circumstances surrounding the confession, was charged as to the voluntariness standard, and was instructed that it could not consider the confession unless it first found it to be voluntary. Under the third alternative, the so-called "New York rule," the determination of voluntariness was left primarily to the jury. The judge would make an initial determination as to whether reasonable persons could differ on

the issue of voluntariness, as where testimony was in conflict or different inferences could be drawn from undisputed facts. Unless there were "no circumstances" under which the confession could be voluntary, the voluntariness issue was passed along to the jury. The jury was instructed on the voluntariness standard and told to consider the confession only if it found it to be voluntary.

In the *Jackson* case, the Court divided 5–4 in holding the New York procedure unconstitutional. The crux of the majority's reasoning in *Jackson*, as later summarized in *Lego v. Twomey*,[2] was

that the New York procedure was constitutionally defective because at no point along the way did a criminal defendant receive a clear-cut determination that the confession used against him was in fact voluntary. The trial judge was not entitled to exclude a confession merely because he himself would have found it involuntary, and, while we recognized that the jury was empowered to perform that function, we doubted it could do so reliably. Precisely because confessions of guilt, whether coerced or freely given, may be truthful and potent evidence, we did not believe a jury could be called upon to ignore the probative value of a truthful but coerced confession; it was also likely, we thought, that in judging voluntariness itself the jury would be influenced by the reliability of a confession it considered an accurate account of the facts.

As also noted in *Lego,* the Court in *Jackson* "cast no doubt upon the orthodox and Massachusetts procedures." As for the latter, the *Jackson* majority found it to be significantly different from the New York procedure because the judge "himself resolves evidentiary conflicts and gives his own answer to the coercion issue," so that the jury only considers those confessions the judge believes to be voluntary.[3] The dozen or so states that had there-

---

§ 10.5

1. 378 U.S. 368, 84 S.Ct. 1774, 12 L.Ed.2d 908 (1964).

2. 404 U.S. 477, 92 S.Ct. 619, 30 L.Ed.2d 618 (1972).

3. The dissenters, on the other hand, responded that this acceptance of the Massachusetts rule revealed the "hollowness" of the Court's holding. They argued that the distinction between the New York and Massachusetts rule was more theoretical than real, and suggested that in

tofore used the New York procedure were thus free to adopt either of the others. The orthodox rule is now followed in the federal courts and in most states, while a substantial minority use the Massachusetts rule. The better view, however, is that the latter rule is inappropriate when the confession has been challenged on *Miranda* grounds, as then the determination that must be made is more complex than a question of voluntariness. But even where the orthodox rule obtains, the defendant must be allowed to put before the jury testimony about the environment in which the police secured his confession so that he may thereby put its credibility into issue. Denial of that opportunity infringes upon the constitutional right to "a meaningful opportunity to present a complete defense," derived from the Fourteenth Amendment due process clause and the Sixth Amendment confrontation and compulsory process clauses.[4]

Only the orthodox rule is generally utilized outside the confession cases. The legality of a search is a matter of law to be determined by the court and not the jury, and this is so even when resolution of the matter depends upon a determination of the credibility of various witnesses and even when the motion was properly made during the course of the trial. Likewise, the admissibility of testimony claimed to be the fruit of unconstitutional identification procedures is a matter to be decided by the court; thereafter, the jury will determine the credibility of the identification by considering the conditions under which the observation was made, the physical ability of the witness to observe the defendant, and any possible problems that could distort the witness' observation powers and judgment. But if a hearing on the admissibility of identification testimony is held in the presence of the jury, this is not per se a violation of due process. In *Watkins v. Sowders*,[5] so holding, the Court distinguished *Jackson* on the theory that when identification

evidence rather than a confession is at issue "no * * * special considerations justify a departure from the presumption that juries will follow instructions."

(b) Presence of Jury. Ordinarily, if the motion to suppress is made before trial, the admissibility issue will be decided before the jury is selected. But if defendant's objection is made initially at trial or the court has delayed a hearing on a pretrial motion to avoid inconvenience to witnesses, it would be possible for the hearing to be conducted in the presence of the jury. Courts have rather consistently ruled this should not be done as to search and seizure claims, reasoning that if suppression was ordered an admonition to the jury to disregard the evidence would hardly suffice. Such reasoning would seem to extend to other suppression hearings as well, and explains why the prevailing practice squares with the Supreme Court's teaching that the most prudent course of action is to hold hearings on the admissibility of confessions[6] and eyewitness identifications[7] out of the presence of the jury. In some jurisdictions, however, it is at least sometimes the practice to hold such hearings while the jury is present, apparently for the reason that this will avoid the necessity of "a replay" of the same testimony later so that the jury can determine the weight to be given the evidence if it is admitted by the judge.

The Supreme Court, dealing only with instances in which the suppression hearing before a jury did *not* result in exclusion of evidence, has declined to hold that there is a per se rule requiring all such hearings be held outside the jury's presence. In *Pinto v. Pierce*,[8] concerning a hearing on whether a confession should be suppressed as involuntary, the Court ruled the trial judge had not acted contrary to *Jackson v. Denno*[9] in holding the hearing in the jury's presence. But the Court placed considerable emphasis upon the fact that defen-

"cases of doubt" a judge operating under the latter was likely to "resolve the doubt in favor of admissibility, relying on the final determination by the jury."

4. Crane v. Kentucky, 476 U.S. 683, 106 S.Ct. 2142, 90 L.Ed.2d 636 (1986).

5. 449 U.S. 341, 101 S.Ct. 654, 66 L.Ed.2d 549 (1981).

6. Pinto v. Pierce, 389 U.S. 31, 88 S.Ct. 192, 19 L.Ed.2d 31 (1967).

7. Watkins v. Sowders, 449 U.S. 341, 101 S.Ct. 654, 66 L.Ed.2d 549 (1981).

8. 389 U.S. 31, 88 S.Ct. 192, 19 L.Ed.2d 31 (1967).

9. 378 U.S. 368, 84 S.Ct. 1774, 12 L.Ed.2d 908 (1964).

dant through his counsel consented to that procedure, and Justice Fortas, concurring, reasoned the result should be otherwise absent such consent: "A telescoped hearing before judge and jury, in which the judge finds voluntariness for purposes of admissibility, in reality reduces the jury function to an echo. Hearing the evidence simultaneously with the judge, the jury is not apt to approach disagreement with him."

More recently, in *Watkins v. Sowders*,[10] the Court held there was no per se rule requiring all hearings into the constitutionality of witness identification procedures to be held outside the presence of the jury. Over a vigorous dissent, the majority reasoned that the notion a jury would not follow instructions to disregard certain evidence, perhaps acceptable in confession cases where a very reliable but coerced confession would be suppressed, had no application in the instant case because if identification evidence were suppressed it would be because of its unreliability. (Such reasoning suggests that in eyewitness identification cases the Court would reach the same result if, as was not the case in *Watkins,* the judge had suppressed the evidence.) As for the claim that the presence of the jury deterred defense counsel from vigorously and fully cross-examining the witnesses, the majority in *Watkins* found no specific instances in which counsel were so deterred and opined that defense counsel in this context runs only the usual risks in cross-examining an adverse witness.

(c) Testimony by Defendant. Often it will be necessary for the defendant to be a witness at a suppression hearing. The defendant may testify in a suppression hearing without waiving his right to decline to take the stand in his own defense at trial or any other rights stemming from his choice not to testify. If he testifies, he may be subjected to cross-examination, but he "does not, by testifying upon a preliminary matter, subject himself to

cross-examination as to other issues in the case."[11] Nonetheless, the cross-examination "may enable the prosecutor to elicit incriminating information beyond that offered on direct examination," and this "might be helpful to the prosecution in developing its case or deciding its trial strategy."[12]

In *Simmons v. United States*,[13] the Court held that testimony given at the hearing by a defendant in order to establish his standing to object to illegally seized evidence may not be used against him at his trial on the question of guilt or innocence. The logic of *Simmons,* namely, that a defendant should not be "obliged either to give up what he believed, with advice of counsel, to be a valid Fourth Amendment claim or, in legal effect, to waive his Fifth Amendment privilege against self-incrimination," indicates that the same protection must be given to any testimony by the defendant at the suppression hearing.

Some courts have read *Simmons* with *Harris v. New York*,[14] holding that a confession obtained in violation of *Miranda* may be introduced at trial for impeachment purposes, so as to permit use of defendant's suppression hearing testimony for impeachment purposes at trial. It may be objected that this conclusion is incorrect in light of *New Jersey v. Portash*,[15] holding that testimony given after a grant of use immunity cannot be admitted even for impeachment purposes because such testimony "is the essence of coerced testimony" in that it was compelled under threat of contempt. So the argument goes, testimony by the defendant at a suppression hearing is likewise "compelled" in light of the Hobson's choice described in *Simmons*. But more recently in *United States v. Salvucci*,[16] a majority of the Supreme Court, while claiming the issue remained open, asserted that "the protective shield of *Simmons* is not to be converted into a license for false representations."

---

10.   449 U.S. 341, 101 S.Ct. 654, 66 L.Ed.2d 549 (1981).

11.   Fed.R.Evid. 104(d).

12.   United States v. Salvucci, 448 U.S. 83, 100 S.Ct. 2547, 65 L.Ed.2d 619 (1980) (dissent).

13.   390 U.S. 377, 88 S.Ct. 967, 19 L.Ed.2d 1247 (1968).

14.   401 U.S. 222, 91 S.Ct. 643, 28 L.Ed.2d 1 (1971).

15.   440 U.S. 450, 99 S.Ct. 1292, 59 L.Ed.2d 501 (1979).

16.   448 U.S. 83, 100 S.Ct. 2547, 65 L.Ed.2d 619 (1980).

(d) Evidentiary Rules. As noted in *United States v. Matlock*,[17] the "rules of evidence normally applicable in criminal trials do not operate with full force at a hearing before the judge to determine the admissibility of evidence." Though it has long been clear that hearsay could be received on the issue of probable cause to search,[18] *Matlock* held that hearsay statements could also be admitted on other issues as well. There, in an effort to show the search was consented to by defendant's roommate, the prosecution sought to put in evidence the roommate's out-of-court statements regarding her joint occupancy of the premises and representation that she was defendant's wife. The Supreme Court held that the trial judge erred in excluding those statements as hearsay, noting that a provision in the proposed (and since adopted) federal evidence rules specifically provided that on a preliminary question, such as the "admissibility of evidence," the trial court "is not bound by the rules of evidence except those with respect to privileges."[19] The Court added that there was "much to be said for the proposition that in proceedings where the judge himself is considering the admissibility of evidence, the exclusionary rules [such as the hearsay prohibition] should not be applicable, and the judge should receive the evidence and give it such weight as his judgment and experience counsel." Even if a trial court could not go that far, the Court declared, it certainly should not exclude hearsay statements where, as here, "the court was quite satisfied that the statement had in fact been made" and "there is nothing in the record to raise serious doubts about the truthfulness of the statements themselves."

(e) Right of Confrontation. As indicated in *McCray v. Illinois*,[20] defendant's right of cross-examination at the suppression hearing may be substantially narrower than that available at trial. *McCray* held that neither due process nor the confrontation clause was violated when the suppression hearing judge refused to allow defense counsel to force the arresting officer, on cross-examination, to reveal the name and address of the informant alleged to have provided probable cause for defendant's arrest. Lower courts similarly have held that the combination of the limited function of the suppression hearing and valid security interests justify receiving certain prosecution evidence in camera (i.e., with the defendant excluded). Courts have stressed, however, that limitations on the opportunity for confrontation must be carefully circumscribed to fit the state's justification for restricted disclosure. And while the court may restrict cross-examination by defense counsel to avoid manipulation of the suppression hearing for discovery purposes, it may not cut off questioning that clearly is relevant to the defense challenge.

(f) Right of Compulsory Process. The constitutional right of compulsory process is essentially a trial right[21]; when the defendant's guilt or innocence is at issue, due process requires that the accused be able to present witnesses in his own defense "to the jury so it may decide where the truth lies."[22] But this right, albeit a "fundamental" one,[23] is not absolute, and thus it may yield to policy considerations such as the interest in the orderly conduct of trials.[24] Whatever lesser right of compulsory process exists at suppression hearings is likewise not absolute, and thus may be outweighed by various policy concerns. Thus, where there is other evidence of probable cause to arrest, the defendant may not call the undercover officer to testify about defendant's drug sale in his presence when such testimony might compromise the undercover officer's safety or the integrity of pending investiga-

17. 415 U.S. 164, 94 S.Ct. 988, 39 L.Ed.2d 242 (1974).

18. Brinegar v. United States, 338 U.S. 160, 69 S.Ct. 1302, 93 L.Ed. 1879 (1949).

19. Fed.R.Evid. 104(a).

20. 386 U.S. 300, 87 S.Ct. 1056, 18 L.Ed.2d 62 (1967).

21. Chambers v. Mississippi, 410 U.S. 284, 93 S.Ct. 1038, 35 L.Ed.2d 297 (1973); Webb v. Texas, 409 U.S. 95, 93 S.Ct. 351, 34 L.Ed.2d 330 (1972).

22. Washington v. Texas, 388 U.S. 14, 87 S.Ct. 1920, 18 L.Ed.2d 1019 (1967).

23. Chambers v. Mississippi, 410 U.S. 284, 93 S.Ct. 1038, 35 L.Ed.2d 297 (1973).

24. Taylor v. Illinois, 484 U.S. 400, 108 S.Ct. 646, 98 L.Ed.2d 798 (1988).

tions. And similarly, at a suppression hearing that has not otherwise produced evidence raising "substantial issues as to the credibility of the lineup," the interest in protecting complainants against harassment has been deemed sufficient to bar the defendant from calling the complainant to inquire about any suggestive actions by the police.

Of course, the right to compulsory process is contingent upon a defense right to present evidence, and a court may conclude under some circumstances, that the receipt of defense evidence is not necessary. That is most likely to occur where the court concludes that even if one accepts the facts alleged in the defense motion and accompanying affidavits, the facts alleged provide no basis for relief. At times, a court also will hold that an evidentiary hearing is not required in light of counter-affidavits filed by the prosecution. This is acceptable where the court concludes that there is no significant dispute between the parties as to the relevant facts, but not where its decision rests on a resolution of disputed fact by reference to the conflicting affidavits.

§ 10.6   The Ruling and Its Effect

(a) Findings. In some jurisdictions the judge ruling on a motion to suppress is required to make specific findings of fact and law, while elsewhere formal findings are not required and it will suffice that a record is made supporting the ruling. In *Sims v. Georgia*,[1] the Supreme Court noted that the due process requirements of *Jackson v. Denno*[2] did not mandate that the judge "make formal findings of fact or write an opinion," though "his conclusion that the confession is voluntary must appear from the record with unmistakable clarity." Appellate courts, however, have urged trial judges to make findings because in their absence appellate review is often more difficult. Indeed, it has been said that findings are all but essential in multi-issue cases where the basis of the trial judge's decision would otherwise be in doubt.

If a defendant puts forward several alternative grounds for suppression, may a judge ruling in his favor on one of them not inquire into the others? There are competing considerations. On the one hand, it would seem superfluous to inquire into the other grounds after a basis for suppression has already been found; on the other, failure to consider the remaining grounds is at odds with the goal of pretrial determination of all such issues. The judge is thus left with considerable discretion in deciding whether judicial economy would best be served by conducting a full hearing on all the grounds urged or by bifurcating the issues. The desirable course of action will depend on a variety of factors, including the number of grounds for the motion to suppress, the number of witnesses expected to be called in support of each ground, and the extent to which the evidence on the first ground pertains to the other grounds.

(b) Recommendations. It is sometimes provided by law that a motion to suppress may be heard by a lesser judicial officer than the judge who has the ultimate responsibility for deciding the matter. Such is the case in the federal system, and in *United States v. Raddatz*[3] the Supreme Court had occasion to assess the respective responsibilities of the hearing magistrate and the district judge. Prior to trial, Raddatz moved to suppress his incriminating statements, and the judge referred the matter to a magistrate for an evidentiary hearing. This was done pursuant to the Federal Magistrates Act, which authorizes a district court to refer such a motion to a magistrate and thereafter to decide the motion based on the record developed before the magistrate, including the magistrate's proposed findings of fact and recommendations, and which also provides that the judge shall make a "de novo determination" of those portions of the magistrate's report, findings or recommendations to which objection is made, and that the judge may accept, reject or modify, in whole or in part, the magistrate's findings or recommendations and that alternatively the judge may

---

§ 10.6

1. 385 U.S. 538, 87 S.Ct. 639, 17 L.Ed.2d 593 (1967).

2. 378 U.S. 368, 84 S.Ct. 1774, 12 L.Ed.2d 908 (1964).

3. 447 U.S. 667, 100 S.Ct. 2406, 65 L.Ed.2d 424 (1980).

receive further evidence or recommit the matter to the magistrate with instructions.[4] Based on his view of the credibility of the testimony, the magistrate found the statements voluntary and thus recommended the motion be denied. The district court accepted that recommendation over defendant's objection, but the court of appeals reversed on the ground Raddatz had been deprived of due process by the district court's failure personally to hear the controverted testimony.

After finding that the statute, by calling for a "de novo determination" rather than a de novo hearing, did not require the district court to rehear the testimony,[5] the Court concluded "that the statute strikes the proper balance between the demands of due process and the constraints of Art. III." As for the Article III question, the *Raddatz* Court concluded that because "the entire process takes place under the district court's total control and jurisdiction," the "delegation does not violate Art. III so long as the ultimate decision is made by the district court." On the due process issue, the Court, after noting that "the guarantees of due process call for a 'hearing appropriate to the nature of the case,'" concluded that "the nature of the issues presented and the interests implicated in a motion to suppress evidence" do not "require that the district court judge must actually hear the challenged testimony." This is because the interests underlying such a hearing "do not coincide with the criminal law objective of determining guilt or innocence."[6]

But there are limits on what the district judge may do with respect to the magistrate's findings and recommendations. It would be a rare case in which a district judge could resolve credibility choices contrary to the recommendations of the magistrate without himself having had an opportunity to see and hear the witnesses testify. And even if matters of credibility are not central to decision of the suppression motion, the district judge may not reject the recommendation of the magistrate without *at least* consulting the transcript of the hearing before the magistrate.

(c) Reconsideration at Trial. Except in those jurisdictions that actually require renewal of a suppression motion at trial,[7] reconsideration at trial of a motion previously denied is a disfavored procedure. Such reconsideration, it is said, defeats the benefits of pretrial motion practice and unfairly imposes upon the prosecution the obligation of proving legality twice. Thus, the trial judge will usually rely upon the prior ruling as the law of the case. However, the law of the case doctrine operates only as a discretionary rule of practice, for to view the pretrial ruling as binding would be to proscribe correction of its own error by the trial court.

A defendant is not likely to obtain reconsideration unless at trial new or additional evidence is produced bearing on the issue or substantially affecting the credibility of the evidence adduced at the pretrial hearing of the motion. The state cases in the main treat such a situation as one in which the court *may* reconsider, while federal cases commonly speak of a *duty* to reconsider where matters appearing at trial cast reasonable doubt on the pretrial ruling. But in light of the fact that a constitutional objection is deemed forfeited absent a showing of good cause for not complying with a pretrial motion rule,[8] it would seem that a defendant is entitled to a redetermination of his claim at trial only if new evidence comes to light that was unavailable at the time of the original hearing on the motion through no fault of the movant.

There is some authority that if defendant's pretrial suppression motion was granted, the

---

4. 28 U.S.C.A. § 636(b)(1).

5. By comparison, in some jurisdictions a full de novo hearing may be provided, as where, following conviction by a lower court, the defendant is by law given a right to a trial de novo that is construed to include relitigation of the suppression issue. But a trial de novo system need not inevitably contain this feature.

6. There were four dissenters. Three of them concluded "that the statute itself required a hearing before the Judge in this case," while three were of the view that due process required a hearing "only in situations in which the case turns on issues of credibility that cannot be resolved on the basis of a record."

7. See § 10.2(b).

8. See § 10.2(a).

prosecution may obtain a reconsideration of that ruling at trial under essentially the same circumstances in which reconsideration would be permitted in the defendant's behalf: where there is new relevant evidence available and good cause is shown as to why that evidence was not introduced at the pretrial hearing. But, while the doctrines of res judicata and collateral estoppel do not bar such reconsideration, the prosecution will not often be able to show cause for reconsideration because it is more able than the defendant to insure a full and fair resolution of any issue at a pretrial proceeding. In jurisdictions where the prosecutor may take an interlocutory appeal from the pretrial granting of a suppression motion, reconsideration at trial may well be barred as to matters that could have been raised by appeal. But there are differences between appellate review and reappraisal of a pretrial ruling at trial, and thus it cannot be said that the availability of interlocutory appeal bars any reconsideration.

(d) Effect of Ruling in Other Cases. If defendant's motion to suppress was granted but the prosecution later seeks to have the same evidence admitted against the defendant at a trial on a different charge, is relitigation of the admissibility issue barred? As a constitutional matter, an argument that the collateral estoppel doctrine of the double jeopardy clause bars relitigation cannot prevail if the charges were dropped in the first case, as then defendant was never placed in jeopardy. But it has been argued that in such circumstances the defendant might prevail because of collateral estoppel protections flowing from the due process clause. Whether the collateral estoppel doctrine has any application here remains in doubt, but if it does apply surely it is necessary that in the first case the state has had an opportunity for a full hearing on suppression and at least one appeal as of right.

Even if the Constitution, either as a general matter or in particular circumstances, does not require that the prosecution be bound by the granting of a suppression motion in another case, it is possible that the law of the jurisdiction will have this effect. This may occur, for example, where a statute declares that if a suppression motion is granted the evidence shall not be admissible "at any trial." In the absence of such law, the judge in the second case might nonetheless not reconsider the matter if he is convinced it was fully explored in the earlier case.

Assume now the reverse situation in which the motion was denied in an earlier case. Though the constitutional doctrine of collateral estoppel regarding a prior verdict in a criminal case does not run both ways,[9] that does not prevent a state from adopting the position that collateral estoppel principles preclude a defendant from obtaining suppression of evidence he unsuccessfully tried to suppress in an earlier case. But even when the earlier denial of the defendants suppression motion does not have such preclusive effect, the judge in the second case may nonetheless accept the admissibility ruling in the earlier case, absent a showing of new evidence or some other basis for reconsideration, provided that the defendant was convicted at the first trial and thus had an opportunity to obtain appellate review of the ruling.

For a ruling on a motion to suppress in a prior case to have either conclusive or presumptive effect in a later case, there must be an identity of parties. Thus, notwithstanding prior suppression by a state court, a federal court may make an independent determination as to admissibility. And if the same evidence is offered in the separate trials of two defendants in the same jurisdiction, the ruling in the first of these cases is not binding in the second.

---

9. Simpson v. Florida, 403 U.S. 384, 91 S.Ct. 1801, 29 L.Ed.2d 549 (1971).

Part Three

THE COMMENCEMENT OF FORMAL PROCEEDINGS

Chapter 11

THE RIGHT TO COUNSEL

Table of Sections

---

§ 11.1   The Constitutional Rights to Retained and Appointed Counsel

(a) Sixth Amendment Rights. The Sixth Amendment provides that "in all criminal prosecutions, the accused shall enjoy the right * * * to have the assistance of counsel for his defense." That this provision guaranteed a right to representation by privately retained counsel was obvious from the outset; that it also included an obligation of the state to provide at public expense defense counsel for the indigent defendant (i.e., the defendant financially unable to retain a lawyer) was far less certain. Unlike the right to retained counsel, a right to appointed counsel lacked any substantial historical grounding. Nonetheless, the Court eventually came to interpret the Sixth Amendment as granting a right to representation by counsel to all defendants, with the state required to provide counsel where the defendant was indigent. Moreover, that Supreme Court precedent also indicated that the proceedings reached by the Sixth Amendment right to counsel were to be precisely the same whether the issue was allowing representation by retained counsel or requiring the state to appoint counsel for the indigent. Indeed, it appears that, as to all basic issues of interpretation (e.g., what constitutes a "criminal prosecution," when is a person an "accused," and what "assistance" is required of counsel), there is but a single Sixth Amendment right to counsel, encompassing both retained and appointed counsel.

The first major Supreme Court discussion of the constitutional right to counsel came in *Powell v. Alabama*,[1] a 1932 ruling that considered the rights of defendants both to utilize retained counsel and to be provided with court appointed counsel. *Powell* was not itself a Sixth Amendment case. It involved a state prosecution and was decided under the then prevailing "fundamental fairness" interpretation of Fourteenth Amendment due process. Nonetheless, it has had continuing significance in the interpretation of the Sixth Amendment. When the Court later discarded the fundamental fairness interpretation in favor of a selective incorporation analysis that made the Sixth Amendment directly applicable to the states (through the Fourteenth Amendment), its interpretation of the Sixth Amendment rested heavily upon an analysis of the need for counsel first suggested by Justice Sutherland in his landmark opinion for the Court in *Powell*.

The Supreme Court had before it in *Powell* a prosecution that was to become a cause celebre in the fight against racial injustice. Nine black youths had been charged with the rape of two white girls in the vicinity of Scottsboro, Alabama. Eight of the youths had been convicted, with the jury imposing the death sentence. On appeal, the defendants raised several constitutional claims, including two relating to a right to counsel. First, they claimed that they had a

§ 11.1
1. 287 U.S. 45, 53 S.Ct. 55, 77 L.Ed. 158 (1932).

constitutional right to retain counsel to represent them at trial and that the trial court had violated this right by failing to give them sufficient opportunity to seek retained counsel. Second, they claimed that, assuming arguendo that they would have been unable to employ counsel even if they had been given that opportunity, the trial court would then have had an obligation to make an effective appointment of counsel. The trial judge at their arraignment had announced that he was appointing "all of the members of the bar" to represent them, but defendants argued that this had been an empty gesture, made in such a haphazard way that the local bar member who eventually stepped forward to represent them at trial (in consultation with an outside attorney) was largely unprepared. The Supreme Court sustained both of defendant's claims, finding that each separately established a denial of due process.

The *Powell* opinion initially considered the trial court's failure to give defendants an adequate opportunity to retain counsel. The opinion concluded that the due process clause of the Fourteenth Amendment guaranteed to defendants a right to be represented by retained counsel, and to implement that right, a trial court must give the defendant reasonable time and opportunity to secure counsel. Justice Sutherland here relied heavily upon the historical developments that had led to the adoption of the Sixth Amendment and similarly worded state provisions. The practice in England had been to allow the complete assistance of retained counsel in misdemeanor trials, but to deny defendants the right to utilize their counsel at felony trials, except for arguments on legal questions. This limitation had not been accepted in the American colonies, where defendants were allowed the full assistance of retained counsel in felony as well as misdemeanor trials. At the time of the adoption of the Constitution, twelve of the thirteen states had rejected the English rule on felony cases, and the Sixth Amendment, not surprisingly, did the same. Justice Sutherland concluded that the right to utilize retained counsel, as reflected in these state and federal provisions, readily fit within the concept of due process.

For due process guaranteed a right to a fair hearing, and such a hearing, "[h]istorically and in practice, in our country at least, has always included the right to the aid of counsel when desired and provided by the party asserting the right."

When the *Powell* opinion turned to the defendants' second claim, asserting an indigent defendant's right to appointed counsel, it did not look to the history underlying the Sixth Amendment or to the early state provisions. This was understandable since the right of the indigent defendant to counsel provided by the state had a much narrower historical base. Where the original states provided for the appointment of counsel, they usually did so only in capital cases. Similarly, Congress, shortly before the ratification of the Sixth Amendment, had adopted a statutory provision requiring an appointment of counsel that was limited to capital crimes. Indeed, at the time of the *Powell* decision, almost half of the states apparently did not provide appointed counsel in most felony cases.

A constitutional right to appointed counsel could be derived, however, if not from historical traditions, from the due process right to a fair hearing. In concluding that the right to retained counsel was an essential element of due process, the first portion of the *Powell* opinion had stressed that the "right to be heard would be, in many cases, of little avail if it did not comprehend the right to be heard by counsel." The indigent defendant, Justice Sutherland reasoned, was as much entitled to a fair hearing as the more affluent defendant who could afford to retain a lawyer. The state accordingly had a due process obligation to provide the indigent defendant with a lawyer where counsel's assistance would be necessary to achieve a fair hearing. Language in the first portion of the opinion might have suggested that a lawyer would almost always be needed to provide a fair hearing. Even the "intelligent and educated layman," Justice Sutherland had noted, needs the "guiding hand of counsel" to cope with the intricacies of the law. The Court's holding on appointed counsel, however, was carefully limited to the type of situation presented in the case before the Court—

"a capital case, where the defendant is unable to employ counsel, and is incapable adequately of making his own defense because of ignorance, feeble-mindedness, illiteracy, or the like."

The *Powell* reasoning suggested that there were two distinct and separately grounded constitutional rights to counsel. First, as a result of the rejection of the English common law rule, the defendant had gained a right to be represented by counsel provided at his own expense. Whether or not a lawyer was needed in the particular case did not matter; that was for the defendant to decide, and the state had to respect his decision, as only his resources were involved. Second, a constitutional right to appointed counsel arose out of the state's obligation to provide a fair hearing. That obligation carried with it an affirmative duty to provide counsel for the indigent defendant where a lawyer's assistance was needed to ensure a fair and accurate guilt-determining process. This right arguably was narrower in scope than the right to retained counsel. Since public funds were being expended, the provision of counsel could be tied to cases where it was actually needed. Thus, the *Powell* ruling on appointed counsel had been restricted to the special circumstances of that case, while its ruling on the right to use retained counsel had spoken of a general right applicable in all felony cases.

Six years after *Powell,* in a federal case, the Supreme Court ruled that the right to appointed counsel, as well as the right to retained counsel, was to be found in the Sixth Amendment. Indeed, Justice Black's opinion for the Court in that case, *Johnson v. Zerbst,*[2] drew no distinction between the two rights. *Johnson* involved a federal prosecution in which two apparently indigent defendants, charged with the felony of counterfeiting, had been refused appointed counsel because theirs was not a capital case. Justice Black held that their trial without counsel violated the Sixth Amendment, which applies by its terms to "all criminal prosecutions." The Sixth Amendment, he noted, "embodies a realistic recognition of the

obvious truth that the average defendant does not have the professional legal skill to protect himself" in a criminal trial. It therefore "withholds from the federal courts, in all criminal proceedings, the power and authority to deprive an accused of his life or liberty unless he has or waives the assistance of counsel." This constitutional prerequisite for a valid conviction applied to all defendants, including those unable to afford counsel.

The *Johnson* opinion did not refer to the historical developments that had been cited in *Powell v. Alabama.* It focused instead upon the language in *Powell* noting that the right to be heard often would be of little value without the assistance of counsel. That language was seen as supporting a reading of the Sixth Amendment that treated representation by counsel as a prescribed prerequisite for the criminal trial, no different than the elements of jury trial, notice, confrontation, and compulsory process. It was the trial court's obligation to ensure that these rights were available to defendant (although, as to the right to counsel, that did not preclude making the defendant bear the financial cost if he was able to do so). If the assistance of counsel otherwise would be unavailable because the defendant lacked funds to retain counsel, then the court had to make that assistance available by appointing counsel. The only exception was when the indigent defendant knowingly and intelligently waived his Sixth Amendment right to appointed counsel.

For a twenty-five year period following *Johnson,* the Supreme Court refused to extend that ruling to state cases. Although *Johnson* had held that the Sixth Amendment required appointed counsel in all cases encompassed by that Amendment, state cases were governed by the "less rigid and more fluid" requirement of the Fourteenth Amendment's due process clause. Relying upon a fundamental fairness analysis, the Court held in *Betts v. Brady*[3] that due process required the appointment of counsel only where the special circumstances of the particular case indicated that the indigent de-

---

2.   304 U.S. 458, 58 S.Ct. 1019, 82 L.Ed. 1461 (1938).

3.   316 U.S. 455, 62 S.Ct. 1252, 86 L.Ed. 1595 (1942). See § 2.4(e).

fendant needed a lawyer to obtain a fair trial. *Powell v. Alabama* and other capital cases presented one illustration of such special circumstances. The need for appointed counsel could also be established by the complicated nature of the offense or possible defenses thereto, events during trial that raised difficult legal questions, and personal characteristics of the defendant, such as youthfulness or mental incapacity. The special circumstances test of *Betts v. Brady* was sharply criticized by commentators, who argued that it was virtually impossible to render a retrospective judgment that a defendant forced to proceed pro se had not been prejudiced by the lack of counsel.

In 1963, in *Gideon v. Wainwright*,[4] the Court rejected the special circumstances rule of *Betts* and extended the right to appointed counsel in state cases to all indigent felony defendants. Unlike *Betts, Gideon* proceeded from the premise, consistent with the selective incorporation doctrine, that the Fourteenth Amendment rendered the Sixth Amendment right to counsel directly applicable to the states as a fundamental right. However, *Gideon* did not reject the *Betts* standard on the ground that the Sixth Amendment imposed a generalized mandate and therefore had a more extensive reach than the case-by-case approach of fundamental fairness. Justice Black, who had dissented in *Betts,* wrote for the Court in *Gideon,* and he stressed that *Betts* had erred in its fundamental fairness analysis by assuming that representation by counsel was not invariably "essential to a fair trial." Relying upon *Powell's* discussion of the value of counsel, Justice Black noted that "reason and reflection require us to recognize that in our adversary system of criminal justice, any person hauled into court, who is too poor to hire a lawyer cannot be assured a fair trial unless counsel is provided for him." The "obvious truth" of this conclusion was evidenced by common experience: "Lawyers to prosecute are everywhere deemed essential * * * [and] there are few defendants * * * who fail to hire the best lawyers they can get to prepare and present their defenses."

Gideon, like *Johnson v. Zerbst*, viewed the Sixth Amendment as prescribing the invariable prerequisites of a fair trial and including the assistance of counsel among those prerequisites.[5] It follows from this premise that no Sixth Amendment distinction should exist between the indigent and affluent defendant as to their basic right to be represented by counsel; both obviously are entitled to a fair hearing. Where a particular proceeding is deemed to be a stage in the "criminal prosecution" for Sixth Amendment purposes, both should have an automatic right to representation by counsel (in the case of the indigent, at state expense). On the other hand, where the proceeding is not within the span covered by the Sixth Amendment's reference to the "criminal prosecution," neither should have a Sixth Amendment right to counsel. Whether a Sixth Amendment right to counsel exists should depend on the nature of the proceeding and not on whether the claim relates to retained or appointed counsel.

Support for such equivalency is found in a series of post-*Gideon* decisions. Initially, there are the cases [discussed in § 11.2(b)] considering whether particular proceedings fall within the coverage of the Sixth Amendment. All involved the denial of appointed counsel for an indigent claimant, but the opinions at no point

---

4. 372 U.S. 335, 83 S.Ct. 792, 9 L.Ed.2d 799 (1963).

5. In a concurring opinion in *Gideon,* Justice Harlan argued that Supreme Court decisions applying the *Betts* special circumstances rule had found such a broad range of circumstances to require the appointment of counsel that the special circumstances limitation had become meaningless; retention of a case-by-case analysis had only led the state courts astray, and it would be to their benefit to adopt a flat requirement that appointed counsel be made available for all "serious criminal charges." Adopting a similar view of the justification for *Gideon's* automatic requirement of appointment of counsel, Justice Powell later described that requirement as "prophylactic"

in nature and created by the Court to ensure that counsel was available where needed to obtain a fair trial. Several later cases, in characterizing the denial of counsel "as presumptively prejudicial," have suggested that the Sixth Amendment itself has this administratively based bright-line quality. The Sixth Amendment, under this view, imposed a flat requirement in recognition both that the denial of counsel's assistance has an "inherently indeterminate" impact and that there exists a substantial likelihood (though hardly a certainty) that a defendant will need counsel to gain a fair adjudication in an adversary process.

suggested that a greater range of proceedings would be subject to the Sixth Amendment were the claim to relate to the assistance of retained counsel. Those cases holding that the Sixth Amendment right to appointed counsel did not apply looked solely to the character of the proceeding—the proceeding either was not part of a "criminal prosecution" or did not present a "critical stage" of the criminal prosecution—which remains the same whether the counsel sought is appointed or retained. So too, in a series of cases discussed in § 11.7(a), the Court did not distinguish between retained and appointed counsel in holding that counsel's ineffective performance did not present a constitutional claim where the proceeding was one as to which an indigent defendant has no constitutional right to appointed counsel.

The end result under this view of the Amendment is that the state has no Sixth Amendment obligation to allow representation by retained counsel in a proceeding as to which it has no Sixth Amendment obligation to appoint counsel for the indigent. It does not necessarily follow, however, that the state has absolute freedom constitutionally to bar representation by retained counsel. As will be seen in the next subsection, due process can provide a constitutional grounding for assistance of counsel where the Sixth Amendment does not apply, and that right may preclude an unreasonable state interference with representation by retained counsel even where there is no constitutional right to appointed counsel.

(b) Due Process Rights. *Powell v. Alabama* recognized due process rights to the assistance of appointed and retained counsel, and while *Powell* recognized those rights in the context of a proceeding that today would be subject to the Sixth Amendment, the concept of a right to counsel grounded on due process has continuing significance for other proceedings not encompassed by the Sixth Amendment. The two leading post-incorporation cases recognizing such a right in the context of the criminal justice process are *Gagnon v. Scarpelli*[6] and *Evitts v. Lucey*.[7] Both involved proceedings not part of the criminal

prosecution itself and therefore not within the Sixth Amendment. *Gagnon* dealt with parole and probation revocation proceedings, and *Evitts* dealt with a first-level appeal granted as a matter of right. In contrast to *Gagnon* and *Evitts*, the Court in a series of other cases (also discussed below), has rejected claims of a due process right to counsel at two other stages of the criminal justice process not within the Sixth Amendment—the application for discretionary, second-tier appellate review and the application for collateral relief.

In *Gagnon,* a due process right to appointed counsel was thought to flow logically from hearing rights that had been mandated previously under the due process clause. Past precedent had established that the parolee or probationer was entitled to substantial procedural safeguards in a revocation hearing, including the rights to present evidence and confront opposing witnesses. *Gagnon* concluded that due process also requires the state to provide appointed counsel where, under the facts of the particular case, counsel is needed to ensure the "effectiveness of the [hearing] rights guaranteed by [due process]." The *Gagnon* Court refused to formulate "a precise and detailed set of guidelines" for determining when counsel was needed to ensure the effective operation of the hearing rights demanded by due process. It did note that counsel ordinarily should be provided where there is a significant factual dispute or the individual relies upon contentions that a layman would have difficulty presenting. At the same time, it cited other situations in which appointment of counsel ordinarily would not be necessary.

Speaking to the possibility of imposing a flat requirement of counsel in all revocation cases, the *Gagnon* Court acknowledged that such a requirement "had the appeal of simplicity." However, "it would impose direct costs and serious collateral disadvantages without regard to the need or the likelihood in a particular case for a constructive contribution by counsel." In most revocation cases, the issue presented simply did not require that expertise of a lawyer. Quite often, "the probationer or

---

6.   411 U.S. 778, 93 S.Ct. 1756, 36 L.Ed.2d 656 (1973).

7.   469 U.S. 387, 105 S.Ct. 830, 83 L.Ed.2d 821 (1985).

parolee has been convicted of committing another crime [which automatically establishes grounds for revocation] or has admitted the charges against him." Although he may still contend that revocation would be too harsh in light of the nature of his violation, "mitigating evidence of this kind is often not susceptible of proof or is so simple as not to require either investigation or exposition by counsel." On the other side, "the introduction of counsel" would "alter significantly the nature of the [revocation] proceeding." The state would respond by retaining its own counsel and the role of the hearing body would become "more akin to that of a judge at trial, and less attuned to the rehabilitative needs of the individual probationer." In addition, the revocation proceedings would be prolonged, and "the financial cost to the State—for appointed counsel, counsel for the State, a longer record and the possibility of judicial review—[would] not be insubstantial."

In contrast to *Gagnon*, which adopted a case-by-case approach similar to that of *Betts*,[8] *Evitts v. Lucey*[9] established a flat right to counsel, following under due process the approach taken in *Gideon* under the Sixth Amendment. At issue in *Evitts* was a due process right to representation by retained counsel, but the Court's ruling extended to both retained and appointed counsel. Prior to *Evitts*, in *Douglas v. California*,[10] the Court had recognized an equal protection right of an indigent defendant to the assistance of appointed counsel on a first appeal granted by state law as a matter of right. *Evitts* held the *Douglas* ruling also had a constitutional grounding in due process and that grounding necessarily established as well a right to be represented by retained counsel. Moreover, the due process right, as indicated in *Douglas*, was not dependant upon the special circumstances of the case, but extended to all first appeals granted of right.

In *Evitts*, unlike *Gagnon*, the Court had not previously set forth a particular due process structure for the proceeding at issue. Indeed, the Court had held that the Constitution imposed no obligation upon a state to grant appeals of right in criminal cases.[11] However, once the state had created such a procedure as " 'an integral part of [its] system for finally adjudicating the guilt or innocence of a defendant,' " it could not, consistent with due process, first structure that procedure so that it was basically a "meaningless ritual" for a defendant lacking the assistance of counsel and then fail to include a right to utilize counsel's assistance. Drawing an analogy to *Gideon*, the Court noted that under a state's appellate procedure, as under its trial procedure, "the services of a lawyer will for virtually every layman be necessary" to effectively present his case. Here too, the defendant faced an "adversarial system of justice" in which "lawyers are 'necessities,' not luxuries." Accordingly, due process, as to the first appeal of right, mandated a right to counsel parallel to the trial-level right established in *Gideon* under the Sixth Amendment.

The imposition of a flat requirement in *Evitts* can be explained on several grounds. The Court indicated that the appellate process was so complicated that here a lawyer always was needed to ensure the appeal was not simply a "meaningless ritual." In this respect the setting was similar to the trial setting presented in *Gideon* where the Court also had rejected applying a case-by-case analysis to determine when counsel was needed. Also, the costs of a flat rule here, in contrast to *Gagnon*, were insubstantial. With *Douglas* already requiring appointed counsel in all first appeals as a matter of right, recognizing a due process right to retained counsel imposed no additional financial burden on the state. As for administrative burdens, recognizing a constitutional right to utilize retained counsel certainly did not alter the character of the proceeding except to allow incompetency challenges by defendants, and as the *Evitts* Court noted, both state courts and lower federal courts had long recognized and adjudicated such claims without "dire consequences." Thus, *Evitts* is readily distinguishable from *Gagnon* and the two

---

8.   See note 3 supra.

9.   See note 7 supra.

10.   See note 24 infra.

11.   See § 27.1(a).

cases, standing alone, could offer significant guideposts on the choice between a case-by-case approach and a flat right to counsel in the application of due process analysis. However, other Supreme Court rulings, rejecting due process claims, introduce additional considerations making that choice far less predictable.

Although the *Evitts* opinion drew an analogy to *Gideon,* the Court in its earlier ruling in *Ross v. Moffitt*[12] had stressed that due process analysis places the convicted defendant seeking appellate review in a quite different position than the defendant who is an "accused" at trial. The defendant at trial has need for an attorney "as a shield to protect him against being 'haled into court' by the State and stripped of his presumption of innocence." On appeal, in contrast, the attorney is to be utilized "as a sword to upset [a] prior determination of guilt." The defendant here is "seeking not to fend off the efforts of the State's prosecutor but rather to overturn a finding of guilt made by a judge or jury below." As one of the factors to be considered under a due process analysis is the "risk of an erroneous deprivation" of the protected liberty interest without the claimed procedural safeguard, a defendant stands in a lesser position when he claims a right to appointed counsel following a conviction at trial. That lesser position, the Court noted in *Ross,* follows from the difference in the constitutional status of the trial and the appeal. "For, while no one would agree that the State may simply dispense with the trial stage of proceedings without a criminal defendant's consent, it is clear that the State need not provide any appeal at all."

As the *Evitts* holding indicates, the defendant's lesser position in a proceeding that challenges a conviction does not necessarily preclude recognition of a due process right to counsel in that proceeding. Indeed, as in *Evitts,* such a due process right can exist without reference to the special needs of the particular defendant. However, as *Ross* indicates, the Court will examine carefully the nature of the particular proceeding, considering both the role that counsel would play and the impor-

tance of the proceeding in protecting against an erroneous deprivation of the liberty interest at stake. Based on those factors, *Ross* and its progeny, as discussed below, concluded that the due process right to counsel does not extend to the preparation of petitions for discretionary appellate review that comes after the first appeal of right or to petitions for collateral challenges that follow the exhaustion of appellate review.

Ross rejected the contention that due process required appointment of counsel to assist indigent defendants in preparing their applications for second-tier, discretionary appellate review. The Court stressed that the defendants in this setting have already received a full appellate review, assisted by counsel, on their first appeal as of right. Accordingly, further assistance of counsel is not necessary to provide "meaningful access" to the higher appellate courts. In considering a defendant's petition for review, those higher courts will have before them the trial transcript, the intermediate court brief prepared by counsel, and in most instances, the opinion of the state's intermediate appellate court. Those materials, supplemented by any personal statement of the defendant, provide an "adequate basis" for determining whether to grant review. This is especially so because of the discretionary nature of the second-tier appellate review. The traditional standard utilized in determining whether to grant such discretionary review is whether the appeal presents issues worthy of high court consideration because of their general legal significance, rather than whether there has been a "correct adjudication of guilt" in the individual.

In *Pennsylvania v. Finley,*[13] the majority characterized the issue before it as whether due process required the state to appoint counsel to assist the respondent in preparing a collateral attack upon her conviction under a state postconviction relief procedure. The state there had appointed counsel, but counsel had then been allowed to withdraw after concluding that the collateral attack lacked arguable

12.   417 U.S. 600, 94 S.Ct. 2437, 41 L.Ed.2d 341 (1974). See also note 28 infra.

13.   481 U.S. 551, 107 S.Ct. 1990, 95 L.Ed.2d 539 (1987).

merit. The Court majority reasoned that the withdrawal procedure would present a constitutional issue only if respondent had an underlying constitutional right to the appointment of counsel (a position rejected by the dissenters). Turning to that question, the Court did not focus on the possible need for counsel. Arguably, a stronger case could be made here than in *Ross,* as collateral challenges in state proceedings commonly present issues that were not raised at trial or on appeal. The *Finley* Court stressed, instead, the place of the collateral attack within the totality of the proceedings for determining guilt. The majority noted that "postconviction relief is even further removed from the criminal trial than is discretionary direct review," is not "part of the criminal proceedings itself," and "normally occurs only after the defendant has failed to secure relief through direct review of his conviction." In such a setting, the Court concluded, "the fundamental fairness mandated by the Due Process Clause does not require that the State supply a lawyer as well."

In *Murray v. Giarratano,*[14] a later collateral relief case, the Court again rejected a due process claim to appointed counsel. *Murray,* however, was not simply a straightforward application of *Finley.* It raised a significant issue as to the level of generality at which a due process claim should be assessed, and produced a split within the Court that left that issue largely unresolved. At issue in *Murray* was the claim of Virginia's death row inmates that they were entitled to appointed counsel to assist them in preparing collateral attack challenges to their convictions and sentences. In upholding that claim, the Fourth Circuit had viewed the inmates' situation as presenting special circumstances that distinguished *Finley.* First, here, unlike *Finley,* the inmates had been sentenced to the death penalty. The Supreme Court had frequently noted that, the finality of the death penalty requires that its imposition be supported by a "greater degree of reliability," and to provide that assurance, it had insisted upon special procedural safeguards in death penalty cases. Second, the district court here had made special factual

findings as to the inmates' need for counsel. That court had concluded "that death row inmates had a limited amount of time to prepare their petitions, that their cases were unusually complex, and that the shadow of impending execution would interfere with their ability to do legal work." While the state did assign "unit attorneys" to each penal institution, the district court had also found that those attorneys could not adequately assist the death row inmates because their role was limited to that of "legal advisor" rather than counsel for the inmate. Those district court findings were seen as providing a case-specific showing of the essentiality of counsel that had not been present in *Finley.*

Speaking for four justices, Chief Justice Rehnquist authored a plurality opinion that flatly rejected both of the distinctions cited by the lower court. While the special quality of the death penalty had been recognized, under both the Eighth Amendment and the due process clause, as requiring additional procedural safeguards, that concern had not been carried beyond the "trial stage of capital adjudication." On both appeal and collateral attack, the Court had refused in various cases to impose special standards for review of capital cases. The reasoning of such rulings "require[d] the conclusion that the rule of *Pennsylvania v. Finley* should apply no differently in capital cases than in noncapital cases." Chief Justice Rehnquist also rejected any attempt to distinguish *Finley* on the basis of case-specific factual findings such as were made here by the district court. To rely upon such findings "would permit a different constitutional rule to apply in a different State if the district court hearing that claim reached different conclusions." The Court's post-*Gideon* rulings on the right to counsel "ha[d] been categorical holdings as to what the Constitution requires with respect to a particular stage of a criminal proceeding in general." This "tack" had been adopted in light of past experience. As the dissenters acknowledged, it had been "the Court's dissatisfaction with the case-by-case approach in *Betts v. Brady* that

---

14. 492 U.S. 1, 109 S.Ct. 2765, 106 L.Ed.2d 1 (1989).

led to the adoption of the categorical ruling * * * in *Gideon.*" There was nothing in the nature of the collateral proceeding that justified departure from the continued use of categorical holdings.

Also speaking for four justices, Justice Stevens' dissenting opinion argued that "particular circumstances" necessarily shape the scope of the due process right to counsel. The dissenters concluded that the circumstances cited by the lower court, as well as additional circumstances, clearly distinguished *Finley.* The "unique nature" of the death penalty had been recognized as shaping due process requirements as far back as *Powell,* which had established an automatic right to appointment of counsel in capital cases while a case-by-case approach was utilized for other felony defendants. The special needs of capital cases necessarily carried over to collateral relief in light of "significant evidence that in capital cases what is ordinarily considered direct review does not sufficiently safeguard against miscarriages of justice." While "federal habeas courts granted relief in only 0.25% to 7% of noncapital cases in recent years," the "success rate in capital cases ranged from 60% to 70%." The district court's findings bolstered this conclusion by establishing the inability of death row inmates to prepare their own petitions. Further support was found in the character of collateral review as applied here: "In contrast to the collateral process discussed in *Finley,* Virginia law contemplate[d] that some claims ordinarily heard on direct review [e.g., incompetency of counsel] will be relegated to postconviction proceedings." Finally, insofar as due process analysis looks to the fiscal and administrative burdens imposed upon the State, here too the special circumstances applicable to the Virginia inmates strengthened their claim. Virginia already appointed counsel to assist death row inmates once their collateral attack petitions were found to assert at least one non-frivolous claim. Accordingly, "the additional cost of providing [Virginia's] 32 death row inmates competent counsel to prepare such petitions should be minimal." That a state could readily bear such cost was evidenced by the fact that Virginia was one of only a handful of capital-

punishment states (out of a total of 37) that "ha[d] no system for appointing counsel for condemned prisoners before a postconviction petition is filed."

With eight justices evenly divided as to the significance of the special circumstances presented by the Virginia inmates, the deciding vote in *Murray* was cast by Justice Kennedy. His very brief opinion appeared to give some weight to special circumstances, although Justice O'Connor found no inconsistency in the Kennedy and Rehnquist opinions and joined both. Justice Kennedy initially accepted Justice Stevens' analysis insofar as it established (1) that "collateral proceedings are a central part of the review process for prisoners condemned to death" and (2) that the "complexity of our jurisprudence in this area * * * makes it unlikely that capital defendants will be able to file successful petitions for collateral relief without the assistance of persons learned in the law." He noted, however, that the necessary assistance can be provided in "various ways" and there was no showing that Virginia's approach had been unsatisfactory. For "no prisoner on death row in Virginia ha[d] been unable to obtain counsel to represent him in postconviction proceedings, and Virginia's prison system is staffed with institutional lawyers to assist in preparing petitions for postconviction relief." Accordingly, Justice Kennedy concurred in the reversal of the lower court ruling based "on the facts and record of this case."

The division of the Court in *Murray* leaves open the extent to which the Court majority will give weight to the special elements of a procedural setting, as it relates to a particular type of litigant, in assessing a due process claim to appointed counsel. Arguably, the division among the justices was limited to the capital case. There was no suggestion that special circumstances could play a role on a discretionary appeal (*Ross*) or a collateral proceeding (*Finley*) in a non-capital case. Yet, there remains *Gagnon v. Scarpelli,* a case utilizing a special-circumstances approach outside of the capital offense context, which was not discussed in any of the *Murray* opinions. Certainly the thrust of the Court's rulings is not so firmly settled as to impose a significant barrier to the adoption in future cases, especially by a Court of changed composition, of an approach that more strongly favors either categorical rulings (e.g., *Evitts, Finley,* and *Ross*) or special-circumstances rulings (e.g., *Gagnon*).

The Court's rulings also leave open the possibility of a due process right to counsel in other proceedings that are not within the coverage of the Sixth Amendment, yet may affect the loss of liberty flowing from a criminal conviction. The Court has not, for example, directly considered whether due process requires appointed counsel where a discretionary appeal is the only appeal available to the defendant (unlike *Ross,* where the discretionary appeal followed a first appeal granted as a matter of right). So too, in *Coleman v. Thompson,*[15] the Court specifically left open the question of whether there exists an exception to *Finley* where state law provides that a claim of ineffective assistance of trial counsel cannot be raised on appeal but must be presented in a state collateral proceeding. In *Coleman,* the defendant had counsel on his state collateral challenge raising the trial counsel ineffectiveness claim, and the issue before the Court was the bearing of that habeas counsel's ineffective performance in failing to properly pursue an appeal from the rejection of the collateral challenge. The Court noted that even if an exception existed and the collateral challenge itself was treated as the equivalent of the appeal in *Evitts v. Lucey,* the subsequent appeal from the rejection of the collateral challenge certainly would not fall within any such exception in light of *Ross v. Moffitt* and *Pennsylvania v. Finley.*

Still another due process issue left in limbo is whether the right to utilize retained counsel may have a broader scope than the right to appointed counsel. Pre–*Gideon* rulings had indicated that the right to representation by retained counsel had a broader due process

grounding that the right to appointed counsel. Thus, during the same period in which the accused's right to appointed counsel in a noncapital felony case was controlled by the special circumstances rule of *Betts,* the right of such a defendant to representation by retained counsel was characterized as "unqualified." Indeed, *Powell v. Alabama*[16] had suggested in dicta that due process would be denied if a court, even in a civil case, "were arbitrarily to refuse to hear a party by counsel, employed by and appearing for him." On the other hand, as previously noted, the later Sixth Amendment rulings have indicated that the rights to appointed and retained counsel are equivalent under that Amendment. The same could be true of due process. Although, one consideration presumably weighed under a due process analysis of the right to appointed counsel would be the burden placed upon the state in providing counsel at its expense, the due process rulings rejecting claims to appointed counsel have tended to emphasize other factors, such as the limited role of postconviction proceedings in ensuring reliability of verdicts. Those other factors could be deemed equally controlling in rejecting claims as to retained counsel—unless the Court recognizes an independent due process interest of the litigant not to be prevented from utilizing his own resources to present his case through counsel if he so chooses.[17] Also, as to almost all proceedings relating to criminal liability that are not themselves part of the criminal prosecution (e.g., appeals and post conviction challenges), there is a longstanding history of allowing representation by retained counsel.

The possibility that a state could refuse to permit retained counsel where it need not appoint counsel was raised in *Gagnon.*[18] After holding that due process required appointment of counsel in probation and parole revocation cases where the circumstances made counsel necessary to ensure the "effectiveness" of due

---

15. 501 U.S. 722, 111 S.Ct. 2546, 115 L.Ed.2d 640 (1991). See also § 11.7 at note 17.

16. See note 1 supra.

17. Because of this distinct grounding, such an independent right to retained counsel would not give rise to a

constitutional right to effective representation by that counsel. See note 6 of § 11.7. See also note 4 of § 8.15, discussing such a grounding as it relates to a grand jury witness.

18. See note 6 supra.

process guaranteed hearing rights, the *Gagnon* Court cited several concerns in refusing to impose a flat requirement of appointed counsel in all revocation cases. Among those concerns was the potentially adverse impact of automatic representation by counsel upon the special nature of the revocation proceeding (where the state typically did not use counsel and the focus often was upon a "predictive and discretionary" determination as to rehabilitative potential). That impact, of course, would flow from frequent representation by retained counsel as well as by appointed counsel. The Court added a warning, however, should a state decide to restrict the use of retained counsel. It stated in a footnote: "We have no occasion to decide in this case whether a probationer or parolee has a right to be represented at a revocation hearing by retained counsel in situations other than those where the State would be obliged to furnish counsel for an indigent." In other contexts, lower courts have noted that should a state seek to bar the assistance of retained counsel in a proceeding that relates to the criminal justice process, it must at least be able to point to the pernicious impact of counsel on the special character of the proceeding. This view finds support in *Wolff v. McDonnell*,[19] where the Court held that prisoners do not have a right to "either retained or appointed counsel" in prison disciplinary proceedings as a result of various difficulties that would arise from the "insertion of counsel" into such proceedings.

(c) Derivative Rights to Counsel. A constitutional right to the assistance of counsel also can be derived from other constitutional guarantees besides the due process right to a fair hearing. Thus, *Miranda v. Arizona*,[20] held that the right to consult with counsel was indispensable to the protection of the self-incrimination privilege of a person subjected to custodial interrogation. The Court there required that the police inform such a person that "he has a right to consult with a lawyer and to have the lawyer with him during interrogation," and that "if he is indigent, a lawyer will be appointed to represent him." This requirement extends beyond the Sixth Amendment right to counsel since custodial interrogation often occurs before the individual is an "accused" in a "criminal prosecution."[21] The *Miranda* approach, requiring an opportunity to consult with counsel as a means of safeguarding another constitutional guarantee, has also been advanced in other situations not encompassed by the Sixth Amendment. In *Kirby v. Illinois*,[22] this approach was urged by the dissenters in arguing that a suspect placed in a lineup should have a right to the presence of retained or appointed counsel, but it was rejected by the majority. In *United States v. Mandujano*,[23] two justices argued that the self-incrimination privilege of a target-witness before a grand jury carried with it a right to consult with retained or appointed counsel prior to questioning. While the Court did not find it necessary to rule on that contention, the *Mandujano* plurality opinion argued against a right to counsel, and later cases have approvingly cited that discussion. Thus, the prospects for recognition of further derivative rights to counsel, beyond that established in *Miranda*, currently appear dim.

(d) Equal Protection and Appointed Counsel. Assume that a state allows a person to be represented by retained counsel in a proceeding as to which neither due process nor the Sixth Amendment requires the appointment of counsel. Does the equal protection guarantee then require the state to provide appointed counsel for indigent persons so as to

19. 418 U.S. 539, 94 S.Ct. 2963, 41 L.Ed.2d 935 (1974).

20. 384 U.S. 436, 86 S.Ct. 1602, 16 L.Ed.2d 694 (1966), discussed in § 6.5.

21. In other respects, the requirement may be tied to Sixth Amendment limitations. In Berkemer v. McCarty, 468 U.S. 420, 104 S.Ct. 3138, 82 L.Ed.2d 317 (1984), holding that *Miranda* warnings were required prior to custodial interrogation of a person arrested for a traffic misdemeanor [see § 6.6(e)], the Court left open for future decision the question of "whether an indigent suspect has a right, under the Fifth Amendment, to have an attorney appointed to advise him regarding his responses to custodial interrogation when the alleged offense about which he is being questioned is sufficiently minor that he would not have a right, under the Sixth Amendment, to the assistance of appointed counsel at trial."

22. 406 U.S. 682, 92 S.Ct. 1877, 32 L.Ed.2d 411 (1972), discussed in § 7.3(b).

23. 425 U.S. 564, 96 S.Ct. 1768, 48 L.Ed.2d 212 (1976), discussed in § 8.15(a).

ensure equal treatment? Supreme Court precedent suggests that the equal protection guarantee might possibly impose an independent obligation upon the state to provide appointed counsel, though any such obligation would appear to be limited to situations in which either due process or the Sixth Amendment would come very close to requiring appointment of counsel. The key cases in assessing the scope of the state's obligation under the equal protection clause are *Douglas v. California*[24] and *Ross v. Moffitt*.[25] An analysis of those rulings, however, must begin with an examination of the earlier case of *Griffin v. Illinois*.[26]

While *Griffin* did not involve the appointment of counsel, it is the seminal ruling on the state's general obligation to provide "equal justice" in the criminal justice process.

Griffin dealt with a state law that gave every defendant the right to appeal, but then conditioned appellate review on defendant's presentation of a trial record that often could not be prepared without a stenographic transcript. Defendant, who was indigent, asked the state to provide him with a free transcript so that he could prepare his appeal, but the state refused to do so. The Supreme Court held that this refusal resulted in a denial of due process and equal protection. Both Justice Black's plurality opinion and Justice Frankfurter's separate concurring opinion acknowledged that the state had no constitutional obligation to provide appellate review of criminal convictions. However, once the state had granted defendants a right to appeal, it could not condition the exercise of that right upon a prerequisite that discriminated against those defendants who were indigent. "In criminal trials," Justice Black noted, "a State can no more discriminate on account of poverty than on account of religion, race, or color" since "the ability to pay costs in advance bears no relationship to defendant's guilt or innocence." Commenting generally upon this country's dedication "to affording equal justice to all," Justice Black added, in an oft-quoted statement: "There can be no equal justice where the kind of trial a man gets depends on the amount of money he has."

Notwithstanding the sweeping language in Justice Black's opinion, it was far from certain that the *Griffin* ruling would be extended to the appointment of counsel for the indigent. By requiring a transcript to perfect an appeal, the state had denied the indigent defendant access to an integral part of its process for ensuring against unjust convictions. In contrast, the indigent defendant denied appointed counsel on appeal still had his right to appellate review. However, in *Douglas v. California*,[27] the Court extended *Griffin* to the right to counsel. *Douglas* held invalid on equal protection grounds an intermediate appellate court's practice of refusing to appoint counsel on appeal when the court, after reviewing the trial record, concluded that "such appointment would be of no value to either the defendant or the court." The majority opinion found this practice inconsistent with the "*Griffin* principle." Here too, there was "discrimination against the indigent," with "the kind of appeal a man enjoys depend[ing] on the amount of money he has." Unlike the indigent, the more affluent defendant was not required to "run [the] gauntlet of a preliminary showing of merit" to have his case presented by counsel. As the Court saw the state's procedure, "the indigent, where the record was unclear or errors were hidden, had only the right to a meaningless ritual, while the rich man had a meaningful appeal."

The *Douglas* opinion (per Justice Douglas) stressed that it was not requiring "absolute equality" throughout the criminal justice process. What was at stake here was the first level of appeal, the "one and only appeal an indigent has as of right." The Court was not here concerned with review "beyond the stage in the appellate process at which the claims have once been presented by a lawyer and passed upon by an appellate court." Left open was the question whether the state would have to pro-

---

24.   372 U.S. 353, 83 S.Ct. 814, 9 L.Ed.2d 811 (1963).

25.   417 U.S. 600, 94 S.Ct. 2437, 41 L.Ed.2d 341 (1974). See also note 12 supra.

26.   351 U.S. 12, 76 S.Ct. 585, 100 L.Ed. 891 (1956), discussed in § 11.2(d).

27.   See note 24 supra.

vide counsel for an indigent defendant seeking to obtain discretionary review from a second-level appellate court.

In stressing the importance of the first appeal, and in characterizing a defendant's presentation of his appeal without counsel as a "meaningless ritual," the *Douglas* opinion cited factors that arguably would have supported a due process right to appointed counsel in that case. Justice Harlan, in his *Douglas* dissent, gave substantial attention to the possibility that due process required appointed counsel on appeal, but concluded that the state's preliminary review procedure for appointing counsel satisfied any such requirement. Traditional due process analysis, Justice Harlan argued, would not recognize an absolute right to counsel, but would focus on the need for counsel in the individual case. Here, the state appellate court had done exactly that in deciding not to appoint counsel. Thus, from Justice Harlan's perspective, *Douglas* took the equal protection guarantee beyond the limits of any due process right to appointed counsel by imposing a flat requirement without regard to the circumstances of the case.

In *Ross v. Moffitt*,[28] the Court refused to extend *Douglas* to indigent defendants seeking appointed counsel to prepare petitions for discretionary appellate review that came after the first appeal. The *Ross* majority opinion looked to both due process and equal protection in reaching that result. *Douglas* itself was described as receiving "some support" from both the due process and equal protection clauses, with "neither clause by itself provid[ing] an entirely satisfactory basis for the result reached." The right it established was characterized as the product of the combined impact of the two clauses, although precisely how they interacted was left unclear. The Court did note that each clause "depend[s] on a different inquiry which emphasizes different factors." For due process the emphasis is on "fairness between the State and the individual dealing with the State, regardless of how other individuals in the same situation may be treated." "Equal protection, on the other hand, empha-

sizes disparity in treatment by a State between classes of individuals."

In refusing to extend *Douglas* to the petition for second-level discretionary review, the *Ross* majority examined separately the impact of the two clauses, and found that neither lent support to the defendant's claim. In discussing the due process element, the Court stressed the quite different relationship of the defendant and the state on an appeal as opposed to a trial. As discussed in subsection (b), the defendant's role as the person pressing the appeal and challenging a determination of guilt reduced the strength of his claim for procedural safeguards. The Court concluded that leaving indigents to pursue on their own a favorable discretionary decision for second-tier review produces "unfairness * * * only if indigents are singled out * * * and denied meaningful access to the appellate system because of their poverty." That question, however, was "more profitably considered under an equal protection analysis."

In finding that there was no denial of meaningful access based on poverty, and therefore no denial of equal protection, the *Ross* majority opinion discussed the ease with which an appellate court could determine whether to grant discretionary review even where the application had not been prepared by counsel. It acknowledged that "a skilled lawyer, particularly one trained in the somewhat arcane art of preparing petitions for discretionary review," could prove helpful to his client. However, the state had no "duty to duplicate the legal arsenal that may be privately retained by a criminal defendant in a continuing effort to reverse his conviction, but only to assure the indigent defendant an adequate opportunity to present his claims fairly in the context of the state appellate process." Here, unlike *Douglas,* that opportunity was available without counsel.

The *Ross* opinion left uncertain the significance of the equal protection component of *Douglas. Douglas* arguably could be read as presenting a situation in which the procedural setting was not sufficient in itself to require

28. See note 25 supra.

counsel as a matter of due process, but the value of the lawyer was significant enough that the disparate treatment of the indigent resulted in an equal protection violation. However, any separate significance of the equal protection clause, at least in the *Douglas* setting, seemed to disappear with the due process ruling in *Evitts v. Lucey*.[29] For the Court there clearly indicated that the right to counsel on the first appeal of right, even as a categorical guarantee as specified in *Douglas,* could also be grounded on due process alone. Consistent with traditional due process analysis, the Court there looked to the extent of defendant's need for counsel as one of the factors to be weighed in determining the demands of due process. The question presented previously under equal protection analysis—whether the lack of counsel rendered the appeal a "meaningless ritual"—was treated in *Evitts* as an aspect of due process analysis. The Court's conclusion was that meaningful access to a first appeal as of right could be achieved only with the effective assistance of counsel. This was a universal requirement, not one geared to the circumstances of the particular case.

Following *Evitts,* the equal protection clause would appear to add nothing to the constitutional right to appointed counsel. Thus, decisions like *Mayer v. Chicago*[30] should not provide a springboard for an equal protection right to counsel where neither due process nor the Sixth Amendment require the appointment of counsel. *Mayer* held that an indigent defendant convicted of an ordinance violation punishable only by fine was entitled under *Griffin* to a free transcript that would permit him to challenge on appeal the sufficiency of the evidence supporting his conviction. Since the defendant was not threatened with the loss of liberty, the interest he advanced was substantially less than that recognized in the due process or Sixth Amendment cases involving the appointment of counsel. The Supreme Court has held, for example, that the Sixth Amendment guarantee does not extend to a defendant charged with a misdemeanor where,

as in *Mayer,* the defendant has at stake no more than a potential fine and a record of a conviction.

Mayer, in contrast, deemed such consequences to be sufficient to justify an equal protection right to a transcript that was, in effect, a prerequisite for obtaining appellate review. The state, having provided for such review, was prohibited from "pricing indigent defendants out of [such review]". But *Mayer* dealt with providing a type of assistance as to which there was no counterpart grounding elsewhere in the Constitution. That counterpart would be available as to the right to counsel, and there, since neither due process nor the Sixth Amendment would view the consequences at stake as sufficient to establish on constitutional right to counsel, the combination of *Ross* and *Evitts* indicates that equal protection similarly should not provide a grounding for appointing counsel. Although *Douglas* initially suggested otherwise, equal protection analysis today does distinguish between providing assistance of the type recognized in *Griffin* and providing the assistance of appointed counsel.

§ 11.2 Scope of the Indigent's Right to Counsel and Other Assistance

(a) Right to Appointed Counsel: Misdemeanor Prosecutions. Prior to the 1972 decision of *Argersinger v. Hamlin,*[1] all of the appointed counsel cases decided by the Supreme Court had involved felony prosecutions. Though the Sixth Amendment refers to "all criminal prosecutions," several lower courts had ruled that the Sixth Amendment right to appointed counsel, like the Sixth Amendment right to jury trial, did not apply to prosecutions for "petty offenses" (basically misdemeanors punishable by no more than six months imprisonment). That position was presented to the Court in *Argersinger,* where it was unanimously rejected. The Court could find no substantial reason for extending the

---

29.   469 U.S. 387, 105 S.Ct. 830, 83 L.Ed.2d 821 (1985), also discussed at note 9 supra.

30.   404 U.S. 189, 92 S.Ct. 410, 30 L.Ed.2d 372 (1971).

§ 11.2

1.   407 U.S. 25, 92 S.Ct. 2006, 32 L.Ed.2d 530 (1972).

petty offense exception to the counsel clause. While there was "historical support" for the jury trial exception, "nothing in the history of the right to counsel" suggested "a retraction of the right in petty offenses, wherein the common law previously did require that counsel be provided." There also was no functional basis for drawing the line at petty offenses. The "problems associated with * * * petty offenses," the Court noted, "often require the presence of counsel to insure the accused a fair trial." It could not be said that the legal questions involved in a misdemeanor trial were likely to be less complex because the jail sentence did not exceed six months. Neither is there less need for advice of counsel prior to entering a plea of guilty to a petty offense. Indeed, petty misdemeanors may create a special need for counsel because their great volume "may create an obsession for speedy dispositions, regardless of the fairness of the result."

Since the defendant in *Argersinger* had been sentenced to jail, the Court found it unnecessary to rule on the defendant's right to appointed counsel where "a loss of liberty was not involved." The opinion laid the foundation, however, for distinguishing between cases involving sentences of imprisonment and those in which only fines are imposed. Both *Johnson v. Zerbst* and *Gideon v. Wainwright*[2] had referred to counsel's assistance as necessary to ensure "the fundamental human rights of life and liberty." The special significance of the loss of liberty to both the accused and society could not be denied. As the *Argersinger* opinion noted: "[T]he prospect of imprisonment for however short a time will seldom be viewed by the accused as a trivial or petty matter and may well result in quite serious repercussions affecting his career and his reputation."

The *Argersinger* opinion also cited the practicability of applying an "actual imprisonment" standard. Responding to the contention that appointment of counsel for minor offenses was beyond the capacity of "the Nation's legal resources," it noted that an actual imprisonment standard would limit significantly the burden imposed upon the states. Although many jurisdictions classified traffic offenses as criminal, only a minute portion of all such offenses were likely to be "brought into the class where imprisonment actually occurs." Indeed, the opinion stated, "the run of misdemeanors will not be affected by today's ruling." Moreover, the Court's ruling continued to leave the classification of crimes to the discretion of the states. It only required that "in those [cases] that end up in the actual deprivation of a person's liberty, the accused will receive the benefit of 'the guiding hand of counsel' so necessary when one's liberty is in jeopardy."

A major objection advanced against an actual imprisonment standard was that it would require the magistrate (who often would also be the trial judge) to "prejudge" the case in determining whether appointed counsel was necessary. The magistrate would have to determine prior to trial whether imprisonment might be imposed if the defendant were convicted. The Court, however, did not see any insurmountable difficulties in requiring the magistrate to make this "predictive evaluation of each case." It apparently assumed that the magistrate's determination would be based in large part upon the general character of the offense charged. The *Argersinger* opinion quoted at length from an ABA report noting that there were many offenses theoretically punishable by imprisonment but so "rarely if ever" resulting in incarceration that "for all intents and purposes the punishment they carry is at most a fine." If the judge had doubts as to whether a particular offense might merit imprisonment, he could always appoint counsel. However, if he failed to do so, that would preclude the imposition of imprisonment no matter what new information came to his attention during the course of the trial.

In *Scott v. Illinois*,[3] the Court refused to carry the Sixth Amendment right to appointed counsel in misdemeanor cases beyond the actual imprisonment standard suggested in *Ar-*

2. See § 11.1 at notes 2 and 4.

3. 440 U.S. 367, 99 S.Ct. 1158, 59 L.Ed.2d 383 (1979).

gersinger. The petitioner there was an indigent defendant who had been convicted of shoplifting. Although that misdemeanor offense was punishable by a maximum sentence of one year in jail and a $500 fine, petitioner had been sentenced to only a fine of $50.00. Referring to both the Sixth Amendment and the Fourteenth Amendment's due process clause, the Supreme Court concluded that the "federal constitution does not require a state trial court to appoint counsel for a criminal defendant such as petitioner." *Argersinger,* the Court stated, had rested on the "conclusion that incarceration was so severe a sanction that it should not be imposed * * * unless an indigent has been offered appointed counsel." It had thereby "delimit[ed] the constitutional right to appointed counsel in state criminal proceedings." The "central premise of *Argersinger*—that actual imprisonment is a penalty different in kind from or the mere threat of imprisonment"—was not altered by the fact that the misdemeanor involved here carried a potential punishment that took it beyond the petty offense category. The key for all misdemeanors is whether the judge imposes a sentence of imprisonment on conviction of the misdemeanor offense. The Court also noted that the actual imprisonment standard "had proved reasonably workable, whereas any extension would create confusion and impose unpredictable, but necessarily substantial, costs in 50 quite diverse states."

Scott was a 5–4 decision, with Justice Powell noting that he had joined the majority opinion only to provide "clear guidance" to the lower courts. However, in light of subsequent cases building upon *Argersinger* and *Scott,* the Court appears firmly committed to utilizing the actual imprisonment standard as the sole Sixth Amendment dividing line for requiring appointed counsel in misdemeanor cases.[4] It has

shown no inclination to build upon Justice Powell's reluctant concurrence, and require appointment of counsel, under a due process analysis, in a particularly compelling non-imprisonment misdemeanor case. Indeed, it has even suggested that the actual imprisonment standard might be incorporated into the right to consult with a lawyer established under *Miranda*.[5]

In *Baldasar v. Illinois*,[6] a per curiam opinion for Court majority, supported by two concurring opinions reflecting the views of five justices, concluded that an uncounseled misdemeanor conviction could not be used under an enhanced penalty statute to raise the level of a subsequently committed offense (and hence to increase the term of imprisonment). Justice Powell, in a dissent for four justices, stressed that the uncounseled conviction was valid under *Scott* because the defendant had not been sentenced to imprisonment upon his conviction, and nothing in *Scott* precluded use of that valid conviction to determine the appropriate length of sentence for the subsequent offense under an enhancement provision. In a subsequent ruling by a differently composed Court, Justice Powell's position was vindicated. *Nichols v. United States*[7] discounted the splintered majority ruling in *Baldasar,* and held that an uncounseled misdemeanor conviction which was valid under *Scott* (no term of incarceration having been imposed) could be used to enhance the imprisonment sentence for a subsequent offense. Since the uncounseled misdemeanor conviction was itself valid, it could be considered by the sentencing court, in much the same fashion as it would consider other aspects of the defendant's criminal record, or even past criminal behavior that did not result in a conviction, in assessing the appropriate sentence for the defendant's current conviction. The enhancement provision

---

4. Of course, the states remain free to provide counsel in situations where the Constitution does not compel appointment. A large group of states require appointment for all offenses that carry an authorized punishment of incarceration. Many others, however, utilize a standard that is tied in some way to actual imprisonment. Some of these states have a statutory standard requiring that counsel be appointed for all misdemeanors carrying an authorized punishment of incarceration unless the judge declares on the record prior to trial that a sentence of

incarceration will not be imposed. Other employ a general directive to appoint counsel if the judge concludes that incarceration is a "practical possibility."

5. See note 21 of § 11.1.

6. 446 U.S. 222, 100 S.Ct. 1585, 64 L.Ed.2d 169 (1980).

7. 511 U.S. 738, 114 S.Ct. 1921, 128 L.Ed.2d 745 (1994).

"did not change the penalty imposed for the earlier conviction," as the Court had recognized in past decisions "sustain[ing] repeat offender laws as penalizing only the last offenses committed by the defendant."

In *Alabama v. Shelton*,[8] the Court refused to extend the *Nichols* analysis to allow a sentence on an uncounseled conviction that "may end up in the actual deprivation of a person's liberty" upon a subsequent revocation of probation. Unlike *Nichols*, where the imprisonment was imposed for the subsequent felony, taking account of the earlier conviction, the imprisonment here would be imposed for the original conviction, as it had produced the underlying sentence that was suspended in conjunction with the probation. Although defendant's imprisonment would be triggered by the probation violation, that violation did not constitute an independent basis for incarceration. Though the *Shelton* opinion also noted that the state's probation revocation proceeding was an informal proceeding, at which the defendant had not right to counsel, it characterized as "more significant" the fact that the defendant in that proceeding, even if provided counsel, could not challenge the validity of the underlying conviction. Thus, the state either had to provide counsel on the original conviction or forgo a conditional sentence that could lead to incarceration.[9]

(b) Right to Appointed Counsel: Stages of the Proceeding. The Sixth Amendment right to appointed counsel applies only to "critical stages" in the criminal prosecution. There is no need for the assistance of appointed counsel unless the "substantial rights of the accused may be affected" at the particular proceeding. Since the trial clearly is a critical stage in the criminal prosecution, most of the cases applying the critical stage test have concerned pretrial proceedings. Applying that test, the Supreme Court has held that an "accused" has the right to the assistance of counsel at a preliminary hearing, at some pretrial identification procedures (but not others), and when subjected to police or prosecutor efforts to elicit inculpatory statements.[10] The first appearance before a magistrate and the arraignment before the trial judge may or may not be a critical stage depending upon the state's treatment of the defendant's actions at that proceeding. Thus, the Supreme Court held that an indigent defendant was entitled to appointed counsel at an arraignment where state law viewed defenses not raised at that point as abandoned.[11] Similarly, the Sixth Amendment right applied where the defendant was asked to enter only a non-binding plea at the first appearance, but his non-binding plea of guilty, though later withdrawn, could still be used against him at trial.[12]

Of course, no matter how significant the particular proceeding, the Sixth Amendment right does not apply if the proceeding is not part of the "criminal prosecution." The starting point for the criminal prosecution is the initiation of "adversary judicial proceedings." It is at that point that the individual becomes an "accused" person entitled to the application of the Sixth Amendment guarantee. Precisely what constitutes the initiation of adversary judicial proceedings is an issue most commonly raised in connection with police investigative procedures, and it has been discussed previously in the chapters on those

---

8. 535 U.S. 654, 122 S.Ct. 1764, 152 L.Ed.2d 888 (2002).

9. This stark alternative led to the majority and dissent sharply debating the questions of: (1) how many states currently did not provide counsel in misdemeanor cases utilizing probationary sentences; (2) whether those states lacked the capacity and resources to provide appointed counsel in such cases, and (3) whether a form of pre-charging probation (i.e., diversion) would adequately serve the state's interests. The state offered its own alternative: treating violation of the probation condition as a form of contempt, and imposing a limited incarceration sanction for that contempt (after a hearing on the con-

tempt with the "full panoply of due process, including the assistance of counsel"). The Court found no need to rule on this concept of a "free standing probation" that was "uncoupled from a prison sentence," as the state had no such system in place.

10. See § 14.2(a) (preliminary hearing); 7.3(a) (lineup); § 6.4(a) (police elicitation).

11. Hamilton v. Alabama, 368 U.S. 52, 82 S.Ct. 157, 7 L.Ed.2d 114 (1961).

12. White v. Maryland, 373 U.S. 59, 83 S.Ct. 1050, 10 L.Ed.2d 193 (1963). As for the right to counsel at the point of setting bail, see § 12.2(3).

procedures.[13] As those discussions indicate, the initiation of adversary judicial proceedings ordinarily requires a formal commitment of the government to prosecute, as evidenced by the filing of charges. This can occur prior to the issuance of an indictment or information, as where the defendant is brought before the magistrate for an "arraignment" or "first appearance" on charges filed in the form of a complaint. In *United States v. Gouveia*[14] the Court reaffirmed, however, that a person has not become an accused for Sixth Amendment purposes simply because he has been detained by the government with the intention of filing charges against him.[15]

Once started, the Sixth Amendment's "criminal prosecution" continues through to the end of the basic trial stage, including sentencing. In the course of ruling upon due process and equal protection claims, *Douglas v. California, Ross v. Moffitt,* and *Evitts v. Lucey* clearly indicated that the "criminal prosecution" has ended where the defendant is pursuing an appeal from his conviction.[16] The status of post-trial proceedings before the trial judge that also challenge the conviction is less clear. The answer may depend, in part, upon the nature of issues presented. If the proceeding involves no more than an extension of a trial ruling, and occurs shortly after trial, as in a post-verdict motion for judgment of acquittal, it should be treated as subject to the Sixth Amendment. On the other hand, a motion for a new trial based on new evidence, which can

occur months after the conviction, might be treated as closer to a collateral attack, which clearly is outside the criminal prosecution.

While timing is a significant factor in assessing post-trial proceedings in the trial court, it is not necessarily conclusive. Thus, a probation revocation proceeding that occurred months after defendant's conviction was held to be a part of the criminal prosecution where that proceeding also involved the setting of the defendant's basic prison term for the crime. In that case, *Mempa v. Rhay,*[17] the trial judge placed the defendant on probation without fixing the term of imprisonment that would be imposed if probation were later revoked. The Supreme Court concluded that the subsequent determination and imposition of a prison sentence at the probation revocation proceeding was as much a part of the criminal prosecution as the sentencing of a defendant immediately after trial. In contrast to *Mempa, Gagnon v. Scarpelli*[18] held that a probation revocation hearing is not part of the criminal prosecution when a prison sentence had previously been imposed but then suspended in favor of probation. The only issue presented in such a hearing is whether to revoke probation, and that determination is based on defendant's subsequent conduct rather than the commission of the original offense.

Of course, even though a proceeding is not part of the criminal prosecution, there may still be a right to appointed counsel drawn

---

13. See §§ 6.4(e), 7.3(b).

14. 467 U.S. 180, 104 S.Ct. 2292, 81 L.Ed.2d 146 (1984).

15. The defendants in *Gouveia* were prison inmates who had been assigned to a special Administrative Detention Unit (ADU) on suspicion that they were responsible for the murder of a fellow inmate. A disciplinary hearing was held shortly thereafter, with the prison officials concluding that defendants had participated in the murder. The defendants remained in the ADU for a substantial period thereafter (19 months in one case) before they were indicted and counsel appointed. They claimed that the government's failure to honor their request for appointment of counsel during their confinement in the ADU constituted a violation of their Sixth Amendment right to counsel. The Court of Appeals sustained their claim. It reasoned that, in prison cases, there existed a substantial possibility that the government might delay the initiation of formal charges, resulting in the loss of evidence that could be preserved through the preindictment investigation of appointed counsel. The Supreme Court ac-

knowledged that the concern of the Court of Appeals was legitimate, but concluded that it was a concern met by other procedural protections (the statute of limitations and the due process protection against prejudicial delay in bringing charges), rather than the Sixth Amendment right to counsel. The Court majority noted that it had "never held that the right to counsel attaches at the time of arrest," and had "never suggested that the purpose of the right * * * is to provide a defendant with a preindictment private investigator." On the contrary, the right was limited by its objective "of protecting the unaided layman at critical confrontations with his adversary," and it therefore demanded the initiation of adversary judicial proceedings, which marked the point at which "the adverse positions of government and defendant have solidified."

16. See § 11.1 at notes 9–12, and 27–29.

17. 389 U.S. 128, 88 S.Ct. 254, 19 L.Ed.2d 336 (1967).

18. See § 11.1 at note 6.

from a constitutional provision other than the Sixth Amendment. Thus, *Douglas* and *Evitts* established an equal protection and due process right to appointed counsel on a first appeal provided as a matter of right, and *Gagnon* established a due process right to appointed counsel under special circumstances in a probation or parole revocation proceeding.[19] On the other hand, *Ross v. Moffitt* held that neither equal protection nor due process required appointment of counsel to assist an indigent convicted defendant in preparing an application for second-level discretionary review of a conviction, and *Pennsylvania v. Finley* and *Murray v. Giarratano* found no constitutional basis for requiring appointment of counsel to assist an indigent prisoner in filing a habeas petition or other collateral attack upon his conviction.[20]

In many states, appointed counsel is provided in various settings where the indigent clearly does not have a constitutional right to appointed counsel. Very often this is a product of practice rather than legal right. Perhaps the most common practice in this regard is appellate courts directing counsel appointed for the first appeal to assist their clients in preparing timely applications for subsequent discretionary review within the state judicial system. States less often establish a legal right to the assistance of appointed counsel where not constitutionally mandated, but such state-created rights are fairly common at some stages of the criminal justice process. In the federal system and numerous states, indigents are entitled to appointed counsel in all probation revocation hearings, without regard to the special circumstances test of *Gagnon v. Scarpelli*. Discretionary authority to provide counsel in a collateral proceeding challenging a conviction is fairly widely recognized, but a statutory right to such assistance—apart from capital cases—is granted only by a much smaller group of states.

(c) The *Anders* Rules. Representing the defendant at trial, the attorney violates no obligation of professional responsibility in forcing the state to prove its case, no matter how clear the defendant's guilt. The defendant has a right to require the state to prove guilt consistent with applicable legal standards and is entitled to the competent representation of counsel in this regard. On appeal, on the other hand, the defendant is presenting a challenge and the lawyer has an ethical obligation not to assert frivolous claims. In *Anders v. California*,[21] the Supreme Court was required to resolve the potential tension between that professional obligation and the indigent defendant's constitutional right to appointed counsel on first appeal of right. The *Anders* Court unanimously agreed that defendant's constitutional right to appointed counsel did not preclude withdrawal where (1) counsel, after "conscientious investigation," concludes that the appeal is "frivolous" and (2) the appellate court "is satisfied that counsel has diligently investigated the possible grounds of appeal, and agrees with counsel's evaluation of the case." However, the *Anders* majority also found that the withdrawal procedure utilized in the case before it, which relied on counsel's conclusory "no merit" letter, failed to provide satisfactory safeguards against undermining the defendant's constitutional right to counsel. Describing the kind of withdrawal procedure that would protect that right, the *Anders* majority set forth the basic elements of what was later characterized as *"Anders' prophylactic framework"* for withdrawal. That framework had four elements: (1) after a "conscientious examination" of the appeal, counsel must determine that it is "wholly frivolous" and "so advise the court and request permission to withdraw"; (2) "that request must be accompanied by a brief referring to anything in the record that might arguably support the appeal"; (3) "a copy of counsel's brief should be furnished the indigent [defendant] and time allowed him to raise any points that he chooses"; and (4) the appellate court, "after a full examination of all the proceedings," must find that "the case is wholly frivolous."

19. See § 11.1 at notes 9, 27, and 6.
20. See § 11.1 at notes 28, 13, and 14.

21. 386 U.S. 738, 87 S.Ct. 1396, 18 L.Ed.2d 493 (1967).

The structure proposed in *Anders* was viewed by some states as imposing administrative burdens that would not be offset by any reduction in frivolous appeals. These states accordingly responded to *Anders* by prohibiting withdrawal by appointed counsel, insisting that counsel file a brief even though regarding the appeal as frivolous. A substantial majority of jurisdictions, however, continued to allow withdrawals, though varying somewhat in their response to what has been described as the *Anders* dilemma—how does counsel, after concluding that the case is "unbriefable" (and that withdrawal is therefore required), then prepare a brief referring to anything in the record "that might arguably support the appeal"?

Some state courts concluded that counsel must present the possible defense contentions strictly as a positive advocate, "leaving it to us to determine whether and to what extent they have merit." Other courts concluded that counsel should present, along with a statement of the strongest possible arguments for the contentions, a brief explanation of the contrary authority that led counsel to conclude that the contentions were frivolous. This procedure was held to be consistent with *Anders* in *McCoy v. Court of Appeals of Wisconsin.*[22] The Supreme Court reasoned that requiring counsel to cite contrary authority could further the interests underlying *Anders* by providing an additional safeguard against attorneys concluding that an appeal is frivolous without diligent research. The basic function of the *Anders* brief, it was noted, was not to serve as "a substitute for an advocate's brief," but to ensure "that counsel had been diligent" in examining the record for meritorious issues and concluding that the appeal is frivolous. Thus, just as *Anders* had concluded that "an attorney can advise the court of his or her conclusion that an appeal is frivolous without impairment of the client's fundamental rights," it should follow that "no constitutional deprivation occurs when the attorney explains the basis for that conclusion."

In *Smith v. Robbins,*[23] the Supreme Court upheld a California withdrawal procedure that dispensed entirely with substantive briefing by appointed appellate counsel. Upon concluding that an appeal would be frivolous, counsel in California files a brief that "summarizes the procedural and factual history of the case with citations of the record." Counsel also "attests that he has reviewed the record, explained his evaluation of the case to his client, provided the client with a copy of the brief, and informed the client of his right to file a pro se supplemental brief." Counsel does not withdraw, but asks the appellate court to independently examine the record for arguable issues, and remains available to brief any such issues designated by the appellate court. The appellate court then thoroughly examines the entire record, and proceeds to affirm if it finds the appeal to be frivolous, but directs further briefing if any nonfrivolous issue is present. A closely divided Supreme Court upheld this procedure as "reasonably ensur[ing] that as indigent's appeal will be resolved in a way that is related to the merit of the appeal."

Anders, the *Smith* majority noted, set forth a "prophylactic framework" for withdrawal, not as a constitutional mandate, but as an illustration of "one method of satisfying the requirements of the Constitution for indigent criminal appeals." The state has leeway to craft other methods that also guarantee a "fair opportunity to obtain an adjudication on the merits of the appeal," with that fairness judged in light of "the underlying goals that the procedure should serve—to ensure that those indigents whose appeals are not frivolous receive the counsel and merits brief required by *Douglas*, and to protect itself so that frivolous appeals are not subsidized and public moneys not needlessly spend." Here the procedure clearly avoided the flaws held in *Anders* and other cases to deprive the indigent appellant of that fair opportunity: (1) it required a determination that the appeal was "frivolous" (as contrasted to rejected state procedures that had asked counsel or court to determine only that the appeal was unlikely to prevail); (2) it

22. 486 U.S. 429, 108 S.Ct. 1895, 100 L.Ed.2d 440 (1988).

23. 528 U.S. 259, 120 S.Ct. 746, 145 L.Ed.2d 756 (2000).

provided "at least two tiers of review" (by counsel and court) of the frivolity issue; (3) it precluded the possibility of counsel withdrawing and the appellate court then being required to rule on the merits of a non-frivolous issue without substantive briefing; and (4) it did not allow counsel to file a "bare conclusion" statement of his analysis, but required a summary of the cases's procedural and factual history, which "both ensures that trained legal eye has searched the record for arguable issues and assists the reviewing court in its own evaluation of the case."

The *Anders* "fair-opportunity" requirement flows from the constitutional right of that indigent to appointed appellate counsel. Thus, *Pennsylvania v. Finley*[24] held that a state could allow withdrawal under a procedure that would have been unacceptable under *Anders* as to the appointed counsel it provided in the state's postconviction collateral attack; since there was no constitutional right to appointed counsel in such proceedings, the state was free to permit withdrawal as it pleased. Similarly in *Austin v. United States*,[25] the Court noted that the federal Courts of Appeal were not bound by *Anders* in shaping court rules that allowed counsel appointed for the first appeal as of right to refuse to also prepare and file a petition for certiorari (discretionary review on which there is no right to appointed counsel) where counsel believed the petition would be frivolous.

Where *Anders* does apply, but an appellate court allows withdrawal without complying with the *Anders* prerequisites, the state cannot escape the *Anders* remedy of a new appeal by arguing that the *Anders* violation was harmless because the appeal lacked merit. As the Supreme Court noted in *Penson v. Ohio*,[26] acceptance of such a harmless error analysis would "render meaningless" the protections afforded by *Anders*.[27]

(d) Transcripts. *Griffin v. Illinois*[28] spawned a long line of Supreme Court and lower court cases dealing with the indigent defendant's right to a transcript provided at state expense. The courts have had no difficulty in extending *Griffin,* which dealt with a trial transcript to be used in presenting an appeal, to transcripts of other proceedings and to other uses of transcripts. Thus, the Supreme Court has held that the "*Griffin* principle" applies to requests for a trial transcript to be used in a collateral attack upon a conviction, for a transcript of a habeas proceeding to be used on appeal from a denial of habeas relief, for a transcript of a habeas proceeding to be used in filing a second habeas petition, and for a transcript of a preliminary hearing to be used in preparing for trial.[29] The Court has also noted, however, that the defendant is not entitled to a transcript simply because he is indigent and might have some use for a transcript. The need for the transcript must reach a level sufficient to impose an equal protection obligation upon the state, and the assessment of that level has frequently produced a division among the justices.

24.　481 U.S. 551, 107 S.Ct. 1990, 95 L.Ed.2d 539 (1987).

25.　513 U.S. 5, 115 S.Ct. 380, 130 L.Ed.2d 219 (1994).

26.　488 U.S. 75, 109 S.Ct. 346, 102 L.Ed.2d 300 (1988), discussed in § 27.6 at note 38.

27.　On the other hand, where counsel utilized a constitutionally acceptable state procedure for placing before the court an appeal which counsel states to be frivolous, but defendant claims on collateral attack that counsel was incompetent in failing to recognize that the appeal actually presented a non-frivolous issue, and the procedure therefore resulted in the erroneous dismissal of the appeal as frivolous, Smith v. Robbins, supra note 23, holds that the defendant must meet the two-pronged standard of a traditional ineffective assistance of counsel claim (see § 11.10), which includes a showing of prejudice. The defendant must show: (1) there existed a nonfrivolous issue which counsel failed to recognize in processing the appeal as frivolous; (2) a reasonably competent counsel would

have recognized that issue as nonfrivolous; and (3) a reasonable probability exists that, but "for counsel's unreasonable failure to file a merits brief [on the issue], [defendant] would have prevailed on his appeal." In this situation, the constitutionally accepted procedure places counsel in the proper adversarial role (so it cannot be said, as in *Penson,* that the procedure, in effect, denied defendant the assistance of counsel), and the burden therefore rests on the defense to show that counsel failed to perform that role and that failure prejudiced the defendant as to actual outcome.

28.　351 U.S. 12, 76 S.Ct. 585, 100 L.Ed. 891 (1956), discussed in § 11.1(d) at note 26.

29.　Thus, an equal protection right to a transcript has been recognized in various proceedings where the Court would not find a due process or equal protection right to appointed counsel. See § 11.1 at note 30.

Griffin itself noted that a transcript need not be provided if the state could "find other means for affording adequate and effective appellate review to indigent defendants." Later cases noted also that "alternative methods of reporting trial proceedings" would be "permissible" if they placed before the appellate court "an equivalent report of the events at trial from which the appellant's contention arose." However, where the grounds of appeal make out "a colorable need" for a transcript, the burden falls upon the state to establish the adequacy of a less costly alternative. Transcripts for use on appeal have generally been required where they were the usual and apparently preferable means of presenting a claim of the type urged by the indigent defendant.

Courts arguably have not been so ready to discount alternatives when the transcript was desired simply for use in preparing for trial. Thus, in *Britt v. North Carolina*,[30] a divided Supreme Court upheld a state court's refusal to grant defendant a transcript of his first trial, which had ended in a mistrial, noting that there was available "an informal alternative which appears to be substantially equivalent." The Court noted that the same counsel had represented defendant at the first trial, only a month before, and that the court reporter would at any time have read back to counsel the stenographic notes of that trial. It added that it was not suggesting that reliance on the memories of the defendant and defense counsel was itself an adequate alternative for trial preparation. In an earlier case, the Court had held that the defense had to be given a transcript of a preliminary hearing at which the major state witnesses had testified, though defendant and his counsel had both been present at the preliminary hearing and defendant had received a transcript of the grand jury testimony of those witnesses.[31]

(e) Assistance of Experts. Relying on the independent content of due process, *Ake v. Oklahoma*[32] held that, "when a defendant has made a preliminary showing that his sanity at the time of the offense is likely to be a signifi-

cant factor at trial, due process requires that a State provide access to a psychiatrist's assistance on this issue, if the defendant cannot otherwise afford one." The *Ake* majority stressed that its ruling was limited to cases in which the defendant's mental condition was "seriously in question" as evidenced by the defendant's "preliminary showing." Moreover, the state's obligation did not go beyond providing defense with the assistance of one competent psychiatrist, and it could provide that psychiatrist as it saw fit (i.e., the defendant's constitutional right did not include the authority "to choose a psychiatrist of his personal liking or to receive funds to hire his own"). The Court noted that it had never held that "a State must purchase for the indigent all the assistance that his wealthier counterpart might buy," but due process did require that the indigent defendant be given the "basic tools" needed to present his defense. Taking into consideration the defendant's interest "in the accuracy of the criminal proceeding," the limited financial burden that would be imposed upon the state under the proposed standard, and the probable value of psychiatric assistance in presenting an insanity defense, a court appointed psychiatrist clearly was such a "basic tool." The psychiatrist was needed "to conduct a professional examination * * *, to help determine whether the insanity defense is viable, to present testimony, and to assist in preparing cross-examination of a state's psychiatric witness."

Lower courts have diverged somewhat in applying *Ake's* threshold requirement that the defendant make a preliminary showing that his mental condition at the time of the offense is "likely to be a significant factor" at trial (also described by *Ake* as a showing that placed defendant's mental condition "seriously in question,"). They generally agree that this requires something more than an assertion that the defense is contemplating raising an insanity defense or even the entry of a not-guilty-by-reason-of-insanity plea. The defense

---

30. 404 U.S. 226, 92 S.Ct. 431, 30 L.Ed.2d 400 (1971).

31. Roberts v. LaVallee, 389 U.S. 40, 88 S.Ct. 194, 19 L.Ed.2d 41 (1967).

32. 470 U.S. 68, 105 S.Ct. 1087, 84 L.Ed.2d 53 (1985).

must be able to point to "substantive supporting facts," usually relating to the character of the crime, the defendant's current behavior, and past psychiatric history. The defendant's psychological history tends to be given the greatest weight in this regard, with a recent competency examination finding no significant evidence of current illness constituting for some courts an almost insurmountable barrier to meeting the threshold standard. As to the substantiality of the showing, lower courts agree that the "likely to be a significant factor" standard does not require a "prima facie case" of insanity, and that the available evidence need not all point in the direction of insanity. Beyond that, however, they offer varying formulations of the strength of the showing. These include establishing "doubt" as to the defendant's insanity at the time of the crime, demonstrating a "substantial basis" for the insanity defense, establishing that insanity is "a 'close' question which may well be decided one way or the other," and showing that "the defendant's insanity is in fact at issue." Finally, the *Ake* opinion at one point spoke of the defense making "an *ex parte* threshold showing to the trial court," and a few courts have addressed the question of whether the defense is entitled constitutionally to insist that its presentation be *ex parte*. Those courts have divided over whether *Ake* mandates an *ex parte* proceeding, but agree that such a proceeding is preferred.

Ake noted that once the necessary showing was made, the state had an obligation to "assure the defendant access to a competent psychiatrist who will conduct an examination and assist in evaluation, preparation, and presentation of the defense." This description of the psychiatrist's role indicates that the defendant is entitled to a psychiatrist who is part of the "defense team" and not simply an "independent expert" who reports back to the court. Several lower court opinions have lent support to that view. *Ake*, they note, does not lend itself to "independent experts" who share their analysis with the prosecution or are otherwise incapable of providing assistance on such matters as cross examination of the state's witnesses on the defendant's mental

capacity. On the other side, a somewhat larger group of courts have held that the due process requirements of *Ake* are not violated when a trial court, in response to a defense request for psychiatric assistance, orders a "disinterested qualified expert" to conduct an examination and submit a report to the court that is then made available to both the defense and the prosecution. However, these rulings may be conditioned upon the context in which the request for assistance was made and the availability of further appointments. The requests in question commonly were made in connection with the defendant's entry of a plea of not-guilty by reason of insanity. The defendant's entry of that plea requires him to submit to a court-ordered examination [see § 20.4(e)], and the court arguably can insist upon taking this step before determining whether a defense psychiatrist is needed. At this point, the defense has no need for the assistance of an expert to challenge the state's expert as there is no certainty that the state will have an expert. Rather what is needed is an initial examination to determine if there exists what *Ake* describes as "the raw materials integral to the building of an effective defense." For this purpose, the disinterested expert is said to be most appropriate because the psychiatric examination is "not an adversary" proceeding, but "an attempt to uncover the truth concerning [defendant's] insanity." Of course, should the neutral expert's examination raise doubts about defendant's insanity, the defense may need further assistance from its own expert to build upon that doubt, but in almost all of the cases concluding that appointment of the disinterested expert satisfied *Ake,* the expert's report lent no support to an insanity claim.

Lower courts also have divided on the question of whether *Ake's* reasoning extends to the appointment of experts other than psychiatrists. Several courts have held that the analysis of *Ake* does not extend beyond providing the assistance of psychiatrists where the defendant's mental condition is placed in issue by the law governing culpability or punishment. Drawing the line here is justified by the special role of defendant's mental condition under the substantive law, standing apart from such fact bound issues as whether defendant committed the act and caused the harm, and the special role of the psychiatrist (as stressed in *Ake*) in gaining a sensible and accurate determination of defendant's mental condition. However, most courts addressing the extension of *Ake* have concluded that psychiatric assistance is not so unique as to invariably exclude from the *Ake* rationale all other types of experts. The question in each case must be not what field of science or expert knowledge is involved, but rather how important is the scientific issue to the case. Applying this standard, courts have concluded that due process, in the appropriate setting, may require the state to provide a psychiatrist or psychologist to assist on issues other than mental condition as an element of the offense or aspect of punishment, forensic experts to assist in the evaluation of physical evidence, a hypnotist needed to challenge the victim's post-hypnotic identification testimony, and an investigator to find critical evidence identified by the defense.

Some support for extending *Ake* to such experts is found in the Supreme Court's post-*Ake* opinion in *Caldwell v. Mississippi*.[33] The Court there rejected the defendant's claim that due process had been denied by the trial judge's refusal to grant appointed counsel's request for the "appointment of a criminal investigator, a fingerprint expert, and a ballistics expert." It noted:

> Given that petitioner offered little more than undeveloped assertions that the requested assistance would be beneficial, we find no deprivation of due process in the trial judge's decision. Cf. *Ake v. Oklahoma,* 470 U.S. 68, 82–83 (1985) (discussing showing that would entitle defendant to psychiatric assistance as matter of federal constitutional law). We therefore have no need to determine as a matter of federal constitutional law what if any showing would have entitled a defendant to assistance of the type here sought.

33. 472 U.S. 320, 105 S.Ct. 2633, 86 L.Ed.2d 231 (1985).

The *Caldwell* discussion at least considers as an open issue the question of whether due process would require the state to provide nonpsychiatric scientific experts under an appropriate showing of need.

Of course, as *Caldwell* indicates, application of the *Ake* analysis to other types of assistance carries with it the requirement of a threshold showing of need, similar to the *Ake* requirement of a showing that defendant's mental condition is "seriously in question." Thus, the *Caldwell* footnote cited to *Ake* in noting that any due process obligation to provide the expert assistance of the type requested in *Caldwell* would be dependent upon a defense showing that went beyond "undeveloped assertions that the requested assistance would be beneficial." Courts uniformly stress that the requisite showing of need must set forth in detail what assistance is being requested and why it is needed. The defense must identify the expert, explain what the expert will do, and explain why that will be important in representing the defendant. There is somewhat less uniformity, however, in characterizing the level of need that must be established by this particularized showing.

Courts recognize that a somewhat different analysis of the requisite need is required once the *Ake* decision is carried beyond psychiatric assistance on the insanity offense. With insanity, once the defense can show that the defendant's mental condition at the time of the crime is "seriously in question," the requisite need follows automatically. Because a mental condition that meets the requirements of the insanity defense thereby relieves the defendant of liability for the crime, it follows from that serious question that defendant's mental condition is most likely to be a "significant factor" at trial. The need for a psychiatrist also follows because, as the Court noted in *Ake,* the testimony of a psychiatrist is " 'a virtual necessity if an insanity plea is to have any chance of success.' " In contrast, as to other issues, there may be a serious factual question on which an expert could provide assistance, but the issue may be one that the defense also could readily contest without the expert or defense success on the issue may not be likely to affect the outcome of the case. Accordingly, while the lower courts often refer to *Ake's* description of the necessary threshold showing, they typically add a broader description of the requisite showing of need that borrows from formulations found in descriptions of the due process obligations of the prosecution in making evidence available to the defense.[34] They speak, for example, of the defendant establishing a "reasonable probability that an expert would aid in his defense, and that denial of expert assistance would result in an unfair trial" or that "the probable value of the assistance sought [is] such that there is a significant risk of error in the proceedings if the assistance is denied." In applying such a due process standard, lower courts look to both the importance of the issue on which the expert will assist and the need for expert assistance in contesting that issue.

In the federal system and a large number of states, statutes or court rules make the assistance of experts available to indigent defendants. In some states, those provisions are limited to psychiatric experts in connection with insanity claims. In some, they cover a broader range of experts but apply only to homicide cases. In the federal system, the Criminal Justice Act of 1964 provides for the finding of "investigative, expert, or other services necessary for adequate representation" when the defendant cannot afford them. A handful of states have similar provisions, and still others recognize a discretionary authority in the trial court to approve state payment for an equally broad range of assistance. Such authority provides a potential for mandating state-funded experts on a less substantial showing of need than is required under *Ake*. State indigent-assistance statutes, for example, speak of granting requests for assistance upon a finding that such assistance is "necessary for an adequate defense," "necessary," "necessary and proper," and "reasonably necessary." In their interpretation of the Criminal Justice Act, the federal appellate courts, though they

stress the need for specificity in applications, and have warned against funding mere "fishing expeditions," do not demand that the expert be as likely to serve a critical role as do the cases applying *Ake* outside the context of insanity and psychiatric assistance. Indeed, they often refer to a "private attorney" standard, which directs the district court to authorize defense services under "circumstances in which a reasonable attorney would engage such services for a client having the independent means to pay." The state courts, on the other hand, have tended to read into their indigent-assistance statutes, and discretionary authority to approve assistance payments, standards very similar to those applied under their reading of *Ake*. Finally, in some jurisdictions, public defenders do not have to look to court authority under either *Ake* or state law to obtain experts as they are provided with a budget that assumes that experts will be utilized in some portion of their representation.

(f) The *Bounds* Right of Access. Although not limited to challenges to convictions or tied to indigency, the right of access recognized in *Bounds v. Smith*[35] provides a major avenue of assistance for indigent defendants. For those defendants who are incarcerated, the state under *Bounds* assumes a special obligation to facilitate at least their constitutional challenges to their convictions. That obligation had its seed in a line of cases which held unconstitutional state interference with prisoner efforts to present constitutional claims to the courts. *Ex parte Hull*[36] struck down a prison authority practice of advance screening of inmate federal habeas petitions so as to allow only those "properly drawn" petitions to be forwarded to the designated court. The necessary quality and content of habeas petitions, the Supreme Court noted, "are questions for [the habeas] court alone." *Johnson v. Avery*[37] later held unconstitutional a prison regulation that forbade prison inmates from seeking assistance from other inmates in preparing legal documents, including habeas corpus applications. The effect of the regulation, the Court

---

34. See § 24.3(b).

35. 430 U.S. 817, 97 S.Ct. 1491, 52 L.Ed.2d 72 (1977).

36. 312 U.S. 546, 61 S.Ct. 640, 85 L.Ed. 1034 (1941).

37. 393 U.S. 483, 89 S.Ct. 747, 21 L.Ed.2d 718 (1969).

noted, was to deny illiterate or poorly educated prisoners the opportunity to exercise their right to utilize the habeas writ. The state could adopt regulations to prohibit the abuses of "jailhouse lawyering" (e.g., demands for payment), but it could not ban the practice altogether unless it provided some other source of assistance for those prisoners unable to proceed on their own. *Wolff v. McDonnell*[38] held that the non-interference principle announced in *Hull* and *Johnson v. Avery* applied as well to prisoners desiring to press claims under the federal Civil Rights Act. "The right of access," the Court noted, extends beyond the inmate's challenge to his confinement: it "assures that no person will be denied the opportunity to present to the judiciary allegations concerning violations of fundamental constitutional rights."

In *Bounds,* the issue presented was whether the state has a constitutional obligation to supply inmates with an adequate library or some alternative state-supported legal assistance program. The prison authorities contended that the previous access cases did no more than prohibit unreasonable restrictions interfering with "inmate communications on legal problems." The state, they argued, had "no further obligation to expend state funds to implement affirmatively the right of access." Rejecting that contention, Justice Marshall's opinion for the *Bounds* majority noted that the "cost of protecting a constitutional right cannot justify its denial." The Court had not hesitated to impose economic burdens upon the states in cases such as *Griffin, Gideon,* and *Douglas.* So too, it was "undisputable that indigent inmates must be provided at state expense with paper and pen to draft legal documents, with notarial services to authenticate them, and with stamps to mail them." A right of access implicitly required "meaningful access," and therefore the critical issue was "whether law libraries or other forms of legal assistance are needed to give prisoners a reasonably adequate opportunity to present claimed violations of fundamental constitu-

tional rights to the courts." Since lawyers could not prepare petitions without adequate libraries, the same would obviously be true for the prisoner proceeding pro se.

Justice Marshall stressed that the Court was leaving the states with considerable flexibility in meeting their constitutional obligation. It demanded only that prison authorities provide "adequate libraries or adequate assistance from persons trained in law," and the latter could be paraprofessionals or law students in clinical programs. One point clearly established in the Court's later interpretations of the *Bounds* right of access is that it cannot be used as a springboard to create a constitutional right to counsel that does not otherwise exist. Thus, in *Murray v. Giarratano,*[39] although the Court was sharply divided as to whether due process required appointed counsel to assist prisoners in challenging capital convictions in collateral proceedings, there was general agreement that *Bounds* was not a source of such a right. Indeed, in *Lewis v. Casey,*[40] the Court concluded that a lower court could not carry *Bounds* so far as to hold a prison library program inherently inadequate simply on a general showing that many prisoners are illiterate. To establish a claim under *Bounds*, individual prisoners would have to show "actual injury" as a result of the inadequacy of the library program as applied to them, with the state officials then given the opportunity "to determine how best to ensure that [these] inmates with language problems have a reasonably adequate opportunity to file nonfrivolous legal claims challenging their convictions or conditions of confinement." Of course, nothing precludes the state from choosing to provide counsel to meet its *Bounds* obligation, and most do so as to capital defendants challenging their convictions.

Neither *Bounds* nor subsequent Supreme Court rulings applying *Bounds* have set forth clearly the constitutional underpinning of the State's obligation to facilitate the prisoner's meaningful access to the courts. The Court has most frequently described the right of access

---

38. 418 U.S. 539, 94 S.Ct. 2963, 41 L.Ed.2d 935 (1974).

39. See note 14 of § 11.1.

40. 518 U.S. 343, 116 S.Ct. 2174, 135 L.Ed.2d 606 (1996).

as a due process right, but it also has cited equal protection cases in its rulings and some justices have characterized the right as "an aspect of equal protection." From the perspective of a due process analysis, the Court has failed to specifically identify the elements weighed in assessing the state's obligation, apart from characterizing access to the courts as a protected liberty interest and noting that the access protected relates only to inmates challenging the validity of their convictions or the constitutionality of the conditions of their incarceration. From an equal protection perspective, it has failed to identify the element that produces an unconstitutional classification in the state's failure to provide inmate-assistance. Undoubtedly, a critical feature under either analysis is the burden imposed upon the individual's access right as a result of his incarceration. For there was no suggestion in *Bounds* or any other access ruling that a similar level of assistance must be afforded the individual who is not incarcerated and desires to pursue a fundamental constitutional claim in the courts (e.g., a parolee who seeks through federal habeas corpus to challenge his conviction or through a civil rights action to present a constitutional claim against the parole agency).

(g) Indigency Standards. Supreme Court opinions speak generally of the rights of an "indigent defendant" without offering any specific definition of "indigency." This vacuum has largely been filled by legislation, court rules, and administrative regulations setting forth (often in considerable detail) standards and procedures to be used in determining indigency. These provisions commonly utilize one or the other of two general standards of indigency—"financially unable to obtain counsel" or "financially unable to obtain adequate representation without substantial hardship for the defendant or the defendant's family." The failure of the first standard to mention a hardship limitation on financial capacity has no substantive significance as legislation and judicial opinions have long established that indigency refers to a capacity to retain counsel after deducting money needed to support the defendant and his dependents. Indeed, a con-

trary position would be constitutionally suspect, as the context of the Supreme Court's opinions clearly indicates that the constitutional right to appointed counsel is not limited to persons who are "destitute."

Almost all (if not all) jurisdictions accept the principle that an individual should not have to choose between posting bond and obtaining the assistance of counsel. The defendant should not be forced to relinquish one constitutional right to obtain another, and the right to counsel should not itself be undercut by denying the defendant "the liberty prior to trial that may be essential to the preparation of his defense." Accordingly, if the expenditure of resources to obtain pretrial release places the defendant at a point where his remaining resources are insufficient to retain counsel without substantial hardship, the defendant will be entitled to appointed counsel just as he would have been if he never had those resources. So too, if defendant has not yet obtained his release, the resources needed to meet the terms set for his release (assuming that is a realistic possibility) should be deducted from the resources calculated to be available for retaining counsel.

While the final say on the indigency determination remains with the court, many jurisdictions assign the initial (and typically uncontested) determination to the public defender, or a court or social service agency. The universal starting point for the determination is the information that the defendant must furnish under oath (typically in the form of an affidavit). The indigency determination statutes in several states provide that the information furnished by the defendant will not be admissible in the subsequent criminal prosecution (except possibly for impeachment). Courts have suggested that should a defendant refuse to submit information on grounds of self-incrimination, but be informed by the court that the information is necessary to determine his indigency, the information subsequently provided will have been "coerced" in violation of the Fifth Amendment and will thereby be inadmissible in the subsequent prosecution. Where the defendant provides information without first claiming the privilege, that is likely to be viewed as a waiver, notwithstanding the absence of self-incrimination warnings. Absent unusual circumstances (e.g., where the defendant is facing charges directly related to his finances, as in a tax fraud prosecution), potential self-incrimination is not anticipated.

(h) Partial Contribution and Recoupment. Where a defendant's resources are sufficient to permit without substantial hardship some payment for counsel, but not enough to meet the anticipated cost of retained counsel, that defendant falls in what is commonly described as the "partially indigent" category. The court will provide an attorney through its usual system of appointment, but the defendant will be required to make payment to the state to cover part of the state's cost. In general this obligation is imposed without regard to the eventual outcome of the case. Indeed, the payment (or series of payments) may be scheduled to start immediately upon counsel's appointment.

Many states also have post-judgment recoupment programs. These programs are conditioned on conviction, and usually involve the entry of a court order that operates in effect as a civil judgment and covers the cost of the aid furnished to the defendant by the state (appointed attorney, transcripts, etc.). Where the defendant possesses property, the state also may impose a lien on that property. Recoupment provisions are aimed primarily at persons thought to be temporarily indigent (e.g., the college student, or the person owning property currently so encumbered that it affords very limited collateral).

In *Fuller v. Oregon*,[41] the Supreme Court upheld a typical recoupment program, applicable only to those indigent defendants who were subsequently convicted. The Court concluded that the distinction drawn between convicted and acquitted defendants "reflect[ed] no more than an effort to achieve fundamental fairness" and therefore did not violate the equal protection guarantee. The Court also rejected the contention that recoupment imposed a substantial burden on the indigent's right to appointed counsel and would therefore "chill"

the exercise of that right. A defendant "who is just above the line separating the indigent from the non-indigent," the Court noted, is also subjected to "considerable financial hardship in retaining a lawyer." The Constitution does not require that "those only slightly poorer must remain forever immune from any [similar] obligation to shoulder the expense of their legal defense."

§ 11.3 Waiver of the Right to Counsel

(a) General Requirements. Just as the right to counsel extends through various stages in the criminal justice process, waiver of that right can occur at each of those stages. In some respects, what is required for a valid waiver will vary with the particular stage. Thus, the standards for a waiver of counsel in the course of a police investigation differ in certain respects from the standards governing a waiver in a judicial proceeding. A judge accepting a waiver at trial, for example, may be required to conduct a type of inquiry as to the defendant's state of mind that simply would not be feasible for a police officer accepting a waiver prior to custodial interrogation. The requisites for a valid waiver in the course of investigatory procedures have been discussed in previous chapters. Our focus in this section is upon waivers in judicial proceedings, particularly at trial.

While the standards governing waiver vary with the nature of the proceeding, there are several general principles that apply to all waivers of the right to counsel. To be valid, a waiver of counsel must be made "knowingly, intelligently, and voluntarily." There must be "an intentional relinquishment or abandonment of a known right or privilege," and it may not be the product of governmental tactics that amount to "coercion."

The Supreme Court repeatedly has warned the lower courts against simply assuming that the defendant has the necessary knowledge and understanding to make a constitutionally acceptable waiver. It has in fact directed those courts to "indulge in every reasonable pre-

---

41. 417 U.S. 40, 94 S.Ct. 2116, 40 L.Ed.2d 642 (1974).

sumption against waiver." Consistent with this approach, a waiver may not be presumed from a "silent record"; the record must show that the defendant was informed specifically of his right to the assistance of appointed or retained counsel and that he clearly rejected such assistance. "No amount of circumstantial evidence that the person may have been aware of his right will suffice to stand" in place of a specific notification of rights. Having been informed of his right, the defendant's relinquishment of that right must be clear and unequivocal. Indeed, some states direct the court to obtain the waiver in writing, if possible.

Finally, a waiver at one stage does not necessarily constitute a waiver for all stages. Thus, the defendant who waives at a preliminary hearing cannot thereby be assumed to have waived for subsequent proceedings before the trial court. Indeed, most jurisdictions place the obligation on the trial court to determine at each new stage that the defendant desires to continue with his waiver. Some, however, adhere to the constitutional minimum of requiring a new determination only if the defendant indicates that he has changed his mind or significantly changed circumstances suggest that his reexamination of the issue is in order.

(b) Waiver at Trial: The Von Moltke Inquiry. Assume that a defendant, having been informed of his right to counsel, states unequivocally that he wishes to proceed without counsel. Is that sufficient to establish that his waiver was made "intelligently" as well as knowingly? While it may be enough for a waiver in the course of police investigatory procedures, an acceptable waiver before the trial court ordinarily requires considerably more. In *Von Moltke v. Gillies*,[1] Justice Black, in a four-justice plurality opinion, maintained that the trial court was constitutionally obligated to undertake a "thorough inquiry," ensuring that the accused has made an informed decision. Justice Black noted:

> This protecting duty imposes the serious and weighty responsibility upon the trial judge of determining whether there is an intelligent and competent waiver by the ac-

cused. To discharge this duty properly in light of the strong presumption against waiver * * *, a judge must investigate as long and as thoroughly as the circumstances of the case before him demand. * * * To be valid such waiver [of counsel] must be made with an apprehension of the nature of the charges, the statutory offenses included within them, the range of allowable punishments thereunder, possible defenses to the charges and circumstances in mitigation thereof, and all other facts essential to a broad understanding of the whole matter. A judge can make certain that an accused's professed waiver of counsel is understandingly and wisely made only from a penetrating and comprehensive examination of all the circumstances.

Von Moltke involved a waiver by a defendant who then proceeded to enter a guilty plea. As the Court subsequently indicated in *Faretta v. California,* discussed in § 11.5, a somewhat different inquiry is required where the defendant intends to waive counsel and proceed to conduct his own trial. There a defendant also must understand the dangers involved in self-representation at trial. On the other side, the understanding arguably can be somewhat more limited than what *Von Moltke* requires where the defendant is waiving counsel only at a first appearance before a magistrate. Some significant rights may be at stake (e.g., to a preliminary hearing), but the defendant will have a subsequent opportunity before the trial court to determine if he should go forward there without counsel. Thus, to the extent that *Von Moltke* sets a constitutional prerequisite, that prerequisite applies basically to the arraignment on the indictment or information before the trial court, where the defendant appears to be making a permanent waiver of counsel presumably with an intent to enter a guilty plea at that time or in a subsequent proceeding. However, *Von Moltke* generally is viewed as not establishing strict constitutional requisites even in that setting.

Perhaps because Justice Black's *Von Moltke* opinion spoke only for a plurality, lower courts

§ 11.3

1.   332 U.S. 708, 68 S.Ct. 316, 92 L.Ed. 309 (1948).

generally have rejected the view "that a waiver, to be [constitutionally] valid, must emerge from a colloquy between trial judge and defendant covering every factor specified by Justice Black." They "have perceived his list as a catalog of concerns for trial court consideration," rather than "as a prescribed litany of questions and answers leading to mandatory reversal in the event that one or more is omitted." The lower courts have frequently noted that an "in-depth inquiry" covering all of the items specified in *Von Moltke* is to be "preferred," but they have also upheld waivers in cases involving very limited inquiries. The critical issue, it has been noted, "is what the defendant understood—not what the court said." Consideration must be given to all of the surrounding circumstances, including not only the statements of the trial judge and defendant, but also the defendant's age, mental condition,[2] and prior experience with the criminal process, previous hearings in the case, and the general nature of the offense charged.

Von Moltke has been challenged not only as to the necessity and scope of the trial court's inquiry, but also as to what the defendant must understand to make a knowing and intelligent waiver. *Von Moltke* spoke of the defendant having an understanding of "possible defenses to the charges and circumstance in mitigation thereof," as well as "the nature of the charges" and the "range of allowable punishments thereunder." Relying on *Von Moltke*, various lower courts have characterized defendant's awareness of possible defenses as a basic element of an acceptable waiver, although their findings of involuntariness have not been based on that factor alone. However, various other courts have virtually discarded that portion of the *Von Moltke* opinion. These courts have spoken of the need only for an understanding of the charges and the range of potential punishment. They apparently view *Von Moltke's* reference to defenses and mitigating factors as more appropriately tied to the acceptance of a guilty plea (also involved in the *Von Moltke* case) than the waiver of counsel. Similarly, in describing what kind of understanding is needed as to the "nature of the charges," some courts have suggested that an understanding of the specific elements of the crime is not needed for waiver of counsel, though it may be needed for acceptance of a guilty plea.

The states are free, of course, to go beyond the minimal constitutional requirements. They may insist, as a matter of state law, that a valid waiver always be conditioned on the trial judge having specifically advised the defendant as to the nature of the offense charged, possible punishments, and related matters. Numerous states have adopted this position through court rule or statute. Several also require an in-depth inquiry on the record.

(c) Forfeiture of the Right. A long line of state and federal cases have sustained trial court rulings that forced defendants to proceed pro se because they failed to obtain counsel prior to the trial date. In these cases, defendants were advised of their right to retain counsel, given ample time to obtain counsel prior to the scheduled trial date, and nevertheless appeared in court on that date without counsel and without a reasonable excuse for

---

2. Where there is some question as to defendant's mental capacity, or where his statements before the court suggest that he is confused, anything short of a complete *Von Moltke* inquiry is likely to result in the waiver being held invalid. In Godinez v. Moran, 509 U.S. 389, 113 S.Ct. 2680, 125 L.Ed.2d 321 (1993), the Supreme Court considered the question of whether a court was required to conduct a further inquiry into defendant's competency where there was some question about his mental state, but he had just been held competent to stand trial. The Court held that an additional competency hearing, as such, was not mandated by due process since a single standard determined both mental competency to stand trial and mental competency to waive counsel (or plead guilty). The standard for competency to stand trial requires that the defendant have a "sufficient present ability

to consult with his lawyer with a reasonable degree of rational understanding" and "a rational as well as factual understanding of the proceedings against him." No greater mental capacity is required for a waiver of counsel, as the right of the defendant to proceed without counsel does not require that he have "greater powers of comprehension, judgment and reason than would be necessary to stand trial with an attorney." On the other hand, as *Godinez* also cautions, a prior determination that a defendant is competent to stand trial does not mean that the defendant has the necessary understanding of the particular decision to waive counsel (or to plead guilty). "In this sense," the Court noted, "there is a heightened standard for pleading guilty and for waiving the right to counsel, but it is not a heightened standard for competence." See § 11.5 at note 6.

having failed to obtain counsel. The courts typically have characterized such conduct by defendant as a "waiver" or "waiver by conduct" of the right to counsel. However, the circumstances in many of these cases clearly did not fit the traditional definition of a defense waiver in the right to counsel context— that is, a defendant's "intentional relinquishment or abandonment of a known right." Initially, the facts strongly suggest that the defendant had not intended to relinquish his right to counsel. Secondly, the trial court in some instances dispensed with even the barest *Von Moltke* inquiry that would have been needed for a true waiver. Finally, even if such an inquiry may be deemed unnecessary where defendant's conduct unequivocally shows an intentional abandonment of his right, that characterization would appear to depend upon a prior warning as to the consequences of failing to have counsel at the time scheduled for trial, and the cases do not always refer to such a warning having been given. Most often, the analysis offered by the courts fits the category of "forfeiture" rather than "waiver." As the Supreme Court explained in *United States v. Olano*,[3] a forfeiture rests on the failure to make "a timely assertion of a right" rather than an intentional abandonment of the right. What these courts have held, in effect, is that the state's interest in maintaining an orderly trial schedule and the defendant's negligence, indifference, or possibly purposeful delaying tactic, combined to justify a forfeiture of defendant's right to counsel in much the same way that the defendant's assault upon his counsel can result in his loss of representation by counsel. Some courts, however, have refused to adopt such an analysis, insisting that there be at least some evidence of a intentional relinquishment in the defendant's failure to retain counsel prior to the scheduled trial date.

§ 11.4   Choice of Counsel

(a) Judicial Discretion in Selecting Appointed Counsel. Courts generally hold that the initial selection of counsel to represent an indigent is a matter resting within the almost absolute discretion of the trial court. The indigent has no right to counsel of his choice even though that attorney is available and his appointment would not be more costly to the state than the appointment of the attorney that the trial court would otherwise select. The trial court's authority to appoint any competent attorney it chooses, without regard to defendant's preference for another attorney, is said to rest on three grounds. First, "judges assume that they can choose a more able attorney than the indigent because they know the abilities of the available local counsel." Second, there is concern that allowing defendant to choose his own attorney will disrupt the "even handed distribution of assignments." Accepting defendant's choice is likely to impose a substantial burden on the more experienced attorneys, as well as give an advantage to repeat offenders, who are most likely to know and select those attorneys. Third, since the Sixth Amendment guarantees the defendant a right only to representation that is competent, and not to that representation that he believes (correctly or not) to be the best, the trial court may value over the defendant's choice the administrative convenience of an appointment system that ignores defendant's preference. Such an appointment system saves time and effort as the court need not determine the availability and competency of the attorney preferred by defendant, or offer an explanation when that attorney is not selected. Also, the government may reduce its costs by utilizing a public defender agency or contracting with private firms for regular representation of indigents.

At least two states have departed from the traditional position that allows a trial court to completely disregard the defendant's preference for a particular counsel. They bar trial courts from adopting an assignment policy that automatically overrides the defendant's request for a particular counsel (where counsel is willing to take the appointment). The court must consider the defendant's preference and give the defendant an opportunity to state the reasons supporting his preference. It retains discretion to reject that preference if defen-

---

3. 507 U.S. 725, 113 S.Ct. 1770, 123 L.Ed.2d 508 (1993).

dant's reasons are matched by "countervailing considerations of comparable weight." Whether administrative factors (e.g., utilization of local lawyers and systemic distribution of assignments) meet that standard depends upon the significance of the reasons advanced by the defendant. The defendant's strongest case is presented where requested counsel previously represented the defendant in similar matters and also has special familiarity with this particular prosecution.

(b) Replacement of Appointed Counsel. Because the indigent defendant has no right to appointed counsel of choice, he also has no right to replace one appointed counsel with another even if that can be done without causing any delay in the proceedings. The defendant has a right to substitution only upon establishing "good cause, such as a conflict of interest, a complete breakdown of communication, or an irreconcilable conflict which [could] lead * * * to an apparently unjust verdict."[1] The mere loss of confidence in his appointed counsel does not establish "good cause." Defendant must have some well founded reason for believing that the appointed attorney cannot or will not competently represent him. Thus the defendant is not entitled to new counsel simply because the attorney told defendant that his chances of being acquitted were slim. Similarly, the defendant cannot insist upon new counsel because he doesn't like the appointed counsel's "attitude," association with the prosecutor, or approach on matters of strategy. Although an irreconcilable conflict establishes good cause, courts warn that defendant cannot manufacture good cause by abusive and uncooperative behavior. Indeed, such behavior may lead to the court allowing coun-

sel to withdraw, and requiring defendant to proceed pro se on the ground that he forfeited or "waived by conduct" his right to counsel.

Since the indigent defendant must be satisfied with a competent (though not preferred) counsel, the Supreme Court in *Morris v. Slappy*[2] recognized a broad discretion in the trial court to force a substitution of counsel where awaiting the availability of the originally appointed and preferred counsel would disrupt the court's schedule. In *Slappy*, the public defender originally assigned to defendant's case was hospitalized for emergency surgery and a replacement was assigned. As the court of appeals read the record, defendant had "timely and in good faith moved for a delay" until the original defender could return to the case. When the replacement attorney acknowledged that he was prepared to go to trial, the trial court denied the defendant's motion. The court of appeals concluded that the denial was contrary to the Sixth Amendment because it violated defendant's "right to a meaningful attorney-client relationship." The Supreme Court held that the court of appeals had (1) misread the record as to the timeliness and purpose of defendant's continuance motion, and (2) erred in concluding that "the Sixth Amendment guarantees an accused a meaningful attorney-client relationship." The majority opinion stressed the "broad discretion that must be granted trial courts on matters of continuance." Thus, its rejection of what it described as the lower court's "novel idea" of a constitutional right to a meaningful client-attorney relationship presumably would not be carried so far as to allow the trial judge to override a defendant's objection and replace a

---

§ 11.4

1. Lower courts have held that a trial court cannot summarily dismiss a defense motion to replace appointed counsel simply because the motion fails to clearly specify one of these grounds. The duty of the trial court is to further inquire to identify the precise cause of the defendant's dissatisfaction. However, in light of the reasoning of Mickens v. Taylor, discussed in § 11.9 at note 8, post-*Mickens* appellate rulings have held that the failure to conduct an adequate inquiry should not result in an automatic reversal on appeal following a conviction. *Mickens* held that, even though a trial judge violated a constitutionally imposed duty by failing to inquire into the possible conflict of interest of counsel, the appropriate

response was not to automatically reverse the defendant's conviction, but to remand to determine whether counsel's performance was adversely affected by a conflict. *Mickens* did recognize an exception, however, where counsel had asked for replacement based on alleged conflict. There the failure to conduct an inquiry did require automatic reversal. See Holloway v. Arkansas, discussed in § 11.9(b). Should appointed counsel call to the court's attention good cause for replacement, such as an actual conflict or a complete and irreparable breakdown in communicating, here too a failure to conduct an inquiry may call for automatic reversal on appeal following a conviction.

2. 461 U.S. 1, 103 S.Ct. 1610, 75 L.Ed.2d 610 (1983).

previously appointed counsel even though continued representation by that counsel did not create any scheduling difficulties. Several lower courts have recognized a protected interest of the defendant in staying with the original appointed counsel in such a situation, in part to preclude substitution from being used as a means of discouraging a presentation that is acceptable to the defendant but not the court.

(c) Choice of Retained Counsel. Where defendant has a Sixth Amendment or due process right to the assistance of counsel, that constitutional guarantee encompasses the "right to retained counsel of his choosing" as an aspect of his " 'right to spend his own money to obtain the advice and assistance . . . of counsel.' " However, since the "essential aim of the [constitutional right to counsel] is to guarantee an effective advocate for each criminal defendant, rather than to ensure that a defendant will inexorably be represented by the lawyer whom he prefers," the right to counsel of choice can be circumscribed by a sufficient overriding interest of the judicial system. Where that interest is directed at precluding representation by a particular individual or category of individuals, it usually will be related to preserving fundamental tenets of the adversary system—such as competent representation by counsel, adherence of counsel to the ethical standards of the legal profession, or preserving an appearance of fairness. Common illustrations of instances in which defendant's right to retain counsel of choice is overridden on such grounds include the denial of defendant's choice to be represented by a person who is not a member of the bar, by an attorney who is not licensed in the particular state, and by a former prosecutor who was involved previously in the prosecution of the same or related charges.

In some instances, categorical prohibitions can be utilized by a court to bar defense representation by a particular person. The court need not assess whether representation by that person in this particular instance would be inconsistent in fact with the requirements of the adversary system. Thus, as the Supreme Court has noted, a court may automatically reject representation by a person not a current member of the bar, "regardless of his persuasive powers." In other instances, as illustrated by *Wheat v. United States*,[3] the court must engage in a case-by-case evaluation of the interests at stake. In *Wheat*, as discussed in § 11.9(c), the Supreme Court sustained the trial court's discretion to preclude representation by an attorney who was also representing codefendants, even though the defendant was willing to waive his right to conflict-free counsel. That discretion was subjected to restrictions, however, that required consideration of a variety of factors as they related to the particular case.

The defendant's capacity to retain counsel of choice may also be restricted by judicial action that is not directed at precluding representation by a particular attorney, but nonetheless has that impact. The classic illustration is the scheduling of the trial at a time when defendant's preferred counsel would be unavailable (usually due to a schedule-conflict). While the judicial interest here is not as significant as the interest in preserving fundamental elements of the adversary system, it nonetheless need not give way entirely to the defendant's preference for particular counsel. The "right to retain counsel of one's choice," appellate courts have frequently noted, "may not be insisted upon in a manner that will obstruct an orderly procedure in courts of justice and deprive such courts of their inherent powers to control the same." At the same time, the appellate courts have also recognized that, under some circumstances, the failure of a trial court to alter its preferred schedule so as to allow defendant to be represented by counsel of choice will result in a constitutional violation.

When will a trial court be required constitutionally to schedule a trial so as to allow representation by defendant's counsel of choice? Perhaps because scheduling accommodations are more readily made in the initial setting of the trial date, appellate decisions considering that issue have in large part dealt with trial court refusals to alter schedules by

---

3. 486 U.S. 153, 108 S.Ct. 1692, 100 L.Ed.2d 140 (1988).

granting continuances that would allow defendants to retain new counsel. As in the replacement of appointed counsel, if the defendant can establish that his current counsel would not be able to give him competent representation (as where a conflict of interest exists), the defendant's constitutional right to the effective assistance of counsel demands granting such continuance as is necessary to substitute new counsel. If the request for a continuance to permit substitution is not justified by good cause grounds for discharging current counsel, the trial court then must undertake the process of balancing the defendant's interest in counsel of choice against the "public's interest in prompt and efficient administration of justice." In reviewing the trial judge's decision not to grant a continuance that would have allowed the substitution of counsel, appellate courts tend to be guided by the due process standard set forth by the Supreme Court in *Ungar v. Sarafite*:[4] "The matter of continuance is traditionally within the trial judge's discretion * * *. There are no mechanical tests for deciding when a denial of a continuance is so arbitrary as to violate [defendant's constitutional rights]. The answer must be found in the circumstances present in every case, particularly in the reasons presented to the trial judge at the time the request is denied."[5]

Restrictions upon the defendant's right to counsel generally flow, as in the continuance cases, from a countervailing governmental interest relating to judicial administration. The impact of the restriction generally is to limit the defendant's choice, but not to eliminate it altogether by forcing the defendant to accept counsel selected by the court. Also, such restrictions are not directed at particular offenses, so their impact ordinarily does not fall disproportionately upon a certain class of defendants. In *Caplin & Drysdale, Chartered v. United States*,[6] the Supreme Court upheld a

restriction on defendant's ability to retain counsel of choice that had none of these characteristics. At issue there were asset forfeiture provisions directed at persons charged and convicted of specific crimes and carrying the potential of rendering a defendant unable to hire any counsel, thereby forcing him to accept court appointed counsel. The Court held that these provisions nonetheless did not impermissibly burden a defendant's Sixth Amendment right to counsel of choice.

The Continuing Criminal Enterprise statute applied in *Caplin & Drysdale* provides that a person engaged in, and subsequently convicted of, specified drug violations forfeits all property "constituting, or derived from," the "proceeds" of those violations. Where such property has been transferred to a third-party, the government can recapture that property unless the third-party was both a bona fide recipient and a person "reasonably without cause to believe" that the property was subject to forfeiture at the time of its receipt. The statute further authorizes the government to obtain a pretrial restraining order against a defendant's transfer of assets upon a showing of probable cause to believe those assets will ultimately be proven forfeitable. The petitioner in *Caplin & Drysdale* was a law firm that had received funds from a defendant after he had been charged in an indictment seeking forfeiture and after a restraining order had been issued freezing his assets. It argued that each of the statute's forfeiture provisions impermissibly burdened a defendant's Sixth Amendment rights. Where a pretrial restraining order was issued, a defendant was deprived of the use of assets that could otherwise be utilized to retain counsel of choice. Even where a restraining order was not obtained by the government, a prospective defense counsel might be reluctant to represent the defendant because his assets might be held forfeited upon conviction and any funds paid to the attorney

---

4. 376 U.S. 575, 84 S.Ct. 841, 11 L.Ed.2d 921 (1964).

5. Since the defendant is relying on a right to counsel of choice, a constitutional violation occurs even though substitute counsel performed competently. However, lower courts are divided as to whether the violation of that right is "structural" and calls for an automatic reversal of a conviction, or is subject to a harmless error standard. See

§ 27.6(d). Courts taking the former position analogize the denial of the right to counsel of choice to the denial of the right to proceed pro se. See § 11.5 at note 4.

6. 491 U.S. 617, 109 S.Ct. 2646, 105 L.Ed.2d 528 (1989).

recaptured by the government. Although a particular defendant might have other assets with which to retain counsel, the Court assessed the constitutionality of the statute under the assumption that "there will be cases" in which the end result of the forfeiture provisions would be to render a defendant "unable to retain the attorney of his choice." Justice White's opinion for the majority concluded, however, that there would be no Sixth Amendment violation even in such a situation.

Justice White's opinion initially cited the well established principle that a "defendant has no Sixth Amendment right to spend another person's money for services rendered by an attorney, even if those funds are the only way that defendant will be able to retain the counsel of his choice." Petitioner had conceded as much, but had argued that the property here was not truly that of another, as would be the case with stolen property. Petitioner maintained that a defendant's use of assets in which others have "a pre-existing property right" should be distinguished from the "fictive property law concept" that underlies the government's claim to forfeitable assets. While the four dissenters found this distinction persuasive, the majority did not. Justice White responded that petitioner's argument failed to recognize the "substantial" property rights of the government under the forfeiture statute. Under the well accepted "taint theory," long recognized in forfeiture law generally, the defendant never had "good title" to the property, as the government obtained a "vested property interest" in the proceeds at the point at which the illegal transaction occurred. Moreover, the government's interest was not limited to simply "separating a criminal from his ill-gotten gains," although Congress obviously has a legitimate interest in "lessen[ing] the economic power of organized crime and drug enterprises" by stripping them of their "undeserved economic power" (including "the ability to command high priced legal talent"). The assets forfeited pursuant to the statute were to be deposited in a fund used to support law-enforcement efforts in various ways, and where the assets came from rightful owners, defrauded of their property, those owners

could seek restitution. Finally, to sustain petitioner's argument here was to cast doubt on such accepted practices as the use of jeopardy assessments in criminal tax cases and to open the door to forfeiture exemptions for defendants desiring to exercise any constitutionally protected freedom that may require the expenditure of funds.

The petitioner in *Caplin & Drysdale* also contended that the forfeiture statute "upset the balance of forces between the accused and accuser" by allowing the prosecution, through its discretion as to the utilization of the forfeiture remedy and the pretrial restraining order, to exercise what the dissenters described as "an intolerable degree of power over any private attorney." The majority saw this claim as analogous to that rejected in *Wheat v. United States,* where government motions to disqualify defense counsel on conflict-of-interest grounds had been challenged as likely to be used by prosecutors to eliminate effective adversaries. Here too, an otherwise permissible procedure would not be struck down because of the potential for abuse. "Cases involving particular abuses," Justice White noted, "can be dealt with by the lower courts, when (and if) any such cases arise."

(d) The Pro Se Alternative. When a court denies a defendant's request for appointment of new counsel or for a continuance to permit the defendant to hire new counsel, it commonly will inform the defendant that he either must proceed with his current counsel or represent himself. Very often the defendant will choose the latter alternative, noting that he does so only because it is the lesser of two evils. If an appellate court concludes on appeal that the trial judge erred in failing to appoint new counsel or in denying the continuance, defendant's choice of proceeding pro se will be viewed as "involuntary" and his conviction reversed. However, if the trial court's decision is upheld, the defendant cannot complain about being "forced into" proceeding pro se. It is not inconsistent with the concept of a voluntary waiver to require a choice between waiver and another option, provided that other option is itself consistent with the protection of his constitutional rights.

Though a defendant's decision to proceed pro se made in response to a proper rejection of his motion to substitute counsel will not be viewed as involuntary, it still may be challenged successfully on appeal if it did not reflect a knowing and intelligent waiver of counsel. Where a defendant appears for trial on the scheduled date without having retained counsel [see § 11.3(c)], requiring the defendant to proceed pro se is the only option open to the court if it is to hold the trial on that date. Accordingly, the need for orderly administration may require that defendant's unreasonable failure to obtain counsel be treated as a forfeiture of his right to counsel. A forfeiture is not necessary, however, where the case can proceed either with the current counsel (for whom the defendant could not successfully substitute) or with the defendant proceeding pro se. Accordingly, courts uniformly insist that the choice to proceed pro se in this situation be tested by the traditional standards applicable to "true waivers" of counsel. Some jurisdictions require that the court inform the defendant on the record of the hazards of proceeding pro se and determine through a colloquy that he has the requisite understanding for a waiver. Others require only that the record establish the defendant's needed understanding in one fashion or another, which sometimes can be done without judicial warnings or an ensuing colloquy. All agree, however, that a pro se decision made as a second choice to a denied substitution of counsel must meet the same waiver standard as the pro se request made as a first choice.

§ 11.5 The Constitutional Right to Self–Representation

(a) The Faretta Ruling. In *Faretta v. California*,[1] the defendant requested, well before trial, that he be allowed to represent himself. After holding a hearing on defendant's ability to conduct his own defense, which raised questions as to defendant's knowledge of such matters as the hearsay rule, the trial court refused defendant's request and appointed counsel to represent him. On appeal from defendant's conviction, the state appellate court found no error, noting that defendant had no constitutional right to proceed pro se. A divided Supreme Court rejected that contention and held that defendant had been denied a right guaranteed by the Sixth Amendment.

Justice Stewart's opinion for the *Faretta* majority relied heavily on the "structure of the Sixth Amendment" and the "English and colonial jurisprudence from which [the Sixth Amendment] emerged." Although the colonial practice had deviated from the English common law in permitting representation by counsel in felony cases, such representation always was at the choice of the defendant. Indeed, the right of self-representation was specifically noted in various state constitutional and statutory provisions that established a right to counsel. While the Sixth Amendment did not refer explicitly to self-representation, that right was "necessarily implied by the structure of the Amendment." The Amendment speaks of confrontation, compulsory process, and notice as rights of "the accused." The implication of this wording, Justice Stewart noted, was that those rights were not merely made available to the defense, but were rights of the accused personally, that he could exercise himself in presenting his own defense. The counsel provision "supplements this design" by referring to the defendant's right to the "assistance" of counsel. The clear purpose of the Amendment, Justice Stewart concluded, was to make "counsel, like the other defense tools guaranteed, * * * an aid to a willing defendant—not an organ of the State interposed between an unwilling defendant and his right to defend himself personally."

The *Faretta* majority acknowledged that a constitutional right to proceed pro se "seems to cut against the grain" of decisions, like *Powell v. Alabama* and *Gideon v. Wainwright,* that are based on the premise that "the help of a lawyer is essential to assure a fair trial."[2] The majority rejected, however, the dissenters' contention that the state's interest in provid-

§ 11.5
1. 422 U.S. 806, 95 S.Ct. 2525, 45 L.Ed.2d 562 (1975).

2. See § 11.1(a).

ing a fair trial permitted it to insist upon representation by counsel. The framers of the Sixth Amendment were well aware of the value of counsel in obtaining a fair trial, but placed on a higher plane the "inestimable worth of free choice." Notwithstanding the lawyer's expertise, "it is not inconceivable that in some rare instances, the defendant may in fact present his case more effectively by conducting his own defense." Since "the defendant, and not his lawyer or the State, will bear the personal consequences of the conviction," he should be free to decide whether his is such a case. Although his decision may not be wise, his "choice must be honored out of that respect for the individual which is the lifeblood of the law."

Having established a constitutional right to self-representation at trial,[3] the Court then turned to the question of whether the defendant in this case had been denied that right. The defendant who proceeds pro se, it noted, must act "knowingly and intelligently" in giving up those "traditional benefits associated with the right to counsel." He should "be made aware of the dangers and disadvantages of self-representation, so that the record will establish that he 'knows what he is doing and his choice is made with eyes open.'" The defendant need not, however, "have the skill and experience of a lawyer in order competently and intelligently to choose self-representation." Here the record showed that the defendant was "literate, competent, and understanding, and that he was voluntarily exercising his informed free will." That he may not have mastered the intricacies of the hearsay rule, or that he lacked other "technical legal knowledge," was "not relevant to an assessment of his knowing exercise of the right

to defend himself." Accordingly, the lower court had erred in forcing him to accept appointed counsel.

The Court in *Faretta,* once it found a trial court error in failing to allow defendant to proceed pro se, reversed defendant's conviction. This disposition suggested that the denial of the right to proceed pro se was not subject to a harmless error analysis, but Justice Blackmun, in his *Faretta* dissent, cited as an issue left open by *Faretta* the possible application of the harmless error rule of *Chapman v. California.* Any doubts raised by Justice Blackmun's dissent were put to rest, however, by a footnote in the later case of *McKaskle v. Wiggins.*[4] The Court there noted: "Since the right of self-representation is a right that when exercised usually increases the likelihood of a trial outcome unfavorable to the defendant, its denial is not amenable to harmless error analysis. The right is either respected or denied; its deprivation cannot be harmless."

(b) Notification. Dissenting in *Faretta,* Justice Blackmun raised the question of whether "every defendant [must] be advised of his right to proceed pro se." The Court had held that notification of the right to counsel is essential; might not a similar requirement apply to the "other side" of defendant's Sixth Amendment right? Lower courts have uniformly assumed that there is no constitutional obligation to inform the defendant of his constitutional right to proceed pro se in the absence of a clear indication on his part that he desires to consider that option. This position is based in part on concern that notification of the right to proceed pro se might undermine the "overriding constitutional policy" favoring the provision of counsel.

3. In Martinez v. Court of Appeal of California, 528 U.S. 152, 120 S.Ct. 684, 145 L.Ed.2d 597 (2000), the Court unanimously refused to extend *Faretta* to self-representation on appeal. *Faretta,* the Court noted, relied on the structure of the Sixth Amendment, but since the Sixth Amendment does not apply once the case has gone beyond the trial stage, a right to self-representation on appeal would have to be based on due process. From the perspective afforded by due process, the Court was "entirely unpersuaded," in light of the "practices that prevail in the nation today," that the "risk of either disloyalty or suspicion of disloyalty [in representation] is of sufficient con-

cern to conclude that a constitutional right of self-representation is a necessary component of a fair appellate proceeding." Also, with defendant's position having shifted from that of an "accused" to a convicted defendant, the "autonomy interests" presented at this point are "less compelling" than in *Faretta.* The Court also examined the colonial and post-revolutionary history relied upon in *Faretta* and found it less than convincing and inapplicable, in any event, to the limited appellate process at that time.

4. 465 U.S. 168, 104 S.Ct. 944, 79 L.Ed.2d 122 (1984), also discussed in § 27.6(d).

Courts are not quite so uniform in describing what constitutes a sufficient indication of a defendant's interest in proceeding pro se to impose upon the trial court a duty to explore that interest. Most courts look to *Faretta*, where the Supreme Court noted that the defendant had "clearly and unequivocally declared to the trial judge that he wanted to represent himself," and hold that no action is required by the trial court absent the defendant's unequivocal expression of a desire to proceed pro se. Some courts have stated, however, that defendant need do no more than state his request "unambiguously" so that "no reasonable person can say the request was not made." This suggests that the request can be "conditional," provided it does speak specifically to self-representation as an alternative, rather than simply addressing a desire for new counsel. Under this position, should the court reject the defendant's preferred alternative of substituting counsel, it must then explore with defendant his back-up position of pro se representation.

(c) Requisite Warnings and Judicial Inquiry. In the course of exercising his constitutional right to proceed pro se, the defendant must necessarily waive his Sixth Amendment right to counsel. Accordingly, *Faretta* stressed that trial courts, before permitting a defendant to represent himself, must determine that he is knowingly and intelligently relinquishing the benefits of representation by counsel. Courts are agreed as to the preferred procedure in making that determination. Initially, the trial court should ascertain that the defendant is aware of the various matters noted in Justice Black's *Von Moltke* opinion.[5] Then, because the defendant here desires to represent himself at trial (rather than to simply plead guilty without a lawyer), the trial court should take special care to advise the defendant as to the pitfalls of self-representation. Appellate opinions have suggested that the defendant should be informed at least of the following: (1) that "presenting a defense is not a simple matter of telling one's story," but requires adherence to various "technical rules" governing the conduct of a trial; (2) that a lawyer has

substantial experience and training in trial procedure and that the prosecution will be represented by an experienced attorney; (3) that a person unfamiliar with legal procedures may inadvertently give the prosecutor a windfall by failing to make objections to inadmissible evidence, may fail to make effective use of such rights as the voir dire of jurors, and may make tactical decisions that produce unintended consequences; (4) that there may be possible defenses and other rights of which counsel would be aware and if those are not timely asserted, they may be lost permanently; (5) that a defendant proceeding pro se will not be allowed to complain on appeal about the competency of his representation; and (6) "that the effectiveness of his defense may well be diminished by his dual role as attorney and accused."

If the defendant persists in his request to proceed pro se, notwithstanding the court's warnings as to the possible disadvantages of self-representation, then the preferred procedure directs the court to ascertain that the defendant understands and appreciates those disadvantages and their possible consequences. This requires, appellate courts note, a "penetrating and comprehensive inquiry," including an interchange with the defendant that produces more than passive "yes" and "no" responses. The trial court should explore the primary factors that might have a bearing on defendant's ability to comprehend, including age, education, social background, mental health history, prior experience or familiarity with criminal trials, and prior consultation with counsel in deciding to proceed pro se.

In most jurisdictions, the preferred procedure described above, as to both warnings and inquiries, is only that; appellate courts describe the procedure as the "better" practice, but do not require that the lower courts adhere to it. However, some jurisdictions do mandate specific warnings and a particular inquiry by statute, court rule, or the exercise of the appellate court's supervisory power. In these jurisdictions, a lack of substantial compliance with the prescribed process ordinarily

---

5. See § 11.3(b).

will result in an appellate reversal without considering whether there also was a Sixth Amendment violation. Thus, courts in such jurisdictions have found it unnecessary to consider the extent to which the Sixth Amendment requires either or both warnings as to the disadvantages of proceeding pro se and an on-the-record inquiry as to the defendant's appreciation of those disadvantages and their possible consequences. As discussed below, courts considering those issues have reached somewhat differing conclusions.

As discussed in § 11.3(b), while it is preferred that the trial court inform the defendant (and inquire into his understanding) as to each of the *Von Moltke* factors, that procedure is not viewed as a constitutional necessity for a waiver of counsel at arraignment. Arguably, *Faretta* suggests otherwise as to informing the prospective defendant of the pitfalls of self-representation. The *Faretta* opinion noted that the defendant "should be made aware of the dangers and disadvantages of self-representation, so that the record will establish that 'he knows what he is doing and his choice is made with his eyes open.' " Relying upon this statement, several courts have suggested that a waiver is not constitutionally acceptable unless the trial judge specifically warns the defendant of the dangers of self-representation. Moreover, the judge's statement must consist of more than "vague, general admonishments, without reference to specific disadvantages," and it must be followed by an inquiry realistically "designed to reveal [defendant's] understanding." Even the most adamant rejection of counsel (including abusive behavior forcing counsel to seek withdrawal) does not excuse the court's failure to make such an inquiry.

Other courts take the position that *Faretta* requires only that the defendant have been aware of the disadvantages of proceeding pro se, and that awareness can be established without regard to any admonitions or colloquies. A waiver is constitutionally acceptable where such factors as defendant's involvement in previous criminal trials, his representation by counsel prior to the trial, and his explanation of his reasons for proceeding pro se indi-

cate that he was fully aware of the difficulties of self-representation. For at least some courts, such factors can serve the same function as an extensive colloquy only when they provide "a compelling case of circumstantial evidence that the pro se defendant knew what he or she was doing." Moreover, the courts generally agree that there is special need for an extensive explanation of the pitfalls of self-representation where the defendant states that he has some doubts about proceeding pro se, but will do so because the court will not replace appointed counsel or grant a continuance permitting him to retain new counsel.

Though the Supreme Court concluded in *Godinez v. Moran*[6] that a defendant found competent to stand trial was thereby mentally competent to waive counsel and proceed to trial, it noted that such mental competency did not in itself ensure the understanding needed for a proper waiver of counsel under *Faretta*. Thus, *Godinez* is fully consistent with demanding special care in questioning the defendant to ensure that he understands the ramifications of his actions where his irrational behavior or medical history suggests that he may be suffering from a mental illness. Of course, once the defendant has been found competent to stand trial and his waiver of counsel is found to be acceptable under *Faretta*, his competency and waiver may again be called into question by his subsequent behavior, but not simply his ineptness in representing himself.

(d) Grounds for Denial. Once a clear and unequivocal request is made, *Faretta* suggests only three possible grounds for denying that request. First, *Faretta* stressed that the request in that case was made "well before the date of trial." This suggests that, at some point, a request might be so disruptive of the orderly schedule of proceedings as to justify rejection on that ground alone. Provided defendant does not demand additional time to prepare, lower courts generally deem pro se motions to be timely as long as they are made before trial. On the other hand, the trial court is recognized as having broad discretion to

---

6. 509 U.S. 389, 113 S.Ct. 2680, 125 L.Ed.2d 321 (1993), also discussed in note 2 of § 11.3.

reject as untimely a request made during the course of the trial.

Second, *Faretta* noted that "the trial judge may terminate self-representation by a defendant who engages in serious and obstructionist misconduct." Ordinarily, this authority would be exercised only after the defendant has begun to represent himself. However, in exceptional situations, the defendant's behavior in the course of seeking to obtain self-representation may in itself be disruptive and thereby justify denying his pro se motion.

Third, by requiring a valid waiver of counsel as a prerequisite for self-representation, *Faretta* recognized the authority of a trial court to refuse to permit self-representation when, despite its efforts to explain the consequences of waiver, defendant is unable to reach the level of appreciation needed for a knowing and intelligent waiver. *Faretta* also makes clear, however, that a defendant does not need legal expertise nor unusual intelligence to meet its standard of awareness of the dangers and disadvantages of self-representation. Indeed, lower courts have read *Faretta* as indicating that, with a proper explanation by the trial judge, a defendant "who is sui juris and mentally competent" should be able to make a knowing and intelligent waiver. Accordingly, trial courts hesitate to deny the request of an adult defendant unless he appears to be suffering from some significant mental disability. Even then, in light of *Godinez*, the disability should only bar pro se representation if it renders the defendant incompetent to stand trial, or unable to make a knowing and intelligent relinquishment of the benefits of representation by counsel.

There also is some authority to support a denial of self-representation where a mental or physical disability renders a defendant unable to communicate in an understandable manner, or unable to abide by the rules of procedure and courtroom protocol. Indeed, a few courts have even suggested that self-representation can be denied where the defendant lacks the intelligence or education needed to present his defense in a coherent fashion. When courts turn to such subjective evaluations, however, they can readily be accused of circumventing the *Faretta* prohibition of denials based on legal ineptitude by looking to proxy weaknesses in communication and organizational skills.

(e) Subsequent Challenge to Ineffective Representation. Commenting upon the limitations of self-representation, the *Faretta* opinion noted:

> Neither is * * * [the right of self-representation] a license not to comply with relevant rules of procedural and substantive law. Thus, whatever else may or may not be open to him on appeal, a defendant who elects to represent himself cannot thereafter complain that the quality of his own defense amounted to a denial of "effective assistance of counsel."

Relying upon this statement, lower courts have consistently rejected claims of defendants that their pro se presentation was so inadequate as to result in a denial of a fair trial. The courts note that the defendant's failure to utilize even the ordinary skills of laymen may in itself be a strategic ploy of a defendant hoping to create grounds for an appellate reversal of an almost certain conviction. They also frequently point to efforts of the trial judge to assist the defendant (though noting that such efforts are not constitutionally mandated) or the availability of consultation with standby counsel (although appointment of such counsel also is not mandatory).

Appellate courts generally have also adhered to the principle that pro se defendants are to be treated on appeal no differently than defendants with counsel as to objections that were not properly preserved at trial. This position is viewed as logically dictated by *Faretta's* comment that pro se defendants are not thereby granted a "license not to comply with relevant rules of procedural and substantive law." Appellate courts also will sustain, as within the trial court's discretion, the refusal to bend rules governing presentation of evidence, especially when those rules serve the important function of ensuring fairness to the opposing party. While the pro se defendant who is incarcerated must have a right of access to legal materials (within limits), he will not be heard to complain on appeal that his ignorance of various procedural requirements should be excused because the jail's law library was inadequate (particularly where standby counsel was available).

(f) Standby Counsel. Justice Stewart noted in *Faretta* that "a state may—even over objection by the accused—appoint a 'standby counsel' to aid the accused if and when the accused requests help, and to be available to represent the accused in the event that termination of the defendant's self-representation is necessary." This statement was viewed by the lower court in *McKaskle v. Wiggins*[7] as restricting the role of standby counsel, in the absence of a defendant's request for assistance, to "being seen but not heard." Counsel's failure to restrict his participation to that limited role was held by the lower court to have violated defendant's *Faretta* right, thereby requiring a new trial. A divided Supreme Court disagreed, holding that the seen-but-not-heard standard was entirely too narrow.

The *McKaskle* majority noted initially that the trial court had the authority, notwithstanding defendant's objection, to both appoint standby counsel and to direct that counsel to "steer defendant through the basic procedures of the trial." It was appropriate for the judge to thereby "relieve [himself] of the need to explain and enforce the basic rules of court room protocol or to assist the defendant in overcoming routine [procedural] obstacles that stand in the way of defendant's achievement of his own clearly indicated goals." Unsolicited and undesired participation by standby counsel did present a difficulty, however, when it went beyond this limited role and involved more than "routine clerical or procedural matters." Even here, however, all such participation did not per se constitute a violation of defendant's right of self-representation. In determining whether such participation undermined defendant's *Faretta* right, the Court would apply a two-pronged test. First, did "standby counsel's participation over defendant's objection effectively allow counsel to make or substantially interfere with any significant tactical decisions, or to control the

questioning of witnesses, or to speak instead of the defendant on any matter of importance"? Such action necessarily undermines the defendant's right of self-representation since it deprives him of the "actual control over the case he chooses to present to the jury." Second, even if the defendant was able to present his case in his own way, did the additional unsolicited participation of counsel "destroy the jury's perception that the defendant is representing himself"? That impact also eviscerates defendant's *Faretta* right since the "defendant's appearance in the status of one conducting his own defense" is an important aspect of the "dignity and autonomy" of the individual protected in *Faretta.* Moreover, "from the jury's perspective, the message conveyed by the defense may depend as much on the messenger as the message itself."

Although appellate courts have suggested that appointment of standby counsel is to be preferred, it is not constitutionally required. The defendant cannot complain because the trial court failed to appoint standby counsel or failed to appoint standby counsel of his choice. The appointment of standby counsel does not relieve the court of the responsibility of ensuring that the choice to proceed pro se meets the standards of *Faretta,* and an improper waiver of counsel cannot be cured by the assistance of standby counsel during the trial.

(g) Hybrid Representation. Under a hybrid form of representation, defendant and counsel act, in effect, as co-counsel, with each speaking for the defense during different phases of the trial. Defendants have claimed that *Faretta's* recognition of self-representation and representation by counsel as "independent constitutional rights" logically establishes a constitutional grounding for hybrid representation. Such representation, they argue, simply is the product of partially waiving each of these rights, no different than the partial waiver allowed with respect to other rights (e.g., the partial waiver of confrontation when the defense cross-examines some witnesses and not others). They note that the Sixth Amendment guarantee speaks of the "assis-

---

7.   465 U.S. 168, 104 S.Ct. 944, 79 L.Ed.2d 122 (1984).

tance" of counsel, a term that readily suggests active participation by both counsel and the defendant himself. Although raised in a substantial number of cases, this contention has failed to persuade either federal or state courts. They have uniformly held that there is no Sixth Amendment right to hybrid representation. The constitutional rights to self-representation and representation by counsel are viewed as mutually exclusive, though the trial court may permit hybrid representation, in its discretion, as "a matter of grace." Of course, since hybrid representation is in part pro se representation, allowing it without a proper *Faretta* inquiry can create constitutional difficulties.

Lower court opinions rejecting defense assertions of a right to hybrid representation have relied on several grounds. Most often cited is the need to grant the trial judge sufficient authority to maintain the "dignity and decorum" of the courtroom and to ensure an orderly and expeditious trial. Another judicial concern is the impact that a right to hybrid representation would have upon the role of counsel as the "manager of the lawsuit." Traditionally, tactical decisions may be made by counsel without even consulting his client. Recognition of a constitutional right to hybrid representation arguably would allow the defendant to force at least appointed counsel to relinquish that authority and accept an "inferior position" as to those portions of the trial in which defendant would proceed pro se. Finally, there is suspicion that hybrid representation would often be used by the defense primarily to permit defendant to present an unsworn statement to the jury. Counsel would carry most of the load, but the defendant would present an opening or closing argument to the jury that would allow him, in effect, to "testify" without being subjected to cross-examination. Although a defendant acting as his own counsel can be restricted to the traditional limits applicable to opening or closing state-

ments, it might be difficult to impose those limitations in a rigid fashion, particularly where he claims a constitutional right to assume this portion of his representation.

§ 11.6 Counsel's Control Over Defense Strategy

(a) "Strategic" vs. "Personal" Decisions. Prior to *Faretta*, a long line of cases had held that a defense counsel had the authority to make various defense decisions on his or her own initiative. Those decisions, commonly characterized as relating to matters of "strategy" or "tactics," were said to be within the "exclusive province" of the lawyer. Counsel had no obligation to consult with the defendant, and if he did consult, had no obligation to follow the defendant's wishes. This was so even where the setting prevented the defendant from obtaining representation by substitute counsel who might follow his wishes. Other defense decisions, however, were said to rest in the ultimate authority of the defendant. As to those decisions, commonly said to require the "personal choice" of the defendant, counsel had to advise the client and abide by the client's directions.[1]

The Supreme Court's decision in *Faretta* was thought by some to have altered this basic division between strategic and personal decisions. The *Faretta* opinion had referred to the "law and tradition" that granted counsel ultimate authority to make "binding decisions of trial strategy in many areas." Indeed it had cited that law and tradition as a factor pointing towards the recognition of an alternative of self-representation where defendant wanted to control his own destiny. The argument was advanced, however, that the overall perspective of the *Faretta* opinion also required that the attorney's ultimate authority be limited, perhaps only to "on-the-spot" decisions where timing considerations precluded consultation with the defendant. *Faretta* had recognized the "personal character" of defendant's "right to

---

§ 11.6

1. The attorney who disagrees with the client's decision on those matters may be allowed to withdraw, depending upon the timing, if the withdrawal will not work to the prejudice of the client. However, if withdrawal is

not allowed because of scheduling difficulties, the attorney must implement the client's directions on a matter within the client's personal control, assuming that implementation does not require the attorney to violate standards of professional responsibility.

make a defense" and this required, as to basic choices shaping the defense, that the final decision be made by the defendant where that was practicable. *Faretta,* it was argued, was "predicated on the view that the function of counsel under the Sixth Amendment is to protect the dignity and autonomy of a person on trial by *assisting* him in making choices that are his to make, not to make choices for him, although counsel may be better able to decide what tactics will be most effective."

In *Jones v. Barnes,*[2] a divided Supreme Court rejected this view of *Faretta. Jones* held that appellate counsel did not have to present a nonfrivolous claim that her client wished to press if counsel believed that the better strategy was to limit her argument and brief to other issues. Counsel was free to follow the time tested advice of countless advocates that inclusion of "every colorable claim" will "dilute and weaken a good case and will not save a bad one." It was for counsel to decide which claims were strong enough to be presented consistent with this strategy. *Faretta* gave the defendant an opportunity to control the presentation of his case by proceeding pro se. Neither it nor decisions defining the obligation of appointed appellate counsel had altered counsel's right to act upon his best professional judgment as to matters of strategy.

The issue of client control was raised in *Jones* through a claim of ineffective assistance of counsel. While that is probably the most common avenue for presenting the issue, questions of client control also may be raised in connection with several other defense contentions. The scope of client control also is presented when an indigent defendant requests appointment of new counsel because his current attorney refuses to accept his directions on an issue that defendant claims should be within his control. The issue similarly is presented when the same ground is advanced by a

defendant seeking a continuance for the purpose of replacing retained counsel. Client control issues often also arise in collateral attacks raising constitutional claims that were not presented at trial. When the state argues that the claim was "waived" by counsel's failure to raise it at trial, the habeas petitioner often responds that a valid waiver of that claim required his personal decision and that counsel had not even consulted with him in deciding not to raise the issue. *Jones* left open whether counsel's strategic decision not to raise on appeal a constitutional claim urged by defendant would bar consideration of that claim on collateral attack. However, various later cases held that a counsel's deliberate decision not to raise a particular claim at trial or on appeal does bar review on collateral attack, provided that decision dealt with a matter subject to counsel's control over strategy.[3]

Although the difference in procedural setting could conceivably influence a court's analysis of the client-control issue, the courts have tended to treat the issue as basically the same whether presented in one procedural context or another. Rulings recognizing attorney or client control with respect to a particular defense decision will be carried over from one procedural context to another. Thus, judicial discussions relating to decision-making authority can appropriately be pieced together, notwithstanding differences in procedural context, in providing a list of those defense decisions that have been categorized as within either defendant's personal choice or defense counsel's strategic control.

The Supreme Court has stated, in dictum or holding, that it is for the defendant to decide whether to take each of the following steps: plead guilty or take action tantamount to entering a guilty plea; waive the right to jury trial; waive his right to be present at trial;

---

2. 463 U.S. 745, 103 S.Ct. 3308, 77 L.Ed.2d 987 (1983).

3. See § 28.4(d), (e). Taylor v. Illinois 484 U.S. 400, 108 S.Ct. 646, 98 L.Ed.2d 798 (1988), reaches a similar conclusion in an analogous procedural context. Defendant there claimed that the trial court had violated his Sixth Amendment rights by refusing to allow the testimony of a defense witness, a sanction imposed because defense counsel had failed to give the prosecution advance notice of the

witness as required by state discovery rules. In rejecting defendant's claim, the Supreme Court viewed as especially significant the defense attorney's authority to adopt, without consulting his client, the tactic of attempting a surprise presentation of a witness in violation of discovery requirements. The Court viewed that decision by counsel as therefore binding upon the defendant in his subsequent challenge. See § 20.6(c).

testify on his own behalf; or forego an appeal. Lower court rulings have added to this group: the waiver of the right to attend important pretrial proceedings; the waiver of the constitutional right to a speedy trial; the refusal (by a competent defendant) to enter an insanity plea; and the decision to withhold defendant's sole defense at the guilt/special circumstances phase of a capital case and use it solely in the penalty phrase. State provisions on waiver of the right to be charged by a grand jury indictment traditionally have also placed that decision in the hands of the defendant.

On the other side, the Supreme Court has indicated, in dictum or holding, that counsel has the ultimate authority in deciding whether or not to advance the following defense rights: barring prosecution use of unconstitutionally obtained evidence; obtaining dismissal of an indictment on the ground of racial discrimination in the selection of the grand jury; wearing civilian clothes, rather than prison garb, during the trial; striking an improper jury instruction; including a particular nonfrivolous claim among the issues briefed and argued on appeal; foregoing cross-examination; calling a possible witness (other than defendant) to testify; providing discovery to the prosecution (even where the failure to do so risks possible sanctions of exclusion); and being tried within the 180 day time period specified in the Interstate Agreement on Detainers. Lower court rulings have added to this list a variety of other determinations, including the following: whether to exercise a peremptory challenge; whether to request or consent to a mistrial; whether to request, or object to, the exclusion of the public from the trial; whether to seek a change of venue, continuance, or other relief due to prejudicial pretrial publicity; whether to seek a continuance and thereby relinquish a statutory right to trial within a specified period of days; whether to seek a competency determination; and choosing among different lines of defense that could produce an acquittal. Lower courts have displayed less certainty, however, as to the proper classification of various other decisions, such as whether to accept a jury of less than twelve, whether to rely upon a partial defense (i.e., a defense that

challenges only the higher level of multiple charges), whether to stipulate to the introduction of prior recorded testimony on a critical issue (or all issues), and whether to pursue an "all or nothing" defense by waiving the right to a jury instruction on lesser included offenses.

Taken together, the various rulings produce a picture that is clear at many points but clouded at others. General agreement exists that the decisions as to guilty plea, jury trial, appeal, defendant's presence at trial, and the defendant testifying are for the defendant, and that decisions on a substantially larger group of matters, such as objecting to inadmissible evidence, are for counsel. As to various other decisions, however, the courts either have not spoken or are divided. Thus, Justice Brennan, dissenting in *Jones,* was on uncertain ground when he suggested that a defendant would have the right to insist that his counsel forego other strategies more likely to produce a dismissal and rely exclusively on a claim of innocence. That assumption, though it relates to an issue basic to the division of responsibility between lawyer and client, is hardly clear under the precedent. Of course, one cannot expect a ruling on each and every decision on which lawyer and client are likely to disagree. The potential for uncertainty is exacerbated, however, by the balancing process that appears to underlie the classification of a particular right as within the domain of defendant or counsel. That process is examined below in subsection (b).

Of course, where the law is unclear, or even where it is clear and places ultimate authority with counsel, a defense lawyer can always follow her client's wishes, provided that path does not require the lawyer to violate standards of professional responsibility. To do so rarely will open the door to a successful postconviction claim of ineffective assistance of counsel based on the attorney's failure to insist upon the attorney's best professional judgment. A lawyer may conclude that, on balance, it is better to go against her best professional judgment, and in accordance with a client's strongly felt views, than run the risk of a breakdown in lawyer-client communications that would be even more likely to preclude a successful defense. Indeed, where the client's preference is not based on a misunderstanding of law or an inability to understand why the lawyer favors an alternative tactic, and that preference does not require the lawyer to forsake "meaningful adversary testing" of the prosecution's case, a lawyer may find justification for following that preference in the client's position as the person who "will bear the personal consequences of the conviction."

In general, the courts have held that where a decision rests with counsel, the lack of consultation with the defendant does not constitute ineffective assistance of counsel. The Third Circuit has warned, however, that in some instances a lack of consultation may in itself fall outside the wide range of constitutionally acceptable performance by counsel.[4] The Supreme Court in its leading competency ruling, *Strickland v. Washington*,[5] referred to counsel's "duties to consult with the defendant on important decisions and to keep the defendant informed in the course of the prosecution." That obligation, the Third Circuit noted, serves four important functions even as to "issues on which counsel has the final word." Consultation will: (1) ensure that counsel receives any factual information relevant to the issue that the defendant might have; (2) give the defendant the opportunity (depending on timing) to consider the possibility of seeking substitute counsel or proceeding pro se; (3) "promote and maintain a cooperative client-counsel relationship"; and (4) give to the attorney the opportunity to shape his or her decision in light of "the client's views and desires concerning the best course to be followed." Of course, where counsel would have insisted upon exercising her authority without regard to the client's wishes, the last function obviously does not alter the character of counsel's representation. However, in particular cases, the failure to meet at least the first two functions of consultation may have an impact so significant as to meet the prejudice prong of the ineffective assistance standard.

(b) Balancing of Interests. The Supreme Court's explanations of why particular decisions are for counsel or client have been brief and conclusionary. Decisions within the client's control are simply described as involving "fundamental rights," while those within the lawyer's control are said to involve matters requiring the "superior ability of trained counsel" in assessing "strategy." While the rights subject to defendant's "personal choice" clearly are "fundamental," the Court has not explained why various rights subject to counsel's authority are not equally fundamental. Arguably, the decision to plead guilty has a special quality because it involves the relinquishment of so many basic rights. But it is more difficult to distinguish the right to be tried before a jury, for example, from the right to present a particular witness or to cross-examine an opposing witness. If the fundamental nature of a right is measured by its importance, its historic tradition, or its current status in constitutional or state law, those rights would appear to be on the same plane.

The Court's emphasis upon the strategic element in those decisions subject to counsel's control also fails to distinguish the different types of decisions. Certainly the decisions to waive a jury or not have the defendant testify also involve substantial strategic considerations. It may be argued that the elements of strategy involved in such decisions are more readily understood by the layman because they do not as frequently rest on technical concerns as many of the tactical decisions made by counsel. But they are hardly distinguishable in this regard from still other decisions made by counsel. For example, counsel's decision not to have a particular witness testify often rests on considerations of the same kind that would lead counsel, if she had such control, to keep the defendant from testifying. Similarly, much the same type of judgment is involved in deciding that a jury should be waived because the trial judge is likely to be the more sympathetic factfinder as in deciding that an unconstitutionally composed jury should not be challenged because discriminatory jury selection

---

4. Government of Virgin Islands v. Weatherwax, 77 F.3d 1425 (3d Cir.1996).

5. See § 11.10 at note 1.

has produced a more sympathetic group of jurors. In sum, just as the fundamental rights characterization could be applied to many of the rights subject to counsel's control, so could the characterization of a decision as strategic and requiring counsel's expertise be applied to certain basic determinations subject to defendant's control. As various lower courts have noted, the determination that particular decisions do or do not require defendant's personal choice has obviously rested on a balancing of several factors including, but not limited to, the fundamental nature of the right involved and the significance of strategic considerations. As discussed below, the other factors considered include: (1) the objective of avoiding disruption of the litigation process; (2) the distinction between objectives and means; (3) the "inherently personal character" of the particular decision; and (4) the need to foster a strong defense bar.

The "practical necessities of the litigation process," although perhaps not dominant, certainly influences the allocation of control between counsel and client. The exercise of defendant's personal choice requires an opportunity for meaningful consultation that often is not practicable. Thus, Justice Brennan, who would have granted defendants far more control than the Supreme Court majority, acknowledged that defense counsel had to be given "decisive authority * * * with regard to the hundreds of decisions that must be made quickly in the course of a trial." Still another concern of judicial administration is that the trial judge be able to establish on the record, without a lengthy disruptive procedure, that the decisions subject to defendant's control were actually made by the defendant. Without such a record, convictions could readily be subject to challenge by defendants claiming that counsel usurped the defendant's authority. Many of the rights within the control of the defendant require a "publicly acknowledged consent of the client" for their waiver.

That is the case for the entry of a guilty plea, for the waiver of the rights to grand jury screening and trial by jury, and for the waiver of the right to a speedy trial. Some jurisdictions require and still others prefer a form of on-the-record defendant acknowledgment of his informed and voluntary relinquishment of the right to testify. There is a ready occasion at which the trial court can determine that such decisions were made by the defendant himself. However, the criminal justice process cannot readily require an open court waiver as to all rights that it deems "fundamental." As to many the trial judge is hardly in a position to "continually satisfy himself that the defendant was fully informed as to, and in complete accord with, his attorney's every action or inaction that involved any possible constitutional right."[6]

Still another factor considered by the courts is the relationship of the procedural decision to the overall concerns of the client. The client, it is often said, must be able to control the "end," while the lawyer determines the "means" for reaching that end. Thus, the defendant must control decisions as to whether or not to contest (e.g., whether to plead guilty or take an appeal) and the lawyer will control the defense presentation when it does contest (e.g., whether to introduce particular evidence and whether to raise particular objections to the prosecution's case).

Not all of the decisions resting in the control of the defendant, however, relate to the question of whether to contest. Some concern the question of how to contest but are so personal in character that they are viewed as critical aspects of the defendant's end object rather than simply a means to achieving that objective. For example, a defendant may have an interest in testifying himself even though he recognizes that doing so may hurt his chances for acquittal (perhaps because cross-examination will reveal his prior convictions). He may

---

6. This is not to say, of course, that a decision will be held to be within counsel's control simply because a record of defendant's personal participation in the waiver is not easily established. The determination as to whether to appeal is for the defendant though the failure of counsel to file an appeal may raise difficult factual questions as to the nature of defendant's participation in that decision. So too, while the exigencies of the trial process will contribute to assignment of certain decisions to counsel's bailiwick, the presence of ample opportunity for consultation does not necessarily mean that the decision will be assigned to defendant's control.

view as more important his opportunity to "tell his story to the public." He may consider an acquittal after a trial in which he did not testify as less than the full vindication that he desires. Similarly, the waiver of a right to a speedy trial (often desirable where delay may weaken the prosecution case) involves personal concerns extending beyond achieving a successful outcome, as the defendant is subject to anxiety and the restraints of bail (or incarceration, where not released on bail) while awaiting trial.

That the exercise or non-exercise of a particular procedural right has this quality, which one court has described as an "inherently personal" character, does not invariably lead it to be classified as within the defendant's control. The defendant's interest in having his guilt determined by members of the community arguably extends not simply to having a jury trial but also the exercise of rights that help to shape the composition of that jury, yet decisions regarding the exercise of those rights are traditionally viewed as strategic and within the control of defense counsel. The personal concerns that lead to requiring the defendant's personal participation in a waiver of the right to a speedy trial arguably also are present in the decision to seek a mistrial, yet the mistrial decision traditionally falls within the exclusive province of the lawyer. Moreover, decisions that most defendants view as relating only to means of best obtaining a favorable outcome may, under exceptional circumstances, be as important to a particular defendant as the outcome itself. Yet courts have indicated that the characterization of a right as "personal" depends on how it might be viewed by the typical defendant in the typical case. None have suggested, for example, that counsel will lose control over whether a suppression motion should be made when the particular defendant's political beliefs make it so important to him that police illegality be revealed that he insists on the motion even though it might work against the possibility of an acquittal.

Finally, courts obviously are concerned that lawyers maintain sufficient control over the case that they not be discouraged from engaging in criminal defense work. A lawyer is not placed in a professionally embarrassing position when she is reluctantly required to try his case before a jury. Neither should she be embarrassed because she is required to go to trial in a weak case, since that decision is clearly attributed to her client. The situation would be somewhat different, however, were a lawyer required to raise a "colorable" claim simply because her client insisted that she do so. A claim may be "nonfrivolous" yet so unlikely to succeed that the lawyer who raises it will be viewed as wasting the time of the court. If the lawyer were forced to raise such a claim because of her client's insistence, she could hardly inform the court that she was presenting the claim only because she was required to do so. So too, if forced to present the testimony of an exceptionally weak witness, the lawyer could hardly inform the jury that the witness was called at her client's direction. In the end, this concern of the courts that the lawyer not be forced to sacrifice her professional reputation while providing no true assistance to her client may explain much of the law governing the division of authority between counsel and client.

(c) Violations of Personal Choice. As discussed in § 11.10, *Strickland v. Washington* ordinarily imposes two prerequisites for reversing a conviction based upon inadequacies in the performance of counsel: (1) a showing that the performance was incompetent as measured by an "objective standard of reasonableness"; and (2) a showing of a potential prejudicial impact, as measured by a "reasonable probability that, but for counsel's unprofessional errors, the result of the proceeding would have been different." Where counsel is alleged to have violated defendant's right to make a procedural decision within defendant's control, the application of each prong of *Strickland* presents issues unique to that claim.

Incompetency. Where counsel violated defendant's clearly expressed choice as to a decision within defendant's control, that action in itself establishes the incompetency of counsel's performance. Counsel's decision may have been tactically sound, but because the decision belonged to defendant, the failure to accept defendant's choice automatically falls below an objective standard of reasonableness. Thus, the first prong of *Strickland* is met where counsel ignores defendant's direction (as where defendant directs counsel to file an appeal, but counsel fails to do so),[7] or where counsel uses coercion to force the client to relinquish his personal choice (as where counsel's mid-trial threat to withdraw kept the client from testifying).[8]

Establishing incompetent performance is not quite so easy, however, where the defendant never was asked and therefore never expressed his choice. The issue then presented is whether counsel was incompetent in failing to inform the defendant of the procedural step and the controlling force of his choice. That issue was considered by the Supreme Court in *Roe v. Flores–Oretega*,[9] where counsel failed to consult and did not take a first appeal as of right (on which defendant has a constitutional right to counsel's effective assistance).

The Court in *Roe v. Flores–Oretega* concluded that, to establish *Strickland's* first prong of professional unreasonableness based upon a failure to consult, it must be shown either that (1) the circumstances of the case were such that a "rational defendant would [have] want[ed] to appeal," or (2) that "this particular defendant reasonably demonstrated to counsel that he was interested in appealing." Thus, the Court noted, a "highly relevant factor would be whether the conviction follows a trial or a guilty plea, both because a guilty plea reduces the scope of potentially appealable issues and because such a plea may indicate that the defendant seeks an end to judicial proceedings." The Court added that where there was a guilty plea, other circumstances also must be considered in assessing whether counsel should reasonably have assumed that the defendant had an interest in an appeal. Those circumstances included "whether the defendant received the sentence bargained for" and

whether the plea "expressly reserved or waived some or all appeal rights."

It remains to be seen whether the *Roe v. Flores–Oretega* analysis will be carried over to other situations in which counsel's inaction without consultation resulted in a failure to exercise a procedural right that is within the defendant's control. Of course, that situation will rarely, if ever, be presented where trial procedure ordinarily requires that the judge ask "the defendant on the record" whether he desires to relinquish that right. However, an on-the-record informed waiver is not typical as to several rights within the defendant's control, and here defendants are likely to raise claims that they were unaware of their options because of a lack of consultation. *Roe v. Flores–Oretega* would indicate that such a claim will fail unless the surrounding circumstances indicate that the defendant would have been interested in the option never discussed. However, because of the special character of a guilty plea as an indicator of the defendant's desire to terminate the proceedings, the relinquishment of the right to appeal following a guilty plea may be treated as *sui generis*, and *Flores–Oretega* readily distinguished. Thus, because defendant has the final say over whether to plead guilty, various lower courts have held that counsel's failure to convey to a defendant the prosecution's offer of a plea bargain establishes incompetency under the first prong of *Strickland* without regard to counsel's conclusion that a rational defendant (and this defendant) would not accept the prosecution's offer.

Prejudice. The *Strickland* standard of ineffective assistance also requires a showing of prejudice, and the Court in *Roe v. Flores–Oretega* held that the failure-to-consult could not be treated as per se prejudicial. Even if "all the information counsel knew or should have known" establishes that the rational defendant would want to appeal or that this

---

7. This applies only to an appeal as to which defendant has a constitutional right to counsel. Where defendant does not have such a right, as in the case of a discretionary second-tier appeal, the failure to file does not give rise to an ineffective assistance claim. See § 11.7(a).

8. The reference here is to preventing the client from testifying on tactical grounds. Where the client intends to

testify falsely, counsel's ethical obligations preclude simply accepting the client's decision. See Nix v. Whiteside, discussed in § 11.10 at note 6.

9. 528 U.S. 470, 120 S.Ct. 1029, 145 L.Ed.2d 985 (2000), also discussed in § 21.3(b).

defendant demonstrated an interest in an appeal, that does not invariably establish that the failure to consult "actually caus[ed] the forfeiture of the appeal." To meet the prejudice prerequisite, the defendant must "demonstrate that there is a reasonable probability that, but for counsel's deficient failure to consult with him about an appeal, he would have timely appealed." The Court acknowledged that this inquiry "is not wholly dissimilar from the inquiry into whether counsel performed deficiently" by failing to consult. Thus, where the defendant shows nonfrivolous grounds for appeal, that will establish both that a "rational defendant would [have] want[ed] to appeal" and a "reasonable probability" defendant would have chosen to appeal after consultation. On the other hand, where the failure to consult constituted deficient performance because defendant had "sufficiently demonstrated to counsel his interest in an appeal," the defendant must also be able to establish that after consultation (where counsel might have suggested that an appeal was fruitless), he would have continued that interest and instructed his counsel to file the appeal.

The court in *Flores–Ortega* concentrated on whether the defendant would have exercised the right of appeal, not on whether the appeal would have been successful. That is consistent with the position the Court has taken where counsel failed to follow a defendant's instruction to file a first appeal as of right. There, the Court has noted, a "defendant is entitled to [an] appeal without showing that his appeal likely would have merit." This is so, the Court has explained, because counsel's deficient performance led to "forfeiture of the proceeding itself." Where a proceeding did occur, a "presumption of reliability" attaches, and to overcome that presumption, the defendant must show specific outcome prejudice. Where no proceeding occurred, there can be "no presumption of reliability" and the defendant need not show he was likely to have succeeded, just as a defendant deprived of counsel at trial need not show that the assistance of counsel would have produced a different result.

Lower courts have divided as to whether a similar analysis applies where counsel, without consultation, took action analogous to entering guilty plea (e.g., conceding defendant's guilt on a lesser offense). Some hold that if defendant can establish that he would have rejected counsel's tactic, prejudice is thereby established. Others have insisted upon the further showing of a reasonable probability that the same result would not have been reached if defendant's choice had been followed. In dealing with still other rights of personal choice, such as the right to testify, courts have regularly held that prejudice is not established unless defendant can establish a reasonable probability that following defendant's choice would have produced a different result in the proceeding.

Denial-of-right-analysis. The client control issue is sometimes presented, not as a claim of incompetency, but a claim that the defendant was denied the underlying right (e.g., the right to testify) by the action of the defense counsel which relinquished that right without defendant's consent. Although it has been argued that the ineffective-assistance claim is the more appropriate vehicle for challenging counsel's action, as a defendant's underlying right can be said to have been "violated" by the "state" only through the action of the trial court or prosecutor (and not by defense counsel), many courts have considered counsel's usurpation of defendant's control as a violation of the substantive right over which the defendant has control. Where the client-control claim is put into this framework, the defendant will not need to show prejudicial impact (unless the substantive right is a due process right and prejudice is a component of its violation). There remains the possibility, however, that the violation still will be deemed a harmless error; but the harmless error standard places the burden on the prosecution to show harmlessness, and it allows for reversal on the basis of a lesser potential for prejudice than the traditional prejudice-prong of the incompetency of counsel standard.[10]

10.　See § 27.6(b), (c).

§ 11.7 The Right to Effective Assistance of Counsel: Guiding Principles

(a) The Prerequisite of a Constitutional Right to Counsel. The Supreme Court first recognized a constitutional right to the effective assistance of counsel in *Powell v. Alabama*.[1] *Powell* noted that where due process requires the state to provide counsel for an indigent defendant, "that duty is not discharged by an assignment at such a time or under such circumstances as to preclude the giving of effective aid in the preparation and trial of the case." Ten years later, in *Glasser v. United States*,[2] the Court held in a federal case that the Sixth Amendment was violated by judicial action that denied defendant's "right to have the effective assistance of counsel." Following its recognition of an equal protection right to appointed counsel on a first appeal of right, the Court held that the defendant also had a constitutional right to the effective assistance of that appointed appellate counsel.[3] In *Evitts v. Lucey*,[4] after concluding that the constitutional right to counsel on a first appeal of right also had a due process grounding and therefore encompassed representation by retained counsel, the Court noted that defendant was entitled *a fortiori* to effective representation by that retained counsel. For "a party whose counsel is unable to provide effective representation is in no better position that one who has no counsel at all."

Taken together, the above cases establish that a constitutional requirement of effective assistance extends to counsel's performance in any proceeding as to which there would be a constitutional right both to appointed counsel for the indigent and to retained counsel for the non-indigent. In other words, a necessary corollary of a constitutional right to counsel that is based on the fair-hearing grounding of the Sixth Amendment, the similar grounding of due process, or the concept of equal protection, is that the retained or appointed counsel not undermine that right by providing ineffective assistance. However, as indicated in the *Torna* and *Finley* cases, discussed below, where there is no constitutional right to the assistance of counsel which is tied to such a grounding, there does not exist a constitutional right to effective representation by counsel.

In *Wainwright v. Torna*,[5] defendant argued that he had been denied the effective assistance of counsel when his retained attorney failed to file a timely application for discretionary review at the state's second-level of appeal. Noting that "*Ross v. Moffitt* [had] held that a criminal defendant does not have a constitutional right to counsel to pursue [such] discretionary state appeals," the per curiam majority opinion concluded that the lawyer's negligence therefore did not violate any constitutional right of the defendant. The Court reasoned: "Since respondent had no constitutional right to counsel, he could not be deprived of the effective assistance of counsel by his retained counsel's failure to file the application timely."[6]

Would the result in *Torna* have been different if the counsel there had been appointed counsel? Although the state would not have had a constitutional obligation to provide counsel on the application for discretionary

§ 11.7
1. 287 U.S. 45, 53 S.Ct. 55, 77 L.Ed. 158 (1932). See also § 11.1(a).
2. 315 U.S. 60, 62 S.Ct. 457, 86 L.Ed. 680 (1942). See also § 11.6(b).
3. Jones v. Barnes, 463 U.S. 745, 103 S.Ct. 3308, 77 L.Ed.2d 987 (1983). See also § 11.1(d).
4. 469 U.S. 387, 105 S.Ct. 830, 83 L.Ed.2d 821 (1985). See also § 11.1(b).
5. 455 U.S. 586, 102 S.Ct. 1300, 71 L.Ed.2d 475 (1982).
6. As discussed in § 11.1 at notes 17–19, in proceedings as to which there is no right to appointed counsel (such as that involved in *Torna*), the defendant nonetheless may have a constitutionally protected interest in being represented by retained counsel which the state

cannot override absent a compelling justification. See also note 4 of § 8.15. *Torna* indicates that, even if such a right to utilize retained counsel were to be recognized as to a particular proceeding, it would not carry with it the guarantee of effective assistance that is a part of the traditional right to counsel. Since a right to retained counsel in these additional proceedings would rest only on the "state's duty to refrain from unreasonable interference with the individual's desire to defend himself in whatever manner he deems best," rather than one on the need for counsel to ensure a fair proceeding, it would not carry with it a state obligation to ensure that counsel was effective. The defendant alone would bear the consequences of his unwise choice of counsel, as he did in *Torna*.

second-tier review, having done so, would it then bear greater responsibility for counsel's performance? That issue was posed in *Pennsylvania v. Finley*,[7] where the Court's narrow ruling suggested only a partial answer. *Finley* involved counsel appointed to represent an indigent prisoner in challenging her conviction through a state postconviction procedure. The appointed counsel advised the habeas court that the prisoner's claim was totally without merit, which resulted in the court-approved withdrawal of counsel and the dismissal of the petition for postconviction relief. Counsel's action had been inconsistent with the withdrawal safeguards prescribed in *Anders v. California* to ensure that appellate counsel appointed pursuant to the constitutional mandate of *Douglas v. California* effectively represent their clients.[8] *Finley* held, however, that the *Anders* safeguards were not constitutionally required in a postconviction proceeding because the state had no constitutional obligation to appoint counsel in such a proceeding. The Court did not go so far as to say that a defendant had no constitutional grounding for complaining about an appointed counsel's ineffective representation where, as in *Finley*, the state voluntarily provided appointed counsel under a state practice, with no constitutional mandate to do so. Rather, the Court simply noted that *Anders* established "a prophylactic framework that is relevant when, and only when, a litigant has a previously established constitutional right to counsel," and that "the procedures followed by respondent's habeas counsel fully comported with 'fundamental fairness.'" However, a later case, *Coleman v. Thompson*,[9] recognized no such limitation in the analysis of *Finley*, and concluded that *Finley* rejects ineffective-assistance claims as a general matter for all proceedings in which there is no constitutional obligation to provide appointed counsel.

It should be noted that both *Torna* and *Finley* involved a proceeding that the state had no constitutional obligation to provide. Where

the state has a constitutional obligation to provide a particular process, but that obligation does not include a duty to appoint counsel, the ineffective performance of counsel, whether retained or appointed, might be successfully challenged by reference to the adequacy of that process. Such a possibility would be presented, for example, by the ineffective assistance of retained counsel at a misdemeanor trial which resulted in the imposition only of a fine (and therefore was not a proceeding at which the Sixth Amendment would guarantee a right to appointed counsel). The defendant could argue here that ineffectiveness of counsel resulted in a proceeding in which defendant was so deprived of his ability to make use of the procedural rights constitutionally guaranteed to him in such a trial that the proceeding itself did not comport with due process. The state might respond that its due process obligation was only to make those hearing rights available to the defendant, and the failure of the defendant to take advantage of those rights due to counsel's incompetency is not the state's responsibility, just as the loss of the appeal was not the state's responsibility in *Torna*. Here, however, what is at stake is the state's basic authority to impose a sanction, which is conditioned constitutionally on a fair determination of liability. In light of that constitutional prerequisite, the state might not so readily be allowed to ignore the actions of counsel, though it had no duty to provide or allow for counsel, where counsel's actions rendered meaningless the rights afforded the defendant to ensure that fair determination of liability.

(b) Retained vs. Appointed Counsel. Prior to the Supreme Court's 1980 decision in *Cuyler v. Sullivan*,[10] many lower courts utilized different standards for reviewing ineffective assistance claims depending upon whether counsel was appointed or privately retained. Some of the earlier cases had refused on an agency rationale to even recognize ineffective-

---

7. 481 U.S. 551, 107 S.Ct. 1990, 95 L.Ed.2d 539 (1987).

8. See § 11.2(c).

9. 501 U.S. 722, 111 S.Ct. 2546, 115 L.Ed.2d 640 (1991). See also note 17 infra.

10. 446 U.S. 335, 100 S.Ct. 1708, 64 L.Ed.2d 333 (1980).

ness claims involving retained counsel. If "there was any error," one court noted in 1935, "it was merely an error of judgment on the part of the defendant in the selection of counsel to represent him." Although the lower courts later came to recognize that the law of agency was misplaced as applied to criminal cases, they often found a basis in the state-action requirement of the Fourteenth Amendment for applying a less stringent standard of review to the alleged incompetency of retained counsel. A constitutional violation, it was argued, required state participation at a sufficient level to render the state responsible for counsel's inadequacies. That responsibility was seen as arising automatically from the trial court's selection of appointed counsel. As for retained counsel, the state bore responsibility for counsel's inadequacies only where they were so obvious that they should have been apparent to the trial court. Other lower courts rejected this distinction. They argued that the necessary element of state action was provided by the trial of the defendant without competent counsel, and that involvement did not hinge on counsel's status as court-appointed or privately retained.

Cuyler put to rest this division among the lower courts. The ineffective assistance claim in *Cuyler* was based upon a retained attorney's multiple representation of codefendants with possibly conflicting interests. Although arguing that counsel was not ineffective, the prosecution also claimed that, in any event, "the alleged failings of * * * retained counsel cannot provide a basis for a * * * [constitutional violation] because the conduct of retained counsel does not involve state action." Rejecting that contention, the Supreme Court noted:

> A proper respect for the Sixth Amendment disarms [the prosecution's] contention that defendants who retain their own counsel are entitled to less protection than defendants for whom the State appoints counsel. * * * The vital guarantee of the Sixth Amendment would stand for little if the often uninformed decision to retain a particular lawyer could reduce or forfeit the defendant's

entitlement to constitutional protection. Since the State's conduct of a criminal trial itself implicates the State in the defendant's conviction, we see no basis for drawing a distinction between retained and appointed counsel that would deny equal justice to defendants who must choose their own lawyers.

Adhering to the obvious thrust of this statement, lower courts have refused to limit the Court's analysis to the multiple representation situation presented in *Cuyler*. Since *Cuyler*, they have uniformly held that the standard of review applied to all types of ineffectiveness claims will not vary with the status of counsel as retained or court-appointed.

(c) The Adversary System Touchstone. Prior to the 1984 rulings in *United States v. Cronic*[11] and *Strickland v. Washington*,[12] the Supreme Court had not sought to articulate a comprehensive conception of ineffective assistance of counsel. Previous rulings had not gone beyond offering standards tied to particular settings likely to result in a lack of effective assistance. Responding to divisions among the lower courts, the opinions for the Court in *Cronic* and *Strickland*, which were announced on the same day, sought to provide a general framework for analysis of ineffective assistance claims. The critical element, both opinions noted, was to evaluate the performance of counsel in light of the underlying purpose of the constitutional right to counsel. Since both cases involved challenges to the performance of counsel at the trial level, the opinions focused on the purpose of the Sixth Amendment right to counsel. However, since the Court indicated that the role of counsel under that Amendment flowed from the adversary nature of the trial process, and that the same principles would apply to other stages of the criminal justice process that are "sufficiently like a trial in its adversarial format and in the existence of standards for decision," the analysis of *Cronic* and *Strickland* should also apply to the various stages of the process at which due

---

11. 466 U.S. 648, 104 S.Ct. 2039, 80 L.Ed.2d 657 (1984).

12. 466 U.S. 668, 104 S.Ct. 2052, 80 L.Ed.2d 674 (1984).

process or equal protection establish a constitutional right to counsel.

The Sixth Amendment right to counsel, the Court noted in *Strickland,* was aimed, like other Sixth Amendment rights, at providing the "basic elements of a fair trial." A key component of that fair trial was an adversarial system of litigation. The Sixth Amendment included a guarantee of assistance of counsel because "it envision[ed] counsel playing a role that is critical to the ability of the adversarial system to produce just results." The " 'very premise of our adversary system * * * is that partisan advocacy on both sides of a case will best promote the ultimate objective that the guilty be convicted and the innocent go free,' " and it was this " 'very premise' that underlies and gives meaning to the Sixth Amendment." Effective assistance therefore must be measured by reference to the functioning of the adversary process in the particular case. "The right to effective assistance," the *Cronic* opinion noted, is "the right of the accused to require the prosecution's case to survive the crucible of meaningful adversary testing. When a true adversarial criminal trial has been conducted—even if defense counsel may have made demonstrable errors—the kind of testing envisioned by the Sixth Amendment has occurred." The critical question therefore is whether counsel's performance was so deficient that the process "lost its character as a confrontation between adversaries," producing an "actual breakdown of the adversary process." Emphasizing this same point of reference, the Court stated in *Strickland:* "The benchmark for judging any claim of ineffectiveness must be whether counsel's conduct so undermined the proper functioning of the adversarial process that the trial cannot be relied on as having produced a just result."

In tying the concept of effective assistance to the functioning of the adversary process, the Court clearly rejected a measurement based solely on a comparison of counsel with his or her peers. The key was not how close counsel came to gaining for defendant the best possible result that an attorney might have realistically achieved. Neither was it the grade counsel might receive as measured against some model

for attorney performance, whether theoretical or reflective of empirical data. Rather the focus was on the presence of the requisite adversarial testing. The most obvious case of ineffectiveness would be that in which counsel simply did not act as an advocate, either because he was prevented from doing so or simply did not make the effort. Where counsel sought to perform as advocate, the question would then be whether his effort provided a "meaningful adversary testing." What was "meaningful" for this purpose would be measured by reference to the operation of the adversary process to achieve its basic objective, ensuring the reliability of the adjudication. Thus, as the *Cronic* opinion noted, a failing to provide adversarial testing as to a single issue, when that issue is critical to a finding of guilt, may in itself produce a breakdown in the adversarial process. On the other hand, as *Strickland* further noted, meaningful adversarial testing hardly requires that challenges be made and investigations directed at each and every point without regard to its likely insignificance in testing the strength of the prosecution's case.

(d) Per Se vs. Actual Ineffectiveness. The adversary system touchstone advanced in *Cronic* and *Strickland* appeared to call for a determination of "actual ineffectiveness" under the facts of the particular case. A constitutional challenge could be found only upon a determination both that counsel had actually failed in some respect to discharge the duties of an advocate in an adversarial system and that counsel's failure so affected the adversary process as to undermine confidence in the result it produced. These determinations suggest a fact-sensitized judgment that evaluates the nature and impact of counsel's representation under the circumstances of the individual case. Not all of the Court's past rulings, however, had adopted such a "judgmental" approach. Some had seemingly relied upon per se standards of ineffective assistance. In cases in which trial courts had prevented counsel from utilizing certain adversarial procedures, the Supreme Court had found ineffective assistance without looking to other aspects of counsel's performance. In cases in which counsel had acted upon a conflict of interest, the Court had also found ineffective assistance without examining all aspects of counsel's performance. Also, in both the restricted assistance cases and the conflict cases, the Court had reversed convictions without looking to the likely impact of counsel's action or inaction upon the outcome of the case.

Numerous commentators and several jurists had applauded this per se approach, and several lower courts had sought to extend it to other settings. They saw the per se (or "categorical") approach as a necessary tool in obtaining quality representation by counsel, particularly for the poor. There was a need, they argued, for prophylactic measures. The courts had to respond to severe institutional restraints impeding effective representation, such as caseload pressures, cut-rate fees for court appointments, and inexperienced defenders. To require a fact-specific finding of actual ineffectiveness was to allow too many cases of incompetency to survive judicial review, as counsel's inadequacies are often hidden in investigative failure and prejudice to the defendant takes forms that are often imperceptible.

Supporters of a per se approach promoted three interrelated positions that would produce a finding of ineffective assistance without examining all of the circumstances of the case. Initially, some settings would be viewed as rendering counsel inherently incapable of providing effective assistance and therefore require reversal of a conviction without examining the specifics of counsel's performance. Thus, a failure to meet prescribed qualifications for appointed counsel—relating to such matters as caseload, time for preparation, and avoidance of conflicts of interest—could be viewed as rendering counsel inherently ineffective (or at least presumptively ineffective). Secondly, guidelines would specify the basic obligations of counsel in providing effective assistance, and a substantial departure from a guideline would be treated as establishing per se that counsel's assistance was ineffective (or, at least, as raising a presumption of ineffectiveness). Finally, as to other elements of

counsel's performance, though judged on the facts of the individual case, once those facts established that the performance fell below a standard of reasonable competency, ineffectiveness would be established without looking further to the impact of that inadequate performance on the outcome of the case. *Cronic* and *Strickland* reviewed lower court rulings that together had lent support to all three of these per se positions. In overturning those rulings, the Supreme Court either flatly rejected or tightly confined each of the three positions.

In *Cronic*,[13] the Court was presented with a case in which the lower court had extended the per se approach to conclude that counsel was inherently incapable of providing effective assistance. The lower court in *Cronic* had sustained defendant's ineffectiveness claim without referring to any specific error or inadequacy in counsel's performance. Instead, it had inferred that "counsel was unable to discharge his duties" based upon the circumstances relating to five factors: "(1) the time afforded for investigation and preparation; (2) the experience of counsel; (3) the gravity of the charge; (4) the complexity of possible defenses; and (5) the accessibility of witnesses to counsel." Justice Stevens' opinion for of the Court concluded that the lower court's adoption of this "inferential approach" lacked support in the Court's prior precedent and was inconsistent with the function of the effective assistance requirement. Those sources made a determination of actual effectiveness the standard prerequisite for sustaining an ineffective assistance claim, with an "inferential approach" of inherent ineffectiveness limited to unique circumstances presented in extreme cases.

Justice Stevens' opinion initially stressed that a judicial evaluation of an ineffectiveness claim must "begin by recognizing that the right to the effective assistance of counsel is recognized not for its own sake, but because of the effect it has on the ability of the accused to receive a fair trial." Accordingly, establishment of an ineffectiveness claim ordinarily requires some showing of an adverse effect on

13. See note 11 supra.

the reliability of the trial process. Moreover, because "we presume that the lawyer is competent," the burden ordinarily rests on the accused to make that showing. "There are, however, circumstances that are so likely to prejudice the accused that the cost of litigating their effect in a particular case is unjustified." In such situations, constitutional effectiveness, amounting to a "breakdown of the adversarial process," could be presumed. However, upon turning to the Court's past decisions, Justice Stevens found only three settings in which such a presumptive approach was justified.

First, there was the situation in which "counsel was either totally absent or prevented from assisting the accused during a critical stage of the proceeding." Falling in this category were cases in which the trial court had unconstitutionally refused to appoint counsel or had restricted counsel's assistance.[14] The second situation was that in which counsel was physically present, but completely absent in effort. As the Court put it, "if counsel entirely fails to subject the prosecution's case to meaningful adversarial testing, then there has been a denial of Sixth Amendment rights that makes the adversary process itself presumptively unreliable."[15] Finally, there were "occasions when, although counsel is available to assist the accused during trial, the likelihood that any lawyer, even a fully competent one, could provide effective assistance is so small that a presumption of prejudice is appropriate without inquiry into the actual conduct of the trial." *Powell v. Alabama*[16] was such a case. The trial court there had utilized such a haphazard process of appointment—ordering admittedly unprepared outstate counsel to proceed with whatever help the local bar, appointed en masse, might provide—that ineffective assistance was properly presumed without further inquiry.

The situations presented in *Powell* and in cases involving an absent, restricted, or completely non-participating counsel were viewed as exceptional. "Apart from circumstances of that magnitude," the *Cronic* opinion noted,

"there is generally no basis for finding a Sixth Amendment violation unless the accused can show specific errors undermining the reliability of the finding of guilt." A footnote cited the conflict-of-interest cases as another setting in which prejudice would be presumed, but there it must be shown either that an actual conflict of interest adversely affected counsel's performance or that the trial court failed to respond as constitutionally required to an apparent conflict. In the case before the Court in *Cronic*, the lower court had not cited any "actual conduct" of counsel at trial indicating "a breakdown in the adversarial process that would justify a presumption that respondent's conviction was insufficiently reliable to satisfy the Constitution." It simply had relied on the surrounding circumstances to "justify a presumption of ineffectiveness * * * without inquiry into counsel's performance at trial." The five circumstances cited to justify that presumption hardly presented a setting "so likely to prejudice" as to be analogous to *Powell* or the cases in which a defendant was denied the assistance of counsel at a critical stage. While all five were "relevant to an evaluation of a lawyer's ineffectiveness in a particular case, * * * neither separately nor in combination [did] they provide a basis for concluding that competent counsel was not able to provide * * * the guiding hand that the Constitution guarantees."

As discussed further in § 11.10(a), the *Strickland* Court had before it a lower court ruling that announced a series of guidelines to be applied in determining whether a trial counsel's failure to conduct a full factual investigation constituted per se ineffective assistance of counsel. The *Strickland* opinion flatly rejected the use of such a guidelines approach, noting that it failed to account for the "countless ways [in which a lawyer could] * * * provide effective assistance in any given case." What was needed was an evaluation that looked to all of the circumstances of the individual case and was highly deferential of counsel's expertise. Moreover once that analysis did

---

14.   See § 11.1 (lack of appointment), § 11.8(a) (trial court restrictions).

15.   See § 11.10 at note 20.

16.   See § 11.8 at note 15.

establish that counsel's performance fell below a reasonable level of competency, a reversal was not in order without a showing of likely prejudicial impact upon the outcome of the adjudication. Prejudice was properly presumed in certain contexts—most notably where counsel was not made available, was prohibited by the trial court from participating in a critical aspect of the proceeding, or acted under a conflict of interest. However, in general, instances in which counsel's actions or inactions arguably fell below a standard of reasonable competency involved far too much variation (indeed "an infinite variety"), including many actions or inactions likely to be "utterly harmless," to employ a presumption of prejudice. Here again, a fact-sensitive judgment, looking to all of the circumstances of the individual case, was needed.

(e) Raising an Ineffectiveness Claim. Appellate courts uniformly note that where a claim of ineffective assistance of trial counsel could be more fully developed by evidence outside the trial record, the preferable procedure is to present it initially in a setting that permits an evidentiary hearing. Three procedural avenues offer that opportunity: (1) a motion for new trial filed with the trial court prior to the initiation of an appeal; (2) a remand or other procedure that will stay a pending appeal and return the case to the trial court; and (3) a post-appeal collateral challenge to the conviction. One factor that may preclude the use of one or all of these opportunities is the continued representation of the defendant by the trial attorney. As numerous courts have noted, a lawyer is most unlikely to look to his or her own ineffectiveness in challenging a conviction. Indeed, a counsel who raises his own ineffectiveness is viewed as having placed himself in a conflict situation, requiring his withdrawal. The same principle is extended by some courts to post-trial representation by a different attorney from the same public defender office as the trial attorney.

Where new counsel is retained or appointed for an appeal, that counsel typically will not be available until after the time limitation runs on filing a motion for new trial. Thus, use of that motion to present an ineffective assis-

tance claim has been described as "more a theoretical than a real possibility." Indeed, the time limitations tend to be so short that even a new counsel retained immediately after the trial very often would not have sufficient time to assess all of the inactions and actions of trial counsel that could provide the grounding for an ineffective assistance claim.

The filing of an appeal typically removes the case from further consideration by the trial court. Some jurisdictions will nonetheless allow the defendant to gain trial court review of an ineffective assistance claim while an appeal is pending. In these jurisdictions, the ineffectiveness claim ordinarily must be raised before the appellate court with a request that it be remanded to the trial court for an evidentiary hearing and ruling on the claim. Indeed, some appellate courts insist that new appellate counsel present all possible ineffectiveness claims on appeal, with the appellate court then determining whether the claim is one that will have to be remanded to the trial court because it may be illuminated by information not within the trial record. Where a remand is ordered, the appellate court may delay disposition of the appeal until the trial court holds the evidentiary hearing and rules on the ineffectiveness claim.

Most jurisdictions prefer not to disrupt the normal processing of appeals to await a trial court evidentiary hearing on an ineffectiveness claim that was not presented on a motion for new trial. The preferred procedure for raising an ineffective assistance claim that might be more fully developed by evidence outside the trial record is the jurisdiction's process for a post-appeal collateral challenge to a conviction (e.g., the writ of habeas corpus). Where the ineffectiveness claim is raised on appeal and its determination could be assisted by an evidentiary hearing, the appellate court will not remand to the trial court. Instead, it will rule on all of the appeals issues other than the ineffective assistance claim and note that the latter claim may be presented by the appropriate collateral remedy. Jurisdictions which thus prefer that ineffective assistance claims be raised by a collateral remedy often draw a distinction as to claims that can be resolved without an evidentiary hearing. Such claims can be raised on appeal, even though not presented to the trial court, at least where the appellate counsel did not have the opportunity to present the claim in a motion for new trial. However, other jurisdictions eschew such a partial review of ineffective assistance claims. They prefer that all such claims, whether apparent on the record or not, be presented together on collateral attack.

The diverse approaches to the issue of when and how ineffective assistance claims should be raised quite naturally has led to diverse rules on when a failure to raise such a claim creates a procedural forfeiture precluding consideration of the claim in later proceedings. The various jurisdictions do have a common starting point. The failure to raise trial counsel ineffectiveness on a motion for new trial or on appeal does not constitute a forfeiture where the defendant is represented at those stages by the trial counsel. That arguably changes where the claim is not raised in the first collateral attack proceeding even though counsel there also was trial counsel. Since the defendant has no constitutional right to the effective assistance of counsel in post-conviction proceedings,[17] the conflict which led the trial counsel not to raise his own ineffectiveness will not be viewed as an excusable "cause" for that failure, and the claim therefore is not likely to be open to a subsequent collateral challenge.

Assuming that defendant was represented by new counsel on appeal, three different positions are taken as to forfeiture by failing to raise an ineffectiveness claim on appeal. First, where the jurisdiction expects the defendant to raise the claim and seek a remand if an evidentiary hearing is needed to fully develop the factual basis of the claim, the failure to raise the claim constitutes a procedural default as to all claims of ineffectiveness by trial counsel. Second, where the jurisdiction requires the defense to present on appeal only those ineffective assistance claims that would not be aided by evidence outside the trial court record, as developed in an evidentiary hearing, only the failure to raise such a claim on appeal constitutes a procedural default. Thus, to present on collateral attack an ineffectiveness claim not presented on appeal, the defense must be prepared to offer extrinsic evidence that does something more than merely affirm what is in the record. Third, where the jurisdiction views all ineffective assistance claims as most appropriately presented through a collateral attack procedure, failure to raise the claim on appeal will not constitute a procedural default.[18] Of course, if the claim of ineffectiveness goes to the performance of the appellate counsel, that obviously could not be raised on appeal and may first be presented in a post-appeal challenge.

§ 11.8　Ineffective Assistance Claims Based Upon State Interference and Other Extrinsic Factors

(a) Restrictions Upon Counsel's Assistance. The "right to the assistance of counsel," the Supreme Court noted in *Herring v. New York*,[1] "has been understood to mean that there can be no restrictions upon the function of counsel in defending a criminal prosecution in accord with the traditions of the adversary factfinding process." Accordingly, state action, whether by statute or trial court ruling, that

---

17. See § 11.1 at note 13. In Coleman v. Thompson, 501 U.S. 722, 111 S.Ct. 2546, 115 L.Ed.2d 640 (1991), the Court left open the question of whether defendant had a constitutional right to counsel on collateral review in order to raise there a trial-counsel ineffectiveness claim where state law does not allow that claim to be raised on indirect appeal (i.e. where state law requires that it be raised on collateral attack). See § 11.1 at note 15. However, the several lower courts considering the issue have uniformly concluded that there is no constitutional right to counsel in the situation left open by *Coleman*.

18. In Massaro v. United States, 538 U.S. 500, 123 S.Ct. 1690, 155 L.Ed.2d 714 (2003), the Supreme Court

rejected a lower federal court ruling which had adopted the second position described above. The Court basically adopted this third position, holding that "an ineffective-assistance-of-counsel claim may be brought in a collateral proceeding under § 2255, whether or not the petitioner could have raised the claim on direct appeal." The Court noted that "a growing majority of states follow (this) rule", but did not suggest that the states were in any way compelled to adopt that position, as opposed to either of the two others discussed above.

§ 11.8
1.　422 U.S. 853, 95 S.Ct. 2550, 45 L.Ed.2d 593 (1975).

prohibits counsel from making full use of traditional trial procedures may be viewed as denying defendant the effective assistance of counsel. In considering the constitutionality of such "state interference," courts are directed to look to whether the interference denied counsel "the opportunity to participate fully and fairly in the adversary factfinding process." If the interference had that effect, then both the overall performance of counsel apart from the interference and the lack of any showing of actual outcome prejudice become irrelevant. The interference in itself establishes ineffective assistance and requires automatic reversal of the defendant's conviction.

Four Supreme Court cases illustrate the type of state imposed restriction upon counsel's performance that will be held to violate the Sixth Amendment. In *Geders v. United States*,[2] the trial court ordered the defendant not to consult with his attorney during an overnight recess which separated the direct-examination and the cross-examination of the defendant. The court of appeals affirmed the conviction because the defendant made no claim of prejudice from the order. The Supreme Court reversed, holding the 17 hour denial of counsel, regardless of demonstrated prejudice, constituted a deprivation of the effective assistance of counsel. In *Herring v. New York*,[3] the Court held that defendant's Sixth Amendment right to counsel was violated by a statute under which the trial court could refuse to permit a closing argument in a bench trial. The Court reasoned that a final summation by counsel was as basic an element of the adversary process in a bench trial as it was in a jury trial. In *Brooks v. Tennessee*,[4] a statute requiring the defendant to testify as the first defense witness or not at all was held to deny due process by depriving the defendant of the " 'guiding hand of counsel' in the

timing of this critical element of the defense." In *Ferguson v. Georgia*,[5] a pre-*Gideon* decision, a statute which allowed the defendant to make an unsworn statement but denied direct examination by his counsel was held to violate due process.

In each of the cases described above, the Court arguably might also have held the particular restriction unconstitutional on the ground that it imposed an undue burden on the exercise of a constitutionally protected trial right.[6] Whether such a ruling would have required a conviction reversal is uncertain, however, because most constitutional violations are subject to the harmless error standard of *Chapman v. California*.[7] The unconstitutional state imposed interference with counsel, in contrast, is presumed prejudicial and therefore requires automatic reversal. In explaining why this presumption is drawn, the Court has cited the similar treatment of Sixth Amendment violations arising from the failure to appoint counsel and counsel ineffectiveness based on a conflict of interest. The fit of both analogies, however, is less than perfect.

As for the failure to appoint counsel, the analogy here rests on the long accepted rule that a violation of *Gideon v. Wainwright* (i.e., a total failure to provide the assistance of counsel) constitutes automatic grounds for reversal. The *Chapman* opinion itself reaffirmed that rule in noting that *Gideon* violations were not appropriately subjected to a harmless error analysis. That position, however, has been explained as following from the inherently indeterminate impact of the lack of counsel's assistance for the entire criminal prosecution. Where the Sixth Amendment violation is based on the failure to appoint counsel only for a particular critical stage of the prosecution,

---

2. 425 U.S. 80, 96 S.Ct. 1330, 47 L.Ed.2d 592 (1976).

3. See note 1 supra.

4. 406 U.S. 605, 92 S.Ct. 1891, 32 L.Ed.2d 358 (1972).

5. 365 U.S. 570, 81 S.Ct. 756, 5 L.Ed.2d 783 (1961).

6. *Brooks* also held that the state rule requiring defendant to testify first, or lose his right to testify, imposed an unconstitutional burden on defendant's free exercise of his Fifth Amendment right not to testify. See § 24.5(a). In *Ferguson*, two justices, in a concurring opinion, argued

that the underlying state statute was unconstitutional in prohibiting the defendant from testifying on his own behalf as a sworn witness. *Geders* might similarly have been viewed as imposing an undue burden upon a defense right to testify. *Herring* might have rested on a due process right to a summation as a necessary element of a fair factfinding process.

7. See § 27.6(d).

that violation has required automatic reversal as to some stages and has been subjected to the *Chapman* standard as to others. While the precise factors that have led to distinguishing between different critical stages for this purpose have not always been clearly identified, one undoubtedly is the ability to isolate the likely impact of the absence of counsel at the particular stage. Thus the harmless error standard has been applied to the denial of counsel at the preliminary hearing because an appellate court can identify those benefits that could have been gained through counsel's assistance and assess whether they could have had a bearing upon the outcome of the subsequent trial.[8] That the same task could be accomplished in the state-interference cases is suggested by the standard that would be applied in assessing an ineffectiveness claim where counsel, rather than being prevented by the state procedure from rendering the particular assistance, had simply failed to render such assistance due to ineptitude. Consider, for example, a case where counsel failed to present a final summation (as in *Herring*) or required defendant to make an early decision as to testifying (as in *Brooks*) because of a mistaken view of the law. There the standard announced in *Strickland* would apply, and the defendant would have to establish the likelihood of actual prejudice.[9] Under the *Strickland* standard, it is readily conceivable that a court could find that such ineffectiveness by counsel had a discrete impact so minimal as not to meet the prejudice prong of the *Strickland* standard.

The above analysis suggests that the critical factor leading to the presumption of prejudice in the state-interference cases does not flow from an inability to assess the impact of the violation, or a likelihood of prejudicial impact so great as to make the cost of litigating that impact unjustified, but rather the role played by the state in restricting counsel's representation. Support for this view may be found in the analogy drawn to the presumption of prejudice applied in the conflict-of-interest cases.

Initially, that analogy too might be distinguished, as the presumption drawn in conflict cases commonly is seen as a product of the potentially indeterminate impact of representation corrupted by an actual conflict acted upon by counsel. However, that presumption also has been justified on the ground that the trial court bears some responsibility for the presence of a conflict problem that it could avoid through a pretrial inquiry and appropriate precautionary action. Indeed, that special responsibility has led the Court to recognize a constitutional violation in some circumstances simply on the trial court's failure to conduct an inquiry.[10] In the interference cases as well, the presumption of prejudice may be described as a prophylactic measure designed to discourage state action that may well preclude effective representation.

(b) State Invasions of the Lawyer–Client Relationship. State invasions of the lawyer-client relationship are unlike the direct impediments involved in cases like *Geders* and *Herring*, in that they do not necessarily restrict the lawyer's performance. Indeed, the circumstances surrounding the invasion may often negate any realistic likelihood that the invasion had any adverse impact upon counsel's performance. In *Weatherford v. Bursey*,[11] the Supreme Court held that, at least in some such cases, it will not find a Sixth Amendment violation. In that case, Bursey, a convicted defendant, brought a civil rights action against Weatherford, a former undercover agent, alleging that Weatherford's actions had denied Bursey the effective assistance of counsel at his criminal trial. In order to maintain Weatherford's undercover status, police had arrested him, along with Bursey, for an offense in which both had participated. Weatherford subsequently attended, at Bursey's request, two pretrial meetings with Bursey and his lawyer. Weatherford did not disclose to his superiors any information derived from those discussions that related to defense plans for the trial. Similarly, when Weatherford was unexpectedly called as a prosecution witness at that trial, he

---

8. See § 14.4 at note 8 and § 27.6 at note 26.

9. See § 11.10(d).

10. See § 11.9(b).

11. 429 U.S. 545, 97 S.Ct. 837, 51 L.Ed.2d 30 (1977).

carefully limited his testimony so as not to touch upon anything he might have learned through the lawyer-client meetings.

The basic issue presented in *Weatherford v. Bursey* was whether the Supreme Court would adopt what it described as a "per se" or "prophylactic rule." The lower court had adopted such a rule. Relying on Supreme Court precedent, it had held that "whenever the prosecution knowingly arranges or permits intrusions into the attorney-client relationship the right to counsel is sufficiently endangered to required reversal and a new trial." A divided Supreme Court held that the lower court had misread the relevant precedent and had adopted a rule that failed to give sufficient weight to the "necessity of undercover work and the value it often is to effective law enforcement." In *Hoffa v. United States*,[12] another case in which an undercover agent had been present during attorney-client conversations, the Court had assumed, without deciding, that a conviction would be overturned if the informer had reported the substance of those conversations to the authorities. Here, however, as in *Hoffa*, the undercover agent had not reported the substance of the lawyer-client conversations and his trial testimony had not related to those conversations. The Court noted that "Bursey would have a much stronger case" if either (1) Weatherford had testified at trial as to those conversations, (2) the "State's evidence [had] originated from those conversations," (3) the "overheard conversations had been used in any other way to the substantial detriment of Bursey," or (4) "even had the prosecution learned from Weatherford * * * the details of the * * * conversations about trial preparations." But with "none of these elements * * * present here," there was no basis for finding a Sixth Amendment violation. The Court would not ignore the fact that Weatherford went to the meetings, "not to spy, but because he was asked and the State was interested in retaining his undercover services on other matters." The protection of defendant's Sixth Amendment rights did not require adoption of a per se rule simply to give

clients and lawyers the assurance that third parties invited to their meetings are not undercover agents, especially when the cost of such a rule may be, "for all practical purposes," to "unmask" the agent.

The reach of the *Weatherford* ruling is uncertain. The case presented an invasion of the lawyer-client relationship that had a significant investigative justification. While *Weatherford* makes clear that such an invasion will not be deemed to violate the Sixth Amendment in the absence of a realistic likelihood of having adversely impacted the defense at trial, the question remains whether that impact will necessarily produce a Sixth Amendment violation. Assuming that the adverse impact is an inevitable byproduct of the state's investigatory need, might that need justify the invasion of the lawyer-client relationship? Lower courts have suggested that the answer may be "yes" in the context of governmental investigations of criminal defense lawyers where the defendant claimed that the investigation impacted the attorney's performance on defendant's behalf.

Weatherford also does not answer the question of whether a per se Sixth Amendment violation is established where the prosecutorial intrusion into the lawyer-client relationship clearly lacks any legitimate justification. The Supreme Court subsequently had such an unjustified invasion before it in *United States v. Morrison*.[13] In that case, D.E.A. agents, although aware that the defendant had been indicted and had retained counsel, met with defendant without defense counsel's knowledge or permission, and while seeking her cooperation, disparaged her retained attorney. The court of appeals held that defendant's right to counsel was violated irrespective of the lack of proof of prejudice to her case, and that the only appropriate remedy was a dismissal of the prosecution with prejudice. The Supreme Court unanimously reversed. The Court found it unnecessary to rule on the government's contention that a Sixth Amendment violation could not be established here without "some [defense] showing of preju-

---

12. 385 U.S. 293, 87 S.Ct. 408, 17 L.Ed.2d 374 (1966).

13. 449 U.S. 361, 101 S.Ct. 665, 66 L.Ed.2d 564 (1981).

dice." Even if it were assumed that there had been a Sixth Amendment violation, the remedy imposed by the lower court was incorrect because it was not "tailored to the injury suffered." Since "[r]espondent has demonstrated no prejudice of any kind, either transitory or permanent to the ability of her counsel to provide adequate representation in these criminal proceedings," there was "no justification" for such "drastic relief" as a dismissal with prejudice.

In declining to reach the government's contention that a showing of prejudice would be needed to establish a Sixth Amendment violation, the *Morrison* opinion left open the possibility that the Court might adopt a per se standard for those state invasions of the lawyer-client relationship that are not supported by any legitimate state motivation. The federal lower courts have divided on this issue on postconviction review of cases in which the prosecution had intentionally obtained, without any legitimate justification, information passed between the defendant and his lawyer. Some have concluded that the intentional invasion of the lawyer-client relationship producing such disclosure constitutes a per se Sixth Amendment violation, with no need to show that the defendant was prejudiced at trial as a result of the disclosure. Others have held that the defendant must show prejudice (e.g., the government's use of the information gained to its advantage), and the First Circuit has taken a "middle position," with the government bearing the "high burden" of showing that it did not use the information against the defendant.

(c) Conditions of Representation. In discussing situations that produce per se ineffective assistance of counsel, the Supreme Court in *United States v. Cronic*[14] mentioned both the state-imposed restriction cases discussed in subsection (a) and the special circumstances presented in *Powell v. Alabama*.[15] In that case, six days before the defendants' trial on capital charges in a hostile community, the judge appointed "all members of the bar"

to represent them at arraignment, leaving ambiguous whether that appointment continued through trial. On the day of the trial, when a lawyer from another state appeared on behalf of persons "interested" in the defendants, noting that he would be willing to represent the defendants only if given time to prepare the case and familiarize himself with local procedure, the court did not grant a continuance. Instead, it appointed that counsel forthwith to represent the defendants at trial, along with whatever help the local bar might provide. The *Powell* Court did not examine the actual performance of counsel at trial, but concluded that "such designation of counsel as was attempted [here] was either so indefinite or so close to trial as to amount to a denial of effective and substantial aid in that regard."

As *Cronic* noted, "*Powell* was * * * a case in which the surrounding circumstances made it so unlikely that any lawyer could provide effective assistance that ineffectiveness was properly presumed without inquiry into actual performance at trial." While *Powell* reached this conclusion in the context of a court appointed counsel, the key to that case, as subsequently read, was the adverse conditions surrounding counsel's representation. The same result presumably would have been reached if the out-of-state counsel in *Powell* had actually been retained only moments before the speedily scheduled trial and the trial judge had then forced that unprepared retained counsel to go to trial forthwith.

Though the lateness of the appointment of counsel obviously was a key element in *Powell*, the Supreme Court, in *Chambers v. Maroney*,[16] declined to "fashion a per se rule requiring reversal of every conviction following tardy appointment of counsel." The Court there stressed the difficulties that would be presented in shaping any hard and fast rules as to the time needed to ensure that counsel is adequately prepared. Indeed, it was not even clear in *Chambers* exactly when counsel had assumed responsibility for representing the defendant. The *Chambers* ruling arguably did

---

14. See § 11.7(d).

15. See § 11.1 at note 1 and § 11.7 at note16.

16. 399 U.S. 42, 90 S.Ct. 1975, 26 L.Ed.2d 419 (1970).

not go so far as to preclude treating a tardy appointment as establishing a non-conclusive presumption of prejudice, shifting to the state the burden of showing that counsel nonetheless performed competently. However, reliance upon such a presumption (adopted by a few lower courts after *Chambers*) was implicitly rejected in *United States v. Cronic.* The *Cronic* opinion warned against using any rule of thumb—such as the time spent by the government in its preparation—in determining how much time was needed for defense preparation. It also stressed that only the most exceptional situations would relieve the accused of the burden of showing ineffectiveness in counsel's actual representation at trial.

Under the prevailing view, at least post-*Cronic,* the time available to counsel to prepare is simply another factor to be considered, under the totality of the circumstances, in determining whether the right to effective assistance of counsel was denied. The defendant must show how that lack of time resulted in deficient performance and how that deficient performance had a probable prejudicial impact, using the *Strickland* standard for both of those prongs of the ineffective-assistance showing. However, though defendant bears the burden of showing counsel's inadequacy, a "belated appointment" is still viewed as "strong evidence in a defendant's behalf," requiring close scrutiny of counsel's performance. In many instances, omissions by counsel that would be viewed as possibly tactical or otherwise within the normal range of competence have been held to constitute ineffective assistance in light of the shortness of the time available for preparation. Also, the courts continue to hold open the possibility that in "very

limited and egregious circumstances," time for preparation may be so inadequate as to establish a per se Sixth Amendment violation.[17]

The one circumstance of representation that frequently has led to application of a per se analysis, without examining actual performance, is the lack of bar certification. On the other hand, courts generally have refused to declare per se ineffective attorneys operating under personal difficulties (e.g., alcohol abuse, cocaine use, or psychological ailments) that might impact the attorney's performance.

§ 11.9 Ineffective Assistance Claims Based Upon Attorney Conflicts of Interest

(a) The Range of Possible Conflicts of Interest. As courts have long noted, the constitutional right to effective assistance of counsel, "entitles the * * * [defendant] to the undivided loyalty of his counsel." The defendant does not receive the full efforts of counsel when the attorney's decisions are influenced by obligations owed to persons other than the defendant. Such a division of loyalty can arise from various different defense arrangements that may subject counsel's representation to conflicting interests.

The arrangement which is most frequently claimed to present such a conflict is the representation of more than one codefendant by the same attorney. The potential for a conflict in the representation of codefendants is so grave that many attorneys simply will not undertake joint representation. A divergence of interests among codefendants may arise throughout the course of the criminal litigation. In the plea bargaining process, the prosecutor may offer a

---

17. Commentators have been especially attracted to the possibility that the level of defense representation could be raised if courts were to adopt a standard of per se ineffectiveness stemming from the heavy caseloads and limited resources often associated with the representation of the indigent. Courts generally have rejected ineffective assistance challenges tied to resource limitations and caseloads, holding in various procedural contexts that ineffective assistance claims must be established on an individualized basis through a showing of deficiency and prejudicial impact in counsel's actual performance. However, in the setting of a pretrial challenge, the Louisiana Supreme Court directed lower courts to thereafter adopt a "rebuttable presumption that indigent * * * [defendants

represented by public defenders in a particular office handling an overload of cases] are receiving assistance of counsel not sufficiently effective to meet constitutionally required standards." State v. Peart, 621 So.2d 780 (La. 1993). The Arizona Supreme Court adopted a similar presumption as to a contract system for representing indigents that failed to take account of caseload burdens and related factors. State v. Smith, 140 Ariz. 355, 681 P.2d 1374 (1984). Other courts have held that appointed counsel must receive greater compensation or that defender offices may not be required to carry a caseload beyond a particular maximum, but have based such rulings on grounds other than a presumed Sixth Amendment violation (e.g., supervisory authority).

reduced charge or dismissal to one defendant in exchange for testimony against the other. At the trial, the potential for conflict is especially high if the defendants are tried together. The codefendants may raise conflicting defenses, with each implicating the other, or they may adopt a joint defense but offer contradictory explanations of relevant factual events. Even if their testimony would be entirely consistent, defendants jointly tried may present a conflict because the advantages and disadvantages of taking the stand may vary substantially as between them. A decision to have them both testify or not testify might work to the disadvantage of one or the other, while a decision to have only one testify will undoubtedly highlight the lack of testimony from the other. In presenting his closing argument, the attorney may again find that the interests of his clients diverge. If the prosecution's evidence is much weaker against one client, that defendant's interests suggest that the comparison be brought to the jury's attention, but the other defendant's interests clearly argue against that tactic. A similar conflict arises at the sentencing stage when the codefendants' roles in the planning and commission of the crime or their backgrounds and prior criminal records vary substantially.

Conflicts of interest may also arise when defense counsel has previously represented, or is currently representing, in another matter, either the victim of the crime or a prosecution witness. Such representation might place the defense counsel in a position where she hesitates to proceed as vigorously as she otherwise might because of a "pecuniary interest in possible future business" or "fail[s] to conduct a rigorous cross-examination for fear of misusing * * * confidential information." A somewhat analogous conflict situation is presented when a third party with some interest in the case pays the legal fees of defense counsel. This situation typically involves the trial of employees for their participation in allegedly illegal acts of a business enterprise, with the defense counsel being paid by the employer. As the Supreme Court has noted, "one risk [presented by this fee arrangement] is that the lawyer will prevent his client from obtaining leniency by preventing the client from offering testimony or from taking other actions contrary to the employer's interest." Still another risk is that the lawyer may fail to raise certain arguments favorable to the employees in order to force a hopefully favorable court ruling on an issue on which the employer has "a long-range interest."

Not all conflicts of interest are between co-defendants or between defendants and third parties. Conflicts of interest also may arise between the defendant and the defense counsel. The key here should be the presence of a specific concern that would divide counsel's loyalties. In some instances, defendants have sought (usually unsuccessfully) to convert general incompetence claims into conflict claims by arguing that the interest of counsel in protecting her reputation, in adhering to a particular philosophy, or in minimizing her effort constituted a conflicting interest that divided her loyalties. Typically, however, courts have looked to cases in which a representation fully devoted to defendant's interest is likely to produce an adverse consequence for counsel unique to the individual case. Thus, the paradigm case is that in which the lawyer representing the defendant fears opening herself up to criminal prosecution because she is under investigation for an offense relating to the same events.

Certain fee arrangements can create such a special conflict, here between counsel's financial interests and the defendant's best interests. Consider, for example, a compensation agreement under which counsel has an interest in the royalties to be received from a movie or book that will portray the trial or related events. Agreements of this kind, the courts have noted, "tempt lawyers, consciously or subconsciously and adversely to the client's interests, to tilt the defense for commercial reasons." The same might be true of a negotiated guilty plea in which the prosecution agrees not to pursue forfeiture on property which would constitute the source of counsel's fee.

A position of conflict also can be created when counsel is required to furnish evidence against the client. Thus, a conflict is likely where statutory or ethical obligations require counsel to deliver to police physical evidence in counsel's possession that will be used against the client, or where counsel is called to testify as a prosecution witness. Indeed, even as to counsel who would be a defense witness, there is a conflict potential. While the broad prohibition against counsel appearing as both a witness and an advocate usually is explained in terms of the public's perception of the lawyer's role and unfairness to the opposing party, it also avoids the potential of counsel promoting her role as a witness over her role as an advocate. Finally, where defense counsel is facing possible criminal or disciplinary consequences as a result of questionable behavior in the representation of defendant, continued representation creates the likelihood that counsel's primary concern will be protecting herself by minimizing the consequences of that behavior rather than serving the defendant's best interests.

The discussion so far has assumed that a setting presenting a possible conflict involves a single lawyer. In general, however, courts do not distinguish the situation in which the lawyer representing the codefendant, the lawyer who currently or formerly represented an interested third party, or the lawyer with a conflicting self-interest unique to the case is the defense lawyer herself or a partner of the defense lawyer. Consistent with the approach of ethic codes, conflicts are vicariously imputed to all members of a law firm. While the Supreme Court has not ruled directly on this approach, it has "assumed without deciding that two law partners are considered as one attorney" in analyzing the conflict potential of representing codefendants.[1] Some courts treat the public defender office in much the same manner. Others, however, view those offices as different, in part because "the salaried government employee does not have the financial interest in the success of the departmental representation that is inherent in private practice." Perhaps also influential is the logical application of the same standard to the prosecutor's office, where disqualification of the en-

tire office can have a substantial disruptive impact if done frequently (e.g., every time a defendant had been represented on a prior charge by an attorney now a member of the prosecutor's staff). In these jurisdictions, where the defender office's potential conflict stems from confidential information received from a past client now a prosecution witness, an appropriate solution is to utilize a "Chinese Wall," which keeps that information away from the attorney representing the defendant. That device tends not to be viewed as sufficient, however, as to codefendants. Defender offices commonly are prohibited from representing indigent codefendants, even when the codefendants seek joint representation; representation is provided through a combination of the defender office representing one codefendant and separate appointed counsel representing each of the others.

While the various conflict settings described above all create a potential for inhibiting counsel's actions on behalf of his client, none do so inevitably. Indeed, few situations creating potential conflicts are viewed as so fraught with the danger of dividing counsel's loyalties as to be absolutely prohibited by prevailing standards of professional responsibility. The ABA's Model Rules,[2] for example, provide that where the lawyer has another client whose interests are "directly adverse" to the defendant, the lawyer may nonetheless represent the defendant if the lawyer "reasonably believes that the lawyer will be able to provide competent and diligent representation to each affected client," and each client consents after full disclosure. So too, a lawyer is not prohibited from representing a client where the representation of that client "will be materially limited by the lawyer's responsibilities to another client, a former client, * * * or by a personal interest of the lawyer" if the lawyer believes the representation will be competent and diligent and there is adequate consultation and consent. Third party payments are acceptable under a similar standard, and even publication agreements are prohibited only where they give the

§ 11.9

1. See Burger v. Kemp, described at note 19 infra.

2. See ABA Model Rules of Professional Conduct, Rule 1.7, 1.8.

lawyer herself the "literary or media rights" to a portrayal based "in substantial part on information relating to the representation."

The profession's willingness to tolerate arrangements that create a high potential for dividing the attorney's loyalty is not based simply upon the fact that those arrangements will not inevitably create a conflict. Its decision not to absolutely prohibit such arrangements is also based in part on the potential value of many of these arrangements to the client. Initially, they may permit the client to obtain the services of the one lawyer that he wants to represent him. Some defendants put their trust in a particular lawyer and would want that lawyer even though he may have previously represented one of the prosecution's witnesses or even the victim. Some would prefer a privately retained lawyer and can afford one only if their employer, a codefendant, or some other interested person will pay that lawyer. Joint representation of codefendants, in particular, may have strategic advantages. Thus the Supreme Court has noted: "Joint representation is a means of ensuring against reciprocal recrimination. A common defense often gives strength against a common attack."

As one might anticipate, the courts have not been willing to adopt prophylactic rules that ban defense arrangements that carry a conflict potential when the profession itself has been unwilling to ban those arrangements. On the other hand, the courts have been willing to view many of those arrangements as suspect. They have recognized also that it is often impossible to reconstruct the precise impact of a divided loyalty upon counsel's performance. In particular, a conflict of interest may have as much bearing on matters that are not reflected in the appellate record (e.g., the failure to interview witnesses or seek a plea bargain) as it does on those acts or omissions at trial that are a part of the record. Very often the only person who knows exactly what the conflict's full ramification might have been is the defense lawyer herself, and courts are naturally wary of the lawyer's disclaimers of influence

(or even the lawyer's acknowledgment of influence, which may be seen as a "last ditch" effort to help the client). One response to these difficulties inherent in a postconviction attempt to trace the impact of a possible conflict has been the development of a trial court obligation to make a pretrial inquiry into possible conflicts.

(b) The Trial Court Duty to Inquire. The Court's initial discussion of the trial court's duty to inquire into possible conflicts of interest came in two cases involving joint representation of codefendants. In the first case, *Holloway v. Arkansas*,[3] a public defender had been appointed to represent three codefendants who were to be jointly tried on charges of robbery and rape. Three weeks before trial, defense counsel requested the appointment of separate counsel for each of the defendants, noting that defendants' statements to him indicated "a possibility of a conflict of interest." The trial court rejected the request and defense counsel continued his joint representation. On the day of the trial, before the jury was empaneled, defense counsel renewed his request. He informed the court that one or two of the defendants might testify, and if they did, he would not be able to cross-examine them on behalf of the other defendants since he had received "confidential information" from each of the defendants. The trial court again denied counsel's request. It directed him to simply "put them on the stand * * * and tell the man to go ahead and relate what he wants to." Each of the defendants subsequently testified, giving unguided narrative testimony without cross-examination by defense counsel. All three alleged that they were not at the scene of the crime. The defendants' ineffective assistance claims were subsequently rejected by the state appellate court on the ground that neither an actual conflict of interest nor prejudice had been demonstrated. The Supreme Court, by a 6–3 majority, reversed the conviction of all three codefendants.

Chief Justice Burger's opinion for the Court initially noted that, as had been previously held, "joint representation is not per se viola-

---

3.   435 U.S. 475, 98 S.Ct. 1173, 55 L.Ed.2d 426 (1978).

tive of constitutional guarantees of effective assistance." Such representation could, under some circumstances, be in the best interest of all of the codefendants. On the other hand, each defendant was entitled to representation free of an actual conflict of interest. Here, however, there was no need to determine whether a conflict in fact existed. The trial judge's failure to properly respond to the possibility of conflicts arising from defendants' "different interests," after that possibility was "brought home to the court" by counsel's requests for separate representation, was sufficient ground in itself for reversal. In *Glasser v. United States*,[4] the Court had held that defendant was denied his Sixth Amendment right to the effective assistance of counsel when the trial court placed his retained attorney in a conflict situation by appointing that attorney to also represent a codefendant. The *Glasser* Court had noted that the trial judge has a duty not to insist that counsel "undertake to concurrently represent interests which might diverge." The trial judge here violated that duty. The defense counsel's request was timely and obviously not made for "dilatory purposes." The trial court should have responded with more than a cursory dismissal of that request. Its failure "either to appoint separate counsel or take adequate steps to ascertain whether the risk [of a conflict] was too remote to warrant separate counsel" violated the defendants' Sixth Amendment rights.

Having responded to the state's claim that no constitutional error could exist without a showing of an actual conflict, the *Holloway* opinion turned to the state's claim that defendants' convictions could not be overturned without a showing of prejudice. *Glasser*, the Court noted, was to the contrary. Although the language of *Glasser* was not without ambiguity, the *Glasser* opinion was properly read as "holding that whenever a trial court improperly requires joint representation over timely objection reversal is automatic." Subsequent to *Glasser*, the Supreme Court had recognized in *Chapman v. California* that certain constitutional violations could constitute harmless

error.[5] However, *Chapman* and its progeny had also recognized that the denial of the right to counsel is "so basic to a fair trial that * * * [it] can never be treated as harmless error." The reasoning of *Glasser*, the *Holloway* opinion concluded, placed in the same category the Sixth Amendment violation created by a failure to inquire where there is a constitutional duty to do so. In "the normal case where [*Chapman's*] harmless-error rule is applied, * * * the reviewing court can undertake with some confidence its relatively narrow task of assessing the likelihood that the error materially affected the deliberations of the jury." But as *Glasser* had suggested, in the case of joint representation of conflicting interests, "the evil * * * is in what the advocate finds himself compelled to *refrain* from doing." While "it may be possible in some cases to identify from the record the prejudice resulting from an attorney's failure to undertake certain trial tasks," to "judge intelligently the impact of a conflict on the attorney's [total] representation of a client," including such matters as potential plea negotiations, "would be virtually impossible." An "inquiry into a claim of harmless error here would require, unlike most cases, unguided speculation." Thus, once the failure to inquire was treated as akin to judicial placement of the attorney in a conflict position, that ended the judicial inquiry and a reversal of the conviction was required.

The fact situation presented in *Holloway* was especially suited for requiring trial court action. As the lower courts later noted, the "imposition upon the state * * * is not heavy" when the trial court has before it a timely objection by counsel, and an appropriate response at that point will avoid the need subsequently for a difficult post-hoc determination as to whether counsel was inhibited by an actual conflict. A more troublesome issue, it was noted, was what "affirmative duty" should be placed upon the trial court to inquire into the propriety of multiple representation when defense counsel fails to request separate representation. That issue produced the Court's second major discussion of the duty to

---

4. 315 U.S. 60, 62 S.Ct. 457, 86 L.Ed. 680 (1942).

5. See § 27.6(c).

inquire, in *Cuyler v. Sullivan*.[6] The defendant Sullivan had been represented by two attorneys, retained by his two codefendants and paid in part by friends of the group. Each defendant had a separate trial, and Sullivan was the only one of the three convicted. Neither defense counsel nor Sullivan objected to the multiple representation. When counsels' effectiveness was challenged in a federal habeas proceeding, the court of appeals held that, in light of *Holloway*, Sullivan had established his claim for relief by showing a possible conflict of interest. The Supreme Court, by a vote of 7–2, ruled that the lower court had misread *Holloway* and applied an improper constitutional standard. The trial court here was not under an obligation to inquire into the possibility of a conflict of interest, and where such an obligation did not exist, a postconviction claim of ineffective assistance required a showing of an "actual" rather than a "potential" conflict.

In ruling that the trial court had no constitutional obligation to inquire into the propriety of counsels' multiple representation, the *Sullivan* Court found *Holloway* clearly distinguishable. The Court reasoned:

Holloway requires state trial courts to investigate timely objections to multiple representation. But nothing in our precedents suggests that the Sixth Amendment requires state courts themselves to initiate inquiries into the propriety of multiple representation in every case. Defense counsel have an ethical obligation to avoid conflicting representations and to advise the court promptly when a conflict of interest arises during the course of trial. Absent special circumstances, therefore, trial courts may assume either that multiple representation entails no conflict or that the lawyer and his clients knowingly accept such risk of conflict as may exist. Indeed, as the Court noted in *Holloway,* trial courts necessarily rely in large measure upon the good faith and good judgment of defense counsel. "An attorney representing two defendants in a criminal matter is in the best position professionally and ethically to determine when a conflict of interest exists or will probably develop in the course of a trial." Unless the trial court knows or reasonably should know that a particular conflict exists, the court need not initiate an inquiry.

The dissenters in *Sullivan* argued that the dangers of multiple representation were so grave that in every case in which two or more defendants were jointly charged or had been joined for trial, the trial court should be under an obligation "to inquire whether there is multiple representation, to warn the defendants of the possible risk of such representation, and to ascertain that the representation is the result of the defendant's informed choice." The majority acknowledged that such a procedure would be desirable. Indeed, under proposed (and subsequently adopted) Federal Rule 44(c), a similar obligation was about to be imposed upon federal trial courts. However, to so substantially extend the essentially prophylactic rule of *Holloway* as a constitutional mandate was another matter. The inquiry that the dissenters would require was not without costs. It would impose a burden on both the trial court and the lawyer-client relationship. Indeed, Chief Justice Burger in *Holloway* had warned that a trial court's attempt to explore the nature of the relationship between jointly represented codefendants, including their potential defenses, could present "significant risks of unfair prejudice" to the defense. It therefore should not be unconstitutional for the state court to seek to limit such costs by relying in general on the professional obligation of counsel to advise the court when an actual conflict arises. Where counsel has not taken that step, the trial court should have a constitutional obligation to act on its own initiative only where it has good cause to believe that counsel may have erred in assuming that there was no actual conflict. Accordingly, the controlling Sixth Amendment standard, the *Sullivan* majority concluded, would be that, in the absence of objection by counsel, an inquiry

---

6.   446 U.S. 335, 100 S.Ct. 1708, 64 L.Ed.2d 333 (1980). Since appellant Cuyler was the prison warden and respondent Sullivan the convicted defendant, this case is most

often is referred to as *"Sullivan,"* although some judges prefer *"Cuyler."*

was not mandated "[u]nless the trial court knows or reasonably should know that a particular conflict exists."

The *Sullivan* opinion did not explain precisely what information would place a trial judge in a position where he "reasonably should know" that a conflict exists. The Court did explain, however, why the *Sullivan* case did not present such a situation. Relevant factors cited were the separate trials of the codefendants, an opening statement that outlined a defense compatible with the view that none of the defendants were involved in the offense, and a suggestion in that statement that counsel were willing to call all relevant witnesses. While the defense later rested without presenting those witnesses, that decision "on its face" appeared to be "a reasonable tactical response" to the weakness of the prosecution's case. *Sullivan's* discussion of the relatively innocuous appearance of the joint representation in that case held open the possibility that a trial judge would constitutionally be required to conduct an inquiry in situations presenting the more common signs of conflict.

Although the Court's ruling was far from clear, *Wood v. Georgia*[7] appeared to be a case in which the Court found that the trial court reasonably should have known of a conflict. The Supreme Court granted certiorari in *Wood* to determine whether a state could constitutionally revoke the probation of defendants who were unable to pay fines imposed for a previous conviction. The case was remanded, however, for an evidentiary hearing on a conflict issue raised by the Court sua sponte. The defendants had been charged with an offense committed in the course of their employment and their counsel had been provided by their employer. They had been sentenced to pay substantial fines on the assumption that the employer would provide them with the necessary funds. When the employer refused to give them the funds, counsel did not immediately move for modification of the fines or ask for leniency. Instead, he pressed the argument that a revocation for the failure to pay fines that were beyond a defendant's means was

unconstitutional, a contention which, if accepted, would work to the long range benefit of the employer. The Supreme Court noted that the record of the revocation proceedings was not sufficiently complete for it to determine whether a conflict actually existed. "Nevertheless," it noted, "the record does demonstrate that the *possibility* of a conflict of interest was sufficiently apparent at the time of the revocation hearing to impose upon the [state] court a duty to inquire further." All of the relevant facts relating to the employer's retention of counsel, the employer's failure to pay the fines, and "counsel's insistence upon pressing a constitutional attack" were known to the state court. Moreover, "any doubt as to whether th[at] court should have been aware of the problem [was] dispelled by the fact that the [prosecutor] had raised the conflict problem."

Notwithstanding the above statements, other aspects of the *Wood* ruling suggested that, perhaps, the Court was not holding that the trial court had violated the *Sullivan* duty to inquire. In a footnote response to the dissent's contention that the *Wood* ruling was moving beyond *Sullivan*, the *Wood* majority stated that "*Sullivan* mandates a reversal when the trial court has failed to make an inquiry even though it knows or reasonably should know that a particular conflict exists!" In *Wood*, the Court was reviewing a probation revocation proceeding, but it did not reverse the trial court's revocation order. Rather, the Court remanded to the lower court with directions to grant a new revocation hearing only if it found that an actual conflict had existed and had not been waived.

In *Mickens v. Taylor*,[8] the Supreme Court spoke to the confusion caused by the *Wood* opinion. The *Mickens* majority concluded that (1) *Wood* had held that the state court there had violated its *Sullivan* duty to inquire, (2) the remand order in *Wood* was consistent with such a finding since the *Sullivan* duty to inquire was distinct from the duty to inquire established in *Holloway*, and (3) while the *Wood* majority did state in a footnote that

---

7. 450 U.S. 261, 101 S.Ct. 1097, 67 L.Ed.2d 220 (1981).

8. 535 U.S. 162, 122 S.Ct. 1237, 152 L.Ed.2d 291 (2002).

Sullivan "mandates a reversal where the trial court has failed [to make] the requisite inquiry," the context of that statement indicated that it should not be read literally. *Mickens* held that where the trial judge failed to make the inquiry mandated by *Sullivan*, a defendant on appeal following conviction must demonstrate that "a conflict of interest affected the adequacy of his representation."

Mickens reaffirmed that a violation of a *Holloway* duty to inquire required automatic reversal, but concluded that the same considerations did not govern as to a *Sullivan* duty of inquiry. Where, as in *Holloway*, defense counsel raises a timely objection to being forced to represent codefendants, and the trial court failed to adequately explore that possible conflict, it is appropriate to presume that there was a "disabling conflict" which "undermined the adversarial process." That presumption is justified, however, only because of the special features of the *Holloway* setting. An objection is raised by a defense attorney, who is "in the best position to determine when a [disabling] conflict exists," and it comes in a setting of joint representation, which is "inherently suspect," and which places on counsel joint obligations that "effectively seal his lips in crucial matters and make it difficult to measure the precise harm arising from counsel's errors."

Mickens concluded that there was no justification for a similar presumption where the duty to inquire arose only from the *Sullivan* requirement of a sua sponte inquiry where the trial court, without counsel's objection, "knows or reasonably should know that a particular conflict exists." Here, on postconviction review, a reversal is required only if the defendant can make the same showing that would be required for reversal where there was no duty to inquire. That showing, as discussed in subsection (d), typically is that there actually was a conflict and that it "significantly affected counsel's performance." Thus, in *Wood*, where the Supreme Court found that the trial judge had violated the *Sullivan* duty in the revocation proceeding, it did not reverse the revocation order, but appropriately remanded to determine whether there existed a conflict that influenced counsel's performance.

The *Mickens* majority added that requiring an automatic reversal where a trial judge violated the *Sullivan* duty to inquire "makes little policy sense." The thrust of the law of ineffective assistance is to tie reversal to a showing of likely prejudice. "The trial court's awareness of a potential conflict renders it no more likely that counsel's performance was significantly altered" by a conflict then a situation in which "the trial judge is not aware of the conflict (and thus not obligated to inquire)." Neither could it be said that the "trial judge's failure to make the *Sullivan*-mandated inquiry often makes it harder for reviewing courts to determine conflict and effect, particularly since these courts may rely on evidence and testimony whose importance only became established at the trial."[9]

After *Mickens*, on review following a conviction, whether the trial court violated the *Sullivan* duty is an issue that need not be decided. For the same standard of review governs whether the *Sullivan* duty applied and was ignored or simply did not apply. Nonetheless, for the trial court, the *Sullivan* obligation still exists, and the court must be aware of the types of situations that trigger the *Sullivan* duty, particularly under the "reasonably-should-know" standard. Apart from identifying *Woods* as presenting circumstances requiring an inquiry, *Mickens* did not contribute

---

9. One of the *Mickens* dissents argued that automatic reversal was necessary to effectively implement the *Sullivan* duty to inquire, but the majority stated that the adoption of such a "sanction," which "risk[s] conferring a windfall upon the defendant," rested on the unproven presumption that judges "need the incentive of an exclusionary rule," and also ignored the "incentive" that the *Sullivan* standard already provides for making an inquiry. Another dissent argued that automatic reversal should be available where, as here, a combination of circumstances—representational incompatibility "egregious on its face,"

the trial court's responsibility for the conflict, and capital punishment—combined to result in a "criminal punishment that will be regarded as fundamentally unfair." The majority responded that the *Holloway/Sullivan* framework itself identified situations on which the conviction "will reasonably not be regarded as fundamentally fair," and that a standard of "*ad hoc* fairness" was inconsistent with the Court's obligation to "lay down rules that can be followed in the innumerable cases we are unable to review."

significantly to identifying such situations. The federal habeas court there had concluded that the *Sullivan* duty applied since the state judge who appointed counsel to represent the defendant on a murder charge had dismissed criminal charges against the homicide victim shortly after his death and had been aware (or should have been aware) from the docket sheet that the counsel now being appointed had represented the victim on those charges. Because the state had not challenged the habeas court's finding, the Supreme Court had no reason to review it, and focused on the consequences of the assumed violation of the *Sullivan* duty.

Pre–*Mickens* lower court rulings that found a duty to inquire under the *Sullivan* standard typically invoked circumstances that made obvious the existence of an actual conflict. The *Sullivan* obligation was held to apply, for example, where the record established that the defense counsel had previously represented a prosecution witness in connection with the same or a related matter, that the defense counsel was facing a disciplinary complaint in connection with the same case, and that the defense counsel had ties to the office of the prosecution that might relate to the current case. The lower courts generally held that the *Sullivan* obligation to inquire did not arise where the circumstances were ambiguous or suggested only a potential conflict (i.e., a conflict that could develop with the occurrence at trial of certain events not necessarily anticipated).

Where the lower courts found that a duty to inquire existed, they also concluded that the inquiry had to be more than perfunctory. They spoke of the need for "probing and specific questions" relating to the apparent conflict, although also noting that the trial court was "entitled to rely on the attorney's representations as to the underlying facts."

Mickens dealt only with the constitutional obligation to inquire, but much the same approach is likely to prevail on postconviction review of an alleged violation of a court rule or statute imposing a duty to inquire. Federal

Rule 44(c) provides for an inquiry whenever defendants have been jointly charged under Rule 8(b) or have been joined for trial under Rule 13 and are represented "by the same counsel or counsel who are associated in the practice of law." The trial court is directed to "promptly inquire about the propriety of the joint representation," and to "personally advise each defendant of the right to the effective assistance of counsel, including separate representation." Moreover, "unless there is good cause to believe that no conflict of interest is likely to arise," the trial court "must take appropriate measures to protect each defendant's right to counsel." Several states impose similar obligations on their trial courts. The Advisory Committee Notes to Rule 44(c) clearly indicated that the failure to comply with Rule 44(c) should not in itself constitute a per se reversible error. Accordingly, on review after a conviction, appellate courts will look to whether the reversal is required under the Sixth Amendment. After *Mickens*, absent the special circumstances of *Holloway*, this will require a defense showing that meets the standard discussed in subsection (d) infra.

(c) Waiver and Disqualification. As a result of pretrial prosecution motions raising possible defense conflicts, automatic inquiries pursuant to provisions like Federal Rule 44(c), and, to a lesser extent, *Sullivan's* inquiry requirement, courts have been forced in recent years to face the question of what should be done when a defendant tells the court to ignore any possible conflict because he or she desires to waive the right to conflict-free counsel. At this point, the Supreme Court noted in *Wheat v. United States*,[10] trial courts could "face the prospect of being 'whipsawed' by assertions of error no matter which way they rule." If the trial court disqualifies the defendant's counsel, the defendant will raise a claim (as did defendant in *Wheat*) that he was denied his Sixth Amendment right to counsel of choice. On the other hand, "if the trial court agrees to the multiple representation, and the advocacy of counsel is thereafter impaired as a result, the defendant may well claim that he did not receive effective assistance of counsel."

10. 486 U.S. 153, 108 S.Ct. 1692, 100 L.Ed.2d 140 (1988).

Wheat recognized that some lower courts had indicated that the defendant's waiver of conflict-free counsel would automatically defeat such a claim (assuming the waiver was "knowing and intelligent"). That position, however, was not universal. The *Wheat* Court also took "note [of], without passing judgment on, the apparent willingness of [other] Courts of Appeals to entertain ineffective assistance claims from defendants who have specifically waived the right to conflict-free counsel." In *Wheat,* the Court sought to reduce this "whipsaw" potential by setting forth the standards under which a trial court constitutionally could refuse to allow multiple representation notwithstanding defendant's waiver.

The *Wheat* majority initially rejected the defendant's contention that "the provision of waivers by all affected defendants cures any problems created by the multiple representation." "No such flat rule," the Court noted, "can be deduced from the Sixth Amendment presumption in favor of counsel of choice." The Sixth Amendment right to choose one's counsel is not absolute; because of countervailing considerations, a defendant cannot insist upon counsel who is not a member of the bar nor can he insist upon representation by an attorney "who has a previous or ongoing relationship with an opposing party, even when the opposing party is the Government." In the conflict situation also, a countervailing consideration is present. The courts "have an independent interest in ensuring that criminal trials are conducted within the ethical standards of the profession and that legal proceedings appear fair to all who observe them." In light of this interest, "where a court justifiably finds an actual conflict of interest, there can be no doubt that it may decline a proffer of waiver and insist that defendants be separately represented."

The *Wheat* majority recognized, however, that the critical situation, as a practical matter, was that in which the trial court found multiple representation to present a "potential" rather than an "actual" conflict. To find an actual conflict, a court must determine that the defense counsel is subject to an obligation or unique personal interest which, if followed, would lead counsel to adopt a strategy other than that most favorable to the defendant. Very often, whether that obligation or interest will come into play, and whether it will lead in a direction other than that most favorable to the defendant, will depend upon future events that may or may not occur (e.g., whether a particular witness testifies). Accordingly, the *Wheat* majority characterized as "rare" any case in which "an actual conflict may be determined before trial"; the "more common" case was that in which the court finds that "a potential for conflict exists which may or may not burgeon into an actual conflict." Because the likely materialization and dimensions of such potential conflicts are "notoriously hard to predict" in the "murkier pretrial context when relationships between parties are seen through a glass darkly," the Court concluded that a trial court can properly find, upon a showing of "a serious potential for conflict," that the presumption favoring defendant's choice of counsel should be overridden.

Wheat further noted that the trial court, in deciding whether to override that presumption, could take into consideration the fact that potential conflicts often reflect "imponderables" that "are difficult enough for a lawyer to assess, and even more difficult to convey by way of explanation to a criminal defendant untutored in the niceties of legal ethics." So too, it need not ignore the reality "that the willingness of an attorney to obtain such waivers from his clients may bear an inverse relation to the care with which he conveys all the necessary information to them." On the other hand, the trial court should also be aware of the possibility that the "government may seek to 'manufacture' a conflict to prevent the defendant from having a particular able counsel at his side." In the end, the trial court, in its evaluation of these and other relevant considerations, must be "allowed substantial latitude in refusing waivers" in cases of potential conflict as well as in cases of actual conflict.

Turning to the case before it, the *Wheat* majority found that the trial court had acted within its discretion in refusing defendant's request to substitute counsel who had been representing two separately charged accomplices of the defendant. The trial court had been "confronted not simply with an attorney who wished to represent two coequal defendants in a straightforward criminal prosecution: rather, [counsel] proposed to defend three coconspirators of varying stature in a complex drug distribution scheme." Moreover, one of the codefendants had pleaded to a lesser count as part of a plea agreement, and the government intended to call him as a prosecution witness at defendant's trial. The other codefendant, although previously acquitted on the drug charges, remained open to a trial on tax evasion and other charges relating to the conspiracy (his offer to plead to those charges had not yet been accepted by the district court and could still be withdrawn), with a distinct likelihood that the defendant Wheat would be called as a government witness at that trial. Thus, counsel in two different situations could have been placed in a setting where he would be cross-examining a former client. Ruling on a motion made "close to the time of trial," the trial court had relied on "instinct and judgment based on experience" in evaluating these factors, and it could not be said to have "exceeded the broad latitude which must be accorded it in making this decision."

In its discussion of the "broad latitude" that must be accorded the trial court, the *Wheat* Court emphasized that this latitude worked both ways—that it also applied to a trial court's determination to allow multiple representation with appropriate waivers. While sustaining the decision of the trial court below to deny multiple representation, the Court noted that other trial courts might have reached an opposite conclusion "with equal justification," and that it was not suggesting one conclusion was "right" and the other "wrong." Moreover, while the circumstances before the trial court here were characterized as establishing "a serious potential for conflict," the Court's discussion of the trial court's two-way discretion referred to both "potential" and "actual" conflicts.

Recognizing this discretion and applying a deferential standard of review, appellate courts have sustained the disqualification of counsel not only in cases involving multiple represen-

tation of codefendants (as in *Wheat*), but also in a broad range of other settings that present a realistic potential for a conflict of interest. These include cases in which: (1) defense counsel currently was representing an anticipated prosecution witness on either a related or different matter; (2) defense counsel has previously represented a prosecution witness on a related matter; (3) defense counsel was a potential witness for the prosecution; (4) defense counsel's participation in events that would be described before the jury could lead to calling her as a defense witness, and would make her an "unsworn" witness for the defense even if she were not called to testify; (5) defense counsel was a former member of the prosecution's staff who had participated in the bringing of these charges or otherwise had access through that position to confidential information relevant to the prosecution; (6) defense counsel was alleged to have been involved in criminal activity or professional misconduct that would bear upon her representation of the defendant; and (7) defense counsel also represented the entity with which defendant was associated (with that entity having interests separate from the defendant).

Of course, trial courts do not invariably require disqualification in all conflict situations. Exercising the discretion recognized in *Wheat*, trial courts often refuse to disqualify, especially in cases that present only a potential conflict, if they can obtain a satisfactory waiver as to that conflict (which may require the participation of third persons as well as the defendant). Although *Wheat* spoke of federal circuits that appeared to allow a defendant to challenge counsel's competency on conflict grounds notwithstanding defendant's waiver of his right to conflict-free counsel, post-*Wheat* circuit court rulings have established that a knowing and intelligent waiver precludes a subsequent competency challenge based on that conflict. There remains for the trial court, however, the need to ensure that the waiver relied upon is in fact a knowing and intelligent waiver.

For reasons noted in *Wheat*, including the pretrial setting, the dilemma inherent in a conflicted counsel advising the client on the dangers of that conflict, and the subtleties of many potential conflicts, trial courts must exercise considerable care if they want to obtain waivers that satisfy the knowing-and-intelligent standard. To assist them in this regard, several appellate courts have set forth fairly detailed instructions for advising defendants of potential and actual conflicts and ensuring that they understand what they are waiving. As an additional safeguard, some courts have also insisted that the defendant considering a waiver first consult with independent counsel. Of course, in the end, whether a waiver was made knowingly and intelligently depends upon the facts of the particular case, including the personal experience and understanding of the defendant, so that a valid waiver can be found even though the trial court did not engage in an extensive colloquy in accepting the waiver.

Although *Wheat* recognized the discretion of the trial court to accept waivers and refuse to disqualify counsel, even in an actual conflict situation, that discretion does not apply to all forms of conflict. *Wheat* involved a conflict situation (the multiple representation of codefendants) in which the primary concern is that the conflict might adversely impact counsel's representation of the defendant, with that potential giving rise, in turn, to a separate "judicial-integrity" concern that the conflict will make the proceeding appear less than "fair." In other conflict situations, however, the conflict also carries with it the potential of giving the defendant an adversarial advantage by depriving the prosecution of "a level playing field," and here the prosecution apparently can insist upon disqualification. "Waiver by the defendant is ineffective in curing the impropriety * * * since he is not the party prejudiced."

The classic illustration of such a conflict situation is that in which defense counsel is a former prosecutor and acquired through that position confidential information relating to the prosecution's case against his current client. An analogous defense advantage is presented where defense counsel formerly represented a prosecution witness, and through that representation obtained confidential information that counsel now intends to use to challenge the witness (against the wishes of the witness). Lower courts also have recognized that the prosecution is placed at a disadvantage where the defense counsel either is called as a defense witness or acts, in effect, as an "unsworn defense witness" because of juror awareness of her participation in the events on which she will examine and cross-examine witnesses. So too, where the prosecution calls the defense counsel as a prosecution witness, counsel's capacity to contradict her own testimony in the course of questioning witnesses or delivering a closing statement gives the defense a weapon that would not be present as to other prosecution witnesses.

(d) Postconviction Review. *Cuyler v. Sullivan*[11] set forth the standard to be applied on postconviction review in determining whether a claim of defense counsel conflict of interest, not presented prior to conviction, requires reversal of the conviction. The conflict there arose from multiple representation in a situation not sufficiently indicative of conflict to impose upon the trial court a constitutional duty to inquire. *Mickens v. Taylor*[12] held that, aside from the special situation of *Holloway* (where defense defense counsel seeks withdrawal on conflict grounds), the *Sullivan* standard also applies where the trial court had a constitutional duty of inquiry, but failed to conduct that inquiry. The Court has not spoken to the situation in which the trial court conducted an inquiry in a non-*Holloway* setting and decided not to disqualify counsel, but the defendant following conviction raised a claim of conflict of interest. Very often, that claim will be defeated by the defendant's pretrial waiver of any conflict, obtained in conjunction with the trial court's decision not to disqualify. However, if no waiver was obtained or the waiver is now determined to be faulty, it seems likely that here too the *Sullivan* standard will apply in determining whether the conviction should be reversed.

11. 446 U.S. 335, 100 S.Ct. 1708, 64 L.Ed.2d 333 (1980), discussed at note 6 supra.

12. 535 U.S. 162, 122 S.Ct. 1237, 152 L.Ed.2d 291 (2002), discussed at note 8 supra.

The Court in *Cuyler v. Sullivan* initially rejected the contention that a defense showing of a potential conflict was enough to require a reversal of a conviction. "A reviewing court," it noted, "cannot presume that the possibility of conflict has resulted in ineffective assistance of counsel. Such a presumption would preclude multiple representation even in cases where a common defense * * * gives strength against a common attack." Accordingly, "to establish a violation of the Sixth Amendment, a defendant must demonstrate an actual conflict of interest adversely affected his lawyer's performance."

The *Sullivan* opinion emphasized that its rejection of a potential conflict standard, in favor of requiring a showing of an actual conflict, should not be taken to suggest that the defendant must establish actual outcome prejudice. As the Court has noted first in *Glasser v. United States* and then again in *Holloway*,[13] "unconstitutional multiple representation is never harmless error." Thus, once a defendant "shows that a conflict of interest actually affected the adequacy of his representation," he is automatically entitled to relief; there is no need to also establish that the Sixth Amendment violation might have adversely affected the outcome of the case.

The *Sullivan* standard requires that the defendant presenting a postconviction challenge "demonstrate [that] an actual conflict of interest adversely affected the lawyer's performance." This requires a showing both that (1) counsel was placed in a situation where conflicting loyalties pointed in opposite directions (an "actual conflict"), and (2) counsel proceeded to act against the defendant's interests ("adversely affect[ing] counsel's performance"). Looking to the Court's explanation of *Glasser's* requirement of automatic reversal upon finding a Sixth Amendment violation, Justice Marshall, in dissent, questioned the second prong of this standard. If the impact of an actual conflict upon the outcome of the case requires an unduly speculative judgment, was not, he asked, the same true of its impact upon counsel's performance? The thrust of the Court's opinion, however, clearly was that

these were two separate determinations of a quite different character. It would not be sufficient for reversal to show only that counsel had faced a situation in which action or inaction that might benefit his client would work to the detriment of another interest that divided counsel's loyalty. There would be no harm to the defendant if counsel actually pursued the route favoring his client, disregarding the conflicting interest. Moreover, even where counsel did not pursue that route, counsel's decision may have been influenced solely by a reasonable determination that the route not taken was inferior to an alternative route, which was more beneficial to his client, putting aside any concern for the conflicting interest. Having identified an actual conflict of interest, defendant should be able to establish as well precisely how counsel acted in response to that conflict. However, once it is shown that counsel was actually influenced by the conflict in one aspect of his performance, it would be inappropriate to measure the impact of that conflict solely by reference to that action or inaction. A court could not assume that counsel so motivated had not also been influenced by the conflict in various other aspects of his representation. Hence, any inquiry into outcome prejudice would be too speculative, and automatic reversal therefore would be required.

The *Sullivan* opinion found support for its requirement of adversely affected counsel performance in *Glasser v. United States* itself. While the Supreme Court there had presumed prejudice when the trial court forced counsel into a conflicted multiple representation, it had also noted that counsel had been required to choose between his two clients, and had made a choice adverse to defendant Glasser. The post-*Cuyler* ruling in *Berger v. Kemp*[14] reaffirmed the need for a showing that counsel had chosen a conflicting interest over that of the defendants. The Court there held that even if an actual conflict existed, the Sixth Amendment would not have been violated, as the lower courts had concluded that counsel's

---

13. See the text following note 4 supra.

14. 483 U.S. 776, 107 S.Ct. 3114, 97 L.Ed.2d 638 (1987), also discussed at note 17 infra.

strategy was motivated not by any conflict, but by his evaluation of what would best serve the defendant.

Two lines of lower court rulings have departed from the *Sullivan* standards relating to the impact of a conflict. *Beets v. Scott*,[15] presenting the most dramatic departure, clearly reflects a minority position. A closely divided Fifth Circuit there concluded that *Sullivan–Glasser* outcome-prejudice presumption should apply only to conflicts presented by "multiple representation" situations (i.e., defense counsel represented codefendants or represented the defendant and witnesses or other interested parties), as opposed to conflicts arising from some self-interest of the attorney. In the latter situation, a claim of ineffective assistance based on a conflict should be treated no differently than any other ineffective assistance claim. Thus, the court should apply the standard of *Strickland v. Washington* (discussed in § 11.10), which requires a showing of prejudicial impact upon the outcome. The *Beets* majority reasoned that attorney ethical conflicts that do not result from obligations owed to current or former clients simply reflect another form of incompetent performance. To allow a "recharacterization of ineffectiveness claims to duty of loyalty claims," thereby importing "*Cuyler v. Sullivan's* lesser standard of prejudice" was to "blu[r] the *Strickland* standard" and undercut its role as the "uniform standard of constitutional ineffectiveness." As the *Beets* court acknowledged, prior to that ruling, "the federal circuits had unblinkingly applied *Cuyler v. Sullivan's* 'actual conflict' and 'adverse effects' standards to all kinds of alleged attorney ethical conflicts." The same was true of state courts, including several that had discussed but rejected the possibility of limiting *Sullivan* to multiple representation cases.

In *Micken's v. Taylor*,[16] the Court left open the possibility of adopting the *Beets* position and even extending it. *Mickens* involved a defense counsel who had formerly represented the person his client was charged with killing. The Court applied the *Sullivan* standard on postconviction review, requiring a defense

showing of a "conflict of interest (that) adversely affected * * * counsel's performance." However, the Court majority went on to state that, "lest today's holding be misconstrued," it was important to note that the case "was argued and presented on the assumption" that the *Sullivan* standard governed if *Holloway* did not. "That assumption," it added, "was not unreasonable in light of the holdings of Courts of Appeals which have applied *Sullivan* 'unblinkingly' to all kinds of alleged attorney conflicts, *Beets v. Scott*, * * * [including] not only when (as here) there is a conflict rooted in counsel's obligations to *former* clients, * * * but even where the representation of the defendant somehow implicates counsel's financial or personal interests, including a book deal, * * * a job with the prosecutor's office, * * * the teaching of classes to Internal Revenue agents, * * * a romantic entanglement with the prosecutor, * * * or fear of antagonizing the trial judge." "It must be said," the Court majority continued, "that the language of *Sullivan* itself does not clearly establish, or indeed even support, such expansive application." Both *Sullivan* and *Holloway* "stressed the high probability of prejudice arising from multiple concurrent representation, and the difficulty of proving that prejudice." Thus, Federal Rule 44(c), imposing a duty to inquire, was limited to that situation. Other conflict settings might not present "comparable difficulties" of proof, and therefore might not require "the prophylaxis" of the *Sullivan* standard, which was designed for a situation "where *Strickland* itself is evidently inadequate to assure vindication of the defendant's Sixth Amendment right to counsel." Whether the *Sullivan* prophylaxis should be extended "even to * * * [cases of] successive representation," as involved in *Mickens*, "remains, as far as the jurisprudence of the Court is concerned, an open issue."

Another line of lower court cases have looked in the opposite direction, creating a presumption of prejudicial impact more extensive than *Sullivan*. They reason that certain conflicts should be deemed "per se conflicts,"

15.   65 F.3d 1258 (5th Cir.1995) (en banc).

16.   See note 8 supra.

requiring automatic reversal once the actual conflict is established, with no need to show some point at which the conflict "adversely effected" the counsel's performance. Placed in this category are conflicts viewed as flagrant and likely to have a widespread influence not focused on a particular action or inaction of counsel. This per se approach has been applied in the federal courts where the attorney is alleged to have engaged in the same criminal activity as the defendant or closely related criminal activity, and where a trial judge indicated to appointed counsel that approval of his fee and future appointments would depend upon counsel "pull[ing] his punches." State courts, perhaps relying upon state law, have applied a per se standard to such conflicts as a lawyer first prosecuting the defendant and then representing him as defense counsel in a probation revocation proceeding on the same charge, a lawyer representing the defendant while also employed by the agency involved in investigating or prosecuting, and a lawyer simultaneously representing the defendant and the victim.

Sullivan itself did not decide whether the defendant there had made a sufficient showing of an actual conflict and adversely affected performance, but it offered as illustrations of sufficient and insufficient showings those presented in *Glasser v. United States*[17] and *Dukes v. Warden*.[18] In *Glasser,* the record showed that counsel had failed to cross-examine a key witness and had failed also to object to "arguably inadmissible evidence." Both omissions were held to have resulted from counsel's desire to diminish the jury's perception of the guilt of a codefendant also represented by counsel. Thus, the *Sullivan* Court noted, an "actual conflict of interest [had] impaired Glasser's defense." In contrast to *Glasser, Dukes v. Warden* had rejected an "actual conflict" claim. Defendant there had relied solely on a showing that the lawyer who advised him to plead guilty had later sought leniency for his codefendants by arguing that their cooperation with the police had induced defendant's

plea. Unlike Glasser, Dukes could not "identify an actual lapse in representation" and "nothing in the record * * * indicated that the alleged conflict resulted in ineffective assistance."

In *Burger v. Kemp,*[19] in a twist upon the usual order of analyzing a postconviction challenge under *Cuyler,* the Court turned first to the question of adversely affected performance, and finding none, concluded that there also had not been an actual conflict. Counsel in *Burger* had prepared the appellate brief for both his trial client (the habeas petitioner in *Burger*) and the client's separately tried accomplice (who had been represented by counsel's partner). The petitioner claimed that this dual responsibility presented an actual conflict of interest for counsel, who was forced to choose between using and discarding a "lesser culpability" argument that would help petitioner but hurt the accomplice. Such an argument had been presented at petitioner's separate trial, but counsel had not raised it on appeal, where both parties were before the same court. In holding that there was no conflict, the Court majority stressed the federal habeas court's complete acceptance of counsel's testimony before that court. Counsel had explained his tactics, noting that he had "in no way tailored his strategy toward protecting [the accomplice]," and the habeas court had rejected any "attribution of [counsel's] motivation to the fact that his partner was [the accomplice's] lawyer or to the further fact that he assisted his partner in that representation." Noting that this finding had been twice sustained by the Eleventh Circuit, the Court concluded that both "respect for the bar and deference to the shared conclusion of two reviewing courts" precluded substitution of "speculation" for the lower courts' "heavily fact-based rulings." Thus, the question of whether a conflict in fact existed was controlled by the factual finding that counsel's actions had been influenced only by his client's interest.[20]

---

17.   See note 4 supra.

18.   406 U.S. 250, 92 S.Ct. 1551, 32 L.Ed.2d 45 (1972).

19.   See note 14 supra.

20.   In Mickens v. Taylor, supra note 8, Justice Kennedy's concurring opinion (joined by Justice O'Connor) stressed that the role of the Supreme Court was to "defer

§ 11.10 Ineffective Assistance Claims Based Upon Lawyer Incompetence

(a) **Guiding Considerations.** Prior to the Supreme Court's 1984 ruling in *Strickland v. Washington*,[1] lower courts had been divided on several issues bearing on those ineffective assistance claims that were grounded on the allegedly incompetent performance of counsel. Some courts adopted specific guidelines for judging defense counsel's performance (typically borrowed from the ABA Standards), with a departure from a guideline constituting "per se incompetency"; others eschewed guidelines and stressed a fact-sensitive analysis that looked to all the circumstances of the case. Among courts that focused on the totality of the circumstances, some applied the traditional test of whether counsel's deficiencies were so great as to have rendered the proceedings a "farce" or "mockery of justice," while others looked to whether counsel's performance fell below that of a "reasonably competent attorney." Most courts further required for reversal a defense showing that counsel's incompetence had a prejudicial impact upon the outcome, but some concluded that a showing of incompetency should shift the burden to the state to show a lack of prejudice, and courts applying categorical performance guidelines typically mandated automatic reversal.

In *Strickland v. Washington,* the Court responded to all of these divisions among the lower courts. Building upon the role of the effective assistance guarantee as discussed in *United States v. Cronic*,[2] the *Strickland* Court held that: (1) to establish ineffective assistance requiring reversal of a conviction, a defendant must show both (i) that "counsel made errors so serious that counsel was not functioning as 'counsel' guaranteed * * * by the Sixth Amendment," and (ii) that the "deficient performance prejudiced the defense"; (2) the "proper standard for [measuring] attorney performance is that of reasonably effective assistance," as guided by "prevailing professional norms" and consideration of "all the circumstances" relevant to counsel's performance; (3) more specific guidelines in applying that standard are "not appropriate"; and (4) the proper standard for measuring prejudice is whether there is a "reasonable probability that, but for counsel's unprofessional errors, the result of the proceedings would be different." Of a significance arguably equal to these rulings, Justice O'Connor's opinion for the Court also discussed at length the basic considerations that should guide a court's judgment on an incompetency claim.

Justice O'Connor noted initially that a court's judgment as to the constitutional inadequacy of counsel's performance was not usefully guided by particularized standards:

> When a convicted defendant complains of the ineffectiveness of counsel's assistance, the defendant must show that counsel's representation fell below an objective standard of reasonableness. * * * More specific guidelines are not appropriate. The Sixth Amendment refers simply to "counsel," not specifying particular requirements of effective assistance. It relies instead on the legal profession's maintenance of standards sufficient to justify the law's presumption that counsel will fulfill the role in the adversary process that the Amendment envisions. The proper measure of attorney performance remains simply reasonableness under prevailing professional norms.

Justice O'Connor acknowledged that competent representation "entails certain basic duties." Counsel had an obligation to "avoid

---

to the District Court's factual findings" as to what motivated counsel, unless those findings are clearly erroneous. In that case, the district court had accepted counsel's explanation that he had assumed that he had owed no obligation to a former client, since the client was now deceased, and while that belief "may have been mistaken, it establishes that the prior representation did not influence the choices he made during the court of the trial." Though the issue before the Court majority was the general applicability of the *Sullivan* standard, and not its appli-

cation to the facts of this case, those facts, the concurring opinion noted, provided "a good example of why a case-by-case inquiry is required, rather than simply adopting an automatic rule of reversal."

§ 11.10

1. 466 U.S. 668, 104 S.Ct. 2052, 80 L.Ed.2d 674 (1984), also discussed in § 11.7(c), (d).

2. See 11.7 at note 11.

conflicts of interest," to "advocate the defendant's cause," to "consult with the defendant on important decisions and * * * keep [him] informed of important developments," and to "bring to bear such skill and knowledge as will render the trial a reliable adversarial testing process." However, the use of these duties or others as a simple "checklist" for determining competency was inappropriate for several reasons:

> [T]he performance inquiry must be whether counsel's assistance was reasonable considering all the circumstances. Prevailing norms of practice as reflected in American Bar Association standards and the like * * * are guides to determining what is reasonable, but they are only guides. No particular set of detailed rules for counsel's conduct can satisfactorily take account of the variety of circumstances faced by defense counsel or the range of legitimate decisions regarding how best to represent a criminal defendant. Any such set of rules would interfere with the constitutionally protected independence of counsel and restrict the wide latitude counsel must have in making tactical decisions. * * * Indeed, the existence of detailed guidelines for representation could distract counsel from the overriding mission of vigorous advocacy of the defendant's cause. Moreover, the purpose of the effective assistance guarantee of the Sixth Amendment is not to improve the quality of legal representation, although that is a goal of considerable importance to the legal system. The purpose is simply to ensure that criminal defendants receive a fair trial. * * *

The availability of intrusive post-trial inquiry into attorney performance or of detailed guidelines for its evaluation would encourage the proliferation of ineffectiveness challenges. Criminal trials resolved unfavorably to the defendant would increasingly come to be followed by a second trial, this one of counsel's unsuccessful defense. Counsel's performance and even willingness to serve could be adversely affected. Intensive scrutiny of counsel and rigid requirements for acceptable assistance could dampen the ardor and impair the independence of defense counsel, discourage the acceptance of assigned cases, and undermine the trust between attorney and client.

In evaluating an attorney's performance, Justice O'Connor concluded, the best approach was to keep in mind the basic Sixth Amendment standard: "Whether, in light of all the circumstances, the identified acts or omissions [of counsel] were outside the range of professionally competent assistance." The lower court had set forth a series of general guidelines for judging the particular deficiency here alleged by defendant—counsel's failure to conduct a full factual investigation. However, the basic standard of professional competency required "no special amplification in order to define counsel's duty to investigate." It was sufficient to say that "counsel has a duty to make reasonable investigations or to make a reasonable decision that makes particular investigation unnecessary." What decisions were reasonable would depend on the total setting, including, in particular, the information the attorney received from his client.

Having established the need for a fact-sensitized judgment. Justice O'Connor looked to much the same concerns in describing the principles that should guide the making of that judgment. Justice O'Connor noted:

> Judicial scrutiny of counsel's performance must be highly deferential. It is all too tempting for a defendant to second-guess counsel's assistance after conviction or adverse sentence, and it is all too easy for a court, examining counsel's defense after it has proved unsuccessful, to conclude that a particular act or omission of counsel was unreasonable. A fair assessment of attorney performance requires that every effort be made to eliminate the distorting effects of hindsight, to reconstruct the circumstances of counsel's challenged conduct, and to evaluate the conduct from counsel's perspective at the time. Because of the difficulties inherent in making the evaluation, a court must indulge a strong presumption that counsel's conduct falls within the wide range of reasonable professional assistance: that is, the defendant must overcome the presumption that under the circumstances, the chal-

lenged action "might be considered sound trial strategy." There are countless ways to provide effective assistance in any given case. Even the best criminal defense attorneys would not defend a particular client in the same way.

Although stressing the need for deference, Justice O'Connor warned that, here too, general principles could not be converted into "mechanical rules." The "ultimate focus must be the fundamental fairness of the proceeding." In every case, the court must retain its concern as to "whether, despite the strong presumption of reliability, the result of the particular proceeding is unreliable because of a breakdown in the adversarial process."

The focus on fundamental fairness, Justice O'Connor noted, logically also required that defendant make a showing of prejudice to gain relief. Since the purpose of the Sixth Amendment guarantee is "to ensure that a defendant has the assistance necessary to justify reliance on the outcome of the proceeding," any deficiency in counsel's performance "must be prejudicial to the defense in order to constitute ineffective assistance under the Constitution." Here, unlike other Sixth Amendment contexts, prejudice could not be presumed: "Attorney errors come in an infinite variety and are as likely to be utterly harmless in a particular case as they are to be prejudicial. They cannot be classified according to a likelihood of causing prejudice."

The defendant's challenge in *Strickland* was to the performance of counsel in a capital sentencing proceeding. After discussing the role of counsel in the adversary adjudication of guilt, the Court noted that the same principles applied to a capital sentencing proceeding as it was "sufficiently like a trial in its adversarial format and in the existence of standards for decisions." In *Smith v. Murray,*[3] the Court later applied the "test of *Strickland v. Washington*" to the alleged incompetency of appellate counsel. *Hill v. Lockhart*[4] similarly held that *Strickland's* two-part test applies to challenges to guilty pleas based on the alleged

ineffectiveness of counsel. Thus, the *Strickland* standard would appear to govern the determination of actual incompetence in all settings where the Constitution requires the effective assistance of counsel. Of course, *Strickland* must be read in conjunction with *Cronic,* which recognized a small window for finding *per se* ineffectiveness as illustrated by the *Powell* ruling. But as discussed in subsection (d), in the absence of counsel's refusal to participate in the proceedings, a claim of incompetency based on performance (as opposed to state interference, a conflict situation, or inherently prejudicial conditions of representation) will be judged by the *Strickland* standards.

(b) The Competency Standard. The *Strickland* opinion, in its initial discussion of the deficient performance component of an incompetency claim, characterized that component as requiring "counsel * * * errors so serious that counsel was not functioning as the 'counsel' guaranteed the defendant by the Sixth Amendment." Since prejudicial impact was a separate component of the claim, the "seriousness" of counsel error apparently was to be measured by reference to the role of counsel in providing what *Cronic* had described as "the kind of [adversarial] testing envisioned by the Sixth Amendment." As *Cronic* had also noted, the level of performance required to fulfill that role does not preclude the presence of "demonstrable errors" by counsel. The critical question is whether, in the context of the particular case, counsel's failing (whether in a single error or a series of errors) kept counsel from meeting the necessary responsibilities of an advocate.

To assist lower courts in making this adversarial performance determination, the Court in *Strickland* set forth a general "standard" for assessing attorney performance. It adopted for this purpose the "reasonably effective assistance" standard that had been advanced by the federal Courts of Appeals. This same standard, it noted, had been "indirectly recognized" as the relevant measure of attorney

---

3. 477 U.S. 527, 106 S.Ct. 2661, 91 L.Ed.2d 434 (1986).

4. 474 U.S. 52, 106 S.Ct. 366, 88 L.Ed.2d 203 (1985). See also § 21.3(b).

competency in the Court's opinion in *McMann v. Richardson.*[5] The Court had there stated that a guilty plea could not be challenged "as based on inadequate legal advice unless counsel was not a 'reasonably competent attorney' and the advice was not 'within the range of competence demanded of attorneys in criminal cases.'" This approach, the Court noted, utilized an "objective standard of reasonableness" for determining whether counsel's representation was "outside the range of professionally competent assistance."

Prior to *Strickland,* several commentators had suggested that the standard used to describe the expected level of counsel performance was far less significant than the attitude and concerns that a court brought to its assessment of counsel's failures. Indeed, the variations among the state and federal courts in formulating that standard, including both the older "farce and mockery" standard and several versions of the newer "reasonably competent" attorney standard, had been characterized as presenting a "semantic merry-go-round." No such standard, it was noted, can be "self-answering"; all must rely, as *McMann* had noted, on the "good sense and discretion of the trial courts." The Court's opinion in *Strickland* lent support to this view. Far more discussion was devoted to the concerns that should guide a court in applying the standard (e.g., the variation in circumstances that render inappropriate a guidelines approach, the need for "deferential" scrutiny that avoids second-guessing, and the importance of considering the totality of the circumstances) than to explaining the standard itself. The Court also refused to attach to the standard such significance as to render suspect lower court rulings that had relied on somewhat differently worded standards. Even cases that had rejected incompetency claims under the farce and mockery standard did not necessarily require reconsideration. If the "guiding inquiry" in the lower court correctly had been whether counsel's failures produced in fact a "breakdown in the adversary process," the difference in the articulation of the standard applied was unimportant.

Justice Marshall, dissenting in *Strickland,* argued that the majority's reasonableness test was subject to "debilitating ambiguity." The Court had failed to address such important issues as whether reasonableness was to be judged by reference to "the adequately paid retained attorney" or to the appointed attorney who had less time and resources to devote to the case. Nor had the Court indicated whether the reference was to the standard of competence of the local bar or of defense lawyers nationally. These concerns, however, appear to be irrelevant under the approach that majority took to its "reasonably effective assistance" standard. There was no suggestion that reasonableness was to be judged by reference to any empirical survey of attorney practices. The majority did characterize the applicable standard as one of "reasonableness under prevailing professional norms," but it also made clear that "prevailing norms of practice" are no more than "guides" to determining what is reasonable. The ultimate point of reference is that performance by counsel needed, under the circumstances of the case, to ensure "the proper functioning of the adversarial process." It is this function of counsel that provides the "objective standard of reasonableness" and determines what is "within the range of competence demanded of attorneys in criminal cases."

In *Nix v. Whiteside,*[6] the Court reaffirmed that what constitutes reasonably effective assistance is not necessarily controlled by standard patterns of practice. The Court there acknowledged that an attorney's performance could conceivably meet the reasonably competent attorney standard even where the attorney breached an "ethical standard of professional responsibility." The critical factor here would be whether the violation was in the interest of the defendant. Of course, ethical standards remain significant guidelines. Indeed, in *Whiteside,* the majority suggested that, where an attorney took a particular action to avoid a breach of professional responsi-

---

5. 397 U.S. 759, 90 S.Ct. 1441, 25 L.Ed.2d 763 (1970). See also § 21.6(a).

6. 475 U.S. 157, 106 S.Ct. 988, 89 L.Ed.2d 123 (1986).

bility, that action would thereby be immune from challenge under *Strickland's* performance standard, but four justices were not willing to accept such a sweeping conclusion. They stressed that it could lead to "blanket rules" of performance, rather than the careful examination of particular circumstances prescribed by *Strickland*.

Strickland and *Nix* make clear that one searching for the content of the reasonably effective assistance standard must look primarily to judicial decisions applying that standard. Generalizations drawn from other sources, whether attorney practice patterns, guidelines proposed by professional organizations, or even standards of professional responsibility, may influence, but will not necessarily control those decisions. The subsection that follows seeks to draw some general lessons from the judicial decisions applying *Strickland's* competency standard.

(c) Applying the Reasonableness Standard. The range of potential claims of allegedly incompetent representation extends throughout the criminal justice process. Defense counsel have been attacked for their failure to investigate, their failure to consult sufficiently with the defendant, their failure to challenge the prosecution on a variety of grounds, their representation in plea bargaining, their failure to challenge the makeup of the jury, their failure to move to suppress illegally obtained evidence, their failure to either raise or properly present various defenses, their failure to object to improper argument by the prosecution, their waiver of opening or closing arguments, their failure to present various postconviction motions, and their representation on sentencing. Space limitations preclude a thorough review of the hundreds of rulings dealing with these and other alleged inadequacies. As might be expected, the rulings are hardly consistent in their treatment of even roughly similar fact situations. Nevertheless, they do suggest some general patterns, at least as to those claims most likely and least likely to be successful.

In general, the defendant is most likely to establish incompetency where counsel's alleged errors of omission or commission are attributable to a lack of diligence rather than an exercise of judgment. Courts will far more readily find incompetency where there has been "an abdication—not an exercise—of professional judgment." The crucial question therefore often becomes, how far will this particular reviewing court go in assuming, in accordance with the general presumption of attorney competence, that counsel's actions were strategic? Since *Strickland* starts with an assumption of competency, it places upon the defendant the burden of showing that counsel's action or inaction was not based on a valid strategic choice.[7]

Whether a counsel's action or inaction was based on a strategic choice is a factual question, on which the defendant should be able to offer evidence when the incompetency challenge is presented in a postconviction proceeding (as often must be the case). However, at least where the setting suggests a possible strategic rationale, some courts are hesitant to call for an evidentiary hearing at which defense counsel will be required to explain his actions. These courts warn that automatically turning to such a hearing to determine why counsel failed to raise a particular objection will place counsel in "the unenviable position where, if he can recall his reasons, and they are good, he is hurting his former client, and if he can't recall his reasons or they are bad, or not very good, he is impugning his professional competence." Still, evidentiary hearings at which counsel explain their actions are common. Where counsel testifies that the decision was tactical, or the decision appears by its nature to be tactical, the defendant must look to surrounding circumstances to establish that the decision in this case actually was the product of inattention rather than strategy. For example, one glaring, obviously non-tactical error may cast doubt on whether counsel's decisions in other matters truly reflected a

---

7. Of course, where the final decision lies in the domain of the defendant, action by defense counsel which takes that decision away from the defendant cannot be justified on the ground that counsel's choice was strategically sound. See § 11.6(c).

tactical choice. Similarly, though counsel's failure to exercise any one of several defense rights might be viewed as tactical, taken together his several omissions may clearly indicate that counsel simply had abdicated his responsibility. That is especially likely where the rights related to different aspects of the prosecution, making it improbable that they are bound by a single strategic goal. Counsel's inconsistency in approach at different points is still another factor that might suggest that there was no overriding strategy guiding counsel's actions, as is also the case where there was "role confusion" among multiple counsel. Where counsel testifies that he or she had no strategy, but simply failed to appreciate the issue, the same factors may be needed to bolster that testimony. An ineffectiveness claim raised on appeal is limited to what the trial record reveals as to the grounding for counsel's actions, and here the court commonly will assume a strategic motivation if any can possibly be imagined.

Of course, a decision apparently based on a tactical judgment is not therefore rendered immune from an incompetency challenge. Courts sometimes speak broadly of matters of "trial strategy and tactics" simply not constituting "grounds for a finding of ineffective assistance of counsel." However, neither *Strickland* nor the lower court rulings go so far. Speaking to the interplay between an attorney's duty to investigate and the making of strategic decisions, the *Strickland* Court did note that "strategic choices made after thorough investigation of law and facts relevant to plausible options are virtually unchallengeable." This "virtually unchallengeable" status obviously requires great deference for strategic choices, but it comes with the important prerequisite of a "complete investigation." That investigation relates to "the law," as well as the facts, and includes a reasonable understanding of the cases and statutes the investigation produced. Thus, lower courts have noted that a strategic decision falls below the *Strickland* performance standard not only where based on a factual assumption not adequately investigated, but also where based on a negligent misunderstanding of the law.

Even where the tactical decision was based on a thorough investigation, the *Strickland* statement did not go so far as to state that such a decision is absolutely unchallengeable. Lower courts have noted that in exceptional situations, strategic judgments may also constitute deficient performance. They stress that such a ruling may not be based "merely [on the fact that] * * * the chosen tactic proves to be ill-advised or turns out to be the wrong decision." The strategy must be so outlandish, some courts have noted, that "no competent attorney would have made such a choice." On choosing among competing strategies, there comes a point "where alternatives not chosen offered a potential for success [so] substantially greater than the tactics actually utilized" as to lack any grounding in "common sense." Courts have found such tactical misuses where counsel took a risk that actually bolstered the prosecution's case or ignored potentially strong positions in favor of a barely plausible position. However, where the defendant's case would well have been viewed as hopeless, deference to strategy has upheld approaches that in other circumstances would most likely have been deemed beyond the pale.

Courts reviewing competency claims frequently stress that, even apart from tactical judgments, they do not demand that counsel's performance be flawless. It must be anticipated that the lawyer will occasionally fail to recognize that a certain course of action may be available to his client. Accordingly, an incompetency claim is most likely to be successful when the defendant can point to a long series of questionable omissions by counsel; this suggests that the lawyer's errors were not simply the product of human fallibility, but the result of a lack of conscientious effort. Very often, however, a single error which was both glaring and related to a matter of obvious significance has been held sufficient to establish incompetency. Although the court must look to the level of counsel's overall performance, clearly negligent treatment of a crucial deficiency in the prosecution's case or an obvious strength of the defense will outweigh the adequate handling of a series of minor matters. Thus, while the issues of prejudicial impact and incompetency are separate prongs of the *Strickland* test, the potential prejudicial impact of the subject dealt with by counsel reaches over into the competency determination, as that potential obviously relates to the care and effort expected from a competent adversary.

Kimmelman v. Morrison,[8] illustrates how the two prongs may overlap in evaluating a single error, so that potential impact leads to a finding of incompetency, but does not necessarily establish prejudice—which rests on actual (not potential) impact. Habeas petitioner Morrison's claim of ineffective assistance rested solely on his counsel's failure to make a timely suppression objection based on an allegedly unconstitutional search and seizure. During Morrison's trial for rape, the state had introduced a sheet seized from his bed and expert testimony concerning stains and hair found on the sheet. Defense counsel had objected on Fourth Amendment grounds, but the trial court refused to consider that objection because there had been no pretrial motion to suppress. Counsel explained that he had not previously been aware of the seizure of the sheet, but the trial judge found that to be no excuse since counsel had not asked for pretrial discovery. Counsel then sought to justify that omission by asserting that it was the state's obligation to inform him of its case against his client and that he had not expected to go to trial since he had been told that the complainant was reluctant to testify. Both justifications were rejected by the trial judge. The first represented a clear misunderstanding of the law and the second ignored the fact that it would have required a court order, not simply the victim's preference, to dismiss the rape indictment.

Rejecting the state's contention that counsel's overall trial performance reflected professionally reasonable representation, notwithstanding his mishandling of the Fourth Amendment objection, the Supreme Court concluded that counsel's failure to request pretrial discovery clearly fell below "prevailing professional norms." The state's attempt to "mini-

mize the seriousness of counsel's errors by asserting that [its] case turned far more on the credibility of witnesses than on the bedsheet and related testimony" was not persuasive. Here, there had been a "total failure to conduct pre-trial discovery," for which counsel offered only "implausible explanations" that reflected a "startling ignorance of the law." Counsel's performance would not be measured by a "hindsight" evaluation of the "relative importance of various components of the State's case"; at the time he failed to seek discovery, counsel "did not * * * know what the State's case would be." While "the relative importance of witness credibility vis-à-vis the bedsheet and related expert testimony [would be] pertinent to the determination of prejudice" (a determination left for lower court consideration on remand), it "shed no light on the reasonableness of counsel's decision not to request discovery."

Lower court rulings suggest several fact patterns that are most likely to result in a finding of incompetency. Perhaps the easiest is that in which the record reveals that counsel failed to make a crucial objection or to present a strong defense solely because counsel was unfamiliar with clearly settled legal principles. *Kimmelman v. Morrison*, described above, is the classic example of such a case. Counsel's misunderstanding of the law also creates ineffective assistance when it leads to reliance on a "defense" that legally doesn't operate as such, or advice on a plea bargain that incorrectly assesses the law governing the available charges or possible sentences. The cases have insisted, however, that counsel's error constitute a misreading of well established, clear legal standards. The *Strickland* standard of reasonableness does not demand that counsel correctly read uncertainties in the law or anticipate likely changes, even when the grant of a writ of certiorari suggests that the change may be right around the corner.

Courts also readily find ineffective assistance when counsel's testimony at a postconviction evidentiary hearing establishes that a failure to act on an important matter was a

---

8. 477 U.S. 365, 106 S.Ct. 2574, 91 L.Ed.2d 305 (1986).

product of inattention. If plausible, the attorney's explanation tends to be treated as the best evidence of why the attorney acted as he did (both where the attorney points to strategy and where the attorney admits to negligence). In one situation, courts are especially likely to find, even without evidentiary hearing testimony, that the attorney acted either out of inattentiveness or a misunderstanding of the law. That is where counsel failed to raise an obviously meritorious objection that would have produced a complete victory for the defense. Strategy may explain why counsel would not raise an objection that would only result in a new indictment (particularly where the alternative is a plea bargain[9]). It may also explain why counsel might not seek to exclude inadmissible evidence when such evidence is not critical to the prosecution's case nor necessarily inconsistent with his client's defense. A possible strategic justification is more difficult to hypothesize, however, where counsel failed to raise a claim of apparent merit which would have resulted in dismissal of the charges with prejudice—such as double jeopardy, the denial of a speedy trial, or the statute of limitations.

Illustrative of incompetency claims that courts often find more difficult to evaluate are those based on counsel's failure to interview possible defense witnesses or otherwise pursue possible sources of helpful information. On the one hand, the lack of pretrial preparation is widely noted to be "the preeminent cause of poor legal performance." On the other, courts also recognize that "the amount of pretrial investigation that is reasonable defies precise measurement." What is satisfactory to meet minimum standards of competency "will necessarily depend on a variety of factors, including the number of issues in the case, the relative complexity of those issues, the strength of the government's case, and the overall strategy of counsel." The Supreme Court in *Strickland* advised that special attention be given in this regard to the "information supplied [to counsel] by the defendant." Counsel has no need to pursue a particular line of investigation, the Court noted, when

"defendant has given counsel reason to believe that pursuing * * * [that line] would be fruitless or even harmful." So, too, "when the facts that support a certain potential line of defense are generally known to counsel because of what the defendant has said, the need for further investigation may be considerably diminished or eliminated altogether." A court is most likely to find counsel's investigation unreasonable when the information available suggested a single line of defense and counsel either failed to make any investigation or conducted only a minimal investigation. Cases finding incompetency on this ground have tended to involve defenses such as alibi and insanity. So too, a deficiency is often found where the defendant offers an explanation of what he did that contradicted the prosecution's theory and the defense counsel failed to investigate known key evidence that could support defendant's explanation.

The measurement of competency becomes more complex where counsel did conduct a substantial investigation into one line of defense, but failed to inquire into others also suggested by information received from his client or other sources. Here, the primary concern is that counsel have had some reasonable basis for focusing on only one avenue of investigation in light of the information and resources available to him, and that his decision not have been based on a desire to prepare for trial with as little effort as possible. Perhaps the failure-to-investigate claims most difficult to establish are those in which counsel did devote substantial effort to the investigation of a particular defense, but the defendant claims that more should have been done. A counsel's decision that further investigation would only produce more of the same is treated very much like a strategic decision.

The difficulties presented in judging the adequacy of counsel's factual investigation are reflected in the quite different perspectives of the majority and dissenting justices in *Burger v. Kemp*.[10] In that case, petitioner's habeas counsel established that there was considera-

---

9. As to ineffective assistance with respect to plea bargains, see § 21.3(b).

10. 483 U.S. 776, 107 S.Ct. 3114, 97 L.Ed.2d 638 (1987).

ble mitigating evidence, relating to petitioner's background, that could have been presented at the capital sentencing hearing. Petitioner's trial counsel had obtained some of that evidence in the course of interviewing petitioner, his mother, and a family friend. Counsel had concluded, however, based on what he had learned from them and from a psychologist's testimony at a suppression hearing, that presenting such evidence would open the door to cross-examination that would reveal petitioner's juvenile record and certain damaging aspects of his personality. Accordingly, trial counsel did not pursue a further investigation that would have produced the other mitigating evidence developed by habeas counsel.

The Court majority in *Burger* noted that petitioner's trial counsel "could well have made a more thorough investigation." Nonetheless, having made "a reasonable professional judgment" in light of information obtained from "all potential witnesses who had been called to his attention," counsel's failure to mount "an all-out investigation into petitioner's background" did not constitute incompetency. As *Strickland* itself had noted, "strategic choices made after less than complete investigation are reasonable precisely to the extent that reasonable professional judgments support the limitations on investigation," and in determining the reasonableness of counsel's decision not to further investigate, a reviewing court should provide "a

heavy measure of deference to counsel's judgments."

The four dissenters in *Burger* saw counsel's performance quite differently. In a capital sentencing proceeding, where petitioner's psychological problems and troubled background were obviously of such great significance, counsel's failure to obtain a complete psychological examination of petitioner could not be excused by his lack of confidence in the local mental hospital, nor could counsel's failure to more fully explore petitioner's background be justified by the petitioner's failure to suggest additional witnesses when asked "whether he could produce evidence of 'anything good about him.'" The dissent saw *Burger* as a case where "further investigation was compelled" under the *Strickland* standard "because there was inadequate information on which the reasonable professional judgment to limit the investigation could have been made."[11]

(d) The Prejudice Element. Prior to the ruling in *Strickland,* lower courts had adopted a confusing array of standards governing the prejudice component of an incompetency claim. *Strickland* replaced those standards with a single test—whether "there is a reasonable probability that, but for counsel's unprofessional errors, the result of the proceeding would have been different." In the course of adopting this test, the Court discussed and rejected various other possibilities. It noted initially that the burden rested with the defen-

---

11. In the later case of Wiggins v. Smith, 539 U.S. 510, 123 S.Ct. 2527, 156 L.Ed.2d 471 (2003), the majority opinion appeared to reflect a perspective very much like that expressed by the *Burger* dissenters. In *Wiggins,* the Court majority (7–2) concluded that the Maryland Court of Appeals had applied the *Strickland* standards in an "objectively unreasonable manner" when it rejected defendant's claim of ineffective assistance at his capital sentencing hearing. The Maryland Court had deferred to counsel's arguably strategic decision not to present evidence of defendant's personal history, but the Court majority held that the investigation leading to that decision had been so inadequate as to violate *Strickland's* "reasonable professional judgment" standard. As the majority read the state court's decision, it had concluded that defense counsel satisfied the *Strickland* standard when they first examined two sources (a presentence investigation report [PSI] and Department of Social Service [DSS] records) that provided "rudimentary knowledge" of the harsh circumstances of the defendant's youth, and then decided (as they later testified) to focus their presentation entirely on disputing

the defendant's direct responsibility for the killing. The Court majority, in finding that conclusion to be unreasonable, noted both that the trial court record strongly suggested that counsel's "failure to investigate thoroughly [defendant's personal history] resulted from inattention, not reasoned strategic judgment," and that "counsel's decision not to expand their investigation beyond the PSI and the DSS records fell short of the professional standards that prevailed in Maryland [at the time of the trial]." In support of the latter conclusion, the majority noted that: (1) the two sources examined suggested a significant potential for mitigation in defendant's personal history; (2) those sources did not suggest offsetting aggravating factors, and thus did not present "the double edge we found to justify limited investigations in other cases, cf. *Burger v. Kemp*"; (3) "standard practice in Maryland in capital cases at the time * * * included the preparation of a social history report" (also the standard under the ABA Guidelines for death penalty representation); and (4) Public Defender funding had been available to obtain such a report.

THE RIGHT TO COUNSEL

dant to establish the prejudice element. Thus, contrary to the suggestion of certain lower courts, it was inappropriate to presume prejudice and shift the burden to the government to establish that counsel's incompetency was harmless error. It was equally inappropriate to adopt a prejudice standard so lenient as to have a similar effect. Thus, to require that defendant show only that counsel's errors "had some conceivable effect on the outcome" was meaningless; "virtually every act or omission of counsel would meet that test."

On the other side, it would require too much to insist that defendant show that counsel's conduct "more likely than not" altered the outcome in the particular case. While such an outcome-determinative test was traditionally applied to motions for new trial based on newly discovered evidence, the situation here was distinguishable. The high standard for newly discovered evidence presupposed an "accurate and fair proceeding," but an "ineffective assistance claim asserts the absence of one of the crucial assurances that the result of the proceeding is reliable." The Supreme Court had also rejected a new-trial standard in its due process analysis assessing the "materiality" of exculpatory evidence that a prosecutor had knowing failed to disclose at trial. It had adopted instead a standard of a "reasonable probability" that the non-disclosure altered the outcome of the trial.[12] A "reasonable probability" standard, *Strickland* noted, was equally suited to showing prejudice due to counsel's incompetent performance. A "reasonable probability" was defined as a "probability sufficient to undermine confidence in the outcome."

The *Strickland* Court also noted that the question of the adequacy of counsel's performance need not be considered before examining the issue of prejudice, and lower courts clearly have been influenced by that suggestion. Indeed, in case after case alleging that counsel's factual investigation was inadequate, the standard response is that there has been no showing of prejudice because defendant has failed

to establish exactly what further evidence existed for counsel to discover if he had investigated more thoroughly. On the other side, very often the showing made in first considering incompetency (including the likely success of an alternative not pursued) will have already established the case as to prejudice.

Application of the *Strickland* prejudice standard can call for quite difficult and subjective judgments, depending upon the character of counsel's alleged incompetency. Where counsel's performance relates to the introduction of evidence, the court can ask what bearing that evidence might have had on the jury's verdict, a question very much like that traditionally applied in harmless error analysis (although the standard is different). Where the allege incompetency relates to some legal claim that would have produced a dismissal or new trial, the court can readily determine whether that objection would have been successful. However, where the alleged incompetency relates to a claim that would have changed the structure of the trial, as opposed to producing a dismissal or altering the evidence before the jury, the task of determining its impact (assuming the claim had merit) is quite different from traditional harmless error analysis. Where a court erred in denying a change of venue, or rejecting a challenge to jury composition, that error results in automatic reversal.[13] If those claims were not presented due to counsel's incompetency, should the court then ask whether there is a reasonable probability that the outcome of the trial would have differed if the trial had been in a different district or before a different jury? Courts have divided in their approach to this issue, with some suggesting that here also prejudice should be automatic.

Broad language in *Strickland* concerning the scope and purpose of the "reasonable probability" standard—such as the references to "confidence in the outcome" and the avoidance of "unjust convictions"—led Justice Powell, concurring in *Kimmelman v. Morrison*,[14] to offer a rather startling interpretation of that standard. It should not be too readily assumed, he

12. See § 24.3(b).

13. See § 27.6(b), (d).

14. See note 8 supra.

argued, that *Strickland's* prejudice prong would be satisfied simply because, but for counsel's incompetence, the outcome might have been different. That might not be the case where counsel's incompetence led to the admission of constitutionally excludable evidence, there was a reasonable probability that the state's use of that evidence affected the jury's verdict, but that evidence was entirely reliable. The improper admission of evidence that harmed the defendant only in allowing the factfinder to render a more well-informed determination of guilt might not be the type of injury that establishes prejudice under *Strickland*.

Notwithstanding the language cited by Justice Powell, his interpretation of *Strickland's* prejudice component would appear to be inconsistent with much of the discussion of that component in *Strickland*. Moreover, it would be difficult to square with Justice Brennan's opinion for the Court in *Kimmelman v. Morrison*, which carefully distinguished between the habeas petitioner's Sixth Amendment rights and his Fourth Amendment claim in dealing with another issue posed in that case.[15] Not surprisingly, with the exception of one Seventh Circuit panel, the federal appellate courts have been unwilling to adopt Justice Powell's analysis. As for the Supreme Court, as Justice Powell noted, the Court did not rule on the prejudice issue in *Kimmelman v. Morrison*, and its other ineffective assistance cases have involved actions of counsel that could not be narrowed in impact to the admission of specific items of excludable evidence. The Court has not had occasion to face the issue in subsequent cases.

In its leading post-*Kimmelman* discussion of *Strickland's* prejudice prong, *Lockhart v. Fretwell*,[16] the Court did note that the "prejudice"

component of the *Strickland* test * * * focuses on * * * whether counsel's deficient performance renders the trial unreliable or the proceeding fundamentally unfair," and that is not necessarily present simply because the reasonable probability standard is met as to the result of the trial. However, the *Lockhart* ruling did not carry this statement beyond the principle that "unreliability or unfairness does not result if ineffectiveness of counsel does not deprive the defendant of any substantive or procedural right to which the law does not entitle him." Thus, in *Nix v. Whiteside*,[17] prejudice could not be established by showing that the outcome would have been different if defendant had been able to present false testimony to the jury. So too, in *Lockhart*, counsel's incompetence did not result in prejudice when it consisted of failing to raise a claim recognized in the precedent prevailing at the time of trial but subsequently rejected as erroneous in a decision that overruled that precedent.[18]

Finally, it should be noted that the *Strickland* discussion of prejudice must be read in light of *Cronic's* recognition of extreme situations in which prejudice will be presumed.[19] One of these situations, as illustrated by *Powell*, requires circumstances of appointment so restrictive that counsel cannot possibly provide effective representation. As discussed in § 11.7(d) and § 11.8(c), this exception is narrowly confined. A second exception—where counsel "entirely fails to subject the prosecutor's case to meaningful adversarial testing"— has been applied by lower courts to a variety of situations in which counsel either was not present during a critical stage in the proceeding or was present but failed to do anything. However, in *Bell v. Cone*,[20] the Supreme Court

---

15. See § 28.3(d).

16. 506 U.S. 364, 113 S.Ct. 838, 122 L.Ed.2d 180 (1993).

17. See note 6 supra.

18. In *Williams v. Taylor*, 529 U.S. 362, 120 S.Ct. 1495, 146 L.Ed.2d 389 (2000), the Court rejected a lower court suggestion that *Lockhart* had "modified or in some way supplemented the rule set down in *Strickland*," and thereby limited reversals to cases of fundamental unfairness. It noted that "[c]ases such as Nix and Lockhart do not justify a departure from a straightforward application of *Strickland* when the ineffectiveness of counsel does

deprive the defendant of a substantive or procedural right to which the law entitles him." See also Glover v. United States, 531 U.S. 198, 121 S.Ct. 696, 148 L.Ed.2d 604 (2001) (rejecting a lower court ruling that had relied in *Lockhart's* reference to fundamental unfairness to hold that counsel's deficient performance did not violate the Sixth Amendment when the only consequence was to increase a sentence of incarceration from 6 to 21 months).

19. See § 11.7 at notes 15 and 16.

20. 535 U.S. 685, 122 S.Ct. 1843, 152 L.Ed.2d 914 (2002).

warned against expansion of this *Cronic* exception. A presumption of prejudice is permissible, the Court noted, only where the "failure is complete," and not where counsel simply failed to take particular steps (important though they might well be) in challenging the prosecution's case. Thus, the federal habeas court there erred in applying that exception to a capital sentencing proceeding because counsel failed to introduce mitigating evidence and waived closing argument. Counsel had challenged the state's case in other respects (including bringing out favorable evidence on cross-examination of the state's witness and calling the jury's attention in an opening statement to mitigating evidence that had been introduced as part of an insanity defense), and the allegations as to mitigating evidence and the closing argument constituted no more than claims of "specific attorney error," which were "subject to *Strickland's* performance and prejudice components."

Chapter 12

PRETRIAL RELEASE

Table of Sections

---

§ 12.1   Pretrial Release Procedures

(a) The Federal Bail Reform Act. The federal Bail Reform Act of 1966, which governed bail and release practices in the federal courts for several years, also served as an important model for reform legislation in the states. Its central theme was that personal recognizance is the preferred method of pretrial release in lieu of the traditional reliance upon money bail as a prerequisite to release. The Act had an immediate impact in terms of the pretrial release rate of federal defendants and the extent of reliance upon personal recognizance as the mode of release. But that Act has now been repealed and replaced by the Bail Reform Act of 1984. The 1984 legislation is in several respects similar to the earlier Act, but it also has many new features. The most

647

significant of them, provisions authorizing preventive detention, are discussed later[1] rather than at this point.

The 1984 Bail Reform Act provides that when a person charged with a crime appears before a judicial officer, the judicial officer "shall order the pretrial release of the person on personal recognizance, or upon execution of an unsecured appearance bond in an amount specified by the court * * * unless the judicial officer determines that such release will not reasonably assure the appearance of the person as required or will endanger the safety of any other person or the community."[2] In the event of such a determination, the judicial officer is then to "order the pretrial release of the person * * * subject to the least restrictive further condition, or combination of conditions, that such judicial officer determines will reasonably assure the appearance of the person as required and the safety of any other person and the community," which may include the condition that the person

(i) remain in the custody of a designated person, who agrees to assume supervision and to report any violation of a release condition to the court, if the designated person is able reasonably to assure the judicial officer that the person will appear as required and will not pose a danger to the safety of any other person or the community;

(ii) maintain employment, or, if unemployed, actively seek employment;

(iii) maintain or commence an educational program;

(iv) abide by specified restrictions on personal associations, place of abode, or travel;

(v) avoid all contact with an alleged victim of the crime and with a potential witness who may testify concerning the offense;

(vi) report on a regular basis to a designated law enforcement agency, pretrial services agency or other agency;

(vii) comply with a specified curfew;

(viii) refrain from possessing a firearm, destructive device, or other dangerous weapon;

(ix) refrain from excessive use of alcohol, or any use of a narcotic drug or other controlled substance * * * without a prescription by a licensed medical practitioner;

(x) undergo available medical or psychiatric treatment, including treatment for drug or alcohol dependency, and remain in a specified institution if required for that purpose;

(xi) execute an agreement to forfeit upon failing to appear as required, such designated property, including money, as is reasonably necessary to assure the appearance of the person as required, and post with the court such indicia of ownership of the property or such percentage of the money as the judicial officer may specify;

(xii) execute a bail bond with solvent sureties in such amount as is reasonably necessary to assure the appearance of the person as required;

(xiii) return to custody for specified hours following release for employment schooling, or other limited purposes; and

(xiv) satisfy any other condition that is reasonably necessary to assure the appearance of the person as required and to assure the safety of any other person and the community.[3]

But it is expressly stated that the "judicial officer may not impose a financial condition that results in the pretrial detention of the person."[4]

The 1984 Act also specifies the factors that, on the basis of "the available information," are to be taken into account in determining which conditions will suffice, namely:

(1) the nature and circumstances of the offense charged, including whether the offense is a crime of violence or involves a narcotic drug;

1. See § 12.3(a).
2. 18 U.S.C.A. § 3142(b).
3. 18 U.S.C.A. § 3142(c).
4. 18 U.S.C.A. § 3142(c).

(2) the weight of the evidence against the person;

(3) the history and characteristics of the person, including—

(A) the person's character, physical and mental condition, family ties, employment, financial resources, length of residence in the community, community ties, past conduct, history relating to drug or alcohol abuse, criminal history, and record concerning appearance at court proceedings; and

(B) whether, at the time of the current offense or arrest, the person was on probation, on parole, or on other release pending trial, sentencing, appeal or completion of sentence for an offense under Federal, State, or local law; and

(4) the nature and seriousness of the danger to any person or the community that would be posed by the person's release.[5]

A release order must include a written "clear and specific" statement of all conditions imposed and advise the person released of the penalties for and other consequences of violating those conditions.[6] The judicial officer may at any time amend the order to impose additional or different conditions.[7] On motion of either the defendant or the government, the release conditions may be reviewed by the court with jurisdiction over the offense charged, and a release order may be appealed to the court of appeals.[8] Violation of a condition of release is punishable by contempt[9] and, in addition, can result in revocation of the release upon a judicial finding that the person is unlikely to abide by any condition of release or that there is no combination of conditions which will assure his appearance or nondanger.[10]

The 1984 Act also provides penalties for failure to appear. A person who "knowingly fails to appear[11] before a court as required by the conditions of release"[12] is to incur a forfeiture of "any property" designated in his bond or forfeiture agreement[13] and, in addition, may be subjected to fine and imprisonment.[14]

(b) State Practice Generally. It is not possible to describe state procedure with the same particularity, for there are obviously significant variations in law and practice among the fifty jurisdictions. The typical state statute declares that the objective of bail is to secure the defendant's attendance at the proceedings against him and to prevent his punishment before conviction. Some of these statutes provide no guidance on what factors may be taken into account, while others provide a detailed list of factors in the manner of the federal Act.

Typically, an arrested defendant is taken to the nearest stationhouse and then transported to the city jail within 24 hours. For defendants charged with a minor offense listed in a fixed bail schedule, the first opportunity for release comes at that time. Those defendants unable to obtain their release at the station must await their appearance before a judicial officer, often the following morning, at which time the judge will set the terms of release. Defendants who obtained their release earlier, if their cases are not immediately disposed of at their subsequent court appearance, may have the amount of their bail revised upward or downward.

Judges are inclined to give primary consideration to the seriousness of the offense charged, most likely because it is a factor that is clear-

5. 18 U.S.C.A. § 3142(g).
6. 18 U.S.C.A. § 3142(h).
7. 18 U.S.C.A. § 3142(c).
8. 18 U.S.C.A. § 3145(a), (c).
9. 18 U.S.C.A. § 3148(c).
10. 18 U.S.C.A. § 3148(b).
11. Under 18 U.S.C.A. § 3146(c) it is an affirmative defense "that uncontrollable circumstances prevented the person from appearing or surrendering, and that the person did not contribute to the creation of such circum-

stances in reckless disregard of the requirement that he appear or surrender, and that he appeared or surrendered as soon as such circumstances ceased to exist."
12. 18 U.S.C.A. § 3146(a).
13. 18 U.S.C.A. § 3146(d).
14. The maximum penalties depend upon the crime charged: 10 years and/or a fine for an offense punishable by death, life imprisonment or a term of 15 years or more; 5 years and/or a fine for an offense punishable by 5 or more but less than 15 years; 2 years and/or a fine for any other felony; 1 year and/or a fine for a misdemeanor. 18 U.S.C.A. § 3146(b).

cut and easy to apply. The strength of the case against the defendant, as communicated by the prosecutor or police, is also an important yardstick in practice. A third factor considered very relevant is the defendant's prior criminal record. In many localities it is unusual for the judge to determine or consider other facts about the defendant's background and character, such as whether he is employed and how long he has resided in the community. The common explanations for this are that the judges believe they are overworked and do not have time to inquire into such matters and that they doubt defendants can be trusted to supply truthful answers to such inquiries. Bail projects, now in operation in many major cities, obtain this information and supply it to the court.

As for the methods by which a defendant may obtain pretrial release in the state courts, one frequently used procedure is cash bail. The defendant may raise the full amount of the bond through personal savings or money supplied by friends and family, in which case the entire amount is usually returned to him if he appears as required. But if, as is often the case, the defendant must rely upon the services of a bail bondsman, then he will have to pay a fee usually not less than 10 per cent of the bond amount, a payment that is not recoverable by the defendant. Another method by which pretrial release may be obtained in many locales is via the 10 per cent plan. The defendant pays 10 per cent of the bond directly to the court and then recovers most or all of that amount if he appears in court as scheduled. Yet another possibility is that a defendant may obtain his release on a property bond, which means he offers property as bail in lieu of cash. Still another possibility is personal bond, sometimes referred to as personal surety or release on recognizance (r.o.r.), which is used when the judge concludes the defendant is sufficiently motivated to show up that he can be released on his own signature without bail. In addition to or in lieu of these methods, some localities utilize daytime release, release to the custody of an approved

individual or organization, or release on conditions.

(c) Counsel at Bail Hearing. If the defendant is represented by counsel at his bail hearing, this greatly improves his chances for either bail set in a modest amount or release on his own recognizance. One reason that the participation of a defense attorney makes such a difference is that he can bring relevant facts about his client's background to the judge's attention. Bail reform in the fashion of the federal Act has, if anything, made participation by defense counsel more significant than ever before. Because modern bail laws permit a variety of alternatives to money bail, defense counsel are rightly expected to present reasonable alternative plans for release and invoke available community resources for this purpose.

Because counsel for the defendant can make such an impact at the bail hearing, there is much to be said for the contention that the Sixth Amendment right to counsel applies at that time. Such a conclusion is certainly consistent with the general notion, as the Supreme Court has put it, that this right comes into play upon "the initiation of adversary judicial criminal proceedings," at which time the "defendant finds himself faced with the prosecutorial forces of organized society, and immersed in the intricacies of substantive and procedural criminal law."[15] Moreover, it finds strong support in *Coleman v. Alabama*,[16] where the holding that a preliminary hearing is a "critical stage" for right to counsel purposes was based in part on the fact that "counsel can also be influential * * * in making effective arguments for the accused on such matters as * * * bail." But even after *Coleman* some courts have held that there is no constitutional right to counsel at a bail hearing.

(d) Proof at Bail Hearing. Information received at a bail hearing need not conform to the rules pertaining to the admissibility of evidence at trial. However, this should not be

---

15. Kirby v. Illinois, 406 U.S. 682, 92 S.Ct. 1877, 32 L.Ed.2d 411 (1972).

16. 399 U.S. 1, 90 S.Ct. 1999, 26 L.Ed.2d 387 (1970).

taken to mean that information must be accepted by the court without regard to its reliability. Thus, whether hearsay is admissible in a bail hearing must ultimately be determined on a case by case basis by asking whether in the particular circumstances it is the kind of evidence on which responsible persons are accustomed to rely in serious affairs.

Questions concerning the burdens of production and persuasion in a bail hearing seldom reach the appellate courts. As a matter of general practice, it is customary for the prosecution to supply such facts as defendant's prior bad record in order to show that this defendant's bail should be higher or the conditions of his release more strict than would typically be true for a person so charged, and for the defense to supply favorable facts about defendant's ties to the community to show the contrary. Thus, each side supplies that information to which it has both ready access and an interest in producing. To some extent at least, the approach of the applicable bail statute may have some influence on who feels compelled to show what; a scheme based on a presumption that personal recognizance is appropriate until the contrary is shown would seem to put the prosecution in a more difficult position.

(e) Defendant's Statements. Sometimes the question has arisen whether defendant's incriminating statements made at the bail hearing are admissible against him at trial. One view of this matter is that because the law favors the release of defendants pending determination of guilt or innocence, a defendant should be encouraged to testify at a hearing on a motion to set bail without the fear that what he says may later be used to incriminate him, which is accomplished by requiring that the defendant's testimony at the bail hearing be excluded from evidence at his later trial. (That reasoning also supports the conclusion that if the defendant makes incriminating statements to a bail agency interviewer charged with the responsibility of gathering facts from the defendant and other sources

relevant to the bail decision, they should likewise be inadmissible.)

Whether that result is mandated by the Constitution is a more difficult matter. A negative answer was given in one case, though the court held on the circumstances there presented that defendant's statements at his bail hearing were inadmissible at trial because the magistrate failed to accurately advise defendant of his *Miranda* rights. The defendant's broader claim, that in any event he was compelled to forfeit his Fifth Amendment right to remain silent, in order to safeguard his Eighth Amendment right to reasonable bail, was based largely upon the Supreme Court's decision in *Simmons v. United States*.[17] The *Simmons* analogy was rejected because in that case the Court emphasized that a defendant who wished to assert a Fourth Amendment objection has been required to show that he was the owner or possessor of the seized property or that he had a possessory interest in the searched premises, while by contrast a defendant at a bail bond hearing need not divulge the facts in his case in order to receive the benefits of the Eighth Amendment right to bail. But there is much to be said for the conclusion that *a* defendant at a bail hearing is confronted with a clearly impermissible compelled election, for the applicable constitutional guarantee is not just the right to bail, but the right to non-excessive bail, and in the case just discussed the defendant not unreasonably concluded that the recommended amount of bail would be determined to be appropriate for him unless he rebutted the government testimony portraying him as a big-time drug dealer.

§ 12.2   Constitutionality of Limits on Pretrial Freedom

(a) Amount of Money Bail. The Eighth Amendment to the United States Constitution, which is also applicable to the states through the Fourteenth Amendment due process clause,[1] provides in part: "Excessive bail shall

---

17. 390 U.S. 377, 88 S.Ct. 967, 19 L.Ed.2d 1247 (1968), discussed in § 10.5(c).

1. In Schilb v. Kuebel, 404 U.S. 357, 92 S.Ct. 479, 30 L.Ed.2d 502 (1971), the Court observed in passing that

not be required." The traditional question raised under this provision is that of what amount of money bail may constitutionally be required of a defendant. The leading case on this point is *Stack v. Boyle*,[2] involving twelve petitioners who had been charged with conspiring to violate the Smith Act, which made it a crime to advocate the overthrow of the government by force or violence. Bail was fixed in the district court in the uniform amount of $50,000 for each petitioner. The petitioners then moved to reduce bail on the ground it was excessive under the Eighth Amendment, and in support submitted statements as to their financial resources, family relationships, health, prior criminal records, and other information. Though the only response of the government was a certified record showing that four other persons previously convicted under the Smith Act had forfeited bail, the district court denied the motion and thereafter denied writs of habeas corpus for the petitioners. The court of appeals affirmed, but the Supreme Court ruled that bail had "not been fixed by proper methods," and then concluded that "petitioners' remedy is by [a renewed] motion to reduce bail" in the district court.

One respect in which the *Stack* decision is important is in its specification of the purpose underlying bail legitimately taken into account in setting the amount. The Court declared:

> The right to release before trial is conditioned upon the accused's giving adequate assurance that he will stand trial and submit to sentence if found guilty. * * * Like the ancient practice of securing the oaths of responsible persons to stand as sureties for the accused, the modern practice of requiring a bail bond or the deposit of a sum of money subject to forfeiture serves as additional assurance of the presence of an accused. Bail set at a figure higher than an amount reasonably calculated to fulfill this purpose is "excessive" under the Eighth Amendment.[3]

In addition, *Stack* stresses that setting an amount of bail that properly serves this single purpose requires an assessment of the facts of the particular case. The Court declared that "standards relevant to the purpose of assuring the presence of that defendant" must "be applied in each case to each defendant." The "traditional standards" recognized by the Court in *Stack* were "the nature and circumstances of the offense charged, the weight of the evidence against him, the financial ability of the defendant to give bail and the character of the defendant." It was relatively easy to find noncompliance with the Eighth Amendment in *Stack*, for (as the Court noted) "bail for each petitioner has been fixed in a sum much higher than that usually imposed for offenses with like penalties and yet there has been no factual showing to justify such action in this case."

As this last comment reflects, the nature of the offense and in particular the "risk" the defendant is running in terms of the potential punishment is an important factor in the Eighth Amendment equation. But *Stack* teaches that it is by no means the only factor. This would indicate that use of a bail schedule, wherein amounts are set solely on the basis of the offense charged, violates the Eighth Amendment except when resorted to as a temporary measure pending prompt judicial appearance for a particularized bail setting. Indeed, such use of a master bond schedule may be constitutionally objectionable on other grounds as well, including that procedural due process requires a hearing in various administrative proceedings,[4] a fortiori, it requires a hearing before depriving a person of his liberty, and that the procedure violates the equal protection clause because it is based upon an erroneous view that a poor person should post precisely the same amount of bail as a rich person.

One question that might be raised under the *Stack* formulation is whether it is possible for

---

"the Eighth Amendment's proscription of excessive bail has been assumed to have application to the States through the Fourteenth Amendment."

2. 342 U.S. 1, 72 S.Ct. 1, 96 L.Ed. 3 (1951).

3. This language was later narrowly construed as not barring preventive detention. See § 12.3(c).

4. Goldberg v. Kelly, 397 U.S. 254, 90 S.Ct. 1011, 25 L.Ed.2d 287 (1970).

there to be circumstances where no amount of bail will suffice to ensure the defendant's appearance at the proceedings against him. This issue has not often been litigated, most likely because a court confronted with a high risk defendant will in all probability proceed to set the bail in an unreachable amount rather than deny bail altogether. But with some defendants, especially those alleged to be major drug dealers, in a position to post bail in amounts up to a million dollars, the question is taking on increasing importance. In *United States v. Abrahams*,[5] the court characterized this issue as "one of first impression" because it had not found a case "that holds directly that a defendant has an absolute right to bail pending trial regardless of the circumstances," and then concluded the instant case was "the rare case of extreme and unusual circumstances that justifies pretrial detention without bail." The defendant in *Abrahams*, charged with fraud (punishable by up to five years imprisonment and a $10,000 fine), had three previous convictions, was an escaped prisoner from New Jersey, had given false information at the previous bail hearing, had failed to appear on the previous bail of $100,000, had failed to appear in a California case and was a fugitive from that state, had used several aliases in the past, and in the last two years had transferred one and a half million dollars to Bermuda. These facts, the court concluded, supported the district court's findings that "none of the five conditions spelled out in" the federal Act, "or any combination thereof, will reasonably assure the appearance of defendant for trial if admitted to bail."

An issue that has been debated more frequently is whether the amount of bail that would suffice to ensure the defendant's appearance in a particular case is constitutionally objectionable because the defendant is indi-

gent and thus cannot come up with bail even in a modest amount. It has been argued that an indigent defendant suffers several constitutional violations under our bail system:

1. He is being denied the fundamental fairness guaranteed by the due process of law because, although he alleges he is innocent, he is being punished by imprisonment before he has been tried.

2. He is being denied procedural due process because detention adversely affects the disposition of his case and thereby deprives him of a fair trial.

3. He is denied equal protection of the law because, solely on account of his poverty, he is being denied pretrial liberty.

4. His right to bail under the eighth and fourteenth amendments is being violated because the proscription against "excessive" bail must be construed in such a way as not automatically to foreclose for indigents the fundamental right to freedom pending trial.[6]

As for the first of these, it cannot be said that there is a constitutional "presumption of innocence" entitling all defendants to pretrial release.[7] The other contentions, however, are worthy of closer attention.

(b) Poverty and Pretrial Release. As for the relevance of the defendant's indigency upon the Eighth Amendment bail question, *Stack v. Boyle*[8] is itself instructive, for it expressly states that "the financial ability of the defendant to give bail" is one of the factors that must be taken into consideration. This is certainly sensible, for an impecunious person who pledges a small amount of collateral constituting all or almost all of his property is likely to have a stake at least as great as that of a wealthy person who pledges a large amount constituting a modest part of his property. But it is a substantial jump from that

---

5. 575 F.2d 3 (1st Cir.1978).

6. Foote, The Coming Constitutional Crisis in Bail, 113 U.Pa.L.Rev. 959, 1125, 1135 (1965).

7. In Bell v. Wolfish, 441 U.S. 520, 99 S.Ct. 1861, 60 L.Ed.2d 447 (1979), the Court concluded as to a related point:

"The presumption of innocence is a doctrine that allocates the burden of proof in criminal trials; it also may serve as an admonishment to the jury to judge an ac-

cused's guilt or innocence solely on the evidence adduced at trial and not on the basis of suspicions that may arise from the fact of his arrest, indictment or custody or from other matters not introduced as proof at trial. * * * But it has no application to a determination of the rights of a pretrial detainee during confinement before his trial has even begun."

8. 342 U.S. 1, 72 S.Ct. 1, 96 L.Ed. 3 (1951).

truism to the proposition that an amount of bail a defendant cannot meet because of his poverty is thereby "excessive" under the Eighth Amendment. Courts have refused to take that leap; they instead continue to adhere to the proposition that bail is not excessive merely because the defendant is unable to pay it.

As for an equal protection claim, note must be taken of the oft-quoted comments of Justice Douglas in *Bandy v. United States.*[9] Observing that the Court had held in *Griffin v. Illinois*[10] "that an indigent defendant is denied equal protection of the law if he is denied an appeal on equal terms with other defendants, solely because of his indigence," Justice Douglas opined that it must be similarly unconstitutional for "an indigent [to] be denied freedom, where a wealthy man would not, because he does not happen to have enough property to pledge for his freedom." Some have argued that this position has been bolstered by such cases as *Williams v. Illinois*[11] and *Tate v. Short,*[12] deemed to provide a close analogy because they held that equal protection bars subjecting indigent defendants to sentences of imprisonment beyond that which other defendants could receive. However, *Williams* and *Tate* did not bar imprisonment for indigents merely because a wealthier defendant would likely escape such a consequence by being fined instead, and *Griffin* has since been given a rather narrow interpretation by the Supreme Court.[13] Thus, notwithstanding the forceful argument by some commentators in support of the equal protection argument, the courts have not been inclined to accept the equal protection argument that bail is unconstitutional when set in an amount a particular indigent defendant cannot meet. But several courts, relying upon *Williams* and *Tate,* have held that failure to grant credit against a

maximum sentence for presentence incarceration imposed because of a defendant's inability to post bail violates the equal protection clause.

Because of bail reform efforts in recent years, the dimensions of the debate concerning the indigent defendant have changed somewhat. Under laws based upon the federal Bail Reform Act of 1966,[14] money bail is but one of several alternative forms of release, and thus the issue is now often cast in terms of the purported "right" of indigent defendants to one of the nonfinancial forms of pretrial release. Where, as was true under the 1966 Act, those nonfinancial alternatives must be considered by the judge, the argument has been made that in the case of an indigent defendant the judge is obligated to select one of those alternatives. But that argument has not prevailed in the courts as a constitutional imperative. It is noteworthy, however, that the successor federal Bail Reform Act of 1984 expressly provides: "The judicial officer may not impose a financial condition that results in the pretrial detention of the person."[15]

A more compelling argument, and one of particular importance in those jurisdictions which have not adopted bail reforms in the manner of the federal Act, is that money bail may no longer be constitutionally viewed as the sole means of pretrial release or even as the preferred means of gaining pretrial freedom. Important here is *Pugh v. Rainwater,*[16] involving a challenge to the Florida bail system, which was construed as making available the same alternatives as the 1966 federal statute but as being different from the federal system in two important respects: (1) there was no presumption in favor of release on recognizance; and (2) the nonfinancial alternatives were not given priority. The court concluded:

---

9. 81 S.Ct. 197, 5 L.Ed.2d 218 (1960).

10. 351 U.S. 12, 76 S.Ct. 585, 100 L.Ed. 891 (1956).

11. 399 U.S. 235, 90 S.Ct. 2018, 26 L.Ed.2d 586 (1970) (defendant unable to pay fine could not be incarcerated beyond maximum term of imprisonment fixed by statute; equal protection requires that "statutory ceiling placed on imprisonment * * * be same for all defendants irrespective of their economic status").

12. 401 U.S. 395, 91 S.Ct. 668, 28 L.Ed.2d 130 (1971) (indigent convicted of offenses punishable by fine only cannot be incarcerated a sufficient time to satisfy fines).

13. See Ross v. Moffitt, 417 U.S. 600, 94 S.Ct. 2437, 41 L.Ed.2d 341 (1974).

14. See § 12.1(a).

15. 18 U.S.C.A. § 3142(c).

16. 557 F.2d 1189 (5th Cir.1977).

Because it gives the judge essentially unreviewable discretion to impose money bail, the rule retains the discriminatory vice of the former system: When a judge decides to set money bail, the indigent will be forced to remain in jail. We hold that equal protection standards are not satisfied unless the judge is required to consider less financially onerous forms of release before he imposes money bail. Requiring a presumption in favor of non-money bail accommodates the State's interest in assuring the defendant's appearance at trial as well as the defendant's right to be free pending trial, regardless of his financial status.

This would mean, as the court later put it,[17] "that in the case of an indigent, whose appearance at trial could reasonably be assured by one of the alternative forms of release, pretrial confinement for inability to post money bail would constitute imposition of an excessive restraint."

As bail reform efforts result in alternative methods of release being provided, other equal protection issues can arise, as is illustrated by *Schilb v. Kuebel*.[18] At issue there was a state statute which provided, as to a defendant not released on his own recognizance, that he could either deposit cash equal to 10% of the bond, in which case 10% of the amount deposited (i.e., 1% of the amount of the bond) would be retained by the state as "bail bond costs" even if defendant appeared as required, or else he could deposit the full amount of the bail, in which event there would be no charge or retention if the defendant appeared as required. Though the defendant claimed this meant a charge was imposed only on the nonaffluent and thus constituted a denial of equal protection, the Court concluded otherwise, finding the distinction drawn by the statute was not "invidious and without rational basis." The defendant's assumption that the affluent would always opt for the full deposit alternative and thus escape the charge was itself doubted by the Court, which noted that "in these days of high interest rates" it would make more sense for an affluent person to post only 10% and earn interest on the balance.

(c) Opportunity to Prepare a Defense. There is little reason to doubt the proposition that pretrial detention has a significant adverse impact upon the ability of a defendant to vindicate himself at trial or secure leniency in sentencing. He cannot contribute either money or labor to pretrial investigation. In particular, he is unable to help locate witnesses or evidence that might be more accessible to him than to any outsider. His contacts with counsel may be impeded, so that he must plan a defense in cramped jail facilities within the limited hours set aside for visitors. The pretrial prison experience may adversely affect his demeanor in court and on the witness stand. Finally, a convicted defendant who has lost his job and been removed from his family will stand a far poorer chance for probation than one who has been employed and maintained strong family ties. Nonetheless, courts have not been particularly receptive to post-conviction claims by defendants that they were entitled to relief because their pretrial incarceration in some way interfered with preparation of their defense.

However, a particularized claim made during the time of pretrial detention will sometimes produce limited relief, as is illustrated by *Kinney v. Lenon*.[19] There the juvenile defendant, in custody awaiting trial on charges arising out of a schoolyard fight, alleged in support of his claim for pretrial release "that there were many potential witnesses to the fight, that he cannot identify them by name but would recognize them by sight, that appellant's attorneys are white though he and the potential witnesses are black, that his attorneys would consequently have great practical difficulty in interviewing and lining up the witnesses, and that appellant is the sole person who can do so." Convinced that there had been "a strong showing that the appellant is the only person who can effectively prepare his own defense," the court concluded that defendant's detention was infringing upon his

---

17. Upon rehearing en banc, 572 F.2d 1053 (5th Cir. 1978).

18. 404 U.S. 357, 92 S.Ct. 479, 30 L.Ed.2d 502 (1971).

19. 425 F.2d 209 (9th Cir.1970).

constitutional right to compulsory process to obtain witnesses in his behalf, which "as a practical matter would be of little value without an opportunity to contact and screen potential witnesses before trial." The court thus held that release of the defendant into the custody of his parents was necessary to protect "his due-process right to a fair trial." In cases of this general type, it would be most appropriate for the court to consider release for limited periods of time and in the custody of some person, such as defendant's lawyer or a law enforcement officer.[20]

(d) Nature of Pretrial Custody. There is yet another sense in which it may be said that constitutional objections may be raised regarding limits on pretrial freedom, and that is when persons unable to obtain their release challenge the circumstances of their pretrial custody. There has been considerable litigation challenging various facets of pretrial detention, which is none too surprising in light of the fact that unconvicted defendants typically receive worse treatment prior to trial than convicted defendants receive after trial. A brief look at this question is nonetheless appropriate, for it adds a perspective to the custody vs. no custody issues addressed in this Chapter.

The Supreme Court first had an opportunity to assess conditions of pretrial incarceration in *Bell v. Wolfish*,[21] a class action brought by detainees in a federally operated short-term custodial facility in New York City. The Court of Appeals, reasoning from the "premise that an individual is to be treated as innocent until proven guilty," concluded that pretrial detainees retain the "rights afforded unincarcerated individuals" and that consequently they could be "subjected to only those 'restrictions and privations' which 'inhere in their confinement itself or which are justified by compelling necessities of jail administration.'" The *Bell* majority disagreed. As for the presumption of innocence, it is "a doctrine that allocates the burden of proof in criminal trials" and thus

"has no application to a determination of the rights of a pretrial detainee during confinement before his trial has even begun." And while clearly "the Due Process Clause protects a detainee from certain conditions and restrictions of pretrial detainment," the question under that provision (that is, where an aspect of the detention "is not alleged to violate any express guarantee of the Constitution") is "whether those conditions amount to punishment of the detainee." The mere fact "that such detention interferes with the detainee's understandable desire to live as comfortably as possible and with as little restraint as possible during confinement" does not itself make the conditions of that confinement "punishment" for due process purposes. Rather, the question is "whether the disability is imposed for the purpose of punishment or whether it is but an incident of some other legitimate governmental purpose." The *Bell* majority also emphasized that while ensuring the detainees' appearance at trial might be the only legitimate purpose of keeping them in custody, it did not follow that this "is the *only* objective that may justify restraints and conditions once the decision is lawfully made to confine a person." Once an individual is lawfully confined, "the effective management of the detention facility" (i.e., maintaining security and order and ensuring that no weapons or illicit drugs reach detainees) is also a permissible objective.

As for the specific complaints, the Court in *Bell* first held that double-bunking did not violate due process where detainees were free to move to a common area, and that the prohibition on receipt of packages of food or personal property did not violate due process even though there might be lesser restrictions which would be "a reasonable way of coping with the problems of security, order, and sanitation." The Court then acknowledged that the First and Fourth Amendment rights of the detainees were not lost by virtue of their pretrial detentions but concluded that "maintain-

---

20. The federal Bail Reform Act of 1984 provides, as to a person ordered detained, that the "judicial officer may, by subsequent order, permit the temporary release of the person, in the custody of a United States marshal or another appropriate person, to the extent that the judicial

officer determines such release to be necessary for preparation of the person's defense or for another compelling reason." 18 U.S.C.A. § 3142(i).

21. 441 U.S. 520, 99 S.Ct. 1861, 60 L.Ed.2d 447 (1979).

ing institutional security and preserving internal order and discipline are essential goals that may require limitation or retraction of the retained constitutional rights." The prohibition against receipt of hardback books unless mailed directly from publishers, book clubs or bookstores was upheld against First Amendment objections because it is "a rational response by prison officials to an obvious security problem," namely, "that hardback books are especially serviceable for smuggling contraband into an institution." Because a detainee's "reasonable expectation of privacy" in his living area under the Fourth Amendment is, at best, "of a diminished scope" in light of "the realities of institutional confinement," the Court held that Amendment was not violated by a practice of irregular "shakedowns" of cells in the inmates' absence. As for the practice of conducting visual body cavity searches as part of strip searches conducted after contact visits with any person from outside the institution, the Court balanced "the significant and legitimate security interests of the institution against the privacy interests of the inmates" and concluded such searches were reasonable.

§ 12.3 Constitutionality of Mandating Pretrial Detention

(a) Preventive Detention in the Federal System. As noted earlier, the *Stack v. Boyle*[1] interpretation of the Eighth Amendment prohibition on "excessive" bail was that in setting pretrial release conditions there is but one legitimate consideration: what is necessary to provide a reasonable assurance that the particular defendant will subsequently appear at the proceedings against him? There is no question, however, but that this legal theory is not always respected in practice and that bail determinations are sometimes influenced by such considerations as the accused's assumed danger to the community. Especially in

earlier days, when there was almost exclusive reliance upon money bail and little opportunity for a defendant to obtain review of his bail setting, this could quite easily occur. Because of the sub rosa character of such action, the concept of "preventive detention" (pretrial custody of a defendant for the purpose of protecting some other person or the community at large) did not receive close scrutiny.

In recent years, by comparison, the subject of preventive detention has been much debated. This is largely attributable to bail reform activities, for from the very beginning of those efforts one of the most serious impediments to bail reform has been the fear that a greater number of pretrial releases would mean a greater amount of serious crime. As alternatives to money bail were implemented and as judicial review of the conditions set for defendants as yet unable to obtain their relief was mandated, it became increasingly likely that those defendants perceived by some as "dangerous" would obtain their freedom pending trial. This concern produced some legislative activity, starting with the District of Columbia preventive detention law, which took effect in 1971.

A preventive detention scheme is also an important part of the federal Bail Reform Act of 1984. A detention hearing is to be held, upon motion of the attorney for the government, where the case involves a crime of violence, an offense for which the maximum penalty is death or life imprisonment, certain serious drug offenses, or any felony by one with two or more convictions of the aforementioned type offenses. Also, such a hearing is to be held on motion of either the attorney for the government or the judicial officer that the case involves a serious risk that the person will flee or will obstruct or attempt to obstruct justice or interfere with a prospective witness or juror.[2] If at the hearing the judi-

§ 12.3

1. 342 U.S. 1, 72 S.Ct. 1, 96 L.Ed. 3 (1951).

2. 18 U.S.C.A. § 3142(f). The Act states that this detention hearing, except upon a grant of a continuance, "shall be held immediately upon the person's first appearance before the judicial officer." "Nothing in § 3142(f) indicates that compliance with the first appearance re-

quirement is a precondition to holding the hearing or that failure to comply with the requirement renders such a hearing a nullity," and thus "a failure to comply with the first appearance requirement does not defeat the Government's authority to seek detention of the person charged." United States v. Montalvo–Murillo, 495 U.S. 711, 110 S.Ct. 2072, 109 L.Ed.2d 720 (1990).

cial officer "finds that no condition or combination of conditions will reasonably assure the appearance of the person as required and the safety of any other person and the community," then detention is to be ordered.[3] A rebuttable presumption in support of such a finding exists in certain circumstances.[4] The Act also makes nonviolation of any federal, state or local crime a condition of any release under the Act,[5] and upon violation of that condition revocation of the release is required upon a finding of probable cause that such a crime was committed while on release, and also a finding that the person is unlikely to abide by any conditions of release or that there is no combination of release conditions that will assure the person will not flee or pose a danger.[6] A person ordered detained may obtain review of the order from the court with original jurisdiction over the offense charged,[7] and may appeal from the detention order.[8]

(b) Preventive Detention and the State Constitutions. The practice in the fifty states regarding preventive detention is quite diverse, largely because of the remarkably different state constitutional provisions to be found on the subject of bail. Generally speaking, it may be said that approximately half of the state constitutions either do not grant a right to bail (which might well present a bar to preventive detention procedures) or else expressly permit some variety of preventive detention, while the right to bail articulated in the constitutions of the remaining states ordinarily permits, at best, only very limits types of preventive detention.

The bail provisions in the state constitutions are conveniently grouped as follows: (1) In nine states, the provision on bail is essentially the same as the Eighth Amendment in the federal constitution; that is, there is an express prohibition upon excessive bail, but not a specific declaration that defendants generally have a right to have bail set in their cases. (2) In 24 states, what might be called the tradi-

tional state constitutional approach is taken, which in its purest form is a provision declaring "All prisoners shall, before conviction, be bailable by sufficient sureties, except for capital offenses, where the proof is evident, or the presumption great." Eighteen states follow this language almost verbatim, while in six others the only difference is that instead of or in addition to the exception for capital cases is an exception for cases where the punishment was once capital, where the punishment is life imprisonment, or where specified serious offenses are charged. (3) In the remaining 17 states there is once again a constitutional declaration of a right to bail as above, typically with an exception for capital cases or some other exception as listed above, but significantly the constitutional provision then, by virtue of an amendment added thereto in relatively recent years, goes on to describe other situations in which a form of preventive detention may be utilized.

The third group may be further subdivided by the kind of preventive detention provision included therein. One type authorizes preventive detention whenever the charge is of a certain type and in addition there is a finding that the defendant, if released, would present a danger to another person or the community. A second grouping requires a certain type of charge plus only some condition precedent, either that the defendant at the time of the alleged crime was already on bail for another offense of a certain type, that he was then on probation or parole, or that at the time of the alleged crime the defendant had previously been convicted of one or (usually) more offenses of a certain type. A third variety of preventive detention constitutional provision combines the features of the other two; that is, the defendant may be detained pending trial only if there was a specified condition precedent and in addition a finding of dangerousness. In these 17 states, then, it may be concluded that preventive detention of the type specifically exempted in their respective consti-

---

3. 18 U.S.C.A. § 3142(e).

4. 18 U.S.C.A. § 3142(e).

5. 18 U.S.C.A. § 3142(b), (c).

6. 18 U.S.C.A. § 3148(b).

7. 18 U.S.C.A. § 3145(b).

8. 18 U.S.C.A. § 3145(c).

tutions from the right-to-bail provisions contained therein are *not* objectionable on the ground that it intrudes upon that right. As with the federal provisions discussed earlier, of course, these state constitutional provisions might well be questioned on federal constitutional grounds, a matter considered later.[9]

Considering now the states in the first of the three groups first mentioned, that is, those in which the constitutional bail provision is like the Eighth Amendment in not expressly declaring a right to bail, these provisions would appear to present no greater bar to preventive detention schemes than does the Eighth Amendment itself. Indeed, most of the states with this variety of constitutional provision have already adopted preventive detention schemes of one kind or another. Some of the statutory provisions in these jurisdictions are of the more limited type, as where a detention-justifying danger to persons or the community may be found or is presumed when the defendant has been charged with a certain crime after conviction for an earlier crime of that type, while on bail or while on probation or parole, or when the defendant has violated some condition of pretrial release. But others are among the most expansive preventive detention provisions to be found, declaring as to a rather broad range of offenses that denial of bail is permissible upon a finding of such danger or upon the defendant's failure to rebut a declared presumption of danger.

Thus, as for those states with either constitutional authorizations for preventive detention or no constitutional declaration of a right to bail, virtually all of them permit such detention in one or more of the forms previously described. There are other variations among the states as well, primarily related to: (1) the crimes subject to preventive detention; (2) the granting of a pretrial detention hearing and other procedural safeguards, such as the right to be represented by counsel at the hearing, the right to call witnesses, and the right to cross-examine adverse witnesses; (3) whether the state must prove probable cause; (4) whether the arrestee or the prosecutor has the burden of proving dangerousness or lack thereof; (5) the standard of proof that is required for the showing of probable cause and dangerousness; (6) whether the judge's specific findings regarding probable cause and danger must be recorded in order to facilitate appellate review; and (7) the length of time the accused may be detained. Most of these state provisions are not as elaborate as the federal provisions discussed earlier, and because of their more abbreviated nature the matter of procedural safeguards is not always developed to the same degree. Because shortcomings in this regard can lead to the invalidation of preventive detention schemes on federal due process grounds, state courts are likely to judicially engraft such protections onto the applicable provisions in the state constitutions, statutes and court rules to forestall such an event.

What remains to be considered here are those 24 states with the "traditional" kind of constitutional bail provision: one expressly granting a right to bail with only a very narrow exception (usually that of a capital charge) and without any additional claim of authority to engage in preventive detention. The question here, as to cases not falling within the specified exception, is whether the state constitutional declaration of a right to bail leaves any room at all for pretrial detention of criminal defendants in the interest of protecting another or the community. Without foreclosing the possibility that some particular state *might* construe its own right-to-bail provision somewhat more narrowly, it is fair to say that the preventive detention possibilities in these jurisdictions are quite limited yet not nonexistent.

Just as it is generally conceded that these right-to-bail provisions foreclose denial of release to a defendant on the ground that no release conditions would suffice to ensure his appearance, it is likewise clear that they do not permit that broader variety of preventive detention authorized in the federal system—that is, detention based upon nothing more than a finding that a certain defendant

---

9. See § 12.3(c)–(g).

charged with a serious offense would be dangerous to some other person or the community if released. As for those preventive detention schemes requiring some sort of a condition precedent, the easiest to deal with here is the case in which the justification is a certain charge accompanied with a record by the defendant of one or more prior convictions of a certain type. There appears to be no basis for concluding that such an approach can be undertaken in one of the right-to-bail jurisdictions. If at the time of the charge the defendant was on probation or parole regarding the prior conviction, the situation is not as certain, although even here it would seem that if the only official response is that of prosecuting the defendant for the new offense, a refusal to set bail on that charge would constitute an impermissible intrusion upon the state's right-to-bail provision. It is common practice, in addition to or in lieu of such new charge, to undertake proceedings to revoke the probation or parole, which would take care of the bail question, as the state-conferred constitutional right-to-bail does not extend to those individuals being held pending a hearing to determine whether probation or parole should be revoked.

What is left for consideration against these state right-to-bail provisions are those preventive detention schemes that rest, in essence, upon the fact that the individual, while on pretrial release, apparently engaged in some form of misconduct, typically criminal conduct but sometimes noncriminal conduct deemed to violate an express or implied condition of the previous release from custody. It is sometimes said that such conduct by the defendant constitutes a forfeiture of his previously-exercised right to bail, which doubtless is the proper conclusion in at least some circumstances. Perhaps the easiest case of this kind is that in which the on-bail defendant's misconduct was an effort to obstruct the fair disposition of the charges against him, as in *In re Mason*,[10] where the trial judge became aware of the defendant's efforts at witness intimidation. In such circumstances, the appellate court concluded, "one the most reasonable ways" for the judge to respond was as he did, "by revoking bail and detaining the person attempting to thwart the proper functioning of the criminal justice system."

But what if the defendant's misconduct during pretrial release was not of that kind, but nonetheless constituted a criminal offense and/or a violation of some condition of release? Some authority is to be found indicating that a state constitutional right to bail does not stand in the way of preventive detention in such circumstances. In *State v. Ayala*,[11] for example, where "an explicit condition placed upon the defendant's release on bail was to refrain from committing any federal, state or local crimes," and "defendant was subsequently arrested on charges that, while on release, he had engaged in an unprovoked brutal assault on Mathews in broad daylight," defendant relied upon the state constitution's right-to-bail clause in challenging the trial court's revocation of his release, but to no avail. The appellate court "agree[d] with the state that the power to enforce reasonable conditions of release is a necessary component of a trial court's jurisdiction over a criminal case," and that consequently the "fundamental right to bail guaranteed under our state constitution must be qualified by a court's authority to ensure compliance with the conditions of release," which in the instant case included "the power * * * to revoke the defendant's release" upon finding probable cause "the defendant had committed this crime."

The broad language in *Ayala*, which could easily be interpreted to mean that a right to bail in the state constitution is subject to a releasing judge's "power * * * to revoke" whenever the defendant commits *any* crime or violates *any* condition of release, must be contrasted with that in *State v. Sauve*,[12] where the court concluded that the "absolute right to bail" in a state constitution means that "liberty must remain the norm" and that exceptions must thus be limited to " 'special circumstances' where the state's interest is 'legiti-

10. 116 Ohio App.3d 451, 688 N.E.2d 552 (1996).
11. 222 Conn. 331, 610 A.2d 1162 (1992).

12. 159 Vt. 566, 621 A.2d 1296 (1993).

mate and compelling.' " The defendant in *Sauve* was on pretrial release after being charged with burglary, unlawful mischief, and trespass for entering the residence of the complaining witness, who continued to carry on an intimate relationship with defendant thereafter. When defendant later was determined to have committed another trespass and to have consumed alcohol, each a violation of an express condition of his release, his release was revoked on the basis of a statutory provision permitting such action for "repeatedly violated conditions of release." But that language, the appellate court concluded, "does not rise to the level of a compelling interest," as even repeated violations do "not show that the judicial process is endangered." For example, those defendants who "violate conditions of release by continuing to use drugs or alcohol" may be "uncooperative" or even "potentially dangerous," but they "will not necessarily threaten justice." Likewise, repeated crimes "may show disrespect for the judicial system, but these violations do not necessarily threaten the integrity of the judicial system, in the constitutionally limited sense that they thwart the prosecution of the defendant." Revocation in the instant case thus violated the state constitution, for to "justify a compelling state interest * * * there must be a nexus between defendant's repeated violations and a disruption of the prosecution."

Because of the infrequency with which the issue under consideration here has been litigated in the appellate courts, it is difficult to generalize from either the *Ayala* or *Sauve* cases. But it does seem that the court in *Sauve* was very right about one thing: if state constitutional declarations of a right to bail are not to be rendered meaningless, exceptions to that right must be extremely limited and must in every instance be grounded in a compelling state interest. This means that bail revocation can never be justified merely because a release condition has been violated or because the person has apparently committed some offense during release; rather, such events must manifest a significant threat to a compelling state interest. Just what qualifies as such an inter-

est is a harder question. *Sauve* represents one possible conclusion; the court there, in essence, declared that since "preventive detention of the potentially dangerous" cannot otherwise be squared with the constitutional right to bail, it was necessary even in the case of new criminal conduct or violation of a release condition that something beyond such dangerousness be shown, i.e., they must "threaten the integrity of the judicial system, in the constitutionally limited sense that they thwart the prosecution of the defendant." But some courts have concluded that dangerousness in a somewhat broader sense should suffice when it is manifested by the released defendant's apparent commission of a serious crime or his violation of a release condition.

(c) The Eighth Amendment Ambiguity. Whether the Eighth Amendment posed a constitutional barrier to preventive detention remained unclear until the Supreme Court addressed the issue in *United States v. Salerno.*[13] True, a literal reading of the relevant language of the Amendment, "Excessive bail shall not be required," suggested the answer was no. But because the pre-*Salerno* utterances of the Court contained language helpful to those on both sides of the debate, lower courts were divided on the issue.

Those holding to the view that the Eighth Amendment does *not* encompass a right to bail found it useful to trace the excessive bail provision back to a comparable provision in the English Bill of Rights of 1689. The latter provision, it was noted, was not prompted by the well established statutory provisions that carefully enumerated which offenses were bailable and which were not, but rather by judicial circumvention of the protections of the Habeas Corpus Act by setting prohibitively high bail for bailable offenses. The English excessive bail clause, therefore, was developed as a specific remedy for judicial abuse of the bail procedure as otherwise established by law and did not, in and of itself, imply any right to bail. This distinction, it was argued, was recognized in the colonies and early states, as reflected by three significant developments: (1) several

---

13. 481 U.S. 739, 107 S.Ct. 2095, 95 L.Ed.2d 697 (1987).

states dealt with the right to bail by statute, thus indicating an understanding that the subject was open to legislative limitation; (2) several states adopted constitutional provisions that were explicitly directed to limiting the power of the judiciary; and (3) several states adopted constitutional provisions that granted a right to bail and also an excessive bail clause, manifesting a recognition that the latter did not encompass the former.

The view that the Eighth Amendment does not confer a right to bail was also claimed to be consistent with the contemporary understanding when the Amendment was considered and adopted. It was pointed out that some of the states proposing an excessive bail clause for the federal Constitution had such a clause and a right to bail provision in their state constitutions, and thus would have proposed both had they desired a constitutional right to bail against the federal government. Also noteworthy is the fact that in the same session in which Congress considered and approved the Bill of Rights, it drafted and enacted the Judiciary Act of 1789, which established a statutory right to bail in noncapital cases. This view of history, it was argued, had been accepted by the Supreme Court, for in *Carlson v. Landon*[14] the Court stated:

> The bail clause was lifted with slight changes from the English Bill of Rights Act. In England that clause has never been thought to accord a right to bail in all cases, but merely to provide that bail shall not be excessive in those cases where it is proper to grant bail. When this clause was carried over into our Bill of Rights, nothing was said that indicated any different concept.

This argument for a narrow reading of the Eighth Amendment concluded with the contention that such an interpretation is consistent with the general constitutional scheme. In response to the objection that it would make little sense to prohibit judicial imposition of excessive bail but not forbid the legislative denial of bail altogether, it was said that such a construction squares with the fact that the chief concern of the Bill of Rights generally is the conduct of the judicial branch of government.

As for those holding to the view that the Eighth Amendment *does* include a constitutional right to bail, they took a somewhat different view as to the significance of the Amendment's English antecedents. They agree that English law denied bail for some offenses, but found no evidence that such a denial was ever permitted for the purpose of protecting the community. Rather, they suggested, the underlying assumption was that certain classes of offenders, particularly those whose lives were at stake, ought to be detained simply to assure their presence at trial. Pretrial release was more readily denied during this period in cases of particularly heinous crimes, but the reason, apart from the fact that such offenses carried heavier penalties and therefore involved a greater temptation to flee, was the fear that persons guilty of especially atrocious offenses might well be killed before they could appear for trial. In any event, so the argument proceeded, the English history is not controlling here because from the very beginning the American concept of bail differed significantly from that of the English. This is reflected by the fact that most states put in their state constitutions a provision that "all persons shall be bailable." And while these state constitutional provisions contain an exception for capital cases, this hardly reflects acceptance of the concept of preventive detention. Rather, these provisions were enacted in this form because it had been thought that most defendants facing a possible death penalty would likely flee regardless of what bail was set.

Those favoring a broader reading of the Eighth Amendment to include a right to bail contended that this was the only logical construction of the bail provision. So the argument proceeded, to read the Amendment as barring judicial setting of excessive bail but not legislative denial of bail would make it virtually meaningless. After all, the interests at stake are identical whether a legislature or a court has made the basic decision resulting

---

14.   342 U.S. 524, 72 S.Ct. 525, 96 L.Ed. 547 (1952).

in the defendant's pretrial imprisonment. Moreover, an interpretation of the bail clause as limited to judicial abuse is inconsistent with the general approach taken in the Bill of Rights, which is concerned primarily with curtailing the powers of Congress. This is evident within the Eighth Amendment itself, for the prohibitions on cruel and unusual punishments and excessive fines have traditionally been viewed as limitations on legislative abuse.

As for the *Carlson* case, it was noted that the language quoted above was dictum set out in the context of a civil rather than a criminal case, in which the actual holding was that bail could be denied to prevent sabotage by alien Communists pending their deportation. More relevant, so the argument proceeded, is the Court's declaration in *Stack v. Boyle*[15] that the

> right to freedom before conviction permits the unhampered preparation of a defense, and serves to prevent the infliction of punishment prior to conviction. * * * Unless this right to bail before trial is preserved, the presumption of innocence, secured only after centuries of struggle, would lose its meaning.

Then came *United States v. Salerno*,[16] involving a facial challenge to the Bail Reform Act of 1984 (meaning, the Court emphasized, that "the challenger must establish that no set of circumstances exists under which the Act would be valid"). The Supreme Court found the *Stack* language "far too slender a reed on which to rest" the argument that the Eighth Amendment grants "a right to bail calculated solely upon consideration of flight," especially when "*Stack* is illuminated by the Court's holding just four months later in *Carlson*." But the Court's brief discussion of the subject concluded with the caution that

> we need not decide today whether the Excessive Bail Clause speaks at all to Congress' power to define the classes of criminal arrestees who shall be admitted to bail. * * * Nothing in the text of the Bail Clause limits

permissible government considerations solely to questions of flight. The only arguable substantive limitation of the Bail Clause is that the government's proposed conditions of release or detention not be "excessive" in light of the perceived evil. Of course, to determine whether the government's response is excessive, we must compare that response against the interest the government seeks to protect by means of that response. Thus, when the government has admitted that its only interest is in preventing flight, bail must be set by a court at a sum designed to ensure that goal, and no more. * * * We believe that when Congress has mandated detention on the basis of a compelling interest other than prevention of flight, as it has here, the Eighth Amendment does not require release on bail.

Thus, there exists in *Salerno* at least the suggestion that under the Eighth Amendment the risk of future crimes by certain types of arrestees could be so insubstantial as to make preventive detention of such persons excessive.

(d) Other Constitutional Objections.[17] The language from *Stack* quoted above has understandably prompted the argument that preventive detention schemes are unconstitutional simply because they run afoul of the presumption of innocence. But while it is now generally accepted that the presumption of innocence has constitutional stature, as currently viewed by the Supreme Court it appears to have no bearing upon the preventive detention issue. The Court in *Bell v. Wolfish*[18] concluded that the presumption "is a doctrine that allocates the burden of proof in criminal trials" and requires the factfinder "to judge an accused's guilt or innocence solely on the evidence adduced at trial and not on the basis of suspicions that may arise from the fact of his arrest, indictment, or custody or from other matters not introduced as proof at trial," and

15. 342 U.S. 1, 72 S.Ct. 1, 96 L.Ed. 3 (1951).

16. 481 U.S. 739, 107 S.Ct. 2095, 95 L.Ed.2d 697 (1987).

17. The reference here is to objections grounded in provisions in the United States Constitution. As for challenges to state preventive detention schemes based upon state constitutional provisions, see § 12.3(b).

18. 441 U.S. 520, 99 S.Ct. 1861, 60 L.Ed.2d 447 (1979).

that it has "no application * * * before his trial has even begun."

Presumption of innocence aside, it is nonetheless possible that a particular preventive detention scheme would be vulnerable to an attack on due process grounds on the theory that it amounts to an impermissible imposition of punishment. As the Supreme Court recognized in *Bell v. Wolfish*,[19] the Constitution "includes freedom from punishment within the liberty of which no person may be deprived without due process of law," so that generally "punishment can only follow a determination of guilt after trial or plea." But the Court in *Bell* deemed it beyond dispute that pretrial incarceration is not inevitably "punishment" within the meaning of this doctrine. As for how to draw the "distinction between punitive measures that may not constitutionally be imposed prior to a determination of guilt and regulatory restraints that may," the Court identified a series of three factors: (1) "whether the disability is imposed for the purpose of punishment or whether it is but an incident of some other legitimate governmental purpose"; (2) absent an intent to punish, whether "an alternative purpose to which [the restriction] may rationally be connected is assignable for it"; and (3) if there is such a purpose, a "legitimate governmental objective," whether the disability "appears excessive in relation to the alternative purpose assigned [to it]."

Applying these factors, the Supreme Court in *United States v. Salerno*,[20] in response to a facial challenge to the Bail Reform Act of 1984,[21] concluded the Act did not violate substantive due process. The legislative history "clearly indicates that Congress did not formulate the pretrial detention provisions as punishment for dangerous individuals"; rather, they serve a legitimate function, as "there is no doubt that preventing danger to the community is a legitimate regulatory goal." As for the third *Bell* factor, the Court concluded that "the incidents of pretrial detention" were not excessive because the Act "carefully limits the circumstances under which detention may be sought to the most serious crimes," the arrestee "is entitled to a prompt detention hearing" at which "the government must convince a neutral decisionmaker by clear and convincing evidence that no conditions of release can reasonably assure the safety of the community or any person," "the maximum length of pretrial detention is limited by the stringent time limitations of the Speedy Trial Act," and the conditions of confinement reflect the regulatory purpose because detainees are, to the extent possible, to be housed separately from convicted defendants. The Court's emphasis upon these characteristics of the Act, together with the assertion that what is involved here is a balancing of the "particularized government interest" against "the individuals's strong interest in liberty," suggests that a more expansive type of preventive detention law would be vulnerable under the *Bell* test.

Next, there is the possibility that a preventive detention scheme could be questioned on equal protection grounds. The traditional standard of review under the equal protection clause requires only that the law be shown to bear some rational relationship to legitimate state purposes,[22] though there are special instances in which a more demanding "strict scrutiny" approach is required. Even assuming the latter test is not applicable here, a matter on which there is not complete agreement, it might be argued that a preventive detention scheme which selects only from those charged with crimes is arbitrary. The reasoning is that there certainly are persons not charged with any crime who give every indication of being at least as dangerous as anyone awaiting trial on a pending charge, and that this being so, it is arbitrary to imprison the man who is about to be tried for a past offense while imposing no restraint on the man who is not facing trial. Obviously relevant to this line of reasoning is

---

19. 441 U.S. 520, 99 S.Ct. 1861, 60 L.Ed.2d 447 (1979).

20. 481 U.S. 739, 107 S.Ct. 2095, 95 L.Ed.2d 697 (1987).

21. Meaning, the Court noted, that "the challenger must establish that no set of circumstances exists under which the Act would be valid."

22. San Antonio Independent School District v. Rodriguez, 411 U.S. 1, 93 S.Ct. 1278, 36 L.Ed.2d 16 (1973).

Jackson v. Indiana,[23] holding that "pending criminal charges" provide no justification for incarcerating incompetents under less demanding standards than apply to mentally ill persons not so charged. *Jackson,* it has been argued, is directly relevant to the preventive detention question. Yet, authority is to be found supporting the conclusion that it is rational for a legislative body to conclude that those charged with a particular type of offense are likely to repeat their crimes and thus to authorize preventive detention as to persons so charged.

Finally, it is well to note that even if a particular preventive detention scheme suffers from none of the previously discussed constitutional defects, it is nonetheless necessary that the procedures whereby it is determined which individuals will actually be confined be fair in a procedural due process sense. Even in a situation in which it is conceded that the defendant has no absolute right to bail, a fair adjudicatory procedure must be followed. Just what constitutes fair procedure for due process purposes depends to some extent upon the circumstances and matter at issue. Thus, in *Gerstein v. Pugh*,[24] concerning the judicial determination of probable cause after a warrantless arrest, the Court held that "the full panoply of adversary safeguards—counsel, confrontation, cross-examination, and compulsory process for witnesses," is not constitutionally required, while in *Morrissey v. Brewer*,[25] concerning parole revocation, the Court ruled the parolee was entitled to notice, an opportunity to present evidence, and a right to confront and cross-examine adverse witnesses. In *United States v. Edwards*,[26] upholding the District of Columbia preventive detention statute, the majority ruled that *Gerstein* rather than *Morrissey* governed because it concerned a hearing with a similar issue: "whether the accused may be detained pending trial." That reasoning is unconvincing. As one of the *Ed-*

wards dissenters noted, it affords "less constitutional protection to an accused at a pretrial detention hearing than the Supreme Court has granted convicted felons facing possible revocation of probation or parole." Moreover, he correctly added, *Gerstein* is hardly analogous because it involves only a probable cause determination, which (1) is not a basis for further detention per se but only for requiring bail; and (2) is much less complicated than the "far more complex, inherently speculative prediction that the accused is likely to be dangerous in the future."

In *United States v. Salerno*,[27] the Court briefly discussed the procedural due process question in upholding the facial constitutionally of the Bail Reform Act of 1984. Seemingly consistent with the discussion above, the Court stressed the procedures mandated by the Act: "a right to counsel at the detention hearing," and a right to "testify in their own behalf, present information by proffer or otherwise, and cross-examine witnesses who appear at the hearing." The Court declared "these extensive safeguards suffice to repel a facial challenge,"[28] but may or may not have intended *Gerstein* as the benchmark in stating enigmatically that these procedures "far exceed what we found necessary to affect limited post arrest detention" in that case.

(e) Detention Where Serious Offense Charged. One variety of preventive detention scheme is that which withholds the right of pretrial release for defendants charged with a certain type of serious offense. Illustrative is the state constitutional provision held unconstitutional in *Hunt v. Roth*;[29] it excepted cases of "sexual offenses involving penetration by force or against the will of the victim * * * where the proof is evident or the presumption great." The court in *Hunt* held that this provision violated the Eighth Amendment, construed to bar an "unreasonable and arbitrary

---

23. 406 U.S. 715, 92 S.Ct. 1845, 32 L.Ed.2d 435 (1972).

24. 420 U.S. 103, 95 S.Ct. 854, 43 L.Ed.2d 54 (1975).

25. 408 U.S. 471, 92 S.Ct. 2593, 33 L.Ed.2d 484 (1972).

26. 430 A.2d 1321 (D.C.App.1981).

27. 481 U.S. 739, 107 S.Ct. 2095, 95 L.Ed.2d 697 (1987).

28. As the Court emphasized, on a facial challenge "the challenger must establish that no set of circumstances exists under which the Act would be valid."

29. 648 F.2d 1148 (8th Cir.1981), judgment vacated for mootness 455 U.S. 478, 102 S.Ct. 1181, 71 L.Ed.2d 353.

denial of bail," but the court's reasoning would also be relevant were the provision instead subjected to a due process or equal protection analysis:

> We do not hold and need not decide that there is a constitutional right in every case to release on bail. As we have discussed, there exists a strong argument that bail may be properly denied without encroaching on constitutional concerns where a judicial officer weighs all the appropriate factors and makes a reasoned judgment that the defendant's past record demonstrates that bail will not reasonably assure his or her appearance or, arguendo, that he or she, because of the overall record and circumstances, poses a threat to the community. The fatal flaw in the Nebraska constitutional amendment is that the state has created an irrebuttable presumption that every individual charged with this particular offense is incapable of assuring his appearance by conditioning it upon reasonable bail or is too dangerous to be granted release. * * * The state may be free to consider the nature of the charge and the degree of proof in granting or denying bail but it cannot give these factors conclusive force.

Because *Salerno,* discussed above, placed great emphasis on the need for proof that the particular "arrestee presents an identified and articulable threat to an individual or the community," it does not put the *Hunt* analysis in doubt.

A *Hunt/Salerno* challenge might be directed at the rather common capital offense exception[30] in the right-to-bail provisions of state constitutions, or especially at variations thereto not so steeped in tradition, such as the constitutional provisions in a few states that go beyond the capital offense exception by including instead or as well certain named noncapital offenses or any offense punishable by life imprisonment. Starting from *Hunt,* the claim might be that any of these provisions applied so as to create an irrebuttable presumption of danger to the community is invalid. Starting from *Salerno,* the contention might be that *all* of these state constitutional provisions violate substantive and/or procedural due process unless the requirements emphasized in that case are engrafted onto these provisions. That is, since *Salerno* deemed it most important that the federal preventive detention statute both (i) was limited to serious offenses and (ii) as to them had careful procedures for assessing dangerousness on a case-by-case basis, these bail exception clauses (which themselves accomplish only the first of these requirements) violate the federal constitution absence procedures for making individual dangerousness assessments. But at least if the state constitutional exception is stated narrowly enough, it would appear that if (1) judicial discretion as to individual cases is preserved and (2) most of the procedural requirements highlighted in *Salerno* are followed, then (3) it is not necessary that the dangerousness inquiry be quite as focused as contemplated by the federal statute.

(f) Detention Upon Individual Finding of Dangerousness. Even if a preventive detention law requires a case-by-case determination of the defendant's dangerousness, as do both the D.C. and federal statutes, it can be argued that there is a fundamental constitutional defect. Whether the question is viewed in terms of an Eighth Amendment right against "unreasonable and arbitrary denial of bail," a due process right under *Bell* to a disability that is not "excessive" in relation to its purpose, or an equal protection right against irrational distinctions, the asserted defect is that there appears to be no simple, reliable technique for predicting which defendants are likely to be dangerous. Various studies show that only 5 percent of the defendants eligible for detention under the District of Columbia preventive detention statute would, if released, be rearrested for dangerous or violent crimes. Moreover, it has also been shown that persons charged with some very serious crimes like homicide, persons arrested while on pretrial release, and persons with prior arrest records all pose no greater release risks than does the average defendant. Still another study concluded that it was not possible to

---

30. Other aspects of which are discussed in § 12.4(a).

develop a reliable set of predictors that could accurately identify the relatively small proportion of released defendants who would be rearrested while on bail. However, the Supreme Court's decision in *Schall v. Martin*,[31] upholding a preventive detention statute for juvenile proceedings, suggests a challenge based upon this uncertainty is unlikely to prevail. The Court there declared "that from a legal point of view there is nothing inherently unattainable about a prediction of future criminal conduct," which "forms an important element in many decisions" regarding sentencing and parole and probation release and revocation.[32] That language was relied upon in *Salerno*, discussed above, upholding the facial constitutionality of the Bail Reform Act of 1984.

But this is not to suggest that the many state provisions of this kind to be found today would pass muster under *Salerno*, as the Supreme Court in that case recognized that any provision of this kind must meet certain substantive and procedural due process requirements. On the substantive side, the Court in *Salerno* deemed it necessary "that the government's regulatory interest in community safety * * * outweigh an individual's liberty interest," which was the case as to the federal statute because (i) "it operates only on individuals who have been arrested for a specific category of extremely serious offenses," (ii) it requires the government to "demonstrate probable cause to believe that the charged crime has been committed by the arrestee," and (iii) in addition the government "must convince a neutral decisionmaker by clear and convincing evidence that no conditions of release can reasonably assure the safety of the community or any person." Certainly state provisions lacking in one or more of these respects are vulnerable.

As for the serious offense limitation, surely it means that a state preventive detention provision permitting denial of bail upon a finding of dangerousness with respect to *all* arres-

tees, without regard to the seriousness of the charge, cannot be upheld. But this is not to suggest that the list of predicate offenses in state legislation must match that in the federal statute; it is sufficient if those offenses are defined somewhat differently but are also limited to serious crimes. As for procedural due process, the Court in *Salerno* placed considerable emphasis upon the fact that "the procedures by which a judicial officer evaluates the likelihood of future dangerousness are specifically designed to further the accuracy of the determinations." Specifically enumerated in this regard were: (i) the detainee's right to counsel; (ii) his ability to testify and otherwise present information; (iii) his right to cross-examine witnesses who appear; (iv) guidance to the judicial officer in the form of a statutory list of relevant considerations; (v) the government must prove its case by clear and convincing evidence; (vi) the judicial officer must make written findings of fact and statement of reasons for detention; (vii) immediate appellate review of a detention decision. Many of the state preventive detention provisions may be vulnerable on this score, as a majority of the state detention provisions contain only some of these minimal protections.

(g) Detention for Misconduct During Release. The one form of preventive detention most likely to pass muster under the federal constitution[33] is that allowing revocation of pretrial release and detention until trial upon a showing that the defendant engaged in misconduct during that release. This is most obviously the case where the defendant has unlawfully tried to thwart his prosecution or conviction by such conduct as threatening, injuring, or intimidating any prospective witness, juror, prosecutor, or court officer. Notwithstanding any constitutional or statutory right to bail, a court has the inherent power to confine the defendant in such circumstances in

---

31. 467 U.S. 253, 104 S.Ct. 2403, 81 L.Ed.2d 207 (1984).

32. The Court also concluded that the governing statute need not specify the factors to be taken into account in making this judgment, as "a prediction of future criminal

conduct is 'an experienced prediction based on a host of variables' which cannot be readily codified."

33. Whether these provisions can be squared with state constitutional provisions guaranteeing a right to bail is a harder question, discussed in § 12.3(b).

the interest of safeguarding the integrity of its own process.

What then of the broader proposition that a defendant may have his bail revoked for any serious criminal conduct engaged in during such release? In support of such a scheme, it may argued that it lacks the defects of outright pretrial detention, where one of the main failings is the fact that the judge has no reliable indicator available by which to determine which defendants will commit further crimes. And thus it is not surprising that there exists even pre-*Salerno* authority to the effect that such a provision is constitutional. But what is the status of these provisions (or indeed any preventive detention provision that substitutes a condition precedent for a case-by-case dangerous determination[34]) under *Salerno*? The question here is whether a requirement that the arrestee be guilty of a prior offense or be charged with committing a crime while out on parole, probation, or pretrial release obviates the need to require that the arrestee be charged with an "extremely serious" crime, that probable cause be shown, or that the state prove clear and convincing evidence of danger. The rationale for an affirmative answer, that the government's interest in detaining repeat criminal offenders is more significant because such individuals pose a statistically greater danger to the community upon release than do first-time offenders, weakens when the arrestee can be detained merely because he is on pretrial release rather than being on parole, probation, or having previously committed a crime. This probably means that if the defendant has been accused twice of relatively insignificant criminal conduct, then this cannot be treated as a sufficient manifestation of dangerousness. By comparison, a statute requiring that the original charge and new conduct both be at the felony level would seem much less vulnerable. Of course, it is also necessary that the revocation hearing be conducted in conformance with the requirements of procedural

due process, but this does not mean that the new crime must be proved beyond a reasonable doubt.

§ 12.4 Special Situations

(a) Capital Cases. In 1818 the State of Connecticut adopted a constitutional provision reading: "All prisoners shall, before conviction, be bailable by sufficient sureties, except for capital offenses, where the proof is evident, or the presumption great." Since that time, forty states have adopted substantially the same clause. Although, as we have seen, there has been considerable uncertainty as to whether the Eighth Amendment creates a right to bail and, if so, to what extent, it has always been generally assumed that the exception in these state constitutional provisions does not offend that Amendment. On the federal level, the Supreme Court declared in *Carlson v. Landon*:[1] "The Eighth Amendment has not prevented Congress from defining the classes of cases in which bail shall be allowed in this country. Thus in criminal cases it is not compulsory where the punishment may be death." It is less certain whether these provisions would in every instance withstand challenge on substantive or procedural due process grounds, although the chance of a successful constitutional challenge would appear to be less in those jurisdictions following the majority view that a sufficient showing of defendant's guilt of the capital offense leaves intact the discretionary power of the court to admit any defendant to bail.

In states with these provisions, legislative abolition of the death penalty has been consistently held to mean that persons charged with offenses formerly subject to capital punishment are in all cases bailable. This conclusion has been reached even when the abolition of capital punishment was accompanied by legislation declaring that persons charged with the offenses so affected were not bailable if the

---

34. As discussed further in § 12.3(b), in some states the condition precedent is merely used to describe a situation in which it is permissible to revoke or deny bail if there is in addition a finding of dangerousness. The issue under these provisions is essentially the same as that discussed in § 12.3(f).

§ 12.4

1. 342 U.S. 524, 72 S.Ct. 525, 96 L.Ed. 547 (1952).

proof was evident or the presumption great. But there has not been agreement as to how these constitutional provisions should be applied when the legislature has provided for the death penalty but has done so in such a way that imposition of the penalty is constitutionally barred.[2] The courts are split, depending upon whether they adopt the penalty theory or the classification theory. The former is that these constitutional provisions are based upon the strong flight urge because of the possibility of an accused forfeiting his life, and thus are inapplicable once that possibility is removed by either the legislature or the courts. The classification theory, on the other hand, is that the underlying gravity of those offenses endures and the determination of their gravity for the purpose of bail continues unaffected by the decision that the death penalty provision is unconstitutional. Which of these two views is correct depends, of course, on the rationale underlying these constitutional provisions. If, as is sometimes assumed, they were adopted to permit pretrial detention because of danger to the community, then the classification theory is correct. But if, as seems more likely, the underlying assumption was that certain classes of offenders, particularly those whose lives were at stake, ought to be detained simply to assure their presence at trial, then the penalty theory is the correct one.

Because these constitutional provisions take away the right to bail only in those capital cases where "the proof is evident or the presumption great," it is not sufficient to bring a capital case within that exception that the defendant has been charged in such a way that he could receive the death penalty. Rather, these provisions contemplate that bail should be denied when the circumstances disclosed indicate a fair likelihood that the defendant is in danger of a jury verdict of an offense punishable by death, for only in instances where such likelihood exists is his life in jeopardy and the well recognized urge to abscond present.

Under the traditional grading of criminal homicide whereby the death penalty can be returned only upon a finding of guilty of murder in the first degree, this means a fair likelihood of such a verdict. But under the Supreme Court's decisions holding unconstitutional a mandatory death penalty for first degree murder[3] but upholding the imposition of a sentence of death where the jury or judge is required to weigh statutory aggravating and mitigating circumstances,[4] it would seem that this fair likelihood exists only if it appears likely one of the requisite aggravating circumstances is present.

Where does the burden of proof lie? One line of cases takes the view that since the defendant is entitled to bail only on application and when he so applies is trying to change the status quo, the burden is rightly on him to show that the proof is not evident or that the presumption is not great. The other and better view is that these constitutional provisions confer a right to bail except under the limited circumstances specified and that the burden should rest on the party relying on the exception, that is, the prosecution. Assuming the latter approach, the next question is what probative force the indictment has with respect to this burden. The decisions on this issue fall into three categories: (1) the burden is on the state to adduce some facts in addition to the indictment in order to satisfy the court that the case against the accused meets the constitutional requirement; (2) the indictment is *prima facie* evidence of a capital offense within the constitutional exception; and (3) the indictment is conclusive against the allowance of bail. Courts have been more receptive to viewing the indictment as prima facie evidence where the grand jury must specify whether the crime charged is murder in the first or second degree. But in light of the Supreme Court's death penalty decisions alluded to above, even such an indictment would not as a matter of logic seem to constitute

---

2. An issue that became especially important because of Furman v. Georgia, 408 U.S. 238, 92 S.Ct. 2726, 33 L.Ed.2d 346 (1972), and its progeny.

3. Woodson v. North Carolina, 428 U.S. 280, 96 S.Ct. 2978, 49 L.Ed.2d 944 (1976).

4. Gregg v. Georgia, 428 U.S. 153, 96 S.Ct. 2909, 49 L.Ed.2d 859 (1976).

prima facie evidence, for the grand jury would not have made a judgment about whether any of the requisite aggravating circumstances were present in the particular case. In any event, another reason for not giving the indictment even prima facie effect is that proceedings of the grand jury are secret and wholly *ex parte.*

A somewhat similar question is whether, in those jurisdictions permitting the institution of even capital offense prosecutions by information rather than indictment, it can be said that the filing of the information raises such a presumption of defendant's guilt as to constitute a prima facie showing. Although some courts have answered this question in the affirmative, that conclusion is open to even greater criticism than reliance upon a grand jury indictment. Such a result is inconsistent with the reasoning in *Gerstein v. Pugh,*[5] where the Supreme Court held an information (as distinguished from an indictment) would not suffice to justify continued custody of a defendant arrested without a warrant. As for whether a probable cause finding by a magistrate at a preliminary hearing should suffice, it would seem not given that it is not customary for the defendant to present evidence at the preliminary hearing.

Assuming the prosecution is obligated to put in proof on the issue at the bail hearing, the question then is how this may be done. Mere representations by the prosecutor that he has and will introduce at trial certain evidence he specifies with particularity is not sufficient. The hearing may well be conducted somewhat informally, as upon affidavits, if the defendant agrees, but affidavits and copies of grand jury testimony may not be received if the defendant objects, as he has a right of cross-examination in this context. Hearsay is not totally barred; the admissibility of such evidence must ultimately be determined on a case by case basis, and receipt of hearsay is proper if it is the kind of evidence on which responsible persons are accustomed to rely in serious affairs. Quite obviously, it is necessary that the nature of the hearsay be such as to indicate that admissible evidence of the same variety will be available at trial (as where a detective indicates what witnesses have told him), for otherwise it does not contribute to the requisite "fair likelihood" determination. By like reasoning it has been held that evidence subject to suppression, such as a confession obtained in violation of *Miranda,* may not be received on this issue, though concern about unduly complicating pretrial proceedings has sometimes prompted the conclusion that the state need only make a prima facie showing of compliance with *Miranda.*

(b) Juvenile Cases. Because state courts have typically relied upon juvenile code safeguards in dealing with pretrial release issues in juvenile cases, there has for some time existed considerable uncertainty as to what extent a constitutional right to bail exists in this context. But under the general "fundamental fairness" approach that the Supreme Court has utilized in determining what rights of adult defendants also apply in juvenile proceedings,[6] it may be concluded that there is no unqualified constitutional right to bail for a juvenile. This is clearly reflected in the fact that the Supreme Court, in the case of *Schall v. Martin,*[7] upheld a preventive detention statute applicable to juvenile court cases.

For one thing, certain problems peculiar to these proceedings make a blanket application of the right to pre-adjudication release upon adequate assurance of future court appearance unworkable and undesirable. Thus an exception to the bail rights an adult would have must be recognized when the child would be endangered by release, as when his parents are not willing to care for the child or if harm will come to the child in his present home situation. More controversial is whether the concept of preventive detention has a place in the juvenile court process, as often contemplated by state law. In *Schall* the Supreme Court upheld a statutory provision authorizing pretrial detention of an accused juvenile delin-

---

5. 420 U.S. 103, 95 S.Ct. 854, 43 L.Ed.2d 54 (1975).

6. McKeiver v. Pennsylvania, 403 U.S. 528, 91 S.Ct. 1976, 29 L.Ed.2d 647 (1971).

7. 467 U.S. 253, 104 S.Ct. 2403, 81 L.Ed.2d 207 (1984).

quent based on a finding that there is a "serious risk" that the child "may before the return date commit an act which if committed by an adult would constitute a crime." The Court, in holding this provision conformed to the "fundamental fairness" demanded by the due process clause, first concluded that the statute served a legitimate state objective, "protecting the community from crime," deemed to be more weighty than the juvenile's countervailing interest in freedom from restraint, which "must be qualified by the recognition that juveniles, unlike adults, are always in some form of custody." As for the added constitutional requirement that the pretrial detention not constitute punishment, the Court concluded there was "no indication in the statute itself that preventive detention is used or intended as a punishment." The Court emphasized in this connection that the challenged provision required a prompt probable cause hearing, an expedited fact-finding hearing for detained juveniles, and nonpunitive conditions of confinement.

Due process also requires adequate procedural safeguards, and thus the Supreme Court in *Schall* also declared that as a constitutional matter it was necessary that the procedures afforded juveniles "provide sufficient protection against erroneous and unnecessary deprivation of liberty." Such procedures were deemed present there, as the juvenile was entitled to a prompt adversarial determination of probable cause of a delinquent act and that the serious risk of a criminal act in the immediate future existed. Because the statute required a finding of facts and statement of reasons supporting preventive detention, the Court concluded the statute need not enumerate the specific factors upon which the juvenile court judge might rely. The Court in *Schall* also emphasized "that from a legal point of view there is nothing inherently unattainable about a prediction of future criminal conduct."

(c) During Trial. Once the defendant's trial has commenced, he is in a somewhat different posture regarding his right to be at large on bail or other form of release. As the Su-

preme Court recognized in *Bitter v. United States*:[8]

> A trial judge indisputably has broad powers to ensure the orderly and expeditious progress of a trial. For this purpose, he has the power to revoke bail and to remit the defendant to custody. But this power must be exercised with circumspection. It may be invoked only when and to the extent justified by danger which the defendant's conduct presents or by danger of significant interference with the progress or order of the trial.

Thus, bail may be revoked during trial where a defendant has made threats to government witnesses, or where he has engaged in obstructive misconduct during the course of the trial. But in *Bitter,* where the revocation was apparently based upon nothing more than "a single, brief incident of tardiness," there was no basis for committing the defendant to custody. Except when the conduct that serves as the basis of the revocation occurred within the observation of the judge, a hearing must be held to determine whether the conduct did take place.

(d) After Conviction. Once the defendant's trial is completed and he has been convicted, his situation with respect to his release, even if he plans to take an appeal, changes significantly. The typical state constitutional provision guaranteeing a right to bail is limited to the time "before conviction," and this distinction is ordinarily observed in state statutes just as it is in the Federal Bail Reform Act of 1984. But the federal Act is especially strict. Pending sentence or appeal, the general rule as to a defendant who could be or has been sentenced to a term of imprisonment is that the court is to order the defendant detained unless the court finds by clear and convincing evidence that he is not likely to flee or pose a danger to the safety of any other person or the community if released under sections 3142(b) or (c).[9] In the pending appeal situation, however, the court must also find that the appeal is not for the purpose of delay and raises a substantial question of law or fact

8. 389 U.S. 15, 88 S.Ct. 6, 19 L.Ed.2d 15 (1967).

9. 18 U.S.C.A. § 3143(a)(1), (b)(1)(A).

likely to result in reversal, an order for a new trial, a sentence that does not include a term of imprisonment, or a reduced sentence less than the time served up to the point when such reduction is ordered.[10] Because a literal reading of that provision would mean release would virtually never be available when the defendant's motion for a new trial had been denied and he was now taking an appeal, it has been construed by the courts in a less absolute fashion.

The post-conviction situation is different as to a person convicted of a crime of violence, a drug offense carrying a statutory maximum sentence of 10 years or more, or an offense for which the maximum sentence is death or life imprisonment. When such a person is awaiting imposition or execution of sentence, he is to be detained unless the court finds by clear and convincing evidence that the person is not likely to flee or pose a danger to any other person or the community,[11] and in addition one of two other events occurs. One is where the court also finds that there is a substantial likelihood that a motion for acquittal or new trial will be granted.[12] The other is where an attorney for the government has recommended no sentence of imprisonment be imposed.[13] But where such a person has filed an appeal or cert. petition, he is to be detained.[14]

The United States Supreme Court held as early as 1894 that there is no constitutional right to bail pending appeal from a conviction.[15] Sometimes this result is explained on the ground that since there is no constitutional right to appeal, there is no constitutional right to be free pending an appeal, which perhaps by itself is not entirely convincing. But the situation is different after conviction in other respects. A defendant who has been convicted and has little hope for reversal might be strongly tempted to flee, and one with greater hope for reversal might be tempted to tamper with witnesses who had been

especially useful to the prosecutor so as to minimize the chances of conviction after remand. Another reason given is that the presumption of innocence and the right to participate in the preparation of a defense to ensure a fair trial are obviously not present where the defendant has already been tried and convicted.

Individual members of the Supreme Court passing upon applications for bail pending disposition of an appeal have sometimes asserted that the "command of the Eighth Amendment that 'Excessive bail shall not be required * * *' *at the very least* obligates judges passing upon the right to bail to deny such relief only for the strongest of reasons."[16] Yet, courts have held that it is permissible for the legislature to exclude certain types of cases from judicial consideration on the question of post-conviction bail, and that it is permissible to impose conditions on post-conviction bail that might not pass muster before conviction, both of which are consistent with the generally accepted proposition that there is no federal constitutional right to bail pending appeal after conviction in a state court. But that proposition has in turn not foreclosed the holding that once a state makes provision for such bail, the Eighth and Fourteenth Amendments require that it not be denied arbitrarily or unreasonably. There is a split of authority as to who must show what on this latter issue. Some courts hold to the view that denial of bail pending appeal without a statement of reasons is arbitrary per se, while others have taken the position that a presumption of regularity attaches to a state court's denial of bail and that the defendant bears the burden of showing that there is no rational basis in the record to support such denial. Under federal procedure, however, it is clear that a statement of reasons is required.

(e) Probation or Parole Revocation. Even assuming a constitutional right to have

---

10. 18 U.S.C.A. § 3143(b)(1)(B).

11. 18 U.S.C.A. § 3143(a)(2)(B).

12. 18 U.S.C.A. § 3143(a)(2)(A)(i).

13. 18 U.S.C.A. § 3143(a)(2)(A)(ii).

14. 18 U.S.C.A. § 3143(b)(2).

15. McKane v. Durston, 153 U.S. 684, 14 S.Ct. 913, 38 L.Ed. 867 (1894).

16. Harris v. United States, 404 U.S. 1232, 92 S.Ct. 10, 30 L.Ed.2d 25 (1971) (Douglas, J.); Sellers v. United States, 89 S.Ct. 36, 21 L.Ed.2d 64 (1968) (Black, J.).

bail set in other circumstances, it does not follow that a defendant held pending a revocation hearing for an alleged violation of probation has a right to bail. As explained in *In re Whitney*:[17]

> The probationer has been convicted of a crime, subjected to the sanctions prescribed by law, and has been granted conditional release in order to serve the interests of society. The interests which the government may protect at this stage of the process are properly much broader than before trial. Since a conviction has been obtained, for example, it is hardly unreasonable to use incarceration pending the revocation hearing to protect society against the possible commission of additional crimes by the probationer. There is no presumption of innocence in the probation revocation process, at least not in the sense in which the phrase is used with reference to the criminal process. Hence, when a probationer is incarcerated pending a hearing, the balance of interests is not the same as that involved in confining an accused who has not been found guilty.

The same is true of a person who is awaiting parole revocation proceedings.

(f) Material Witnesses. The federal Bail Reform Act of 1984 provides that if the testimony of a person is material in a criminal proceeding and it is shown "that it may become impracticable to secure the presence of the person by subpoena," then the release conditions otherwise provided for in that Act shall be utilized. Detention of a material witness for inability to comply with the conditions set is not allowed "if the testimony of such witness can adequately be secured by deposition, and further if detention is not necessary to prevent a failure of justice," and in such case release may be delayed "for a reasonable period of time until the deposition of the witness can be taken."[18] In the context of increased reliance upon this authority post–9/11/01, one court has reaffirmed that the term "criminal proceedings" in the statute includes a grand jury, and that it is unobjec-

tionable that "grand jury secrecy requires the judge to rely largely on the prosecutor's representations about the scope of the investigation and the materiality of the witness's testimony."[19]

Nearly all states have enacted provisions dealing with the pretrial confinement of material witnesses. Typically these statutes provide that a prospective witness in a case involving a felony or major crime can be brought before a judge on application of counsel, generally the prosecutor. The magistrate determines the importance of the witness to the case and gives the witness the option of posting some form of bail or recognizance, either personal or with sureties. If the witness must post bail but refuses or fails to do so, he can be confined until he has given his testimony or the case is dismissed. Several states authorize the taking of depositions for preserving testimony so that the witness may be released when the deposition is obtained. Some jurisdictions have adopted alternatives to incarceration, such as placing the witness in the custody of a designated person or organization, placing restrictions on his travel, association, or place of abode during the period of release, or requiring the witness to return to custody after daylight hours, or requiring the execution of an appearance bond.

§ 12.5   Alternatives to Arrest

(a) Summons in Lieu of Arrest Warrant. Another avenue of reform in the efforts to prevent unnecessary pretrial detention, especially in minor cases, is invocation of the criminal process against a person without even taking custody in the first place. One way in which this may be done is by a judicial officer issuing a summons instead of an arrest warrant, as is now authorized by the law in most jurisdictions. There is considerable variation in these laws. A few permit the magistrate to issue a summons instead of an arrest warrant only if the prosecutor so requests, while many others merely indicate that the magistrate has

---

17.   421 F.2d 337 (1st Cir.1970).

18.   18 U.S.C.A. § 3144.

19.   United States v. Awadallah, 349 F.3d 42 (2d Cir. 2003).

the option of utilizing either a warrant or a summons without in any way indicating that the latter alternative is to be preferred. Still others appear to tilt in favor of the warrant alternative by indicating that a summons may or shall be utilized only upon the finding of some specified justification. In contrast to all of these provisions are those statutes and rules of court that manifest a preference for the summons alternative, usually by asserting that a summons "shall" be utilized (at least as to lesser offenses) unless there exists a basis for concluding that one of various adverse consequences would thereby result.

It is fair to say that those provisions not falling into the very last category have had little impact in decreasing the number of arrests. For one thing, arrest warrants are seldom required and are seldom sought, so that the occasion for choosing between a warrant and summons rarely arises. For another, it is generally the practice (even when not required) for the magistrate to rely upon the prosecutor or police officer to ask for a summons, and such requests are seldom made. Moreover, it is unlikely that information relevant to a judicial determination of the likelihood of the person's appearance in response to a summons will be tendered to the court. This suggests that summons statutes and rules should be drafted so as to make it clear that the magistrate is responsible for making an intelligent choice between the two modes of proceeding, and that in minor cases the summons is presumed to be the preferred alternative.

(b) Citation in Lieu of Arrest Without Warrant. Despite the success of the long-standing practice of having the police issue citations for all but the most serious traffic violations, for years there was very little movement to extend these procedures to more ordinary criminal cases. As of 1960 only four states had adopted police citation statutes that extended beyond traffic offense cases, though more recently the number has increased dra-

matically. Many of the relevant statutes and rules of court do not require the police to utilize the citation alternative in any particular circumstances. A great many of them do nothing more than declare that the officer is allowed either to arrest or to issue a citation for certain offenses, without any suggestion that citation is the preferred alternative. Some other provisions make issuance of a citation the disfavored alternative by setting out certain circumstances that must exist before the officer may give a citation instead of or just after making an arrest. By comparison, certain other grants of authority to utilize the citation alternative seem to encourage that alternative somewhat more by instead reciting those circumstances which, if established, would bar the citation alternative or mandate the arrest alternative. But all of the foregoing must be distinguished from the final category, that in which the statute or court rule expressly and unequivocally declares that the citation alternative "shall" be used unless certain circumstances (e.g., inability of the person to provide satisfactory identification) are present.

Because this last variety of provision is bound to have a much more profound impact in terms of ensuring that police more frequently utilize the citation alternative, the proposal has been made that what is needed in all jurisdictions is mandatory resort to the noncustody alternative in lesser cases absent unusual circumstances. The Supreme Court has declined to impose such a requirement as a matter of Fourth Amendment reasonableness,[1] and in doing so has opined that the common system in which the officer has the power to opt for "the discretionary leniency" of a citation in lieu of custodial arrest is adequate because "it is in the interest of the police to limit petty-offense arrest."

However, the situation is complicated by the fact that a warrantless arrest may and often does provide an opportunity for the officer to make a lawful search of the defendant and the

---

§ 12.5

1. Atwater v. City of Lago Vista, 532 U.S. 318, 121 S.Ct. 1536, 149 L.Ed.2d 549 (2001), discussed further in § 3.5(a).

surrounding area. In *United States v. Robinson*,[2] the Supreme Court held that a search of the person could be conducted incident to "a lawful custodial arrest," and in *New York v. Belton*[3] the Court held that the passenger compartment of an automobile may be searched incident to the "lawful custodial arrest" of an occupant. Thus, here as well it would seem that unless the right to search is somehow disentangled from the right to arrest, the need (or, in some cases, just the opportunity) to conduct a search will discourage resort to the citation alternative. A few jurisdictions have attempted to address this problem with a statutory declaration to the effect that the officer's election of the arrest-release on citation sequence does not adversely affect his authority to search.

But, as is made clear by *Knowles v. Iowa*,[4] such statutory provisions would, at best, appear to provide a basis for a search in relatively few circumstances. In *Knowles*, an officer stopped Knowles for speeding and then, pursuant to a statute authorizing but not requiring him to issue a citation in lieu of arrest for most bailable offenses, issued a citation. The officer then made a full search of Knowles' car and found a bag of marijuana. That search was upheld by the state courts on the ground that because a state statute declared that issuance of a citation in lieu of arrest "does not affect the officer's authority to conduct an otherwise lawful search," it sufficed that the officer had probable cause to make a custodial arrest. A unanimous Supreme Court reversed on the ground that the two search-incident-arrest rationales discussed in *Robinson* did not justify the search in the instant case. The "threat to officers safety from issuing a traffic citation * * * is a good deal less than in the case of a custodial arrest," where (as it was put in *Robinson*) there is "the extended exposure which follows the taking of a suspect into custody and transporting him to the police station."

And thus the "concern for officer safety" incident to a traffic stop is sufficiently met by the officer's authority under existing decisions of the Court: he could order the driver and passengers out of the car,[5] "perform a 'patdown' of a driver and any passengers upon a reasonable suspicion they may be armed and dangerous,"[6] and conduct a patdown "of the passenger compartment of a vehicle upon reasonable suspicion that an occupant is dangerous and may gain immediate control of a weapon."[7] As for the "need to discover and preserve evidence," the Court continued, there was no such need in the instant case, as "no further evidence of excessive speed was going to be found on the person of the offender or in the passenger compartment of the car."

The statute in *Knowles*, of course, was different than those alluded to previously, as the *Knowles* legislation addressed a citation-*instead-of*-arrest situation rather than an citation-*following*-arrest situation. But the rationale of *Knowles* would seem applicable in either instance, that is, in any case where a custodial arrest is lacking. This being the case, it is especially important to note that the Court in *Knowles* only passed on "the search at issue" and did not invalidate the statute the state courts had relied upon; indeed, the Court emphasized that Knowles "did not argue * * * that the statute could never be lawfully applied." As for when such a statute *might* be lawfully applied, the only possibility would seem to be the case in which the offense was one for which there *could* be evidence on the offender's person or in his vehicle. The issue there, it would seem, is whether, in the interest of not discouraging resort to the citation alternative in such cases, officers opting for the citation alternative should be given the same opportunity to discover evidence they would have by electing the more severe alternative of custodial arrest, or whether instead searches contempora-

---

2. 414 U.S. 218, 94 S.Ct. 467, 38 L.Ed.2d 427 (1973).

3. 453 U.S. 454, 101 S.Ct. 2860, 69 L.Ed.2d 768 (1981).

4. 525 U.S. 113, 119 S.Ct. 484, 142 L.Ed.2d 492 (1998).

5. As authorized in Maryland v. Wilson, 519 U.S. 408, 117 S.Ct. 882, 137 L.Ed.2d 41 (1997) (passengers); Penn-

sylvania v. Mimms, 434 U.S. 106, 98 S.Ct. 330, 54 L.Ed.2d 331 (1977) (driver). See §§ 3.5(b), 3.8(e).

6. As authorized by Terry v. Ohio, 392 U.S. 1, 88 S.Ct. 1868, 20 L.Ed.2d 889 (1968). See § 3.8

7. As authorized by Michigan v. Long, 463 U.S. 1032, 103 S.Ct. 3469, 77 L.Ed.2d 1201 (1983). See § 3.8(e).

neous with use of the citation alternative should be permitted only on probable cause of finding such evidence, which will often but not inevitably be present in this kind of case.

The impact of *Knowles* upon future use of the citation alternative is less than clear. Because Iowa officers apparently have full discretion to opt for either citation or custodial arrest, it might be thought that they would now shift to the latter so as not to lose the search opportunities they had been afforded by the statute. But this seems unlikely; the political costs of making custodial arrest the usual choice for traffic offenses would be great, as would the cost in terms of police manpower. Somewhat more likely is that the citation alternative will usually be used but that police will opt for custodial arrest on occasion when, perhaps only because of a "hunch," they want an excuse to search, for under *Whren v. United States*[8] the existence of probable cause for arrest makes any arbitrary selection of violators to be arrested immune from Fourth Amendment challenge. Yet another possibility is that police will attempt to circumvent *Knowles* by making searches as before but without first manifesting any decision as to citation versus arrest and then follow productive searches with custodial arrests, so that the search can be rationalized under the *Rawlings v. Kentucky*[9] principle that a search "incident" to arrest may come before the formal making of an arrest if the grounds for arrest existed at the time the search was made.

8. 517 U.S. 806, 116 S.Ct. 1769, 135 L.Ed.2d 89 (1996).

9. 448 U.S. 98, 100 S.Ct. 2556, 65 L.Ed.2d 633 (1980).

Chapter 13

THE DECISION WHETHER TO PROSECUTE

Table of Sections

§ 13.1 Nature of the Decision

(a) In General. The charging decision, involving a determination of whether a person should be formally accused of a crime and thus subjected to trial if he does not first plead guilty, is a vitally important stage in the criminal process with serious implications for the individual involved. A decision to charge will result in the defendant's loss of freedom pending and during trial or at best release only upon financial or other conditions, and will confront him with the economic and social costs of a trial. Whatever the outcome at trial, the charge itself can be and often is damaging to reputation and imposes upon the defendant the considerable expense of preparing a defense. Charging decisions, viewed collectively, are also of obvious importance to the community. Among other things, the manner in which these decisions are made permits adjustment of the criminal justice process to local conditions. In this way, it is possible to take account of the marked variations in the crime problem and in the community resources available to combat it that often exist from area to area.

Although the charging decision is not inevitably so complex, it frequently involves several of the following potentially difficult determinations: (1) whether there is sufficient evidence to support a prosecution; (2) if so, whether there are nonetheless reasons for not subjecting the defendant to the criminal process; (3) if so, whether nonprosecution should be conditioned upon the defendant's participation in a diversion program; and (4) if prosecution is to be undertaken, with what offense or offenses the defendant should be charged.

In minor cases, most notably those involving lesser traffic offenses, this decision is commonly made exclusively by police. The "ticket" given the violator serves as the charge, and the case goes directly to court for trial or plea without prosecutorial review. In other cases, however, it is usually the prosecutor who plays the central role, although this is not inevitably so. Even when the prosecutor does play the central role, other actors may play a significant part. The police, for example, nonetheless exercise considerable influence in both a negative and positive sense. The overwhelming majority of cases that reach the prosecutor are brought to his attention by police after they have made an arrest, a decision as to which they exercise vast and largely uncontrolled discretion. Thus, if in a particular instance an officer decides not to arrest, doubting whether the evidence is sufficient or whether any good purpose would be served by invoking the criminal process, he has in effect virtually assured that there will be no prosecution. As for positive influence, police sometimes accomplish this by an especially solid presentation of their evidence or by articulation of some law enforcement interest that presumably would be served by prosecution.

Another actor who may play an important part is the victim. In many locales certain crimes such as nonsupport and the passing of bad checks are unlikely to come to official attention unless reported directly to the prosecutor's office by a concerned citizen. Here again, a decision not to bring the matter before the prosecutor virtually assures no charge. As for positive influence, in these kinds of cases (and, to a lesser extent, in cases first handled by the police) the complainant may prompt a charge by expressing strong interest in, or promising full cooperation in, the prosecution. The traditional view is that the victim is not—and should not be—entitled to participate formally in the charging process. But one outgrowth of the recent victims' rights movement has been the suggestion that the victim should have a formal, albeit limited, role.

It has been asserted that the defendant should also have some opportunity for input into the charging decision, and that defense counsel has an important role to play at this stage. But except where the concept of a screening conference has been adopted, such participation in the charging decision does not ordinarily occur on a regular basis.

In most jurisdictions there are institutional checks upon the prosecutor's charging power in serious cases, so that he exercises this power affirmatively only with the concurrence of another agency. In the federal system as a Fifth Amendment requirement and in about a third of the states as a matter of state law, a felony charge must be approved by a grand jury unless the defendant has waived that right. And unless the grand jury has first acted, most jurisdictions require that a felony charge be approved by a judicial officer at a preliminary hearing, again unless the defendant has waived that protection.

(b) Evidence Sufficiency. It is not possible to state categorically how much evidence is required before the prosecutor is justified in charging a suspect with a crime, as the law does not expressly provide a distinct probability of guilt standard for the charging decision. Although the prosecutor's decision to charge is often reflected in the post-arrest issuance of an arrest warrant, and though it is clear that such a warrant may issue only upon "probable cause," that phrase has been interpreted by courts only in cases where the warrant was challenged as a basis for arrest rather than as a basis for the decision to charge. An arrest, the Supreme Court declared in *Brinegar v. United States*,[1] may be based upon "the factual and practical considerations of everyday life on which reasonable and prudent men, not legal technicians, act." But it does not necessarily follow that charging would be proper on the same quantum of evidence, if for no other reason than that the prosecutor, as a legal technician, will have to consider whether his decision to charge will withstand review at the preliminary hearing and before the grand jury.

As a practical matter, the prosecutor is likely to require admissible evidence showing a high probability of guilt, that is, sufficient evidence to justify confidence in obtaining a conviction. This, however, may vary from case to case, based upon the prosecutor's experience with juries in that locale. For example, one former federal prosecutor has reported that in his office it was the practice to require a higher quantum of proof in receipt of stolen goods cases, where the prosecution witnesses were usually admitted thieves and the defendant would usually come from the middle class and not have a prior criminal record, than in narcotics cases, where jury acquittals were rare and defendants were usually persons of lower class. Even in the latter category of cases, however, it was the practice to insist upon a high quantum of evidence in order to continue the 100% conviction record for these offenses and thereby induce pleas of guilty.

(c) Screening Out Cases. Even when it is clear there exists evidence that is more than sufficient to show guilt beyond a reasonable doubt, the prosecutor might nonetheless decide not to charge a particular individual with a criminal offense. Such discretionary enforcement of the criminal law has traditionally been an important part of the American prosecutor's function. Whether this exercise of discretion at the charging stage is a vice or a virtue is a matter on which there is not complete agreement. It does seem fair to say, however, that something less than full enforcement of the law by the prosecutor is an absolute necessity. As one judge once noted, if every prosecutor "performed his * * * responsibility in strict accordance with rules of law, precisely and narrowly laid down, the criminal law would be ordered but intolerable."[2] But this is not to suggest that there does not reside in the prosecutorial screening function considerable potential for abuse. The danger, of course, is that the screening process is so informal and invisible and so lacking in adequate information and policy guidance or rules that it may neither operate fairly upon those individuals subjected to the process nor accurately identify those who should be prosecuted.

§ 13.1
1. 338 U.S. 160, 69 S.Ct. 1302, 93 L.Ed. 1879 (1949).

2. Breitel, Controls in Criminal Law Enforcement, 27 U.Chi.L.Rev. 427 (1960).

(d) Diversion. The choices for the prosecutor when making the charging decision are not merely those of prosecution or no action at all. An intermediate course, commonly referred to as deferred prosecution or pretrial diversion, may be available. Diversion is the disposition of a criminal complaint without a conviction, the noncriminal disposition being conditioned on either the performance of specified obligations by the defendant, or his participation in counselling or treatment. Typically, the effect of diversion is to stop the clock on criminal prosecution while the defendant is offered counselling, career development, education and supportive treatment services. If he participates and responds as required for a specified period of time, then the charges are dismissed without trial. But if the defendant does not meet his obligations then he may be subjected to prosecution on the deferred charge.

The extent to which diversion exists as a meaningful alternative depends upon a number of factors. In many communities the resources for dealing with offenders and their problems are totally inadequate, and even if these resources exist, there may be little liaison between the prosecutor and community agencies that could assist an offender. Even with sufficient liaison, there may be pressures to divert only defendants who will represent the lowest risk to the community, in which case that diversion will bring many people into the criminal process who either would not have been processed at all or would have been screened out at an early stage.

(e) Selection of the Charge. If the prosecutor has decided upon prosecution, there often remains the question of what the charge should be. Sometimes it is simply a matter of whether the charge should be of a greater or lesser crime—for example, felony burglary versus misdemeanor breaking and entering. This involves judgments about both evidence sufficiency (whether the greater crime can be proved at trial) and enforcement policy (whether prosecution for the greater crime

would be unduly harmful to this defendant). However, sometimes the prosecutor will initially charge a defendant with a higher offense than can be proved or than would be "just," hoping to use that charge as leverage to obtain a guilty plea to a lesser crime.

Sometimes the defendant's conduct will appear to violate more than one criminal statute, in which case the prosecutor will need to decide whether the defendant is to be charged with more than one offense. This occurs (1) when it appears the defendant has committed a series of acts, such as a number of burglaries, over a period of time; or (2) when it appears the defendant violated more than one statute during a single course of conduct, as where a burglary is followed by theft of property. Resort to multiple charges is most common when undertaken to encourage a plea of guilty to one of the crimes or when deemed necessary to provide the judge with a sufficient range of sentencing options.

§ 13.2 Discretionary Enforcement

(a) The Prosecutor's Discretion. The notion that the prosecuting attorney is vested with a broad range of discretion in deciding when to prosecute and when not to is firmly entrenched in American law. Prosecutors in this country have long exercised this discretionary authority, but it would be in error to assume that discretionary enforcement by prosecutors is essentially the same in all locales. The extent of and reasons for nonenforcement vary considerably from place to place, often because of factors over which the individual prosecutor has no control. It is nonetheless possible to identify the most common explanations:

(1) Because of legislative "overcriminalization." As one commentator has said, "The criminal code of any jurisdiction tends to make a crime of everything that people are against, without regard to enforceability, changing social concepts, etc. The result is that the criminal code becomes society's trash bin."[1] Exami-

§ 13.2

1. Statement by a representative of the FBI, quoted in President's Comm'n on Law Enforcement and Administration of Justice, Task Force Report: The Courts 107 (1967).

nation of the typical state code of criminal law supports this judgment. Included therein are likely to be crimes that are over-defined for administrative convenience (e.g., the gambling statute that bars *all* forms of gambling so as "to confront the professional gambler with a statutory facade that is wholly devoid of loopholes"[2]); crimes that merely constitute "state-declared ideals"[3] (e.g., the crime of adultery, which is "unenforced because we want to continue our conduct, and unrepealed because we want to preserve our morals"[4]); and now-outdated crimes that found their way into the law because of the mood that dominated a tribunal or a legislature at strategic moments in the past, a flurry of public excitement on some single matter.

(2) Because of limitations in available enforcement resources. No prosecutor has sufficient resources available to prosecute all of the offenses that come to his attention. To deny the authority to exercise discretion under these circumstances, it is said, is "like directing a general to attack the enemy on all fronts at once."[5] Thus, so the argument goes, the prosecutor must remain free to exercise his judgment in determining what prosecutions will best serve the public interest.

(3) Because of a need to individualize justice. A criminal code can only deal in general categories of conduct. "No lawmaker has been able to foresee more than the broad outlines of the clash of interests or more than the main lines of the courses of conduct to which the law even of his own time must be applied. Moreover, a legal system that seeks to cover everything by a special provision becomes cumbrous and unworkable."[6] Individualized treatment of offenders, based upon the circumstances of the particular case, has long been recognized in sentencing, and it is argued that such individualized treatment is equally appropriate at the charging stage so as to relieve deserving defendants of even the stigma of prosecution.

Decisions not to prosecute, when not motivated by doubts as to the sufficiency of the evidence, usually fall within one of these three broad categories. A closer look at the practice makes it possible to particularize further those situations in which prosecutors most commonly decline to prosecute. They are:

(i) When the victim has expressed a desire that the offender not be prosecuted. Particularly in assault cases involving a dispute between spouses or prior acquaintances, the victim's disinterest in prosecution is often determinative. The assumption apparently is that uncoerced forgiveness reflects a lack of importance attached to the incident by the victim (and, perhaps, by the aggressor), so that nonprosecution is not contrary to the statutory policy of discouraging the settlement of disputes by force.

(ii) When the costs of prosecution would be excessive, considering the nature of the violation. Most significant here are those cases that would involve unusual costs, as where the offender is now known to be in a distant state and could be extradited and returned only at considerable expense. Prosecution of certain offenders who would be prosecuted if they were in custody within the jurisdiction (e.g., professional bad check passers), is abandoned under these circumstances.

(iii) When the mere fact of prosecution would, in the prosecutor's judgment, cause undue harm to the offender. For example, when it was learned that a married woman had filed a false report of rape with the police and that she had done so to conceal her indiscretion from her husband, it was decided that prosecution for filing a false crime report would be unwise because it would jeopardize her marriage.

(iv) When the offender, if not prosecuted, will likely aid in achieving other enforcement goals. Nonprosecution is used as an inducement to make informants out of offenders, and also as an inducement for present informers to take on additional duties. This occurs most

---

2. 2 A.B.A. Comm'n on Organized Crime, Organized Crime and Law Enforcement 75 (1952).

3. R. Pound, Criminal Justice in America 67 (1930).

4. T. Arnold, The Symbols of Government 160 (1935).

5. Id. at 153.

6. R. Pound, supra note 3, at 40–41.

frequently when the individual is in a position to aid in vice enforcement, particularly against the sale of narcotics.

(v) When the "harm" done by the offender can be corrected without prosecution. The best example is the frequent decision not to prosecute persons who have committed minor property crimes, such as writing bad checks, if full restitution to the victim is made.

A full appreciation of the extent of the prosecutor's power, however, requires consideration of the fact that his discretion may be exercised in the other direction. A particular individual may be selected out for prosecution notwithstanding the fact that the case is one which ordinarily would not result in an affirmative charging decision. Such selection may occur in response to press and public pressure for "law and order," to rid society of certain "bad actors" who are thought to have committed more serious crimes, and for similar reasons.

(b) Police Discretion. Although the principal concern here is with the exercise of discretion by the prosecutor, note must also be taken of discretionary enforcement by the police, for it is clear beyond question that discretion is regularly exercised by the police in deciding when to arrest and that such decisions have a profound effect upon prosecution policy. This is so for the simple reason that for the most part the police determine what cases come to the attention of the prosecutor.

As a general matter, it may be said that the exercise of discretion by the police at the arrest stage occurs for much the same reasons as the charging discretion of the prosecutor described above. This police discretion is in a practical sense even less restricted than the prosecutor's discretion, for it is exercised at an earlier and generally less visible stage of the criminal process. But in the eyes of the law, discretion by the prosecutor is considered proper while discretion by the police is with rare exception viewed with disfavor. Arrest statutes are commonly drafted in mandatory terms, and on the infrequent occasions when courts are called upon to speak to the question they typically assert that the police lack authority not to invoke the criminal process when the evidence is sufficient to arrest.

One reason for police nonenforcement, as with prosecutor nonenforcement, is legislative "overcriminalization." A second is because of limitations in available enforcement resources, while a third reason involves the judgment that even arrest would be unduly harmful to the offender. There is every reason to believe that police discretion is absolutely essential and cannot be eliminated. That conclusion, however, is entirely consistent with two other essential propositions—that excessive or unnecessary discretion can and should be eliminated, and that necessary discretion should be properly controlled.

(c) Jury and Judge Discretion. The prosecutor does not function in a vacuum, and thus a decision not to prosecute is often based upon the expectation that the judge or jury would refuse to convict notwithstanding proof of guilt beyond a reasonable doubt. A full understanding of the prosecutor's discretion, therefore, necessitates an awareness of the discretion that may be exercised at the trial stage by a jury, and at a pretrial or trial stage by the judge.

The jury in a criminal case has uncontrolled discretion to acquit the guilty. An empirical study has shown that juries acquit the guilty because: (1) they sympathize with the defendant as a person; (2) they apply personal attitudes as to when self-defense should be recognized; (3) they take into account the contributory fault of the victim; (4) they believe the offense is de minimis; (5) they take into account the fact that the statute violated is an unpopular law; (6) they feel the defendant has already been punished enough; (7) they feel the defendant was subjected to improper police or prosecution practices; (8) they refuse to apply strict liability statutes to inadvertent conduct; (9) they apply their own standards as to when mental illness or intoxication should be a defense; and (10) they believe the offense is accepted conduct in the subculture of the defendant and victim.

Because there is not agreement on whether such discretionary action by a jury is a desirable safety valve in the criminal justice system or an unavoidable evil, it is a debatable point whether it is proper for the trial judge to act in a similar fashion when a case is tried before him without a jury. The law generally seems to take the view that it is not the business of a judge trying a case without a jury to act "like" the jury could be expected to act. Yet judges acquit guilty defendants for the same reasons as juries.

That situation must be distinguished from one in which the judge attempts to foreclose conviction on policy rather than evidentiary or legal grounds without the defendant even standing trial. The prevailing view is that the judge does not have authority either to dismiss charges or to reduce charges merely because the prosecutor, had he been so disposed, could have dealt with the case in such a fashion at the time of charging. However, about a dozen states have statutes or court rules that authorize a trial judge to dismiss criminal charges sua sponte in furtherance of justice. While some states have construed such a provision to mean that the court may dismiss a prosecution only upon a showing of arbitrary action or government misconduct, elsewhere the trial court's authority has not been so limited but yet has withstood challenge under the separation-of-powers doctrine. Those provisions must be distinguished from those found in five states authorizing the court to dismiss a prosecution when it is of a de minimis infraction.

(d) The "Problem" of Discretion. It is tempting to view discretionary enforcement in general and charging discretion by the prosecutor in particular as practices that need not be a matter of concern. After all, what harm can there be in the benign act of not invoking the criminal process against one who has violated an obsolete or overbroad law, one whose conduct is not serious enough to warrant the expenditure of scarce enforcement resources, or one who has committed a crime under strongly mitigating circumstances? But this vast and largely uncontrolled discretion cannot be dismissed on the notion that only acts of leniency are involved. Absent procedures that

ensure that the "right" decisions are being reached regarding who should receive leniency and when, society at large and also the individuals dealt with by the criminal justice system are jeopardized.

As for society at large, the fundamental point is that what is characterized as the bestowal of leniency can sometimes work contrary to the public interest in effective law enforcement. As for the individuals involved, the basic point is that the discretionary power to be lenient is an impossibility without a concomitant discretionary power not to be lenient, so that the power to be lenient is the power to discriminate. If provable cases against A, B, C, and D cross the prosecutor's desk and he elects not to prosecute D, it cannot be said that the rationality of that decision is of no moment because A, B, and C are guilty and thus deserving of conviction. Rather, if we strive for equal justice it is important that this discretion have been exercised reasonably, so that D has escaped prosecution for a legitimate reason not also applicable to A, B, or C. Sometimes the process is viewed more in terms of a selection of those who *will* be prosecuted. It is said, for example, that the substantive criminal law amounts to "an arsenal of weapons to be used against such persons as the police or prosecutor may deem to be a menace to public safety."[7] From this perspective, the potential for arbitrary and discriminatory enforcement stands out more starkly.

While it is thus fair to say that discretionary enforcement in the charging process is a significant problem in current criminal justice administration, clearly the answer does not lie in depriving the prosecutor of any discretion whatsoever. Full enforcement is neither possible nor tolerable; discretion is necessary in criminal justice administration because of the immense variety of factual situations faced at each stage of the system and the complex interrelationship of the goals sought. The issue is not discretion versus no discretion, but rather how discretion should be confined, structured, and checked.

7. Arnold, Law Enforcement—An Attempt at Social Dissection, 42 Yale L.J. 1, 17 (1932).

(e) Confining the Prosecutor's Discretion. Because a major source of excess prosecutorial power is the loose drafting and overly casual definition of conduct as criminal that characterize the nation's penal codes, adequate reform of the substantive criminal law would eliminate many cases now screened out only at the option of the prosecutor. Clearly, some significant portion of the prosecutor's discretion could be rendered unnecessary if obsolete or largely unenforceable statutes were repealed. In addition, some statutes could be more narrowly drawn, again eliminating certain cases that are now screened out only at the will of the prosecuting attorney, and some statutes could be subdivided so as to reflect degrees of severity, thus providing a clear basis upon which the prosecutor could determine whether a greater or lesser charge is called for.

But there are limits on what can be achieved in this way, and thus no one would seriously contend that the prosecutor's discretion could be entirely eliminated by penal law reform. Framing statutes that identify and prescribe for every nuance of human behavior is impossible, and even to the extent that the numerous operative factors *could* be expressed in a substantive criminal statute, there may be reasons for not doing so. There is a need to confront those at whom the law is aimed "with a statutory facade that is wholly devoid of loopholes,"[8] and in any event a need to avoid unduly complicating criminal statutes.

(f) Structuring the Prosecutor's Discretion. Three basic needs must be met before the prosecutor's charging discretion can become more structured and thus more rational. They are:

(i) The need for more information. More detailed background information about the offender is needed so that it may be determined whether he is a dangerous or only marginal offender. (In the absence of any information, or only the limited information provided by a brief police report, the temptation is great to resort to rule-of-thumb policies based only upon the nature of the crime.) In addition, most prosecutors lack sufficient information about alternative treatment facilities and programs in the community to be able to make a rational determination of whether there exists some better course than prosecution.

(ii) The need for established standards. What is needed is for each prosecutor's office to develop a statement of general policies to guide the exercise of prosecutorial discretion, particularizing such matters as the circumstances that properly can be considered mitigating or aggravating, or the kinds of offenses that should be most vigorously prosecuted in view of the community's law enforcement needs. Such rulemaking can aid in the training of new assistant prosecutors and in the internal review of all prosecution decisions, so that office policy is consistently and efficiently carried out. Such an administrative law approach, to be helpful, requires standards that are fairly specific, though certainly the exactitude to be expected in a criminal statute would be neither necessary nor always possible in this rulemaking context. Some prosecutors' offices have undertaken the drafting of such rules and have found it feasible to express enforcement policy in these ways.

Whether these standards should generally be available to the public presents a most difficult issue. On the one hand, it is said they should be because defendants and complainants and the public at large are entitled to know and be able to question such rules and whether they have been complied with. However, reasons have sometimes been advanced for not making them available to the public, including the following: (1) that publication will reduce the legitimate moralizing and deterrent effects of the criminal law; (2) that publication will inevitably result in more frequent attempts to invoke judicial review of prosecution policy and decisions, thereby further clogging an already overburdened court system; (3) that if prosecutors knew their policy would be published, they would be reluctant to formulate it; and (4) that if potential defendants in minor cases knew in advance they would not be prosecuted they would not cooperate with law enforcement agents in the in-

---

8. 2 ABA Comm'n on Organized Crime, Organized Crime and Law Enforcement 74 (1952).

vestigation and prosecution of more serious offenders.

(iii) The need for established procedures. These procedures might include a "precharge conference" at which the prosecutor and defense counsel could discuss the appropriateness of a noncriminal disposition. Such a practice would make it less likely that favored defense counsel or clients will have the sole opportunity to discuss their cases with the prosecutor and receive the benefits of such exchanges, and would also provide a natural occasion for an exchange of information that might be useful to each side in deciding whether to agree on a disposition. In addition, it might be well if a decision not to prosecute was supported by a written statement of the underlying reasons. Such a procedure has been found to facilitate internal review and to produce fairly consistent results.

(g) Checking the Prosecutor's Discretion. Although the American criminal justice system has reasonably effective controls to ensure that the prosecutor does not abuse his power by prosecuting upon less than sufficient evidence, there are—as a practical matter—no comparable checks upon his discretionary judgment of whether or not to prosecute one against whom sufficient evidence exists. The prosecution function has traditionally been decentralized, so that state attorneys-general exercise no effective control over local prosecutors. Actions such as impeachment and quo warranto have only served to reach extreme cases of continued and flagrant abuse. If a specific instance of nonenforcement is challenged in the courts by way of mandamus action, the usual response is that the matter rests with the executive rather than the judicial branch of government. This is also the typical reaction if a specific instance of enforcement is challenged as being grounded in an "improper motive." Or, if a specific instance of enforcement is called into question

as an arbitrary deviation from a general pattern of nonenforcement, the complaining prospective defendant can seldom overcome the several hurdles to establishing his denial-of-equal-protection claim. And while the local prosecutor is in theory responsible to the electorate, the public can hardly assess prosecution policies that are kept secret.

While it may be apparent that this is an unfortunate state of affairs, it is not so apparent how the situation might be best remedied. Some have suggested close administrative review, modeled after what is said to be the practice in Germany. But such administrative review would require a hierarchial arrangement quite different from the present structure of most state governments. Whether such a significant change in structure would be an improvement is not readily apparent. Moreover, some have questioned the conclusion that the German experience shows such administrative controls work.

Another possibility is judicial review of the prosecutor's discretionary enforcement decisions. One proposal is that decisions by a prosecutor not to prosecute be subjected to regular review by a judicial officer, who would determine whether the prosecutor's decision conformed to his pre-existing written standards. In support of such judicial screening, it is argued that it would ensure uniformity of treatment and would enhance the various benefits to be derived from giving the prosecutor's enforcement policies greater publicity. Others have suggested that judges would be unable to review prosecution policies because of the practical difficulties of evaluating the allocation of scarce prosecution resources, and would be unable to achieve meaningful review of prosecution decisions because the court would be unable to go behind the record to determine that there was an insufficient factual basis for the reasons the prosecutor has provided. The Supreme Court has expressed the latter view.[9]

---

9. In Wayte v. United States, 470 U.S. 598, 105 S.Ct. 1524, 84 L.Ed.2d 547 (1985), the Court asserted "that the decision to prosecute is particularly ill-suited to judicial review. Such factors as the strength of the case, the prosecution's general deterrence value, the Government's enforcement priorities, and the case's relationship to the

Government's overall enforcement plan are not readily susceptible to the kind of analysis the courts are competent to undertake. Judicial supervision in this area, moreover, entails systematic costs of particular concern. Examining the basis of a prosecution delays the criminal proceeding, threatens to chill law enforcement by subject-

A more limited form of judicial review would focus upon the prosecutor's decisions *in favor of* prosecution by permitting defendants in a pretrial setting to question whether their selection squares with existing prosecution policies. The policies themselves would be subjected only to limited scrutiny to see if they drew arbitrary or capricious distinctions or were too vague to enable review of specific cases, and the decision in the particular case would be examined to see if it amounted to a significant deviation from these policies for which the prosecutor is unable to give a permissible reason. Quite obviously, meaningful review even in this context would be possible only if the reforms discussed earlier, written prosecution policies and written reasons for prosecution decisions, were first adopted. Finally, it is well to note that the written policies and written decisions reforms, if those documents are given publicity, might be said to provide another kind of check upon the prosecutor in the sense of making political accountability a reality.

(h) Mandating the Prosecutor's Discretion. Given the well established principle that a prosecutor possesses vast discretion in the enforcement of the criminal law, does it follow that he is obligated to exercise it? At least one court has answered in the affirmative. In *State v. Pettitt*,[10] the defendant, after his conviction for taking a motor vehicle without permission, was charged under the habitual criminal statute pursuant to the prosecutor's "mandatory policy of filing habitual criminal complaints against all defendants with three or more prior felonies." The defendant, who had prior convictions for taking a motor vehicle without permission, second degree burglary, and unauthorized use of a vehicle, argued that "a policy which prevents the prosecutor from considering mitigating factors is a failure to exercise discretion, which may, as in this case, result in an unfair and arbitrary result." The court agreed:

> In the present case, the prosecutor (now former prosecutor) admitted that he relied

on the record alone in deciding to file the habitual criminal information. He testified that he did not consider any mitigating circumstances in reaching his decision, and that he could imagine no situation which would provide for an exception to the mandatory policy.

> In our view, this fixed formula which requires a particular action *in every case* upon the happening of a specific series of events constitutes an abuse of the discretionary power lodged in the prosecuting attorney.

Given the draconian nature of full enforcement of habitual criminal laws, the result in *Pettitt* is an appealing one. But it does not necessarily follow that full enforcement of any particular criminal statute is inevitably an abuse of discretion. There may well be statutes that are so narrowly drawn and that encompass conduct so serious that a prosecutor would be justified in fully enforcing them.

§ 13.3 Challenges to and Checks Upon the Decision Not to Prosecute

(a) Mandamus. It sometimes happens that one or several private citizens will attempt to force a reluctant prosecutor to initiate a criminal prosecution by asking a court to issue a writ of mandamus—an order directing the prosecutor to take affirmative action with respect to a particular case. It is unlikely that this effort will succeed, as mandamus is available only to compel performance of a duty owed to the plaintiff and not to direct or influence the exercise of discretion in the making of a decision. This means, of course, that because of the longstanding acceptance of the notion that a prosecutor does have discretion in deciding when to prosecute, mandamus is deemed an inappropriate remedy in this context. The force of this principle is highlighted by the fact that it applies even when a serious question had been raised in the complaint as to the fair administration of the criminal justice system, and also when a statute declared

ing the prosecutor's motives and decisionmaking to outside inquiry, and may undermine prosecutorial effectiveness by revealing the Government's enforcement policy. All these are substantial concerns that make the courts

properly hesitant to examine the decision whether to prosecute."

10. 93 Wash.2d 288, 609 P.2d 1364 (1980).

that prosecutors are "required * * * to institute prosecutions against all persons" violating the criminal statutes in question.

Other reasons commonly given for this result are that it is compelled by the separation of powers doctrine, that is, the notion that courts are not to interfere with exercise of discretion by the executive branch of government, and that judicial review of prosecutorial action is simply impractical. But some commentators have criticized this "hands off" approach and the reasons given for it. Most vulnerable is the separation of powers argument, for many Supreme Court decisions state that it is the function of the judiciary to review the exercise of executive discretion. As for the practical problems, they might be largely overcome if prosecutors moved to a system of written prosecution guidelines and written reasons for nonprosecution decisions.

(b) Private Prosecution; Qui Tam Actions. It has sometimes been argued that private prosecution is desirable and ought to be recognized by more jurisdictions. But the generally accepted view is that the prosecution function should be performed by a public prosecutor because prosecution by a private party without authorization or approval of the prosecutor presents a serious danger of the vindictive use of the criminal law process. Thus, even in the face of apparent authority in the law permitting private prosecution, it has been refused on the ground that it is desirable to seek uniformity of prosecutorial policy. Indeed, it has often been held that private attorneys may constitutionally be involved in a criminal prosecution *only* if the prosecutor maintains substantial control over the case.

A criminal prosecution brought by a private individual must be distinguished from a *qui tam* legal action, so called because the plaintiff in this civil action states that he sues *as well* for the state as for himself. It is an action that may be brought only when specifically authorized by a statute providing a penalty for the commission or omission of a certain act and further providing that this penalty may be recovered in a civil action, with part of it to go to the person bringing such action and the remainder to the state.

Qui tam statutes were once an important part of the law enforcement scheme, but this was before the time of organized police forces and effective conventional law enforcement procedures. They have been abolished in England, and are seldom to be found in this country. The virtual demise of the *qui tam* action is certainly understandable. The legislature may well prefer to have no citizen enforcement at all rather than a complete *qui tam* enforcement scheme that is susceptible to abuse. Similarly, courts are disinclined to construe statutes providing for informer fees as allowing *qui tam* suits, reasoning that prosecutors must be immune from interference by private citizens in exercising discretion whether to prosecute.

(c) Judicial Approval of Nolle Prosequi. An initial decision not to prosecute may be reached by the prosecutor without his being required as a matter of course to explain his decision to or obtain the approval of a judicial officer. The situation may change, however, after some initial steps toward prosecution have been taken. The common law view was that a prosecutor was free to nol pros (from the Latin phrase *nolle prosequi*—an entry on the record by the prosecutor declaring that he will not prosecute) even after a formal charge was embodied in an indictment or information lodged against the defendant. Concern over this unbridled discretion in the prosecutor resulted in legislation or rules of court in many jurisdictions intended to restrain the nol pros power of the prosecutor. These provisions, at a minimum, forced the prosecutor to explain his reasons for doing so in writing, thus assuring greater visibility of the manner in which the prosecutor acted; at a maximum they required that he receive judicial approval to make his decision effective. Most jurisdictions have imposed such restraints only after formal accusation by indictment or information, but some others apply them to all cases that have passed the preliminary hearing stage. Doubtless the effect of these restrictions varies from place to place, depending upon established custom, but at least in some locales they are of little significance. A requirement of a statement of reasons may result in boilerplate "in the interests of justice" explanations, and where required judicial approval may be given perfunctorily.

Where the law requires judicial approval of a nolle prosequi, the next question is what standard the judge is to apply in passing upon the prosecutor's request. Although this question can be answered with precision only by carefully examining the applicable statute or court rule and cases in the particular jurisdiction where the issue arises, the law on the federal level is fairly representative. A United States Attorney may file a dismissal of an indictment, information or complaint only "with leave of court."[1] As the Supreme Court has noted, the "principal object" of this "requirement is apparently to protect a defendant against prosecutorial harassment, e.g., charging, dismissing and recharging, when the Government moves to dismiss an indictment over the defendant's objection."[2] But this does not mean that the court must concur whenever the defendant does not object to the proposed dismissal, for this requirement of court approval is intended to clothe the federal courts with a discretion broad enough to protect the public interest in the fair administration of criminal justice. This means that the executive branch's exercise of its discretion with respect to the termination of pending prosecutions should not be judicially disturbed unless clearly contrary to manifest public interest.

(d) Grand Jury. Most jurisdictions permit the grand jury to initiate prosecution by indictment even though the prosecutor opposes prosecution. Some require only that the foreman, acting on behalf of the grand jury, sign the indictment, while others require the prosecutor's signature but view that requirement as mandating only a "clerical act" by the prosecutor. However, it takes a most unusual case for a grand jury to act as a "runaway" and indict notwithstanding the prosecutor's opposition. It is fair to conclude, therefore, that the grand jury is not a meaningful check upon the prosecutor's decisions not to prosecute.

Especially noteworthy because of the variety of views expressed therein is *United States v. Cox*,[3] where the court reviewed a district judge's action in holding a U.S. Attorney in contempt for refusing, upon instructions from the Acting Attorney General, to prepare or sign indictments charging with perjury two blacks who had testified in a civil rights action against a voting registrar. Three members of the court concluded the U.S. Attorney was not obligated to either prepare or sign the indictments because the "role of the grand jury is restricted to a finding as to whether or not there is probable cause" and does not extend to matters of enforcement policy. Three others concluded he was required to prepare and sign the indictments, after which he could refuse to go forward "in open court and not in the secret confines of the grand jury room," at least upon "a showing of good faith, and a statement of some rational basis for dismissal." The seventh member of the court concluded the U.S. Attorney must prepare (but need not sign) the indictments so as to "reveal the difference of view as between the Grand Jury and the prosecuting attorney."

(e) Attorney General. In most jurisdictions the state Attorney General may initiate local prosecutions in at least some circumstances. This authority ranges from power concurrent with that of the local prosecutor, to power to initiate prosecution under certain circumstances, such as at the request of certain officials or in order to enforce specified statutes. In addition, most states allow the Attorney General to intervene in a local prosecution. About half the states give the Attorney General broad authority to intervene on his own initiative, while some others allow intervention only at the direction or request of another official. In theory, at least, the power of the Attorney General to initiate a local prosecution is a check upon the local prosecutor's exercise of discretion in deciding not to undertake a prosecution. In practice, however, initiation of prosecution by Attorneys General

§ 13.3

1. Fed.R.Crim.P. 48(a). This language was added to the rule by the Supreme Court without explanation.

2. Rinaldi v. United States, 434 U.S. 22, 98 S.Ct. 81, 54 L.Ed.2d 207 (1977).

3. 342 F.2d 167 (5th Cir.1965).

only rarely occurs. Moreover, the great majority of interventions come at the request of the local prosecutor, though occasionally the Attorney General will prosecute where it appears the local prosecutor has failed to act because of a conflict of interest.

(f) Removal; Special Prosecutor. Various mechanisms are available in the several states by which a local prosecutor might be removed from office. Impeachment is the most common method of removal, but some states have provided for removal by the governor, removal by a court, removal on recommendation of the Attorney General, impeachment by the legislature, or recall by the electorate. The grounds for removal vary among the states, and include such causes as "malfeasance, misfeasance, nonfeasance, or nonadministration in office," "incompetency, neglect of duty or misuse of office when such incompetency, neglect of duty or misuse of office has a material adverse effect upon the conduct of such office," and "incompetency, corruption, malfeasance or delinquency in office, or other sufficient cause." Disbarment and conviction of a serious crime are other common grounds for removal. Removal proceedings are seldom utilized, and the same may be said for criminal prosecution of a prosecutor for nonfeasance, misfeasance, or malfeasance in office. The risk of such sanctions, it is fair to say, has only a limited effect upon the making of decisions not to prosecute.

Another possibility is that a prosecutor will be replaced with respect to a particular case by a special prosecutor. Considerable authority is to be found in support of the validity of an appointment of a special prosecutor under some circumstances. The need for the services of a special prosecutor may arise because the prosecuting attorney is legally precluded from proceeding due to a conflict of interest, because he is faced with a difficult case beyond his investigative and legal abilities, or because

public confidence requires an "uninvolved" outsider to investigate and prosecute corruption within the judicial/governmental system. It does not appear that the special prosecutor mechanism constitutes a meaningful check upon the decision not to prosecute.

A federal statute requiring the Attorney General to conduct a preliminary investigation of allegations that enumerated high-ranking federal officials have committed a crime and, unless the allegations prove insubstantial, to ask a special three-judge panel to appoint an "independent counsel" to complete the investigation and conduct any prosecutions, was upheld in *Morrison v. Olson*.[4] The provision in the law restricting the Attorney General's power to remove the independent counsel to instances in which he can show "good cause" does not violate the constitutional principle of separation of powers, as the President's need to control the exercise of discretion by that counsel is not "so central to the functioning of the Executive Branch as to require as a matter of constitutional law that the counsel be terminable at will by the President." The statute was allowed to lapse, doubtless because a majority in Congress agreed with the contentions made in the dissent in *Morrison*.[5]

§ 13.4　Challenging the Decision to Prosecute: Equal Protection

(a) Discriminatory Prosecution. The Fourteenth Amendment to the United States Constitution prohibits any state from taking action that would "deny to any person within its jurisdiction the equal protection of the laws." Though there is no comparable language in the Constitution applicable to the federal government, it has been held that the Fifth Amendment due process clause imposes a similar restraint upon actions by the national government.[1] This guarantee, which of course applies with respect to the enactment of

---

4. 487 U.S. 654, 108 S.Ct. 2597, 101 L.Ed.2d 569 (1988).

5. Scalia, J., dissenting, noted that various independent counsel were collectively spending an equivalent of 10% of the Criminal Division's budget, and complained that the Act permits investigations and prosecutions even when the executive branch might conclude they are not

"worth the cost in money and in possible damage to other governmental interests."

§ 13.4

1. Bolling v. Sharpe, 347 U.S. 497, 74 S.Ct. 693, 98 L.Ed. 884 (1954).

laws by the legislative branches,[2] also extends to the conduct of the executive branches in the enforcement of these laws.[3]

Although the United States Supreme Court has never had occasion to hold that a prosecutor's charging decision was in violation of the equal protection clause, the Court has in several instances indicated that a charging decision could suffer such a defect.[4] In *Oyler v. Boles*,[5] for example, though the Court found the defendant had not established that the state habitual criminal statute had been discriminatorily enforced against him, a distinction was drawn between the permissible "conscious exercise of some selectivity in enforcement" and an impermissible selection "deliberately based upon an unjustifiable standard such as race, religion, or other arbitrary classification." In recent years, therefore, a host of federal and state courts have entertained claims of discriminatory prosecution. These claimants have seldom prevailed because of their heavy burden to overcome the presumption of legal regularity in enforcement of the penal law[6] by proving the three essential elements of a discriminatory prosecution claim: (1) that there was a "discriminatory effect," i.e., that the enforcement in question falls disproportionately on the group alleged to be the subject of the discrimination and in addition that other violators similarly situated are generally not prosecuted; (2) that there was a "discriminatory purpose," i.e., that the selection of the claimant was "intentional or purposeful"; and (3) that the selection was pursuant to an "arbitrary classification."

Although some authority is to be found that a discriminatory prosecution claim is a "defense" to be raised during the course of the trial and sent to the jury as part of the case just as with, say, a defense of self-defense, this is not a sound procedure. Because the question of discriminatory prosecution relates not to guilt or innocence but rather to an alleged constitutional defect in the institution of the prosecution, the claim should be treated as an application to the court for dismissal of the prosecution to be decided by the court. As for the remedy of injunction, although it is of limited utility because of the common restrictions that it is available only if the party suing for injunctive relief has clean hands. In any event, an attempt to obtain injunctive relief is likely to be met with the response that resolution of the matter would be premature and unnecessary because the person can raise the issue in the context of the criminal prosecution if and when it is actually brought.[7]

(b) Problems of Proof. The defendant bears the ultimate burden of proof as to all elements of a discriminatory prosecution claim. In the *Armstrong* case, discussed below, the Supreme Court declared that the defendant, to overcome the presumption of regularity, must present "clear evidence to the contrary," which has been read by lower courts as requiring application of the "clear and convincing evidence" standard. Some of the pre-*Armstrong* cases speak of the burden shifting to the government at some point, which has prompted some uncertainty as to when this ought to occur and exactly what kind of burden is then on the government.[8]

2. Skinner v. Oklahoma ex rel. Williamson, 316 U.S. 535, 62 S.Ct. 1110, 86 L.Ed. 1655 (1942).

3. Yick Wo v. Hopkins, 118 U.S. 356, 6 S.Ct. 1064, 30 L.Ed. 220 (1886).

4. United States v. Armstrong, 517 U.S. 456, 116 S.Ct. 1480, 134 L.Ed.2d 687 (1996); United States v. Batchelder, 442 U.S. 114, 99 S.Ct. 2198, 60 L.Ed.2d 755 (1979); Oyler v. Boles, 368 U.S. 448, 82 S.Ct. 501, 7 L.Ed.2d 446 (1962); Two Guys from Harrison–Allentown, Inc. v. McGinley, 366 U.S. 582, 81 S.Ct. 1135, 6 L.Ed.2d 551 (1961).

5. 368 U.S. 448, 82 S.Ct. 501, 7 L.Ed.2d 446 (1962).

6. This "presumption of regularity," which exists "in the absence of clear evidence to the contrary," is a type of "judicial deference" that "rests in part on an assessment of the relative competence of prosecutors and courts"

regarding the facts that enter into enforcement policy and "also stems from a concern not to unnecessarily impair the performance of a core executive constitutional function." United States v. Armstrong, 517 U.S. 456, 116 S.Ct. 1480, 134 L.Ed.2d 687 (1996).

7. Two Guys from Harrison–Allentown, Inc. v. McGinley, 366 U.S. 582, 81 S.Ct. 1135, 6 L.Ed.2d 551 (1961).

8. In Wayte v. United States, 470 U.S. 598, 105 S.Ct. 1524, 84 L.Ed.2d 547 (1985), the district court dismissed the indictment on the ground that the defendant had made out a prima facie case of selective prosecution entitling him to discovery of government documents and testimony of government officials, which the prosecution refused to supply. The Supreme Court decided the case without dealing with these problems of proof, much to the chagrin of the two dissenters.

One such case is *United States v. Crowthers*,[9] where the defendants were convicted of disturbing the peace by their conduct in holding several "masses for peace" in the Pentagon public concourse. It was shown that in the months immediately preceding the masses the area had been used 16 times for various religious, recreational and award assemblies, including band recitals and a speech by the Vice President. The court concluded that

> when the record strongly suggests invidious discrimination and selective application of a regulation to inhibit the expression of an unpopular viewpoint, and where it appears that the government is in ready possession of the facts, and the defendants are not, it is not unreasonable to reverse the burden of proof and to require the government to come forward with evidence as to what extent loud and unusual noise and obstruction of the concourse may have occurred on other approved occasions. It is neither novel nor unfair to require the party in possession of the facts to disclose them.

This language is especially significant when it is considered that the record also showed that the defendants had "created loud and unusual noise," for this left it quite unclear whether the defendants' conduct had been singled out from the 16 previous events on the legitimate basis that it had been noisier or on the improper basis of the defendants' opposition to government policy. Despite this defect in the defendant's showing of discriminatory prosecution, the court deemed it appropriate to call upon the government for clarification because the government had unique access to the relevant facts. Some other cases have taken this approach, though it is fair to say that *Crowthers* is not typical of how courts have treated discriminatory prosecution claims.

If the problem is that the critical facts are often in the hands of the prosecutor rather than the defendant, an alternative approach is to afford the defendant more ready access to those facts. One longstanding difficulty, of course, is that prosecution policies are not reduced to writing and made available to the public. In lieu of or in addition to that information, it would be helpful to the defendant if he could require the prosecutor to give testimony concerning the reasons underlying his inaction in other cases or his affirmative action in the instant case, but courts are understandably reluctant to require prosecutors to so testify even when this might be the only way the defendant could establish his claim. Similarly, government documents about the particular case that might reveal motivation may also be very helpful, but courts are likewise reluctant to order such discovery. Here again, the result may be that the discovery will be denied even when it would be the only way the defendant could be expected to establish his claim.

Instructive on this matter of discovery is *United States v. Armstrong*,[10] where the Supreme Court imposed a "rigorous standard for discovery in aid of" a selective prosecution claim. The Court explained that the reasons for the presumption of regularity re the prosecutor's actions also have significance at the discovery stage, for if discovery is ordered that event itself will "divert prosecutors' resources and may disclose the Government's prosecutorial strategy." Moreover, a demanding standard re discovery was seen as "a significant barrier to the litigation of insubstantial claims." And thus the Court in *Armstrong* concluded that even to obtain discovery a defendant must first produce "some evidence tending to show the existence of the essential elements of the defense," that is, both discriminatory intent and discriminatory effect. Because of the latter element, this required threshold includes "a credible showing of different treatment of similarly situated persons."[11]

---

9. 456 F.2d 1074 (4th Cir.1972).

10. 517 U.S. 456, 116 S.Ct. 1480, 134 L.Ed.2d 687 (1996).

11. In United States v. Bass, 536 U.S. 862, 122 S.Ct. 2389, 153 L.Ed.2d 769 (2002), the Court summarily reversed a lower court holding that defendant had made a "credible showing" that "similarly situated individuals of a different race were not prosecuted," based on nationwide statistics demonstrating that "[t]he United States charges blacks with a death-eligible offense more than twice as often as it charges whites," stating: "Even assuming that the *Armstrong* requirement can be satisfied by a

Statistical evidence can be of some assistance to a defendant who is trying to establish a discriminatory enforcement defense. Illustrative is *United States v. Ojala*,[12] where the defendant made what the court characterized as "a strong showing" of his selection for enforcement within a general pattern of nonenforcement. This was done by statistical evidence showing that in a two year period there were about 51,000 tax delinquency investigations in the state, that about 4,000 of them were referred to the IRS Intelligence Division, and that only nine criminal prosecutions for failure to file were recommended. But most courts have found statistical evidence insufficient to establish a prima facie case of intentional discrimination. For example, evidence comparing the percentage of blacks in the population with the percentage of prosecutions for certain kinds of offenses involving black defendants has been held insufficient because it reveals nothing about the number of minority and majority group members who in fact have committed the particular crimes or about how many violations by each group are known to law enforcement authorities. (Statistical evidence can also be used against the defendant.[13])

(c) "Arbitrary Classification." In *Oyler v. Boles*,[14] the Supreme Court emphasized that "the conscious exercise of some selectivity in enforcement is not in itself a federal constitutional violation," and that to prevail on an equal protection claim a defendant would have to show that he was selected pursuant to an "arbitrary classification" such as "race" or "religion." Notwithstanding the number of appellate cases in which a discriminatory enforcement claim has been raised (usually without success), it is far from clear just what constitutes an "arbitrary classification" in this

context. The lower court cases indicate that a rather limited number of classifications have been rather readily held or assumed to be "arbitrary." Included are those instances in which the selection for prosecution was based upon race, national origin, sex, political activity or membership in a political party, union activity or membership in a labor union, or more generally the exercise of First Amendment rights.

But while at least as to some of these categories it may be highly unlikely if not impossible that there could ever be a sufficient explanation for an enforcement policy so limited, it must be stressed that the classification in question cannot be looked at only in the abstract. Rather, it must be examined as it relates to legitimate law enforcement objectives. Under traditional equal protection analysis, the question that *usually* must be asked is whether there is a "rational relationship" between the classification and those objectives. (A few classifications, such as those based on race or national origin or those restricting the exercise of fundamental constitutional rights, are subjected to a more demanding strict scrutiny-compelling interest test, while a few others, such as those based on gender, are subjected to an intermediate level of scrutiny.)

Consider, for example, a classification that is or appears to be based upon the sex of the offender, sometimes challenged with respect to enforcement of the prostitution laws. With rare exception, courts have not been receptive to equal protection claims directed to enforcement practices that bring about the prosecution of female prostitutes but not their male customers. The prostitute-customer distinction, which could be made by the legislature, has been deemed appropriate in light of legiti-

nationwide showing (as opposed to a showing regarding the record of the decisionmakers in respondent's case), raw statistics regarding overall charges say nothing about charges brought against similarly situated defendants. And the statistics regarding plea bargains are even less relevant, since respondent was offered a plea bargain but declined it. Under *Armstrong*, therefore, because respondent failed to submit relevant evidence that similarly situated persons were treated differently, he was not entitled to discovery."

12. 544 F.2d 940 (8th Cir.1976).

13. In United States v. Armstrong, 517 U.S. 456, 116 S.Ct. 1480, 134 L.Ed.2d 687 (1996), evidence tending to show that a federal prosecutor had prosecuted only blacks for crack dealing was deemed insufficient even to justify discovery; significantly, the Court disapproved of the court of appeals' resort to a "presumption that people of all races commit all types of crimes" because such a presumption is "at war with presumptively reliable statistics" of the federal Sentencing Commission.

14. 368 U.S. 448, 82 S.Ct. 501, 7 L.Ed.2d 446 (1962).

mate law enforcement interests. The use of male "decoys" to catch prostitutes without equivalent use of female "decoys" to catch persons seeking prostitutes has been upheld as a rational way to maximize the deterrent effect of the law and to utilize resources in a way most likely to lead to convictions. By comparison, if the policy was to enforce the prostitution laws against female prostitutes but not against male prostitutes, then it seems much more likely a court would conclude there was a denial of equal protection.

The broader point is that a prosecutor's enforcement classification is "arbitrary" only if people have been classified according to criteria that are clearly irrelevant to law enforcement purposes. There is certainly nothing wrong, for example, with a decision to employ the statute against only those kinds of conduct that present a threat to the central interests intended to be protected by the law. Illustrative of enforcement policies deemed to fit this description are the following: enforcement of gambling laws against bookmakers but not those placing bets with them, prosecuting draft evaders but not those who abet them, prosecuting those who violate the law against selling securities without a license only if they have sold 10 or more securities, and enforcement of the law prohibiting public officials from accepting money only against those receiving over $100. By comparison, in *United States v. Robinson*[15] a policy to enforce the statutes prohibiting wiretapping against private detectives but not government officials was deemed arbitrary, for such a distinction could not serve a legitimate enforcement purpose. There was simply no basis upon which it could be rationally argued that illegal intrusions into privacy are less serious when done by those working for the government. Similarly, in *People v. Acme Markets, Inc.*,[16] a denial of equal protection was found where the Sunday closing laws were enforced only upon complaint and the complaints in question were motivated by a dispute between a union and certain businesses. The court in *Acme* stressed

that in these circumstances the motives of the private complainants must be taken to be the motives of the state for purposes of applying the "rational relation" test.

Some cases are a bit more difficult, as where it is arguable that the persons selected for enforcement were chosen because of their personal characteristics rather than the nature of their conduct. It has been held, however, that selective enforcement may be justified when a striking example or a few examples are sought in order to deter other violators, and on this basis it has been deemed permissible to proceed against the most notorious violators or the most prominent persons who are violating a particular law. Sometimes the notoriety of the person selected for prosecution is largely attributable to his public stands on issues, in which case the matter must be scrutinized more closely. As stated in *United States v. Steele*[17]: "An enforcement procedure that focuses upon the vocal offender is inherently suspect, since it is vulnerable to the charge that those chosen for prosecution are being punished for their expression of ideas, a constitutionally protected right." The defendant in *Steele* prevailed when he showed that he was one of only four persons in the state prosecuted for refusing to answer questions on the census form and that all four had publicly participated in the census resistance movement. But in *Steele* the government denied it had exercised any selectivity at all; the court might have come out differently if the government had instead argued that its selection standard was to prosecute only those offenses that were likely to have a strong deterrent effect on potential offenders and that offenses by vocal census resistors would have a broader impact than would offenses by ordinary citizens.

One way of looking at the issue of what constitutes an "arbitrary classification" for discriminatory enforcement purposes is to inquire whether that question is different than when it is asked whether a criminal statute

15.   311 F.Supp. 1063 (W.D.Mo.1969).

16.   37 N.Y.2d 326, 372 N.Y.S.2d 590, 334 N.E.2d 555 (1975).

17.   461 F.2d 1148 (9th Cir.1972).

employs a classification that violates the equal protection clause. Courts have sometimes upheld an enforcement classification on the ground that it would have been permissible for the legislature to draft a statute matching the actual enforcement practice, yet some decisions have held invalid enforcement policies identical to those which have been permitted when expressed in criminal statutes. Except perhaps for highly sensitive issues better left to the political-legislative process, the former is the better view. Surely if the legislature encompasses more conduct than can be reasonably reached by available enforcement resources, then those responsible for making enforcement policy must likewise be allowed to focus on those aspects of the problem that are most serious, just as the legislature could have done initially.

Another issue, essentially the reverse of that put above, is whether an enforcement scheme employed by a prosecutor is inevitably "arbitrary" whenever the applicable criminal statute could not have been lawfully drawn in a fashion that would square precisely with the enforcement practice. The answer is no. One reason that discretionary enforcement is necessary is because the inherent limitations upon the effective use of language in criminal statutes make it impossible to state exactly and completely all that is to be included and excluded. This being so, an enforcement policy is not constitutionally invalid merely because it could not have been expressed in the criminal statute without running afoul of equal protection or void for vagueness limitations. The most obvious example is the policy discussed earlier of maximizing deterrence by enforcing certain laws against notorious or prominent violators.

Yet another important issue regarding the meaning of the "rational relationship" test in this context concerns the subject matter against which the classification must appear to be rational. Is it sufficient that the classification bears a rational relationship to *some* permissible governmental purpose, or must

the classification be rationally related to the purposes of the criminal law under which the defendant is charged? The answer may depend on the circumstances. Consider, for example, *United States v. Sacco*,[18] where the defendant objected that he was singled out, "based on his suspected role in organized crime," for investigation and prosecution under the alien registration laws. That this was the basis of selection was not disputed, yet the court unhesitantly held that it "cannot be said that that standard for selection is not rationally related to the purposes of * * * the alien registration laws." In other words, it is quite rational, considering the purposes underlying the alien registration statute, to focus upon those aliens suspected not to be law-abiding. One might well doubt whether the result would be the same were Sacco singled out on the same basis for prosecution under a generally nonenforced criminal adultery statute; there is nothing relating to the policies underlying *that* law which would explain a focus upon those suspected of organized crime. Yet, authority is to be found that would seemingly produce the same result on those facts.

(d) "Intentional or Purposeful." In *Oyler v. Boles*,[19] the Supreme Court declared that there is no equal protection violation unless "the selection was *deliberately* based upon an unjustifiable standard."[20] In support, the Court cited *Snowden v. Hughes*,[21] wherein it is stated: "The unlawful administration by state officers of a state statute fair on its face, resulting in its unequal application to those who are entitled to be treated alike, is not a denial of equal protection unless there is shown to be present in it an element of intentional or purposeful discrimination." It is not immediately apparent, however, precisely what that language means.

In *Snowden,* the words were used in a way that implied bad faith, or awareness of the unjustifiability of the standard of selection. Given the context in which the matter arose in that case, this is not surprising. *Snowden* in-

---

18.   428 F.2d 264 (9th Cir.1970).

19.   368 U.S. 448, 82 S.Ct. 501, 7 L.Ed.2d 446 (1962).

20.   Emphasis added.

21.   321 U.S. 1, 64 S.Ct. 397, 88 L.Ed. 497 (1944).

volved a civil suit to recover damages for infringement of civil rights, and it is understandable that the Court might not have wished to have an administrative official held personally liable in damages for a good faith mistake on his part. But this sensible notion that a non-malicious official should not be required to pay out damages clearly has no application when a defendant in a criminal prosecution is seeking dismissal of the charges against him because of the basis upon which he was selected for prosecution. In such a case, the question ought to be whether the classification used by the prosecutor is *in fact* arbitrary, not whether the prosecutor was personally aware that it was arbitrary. This principle is unquestionably sound, but it cannot be said with assurance that it is always grasped by the courts or applied by them.

But if malice ought not be required when a discriminatory prosecution defense is interposed, then in what sense can it be said that there must be "intentional or purposeful discrimination"? The answer, which is fully consistent with the more generalized development of equal protection doctrine, is that it is not enough that a particular enforcement policy has the *effect* of singling out those who happen to be in an impermissible class; there must have been an *intent* to single out that class.[22] A decision to prosecute black gamblers but not white gamblers would clearly be impermissible, but this is not also true of a decision to focus upon the numbers racket rather than poker in private clubs because of the former's ties to organized crime. Nor does this latter policy become arbitrary merely because it has the effect that most of the defendants prosecuted for gambling are black. By the same

token, the mere fact that the latter policy would be legitimate does not mean that enforcement intended to discriminate against blacks can be "papered over" by this other reason. This highlights the significance of the earlier discussion of burden of proof, and in particular the important question of whether a defendant who has succeeded in showing a discriminatory effect should be deemed to have shifted the burden to the prosecution to establish that this effect was not deliberate but instead was an incidental consequence of a legitimate enforcement policy.

(e) Nonprosecution of Others. Many cases reflect the view that a defendant cannot prevail on a discriminatory prosecution claim unless he shows, inter alia, that the law in question is generally not enforced against others similarly situated. Whether this is a sensible limitation is a matter on which there is a difference of opinion. Consider, for example, the situation alleged in *People v. Walker*,[23] namely, that closely following her exposure of corrupt practices in the Department of Buildings, defendant was charged with violating several building code provisions which were generally enforced. One view is that once

> it is recognized that the equal protection clause requires each state to enact and enforce its laws in an impartial manner, it follows that Miss Walker should be given the opportunity to prove that even though there was general or random enforcement of the statute in question she would not have been prosecuted but for the purposeful discrimination on the part of the borough superintendent. For example, assume that the superintendent has a list of 1,000

22. Illustrative is Wayte v. United States, 470 U.S. 598, 105 S.Ct. 1524, 84 L.Ed.2d 547 (1985), involving a challenge of the government's passive enforcement policy as to nonregistration for the draft, under which it would investigate and prosecute only those who had advised Selective Service that they had failed to register or who were reported by others as having failed to register. The Court concluded the government had not thereby subjected "vocal nonregistrants to any special burden," but then added:

"Even if the passive policy had a discriminatory effect, petitioner has not shown that the Government intended such a result. The evidence he presented demonstrated only that the Government was aware that the passive

enforcement policy would result in prosecution of vocal objectors and that they would probably make selective prosecution claims. As we have noted, however, 'purpose' ... implies more than ... intent as awareness of consequences. It implies that the decisionmaker ... selected or reaffirmed a particular course of action at least in part 'because of,' not merely 'in spite of,' its adverse effects upon an identifiable group. * * * In the present case, petitioner has not shown that the Government prosecuted him *because of* his protest activities. Absent such a showing, his claim of selective prosecution fails."

23. 14 N.Y.2d 901, 252 N.Y.S.2d 96, 200 N.E.2d 779 (1964).

known violators and reasonably exercises his discretion to enforce the law selectively by prosecuting every other person on the list, namely, even numbers. If Miss Walker's name is 149th on the list and the superintendent admits deviating from his selective enforcement formula in order to vent his personal prejudice against her, she has been deprived of equal protection of the laws and should be permitted to quash the prosecution.[24]

Although, at least in abstract terms, that is a most appealing position, it has frequently been challenged on practical grounds. It is argued that general nonenforcement must remain an essential prerequisite of a discriminatory prosecution defense so that it cannot be too readily invoked. "Were the law otherwise all enforcement proceedings could be turned into subjective expeditions into motive without the stabilizing, objectively verifiable, element of an unequal pattern of enforcement."[25] Moreover, so the argument proceeds, a prosecutor ought not to be obligated to forego prosecuting a violator whom he believes to be guilty, merely because of some personal feeling or antagonism he has toward that violator. And then there is the possibility that the personal animus did not actually make a difference, given the general pattern of enforcement. The point is that even if it can be proved that the prosecution might have been improperly motivated, it will be exceedingly difficult to prove that the defendant would not have been selected for prosecution in the normal course of events.

§ 13.5   Other Challenges to the Decision to Prosecute

(a) Vindictive Prosecution. In *Blackledge v. Perry*,[1] where defendant was convicted of misdemeanor assault, exercised his right to trial de novo, and then was charged with felony assault based upon the same conduct, the Court held that a person "is entitled to pursue

his statutory right to a trial *de novo*, without apprehension that the State will retaliate by substituting a more serious charge for the original one." The felony charge was thus barred on due process grounds. *Blackledge* emphasized that this result was necessary even absent "evidence that the prosecutor in this case acted in bad faith or maliciously," because it was the appearance of vindictiveness that would chill the right to appeal. But in *United States v. Goodwin*,[2] the Court declined "to apply a presumption of vindictiveness" in a pretrial setting because a realistic likelihood of vindictiveness was deemed not to exist at that stage. The Court added, however, that it did not "foreclose the possibility that a defendant in an appropriate case might prove objectively that the prosecutor's charging decision was motivated by a desire to punish him for doing something that the law plainly allowed him to do."

That an initial decision to prosecute might be undertaken to chill the exercise of rights cannot be denied, as is illustrated by *Dixon v. District of Columbia*.[3] Dixon, a black retired detective sergeant, was stopped by two white police officers for alleged traffic violations. He filed a complaint with the police department concerning the conduct of the officers, after which the prosecutor entered into a tacit agreement with Dixon that if he proceeded no further with his complaint the government would not prosecute the traffic charges. Dixon later filed a complaint with the Council on Human Relations, and he was then charged and convicted for the traffic offenses.

Though the court in *Dixon* relied upon its supervisory power to grant relief because of government misconduct, it was recognized that constitutional considerations were lurking very close to the surface:

Of course prosecutors have broad discretion to press or drop charges. But there are limits. If, for example, the Government had

---

24. Recent Case, 78 Harv.L.Rev. 884, 885–86 (1965).

25. Burke, J., dissenting in *Walker*.

§ 13.5

1. 417 U.S. 21, 94 S.Ct. 2098, 40 L.Ed.2d 628 (1974).

2. 457 U.S. 368, 102 S.Ct. 2485, 73 L.Ed.2d 74 (1982).

3. 394 F.2d 966 (D.C.Cir.1968).

legitimately determined not to prosecute appellant and had then reversed its position solely because he filed a complaint, this would clearly violate the first amendment. The Government may not prosecute for the purpose of deterring people from exercising their right to protest official misconduct and petition for redress of grievances.

The court then noted that the instant case was "more complicated" because the government's initial decision not to prosecute was improper because based upon Dixon's tentative agreement to drop his complaint; "if the Government should have prosecuted Dixon in the first place, there is arguably no reason why it should be barred from prosecuting him now." But the court concluded there was a countervailing consideration of greater importance, namely, the need not to "suppress complaints against police misconduct which should be thoroughly aired in a free society."

If this is so, then it well might be asked whether it is essential that there first have been a decision not to charge. Should not a defendant prevail simply by showing that he was selected for charging by a vindictive prosecutor who was annoyed by the defendant's exercise of his first amendment rights in complaining about government policy or the conduct of government officials? Where this has occurred with respect to a statutory provision not generally enforced as to those similarly situated, a prerequisite to an equal protection claim, defendants making such a showing have prevailed on a discriminatory prosecution theory. But it has been suggested that these cases truly are not so much equal protection cases as

they are cases in which the defendants have been deemed entitled to relief because prosecutors have retaliated against specially protected actions by defendants, such as the exercise of First Amendment rights. If this is so, then presumably a defendant should likewise prevail upon a showing that the authorities focused upon him because of his exercise of First Amendment rights *even when* the law under which he is charged is generally enforced against others, a result certainly not favored by the Supreme Court.[4]

Whether a vindictive prosecution defense this broad will ever be generally accepted by the courts is not entirely clear. There will likely be considerable resistance to such a development, primarily because of a perceived need to impose some limits on the number of criminal prosecutions in which a defendant would be entitled to put the prosecutor's motivations and intentions into issue. In the equal protection area, that objective is largely served by the requirement that the defendant show the law in question is not being enforced against others similarly situated. In the *Blackledge–Goodwin–Dixon* line of vindictive prosecution cases, so the argument goes, this "stabilizing, objectively verifiable, element" is provided by the necessity of the defendant establishing an exercise of a right by him that was *both* preceded by a favorable charging decision and followed by an unfavorable one.

Another issue that can arise in a *Dixon* type of case is whether all charging decisions intended to foreclose or discourage a complaint by the defendant are improper. In *MacDonald*

---

4. In Wayte v. United States, 470 U.S. 598, 105 S.Ct. 1524, 84 L.Ed.2d 547 (1985), the defendant challenged the government's passive enforcement policy re the draft registration laws on the ground that it infringed upon his First Amendment right to protest registration. In rejecting that claim, the Court noted:

"We think it important to note as a final matter how far the implications of petitioner's First Amendment argument would extend. Strictly speaking, his argument does not concern passive enforcement but self-reporting. The concerns he identifies would apply to all nonregistrants who report themselves even if the Selective Service engaged only in active enforcement. For example, a nonregistrant who wrote a letter informing Selective Service of his failure to register could, when prosecuted under an

active system, claim that the Selective Service was prosecuting him only because of his 'protest.' Just as in this case, he could have some justification for believing that his letter had focused inquiry upon him. Prosecution in either context would equally 'burden' his exercise of First Amendment rights. Under the petitioner's view, then, the Government could not constitutionally prosecute a self-reporter—even in an active enforcement system—unless perhaps it could prove that it would have prosecuted him without his letter. On principle, such a view would allow any criminal to obtain immunity from prosecution simply by reporting himself and claiming that he did so in order to 'protest' the law. The First Amendment confers no such immunity from prosecution."

v. Musick,[5] for example, the prosecutor moved to dismiss a drunken driving charge against the defendant but then, when defendant declined to stipulate that there was probable cause for his arrest, the prosecutor not only withdrew that motion but amended the charge by adding a resisting arrest count, on which defendant was convicted. The prosecutor explained his actions by saying that one of his duties was "to protect the police officers" and that he thus had properly sought the stipulation "so that the defendant cannot sue the police department." But the federal court disagreed, stating it "is no part of the proper duty of a prosecutor to use a criminal prosecution to forestall a civil proceeding by the defendant against policemen, even where the civil case arises from the events that are also the basis for the criminal charge." At least one court has reached a contrary result. In *Hoines v. Barney's Club, Inc.*,[6] the court enforced the plaintiff's agreement with the prosecutor that the charge against him for disturbing the peace would be dropped in exchange for his release from any civil liability of the private persons who arrested him. In concluding that such an agreement did not contravene public policy, the court likened what had occurred in the instant case to legitimate plea bargaining. But as the *Hoines* dissenters noted, this analogy is faulty. The agreement in the instant case did "not achieve any legitimate function of the criminal process," while proper plea bargaining does, as there "the state benefits by saving the expense of trial and expediting the disposition of the criminal case."

In *Town of Newton v. Rumery*,[7] the issue was whether "a court properly may enforce an agreement in which a criminal defendant releases his right to file a § 1983 action in return for a prosecutor's dismissal of pending criminal charges." The Court concluded that

waiver of a right to sue under a federal statute was itself a matter of federal law, as to which the "relevant principle is well-established: a promise is unenforceable if the interest in its enforcement is outweighed in the circumstances by a public policy harmed by enforcement of the agreement." The waiver in the instant case, by a sophisticated businessman represented by an experienced lawyer, was voluntary, and "the possibility of coercion in the making of similar agreements" was deemed "insufficient by itself to justify a *per se* rule against release-dismissal bargains." Moreover, all such agreements do not offend public policy, for they "protect public officials from the burdens of defending * * * unjust claims." The prosecutor had acted properly in the instant case, the Court concluded, for he "had an independent, legitimate reason to make this agreement directly related to his prosecutorial responsibilities, namely, sparing a sexual assault victim the public scrutiny and embarrassment she would have endured if she had to testify in either" the criminal or § 1983 trial. O'Connor, J., who supplied the necessary fifth vote,[8] wrote separately "to emphasize that it is the burden of those relying upon such covenants to establish that the agreement is neither involuntary nor the product of an abuse of the criminal process."

(b) Reneging on a Promise. In *United States v. Bethea*,[9] the United States attorney agreed with defendant that he would not be prosecuted for his failure to report for induction if defendant now submitted himself for induction; the defendant did so but the Army refused to induct him on moral grounds, after which defendant was prosecuted for his earlier failure to report. The defendant relied upon *Santobello v. New York*,[10] holding a plea bar-

---

5. 425 F.2d 373 (9th Cir.1970).

6. 28 Cal.3d 603, 170 Cal.Rptr. 42, 620 P.2d 628 (1980).

7. 480 U.S. 386, 107 S.Ct. 1187, 94 L.Ed.2d 405 (1987).

8. The four dissenters objected that the fact a criminal defendant "made a knowing and voluntary choice to sign a settlement agreement should not be determinative," for a prosecutor's offer to drop charges in this context "is inherently coercive," "exacts a price unrelated to the character of the defendant's conduct" (unlike plea bar-

gaining), and conflicts with the public entitlement that the decision whether to prosecute be made independently of "concerns about the potential damages liability of the police department." They concluded the "strong presumption against the enforceability of such agreements" had not been overcome in the instant case.

9. 483 F.2d 1024 (4th Cir.1973).

10. 404 U.S. 257, 92 S.Ct. 495, 30 L.Ed.2d 427 (1971).

gain enforceable against the government, but the court ruled it was not controlling here:

> The concern of *Santobello* was to protect a defendant who by pleading guilty has surrendered valuable constitutional rights in exchange for the prosecution's assurances. That concern has no application to the facts of this case. Appellant's submission for induction surrendered none of the rights protected by *Santobello*. In the context of this case, Bethea's conduct was at most only a factor to be considered by the prosecutor in deciding whether or not to prosecute, a decision not reviewable here.

Bethea, which requires that the unkept promise have produced a waiver of constitutional rights, means a defendant would prevail only in limited circumstances, such as those in which the agreement is that the charges will be dropped if defendant passes a lie detector test but that otherwise defendant will plead guilty or otherwise the results of the test will be admissible against defendant at trial.

The soundness of the *Bethea* rule is to be doubted, and has been rejected by those courts that have enforced prosecution agreements for charges to be dropped if the defendant passed a polygraph examination or aided a criminal investigation in some way. Sometimes this has been achieved by utilizing contract principles and focusing upon the "consideration" the defendant has supplied, and sometimes this has resulted from application of the even broader principle that a pledge of public faith is enforceable in any event. The result might be otherwise, of course, if the prosecutor is misled by force of defendant's connivance into a disadvantageous agreement or where facts not within the fair contemplation of the agreement have come to light. Moreover, a promise not to prosecute is unlikely to be enforced if made by an official unauthorized to make such a commitment (especially if defendant's reliance can be accommodated in some other way), or if defendant failed to keep his side of the bargain (as to which the prosecutor must obtain a judicial determination unless the agreement indicates otherwise, in which case the court is limited to determining whether the prosecutor's decision in this regard was reached honestly and in good faith).

(c) Desuetude and Lack of Fair Notice. Virtually every jurisdiction has some criminal statutes that, as a practical matter, have become ineffective without any legislative or judicial action invalidating or repealing them. These statutes have been long unenforced, and are totally ignored by those charged with enforcing the law and by the public at large. But it sometimes happens that these old laws are resurrected and enforced by a prosecutor, in which case the question may arise as to whether the defendant so proceeded against can object. One possibility is a discriminatory prosecution defense grounded in the equal protection clause, but such a defense is seldom successful, and will not necessarily prevail merely because of the prior period of nonenforcement.

There is a doctrine in the civil law, called desuetude, whereunder a statute is abrogated by reason of its long and continued nonuse. But no such rule exists in English law, and it is commonly assumed that the concept of desuetude has no place in American law. Such was the conclusion of the Supreme Court in *District of Columbia v. John R. Thompson Co.*[11] The lower court, though holding a criminal statute on refusal to serve blacks unenforceable on other grounds, asserted that "the enactments having lain unenforced for 78 years, in the face of a custom of race disassociation in the District, the decision of the municipal authorities to enforce them now, by the prosecution of the instant case, was, in effect, a decision legislative in character." The Supreme Court responded:

> The repeal of laws is as much a legislative function as their enactment. * * *
>
> Cases of hardship are put where criminal laws so long in disuse as to be no longer known to exist are enforced against innocent parties. But that condition does not bear on the continuing validity of the law; it is only an ameliorating factor in enforcement.

---

11. 346 U.S. 100, 73 S.Ct. 1007, 97 L.Ed. 1480 (1953).

This analysis has not escaped criticism. For one thing, it has been questioned whether the prosecutor's conduct in now enforcing the long dormant law can fairly be said to be nothing more than a carrying out of the wishes of the legislative branch of government. More significant, however, for present purposes, is the argument that these "innocent parties" will sometimes have available a lack-of-fair-notice defense under the due process clause. The notion is that a penal enactment that is linguistically clear, but has been notoriously ignored by both its administrators and the community for an unduly extended period, imparts no more fair notice of its proscriptions than a statute that is phrased in vague terms. From this, it has been argued that a person should have a valid defense when he believed his conduct was not criminal and acted in reasonable reliance upon a clear practice of nonenforcement of the statute or other enactment defining the offense by the body charged by law with responsibility for enforcement, unless notice of intent to enforce the statute or other enactment is reasonably made available prior to the conduct alleged. No case expressly recognizing such a defense has been found, although courts have occasionally suggested that given the right set of circumstances the due process lack of notice defense would prevail here. Apparently, it would be necessary that there have been a long period of nonenforcement and also that defendant's conduct have acquired the status of customary usage.

(d) Federal Relief From State Prosecution: Removal. In limited circumstances, pretrial relief in federal court is available to defendants who establish a possibility or probability of certain sorts of impropriety in the commencement of a state prosecution. One possibility is removal of the criminal case from the state court to the federal court for trial there. A federal officer or a person acting under him[12] or a member of the armed forces,[13] if charged in a state court for acts done under color of office, is entitled to such removal. The constitutional basis for such legislation "rests on the right and power of the United States to secure the efficient execution of its laws and to prevent interference therewith, due to possible local prejudice, by state prosecutions instituted against federal officers in enforcing such laws, by removal of the prosecutions to a federal court to avoid the effect of such prejudice."[14] A person petitioning for removal under these statutes need not admit the acts charged or establish his innocence,[15] but must be "candid, specific and positive in explaining his relation to the transaction growing out of which he has been indicted, and in showing that his relation to it was confined to his acts as an officer."[16] But the "color of office" requirement means "that federal officer removal must be predicated on the allegation of a colorable federal defense," and thus removal is unavailable where federal employees are charged "with traffic violations and other crimes for which they would have no federal defense in immunity or otherwise."[17]

Yet another statute permits removal to federal court of a state criminal prosecution brought against "any person who is denied or cannot enforce in the courts of such State a right under any law providing for the equal civil rights of citizens of the United States, or of all persons within the jurisdiction thereof."[18] The circumstances that will support removal under this provision are quite limited. Thus, removal was denied in *City of Greenwood v. Peacock*,[19] where the petitioners alleged that they were arrested and charged with various state offenses because they were blacks or were helping blacks assert their rights, that they were innocent of the charges, and that they would be unable to obtain a fair trial in state court. The Court reasoned:

---

12. 28 U.S.C.A. § 1442.

13. 28 U.S.C.A. § 1442a.

14. Maryland v. Soper, 270 U.S. 9, 46 S.Ct. 185, 70 L.Ed. 449 (1926).

15. Willingham v. Morgan, 395 U.S. 402, 89 S.Ct. 1813, 23 L.Ed.2d 396 (1969).

16. Maryland v. Soper, 270 U.S. 9, 46 S.Ct. 185, 70 L.Ed. 449 (1926).

17. Mesa v. California, 489 U.S. 121, 109 S.Ct. 959, 103 L.Ed.2d 99 (1989).

18. 28 U.S.C.A. § 1443.

19. 384 U.S. 808, 86 S.Ct. 1800, 16 L.Ed.2d 944 (1966).

It is *not* enough to support removal * * * to allege or show that the defendant's federal equal civil rights have been illegally and corruptly denied by state administrative officials in advance of trial, that the charges against the defendant are false, or that the defendant is unable to obtain a fair trial in a particular state court. The motives of the officers bringing the charges may be corrupt, but that does not show that the state trial court will find the defendant guilty if he is innocent, or that in any other manner the defendant will be "denied or cannot enforce in the courts" of the State any right under a federal law providing for equal civil rights. The civil rights removal statute does not require and does not permit the judges of the federal courts to put their brethren of the state judiciary on trial. * * * [T]he vindication of the defendant's federal rights is left to the state courts except in the rare situations where it can be clearly predicted by reason of the operation of a pervasive and explicit state or federal law that those rights will inevitably be denied by the very act of bringing the defendant to trial in the state court.

Illustrative of that rare situation is the companion case of *Georgia v. Rachel*,[20] where removal was permitted because the relevant federal civil rights statute "specifically and uniquely" barred "any prosecution" and thereby granted immunity from the institution of a state prosecution based upon petitioners' sit-in activities.

(e) Federal Relief From State Prosecution: Injunction and Declaratory Judgment. In *Dombrowski v. Pfister*,[21] a divided Court held that the district court erred in dismissing on abstention grounds a complaint seeking to enjoin state officials in Louisiana from prosecuting or threatening to prosecute petitioners for alleged violations of the state Subversive Activities and Communist Control Law and the Communist Propaganda Control Law. The Court noted, inter alia, that there was no readily apparent construction that would render the statute constitutional, and that the complaint alleged bad faith of the prosecutor in threatening further prosecutions, holding public hearings on petitioner's activities, and the like.

But in *Younger v. Harris*,[22] the *Dombrowski* case was given a narrow interpretation. The Court in *Younger* stressed the concept of "Our Federalism," which represents "a system in which there is sensitivity to the legitimate interests of both State and National Government, and in which the National Government, anxious though it may be to vindicate and protect federal rights and federal interests, always endeavors to do so in ways that will not unduly interfere with the legitimate activities of the States." Thus, "a federal court should not enjoin a state criminal prosecution begun prior to the institution of the federal suit except in very unusual situations, where necessary to prevent immediate irreparable injury,"[23] that is, only on a "showing of bad faith, harassment, or any other unusual circumstance that would call for equitable relief." The possibility of a "chilling effect" on First Amendment rights is not enough to justify federal intervention, and the testing of the constitutionality of a statute "on its face" is "fundamentally at odds with the function of the federal courts in our constitutional plan," as it requires detailed analysis of statutes without the focus of their application to specific facts previously established in a criminal trial. There are thus only "narrow exceptions"[24] to the *Younger* bar to federal injunctive relief, and litigants have rarely been successful in trying to bring themselves within them.

Younger emphasized that the barriers it erected governed whenever there was a prosecution pending in the state courts, for that pendency meant that federal action would interfere with this state activity and also that

---

20. 384 U.S. 780, 86 S.Ct. 1783, 16 L.Ed.2d 925 (1966).

21. 380 U.S. 479, 85 S.Ct. 1116, 14 L.Ed.2d 22 (1965).

22. 401 U.S. 37, 91 S.Ct. 746, 27 L.Ed.2d 669 (1971).

23. As the court characterized the *Younger* holding in the companion case of Samuels v. Mackell, 401 U.S. 66, 91 S.Ct. 764, 27 L.Ed.2d 688 (1971).

24. Huffman v. Pursue, Limited, 420 U.S. 592, 95 S.Ct. 1200, 43 L.Ed.2d 482 (1975).

the individual would soon have an opportunity to raise his objections in the context of the state criminal trial.[25] Not surprisingly, the Court also held that in such circumstances relief by way of a declaratory judgment is also barred.[26] But a unanimous Court in *Steffel v. Thompson*[27] concluded that "regardless of whether injunctive relief may be appropriate, federal declaratory relief is not precluded when no state prosecution is pending and a federal plaintiff demonstrates a genuine threat of enforcement of a disputed state criminal statute, whether an attack is made on the constitutionality of the statute on its face or as applied." This was not at all inconsistent with *Younger*; a person against whom state criminal charges are pending may be able to vindicate his rights in defense of a single criminal action, but the person against whom no charges are pending would have no remedy, except that provided by *Steffel*. From this it follows, as the Court shortly thereafter concluded, that *Steffel* rather than *Younger* governs where federal action for injunctive relief was sought prior to the commencement of state criminal proceedings.[28]

But then came *Hicks v. Miranda*,[29] involving federal action for declaratory and injunctive relief, where the Court recognized two exceptions to *Steffel*. The first is that the federal plaintiff against whom state proceedings are *not* pending is nonetheless bound by the *Younger* limitations if his interests "were intertwined" with those of others against whom state criminal proceedings have been commenced.[30] The second and more controversial is "that where state criminal proceedings are begun against the federal plaintiffs after the federal complaint is filed but before any proceedings of substance on the merits have taken place in the federal court, the principles of *Younger v. Harris* should apply in full force." The four dissenters in *Hicks* objected that the majority "virtually instructs state officials to answer federal complaints with state indictments," and noted, which is still the case, that it was quite unclear what constitutes "proceedings of substance on the merits."

(f) Federal Relief From State Prosecution: Habeas Corpus. By statute, federal habeas corpus is provided for a prisoner "in custody in violation of the Constitution or laws or treaties of the United States."[31] Another provision says that an application for such a writ "in behalf of a person in custody pursuant to the judgment of a State court shall not be granted unless it appears that the applicant has exhausted the remedies available in the courts of the State, or that there is either an absence of available State corrective process or the existence of circumstances rendering such process ineffective to protect the rights of the prisoner."[32] Despite the "in custody pursuant to the judgment of a State court" language, the requirements of this latter statute also govern instances of pretrial applications for habeas relief. This means that constitutional objections to pending state prosecutions can sometimes be heard and decided in federal court via habeas corpus,[33] though often this will not be the case because of the petitioner's inability to satisfy the "custody" and "exhaustion" requirements, which are discussed elsewhere herein.[34]

(g) Civil Action Against Prosecutor. In the event that a defendant in a criminal case later brings a tort action for malicious prosecution against the prosecutor on the ground that the latter's decision to prosecute was improper, the action will be dismissed on the ground that the prosecutor is absolutely im-

---

25. And thus, notwithstanding *Younger*, state criminal procedures can be challenged in federal court if the relief sought is not directed to the prosecution as such and if the federal claim is one which cannot be raised in defense of the state prosecution. See, e.g., Gerstein v. Pugh, 420 U.S. 103, 95 S.Ct. 854, 43 L.Ed.2d 54 (1975).

26. Samuels v. Mackell, 401 U.S. 66, 91 S.Ct. 764, 27 L.Ed.2d 688 (1971).

27. 415 U.S. 452, 94 S.Ct. 1209, 39 L.Ed.2d 505 (1974).

28. Village of Belle Terre v. Boraas, 416 U.S. 1, 94 S.Ct. 1536, 39 L.Ed.2d 797 (1974).

29. 422 U.S. 332, 95 S.Ct. 2281, 45 L.Ed.2d 223 (1975).

30. Such was the case in *Hicks,* for the federal plaintiffs were a theater owner and his corporate alter ego, but state charges were pending against two employees of the theater following police seizure of allegedly obscene films there.

31. 28 U.S.C.A. § 2241(c)(3).

32. 28 U.S.C.A. § 2254(b).

33. Braden v. 30th Judicial Circuit Court, 410 U.S. 484, 93 S.Ct. 1123, 35 L.Ed.2d 443 (1973).

34. See §§ 28.3(a), 28.5(a).

mune. This is the clear majority view in the state courts and is also the rule adopted by the Supreme Court for application when such a suit is brought against a federal prosecutor.[35] This common-law immunity of a prosecutor is grounded in "concern that harassment by unfounded litigation would cause a deflection of the prosecutor's energies from his public duties, and the possibility that he would shade his decisions instead of exercising the independence of judgment required by his public trust."[36]

In *Imbler v. Pachtman*,[37] the Supreme Court relied upon this concern in holding that such absolute immunity also exists when a federal civil rights action is brought against a state prosecutor in federal court. The Court stressed that this did "not leave the public powerless to deter misconduct or to punish that which occurs," for the prosecutor could be criminally prosecuted for willful denial of constitutional rights and could be subjected to professional discipline. The holding in *Imbler* was confined to circumstances in which the prosecutor's activities "were intimately associated with the judicial phase of the criminal process," such as the prosecutor's actions "in initiating a prosecution and in presenting the State's case." The Court in *Imbler* added it was not deciding whether like immunity existed "for those aspects of the prosecutor's responsibility that cast him in the role of an administrator or investigative officer rather than that of advocate." More recently, the Court has held that the prosecutor has only qualified immunity with respect to his actions in giving legal advice to the police on whether there exists probable cause to arrest,[38] in conducting investigative work to determine whether a suspect may be arrested,[39] and in swearing to the truthfulness of the facts set forth to establish probable cause for issuance of an arrest warrant.[40]

(h) Recoupment of Litigation Expenses. In 1997 Congress enacted legislation whereby the defendant in a federal criminal case could sometimes collect for his attorney's fees and litigation expenses, to be paid from the regular budget of the prosecuting agency. To prevail, the claimant must prove that: (1) he was not represented by assigned counsel paid for by the public; (2) he was the prevailing party; (3) the prosecution was "vexatious, frivolous, or in bad faith"; (4) the attorney's fees were reasonable; and (5) no special circumstances exist that would make such an award unjust. The most critical and difficult issue ordinarily confronted in proceedings brought under this legislation is whether there is a basis for finding the government's position to be "vexatious, frivolous, or in bad faith." The legislative history is of little help in indicating the meaning of those words in this context, except in a negative sense. For one thing, recovery is contemplated in a broader range of cases than those that would amount to the common law tort of malicious prosecution, which requires the acquitted defendant to prove there was no probable cause, as Congress indicated recovery under this legislation would not be foreclosed by a grand jury finding of probable cause to support the indictment. On the other hand, Congress clearly intended to impose a more demanding standard than the Equal Access to Justice Act, authorizing recoupment against the government in civil cases unless the government shows its position was "substantially justified," which has been interpreted as referring to a "reasonable basis in law and fact."

§ 13.6   Challenges to the Decision to Forego or Terminate Diversion

(a) The Diversion Process. For years, individual prosecutors have in a very informal

---

35. Yaselli v. Goff, 275 U.S. 503, 48 S.Ct. 155, 72 L.Ed. 395 (1927).

36. Imbler v. Pachtman, 424 U.S. 409, 96 S.Ct. 984, 47 L.Ed.2d 128 (1976).

37. 424 U.S. 409, 96 S.Ct. 984, 47 L.Ed.2d 128 (1976).

38. Burns v. Reed, 500 U.S. 478, 111 S.Ct. 1934, 114 L.Ed.2d 547 (1991).

39. Buckley v. Fitzsimmons, 509 U.S. 259, 113 S.Ct. 2606, 125 L.Ed.2d 209 (1993).

40. Kalina v. Fletcher, 522 U.S. 118, 118 S.Ct. 502, 139 L.Ed.2d 471 (1997) (prosecutor's activities in preparing and filing the information, the motion for an arrest warrant, and the probable cause certification "are protected by absolute immunity," but such immunity does not extend to "her act in personally attesting to the truth of the averments in the certification," for then "she was acting as a complaining witness rather than a lawyer").

and often haphazard way permitted diversion in some circumstances, agreeing not to proceed with prosecution of a defendant if he in return makes restitution to the victim or does some other act. Of primary concern here, however, is the kind of diversion that is now becoming quite common: a formalized procedure authorized by legislation or court rule whereby persons who are accused of certain criminal offenses and meet preestablished criteria have their prosecution suspended for a three month to one year period and are placed in a community-based rehabilitation program, after which the case is dismissed if the conditions of the diversion referral are satisfied. In the earlier and informal days of pretrial diversion, it was perceived as just another aspect of the prosecutor's discretion, meaning that the prosecutor's decisions on when to divert and when to terminate a diversion were largely uncontrolled. That is still the case in some jurisdictions, although there is a noticeable trend toward limiting the prosecutor's discretion in these respects as diversion programs become more formalized.

(b) Statutory Standards for Diversion. One consequence of the greater attention now given to the pretrial diversion alternative is that efforts have been made to identify criteria by which to select those defendants who are the most likely candidates for diversion. Sometimes these criteria are set out in statutes or rules of court. It has occasionally been claimed that such provisions are unconstitutional attempts to limit the prosecutor's discretion, barred by the separation of powers doctrine, but such challenges have been rejected where the legislation does not destroy or unreasonably restrict the prosecutor's discretion. If the statute provides that the courts are to administer the program or if the program was adopted by rule of court, then it is clear that the setting of standards does not encroach upon the executive power because then a judicial function is involved.

If a particular defendant was made ineligible for a pretrial diversion program by virtue of certain criteria in a statute or rule of court, a defendant might attack those criteria on equal protection grounds. Except in extraordinary circumstances, however, it is unlikely that such a challenge will prevail. In *Marshall v. United States*,[1] for example, the Supreme Court held there was no equal protection denial in the statutory exclusion from the treatment alternative under the Narcotic Addict Rehabilitation Act of those persons with two prior felony convictions. The Court reasoned that it was not "unreasonable or irrational for Congress to act on the predicate * * * that a person with two or more prior felonies would be less likely to adjust and adhere to the disciplines and rigors of the treatment program and hence is a less promising prospect for treatment than those with lesser criminal records." Various other classifications would appear to be legally defensible, even if seemingly unwise or not fully supported by empirical evidence, such as those denying eligibility to felons, perpetrators of violent crimes, recidivists, juveniles, youthful offenders, addicts or alcoholics.

(c) Decision Not to Divert. A decision by the prosecutor not to divert a particular defendant and instead to proceed with prosecution on the pre-existing charge is, in essence, a decision to prosecute, and thus at a minimum is subject to challenge in the same way as any other decision to prosecute. One possibility, therefore, is that a nondiversion decision will be contested as a discriminatory decision to prosecute violating the equal protection clause. As we have already seen, defendants seldom are successful in bringing such a challenge. If it is brought within the context of a formalized diversion program, the defendant's chances may be somewhat better in the sense that he may find it easier to carry his heavy burden of proof. Because of the established criteria in a statute, rule of court or a prosecutor's policy statement, the defendant may be able to establish more readily that others similarly situated are not being prosecuted and that he was singled out on an arbitrary basis.

Another possible basis upon which to challenge a decision to charge is that the prosecu-

§ 13.6
1. 414 U.S. 417, 94 S.Ct. 700, 38 L.Ed.2d 618 (1974).

tion is vindictive or has the appearance of vindictiveness. As already noted, the *Blackledge v. Perry*[2] presumption-of-vindictiveness was held inapplicable in a pretrial setting in *United States v. Goodwin*.[3] Although this means that in such circumstances the defendant cannot prevail without proving the existence of a vindictive motive, the chances of a defendant carrying that burden would seem somewhat greater when the prosecution does not square with established diversion criteria. Illustrative is *State v. Eash*,[4] where the prosecutor exercised his statutory veto of defendant's diversion application because of dissatisfaction with the breadth of defendant's waiver of speedy trial. Upon application of the defendant, the court then ruled that defendant's waiver was sufficient under the diversion statute, which contemplated waiver only "for the period of his diversion." The prosecutor persisted in his refusal to consent to diversion, and "admitted that the sole basis for refusing to accept such a waiver was that such a ruling conflicted with [his] 'total waiver' policy with regard to speedy trial waivers in pretrial intervention situations." The *Eash* court ruled that refusal on this basis was constitutionally impermissible: "Such conduct on the part of the state is tantamount to coercion and has a chilling effect upon the exercise of the right to a vigorous defense."

Seemingly inconsistent with *Eash* is *United States v. Smith*,[5] where defendant moved to dismiss a marijuana possession charge on cruel and unusual punishment grounds and the motion was granted but that ruling was reversed on appeal, after which the prosecutor refused to divert the defendant because it was his policy to deny such treatment to defendants who had chosen to litigate any issues in their case. The lower court found this objectionable and dismissed the charge, but the appellate court disagreed. The court asserted "that a policy intended to deter defendants from exercising their legal rights cannot be tolerated in the name of prosecutorial discretion," but that

this was not such a case because "if a defendant applies for, is accepted into the program, and successfully completes the requisite activities, charges are dropped without his having to go to court, and no conviction or criminal record results." Thus, the court concluded, the "beneficiary of such a disposition of charges against him can scarcely be said to be deterred from exercising his right to defend himself, for, by dismissing such charges, the government has done away with any reason for him to do so."

Whether the *Smith* result is constitutionally objectionable is not entirely clear. *Smith* certainly is not as serious a matter as *Eash,* for the defendant in the latter case was confronted with the necessity of making a total and permanent waiver of Sixth Amendment speedy trial rights with respect to that charge, while Smith apparently could have opted for diversion initially and then, if his diversionary status was later terminated, moved to dismiss the charge on whatever theory he had previously entertained. There is also the argument that the prosecutor's policy in *Smith* should be upheld because it is totally consistent with one of the two objectives of diversion programs, namely, reducing the litigation burden in the courts. This is apparently what the *Smith* court had in mind when it asserted that if "it is permissible, in plea bargaining, to induce a defendant to plead guilty and waive his right to trial, *a fortiori* no substantial constitutional question is presented when a prosecutor offers to drop all charges provided the accused conforms to certain conditions, including, *inter alia,* forgoing the filing of any motions or pleas in defense." But it is this analogy which suggests that *Smith* may be somewhat vulnerable, for there is authority that even in a plea bargaining context there are limits upon what conditions the prosecutor may impose in terms of surrender of rights.[6]

Though it has been argued that the decision by the prosecutor not to divert a particular

---

2. 417 U.S. 21, 94 S.Ct. 2098, 40 L.Ed.2d 628 (1974).

3. 457 U.S. 368, 102 S.Ct. 2485, 73 L.Ed.2d 74 (1982).

4. 367 So.2d 661 (Fla.App.1979), disapproved in Cleveland v. State, 417 So.2d 653 (Fla.1982).

5. 354 A.2d 510 (D.C.App.1976).

6. See § 21.3(c).

defendant should not be subject to judicial review, and though it seems clear that such a decision does not implicate rights entitling the defendant to a hearing as a matter of course, as a general matter it is fair to say that such decisions, at least when they occur within the context of a formalized diversion program, are likely to be subject to somewhat greater judicial scrutiny than the usual decision to charge. The extent to which this is so, however, will depend upon the exact nature of the diversion program. A program created by court rule is likely to be construed to includes judicial power to interpret and enforce the rules. Under such a scheme an "abuse of discretion" standard is likely to be used upon review, which prompts somewhat closer scrutiny than under the equal protection arbitrariness test. Greater court control is also likely if a diversion program is interpreted to be an aspect of the court's sentencing function or if the applicable statute expressly assigns responsibility for the program to the courts. Also, if the statute puts the program in the hands of the prosecutor but says that he "shall consider" certain enumerated factors, a defendant might prevail upon a showing of a substantial departure from them.

(d) Decision to Terminate by Prosecution. If a defendant is accepted into a diversion program, the operating assumption is that if he carries out his responsibilities under the program the charges against him will be dropped. But this gives rise to the question of how free the prosecutor is, on his own, to decide that the "deal is off" or to conclude that the defendant has defaulted in some respect. In *United States v. Bethea*,[7] which might be viewed as an unusual type of diversion case, the prosecutor promised that he would drop the charges against defendant for failure to report for induction in the Army if defendant submitted himself for induction. The defendant complied, but the Army rejected him on moral grounds, after which the prosecutor proceeded with the prosecution. Relying upon the

plea bargaining case of *Santobello v. New York*,[8] defendant tried to enforce the agreement in court, but the court ruled the prosecutor's decision was "not reviewable here" because, unlike the situation in *Santobello,* the defendant had not "surrendered valuable constitutional rights in exchange for the prosecution's assurances." But there is much to be said for the proposition, which has been accepted in a related context,[9] that such contract law analysis is inappropriate here and that the government should be required to keep its word without regard to whether the defendant has supplied "consideration." And even if the premise underlying *Bethea* is sound, it would seem not to govern the more typical diversion case. As held in *United States v. Garcia*,[10] *Santobello* is controlling where, "by entering into the deferred prosecution agreement, [the defendant] waived his valuable right to a speedy trial."

Even assuming it is clear that the prosecutor cannot simply renege on the agreement, obviously the defendant cannot complain about now being subjected to prosecution if he failed to carry out his part of the bargain. But whether there has been such a failure in a particular case may not be entirely clear. This being so, the question naturally arises as to how the prosecutor is to make that decision and whether the decision is subject to review. One view is that the prosecutor should have the discretionary authority to determine whether the offender is performing his duties adequately under the agreement and, if he determines that the offender is not, to reinstate the prosecution. But there is much to be said for the procedural scheme advocated in the Model Code of Pre–Arraignment Procedure, by which the defendant is entitled to "a hearing before the prosecutor to determine" whether defendant "violated a material term of the agreement or * * * made a misrepresentation materially affecting the agreement" and, "if so, whether the prosecution should be

---

7. 483 F.2d 1024 (4th Cir.1973).

8. 404 U.S. 257, 92 S.Ct. 495, 30 L.Ed.2d 427 (1971), discussed in § 21.2(d).

9. See § 13.5(b).

10. 519 F.2d 1343 (9th Cir.1975).

reinstated or the agreement modified."[11] If the prosecutor decides to reinstate the prosecution, the defendant may move in court for continuation of the diversion "on the ground that the record does not support the prosecutor's determination or that the prosecutor has not complied with the provisions" governing the aforementioned hearing.[12]

Indeed, it would seem that some sort of hearing is ordinarily required in this context as a matter of procedural due process. Revoking a person's diversion status is quite similar to parole revocation and probation revocation, and this has prompted some courts to conclude that the procedures mandated in *Morrissey v. Brewer*[13] and *Gagnon v. Scarpelli*[14] with respect to the latter revocations are equally necessary here. Those procedures are: (1) written notice of the claimed violation; (2) disclosure to the defendant of the evidence against him; (3) an opportunity to be heard in person and to present witnesses and documentary evidence; (4) the right to confront and cross-examine adverse witnesses, unless good cause is found for not allowing such confrontation; (5) a "neutral and detached" hearing body; and (6) a written statement by the factfinders as to the reasons for revocation. Whether this is so as to every type of diversion program is hard to say. In *Meachum v. Fano*,[15] holding no hearing was needed regarding transfer of a convict for alleged misconduct from a medium to a maximum security prison, the Court reasoned (1) that the prisoner's fundamental interest in liberty had been protected by his prior criminal trial, and (2) that state law had not conferred upon the prisoner any right to remain in the prison where he was assigned. From this, it is argued that the once-diverted defendant's liberty interest will be protected by his forthcoming criminal trial and that therefore a hearing regarding the termination of diversion status is constitutionally required only if diversion is a statutorily created entitlement. This in turn depends upon whether the statutory language creates an expectancy in the defendant that diversion will continue until the fact of violation of the agreement's explicit conditions has been found.

§ 13.7   Challenges to the Charge Selection

(a) Duplicative and Overlapping Statutes. Sometimes a defendant's challenge to a prosecutor's charge selection in a particular case is directed to the statutory scheme under which the prosecutor acted. This occurs when the defendant claims that the legislature has bestowed unnecessary discretion upon the prosecutor by defining the same criminal conduct in two different statutes carrying different penalties. Such a challenge reached the Supreme Court but was rejected by a unanimous Court in *United States v. Batchelder*.[1]

The defendant in *Batchelder* was convicted under a statute making it a crime for various persons, including one who "has been convicted in any court of a crime punishable by imprisonment for a term exceeding one year," to "receive any firearm * * * which has been shipped or transported in interstate or foreign commerce." He objected to his five year prison term, the maximum under this provision, because another statute carrying a two year maximum covers any person, among others, who "has been convicted by a court of the United States or of a State or any political subdivision thereof of a felony * * * and who receives, possesses, or transports in commerce or affecting commerce * * * any firearm." The Court of Appeals ruled he could receive no more than the two year maximum provided under the latter statute because of doubts as to whether Congress had intended the two penalty provisions to coexist, and add that without such a construction the statute might (1) be void for vagueness, (2) implicate "due process and equal protection interest[s] in avoiding excessive prosecutorial discretion and

11. ALI Model Code of Pre–Arraignment Procedure § 320.9(1)(1975).

12. Id. at § 320.9(2).

13. 408 U.S. 471, 92 S.Ct. 2593, 33 L.Ed.2d 484 (1972).

14. 411 U.S. 778, 93 S.Ct. 1756, 36 L.Ed.2d 656 (1973).

15. 427 U.S. 215, 96 S.Ct. 2532, 49 L.Ed.2d 451 (1976).

§ 13.7

1. 442 U.S. 114, 99 S.Ct. 2198, 60 L.Ed.2d 755 (1979).

in obtaining equal justice," and (3) constitute an impermissible delegation of congressional authority. But the Supreme Court construed the statute otherwise and, in the process, found "no constitutional infirmities" in such a statutory scheme.

As for the vagueness issue, the Court acknowledged that lack of fair notice as to the potential punishment might well violate due process, but concluded that the provisions at issue were not deficient because, though they created "uncertainty as to which crime may be charged and therefore what penalties may be imposed, they do so to no greater extent than would a single statute authorizing various alternative punishments." As for the Court of Appeals' concern that the legislative redundancy left the prosecutor with "unfettered" discretion, the Court responded that

> there is no appreciable difference between the discretion a prosecutor exercises when deciding whether to charge under one of two statutes with different elements and the discretion he exercises when choosing one of two statutes with identical elements. In the former situation, once he determines that the proof will support conviction under either statute, his decision is indistinguishable from the one he faces in the latter context. The prosecutor may be influenced by the penalties available upon conviction, but this fact standing alone does not give rise to a violation of the Equal Protection or Due Process Clauses.

On the delegation point, the *Batchelder* Court concluded that because the provisions at issue "plainly demarcate the range of penalties that prosecutors and judges may seek and impose," this meant "the power that Congress has delegated to those officials is no broader than the authority they routinely exercise in enforcing the criminal laws."

In assaying the *Batchelder* reasoning, it is useful to think about three types of situations in which a defendant's conduct may fall within two statutes. They are: (1) where one statute defines a lesser included offense of the other and they carry different penalties (e.g., whoever carries a concealed weapon is guilty of a misdemeanor; a convicted felon who carries a

concealed weapon is guilty of a felony); (2) where the statutes overlap and carry different penalties (e.g., possession of a gun by a convicted felon, illegal alien or dishonorably discharged serviceman is a misdemeanor; possession of a gun by a convicted felon, fugitive from justice, or unlawful user of narcotics is a felony); (3) where the statutes are identical (e.g., possession of a gun by a convicted felon is a misdemeanor; possession of a gun by a convicted felon is a felony). The Court in *Batchelder* had before it a situation falling into the second category, but seems to have concluded that the three statutory schemes are indistinguishable for purposes of constitutional analysis. But in terms of either the difficulties confronted at the legislative level in drafting statutes or in the guidance given to a prosecutor by the legislation, the three schemes are markedly different.

The first of the three is certainly unobjectionable. Such provisions are quite common (robbery-armed robbery; battery-aggravated battery; joyriding-theft; housebreaking-burglary), and usually are a consequence of a deliberate attempt by the legislature to identify one or more aggravating characteristics that in the judgment of the legislature should ordinarily be viewed as making the lesser crime more serious. They afford guidance to the prosecutor, but—as noted in *Batchelder*—do not foreclose the prosecutor from deciding in a particular case that, notwithstanding the presence of one of the aggravating facts, the defendant will still be prosecuted for the lesser offense.

By contrast, the third of the three is highly objectionable. It is likely to be a consequence of legislative carelessness, and even if it is not such a scheme serves no legitimate purpose. There is nothing at all rational about this kind of statutory scheme, as it provides for different penalties without any effort whatsoever to explain a basis for the difference. It confers discretion that is totally unfettered and totally unnecessary. And thus the Court in *Batchelder* is less than convincing in reasoning that this third category is unobjectionable simply because in other instances, falling into the first category, the need for discretionary judgments by the prosecutor has not been and cannot be totally eliminated.

The second of the three categories presents a harder case. Here as well, the dilemma is likely to have been created by legislative carelessness, though this is not inevitably so. In the illustration given above, where the possession of a gun by a felon is listed in both misdemeanor and felony statutes that otherwise cover distinct circumstances, carelessness in the legislative process seems the most likely explanation. However, overlapping statutes are very common at both the federal and state level, and it can hardly be said that in every instance they are a consequence of poor research or inept drafting. Drafting a clear criminal statute and still ensuring that in *no* instance could it cover conduct embraced within any existing criminal statute in that jurisdiction can be a formidable task. (This fact alone may make courts somewhat reluctant to find overlap per se unconstitutional, although the consequence of such a finding, limiting punishment to that under the lesser of the two statutes until such time as the legislature decides what to do about the now-identified overlap, is hardly a cause for alarm.) Moreover, in the overlap scheme the two statutes will at least *sometimes* assist the prosecutor in deciding how to exercise his charging discretion. To the extent of the overlap, however, the conduct is the same, and thus the guidance afforded here falls considerably short of that in the first of the three categories.

Just how broad the *Batchelder* holding is in other respects is not entirely clear. Of particular importance is the question of whether more dramatic or more certain disparities between the sentences allowed or required under the two statutes at issue makes a difference. In response to the Court of Appeals' objection that the prosecutor was given unfettered discretion in "selection of which of two penalties to apply," the Supreme Court answered that the government had not been allowed "to predetermine ultimate criminal sanctions" but instead had simply enabled "the sentencing judge to impose a longer prison sentence." That is, the prosecutor's choice of the statute that allowed imprisonment "not more than

five years" rather than the one providing for imprisonment "not more than two years" had simply added to the judge's sentencing discretion. But what if, for example, one statute permitted imprisonment up to ten years and the other made ten years the mandatory minimum? In such a case, where the prosecutor actually makes a sentencing decision without either sentencing information or expertise in sentencing, there is more force to the equal protection argument.

Notwithstanding these arguments, the advent of strict sentencing guidelines and the increased use of mandatory minimum sentences have significantly eroded judicial discretion over sentencing and thus enhanced the importance of charge selection by the prosecutor. Since judges now have less discretion over sentencing, prosecutors virtually dictate the punishment for a given defendant when they select the charge to prosecute. This shift in sentencing discretion from judge to prosecutor has been challenged as a violation of due process, but courts, relying on *Batchelder*, have refused to restrain the discretion of prosecutors over charge selection.

Prior to *Batchelder*, some states held unconstitutional statutes providing different punishment for exactly the same conduct. Some of the decisions went so far as to also cover criminal statutes that merely overlapped with one another. Though the reasoning in these cases was often similar to that found wanting in *Batchelder*, meaning that decision has created some chance that the courts so holding will retreat from their earlier position, a state might well reject *Batchelder* as a matter of state constitutional law. And of course there remains open the possibility that a court will be able to avoid the problem entirely by utilizing canons of statutory construction, such as that a later statute should prevail over the earlier one with which it would otherwise overlap, or that the more specific statute should prevail over the more general one with which it would otherwise overlap.

(b) Discriminatory Charge Selection. Even if the statutory scheme whereunder the prosecutor selected the charge is not objectionable, the defendant might nonetheless claim that the seriousness of the charge or number of charges lodged against him are the result of discriminatory enforcement. In *United States v. Batchelder*,[2] the Court expressly noted that the prosecutor's conduct in selecting the charge is "subject to constitutional constraints," in particular the equal protection clause's prohibition upon "selective enforcement 'based upon an unjustifiable standard such as race, religion, or other arbitrary classification.'" As for exactly what must be shown to make out an equal protection claim, what was said on this matter earlier regarding the decision to charge[3] is generally applicable in this context as well. Here, as there, it is extremely difficult to make out a successful equal protection claim.

(c) Vindictive Charge Selection. A defendant who cannot make out an equal protection claim might nonetheless, given the right sequence of events, prevail on a due process vindictiveness theory under *Blackledge v. Perry*.[4] There, defendant was convicted in district court of misdemeanor assault, exercised his right to trial de novo in the superior court, and was then charged with the felony of assault with a deadly weapon with intent to kill. Relying upon *North Carolina v. Pearce*,[5] holding that due process prohibits a judge from imposing a more severe sentence upon retrial for the purpose of discouraging defendants from exercising their statutory right to appeal, defendant claimed the felony charge deprived him of due process. The Supreme Court agreed:

> There is, of course, no evidence that the prosecutor in this case acted in bad faith or

maliciously in seeking a felony indictment against Perry. The rationale of our judgment in the *Pearce* case, however, was not grounded upon the proposition that actual retaliatory motivation must inevitably exist. Rather, we emphasized that "since the fear of such vindictiveness may unconstitutionally deter a defendant's exercise of the right to appeal or collaterally attack his first conviction, due process also requires that a defendant be freed of apprehension of such a retaliatory motivation on the part of the sentencing judge." We think it clear that the same considerations apply here. * * * A person convicted of an offense is entitled to pursue his statutory right to a trial *de novo*, without apprehension that the State will retaliate by substituting a more serious charge for the original one, thus subjecting him to a significantly increased potential period of incarceration.

Because the Court in *Blackledge* did not require proof of "actual retaliatory motive," the defendant there prevailed merely by showing that he exercised a "right" and that this was followed by "a more serious charge" by the same prosecutor.[6] The right in *Blackledge* was the right to appeal and the more serious charge was lodged after he had been once tried and convicted, but lower courts often took the same approach when the defendant's exercise of the right and the prosecutor's escalation of the charge all occurred in a pretrial setting. However, the Supreme Court rejected such an extension of *Blackledge* in *United States v. Goodwin*.[7] There, defendant was charged with several misdemeanor and petty offenses that

---

2. 442 U.S. 114, 99 S.Ct. 2198, 60 L.Ed.2d 755 (1979).

3. See § 13.4.

4. 417 U.S. 21, 94 S.Ct. 2098, 40 L.Ed.2d 628 (1974).

5. 395 U.S. 711, 89 S.Ct. 2072, 23 L.Ed.2d 656 (1969), discussed in § 26.8(a).

6. In Thigpen v. Roberts, 468 U.S. 27, 104 S.Ct. 2916, 82 L.Ed.2d 23 (1984), where the relevant facts were essentially identical to those in *Blackledge* except that in the instant case the first trial was the responsibility of the county prosecutor while the indictment and trial on the felony was the responsibility of the district attorney, the Court noted: "It might be argued that if two different prosecutors are involved, a presumption of vindictiveness, which arises in part from assumptions about the individual's personal stake in the proceedings, is inappropriate.

* * * On the other hand, to the extent the presumption reflects 'institutional pressure that ... might ... subconsciously motivate a vindictive prosecutorial ... response to a defendant's exercise of his right to obtain a retrial of a decided question,' * * * it does not hinge on the continued involvement of a particular individual. A district attorney burdened with the retrial of an already-convicted defendant might be no less vindictive because he did not bring the initial prosecution." But the Court then found it unnecessary to "determine the correct rule when two independent prosecutors are involved," for here the county prosecutor participated fully in the later proceedings, as was his statutory duty, and thus "the addition of the district attorney to the prosecutorial team changes little."

7. 457 U.S. 368, 102 S.Ct. 2485, 73 L.Ed.2d 74 (1982).

were scheduled for trial before a federal magistrate until defendant exercised his right to have them tried by jury in district court. The case was accordingly transferred to another prosecutor, who upon review of it obtained a felony indictment. The defendant's subsequent felony conviction was overturned on appeal on the theory that the more serious charge was barred under *Blackledge* even absent proof of actual vindictiveness. The Supreme Court disagreed and reversed.

The *Goodwin* majority, characterizing *Blackledge* as a case in which the Court "found it necessary to 'presume' an improper vindictive motive," concluded that such a presumption was "not warranted in this case" because actual vindictiveness was so unlikely on these facts. One major consideration, the Court explained, was "the timing of the prosecutor's action in this case":

> There is good reason to be cautious before adopting an inflexible presumption of prosecutorial vindictiveness in a pretrial setting. In the course of preparing a case for trial, the prosecutor may uncover additional information that suggests a basis for further prosecution or he simply may come to realize that information possessed by the State has a broader significance. At this stage of the proceedings, the prosecutor's assessment of the proper extent of prosecution may not have crystallized. In contrast, once a trial begins—and certainly by the time a conviction has been obtained—it is much more likely that the State has discovered and assessed all of the information against an accused and has made a determination, on the basis of that information, of the extent to which he should be prosecuted. Thus, a change in the charging decision made after an initial trial is completed is much more likely to be improperly motivated than is a pretrial decision.

A second consideration the *Goodwin* Court deemed relevant in determining the reach of the *Blackledge* rule was the "nature of the right asserted" by the defendant:

> As compared to the complete trial *de novo* at issue in *Blackledge,* a jury trial—as opposed to a bench trial—does not require duplica-

tive expenditures of prosecutorial resources before a final judgment may be obtained. Moreover, unlike the trial judge in *Pearce,* no party is asked "to do over what it thought it had already done correctly." A prosecutor has no "personal stake" in a bench trial and thus no reason to engage in "self-vindication" upon a defendant's request for a jury trial. Perhaps most importantly, the institutional bias against the retrial of a decided question that supported the decisions in *Pearce* and *Blackledge* simply has no counterpart in this case.

It thus appears unlikely that the *Blackledge* prophylactic rule has any application whatsoever in a pretrial setting. (There is some dispute as to whether the *Blackledge* prophylactic rule applies beyond the pretrial setting when there was not a conviction and appeal.)

In a case falling within *Blackledge,* where again the defendant is not obligated to prove actual vindictiveness, should the prosecutor be allowed to make some showing that there was a valid reason for his "adjustment" of the charges against the defendant? In *Pearce,* on which *Blackledge* is grounded, the Court held a judge could impose a higher sentence on retrial only if based upon "identifiable conduct on the part of the defendant occurring after the time of the original sentencing proceeding." This very strict rule, not even allowing a higher sentence on retrial based upon very relevant preexisting facts simply not brought to the attention of the judge at the first trial (e.g., an earlier conviction of the defendant for some other crime), was deemed necessary "to assure the absence of" an improper motivation. If that approach were carried over to all *Blackledge*-type cases, where the concern is with prosecutorial rather than judicial vindictiveness, then there would likewise be only one situation in which a higher charge would be permitted. Significantly, it is the one situation specifically mentioned by the Court in *Blackledge*: where the prosecutor has "shown that it was impossible to proceed on the more serious charge at the outset," as where the defendant was originally tried for assault and battery but was later tried for murder after the victim died.

The courts have not held the line there, however, which is none too surprising in light of intervening events. The Supreme Court has now taken a broader view of *Pearce*[8] and has also asserted somewhat ambiguously that "the *Blackledge* presumption is rebuttable"[9] and "could be overcome by objective evidence justifying the prosecutor's action."[10] But there is not complete agreement as to what other showing by the prosecutor will suffice. One approach, apparently limited to where the prosecutor has added charges, is merely to require the prosecutor to present a nonvindictive reason. This approach is objectionable because it makes it too easy to conceal actual vindictiveness and creates an atmosphere in which other defendants will be most reluctant to exercise their rights. Under another approach it is necessary that the prosecutor dispel any appearance of prosecutorial vindictiveness. At least if taken literally, this seems a too demanding test, for an appearance of vindictiveness arises every time a defendant asserts a right and a prosecutor subsequently takes a position contrary to the defendant's interests. An attractive middle ground is provided by *United States v. Andrews*,[11] which holds that in the case of added counts the question is "whether a reasonable person would think there existed a realistic likelihood of vindictiveness," so that the prosecutor must come up with an "objective explanation" for his actions (e.g., governmental discovery of previously unknown evidence). This approach

(1) takes account of the due process value stressed in *Blackledge* that defendants be "freed of apprehension of such a retaliatory motivation" by the prosecutor; (2) is a realistic way to police vindictiveness, for a determination of actual motivation (as the Court said in *Pearce*) would "be extremely difficult to prove in any individual case"; and (3) "allows the judge to avoid the 'Hobson's choice,' which the actual vindictiveness test presents, of either allowing the extra charge or making an explicit finding of prosecutorial bad faith."

In any event, the situation is quite different in a case governed by *Goodwin* rather than *Blackledge,* for the Court in the former case said that when the "presumption of vindictiveness" is not applicable it is then necessary for the defendant to "prove objectively that the prosecutor's charging decision was motivated by a desire to punish him for doing something that the law plainly allowed him to do." The Court made it quite clear that it would be most difficult for the defendant to meet this burden.

As for the "more serious charge" element of *Blackledge,* in that case it was a shift from misdemeanor assault to felony assault which, the Court noted, subjected defendant "to a significantly increased potential period of incarceration." The charge is "more serious" for *Blackledge* purposes even when the change is only to a higher sentence, where the prosecutor has increased the number of charges, and when the new charge entails more serious collateral consequences. But, where the

8. Texas v. McCullough, 475 U.S. 134, 106 S.Ct. 976, 89 L.Ed.2d 104 (1986); Wasman v. United States, 468 U.S. 559, 104 S.Ct. 3217, 82 L.Ed.2d 424 (1984). Both cases are discussed in § 26.8(b).

9. Thigpen v. Roberts, 468 U.S. 27, 104 S.Ct. 2916, 82 L.Ed.2d 23 (1984) (a footnote observation which, however, cites back to the footnote in *Blackledge* referring to the situation where it was impossible to proceed on the more serious charge originally).

10. United States v. Goodwin, 457 U.S. 368, 102 S.Ct. 2485, 73 L.Ed.2d 74 (1982) (a footnote observation which, however, is followed by quotation of the footnote in *Blackledge* referring to the situation where it was impossible to proceed on the more serious charge originally). In Wasman v. United States, 468 U.S. 559, 104 S.Ct. 3217, 82 L.Ed.2d 424 (1984), concerning the *Pearce* rule and thus discussed more fully in § 26.8(b), a four-Justice plurality asserted that both *Pearce* and *Blackledge* involve only a presump-

tion of vindictiveness and that "where the presumption applies, the sentencing authority or the prosecutor must rebut the presumption that an increased sentence or charge resulted from vindictiveness." Five members of the Court declined to join that part of the opinion because, as Justice Powell put it, the *Pearce–Blackledge* presumption "is not simply concerned with actual vindictiveness, but also was intended to protect against reasonable apprehension of vindictiveness that could deter a defendant" from exercising his rights. But in Texas v. McCullough, 475 U.S. 134, 106 S.Ct. 976, 89 L.Ed.2d 104 (1986), also discussed more fully in § 26.8(b), a majority of the Court made it clear that "even if the *Pearce* presumption were to apply here" it could be overcome "by objective information * * * justifying the increased sentence."

11. 633 F.2d 449 (6th Cir.1980).

charges are not more severe in the above senses, it is not objectionable that the later charge is different in a way enhancing the probability of conviction.

Chapter 14

THE PRELIMINARY HEARING

Table of Sections

§ 14.1 Functions of the Preliminary Hearing

(a) Screening. The preliminary hearing (also referred to as the "preliminary examination," the "probable cause" hearing, and the "bindover" hearing) is a judicial proceeding, commonly conducted before a magistrate court (i.e., a court of limited jurisdiction) as to felony charges only. At that proceeding, the prosecution in an open and adversary hearing must establish that there is sufficient evidence supporting its charge to "bind the case over" to the next stage in the process (either review by the grand jury or the filing of an information in the trial court). In determining whether the prosecution has made such a showing, the magistrate judge provides an independent screening of the prosecution's decision to charge. Indeed, most courts view this screening objective as the sole legally cognizable purpose of the preliminary hearing. The independent review by the magistrate is said "to prevent hasty, malicious, improvident, and oppressive prosecutions, * * * to avoid both for the defendant and the public the expense of a public trial, and to save the defendant from the humiliation and anxiety involved in public prosecution."

The actual effectiveness of the preliminary hearing screening in achieving these ends is a matter of dispute. To some extent the different conclusions may be explained by differences in the preliminary hearings being evaluated. Substantial variations exist in the hearing's legal structure from one jurisdiction to another, and because of considerable discretion given to magistrates, great variations can exist under the same legal structure from one magistrate court to another. These variations obviously can produce differences in screening effectiveness. Thus, studies of the preliminary hearing in different jurisdictions have produced quite disparate statistics on preliminary hearing dispositions. The percentage of dismissals to the total number of hearings have ranged from 2% to more than 30%.

A variety of differences have been cited as possibly contributing to the variations in the rate of preliminary hearing dismissals. Those differences relate not only to the legal standards governing the preliminary hearing, but also to the institutional structure and the practice of participants in the hearing. Among the factors mentioned are the following: (1) whether there is extensive prosecutorial screening before the case reaches the preliminary hearing stage (as in jurisdictions where 30–50% of the cases presented by the police do not result in the filing of charges); (2) whether prosecutors are assigned horizontally to cases (with different prosecutors responsible for initial screening, preliminary hearing presentation, and trial) or vertically (with the same prosecutor responsible for the case from initial presentation to final disposition); (3) whether the prosecutor may bypass the preliminary hearing by taking the case directly to the grand jury, and whether the prosecutor regularly uses the bypass alternative (so that preliminary hearings are used in only a small group of cases) or regularly utilizes the preliminary hearing; (4) whether the use of the bypass procedure is tied to the strength of the particular case; (5) whether the magistrates conducting the hearings are lay persons or lawyer/judges; (6) whether the magistrates operate under heavy or light caseloads; (7) whether the caseload at the trial level makes difficult the disposition there of all cases which could justifiably be boundover, and the trial

courts therefore encourage the magistrate court to reduce charges and accept guilty pleas in cases more appropriately disposed of at the misdemeanor level; (8) whether prosecutors seek to settle cases by plea bargains prior to the preliminary hearing stage or plea bargaining begins and cases are settled largely after the case is boundover to the trial level; (9) whether defense counsel regularly insist upon a preliminary hearing even in open and shut cases (largely to obtain discovery) or usually waive the hearing in such cases; (10) whether the proof standard governing the magistrate's decision to bindover is essentially the same probable cause standard applied on the issuance of an arrest warrant or is a standard comparable to that imposed by a trial judge in determining whether there is sufficient evidence to send a case to the jury; (11) whether the prosecutor must meet the bindover standard through evidence that would be admissible at trial or may rely instead on hearsay and other evidence generally inadmissible at trial; (12) whether the prosecution, even though not required to do so in order to satisfy the bindover standard, follows the practice of presenting all of its key witnesses, or instead seeks to limit defense discovery and reduce the burden on its witnesses by introducing just enough evidence to meet the bindover standard; (13) whether the magistrate has the same leeway as a trial court factfinder in judging credibility; (14) whether the scope of defense presentations is limited—e.g., whether the defense may establish affirmative defenses, and whether the leeway granted the defense in cross-examining prosecution witnesses and presenting defense witnesses generally approximates, or is considerably narrower than, that granted at trial; and (15) whether the practical impact of a magistrate's order of dismissal is to end the case unless new evidence is uncovered, or the prosecutor frequently reinitiates prosecution without additional evidence by either taking the case to the grand jury or refiling when another judge is sitting as preliminary hearing magistrate.

(b) Discovery. In meeting the evidentiary standard for a bindover, the prosecutor will necessarily provide the defense with some discovery of the prosecution's case. The defendant may obtain even more discovery by cross-examining the prosecution's witnesses at the hearing and by subpoenaing other potential trial witnesses to testify as defense witnesses at the hearing. The extent of the discovery obtained in this manner will depend upon several factors, including: (1) whether the prosecution can rely entirely on hearsay reports and thereby sharply limit the number of witnesses it presents; (2) whether, even assuming hearsay cannot be used, the bindover standard may be satisfied by the presentation of a minimal amount of testimony on each element of the offense; (3) whether, notwithstanding the ease with which the standard is met, the prosecution still follows a general practice of presenting most of its case; (4) whether the defendant is limited, both in cross-examination and in the calling of witnesses, to direct rebuttal of material presented by the prosecution; (5) whether limited discovery procedures apply to the preliminary hearing or can be made applicable to the preliminary hearing at the discretion of the magistrate; and (6) whether the defendant is willing to bear the tactical costs that may be incurred in utilizing his subpoena and cross-examination authority for discovery purposes.

In many jurisdictions, several of these factors combine to make preliminary hearing discovery quite limited, but in other jurisdictions, other factors shape a preliminary hearing that gives the defense a fairly good preview of the prosecution's case. Whether preliminary hearing discovery is narrow or broad, its importance to the defense will depend in large part on how that discovery compares to what is available under the jurisdiction's pretrial discovery. Where the identity of prosecution witnesses, their prior statements to the police, and all material physical evidence is available through pretrial discovery, even the broadest preliminary hearing discovery will add only the opportunity to learn more about some prosecution witnesses by cross-examining them under oath (and even that advantage disappears if the jurisdiction also provides pretrial discovery depositions). On the other hand, where pretrial discovery does not reveal even the names of prosecution witnesses, and where discovery from witnesses known to the defense depends on their willingness to be interviewed, even fairly narrow preliminary hearing discovery may be so important to the defense that it will seek a preliminary hearing even where a bindover is almost certain. Also, though pretrial discovery may be quite broad, if that discovery is not available until after the critical time for plea settlements has passed, the preliminary hearing may still serve as the primary discovery vehicle for the substantial percentage of cases resolved by guilty pleas.

For all but a few jurisdictions, the defense discovery available through the hearing is treated as an incidental "byproduct", rather than a basic function, of the hearing. Indeed, if the defense's use of cross-examination or subpoena authority seems aimed basically at discovery, rather than challenging the sufficiency of the prosecution's evidence, the magistrate may prohibit such use. So too, where some magistrate error is found to have had no bearing on defendant's right to a fair finding on evidentiary sufficiency, a defense showing that the error cost it the opportunity for discovery will not justify relief. Both legislatures and courts have been unreceptive to the suggestion that discovery should be recognized as a basic function of the preliminary hearing and its procedures shaped accordingly. The preliminary hearing, it is noted, imposes significant burdens on witnesses and is a costly use of the time of prosecutor, defense counsel, and magistrate. It makes no sense to expand its use to serve a function that can be fulfilled more expeditiously and with more appropriate timing through traditional discovery procedures.

(c) Future Impeachment. Extensive cross-examination of prosecution witnesses at the preliminary hearing may be of value to the defense even though there is little likelihood of successfully challenging the prosecution's showing of evidentiary sufficiency and little to be gained by way of discovery. This is because, as the Supreme Court has noted, "the skilled interrogation of witnesses [at the preliminary examination] by an experienced lawyer can fashion a vital impeachment tool for use in cross-examination of the State's witnesses at the trial."[1] In many instances, witnesses are more likely to make damaging admissions or contradictory statements at the preliminary hearing because they are less thoroughly briefed for that proceeding than they are for trial. Also, with respect to some witnesses, the more they say before trial, the more likely that there will be some inconsistency between their trial testimony and their previous statements. Arguably, the jury may view such inconsistencies as more damaging to the witness' credibility when the inconsistency is with preliminary hearing testimony, as opposed to prior statements given to the police, since the preliminary hearing testimony was given under oath in a judicial setting. Moreover, in some jurisdictions, the use of the inconsistent statement is not limited to impeachment; it may be used as well as substantive evidence.

As with discovery, the opportunity to prepare for future impeachment of prosecution witnesses is a "by-product of a preliminary hearing," but not the "reason for the hearing." Thus, the defendant has no right to insist that key prosecution witnesses be called so that they can be cross-examined. Also, should probable cause otherwise be established (e.g., by an intervening grand jury indictment), defendant ordinarily is not entitled to relief because he was restricted in his opportunity to develop impeachment material through cross-examination at the preliminary hearing.

(d) The Perpetuation of Testimony. Preliminary hearing testimony traditionally has been admitted at trial as substantive evidence, under the "prior testimony" exception to the hearsay rule, where the witness is not available to testify at trial.[2] Thus, the hearing perpetuates the testimony of witnesses, ensuring that it may be used even if the witness should die, disappear, or otherwise become unavailable to testify. For reasons discussed in § 14.4(d), the defense rarely will have its own witnesses testify at the preliminary hearing. Accordingly, the perpetuation of testimony is of practical significance primarily as it relates to prosecution witnesses, and the possibility of perpetuation tends to by viewed by the defense as a negative feature of the hearing.

The admission of the preliminary hearing testimony of a prosecution witness who is unavailable at trial (and therefore is not subject to trial cross-examination) must be reconciled with the defendant's Sixth Amendment right of confrontation. *California v. Green*[3] established the basic guidelines for admitting such testimony consistent with defendant's Sixth Amendment right. The Court there upheld the constitutionality of admitting preliminary hearing testimony over a defense objection that it should not be admissible where the prosecution witness was "unavailable" solely because of a claimed loss of memory. The defendant in *Green* had been charged with furnishing marijuana to a minor, Porter.

§ 14.1

1. See Coleman v. Alabama, discussed in § 14.4 at note 1. Cross-examination designed to lay the foundation for future impeachment carries with it certain dangers for the defense. If the cross-examination focuses too much on potential weaknesses in the witness' testimony, it may educate the witness as to those weaknesses. The witness may "rehabilitate himself for the trial and state that at the hearing he was confused, but that everything is now clear in his mind." If the witness is one who otherwise might "soften" his view of the facts as time passes and his emotional involvement lessens, extensive cross-examination at the preliminary hearing may only harden his position and make him less able to retreat to a more friendly position. Finally, if the witness becomes unavailable at trial, the defense may find that it has perpetuated testimony more damaging than that which would have existed without the cross-examination.

2. Federal Evidence Rule 804(a) sets forth the traditional grounds of unavailability: "Unavailability as a witness" includes situations in which the declarant (1) is exempted by ruling of the court on the ground of privilege from testifying concerning the subject matter of declarant's statement; or (2) persists in refusing to testify concerning the subject matter of declarant's statement despite an order of the court to do so; or (3) testifies to a lack of memory of the subject matter of declarant's statement; or (4) is unable to be present or to testify at the hearing because of death or then existing physical or mental illness or infirmity; or (5) is absent from the hearing and the proponent of a statement has been unable to procure the declarant's attendance * * * by process or other reasonable means. * * *. It should be noted in connection with this 5th ground that persons located outside the trial jurisdiction will not for that reason alone be "unavailable." If the former witness can be located, even though the location is in another state, the witness ordinarily will be subject to compulsory process under the Uniform Act to Secure The Attendance of Witnesses From Without A State In Criminal Proceedings.

3. 399 U.S. 149, 90 S.Ct. 1930, 26 L.Ed.2d 489 (1970).

When Porter was called to testify, he was evasive and uncooperative on the stand, claiming a lapse of memory. The prosecution then introduced two prior statements of Porter, including his preliminary hearing testimony, "to prove the truth of the matter asserted in the statements." The state court held that admission of these statements as substantive evidence violated defendant's right to confrontation, but the Supreme Court reversed.

The Court in *Green* initially held that if Porter was subject to cross-examination as to the statements at the trial, then the confrontation clause was not violated by admission of the statements as substantive evidence. The Court added, however, that there was a question as to whether Porter was subject to effective cross-examination at trial in light of his lapse of memory. It accordingly went on to consider the admissibility of the preliminary hearing testimony on the assumption that Porter was, in effect, an "unavailable" witness at trial. This made "Porter's preliminary hearing testimony * * * admissible as far as the Constitution is concerned * * * [because that testimony] had already been given under circumstances closely approximating those that surround the typical trial. Porter was under oath; [the defendant] was represented by counsel—the same counsel in fact who later represented him at the trial; [the defendant] had every opportunity to cross-examine Porter as to his statement; and the proceedings were conducted before a judicial tribunal, equipped to provide a judicial record of the hearings."

As various lower courts have noted, *Green* requires "an opportunity to effectively cross-examine and merely providing an opportunity to cross-examine at the preliminary hearing is not per se an adequate opportunity." In his *Green* dissent, Justice Brennan cited a series of factors that might inhibit cross-examination at the typical preliminary hearing. Since the issue presented there is one of probable cause, counsel may view cross-examination to be of little value. Counsel may also be concerned that cross-examination will give the prosecutor discovery, that the magistrate will not look

kindly on extending the length of the hearing, and that the short time for preparation makes cross-examination too risky at this point. The Court majority did not find persuasive Justice Brennan's reliance on these potential restraints, noting that Justice Brennan nonetheless acknowledged that the preliminary hearing testimony could be used where the witness was unavailable for reasons (e.g., death) that would have prevented his appearance. *Green* accordingly was viewed by lower courts as establishing that, for confrontation clause purposes, the "adequacy of [the] opportunity to conduct meaningful cross-examination focus primarily not on the practical realities facing counsel at the preliminary hearing * * *, but rather upon the scope and nature of the opportunity for cross-examination permitted by the [magistrate at the preliminary hearing]." The *Green* majority had noted simply that defense counsel there had not been "significantly limited in any way in the scope or nature of his cross-examination of the witness Porter at the preliminary hearing."

Lower courts subsequent to *Green* held that the prior testimony could be used even where the defense had decided for strategic reasons not to cross-examine at the preliminary hearing. Subsequently, in *Ohio v. Roberts*,[4] the Supreme Court raised the possibility that *Green* might be limited to cases in which the opportunity to cross-examine had been extensively utilized. The Court there held that *Green* permitted admission of the preliminary hearing testimony of an unavailable prosecution witness who had been called by the defense at the preliminary hearing, but had been examined, in effect, as a hostile witness. The Court noted that counsel, in his "direct examination," had challenged the witness' perception of events and her veracity, and had not been limited "in any way" in this line of questioning. The end result was, as in *Green*, a "substantial compliance with the purposes behind the confrontation requirement." The Court added that, in light of the facts before it, there was no need to determine whether *Green* applied where a defense counsel had not actually cross-examined the witness or had en-

---

4.   448 U.S. 56, 100 S.Ct. 2531, 65 L.Ed.2d 597 (1980).

gaged in only "de minimis questioning." It acknowledged that passages in *Green* "suggest that the opportunity to cross-examine at the preliminary hearing—even absent actual cross-examination—satisfies the Confrontation Clause." Yet, the Court there also recognized that "defense counsel in fact had cross-examined Porter." As defense counsel here had acted similarly, it would leave for another day the question of whether "the mere opportunity to cross-examine render[s] the prior testimony admissible."

Post–*Roberts* lower court rulings have focused upon the adequacy of the opportunity that had been available to counsel to cross-examine the now unavailable witness, rather than whether counsel actually utilized that opportunity. Lower courts stress that the opportunity to cross-examine at the preliminary hearing inherently provides other indicia of reliability. The preliminary hearing presents "substantially the same issues" as the trial and the defendant's "motive to cross-examine a witness * * * [is] similar to * * * [that] at trial." Accordingly, the critical question becomes whether the opportunity for cross-examination was "sufficient," which does not require that it have been equal to the cross-examination opportunity at trial. Ordinarily, the opportunity is deemed adequate unless the magistrate imposed some significant restriction on the preliminary hearing cross-examination. Courts have rejected the contention that the opportunity is insufficient because defense counsel had limited time to prepare for the hearing and did not have available the tool of pretrial discovery to develop potential lines of impeachment. However, courts have suggested that insufficiency may be established by showing that defense counsel at the preliminary hearing lacked crucial information that would have altered the entire character of the cross-examination.

(e) Other Functions. In a particular jurisdiction the preliminary hearing may be utilized to serve other incidental functions, such as to gain reduction of bail or other terms of

pretrial release. This is particularly true where bail is set at the initial appearance largely on the basis of a schedule tied to the offense charged, and the preliminary hearing provides the magistrate court with its first extensive examination of the facts of the individual case. The preliminary hearing also may serve as an integral part of the plea bargaining process, particularly where negotiations have been undertaken prior to the hearing. The hearing may then provide a valuable "educational process" for the defendant who is not persuaded by his counsel's opinion that the prosecution has such a strong case that a negotiated plea is in the defendant's best interest. As discussed in § 14.4(b), the hearing in some jurisdictions offers the initial point at which the constitutional validity of police acquisition of evidence may be challenged, and under some circumstances, it may offer sufficient advantages over the pretrial motion to suppress that defense counsel will insist upon a preliminary examination for this purpose alone. The preliminary hearing also may be utilized to establish mitigating circumstances that can then be presented at sentencing through the preliminary hearing transcript.

§ 14.2 Defendant's Right to a Preliminary Hearing

(a) The Federal Constitution. In *Hurtado v. California*,[1] the Supreme Court held that the Fifth Amendment guarantee of prosecution by grand jury indictment was not a fundamental right applicable to the states through the due process clause of the Fourteenth Amendment. The procedure challenged in that case provided for charging by prosecutor's information rather than by indictment, but it also required a magistrate's determination of probable cause at a preliminary hearing. In *Lem Woon v. Oregon*,[2] however, the Court was faced with a procedure permitting direct filing of an information without "any examination of commitment by a magistrate * * * or any verification other than [the]

§ 14.2

1. 110 U.S. 516, 4 S.Ct. 111, 28 L.Ed. 232 (1884), also discussed in § 15.1(c).

2. 229 U.S. 586, 33 S.Ct. 783, 57 L.Ed. 1340 (1913).

prosecutor's official oath." A unanimous Supreme Court held that the lack of a preliminary hearing caused no due process difficulties. Having held earlier in *Hurtado* that a grand jury indictment was not required, the Court was "unable to see upon what theory it can be held that an examination or the opportunity for one, prior to the formal accusation by the district attorney, is obligatory upon the States." The Court has continued to adhere to the *Lem Woon* holding, and in *Gerstein v. Pugh*,[3] the Court rejected the contention that a preliminary hearing is required by the Fourth Amendment. Though the Court in *Gerstein* did hold that a reasonably prompt "judicial determination of probable cause [is] a prerequisite to extended restraint on liberty following [a warrantless] arrest," it concluded this could be done in a nonadversary proceeding (as opposed to a preliminary hearing).[4]

Though the Constitution does not require that the defendant be afforded a preliminary hearing, once a jurisdiction provides for a preliminary hearing, it may not then restrict the defendant's right to that hearing in a manner that would violate constitutional protections. Thus, *Coleman v. Alabama*[5] held that a state cannot grant defendants a right to a preliminary hearing and then refuse to appoint counsel to represent an indigent defendant at that hearing. For reasons discussed at § 14.4(a), *Coleman* held that the preliminary hearing, though not itself constitutionally required, is a "critical stage" in the criminal prosecution, rendering applicable a defendant's Sixth Amendment right to counsel. So too, by analogy to cases dealing with other rights that have only a state law grounding, due process would prohibit prosecutorial vindictiveness in charging or judicial vindictiveness in sentencing that was directed against a defendant because

the defendant refused to waive a state law right to a preliminary hearing. A state also could not engage in discrimination that would violate the equal protection clause in determining which groups of defendants will be entitled to a preliminary hearing.

(b) The Federal Practice. In the federal system, the Fifth Amendment requires grand jury screening (unless waived) in all felony cases. Nonetheless, federal law has for many years granted to the felony defendant a right to a preliminary hearing. That right was established because, in many parts of the country, charges were not presented to the grand jury until weeks after a defendant's arrest. An earlier review procedure was needed to ensure that a person was not held in custody, or subjected to the continued burdens associated with release on bail, without a fairly prompt prosecutorial showing of probable cause. While the magistrate made a probable cause determination where a warrant was issued, the *Gerstein* requirement of a similar determination for warrantless arrests had not yet been imposed, and the warrant determination was, in any event, based solely on affidavits.

The preliminary hearing screening, however, remained subordinate to the eventual screening by the grand jury. Thus, where a grand jury indictment was issued prior to the time set for the preliminary hearing, the defendant's right to a hearing was "mooted." The return of the indictment established probable cause, so there was nothing left for the preliminary hearing magistrate to decide. The Federal Rules of Criminal Procedure subsequently incorporated this analysis. Federal Rule 5.1(a) requires a preliminary hearing for a felony prosecution, but then recognizes an exception where the "defendant is indicted."[6] That ex-

---

3. 420 U.S. 103, 95 S.Ct. 854, 43 L.Ed.2d 54 (1975), also discussed in § 3.5(a) at note 8.

4. *Gerstein* established that, apart from the application of Fourth Amendment safeguards stemming from the defendant being subjected to restraints on his liberty pending trial, Fourteenth Amendment due process does not impose any procedure prerequisites for initiating a prosecution and subjecting a person to trial. In particular, the burdens of accusation and litigation do not demand that some neutral body—grand jury or magistrate—find that the charge has some minimal evidentiary support. Indeed,

in *Albright v. Oliver*, 510 U.S. 266, 114 S.Ct. 807, 127 L.Ed.2d 114 (1994), the Court majority concluded that substantive due process (as distinct from the Fourth Amendment) offers no protection against the government's initiation of a prosecution where probable cause is obviously lacking. See also note 45 of § 2.7(d).

5. 399 U.S. 1, 90 S.Ct. 1999, 26 L.Ed.2d 387 (1970), discussed in § 14.4(a).

6. Rule 5.1 initially requires a preliminary hearing if a defendant is "charged with an offense other than petty offense," but then lists five exceptions, including the pri-

ception allows the prosecutor to preclude a preliminary hearing by simply obtaining a grand jury indictment prior to the scheduled date of the hearing. As to that date, Rule 5.1 requires that the hearing be held "within a reasonable time, but not later than 10 days after the initial appearance if the defendant is in custody and no later than 20 days if not in custody," although extensions of these time limits are possible on a prosecution showing "that extra-ordinary circumstances exist and justice requires the delay."

In many federal districts, the "prior-indictment" exception has been used to eliminate virtually all preliminary hearings. Where a grand jury sits daily and can promptly dispose of submitted cases, there are no administrative barriers to regularly mooting scheduled preliminary hearing by obtaining prior indictments. Very often, such districts will have no more than two or three preliminary hearing for every hundred felonies defendants processed. In other districts, it is more difficult to obtain indictments within the prescribed time limits and preliminary hearings are thus mooted only in a small portion of all cases. Over the federal system as a whole preliminary hearings are held in roughly 15–18% of the felony prosecutions filed in the federal district court.

(c) Indictment States. Eighteen states, as in the federal system, require prosecution by indictment (unless waived) for all felonies.[7] All of these "indictment states" also have statutes or court rules granting the defendant a right to a preliminary hearing within a specified period after his arrest. The common pattern in these jurisdictions is to allow bypassing without restriction, as in the federal system. In several, the state preliminary hearing provision contains a proviso, identical to that in federal law, stating that the hearing shall not be held if an indictment is returned prior to the scheduled hearing. In others, that result has been reached by judicial ruling. Where prosecutors intend to bypass but cannot obtain

an indictment with sufficient promptness, some courts permit them to obtain continuances or gain dismissal of the complaint without prejudice so to ensure that the indictment precedes the preliminary hearing.

While the ready availability of an indicting grand jury leads to more frequent use of the bypass procedure in indictment states than in information states, that use still tends to be far less than in the federal system. In some districts, prosecutors regularly bypass but recognize exceptions for certain types of cases. Like federal prosecutors, they see no reason to provide dual screening procedures, but unlike federal prosecutors, they regularly create exceptions when special circumstances would make a showing of proof in an open proceeding desirable from the prosecutor's perspective. Those special circumstances can include: (1) the need to perpetuate the testimony of a witness who might well be unavailable at trial; (2) some special reason for putting a prosecution witness to the test of testifying in public; (3) promoting the victim's interest in pursuing the matter by presenting it in a public forum; (4) gaining the defense perspective as to the events involved where there is some uncertainty as to what actually happened and the defense has indicated a willingness to present its side of the story at the preliminary hearing; (5) gaining a further identification of the suspect by having the witness make that identification at the hearing; and (6) promoting public confidence in a sensitive prosecutorial decision by having the evidence presented in a public forum and the decision to proceed ratified by a magistrate (or if the case is likely to be dismissed, by inviting dismissal in an open proceeding rather than a grand jury proceeding, where the prosecutor might be accused of having "dumped" the case due to political pressures).

In other indictment districts, bypassing is the exception, rather than the general rule.

or-indictment exception. Two of the exceptions relate to misdemeanors that are not petty-offenses (where the defendant consents to trial before a magistrate judge and where the prosecution files an information, which is regularly done to eliminate preliminary hearings in misdemeanor cases). Two other exceptions apply to felonies and

involve waivers (where the defendant waives the preliminary hearing, and where the prosecution charges a felony by information, which can be done only where the felony defendant waives a right to prosecution by indictment).

7. See § 15.1(d).

This may be a product of practical necessity, as where the grand jury meets too infrequently to obtain indictments prior to preliminary hearings as a regular matter. However, presenting cases initially at a preliminary hearing and then before the grand jury is also the common practice in many districts where grand jury review could readily be obtained prior to the scheduled preliminary hearing. Here, the limited use of the bypass procedure may be the product of a tradition established when prompt grand jury review was not as readily available. It may also reflect the prosecutor's conclusion that the extra expenditure of effort in having a preliminary hearing will be offset in the long run by advantages gained from the preliminary hearing (e.g., the better preparation for trial of witnesses and prosecutors, and the facilitation of plea bargaining by impressing upon defendants the strength of the prosecutor's case).

Where the common practice is to go forward with the preliminary hearing, approaches vary in identifying those exceptional cases in which mooting will be utilized. Uniformly, the indictment will come first (with the preliminary hearing thereby precluded) on those charges that are developed through a grand jury investigation. Indeed, the indictments in such cases are often issued even before the defendant is arrested. The indictment will also come before arrest where the defendant is a fugitive or outside the jurisdiction. Beyond this, prosecutors differ as to the need for further exceptions. Some will bypass in particular cases or particular types of cases in which they find special justification for limiting the number of instances in which the victim will be forced to testify in public. Thus, a prosecutor's office may regularly bypass in all sex offense prosecutions. Some prosecutors will bypass where the preliminary hearing process would be protracted due to the number of exhibits or witnesses or the number of separate hearings that would have to be held for factually linked defendants. Thus, where a single agent is the key witness on a number of separate drug buys, the prosecutor may go directly to the grand jury (where the agent can testify as to all of the drug buys in a single presentation) rather than have the agent be forced to testify at each of the separate preliminary hearings that the individual defendants would demand.

Finally, many prosecutors will bypass where they judge the discovery inherent in a preliminary examination to be too costly. Some will limit that judgment to the most pressing case for avoiding discovery, as where a key witness is an informer whose identity must be shielded until the last possible moment. Others also will bypass in particular types of cases likely to present an especially broad range of discovery (e.g., homicide prosecutions based on extensive circumstantial and forensic evidence), especially where that discovery would not be available under pretrial discovery procedures or would be available only if the defense granted reciprocal discovery to the prosecution. Critics of the bypass tactic, viewing the grand jury as by far the easier screening procedure, suggest that prosecutors are most likely to bypass where the prosecution's case is weak, but the various studies do not support that contention.

(d) Information States. Almost two-thirds of the states permit felony prosecutions to be brought by either information or indictment (although several in this group allow only for indictments for capital or life-sentence felonies). These states are commonly described as "information states" (although technically they are "option" states) because the overwhelming choice of prosecutors is to use the information alternative. Almost all of these states also provide for a preliminary hearing. In several information states, the possibility of bypassing the preliminary hearing by first obtaining an indictment is precluded. Some have eliminated the indicting grand jury and others require a preliminary hearing even after an indictment has issued. The vast majority of the information states, however, hold open the possibility of bypassing the preliminary hearing by obtaining an indictment prior to the scheduled hearing.

In many prosecutorial districts in information states, the possibility of a bypassing by indictment is largely theoretical. These districts do not have regularly sitting grand juries, and in some, grand juries have not been used for decades. In many other districts, while a grand jury is available, it is utilized almost exclusively for situations in which the grand jury's investigative power is needed. Those situations typically produce a bypass of the preliminary hearing as the investigating grand jury will also issue indictments, typically before the defendant is even arrested. In still other prosecutorial districts, a regularly sitting grand jury is utilized to bypass the preliminary hearing in a variety of cases, but still amounting to less than 10% of all felony prosecutions. Where prosecutors engage in such limited mooting, they usually use this route for the same reasons [discussed in subsection(c)] as prosecutors in indictment states who bypass as the exception rather than the general rule. Finally, in occasional districts in information states, prosecutors have sought to make the grand jury indictment the standard mode of charging, rejecting the conventional wisdom that leads to the overwhelming choice of the information alternative in the "information" (i.e. option) states. In these districts, bypassing is the common practice, and preliminary hearings become the exception rather than the general rule.

Equal protection challenges to prosecutorial bypassing of the preliminary hearing generally have failed. In a unique ruling, subsequently overturned by a state constitutional amendment, the California Supreme Court held that the preliminary hearing afforded the defendant so much greater screening protection than the grand jury that prosecutorial bypassing by obtaining a prior indictment constituted a per se violation of the state constitution's equal protection clause, without regard to the prosecutor's purpose in bypassing in the particular case. The Oregon Supreme Court refused to go that far, but held that "a constitutional claim for equal treatment is made out when the accused shows that preliminary hearings are offered or denied to individual defendants, or to social, geographic, or other classes of defendants * * * purely haphazardly or otherwise in terms that have no satisfactory explanation." However, the dominant view is that selectivity in the exercise of the bypass tactic only violates equal protection where the defendant can show "discriminatory purpose," as required under the Supreme Court's leading selective enforcement rulings. This requires, in effect, that the decision to bypass be motivated by race, religion, or some similar arbitrary classification.[8]

Most information states make a preliminary hearing bindover (or a waiver of the hearing) a prerequisite to charging by information in a felony case. Indeed, in many of these states, that requirement is imposed by the state constitution. However, a handful of states accept what is sometimes described as the "direct filing" of an information (i.e., the prosecutor may file the information in the trial court without first obtaining a preliminary hearing bindover or a defense waiver of that screening). Some of these states have abolished the preliminary hearing. Others provide for a preliminary hearing but allow a prosecutor to bypass by a direct filing prior to the scheduled hearing. Special safeguards are added to ensure that the information so filed has adequate evidentiary support. The direct filing procedure may require, for example, that the trial court approve the filing and that the information be accompanied by affidavits establishing probable cause. Another approach is to allow the defendant, after obtaining complete discovery, to move for dismissal on the ground that the evidence available to the prosecution, even if taken as undisputed, fails to establish a prima facie case. That motion is utilized to screen cases in a fashion roughly analogous to the motion for summary judgment in civil cases.

(e) **Waiver and Demand.** While many states condition the defendant's right to a preliminary hearing upon a timely demand for the hearing, the majority position appears to be that the right can be lost only by an affirmative waiver reflecting a voluntary and knowledgeable choice by the defendant. To obtain a knowledgeable waiver, caution would direct the magistrate to explain the purpose of the hearing, the rights available at the hearing, and the nature of the charges on which the hearing would be held. However, in con-

---

8. See § 13.4.

trast to the waiver of other rights, neither statutory provisions nor case law prescribe a particular litany for an affirmative waiver of a preliminary hearing. Statutes and court rules typically require that the magistrate advise the arrested person of the "right" to a preliminary hearing, with only a few also mandating a description of the "nature" of the hearing. Courts have held that a waiver should be judged in light of the circumstances of the individual case, including the defendant's familiarity with the criminal justice process. A critical factor here may be whether the defendant was assisted by counsel in making the waiver. Indeed some states require that the waiver acknowledge the advice of counsel.

Where states require a preliminary hearing unless waived, magistrates often will seek to determine whether defendant desires to waive at the first appearance, with defendant not yet having either retained or appointed counsel. A few courts have suggested that a defendant may knowingly waive a preliminary hearing without the assistance of counsel or an on-record waiver of the right to counsel that meets Sixth Amendment standards. However, since the Supreme Court has held that the preliminary hearing is a stage in the process to which the Sixth Amendment applies, it would seem that the defendant is entitled constitutionally to counsel's assistance in deciding whether to waive such a hearing, and a waiver without counsel therefore can be sustained only with a waiver of counsel's assistance as well. Accordingly, a waiver by a defendant who has yet to obtain counsel should be treated as subject to withdrawal should subsequently appointed or retained counsel request the hearing. In jurisdictions that condition the right to a preliminary hearing on a defense demand within a specified number of days, that time period should give the defendant enough time to obtain and consult with counsel before a choice is made.

Practice manuals generally urge defense counsel not to waive a preliminary hearing unless circumstances suggest that the hearing would pose a substantial danger to the defense that outweighs its value. Such circumstances include: (1) an essential prosecution witness is able to testify at the preliminary hearing but may well be unavailable at trial; (2) a complainant appears likely to "mellow" with time if not required at this point to put his or her testimony "on the record"; (3) the preliminary hearing may add to adverse publicity that will make it difficult to obtain a fair trial; (4) the preliminary hearing will call the prosecutor's attention to a curable defect in the prosecution's case that otherwise would not be noticed until trial, when it would be too late to correct it; and (5) the preliminary hearing will alert the prosecutor to the fact that the defendant is undercharged.

The potential value of the preliminary hearing to the defense might suggest that waiver of the hearing would be rare. In fact, waivers by the defense exceed fifty percent in a substantial number of jurisdictions which provide quite extensive preliminary hearings. A variety of factors may influence the waiver rate in a particular jurisdiction, including: (1) the availability of alternative discovery devices; (2) the inadequacy of the payment schedule of appointed counsel for representation at a preliminary hearing; (3) a prosecution practice of offering significant concessions to defendants who waive their preliminary hearings; and (4) the conventional wisdom of the local defense bar that the preliminary hearing is (i) unnecessary where the prosecution has a strong case and defendant intends to plead guilty, or (ii) an inherently risky process because the disadvantages noted above often cannot be foreseen until after the hearing is underway.

In many jurisdictions, the prosecutor has a right to insist upon the preliminary hearing even though the defendant desires to waive the hearing. The prosecutor's right is based on the premise that the state has an interest, independent of the defendant, in determining whether or not there is sufficient cause to proceed. Usually, the prosecutor will only insist upon a hearing where it offers a special advantage akin to that which may lead a prosecutor not to bypass in a district in which bypassing is the general rule.

§ 14.3   The Bindover Determination

(a) The Applicable Standard. The standard to be applied by the magistrate in determining whether the defendant will be bound-over typically is set forth in the statute or court rule that establishes the right to the hearing. The dominant formulation of that standard directs the magistrate to determine whether "there is probable cause to believe that an offense has been committed and that the defendant committed it." Another common formulation directs the magistrate to determine whether "it appears that an offense has been committed and there is probable cause to believe that the defendant committed it." Although the "offense has been committed" phrasing suggests that more than probable cause is needed to establish the corpus delecti, that distinction appears to have been lost in most, if not all, of these jurisdictions.

Exactly what probable cause means in the context of the preliminary hearing has been left to judicial development. Courts typically have followed one of three approaches in their descriptions of the probable cause requirement. Perhaps the most common is to look to the Fourth Amendment standard of probable cause as formulated in cases involving probable cause to arrest. Thus, courts speak of evidence that is "sufficient to induce a person of ordinary prudence and caution to entertain a reasonable belief that the defendant committed the crime charged," evidence that would lead "a man of ordinary caution or prudence * * * to believe and conscientiously entertain a strong suspicion of the guilt of the accused," and evidence establishing "a reasonable ground of suspicion, supported by circumstances sufficiently strong in themselves to warrant a cautious person in the belief that the accused is guilty of the offense charged." Another approach is to focus on the character of the evidence needed to establish probable cause at the preliminary hearing. Courts here note that, as to each element of the crime, there need only be "some evidence" from which a reasonable person could infer the presence of that element. Some courts using this standard may require evidence establishing no higher probability than that needed to

arrest. For others, however, to infer the "presence" of an element may require more than establishing a "fair probability" as to that element. A third approach is to stress what probable cause in the preliminary hearing context does not require. Thus, courts will note that it does not require proof beyond a reasonable doubt, and some will add that it also does not require proof that meets the preponderance of the evidence standard. Again, some of these courts may have in mind only the arrest standard of probability, but others may have in mind a somewhat higher showing of probability.

The use of the Fourth Amendment arrest standard in describing probable cause at a preliminary hearing indicates equivalence only in the requisite degree of probability. It does not mean that the magistrate's ruling will merely duplicate the decision made in the same case (often by the same magistrate) in the issuance of an arrest warrant or in the ex parte post-arrest finding of probable cause made pursuant to the *Gerstein* requirement.[1] The difference in context will necessarily lend a different shading to the preliminary hearing determination. Here, the assessment of probable cause will be made at an adversary rather than an ex parte proceeding. Even where use of hearsay is permitted, that hearsay will be presented through the testimony of a witness, who can be cross-examined as to the source of the hearsay, rather than through a showing based entirely on affidavits. Also, the arrest standard, directed primarily at police, is expressed in terms of "the factual and practical distinctions of everyday life in which reasonable and prudent men, not legal technicians act," while the charging decision being reviewed at the preliminary hearing is, by its nature, one involving the "legal technicians" of the prosecutor's office. Under the arrest standard, considerable uncertainty must be tolerated on occasion because of the need to allow the police to take affirmative action in ambiguous circumstances, but no comparable

---

§ 14.3

1. As to this requirement, see § 3.5(a) at note 8, and § 14.2 at note 3.

exigencies are presented when the charging decision is made. Thus, a police officer may make an arrest where the circumstances suggest that the property possessed by the suspect may have been stolen, but the prosecutor ordinarily has no justification for proceeding to charge without first determining that a theft actually did occur.

When courts indicate that probable cause at a preliminary hearing requires "more" than the probable cause needed for an arrest or search warrant, they may have in mind nothing more than the differences in the type of evidence required at each stage. However, commentators have suggested that the preliminary hearing has a "forward looking" component that logically should require a higher and different degree of probability than that applied to the review of an arrest or search. Consider, for example, the classic hypothetical in which the evidence known to the police establishes beyond a reasonable doubt that one of two independent actors committed a crime, but does not distinguish between the two. The usual view of Fourth Amendment probable cause would allow an arrest of both actors, but arguably the same should not be said for a preliminary hearing bindover, assuming no further evidence has been produced. The arrest standard looks only to the probability that the person committed the crime as established at the time of the arrest, while the preliminary hearing looks both to that probability as of the time of the hearing *and* to the probability that the government will be able to establish guilt at trial. If the police have been unable to develop further evidence pointing to the guilt of one of the actors, and there is not a reasonable likelihood that such evidence will be forthcoming, it arguably would be contrary to the screening function of the preliminary hearing to bindover either actor.

This view of probable cause as encompassing consideration of the prosecution's likely future development finds support in occasional language in appellate opinions and magistrate explanations of bindover rejections. However, a "forward looking" interpretation of probable cause has been rejected by the few courts speaking directly to the issue, and has not

been suggested in the many decisions speaking generally of the character of probable cause. The adoption of a probable cause standard, courts have noted, carries with it an automatic presumption that the prosecution may be able to "strengthen its case at trial," which is not subject to reevaluation by the magistrate in the individual case.

Several states clearly have departed from this traditional preliminary hearing perspective, as they shape the hearing to test the likelihood of the prosecution being able to succeed at trial. A few have done this by moving to a bindover standard that is roughly analogous to the standard applied by a trial judge in deciding whether the prosecutor's case is strong enough to send to the jury. These jurisdictions require that the prosecution establish a "prima facie case" at the preliminary hearing—that is, the evidence presented, taken in the light most favorable to the prosecution, must be sufficient to allow a reasonable finder of fact to convict the defendant at trial. Such a standard is also applied by the grand jury in a much larger group of states. Of course, in the grand jury context, the prima facie case standard is applied somewhat differently because the grand jury sees only the prosecution's evidence and its witnesses are not subject to cross-examination. In the preliminary hearing, where cross-examination is allowed and the defense can present its own evidence, the application of this standard comes closer to the ruling on a motion for directed verdict at the close of all the evidence.

Another approach to increasing the rigor of preliminary hearing screening looks not so much to the bindover standard as to the procedural characteristics of the hearing. The emphasis here is on providing what is commonly described as a "mini-trial" type of preliminary hearing. The prosecution is limited to use of evidence that would be admissible at trial, and the defense is allowed full scope in cross-examination and the presentation of defense evidence. Though the mini-trial hearing fits naturally with a bindover standard requiring a prima facie case, it is seen as having value as well in a jurisdiction applying a probable cause standard requiring a degree of probability similar to an arrest warrant. A mini-trial hearing, particularly if combined with the magistrate's capacity to judge witness credibility, provides a screening procedure that arguably is much more exacting even though it requires no greater degree of probability.

A substantial majority of jurisdictions reject both the prima facie standard and the mini-trial type of preliminary hearing. These attributes are deemed inconsistent with various provisions of the typical statute or court rule establishing the preliminary hearing. The bindover standard is described in terms of "probable cause," in contrast to provisions on the grand jury which do refer to a prima facie case standard. The timing requirements are stringent and do not suggest affording the prosecution adequate time to bring together its full case in the form of admissible evidence. Indeed, the basic thrust of reform in preliminary hearing procedure has been to shorten time periods and preclude continuances so as to ensure that no person is being held in custody or otherwise subjected to significant restraints on his liberty where the state does not have some reasonable grounding for its charge. Consistent with this purpose, many states also provide that the prosecutor is not limited by the rules of evidence and may rely entirely upon hearsay. Viewing the preliminary hearing from the perspective suggested by such provisions, judicial imposition of either a mini-trial approach or a prima facie evidence test is deemed inappropriate. Although the provisions indicate that the hearing should be somewhat more rigorous in its procedural attributes than the issuance of an arrest or search warrant, that objective can be achieved without applying trial standards or requiring a level of probability substantially greater than the traditional Fourth Amendment standard.

Finally, there is the question of whether it is permissible for the magistrate to consider factors other than the technical sufficiency of the evidence—e.g., the likelihood that a trial jury will not convict because of sympathy for the defendant, or disagreement with the substantive law, or the availability of civil remedies that the magistrate views as more appropriate for resolving disputes of this type. Opinions have noted that "it is not the function of the * * * magistrate at a preliminary hearing to determine the wisdom of the prosecuting attorney's decision to file * * * or to conclude that there should be no prosecution because the possibility of a conviction may be remote or virtually nonexistent" notwithstanding the sufficiency of the evidence. The preliminary hearing screening function, even under a forward looking prima facie case standard, no more puts the magistrate in the shoes of the jury or prosecutor than does the function of a trial judge in ruling on a motion to dismiss or a motion for a directed verdict of acquittal. However, a leading study of preliminary hearings found that magistrates do sometimes engage in such "nullification screening."

(b) Assessment of Credibility. Closely related to the definition of the applicable bindover standard is the extent of the magistrate's authority to pass judgment on the credibility of witnesses in applying that standard. Courts almost uniformly recognize that the magistrate has authority to judge credibility. If that were not so, there would be no reason for allowing the defense to cross-examine prosecution witnesses and present contradicting evidence of its own. The critical issue is how much leeway is granted to the magistrate in judging credibility. Consider, for example, a case in which the prosecution's proof of a particular element rests primarily on the testimony of a single witness. Assume also that the magistrate concludes that reasonable persons could conceivably believe that the witness is telling the truth, but the magistrate's own judgment is that the witness is very likely lying or mistaken. A leading study found that magistrates commonly will not refuse to bindover based on such credibility judgements, but not necessarily because that would be beyond their authority under the applicable legal standards.

In those jurisdictions with mini-trial type hearings, where appellate courts describe most broadly the magistrate's authority to judge credibility, a magistrate arguably would have authority to refuse to bindover in such a case. Thus, the Michigan courts speak of the magistrate having a "duty to pass judgment on the credibility of witnesses as well as the weight and competency of the evidence." They note in this regard that a proper case for a bindover is not presented simply because the "prosecution has presented evidence on each element of the offense," as the magistrate must weigh "the whole of the matter," resting "his conclusion on what he believes". Thus, a magistrate may refuse to bind over on a murder charge where the use of a weapon and other circumstances suggest that defendant had the necessary mens rea, but the magistrate finds believable the testimony of defense witnesses that refute the presence of that mens rea. On the other hand, the same courts have noted that the magistrate should not assume the role of the "ultimate finder of fact" and should bindover for jury consideration where "the evidence conflicts and raises a reasonable doubt regarding the defendant's guilt."

Other jurisdictions clearly would not allow the magistrate to refuse to bindover on a credibility judgement in the hypothetical posed above. Thus, both the Colorado and Wisconsin high courts have held that the magistrate has a very narrow capacity to judge credibility. The Colorado Supreme Court, after pointedly noting that the Colorado preliminary hearing was not a mini-trial type hearing, analyzed the magistrate's authority to judge credibility in light of the limited probability required under the traditional probable cause bindover standard. It concluded that a "judge in a preliminary hearing has jurisdiction to consider the credibility of witnesses only when, as a matter of law, the testimony is implausible or incredible. When there is a mere conflict in testimony, a question of fact exists for the jury, and the judge must draw the inference favorable to the prosecution." A slightly broader standard would allow the magistrate to resolve conflicts in testimony, "but only 'where the evidence is overwhelming.'"

(c) Consequences of a Dismissal. As with prosecution appeals in general, a prosecution appeal of a magistrate's dismissal at a preliminary hearing must be grounded on specific statutory authorization. Traditionally, that authorization has been lacking. Where statutes authorized prosecution appeals from

"final judgments," the magistrate's dismissal commonly was held not to fit that characterization because the dismissal did not preclude the prosecution from simply refiling the complaint on the same evidence before another magistrate. Other statutes provided for prosecution appeals from the dismissal of an "indictment or information," which did not include the preliminary hearing dismissal because the charging instrument dismissed there was a complaint. Today, however, at least a dozen states specifically provide for a prosecution appeal of a magistrate's refusal to bind over, with that appeal going initially to the trial court as the next highest court.

In the many states in which the prosecution lacks a right of appeal, appellate review may still be possible by application for an extraordinary writ (e.g. mandamus). However, the state may limit those writs in general to jurisdictional excess, thereby requiring the prosecution to show that the magistrate applied an incorrect legal standard. Even where the jurisdiction otherwise allows use of the writs to challenge an erroneous application of the law, it may refuse to do so in the preliminary hearing setting because of the availability to the prosecutor of the alternatives of refiling or seeking an indictment. If those possibilities do not preclude use of the writ, the prosecution still must meet the standard of establishing a "gross abuse" of discretion in the refusal to bind over.

In most jurisdictions, whether or not appellate review is available, a prosecutor will look to alternative procedures to obtain a "reversal" of a dismissal. The dismissal occurs before jeopardy has attached, and the Fifth Amendment does not bar initiation of a new prosecution for the same offense. Where prosecutions commonly are brought by indictment, the prosecutor most often will take the same charge directly to the grand jury. The grand jury may indict notwithstanding the magistrate's refusal to bind over and the defendant may be rearrested on the indictment. Where a grand jury is not available, the prosecutor may refile the complaint and attempt to obtain a bindover at a subsequent preliminary hearing (possibly before a different magistrate).

As discussed below, a handful of state courts have concluded that refiling undermines the magistrate's authority and therefore should not be permitted unless the prosecution offers substantial additional evidence. A few others have adopted provisions that preclude refiling, but give the trial court authority to allow the filing of an information notwithstanding the magistrate's rejection of a bindover, upon a factually supported allegation of sufficient evidence. The vast majority, however, permit refiling at will, including refiling on the same evidence before a different magistrate, absent proof that the prosecutor's purpose is to harass the defendant. Although rulings sustaining such authority commonly point to the prosecution's lack of authority to appeal the dismissal in the particular state, the authority to refile without new evidence is also recognized in some of the states that allow a prosecution appeal. In many jurisdictions, support for unlimited refiling also is found in preliminary hearing provisions which specifically state that a dismissal "shall not preclude the state from instituting a subsequent prosecution for the same offense."

Where state law allows refiling only with "additional evidence," the question arises as to what will satisfy that requirement. The most rigorous standard is that imposed in Oklahoma, which contains four prerequisites for refiling: (1) the prosecution must "make an offer of additional evidence or prove other good cause to justify another preliminary examination"; (2) such "additional or new evidence does not mean that which was known to the state at the time of the first preliminary or which could have been easily acquired"; (3) the refiling with additional evidence "must * * * [be brought] before the same magistrate who dismissed the charge, or in his absence, another magistrate, setting forth the dismissed case number"; and (4) "the magistrate at the subsequent preliminary examination * * * should not consider the matter anew as on first impression," but should ask only whether "the additional competent evidence" operates to "overcome" the prior dismissal. One consequence of this standard is to deter the prosecutorial strategy of presenting just so much of its

evidence as is needed to meet the bindover standard. Should the prosecution miscalculate and the magistrate hold its evidence insufficient, it must seek a continuance so that it can produce the evidence it has in reserve (and that evidence must be promptly available). That continuance tactic is not necessary in jurisdictions that require new evidence for a refiling, but do not limit the additional evidence to that which could not previously have been presented.

(d) Consequences of a Bindover. In an indictment jurisdiction, the magistrate binds over for consideration by the grand jury. However, the grand jury is in no way bound by the magistrate's action, but must make its own determination based on the evidence presented to it, which may not be the same evidence presented before the magistrate. Indeed, it would be inconsistent with the grand jury's independence for the prosecutor to urge it to return a charge because the magistrate had found probable cause on that charge. Should the grand jury indict on that same charge, that indictment serves as the basis for further proceedings and sufficiency of the evidence supporting the bindover is no longer in issue.

In information states, where a preliminary hearing bindover (or waiver) is a prerequisite for the filing of an information, the information ordinarily is limited to the offense on which the magistrate found probable case and bound over. Thus, should a magistrate bind over on a lesser offense than that requested, a prosecutor still seeking to pursue the higher charge must look to the same alternatives that would be utilized where the magistrate dismisses the complaint. If a grand jury is available, the magistrate may seek an indictment on the higher charge. If the state allows for an appeal from a dismissal (and the rejection of the higher offense is treated as a dismissal of that charge), or extraordinary writs are available, the prosecutor may seek appellate review of the magistrate's rejection of the higher charge. Finally, the prosecution may seek to have the complaint dismissed without prejudice, which would permit it (in most jurisdictions) to refile on the higher charge and obtain a "second chance" through a new preliminary hearing.

Not all information states limit the information to the offenses on which the magistrate finds probable cause. Several states have statutes authorizing the prosecutor to charge any offense transactionally related to the bindover offense, although at least one requires that the evidence at the preliminary hearing establish probable cause as to the added charge. However, courts construing such provisions have divided as to whether they permit the information to add to the bindover offense a related charge that had been dismissed by magistrate.

Pending the filing of an information or indictment, the defendant may be able to challenge the bindover decision by writ of habeas corpus. When the bindover is followed by an information, the appropriate challenge usually is by a motion to dismiss or quash the information, which must be made pretrial, and in some states, prior to pleading to the information. Courts reviewing a bindover decision often stress that they may not substitute their judgement for that of the magistrate who saw and heard the testimony. Here too, courts often state that the magistrate's decision will only be overturned when there has been a clear abuse of discretion. Accordingly, the magistrate's decision (ordinarily not accompanied by opinion or findings of fact) is most likely to be reversed when a misinterpretation of substantive law (or perhaps oversight) resulted in a total absence of proof on a particular element of the offense. On occasion, however, bindover decisions also are rejected on the ground that, without attempting to reconcile conflicts or judge the credibility of witnesses, the inferences drawn from the evidence simply are not sufficient to support a probable cause finding.

Assume now that a magistrate binds over on a record that clearly fails to establish probable cause, after which the prosecutor files an information based on that bindover. If a timely challenge in the trial court is rejected, as to which interlocutory appeal is unavailable, and the defendant is then convicted at trial, may defendant raise again the improper bindover issue on his appeal? In several states, a proper bindover is viewed as a jurisdictional prerequisite to the filing of an information, and therefore a new trial is required if it is shown on appeal that the bindover was not supported by sufficient evidence. Most states hold, however, that the magistrate's error in binding over, and the trial court's error in failing to quash the information, are rendered harmless by the introduction of sufficient evidence to convict at trial. With the state having established guilt beyond a reasonable doubt, the probable cause issue is rendered "moot", and a claim limited only to that issue offers no suggestion of having impacted the fairness of defendant's trial. Where the state appellate courts do not readily accept defense petitions for interlocutory review, this position results, as a practical matter, in typically rendering unreviewable trial court rulings rejecting motions to quash.

§ 14.4 Preliminary Hearing Procedures

(a) Right to Counsel. In *Coleman v. Alabama*,[1] the Supreme Court held that the Sixth Amendment right to counsel extends to the preliminary hearing and therefore grants to the indigent defendant a right to the appointment of counsel for that hearing. The Sixth Amendment right only applies to critical stages in the proceedings so the Court had to determine whether the preliminary hearing is a stage where counsel's assistance was "necessary to preserve the defendant's basic right to a fair trial." The Court majority was not persuaded by the argument of the state (and the dissenters) that counsel was not needed because state law protected the unrepresented accused by prohibiting the prosecution's use at trial of "anything that occurred" at the preliminary hearing. The majority responded by reciting the various significant steps which counsel could take at the preliminary hearing. These steps included: "exposing fatal weaknesses in the State's case that might lead the magistrate to refuse to bind the accused over"; fashioning through preliminary hearing cross-examination "a vital impeachment tool" for

§ 14.4
1. 399 U.S. 1, 90 S.Ct. 1999, 26 L.Ed.2d 387 (1970).

the trial; discovery of the prosecution's case; preserving the testimony of favorable witnesses who might became unavailable at trial; and making arguments on such matters as "the necessity for an early psychiatric examination or bail." *Coleman* was written with reference to a state in which the ultimate prosecution screening was to be by the grand jury in considering an indictment, so its first cited significant step (precluding a bindover) arguably would be even more telling in an information state. Accordingly, *Coleman* has uniformly been read as requiring the appointment of counsel at the preliminary hearing in both indictment and information jurisdictions.

(b) Application of the Rules of Evidence. While all jurisdictions require magistrates to recognize testimonial privileges at the preliminary hearing, from that point on they vary considerably in their treatment of the applicability of the rules of evidence. With a modest degree of overgeneralization, the various positions can be divided into three basic approaches: (1) full applicability; (2) inapplicability with varying magistrate discretion to exclude evidence that would not be admissible at trial; and (3) general applicability with exceptions for certain types of evidence not admissible at trial.

Only a handful of states require full application of the rules of evidence, restricting the preliminary hearing evidence to that which would also be admissible at trial. These jurisdictions will not reject a bindover, however, simply because the magistrate erroneously admitted incompetent evidence. If the reviewing court concludes that there was sufficient admissible evidence before the magistrate to meet the bindover standard, the bindover will be upheld. The magistrate's error in admitting the incompetent evidence will be treated, in effect, as per se harmless error.

A much larger group of jurisdictions, perhaps a majority, start from the premise that the rules of evidence do not apply to the preliminary hearing. Most of these jurisdictions have provisions similar to Rule 1101(d) of the Federal Rules of Evidence, which states that the evidentiary rules, "other than with respect to privileges, do not apply in * * * preliminary

examinations in criminal cases." Such provisions clearly allow the magistrate to admit and rely upon evidence that would not be admissible at trial where the magistrate views such evidence as sufficiently reliable for a probable cause determination. At the same time, these provisions do not restrict the magistrate's authority to insist upon adherence to the rules of evidence where the magistrate believes that the offered incompetent evidence is not sufficiently reliable. However, in the federal system and in most of the states with Rule 1101(d)-type provisions, the preliminary hearing provisions at least somewhat restrict the magistrate's discretion with respect to two categories of evidence that would be inadmissible at trial.

The restrictive provisions typically state that "the finding of probable cause may be based on hearsay in whole or part," and that "objections to evidence on the ground that it was acquired by unlawful means are not properly made at the preliminary hearing." Although the hearsay provision is stated as permissive, it appears to at least give the prosecution the right to gain admission of its hearsay evidence. Its permissiveness does come into play, however, in the probable cause determination; the provision does not also require that the magistrate ignore the weaknesses of hearsay evidence in determining what weight should be given to that evidence. The provision on evidence obtained by unlawful means similarly appears to require that such evidence not be excluded for that reason. Since the illegal acquisition ordinarily would not bear upon the reliability of the evidence, that factor ordinarily should have no bearing upon the weight given to the evidence by the magistrate. An exception would be the case in which coercive methods of obtaining statements from persons cast doubt upon the reliability of those statements.

A third group of jurisdictions, consisting of roughly a dozen states, hold the rules of evidence generally to be applicable to preliminary hearings, but creates exceptions for certain categories of evidence that would be inadmissible at trial. The two most common exceptions relate to particular classes of hearsay[2] and to evidence obtained by police methods that could lead to suppression at trial, although other exceptions also are specified in particular states (e.g., to the best evidence rule). The exceptions typically take one of two forms. Some provisions state that a particular class of evidence "shall" or "may" be admitted. Others state that the probable cause finding may be based on specified categories of evidence that would be inadmissible at trial. At least the latter provisions suggest that the magistrate has discretion to give the evidence less weight if the factors that lead to its inadmissibility at trial suggest that it is less reliable.

Provisions prohibiting a preliminary hearing objection to the admission of evidence obtained through unlawful means are found in the vast majority of jurisdictions. However, objections based on the unlawful acquisition of evidence are recognized in the handful of states that limit the bindover decision to evidence that would be admissible at trial, and in several of the states that generally apply the rules of evidence subject to specified exceptions. Also, because electronic surveillance statutes, in accordance with federal law, provide for suppression of the contents of illegal interceptions in any "hearing", the exclusion of such evidence may be required even where the preliminary hearing provision generally precludes objections based on the unlawful acquisition of evidence. Where the objection based upon unlawful acquisition is available at the preliminary hearing, it operates somewhat differently than the pretrial motion to suppress made in the trial court. Unlike the pretrial suppression motion, which is made in anticipation of the prosecution's use of illegally acquired evidence, the preliminary hearing objection is tied to the prosecutor's attempt to actually use that evidence at the hearing. Thus, if the prosecution has sufficient evidence to support a bindover without using the fruits of an arguably unconstitutional police activity, it can avoid an exclusionary rule challenge by limiting the evidence it uses at the hearing.

Like all evidentiary rulings at a preliminary hearing, the ruling on a challenge to evidence as illegally acquired will not be binding upon the trial court. The preliminary hearing ruling can nonetheless have a significant bearing in several ways on the subsequent proceedings. If the magistrate should exclude the evidence and find insufficient remaining evidence to bindover, the prosecution will be required to either refile or gain an appellate reversal of the magistrate's ruling. As discussed in § 14.3(c), either alternative may present significant obstacles. In particular, should the prosecutor gain appellate review by the trial court, either through an extraordinary writ or a statutory right of appeal, that court will ordinarily accept the magistrate's factual findings as to the acquisition of the evidence and reinstate the complaint only if the magistrate erred in applying the applicable law to those findings. If the prosecutor refiles before another magistrate, that magistrate may likewise rule that the evidence is inadmissible and refuse to bind over. Should the defendant lose the suppression objection before the magistrate, the defendant will be able to renew the motion before the trial court, but may be limited to the transcript of the preliminary hearing, in effect giving the defendant a single opportunity as to the evidentiary showing of illegal acquisition.

(c) The Defendant's Right of Cross-Examination. All jurisdictions grant the defense a right to cross-examine those witnesses presented by the prosecution at the preliminary hearing. This right is based on local law; the

---

2. The narrowest hearsay exceptions are limited to one or both of two categories of hearsay unlikely to pose reliability difficulties. They allow for admission of the reports of experts without the experts testifying and admission of written statements of persons attesting to such matters as their ownership of property that was stolen, damaged, or broken into, to their lack of consent to the taking of property, and to the authenticity of their signature on a written instrument. Somewhat broader provisions apply to any type of hearsay statement, but impose certain prerequisites before the statement may be admitted. Thus, the prosecutor may be required to establish initially that there is "reasonable ground to believe that the declarant will be personally available at trial," or that "it would impose an unreasonable hardship on one of the parties or on a witness to require that the primary source of the evidence be produced" and that "there is a substantial basis for believing the source of the hearsay is credible and for believing that there is a factual basis for the information furnished."

Supreme Court has long held that cross-examination at a preliminary hearing is not required by the confrontation clause of the Sixth Amendment. The relevant provisions typically describe the right in general terms, leaving to the judiciary the formulation of applicable limitations. As would be expected, the courts uniformly agree that cross-examination at the preliminary hearing should at least be subject to those restrictions that the particular jurisdiction imposes on trial cross-examination. Most also apply, however, one or more additional limitations that stem from the limited screening function of the preliminary hearing and therefore would not be applicable in the trial setting.

A common restriction tied to the function of the preliminary hearing permits the magistrate to cut-off examination that seems to be aimed more at obtaining pretrial discovery than at challenging the witness' testimony. The possible use of cross-examination for discovery purposes is not a significant concern at trial, where the defense has already obtained discovery and presumably has its case fully prepared. In contrast, magistrates are well aware that defense counsel may utilize the preliminary hearing primarily for discovery purposes. Questions most likely to be challenged on this score are those asking about other sources of evidence (e.g., the names of known eyewitnesses) or exploring the range of investigative procedures that were utilized by the police. Also, where a jurisdiction holds that a particular defense is not cognizable at a preliminary hearing, as discussed in subsection (d) infra, cross-examination apparently designed to bring forth information relating to such a defense will be prohibited either as an attempt at discovery or as failing to relate to an issue properly before the magistrate. Questions that seem to be fishing for possible lines of defense, rather than supporting a particular defense that defendant intends to present at the hearing, also may be rejected as aimed at discovery.

Since the issue for determination at the preliminary hearing is only that of probable cause, a magistrate may also have authority to bar cross-examination that clearly challenges the prosecution's case but is deemed not to carry sufficient force to upset the prosecution's showing of probable cause. Thus, courts sometimes state that while cross-examination must be permitted to challenge the witness' credibility as to the events described in his or her testimony, the magistrate may bar cross-examination aimed at challenging only the witness' "general trustworthiness." So too, where the magistrate takes the position that credibility judgments at the preliminary hearing should be limited only to apparent falsehoods, and the initial questioning indicates that the witness will not retreat from her testimony, a magistrate may cut-off all further questioning as unlikely to alter the magistrate's judgment on probable cause. Critics of this practice respond that even if the magistrate has an extremely limited authority to judge credibility, there always exists the possibility that a defense counsel allowed to conduct a probing cross-examination could eventually force the witness to retreat or produce inconsistencies so significant as to totally undermine the witness' credibility.

At noted in § 14.1(d), the preliminary hearing testimony of a witness who later becomes unavailable at trial may be admitted there as substantive evidence, provided the defendant was given an adequate opportunity to cross-examine the witness at the preliminary hearing. Restriction of cross-examination by the magistrate thus often carries with it the risk of later being deemed to have denied the defense that adequate opportunity. While a bar against questions apparently aimed at discovery is not likely to cause difficulties, the preclusion of questions referring to defenses not cognizable at the preliminary hearing conceivably could constitute such a bar should those defenses be presented at trial. Restrictions on questions relating to the witness' credibility are most likely to be seen as having a bearing on the adequacy issue as they go directly to the function of cross-examination. Thus, very often, the magistrate must decide, even where the authority to restrict cross-examination is clear, whether the imposition of that restriction is justified if its cost may be to preclude possible trial use of the witness' testimony.

The critical factor here may be whether the prosecution requests that the magistrate restrict the cross-examination. If the prosecutor is willing to risk the possible inability to use the testimony at trial, the magistrate's obligation arguably is to impose the restriction; but where the prosecution would prefer to allow the cross-examination, a magistrate should be hesitant to insist upon the restriction. While the magistrate has an independent interest in properly confining cross-examination so as to avoid a hearing more lengthy than it need be, the prosecution may be seen as having an equally weighty interest in being able to perpetuate the testimony of its witnesses. This is especially true where the jurisdiction's deposition procedure is limited in availability on the assumption that the preliminary hearing ordinarily will be used to perpetuate testimony.

At trial, the defense has available for use in cross-examination any prior recorded statements of the prosecution witness. In some jurisdictions those statements are given to the defense as part of pretrial discovery, while others make them available under Jencks-type provisions following the witness' direct testimony.[3] Where availability is tied to pretrial discovery, the prior recorded statement ordinarily is not available at the preliminary hearing. A few jurisdictions do hold that the magistrate has discretionary authority to order discovery restricted to defense needs in challenging the prosecution's showing of probable cause, but most reason that pretrial discovery cannot be ordered by the magistrate, as discovery provisions do not take effect until the prosecution reaches the trial court. Where the jurisdiction utilizes a Jencks-type provision, that provision most often will be specifically limited to trial witnesses, but several such jurisdictions, including the federal, do extend the required disclosure of a witness prior recorded statements to various pretrial proceedings, including the preliminary hearing.

In a few jurisdictions, courts have held or suggested that the prosecutor's constitutional duty under the *Brady* doctrine to disclose material, exculpatory evidence within its control extended to the preliminary hearing, as well as the trial.[4] As applied at trial, the *Brady* obligation has encompassed disclosure of critical impeachment material as to key witnesses. However, that extension of *Brady* obligation to the preliminary hearing is dubious as a matter of federal constitutional law. *Brady* constitutes one of numerous due process requirements designed to safeguard against the conviction of the innocent, which is a basic due process objective. As discussed in § 14.2(a), no similar due process objective has been recognized with respect to forcing an innocent person to face trial even where the state's case falls below probable cause (although such an objective does have a state constitutional grounding in those states that require a preliminary hearing bindover as a constitutional prerequisite for filing an information). Moreover, since the *Brady* standard requires a reasonable probability that the exculpatory evidence would alter the outcome, its applicability to the preliminary hearing would require only prosecutorial disclosure of evidence that comes close to completely destroying the prosecution's case, thereby precluding even a finding of probable cause.

(d) The Right to Present Defense Witnesses. All jurisdictions recognize at least a conditional defense right to call its own witnesses at the preliminary hearing, but the limitations placed upon that right are only infrequently tested. The conventional wisdom frowns upon defense presentation of its own witnesses at a preliminary hearing absent most unusual circumstances. Most often, the defense anticipates a bindover and is utilizing the hearing to obtain discovery of the prosecution's case and to lay the groundwork for impeachment of the prosecution's witnesses at trial. If counsel should conclude that the opportunity exists to shake the prosecution's showing, that will usually be attempted through vigorous cross-examination of the prosecution's witnesses. Producing defense testimony contradicting the prosecution's case is deemed to carry costs that ordinarily far

---

3. See § 24.3(c).

4. The *Brady* doctrine is discussed in § 24.3(b).

outweighs its benefits. Unless the credibility of prosecution witnesses has been shaken substantially on cross-examination, the contrary testimony of defense witnesses is likely to be viewed by the magistrate as simply presenting the kind of credibility conflict that should be resolved by the factfinder at trial. On the other hand, by presenting the defense witness at the preliminary hearing, the defendant runs the risk of making that witness' testimony less effective at trial. Just as the defense may use its cross-examination of prosecution witnesses to gain discovery and to prepare for future impeachment, the prosecution may use its cross-examination of the defense witnesses to achieve those same goals. Much the same analysis argues against presenting witnesses whose testimony will not directly challenge the prosecution's showing as to the elements of the offense, but will point to additional factors that would excuse or justify the actor's behavior.

The preliminary hearing provisions in a handful of states specifically condition the defense presentation of witnesses upon the approval of the magistrate. In these jurisdictions, the defense ordinarily must make an offer of proof as to the anticipated testimony of its proposed witness, and the witness then is allowed to testify only if the magistrate concludes from that showing that the anticipated testimony could rebut successfully the prosecution's showing of probable cause. In most jurisdictions, the preliminary hearing provisions simply state that the defendant "may introduce evidence on his own behalf." As with the similarly described defense right of cross-examination, the defense right to call witnesses is subject not only to the limits placed upon the trial right to call witnesses, but also to a broad discretion of the magistrate to restrict preliminary hearing presentations in accordance with the limited purposes of that hearing. The primary restrictions imposed under that authority relate to the calling of witnesses for the purposes of obtaining discovery and the refusal to hear defense witnesses upon the conclusion that further testimony would do no more than raise a credibility issue.

Where the magistrate has reason to believe that the defense is calling a witness to obtain further discovery of the prosecution's case, the magistrate may require the defense to make an offer of proof as to what will be obtained from the witness' testimony. This prerequisite is most likely to be imposed where the person called to testify is likely to be a prosecution witness at trial—as where the prosecution's probable cause showing consisted in part of the investigating officer's hearsay testimony as to the statements of the victim and the defense then seeks to call the victim. Typically, all the defense can do at this point is to identify possible lines for challenging the victim's statement as related by the police officer. Whether that is sufficient is often committed to the magistrate's discretion, although an appellate court troubled by the prosecution's use of hearsay is more likely to conclude that the defense should be given an opportunity to challenge the complainant directly as to critical matters such as eye witness identification. Even such a court may well sustain a refusal to call the victim, however, when testifying would impose a hardship upon the victim.

Courts note that the magistrate may appropriately prevent the preliminary examination from becoming an "endless wrangle relating to the existence of probable cause." Accordingly, even where statutes do not refer to refusing to hear defense witnesses whose testimony would not successfully rebut the prosecution's case, magistrates are assumed to have that authority. Its exercise may be difficult to sustain, however, in a mini-trial jurisdiction that directs the magistrate to resolve issues of credibility.[5] Where the magistrate's evaluation of credibility is limited, the magistrate can more readily conclude that the witness' testimony would only present a conflict in testimony to be resolved at trial.

Another limitation that may be imposed upon the defense presentation of witnesses relates to the presentation of "affirmative defenses." Because presenting such a defense at the preliminary hearing is contrary to conven-

5. See § 14.3(b).

tional wisdom, case law on the subject is sparse. Not surprisingly, the leading cases deal with attempts to present a defense of entrapment. Under the majority view that treats entrapment as an issue of substantive law to be resolved by the jury, rather than an issue of police impropriety to be resolved by the court, the presentation of that defense at trial is a highly risky venture. As a result, counsel might readily conclude that the entrapment defense should be presented at the preliminary hearing with an eye towards not repeating it as a trial defense should it not persuade or come close to persuading the magistrate. Entrapment also has special qualities that might make the defense more appealing to a magistrate of a certain disposition than to the typical jury.

Occasional decisions bar presenting an entrapment offense because it is deemed an "affirmative defense". Those rulings are not readily extended to all defenses that are "affirmative" in the sense that the defenses do not negate the basic elements of the crime. No court has suggested, for example, that a defendant can be precluded from introducing evidence of self-defense at a preliminary hearing (although such a tactic most likely will do no more than raise a credibility issue that the magistrate will not resolve). However, the entrapment rulings could readily be extended to all defenses that are "affirmative" in the sense that they place upon the defense the burden of proof.[6] Application of the traditional probable cause standard suggests that once the defense has established some evidentiary basis for a defense (e.g., self-defense) at the preliminary hearing, the prosecution must make a probable cause showing that the elements of the defense are not present. This proceeds from the assumption, however, that the prosecutor at trial would have the burden of negating the defense by proof beyond a reasonable doubt.

As to a defense on which the defendant carries the burden of proof, the prosecution might argue that there is no need for it to make an affirmative probable cause showing. At trial, even though the prosecution has not produced substantial contradictory evidence, a jury could always find for the prosecution on the ground that the defense witnesses were not sufficiently credible to carry the defense's burden of proof. Thus, the issue automatically becomes one which should go forward to a trial determination.

(e) Challenging Procedural Rulings. If a magistrate makes an improper procedural ruling at a preliminary hearing and subsequently binds over, and the defendant then moves to dismiss the ensuing information because of the magistrate's procedural error, what weight should be given to the strength of the prosecution's case in determining whether that error requires rejection of the bindover? Three different approaches may be taken here. As noted previously in subsection (b), in jurisdictions holding the rules of evidence applicable to the preliminary hearing, a magistrate error in admitting incompetent evidence will be viewed as harmless if there remained sufficient competent evidence to support a bindover. A similar analysis can also be applied to other errors, such as the improper curtailment of cross-examination or the refusal to allow a defense witness. Here, however, since the defense was not allowed to proceed, the court may be required to give the defense the benefit of the doubt as to what would have been shown if the magistrate had not erred. It can nonetheless find that the prosecution's evidence would have been sufficient even with that showing and therefore sustain the bindover notwithstanding the magistrate's error.

A variation of the above approach would look to a harmless error standard similar to that applied by the Supreme Court in evaluat-

---

6. Another factor that distinguishes the entrapment offense is that it often deals with events that occurred apart from the commission of the crime and therefore would not be included in the investigation of the crime. Thus, considering the lack of advance notice and the short time span for preparation, the prosecution should not be expected to respond to such a defense in its probable cause presentation. This justification for precluding consider-

ation of an entrapment defense at a preliminary hearing would be equally applicable to other "defenses" (e.g., insanity and alibi) as to which pretrial advance notification by the defense typically is required. The appellate courts have not dealt with this issue, presumably because defendants have had no interest in presenting such defenses at a preliminary hearing.

ing the impact of non-constitutional errors which restrict the defense's presentation at trial. The Court there holds that a reversal will not be required if the appellate court concludes, with fair assurance, that the jury would not have been substantially influenced in its decision by the presentation the defense would have made had it not been erroneously restricted. In the context of the preliminary hearing, the trial court would ask whether the magistrate clearly would have reached the same result if the defense had made the showing that was precluded by the magistrate's error. The strength of the prosecution's case would remain significant, but the question would not be whether it merely would be "adequate" for a bindover even with the added defense showing, but whether it was so strong (or the additional defense showing so weak) that the magistrate would not have been substantially swayed by the added defense presentation.

A third approach holds that automatic reversal of a bindover is required where the magistrate's erroneous ruling deprived the defendant of a "substantial right," such as his right to cross-examine or to present witnesses. In determining whether the right denied is substantial, the court will look to its potential significance and the scope of the denial. Thus, such a violation was found in the denial of the cross-examination of a key witness that went "directly to the matter at issue." The analysis here does not look to the strength of the prosecution's case, but simply to the character of the error. Applying such a standard for reversal, apparently more rigorous than the harmless error standard applied at trial, is supported by the argument that redoing a preliminary hearing imposes substantially less of a burden on the judicial system than redoing a trial.

Assume that a magistrate improperly curtails cross-examination or denies a request to present a defense witness, but an indictment is issued before the magistrate's ruling can be challenged in the trial court. Has the defendant lost his right to relief even though the magistrate's ruling clearly resulted in an erroneous bindover? The tradition rule is that all "defects" in the preliminary hearing are "cured by the subsequent indictment." The rationale here is similar to that underlying the practice of mooting the defendant's right to a preliminary hearing by obtaining a prior indictment: "Once an indictment has been issued, the preliminary hearing proceedings are no longer subject to either direct or collateral attack because the defendant has been afforded an independent determination that probable cause exists, which overrides any decision that the magistrate might render at a new preliminary hearing." However, where the alleged preliminary hearing error had an impact extending beyond the bindover itself, arguably impacting the defense's trial preparation, a few courts have suggested that the trial judge has discretion to fashion a remedy that will grant the defense similar preparatory assistance (e.g., a right to depose the witness that the magistrate refused to hear). This position stands in stark contradiction to the numerous cases stating that the only cognizable function of the preliminary hearing is determining probable cause.

Assume next that the magistrate erroneously restricts defendant's right to cross-examination or to present evidence at a preliminary hearing. The magistrate subsequently binds over and an information is filed. The defense challenges the information as based on a defective preliminary hearing, but the trial court erroneously finds that the magistrate's rulings were proper. Interlocutory review is not available, so defendant next raises the issue on appeal following conviction. At this point, the information jurisdictions are divided. Most take the view that the conviction should be treated as having automatically rendered harmless the magistrate's error. The function of the preliminary hearing, they note, is to determine whether probable cause exists, and that issue obviously is closed by a finding of guilt beyond a reasonable doubt at a fairly conducted trial. This means, as a practical matter, that relief for magistrate errors at preliminary hearings will largely be limited to trial court rulings, as interlocutory review of a trial court's acceptance of a bindover is rarely available. Courts treating the trial conviction as rendering preliminary hearing errors per se harmless recognize this procedural difficulty, but reason that it does not justify disregard "of the rule that the remedy should be appropriate to the violation." Granting the defendant a reversal of the conviction and a new preliminary hearing "would be to give him an entirely disproportionate remedy"—"a windfall * * * not in the public interest."

A closely related but distinct position agrees that preliminary hearing errors are mooted insofar as they relate only to the bindover determination, but recognizes that those errors could also impact the trial. Thus, these courts start from the assumption that the error will be harmless, but will reverse a conviction if the defendant can rebut that assumption by showing "that he was denied a fair trial or otherwise suffered a prejudice as a result of the error at the preliminary examination." The cases typically have announced this standard in the course of rejecting a defense argument for automatic reversal, so they have not had occasion to explore what would constitute an adequate showing of trial prejudice. It has been suggested that the loss of a critical witness would be sufficient (e.g., where the magistrate refused to allow the witness to testify at the preliminary hearing and the witness then proved to be unavailable at trial), and that the lack of additional preparation for trial through the hearing would not be sufficient. The Supreme Court's decision in *Coleman v. Alabama*, discussed below, is sometimes cited as recognizing an analogous harmless error approach in the context of a constitutional violation at a preliminary hearing.

On the other side of the spectrum, several courts, viewing a proper bindover as a jurisdictional prerequisite to the filing of an information, apparently will require a new trial whenever the preliminary hearing error could have altered the magistrate's decision to bind over. *Mascarenas v. State*[7] is illustrative. The court there concluded that an improper restriction of cross-examination of a key witness amounted, in effect, to a "denial of a preliminary

examination"; accordingly, since state law required a preliminary hearing as a prerequisite to "holding any person on an information," the trial court was "without jurisdiction" and the subsequent conviction was invalid. This position also has been justified as necessary to ensure that the preliminary hearing does not become "a right without an effective remedy."

In *Coleman v. Alabama*,[8] the Supreme Court spoke to the impact of a subsequent conviction upon a constitutional violation at the preliminary hearing. After defendants there had been denied unconstitutionally the assistance of appointed counsel at their preliminary hearing, they had been indicted by a grand jury and convicted at a trial in which they were represented by counsel. The state contended that the subsequent conviction at trial rendered harmless per se the failure to appoint counsel at the preliminary hearing. The defendants, in response, argued that denial of the Sixth Amendment right to counsel required an automatic reversal of any subsequent conviction, as the Court had held where counsel was denied at trial. The Supreme Court took a middle position, remanding the case for consideration as to whether the denial of counsel at the preliminary hearing had been a harmless error under the standard of *Chapman v. California*.[9] The Court noted in this regard that while the "trial transcript indicates that the prohibition against use by the State at trial of anything that occurred at the preliminary hearing was scrupulously observed," the record before it did not reflect "whether or not petitioners were otherwise prejudiced by the absence of counsel at the preliminary hearing." Justice Harlan, in a separate opinion, sought to add specificity to the remand order, which he viewed as "too broad and amorphous." Reversal should not follow, he argued, "unless petitioners are able to show on remand that they have been prejudiced in their defense at trial, in that favorable testimony that might otherwise have been preserved was irretrievably lost by virtue of not having counsel to help present an affirmative case at the preliminary hearing." Similarly, Justice White asserted

---

7. 80 N.M. 537, 458 P.2d 789 (1969).

8. See note 1 supra.

9. See § 27.6(c).

that because "petitioners had been tried and found guilty by a jury," the denial of counsel at the preliminary hearing "was harmless beyond a reasonable doubt" (the *Chapman* standard) unless "important testimony of witnesses unavailable at the trial could have been preserved had counsel been present to cross-examine opposing witnesses or to examine witnesses for the defense." It would be inappropriate, he noted, for a lower court to hold that the constitutional error had not been harmless on the speculative assumptions either "(1) that the State's witnesses at the trial testified inconsistently with what their testimony would have been if petitioner had counsel to cross-examine them at the preliminary hearing, or (2) that counsel, had he been present at the hearing, would have known so much more about the State's case than he actually did when he went to trial that the result of the trial might have been different."

Although the failure of the *Coleman* majority opinion to respond to the concurring opinions creates some ambiguity as to the exact nature of the required harmless error inquiry, all of the opinions clearly indicated that the inquiry was to take account of at least some incidental benefits that the hearing could have provided the defense at trial. Lower courts applying *Coleman* have consistently looked to those incidental benefits in determining whether the denial of counsel at a preliminary hearing required reversal of a subsequent conviction. Most have adopted an analysis similar to that suggested by Justices Harlan and White in *Coleman*, refusing to find a reasonable doubt as to possible prejudice based on the assumption that counsel's trial presentation would have been helped if counsel had been present at the preliminary hearing and therefore able to use it as an impeachment and discovery device. A few, however, have suggested that counsel's lack of opportunity to obtain such benefits as to critical preliminary hearing witnesses automatically creates a reasonable doubt, absent a state showing that later procedures gave counsel that same opportunity.

As discussed above, many state courts have not looked to these same incidental benefits in determining whether errors in other aspects of the preliminary hearing should require a reversal on review of a conviction. In that context, they treat the probable cause determination as the critical function of the hearing, conclude that it is mooted by the finding of guilt beyond a reasonable doubt, and refuse to consider the loss of incidental tactical advantages as sufficient in itself to overturn an indictment or a subsequent conviction. *Coleman's* broader inquiry is treated as a special attribute of a Sixth Amendment right to counsel, which is granted to ensure a fair trial, and therefore not controlling as to the treatment of a denial of defendant's rights under local law to cross-examine prosecution witnesses and present defense witnesses, which are granted to facilitate the screening function of the preliminary hearing.

Chapter 15

GRAND JURY REVIEW

Table of Sections

---

§ 15.1　Defendant's Right to Prosecution by Indictment

(a) The Fifth Amendment Right: History. As described in § 8.2, the English grand jury was established to assist the Crown in uncovering crime and apprehending offenders, but by the end of the seventeenth century, it had come to be valued in England as a shield against the arbitrary initiation of prosecution by the Crown. In the American colonies, the "shielding role" of the grand jury was equally revered, in part because of colonial grand juries which had refused in several highly celebrated cases to indict persons opposed to the Crown. As the Supreme Court has stated, "[u]ndoubtedly the framers of [the Bill of Rights] * * * had for a long time been absorbed in considering the arbitrary encroachments of the crown on the liberty of the subject and were imbued with common law estimate of the value of the grand jury as part of the system of criminal jurisprudence." They viewed the grand jury in a light aptly summarized in *Wood v. Georgia*:[1] "Historically, this body [the grand jury] has been regarded as a primary security to the innocent against hasty, malicious and oppressive persecution; it serves the invaluable function in our society of standing between the accuser and the accused, whether the latter be an individual, minority group, or other, to determine whether a charge is founded upon reason or was dictated by an intimidating power or by malice and personal ill will."

This important role of the grand jury was guaranteed as a constitutional command though the adoption of the first clause of the Fifth Amendment, which provides:

> No person shall be held to answer for a capital, or otherwise infamous crime, unless on a presentment or indictment of a grand Jury, except in cases arising in the land or naval forces, or in the Militia, when in actual service in time of War or public danger.

The net effect of this provision is to grant to an individual accused of an infamous crime not arising in the military the right not to be proceeded against unless that accusation has been approved by an affirmative vote of a grand jury. The individual has a right to insist that the charges against him be brought by presentment or indictment, either of which has to be issued by the grand jury. The presentment historically differed from the indictment in that it was a charge issued by the grand jury on its own initiative, commonly on the basis of the jurors' own knowledge, but sometimes based on information provided by a private complainant. The indictment, in contrast, was a charge issued by the grand jury after that charge was put before it by a crown official. In either case, the charge could issue only if agreed to by at least 12 grand jurors (a bare majority, if the grand jury was at its maximum size of 23 jurors).

§ 15.1
1.　370 U.S. 375, 82 S.Ct. 1364, 8 L.Ed.2d 569 (1962).

(b) The Fifth Amendment Right: Scope. As evidenced by its language, the Fifth Amendment was not intended to give the benefit of grand jury screening to all persons charged with all crimes in all kinds of cases. Neither was it intended to prohibit application of all aspects of the criminal process before persons entitled to that screening would be due to receive it. The grand jury clause applies to a "person" who is proceeded against on a "capital or otherwise infamous crime," provided the "case" did not arise "in the land or naval forces or in the Militia, when in actual service in time of War or public danger." Moreover, as to persons who meet these criteria, the right to insist that the charge be made by the grand jury (on a presentment or indictment) only applies as of that point where they are "held to answer." Each of these limitations is discussed below.

"Persons". The word "person" is used to describe the subject of each of the criminal procedure rights specified in the Fifth Amendment—the right to be charged by the grand jury, the right not to be twice put in jeopardy, the right not to be compelled to be a witness against oneself, and the right not to be deprived of life, liberty, and property without due process of law. The term "person" is to be distinguished from "citizen", and therefore courts have consistently held that these rights are available to aliens as well citizens. "Person" can be read to refer only to natural persons or to include, as well, collective entities (e.g., corporations). The Supreme Court has held that the privilege against self-incrimination does not apply to entities, in part because that privilege is based on respect for attributes of the human personality which are foreign to an artificial being. On the other hand, the Court has long held that the due process clause does protect entities, and it has more recently applied the double jeopardy prohibition to an entity. The Court has not had occasion to consider the applicability of the grand jury clause to entities but the function of grand jury review—"to stand between the prosecutor and the accused"—would appear as appropriately directed to an entity as a natural

person. However, Ninth Circuit cases have held the grand jury clause does not protect corporations because they cannot be incarcerated and therefore are not being prosecuted for crimes that should be deemed "infamous" as applied to them.

"Infamous crime." Ex parte Wilson[2] set forth what has become the standard analytical framework for determining the content of the "infamous crime" category. *Wilson* held that all crimes carrying the potential of an infamous punishment are infamous crimes even though a lesser punishment is imposed in the particular case. As for what constituted infamous punishment, that could "be affected by the changes of public opinion from one age to another." However, history clearly indicated that "imprisonment at hard labor" in a "prison or penitentiary" or "other similar institution" constituted an infamous punishment. Later cases held that even imprisonment in a workhouse for a term of less than a year constituted infamous punishment when designated as "at hard labor," and incarceration in a penitentiary, even if not so designated, constitutes an infamous punishment.

When the Federal Rules of Criminal Procedure were adopted, the draftsmen sought to incorporate these rulings. Rule 7 originally set forth three categories of offenses that had to be prosecuted by indictment (assuming no waiver): (1) offenses punishable "by death"; (2) offenses punishable "by imprisonment for a term exceeding one year"; and (3) offenses punishable "at hard labor." The Advisory Committee's notes to Rule 7 explained that the second category simply restated the standard of penitentiary imprisonment, as a sentence to a term exceeding one year, under federal sentencing law, is a sentence of potential imprisonment in a penitentiary. The third category later was removed from the Rule when federal statutes no longer provided for punishment at hard labor. Also, an exemption was created for criminal contempt prosecutions, which historically can be initiated by judicial complaint.

---

2.   114 U.S. 417, 5 S.Ct. 935, 29 L.Ed. 89 (1885).

"Military cases." The Fifth Amendment's exemption for what may be loosely described as "military cases" reflects recognition of the separate jurisdiction of military tribunals and the use by these tribunals of procedures quite distinct from those of civilian courts. A major purpose of the exception "was to preserve the separation of military law from the requirements of civil law." Accordingly, the Supreme Court has held that the exemption is limited to actual members of the armed forces. It does not apply to civilian dependents of servicemen living overseas in military housing, even where the crime is committed on the military base and affects the military community. With respect to the militia, active membership in itself is not sufficient as the case must arise when the member is "in actual service in time of war or public danger." That same requirement does not apply to the military, so its members can be prosecuted by court martial for offenses committed during peacetime. However, they must be prosecuted while still in the military, and the offense must be "service connected." A long list of factors are considered in determining whether an offense is service connected, but crimes typically not within that category would be off-base felonies committed in the United States against civilians by servicemen properly absent from the base.

"Held to answer". Judicial opinions finding violations of the Fifth Amendment's grand jury clause have largely bypassed identifying that point at which the defendant was "held to answer" without the required indictment or presentment. In today's vernacular, a person is "held to answer" when, following his arrest, he is brought before a magistrate who sustains his continued custody (or release on bail) and directs that the charges against him be sent forward for consideration by the grand jury (or a preliminary hearing where that is the next step in the process). It seems unlikely that this was the stage that the framers of the grand jury clause had in mind since it typically occurs prior to the issuance of the grand jury's charge and the clause requires that the grand jury charge exist before the person is held to

answer. It is far more likely that "be[ing] held to answer" referred to being required to enter a plea at the arraignment before the trial court, although it also could have been intended simply to refer to the person being put to trial.

(c) Fourteenth Amendment Due Process. The Fifth Amendment imposes its constitutional command only upon the federal government. That the states were not bound by the Amendment's grand jury clause was hardly critical at the time of its adoption, since all of the original states had their own laws giving defendants a right to insist upon a grand jury charge when being prosecuted for a serious offense. It was not until the middle of the nineteenth century that a state completely did away with the right to a grand jury charge. Michigan, in 1859, authorized prosecutors to bring all felony prosecutions by information. Several states, including California, soon followed Michigan's lead. This development posed no legal difficulties under the Fifth Amendment, but the post civil war adoption of the Fourteenth Amendment did present a possible constitutional bar. That Amendment clearly applied to the states, and it prohibited them from denying "life, liberty or property" (thereby encompassing the full range of criminal sanctions) without "due process of law." The due process clause was commonly viewed as the equivalent of the "law of the land" guarantee in the Magna Charta, which, in turn, had been interpreted by Coke and others as requiring prosecution by indictment or presentment for all serious offenses.[3]

In 1884, the due process issue reached the Supreme Court in *Hurtado v. California*,[4] a case in which the defendant had been prosecuted for murder, in accordance with state law, by a prosecutor's information issued upon a preliminary hearing bindover. In holding that this procedure did not violate due process, the Supreme Court adopted what came to be known as the "fundamental fairness" interpretation of the Fourteenth Amendment. The critical question, the *Hurtado* Court noted,

---

3. See § 2.4(b).

4. 110 U.S. 516, 4 S.Ct. 111, 28 L.Ed. 232 (1884), also discussed in § 2.4 at note 1, and in § 14.2 at note 1.

was whether the California legislature had procedures that were "within the limits of these fundamental principles of liberty and justice which lie at the base of all our civil and political institutions." While a major component of those principles was providing adequate safeguards against the arbitrary exercise of government power, and the grand jury certainly provided such a safeguard, its role in this regard was not so essential as to be commanded by due process. Other modes of proceeding could also satisfy this core value of fundamental fairness. The Court stressed in this regard historical evidence indicating that prosecution by indictment or presentment had never been viewed as the only means for initiating prosecutions in accord with the core values of the common law.

In the years since *Hurtado* was decided, the Supreme Court has dramatically altered its approach to Fourteenth Amendment due process issues.[5] It has adopted the position that the very presence of a guarantee in the Bill of Rights strongly suggests that the guarantee is one of those "fundamental principles of liberty and justice which lie at the base of all our civil and political institutions." As a result, it has found Fourteenth Amendment due process to encompass almost all of the guarantees relating to criminal procedure that are in the Bill of Rights. Indeed, the only other guarantees, besides the grand jury clause, not definitely within the protection of due process are those as to which the Court has not had occasion to rule. Nonetheless the Supreme Court has reaffirmed its *Hurtado* ruling that due process does not require a state to initiate prosecution by a grand jury indictment or presentment in a capital case or any other criminal case.

(d) Indictment Jurisdictions. Jurisdictions are commonly described as "indictment jurisdictions" if they grant to the accused a right not to be held to answer a felony charge unless that charge has been issued by a grand jury through an indictment (or a presentment, where the jurisdiction retains the presentment process). Currently, the federal criminal justice system, the District of Columbia, and eigh-

teen states are indictment jurisdictions. These jurisdictions vary somewhat in defining the precise scope the right to a grand jury accusation, but there is unanimity as to remedy for its violation. Where a defendant was entitled to be prosecuted on a grand jury charge but was prosecuted instead on an information, and an objection was timely raised, the remedy on review of the conviction is the automatic reversal of that conviction—the error will not be deemed "harmless."

The federal system. In the federal system, the accused's right to a grand jury accusation is established and defined through the combination of the Fifth Amendment and Rule 7 of the Federal Rules of Criminal Procedure. The scope of the Fifth Amendment's grand jury clause has been discussed above in subsection (a). Federal Rule 7 does not extend the right to a grand jury accusation beyond the Fifth Amendment guarantee. However, it does differ from the Fifth Amendment in an important respect; its guarantee refers to prosecution only by indictment, rather than by indictment or presentment.

Rule 7 thus rejected the view that the grand jury had the authority to force a prosecution on its own initiative. Although federal grand juries apparently had such authority, through the issuance of presentments, at the time of the adoption of the Constitution, as the executive branch later moved to assert a monopoly over the prosecutorial function, federal prosecutors came to reject the view that they were obliged to convert presentments into indictments. They assumed an authority to veto the initiation of prosecution by the grand jury, and Rule 7 recognized that authority.

Rule 7(c) mandated that the indictment be "signed by the attorney for the government." Thus, for an indictment to be valid, not only did it have to be approved by the grand jury, but the prosecutor also had to signify approval by her signature. Lower courts subsequently held that the prosecutorial act of signing (and thereby completing) an indictment was discretionary rather ministerial; the United States Attorney has no obligation to convert an accu-

5.   See § 2.4(d),(e), and § 2.6(a).

sation favored by the grand jury into a formal charge and to thereby initiate prosecution.[6]

States. Eighteen states grant to persons accused of serious crimes the right to insist that those charges be issued by a grand jury. These states are Alabama, Alaska, Delaware, Georgia, Kentucky, Maine, Massachusetts, Mississippi, New Hampshire, New Jersey, New York, North Carolina, Ohio, South Carolina, Tennessee, Texas, Virginia, and West Virginia. Fourteen of these states have constitutional provisions guaranteeing a right to a grand jury charge. One reads a Magna Charta type "law of the land" clause as incorporating such a right, and three establish the right as a statutory or common law guarantee. These "indictment states" vary in their description of the offenses as to which the defendant may insist upon a grand jury accusation. Except for minor variations in a few states, however, those different descriptions all add up to requiring a grand jury charge for offenses meeting the traditional definition of felonies.

In eight of the indictment states, the grand jury clause in the state constitution refers specifically to a grand jury presentment as an alternative to an indictment. However, in all but one of these states, plus most of the other indictment states, a statute or court rule provides that prosecution shall be initiated by indictment, with no reference made to a presentment. In at least a few jurisdictions, these provisions clearly were intended to establish that grand juries could not charge on their own initiative by presentment and could not achieve the same objective by issuing an indictment over the objection of the prosecutor. However, as to others, the consequence of eliminating presentment authority is far from certain. The lack of reference to a presentment in the statute or court rule on charging instruments may simply reflect recognition of a practice under which a presentment is converted by the prosecutor into a draft indictment which is then issued by the grand jury. Indeed, some of these states recognize by statute or court rule an obligation of the prosecutor to draft indictments upon request of the grand

jury. So too, where the prosecutor's signature is required, that may simply be as an act of attesting to the grand jury's issuance of an indictment. In three indictment states, presentment authority is specifically recognized in the statutory law governing charging instruments.

(e) Limited Indictment Jurisdictions. Four states require prosecution by indictment only as to the most severely punished felonies. Although sometimes described as indictment states, they are more appropriately placed in a separate category, as they do not require grand jury screening for the vast majority of felony charges. Two of the four, Louisiana and Rhode Island, grant to the accused the right to insist upon a grand jury's charge as to any capital offense and any offense punishable by life imprisonment. Florida limits its guarantee to capital offenses, while Minnesota, not having capital offenses, extends its guarantee simply to offenses that are punishable by life imprisonment. In all four states, the need for a grand jury charge is measured by the potential punishment carried by the offense, so it matters not that the prosecutor is not seeking that punishment or that a lesser punishment is imposed. Where the right to a grand jury charge is violated, the consequence is to render invalid any conviction obtained at the subsequent trial on the improper charging instrument.

(f) Waiver in Indictment and Limited–Indictment Jurisdictions. The grand jury clause of the Fifth Amendment, and similar clauses in state constitutions do not refer to the possibility of waiving the requirement of a grand jury charge, but then neither do the constitutional clauses establishing other procedural guarantees, and those guarantees regularly have been held to be waivable by the defendant. Relying in part on that analogy, a substantial majority of the courts that have considered the issue have held that such constitutional grand jury clauses establish a "personal right" of the defendant, which accordingly is subject to waiver by the defendant.

---

6. See § 13.3 at note 3.

The lack of a constitutional barrier to waiver does not necessarily mean that waiver is thereby acceptable under the law of the jurisdiction. A few courts have suggested that, since waiver of prosecution by a grand jury charge was not recognized at common law, it should be allowed only if authorized by the legislature, and two states, by their constitutions, provide for waiver only if authorized by the legislature. Today all of the indictment jurisdictions have constitutional, statutory, or court rule provisions explicitly authorizing waivers, so the question of whether waiver could be recognized without such authorization has been rendered moot in these jurisdictions. However, three of the "limited indictment states" are without a provision explicitly authorizing waiver, and prosecution by indictment therefore is viewed in those states as non-waivable as to the special offenses (capital and life imprisonment) covered by the state's grand jury guarantee.

Fewer than a third of the current provisions authorizing waiver allow waiver as to all offenses and all situations in which the defendant has a right to insist upon a grand jury charge. Eleven of those provisions do not allow waiver as to capital offenses. Indeed, only a few of the states in the combined group of indictment and limited-indictment jurisdictions permit waiver in capital cases. The general prohibition against waiver for capital offenses apparently reflects the position, also reflected in provisions relating to the role of the petit jury in capital cases, that the agreement of lay participants should be a prerequisite to a final determination to impose the death penalty. Of course, the grand jury, unlike the trial jury, is not deciding on whether to impose the death penalty, but it provides an initial screening by a lay body in determining whether the offense charged should be one subject to the death penalty. The prohibition found in several states against waiver for life imprisonment offenses probably is derived from the capital punishment prohibition. When states either abolished capital punishment, or had the death penalty at least temporarily barred by the invalidation of their capital punishment statutes, they often carried

over to their former capital punishment offenses (now usually punished by life imprisonment) the procedural guarantees previously applied to capital offenses.

Of course, as with other trial rights, the waiver of the right to be proceeded against by a grand jury charge must be made "voluntarily, knowingly, and intelligently." In addition, the waiver must meet any further prerequisites specified in the provision authorizing waiver. Federal Rule 7 requires that the waiver must be made by defendant "in open court" and "after being advised of the nature of the charge and of the defendant's rights." Several indictment states have similar requirements in their waiver provisions. These requirements are treated as safeguards designed to ensure, in particular, that waivers are made knowingly and intelligently. In this connection, they serve a function much like the guilty plea prerequisites set forth in Federal Rule 11, although federal courts have noted that, since "a waiver of indictment, being merely a finding of probable cause by a grand jury is of relatively less consequence as compared with a waiver of trial, * * * [it] does not call for all of the protections surrounding entry of a guilty plea." This presumably means the advice as to rights need not be as extensive, since the only rights that the defendant relinquishes are those relating to the indictment process, and arguably the inquiry by the court as to the defendant's understanding need not be as extensive. State provisions on waiver commonly also include requirements that go beyond Federal Rule 7. All but a few of the indictment states require that the waiver be in writing. This precludes accepting an implied waiver (as has been done in the federal courts).

Waivers are most frequently made where the defendant pleads guilty. In many instances, the waiver will come at the prosecutor's request, as part of the plea bargain; but defendants intending to plead guilty are likely to waive on their own initiative simply to speed up the process. Where the defendant intends to go to trial, the conventional wisdom argues against waiver even where it is certain that grand jury review will not help the defendant (i.e., where the grand jury undoubtedly will indict). Prosecution by indictment may offer the defense a potential procedural advantage since an indictment may be subject to more rigorous pleading standards, and pleading defects in an indictment cannot be cured as readily by amendment as similar defects in an information. Also, if the jurisdiction precludes the use of hearsay before the grand jury, key witnesses will have to testify before the grand jury and that testimony ordinarily will be available for impeachment use at trial. Other considerations, however, may prevail and lead counsel to favor waiver. In some instances, the defense may be concerned that the prosecutor will gain valuable preparation for trial in presenting prospective trial witnesses before the grand jury. Defendant also has an incentive to waive if he is in jail or would otherwise be inconvenienced by delay and his case cannot promptly be presented to the grand jury. Some defense counsel also prefer that charges be presented by information because they believe that trial jurors, contrary to the court's instructions, do give weight to the fact that another group of lay persons reviewed the case and issued an indictment.

(g) Information States. Over the years, the number of states allowing felony prosecutions by information (usually only after a preliminary hearing bindover), has grown. Because these states recognize the information as an alternative to the indictment, they commonly are described as "information states." Today, 28 states fall in this category. Each of these states has a constitutional, statutory, or court rule provision authorizing the prosecution of any felony offense to be brought by information. All 28 states also have provisions stating that prosecutions may be brought by indictment. Thus, the prosecutor is given an option to proceed by indictment or information (leading some to describe the "information" states as "information-option" states). In several information states, this option is entirely theoretical, as the prosecution has no way of obtaining a grand jury from which it can seek an indictment. These include two jurisdictions in which the provisions for creating an indicting grand jury have been repealed and others in which grand juries have not been used for

so many years that the indicting grand jury is considered an extinct institution.

In most information jurisdictions, convening a grand jury which may issue an indictment is at least a realistic possibility (if not a standard practice), so the prosecutor does have a true option of proceeding by indictment rather than information. The extent to which that option is utilized varies tremendously from one information state to another, and even from one prosecution district to another within the same state. In some prosecutorial districts, the grand jury is the screening agency of choice, and here the percentage of cases instituted by indictment may come close to that of a indictment jurisdiction (particularly one with a high waiver rate). For the vast majority, however, the grand jury is not used as the standard practice, but as an alternative employed when grand jury screening and the indictment process is thought to be especially helpful under the circumstances of the particular case. Here, the percentage of felony cases charged by indictment commonly is less 5%, although individual prosecutors could take it to the 20% range in some districts.

A variety of factors may lead a prosecutor to categorize a case as one that should be taken before the grand jury rather than prosecuted by information. In many instances of prosecution by indictment in information jurisdictions, the case was originally brought to the grand jury because the prosecutor had need for the grand jury's investigative power in developing the case. Once the grand jury investigation has developed sufficient additional evidence to support a prosecution, the proposed charge was presented to the grand jury for indictment. While the prosecutor could conceivably have asked the grand jury to do no more than investigate, and then have proceeded by information, that hardly serves to gain the cooperation of the grand jury in further investigations. Thus, once a case goes before the grand jury for investigation, it invariably will stay there through the process of determining whether or not to indict.

Where a case is fully investigated, prosecutors in information states are less likely to utilize the grand jury, but special circumstances may lead the prosecutor in that direction. In certain types of cases, for reasons of efficiency or to obtain tactical advantages, the prosecutor may desire to avoid a preliminary hearing, and as discussed in § 14.2(d), that can be achieved by taking the case to a grand jury and obtaining an indictment prior to the point when a preliminary hearing otherwise would be held. In politically sensitive situations, the prosecutor may turn to the grand jury to use it as a buffer against adverse public reaction. Recognizing that a decision to prosecute or not prosecute will give rise to substantial controversy, the prosecutor may seek to share the responsibility for that decision with the grand jury. Occasionally, the prosecutor may truly want the independent judgment of the jurors as to whether to proceed. Thus, the prosecutor may feel that the equities of the case are closely balanced and the final determination should rest on the grand jury's sense of community standards. Similarly, the prosecutor might have difficulty with the credibility of a key witness and not want to proceed unless the grand jurors view the witness as truthful.

§ 15.2 The Structure of Grand Jury Screening

(a) Grand Jury Composition. The grand jury, like the petit jury, speaks as "the voice of the community," and typically the grand jury venire is as representative of the community as the petit jury venire. Indeed, in all but a handful of jurisdictions, the system used to select those persons called for grand jury service is identical to that used to select those persons called for petit jury service.[1] However, as discussed in § 8.4(a), because of the more liberal use of hardship excuses (to compensate for the longer grand jury term), grand juries in many jurisdictions tend to be somewhat less representative of the community than petite juries.

(b) Control Over Proof. As discussed in § 8.4(b), the prosecution, through its ex parte presentation of the case against the prospective defendant, exercises primary control over the proof that will be presented to the grand jurors. As a practical matter, that primary control may be converted to exclusive control, but the legal structure of the grand jury certainly does not delegate such complete authority to the prosecutor. It subjects the prosecutor's control over the proof presented to several at least theoretically important limitations, stemming from the independence of the jurors, the supervisory authority of the court, and the general responsibility of the prosecutor to seek justice rather than simply victory.

Initially, most jurisdictions, in keeping with historical tradition, allow the grand jurors to go beyond the prosecution's presentation and consider any information the grand jurors personally have obtained regarding the events in question. Of course, that authority has limited practical significance in the larger communities of today. Apart from the unusual case in which the alleged offense itself occurred before the grand jury (e.g., perjury in grand jury testimony), jurors are unlikely to have personal knowledge of the events brought before them by the prosecutor.

Grand jurors also can go beyond the prosecutor's presentation of evidence by asking their own questions of witnesses offered by the prosecutor. Prosecutors sometimes request that the grand jurors pass their questions through the prosecutor to ensure that the questions are proper as to form and content. Where the prosecutor and a grand juror disagree on the appropriateness of a question put forth by the juror, the foreperson may resolve the issue as the presiding officer, although that may call for a vote of the jurors. Of course, in the end, the dispute may be taken to the supervising judge.

Grand jurors also may seek to go beyond the prosecutor's evidence by insisting that additional witnesses or physical evidence (e.g., documents) be subpoenaed. Such a demand fits within the grand jury's well established authority to set the scope of its investigation and therefore to obtain all relevant evidence. Indeed, in more than a dozen jurisdictions, when the grand jury "has reason to believe that

---

§ 15.2

1. See § 22.2(a), (b).

other evidence within its reach will explain away the charge," it has a statutory obligation "to order the evidence to be produced." As a practical matter, however, jurors are most unlikely to make a demand for additional evidence. Most often, they will not be aware of those persons who might provide additional relevant evidence, particularly exculpatory evidence. Moreover, even where the grand jury learns from one source or another that a certain individual might possess exculpatory information, the jurors ordinarily will lean in the direction of accepting the prosecutor's explanation as to why that witness should not be called to testify.

In most jurisdictions, the prosecutor's control over the proof presented may also be overridden by the supervisory authority of court acting on its own initiative. The supervising judge (usually the judge who impaneled the grand jury) generally is recognized to have the authority to insist that the grand jury consider particular evidence where that is necessary to prevent a "miscarriage of justice." The supervising judge, however, is even less likely to be aware of such evidence than the grand jury. Absent a communication from the prosecutor, jurors, or prospective defendant, the judge ordinarily will have no knowledge of what evidence is (or is not) being presented to the grand jury.

A much more likely restraint upon the prosecutor's control over the proof presented comes from the prosecutorial obligation to produce known exculpatory evidence. As noted in § 15.7(f), not all jurisdictions recognize such an obligation and its scope varies in those jurisdictions in which it is recognized. In general, the obligation requires presentation of evidence known to the prosecutor that could readily be viewed by the grand jury as negating the guilt of the prospective defendant. Jurisdictions recognizing the obligation commonly give it teeth by allowing a defense challenge to any subsequent indictment based upon the prosecutor's failure to inform the grand jury of such exculpatory evidence. The threat of such a challenge could induce the prosecutor to proceed with extreme caution, presenting potentially exculpatory evidence even where he has doubts as to whether the evidence is sufficiently significant to fall within the obligation. Even should a prosecutor so respond, however, the obligation is likely to have limited significance, as the prosecutor often will not be aware of the existence of exculpatory evidence. Very often, as with the other limitations upon the prosecutor's control over proof, a critical factor will be whether the prospective defendant is willing to call potentially exculpatory evidence to the attention of the prosecutor and request its presentation before the grand jurors. As a practical matter, the prospective defendant is unlikely to do that.

(c) The Prospective Defendant's Testimony. In all but a handful of jurisdictions, a prospective defendant's request that he be allowed to testify before the grand jury is treated legally no differently than a prospective defendant's request that any other evidence be presented before the grand jury. Indeed, here the prosecutor and the grand jury are most likely to have absolute discretionary authority in responding to the request, for the self-serving nature of a prospective defendant's testimony makes it highly unlikely that such testimony will be characterized as critical exculpatory evidence under statutes requiring the prosecutor to present, or the grand jury to call for, exculpatory evidence known to them. Thus, both caselaw and statutes commonly note that the defendant has no right to testify and a request to do so may be denied at the discretion of the grand jury.

As a matter of practice, however, prosecutors are most likely to accede to a prospective defendant's request to give testimony himself—if for no other reason than that prosecutor's cross-examination of the prospective defendant will provide an excellent opportunity to lay the ground work for impeachment at trial and may even produce incriminating statements. Those prosecutorial advantages are not lost on defense counsel, however. Few will advise the prospective defendant to run the risks presented in submitting to the cross-examination of the prosecutor in a setting in which neither the defense counsel (in most jurisdictions) nor the judge (in all jurisdictions) will be present. But this general rule of strategy, like any other, is subject to exceptions. At least in those jurisdictions in which the witness is entitled to have counsel present (see § 8.15), special situations will arise in which the risks of testifying are offset by its potential advantages.

In a small group of states, statutory provisions give to any person an opportunity to obtain a court order directing the grand jury to receive that person's testimony. While such provisions were enacted primarily to ensure that complainants could call to the grand jury's attention alleged crimes not been pursued by police and prosecutor, their broad phrasing could easily encompass a prospective defendant. Another handful of states have provisions specifically granting to the prospective defendant a right to testify before the grand jury upon making a timely request. The only indictment state with such a provision is New York. The prospective defendant's exercise of the right to testify is not a rare event in that state. One consequence is public awareness of the right, heightened by media coverage in cases of public interest of the prospective defendant's decision to testify or not testify before the grand jury. This arguably casts in a different light the weight given by the public (including prospective jurors) to the issuance of an indictment. Proponents of the right contend that its value offsets this potential disadvantage. They argue that the right's impact on improving grand jury screening is not limited to cases in which the prospective actually testifies. Knowing that the prospective defendant can insist upon testifying, the prosecution, it is argued, will be more cautious in its presentation of evidence to the grand jury.

(d) Evidentiary Rules. All jurisdictions require that a witness' testimonial privileges be recognized in grand jury proceedings, but there is substantial variation as to the applicability of the remaining rules of evidence to grand jury proceedings. No more than thirteen states make the rules of evidence fully applicable to grand jury proceeding. A somewhat smaller group make most of the rules applicable, but create limited exceptions (allowing the substitution of hearsay, for example, where the witness' personal appearance is not likely to be critical, as in the case of a scientific expert reporting on physical evidence). The remainder—the vast majority—adhere only to testimonial privileges, and allow complete use of hearsay.

The contentions advanced for and against the various state positions on the use of inadmissible evidence are much the same as the contentions presented in the debate over the applying the rules of evidence to the preliminary hearing [see § 14.4(b)]. Those favoring application of the rules contend that the grand jury must be given admissible evidence if it is to serve the task of preventing unwarranted prosecutions. The grand jury can hardly assess the strength of the prosecution's case, they argue, where it is allowed to rely upon evidence that cannot be used at trial. Those opposing application of the rules of evidence maintain that insistence upon admissible evidence is not necessary for, and indeed is inconsistent with, the grand jury's fulfillment of its various functions. They note that: (1) grand jurors who may have doubts about the witness summaries provided by the prosecution can always request that the actual witnesses be presented before them; (2) to perform its varied functions—which include both investigation and possible consideration of grounds for nullifying notwithstanding sufficient evidence—the grand jury must be able to ask for, and receive, material that would not be admissible at trial; and (3) busy prosecutors are not interested in obtaining an indictment through incompetent evidence which cannot be replaced at trial with admissible evidence, as their concern is with gaining a conviction rather than gaining an indictment that has no chance of success at trial. Also advanced against applying the evidentiary rules are a series of administrative difficulties, including (1) the increased length of the grand jury proceeding and inconvenience to witnesses, (2) the absence of opposing counsel, who at trial would make the prosecution aware of potential evidentiary objections and thereby facilitate the prosecution's substitution of other evidence that would not be objectionable, and (3) the unavailability of a judicial officer to provide a prompt ruling on admissibility where the prosecutor is aware of evidentiary uncertainty.

(e) Legal Advice. The prosecutor serves not only as the state's advocate in presenting its case to the grand jury, but also as the primary legal advisor to the grand jury. The tension produced by these seemingly conflicting roles tends to be moderated, however, by the character of the legal advice that must be given as well as other features of the process. The two most significant portions of prosecutorial legal advice are the explanation of the grand jury's authority and the explanation of the required elements of the crimes that might be charged in a particular case. As to the former, the grand jury also is given extensive direction by the supervising court in its charge to the jury upon its impanelment. That charge commonly will speak to such matters as the grand jury's obligation to act as an independent body in screening charges, juror recognition that the prosecutors present evidence as "advocates for the government," the authority of the grand jury to have appropriate questions put to witnesses and to request the production of additional witnesses, the need for the jurors to make their own judgment of the credibility of witnesses, the possible limitations of hearsay evidence (where such evidence is allowed), and the level of proof needed to indict. In the course of offering further legal advice on the grand jury's authority, the prosecutor must maintain a consistency with the court's charge. Indeed, in some jurisdictions, the jurors are informed in that charge that they may return to the court for additional instructions if they should find an inconsistency, or otherwise lack confidence, in the further legal advice provided by the prosecutor.

While the court's charge ordinarily will not touch upon the elements of particular offenses, prosecutorial leeway here commonly is limited by the practice of utilizing the same jury instructions that would be presented by a trial judge in charging a jury. The prosecutor need not give instructions nearly as detailed as those given to a petit jury, and thus can readily rely upon standard jury instructions or instructions otherwise well established under state law. Role conflicts are likely to be felt only where the prosecutor must decide whether the instructions should go beyond the offense itself to encompass excuses or justifications or where the prosecutor is asked by jurors to expand upon the instructions. As discussed in § 15.7(g), where the prosecutor errs in his judgment on these matters, the result can be the quashing of the indictment issued by the grand jury. In explaining the elements of the crimes that might be charged, the prosecutor may be required to make reference to the evidence in the case as it relates to the proof of each element. As discussed in § 15.7(b) most jurisdictions allow the prosecutor to express a legal opinion on the sufficiency of the evidence, but there is a division on how far the prosecutor can carry such commentary.

(f) Quantum of Proof. There is a sharp division among the states as to the quantum of proof needed to indict. Approximately a third of the states provide for indictment upon a finding of "probable cause" to believe that the accused has committed the crime charged. A slightly smaller group of states utilize a "prima facie evidence standard," authorizing indictment only "when all the evidence taken together, if unexplained or uncontradicted, would warrant a conviction of the defendant." Another group of states, consisting largely of information states, have no clear precedent as to the applicable standard. In the federal courts, the governing standard apparently is the probable cause standard, but some judges use a prima facie instruction. Since the trial jury may convict only if convinced of the accused's guilt beyond a reasonable doubt, it generally is assumed that the prima facie evidence standard is a substantially more rigorous test than the traditional probable cause standard. However, where the supervising judge follows the common charging practice of simply quoting the prima facie standard, without explaining the degree of proof needed to "warrant a conviction," that greater rigor will be lost.

(g) The Indictment Decision. At common law, a decision to indict required the affirmative vote of a majority of the grand jurors. The grand jury had 23 members and at least 12 had to support a decision to indict. If majority did not support a decision to indict, the grand jury returned a finding of "ignoramus" (we ignore it) or "no bill" in response to the proposed charge put before it by the prosecution.

The federal system today still provides for a grand jury of a maximum size of 23, and requires 12 affirmative votes for an indictment. Because federal grand jurors sit for a lengthy term, absences and withdrawals can readily reduce the number below 23. Federal Rule 6(a) accommodates this possibility by requiring that the grand jury have at least 16 members and no more than 23 members. Of course, when jury size is reduced, 12 votes are still required for an indictment, so that with a jury reduced to 16, a three-fourths affirmative vote becomes necessary for an indictment. A handful of states also provide for a maximum jury size of 23 and an affirmative vote of 12 for an indictment; most, however, have smaller grand jurors and require a two/thirds or three/fourths vote for indictment.

The grand jury retains complete independence in refusing to indict. That includes the authority to refuse to indict even where the evidence presented clearly met the quantum of proof needed for indictment. This authority of the grand jury to "nullify" the law arguably was the most important attribute of grand jury review from the perspective of those who insisted that a grand jury clause be included in the Bill of Rights. That authority and its historical grounding have frequently been noted in appellate opinions discussing the grand jury's screening function. Contrary to the dominant position taken with respect to the petit jury, judges sometimes will inform the grand jurors of their authority to nullify in the course of the judge's charge to the grand jury upon impanelment. This appears to be a minority position, however, and is nowhere statutorily required.

(h) Resubmission. Jeopardy not having attached, a grand jury's refusal to indict does not inherently preclude returning to a new grand jury (or even the same grand jury) to seek an indictment. Jurisdictions vary in their treatment of the prosecutor's authority to resubmit a proposed indictment to a grand jury.

The division here, as in the case of resubmission following a preliminary hearing dismissal, clearly favors unrestricted resubmission, but a significant minority group of jurisdictions do impose limitations. These usually came through statutory provisions requiring judicial approval for resubmissions. Though most of these provisions do not set forth any standard as to when the court should allow resubmission, where the provisions do include a standard, they typically require a showing of newly discovered additional evidence.

(i) Secrecy Requirements. Grand jury secrecy requirements bear upon two aspects of grand jury screening. Initially, those requirements provide a protective buffer for the grand jury in deciding whether or not to indict. Secondly, those requirements may sharply limit the capacity of the indicted defendant to learn of deficiencies in the screening process that could lead to a successful challenge to the indictment.

The protective buffer. As discussed in § 8.5(a), grand jury secrecy requirements are designed in large part to strengthen the grand jury's investigative function. However, secrecy requirements also are designed "to protect the independence of the grand jury" in its decision as to whether to indict. They do this by providing two types of shields for the jurors. First, insofar as secrecy requirements keep secret the subject of the grand jury's inquiry while it is considering the possible issuance of an indictment, they serve to ensure that deliberations are free from the pressures that otherwise might be imposed by the potential defendant and his friends or opponents. This depends, of course, on keeping such persons in the dark as to both the events and individuals on the grand jury's agenda. Very often, that cannot be done. Where the grand jury is used simply for screening (rather than investigation and screening), police usually arrest the suspect as soon as they have probable cause and then take the case to the grand jury. In an indictment jurisdiction, the arrested person and anybody else aware of the arrest knows that the case will be going to the grand jury, and in an information state, those persons familiar with local prosecutorial practice can usually estimate fairly accurately whether the prosecutor is likely to charge by information or seek an indictment. Even in those cases where the prosecutor seeks an indictment before any arrest is made, suspects often know that the grand jury is considering their possible indictment. For example, as discussed in § 8.5(d), the target of a grand jury investigation often learns of that investigation from persons who have been subpoenaed to provide testimony or documents.

Grand jury secrecy requirements may be somewhat more successful in providing a second shield, precluding public scrutiny (and criticism) when the grand jury refuses to indict. In some instances the public will not even be aware that the grand jury was considering the indictment of a particular person. More often, the public will be aware (as when the person was first arrested), but arguably will be hesitant to criticize the grand jury's decision because it recognizes that the grand jury may have received exculpatory evidence which is blocked from its view by grand jury secrecy. Grand jury secrecy also helps the grand jury in this regard by restricting the comments of the disappointed prosecutor (who cannot reveal what evidence was before the grand jury). However, grand jury secrecy does not restrict the disappointed victim, and the prosecution may be able with some ingenuity to have a fair amount of its case against the individual made public.

Restricting challenges. In most jurisdictions, grand jury secrecy requirements keep from the indicted defendant most of the deficiencies that may have occurred in the course of grand jury screening. Where the defendant furnished evidence to the grand jury (in the form of testimony or a subpoenaed document or other tangible item), the defendant obviously is aware of the grand jury's consideration of that evidence. If other persons furnishing evidence to the grand jury are friendly to the defendant, they may be willing to share with the defendant their experiences before the grand jury. Apart from these limited sources, however, the defendant must depend upon exceptions to the general requirement of grand jury secrecy to learn what occurred in the process that led to his indictment. The two exceptions offering the most potential in this regard are those authorizing disclosure as part of pretrial discovery and in connection with a motion to dismiss an indictment.

In most jurisdictions, the defense's right to pretrial discovery of grand jury material is limited to the recorded grand jury testimony of the defendant and of the witness who will be called by the prosecution at trial, insofar as the jurisdiction generally provides for the disclosure of the prior recorded statements of defendants and witnesses (universal as to the former and fairly common as to the latter). Such discovery can be useful in identifying deficiencies in the screening process, but its potential is limited. The disclosure does not encompass all of the testimony presented before the grand jury (not all grand jury witnesses will necessarily be called to testify at trial), and the recorded testimony of witnesses will not necessarily identify documents and other exhibits that were presented to the grand jury. Also, the disclosure does not include comments of the prosecutor or grand jurors except as they are made as part of the examination of the witness.

Roughly a dozen states grant to the defendant pretrial discovery of the transcript of the grand jury proceedings that produced the indictment of the defendant. Most of these jurisdictions are information jurisdictions and make infrequent use of indictments. However, four of the states in this group are indictment jurisdictions. A handful of additional states (all information jurisdictions) provide for pretrial disclosure of the entire grand jury transcript at the discretion of the court. Not all of these jurisdictions, however, require a transcription that goes beyond the "testimony of all witnesses" before the grand jury.

In the federal system and in most other jurisdictions that do not provide for pretrial discovery of grand jury transcripts, grand jury secrecy provisions allow for disclosure of relevant grand jury material in support of a defense motion to dismiss the indictment because of defects in the screening process. Federal Rule 6(e)(3) provides that a court may order disclosure of grand jury materials upon a showing that "a ground may exist to dismiss the indictment because of a matter that occurred before the grand jury." Numerous states have similar provisions. The key to the applicability of these provisions is the required initial showing of a potential irregularity that would justify dismissing the indictment.

In applying provisions like Rule 6(e)(3), courts apparently take into consideration the distinct possibility that a defense motion may be characterized as aimed at supporting a motion to dismiss when its actual purpose is to gain valuable discovery that goes beyond what the pretrial discovery rules would allow. They also recognize that the nature of many of the irregularities that justify dismissal, along with the need to show that the irregularity had a prejudicial impact, commonly would require that any disclosure cover the entire proceeding that led to the indictment. The transcript made available to the defense therefore will often include witnesses and information that will not be presented at trial and thereby seriously breach the promise of secrecy that encourages "free and untrammeled" disclosure by grand jury witnesses. Accordingly, a typical standard for court ordered disclosure is that the defense establish preliminarily "a substantial likelihood of gross or prejudicial irregularities in the conduct of the grand jury."

Applying such a standard, courts universally find insufficient a showing that does no more than point to surrounding circumstances that evidence a "potential" for irregularities. They suggest that to be successful, the defendant must be able to produce such "hard evidence" as the affidavit of a witness who was present when misconduct occurred or the clear suggestion of impropriety in a portion of the transcript released to defendant in the course of pretrial discovery. Of course, such sources of "direct proof" are rarely available, leading

courts to acknowledge that the preliminary showing requirement places the defendant in "something of a 'catch 22' [situation]." Courts do have discretion, however, to review the transcript in camera without the requisite preliminary showing, and a small group of reported cases note the exercise of this authority (typically with the court then finding no substantial basis for challenging the indictment).

(j) Transcription. The transcription of grand jury proceedings also bears upon both the screening process itself and the indicted defendant's capacity to challenge the screening process. Where the screening process extends over a significant period of time (quite common in situations where the grand jury is also used for investigation), the transcript assists the jurors in reviewing the evidence and enables jurors who missed sessions to nonetheless gain a complete picture of the evidence presented. Recordation arguably also has a bearing in how at least some witnesses approach the giving of testimony, arguably encouraging their truthfulness. So too, it is seen as dampening any prosecutorial inclination to abuse the grand jury process.

For the indicted defendant, recordation is often crucial to gaining the information needed to determine if the screening process was tainted by irregularities. Provisions authorizing pretrial discovery of grand jury material assume that the testimony in question has been recorded. Where discovery is limited and the defendant looks to a Rule 6(e)(3)–type motion, a successful preliminary showing is often of little value if the grand jury proceedings were not recorded.

The federal system and a bare majority of the states currently require that grand jury proceedings be recorded.[2] Among the 18 indictment states, only about a third require recordation. In a few other indictment jurisdictions and some information jurisdictions, the authority to require recordation is vested specifically in the court, which apparently can re-

---

2. Where recordation is mandatory, jurisdictions commonly require, as in Federal Rule 6, that the transcription extend all proceedings except grand jury voting or deliberations. Thus, they require recordation of "any explanation or instructions of the prosecutor and any comments made

by the prosecutor or other persons in the presence of the grand jury." Several states, however, limit the required transcription to "all of the testimony before the grand jury."

quire recordation as a regular practice. In still other jurisdictions, recordation is deemed an issue of grand jury discretion. As the grand jury is likely to follow the lead of the prosecutor, the choice between transcribing and not transcribing tends to rest on whether the prosecutor sees the greater advantage in having available a transcript of the witness' testimony for prosecutorial use (including facilitating an identical recollection in the witness' trial testimony) or in not providing the defense with a transcription that it can use in preparing for that testimony or impeaching the witness.

§ 15.3　The Effectiveness of Grand Jury Screening

(a) **The Ongoing Debate.** The value of grand jury review has been a subject of ongoing debate in this country ever since American law reformers, following the lead of Bentham in England, launched the first major attack upon prosecution by indictment in the mid–1800s. During the twentieth century, periods of heated debate were sparked by reports of National Commissions, issued in the 1930s and the 1970s, urging elimination of statutory and constitutional provisions requiring prosecution by indictment. In recent years, the debate has been one-sided, at least in legal periodicals. Academic commentators have almost uniformly been critical of relying upon grand jury screening in its current form to eliminate prosecutions that are weak and arbitrary.

Grand jury critics tend to fall in three categories: (1) those who would abolish grand jury screening; (2) those who would reform the grand jury and retain it as a major screening agency; and (3) those who would substitute the preliminary hearing or some other procedure as the primary screening agency, although retaining the grand jury as a screening agency to be used in special circumstances.

Critics in the first two groups share the view that grand jury screening, as currently practiced, is essentially worthless. Grand juries, they argue, are no more than a "rubber stamp" for the prosecutor. They cite statements of former prosecutors who note that a prosecutor, if he so desires, "can indict any-

body, at any time, for almost anything before a grand jury." They cite as well the complaints of former grand jurors that prosecutors, by virtue of their expertise in maintaining rapport with the jurors and the inclination of most jurors to simply "move on", were able to obtain indictments even when many grand jurors had serious reservations about a case. Available statistics, they argue, support such accounts of those who have participated in the process. They point in particular to the statistics on grand jury screening in the federal system (the most comprehensive statistics available), which show that grand jurors refuse to indict in less than two percent of the cases presented to them.

The second group of critics believe that reforming grand jury procedures can turn the grand jury into a fairly effective screening body. They call primarily for the following reforms (already in place in at least some jurisdictions): (1) requiring the court to fully inform the grand jurors of their independent authority and to impress upon them their obligations to screen out unworthy prosecutions; (2) giving the grand jury its own counsel, to whom it can turn for independent legal advice; (3) giving the target the right to testify before the grand jury; (4) requiring the prosecutor to present all available exculpatory evidence; (5) forbidding the prosecutor's use of evidence which would be constitutionally inadmissible at trial; (6) prohibiting the use of hearsay testimony to support an indictment, except under narrowly defined circumstances; (7) prohibiting prosecutorial resubmission of a case to another grand jury following a first grand jury's decision not to indict, absent the production of substantial additional evidence; and (8) providing for a post-indictment pretrial hearing at which a judge or magistrate will review the transcript to ensure that there were no significant procedural violations and that the indictment was supported by sufficient evidence.

Critics in the first group view such reforms as insufficient to justify retention of grand jury screening. The basic problem, as they see it, lies not in any particular aspect of the process (e.g., in the reliance upon hearsay evidence), but in the very structure of grand jury screening. That structure asks a group of laypersons to apply a totally unfamiliar legal standard to a one-sided case presented in a process that is non-adversary, that allows the prosecutor to establish a close rapport with the jurors, and that forces the jurors to rely largely on the prosecutor's investigate resources and legal advice. The proposed reforms would modify that structure only slightly. They would not provide the jurors with the experience, the adversarial debate, and the access to all relevant information that is needed to meet the objective of an effective screening process.

The third group of critics view grand jury screening as having some value, but not enough to require it in every case. They argue that grand jury screening, even though adequate, is less effective and less efficient than screening by a magistrate at a preliminary hearing. Since they reject use of both screening procedures as unnecessary duplication, these critics would reserve grand jury review for exceptional situations, as determined by the prosecutor in his discretion. Those exceptional situations would consist largely of cases in which the prosecutor has need for the grand jury's investigative authority or the special qualities that layperson evaluation can bring to the charging decision. In all other cases, the preliminary hearing would be the exclusive screening device and the prosecution would charge by information. Critics in this third group maintain that the preliminary hearing, because it is an adversary proceeding, generally provides a better safeguard against unwarranted prosecutions, even if one assumes that grand jurors do exercise independent judgment. These critics also stress the preliminary hearing's value as an open screening procedure, as opposed to the secret grand jury proceeding. This feature is particularly important today, they say, when so many cases are resolved by guilty plea rather than by trial. Finally, they argue, the preliminary hearing is preferable simply because it is more efficient. Impaneling and servicing a grand jury is costly in terms of space, manpower, and money. The grand jury also adds to the delay in processing

cases since grand juries, particularly in rural areas, are not as readily available as magistrates.

Supporters of grand jury review reject the contentions of all three groups of critics. Initially, they maintain that the grand jury is a highly effective screening agency. They cite prosecutors who have characterized the grand jury as a valuable sounding board with a mind of its own. They cite studies suggesting that grand juries will reject a substantial portion of the cases presented to them if prosecutors fail to carefully screen their cases in anticipation of grand jury review.

Supporters of grand jury review also reject the contention that the preliminary hearing is a superior screening agency. First, the grand jury brings a layperson's sense of reality to the evaluation of the circumstances surrounding the alleged offense. Though critics contend that grand jurors tend to "just sit there, like a bump on a log," prosecutors and others report that they do ask questions when testimony does not "ring true." Secondly, supporters argue, the strength of grand jury review lies exactly where independent screening is most needed—in those cases in which special factors, e.g., the involvement of politics or racial animosity, are likely to result in unjust accusations. Such cases require a screening agency that can carefully judge credibility and can give consideration to community notions of fairness and justice. The preliminary hearing magistrate is restricted in her judgment of credibility, whereas the grand jury can weigh credibility in much the same fashion as a trial jury. Unlike the magistrate, the grand jury also has a recognized authority to disregard legally sufficient evidence and indict for a lesser offense or refuse to indict altogether. As a group selected from the community, it can and will act to leaven the rigidity of the law.

Supporters of the grand jury originally contended that the nullification and other screening advantages of layperson review justified any additional costs associated with grand jury review. Today, they argue that the grand jury actually is less costly than the preliminary hearing. The modern preliminary hearing, they note, has developed into a time consuming mini-trial. The major cost factor in the grand jury process, the use of jurors, is more than offset by the extra costs of the preliminary hearing—the participation of the defense counsel and the magistrate, and the investment of far more time by the prosecutor and witnesses.

Finally, supporters contend that grand jury review clearly comes out ahead when the symbolic impact of the information and indictment processes are compared. What the grand jury loses through a non-adversary, secret proceeding is more than offset by its inclusion of community representatives in the screening process. Participation of laypersons contributes to public confidence in the criminal justice system and thereby justifies grand jury review even in cases that are "open and shut." Supporters note that, in a system where most cases do not go to trial, it is especially important that "private citizens" are given an "active role" in the "front lines" of the criminal justice process.

(b) Statistics. As suggested above, both proponents and critics of the grand jury seek support for their respective positions in the available statistics that arguably might measure grand jury performance. The statistic most commonly cited is the "no-bill" rate, i.e., the percentage of cases in which the grand jury refuses to indict. That statistic, however, is not regularly available even for indictment jurisdictions. Thus, the proponents and critics often have found themselves dealing with limited data contained in sporadic studies of grand jury actions in a single jurisdiction (sometimes a single county) for a single year. Among all indictment jurisdictions, the only one with comprehensive grand jury statistics is the federal system, which offers data for all its judicial districts covering many years.

Reports on screening by state grand juries cite some no-bill rates as high as 10–20 percent. Supporters of grand jury screening point to such statistics as proof that the grand jury is hardly a "rubber stamp". Critics, however, question whether such rates largely reflect a prosecution practice of bringing to the grand jury both cases in which it wants to prosecute and cases in which it would prefer not to

charge, but finds it more convenient to run that decision through the grand jury. Once a case has proceeded beyond a certain point (e.g. an arrest, the filing of a complaint, or a preliminary hearing bindover a waiver), a prosecutor desiring not to proceed may find an invited grand jury no-bill offers advantages over filing a *nolle prosequi* with the court. Thus critics argue that high no-bill rates must be examined more closely to determine what percentage of those no-bills reflect a disagreement between the prosecutor and the grand jury. The one major study on the degree of disagreement dates back to a different era, and it showed prosecutors and grand juries disagreeing in approximately five percent of the case surveyed.

Critics of grand jury screening point to the no-bill rate in the federal system which regularly falls below two percent of the cases presented to the grand jury. They also point to studies of state grand juries that report similar low rates. The supporters of grand jury screening respond that these minuscule no-bill rates do not reflect inadequacies in the grand jury's efforts, but that the prosecution is itself weeding out weak cases in anticipation of grand jury review. The better test, they argue, is the disposition of indictment cases when challenged by a defense motion alleging the insufficiency of the evidence to let the case reach the jury. Here again, available statistics are limited, since jurisdictions ordinarily do not breakdown statistics on successful defense motions so as to identify those based on an insufficiency of the evidence. Supporters of grand jury screening point out, however, that dismissals on all grounds—including insufficiency of the evidence—rarely exceed two percent.

The critics respond, in turn, that this low percentage of dismissals on defense motions is deceptive for two reasons. First, a substantially higher percentage of cases are dismissed post-indictment on a *nolle prosequi* motion, and many of those presumably are based on the prosecution's realization that the screening process failed to identify a weak case. Second, many cases are resolved by guilty pleas to a lesser offense than that charged by the grand jury, and while some of these reductions may reflect prosecutorial concessions responsive to a guilty plea, others may be required by an initial overcharge that was approved by the grand jury.

Finally, critics and supporters agree that the statistics say little about the performance of the grand jury in reflecting the community's sense of justice and rejecting prosecutions deemed inappropriate notwithstanding arguably sufficient evidence. Such cases obviously will be low in number. Here the debate must turn on an evaluation of decisions to indict or not-indict in particular cases thought to raise substantial issues regarding the community's sense of justice. By and large, the focus here is upon cases that achieved some degree of notoriety. Where the grand jury decided not to indict, it is not always clear that this decision reflected grand jury "nullification". Grand jury secrecy commonly precludes a fully informed judgment as to whether the grand jury's decision reflected inadequacies of proof or a grand jury conclusion that applying criminal sanctions in the particular case would be contrary to the community's sense of justice. Where the decision was to charge, supporters and critics are likely to divide over whether that decision reflects an inability of the grand jury to exert its independence or simply a grand jury decision that nullification was not appropriate under the circumstances.

(c) Screening Variations. Both supporters and critics sometimes characterize grand jury screening as if the grand jury's processes were largely uniform throughout the country. There are, however, numerous variations that relate to both grand jury independence and standards for indictment. These include variations in: (1) the pool that provides the grand jury venire; (2) the length of the grand jury term, which may lead in a jurisdiction with a longer term (e.g., 12 or 18 months) to more frequent excusals on hardship grounds and a different mix of jurors; (3) the recognition of bias challenges to jurors; (4) the size of the jury and the proportion of the jurors that must vote in favor of indictment; (5) the authority of the prosecutor to present and examine witnesses over grand juror objection and the au-

thority of the grand jury to call for further evidence over the prosecutor's objection; (6) the recognition of an obligation of the prosecutor to present known exculpatory evidence or the grand jury to call for such evidence; (7) the recognition of a right of a prospective defendant to testify; (8) the extent of the application of the rules of evidence to grand jury proceedings; (9) the scope of the court's initial charge upon impaneling the grand jury and use of standard instructions in the prosecutor's charge on the legal elements of the offenses considered; (10) the use of a "probable cause" or "prima facie case" standard as to the quantum of proof required for indictment; (11) the scope of the prosecutor's authority to resubmit following a grand jury refusal to indict; (12) the availability of trial court review of the sufficiency of the evidence before the grand jury to support its indictment; (13) the scope of the trial court's review of alleged prosecutorial misconduct before the grand jury; and (14) the scope of appellate review of alleged errors in a grand jury proceeding where there has been an intervening conviction on the indictment.

(d) Judicial Responses. While the debate over the effectiveness of grand jury review has been aimed primarily at legislative reform, it has not gone unnoticed by the courts. Several courts have suggested that the critics probably are correct in concluding that grand jury review almost always is a rubber stamp operation. Their response has been to downplay in various respects the significance of the indictment process. Still other courts have expressed concern as to the possible loss in effectiveness of grand jury review, but have cited that concern as a basis for insisting upon procedural safeguards designed to offset prosecutorial dominance. Finally, many other courts largely reject the criticism of grand jury screening. They view grand jury review as continuing to function effectively, although that judgment may rest upon a view of the process as designed to provide screening less finely tuned than that envisaged by many of those most critical of the process. The Supreme Court of the United States has stressed, in particular, the capacity of the grand jury to either refuse to indict or to charge in a lesser offense even when probable cause exists.

These differences in judgment as to the potential value of grand jury screening are reflected in the judicial treatment of almost all of the various grounds urged for challenging an indictment. While some opinions treating such challenges openly discuss the merits of grand jury review, most do not speak to the issue directly. Very often the court's underlying policy perspective will be obvious from the result it reaches. At times, however, the same ruling might be supported by either of two quite different judgments as to the value of grand jury review. Thus, a court rejecting a challenge to an indictment that was based in part on illegally obtained evidence may be guided by the conclusion that: (1) even if use of such evidence were prohibited, the grand jury still would almost always indict upon the prosecutor's request, so adding a prohibition against such use would simply cause delay without significant gain for an inherently weak screening process; or (2) the grand jury is functioning well as a rough screening body guided by a community sense of justice and the addition of prohibitions against the use of illegally obtained evidence is not needed for effective performance of its assigned role.

§ 15.4 Indictment Challenges Based Upon Grand Jury Composition

(a) Grand Jury Selection Procedures. As will be seen in the subsections that follow, the law governing the composition of the grand jury differs in several respects from that governing the composition of the petit jury. Those differences are shaped primarily by the different roles of the grand and petit juries, but they also are shaped by differences in the procedures utilized in selecting the two juries. As noted in § 15.2(a), the first step in the jury selection process—the summoning of prospective jurors (commonly described as the "calling of the array" or the "selection of the venire")—tends to be the same for both the grand jury and the petit jury. The same representative list (e.g., a voter registration list) will provide the pool from which the grand jury venire will be randomly selected. The same

basic qualifications for jury service (e.g., residency, age, and citizenship) will be applicable, and the unqualified jurors will be eliminated by the court or jury commissioners either before or after the prospective jurors are summoned. Those persons statutorily exempted from jury service will be eliminated in a similar fashion.

Once the venire of qualified and non-exempt prospective jurors is established, the selection procedures for grand juries and petit juries begin to vary. Initially, because the grand jury sits for a longer term, a larger group of prospective jurors is likely to be excused on hardship grounds. Following the excusals, in the selection of the petit jury, the next steps will be the voir dire and the exercise of peremptory challenges and challenges for cause by both the prosecution and the defense. In the grand jury process, in contrast, there is no voir dire or peremptory challenge. As for challenges for cause, some jurisdictions do allow something akin to such a challenge, but as discussed in subsection (b), these challenges ordinarily can be made by prospective defendants only if held to answer before the grand jury is impaneled.

Though the grand jury process does not utilize a voir dire, the supervising judge may on occasion ask the jurors about their background as it relates to a particular type of case (e.g., drug offenses) or a particular case. That is most likely to be done where the prosecution has announced its intention to use the grand jury to conduct an investigation of particular events or a particular type of criminal activity. Where the juror's background suggests that he or she might have some involvement with the activities or persons to be investigated, or the juror responds with comments indicating an inability to approach the case impartially, the court may excuse the juror on its own initiative.

Once the petit jury is impaneled, the composition of the jury is set, apart from the dismissal of any alternate jurors prior to deliberations. The composition of the grand jury, on the other hand, can readily shift over the term of the jury. Particularly in those jurisdictions in which grand juries sit for a long term, one or more jurors are likely to be excused over the course of the term. Ordinarily, jurors are excused because of changed circumstances that make continued service a hardship or render the juror ineligible for service (e.g., a change in residence). Less commonly, a juror will respond affirmatively to the prosecutor's standard query as to whether any reason exists for a juror not to participate in the matter about to be presented, with the supervising judge then excusing that juror on request of the prosecutor. Occasionally, the court, on recommendation of the prosecutor, will dismiss a juror for "cause shown," which includes both actual misconduct and an extreme lack of diligence (e.g., excessive absences or frequent dozing during proceedings). Where the number of remaining jurors is still sufficient to meet the statutory minimum, the excused juror may not be replaced. Very often, however, the court will find it necessary or desirable to add replacements. Those persons will then be selected in accordance with the procedure used in selecting the original jurors.

(b) Objection Procedures and Timing. *Pre-indictment challenges.* At common law, in the federal system and in at least some of the states, a person threatened with grand jury indictment could challenge the composition of the grand jury prior to its issuance of the indictment. Today, most indictment and information jurisdictions have statutes or court rules that build upon but modify the common law in providing for pre-indictment challenges to grand jury composition. They typically provide for a pre-indictment challenge to the array "on the ground that the grand jury was not lawfully selected, drawn or summoned" and for a pre-indictment challenge to an individual juror on the ground that "the juror is not legally qualified." In some of these jurisdictions, the pre-indictment challenge may be made at any time prior to the indictment by either the prosecutor or "a defendant." In most, however, the defense challenge is limited to the "defendant who has been held to answer," and the challenge by prosecution or defense must be made before the grand jury is impaneled. These two prerequisites limit defense challenges to a narrow band of "defen-

dants"—persons arrested and bound over for grand jury consideration by the magistrate (with or without a preliminary hearing) either during the interim between the expiration of the term for one grand jury and the start of the term for the next or at a point so close to the end of the term of the currently sitting grand jury as to require the case to be passed on to a grand jury yet to be impaneled.

The pre-empanelment requirement make the pre-indictment challenge virtually useless for most arrestees, but even in jurisdictions that do not impose such a requirement (such as the federal), arrestees will find it difficult to investigate and present a composition challenge prior to indictment. Thus, not surprisingly, the motion to dismiss—and not the pre-indictment challenge—has become the standard vehicle for raising defense objections to grand jury composition. Indeed, several states have retained the pre-indictment challenge only for prosecutors and designated the post-indictment motion to dismiss as the exclusive vehicle for raising defense objections. The motion to dismiss also is the exclusive means for raising defense objections to grand jury composition in those states (roughly a third) that simply do not provide for pre-indictment challenges by either side.

Motions to dismiss. In the federal system and in almost all of the states that require pre-indictment defense challenges to be made before the jury is empaneled, the opportunity to make such a challenge does not preclude the defense from choosing instead to make a post-indictment objection through a motion to dismiss the indictment. In these jurisdictions, court rules or statutes authorize use of a motion to dismiss simply as an alternative vehicle for objecting to composition, standing alongside the pre-indictment challenge. A small group of jurisdictions, however, allow the motion to dismiss only where the defendant can show that he lacked a reasonable opportunity to utilize that jurisdiction's procedure for a pre-indictment challenge. These jurisdictions typically allow for pre-indictment challenges made after the grand jurors have been sworn, but do limit that challenge to those defendants who have been "held to answer" prior to indictment. Thus, a reasonable opportunity is assumed to exist where, at the time of being held to answer, the defendant had reason to know that the grand jury would not consider his indictment for several days, during which he could have filed his pre-indictment challenge.

The required timing for a motion to dismiss based on composition grounds starts with the longstanding rule that motions based upon "a defect in the institution of the prosecution" must be brought before trial. Of course, the trial judge may relieve the defendant of the "waiver" or "forfeiture" produced by failing to make the motion until after the trial has started, but that requires "good cause shown," (such as where governmental deception or other circumstance prevented the defense from discovering before trial the factual basis for its claim). Trial courts commonly are given authority to implement the requirement of a pretrial filing by setting a specific deadline prior to trial before which the motion must be filed, and in a fair number of states, the statute or court rule itself establishes a specific timetable (e.g., within 30 days after arraignment or before trial, whichever is earlier).

Two additional requirements may cut even shorter the time for filing a motion to dismiss based on composition grounds. First, the federal system and several states require that certain such motions be filed promptly after the defense becomes aware or should have become aware of the grounds for the objection (but no later than the start of trial in any event). The federal provision, which applies only to violations of the Federal Jury Selection Act, requires that a "motion to dismiss the indictment on the ground of substantial failure to comply with the provisions of this title in selecting the grand * * * jury" must be made "before the voir dire examination [of the petit jurors] begins, or within seven days after the defendant discovered or could have discovered, by the exercise of diligence, the grounds therefore, whichever is earlier."

Second, the time allowed for filing a motion to dismiss may be even further shortened by a requirement that any objection to the charging process be made prior to the entry of a plea to

the charge. Such a requirement was fairly widespread prior to the mid–1900s, reflecting the common law notion that "a plea to an indictment admits the validity of the indictment." At common law, a defendant who wished to reserve his right to challenge the indictment process could do so by standing "mute" at the arraignment, which resulted in the court itself entering the plea of "not guilty." Jurisdictions continuing to require the motion to be made at or before the entry of the plea ordinarily recognize some similar means of reserving the objection notwithstanding the plea, although its use may depend upon the permission of the court.

Insofar as states impose more restrictive time restraints on objections to the composition of the grand jury than on other objections relating to the institution of the prosecution, they commonly cite two justifications. First, motions challenging the selection process often require more substantial hearings than motions based upon other alleged defects in the grand jury process, which usually can be resolved on the basis of a review of the grand jury transcript. Second, an error in grand jury selection is likely to have an impact beyond the immediate case, and therefore should be brought to the attention of the court as soon as possible. Such an error ordinarily will extend to all indictments issued by the particular grand jury, and very often concerns an irregularity in the general selection process that applies to other grand juries as well.

Exceptionally restrictive timing requirements may be challenged as imposing an undue burden on a defendant's right to contest selection procedures that violate the federal constitution. The Supreme Court has held that restrictive requirements are constitutionally acceptable, however, provided that, as applied, they do not deny the defendant a reasonable opportunity to raise his constitutional claim. Applying this standard, the Court held valid "on its face" a state rule requiring that objections be raised within three days after the end of the grand jury term (or before trial, if it came earlier). Although defendants indicted on the last day of the grand jury term would have only three days within which to raise the claim, that period was deemed not per se unreasonable.[1] However, a requirement that the challenge be made prior to indictment was held invalid as applied to an indigent defendant who was not provided with appointed counsel until the day after his indictment.[2]

(c) Equal Protection Claims. Not long after the adoption of the Fourteenth Amendment, its equal protection clause was held to prohibit racial discrimination by the state in the selection of grand juries, as well as petit juries. Though a defendant in a state prosecution has no federal constitutional right to grand jury review, he does have "a right to equal protection of the laws [which is] denied when he is indicted by a grand jury from which members of a racial group purposefully have been excluded." Provided a timely objection is made, an indictment issued by such a grand jury cannot stand, without regard to the sufficiency of the evidence before the grand jury, since the racial discrimination "strikes at the fundamental values of our judicial system and our society as a whole." Under the Fifth Amendment's due process clause, the same prohibition applies to racial discrimination in the selection of grand juries in federal cases.

An equal protection challenge to the selection of the grand jury will be analyzed under the same standards as apply to equal protection challenges to the selection of the petit jury. This means that the Supreme Court rulings discussed in § 22.2(c), relating to the basic elements of an equal protection challenge to the selection of the petit jury, also set the standards for equal protection challenges to grand jury selection. The same basic elements—a discriminatory impact upon "a recognizable distinct class", and a "discriminatory purpose"—are required to establish the equal protection claim. Here as well, those elements typically are established through the combination of a statistical showing of under-

representation of a suspect class in jury service and a showing that the selection system is susceptible to manipulation. Also, as established in *Campbell v. Louisiana*,[3] the standing doctrine of *Powers v. Ohio*[4] applies equally to grand jury selection, allowing a defendant who is not a member of the excluded group to challenge an alleged equal protection violation in the discrimination against that group. As the Court there noted, the equal protection violation basically lies in the denial of the prospective juror's right not to be discriminated against, not in any loss of potential favoritism for the person whose case is being considered by the jury.

(d) The "Fair Cross–Section" Requirement. The Sixth Amendment right to jury trial requires that a petit jury be drawn from a "fair cross-section of the community." This requirement overlaps to a substantial extent with equal protection restrictions upon jury selection, but the two guarantees are distinct.[5] Equal protection prohibits discrimination against a "cognizable group," while the fair cross-section requirement prohibits the exclusion of a "distinct" group that leaves the venire less than reasonably representative. The character of a distinct group for cross-section purposes may be somewhat different than that of a cognizable group for equal protection purposes. Also, equal protection prohibits only intentional discrimination, while a fair cross-section can reach the systemic underrepresentation of a distinct group even where there was no intent to under-represent that group. Although the state may justify such underrepresentation as an incidental byproduct of serving an important governmental interest, it must show that the resulting exclusion from jury service is not broader than necessary to serve that interest.

---

§ 15.4

1. See Michel v. Louisiana, 350 U.S. 91, 76 S.Ct. 158, 100 L.Ed. 83 (1955) (upholding this provision even as applied to a defendant not provided with appointed counsel until the day the term ended, where the objection was not filed until several days thereafter).

2. Reece v. Georgia, 350 U.S. 85, 76 S.Ct. 167, 100 L.Ed. 77 (1955).

3. 523 U.S. 392, 118 S.Ct. 1419, 140 L.Ed.2d 551 (1998).

4. 499 U.S. 400, 111 S.Ct. 1364, 113 L.Ed.2d 411 (1991), discussed in § 22.2(c) at note 5.

5. See § 22.2(d).

Insofar as a federal constitutional cross-section requirement applies to the grand jury venire, it would appear to impose largely the same standards as the cross-section requirement applied to the selection of the venire for the petit jury. The critical question here is whether the Fourteenth Amendment's due process clause imposes upon the states a cross-section requirement for the grand jury venire, or whether the cross-section requirement is strictly a Sixth Amendment concept made applicable to the states only for the petit jury venire. In many states, that issue will not be reached because a cross section requirement is included in the statute governing the selection of the venire for both the grand jury and the petit jury.

In *Peters v. Kiff*,[6] a case decided at a time when a white defendant could not raise an equal protection challenge to the exclusion of blacks (i.e., pre *Powers v. Ohio*), Justice Marshall's opinion for three justices reasoned that due process was violated by racial discrimination in the selection of the grand jury and the petit jury. The opinion noted initially that the racial discrimination in the selection of the jurors clearly violated the prospective jurors' rights under the equal protection clause. That denial also had an impact on defendants, however, that extended beyond the "issue of race." For "due process is denied by circumstances that create the likelihood or appearance of bias," and the arbitrary exclusion of a "substantial and identifiable class of citizens" creates a "risk of bias" that impacts all defendants "indicted or * * * [tried] by a jury * * * [so selected] * * * in violation of the Constitution."

In *Hobby v. United States*,[7] without substantial discussion, the Court appeared to convert into a majority position Justice Marshall's due process analysis in *Peters*. In the course of measuring the constitutional impact of racial and gender discrimination in the selection of the grand jury foreperson, the Court characterized the issue presented as whether that discrimination violated the "representational

due process values expressed in *Peters*." Although a footnote explained that those values had been set forth originally in an opinion for three justices, there was no suggestion that the Court majority was merely assuming arguendo that they applied to grand jury selection. Moreover, the representational due process values were described as requiring that "no large and identifiable segment of the community [be] excluded from jury service." Here again, however, the discrimination related to groups historically discriminated against and long protected under equal protection. Also, though speaking of "representational due process values," the *Hobby* opinion did not refer to the fair cross-section cases (although it did cite the cross-selection mandate of the Federal Jury Selection Act). Arguably, the *Hobby* analysis was meant to apply only to intentional discrimination that violated the equal protection clause, and to provide through due process an avenue for challenge for defendants not of the group discriminated against—an avenue no longer needed today in light of *Powers* and *Campbell v. Louisiana*.[8]

In *Campbell*, the white defendant challenging the exclusion of blacks from the grand jury raised both an equal protection objection and a due process objection based on *Hobby* and *Peters v. Kiff*. Finding that the court below had erroneously concluded that the defendant lacked standing, the Supreme Court remanded for consideration of those claims on their merits. The Court noted that it was "unnecessary here to discuss the nature and full extent of due process protection in the context of grand jury selection," and spoke of "that issue, to the extent it is still open based upon our earlier precedents," as distinguishable from both defendant's equal protection claim and a "fair cross-section claim" that had not been properly presented to the state courts. Although *Campbell* certainly leaves open the possibility that a due process objection will have a content that differs from the equal protection objection now available to all defendants, it also appears to assume that the content of due process, as it relates to "represen-

---

6. 407 U.S. 493, 92 S.Ct. 2163, 33 L.Ed.2d 83 (1972).

7. 468 U.S. 339, 104 S.Ct. 3093, 82 L.Ed.2d 260 (1984).

8. See the text at notes 3–4 supra.

tational values," somehow differs from the content of a cross-section requirement.

(e) Constitutional Challenges to the Selection of the Foreperson. Typically, the foreperson of the grand jury, unlike the foreperson of the petit jury, is appointed by the court rather than elected by the jurors. Since the judge makes the appointment fully aware of the juror's race, the selection procedure is naturally suspect where the number of minority foreperson has been substantially disproportionate to the representation of minorities on the grand jury panels. Such a showing can establish a prima facie case of an equal protection violation, shifting to the prosecution the obligation of showing that there was not intentional discrimination. Of course, that presumption can then be rebutted by the prosecution showing that the impaneling court looked only to other racially neutral factors in selecting the foreperson, so there was no intentional discrimination (the disproportionate underrepresentation of a particular race constituting an incidental impact of reliance on those factors).

Assuming that there has been an adequate showing of discrimination, the question remains as to whether the appropriate remedy is dismissal of the indictment. That issue was first put to the Supreme Court in *Rose v. Mitchell*.[9] The Court there found no need to reach the issue because the defendant had failed to make out a prima facie case of discrimination. It noted as to the remedy issue only that it would "assume without deciding that discrimination with regard to the selection of only the foreman requires that an indictment be set aside, just as if the discrimination proved had tainted the selection of the entire grand jury venire." In *Hobby v. United States*,[10] the issue was again raised, but the context was different. The defendant in *Hobby*, not being a member of the classes discriminated against (blacks and women), relied on the due process analysis of *Peters v. Kiff*, rather than an equal protection claim.

The Court in *Hobby* unanimously agreed that the alleged "purposeful discrimination against Negroes or women in the selection of

federal grand jury foreman is forbidden by the Fifth Amendment." It split, however, as to whether such a constitutional violation invariably required dismissal of an ensuing indictment. The dissenters argued that the "injury caused by race and sex discrimination * * * is measured not only in terms of actual prejudice caused to individual defendants but also in terms of the injury done to public confidence in the judicial process," and it therefore required the deterrent impact of automatic dismissal of the indictment. The majority responded that dismissal was appropriate only if the discrimination adversely affected the defendant's personal due process interests as set forth in Justice Marshall's opinion in *Peters*. Absent such an injury to defendant, "less draconian measures" would suffice to ensure that "no citizen is excluded from consideration for service [as foreperson] * * * on account of race, color, religion, sex, national origin or economic status."

The *Hobby* majority concluded that dismissal there was not required, as the defendant's due process interests could not have been violated by intentional discrimination that was limited to the appointment of the foreperson. *Peters* had recognized "representational due process values" that granted to the defendant a right not to be indicted by a grand jury unfairly selected through the exclusion of any "large and identifiable segment of the community." Here, however, no such exclusion had been applied to the grand jury *as a whole*, but simply to the grand jury member performing the additional duties of the foreperson. Unlike the situation presented in *Rose*, the foreperson here was a member of the randomly selected panel, so all of the persons voting on the indictment had been fairly selected. Neither could the discrimination have "impugn[ed] the fundamental fairness of the [grand jury] process itself," as one foreperson could make no appreciable difference from another. Again in contrast to *Rose*, the foreperson on a federal grand jury performed basically ministerial

9. 443 U.S. 545, 99 S.Ct. 2993, 61 L.Ed.2d 739 (1979).

10. See note 7 supra.

duties that would have no bearing upon the substantive decisions of the grand jury.

The *Hobby* majority distinguished *Rose* on three grounds: (1) the foreman in *Rose* had been appointed from outside the randomly selected panel; (2) the foreman in *Rose* had substantial duties and powers that gave him "virtual veto power over the indictment process" (e.g., the authority to issue subpoenas for witnesses and the requirement of his endorsement for a valid indictment); and (3) *Rose* did not present a due process objection, but "a claim brought by two Negro defendants under the Equal Protection Clause." In *Campbell v. Louisiana*,[11] only the second factor could be called upon to distinguish *Rose*. The defendant there, like the defendants in *Rose*, had raised an equal protection claim (although unlike the defendants in *Rose*, he was not a member of racial group allegedly discriminated against). As in *Rose* also, the foreperson came from outside the randomly selected grand jury panel; the foreperson was selected by the judge from the venire prior to the random selection of the remaining members of the grand jury panel. The state court had nonetheless held that *Hobby* should still control because the foreperson's duties were basically ministerial. The Supreme Court responded that the foreperson's functions were irrelevant, since the foreperson also was a member of the panel and voted on the indictment. Hence, if the judge discriminated in selecting the foreperson, there had been discrimination in the selection of the grand jury panel itself. The governing cases were those dealing with discrimination in the composition of the grand jury, not *Hobby*, and they clearly required dismissal of the indictment.

The *Campbell* ruling, like *Rose*, deals with a situation found in only a small group of states that allow for selection of the foreperson from outside the randomly selected panel. The second factor distinguishing *Rose* from *Hobby* similarly applies to only a few states. Among the states in which the judge chooses the foreperson from the randomly selected panel, a small group give to the foreperson more exten-

sive powers than the federal system, but few grant powers that reach the level found in *Rose*. Lower courts addressing the issue have uniformly concluded that the foreperson's role remains "ministerial" and *Hobby* controls, unless the foreperson has the kind of decisive authority attributed to the foreperson in the *Rose* case.

Hobby's third ground of distinction has much greater potential significance. *Campbell* did not have to consider whether that ground, when standing alone, would distinguish *Hobby*. If the foreperson is selected from the panel, has only ministerial duties, but panel members of the same distinct group as the defendant are intentionally excluded from that position by the judge, does an equal protection claim require dismissal? Speaking to the distinct nature of the racial discrimination claim raised in *Rose*, the *Hobby* majority noted: "As members of the class allegedly excluded from service as the grand jury foreman, the *Rose* defendants had suffered the injuries of stigmatization and prejudice associated with racial discrimination." The majority did not seek to explain, however, precisely what prejudice was involved, or how such prejudice and stigmatization would justify a remedy of dismissal without regard to the limited functions of the foreperson. Nonetheless the suggestion was clear that the *Hobby* ruling might not be extended to equal protection claims because of the impact of the discrimination upon a defendant who (unlike defendant Hobby) belonged to the same distinct group as the persons excluded.

In referring to the *Rose* defendants as having suffered the injuries of "stigmatization and prejudice," the *Hobby* Court may have had in mind the possibility that the discrimination, even under the conditions involved in *Hobby* (with the foreperson being drawn from the panel and having only ministerial duties), was more likely to affect the outcome of the proceeding where the defendant was a member of the class discriminated against. When the judge selecting the foreperson has discriminated against a class of jurors on the basis of

11. See note 3 supra.

their race, that may suggest that the same prejudice has been carried over by that judge (and perhaps even by the grand jurors, if they recognized the discrimination) in the treatment of other aspects of the grand jury process as they related to a defendant of the same race. On the other hand, subsequent equal protection rulings in *Campbell* and *Powers* recognized the equal protection standing of a defendant, whether or not a member of the race discriminated against, on the theory that the defendant is simply vindicating the rights of the excluded jurors, not implementing his own rights (in contrast to the reasoning of *Hobby*). This suggests that if equal protection claims are to be treated differently than the due process claim presented in *Hobby*, then that distinction would be applicable to all defendants raising equal protection claims. Not surprisingly, since *Hobby* simply noted a possibility of distinguishing equal protection claims, since the ground it offered focused on a same-race qualification later rejected in *Powers* and *Campbell*, and since *Powers* introduced its entirely different analysis in a different context (selection of the petit jury), lower courts have divided over whether an equal protection violation in selecting a foreperson requires dismissal of the indictment even though the foreperson was discriminatorily chosen from among the randomly selected grand jury members and played only a ministerial role as foreperson.

(f) Statutory Violations. Although a few jurisdictions will not allow a challenge to an indictment based on nonconstitutional grounds, the vast majority hold that at least some violations of statutory selection procedures will require dismissal of an indictment though falling short of constitutional error. Ordinarily those violations must be so "substantial" as to violate a fundamental policy of the statutory procedure. In the federal system, the primary focus in this regard is on whether the statutory failure affected the random nature and objectivity of the selections. Perhaps the most common violation is the seating of a juror who does not meet the statutory qualifications for service, such as residency or citizenship. Dismissal will be granted in such cases only if, after deducting the number of jurors not legally qualified, the number of votes supporting the indictment does not meet the statutory prerequisite.

(g) Juror Bias. Grand jurors are commonly advised, at the time of their impanelment, that they should not participate in the review of a particular case if their vote is likely to be motivated "on the basis of friendship or hatred or some other similar motivation." If the prosecutor has reason to believe that a particular juror may be biased due to a special relationship to the victim or target, he may ask the court to excuse that juror. However, less than half of the states have statutes disqualifying jurors on grounds relating to bias. About half of those provisions are limited to persons who have a special relationship to the case (e.g., complainants, victims, persons related to complainants or targets, and witnesses for the prosecution). About half are broader provisions that disqualify based on a state of mind that will prevent the juror from "acting impartially." Only one of the states with this type of provision is an indictment jurisdiction.

Statutes disqualifying on bias related grounds may be used to challenge the individual juror, but challenges must be presented prior to indictment, and in many jurisdictions, prior to the juror being sworn. Thus, as a practical matter, the bias-disqualification statutes are most likely to be utilized as the grounding for a motion to dismiss the indictment. Not all states with disqualification statutes, however, view those provisions as authorizing a motion to dismiss. Some states read their disqualification provisions as allowing only for preindictment challenges to the juror or for discharge of the juror on the court's own motion. On the other hand, several state courts have recognized a defense right to dismissal of an indictment on bias grounds without the support of a bias-disqualification statute.

Where the motion to dismiss is available, its successful use is subject to two major hurdles. The first is establishing that the juror was disqualified. This requirement may operate in practice to largely limit the defendant to challenging jurors who have a personal relationship to some person involved in the case, even where the statute extends to all persons whose "state of mind prevent[s] him from acting impartially." Without showing such a relationship, courts are unlikely to allow the defendant to question the juror as to his or her state of mind, notwithstanding the bias provision. They clearly will not allow a general post-indictment voir dire since it threatens the "traditional secrecy" of grand jury deliberations. Even should the defendant establish that the juror should have been disqualified under the bias-disqualification statute, there remains the obstacle of provisions that prohibit dismissal of the indictment if there were a sufficient number of votes to indict, not counting the votes of any jurors who should have been disqualified.

The majority of jurisdictions do not have bias disqualification provisions and do not permit a challenge to an indictment based on the alleged bias of a particular grand juror. Thus, courts have refused to dismiss indictments where the grand jury included relatives of the victim, persons who had an ongoing relationship to the prosecutor's office, persons who were likely to be witnesses for the prosecution at trial, and persons who were political opponents of the accused. Those courts basically hold that the defendant has no right to an unbiased grand jury under either the law of the jurisdiction or the federal constitution. They do recognize the authority of the judge to discharge jurors who are likely to be biased. That power is said to be derived, however, not from any rights of persons subjected to grand jury screening, but from the authority of the court to ensure that jurors abide by their oath not to indict out of hatred or malice.

Some of the courts following this traditional position express concern that bias objections would be procedurally cumbersome and would inevitably lead to a post-indictment voir dire of the grand jurors that would be time consuming and would adversely impact grand jury deliberations. They more frequently argue, however, that such an objection simply is inconsistent with the function of the grand jury.

They note in this regard that: (1) grand juries historically could indict based upon the personal knowledge of the jurors; (2) the Sixth Amendment refers to a right to an "impartial jury", but the Fifth Amendment includes no such impartiality provision; and (3) the role of the grand jury as an accusatory body, not making a final determination of guilt, does not demand the assurances of open-mindedness applied to a trial jury.

In the leading Supreme Court case speaking directly to the issue of grand juror bias, *Beck v. Washington*,[12] the Court noted that "[i]t may be that the Due Process Clause of the Fourteenth Amendment requires the State, having once resorted to a grand jury procedure, to furnish an unbiased grand jury." The *Beck* plurality found it unnecessary to reach that issue, but Justice Douglas, in dissent, argued that the state clearly did have such an obligation. The requirement that a grand jury be unbiased, he argued, followed from the language and reasoning of various prior decisions, particularly the equal protection decisions regulating the grand jury selection process. The "systematic exclusion of Negroes from grand jury service" was barred because it "infects the accusatory process * * * [with] unfairness" in much the same way as juror bias infects the process. Surely, he noted, the Court would not sustain an indictment "where the grand jury that brought the charge was composed of the accused's political enemies."

If the issue left open in *Beck* is eventually resolved with a ruling rejecting the traditional majority position, the Supreme Court will then have to decide what steps a court must take to ensure that a grand jury is not biased. The alleged bias in *Beck* stemmed from extensive preindictment publicity, and the issue that divided the Court was whether the judge impaneling the jury had gone far enough in determining "whether any prospective [grand] juror had been influenced by the adverse publicity." The plurality found that the judge had done so when he asked the prospective jurors whether they were conscious of any prejudice and excused three who acknowledged possible

---

12.   369 U.S. 541, 82 S.Ct. 955, 8 L.Ed.2d 98 (1962).

bias. Assuming arguendo that due process requires the state to furnish an unbiased grand jury, *Beck* suggests that the presiding judge nevertheless has only a limited obligation to inquire into possible prejudice. *Beck* involved an unusual situation in which the judge was aware of the potential source of bias prior to impaneling the grand jury. Ordinarily, the issue of bias will not be called to the court's attention until after an indictment has been issued. At that point, an inquiry that goes beyond considering bias inherent in a juror's special relationship to the parties (as where the juror is a relative of the complainant) runs the risk of invading the secrecy of the juror's deliberations in casting his vote. This danger, combined with the limited inquiry found acceptable in *Beck,* suggests that an extensive investigation of the juror's state of mind (through, for example, a post-indictment voir dire) is not likely to be required by due process even if the traditional position eventually is rejected by the Supreme Court.

(h) Preindictment Publicity. Another question that would arise with the rejection of the traditional position is whether a showing of extensive prejudicial pretrial publicity would be sufficient to establish the degree of bias necessary to require dismissal of the indictment. So far, the lower courts have uniformly rejected motions to dismiss based on the inflammatory character of preindictment publicity. Even those courts accepting the premise of a defense right to an unbiased grand jury have nevertheless concluded that such a right does not allow application of the concept of inherently prejudicial publicity, which is available at the trial stage to presume juror bias and require a change of venue.[13] In the grand jury setting, these courts insist upon a specific showing of actual bias on the part of the seated jurors. Moreover, they hold that the defendant, with no right to voir dire, must establish a significant likelihood of actual bias, based upon more than the character of the publicity alone, to justify an evidentiary hearing. With access to the grand jury transcript difficult to obtain in most jurisdictions, and

not very likely to reveal juror bias in any event, this required showing has been aptly characterized as rendering preindictment publicity claims almost "inevitably doomed as a matter of law."

The imposition of such a substantial burden on defendants raising preindictment publicity claims is justified on several grounds. First, the "role of the grand jury historically has differed from that of a petit jury" in a way that does not require that it have "the same freedom from outside influences." The grand jury, as an investigative body, is allowed to look to "rumor, tips, and hearsay," which would include much of the material found in preindictment publicity. Second, "if preindictment publicity could cause the dismissal of an indictment, many persons, either prominent or notorious, could readily avoid indictment, a result detrimental to the system of justice." The impact of pretrial publicity upon the petit jury can be eliminated or alleviated by a change of venue, but an indictment can be returned only by a grand jury of the judicial district in which the offense occurred. Finally, courts note that the prospective defendant has other safeguards. In cases of extensive preindictment publicity, the prospective defendant is likely to be aware that the case against him will go to the grand jury, and he can always request that the supervising judge conduct a brief inquiry into the open-mindedness of the prospective jurors, as was done in *Beck*.

(i) Postconviction Review. Assume that a defendant makes a timely objection to the composition of the grand jury, but that objection is denied by the trial judge. Assume also that the defendant is subsequently convicted by a properly selected petit jury. On appeal from a subsequent conviction, should the illegality of the grand jury's composition be treated as harmless error? In *Rose v. Mitchell*,[14] Justice Stewart, dissenting, argued that "any possible prejudice" to a defendant from racial discrimination in the selection of the grand jury "disappears when a constitutionally valid trial jury later finds him guilty beyond a rea-

13. See § 23.2(a).

14. See note 9 supra.

sonable doubt." The majority rejected this contention, noting that it was inconsistent with a long line of cases and failed to give adequate consideration to the varied interests at stake in prohibiting racial discrimination in the selection of the grand jury. "[B]ecause discrimination on the basis of race * * * strikes at the fundamental values of our judicial system and our society as a whole," it was entirely appropriate to "revers[e] the conviction * * * in such cases without inquiry into whether the defendant was prejudiced in fact by the discrimination at the grand jury stage." While there were "costs associated with this approach," those costs (basically the reindictment and retrial of the defendant) were "outweighed by the strong policy the Court consistently has recognized of combating racial discrimination in the administration of justice."

In *Vasquez v. Hillery*,[15] the Court reaffirmed the *Rose* ruling and added another ground for failing to treat the conviction before a fairly selected petit jury as "curing" the racial discrimination in the selection of the grand jury. The grand jury, the Court noted, "does not determine only that probable cause exists," but also "has the power to charge * * * a lesser offense" than the evidence might support. "Thus even if a grand jury's determination of probable cause is confirmed in hindsight by a conviction on the indicted offense, that confirmation in no way suggests that the discrimination did not impermissibly infect the framing of the indictment and consequently,

the nature or existence of the proceedings to come."[16]

In *United States v. Mechanik*,[17] which held that other errors in the grand jury process did not survive an intervening conviction at a fair trial, the Court distinguished the claim presented in *Rose* and *Vasquez*. The Court noted that the considerations that led to the setting aside of a "final judgment of conviction" in those cases "have little force outside the context of racial discrimination in the composition of the grand jury." Those considerations were said to include a long line of precedent "directly applicable to the special problem of racial discrimination" and the belief that "racial discrimination in the selection of grand jurors is so pernicious and other remedies so impractical, that the remedy of automatic reversal was necessary as a prophylactic means of deterring grand jury discrimination in the future." This explanation of the racial discrimination cases might suggest that other constitutional objections to grand jury composition would not be subject to the automatic reversal rule of the racial discrimination cases. However, the rationale of *Rose* and *Vasquez* was not viewed as so limited in the later case of *Bank of Nova Scotia v. United States*.[18] In discussing *Rose* and *Vasquez,* the Court there noted that it had appropriately "reached a like conclusion in *Ballard v. United States*,[19] when women had been excluded from the grand jury." The key in such cases, the *Bank of Nova Scotia* Court noted, was that "the nature of the violation allowed a presumption that the defendant was prejudiced, and any inquiry into harmless er-

15. 474 U.S. 254, 106 S.Ct. 617, 88 L.Ed.2d 598 (1986).

16. The dissenters in *Vasquez* found unpersuasive the majority's hypothesis of possible grand jury nullification. The dissenters argued that the long line of cases recognizing the challenges of black defendants to racial discrimination in the selection of the grand jury had never been based on the assumption that an "all white grand jury from which blacks are systematically excluded might be influenced by race in determining whether to indict and on what charge." Subsequent support for their position was found in *Powers v. Ohio,* supra note 4. *Powers'* analysis would seem to push to the forefront the *Rose* justification for the automatic reversal rule. Arguably, still further support for the predominance of *Rose's* "integrity analysis" is found in the remedy imposed in *Vasquez.* As commentators have noted, that remedy was not geared strictly to the possibility that the grand jury might have been more lenient in charging if blacks had not been

excluded. If that were the Court's only concern, rather than dismissing the indictment and requiring a new trial, it might simply have remanded for a reconsideration of the charges by a fairly selected grand jury. If such a grand jury should indict on the same charge, there would be no reason for a new trial. Of course, while such a limited remedy would meet the concern that a fairly composed grand jury might have nullified, it might not have been viewed as a satisfactory to serve the *Rose* objective of protecting the integrity of the process.

17. 475 U.S. 66, 106 S.Ct. 938, 89 L.Ed.2d 50 (1986), also discussed in § 15.6(f).

18. 487 U.S. 250, 108 S.Ct. 2369, 101 L.Ed.2d 228 (1988).

19. 329 U.S. 187, 67 S.Ct. 261, 91 L.Ed. 181 (1946).

ror would have required unguided speculation." Interestingly, *Ballard* was a ruling based on a federal statute and the exercise of the Court's supervisory power to fashion a remedy for its violation, rather than on constitutional grounds. However, the group excluded there would also be one protected under an equal protection analysis.

Of course, even if the reasoning of *Rose* and *Vasquez* does not require post-conviction appellate court consideration of constitutional errors in the grand jury selection process apart from racial or gender discrimination, a state court always remains free to treat the issue as open to consideration under state law. Many state courts have done exactly that for a wide range of challenges to the composition of the grand jury. Indeed, appellate opinions commonly consider such objections on the merits without even taking note of the fact that the alleged error undoubtedly had no impact upon the fairness of the trial itself (the petit jury having been fairly selected). This position may rest on the rationale that an illegally composed grand jury is itself a nullity and therefore its indictment fails to provide a jurisdictional grounding for the subsequent conviction. It may also reflect the concern that treating the subsequent trial as having purged the illegality in grand jury composition would effectively preclude appellate review of such errors, at least in jurisdictions barring interlocutory appeals. A similar concern has led appellate courts in many jurisdictions to consider on appeal from a conviction other errors in the grand jury process that do not have a bearing on trial fairness even where those errors clearly did not relate to the legality of the grand jury itself (e.g., prosecutorial misconduct in questioning witnesses).[20]

§ 15.5 Indictment Challenges Based Upon Evidentiary Grounds

(a) The Federal Standard: The *Costello* Rule. *Costello v. United States*[1] is the seminal Supreme Court ruling on defense challenges to a federal grand jury indictment based on the alleged incompetency or insufficiency of the evidence before the grand jury. *Costello* involved a tax-evasion prosecution in which it was discovered at trial that the prosecution before the grand jury had relied entirely on the testimony of three government agents who summarized what later became the testimony of 144 witness at trial. Defendant then moved to dismiss the indictment on the ground that the grand jury had before it only hearsay testimony that would not have been admissible at trial and therefore lacked sufficient evidence to support the indictment. On review following defendant's conviction, the Supreme Court held that the trial correctly denied the motion because the Fifth Amendment did not preclude an indictment based "solely on hearsay" and it would be inappropriate for the Court to impose such a prohibition in the exercise of its supervisory power over procedure in the federal courts. The Court, in an opinion by Justice Black, also spoke generally of the unavailability of any indictment challenge grounded upon the "competency and adequacy of the evidence before the grand jury."

The *Costello* opinion placed considerable stress upon the "history" and "traditions" of the grand jury. The Fifth Amendment's grand jury provision assumed a grand jury that "operates substantially like its English progenitor." The English grand jurors were not "hampered by rigid procedural or evidentiary rules," but could act on "such information as they deemed satisfactory," including "their own knowledge." They acted independently and were "free from control by the Crown or the judges." This tradition of a "body of laymen, free from technical rules" was recognized in early decisions in this country holding that a court could not "revis[e] the judgment of the grand jury upon the evidence, * * * whether or not [the grand jury's] finding was founded upon sufficient proof." Thus, defendant's Fifth Amendment claim was contrary to "the whole history of the grand jury institution."

Justice Black also noted, partially in response to defendant's suggestion that the

20. See § 15.6(f) prior to note 11.

§ 15.5
1. 350 U.S. 359, 76 S.Ct. 406, 100 L.Ed. 397 (1956).

Court look to its supervisory authority, that allowing challenges of the type urged by the defendant would impose unacceptable administrative costs. "If indictments were to be held open to challenge on the ground that there was inadequate or incompetent evidence before the grand jury, the resulting delay would be great indeed." Such a rule would allow defendants in every case to "insist on a kind of preliminary trial to determine the competency and adequacy of the evidence before the grand jury." The indicted defendant would later obtain at trial "a strict observance of all the rules designed to bring about a fair verdict." There was no need to adopt "a rule which would result in interminable delay, but add nothing to the assurance of a fair trial."

The reasoning and language of *Costello* went far beyond the particular evidentiary challenge presented there. The challenge in *Costello* was to hearsay, and the lower court had stressed the special characteristics of hearsay evidence. It had noted that hearsay often is quite reliable, and that the primary reason for its exclusion, the inability to cross examine the declarant, had no bearing in the ex parte process of the grand jury. Justice Black's opinion, however, relied upon none of these limiting features. Indeed, it spoke of the grand jury's freedom to rely on incompetent evidence in general, and not simply to the use of hearsay.

The *Costello* opinion, moreover, rejected challenges not only to the competency of the evidence, but also of its sufficiency to establish the quantum of proof needed for an indictment. The two issues might well have been separated. A court might allow use of evidence that would be inadmissible at trial, but then insist that such evidence have sufficient probative weight to establish probable cause. Justice Black's opinion, however, viewed the challenges to sufficiency and competency as equally inconsistent with the historical role of the grand jury. Indeed, his opinion was written so broadly as to suggest that federal courts would be powerless to dismiss an indictment even in the extreme case in which the grand jury had received absolutely no evidence that was pro-

bative. Thus, Justice Black noted that the judicial response to an indictment should be governed by a single, overriding principle: "An indictment returned by a legally constituted and unbiased grand jury, like an information drawn by the prosecutor, if valid on its face, is enough to call for a trial of the charge on the merits." Responding to the implications of that principle, Justice Burton concurred separately, seeking to establish a narrow exception that would justify minimal judicial review of the grand jury evidence. Noting that the Court's opinion apparently "would not preclude an examination of grand jury action to ascertain the existence of bias or prejudice in an indictment," Justice Burton contended that an indictment likewise should be quashed "if it is shown that the grand jury had before it no substantial or rationally persuasive evidence."

Subsequent Supreme Court cases have not put before the Court the situation hypothesized by Justice Burton, but they have produced general reaffirmations of the breadth of the *Costello* principle. Thus, a series of rulings have stated that an indictment will not be subject to challenge in the federal courts even when based on unconstitutionally obtained evidence. In the latest of those rulings, *United States v. Calandra*,[2] the Court relied upon the *Costello* principle in refusing to fashion a remedy that would preclude grand jury consideration of evidence obtained through an unconstitutional search and seizure. Citing *Costello* and the broad reading of *Costello* in later cases, the *Calandra* Court noted:

> The grand jury's sources of information are widely drawn and the validity of an indictment is not affected by the character of the evidence considered. Thus, an indictment valid on its face is not subject to challenge on the ground that the grand jury acted on the basis of inadequate or incompetent evidence; or even on the basis of information obtained in violation of a defendant's Fifth Amendment privilege against self-incrimination.

(b) The Federal Standard: The Rise and Demise of the "Misconduct Exception" to *Costello*. Many lower federal courts

---

2. 414 U.S. 338, 94 S.Ct. 613, 38 L.Ed.2d 561 (1974).

were not entirely comfortable with the breadth of the *Costello* ruling. They expressed appreciation for "Mr. Justice Black's fear of minitrials for indictments," but noted that there also was a need to respond to the "growing use of the grand jury as a pawn or 'mere tool' of the prosecutor." These courts sought to establish a half-way station between full review of the competency and adequacy of evidence and a refusal to consider evidentiary challenges under any circumstances. That half-way station was founded on the doctrine of supervisory control over prosecutorial misconduct. *Costello*, it was argued, did not take from the lower federal courts their traditional authority to "preserve the integrity of the judicial process" by dismissing indictments that were the product of "flagrantly abusive prosecutorial conduct" before the grand jury. Indeed, support for exercising that authority was found in *Costello's* caveat that an indictment must be returned by "an unbiased grand jury" in order to be enough in itself "to call for trial." Abusive prosecutorial practices, such as insults and insinuations directed against the target, traditionally had been held inconsistent with this requirement since they "serv[ed] no purpose other than to have the grand jury indict out of bias." The same could be true, the lower courts reasoned, of prosecutorial misconduct in inappropriately presenting certain types of evidence to the grand jury. While historical tradition allowed the federal grand jury to consider all types of evidence, that should not allow the prosecutor to attempt to pressure the jurors into issuing an indictment by deception or other improprieties in introducing evidence.

The assumption of the lower courts that *Costello* did not preclude dismissals based on prosecutorial misconduct in presenting evidence was open to question. Justice Black had noted that the judiciary traditionally lacked authority to impose "procedural or evidentiary rules" upon the grand jury process. Restrictions imposed upon prosecutorial actions before the grand jury would constitute, in effect, judicially imposed "procedural rules" for the

process. Very often such a rule would simply restate in another fashion an evidentiary standard. A court could say, on the one hand, that an indictment must be supported by some substantive evidence (as Justice Burton argued) or, on the other, that a prosecutor engaged in misconduct by seeking an indictment without any substantive evidence. Judicial intervention to enforce either rule would involve what *Costello* warned against—"revising the judgment of the grand jury upon the evidence." Moreover, allowing challenges to indictments to enforce judicially imposed rules governing prosecutorial conduct before the grand jury would open the door to the delays and disruptions in the process that *Costello* viewed as intolerable.

Some lower courts ignored these inconsistences, while others sought to distinguish misconduct challenges as imposing a lesser burden on the process. All accepted the concept that they had authority to create and enforce (by indictment dismissal) standards governing the prosecutor's presentation of evidence. For roughly thirty years the Supreme Court did not speak to the issue, and during that period the lower courts developed an extensive "common law" of prosecutorial misconduct in presenting evidence. Then in *United States v. Williams*,[3] the Court undercut at least a substantial portion (if not all) of the doctrinal foundation of such rulings.

For reasons discussed in § 15.6(b), the *Williams* majority concluded that, "as a general matter at least," federal courts lacked the authority to independently prescribe standards of appropriate prosecutorial conduct before the grand jury. Federal courts could utilize their supervisory authority "as a means of enforcing or vindicating legally compelled standards of prosecutorial conduct before the grand jury," but those standards were to be found basically in statutes, the Federal Rules of Criminal Procedural, and any constitutional prohibitions. Federal courts were not free to create on their own initiative additional limits based on their independent judgment of what was needed to

---

3. 504 U.S. 36, 112 S.Ct. 1735, 118 L.Ed.2d 352 (1992), also discussed in § 15.6(b).

ensure the proper functioning of the grand jury.

Looking to this limited authority, the *Williams* majority held that the supervisory authority of the federal courts did not extend to imposing upon the prosecutor an obligation to disclose known exculpatory evidence to the grand jury. The Court noted in the regard that the imposition of such an obligation not only was not authorized by statute, court rule, or constitutional command, but also was contrary to *Costello*. "It would make little sense," the Court noted, "to abstain from reviewing the evidentiary support for the grand jury's judgment while scrutinizing the sufficiency of the prosecutor's presentation." This was so because "a complaint about the quality or adequacy of the evidence can always be recast as a complaint that the prosecutor's presentation was 'incomplete' or 'misleading'." As an illustration, the Court cited one of the more extensive lower court rulings on supervisory authority, which it described as directing that the "prosecutor should not introduce hearsay evidence before the grand jury when direct evidence was available." That directive, the Court noted, simply reflected a shift from "complaining about the grand jury's *reliance* upon hearsay evidence" to "complain[ing] about the prosecution's *introduction* of it."

Williams thus cast considerable doubt upon the continuing vitality of most, if not all, of the lower court rulings dismissing indictments based on prosecutorial misconduct in presenting evidence. Those rulings, in general, made no effort to tie the misconduct standards they recognized to a statutory prohibition, a court rule, or a constitutional command, but relied on precisely the authority to prescribe general standards of fairness that *Williams* rejected. Arguably, some of those misconduct standards can be preserved by reference to statutory prohibitions. The Court cited a list of illustrative court rules and statutory provisions that could be "enforced or vindicated" through the federal courts' supervisory power. Those statutory provisions included the provisions restricting use of immunized testimony, the pro-

vision prohibiting grand jury use of unlawfully intercepted oral communications, and provisions described in *Williams* as "criminalizing false declarations before [the] grand jury" and "criminalizing subornation of perjury" The provision barring government use of immunized testimony against the immunized person can certainly provide the requisite statutory violation to sustain pre-*Williams* rulings that consideration of such testimony by the indicting grand jury constituted grounds for dismissing the indictment. As discussed in § 15.7(e), the provisions on false testimony and suborning perjury can do the same for the pre-*Williams* misconduct rulings justifying dismissal of an indictment on the basis of the prosecutor's knowing use of perjured testimony before the grand jury.

Even should the prosecutions's presentation of evidence violate a statute or court rule, *Williams'* warning against the use of the misconduct rational to subvert *Costello* affords a basis for rejecting dismissal as an appropriate remedy. That possibility is illustrated by the Supreme Court's interpretation of the federal wiretap statute, one of the provisions cited by *Williams* as illustrative of congressional regulation of grand jury procedures. In *Gelbard v. United States*,[4] a pre-*Williams* ruling, the Supreme Court held that a grand jury witness could invoke the statutory prohibition against use of illegally intercepted communications in grand jury proceedings to challenge grand jury questioning based upon any such communication. At the same time, the Court construed that statute as not designed to allow a defendant to challenge an indictment where the grand jury had considered illegally intercepted conversations, as Congress had indicated that the statute's exclusionary rule was not intended to create an exception to *Costello* and its progeny. The *Costello*-type concerns that led Congress to deem dismissal an inappropriate remedy for prosecutorial violation of the wiretap statute's prohibition could also convince a court that its supervisory authority should not be used to create a dismissal sanction for prosecutorial violation of other statutes that relate

---

4. 408 U.S. 41, 92 S.Ct. 2357, 33 L.Ed.2d 179 (1972).

to the presentation of evidence before the grand jury.

(c) State Standards. A substantial majority of the states agree with *Costello* that an indictment should not be subject to dismissal because the grand jury relied upon evidence that would be inadmissible at trial. Included in this group are all but a few of the states that regularly use indictments to charge. Today, many of the "*Costello* states" have statutory provisions stating that the rules of evidence do not apply to the grand jury, but their adherence to the *Costello* position commonly predates the adoption of those provisions. In several *Costello* states, statutes require adherence to all or most of the rules of evidence in grand jury proceedings. Nonetheless, the *Costello* position prevails because of statutory provisions which preclude evidentiary challenges or judicial rulings adopting the *Costello* arguments against allowing "judicial revision" of the "judgement of the grand jury" and thereby opening the door to "interminable delays."

Most of the states adopting the *Costello* position on challenges to the competency of the evidence before the grand jury also follow *Costello* in refusing to recognize challenges to the sufficiency of the evidence supporting the indictment. Several, however depart somewhat from this prong of *Costello*, allowing challenges based on the total absence of evidence on a necessary element of the crime, or challenges based on the absence of any testimony from a witness competent to testify.

In both states that completely adhere to *Costello*, and states that slightly modify *Costello's* sufficiency prohibition, courts will recognize at least a limited "misconduct exception" to the *Costello* prohibitions. In some states, where statutory provisions on challenges do not recognize misconduct objections, claims of misconduct in presenting evidence will only be cognizable where presented as a constitutional claim. In others, the misconduct analysis extends to various actions characterized as misrepresenting the strength of the evidence. Those state rulings are discussed in § 15.7(e).

Approximately a dozen states flatly reject the positions taken in *Costello*. Most of these states are information jurisdictions, but a few are indictment states. Jurisdictions rejecting *Costello* allow challenges both to the sufficiency and competency of the evidence underlying an indictment. Several do so by statutory command, but others have reached this position through judicial decision. The broad rule of *Costello*, it is argued, can be justified only "if the institution of the grand jury is viewed as an anachronism." If the grand jury is to "protect * * * the innocent against oppression and unjust prosecution," a defendant "with substantial grounds for having an indictment dismissed should not be compelled to go to trial to prove the insufficiency."

Jurisdictions rejecting *Costello* uniformly insist that the trial court act with caution in reviewing the sufficiency of the evidence before the grand jury. They stress that "every legitimate inference that may be drawn from the evidence must be drawn in favor of the indictment," and note that "probable cause * * * may be based on 'slight' or even marginal evidence." As a result, most of the successful sufficiency challenges arise from the prosecution's failure to offer any evidence on a particular element of the crime charged.

Although several of the non-*Costello* states apparently make the rules of evidence fully applicable to the grand jury, not all are so restrictive as to what the grand jury considers. Several make the rules generally applicable, but create special exemptions allowing admission of hearsay evidence to replace the personal appearance of youthful witnesses and persons whose testimony ordinarily should not be critical. A few allow considerable evidence that would not be admissible at trial. Indeed, in these states, the rejection of *Costello* applies basically to sufficiency review rather competency review.

Review of the competency of the evidence before the grand jury does not mean that indictments will be dismissed wherever the grand jury considered evidence deemed inadmissible for indictment purposes. Ordinarily, the indictment will be sustained if there was sufficient admissible evidence before the grand jury to support the charge. However, where the inadmissible evidence was so prejudicial as to necessarily have influenced the grand jury, the indictment may be dismissed notwithstanding otherwise sufficient legal evidence. This result can also be reached under a misconduct rationale where the prosecution sought to manipulate the grand jury through the use of evidence known to be inadmissible.

Where the trial court erroneously fails to grant a motion to dismiss based on the incompetency or insufficiency of the grand jury evidence, that ruling is likely to come before the appellate court only after conviction. At that point, some non-*Costello* states treat the sufficiency of the grand jury evidence as a moot issue, as the conviction at trial has clearly established the presence of more than enough admissible evidence to meet the indictment standard. Other states, however, will consider the denial of the motion to dismiss on a post-conviction appeal, and reverse the conviction if the trial judge clearly erred in that ruling. The Alaska Supreme Court has noted that postconviction review and reversal is necessary to ensure that proper standards are applied by the grand jury (and by the prosecutor in presenting evidence to the grand jury).

To assist the defendant in presenting an evidentiary challenge, most of the jurisdictions rejecting *Costello* grant defendant an automatic right to inspect the grand jury transcript.[5] New York, however, provides initially only for an in camera inspection by the trial court, with the court having authority to deny defense inspection if it "determines there is not reasonable cause to believe that the evidence before the grand jury may have been legally insufficient." This authority is viewed as necessary to preclude use of the evidentiary challenge as a delaying tactic or as a means of obtaining pretrial discovery. Courts in other non-*Costello* jurisdictions have argued, however, that an automatic right of inspection "is essential to give meaning to the defendant's right to challenge the indictment." Requiring a prior showing is condemned as unlikely to reach numerous deficiencies that will not be detectable on the face of the proceedings. In camera inspection has been rejected on the grounds that the court needs the "assistance of counsel for both sides if it is to judge wisely."

§ 15.6 Misconduct Challenges: General Principles

(a) **Prosecutorial Misconduct.** In almost every jurisdiction making more than occasional use of the grand jury, appellate opinions recognize a trial court authority to dismiss an indictment, under at least some circumstances, based upon prosecutorial "misconduct" in the grand jury proceedings. Whether such authority exists in the remaining states is unclear. The lack of precedent is probably due to the infrequent use of the grand jury. However, it may also rest on the assumption that consideration of possible misconduct is precluded by the *Costello* principle that indictments valid on their face, if issued by a properly selected grand jury, are not subject to judicial review.

In perhaps a dozen states, the authority to dismiss based upon misconduct is shaped by statutes setting forth the grounds for dismissal of an indictment. In a few states, those provisions authorize a motion to dismiss based upon a violation of the various statutory provisions regulating grand jury practice (including provisions defining the role of the prosecutor), subject to a prejudice or potential prejudice prerequisite. In most instances, however, the provisions set forth very narrow grounds (apart from composition challenges) that encompass only a single type of misconduct provision—the presence of an authorized person during the grand jury proceedings. Where such provisions are viewed as exclusive, they sharply restrict the court's capacity to dismiss based upon improprieties in the grand jury proceedings. Of course, the legislature cannot immunize a constitutional violation, so courts facing such statutes have turned to the question of whether the alleged misconduct before them violates the state or federal constitution.

Where a state has a constitutional guarantee of prosecution by indictment, a constitutional challenge to prosecutorial misconduct may be based on that guarantee. However, state cases

---

5. See § 15.2(i).

analyzing constitutional challenges most frequently have done so under the due process clause of the state or federal constitution. Of course, due process has been held not to require a grand jury screening, but courts have assumed that the state cannot provide such a proceeding and then allow such basic unfairness as to render it worthless. They note that when the indictment mechanism is employed, it must be through a grand jury which is "unbiased", and prosecutorial misconduct can produce a grand jury which is no longer unbiased. This analysis can be challenged as reading into due process a prohibition that has been rejected in other contexts [e.g., in allowing grand jurors who have a personal interest in the case, see § 15.5(g)].

In applying due process to misconduct challenges, courts have looked to the traditional fundamental fairness standard of due process and the application of that standard at trial. Thus, they require that the prosecutor not have coerced, deceived, or inflamed the grand jury through actions that would be deemed a due process violation at trial if done to manipulate a trial jury. Due process violations have been found, for example, in flagrant improprieties in argument before the grand jury, similar to the arguments that would violate due process at trial. Courts have also found due process violations in the knowing use of perjured testimony and similar deceptions of the grand jury that parallel deceptions constituting due process violations at trial. So too, although the historical tradition of grand jury proceedings has led courts to reject the contention that a prosecutor's due process obligation to disclose exculpatory materials can be carried over to the grand jury, it was noted by one court rejecting such an obligation that "under certain circumstances, a prosecutor's intentional withholding of such evidence could result in a denial of a defendant's right to due process." Such rulings and suggestions may be reexamined in light of the Supreme Court's ruling in *Albright v. Oliver*,[1] holding that substantive due process afforded no protection against governmental initiation of a prosecution based on information known to be unreliable.

Where statutes do not restrict the grounds for dismissing an indictment, state courts generally have found no need to turn to constitutional guarantees to find judicial authority to dismiss indictments deemed to be the product of prosecutorial misconduct. They have found an ample grounding for such dismissals in what is characterized as the "common law", "inherent", or "supervisory" authority of the court to protect the "integrity" of the grand jury's decision-making function. They note that, though courts must give "due deference to the grand jury's status as an independent body," courts also have a responsibility not to accept indictments that are the product of the prosecutor's subversion of that body. In describing the touchstone for the exercise of this responsibility, courts frequently speak of prosecutorial conduct that substantially undercuts the grand jury's independent decision making function. Other courts, however, speak of actions that deprive the grand jury process of its "fairness and impartiality."

State courts have looked to a variety of sources in determining what constitutes "misconduct" which may justify a dismissal nonconstitutional grounds. Thus, misconduct may be found where there has been: (1) a violation of a statutory standard governing grand jury proceedings; (2) a grand jury violation of the rights of the target (as a witness or otherwise) where that violation contributes to the indictment; (3) the failure of the prosecutor to fulfill the prosecutor's obligations as legal advisor to the grand jury; (4) actions that prevent the grand jury from exercising its independent authority; (5) a presentation of evidence that puts before the jury a deceptive or false case as compared to the evidence known to prosecutor; and (6) advocacy that goes substantially beyond the traditional limits as developed largely in the trial context, but modified somewhat for the grand jury setting.

---

§ 15.6

1.   510 U.S. 266, 114 S.Ct. 807, 127 L.Ed.2d 114 (1994), discussed in § 14.2 at note 4, and note 45 of § 2.7(d).

The range of prosecutorial behavior that may be challenged by reference to the above guideposts is extremely broad. Those actions most frequently challenged by defendants will be considered in greater detail in § 15.7. While each has its own analytical shading, three overriding considerations provide a common structure for the claims discussed there and all other misconduct claims. First, as discussed in subsection (g), the defendant bears the burden of establishing the existence of the misconduct within the restrictions imposed by grand jury secrecy requirements. Second, as discussed in subsections (d) and (e), prosecutorial misconduct ordinarily will not justify a dismissal absent some showing of likely prejudice. Third, as discussed below, to establish most forms of misconduct, the defendant will be required to show that the prosecutor acted with some measure of scienter.

While the term "misconduct" might suggest an element of prosecutorial culpability, a mental element commonly associated with wrongdoing is not invariably required by all courts to establish prosecutorial "misconduct". For example, some courts find prosecutorial misconduct in the erroneous charging of the grand jury as to the elements of an offense even though the prosecutor adopted an interpretation of the offense that was arguable, but later held to be erroneous. Yet even as to improper legal advice, some courts will take into account that the prosecutor was not acting in a "deliberately improper fashion". Where courts view misconduct dismissals as reserved for "very limited and very extreme cases", scienter often becomes an important factor in determining whether action of the prosecutor was "egregious" or "flagrant". Thus, as to the introduction of false testimony before the grand jury, these courts indicate that misconduct requires prosecutor knowledge of its falsity. Where jurisdictions recognize a broad range of misconduct, they are likely to require no more than a certain degree of recklessness or gross negligence as to certain types of misconduct. Here, a prosecutor may be held responsible for deceptive presentations of evidence by government agents where the prosecutor should have recognized that the presentations were deceptive.

(b) The Federal Standard; The *Williams* Limits. Prior to the Supreme Court's 1992 decision in *United States v. Williams*,[2] the lower federal courts had found prosecutorial misconduct calling for an indictment dismissal to encompass a broader range of actions than almost any other jurisdiction. Such misconduct included: various actions or inactions relating to the presentation of false evidence, misleading evidence, hearsay evidence, and exculpatory evidence; the prosecutor operating under a conflict of interest; the prosecutor giving incorrect legal advice; the prosecutor testifying as a witness; the prosecutor making inflammatory comments relating to the case; the prosecutor expressing a personal opinion as to guilt; the prosecutor presenting to a grand jury an indictment that is pre-signed (thereby indicating the prosecutor's opinion); allowing an unauthorized person to be present while a witness gave testimony; the prosecutor commenting on the exercise of the privilege against self-incrimination by the target or an allied witness, or presenting before the grand jury the target's immunized testimony; various violations of the Rule 6(e) provisions governing disclosure of grand jury matter; and a totality of circumstances analysis considering the combined impact of a variety of improprieties. However, *United States v. Williams* produced a sea change in the authority of federal courts to characterize prosecutorial actions as misconduct that can produce an indictment dismissal.

The *Williams* majority rejected a Tenth Circuit ruling sustaining a pretrial dismissal because of the prosecution's failure to present before the grand jury exculpatory evidence within the possession of the government. In so doing, the Court largely limited federal courts to misconduct challenges that involve either constitutional violations or violations of "one of those few clear rules which were carefully drafted and approved by this Court and by Congress to ensure the integrity of the grand jury's functions." It rejected the contention

2. 504 U.S. 36, 112 S.Ct. 1735, 118 L.Ed.2d 352 (1992), also discussed in § 15.5 at note 3.

"that the [federal] courts' supervisory power could be used, not merely as a means of enforcing or vindicating legally compelled standards of prosecutorial conduct before the grand jury, but as a means of prescribing those standards of prosecutorial conduct in the first instance."

Williams acknowledged that the supervisory authority of the federal courts had been utilized to "establish standards of prosecutorial conduct before the courts themselves", but concluded that, "because the grand jury is an institution separate from the courts, over whose functioning the courts do not preside, * * * [it is] clear that, as a general matter at least, no such 'supervisory' judicial authority exists [as to grand jury proceedings]." In support of this conclusion, Justice Scalia cited various aspects of the grand jury's "functional independence from the judicial branch," including its broad investigative authority and its "operational separateness." While it was "true [that] the grand jury cannot compel the appearance of witnesses and the production of evidence, and must appeal to the court when such compulsion is required," that link to judicial subpoena authority had served as the grounding for only limited judicial supervision which had been directly related to the use of the subpoena power (as when a court "refuse[s] to lend its assistance when the compulsion the grand jury seeks would override rights accorded by the Constitution * * * [or] * * * testimonial privileges recognized by the common law"). A quite different challenge to grand jury independence was presented where, as here, the federal courts were being asked to use their "judicial supervisory power as a basis for prescribing modes of grand jury procedure."

The *Williams* majority stressed that federal courts had only limited authority to formulate procedural rules "not specifically required by the Constitution or Congress" when those rules do not "deal strictly with the courts' power to control their own procedures," and further stressed that the exercise of that limited authority was most appropriately restricted as to the institution of the grand jury, which was a "constitutional fixture in its own right."

Nonetheless, the Court did not absolutely foreclose the application of that limited authority to the grand jury process under any and all circumstances. The Court noted that "as a general matter at least," no supervisory authority existed to independently create standards for judging prosecutorial conduct before the grand jury. Past Supreme Court precedent was described as "suggest[ing] that any power federal courts may have to fashion, on their own initiative, rules of grand jury procedure is a very limited one." Moreover, after suggesting by these statements that the federal courts might not totally lack authority to establish independently misconduct standards for grand jury proceedings, the Court echoed that possibility in its subsequent discussion of the respondent's contention that requiring prosecutorial disclosure of exculpatory evidence should be recognized "as a sort of Fifth Amendment common law." The Court rejected that contention as inconsistent with the "grand jury's historical role" as an "accusatory body," and as requiring "judicial reshaping of the grand jury institution, substantially altering the traditional relationships between the prosecutor, the constituting court, and the grand jury itself." The Court did not, however, flatly rule out the possibility of courts recognizing some Fifth Amendment common law of grand jury proceedings. It stated only that any power of federal courts to fashion such "common law" standards "certainly would not" extend to such a fundamental change.

Thus, the Court appeared to leave the door open for prohibiting prosecutorial conduct that may not be "specifically proscribed by Rule, statute, or the Constitution," but nonetheless has long been deemed contrary to "the traditional functions of the [grand jury] institution." That might well be the case, for example, of prosecutorial action that intentionally keeps from the grand jury potentially exculpatory evidence that the grand jury itself specifically requested. Yet, even should *Williams* eventually be read to sustain a prohibition of this type, federal supervisory authority seems likely to remain restricted in large part, if not exclusively, to responding to prosecutorial action that contradicts either the Constitution or the specific limitations set forth in Federal Rule 6 and in the United States Code.

The *Williams* Court noted in its footnote 6 that Federal Rule 6 contains a number of grand jury standards, including strict controls on prosecutorial disclosure of matters occurring before the grand jury (see § 8.5) and a prohibition against outsider presence during deliberations or voting. It also cited as illustrative of statutory provisions applicable to grand jury procedures those statutes governing the granting of immunity to witnesses, criminalizing false declarations and subornation of perjury, and prohibiting use of unlawfully intercepted wire and oral communications before the grand jury.

Post–*Williams* lower court rulings have recognized that "*Williams* was not confined to exculpatory evidence" or even to misconduct claims that relate to the "quality" of the evidence placed before the grand jury. These rulings generally view misconduct dismissals as likely to have a sound footing "only where violations of positive law embodied in a rule of criminal procedure, a statute, or the Constitution are raised." As discussed in § 15.5(b) and § 15.7(e), *Williams* has been read as overriding various pre-*Williams* supervisory-authority rulings relating to the presentation of evidence, and the same should be the case for most of the pre-*Williams* rulings discussed at the start of this subsection. Such "misconduct" as incorrect legal advice, conflicts of interest, inflammatory comments, and expression of personal opinions as to guilt are unlikely to involve violations of a court rule or statute.

(c) Juror Misconduct. While claims of juror misconduct are raised far less frequently than claims of prosecutor misconduct, those courts considering such claims uniformly recognize the authority of a trial court to dismiss an indictment on the basis of juror misconduct. In a jurisdiction that follows *Costello* and refuses to allow challenges to the sufficiency of the grand jury's evidence, challenges to juror misconduct may be seen as distinguishable for much the same reason that challenges to the grand jury's composition are distinguishable. The *Costello* principle, it may be argued, precludes judicial review of the correctness of a juror's judgment of the evidence, but actions by the jurors that take them outside of their role can be identified and reviewed apart from that judgment.

Since grand jurors, like petit jurors, are sharply restricted in their capacity to testify as to their deliberations, juror misconduct claims usually relate to juror activities outside the jury room. Thus, courts have sustained challenges to indictments where jurors engaged in off-the-record substantive discussions with witnesses during recesses or visited the site of the crime on their own initiative. Where the grand jury is limited to receiving sworn testimony, the juror who engages in such independent evidence gathering clearly engages in misconduct. But where the jurisdiction does not seek to restrict the common law authority of grand jurors to act on the basis of their own knowledge, one might question that conclusion. Of course, other "outside influences," such as threats or bribes, would be grounds for challenging an indictment in any jurisdiction.

In part because of the limitation upon the jurors capacity to testify about their deliberations, and in part because of the implications of *Costello*, courts have rejected challenges to the character of the grand jury's evaluative process in deciding to indict. Thus, indictments will be sustained without regard to the time spent by the jurors in evaluating the case. So too, a court will not stop to determine whether a careful evaluation would have required separate votes on different counts in the indictment rather than a single vote approving all of the charges together.

Defendants have argued that an issue separable from the evaluative process is presented when an indictment is sustained by the votes of jurors who were absent when a substantial portion of the evidence was presented. The federal courts, looking to the implications of *Costello*, have consistently rejected such challenges. They reason that each juror heard what he or she considered to be sufficient evidence to indict during the sessions attended, and the court cannot question that judgment under *Costello*. While it is possible that the absentee juror may have missed some exculpatory evidence, that possibility is too remote to either bar the juror from voting or require a review of the evidence to determine what was missed. Moreover, significant exculpatory evidence is likely to be noted in the course of the jury discussion and the absentee juror can decide for herself whether that evidence might have been so influential that she should not participate without having heard it.

(d) The Requirement of Prejudice. Assuming misconduct is established, must there be some showing of prejudicial impact upon the grand jury's decision to indict before a trial court can dismiss the indictment? Prior to the Supreme Court's ruling in *Bank of Nova Scotia v. United States*,[3] several lower federal courts had suggested that, in the exercise of their supervisory powers, trial courts could dismiss an indictment even where the defendant clearly had suffered no prejudice. The courts had authority, they argued, to dismiss an indictment simply as a "prophylactic tool" designed to deter prosecutorial misconduct, at least where that misconduct was "flagrant and entrenched." The *Bank of Nova Scotia* ruling, as discussed in the next subsection, rejected the use of the supervisory authority in this fashion. Although the propriety of prophylactic dismissals has not been widely considered in the state courts, a similar result presumably would be reached in the vast majority of the states.

In some states, the rejection of prophylactic dismissals would seem to follow *a fortiori* from their reading of their state statute governing dismissals as barring supervisory dismissals of indictments on misconduct grounds. As noted in subsection (a), jurisdictions so construing their statutes allow dismissals only for misconduct that reaches the level of a constitutional violation. One element of a constitutional violation, particularly a due process violation, is a showing of actual or potential prejudicial impact upon the decision to indict. In other states, statutory provisions specifically authorize dismissals based upon misconduct in the grand jury process, but include a requirement

of likely prejudicial impact. Here again, a prophylactic dismissal would be barred by the directly applicable statute.

Finally, in *Bank of Nova Scotia*, the Court concluded that prophylactic supervisory dismissals, because they operated without regard to prejudice, were inconsistent with the general statutory command of Federal Rule 52(a), which bars reversal of an adjudication based on an error that was "harmless" in its impact. All states have similar harmless error statutes or rules. However, a few state courts have suggested that a traditional Rule 52(a) harmless-error analysis should not apply to prosecutorial misconduct before the grand jury when its application would render "toothless" the prohibitions violated by the prosecutor's misconduct. In such cases, they note, a prophylactic dismissal would be appropriate to ensure that "today's harmless error" does not become "the standard practice of tomorrow."

In limited situations, states which have rejected a prophylactic dismissal authority will employ an "inherent prejudice" concept to justify misconduct dismissals without a specific showing of prejudice. That concept disposes with the need for a case-by-case showing of prejudicial impact and treats a particular type of misconduct as presumptively prejudicial and therefore automatically calling for a dismissal. Courts have offered two rationales in characterizing misconduct as inherently prejudicial. One is that the impact of the misconduct is too difficult to ascertain and the defendant therefore must be given the benefit of the doubt, with the court conclusively assuming the defendant was prejudiced. The other is that the flaw in the grand jury proceeding constituted a "structural defect", which deprived the grand jury of the authority to act. Both rationales draw in part from the treatment of racial discrimination in the selection of the grand jury as inherently prejudicial.[4] Both rationales also are said to be distinguishable from the imposition of a prophylactic sanction of dismissal, although the postconviction reversal of convictions based upon racial discrimination

---

3. See note 6 infra.   **4.** See § 15.4(h).

limited to the selection of the grand jury has sometimes been characterized as prophylactic in character.

The inherent prejudice concept has been applied to only a small group of improper actions in grand jury screening. Foremost among these are misconduct in the grand jury voting process, such as failing to put before the grand jury the indictment which it supposedly approved or having the prosecutor present when the grand jury deliberated and voted. As discussed in § 15.7(h), the states are divided on whether unauthorized presence in general should be deemed inherently prejudicial, with the courts supporting that position arguing that any inquiry into likely prejudice would be too speculative and those opposing that position arguing that a variety of concrete indicators (e.g., who was present and what happened during that presence) can certainly identify many cases in which there clearly was not prejudicial impact. Courts similarly are divided as to whether the presentation of the case by a prosecutor subject to a conflict of interest or lacking proper authorization should be deemed per se prejudicial. Certain errors relating to the structure of the proceedings (e.g., the failure to record) are so unlikely to impact the grand jury decision's to indict that they readily have been recognized as inappropriate candidates for treatment as inherently prejudicial.

Jurisdictions requiring a showing of actual prejudice do not require that the defense show by a preponderance that the grand jury would not have indicted but for the error. Rather, most apply a standard similar to that adopted by the Supreme Court in *Bank of Nova Scotia*, which requires dismissal if there is a "grave doubt" as to whether the decision to indict was "free from the substantial influence" of the alleged misconduct. As discussed in subsection (e), that standard focuses on the impact of the error, which may require reversal notwithstanding evidence before the grand jury that would easily support on indictment. However, for some state courts, the presence of substantial evidence supporting an indictment appears

to automatically render any error non-prejudicial.

(e) The Prejudice Standard of *Bank of Nova Scotia*. Although the lower federal courts had for many years considered misconduct challenges under their supervisory authority, the Supreme Court did not speak to the prejudice issue until 1986, when it decided *Mechanik v. United States*.[5] *Mechanik*, however, considered the prejudice question in the special context of judicial review following an intervening conviction, discussed below in subsection (f). One year later, in *Bank of Nova Scotia v. United States*,[6] the Court had before it a misconduct challenge to be resolved prior to trial. The prejudice issue came before the Court in *Bank of Nova Scotia* as a result of a trial court's pretrial dismissal of an indictment, and a prosecutor's decision to appeal that ruling rather than seek a new indictment from another grand jury. The trial court's ruling had been based on its finding of several violations of the Rule 6 provisions governing grand jury proceedings, and its additional finding that the "totality of the circumstances," as reflected in various additional acts of misconduct, had resulted in a prosecutorial undermining of the integrity of the grand jury process. The Court of Appeals found that some of the alleged acts of misconduct had been mischaracterized and those that remained did not justify a dismissal since they had not "significantly infring[ed] on the grand jury's ability to exercise independent judgment." A dissenting judge argued, however, that the trial court had supervisory authority to dismiss without any such showing of "prejudice" where there was, as here, "egregious prosecutorial misconduct." Such misconduct, the dissent argued, justified the use of dismissal as a prophylactic measure to "safeguard the integrity of the judicial process."

The Supreme Court initially considered and rejected the use of a prophylactic dismissal. The Court had previously ruled that the supervisory power may not be used in conflict with either constitutional or statutory command. Among the statutory commands held to limit

---

5. 475 U.S. 66, 106 S.Ct. 938, 89 L.Ed.2d 50 (1986), also discussed at note 11 infra.

6. 487 U.S. 250, 108 S.Ct. 2369, 101 L.Ed.2d 228 (1988).

the use of the supervisory power was that of Federal Rule 52(a). That rule requires federal courts to disregard any error or irregularity that "does not affect [the] substantial rights" of the accused. The "harmless error" standard of Rule 52(a) had been held to preclude the prophylactic reversal of a conviction even where the prosecutorial misconduct at trial was systemic and involved constitutional error. The same limitation, the Court reasoned, surely should also govern a nonconstitutional error in the grand jury setting. As applied to the grand jury, the harmless error standard required that the alleged prosecutorial misconduct present a sufficient potential for having harmed the defendant in the grand jury's decision to indict. In the absence of a finding of such potential prejudice, the misconduct must be deemed "harmless" and dismissal therefore barred by Rule 52(a).[7]

Turning to the standard to be utilized in applying Rule 52(a), the Court adopted the following measure of the necessary showing of prejudice: "Dismissal of the indictment is appropriate only 'if it established that the violation substantially influenced the grand jury's decision to indict,' or if there is 'grave doubt' that the decision to indict was free from the substantial influence of such violations." This standard was derived from the traditional federal harmless error standard governing the reversal of a conviction based on a nonconstitutional trial error, as set forth in *Kotteakos v. United States*.[8] The Court there had held that a conviction could not be overturned unless a reviewing court concludes "after examining the record as a whole, * * * that an error may have had 'substantial influence' on the outcome of the proceeding."

By looking to *Kotteakos*, the *Bank of Nova Scotia* Court gave content to at least the "substantial influence" element of its harmless error standard for grand jury proceedings. The *Kotteakos* opinion made clear that influence of the error was to be measured by its impact on the decision of the adjudicator, regardless of the correctness of the result reached by the adjudicator. Thus, the presence of sufficient evidence to convict would not necessarily render the error harmless; the question to be asked was whether "even so, * * * the error itself had substantial influence." The particular error may have been so influential as to have played an important role in the jury's decision to convict even though it was most likely that the same result would have been reached by another jury not exposed to the error. In the grand jury setting, the federal court similarly must go beyond the question of whether the grand jury had before it sufficient evidence of guilt. Misconduct may be so influential as to make it likely that the grand jury gave it great weight in deciding to indict notwithstanding that the untainted remainder of the prosecution's presentation would have been sufficient to support indictment.

The Court's reliance on *Kotteakos* offered less direction as to the second element of the *Bank of Nova Scotia* standard—the requisite likelihood that the misconduct had a substantial influence. *Kotteakos* stated that the critical issue was whether the appellate court could "say, with fair assurance * * * that the [jury's] judgment was not substantially swayed by the error" or could hold a "conviction [which] is sure that the error did not influence the jury, or had but very slight effect." *Bank of Nova Scotia* reformulated that standard to require that it either be "established that the violation substantially influenced the grand jury's decision to indict" or that there exist a " 'grave doubt' that the decision to indict was free from the substantial influence of [the]

---

7. Justice Marshall, in dissent, argued that defense discovery of prosecutorial misconduct before the grand jury was already made difficult by grand jury secrecy requirements and "to afford the occasional revelation of prosecutorial misconduct the additional insulation of harmless error analysis leaves Rule 6 toothless." The majority noted, however, that where misconduct did not have a prejudicial effect on the grand jury's decision to change, there remained other means of deterrence, more narrowly tailored than dismissal. It cited in this regard the use of the contempt power to punish a knowing violation of Rule 6, the "chastis[ing]" of the prosecutor in a published opinion, and the disciplinary processes of the bar and the Justice Department. "Such remedies," the court noted, "allow the court to focus on the culpable individual rather than granting a windfall to the unprejudiced defendant."

8. 328 U.S. 750, 66 S.Ct. 1239, 90 L.Ed. 1557 (1946), discussed in § 27.6(b).

violations." The second prong of this standard obviously is the easier to meet. Indeed, the first prong presumably is encompassed by the second. Where the defense has "established" that the error substantially influenced the grand jury's decision, the court obviously goes well beyond merely having a "grave doubt" as to whether that decision was free from substantial influence; since the misconduct's actual influence has been "established," the court presumably is convinced that it is more likely than not that the decision was not free from such influence. Thus, the critical issue under the Court's standard will be what degree of likelihood of substantial influence creates a "grave doubt," and on that issue, neither *Kotteakos* nor *Bank of Nova Scotia* provides a precise answer.

Kotteakos spoke of a court being able to say with "fair assurance" that the jury was not "substantially swayed by the error." Lower courts have disagreed as to the precise degree of likelihood suggested by this "fair assurance" language. They do agree, however, that a fair assurance can be present notwithstanding the minimal contrary indicators that would establish a "reasonable doubt" as to prejudicial impact. A reasonable doubt is all that is necessary to preclude a finding of harmless error for constitutional violations under the standard of *Chapman v. California*,[9] but *Kotteakos* is seen as requiring a greater likelihood of prejudice to preclude such a finding for nonconstitutional trial errors. The "grave doubt" language of *Bank of Nova Scotia* similarly suggests a doubt with a more substantial basis than that necessary merely to create a reasonable doubt. Beyond this, the only additional direction offered as to the substantiality

of a "grave doubt" came from a single comment to the effect that a "grave" doubt required more than simply raising a "substantial question" as to likely impact in the mind of the reviewing court.

Although applying its reformulation of the *Kotteakos* standard to the full range of prosecutorial misconduct in the case before it, the *Bank of Nova Scotia* opinion contained language suggesting that this prejudice standard might not govern in all situations. At the outset of its opinion, the Court majority stated that it was holding that, "*as a general matter*, a district court may not dismiss an indictment for errors in grand jury proceedings unless such errors prejudiced the defendants" (emphasis added). Subsequently, the opinion noted that the Court did not have before it a case in which either (1) "constitutional error occurred during the grand jury proceedings," (2) the "grand jury's independence was infringed," or (3) there was a history of systemic prosecutorial misconduct spanning several cases and raising a "serious question" of "fundamental fairness." The applicability of the reformulated *Kotteakos* standard to those three situations accordingly may be treated as an open question, although the context of the discussion of the latter two situations arguably indicates that they are subject to that standard and distinctive only in providing inferences in its application.[10]

(f) Postconviction Review. In *Bank of Nova Scotia*, the misconduct challenge was presented before trial and was considered in a preconviction context by both the trial and the appellate courts. It is not unusual, however, for a misconduct challenge to be considered by the trial or appellate court only after the de-

---

9. See § 27.6(c).

10. With respect to constitutional claims, the Court's discussion of two such claims suggested the potential for treating those claims somewhat differently. First, the Court noted that a case-specific showing of prejudice had not been required for constitutional challenges to the composition of the grand jury, but it distinguished those violations from the misconduct challenges before it. The composition challenges involved a violation of the "structural protections of the grand jury," leading to an automatic "presumption of prejudice." They were thus "isolated exceptions to the harmless error rule." Second in discussing the one constitutionally grounded misconduct

exception presented in the case before it, the Court looked to a Fifth Amendment principle similar to that which applies at trial (the prosecution may not seek to draw an adverse inference from the exercise of the privilege against self-incrimination). While the Court found no violation of that principle and therefore had no need to determine the consequences of such a violation, continuation of the same analogy would produce a more stringent standard for a finding of harmless error. At trial, a violation of that Fifth Amendment principle would be tested by the *Chapman* harmless error standard, requiring reversal unless the court could conclude beyond a reasonable doubt that the violation had not contributed to the jury's verdict.

fendant has gone to trial and has been convict-ed. Ordinarily, the defense must raise the ob-jection before trial or risk its forfeiture, but the defense will be excused in making a late objection where it could not reasonably discov-er the misconduct at an earlier point. Such excused late objections commonly will come during trial, often as a result of information learned at trial, but the trial court is likely at this point to postpone considering the objec-tion until after the trial is completed and the jury has rendered its verdict. Thus, where the objection is not made before trial, even if it is presented prior to the completion of the trial, rulings by both the trial and appellate court ordinarily are made only after the defendant has been convicted. Indeed, even where the objection is made before trial, only the trial court is certain to rule on it prior to the conviction. If that court rejects the challenge, a preconviction appellate review of that ruling is most unlikely. In most jurisdictions, defen-dant will not be able to gain interlocutory review of a pretrial ruling against his motion to dismiss, so appellate review will be available only in connection with the appeal from the conviction.

Where a misconduct challenge is reviewed following a conviction, the court must consider whether the element of prejudice should be analyzed in light of that conviction. State courts are divided on this issue. Most hold that misconduct which had sufficient impact to jus-tify a dismissal prior to trial will also require dismissal of the indictment upon review fol-lowing a conviction. Under this view, the in-dictment must be dismissed because the grand jury process was inadequate and the conviction reversed because it was based upon an invalid indictment. Thus, even though the prosecution may have proven the offense in a fair trial, it must start over again with the issuance of a new indictment and a retrial of the charge.

A contrary position holds that the defen-dant's conviction at a fairly conducted trial renders "moot" or "harmless" any misconduct in the indictment process. Since the grand jury's task was to determine whether there

was sufficient evidence to meet the standard for indictment, and since the trial jury has now found the evidence sufficient to meet the higher standard of proving guilt beyond a rea-sonable doubt, any misconduct that influenced the grand jury can no longer be said to have had a substantial bearing on the outcome of the case. Unlike a constitutional violation in the selection of the grand jury, prosecution or juror misconduct does not justify reversal of a conviction under either a theory of presumed prejudice affecting the conviction or the use of reversal as a deterrent sanction.

In *United States v. Mechanik*,[11] the Supreme Court held the latter approach to govern in federal cases. Whether that holding extends to all types of misconduct or only certain kinds of misconduct remains an open issue. *Mechanik* presented an alleged violation of the Federal Rule 6(d) provision that allows only specified persons, including "the witness under exami-nation," to be present before the grand jury. The prosecutor had presented before the grand jury two government witnesses who appeared together and testified in tandem. The defen-dants' motion to dismiss was presented mid-way through the trial, but there was good cause for the late objection (the defendants had been unable to discover that the two wit-nesses appeared simultaneously until the de-fense gained impeachment discovery of the witnesses' grand jury testimony at trial). The district judge delayed ruling on the defen-dants' motion until after the trial was complet-ed and the defendants had been convicted. The district judge then found that there had been a Rule 6(d) violation, but also concluded that dismissal was inappropriate since the particu-lar circumstances of the case suggested that the violation had not affected the grand jury's indictment decision. The Fourth Circuit, on appeal from the conviction, agreed that Rule 6(d) had been violated, but concluded that the violation did require reversal of the conviction and dismissal of the indictment. The Supreme Court reversed that ruling.

The *Mechanik* majority "assumed arguen-do" that there had been a Rule 6(d) violation,

11.   475 U.S. 66, 106 S.Ct. 938, 89 L.Ed.2d 50 (1986).

and that the trial court "would have been justified in dismissing * * * the indictment on that basis had there been actual prejudice and had the matter been called to its attention before the commencement of the trial." However, since the violation was ruled upon after the defendants had been convicted on the indictment at a fair trial, it should have been treated by the lower courts as a per se harmless error. The Court (per Rehnquist, J.) explained:

> Both [courts below] observed that Rule 6(d) was designed in part, "to ensure that grand jurors, sitting without the direct supervision of a judge, are not subject to undue influence that may come with the presence of an unauthorized person." The Rule protects against the danger that a defendant will be required to defend against a charge for which there is no probable cause to believe him guilty. * * * But the petit jury's subsequent guilty verdict not only means that there was probable cause to believe that the defendants were guilty as charged, but that they are in fact guilty as charged beyond a reasonable doubt. Measured by the petit jury's verdict, then, any error in the grand jury proceedings connected with the charging decision was harmless beyond a reasonable doubt. * * * It might be argued in some literal sense that because the Rule was designed to protect against an erroneous charging decision by the *grand jury*, the indictment should not be compared to the evidence produced by the Government at trial, but to the evidence produced before the grand jury. But even if this argument were accepted, there is no simple way after the verdict to restore the defendant to the position in which he would have been had the indictment been dismissed before trial. He will already have suffered whatever inconvenience, expense, and opprobrium that a proper indictment may have spared him. In courtroom proceedings as elsewhere, "the moving finger writes, and having writ moves on."

The key to the above analysis, as the Court recognized, lies in the conclusive significance attached to the jury's finding of guilt. The Court assumes that the misconduct could not have influenced the outcome of the case because the defendant in any event would have been convicted of the offense. Even if the original grand jury would not have indicted but for the misconduct, another grand jury, presented with the same evidence that led the petit jury to convict, surely would have indicted. As it relates to the grand jury's decision to indict, the Court analysis focuses on a correct-result evaluation rather than the effect-on-the-judgment evaluation suggested by the *Kotteakos*-derived standard of *Bank of Nova Scotia*. That is considered appropriate because the reviewing court is not substituting its own evaluation of the strength of the prosecution's case, but that of the petit jury.

The *Mechanik* majority acknowledged that a quite different approach had been adopted in considering claims of racial discrimination in the selection of the grand jury. There, even though the indictment had been followed by the defendant's conviction by a fairly selected petit jury, the Court had applied a rule of automatic reversal of the conviction and dismissal of the indictment. That position was explained as based on grounds that had no bearing on the situation presented in *Mechanik*. The "remedy of automatic reversal was necessary as a prophylactic means of deterring grand jury discrimination in the future" and "one could presume that a discriminatorily selected grand jury would treat defendants of excluded races unfairly." Such considerations had "little force outside the context of racial discrimination in the composition of the grand jury." Here, in contrast, a prophylactic sanction could not be imposed consistent with the harmless error standard of Rule 52(a), and it was appropriate to conclude that "reversal of a conviction after a trial free from reversible error cannot restore to the defendant whatever benefit might have accrued to him from a trial on an indictment returned in conformity with Rule 6(d)."

Read broadly, the *Mechanik* reasoning would characterize as per se harmless almost all forms of prosecutorial misconduct before the grand jury where there has been an intervening conviction. The only possible exception would be the unusual situation in which one could say with fair assurance that a grand jury could well have not indicted, or have indicted on a lesser charge, even if it had before it the evidence presented at trial (i.e., the grand jury would have nullified). Only there could it be said that reversal of the conviction and dismissal of the indictment could possibly restore to the defendant a benefit that he might have received except for such misconduct before the grand jury. The *Mechanik* reasoning otherwise should apply to all types of prosecutional misconduct, even that which reaches the level of a constitutional violation.

The lower federal courts have divided as to whether *Mechanik* should be read so broadly. Courts rejecting that reading argue that the "*Mechanik* [ruling] was carefully crafted along very narrow lines" and involved misconduct that "at worst, was technical, and at most, would have affected only the grand jury's determination of probable cause." These courts hold *Mechanik* inapplicable to misconduct that goes to "fundamental fairness," but they do not limit this concept to misconduct amounting to a denial of due process. Thus the Tenth Circuit has noted that "conduct that might properly be characterized as transgressing a defendant's right to fundamental fairness [for this purpose] would include, for example, an attempt by the government to 'unfairly sway the grand jury' * * * or a pervasive attempt to charge without cause or to undermine the defense." Under this standard, postconviction review has been held available for many of the usual misconduct claims, including those alleging prosecutorial argument calculated to arouse prejudice, the perjury of government agents, and the typical "totality of the circumstances" claim alleging a series of improper prosecutorial actions. Of course, after *Williams*, some of these claims may not be available without regard to the application of *Mechanik*.

Other courts have adopted a much broader reading of *Mechanik* and have held it to bar consideration of a wide range of traditional misconduct objections on postconviction review. They note that the rationale of *Mechanik* did not depend on the "technical * * * nature

of the rule at hand; [for] the Court assumed that the violation was sufficiently substantial to permit the dismissal of the indictment." *Mechanik*, it is said, "proceeds by identifying the purpose of the rule (to protect the innocent from being indicted) and then says that a rule with this purpose should not be enforced by reversing a conviction after trial—because we know, as surely as courts 'know' anything, that the convicted defendant is not a member of the class of the beneficiaries of the rule." These courts, if they would recognize any exception to the *Mechanik* approach, would limit that exception to misconduct reaching the level of a constitutional violation.

(g) Establishing Misconduct. The best source for determining what happened before the grand jury ordinarily would be the transcript of the grand jury proceedings. However, as noted in § 15.2(j), many jurisdictions do not require recordation of grand jury proceedings, and some of the states requiring recordation limit that requirement to the recording of witness testimony. Of course, the existence of a transcript does not thereby make it available to the defendant. As discussed in § 15.2(i), automatic defense access to the transcript is limited to roughly a dozen states that permit challenges to the sufficiency of the evidence before the grand jury [the non-*Costello* states described in § 15.5(c)]. In the federal system and most states, the defendant must make a preliminary showing of likely misconduct before a court will order disclosure. As discussed in § 15.2(i), this prerequisite often places the defendant in a "catch 22" situation.

Where misconduct occurred while a witness was present, the defense has its best opportunity to meet the preliminary showing requirement needed to gain access to the transcript. The witness, not being sworn to secrecy, may be willing to assist the defense by providing the necessary affidavit as to what occurred. Even where the witness is not cooperative, if the witness later testifies at trial, the defense is likely to obtain a transcript of the witness' grand jury testimony [see § 8.5(g)], which would include the questions and comments of the prosecutor directed to the witness. In some jurisdictions, that transcript will be made available as part of the defense's pretrial discovery from the prosecutor, but in other jurisdictions, the transcript will first be made available at trial for use in impeaching the witness. In the latter situation, as occurred in the *Mechanik* case, the defense will not be able to utilize the transcript in providing the basis for a misconduct challenge until after the trial has begun, and the trial court may then put off consideration of the motion for disclosure of the complete transcript (to uncover further misconduct) until after the trial is completed and jury renders its verdict. Of course, postponing consideration in that fashion will effectively render the motion moot in a jurisdiction that follows *Mechanik*. An acquittal will have eliminated any need for the challenge and a conviction is likely to be viewed as having rendered any misdconduct per se harmless error.

If only the jurors and prosecutor were present when prosecutorial misconduct occurred, the defendant faces an almost insurmountable task in making the type of showing ordinarily needed to gain access to the transcript. In general, secrecy requirements will prevent the jurors from revealing what happened during the proceedings, except with the permission of the court, and that permission will not be granted without the defense first making an independent showing of possible misconduct. Here the best hope of establishing prosecutorial misconduct is through the trial court's exercise of discretion to examine the transcript *in camera*, and that is unlikely to occur without some initial defense showing that creates doubt as to the regularly of the grand jury proceedings.

§ 15.7   Common Prosecutorial Misconduct Claims

(a) The Range of Objections. Any attempt to categorize misconduct objections necessarily loses sight of a substantial number of objections that fail to fit any common mold. Nonetheless, the objections discussed in the reported cases seem to cluster around certain basic categories of misconduct. The sections that follow discuss these general types of misconduct. Not considered in this discussion are

various types of misconduct that ordinarily would not have an impact upon the grand jury's evaluation of the case presented by the prosecution. Included in this category are such actions as the unauthorized disclosure of grand jury material to business associates of the target and the misuse of the grand jury process to develop civil suits or to gain discovery relevant to a pending criminal prosecution. In *Bank of Nova Scotia*, the Court found that several such acts of misconduct could not justify a dismissal because they could not, by their nature, have influenced the grand jury's decision to indict. Most jurisdictions apparently adhere to this viewpoint, although some courts might take such misconduct into consideration in determining whether the totality of the circumstances reflect a prosecutorial undermining of the integrity of the grand jury.

(b) Prejudicial Comments and Information. The American Bar Association standards provide that the prosecutor, in his appearances before the grand jury, "should not make statements or efforts to influence grand jury action in a manner which would be impermissible at trial before a petit jury." This standard applies both to impermissible prosecution arguments and impermissible references to prejudicial information in the examination of witnesses and the introduction of evidence. Although courts frequently have cited the A.B.A. standard with approval, their rulings suggest that its incorporation of the standards applicable to trial presentations will not be strictly applied. The prosecutor in the grand jury setting wears several hats that are not worn by the trial prosecutor, and these additional roles should be taken into consideration in determining what constitutes misconduct before the grand jury. The grand jury prosecutor serves as the legal advisor to the grand jury and his performance in that role may give him leeway to make comments that would not be permitted of a trial attorney, who acts strictly as an advocate and leaves the giving of legal advice to the trial judge. So too, the prosecutor occupies a leadership role in the exercise of the grand jury's investigative authority and that role may require a reference to matters that could not be put before the petit jury by a trial prosecutor. Finally, in the federal system, operating under the limitation of *Williams*,[1] courts cannot look to the trial standards referred to in the ABA standards unless they reflect statutory, court rule, or constitutional standards applicable to the grand jury.

One trial limitation that courts readily apply to the prosecutor in the grand jury setting is the prohibition of arguments or references that are calculated to inflame the passions or prejudices of the grand jury or to inject broader issues than the guilt of the particular defendant under the controlling law. Thus, courts have characterized as misconduct such actions as the following: (1) asking a witness who is a prospective defendant questions about irrelevant personal matters in an effort to "discredit and impugn her in the eyes of the jurors"; (2) informing the grand jurors that the target is suspected of other serious crimes that are not before them; (3) referring to the target's criminal record where it is irrelevant to the offense; (4) referring to the defendant's refusal to take a polygraph test; (5) inviting the jurors, through unfounded references in questions put to witnesses, to "associate the defendants with a disfavored criminal class [Cosa Nostra leaders]"; (6) informing the grand jurors that the target had sought to plea bargain; and (7) appealing to the grand jurors' personal pride in their office. Of course, one aspect of reaching such a ruling is concluding that the material in question is irrelevant to the task of the grand jury, and that issue is not always so readily resolved by reference to trial standards.

In light of the grand jury's additional role as an investigative body, and its broad screening function which goes beyond the mere sufficiency of the evidence, not every prosecutorial reference to material that would be deemed irrelevant at trial necessarily falls in the same category in the grand jury setting. Thus, where a defendant charged with sexual abuse claimed prosecution misconduct in introducing testimony of "other bad acts" that would not have been admissible at trial, the court responded that the grand jury had a responsibility to investigate all possible offenses, including even those suggested by rumors. So too, because the prosecutor can appropriately provide "general background and investigative information" to a grand jury, a prosecutor might find a need to refer to connected offenses committed by others that are part of the investigation (while advising the jurors as to defendant's lack of involvement in those offenses), or to explain that the witnesses about to be called might have memory difficulties (being sympathetic of the defendant), but it was important to find out "what they know or what they don't know," and a lack of recollection was "not all bad" because that would undermine their credibility if they later had sudden recollections favorable to the defendant. Similarly, while a prosecutor at trial could hardly tell a testifying defendant that he just committed perjury, that comment could be appropriate in examining a grand jury witness if the prosecutor's purpose was not to convey to the jurors her personal evaluation of the witness' credibility, but to facilitate the inquiry by suggesting to the witness that he reconsider his testimony and come forward with the truth. So too, the prosecutor at trial could not tell a petit jury that this was a retrial of a case in which the previous jury convicted, but a prosecutor in a grand jury proceeding can rely on the transcripts of testimony before a previous grand jury, telling the grand jury that the prosecution is seeking "a re-indictment of a previous indictment voted by another grand jury."

Still another feature that distinguishes what is appropriately presented before a grand jury is the capacity of the grand jury to ask questions and expect answers on such matters as the thoroughness of the government's investigation. Such questioning can lead to the prosecutor revealing, for example, that the target had been given the opportunity to make a statement, but had exercised his *Miranda* rights. In another case, such juror questioning led the investigating officer to inform the grand jury that the photo of the defendant used in presenting a photo array to the two crime victims had come from the files of an-

§ 15.7

1. See § 15.6(b).

other police department, that the drug stolen was commonly used by heroin addicts, and that he believed defendant to be a heroin addict.

A critical feature in determining whether the prosecutor engaged in misconduct in presenting information that would be deemed irrelevant and prejudicial at trial is the prosecutor's purpose in presenting the information and subsequent use of the information. Where the prosecutor did not rely on the information in urging the grand jury to indict, the prosecutor commonly will be presumed to have acted in good faith. Thus, where the prosecutor admonishes the jurors not to consider particular irrelevant evidence, that admonishment will not be viewed skeptically as a strategic tactic designed to remind the grand jury of that evidence. On the other hand, where the prosecutor places substantial emphasis upon improper material and clearly uses it as part of an appeal to indict, the court is far more likely to find misconduct at a level sufficient to dismiss the indictment. Indeed, even improper comments that might otherwise be viewed as comparatively innocuous are likely to require dismissal where aimed at prodding a grand jury that has clearly indicated its reluctance to indict.

In one aspect of prosecutorial commentary, many jurisdictions conclude that the prosecutor's role as a legal advisor justifies a form of comment that clearly would not be allowed at trial. Many jurisdictions will allow the prosecutor to convey to the grand jury his or her personal opinions as to the sufficiency of the government's case. Thus the ABA Standards note that the prosecutor may "express an opinion on the legal significance of the evidence," though adding that such expression "should give due deference to [the grand jury's] status as an independent legal body." Indeed, the ABA Standards require the prosecutor to recommend to the grand jury that it not indict where "he believes the evidence presented does not warrant an indictment under governing law." While the latter principle is well accepted, not all courts acknowledge a the prosecutor's authority also to express a personal opinion on the evidence which is ad-

verse to the defendant. Some courts will not allow the prosecutor to go beyond presenting the same type of general argument for the sufficiency of the evidence as would be allowed at trial. Statements as to the overall strength of the evidence are permissible, but not in the form of a personal conclusion or a personal recommendation to indict. This position apparently rests on the premise that the prosecutor's role of legal advisor simply places him in the same position as the charging judge, who would not be allowed to express such personal opinions. Courts rejecting this position, and allowing an expression of personal opinion, view the giving of legal "advice" as extending to the applicability of the law to the facts presented. These courts also see little harm in the expression of a personal opinion on evidentiary sufficiency, particularly where the prosecutor reminds the grand jury that it is not bound by his opinion and should exercise its own independent judgment. Since grand jurors realize that the case is being presented precisely because the prosecutor believes the grand jury should indict, a statement of opinion on the sufficiency of the evidence arguably does no more than openly convey what otherwise is implicit. Similarly, in many jurisdictions, the presentation of a proposed indictment already signed by the prosecutor is not itself viewed as misconduct.

Although "most jurisdictions agree that the grand-jury proceeding is a one-sided affair that affords prosecutors great latitude in their comments" relating to the case for indicting, they also agree that prosecutors may not seek to "pressure" or "coerce" the grand jury into issuing an indictment. The prosecutor may not tell the grand jury that it is under an obligation to indict, or inform the grand jury after it refused to indict that its decision was "wrong", and encourage reconsideration. The prosecutor's continued presence during the grand jury's deliberation and voting commonly is viewed as a form of pressure, particularly where the prosecutor used that occasion to urge the grand jury to indict. A few courts have suggested that prosecutorial comments implicitly suggesting the grand jury view itself as part of the prosecutorial team also can produce pressures that render an indictment invalid.

(c) The Prosecutor's Assumption of Other Roles. Certain misconduct claims arise not so much from the prosecutor misusing authority that is part of the prosecutor's role as assuming different roles that are inconsistent with the prosecutorial role. One such situation is presented when the grand jury prosecutor is alleged to have a conflict of interest because of the prosecutor's relationship to a party that arguably could benefit from a successful investigation and prosecution. Thus, defendants have argued that administrative agency attorneys who served as special prosecutors before grand juries assumed conflicting roles by virtue of their continuing interest in assisting the agency's civil proceedings as well as the grand jury's criminal investigation. Although a few courts have found merit in that contention, at least as to an agency lawyer who was involved in the initial agency investigation and recommended that the case be prosecuted, other courts have noted that such a conclusion ignores statutory and court rule provisions adopted for the very purpose of allowing United States Attorneys to designate agency attorney as grand jury attorneys and thereby gain the advantage of their expertise. Particularly after *Williams*, federal courts cannot override legislative and rule authorization by applying court created notions as to what should constitute a conflict of interest. Where a true conflict is held to exist, courts often will treat the conflicted prosecutor as lacking authority to operate before the grand jury, and thereby creating a situation in which an unauthorized person (the conflicted prosecutor) has been present during grand jury sessions.

A conflict-type analysis also has been utilized by courts finding misconduct in the prosecutor acting as a witness before the grand jury as well as its legal advisor. That practice not only conveys the appearance of professional impropriety, but it also creates the risk that the jury will give undue weight to the prosecutor's testimony because of the prestige of his office. Some courts have suggested, that there is no misconduct when the testimony does not come from the prosecutor's personal knowl-

edge, as where the prosecutor merely reads to the grand jury the transcript of testimony before a previous grand jury. While the Code of Professional Responsibility provides that counsel should not assume the role of both advocate and witness, its provisions speak to the trial and exclude the situation in which the testimony relates to an "uncontested issue." Courts note that the prohibition against giving testimony and serving as the grand jury's legal advisor should extend to unsworn as well as sworn testimony, leaving open the possibility that the prosecutor will violate the dual role prohibitions through comments on evidence and questions put to witnesses that convey additional information presumably known to the prosecutor.

(d) Violation of the Defendant's Witness–Rights. Various courts have either held or suggested that a subsequent indictment can be challenged because of grand jury violations of what might be characterized as the defendant's "witness-rights"—that is, rights relating to the defendant having given testimony or having refused to give testimony before the grand jury. Perhaps the most well established of those violations involves a defendant who gives immunized testimony before a grand jury and later is indicted by the same grand jury. The federal immunity statute provides that testimony given by a witness under an order of immunity may not be "used against the witness in any criminal case" (with an exception for establishing perjury in that testimony). Relying on this prohibition and its Fifth Amendment grounding (and thereby establishing a source of authority consistent with *Williams*), federal courts have held that a grand jury indictment is subject to dismissal if the grand jury had before it the immunized testimony of the person it indicted (apart from a perjury indictment). However, they have divided as to the showing needed for a dismissal. One view is that automatic dismissal is required in light of the difficulties involved in determining what weight was given to the immunized testimony. The other finds it is sufficient to shift to the government the burden of showing at an evidentiary hearing that the indictment was based on "independent evidence", with the indictment dismissed if the government cannot meet that burden.

A few courts have suggested that where the grand jury violated the defendant's self-incrimination or other constitutional rights in obtaining his testimony as a witness before the grand jury, a dismissal of the subsequent indictment may be appropriate. They distinguish *Costello's* acceptance of an indictment based on unconstitutionally obtained evidence; here, it is argued, the grand jury itself violated the rights of the defendant. Other courts, however, have viewed the appropriate remedy for the grand jury's violation of a defendant's witness-rights to be the suppression of that testimony at trial, not a dismissal of the indictment. In *Williams*, the Supreme Court noted that, "while a grand jury may not force a witness to answer questions in violation of the Fifth Amendment's constitutional guarantee, * * * other cases suggest that an indictment obtained through the use of evidence previously obtained in violation of the privilege against self-incrimination is nevertheless valid." Arguably, even when the indicting grand jury itself obtained the unconstitutionally compelled evidence, it was "previously obtained" at the point of indictment. Taking a contrary position, it is noted, would adopt an artificial distinction between indictments issued by grand juries which compelled the testimony and indictments issued by other grand juries based on that same testimony.

Courts also recognize as misconduct, possibly calling for dismissal of the indictment, the prosecution's adverse comment on the defendant's refusal to testify before the grand jury. Such a comment falls within the general category of irrelevant and prejudicial commentary by the prosecution. Thus, in *Bank of Nova Scotia*, the Supreme Court took note of a challenge based upon a similar claim with respect to a grand jury witness—that the prosecution had called as witnesses several associates of the prospective defendant, despite their "avowed intention to invoke the self-incrimination privilege", in order to suggest that they had something to hide. The Court found no

factual support for the claim and thus did not have to decide whether such action provided a grounding for dismissal of an indictment in the federal courts. After *Williams*, such a dismissal could arguably be justified as an implementation of a constitutional prohibition against adverse prosecutorial comments on the exercise of the privilege, but that would require extending to the grand jury setting a constitutional prohibition recognized as a trial right.[2]

(e) Deception in Presenting Evidence. The Supreme Court has held that the prosecution at trial has a due process obligation to correct any material false evidence presented by its witnesses when the prosecution knows that the evidence is false. While the courts generally have agreed that the basic components of this obligation also apply to the grand jury setting, its exact grounding is on matters of some dispute. Several courts have relied upon due process, looking to the due process rulings at trial. Many others have preferred to treat the prosecution's knowing reliance upon false testimony as action clearly inconsistent with the prosecutor's roles both as advocate and legal advisor and therefore subject to the general judicial authority to dismiss indictments based upon prejudicial prosecutorial misconduct. Some express doubt as whether the Supreme Court's due process rulings governing the use of false testimony at trial, where that testimony relates to the issue of conviction, can readily be carried over to the grand jury's decision to indict. They note the limited function of the indictment and the continued availability of the trial "to correct errors before the grand jury."

Courts also disagree as to the precise element of scienter needed for prosecutorial misconduct in the use of false testimony. Prior to *Bank of Nova Scotia v. United States*, most federal courts found misconduct only where the prosecution knowingly relied upon false testimony, but several courts extended that responsibility to situations in which the prosecution clearly should have been aware that the testimony was false. State courts similarly

2. See § 24.5(b).

tend to insist upon prosecution knowledge, although an occasional case will suggest that a dismissal can be based upon a reckless disregard as to falsity. In *Bank of Nova Scotia*, the Court appeared to require knowledge as a prerequisite for a misconduct finding in the federal courts. Moreover, in light of *United States v. Williams*, a misconduct claim in the federal courts, if not based on a constitutional violation, must be based on the violation of a statute or court rule. The most likely candidate in the use of perjured testimony would be statutes criminalizing the subornation of perjury or false declarations. Such provisions would appear to require actual knowledge of falsity at the time that the false testimony is being presented to the grand jury.

Still another issue dividing the courts is whether the introduction of testimony that is known to be misleading but not false should be treated in the same manner as the knowing introduction of false testimony. That issue most often arises in reading to the grand jury selected portions of the transcript of testimony given to a previous grand jury or in presenting hearsay without clearly indicating that it is hearsay. Prior to *Williams*, many federal courts treated such presentations as the equivalent of presenting perjury. Indeed, some cases found misconduct in introducing clearly labeled hearsay if there was a "high probability" that the jury would have viewed differently eyewitness testimony, or if the prosecution failed to at least inform the grand jury that the first-hand witness could be subpoenaed on the grand jury's request. As several federal lower courts have noted, such rulings cannot survive *Williams*. In the absence of known perjury in presenting the testimony (e.g., where the prosecutor knowingly allowed a witness to portray himself a an eyewitness when he actually was recounting the observation of others), neither federal statutes nor federal court rules prohibit using hearsay which may mask weaknesses in the accounts of the underlying first-hand observers.

Several state courts have characterized as misconduct the uses of hearsay that were barred by the pre-*William* federal rulings. Others, however, view the concept of a "misleading" or "deceptive" use of evidence as a perniciously open-ended grounding for finding misconduct. They also view its application in the grand jury setting as inconsistent with cases holding that the prosecution may introduce the evidence it chooses, without also presenting evidence that contradicts or undercuts its chosen evidence.

(f) Failure to Present Known Exculpatory Evidence. Appellate courts in over twenty states and the federal system have addressed the question of whether the prosecution has an obligation to present to the grand jury at least some types of known exculpatory evidence. As a result, roughly a third of the states now have appellate opinions recognizing such an obligation. While some of those opinions relied upon statutory provisions requiring the grand jury to consider "evidence within its reach which will explain away the charge," others relied upon a due process analysis or the court's common law authority over grand jury procedures. The due process grounding is drawn by analogy from the *Brady* line of cases requiring the prosecution to disclose known exculpatory material at trial[3]—an analogy implicitly rejected by the Supreme Court in *Williams*. State courts looking to their common law authority or supervisory power often draw an analogy to the dismissal of an indictment where the prosecutor knowingly relied upon perjured testimony.

The Supreme Court's ruling in *United States v. Williams* constitutes the leading precedent rejecting a prosecution obligation to disclose known exculpatory evidence to the grand jury. Resolving a conflict among the federal lower courts, *Williams* held that the federal court's supervisory authority could not be utilized to dismiss an indictment based upon the prosecution's failure to have presented the grand jury "substantial exculpatory evidence" within its possession. As discussed in § 15.6(b), the *Williams* ruling rested on the premise that federal courts, in general, lack authority to prescribe grand jury procedures

---

3. See § 24.3(b).

and to dismiss indictments apart from the prosecution's violation of procedural rules derived from either the Constitution, statutes, or the Federal Rules of Criminal Procedure. However, the Court clearly indicated that establishing a prosecutorial obligation to present exculpatory evidence to the grand jury would not be justified even if the federal courts had authority to prescribe grand jury procedures as part of a "sort of common law of the Fifth Amendment." Requiring disclosure of even the most substantial exculpatory evidence "would neither preserve nor enhance the traditional functioning" of the federal grand jury, but instead "alter the grand jury's historical role, transforming it from an accusatory body to an adjudicatory body."

"The grand jury", the *Williams* Court noted, "sits not to determine guilt or innocence, but to assess whether there is adequate basis for bringing a criminal charge". For that purpose, it traditionally has been sufficient for the grand jury "to hear only the prosecutor's side." Requiring the production of exculpatory evidence would, in effect, give the prospective defendant a voice in the proceedings, contrary to both grand jury function and history. It would surely "invite the target to circumnavigate the system by delivering the exculpatory evidence to the prosecutor, whereupon it would have to be passed on to the grand jury— unless the prosecutor is willing to take the chance that a court will not deem the evidence important enough to qualify for mandatory disclosure." Moreover, allowing a challenge to the indictment based on the prosecutor's failure to present known exculpatory evidence would undercut the *Costello* prohibition, as "a complaint about the quality or adequacy of the evidence can always be recast as a complaint that the prosecutor's presentation was 'incomplete' or 'misleading'."

State courts recognizing a prosecutorial obligation to present to the grand jury known exculpatory evidence have varied in their description of the scope of that obligation. All agree that the evidence must be "known" to the prosecutor, but some have suggested that here, in contrast to the obligation imposed at trial, the knowledge of the prosecution may be limited to the knowledge of the individual prosecutors presenting the case to the grand jury. The primary area of variation, however, relates to describing what falls within the category of "exculpatory evidence" for the purpose of this obligation. In general, that category has been defined much more narrowly than the due process standard of material exculpatory evidence that must be disclosed at trial.[4] Four considerations are said to require a narrower definition in the grand jury setting. First, the prosecutor at this stage of the proceedings ordinarily does not have the advantage of defense motions identifying those items that the defense views as potentially exculpatory. It would impose an intolerable burden on the government to require it to "sift through all the evidence to find statements or documents that might be exculpatory." Second, at this preliminary stage of the proceeding, where both the possible charges and defenses may be uncertain, the prosecutor is likely to have greater difficulty in determining what evidence is exculpatory. Third, consideration must be given to the "unique role of * * * grand jury [review] as a flexible and non-adversarial process." It is a basic premise of grand jury screening that the "prosecutor does not have a duty to present defendant's version of the facts." Finally, taking a page from *Costello*, some courts have stressed the need to avoid "convert[ing] a grand jury proceeding from an investigative one into a mini-trial of the merits."

(g) Erroneous Legal Advice. As legal advisor to the grand jury, the prosecutor has an obligation to give the grand jury sufficient information concerning the applicable law "to

---

4. State decisions have offered various formulations of this narrower disclosure requirement. They state, for example, that the obligation to disclose only applies to evidence which "clearly negates guilt", "which directly negates * * * guilt", which "objectively refutes * * * the state's evidence", which "directly negate[s] guilt and * * * also [is] clearly exculpatory", which "would * * *

materially affect the grand jury determination", which "greatly undermines the credibility of evidence likely to affect the grand jury's decision to indict", which would "be of such weight * * * [as to] deter the grand jury from finding probable cause", and which "would preclude issuing an indictment."

enable it intelligently to decide whether a crime has been committed." Only a handful of states, however, have precedent dealing with that obligation. This may be due in part to practical obstacles to challenging instructions. The instructions are not transcribed in some jurisdictions, and the transcription is not likely to be available to the defense in any event, apart from those jurisdictions that provide for automatic disclosure.[5] The sources that might be helpful in making the preliminary showing ordinarily needed to obtain disclosure are most unlikely to be able to refer to the prosecutor's instructions. Perhaps even more significantly, in jurisdictions that adhere to the *Costello* limitation of judicial review, error in the prosecution's charge on the offense is not likely to be viewed as an exception to that limitation. Reviewing a challenge to the prosecutor's explanation of the elements of the crime often requires examination of the proof offered to establish those elements, running directly into the review proscribed by *Costello*. Moreover, any such errors are unlikely to be a product of the kind of intentional deception which often is cited to distinguish misconduct challenges from the challenges barred by *Costello*. Thus, pre-*Williams* federal decisions suggested that erroneous instructions were likely to provide a grounding for challenging an indictment only if "so flagrantly erroneous that the grand jury was deceived in some significant way." After *Williams*, a federal court presumably would lack authority even to dismiss on that ground unless such instructions violated a statute, court rule, or constitutional command.

Among those states recognizing challenges to the prosecutor's legal instructions, all agree that the prosecutor need not give instructions even roughly approximating the comprehensiveness of the trial judge's charge to the petit jury. They also agree, however, that an instruction may be "so misleading," due to mistakes or omissions, that the ensuing indictment "will not be permitted to stand even though it is supported by legally sufficient evidence." In some states, courts ask whether the instruction was sufficient to permit the jury to determine whether the evidence before

it was legally sufficient. In others, courts speak of whether the instructions were so erroneous or lacking in need substance as to constitute "flagrant and overbearing misconduct", or operate to "compromise" the "fundamental integrity of the indictment process."

Courts addressing the issue generally have found that the prosecutor satisfactorily explains the offense to be charged by simply reading the statute to the grand jury. They note a reluctance to grant dismissals based upon the failure to provide further content. At trial, the court may be required to provide further definition of particular elements, or to call the jury's attention to special proof requirements, but the trial court can rely upon defense counsel to call to its attention the need for such instructions where they are critical in light of the character of the case the prosecution has presented. The prosecutor cannot readily be expected to make the same judgement as to what additional instructions will bear upon the case he or she is presenting to the grand jury. In some settings, however, courts will hold prosecutors responsible to provide instructions on aspects of the law favoring the defense. While prosecutors are not ordinarily required to inform the grand jury of lesser included offenses, an explanation of such an offense may be necessary where the grand jurors themselves indicated that they want to consider such a charge. A prosecutor also may have the obligation to charge on a defense, provided the evidence before the grand jury "clearly establishes" the defense and the defense is complete.

The prosecutor's instruction on the law is most likely to require a dismissal where it incorrectly informs the grand jury that it lacks some authority in which the grand jury has indicated an interest. Such instructions, such as erroneously informing the grand jury that it could not call a particular witness, are viewed as classic cases of misconduct, depriving the grand jury of its independence. Indeed, grounds for dismissal will be present when the prosecutor simply takes action to deprive the grand jury of such authority without relying

---

5. See § 15.2(i), (j).

on a legal instruction. Instructions that improperly state the role of the grand jury in indicting, suggesting that it lacks the authority to make an independent determination or should be influenced by inappropriate factors, also are likely to justify a dismissal.

(h) Presence of Unauthorized Persons. Grand jury secrecy provisions commonly provide that no person other than the grand jurors may be present during deliberations and voting, while only the jurors, prosecutors, supporting personnel (e.g., stenographers) and the witness under examination may be present during any other portion of the proceedings. It is uniformly accepted that a violation of the provisions on presence may justify a pretrial dismissal of an indictment, but a division exists as to whether dismissal here should be conditioned on the usual requirement of a case-specific showing of likely prejudice. Courts requiring such a showing see no basis for distinguishing the presence of an unauthorized person from other irregularities in grand jury proceedings (e.g., improper comments by the prosecutor). In determining whether an unauthorized presence presents a sufficient likelihood of prejudicial impact, these courts look to such factors as: (1) the relationship of the person improperly present to the prosecution of the offense (e.g., whether that person was the complainant, whose very presence might impose pressure on the jurors, or merely a clerk); (2) the stage at which that person was improperly present (i.e., during deliberations and voting, or simply during the presentation of evidence or argument); (3) where a person was improperly present during the presentation of testimony, whether that person had a relationship to the witness that could have influenced the witness' testimony; (4) the length of the unauthorized presence; and (5) whether the individual made any overt attempt to influence the grand jurors or a witness. Not surprisingly, courts differ in their evaluation of arguably similar factors. One court might view a mother's presence when her minor child testified as to an alleged sexual assault as merely providing "emotional support", while another might view it as presenting a significant potential for shaping the

child's testimony to fit what she had previously told her mother.

A substantial number of state courts treat unauthorized presence as a per se ground for dismissal (a position rejected as to federal courts in *Bank* of *Nova Scotia*). A per se approach is required, these courts argue, because dismissal only upon a showing of likely prejudice would offer "too great a possibility for the exercise of undue influence to be condoned." A prejudicial impact is so difficult to determine that it often would be missed. In most cases, the precise influence of the unauthorized presence would not be apparent on the face of the grand jury transcript. "A change in expression, a pressure on the hand or a warning glance would not be shown upon the minutes, but might well influence, suppress, or alter testimony to the prejudice of the defendant." A court could attempt to assess the influence that the presence of a particular person is likely to have had upon the witness or jurors, but such a determination would be too speculative to afford the defendant proper protection. How could one be certain, for example, that the unauthorized presence of custodial officers might not have influenced the testimony of the prisoner-witness the officers were guarding? Where two witnesses appeared simultaneously before the grand jury, isn't there always the possibility that each was hesitant to repudiate what was said by the other in the presence of that person? The appropriate approach, these courts argue, is to hold that even "the slightest intrusion of an unauthorized person into a grand jury proceeding voids the indictment."

While the determination of likely prejudice stemming from an unauthorized presence obviously entails some difficulty, it is doubtful whether that determination is substantially more speculative than the determination of prejudice made by courts considering whether other types of irregularities require dismissal of indictments. The adoption of a per se approach may be explained, however, by additional factors that more readily distinguish the unauthorized presence violation. In most jurisdictions, a per se approach was adopted when transcripts were unavailable and an unauthorized presence therefore was one of the few grand jury irregularities that could readily be established by the defendant. An automatic dismissal was seen as a sanction that would send an important message as to the need for regularity in grand jury proceedings and there was no concern about its application to a much wider range of misconduct. Courts also have noted that an unauthorized presence should be a rare occurrence if the prosecutor exercises proper control over access to the grand jury chambers. The rules governing presence are clear and most violations are the product of the prosecutor's failure to adopt proper safeguards to ensure compliance. Assuming that unauthorized presence could readily be avoided, a per se approach has been justified on the ground that "a standard of actual or even potential prejudice would impose upon the court a difficult burden that would outweigh the benefits to be derived."

Chapter 16

THE LOCATION OF THE PROSECUTION

Table of Sections

§ 16.1   Venue: General Principles

(a) Distinguishing Venue From Jurisdiction. The term "venue" refers to the locality of the prosecution; venue sets the particular judicial district in which a criminal charge is to be filed and in which it will be tried. Venue is to be distinguished from "jurisdiction," which refers to the authority or power of the court to take action on a particular charge. The concept of jurisdiction encompasses several different types of limitation upon judicial authority. One of those limitations commonly restricts enforcement authority by reference to the geographical location of the offense, and thereby requires an analysis similar to that applied in determining venue. The consequence of that analysis, however, is quite different from its application in determining venue.

The jurisdictional limitation which, like venue, seeks to determine the place of crime, stems from the limited territorial reach of a government's legislative power. If the events that would give rise to a criminal charge occurred beyond that territorial reach, then the government cannot grant to its courts the authority to apply its criminal laws to those events. If the government's legislative power could reach those events, then the judiciary of that government is said to have "jurisdiction" over the offense. To say that the judiciary has such jurisdiction, however, is not to say that every judicial district within that judiciary is a proper locality for the prosecution of the offense. The determination of proper locality is what the setting of venue is about. It looks to the convenience of the forum rather than the territorial reach of the government's legislative power.

The reach of a political entity's legislative power need not be limited to the geographical boundaries of the entity. As evidenced by certain federal statutes applicable to conduct committed abroad, a government can extend its authority beyond its territory based on its power to regulate the conduct of, and to provide protection for, its citizens. At the state level, however, the common law established, and states continue to adhere to, a territorial principle as the jurisdictional foundation for the reach of state laws. Under that principle, states have power to make conduct a crime only if that conduct takes place, or its results occur, within the state's territorial borders. The application of this territorial limitation often raises issues quite similar to those presented in determining venue under the "crime committed" formula, which is discussed in subsections (c) and (d) below and in § 16.2.

Initially, both the territorial principal and the crime committed formula require the court to assess whether the particular crime is "continuing" in nature or otherwise capable of having been started in one location and finished in another. At common law, the territorial principle was governed in its application by an assumption that all but a small group of crimes had a single situs. In general, that situs was the place where the act (or omission) occurred if the crime was defined only in those terms, and the place of an event which combined act and consequence when the offense was so defined. Thus, a murder occurred in the state where the fatal force struck the victim and produced his death, even though that force may have been initiated in another state. The common law did recognize an exception, however, for crimes that were "continuing"

(e.g., kidnapping). Those crimes could be committed in more than one place and prosecuted in more than one state. In determining whether an offense is a continuing crime, so that more that one state has jurisdiction, a court makes a determination analogous to that made in establishing venue. There too, as discussed in subsection (d), a crime may be deemed "continuing," so that venue lies in more than one district under the crime committed formula.

Even as to crimes that do not traditionally fall in the continuing category, many states today have legislation that recognizes more than one territorial situs for the crime. The territorial principle does not demand a single situs; it recognizes the state's authority to reach criminal conduct performed partly within and partly without the state, conduct performed within the state that results in harm outside the state, and conduct performed outside the state that produced harm within. Where states have sought to carry the territorial principle to its full reach through such "territorial scope" legislation, the issues presented again tend to be analogous to those presented in establishing venue. There too, as discussed in subsection (d), the crime committed formula allows for multi-venue as to an offense "begun in one district and completed in another." Thus, where the defendant ships poisoned candy from State A, the victim receives the candy in State B, eats it in State C, and dies in State D, and all the states involved have broad territorial scope provisions, the issue as to whether each has jurisdiction closely resembles that which would be presented if everything occurred within four different judicial districts in a single state and the issue was whether the prosecution could be brought in any of the four districts.

Though the issues presented in applying the crime committed formula of venue and the territorial principle of jurisdiction often are quite similar, important distinctions exist. First, the governing language of a territorial scope provision typically is not the same as that of a multi-venue provision, and that difference may produce different results in assessing the multi-site potential of the same criminal conduct. Second, and more significantly, the interests at stake in determining which state may prosecute are quite different from those at stake in determining where the trial will be held within a state. This is evidenced by the absence of any provision for transfer from a state with jurisdiction to a state without jurisdiction, in contrast to venue transfer provisions, which allow for transfer from a district in which the crime committed formula sets venue to another district in which it would not apply. Similarly, whereas venue limitations are subject to voluntary waiver or to forfeiture by failure to raise a timely objection, jurisdictional limitations are not subject to waiver and can be raised at any point in the proceeding.

(b) Distinguishing Vicinage. Venue also should be distinguished from "vicinage." Both venue and vicinage refer to locality as defined by a particular geographical district, but they identify that locality for different purposes. Whereas venue refers to the locality in which charges will be brought and adjudicated, vicinage refers to the locality from which jurors will be drawn. Also, while the concept of venue does not inherently point to a particular district, but rather requires simply that a district be designated in a venue provision (constitutional or statutory), the concept of vicinage in itself identifies a particular geographical district and arguably limits the territorial scope of that district. The vicinage concept requires that the jurors be selected from a geographical district that includes the locality of the commission of the crime, and it traditionally also mandates that such district not extend too far beyond the general vicinity of that locality. Thus, while a venue provision must specify how the appropriate district for trial is to be determined (or even identify that district by name), a vicinage provision can merely state that the defendant has a right to a jury "of the vicinage." That language will be taken to designate automatically, as the appropriate district for jury selection, the judicial district that includes the place of the offense.

Occasionally, vicinage and venue are treated together in the same provision, but that is hardly necessary for each subject to bear upon the other. Though a provision may speak only to vicinage or only to venue, it typically builds upon the assumption that the locality requirements of venue and vicinage will go hand in hand. Thus, a provision giving to the defendant a right to a jury selected from a judicial district constituting the vicinage commonly will also grant, by implication, a parallel right to be tried in that judicial district; for unless the legislature specifically provides otherwise, the prevailing assumption is that the trial should be held in the district from which the jury is selected. So too, since venue provisions commonly provide for trial in the judicial district in which the alleged offense was committed, which often coincides with the vicinage, venue provisions frequently operate by implication to require that jurors be selected from the vicinage; for it is assumed also that the jury will be drawn from the judicial district in which the trial takes place.

The overlap of venue and vicinage, however, is not inevitable. First, there exists the possibility (largely theoretical) of prescribing different districts under the two concepts. This could be done by providing for a jury selected from the district of the crime, as required by the concept of vicinage, while setting the venue for the trial elsewhere. Secondly, even where, as is almost always the case, the venue provision refers to the district in which the crime was committed, and thereby encompasses the vicinage, the vicinage concept can demand a smaller geographical unit than that required by the venue provision alone. Traditionally, the vicinage concept demands that the geographical boundaries of the district of jury selection not extend substantially beyond the general vicinity of the place of the crime. Tying a venue provision to the district of the crime, on the other hand, says nothing about the boundaries of the district except that the district include the locality of the crime.

The distinction between venue and vicinage underlies the adoption of separate jury selection and venue provisions in the federal constitution and in Congress' initial legislation implementing those constitutional provisions. Though the framers of the Constitution initially saw no need to safeguard by constitutional provision the basic rights of the individual (a position later altered with the agreement to add the Bill of Rights), they nonetheless did include in the body of the Constitution certain requirements of criminal procedure that would protect the accused. Not surprisingly, one of those safeguards guaranteed that the accused would not be forced to trial outside of the state in which the charges against him arose. Appropriate venue had been a matter of great concern to the colonists. They had fiercely opposed Acts of Parliament that allowed the Crown to take colonists to England or to another colony for trial on various capital offenses. Article III, Section 2, of the Constitution prohibited the federal government from engaging in a similar practice. It provided: "The Trial of all Crimes, except in Cases of Impeachment, shall be by Jury, and such Trial shall be held in the State where said Crimes shall have been committed; but when not committed within any State, the Trial shall be at such Place or Places as the Congress may by Law have directed."

Article III, Section 2, did not guarantee that an accused would be tried in the location most convenient for him. An accused charged with committing a crime in one part of a state could be tried in any other part of the state, notwithstanding its distance from the place of the crime. Still, the constitutional guarantee would not allow the bringing of the defendant to trial in what was basically the alien setting of another state. In allowing for flexibility in the fixing of venue within the state. Article III took account of the fact that, if a federal trial judiciary were created, the federal judges obviously would be too few to sit in every county within every state.

When the Constitution came before the states for ratification, Article III was strongly criticized for failing to guarantee to the accused a jury drawn from the vicinage. The vicinage concept had arisen out of the earliest function of the jury, which was to present accusations based on the jurors' personal knowledge or on information they had gathered from their neighbors. This function required that the jurors be chosen from the vicinity of the crime, as residence in that area

was essential to gaining the knowledge of local crimes that the jurors were assumed to possess. Although the function of the jury later changed, with the jurors becoming a body adjudicating guilt based upon evidence presented by the parties, the selection of the jury from the vicinity of the crime remained the norm in England. Residence in the community provided a better background for judging the evidence presented and ensured that the criminal law was applied in accord with customs, habits, and values of the local community. Imposing a vicinage requirement also prohibited the prosecutor from "jury-shopping" by selecting that community most likely to produce jurors receptive to the prosecution's point of view. Although not always adhered to in practice within the colonies, the selection of the jury from the vicinage of the crime was commonly characterized as an essential element of the right to jury trial.

Article III, Section 2, provided for a right to jury trial, but it said nothing about the selection of the jury. Supporters of the proposed Constitution noted that Article III's venue provision guaranteed a trial in the state in which the alleged crime was committed, so the defendant, by implication, would also have a jury of that state. That assurance did not satisfy proponents of a vicinage requirement, for the jurors could come from anywhere in the state. While they were most likely to come from that area of the state in which the trial would be held, there was no assurance that area would even include the place of the crime. Moreover, even it it did, the selection of jurors from the entire area might extend beyond the vicinage. The vicinage concept had been described variously as referring to the "vicinity," the "neighborhood," and the "county" of the offense, but none of those terms could be stretched to include an entire geographical region of a large state.

Responding to the criticism of the ratification conventions, Madison presented to the House of Representatives in the First Congress a proposed amendment of Article III. The Madison proposal spelled out in greater detail various aspects of the right to a jury trial. Included was a requirement that the trial be to an "impartial jury of freeholders of the vicinage." The Madison proposal indicated that the "vicinage" for this purpose was to be the county in which the crime was committed, for it added an exception allowing for trial "in some other county of the same state, as near as may be to the seat of the offense," if the county of the offense should be "in the possession of an enemy" or in a state of "general insurrection." The House of Representatives approved Madison's proposal, although it replaced the word "county" with the less definite word "place" in the clause providing for a change in venue in instances of enemy occupation or insurrection. The Senate, however, flatly rejected the House proposal. Madison subsequently described the Senate's opposition as resting on the ground that the term "vicinage" was "either too vague or too strict a term, too vague if depending on limits to be fixed by the pleasure of the law, too strict if limited to the County." The latter difficulty, he noted, arose from the variety of jury selection practices found among the states. In some, "jurors * * * [were] taken from the State at large; in others from districts of considerable extent; in very few from the county alone." Moreover, the Congress had decided, in the proposed Judiciary Bill, to create a federal trial court, with the judges "riding circuit." Since it would be impossible for the 13 judges of the newly created district court and for the Supreme Court Justices (who also rode circuit) to sit in every portion of every state, the goal had been simply to ensure that trial judges would sit in centrally located sites in each of the states. In addition, the Judiciary Bill had encouraged their sitting with jurors selected from that locality. The Senate agreed that the prosecution should not be allowed to determine the geographical source of the jury at its pleasure, but it believed "that the provisions for vicinage in the Judiciary Bill, will sufficiently quiet the fears that called for an amendment on that point."

The opposition of the Senate did not end the matter, as a compromise was eventually reached and a new jury provision included in the Sixth Amendment of the Bill of Rights. That provision granted to the accused a right to trial "by an impartial jury of the State and district wherein the crime shall have been committed, which district shall have been previously ascertained by law." Unlike Article III, Section 2, the Sixth Amendment specifically recognized a right to have the jury selected from a particular district. That right was no longer left to the implication of a venue provision. However, the geographical boundaries of the particular district were not defined in the Constitution, nor were they left to a judicial determination that might look to the vicinage concept. Certainty was to be provided, and prosecution discretion thereby limited, by the requirement that the district be "previously ascertained" by legislation. The districts set by the Congress could be as large as the state itself, but they also could be smaller, and therefore more in keeping with the traditional view of the vicinage. In the First Judiciary Act, passed one day before the Bill of Rights was sent to the states for ratification, Congress also adopted a compromise as to the size of the districts, distinguishing between different states and between capital and non-capital offenses.

The Judiciary Act initially established judicial districts for each of the newly established federal trial courts. Those districts coincided with the boundaries of the individual states, except for two states which were subdivided into two districts each. The district and circuit courts were required to sit in each of the districts, and as to some districts, the courts were required to sit alternately at two different cities. The selection of jurors was controlled by Section 29, which required that the jurors be summoned from the particular district, but afforded flexibility within that requirement. Section 29 provided that the jurors be summoned "from such parts of the district from time to time as the court shall direct, so as shall be most favorable to an impartial trial, and so as not to incur an unnecessary expense, or unduly to burden the citizens of any part of the district with such services." A more restrictive provision was added, however, for capital offenses, which constituted a significant portion of all federal crimes.

Under Section 29, the trial of capital offenses was to be held in "the county where the offence was committed" if that could be done "without great inconvenience." But even where such inconvenience required that the trial be moved to some other county within the district, the court was directed to summon "twelve petit jurors at least" from the county where the offense was committed. Thus, as to capital offenses, the Judiciary Act largely guaranteed a jury consistent with even the most geographically confining view of the "vicinage." Where the trial was to be held in the county of the offense, the defendant would receive a jury selected entirely from that county. Where a change in venue was required due to great inconvenience, the venire would be mixed, but at least 12 prospective jurors would still be summoned from county of the offense, with those persons then being transported to the place of the trial.

The Judiciary Act brought home several lessons relating to the linkage between venue and vicinage that had been recognized as well in the debates regarding Article III and the Sixth Amendment. First, a narrower jury selection district, with nothing further stated as to the place where the jurors may sit, will operate to limit a broader venue provision. Thus, though Article III, Section 2, required only that an offense be tried within the state of its commission, where Congress divided the state into more than one judicial district, that Congressional designation rendered this smaller geographical unit not only the district from which the jury was to be selected under the Sixth Amendment but also the district in which the case was to be tried. There being no provision made for a trial in one district by a jury selected in another, venue was assumed to be placed in that district in the state from which the jury was to be selected.

Second, the legislature could make effective a broader venue provision, notwithstanding a vicinage provision, by simply providing that the jurors could sit for the trial outside the community of the vicinage. Thus, in capital cases, Section 29 allowed the trial to take place outside the county of commission, but insisted that at least 12 jurors be drawn from that county. Section 29 was, however, a quite unusual provision. Over the history of federal and state provisions dealing with venue and jury selection, only a very small group of jurisdictions have sought to separate the place of jury selection from the place of trial.[1]

Third, even though the jury will be drawn from the venue district, and even though that venue district must include the locality of the offense, that hardly ensures that the jury will be drawn from the general vicinity of crime. Thus, a major criticism directed against Article III was that it said nothing about jury selection, allowed for trial anywhere in the state, and thereby allowed for a jury drawn from a portion of the state that did not include the community in which the offense was committed. Indeed, as illustrated by the Sixth Amendment, even a provision speaking directly to jury selection provides no assurance that the jurors will come from the general locality of the crime where that provision fails to either specifically adopt a vicinage requirement or sharply confine the geographical boundaries of the district of selection. Thus, the Sixth Amendment did not bar the provisions of Section 29 that clearly allowed in a non-capital case for the selection of a jury that could have no relationship to the locality of the crime. The only limitations imposed by the combination of Article III and the Sixth Amendment were that the case be tried within, and the jury selected from, a district defined by Congress that did not encompass more than an entire state. Under those limitations, Congress could (and did) authorize the trial court to summon jurors and try the case in any portion of a state-wide district, without regard to the particular location of the crime in that district. Under Section 29, a trial judge sitting in one of the designated cities within the district could direct that all persons charged with non-capital offenses throughout the district be tried at that site and could summon juries for trials solely from residents of that city. Although often described as a "vicinage provision," the Sixth Amendment, because it left to Congress

§ 16.1

1. See § 23.2(c).

whether the jury selection district would be smaller than the entire state, operated only to ensure that the jury came from the state in which the offense was committed, and thereby guaranteed what was implicit in Article III. Of course, Congress could insist upon a jury of the vicinage, as it did for capital offenses, but it could also do otherwise, as it did for non-capital offenses.

In contrast to the Sixth Amendment, many states have constitutional vicinage provisions which are true to the common law in limiting jury selection to a geographical area that might legitimately be described as the "vicinity" or "neighborhood" of the crime. Three give the defendant a right to a jury "of the vicinage." Almost a dozen provide for a right to a trial by jury "of the county in which the crime shall have been committed." A slightly smaller number speak of a jury "of the county or the district," allowing legislative creation of multi-county districts, but with districts still much smaller than the federal districts and more consistent with the common law vicinage concept (which recognized that "the vicinity" could extend beyond a single county). Because the place of juror residence is assumed to be the intended place of trial (absent a legislative directive to the contrary), these vicinage provisions also operate as limitations on venue. Thus, legislation that arguably allows venue outside the judicial district of the commission of the crime will be tested against the constitutional vicinage provision, as will be legislation that allows for a change in venue (without defense waiver) from that district.

(c) The "Crime–Committed" Formula. The standard formula for setting venue calls for dividing the territory of the political entity (i.e., the state or nation) into geographical districts and then selecting as the appropriate venue that district in which the alleged crime was committed. Those districts either are drawn specially solely for the division of judicial authority, as illustrated by the federal judicial districts, or are traditional political entities, such as counties or parishes. Though American jurisdictions vary in their use of these two types of districts, they all utilize the same formula for designating the particular

district in which the prosecution must be initiated and trial held—that district in which the "crime shall have been committed." As discussed in subsection (e), special venue provisions may otherwise identify the district of venue for particular crimes, but for most offenses, the general venue provision governs and sets venue according to the crime-committed formula.

The "crime-committed" formula is imposed as a constitutional requirement in the federal system under Article III. Only a handful of states have constitutional venue provisions (all of which impose the crime-committed formula), but many additional states make the location of the trial in the district of the crime a constitutional command through the combination of a constitutional vicinage provision requiring the jury to be selected from the county in which the crime was committed, and the absence of legislation authorizing jury selection in a district other than the venue district. Where venue is challenged in such jurisdictions as not meeting the crime committed formula, a constitutional claim is inherent in that challenge because the jury is not being selected from the district in which the crime was committed. In both jurisdictions with and without constitutional adoptions of the crime-committed formula, that formula will be set forth as the general venue standard in either the code of criminal procedure or the court rules of criminal procedure.

Although not always followed by the English, the crime-committed formula was well established in English common law at the time of the adoption of the United States Constitution. As in the case of the vicinage requirement, the use of the crime-committed formula in placing venue is commonly traced to the use of the early jury as a factfinding body that relied upon its own knowledge. However, the formula arguably follows from the even earlier established role of the grand jury as a charging body, and the restriction of the grand jury to the inquiry into crimes that occurred in the county for which it was sworn. That restriction arguably stemmed from the notion of a territorial limit on the community's interest in presenting charges, as well as the grand jury's assumed knowledge of the community for which it spoke. Whatever its grounding, that restriction naturally served also to place trials in the county in which the crime had been committed. The charge was brought by a grand jury in the county in which the crime was committed, and it was thought to follow naturally that the trial should be in the same place, before the court to which the indictment was returned.

Though the crime-committed formula often facilitated use of a jury of the vicinage, that formula was commonly praised as also serving the independent value of providing a forum convenient to the accused in presenting his defense. Relevant evidence would most readily be accessible at the place where the incident constituting the alleged offense had occurred. Any witnesses to the incident were most likely to live in the vicinity and any relevant tangible evidence was most likely to be found there. Trial in a distant place would impose upon the defendant the often serious hardship of arranging for the transportation of such witnesses and tangible evidence. Of course, the trial could still be in a distant place if the district of the offense were large, as the trial could take place anywhere in the district, but that still was better than having all of a nation's or state's trials in a single place (e.g., its capital).

At the time of the adoption of the Constitution, mobility of individuals still was quite limited, and the place of the commission of the crime was most likely also be at or near the accused's place of residence. This added to the convenience of trial in the district of the offense. It was in the place of his residence that the accused was most likely to find witnesses willing to vouch for his character, and a trial there avoided the need to arrange for the transportation of those witnesses to some other location. An accused tried in the vicinity of his residence also would have the benefit of friends and relatives being close at hand. Those persons could not only provide moral support, but they also could assist in preparing for trial. They could, for example, both help in investigation and provide insights that might be useful in challenging jurors, who would ordinarily come from the same community. So too, an accused tried at his place of residence was more likely to know the local attorneys and thereby have greater confidence in his selection of counsel.

Of course, there would be instances in which the accused would have traveled to another district and be accused there of having committed a crime. In that situation, the crime-committed formula would deprive him of the convenience of being tried in his home district. The choice nonetheless was made for the place where the critical events had occurred. That choice may have reflected a belief that greater convenience to the accused was in a trial where the witnesses to the events were located rather than the place of his residence. It may also have been based, however, on other considerations related less to the convenience of the accused and more to the concerns of the community in which the crime took place.

If only the defendant's interests were at stake, the defense could have been given the choice of having the case tried either in the district of the offense or the district of the defendant's residence. However, the defendant was never given such a choice, and even today's more liberal change of venue provisions do not provide for a change based simply on a particular place being most convenient for the defendant. Thus, the crime-committed formula has come to be characterized as grounded as much on serving the interest of the public in the fair and efficient enforcement of the criminal law as on the defendant's interest in being tried in a convenient forum. Some support for this characterization is found in the form of the constitutional, statutory, and court rule provisions imposing the crime-committed formula. Unlike the vicinage provisions, which refer to a right of the defendant to a particular type of jury, the crime-committed provisions simply state where the prosecution shall be brought, utilizing the form of a directive to the courts and prosecution. History, however, casts doubt on making much of that distinction.

Whether or not the crime-committed formula was designed in part to promote the public interest in law enforcement, it certainly supports that interest in several ways. Since the place in which the crime is committed typically also is the place that suffered from the crime, the crime-committed formula locates the prosecution in the community that has the greatest interest in enforcing the law. So too, since the act and its consequences are most likely to have occurred in the district of the crime, insofar as the legal system seeks to judge those acts and consequences by reference to community standards, that district has the strongest claim for utilizing its community standards (as applied by a local jury). The crime committed formula also designates the district of most likely convenience for the prosecution. Its primary witnesses (including the complainant) are likely to be located in the place where the crime occurred and therefore can more easily be presented at a trial in that district. Also, the defendant most frequently will have been arrested at the place of the offense, and a trial in the same district will avoid the necessity of transporting him a long distance.

(d) Multi–Venue Offenses. When the framers of the Constitution included the crime-committed formula in both Article III, Section 2, and the Sixth Amendment, they referred in the singular to the "state" and the "district" in which the crime "shall have been committed." This reflected the assumption that a crime ordinarily would be committed in a single place. At a time when travel was difficult and slow, and communications systems were rudimentary, all of the action constituting an offense and all of the immediate harm flowing from that action commonly occurred within a limited geographic area. Even at that time, however, there were certain federal offenses that could occur in more than one place and those two or more places would occasionally be in two different states. At the state level, where the judicial districts typically were counties, it was even more likely that some offenses would be committed in more than one judicial district.

The offenses most likely to be multi-venue offenses were those commonly described as "continuing offenses." These were offenses having basic elements that continued (or, as some would say, "repeated themselves") over

a period of time as part of a single crime. A prime illustration is kidnapping, which starts when the victim is taken into custody and continues until the victim is no longer under the control of the kidnappers. If the kidnapped victim was moved from one district to another in the course of the kidnapping, the offense was committed in each of those districts. At common law, larceny was placed in the same category as the continued possession of the stolen property by the thief was viewed as a continuation of the trespassory taking.

A crime could also occur in more than one place when it had two or more distinct parts. Such offenses created a multi-venue potential when they required two separate elements that could occur at separate places. A criminal statute, for example, might define the offense as requiring first the doing of a prohibited act and then the causing of a certain victim response, with the act and response capable of occurring in two different localities. Similarly a statute may require two distinct acts by the defendant which can occur in different places. The classic example here is the crime of conspiracy where it requires both an agreement and an overt act in furtherance of that agreement. Some courts have placed forcible rape in the same category, concluding that venue can apply both in the place where the defendant placed the victim in fear through force or threats of force and the place the defendant engaged in the sexual act involved.

Multi-venue also was possible where the offense could be committed by a single act that could start in one place and finish in another. Thus, the "making" of a false claim might start with the placing of that claim in motion and end with its actual presentation. Some courts view the act of conversion as one that can start with the decision to convert a financial account or instrument held in trust to one's own use and end when that scheme is fulfilled by obtaining funds for defendant's use. So too, the attempted evasion of tax liability might start with the arrangement of a false transaction and end with the filing of a false return utilizing that transaction. While these offenses are distinguishable from those in which the act is repetitive, such as kidnapping, they are sometimes also characterized as capable of "continuation" in the sense that the prohibited action, as it involves multiple components, may start at one place and finish elsewhere.

The possibility of a multi-venue commission of an offense was recognized as early as the sixteenth century, when Parliament adopted a provision governing homicides committed through actions in one county that resulted in death in another. Crimes committed in more than one district were rare, however, and they were limited to a small group of offenses. By the mid-nineteenth century, however, with significant advances made in transportation and communications, crimes committed in more than one judicial district became much more common. This was particularly true for the federal system, which dealt with many crimes relating to commerce. In 1867, Congress adopted a general provision governing offenses committed in more than one district. That provision, in a slightly modified form, is now contained in Section 3237 of the federal criminal code. It provides:

> Except as otherwise expressly provided by enactment of Congress, any offense against the United States begun in one district and completed in another, or committed in more than one district, may be inquired of and prosecuted in any district in which such offense was begun, continued, or completed.[2]

Most states also have adopted provisions, similar to § 3237, authorizing multi-district venue when the commission of an offense involves more than one district. These provisions typically refer to offenses "committed partly" in more than one district. Several state provisions refer as well to "acts or effects thereof constituting or requisite to the consummation of the offense" occurring in more than one district. Others provide for multi-venue based on "acts," "conduct," and "results" that are elements of the offense occurring in more than one district. While these different formulations could be viewed as offering somewhat different standards for determining whether venue lies in more than one district, they all are inter-

preted to encompass the same general types of multi-venue offenses. Indeed, multi-venue for such offenses is now recognized even without statutes specifically referring to crimes committed in part in different districts. As a result, all jurisdictions now recognize multiple venue is possible for offenses that occur in more than one district because of repetitive action or harm, offenses containing multiple elements that may occur in different places, and offenses containing an element that may be established by conduct starting in one place and finishing in another. Exceptions may exist, however, where special legislation restricts venue for a particular offense in this category to the district in which a particular aspect of the offense occurred.

As will be seen in § 16.2, courts often have experienced difficulties in determining whether an offense was committed in more than one place. The legislature, however, can readily shape the offense so that it clearly will fall in the multi-venue category. For example, though the crime of "sending" an item to another state might be limited to the place at which the item was placed in the stream of transportation, the crime of "transporting" would occur in any district through which the item is carried. Where a jurisdiction has a constitutional provision that incorporates the crime committed formula, establishing multi-venue in this fashion often is preferable to special venue legislation which might present constitutional difficulties.

Where a criminal activity is likely to have ramifications that extend over time and space, legislatures commonly have responded to this potential by defining the offense so that it clearly can be committed in more than one place. That is especially the case for federal crimes enacted by Congress under its authority to regulate interstate commerce. Article III and the Sixth Amendment hardly impose a significant limitation on Congress' capacity to allow for a substantial choice of venues for such offenses. By defining offenses so that they can be committed in more than one place, Congress can provide for extremely flexible

---

2. 18 U.S.C.A. § 3237.

venue consistent with the crime-committed formula imposed by those constitutional provisions. Indeed, as to most commercial activities affecting products distributed throughout the United States, Congress may, if it so chooses, provide for what is, in effect, nationwide venue. As discussed in § 16.2(e), precisely that strategy has been employed for certain federal offenses.

(e) Special Legislation. The most common special legislation deals with situations in which the crime-committed formula will not produce a venue. One such situation is presented by the crime committed within the territorial reach of the government but not within the territorial boundaries of any judicial district. The federal constitution recognized that difficulty when it provided in Article III that Congress could designate the "place or places" of trial when the crime "was not committed within any State." In its exercise of that authority, Congress has adopted a special provision governing the trial of offenses committed upon the high seas "or elsewhere outside the jurisdiction of any particular state or district." That provision sets venue "in the district which the offender, or any one of two or more joint offenders, is arrested or is first brought; but if such offender or offenders are not so arrested or brought into any district, an indictment or information may be filed in the district of the last known residence of the offender or of any one of two or more joint offenders, or if no such residence is known the indictment or information may be filed in the District of Columbia."

Another troubling situation under the crime-committed formula is that in which it is extremely difficult or impossible to establish exactly where the events in question occurred. Several different legislative approaches are used to meet such situations. Recognizing that the exact location of a particular event is often difficult to prove, states have adopted "either county legislation" for offenses alleged to have been committed within a specified distance (e.g., 500 yards) of the boundary between two counties. Some of these provisions are conditioned on the prosecution's inability to readily determine the precise location of the crime

within the boundary area, but others do not include that prerequisite. The difficulty of proving the exact location of a homicide has led to statutes allowing trial in the place where the body of the victim is found, sometimes automatically and sometimes only where the place of death or mortal wound cannot readily be determined. Similarly, because victims of crimes committed in moving vehicles often are uncertain as to where the crime occurred, several states provide as to such crimes that, if the place of the offense cannot readily be determined, venue will be in any county through which the vehicle passed on the journey in question. Even broader legislation provides that where an attorney general concludes that an offense was committed somewhere within the state, but "it is impossible to determine in which county it occurred, the offense may be alleged in the indictment to have been committed and may be prosecuted * * * in such county as the attorney general designates."

In some instances, legislatures apparently have found troubling the breadth of the multivenue consequences of applying the crime-committed formula and have responded with legislation limiting venue to the district in which a particular aspect of the crime was committed. Thus, Congress has provided that the prosecution of a fugitive felon for flight in interstate commerce may be brought only in the district "in which the original crime was alleged to have been committed, or in which the person was held in custody or confinement, or in which an avoidance of service of process or a contempt [for disobedience of process] * * * is alleged to have been committed." Without that provision, the flight, as a continuing offense, might provide venue in any district through which the felon traveled. So too, to preclude an interpretation of homicide as having occurred both in the district where the fatal blow was struck and the district in which the victim died, several states provide that venue will be only in the district of the fatal blow.

More frequently, special legislation is geared to ensuring that offenses will be viewed as allowing for venue in more than one district. A federal statute, for example, provides that a prosecution for illegal entry into the country may be prosecuted in the district in which the accused was apprehended even though that was not the district in which he illegally crossed the border. State statutes provide that not only larceny, but other offenses involving the taking of property, such as robbery and burglary, also produce venue in any county into which the thief takes the stolen property. Most such provisions, even though going beyond the common law application of the crime-committed formula, can be characterized as the equivalent of a legislative redesignation of the elements of the crime that would produce the same multi-venue under the crime-committed formula. Such a characterization is not as readily advanced, however, for some special legislation. Thus, a Minnesota statute provides for prosecution of child abuse "either in the county where the alleged abuse occurred or the county where the child is found," and an Illinois statute provides that "a person who commits the crime of cannabis trafficking or controlled substance trafficking may be tried in any county."[3]

Where a state has either a constitutional venue guarantee of a right to trial in the county in which the offense was committed or a constitutional guarantee of a jury of the vicinage, special venue legislation can pose constitutional difficulties insofar as it can be seen as going beyond the implementation of the crime-committed formula. Of course, the crime-committed formula was not designed to impose a requirement so rigid as to preclude a trial anywhere within the state. Thus, courts have no difficulty in squaring with such constitutional guarantees special legislation governing offenses committed in border waters or governing situations in which the location of the critical conduct cannot readily be determined. However, state courts have struck down provisions that allowed for venue in either county for crimes committed close to their mutual boundary when that venue was not justified by the inability to readily determine precisely where the crime occurred within the boundary area. If the locus of the crime readily

can be placed within county A, allowing the trial in county B is held to violate a constitutional vicinage or venue provision tied to "the county in which the crime was committed." A contrary position treats the legislature as merely having extended slightly the boundaries of both counties for venue purposes where the crime was committed in what then becomes overlapping territory. The venue district is more than slightly expanded by the application of in-transit statutes, extending venue for crimes committed in moving vehicles to include each county through which the vehicle traveled on the trip in question. Accordingly, such statutes have consistently been held to violate constitutional vicinage and venue provisions when not conditioned on an inability to determine the locus of the crime within a single county.

As noted in § 2.6(b), the Supreme Court has not yet squarely ruled on whether the "vicinage clause" of the Sixth Amendment ("requiring a jury of the state and district wherein the crime shall have been committed") is applicable to the states via the Fourteenth Amendment's due process clause. Lower courts considering the issue in a venue context have split on whether the vicinage clause should be viewed as a fundamental aspect of the Sixth Amendment jury clause and therefore applicable to the states. Assuming that the clause does apply, the question arises as to what geographical unit constitutes the appropriate "district" for Sixth Amendment purposes "wherein the crime shall have been committed." The California courts have stated that the Sixth Amendment district as applied to that state is the county, California's traditional local judicial district. Under this view, special legislation arguably departing from the crime-committed formula as applied to a state's standard judicial district (whether a county or a multi-county district) would present a Sixth Amendment issue. As a result, the questions of constitutionality previously thought applicable only to states which had their own constitutional venue and vicinage

---

3. See Minn.Stat.Ann. § 627.15; Ill. Smith–Hurd Ann. Ch. 750, ILCS § 511–6(r).

provisions would now be applicable to all states under the Sixth Amendment.

Other courts, however, have treated the Sixth Amendment's district as not nearly so restrictive. The Sixth Amendment "vicinage" provision is not a true vicinage requirement as it has never required a jury from the "vicinity" or "neighborhood." The original federal judicial districts typically covered the territory of an entire state, and any venue chosen by state legislation would be within the state. Arguably, the key to the Sixth Amendment clause as applied to the state is the prior legislative designation of the district, but that clearly is satisfied by special legislation. Under this view, application of the Sixth Amendment clause to the states poses no significant difficulty for special legislation, even where that legislation authorizes venue in every county in the state.

(f) Joinder and Venue. Unless the statute or court rule establishing permissive joinder explicitly states otherwise, venue requirements are assumed to override that provision's allowance for joinder at the prosecutor's option. As a result, two offenses that could readily have been joined in a single prosecution if committed in a single district will have to be brought separately when committed in different districts. In the federal system, for example, rule 8(a) allows joinder of multiple offenses if they are of the "same or similar character" or "parts of a common scheme." Thus, if a defendant should rob several federally insured banks in the same district, all of those robberies can be charged in the same prosecution; if sufficiently interrelated, the robberies might be deemed parts of a common scheme, but in any event, they are offenses of "the same character." However, if those robberies are committed in several different states, they are venue-barred from being presented in a single prosecution. That is so even though the robberies may be so closely connected in time and circumstance of commission that they could be deemed part of a single criminal episode and evidence of one could be introduced in the proof of the other.

Of course, where multiple offenses are so closely related as to be part of the same criminal episode, they are likely to have an overlapping venue in a single district if they also are offenses that can be committed in part in different places. However, many offenses are deemed committed by a single act in a single place, and here venue requirements commonly will preclude a single prosecution even for closely related crimes if they involved separate venue districts. State prosecutions are more likely to face such venue-bars than federal prosecutions since the state venue districts (typically counties) are much smaller than the federal districts and state offenses less frequently contain elements, such as the use of interstate commerce, that may link an offense to more than one district.

Most jurisdictions do not have compulsory joinder provisions. A substantial minority group of states, however, do impose a mandatory joinder requirement by statute, court rule, or judicial decision.[4] Almost all of these jurisdictions require joinder of offenses arising out of the same "transaction" or "criminal episode." Because such provisions compel joinder, they are viewed as creating a direct conflict with venue limitations (in contrast to permissive joinder provisions), and therefore commonly speak to the situation in which crimes that are part of the same episode are committed entirely in different venue districts. In general, states requiring same transaction joinder restrict that obligation to offenses that have venue in a single judicial district. However, in several states, when the crime committed formula gives a trial court the authority to try one of several offenses that are part of the same transaction, that court also has the authority to try all other offenses that were a part of that transaction even if those offenses were committed in other counties. Here compulsory joinder trumps venue limitations.

(g) Proof of Venue. Only a handful of jurisdictions treat venue in much the same manner as other procedural prerequisites for prosecution (e.g., a valid preliminary hearing bindover, or a grand jury charge). In those

---

4. See § 17.4(c).

jurisdictions, the defendant must put the venue prerequisite in issue by a pretrial motion to dismiss, with the court then making a determination that venue does or does not exist. If an issue of fact is presented, it is resolved at a pretrial evidentiary hearing conducted by the court, with the prosecution bearing the burden of proof under a preponderance of the evidence standard. Presumably, if the court holds pretrial that venue is proper, but newly available evidence at trial undercuts that determination, the court may reverse itself.

In the federal system and the vast majority of the states, venue is not simply a prerequisite that the defendant may choose to challenge pretrial; it is viewed as part of the case that the prosecution must prove at trial. These jurisdictions offer a variety of explanations for requiring that venue be established at trial. Venue is described as: "a jurisdictional fact put in issue by a plea of not guilty"; a "material allegation of the indictment" which must be proven along with other indictment allegations; an "element of the crime" to be treated no differently than the substantive elements of the offense; and an "issuable fact" most appropriately addressed in the course of the proof of the offense and presented to the finder of fact.

As might be expected from the above explanations, all but a few of these jurisdictions treat venue as a factual question to be decided by the jury in a jury trial. The court has the responsibility for determining whether, as a matter of law, the events alleged to have occurred in a particular place could be sufficient to establish that the crime was committed at least in part in that district (or whether venue could otherwise be justified under special legislation). The jury then decides the underlying factual issue, such as whether a particular act did occur in the district, or whether an act had the objective or other quality that the court deems necessary to characterize it as locating the commission of the crime. The jury can take into account not only the evidence presented in the case, but also such geographical facts as the court directs it to consider via judicial notice. The judge may charge the jury, for example, that Manhattan is within the Southern District of New York, leaving to the jury only the question as to whether the events identified as critical did occur there.

Though most jurisdictions treat proof of venue as a jury issue, they ordinarily do not view venue as one of those matters that must invariably be submitted to the jury. Courts frequently state that a charge on venue is required only "when trial testimony puts venue in issue." Thus, a jury charge on venue is not required "where the entirety of the defendant's illegal activity is alleged to have taken place within the trial * * * [district] and no trial evidence is proffered that the illegal act was committed in some other place or that the place alleged is not within the * * * [district]." One explanation of this "in issue" requirement is that the lack of venue, like various substantive defenses on which the prosecution will ultimately carry the burden of proof, must first be placed in contention by an initial defense showing that raises doubts on the issue. Another explanation is that an instruction on venue simply is not necessary where the jury, in order to conclude that the defendant committed the crime, must rest that conclusion on illegal acts that indisputably occurred in the district.

Courts also have concluded that the failure to charge the jury on venue should not constitute error, even when the evidence puts venue in issue, where the defendant failed to request a charge on venue. A jury finding on venue is not so basic to the determination of guilt as to justify departing from the "usual, salutary requirement that one complaining about an omitted instruction must have tendered a request and objected to its omission." Indeed, in some jurisdictions requiring proof of venue at trial, an objection pretrial also may be required. Where the prosecution has set forth pretrial its theory of venue, and the defense challenge is to whether that theory is correct in its placement of venue, rather than whether the prosecution can prove the facts necessary to support that theory, a failure to object pretrial can also forfeit a venue objection.

Jurisdictions requiring prosecution proof of venue at trial are divided as to the level of persuasiveness of the prosecution's proof of venue. The federal courts and a substantial number of state courts hold that the facts supporting venue only need be established by a preponderance of the evidence. They take the position that venue is not a true element of the crime (which elements constitutionally must be established by proof beyond a reasonable doubt), as it does not relate even remotely to the issues of guilt or innocence or the level of culpability. At most, they note, it is simply a "jurisdictional fact." As the preponderance standard is satisfactory for determining factual issues relating to other aspects of the trial structure (e.g., juror disqualification) and even to constitutional violations in the government's acquisition of evidence, it should also be satisfactory, they maintain, on the issue of venue. Other states disagree with this analysis, and require that venue be proved beyond a reasonable doubt. Courts explaining this higher proof requirement point to state law that treats venue as an "element of the offense," the characterization of venue as a "material allegation" of the charging instrument, and the status of venue as a jurisdictional prerequisite and therefore requiring the same standard proof as traditionally applied to proof of the territorial jurisdiction of the state.

§ 16.2 Applying the Crime–Committed Formula

(a) Recurring Questions. When all the acts of the defendant and all the consequences of those acts occur in the same district, application of the crime-committed formula is straightforward and simple. Complexities began to arise, however, where the acts occur in one district and the consequences in another. They increase where the acts as well as consequences are spread over several districts. In applying the crime-committed formula to such cases, courts must determine initially whether the offense is one that can be committed only in a single place or an offense that can be committed in more than one place. If the answer is that the offense can be committed only in one place, the court must then identify the act or consequence that marks that place. If the answer is that the offense can be committed in more than one place, then the court must determine the point at which the offense starts and the point at which it finishes. These are recurring questions that arise in the context of both traditional common law offenses and newly created statutory offenses.

The offenses and situations presenting these recurring questions are too diverse to be placed in a few basic groupings or otherwise categorized. A few illustrations will have to suffice in suggesting their range. Consider first a comparatively simple case. Defendant makes a false pretense to the victim in district A and the victim responds by transferring funds to the defendant in district B. On a charge of false pretenses, does venue lie only in district A, only in district B, or in both districts A and B? The possibilities are more numerous in a classic homicide hypothetical. Defendant manufactures a bomb in district A, places it in the victim's car in district B, the bomb explodes and injures the victim while he is driving in district C, and the victim dies in the hospital to which he is taken in district D. Is the homicide offense one that starts with the manufacture of the bomb and finishes with the death of the victim, so that it is committed in all four districts? Does it start with the placing of the bomb in the car, so that district A is excluded, or only with the infliction of the injury, so that districts A and B are both excluded? Is homicide a crime that cannot start at one place and finish at another, so that venue lies in only one district? If so, is the single place of the crime that where the injury occurs or that where the victim dies? Courts have struggled with such cases for years.

As to false pretenses, there is a general agreement that the offense has multiple parts and occurs both where the misrepresentation is made and funds obtained. As to homicide, there is less uniformity. Some courts have viewed the offense as committed only where the fatal injury was inflicted, while others have viewed it as an offense that can be committed in more than one district, so that the place of death and the starting point for the act inflicting injury are also proper venues. As to the appropriate starting point, some courts would start with significant preliminary acts such as manufacture of the bomb, while others would start only where defendant has actually set in motion the agency of death, as in the placing of the bomb in the car.

Although there may not be agreement among the various jurisdictions, the basic venue questions should be firmly settled in any particular jurisdiction as to a traditional offense. Indeed, in many jurisdictions, special venue legislation has been adopted to ensure that a particular position is taken as to specified traditional offenses. However, as to each new offense, these questions must be considered anew (assuming the legislature does not add a provision specifically identifying the district of venue for that offense). Very often, analogies can be drawn to similar common law offenses, but these can be deceiving as the very purpose of the new offense may be to change the nature of the traditional offense in a way that may be critical for venue purposes. On occasion, the new offense will have no counterpart among the common law offenses. Especially for such offenses, the end result is likely to be a substantial period of uncertainty until the courts finally provide definitive answers as to each of the critical questions for that particular offense.

Some state venue provisions seek to offer directions on what will produce an offense committed partly in one district and partly in another. These provisions typically state that, for a crime to have been committed in part in a district, events of a certain type must have occurred there. Thus, the provision may state that a crime is committed in a district if there occurs in that district: "an act in furtherance of the offense"; "conduct constituting an element of the offense or a result of such conduct"; "conduct or results which constitute elements of the offense"; or "acts or effects thereof constituting or requisite to the consummation of the offense." Of course, such provisions are hardly self defining, but they do establish some basic starting points (e.g., whether situs is determined by reference to both acts and results; whether either, to qualify, must in itself establish an element of the offense, as opposed to simply leading to other acts or results that establish elements of the offense).

The primary federal venue provision, and the venue provisions of most states, in contrast, simply recognize that crimes will have multiple venues if committed in part in multiple districts. Here courts are left to develop their own standards for determining whether an offense has that quality. The federal courts have been a leader in this task, in part because federal offenses so often implicate more than one place, and at the same time, lack precise counterparts in traditional common law crimes. Although the large body of federal caselaw on the subject defies ready categorization, it does suggest at least three distinctive modes of analysis for responding to the recurring questions presented by potential multi-venue situations. Those three are: (1) looking to a technical analysis of the language of the statute; (2) looking to the "nature" of the offense, as determined primarily by its elements; and (3) a multifaceted "substantial contacts" analysis that takes account of a series of different interests. Added to these approaches, at least where they produce no clear-cut answer, is the consideration of overriding venue "policy." Though hardly unique to the federal courts, these modes of analysis have been most fully discussed and distinguished from each other in federal opinions. Accordingly, the description of each in the subsection that follows relies primarily on the federal caselaw.

(b) Literalism. The crux of the literalist approach to the application of the crime-committed formula is the assumption that most crimes contain a key verb that describes the core of the crime and thereby identifies the act which sets venue. While all would agree that a "key verb" often helps to sets venue, the critical question is whether that verb should almost invariably be viewed as providing an answer in itself. The Supreme Court's ruling in *United States v. Lombardo*[1] came close to responding in the affirmative, although the *Lombardo* opinion also contained additional

§ 16.2
1.   241 U.S. 73, 36 S.Ct. 508, 60 L.Ed. 897 (1916).

reasoning suggesting that policy concerns were not totally ignored.

The defendant in *Lombardo*, the operator of a house of prostitution in Seattle, was charged in the Western District of Washington with failing to comply with a federal statute requiring any person who harbored an alien for the purpose of prostitution to report that alien's identity to the Commissioner General of Immigration. The district court sustained a demurrer to the indictment on the ground that the offense was not committed in Seattle, but in the District of Columbia, where the offices of the Commissioner General were located. Affirming that ruling, the Supreme Court initially quoted with approval from the district court's analysis of the critical statutory verb:

> "The word 'file' was not defined by Congress. No definition having been given, the etymology of the word must be considered and ordinary meaning applied. The word 'file' is derived from the Latin word 'filum,' and relates to the ancient practice of placing papers on a thread or wire for safekeeping and ready reference. Filing, it must be observed, is not complete until the document is delivered and received. 'Shall file' means to deliver to the office and not send through the United States mails. A paper is filed when it is delivered to the proper official and by him received and filed."

The Court then rejected the government's response that this was an unduly narrow reading of the term "shall file." The government contended that a filing could begin in the place where the document was sent and therefore the defendant's failure to send the document from Seattle marked the beginning of the crime. The Court's answer to this contention was that it "was constrained by the meanings of the words of the statute." The requirement of a filing demanded delivery in a specific place; it had never been deemed satisfied by "a deposit in a post office at some distant place." The statute thus was quite distinct from one that imposed a "general duty" upon a person, such as the "duty of the father to support his children," which could be enforced both

"where the 'actor' is and where the 'subject' is." Here, in contrast, there was a specific duty that required an action at a single place.

While the *Lombardo* opinion stressed what it viewed as the clear meaning of the verb "file," it also offered several administrative justifications for the interpretation it adopted. These included difficulties relating to proof of the mailing (or the lack thereof) and to setting the "instant of time" for compliance if a mailing was to be taken as compliance in itself. In *Travis v. United States*,[2] the Supreme Court relied upon *Lombardo* but offered no reasons other than the language of the statute to support its reading of the offense involved there as capable of being committed only in one place.

The defendant in *Travis*, a union official in Colorado, was charged under a statute applicable to any person who, "in a matter within the jurisdiction of any department or agency of the United States," knowingly "makes" any false statement. The false statements at issue were non-Communist affidavits executed and mailed in Colorado to the offices of the N.L.R.B. in Washington, D.C. The defendant contended, and the Court majority agreed, that the government had erred in bringing the prosecution in Colorado as the offense only could be committed in the District of Columbia. Justice Douglas' opinion's stressed that the offense required that the false statement be "within the jurisdiction" of the N.L.R.B. Section 9(h) of the National Labor Relations Act did not require union officers to file non-Communist affidavits, but provided for their voluntary filing as a prerequisite to invoking the Board's authority in the investigation and issuance of complaints against employers. Accordingly, Justice Douglas reasoned, "filing [of the affidavit] must be completed before there is a 'matter within the jurisdiction' of the Board." *Lombardo* had held that "when a place is explicitly designated where a paper must be filed, a prosecution for failure to file lies only at that place." The same was true for an actual filing. Accordingly, the charge could be

2. 364 U.S. 631, 81 S.Ct. 358, 5 L.Ed.2d 340 (1961).

brought only in the District of Columbia, where the affidavit was filed.

The *Travis* majority acknowledged that "Colorado, the residence of the [defendant] might offer conveniences and advantages to him which a trial in the District of Columbia might lack." It did not disagree with Justice Harlan's contention in dissent that "the witnesses and relevant circumstances surrounding the contested issues in such cases more probably will be found in the district of the execution of the affidavit than at the place of filing." Its response was that the "constitutional requirement is as to the locality of the offense and not the personal presence of the offender," and here the language of the offense set that locality in only one place. To argue, as the government did, that the offense started in Colorado because the defendant there "irrevocably set in motion and placed beyond his control the train of events which would normally result (and here did result) in the consummation of the offense" was to ignore that Congress here "has so carefully indicated the locus of the crime." That was done in the "explicit provision of 9(h)" conditioning N.L.R.B. authority, which combined with the "agency jurisdiction" requirement of the false statement statute to render the crime incapable of commission until the affidavit was delivered to the N.L.R.B.[3]

Commentators have criticized the frequent reliance of federal courts on a "key verb" analysis. They note that there is only so much weight that language can carry in deciding a question that the legislature most likely did not have in mind in its choice of language. Should it be determinative, for example, whether a statute states that it is a crime to "obtain" property through a false pretense or states that the crime consists of the "making" of a false pretense and thereby "obtaining" the transfer of property? Very often, it is argued, differences in phrasing are the product of drafting goals that have little to do with clearly indicating the gist of the crime. Where the legislature has in mind a specific venue, it can append an explicit venue provision to the substantive criminal provision. Absent that, it is argued, a court should consider along with language a variety of factors that help to identify the character of the offense, and where ambiguity exists, adopt an interpretation that suits the ends of appropriate venue policy.

Lower courts commonly are not quite as willing as the commentators to look beyond the language of the statute. Thus, "examin[ing] * * * the verbs employed in the statute" is still described by many courts as the "usual method" for determining where venue will lie. The federal courts taking this approach must acknowledge, however, that the Supreme Court has clearly stated that key verb is not the exclusive touchstone for determining venue. In *United States v. Anderson*,[4] the Court spoke of the "locus delecti * * * [being] determined from the nature of the crime alleged and the location of the acts or acts constituting it." As illustrated in *United States v. Rodriguez–Moreno*,[5] this inquiry may point in a direction other than that indicated by the key verb.

At issue in *Rodriguez–Moreno* was the multi-venue potential of a criminal statute prohibiting the "use" or "carry[ing]" of a firearm "during and in relation to any crime of violence." The defendant there, who had participated in a kidnaping that extended over sever-

---

3. Dissenting in *Travis*, Justice Harlan found no such clear designation in the statutory language. At the least, the statutory language was just as readily read as creating an offense that could be started in one place and finished in another. The prohibited act was the "making" of a false statement to the government, which certainly could "begin at the place where the false affidavit is actually made, sworn, and subscribed"; it was with the bringing of the statement within the jurisdiction of the N.L.R.B., through its filing, that the other necessary element was added and the crime completed. The dissent maintained that "the appropriate venue should be determined by reference to the 'nature of the crime alleged' and the 'location of the act or acts constituting it.' " From that perspective, it would be difficult to distinguish the case in which the affidavit was within the N.L.R.B.'s jurisdiction at the time of execution because the official had an obligation to file and the situation presented in *Travis*. Yet Justice Douglas had noted that if § 9(h) had mandated the filing of the non-Communist affidavits, rather than making it optional, "the whole process of filing, including the use of the mails, might logically be construed to constitute the offense."

4. 328 U.S. 699, 66 S.Ct. 1213, 90 L.Ed. 1529 (1946).

5. 526 U.S. 275, 119 S.Ct. 1239, 143 L.Ed.2d 388 (1999).

al districts, argued that the prosecution for this firearms offense could be brought only in the district in which he threatened the victim with a weapon, and not in other districts where the kidnaping had occurred without the weapon. Relying on what it called the "verb test," the Third Circuit sustained that contention, reasoning that venue for this part of the overall criminal transaction was tied to where the firearm was either used or carried. The Supreme Court rejected that conclusion, looking to the standard of *Anderson*. It noted that "the 'verb test' certainly has value as an interpretive tool," but should "not be applied rigidly, to the exclusion of other relevant statutory language." Such language here established that the underlying violence offense itself was another element of the firearms crime. Thus, the crime had the character of an offense with "two distinct elements." This was so even though "the crime of violence element * * * is embedded in a prepositional phrase and not expressed in verbs." Also, contrary to the dissent, the majority found nothing in the character or language of the firearm offense suggesting that it was intended to be an offense which did not begin until the two elements combined. "Congress prescribed both the use of firearm and the commission of the acts that constitute the violent crime," and either provided an appropriate venue for the crime that was the product of the two. Therefore, venue was proper in a district in which the kidnaping occurred even though the weapon was not used there.

(c) Nature of the Offense. In recent years, the Supreme Court, in *Anderson* and other cases, has emphasized a venue inquiry that focus on the "nature of the offense." The two leading applications of this inquiry are *United States v. Rodriguez–Moreno*, described above, and *United States v. Cabrales*.[6]

Cabrales involved a prosecution under a money laundering statute making it a crime to "knowing[ly] * * * conduct * * * a financial transaction which * * * involves proceeds of specified unlawful activity * * * knowing that the transaction is designed * * * to avoid a

transaction reporting requirement." The prosecution was brought in Missouri, where drug trafficking had produced the criminally derived funds, but the alleged financial transactions were deposits and withdrawals made in Florida (and it was not alleged that the defendant had transported the funds from Missouri to Florida). The government argued that venue in the district of the underlying criminality (here Missouri) was proper because (1) the underlying crime producing the funds is an essential element of the money laundering offense, (2) the laundering activity impacts the underlying criminal activity by making it profitable and impeding its detection, and (3) the district of the underlying offense is a most appropriate district for trial because of the need to prove that the funds were criminally derived and the "interests of the community victimized by [the] drug dealers." The Supreme Court, in a unanimous ruling, found these arguments unpersuasive.

The *Cabrales* opinion looked to the "general guide" of *Anderson* that venue "be determined from the nature of the crime alleged and the location of the acts or acts constituting it." The money laundering offense, it noted, was "defined in statutory proscriptions * * * that interdict only the financial transactions (acts located entirely in Florida), not the anterior criminal conduct that yielded the funds allegedly laundered." To be criminally liable, "the money launderer must know she is dealing with funds [criminally] derived," but "it is immaterial whether * * * [she] knew where the first crime was committed." Admittedly, "whenever a defendant acts 'after the fact' to conceal a crime, * * * it might be said that the first crime is an essential element of the second, * * * and that the second facilitated the first," but that does not establish the venue for the second in the district of the first. The government had available to it the potential for trial in the district of drug trafficking if it charged the defendant with a conspiracy with the drug dealers and treated the money laundering as an overt act.[7] It could not use charges of money laundering, which "describe

---

6. 524 U.S. 1, 118 S.Ct. 1772, 141 L.Ed.2d 1 (1998).

7. See subsection (g) infra.

activity" of the "[defendant] alone, untied to others," as a substitute for a conspiracy charge.

Looking to the essential character of the crime created by Congress, *Cabrales* and *Rodriguez–Moreno* found that one crime treated related criminal conduct as no more than an anterior factor giving rise to a separate offense, and the other treated such conduct as critical element of the crime itself. *Cabrales* held that the element that characterized the money laundering offense was the laundering element, and though an illegal source of the funds to be laundered also was an element, the criminal conduct creating that status was simply an anterior factor. *Rodriguez–Moreno* held that the ongoing crime of violence was a "critical" conduct element of a crime prohibiting the use of a firearm "during and in relation to" that crime; the predicate crime stood alongside the use of the firearm itself, thereby creating venue in any district on which the predicate crime occurred (whether or not the firearm also was used there).

Both *Cabrales* and *Rodriguez–Moreno* emphasize the need to look to elements of the crime in determining the "nature" of the crime. They also make clear, however, that not all elements are equal. *Rodriguez–Moreno* distinguished *Cabrales* as a case in which the government sought to base venue on a "circumstance element," rather than a "conduct element" that was an integral part of the offense. The anterior crime in *Cabrales* simply identified the source of the money; the conduct proscribed by the laundering statute occurred "after the fact" as an offense "begun and completed by others." The predicate crime in *Rodriguez–Moreno*, on the other hand, was ongoing, and one of "two distinct conduct elements" required of the defendant for liability. In effect, the Court viewed the crime in *Rodriguez–Moreno* as a type of aggravated crime of violence, and the crime in *Cabrales* as an offense which looked to a status created by an earlier offense, but was completely separate from that offense (akin to the relationship of the crime of dealing in stolen property to the crime of theft).

Though analysis in *Cabrales* and *Rodriguez–Moreno* looked in part to the purpose of the criminalization, that inquiry was shaped by the specific function of the offense as evidenced by its definition, not some secondary goal of the legislature in creating the offense. Money laundering certainly is aimed at restricting the profit derived from the commission of the underlying offense, but its definition does not include an offender purpose of facilitating (and, in effect becoming an accomplice to) those who committed the original offense. In contrast, the criminal prohibition in *Rodriguez–Moreno* was aimed through its definition at those who engaged in violent crime and also utilized a weapon.

(d) Substantial Contacts. The analysis employed in *Cabrales* and *Rodriguez–Moreno* casts doubt on the continuing use in federal courts of what had come to be known as the "substantial contacts" analysis of venue. That analysis arguably finds support in numerous federal lower court rulings holding venue appropriate in more than one district notwithstanding proscribed conduct that might have been viewed as pointing only to one district.[8] Elements of the substantial contacts analysis also are found in state court rulings and state venue provisions.

In *United States v. Reed*,[9] the leading pre-*Cabrales* discussion of the substantial contacts analysis, the Second Circuit described that analysis as "tak[ing] into account a number of factors—the site of the defendant's acts, the elements and nature of the crime, the locus of the effect of the criminal conduct, and the suitability of each district for accurate fact-finding." The first factor—the site of the de-

---

8.　These included: (1) holdings that a statute prohibiting the making of a false statement "in any proceeding ancillary to" an ongoing judicial proceeding established venue both where the false statement was made and where the parent proceeding was conducted; (2) holdings that a bail jumping statute established venue in both the district in which the defendant failed to appear and the

district in which he was released; and (3) holdings that fraud provisions established venue in the districts where the fraudulent communications were sent and received and in the district in which the subject matter of the scheme was located.

9.　773 F.2d 477 (2d Cir.1985).

fendants acts—was viewed as generally fixing the first permissible place of venue. The presence of the "alleged criminal acts" in itself "provide[s] substantial contact with the district" and ensures that the district "is usually as suitable for factfinding as any other." Of course, not all the defendant's actions would be viewed as criminal conduct for this purpose. The focus was on acts that are "part of the offense" rather than mere "preparatory acts."

The second factor cited in *Reed*—the elements and nature of the crime—looked beyond defendant's conduct, to events and consequences that were also a prerequisite for criminal liability. Thus, where a statute makes interstate transportation a jurisdictional prerequisite, the districts of transportation could provide an additional venue. The third *Reed* factor—the locus of the effect of the criminal conduct—would overlap with the second factor where a specific harm was an element of the offense. However, it suggested another appropriate venue even where the criminal statute did not itself refer to some specific harm in another district. Thus, in criminal contempt proceedings, venue was permitted both in the district in which the act violating the court order occurred and the district in which the court order was issued. *Reed's* fourth factor—the suitability of the district for accurate factfinding—looked to the likely location of evidence as measured by the general nature of the offense. It did not provide an independent basis for finding venue, but could provide support for a finding of permissible venue under one of the other three factors.

While the substantial contracts analysis was advanced, in part, as a means of complying with the Supreme Court's directive to examine the "nature of the crime," it offered a much broader conception of that inquiry than did *Cabrales* and *Rodriguez–Moreno*. The substantial contacts analysis looked beyond the elements of the crime, and as to elements, give weight to "circumstance" as well as "conduct" elements. Thus, not surprisingly, a leading lower court ruling applying a substantial contacts analysis had supported the position that

the government advanced in *Cabrales*. In rejecting that position, the *Cabrales* Court did not mention the substantial contacts position as such, but it clearly refused to go beyond the elements of the crime in determining its nature, and as to elements, discounted the circumstance element of anterior criminality. In a post-*Cabrales* decision, the Second Circuit noted that the nature of an offense is to be determined in light of the guidelines suggested in *Cabrales* and *Rodriguez–Moreno*, and the "substantial contacts rule [then] offers guidance on how to determine whether the location of venue is constitutional, especially in those cases where the defendant's acts did not take place in the district."[10]

(e) Constitutional Policy. Whether applying an analysis that focuses on the key verb or the nature of the crime, the Supreme Court, in both majority and dissenting opinions, has often noted the importance of turning to the policies underlying the Constitution's venue and vicinage provisions where the language and structure of the crime do not clearly fix venue. Indeed, no statement on venue determination is more frequently cited than the admonition in one such case, *United States v. Johnson*,[11] where the Court stated that "questions of venue in criminal cases" should not be viewed as presenting "merely matters of formal legal procedure," but as "rais[ing] deep issues of public policy in light of which legislation must be construed." However, as both commentators and lower courts have noted, the Supreme Court has been unable to achieve a consistent consensus on the precise content of those policies.

Although the Court had referred occasionally to policy considerations in earlier opinions, the 1944 opinion in *Johnson* clearly constitutes the seminal Supreme Court discussion of the guidance provided by "constitutional venue policy" in applying the crime-committed formula. Prosecution there was brought under a statute prohibiting the "use of the mails * * * for the purpose of sending or bringing into" any state a denture the cast of which

---

10. United States v. Saavedra, 223 F.3d 85 (2d Cir. 2000).

11. 323 U.S. 273, 65 S.Ct. 249, 89 L.Ed. 236 (1944).

was taken by a person not licensed to practice dentistry in that state. The defendant, the sender of the dentures, objected to his prosecution in the state of delivery, arguing that the offense was committed only where the dentures were deposited in the mail. The government countered that the statute prohibited the use of the mails and the offense therefore was committed "in every state through which the dentures were carried" by the mails, including the state of delivery. Responding to that argument, Justice Frankfurter noted for a 5–4 majority:

> An accused is so triable, if a fair reading of the Act requires it. But if the enactment reasonably permits the trial of the sender of outlawed dentures to be confined to the district of sending, and that of the importer to the district into which they are brought, such construction should be placed upon the Act. Such construction, while not required by the compulsions of Article III, § 2 of the Constitution and of the Sixth Amendment, is more consonant with the considerations of historic experience and policy which underlie those safeguards in the Constitution regarding the trial of crimes. * * * Aware of the unfairness and hardship to which trial in an environment alien to the accused exposes him, the Framers wrote into the Constitution * * * [Article III, § 2 and the Sixth Amendment provision on jury selection]. * * * By utilizing the doctrine of a continuing offense, Congress may, to be sure, provide that the locality of a crime shall extend over the whole area through which force propelled by an offender operates. * * * Plainly enough, such leeway not only opens the door to needless hardship to an accused by prosecution remote from home and from appropriate facilities for defense. It also leads to the appearance of abuses, if not to abuses, in the selection of what may be deemed a tribunal favorable to the prosecution. * * * If an enactment of Congress equally permits the underlying spirit of the constitutional concern for trial in the vicinage to be respected rather than to be disrespected, construction should go in the direction of constitutional policy even though not commanded by it.

The *Johnson* majority concluded that the statute presented there did not demand a reading that would allow venue in any district in which the mails were used. When Congress in the past had desired to give the government such a broad choice of venue, it had done so by a specific venue provision. There was no such provision here. Moreover, the statutory language did not make it a crime to "transport" the unlawful dentures, but instead referred to use of the mails for sending or importing the denture. A "strained construction" was not needed to hold that the "crime of the sender is complete when he uses the mails in Chicago, and the crime of the unlicensed dentist in California or Florida or Delaware, who orders the denture from Chicago, is committed in the State into which he brings the dentures." Not only was such an interpretation favored by constitutional venue policy, but "no considerations of expediency" required otherwise. Allowing prosecution of the sender in the state of delivery was not needed to safeguard against the possible reluctance of a local prosecutor in the sending district to press charges on an offense that had no local victim. All United States Attorneys were subject to the "general supervision of the Attorney General," which ensured a broader perspective. "While it might facilitate the Government's prosecution in a case like this to have its witnesses near the place of trial," there should be "balanced against * * * [that interest] the serious hardship of defending prosecutions in places remote from home (including the accused's difficulties, financial and otherwise, of marshalling witnesses) as well as the temptation to abuses" of possible prosecutorial forum-shipping. Four dissenters in *Johnson* found unpersuasive Justice Frankfurter's policy arguments. They responded that "the Court misapprehends the purpose of constitutional provisions. We understand them to assure a trial in the place where the crime is committed and not to be concerned with domicile of the defendant nor with his familiarity with the environment of the place of trial."

In the years since *Johnson*, the Court has continued to divide over whether it should apply a preference for a reading of the crime-committed formula that would allow prosecution in the district where the defendant was physically present, which most often will be his "home" district—*i.e.*, the district of his residence. In *Johnston v. United States*,[12] the Court majority held that persons charged with the failure to report to hospitals for civilian work as ordered by their local draft boards could be prosecuted only in the districts where the hospitals were located and not in the districts where they lived and their draft boards were located. Speaking for the majority, Justice Reed, a dissenter in *Johnson*, stated that the case was governed by the "general rule that where the crime charged is a failure to do a legally required act, the place fixed for its performance is the situs of the crime." Justice Reed added: "This requirement of venue states the public policy that fixes the situs of the trial in the vicinage of the crime rather than the resident of the accused." Here, it was the dissenters who responded that they would have preferred "to read the statute with an eye to history and try the offenders at home where our forefathers thought that normally men would receive their fairest trial."

Only two years later, in *United States v. Cores*,[13] the Court majority, in construing an immigration law violation to be continuing in nature, noted that an advantage of that construction was to produce a result "in keeping with the policy of relieving the accused, where possible, of the inconvenience incident to prosecution in a district far removed from his residence." *Cores* involved the prosecution of an alien seaman for "willfully remain[ing]" in the United States beyond the time permitted under his landing permit. If the prosecution were limited to the district in which the seaman was located at the moment the permit expired, that often would not be the district in which he eventually took up residence. While construing the offense to be continuing in nature did not ensure that the government would bring the prosecution in his place of residence, the prosecution was most likely to be brought where the defendant was apprehended (as it was in this case) and that was most likely to be his district of residence. Moreover, at the time, Rule 21(b) allowed convenience transfers only to a district "in which the offense was committed," so only a construction of the offense as continuous would allow the defendant to seek a change of venue to his district of residence should the prosecution happen to be brought in the district of his location when the permit expired.

Cores, however, was followed by a contrary construction of the false statements statute in *Travis v. United States*,[14] discussed in subsection (b). The Court majority there refused to adopt an application of the crime-committed formula that would have allowed the government to bring the prosecution in district of the execution of the false affidavit (as it had done in that case), which ordinarily would be the district of the affiant's residence. *Travis* also was decided at a time when Rule 21(b) allowed transfer only to a district where the crime was committed, and by holding that the offense occurred only in the District of Columbia, it precluded a defendant prosecuted there from obtaining transfer to his home district where he had executed and mailed the false affidavit.

In *Johnson*, Justice Frankfurter argued in favor of an application of the crime-committed formula that would both establish venue in the place of the accused's residence and avoid granting the government a broad choice of venues that would "lead to the appearance of abuses, if not to abuses," in its decision to prosecute in one district rather than another. In that case, those two values would be served by the same reading of the Federal Denture Act, as the limitation of venue to the single district of the mailing typically also would produce the district of the sender's residence. In other instances, as in *Cores* and *Travis*, the two goals suggested opposite readings. If the offense were held to be committed in only one district, that district would not be the most likely site of the accused's residence. The dis-

12.   351 U.S. 215, 76 S.Ct. 739, 100 L.Ed. 1097 (1956).
13.   356 U.S. 405, 78 S.Ct. 875, 2 L.Ed.2d 873 (1958).

14.   See note 2 supra.

trict of residence could only be made an allowable venue by holding that the crime was committed in more than one district and thereby granting to the prosecution an opportunity to choose between districts according to its own interests.[15] The outcomes in *Travis* and *Cores*—with the former limiting the prosecution to a single district and the latter deciding in favor of multi-venue that would include the district of residence—indicate no clear choice in balancing the two goals. Indeed, it is unclear whether those cases were seen by the Court majority as involving a choice between those goals.

In general, federal lower courts discussing venue policy have spoken less frequently of the goal of narrowing venue in order to restrict the prosecutor's choice than of the goal of providing a venue most likely to coincide with defendant's residence. At the state level, a lack of concern for limiting prosecutorial options is explained by the typical division of prosecutorial authority. Each judicial district is likely to have its own independent prosecutor, so the scenario of a coordinated prosecutorial decision to bring charges in the district most likely to present a "favorable tribunal" does not seem realistic. If more than one prosecutor has an interest in the case, the primary concern is an unseemly race to file charges rather than a plot to select the most favorable venue.

(f) Transportation Offenses. At common law, the paradigm multi-venue offenses were those in which the proscribed criminal conduct included the movement of an item or person (e.g., kidnapping and larceny). Because the offense continued with the movement, venue was available in all of the different districts in which the movement took place. With rare exceptions, those were districts in which the

defendant was physically present as the item or person moved would have been within his personal control. Modern counterparts of those offenses include crimes such as driving while intoxicated, where the basic wrongdoing lies in the transportation itself. However, the same principle has been utilized to create broad venue by making transportation an element of the offense even though the basic wrongdoing relates more to events occurring before or after the transportation than the transportation itself. Section 3237 of the federal criminal code establishes such a broad venue in its second paragraph, which provides:

> Any offense involving the use of the mails, transportation in interstate or foreign commerce, or the importation of an object or person to the United States is a continuing offense and, except as otherwise expressly provided by enactment of Congress, may be inquired of and prosecuted in any district from, through, or into which such commerce, mail matter, or imported object or person moves.[16]

This second paragraph was added partially in response to the Supreme Court's reliance in *United States v. Johnson*[17] on the absence of any provision in the Denture Act specifically providing for venue in any district through which the illegally shipped dentures passed. With the amendment of § 3237, the courts were now to be directed by a single provision applicable to all "mailing" and "transportation" offenses. In *Travis v. United States*,[18] the Supreme Court apparently concluded that the second paragraph's reference to offenses "involving the use of the mails" does not apply to the situation in which the offender happens to use the mails but such use is not a specified element of the crime. Section 3237's second

---

15. As noted above, at the time of those decisions, a ruling that the crime was committed in more than one district, including the likely district of the defendant's residence, was necessary for the defendant to obtain a change of venue to that district where it was not the venue chosen by the prosecutor. That is not the case under current Rule 21(b), which does not limit a change of venue to a district in which the crime was committed. See § 16.3(c). However, as a practical matter, the defendant cannot gain a change of venue simply by showing that trial in his "home district" would be more convenient. In the settings of *Travis* and *Cores*, the strongest likelihood

that the defendant will be tried in his home district still comes from a multi-venue ruling which includes the district most likely to be that of defendant's residence, although there is no assurance that the prosecution will select that district (although that was done in both *Travis* and *Cores*).

16. See § 16.1 at note 2 for the first paragraph of § 3237.

17. See note 11 supra.

18. See note 12 supra.

paragraph could not be used there to expand the venue of a false statement prosecution, otherwise available only where the government received the false document, simply because the defendant chose to make delivery by mail.

Section 3237's second paragraph does provide broader venue, however, for such offenses as mail fraud, wire fraud, and transportation of stolen goods, which require use of the mails or interstate transportation or communications as an element of the offense. The second paragraph also has been held applicable to offenses that do not refer to interstate transportation, but render such transportation inherent in the commission of the offense. As a practical matter, however, the second paragraph of § 3237 appears rarely to be utilized by the government to bring a prosecution in a district that has no greater relationship to the offense than an item having passed through the district on its way to delivery. The provision is utilized primarily as an alternative justification for venue placed in a district that arguably might not satisfy the requirement of an "in-part commission" because the defendant had not been present in the district and, though the defendant's conduct did have an impact in the district, that impact might not be sufficient to establish venue under a "key verb" or "nature of the offense" analysis.

(g) Multiple Participants. Where multiple parties participate in a criminal transaction, venue often can be extended through the special venue rules applicable to accomplice liability and the offense of conspiracy. As to accomplices, the acts of the accomplice constituting the aiding and abetting may have occurred in a different district than the commission of the crime. In such a case, the prosecutor can choose between those districts in the prosecution of the accomplice. The abolition of the distinction between principal and accomplice means the accomplice may be treated as a principal and prosecuted where the crime occurred, but he may also be treated as an accomplice and prosecuted where the accessorial acts occurred (the traditional common law position).[19]

As to conspiracy, the formation of the conspiratorial agreement may have occurred in one district and overt acts in furtherance of the conspiracy may have occurred in other districts. Here, the prosecution has the option of proceeding against all the conspirators in the district of formation or in any district in which an overt act occurred. This venue standard is sometimes described as the *Hyde* rule, based on the 1912 Supreme Court ruling that first established the standard in the federal courts. It subsequently became the prevailing standard in state as well as federal courts.

The majority opinion in *Hyde v. United States*[20] reasoned that conspiracy was a continuing crime committed wherever an overt act furthering the conspiracy was performed. The Court noted that the federal conspiracy offense required as its elements both the conspiratorial agreement and at least one overt act by a conspirator in furtherance of the conspiratorial objective. Accordingly, each such overt act constituted a partial execution of the offense, allowing the prosecution of the conspiracy at that place under the crime-committed formula. While the remaining conspirators

---

19. The concept of accomplice liability may not be twisted in such a way, however, as to render the principle an accomplice and thereby establish venue that bypasses the crime-committed formula. The Fourth Circuit ruling in United States v. Walden, 464 F.2d 1015 (4th Cir.1972), is illustrative. In that case, the ten defendants were charged in South Carolina with a conspiracy to rob federally insured banks and with the substantive counts of robbing those banks, which were located in states other than South Carolina. Venue on the conspiracy count presented no difficulties as the conspiracy had been formed in South Carolina. However, since the bank robberies had not been committed there, the government had to support venue on the substantive counts under the theory that the defendants were being prosecuted as accomplices who committed their accessorial acts in South Carolina. The court accepted arguendo the government's contention that the acts involved in the formation of the conspiracy in South Carolina could be deemed accessorial acts, but concluded that venue on the substantive counts nonetheless failed because of the defendants' further activities in the other states in robbing the banks. Acceptance of the government's accessorial theory, the court noted, would present "the conceptual difficulty of a bank robbery * * * being perpetrated entirely by accessories in South Carolina without the assistance of principals" at the scene of the robberies, notwithstanding that these persons were, in fact, the principals.

20. 225 U.S. 347, 32 S.Ct. 793, 56 L.Ed. 1114 (1912).

may not have been physically present in the district when their associate committed the overt act, they had a "constructive presence" there based on the vicarious liability of conspirators.

Although the *Hyde* opinion stressed the overt act element of the federal conspiracy offense, it cited various common law rulings that had reached a similar result under a conspiracy offense that did not require an overt act in addition to the conspiratorial agreement. The reasoning of those rulings was that the overt act, although not an element of the offense, constituted a "renewal" or "continuation" of the agreement and thus carried its commission into the district of that act. In later years, the *Hyde* reasoning came to be viewed as incorporating both rationales, and the *Hyde* rule was applied, in both state and federal systems, to conspiracy offenses that did not require an overt act. This suggests that perhaps the key to the *Hyde* opinion was the pragmatic justification offered by the Court for the standard adopted there. The dissenters in *Hyde* (per Holmes, J.) had argued that venue should be limited to that place "where the conspiracy exists in fact"—i.e., the place where the agreement was formed or where the conspirators continued its operation by acting together. The Court majority responded that this approach might make it impossible to establish venue. With conspirators often meeting in secret, it would impose too great a burden on the government to require it to establish precisely where and when the conspirators reached an agreement. Often the primary evidence of the conspiracy was the coordinated action by individuals indicating the obvious presence of an agreement. Moreover, it was not "an oppression in the law to accept the place where an unlawful purpose is attempted to be executed as the place of its punishment, and rather conspirators be taken from their homes than the witnesses and victims of the conspiracy be taken from theirs."

Although the *Hyde* case itself involved substantial overt acts, the *Hyde* rule has been held to impose only a few basic limitations upon the overt acts that will suffice to estab-

lish venue. The act must occur subsequent to the formation of the conspiracy agreement and prior to or in completion of the conspiratorial objective. It also must have been done in furtherance of the accomplishment of that objective, but that requirement is readily satisfied. No distinctions are drawn based on the importance of the act to the accomplishment of the objective or on the legality of the act. A simple and commonplace legal activity may be sufficient, even though the action may be one that would have been taken in any event even had there been no illegal purpose. The act can be that of a single conspirator or even an innocent agent who is acting at his direction. The other conspirators need not have counseled the commission of the act nor even have been aware that it was to be done.

Where a conspiracy involves a large number of conspirators, spread throughout the country with each performing at least some small act in furtherance of the conspiracy, the *Hyde* doctrine can give to the prosecutor enormous opportunities for venue-shopping. Conspirators from major cities throughout the nation, engaged in some organized criminal activity such as illegal gambling or drug trafficking, conceivably could find themselves prosecuted in some rural district in a remote part of the country where one of the conspirators happened to make a "business related" telephone call while on a fishing trip. In his oft-quoted discussion of the potential for prosecutorial excesses in the use of conspiracy,[21] Justice Jackson noted that "the Government may, and often does, compel one to defend at a great distance from any place he ever did any act because some accused confederate did some trivial and by itself innocent act in the chosen district." "The leverage of the conspiracy charge," he argued, "lifts [the Sixth Amendment's venue] limitation from the prosecution and reduces its protection to a phantom."

Justice Jackson's primary complaint related to prosecutorial use of conspiracy, an inchoate offense, in cases in which the criminal objectives of the conspiracy had been completed. At least in that situation, however, there are cer-

---

21. Krulewitch v. United States, 336 U.S. 440, 69 S.Ct. 716, 93 L.Ed. 790 (1949) (Jackson, J. concurring).

tain practical restraints upon the government's selection of the district of some trivial and innocent act as the site of the prosecution. Because conspiracy commonly carries a lower penalty than the substantive felony offense, the preferable prosecution in such cases is for the conspiracy combined with the substantive offenses. The addition of a conspiracy count to the substantive counts offers the prosecution several advantages: a wider range of admissible evidence, a grounding for broader joinder of the various substantive offenses and defendants, possible cumulative punishment for the conspiracy and the substantive count, and the complicity liability of each conspirator for all of the substantive crimes committed in furtherance of the conspiracy. Joining the substantive counts with the conspiracy count is not a simple matter, however, under the crime-committed formula. Venue in the district of prosecution must be appropriate for each of the substantive counts as well as the conspiracy count. Accordingly, the choice of overt act for setting the venue on the conspiracy count often will be determined by the substantive counts. Selection of a district in which none of the substantive crimes were committed will not permit the joinder of a substantive count with the conspiracy count. To gain the fullest possible joinder, the prosecution for the conspiracy count will be brought not where some insubstantial overt act occurred, but where the greatest number of substantive offenses occurred. While that may be a district in which many of the conspirators were not physically present, it will nonetheless be a district in which they anticipated the accomplishment of their criminal objective and where they might well have been prosecuted simply as accomplices to the crimes committed there.

§ 16.3   Change of Venue

(a) Variations. All fifty-two jurisdictions have either statutes or court rules (or both) authorizing a trial court to order that a case be moved from its original district of prosecution, proper under the jurisdiction's venue

laws, to a district that otherwise would not be proper under those laws. In some states, additional authorization is provided through the recognition of an inherent judicial authority to order a change of venue, which supplements the statutory authorization. Together, these sources establish a quite varied law governing venue changes, differing significantly among the fifty two jurisdictions as to several key elements.

Initially, the jurisdictions divide as to the grounds that justify ordering a venue change. Some limit changes to ensuring that the ensuing trial will be fair, while others add to that ground, allowing changes in the interest of witness convenience or sound judicial administration. Jurisdictions also vary as to whether changes are allowed only on motion of the defendant, on the motion of the prosecution as well as the defendant, and on the courts own initiative over the objections of one or both parties. Subsections (b)–(f) below consider the most common combinations of these different elements, as well as lesser differences among jurisdictions that share the same position on a basic feature. Subsection (g) considers still another topic on which the jurisdictions vary— the extent to which judges are given discretion in selecting the district to which the case will be transferred.

(b) "Fair Trial" Venue Changes on Defense Motion. All fifty-two jurisdictions recognize judicial authority to grant a change of venue on a timely defense motion where needed to ensure that the defendant receives a fair trial. Indeed, *Groppi v. Wisconsin*[1] holds that a state is constitutionally bound to allow a change of venue if a fair trial cannot be had in the district in which the prosecution is brought. The Supreme Court there struck down a state law that prohibited venue changes in misdemeanor cases as applied to a defendant who claimed that a venue change was needed because community prejudice would preclude selection of an unbiased jury. The Court noted that "under the Constitution a defendant must be given an opportunity to show that a change of venue *is* required in *his*

1.   400 U.S. 505, 91 S.Ct. 490, 27 L.Ed.2d 571 (1971).

case." In some situations, a change of venue might be the only means of gaining a fair trial, and the defendant in such a case could not be denied that remedy.

Court rules and statutes authorizing "fair trial" venue changes vary in their description of the grounds that justify such a change. Some simply set forth the ultimate standard, stating that a change is required where "a fair and impartial trial cannot be had" in the district of prosecution. Others, like Federal Rule 21, speak of the inability to obtain a fair trial because of "prejudice against the defendant" in the district of prosecution. A few speak of the inability to obtain a fair trial because circumstances preclude selection of an impartial jury. All of these provisions will readily cover the ground most commonly advanced for a "fair trial" change of venue—that adverse pretrial publicity precludes selection of an unbiased jury. That ground is discussed in § 23.2(a), and as noted there, it often requires determining whether strong community sentiments may bear upon decisionmaking by otherwise fair minded jurors. However, a community uproar may operate to deprive the defendant of a fair trial apart from its impact upon the jury, e.g., by threatening disruption of the trial, violence against the accused, or the intimidation of witnesses. In light of *Groppi*, such threats should be recognized as appropriate grounds for changing venue even in jurisdictions with somewhat more narrowly drawn statutory provisions.

Provisions authorizing a venue change to ensure a fair trial also vary in their description of the requisite likelihood that a fair trial cannot be obtained in the district of prosecution. A handful of states have provisions requiring a "reasonable likelihood" that a fair and impartial trial cannot be achieved in that district. That standard has been held to require a likelihood less than "more probable than not." A substantial majority of provisions, in contrast, direct that the change be granted where the court "determines," or "is satisfied," or concludes that it "appears" that the defendant "cannot obtain" a fair and impartial trial in the district of prosecution. Interpreted literally, such provisions would re-

quire that the court find under the appropriate proof standard (presumably, the preponderance of the evidence standard) that a fair and impartial trial is not a realistic possibility. Various opinions applying such provisions do speak of a need for the defendant (as the party bearing the burden of proof) to show that a fair trial is "impossible." However, federal courts and various state courts, also applying such provisions, have stated that the defendant must show only a "reasonable" or "substantial" likelihood that a fair and impartial trial cannot be obtained in the district of prosecution.

(c) Convenience Venue Changes on Defense Motion. Federal Rule 21(b) authorizes the granting of a defense motion seeking a change of venue "for the convenience of the parties and witnesses and in the interest of justice." Most state venue provisions do not authorize a change on convenience grounds, but a substantial minority have provisions similar to Rule 21(b). These provisions are designed to allow transfer to a clearly more convenient forum. However, the inclusion of the phrase "and in the interest of justice" makes clear that concerns of judicial administration are to be taken into account along with the convenience of the parties and witnesses. Moreover, unlike "fair trial" venue changes, here the defendant does not become entitled to a change by making a certain showing. Provisions authorizing convenience transfers typically state that the court "may transfer" on convenience grounds, and courts recognize that such a transfer lies in the discretion of the trial court, subject only to the prohibition against arbitrary or capricious exercise of that discretion. Federal courts have noted, with respect to Federal Rule 21(b), that it does not place on the defendant "the burden of establishing truly compelling circumstances for such a change. The Court may grant a change if it determines, all relevant things considered, the case would better off transferred to another district."

What factors are relevant in determining whether another district would be a more convenient forum and a transfer to that district would be in the interest of justice? In the leading Supreme Court ruling on Federal Rule 21(b),[2] the Court cited a ten factor list that had been considered by the district court, and while the Court's ruling related to another point, it did add that both the parties and the appellate court had agreed that the consideration of those ten factors was "appropriate." Those ten factors, frequently relied upon in subsequent federal lower court decisions, were: "(1) location of the corporate defendant [which was the apparent counterpart of the location of one's residence for an individual]; (2) location of possible witnesses; (3) location of events likely to be in issue; (4) location of documents and records likely to be involved; (5) disruption of defendant's business unless the case is transferred; (6) expense to the parties; (7) location of counsel; (8) relative accessibility of place of trial; (9) docket condition of each district or division involved; and (10) any other special elements which might affect the transfer." In a jurisdiction with victims' rights legislation, consideration would also have to be given to any logistical difficulties that a transfer would create for a victim who sought to regularly attend the trial.

In considering a change of venue to promote convenience, courts largely weigh the comparative burdens that would be imposed upon both the prosecution and the defense in changing and not changing venue, but as to some factors, the burden imposed upon the prosecution may be downgraded in light of the government's greater resources. Thus, in the federal system, with U.S. Attorneys' offices spread across the country, the government's burden in moving lawyers to another district (or even shifting to different lawyers) may be considered less significant than imposing a similar burden upon the defense. One factor not considered under Rule 21(b) is the potentially greater sympathy of the jury to one side or another in the district of possible transfer. The defendant cannot gain a transfer on the ground that the jury in the transfer district would be more sympathetic to the defense, and a transfer justified on grounds of convenience cannot be denied because the prosecution believes that the jury in that district would be less sympathetic to its position. On the other hand, where the offense requires the jury to apply community standards, the prosecution may properly emphasize the importance of having a jury selected from the community in which the offense occurred.

(d) "Fair Trial" Venue Changes on Prosecution Motion. Federal Rule 21(a) and most state provisions on "fair trial" venue changes provide for a change of venue on motion of the defendant, with no mention of a similarly granted change on motion of the prosecution. Such provisions generally are held to preclude granting a change of venue on motion of the prosecution. However, a substantial group of states recognize prosecution authority to obtain a change of venue where it cannot obtain a fair trial in the district of prosecution. Almost all rely on statutes explicitly authorizing prosecution as well as defense motions. However, caselaw suggests that where the venue statute does not refer to either party in authorizing a venue change, a motion by the prosecution may be recognized as consistent with a general directive to ensure a "fair trial."[3]

Courts in states with constitutional vicinage provisions[4] have divided over the constitutionality of legislation authorizing a change of venue upon a prosecution showing that it cannot obtain a fair trial in the district of prosecution. A majority of the courts considering the issue have upheld such legislation as consistent with the background and objective of the state constitutional vicinage provisions. Those courts have pointed to: (1) a common law authority of courts to order a change of venue upon prosecutorial application where needed

2. Platt v. Minnesota Mining and Manufacturing Co., 376 U.S. 240, 84 S.Ct. 769, 11 L.Ed.2d 674 (1964).

3. Reported cases suggest that successful prosecution motions to change venue on "fair trial" grounds are less frequently based on media publicity than defense venue change motions. Prosecution requested changes are more likely to be based on the defendant's prominence and influence in a small community, or past efforts to sway or intimidate prospective jurors. A fair trial may also be threatened by difficulties in maintaining order in the courtroom and the general courthouse area because of the activities of groups favoring the defendant.

4. See §§ 16.1(b), 22.2(e).

to ensure a "fair and impartial" trial; (2) the presence of the vicinage provision in a jury trial guarantee which also speaks to providing an "impartial jury" of the county or district of the offense (thereby suggesting that a transfer is permissible when such a jury cannot be obtained in that district); and (3) the principle that the Constitution not be construed so as to nullify the prosecution's authority to enforce the law, which is said to be the consequence of forcing it to trial in a district where a jury is motivated by prejudice or fear to reject any case the prosecution might present. Courts rejecting this analysis rely on what they describe as the "clear language" of the vicinage provision (granting defendant a right to a jury from the district of the crime's commission), a different reading of the common law practice and its significance, a reading of the constitutional reference to jury impartiality as aimed solely at precluding a jury prejudiced against the defendant, and the view that the vicinage provision places ahead of any state interest in jury impartiality the defendant's interest in a trial in the vicinage, where he is most likely to be able to benefit from his good standing with his neighbors.

As noted in § 16.1(e), lower courts are divided on the question of whether the Fourteenth Amendment's due process clause incorporates and makes applicable to the states the Sixth Amendment's vicinage clause (requiring a jury "of the State and district wherein the crime has been committed"). Various federal lower courts have suggested that Sixth Amendment provision would prohibit Congress from authorizing a venue change on the motion of anyone other than the defendant. Assuming arguendo that the Sixth Amendment applies to the states and that the lower federal courts have correctly interpreted that Amendment as not permitting any exceptions apart from a defense waiver, the state provisions allowing a venue change on prosecution motion may nonetheless be in accord with the federal constitution. If the Sixth Amendment "district" as applied to the state encompasses the territory of the whole state (as did the original federal districts), then the change in venue on the motion of the prosecution would still be within

the same "district." The requirement of prior legislative designation of the district would also be met by treating the legislative authorization of the venue change as expanding the district to include counties outside of the county of the crime's commission where the conditions specified for transfer are met. On the other hand, if the Sixth Amendment district as applied to the states should be limited to the county or a similar state judicial district, then the prosecution venue change provisions could only be sustained by a reading of the Sixth Amendment similar to that which state courts have relied upon in rejecting challenges under state constitutional vicinage provisions.

(e) Convenience Venue Changes on Prosecution Motion. Only a few states have provisions broad enough to authorize a change of venue to further the convenience of the prosecution and its witnesses. The failure of more states to provide for a prosecutorial requested change of venue on convenience grounds is probably attributable to a combination of constitutional concerns and lack of practical need. In those states with constitutional vicinage or venue provisions, the arguments utilized to sustain a change to preserve the prosecution's ability to obtain a fair trial would not carryover to a convenience transfer. Convenience transfers to assist the prosecution would most likely be unconstitutional. The lack of a significant practical need for prosecutorial-convenience stems in large part from the general effectiveness of the crime-committed formula in identifying the district most convenient from a prosecutorial perspective. The district of the defendant's actions usually is the district in which the prosecution's evidence is located, and where that is not the case, the offense is likely to have a multi-venue potential that includes the district providing the prosecution's evidence.

Perhaps the most telling case for a venue change to promote prosecutorial convenience arises where the defendant commits multiple crimes of a type that could otherwise be joined in a single trial. Consider, for example, the case in which the defendant is charged with separate burglaries in different counties and the primary evidence against him is that found through a search of his residence in one of those counties and his subsequent confession given there to the local police. Considerable savings might be obtained if the trial of the burglaries committed in the other counties could be transferred to the county of defendant's residence, where the charges could be consolidated for a single trial relying heavily on the evidence obtained there. It is not clear, however, that such a consolidation would be sought even if prosecutorial-convenience changes were authorized.

Initially, sentencing law may be such that a conviction on multiple counts would bring no greater sentence than a conviction on a single count. Thus, if a conviction is obtained in the county where the evidence was found, the charges in the other counties might simply be dismissed. Moreover, even if there is an advantage to multiple convictions, the incentive to coordinate might not be sufficient to produce a consolidated proceeding. In almost all states, the burglaries committed in different judicial districts also would have been committed within the bailiwicks of separate prosecutors, each having an immediate interest only in the prosecution of the burglary of that county.

In the federal system, where there is a single prosecutorial authority and, perhaps, greater interest in consolidating prosecutions, the availability of offenses framed so as to allow overlapping venue for harms occurring in different places substantially reduces the need for a venue transfer to achieve a single trial in such cases. For example, where the multiple crimes involved the use of the mails or interstate transportation, and that use included an overlapping district (e.g., the same point of mailing or the same starting point in travelling to the separate site of each crime), federal offenses tied to such use (e.g., the mail fraud statute or the Travel Act) ordinarily will permit the prosecution to reach all of those criminal activities through a single prosecution brought in that district. Also, where prosecutions are brought in separate districts and the defendant desires to dispose of all charges through a guilty plea, Federal Rule 20 does allow for a transfer to the district where the defendant is located upon motion of the defendant and approval of the prosecutors in the different districts.

(f) Venue Changes on the Court's Own Motion. Roughly a dozen states have provisions authorizing the court to grant a change of venue on its own motion, notwithstanding the objections of the parties. Those provisions differ dramatically in the grounds they accept for the change. Among the grounds recognized in one or more states are: (1) the threat of violence against the defendant or disruption of the proceedings; (2) the exhaustion of so many jury panels as to clearly indicate that "it will be impossible to secure a jury to try the cause in the county"; (3) a community "so prejudiced against the defendant that a fair and impartial trial cannot be had" in the county of prosecution; (4) "a trial, alike fair and impartial to the accused and to the State, cannot, from any cause, be had in the county in which the case is pending"; and (5) the interest of "sound judicial administration", which encompasses concerns relating to providing a fair trial, witness convenience, and such matters as court congestion. In several states, an inherent judicial authority to change venue is recognized as to a change needed to obtain a fair and impartial trial. Most states, however, view the absence of a statutory authorization as having abrogated any authority for sua sponte venue changes that existed at common law.

As in the case of venue changes granted on the prosecution's motion, venue changes ordered sua sponte have been challenged under state constitutional vicinage provisions. An additional consideration is presented here, however, when the court orders the change in venue to ensure that the defendant receives a fair trial. Courts have argued that they have an obligation to ensure that the defendant receives a fair trial even if the defendant objects, especially where that objection is part of a strategy to prevent any trial because an impartial jury cannot be selected. Other courts have concluded that a state constitutional vicinage provision places in the defendant the final responsibility for choosing to proceed in the district of the crime notwithstanding possible bias, and places the obligation on the state to continue with the jury selection process until it can find a jury in that district that is impartial.

(g) Selection of the Transfer District. Where a change of venue is based upon the greater convenience presented by another district, the very grounds for the change identify the district of transfer. Where the change is based, however, on fair trial grounds, there likely will be numerous districts not subjected to the influences that require the transfer. Most jurisdictions simply leave the choice of the district of transfer to the discretion of the court ordering the venue change. Their provisions on "fair trial" venue changes simply state that the case shall be transferred to "any [judicial district] where a fair trial may be had." That district may or may not be a district requested by the moving party. The court is to exercise its own independent judgment in selecting the district. Of course, the first consideration is that the district be one not also subject to influences that are likely to prevent a fair and impartial trial. Beyond that, the court will consider the convenience of the parties and witnesses, and the availability of facilities that will permit a speedy trial. The trial court's discretion in this regard is broad and will not be overturned by an appellate court absent a clear showing of reliance on improper factors.

A substantial minority of the states seek to narrow the trial judge's discretion by setting forth a formula for selection of the district of transfer. Some direct the trial court to select the "nearest" judicial district that is "free from exception." Others direct that the transfer be to an "adjoining" district unless a fair trial cannot be obtained there. While such provisions reduce the potential for forum-shopping, they also fail to take account of factors beyond proximity to the original district that are relevant to sound judicial administration, (e.g., court congestion).

During the 1990s, highly publicized changes of venue in prosecutions of police officers charged with using excessive force against minority arrestees spurred a movement to have

courts choose transfer districts similar in racial composition to the initial district of prosecution. The issue posed is hardly new. Scattered rulings, dating back to the 1960s, have held that a court ordering a change of venue has no obligation to consider the comparative racial composition of the original district and potential transfer districts in selecting the transfer district. Indeed, it has been suggested that a race conscious selection runs the risk of violating the equal protection clause, at least insofar as it forces the court to choose between districts that will "favor" either the race of the victim or the defendant as compared to the original district. Critics of this traditional appellate court response argue for an effort to match the total demography of the original district, with race being only one component. They argue that requiring the trial court to select a transfer district that comes reasonably close to the demographic character of the original district follows from the policy underlying the common law vicinage requirement. Demographic similarity is viewed as a means of preserving the interests of the defendant, and of the community in which the crime was committed, in having the alleged criminality judged by reference to that community's values. So far, at least one appellate court and one legislature have found this argument persuasive. In *People v. Goldswer*,[5] the New York Court of Appeals, in the course of upholding a "fair trial" venue change on motion of the prosecution, stressed that the venue change statute "is designed to ensure a neutral forum." "Thus," the Court noted, "within reasonable limits, the community to which the trial is transferred should reflect the character of the county where the crime was committed." Florida, in its statute on venue changes, directs a court ordering a change of venue to "give priority to any county which closely resembles the demographic composition of the county wherein the original venue would lie."[6]

The vast majority of jurisdictions apparently continue to take the position that a demographic comparison either may be utilized or not at the discretion of the trial court, or

5. 39 N.Y.2d 656, 385 N.Y.S.2d 274, 350 N.E.2d 604 (196).

6. West's Fla.Stat.Ann. § 910.03(2).

simply is not a factor properly considered in selecting a transfer district. The latter position would follow from a statute that requires transfer to a specific district (e.g., the nearest district not subject to exception), or the view that consideration of demographic factors inappropriately assumes that defense and prosecution have some type of vested interest in the character of the community of the vicinage. Where discretion exists, the jurisdiction may allow the defendant to condition his motion for a change of venue on the selection of a particular transfer district. However, some jurisdictions recognizing an authority to order a change on motion of the defendant insist that such a motion be unconditional, and others recognize judicial authority to order a change of venue over a defense objection if that change is needed to ensure a fair and impartial trial.

Although potential jurors from other districts presumably have no constitutionally protected interest in having their district designated as the transfer district, a venue change decision may be viewed as analogous to a peremptory strike and therefore subject to an equal protection challenge when designed to exclude a particular racial group from the defendant's future jury. In *Mallett v. State*,[7] the Missouri Supreme Court recognized such a challenge, but also made clear that it had little chance of success. That case involved a change of venue granted on the motion of an African-American defendant accused of killing a white police office in a southeastern Missouri district with a roughly 6.5% African-American population. Although defense counsel "expressed a concern that venue be moved to a community where there was a possibility of blacks appearing on the jury," the trial court selected as the transfer district a rural county, located in the northernmost part of the state, in which only three African-Americans resided. The Missouri Supreme Court concluded that, in light of cases such as *Batson v. Kentucky*,[8] the choice of venue would constitute a denial of equal protection if the product of purposeful racial discrimination. The Court also concluded, however, that the *Batson* standard for establishing a prima facie case of intentional discrimination was of "limited usefulness" because of differences in the character of prosecutorial discretion in exercising peremptory challenges and judicial discretion in selecting a transfer district. A prima facie case was not otherwise established because the facts surrounding the transfer indicated that the judge's objective simply was "to get the case moved as far north as possible where reports of Trooper Froemsdorf's killing may have received less attention." Since "there was not the slightest suggestion that race was a consideration in the decision to change venue," there was no need to rely on the trial judge's affidavit, explaining the change, but that affidavit, the Missouri Court noted, would have constituted "extremely forceful rebuttal evidence" to any prima facie case. Dissenting from a denial of certiorari in *Mallet*,[9] United States Supreme Court Justice Thurgood Marshall (joined by Justices Blackmun and Brennan) concluded that the *Batson* standard for establishing a prima facie case applied under the circumstances of the case. However, as long as the trial court is deemed to have no obligation to seek out a county with a jury pool similar to that of the county of the crime, that court certainly would have rebutted such a prima facie case with an appropriate "race neutral explanation" if, as the Missouri Supreme Court concluded, the court simply had sought to move the trial as far away from the source of adverse publicity as possible.

7.   769 S.W.2d 77 (Mo.1989).

8.   See § 22.3(d).

9.   494 U.S. 1009, 110 S.Ct. 1308, 108 L.Ed.2d 484 (1990).

Chapter 17

THE SCOPE OF THE PROSECUTION: JOINDER AND SEVERANCE

Table of Sections

§ 17.1 Joinder and Severance of Offenses

(a) Joinder: Related Offenses. It is commonly provided that offenses committed at the same time and place or are otherwise related to one another may be joined together so that the defendant may be prosecuted for all of them in a single trial. In the federal system, for example, offenses may be so joined if they are "based on the same act or transaction, or are connected with or constitute parts of a common scheme or plan."[1] The overwhelming majority of states have adopted the federal language or something very close to it, while most of the other jurisdictions either use some other formulation to describe offenses that may be joined because related in their commission or else ensure related offense joinder by virtue of some much broader joinder rule.

§ 17.1

1. Fed.R.Crim.P. 8(a).

A brief look at the manner in which the federal provision has been interpreted provides some insight into what are likely to be viewed as related offenses for joinder purposes. Under the "same transaction" test, it is proper to join a conspiracy charge with a substantive offense committed in furtherance of the conspiracy, or to join offenses that are closely related in that they were interrelated parts of a particular criminal episode. But under the general notion that the offenses must arise out of the same sequence of events, it is sufficient that they were occurring simultaneously but yet not part of a common scheme. As for the "common scheme or plan" part of the federal provision, it will permit joinder of offenses that may not be close together in a time-space sense but that may be viewed as facets of a general criminal undertaking. The "connected with" part of the test, by contrast, focuses more upon the time-space relationship between the crimes and does not require that the crimes be connected in terms of their motivation.[2]

The provisions permitting joinder of related offenses have generally been viewed with favor by both the prosecution and the defendant: The state can avoid the duplication of evidence required by separate trials, reduce the inconvenience to victims and witnesses, and minimize the time required to dispose of the offenses. The defendant can avoid the harassment, trauma, expense, and prolonged publicity of multiple trials, obtain faster disposition of all cases, and increase the possibility of concurrent sentences in the event of conviction.

(b) Joinder: Offenses of Similar Character. In the federal system, it is also permissible to join offenses for disposition in a single trial of the defendant if those offenses are "of the same or similar character."[3] About half of the states have adopted the federal language, while a few others utilize language that should produce nearly the same result.

Under a provision allowing joinder of offenses of the same or similar character, it is permissible to join together several instances of the same crime, such as bank robbery, though they were committed by the defendant at distinct times and places and not as part of a single scheme. But the mere fact that the crimes carry different labels is not determinative of the joinder issue, as if they have "a general likeness" they are still of similar character.

Joinder of offenses of the same or similar character has its advantages. For one thing, it also helps save judicial and prosecutorial resources. The defendant may prefer the disadvantages of joinder to the delay, and expense of multiple prosecutions especially because disposal of all of the charges in a single prosecution may facilitate concurrent sentencing and will avoid the possibility of a detainer being filed against him for offenses not tried. But some have strongly criticized this form of joinder. It is said that the savings to the government are substantially reduced because unrelated offenses normally involve different times, separate locations, and distinct sets of witnesses and victims. Moreover, the joint trial of offenses creates a significant risk that the jury will convict the defendant upon the weight of the accusations or upon the accumulated effect of the evidence.

(c) Severance: Separate Defenses. In the federal system, offenses which have been joined for trial will be severed, so that they will be tried separately, if the joinder "appears to prejudice a defendant or the government."[4] State laws also provide for severance of offenses where otherwise a party would be prejudiced or where it would be in the interest of justice and for good cause shown. With respect to prejudice of the defendant, it is likely to fall into one of three categories: (1) he may become embarrassed or confounded in presenting separate defenses; (2) the jury may use the evidence of one of the crimes charged to infer

---

2. While a literal reading of rule 8(a) in its present form, quoted in note 1 supra, would not appear to produce this conclusion, such a result was reached under earlier language covering "acts or transactions connected togeth-er," and the subsequent change in the rule's language was intended to be stylistic only.

3. Fed.R.Crim.P. 8(a).

4. Fed.R.Crim.P. 14.

a criminal disposition on the part of the defendant from which is found his guilt of the other crime or crimes charged; or (3) the jury may cumulate the evidence of the various crimes charged and find guilt when, if considered separately it would not so find.

As for the first of these, one type of case is that discussed in *Cross v. United States*[5]:

> Prejudice may develop when an accused wishes to testify on one but not the other of two joined offenses which are clearly distinct in time, place and evidence. His decision whether to testify will reflect a balancing of several factors with respect to each count: the evidence against him, the availability of defense evidence other than his testimony, the plausibility and substantiality of his testimony, the possible effects of demeanor, impeachment, and cross-examination. But if the two charges are joined for trial, it is not possible for him to weigh these factors separately as to each count. If he testifies on one count, he runs the risk that any adverse effects will influence the jury's consideration of the other count. Thus he bears the risk on both counts, although he may benefit on only one. Moreover, a defendant's silence on one count would be damaging in the face of his express denial of the other. Thus, he may be coerced into testifying on the count upon which he wished to remain silent.

In *Cross,* the court was satisfied that the defendant was "embarrassed or confounded," for his alibi testimony as to one robbery charge led to his acquittal, but "to avoid the damaging implication of testifying on only one of the two joined counts" he had given "dubious testimony" concerning the other robbery count and had been convicted of that charge. However, *Cross* has not been interpreted as requiring the granting of a severance whenever a defendant asserts a desire to testify on one count and not another. Absent prejudice, it is not a violation of the Fifth Amendment privilege against self-incrimination to require a defendant to elect to testify as to both charges or to none at all. And the burden is on the defendant to show that a joint trial would be prejudicial, so that no need for a severance exists until the defendant makes a convincing showing that he has both important testimony to give concerning one count and strong need to refrain from testifying on the other.

(d) Severance: Evidence of Other Crimes. As a general matter, the prosecution may not admit at the trial of a defendant on one charge evidence that this defendant has on another occasion committed some other crime. This established rule of evidence[6] rests upon two very legitimate concerns: (1) that the jury may convict a "bad man" who deserves to be punished because of his other misdeeds; and (2) that the jury might infer from the defendant's other crimes that he probably committed the crime charged as well. Because the same dangers exist when two crimes are joined for trial, courts have had to confront the question of whether a defendant must be granted a severance so that the jury trying the defendant on each of the crimes charged does not have available to it evidence of these other crimes. A leading case on this issue is *Drew v. United States,*[7] concluding that the answer depends upon (i) whether evidence of the other crimes would be admissible even if a severance was granted; and (ii) if not, whether the evidence of each crime is simple and distinct.

As for the first of these, the essential point is that there are several limited exceptions to the other-crimes-as-evidence prohibition, and that if one of the exceptions applies to the case in question then (as the court put it in *Drew*) "the prejudice that might result from the jury's hearing the evidence of the other crime in a joint trial would be no different from that possible in separate trials." These exceptions are where the evidence of the other crime is offered as proof of motive, opportunity, intent, preparation, plan, knowledge, identity, or absence of mistake or accident, in which instances the evidence is admissible unless its probative value is substantially outweighed by the risk that its admission will result in unfair prejudice to the accused. In *Drew,* therefore,

---

5. 335 F.2d 987 (D.C.Cir.1964).

6. Fed.R.Evid. 404(b).

7. 331 F.2d 85 (D.C.Cir.1964).

where the two charges were of robbery and attempted robbery, respectively, of two High's neighborhood stores a few weeks apart, the first task of the court was to determine whether any of the aforementioned exceptions applied. The court concluded that the facts of the two crimes did "not show such a close similarity in the manner of committing the crimes as would make them admissible in separate trials," and thus further inquiry into defendant's prejudice claim was necessary. Had it been determined that evidence of the joined offense would have been received in any event under an exception to the "other crimes" rule, that would be the end of the inquiry.

As for the "simple and distinct" part of the inquiry, the court in *Drew* explained that it rested "upon the assumption that, with a proper charge, the jury can easily keep such evidence separate in their deliberations and, therefore, the danger of the jury's cumulating the evidence is substantially reduced." But because the record in the instant case reflected repeated confusion as to which of the two crimes was being referred to, the court concluded defendant had been prejudiced by the joinder. By contrast, in other cases where the crimes charged were sufficiently distinct in nature that such confusion did not occur, no prejudice has been found.

(e) Severance: Cumulation of Evidence. Although the possibility that the joinder may have prejudiced the defendant by causing the jury to cumulate the evidence against him has been recognized in *Drew* and other cases, relief is seldom obtained on this basis. If the trial judge is not moved to grant a severance on this basis, it is especially unlikely that appellate relief will be forthcoming; weighing the danger of confusion and undue cumulative inference is a matter for the trial judge within his sound discretion. The defendant's chances may be somewhat better if in addition it is shown that he was convicted on a count as to which the evidence was relatively weak. Absent that, appellate courts are inclined to accept unquestionably the notion that an instruction to the jury not to cumulate the evidence will avoid any prejudice.

(f) Severance as of Right. Defendants generally have not fared very well under rules and statutes permitting them to obtain a severance of offenses only upon proof of prejudice. For one thing, it is very difficult for the trial judge to make a finding on the prejudice issue before trial, for it involves speculation about many things that may or may not occur. Also, judges are understandably reluctant to make a finding of prejudice during trial, after the prosecution has put in most or all of its proof. And if the trial judge denies defendant's severance motion on the ground that a showing of prejudice has not been made, experience has shown that it is virtually impossible for the defendant to prevail on appeal. This has given rise to the proposal, reflected in recent law reform efforts, that severance of offenses should exist as a matter of right in many instances, which some states have adopted.

§ 17.2   Joinder and Severance of Defendants

(a) Joinder of Defendants. Statutes and rules of court commonly provide for the joinder of defendants, whereby two or more persons may together be prosecuted in a single trial. For example, in the federal courts the "indictment or information may charge 2 or more defendants if they are alleged to have participated in the same act or transaction, or in the same series of acts or transactions, constituting an offense or offenses. The defendants may be charged in one or more counts together or separately. All defendants need not be charged in each count."[1] The statutes and court rules in over a third of the states utilize this same language, while some others either add to that language or else employ wording of about the same specificity permitting either somewhat broader or somewhat narrower joinder than in the federal system. In other states, the effort has been to identify more specifically the situations in which joinder of defendants is permissible.

§ 17.2

1. Fed.R.Crim.P. 8(b).

A brief look at the way in which the federal provision quoted above has been construed will provide some insight into the kind of joinder of defendants likely to be permitted. At the outset, it is important to understand that the previously discussed joinder-of-offenses provision cannot somehow be read into the just-quoted joinder-of-defendants provision so as to produce the result that all offenses which could be joined as to a single defendant may likewise be joined as to multiple defendants. This means, the courts have held, that though defendant X could be jointly charged with crimes A and B because they are of the same or similar character, defendant X and Y may not together be jointly charged with crimes A and B. Assuming one accepts the principle of similar offense joinder, it is difficult to see why it is unobjectionable only when a single defendant is charged.

One fairly common situation falling within the federal joinder-of-defendants provision is that in which the several defendants are connected by virtue of a charged conspiratorial relationship. Thus, where the joined defendants are all charged in the conspiracy count and they or some of them are also charged with various substantive offenses alleged to have been committed in furtherance of the conspiracy, joinder is proper. But it would not be proper also to join offenses alleged to have been committed outside the conspiracy period or by defendants not parties to the conspiracy. Joinder where there are multiple conspiracies has been particularly troublesome. Such joinder is improper where nothing is shown except for a slight membership overlap between the conspiracies. But even a single common conspirator will suffice where in addition it appears that the two conspiracies are a series of acts or transactions, as where they both related to the common conspirator's gambling operations. In support of permitting joinder of several conspiracies involving different parties when they are so related that they constitute different aspects of a scheme of organized criminal conduct, it is argued that in the case of complex and far-flung networks of crime,

such a presentation may be essential to an understanding of the entire operation and the role played by each participant.

Even absent a conspiracy count, defendants may be joined together when their acts were part of a common plan, as where the offenses charged to less than all of the joined defendants were tied in with an underlying joint crime. This point can best be made by comparing the cases of *United States v. Roselli*[2] and *United States v. Granello*,[3] both involving the joinder of separate counts of income tax evasion against multiple defendants. The joinder was upheld in *Roselle* because the unreported income was derived from the defendants' joint gambling and racketeering activities. But in *Granello*, where each of the two defendants individually failed to report income from their lawful joint business venture, joinder was improper because the individual instances of nonreporting could not be said to be part of the "same series of acts or transactions."

Yet another basis for joining defendants is where their crimes are so closely connected in respect of time, place and occasion, that it would be difficult, if not impossible, to separate the proof of one charge from the proof of the other. This close connection is deemed a basis for joinder even absent proof of a common scheme—indeed, even when it is apparent that no such scheme exists. Thus, where the driver of a bus and the driver of an automobile have both been charged with the negligent homicide of a motorist whose car was struck by the other vehicles, these charges are properly joined. This is not to suggest, however, that joinder is proper whenever two defendants have separately committed similar crimes at about the same time and place. Thus, two defendants who happen to live in the same apartment building and who separately sold cocaine to the same individual may not be jointly charged.

(b) Severance: Codefendant's Confession Incriminates. Assume a case in which defendants A and B have been lawfully joined for trial, but at that trial the prosecution in-

2.   432 F.2d 879 (9th Cir.1970).

3.   365 F.2d 990 (2d Cir.1966).

tends to offer against *A* a confession by him stating, in effect, that he and *B* committed the crime. Although this confession is admissible only against *A* and not against *B*, a point on which the jury will be cautioned, is *B* entitled to a severance or some other relief? In *Delli Paoli v. United States*,[4] the Supreme Court answered this in the negative, reasoning that the jury could be trusted to follow these instructions. But *Delli Paoli* was later overruled in *Bruton v. United States*.[5] The Court in *Bruton* first noted it was dealing with a constitutional right, namely, the right of cross-examination, which it had previously held "is included in the right of an accused in a criminal case to confront the witnesses against him"[6] secured by the Sixth Amendment. That right would be violated if *A*, by his confession, was a witness against *B* but could not be cross-examined. Whether *A* was, in effect, such a witness depended upon the correctness of the assumption in *Delli Paoli*, which the Court now concluded was in error. As the Court explained,

> there are some contexts in which the risk that the jury will not, or cannot, follow instructions is so great, and the consequences of failure so vital to the defendant, that the practical and human limitations of the jury system cannot be ignored. * * * Such a context is presented here, where the powerfully incriminating extrajudicial statements of a codefendant, who stands accused side-by-side with the defendant, are deliberately spread before the jury in a joint trial. Not only are the incriminations devastating to the defendant but their credibility is inevitably suspect, a fact recognized when accomplices do take the stand and the jury is instructed to weigh their testimony carefully given the recognized motivation to shift blame onto others. The unreliability of such evidence is intolerably compounded when the alleged accomplice, as here, does not testify and cannot be tested by cross-examination. It was against such threats to a fair

trial that the Confrontation Clause was directed.

A significant limitation upon the *Bruton* rule was later recognized by a plurality of the Court in *Parker v. Randolph*,[7] a case involving what the court below had called "interlocking inculpatory confessions." Each of the three respondents had given confessions implicating the others, and all of these confessions had been admitted at the trial, which the plurality concluded made cross-examination something less than a constitutional imperative. The plurality reasoned that because "one can scarcely imagine evidence more damaging to his defense than his own admission of guilt," "the incriminating statements of a codefendant will seldom, if ever, be of the 'devastating' character referred to in *Bruton*." But the Court held otherwise in the 5–4 decision of *Cruz v. New York*,[8] reasoning:

> In fact, it seems to us that "interlocking" bears a positively inverse relationship to devastation. A codefendant's confession will be relatively harmless if the incriminating story it tells is different from that which the defendant himself is alleged to have told, but enormously damaging if it confirms, in all essential respects, the defendant's alleged confession. It might be otherwise if the defendant were *standing by* his confession, in which case it could be said that the codefendant's confession does no more than support the defendant's very own case. But in the real world of criminal litigation, the defendant is seeking to *avoid* his confession—on the ground that it was not accurately reported, or that it was not really true when made. * * * Quite obviously, what the "interlocking" nature of the codefendant's confession pertains to is not its *harmfulness* but rather its *reliability*: If it confirms essentially the same facts as the defendant's own confession it is more likely to be true. Its reliability, however, may be relevant to whether the confession should (despite the lack of oppor-

---

4. 352 U.S. 232, 77 S.Ct. 294, 1 L.Ed.2d 278 (1957).

5. 391 U.S. 123, 88 S.Ct. 1620, 20 L.Ed.2d 476 (1968).

6. Pointer v. Texas, 380 U.S. 400, 85 S.Ct. 1065, 13 L.Ed.2d 923 (1965).

7. 442 U.S. 62, 99 S.Ct. 2132, 60 L.Ed.2d 713 (1979).

8. 481 U.S. 186, 107 S.Ct. 1714, 95 L.Ed.2d 162 (1987).

tunity for cross-examination) be *admitted as evidence* against the defendant, but cannot conceivably be relevant to whether, assuming it cannot be admitted, the jury is likely to obey the instruction to disregard it, or the jury's failure to obey is likely to be inconsequential.

The Court in *Bruton*, emphasized the fact that "the hearsay statement inculpating petitioner was clearly inadmissible against him under traditional rules of evidence," and thus lower courts have concluded *Bruton* has no application when a statement by defendant's partner in crime is received under some exception to the hearsay rule. Illustrative are cases where the evidence was admissible because the statement was made by a co-conspirator during the course of and in furtherance of the conspiracy, was made in defendant's presence in circumstances where if it were not true a person would be expected to deny it (i.e., an "implied admission"), or fell within the admission against interest, spontaneous exclamation or business record exceptions to the hearsay rule. These decisions seem correct in light of *Dutton v. Evans*,[9] where the Supreme Court upheld the use of hearsay evidence in the form of a statement by a co-conspirator not on trial made during the concealment phase of the conspiracy.[10] Distinguishing *Bruton* because the instant case did not involve evidence that was "devastating" or "a confession made in the coercive atmosphere of official interrogation," the Court in *Dutton* held the admitted statement was "sufficiently clothed with 'indicia' of reliability" that it was properly "placed before the jury though there is no confrontation with the declarant." In short, the "right of confrontation * * * is not absolute."

Because *Bruton* is grounded upon denial of the constitutional right of confrontation, it governs only in those instances in which "effective confrontation" was not possible. Such was the case in *Bruton*, for the codefendant who made the confession did not take the stand. Though language in that case suggested that a sufficient confrontation opportunity would exist only if the codefendant took the stand *and* "affirmed the statement as his," that position was later rejected in *Nelson v. O'Neil*.[11] There, the codefendant took the stand, denied making the confession, and asserted that the substance of it was false, and the Court reasoned that this placed defendant in a "more favorable" situation than if the codefendant had affirmed the statement as his. The Court in *Nelson* thus held "that where a codefendant takes the stand in his own defense, denies making an alleged out-of-court statement implicating the defendant, and proceeds to testify favorably to the defendant concerning the underlying facts, the defendant has been denied no rights protected by the Sixth and Fourteenth Amendments."[12] But whether the codefendant admits or denies having made the statement, it has been questioned whether the opportunity for cross-examination sufficiently deals with the incriminated defendant's dilemma. So the argument goes, severance would be a much better remedy, for otherwise the fact remains that the jury will be considering as to that defendant evidence not admissible against him that has actually been highlighted by the cross-examination. Indeed, the cross-examination of one defendant by another may sometimes involve such conflict and antagonism between them that a severance will thereby be necessary.

---

9. 400 U.S. 74, 91 S.Ct. 210, 27 L.Ed.2d 213 (1970).

10. On the other hand, the statement of a co-conspirator not on trial is not admissible where given in response to police interrogation upon being told he had been implicated by another, as "a reality of the criminal process [is] that once partners in a crime recognize that the 'jig is up,' they tend to lose any identity of interest and immediately become antagonists, rather than accomplices." Lee v. Illinois, 476 U.S. 530, 106 S.Ct. 2056, 90 L.Ed.2d 514 (1986).

11. 402 U.S. 622, 91 S.Ct. 1723, 29 L.Ed.2d 222 (1971).

12. *Nelson* must be distinguished from *Lilly v. Virginia*, 527 U.S. 116, 119 S.Ct. 1887, 144 L.Ed.2d 117 (1999), where petitioner's accomplice in a 2–day crime spree, *not*

joined for trial with petitioner, was called by the prosecution as a witness and invoked his privilege against self-incrimination, after which the court admitted his confession to police, blaming petitioner for the homicide occurring during the spree, as a declaration of an unavailable witness against penal interest. While the state court affirmed defendant's confession on the ground that the accomplice's confession fell within an exception to the hearsay rule, the Supreme Court, although divided as to the breadth of the applicable rule, concluded that "admission of the untested confession" in such circumstances "violated petitioner's Confrontation Clause rights."

Though the lesson of *Nelson* is that ordinarily any *Bruton* problem is avoided if the maker of the confession testifies at trial, this is not inevitably the case. For example, if the two defendants are represented by the same attorney, he can hardly engage in effective cross-examination on behalf of one client without discrediting the other, and thus his decision not to cross-examine or to do so only pro forma would constitute a violation of the *Bruton* rule. Notwithstanding *Nelson,* it has been held that a sufficient opportunity for cross-examination may have been afforded even if the maker of the confession does not testify at the criminal trial. Specifically, such opportunity has been held to be present where the confessing codefendant testified at an earlier proceeding, such as a hearing on his motion to suppress the confession, and could have been cross-examined about the confession at that time. This result is supported by *California v. Green,*[13] where the Supreme Court held that a witness' "preliminary hearing testimony was admissible as far as the Constitution is concerned wholly apart from the question of whether respondent had an effective opportunity for confrontation at the subsequent trial," in that his "statement at the preliminary hearing had already been given under circumstances closely approximating those that surround the typical trial." Though there is language in *Green* supporting the dubious proposition that an earlier "opportunity to cross-examine" would suffice, the Court has more recently cautioned that it has not yet decided what the result should be where in fact there was no questioning or only de minimis questioning.[14] And in *Lee v. Illinois,*[15] the state's argument that it was sufficient that defendant could have examined the maker of the confession at the suppression hearing was rejected; because the "function of a suppres-

sion hearing is to determine the voluntariness * * * of a confession," as to which the "truth or falsity of the statement is not relevant," there really "was no opportunity to cross-examine [the maker] with respect to the reliability of that statement."

Because the *Bruton* rule was stated in terms of "a codefendant's confession inculpating the defendant," sometimes the question is whether that has occurred. The courts are generally rather demanding in that regard, insisting that the challenged statements must be clearly inculpatory. It is not enough, the Court concluded in *Richardson v. Marsh,*[16] that the codefendant's confession provides "evidentiary linkage," that is, information which by itself does not incriminate the other defendant but which does have some tendency to link him to the crime when considered together with other evidence admitted at the trial (there, that an intent-to-kill statement was uttered by an accomplice on the way to the crime while the implicated defendant was, by his own testimony, in the car with the others). In refusing to extend *Bruton* to such a situation, the majority reasoned (i) that jury instructions, deemed insufficient in a true *Bruton* situation, would suffice as to the risk of mere "inferential incrimination"; (ii) that the pretrial redaction solution would not work in an "evidentiary linkage" case because the linkage would be apparent only at the conclusion of the case; and (iii) that the solution of severance in all cases of potential "evidentiary linkage" "would impair both the efficiency and the fairness of the criminal justice system."

Assuming now that a case falling within *Bruton* is identified in a pretrial setting, the question remaining is what alternative remedies exist.[17] One, of course, is severance of the

13. 399 U.S. 149, 90 S.Ct. 1930, 26 L.Ed.2d 489 (1970).

14. Ohio v. Roberts, 448 U.S. 56, 100 S.Ct. 2531, 65 L.Ed.2d 597 (1980).

15. 476 U.S. 530, 106 S.Ct. 2056, 90 L.Ed.2d 514 (1986).

16. 481 U.S. 200, 107 S.Ct. 1702, 95 L.Ed.2d 176 (1987).

17. In slightly different circumstances there may be no remedy other than jury instructions. Illustrative is Tennessee v. Street, 471 U.S. 409, 105 S.Ct. 2078, 85 L.Ed.2d

425 (1985), where Street testified at trial that his confession to murder and burglary had been coerced by the sheriff reading to him the prior confession of severed codefendant Peele and then directing Street to say the same thing. Peele's confession was then admitted in rebuttal to show the several differences in the two confessions. The Court, after concluding that use of Peele's confession for this "legitimate, nonhearsay purpose" itself "raises no Confrontation Clause concerns," noted that the "only similarity to *Bruton* is that Peele's statement, like the codefendant's confession in *Bruton,* could have been mis-

implicated defendant. Another is a joint trial at which the prosecution elects to make no use of the confession. Yet another possibility is a joint trial at which the confession is admitted after it has been "redacted," that is, edited so as to delete any reference to the other defendant. But this solution will often not be feasible. For one thing, the maker of the confession is entitled to object if it is edited in such a way as to change its sense to his detriment, as where the deletion would leave out his claim of a valid defense. For another, the deletion must be effective in terms of removing a reference that will be perceived by the jury as referring to the codefendant. And thus in *Gray v. Maryland*,[18] the Court held that a "redaction that replaces a defendant's name with an obvious indication of deletion, such as a blank space, the word 'deleted,' or a similar symbol, still falls within *Bruton's* protective rule." This, the Court explained, is because (i) "a jury will often react similarly to a unredacted confession and a confession redacted in this way, for the jury will often realize that the confession refers specifically to the defendant"; (ii) "the obvious deletion may well call the juror's attention specially to the removed name," thus "encouraging the jury to speculate about the reference"; and (iii) "*Bruton's* protected statements and statements redacted to leave a blank or some other similar obvious alteration, function the same way grammatically," as both "are directly accusatory." As for the state's reliance on *Richardson*, the Court distinguished that case because it involved practical problems not present here and its "inferences involved statements that did not refer directly to the defendant," while the "inferences at issue here involve statements that, despite redaction, obviously refer directly to someone, often obviously the defendant."

Still other remedies for a *Bruton*-type confession have been used on occasion but have not been viewed with enthusiasm by appellate courts. One is a bifurcated joint trial at which the confession is withheld until the jury returns a verdict as to the implicated codefendant, and another is a joint trial utilizing a separate jury for each defendant that is allowed to be present only when evidence admissible against that defendant is received.

(c) Severance: Codefendant's Testimony Would Exculpate. A situation in some respects the reverse of that just discussed involves a request by one defendant for the severance of another defendant so that the latter can be called as a defense witness in the trial of the former. Even assuming such testimony is needed, the granting of a severance may be the only way by which it can be obtained. One defendant may not compel another defendant to testify in a joint trial. Moreover, the other individual is unlikely to want to give favorable testimony for his codefendant in a joint trial, for there are many tactical reasons why a defendant would wisely elect not to take the stand.

The seminal case on this subject is *United States v. Echeles*,[19] which provides a useful illustration. An attorney and his client were jointly charged with suborning perjury and perjury, respectively. In earlier proceedings involving the client, he had said that the attorney had not advised him to commit perjury. Consequently, the attorney asked for a severance so that the client could so testify at his trial, but the government opposed the motion and argued that there was no assurance the client would give such testimony even if the severance were granted. The appellate court held it was error to deny the attorney's severance motion, stating that "a fair trial for Echeles necessitated providing him the *oppor-*

used by the jury." However, the Court concluded that in the present context the trial court's limiting instruction—that Peele's confession was to be considered "for the purpose of rebuttal only"—constituted an "appropriate way to limit the jury's use of that evidence in a manner consistent with the Confrontation Clause." This was because here, "unlike the situation in *Bruton*, there were no alternatives that would have both assured the integrity of the trial's truthseeking function and eliminated the risk of

the jury's improper use of evidence." The already-granted severance did not solve the problem, and redaction of Peele's confession "would have made it more difficult for the jury to evaluate" Street's claim that his confession was a coerced imitation of Peele's.

18. 523 U.S. 185, 118 S.Ct. 1151, 140 L.Ed.2d 294 (1998).

19. 352 F.2d 892 (7th Cir.1965).

tunity of getting the [client's] evidence before the jury, regardless of how we might regard the credibility of that witness or the weight of his testimony."

Although some other courts have viewed such severance requests sympathetically, in the main courts have viewed such tactics as an alibi-swapping device not to be encouraged. As a consequence, most courts place a much heavier burden upon the requesting defendant, typically requiring him to show that he would call the codefendant at a severed trial, that the codefendant would in fact testify, and that the testimony would be favorable to the moving defendant. This often is not an easy burden to meet. For one thing, the severance would not likely produce the testimony unless the defendant who is to give the testimony has already been tried, for if he has not yet been tried his testimony could be used against him at his later trial even if he does not then take the stand. By the simple device of declaring that a defendant seeking a severance has no right to dictate the order in which the two cases would be tried if severed, courts have been able to conclude that the requesting defendant has not carried his burden. Moreover, even if the testifying defendant *is* tried first, this alone will not inevitably wipe out any basis for his later claiming reliance upon the privilege against self-incrimination, and it does not seem that this defendant can somehow be forced to waive his privilege and promise to testify as a condition of the severance being granted. Based upon such considerations, courts often deny these severance motions because it has not been shown that the severed defendant would in fact testify when called upon to do so. Secondly, the moving defendant may be unable even to show the testimony sought would be favorable. *Echeles* was a unique case because the codefendant's exoneration of his attorney was already a matter of record. Absent that, the moving defendant will have to do more than file conclusory affidavits that exculpatory testimony would be forthcoming, but may be confronted by the other defendant's reluctance to reveal the nature of his testimony. Finally, the moving defendant may

be unable to establish that the testimony is sufficiently important, which is especially likely when courts reach the highly questionable conclusion that it is not enough that the testimony would corroborate other defense evidence.

(d) Severance: Conflicting Defenses and Strategies. The joint trial of defendants who truly have antagonistic defenses is most unfair, and thus the remedy of severance is needed to prevent the kind of trial described by one appellate court: "The trial was in many respects more of a contest between the defendants than between the people and the defendants. It produced a spectacle where the people frequently stood by and witnessed a combat in which the defendants attempted to destroy each other."[20] This is not to suggest, however, that a severance will necessarily be granted even when there is a rather significant difference between the defensive posture of the several defendants. It is common doctrine that a severance is necessary only if the defenses are mutually exclusive (i.e., that belief of one compels disbelief of the other), and that the mere fact that there is hostility between defendants or that one may try to save himself at the expense of another is alone not sufficient grounds to require separate trials. Similarly, it has been asserted that the fact the defendants have conflicting versions of what took place or the extent to which they participated is a reason for rather than against a joint trial because it is easier for the truth to be determined if all are required to be tried together. Though courts in some jurisdictions are more sympathetic to antagonistic defense claims, often a failure to grant a severance motion will not be deemed error unless the defendants were directly accusing one another. The mere fact that the joined defendants have conflicting strategies is unlikely to be viewed as mandating an affirmative ruling on a severance motion.

As for a federal defendant's right to severance under Fed.R.Crim.P.14, the Supreme

---

20. People v. Braune, 363 Ill. 551, 2 N.E.2d 839 (1936).

Court in *Zafiro v. United States*[21] took a strict view: "Defendants are not entitled to severance merely because they may have a better chance of acquittal in separate trials" or "whenever codefendants have conflicting defenses." Rather, a court should grant a severance "only if there is a serious risk that a joint trial would compromise a specific trial right of one of the defendants, or prevent the jury from making a reliable judgment about guilt or innocence." Moreover, the Court added, even if a defendant makes out a showing of "some risk of prejudice," the remedy of severance is unnecessary if that prejudice "is of the type that can be cured with proper instructions," which "juries are presumed to follow."

Another kind of conflict situation is represented by *De Luna v. United States*.[22] There, de Luna and Gomez, after denial of a severance motion, were jointly tried on a narcotics charge. They were the occupants of a moving car from which police had seen Gomez throw a package of narcotics. Gomez testified that he was innocent, explaining that de Luna had thrown the package to him and told him to throw it out the window when the police approached. De Luna did not testify, but his lawyer argued that Gomez had the package at all times. Gomez's attorney commented on de Luna's failure to take the stand, and Gomez was acquitted but de Luna was convicted. On appeal his conviction was reversed because of the violation of his privilege against self-incrimination. But two members of the court went on to say that under these circumstances the proper result below would have been to permit the comment and grant severance. This was because Gomez's "attorneys should be free to draw all rational inferences from the failure of a co-defendant to testify, just as an attorney is free to comment on the effect of any interested party's failure to produce material evidence in his possession or to call witnesses who have knowledge of pertinent facts."

But *De Luna* has had a limited impact. For one thing, it has been deemed not to require a severance when the defense attorney for the other defendant has merely called attention to the fact that his client had taken the stand, for in such instance it is thought to be a sufficient remedy that the defendant who elected not to testify could have a jury instruction in support of his exercise of the privilege. For another, some courts have held that "*De Luna* applies only when it is counsel's *duty* to make a comment" and that such duty arises only when the defenses are clearly antagonistic. Still others have rejected *De Luna* on the ground that its reasoning is defective. So the argument goes, there are no "rational inferences" to be drawn from a codefendant's silence, for, as the Supreme Court instructed in *Griffin v. California*,[23] even one "entirely innocent of the charge against him" might have a good reason[24] for staying off the stand. Moreover, a similar tactic could not have been utilized had there been a severance at the outset, for it is improper to call a witness it is known will claim his privilege against self-incrimination and then require him to make that claim in the presence of the jury.

(e) Severance: Guilt by Association. One of the inherent risks attending the joint trial of criminal defendants is that some defendants might be convicted only because of their association with others who were proved guilty at that trial. As Justice Jackson stated in his oft-quoted opinion in *Krulewitch v. United States*[25]: "There generally will be evidence of wrongdoing by somebody. It is difficult for the individual to make his own case stand on its own merits in the minds of jurors who are ready to believe that birds of a feather are flocked together." This is obviously so, but it is equally obvious that a defendant who shows no more than this common risk will not have

---

21. 506 U.S. 534, 113 S.Ct. 933, 122 L.Ed.2d 317 (1993).

22. 308 F.2d 140 (5th Cir.1962).

23. 380 U.S. 609, 85 S.Ct. 1229, 14 L.Ed.2d 106 (1965).

24. "Excessive timidity, nervousness when facing others and attempting to explain transactions of a suspicious character, and offenses charged against him, will often confuse and embarrass him to such a degree as to increase rather than remove prejudices against him." Wilson v. United States, 149 U.S. 60, 13 S.Ct. 765, 37 L.Ed. 650 (1893), quoted in *Griffin*.

25. 336 U.S. 440, 69 S.Ct. 716, 93 L.Ed. 790 (1949).

established the prejudice which would entitle him to a severance. The harm from being so tainted would seem to be greatest as to relatively minor participants, but, while they may occasionally be held entitled to relief, there is certainly no general willingness to free minor figures from the risks and burdens of standing trial with more culpable associates.

A guilt-by-association claim takes on somewhat more substance when it is shown that highly prejudicial evidence admissible only against a co-defendant was or will be admitted at the joint trial. One situation is where a defendant is joined with another defendant whose substantial criminal record was admitted or will be admitted at trial. A few jurisdictions mandate severance in such circumstances, but most states approach the problem on an ad hoc basis and require the defendant to show actual prejudice before compelling severance. A *Bruton*-type analysis[26] would seem appropriate here, though it is well to note that unlike a *Bruton* confession, prior act evidence is not so inevitably prejudicial to co-defendants that the worth of limiting instructions can be totally discounted.

(f) Severance: Confusion of Evidence. Yet another basis upon which a severance of defendants might be sought is to avoid confusion by the fact-finder. If the case is so confusing that the trier of fact cannot be expected to keep straight the evidence relating to the various defendants and counts, then surely a severance should be granted. But in face of the almost certain lack of evidence that the jury was actually confused, a defendant's complaint on appeal is likely to be dismissed as in *Opper v. United States*[27]: "To say that the jury might have been confused amounts to nothing more than an unfounded speculation that the jurors disregarded clear instructions of the court in arriving at their verdict." A claim of confusion may receive somewhat readier acceptance as the other disadvantages of joinder, such as guilt by association, also become apparent.

(g) Severance as of Right. At one time, nearly half of the jurisdictions granted crimi-

nal defendants a severance as a matter of right, but now only a very few statutes so provide. Some have argued, however, that the uncertain benefits of joint trials and the mischief they so frequently work justify a statute or rule of court giving defendants rights to separate trials. Underlying the assumption that joint trials are more economical and minimize the burden of witnesses, prosecutors, and courts is the expectation that if defendants had a right of severance then each defendant would undergo a separate trial. But experience in at least one jurisdiction is to the contrary; what has ordinarily happened there is that upon conviction of one defendant at the first trial the severed defendants are induced to negotiate a guilty plea. Another consideration is that defendants generally have not fared well under rules requiring proof of prejudice: it is difficult to ascertain the degree of prejudice in advance of trial; once the trial is under way there is great reluctance to grant a severance and allow some defendants a fresh start; and on appeal there is even greater reluctance to find the trial judge's denial of the motion erroneous.

§ 17.3 Joinder and Severance: Procedural Considerations

(a) Court's Authority to Consolidate and Sever. Whether offenses or defendants are initially joined together for trial is a matter determined by the prosecuting attorney (or, in the case of an indictment, the prosecutor and the grand jury). If a defendant believes that the prosecutor has joined together offenses or defendants beyond that permitted by law, he may by motion challenge the prosecutor's action as misjoinder. Or, as we have seen, if a defendant believes the lawful joinder would be prejudicial to him in some way, he may seek a severance of offenses or of defendants. On occasion, the prosecutor may move for severance of offenses or defendants he had originally joined. Although it has occasionally been held that a prosecutor should not be granted a severance for lack of evidence, that

---

26. See § 17.2(b).

27. 348 U.S. 84, 75 S.Ct. 158, 99 L.Ed. 101 (1954).

position has been strongly criticized as running contrary to speedy trial interests.

Though the court must of course rule upon motions made by the prosecutor and defendant, the court also has authority of its own in determining what the scope of a pending trial will be. For one thing, the court will likely be empowered to consolidate existing charges. In the federal system, for example, the court "may order that separate cases be tried together as though brought in a single indictment or information if all offenses and all defendants could have been joined in a single indictment or information."[1] Many states have comparable provisions, while elsewhere case law recognizes this authority as within the inherent power of the court. Under the better view, the court also has the power to order a severance, even when such action has not been specifically requested by either the prosecution or a defendant, because of the court's responsibility for the orderly progress of the trial.

(b) Misjoinder. The term "misjoinder" refers to the inclusion within a single charge of offenses or defendants the law does not permit to be joined together. An apt illustration under the law of virtually all jurisdictions would be an instance in which a single indictment includes two offenses that are neither similar in character nor part of a single scheme or otherwise connected together in their commission. Misjoinder must be distinguished from certain other charging defects. It is different from "duplicity," the joining in a single count of two or more distinct and separate offenses, and from "multiplicity," the charging of a single offense in several counts. As to these latter two defects, the defendant is entitled upon timely demand to require the prosecution to elect which offense or which count, respectively, will be relied upon. By contrast, in the case of misjoinder the remedy is a separate trial of the misjoined offenses or defendants. What these three defects have in common is that neither duplicity, multiplicity,

nor misjoinder constitutes grounds for dismissal of the charge.

Where a misjoinder has been shown to exist, in contrast to the case in which the joinder was initially proper but a severance is sought on grounds of prejudice, the trial judge has no discretion to deny a motion for severance. But there is not complete agreement on the question of whether a failure to grant the motion should inevitably require reversal on appeal. There was for years a split in the federal courts, but this conflict was resolved in *United States v. Lane*,[2] holding that "misjoinder under rule 8 of the Federal Rules of Criminal Procedure is subject to the harmless-error rule." The Court stressed that the argument for harmless error, applicable to most constitutional violations,[3] "is even stronger [here] because the specific joinder standards of Rule 8 are not themselves of constitutional magnitude"; and rather questionably opined that *Schaffer* (discussed below) applied here because in that case, once the court found the evidence to be insufficient on the count supporting joinder, there was "at that point in the trial * * * a clear error of misjoinder."

(c) Failure to Prove Joinder Basis. The misjoinder situation discussed above, must be distinguished from that in which the charge is not defective on its face but at trial there is a failure to prove some fact on which the joinder rested. This might be the case, for example, where the conspiracy charge fails completely, or as to a particular defendant, the conspiracy charged turns out to be several unrelated conspiracies, or two offenses alleged to be related turn out to be independent of one another. In such circumstances, it must be asked whether an affected defendant is entitled to relief equivalent to that in the misjoinder situation, to consideration for relief under some less demanding standard, or is entitled to no relief at all.

This question split the Supreme Court 5–4 in *Schaffer v. United States*.[4] The four-count indictment in that case charged: (1) that peti-

§ 17.3
1. Fed.R.Crim.P. 13.
2. 474 U.S. 438, 106 S.Ct. 725, 88 L.Ed.2d 814 (1986).

3. See § 27.6(c).
4. 362 U.S. 511, 80 S.Ct. 945, 4 L.Ed.2d 921 (1960).

tioners and the Stracuzzas transported stolen goods; (2) that Marco and the Stracuzzas transported other stolen goods; (3) that Karp and the Stracuzzas transported still other stolen goods; and (4) that all of them were joined in a single conspiracy to commit such offenses. At the close of the government's case the court dismissed the conspiracy count, but permitted the trial to proceed on the other counts. In affirming the petitioners' conviction, the *Schaffer* majority asserted that the validity of the joinder was to be determined solely by the allegations in the indictment and that consequently the issue was not one of misjoinder but rather whether a severance should have been ordered on grounds of prejudice. Because "the proof was carefully compartmentalized as to each petitioner," the Court concluded that the trial judge properly concluded no prejudice was present. While cautioning that in such circumstances "a trial judge should be particularly sensitive to the possibility of such prejudice," the majority in *Schaffer* declined to adopt "a hard-and-fast formula that, when a conspiracy count fails, joinder is error as a matter of law." The four dissenters, on the other hand, while stressing the potential for prejudice in such circumstances, challenged the majority's major premise. For them, an allegation in the charge is a sufficient basis for judging the validity of joinder only "at the preliminary stages," as "once it becomes apparent during the trial that the defendants have not participated 'in the same series' of transactions, it would make a mockery of Rule 8(b) to hold that the allegation alone, now known to be false, is enough to continue the joint trial."

One view of the *Schaffer* rule is that it may have the effect of encouraging an unscrupulous prosecutor to frame a baseless conspiracy count in order that several defendants, accused of similar but unrelated offenses, may be tried together. This is a legitimate concern, also reflected in the post-*Schaffer* authority that reversal would be required if bringing the conspiracy charge constituted bad faith on the part of the prosecutor in the sense that he lacked a reasonable expectation that sufficient proof of the charge would be forthcoming at

trial. It is not easy for a defendant to show such bad faith.

The other view is that the *Schaffer* minority's position is unsound because such a rigid sanction would require the prosecutor to undertake new trials even when there had been no prejudice. Moreover, the dissent's argument, in practice, might militate against the very result it seeks to achieve as a trial judge facing such a rigid rule might be extremely reluctant to dismiss the charge upon which joinder is founded.

The *Schaffer* situation must be distinguished from that in which the evidence *was* sufficient to go to the jury, but the jury then acquitted on the count that was the basis upon which the other counts were joined. In such circumstances, it is clear that the acquittal does not affect the propriety of joinder. As was conceded by the *Schaffer* dissenters, in such a case there "is then no escape from the quandary in which defendants find themselves. Once the conspiracy is supported by evidence, it presents issues for the jury to decide. What may motivate a particular jury in returning a verdict of not guilty on the conspiracy count may never be known."

(d) Waiver or Forfeiture. A defendant can lose his rights under joinder and severance law by failing to assert them in a timely fashion. This is true even in the instances of misjoinder; a defendant is thus well advised to raise that issue by pretrial motion, though a motion at trial would suffice at least when the circumstances establishing the misjoinder only then emerged. Misjoinder claims raised for the first time on appeal will not ordinarily be considered, though an exception may be made when the record reveals some circumstance explaining why the issue was not raised earlier.

Likewise, a claim that a severance should have been granted to avoid prejudice may be lost for failure to assert it in a timely fashion. Certainly a motion for severance is appropriate in advance of trial. However, in a pretrial setting the motion often can be assessed only in terms of the potential for prejudice, while events later occurring at trial may provide something more concrete in terms of actual prejudice. Thus the fact a pretrial motion has been denied is no reason for not renewing the motion during the course of the trial. Indeed, failure to do so may operate to the defendant's detriment in one of several ways. While the Supreme Court in *Schaffer v. United States*[5] spoke of the trial judge's "continuing duty at all stages of the trial to grant a severance if prejudice does appear," this does not mean that a pretrial severance motion previously ruled upon somehow remains open for reconsideration without further efforts by the defendant. Failure to renew the motion at trial may be treated as a waiver of any severance claim, or at a minimum is likely to limit appellate review to the question of whether the judge properly decided the pretrial motion on the facts then available to him.

(e) Appellate Review of Prejudice Claim. On appeal, the defendant has the burden of showing that he was prejudiced by the joinder, and a reversal will ordinarily be forthcoming only if it appears there was a clear abuse of discretion by the trial judge. Appellate courts have traditionally relied on four doctrines to support a finding of absence or prejudice through joinder and to justify denial of relief. One is that the judge's instructions sufficed to confine the evidence to one offense or one defendant. But the Supreme Court has rejected it in one setting,[6] and it is dubious in other joinder contexts as well. It is not generally realistic to expect jurors to ignore relevant data once they have heard it, and limiting instructions are likely to do more harm by emphasizing the challenged evidence than good by erasing it. A second doctrine is that if the jury convicted as to some counts or defendants but not as to others, this shows that the jury carefully examined each count as to each defendant and rendered its verdict accordingly. But this ignores the possibility that absent the prejudicial joinder the jury might have acquitted on more counts or on all counts, and the same may be said for the third doctrine that any prejudice has been cured by concurrent

sentencing. The fourth doctrine is that any prejudice is deemed harmless if, putting the prejudicial information to one side, defendant *could* still have been convicted on the balance of the evidence. But this involves considerable speculation as to what the jury would have done under other circumstances.

§ 17.4 Failure to Join Related Offenses

(a) Collateral Estoppel. Usually the prosecutor will be in favor of as much joinder of offenses and defendants as he can get, while the defendant will want as much severance as can be obtained. But sometimes the prosecutor will want to maintaining the opportunity to proceed with multiple trials, while the defendant prefers a prompt and unified disposition of all charges—or, if such a disposition is not undertaken, a bar to any subsequent related prosecutions. One possibility, discussed in the following subsections, is that on constitutional or other grounds a prosecution will be barred because of the failure of the prosecutor to join that charge with one earlier prosecuted. Another, of concern here, is that a verdict or finding of guilty in the second prosecution will be barred because it would be inconsistent with the result reached in the first prosecution.

This last notion, which goes by the name of "collateral estoppel," was given constitutional status in *Ashe v. Swenson*.[1] There, four armed men broke into the basement of a house and robbed six poker players and then fled in the car belonging to one of the victims. Ashe and three others were arrested shortly thereafter, and he and the others were charged with seven separate offenses—robbery of each of the poker players and theft of the car. Ashe was put on trial for robbery of victim Knight. The proof that the robbery had occurred was unassailable, but the evidence that Ashe was one of the robbers was weak. The defense never questioned the testimony about the occurrence of the robbery, but concentrated on exposing

5. 362 U.S. 511, 80 S.Ct. 945, 4 L.Ed.2d 921 (1960).

6. Bruton v. United States, 391 U.S. 123, 88 S.Ct. 1620, 20 L.Ed.2d 476 (1968).

§ 17.4

1. 397 U.S. 436, 90 S.Ct. 1189, 25 L.Ed.2d 469 (1970).

weaknesses in the identification of Ashe. The case went to the jury with instructions that if Ashe was in the group participating in this scheme he would be guilty whether or not he personally took the money from this particular victim; the jury returned a verdict of not guilty. Over his objection, Ashe was then tried for robbery of victim Roberts. The witnesses, essentially the same as in the prior trial, were now more certain of Ashe's identity, and Ashe was convicted. The Supreme Court reversed, reasoning:

> "Collateral estoppel" is an awkward phrase, but it stands for an extremely important principle in our adversary system of justice. It means simply that when an issue of ultimate fact has once been determined by a valid and final judgment, that issue cannot again be litigated between the same parties in any future lawsuit. Although first developed in civil litigation, collateral estoppel has been an established rule of federal criminal law [for] more than 50 years. * * *
>
> Straightforward application of the federal rule to the present case can lead to but one conclusion. For the record is utterly devoid of any indication that the first jury could rationally have found that an armed robbery had not occurred, or that Knight had not been a victim of that robbery. The single rationally conceivable issue in dispute before the jury was whether the petitioner had been one of the robbers. And the jury by its verdict found that he had not. The federal rule of law, therefore, would make a second prosecution for the robbery of Roberts wholly impermissible.
>
> The ultimate question to be determined, then, * * * is whether this established rule of federal law is embodied in the Fifth Amendment guarantee against double jeopardy. We do not hesitate to hold that it is. For whatever else that constitutional guarantee may embrace, * * * it surely protects

a man who has been acquitted from having to "run the gauntlet" a second time.

Although *Ashe* represents an important principle, it must be recognized at the outset that this collateral estoppel defense will not often be available to a criminal defendant, for it is seldom possible to determine how the judge or jury has decided any particular issue. For example, in the not atypical criminal case in which the crime consists of elements *A, B, C* and *D* and the defendant interposes defenses *X* and *Y,* and the case goes to the jury on instructions to convict only if it is found that facts *A, B, C* and *D* all exist and that neither *X* nor *Y* exist, the jury's verdict of "not guilty" will not itself reveal what the jury decided as to *A, B, C, D, X* or *Y.* In such a situation, the Court in *Ashe* instructed, it will be necessary to "examine the record of a prior proceeding, taking into account the pleadings, evidence, charge, and other relevant matter, and conclude whether a rational jury could have grounded its verdict upon an issue other than that which the defendant seeks to foreclose from consideration." But unless this inquiry shows, as in *Ashe,* that there was but one "rationally conceivable issue in dispute" at the first trial, that will be the end of the collateral estoppel claim. If the first trial was for multiple charges and ended with mixed results, and the question concerns whether a charge not resulting in acquittal in the first trial may be brought again, the assessment becomes more complicated.[2]

If a defendant at the first trial wishes to act in a fashion that will maximize his chances of being able to make a collateral estoppel defense later, he is placed in a dilemma. He must either put only a few of his defenses in issue, thereby assuring a collateral-estoppel effect in any future proceedings but at the same time increasing the risk of a conviction in this trial, or he must put all the defenses he has before

---

2. While an acquittal accompanied by a failure to reach a verdict may appropriately give rise to collateral estoppel if the acquittal necessarily determines facts in the defendant's favor, an acquittal accompanied by conviction on the count sought to be retried does not have a similar preclusive effect; the conviction casts doubt on whatever factual findings might otherwise be inferred from the

related acquittal. But because the primary purpose of the doctrine of collateral estoppel is to protect an accused from the unfairness of being required to *relitigate* an issue that has once been determined in his favor by a verdict of acquittal in a *second proceeding*, inconsistent verdicts in a single case are not objectionable on collateral estoppel grounds.

the jury, thereby better shielding himself against a conviction but destroying the possibility of any future collateral-estoppel effect on the issues raised. It has been suggested that the solution is to utilize special verdicts in criminal cases, but this procedure is generally not available and is disadvantageous to a criminal defendant in other respects. In some jurisdictions a defendant tried by the court may upon request have the judge find the facts specially,[3] and it has been suggested that this is another way by which the defendant can overcome this problem at the price of surrendering his right to jury trial.

In trying to determine whether a particular factual matter has been determined adversely to the prosecution, it is especially important to consider the legal theory underlying the prior trial. Illustrative is *Turner v. Arkansas*,[4] where, some time after petitioner, his brother, Yates and a fourth person played poker, Yates was robbed and murdered. Turner was charged with murder on a felony-murder theory and acquitted, after which he was charged with the robbery. The state's theory was that this second prosecution was not foreclosed by the earlier acquittal, for it might have occurred because the jury concluded that both Turner and his brother robbed Yates but that only the brother actually committed the murder. But the Court responded that if the jury had "found petitioner present at the crime scene, it would have been obligated to return a verdict of guilty of murder" even in those circumstances, as revealed by the judge's instructions that any party to the felony would be guilty of felony-murder. Of course, even if it is correct to say that the jury was "obligated" to convict on such facts,[5] it is possible that the jury in the first trial disregarded those instructions and acquitted because it believed Turner should not be convicted of murder merely because of his participation in a robbery where his brother actually did the killing. Thus *Turner* indicates, in effect, that such possibilities are not to be taken into account in applying the *Ashe* rule. By like token, *Ashe* has been

applied even where the first trial involved only "an implicit acquittal," that is, where the jury returned no verdict on the offense charged but did return a guilty verdict on a lesser included offense. But, as the Court later held in *Schiro v. Farley*,[6] the "failure to return a verdict does not have collateral estoppel effect * * * unless the record establishes that the issue was actually and necessarily decided in the defendant's favor." In that case, defendant's trial for a single killing resulted in the jury being given ten possible verdicts, including three murder counts ("knowingly" killing, rape felony-murder, deviate conduct felony-murder), voluntary and involuntary manslaughter, guilty but mentally ill, not guilty by reason of insanity, and not guilty. Because the jury returned a guilty verdict as to rape felony-murder and left the other verdict sheets blank, defendant claimed the state was collaterally estopped from now showing intentional killing as an aggravated factor supporting a death sentence. The Court disagreed, concluding that because the jury (i) was not instructed to return more than one verdict but (ii) was instructed that intent was required for each variety of murder, defendant had "not met his 'burden . . . to demonstrate that the issue whose relitigation he seeks to foreclose was actually decided' in his favor."

In *Ashe,* the Court made note of the fact that the prosecutor there "frankly conceded" that "it treated the first trial as no more than a dry run for the second prosecution." But this does not mean that *Ashe* is inapplicable just because the prosecution's conduct can be viewed somewhat more sympathetically. The Court so held in *Harris v. Washington*,[7] in which the state court had declined to apply *Ashe* where the issue of identity had not been "fully litigated" at the first trial because the trial judge had excluded evidence on grounds having "no bearing on the quality of the evidence." The Court reversed, holding that "the constitutional guarantee applies, irrespective of whether the jury considered all

---

3. Fed.R.Crim.P. 23(c).

4. 407 U.S. 366, 92 S.Ct. 2096, 32 L.Ed.2d 798 (1972).

5. On jury nullification, see § 21.1(g).

6. 510 U.S. 222, 114 S.Ct. 783, 127 L.Ed.2d 47 (1994).

7. 404 U.S. 55, 92 S.Ct. 183, 30 L.Ed.2d 212 (1971).

relevant evidence, and irrespective of the good faith of the State in bringing successive prosecutions." But this last observation should not be taken to mean that a defendant who himself is responsible for the separate disposition of the several charges against him may invoke the *Ashe* rule. In *Ohio v. Johnson*,[8] where defendant, charged with both murder and manslaughter based on the same killing and robbery and theft based on the same taking, entered a guilty plea over the state's objection to manslaughter and theft, the Supreme Court held that he could not rely on *Ashe* even if those offenses were mutually exclusive of the murder and robbery charges still pending. The Court explained that "in a case such as this, where the State has made no effort to prosecute the charges seriatim, the considerations of double jeopardy protection implicit in the application of collateral estoppel are inapplicable." This means a defendant may not even take advantage of his own prior acquittal if the second trial is for an offense severed from the first trial at defendant's request.

Because the Court in *Ashe* said that once "an issue of ultimate fact has once been determined * * * that issue cannot again be litigated," it is of course necessary to consider whether the issue in the second proceedings is actually the same as the issue decided in the earlier criminal trial. This requires, for one thing, consideration of the burden and standard of proof applicable in the two proceedings, as is indicated by *One Lot Emerald Cut Stones v. United States*.[9] One Klementova had been acquitted on charges of smuggling certain goods into the United States, after which the government instituted a civil forfeiture action with respect to those goods. In holding that he had no valid *Ashe* defense to this action, the Court reasoned that

the difference in the burden of proof in criminal and civil cases precluded application of the doctrine of collateral estoppel. The acquittal of the criminal charges may have only represented " 'an adjudication that the proof was not sufficient to overcome all reasonable doubt of the guilt of the accused.' " * * * As to the issues raised, it does not constitute an adjudication on the preponderance-of-the-evidence burden applicable in civil proceedings.[10]

Thus, the acquittal only is a bar to a later determination that there is *not* a reasonable doubt on the same fact issue. This is why jurisdictions that have passed on the issue have held an acquittal in a criminal proceeding does not bar revocation of parole or probation on the underlying charge. The failure to prove guilt beyond a reasonable doubt does not foreclose proof of the same crime by a preponderance of the evidence at the later revocation proceedings. (From this it might be thought that if the revocation proceedings come first and not even the preponderance standard is met, then the government is barred by *Ashe* from trying to show the same crime beyond a reasonable doubt in a criminal prosecution, but this is not so for the reason that no jeopardy attached at the revocation proceeding.) Special circumstances may produce different results; thus, where at the prior criminal trial the defendant successfully defended on grounds of entrapment, as to which he had the burden of proof by a preponderance of the evidence, this is a bar to a later determination in a revocation hearing that he did commit the crime. On similar reasoning, it was held in *Dowling v. United States*[11] that notwithstanding a defendant's prior acquittal of a certain crime, evidence of that crime may be received in a later prosecution under some exception to the "other crimes" rule (e.g., that it helps show identity or motive in the instant case). In

8. 467 U.S. 493, 104 S.Ct. 2536, 81 L.Ed.2d 425 (1984).

9. 409 U.S. 232, 93 S.Ct. 489, 34 L.Ed.2d 438 (1972). See also United States v. One Assortment of 89 Firearms, 465 U.S. 354, 104 S.Ct. 1099, 79 L.Ed.2d 361 (1984), reaching the same result and expressly disapproving of Coffey v. United States, 116 U.S. 436, 6 S.Ct. 437, 29 L.Ed. 684 (1886), to the extent it suggested otherwise.

10. To the same effect is United States v. One Assortment of 89 Firearms, 465 U.S. 354, 104 S.Ct. 1099, 79 L.Ed.2d 361 (1984).

11. 493 U.S. 342, 110 S.Ct. 668, 107 L.Ed.2d 708 (1990). The Court also rejected the contention that introduction of that evidence failed the due process test of "fundamental fairness."

such a situation, proof of the prior crime is an "evidentiary fact" rather than an "ultimate fact" in the second prosecution, and as such it is not a matter the prosecution must now prove beyond a reasonable doubt but rather is a matter that, if proved by a preponderance of the evidence, can contribute to a conviction beyond a reasonable doubt for the second crime.

Burden of proof issues aside, it still must be determined whether there is an identity of issues in the two proceedings, for only if there is can *Ashe* be used as a defense. The *One Lot Emerald Cut Stones* case also provides a useful illustration of this point. At the earlier criminal trial for smuggling, the government had to prove both the physical act of unlawful importation and the mental state of intent to defraud, and in the trial to the court the judge expressly found that the government had failed to establish intent. That being so, the acquittal could in no event bar the later forfeiture proceedings at which there was no need to prove such intent. Ascertaining whether the issues in the two cases are identical is not always that easy, as is illustrated by those decisions on whether two killings were sufficiently proximate that a finding of not guilty by reason of insanity in the first murder trial foreclosed conviction in the second murder trial. The same may be said of those decisions on whether an acquitted defendant may be prosecuted for perjury based upon his exonerating testimony given at the earlier trial, where the exact nature and breadth of the testimony is likely to be determinative (although some courts deem the perjury situation not within *Ashe* in any event).

Some other limitations upon the *Ashe* collateral estoppel rule remain to be briefly noted. For one thing, there must have been a valid final judgment in the earlier case, which means, for example, that no estoppel can be based upon an informal probation-like disposition involving neither verdict nor judgment or upon a judge's dismissal on the merits beyond his power because done in the absence of a

waiver of jury trial. But the judgment need not be one of acquittal as in *Ashe,* and thus a defendant may not be prosecuted for an assault occurring during a robbery after he was convicted of receiving the fruits of that robbery from another party. Perhaps the result is otherwise if the conviction is on a guilty plea, for in the *Johnson* case[12] the Court in rebuffing defendant's collateral estoppel claim asserted that "the taking of a guilty plea is not the same as an adjudication on the merits after full trial, such as took place in *Ashe.*" As for the "issue of ultimate fact" requirement, this means that a defendant cannot use *Ashe* to foreclose a ruling on an issue of law contrary to that made in the earlier case, or to prevent a factual determination contrary to one which was not of the "ultimate" kind in the first trial (e.g., that a certain witness was not credible). And the "same parties" requirement means that under *Ashe* one defendant cannot take advantage of another defendant's prior acquittal, just as one sovereign cannot be barred from prosecuting because of a factual determination concerning the same defendant in a trial by another sovereign, or in a trial within the jurisdiction to which the government was not a party. And even if the government *was* a party to the prior proceedings, an *Ashe* collateral estoppel claim (because it is grounded in the double jeopardy clause[13]) cannot be based on the outcome of those earlier proceedings, whether administrative or judicial, when they were not undertaken for the purpose of imposing of punishment, or even upon an earlier criminal prosecution, where no single court had jurisdiction over the prior and present charge.

Can collateral estoppel operate against the defendant, so that if defendant Ashe had been convicted at his first trial he would have been barred from making a mistaken identity defense at the second trial? The prevailing view is no, and the Supreme Court has assumed that the result in such circumstances is so apparent as not to require extended discus-

---

12. See text at note 8 supra.

13. On the double jeopardy clause limitation to instances of punishment, see § 17.4(b).

sion. In *Simpson v. Florida*,[14] where two men entered a store and robbed the manager and a customer, Simpson was convicted of robbing the manager; when that conviction was overturned for a defect in jury instructions he was acquitted of robbing the manager, and then he was prosecuted for robbing the customer. The state court characterized the two prior trials as presenting a "double collateral estoppel" that presumably left both sides free to dispute whether or not Simpson was one of the robbers. In rejecting that line of reasoning as "plainly not tenable," the Court noted that "had the second trial never occurred, the prosecutor could not, while trying the case under review, have laid the first jury verdict before the trial judge and demanded an instruction to the jury that, as a matter of law, petitioner was one of the armed robbers in the store that night."

Finally, it must be emphasized that the foregoing comments are directed only at the *Ashe* collateral estoppel doctrine, grounded in the Fifth Amendment guarantee against double jeopardy. Issue preclusion in a criminal law context may occur for other reasons. For one thing, it has been suggested that there may be another constitutionally-based collateral estoppel rule, this time derived from the due process clause, upon which a defendant could rely even as to pretrial rulings not governed by *Ashe* because jeopardy had not attached. And then of course there is the real possibility that the jurisdiction in question may have developed a good deal of law on collateral estoppel not grounded in the constitution at all but that nonetheless could be utilized to advantage by a criminal defendant. This largely explains why collateral estoppel decisions going beyond those heretofore discussed are to be found. Illustrative are decisions finding collateral estoppel even though the sovereign or defendant was not the same in the two cases, or even though the second proceeding involved a lower burden of proof on the government than the earlier criminal prosecution. It also explains why, at least as to matters not going to guilt

or innocence, principles of collateral estoppel are sometimes applied both against and in favor of criminal defendants.

(b) Double Jeopardy: Same Offense. A second way in which the Constitution prohibits a prosecution because of a failure to join the charge in an earlier trial is illustrated by *Brown v. Ohio*.[15] On November 29 Brown stole a car from a parking lot in one Ohio county and on December 8 was apprehended while driving the car in another Ohio county. Charged there with joyriding on that date, Brown pled guilty, after which he was indicted in the first county for auto theft and joyriding on November 29, and his conviction for the latter crimes was affirmed by the state court despite his double jeopardy objection. The Supreme Court first set out to interpret the double jeopardy clause of the Fifth Amendment, which states that no person shall "be subject for the same offence to be twice put in jeopardy of life or limb," and concluded that offenses could be the "same" for jeopardy purposes without being "identical." The Court then took note of the longstanding *Blockburger* test,[16] which originated as a device for determining congressional intent as to cumulative sentencing: "The applicable rule is that where the same act or transaction constitutes a violation of two distinct statutory provisions, the test to be applied to determine whether there are two offenses or only one, is whether each provision requires proof of an additional fact which the other does not." And the Court in *Brown* then held:

> If two offenses are the same under this test for purposes of barring consecutive sentences at a single trial, they necessarily will be the same for purposes of barring successive prosecutions. * * * Where the judge is forbidden to impose cumulative punishment for two crimes at the end of a single proceeding, the prosecutor is forbidden to strive for the same result in successive proceedings.

Having adopted the *Blockburger* test, the Court in *Brown* then proceeded to apply it to the facts of the particular case. Looking to the

---

14.   403 U.S. 384, 91 S.Ct. 1801, 29 L.Ed.2d 549 (1971).

15.   432 U.S. 161, 97 S.Ct. 2221, 53 L.Ed.2d 187 (1977).

16.   Blockburger v. United States, 284 U.S. 299, 52 S.Ct. 180, 76 L.Ed. 306 (1932).

definitions of joyriding and auto theft under Ohio law, the Court determined that the former consists of taking or operating a vehicle without the owner's consent and the latter of joyriding plus intent permanently to deprive the owner of possession. That is, the relationship of the two offenses was that of concentric circles rather than overlapping circles, and thus they were the "same" under *Blockburger* unless the time factor dictated a different result. Though the state court had concluded that the two prosecutions were distinct because based upon separate acts nine days apart, the Supreme Court responded that as a matter of Ohio law only a single continuing offense was involved. This somewhat dubious characterization of Ohio law, seemingly critical to the outcome in view of the Court's apparent concession that the result would be otherwise if Ohio law made each day of joyriding a separate offense, may have been made in order to avoid other difficult issues.

The Court in *Brown* commented at one point that "the sequence is immaterial," and

this proved to be true in the subsequent case of *Harris v. Oklahoma*.[17] There Harris was convicted of felony murder on proof that his companion shot and killed a clerk during a robbery of a store by two men. Though proof of the underlying felony of robbery with firearms was necessary for the felony murder conviction, Harris was thereafter tried and convicted of that felony. The Supreme Court reversed, holding that "the Double Jeopardy Clause bars prosecution for the lesser crime after conviction of the greater one." (It should also be noted that when only the greater offense has been charged, as in *Harris*, a well-established rule of procedure sometimes produces a joinder; under that rule, a defendant is entitled to a jury instruction on the uncharged lesser included offense whenever such an alternative disposition is rationally justified by the evidence in the case.[18])

With respect to the *Blockburger* test, the Court in *Brown* asserted the critical question is "whether each provision requires proof of

---

17. 433 U.S. 682, 97 S.Ct. 2912, 53 L.Ed.2d 1054 (1977).

18. As noted in Beck v. Alabama, 447 U.S. 625, 100 S.Ct. 2382, 65 L.Ed.2d 392 (1980): "In the federal courts, it has long been 'beyond dispute that the defendant is entitled to an instruction on a lesser included offense if the evidence would permit a jury rationally to find him guilty of the lesser offense and acquit him of the greater.' Similarly, the state courts that have addressed the issue have unanimously held that a defendant is entitled to a lesser included offense instruction where the evidence warrants it." Citing state authority in support, the Court in *Beck* added: "Although the States vary in their descriptions of the quantum of proof necessary to give rise to a right to a lesser included offense instruction, they agree that it must be given when supported by the evidence." By way of describing the benefits of this procedure, the Court noted: "This rule [that the jury was permitted to find the defendant guilty of a necessarily included lesser offense] originally developed as an aid to the prosecution in cases in which the proof failed to establish some element of the crime charged. But it has long been recognized that it can also be beneficial to the defendant because it affords the jury a less drastic alternative than the choice between conviction of the offense charged and acquittal."

In *Beck*, concluding that "the nearly universal acceptance of the rule in both state and federal courts establishes the value to the defendant of this procedural safeguard," which is "especially important * * * when the evidence unquestionably establishes that the defendant is guilty of a serious, violent offense—but leaves some doubt with respect to an element that would justify conviction of a capital offense," the Court held as a matter of due process that when "the unavailability of a lesser included

offense instruction enhances the risk of an unwarranted conviction," that option may not be withdrawn from the jury in a capital case. The *Beck* rule does not require a state court to instruct the jury on offenses that, under state law, are not considered lesser included offenses of the crime charged. Hopkins v. Reeves, 524 U.S. 88, 118 S.Ct. 1895, 141 L.Ed.2d 76 (1998) (second-degree murder, which requires intent, is not lesser included offense of felony-murder, which does not).

In Carter v. United States, 530 U.S. 255, 120 S.Ct. 2159, 147 L.Ed.2d 203 (2000), the defendant charged with violating 18 U.S.C.A. § 2113(a), punishing whoever, "by force and violence, or by intimidation, takes * * * any * * * thing of value [from a] bank," sought a jury instruction as a lesser included offense on 18 U.S.C.A. § 2113(b), punishing whoever "takes and carries away, with intent to steal or purloin, any * * * thing of value exceeding $1,000 [from a] bank." Applying the rule in Schmuck v. United States, 489 U.S. 705, 109 S.Ct. 1443, 103 L.Ed.2d 734 (1989), that a defendant requesting an instruction on a lesser offense must demonstrate that "the elements of the lesser offense are a subset of the elements of the charged offense," the Court held that request was properly denied, as the latter offense has three elements not required by the former. The defendant's claim that the $1,000 valuation requirement was a sentencing factor rather than an element was rejected in *Carter*, and shortly thereafter the Court held in Apprendi v. New Jersey, 530 U.S. 466, 120 S.Ct. 2348, 147 L.Ed.2d 435 (2000), that any fact other than prior conviction that raises the statutory maximum sentence is an element rather than a sentence enhancement, meaning that such facts must now be factored into the *Schmuck* analysis as elements.

an additional fact which the other does not." In *Brown* itself, this involved nothing more than a comparison of the statutory elements of the two crimes; as noted earlier, auto theft was simply joyriding with the additional element of intent to permanently deprive. But, does this mean that if two statutory provisions are such that violation of one does not inevitably involve a violation of the other that the offenses are not the "same" under *Brown*? No, the Court answered in *Illinois v. Vitale*,[19] citing the *Harris* decision as an illustration. In *Harris,* as the Court now explained it, the "felony murder statute on its face did not require proof of a robbery to establish felony murder, other felonies could underlie a felony-murder prosecution," but yet the Court held the subsequent robbery prosecution barred because of the earlier felony-murder prosecution where that same robbery was used as the necessary felony. In essence, *Harris* indicated that in comparing "each provision" as *Brown* required, some attention to the theory of the prosecutions was also necessary: once it appeared that the robbery was the felony relied upon in the earlier felony-murder prosecution, that felony became a lesser included "same" offense under *Brown–Blockburger.*

But then came *Grady v. Corbin*,[20] in which the Court asserted that *Blockburger* itself involved only "a technical comparison of the elements of the two offenses" and that *Harris* in fact illustrated that the Court had "not relied exclusively on the *Blockburger* test to vindicate the Double Jeopardy Clause's protection against multiple prosecutions." The Court in *Corbin* thus held that "the Double Jeopardy Clause bars any subsequent prosecution in which the government, to establish an essential element of an offense charged in that prosecution, will prove conduct that constitutes an offense for which the defendant has already been prosecuted."[21] To distinguish

Dowling v. United States,[22] the Court stressed that the "critical inquiry is what conduct the State will prove, not the evidence the State will use to prove that conduct." This expanded version of the double jeopardy protection, the *Corbin* majority explained, was necessary to protect criminal defendants from the ordeal of multiple prosecutions that would give "the State an opportunity to rehearse its presentation of proof, thus increasing the risk of an erroneous conviction for one or more of the offenses charged."

Corbin illustrates application of the new rule to a clearly non-*Blockburger* situation. The defendant was involved in an automobile accident in which one person was killed and another injured. He received traffic tickets for driving while intoxicated and crossing the median, pleaded guilty to those offenses a few weeks later, and then raised a double jeopardy objection when he was later indicted for, inter alia, criminally negligent homicide and reckless assault. The prosecution's bill of particulars specified the negligent and reckless acts as (1) driving under the influence, (2) crossing the median, and (3) driving too fast for conditions. The Court ruled that because the state had thus "admitted that it will prove the entirety of the conduct for which Corbin was convicted [earlier] to establish essential elements of the homicide and assault offenses," the double jeopardy clause barred the prosecution. But, the Court added, this prosecution would not be barred if the state were to amend its bill of particulars to rely "solely on Corbin's driving too fast."

Corbin was soon overruled in *United States v. Dixon*,[23] which involved two consolidated cases in which the defendants were charged with crimes following their trials for criminal contempt based on the same conduct. After concluding that the double jeopardy protection

19. 447 U.S. 410, 100 S.Ct. 2260, 65 L.Ed.2d 228 (1980).

20. 495 U.S. 508, 110 S.Ct. 2084, 109 L.Ed.2d 548 (1990).

21. When, as in *Harris,* the greater offense is prosecuted first, the proposition must be stated somewhat differently. As *Corbin* put it: "if in the course of securing a conviction for one offense the State necessarily has proved

the conduct comprising all of the elements of another offense not yet prosecuted * * *, the Double Jeopardy Clause would bar subsequent prosecution of the component offense."

22. 493 U.S. 342, 110 S.Ct. 668, 107 L.Ed.2d 708 (1990).

23. 509 U.S. 688, 113 S.Ct. 2849, 125 L.Ed.2d 556 (1993).

is applicable "in nonsummary criminal contempt prosecutions just as * * * in other criminal prosecutions,"[24] Justice Scalia[25] proceeded to assay the situations presented under the *Brown–Blockburger* test. Dixon's prosecution for cocaine possession was deemed barred by his earlier contempt conviction for violation of a pretrial release condition that he not commit "any criminal offense," as the contempt was the very same cocaine possession; and Foster's prosecution for simple assault was likewise deemed barred by his earlier contempt trial for several alleged violations of a civil protection order requiring that he not "assault * * * or in any manner threaten" his estranged wife, including the very same assault. The possession and assault crimes were each seen as having the same relationship to the contempt as the robbery had to the felony murder in *Harris*: "a species of lesser-included offense."[26] However, the other charges against Foster, assault with intent to kill and several threats with intent to injure, were deemed to be barred under the *Corbin* test but not under *Brown–Blockburger* because of mutually exclusive elements: the aforementioned mental states were not required for criminal contempt, while on the other hand only the contempt required knowledge and willful violation of the civil protection order. With the case in this posture, the Court decided to overrule *Corbin* because (i) it "lacks constitutional roots" by virtue of being "wholly inconsistent with earlier Supreme Court precedent and with the clear common-law understanding of double jeopardy"; (ii) it "has already proved unstable in application," as manifested by the fact that in less than two years the Court had recognized "a large exception" thereto grounded in "longstanding authority";[27] and (iii) it

would otherwise be "a continuing source of confusion."

Four other Justices in *Dixon* wanted to retain the *Corbin* "same-conduct" test. The principal argument in favor of retention was that while the *Brown–Blockburger* focus on statutory elements was sufficient as to that branch of double jeopardy law having to do with when cumulative punishments are prohibited, it was insufficient on the issue of when successive prosecutions should be prohibited, where there is a need "to prevent repeated trials in which a defendant will be forced to defend against the same charge again and again, and in which the government may perfect its presentation with dress rehearsal after dress rehearsal." The *Dixon* majority responded to this with three points: (i) the concern expressed by the dissenters was "unjustified" because the government would be deterred from bringing successive prosecutions "by the sheer press of other demands upon prosecutorial and judicial resources"; (ii) in any event, that concern could not be met by the *Corbin* "same-conduct" test, but only by an even broader "same-transaction" test, theretofore rejected by the Court[28]; and (iii) no departure from *Brown–Blockburger* was possible, for (contrary to the assumption of some of the dissenters) the successive prosecution strand of the double jeopardy clause cannot have a meaning different from the multiple punishment strand—it is "embarrassing to assert that the single term 'same offence' * * * has two different meanings."

Although, as noted earlier, this latter conclusion was also reached in *Brown*, it is important to note that in the interim significant developments have occurred with respect to the cumulative punishment branch of double

24. Only Blackmun, J., expressed disagreement on this score; he feared that the Court's willingness "to overlook the unique interests served by contempt proceedings not only will jeopardize the ability of trial courts to control those defendants under their supervision but will undermine their ability to respond effectively to unmistakable threats to their own authority and to those who have sought the court's protection," as in the case of battered women.

25. Who was joined as to all aspects of this assessment only by Kennedy, J.

26. Noting *Harris* was so characterized in Illinois v. Vitale, 447 U.S. 410, 100 S.Ct. 2260, 65 L.Ed.2d 228 (1980).

27. The reference is to United States v. Felix, 503 U.S. 378, 112 S.Ct. 1377, 118 L.Ed.2d 25 (1992), where defendant's double jeopardy claim failed "because of long established precedent in this area," namely, "the rule that a substantive crime, and a conspiracy to commit that crime, are not the 'same offence' for double jeopardy purposes."

28. See § 17.4(c).

jeopardy law. In *Albernaz v. United States*,[29] the Court treated *Blockburger* as only a method for ascertaining legislative intent when nothing more concrete was available. It was said that "the question of what punishments are constitutionally permissible is not different from the question of what punishment the Legislative Branch intended to be imposed." Thus, as the Court later put it in *Missouri v. Hunter*,[30] where "a legislature specifically authorizes cumulative punishment under two statutes, regardless of whether those two statutes proscribe the 'same' conduct under *Blockburger*, a court's task of statutory construction is at an end and the prosecutor may seek and the trial court or jury may impose cumulative punishment under such statutes in a single trial." What this means, of course, is that in a case such as *Harris*, cumulative punishment for the robbery and murder would be constitutionally permissible if the legislature so provided. But if this is so, and if in addition the *Dixon* decision really means that the two strands of the double jeopardy clause must be given precisely the same meaning, then the actual holding in *Harris* would likewise be open to circumvention by such legislative action. Should this be so, then surely (as one of the *Dixon* dissenters put it) "the same-elements test is an inadequate safeguard, for it leaves the constitutional guarantee at the mercy of a legislature's decision to modify statutory definitions."

With *Corbin* gone, future battles in this area may well revolve around the question of just how it is to be determined under *Brown–Blockburger* "whether each offense contains an element not contained in the other." Recall that *Corbin* characterized *Blockburger* as permitting only "technical comparison" of the offenses and, in that connection, viewed *Harris* as inexplicable under *Blockburger*. What remains to be seen is whether, with the *Corbin* "same-conduct" test now abandoned, *Blockburger* will be interpreted more generously

than it was in *Corbin*, so that at least *Harris* survives. The *Dixon* majority seems to have taken a step in that direction by rejecting the dissenters' claim that *Harris* manifested a beyond-*Blockburger* rule in operation. But the *Dixon* case also shows that the Justices are not in agreement as to just how *Brown–Blockburger* should be applied. The Scalia application of *Brown–Blockburger* in that case was supported in its entirety by only one other Justice; three others felt Scalia's application was too generous to the defendants, while two others believed it was not generous enough. While it is doubtless true that *Dixon* presented some unusual problems regarding the *Brown–Blockburger* test because of the criminal contempt context, that case nonetheless manifests that subtle differences in the approach to making the same-offense calculation can produce profound changes in the scope of the double jeopardy guarantee. On the fundamental question of whether it is the indictments or the statutes that are to be examined in applying *Brown–Blockburger* test, lower courts often focus on the statutory elements to ensure that separate prosecutions are not unnecessary barred by averments going beyond the statutory elements, but sometimes look to the allegations in the indictments when (much like the situation in *Dixon*) one of the statutes covers a broad range of conduct.

The *Brown* rule, barring the prosecution in separate trials of several crimes that are the "same" for double jeopardy purposes, is not absolute. As noted in *Brown*, an exception "may exist where the State is unable to proceed on the more serious charge at the outset because the additional facts necessary to sustain that charge have not occurred or have not been discovered despite the exercise of due diligence." The Court cited *Diaz v. United States*,[31] which is an apt illustration, for there the victim died after the defendant was convicted of assault and battery. Despite the tentative nature of the language used in *Brown*,

---

29. 450 U.S. 333, 101 S.Ct. 1137, 67 L.Ed.2d 275 (1981).

30. 459 U.S. 359, 103 S.Ct. 673, 74 L.Ed.2d 535 (1983). See also Garrett v. United States, 471 U.S. 773, 105 S.Ct. 2407, 85 L.Ed.2d 764 (1985).

31. 223 U.S. 442, 32 S.Ct. 250, 56 L.Ed. 500 (1912).

such an exception is sound, for in such circumstances the inconvenience to the defendant is clearly outweighed by the public's interest in assuring that the defendant does not fortuitously escape responsibility for his crimes.

But a plurality of the Supreme Court has now indicated its willingness to extend this exception beyond instances of actual necessity. In *Garrett v. United States*,[32] the defendant, two months after pleading guilty to importing marijuana, was charged with engaging in a continuing criminal enterprise, which requires proof of three or more successive violations of a certain type within a set period of time. At trial, the government's proof in that respect included the earlier importation offense, which the plurality deemed permissible under *Brown* simply because "the continuing criminal enterprise charged against Garrett in Florida had not been completed at the time that he was indicted" on the importing charge. While the dissenters[33] objected the exception was not applicable because all the facts needed to prove a continuing criminal enterprise of shorter duration existed prior to that indictment, the plurality deemed it irrelevant "whether the Government could [at the time of the importing charge] have successfully indicted and prosecuted Garrett for a different continuing criminal enterprise" of less expansive temporal dimensions. For them, the exception in *Brown* is not limited to instances in which the government absolutely could not have charged the offenses together, but rather is based also on the notion that "one who at the time the first indictment is returned is continuing to engage in other conduct found criminal" cannot complain about multiple prosecutions. *Garrett* thus lends no support to the claim that mere prose-

cutorial oversight falls within the *Diaz* exception. Consequently, in the previously-discussed *Corbin* case the Court deemed it of no significance that the assistant prosecutor who was handling the traffic charges to which defendant pleaded guilty was unaware there had been a fatality, then under investigation by another assistant prosecutor.[34]

The Court also cautioned in *Brown* that the case did not "raise the double jeopardy questions that may arise * * * after a conviction is reversed on appeal." Stressing that in *Brown* the defendant did not overturn the first conviction but rather served the sentence assessed for that crime, the Court held in *Montana v. Hall*[35] that if a defendant does obtain a reversal of the first conviction, then he may thereafter be prosecuted for another crime which is the "same" offense for double jeopardy purposes.[36] Such a case, the Court reasoned, "falls squarely within the rule that retrial is permissible after a conviction is reversed on appeal."[37]

Because of the separate sovereigns exception to the double jeopardy clause,[38] clearly no *Brown* issue is presented when the crime involved in the earlier prosecution, no matter how similar in its elements to the present one, was an offense against another sovereign. What remains unclear, however, is whether when the sovereign is the same the failure to join the "same" offenses in the first prosecution may be excused because the court in which the first prosecution was commenced could not have tried the other offense. On the subject of exceptions, *Brown* cites to a footnote in Justice Brennan's concurring opinion in

---

32. 471 U.S. 773, 105 S.Ct. 2407, 85 L.Ed.2d 764 (1985).

33. Stevens, J., joined by Brennan and Marshall, JJ. O'Connor, J., concurring, found "merit to this position" of the dissenters, but reached "a different conclusion upon balancing the interests protected by the Double Jeopardy Clause," including the desirability of allowing the government to decide prosecution is warranted whenever "the defendant continues unlawful conduct after the time the Government prosecutes him for a predicate offense." Powell, J., took no part in the decision.

34. The Court stated: "With adequate preparation and foresight, the State could have prosecuted Corbin for the

offenses charged in the traffic tickets and the subsequent indictment in a single proceeding."

35. 481 U.S. 400, 107 S.Ct. 1825, 95 L.Ed.2d 354 (1987).

36. At the first trial, defendant was convicted of incest, but that conviction was reversed on appeal because at the time of defendant's conduct the incest statute was not applicable to sexual assaults upon stepchildren. Relying upon *Brown*, the state supreme court ruled that retrial on a charge of sexual assault, grounded in the very same conduct, was barred.

37. See § 25.4(a).

38. See § 25.5.

Ashe v. Swenson[39] recognizing the *Diaz* type of exception and then stating: "Another exception would be necessary if no single court had jurisdiction of all the alleged crimes." It is unfortunate that the issue went unrecognized in *Brown,* for the facts of that case reveal the nature of the problem. Though never mentioned by the Court, the first prosecution was in a different county than the second one, and it would appear that while the county of the first prosecution could as it did prosecute there for the continuing crime of joyriding, it probably could not prosecute for the crime of theft in the other county. Presuming that to be so, it might be asked whether the defendant should be entitled to complain about the impossible failure to join the theft charge in the first trial.

One way to look at that problem, especially if a change of venue to the county in which both offenses occurred was a possibility, is whether the lack of joinder should be placed at the feet of the prosecutor or the defendant. That this is a relevant inquiry was recognized by the Court in *Jeffers v. United States.*[40] There, defendant was charged in two separate indictments with conspiracy to distribute drugs and conducting a continuing criminal enterprise to violate the drug laws, respectively. The government moved to join the charges for trial, but defendant objected on the ground that much of the evidence admissible on the conspiracy count would not be admissible on

the other charge, and thus the court denied the defendant's motion. In upholding defendant's subsequent separate convictions for these two offenses, the Court stated: "If the defendant expressly asks for separate trials on the greater and the lesser offenses,[41] or, in connection with his opposition to trial together, fails to raise the issue that one offense might be a lesser included offense of the other, [an] exception to the *Brown* rule emerges." Because "he was solely responsible for the successive prosecutions," his "action deprived him of any right that he might have had against consecutive trials." The exact scope of the *Jeffers* rule is uncertain.[42] For one thing, the Court by footnote said that the "considerations relating to the propriety of a second trial obviously would be much different if any action by the Government contributed to the separate prosecutions." This indicates, at a minimum, that where defendant is not "solely responsible," as where the government obtains separate indictments and defendant merely fails to seek their joinder for trial, *Jeffers* is not controlling. Secondly, the Court noted that in the instant case "trial together of the [two] charges could have taken place without undue prejudice to petitioner's Sixth Amendment right to a fair trial," thus indicating that the result would be different if defendant's waiver of his rights under *Brown* was necessitated by the need to protect some other constitutional right.[43]

39.　397 U.S. 436, 90 S.Ct. 1189, 25 L.Ed.2d 469 (1970).

40.　432 U.S. 137, 97 S.Ct. 2207, 53 L.Ed.2d 168 (1977).

41.　In *Jeffers,* the Court merely "assumed, *arguendo,*" that such a relationship existed between these two crimes. The Court later held this was the case. Rutledge v. United States, 517 U.S. 292, 116 S.Ct. 1241, 134 L.Ed.2d 419 (1996).

42.　The Court has more recently decided a case that did not clarify matters because it involved a situation the Court rightly declared was "an even clearer case than *Jeffers.*" In Ohio v. Johnson, 467 U.S. 493, 104 S.Ct. 2536, 81 L.Ed.2d 425 (1984), where defendant was charged in a single indictment with both murder and manslaughter for the same killing and robbery and theft for the same taking, and defendant entered a guilty plea to the two lesser offenses and thus "offered only to resolve part of the charges against him, while the State objected to disposing of any of the counts against respondent without a trial," the Court held *Brown* inapplicable because "respondent's efforts were directed to separate disposition of counts in the same indictment where no more than one trial of the offenses charged was ever contemplated."

In light of *Johnson,* what then if the defendant pleaded guilty to a minor offense before the state got around to charging (and possibly joining) a greater offense? In Grady v. Corbin, 495 U.S. 508, 110 S.Ct. 2084, 109 L.Ed.2d 548 (1990), the defendant pleaded guilty to traffic offenses without revealing that the accident had resulted in a fatality (unknown to the assistant prosecutor handling the traffic charges, but then under investigation by another assistant prosecutor). The Court accepted the state court's "characterization of the proceedings," namely, that defendant and his counsel "should not be expected to *volunteer* information that is likely to be highly damaging," but cautioned it "need not decide whether our double jeopardy analysis would be any different if affirmative misrepresentations of fact by a defendant or his counsel were to mislead a court into accepting a guilty plea it would not otherwise accept."

43.　See Simmons v. United States, 390 U.S. 377, 88 S.Ct. 967, 19 L.Ed.2d 1247 (1968) (defendant cannot be "obliged either to give up what he believed, with advice of counsel, to be a valid Fourth Amendment claim or, in legal effect, to waive [his] privilege against self-incrimination").

Finally, while the mandatory joinder issue under *Brown–Blockburger* usually involves two criminal charges, it will occasionally involve a criminal charge and another type of proceeding. Although it has long been clear that the Double Jeopardy Clause protects only against the imposition of multiple *criminal* punishment, the Supreme Court has experienced difficulty over the years in deciding how to go about making the civil-criminal distinction. One approach, under which the outcome depended primarily on whether the sanction imposed served the traditional "goals of punishment," namely "retribution and deterrence,"[44] was abandoned in *Hudson v. United States*,[45] where the Court rejected the contention of bank officers indicted for misapplication of bank funds that the prosecution was barred because monetary penalties and occupation debarment had previously been imposed upon them by the Office of Comptroller of Currency. Under *Hudson*, the controlling question is whether the legislature intended to establish a civil penalty, except upon "the clearest proof" that the statutory scheme is "so punitive either in purpose or effect" as to transform what was intended as a civil remedy into a criminal penalty. The Court in *Hudson* then set out some "useful guideposts" for making the latter determination: "(1) [w]hether the sanction involves an affirmative disability or restraint; (2) whether it has historically been regarded as a punishment; (3) whether it comes into play only on a finding of scienter; (4) whether its operation will promote the traditional aims of punishment—retribution and deterrence; (5) whether the behavior to which it applies is already a crime; (6) whether

an alternative purpose to which it may rationally be connected is assignable for it; and (7) whether it appears excessive in relation to the alternative purpose assigned."[46] And thus lower courts have held that separate proceedings are not barred under the double jeopardy clause when the prosecuted crime was also the subject of certain nonpunitive proceedings, such as forfeiture of goods, suspension or revocation of a driver's license or a business or professional license, revocation of a scholarship, debarment from participation in government programs, withholding of government payments, penalties and interest for underpayment of taxes, various administratively-imposed fines, revocation of conditional release, prison discipline, commitment of a sexually dangerous person, and even imposition of a civil penalty for a minor traffic offense. As for statutes imposing a tax upon certain criminal activity (e.g., drug possession, gambling), one such statute was found to be punitive by the Supreme Court in a pre-*Hudson* case,[47] but various results have been reached in subsequent lower court cases.

(c) "Same Transaction" Joinder. In *Ashe v. Swenson*,[48] Justice Brennan, joined by two other members of the Court, indicated he would resolve the issue at hand (whether a defendant acquitted of one robbery on mistaken identity grounds could be tried for another robbery occurring at the same time and place and obviously committed by the same person) by redefining the "same offence" part of the double jeopardy clause to mean "same transaction" rather than "same evidence." The latter, traditional definition, he objected,

---

44. United States v. Halper, 490 U.S. 435, 109 S.Ct. 1892, 104 L.Ed.2d 487 (1989).

45. 522 U.S. 93, 118 S.Ct. 488, 139 L.Ed.2d 450 (1997).

46. In applying these factors, derived from Kennedy v. Mendoza–Martinez, 372 U.S. 144, 83 S.Ct. 554, 9 L.Ed.2d 644 (1963), the Court in *Hudson* stated that though "the conduct for which OCC sanctions are imposed may also be criminal" and though the sanctions will serve to deter others, "a traditional goal of criminal punishment," neither of those factors "renders such sanctions 'criminal' for double jeopardy purposes." *Hudson* produced four concurring opinions by six Justices. All but one of them agreed that a departure from pre-*Hudson* doctrine was necessary, but three expressed reservations about the extent of the departure expressed in the opinion of the Court.

In Seling v. Young, 531 U.S. 250, 121 S.Ct. 727, 148 L.Ed.2d 734 (2001), the Court held that a provision deemed civil under the *Hudson* approach, which requires a focus upon several factors considered in relation to the statute on its face, cannot be deemed punitive "as applied" to a single individual, for an "as applied" approach would be unworkable in that it could never be fully determined whether a scheme was valid under the double jeopardy clause.

47. Department of Revenue of Montana v. Kurth Ranch, 511 U.S. 767, 114 S.Ct. 1937, 128 L.Ed.2d 767 (1994).

48. 397 U.S. 436, 90 S.Ct. 1189, 25 L.Ed.2d 469 (1970).

does not enforce but virtually annuls the constitutional guarantee. For example, where a single criminal episode involves several victims, under the "same evidence" test a separate prosecution may be brought as to each. * * * The "same evidence" test permits multiple prosecutions where a single transaction is divisible into chronologically discrete crimes. * * * Even a single criminal act may lead to multiple prosecutions if it is viewed from the perspective of different statutes. * * * Given the tendency of modern criminal legislation to divide the phases of a criminal transaction into numerous separate crimes, the opportunities for multiple prosecutions for an essentially unitary criminal episode are frightening. And given our tradition of virtually unreviewable prosecutorial discretion concerning the initiation and scope of a criminal prosecution, the potentialities for abuse inherent in the "same evidence" test are simply intolerable. * * *

In my view, the Double Jeopardy Clause requires the prosecution, except in most limited circumstances, to join at one trial all the charges against a defendant which grow out of a single criminal act, occurrence, episode, or transaction. This "same transaction" test of "same offence" not only enforces the ancient prohibition against vexatious multiple prosecutions embodied in the Double Jeopardy Clause, but responds as well to the increasingly widespread recognition that the consolidation in one lawsuit of all issues arising out of a single transaction or occurrence best promotes justice, economy, and convenience.

Although a majority of the Court has refused to accept the "same transaction" test as a constitutional imperative,[49] several states

have adopted that standard as a matter of local law. By statute, court rule or by judicial decision, a number of jurisdictions now provide that the prosecutor must join (or, that on motion of the defendant, there must be joined) all offenses arising out of the same transaction. But some have criticized this trend:

> The absurdity of the "same transaction" standard can be easily illustrated. Assume that one breaks and enters a building to commit larceny of an automobile, does thereafter in fact steal the automobile and drive away, killing the night watchman in the process, and two blocks away runs a red light which brings about his arrest by the municipal police. Could it be said with any logic that a plea of guilty to breaking and entering would bar a subsequent prosecution for murder? If so, presumably a plea of guilty to the traffic offense would likewise, since all arise out of the "same transaction."[50]

However, this problem and others which might arise from an unqualified application of the "same transaction" standard can be overcome by various limitations upon its use, such as: that the offenses must be within the jurisdiction of a single court; that the offenses must have been known by the prosecutor at the time he commenced the first prosecution; that as to offenses charged the burden is on the defendant to move for joinder; that entry of a plea of guilty or nolo contendere does not bar later prosecution for other offenses part of the same transaction; that the court may permit a later trial of the related offense if the prosecutor did not have sufficient evidence to try it at the time of the first trial; or that the court may permit a later trial of the related offense to serve the ends of justice.

49. Brown v. Ohio, 432 U.S. 161, 97 S.Ct. 2221, 53 L.Ed.2d 187 (1977).

50. State v. Conrad, 243 So.2d 174 (Fla.App.1971).

Chapter 18

SPEEDY TRIAL AND OTHER
PROMPT DISPOSITION

Table of Sections

§ 18.1 The Constitutional Right to Speedy Trial

(a) Generally. The Sixth Amendment provides that "[i]n all criminal prosecutions, the accused shall enjoy the right to a speedy * * * trial." This right, the Supreme Court has noted, "is as fundamental as any of the rights secured by the Sixth Amendment."[1] For one thing, the right to speedy trial "has its roots at the very foundation of our English law heritage."[2] Recognition of a right to speedy justice

§ 18.1

1. Klopfer v. North Carolina, 386 U.S. 213, 87 S.Ct. 988, 18 L.Ed.2d 1 (1967).

2. Ibid. Even if the proceeding is not within the "criminal prosecutions" category of the Sixth Amendment, its nature may be such that as a matter of due process comparable protection is provided by the Constitution. See

United States v. Eight Thousand Eight Hundred and Fifty Dollars, 461 U.S. 555, 103 S.Ct. 2005, 76 L.Ed.2d 143 (1983) (in forfeiture action under 31 U.S.C.A. § 1102(a), whether post-seizure delay violates due process is not to be determined by the *Lovasco* rule for pre-arrest/charge delay in criminal cases, discussed in § 18.5(b), as the "more apt analogy is to a defendant's right to a speedy

has been traced back to the twelfth century, and it was articulated in Magna Carta. The importance of this right was acknowledged in the earliest days of this nation, and today virtually all state constitutions also expressly guarantee the right. It is not surprising, therefore, that the Sixth Amendment right applies not only to prosecutions in the federal courts,[3] but also to state prosecutions through the Fourteenth Amendment due process clause.[4]

(b) Interests Involved. As the Supreme Court explained in *Smith v. Hooey*,[5] the constitutional right to speedy trial protects "at least three basic demands of criminal justice in the Anglo–American system: '[1] to prevent undue and oppressive incarceration prior to trial, [2] to minimize anxiety and concern accompanying public accusation and [3] to limit the possibilities that long delay will impair the ability of an accused to defend himself.' " As for the first on the list, clearly the disadvantages for the accused who cannot obtain his pretrial release are most serious. The time spent in jail awaiting trial often means loss of a job; it disrupts family life; and it enforces idleness. Moreover, if a defendant is locked up, he is hindered in his ability to gather evidence, contact witnesses, or otherwise prepare his defense. The second interest on the list concerns even the defendant who has been able to secure his release on bail. While the criminal charges are outstanding, he may be subjected to public scorn, deprived of employment, and chilled in the exercise of his First Amendment rights of speech and association. But of the

three interests, "the most serious is the last, because the inability of a defendant adequately to prepare his case skews the fairness of the entire system. If witnesses die or disappear during a delay, the prejudice is obvious. There is also prejudice when defense witnesses are unable to recall accurately events of the distant past."[6] In *Doggett v. United States*,[7] the Court held that prejudice to this third interest, standing alone, was a basis for finding a Sixth Amendment speedy trial violation.[8]

In *Barker v. Wingo*,[9] the Court declared that the right to a speedy trial "is generically different from any of the other rights enshrined in the Constitution for the protection of the accused" because

> there is a societal interest in providing a speedy trial which exists separate from, and at times in opposition to, the interests of the accused. The inability of courts to provide a prompt trial has contributed to a large backlog of cases in urban courts which, among other things, enables defendants to negotiate more effectively for pleas of guilty to lesser offenses and otherwise manipulate the system. In addition, persons released on bond for lengthy periods awaiting trial have an opportunity to commit other crimes. * * * Moreover, the longer an accused is free awaiting trial, the more tempting becomes his opportunity to jump bail and escape. Finally, delay between arrest and punishment may have a detrimental effect on rehabilitation.

trial," and thus the *Barker* balancing test, discussed in § 18.2, governs). Applying *$8,850*, the Court held in United States v. Von Neumann, 474 U.S. 242, 106 S.Ct. 610, 88 L.Ed.2d 587 (1986), that the owner of a car seized at the border for failure to declare it had no constitutional right to a speedy disposition of his remission petition without awaiting a forfeiture proceeding.

3. Beavers v. Haubert, 198 U.S. 77, 25 S.Ct. 573, 49 L.Ed. 950 (1905).

4. Klopfer v. North Carolina, 386 U.S. 213, 87 S.Ct. 988, 18 L.Ed.2d 1 (1967).

5. 393 U.S. 374, 89 S.Ct. 575, 21 L.Ed.2d 607 (1969).

6. Barker v. Wingo, 407 U.S. 514, 92 S.Ct. 2182, 33 L.Ed.2d 101 (1972).

Some doubt that the right to speedy trial effectively safeguards the defendant from stale evidence, noting that "prejudice to the defense stems from the interval between *crime* and trial, which is quite distinct from the interval

between *accusation* and trial." Doggett v. United States, 505 U.S. 647, 112 S.Ct. 2686, 120 L.Ed.2d 520 (1992) (Thomas, J., dissenting).

7. 505 U.S. 647, 112 S.Ct. 2686, 120 L.Ed.2d 520 (1992).

8. The Court in *Doggett* requested argument on whether there is a fourth interest, repose, i.e., to be free of disruption of one's life well after the criminal events at issue, but the Court found it unnecessary to decide this issue. Three of the four dissenters in *Doggett* did speak to this issue. They concluded, correctly it would seem, that the Sixth Amendment right does not "protect a right to repose," which was not recognized at common law but *is* recognized "in any number of specific statutes of limitations enacted by the federal and state legislatures."

9. 407 U.S. 514, 92 S.Ct. 2182, 33 L.Ed.2d 101 (1972).

If an accused cannot make bail, he is generally confined * * * in a local jail. This contributes to the overcrowding and generally deplorable state of those institutions. Lengthy exposure to these conditions "has a destructive effect on human character and makes the rehabilitation of the individual offender much more difficult." At times the result may even be violent rioting. Finally, lengthy pretrial detention is costly. * * * In addition, society loses wages which might have been earned, and it must often support families of incarcerated breadwinners.

But, while this is a useful explanation of why society should be interested in the prompt disposition of criminal cases, it is rather misleading to say, as it is put in *Barker,* that this "societal interest" is somehow part of the right. The fact of the matter is that the Bill of Rights, does not speak of the rights and interests of the government. Moreover, to assert that this "societal interest" might well be disserved if the defendant was to surrender his right (or, indeed, even to insist that it not be honored) is not to point out anything that makes the speedy trial right different from other Sixth Amendment rights.

(c) When Right Attaches. In *United States v. Marion,*[10] the Court was called upon to determine when the speedy trial right attaches. The government appealed the dismissal of a business fraud indictment two months following its return based upon the defendants' claim that the 38–month delay between the end of the scheme charged and the indictment violated their speedy trial right. The Supreme Court reversed. It was first noted that the Sixth Amendment on its face applies "only when a criminal prosecution has begun and extends only to those persons who have been 'accused' in the course of that prosecution," and thus "would seem to afford no protection to those not yet accused, nor would [it] seem to require the Government to discover, investigate, and accuse any person within any particular period of time." More-

over, the position of the defendants was "at odds with longstanding legislative and judicial constructions of the speedy trial provisions in both national and state constitutions." Most important, however, was the fact that the defendant's position did not square with the previously noted purposes of the speedy trial guarantee:

Arrest is a public act that may seriously interfere with the defendant's liberty, whether he is free on bail or not, and that may disrupt his employment, drain his financial resources, curtail his associations, subject him to public obloquy, and create anxiety in him, his family and his friends. * * * So viewed, it is readily understandable that it is either a formal indictment or information or else the actual restraints imposed by arrest and holding to answer a criminal charge that engage the particular protections of the speedy trial provisions of the Sixth Amendment.

Invocation of the speedy trial provision thus need not await indictment, information, or other formal charge. But we decline to extend the reach of the amendment to the period prior to arrest. Until this event occurs, a citizen suffers no restraints on his liberty and is not the subject of public accusation: his situation does not compare with that of a defendant who has been arrested and held to answer. Passage of time, whether before or after arrest, may impair memories, cause evidence to be lost, deprive the defendant of witnesses, and otherwise interfere with his ability to defend himself. But this possibility of prejudice at trial is not itself sufficient reason to wrench the Sixth Amendment from its proper context. Possible prejudice is inherent in any delay, however short; it may also weaken the Government's case.[11]

Because in *Marion* "the indictment was the first official act designating appellees as accused individuals," the speedy trial right attached at the time of indictment. But, as the

---

10. 404 U.S. 307, 92 S.Ct. 455, 30 L.Ed.2d 468 (1971).

11. But, as the Court later said in United States v. Lovasco, 431 U.S. 783, 97 S.Ct. 2044, 52 L.Ed.2d 752

(1977), in such circumstances "the Due Process Clause has a limited role to play in protecting against oppressive delay." On just how limited it is, see § 18.5(b).

language quoted above makes apparent, had an arrest preceded the formal charge the right would have attached at the time of that arrest.[12]

The general rule that the speedy trial right attaches at the time of arrest or formal charge, whichever comes first, is easy to apply in most cases, but on occasion it may be unclear exactly what point in time governs. If the first critical event is indictment but the indictment is sealed until some later time, the Sixth Amendment right attaches on the date of unsealing, as there has been neither oppressive incarceration nor public accusation until then. The assumption seems to be that the possibility of prejudice to the defense from such delay is standing alone not enough to invoke the speedy trial right. A charging document short of an indictment, such as a complaint, will suffice *if* it alone gives the court jurisdiction to proceed to trial. In the event of reindictment following dismissed of the charge, the prevailing view is that the date of the original arrest or charge is still controlling, but that the time between the dismissal and recharging are not counted, provided of course that the defendant is not held in custody in the interim awaiting the new charge. But if the original charge was dismissed on motion of the defendant, some courts simply begin counting again as of the date of recharging. Problems can arise where after the initial charge some other charge is filed against the same defendant. It is difficult to generalize about this situation, except to say that the date of the first charge is more likely to be deemed controlling if the second charge by the same sovereign[13] is a refinement of the first rather than a charge of different crimes arising out of the same incident. In any

event, continuous custody of the defendant between the two charges when there is some relationship between them makes it more likely the earlier date will be deemed controlling.

When the first event is arrest,[14] the question may be whether in a nature-of-the-offense sense that arrest is sufficiently related to the later formal charge to be viewed as part of the same criminal prosecution for speedy trial purposes. Though it would be absurd in the extreme if an arrest on one charge triggered the Sixth Amendment's speedy trial protection as to prosecutions for any other chargeable offenses, the result may well be otherwise if the crimes ultimately prosecuted really only gild the charge underlying his initial arrest. A variation of the problem arises when the arrest is made by a jurisdiction other than that which later returns the charge, as where state officers apprehend a person for a violation of local law but that individual is later turned over to federal authorities for prosecution based upon the same or related conduct. Where the initial arrest is solely for violation of state law, then it is generally accepted that this arrest does not mark the commencement of the speedy trial right as to a subsequent federal charge even if based on the same activity, a result which is consistent with the dual sovereignty limitation upon the double jeopardy guarantee.[15] But where there is close state-federal cooperation in the investigation preceding the arrest or significant federal involvement promptly after the arrest, a contrary result may be justified.

(d) Waiver or Forfeiture of the Right. A defendant's claim that his Sixth Amendment

---

12. Dillingham v. United States, 423 U.S. 64, 96 S.Ct. 303, 46 L.Ed.2d 205 (1975).

13. In United States v. MacDonald, 456 U.S. 1, 102 S.Ct. 1497, 71 L.Ed.2d 696 (1982), the Court stated that "indictment by one sovereign would not cause the speedy trial guarantee to become engaged as to possible subsequent indictment by another sovereign."

14. Sometimes the question is whether there has been an "arrest" or something that ought to be viewed as comparable for speedy trial purposes. In United States v. Gouveia, 467 U.S. 180, 104 S.Ct. 2292, 81 L.Ed.2d 146 (1984), holding prison inmates suspected of murder in prison were not entitled to appointment of counsel while they were in administrative segregation before adversary

judicial proceedings had been initiated against them, the Court observed that the lower court's "attempt to draw an analogy between an arrest and an inmate's administrative detention pending investigation may have some relevance in analyzing when the speedy trial right attaches in this context." But the Court by footnote cautioned it was expressing "no view as to when the Sixth Amendment speedy trial right attaches in this context because that issue is not before us," and noted numerous circuits had "held that the segregation of an inmate from the general population pending criminal charges does not constitute an 'arrest' for purposes of the speedy trial right."

15. See § 25.5.

right to speedy trial was violated must be brought before the trial court by a timely motion to dismiss the charges. If the defendant fails to so move and instead enters a guilty plea or submits to trial, he may not raise the issue for the first time on appeal. The right is that of the defendant rather than his attorney, and thus counsel cannot waive this constitutional right over his client's objection. Failure of defense counsel to raise a speedy trial objection could in some circumstances constitute ineffective assistance of counsel, which perhaps explains why appellate courts not infrequently assess speedy trial claims even when there was no timely motion for dismissal below. If a defendant made a timely motion for dismissal on speedy trial grounds but it was denied, and the defendant thereafter entered a plea of guilty or nolo contendere, then under the traditional view he may not ordinarily obtain appellate review of the speedy trial claim. This rule has been criticized on the ground that a defendant who has interposed what he believes to be a valid speedy trial objection should not have to surrender it in order to obtain whatever benefits are to be derived from pleading guilty, and has been put into serious question by the Supreme Court's decisions on what rights are forfeited by a guilty or nolo plea.[16]

(e) Remedy for Violation. In *United States v. Strunk*,[17] where defendant's denial of a speedy federal trial occurred while he was serving a state prison sentence, the court concluded:

> The remedy for a violation of this constitutional right has traditionally been the dismissal of the indictment or the vacation of the sentence. Perhaps the severity of that remedy has caused courts to be extremely hesitant in finding a failure to afford a speedy trial. Be that as it may, we know of no reason why less drastic relief may not be granted in appropriate cases. Here no question is raised about the sufficiency of evidence showing defendant's guilt, and, as we

have said, he makes no claim of having been prejudiced in presenting his defense. In these circumstances, the vacation of the sentence and a dismissal of the indictment would seem inappropriate.

The court thus ordered that defendant receive credit on his sentence for the period of impermissible delay, reasoning that this would compensate him for the lost opportunity to serve part of the federal sentence concurrently with the state sentence. But a unanimous Supreme Court reversed, noting that delay even in a situation such as this "may subject the accused to an emotional stress" and that as a result "the prospect of rehabilitation may also be affected." The Court thus concluded: "In light of the policies which underlie the right to a speedy trial, dismissal must remain * * * 'the only possible remedy.' "[18]

§ 18.2 The Constitutional Balancing Test

(a) The *Barker* Case. Manning and Barker were arrested in July of 1958 for killing an elderly couple and were indicted in September. The prosecution believed it had a stronger case against Manning and that Barker could not be convicted unless Manning testified against him, so Manning was prosecuted first, but it took six trials until finally, in December of 1962, he had been convicted of the two murders. In the meantime, a series of continuances were granted as to Barker, who after 10 months in jail obtained his release on bond. Barker raised no objection until the twelfth continuance was sought in February 1962 and he failed to object to some later continuances, though he did object to continuances granted in March and June of 1963 because of the unavailability of a prosecution witness. He was tried over objection in October 1963 and convicted, and his speedy trial contention was later rejected by the state and lower federal courts. The Supreme Court affirmed in *Barker v. Wingo*,[1] but in the process "attempted to set

---

16. See § 21.6(a).

17. 467 F.2d 969 (7th Cir.1972).

18. Strunk v. United States, 412 U.S. 434, 93 S.Ct. 2260, 37 L.Ed.2d 56 (1973).

§ 18.2

1. 407 U.S. 514, 92 S.Ct. 2182, 33 L.Ed.2d 101 (1972).

out the criteria by which the speedy trial right is to be judged."

Noting first the "amorphous quality of the right," the Court examined "two rigid approaches" urged "as ways of eliminating some of the uncertainty." One, the proposal that the Court "hold that the Constitution requires a criminal defendant to be offered a trial within a specified time period," was rightly rejected on the ground that it "would require this Court to engage in legislative or rulemaking activity." The other proposal was that the Court adopt "the demand-waiver doctrine," which "provides that a defendant waives any consideration of his right to speedy trial for any period prior to which he has not demanded a trial." This was rejected as "inconsistent with this Court's pronouncements on waiver of constitutional rights," whereunder the test is whether there has been "an intentional relinquishment or abandonment of a known right or privilege."[2] Mere lack of demand does not evidence such a waiver, especially because defense counsel is often "in an awkward position" in deciding whether and when to make such a demand. Moreover, nonapplication of the waiver doctrine to this particular constitutional right on the ground "that delay usually works for the benefit of the accused" would be improper, as "it is not necessarily true that delay benefits the defendant."

The Court in *Barker* thus proceeded to adopt "a balancing test, in which the conduct of both the prosecution and the defendant are weighed," and to "identify some of the factors which courts should assess in determining whether a particular defendant has been deprived of his right." They are: (1) the length of the delay; (2) the reason for the delay; (3) whether and when the defendant asserted his speedy trial right; and (4) whether defendant was prejudiced by the delay. In finding no constitutional denial in the instant case, the Court utilized these factors as follows: (1) the delay, well over five years, "was extraordinary"; (2) there was good reason for 7 months of delay while a witness was unavailable, and some delay so that Manning could be tried

first was proper, but a 4–year delay for the latter reason was too long given the state's failure or inability to try Manning promptly; (3) for a long time defendant did not assert his right, and this was a calculated tactical decision based on the hope that Manning would be acquitted and the case against him dropped; (4) the prejudice "was minimal," as though he lived "for over four years under a cloud of suspicion and anxiety," most of this time he was free on bail, and there was no showing his defense at trial was prejudiced.

(b) The Length of the Delay. With respect to this first factor, the Court in *Barker* declared that "length of the delay is to some extent a triggering mechanism," so that "[u]ntil there is some delay which is presumptively prejudicial, there is no necessity for inquiry into the other factors that go into the balance." The reference to "delay which is presumptively prejudicial" is somewhat confusing, but viewing the case in its entirety it seems fair to say that this phrase does *not* mean a period of time so long that it may actually be presumed the defense at trial would be impaired.[3] Nor does it mean that once a sufficient time has been shown the prosecution has the burden of establishing that in fact there was no prejudice. The Court apparently meant that a claim of denial of speedy trial may be heard after the passage of a period of time that is, prima facie, unreasonable in the circumstances.

The Court in *Barker* says that this length of time is "dependent upon the peculiar circumstances of the case," and by way of example it is added that "the delay that can be tolerated for an ordinary street crime is considerably less than for a serious, complex conspiracy charge." What this illustration is intended to reveal about the kind of "peculiar circumstances" deserving of notice is far from clear. Perhaps it is meant to show that it takes more time to trigger further inquiry when the nature of the case is more complex and thus in need of more trial preparation. But if that is the point, then it may be criticized on two

---

2. Johnson v. Zerbst, 304 U.S. 458, 58 S.Ct. 1019, 82 L.Ed. 1461 (1938).

3. See Doggett v. United States, 505 U.S. 647, 112 S.Ct. 2686, 120 L.Ed.2d 520 (1992).

counts: the example really does not reflect such a distinction; and to the extent the prosecutor by reason of the nature of the charge or otherwise is hampered by special difficulties, this could best be taken into account under the reason-for-delay factor. The lower courts have been inclined to apply this first *Barker* factor without any extensive assessment of the unique facts of the particular case. Rather, the courts have usually tried to settle upon some time period after which, as a general matter, it makes sense to inquire further into why the defendant has not been tried more promptly. Generally, any delay of eight months or longer is deemed "presumptively prejudicial," any delay of less than five months is not, while there is judicial disagreement as to the six to seven month range.

In determining whether the requisite period of time has passed, it is necessary of course to know how the counting is to be done. In the usual case, this is simply a matter of calculating the time that has elapsed from when the Sixth Amendment right attached[4] until trial (or, until the pretrial motion to dismiss on this ground is determined). But when the situation is out of the ordinary it may be necessary, as to certain portions of this intervening period, to determine whether the circumstances then prevailing were such that the interests protected by the Sixth Amendment right[5] were implicated. Such was the approach taken in *Klopfer v. North Carolina*,[6] where defendant was indicted in February 1964 for criminal trespass but the prosecutor in August 1965 obtained a "*nolle prosequi* with leave," which served to toll the statute of limitations but left the prosecutor free to reinstate the prosecution on that indictment at some future date. Though the state court ruled that the subsequent delay was not relevant to defendant's speedy trial claim, the Supreme Court disagreed, noting that even though the defendant was free without recognizance he was nonetheless subject to "anxiety and concern" because of the continuing pendency of the indictment.

But in *United States v. MacDonald*,[7] the Court held that the time between dismissal of military charges and the subsequent indictment on civilian charges may not be considered in determining whether the delay in bringing the defendant to trial violated his Sixth Amendment right to speedy trial. The majority reasoned that once charges are dismissed the person is no longer a subject of public accusation and has no restraints on his liberty, a situation analogous to that in *United States v. Marion*,[8] holding the Sixth Amendment protection inapplicable in a pre-arrest, pre-indictment situation. *Klopfer* was distinguished as a case in which the charges were suspended rather than dismissed.

MacDonald rather than *Klopfer* was deemed controlling in *United States v. Loud Hawk*,[9] holding that the time during which the government appealed the district court's dismissal of the indictment, while the defendants were not incarcerated and not subject to bail (and could not have been subjected to any actual restraints without further judicial proceedings), was not to be counted. This was because there was neither public accusation nor restraint of liberty during that period; mere "public suspicion" flowing from the fact that "the Government's desire to prosecute them was a matter of public record" was not deemed sufficient to trigger Sixth Amendment protections.

(c) Reason for Delay. As for the second *Barker* factor, "the reason the government assigns to justify the delay," the Court cautioned that "different weights should be assigned to different reasons." Three categories of reasons were then listed: (1) a "deliberate attempt to delay the trial in order to hamper the defense," which "should be weighted heavily against the government"; (2) a "more neutral reason such as negligence or overcrowded courts," which "should be weighed less heavily but nevertheless should be considered since the ultimate responsibility for such

---

4. See § 18.1(c).

5. See § 18.1(b).

6. 386 U.S. 213, 87 S.Ct. 988, 18 L.Ed.2d 1 (1967).

7. 456 U.S. 1, 102 S.Ct. 1497, 71 L.Ed.2d 696 (1982).

8. 404 U.S. 307, 92 S.Ct. 455, 30 L.Ed.2d 468 (1971).

9. 474 U.S. 302, 106 S.Ct. 648, 88 L.Ed.2d 640 (1986).

circumstances must rest with the government"; and (3) "a valid reason, such as a missing witness," which "should serve to justify appropriate delay."

The initial question that must be asked is where the burden lies to supply the reasons in a particular case. The reference to "the reason the government assigns" indicates that the burden is on the government. As a practical matter, however, this is likely to mean that the prosecution is afforded an opportunity to show a reason falling in the "valid" category, failing which the case will be treated as if there was a "more neutral reason." This is because a reason that is to be heavily weighted against the government will rarely be admitted or otherwise apparent from the record. And when the government simply offers no explanation at all, it has been held that the court can presume neither a deliberate attempt to hamper the defense nor a valid reason for the delay.

Although the first of the three categories put in *Barker* might be objected to on the ground that the balancing procedure should not continue once an inexcusable breach of the state's acknowledged duty appears, the lower courts, in compliance with *Barker,* proceed with the balancing even when it is determined that there is present in the case a reason for the delay that is to be weighed heavily against the government. With respect to the second category, the illustration of "negligence" has been questioned on the ground that it seems more logically joined to the invalid reason than to the unavoidable condition of docket crowding. But it is well to remember that this second category, involving such reasons as negligence,[10] court congestion, and an understaffed prosecutor's office,[11] should not be described (as sometimes is the case) as the "neutral reason" category; after all, "the duty of the charging authority is to provide a prompt trial,"[12] and thus such reasons weigh against the government albeit "less heavily than intentional delay."[13]

It must be stressed, as to the Court's third category, that while it is called "a valid reason" this does not mean that existence of a reason falling within this grouping will necessarily compel the conclusion that defendant's speedy trial rights were not violated. This is but one of the four factors in the balancing test, and as is highlighted by the Court's statement that such a reason will "justify appropriate delay," even a valid reason does not necessarily permit delay indefinitely. And certainly a close look at the circumstances of the particular case is in order. To take, for example, the Court's hypothesis of a missing witness, it is appropriate to determine how important the witness is, why he is missing, and how hard the government has looked to find him. Courts have recognized several other situations falling within the "valid reason" category, such as incompetency of the defendant, unavailability of the defendant, the unavailability of a codefendant in a joint trial situation, interlocutory appeal by the prosecution, and the necessity to rule on defendants pretrial motions.

The reason-for-delay factor was assessed with respect to interlocutory appeals "when the defendant is subject to indictment or restraint"[14] in *United States v. Loud Hawk.*[15] As for the rare case in which such an appeal may be and is taken by a defendant, the Court stated that where the defendant's claim is clearly without merit he cannot complain about appellate delay, and that even if it was "meritorious" he would have a "heavy burden of showing an unreasonable delay," for a defendant "normally" cannot complain about the very process he invoked. As for government appeal, the Court said it "ordinarily is a valid reason that justifies delay" (i.e., in *Barker* category (3)), but seemed to acknowledge

---

10. See, e.g., Doggett v. United States, 505 U.S. 647, 112 S.Ct. 2686, 120 L.Ed.2d 520 (1992):

11. The latter was added to the second category in Strunk v. United States, 412 U.S. 434, 93 S.Ct. 2260, 37 L.Ed.2d 56 (1973).

12. Dickey v. Florida, 398 U.S. 30, 90 S.Ct. 1564, 26 L.Ed.2d 26 (1970).

13. Strunk v. United States, 412 U.S. 434, 93 S.Ct. 2260, 37 L.Ed.2d 56 (1973).

14. On this limitation, see the discussion of *Loud Hawk* in § 18.2(b).

15. 474 U.S. 302, 106 S.Ct. 648, 88 L.Ed.2d 640 (1986).

that a particular case could fall into category (2) because of crowded appellate courts or into category (1) if the prosecution misused the appellate process. Thus, courts must consider "the strength of the Government's position on the appealed issue, the importance of the issue in the posture of the case, and—in some cases—the seriousness of the crime."

(d) Defendant's Responsibility to Assert the Right. Although *Barker* rejected the notion that failure to demand a speedy trial constitutes a waiver of that right, the Court hastened to add that this "does not mean, however, that the defendant has no responsibility to assert his right." The Court thus held that "the defendant's assertion of or failure to assert his right to a speedy trial is one of the factors to be considered." Assertion of the right, the Court said, "is entitled to strong evidentiary weight," but yet it was cautioned that not all demands need to be assessed in the same way; the "frequency and force of the objections" should be taken into account. Thus, a mere pro forma demand will not count for much, and even a more substantial demand is weakened where the defendant subsequently engaged in delaying tactics or indicated a desire not to be tried promptly.

The Court in *Barker* deemed it important to "emphasize that failure to assert the right will make it difficult for a defendant to prove that he was denied a speedy trial." Consequently, lower courts rather readily assume that a lack of demand indicates that the defendant really did not want a prompt trial. It is important, however, to examine carefully the circumstances of the particular case. As the Court cautioned in *Barker,* a case in which the defendant knowingly fails to object to ongoing delay is quite different from "a situation in which his attorney acquiesces in long delay without

adequately informing his client, or from a situation in which no counsel is appointed." Moreover, failure to make a demand can hardly be counted against the defendant during those periods when he was unaware that charges had been lodged against him or when he was incompetent.[16]

(e) Prejudice. As for the final factor of prejudice, *Barker* teaches that it must "be assessed in the light of the interests of defendants which the speedy trial right was designed to protect": (i) to prevent oppressive pretrial incarceration; (ii) to minimize anxiety and concern of the accused; and (iii) to limit the possibility that the defense will be impaired. As with the previous three factors, *Barker* treats prejudice as neither "a necessary or sufficient condition to the finding of a deprivation of the right of speedy trial," and thus, as the Court later held, it is a "fundamental error" to say that a defendant cannot prevail unless he makes an affirmative showing of prejudice.[17] (More recently, however, the Court itself appears to have made precisely such an error.[18]) Just when a defendant will succeed without such a showing is a matter on which the courts are not in complete agreement. It is sometimes said that defendant must have shown bad motives by the prosecutor, sometimes that the other three factors must be in defendant's favor, and sometimes that they must weigh heavily in his favor.

As for prejudice of the first type, it is noteworthy that in *Barker* the defendant's incarceration for 10 months was not deemed sufficiently oppressive to call for a ruling in his favor. Lower courts have reached the same conclusion as to substantially longer periods of imprisonment. As for the second type of prejudice, it is always present to some extent, and

16. Thus in Doggett v. United States, 505 U.S. 647, 112 S.Ct. 2686, 120 L.Ed.2d 520 (1992), where defendant was unaware he had been charged until he was arrested 8½ years later, he "is not to be taxed for invoking his speedy trial right only after his arrest."

17. Moore v. Arizona, 414 U.S. 25, 94 S.Ct. 188, 38 L.Ed.2d 183 (1973).

18. In Reed v. Farley, 512 U.S. 339, 114 S.Ct. 2291, 129 L.Ed.2d 277 (1994), the Court held that a state court's failure to observe the 120–day time-for-trial rule of the Interstate Agreement on Detainers was not cognizable on

federal habeas corpus when, as here, the defendant registered no objection to the trial date when it was set and suffered no prejudice from the delay. In responding to Reed's argument the result should be otherwise because the IAD's speedy trial provision "effectuates" the Sixth Amendment speedy trial guarantee, the Court asserted, citing *Barker*: "A showing of prejudice is required to establish a violation of the Sixth Amendment Speedy Trial Clause, and that necessary ingredient is entirely missing here."

thus absent some unusual showing is not likely to be determinative in defendant's favor. The third type of prejudice, as the Court stressed in *Barker,* is "the most serious." One kind of situation described by the Court is where witnesses die or disappear. As to this, some substantiation is required; generally, it may be said that the defendant must show that the witness truly is now unavailable, that he would have been available for a timely trial, and that his testimony would have been of help to the defendant. Another variation of the third type of prejudice noted in *Barker* is where "defense witnesses are unable to recall accurately events of the distant past." As to this, special note must be taken of the Court's caution that loss of memory "is not always reflected in the record because what has been forgotten can rarely be shown." This suggests, at a minimum, that courts should not be overly demanding with respect to proof of such prejudice.

Doggett v. United States[19] makes it clear that, with respect to that third type of prejudice, the prejudice factor of *Barker* may sometimes be placed on the defendant's side of the scales even though the defendant "failed to make any affirmative showing that the delay weakened his ability to raise specific defenses, elicit specific testimony, or produce specific items of evidence." That is, "affirmative proof of particularized prejudice is not essential to every speedy trial claim," as "excessive delay presumptively compromises the reliability of a trial in ways that neither party can prove or, for that matter identify." The *Doggett* Court then concluded, as to the eight and a half year delay in that case, that prejudice would not be presumed had the delay been for a valid reason; that it would be presumed and "would present an overwhelming case for dismissal" if the delay had been deliberate; and that it would be presumed where, as in the instant case, the government's negligence amounted to "egregious persistence in failing to prosecute."

§ 18.3   Statutes and Court Rules on Speedy Trial

(a) The Need. It is apparent that the *Barker* speedy trial doctrine is not standing alone adequate to deal with the matter of prompt disposition of criminal cases. For one thing, *Barker* and related cases "have * * * tended to convert the right of every criminal defendant to have a speedy trial into a very different sort of right: the right of a few defendants, most egregiously denied a speedy trial, to have the criminal charges against them dismissed on that account."[1] Quite obviously, criminal defendants as a class need some additional basis upon which to compel the government to try them promptly. Secondly, the *Barker* balancing test, as the Court fully recognized, of necessity has an "amorphous quality" to it, for unlike what can be done via "legislative or rulemaking activity," there is "no constitutional basis for holding that the speedy trial right can be quantified into a specified number of days or months." Finally, notwithstanding the articulation in *Barker* of the "societal interest" in speedy trial, it is clear from the manner in which the Court proceeds to describe the factors to be placed in the balance (especially "the defendant's responsibility to assert his right") that this societal interest will not be sufficiently protected by the Sixth Amendment alone.

All of this points up the need for and significance of other law dealing with the subject of speedy trial. Such other law exists in all jurisdictions. On the federal level, there is the Speedy Trial Act of 1974; as for the states, rules of court or statutes impose prompt trial requirements. These rules and statutes are sometimes rather complex, as is true of the federal legislation, and elsewhere contain little detail, in which case a process of "fleshing-out" by court decision has typically occurred.

(b) Federal Speedy Trial Act of 1974. The Speedy Trial Act of 1974[2] imposes time

---

19.   505 U.S. 647, 112 S.Ct. 2686, 120 L.Ed.2d 520 (1992).

§ 18.3

1.   Amsterdam, Speedy Criminal Trial: Rights and Remedies, 27 Stan.L.Rev. 525 (1975).

2.   18 U.S.C.A. §§ 3161–3174. The Act was amended in

requirements for the trial of criminal cases in the federal courts. Because this Act worked a rather dramatic change in federal law in this respect, a five-year transition period was provided for; the final time limits and sanctions became effective only at the end of that time. This transition period allowed the federal courts to engage in research and planning facilitating compliance with the statutory requirements and providing a basis for recommending changes in the Act.

As for the time limits provided under the Act, an indictment or information is to "be filed within thirty days from the date on which such individual was arrested or served with a summons in connection with such charges," except that if in a felony case no grand jury was in session during that time the period "shall be extended an additional thirty days." As for trial, it is to "commence within seventy days from the filing date (and making public) of the information or indictment, or from the date the defendant has appeared before a judicial officer of the court in which such charge is pending, whichever date last occurs." The Act also protects the defendant from undue haste, for absent defendant's consent "the trial shall not commence less than thirty days from the date on which the defendant first appears through counsel or expressly waives counsel and elects to proceed pro se."[3]

The Act specifies the point at which the counting of the time to charge and to trial is to be commenced in certain special circumstances. If the charge was dismissed on motion of the defendant but he is later charged "with the same offense or an offense based on the same conduct or arising from the same criminal episode," then the time is to be calculated "with respect to such subsequent complaint, indictment, or information, as the case may be." If a charge was dismissed but reinstated following an appeal, then trial must ordinarily commence "within seventy days from the date the action occasioning the retrial becomes final." As for a second trial occasioned by a mistrial, order for new trial, appeal or collateral attack, again the retrial must ordinarily begin "within seventy days from the date the action occasioning the retrial becomes final."

As for the "periods of delay" that "shall be excluded in computing the time" for charge or trial, the Act specifies the following:

(1) any "period of delay resulting from other proceedings concerning the defendant," such as examinations and other proceedings to determine competency to stand trial, trial of other charges, interlocutory appeal, transfer to another district, consideration of a proposed plea agreement, "delay resulting from any pretrial motion, from the filing of the motion through the conclusion of the hearing on, or other prompt disposition of, such motion," and delay up to 30 days "during which any proceeding concerning the defendant is actually under advisement by the court."

(2) any "period of delay during which prosecution is deferred" by agreement of the prosecutor, defendant and court.

(3) any "period of delay resulting from the absence or unavailability of the defendant[4] or an essential witness." A person is absent "when his whereabouts are unknown and, in addition, he is attempting to avoid apprehension or prosecution or his whereabouts cannot be determined by due diligence," and is unavailable "whenever his whereabouts are known but his presence for trial cannot be obtained by due diligence or he resists appearing at or being returned for trial."

1979 and 1988. The discussion following is of the Act as amended and without reference to provisions that are of no effect after the transitional period.

3. In United States v. Rojas–Contreras, 474 U.S. 231, 106 S.Ct. 555, 88 L.Ed.2d 537 (1985), the Court held that this 30–day period does not begin to run anew upon the filing of a superseding indictment; that the authority of the court under § 3161(h)(8) to grant an "ends of justice" continuance "should take care of any case in which the Government seeks a superseding indictment which operated to prejudice a defendant"; and that there was no prejudice in the instant case because the superseding indictment merely corrected the date of a prior conviction.

4. Pursuant to a 1988 amendment to the Act, if a defendant is absent on the date set for trial and later appears before the court not more than 21 days later, the time limit as otherwise extended is extended by 21 days. If the defendant's appearance is more than 21 days later, the date of that appearance is to be treated as defendant's first appearance before a judicial officer for purposes of calculating that defendant's statutory speedy trial right.

(4) any "period of delay resulting from the fact that the defendant is mentally incompetent or physically unable to stand trial."

(5) any "period of delay resulting from the treatment of the defendant" under the Narcotics Addict Rehabilitation Act.

(6) "any period of delay from the date the charge was dismissed to the date the time limitation would commence to run as to the subsequent charge had there been no previous charge," provided the dismissal was on motion of the prosecutor.

(7) a "reasonable period of delay when the defendant is joined for trial with a codefendant as to whom the time for trial has not run and no motion for severance has been granted."

(8) a "period of delay resulting from a continuance granted by any judge on his own motion or at the request of the defendant or his counsel or at the request of the attorney for the Government," provided the judge makes findings for the record as to why "the ends of justice served by the granting of such continuance outweigh the best interests of the public and the defendant in a speedy trial." The judge is to consider whether failure to grant the continuance would likely "make a continuation of such proceeding impossible, or result in a miscarriage of justice"; whether the case is so complex "that it is unreasonable to expect adequate preparation for pretrial proceedings or for the trial itself within the time limits"; whether, as to preindictment delay, it is "because the facts upon which the grand jury must base its determination are unusual or complex"; and whether failure to grant the continuance would deny defense counsel or prosecutor "the reasonable time necessary for effective preparation, taking into account the exercise of due diligence." In addition, the statute expressly forbids the granting of a continuance "because of general congestion of the court's calendar, or lack of diligent preparation or failure to obtain available witnesses on the part of the attorney for the Government." This provision on continuances, virtually un-

precedented in prior speedy trial statutes and rules, is the heart of this statutory scheme.

(9) a "period of delay, not to exceed one year, ordered by a district court upon an application of a party and a finding by a preponderance of the evidence that an official request * * * has been made for evidence of any such offense and that it reasonably appears, or reasonably appeared at the time the request was made, that such evidence is, or was, in such foreign country."

As for sanctions, the Act provides that if the charge is not filed within the 30 day limit extended by any excluded periods or if defendant has moved for dismissal because trial did not commence within the 70 day limit extended by any excluded periods, then the case or charge shall be dismissed. "In determining whether to dismiss the case with or without prejudice, the court shall consider, among others, each of the following factors: the seriousness of the offense; the facts and circumstances of the case which led to the dismissal; and the impact of a reprosecution on the administration of this chapter and on the administration of justice." This "with or without prejudice" provision, the result of an amendment on the floor of the House, is not only anticlimactic but also very unclear. The legislative history indicates, however, that dismissal with prejudice is permitted under circumstances which would not require dismissal under the Sixth Amendment, and that the extent of prejudice to the defendant, government "fault," and defense "fault" are other factors to be weighed in the balance. But, "Congress did not intend any particular type of dismissal to serve as the presumptive remedy for a Speedy Trial Act violation."[5] A "district court must carefully consider [the aforementioned] factors as applied to the particular case and, whatever its decision, clearly articulate their effect in order to permit meaningful appellate review," during which the appellate court can "ascertain whether a district court has ignored or slighted a factor that Congress has deemed pertinent to the choice of remedy."[6]

---

5. United States v. Taylor, 487 U.S. 326, 108 S.Ct. 2413, 101 L.Ed.2d 297 (1988).

6. Ibid.

Finally, it must be noted that the federal Act expressly provides for punishment of any prosecutor or defense attorney who "(1) knowingly allows the case to be set for trial without disclosing the fact that a necessary witness would be unavailable for trial; (2) files a motion solely for the purpose of delay which he knows is totally frivolous and without merit; (3) makes a statement for the purpose of obtaining a continuance which he knows to be false and which is material to the granting of a continuance; or (4) otherwise willfully fails to proceed to trial without justification." The punishment may be a fine up to $250 on the prosecutor or up to 25% of the compensation due appointed or retained defense counsel, denial of the right to practice before that court for up to 90 days, or filing of a report with the appropriate disciplinary committee.

(c) State Provisions. Virtually all states have provisions in their own constitutions safeguarding the right to speedy trial. Usually the language is identical to that in the Sixth Amendment, and thus the tendency of state courts is to use the balancing test of *Barker v. Wingo*[7] in construing those provisions. In addition, all but a few states have adopted statutes or rules of court on the subject of speedy trial. These provisions usually provide protection beyond the state constitutional guarantee, and thus, to understand fully the speedy trial situation in any particular jurisdiction, it is necessary to examine the applicable court rule or statute and the case law that has developed from it. The objective here is the more modest one of providing a general description of those provisions collectively.

Most of the state provisions declare that trial must commence within a specified period of time from a specified event. These time limits range up to one year, with the most common time limit being six months. As for the event that will start the specified time running, these provisions usually state that where the defendant was indicted prior to arrest or, where indictment is not required, a complaint, affidavit, or information was filed before arrest, the time runs from the date the

charge was filed, and otherwise the time runs from the date of arrest or first appearance before a judicial officer; some states, however, have provided (usually shorter) limits running from some later event, such as the defendant's arraignment, plea of not guilty, or demand for trial.

Some of the more elaborate speedy trial statutes and court rules specify other starting times for special situations. Most common is the declaration that if there is to be a retrial following a mistrial, order for a new trial, appeal or collateral attack, then the counting begins on the date of mistrial, order or remand. Statements that the counting of the time is to begin anew following defendant's withdrawal of a guilty plea or termination from a pretrial diversion program are encountered much less frequently. As for trial on a charge earlier dismissed, those statutes and court rules specifically addressing this situation often ensure that the prosecutor cannot circumvent speedy trial requirements by a process of dismissal and recharging, typically by asserting that the time does not begin running anew (as might well be the case if dismissal was on motion of the defendant) but instead is merely interrupted between dismissal and recharging. When these matters are not addressed in the speedy trial statute or court rule, then they must be addressed by the courts when such situations arise, which can produce various results; especially as to the troublesome matter of prosecutor dismissal and recharging, there is no uniformity in approach.

In the case of the typical speedy trial provision, determining the time within which the trial must begin is not merely a matter of identifying the proper starting point for counting the time and then adding on the number of days or months specified in the applicable court rule or statute. It is also necessary to add on any excluded periods. Some of these provisions define those excluded times in some detail, usually encompassing periods of delay resulting from (1) other proceedings concerning the defendant; (2) a continuance granted

---

7. 407 U.S. 514, 92 S.Ct. 2182, 33 L.Ed.2d 101 (1972).

at the request of the prosecution or at the request of or with the consent of the defendant; (3) the absence or unavailability of the defendant; and (4) the defendant being joined for trial with a codefendant as to whom the time for trial has not run, where there is good reason for not granting a severance. Where such detail is given, it is sometimes the case that the statutory or court rule list of exclusions constitutes the only bases for extending the time, and sometimes the case that the provision contains a residual "good cause" category conferring upon the judge in the particular case the authority to find other bases for delay. Several other states have provisions with shorter or less detailed lists of excluded periods, again either with or without a "good cause" residual category. It is a fair generalization that those provisions having very long time periods to start with or not providing for a dismissal remedy in the event the trial is not commenced on time are likely to have the fewest and narrowest excluded times. Still other speedy trial provisions are quite different; no excluded periods are defined in the statute or rule of court, which instead confers upon the judge the authority to permit delay for "good cause" or pursuant to some similar general standard. Finally, there are provisions that seem to contemplate no excluded periods because they neither set out such a general standard or describe particular situations justifying exclusion.

In dealing with court congestion, these state rules and statutes come down on both sides of the issue, some effectively excluding such delay from consideration in measuring expiration of time-precise periods, while others do not. As for continuances, many of the statutes and court rules state that such continuances when sought by the defendant toll the running of the time for trial or simply make such time limits inapplicable, yet do not in any way suggest that restraint and caution should be exercised in granting them. These provisions appear to encourage rather than discourage the routine granting of defense continuances, to the detriment of the public interest in speedy trial. Several other states forbid the routine granting of defense continuances by requiring that such continuances be permitted only upon a showing of "good cause" or "extraordinary" or "exceptional" circumstances, or, even better, by requiring the judge to weigh the defendant's reasons against the public interest in prompt disposition. As for a continuance requested by the prosecution, it is commonly made clear that the request can be granted only upon a showing of need, and the applicable provision usually states what is needed in rather specific and narrow terms.

As for the applicable sanction when a defendant by timely motion has shown that the time specified by a statute or court rule has run, the prevailing view is that only dismissal with prejudice will suffice, meaning that the defendant may not later be charged with the same offense (or, some of the provisions specify, with any related offense). Ambiguous statutes have usually been interpreted as mandating dismissal with prejudice, and only rarely as either permitting only dismissal without prejudice or placing the choice of the form of dismissal in the hands of the judge. This last alternative is also specifically provided for in a few other states, while a few other jurisdictions provide for dismissal with prejudice only for lesser offenses. But some states do not utilize dismissal of the charges in any form. In the remaining states, the only means of relief mentioned in the applicable provisions is release of the defendant from custody upon the running of the time for trial.

§ 18.4   The Imprisoned Defendant

(a) Constitutional Right. Despite numerous prior lower court decisions to the contrary, the Supreme Court in *Smith v. Hooey*,[1] held that prisoners also have Sixth Amendment speedy trial rights and that consequently upon demand by the prisoner the charging jurisdiction "had a constitutional duty to make a diligent, good-faith effort to bring him before the * * * court for trial." This result was assured once the Court in *Smith* concluded that the interests protected by the constitu-

---

§ 18.4

1. 393 U.S. 374, 89 S.Ct. 575, 21 L.Ed.2d 607 (1969).

tional right are especially threatened "in the case of an accused who is imprisoned by another jurisdiction." As for the interest in preventing undue and oppressive incarceration prior to trial, delay as to an imprisoned defendant may "result in as much oppression as is suffered by one who is jailed without bail upon an untried charge":

> First, the possibility that the defendant already in prison might receive a sentence at least partially concurrent with the one he is serving may be forever lost if trial of the pending charge is postponed. Secondly, under procedures now widely practiced, the duration of his present imprisonment may be increased, and the conditions under which he must serve his sentence greatly worsened, by the pendency of another criminal charge against him.

The reference is to the fact that the filing of a detainer[2] on a prisoner may have adverse effects upon the prisoner's situation.[3] As for the interest in minimizing the anxiety and concern accompanying public accusation of crime, the Court in *Smith* noted that delay could be particularly harmful to a prisoner in this respect, for it would tend to thwart efforts at rehabilitation. Likewise, the interest in preventing impairment of the ability to defend is especially strong as to a prisoner, for he "is powerless to exert his own investigative efforts to mitigate [the] erosive efforts to the passage of time."

A year later, in *Dickey v. Florida*,[4] the Court had occasion to apply *Smith* and actually hold that a particular prisoner's speedy trial right had been violated. Although *Dickey* preceded

the Court's announcement of the four-pronged balancing test in *Barker v. Wingo*,[5] the holding in *Dickey* can easily be placed into the *Barker* framework. In holding that the defendant's Sixth Amendment right to a speedy trial had been violated, the Court emphasized: (1) the length of the delay, here a "seven-year period"; (2) the reason for the delay, here that "no tenable reason" was ever offered for not seeking to obtain custody of defendant from a federal prison; (3) that over this period defendant made "diligent and repeated efforts * * * to secure a prompt trial"; and (4) prejudice was apparent, for in the interval "two witnesses died and another potential witness is alleged to have become unavailable," and "[p]olice records of possible relevance have been lost or destroyed."

More recently and quite correctly, lower courts have applied the *Barker* formula to prisoner cases in much the same way as in other cases. What this means, with respect to the reason for the delay, is that the government has the burden of showing that the reason is something other than a failure (as stated in *Smith*) to "make a diligent, good-faith effort to bring him before the * * * court for trial." If the government makes no such showing, this counts against the government, but not as heavily as it would if an actual intent to hamper the defense were shown. And *Smith*, which stresses the "increased cooperation between the States themselves and between the States and the Federal Government," makes it perfectly clear that the fact the charging jurisdiction lacks the power to compel the defendant's return is not a valid reason for failing to make the effort. But there is no need to

---

2. A detainer, or hold order, may be filed by a prosecutor, court, police chief or any other official empowered to take persons into custody, and it need not be supported by an indictment or information. A detainer notifies the incarcerating authorities that the prisoner is wanted, and requests that the authorities desiring custody be forewarned of the prisoner's release date so that they can arrange to pick him up at the institution. Filing a detainer is an informal process; it does not bind the requesting authority to act (and roughly half are never acted upon), nor does it bind the incarcerating authorities to hold the prisoner, although this is usually done as a matter of comity between sovereigns.

3. The existence of a detainer may have several adverse effects upon the prisoner. He may, for that reason, be held under maximum security or be denied opportunities open to other prisoners, such as transfer to a minimum security area, the privilege of being a trusty, or assignment to a job involving a degree of trust. The detainer makes the prisoner's future uncertain, and thus renders more difficult the formulation of an effective rehabilitation program. Many parole boards will not consider parole for a prisoner who has a detainer lodged against him, although some jurisdictions are now using the parole-to-detainer device, which allows release of the detainee while he serves another sentence or answers other charges

4. 398 U.S. 30, 90 S.Ct. 1564, 26 L.Ed.2d 26 (1970).

5. 407 U.S. 514, 92 S.Ct. 2182, 33 L.Ed.2d 101 (1972).

make this effort when the other jurisdiction is holding the defendant pending or during trial and sentencing, for return during such period would not occur. And there is some tendency not to be as demanding when the defendant is being held in a foreign country, in which case presumably the chances of cooperation may at least sometimes be diminished.

Although, as in other situations governed by *Barker,* a defendant who fails to demand a prompt trial is ordinarily unlikely to prevail, note must be taken of two special circumstances that may be present in the prisoner case. On occasion, especially where the charging authorities have not filed a detainer against the prisoner, the prisoner may be unaware of the outstanding charge, in which case his lack of demand can hardly be counted against him. And when he is aware, as is more commonly the case, the imprisoned defendant is unlikely to have the assistance of counsel, which has influenced courts to be fairly generous in deciding exactly what constitutes a demand. Finally, it should be noted that the presence of a demand may also have an important bearing on the reason-for-delay factor, as it will deprive the charging jurisdiction of the excuse which otherwise might be valid: that the defendant's whereabouts were unknown.

As for the prejudice factor, it is unlikely to weigh heavily in the prisoner's favor unless he makes the kind of showing accepted by the Court in *Dickey.* Something more than mere speculation is ordinarily required to establish impairment of the defense. As for the anxiety factor, it will count substantially in defendant's favor only if it is shown that there was a rather special situation giving rise to an inordinate amount of anxiety. Similarly, courts often do not take favorably to speculative assertions of loss of concurrent sentencing.

If a person serving a prison term in state *A* has a detainer filed against him by state *B* because of an outstanding charge there, but state *B* has failed to act upon that person's demand for a prompt trial, the prisoner may seek relief via federal habeas corpus. In such circumstances, the prisoner is in a unique situation whereby he has a choice of the federal court in which to file his habeas petition. It may be filed in *either* the federal district where he is presently incarcerated *or* the federal district of the outstanding charge, though either district could transfer the case to the other if it proved to be a more convenient forum.[6]

(b) Federal Speedy Trial Act of 1974. This Act deals specially with the situation in which the prosecutor knows that a person charged with a federal offense is serving a term of imprisonment in any penal institution. In such a case, the prosecutor has the option of "promptly" doing either of two things: (1) he may undertake to obtain the prisoner's presence for trial; or (2) he may cause a detainer to be filed with the person having custody of the prisoner and request him to so advise the prisoner and to advise him of his right to demand trial. If, in the latter instance, the prisoner informs the person having custody that he does demand trial, this person is to cause that notice to be sent promptly to the prosecutor who caused the detainer to be filed. Upon receipt of that notice, the prosecutor must "promptly seek to obtain the presence of the prisoner for trial."[7]

Because under the Act generally it does not take a demand by the defendant to start the speedy trial clock running, it might be asked why an exception has been made in this particular case. A part of the explanation is that the public interest in speedy trial is not as intense in the situation just discussed; there is no additional cost associated with such correctional custody, nor any of the risks associated with pretrial release. But more important is the fact that this exception opens up an important tactical choice for the prisoner. Absent a desire by the prosecutor to go to trial, the prisoner then retains the option of demanding trial in order to overcome whatever disadvantages may flow from the fact that a detainer has been lodged against him or of not making the demand in the hope that the charges will be

---

6. Braden v. 30th Judicial Circuit Court, 410 U.S. 484, 93 S.Ct. 1123, 35 L.Ed.2d 443 (1973).

7. 18 U.S.C.A. § 3161(j).

dropped before or at the time the prisoner completes his sentence.

(c) Interstate Agreement on Detainers.

Under the Uniform Criminal Extradition Act,[8] which has been adopted in the overwhelming majority of the states, procedures are set out whereby a person imprisoned in another state may be extradited for purposes of criminal prosecution. However, the necessity for extradition often can be avoided by proceeding under the Interstate Agreement on Detainers,[9] a Compact adopted by the federal government and virtually all the states. The IAD provides that a prisoner against whom a detainer has been filed must be promptly notified of that fact and of his right to demand trial, and if he demands trial then trial must be had within 180 days thereafter; the request is a waiver of extradition by the prisoner, and the state by adopting the Compact has agreed to surrender the prisoner under such circumstances; if trial is not had within 180 days and good cause for delay is not shown, the charges are dismissed with prejudice.

The prosecutor is certainly an appropriate officer to file the detainer, though in practice the filing might be by a court clerk or police official. Failure of the custodian to notify the prisoner of the detainer is a serious matter, but the IAD has no sanction for failure to notify timely an inmate about a detainer. As for the inmate's demand for trial, some courts are quite particular and thus have held that a motion for speedy trial is insufficient or that a request not sent through channels is inadequate compliance with the Compact, while oth-

ers are less demanding. In *Fex v. Michigan*,[10] the Court held that the 180 days begins running "when the prisoner's request for final disposition of the charges against him has actually been delivered to the court and prosecuting officer of the jurisdiction that lodged the detainer against him." The Court reasoned the alternative construction of the IAD, that the prisoner's delivery to the custodial authorities should suffice and that their "negligence or even malice" in failing or delaying to forward the request should count against the prosecutor rather than the prisoner, would produce an "undesirable result." The 180 days can be tolled in some circumstances, as where the prisoner is standing trial in another state, and can be extended by continuances for good cause, as where a witness is unavailable.

If trial of the charge is not commenced on time and defendant (or his counsel[11]) has not waived the time limit, then the court is to "enter an order dismissing the same with prejudice, and any detainer based thereon shall cease to be of any force or effect." Also, if the inmate is returned to his original place of imprisonment without trial, the charge "shall not be of any further force or effect." But, while some courts had held that the purpose of that provision is to prevent significant interference with the inmate's rehabilitation and that consequently dismissal is not required when the violation of the antishuttling provision is "technical," "harmless," or "*de minimis*," the Supreme Court ruled otherwise in *Alabama v. Bozeman*.[12] A unanimous Court held that because the language of the Agree-

---

8. 11 U.L.A. 59 (1974).

9. 11 U.L.A. 323 (1974). Article III of the IAD, which by its terms applies to detainers based on an "indictment," "information," or "complaint," refers to documents charging a person with a criminal offense, and thus is not applicable to a detainer based on probation violation charges. Carchman v. Nash, 473 U.S. 716, 105 S.Ct. 3401, 87 L.Ed.2d 516 (1985).

10. 507 U.S. 43, 113 S.Ct. 1085, 122 L.Ed.2d 406 (1993).

11. In New York v. Hill, 528 U.S. 110, 120 S.Ct. 659, 145 L.Ed.2d 560 (2000), a unanimous Court held that "defense counsel's agreement to a trial date outside the time period required by Article III * * * bars the defendant from seeking dismissal because trial did not occur within that period." The Court reasoned that "[s]cheduling matters are plainly among those for which agreement

by counsel generally controls," for "only counsel is in a position to assess the benefit or detriment of the delay to the defendant's case," and "only counsel is in a position to assess whether the defense would even be prepared to proceed any earlier." As for defendant's claim "that the IAD benefits not only the defendant but society generally, and that the defendant may not waive society's rights," the Court responded that "some social interests served by prompt trial are less relevant here than elsewhere": "because the would-be defendant is already incarcerated in another jurisdiction, society's interests in assuring the defendant's presence at trial and in preventing further criminal activity (or avoiding the costs of pretrial detention) are simply not at issue."

12. 533 U.S. 146, 121 S.Ct. 2079, 150 L.Ed.2d 188 (2001).

ment is absolute it permitted no implied exceptions. Consistent with the fact that the IAD refers to the receiving state having "temporary custody" of the prisoner, the usual practice if the inmate is now convicted and sentenced in the receiving state is that he is returned to the sending state to complete his sentence there, after which he is extradited to the receiving state to then serve the previously-imposed sentence there. However, the inmate has no legally protected interest in having that procedure followed, and thus, for example, if the sentence was a term of years in the sending state and death in the receiving state, the sending state may waive its right to have the inmate returned so that the death penalty may be carried out in the receiving state.

(d) Uniform Mandatory Disposition of Detainers Act. Seven states have adopted this Act,[13] and several others have enacted similar legislation. The UMDDA provides that the inmate's custodian must promptly inform him of any charges against him by that jurisdiction of which the custodian has knowledge or notice and of his right to request disposition of such charges. If a detainer has been filed against the inmate, failure of the custodian to advise the inmate of the detainer within a year of the filing entitles the inmate to dismissal of the charge with prejudice. An inmate can request disposition of any outstanding charge, and this request is to be forwarded by the custodian to the appropriate court and prosecutor. Failure of the custodian to perform that responsibility would entitle the prisoner to relief. Trial is to commence within 90 days of the time the court and prosecution receive the request, though additional time can be granted for good cause. The defendant has no further burden to seek a timely trial, and if the prosecutor does not ensure that the trial starts on time the defendant is entitled to dismissal with prejudice.

§ 18.5　The Right to Other Speedy Disposition

(a) Statutes of Limitations. In *United States v. Marion*,[1] in the course of holding that the Sixth Amendment right to speedy trial had no application to delay preceding both arrest and charge, the Court noted that statutes of limitations provide "the primary guarantee against bringing overly stale criminal charges."[2] As the Court earlier noted in *Toussie v. United States*:[3]

> The purpose of a statute of limitations is to limit exposure to criminal prosecution to a certain fixed period of time following the occurrence of those acts the legislature had decided to punish by criminal sanctions. Such a limitation is designed to protect individuals from having to defend themselves against charges when the basic facts may have become obscured by the passage of time and to minimize the danger of official punishment because of acts in the far-distant past. Such a time limit may also have the salutary effect of encouraging law enforcement officials promptly to investigate suspected criminal activity.

Other objectives are served by these statutes. They prevent prosecution of those who have been law abiding for some years, avoid prosecution when the community's retributive impulse has ceased, and lessen the possibility of blackmail. But foremost is the desirability of requiring that prosecutions be based upon reasonably fresh evidence so as to lessen the possibility of an erroneous conviction. Thus, these statutes share an important common purpose with speedy trial protections, and to that end are liberally construed in favor of criminal defendants.

All jurisdictions make a distinction between serious and minor offenses, permitting longer lapses of time for prosecution of the former. For felonies the times usually range between three and six years; for misdemeanors they are ordinarily somewhere between one and three

---

13.　11 U.L.A. 328 (1974).

§ 18.5

1.　404 U.S. 307, 92 S.Ct. 455, 30 L.Ed.2d 468 (1971).

2.　Quoting from United States v. Ewell, 383 U.S. 116, 86 S.Ct. 773, 15 L.Ed.2d 627 (1966).

3.　397 U.S. 112, 90 S.Ct. 858, 25 L.Ed.2d 156 (1970).

years. The assumption appears to be that a longer time is justified for serious crimes because in such instances there is a greater need for deterrence, a greater likelihood the perpetrator is a continuing danger to society, and a lesser likelihood that the perpetrator would reform on his own. It is commonly provided that a few of the most serious offenses, usually murder and treason, have no statute of limitations.

Virtually all jurisdictions provide that the period of limitation begins to run with the commission of the crime, that is, when every element in the statutory definition of the offense has occurred. Certain crimes are properly characterized as continuing offenses, and as to them the time begins to run only when the course of conduct or defendant's complicity therein terminates. Illustrative of continuing offenses are possession-of-contraband crimes, falsification schemes continuing to produce fruits, and of course conspiracy (where the counting begins with the last overt act or, with respect to a particular conspirator, his effective withdrawal from the enterprise).

It is common to deal with certain special situations by provisions that allow either for tolling of the time or for the time to commence at some time later than commission of the offense. The assumption underlying the rules usually applicable is that most offenses are known at least to the victim at the time of or soon after its commission, or that the offense can be discovered by adequate investigation by enforcement officials. But this is not likely to be true of cases involving fraud or breach of fiduciary obligation or those involving misconduct by a public officer or employee, and thus some statutes provide that the times for such offenses run from the date of discovery or

departure from office, respectively. Many statutes more generally provide that the time does not run when commission of the crime has been concealed; these provisions are narrowly construed, for efforts at concealment are so common that literal application of such provisions would deprive the statute of limitations of most of its effect. Limitations statutes also usually provide for tolling during the period of nonavailability of the defendant.

Though the purpose of these statutes is to ensure a timely commencement of prosecution, there is not agreement on what act will suffice to show such commencement. Some legislation expressly requires that an indictment be found or an information filed, but where this is not the case it is generally held sufficient that an arrest warrant has issued or that a complaint has been filed. Assuming diligence in arresting the defendant or notifying him of the complaint, these latter interpretations square with the assumption that the basic purpose of a statute of limitations is to insure that the accused will be informed of the decision to prosecute and the general nature of the charge with sufficient promptness to allow him to prepare his defense before evidence of his innocence becomes weakened with age. So as not to foreclose recharging after proceedings terminated prior to final adjudication, it is commonly provided that the statute is tolled during the time a prosecution was pending for the same offense or, as it is put in some jurisdictions, for an offense arising out of the same transaction. If the original charge, timely brought, resulted in conviction for a lesser offense as to which the time had run before the original charge was brought, this conviction is barred by the statute of limitations (unless waived by the defendant[4]) for the rea-

---

4. A variation of this problem reached the Supreme Court in *Spaziano v. Florida,* 468 U.S. 447, 104 S.Ct. 3154, 82 L.Ed.2d 340 (1984), where at defendant's trial for the capital offense of first-degree murder the trial judge refused to instruct on the lesser included offenses of attempted first-degree murder, second-degree murder, third-degree murder, and manslaughter because defendant refused to waive the statute of limitations, which had already run on those offenses. Defendant claimed this violated the Supreme Court's ruling in *Beck v. Alabama,* 447 U.S. 625, 100 S.Ct. 2382, 65 L.Ed.2d 392 (1980), that in a capital trial a lesser included offense instruction is a

necessary element of a constitutionally fair trial, but the Supreme Court disagreed. *Beck,* the Court explained, was intended "to eliminate the distortion of the fact-finding process that is created when the jury is forced into an all-or-nothing choice between capital murder and innocence," but requiring "that the jury be instructed on lesser included offenses for which the defendant may not be convicted * * * would simply introduce another type of distortion into the fact-finding process." The Court concluded a proper compromise of the defendant's and prosecution's interests would be to give the defendant "a choice between having the benefit of the lesser included offense instruc-

son that otherwise the prosecutor might over-charge to avoid the limitation period on the lesser offense.

Three different views are to be found as to the effect of the running of the applicable statute of limitations in a criminal case. One is that once the time has run the court is without jurisdiction to try the offense, which means the defendant need not raise the issue in a pretrial motion and is entitled to relief notwithstanding his otherwise valid plea of guilty or his raising of the issue for the first time on appeal. The second is that this is a matter of affirmative defense which may be waived by either the defendant's failure to raise it in a pretrial motion or the defendant's entry of a guilty plea. The third variation is that the statute of limitations is waivable, but that only an intentional relinquishment of the right will suffice.

(b) Unconstitutional Pre-accusation Delays. In *United States v. Marion*,[5] the Court cautioned that "the statute of limitations does not fully define the appellees' rights with respect to the events occurring prior to indictment," and noted that the government conceded that the due process clause "would require dismissal of the indictment if it were shown at trial that the pre-indictment delay in this case caused substantial prejudice to appellees' rights to a fair trial and that the delay was an intentional device to gain tactical advantage over the accused." Because the posture of the case was such that defendants' due process claims were "speculative and premature," the Court did not elaborate on this due process test.

The contours of the test were elucidated to some extent in the later case of *United States v. Lovasco*,[6] overturning the lower court's ruling that defendant's rights were violated where he established actual prejudice (loss of the testimony of a significant witness) and the government's explanation for the 17–month delay was the desire for further investigation notwithstanding the presence of sufficient evidence to support a charge. The Court first rejected unequivocally the contention that a due process violation exists whenever pre-charge delay actually prejudices the defendant. Prejudice, the court concluded, "is generally a necessary but not sufficient element of a due process claim," and its existence merely "makes a due process claim concrete and ripe for adjudication." What remains to be assessed in such circumstances are "the reasons for the delay," and so the Court in *Lovasco* turned to this question and concluded that no due process violation exists in the case of "investigative delay." As for just what is encompassed within that term, the Court explained: (1) that it unquestionably covers the case where probable cause was lacking, because "it is unprofessional conduct for a prosecutor to recommend an indictment on less than probable cause"; (2) that it also covers the case where probable cause existed, for "prosecutors are under no duty to file charges * * * before they are satisfied they will be able to establish the suspect's guilt beyond a reasonable doubt," as such charging would "increase the likelihood of unwarranted charges being filed," cause "potentially fruitful sources of information to evaporate," and "cause scarce resources to be consumed on cases that prove to be insubstantial"; and (3) that it even covers the case where there is "evidence sufficient to establish guilt," for to compel immediate charging upon such evidence "would preclude the Government from giving full consideration to the desirability of not prosecuting in particular cases," and also "would cause numerous problems in those cases in which a criminal transaction involves more than one person or more than one illegal act," for "an immediate arrest or indictment would impair the prosecutor's ability to continue his investigation" and thus might result

---

tion or asserting the statute of limitations on the lesser included offenses."

5. 404 U.S. 307, 92 S.Ct. 455, 30 L.Ed.2d 468 (1971).

6. 431 U.S. 783, 97 S.Ct. 2044, 52 L.Ed.2d 752 (1977). In United States v. Eight Thousand Eight Hundred and Fifty Dollars, 461 U.S. 555, 103 S.Ct. 2005, 76 L.Ed.2d 143

(1983), the government argued *Lovasco* provided the standard by which to test post-seizure delay in a forfeiture proceeding under 31 U.S.C.A. § 1102(a), but the Court concluded that a "more apt analogy is to a defendant's right to a speedy trial," and thus applied the *Barker* balancing test discussed in § 18.2.

in other illegal acts or other participants not being prosecuted or being prosecuted too late to permit joinder in a single trial.

With respect to what reasons for delay are "bad," in the sense that their coexistence with actual prejudice would entitle the defendant to prevail on his due process claim, the *Lovasco* Court declined to deal with that question "in the abstract." The Court did note that the government had renewed its concession in *Marion* that dismissal would be required if the delay was undertaken solely "to gain tactical advantage over the accused," and then in a footnote observed that the government had now broadened its concession by stating: "A due process violation might also be made out upon a showing of prosecutorial delay incurred in reckless disregard of circumstances, known to the prosecution, suggesting that there existed an appreciable risk that delay would impair the ability to mount an effective defense."

Under the two-pronged test of *Lovasco*, as interpreted by the lower courts, it will be extremely difficult for a defendant to prevail on his due process claim.[7] As for the prejudice prong, though *Lovasco* contains the somewhat qualified statement that "proof of prejudice is generally a necessary * * * element," the lower courts take the view that prejudice must always be shown. The burden of proof is on the defendant to show prejudice by a preponderance of the evidence; actual prejudice must be established, for courts are disinclined to presume prejudice no matter what the reason for delay or length of delay, and some courts also insist that the prejudice must be substantial in degree. As for what it takes to meet this burden, it is not enough that the defendant is unable to recall or reconstruct the events in question, for he must show an actual loss of a witness or physical evidence. And it must be established that this loss was prejudicial. This

means, for example, that in the case of a lost witness it must be shown that the witness would have been available at an earlier time, would have testified for the defendant, and would have aided the defense.

As for the reason-for-delay prong, it is unclear where *Lovasco* places this burden. The government gave no explanation for the delay in the district court, and the Supreme Court proceeded as had the Court of Appeals to accept the government's representations as to the motivation for the delay set out in the government's appellate brief. Some lower courts have read *Lovasco* to mean that once the defendant proves prejudice, then "the burden shifts" to the prosecution to show a valid reason for the delay. This is a sensible allocation of the burden, for the reasons underlying the delay are peculiarly within the knowledge of the prosecution. Nonetheless, the prevailing view is that the defendant must shoulder this burden as well. It is not an easy burden to meet, especially because there is no discernible inclination of the lower courts to treat anything except an intent to hamper the defense as an improper reason.

It can certainly be argued that the *Lovasco* rule is too demanding. "Loss of memory," the Supreme Court noted in *Barker v. Wingo*,[8] "is not always reflected in the record because what has been forgotten can rarely be shown." That being so, it would not be inappropriate to require the prosecution to establish that no such harm has occurred when it has acted for the purpose of hampering the defense. Indeed, it has been argued that the *Lovasco* test should be restated "in a disjunctive fashion, so that constitutional guarantees of due process of law would mandate dismissal if the delay were perpetrated by the state to gain a tactical advantage over the accused, or if the accused

---

7. In an apparent effort to avoid such difficulties, the defendants in United States v. Gouveia, 467 U.S. 180, 104 S.Ct. 2292, 81 L.Ed.2d 146 (1984), argued without success that the Sixth Amendment required appointment of counsel prior to the initiation of adversary judicial proceedings against indigent inmates who are confined in administrative detention for lengthy periods while being investigated for crimes committed in prison, for the reason that counsel could minimize the risks which attend a delay in the

bringing of charges. The Court concluded that though these concerns were "certainly legitimate," the protections of the statute of limitations and the *Lovasco* due process rule were sufficient that it was not necessary "to depart from our traditional interpretation of the Sixth Amendment right to counsel in order to provide additional protections."

8. 407 U.S. 514, 92 S.Ct. 2182, 33 L.Ed.2d 101 (1972).

demonstrated that he had suffered actual, substantial and irremediable prejudice."

(c) Post–Trial Delays. Even if the criminal trial has commenced on time, the defendant might object to delays occurring thereafter. If the case was tried without a jury, the objection, as in *Campodonico v. United States*,[9] might be that the trial judge unduly delayed his findings as to defendant's guilt or innocence. In that case, where the criminal trial lasted only 14 hours but defendant was adjudged guilty more than a year after commencement of that trial, he claimed this delay violated his Sixth Amendment right to a speedy trial. The court, though not questioning the applicability of the constitutional right to a speedy trial in this context, ruled against the defendant on the theory that he could not now complain in light of his failure "to press the trial court for a quick decision." Both that result and the assumption that the Sixth Amendment right was applicable are consistent with the later analysis in *Barker v. Wingo*.[10]

As for delays in sentencing, the Supreme Court in *Pollard v. United States*[11] assumed that the Sixth Amendment right to speedy trial was applicable to such delays. This is also consistent with the later analysis in *Barker*, where the Court stressed that delay in punishment "may have a detrimental effect on rehabilitation" and thus be harmful to the particular defendant and to society at large. Other courts have rather consistently held that the Sixth Amendment right applies to sentencing delay, but then have typically ruled against the defendant because of his failure at any time during the interval between conviction and sentence to request prompt sentencing. A due process violation may occur because of delay in *execution* of the sentence, but this requires a

showing of something more than mere negligence by the government.

Because appeals are not a part of the "criminal prosecutions" to which Sixth Amendment rights attach,[12] it seems clear that a speedy trial claim may not be made with respect to delays in the appellate process.[13] But, while the Constitution apparently does not require the states to afford a right to appellate review of a criminal conviction, when a state does provide the right it must do so in a manner meeting the requirements of due process and equal protection.[14] As concluded in *Rheuark v. Shaw*,[15] "due process can be denied by any substantial retardation of the appellate process, including an excessive delay in the furnishing of a transcription of testimony necessary for completion of an appellate record." Though this might suggest that the *Lovasco* decision concerning pre-charge delays in violation of due process would provide the best analogy for purposes of analysis, the court in *Rheuark* concluded this was not the case. Noting that "the reasons for constraining appellate delay are analogous to the motives underpinning the Sixth Amendment right to a speedy trial," the court decided that application of the four factors in *Barker* was the best way "to determine whether a denial of due process has been occasioned in any given case."

Proceedings to revoke probation or parole, while likewise not a part of the "criminal prosecutions" covered by the Sixth Amendment,[16] are subject to due process limits. In *Morrissey v. Brewer*,[17] dealing exclusively with the due process protections attending the parole revocation process, the Court concluded a parolee is entitled to two hearings, a preliminary hearing and a final revocation hearing, and that both must be conducted in a timely fashion. Because the latter might occur after

---

9. 222 F.2d 310 (9th Cir.1955).

10. 407 U.S. 514, 92 S.Ct. 2182, 33 L.Ed.2d 101 (1972).

11. 352 U.S. 354, 77 S.Ct. 481, 1 L.Ed.2d 393 (1957).

12. Douglas v. California, 372 U.S. 353, 83 S.Ct. 814, 9 L.Ed.2d 811 (1963).

13. Except in the case of interlocutory appeal "when the defendant is subject to indictment or restraint." See the discussion of the *Loud Hawk* case in § 18.2(c).

14. Douglas v. California, 372 U.S. 353, 83 S.Ct. 814, 9 L.Ed.2d 811 (1963).

15. 628 F.2d 297 (5th Cir.1980).

16. Except when sentencing has been deferred to the time of probation revocation. Mempa v. Rhay, 389 U.S. 128, 88 S.Ct. 254, 19 L.Ed.2d 336 (1967).

17. 408 U.S. 471, 92 S.Ct. 2593, 33 L.Ed.2d 484 (1972).

"a substantial time lag" and at a place distant from where the alleged violation of parole occurred, the Court concluded that "due process would seem to require that some minimal inquiry be conducted at or reasonably near the place of the alleged parole violation or arrest and as promptly as convenient after arrest while information is fresh and sources are available." As for the final hearing, the Court in *Morrissey* declared that it "must be tendered within a reasonable time after the parolee is taken into custody," but added that a "lapse of two months * * * would not appear to be unreasonable." Later in *Gagnon v. Scarpelli*,[18] the Court held that a probationer "is entitled to a preliminary and final revocation hearing, under the conditions specified in *Morrissey*," and thus a probationer also has a due process right to timely hearings.

An exception was recognized in the later case of *Moody v. Daggett*,[19] holding that a federal parolee was not constitutionally entitled to a prompt parole revocation hearing under the facts of that case. The parolee killed two people while he was on parole, for which he was convicted and sentenced to two concurrent 10–year terms. A parole violator warrant was then issued and lodged with prison officials as a detainer, which thus was to be executed only at the end of the new sentences, and the parolee then unsuccessfully sought dismissal of the warrant on the ground he had been denied a prompt hearing. The Court affirmed, ruling that *Morrissey* was not controlling because the parolee was not presently in custody as a parole violator: not even his opportunity for parole on the intervening sentences was affected by the outstanding warrant, and the question of whether the new sentences should run concurrently with the balance of the old one could be addressed whenever revocation was undertaken. Moreover, the Court was strongly influenced by the fact that in this particular situation there was a "practical aspect" making delay of the revocation issue a preferable course of action. Because the parolee had been convicted of new crimes obviously amounting to a violation of his parole, "the only remaining inquiry is whether continued release is justified notwithstanding the violation." Given "the predictive nature" of such a determination, as to which "a parolee's institutional record can be perhaps one of the most significant factors," it "is appropriate that such hearing be held at the time at which prediction is both most relevant and most accurate—at the expiration of the parolee's intervening sentence."

18. 411 U.S. 778, 93 S.Ct. 1756, 36 L.Ed.2d 656 (1973).

19. 429 U.S. 78, 97 S.Ct. 274, 50 L.Ed.2d 236 (1976).

Part Four

THE ADVERSARY SYSTEM AND THE DETERMINATION OF GUILT AND INNOCENCE

Chapter 19

THE ACCUSATORY PLEADING

Table of Sections

---

§ 19.1   The Liberalization of Pleading Requirements

(a) Common Law Technicalities. As first developed, the accusatory pleading was a simple document. In the early fourteenth century, it was sufficient to allege that "A stole an ox, B burgled a house, C slew a man." Over the next few centuries, however, as the criminal law grew more complex and defendants were allowed to use counsel to challenge indictments, courts came to demand that the pleading contain a full statement of the facts and legal theory underlying the charge. Pleading requirements for particular crimes often paralleled in their complexity and formalism the

882

special civil pleadings required for the different forms of action. Indictments were lengthy, highly detailed, and filled with technical jargon. An indictment charging forcible entry had to include the words "with strong hand" and one alleging an assault had to include the phrase "*vi et armis*." In a perjury indictment, it was necessary to allege both that the statement was made under oath and that the oath was given before a proper person, and a murder charge had to describe not only the means used but also the nature and extent of the wound inflicted.

For many years, American courts demanded strict adherence to the technical niceties of common law pleading rules. Indictments were not infrequently quashed for the most picayune errors in form. As the Supreme Court later noted, the courts were unwilling "to understand or accept a pleading that did not exclude every misinterpretation capable of occurring to an intelligence fired with a decision to pervert." Moreover, defects in an indictment were not waived by defendant's failure to object before trial; most defects could also be challenged after conviction by a motion in arrest of judgment. As a result, courts were striking down convictions fully supported by the evidence simply because indictments were inartfully drawn, awkwardly worded, or failed to include evidentiary detail. Two North Carolina rulings of the early 1800s illustrated just how far courts could go in this regard. One reversed a conviction in a murder case because the indictment, in specifying the location of the wound, spelled "breast" as "brest," and the other overturned a murder conviction because the indictment "did not set forth the length and depth of the mortal wounds."

A conviction could also be reversed because the evidence at trial varied from facts alleged in the indictment. Here too, the courts generally were strict, except for variance as to the date of the offense. Thus, an 1840s Delaware decision reversed a conviction under an indictment alleging the theft of a "pair of shoes" because the evidence established that both of the shoes stolen were for the right foot and therefore did not constitute a pair.

While the formalism and detail mandated by the common law pleading rules were designed in part to provide notice to the accused, they clearly went beyond what was needed to provide notice alone. Indeed, it has been suggested that the "common law indictment, replete with archaic terminology and ritualistic formulae, was a lengthy and tortuous document, which * * * served more to mystify than to inform the defendant." As Sir James Stephen observed, a major function of the "strictness and technicality" in indictments was to guard against "looseness in the legal definitions of crimes." At a time when "the concepts and definitions of offenses took form largely through the experience of administration and without the aid of definitive statutes," the requirement that the offense be stated according to a particular formula, specifying in detail each element of the crime, was seen as providing assurance both that the grand jury understood what was necessary to establish an offense and that the courts did not engage in unanticipated extensions of the substance of the offense. Courts in later years suggested that perhaps an equally significant function of the complex common law requirements was to supply the judiciary with grounds that were readily available for reversing convictions in cases in which the harsh punishments of the day (which were non-reviewable) did not fit the offender or his offense.

(b) Initial Attempts at Reform. By the mid–1800s, with the increasing codification of the substantive criminal law and the sharp reduction in the number of capital offenses, many courts no longer insisted upon strict adherence to the technical rules of pleading. The judiciary, they noted, should "no longer permit the guilty man to escape punishment by averring that he cannot comprehend * * * what is palpable and evident to the common sense of everybody else." Many rulings were not consistent with this philosophy, however, as well established precedent proved difficult to discard. Indeed, a substantial number of courts not only continued to adhere to the technical rules of common law pleading, but also extended those rules to informations where the jurisdiction now allowed felony prosecutions to be brought by information rather than indictment. The nineteenth-century appellate courts rendering such decisions argued that the exactness they demanded in criminal cases was not "an idle technicality," but "a safe and salutary policy * * * supported by the weightiest of evidence." Because "the harmless decision of today becomes the dangerous precedent of tomorrow," the "people [could] have no better security than in holding the officers of the state to a reasonable degree of care, precision, and certainty in prosecuting a citizen for a violation of law."

State legislatures tended to view reversals on technical pleading errors as more reflective of "record worship" than a concern for fairness. They responded with legislative reform enactments carrying such titles as the "Common Sense Indictments Act." In general, the new legislation was directed at relaxing specific common law requirements. Thus, it was provided that a murder charge need not allege the manner or means of causing death, that there was no need to specify the denomination or species of money taken in a theft, and that the absence of specified phrases, such as "with force and arms," did not render an indictment invalid. More general provisions stated that variances would not be fatal unless they were "material," and that indictments should not "be deemed insufficient * * * by reason of any defect or imperfection in form only, which shall not tend to the prejudice of the defendant." The judicial response to the new legislation was mixed. Although most jurisdictions had adopted some form of pleading reform by the start of the twentieth century, courts in many states continued to insist that offenses be charged with technical accuracy and nicety of language. This led to the of broader pleading reform legislation discussed below.

(c) The Short–Form Pleading Movement. One legislative avenue to the liberalization of pleading requirements was the authorization of "short-form" pleadings. The authorizing statute would specify the particular language to be used in alleging the most common criminal offenses. That language would present an extremely truncated description of the criminal conduct. A murder plead-

ing, for example, would allege only that "A.B. murdered C.D." If the defendant wanted more information, he was entitled to a "bill of particulars setting up specifically the nature of the offense charged." The theory underlying the short-form pleading was that the pleading would be immune from attack (assuming the specified language was followed) and the defendant would receive his notice through the bill of particulars. The only post-conviction challenge available to the defendant would be based on the sufficiency of that notice, and such a challenge would be lost if the defendant had not specifically indicated before trial exactly what additional information was needed.

In general, the short form process survived constitutional challenges. There was a persistent concern, however, that it would be held inconsistent with the indictment process since the bill of particulars was provided by the prosecutor and did not necessarily reflect the thinking of the grand jury. Also, even in information states, prosecutors had reservations about the litigation consequences of short-form pleading. Precisely how much information had to be included in the bill of particulars was uncertain. If the prosecutors there were required to furnish as much detail as formerly was included in the common law pleadings (or even more), that would create a substantial risk of fatal variance between the trial proof and the bill. The end result was that the short-forms were eventually discarded in many of the states where initially authorized. However, such pleadings are still authorized and used today in a handful of states.

(d) The Mid–1900s Reforms. The legislative effort that eventually did succeed in liberalizing pleading requirements centered upon the enactment of three interrelated reforms: (1) a single simplified pleading standard; (2) official forms for the most commonly prosecuted crimes; and (3) an expanded waiver rule. These reforms, which had already been instituted in a fair number of states, were included in the Federal Rules of Criminal Procedure, when the Federal Rules were initiated in 1946. Today, they are found in almost all jurisdictions, with many states having provisions that are almost verbatim copies of the Federal Rules provisions. In many jurisdictions, these reforms did not replace, but were added to the earlier reforms, which modified common law requirements as to specific offenses and prohibited dismissals for specified technical imperfections or for any "defect or imperfection in the matter of form which does not tend to prejudice the substantial rights of the defendant upon the merits."

Federal Rule 7(c) sets forth the most common formulation of a simplified pleading standard. It requires that the "indictment or information * * * be a plain, concise, and definite written statement of the essential facts constituting the offense charged." This standard—followed verbatim or in substance in the vast majority of states—offered several advantages over the provisions adopted in the first wave of pleading reforms. Many of those provisions dealt either with a specific common law pleading requirement or a particular crime. Rule 7(c), on the other hand, established a single standard, applicable to the pleading of all crimes and to all elements of the pleading. Moreover, the description of that standard was quite similar to the description that reformers had used to obtain simplified pleadings in civil cases (though the Rule 7(c) reference to pleading "facts" more closely resembled the earlier code pleading reforms than the more liberal Federal Rules of Civil Procedure). The incorporation of the basic thrust of an already achieved reform provided clear indication of direction even if the parallel between the civil complaint and the criminal pleading was far from perfect. Finally, apart from any analogy to the reform of civil pleadings, the language of the Rule 7(c) standard, combined with other provisions speaking to specific parts of the pleading, clearly evidenced a rejection of the formalism and verbosity of common law pleadings. What was required was merely a statement "setting forth, in factual terms, the elements of the offense sought to be charged."

That Rule 7(c) did not require all of the detail found in the common law pleading was apparent from its reference to a "concise" statement of the "essential" facts. On the oth-

er hand, the Rule 7(c) standard also rejected the truncated short-form pleading of "A murdered B," since it required allegation of all of the "essential facts" that "constitut[e] the offense charged." Exactly how little detail was needed apparently would vary with the offense, and most jurisdictions adopting the Rule 7(c) formulation initially adopted official forms, which provided both specific and general guidance.

The Federal Rules originally included forms for 11 different crimes, which many years later were deleted as no longer necessary. The states adopting forms often did so for a much larger group of offenses. In addition to providing the prosecutor with a safe path for pleading the listed offenses, the forms seek to "illustrate the simplicity of statement which the Rules are designed to achieve." Thus, Federal Rule Form 1, for the offense of murder in the first degree of a federal officer, stated:

> On or about the _____ day of _____, in the _____ District of _____, John Doe with premeditation and by means of shooting murdered John Roe, who was then an officer of the Federal Bureau of Investigation of the Department of Justice engaged in the performance of his official duties.

The third element of pleading reform incorporated in the Federal Rules was an expansive waiver doctrine that forced most pleading objections to be raised before trial. The original version of Federal Rule 12(b) provided that "defenses and objections based on defects * * * in the indictment or information other than it fails to show jurisdiction in the court or to charge an offense may be raised only by motion before trial." Rule 12(b) further stated that the failure to present any such objection pretrial constituted a "waiver," although the court "for good cause shown" was given discretion to "grant relief from the waiver." The only exceptions, the waiver provision noted, were the failure to show jurisdiction or to charge an offense. Those defects were to "be noticed by the court at any time during the pendency of the proceeding."

The Rule 12(b) provision sharply restricted the defense tactic of "sandbagging" that was available in many jurisdictions under common law pleading. Recognizing that there was a defect in the pleading, defense counsel in those jurisdictions often would forego raising the defect before trial, when a successful objection would merely result in an amendment of the pleading (or a new pleading). If the trial ended in a conviction, counsel would then raise the defect on a motion in arrest of judgement and obtain a new trial. Federal Rule 12(b) eliminated this tactic as to all pleading objections except the failure to show jurisdiction or to charge an offense. While those objections could be raised for the first time at any point in the proceeding, which included the appeal following conviction, any lesser objection to the pleading would be lost if not raised before trial (absent a showing of good cause and a favorable exercise of trial court discretion). States with court rules modeled on the Federal Rules typically have incorporated verbatim a later (but substantively identical) version of this Federal Rule 12(b) provision, and other states have similar provisions requiring most pleading objections to be raised before trial (and in some states, before entry of a plea).

Of course, the requirement that the objection be raised before trial did not preclude the possibility that a conviction would be reversed on appeal due to a pleading error. The trial court might reject the pretrial objection, and continue through the trial and subsequent conviction, only to have an appellate court reverse the conviction because the ruling on the pleading objection was erroneous. However, the requirement of a pretrial objection did put the prosecutor in a position where she could take steps to preclude that possibility. If the prosecutor had any doubt as to the validity of the challenged pleading, she could always avoid the possibility of a reversal on appeal by substituting a new pleading that eliminated the alleged flaw. Of course, since the requirement of pretrial objection was not absolute, that opportunity was not guaranteed. A late objection could be excused under the good cause exception, but that was not likely as to

pleading objections (in contrast to other defects in the institution of the prosecution, which might not be apparent on the record). Of more concern was the failure of the pleading to "charge an offense," as that was a fairly common objection, and Rule 12(b) required that it be "noticed * * * at any time during the pendency of the proceeding."

While the requirement of a pretrial objection hopefully would reduce the number of convictions that were reversed due to pleading defects, it did not respond to the problem of convictions reversed due to a variance between the allegations contained in a proper pleading and the proof introduced at trial. Many states, seeking to preclude application of the rather strict common law view of variance, adopted legislation permitting the pleading to be amended at trial to conform to the proof (thereby "curing" the variance), provided the defendant was not prejudiced by the amendment. The Federal Rules did not include such a provision as to indictments, although it did allow liberal amendment of an information.

(e) **Recent Reforms.** Over roughly the past decade, rulings in Texas, Oklahoma, and several federal courts may have sown the seeds for a new round of widespread pleading reforms. These rulings related to the consideration of pleading errors on appellate review following a conviction. As to pleading objections raised before trial and rejected by the trial court, the traditional position has been that, as to most such objections, a finding that the trial court erred in failing to dismiss the pleading requires a reversal of the defendant's conviction. Oklahoma has taken the position, however, that the conviction will be overturned only if the pleading defect resulted in prejudice to the defendant due to a lack of notice.[1] As discussed in § 19.3(a), several federal courts have held that an erroneous trial ruling on even a failure to charge an offense will not require reversal on appeal if the error is deemed "harmless." Reversal is no longer

---

§ 19.1

1. Parker v. State, 917 P.2d 980 (Okla.Cr.App. 1996) (court in considering prejudice from lack of notice will go beyond the pleading and ask whether the notice lacking in the pleading was a otherwise provided).

automatic, but depends upon the possible impact of error on the trial proceedings.

Where a pleading objection was not raised pretrial, Rule 12(b) and similar state provisions deem the object forfeited, except for the "failure to show jurisdiction * * * or to charge an offense." As to those objections, the traditional position is that they can be raised for the first time on appeal, and if the objection is well taken, the conviction must be reversed. The practical impact of this position is largely limited to the failure to charge an offense (i.e., the failure to allege all essential elements of the offense), as pleadings will rarely be challengeable for failing to invoke jurisdiction. As discussed in § 19.3(e), appellate courts subject to special scrutiny essential elements objections that were first raised on appeal, but traditionally have automatically reversed a conviction on finding a complete failure to charge an essential element. Texas was the first jurisdiction to flatly reject this position, as it came to hold that pleading defects in form or substance, including "missing element" defects, are forfeited if not raised before trial.[2] Subsequently, as discussed in § 19.3(e), the federal courts moved in the same direction. The Supreme Court in *United States v. Cotton*[3] held that at least one type of essential elements defect, if not raised before trial, could only be considered on appeal if it met the rigid requirements of the plain error rule. This position has been extended by several federal lower courts to preclude consideration of all essential elements objections first raised on appeal.

It remains to be seen whether the new positions taken by a scattering of federal courts as to applying the harmless error and plain error standards to pleading defects will be accepted throughout the federal system. It also remains to be seen whether a large number of states will similarly reject the traditional positions on appellate review of pleading objections properly presented in the trial court and essential

elements objections first raised after conviction. Particularly with respect to the application of a harmless error analysis, there is potential as well for extending this new position to other types of objections. As discussed § 19.5 and § 19.6, jurisdictions accepting that position could readily extend harmless error analysis to the appellate review of claims that the trial court erroneously permitted an amendment of the charging instrument or erroneously disregarded a variance from the pleading in permitting the prosecution to advance a particular line of proof.

§ 19.2   Pleading Functions

(a) Functional Analysis. Courts frequently note that under modern pleading philosophy, the accusatory instrument should be tested by reference to the basic functions that a pleading should perform rather than by reference to technical pleading requirements. The reforms incorporated in the Federal Rules and similar state provisions were designed to allow simplified pleadings, but they were not intended to modify the fundamental functions of the written charge. Accordingly, it is noted, the sufficiency of an indictment or information should ultimately depend on whether it fulfills those functions. The Supreme Court has consistently adhered to this "functional approach," which it utilized even before the Federal Rules were adopted. In *Hamling v. United States*,[1] it set forth the following standard for testing pleading sufficiency, based on a long line of cases applying a functional analysis:

> Our prior cases indicate that an indictment is sufficient if it, first, contains the elements of the offense charged and fairly informs a defendant of the charge against which he must defend, and, second, enables him to plead an acquittal or conviction in bar of future prosecutions for the same offense.

Although sometimes described as a two-pronged test, the *Hamling* standard actually

---

2. See Studer v. State, 799 S.W.2d 263 (Tex.Crim.App. 1990) (relying on a 1985 Texas constitutional amendment).

3. 535 U.S. 625, 122 S.Ct. 1781, 152 L.Ed.2d 860, also discussed in § 19.2 at note 6, § 19.3 at note 16, § 19.5 at note 5, and § 19.6 at note 9.

§ 19.2

1. 418 U.S. 87, 94 S.Ct. 2887, 41 L.Ed.2d 590 (1974).

includes three requirements: (1) inclusion of the elements of the offense; (2) providing adequate notice as to the charge; and (3) providing protection against double jeopardy. These three requirements have been cited repeatedly by both federal and states courts. They are widely treated as providing the basic analytical framework for determining whether a particular pleading sets forth a "plain, concise, and definite * * * statement of the essential facts constituting the offense charged," as required by Federal Rule 7(c) and similar state provisions.

The second and third requirements of *Hamling* clearly identify basic functions of the accusatory pleading. The need for notice and protection against double jeopardy are commonly accepted as pleading goals and regularly are looked to in evaluating alleged pleading deficiencies. The first requirement of *Hamling*—that the pleading set forth the presence of each of the essential elements of the offense—is less helpful. That requirement clearly identifies what must be included in the pleading, but does not explain why that content is needed. Nonetheless courts quite often refer to the "essential elements" requirement as a pleading objective in itself, without seeking to explore what lies beneath that requirement. That is unfortunate, as it is in the application of the essential elements requirement that the functions of the pleading are most fully discerned. For that requirement, as *Hamling* implicitly suggests, may find part of its grounding in functions that exist apart from providing notice and protection against double jeopardy. In particular, in discussing the essential elements requirements, courts have pointed to three other functions of a pleading—(1) informing the court of the elements that the prosecution intends to prove, so that it can determine whether they are legally sufficient to constitute a crime; (2) ensuring that grand jury took all the elements into consideration in voting to indict (a function limited to indictments); and (3) providing a formal record upon which the prosecution can proceed.

The discussion of pleading functions that follows focuses primarily upon the relationship of pleading functions to the essential elements requirement. This should not be taken to suggest that a functional analysis is less helpful in determining the scope of other pleading requirements. Courts utilize a functional analysis in applying all four of the basic pleading standards discussed in § 19.3—the essential elements requirement, the requirement of sufficient factual specificity, the prohibition against duplicity (i.e., charging separate offenses in a single count), and the prohibition against multiplicity (i.e., charging a single offense in more than one count). Indeed, the functions underlying the latter three standards are more readily identified and therefore more readily lead to a functional analysis in the judicial application of those standards.

(b) Double Jeopardy Protection. Protecting the defendant against multiple jeopardy for the same offense was a pleading function given considerable attention at common law. Perhaps its most obvious influence is in the prohibition against multiplicity (i.e., charging a single offense on multiple counts), a practice which could lead to multiple punishments for a single offense in violation of the double jeopardy prohibition. However, the double jeopardy function is also cited as a source of the requirement that the pleading sets forth the essential elements of the offense.

The link between the essential elements requirement and protection against multiple jeopardy is found in the double jeopardy clause's reliance upon the *Blockburger*-elements standard to determine whether prosecutions for different statutory crime are nonetheless prosecutions for the "same offence" under the double jeopardy clause.[2] If each charging instrument sets forth all of the elements of offense charged, a court can determine by reference to those pleadings whether each crime charged contains an element not found in the other and therefore constitutes a separate offense for double jeopardy. Of course, even if the crimes charged in a first and second prosecution do not each present a separate element,

2. See § 17.4(b).

that does not invariably mean that they present the same offense. The facts sustaining the elements may have been different, producing different offenses, as where the defendant in the same criminal episode commits the same crime against different victims or on separate occasions commits the same crime against the same victim. Thus, to allow a court to determine on the face of two pleadings that the same offense is charged in both, the pleadings must provide considerable factual specificity as to the elements of the crime, covering such matters and the time, place, conduct, and victim's identity.

As applied over the years, neither the essential elements requirement nor the requirement of adequate factual specificity have been tied to what is necessary to ensure that a court can determine, simply by comparing allegations, whether two pleadings charge the same offense. As for informing the court of the elements of the crime being charged, where those elements are clearly stated in the statutes defining the crimes, a pleading's inclusion of statutory citations should be enough to allow the court to compare the elements of two crimes. However, such a reference typically is not enough to satisfy the essential elements requirement, which will reject a pleading for failing to allege a particular element even though any court reviewing the pleading obviously would be aware that proof of the element not alleged would be necessary to obtain a conviction. As to factual specificity, such crucial matters as precise time and place traditionally have not been required, even though they may be critical in determining whether two pleadings charging violations of the same criminal code provision are also charging the same offense for double jeopardy purposes. Thus, even at a time when the charging instrument was the primary record of the trial, it is questionable whether the double jeopardy function gave to those pleading requirements any special content above and beyond that demanded by other pleading functions.

More significantly, the determination of double jeopardy—especially with the introduction of the doctrine of collateral estoppel—is no longer a matter that courts expect to resolve on the basis of matching charging instruments in the first and second prosecutions. Transcriptions of trial proceedings are available to determine exactly what was put before the jury in the first case and the prosecution can be expected, in response to a defense objection, to explain how the anticipated proof in the second case will differ. Thus, commentators and a few courts have questioned whether the double jeopardy function of pleadings has any modern relevancy, as related either to the essential elements requirement or the sufficient specificity requirement. Most courts continue, however, to cite the double jeopardy function in discussing both of those pleading requirements, but then give that function no special content, assuming that a pleading satisfactory in fulfilling the notice function will also be satisfactory in fulfilling the double jeopardy function.

(c) Providing Notice. Discussions of pleading functions almost invariably start by noting that the pleading must "fairly inform" the accused of charges against him. Indeed, the notice function has been characterized by the Supreme Court as tied to the defendant's Sixth Amendment right "to be informed of the nature and cause of the accusation." Some courts therefore have suggested that the essential elements requirement is demanded by the Sixth Amendment—i.e., a failure to include reference to an essential element in a pleading constitutes a violation of the defendant's constitutional right to adequate notice of the charge against him. However, such statements typically are made in connection with interpretations of a Rule 7(c)-type pleading provision, with the court having no need to rely upon the Sixth Amendment. In applying the Sixth Amendment notice requirement to other objections related to pleadings, courts have looked to (1) the actual notice provided in light of the totality of the information available to the defendant and (2) the likelihood of the defendant having actually been prejudiced in defending against the charges. These rulings suggest that compliance with the Sixth Amendment notice requirement looks beyond the face of the pleadings, which the essential elements requirement and other pleading requirements do not do.

While the Sixth Amendment may not require that the pleading in itself provide adequate notice of the offense charged, Federal Rule 7(c) and counterpart state provisions clearly do require that the charging instrument provide such notice. However, disagreement exists both as to those features of the crime as to which notice is needed and the degree of particularization that should be required in providing notice as to those features. The Rule 7(c) notice function clearly requires that the pleading identify the conduct of the defendant alleged to have constituted a crime. The primary disagreement here, as discussed in § 19.3(b), concerns the amount of factual detail that must be included in describing that conduct. Whether the Rule 7(c) notice function also underlies the essential elements pleading requirement is not so clear. Some courts state that the essential elements requirement springs from the need to apprise the defendant of the charges being brought, apparently assuming that the Rule 7(c) notice function requires notification of the prosecution's theory of the legal content of the offense. Other courts suggest that the essential elements requirement stands apart from the pleading's notice function, as they note that a pleading must both allege the essential elements and provide notice of the charge. They view the essential elements requirement as resting on other functions of the pleading, as discussed in subsections (d), (e), and (f) infra.

Whether the essential elements requirement springs from the notice function is not simply of theoretical significance. Where a pleading requirement is viewed as tied solely to the notice function, courts are more likely to treat an objection based on the pleading's alleged failure to meet that requirement as "forfeited" or "waived" by the defendant's failure to raise the objection before trial (that lack of objection suggesting that the defendant did not see the need for further notice in preparing for trial). Moreover, where notice is the key to a pleading requirement, courts are more likely to look to the availability of other means of obtaining notice, such as the bill of particulars, in determining the degree of particularity that satisfies that requirement. Finally, on appellate review following a conviction, a pleading defect based on the failure to provide notice is more likely to be treated as harmless since the trial record will often suggest that defendant was not surprised or otherwise prejudiced by his lack of notice (notwithstanding his objection). As discussed in § 19.3, traditionally none of these limitations have been applied to the essential elements requirement. Under the prevailing view, the failure to allege essential elements is cognizable even if not raised before trial; it is not cured by an allegation in a bill of particulars or the defense otherwise being made aware of the missing element; and it constitutes a per se ground for reversing a conviction.

(d) Facilitating Judicial Review. Commentators have argued, with considerable force, that the essential elements requirement is based primarily upon a third pleading function, sometimes characterized as the "judicial review" function. That function has been described by the Supreme Court as "inform[ing] the [trial] court of the facts alleged, so that it may decide whether they are sufficient in law to support a conviction, if one should be had." Although this "judicial review" function is mentioned far less frequently than the "notice" and "double jeopardy" functions, it remains a cornerstone of both federal and state pleading requirements.

One objective of the judicial review function is to permit the trial court to rule before trial on the sufficiency of the prosecution's theory of the statutory elements. Consider, for example, a situation in which the statute does not include a particular mens rea element, and there is some question as to the level of mens rea required. The pleading's inclusion of a specific mens rea allegation could be helpful in settling that issue in advance of trial and possibly even in avoiding an unnecessary trial. Thus, if the trial court were to decide, on a motion to dismiss, that the offense requires actual intent rather than some lower level of mens rea alleged in the pleading, the prosecution might conclude that its evidence would be insufficient and not even seek to return with a new pleading alleging the required intent.

This aspect of the review function also explains why courts sometimes have insisted upon more factual specificity as to the elements of a particular offense most likely to raise difficult legal questions. *Russell v. United States*[3] is a classic illustration. The Supreme Court there held insufficient an indictment charging a violation of a federal statute which makes it a crime for a witness to refuse to answer before a Congressional Committee "any question pertinent to the * * * [subject] under inquiry." The indictment was held defective because it failed to specifically identify the subject of the Committee's inquiry, which had to be known to determine whether the questions asked (which were set forth in the indictment) met the statutory requirement of pertinency. The Court noted that the pertinency element had been the subject of frequent litigation, with the lower courts often beset with "difficulties and doubts" in identifying the inquiry subject. Since this "critical and difficult question could be obviated by a simple averment," the prosecution would not be allowed to simply describe the question asked as "pertinent," but had to also identify the particular subject under inquiry to which the question was allegedly pertinent.

Though the judicial review function readily explains pleading rulings in cases like *Russell*, it does not provide a satisfactory justification for the many rulings that have found charging instruments deficient for failing to clearly allege elements of the crime notwithstanding that: (1) those elements obviously were a part of the offense under prevailing law (so that both sides would have been well aware that they had to be proved), (2) the deficiency produced no pretrial objection by the defense, and (3) the element was presented before the jury (with no objection) and adequately proven at trial. Such rulings can be viewed as serving a prophylactic function, insisting that the prosecution clearly set forth the essential elements in all cases so that they are not missed in those situations, like *Russell*, where the judicial review function is needed. Such a remedy,

however, would be contrary to the usual rule that a conviction not be reversed where the error in pretrial or trial proceedings was harmless under the facts of the particular case. Moreover, the need for reversal as a prophylactic remedy is especially questionable in those jurisdictions where pretrial review of the adequacy of the prosecution's theory is readily available through procedures other than a challenge to the pleadings, as where the defense has available a challenge to the sufficiency of the evidence supporting a preliminary hearing bindover, a challenge to the sufficiency of the grand jury evidence supporting an indictment, or a post-discovery motion for dismissal for lack of sufficient evidence to proceed to trial. Thus, what seems to be at stake in rulings sustaining essential elements challenges on appeal from a conviction supported by adequate evidence, particularly where no previous objection was made, is some pleading function that goes beyond facilitating pretrial clarification of the substance of the law. That additional component arguably is to ensure that there is a jurisdictional grounding for the issuance of the trial court's judgment. Judicial review for this purpose flows from the concept, discussed below, that an adequate pleading is necessary to provide a formal basis for the exercise of court authority.

(e) Providing a Jurisdictional Grounding. The common law viewed the accusatory instrument as "providing a formal basis for the judgment, so that the indictment or information * * * [was required to] set forth everything necessary for a complete case on paper." This function of the pleading has been challenged as unnecessary now that complete trial records are available. That record, whether defendant enters a guilty plea or is convicted after a trial, should contain a judicial acknowledgment of the presence of the elements that support the entry of a judgment of conviction for the particular offense. Of course, prior to trial, the evidentiary grounding for jurisdiction has not yet been put before the court, but there is nothing inherently offensive to the concept of jurisdiction in allowing a judge to

---

3. 369 U.S. 749, 82 S.Ct. 1038, 8 L.Ed.2d 240 (1962). See also § 19.3 at note 5.

proceed to the adjudication stage simply on an initial allegation that the defendant has committed a crime that is within the jurisdiction of the court. Such a general allegation could be presented, of course, without also setting forth the presence of each of the essential elements of the crime. Thus, it is argued that, with the availability of the trial record, the demands upon the pleading to provide a jurisdictional grounding have diminished to the point where a pleading that simply identifies the offense and its location should be sufficient.

Notwithstanding the above arguments, all but a few jurisdictions continue to view a pleading that "charges an offense" as a necessary precondition for a conviction. Admittedly, only a small group of jurisdictions continue to describe an indictment that fails to allege "each and every element of the offense" as importing a "jurisdictional defect" that renders "void ab initio" any subsequent conviction, notwithstanding the adequacy of the evidence produced at trial. Indeed, in recent years, a growing list of states have withdrawn from earlier rulings characterizing the failure to allege all material elements as a jurisdictional defect. However, almost all jurisdictions continue to treat a pleading alleging the essential elements as a prerequisite for a judgment of conviction. Where the pleading defect was challenged below, the appellate court will reverse the subsequent conviction without considering whether the charging instrument's failure to include a particular element prejudiced the defense in contesting the prosecution's proof of that element at trial. Rather, it will simply be noted that the trial court erred in failing to dismiss the charging instrument on defendant's objection, and therefore the subsequent conviction cannot stand. So too, while other pleading objections must be raised before trial, the failure to charge an offense is an objection that can first be raised postconviction on a motion for arrest of judgement or on appeal. The object cannot be lost, it is argued, because the defendant has a fundamental right not to be put to trial on an indictment or information that fails completely to charge an offense. Where the objection was

not raised below, the prosecution will be given the benefit of a liberal construction of the pleading, but if it nonetheless is found not to include all essential elements, the conviction must be overturned. Indeed, in some jurisdictions, the clear failure to allege an essential element will require the overturning of a conviction notwithstanding a guilty plea. The explanation here is that the guilty plea does not waive a claim that goes to the trial court's basic authority to proceed.

In the federal system, the Supreme Court's ruling in *Apprendi v. New Jersey*[4] has led to a reexamination of such positions and the rationales supporting them. The Supreme Court's decision in *Apprendi*, in the year 2000, was a seminal ruling not on pleading, but on the issues that must be presented to the jury. One of its side effects, however, was a reexamination of the consequences of failing to allege an essential element in an indictment.

Apprendi, held that a factor which increases the allowable maximum sentence is an element of the crime, and in treating that element as a sentencing factor to be decided by the judge rather than the jury, the state violated the Sixth Amendment. The federal system had a significant group of statutes in which maximum-enhancing factors had been treated as sentencing factors, leading to a deluge of cases challenging enhanced sentences under those statutes. The defendants soon learned that they faced serious obstacles in gaining relief. Where the defendant had pled guilty, that plea eliminated the Sixth Amendment issue because the defendant had not sought a jury trial. Where the defendant went to trial before a jury, but failed to object to the court's failure to submit the maximum-enhancing factor to the jury, the error was forfeited by the lack of objection and could only be considered on appeal if it met the narrow exception of the "plain error" rule. Where the defendant had anticipated *Apprendi* and objected at trial, the appellate court could still find the error to be harmless. All of these obstacles could be avoided, however, by grounding the defense chal-

---

4. 530 U.S. 466, 120 S.Ct. 2348, 147 L.Ed.2d 435 (2000), also discussed in § 26.4 at note 55.

lenge on the failure of the indictment to allege the maximum-enhancing factor .

While *Apprendi* had ruled only on the jury issue, a factor that is element of the crime for Sixth Amendment purposes should also be an essential element for pleading purposes. Indeed, Justice Thomas' concurring opinion in *Apprendi* had suggested that the failure to allege such an element in the indictment constituted a violation of the grand jury clause of the Fifth Amendment. Basing the challenge on the indictment deficiency, rather than the *Apprendi* error, the defendant could look to traditional federal remedial law as to essential elements objections to avoid all of the obstacles facing *Apprendi* claims. If the defendant objected at trial, the failure to plead an essential element required automatic reversal; it was not subject to a harmless error analysis. If the defendant was raising the issue for the first time on appeal, Rule 12(b) bypassed the difficult prerequisites and discretionary character of the plain error doctrine. It provided that the indictment's failure to charge an offense "shall be noticed by the court at any time during the pendency of the proceeding." This language had been read as requiring that an essential elements objection be considered even if first raised on appeal, without regard to the plain error rule, which was designed for objections that would otherwise be forfeited by the failure to have presented the objection in a timely fashion. As for a guilty plea, several federal courts had held that the failure to allege all essential elements was a jurisdictional type of defect and therefore survived a guilty plea.

The government offered a two-pronged response to these pleading claims. First, as to objections to the indictment that had been properly raised before the trial court (in anticipation of *Apprendi*), a harmless error analysis should apply. The government recognized that harmless error analysis traditionally had not been applied to a failure of the indictment to allege the essential elements of the charged offense. It argued initially that the failure to allege an *Apprendi*-type element was not such a failure. The indictment here did allege the

essential elements of an offense, albeit an offense carrying a lesser maximum than the offense on which the defendant was sentenced The true source of the error, it argued, was in the sentencing process, and such errors were subject to harmless error analysis on appellate review. The government also contended that, even if the error was viewed as a pleading error, that should not preclude application of a harmless error analysis. While previous Supreme Court rulings had reversed convictions automatically on finding that the indictment failed to allege an essential element, those rulings came before *Chapman v. California*,[5] at a time when all constitutional violations (including violations of the Fifth Amendment's grand jury clause) were viewed as requiring automatic reversal on appellate review. The Supreme Court subsequently had held that almost all constitutional errors were subject to a harmless error analysis.

The government's position largely prevailed in the limited number of cases in which defendants had anticipated *Apprendi* and made a timely objection to the indictment's failure to allege an *Apprendi*-type element. Various circuits held that this failure was subject to a harmless-error standard of review, although some also concluded that, under the circumstances of the case, the error was not harmless. Moreover, as discussed in § 19.3(a), several circuits, relying essentially on the government's argument as to post-*Chapman* developments, suggested that harmless error analysis should also apply to an indictment's failure to allege any essential element, and not just an *Apprendi*-type element. Thus, the failure to charge an offense would no longer require automatic reversal, but would be subject to harmless error review. Others federal courts, however, have limited their application of the harmless error standard to the failure to allege an *Apprendi*-type element.

Where the indictment challenge had not been presented to the trial court, the government argued that the standard of review should be more rigorous than the harmless

---

5. See § 27.6(c) at note 10.

error standard. Rather, reversal should be required only if the defendant could meet the prerequisites of the "plain error" standard of Federal Rule 52(b). That standard had been applied by the Supreme Court to the failure to submit an element to the jury where an objection had not been timely presented. The same should be true, the government argued, of a failure to allege an *Apprendi*-type element in an indictment. This prong of the government's position received the support of a substantial group of the federal lower courts. The Fourth Circuit disagreed, however, leading to the Supreme Court's consideration of the issue in *United States v. Cotton*.[6]

The defendants in *Cotton* were indicted and convicted under a federal statute making a conspiracy to distribute cocaine base a 20–year offense, but raising the maximum sentence to life imprisonment if the offense involve 50 or more grams of cocaine base. At the time of the indictment and trial, the enhancement element of drug quantity was viewed as a sentencing factor, and it therefore was not included in the indictment nor presented to the jury (although defendants knew from the outset that the prosecution intended to establish the enhancement at sentencing, which it did). On appeal, relying on the intervening Supreme Court ruling in *Apprendi*, defendants argued that their sentences in excess of 20 years were invalid because the issue of drug quantity was neither alleged in the indictment nor submitted to the petit jury. The government acknowledged both errors, but argued that, since the objections had not been timely presented before the district court, they were cognizable on appeal only if they met the prerequisites for recognition as "plain errors" under Rule 52(b) and neither error fulfilled those prerequisites. Relying basically on language in the Supreme Court's ruling in *Ex parte Bain*,[7] the Fourth Circuit held that an indictment's failure to include an essential element of an offense was a "jurisdictional" defect, and therefore the enhanced sentence had to be vacated even though not timely challenged below. Rejecting

that reasoning, a unanimous Supreme Court held that the indictment defect was not jurisdictional and should be cognizable only if it met the rigorous standards of the plain error doctrine (which was not the case, here, as the evidence supporting the sentencing enhancement factor was "overwhelming" and "essentially uncontroverted").

The Supreme Court in *Cotton* rejected *Bain's* broad conception of jurisdiction as an outdated "product of an era in which the [Supreme] Court's authority to review criminal convictions was greatly circumscribed." Subsequent rulings, it noted, had properly limited the concept of jurisdictional defects (i.e., defects that "require correction regardless of whether the error was raised in [the] district court") to "defects in subject-matter jurisdiction." Thus, post-*Bain* rulings had rejected "the claim that the [district] court had no jurisdiction because the indictment does not charge an offense against the United States." Since such defects were not jurisdictional, there was no reason to exempt them from the usual rule that, where first raised on appeal, they were not reviewable unless they constituted "plain error."

As discussed in § 19.3(e), *Cotton's* flat rejection of a jurisdictional grounding for indictment defects, including the failure to "charge an offense," has led federal lower courts not to restrict the *Cotton* ruling to the failure to allege an *Apprendi*-type element. The "plain error" prerequisite has been applied to the appellate review of traditional essential elements objections that were first raised on appeal. Indeed, as discussed in § 19.5 and § 19.6, *Cotton* could well lead to a reexamination of the standards of appellate review applied to other objections relating to pleadings, including improper amendments and variances.

(f) Safeguarding Defendant's Right to Prosecution by Indictment. In recent years, courts have cited yet another pleading function, relevant only to the indictment, that may also contribute to the categorization of

---

6. 535 U.S. 625, 122 S.Ct. 1781, 152 L.Ed.2d 860 (2002), also discussed in § 19.3 at note 16, § 19.5 at note 5, and § 19.6 at note 9.

7. 121 U.S. 1, 7 S.Ct. 781, 30 L.Ed. 849 (1886), discussed in § 19.5(d).

certain pleading defects as jurisdictional in nature. As the Supreme Court has long noted, the indictment is the product of the grand jurors and the defendant is entitled to be tried only on the offense that the jurors desired to charge. To allow a defendant "to be convicted on the basis of facts not found by, and perhaps not even presented to, the grand jury which indicted him" is to deprive him "of a basic protection which the guaranty of the intervention of the grand jury was designed to secure." This concern is said to be reflected in "the prohibition against the amendment of indictments except by resubmission to the grand jury, and the bar against 'curing' of defective indictments by issuance of a bill of particulars."

Some courts have suggested that the preservation of the defendant's right to be tried only upon a charge properly found by the grand jury underlies many of the basic requirements for a pleading. The essential elements requirement, in particular, is commonly attributed to this function. The inclusion of each of the essential elements in the indictment tends to structure the grand jury's charging decision, focusing its attention on the specific requirements for criminal liability rather than a general sense of the accused's wrongdoing. Without a specific reference to an element, the "indictment contains no assurance that the grand jury deliberated or even considered whether [the facts established that element]."

The Supreme Court has suggested that the requirement of factual specificity sufficient to provide adequate notice also serves to safeguard the grand jury's charging function. Indeed, the Court majority in *Russell v. United States*[8] spoke of the factual allegations in the indictment serving to preclude (through the prohibition against variance) conviction of the defendant on "the basis of facts not found by, and perhaps not even presented to, the grand jury." Of course, as Justice Harlan noted in response, it is neither practicable nor demanded by the grand jury's screening role that the prosecution be limited at trial to precisely the same facts that were put before the grand

jury. The prosecution cannot be expected to go back to grand jury every time subsequent information reveals additional incriminatory information, and to do so would hardly benefit the defendant. The cases suggest, however, that the prosecution should be limited to proceeding on the same basic factual theory that was before the grand jury—i.e., using facts that are consistent with "what was in the minds of the grand jury as to the essential elements of the specific offense charged." Arguably, however, this requires a degree of specificity no greater than that needed to provide notice.

In the federal system and several states, the grand jury function also plays a major role in shaping the prohibition against evidentiary variances from the pleading, with a far more rigorous standard applied to variances from an indictment than variances from an information. The prohibition against duplicity is still another pleading rule sometimes described as implementing the grand jury's screening role. It ensures that the grand jury recognized the distinction in the necessary elements of separate crimes and found sufficient evidence to indict on each.

At a time when grand jury proceedings were not transcribed, the indictment furnished the only evidence of what was before the grand jury and what it had decided. Today, however, such transcriptions are available in many jurisdictions and could be used to ensure both that the grand jury was made aware of each of the distinct elements of the crime and that the prosecution is not seeking at trial to establish the offense by reference to a factual theory different than that presented to the grand jury. With that record available, the continued use of pleading requirements as an indirect means of safeguarding the defendant's right to grand jury screening has been questioned.

Also questioned is the standard applied on the appellate review of pleading defects following a conviction. Even if the failure to allege an essential element is viewed as a proxy for the grand jury's failure to have considered that element, why should that omission re-

---

8. See note 3 supra.

quire automatic reversal of a subsequent conviction on appeal? In many jurisdictions, including the federal, most errors in grand jury screening are viewed as "mooted" by the petit jury's finding of guilt beyond a reasonable doubt.[9]

Of course, some grand jury errors are deemed "structural" and require automatic reversal of a conviction (at least where timely raised). That is the case as to a charge brought by information when an indictment was required or an indictment issued by a grand jury that had been selected through racial or gender discrimination.[10] Perhaps a flaw as significant as failing to consider an essential element could also be put in the same category. However, the Supreme Court's analogous ruling in *Neder v. United States*[11] strongly suggests otherwise. In *Neder*, the Court rejected the contention that a failure to submit an element of the charged offense to the jury (the trial court erroneously classified the element as an issue for the court) was structural, comparable to having no jury. The Court held instead that the error was subject to harmless error review, and was harmless where the evidence on the element not submitted was overwhelming and uncontroverted. If the failure to submit an essential element to the petit jury can be a harmless error, should not the same be true of the failure to submit an element to the grand jury (as reflected in an indictment which fails to charge that element)? The showing at trial of guilt beyond a reasonable doubt as to the element not charged in the indictment certainly suggests the grand jury would have had no difficulty finding probable cause on that element if asked to do so. As discussed in § 19.3(a), in the post-*Apprendi* reexamination of pleading issues, several federal courts have asked precisely these questions and found the *Neder* analogy persuasive.

§ 19.3 Basic Pleading Defects

(a) Failure to Allege Essential Elements. *Significance.* As a cornerstone of

common law pleading, the requirement that a pleading allege each essential element of the offense charged quite naturally was carried over to the modern pleading standard requiring a statement of the "essential facts constituting the offense charged." Indeed, as discussed in § 19.2(c), various courts have suggested that the pleading of all essential elements is mandated by the notice requirement of the Sixth Amendment, although that is a dubious proposition.

From the prosecution's perspective, the essential elements requirement clearly is the most critical pleading requirement. The failure to allege an essential element is not cured by a bill of particulars that covers the missing element or any other procedure or circumstance that makes the defendant aware that the government would have to establish that element. Where the objection was timely made pretrial, but rejected by the trial court, the subsequent trial may be wasted if an appellate court should disagree with trial court and agree with the defendant that all elements were not pleaded. Under the traditional position, an appellate court finding that the pleading failed to allege an essential element requires automatic reversal of the conviction, even though the element not pleaded was proven at trial and submitted to the jury with proper instructions. Indeed, under another prong of the traditional position, even where the lack of an element in the pleading was not challenged prior to trial, caused no confusion at trial, and was properly presented to the jury, it can nevertheless be raised on appeal, and can result (when sufficiently glaring) in a reversal of a conviction.

Not surprisingly, no pleading defect has resulted in more dismissals of indictments and informations and more reversals of convictions than the failure to allege all of the essential elements of the offense. On occasion, the absence of an essential element in a charging instrument appears to have been the product of a calculated drafting decision; the prosecutor apparently reached the conclusion (later

---

9. See § 15.6(f). This includes errors in instructing the grand jury on the content of the charged elements. See § 15.6(g).

10. See §§ 15.1(d), 15.4(i).

11. 527 U.S. 1, 119 S.Ct. 1827, 144 L.Ed.2d 35 (1999), discussed in § 27.6 at note 56.

rejected by the court) that the offense simply did not encompass that element or that the element was a defensive matter rather than an affirmative prerequisite for criminal liability. In many other instances, however, the element clearly was part of the offense and the failure to allege it properly appears to have resulted simply from a lack of care in the drafting of the charge.

Necessary content. The essential elements requirement demands that the pleading allege the presence of each of the basic elements required for the commission of the offense—in general, the elements of mental state, criminal conduct, and resulting harm. It does not demand, however, that the pleading negate exemptions, excuses, or justifications that relieve one of liability notwithstanding the presence of the basic elements. It is not always clear, however, whether a circumstance mentioned in the statute is a defense (i.e., an excuse or justification) or an element of the offense. Consider, for example, a state statute which prohibits the distribution of a particular substance unless prescribed by a physician. If the absence of a prescription is an element of the offense, it must be alleged in the accusatory pleading. If the presence of a prescription is an exception to be established by the defense, it need not be negated in the pleading. Courts look to various factors to distinguish between defenses and elements of the offense. These include: (1) whether the exception was treated as a defense at common law; (2) whether the exception was "so incorporated in the language of the statute defining the crime that the elements of the offense cannot be accurately described if the exception is omitted"; and (3) whether the exception appears in the enacting law of the statute (suggesting it is an element of the offense) or is located in a subsequent clause (suggesting it is a defense).

To avoid omitting a crucial element of the offense, prosecutors frequently draft pleadings that track the language of the criminal statute, adding appropriate factual references (e.g., the victim's name) along the way. Reliance upon the statutory language will be acceptable, however, only if "the words of [the statute] themselves fully, directly, and expressly, without any uncertainty or ambiguity, set forth all the elements necessary to constitute the offence." In many instances, that will not be the case, and the use of the statutory language will be inadequate. If the statute fails to refer to an essential element, such as *mens rea*, then that element must be added to the tracked statutory language in framing the pleading. Similarly, if courts have added a significant refinement in the interpretation of a particular statutory element, that element often must be pleaded as interpreted rather than as stated in the statutory language, especially if the judicial interpretation substantially limits the scope of the statutory language.

Most failures to allege essential elements are found in pleadings which do not track the statutory language (either because that language is not sufficient in itself or because the prosecutor prefers to set forth the substance of the statute in other terms). The critical issue presented in challenges to such pleadings often is whether a particular element, though not set forth explicitly, is nevertheless included by implication. Courts tend to be more willing to find certain elements alleged by implication than others. Thus, indictments for murder need not state that the victim was a human being; the courts have long held that the very nature of the charge of "murder" suggests the presence of that element. On the other hand, the element of *mens rea* ordinarily will require a more explicit allegation. For example, in a typical ruling, one court held that an allegation that defendant "unlawfully sold" a pornographic magazine was insufficient to allege that defendant acted with scienter. If the activity would have been one that inherently encompassed the *mens rea* (as in the case of "assaulting" another, which implies an intent to do bodily harm), the description of the act might have been sufficient in itself to allege the necessary mental element.

Where the pleading refers to the mental element in a general fashion, using terms other than those specified in the statute, courts sometimes draw fairly fine lines in determining whether the general reference is a fair equivalent of the statutory language. Thus, an indictment charging that defendant "stole" property was held sufficient to allege the specific intent required for larceny (to permanently deprive another of his property), but an indictment charging a postal employee with having "converted" postal funds "without authorization by law" was held inadequate to charge "larcenous intent." In cases such as these, much will depend upon the outlook of the particular court. A judge who looks primarily to the presence of adequate notice is more likely to sustain the pleading since the elements of the offense usually are well known and the absence of an explicit reference is unlikely to confuse a defendant represented by counsel. Similarly, while it is commonly stated that an indictment's citation to the statute violated will not cure the failure of to allege an element specified in that statute, a judge who looks primarily to notice may rely upon that statutory reference, where the indictment language is sufficient for an implicit allegation, to hold that the defendant obviously was on notice notwithstanding the lack of an explicit statement of the element in the indictment.

Although a pleading must contain the "essential facts" constituting the offense, the need for factual detail generally stems from the factual specificity pleading requirement (discussed in subsection (b) infra) rather than the essential elements requirement. An element of a crime very often can be pleaded without providing any specific factual reference. Thus, a defendant can be alleged to have acted with "depraved indifference" without further alleging an awareness of specific circumstances that produced that level of *mens rea*. So too, if the aggravated assault statute requires the infliction of a "serious bodily injury," that element can be alleged in the very terms of the statute. If the pleading should require an identification of the particular injury, that additional detail commonly is seen as flowing from the factual specificity requirement rather than the essential elements requirement. A minority position, however, will

categorize a failure to provide basic factual identification as to an element of the crime as an essential elements deficiency. This conclusion appears to stem from a combination of treating the factual specificity requirement as limited to ensuring adequate notice and viewing the failure to provide such factual identification of the element as undercutting other pleading functions, such as affording protection against double jeopardy and safeguarding the grand jury's screening role, which are associated with the essential elements requirement.

Most courts will view a somewhat different type of a failure to provide greater specificity as producing an essential elements deficiency, and that is the failure to describe an element with sufficient specificity to distinguish between alternative legal components of the element. As the Supreme Court noted in *United States v. Cruikshank*,[1] where the statute uses "generic terms," the accusatory instrument must go beyond those terms and "descend to particulars," and the failure to do so means the element has not been pleaded.[2] The primary illustration of this principle is found in offenses that prohibit certain action when tied to the commission or attempted commission of another crime. Although some courts disagree, the charge here ordinarily may not simply allege in a generic form that a relationship existed to other criminality (e.g., in burglary, alleging that the illegal entry was with an "intent to commit a felony"); it must specify the particular ulterior offense that fulfills the relationship in this case (e.g., by alleging an entry with "an intent to commit theft"). Similarly, where a statute specifies several different ways in which the crime can be committed, some jurisdictions hold that the pleading must refer to the particular alternative presented in the individual case. Simply using a verb that encompasses all of the statutorily proscribed methods of commission may be deemed too

---

§ 19.3

1. 92 U.S. (2 Otto) 542, 23 L.Ed. 588 (1876).

2. In *Cruikshank,* the Supreme Court held invalid an indictment which charged defendants, in the language of the applicable criminal provision, with having intentionally hindered certain citizens in their "free exercise and

enjoyment * * * of the several rights and privileges granted and secured to them by the constitution." This pleading was defective because the defendants had not received adequate notice of which of the many constitutional rights of citizens had been taken from the alleged victims.

conclusory where the statute itself uses that verb in describing the crime but then sets forth the different methods encompassed in its definition section (e.g., where the statute refers to "compulsion", but then defines that term as including both the use of physical force and the use of particular types of threat). Indeed, this remains so even though the defendant today gains very little as the prosecution is not forced to chose a single method. Most jurisdictions allow the use of disjunctive pleadings, and in others, conjunctive pleading will be allowed, even as to inherently inconsistent means, with the conviction being sustained if any means is proven, notwithstanding the pleading of the conjunctive.

Consequences of error. Should a trial court find that the indictment or information fails to allege an essential element, it must dismiss the pleading. An amendment of the pleading ordinarily is not permissible. Since no offense has been charged, an amendment adding the missing element charges a new offense, and such amendments traditionally are not allowed.[3] If a failure to allege an element of the offense could be cured by an amendment adding the missing element, a basic function of the essential elements requirement—ensuring that all elements were found to be supported by sufficient evidence by the appropriate screening agency (i.e., the grand jury in an indictment jurisdiction, and the preliminary hearing magistrate in most information jurisdictions)—would be lost. The prosecutor would be adding elements to the charge even though they were never considered by the screening agency.

Where an essential elements objection is timely raised pretrial, rejected by the trial court, and then raised on appeal, the appellate court will determine *de novo* whether the element was properly alleged, applying the same standard as the trial court. This standard is more rigorous than that applied when objection was not timely raised; there, as noted in subsection (e), a standard of liberal construction is applied in determining whether the pleading failed to allege an essential element. Should the appellate court find that the charging instrument failed to allege an essential element, the traditional position is that this defect requires automatic reversal of the conviction. It matters not that the defense was in no way confused by the failure to allege the element (it being understood from the outset that the prosecution would have to prove the element), and that the element was properly presented to the jury in its finding guilt.

As noted in § 19.1(e), and 19.2(e), several federal circuits have held or otherwise indicated that a timely challenge to an indictment's failure to allege an *Apprendi*-type element (i.e., an element that raises the allowable maximum sentence) will be reviewed on appeal following a conviction under a harmless error standard. That position has been advanced in some instances on grounds distinctive to the *Apprendi*-element. Here, it argued, the indictment still charged an offense (albeit an offense carrying a lesser maximum than that opposed). Thus, harmless error is being applied to what in effect is sentencing error, rather than an essential elements error.[4] These courts therefore do not see their rulings on *Apprendi*-type elements as logically also requiring application of a harmless error analysis to the failure of an indictment to charge any offense. They have continued to treat the failure to allege all essential elements as requiring automatic reversal on appeal where the objection had been raised pretrial.

---

3. See § 19.5(b).

4. Other courts have reasoned, however, that where a judge imposes a sentence on the basis of an element not alleged, that action can be viewed as operating in effect as a prohibited constructive amendment of the indictment, and a constructive amendment, where timely challenged on the trial level, traditionally has required automatic reversal on appeal, without considering whether the error might be deemed harmless. See § 19.6 at note 8 (discussing Stirone v. United States). They nonetheless apply harmless error analysis, as they discount those earlier

constructive amendment cases, such as *Stirone*, as rulings that come before Chapman v. California's introduction of the harmless error doctrine into constitutional jurisprudence. See § 27.6. This line of analysis arguably should extend beyond *Apprendi*-type elements to encompass generally the failure to allege an essential element. If the earlier constructive amendment cases give way to a harmless error analysis the same should be true of the pre-*Chapman* essential element cases that applied the traditional position of automatic reversal.

A few circuits, however, have reached a contrary conclusion. In the leading ruling of *United States v. Prentiss*,[5] a divided Tenth Circuit (sitting en banc) held that the failure to allege the essential elements needed to constitute a crime could be a harmless error. The defendant in *Prentiss* was convicted of the crime of committing arson in Indian country, but the indictment failed to allege the Indian/non-Indian statuses of the victim and defendant (a prerequisite for the application of the offense). Anticipating the reasoning of *Cotton v. United States*, the *Prentiss* majority noted initially that the failure to allege an essential element did not deprive the trial court of jurisdiction. Thus, harmless error analysis applied on appellate review unless the error was deemed "structural," and the Supreme Court had indicated that the only structural error relating to grand jury proceedings was discrimination in the selection of the grand jury.[6] Moreover, the majority reasoned, the Supreme Court in Neder v. United Statees[7] had applied a harmless error analysis to the failure to submit an element of a crime to a petit jury. Here, the underlying analogous error was the failure to submit an element to the grand jury.

As discussed in § 19.2(e),[8] the Supreme Court's subsequent ruling in *Cotton* agreed with *Prentiss* as to the non-jurisdictional character of pleading errors, referring not only to the failure to allege an *Apprendi*-type element, but also the failure of the indictment to "charge a crime." However, *Cotton* did not address the standard of review applicable when a challenge to the pleading had been timely presented in the trial court. The government argued in its brief that prior rulings requiring automatic dismissal for timely challenged pleading errors (such a *Russell* and *Stirone*[9]) predated the introduction of harmless error analysis to constitutional errors,[10] but the *Cotton* opinion, in distinguishing *Rus-*

sell and *Stirone* from the situation before the Court, noted only that those were cases in which "proper objection had been made in the District Court to the sufficiency of the indictment."

(b) Factual Specificity. As courts repeatedly note, "an indictment [or information] must not only contain all the elements of the offense charged, but must also provide the accused with a sufficient description of the acts he is alleged to have committed to enable him to defend himself adequately." Precisely how much factual specificity is needed to meet that standard will necessarily vary from one case to another. Relevant factors include the nature of the offense, the likely significance of particular factual variations in determining liability, the ability of the prosecution to identify a particular circumstance without a lengthy and basically evidentiary allegation, and the availability of alternative procedures for obtaining the particular information. It generally is agreed that the issue is not whether the alleged offense could be described with more certainty, but whether there is "sufficient particularity" to enable the accused to "prepare a proper defense."

The leading specificity case, *Russell v. United States*,[11] clearly indicates that specificity requirements can be driven by more than simply providing notice. The defendants there were charged with violating a federal statute making it a crime for a witness to refuse to answer before a Congressional Committee "any question pertinent to the * * * [subject] under inquiry." The indictments set forth the precise questions that each defendant had refused to answer before the House Un–American Activities Committee (HUAC), and alleged that those questions were "pertinent to the question [i.e., subject matter] then under inquiry," but did not identify that subject

---

5. 256 F.3d 971 (10th Cir.2001) (en banc).

6. See § 15.4(i), 15.6(f). The *Stirone* case, see § 19.6 at note 8, was distinguished as involving a shift in the basic character of the offense charge, while the "indictment in this case, although it failed to expressly set forth all elements of the crime, sought to charge the defendant with the sole crime for which the jury sentenced him."

7. See § 19.2 at note 11.

8. See § 19.2 at note 6.

9. See § 19.3 at note 11 (*Russell*); § 19.6 at note 8 (*Stirone*).

10. See § 27.5(d).

11. 369 U.S. 749, 82 S.Ct. 1038, 8 L.Ed.2d 240 (1962). See also § 19.2 at note 3.

matter. In finding that the indictments were defective because they failed to specify the particular subject under inquiry, the Court did rely, in part, on notice considerations. The HUAC investigations dealt with Communism, but their precise interest in Communism was not readily ascertained from either the Committee's authorization or "the widely meandering statements" of its members defining its mission. Guilt here depending largely on a "specific identification of fact" (the subject under inquiry), yet a defendant was not likely to be apprised of the governments premise as to that fact unless it was set forth in indictment. An examination of HUAC's recorded proceedings provided no obvious, single subject matter, which could lead to a shifting prosecution and judicial identification of the subject matter as the prosecution progressed (a potential that had in fact materialized in one of the cases before the Court).

The potential for a shifting identification of the subject under inquiry led the *Russell* Court to a second reason for the specificity requirement it was imposing—to ensure that the government's theory of prosecution was that upon which the grand jury issued its indictment. Even if the prosecution had clearly provided the defendant with notice of its view of the subject under inquiry (e.g., by a bill of particulars), that would not have ensured that the prosecution was following the grand jury's view of that critical element. Only an allegation in the indictment would be sufficient for this purpose. Still a third justification related to another pleading function. The pertinency of the questions asked to the subject under inquiry presented a "critical" legal issue, usefully reviewed by a court pretrial to eliminate any prosecutions that might fail as a matter of law. This "judicial review" function of the indictment would also be served by simply adding the specific subject under inquiry to the verbatim listing of the questions already in the indictment.

Presumably because functions beyond notice required the additional specificity, *Russell* viewed the pleading defect in that case as akin

to a failure to state an element of the offense. It noted that a bill of particulars could not have cured the defect, and relied upon the Court's earlier *Cruikshank* ruling.[12] State courts, however, often view specificity objections as tied strictly to a notice requirement. Thus, they hold that the bill of particulars (or sometimes even other sources of notice) must be considered in assessing the needed degree of specificity in the charging instrument. Similarly, if the issue is not raised pretrial, it generally will be viewed as waived. On appellate review (where properly raised), the courts will look to discovery that was given (or could have been requested), and ask whether the defendant was actually taken by surprise, and if so, whether prejudice resulted.

In applying a notice perspective to the factual specificity of a charging instrument, courts start from the assumption that the defendant is innocent and consequently "has no knowledge of the facts charged against him." But even from the perspective of the innocent person, comparatively little information is needed to prepare a defense for some crimes. A charge of assault, for example, provides enough information if it identifies who was assaulted and when and where the assault occurred. There is no need to inform the defendant of how the assault occurred (assuming the charge is simple assault and not assault with a deadly weapon). If the defendant wasn't there, the manner of assault will be irrelevant to his defense, and if he was present, he will be aware of the circumstances. Greater specificity will be required, however, where the crime encompasses more factual variations. Thus, if the defendant is charged with fraud arising from a series of statements made to the victim, he ordinarily must be informed as to which of his representations is alleged to be false. On the other hand, the defendant need not also be furnished with a factual explanation as to why those statements were both false and material to the transaction. To insist that the charge include such matter would be "tantamount to requiring that supporting evidence be alleged" and could often require a lengthy and highly detailed allegation. For federal offenses requir-

12.   See note 1 supra.

ing a nexus to interstate commerce, some courts similarly require greater specificity because of the multiple connections that may be cited.

Traditionally, time and place have been viewed as not requiring great specificity because they ordinarily do not involve proof of an element of crime. Thus, the time allegation can refer to the event as having occurred "on or about" a certain date and, within reasonable limits, proof of a date before or after that specified will be sufficient, provided it is within the statute of limitations. Of course, when the time is a material element of the offense, it ordinarily must be charged as to a particular day. In exceptional cases, however, where the defendant would have difficulty in identifying the timing of specific acts, a substantial time span may be prohibited. While an allegation of place is necessary, it too may be flexible. Thus, the allegation of place may state only that the event occurred within a geographical area that would establish proper venue and jurisdiction (e.g., within a particular county).

The looseness of pleading permitted as to time and place certainly could result in failing to give the defendant adequate notice in particular cases. Yet courts have rejected attempts to tighten the traditional rules, noting that the bill of particulars always remains available to get such information when needed. While the bill of particulars will not cure the failure to allege an essential element, it is a factor given weight in determining whether greater factual specificity is required. Courts frequently cite the availability of the bill (and sometimes the availability of pretrial discovery) in refusing to require specificity that goes beyond a basic identification of the underlying event. In most instances, the end result is pleading substantially less detailed than that required at common law. Not all courts, however, are fully convinced by this approach. Pleading requirements that demand specificity similar to that found in common law pleadings, even as to matters irrelevant to the essential elements of the crime, are still imposed in several states.

At common law, pleadings in the disjunctive were frowned upon, and the same was true of pleadings in the conjunctive where conjunctive elements were contradictory. The prosecutor's obligation was to pick the alternative that applied rather than leaving uncertain what would be established at trial. One of the major pleading reforms of the early 1900s was to authorize pleadings alleging that the offense was committed by one or more specified means. Where these provisions did not specify that the different means could be alleged in the alternative, some courts continued to prohibit disjunctive pleadings, but allowed conjunctive pleadings of contradictory means, and did not view the failure to prove both as a fatal variance. The net effect of those rulings, as well as the rulings allowing alternative pleading, was to relieve the prosecution of need to make a choice at the pleading stage. Moreover, the allowance of such conjunctive or disjunctive pleading was not necessarily limited to instances in which the statute itself listed alternative means of committing the offense. It also permitted prosecutors to refer to alternative mental elements, results, and acts.

(c) Duplicity and Multiplicity. Duplicity is the charging of separate offenses in a single count. This practice is unacceptable because it prevents the jury from deciding guilt or innocence on each offense separately and may make it difficult to determine whether the conviction rested on only one of the offenses or both. Duplicity can result in prejudice to the defendant in the shaping of evidentiary rulings, in producing a conviction on less than a unanimous verdict as to each separate offense, and in limiting review on appeal. Also, where the jury is not able to reach a verdict or renders a guilty verdict that is later overturned, the defendant may be subjected to a second trial that exposes him to double jeopardy insofar as it includes an offense on which the original jury would have acquitted if required to render separate verdicts.

Duplicity usually occurs because of prosecutor error in assuming that a particular statute creates a single offense which may be committed by multiple means (properly chargeable in a single count), rather than separate offenses. A valid duplicity objection raised before trial will force the government to elect the offense upon which it will proceed, but will not require the dismissal of the indictment. If the trial court erroneously rejects the duplicity objection, on appeal follow a conviction, the conviction will be reversed unless the duplicity is found to be harmless error in light the instructions given to the jury. A duplicity objection is forfeited, however, if first raised on appeal.

A multiplicitous indictment charges a single offense in several counts. It often is the product of a prosecutor's mistaken assumption that a particular statute creates several separate offenses rather than a single crime that can be accomplished through multiple means. A multiplicity issue is also presented when a series of repeated acts are charged as separate crimes but the defendant claims they are part of a continuous transaction and therefore a single crime. The principle danger in multiplicity is that the defendant will receive multiple sentences for a single offense, although courts have noted that multiple counts may also work against defendant by leading the jury to believe that defendant's conduct is especially serious because it constitutes more than one crime. Multiplicity does not require dismissal of the indictment. The court may respond to a successful objection by requiring the prosecutor to elect one count, consolidating the various counts, or simply advising the jury that only one offense is charged. If the objection is first raised after conviction, the defendant will be entitled to relief from an improperly imposed multiple sentence, but he cannot object to the possible impact of the multiplicity upon the jury's assessment of his guilt. Even if the objection was timely made and erroneously rejected by the trial court, the result is likely to be the same, as the error generally will be viewed as harmless with respect to its possible impact upon the jury's deliberations.

(d) Defects in Form. Defects in form tend to be remedied by amendment, even in jurisdictions that sharply limit the amendment of an indictment. No longer are charges dismissed because they fail, for example, to allege that the offense was committed "against the peace and dignity of the state." Errors in the

caption were the first to be recognized as not requiring dismissal, as the caption came to be treated as surplusage, with the body of the instrument controlling as to the allegation of the offense. Technical errors in the body of the indictment did produce dismissals for a much longer period, but courts eventually came to measure those errors by reference to pleading functions, which commonly resulted in the conclusion that the particular error was harmless. Thus, though the statutory provision governing the pleading may require citation to the applicable statute, the lack of citation or error in citation will not require dismissal if the offense is otherwise identified through the allegations of the charge. Similarly, the misspelling of the defendant's name or the use of the wrong middle name usually will present difficulties only where there is some confusion as to whether the defendant was the person in fact charged. A few courts, however, adhere to the doctrine of *idem sonans*, rendering the charge fatally flawed unless the pronunciation of the misspelled name would be difficult to distinguish from the pronunciation of defendant's true name. Many jurisdictions have pleading provisions stating that a variety of defects in form shall not be a basis for dismissal.

(e) Late Objections. As noted in § 19.1(d), a critical element of the mid–1900's pleading reforms was to provide for a "waiver" or "forfeiture" of pleading objections that were not raised before trial. That reform was not carried over, however, to what original Federal Rule 12(b) and similar state provisions describe as the "failure to show jurisdiction in the court" and the failure "to charge an offense." Those two defects, the Rule 12(b)-type provisions noted, "shall be noticed * * * at any time during the pendency of the proceeding." The caselaw applying that "waiver exception" tended to focus on the "failure to charge on offense," at it was the much more common error. That defect commonly was read as limited to a failure of the pleading to allege the essential elements of the offense.[13]

---

13. Appellate courts frequently note that the lack of factual specificity does not in itself result in a "failure to

charge an offense" and therefore a deficiency in specificity is lost by the defense's failure to raise the objection before

The court's obligation to notice that failure at "any time during the pendency of the proceeding" included review of an objection first raised on appeal.[14]

Why was this pleading requirement singled out and basically exempted from the timely-objection rule. Very often courts have simply applied the provisions recognizing the exception without explaining their grounding. The explanations that have been offered point in various different ways to the non-notice functions of the essential elements requirement. Particular emphasis has been placed on a pleading serving as the formal basis of the judgment of conviction [see § 19.2(e)]. That explanation arguably finds support in the common pairing of the "failure to charge an offense" with the "failure to show jurisdiction." In jurisdictions lacking a provision like the original Rule 12(b), courts reach the same result, holding that the failure to allege an essential element is such a fundamental defect that it must be open for review on appeal even though not raised below.

Allowing the essential elements requirement to be raised for the first time after conviction, even though previously known to the defense, arguably provides an incentive to the defense to delay making the objection. Where made before trial, a successful objection is likely to result only in the production of a new indictment or information which cures the defect by correctly alleging all of the elements. While the delay resulting from the process of forcing the prosecution to start over again may be of value to the defense under certain circumstances, that advantage hardly compares to the value of overturning a conviction. Here too, the prosecution is likely to return with a new indictment or information that now alleges all of the elements, but the defense has gained a second opportunity to avoid a conviction (and sometimes a somewhat stronger plea-bargaining position where the prosecution prefers not to force upon the complainant and other witnesses the inconvenience of another trial).

In considering essential elements objections first raised after conviction, appellate courts are fully aware of the defense incentive to sandbag and they often react accordingly. Noting that the failure of the defense to raise the objection at an earlier point suggests that it was hardly misled, the courts repeatedly state that the charging instrument not previously challenged "should be construed liberally in favor of sufficiency, absent any prejudice to the defendant." Indeed, it is said that the pleading will be held sufficient unless it is "so defective that it does not by any reasonable construction" charge the necessary elements. Nonetheless, there is considerable variation to be found from one appellate court to another in its willingness to stretch the language of the pleading to find that an allegedly missing element was sufficiently set forth "by implication." One will find satisfactory, against a late objection, a pleading that simply alleged "the commission of a battery," without referring to any of the elements of the crime. Another will hold invalid a murder indictment that alleged

---

trial. Thus, United States v. Varkonyi, 645 F.2d 453 (5th Cir.1981), carefully distinguished between two alleged defects, raised for the first time on appeal, in an indictment charging the defendant with the crime of interfering with a federal official. The defendant could raise the indictment's failure to allege that the victim of defendant's assault was a federal official, because that went to the pleading of an element of the crime. The defendant could not raise, however, the failure of the allegation of "forcible interference" to spell out how defendant had interfered with the official's performance of his governmental duties as that merely related to providing notice through factual specificity. Appellate courts, however, do not always find the distinction between an essential elements defect and a factual specificity defect so easy to apply. Thus, disagreements may be found on precisely the same pleading defect—as where one court holds that the failure to identify the ulterior offense in charging burglary (i.e., charging

only entry with "an intent to commit a crime") is an elements defect requiring reversal even where first raised on appeal, and another holds that it is a specificity defect lost because it was not raised before trial. See also United States v. Cruikshank at note 1 supra.

14. In a 2002 revision of Federal Rule 12(b), the relevant language was changed from "*shall* be noticed by the court at any time during the pendency of the proceeding" to "at any time while the case is pending, the court *may* hear a claim that the indictment or information fails to involve the court's jurisdiction or to state an offense" (emphasis added). Although the shift from "shall" to "may" would seem to indicate that a federal court now has discretion to refuse to consider either defect when not timely raised, the Advisory Committee Note described the new phrasing as a stylistic change and added that "[n]o change in practice is intended."

that the defendant "unlawfully, willfully, deliberately and with premeditation" killed a particular person, reasoning that such language could not reasonably be construed as alleging the necessary element of "malice aforethought." One will find an allegation that defendant carried and used a firearm during a drug crime sufficient to imply that he did so "knowingly and willfully," while another will find an indictment alleging a postal employee "did convert * * * without authorization of law" certain postal moneys insufficient to find implicit the element of criminal intent.

Should a pleading fail to allege an essential element of the offense of conviction, notwithstanding a liberal construction in favor of sufficiency, the traditional position is that reversal of the conviction is automatic, just as it would be if the pleading objection had been properly presented at trial and erroneously rejected there. That position continues to prevail in all but a few states.[15] In the federal courts, however, the Supreme Court's ruling in *United States v. Cotton*[16] has sparked on ongoing reexamination of that position.

As discussed previously[17] *Cotton* presented a challenge to an indictment based upon the indictment's failure to include an *Apprendi*-element which had been utilized in increasing the defendant's maximum sentence. The defense first raised this issue on appeal, but argued that its challenge was nonetheless cognizable because the trial court had exceeded the scope of its sentencing jurisdiction as set by the indictment. Responding to the government's contention that plain error analysis should apply, the defense argued that the "discretionary nature" of such review is "logically incompatible with jurisdictional error," as reflected in "Federal Rule 12(b)(2) * * * [which then stated] that a court 'shall' notice at any time an error if the indictment 'fails to show jurisdiction in the court or to charge an offense.'" Agreeing with the defense's general position, the Fourth Circuit mentioned the

Rule 12(b)(2) exception, but relied basically on language in the Supreme Court's opinion in *Ex parte Bain*,[18] which spoke to the jurisdictional limitation imposed by the offense charged in the indictment. The Supreme Court, in a unanimous opinion, found this reasoning unpersuasive.

The Supreme Court in *Cotton* rejected *Bain's* broad conception of jurisdiction as outdated, noting that subsequent decisions had restricted the concept of a "jurisdictional defect" (i.e., a defect that "require[s] correction regardless of whether the error was raised in [the] district court") to "defects in subject-matter jurisdiction." It noted that post-*Bain* rulings had "rejected the claim that the [district] court had no jurisdiction because the indictment had not charged a crime against the United States," and while *Bain* had been relied upon in *Russell v. United States*[19] and *Stirone v. United States*[20] (both imposing automatic reversal for indictment defects), the defects there had been timely challenged in the district court. Here, with no timely challenge and no jurisdictional defect, the appropriate standard for appellate review was the plain error standard prescribed by Federal Rule 52(b).

The *Cotton* opinion did not refer to the waiver exception that was then in Rule 12(b)(2)[21], and that omission might indicate that the Court did not view the failure to allege an *Apprendi*-type element as the equivalent of a "failure to charge an offense." The government in its brief argued that Rule 12(b)(2) was not applicable since the indictment here did allege an offense (which existed without the sentencing-enhancement factor) and the critical error therefore "occurred at sentencing." Accepting that analysis of the error in *Cotton* would limit the ruling there to the failure to allege an *Apprendi*-type element. The reasoning of *Cotton*, however, was not so limited. In discussing the flaws in *Bain's* juris-

---

15. See § 19.1(e) as to the exceptions.

16. 535 U.S. 625, 122 S.Ct. 1781, 152 L.Ed.2d 860 (2002).

17. See § 19.2 at note 6, and § 19.3 at note 8 supra.

18. See § 19.5(d).

19. See § 19.3 at note 11.

20. See § 19.6 at note 8.

21. As to the subsequent change in that provision, see note 14 supra.

dictional analysis, the *Cotton* opinion specifically referred to the failure of an indictment to "charge a crime" as not presenting a jurisdictional flaw.

Recognizing that its rationale would leave the traditional reading of Rule 12(b)(2) without a solid theoretical grounding, the government in its *Cotton* brief also advanced an argument that would apply the same standards of appellate review to both the failure to allege an *Apprendi*-type element and the failure to allege any offense. The government argued that Rule 12(b) sets forth a general rule of waiver for pleading defects not raised before trial, and the function of its provision on the two exceptions simply was to indicate that they were not waived by the failure to present them at any earlier point in the proceeding. Rule 12(b)'s provision on the two exceptions, the government argued, did not address the consequence of a determination that the untimely, but not waived objection had merit (e.g., that the pleading did fail to state an offense), for doing so would take it into the sphere regulated by Rule 52(b). That Rule had to be accorded "equal dignity," and therefore should govern as to this objection, just as it would to any other objection not properly presented to the trial court. Rule 12(b)'s provision on exceptions merely served to make certain that the waiver provision of Rule 12(b) did not operate to preclude application of Rule 52(b), as plain error only authorizes possible review for non-waived objections.

The government's argument as to the interface of Rules 52 and Rule 12(b) was inconsistent with a long line of federal lower court cases dealing with essential element objections that had not been raised before the trial court. On the other hand, limiting *Cotton* to pleadings missing *Apprendi*-type elements would cut out the heart of the essential-elements pleading requirement by separating it from the level of the offense of conviction. Thus, it is not surprising that several lower courts have discarded their earlier rulings and applied *Cotton* to pleadings that omitted more traditional elements of an offense and thereby failed to

charge any crime. Not surprisingly also, these courts have found that the failure of the indictment to allege all essential elements did not qualify as plain error as that requires a showing both of actual prejudice and an adverse impact upon the fairness and the integrity of the proceeding.[22]

§ 19.4 Bill of Particulars

(a) Nature of the Bill. The motion for a bill of particulars requests that the prosecution be directed to furnish further information (i.e., "particulars") concerning the offense charged in the information or indictment. The motion ordinarily lists a series of questions concerning the events cited in the charge that the defense would have the prosecution answer. Thus, if an indictment charging the obstruction of a public official has simply tracked the language of the statute, the motion might ask for the answers to such questions as what official duties were obstructed and how did the obstruction occur. So too, where a defendant is charged with driving under the influence of alcohol, the defense may ask for particulars relating to the exact manner of the defendant's driving and the administration of the breath analyzer or other tests to determine the defendant's level of intoxication.

Assuming that the defense motion is granted, the status of the prosecution's response falls somewhere between a pleading and a discovery response. The factual allegations contained in the bill of particulars will limit the government's case at trial in the same manner as factual allegations in an original charging instrument. The rules governing variance between proof and pleading apply to the bill of particulars just as they do to an indictment or information. The allegations of the bill of particulars are not treated as equivalent to those in the original charging instrument, however, when it comes to meeting basic pleading requirements. If an indictment or information does not state all of the essential elements, it cannot be cured by a bill of particulars that alleges facts establishing the miss-

---

22. See § 27.5(d).

ing element. In *Russell v. United States*,[1] where the pleading lacked sufficient specificity, the Supreme Court described as "the settled rule" that "a bill of particulars cannot save an invalid indictment." However, *Russell* involved a specificity deficiency that was treated as a failure to allege the offense, and where the issue is simply a lack of factual detail, with elements of the offense alleged, the bill of particulars clearly counts. As discussed in 19.3(b), the availability of the bill of particulars frequently leads courts to conclude that the charging instrument is sufficient, notwithstanding the generality of its allegation.

(b) Standards for Issuance. The bill of particulars is available in all but a small group of states. In most of those states, its issuance is governed by common law principles. Some states do not have a court rule or statute governing the bill of particulars, and recognize it as a common law motion. Others have provisions like Federal Rule 7(f), which simply notes that the "court may direct the filing of a bill of particulars," and leaves to the courts the development of standards governing issuance. Still other states have rules setting forth standards, but those standards are exceptionally flexible. Only a small group of states have provisions that are specific in identifying at least some of the particulars that may be needed. They refer, for example, to providing: "reasonable notice of the crime charged, including time, place, manner or means"; "factual information * * * which pertains to the offense charged * * * including the substance of each defendant's conduct * * *, and whether the people intend to prove that defendant acted as a principal or accomplice or both"; and the "essential facts of the alleged offense."

Most jurisdictions hold that the issuance of the bill of particulars is discretionary. In several additional states, statutory provisions make issuance of the bill mandatory, but condition that obligation on broadly stated standards that give the trial judge considerable leeway in deciding whether they apply. Accordingly, in the vast majority of jurisdictions, appellate courts will give considerable weight to the trial

court's judgment when reviewing its decision not to grant a bill of particulars (in part, perhaps, because the trial court's ruling ordinarily is challenged on an appeal following a conviction). Appellate courts do, however, offer various guidelines to trial courts as to where the bill should or should not be granted. Unfortunately, those guidelines tend to be overgeneralizations that provide limited assistance in individual cases.

As noted above, the traditional common law standard, and a common statutory standard, for issuing the motion looks to "whether it is necessary that defendant have the particulars sought in order to prepare his defense and in order that prejudicial surprise will be avoided." Taken literally, this standard might require that defendant gain disclosure of everything in the prosecution's files, because only such broad discovery can assure that defendant will not be subjected to "prejudicial surprise." But the bill relates to the pleading, and the concern therefore should be with surprise only as to the particular acts or events that underlie the pleading, not with the manner in which they will be established at trial. Its function is only to give the defendant somewhat more factual detail, if needed, as to what will constitute the elements of the offense. Yet, at the same time, in recognizing defendant's need for particulars to "prepare his defense," trial courts often allow the bill to go somewhat beyond what would be obtained in even the most detailed pleading of the charges. Indeed, some courts have been willing to include an especially broad range of circumstances among the required particulars regarding the acts that constituted the crime (e.g., the names of non-participant eyewitnesses to the acts), but most have resisted efforts to expand the bill beyond the basics of who, what, where, and how.

In light of the bill's relationship to the pleading, it is not surprising that the courts repeatedly state that "a bill of particulars may not call for evidentiary matter." The discovery of the prosecution's evidence is a task for the procedures of pretrial discovery, which often

§ 19.4

1. See § 19.3 at note 11.

require a certain degree of reciprocal disclosure from the defense. Yet, in many instances, a request for more information relating to the factual elements of the charge necessarily also provides information about the government's evidence. Moreover, as courts place more emphasis upon the defense's use of the bill to facilitate its own investigation of the underlying events, the overlap becomes greater. In the end, the issue may not be whether granting the motion will disclose the government's evidence but whether the formulation of the defendant's request fits the basic function of the bill. Thus, a court may be willing to grant a motion asking that the government identify those persons who participated in the conduct it seeks to establish, but not a motion asking for a list of the government's witnesses.

Matching the prohibition against disclosure of evidentiary matter—and raising similar problems in application—is the prohibition against disclosure of the government's legal theory. Here again, an absolute prohibition must fail if the bill is to serve its purpose. A bill that provides the detail behind a very general factual allegation will often suggest a legal theory not apparent from the original allegation. Thus, where a court required the government to state in what respects defendants charged with a civil rights violation had acted "under color of law," the government response could well suggest its legal theory as to the scope of the actor's official status as well as the nature of his behavior. The key here was that the requested bill did not ask for a description of legal theory as such, but an explanation as to the official position held by the actor and how he utilized that position.

In ruling upon a defense motion for a bill of particulars, a trial court must also take into consideration the scope of the pretrial discovery that will be available to the defense. The government will often cite discovery opportunities as providing the defense with ample protection against prejudicial surprise at trial and adequate leads for preparing a meaningful defense. It will note also that discovery procedures, in contrast to the bill of particulars, will often require reciprocal disclosure from the defense. The defense, on the other hand, is

likely to argue that even the most complete discovery, if combined with a broadly stated accusatory instrument, is likely to be of limited use because it may suggest several different directions in which the prosecution may proceed. Only the bill of particulars, the defense will argue, serves to limit the shape of the case, and thereby allow the defense to properly focus its limited investigatory resources. To this contention the prosecution will respond that it should not be required before trial to virtually set its case in stone so that the differences that almost invariably occur between pretrial investigation and trial testimony can become the source of a constant stream of defense challenges to variances between the trial proof and the particulars.

The evaluation of the above arguments requires consideration of several additional factors, including the nature of the offense involved, the nature of the events that serve as the basis for the charge, and the breadth of the pleading. Consideration must be given, in particular, to the complexity of the offense, the range of activities it encompasses, and the time span it covers. Massive indictments, sprawling over many years and implicating a large number of defendants, obviously present a stronger case for a bill of particulars. Offenses using loose concepts do the same. Thus, as has been noted with respect to the RICO offense, "with the wide latitude accorded the prosecution to frame a charge that a defendant has 'conspired' to promote the affairs of an 'enterprise' through a 'pattern of racketeering activity' comes an obligation to particularize the nature of the charge to a degree that might not be necessary in the prosecution of crimes of more limited scope."

§ 19.5 Amendments of the Pleading

(a) Varied Uses. Various circumstances may lead the prosecution to propose an amendment to a charging instrument. The prosecution may find a technical irregularity in the indictment or information (e.g., an improper statutory citation) and utilize an amendment to make a correction even though the error would not render the pleading fatally defective. The prosecution may conclude on its own initiative (or in response to a defense motion to dismiss) that the charge fails to include a necessary element or lacks needed specificity and seek to cure that fatal defect with an amendment. Either before or during trial the prosecution may anticipate that its evidence will vary from the allegations in the pleading, giving the defense grounds for objection, and seek to preclude any such objection by an amendment that renders the pleading consistent with such evidence. Where the variance was not anticipated, the evidence was offered, and the defense objected on variance grounds, the prosecution may seek an amendment to meet that objection.

The prosecution may also move to amend following the completion of the introduction of evidence, and before the case is submitted to the jury. Evidence may have been introduced at variance with the pleading without a defense objection, and the prosecution may move to amend to conform the pleading to the proof, and thereby meet any objection to charging the jury on a theory of liability suggested by that evidence. So too, some aspect of the pleading may not have been supported by the prosecution's evidence, and the prosecution may move to delete that portion of the charge and have only the remainder presented to the jury.

Whether amendments will be allowed to achieve these different objectives will depend upon the standard governing amendments that is applied in the particular jurisdiction. The discussion below considers the most common variations in those standards and their application.

(b) The Prejudice/Different–Offense Standard. The dominant standard governing amendments is the two-pronged standard that permits an amendment provided it does not either (1) result in prejudice to the accused or (2) charge a different crime. This standard is set forth in Federal Rule 7(e), which provides:

> Unless an additional or different offense is charged or a substantial right of the defendant is prejudiced, the court may permit an information to be amended at any time before the verdict or finding.

Although Federal Rule 7(e) is limited to amendments of the information, most states apply its two-pronged limitation on amendments to both indictments and informations. The federal practice of utilizing different standards for amendments of the information and the indictment, while not unique, reflects a minority position.

Of the two limitations imposed under the dominant standard, the prejudice limitation clearly has produced the greater consistency in interpretation among the various state and federal courts. General agreement exists that the concept of "prejudice" to the "substantial rights" of the accused requires an inquiry that focuses on the element of surprise. Ordinarily, the defense, in opposing an amendment, must make some showing that the proposed change introduces an element of surprise that will interfere with the defense's ability to defend against the charges. Courts often note that timing is the key here, with a critical distinction drawn between amendments made before and during trial. Prior to trial, prejudice in preparation ordinarily may be avoided by granting a continuance, and courts are hesitant to find prejudice if a continuance was granted, offered and refused, or not requested. Since continuances during trial (particularly a jury trial) are less likely to be granted, the prosecution faces a much more difficult task in overcoming a defense claim of surprise as to an amendment offered during trial. Such amendments are most likely to be accepted where the prosecution can show that the amendment does not change substantially the factual basis of the offense as set forth in the original pleading, the bill of particulars, or the discovery made available to the defense. However, the critical test here is whether the defense's challenge to the prosecution's evidence and the defense's presentation of its own evidence will have the same bearing upon the amended pleading as upon the original pleading, and that may not always be the case even when the defense was previously aware of the factual basis of the amendment.

The prohibition against amendments that charge a different or additional offense has produced somewhat greater divergence in its interpretation. There is general agreement that this prohibition stands without regard to the absence of prejudicial surprise. Courts recognize two different types of amendments that can result in the charging of a different or additional offense. The first, producing what is commonly described as a "factually different offense," is the amendment that alters the facts alleged, but continues to allege a violation of the same substantive crime as the original pleading. The second, creating what is described as "legally separate offense," is the amendment that alters the substantive crime alleged to have been violated, usually relying upon a different code provision. Where an amendment both changes the facts alleged and the statutory violation, it must be analyzed under the standards applied to both types of changes.

In determining whether a factual change produces a new offense, most courts ask whether the amendment moves to what is basically a different factual event. Thus, a court may ask whether "the prosecution is relying [through the amendment] on a complex of facts distinctly different" from that set forth in the original pleading, or whether the crime specified in the original pleading "evolved out of the same factual situation as the crimes specified in the amended indictment or information." In applying such standards, courts do not find critical factual shifts that would produce a separate offense for the purpose of applying the double jeopardy clause (as where each assault victim produces a different offense). If the remaining characteristics of the event (e.g., time, place, behavior, and consequence) are constant, an amendment identifying a different victim of an offense (e.g., a different owner of the stolen property) does not allege a different offense. Similarly, different offenses are not changed by amendments that change the identification of the property stolen, the description of the sexual contact with the victim of a sexual assault, or different means of committing the offense. So too, though a change in the alleged date of the offense may raise difficulties in terms of prejudice (e.g., rendering irrelevant the defendant's alibi), it will not create a different offense

unless it refers to an event different than that originally alleged. Some courts suggest, however, that even though the basic incident remains the same, an amendment altering the facts alleged will be deemed to allege a different offense if it changes the "theory of the prosecution."

Where the amendment alleges violation of a different substantive criminal prohibition, most courts will apply the traditional double jeopardy standard that looks to the elements of crime in determining whether two statutes proscribe the same offense. Under that standard, an amendment will be accepted if it merely alleges a lesser included offense, but not if it alleges a more serious offense with additional elements or even a similarly graded offense with different elements. Some courts, however, will accept amendments charging a crime of similar gravity with different elements if the core elements of that crime are the same as that of the crime originally charged (e.g., the same assault with different aggravating circumstances).

Courts have divided in applying the same offense standard to the amendment of the allegation stating the means of commission of the crime from one statutory prescribed alternative to another. A minority position views such a change as charging a separate offense even though the same statutory provision is relied upon. They view the alternatives, at least where distinct in character, as establishing offenses that are separate in function, though having the same consequence. The majority position rejects that analysis and views such a shift as not changing the offense charged. These courts treat the amendment as merely shifting the facts that will be relied upon to establish the same basic element of the crime. From this perspective, to disallow the amendment would be to draw a functionally unpersuasive distinction between basically similar amendments depending upon whether the statute describes an element generally (e.g., simply uses the term "narcotics") or specifies various alternatives that will satisfy that element (e.g., by listing different types of narcotics). If a shift from one alternative to another does not change the element of the offense (and therefore does not allege a new offense) under the first type of statute, neither should it do so under the second type of statute. Carrying the single-element analysis to its logical extreme, these courts have allowed a shift in a first degree murder charge from premeditated killing to a killing in the course of a felony since all that was altered was means of establishing the mens rea element for a single statutory offense.

Divergence in the judicial interpretation of the prohibition against amendments alleging a different offense may be the product of quite different perspectives on the purpose of that prohibition. One characterization of the prohibition is that of a flat rule safeguarding against prejudicial surprise. If the concept of a different offense is limited to different underlying criminal events or statutory prohibitions involving different core elements, then it can readily be assumed that a shift to a different offense, even before trial, ordinarily will create a substantial possibility of surprise and prejudice. On the other hand, the different-offense prohibition may be seen as an attempt to protect the role of the agency that screened the charge, whether the grand jury in the case of an indictment or the magistrate in the case of an information. From this perspective, the confines of an "offense" arguably should be narrower. While one might not demand that the precise evidentiary basis presented to the screening agency be the grounding for the charge presented by amendment, the basic factual theory of the offense arguably should remain the same or the defendant has not truly had the particular charge against him screened by that agency.

The different offense standard, however, provides an awkward vehicle for protecting the screening agency's role. First, changes that fall far short of altering the offense may still alter the theory of prosecution presented to the screening agency. Second, the different offense standard is designed to apply to amendments of all charging instruments, including those that were never screened by a screening agency. It applies, for example, to amendments of misdemeanor charges and to amendments of felony charges set forth in informations that

were the product of a waiver of an indictment or the waiver of a preliminary hearing. A jurisdiction concerned primarily with protecting the role of the screening agency would more appropriately shape it standard to speak directly to altering the screening agency's determination. Thus, New York's amendment provision on indictments states that an amendment is not permitted where it "change[s] the theory or theories of the prosecution as reflected in the evidence before the grand jury." Similarly, California's provision on the amendment of an information insists that any offense charged by an amendment "was shown by the evidence taken at the preliminary examination."

(c) The Form/Substance Distinction. A substantial group of states adhere to the formulation that permits amendment as to "form," but not as to "substance." Some of these states allow amendments as to substance prior to trial (provided they do not allege a different or additional defense), but then permit only amendments as to form after the trial has started. Others simply provide for amendments as to form at any time before verdict. Although the limitation of the amendment to matters of form might be seen as precluding the possibility of prejudice or changing the offense charged, some provisions add prohibitions against amendments having those results. Typically, the provisions apply to the amendment of indictments as well as informations.

While provisions adopting a form/substance distinction may offer illustrations of formal defects that may be cured by indictment (e.g., miswritings, surplusage, and the failure to state time or place where "not of the essence of the offense"), they do not attempt to describe what constitutes a substantive amendment. Not surprisingly courts have varied in their interpretation of that standard. A few view substantive changes as largely limited to those which charge what would constitute a different offense under a Rule 7(e)-type standard. Most, however, find substantive changes in amendments that would be acceptable (assuming no prejudice) under the narrowest interpretation of a Rule 7(e)-type standard.

Amendments are said to be substantive if they change any "essential facts that must be proved to make the act complained of a crime." Thus, a jurisdiction adopting a restrictive interpretation of the form/substance distinction is likely to bar automatically an amendment that substantially changes the pleading's description of the criminal act, the mens rea accompanying that act, or the consequences of that act. Such rulings have prohibited amendments that changed the original allegation that defendant defrauded an automobile dealer of a dollar amount to defrauding the dealer of an automobile selling for that amount, that changed the action involved in shoplifting from altering the price tag to removing the price tag, and that added robbery by reasonably appearing to be armed to an indictment that alleged defendant was actually armed. Courts also have characterized as substantive an amendment alleging the assault was against a different victim, an amendment deleting the name of one of several named robbery victims, and even an amendment altering an allegation as to the ownership of the property that was stolen. Other courts, however, have accepted as non-substantive similar changes in the name of the victim where that change did not look to a different event and did not alter the "character" of the modus operandi.

(d) The _Bain_ Rule. As previously noted, most jurisdictions treat the amendment of an indictment no differently than the amendment of an information. However, the federal courts and several states draw a sharp distinction between the amendment of the information and the indictment. While utilizing the liberal Rule 7(e) standard for amendments to the information, they apply a much more stringent standard to amendments of the indictment. The permissible scope of an amendment of an indictment in federal courts is controlled by the _Bain_ rule, which is based on the Supreme Court's ruling in _Ex parte Bain_.[1] The _Bain_ ruling relied on common law principles that treated the indictment as the sole product of the grand jury, subject to alteration only by that body. As originally announced, the _Bain_

rule imposed a prohibition against amending indictments that arguably was more restrictive than even the most stringent interpretation of the form/substance distinction. A few states that continue to look to the same common law principles (and thus are described as "_Bain_ jurisdictions") have retained that original prohibition. In the federal courts, however, the _Bain_ rule is now held to allow some limited amendments to the indictment, though under a standard not nearly as broad as the Rule 7(e) standard applicable to informations. In many respects, the federal rulings on amending indictments are similar to state rulings that significantly restrict amendments under a "form/ substance" standard.

Bain was decided in 1887, at a time when several states had started to depart from the early common law rule that "indictments could not be amended." The Supreme Court noted, however, that its ruling was "not left to the requirements of the common law," but was controlled by the "positive and restrictive language" of the Fifth Amendment guarantee of indictment by grand jury. That guarantee, the Court noted, entitles the defendant to be tried on the indictment as issue by the grand jury, not as amended by the prosecutor with permission of the trial court. A trial court could not allow alteration even as to matter that it deemed "surplusage" and therefore not critical to the grand jury's decision to indict. That prohibition followed, the Court reasoned, from the constitutional obligation to preserve the Fifth Amendment right to grand jury review. A court could not "change the charging part of an indictment to suit its own notions of what it ought to have been, or what the grand jury would probably have made if their attention had been called to suggested changes," for the charge was then that of the court rather than the grand jury.

Read broadly, Justice Miller's opinion in _Bain_ would have barred any amendment to what he described as the "body of the indictment." His discussion of common law authority included cases that refused to permit

<hr/>

§ 19.5

1. 121 U.S. 1, 7 S.Ct. 781, 30 L.Ed. 849 (1886).

amendments to correct a misnomer or even amendments offered with the consent of the defendant. Modern federal cases have refused to read the *Bain* prohibition against amendment as so absolute. Consent to an amendment generally makes the prohibition inapplicable, at least in those cases where the right to an indictment could be waived altogether. Federal courts also have allowed amendments that deal with matters of "form" rather than substance. This includes corrections of misnomers or typographical errors. *Bain* itself continues to be cited, however, as an illustration of the type of change, relating to the substance of the crime, that cannot be permitted even though there is no suggestion that the change will affect the preparedness of the defendant.

The indictment in *Bain* charged the defendant with having made a false statement "with intent to deceive the Comptroller of the Currency and the agent appointed to examine the affairs of said association." The trial court sustained a demurrer to the indictment, apparently on the ground that the statute applied only to deception of the person who actually examined the records, and therefore did not prohibit the derivative deception of the Comptroller. Under the pleading rule then prevailing, an offense was not charged if any of the alternative actions cited in the indictment did not constitute a crime. Responding to the trial court's ruling, the government, with the permission of the trial court, then "corrected" the indictment by deleting the reference to the Comptroller of the Currency. The Supreme Court held that this amendment was impermissible and the defendant's subsequent conviction on that amended indictment therefore had to be reversed. The Court rejected the view that the reference to the Comptroller was merely "surplusage" that had no bearing on the grand jury's view of the case. It reasoned:

> While it may seem to the court with its better instructed mind in regard to what the [criminal] statute requires * * *, that it was neither necessary nor reasonable that the grand jury should attach importance to the fact that it was the Comptroller who was to

be deceived, yet it is not impossible nor very improbable that the grand jury looked mainly to that officer as the party whom the prisoner intended to deceive by a report which was made upon his requisition and returned directly to him. * * * How can the court say that there may not have been more than one of the jurors * * * who was satisfied that the report was made to deceive the Comptroller, but was not convinced that it was made to deceive anybody else. And how can it be said that, with those words stricken out, it is the indictment which was found by the grand jury.

In its most recent interpretation of *Bain*, *United States v. Miller*,[2] the Supreme Court stated that *Bain* today stands only for "the proposition that a conviction cannot stand if based on an offense that is different from that alleged in the grand jury indictment." In *Miller*, the indictment had alleged that the defendant defrauded an insurance company by both arranging for a burglary at his place of business and by lying to the insurer as to the value of the loss, but the evidence at trial established only the lying. Although there was no element of surprise involved, the trial court denied the government's motion to amend the indictment by striking the allegation of the defendant's prior knowledge of the burglary. After the case was submitted to the jury on the full indictment, and the defendant was convicted, the defense challenged the conviction on the ground that the government's proof had fatally varied from the scheme alleged in the indictment by failing to cover both aspects of that scheme. In the course of rejecting that contention, the Supreme Court noted that the government's proposed amendment, which would have limited the indictment to the proof presented, would have been permissible under a proper reading of *Bain*. The Court acknowledged that language in *Bain* quoted above could "support the proposition that the striking out of part of an indictment invalidates the whole of the indictment, for a court cannot speculate as to whether the grand jury had meant for any remaining offense to stand independently, even if that re-

2. 471 U.S. 130, 105 S.Ct. 1811, 85 L.Ed.2d 99 (1985).

maining offense clearly was included in the original text." However, later cases had implicitly rejected that proposition by holding that, "as long as the crime and elements of the offense that sustain the conviction are fully and clearly set out in the indictment, the right to a grand jury is not normally violated by the fact that the indictment alleges more crimes or other means of committing the same crime." In light of these rulings, *Miller* noted, where an indictment alleges two separate offenses or two separate means of committing the same offense, *Bain* should not be read to prohibit dropping from the indictment those allegations concerning the one offense or one means that was not supported by the evidence at trial.

As it relates to the deletion of allegations, the *Miller* reading of *Bain* presents a principle fairly easily applied. Indeed, perhaps the only complexity is how that principle can be squared with the *Bain* holding on the facts presented there. The answer may be that the *Miller* analysis would call for a different ruling on the *Bain* facts today, but it is nonetheless consistent with the *Bain* ruling in light of the pleading rules applied in 1887. The trial court in *Bain* had viewed the indictment as fatally defective under the then-prevailing view of the essential elements requirement. Under that view, an indictment was fatally flawed if it alleged one method of committing the offense (deceiving the Comptroller) that did not violate the statute. With the indictment therefore failing to charge an offense in the first instance, any amendment was, as the Court noted in *Miller*, setting forth a "different offence." Today, the *Bain* indictment could be viewed, in the terms of *Miller*, as alleging "two separate means of committing the offense," with one being defective. Under the analysis of *Miller*, which treats the grand jury as having made an independent judgment as to each, there would be no difficulty in dropping that means held to be deficient and relying on the other, which clearly did set forth criminal conduct. In this regard, *Miller* specifically noted:

> To the extent *Bain* stands for the proposition that it constitutes an unconstitutional amendment to drop from an indictment

those allegations that are unnecessary to an offense that is clearly contained within it, that case has simply not survived. To avoid further confusion, we now explicitly reject that proposition.

Miller had no need to discuss the application of the *Bain* rule to amendments that would add or substitute new factual allegations. It noted only that *Bain* continues to stand for the proposition "that a conviction cannot stand if based on an offense that is different from that alleged in the grand jury's indictment." The Court had no reason to explore the question of what new matter results in alleging an offense "different" from that originally charged. It described as "the most important reaffirmation" of this aspect of *Bain* the Court's ruling in *Stirone v. United States*.[3] In that case, as discussed in § 19.6(c), the Court found that the trial court's admission of evidence establishing a factual theory of liability at variance with that alleged in the indictment resulted in a prohibited "constructive amendment" of the indictment. The indictment there alleged that the element of interference with interstate commerce had been produced through one consequence of defendant's extortion activities while the trial evidence and jury instruction allowed for the finding of interference based on a different consequence.

In a jurisdiction that applied the dominant two-pronged standard discussed in subsection (b), the new factual theory allowed by the trial court in *Stirone* would not have been viewed as alleging a different offense. The constructive amendment simply introduced a new factual alternative for establishing one element of the crime. *Stirone*, however, viewed the new theory as an impermissible departure from the original indictment because it broadened the factual basis for liability; it mattered not that this "constructive amendment" did so without creating what would be considered a separate crime for double jeopardy purposes. The *Miller* opinion also cited language in still other federal rulings that similarly indicated that changes which would fall short of producing a new offense under a Rule 7(e)-type standard will

---

3. 361 U.S. 212, 80 S.Ct. 270, 4 L.Ed.2d 252 (1960), discussed in § 19.6 at note 8.

nonetheless be prohibited under the *Bain* rule as alleging an offense "different" from that originally charged. Thus reference was made to the impermissible broadening of the grand jury's determination of the "means" of committing a crime.

Lower federal courts applying the *Bain* rule accordingly have drawn a distinction between acceptable amendments that merely explain or expand upon factual elements originally alleged (e.g., by more specifically identifying an altered commercial draft) and impermissible amendments that alter the factual theories establishing elements of the same offense. Thus, courts have rejected amendments that added a different drug to the list of drugs possessed by defendant with an intent to distribute, and that shifted the deadly weapon under a charge of possession during a felony from a "chair" to a "chair and/or table."

For the federal prosecutor who wishes to avoid repeated trips to the grand jury, the *Bain* rule, as modified by *Miller*, offers two obvious lessons. First, all possible factual theories of liability should be included in the initial indictment. If post-indictment investigation should reveal that a theory is not worthy of carrying forward at trial, it may always be deleted; on the other hand, if a factual theory originally is omitted on the ground that it is not as strong as other theories, and post-indictment investigation reveals its strength was underestimated, the addition of that theory will require a new indictment under the *Bain* rule. Second, there is an advantage in utilizing less specificity so that allegations can cover more factual variations that might arise as a result of post-indictment investigation. In case after case, federal prosecutors have avoided *Bain* difficulties as a result of broad initial descriptions of essential elements. Of course, the prosecution often walks a fine line in adopting this tact, as the lack of factual specificity, as discussed in § 19.3(b), may provide a basis for a successful defense challenge to the sufficiency of the pleading.

Where an appellate court finds that the trial court erred by permitting an amendment that violated the *Bain* limitation, the consequence traditionally has been a reversal of defendant's conviction, without inquiry as to whether the error had a prejudicial impact upon the trial. The rejection of *Bain's* jurisdictional characterization of pleading errors in *United States v. Cotton*[4] may call for reexamination of this position. While *Cotton* distinguished the automatic reversal in *Stirone* as arising in a case in which, unlike *Cotton*, the objection had been properly presented at trial,[5] those lower federal courts that have viewed *Cotton* as lending support to applying a harmless error standard to a properly presented claim that the indictment failed to charge an offense presumably would find the harmless error standard applicable as well to a properly presented claim that the trial court permitted an amendment prohibited by *Bain*.[6]

§ 19.6   Variances

(a) Challenging Variances. A variance arises when the proof offered at trial departs from the allegations in the indictment or information. A defense objection to a variance may be made initially at the point that the prosecution introduces its proof, with the defense arguing that the prosecutor's evidence is irrelevant to the charges. Very often that objection may have escaped the defense's notice, or the evidence may have had relevance to a similar happening or transaction, and the defense objection will first be raised in opposition to the prosecution's request for a jury instruction resting liability on a theory supported only by the proof which departs from the pleading. The defendant objecting at this point states, in effect: "The state may have introduced evidence sufficient to establish a crime, but it is not the crime alleged in its accusatory pleading and I therefore am entitled to an acquittal." If the state has introduced evidence covering the allegations in its pleading and the variance relates to evidence establishing an additional theory of liability, then the defense

---

4.   See § 19.2 at note 5, and § 19.3 at note 16.

5.   See § 19.3 at note 20.

6.   See note 4 of § 19.3 and § 19.3 at note 5.

objection is to allowing the jury to find liability based on this additional theory. Frequently, the prosecution, recognizing the existence of a variance, will seek to amend the pleading to conform to the evidence. If this is permitted, and the defendant is convicted, then the issue raised on appeal will be whether the amendment was properly allowed. If the trial judge does not allow the amendment (or no request for amendment is made), and the case is sent to the jury over the defendant's variance objection, then the defendant, if convicted, will contend on appeal that allowance of the variance constitutes reversible error.

If the trial judge upholds the defense objection to a variance and does not allow an amendment, then the issue basically is removed from the case. The defense has no reason to object, and the prosecution will be unable to gain appellate review of the trial court's ruling. If there is insufficient evidence to convict without the variance, and the defendant is acquitted, the prosecution cannot challenge that verdict. The prosecution may obtain a new charge based upon the material that had been excluded on a variance theory, but if the court should then conclude that the new material sets forth the same offense for double jeopardy purposes as the prior charge, the acquittal on that charge constitutes a bar to the new prosecution. Numerous states have provisions stating that "if the defendant is acquitted on the ground of a variance between the charge and the proof, * * * it is not an acquittal of the crime and does not bar a subsequent prosecution for the same crime." These provisions seek to treat the acquittal as the equivalent of a dismissal, but that position probably is unacceptable in light of the double jeopardy definition of an "acquittal."[1]

(b) The *Berger* Standard. Without doubt, the most frequently cited analysis of the law governing variances is that of Justice Sutherland in *Berger v. United States:*[2]

> The true inquiry, * * * is not whether there has been a variance in proof, but whether there has been such a variance as to "affect

the substantial rights" of the accused. The general rule that allegations and proof must correspond is based upon the obvious requirements (1) that the accused shall be definitely informed as to the charges against him, so that he may be enabled to present his defense and not be taken by surprise by the evidence offered at the trial; and (2) that he may be protected against another prosecution for the same offense.

Justice Sutherland's analysis has been adopted by various state courts as the sole measure for testing the acceptability of a variance. Under what is described as the *"Berger* standard," a variance requires reversal of a conviction only when it deprives the defendant of his right to fair notice or leaves him open to a risk of double jeopardy.

In applying the notice element of the *Berger* standard, courts look to the record to determine whether it suggests "a possibility that the defendant may have been misled or embarrassed in the preparation or presentation of his defense." A failure to object to the variance at trial generally is viewed as a waiver of a claim of prejudice, and an eleventh hour objection is taken as strong evidence belying any such claim. If the defendant was previously aware of the prosecution's proof as a result of pretrial discovery or a preliminary hearing, that factor also will weigh against a finding of prejudice. The court also will look to the relationship of the variance to the defense presented by the defendant. Thus, a variance in date or location is not likely to have misled a defendant who raised an affirmative defense or claimed a lack of mens rea, as those defenses acknowledge the defendant's participation in the alleged event.

The possibility of actual prejudice at trial is put aside when courts test a variance against the risk of exposing the defendant to double jeopardy. The only element considered here is the extent to which the variance alters the scope of the charge. Indeed, a challenge based on this ground may be raised by a defendant who failed to object to the variance at trial.

§ 19.6

1. See § 25.3(b), (c).

2. 295 U.S. 78, 55 S.Ct. 629, 79 L.Ed. 1314 (1935).

The concern of *Berger* apparently was that if defendant were tried on the proof presented in the variance and the jury concluded that such proof did not establish the offense charged, the record would be such that a reprosecution on the theory of the variance would not necessarily be barred. The original pleading would establish the scope of the jeopardy that attached at the first trial and it would not bar a second trial on the theory of the variance if that theory established a different offense. Today, however, the pleading alone would not control the scope of the jeopardy that attached at the original proceeding, as the trial record would be available to show that the defendant had been placed in jeopardy on the theory of the variance. Since the defendant went to trial on the original pleading, a reprosecution on that charge alone would also be barred. Thus, it is questionable whether the implementation of the double jeopardy bar continues to demand the prohibition against variances establishing a new offense.

Assuming, however, that the focus on the pleading as a protection against multiple jeopardy remains viable, then the double jeopardy prong of *Berger* still should not bar a variance unless it constitutes a separate offense for double jeopardy purposes. Yet, courts have barred, presumably under *Berger's* double jeopardy prong, variances that changed the offense only by alleging a different means of commission as part of the same incident or a different ultimate victim of a property offense. In many such cases, the distinction between what was alleged in the initial charge and what was established through the variance clearly would not produce different offenses under the currently prevailing double jeopardy standard of *Blockburger*.[3] Such rulings, may reflect an outdated view of separate offenses for double jeopardy purposes, but they seem more likely to reflect the state's conversion of the second prong of *Berger* into a constructive amendment limitation as discussed in the next subsection.

(c) **The Constructive Amendment Limitation.** The Supreme Court, in its treatment of variances, has looked to both the *Berger* standard and the limitations that apply to amendments of the charge, particularly as to indictments. The Court accordingly has drawn a distinction between trial court allowance of departure in the proof from the indictment so great as to be regarded as a "constructive amendment," which constitutes a reversible error in itself, and a "mere variance," which is reversible error only if it is likely to have caused surprise or otherwise been prejudicial to the defense. The analysis underlying this distinction was described by Circuit Judge Gibbons as follows:

It is, of course, elementary that neither the prosecutor nor the trial court may constitutionally amend a federal indictment. *Ex parte Bain*. The Supreme Court has recognized, however, that if there is no amendment of the indictment, but only a variance between the facts alleged in the indictment and the evidence offered at trial, the problem is not one of usurping the constitutionally guaranteed role of the grand jury, but one of promoting the fairness of the trial and ensuring the defendant notice and an opportunity to be heard. See e.g., *Kotteakos v. United States*; *Berger v. United States*. The variance rule, to the extent that it is constitutionally required, is more of a due process rule than is the flat fifth amendment prohibition against being tried on an indictment which a grand jury never returned. In *Stirone v. United States*, however, the Supreme Court recognized that even though a trial court did not formally amend an indictment, it could accomplish the practical result of trying a defendant on a charge for which he was not indicted by a grand jury if it permitted proof of facts on an essential element of an offense which were different than those charged in the indictment. The trial court would not be permitted, in the guise of a variance, to accomplish a constructive amendment so as to modify the facts which the grand jury charged as an essential element of the substantive offense. * * * The consequence of a constructive amendment is that the admission of the

---

3.　See § 17.4(b).

challenged evidence is per se reversible error, requiring no analysis of additional prejudice to the defendant.[4]

The three Supreme Court rulings cited by Judge Gibbons offer the best illustration of the distinction between "mere variance" and a variance that amounts to a "constructive amendment." Both *Berger* and *Kotteakos* involved situations in which one large conspiracy was charged but proof at trial established a series of separate conspiracies. The Court in each case applied the *Berger* standard. Since the variances did not create double jeopardy difficulties, the focus was on whether the distinction in proof resulted in prejudice, with the Court finding that it had in one case but not in another. *Berger*[5] held that the variance was not prejudicial when it established two conspiracies involving contemporaneous transactions rather than a single conspiracy. *Kotteakos v. United States*,[6] held otherwise as to a situation "in which one conspiracy only is charged and at least eight having separate though similar objects are made out * * * and in which the more numerous participants in the different schemes were, on the whole, except for one, persons who did not know or have anything to do with one another." There, thirteen parties were jointly tried, and as to all but one defendant, the variance resulted in the jury having before it evidence of additional conspiracies which had no bearing on individual defendant's liability.

Neither *Berger* nor *Kotteakos* spoke to whether, if amendments had been allowed to reshape the conspiracies to fit the prosecution's evidence, those amendments would have violated the *Bain* rule. However, the Court later suggested in *United States v. Miller*[7] that the *Berger* and *Kotteakos* rulings were consistent with the amendment principle announced in *Bain*. The more confined conspiracies of which the defendants were convicted were described in *Miller* as "technically included" within the broader conspiracy originally alleged. Thus, if the variances were treated as

amendments, they would have reduced the scope of the charges, rather than have added new material and therefore would not have violated *Bain* as interpreted in *Miller*. That was not the case in *Stirone v. United States*.[8]

In *Stirone*, the indictment charged a violation of the Hobbs Act through extortion that obstructed interstate commerce by preventing the victim (Rider) from importing sand that was shipped from another state. At trial, over the defendant's objection, the court admitted evidence (and charged the jury) on obstruction of interstate commerce that resulted from Rider's inability to supply concrete for the construction of a local steel plant which had intended to ship its product in interstate commerce. The lower court found that this variance had not been fatal since defense counsel had been prepared for the introduction of that evidence. Without disturbing this finding of no prejudice, the Supreme Court reversed. Justice Black, speaking for a unanimous Court, noted:

> The grand jury which found this indictment was satisfied to charge that Stirone's conduct interfered with interstate importation of sand. But neither this nor any other court can know that the grand jury would have been willing to charge that Stirone's conduct would interfere with interstate exportation of steel from a mill later to be built with Rider's concrete. * * * Although the trial court did not permit a formal amendment of the indictment, the effect of what it did was the same. And the addition charging interference with steel exports here is neither trivial, useless, nor innocuous.

The variance in *Stirone* would not have created a "new offense" for double jeopardy purposes. The act of extortion was the same under both theories, with the variation extending only to the consequences establishing the element of harm (i.e., the obstruction of interstate commerce). However, as noted in § 19.5, many jurisdictions apply a much more restric-

---

4.   United States v. Crocker, 568 F.2d 1049 (3d Cir. 1977)

5.   See note 2 supra.

6.   328 U.S. 750, 66 S.Ct. 1239, 90 L.Ed. 1557 (1946).

7.   See § 19.5 at note 3.

8.   361 U.S. 212, 80 S.Ct. 270, 4 L.Ed.2d 252 (1960).

tive view of what constitutes a different offense in the context of limiting amendments. The federal system, under the *Bain* rule, certainly falls within this group. Under that rule, an amendment adding the theory of harm advanced by the *Stirone* variance clearly would not have been permitted. The variance altered a substantial element of the crime, providing an entirely different theory of impact upon interstate commerce. In contrast to *Berger* and *Kotteakos*, it added a new factual element rather than simply rearranging the elements alleged in the original indictment. Moreover, it was a new factual element substantially different from that previously presented; the possible interference with prospective steel shipments had a much more remote and speculative impact upon interstate commerce than the interference with the importation of sand. Under these circumstances, as various lower courts have noted, there was a "substantial likelihood that a defendant may have been convicted of an offense other than the one the grand jury had in mind."

Stirone appeared to draw an absolute parallel between the *Bain* prohibition of amendments and the prohibition of variances as constructive amendments. A strict application of the *Bain* prohibition could certainly bar variances far less extreme than that in *Stirone*. Some federal lower courts, however, have looked to *Stirone* as the prototype of the variance that will be barred automatically, as a constructive amendment. They have suggested that the variance must change the basic character of an element of the offense, producing a

modification that could possibly have affected the grand jury's assessment of the charges. Others have taken a position arguably more consistent with *Bain* and construed as a constructive amendment any variance that basically alters the prosecution's factual theory as to any element. In states that adhere to a restrictive form/substance limitation on amendments, the constructive amendment doctrine has barred even the most minor variances. Thus, one court rejected a variance where the indictment charged armed robbery with a pistol and evidence was that defendant had used a rifle.

As previously noted, a constructive amendment has traditionally called for automatic reversal on appellate review. The combination of *United States v. Cotton*[9] and the federal lower court rulings applying a harmless error analysis to an indictment's failure to charge an offense is likely to lead to a reconsideration of this position. While *Cotton* distinguished the automatic reversal in *Stirone*[10] it rejected the *Bain* perspective as to the jurisdictional quality of a proper indictment—a perspective that arguably also influenced Stirone. Also, as the government noted in its *Cotton* brief, *Stirone* was decided before the Court introduced its harmless error jurisprudence as applied to constitutional errors.[11] If the grand jury's failure to consider all the elements of the charged offense (as reflected in its indictment) is subject to harmless error review, then arguably the same should be true of the grand jury's failure to consider the factual variance that constituted a constructive amendment.

---

9. See § 19.2 at note 5, and § 19.3 at note 16.

10. See § 19.3 at note 20.

11. See § 19.1 at note 5.

Chapter 20

DISCOVERY AND DISCLOSURE

Table of Sections

§ 20.1 The Expansion of Discovery

(a) The Break From the Common Law. Although the English common law may not have been quite so absolute, American courts, relying on the English precedent, adopted a common law rule holding that the judiciary lacked any inherent authority to order pretrial discovery in criminal cases. Absent specific legislative authorization, a trial court could not order the prosecution to make a pretrial disclosure of its evidence to the defense or the defense to make a pretrial disclosure of its evidence to the prosecution. Well into the early 1900s, in all but the few states that had legislatively authorized pretrial discovery, the only pretrial discovery available to the parties was that which was obtained informally through the mutual exchange of information or incidentally in the course of such pretrial proceedings as the preliminary hearing. By the late 1930s, however, formal pretrial discovery had come onto the scene in a substantial number of jurisdictions, and that number grew to include a majority of the states over the next decade. Many states came to accept Professor Wigmore's position that the common law prohibition was a rule "of policy, not of power." They recognized a discretionary authority of the trial court, in the exercise of its inherent authority to control the trial process, to require the prosecution to make a pretrial disclosure of specified evidence to the defense. Also, many adopted statutes requiring the accused to give advance notice of the intent to present an alibi defense along with specific information relating to that defense.

During the 1930s and 1940s, through court rules and legislation, the vast majority of jurisdictions adopted procedures designed to promote full and open pretrial discovery in civil cases. By providing for depositions, interrogatories, production of documents, inspection of intangible items, and physical and mental examinations, civil discovery provisions sought to give each side pretrial access to almost all relevant information within the knowledge of the other side. The success of this liberalization of civil discovery naturally led courts and legislatures to consider whether a similar expansion of discovery should be attempted in criminal cases. The proposals for expansion in the criminal area did not utilize precise counterparts to the civil vehicles for discovery, but sought to achieve the same basic end—avoidance of "trial by surprise"—through somewhat different procedures. The primary distinctions were in the focus on discovery only as to one side, the defense, and the use of different forms of disclosure.

Since prosecution discovery from the defense was thought to be largely prohibited by the defendant's privilege against self-incrimination, and many states already had alibi-discovery provisions (arguably meeting the prosecution's greatest need for disclosure), the proposals for expansion looked primarily to granting to the defense broader discovery from the prosecution. For reasons noted in § 20.2(e), the deposition of possible witnesses for the opposition, a primary tool of discovery in civil cases, was thought ill-suited for the criminal arena. Since the prosecution, unlike the plaintiff in the civil case, was not a participant in any of the events involved, an interrogatory procedure (commonly used to probe the opposing party's knowledge) also was deemed inappropriate. Instead, the proposals for expansion focused on requiring the prosecutor to make available for defense inspection the critical information in its files that related to the case it intended to present at trial. Thus, the prosecution would be required to disclose statements it had obtained from the defendant, his codefendant, and any witnesses it intended to present. It would also be required to make available to the defense, as in civil discovery, relevant documents and tangible items. Finally, it would be required to inform the defense of certain information (e.g., the names and addresses of potential prosecution witnesses) that ordinarily was obtained in civil cases through interrogatories.

Though the proposed vehicles for disclosure and the one-sided focus differed from the expansion that had occurred on the civil side, the possible expansion of discovery in criminal cases was thought, at least by its proponents, to raise basically the same policy concerns as had been encountered in the dramatic expansion of civil discovery. Critics disagreed, and there occurred during the 1950s and 1960s one of the classic debates in the field of criminal procedure. Today the issues raised in that debate have been largely resolved in each jurisdiction by court rules or statutes which detail that discovery which must (or may) be given to the defense. However, an understanding of that debate provides a useful guidepost in the interpretation of current discovery provisions. Indeed, though the debate focused on defense discovery, the policy considerations advanced there are currently cited not only in opinions interpreting the provisions on defense discovery, but also in opinions interpreting the provisions governing prosecution discovery from the defense.

(b) The Debate. An extensive exploration of the numerous arguments and counter-arguments presented in the discovery debate would occupy far more space than the purposes of this hornbook allow. What follows is a brief review of the major contentions advanced by proponents and opponents. It is limited primarily to those policy considerations that have been stressed in judicial opinions commenting upon the discovery question.

The need to eliminate "trial by surprise." Proponents of liberal defense discovery emphasize the need to make the trial "less a game of blind man's bluff and more a fair contest with the basic issues and facts disclosed to the fullest practicable extent." The recent experience with discovery reforms in the field of civil discovery, proponents maintained, clearly had established that this objective was best achieved by providing expansive pretrial discovery. The end result there had been better marshalling of all available evidence and trials that were far more effective in revealing the truth.

Opponents of expansive defense discovery accepted the premise that a trial should be a quest for truth rather than a "sporting event." Neither did they quarrel with the premise that expansive discovery in civil cases had reduced surprise and thereby permitted a more complete presentation of all relevant evidence. They argued, however, that three factors distinguished criminal discovery from civil discovery and made expansive criminal discovery far less desirable. Those factors were: (1) the criminal defendant's privilege against self-incrimination, which would not permit the fully reciprocal discovery found in civil practice; (2) the greater likelihood that defense discovery in criminal cases would be used to facilitate successful perjury; and (3) the greater likelihood that criminal defense discovery would lead to the intimidation of witnesses. Opponents of expansive criminal discovery argued that when these three factors were taken into account, along with the availability of alternative procedures that served to combat unfair surprise, the costs of expansive defense discovery would clearly outweigh its benefits. Proponents of expansive discovery responded that such costs either did not exist or were exaggerated and that alternative procedures for combating surprise were ineffective.

The "reciprocity argument." Critics of liberal defense discovery contended that discovery would not be an effective tool in developing the truth unless it was a "two-way street" (as in civil discovery), but that was not feasible in the criminal justice process because the defendant's constitutional rights—particularly the privilege against self-incrimination—stood in the way of providing equal discovery from the defense to the prosecution. In response, some supporters of liberal defense discovery rejected the contention that the Constitution prohibited granting reciprocal discovery to the prosecution. Most, however, assumed that reciprocity was prohibited, and argued that expansive defense discovery would be a useful tool in the truth-seeking process even though similar discovery was not available to the prosecution. If the privilege against self-incrimination created a discovery imbalance in favor of the defense, that imbalance would be consistent with the intent of the framers; the defendant should not be denied a procedure essential to the protection of the innocent in an attempt to offset a protection granted by the Constitution.

Critics of liberalized defense discovery responded that even if such discovery did contribute somewhat to the protection of the innocent, notwithstanding the lack of reciprocity, the defendant already was given a multitude of advantages (e.g. the self-incrimination privilege and the requirement of proof beyond a reasonable doubt) that provided ample protection of the innocent. There was no need to add another advantage, particularly one capable of misuse to protect the guilty. Proponents of expanded defense discovery challenged this position as looking at the process as a sporting contest that requires overall adversary equality and ignoring the need to take every precaution to ensure that the innocent are not convicted. In any event, as they viewed the "realities of administration," the alleged advantage of the defendant was largely a myth. Even at trial, where the defendant supposedly possesses his greatest advantage, many of his rights, such as the right not to testify, are of limited practical significance. Moreover, at the most significant stage, the pretrial preparation of the case, the state has all of the advantages. Its investigators will be first at the scene of the crime, and they will have greater resources, including search and grand jury subpoena authority and capacity to obtain voluntary cooperation of witnesses that the defense rarely can match. Moreover, those investigators often could gain considerable information from the accused through interrogation following his arrest that reached "up to the point of coercion." Indeed, the proponents of discovery argued, the typical defense counsel operates at such an investigative disadvantage that the adversary system is substantially undermined without the partial equalization provided by liberal defense discovery.

The perjury argument. Opponents of liberal discovery also contended that pretrial disclosure of the prosecution's evidence would greatly facilitate a defendant's use of perjury. If a defendant learns in advance of the state's evidence, he can carefully tailor his testimony, both to minimize conflict with the prosecution's evidence and to take advantage of the weakest point in the prosecution's evidence. Proponents of expansive defense discovery responded that this claimed facilitation of perjury was an "old hobgoblin" based on "untested folklore." They argued that civil discovery had proven successful notwithstanding similar objections. The opponents of liberal defense discovery responded in turn that criminal defendants were more likely as a class to engage in perjury because: (1) many were criminals, (2) all were facing the potential of criminal sanctions, and (3) the criminal justice process lacked the pretrial deposition procedure that permitted a party in a civil case to "freeze" the opposing party's story before the opposing part could take advantage of discovery to fabricate.

Proponents of expansive defense discovery rejected the assumptions that there necessarily is a greater incentive for perjury in a criminal case and that criminal defendants are more prone to utilize perjury. They also stressed that the prosecution, though it cannot depose the defendant, uses various other devices (e.g., police interrogation) to "pin down" the defendant. In any event, they noted, the proper safeguard against perjury "is not to refuse to permit any inquiry at all, for that will eliminate the true as well as the false, but the inquiry should be conducted so as to separate and distinguish the one from the other."

The intimidation argument. The arguments relating to possible intimidation of witnesses followed much the same lines as the arguments relating to perjury. Opponents of liberal discovery contended that a defendant armed with knowledge of the prosecution's case could "take steps to bribe or frighten [witnesses] into giving perjured testimony or into absenting themselves so that they are unavailable to testify." Admittedly, not all defendants would use such tactics, but enough would do so, it was argued, to make many witnesses reluctant to come forward to assist the police. Witnesses, it was argued, were already under considerable pressure, and even aggressive discovery efforts by defense counsel were likely to prove frightening.

In response, supporters of liberal discovery noted that a similar contention had been rejected in the expansion of civil discovery. They again denied that criminal cases were likely to present a greater problem than civil cases. Where there was a realistic likelihood of actual intimidation, an ample safeguard was presented by the trial court's authority to issue a protective order restricting discovery (a procedure which opponents of liberal discovery deemed inadequate because it placed an impracticable burden on the prosecution of establishing a defendant's intent to intimidate). Proponents of discovery also rejected arguments based on a general concern for accommodating witnesses. The search for truth should not be made more difficult, they argued, simply because witnesses have unfounded fears or don't want to be "bothered" by the investigative efforts of defense counsel.

Other means of discovery. In evaluating the need for liberal rules of discovery, opponents and proponents frequently disagreed as to the value of other means of obtaining discovery, such as the preliminary hearing and the bill of particulars. Of course, not all of these procedures are available in every case. Also, as discussed in § 20.2(d), each has distinct limits as a discovery device. Opponents of liberal defense discovery nonetheless claimed that, even with such restrictions, these alternative procedures provided more than enough discovery to avoid unfair surprise. Proponents of discovery disagreed, but they also argued that, in any event, the law should not encourage defense manipulation of these procedures to achieve a discovery objective they were not designed to fulfill.

In many jurisdictions, prosecutors, as a matter of local practice, often provided defense counsel with substantial pretrial discovery. Indeed, today, in some jurisdictions, prosecutors have adopted an "open file" policy that gives the defense greater access to certain types of

material than would be available under even the most liberal discovery statutes. Where such extensive "informal discovery" is widely available, it adds an extra dimension to the traditional discovery debate. Opponents of expansive discovery requirements commonly argue that informal discovery practices serve all legitimate needs of the defense while avoiding most of the dangers that may accompany formal discovery requirements. Under an informal discovery practice, the prosecutor readily can deny discovery where there is substantial likelihood that the defendant will use it to fabricate a defense or to intimidate witnesses. Similarly, where the prosecutor is concerned that discovery will upset the balance of the adversary system, he or she can condition an offer of discovery on the defendant's willingness to reciprocate. The end result, it is argued, is a system that is preferable to formal discovery requirements, at least where prosecutors are acting in an even-handed manner.

Proponents of expansive discovery requirements typically respond that discovery is too significant to be left to the discretion of the prosecutor. The "ultimate responsibility" for the fairness of the trial process lies with the court, and therefore, they argue, the court also must bear the "responsibility for the exercise of judgment as to the merit of the grounds for withholding disclosure in a particular case." Too often, it is contended, the availability of informal discovery varies with the particular assistant prosecutor in charge of the individual case. Also, it is argued, prosecutors may insist upon reciprocity that goes beyond what any statute or court rule would or could permit, using the threat to withdraw all discovery to force the defense to give disclosure that the state could not compel consistent with the defendant's self-incrimination privilege.

(c) The Outcome. The debate over the merits of expanding defense discovery produced a reassessment of discovery law both in the federal system and the states. The response uniformly was to provide for defense discovery where it did not previously exist or expand that discovery which had previously been established. As far back as 1966, the

Supreme Court spoke of "the growing realization that disclosure, rather than suppression, of relevant materials ordinarily promotes the proper administration of criminal justice," and referred to "the expanding body of materials, judicial and otherwise, favoring disclosure in criminal cases analogous to the civil practice." That there is to be defense discovery in criminal cases in now taken as a matter of course. The issues that divide the various jurisdictions today relate only to exactly how far that discovery should be carried. Moreover, the trend has been in the direction of consistently broadening the reach of defense discovery, as illustrated by the changes over the years in Federal Rule 16. As originally adopted in 1946, Rule 16 simply allowed the defendant access, on a showing of materiality, to documents obtained by the government. In 1966, Rule 16 was completely revised to grant the trial court discretion to order discovery of a broad range of items (basically written or recorded statements of the defendant, reports of physical and medical examinations, and relevant documents and "other tangible objects"). In 1975, there was still another revision of Rule 16 which produced essentially the current provision. That revision further broadened the range of discoverable statements (including, for example, the substance of oral statements of the defendant) and made prosecutorial disclosure mandatory (rather than leaving it to the discretion of the trial court). The original draft of the 1975 revision, as approved by the Supreme Court, would also have required disclosure of the names, addresses, and felony conviction records of all prosecution witnesses, but Congress struck that provision from the Rule as it was eventually adopted.

In contrast to Congress, many states have been willing to take defense discovery several steps beyond current Rule 16. The American Bar Association, in 1970, recommended adoption of discovery provisions extending substantially beyond even the broadest federal proposal, and a large number of states revised their discovery provisions in accordance with the ABA's proposed standards. They provided for defense discovery of a wide range of items, including not only the names of prospective prosecution witnesses, but also any statements they had given to the police. The second edition of the ABA Standards expanded upon the first edition and proposed "open file" discovery. The prosecutor's disclosure obligation, under that later standard, extended to "all the material and information within the prosecutor's possession or control." So far, however, not even the most liberal discovery jurisdiction has been willing to adopt such an open-ended provision, and the ABA has somewhat modified that proposal in the third edition of the Standards. Also, many proponents of defense discovery commonly argue that even requiring disclosure of the complete prosecutorial file is not sufficient because it relies on information that the prosecution has obtained and fails to give the defense the capacity to obtain its own information through a discovery deposition procedure similar to that found in civil cases. As discussed in § 20.2(e), less than a dozen states provide for discovery depositions.

(d) The "Two–Way Street" Movement. The expansion of defense discovery led prosecutors, not unexpectedly, to insist that the government be given equally broad discovery from the defense. The avoidance of trial by surprise, they argued, necessarily required that both parties be aware of the evidence to be introduced by its adversary. Discovery, as evidenced by the form it took in civil cases, was designed to be a two-way street. This concept of requiring the defense to show its case to the prosecution was not new. Alibi-notice provisions (requiring the defense to give pretrial notice regarding its use of an alibi defense) had been in place in more than a dozen states before the discovery debate even started. Some had thought, however, that such provisions had a special character that provided a stronger foundation for meeting defense challenges based on the self-incrimination privilege than would broader forms of compulsory defense disclosure to the prosecution. However, in 1970, the Supreme Court in *Williams v. Florida*[1] upheld the constitutionality of an alibi-notice provision under a ratio-

1. See § 20.4 at note 1.

nale that could readily be seen as extending to a much broader range of prosecutorial discovery. That decision, in effect, removed the primary obstacle to the long-standing prosecutorial effort to make discovery a two-way street. Reading the *Williams* case broadly, the ABA, in its first set of discovery standards, proposed prosecution discovery rights that would go substantially beyond alibi-notice, although stopping short of full reciprocity. Post–*Williams* amendments to the Federal Rules similarly extended its preexisting prosecution discovery provisions. Allowing discovery only slightly narrower than the ABA proposal, the Federal Rules actually came somewhat closer to full reciprocity because of the Federal Rules' narrower provisions on defense discovery.

The response of the states to the ABA proposal and the Federal Rules amendments was quite positive. Indeed, many expanded upon the ABA and Federal Rules models to make prosecution discovery more fully equivalent to defense discovery. The end result is that the number of states with some form of prosecutorial discovery provision has increased dramatically (from roughly a third pre-*Williams* to all but a few today). Still, the majority of the states have provisions much narrower in scope than their defense-discovery provisions. To some extent that narrower scope may flow from lingering doubts as to the constitutionality and policy justifications for certain types of prosecution discovery. However, since prosecution discovery, apart from alibi-notice provisions, is a much more recent innovation than defense discovery, the narrower prosecution-discovery provisions may simply reflect the same type of caution in first round efforts as dominated the development of defense discovery.

§ 20.2 The Structure of Discovery Law

(a) "Common Law" Jurisdictions. Although statutes and court rules came to dominate criminal discovery by mid-twentieth-century, as late as the mid–1970s, a substantial group of states still treated discovery as a common law subject. Of course, none of these "common law" jurisdictions still adhered to

the early common law rulings holding that the judiciary lacked the power to order discovery in the absence of legislative authorization. All recognized a trial court's inherent authority to require pretrial discovery as an element of its control over the trial process and relied primarily on that authority to define available discovery. Today, common law jurisdictions have all but disappeared. Almost all jurisdictions have statutes or court rules determining what items are discoverable and under what conditions. However, in some jurisdictions, courts retain the inherent authority to prescribe discovery standards where statutes or court rules leave gaps. Also, as to certain subjects (e.g., sanctions), courts commonly are interpreting statutes so loosely formulated as to depend largely upon judicial development of more specific guidelines.

(b) Court Rules and Statutes. Although the statutes or court rules governing discovery vary in content, they tend to be similar in structure. Typically, the basic statute or court rule performs the following major tasks: (1) it establishes a procedure by which the defense and the prosecution can put into effect the other side's obligation to make pretrial disclosure; (2) it designates those items which shall or may (upon court order) be disclosed by the prosecution to the defense; (3) it designates those items that shall or may (upon court order) be disclosed by the defense to the prosecution; (4) it establishes certain exemptions from disclosure based upon content (e.g., work product) or, in some instances, based on the nature of the item (e.g., witness' statements); (5) it authorizes the trial court to issue under special circumstances a protective order that will bar or limit disclosures that would otherwise be required; (6) it imposes a continuing duty to disclose discoverable items so that the process automatically encompasses items acquired after the initial disclosure; and (7) it provides a procedure for judicial administration and enforcement of the discovery provisions, including the imposition of sanctions.

As to content, discovery provisions can be loosely categorized by reference to three basic coverage patterns as to first defense and then prosecution discovery. Allowable defense discovery can be helpfully categorized by comparison to the Federal Rules and the 1970 ABA Standards. The narrowest major grouping of state provisions roughly provide the same discovery as the Federal Rules. Approximately a dozen states fall within this category. A somewhat larger grouping follows fairly closely the ABA model, which provides the broadest defense discovery. The remaining states fall somewhere in between the two models.

The Federal Rules model also provides the standard for the narrowest range of prosecution discovery, taking account of the conditional nature of such discovery (dependent upon the defense requesting similar discovery from the prosecution) and the items that are discoverable. Since the original ABA Standards were roughly akin to the Federal Rules on prosecution discovery, it is not surprising that almost half of the states with comprehensive discovery provisions can be placed in this category. The broadest discovery standards are found in states that utilized the ABA Standards for defense discovery and then sought to provide the prosecution with roughly equivalent discovery (excluding discovery of the defendant's personal knowledge). Perhaps a dozen states can be placed in this group. A slightly larger group utilize the ABA standards for defense discovery, and go beyond the Federal Rules and the original ABA Standards for prosecution discovery, but still fall short of even roughly reciprocating defense discovery.

(c) The Operation of Discovery Provisions. Discovery statutes and court rules commonly apply only to proceedings before the court of general jurisdiction. This means that the basic discovery provisions will govern only felonies and such high level misdemeanors as fall within the jurisdiction of the general trial court. Also, those provisions ordinarily do not take effect prior to the filing of charges in the court of general jurisdiction. Thus, they are not available during the course of the preliminary proceedings in the magistrate court, such as the preliminary hearing and the bail hearing.

Once the discovery provision takes effect, that discovery which is granted as a matter of

right, in all but a small group of jurisdictions, is provided without resort to judicial action. A motion seeking a court order directing a party to provide discovery is required only where there is a dispute as to what must be disclosed as a matter of right or the particular item is discoverable only at the discretion of the court. Under many state discovery provisions, the prosecution has an automatic obligation to disclose the items discoverable as of right within a specified number of days following the filing of the indictment or information. Under other discovery provisions, the defense must make a request of the prosecutor. That request, however, need contain no more than a listing of those categories of items specified in the discovery provision as to which disclosure is desired. A major function of the request requirement is to relieve the prosecutor of the burden of collecting and disclosing items listed in the discovery provision that may not be needed in the particular case.

Where the prosecution's right to discovery is conditioned on the defense having received similar discovery, the request also serves to trigger the prosecution's authority to seek parallel discovery. In other jurisdictions, the prosecution's right is not so conditioned, and the defense, like the prosecution, has an automatic obligation to provide disclosure within a specified period following the filing of the indictment or information.

(d) Other Discovery Vehicles. In almost all jurisdictions there will be available to the defense, and to a lesser extent, to the prosecutor, various other procedures through which some degree of pretrial discovery may be obtained. Unlike the discovery provisions, these procedures are not designed specifically to gain disclosure of the evidence possessed by the other side, but they nonetheless reveal incidentally part of that evidence. Procedures providing such a discovery potential include the bail hearing (particularly where the prosecution seeks preventative detention), the preliminary hearing, the challenge to the sufficiency of the evidence before the grand jury (available in only a small group of states), and hearings on various pretrial motions, such as the motion to suppress. Some discovery may be available outside of the criminal justice process, although the primary vehicle here, the Freedom of Information Act, typically will include an exemption for records "compiled for law enforcement purposes" where disclosure could reasonably be expected to "interfere" with enforcement proceedings.

In exploring the range of pretrial discovery that may be available, counsel must take account of all such alternative avenues for gaining discovery. In some instances, they will reach information not available through the jurisdiction's discovery provision. In other instances, even though they reach the same items as the discovery provisions, they often offer certain advantages. Thus, the defense may find that other procedures will provide earlier disclosure or will provide disclosure without the requirement of reciprocal defense disclosure found in the discovery provision.

(e) Depositions. In civil cases, the deposition is a major discovery device. Both parties may subject to a deposition any person thought to have relevant information, including the opposing party. The deposition may be taken without court order, on notice to the other party. A party simply obtains a subpoena from the clerk of the court and serves it on the deposition witness, directing him to appear at certain place for that purpose. At the deposition, the witness is placed under oath, and subjected to questioning by the party taking the deposition, with the opportunity given to the adversary to cross-examine and to object to improper questions. The deposition is stenographically transcribed and in many jurisdictions may also be videotaped.

In criminal cases, the form of the deposition is quite similar, but the availability of the deposition is much more restricted. Only about ten states allow for the use of depositions as a basic discovery procedure. In the vast majority of the states and in the federal system, the deposition is available in criminal cases primarily for the purpose of preserving the testimony of a witness likely to be unavailable at trial. To obtain a deposition to perpetuate testimony, a party must make a showing that the deponent is a prospective material witness and is likely not to be available to testify at trial. A typical statutory formulation requires a showing "that a prospective witness may be unable to attend or be prevented from attending a trial or hearing, that the witness' testimony is material, and that it is necessary to take the witness' deposition in order to prevent a failure of justice."

Considerable variation exists as to the availability of depositions in that small group of states that treat the deposition as a vehicle for discovery as well as a means for preserving testimony. In general, the discovery deposition is available to both the defense and prosecution. Consistent with the focus on discovery, and in contrast to the deposition limited to preserving testimony, a party may depose persons expected to be a trial witness for the other side. The one exception, of course, is that the prosecution may not depose the defendant. In jurisdictions allowing the broadest use of discovery depositions, there is no need for prior approval from the court. In other jurisdictions, the utilization of a discovery deposition requires court approval upon a special showing of need. Jurisdictions with discovery depositions often carve out special categories of witnesses who are not subject to that procedure. Those categories include witnesses of a tender age, witnesses who provide only "foundation" testimony or testimony relating to a "ministerial act," and witnesses "adequately examined at a preliminary hearing." Since the objective of the deposition is to provide discovery, rather than to preserve testimony, there is no need that the defendant be present at the deposition (a significant administrative obstacle where the defendant remains in custody).

Several factors help to explain why the discovery deposition, a mainstay of civil discovery, is unavailable in criminal cases in the vast majority of jurisdictions. In many jurisdictions, the parties do not receive a listing of witnesses for the other side, and very few require a listing of all persons known to have relevant information. Such listings are available through interrogatories in the civil process and provide the foundation for obtaining discovery through depositions.

Still another factor is the available discovery of the prior recorded statements of potential witnesses in many jurisdictions. In civil pretrial discovery, those statements are not available except under special circumstances, as it is expected that each party will depose the other's potential witnesses, rather than rely upon statements the other side obtained in the course of its trial preparation. Of course, such statements are far from a perfect substitute for a deposition, as they provide only the witness' responses in an interview conducted by the opposite side. Nonetheless, the availability of the witness' prior statement contributes to the argument that there is less need for discovery depositions in the criminal justice process and therefore the value of such further disclosure is more readily out-weighed by the burden imposed upon the deposed witness (particularly the victim, who might be placed in the awkward position of testifying in the presence of the alleged offender). A somewhat stronger argument along these lines is that discovery depositions are unnecessary where the jurisdiction utilizes the preliminary hearing as a screening device. Of course, the timing of the preliminary hearing makes it a far from perfect substitute, as both sides may be unaware of relevant witnesses at that point.

The potential cost of the discovery deposition is still another concern that may have contributed in many states to the decision to limit depositions to the exceptional case requiring the preservation of testimony. The Commentary to the 1970 ABA Standards expressed that concern, noting as to defense depositions: "There is no inherent limitation of cost on the conduct of unnecessary depositions, because in many cases the cost of the defense must be borne by the state * * * [and] if stated as a right, the need to take depositions might be construed as part of the adequacy of representation required by the constitutional right to counsel." It is true that in civil discovery the deposition is one of the most costly and time-consuming elements of pretrial proceedings. However, jurisdictions that utilize discovery depositions in criminal cases have not found the burden imposed by their use to outweigh their value.

§ 20.3   Defense Discovery

(a) Prosecution Possession or Control. An element bearing on almost all portions of a typical defense discovery provision is the scope of the prosecution's obligation to obtain and make available for discovery items that are not within its immediate possession. As to each item designated as subject to discovery, apart from those obviously within the prosecution's possession (e.g., items to be used at trial), the discovery provision will attach a clause describing the necessary connection of the prosecution to the particular item. States with ABA-type discovery provisions commonly describe the prosecutor's discovery obligation as extending to specified "material and information" that is "within the possession or control of the prosecuting attorney." Federal Rule 16 applies its basic discovery provisions to items "within the government's possession, custody, or control." However, it also adds as to most items that the government does not intend to use in evidence the further requirement "that the attorney for the government knows—or through reasonable diligence should know— that the * * * [item] exists."

Courts interpreting typical "scope" clauses uniformly have held that the basic obligation to disclose extends to items within the files of those investigative agencies of the same government (federal or state) that have participated in the development of the particular prosecution. Their files are deemed within the "control" of the prosecution under the ABA-type provision, or "within the possession of the 'government'" and having an existence that should be known to the prosecutor under the federal-type provision. Some state courts have held that the prosecutor's control extends to records in the possession of "any * * * prosecutorial or law enforcement office" of the particular state, whether or not involved in the investigation or ordinarily reporting to the particular prosecutor. This position is easier to sustain as applied to specific obligations that by their very nature appear to encompass all law enforcement agencies (e.g. an obligation to provide the criminal records of government witnesses) than to a provision dealing with a broad category of materials (e.g., "documents") subject to discovery under a general standard of relevancy. Under the broad language of Federal Rule 16, material which is possessed by any agency of the "government," whether or not investigatory, should be discoverable if it is identified by reference to its likely location in the defense request (and thereby made "known" to the "attorney for the government"). However, "government" for this purpose arguably does not extend to agencies outside of the executive branch (e.g., a probation department).

(b) Written or Recorded Statements. Another issue that has a bearing on several parts of a typical defense discovery provision is the reach of the phrase "written or recorded statement." All discovery provisions provide for discovery of written or recorded statements of the defendant, and many allow for discovery of written or recorded statements of codefendants and prosecution witnesses as well. Where the prosecution has within its possession, custody, or control the substance of statements that were not "written or recorded," that information may not be discoverable or may be discoverable pursuant to separate provisions imposing special limitations. Thus, whether a statement was "written or recorded" may be critical in determining its discovery status.

Neither the original ABA Standards nor the Federal Rules sought to define the phrase "written or recorded statement." The drafting committees in both instances recognized the possible incorporation of the definition of "statement" used in the Jencks Act.[1] That Act, which applies only to federal courts, gives the defendant a right to inspect the prior statements of a prosecution witness, following that witness' testimony at trial, for the purpose of possible impeachment of the witness. The Jencks Act defines "statement" for this purpose as (1) "a written statement made by said witness and signed or otherwise adopted by him," (2) "a stenographic, mechanical, electrical or other recording, or a transcription

thereof, which is a substantially verbatim recital of an oral statement made by said witness and recorded contemporaneously with the making of such oral statement," and (3) grand jury testimony. The drafters of both the original ABA Standards and Federal Rule 16 agreed that the "written or recorded statement" phrase in their respective discovery provisions should include all statements that fell within the Jencks Act definition of "statement." The unresolved issue was whether the discovery provision should have a broader scope. Since the character of a written statement is fairly clear (basically including statements written or signed or otherwise approved by the individual), the primary issue of interpretation centered upon possibly going beyond the Jencks Act limitations as to a "recording" of an oral statement—i.e., not insisting that the recording be substantially verbatim and be recorded contemporaneously with the making of the oral statement.

Because the ABA Standards provide for prosecution disclosure of the substance of oral statements of the defendant, in addition to disclosure of the written or recorded statements of the defendant, the judicial definition of the phrase "recorded statement" is of critical importance in an ABA jurisdiction primarily as to the statements of witnesses, where discovery is limited to written or recorded statements. If a court should adopt the Jencks Act definition and hold that the recordation of a defendant's comments was not sufficiently complete or sufficiently promptly recorded to constitute a "recorded statement" of the defendant, the content of that recordation will still be discoverable under the provision calling for the prosecution to disclose the substance of any oral statement of the defendant, although that discovery may be limited to oral statements the prosecution intends to use at trial. On the other hand, if the recordation of a witness' statement was not sufficiently complete or promptly recorded to constitute a "recorded statement", the ABA Standards pro-

§ 20.3

1. 18 U.S.C.A. § 3500(a), discussed in § 24.3(c). The Jencks Act definition is also applied on Fed.R.Crim.P.

26.2(f), governing production at trial of prior recorded statements of both prosecution witnesses (as in the Jencks Act) and defense witnesses.

vide no alternative route requiring disclosure of its substance.

When the Federal Rules Advisory Committee similarly decided not to take a position on the incorporation of the Jencks Act definition, that decision, in contrast, had a bearing only on the discovery of a defendant's statement. The Federal Rules do not provide for pretrial discovery of a witness' statement, as the Jencks Act specifically prohibits disclosure of statements of the witness until after the witness has testified. The "written or recorded" standard is used in Federal Rule 16 only with respect to the defendant's own statements. While Rule 16 (and similar state provisions) also provide for the disclosure of (1) a written record containing the substance of any oral statement, and (2) the substance of an unrecorded oral statement that will be used at trial, those disclosures are limited to oral statements made by defendant in response to interrogation by a person he knows to be a government agent. That limitation as to the context in which the statement was made does not apply to the written or recorded statement of a defendant. Thus, if the Jencks Act definition of statement is applied under Rule 16, and the defendant's statement was memorialized in a context that did not involve responding to interrogation by a known government agent (e.g., in the context of speaking to an associate or an undercover agent), if that written record fails to come within the Jencks definition, either because it was not sufficiently complete or not contemporaneously recorded, there is no alternative route through which defendant will have a right to discover the contents of that statement.

Although several earlier federal decisions went beyond the Jencks Act definition to describe as recorded statements all written "summaries of the defendant's [oral] statements," the more recent federal decisions have turned to a Jencks-type standard in the two key settings where the distinction controls the discovery issue. The first involves requests for the rough notes of investigative agents relating to their interrogation of the defendant in settings where the agents were not known to be government agents (e.g., where they were

undercover agents). The lower courts have assumed that the applicability of Rule 16's recorded statement provision to those notes should be controlled by the same standard applied in determining whether rough notes of a witness' statement have to be disclosed at trial pursuant to the Jencks Act. That standard requires consideration of such factors as the extent to which the language in the notes was intended to conform to the precise language of the defendant, the length of the notes in comparison to the length of the statement, and the lapse of time between the interview and the making of the notes. The second setting involves the subsequent "memorialization" of a private conversation of the defendant, typically by the other participant in the conversation subsequently providing his written recollection of the statement to a police officer. Courts here have held that the subsequent memorialization, even where it sought to repeat verbatim what the defendant said in the conversation, will not constitute a recorded statement of the defendant because it was not recorded contemporaneously.

(c) Defendant's Statements. Perhaps no item is more readily discoverable by the defense than the defendant's written or recorded statement. In the federal system and all but a handful of the states, such discovery is granted as a matter of right. The remaining states allow discovery of the defendant's written or recorded statements at the trial judge's discretion. In many of these jurisdictions, however, the disclosure of such statements is almost automatic. Disclosure generally is granted without any showing of need beyond defendant's allegation that inspection is "necessary to refresh his recollection" of the statement.

Providing automatic discovery of a defendant's recorded statement has been supported on the grounds that: (1) the precise wording of defendant's statement is especially helpful to defense counsel in preparing for trial or in determining whether a guilty plea is advisable; (2) disclosure does not pose a substantial threat of successful perjury since the defendant may be impeached effectively by reference to his statement; (3) disclosure of defendant's statement does not create a reciprocity problem since the state obviously gained discovery from the defendant in obtaining the statement from him originally; and (4) if disclosure is not granted directly, the defendant will simply use the motion to suppress as an indirect discovery device. The last ground also serves as a practical limitation upon prosecution opposition to disclosure in those jurisdictions where defendant does not have an absolute right to discovery. As a result, the prosecution is only likely to oppose disclosure in a discretionary-disclosure jurisdiction (usually on the grounds of a lack of relevancy or lack of defense need) where it does not intend to use the defendant's statement in its case-in-chief.

The ABA Standards impose no prerequisite that the defendant's prior recorded statement be "relevant" to the subject of the criminal prosecution. The apparent assumption here is that the statements will almost always be relevant; if they are within the possession or the control of the prosecutor, they are most likely to have some potential value to the defense even if the prosecutor does not intend to use them in evidence. In any event, to occasionally require disclosure of some unrelated material is deemed a lesser cost than to open the door to potentially burdensome litigation over what is relevant and what is not. Federal Rule 16(a)(1)(A), on the other hand, does impose a requirement of "relevancy," and a similar restriction is found in some state provisions modeled after Rule 16. Most courts have taken a broad view of "relevancy" for this purpose, basically assuming that any statement made by the defendant during the course of the investigation was relevant. This position is consistent with the assumption that the relevancy requirement exists primarily as a safeguard against imposing upon the prosecution the obligation of collecting and disclosing the countless forms and other written statements that a defendant may have submitted in the regular course of business to a government regulatory agency that also happens to be the investigating agency in the particular case.

All of the state discovery provisions modeled after the ABA Standards and most of those modeled after Federal Rule 16 also require disclosure of the substance of certain oral statements of defendant known to the prosecution. As noted in subsection (b), where these provisions apply, they eliminate dispute over whether a particular documentation of an oral statement is sufficient in quotation and time of recording to fall within the recorded statement provision; the government must disclose the substance of the comments in any event. However, the oral statement provisions often are much narrower in scope than the recorded statement provisions. Some of the ABA-type provisions do apply to all oral statements within the prosecution's possession or control. Many other states, however, will require disclosure only as to oral statements that the prosecution "intends to offer in evidence at the trial." This limitation stems from the concern that the range of oral statements known to the police, including those between the defendant and investigators and between defendant and police interviewees who recounted defendant's past statements, is too broad to impose an obligation of disclosure without regard to the possible use of those statements at trial. Indeed, the limitation to oral statements to be "offered in evidence" arguably goes so far as to relieve the prosecution of the task of anticipating what oral statements might be used only for impeachment, if at all.

A 1991 amendment of Federal Rule 16 discarded the intended use requirement as to a written record containing the substance of defendant's oral statements (although intended use remains a prerequisite for disclosing oral statements where there is no such writing). However, Federal Rule 16 here retains a second fairly common limitation—the oral statement summarized in the writing must have been made "in response to interrogation by a person the defendant knew was a government agent." This limitation allows the prosecution to keep from the defense the fact that the persons he conversed with were undercover agents or non-agent witnesses who will be testifying against him at trial. It is seen as flowing from concerns relating to the defendant's misuse of that information which are similar to those concerns—discussed in subsections (h) and (i)—that have led these same jurisdictions not to provide for witness-disclosure and to bar pretrial disclosure of witness statements. Accordingly, the Federal Rules (and similar state provisions) apply the "known agent" limitation even to oral statements that the prosecution intends to use in its case-in-chief.

(d) Codefendant's Statements. Required disclosure of codefendants' statements has been urged on the grounds that such statements: "(1) * * * are potentially important to defense counsel in preparing to meet the government's case and developing evidence on defendant's behalf; (2) * * * aid defense counsel in deciding whether to make a severance motion and in assisting the judicial determination of such a motion; and (3) * * * mitigate the well-known proclivities of some criminal defendants not to give their own lawyers a truthful account of their actions." These grounds have not proven as convincing to the drafters of discovery provisions as the grounds supporting the required disclosure of the defendant's own statements. Here, there is substantially greater division as to whether and under what conditions disclosure should be required.

Only slightly over one-third of the states have provisions requiring disclosure of a codefendant's statement, and those provisions vary substantially in coverage. Several states provide for the disclosure of recorded or oral statements of codefendants without limitation. Others, following the original ABA model, restrict the required disclosure of a codefendant's recorded or oral statements to cases in which the codefendants will be jointly tried. The focus here is basically on the second ground noted above—giving the defense that information which will be critical in its determination as to whether to seek a severance. Of course, if the codefendant is a coconspirator and his statement was made in the course of the conspiracy, that statement will be admissible against the defendant, and it therefore may well be discoverable, even though the two are not tried together, in those jurisdictions that grant disclosure of the statements of prosecution witnesses. Some jurisdictions, to ensure that disclosure is made in such situations,

include a specific provision requiring disclosure of a codefendant's statement when the prosecution intends to use it at trial (without regard to whether the two are jointly tried).

Federal Rule 16 does not include a provision requiring disclosure of a codefendant's statements, but federal courts have held that they have discretion to order such disclosure. However, that discretion is limited by the prohibition against disclosure of the statements of prospective government witnesses. Thus, the court may not order disclosure of the codefendant's statement when the prosecution intends to use it at trial, because that will require disclosure of the statement of the witness who will testify to the codefendant's statement. This prohibition has been held to encompass even the coconspirator's statement made in the course of the conspiracy. Although its admissibility is based in part on the theory that each coconspirator speaks for the other, federal courts have rejected the contention that the coconspirator's statement should be treated as another form of statement of the defendant himself rather than as a statement of a prosecution witness. Of course, nothing prevents each codefendant from obtaining discovery of his own statement and sharing that information with the others.

(e) Criminal Records. Federal Rule 16 and a substantial majority of the state discovery provisions grant the defendant a right to discovery of his criminal record. Disclosure of the prior record does not disadvantage the prosecution while the contents of the record are important to the defense on various issues (e.g., whether the defendant should testify at trial, or should move to restrict the use of prior convictions for impeachment purposes). The prior record also will show whether the defendant faces sentencing under enhanced sentencing provisions. In general, pretrial discovery provides a very limited vehicle for making a sentencing assessment. Much of the material that would be considered relevant under sentencing guidelines will be unrelated to the proof of the crime charged and therefore not be discoverable pretrial under even the broadest discovery provisions. Thus, the primary function of the disclosure of the criminal record relates to potential impeachment. Accordingly, jurisdictions which provide for disclosure of the names of prosecution witnesses commonly also require disclosure of their criminal records.

(f) Scientific Reports. Federal Rule 16 and almost all state discovery provisions provide for the disclosure of various reports of medical and physical examinations, scientific tests, and experiments. Most jurisdictions encompass all such reports that are "made in connection with the particular case." Several require that the reports be intended for use by the government at trial, while several follow the federal formula of requiring that they are either "material to preparing the defense" or intended to be used by the government "in its case-in-chief at the trial." Most of those provisions apply to all the covered reports that are in the possession or control of the prosecutor, but some add a requirement that the prosecutor either knew of the report or had the capacity to do so through due diligence. Among the reports commonly sought under these provisions are those relating to the physical examination of the victim (e.g., autopsy reports) or the analysis of evidence found at the scene of the crime (e.g., fingerprint comparisons and tests on seized drugs).[2] Automatic disclosure of scientific reports is justified on several grounds. Once the report is prepared, the scientific expert's position is not readily influenced, and therefore disclosure presents little danger of prompting perjury or intimidation. Very often such disclosure is needed to "lessen the imbalance which results from the State's early and complete investigation in contrast to [defendant's] * * * late and limited investigation." Also, a scientific report typically cannot be challenged adequately at trial without the opportunity to examine it closely and seek the assistance of defense experts, which requires disclosure well in advance of trial.

(g) Documents and Tangible Objects. The federal system and a substantial majority of the states have mandatory disclosure provisions governing documents and tangible objects. The remaining jurisdictions allow for disclosure at the discretion of the trial court with allowance of disclosure decidedly favored. All provisions encompass at least two categories of documents and tangible objects: (1) items "which the prosecution will use at trial", and (2) items "which were obtained from or purportedly belong to the defendant."

The justification for requiring disclosure of the items to be used at trial is similar to that for disclosure of scientific reports. Here too, there is no substantial threat of perjury and an inspection in advance of the trial often will be necessary to challenge the evidence. In many instances, the defense may have need to have its own experts examine the documents or tangible items. The justification for requiring disclosure of items obtained from or belonging to the defendant lies largely in recognizing the defense's right to sources of information that it originally possessed. Even if the prosecution does not intend to use the particular items at trial, they may be helpful to the defense, and they presumably are relevant by virtue of their very acquisition by the government through methods such as subpoena or seizure. In particular, items seized illegally from the defendant may be used only for impeachment (and therefore would otherwise not be discoverable where the concept of intended "use at trial" is limited to the prosecution's case-in-chief); thus, this category of disclosure can be especially helpful to the defense in anticipating a possible source of impeachment.

---

2. Scientific reports provisions have been held to apply only to preexisting reports; they do not require that the expert create a particular document at the defense's request. Although a written report will be needed for many types of examinations and tests, experts in some instances will be able to testify on the basis of their notes alone, and here a prosecutor could avoid pretrial disclosure under a provision restricted to written reports. Federal Rule 16(a)(1) responds to such a tactic by requiring the government to disclose a written summary of the testimony that it intends to introduce under the Federal Rules of Evidence provisions governing expert testimony. The summary must "describe the witnesses' opinions, the basis and reasons for those opinions and the witnesses' qualifications." This provision applies only to expert testimony that the prosecution intends to use at trial, whereas Federal Rule 16(a)(1)'s provision on scientific reports also encompasses those which are "material to preparing of the defense."

The Federal Rules and state provisions modeled after the Federal Rules include a third category of discoverable documents and objects—those "which are material to preparing the defense." Here the burden is on the defendant to demonstrate the requisite materiality. Moreover, the use of the term "material" suggests that more than a showing of potential relevancy is demanded. Where a specific document is requested, the trial court may, if it so chooses, examine the requested item in camera to determine whether it has that potential significance. Of course, the court must be wary of underestimating the possible bearing of the evidence at it relates to a defense posture still to be developed (and not yet fully disclosed), but it can determine whether the item deals with the particular subject matter or otherwise has the type of content on which the defense bases it claim of materiality. Where the defense makes a general request for "material" documents, failing to identify materiality by document function (e.g., "sales receipts") or specific document content, and subsequently claims a Rule 16 violation during or after trial based on the prosecutor's failure to disclose a particular document, courts tend to impose a very high standard of materiality. Indeed, it has been stated that a violation will be found only where there was "some indication that disclosure of the disputed evidence would have enabled the defendant significantly to alter the quantum of proof in his favor."

The provision allowing discovery of documents "material to preparing the defense" commonly is used in white collar cases to gain disclosure of documents that the government subpoenaed or otherwise obtained from third parties but does not intend to use at trial. However, inventive counsel also may seek to obtain through that provision various documents in the government's possession that were not obtained or prepared in the course of the government's investigation. Thus, a defendant charged with assaulting a police officer might claim that, to prepare a defense of self-defense, he should be allowed to inspect personnel records which would indicate whether the officer had previously been reprimanded for unnecessary use of force. So too, a defendant might seek the "rap sheet" listing prior convictions of the state's chief witnesses in a jurisdiction in which the criminal records provision speaks only of the defendant's criminal records.[3]

(h) Witness Lists. State provisions patterned after the ABA Standards generally require the prosecution to provide the defense with "the names and addresses of persons whom the State intends to call as witnesses." A few states with ABA-type provisions have a broader standard requiring the prosecutor to list the names and addresses of all persons "known by the government to have knowledge of relevant facts" without regard to whether they will be called as witnesses. Although the Federal Rules do not include a witness disclosure provision, various states which started with provisions similar to the Federal Rules added witness-list disclosure in accordance with the proposed amendment to the Federal Rules that Congress rejected in 1975. Most of the mandatory disclosure provisions require the prosecution to list only those witnesses that it expects to present in building its case-in-chief. Here, if the prosecution expects that the defendant will raise a certain contention that might call for rebuttal witnesses, it need not list those witnesses even if fairly certain as to who they will be. In other jurisdictions, however, the prosecution must also list rebuttal witnesses when it can anticipate who they will be. Of course, as with all disclosure obligations, the duty is continuing, so the prosecution must add to the list as it discovers new witnesses. Also the prosecution may not purposely "overlist" so as to effectively hide the names of those persons it intends to call.

---

3. In United States v. Armstrong, 517 U.S. 456, 116 S.Ct. 1480, 134 L.Ed.2d 687 (1996), the Supreme Court held that such Rule 16 "materiality" requests did not go beyond documents material to a "defense against the government's case-in-chief." Thus, discovery of documents desired to establish a defense of discriminatory prosecution was not governed by Rule 16, but standards arising out of the law shaping that constitutional objection to the initiation of prosecution. See § 13.4 at note 10. Rule 16 apparently also would not govern disclosure of documents helpful in raising the broad range of other objections that are not "substantive" in nature, but challenge the institution of the prosecution.

The states that do not mandate pretrial disclosure of witness lists generally allow the trial court to order such disclosure at its discretion. In some jurisdictions, discovery provisions specifically recognize this discretionary authority, while other jurisdictions rely upon the inherent discovery authority of the trial court. Disclosure of witness lists in the federal courts, aside from capital cases (where a statute requires such disclosure), rests on the latter authority. Since the Federal Rules do not contain any reference to witness lists, and since Congress in 1975 rejected only a proposed amendment that would have made such disclosure mandatory, federal courts have held that Rule 16 does not preclude the exercise of their inherent authority to require pretrial disclosure of witness identities where such disclosure is justified by the circumstances of the particular case.

Where disclosure of witness lists lies in the discretion of the trial court, the defendant usually must make some showing of need to obtain disclosure. In many of these jurisdictions, including the federal system, the burden placed on the defendant is especially heavy, with the courts starting from the presumption that witness-list disclosure generally is not available. Factors that courts have considered in determining whether the defense should gain witness identification include: (1) whether the crime charged is one of violence; (2) whether the defendant has a past history of violence; (3) whether the evidence in the case consists largely of material that cannot readily be altered (e.g., documents); (4) whether a realistic possibility exists that the government witnesses might not appear or might be unwilling to testify at trial; (5) whether the offense charged covers a long time span, making more difficult the defendant's recollection of all potential witnesses; and (6) whether the defense has only limited resources available for investigation and trial preparation.

The primary objection to presumptive or mandatory disclosure of witness lists is the potential for intimidation of witnesses. In opposing the proposed 1975 amendment to the Federal Rules, the Department of Justice offered a study listing more than 700 instances of witness intimidation ranging from assault to assassination. Concern has also been expressed that even in cases far removed from violence, such as white collar cases, there remains a potential for the use of economic coercion against witnesses. The basic response of the proponents of broad discovery is that a realistic potential of such intimidation or coercion exists in only a relatively small portion of all cases and the proper response therefore is the " 'scalpel' of the protective order," which would allow disclosure in the vast majority of cases, rather than a policy that allows disclosure only in the most exceptional cases. Opponents of the regular disclosure of witness lists reply that the protective order is not a sufficient answer. They note that the protective order procedure puts the government in the position of having to make a special showing, which itself creates difficulties in protecting witnesses, and that the judicial emphasis upon protective measures short of denying disclosure often produces an insufficient safeguard. Another concern is that allowing disclosure as a regular matter, even with a broad exception for cases presenting any threat of intimidation, would inevitably reinforce the natural reluctance of many persons to willingly come forward and testify in criminal cases.

(i) Witness Statements. American jurisdictions can be divided into three groups in their treatment of pretrial disclosure of the written or recorded statements of prosecution witnesses. One group requires the prosecution to disclose all such statements within its possession or control; another allows the trial court to order such disclosure at its discretion; and a third specifically prohibits such orders. While these groups are of roughly equal size, most of the jurisdictions recognizing a discretionary authority tend to frown upon the exercise of that authority, and pretrial discovery of witness statements therefore is readily available in no more than twenty states.

Jurisdictions barring pretrial discovery of witness statements ordinarily include in their discovery rules a specific prohibition similar to that found in Federal Rule 16(a)(2). That provision states that Rule 16 "does not authorize the discovery or inspection of statements made by prospective government witnesses except as provided in 18 U.S.C. § 3500." The cited exception is to the Jencks Act (18 U.S.C. § 3500), which was designed to ensure that prior recorded statements of witnesses are available for impeachment use, but not subject to pretrial discovery. The Jencks Act provides that after a government witness testifies on direct examination, the government shall make available his prior recorded statement insofar as that statement relates to the subject matter of the defendant's testimony, but it also adds: "[N]o statement * * * in the possession of the United States which was made by a Government witness or prospective Government witness (other than the defendant) shall be the subject of subpoena, discovery, or inspection until said witness has testified on direct examination in the trial of the case."

Among jurisdictions leaving disclosure to the discretion of the trial judge, some have basic discovery provisions which explicitly makes witness statements a subject of discretionary discovery, while others have provisions that make no mention of such statements and thereby render disclosure subject to the court's inherent power to require discovery. Most of the jurisdictions relying upon the trial judge's discretionary authority assume that disclosure of witness statements should not ordinarily be available, so a trial court's refusal to order discovery will rarely be deemed an abuse of discretion. General requests for the disclosure of the written or recorded statements of all prospective prosecution witnesses are commonly condemned as "fishing expeditions" or attempts to require the prosecutor to "open his files to the attorney for the accused." To be successful, the defense ordinarily must show a special need for the statement of a particular witness and convince the trial court that the later disclosure of that statement at trial (for use in cross-examination) is not a satisfactory alternative.

Jurisdictions with provisions patterned after the ABA Standards generally include witness statements among the required items of disclosure. In most of these jurisdictions, disclosure is limited to "relevant written or recorded statements." Several of these states also in-

clude written summaries of oral statements. A few states go beyond the witness category and require pretrial disclosure of the written or recorded statements of all persons known to have knowledge of relevant facts.

The division among the states in their treatment of witness statements follows in part from their division on the disclosure of witness lists. A jurisdiction that does not grant witness lists as a matter of right will not make witness statements available as a matter of right. However, there are jurisdictions that grant discovery of witness lists as a matter of right but do not do the same for witness statements. One factor said to support a narrower position on witness statements is the potential misuse of the statement to facilitate defense perjury. Providing the defendant with a witness' recorded statement is seen as more likely to facilitate his use of perjury than any other item of discovery. Very often, however, the advocates of a complete bar on discovery of witness statements rely on other justifications as well. They argue that: (1) defendant has an ample opportunity to challenge the testimony of prosecution witnesses at trial since the witness' prior recorded statement may be obtained at that point under state provisions similar to the Jencks Act or common law rules on witness impeachment; (2) where witness lists are available or the defense is otherwise aware of likely prosecution witnesses, defense counsel has ample opportunity for pretrial preparation by interviewing those witnesses, and it will be in the best interests of defendant to encourage defense counsel to conduct his own investigation through such interviews rather than rely on the prosecution's investigative efforts; and (3) recorded statements of witnesses ordinarily are within the work product privilege since they are obtained by prosecutors or their agents (police officers) "in anticipation of litigation," and a blanket exemption avoids the need to litigate the work product issue on a case-by-case basis.

As might be expected, proponents of the ABA-type provisions find none of the above arguments persuasive. Disclosure at trial pursuant to a Jencks-type provision is viewed as an unsatisfactory alternative. It is said that, "for adequate preparation and to minimize surprise," disclosures must be made prior to trial. The opportunity to interview a witness is also considered an inadequate substitute for pretrial discovery of witness statements. Witnesses frequently either refuse to talk to defense counsel or insist upon very limited interviews. Courts have consistently held that prosecutors cannot encourage witnesses in this regard by advising or directing them not to cooperate with defense counsel. But they have also stated that since "the witness is free to decide whether to grant or refuse an interview, * * * it is not improper for the government to inform the witness of that right." Moreover, even if the witness is willing to cooperate fully (or the defense has the right to depose the witness under state law), the interview will not come nearly as promptly after the event as the initial police investigation. The witness is likely to have forgotten details that were included in his initial statement, and those details might provide helpful leads for further defense investigation. For similar reasons, it is argued, counsel who obtains a witness' statement is not likely to "ride the coattails" of the prosecution's investigative efforts. Since there may be more to be learned than is contained in the statement, counsel will still want to interview the witness if the witness is willing to cooperate. Reliance upon the work product doctrine to bar discovery of a witness' statements is also challenged. As discussed in the next subsection, the work product doctrine generally is not viewed as so broad as to automatically encompass all prior recorded witness statements in whatever form they might take.

(j) The Work Product Exemption. States with provisions requiring the prosecution's mandatory pretrial disclosure of a prospective witness' recorded statement commonly also include a specific exemption for "work product." Where courts have discretionary authority to order disclosure, a common law work product exemption similarly restricts the exercise of that discretion. As developed in civil discovery, the work product doctrine seeks to preserve

against discovery materials developed in the course of preparing for litigation. The underlying purpose of the doctrine, as set forth in the leading case of *Hickman v. Taylor*,[4] is to preclude "unwarranted inquiries [through discovery] into the files and mental impressions of an attorney." *Hickman* did not absolutely bar civil discovery of "written materials obtained or prepared by an adversary's counsel with an eye toward litigation," but it did recognize a "general policy" against discovery of such "work product" of counsel. As incorporated in the Federal Rules of Civil Procedure, Rule 26(b)(3), the *Hickman* work product doctrine (1) encompasses documents and tangible things prepared in anticipation of litigation, (2) allows discovery of such items only upon a showing of "substantial need" and inability without "undue hardship" to obtain equivalent materials, but (3) also requires the court ordering such discovery to "protect against disclosure of the mental impressions, conclusions, opinions, or legal theories of an attorney or other representative of a party concerning the litigation."

Application of the work product doctrine to the criminal justice process raises a series of issues. First, there is the question of whether the interests protected by the doctrine are sufficiently strong that they should even be recognized in the context of criminal procedure. The doctrine's basic objective is to protect the adversary system by affording counsel free rein in the development of litigation materials and the analysis that development reflects. This is to be done by providing assurance that those materials will not automatically be available to counsel's adversary and that counsel's mental processes (i.e., "mental impressions, conclusions, opinions or legal theories") will be given close to absolute protection from discovery by an adversary. Several commentators have argued that a work product exception is inappropriate as to the trial preparation material of the prosecutor. The prosecutor, they note, is not simply an adversary, but a representative of the people who bears a duty to "promote justice,"

---

4.   329 U.S. 495, 67 S.Ct. 385, 91 L.Ed. 451 (1947).

which points toward full discovery and avoidance of trial by surprise. Both courts and legislatures, have consistently rejected the view that the prosecutor's broader role renders the work product privilege irrelevant. Thus, the Supreme Court, in *United States v. Nobles*,[5] expressed no qualms in holding the work product doctrine applicable in federal criminal cases as a basic common law doctrine. Indeed, the Court noted that the work product doctrine was "even more vital" in the criminal justice system than in civil litigation for "the interests of society and the accused in obtaining a fair and accurate resolution of the question of guilt or innocence demand that adequate safeguards assure the thorough preparation and presentation of each side of the case."

A second issue is whether, as in civil cases, the doctrine will operate to require a showing of special need for what is commonly described as "fact" or "ordinary" work product—i.e., the content of a trial preparation document apart from that which reflects counsel's mental processes. In the civil setting, fact work product is given less protection than mental process work product (often called "opinion" work product), but disclosure of fact work product does require a showing of need and unavailable alternatives. As to a recorded statement of a witness, the party seeking discovery must show, at the least, that the deposition process is unavailable or otherwise unsatisfactory. In the criminal justice process, of course, the deposition process ordinarily is not available as a discovery tool, but there remain other alternatives, such as interviewing the witness. In jurisdictions providing for discretionary discovery of a prosecution witness' statement, the showing required to gain discovery of that statement often will parallel if not surpass the showing mandated in civil cases to obtain fact work product. Jurisdictions with ABA-type provisions, however, view the witness' statement as so important to defense preparation that they simply dispatch with a showing of need and automatically make it available insofar as it contains no more than "fact" work product.

All jurisdictions allowing disclosure of witness statements do protect, however, "opinion" work product. The primary issue here is whether what is to be protected is solely the mental impressions of the prosecution's legal staff, or also the mental impressions of their investigators—the police. In civil cases, as the Supreme Court noted in *Nobles*, the work product doctrine has developed "as an intensely practical one, grounded on the realities of litigation," and one of those realities is that "attorneys often must rely on assistance of their investigators." *Nobles* concluded that the federal work product rule in criminal cases should also extend to statements taken by investigators. Many states do likewise, often with specific reference made to "police officers," but other states follow the ABA model, which is limited to opinions, theories, or conclusions of the "prosecuting attorneys or members of his legal staff." The difference in coverage is unlikely to have great practical significance, however, as applied to most prior recorded statements of witnesses. Statements obtained by police officers ordinarily will not reflect a significant amount of "opinion" work product. Very often, the statement will consist of little more than the witness' narrative of events in response to an open-ended question. On occasion, the interrogator's questions may reflect some legal theory or factual judgment, but such material often can be deleted without detracting from the flow of the witness' statement. Indeed, courts have held that even a prosecutor's notes on witness interviews, selectively recording particular comments or summarizing the substance of the witness' statement, do not constitute opinion work product.

Federal Rule 16 and similar state provisions do not contain a work product provision as such. Instead, they have a provision prohibiting discovery of "reports, memoranda, or other internal government documents made by the attorney for the government or any other government agent investigating or prosecuting the case." This provision clearly covers all opinion work product and most fact work

5. 422 U.S. 225, 95 S.Ct. 2160, 45 L.Ed.2d 141 (1975), also discussed in § 20.4(b) and § 20.5(f).

product as well.[6] It does not recognize an exception based upon a showing of need as to either, and it covers police officers as well as prosecutors. It is not tied to the traditional definition of work product, and presumably is not subject to traditional work product exceptions such as waiver. Accordingly, it renders unnecessary the inclusion of a work product provision.

(k) Police Reports. Police investigative reports may fall in one or more of several categories of discoverable material. Where the report contains a recital of the comments of a defendant, codefendant or witness sufficiently complete to constitute a recorded statement of that person, that portion of the report may be subject to discovery under the appropriate provision for recorded statements. So too, an abridged description of a statement may be subject to discovery when state law requires disclosure of summaries of oral statements of defendants or codefendants. Most often, the police report will contain considerable additional information that would not fall under the provisions governing recorded or oral statements. This would include the officer's own observations and comments and references to conversations with persons whose statements are not subject to disclosure. In many jurisdictions, one or more discovery provisions could conceivably reach this portion of the report. These include: (1) provisions for discovery of documents "which are material to the preparation of the defense"; (2) provisions requiring disclosure of statements of persons having knowledge of relevant facts; (3) provisions requiring disclosure of statements of prosecution witnesses where the officer himself will testify at trial; and (4) provisions

authorizing discretionary disclosure of "relevant material and information" not otherwise listed in the discovery rule.

A substantial number of jurisdictions specifically exempt police reports and similar documents from discovery under most of the provisions noted above. Many do so under provisions that protect from discovery "reports, memoranda, or other internal documents" made by government agents in connection with "the investigation or prosecution of the case."[7] Many states similarly have provisions that exempt police reports from discovery except for that portion of the report that is discoverable as a recordation of a defendant's or witness' statement. Others have achieved the same result through rulings that hold other portions of the report to automatically constitute work product. Still others, however, have no specific exemption provision and offer little or no protection under the work product doctrine (either because most parts of the police report are not deemed to reveal "the mental impressions, conclusions, opinions, or legal theories" of the police officer, or the work product exemption is limited to "opinion" work product of the legal staff). In these jurisdictions, if the investigative report otherwise fits within one of the categories of material subject to pretrial disclosure, it has no special protection.

(l) Protective Orders. All jurisdictions with an extensive statute or court rule governing discovery include a provision authorizing the issuance of a protective order. In common law jurisdictions, the trial court's discretionary authority similarly permits it to defer or deny discovery for protective purposes. Federal Rule

---

6. Indeed the protective sweep of the "internal memoranda" category is so broad that such provisions usually recognize exceptions as to several items specifically made discoverable under the rules. Thus, an exception is made for the recorded statement of the defendant, even though it may be contained in an internal report. Federal Rule 16 for many years created exceptions for items discoverable under its provisions on defendant's written statements, defendant's prior record, reports of examinations and tests, and expert witness materials. It did not contain an exceptions for the provision on the discovery of documents as that provision extended to documents "material to preparing the defense" and many forms of internal memoranda would meet that standard (e.g., investigative re-

ports). In 2002, a revision of Rule 16(a)(2) broadened the initial exception in the internal memoranda provision to read, "except as provided in Rule 16(a)(1)." This would appear to extend the exception to the discovery of documents as authorized in Rule 16(a)(1)(E), which includes items "material to preparing the defense." However, the Advisory Committee Note indicated that the Rule 16 changes were "intended to be stylistic only."

7. This clearly was the case under the Federal Rules prior to the 2002 revision, discussed in note 6 supra, which extended the exception at the outset of Rule 16(a)(2) to material discoverable under Rule 16(a)(1)(E). See note 6 supra.

16(d) and various state protective-order provisions authorize the trial court to "deny, restrict, or defer" discovery otherwise available. Other states, however, limit protective orders to restricting or deferring discovery and add the requirement that "all material and information to which a party is entitled must be disclosed in time to make beneficial use thereof."

What constitutes appropriate grounds for the issuance of a protective order? Federal Rule 16(d) simply notes that the order shall be issued "for good cause." Several state provisions list various interests that may be weighed against the value of disclosure to the defendant. These include: protection of witnesses and others from "physical harm, threats of harm, bribes, economic reprisals and other intimidation"; maintenance of secrecy regarding informants; and "protection of confidential relationships and privileges recognized by law." In the end, the court must determine "that the disclosure would result in a risk or harm outweighing any usefulness of the disclosure."

The burden of establishing a need for a protective order rests, of course, on the government as the party seeking that order. Protective order provisions commonly authorize the prosecution to make its showing in camera. This procedure is often necessary to avoid disclosing to the defense that information which the government seeks to protect under the order. If the court enters the order, the record of the showing is sealed and made available for review on appeal. In light of the broad discretion granted the trial judge and the fact that appellate review is ordinarily not available prior to an appeal from a conviction, the protective order is likely to either be sustained on appeal as within the trial judge's discretion or held to constitute harmless error even if its issuance was an abuse of discretion.

(m) Constitutional Overtones. The major portion of defense discovery focuses on avoiding "trial by surprise" by giving the defense advance notice of the evidence that the prosecution intends to use at trial. This aspect of defense discovery has been viewed as a matter to be determined by local legislative or judicial policy, with the Constitution imposing no significant requirements as to what must be disclosed before trial. The Supreme Court has noted, for example, that while it may be the "better practice" to grant the defendant pretrial discovery of his confession where the prosecution intends to use it at trial, the failure to follow that practice does not violate due process. So too, in a case in which the prosecution failed to inform defendant that his associate and codefendant had become an informant and would testify for the police, the Court, in rejecting defendant's constitutional objection, noted: "There is no general constitutional right to discovery in a criminal case."[8] Still, exceptional cases do arise, and state courts have occasionally found due process violated where the prosecution's failure to disclose certain critical portions of its evidence before trial deprived the defendant of an adequate opportunity to prepare to meet the prosecution's case (as where that evidence was a scientific report that would have required consultation with an expert).

As discussed in § 24.3(b), the Supreme Court, in a series of cases starting with *Brady v. Maryland*,[9] has established a constitutional obligation of the prosecution to disclose exculpatory evidence within its possession when that evidence might be material to the outcome of the case. The Supreme Court's *Brady* rulings have involved situations in which exculpatory material has not been disclosed and therefore the Court has not dealt with the necessary timing of a *Brady* disclosure. Lower courts generally have agreed that the prosecutor's *Brady* obligation is satisfied if the exculpatory material is disclosed "in time for its effective use at trial," and for many types of exculpatory evidence, disclosure at trial itself will be satisfactory. The ultimate issue under *Brady*, where the exculpatory evidence is produced at trial, is whether delay in production resulted in a violation of the *Brady* "materiali-

---

8. Weatherford v. Bursey, 429 U.S. 545, 97 S.Ct. 837, 51 L.Ed.2d 30 (1977).

9. See § 24.3(b) at note 7.

ty standard"—that is, whether there is a reasonable probability that, had the evidence been disclosed to the defense pretrial (assuming it was then within the prosecution's possession or control), the "result of the proceeding would have been different."

The range of possible *Brady* material is so broad that it can readily encompass material that the discovery rule either implicitly or explicitly excludes from pretrial disclosure. Thus, *Brady* may reach impeachment material to be found in the prior recorded statement of a prospective government witness, but the jurisdiction's "Jencks Act" provision may preclude disclosure of that statement until the witness testifies at trial. *Brady* would also require disclosure of incentives given to prosecution witnesses, but requiring pretrial disclosure of the relevant documents (e.g., plea agreements) would be contrary to the protection of internal documents and would be inconsistent with a discovery provision that ordinarily seeks to withhold pretrial the identity of the prosecution's witnesses.

Federal courts have divided in treating such potential conflicts between *Brady* and the limits placed on federal pretrial discovery. Many conclude that no conflict is presented since *Brady* will be satisfied by producing such exculpatory material at trial. Others have argued that disclosure at trial could be insufficient, and the trial court therefore has the authority to "trump" the Jencks Act and order disclosure pretrial of prior statements of witnesses insofar as they contain exculpatory material. Some would do this automatically and others would do so based on the character of the exculpatory evidence and the likely need for pretrial disclosure to permit the defense to use it effectively (distinguishing in this regard between impeachment material and other exculpatory material). One court has suggested, however, that even assuming arguendo that *Brady* may be violated by failing to reveal until trial exculpatory material within a witness' prior recorded statement (notwithstanding the court's capacity to grant a recess at that point if the defense needs more time to explore that material), the *Brady* doctrine does not thereby give the trial court the authority to override Jencks and order pretrial disclosure. *Brady* imposes an obligation upon the prosecution and leaves to the prosecution the initial determination of when to disclose. If it fails to comply adequately, "it acts at its own peril." Under this view, Jencks is not necessarily compatible with *Brady* under all circumstances, and clearly does not "trump" *Brady*, but does leave to the government the opportunity to control the timing of its disclosure, with the court determining after the case is completed whether a delay in disclosure so prejudiced the defendant as to deny due process.[10]

§ 20.4 Constitutional Limitations Upon Pretrial Discovery for the Prosecution

(a) Due Process. The constitutionality of pretrial discovery for the prosecution was first considered by the Supreme Court in *Williams v. Florida*[1]. That case considered a challenge to a typical alibi-notice provision. It required the defendant, on written demand of the prosecutor, to give notice in advance of any claim of alibi, to specify the place where he claims to have been at the time of the crime, and to provide the names and addresses of alibi witnesses. The prosecution was required, in return, to notify the defense of any witnesses it proposed to offer in rebuttal of the alibi. The possible sanction for violation of these disclo-

---

10. The Supreme Court's reasoning in United States v. Ruiz, 536 U.S. 622, 122 S.Ct. 2450, 153 L.Ed.2d 586 (2002), arguably lends support to refusing to interfere with prosecutorial discretion in weighing the benefits and risks of not disclosing until trial. In sustaining the government's policy of requiring a defendant's waiver of the receipt of impeachment material as part of a fast-track guilty plea (see § 21.3 at note 22), the Court acknowledged that the impeachment material could be exculpatory under *Brady*, but stressed that *Brady* created a trial right and the prosecutor had valid reasons for refusing to make

disclosure pre-plea. These reasons related primarily to the plea-bargaining process, but the Court did point to various costs of pretrial disclosure generally, including disrupting investigations, exposing potential witnesses to harm, and increasing the resources devoted to cases that might eventually result in guilty pleas.

§ 20.4

1. 399 U.S. 78, 90 S.Ct. 1893, 26 L.Ed.2d 446 (1970).

sure obligations by the prosecution or defense was the exclusion of its alibi witnesses (although the defendant himself remained free to testify as to the alibi). The defendant in *Williams* had complied with the alibi-notice requirement, providing the prosecution with the name and address of his alibi witness. The prosecution then deposed that witness, and when she testified at trial, used that deposition to challenge her alibi testimony. The prosecution also introduced the testimony of an investigator who stated that the witness herself had been at still a different place during the time when she claimed to have been with the defendant.

The defense challenge to the alibi-notice rule in *Williams* rested on three grounds: violation of due process by altering the balance of the adversarial process; violation of the Fifth Amendment privilege against self-incrimination by forcing the defendant to furnish the state with information (the name and address of his alibi witness) that was useful to the state in convicting him; and violation of the Sixth Amendment by providing for a sanction of exclusion under which the defendant could be denied the right to present alibi witnesses if he failed to provide pretrial notice as required by the alibi rule. The Supreme Court found it unnecessary to consider the Sixth Amendment issue since the defendant had complied with the alibi-notice requirement and the exclusion sanction had not been applied in his case. The constitutionality of that sanction was later upheld in *Taylor v. Illinois* (discussed in § 20.6) as applied to the circumstances there presented. The Court considered and rejected the defendant's due process and self-incrimination arguments. The *Williams* opinion, by Justice White, treated the self-incrimination issue (discussed in subsection (c) infra) as the "petitioner's major contention." The due process issue was treated as not very troublesome and disposed of in a paragraph.

The Court saw nothing in the Florida alibi-notice rule that unfairly affected the adversarial process. Given "the ease with which an alibi can be fabricated," the government's interest

in "protecting itself against an eleventh hour defense" was characterized as "both obvious and legitimate." The adversary system was not "a poker game in which players enjoy an absolute right always to conceal their cards until played." There was "ample room in that system" for a notice requirement "designed to enhance the search for truth * * * by insuring both the defendant and the State ample opportunity to investigate certain facts crucial to the determination of guilt or innocence." The Florida rule, the Court stressed, was fairly constructed to meet that end. Florida law generally provided liberal discovery to the defendant and the alibi rule was "carefully hedged with reciprocal duties requiring state disclosure to the defendant."

The critical nature of the reciprocal disclosure provided by the Florida alibi rule was subsequently brought home in *Wardius v. Oregon*.[2] Distinguishing *Williams*, the Court there held that an alibi rule which failed to provide reciprocal discovery by the prosecution of its rebuttal alibi witnesses violated due process. The Court noted: "The State may not insist that trials be run as a 'search for the truth' so far as the defense witnesses are concerned, while maintaining 'poker game secrecy' for its own witnesses." "Due process," it added, has "little to say regarding the amount of discovery which the parties must be afforded, [but] it does speak to the balance of force between the accused and his accuser." It was "fundamentally unfair" for the state to "require a defendant to divulge the details of his own case while at the same time subjecting him to the hazard of surprise concerning refutation of the very pieces of evidence which he disclosed to the State."

The reciprocity required by *Wardius* is now commonly found in all aspects of prosecution discovery. Moreover, the range of items that the prosecution must disclose is always equal to or broader than the range of items the defense must disclose. Of course, this does not necessarily mean that the defense disclosure will always be matched in type by prosecution disclosure, as the prosecutor may not have in

---

2. 412 U.S. 470, 93 S.Ct. 2208, 37 L.Ed.2d 82 (1973).

its possession the same type of evidence as the defense.

(b) Self–Incrimination: Non–Defendant and Non–Testimonial Disclosures. Consistent with standard self-incrimination doctrine, as discussed in § 8.12, a compelled disclosure will not violate the defendant's privilege against self-incrimination unless it requires a testimonial disclosure by the defendant. Although the Supreme Court's ruling in *United States v. Nobles*[3] did not involve pretrial discovery, its reasoning clearly establishes that many types of prosecution discovery do not present self-incrimination difficulties because they do not demand a testimonial communication by the defendant. *Nobles* upheld the required defense disclosure at trial of its prior recorded statement of a defense witness. When the defense there called its investigator to testify to his conversations with two prosecution witnesses, the trial court granted the prosecutor's request to inspect that portion of the investigator's written report that had recorded the essence of those conversations. The Supreme Court, in an unanimous ruling, held that the inspection order had not violated the defendant's privilege against self-incrimination. The defendant had not "prepared the report, and there [was] no suggestion that the portions subject to the disclosure order reflected any information that he conveyed to the investigator." Although the witnesses' recorded statements "were elicited by a defense investigator on defendant's behalf," that "did not convert them into defendant's personal communications." Accordingly, the Court concluded, "requiring their production from the investigator would not in any sense compel defendant to be a witness against himself or extort communications from him." This rationale would sustain equally a pretrial discovery order requiring pretrial defense production of a known document not prepared by the defendant and not reflecting information conveyed by the defendant.

Nobles focused on the character of the document and its relationship to defendant's communications. One year later, however, in *Fisher v. United States*,[4] the Court held that a person's act of producing a document written by another, in response to a court order, could constitute a testimonial communication of the person producing the document and therefore be covered by the privilege. As discussed in § 8.13(a), this testimonial component exists only insofar as the act of production acknowledges the existence and possession of the document and provides authentication evidence and those issues are not otherwise a foregone conclusion. For at least two reasons, this act-of-production doctrine does not present self-incrimination difficulties for a *Nobles*-type discovery order. Initially, it is the lawyer rather than the client who is being compelled to disclose the document. *Fisher* did recognize that a lawyer, relying on the attorney-client privilege, can object to compelled production of a document received from a client where the client could successfully have challenged on self-incrimination grounds a court order directing the client to produce that document. However, unlike *Fisher*, the lawyer responding to a *Nobles*-type discovery order typically is not being compelled to produce a document that a client has given to him for the purpose of seeking legal advice. Secondly, even if the production order is viewed as directed to the client/defendant, the act of production lacks the elements needed to present a testimonial component, for the elements of possession and existence fall within the foregone conclusion analysis of *Fisher*. In seeking discovery of a particular document (e.g. the recorded statement of a known witness), the government establishes that it already knows of existence and possession (established in *Nobles* through the investigator's own testimony). So too, the known author of the document (e.g., the investigator or expert) can serve as the source of authentication, rendering irrelevant the production by the defendant, who was not even present when the document was prepared. Moreover, since the prosecution's objective in obtaining discovery commonly does not include

---

3. 422 U.S. 225, 95 S.Ct. 2160, 45 L.Ed.2d 141 (1975).

4. 425 U.S. 391, 96 S.Ct. 1569, 48 L.Ed.2d 39 (1976), discussed in § 8.12(f), 8.13(a).

introducing the document into evidence, authentication often is not even in issue.[5]

(c) Self–Incrimination: Defendant's Testimonial Disclosure. In *Williams v. Florida*,[6] the Court treated the Florida alibi-notice provision before it as requiring a testimonial disclosure of the defendant. That provision imposed an obligation upon "a defendant" who intended to offer a defense of alibi to give pretrial notice of (1) "his intention to claim such alibi," (2) "specific information as to the place at which the defendant claims to have been," and (3) "the names and addresses of the witnesses by whom he proposes to establish such alibi." Justice White did comment in a footnote that "it might be argued that the 'testimonial disclosures' protected by the Fifth Amendment include only the statements relating to the historical facts of the crime, not statements relating solely to what a defendant proposes to do at trial." There was no need to further explore this possibility because (as discussed in subsection (d) infra) the Court found no element of compulsion. Moreover, the defendant clearly is being asked to cite an historical fact in identifying the place at which he claims to have been at the time of the crime. The identification of the alibi witnesses also incorporates an historical fact, in addition to describing defendant's intended future behavior, as it states that these are persons who were in that same place at the same time.

The disclosure of an intent to raise an alibi defense, standing alone, would most likely to be viewed as non-testimonial under the distinction suggested in the *Williams* footnote. The same would be true of broader provisions, requiring the defense to give pretrial notice as to a wide range of defenses. However, that characterization may be altered if notice of the intended defense is treated like any other statement of a party (i.e., as a party admission) and is available to the prosecution to be used to impeach the defendant should he shift to another defense in his testimony at trial. Where that use is not allowed, as is true in many states, whether the notice is characterized as testimonial or not tends to be unimportant, since the information conveyed is so limited that it is likely not to be sufficiently incriminating to implicate the Fifth Amendment. Ordinarily, for example, a notice of alibi standing by itself would hardly pose a realistic threat of providing the prosecution with a true link in the development of a chain of incriminating evidence.

The alibi-notice provision in *Williams* required disclosure by the defendant, but many discovery provisions place the obligation of disclosure on the defense counsel. Of course, if the defense counsel can respond based on his or her own knowledge obtained in the course of the investigation, then the response may be subject to challenge on grounds other than self-incrimination (e.g., as demanding work-product), but it would not require the testimony of the defendant. On the other hand, if the disclosure can be made by counsel only by obtaining the information from the defendant, the formal structure of the disclosure obligation should not alter the treatment of the disclosure as a testimonial communication of the defendant. Indeed, in jurisdictions that treat a defendant's discovery response as a party admission, a response will be treated as an admission by the defendant, even though made by counsel, and not invariably based upon information provided by the defendant. Surely any compelled statement of the attorney that will be treated as a party admission by the client must also be viewed, for Fifth

---

5. The above analysis assumes that the prosecution can identify the specific document it seeks—as it did in *Nobles* where it sought the investigator's report on the interview of specific witnesses. Where the prosecution does not know that the document exists and cannot identify it by reference to author and content, there may be a testimonial communication inherent in the act-of-production that does present self-incrimination difficulties. For example, in producing the written or recorded statements of persons described in a discovery request simply by a generic category (e.g., all experts consulted, or all persons

at the scene of the crime), the defense is being asked to identify specific persons as falling within those categories. Of course, that testimonial element is not necessarily protected by the defendant's privilege. First, as in *Nobles*, it need not necessarily be viewed as a testimonial disclosure by the defendant himself. Second, under the acceleration doctrine discussed in subsection (d), it will not be viewed as a "compelled" testimonial disclosure if the defense intends to use the document at trial.

6. See note 1 supra.

Amendment purposes, as the compelled statement of the client.

Thus, it ordinarily would not matter whether counsel or the defendant is required to identify the place of the alibi or the alibi witness, as such information would obviously come from the defendant and thereby present a self-incrimination issue. The same would commonly be true of the notification of various defenses (e.g., self-defense) or the listing of witnesses who might support those defenses. As to the identification of many other witnesses, however, the information is more likely or just as likely to come from counsel. Thus, where the defense must list experts consulted to conduct scientific tests, the listing would ordinarily be that of the defense counsel, not the defendant speaking through the defense counsel. Where the required disclosure does not indicate by its nature that the defendant is the almost inevitable source of the required response, the burden should be on the defendant, as the party claiming the privilege, to allege that the requested answer would require the defendant to provide testimony through the response by counsel to the prosecution's discovery request.

(d) Self–Incrimination: The Acceleration Doctrine. Although the disclosure under the alibi-notice rule challenged in *Williams v. Florida*[7] clearly required a testimonial communication by the defendant, the Court there rejected defendant's self-incrimination claim. It concluded that the alibi-notice rule did not meet an additional prerequisite for a successful self-incrimination claim. The pressure imposed to disclose was not the kind of "compulsion" against which a person is protected by the Fifth Amendment privilege.

Speaking for the *Williams* majority, Justice White reasoned that the alibi-notice provision imposed no greater compulsion than would be present at trial when the defendant eventually had to decide whether or not to raise the alibi defense. At that point, if the defendant decided to present his alibi witnesses, he would be forced to "reveal their identity and submit them to cross-examination which in itself may

prove incriminating or which may furnish the State with leads to incriminating rebuttal evidence." In deciding whether to take this risk, the defendant might be subject to "severe pressures" generated by the strength of the government's evidence, but such pressures had never been viewed as prohibited by the Fifth Amendment. The alibi-notice requirement simply imposed "very similar constraints" upon the defendant. It did no more than "accelerate the timing of his disclosure, forcing him to divulge at an earlier date information which * * * [he] planned to divulge at trial." Moreover, it was only the disclosure rather than the final choice that was accelerated. The defendant could give an alibi notice before trial, but then decide not to raise the defense at trial. Nothing in the Florida procedure prevented him "from abandoning the defense" in his "unfettered discretion."

The defendant in *Williams* argued that the accelerated disclosure in itself violated the privilege because it forced him to make his decision before the state had presented its case-in-chief. Justice Black, in dissent, found that argument persuasive. The dissent noted: "When a defendant is required to indicate whether he might plead alibi in advance of trial, he faces a vastly different decision than that faced by one who can wait until the state has presented the case against him before making up his mind." The majority responded, however, that the defendant had no constitutional right to insist that his decision to disclose be delayed until trial. The Court stated:

> Nothing in the Fifth Amendment privilege entitles a defendant as a matter of constitutional right to await the end of the State's case before announcing the nature of his defense, any more than it entitles him to await the jury's verdict on the State's case-in-chief before deciding whether or not to take the stand himself. * * * Petitioner concedes that absent the notice-of-alibi rule the Constitution would raise no bar to the court's granting the State a continuance at trial on the grounds of surprise as soon as the alibi witness is called. Nor would there

---

7. See note 1 supra.

be self-incrimination problems if, during that continuance, the State was permitted to do precisely what it did here prior to trial: to depose the witness and find rebuttal evidence. But if so utilizing a continuance is permissible under the Fifth and Fourteenth Amendments, then surely the same result may be accomplished through pretrial discovery as it was here, avoiding the necessity of a disrupted trial."

The key to the *Williams* ruling clearly was this conclusion that accelerated disclosure did not violate the Fifth Amendment. How far that ruling extends has been a subject of considerable debate among commentators and, to a much lesser extent, among lower courts.

Williams clearly found no self-incrimination difficulties in two of the primary advantages that accelerated disclosure provides to the prosecution over disclosure at trial. Initially, by indicating the direction that the defense is likely to take, accelerated disclosure permits the prosecution to husband its resources and focus on the primary areas of dispute. *Williams* obviously viewed that advantage as one the state could demand consistent with defendant's self-incrimination privilege. Another advantage placed in the same category was the primary focus of the Court's opinion. The information furnished in the defense disclosure, such as the names of defense witnesses, could be used, as it was in *Williams*, to develop grounds for impeaching that evidence and otherwise rebutting defendant's alibi defense. It often would be much more difficult for the prosecution to attempt to investigate the alibi defense when that defense first is revealed at trial, even when it could obtain a continuance for that purpose. *Williams* clearly concluded that the defendant had no constitutionally protected right to a "surprise element" that would restrict the prosecution's investigative capacity in this regard.

The status of a third potential advantage of accelerated disclosure—that of using the disclosure to prepare an affirmative case rather than simply to rebut a defense—is the primary source of division among the commentators. Accelerated disclosure, they agree, is not always the same as the disclosure that would be made at trial. Indeed, there exists the possibility of forcing the defense pretrial to make a choice that it would never even face at trial. That could occur where the prosecution would otherwise not be able to establish a prima facie case in its case-in-chief (resulting in a directed acquittal and no need for the defendant to present any defense), but the pretrial disclosure by the defense gives the prosecution leads that allow it to sufficiently bolster its case-in-chief to avoid a directed acquittal. Here, it is argued, the defendant is not simply being asked to accelerate a decision that otherwise must be assessed at trial, but to risk assisting the state in fulfilling its basic obligation of establishing a prima facie case. The disclosure requirement is not being used simply to avoid the element of surprise that might make it more difficult for the prosecution to rebut the defendant's defense, but to allow the state to shore up a weak prosecution case on the basic elements of the offense. Some commentators see an analogous difficulty where the defendant's disclosure may be used to connect the defendant with other crimes.

Does the accelerated disclosure doctrine of *Williams* take into account the potential for such disclosure being utilized by the prosecution to obtain evidence of the formative elements of the crime that would not have been obtained if disclosure was required only after the prosecution established a prima facie case? Commentators taking a narrow view of *Williams* argue that it does not and that the Court would distinguish *Williams* if fairly faced with such a case. *Williams*, they note, simply did not present a situation in which pretrial disclosure would "accelerate" a choice that would otherwise never have to be made because the prosecution, without leads provided by the disclosure, would not have established a prima facie case in its case-in-chief. Indeed, they argue, the facts there clearly negated such a possibility. In describing the prosecution's use of the alibi disclosure, the Court noted that the prosecution had responded by laying the groundwork for impeaching the alibi witness and establishing by independent evidence the falseness of her testimony. Although Justice Black in dissent raised the possibility that an accelerated disclosure might be used directly or derivatively to enhance the strength of the prosecution's case-in-chief, there was no suggestion in the facts presented by the majority that such had been the case and, indeed, no such claim had been made by the defendant. Moreover, the very nature of an alibi defense, the commentators note, made such use largely unlikely. Alibi witnesses, as persons who were elsewhere, are not likely to be helpful sources to the prosecution in proving the elements of the offense. While they conceivably could have some relevant information on that score in unusual cases, that possibility as a general matter falls far below the requirement of a "real and appreciable danger"—the standard commonly used in determining whether the likelihood of incrimination is sufficient to raise a legitimate self-incrimination claim.

The likelihood of incrimination would be far greater, these commentators note, as to other types of defense witnesses, particularly those who would be present at the scene (as in the case of witnesses supporting a claim of self-defense). Where a pretrial discovery rule would require disclosure of the identity of such witnesses, the Court might be far less willing to accept the disclosure requirement by drawing an analogy between the pretrial and the trial choice to disclose. At the least, it is argued, the Court might hold that pretrial discovery could not be ordered where the defense can establish in camera that there exists a real and appreciable danger that its disclosure could be used by the prosecution in developing its case-in-chief. Arguably disclosure also would not be required where the defense could make a showing in camera that its disclosure would be incriminating with respect to some unrelated offense. Here too, the defense would not be required to decide whether the disclosure is worth the risk until it is clear that the prosecution can meet its burden of establishing its case-in-chief.

Other commentators contend that there is no limitation to the Court's acceptance of the accelerated disclosure concept in *Williams*. The *Williams* ruling demands at most that the

defense be given broad discovery of the prosecution's case, as was true in Florida, so it can make a reasoned tactical judgment as it would at trial. *Williams* then allows the state leeway in structuring the timing of that judgment provided its timing requirement is justified by a reasonable state interest that satisfies due process. The choice may be somewhat more difficult at an earlier stage, but that does not so alter the character of the pressure exerted as to justify characterizing as Fifth Amendment "compulsion" at the pretrial stage the same type of pressure, produced by the strength of the prosecution's case, as has long been accepted at the trial stage. As *Williams* noted, were the state to have a Fifth Amendment obligation to minimize such pressure, there would be no ending point; the defendant could claim that the state must provide a tentative jury verdict on the prosecutor's case-in-chief so that defendant would not be required to present a defense until he was certain that the jury would otherwise convict.

In assessing the scope of *Williams'* accelerated disclosure doctrine, commentators sometimes look to *Brooks v. Tennessee*,[8] a case decided after *Williams*. The Court there held unconstitutional, as imposing an impermissible burden on defendant's right not to testify, a state rule that defendant could testify on his own behalf only if he testified before any other defense witnesses gave testimony. The majority in *Brooks* did not refer to *Williams*, but the dissent cited *Williams*, among other cases, in arguing that the burden imposed upon the defendant by shifting the time of his decision was no worse than the analogous burdens upheld in past cases. Commentators favoring a narrower reading of *Williams* see *Brooks* as acknowledging that the mandated timing of a decision to present evidence can trigger the compulsion element of self-incrimination. The majority's decision without any reference to *Williams* (despite the dissent's reliance on that case) indicates, it is argued, that the accelerated disclosure doctrine was viewed as limited to the special situation presented in the alibi-notice context of *Williams*. Commentators on

---

8.   406 U.S. 605, 92 S.Ct. 1891, 32 L.Ed.2d 358 (1972), also discussed in § 24.5(a) at note 8.

the other side see *Brooks* as presenting a situation quite distinct from any discovery requirement. What was involved, they note, was not compulsion that forced the defendant to disclose a prospective defense witness who might also be a source of incriminatory evidence, but a restriction on defendant's unfettered choice in deciding whether to exercise his personal right to testify. Moreover, the defendant there was not asked to make an initial decision from which he could withdraw (as in *Williams*), but an accelerated final decision on whether to testify. *Brooks* is therefore seen as in no way detracting from the *Williams* analysis upholding a state requirement of accelerated defense disclosure of the evidence from others that the defendant intends to use at trial.

Initially, some lower courts were cautious in their reading of *Williams*, particularly in its application to provisions requiring the disclosure of all defense witnesses. Such provisions were challenged on self-incrimination grounds in light of their potential for requiring disclosure of the names of defense witnesses who were likely to have knowledge that might help the prosecution its case-in-chief (e.g., witnesses on a claim of self-defense). Though rejecting such challenges, which sought to have the discovery provision held unconstitutional on its face, these courts left open the possibility of exempting the defense from its discovery obligation upon a showing that the prosecution "was seek[ing] information that might serve as an unconstitutional link in a chain of evidence tending to establish the accused's guilt." A growing group of subsequent rulings, however, have sustained reciprocal disclosure requirements without regard to the possibility that the information provided might assist the prosecution in building its case-in-chief. They have accepted the accelerated disclosure rationale of *Williams* as refuting self-incrimination claims with respect to all aspects of the advance disclosure of evidence the defendant intends to introduce at trial (except for the defendant's own testimony). Thus, the narrower reading of *Williams* advanced by the commentators has virtually no support in the more recent case law.

(e) Self–Incrimination: The Special Case of the Insanity Defense. Even under the broadest reading of *Williams, Nobles,* and *Fisher*, self-incrimination doctrine still should preclude a discovery provision that requires the defendant himself to make a testimonial disclosure where that disclosure creates a realistic danger of providing a link in the chain of evidence that will be used against him and does not merely accelerate revealing information that would be forthcoming at trial in the presentation of the defense's evidence. In one area, however, the defendant commonly is required personally to make a statement for possible prosecution use that he otherwise would not make. Where a defendant intends to rely upon a defense of insanity, or to introduce expert testimony on another mental-condition defense (e.g., diminished responsibility), he commonly is required not only to make accelerated disclosure of that defense, but also to submit to a psychiatric examination by a psychiatrist designated by the court. Statements made by the defendant during that psychiatric examination may not be used for other purposes, but the psychiatrist, relying on those statements, can testify that the defendant was sane or had sufficient mental capacity to meet the prescribed mens rea and thereby convince the jury to reject the defendant's insanity or mental-condition defense. Thus, a defendant required to submit to a court-order psychiatric exam clearly is participating in the development of evidence that may be used against him (albeit on a single issue) by offering information in response to the psychiatrist's questions that he otherwise would not offer at trial.

Lower courts have uniformly upheld the required participation of the defendant in a psychiatric exam, although they have varied somewhat in their reasoning. At one time, it had been suggested that the defendant's statements during the examination were not testimonial, but that contention is contrary to the Supreme Court's analysis in *Estelle v. Smith,*[9] which considered in another context the allowable use of psychiatric testimony that was the fruit of a compelled examination. The Court

---

9. 451 U.S. 454, 101 S.Ct. 1866, 68 L.Ed.2d 359 (1981).

there reasoned that the defendant's responses during the psychiatric examination were testimonial where the doctor was relying not on his observation of the defendant's behavior but on the substance of defendant's responses. Some courts have stressed that the defendant's responses, though testimonial, will be used only on the issue of insanity, which is characterized as an "objective" medical issue that relates to the appropriateness of a special type of verdict rather than to the basic issue of whether the defendant committed the crime. However, as other courts have noted, this makes the examination offered by the prosecution in establishing defendant's sanity no less incriminating than evidence rejecting any other defense, for the defendant's statements are still being used against him to avoid an acquittal (albeit of a special character) and to produce a conviction.

Perhaps the most widely accepted rationale as to why a court-ordered psychiatric examination does not violate the Fifth Amendment is that of waiver. Of course, the waiver here is not the traditional waiver by an entirely voluntary relinquishment, but waiver that is produced by conditions that the state attaches to the defendant's use of experts on the psychiatric issue. The state may duly be concerned about allowing the use of fully informed expert testimony on one side only, and therefore may insist that each side's expert have access to the subject of the examination (here the defendant) just as they might insist that a defendant who offers expert testimony on the physical characteristics of a tangible object within the defendant's possession also make that object available for examination by the prosecution's experts. The defendant, in choosing to use his own expert testimony, is taken as agreeing to submit the subject of that testimony to the other side for the same use as has been made by his experts.

(f) Sixth Amendment Limitations. Sixth Amendment challenges to prosecution discovery have been raised primarily where (1) the defense is required to disclose information it does not intend to offer at trial, (2) that information was developed by defense counsel or defense investigative agents but is not exempted from discovery under the particular jurisdiction's work-product exemption, and (3) the information does not reveal lawyer/client communications and therefore is not protected against discovery by the attorney-client privilege. The discovery orders that most often have caused courts to give serious consideration to Sixth Amendment challenges have been those directing the defense to produce for prosecution inspection items such as the following: the reports of non-testifying experts who were consulted on a scientific issue that the defense intends to raise at trial through different experts; recordations of statements made by anticipated defense and prosecution witnesses during interviews by defense investigators; and physical evidence relating to the crime that was either given to counsel or was discovered in the course of counsel's investigation, often apart from any communication by the client.[10] As to some of those orders, some jurisdictions would find work-product or lawyer-client protection, but many other jurisdictions would not.[11]

The basic rationale of the Sixth Amendment objection to required pretrial disclosure of such information is that the disclosure has a chilling effect upon the investigative efforts of counsel and therefore undermines the defendant's right to the effective assistance of counsel. Defense counsel, it is argued, must be afforded the "maximum freedom" to pursue various avenues of inquiry, including consultation with experts, interviews of possible prosecution and defense witnesses, and the collection of physical evidence, without fearing that any unfavorable material thereby obtained will be used against the defendant. If the attorney cannot be ensured of the absolute confidential-

---

10. Of course, the Sixth Amendment issue is not reached if the defendant's privilege against self-incrimination prohibits compelling the disclosure. Since the information in question here is not to be introduced at trial, the accelerated disclosure doctrine does not eliminate self-incrimination difficulties. However, the self-incrimination clause typically will not apply to such disclosures because

(1) the disclosure involves a known document and the act of production therefore is not testimonial or (2) the disclosure is made by counsel and does not reveal communications of the defendant. See subsections (b) and (c) supra.

11. See § 20.5(f), (h).

ity of the fruits of such efforts, then she may very well refuse to pursue such avenues and miss the opportunity to uncover exculpatory evidence.

Judicial responses to such a Sixth Amendment contention have varied with the court and the type of disclosure demanded. Lower courts are divided on requiring defense disclosures of the reports of non-testifying experts. Courts sustaining a Sixth Amendment challenge have argued that the "confidentiality and loyalty of expert consultants traditionally enjoyed by defendants and defense counsel is a crucial element in the effective legal representation of the defendant." Courts on the opposite side have responded with rationales similar to those advanced to support the constitutionality of requiring an insanity defense defendant to submit to a psychiatric exam. They note that the defendant has put into issue the scientific claim on which the non-testifying expert reported and will introduce other expert testimony on that claim. The state, in the interest of having objective scientific evidence freely available to all sides, may insist that the defense, once it raises the issue, make all of its experts available, just as it allows the defense discovery of the reports of all experts consulted by the prosecution, including those that the prosecution may later decide not to use at trial. This rationale, which is commonly described as resting on a "waiver" by the defense, would not extend to the situation in which the defense has decided (perhaps as a result of the expert's negative report) not to challenge on a certain issue, but the prosecution still wants disclosure because it must prove each element of crime, whether or not challenged by the defense, and the defense expert's report might be helpful in that regard.

Sixth Amendment challenges have been considerably less persuasive outside of the context of disclosure of non-testifying defense experts. The tendency here is to look to the work-product exemption and the attorney-client privilege as providing sufficient protection of defense counsel's role and not to impose fur-

ther limitations upon otherwise prescribed disclosures through the Sixth Amendment. Thus, where counsel discovers and takes possession of physical evidence of a crime even as a result of a confidential communication with his client, disclosure will be required. The communication will be protected, perhaps even by prohibiting any reference to counsel as the source of the evidence, but the tangible item itself will be treated no differently than if it were in the hands of some third party. The adversary role of counsel, the courts note, may not turn counsel's office into a sanctuary for evidence that the government could otherwise have obtained from its original location by seizure or subpoena. So too, courts have uniformly rejected Sixth Amendment challenges to the required production of the defense's prior recorded statements of witnesses (other than defendant) who will testify at trial.

(g) Conditional Discovery. Many state discovery provisions give the prosecution an automatic right to discovery of specified items, similar to the automatic right given to the defendant. In the federal system and in roughly half of the states, prosecution discovery, apart from that on insanity and alibi, is "conditional"—i.e., dependent upon the defendant's exercise of a right to discovery rather than existing as an independent right of the prosecutor. Unlike the defense, the prosecutor cannot simply institute a demand for disclosure of the items specified in the applicable discovery provision. The prosecutor may only insist upon disclosure if the defendant has demanded and received disclosure of material within the possession or control of the prosecution. Federal Rule 16(b)(1), for example, permits the prosecution to seek from the defense scientific reports made in connection with the case only after the defendant has used the corresponding provision in 16(a)(1) to obtain scientific reports from the government.

Conditional discovery is not needed to meet the reciprocity requirement of *Wardius*[12]. It is sufficient that the discovery available to the defense is at least as broad as the discovery it may be required to give the prosecution. Sup-

---

12. See note 2 supra.

porters of conditional discovery contend that, by giving the defendant the capacity to foreclose prosecution discovery, conditional discovery minimizes the risk that prosecution discovery will be held to violate defendant's constitutional rights. They argue that defendant's decision to seek discovery from the prosecution may be treated as a waiver of his privilege against self-incrimination or of any other constitutional objection to reciprocal discovery. Defense has no constitutional right to discovery of the prosecution's evidence, and the state can appropriately condition the grant of such discovery to the defense on a defense obligation to make reciprocal discovery.

Although a substantial number of jurisdictions utilize conditional discovery, the courts have said very little about the impact of the conditional element upon the constitutionality of mandating defense disclosure to the prosecution. Decisions in conditional discovery jurisdictions that have considered constitutional challenges to prosecution discovery usually have moved directly to the constitutional question without reference to the conditional nature of the discovery. Since those courts then upheld the discovery provisions, they never had to decide whether the conditional nature of the discovery provision would have saved the provision where a compelled disclosure would have been unconstitutional. Their failure to turn initially to the conditional feature may reflect doubts as to whether the discovery being conditional actually makes a difference on the constitutional issue. One court has expressed such doubts based upon a series of Supreme Court rulings holding unconstitutional governmental action that operates to penalize the exercise of a constitutional right (e.g., the disbarment of lawyers who have exercised the self-incrimination privilege). Here, however, the state is not telling the defendant that the exercise of a constitutional objection in response to some governmental inquiry will result in the deprivation of some governmental benefit the individual otherwise would receive. Rather, it offers to the defendant an advantage he otherwise would not receive on condition that the defendant, in turn, relinquishes any

constitutional restraint that would keep the prosecution from receiving a reciprocal advantage. One possible analogy is the process of plea bargaining, which accepts the state's offering of sentencing or charge inducements in return for the defendant's waiver of trial rights. However, the waiver process involved in plea bargaining finds support in its tradition and necessity, as well as requisite judicial inquiry to ensure that the waiver has been made knowingly and voluntarily. The "discovery bargain" arguably is distinguishable on all three counts.

§ 20.5 Prosecution Discovery Provisions

(a) Variations in Approach. Few courts or legislatures would disagree with the general proposition that, consistent with restraints imposed by constitutional limitations, discovery should be a "two way street" that accords neither party an "unfair advantage" and seeks to promote the determination of the truth. The difficulty arises in determining precisely what this proposition should produce in the way of prosecution discovery from the defense. As suggested in the preceding section, some disagreement exists over the extent to which the defendant's constitutional rights preclude granting the prosecution full reciprocity in discovery. But even more substantial disagreements arise in deciding how much reciprocity is needed to provide a fair adversarial balance as to the prosecution. Some argue that, even where the defense receives exceptionally broad discovery, the prosecution need be given very little discovery since it already has an "advantage over the accused through its use of the subpoena power, the grand jury, and the right to make reasonable searches and seizures for discovery purposes and through the use of the police as an investigative resource to obtain statements." Others disagree both with this conclusion and with the suggestion that an unfair advantage exists unless each party can precisely match the other in its investigative authority. They note that the government, even with all of its investigative resources, cannot be expected to uncover on its own every relevant piece of information that the defense might learn from its special resources (even apart from the defendant), so the prosecution is placed at a disadvantage where required to disclose almost all relevant information within its file without being given full reciprocity. Moreover, they argue, even if the prosecution has uncovered on its own all relevant factual information, it cannot make use of that evidence, to best ensure determination of the truth, without pretrial notice of the evidence that the defendant will use at trial. Here, they argue, the value of complete disclosure to both sides, so as to avoid a battle by surprise, stands apart from any balancing of investigative capacity.

As might be expected, the division on these issues has led to considerable variation in prosecution discovery in comparison to defense discovery. While one court rule or statute will allow the prosecution discovery that roughly parallels defense discovery, at least as to the evidence that the defense intends to use at trial, another will provide the prosecution with far less disclosure than is granted the defense. Moreover, these differences in coverage most often will not be subject to modification by the trial judge's inherent authority to grant discovery beyond that specifically authorized in the discovery provision. In the area of prosecution discovery, in contrast to defense discovery, statutory provisions commonly are viewed as preemptive. The failure of the state's discovery provisions to specifically authorize a particular type of disclosure is taken as indicating the draftsmen did not intend to allow the prosecution such discovery.

Another element of variation in prosecution discovery provisions arises from the separate treatment of the insanity and alibi defenses. Even before the states had adopted general discovery provisions, many had legislation allowing prosecution discovery as to these two defenses. In many jurisdictions, the two are still governed by a separate statute or court rule, while other aspects of prosecution discovery are covered in the general discovery provision (which also governs defense discovery). Those general provisions often differ in several aspects of their structure from the alibi and insanity provisions. While alibi and insanity disclosure obligations tend to be automatic,

the general discovery provision may be conditional, allowing for prosecution discovery only where the defense has first requested discovery. The separate alibi and insanity provisions also tend to have somewhat differently worded remedy provisions as well as different timing provisions.

(b) Alibi Defense Provisions. Unlike the practice in civil pleadings, the criminal law traditionally has not required the defendant to plead specifically his defense. A plea of "not guilty" ordinarily brings into issue all possible defenses to the substantive charge. However, the federal system and more than forty states require the defendant to give advance notice of his intent to raise an alibi defense. Several characteristics of the alibi defense are said to make a more pressing case for advance notice of alibi than for most other defenses. These include: (1) alibi is a "hip pocket" defense, easily prepared for introduction in the final hours of trial and therefore more likely to catch the prosecutor by surprise; (2) a false alibi defense will be based on perjured testimony of third parties, which can be readily discouraged by affording the prosecution an opportunity to prepare for their testimony; (3) alibi requires an independent investigation by the prosecutor, and the failure to facilitate that investigation before trial will often necessitate a continuance during trial; and (4) alibi is the type of defense which will lead the prosecution to dismiss the charges if it determines from its pretrial investigation that the alibi witnesses are not lying.

Most alibi provisions are similar in procedure and scope to Federal Rule 12.1. Initially, the government must issue a demand for notification, stating therein the time, date, and place of the alleged offense. If the defendant intends to raise the defense, he is required to respond within a specified number of days. His response must state the specific place or places where he claims to have been at the time of the alleged offense and the names and addresses of the witnesses upon whom he intends to rely to establish his alibi. The prosecution is then required, within a specified period, to list those witnesses who will be used to establish the defendant's presence at the scene of the crime and any other witnesses who will be used to rebut the alibi defense. As with other discovery obligations, there is a continuing duty to disclose on both sides; if either side finds an additional witness that it intends to use, that person must be added to its list. For good cause shown, the trial court may grant an exception or modification to any of the above requirements. Good cause exceptions most often are requested by the prosecution on grounds similar to those that would justify a protective order under the general discovery provisions.

Federal Rule 12.1 also provides that "evidence of an intention to rely on an alibi defense, later withdrawn, or of a statement made in connection with that intention, is not * * * admissible against the person who gave notice of the intention."[1] Such provisions also have been viewed as prohibiting the prosecution from commenting upon the defendant's failure to call a listed witness in presenting the alibi defense at trial. Courts have held, however, that the notice of alibi can be used to impeach a defendant who testifies as to an alibi defense inconsistent with that contained in the notice of alibi. Here, the defendant has violated the notice requirement by failing to give notice of the alibi he is now claiming, and the court is allowing impeachment as a remedy.

(c) Insanity and Related Defenses. The federal system and almost all of the states have provisions requiring the defendant to give advance notice if he intends to rely upon the defense of insanity. In many states, as under Federal Rule 12.2(b), the obligation of notice is extended beyond insanity to encompass the introduction of expert testimony "relating to a mental disease or defect or any other mental condition of the defendant bearing on either (1) the issue of guilt or (2) the issue of punishment in a capital case." Such provisions have been held to apply to the use of psychiatric experts to support such defense

claims as diminished responsibility, "brain-washing," and the innate lack of aggressiveness needed to purposely place another in fear. Indeed, it seems unlikely that any psychiatric testimony would escape its reach except that which is utilized only as to non-capital sentencing.

Where the defendant enters a notice of insanity or other mental condition defense, he remains free to change his mind and proceed at trial with another defense. The prosecution is prohibited from using the withdrawn notice in any fashion. Although a few jurisdictions do allow a withdrawn notice of alibi to be used to impeach a defendant, notice on insanity is viewed as a different matter. It does not set forth a fact within the defendant's knowledge, but simply reflects a legal judgment as to the defendant's mental condition, a judgment which may be subject to reconsideration in light of additional psychiatric information. A similar restriction on uses applies to the court-ordered psychiatric exam to which the defendant must submit as a result of filing a notice of intent to raise an insanity defense. The responses given in any court-ordered psychiatric exam can be introduced only on the mental condition issues raised by the defense. Neither the defendant's statements during the examination, nor the fruits of those statements, can be used by the prosecutor in any other fashion. That safeguard is usually specified in the discovery provision, and it is held to follow, in any event, from the rationale underlying the acceptance of the court-ordered examination as consistent with the defendant's self-incrimination privilege.

(d) Identification of Defenses. Approximately a dozen states require the defendant to give notice in advance of trial of various defenses beyond alibi and insanity that defendant intends to raise at trial. These provisions sometimes are designed to encompass all defenses and sometimes are limited to a series of

§ 20.5

1. In a few states, lacking provisions like Rule 12.1, courts have suggested that prosecutors may use a withdrawn alibi notice to impeach a defendant who takes an inconsistent position in his trial testimony. As noted in § 20.5(a), Williams v. Florida was decided on the premise

that the notice of alibi there "in no way 'fixed' " the defendant's choice of defense, and allowing impeachment use in this fashion certainly has a "fixing" tendency. However, the *Williams* court also stated that it did "not mean to suggest * * * that such a procedure might necessarily raise serious constitutional problems."

enumerated offenses. Even when all defenses are included, the statutory provision may include an illustrative listing of the types of defenses which a defendant is expected to identify. Typical examples cited are a claim of authority (such as ownership of the property involved), the justifiable use of force, entrapment, duress, intoxication, and the lack of the requisite mens rea. The defense-notice provisions are interpreted as encompassing only those defense claims on which testimony will be offered. The defendant need not include matters on which the state's case simply will be challenged as insufficient on its face. The function of the defense-notice requirement is to make the prosecution aware of the areas as to which the defense is likely to introduce evidence and the prosecution therefore might need to look for rebuttal evidence.

Many of the jurisdictions requiring notification of defenses also mandate disclosure of witness lists (discussed in subsection (e) infra). The two discovery requirements are designed to supplement each other. Simply knowing the identity of the witnesses does not necessarily disclose the defense to which they will testify, and defense witnesses will not necessarily be willing to speak to the prosecution. The notice of defenses ensures that the prosecution will nonetheless have a general idea as to the subject of their testimony. Some jurisdictions provide even better notice in this regard by requiring disclosure of the recorded statements of defense witnesses or allowing discovery depositions of those witnesses. In light of the information available through that discovery, those jurisdictions commonly have found it unnecessary to also require a general notice of defenses.

(e) Witness Lists. Roughly half the states authorize court-ordered defense disclosure of the names and addresses of the witnesses that the defendant intends to introduce at trial. In some of these jurisdictions, the prosecution has an independent right to such discovery. In some, discovery is conditional upon the defense having first sought discovery, and in still others, the trial court has discretion as to whether to order witness-list disclosure. In all of the jurisdictions, the defendant is entitled to a listing of the witnesses that the prosecution intends to call.

The primarily legal question presented in the application of the witness-list provisions is what degree of likelihood as to calling a person as a witness creates an obligation to list that person. The defense has no obligation to list every person who has come to defense counsel's attention as a "possible witness," especially where counsel has not interviewed or otherwise confirmed that the person has helpful information. Indeed, to provide such a listing would often undercut the function of the notice requirement by forcing the prosecution to sift through a long list of potential witnesses. On the other hand, if the defense counsel knows that a person's testimony will support a point that the defense desires to make in challenging a prosecution witness, and it is "reasonably predictable" that the prosecution witness will deny that point, the defense cannot omit that person from its list because the prosecution witness might admit the point and the witness therefore would be unnecessary. The witness must be listed not only where the defense feels certain that the witness will be called, but also where it "reasonably anticipates it is likely to call" the witness.

(f) Witness Statements. More than a dozen states have provisions requiring defense disclosure of its recorded statements of the witnesses listed in its witness list. In general, a "recorded" statement for this purpose follows the Jencks Act definition, but some states utilize broader definitions that encompass written summaries of the witness' oral statement. In all jurisdictions requiring disclosure of recorded witness statements, the defendant has a right to receive from the prosecution the recorded statements, similarly defined, of the prosecution's witnesses.

As noted in § 20.4(b), the Supreme Court in *United States v. Nobles* rejected a self-incrimination objection to court-ordered disclosure at trial of a defense witness' recorded statement. At the same time, however, the Court laid the ground work for what has proven to be the major limitation upon the required pretrial disclosure of the recorded statements of defense witnesses. The defendant in *Nobles* also objected to the court order there on the basis of the work product doctrine, and while the Court rejected that claim, its analysis generally has been viewed as favorable to those opposing pretrial disclosure of a defense witness' recorded statement. The *Nobles* Court noted initially that the doctrine in the federal courts was not limited to reports prepared by defense counsel, but could also apply to a report written by a defense investigator. This would include the investigator's report on the interview of a prospective witness. The work product claim in *Nobles* ultimately failed, however, because of waiver. The protection of the doctrine had been waived as to that portion of the investigator's report covered by the investigator's testimony when the defense elected to have him testify.

Relying upon *Nobles*, several state courts have held that the work product doctrine bars pretrial disclosure of a defense witness' statement that was prepared by either counsel or an investigator working under the direction of counsel. While *Nobles* sustained disclosure based on the waiver that occurs once the witness testifies, the waiver doctrine cannot operate pretrial on the anticipation that the witness will testify at trial. The primary function of the work product rule, it is noted, is basically to protect against pretrial disclosure; it is such disclosure which permits the opposing attorney to build upon his opponent's efforts. Where the work product is extended so far as to preclude defense discovery of all prosecution internal memoranda (including police reports), a similar protection must be afforded to the defense, which includes its reports of witness' statements.

Other jurisdictions, including most of those with discovery provisions specifically requiring defense disclosure of its witnesses' statements, take a contrary position. Though acknowledging the need to preclude pretrial disclosure of the defense's work product, they view the *Nobles* concept of work product as overly broad. Since that concept was not constitutionally based, the states are free to reject it. In criminal cases, it is noted, the interest in reciprocal disclosure overrides the protection of

"fact" (i.e., non-opinion) work product. This is justified, in particular, where the pretrial discovery does no more than accelerate disclosure of the prior recorded statements of a defense witness that would otherwise become available to the prosecution at trial for use in impeaching the witness. However, it also is held to override the protection of fact work product as to the defense's recordation of interviews with prosecution witnesses in the few jurisdictions that require the defense to disclose the recorded statements in its possession of all persons who will testify at trial.

Courts rejecting a work product exemption to the required defense disclosure of the statements of witnesses do recognize a work product protection limited to the "opinions, theories, and conclusions" of defense counsel (and in some states, defense investigators as well). Thus, where the defense's recordation or summary of a statement goes beyond relating the words of the witness, including, for example, comments on the witness' appearance or demeanor, the defense counsel may redact those portions of the disclosed statement. If the prosecution questions the redaction, the court will review the unredacted record in camera to ensure that the redaction was appropriate.

(g) Documents and Tangible Objects. Almost all of the jurisdictions with general discovery provisions authorize prosecution discovery of documents and tangible objects which the defense intends to introduce in evidence. In some jurisdictions, the prosecution has an independent right to such discovery, while in others, discovery is conditioned on the defendant first requesting discovery from the prosecution. The types of items encompassed are the same as under similar provisions authorizing defense discovery of documents and tangible objects. The primary difference between the defense and prosecution provisions is that the prosecution's obligation to disclose often goes beyond items the prosecution intends to use as evidence.

(h) Scientific Reports. Almost all jurisdictions with general discovery provisions allow for prosecution discovery of reports and results of medical and physical examinations, scientific tests, and experiments made in connection with the particular case. Most of these provisions, like Federal Rule 16(b)(1), apply "only if the defendant intends to use the item in the defendant's case in chief at the trial or intends to call the witness who prepared the report and the report relates to the witness's testimony." While some courts would view as work product reports of experts prepared under the supervision of the defense counsel, the mental impressions of counsel will not be involved, and the interest in reciprocal disclosure will override any non-opinion work product protection, as in the case of the pretrial disclosure of the statements of defense witnesses.[2]

Defense discovery of scientific reports in the possession of the prosecution typically extends beyond that material the prosecution will use at trial. It commonly encompasses all reports and results on scientific tests and examinations made in connection with the case, whether or not they will be used at trial. Similar prosecution discovery from the defense may be available under occasional provisions that are broader than Federal Rule 16(b)(1) or under catch-all provisions allowing the trial court to order additional discovery as to items that are material and not otherwise available to the prosecution[3]. As discussed in § 20.4(f), such orders have been successfully challenged on Sixth Amendment grounds. Where the item sought is the interpretative report of an expert, rather than simply a test result, the attorney-client privilege may also come into play, depending upon the content of the report, the communications of the attorney or client to the expert, and the view of the privilege taken in the particular jurisdiction. Some limit that privilege to communications between the attorney and the client, and there-

fore would not include reports of experts, without regard to the nature of the communications relied upon by the expert. Other jurisdictions recognize that the privilege extends to experts acting as counsel's agent as to the defendant, but thereby limit the privilege to the communications the experts had with the client directly or with counsel who revealed private information coming from the client. A third position would include within the privilege the entire report of an expert who relied upon information from the client or attorney, including information from the attorney that was only indirectly derived from client communications. Even that broad view, however, will not cover the full range of experts that may be involved in criminal cases.

§ 20.6   Sanctions

(a) Range. Federal Rule 16(d)(2) provides that, "if a party fails to comply with Rule 16", the court may (1) order the party to permit discovery or inspection as specified by the court, (2) "grant a continuance", (3) "prohibit that party from introducing the undisclosed evidence," or (4) "enter any other order that is just under the circumstances." State statutes or court rules authorizing discovery contain similar provisions, and common law jurisdictions recognize that appropriate sanctions or remedies may be imposed as part of the trial court's inherent authority to order discovery. The measures noted in Rule 16(d)(2)—ordering immediate disclosure, granting a continuance, and excluding evidence—are the three most commonly imposed remedies. However, judicial opinions and statutory provisions also recognize several other sanctions or remedies, including (1) a charge directing the jury to assume certain facts that might have been established through the nondisclosed material,

---

2. See § 20.3(j) and 20.5(f).

3. The issues discussed below also arise, apart from discovery, where the prosecution learns on its own of an expert consulted by the defense who produced a report adverse to the defendant and seeks to have that expert testify as a prosecution witness. In addition to the Sixth Amendment and the attorney client privilege, such use may also be precluded by a privilege attending consultation with the particular expert (e.g., doctor/patient privilege) or a work product exemption. As to potential application of the work product exemption, see § 20.3(j) and

20.5(f). Some states deem the introduction of an insanity defense to constitute a waiver of privileges that might otherwise preclude prosecution use of a defense expert. They view the defendant's submission to examination by a state expert as insufficient to achieve a fair balance on the insanity issue, noting that the defense psychiatrist's examination has the advantage of a greater degree of cooperation by the defendant and often being closer in time to the offense.

(2) granting a mistrial, (3) holding in contempt the party responsible for the nondisclosure, and (4) dismissal of the prosecution.

Alibi-notice and insanity-notice statutes usually have their own sanction provisions, which sometimes appear to be more narrowly confined than the general discovery provisions. In several states, the alibi statute states that the trial court shall exclude the testimony of any unlisted witness "except for good cause shown." This language might arguably give the trial court less leeway in the selection of a sanction than the typical general discovery provision, which will merely note that the court "may enter such order as it deems just under the circumstances." However, the "good cause" language tends to be interpreted to provide essentially the same flexibility as is found in the general provisions. On the other hand, alibi-notice and insanity-notice provisions may contain explicit restrictions that bar the use of certain sanctions. Thus, alibi-notice provisions commonly provide that the exclusion sanction as to undisclosed alibi witnesses "shall not limit the right of the defendant to testify on his own behalf," and an insanity-notice provision may allow for exclusion only of expert witnesses.

(b) Prosecution Violations. *Violations discovered before or at trial.* Perhaps no defense claim relating to discovery is more frequently raised on appeal than the claim that the trial court failed to utilize the proper remedy when the defendant discovered shortly before or during trial that the prosecution had breached a discovery order. The claim usually relates to the prosecution's presentation of a witness who was not endorsed on its witness list or its introduction into evidence of a previously undisclosed statement of the defendant or a scientific report. On occasion, it will be based upon the late disclosure of discoverable material that was not used as prosecution evidence, but which might have been helpful to the defense, if disclosed earlier, in developing its own case or in impeaching a prosecution witness. The usual defense complaint is that the trial court should have excluded the evidence or declared a mistrial as opposed to granting some lesser remedy, such as simply

ordering immediate disclosure, or combining such disclosure with a brief continuance. Appellate courts frequently note that a trial court must be given "broad latitude" in its selection of an appropriate remedy. Nevertheless, they also have advanced certain guidelines for the exercise of that discretion, and reversals for the failure to follow those guidelines are not infrequent.

Once the trial court learns of the prosecution's non-compliance, it is expected initially to conduct an inquiry into the background, character, and impact of the nondisclosure. In some jurisdictions, the trial court's failure to conduct an appropriate inquiry (e.g., by not offering the defense counsel an opportunity to show possible prejudice) will constitute a sufficient ground in itself for an appellate reversal. Thus, if the trial court simply orders immediate disclosure without conducting an inquiry to assess whether other sanctions also are needed, the appellate court will automatically reverse a subsequent conviction, without attempting any post hoc determination as to whether other sanctions should have been ordered or whether the failure to utilize those sanctions might have had a bearing on the outcome of the trial. The standard directive to trial courts, in conducting the needed inquiry, is to "take into account the reasons why disclosure was made, the extent of prejudice, if any, to the opposing party [here the defendant], the feasibility of rectifying the prejudice by a continuance, and any other relevant circumstance."

In general, the concept of "prejudice" in this context is limited to an adverse impact upon the defense's ability to prepare and present its case. Some courts, moreover, will not give weight to all types of adverse impact. In particular, they will not consider harm to the defendant's presentation that flows from a defense choice of a strategy designed to mislead the jury. The function of discovery, these courts note, is to permit the defense to marshall its evidence so as to challenge the possible falsity of the prosecution's evidence. Prejudice, they argue, therefore should be limited to restrictions on the defense's capacity to present such a challenge, and should not encompass self-inflicted wounds resulting from the defendant's unsuccessful attempt to use a fabricated defense. Thus, where the prosecution negligently failed to disclose pretrial that it possessed a document written by defendant, and the defendant then gave apparently false testimony that was clearly contradicted by that document, the defense was not allowed to look to the harm it obviously suffered when the prosecution subsequently used the document to impeach the defendant. The court reasoned that, just as the unconstitutional seizure of evidence does not bar use of that evidence to impeach the defendant, a discovery violation should not bar impeachment use of defendant's own written statement simply because it was not disclosed in a timely fashion; the defendant knew fully well that the written statement existed and that it refuted his testimony, and he should not be allowed to claim harm based on his supposition that the prosecution was not aware of the written statement and that he therefore could contradict it with impunity.

Decisions holding that the prejudice element will not encompass the prosecution's contradiction of a fabricated defense through evidence that should have been disclosed pretrial have not dealt with instances of purposeful prosecutorial "sandbagging." The discovery violations involved could be characterized as resulting from negligence or good faith misreadings of discovery obligations. Arguably a different result would be reached where the defendant was lured into "ensnaring himself in his self-made trap" by a purposeful prosecutorial nondisclosure. Indeed, other courts have indicated that the defense should be viewed as prejudiced and entitled to relief whenever a position taken by the defense is contradicted by prosecution evidence that was not properly disclosed during pretrial discovery, even though the defendant was fully aware that reliable evidence contradicted that position and proceeded because he assumed that the prosecution was unaware of that evidence. These courts note that while defendant has no right to fabricate a defense, the purpose of discovery is to avoid "trial by surprise," and to simply allow the trial to proceed, with the defense suffering from a presentation it would not have made with proper discovery, is to undercut that objective. While it would be inappropriate to bar impeachment use of the previously nondisclosed evidence and thus allow what appears to be false testimony to stand, the court may utilize a remedy that would restore the parties to where they would have been if timely disclosure had been made as required by the discovery rules—declaring a mistrial and disallowing prosecution use at the second trial of the defendant's inconsistent testimony of the first trial.

Very often, the discovery violation is called to the attention of the trial court during the prosecution's case-in-chief. Commonly, the prosecution will attempt to introduce a document or a witness that was not noted in pretrial discovery, with either the prosecutor acknowledging a discovery violation or the court determining that disclosure should have been given under the general discovery provision or the court's specific discovery directive. At other times, the defense will learn in cross-examining the witness that there exists some relevant evidence that should have been made available to it under the applicable discovery standard. The likely prejudice here ordinarily flows from the defense lacking sufficient time to digest and prepare either to meet or to use the previously undisclosed evidence. Many courts therefore view the continuance as playing a critical role in assessing the potential for prejudice. Indeed the preferred remedy, at least where the prosecution has acted in good faith, is to order immediate compliance with discovery requirements, and offer the defense a continuance so that it can take advantage of the delayed discovery.

Where the defense is truly surprised, it will be expected to demand a continuance or at least accept a court offer of a continuance. Thus, the lack of a demand, or the rejection of the trial court's offer, is often taken as strong evidence that the discovery violation has not been prejudicial. Where a demand for a continuance is made, that tends to support the defense claim of likely prejudice, but it is not conclusive. Courts recognize that continuances are not always needed, and defendants may seek a continuance for purposes unrelated to true surprise (including imposing pressure on the trial court to look to the alternative of a mistrial where the continuance would not be convenient). Accordingly, a trial court is not forced to grant a continuance request, but it must have a sound basis for concluding that the defense will be able to present its case as effectively notwithstanding the lack of earlier notice of the previously undisclosed evidence.

Courts also recognize that there are occasions in which a continuance will not eliminate potential prejudice even though the previously undisclosed evidence comes to light during the prosecution's case-in-chief. The defense may already have committed itself—in opening statement or in cross-examination—to a line of attack that it would not have utilized if aware of the undisclosed testimony. Such a defense predicament is not limited to the situations discussed above in which the defendant sought to fabricate a defense later shown to be false by evidence that should have been disclosed pretrial. It can also arise when the prosecution is now coming forward with previously undisclosed evidence filling gaps in its case that had been the focus of the defense's initial challenge to the prosecution's proof. While the defense here is not placed in the embarrassing position of having the defendant's testimony revealed to be false, it still suffers from the impression that it simply is fishing for a line of attack, shifting its challenge from one unfounded ground to another. Where the circumstances clearly could convey that impression to the jury, the court may be forced to recognize that the continuance will be a less than complete remedy, and that the potential prejudice to the defense can be eliminated only by a mistrial or by precluding the use of the new evidence. The defense, however, cannot readily characterize a discovery violation as presenting such irreversible prejudice merely by offering speculative theories as to how its challenge might have differed if it had learned earlier of all information that is only now being disclosed.

Consistent with their advice to trial courts to first look to the continuance as a remedy,

appellate courts frequently warn against the unnecessary use of the preclusion sanction. The trial court, it is noted, "should seek to apply sanctions that affect the evidence at trial and the merits of the case as little as possible." Sanctions generally should not have "adverse effects on the rights of the parties rather than the offending attorneys themselves," and preclusion necessarily has such an adverse effect on the interests of the community, the party represented by the prosecutor. Accordingly, some courts treat preclusion as a remedy that should be available only where there was actual prejudice and where no other remedy will respond adequately to that prejudice. It is a "remedy of last resort," to be used only where absolutely needed. That may sometimes be the case, however, because of the prejudicial costs to the defense resulting from a continuance, such as a delay that would impact defendant's right to a speedy trial or a delay that would require a mistrial and thereby deprive the defendant of his interest in proceeding with the already selected jury.

Other jurisdictions, while viewing preclusion as a remedy to be used sparingly, will not place the trial court in a position where it can exclude previously undisclosed evidence only upon finding that lesser sanctions could not eliminate the prejudice to the defense. Here, the trial court is given considerably greater leeway. It may, for example, chose preclusion over a continuance where a continuance is deemed to impose substantial burdens on an already congested docket or the continuance simply would not provide the same degree of assurance that the prejudice would be eliminated. Prosecution bad faith might also justify selection of preclusion over a continuance even though the continuance would be equally effective in responding to a prejudicial impact.

The jurisdictions also are divided as to the possible use of preclusion simply as a deterrent, without regard to the presence of prejudice. Some courts would allow such use where the trial court finds that the discovery violation was intentional or reflects a recurring disregard for discovery obligations. These courts view exclusion as offering the same prophylactic impact in the enforcement of discovery rules as the exclusion of illegally seized evidence offers in the enforcement of the Fourth Amendment. Indeed, a few courts have gone beyond that position and approved the use of a dismissal with prejudice to respond to glaring prosecutorial discovery violations that suggest either gross negligence or purposeful misconduct. Other jurisdictions would allow exclusion to be used only where needed to respond to prejudice. Similarly, dismissal would be allowed only where the prosecution is ordered to provide discovery as to a certain item and prefers dismissal to complying with the court's order. Where the trial court believes that there is need for a deterrent measure, it is directed to make use of contempt orders directed against the offending prosecutor. A sanction, they note, should "not be regarded as a bonus awarded without regard to its need in the furtherance of fair trial rights."

Violations discovered post-trial. When the prosecution has an obligation to disclose information or matter other than that which it will use at trial, its failure to comply with that discovery obligation may be uncovered only after the trial is completed. Thus, the defense may learn only after the defendant was convicted that the prosecution had violated its duty to disclose prior recorded statements of a witness or scientific tests which were made in connection with the case but not used at trial. At this point, the analysis adopted in determining the appropriate remedy is somewhat different than that applied to a discovery violation uncovered shortly before or during trial. Standard remedies like ordering immediate disclosure and providing a continuance or excluding evidence no longer are available. The issue before the court is whether the defendant's conviction must be overturned and a new trial granted, with the defense now having the benefit of the discovery to which it is entitled.

Since the undisclosed discoverable matter was not used by the prosecution at trial, the defense is likely to argue that it would have had an exculpatory rather than incriminating

potential. This brings into consideration the possibility of a violation of the prosecutor's constitutional obligation under *Brady v. Maryland* to disclose exculpatory evidence.[1] While the *Brady* doctrine often does not mandate pretrial disclosure, it does require that exculpatory evidence which meets the requisite test of materiality at least be disclosed at trial. Accordingly, a court ruling on a discovery violation uncovered only after trial must first determine whether there also has been a *Brady* violation, which would require a new trial as a matter of due process. If it is determined that the nondisclosure did not constitute a *Brady* violation, then whether a new trial will be granted is said to rest on a balancing of the likely prejudice to the defense against "the extent of the Government's culpability" for its failure to have complied with the discovery rules. Since the court has already determined that the nondisclosed information was not sufficiently exculpatory to establish a *Brady* violation, the potential for prejudice is not likely to be substantial enough to require relief where the government's omission was "merely inadvertent or negligent." On the other hand, if the nondisclosed matter was potentially favorable, though not so significant as to meet the *Brady* standard of materiality, that potential may well be sufficient to require a new trial where the failure to disclose was "deliberate" or the result of "gross negligence." Especially where the government's action reflects a bad-faith attempt to gain a tactical advantage, the court may prefer to give the defendant "the benefit of the doubt" rather than "let the Government reap even a slight possibility of benefit" from its wrongdoing.

Lost or destroyed evidence. Where the government's failure to disclose stems from the loss or destruction of discoverable material, the motivation of the responsible government officials may again be controlling in determining what sanctions, if any, should apply. As a matter of due process, the loss or destruction of evidence by police or prosecutor presents a constitutional violation only where the evidence had an apparent exculpatory value distinct from comparable evidence reasonably

§ 20.6

1. See § 24.3(b).

available to the defendant and its loss or destruction was the product of a "bad faith" failure to preserve evidence known to be potentially exculpatory.[2] States are free, however, to impose a less rigorous standard based on the violation of the government's obligations under the law of discovery.

Initially, there is general agreement that the prosecution's duty to disclose carries with it an obligation to preserve material within its possession that is clearly relevant and discoverable. The prosecution's failure to meet this obligation, however, differs in two important respects from other discovery violations. First, since the nondisclosed material cannot be produced for inspection, it may be difficult to ascertain what its value to the defendant would have been. Second, the sanctions imposed must necessarily be much more severe than those imposed when the nondisclosed evidence is still available. Here the failure to disclose cannot be remedied by a continuance or even a new trial. Ordinarily, the only remedies available are dismissal of the prosecution or, if the nondisclosed evidence would have been relevant only to challenge particular evidence of the prosecution, exclusion of that evidence. In light these distinctions, courts note their preference for a "pragmatic balancing approach" in determining whether the loss or destruction of discoverable material requires the imposition of sanctions.

One factor given substantial weight is the character the government's culpability for the loss or destruction. If the evidence was destroyed for the very purpose of hindering the defense, such conscious impropriety creates an inference in itself that the matter was *Brady* material, and its destruction constituted a due process violation. Accordingly, cases considering the appropriateness of imposing sanctions under the discovery rules, apart from due process requirements, are more likely to involve negligent loss or intentional destruction without any bad-faith motivation. Where the loss was inadvertent, and did not involve gross negligence, discovery sanctions are not likely to be imposed. On the other hand, where the

destruction is deliberate, although not suggesting the "evil motive" or "foul play" needed for a due process violation, some courts hold that "sanctions will normally follow, * * * unless the Government can bear the heavy burden of demonstrating that no prejudice resulted to defendant." That burden may be met, for example, by a showing from related evidence that there is "no reason to believe" that the destroyed material "would have been favorable to the defense." Other courts, however, will not shift the burden to the government simply because the destruction was deliberate. The defendant still must show that "he was prejudiced by the loss or the destruction of the evidence."

(c) Defense Violations. In many jurisdictions, the judicial treatment of sanctions is quite similar for discovery violations by both the defense and the prosecution. Of course, differences will exist as to violations first uncovered after trial, due to the prosecutor's quite different procedural posture in the post-verdict setting. Unlike the defense, if the trial resulted in an adverse verdict to the prosecution (i.e., an acquittal), the prosecution will not be able to challenge that verdict even if it can be attributed in part to the defense's discovery violation. At this point, the only sanction available to the court will be holding the responsible person in contempt if the violation was purposeful.

Where the defense's discovery violation is brought to the court's attention before or during trial, the court can look to the same sanctions that are imposed for prosecution violations. The one major distinction is the bearing of the Sixth Amendment upon the sanction of precluding defense use of the evidence that it should have disclosed pretrial under its discovery obligations. The Supreme Court in *Williams v. Florida*[3] had no need to determine whether the alibi-notice statute at issue there constitutionally could be enforced by excluding a witness who had not been listed during pretrial disclosure as required by the discovery rules. The Court did answer that question,

---

2. See § 24.3(e).

3. See § 20.4 at note 1.

however, in *Taylor v. Illinois*.[4] Although *Taylor* rejected the contention that the preclusion sanction constituted a per se violation of the defendant's Sixth Amendment right to compulsory process and upheld the sanction as applied in the circumstances of that case, it also indicated that the preclusion sanction might not be used against the defendant quite as freely as some courts have allowed it to be used against the prosecution.

Taylor involved the exclusion of the testimony of a defense witness after defendant had failed to list that witness in responding to a prosecution discovery request (the state discovery rule authorizing the request itself not being challenged). The facts there, as recounted by the Court, revealed a clear discovery violation by a counsel who sought to mislead the trial judge, apparently in a last ditch effort to gain admission of dubious testimony that might save a failing defense. After having listed four witnesses in response to a prosecution discovery request for a listing of all defense witnesses, and having called only two of those witnesses, who testified favorably but were obviously afraid of the defendant, defense counsel, on the second day of trial, sought to add two additional witnesses. Defense counsel initially claimed that he had just been informed about the witnesses and that they had probably seen the shooting incident upon which the charge against defendant was based. Responding to an inquiry by the trial judge, counsel then acknowledged that defendant had told him about the witnesses, but said he had been unable previously to locate one of them (Wormley). The judge then directed counsel to bring both witnesses to court on the next day, at which time he would decide whether they could testify. Counsel appeared the next day only with witness Wormley, who was then voir dired in an offer of proof. Wormley's testimony revealed that he had been visited by counsel during the week before the trial began, and that he had not actually seen the shooting incident. He stated that prior to the incident, he had "run into" the defendant and had warned him that the victim was armed and

after the defendant (although he also stated on cross-examination that he had first "met" the defendant over two years later). The trial judge concluded initially that the failure to list the witness was a "blatant" and "willful" violation and exclusion would be required. He also noted: "For whatever value it is, because this is a jury trial, I have a great deal of doubt in my mind as to the veracity of this young man."

The Supreme Court in *Taylor* initially rejected the claim of the defendant that the compulsory process clause established an "absolute bar" to the exclusion of a witness. While it was true that that clause embraced the right to have the witness' testimony heard (and not simply the right to compel the witness' attendance by subpoena), that right was not without limits (as evidenced by the fact "the accused does not have an unfettered right to offer testimony that is incompetent, privileged, or otherwise inadmissible under standard rules of evidence"). Indeed, in *Nobles*,[5] the Court had upheld the exclusion of the testimony of a defense witness where the defense refused to comply with an order to disclose the witness' prior recorded statement. *Nobles* had reasoned that exclusion was an appropriate sanction since the defense's refusal had restricted the prosecution's opportunity for effective cross-examination of the witness. The petitioner Taylor argued that the exclusion of an unlisted witness was different, since "a less drastic sanction" would always be available: where a disclosure is made, though late, prejudice to the prosecution "[can] be minimized by granting a continuance or mistrial * * * [and] further violations can be deterred by disciplinary sanctions against the defendant or defense counsel." The Court responded that, while "it may well be true that alternative sanctions are adequate and appropriate in most cases * * *, it is equally clear that they would be less effective than the preclusion sanction" and would sometimes "perpetuate rather than limit the prejudice to the State." A primary purpose of discovery rules, the Court reasoned, is to "minimize the

---

4. 484 U.S. 400, 108 S.Ct. 646, 98 L.Ed.2d 798 (1988).

5. See § 20.4 at note 3.

risk that fabricated testimony will be believed." Quite often, it is "reasonable to presume that there is something suspect about a defense witness who is not identified until after the eleventh hour has passed." Where "a pattern of discovery violations is explicable only on the assumption that the violations were designed to conceal a plan to present fabricated testimony, it would be entirely appropriate to exclude the tainted evidence regardless of whether other sanctions would also be merited."

To reject petitioner's claim "that preclusion is never a permissible sanction," the Court noted, it was "neither necessary nor appropriate * * * to attempt to draft a comprehensive set of standards to guide the exercise of discretion" as to the permissible use of that sanction. It was sufficient to recognize that, while "a trial court may not ignore the fundamental character" of the defendant's right to present evidence, the "mere invocation of that right cannot automatically and invariably outweigh countervailing public interests." Also to be "weigh[ed] in the balance" were: "the integrity of the adversary process, which depends both on the presentation of reliable evidence and the rejection of unreliable evidence; the interest in the fair and efficient administration of justice; and the potential prejudice to the truth-determining function of the trial process." Thus, where the defense failed to comply with a discovery requirement and "that omission was willful and motivated by a desire to obtain a tactical advantage that would minimize the effectiveness of cross-examination and the ability to adduce rebuttal testimony, it would be entirely consistent with the purposes of the Confrontation Clause simply to exclude the witness' testimony." Also "relevant" in this regard was the "simplicity of compliance with the discovery rule," as the burden of compliance "adds little" to the routine demands of trial preparation that naturally fall upon defense counsel.

Turning to the case before it, the Court also found unpersuasive the defendant's claim that preclusion was unnecessarily harsh since the

trial court, prior to applying the sanction, had conducted a voir dire examination of the unlisted witness which "adequately protected the prosecution from any possible prejudice resulting from surprise." "More is at stake," the Court noted, "than possible prejudice to the prosecution." Also of concern was "the impact of this conduct on the integrity of the judicial process itself." Here, the judge found that the defense counsel's failure to list the witness was "both willful and blatant." Thus, "regardless of whether prejudice to the prosecution could have been avoided * * *, it [was] plain that the case fits into the category of willful misconduct in which the severest sanction is appropriate." The Court also rejected the contention, strongly advanced by the dissent, that exclusion was inappropriate because defendant had not participated in the discovery violation and the "sins of the lawyer" should not be visited on his client. The Court responded that the right involved here was not one of those which could be waived only with the consent of the client and given the "protections afforded by the attorney-client privilege * * *, it would be highly impracticable to require an investigation into the * * * relative responsibilities [of attorney and client] before applying the sanction of preclusion."[6]

The *Taylor* opinion arguably raises as many questions as it answers. At the least, it lacks the kind of clear directive that is necessary to shape a lower court consensus on the bounds of the constitutionally permissible use of the preclusion sanction. Lower courts have had the least difficulty with cases that fit the *Taylor* description of a "willful [violation] * * * motivated by a desire to obtain a tactical advantage." Such willful misconduct is seen as sufficient in itself to justify the preclusion sanction. It calls upon the combined judicial interests of deterring willful violations of discovery rules and avoiding a possible affront to the integrity of the trial process through the offering of probably perjured testimony.

Some courts suggest that the tactically motivated willful violation may be the only situation in which preclusion is constitutionally ac-

---

6. See also note 3 of § 11.6.

ceptable. Others, noting the broad range of interests cited by *Taylor* as relevant to the constitutional balancing process, have looked to several additional factors that may justify imposing the preclusion sanction. They would consider the degree of fault in the violation that was not intentional (asking, for example, whether the discovery requirement was clear and whether compliance was relatively simple), the degree of prejudice suffered by the prosecution, the impact of preclusion upon the total evidentiary showing (including consideration of factors suggesting that the precluded evidence is unreliable), and the degree of effectiveness of less severe sanctions. Arguably also, at least in certain contexts, the extent of the defendant's personal responsibility for the omission also would be considered. The balance struck by reference to these factors could conceivably justify preclusion in a case that did not involve a willful violation designed to gain a tactical advantage.

Of course, a state may prohibit the use of the preclusion sanction even where its use would be permissible under the Sixth Amendment, and some state courts have done exactly that. They view judicial adoption of a "conscious mandatory distortion of the fact-finding process" as especially inappropriate where the risk taken (by excluding evidence that defendant claims to be exculpatory) is the possible conviction of the innocent. Accordingly, they allow use of the preclusion sanction only where the prosecution shows an actual prejudice attributable to the defense's discovery violation which cannot be cured by any other remedy.

One limitation commonly found in state law is the prohibition against excluding the defendant's own alibi testimony even where there has been a purposeful violation of the requirement of advance notification as to alibi witnesses. This limitation also has been adopted by courts on their own initiative. The exemption of the defendant's own testimony from the exclusion sanction has been justified on various grounds. Allowing the defendant himself to testify as to the alibi, even though the prosecution did not receive advance notice and therefore is limited to on-the-spot cross-examination, is seen as having a limited prejudicial impact upon the prosecution. Initially, the surprise element is not the same as when the defense presents some other witness previously unknown to the prosecution. The prosecution is aware that the defendant might testify and should be prepared to challenge his credibility. Moreover, the defense must overcome a significant credibility hurdle in presenting an otherwise unsupported alibi. As one court put it: "The optimistic defendant who hopes to convince the jury through his own unsupported testimony that he was not in the vicinity of the crime has sufficient credibility problems to offset any disadvantage to the state from surprise." Another grounding is that the defendant's right to testify requires greater protection than his right to present the testimony of others, as it has significance beyond the content of his testimony. It is also argued that the exclusion of the defendant's own testimony has greater impact with respect to the alibi defense itself. Where only other witnesses are excluded, the defendant is not barred entirely from presenting the defense, as he can testify himself. If the preclusion sanction is extended to the defendant as well, then the defense simply cannot be presented.

Chapter 21

PLEAS OF GUILTY

Table of Sections

§ 21.1   The Plea Negotiation System

(a) Forms of Plea Bargaining. In the United States, the great majority of criminal cases are disposed of by plea of guilty rather than by trial. Sometimes this plea is the result of nothing more than implicit plea bargaining in that the defendant enters his plea merely because it is generally known that this is the route to a lesser sentence. But more common is explicit bargaining in which the defendant enters a plea of guilty only after a commitment has been made that concessions will be granted (or at least sought) in his particular case.

One common form of plea negotiation consists of an arrangement whereby the defendant and prosecutor agree that the defendant should be permitted to plead guilty to a charge less serious than is supported by the evidence. There are several reasons why this kind of "deal" may seem advantageous to the defendant. For one, the less serious offense is likely to carry a lower statutory maximum penalty than the offense actually committed, so that the defendant has an assurance at the time of his plea that the judge's sentencing discretion will be limited. Or, the plea to the lesser offense may instead maximize the judge's sentencing discretion; by his plea, the defendant may avoid a high statutory minimum sentence or a statutory bar to probation. A third reason why defendants bargain as to the charge is to avoid a record of conviction on the offense actually committed. Sometimes the desire is to avoid a repugnant conviction label, as where a defendant charged with a sex offense is permitted to plead to the nondescript charge of disorderly conduct. On other occasions, the purpose is to avoid conviction on a felony charge, which would carry with it certain undesirable collateral consequences (e.g., loss of certain civil rights, loss of eligibility for certain types of employment).

A second form of plea bargaining involves an agreement whereby the defendant pleads "on the nose," that is, to the original charge, in exchange for some kind of promise from the prosecutor concerning the sentence to be imposed. The prosecutor may agree in a general way to seek leniency, or he may promise to ask for some specific disposition, such as probation. On occasion the prosecutor may do no more than promise that he will refrain from making any recommendation to the judge, or that he will not oppose a request for leniency put to the judge by the defendant. Or, the prosecutor may be so bold as to promise a certain sentence upon a guilty plea, a promise he may know he can fulfill because of the trial judge's practice of following the prosecutor's recommendations. Sentence bargaining carries with it a somewhat greater risk than charge bargaining, as there remains some possibility (slight in most locales) that in this case the trial judge will not follow the prosecutor's recommendations.

Another form of plea negotiation is the on-the-nose plea of guilty to one charge in exchange for the prosecutor's promise to drop or not to file other charges. Multiple charges, either actual or potential, against a single defendant are not uncommon; a single criminal episode may involve violation of several separate provisions of the applicable criminal code, or investigation of the defendant may show that he was responsible for several unrelated crimes (e.g., several burglaries committed in the course of many months). This kind of bargain is most likely to be illusory, in that multiple charges are seldom brought against the defendant who does not plead guilty, and, if brought, often result in concurrent sentencing.

(b) Development of Plea Bargaining. The practice of plea bargaining, though not limited exclusively to the United States, is doubtless more firmly established here than in any other country. It began to appear during the early or mid-nineteenth century, and became institutionalized as a standard feature of American urban criminal courts in the last third of the nineteenth century. One common explanation is that plea bargaining came about and exists because of crowded court dockets. But this is certainly not the only reason, for plea negotiation practices have developed at times and places where there was no serious court congestion. Other important reasons why the plea negotiation system has reached its present proportions in this country are: (1) the rise of professional police and prosecutors who developed and selected their cases more carefully, so that there are relatively few genuine disputes over guilt or innocence left to be resolved by juries; (2) the rise of specialization and professionalism on the defense side and broadening of the right to counsel, meaning that many more defendants had counsel and that those attorneys appreciated they could be of assistance to their clients at the pretrial stage; (3) changes in the jury trial process from a relatively simple proceeding to one so cumbersome and expensive that our society refuses to provide it; (4) the due process revolution, which made additional demands on the prosecutor's office in pretrial and post-conviction proceedings and gave the defendant additional rights strengthening his bargaining position; (5) the expansion of the substantive criminal law, and in particular new criminal legislation that did not always have the full weight of the community behind it; and (6) the desire of prosecutors and judges to reach a sentence that, in their view, would be more appropriate for the needs of the individual offender than that otherwise permissible under rigid sentencing statutes. Some years ago, there was a widely held view that prosecutors never bargain, but in recent times the practice has become highly visible, and the United States Supreme Court has now upheld the practice as necessary and proper.[1]

(c) Administrative Convenience. The most commonly asserted justification of plea bargaining is its utility in disposing of large numbers of cases in a quick and simple way. The assumption is that the system can function only if a high percentage of cases are disposed of by guilty plea and that this will happen only if concessions are granted to induce pleas. So the argument goes, our present criminal justice system is "based on the premise that approximately 90 per cent of all defendants will plead guilty, leaving only 10 per cent, more or less, to be tried," meaning that even a small reduction in the percentage of pleas received would have a tremendous impact. "A reduction from 90 per cent to 80 per cent in guilty pleas requires the assignment of twice the judicial manpower and facilities— judges, court reporters, bailiffs, clerks, jurors and courtrooms."[2]

One view is that society should and can pay the price for whatever increase in the number of trials would be brought about by ending plea bargaining. But it has sometimes been questioned whether an increase in funding and staffing for this purpose would, in the broad view of things, be beneficial. Even if the money were readily available, it is unclear that we could call upon sufficient numbers of competent personnel. Moreover, funds and personnel might be diverted from other segments of the criminal process where they are needed.

The issue is further complicated by the fact that it is unclear whether bringing plea negotiations to an end would significantly increase the burdens on the criminal justice system. Some argue that eliminating plea bargaining would eliminate the incentive for prosecutors to overcharge or otherwise inappropriately charge, meaning defendants would plead guilty in the many cases in which they and their attorneys conclude that the prosecutor's charge reflects the likely result at trial. It has also been contended that barring plea bargaining would lift those burdens attributable to bargaining: defense strategies whose only utility lies in the threat they pose to the court's and the prosecutor's time.

(d) Accurate and Fair Results. Another concern expressed about the plea negotiation system is that, by its nature, it is likely to produce unfair or inaccurate results. The objection is that the disposition of cases is influenced by factors irrelevant to the correctional

§ 21.1

1. E.g., Bordenkircher v. Hayes, 434 U.S. 357, 98 S.Ct. 663, 54 L.Ed.2d 604 (1978), Santobello v. New York, 404 U.S. 257, 92 S.Ct. 495, 30 L.Ed.2d 427 (1971).

2. Address of Chief Justice Burger at ABA Annual Convention, N.Y. Times, Aug. 11, 1970, p. 24, col. 4.

needs of the defendant or the requirements of law enforcement, such as court and prosecutor workload or the aggressiveness of the lawyers, so that either of two undesirable consequences may occur: (1) a serious offender may escape with undeserved leniency; or (2) an innocent person may be convicted.

The possibility of the first of these consequences is somewhat greater in those urban centers where the pressures to move the docket are most intense. Criticism of plea bargaining on this ground is sometimes made by the police, but it is often difficult to ascertain whether excessive leniency actually exists in a particular jurisdiction. As for the second of these consequences, the fear is that even an innocent person might be tempted to plead guilty and receive the tendered concessions rather than risk conviction at trial and a more severe penalty. But we just do not know how common such a situation is, nor do we know how often innocent persons are convicted at trial. The latter possibility must also be taken into account here if the matter is to be kept in proper perspective, for the significant question is whether there is a likelihood that innocent people who would be (or have a fair chance of being) acquitted at trial might be induced to plead guilty.

Indeed, it has been argued that in some instances plea negotiation leads to more intelligent results than could be obtained at trial. The premise is that the categories of guilt and innocence are not always simple and clear-cut, that instead of a black-or-white dichotomy there are many gray areas at the boundaries of criminal culpability. This being so, the reasoning proceeds, in a case in which the defendant's conduct falls into one of these gray areas it is preferable to achieve an intermediate judgment via plea bargaining than to undertake a trial at which only an all or nothing result is possible. Thus, because the line between responsibility and irresponsibility due to insanity is not as sharp as the alternatives posed to a jury would suggest, some view it not at all irrational that a negotiated compromise might be reached in a case in which the defen-

dant, charged with murder, has raised an insanity defense that might or might not succeed at trial. Others find it inconceivable that whatever is at stake in the insanity defense should be left to defendants and prosecutors to negotiate away.

The notion that a bargained plea may produce a fairer result is grounded in the supposition that the flexibility of plea bargaining as a dispositional device has substantial advantages over the formal rigidities of the jury trial. Opponents of plea bargaining offer two responses to this. One is that unjustifiably harsh provisions in the substantive law can be avoided without plea bargaining by the simple expedient of more careful and considerate initial charge selection. The other, doubtless unappealing to the defendants who would be sacrificed, is that unjustifiably harsh and otherwise unavoidable provisions of the substantive criminal law should be applied strictly in order to influence changes in the formal law producing greater flexibility.

(e) The Problem of Disparity. Because the plea negotiation system is grounded in the granting of concessions in exchange for guilty pleas, it raises the fundamental question of whether the fact that the defendant has pleaded guilty should have any legitimate bearing on the punishment he receives. The issue is exposed by the case of *People v. Snow*,[3] where the defendant, tried and convicted of prison escape by a jury, received a sentence of 2 to 5 years. On appeal he showed that of 234 prison escape cases in the county over a 26–month period, 207 pled guilty and (except in 5 cases where aggravated circumstances were present) received minimum sentences of one and a half years or less, while 13 were tried by a jury and (except in one case in which the defendant entered a guilty plea during trial) received sentences of two years or more. The court concluded that because "in the usual escape case a minimum sentence of 1½ years has been deemed appropriate by the sentencing judge" and "examination of the record in this case fails to reveal a single fact that would place this defendant in a different category," the

---

3.   386 Mich. 586, 194 N.W.2d 314 (1972).

case should be remanded for resentencing. But, while *Snow* thus seems to view sentencing concessions for pleas to be improper, the courts generally do not take this view, and certainly the Supreme Court's excursions into the plea bargaining area lend little support to the *Snow* position.[4]

One view is that dispositional disparity between guilty plea and trial defendants, arising out of and essential to a plea negotiation system, is proper so long as it is achieved without being unduly harsh to the latter category of defendants. Thus, it is argued that it is proper for guilty plea defendants to receive concessions so long as a court does not impose any sentence in excess of that which would be justified by any of the protective, deterrent, or other purposes of the criminal law upon a defendant who has chosen to require the prosecution to prove guilt at trial rather than to enter a plea of guilty. Others object that the normal sentence is the average sentence for all defendants, so that if we are lenient toward those who plead guilty we are by precisely the same token more severe toward those who do not.

The disparity in treatment of guilty plea and trial defendants has sometimes been explained on the ground that the circumstances of a trial are often such as to justify a more severe sanction than would have been imposed had the defendant entered a guilty plea. Thus a defendant who goes to trial may be punished more severely because the brutal circumstances of the crime are more vividly portrayed if there is a trial. Others argue that this is not a valid reason because if these circumstances are relevant to sentencing they should be revealed in the presentence report of a pleading defendant. A second reason why a defendant who goes to trial may receive a higher sentence is because the judge is convinced he committed perjury in the course of his defense. In *United States v. Grayson*,[5] the Supreme Court held that perjury by the defendant has a proper bearing on the sentence to be imposed and that consideration of it by the judge does

not infringe upon the defendant's right to testify on his own behalf. More troublesome is a third and broader reason given in the survey, that a higher sentence is justified when the defendant has presented a frivolous defense. Some object that a defendant whose punishment has been increased for demanding what the court considers a useless trial is in effect being penalized for asserting his constitutional rights.

Still another approach is to explain the disparity in terms of factors likely to call for leniency when a guilty plea is entered. There is considerable disagreement, however, as to the legitimacy of various factors that have been put forward, as may be best seen by examining the list of six factors in the original ABA Standards:[6]

"(i) that the defendant by his plea has aided in ensuring the prompt and certain application of correctional measures to him." Although this factor is fully consistent with the long-standing principle that punishment need not be as severe if it is certain and prompt in application, it has been criticized because of its universal applicability to all guilty pleas. It was omitted from the reformulated Standards on the ground that standing alone this factor is not sufficient to justify lesser punishment.

"(ii) that the defendant has acknowledged his guilt and shown a willingness to assume responsibility for his conduct." This factor is consistent with accepted sentencing criteria, which emphasize the relevance of the attitudes of the defendant and his willingness to assume responsibility for his actions. But its use has been criticized on the ground that because of plea bargaining guilty pleas are often tendered for reasons other than repentance and that it is not feasible to distinguish the truly repentant from those merely bargaining in the marketplace.

"(iii) that the concessions will make possible alternative correctional measures which are better adapted to achieving rehabilitative, pro-

---

4. See cases discussed in § 21.2.

5. 438 U.S. 41, 98 S.Ct. 2610, 57 L.Ed.2d 582 (1978), also discussed in § 26.4 at note 8.

6. ABA Standards Relating to Pleas of Guilty § 1.8(a) (Approved Draft, 1968).

tective, deterrent or other purposes of correctional treatment, or will prevent undue harm to the defendant from the form of conviction." Some support this notion that plea bargaining can provide needed flexibility, especially when the judge's sentencing discretion is unduly limited. It has been objected, however, that whatever concessions are appropriate in this respect could be achieved without exacting the plea in exchange for the concession. But sometimes the concession is possible only if there is a plea because it would be unavailable if at a trial the true legal nature of defendant's conduct were established.

"(iv) that the defendant has made public trial unnecessary when there are good reasons for not having the case dealt with in a public trial." Illustrative are cases in which the defendant by his plea has made unnecessary a rape or indecent liberties trial at which the victim would have to testify or an espionage trial at which secret information would have to be disclosed. But there is some authority that this is not a legitimate sentencing consideration.

"(v) that the defendant has given or offered cooperation when such cooperation has resulted or may result in the successful prosecution of other offenders engaged in equally serious or more serious criminal conduct." The notion here is that if complete immunity can be granted in exchange for testimony, as is sometimes essential as a Fifth Amendment matter, then surely "partial immunity" by sentencing concessions is appropriate. It has sometimes been asserted that this is not a factor properly taken into account at sentencing, but the Supreme Court has decided otherwise.[7]

"(vi) that the defendant by his plea has aided in avoiding delay (including delay due to crowded dockets) in the disposition of other cases and thereby has increased the probability of prompt and certain application of correctional measures to other offenders." This factor reflects the view that in localities with a significant court congestion problem, guilty plea defendants as a class make a meaningful contribution toward the attainment of the objectives of the criminal justice system, and thus are entitled to concessions because they have increased both the proximity and probability of punishment for other defendants. But this provision is omitted from the reformulated standards on the ground that the solution for crowded criminal dockets is the availability of sufficient personnel and other resources.

It has been forcefully argued that plea bargaining is legitimate and noncoercive if and only if it is responsive to a substantial uncertainty concerning the likely outcome of a trial. As Judge Bazelon explained in *Scott v. United States*[8]:

> Superficially it may seem that even in such a case the defendant who insists upon a trial and is found guilty pays a price for the exercise of his right when he receives a longer sentence than his less venturesome counterpart who pleads guilty. In a sense he has. But the critical distinction is that the price he has paid is not one imposed by the state to discourage others from a similar exercise of their rights, but rather one encountered by those who gamble and lose. After the fact, the defendant who pleads innocent and is convicted receives a heavier sentence. But, by the same token, the defendant who pleads innocent and is acquitted receives no sentence. To the extent that the bargain struck reflects only the uncertainty of conviction before trial, the "expected sentence before trial"—length of sentence discounted by probability of conviction—is the same for those who decide to plead guilty and those who hope for acquittal but risk conviction by going to trial.

7. Roberts v. United States, 445 U.S. 552, 100 S.Ct. 1358, 63 L.Ed.2d 622 (1980), where the Court held that the district court properly considered, as one factor in imposing consecutive sentences on a petitioner who had pleaded guilty to two counts of using a telephone to facilitate the distribution of heroin, petitioner's refusal to cooperate with government officials investigating a related criminal conspiracy to distribute heroin in which he was a confessed participant. Citing this provision in the ABA Standards, the majority expressed "doubt that a principled distinction may be drawn between 'enhancing' the punishment imposed upon the petitioner and denying him the 'leniency' he claims would be appropriate if he had cooperated."

8.   419 F.2d 264 (D.C.Cir.1969).

Whether one accepts or rejects this line of reasoning is likely to depend upon how one views some rather fundamental questions about the plea negotiation process. One such question is that of what kinds of cases are best disposed of by plea and what kinds by trial. Some see plea bargaining as a device to screen out those cases where there is no real dispute, but under the *Scott* approach bargaining would be limited to cases in which there is a substantial uncertainty concerning the likely outcome of a trial. Under the latter approach, it is objected, trials would tend to be limited to open-and-shut cases. Moreover, if the *Scott* theory is otherwise valid, there is the troublesome question of whether it should make any difference why there is a substantial uncertainty concerning the likely outcome of a trial. For example, when the uncertainty is whether the prosecutor has enough evidence to convict, should the tendering of concessions be limited to instances in which guilt is fairly certain but unprovable (e.g., where defendant's accomplice, having made a full, substantiated confession implicating the defendant, cannot now be found) or may it be legitimately extended to cases in which guilt is in real doubt (e.g., where there has been a shaky eyewitness identification of the defendant)?

(f) Other Attributes and Consequences. Even if the plea negotiation process is seen as having certain positive attributes, such as facilitating the processing of criminal cases and permitting needed flexibility in sentencing, there remains the difficult question of whether those attributes are outweighed by certain undesirable consequences of plea bargaining. One of these consequences, it is claimed, is an unhealthy relationship between the prosecutor and defense counsel, especially when the latter is the public defender. A related concern is the effect that plea bargaining has on the criminal defense bar. Some have concluded that the plea negotiation system subjects defense attorneys to serious temptations to disregard their clients' interests. Finally and consequently, there is the fact that plea bargaining often gives the defendant an image of corruption in the system, or at least an image of a system lacking meaningful purpose and subject to ma-

nipulation by those who are wise to the right tricks.

(g) Prohibiting Plea Bargaining. In the eyes of some, the practice of plea bargaining as it has developed in this country is undesirable and ought to be abolished entirely. What is not known is whether, assuming the plea negotiation process could be and was entirely eliminated, we would end up with a criminal justice system better (or worse) than we have now. For one thing, it is unclear whether abolition would produce intolerable congestion in the courts and unsatiable demands upon available resources. For another, it is not known whether without any form of plea bargaining to mitigate mandatory or excessive sentencing laws, the dispositions as to some types of criminal defendants would be unduly harsh.

There is a considerable body of thought that it is unnecessary to ponder such matters for the simple reason that it is not possible to abolish plea bargaining. Some believe that though it might be possible to proscribe explicit negotiation between prosecutor, defense attorney, and judge, it would be impossible to proscribe implicit plea bargaining agreement among all court actors that most guilty defendants should plead guilty and be rewarded for their plea. Some foretell a somewhat different accommodation in a system where plea bargaining is prohibited, such as that there would result increased pre-indictment plea adjustments. The notion is that eliminating discretion at one stage of the process fosters it at others, so that efforts to eliminate plea bargaining will be counterproductive by serving to shift the discretion to some other, usually less visible stage. Some empirical studies lend support to this thesis.

Some plea bargaining abolitionists believe abolition will work *if* the system is structured so as to encourage a large volume of *jury* trial waivers. They see jury waiver bargaining as superior to plea bargaining because the defendant retains most of his adversary trial rights. For this to be a viable alternative, it must be concluded that the Sixth Amendment right to jury trial is not absolute and thus may be lawfully discouraged by such tendering of concessions for its surrender. This conclusion finds support in the fact that the present system of plea bargaining has withstood attack even though it involves waiver of jury trial with other rights.

In a few jurisdictions, the law forbids the prosecutor from engaging in plea bargaining in certain circumstances or with regard to certain offenses. If the defendant enters a guilty plea pursuant to a bargain the prosecutor has struck in violation of such a statute, courts are disinclined to allow the defendant to overturn his plea because of the prohibition.

(h) Plea Bargaining and the Federal Sentencing Guidelines. The Federal Sentencing Guidelines,[9] which became effective in 1987, were expected to have a positive, rationalizing impact upon plea agreements in the federal system. In actuality, the Guidelines have even had an effect upon "implicit" bargaining, where even absent any negotiations it was common for federal judges to sentence defendants who entered a guilty plea less severely than defendants who were convicted at jury trials. The Guidelines seek to channel and control such bargaining by providing for decrease of the offense level by two levels when "the defendant clearly demonstrates acceptance of responsibility for his offense."[10]

In the federal system, there are two varieties of sentence bargaining: (1) an agreement between the parties "that a specific sentence or sentencing range is the appropriate disposition of the case,"[11] which the court may then accept or reject, though if it is rejected then the defendant must be allowed to withdraw his plea; and (2) an agreement that in exchange for the defendant's plea the government will "recommend, or agree not to oppose the defendant's request, that a particular sentence or sentencing range is appropriate,"[12] which is not binding on the court, necessitating a warning to the defendant that if the court imposes

a different sentence the defendant nevertheless may not withdraw his plea. As to both, the Guidelines provide that the court may impose the sentence contemplated by the agreement only if it is satisfied that such sentence is either "within the applicable guideline range" or "departs from the applicable guidelines range for justifiable reasons." Though there is inter-circuit disagreement on this point, under one view this means that the existence of the plea agreement is not itself a mitigating circumstance and that in determining the proper sentence the court must, for the most part, proceed just as it would had the defendant pled not guilty and been convicted after a trial. If the guilty plea defendant gets a lighter sentence, this is most likely to occur by application of at least one of two sentencing factors with special significance in the guilty plea context: (i) the previously discussed decrease in the offense level by two levels because the defendant "clearly demonstrates acceptance of responsibility for his offense," which in the case of a prompt guilty plea can actually result in a decrease by a total of three levels because of defendant's conduct in "timely notifying authorities of his intention to enter a plea of guilty, thereby permitting the government to avoid preparing for trial and permitting the court to allocate its resources efficiently"; and (ii) a departure from the Guidelines because of a "motion of the government stating that the defendant has provided substantial assistance in the investigation or prosecution of another person," though not all defendants who believe such a motion will be forthcoming in fact benefit from this provision.[13]

Mention must next be made of fact stipulation agreements, though they are not truly a distinct variety of plea bargaining but rather a device that can be used to support one of the other types of agreements discussed here. Fact bargaining predated the Guidelines, for it was

---

9. See § 26.3(e) for a brief description.

10. This two-level reduction is likely to be about a 20% reduction, something less than the pre-Guidelines "discount" for pleading guilty.

11. Fed.R.Crim.P. 11(c)(1)(C), adding also where the parties agree "that a particular provision of the Sentencing Guidelines, or policy statement, or sentencing factor does or does not apply."

12. Fed.R.Crim.P. 11(c)(1)(B), adding also where the prosecutor agrees to recommend or not oppose "that a particular provision of the Sentencing Guidelines, or policy statement, or sentencing factor does or does not apply."

13. This point is considered in § 21.2(d).

often a useful device for convincing the judge that the contemplated charge or sentence concessions were appropriate. The Guidelines provide that a plea agreement "may be accompanied by a written stipulation of facts relevant to sentencing," which "shall (1) set forth the relevant facts and circumstances of the actual offense conduct and offender characteristics; (2) not contain misleading facts; and (3) set forth with meaningful specificity the reasons why the sentencing range resulting from the proposed agreement is appropriate." While it thus appears that a stipulation must fully disclose all relevant historic facts of the case, as a practical matter this provision may not prevent all shading of the facts by bargaining prosecutors and defense attorneys. The parties are bound by a stipulation of facts, but "the court is not bound by the stipulation."[14]

As for charge bargaining, there is that variety of charge bargaining specifically enumerated in rule 11: a plea of guilty to one count in exchange for the government's promise that it will "not bring, or will move to dismiss, other charges."[15] It has been said that the advantage of charge bargaining is that the defendant can pick the crime with the most favorable sentencing scheme under the Guidelines, thereby determining the sentence range. To some extent this is true, but the opportunities to affect the sentence via plea bargaining are limited by the Guidelines instructions to judges that such an agreement should be accepted only upon a determination "for reasons stated on the record, that the remaining charges adequately reflect the seriousness of the actual offense behavior and that accepting the agreement will not undermine the statutory purpose of sentencing or the sentencing guidelines."

While this provision appears to give sentencing courts wide latitude in deciding whether to accept charge bargains, there are other provisions in the Guidelines that further limit the opportunities for the judge to reduce the defendant's sentence as a result of the dropping of some counts. The above quoted provision

goes on to say that dismissal of a charge "shall not preclude the conduct underlying such charge from being considered" as relevant conduct. What this means is that whenever "the offense level is determined largely on the basis of the total amount of harm or loss, the quantity of a substance involved, or some other measure of aggregate harm, or if the offense behavior is ongoing or continuous in nature and the offense guideline is written to cover such behavior," then such matters as the base offense level, specific offense characteristics and adjustments are to be determined on the basis of "all acts and omissions * * * that were part of the same course of conduct or common scheme or plan as the offense of conviction."[16] This includes conduct underlying counts dismissed pursuant to a plea bargain. For example, in a drug case involving five counts of distributing heroin, the offense level is determined primarily by the quantity of drugs involved, thus if a plea agreement is reached involving a plea to one count, the offense level will still be calculated based on all the drugs of that common drug scheme.

These constraints can be overcome to some degree by moving the bargaining back to the pre-indictment stage. Although the Department of Justice in 1989 adopted the policy that a federal prosecutor should initially charge the most serious, provable offense or offenses consistent with the defendant's conduct, that policy has not always been followed and has more recently been ameliorated to some degree.[17] Defense attorneys are advised that they should become part of the process as early as possible and should initiate negotiations as soon as they are familiar with the facts of the case. The prosecutor may be more flexible at this pre-charge stage precisely because no formal position on a charge has yet been taken, and is more likely to have the authority to reach an agreement on the matter, as compared with the review process that might well be necessary if the proposal were to drop existing

---

14. U.S.S.G. § 6B1.4(d).

15. Fed.R.Crim.P. 11(c)(1)(A).

16. U.S.S.G. § 1B1.3(a)(2).

17. The policy was amended in 1993 so as to allow "federal prosecutors to take the circumstances of a particular case into account when making charging decisions and negotiating plea agreements."

charges. And most important, dealing with the matter at this earlier stage reduces the probability that facts disadvantageous to the defendant will emerge and bar the contemplated concessions. The facts supporting the charged offenses can be presented in a much more limited scope to the court and the probation officer because no other charges have been listed.

§ 21.2　Kept, Broken, Rejected and Non-existent Bargains

(a) Statutory Inducements to Plead Guilty. One troublesome aspect of the plea negotiation system is the disparity that can result between the sentences imposed upon defendants who plead guilty and those given to defendants who choose to go to trial. But the problem is by no means limited to situations in which bargaining on a case-by-case basis occurs, for it is possible that the disparity will be facilitated or mandated by sentencing laws. This occurs when a sentencing provision requires or allows a certain kind or degree of sentence to be imposed upon a defendant who stands trial, but does not require or allow that same punishment to be inflicted upon another defendant, charged with the same offense, who enters a trial-avoiding plea. Under such a statutory scheme, it may legitimately be asked: (1) whether a defendant who elects to go to trial is being punished to an unconstitutional extent or in an unconstitutional manner; and (2) whether a defendant who elects to forego trial has, by virtue of the statute, entered a coerced and thus involuntary plea.

The first of these issues reached the Supreme Court in *United States v. Jackson*,[1] where a defendant who had not opted to plead guilty challenged the Federal Kidnaping Act because of its provision that the punishment of death could be imposed only "if the verdict of the jury shall so recommend." This meant, the Court noted, that "the defendant who abandons the right to contest his guilt before a jury is assured that he cannot be executed; the defendant ingenuous enough to seek a jury

acquittal stands forewarned that, if the jury finds him guilty and does not wish to spare his life, he will die." Because the legitimate goal of this statute, "limiting the death penalty to cases in which a jury recommends it," could be accomplished in other ways, and because the "inevitable effect" of the provision was "to discourage assertion of the Fifth Amendment right not to plead guilty and to deter exercise of the Sixth Amendment right to demand a jury trial," the Court in *Jackson* concluded that the death penalty provision in the statute "needlessly penalizes" the assertion of those constitutional rights and thus was unconstitutional. The Court continued:

> It is no answer to urge, as does the Government, that federal trial judges may be relied upon to reject coerced pleas of guilty and involuntary waivers of jury trial. For the evil in the federal statute is not that it necessarily *coerces* guilty pleas and jury waivers but simply that it needlessly *encourages* them. A procedure need not be inherently coercive in order that it be held to impose an impermissible burden upon the assertion of a constitutional right. Thus the fact that the Federal Kidnaping Act tends to discourage defendants from insisting upon their innocence and demanding trial by jury hardly implies that every defendant who enters a guilty plea to a charge under the Act does so involuntarily. The power to reject coerced guilty pleas and involuntary jury waivers might alleviate, but it cannot totally eliminate, the constitutional infirmity in the capital punishment provision of the Federal Kidnaping Act.

This language suggested, as the Supreme Court subsequently held, that a defendant who challenged a guilty plea entered under such a sentencing scheme would not necessarily prevail. In *Brady v. United States*,[2] a defendant who had entered a guilty plea under this same Act prior to the *Jackson* decision and who had been sentenced to a 30 year term, unsuccessfully claimed that his plea was invalid. Declaring that *Jackson* "neither fashioned a

---

1. 390 U.S. 570, 88 S.Ct. 1209, 20 L.Ed.2d 138 (1968).

2. 397 U.S. 742, 90 S.Ct. 1463, 25 L.Ed.2d 747 (1970).

new standard for judging the validity of guilty pleas nor mandated a new application of the test theretofore fashioned by courts and since reiterated that guilty pleas are valid if both 'voluntary' and 'intelligent,' " the Court concluded (a) that a guilty plea is not rendered unintelligent merely "because later judicial decisions indicate that the plea rested on a faulty premise"; and (b) that a guilty plea is not rendered involuntary "merely because entered to avoid the possibility of a death penalty."

Although *Brady* did not involve a bargained plea in the true sense of that term, it appears that the Court was influenced to some degree by a perceived need to reach a result not casting doubts upon the plea negotiation process. The same may be said of the later case of *Corbitt v. New Jersey*,[3] which unlike *Brady* and like *Jackson* involved a defendant who had elected to stand trial. Defendant was tried and convicted of first degree murder and sentenced to the mandatory punishment of life imprisonment. Had he entered a plea of non vult or nolo contendere,[4] then by state law the punishment would have been "either imprisonment for life or the same as that imposed upon a conviction of murder in the second degree," i.e., a term of not more than 30 years. The defendant thus claimed that this scheme was unconstitutional under *Jackson,* but the Court responded that the more recent case of *Bordenkircher v. Hayes*[5] provided the better analogy. For one thing, there were deemed to be "substantial differences between this case and *Jackson*" in that the instant case (a) did not involve the death penalty and (b) did not involve a scheme whereby the maximum penalty was reserved exclusively for those who insisted on a jury trial. For another, the *Corbitt* majority saw "no difference of constitutional significance" between the instant case and *Bordenkircher,* approving a prosecutor's conduct in having defendant charged and convicted as a habitual criminal and subjected to the mandatory sentence of life imprisonment because the defendant refused to plead guilty to the original forgery charge punishable by 2–10 years.[6]

Here, as there, the defendant was free to choose either "to go to trial and face the risk of life imprisonment" or to enter a plea making possible a lesser penalty.

Lying at the heart of the *Corbitt* decision, it appears, is the debatable assumption that no constitutional distinction can be drawn between the tendering of concessions for pleas as a result of negotiations on a case-by-case basis and the wholesale tendering of concessions by statute. The majority saw both as serving a legitimate function, "the encouragement of guilty defendants not to contest their guilt," and declared that the Court could not permit bargaining by a prosecutor "and yet hold that the legislature may not openly provide for the possibility of leniency in return for a plea." To this, the author of *Bordenkircher*—Justice Stewart—objected that "there is a vast difference between the settlement of litigation through negotiation between counsel for the parties, and a state statute such as is involved in the present case," for the prosecutor "necessarily must be able to settle an adversary criminal lawsuit through plea bargaining with his adversary," while "a state legislature has a quite different function to perform." That is, while it cannot be said that authorizing plea bargaining "needlessly penalizes" the assertion of constitutional rights under the *Jackson* test, it hardly follows, as the *Corbitt* majority assumed, that this statutory scheme "is at the very heart of an effective plea negotiation program." Moreover, as the three *Corbitt* dissenters noted: "In the bargaining process, individual factors relevant to the particular case may be considered by the prosecutor in charging and by the trial judge in sentencing, regardless of the defendant's plea; the process does not mandate a different standard of punishment depending solely on whether or not a plea is entered."

Just how far *Corbitt* undercuts *Jackson* is unclear. The majority cautioned it was not suggesting "that every conceivable statutory sentencing structure" would be constitutional,

---

3.   439 U.S. 212, 99 S.Ct. 492, 58 L.Ed.2d 466 (1978).

4.   On the difference between such a plea and a plea of guilty, see § 21.4(a).

5.   434 U.S. 357, 98 S.Ct. 663, 54 L.Ed.2d 604 (1978).

6.   For further discussion of this case, see § 21.2(b).

and upheld the challenged statute because it was "unconvinced" that it "exerts such a powerful influence to coerce inaccurate guilty pleas that it should be deemed constitutionally suspect." Certainly there is such a "powerful influence" when it is the risk of the death penalty, "unique in its severity and irrevocability,"[7] that is involved, but the Court in *Corbitt* denied it was holding "that the *Jackson* rationale is limited to those cases where a plea avoids any possibility of the death penalty being imposed." Lower courts continue to apply *Jackson* even where the death penalty has not been involved.

Corbitt also distinguished *Jackson* because there "any risk of suffering the maximum penalty could be avoided by pleading guilty," but it is debatable whether this ought to be determinative. It is far from apparent that a may/cannot system (i.e., defendant *may* get the maximum if he goes to trial, but *cannot* if he pleads guilty) is more coercive than a must/may system (i.e., defendant *must* get the maximum if he goes to trial, and *may* if he pleads guilty). This is especially true when, as was the case under the New Jersey statute challenged in *Corbitt,* the statutory scheme is accompanied by an established practice of not giving the maximum to a pleading defendant. Moreover, there is a sense in which the must/may system is more pernicious, for under it the price for exercising constitutional rights is the total loss of any chance of sentencing leniency.

The *Corbitt* decision may actually reflect a broader point, namely, that statutory inducements to plead guilty are to be assessed in terms of the extent to which they make the choice between plea and trial determinative and remove discretion from the prosecutor and court.[8] This would mean that Justice Stewart was correct in asserting it would be "clearly unconstitutional" for a state legislature to provide "that the penalty for every criminal offense to which a defendant pleads guilty is to be one-half the penalty to be imposed upon a defendant convicted of the same offense after a not guilty plea."

(b) Inducements by the Prosecutor. The plea bargaining system as it has developed in this country depends not upon such statutory inducements but rather upon inducements frequently put forward by prosecutors in individual cases. In *Brady v. United States,*[9] upholding as voluntary and intelligent a guilty plea entered under the statutory scheme found unconstitutional in *Jackson,* the Court cast its decision in terms that appeared calculated to lend support to some forms of plea bargaining:

> We decline to hold, however, that a guilty plea is compelled and invalid under the Fifth Amendment whenever motivated by the defendant's desire to accept the certainty or probability of a lesser penalty rather than face a wider range of possibilities extending from acquittal to conviction and a higher penalty authorized by law for the crime charged.

> The issue we deal with is inherent in the criminal law and its administration because guilty pleas are not constitutionally forbidden, because the criminal law characteristically extends to judge or jury a range of choice in setting the sentence in individual cases, and because both the State and the defendant often find it advantageous to preclude the possibility of the maximum penalty authorized by law. For a defendant who sees slight possibility of acquittal, the advantages of pleading guilty and limiting the probable penalty are obvious—his exposure is reduced, the correctional processes can begin immediately, and the practical burdens of a trial are eliminated. For the State there are also advantages—the more promptly imposed punishment after an admission of guilt may more effectively attain the objectives of punishment; and with the

---

7. Gregg v. Georgia, 428 U.S. 153, 96 S.Ct. 2909, 49 L.Ed.2d 859 (1976).

8. The *Corbitt* majority emphasized that the statute "leaves much to the judge and to the prosecutor," in that "pleas may be rejected even if tendered" and when accepted "there is discretion to impose life imprisonment," and

that as for the defendant who does go to trial it is "true that under normal circumstances, juries in New Jersey may find a defendant guilty of second-degree murder rather than first."

9. 397 U.S. 742, 90 S.Ct. 1463, 25 L.Ed.2d 747 (1970).

avoidance of trial, scarce judicial and prosecutorial resources are conserved for those cases in which there is a substantial issue of the defendant's guilt or in which there is substantial doubt that the State can sustain its burden of proof. It is this mutuality of advantage which perhaps explains the fact that at present well over three-fourths of the criminal convictions in this country rest on pleas of guilty, a great many of them no doubt motivated at least in part by the hope or assurance of a lesser penalty than might be imposed if there were a guilty verdict after a trial to judge or jury.

Of course, that the prevalence of guilty pleas is explainable does not necessarily validate those pleas or the system which produces them. But we cannot hold that it is unconstitutional for the State to extend a benefit to a defendant who in turn extends a substantial benefit to the State and who demonstrates by his plea that he is ready and willing to admit his crime and to enter the correctional system in a frame of mind which affords hope for success in rehabilitation over a shorter period of time than might otherwise be necessary.

That theme was sounded by the Court on other occasions, but again in circumstances where the prosecutor's bargaining tactics were not directly at issue.[10] Moreover, the Court gave no indication it was extending wholesale approval to all forms of prosecutorial inducements. In *Brady*, for example, the Court spoke approvingly only of the prosecutor allowing the defendant "to plead guilty to a lesser offense included in the offense charged" or "with the understanding that other charges will be dropped," but indicated a guilty plea could not stand if "induced by threats (or promises to discontinue improper harassment), misrepresentation (including unfulfilled or unfulfillable promises), or perhaps by promises that are by their nature improper as having no proper relationship to the prosecutor's business (e.g., bribes)."

But this left unsettled exactly where the line should be drawn between the permissible tender of concessions and impermissible "threats." What if the prosecutor confronted the defendant with dramatically different punishment consequences depending upon whether or not he entered a guilty plea? What if the prosecutor indicated that failure of the defendant to plead guilty would result in the filing of more serious charges against the defendant? Such were the issues in *Bordenkircher v. Hayes*,[11] for there the prosecutor carried out his threat that if the defendant did not plead guilty to the existing charge of uttering a forged instrument, punishable by two to 10 years, he would be indicted under the Habitual Criminal Act, which would subject defendant to a mandatory sentence of life imprisonment by reason of his two prior felony convictions. On federal habeas corpus, the court of appeals had held that defendant's prosecution and conviction under that Act violated the principles of *Blackledge v. Perry*,[12] where a prosecutor's escalation of charges against a defendant who had exercised his right to appeal was held to violate due process because there was a "realistic likelihood of 'vindictiveness'" in such circumstances.[13]

The Supreme Court, in a 5–4 decision, reversed the court of appeals. The majority reasoned that while in *Blackledge* and related cases "the Court was dealing with the State's unilateral imposition of a penalty upon a defendant who had chosen to exercise a legal right to attack his original conviction," that situation was "very different from the give-and-take negotiation common in plea bargaining between the prosecution and the defense, which arguably possess relatively equal bargaining power." In the latter circumstances, the Court asserted, "there is no such element of punishment or retaliation so long as the accused is free to accept or reject the prosecution's offer." And consequently, the Court concluded, "the course of conduct engaged in by

---

10. E.g., *Blackledge v. Allison*, 431 U.S. 63, 97 S.Ct. 1621, 52 L.Ed.2d 136 (1977); *Santobello v. New York*, 404 U.S. 257, 92 S.Ct. 495, 30 L.Ed.2d 427 (1971).

11. 434 U.S. 357, 98 S.Ct. 663, 54 L.Ed.2d 604 (1978).

12. 417 U.S. 21, 94 S.Ct. 2098, 40 L.Ed.2d 628 (1974).

13. For further discussion of this principle, see § 13.5(a).

the prosecutor in this case, which no more than openly presented the defendant with the unpleasant alternatives of foregoing trial or facing charges on which he was plainly subject to prosecution, did not violate the Due Process Clause of the Fourteenth Amendment." The majority treated this result as a foregone conclusion in light of the Court's earlier favorable words concerning the institution of plea bargaining. Because "acceptance of the basic legitimacy of plea bargaining necessarily implies rejection of any notion that a guilty plea is involuntary in a constitutional sense simply because it is the end result of the bargaining process," it was said by way of explanation, it "follows that, by tolerating and encouraging the negotiation of pleas, this Court has necessarily accepted as constitutionally legitimate the simple reality that the prosecutor's interest at the bargaining table is to persuade the defendant to forego his right to plead not guilty."

Given the fact that this left the defendant with the life sentence he had received for failing to plead guilty to a charge carrying a 10 year maximum, the Court's decision in Bordenkircher is, at best, unsettling. The tensions that contributed to this troublesome result can best be seen by considering the alternative courses the Court might have taken. One, that taken by the court below and urged by three of the dissenting Justices, is that the original charge should be presumed to reflect the prosecutor's judgment of what would be an appropriate disposition in the case, so that in the event of a subsequent enhancement of the charge the prosecutor would have to justify his action on some basis other than discouraging the defendant from exercising his constitutional rights. But as the dissenters acknowledged, such a ruling "merely would prompt the aggressive prosecutor to bring the greater charge initially in every case, and only thereafter to bargain." They went on to note that the "consequences to the accused would still be adverse, for then he would bargain against a greater charge, face the likelihood of increased

bail, and run the risk that the court would be less inclined to accept a bargained plea."

Judicial scrutiny of the motives underlying even initial charging decisions, particularly with a view to determining whether the charges brought were filed to gain bargaining leverage, is not feasible either. "Normally," the Bordenkircher dissenters observed, "it is impossible to show that this is what the prosecutor is doing, and the courts necessarily have deferred to the prosecutor's exercise of discretion in initial charging decisions." Moreover, if, as the dissenters seem to suggest, "a prosecutor ought not to bring charges more serious than he thinks 'appropriate for the ultimate disposition of a case' without any consideration of plea bargaining leverage," then "there would be little meaningful bargaining," for the only way to induce a plea would be for the prosecutor to accept a plea at a level *below* what the prosecutor thinks appropriate for the ultimate disposition of the case.

A third approach to the Bordenkircher situation would focus upon sentences that technically lie within the legal range of sentence options but violate our sense of fairness. Perhaps the most disturbing part of the case is the extreme severity of the sentence under the circumstances. As Justice Powell noted in his separate dissent: "Although respondent's prior convictions brought him within the terms of the Habitual Criminal Act, the offenses themselves did not result in imprisonment; yet the addition of a conviction on a charge involving $88.30 subjected respondent to a mandatory sentence of imprisonment for life. Persons convicted of rape and murder often are not punished so severely." But for the Court to take on this issue would involve the judiciary in the sensitive and difficult task of making judgments about the constitutionality of legislative action in setting the permissible range of imprisonment for a variety of offenses. The Court is understandably reluctant to go this route, as is illustrated by *Ewing v. California*.[14]

---

14. 538 U.S. 11, 123 S.Ct. 1179, 155 L.Ed.2d 108 (2003), holding that where defendant, convicted of felony grand theft for stealing three golf clubs, was sentenced under California's three-strikes law to 25 years to life

because he had previously been convicted of several serious or violent felonies, the sentence did not violate the Eight Amendment's prohibition on cruel and unusual punishment.

Still a fourth approach would be to view the prosecutor's conduct in *Bordenkircher* as outside the boundaries of permissible plea bargaining tactics because of the degree of leverage utilized by him. This is where Justice Powell came out; he was prepared to intrude upon the prosecutor's bargaining discretion only "in the most exceptional case," and he found the instant case to fall within this limited exception because the prosecutor proceeded "to penalize with unique severity [the defendant's] exercise of constitutional rights." The Court's reluctance to take on this issue is also understandable, for it would have been almost impossible for the Court to articulate how great a sentence differential was too great. A holding that the difference in *Bordenkircher* was excessive thus might have plunged the Court into a review of innumerable other sentences that defendants had received after rejecting prosecutorial offers of lenient treatment in exchange for pleas of guilty.

Understandably, the *Bordenkircher* case has been treated as encompassing all of the typical charge bargain situations, where the prosecutor offers to allow the defendant to plead guilty to a lesser offense or a lesser number of offenses than originally charged or to plead guilty to the original charge and thus escape charges for other crimes or a charge of a higher degree of offense than originally charged. Presumably *Bordenkircher* also extends to the prosecutor's involvement in sentence bargaining, though it is well to note that in *Brady* the Court expressly declined to give approval to a situation in which the defendant is "threatened * * * with a harsher sentence if convicted after trial in order to induce him to plead guilty."[15] But, as a practical matter, that was the effect of what the prosecutor was allowed to do in *Bordenkircher*.

Bordenkircher should not be read as declaring that a defendant who refuses to plead guilty and then is convicted on added charges is never entitled to relief. The Court emphasized that it did not have before it a case "where the prosecutor without notice brought an additional and more serious charge after plea negotiations relating only to the original indictment had ended with the defendant's insistence on pleading not guilty," and the holding in the case was stated in terms of the prosecutor having "openly presented the defendant with the unpleasant alternatives" he faced. This suggests that if the prosecutor fails to tell the defendant that there is a price attached to his refusal to plead guilty or only makes an unspecified threat of increased criminal liability, so that defendant has no means by which to weigh the potential liabilities of that refusal, the prosecutor might be barred from thereafter upping the ante because the defendant refuses to plead guilty.

Another way to look at *Bordenkircher* is to ask what significance the case has, if any, in a situation where the defendant *does* plead guilty. That is, what if the defendant in that case, upon being confronted with the prospect of life imprisonment from an added charge under the Habitual Criminal Act, had entered a guilty plea to the forgery charge and then later challenged that plea as coerced? Strictly speaking, *Bordenkircher* should not be viewed as foreclosing a finding of involuntariness, for the Court was only addressing the vindictive prosecution issue raised by a defendant who did not give in to the pressure. Yet, a reading of *Bordenkircher* with *Brady* indicates the defendant is not likely to prevail. The former case establishes that the prosecutor's conduct does not involve an improper threat or promise, and the latter seems to say that in such circumstances the plea is voluntary if the defendant was aware of "the actual value of any commitments made to him." But that phrase, together with the strong emphasis in *Bordenkircher* upon the prosecutor having charging discretion "so long as the prosecutor has probable cause," indicates the defendant's attack would be strengthened if the threatened charge in fact could not have been brought.

Bordenkircher should not be read as manifesting approval of any type of threat or prom-

---

15. However, this reference was to a threat by "the trial judge," which might be viewed differently. See § 21.2(c).

ise made by the prosecutor in a plea bargaining context. In a footnote the Court cautioned that the case did not "involve the constitutional implications of a prosecutor's offer during plea bargaining of adverse or lenient treatment for some person *other* than the accused, which might pose a greater danger of inducing a false guilty plea by skewing the assessment of the risks a defendant must consider." It has been forcefully argued that such inducements present a special risk that an innocent defendant will plead guilty and that a guilty defendant will receive treatment that does not meet his correctional needs, but the courts have rather consistently held that there is no intrinsic infirmity in broadening plea negotiations to permit third party beneficiaries. However, guilty pleas made in consideration of lenient treatment to third persons pose a greater danger of coercion than purely bilateral plea bargaining and thus deserve close scrutiny.

A prosecutor's bargaining tactics may come under attack because of commitments exacted from the defendant in addition to the guilty plea. Illustrative is a plea bargain that included a promise by defendant to leave the state for ten years, a commitment held unenforceable because contrary to public policy; one that included a promise by defendant not to testify in favor of a codefendant, unenforceable because a violation of the codefendant's right to compulsory process; or one that required defendant to testify in another's case consistently with statements previously given the police, unenforceable because it taints the truth-seeking function of the courts. Courts are not in agreement concerning a prosecutor-induced commitment by the defendant not to take an appeal. One view is that such a bargain is a proper method of making a plea agreement enforceable,[16] while another treats the right to appeal as non-negotiable because otherwise plea bargains could be insulated from appellate review. A middle view is that such a waiver is neither inherently coercive or fully enforceable, so that a defendant remains free to file a timely appeal, which relieves the state of its part of the bargain.

(c) Inducements by the Judge. As discussed later,[17] there exists a considerable difference of opinion as to how the plea negotiation process should be structured in terms of judicial involvement, and in particular with whether it is better that the judge participate directly in negotiation sessions or remain completely aloof from them. Some jurisdictions have adopted the latter position; the federal rule is that the "court must not participate in these discussions,"[18] and several states are in accord. If in one of those jurisdictions a defendant brings his guilty plea into question by showing that it was preceded by some inducements from the judge, the case might well be disposed of in the defendant's favor without any determination of whether the judge's involvement in the particular case was so extreme as to make the plea involuntary. That is, it might well be concluded that this absolute prohibition upon judicial involvement can best be enforced by permitting a defendant to withdraw his plea without first showing that actual prejudice resulted from the judge's participation.[19]

In a jurisdiction not taking that view, the question then to be considered is whether the nature and circumstances of the judge's participation was such that the defendant's plea was coerced and thus invalid. The generally accepted view is that such participation, in and of itself, does not require setting a guilty plea aside as a constitutional matter. Rather, there must be a more particularized assessment of the individual case, during which the trial judge's participation in the plea bargaining process must be carefully scrutinized.

---

16. In support, it is sometimes argued that the right to appeal is no more fundamental than other rights waived by a guilty plea, which raises the question whether such waiver should be addressed by the judge in receiving the plea, as with waiver of other important rights, see § 21.4(e). By virtue of the recent addition of what is now Fed.R.Crim.P. 11(b)(1)(N), there has been added to the list of items about which the judge must inform the defendant and determine that the defendant understands the following: "the terms of any plea-agreement provision waiving the right to appeal or to collaterally attack the sentence."

17. See § 21.3(d).

18. Fed.R.Crim.P. 11(c)(1).

19. United States v. Adams, 634 F.2d 830 (5th Cir. 1981).

There remains considerable uncertainty, however, as to exactly what kind of involvement by the judge will make the defendant's plea involuntary. The Supreme Court has not had occasion to address the issue directly, though in *Brady v. United States*,[20] indicating approval of prosecutor bargaining, the Court in a cautionary footnote observed that those remarks were not intended to encompass a case "where the prosecutor or judge, or both, deliberately employ their charging and sentencing powers to induce a particular defendant to tender a plea of guilty." Of course, the Court has since approved such action by the prosecutor,[21] but it is unclear whether that has any significance as to judicial involvement. One view is that judicial participation has a substantially different effect than negotiations between the parties because of the unequal positions of the judge and the accused and the judge's awesome power to impose a substantially longer or even maximum sentence if the defendant rejects the court's proposals. In response, it may be argued that this assertion is inconsistent with the Supreme Court's teachings as to what is a voluntary plea,[22] and also with the fact that because the prosecutor has many means not available to the judge of putting pressure upon the defendant, this disparity of positions may be even greater between prosecutor and defendant.

Examination of the decisions assessing the voluntariness of a plea entered subsequent to some judicial involvement in the negotiation process sheds some light on the factors that may influence a determination that the plea is or is not valid. Certainly the defendant's plea cannot be upheld where the judge significantly overstated the defendant's predicament were he to stand trial, as where the judge erroneously indicated that in such circumstances he would have no choice but to sentence defendant to prison. Also, a plea is likely to be held involuntary where the judge was the moving force in pressing for a guilty plea after defendant had manifested a desire not to so plead or where the judge indicated conviction at trial was a foregone conclusion. On the other hand, the judge's involvement is not likely to be deemed coercive where the bargaining was not initiated by the judge, where the judge merely said he would abide by the agreement previously reached by the parties, or where the judge only suggested a compromise position between the different sentencing proposals of the defendant and prosecutor. Nor is it coercive for the judge, after jury selection had begun, to put a time limit on how long thereafter the parties had to negotiate an plea agreement, as eleventh hour settlements are properly discouraged.

Assume now a different scenario, one in which again there has been judicial involvement in the bargaining process (e.g., a promise of a 5 year sentence if defendant pleads guilty) but the defendant elected to stand trial, was convicted, and then received a more severe sentence (e.g., a 7 year sentence). Even if we are prepared to say that this defendant's plea would have been voluntary had he accepted the judge's proposal, it does not necessarily follow that the defendant in the above scenario lacks a valid constitutional claim, for the Supreme Court in a related context has made it unmistakably clear that the two situations are different and necessitate different analysis.[23] In the above scenario the defendant's argument will be that these events amount to a violation of due process because of the vindictiveness—or, at least, the appearance of vindictiveness—against the defendant for his exercise of his constitutional right to stand trial. So the argument goes, if, as the Supreme Court held in *North Carolina v. Pearce*,[24] due process "requires that vindictiveness against a defendant for having successfully attacked his first conviction must play no part in the sentence he receives after a new trial," then sure-

20. 397 U.S. 742, 90 S.Ct. 1463, 25 L.Ed.2d 747 (1970).

21. Bordenkircher v. Hayes, 434 U.S. 357, 98 S.Ct. 663, 54 L.Ed.2d 604 (1978).

22. Brady v. United States, 397 U.S. 742, 90 S.Ct. 1463, 25 L.Ed.2d 747 (1970), asserting that a plea of guilty is generally to be deemed voluntary if "entered by one fully aware of the direct consequences, including the actual value of any commitments made to him by the court."

23. See the discussion of the *Jackson* and *Brady* cases in § 21.2(a).

24. 395 U.S. 711, 89 S.Ct. 2072, 23 L.Ed.2d 656 (1969).

ly the same is true as to a defendant's exercise of a constitutional right.

That argument, of course, bears a distinct similarity to that made with respect to prosecutorial inducements and rejected by the Supreme Court in *Bordenkircher v. Hayes*.[25] The defendant's position there was that if, as the Court had previously held,[26] the prosecutor could not ordinarily escalate the charges after defendant had exercised his right to appeal, then he likewise could not do so after defendant had rejected the prosecutor's plea inducements and exercised his constitutional right to trial. But, as we have seen,[27] the Court declined to apply the vindictiveness concept to plea negotiations, reasoning that "in the 'give-and-take' of plea bargaining, there is no such element of punishment or retaliation so long as the accused is free to accept or reject the prosecution's offer."

Whether that analysis carries over to cases of judicial involvement is a matter on which there is a difference of opinion, as is revealed by the en banc decision in *Frank v. Blackburn*.[28] Prior to and during defendant's state trial the trial judge conducted plea bargaining sessions in his chambers at which he stated the sentence would be 20 years if defendant were to plead guilty, but defendant rejected those offers and was convicted of armed robbery, after which the judge sentenced him to a term of 33 years. On federal habeas corpus, a majority of the court of appeals read *Bordenkircher* as making "it clear that a state is free to encourage guilty pleas by offering substantial benefits to a defendant, or by threatening an accused with more severe punishment should a negotiated plea be refused," necessitating the finding that "the rule of *North Carolina v. Pearce* [is] completely inapplicable to post-plea bargain sentencing proceedings." But the dissenters in *Frank* reasoned that *Bordenkircher* had merely declined to apply the vindictiveness doctrine to plea bargaining between the parties because a contrary result

would have, in effect, foreclosed what the Court had repeatedly said was a necessary aspect of the criminal process. Judicial participation, they reasoned, had no such credentials and thus was not equally deserving of exemption from the *Pearce* rule. The dissenters also noted that the opinion in *Bordenkircher* had been carefully crafted to make it unmistakably clear that it did not extend to judicial involvement. Specifically, the Supreme Court emphasized that the *Pearce* rule had been applied in situations "very different from the give-and-take negotiations common in plea bargaining between the prosecution and the defense, which arguably possess relatively equal bargaining power." Be that as it may, a defendant today would find it difficult to prevail in this setting on a *Pearce* theory, for it now appears such a defendant would not have available the *Pearce* presumption and thus would have the burden of establishing actual vindictiveness. In *Alabama v. Smith*,[29] the Supreme Court ruled that because there does not exist a "reasonable likelihood" of vindictiveness in the case of a vacated guilty plea and higher sentence after a subsequent trial and reconviction, no presumption of vindictiveness exists in such circumstances.

Even assuming the majority is correct in *Frank,* there remains here (as with prosecutorial inducements) the troublesome question of whether certain inducements are improper simply because of the substantial disparity between the contemplated disposition depending upon whether the defendant opts to plead guilty or go to trial. In the *Frank* case, for example, one might well ask what legitimate objective of the plea bargaining system is served by a sentencing differential of 13 years. An even more dramatic illustration is provided by *People v. Dennis*,[30] where the judge offered defendant a term of either 2–4 or 2–6 years if he would plead guilty, the defendant elected to stand trial and was convicted, and that judge then sentenced him to a term of 40–80 years.

25. 434 U.S. 357, 98 S.Ct. 663, 54 L.Ed.2d 604 (1978).

26. Blackledge v. Perry, 417 U.S. 21, 94 S.Ct. 2098, 40 L.Ed.2d 628 (1974).

27. See § 21.2(b).

28. 646 F.2d 873 (5th Cir.1980).

29. 490 U.S. 794, 109 S.Ct. 2201, 104 L.Ed.2d 865 (1989), discussed in § 26.8(c).

30. 28 Ill.App.3d 74, 328 N.E.2d 135 (1975).

The appellate court, noting that the judge at sentencing had before him no relevant facts of which he had been unaware at the time of his plea offer, reduced defendant's sentence to 6–18 years. As one critic asked, does this mean "that a defendant may be penalized for exercising his right to trial by a sentence three times more severe than that he could have secured by pleading guilty, but not by a sentence twenty times more severe"?[31] Certainly this is an important question, central to the entire plea negotiation process, but it is one that courts are understandably reluctant to address.

(d) The Broken Bargain. In *Santobello v. New York*,[32] the Supreme Court ruled that it was constitutionally impermissible to hold a defendant to his negotiated plea when the promises upon which it was based were not performed. The defendant in that case entered a guilty plea to a lesser included offense upon the prosecutor's promise to make no recommendation as to sentence, but at the sentencing hearing some months later that prosecutor's successor recommended the maximum sentence, which the judge imposed. After speaking approvingly of the plea negotiation system, the Court concluded:

> This phase of the process of criminal justice, and the adjudicative element inherent in accepting a plea of guilty, must be attended by safeguards to insure the defendant what is reasonably due in the circumstances. Those circumstances will vary, but a constant factor is that when a plea rests in any significant degree on a promise or agreement of the prosecutor, so that it can be said to be part of the inducement or consideration, such promise must be fulfilled.

The Court in *Santobello* thus remanded the case to the state court for a determination of whether the defendant should be given the relief he sought, withdrawal of his plea, or whether instead he should be granted specific performance by resentencing before another judge. (The Court in *Santobello* declined to

find harmless error because of the sentencing judge's statement that the prosecutor's recommendation did not influence him.)

The first step in applying the *Santobello* rule is to determine if promises were made and, if so, precisely what they were. If the plea agreement is ambiguous, then courts are inclined to apply the law of contracts to resolve the ambiguity. However, because the defendant's "contract" right is constitutionally based, the prosecution is held to a greater degree of responsibility than the defendant for ambiguities, especially when the prosecutor has proffered the terms or prepared a written agreement.

One kind of promise is a commitment by the prosecutor that he will recommend or at least not oppose a particular sentence sought by the defendant. If the prosecutor does recommend or not oppose that sentence but the judge imposes a more severe sentence, the defendant is not entitled to relief under *Santobello*, for the promise to seek or not oppose the lesser sentence has been kept. However, some jurisdictions as a matter of state law have adopted the contrary position apparently on the assumption that there is an element of unfairness in holding the defendant to his plea when there was such uncertainty as to the actual result.

If as a part of the plea agreement the prosecutor has promised to recommend a particular disposition, then certainly there has been a broken bargain if the prosecutor fails to make that recommendation or makes a contrary recommendation. Some lower courts had held that such agreements include an implied promise of effective advocacy of the recommendation that, should it not occur, would also entitle the defendant to relief. But in *United States v. Benchimol*,[33] where the prosecutor engaged in no advocacy of and gave no reason for his promised probation recommendation, the Supreme Court rejected the court of appeals' conclusion that there had been a breach. It "was error," said the Court, "for the Court

---

31. Alschuler, The Trial Judge's Role in Plea Bargaining, Part I, 76 Colum.L.Rev.1059, 1134 (1976).

32. 404 U.S. 257, 92 S.Ct. 495, 30 L.Ed.2d 427 (1971).

33. 471 U.S. 453, 105 S.Ct. 2103, 85 L.Ed.2d 462 (1985).

of Appeals to imply as a matter of law a term which the parties themselves did not agree upon." The Court in *Benchimol* emphasized that the instant case was not one in which the government had made an express commitment either to make the recommendation enthusiastically or to state reasons for it, and distinguished those lower court cases in which "the Government attorney appearing personally in court at the time of the plea bargain expressed personal reservations about the agreement to which the Government had committed itself." If the prosecutor promises to recommend a certain sentence and does so, he has not breached the bargain by also bringing all relevant facts to the attention of the court.

If, on the other hand, the plea bargain was that the prosecutor would not recommend a sentence or would not oppose defendant's recommendations, it may be claimed that the prosecutor did too much. Certainly if the prosecutor promised to make no recommendation, there is a breach of the agreement when the prosecutor later recommends that the defendant be given the maximum possible sentence. By contrast, it is generally accepted that a promise of this limited nature is not broken merely by the prosecutor's conduct in supplying relevant facts at the sentencing hearing. But if the prosecutor has entered into a broader commitment, stated in terms of remaining silent or taking no position whatsoever with regard to the sentence, this may be construed as meaning that the prosecutor is barred from volunteering any information detrimental to the defendant. However, there is a disinclination to interpret such promises as commitments to remain silent under all circumstances, and thus it has been held that the prosecutor is free to speak for the purpose of correcting misstatements by the defense or in response to a question from the court, and that he is likewise free to follow his customary practice of responding to requests from the probation office for information on defendant's background and character to be included in the presentence report, and also that he may respond to the standard request from the parole commission as to his recommendation regarding parole.

If the prosecutor has made a promise to recommend or not oppose a certain sentence, the question may arise whether that commitment extends beyond the sentencing hearing and imposition of sentence. For example, if the prosecutor kept that promise at the sentencing hearing but nonetheless the judge imposed a higher sentence than was sought by the defendant, is the prosecutor bound to maintain the same posture if the defendant thereafter moves for a reduction in sentence? This depends upon what the parties to this plea bargain reasonably understood to be the terms of the agreement, A promise not to oppose a certain lenient sentence might well be construed as creating in the defendant's mind a reasonable expectation that the benefits of that promise would be available throughout the proceedings including the hearing on defendant's motion to reduce the sentence. But the same might not be true where the prosecutor's promise was to make no recommendation or to make a particular recommendation. And even a promise to "stand silent at sentencing" does not bar the prosecution from arguing against leniency at a subsequent probation revocation hearing.

In the case of charge bargaining, where the defendant enters a guilty plea to a lesser charge or fewer charges than originally brought, the more obvious types of broken bargain situations rarely occur because typically the more serious or additional charges are dismissed at the very time of defendant's plea. But defendants sometimes claim a violation of the *Santobello* rule when either the court or parole agency takes into account an aspect of defendant's conduct encompassed within a charge dropped pursuant to a plea bargain. Illustrative is a case in which the negotiated plea was to robbery in lieu of the original charge of armed robbery, but at sentencing the judge considered the fact that the defendant had been armed. In these and like circumstances (including when dismissed counts are used to determine the offense level under the federal sentencing guidelines), courts have consistently held that there has been no breaking of the plea bargain. It is emphasized that these facts have obvious and direct relevance to the matters to be decided, so that it would be detrimental to the sentencing and parole release processes if it were necessary to disregard them totally. Moreover, permitting their use is deemed not inconsistent with the terms of the agreement, as a bargain that involves dropping charges is attractive to a defendant primarily because the total length of time to which he can be sentenced is reduced.

Some authority is to be found to the effect that a defendant may be disentitled from prevailing on a broken bargain claim because of his own misconduct. One type of situation is that in which the defendant was able to obtain a promise of concessions by misrepresenting the material facts. Thus, it has been held that where a defendant claiming to have no prior convictions was promised probation but it was later determined he had an out-of-state felony conviction, making him ineligible for probation as a matter of state law, a sentence of imprisonment was properly imposed on the basis of the guilty plea. (If the defendant enters a plea to a lesser offense before his misrepresentation is discovered, some courts treat this as a "misplea," a guilty plea equivalent to a "mistrial" that permits the plea to be rescinded and the higher charge reinstated.) A second situation is that in which additional criminal conduct by the defendant occurs prior to the time of sentencing, which has been held to be a sufficient change in circumstances to justify the state in retreating from the promised recommendation. Certainly the defendant should not be entitled to enforce the bargain in this latter situation, but it is less apparent that permitting withdrawal of the plea would be inappropriate.

Yet another variation of the changed circumstances problem is that in *State v. Thomas*,[34] where the defendant was initially charged with atrocious assault and battery, assault with intent to rob, and robbery of one Murray. A negotiated plea was entered to the first count in exchange for the prosecutor's promise to dismiss the remaining counts, and they were subsequently dropped, but after Murray died the defendant was charged with murder. On defendant's motion to dismiss, the court ruled that under the collateral estoppel rule of *Ashe v. Swenson*[35] the defendant could not be prosecuted on a felony-murder theory. The court reasoned that the "dismissal of the two counts must be treated as a general verdict of acquittal" and that "two issues can be deemed already litigated and decided—defendant did not assault Fannie Murray with intent to rob her nor did he rob her." But this analysis is faulty. Collateral estoppel, as defined in *Ashe*, "means simply that when an issue of ultimate fact has once been determined by a valid and final judgment, that issue cannot again be litigated between the same parties in any future lawsuit," but the dynamics of plea bargaining are such that the dropping of the two counts can hardly be said to rest upon a factual determination that the defendant did not commit the robbery or assault with intent to rob. Moreover, even the concurring Justices in *Ashe*, who preferred a considerably broader rule, acknowledged that any double jeopardy requirement that related crimes be disposed of together did not apply "where a crime is not completed or not discovered, despite diligence on the part of the police, until after the commencement of a prosecution for other crimes arising from the same transaction."

Finally, there is the case in which the government is relieved of the obligation to carry out its promise (or, in some circumstances, is entitled to the remedy of specific performance) because the defendant failed to carry out some obligation under the plea agreement beyond entering the plea. Illustrative is *United States v. Simmons*,[36] where part of the agreement was that the government would recommend a sentence of 15 years "in exchange for the defendants' full, complete, and truthful cooperation regarding this bank robbery." The court held that "in a plea bargain the government's obligation to make a recommendation arises only if defendant performs his obligation

34. 114 N.J.Super. 360, 276 A.2d 391 (1971), order modified 61 N.J. 314, 294 A.2d 57, by rejecting the collateral estoppel analysis and instead reasoning that defendant's plea bargain, entered into with knowledge the victim likely to die, should be enforced so as to "not disappoint a defendant's reasonable expectations."

35. 397 U.S. 436, 90 S.Ct. 1189, 25 L.Ed.2d 469 (1970).

36. 537 F.2d 1260 (4th Cir.1976).

(in this instance, full disclosure)," but then added the important caveat that under *Santobello* "the question whether defendant did in fact fail to perform the condition precedent is an issue not to be finally determined unilaterally by the government, but only on the basis of adequate evidence by the Court." Indeed, even if the agreement expressly declared that the government had "sole discretion" to decide whether defendant had cooperated, the court which approved the bargain has a duty to inquire whether the terms have been followed, and should not permit the government to use its "sole discretion" to disregard its contractual commitments. And even assuming it is clear that the defendant has failed to perform, *Simmons* does not mean that the government will inevitably be able to forego its own obligations under the plea agreement *and* in addition hold the defendant to his plea. Illustrative is *United States v. Fernandez,*[37] where a plea agreement specified the sentence to be imposed as a 6–year term of imprisonment but added that if the defendant did not cooperate as specified "the agreement shall be null and void." When the defendant failed to cooperate, the prosecutor took the position that a sentence over 6 years was now possible and that defendant could not then withdraw his plea. The court disagreed, noting that the defendant "could only have reasonably understood [the above quoted language] to mean that if he failed to live up to his end of the bargain, the entire plea agreement would be null and void."

However, cases of this genre arising under the federal sentencing guidelines, which per § 5K1.1 recognize that the prosecution may make a downward departure motion because of the defendant's substantial assistance to the government, have received somewhat different treatment. This is attributable to the Supreme Court's decision in *Wade v. United States,*[38] where it was held (i) that a sentencing court may not grant defendant a downward departure under § 5K1.1 in the absence of a government motion for same, and (ii) that whether to

make such a motion is discretionary with the government, so that even a defendant who provides substantial assistance is not entitled to a remedy unless an unconstitutional motive underlies the government's refusal to so move. But the Court then made an important qualification, namely, that the government could sacrifice its discretion and obligate itself to move for downward departure in exchange for a plea, and cited as an example *United States v. Watson,*[39] where the plea agreement said that if defendant gave substantial assistance the government "would" so move. After *Wade*, it has become common procedure for federal prosecutors drafting plea agreements with a cooperation-by-defendant ingredient to specifically state therein that the government reserves the "sole discretion" whether or not to file a downward departure motion. Faced with such language, the courts have simply applied the *Wade* holding, meaning that a guilty plea defendant who enters into such an arrangement may receive concessions via downward departure, no matter what the quality and extent of his cooperation, only if the prosecutor later decides to make the requisite motion. This is, at best, an unsettling state of affairs, for under such one-sided agreements the defendant might well provide the promised substantial assistance and still end up with nothing in return.

The defendant may not escape the consequences of his nonperformance merely because the quid pro quo was a concession already given up by the prosecution, such as allowing the defendant to enter a plea to a lesser offense. In *Ricketts v. Adamson,*[40] where defendant, charged with first degree murder, was allowed to plead guilty to second degree murder in exchange for his promise to testify against his confederates, and the agreement specified that if defendant refused to testify "this entire agreement is null and void and the original charge will be automatically reinstated" and the parties "returned to the positions they were in before this agreement," the

---

37.   960 F.2d 771 (9th Cir.1992).

38.   504 U.S. 181, 112 S.Ct. 1840, 118 L.Ed.2d 524 (1992).

39.   988 F.2d 544 (5th Cir.1993).

40.   483 U.S. 1, 107 S.Ct. 2680, 97 L.Ed.2d 1 (1987).

Court held there was no double jeopardy barrier to vacating the second degree murder conviction and prosecuting defendant for first degree murder. This is because "the Double Jeopardy Clause * * * does not relieve a defendant from the consequences of his voluntary choice."[41]

Though that conclusion is not objectionable, the manner in which the Court applied it in *Ricketts* is troublesome. The defendant *did* testify against his confederates and they were convicted, but after their convictions were reversed he refused to testify a second time on the not totally implausible contention that he had already fulfilled completely his part of the bargain.[42] Once the state supreme court ruled defendant's construction of the agreement was in error, defendant offered to testify in the pending retrial of his confederates, but the prosecution rejected that offer in favor of prosecuting defendant for first degree murder. As the four dissenters cogently reasoned, the "logic of the plea bargaining system requires acknowledgment and protection of the defendant's right to advance against the State a reasonable interpretation of the plea agreement." Thus, if the defendant and state disagree as to how the agreement is to be interpreted, the state should not be allowed to treat this as a breach by the defendant, permitting the state to revoke the agreement; rather, at that point "either party may seek to have the agreement construed by the court in which the plea was entered." In light of *Ricketts,* defense counsel would be well advised to insist that plea agreements of this type include an express provision mandating judicial construction of it in the event of a disagreement.

(e) Remedy for Broken Bargain. Assuming now a broken bargain not excused because of the defendant's misconduct or subsequent events, the next question concerns the relief to which the defendant is entitled. This is a matter of some uncertainty, for while the Supreme

Court was unequivocal in ruling in *Santobello v. New York*[43] that there was a constitutional right to relief, that decision is less explicit on the constitutional source of that right and on what remedy is required under what circumstances. The opinion of the Court, joined in by three Justices, makes reference to the requirement that guilty pleas be "knowing and voluntary" and says defendant was entitled to relief in the "interests of justice." The choice of remedy was left to the state court in the first instance, but there is an unexplained intimation that either specific performance or plea withdrawal might be "required" by the "circumstances of the case." Justice Douglas, concurring, indicated that the choice of remedy was itself a constitutional matter, and he asserted that the defendant's preference should be given "considerable, if not controlling, weight." The three remaining members of the Court[44] were no more certain as to the source of the right. They claimed that a breaking of the bargain constitutes "ample justification for rescinding the plea" if the defendant wishes and that if he prefers "it may be appropriate to permit the defendant to enforce the plea bargain."

As for the source of the right, most certainly it is not the requirement that guilty pleas be voluntary, for without regard to subsequent events a plea is either voluntary or involuntary at the time it is made. Perhaps the source is the constitutional requirement that guilty pleas be intelligent, for that requirement reflects the notion that the defendant has a constitutional interest in making an informed choice and that the state cannot mislead the defendant into making a disadvantageous choices. But if this is all there is to *Santobello,* then the intimation therein that a particular remedy might be required in certain unspecified circumstances cannot be taken seriously. By affording the defendant an opportunity to

41. Quoting from and analogizing to United States v. Scott, discussed in § 25.3(a).

42. As the dissenters noted, that was not an unreasonable interpretation of the agreement because it referred to defendant being sentenced "at the conclusion of his testimony" and remaining in the sheriff's custody "until the conclusion of his testimony," but by the time the state

demanded defendant's testimony on retrial the defendant had been sentenced and was no longer in the sheriff's custody.

43. 404 U.S. 257, 92 S.Ct. 495, 30 L.Ed.2d 427 (1971).

44. The Supreme Court had only seven members sitting at the time of the decision.

choose again on the basis of accurate information, the court fully protects the defendant's opportunity to make a meaningful choice, while the remedy of specific performance gives the defendant the full benefit of his original choice and thus suffices to vindicate his constitutional interest in deciding what course is best. This suggests another interpretation of the case: that it extends constitutional protection to the personal expectations created in defendants by plea agreements, on the notion that it is fundamentally unfair for the state to create and then destroy a defendant's expectations.

Although federal courts finding a *Santobello* violation on habeas corpus by a state prisoner ordinarily give the state court the opportunity to decide which remedy is more appropriate, federal courts ruling on claims by federal prisoners and state courts ruling on claims of state defendants rather regularly opt for the remedy of specific performance. This may be taken as some support for the protection-of-expectations theory noted above, which would generally call for such a remedy, or it may only reflect that these courts have perceived that as a policy matter specific performance is usually the most appropriate remedy, one which serves the state's interest in the continued vitality of the process of plea negotiation. Whichever is the case, clearly specific performance is usually the remedy to be preferred, which may be seen by a closer look at two situations: that in which the defendant's preference for vacatur of the plea is contested; and that in which his preference for specific performance is challenged.

Assume first a case in which the plea bargain was not kept and consequently the defendant asks that he be allowed to withdraw his plea, but the prosecution counters that withdrawal should not be permitted because it is prepared to carry out the remedy of specific performance. Four members of the Court in *Santobello* appeared to conclude that in such circumstances withdrawal of the plea and trial on the original charges[45] should be ordered,

but their explanations for this conclusion are less than compelling. Justice Douglas offered only the non sequitur that because it is the defendant's rights which were violated it must be the defendant's choice of remedy which is given preference, while the three dissenters asserted that the breaking of the bargain "undercuts the basis for the waiver of constitutional rights implicit in the plea" and thus allows those rights to be reclaimed by the defendant. But whether the constitutional basis for *Santobello* is to protect defendants from entering guilty pleas that are not intelligent or to enforce their state-created expectations, the defendant need not be given an option to rescind if the state agrees to give him the benefit of the original bargain. Both the intelligent-plea interest and the protection-of-expectations interest can be satisfied by specific performance because it gives the defendant everything on which he relied in entering the plea.

Although some authority is to be found supporting the proposition that the defendant is entitled to elect the remedy of recission, these cases do not indicate that the prosecutor had any objection. It has also been held that there is no right to the remedy of plea withdrawal, and on remand in *Santobello* the court ruled such a remedy was inappropriate where the prosecution objected because due process and the interest of justice would be fully served by specific performance of the prosecutor's promise. The court emphasized that the facts of the case did not produce an "outraged sense of fairness," perhaps a reference to the inadvertence of the prosecution's noncompliance. From this, it might be argued that in the case of a deliberate breaking of the plea agreement by the prosecutor it would be justifiable to "punish" the prosecutor by allowing the defendant to withdraw the plea if he wishes, for a belated specific performance only requires the prosecutor to do what he had agreed to do in the first place. But because in most cases the state's breach is either inadvertent or arguably justified by some change in circumstances, this punishment theory would be use-

---

45. On the question of whether, after plea withdrawal, trial on the previously dismissed charges is permissible, see § 21.5(e).

ful in a relatively few cases and might not be worth the added burden of a specific determination regarding the character of the prosecutor's conduct.

Assume now the reverse situation, where again the plea bargain was not kept but the defendant wants specific performance while the prosecution takes the position that only withdrawal of the plea should be permitted. When the breach was a failure by the prosecutor to carry out a promise that was fulfillable, then certainly the defendant's request for specific performance should be honored. This is most certainly the case when the defendant has relied on the promise to his detriment, as where a prosecutor failed to keep his promise as to what sentence recommendation he would make if the defendant first were to plead guilty and spend 60 days at a correctional center for evaluation. Though it has occasionally been held that withdrawal is the preferred remedy in the absence of such irrevocable prejudice, that position is unsound. Even absent a showing of prejudice, there is no reason why a prosecutor who has failed to keep his fulfillable plea bargain promise should be allowed to force the defendant into a withdrawal of the plea and thus, presumably, a permanent breach of the bargain. The same may be said of the case in which the breach is by the court in reneging on its earlier acceptance of a lawful plea agreement, or in which the court exceeded its authority in not permitting the prosecutor to carry through on a charge bargain.

A defendant who objects to the breach of his bargain by the prosecutor or the court is not entitled to more performance than he should have received the first time around. For example, if an appellate court finds that the prosecutor failed to recommend a certain sentence as promised in the plea agreement, that court should not remand with an order that the recommended sentence be imposed. But sometimes the procedure the second time around must be somewhat different to ensure that the taint of the prior breach is overcome. Lower courts often follow the suggestion in *Santobel-*

lo v. New York[46] that specific performance requires remand for sentencing by a different judge, one not exposed to the prosecution's more harsh recommendations made in breach of the agreement.

Much more difficult are those cases in which the promise that was made by the prosecutor or some other agent of the state is "unfulfillable" in the sense that it is a commitment to produce a result not authorized by law or beyond the power of the promisor to produce. Illustrative of the latter are where the prosecutor makes commitments as to the sentence actually to be imposed, the time of release on parole, nonprosecution outside his county or district or even in another jurisdiction, nonextradition to another country, termination of civil proceedings against the defendant, or favorable action by an administrative agency. In such circumstances the court faces an unpleasant choice: order specific enforcement of the unauthorized promise and thus bind officials who took no part in the plea negotiations, or merely allow withdrawal of the guilty plea and thereby ignore defendant's reliance on the bargain. But when that reliance is nothing more than an expectation that the promise would be kept and withdrawing the plea will approximate the *status quo ante,* there is good reason to deny the defendant his desired remedy of specific performance. Otherwise there would be unnecessary encroachment upon established doctrine on the allocation of authority, such as that the prosecutor cannot bind the judge as to the sentence and cannot bind decisionmakers in another jurisdiction as to charging, sentencing, or release from incarceration.

When the defendant's reliance is more substantial, then a more delicate balancing process is required. One factor that must be considered is the precise nature and extent of the detrimental reliance. If the defendant has served a period of imprisonment under the plea, has provided information to the authorities as part of the plea agreement, or has been jeopardized as to his defense by the turn of events, a court may be more willing to turn to specific enforcement even though the neces-

---

46.   404 U.S. 257, 92 S.Ct. 495, 30 L.Ed.2d 427 (1971).

sary consequence is to limit the discretion of persons who were not even parties to the plea agreement. A second factor that appears to enter into the resolution of these cases is the extent to which it is important to preserve the independence of the other agency that would be required to act in a certain way if specific performance were ordered. One would expect, therefore, that in the case of significant detrimental reliance a court would be more ready to grant specific performance that estopped charges by another prosecutor serving a different county or district of the same jurisdiction than such a remedy that barred charges in a different jurisdiction. Such analysis is also useful as to the so-called illegal promise. For example, if the prosecutor has promised a sentence that the law does not allow under the circumstances, it is not unthinkable that some manipulation of the defendant's sentence to produce a comparable benefit might occur.

(f) The Withdrawn Offer. The thrust of the preceding discussion is that once the defendant enters his negotiated plea the prosecutor may not now withdraw his offer, even if he does so prior to sentencing, the time when the prosecutor was to deliver on his promises. This is not to suggest, however, that withdrawal prior to the defendant's plea is inevitably permissible. The prevailing doctrine is that the state may withdraw from a plea bargain agreement at any time prior to, but not after, the entry of the guilty plea by the defendant or other action by him constituting detrimental reliance upon the agreement (e.g., giving a self-incriminating deposition).

Going well beyond that position is *Cooper v. United States*,[47] holding that unless the prosecutor's plea proposal is properly conditioned it is enforceable by a defendant who, prior to the prosecutor's withdrawal of the offer, had neither entered a guilty plea nor relied to his detriment on the bargain. Counsel for Cooper, charged with two counts each of bribery of a witness and obstruction of justice, was told by an assistant U.S. Attorney that if his client would plead guilty to one count, remain in jail

and testify in upcoming narcotics trials, then the government would dismiss the other charges and bring Cooper's cooperation to the attention of the sentencing judge. Counsel immediately communicated this proposal to Cooper, who accepted, but when he finally was able to reach the prosecutor by phone a few hours later counsel was told that the offer was withdrawn. Cooper was thereafter convicted on all counts, but on appeal it was held "that the defendant's constitutional rights were here violated by the government's failure to honor its plea proposal." The court declared that there were "two distinct sources" for that ruling: (1) the Sixth Amendment right to effective assistance of counsel, involved here because to "the extent that the government attempts through defendant's counsel to change or retract positions earlier communicated, a defendant's confidence in his counsel's capability and professional responsibility * * * are necessarily jeopardized and the effectiveness of counsel's assistance easily compromised"; and (2) a due process right to enforcement of the plea proposal "on the basis alone of expectations reasonably formed in reliance upon the honor of the government in making and abiding by its proposals" where, as here, the offer was unambiguous and not unreasonable and was promptly assented to by the defendant and no "extenuating circumstances affecting the propriety of the proposal" intervened.

A unanimous Supreme Court rejected the *Cooper* approach in *Mabry v. Johnson*.[48] As for the right to counsel argument, the Court stated it failed "to see how an accused could reasonably attribute the prosecutor's change of heart to his counsel any more than he could have blamed counsel had the trial judge chosen to reject the agreed-upon recommendation, or, for that matter, had he gone to trial and been convicted." Moreover, there was no guilty plea obtained in violation of due process. When his agreement to accept the prosecution's offer of a 21-year concurrent sentence for a murder plea resulted in that offer being withdrawn as "a mistake" and replaced by an offer of a 21-year consecutive sentence, the

---

47.　594 F.2d 12 (4th Cir.1979).

48.　467 U.S. 504, 104 S.Ct. 2543, 81 L.Ed.2d 437 (1984).

defendant accepted the second offer after the trial began. Noting that this plea "was in no sense induced by the prosecutor's withdrawn offer," the Court concluded that defendant's "inability to enforce the prosecutor's offer is without constitutional significance" because that offer "did not impair the voluntariness or intelligence of his guilty plea." (Because there was neither a guilty plea *nor* any other form of detrimental reliance in *Mabry*, that decision does not address the question whether reliance short of a plea or other waiver of constitutional rights would be the basis for a due process objection.) As for the prosecutor's possible negligence or culpability in making and withdrawing the first offer, the Court deemed that irrelevant because the due process clause "is not a code of ethics for prosecutors" but is concerned "with the manner in which persons are deprived of their liberty."

A variation of the withdrawn offer issue arises when a defendant declines to accept a plea bargain tendered by the prosecutor before trial and then, some time after the trial is under way or even after conviction and at the time of sentencing, the defendant asserts a right to receive the concessions earlier tendered. A defendant is even less likely to prevail in such circumstances, for if the concessions offered earlier had to remain available there would be little point in a defendant not going to trial and taking his chances on acquittal. Once a trial begins, a prosecutor has less reason to negotiate a plea bargain than prior to trial, and thus a decision by a prosecutor to cut off plea bargaining at the time trial begins follows logically from one reason for engaging in plea bargaining: judicial economy through the avoidance of trials.

(g) The Unrealized Expectation. As a general matter, it may be said that a guilty plea defendant is not entitled to relief merely because the sentence that he received is greater than he had hoped or anticipated would be imposed in his case. And this is so even if the defendant's hope or anticipation was attributable to comments made by his attorney.

For example, where defense counsel told the defendant that he believed a two-year sentence would be imposed but this was related to the defendant in equivocal terms of what "could" or "perhaps" happen, but the defendant was thereafter sentenced to eight years, the guilty plea is valid. The rule in *Santobello v. New York*[49] to the effect that the Constitution compels relief in the case of a broken plea bargain has no application here. However, if the defense attorney's "prediction" is stated in more definite terms and, as it turns out, is significantly inaccurate, there is the possibility that the defendant will be able to mount a successful attack upon his plea on the ground that he was denied the effective assistance of counsel.

Such cases must be distinguished from those in which the defendant is led to believe, most likely because of comments made by defense counsel, that a plea agreement has actually been reached with the prosecutor or the judge, but in fact there is no such agreement and the defendant does not thereafter receive the concessions contemplated under the nonexistent plea agreement. In such circumstances the courts have rather consistently held that the plea is involuntary, although it is more precise to say that the guilty plea is constitutionally defective because not "intelligent" due to the defendant's misunderstanding of what the consequences of his plea were to be. But the fundamental point is that in such a case the defendant was "entitled to credit his attorney's representation as to the fact of such an agreement, and to rely on it. So that he is entitled to relief if his guilty plea was induced by such a representation."

That situation must likewise be distinguished from yet another, where the defendant had a belief that there existed a plea bargain including certain concessions he did not thereafter receive, but that belief was erroneous and was based upon comments by the defense attorney or others not specifically stating a plea agreement with those concessions had been reached. Purely as a matter of logic, this case would seem to be no different than the

49. 404 U.S. 257, 92 S.Ct. 495, 30 L.Ed.2d 427 (1971).

preceding one. As explained in *United States ex rel. Thurmond v. Mancusi:*[50]

> If, at the time he pled guilty, the defendant believed that a coercive promise or threat had been made by either the court or the prosecutor, though in fact no such promise or threat had been made, and his plea was induced by this belief, it is an involuntary and void plea. This conclusion necessarily follows from the fact that voluntariness connotes a state of mind of an actor. If the actor—i.e., the defendant—believes that a promise has been made, the effect on his state of mind is exactly the same as if such a promise had in fact been made. Thus, any test of whether a person acts voluntarily is necessarily "subjective."

But that is not the prevailing view. Rather, state and federal courts have taken the position that the defendant must in addition show that his belief was a reasonable one under the circumstances. This burden of showing a reasonable belief has been imposed because of a fear that otherwise the granting of a motion for plea withdrawal would be automatic upon the movant's assertion that his guilty plea resulted from a subjectively mistaken belief, for it could not be established whether in fact this misunderstanding was actual or feigned. Some argue, however, that those fears are unwarranted and do not justify abandonment of the subjective test which, on principle, is correct. They believe that issues of fact such as a person's state of mind can be accurately decided on the basis of reasonable inferences drawn from the known surrounding facts and circumstances.

In any event, a valid unrealized expectation claim should be rare under the reforms that have been adopted regarding receipt of guilty pleas. The practice of having any plea bargain placed on the record and of making specific inquiry of the defendant regarding his expectations and understandings[51] will make it highly unlikely, albeit not impossible, that under either a subjective or reasonableness test a defendant can make out a plausible mistaken

belief claim thereafter.[52] If such a claim is made out, it must be remembered that this is not a broken bargain under the *Santobello* case and that consequently the defendant is not entitled to demand specific performance of a promise in fact never made; the remedy is withdrawal of the plea. However, if the prosecution is able to alter the disposition so that it conforms to the defendant's expectations and elects to do so, then the defendant will obtain all he says he was promised and can then have no right to withdraw his plea.

(h) Admission of Statements Made During Bargaining. The modern trend to hold inadmissible the defendant's offer to plead guilty, the plea agreement or statements made in the course of plea negotiations when no guilty plea is subsequently entered or if entered is withdrawn makes obvious sense. A contrary rule would discourage plea negotiations and agreements, for defendants would have to be constantly concerned whether, in light of their plea negotiation activities, they could successfully defend on the merits if a plea ultimately was not entered.

There has been some dispute as to how broad this rule ought to be, and in particular whether it should ever extend to admissions by the defendant to someone other than the prosecutor. The current federal rule covers only statements made by the defendant in court when a plea is tendered or during plea discussions with the prosecutor. The theory is that such a rule fully protects the plea discussion process authorized by federal law without attempting to deal with confrontations between suspects and law enforcement agents, which involve problems of quite different dimensions best resolved by that body of law dealing with police interrogations. Some have criticized this view on the ground that it fails to provide protection for defendants who plea bargain under the reasonable belief that the agent has bargaining authority, as where representations by the law enforcement officer or other circumstances lead the defendant to conclude that the officer is the proper person with

---

50.   275 F.Supp. 508 (E.D.N.Y.1967).

51.   See § 21.4(b).

52.   See § 22.5(d).

whom to negotiate. At least some states follow the broader view.

The rule regarding statements made during plea negotiations must be distinguished from that concerning statements made subsequent to a plea later withdrawn. The Supreme Court dealt with such a situation in *Hutto v. Ross*,[53] reversing the holding below that defendant's confession, given subsequent to a negotiated plea agreement from which the defendant later withdrew, was involuntary because it would not have been made "but for the plea bargaining." Noting that "causation in that sense has never been the test of voluntariness," the Court concluded:

> The existence of the bargain may well have entered into respondent's decision to give a statement, but counsel made it clear to respondent that he could enforce the terms of the plea bargain whether or not he confessed. The confession thus does not appear to have been the result of "any direct or implied promises" or any coercion on the part of the prosecution, and was not involuntary.

A different result has been reached with respect to post-plea statements made by the defendant in compliance with a commitment made in the plea bargain or on the representation of defense counsel that they were necessary to comply with the plea agreement.

Assuming now a statement made during plea discussions under circumstances that would as a general matter make it inadmissible against the defendant, a question may arise as to whether the rule of inadmissibility is absolute. What, for example, if the statement is offered for the limited purpose of impeachment? Although it has been argued by analogy to *Harris v. New York*,[54] holding admissible for impeachment purposes a voluntary statement obtained in violation of *Miranda*, that the answer should be yes, the courts have quite properly rejected that argument. *Harris,* has no application in a plea

bargaining context in which a waiver of the privilege against self-incrimination is an aspect of the plea obtained by active participation of the prosecution. A better analogy is *New Jersey v. Portash*,[55] holding that testimony obtained by a grant of immunity involves "the constitutional privilege against compulsory self-incrimination in its most pristine form" and does not permit a balancing that takes into account the need to prevent perjury. A contrary rule in the plea bargaining context, even if constitutionally permissible, would be unwise, for it would have a strong chilling effect on plea negotiations.

But the rule of inadmissibility is *not* absolute in another sense, for in *United States v. Mezzanatto*[56] the Court held the aforementioned federal plea-statement rule does not "depart from the presumption of waivability" that exists as to "legal rights generally, and evidentiary provisions specifically." And thus, concluded the Court, a defendant at the outset of plea discussions could agree that any statement he made could be used to impeach any contradictory testimony if the case went to trial.[57] In rejecting the defendant's claim that such waiver is inconsistent with the rule's goal of encouraging voluntary settlement, the Court reasoned it "makes no sense to conclude that mutual settlement will be encouraged by precluding negotiation over an issue that may be particularly important to one of the parties to the transaction."

§ 21.3 Plea Negotiation Responsibilities of the Attorneys and Judge

(a) Right to Counsel During Plea Bargaining. The Sixth Amendment right to counsel in criminal cases applies not only at the criminal trial, but also at various other "critical stages" of the criminal process. For one thing, this means that the defendant has a right to counsel at the arraignment, the time

---

53. 429 U.S. 28, 97 S.Ct. 202, 50 L.Ed.2d 194 (1976).

54. 401 U.S. 222, 91 S.Ct. 643, 28 L.Ed.2d 1 (1971).

55. 440 U.S. 450, 99 S.Ct. 1292, 59 L.Ed.2d 501 (1979).

56. 513 U.S. 196, 115 S.Ct. 797, 130 L.Ed.2d 697 (1995).

57. Perhaps that marks the limits of permissible waiver. Two Justices dissented in *Mezzanatto*, while three others speculated "that a waiver to use such statements in the case-in-chief would more severely undermine a defendant's incentive to negotiate, and thereby inhibit plea bargaining."

when the defendant is called upon to enter his plea.[1] For another, it means that there is a constitutional right to counsel at extrajudicial proceedings occurring after "the initiation of adversary judicial criminal proceedings" whenever "a defendant finds himself faced with the prosecutorial forces of organized society, and immersed in the intricacies of substantive and procedural criminal law."[2]

Applying this test, it is clear that there is a Sixth Amendment right to the assistance of counsel at a plea negotiation session with the prosecutor or his agents. For a prosecuting attorney to talk with the defendant in the absence of his counsel and attempt to have him change a plea of not guilty is to deprive the defendant of the effective assistance of counsel at a time when it was needed. And if such a violation of the defendant's Sixth Amendment right to counsel occurs, it cannot be dismissed on the supposition that the defendant effectively represented himself at the bargaining session. (But as to pre-indictment bargaining, increasingly common because of the federal Sentencing Guidelines,[3] one court concluded that under the Supreme Court's rulings it had no choice but to hold that no Sixth Amendment right to counsel existed at that time, a result the court deemed most unfortunate.)

What is less clear is how the situation is to be handled when defense counsel reenters the case at some later point. What if, for example, the prosecutor improperly meets with defendant in the absence of defense counsel and engages in plea bargaining with him but the plea of guilty subsequently entered by the defendant is pursuant to a bargain defendant's counsel was aware of and had discussed with defendant prior to the entry of his plea? One view is that pursuant to *McMann v. Richardson*[4] the defendant's constitutional claim must focus upon whether, as the Supreme Court put

it in that case, counsel's advice "was within the range of competence demanded of attorneys in criminal cases." But it is more precise to say that in such circumstances there exists *both* the question of the voluntariness of the plea and of the effectiveness of counsel's representation; the uncounseled bargaining session may not be divorced from any effect it had on the adequacy of defense counsel's subsequent performance or defendant's subsequent volition.

As for waiver of the constitutional right to counsel in the plea bargaining context, it has been argued that such waiver should not be permitted because (unlike the possible tactical advantage at trial) there is nothing for a defendant to gain by being unrepresented in the guilty plea context. This may explain why a few jurisdictions, at least in the past, have taken the position that felony defendants may not plead guilty without counsel. But in light of the Supreme Court's recognition in *Faretta v. California*[5] of a constitutional right to proceed pro se, which presumably is applicable in the guilty plea context as well, it appears that waiver must be permitted.

Waiver of counsel, to be effective, must be "intelligent and competent."[6] Certainly a defendant who is contemplating waiver of his constitutional right to counsel "should be made aware of the dangers and disadvantages of self-representation,"[7] and surely this requires an especially careful procedure in a guilty plea context because of defendant's likely ignorance of what assistance counsel can provide even if there will be no trial. Yet some courts have reached the remarkable conclusion that when the defendant was informed of the charge against him and of his right to appointed counsel and responded that he desired to plead guilty, this was an implicit waiver of counsel. Equally troubling is the occasional ruling that the right to counsel at a plea

§ 21.3

1. Cf. White v. Maryland, 373 U.S. 59, 83 S.Ct. 1050, 10 L.Ed.2d 193 (1963).

2. Kirby v. Illinois, 406 U.S. 682, 92 S.Ct. 1877, 32 L.Ed.2d 411 (1972).

3. See § 21.1(h).

4. 397 U.S. 759, 90 S.Ct. 1441, 25 L.Ed.2d 763 (1970).

5. 422 U.S. 806, 95 S.Ct. 2525, 45 L.Ed.2d 562 (1975).

6. Johnson v. Zerbst, 304 U.S. 458, 58 S.Ct. 1019, 82 L.Ed. 1461 (1938).

7. Faretta v. California, 422 U.S. 806, 95 S.Ct. 2525, 45 L.Ed.2d 562 (1975).

bargaining session was waived because it was the defendant, rather than the prosecutor or his agent, who initiated the meeting at which defense counsel was absent.

(b) Effective Assistance by Defense Counsel. The Sixth Amendment right of a guilty plea defendant to is to the *effective* assistance of counsel, which is to be determined not by a hindsight assessment of whether the attorney's actions and conduct were right or wrong, but rather by an inquiry into whether they fell "within the range of competence demanded of attorneys in criminal cases."[8] There is greater uncertainty as to what this means in a guilty plea context as compared to a trial context, perhaps because until recent years courts were disinclined to acknowledge either the existence or the legitimacy of plea negotiations. In any event, there is an additional requirement that the defendant have been prejudiced by the ineffective assistance,[9] and what this means in a guilty plea context is that the defendant must show "a reasonable probability that, but for counsel's errors, he would not have pleaded guilty and would have insisted on going to trial."[10] If the ineffective assistance resulted in the defendant *rejecting* a plea bargain and not pleading guilty, then, of course, the prejudice question is whether, absent the ineffective assistance, the defendant *would* have entered a guilty plea.

There is not complete agreement by the courts as to the defense attorney's responsibility to conduct an investigation of the relevant facts when his client has indicated a disposition toward a plea of guilty. One view is that an extensive, independent investigation would be superfluous in such circumstances, but this overlooks the fact that in an adversary system, it is not the role of counsel merely to acquiesce in a guilty plea decision made independently by his client. Thus it is the responsibility of the defense attorney in that setting to conduct a prompt investigation of the circumstances of

the case and to explore all avenues leading to facts relevant to the merits of the case and the penalty in the event of conviction. Courts in recent years have been more inclined to find that a defense attorney's failure to interview witnesses or otherwise investigate the case falls short of effective assistance, and that the defendant's guilty plea cannot stand where it appears such investigation would have uncovered facts significantly strengthening the defense case or where the absence of such investigation prejudiced the defendant's ability to make an intelligent and voluntary plea of guilty.

This responsibility to investigate is related to defense counsel's broader obligation to confer with his client and to give him advice. It is essential that the attorney advise the defendant of the available options and possible consequences, though there is not complete agreement on the extent of a defense attorney's responsibilities in this regard. For example, there is a split of authority on the question of when, if ever, a defense attorney is responsible for alerting an alien defendant of the fact that conviction could result in deportation. The view that if deportation is a "collateral consequence" about which the judge receiving the plea need not warn, then it follows defense counsel is not rendering ineffective assistance in failing to admonish the defendant, is certainly open to question. It is not apparent why a defense counsel's obligations should be deemed to be no more extensive than those of the judge.

It is quite proper for the attorney to express a view on the appropriate course of action, including whether a particular plea appears to be desirable. But it is for the client to decide what plea should be entered. Courts have held that defense counsel coerced defendant's plea where he threatened to withdraw from the case if a guilty plea was not entered and where

---

8. McMann v. Richardson, 397 U.S. 759, 90 S.Ct. 1441, 25 L.Ed.2d 763 (1970).

9. Strickland v. Washington, 466 U.S. 668, 104 S.Ct. 2052, 80 L.Ed.2d 674 (1984), discussed in § 11.10.

10. Hill v. Lockhart, 474 U.S. 52, 106 S.Ct. 366, 88 L.Ed.2d 203 (1985). For example, the Court elaborated, if

the error was a failure to discover potentially exculpatory evidence, the question is whether "discovery of the evidence would have led counsel to change his recommendation as to the plea," which in turn depends on "whether the evidence likely would have changed the outcome of a trial."

the lawyer's advice was so strongly worded as to constitute a threat.

Sometimes the question is whether the particular recommendation of defense counsel constitutes ineffective assistance under the circumstances of the case. For example, what of a recommendation to accept a plea bargain made to a defendant who has asserted his innocence? One view is that it is unreasonable for counsel to recommend a guilty plea to a defendant without first cautioning him that, no matter what, he should not plead guilty unless he believed himself guilty, for our judicial system has so many safeguards that it may not be assumed that an innocent person will be convicted. The contrary view is that if a fair assessment of the prosecution's case indicates a substantial likelihood of conviction and severe sanctions, then defense counsel should not be barred from recommending the negotiated plea route merely because the defendant might in fact be innocent or because the defendant cannot bring himself to acknowledge his guilt. The latter position draws support from *North Carolina v. Alford*,[11] where the Supreme Court ruled it was constitutionally permissible to accept a guilty plea from a defendant who claimed to be innocent if there was a "strong factual basis for the plea." Even more troublesome is somewhat the reverse situation, where an apparently guilty defendant has entered a guilty plea on advise of counsel notwithstanding the likelihood that defendant would not have been convicted if he had gone to trial. The fundamental dilemma is whether defense counsel's duty to his client should be viewed solely in terms of obtaining for him as lenient a sentence as possible, or whether instead the attorney should advise his client in terms of what appears to be an appropriate correctional disposition.

A defendant has no right to be present at a plea negotiation conference between his attorney and the prosecutor, and typically he will not be present. As a result, problems can arise concerning communication or lack thereof to the defendant of any plea bargain offer put forward by the prosecutor. One difficulty, discussed earlier,[12] is that the defense attorney may intentionally or inadvertently cause the defendant to believe the prosecutor (or, if he is involved in the negotiation process, the judge) has agreed to certain concessions in exchange for defendant's plea when in fact that has not occurred. Another, in a sense the opposite of this, is that the defense attorney may fail to communicate to the defendant a plea offer. It has been held that just as a defendant has the right to make a decision to plead not guilty, he also has the right to make the decision to plead guilty, which has been denied if his attorney has not informed him of the concessions offered. A more difficult case would be that in which defense counsel did not convey the offer because he feared that the defendant, who theretofore had asserted his innocence, would unwisely accept it, but even there it would seem that the better course is for counsel to communicate the offer and then give his professional opinion as to whether it should be accepted.

Another question is whether in the absence of such overtures by the prosecutor it is always or sometimes an obligation of defense counsel to sound out the prosecutor as to what concessions would be granted in exchange for a plea of guilty by his client. One view is that at least when the lawyer concludes, on the basis of full investigation and study, that under controlling law and the evidence, a conviction is probable, he should so advise the accused and seek his consent to engage in plea discussions with the prosecutor. Indeed, it has been asserted that such plea discussions should be considered the norm and that failure to seek them is excusable only when defense counsel concludes that sound reasons exist for not doing so. But just when a failure of defense counsel to take the initiative in this way constitutes ineffective assistance is not entirely clear, as the issue has seldom reached the courts. It has been held, however, that defendant's guilt is not by itself an excuse for not exploring plea bargaining opportunities, and that the failure to initiate plea bargain negotiations is inexcusable when

---

11. 400 U.S. 25, 91 S.Ct. 160, 27 L.Ed.2d 162 (1970), discussed in § 21.4(f).

12. See § 21.2(g).

there is a fairly apparent weakness in the prosecution's case.

If plea negotiations are undertaken, there are ethical and tactical questions that can arise concerning defense counsel's dealings with the prosecutor or the judge. Unquestionably it is unethical for the defense attorney to circumvent the prosecutor and in a secret ex parte proceeding attempt to extract a promise of concessions from the judge. As for his dealings with the prosecutor, certainly some degree of "bluffing" is engaged in by both the prosecutor and the defense attorney. Excesses in this regard by the prosecutor can amount to a denial of due process, but as a matter of professional ethics it is improper for defense counsel to knowingly make false statements concerning the evidence in the course of plea discussions with the prosecutor. Such action is also counterproductive, for it severely handicaps counsel's usefulness to the accused and to future clients. But the defense attorney is not obligated to reveal evidence to the prosecution; counsel must preserve the client's confidences unless granted consent to make disclosures for this purpose. Informal discovery in the plea bargaining context is often treated by defense attorneys as a two-way street, on the ground that they thereby establish with the prosecutor a good working relationship from which ultimately will flow substantial benefits to the defendant.

Yet another aspect of the Sixth Amendment right to the effective assistance of counsel is that defendant is entitled to be represented by an attorney who is not hampered by a conflict of interest. The mere existence of a conflict does not inevitably mean that a particular defendant has received less than adequate representation, but the problem is that it is extremely difficult to ascertain whether the conflict had any impact upon the attorney's representations. Indeed, as the Supreme Court has noted, "to assess the impact of a conflict of interests on the attorney's options, tactics and decisions in plea negotiations would be

virtually impossible."[13] Joint representation is not per se a violation of the constitutional guarantee of effective assistance by counsel,[14] but conflicts most frequently arise out of such arrangements. Illustrative are these situations: (1) where there was a "package deal" in which defense counsel could obtain a favorable disposition for one client only if the other defendants in the case, also represented by him, also plead guilty; (2) where defense counsel was representing one client who implicated others in the hope of favorable treatment, and also one of those implicated, whose plea of guilty as recommended by counsel served to build a record of cooperation by the first client; (3) where defense counsel, representing two persons charged with joint possession of marijuana, stressed the relatively minor role of one defendant and consequently made the other appear more culpable; and (4) where defense counsel advised against a plea bargain contemplating the defendant would then testify at the trial of another defendant, also represented by this attorney. Conflicts may arise for other reasons as well, as where counsel might advise against a negotiated plea because his fee is collectible only if the defendant is acquitted.

Once the defendant establishes that "a conflict of interest actually affected the adequacy of his representation," he is entitled to relief without also establishing the proof of prejudice required in other circumstances.[15] In the guilty plea context, this means, for example, that if an attorney's multiple representation caused him to forego plea negotiations for one defendant, that defendant is entitled to relief without any showing separate counsel would have brought about a more advantageous disposition of the case.

If a defense attorney has brought about a negotiated plea, does he nonetheless have an obligation to apprise the defendant of his right to appeal following his guilty plea? At least sometimes, for the Court in *Roe v. Flores–*

13. Holloway v. Arkansas, 435 U.S. 475, 98 S.Ct. 1173, 55 L.Ed.2d 426 (1978)

14. Holloway v. Arkansas, 435 U.S. 475, 98 S.Ct. 1173, 55 L.Ed.2d 426 (1978).

15. Holloway v. Arkansas, 435 U.S. 475, 98 S.Ct. 1173, 55 L.Ed.2d 426 (1978).

Ortega[16] held that an obligation to give such advice exists when either (1) the defendant has reasonably demonstrated to counsel his or her interest in filing an appeal, or (2) a rational defendant would want to appeal under the circumstances.[17] A "highly relevant factor" in making this determination, the Court added, is that there was a plea of guilty, for "a guilty plea reduces the scope of potentially appealable issues and * * * may indicate that the defendant seeks an end to judicial proceedings."

(c) The Prosecutor's Bargaining Tactics. In considering the prosecutor's role in the plea negotiation process, a logical first inquiry is whether there is some obligation upon the prosecutor to engage in bargaining with defendants. The courts have rather consistently answered in the negative. As the Supreme Court declared in *Weatherford v. Bursey*,[18] "there is no constitutional right to plea bargain; the prosecutor need not do so if he prefers to go to trial. It is a novel argument that constitutional rights are infringed by trying the defendant rather than accepting his plea of guilty." This is because plea bargaining is an aspect of the prosecutor's broad charging discretion whereunder he is permitted to decide when and whether to institute criminal proceedings, or what precise charge shall be made, or whether to dismiss a proceeding once brought.

But it would not be correct to say that a court should in no circumstances become involved in assessing the prosecutor's refusal to bargain. For example, if a prosecutor were to adopt a practice of refusing to bargain with any defendants represented by certain attorneys, disciplining of the prosecutor would certainly be appropriate. Moreover, just as is true of the prosecutor's charging decision,[19] a court is entitled to grant relief to a defendant when he shows that the prosecutor's conduct is so arbitrary as to constitute a denial of equal protection of the laws under the Fourteenth

Amendment. But as we have already seen with respect to the charging decision, a defendant is likely to prevail on an equal protection claim only rarely and in extraordinary circumstances. Constitutional inequality is not demonstrated by the mere fact that two or more individuals are charged with the same or similar offenses and a plea-offer was not extended to all of them.

This notion that plea bargaining is simply an aspect of the prosecutor's charging discretion and thus subject to no greater judicial supervision has sometimes been questioned. So the argument goes, prosecutors may usually be trusted when they exercise a unilateral discretion in deciding whether and what to charge, but there is greater reason for mistrust when it comes to plea negotiations because then prosecutors gain something of value for deciding that a certain punishment is adequate. But whether there is judicial supervision or not, prosecutors should affirmatively act to ensure that their plea bargaining practices are rational. Certainly similarly situated defendants should be afforded equal plea agreement opportunities, though a more common problem may be that equal bargaining opportunities and concessions will be made available to defendants whose situations are only superficially similar. A plea negotiation process which is fair, which is perceived to be fair, and which permits the attainment of desirable correctional goals can therefore be achieved only if the prosecutor establishes policy guidelines and procedures for bargaining and ensures that facts relevant to determining the appropriate disposition are at hand at the time the bargaining occurs.

If a prosecutor were to bring a greater charge against the defendant than is supported by the evidence in order to increase his plea bargaining leverage, this would unquestionably be improper. More controversial, however, is the not uncommon practice of "overcharging" in another sense, as where the

16. 528 U.S. 470, 120 S.Ct. 1029, 145 L.Ed.2d 985 (2000).

17. The Court noted, however, that for a failure to apprise to be prejudicial, there must be a reasonable

likelihood that the defendant, had he been apprised, would have opted for appeal.

18. 429 U.S. 545, 97 S.Ct. 837, 51 L.Ed.2d 30 (1977).

19. See § 13.4.

prosecutor files a felony charge supported by the evidence in the hope of inducing a plea to a misdemeanor when, as a matter of general prosecutive policy, the case would actually be tried only on a misdemeanor charge. Although the Supreme Court held in *Bordenkircher v. Hayes*[20] that such conduct was not unconstitutional, there is a division of opinion as to whether this charging practice is ethical and proper.

Yet another practice a prosecutor may engage in during plea negotiations is some degree of "bluffing" concerning the strength of his case against the defendant at the present time. The range of possibilities here is substantial, all the way from withholding exculpatory evidence to not volunteering the immediate unavailability of a certain witness, though most prosecutors feel obligated to produce evidence indicating factual innocence. The Supreme Court, albeit dealing with cases that *had* gone to trial, has held that it is a violation of due process for a prosecutor to withhold favorable evidence whenever "there is a reasonable probability that, had the evidence been disclosed to the defense, the result of the proceeding would have been different."[21] Courts have been inclined to find that due process mandates some disclosure in guilty plea cases as well, especially as to evidence that is clearly exculpatory. This means, for example, that a prosecutor should reveal to a defendant contemplating a plea to possessing an incendiary device that prior to the time of the possession the dynamite had been replaced with sawdust. By contrast, it is constitutionally permissible for a prosecutor to negotiate a robbery plea without revealing that the victim had since died and thus could not testify, for the prosecutor is not obliged to share his appraisal of the weaknesses of his own case (as opposed to specific exculpatory evidence) with defense counsel.

However, in *United States v. Ruiz*,[22] the Court concluded that at least *some* of the constitutionally-based disclosure requirements existing as to cases going to trial do not likewise apply to guilty plea cases. In *Ruiz*, the prosecutor offered the defendant a plea bargain, by which she could have obtained a reduction in sentence, but she rejected the bargain because she would not agree, as the plea agreement necessitated, to waive her right to receive "impeachment information relating to any informants or other witnesses" as well as her right to receive information supporting any affirmative defense. The defendant later entered a guilty plea without any plea agreement, and then appealed when she did not obtain a reduction in sentence like that the prosecutor had included in the rejected plea agreement. The court of appeals concluded that the prosecutor's disclosure obligations at trial were equally applicable in a guilty plea context, and that consequently the prosecutor's proposed plea agreement was unlawful, but the Supreme Court disagreed.

In holding that the Constitution does not require the pre-guilty plea disclosure of impeachment information, the Court reasoned: (1) that "impeachment information is special in relation to the *fairness of a trial*, not in respect to whether a plea is *voluntary*," for rights may be waived (as by guilty plea) even by those who "may not know the *specific detailed* consequences" of invoking them; (2) that the Court's prior cases make it clear that a court may "accept a guilty plea, with its accompanying waiver of various constitutional rights, despite various forms of misapprehensions under which a defendant might labor"[23];

20. 434 U.S. 357, 98 S.Ct. 663, 54 L.Ed.2d 604 (1978).

21. United States v. Bagley, 473 U.S. 667, 105 S.Ct. 3375, 87 L.Ed.2d 481 (1985). Brady v. Maryland, 373 U.S. 83, 83 S.Ct. 1194, 10 L.Ed.2d 215 (1963), dealt only with requested evidence, and the Court thereafter developed a different test where there was no request or only a generalized request, United States v. Agurs, 427 U.S. 97, 96 S.Ct. 2392, 49 L.Ed.2d 342 (1976), but *Bagley* merged *Brady* and *Agurs* and the knowing-use-of-perjured-testimony cases into a single test.

The phrase "the proceeding" in *Bagley* clearly refers to a criminal trial, and thus *Bagley* cannot be readily converted, in a guilty plea context, to cover any information which, if known by defendant, would have changed his guilty plea decision. This is highlighted by the *Bagley* Court's repeated and consistent characterization of the withheld information as "evidence."

22. 536 U.S. 622, 122 S.Ct. 2450, 153 L.Ed.2d 586 (2002), also discussed in § 24.3 at note 20.

23. The Court referred to its prior decisions indicating a guilty plea would be valid notwithstanding the fact the

and (3) that, as to the due process considerations of the value of the purported right and its adverse impact on the government's interests, it may be concluded (a) that the risk was slight that "in the absence of impeachment information, innocent individuals, accused of crimes, will plead guilty," considering the "guilty-plea safeguards" in Fed.R.Crim.P. 11 and the fact that the proposed plea agreement expressly incorporated a continuing duty on the prosecutor to provide "any information establishing the factual innocence of the defendant," while (b) "premature disclosure of Government witness information * * * could 'disrupt ongoing investigations' and expose prospective witnesses to serious harm." The Court then concluded that most of the foregoing reasons also applied to information regarding "affirmative defenses."[24] Because it was the above-stated "considerations, taken together," that the Court felt supported its result, *Ruiz* hardly settles what the prosecutor's disclosure obligations are as to other types of withheld information. In particular, the Court's emphasis upon the prosecutor's recognition of his continuing duty to disclose information regarding the defendant's "factual innocence" indicates that *Ruiz* is not incompatible with the principles underlying the decision in the incendiary device case described above.

In further considering the impact of *Ruiz* upon the prosecutor's disclosure responsibilities in the guilty plea context, as compared to the trial context, it is necessary to take into account the fact that a violation of the due process disclosure requirements, when occurring in the former context, has sometimes been characterized in terms of a guilty plea constitutionally defective because not intelli-

gently made. Especially if, as the Supreme Court once intimated, for a guilty plea to be valid the defense must be aware of "the actual value of any commitments made,"[25] which is not possible if there exists a significant misperception of the likelihood that the prosecution could succeed at trial, then it may be that the prosecutor is obligated to make disclosures during plea bargaining beyond those otherwise mandated, in order to satisfy the intelligent plea requirement. To put the matter somewhat differently, if (as seems to be indicated from the Supreme Court's decisions[26]) the legitimacy of the negotiated plea process rests upon the consent of defendants to surrender their chance of acquittal at trial in exchange for concessions, then it is essential that the defendant have had a meaningful opportunity to make a rational prediction of what the outcome at trial would be. From this would derive a broad pre-plea duty to disclose to the defendant all information bearing on the likelihood of trial conviction.

While *Ruiz* certainly indicates that there is no obligation on the prosecutor to disclose "all information" bearing on the likely outcome at trial, *Ruiz* does *not* assert that the prosecutor can withhold important information from the defendant when, as a consequence, the defendant will be misled into thinking that the "concessions" offered by the prosecutor are valuable when, in fact, they are not. *Ruiz*, after all, was *not* a case involving a defendant who *had* accepted a plea agreement and who *had* in fact been misled because such information was withheld. Consequently, that decision ought not be viewed as foreclosing a defendant's claim that a prosecutor offered illusory concessions and then concealed their true character by withholding information from the

---

defendant "misapprehended the quality of the State's case," misapprehended "the likely penalties," failed to "anticipate a change in the law regarding" relevant "punishments," "misjudged the admissibility" of a "confession," or was unaware of a potential defense or of a potential constitutional infirmity in grand jury proceedings.

24. "That is to say, in the context of this agreement, the need for this information is more closely related to the *fairness* of a trial than to the *voluntariness* of the plea; the value in terms of the defendant's added awareness of relevant circumstances is ordinarily limited; yet the added

burden imposed upon the Government by requiring its provision well in advance of trial (often before trial preparation begins) can be serious, thereby significantly interfering with the administration of the plea bargaining process."

25. Brady v. United States, 397 U.S. 742, 90 S.Ct. 1463, 25 L.Ed.2d 747 (1970), quoting Shelton v. United States, 246 F.2d 571 (5th Cir.1957).

26. See, e.g., Santobello v. New York, 404 U.S. 257, 92 S.Ct. 495, 30 L.Ed.2d 427 (1971); North Carolina v. Alford, 400 U.S. 25, 91 S.Ct. 160, 27 L.Ed.2d 162 (1970).

defendant. In any event, there is much to be said for more openness in plea negotiations; it would permit the defendant to play a more meaningful role in the negotiation process, produce fairer bargains, and minimize the risk of duress and mistake.

(d) Judicial Involvement in Negotiations. Some years ago there was a general consensus that trial judges should not participate in the pretrial negotiations which influence a great many defendants to plead guilty. But as a matter of current practice, considerable variation is to be found. Four different kinds of plea bargaining systems have been identified: (1) no judicial involvement of any kind, (2) involvement through unannounced but known sentencing breaks to those who plead guilty, (3) involvement by the judge in sentencing discussions in an occasional, vague, and inconsistent manner, and (4) direct participation in which the judge makes a sentence commitment before the defendant pleads. In some localities the judicial involvement has become formalized to the extent that as a routine matter the parties often meet with the judge at a pretrial settlement conference. Elsewhere, by contrast, there is no established routine, but at least some judges on occasion will become involved in the negotiation process beyond merely being advised of the agreement at arraignment when the defendant's negotiated plea is tendered.

There is also considerable variation among jurisdictions as to the legal position on judicial involvement in plea negotiations. Some jurisdictions have by statute or court rule absolutely prohibited such involvement, and it is claimed that these provisions have in fact substantially deterred judicial involvement. These provisions mean the sentencing judge is to take no part whatever in any discussion or communication regarding the sentence to be imposed prior to the entry of a plea of guilty or conviction, or at least the submission to him of a plea agreement. The law in some states gives express approval to at least limited involvement by the judge in plea negotiations, and further movement in this direction can be expected. This reflects growing acceptance of the view that the "evils" of judicial participation are not as substantial as had once been commonly assumed and that they are, in any event, outweighed by certain benefits that can be achieved by having the judge more actively involved in the negotiation process. Judicial guidance is more likely to pass muster if it is limited in nature and occurs only after the parties tendered a plea bargain to the court that the court found unacceptable.

One reason often given for keeping the judge out of the negotiation process is that his participation would have a coercive effect upon the defendant. As stated in *United States ex rel. Elksnis v. Gilligan*[27]:

> The unequal positions of the judge and the accused, one with the power to commit to prison and the other deeply concerned to avoid prison, at once raise a question of fundamental fairness. When a judge becomes a participant in plea bargaining he brings to bear the full force and majesty of his office. His awesome power to impose a substantially longer or even maximum sentence in excess of that proposed is present whether referred to or not. A defendant needs no reminder that if he rejects the proposal, stands upon his right to trial and is convicted, he faces a significantly longer sentence.

So the argument goes, the situation is quite different when only the prosecutor is involved, as the prosecutor's threat is highly diluted because he lacks power to sentence. But this line of reasoning has not gone unchallenged; in response it is contended that because the prosecutor has many means not available to the judge of putting pressure upon the defendant, the disparity of positions may be even greater between prosecutor and defendant than between judge and defendant. Specifically, it has been noted that prosecutorial sentence recommendations are so universally followed that their effect is virtually indistinguishable from that of judicial promises of specific sentences.

27. 256 F.Supp. 244 (S.D.N.Y.1966).

A second concern underlying the traditional position is that if a judge was involved in the bargaining but the negotiations did not result in a guilty plea, then it would be difficult for that judge to conduct a fair trial thereafter. But the case law has generally rejected the notion that unfairness is inherent in such circumstances. It is reasoned that if the case goes to jury trial the judge will have little opportunity to influence the outcome, and that if there is a bench trial the judge will likely understand that the fact a defendant has engaged in plea bargaining says nothing at all about his guilt. Any actual or perceived risk of unfairness could be overcome by having the judge who participated in the bargaining recuse himself from the trial, but this practice would have to be carefully controlled to ensure against judge-shopping in cases plainly headed for trial and also offer-shopping in guilty plea cases.

A third objection to judicial participation in plea negotiations is that such activity is inconsistent with the judge's responsibilities at the arraignment. As stated in *Elksnis,*

> a bargain agreement between a judge and a defendant * * * impairs the judge's objectivity in passing upon the voluntariness of the plea when offered. As a party to the arrangement upon which the plea is based, he is hardly in a position to discharge his function of deciding the validity of the plea—a function not satisfied by routine inquiry, but only, as the Supreme Court has stressed, by "a penetrating and comprehensive examination of all the circumstances under which such a plea is tendered."

In response, it is argued that the inquiry could be by another judge if this is a problem and that the judge's presence at the negotiations rather than his after-the-fact inquiry into them provides greater assurance of voluntariness.

Still another objection is that judicial participation to the extent of promising a certain sentence is inconsistent with the theory behind the use of the presentence investigation report. A possible solution lies in ordering the preparation of a presentence report prior to the initiation of plea bargaining, as is the practice in some jurisdictions. But this procedure poses some dangers, as an interview with the defendant is typically part of a presentence investigation. Absent rigorous safeguards to insure against even the indirect use of a defendant's statements at trial, it would violate the privilege against self-incrimination to require him to answer questions about his alleged crime at this early stage.

Finally, there is the concern over the unseemliness of judicial plea bargaining—that the procedure leads defendants to think of the judge as just one more official to be bought off. In response it has been said that it is better for judges to administer our system of justice—however indecorous that system is—than for them to leave the task to prosecutors, especially since a regime of prosecutorial plea bargaining cannot be successful unless judges substantially abdicate their power.

Because the reasons given for nonparticipation in plea negotiations by the judiciary are not entirely without merit and substance, another important consideration is that of what is to be gained by greater judicial involvement. These benefits have been identified: (1) it would restore the sentencing function to the judiciary, in contrast to the prevailing practice that causes some judges to ratify agreements they would not have formulated had they participated in the negotiations; (2) it would facilitate the flow of information relevant to sentencing to the judge; (3) it would remove the cloak of uncertainty whereby the defendant is required to plead in the dark in the sense of not knowing whether the judge will grant the concessions the prosecutor has promised to seek; (4) it would cause the prosecutor to open his file and to freely discuss the strength of his case; (5) it would ensure that the various sentencing provisions applicable are discussed and understood; and (6) it would permit the judge to perform as an effective check on prosecutorial power, police behavior, and defense counsel effectiveness, and thus equalize the opportunity of all defendants to negotiate.

It has also been proposed that all plea negotiations occur at an on-the-record pretrial conference held on motion of the defendant. In attendance would be the defendant and his attorney, the prosecutor and the judge. A limited presentence investigation, not including an interview with the defendant, would be conducted in advance of the conference and a presentence report would be available. The judge should permit the defense and prosecution to discuss the circumstances of the case, present one or more proposals for disposition, and argue in support of them, after which the judge would indicate the sentence he would impose if the defendant enters a plea of guilty and, when necessary to that result, how the charges would be reduced. If the defendant decided to plead guilty, that judge would conduct the arraignment; otherwise the matter would be assigned to another judge. Such a system contemplates a much more central role for the judge in the plea negotiation process than presently is permitted in many jurisdictions. It stands in especially sharp contrast to the view that the defendant should be able to bargain only for a sentence recommendation, and to the even more extreme view that judicial sentencing should occur even without knowledge of what the plea bargain contemplates. But it is also quite different from the more common current view that the judge has no business tendering sentence concessions or granting charge concessions without the prosecutor's approval.

(e) Judicial Evaluation of Contemplated Concessions. Even if the judge does not become involved in the plea negotiation process, he will usually have a critical role to play whenever the defendant tenders a plea as a consequence of the negotiations. If the plea agreement contemplates the granting of sentence concessions to the defendant, then quite obviously the judge will play an essential part, for sentencing is the responsibility of the judge. In those many jurisdictions where charges that have been filed may be dropped only with the consent of the court, the judge will likewise perform a necessary part whenever the plea agreement contemplates the reduction of the charge or the dropping of some counts. In all of these circumstances, quite clearly the judge is under no obligation to

grant the contemplated concessions merely because the parties are agreeable. Nor, under the better but not prevailing view, is the judge free to refuse to give any consideration to the agreement reached by the parties. Rather, the judge should give the agreement due consideration, but notwithstanding its existence should reach an independent decision on whether to grant charge or sentence concessions.

Just how much "consideration" should be given to the disposition agreed to by the prosecutor and just how "independent" the judge should be in these circumstances is a most difficult issue, seldom addressed in the cases. Rather unique is *United States v. Ammidown*,[28] where defendant appealed his first degree murder conviction, based upon proof that he hired the man who killed his wife, because the trial was necessitated by the judge's rejection of a plea bargain contemplating defendant would enter a plea to second degree murder and testify against the killer. In reversing and remanding for acceptance of a plea to second degree murder, the court seemed to view the judge as having a rather limited function to perform with respect to charge reduction bargains. The court declared that

> the trial judge must provide a reasoned exercise of discretion in order to justify a departure from the course agreed on by the prosecution and defense. This is not a matter of absolute judicial prerogative. The authority has been granted to the judge to assure protection of the public interest, and this in turn involves one or more of the following components: (a) fairness to the defense, such as protection against harassment; (b) fairness to the prosecution interest, as in avoiding a disposition that does not serve due and legitimate prosecutorial interest; (c) protection of the sentencing authority reserved to the judge.

Noting that the first of these, concerning "protecting a defendant from harassment, through a prosecutor's charging, dismissing without having placed a defendant in jeopardy, and commencing another prosecution at a dif-

28. 497 F.2d 615 (D.C.Cir.1973).

ferent time or place deemed more favorable to the prosecution," was not involved in the instant case, the court elaborated on the second component:

> As to fairness to the prosecution interest, here we have a matter in which the primary responsibility, obviously, is that of the prosecuting attorney. The District Court cannot disapprove of his action on the ground of incompatibility with prosecutive responsibility unless the judge is in effect ruling that the prosecutor has abused his discretion. The requirement of judicial approval entitles the judge to obtain and evaluate the prosecutor's reasons. * * * The judge may withhold approval if he finds that the prosecutor has failed to give consideration to factors that must be given consideration in the public interest, factors such as the deterrent aspects of the criminal law. However, trial judges are not free to withhold approval of guilty pleas on this basis merely because their conception of the public interest differs from that of the prosecuting attorney. The question is not what the judge would do if he were the prosecuting attorney, but whether he can say that the action of the prosecuting attorney is such a departure from sound prosecutorial principle as to mark it an abuse of prosecutorial discretion.

The court in *Ammidown* then went on to assert, with respect to the third component, "that the judge is free to condemn the prosecutor's agreement as a trespass on judicial authority only in a blatant and extreme case," and explained:

> When we come to the possible ground of intrusion on the sentencing function of the trial judge, we have a consideration that is interdependent of the other. That is to say, a dropping of an offense that might be taken as an intrusion on the judicial function if it were not shown to be related to a prosecutorial purpose takes on an entirely different coloration if it is explained to the judge that there was a prosecutorial purpose, an insufficiency of evidence, a doubt as to the admissibility of certain evidence under ex-

clusionary rules, a need for evidence to bring another felon to justice, or other similar consideration.

Under the *Ammidown* approach, then, the trial judge is clothed with a discretion to determine whether the dismissal of these charges was clearly contrary to the public interest, but this is a limited discretion subjected to rather strict appellate review. However, as elaborated earlier,[29] federal trial judges now have somewhat greater authority in this respect, as the Sentencing Guidelines permit a judge to accept a plea agreement including a government commitment to dismiss or not bring certain charges only "if the court determines, for reasons stated in the record, that the remaining charges adequately reflect the seriousness of the actual offense behavior and that accepting the agreement will not undermine the statutory purposes of sentencing or the sentencing guidelines."

If the plea bargain agreed to by the prosecution and the defendant were to deal directly with sentence concessions, rather than charge concessions as in *Ammidown,* it is beyond dispute that the trial judge is in a quite different position. This is particularly true in the federal system, where the judge can go so far as to not even give consideration to the contemplated sentence concessions. Or, the judge may grant more generous sentencing concessions than are recommended in the agreement, though no such power exists as to a type (C) plea agreement (i.e., that "a specific sentence is the appropriate disposition").

The *Ammidown* approach has not escaped criticism. It is argued that there is insufficient screening and supervision within the executive branch to ensure that the interests of the public and the defendant have been properly balanced, and that under *Ammidown* many highly imprudent plea agreements would survive judicial scrutiny if the impropriety were not sufficiently blatant to support a finding of abuse of prosecutorial discretion. Moreover, it has been pointed out that to distinguish between charge bargains and sentence bargains in determining the range of the judge's discre-

29. See § 21.1(h).

tion in deciding whether the contemplated concessions should be granted assumes a difference that does not exist, as the primary significance of the charge-reduction process plainly lies in its effect on the sentence the defendant will receive. This being so, the argument proceeds, *Ammidown* is in error because it, in effect, amounts to a formal recognition of the prosecutor's authority over sentencing. Decisions are to be found on both the state and federal level accepting this latter view and thus recognizing broader discretion in the judge to determine whether a charge bargain with sentencing consequences should be approved.

§ 21.4 Receiving the Defendant's Plea

(a) Arraignment; Pleading Alternatives. The word "arraignment" is sometimes used to refer to the defendant's first appearance in court before a magistrate. The defendant will not normally be called upon to plead at that time unless the offense charged is a minor one. The more common use of the word "arraignment" is to refer to a later appearance in the court of trial jurisdiction, when the defendant is advised of the formal charge and called upon to enter a plea. Typically this will occur weeks or even months after the initial appearance, and thus the defendant will have had adequate time to consult with counsel and to reflect on what his plea should be. On occasion, however, a defendant is brought into court after arrest, where he waives all rights and procedures that would delay the proceedings (right to counsel, preliminary hearing, grand jury indictment) and then immediately enters a guilty plea. Some courts have upheld this practice, while others have criticized it. Certainly the better view is that even a defendant who has waived his other rights should not be called upon to decide on his plea so promptly.

When the defendant is called upon to enter his plea at arraignment, he may enter a plea of (1) not guilty, (2) guilty, (3) guilty but mentally ill (in a few jurisdictions where such a plea permits a sentenced defendant to receive mental health treatment), (4) not guilty by reason of insanity (in a few jurisdictions where such a plea is a prerequisite to the presentation of an insanity defense at trial), or (5) nolo contendere (in the federal system and about half of the states). A plea of nolo contendere—sometimes referred to as a plea of non vult contendere or of non vult—is simply a device by which the defendant may assert that he does not want to contest the issue of guilt or innocence. Such a plea may not be entered as a matter of right, but only with the consent of the court. Although the prevailing view is that the consent of the prosecutor is not also required, it is common practice for the court to determine the views of the prosecutor and to give them considerable weight in deciding whether to accept the nolo plea.

Although some minor variations are to be found from jurisdiction to jurisdiction, a plea of nolo contendere usually has the following significance: (1) Unlike a plea of guilty or a conviction following a plea of not guilty, a plea of nolo contendere may not be put into evidence in a subsequent civil action as proof of the fact that the defendant committed the offense to which he entered the plea. (2) Judgment following entry of a nolo contendere plea is a conviction, and may be admitted as such in other proceedings where the fact of conviction has legal significance (e.g., to apply multiple offender penalty provisions, to deny or revoke a license because of conviction, or to claim double jeopardy in a subsequent prosecution). (3) When a nolo contendere plea is accepted, it has essentially the same effect in that case as a guilty plea. The procedures for receiving the plea are the same, the defendant may receive the same sentence, and the nolo plea is like a guilty plea in terms of its finality, its effect as a waiver of claims unrelated to the plea, and the circumstances in which withdrawal of the plea would be permitted.

Opinions differ as to whether it is desirable to have the nolo contendere pleading alternative. Some say there should not be such an "in between" plea, for if a defendant is innocent he should go to trial and if he is guilty he should be required to acknowledge that guilt if he is not prepared to stand trial. The assumption is that existence of the nolo plea as an alternative will have two undesirable effects: (i) some innocent persons will so plead just to avoid the expense and notoriety of trial; and (ii) some guilty persons will be allowed to so plead and thereby receive the unwarranted benefit of freedom in subsequent civil proceedings to deny the facts regarding their crimes. The contrary view is that the nolo plea serves an important function in certain circumstances, such as where the charge is a criminal antitrust violation, in that otherwise the defendant would impose upon the system the need for a costly and lengthy trial solely in an effort to avoid the collateral civil consequences of a guilty plea.

It is in the discretion of the court to reject or accept such a plea, and no criteria have been established to guide exercise of this discretion. Some courts operate under the assumption that the plea should be accepted in the absence of some compelling reason to the contrary, while others take the view that the plea should be rejected unless a compelling reason for acceptance is established. The question of whether to accept a nolo plea, it would seem, is similar to that of whether a defendant should be given concessions in a plea bargaining context. Of particular relevance is whether the nature of the case is such that having the defendant admit guilt or be convicted at trial is desirable in order to maximize the deterrent or rehabilitative effects of the prosecution, and whether enhancing the likelihood of the defendant being held liable in damages in collateral civil proceedings would further the goals of the criminal prosecution.

In the material that follows, the concern is with what procedures are appropriate when a judge conducts an arraignment at which the defendant enters a plea of guilty or nolo contendere. Statutes or rules of court often prescribe a set of procedures for such a situation. At least some of those procedures are constitu-

tionally required, though it remains unclear in many respects just how much of the usual plea-receiving process is constitutionally mandated.

(b) Determining Voluntariness of Plea and Competency of Defendant to Plead. When a defendant tenders a plea of guilty or nolo contendere in court at arraignment, one important responsibility of the court is to determine whether the plea is voluntary. Consistent with the Supreme Court's standard as to what constitutes a voluntary plea,[1] this means the court will inquire whether the tendered plea was the result of any threats or promises. At an earlier time, when the legitimacy of plea bargaining was in doubt, the general practice was not to reveal in court that a bargain had been struck, but today the prevailing practice is for the voluntariness inquiry to include a determination of whether a plea agreement has been reached and, if so, what it is. Depending upon the nature of the agreement, the judge will then advise the defendant of the effect of the agreement.

Although it is the responsibility of the judge presiding at the arraignment to reject a guilty or nolo plea that is not voluntary, it is well to note that a judge who is unduly demanding with respect to the voluntariness determination may harm a defendant rather than protect him. Illustrative is *United States v. Martinez*,[2] where defendant was indicted for conspiracy to import marijuana, importation of marijuana, possession of marijuana with intent to distribute it, and assault upon a federal officer. Martinez tendered a plea to the second count as a result of an agreement with the prosecution that the other charges would then be dismissed. Upon inquiry into the voluntariness of the plea, the judge learned that Martinez' waiver of his *Miranda* rights had been obtained by a promise that

---

§ 21.4

1. In Brady v. United States, 397 U.S. 742, 90 S.Ct. 1463, 25 L.Ed.2d 747 (1970), the Court accepted the standard first set out in Shelton v. United States, 246 F.2d 571 (5th Cir.1957), reversed on other grounds 356 U.S. 26, 78 S.Ct. 563, 2 L.Ed.2d 579 (1958): "[A] plea of guilty entered by one fully aware of the direct consequences, including the actual value of any commitments made to

him by the court, prosecutor, or his own counsel, must stand unless induced by threats (or promises to discontinue improper harassment), misrepresentation (including unfulfilled or unfulfillable promises), or perhaps by promises that are by their nature improper as having no proper relationship to the prosecutor's business (e.g. bribes)."

2. 486 F.2d 15 (5th Cir.1973).

nothing would happen to him, and thus declined the plea as involuntary notwithstanding counsel's efforts to persuade him that the government possessed sufficient evidence to convict independent of Martinez' statement. Martinez was then tried and convicted of all four counts, but on appeal all but the second count was vacated. The appellate court viewed the action of the district court as improper because he rejected a guilty plea that was not involuntary merely "because of the possibility of later collateral attack on the judgment to be entered upon the plea." It thus appears that a judge must proceed with special care when rejecting defendant's plea if, as a consequence, the defendant would be deprived of bargained-for concessions.

The voluntariness determination does not include, as a matter of course, an inquiry into the defendant's competency to plead. However, in much the same way that a trial judge has a constitutional responsibility to act upon circumstances suggesting a defendant is not competent to stand trial,[3] a judge must defer acceptance of defendant's guilty or nolo plea whenever he has a reasonable ground to doubt the defendant's competence. Then he must put into motion the process whereby the defendant's mental condition may be inquired into and determined. Whether the standard for competence to stand trial, that the defendant "has sufficient present ability to consult with his lawyer with a reasonable degree of rational understanding—and whether he has a rational as well as factual understanding of the proceedings against him,"[4] also applies in this context was long a matter of dispute. But in *Godinez v. Moran*,[5] the Court held that standard did apply and thus rejected a lower court holding that in a guilty plea context a defendant's competency was to be tested by the higher standard of whether he had "the capacity for 'reasoned choice' among the alternatives available to him." In support of a single standard for both trial and guilty plea cases, the Court stressed that a "defendant who

stands trial is likely to be presented with choices that entail relinquishment of the same rights that are relinquished by a defendant who pleads guilty" (e.g., to jury trial, right of confrontation, privilege against self-incrimination).

(c) Determining Understanding of Charge. Yet another responsibility of the judge at an arraignment at which a guilty or nolo plea is tendered is to determine that the defendant understands the charge to which he is pleading. In federal court, "the court must address the defendant personally in open court" and "must inform the defendant of, and determine that the defendant understands, * * * the nature of each charge to which the defendant is pleading."[6] Similar requirements are to be found in state procedure. As the Supreme Court explained in *Henderson v. Morgan*,[7] a plea of guilty

> cannot support a judgment of guilt unless it was voluntary in a constitutional sense. And clearly the plea could not be voluntary in the sense that it constituted an intelligent admission that he committed the offense unless the defendant received "real notice of the true nature of the charge against him, the first and most universally recognized requirement of due process."

The better practice is for the judge to inform the defendant of the nature and elements of the offense to which the plea is offered, that is, the acts and mental state and attendant circumstances that the prosecution would have to prove in order to establish guilt at trial. However, the *Henderson* case indicates that the constitutional requirement does not in all instances go this far. The defendant there was indicted for first degree murder. His attorneys unsuccessfully sought to have the charge reduced to manslaughter, but were able to obtain a bargained plea to second degree murder. The attorneys did not tell defendant that the new charge had a required element of intent to

---

3. Pate v. Robinson, 383 U.S. 375, 86 S.Ct. 836, 15 L.Ed.2d 815 (1966).

4. Dusky v. United States, 362 U.S. 402, 80 S.Ct. 788, 4 L.Ed.2d 824 (1960).

5. 509 U.S. 389, 113 S.Ct. 2680, 125 L.Ed.2d 321 (1993).

6. Fed.R.Crim.P. 11(b) (1).

7. 426 U.S. 637, 96 S.Ct. 2253, 49 L.Ed.2d 108 (1976).

kill, and no reference was made to this element at the time of the defendant's plea. The opinion of the Court[8] concluded that this oversight constituted a violation of due process where, as in the instant case, there was no indication that the defendant was otherwise aware that the offense to which he was pleading had an intent-to-kill element. But the Court then dropped this cautionary footnote:

> There is no need in this case to decide whether notice of the true nature, or substance, of a charge always requires a description of every element of the offense; we assume it does not. Nevertheless, intent is such a critical element of the offense of second-degree murder that notice of that element is required.

Just what makes an element "critical" within the meaning of *Henderson* is far from clear, though it appears that the Court in that case deemed the "design to effect the death of the person killed" critical because it was the element which differentiated the offense of second degree murder from that of manslaughter. Lower courts, in declaring a certain element to be critical in the *Henderson* sense, have often rested this conclusion upon the fact that the omitted or unexplained element was one elevating the degree and seriousness of the crime to which the plea was offered above some other offense. Courts have also taken into account whether or not the charge is a self-explanatory legal term or so simple in meaning that it can be expected or assumed that a lay person understands it. On this basis it has been held, for example, that the elements of a conspiracy charge should be explained but that an element-by-element parsing of such offenses as escape and altering a check is unnecessary. With regard to possible affirmative defenses, the judge is not obligated to mention or explain them unless made aware of facts that would constitute such a defense.

Even if the defendant was presumptively informed of the charge sufficiently via the indictment, a constitutional violation of the notice requirement may occur if prior to defendant's plea the trial court *mis*informs the defendant regarding an element of the offense. Illustrative is *Bousley v. United States,*[9] where the defendant's guilty plea to "using" a firearm in violation of 18 U.S.C. § 924(c)(1) came a few years before the Supreme Court's holding in *Bailey v. United States*[10] that proof of such an offense requires a showing of "active employment of the firearm." Because *Bailey* is retroactive, the defendant in *Bousley* claimed that in light of that decision the district court had misinformed him of the elements of a § 924(c)(1) offense, and "that neither he, nor his counsel, nor the court correctly understood the essential elements of the crime with which he was charged." "Were this contention proven," the Supreme Court held in *Bousley*, "petitioner's plea would be * * * constitutionally invalid" notwithstanding the fact that defendant's receipt of a copy of the indictment charging him with "using" a firearm would, "standing alone, give rise to a presumption that the defendant was informed of the charge against him."

Due process is denied only if the defendant was actually unaware of the nature of the charge. Thus, essential to the result in *Henderson* was the fact that defendant's attorneys did not tell him that intent to kill was required for second degree murder or "explain to him that his plea would be an admission of that fact." It is not surprising, therefore, that lower courts have often denied relief upon a showing that defense counsel had explained the elements of the offense charged to the defendant. In *Henderson* it is noted that the record in a guilty plea case will normally contain "either an explanation of the charge by the trial judge, or at least a representation by defense counsel that the nature of the offense has been explained to the accused," thereby suggesting that either will suffice. More troublesome, however, is the Court's added com-

---

8. By Stevens, J., which did not command the unqualified support of a majority of the Court. Two Justices dissented, and four others joined in a concurring opinion.

9. 523 U.S. 614, 118 S.Ct. 1604, 140 L.Ed.2d 828 (1998).

10. 516 U.S. 137, 116 S.Ct. 501, 133 L.Ed.2d 472 (1995).

ment that "even without such an express representation, it may be appropriate to presume that in most cases defense counsel routinely explain the nature of the offense in sufficient detail to give the accused notice of what he is being asked to admit." Though lower courts have sometimes entertained such a presumption in order to defeat a defendant's *Henderson* claim, this is a highly questionable result. Of course, when the defendant was not represented by counsel it cannot be presumed that any part of this function of informing defendant of the charge was performed by the defense attorney, and thus the court should make a more exacting inquiry to assure a defendant's understanding of the charge in such a case.

Yet another troublesome aspect of the Court's opinion in *Henderson* is the assumption that if a defendant admits facts amounting to an element of the offense to which he entered his plea, then he cannot complain about not being told that the offense contained that element. The Court asserted that proof at trial that defendant had "repeatedly stabbed" the victim would not inevitably have led the jury to infer intent to kill, and that consequently "an admission by respondent that he killed Mrs. Francisco does not necessarily also admit that he was guilty of second-degree murder." This was followed with the conclusion that the unadvised defendant's plea could not be deemed voluntary "in these circumstances," namely, where "he made no factual statement or admission necessarily implying that he had such intent." From this, lower courts have understandably concluded that factual statements or admissions by the defendant necessarily implying the existence of unexplained elements of the crime are sufficient.

To the extent that the due process requirement of notice of the charge is grounded upon a need, absent some other showing of guilt, for defendant to admit that he committed the crime, this is an understandable result. That is, if having the judge tell the defendant that second degree murder requires an intent to

kill is important so that when the defendant says "I plead guilty" this may be taken to mean "I admit that I killed while acting with an intent to kill," then the presence of such a specific admission is a suitable substitute for the advise from the judge. But it would seem that the notice requirement serves another important function, one of particular significance in a system authorizing plea bargaining: it ensures that the defendant understands that if he pleads not guilty the state will be required to prove certain facts, thus permitting the defendant to make an intelligent judgment as to whether he would be better off accepting the tendered concessions or chancing acquittal if the prosecution cannot prove those facts beyond a reasonable doubt. If that is so—which would seem to be what the Supreme Court meant when it said in *McCarthy v. United States*[11] that a guilty plea cannot be voluntary "unless the defendant possesses an understanding of the law in relation to the facts"—then admissions by the defendant are not an adequate substitute for advice from the court as to the elements of the offense.

(d) Determining Understanding of Possible Consequences. If the defendant offers a plea of guilty or nolo contendere at arraignment, yet another responsibility of the judge is to advise the defendant of certain consequences that could follow if the plea is accepted. The conventional wisdom is that this obligation extends to those consequences that are "direct" but not to those that are only "collateral" in nature. There is not complete agreement, however, as to the manner in which it should be determined whether a particular consequence is of the direct or collateral type. The distinction between these two categories, it is sometimes said, turns on whether the result represents a definite, immediate and largely automatic effect on the range of the defendant's punishment. That is a useful albeit not foolproof test, and considerable variation is to be found in both federal and state cases on the direct-collateral dichotomy.

Matters concerning the nature of the sentence that could be imposed are most likely to

---

11.   394 U.S. 459, 89 S.Ct. 1166, 22 L.Ed.2d 418 (1969).

be viewed as direct consequences. Traditionally, the emphasis in the case law has been upon the requirement that the judge inform the defendant of the maximum possible punishment. But the current requirement in federal practice is that the judge advise the defendant not only of "any maximum possible penalty, including imprisonment, fine, and term of supervised release," but also "any mandatory minimum penalty,"[12] and several states have adopted comparable requirements. This is a welcome change, for advising the defendant in this way gives him a more realistic picture of what might happen with regard to sentencing. It has also been suggested that the defendant should be expressly warned in multiple charge situations of the possibility of consecutive sentences, but the cases reflect a split of authority on this point. The courts are even less demanding with respect to possible elaboration of how low the sentence might be; it has been held that the defendant need not be told that some of the multiple charges might be merged for sentencing purposes or that there is an included offense carrying a lesser penalty of which he might be convicted were he to stand trial.

The better view is that the maximum possible sentence about which the defendant should be warned includes punishment possible by virtue either of the sentence provisions of the statute under which the charge is brought or of other statutes that authorize added penalties because of special circumstances in the case, as where a statute provides for added punishment of persons who commit crimes while armed. Under this approach, it has been concluded a defendant should be advised of the maximum permissible "restitution" that may be ordered as a consequence of legislation permitting such disposition in a criminal case. Equally desirable is a warning to the defendant of the fact, where the law so provides, that the sentencing provisions of the statute under which he is charged or a more general multiple offender statute provides for specified

higher penalties if the instant offense puts the defendant into the repeater category. With respect to parole and probation, there is no need specifically to advise the defendant that if he achieves such conditional release status then any violation of a condition of the release could result in revocation. But because the availability of parole is assumed by the average defendant, the better view is that the defendant should be so advised if the offense to which he is pleading may not lead to parole.

As for the collateral consequences of which the defendant need not be warned, they include such matters as the possible evidentiary use of defendant's plea in later proceedings, the diminished reputation or other adverse social consequences that may follow conviction, loss of the right to vote, loss of a passport and the opportunity to travel abroad, loss of the right to possess a firearm, and loss of public employment, a business license or driver's license. The majority view is that deportation is a collateral consequence and that consequently an alien defendant is not entitled to be advised by the judge of that consequence. It has been argued rather unconvincingly that this is so even when deportation is automatic upon conviction of the charged offense. Some courts view deportation as such a serious consequence that the alien defendant is entitled to be aware of it before entering his plea.

In cases involving the question of whether various consequences deserve to be characterized as direct or collateral, two considerations, though seldom articulated, seem to influence the courts: (1) that it is simply impracticable for a trial judge to advise the defendant of all possible consequences, especially because often the judge will not be aware at the time of the plea of the special circumstances which would make some of those consequences possible; and (2) that defense counsel should be expected to discuss with his client the range of risks attendant his plea.

If a judge fails to advise the defendant of certain direct consequences of his plea and

---

12. Fed.R.Crim.P. 11(b)(1), adding that the advise shall also cover "any applicable forfeitures," "the court's authority to order restitution," "the court's obligation to impose a special assessment," and "the court's obligation to apply the Sentencing Guidelines, and the court's discretion to depart from those guidelines under some circumstances."

thus violates the obligation imposed upon him by statute, court rule, or court decision, does it follow that this failure amounts to a violation of due process? Although some courts have answered in the affirmative, the prevailing view is to the contrary, which accords with the Supreme Court's position on the matter.[13] Thus, while due process might be violated because of the failure of the judge taking the plea to tell defendant of the maximum sentence or any mandatory minimum sentence, the constitutional issue can be resolved only by considering other matters. Certainly there is no due process violation if the defendant was otherwise aware of the sentencing possibilities. If he was not aware, then the question is whether the defendant was prejudiced by the lack of information or by misinformation, which usually comes down to whether having the accurate information would have made any difference in his decision to enter the plea. (Where the government is responsible for defendant's lack of the correct sentencing information at the time of his plea, then it is quite appropriate to place upon the government the burden of showing that having the accurate information would not have made any difference.) If the defendant received a sentence longer than he knew could be imposed, then surely the judge's failure does amount to a due process violation. On the other hand, a defendant is not likely to prevail on his constitutional claim if he knew he could receive the sentence he did receive but lacked correct or certain knowledge of what maximum above that was possible. In the latter situation, however, it would seem that a significant overstatement of the maximum possible punishment would be objectionable whenever it skewed defendant's understanding of the value of his plea bargain.

(e) Determining Understanding of Rights Waived. *Boykin v. Alabama*[14] concerned a defendant who had pleaded guilty in state court to five armed robbery indictments and thereafter received the death penalty. At arraignment, "so far as the record shows, the judge asked no questions of petitioner concerning his plea, and petitioner did not address the court." The Supreme Court reversed, concluding that it "was error, plain on the face of the record, for the trial judge to accept petitioner's guilty plea without an affirmative showing that it was intelligent and voluntary." Noting that it had earlier established in another context the "requirement that the prosecution spread on the record the prerequisites of a valid waiver," the Court in *Boykin* asserted:

> We think that the same standard must be applied to determining whether a guilty plea is voluntarily made. For, as we have said, a plea of guilty is more than an admission of conduct; it is a conviction. Ignorance, incomprehension, coercion, terror, inducements, subtle or blatant threats might be a perfect coverup of unconstitutionality. The question of an effective waiver of a federal constitutional right in a proceeding is of course governed by federal standards. * * *

> Several federal constitutional rights are involved in a waiver that takes place when a plea of guilty is entered in a state criminal trial. First is the privilege against compulsory self-incrimination guaranteed by the Fifth Amendment and applicable to the States by reason of the Fourteenth. * * * Second is the right to trial by jury. * * * Third, is the right to confront one's accusers. * * * We cannot presume a waiver of these three important federal rights from a silent record.

(In *Mitchell v. United States*,[15] the Court later clarified that, at least in federal procedure, the waiver of rights occurring upon entry of a guilty plea is a "waiver of a right to trial with its attendant privileges" and "not a waiver of the privileges which exist beyond the confines of the trial." That being the case, the Court in *Mitchell* concluded that the defendant's guilty plea did not amount to "a waiver of the privilege [against self-incrimination] at sentenc-

13. United States v. Timmreck, 441 U.S. 780, 99 S.Ct. 2085, 60 L.Ed.2d 634 (1979), discussed in § 21.5(c).

14. 395 U.S. 238, 89 S.Ct. 1709, 23 L.Ed.2d 274 (1969).

15. 526 U.S. 314, 119 S.Ct. 1307, 143 L.Ed.2d 424 (1999), also discussed in § 24.5 at note 14, and § 26.4 at note 10.

ing," which "would be a grave encroachment on the rights of defendants."[16])

In the wake of *Boykin,* most jurisdictions revised their procedures for taking pleas so that defendants were specifically warned of the constitutional rights lost by entry of a plea other than not guilty.[17] Although this is a desirable procedure, does *Boykin* mean that a guilty plea is constitutionally defective whenever the judge failed to articulate specifically the constitutional rights listed in the *Boykin* case? Some courts have answered in the affirmative, reasoning that there cannot be a knowledgeable waiver of those rights unless the defendant was so informed of them. But most courts, often stressing the uniqueness of *Boykin* in that the defendant had been sentenced to death and his plea had apparently been accepted without any admonishments or inquiry whatsoever, have reached the contrary conclusion. The latter view is supported by Supreme Court decisions subsequent to *Boykin*: *Brady v. United States*,[18] citing *Boykin* but upholding a guilty plea even though defendant had not been specifically advised of the three rights discussed in *Boykin*; and *North Carolina v. Alford*,[19] stating that in determining the validity of guilty pleas the "standard was and remains whether the plea represents a voluntary and intelligent choice among the alternative courses of action open to the defendant."

(f) Determining Factual Basis of Plea. In recent years, many jurisdictions have imposed an added obligation upon the judge receiving a plea of guilty, which is to make a

determination regarding the accuracy of the plea. In federal procedure, for example, "[b]efore entering judgment on a guilty plea, the court must determine that there is a factual basis for the plea."[20] Many states have adopted a comparable provision. Generally, these provisions leave the judge free to decide in the particular case how this determination can best be made; the factual basis is most commonly established by inquiry of the defendant, inquiry of the prosecutor, or defense counsel, examination of the plea agreement, presentence report or preliminary hearing transcript, testimony by police, or a combination of those methods. Nor do these provisions attempt to establish a precise quantum of evidence that must be met.

In the previously-discussed *Mitchell* case, the Supreme Court focused upon the self-incrimination aspects of inquiry of the defendant to establish, at least in part, the factual basis for a plea. For one thing, because (as noted above) *Mitchell* holds the entry of the plea is itself not a waiver of the privilege other than as an at-trial right lost by not standing trial, a defendant to whom a factual basis inquiry is made *could* decline to answer on Fifth Amendment grounds, but by doing so he "runs the risk the district court will find the factual basis inadequate." Secondly, the guilty plea and statements made in the plea colloquy, including the factual basis inquiry, "are later admissible against the defendant," for example, at sentencing. Thirdly, the fact the defen-

---

16. The Court elaborated: "Were we to accept the Government's position, prosecutors could indict without specifying the quantity of drugs involved, obtain a guilty plea, and then put the defendant on the stand at sentencing to fill in the drug quantity. The result would be to enlist the defendant as an instrument in his or her own condemnation, undermining the long tradition and vital principle that criminal proceedings rely on accusations proved by the Government, not on inquisitions conducted to enhance its own prosecutorial power."

17. See, e.g., Fed.R.Crim.P. 11(b)(1)(N), where there has been added to the list of items about which the judge must inform the defendant and determine that defendant understands the following: "the terms of any plea-agreement provision waiving the right to appeal or to collaterally attack the sentence."

18. 397 U.S. 742, 90 S.Ct. 1463, 25 L.Ed.2d 747 (1970).

19. 400 U.S. 25, 91 S.Ct. 160, 27 L.Ed.2d 162 (1970).

20. Fed.R.Crim.P. 11(b)(3).

Libretti v. United States, 516 U.S. 29, 116 S.Ct. 356, 133 L.Ed.2d 271 (1995), involving very similar language then in Rule 11(f), held it did not require a factual basis showing for a stipulated asset forfeiture embodied in a plea agreement: "Forfeiture is an element of the sentence imposed *following* conviction or, as here, a plea of guilty, and thus falls outside the scope of rule 11(f)." The Court cautioned it did "not mean to suggest that a district court must simply accept a defendant's agreement to forfeit property, particularly when that agreement is not accompanied by a stipulation of facts supporting forfeiture," but added that in the instant case it "need not determine the precise scope of a district court's independent obligation, if any, to inquire into the propriety of a stipulated asset forfeiture embodied in a plea agreement," for here the judge acted upon "ample evidence that * * * the statutory requisites for criminal forfeiture * * * were satisfied."

dant has made incriminating statements at the factual basis inquiry does not itself constitute a waiver of the privilege at later proceedings such as sentencing. This is so, the Court explained, because that situation is unlike the case of a witness at a single proceeding, who "may not testify voluntarily about a subject and then invoke the privilege against self-incrimination when questioned about the details," thereby "diminishing the integrity of the factual inquiry." Such a concern is "absent at a plea colloquy," as "the defendant who pleads guilty puts nothing in dispute regarding the essentials of the offense" but rather "takes those matters out of dispute, often by making a joint statement with the prosecution or confirming the prosecution's version of the facts," in which case "there is little danger that the court will be misled by selective disclosure."

This inquiry into the factual basis serves a number of worthwhile functions. Most importantly, it should protect a defendant who is in the position of pleading voluntarily with an understanding of the nature of the charge but without realizing that his conduct does not actually fall within the charge. As the cases indicate, this does happen on occasion. In addition, the inquiry into the factual basis of the plea provides the court with a better assessment of defendant's competency and willingness to plead guilty and his understanding of the charges, increases the visibility of charge reduction practices, provides a more adequate record and thus minimizes the likelihood of the plea being successfully challenged later, and aids correctional agencies in the performance of their functions.

Difficulties with regard to establishing a factual basis matching the offense to which the plea is entered occasionally arise when the plea is the result of charge bargaining. Sometimes a defendant apparently guilty of a greater offense will be permitted to plead guilty to a logical included offense, in which case presumably the factual basis for the latter can be easily established by disclosing so much of the full occurrence that would constitute the lesser

offense. But sometimes the offense to which the plea is made is not a logical included offense of the crime committed. For example, in a jurisdiction with an offense of breaking and entering in the nighttime (a nonprobationable offense with a 15-year maximum) and an offense of breaking and entering in the daytime (a probationable offense with a 5-year minimum), a bargained plea to the latter offense might be tendered although the facts show that the crime occurred at midnight. Or, the plea might be to a hypothetical crime that produces the range of sentencing possibilities the parties are agreeable to, as where a defendant charged with manslaughter is allowed to plead guilty to attempted manslaughter. Even in the hypothetical crime situation, an appellate court called upon to overturn the plea is not likely to do so, reasoning that the anomalous situation was sought by defendant as part of a bargain struck for his benefit. But an appellate court which applies the factual basis requirement literally might overturn a plea even in the face of a clear factual basis for the more serious charge dropped as a part of the plea bargain.

Although as a general matter the determination of a factual basis for the plea is not constitutionally required, the situation is otherwise in one special set of circumstances as a result of *North Carolina v. Alford*.[21] Alford, indicted for first degree murder, pleaded guilty to second degree murder but then took the stand and declared he had not committed the murder and was pleading guilty to avoid the risk of the death penalty. Because he persisted in his plea and because a summary of the state's case indicated Alford had taken a gun from his house with the stated intention of killing the victim and had later returned with the declaration that he had carried out the killing, the judge accepted the plea. The Supreme Court upheld the plea, reasoning that

while most pleas of guilty consist of both a waiver of trial and an express admission of guilt, the latter element is not a constitutional requisite to the imposition of criminal penalty. An individual accused of crime may

21.   400 U.S. 25, 91 S.Ct. 160, 27 L.Ed.2d 162 (1970).

voluntarily, knowingly, and understandingly consent to the imposition of a prison sentence even if he is unwilling or unable to admit his participation in the acts constituting the crime.

* * * Confronted with the choice between a trial for first-degree murder, on the one hand, and a plea of guilty to second-degree murder, on the other, Alford quite reasonably chose the latter and thereby limited the maximum penalty to a 30–year term. When his plea is viewed in light of the evidence against him, which substantially negated his claim of innocence and which further provided a means by which the judge could test whether the plea was being intelligently entered, its validity cannot be seriously questioned. In view of the strong factual basis for the plea demonstrated by the State and Alford's clearly expressed desire to enter it despite his professed belief in his innocence, we hold that the trial judge did not commit constitutional error in accepting it.

The Court did not state just how strong this factual basis must be, but it would appear that when a pleading defendant denies the crime the factual basis must be significantly more certain than will suffice in other circumstances.

The Court in *Alford* observed that some courts require trial judges to reject pleas in such circumstances, and then in an oft-quoted footnote indicated no intention to foreclose such a result:

Our holding does not mean that a trial judge must accept every constitutionally valid guilty plea merely because a defendant wishes to so plead. A criminal defendant does not have an absolute right under the Constitution to have his guilty plea accepted by the court, although the States may by statute or otherwise confer such a right. Likewise, the States may bar their courts from accepting guilty pleas from any defendants who assert their innocence.

This language has been cogently criticized on the ground that it would permit a trial judge for no good reason to deny a defendant such as Alford the opportunity to obtain concessions via plea bargaining unless he misrepresents his own perception of the circumstances. This same footnote in *Alford* goes on to say that the Court "need not now delineate" the scope of a federal judge's discretion in this regard, but since that time at least one court has held that when there is strong factual evidence implicating defendant it is an abuse of discretion to refuse a guilty plea solely because the defendant does not admit the alleged facts of the crime.

(g) Acting on the Plea Bargain. In any case in which the tendered plea of guilty or nolo contendere is the result of a plea bargain, the judge receiving the plea will have added responsibilities. In some circumstances, at least, he will have to advise the defendant of the legal effect of the bargain, and he will of course have to decide whether or not to approve the terms of the bargain to which the parties have agreed.

In federal procedure, for example, there are three recognized types of plea bargains. The parties may agree that if

the defendant pleads guilty or nolo contendere to either a charged offense or a lesser or related offense, the plea agreement may specify that an attorney for the government will:

(A) not bring, or will move to dismiss, other charges;

(B) recommend, or agree not to oppose the defendant's request, that a particular sentence or sentencing provision of the Sentencing Guidelines, or policy statement, or sentencing factor does or does not apply (such a recommendation or request does not bind the court); or

(C) agree that a specific sentence or sentencing range is the appropriate disposition of the case, or that a particular provision of the Sentencing Guidelines, or policy statement, or sentencing factor does or does not apply (such a recommendation or request binds the court once the court accepts the plea agreement).[22]

A critical distinction, which determines the nature of the judge's responsibilities in a particular case, is that an agreement of the (B) type involves only a promise by the prosecution to seek or not oppose a certain result, while an agreement of either of the other two types involves a promise to actually bring about a certain result. This means that when the judge learns that an agreement of the (B) type has been made, he must tell the defendant of his precarious position; "the court must advise the defendant that the defendant has no right to withdraw the plea if the court does not follow the recommendation or request."[23] No such caution is required as to the other two types of agreements, for they do not carry this risk. Rather, as to them the court may simply proceed to "accept the agreement, reject it, or defer a decision until the court has reviewed the presentence report."[24] But if the court ultimately rejects a type (A) or type (C) agreement, it must so advise the parties, "give the defendant an opportunity to withdraw the plea," and "advise the defendant personally that if the plea is not withdrawn, the court may dispose of the case less favorably toward the defendant than the plea agreement contemplated."[25]

Somewhat similar procedures are required by state law, though there is some variation to be found as to when the defendant is to be informed that if he persists in his plea he has no assurance of the anticipated concessions and when he is to be told that he retains the right to withdraw his plea if those concessions are not granted. In large measure, the disparity is attributable to the fact that the states are not in agreement on how to deal with what in federal practice is known as a type (B) agreement. In some states that type of agreement is

recognized as a situation in which the defendant assumes the risk that the prosecutor's recommendation will not be followed, which means that the judge is obligated to advise the defendant of the risk he is taking. In some other states, however, that type of agreement is not viewed as calling for different treatment. In those jurisdictions no advance warning is required; if the judge ultimately decides not to accept the prosecutor's recommendation, the defendant must then be so advised and be given an opportunity to withdraw his plea. Which of these two systems is preferable is understandably a matter as to which there is disagreement. In favor of the first approach, it is argued that there is nothing inherently unfair in permitting a defendant to bargain for nothing more than a calculated risk that the punishment meted out by the court might be less severe than he would receive upon a trial. In support of the second approach, it is argued that the first one allows for at least the taint of false inducement even when the trial court properly advises the accused that the trial court is not bound by the prosecutor's dispositional recommendation.

Under either system, of course, the judge has an independent responsibility to pass upon the merits of all plea bargains contemplating certain consequences that can be achieved only by the judge or with his approval. If the bargain goes to the sentence to be imposed, quite obviously this is a matter ultimately to be decided by the judge. If the bargain necessitates the dropping of other charges where, as is common, this can be accomplished only with the judge's approval, there is at least a limited role for the judge to perform here as well.[26]

Assume a case in which the judge acting on the plea bargain, if he were to impose a sen-

---

22. Fed.R.Crim.P. 11(c)(1).

23. Fed.R.Crim.P. 11(c)(3)(B).

24. Fed.R.Crim.P. 11(c)(3)(A). If the court accepts a Type (A) or (C) agreement, it "must inform the defendant that * * * the agreed disposition will be included in the judgment." Fed.R.Crim.P. 11(c)(4).

25. Fed.R.Crim.P. 11(c)(5). Then-existing similar language was relied upon in United States v. Hyde, 520 U.S. 670, 117 S.Ct. 1630, 137 L.Ed.2d 935 (1997), holding that when a federal defendant has entered into a type (A) or

type (C) agreement and has then entered a guilty plea though the judge has deferred decision on the plea agreement, that defendant may not withdraw his plea as a matter of right merely because the judge has not yet acted on the plea bargain. The Court added that the court of appeals' decision to the contrary "would degrade the otherwise serious act of pleading guilty into something akin to a move in a game of chess."

26. See the further discussion of the judge's responsibility in this regard in § 21.3(e).

tence higher than contemplated by the plea agreement, would be required to allow the defendant to withdraw his plea. In these circumstances, may the judge impose a *lower* sentence than the agreement contemplates without affording the prosecution an equivalent opportunity to withdraw? At least in the federal system regarding type (C) agreements, the answer clearly is no, for the legislative history unequivocally shows that this was the intent of the revision of rule 11 allowing type (C) agreements. The situation is not as clear at the state level. One view is that the state, if it is to bargain freely and on equal terms with the defendant, must also be allowed to timely withdraw from a plea agreement when it is apparent that the court does not wish to abide by its terms. The contrary view rests upon the conclusion that though notions of fairness apply to each side, the defendant's constitutional rights and interests weigh more heavily on the scale.

When the defendant's plea of guilty is inextricably connected to a specific disposition contemplated by the plea agreement, does the court's statement that it "accepts" the plea constitute an irrevocable decision to accept the plea agreement terms as well, so that the judge is bound to that disposition even if the presentence report later reveals that such a disposition would be inappropriate? There are many situations in which it is clear that the answer is no. One is where the trial judge has cautiously conditioned the plea acceptance upon his later agreement with the terms of the plea agreement, and another is where the law of the jurisdiction declares that a plea of guilty is not deemed to be "accepted" until certain other specified events have transpired. But the answer should be no in other situations as well under any modern system in which the judge's responsibility is recognized to include acceptance or rejection of both (i) the plea, and (ii) the plea agreement.

On the other hand, once the court has accepted the plea agreement, it may not—absent a fraud on the court—change its mind because

of the discovery of new facts. Were courts free to re-examine the wisdom of plea bargains with the benefit of hindsight, the agreements themselves would lack finality and the benefits that encourage the government and defendants to enter into pleas might prove illusory.

§ 21.5   Challenge of Guilty Plea by Defendant

(a) Withdrawal of Plea. The prevailing view is that plea withdrawal between the time of the guilty plea and sentencing is not granted as a matter of right. But it is also clear that a defendant may withdraw a guilty plea as a matter of right before it is accepted by the court, which naturally gives rise to the question of whether a guilty plea should be deemed "accepted" when the judge who received the defendant's plea has not yet decided whether to accept the underlying plea agreement, especially when the plea agreement contemplates a specific disposition and not just a recommendation. This was the nature of the question confronting the Supreme Court in *United States v. Hyde*,[1] where the court of appeals reasoned that the guilty plea and plea agreement are "inextricably bound up together," so that deferral of the decision whether to accept the plea agreement constitutes deferral of acceptance of the plea as well. A unanimous Supreme Court reversed, noting that the court of appeals' reasoning runs counter to the language in Rule 11(e), which expressly states that in the case of a type (A) or type (C) agreement (i.e., for a specific sentence or dropping of charges) the judge may defer acceptance of the agreement in order to consider the presentence report, and then goes on to permit plea withdrawal *only* in the event that the court ultimately rejects the plea agreement. Moreover, the Court added, the court of appeals' holding "also debases the judicial proceeding at which a defendant pleads and the court accepts his plea," and "would degrade the otherwise serious act of pleading guilty into something akin to a move in a game of

1. 520 U.S. 670, 117 S.Ct. 1630, 137 L.Ed.2d 935 (1997).

chess." Some states have taken the contrary position, while others are in accord with *Hyde*.

Even when a plea cannot be withdrawn as a matter of right, a defendant who enters a plea of guilty is not foreclosed from subsequently challenging that plea or his disposition pursuant thereto. Procedurally, one means commonly employed in an effort to "undo" a plea of guilty is a motion to withdraw the plea. Contrary to earlier practice, such a motion may now be made in the federal system only before sentencing,[2] when withdrawal is permitted for "a fair and just reason."[3]

There is considerable variation on the state level. In some jurisdictions plea withdrawal is allowed only before sentence or only before "judgment" (which may refer to the time of sentencing or some earlier time). Many states follow the former federal approach and thus recognize that withdrawal of a plea is possible both before and after sentence and judgment. In these latter jurisdictions, there has been a distinct trend in the direction of utilizing the terminology that had been used in the federal cases. Where the defendant seeks to withdraw his guilty plea before sentence, he is generally accorded that right if he can show any fair and just reason, but where the guilty plea is sought to be withdrawn by the defendant after sentence, it may be granted only to avoid manifest injustice. The prevailing approach of utilizing a more demanding standard after imposition of sentence is based upon (i) the fact that after sentence the defendant is more likely to view the plea bargain as a tactical mistake and therefore wish to have it set aside; (ii) the fact that at the time of sentencing, other portions of the plea bargain agreement will often be performed by the prosecutor (e.g., dismissal of additional charges), which might be difficult to undo if the defendant later attacks his plea and (iii) the policy of giving finality to criminal sentences resulting from a voluntary guilty plea.

As for the presentence "fair and just reason" test, some courts proceed as if any desire to withdraw the plea before sentence is "fair and just" so long as the prosecution fails to

establish that it would be prejudiced by the withdrawal, while others take the position that there is no occasion to inquire into the matter of prejudice unless the defendant first shows a good reason for being allowed to withdraw his plea. The latter is the sounder and prevailing view. Given the great care with which guilty pleas are now taken—including placing the plea agreement on the record, making full inquiry into the voluntariness of the plea, advising the defendant in detail concerning his rights and the consequences of his plea, determining that the defendant understands these matters, and determining that the plea is accurate—there is no reason to view pleas so taken as merely "tentative," subject to withdrawal before sentence whenever the government cannot establish prejudice.

Under the "fair and just" test, whether the movant has asserted his innocence is an important factor to be weighed, as is the explanation for why the reason now asserted was not put forward at the time of the original pleading. The amount of time that has passed between the plea and the motion must also be taken into account. Illustrative of a reason that would meet this test but not the post-sentence "manifest injustice" standard is where the defendant now wants to pursue a certain defense he for good reason did not put forward earlier. If the defendant establishes such a reason, its strength must be balanced against any prejudice that would be suffered by the government if the plea were withdrawn.

The "manifest injustice" test is not self-defining, and doubtless does not mean precisely the same thing in every jurisdiction. But it may generally be said that withdrawal is necessary to correct a manifest injustice if

(A) the defendant was denied the effective assistance of counsel guaranteed by constitution, statute, or rule;

(B) the plea was not entered or ratified by the defendant or a person authorized to so act in the defendant's behalf;

2. Fed.R.Crim.P. 11(e).

3. Fed.R.Crim.P. 11(d)(2).

(C) the plea was involuntary, or was entered without knowledge of the charge or knowledge that the sentence actually imposed could be imposed;

(D) the defendant did not receive the charge or sentence concessions contemplated by the plea agreement and the prosecuting attorney failed to seek or not to oppose these concessions as promised in the plea agreement;

(E) the defendant did not receive the charge or sentence concessions contemplated by the plea agreement, which was either tentatively or fully concurred in by the court, and the defendant did not affirm the plea after being advised that the court no longer concurred and after being called upon to either affirm or withdraw the plea; or

(F) the guilty plea was entered upon the express condition, approved by the judge, that the plea could be withdrawn if the charge or sentence concessions were subsequently rejected by the court.[4]

The courts commonly treat the "manifest injustice" test as being no broader than the available grounds for relief upon collateral attack. If the defendant shows a manifest injustice, under the better view it is unnecessary that he also assert his innocence. The defendant has the burden of satisfying the trial judge that there are valid grounds for withdrawal. Courts rarely articulates the extent of this burden; it is sometimes said to be a showing of a basis of relief "by clear and convincing evidence," and sometimes a showing by a "preponderance of the evidence."

(b) Other Challenges to Plea. A defendant who has entered a plea of guilty might also challenge that plea by resorting to certain procedures likewise utilized by defendants convicted at trial, such as appeal, habeas corpus or a statutory post-conviction hearing. These procedures are discussed in more detail later,[5] and thus it will suffice here to make brief note of the limits on their use by defendants who have previously pled guilty.

In federal procedure, a defendant may take a direct appeal from a guilty plea conviction. Direct appeal offers the plea-convicted defendant a significant advantage over collateral attack, as the appeal is reviewed by a three-judge panel of the court of appeals that can overturn the plea conviction on a finding of error less than constitutional, jurisdictional, or fundamental magnitude. The states also generally allow an appeal to be taken from a guilty plea, where again there is this advantage. But the appeal alternative is more limited in that the appeal must be taken promptly after the plea, and the only matters properly raised are those that can be resolved on the basis of the record in the case—mainly the transcript of the proceedings at which the defendant's plea of guilty was received.

A state guilty plea defendant will also have available state habeas corpus or a statutory post-conviction hearing procedure in lieu thereof. These avenues, in contrast to direct appeal, provide an opportunity for a hearing at which additional facts supporting (or refuting) defendant's claim may be adduced. However, relief is unlikely to be available unless any defect shown is of constitutional magnitude. As for the federal defendant, he may resort to the post-conviction procedures provided for in 28 U.S.C.A. § 2255. If he does so, he will prevail only by showing "a fundamental defect which inherently results in a complete miscarriage of justice" or "an omission inconsistent with the rudimentary demands of fair procedure."[6] Finally, mention must be made of the fact that the state defendant may ultimately end up in federal court raising constitutional objections via federal habeas corpus.

(c) Significance of Noncompliance With Plea–Receiving Procedures. One issue that arises with some frequency when a defendant moves to withdraw or otherwise challenges his guilty plea is whether a failure to comply fully with the established procedures for receiving the plea is inevitably a basis for relief. The answer may turn to some

---

4. 3 ABA Standards for Criminal Justice § 14–2.1(b)(ii) (2d ed. 1980).

5. See chs. 27 and 28.

6. Hill v. United States, 368 U.S. 424, 82 S.Ct. 468, 7 L.Ed.2d 417 (1962).

extent upon the procedural context in which that issue is raised.

If, for example, that question is asked regarding a federal defendant's attack upon his guilty plea in a § 2255 proceeding, the answer given by the Supreme Court in *United States v. Timmreck*[7] is no. In *Timmreck*, the judge at the rule 11 hearing told defendant that he could receive a sentence of 15 years imprisonment but failed to add that there was a mandatory special parole term of at least 3 years. He then accepted defendant's guilty plea and thereafter sentenced him to 10 years imprisonment plus a special parole term of 5 years. The district court concluded the rule 11 violation did not entitle defendant to § 2255 relief because he had not suffered any prejudice, as his sentence fell within that described to him when the plea was accepted, but the court of appeals disagreed and concluded that "a Rule 11 violation is per se prejudicial." A unanimous Supreme Court rejected the latter view. Noting that relief under § 2255 is available only when "the error resulted in a 'complete miscarriage of justice' or in a proceeding 'inconsistent with the rudimentary demands of fair procedure,'" the Court concluded this could hardly be the case when there has been merely "a technical violation of the rule" rather than one which "occurred in the context of other aggravating circumstances." The Court added that this result made good sense, given the fact that "the concern with finality served by the limitation on collateral attack has special force with respect to convictions based on guilty pleas."[8] (States have often reached the same result as a matter of state practice.)

The Court in *Timmreck* intimated that the result might have been otherwise had the defendant raised the claim on direct appeal, and cited *McCarthy v. United States*[9] in support. In *McCarthy,* the trial judge failed to address the defendant personally and determine that his plea was made voluntarily and with an understanding of the nature of the charge, as required by rule 11, and defendant raised that omission on appeal. In rejecting the government's contention that in such circumstances the government should still be allowed to prove that defendant in fact pleaded voluntarily and with an understanding of the charge, the Court concluded

> that prejudice inheres in a failure to comply with Rule 11, for noncompliance deprives the defendant of the Rule's procedural safeguards, which are designed to facilitate a more accurate determination of the voluntariness of his plea. Our holding that a defendant whose plea has been accepted in violation of Rule 11 should be afforded the opportunity to plead anew not only will insure that every accused is afforded those procedural safeguards, but also will help reduce the great waste of judicial resources required to process the frivolous attacks on guilty plea convictions that are encouraged, and are more difficult to dispose of, when the original record is inadequate.

Read narrowly, *McCarthy* says that a defendant's violation-of-rule-11 complaint on appeal cannot be defeated by the government's claim that *if* it could produce more facts by an evidentiary hearing it could show the violation was insignificant. But the above language was given a broader reading by some courts, which have held that on direct appeal a defendant's conviction *must* be reversed whenever the there was not full adherence to the procedure provided for in rule 11. In support of this automatic reversal standard, it was asserted that it better protects the defendant's rights and conserves judicial resources. Other federal courts took the harmless error approach on direct appeal when it appeared that the nature and extent of the deviation from rule 11 was such that it could not have had any impact on the defendant's decision to plead or the fairness in now holding him to his plea. On the

---

7.   441 U.S. 780, 99 S.Ct. 2085, 60 L.Ed.2d 634 (1979).

8.   In Bousley v. United States, 523 U.S. 614, 118 S.Ct. 1604, 140 L.Ed.2d 828 (1998), the Court added that even where the noncompliance presented a constitutional claim, it would be deemed procedurally defaulted where it did not depend upon facts that had to be developed apart from the

record and was not raised on appeal. Such a claim, first presented on collateral attack, would only be considered if the defendant met the "actual innocence" standard applied to procedurally defaulted claims. See § 28.4(f).

9.   394 U.S. 459, 89 S.Ct. 1166, 22 L.Ed.2d 418 (1969).

notion that it exalts form over substance to ignore what has been established to be a truly harmless error, this latter position has now been incorporated into the federal rules.[10] (Although that change in rule 11, unlike the more general harmless error provision in rule 52, does not also contain a plain-error provision, this does not relieve a guilty plea defendant who raises a rule 11 issue for the first time on appeal of the burden of showing plain error affected his substantial rights, as the rule 11 change did not "implicitly repeal Rule 52 so far as it might cover a Rule 11 case."[11]) One possible consequence of the harmless error doctrine is that if on appeal the error is *not* harmless, the government might convince the appellate court not to reverse but to remand for such modification in the disposition as would then make the error harmless.

In *McCarthy*, the Supreme Court at one point stated that "[t]here is no adequate substitute for demonstrating *in the record at the time the plea is entered* the defendant's understanding of the nature of the charge against him." This language, the Court conceded in *United States v. Vonn*,[12] "ostensibly supports" the position of the court of appeals in the instant case, namely, that in considering defendant's challenge to his guilty plea on the ground the judge had skipped the advice required by what is now rule 11(b)(1)(D) about the right to assistance of counsel, only the record at "the plea proceeding" would be considered. But the Supreme Court then noted that in *McCarthy* the "only serious alternative" to the plea record would have been "an evidentiary hearing for further factfinding by the trial court," while in the instant case "there is a third source of information," namely, that "part of the record" showing defendant was advised on his right to counsel "during his initial appearance" and "at his first arraignment." "Because there are circumstances in which defendants may be presumed to recall information provided to them prior to

the plea proceeding," the *Vonn* Court concluded that third source should have been considered by the court of appeals

States are not obligated to grant relief whenever a failure to follow plea-receiving procedures has been established. True, in *Boykin v. Alabama*[13] the Court noted that "so far as the record shows, the judge asked no questions of petitioner concerning his plea, and petitioner did not address the court," and then concluded that it "was error, plain on the face of the record, for the trial judge to accept petitioner's guilty plea without an affirmative showing that it was intelligent and voluntary." But in *North Carolina v. Alford*[14] the Court explained that it would suffice if at a hearing on a post-conviction petition it was established that defendant's plea was in fact knowing and voluntary. It of course follows that this is the case if a state defendant challenges his plea by federal habeas corpus.

(d) Significance of Compliance With Plea–Receiving Procedures. An issue in a sense the converse of that just discussed is whether full compliance with all the established procedures for taking a plea of guilty should foreclose any subsequent attack upon the plea that would necessitate a factual determination contrary to the one made when the plea was taken. The Supreme Court has confronted this question on two occasions, first in *Fontaine v. United States*.[15] The Court there held that upon a federal defendant's § 2255 motion to vacate his sentence on the ground that his plea of guilty had been induced by a combination of fear, coercive police tactics, and illness (including mental illness), a hearing was required "on this record" notwithstanding full compliance with rule 11, as § 2255 calls for a hearing unless "the motion and the files and records of the case conclusively show that the prisoner is entitled to no relief." The Court, in concluding such was not the case, noted that the objective of rule 11 "is to flush

---

10.   Fed.R.Crim.P. 11(h).

11.   United States v. Vonn, 535 U.S. 55, 122 S.Ct. 1043, 152 L.Ed.2d 90 (2002). The Court added that "the incentive to think and act early when Rule 11 is at stake," the objective of then rule 32(e), now rule 11(d) and (e), "would prove less substantial if Vonn's position were law."

12.   535 U.S. 55, 122 S.Ct. 1043, 152 L.Ed.2d 90 (2002).

13.   395 U.S. 238, 89 S.Ct. 1709, 23 L.Ed.2d 274 (1969).

14.   400 U.S. 25, 91 S.Ct. 160, 27 L.Ed.2d 162 (1970).

15.   411 U.S. 213, 93 S.Ct. 1461, 36 L.Ed.2d 169 (1973).

out and resolve all such issues, but like any procedural mechanism, its exercise is neither always perfect nor uniformly invulnerable to subsequent challenge calling for an opportunity to prove the allegations." But because one of the defendant's allegations in *Fontaine* concerned whether he had been mentally ill, a matter not routinely explored in a rule 11 proceeding, the case does not settle whether a hearing would be required if defendant's factual allegations were in all respects contrary to what had been determined at the time the plea was received.

In the second case, *Blackledge v. Allison*,[16] Allison had pled guilty to attempted safe robbery in North Carolina, answered that he understood the judge's advise that he could receive 10 years to life, and responded in the negative when asked by the judge if anyone "made any promises or threats to you to influence you to plead guilty in this case." The only record of the proceedings was the executed form from which the judge had read those and other questions. Allison, later sentenced to 17–21 years, sought relief via federal habeas corpus; he claimed that his lawyer had told him that the prosecutor and judge had agreed to a sentence of 10 years but that he should nonetheless answer the questions at the arraignment as he did. The district court denied the petition on the ground that the form "conclusively shows" no constitutional violation and thus met the *Fontaine* standard, but the court of appeals' reversal was upheld by the Supreme Court. The Court declared: "In the light of the nature of the record of the proceeding at which the guilty plea was accepted, and of the ambiguous status of the process of plea bargaining at the time the guilty plea was made, we conclude that Allison's petition should not have been summarily dismissed."

The Court in *Allison* clearly signaled that if the plea had been received at another time with a more complete record, the result would be otherwise. It was emphasized that the plea here was entered in 1971, at a time when there were "lingering doubts about the legitimacy of the practice" of plea bargaining and

thus reason not to disclose bargains in court, and that the only record was the printed form, which did not disclose whether the judge "deviated from or supplemented the text of the form" or what others at the hearing had said regarding promised sentence concessions. Most significantly, the Court observed:

North Carolina has recently undertaken major revisions of its plea bargaining procedures in part to prevent the very kind of problem now before us. Plea bargaining is expressly legitimate. * * * The judge is directed to advise the defendant that courts have approved plea bargaining and he may thus admit to any promises without fear of jeopardizing an advantageous agreement or prejudicing himself in the judge's eye. Specific inquiry about whether a plea bargain has been struck is then made not only of the defendant, but also of his counsel and the prosecutor. * * * Finally, the entire proceeding is to be transcribed verbatim. * * *

Had these commendable procedures been followed in the present case, Allison's petition would have been cast in a very different light. The careful explication of the legitimacy of plea bargaining, the questioning of both lawyers, and the verbatim record of their answers at the guilty plea proceedings would almost surely have shown whether any bargain did exist and, if so, insured that it was not ignored.

Although lower courts before *Allison* were inclined to give little credence to the record made when the guilty plea was received, this is much less true today. Of course, there are still some circumstances in which a court must conduct an evidentiary hearing to resolve a challenge to a guilty plea even when the earlier proceedings were flawless. This is certainly true when the allegation goes to a matter, such as incompetence in representation by defense counsel, which is not likely to be disproved by the record made when the plea is received, or to unusual or extreme pressures that could be expected to "carry over" to the plea proceedings and influence the defendant to give false or incomplete responses. But in

16.   431 U.S. 63, 97 S.Ct. 1621, 52 L.Ed.2d 136 (1977).

the more common situations in which the defendant asserts a prior misperception of the possible consequences of his plea, of whether there was a bargain, or of the terms of the bargain, and the record of the plea proceedings clearly indicate otherwise, courts are now inclined to hold that relief can be denied without an evidentiary hearing.

(e) Effect of Withdrawn or Overturned Plea. If a defendant entered a plea of guilty in exchange for certain concessions (for example, reduction of the charge from murder to manslaughter) but thereafter managed to withdraw or overturn that guilty plea, so that the matter will now go to trial, is the prosecutor somehow "bound" by the concessions given earlier? Although the Supreme Court in *Santobello v. New York*[17] assumed that the answer was no, some lower courts have found this issue to be a very difficult one. Two conflicting points of view have been expressed. One is that by his earlier action in giving the defendant concessions the prosecutor vouched that the ends of justice will be served by such a disposition, so that he is now foreclosed from asserting the contrary. The other and prevailing view is that holding the prosecutor to his end of the bargain while allowing the defendant to extricate himself from his plea, so that the defendant takes nothing more than a "heads-I-win-tails-you-lose" gamble, would restrain prosecutors from entering plea bargains, and judges from exercising their discretion in favor of permitting withdrawal of a guilty plea.

One question is whether that position conflicts with the protections of the double jeopardy clause. Defendants have argued that it does, relying upon *Green v. United States*,[18] holding a defendant may not be prosecuted again for first degree murder following reversal of his conviction upon a jury verdict of guilty of second degree murder, returned at the conclusion of an earlier prosecution for first degree murder. The Court ruled that for double jeopardy purposes that jury verdict constituted "an implied acquittal on the charge of

first degree murder," barring further prosecution for that offense. It has occasionally been held that when in a guilty plea context a judge finds a factual basis for the lesser offense to which the defendant is pleading and dismisses the higher charge at the state's request, this provides defendant with the same double jeopardy protection as the jury verdict in *Green*. But the great weight of authority is to the contrary, and rightly so. The other view ignores the importance of the plea milieu and the fact that acceptance of the guilty plea does not constitute an inferential finding of not guilty of the higher charge, in that no trier of fact was presented with a choice between the greater and lesser charge.

Yet another line of attack is to assert that trial on the greater charge after the guilty plea is withdrawn or overturned amounts to a violation of due process under *Blackledge v. Perry*.[19] In that case, where defendant was prosecuted on a felony assault charge after he exercised his right to trial de novo on a misdemeanor assault charge based upon the same incident, the Court held it was constitutionally impermissible for the state to respond to defendant's invocation of his statutory right to appeal in that way. Without regard to whether the prosecutor was acting in bad faith, due process "requires that a defendant be freed of apprehension of such a retaliatory motivation." But surely *Blackledge* has no application when all that the prosecutor has done is to return to the original charge, for there is no appearance of retaliation when a defendant is placed in the same position as he was before he accepted the plea bargain. It may be, however, that this "same position" must include a continuing opportunity for the defendant to enter a guilty plea to the same reduced charge as before.

But what if the prosecutor really does "up the ante" after defendant withdraws or overturns his guilty plea, now filing more charges or a more serious charge than had been brought originally? Here, courts are more like-

---

17.   404 U.S. 257, 92 S.Ct. 495, 30 L.Ed.2d 427 (1971).

18.   355 U.S. 184, 78 S.Ct. 221, 2 L.Ed.2d 199 (1957), discussed in § 25.4(d).

19.   417 U.S. 21, 94 S.Ct. 2098, 40 L.Ed.2d 628 (1974).

ly to find that *Blackledge* applies and that due process has been violated, in that the charge enhancement has the appearance of vindictiveness in response to defendant's successful challenge of his guilty plea. As discussed elsewhere herein,[20] there exists considerable uncertainty as to what kind of showing by the prosecutor will suffice to justify the escalation of charges. But, even assuming some such limits otherwise govern, it is unclear whether they are applicable in a plea bargaining context. In *Bordenkircher v. Hayes*,[21] where the prosecutor carried out his threat to prosecute defendant as a habitual offender because of his unwillingness to plead guilty to a forgery charge, the Court concluded that this conduct was not barred by *Blackledge* because the vindictiveness rationale of that case had no application to "the 'give-and-take' of plea bargaining." If that is so, then it would seem to follow that if the defendant had instead entered a guilty plea on the original forgery count but then later overturned that plea, the prosecutor would again be free to threaten prosecution under the habitual offender law and to carry out the threat if defendant did not again plead guilty to forgery.

In some cases, the due process objection may be stated somewhat differently and be grounded in *North Carolina v. Pearce*.[22] In that case, two defendants who had successfully challenged their original convictions were reprosecuted and convicted of the same offense but received higher sentences the second time around. The Court held that due process bars vindictive sentencing in response to exercise of the statutory right to appeal and also necessitates that defendants be free of "the fear of such vindictiveness," and thus concluded that a higher sentence could be imposed only if "based upon objective information concerning identifiable conduct on the part of the defendant occurring after the time of the original sentencing proceeding." In the guilty plea context, *Pearce* has not been read as barring a

higher sentence where the prosecutor properly filed a higher charge after vacation of the guilty plea. As for when the sequence was plea of guilty, a setting aside of that plea, prosecution and conviction on the same charge to which the plea was entered, and imposition of a higher sentence, there was a split of authority until the Supreme Court decision in *Alabama v. Smith*.[23] The Court held that the *Pearce* presumption, limited to circumstances presenting a " 'reasonable likelihood' that the increase in sentence is the product of actual vindictiveness," did not apply in this situation for two reasons: (i) because plea bargaining may "be pursued * * * by providing for a more lenient sentence if the defendant pleads guilty"; and (ii) because of "the greater amount of sentencing information that a trial generally affords as compared to a guilty plea." By contrast, the *Pearce* presumption *is* applicable if the defendant also pleads guilty the second time around but receives a higher sentence than he received after the first plea.

Finally, it is necessary to return to the charge bargaining situation in order to focus specifically upon the situation in which the defendant's guilty plea to one or more charges was in exchange for the prosecutor's promise to dismiss or not bring certain other charges. If the defendant thereafter challenges successfully the conviction or sentence on one count to which he had pleaded guilty (especially if the nature of the challenge is such that reconviction or resentencing on that particular count is impossible or unlikely), may he continue to enjoy the benefits of his plea bargain after having thus ended the burden? This issue has arisen with some frequency after *Bailey v. United States*,[24] where the Supreme Court held, contrary to the then common view, that a conviction for "use" of a firearm during or in relation to a drug trafficking offense under 18 U.S.C. § 924(c)(1) requires evidence that the defendant "actively employed the firearm in relation to the predicate offense."[25]

20. See § 13.7(c).

21. 434 U.S. 357, 98 S.Ct. 663, 54 L.Ed.2d 604 (1978).

22. 395 U.S. 711, 89 S.Ct. 2072, 23 L.Ed.2d 656 (1969).

23. 490 U.S. 794, 109 S.Ct. 2201, 104 L.Ed.2d 865 (1989).

24. 516 U.S. 137, 116 S.Ct. 501, 133 L.Ed.2d 472 (1995).

25. The Supreme Court has since held that *Bailey* applies retroactively and can be invoked notwithstanding a plea of guilty, Bousley v. United States, 523 U.S. 614, 118

Illustrative is *United States v. Barron*,[26] where defendant pleaded guilty to being a felon in possession of a firearm (count #1), possession of cocaine with intent to distribute (count #2), and use of a firearm during drug trafficking (count #3), and was sentenced to concurrent terms of 120 months on counts 1 and 2 and a consecutive term of 60 months on count 3, to be followed by an 8–year period of supervised release, pursuant to a plea agreement in which the government promised to refrain from bringing any other charges arising from the facts underlying the indictment, to refrain from seeking an enhanced penalty, and to recommend a 2–point reduction for acceptance of responsibility. After *Bailey* was decided, the defendant filed a section 2255 petition seeking only to vacate his § 924(c)(1) conviction and 60–month consecutive sentence. On the "difficult question" of the remedy in such circumstances, the court first noted that

> there are three possibilities. (1) The district court could treat the section 924 conviction and sentence in isolation, vacate them, and leave the remainder of the convictions, sentence and plea bargain intact. This is Barron's preference. (2) It could vacate the section 924 conviction, leave the other convictions intact, and resentence Barron de novo on all remaining convictions. This has been the most common response in the case law and is perhaps most appropriate where no counts were dismissed or uncharged pursuant to the plea agreement. * * *. (3) It could vacate the entire plea agreement, including the guilty pleas on all counts, and restore the parties to the *status quo ante* the agreement. This might be appropriate where charges in the indictment were dismissed pursuant to the plea agreement or where the plea negotiations included potential charges and enhancements not included in the indictment. The district court held it would apply this rem-

edy if Barron pursued his section 2255 petition.

As for the defendant's claim that because he had only challenged his § 924(c)(1) conviction and sentence the district court lacked jurisdiction to vacate his unchallenged convictions, the court in *Barron* took note of the unanimous view "that section 2255 confers jurisdiction on district courts to resentence a defendant on unchallenged counts of conviction after vacating a challenged 924(c) count, at least where the aggregate sentence can be viewed as a 'package.'" The court then cogently concluded that the " 'sentencing package' concept," namely, "that when a petitioner attacks one of several interdependent sentences, he in effect challenges the aggregate sentencing scheme," "applies with equal force here":

> Given the realities of plea bargaining, it makes good sense to apply the sentence package concept when a petitioner challenges one of multiple convictions obtained under a plea agreement. A set of convictions and sentences entered pursuant to a plea agreement may be viewed as part of a "package" deal, considered and approved by the court. Because the government agreed to refrain from bringing other charges arising out of the same general facts in exchange for Barron's agreement to plead guilty to the charges in the indictment, it is possible, perhaps likely, that Barron would have faced other charges had he not pleaded guilty to the section 924(c) count. Because the district court cannot possibly know what convictions or sentences Barron would have received had he not pleaded guilty to the section 924(c) count or had the district court refused to accept his defective plea, an appropriate remedy is to put Barron in the position he was in before he entered into the plea agreement or before the district court accepted the plea based on conduct which did not constitute the crime charged.

S.Ct. 1604, 140 L.Ed.2d 828 (1998), and thus *Bailey* means that a plea to such a "use" count is vulnerable as lacking a factual basis or for want of sufficient notice of the charge.

26. 127 F.3d 890 (9th Cir.1997).

The court then concluded that this result, which could be reached without characterizing defendant's 2255 challenge as a breach of the plea agreement, did not subject the defendant to double jeopardy.

However, upon rehearing en banc, that decision was reversed.[27] The court, looking first at the district court's reasoning, concluded:

> Although Barron did not seek a new trial, the district court chose that option on the ground that Barron's plea agreement had forfeited an appeal on the basis of "a favorable intervening change in the law," so that the only way Barron's motion could be granted was by construing it as an attack on the plea agreement. In this analysis the district court was mistaken for three reasons. First, Barron was not appealing. Second, *Bailey* was not "a favorable intervening change in the law"; it was a determination that at no time had the law forbidden use of a gun in the sense Barron had used a gun. Third, granting a new trial was not necessary to granting his motion. To grant his motion, the district court did not need to construct an argument against the plea agreement. The district court needed only to resentence.

> Barron's motion purely and simply asked the district court to vacate a conviction that was void as a matter of law. The motion did not attack the plea agreement in any way.

As for the panel's "package" concept, the court concluded that "the argument that plea bargains must be treated as a package logically applies only in cases in which a petitioner challenges the entire plea as unknowing or involuntary." The court added that the "drafter of the plea agreement could have anticipated the contingency that has arisen and included a provision protecting the government's interest in the event that Barron's conviction was vacated." Because the government had not done so, the appellate court concluded, the district court may only "vacate the judgment and resentence Barron on the two counts of conviction that still stand."

(f) Admissibility of Withdrawn or Overturned Plea and Related Statements. In the past, some courts have held that if a defendant's plea of guilty is subsequently withdrawn or otherwise vacated, the fact of that plea may nonetheless be admitted into evidence against the defendant at his later trial because it constitutes conduct inconsistent with innocence and is comparable to an extrajudicial confession to the crime. The federal rule has long been otherwise,[28] and the more recent state decisions have consistently held that such a plea is not admissible. This is as it should be, as the privilege extended to withdrawing the plea would be an empty one if the withdrawn plea could be used against the defendant on his trial.

It is not uncommon for a defendant to make incriminating statements in connection with the entry of a guilty plea, especially when he is called upon to supply information establishing a factual basis for the plea. If that plea has been vacated, then those statements are not admissible in evidence against the defendant either. When the nature of the statements is such as to make it evident that a guilty plea was entered, then this result is an inevitable consequence of the rule that the vacated plea is itself inadmissible. But the result is just as compelling when the statements are incriminating but do not disclose that they were given in connection with a plea of guilty. A contrary rule would discourage the giving of information needed by the court in the plea receiving and sentencing process. Sometimes limited exceptions have been recognized or urged to this rule on the nonadmissibility of statements given in connection with a since vacated plea. One is that such statements may be admitted against a defendant in a criminal proceeding for perjury or false statement if the statements were made by the defendant under oath, on the record, and in the presence of counsel; and another is that the statements may be used for impeachment purposes.

§ 21.6 Effect of Guilty Plea

(a) Rights Waived or Forfeited by Plea. A valid plea of guilty generally bars the defen-

---

27. United States v. Barron, 172 F.3d 1153 (9th Cir. 1999).

28. Kercheval v. United States, 274 U.S. 220, 47 S.Ct. 582, 71 L.Ed. 1009 (1927).

dant from subsequently raising objections that might well be a basis for overturning his conviction had he gone to trial. Why this should be so and the extent to which it is so was first addressed by the Supreme Court in *McMann v. Richardson*[1] and two companion cases. In *McMann,* a federal court of appeals ordered evidentiary hearings for three petitioners who had entered pleas of guilty some years earlier in New York but now asserted their pleas had been motivated by confessions coerced from them. Although those pleas had been received prior to the Court's decision in *Jackson v. Denno,*[2] holding unconstitutional the New York procedure requiring submission of the admissibility-of-a-confession issue to the jury, and though *Jackson* had been applied retroactively to the benefit of defendants who had gone to trial, the Court nonetheless concluded these petitioners were not entitled to relief:

> A conviction after trial in which a coerced confession is introduced rests in part on the coerced confession, a constitutionally unacceptable basis for conviction. * * * The defendant who pleads guilty is in a different posture. He is convicted on his counseled admission in open court that he committed the crime charged against him. The prior confession is not the basis for the judgment, has never been offered in evidence at a trial, and may never be offered in evidence.

The Court added that a contrary rule "would be an improvident invasion of the State's interest in maintaining the finality of guilty plea convictions which were valid under constitutional standards applicable at the time," and concluded: "It is no denigration of the right to trial to hold that when the defendant waives his state court remedies and admits his guilt, he does so under the law then existing; further, he assumes the risk of ordinary error in either his or his attorney's assessment of the law and facts."

In the companion case of *Brady v. United States,*[3] defendant had entered a guilty plea to violating the Federal Kidnapping Act, later held to contain an unconstitutional penalty provision whereby only those exercising their constitutional right to jury trial could receive the death penalty. Although assuming "that Brady would not have pleaded guilty except for the death penalty provision," the Court ruled he was not entitled "to withdraw his plea merely because he discovers long after the plea had been accepted that his calculus misapprehended the quality of the State's case or the likely penalties attached to alternative courses of action." In the third case in the trilogy, *Parker v. North Carolina,*[4] both the death penalty and coerced confession issues were held to be foreclosed by defendant's guilty plea. Similarly, just a few years later the Court in *Tollett v. Henderson*[5] held that a defendant who had pled guilty to murder could not subsequently challenge the racial composition of the grand jury that had indicted him, as "a guilty plea represents a break in the chain of events which has preceded it in the criminal process. When a criminal defendant has solemnly admitted in open court that he is in fact guilty of the offense with which he is charged, he may not thereafter raise independent claims relating to the deprivation of constitutional rights that occurred prior to the entry of the guilty plea."

Any thought that this was an absolute rule, extending to *all* constitutional rights, was soon dispelled. In *Blackledge v. Perry,*[6] holding that escalation of the charge against defendant from misdemeanor to felony following defendant's assertion of his right to trial de novo violated due process, the Court explained why defendant's guilty plea to the felony was no bar:

> Although the underlying claims presented in *Tollett* and the *Brady* trilogy were of constitutional dimension, none went to the very power of the State to bring the defendant into court to answer the charge brought against him. * * * Unlike the defendant in

§ 21.6

1. 397 U.S. 759, 90 S.Ct. 1441, 25 L.Ed.2d 763 (1970).

2. 378 U.S. 368, 84 S.Ct. 1774, 12 L.Ed.2d 908 (1964).

3. 397 U.S. 742, 90 S.Ct. 1463, 25 L.Ed.2d 747 (1970).

4. 397 U.S. 790, 90 S.Ct. 1458, 25 L.Ed.2d 785 (1970).

5. 411 U.S. 258, 93 S.Ct. 1602, 36 L.Ed.2d 235 (1973).

6. 417 U.S. 21, 94 S.Ct. 2098, 40 L.Ed.2d 628 (1974).

Tollett, Perry is not complaining of 'antecedent constitutional violations' or of a 'deprivation of constitutional rights that occurred prior to the entry of the guilty plea.' Rather, the right that he asserts and that we today accept is the right not to be hailed into court at all upon the felony charge.

Thereafter, in *Menna v. New York,*[7] defendant's previously asserted claim that his indictment should be dismissed on double jeopardy grounds was held not to be "waived" by his guilty plea. The Court explained in a footnote

> that a counseled plea of guilty is an admission of factual guilt so reliable that, where voluntary and intelligent, it *quite validly* removes the issue of factual guilt from the case. In most cases, factual guilt is a sufficient basis for the State's imposition of punishment. A guilty plea, therefore, simply renders irrelevant those constitutional violations not logically inconsistent with the valid establishment of factual guilt and which do not stand in the way of conviction if factual guilt is validly established.

The dissenters in the *Brady* trilogy and in *Tollett* objected that those decisions cannot be squared with established doctrine on the waiver of constitutional rights, whereunder there is no effective waiver absent an "intentional relinquishment or abandonment of a known right or privilege."[8] But as a unanimous Court later pointed out, "these decisions did not rest on any principle of waiver,"[9] but instead reflect the fact that constitutional rights can be "forfeited" by entering a plea of guilty just as they can be forfeited by a failure to raise them in a timely fashion.

Whether a guilty plea *ought* to be so viewed is another matter, which inevitably leads into the issue of how one determines what constitutional rights can be lost in this fashion. The Supreme Court has not been particularly help

ful on this question, but surely the *Blackledge* "power of the State" test cannot mean that a guilty plea defendant may later challenge his conviction on any constitutional ground that, if asserted before trial and left uncorrected, would have left the state with no power to obtain a valid conviction against him at trial, for if that were the rule, the defense in *Tollett* would have survived. Nor can it mean that a defendant who has been convicted on a plea of guilty may challenge his conviction on any constitutional ground that would preclude the state from obtaining a valid conviction without regard to whether the defendant asserts it as a defense, as such a rule would not cover the defense in *Blackledge.* As for the "factual guilt" theory of *Menna,* it cannot be squared with *Tollett,* where the defendant was barred even though he was asserting a claim independent of his factual guilt. Nor can the matter be resolved by saying that whether constitutional claims survive a guilty plea depends on whether they are "jurisdictional," for this simply begs the question.

One commentator has articulated the *Blackledge–Menna* exception as follows: "a defendant who has been convicted on a plea of guilty may challenge his conviction on any constitutional ground that, if asserted before trial, would forever preclude the state from obtaining a valid conviction against him, regardless of how much the state might endeavor to correct the defect. In other words, a plea of guilty may operate as a forfeiture of all defenses except those that, once raised, cannot be 'cured.' "[10] Where an error can be cured, the entry of the plea itself may have impaired the state's ability thereafter to prove the defendant guilty at trial. And it is not unfair to assume that the state relied on the plea to its detriment, particularly because the entry of the plea has itself made the issue so difficult to resolve later. But when the constitutional error is incurable the state is in precisely the

7. 423 U.S. 61, 96 S.Ct. 241, 46 L.Ed.2d 195 (1975).

8. Johnson v. Zerbst, 304 U.S. 458, 58 S.Ct. 1019, 82 L.Ed. 1461 (1938).

9. Haring v. Prosise, 462 U.S. 306, 103 S.Ct. 2368, 76 L.Ed.2d 595 (1983), holding that consequently the respondent's damages action under 42 U.S.C.A. § 1983 against police who allegedly subjected him to an illegal search was

not barred by his earlier plea of guilty to the offense discovered by that search.

10. Westen, Away From Waiver: A Rationale for the Forfeiture of Constitutional Rights in Criminal Procedure, 75 Mich.L.Rev. 1214, 1266 (1977).

same position after the entry of the guilty plea as it occupied beforehand with respect to its ability to prove the defendant guilty at trial: the error would always have prevented it from obtaining a valid conviction at trial. This reasoning conforms to the results in the Supreme Court's decisions. In *Tollett* the alleged defect could have been cured by reconstituting the grand jury and obtaining a proper indictment, but the due process claim in *Blackledge* and the double jeopardy claim in *Menna* involved errors that could not be cured. Other constitutional defenses of this character, which likewise should not be deemed forfeited by a guilty plea, include the Sixth Amendment right to speedy trial, the right not to be convicted of conduct that cannot constitutionally be made criminal, and perhaps the right not to be selectively prosecuted in violation of the equal protection clause.

This is not to suggest, however, that a constitutional defense of that special character will in all instances survive a guilty plea, for *United States v. Broce*[11] holds to the contrary. The defendants pleaded guilty to two conspiracy indictments charging the rigging of bids on two highway projects but later, relying on a ruling re other defendants who did *not* plead guilty, interposed the double jeopardy claim that only one conspiracy was involved. The Court ruled that "a defendant who pleads guilty to two counts with facial allegations of distinct offenses concede[s] that he has committed two separate crimes," and thereby has relinquished any "opportunity to receive a factual hearing on a double jeopardy claim." The *Broce* Court distinguished *Blackledge* and *Menna* as cases that "could be (and ultimately were) resolved without any need to venture beyond [the] record,"[12] while in the instant case the defendants "cannot prove their claim by relying on [the] indictments and the existing record" or, indeed, "without contradicting those indictments, and that opportunity is foreclosed by the admissions inherent in their guilty pleas."

Even if the constitutional violation has produced an incurable defect so that the right is not automatically forfeited by a plea of guilty, there still might occur an enforceable waiver of that same right in a particular case. For example, what if a defendant is charged with count one (as to which he has a colorable speedy trial defense) and with count two (as to which he has no apparent defense), but as a result of negotiations with the prosecutor he agrees to plead guilty to count one, which carries a lower sentence, in exchange for dismissal of count two? Because the state has given up something of value, in that its prosecutorial position on count two would have deteriorated because of its reasonable assumption that it would never have to go to trial on that charge, the state's interest in preserving its opportunity to prosecute the defendant justifies foreclosing him from asserting his constitutional claim. This conclusion conforms to the Supreme Court's declaration in *Menna* that it was not holding "that a double jeopardy claim may never be waived."

If the right in question is one that *is* subject to forfeiture under the line of Supreme Court cases discussed above, this does not inevitably mean the defendant's attack upon his guilty plea will be unsuccessful. As the Court emphasized in *McMann,* it means that to prevail the defendant must "allege and prove serious derelictions on the part of counsel sufficient to show that his plea was not, after all, a knowing and intelligent act." The Court then said this depends "not on whether a court would retrospectively consider counsel's advice to be right or wrong, but on whether that advice was within the range of competence demanded of attorneys in criminal cases." But the advice by counsel in *McMann* was deemed to be within that range, for the New York procedure not challenged had theretofore been upheld by the Supreme Court. In *Tollett,* by contrast, it appears that defense counsel had not even investigated the facts upon which a claim of unconstitutional selection of the grand jury could

---

11. 488 U.S. 563, 109 S.Ct. 757, 102 L.Ed.2d 927 (1989).

12. The three dissenters argued that "nothing in *Blackledge* or *Menna* indicates that the general constitu-

tional rule announced in those cases was dependent on the fortuity that the defendants' double jeopardy claims were apparent from the records below without resort to an evidentiary hearing."

have been grounded, yet the Court also declined to treat that as beyond the range of competence required. The Court emphasized, however, that had counsel done otherwise he could at best "only delay the inevitable date of prosecution," which suggests a more rigorous standard might well be applied if counsel failed to explore possible constitutional objections more likely to affect the outcome of a case.

As the Court later concluded in *Hill v. Lockhart*,[13] the two-part ineffective assistance of counsel test of *Strickland v. Washington*[14] applies in a guilty plea context. The first half of that test is "nothing more than a restatement of the standard of attorney competence" stated in *Tollett* and *McMann* and discussed above, while the second or "prejudice" part "focuses on whether counsel's constitutionally ineffective performance affected the outcome of the plea process." What the defendant must show is "a reasonable probability that, but for counsel's errors, he would not have pleaded guilty and would have insisted on going to trial." This means, the Court elaborated, that if the error was a failure to discover potentially exculpatory evidence, the question is whether "discovery of the evidence would have led counsel to change his recommendation as to the plea," which in turn depends on "whether the evidence likely would have changed the outcome of a trial." Similarly, if the error was failure to advise defendant of an affirmative defense it must be asked "whether the affirmative defense would likely have succeeded at trial." In *Hill*, where the error was a failure by counsel to advise defendant correctly on his parole eligibility under the plea bargain, prejudice was not shown because it did not appear defendant "placed particular emphasis on his parole eligibility in deciding whether or not to plead guilty."

Finally, it must be emphasized that the forfeiture rule discussed above has no application to defects going directly to the guilty plea itself. This includes not only defects concerning advice of counsel, as just noted, but also defects in the procedure by which the plea was received or circumstances making the plea other than voluntary, knowing and intelligent.[15] As the Court noted in *McMann*, it is beyond dispute that "a guilty plea is properly open to challenge" if, for instance, "the circumstances that coerced the confession have abiding impact and also taint the plea." Moreover, a defendant after his plea of guilty remains free to raise objections regarding the sentence subsequently imposed, at least when the sentence now objected to was not itself a part of the plea agreement.

(b) Conditional Pleas. There are many defenses and objections that a defendant must ordinarily raise by pretrial motion, and if that motion is denied interlocutory appeal of the ruling by the defendant is seldom permitted. As noted above, a plea of guilty is with rare exception treated as a waiver or forfeiture of such claims. This is also true of a plea of nolo contendere, which means that in most jurisdictions a defendant who wishes to preserve his pretrial objections for appeal must go to trial. A few jurisdictions have provided for a contrary result by court rules or statutory provisions to the effect that certain pretrial motions, such as suppression motions, may be reviewed upon appeal from an ensuing conviction notwithstanding the fact that such judgment is based upon the defendant's plea rather than a finding of guilty after trial.

These provisions serve to avoid the necessity for trials undertaken for the sole purpose of preserving pretrial objections. As the Supreme Court put it in *Lefkowitz v. Newsome*,[16] holding that such a provision has the effect of preserv-

---

13.   474 U.S. 52, 106 S.Ct. 366, 88 L.Ed.2d 203 (1985).

14.   466 U.S. 668, 104 S.Ct. 2052, 80 L.Ed.2d 674 (1984), discussed in § 11.10.

15.   Thus in Bousley v. United States, 523 U.S. 614, 118 S.Ct. 1604, 140 L.Ed.2d 828 (1998), where defendant claimed "that his guilty plea was unintelligent because the District Court subsequently misinformed him as to the elements of [the] offense," and further contended that "the record reveals that neither he, nor his counsel, nor

the court correctly understood the essential elements of the crime with which he was charged," the Court declared he was not barred by *Brady*, *McMann* and *Parker*, discussed in the text supra, as "those cases involved a criminal defendant who pleaded guilty after being correctly informed as to the essential nature of the charge against him."

16.   420 U.S. 283, 95 S.Ct. 886, 43 L.Ed.2d 196 (1975).

ing the claim for federal habeas corpus review as well, it constitutes a "commendable effort to relieve the problem of congested trial calendars in a manner that does not diminish the opportunity for the assertion of rights guaranteed by the Constitution." The four major arguments made against such conditional pleas, that the procedure encourages a flood of appellate litigation, militates against achieving finality in the criminal process, reduces effectiveness of appellate review due to the lack of a full trial record, and forces decision on constitutional questions that could otherwise be avoided by invoking the harmless error doctrine, are less than compelling.

In the great majority of jurisdictions that have not enacted such statutes, the parties in a particular case may be able to create a situation whereby the defendant's plea of guilty or nolo contendere does not foreclose appeal of the denial of a pretrial motion. In recent years there has developed a practice whereby a defendant will enter such a plea but expressly reserve his right to appeal a specified pretrial ruling. Some appellate courts, either because they view this plea-with-reservation procedure to be a desirable alternative to an otherwise unnecessary trial or because they feel bound to honor the plea agreement made below, proceed to decide the reserved issue. Others, most often because they believe conditional pleas are undesirable and should be discouraged, refuse to decide the reserved question and remand so that the defendant may be permitted to withdraw his plea.

(c) Trial on Stipulated Facts. Yet another device sometimes utilized to avoid both the necessity for a full trial and the waiver-forfeiture consequences attending a nolo or guilty plea is a trial on stipulated facts. Under this procedure, the defendant enters a plea of not guilty, after which the case is submitted to the judge for decision upon the preliminary hearing transcript or other statement of facts agreed to by the parties. If the judge finds the defendant guilty, the defendant will have retained his usual right to appeal. But the conditional plea is a better procedure: it saves time by avoiding the need for even a short trial; it is more likely to be understood by the defendant; and there is a risk that in some circumstances the stipulation procedure will be viewed by an appellate court as foreclosing the very issue the defendant sought to preserve.

Chapter 22

TRIAL BY JURY AND IMPARTIAL JUDGE

Table of Sections

---

§ 22.1 The Right to Jury Trial

(a) Generally; Applicable to the States. Royal interference with jury trial in the colonies was deeply resented, and thus it is not surprising that the constitutions of the original states (and every state entering the Union thereafter) guaranteed jury trial, and that the United States Constitution commanded from the outset: "The Trial of all Crimes, except in Cases of Impeachment, shall be by Jury; and such Trial shall be held in the State where the said Crimes shall have been committed."[1] That language was criticized as inadequate, and thus the Bill of Rights specifically provided for jury trial in civil cases,[2] grand jury indictment

§ 22.1
1. U.S. Const. art. III, § 2.

2. "In suits at common law, where the value in controversy shall exceed twenty dollars, the right of jury trial

in criminal cases,[3] and in the Sixth Amendment that in "all criminal prosecutions" the defendant was entitled to trial "by an impartial jury of the State and district wherein the crime shall have been committed."

The Supreme Court on several occasions indicated that this Sixth Amendment right was not applicable to the states via the Fourteenth Amendment due process clause.[4] When the incorporation issue was resolved by asking whether "a fair and enlightened system of justice would be impossible without" the right in question,[5] that conclusion seemed beyond dispute, for then (as now) jury trial was not utilized in most countries. But when, as the Court put it in *Duncan v. Louisiana*,[6] it was deemed more appropriate to settle the incorporation question by asking whether the right "is necessary to an Anglo–American regime of ordered liberty," then it was apparent that the Sixth Amendment right to jury trial was also applicable to the states. As the Court explained in *Duncan*: "[p]roviding an accused with the right to be tried by a jury of his peers [gives] him an inestimable safeguard against the corrupt or overzealous prosecutor and against the compliant, biased, or eccentric judge." The *Duncan* majority conceded that jury trial has "its weaknesses and the potential for misuse," but concluded it was well established that in criminal cases "juries do understand the evidence and come to sound

conclusions in most of the cases presented to them."

The right recognized in *Duncan* is to have a jury pass on the ultimate question of guilt or innocence. This means that though it is for the judge to "instruct the jury on the law and to insist that the jury follow his instructions,"[7] "the jury's constitutional responsibility is not merely to determine the facts, but to apply the law to those facts and draw the ultimate conclusion of guilt or innocence."[8] But the right to jury trial does not include the matter of sentencing.[9] As stated in *Spaziano v. Florida*,[10] the Sixth Amendment "never has been thought to guarantee a right to a jury determination" of "the appropriate punishment to be imposed on an individual." The Court there held that this was so even as to the death penalty, and that consequently there was no constitutional prohibition upon a sentencing scheme permitting a trial judge to override a jury's recommendation of a life sentence instead of the death penalty. In response to the claim that because "the jury serves as the voice of the community, the jury is in the best position to decide whether a particular crime is so heinous that the community's response must be death," the Court declared that the "community's voice is heard at least as clearly in the legislature when the death penalty is authorized and the particular circumstances in which death is appropriate are defined."[11]

shall be preserved, and no fact tried by jury, shall be otherwise re-examined in any Court of the United States, than according to the rules of the common law." U.S. Const. amend. 7.

3. "No person shall be held to answer for a capital or otherwise infamous crime, unless on a presentment or indictment of a Grand Jury." U.S. Const. amend. 5.

4. Palko v. Connecticut, 302 U.S. 319, 58 S.Ct. 149, 82 L.Ed. 288 (1937); Snyder v. Massachusetts, 291 U.S. 97, 54 S.Ct. 330, 78 L.Ed. 674 (1934); Maxwell v. Dow, 176 U.S. 581, 20 S.Ct. 448, 44 L.Ed. 597 (1900).

5. Palko v. Connecticut, 302 U.S. 319, 58 S.Ct. 149, 82 L.Ed. 288 (1937).

6. 391 U.S. 145, 88 S.Ct. 1444, 20 L.Ed.2d 491 (1968).

7. United States v. Gaudin, 515 U.S. 506, 115 S.Ct. 2310, 132 L.Ed.2d 444 (1995), relying on Sparf & Hansen v. United States, 156 U.S. 51, 15 S.Ct. 273, 39 L.Ed. 343 (1895), so holding.

8. United States v. Gaudin, 515 U.S. 506, 115 S.Ct. 2310, 132 L.Ed.2d 444 (1995) (in prosecution of defendant

for making false statement, as to which "materiality" an element of the offense, trial judge erred in instructing jury that statements in instant case were material).

9. However, as further discussed in § 26.4(i), the constitutional rights to due process and to trial by jury necessitate one very important exception: "Other than the fact of a prior conviction, any fact that increases the penalty for a crime beyond the prescribed statutory maximum must be submitted to a jury, and proved beyond a reasonable doubt." Apprendi v. New Jersey, 530 U.S. 466, 120 S.Ct. 2348, 147 L.Ed.2d 435 (2000).

10. 468 U.S. 447, 104 S.Ct. 3154, 82 L.Ed.2d 340 (1984).

11. Stevens, J., joined by Brennan and Marshall, JJ., dissenting in part, concluded: "The same consideration that supports a constitutional entitlement to a trial by a jury rather than a judge at the guilt or innocence stage—the right to have an authentic representative of the community apply its lay perspective to the determination that must precede a deprivation of liberty—applies with special force to the determination that must precede a deprivation of life. In many respects capital sentencing resembles a

However, as discussed in more detail elsewhere herein,[12] the Supreme Court held in *Apprendi v. New Jersey*[13] that any fact (other than the fact of a prior conviction) that increases the penalty for a crime beyond the prescribed statutory maximum is, in effect, an element of the crime, which must be submitted to a jury and proved beyond a reasonable doubt. Applying *Apprendi*, the Court later ruled in *Ring v. Arizona*[14] that where the death penalty may be imposed only upon a finding of enumerated aggravating factors operating as "the functional equivalent of an element of a greater offense," then the Sixth Amendment requires that they be found by a jury as well.

(b) Petty Offenses. The Court in *Duncan* noted in passing that "there is a category of petty crimes or offenses which is not subject to the Sixth Amendment jury trial provisions and should not be subject to the Fourteenth Amendment jury trial requirement here applied to the States." Shortly thereafter, in *Baldwin v. New York*,[15] where appellant had been denied a jury trial when convicted of a misdemeanor punishable by imprisonment up to one year, a 5–3 majority held that "no offense can be deemed 'petty' for purposes of the right to trial by jury where imprisonment for more than six months is authorized." Justice White's opinion stressed that in the federal system petty offenses had long been "defined as those punishable by no more than six months in prison and a $500 fine," that "crimes triable without a jury in the American States since the late 18th century were also generally punishable by no more than a six-month prison term," and that after *Duncan* "New York City alone denies an accused the right to interpose between himself and a possi-ble prison term of over six months, the common sense judgment of a jury of his peers." He concluded: "This near-uniform judgment of the Nation furnishes us with the only objective criterion by which a line could ever be drawn—on the basis of the possible penalty alone—between offenses which are and which are not regarded as 'serious' for purposes of trial by jury."

Two points must be emphasized regarding the *Baldwin* test. For one thing, it should be noted that the Court used the word "punishable," so that the right to jury trial (unlike the right to counsel[16]) is to be determined on the basis of the punishment which *could* be imposed rather than that which it turns out is actually imposed in the particular case. This is because the maximum penalty authorized by the legislature is a truer indicator of society's judgment as to the seriousness of the crime charged. But where the legislature has not set any maximum penalty, as is typically the case as to criminal contempt, the Supreme Court has held that in such circumstances the "petty offense" distinction must be made on the basis of the penalty actually imposed.[17] In that connection, the Court ruled in *Frank v. United States*[18] that where petitioner was convicted of criminal contempt without a jury and received a suspended sentence and probation for three years, and the government conceded that he could receive not more than six months imprisonment if he violated the terms of probation, the contempt was a petty offense for jury trial purposes. The Court in *Frank* stressed that conditional release is a much lesser imposition than incarceration, and noted that in "noncontempt cases, Congress has not viewed the possibility of five years' probation as oner-

---

trial on the question of guilt, involving as it does a prescribed burden of proof of given elements through the adversarial process. But more important than its procedural aspects, the life-or-death decision in capital cases depends upon its link to community values for its moral and constitutional legitimacy."

12. See text in § 26.4 at note 55.

13. 530 U.S. 466, 120 S.Ct. 2348, 147 L.Ed.2d 435 (2000).

14. 536 U.S. 584, 122 S.Ct. 2428, 153 L.Ed.2d 556 (2002), discussed further in § 26.4 at note 55.

15. 399 U.S. 66, 90 S.Ct. 1886, 26 L.Ed.2d 437 (1970).

16. See § 11.2(a).

17. Dyke v. Taylor Implement Manufacturing Co., 391 U.S. 216, 88 S.Ct. 1472, 20 L.Ed.2d 538 (1968) (jury trial not required where maximum sentence authorized by statute is 10 days in jail and a $50 fine); Bloom v. Illinois, 391 U.S. 194, 88 S.Ct. 1477, 20 L.Ed.2d 522 (1968) (no statutory limits; denial of requested jury trial to defendant sentenced to imprisonment for 24 months constitutional error).

18. 395 U.S. 147, 89 S.Ct. 1503, 23 L.Ed.2d 162 (1969).

ous enough to make an otherwise petty offense 'serious.'"

Secondly, it is important to note that *Baldwin* describes a particular situation (i.e., offense punishable by more than six months' imprisonment) in which the offense is not petty, but did not hold that all other situations qualify as petty offenses. Thus, it was then open to contention that some such situations did *not* qualify, because of either (a) the very nature of the offense charged, or (b) the magnitude of other punishment (e.g., a fine) authorized by statute. Well before the *Baldwin* decision, the Supreme Court had refused to view the maximum potential sentence as the sole criterion for determining whether or not an offense was petty for jury trial purposes. Rather, the Court looked to the nature of the offense, considering such factors as whether it was indictable at common law,[19] whether it was morally offensive,[20] and whether it was *malum in se* rather than *malum prohibitum*.[21]

But that approach was abandoned in *Blanton v. City of North Las Vegas*.[22] Noting that the earlier "common law approach has been undermined by the substantial number of statutory offenses lacking common law antecedents," the Court in *Blanton* declared: "The judiciary should not substitute its judgment as to seriousness for that of a legislature, which is 'far better equipped to perform the task, and [is] likewise more responsive to changes in attitude and more amenable to the recognition and correction of their misperceptions in this respect.'"

The focus, therefore, is upon the various penalties that the legislature has attached to the offense in question. As a unanimous Court explained in *Blanton*:

Although we did not hold in *Baldwin* that an offense carrying a maximum prison term of six months or less automatically qualifies as a "petty" offense, and decline to do so today, we do find it appropriate to presume for purposes of the Sixth Amendment that society views such an offense as "petty." A defendant is entitled to jury trial in such circumstances only if he can demonstrate that any additional statutory penalties, viewed in conjunction with the maximum authorized period of incarceration, are so severe that they clearly reflect a legislative determination that the offense in question is a "serious" one. This standard, albeit somewhat imprecise, should ensure the availability of a jury trial in the rare situation where a legislature packs an offense it deems "serious" with onerous penalties that nonetheless "do not puncture the 6–month incarceration line."

The Court then applied those principles in the instant case, involving defendants charged with driving under the influence, and concluded they were not entitled to jury trial, as (1) the maximum authorized prison sentence did not exceed six months;[23] (2) the 2–day mandatory minimum is "immaterial," as in drawing the constitutional line the Court has "assumed that a defendant convicted of the offense in question would receive the *maximum* authorized prison sentence"; (3) the mandatory 90–day license suspension "will be irrelevant if it runs concurrently with the prison sentence, which we assume for present purposes to be the maximum of six months"; (4) the alternative sentence of 48 hours community service while dressed in clothing identifying the defendant as a DUI offender "is less embarrassing and less onerous than six months in jail";[24]

19. District of Columbia v. Clawans, 300 U.S. 617, 57 S.Ct. 660, 81 L.Ed. 843 (1937).

20. Schick v. United States, 195 U.S. 65, 24 S.Ct. 826, 49 L.Ed. 99 (1904).

21. District of Columbia v. Colts, 282 U.S. 63, 51 S.Ct. 52, 75 L.Ed. 177 (1930).

22. 489 U.S. 538, 109 S.Ct. 1289, 103 L.Ed.2d 550 (1989).

23. See also United States v. Nachtigal, 507 U.S. 1, 113 S.Ct. 1072, 122 L.Ed.2d 374 (1993) (*Blanton* presumption applies where Congress set 6 months as maximum

penalty; that determination is "legislative" in character though Secretary of Interior had final authority to decide, within limit set by Congress, as to whether maximum should be 6 months or something less and Secretary had opted for 6 months).

24. See also United States v. Nachtigal, 507 U.S. 1, 113 S.Ct. 1072, 122 L.Ed.2d 374 (1993) (offense is petty offense despite alternative sentence of probation up to 5 years, even if attended by various conditions, as these conditions "do not approximate the severe loss of liberty caused by imprisonment for more than six months").

and (5) as for the possible additional penalty of a $1,000 fine, "it is well below the $5,000 level set by Congress in its most recent definition of a 'petty' offense,"[25] and is not "out of step with state practice for offenses carrying prison sentences of six months or less."

Special problems are presented in cases involving defendants other than individuals, as in *Muniz v. Hoffman*,[26] where a labor union contended it was entitled to a jury trial in a criminal contempt proceeding for violating temporary injunctions, which resulted in the imposition of a fine of $10,000 on the union. The Court, after finding no statutory right to jury trial in such circumstances, went on to consider the constitutional right and in that connection declined to

> accept the proposition that a contempt must be considered a serious crime under all circumstances where the punishment is a fine of more than $500, unaccompanied by imprisonment. It is one thing to hold that deprivation of an individual's liberty beyond a six-month term should not be imposed without the protections of a jury trial, but it is quite another to suggest that, regardless of the circumstances, a jury is required where any fine greater than $500 is contemplated. From the standpoint of determining

the seriousness of the risk and the extent of the possible deprivation faced by a contemnor, imprisonment and fines are intrinsically different. It is not difficult to grasp the proposition that six months in jail is a serious matter for any individual, but it is not tenable to argue that the possibility of a $501 fine would be considered a serious risk to a large corporation or a labor union. Indeed, * * * we cannot say that the fine of $10,000 imposed on Local 70 in this case was a deprivation of such magnitude that a jury should have been interposed to guard against bias or mistake. This union, the Government suggests, collects dues from some 13,000 persons; and although the fine is not insubstantial, it is not of such magnitude that the union was deprived of whatever right to jury trial it might have under the Sixth Amendment.

Assuming (as the Supreme Court later held[27]) that in some circumstances there is a right to jury trial when a fine for criminal contempt is imposed on a labor union or corporation, the result in *Munoz* is nonetheless unobjectionable, for the fine came to less than a dollar per member. Other courts, expressing doubts as to whether there was a right to jury trial in any event in such circumstances, have

---

25. 18 U.S.C.A. § 1. See also United States v. Nachtigal, 507 U.S. 1, 113 S.Ct. 1072, 122 L.Ed.2d 374 (1993) (offense petty though "offense carries a maximum fine of $5,000").

26. 422 U.S. 454, 95 S.Ct. 2178, 45 L.Ed.2d 319 (1975).

27. International Union, UMW v. Bagwell, 512 U.S. 821, 114 S.Ct. 2552, 129 L.Ed.2d 642 (1994), which illustrates that the distinction between a criminal contempt and a civil contempt, as to which there is no right to jury trial, is often difficult to draw. In that case, a state court enjoined the union from conducting unlawful strike-related activities against certain mining companies, later fined the union for its disobedience and announced the union would be fined for any future breaches according to a specified fine schedule, and still later levied fines against the union totalling over $64,000,000. The state supreme court held these fines were civil and thus could be imposed without jury trial, but a unanimous Supreme Court reversed. The Court, per Blackmun, J., stressed these points: (1) While a contempt fine is civil if it merely compensates the complainant for losses sustained, such was not the case here, as the unions neither requested compensation nor presented evidence regarding their injuries. (2) While traditionally a contempt fine has been considered civil if it forced a defendant into compliance with a court order, this does *not* mean (a) that the fines here were civil because there was a prospective fine sched-

ule, for the "union's ability to avoid the contempt fines was indistinguishable from the ability of any ordinary citizen to void a criminal sanction by confirming his behavior to the law"; or (b) that the fines are criminal where they prohibit conduct but not when they mandate affirmative actions, as often "injunctive provisions containing essentially the same command can be phrased either in mandatory or prohibitory terms." (3) While direct contempts in the presence of the court are subject to immediate summary adjudication without jury trial, the union's conduct did not occur in the court's presence. (4) Civil contempt without jury trial is appropriate for certain indirect contempts, "such as failure to comply with document discovery, [which] impedes the court's ability to adjudicate the proceedings before it," but the union's conduct was also not of that variety. (5) Because the state court "levied contempt fines for widespread, ongoing, out-of-court violations of a complex injunction," and thereby "effectively policed petitioner's compliance with an entire code of conduct that the court itself had imposed," resulting in fines that "unquestionably" were not at the petty offense level, the contempt must be deemed criminal, as in "such circumstances disinterested factfinding and even-handed adjudication were essential," and thus "petitioners were entitled to a criminal jury trial."

also looked at the impact per member in holding, for example, that it is not objectionable that the fine on a union amounted to $50 per member or to no more than a member's weekly union dues for each day of the contempt. Similar uncertainty exists as to corporate defendants. Fines of $1,000 have been upheld almost routinely, and fines well in excess of that have been allowed when the corporation's illicit activity produced much revenue.

Finally, there is the question of whether in the joint trial of several petty offenses there is a right to jury trial if the cumulative penalty that could be imposed exceeds the petty offense limits. One aspect of this problem reached the Supreme Court in *Codispoti v. Pennsylvania*.[28] The Court there held that in the case of post-verdict adjudications of various acts of contempt committed during trial, the Sixth Amendment requires a jury trial if the sentences imposed[29] aggregate more than six months, even though no sentence for more than six months was imposed for any one act of contempt, as "the salient fact [is] that the contempts arose from a single trial, were charged by a single judge and were tried in a single proceeding."

But in *Lewis v. United States*,[30] the five-Justice majority opinion distinguished *Codispoti*[31] and concluded: "Here, by setting the maximum authorized prison term at six months, the legislature categorized the offense of obstructing the mail as petty. The fact that the petitioner was charged with two counts of a petty offense does not revise the legislative judgment as to the gravity of that particular offense, nor does it transform the petty offense into a serious one, to which the jury-trial right would apply." Two other Justices reasoned that the right to jury trial protects against both (i) the stigma attaching to conviction of

an offense the legislature has deemed serious and (ii) serious deprivation of liberty, and that the latter concern would require jury trial in the instant case but for the fact that the trial judge ruled at the outset that no more than six months imprisonment would be imposed for the combined petty offenses. The remaining two Justices dissented, reasoning that the stigma concern was applicable in the instant case notwithstanding the trial judge's action, as there is "no basis for assuming that the dishonor associated with multiple convictions for petty offenses is less than the dishonor associated with conviction of a single serious crime." Under *Lewis*, if a petty offense is joined with a nonpetty offense, there is no inherent barrier to having the guilty/not guilty determination made, respectively, by the judge and the jury, although due process considerations require both charges go to the jury whenever the petty offense is a lesser included offense of the joined nonpetty offense.

(c) Noncriminal Trials. Although the Sixth Amendment right to jury trial by its own terms extends only to "criminal prosecutions," it has been argued from time to time that the right extends also to other proceedings bearing some similarity to criminal trials. Courts have generally not been receptive to this contention. It has been held, for example, that this right does not extend to suits by the government to collect civil penalties, sexual psychopath proceedings, or paternity actions. In *McKeiver v. Pennsylvania*,[32] the Supreme Court held that "trial by jury in the juvenile court's adjudicative stage is not a constitutional requirement," reasoning that compelling jury trial might make the proceeding fully adversary and deprive it of its informal and protective character."

---

28. 418 U.S. 506, 94 S.Ct. 2687, 41 L.Ed.2d 912 (1974).

29. Again, the sentence actually imposed governs when there is no legislative maximum. This means that in a criminal contempt case several contempts that are individually petty because of the sentence imposed for each do not become serious when tried together if the sentences are directed to run concurrently. Taylor v. Hayes, 418 U.S. 488, 94 S.Ct. 2697, 41 L.Ed.2d 897 (1974).

30. 518 U.S. 322, 116 S.Ct. 2163, 135 L.Ed.2d 590 (1996).

31. On two grounds: (1) there "the legislature had not set a specific penalty for criminal contempt," in which case "courts use the severity of the penalty actually imposed as the measure of the character of the particular offense," and (2) the "benefit of a jury trial," as a protection against the arbitrary exercise of official power, "was deemed particularly important in [the criminal contempt] context."

32. 403 U.S. 528, 91 S.Ct. 1976, 29 L.Ed.2d 647 (1971).

(d) Size of Jury. Although the Supreme Court had originally ruled that the right guaranteed by the Sixth Amendment was a trial by the traditional jury of 12 persons,[33] in *Williams v. Florida*[34] the Court held that the Sixth Amendment was not violated by use of 6–person juries. Justice White explained:

> The purpose of the jury trial, as we noted in *Duncan,* is to prevent oppression by the Government. * * * Given this purpose, the essential feature of a jury obviously lies in the interposition between the accused and his accuser of the common-sense judgment of a group of laymen, and in the community participation and shared responsibility which results from that group's determination of guilt or innocence. The performance of this role is not a function of the particular number of the body which makes up the jury. To be sure, the number should probably be large enough to promote group deliberation, free from outside attempts at intimidation, and to provide a fair possibility for obtaining a representative cross section of the community. But we find little reason to think that these goals are in any meaningful sense less likely to be achieved when the jury numbers six, than when it numbers 12—particularly if the requirement of unanimity is retained. And, certainly the reliability of the jury as a factfinder hardly seems likely to be a function of its size.[35]

He went on to assert that a 12–person jury was not "necessarily more advantageous to the defendant" in that a smaller group reduced the chances of a holdout juror on either side, and that the cross section objective would not be "significantly diminished" by a 6–person jury if arbitrary exclusions from the jury rolls were forbidden.

The analysis in *Williams* has frequently been criticized. It is argued that 6–person juries are significantly less reliable than 12–person juries, and support for this conclusion is drawn from studies showing that civil juries of six are more erratic in their awarding of damages. There are also studies indicating that use of smaller juries does not result in significant savings of time, although it is true that smaller juries "hang," necessitating retrial, less often. That might be viewed as a mark of efficiency by some, but not those who see the hung jury as representing the legal system's respect for the minority viewpoint. It has also been shown that as a statistical matter a 6–person jury is much less likely to represent diverse groups in the community. Some of these studies were relied upon by the Court in *Ballew v. Georgia,*[36] where it was unanimously held[37] that petitioner's trial before a 5–member jury deprived him of his constitutional right to jury trial. Although the Court did "not pretend to discern a clear line between six members and five," this data was deemed to justify the conclusion that "any further reduction" in jury size "attains constitutional significance," especially in light of the fact that there is "no significant state advantage in reducing the number of jurors from six to five."

(e) Unanimity. In *Apodaca v. Oregon,*[38] where petitioners had been convicted of felonies by 11–1 and 10–2 votes, the Supreme Court overruled earlier decisions and held that the Sixth Amendment does not require jury unanimity. As in *Williams,* the Court began the analysis with the assertion that "the essential feature of a jury obviously lies in the interposition between the accused and his ac-

---

33. Thompson v. Utah, 170 U.S. 343, 18 S.Ct. 620, 42 L.Ed. 1061 (1898).

34. 399 U.S. 78, 90 S.Ct. 1893, 26 L.Ed.2d 446 (1970).

35. Harlan, Stewart, Black and Douglas, JJ., concurred in the result. Blackmun, J., took no part in the case. Marshall, J. dissenting, adhered "to the decision of the Court in *Thompson v. Utah* that the jury guaranteed by the Sixth Amendment consists 'of twelve persons, neither more nor less.'"

36. 435 U.S. 223, 98 S.Ct. 1029, 55 L.Ed.2d 234 (1978).

37. Stevens, J., joined the Blackmun opinion. White, J., concurred in the judgment. Powell, J., joined by the Chief Justice and Rehnquist, J., concurred in the judgment but expressed "reservations as to the wisdom—as well as the necessity—of Mr. Justice Blackmun's heavy reliance on numerology derived from statistical studies." Brennan, J., joined by Stewart and Marshall, JJ., joined the Blackmun opinion "insofar as it holds that the Sixth and Fourteenth Amendment require juries in criminal trials to contain more than five persons."

38. 406 U.S. 404, 92 S.Ct. 1628, 32 L.Ed.2d 184 (1972).

cuser of the commonsense judgment of a group of laymen,'' and then concluded:

> A requirement of unanimity, however, does not materially contribute to the exercise of this commonsense judgment. As we said in *Williams,* a jury will come to such a judgment as long as it consists of a group of laymen representative of a cross section of the community who have the duty and the opportunity to deliberate, free from outside attempts at intimidation, on the question of a defendant's guilt. In terms of this function we perceive no difference between juries required to act unanimously and those permitted to convict or acquit by votes of 10 to two or 11 to one. Requiring unanimity would obviously produce hung juries in some situations where nonunanimous juries will convict or acquit. But in either case, the interest of the defendant in having the judgment of his peers interposed between himself and the officers of the State who prosecute and judge him is equally well served.

The plurality opinion in *Apodaca* also rejected the contention, raised without success in the companion case of *Johnson v. Louisiana,*[39] that unanimity was required to effectuate the constitutional requirement that the defendant be proved guilty beyond a reasonable doubt. It was noted that the reasonable doubt standard developed separately from the jury trial right and that, in any event, lack of unanimity was not the equivalent of a reasonable doubt. As for the claim that unanimity was a necessary precondition for effective application of the requirement that jury panels reflect a cross section of the community, the *Apodaca* plurality opinion rejected the assumption that "minority groups, even when they are represented on a jury, will not adequately represent the viewpoint of those groups simply because they may be outvoted in the final result." The

Court did not say in *Apodaca* and *Johnson* how great a departure from unanimity would be tolerated, but in a brief concurring opinion Justice Blackmun, noting the assertion in *Johnson* that "a substantial majority of the jury" are to be convinced, declared that "a 7–5 standard, rather than a 9–3 or 75% minimum, would afford me great difficulty." Justice Powell, who supplied the critical fifth vote in *Apodaca,* explained in his concurrence that he based it upon his conclusion that unanimity was a part of the jury trial right not incorporated by the due process clause. This meant that *Apodaca* had no significance for federal trials.

With *Williams* having declared that there is no right to a jury of 12 and *Apodaca* that there is no right to unanimity, it was perhaps inevitable that the Court would ultimately have to consider the extent to which both variations from the traditional jury could be simultaneously permitted. *Burch v. Louisiana*[40] presented such a question, for at issue there was a provision that misdemeanors punishable by more than 6 months "shall be tried before a jury of six persons, five of whom must concur to render a verdict." A unanimous Court struck down that provision. Noting "that lines must be drawn somewhere if the substance of the jury trial right is to be preserved," the Court concluded that the "near-uniform judgment of the Nation," reflected by the fact that only two states allowed nonunanimous verdicts by 6–person juries, "provides a useful guide in delimiting the line between those jury practices that are constitutionally permissible and those that are not."[41]

(f) Trial De Novo. In *Callan v. Wilson,*[42] the Supreme Court held that the Sixth Amendment right to jury trial barred procedures whereby a trial was held in the first instance without a jury but at the first appel-

---

39. 406 U.S. 356, 92 S.Ct. 1620, 32 L.Ed.2d 152 (1972), involving a 9–3 verdict. There, the case had been tried before *Duncan,* so appellant conceded that the Sixth Amendment was not applicable and instead argued he must prevail in order to give substance to the proof beyond a reasonable doubt standard. *Apodaca* involved the slightly different contention that the Sixth Amendment right to jury trial should be read as requiring unanimity so as to give support to the reasonable doubt standard.

40. 441 U.S. 130, 99 S.Ct. 1623, 60 L.Ed.2d 96 (1979).

41. The Court also concluded that the state's claims that nonunanimous 6–person juries saved considerable time "are speculative, at best."

42. 127 U.S. 540, 8 S.Ct. 1301, 32 L.Ed. 223 (1888).

late stage a de novo trial by jury was provided. But in *Ludwig v. Massachusetts*,[43] involving a two-tier system of trial courts in which there was a right to jury trial only at the second tier, available after a conviction upon a trial without a jury at the first tier, the Court, in upholding that particular system, placed considerable emphasis upon the fact that the right to jury trial was not burdened by the cost of an additional trial. This was because under the Massachusetts system a defendant may reach the second tier by "admitting sufficient findings of fact," meaning he "need not pursue, in any real sense, a defense at the lower tier." It was thus different than the District of Columbia system found wanting in *Callan*, where it was necessary for the defendant to be "fully tried" in the first tier.

The Court in *Ludwig* also concluded that the right to jury trial was not unconstitutionally burdened by the danger of a harsher sentence at the second tier. This was because the Court's prior decisions[44] effectively guarded against that possibility. Finally, the Court declared that it had not been established that the right to jury trial was unconstitutionally burdened by the psychological and physical hardships of the two trials, as appellant "has not presented any evidence to show that there is a greater delay in obtaining a jury in Massachusetts than there would be if the Commonwealth abandoned its two-tier system." But this did not require reconsideration of *Callan*, the Court cautioned, for that decision also rested upon Article 3, § 2, clause 3 of the Constitution, which is not applicable to the states.

(g) Jury Nullification. Except in a few states where a constitutional provision provides that in criminal cases the jury shall be entitled to determine both the law and the facts, the function of the jury is commonly said to be that of ascertaining the facts and then applying the law, as stated by the judge, to those facts. Indeed, it is not at all unusual for a jury in a criminal case to be instructed that it has the "duty" to proceed in such a fashion. But it is nonetheless true that a jury in a criminal case has the power to acquit even when its findings as to the facts, if literally applied to the law as stated by the judge, would have resulted in a conviction. This is because a jury verdict of not guilty is not subject to reversal or to review in any manner whatsoever. On occasion, juries exercise this power by acquitting defendants who are charged with violating an unpopular law and defendants otherwise viewed sympathetically.

This practice, usually referred to as jury nullification, would seem to be part of the right to jury trial guaranteed by the Sixth Amendment. At least, the language the Supreme Court has used to describe that right appears to encompass the nullification process. In *Duncan v. Louisiana*,[45] holding that right applicable to the states, the Court declared that in the view of the framers "[i]f the defendant preferred the commonsense judgment of a jury to the more tutored but perhaps less sympathetic reaction of the single judge, he was to have it." Similarly, in emphasizing the need for juries drawn from a cross-section of the community the Court later asserted: "The purpose of a jury is to guard against the exercise of arbitrary power—to make available the commonsense judgment of the community as a hedge against the overzealous or mistaken prosecutor and in preference to the professional or perhaps overconditioned or biased response of a judge."[46] And in ruling a defendant is entitled to a fairly selected jury sufficiently open-minded on the death penalty issue, the Court explained that "one of the most important functions any jury can perform * * * is to maintain a link between contemporary community values and the penal system."[47] However, there is not complete agreement even on this point. In *United States v. Thomas*,[48] holding that a juror's intent to acquit regardless of

---

43. 427 U.S. 618, 96 S.Ct. 2781, 49 L.Ed.2d 732 (1976).

44. See § 26.8(c).

45. 391 U.S. 145, 88 S.Ct. 1444, 20 L.Ed.2d 491 (1968).

46. Taylor v. Louisiana, 419 U.S. 522, 95 S.Ct. 692, 42 L.Ed.2d 690 (1975).

47. Witherspoon v. Illinois, 391 U.S. 510, 88 S.Ct. 1770, 20 L.Ed.2d 776 (1968).

48. 116 F.3d 606 (2d Cir.1997).

the evidence constitutes a basis for the juror's removal during the deliberations, the court used strong language to the contrary: "Nullification is, by definition, a violation of a juror's oath to apply the law as instructed by the court * * * We categorically reject the idea that, in a society committed to the rule of law, jury nullification is desirable or that courts may permit it to occur when it is within their authority to prevent."

But even assuming that *Thomas* is wrong on this point, does it follow that the jury should be told specifically that it has this power? The prevailing view today—that it should not be so informed—is often attributed to *Sparf and Hansen v. United States*,[49] upholding a jury instruction that "a jury is expected to be governed by law, and the law it should receive from the court." But *Sparf* did not settle the jury nullification issue, for the Court did not address the specific question whether jurors should be told they can refuse to enforce the law's harshness when justice so requires. But lower courts have rather consistently ruled that no such instruction should be given. The leading case is *United States v. Dougherty*,[50] where the court concluded that the "jury system has worked out reasonably well overall" without resort to a nullification instruction, "with the jury acting as a 'safety valve' for exceptional cases, without being a wildcat or runaway institution." This is because, the court explained, the jury "gets its understanding as to the arrangements in the legal system" not only from the judge's instructions but also through "the informal communication from the total culture," and the "totality of input generally convey adequately enough the idea of prerogative, of freedom in an occasional case to depart from what the judge says." The court expressed the fear that a nullification instruction would upset the existing balance and produce many more hung juries. Finally, the court in *Dougherty* declared that such an instruction would deprive the individual juror of an important protection he now enjoys and

to which he is entitled: that "when he takes action that he knows is right, but also knows is unpopular, either in the community at large or in his own particular grouping, that he can fairly put it to friends and neighbors that he was merely following the instructions of the court."

There is considerable commentary supporting the *Dougherty* position, although the contrary position has also been vigorously argued. In opposition, it is contended that there is no reason to assume that juries will act in a different and less desirable way if informed about their nullification power, that there are political advantages to be gained by not lying to the jury, and that a nullification instruction would serve to discourage acquittals based on prejudice instead of encouraging them because it sets justice and conscience as the standards for acquittal rather than leaving the jurors to use their own biases as standards.

(h) Waiver of Jury Trial. Contrary to earlier practice, waiver of jury trial is now generally permitted except when expressly prohibited by a constitutional or statutory provision, as is the case in a few jurisdictions with respect to capital cases. A major influence in bringing about this shift was *Patton v. United States*,[51] settling that waiver of jury trial was permissible in a federal criminal trial.[52] In support of this conclusion, the Court in *Patton* pointed out that: (1) constitutional provisions as to jury trials are primarily for the protection of the accused, and thus waiver by the party sought to be benefited should be possible; (2) absence of a jury does not affect the jurisdiction of the court; (3) the argument that public policy requires jury trials is fallacious, as a defendant may plead guilty and thus dispense with trial altogether; and (4) the common law rule not permitting waiver was justified by conditions that no longer exist.

The Court in *Patton* emphasized that for a waiver of jury trial to be effective there must be "the express and intelligent consent of the

49.   156 U.S. 51, 15 S.Ct. 273, 39 L.Ed. 343 (1895).

50.   473 F.2d 1113 (D.C.Cir.1972).

51.   281 U.S. 276, 50 S.Ct. 253, 74 L.Ed. 854 (1930).

52.   Although *Patton* concerned only defendant's waiver of trial by a jury numbering 12 persons, the Court was of the view that no distinction should be drawn between such a waiver and a complete waiver of jury trial.

defendant." Waiver cannot be presumed from a silent record, and thus the better practice is for the defendant to be specifically advised by the court of his right to jury trial and for the waiver to be by the defendant personally either in writing or for the record in open court. Whether to be tried by a jury is an important matter to be decided by the defendant personally; it is not merely a tactical decision that may be left to defense counsel. In the federal courts and in several states waiver of jury trial must be in writing. Jury waiver tends to vary depending upon the offense category, and the pattern is similar to that for guilty pleas, suggesting that the motivations are similar: the expectation of a lesser sentence. If a "jury waiver agreement" is entered into contemplating concessions to the defendant for his jury waiver, questions of alleged breach of the agreement are dealt with in essentially the same way as with plea bargains.

However, only a minority of states give the defendant an unconditional right to trial without a jury; elsewhere the defendant must also obtain the consent of the court, the consent of the prosecution, or both. In the federal system, it is necessary that "the government consent" and "the court approves" regarding defendant's jury waiver.[53] In support of requiring the consent of the prosecutor, it is argued that the state and defendant should have an equal voice as to the method of trial, that the prosecutor should be allowed to prevent trial before a biased judge, that the prosecutor should be entitled to prevent a defendant from waiving his rights when it is against his best interests, and that the prosecutor is also entitled to protect the public interest in maintaining the role of the jury in the criminal process. In favor of requiring the court's consent, it is asserted that the judge should be so involved so that he can protect the defendant, protect himself from criticism regarding the outcome of the case, obtain valuable input on matters of witness credibility and community standards, and ensure that juries continue to have a role in criminal proceedings. On the other hand, in favor of an unconditional right to

waive jury trial it has been contended that such waiver should suffice because jury trial is solely for the protection of the accused, that waiver of a jury may sometimes be important to ensure a fair and impartial trial, that either the prosecutor or the court might refuse consent for unjustified reasons, that prosecutor and court consent can impede the public interest in more efficient and less expensive trials, and that jury trial is like other constitutional safeguards which can be waived by the defendant alone.

In *Singer v. United States*,[54] the Court found "no constitutional impediment to conditioning a waiver of this right on the consent of the prosecuting attorney and the trial judge when, if either refuses to consent, the result is simply that the defendant is subject to an impartial trial by jury—the very thing that the Constitution guarantees him." The Court emphasized that there was no common law right to trial by the court, that generally the "ability to waive a constitutional right does not ordinarily carry with it the right to insist upon the opposite of that right," and that jury trial is the "normal and * * * preferable mode of dispensing of issues of fact in criminal cases." But the Court concluded with this cautionary note:

> We need not determine in this case whether there might be some circumstances where a defendant's reasons for wanting to be tried by a judge alone are so compelling that the Government's insistence on trial by jury would result in the denial to a defendant of an impartial trial. Petitioner argues that there might arise situations where "passion, prejudice * * * public feeling" or some other factor may render impossible or unlikely an impartial trial by jury. However, since petitioner gave no reason for wanting to forgo jury trial other than to save time, this is not such a case, and petitioner does not claim that it is.

Experience has shown that defendants relying upon this passage have generally been unable to convince the court that their reasons for wanting a trial by the court alone are suffi-

---

53. Fed.R.Crim.P. 23(a).

54. 380 U.S. 24, 85 S.Ct. 783, 13 L.Ed.2d 630 (1965).

ciently "compelling" that defendant's waiver motion must be granted despite the prosecution's opposition.

Finally, note should be taken of the possibility of a "partial" waiver of the right to jury trial. The *Patton* case actually involved such a situation, for the waiver upheld there concerned only the requirement that the jury consist of 12 persons. Some states expressly provide for pretrial election by the defendant to be tried by a smaller jury. Waiver of the number of jurors also occurs when the defendant agrees in advance or at the time of the event that the trial may continue with some lesser number of jurors when otherwise a mistrial would be necessitated by the excusal of some jurors during the trial or deliberations. In contrast to the situation in *Patton,* courts are generally not inclined to permit waiver by a defendant of his right to a unanimous verdict.

§ 22.2 Selection of Prospective Jurors

(a) Federal Jury Selection Procedures. Jury selection in the federal courts is governed by the Federal Jury Selection and Service Act of 1968.[1] The purpose of this Act is to ensure that juries are "selected at random from a fair cross section of the community in the district or division wherein the court convenes" and that "[n]o citizen shall be excluded from service as a grand or petit juror in the district courts of the United States on account of race, color, religion, sex, national origin, or economic status." Each district court is required to devise and implement a jury selection plan designed to achieve those objectives.

Each plan must: (1) either establish a jury commission (consisting of one citizen and the clerk of the court) or authorize the clerk to manage the jury selection process; (2) specify whether the names of prospective jurors are to be selected from voter registration lists or the lists of actual voters of the political subdivisions within the district or division, and prescribe other sources when necessary to achieve the objectives stated above; (3) specify procedures for selecting names from those sources designed to ensure that each political subdivi-

sion is substantially proportionally represented in the master jury wheel; (4) provide for a master jury wheel into which the names of at least one-half of 1 per cent of the names on the source lists are placed; (5) specify those groups of persons or occupational classes whose members shall on individual request be excused from jury service because such service would entail undue hardship or extreme inconvenience; (6) specify that active members of the armed forces, members of fire or police departments, and members of the executive, legislative or judicial branches of government who are actively engaged in the performance of official duties are barred from jury service on the ground that they are exempt; (7) fix the distance beyond which jurors shall on individual request be excused from jury service on the ground of undue hardship in traveling to where court is held; (8) fix the time when the names drawn from the jury wheel shall be disclosed to the parties and to the public; and (9) specify the procedure for assigning persons whose names have been drawn from the jury wheel to jury panels.

From time to time as directed by the district court, the clerk or a district judge is publicly to draw at random from the jury wheel the names of as many persons as may be required for jury service. A juror qualification form is to be sent to each person drawn. A district judge is to determine whether a person is unqualified for, or exempt, or to be excused from jury service. A person is deemed qualified unless he "(1) is not a citizen of the United States eighteen years old who has resided for a period of one year within the judicial district; (2) is unable to read, write, and understand the English language with a degree of proficiency sufficient to fill out satisfactorily the juror qualification form; (3) is unable to speak the English language; (4) is incapable, by reason of mental or physical infirmity, to render satisfactory jury service; or (5) has a charge pending against him for the commission of, or has been convicted in a State or Federal court of record of, a crime punishable by imprisonment

§ 22.2
1. 28 U.S.C.A. §§ 1861–1869.

for more than one year and his civil rights have not been restored."

The names of all persons drawn from the master jury wheel who are determined to be qualified as jurors and not exempt or excused are to be placed in a qualified jury wheel, from which the names of persons to be assigned to jury panels are to be publicly drawn from time to time. Summonses for those persons are then to be issued. A person drawn is not to be disqualified, excluded, excused or exempted from service except as indicated above, provided that a person summoned may be "(1) excused by the court, upon a showing of undue hardship or extreme inconvenience, for such period as the court deems necessary * * *, or (2) excluded by the court on the ground that such person may be unable to render impartial jury service or that his service as a juror would be likely to disrupt the proceedings, or (3) excluded upon peremptory challenge as provided by law, or (4) excluded pursuant to the procedure specified by law upon a challenge by any party for good cause shown, or (5) excluded upon determination by the court that his service as a juror would be likely to threaten the secrecy of the proceedings, or otherwise adversely affect the integrity of jury deliberations."

Before the voir dire examination begins, or within seven days after the grounds therefor were discovered or could have been discovered by the exercise of diligence, the defendant or Attorney General may move to stay the proceedings for failure to comply with the above procedures in selecting the jury. If the motion contains a sworn statement of facts that, if true, would constitute a substantial failure to comply with the provisions of the Act, the movant is entitled to submit supporting proof. If the court determines that there has been such substantial failure, the court is to stay the proceedings pending proper jury selection.

(b) State Jury Selection Procedures. Largely as a result of changes adopted in recent years, virtually all states now follow procedures similar to those described above in an effort to select jurors at random from some standard list. Lists of voters are most commonly used, although some states instead or in addition utilize other lists, such as a local census, the tax rolls, city directories, telephone books, and drivers' license lists. Few if any states still authorize the key-man system in one form or another. Under this system, political and civic leaders (the "key men") are asked for suggestions of prospective jurors. They are likely to recommend persons they know, and as a result the list of prospective jurors is not likely to be representative of the community at large. Such selection procedures have understandably been the source of virtually continuous litigation over the years.

A high percentage of those persons whose names are drawn for state jury service seek to be excused, and in many states excuses are rather readily granted. The courts have generally found it easier, administratively and financially, to excuse unwilling people from service on juries than to try to ensure that all qualified jurors are able to serve. Especially in those states requiring jurors to serve for a considerable period of time at low pay, excuses for economic hardship are quite common. Others are excused because of poor health, advanced age, a need to care for small children, or the distance they live from the courthouse. In addition, state jury selection statutes typically list those persons who are disqualified from serving as jurors (e.g., persons not of voting age, persons who have not resided in the jurisdiction some minimum time, persons unable to read and write English, and persons with a felony conviction) and those who are exempted from jury service because of their occupations (e.g., doctors, pharmacists, teachers, clergy, and certain public employees).

(c) Denial of Equal Protection. Long before the Sixth Amendment right to jury trial was applied to the states, state jury selection procedures were subjected to constitutional challenge on the ground that they violated the equal protection clause of the Fourteenth Amendment. Just a few years after the Amendment was adopted, the Supreme Court held in *Strauder v. West Virginia*[2] that it was a

2.   100 U.S. 303, 25 L.Ed. 664 (1879).

denial of equal protection for a state to try a black defendant before a jury from which all members of his race has been excluded pursuant to a statute limiting jury service to "white male persons." A year later, in *Neal v. Delaware*,[3] the principle was extended to the discriminatory administration of ostensibly fair jury selection laws to achieve the same result. Under the *Strauder–Neal* equal protection approach, it was long accepted that the constitutional challenge could be made only by a defendant who was a member of the excluded class.[4] But in *Powers v. Ohio*[5] the Court held that the defendant in a criminal case has standing to raise the equal protection rights of excluded jurors, who would themselves confront "considerable practical barriers" to challenging their exclusion.

An equal protection challenge can succeed only upon a sufficient showing of intentional or deliberate discrimination. For many years, defendants seldom succeeded in making the requisite showing; the state action was presumed constitutional and the lower court findings were presumed to be true unless the defendant proved the contrary.[6] But then came the important decision in *Norris v. Alabama*,[7] where the Supreme Court held that a defendant in a criminal case could make out a prima facie case of discriminatory jury selection by showing (i) the existence of a substantial number of blacks in the community, and (ii) their total or virtual exclusion from jury service. Once such a prima facie case is established, the burden then shifts to the state to prove that the exclusion did not flow from intentional discrimination,[8] which is not met merely by testimony from a jury commissioner that he

did not intend to discriminate or that he did not know any qualified blacks.[9]

Much of the litigation that followed *Norris* concerned the question of what constitutes a "prima facie case" of discrimination and what the government must do to rebut such a case. The Supreme Court's initial approach to this question was troublesome at best. *Swain v. Alabama*,[10] for example, was rightly criticized because of the Court's willingness to accept the statements by the jury commissioners of a nondiscriminatory intent at face value and because of the Court's primitive statistical analysis. The post-*Swain* decisions of the Court reflect more careful and sophisticated analysis. While the Court has declined to hold that a statute is unconstitutional merely because it requires jury commissioners to apply rather subjective criteria providing some opportunity for discrimination,[11] that opportunity plus a significant statistical disparity will constitute a prima facie case. Thus in *Turner v. Fouche*,[12] a prima facie case was made out by showing that 60% of the county population was black, that only 37% of those on the jury list were black, and that 171 of the 178 persons disqualified for lack of "intelligence" or "uprightness" were black, so that "the disparity originated, at least in part, at the one point in the selection process where the jury commissioners invoked their subjective judgment rather than objective criteria." Similarly, in *Alexander v. Louisiana*,[13] where 21% of the population was black, and jury questionnaires with a racial designation on them were returned by 7,000 persons 14% of whom were black, and the pool was then reduced to 400, of which 7% were black, this was deemed to constitute a prima facie case which was not rebutted by testimony

---

3.　103 U.S. 370, 26 L.Ed. 567 (1880).

4.　The same principle was applied to an equal protection claim regarding selection of grand jurors. See, e.g., Castaneda v. Partida, 430 U.S. 482, 97 S.Ct. 1272, 51 L.Ed.2d 498 (1977) ("to show that an equal protection violation has occurred * * *, the defendant must show that the procedure employed resulted in substantial underrepresentation of his race, or of the identifiable group to which he belongs").

5.　499 U.S. 400, 111 S.Ct. 1364, 113 L.Ed.2d 411 (1991).

6.　See, e.g., Thomas v. Texas, 212 U.S. 278, 29 S.Ct. 393, 53 L.Ed. 512 (1909).

7.　294 U.S. 587, 55 S.Ct. 579, 79 L.Ed. 1074 (1935).

8.　Avery v. Georgia, 345 U.S. 559, 73 S.Ct. 891, 97 L.Ed. 1244 (1953).

9.　Eubanks v. Louisiana, 356 U.S. 584, 78 S.Ct. 970, 2 L.Ed.2d 991 (1958); Hill v. Texas, 316 U.S. 400, 62 S.Ct. 1159, 86 L.Ed. 1559 (1942), respectively.

10.　380 U.S. 202, 85 S.Ct. 824, 13 L.Ed.2d 759 (1965).

11.　Carter v. Jury Commission of Greene County, 396 U.S. 320, 90 S.Ct. 518, 24 L.Ed.2d 549 (1970).

12.　396 U.S. 346, 90 S.Ct. 532, 24 L.Ed.2d 567 (1970).

13.　405 U.S. 625, 92 S.Ct. 1221, 31 L.Ed.2d 536 (1972).

of one commissioner that race was no consideration in reducing the pool. More recently, in *Castaneda v. Partida*,[14] the Court held that a showing the population was 79% Mexican–American but that over an 11–year period only 39% of the persons summoned for jury service were Mexican–American established a prima facie case, which was unrebutted absent evidence that racially neutral qualifications produced the disparity.

The Court in *Castaneda* emphasized that "an official act is not unconstitutional *solely* because it has a racially disproportionate impact." Discriminatory intent must be shown, but a prima facie case of such intent may be shown by "substantial underrepresentation," for when "a disparity is sufficiently large, then it is unlikely that it is due solely to chance or accident, and, in the absence of evidence to the contrary, one must conclude that racial or other class-related factors entered into the selection process." Because, as the Court also noted, "a selection procedure that is susceptible of abuse or is not racially neutral supports the presumption of discrimination raised by the statistical showing," it would seem that a somewhat smaller disparity will suffice when it occurs within a selection process containing subjective selection criteria.

(d) The "Fair Cross Section" Requirement. In *Glasser v. United States*,[15] the defendant claimed but did not prove that all the names of women placed in the box from which the federal jury panel was drawn were taken from a list of the members of the Illinois League of Women Voters. The Court indicated that if the allegations had been proved all the petitioners would be entitled to a new trial. Because "the proper functioning of the jury system, and, indeed, our democracy itself, requires that the jury be a 'body truly representative of the community', and not the organ of

any special group or class," the Court declared that jury officials "must not allow the desire for competent jurors to lead them into selections which do not comport with the concept of the jury as a cross-section of the community." In other cases also involving federal juries, the Court held it improper to exclude women[16] or day laborers.[17]

By contrast, efforts during that era to upset state juries on grounds other than racial exclusion did not meet with success. The Court early on held that states could exempt certain occupational groups from jury service,[18] and later in *Fay v. New York*[19] and *Moore v. New York*[20] held that the mere fact of disproportionate economic representation, resulting from character, literacy, and property requirements for jurors, did not violate the due process or equal protection clauses, even when this was accomplished by the use of special "blue-ribbon" juries for some cases. The majority in these cases emphasized that the Sixth Amendment right to jury trial was not applicable to the states and that *Glasser* and other cases concerned with federal juries were based upon the Court's supervisory power over federal courts.

When the Supreme Court thereafter, in *Duncan v. Louisiana*,[21] held that the Sixth Amendment right to "an impartial jury" was applicable to the states through the Fourteenth Amendment due process clause, it appeared very likely that this meant the cross-section requirement was now applicable to the states as a part of that right. A majority of the Court so indicated a few years later,[22] and a square holding to that effect came in *Taylor v. Louisiana*.[23] The Court in *Taylor* declared that the purpose of a jury, "to guard against the exercise of arbitrary power," is not served "if the jury pool is made up of only segments of the populace or if large, distinctive groups are

14. 430 U.S. 482, 97 S.Ct. 1272, 51 L.Ed.2d 498 (1977).

15. 315 U.S. 60, 62 S.Ct. 457, 86 L.Ed. 680 (1942).

16. Ballard v. United States, 329 U.S. 187, 67 S.Ct. 261, 91 L.Ed. 181 (1946).

17. Thiel v. Southern Pacific Co., 328 U.S. 217, 66 S.Ct. 984, 90 L.Ed. 1181 (1946).

18. Rawlins v. Georgia, 201 U.S. 638, 26 S.Ct. 560, 50 L.Ed. 899 (1906).

19. 332 U.S. 261, 67 S.Ct. 1613, 91 L.Ed. 2043 (1947).

20. 333 U.S. 565, 68 S.Ct. 705, 92 L.Ed. 881 (1948).

21. 391 U.S. 145, 88 S.Ct. 1444, 20 L.Ed.2d 491 (1968).

22. See Apodaca v. Oregon, 406 U.S. 404, 92 S.Ct. 1628, 32 L.Ed.2d 184 (1972).

23. 419 U.S. 522, 95 S.Ct. 692, 42 L.Ed.2d 690 (1975).

excluded from the pool." To prevail under *Taylor*, the Court later elaborated in *Duren v. Missouri*,[24] the defendant must show "(1) that the group alleged to be excluded is a 'distinctive' group in the community; (2) that the representation of this group in venires from which juries are selected is not fair and reasonable in relation to the number of such persons in the community; and (3) that this underrepresentation is due to systematic exclusion of the group in the jury-selection process."

Several points must be emphasized concerning the fair cross section requirement adopted in *Taylor*. For one thing, the requirement is simply that juries "must be drawn from a source fairly representative of the community"; the earlier rule that defendants are not entitled to a jury of any particular composition[25] still obtains.[26] Secondly, this fair cross section requirement is a right of *all* defendants,[27] Thus, in *Taylor* a male defendant prevailed though the constitutional violation was the exclusion of women, just as in *Peters v. Kiff*[28] a white man was entitled to claim that blacks had been systematically excluded. Thirdly, in contrast to the limitations that exist when there is an equal protection challenge, a defendant raising a cross section objection can prevail without showing purposeful discrimination; he "need only show that the jury selection procedure 'systematically exclude[s] distinctive groups in the community and thereby fail[s] to be reasonably representative thereof.' "[29] But the "systematic exclusion" requirement, repeatedly stressed in *Taylor,* would seem to mean that a constitutional

violation is not made out by a showing that on a particular occasion a member of a distinct group happened to be mistakenly excused. On the other hand, as the Court made clear in *Duren v. Missouri*,[30] a cross section violation can occur without there being total exclusion of a distinct group, though even total exclusion is not necessarily "systematic."

Next, it would appear that exclusion of only certain kinds of groups conflicts with the cross section objective. However, the Court in *Taylor,* while concluding that women were such a class, did not establish with clarity just what the nature of the excluded group must be. Reference is made to "large, distinctive groups" and "identifiable segments playing major roles in the community," and the Court asserts that "women are sufficiently numerous [53% of the citizens eligible for jury service] and distinct from men that if they are systematically eliminated from jury panels, the Sixth Amendment's fair cross section requirement cannot be satisfied." This suggests that some groups may be so small as to not come within *Taylor* and that some groups may be insufficiently "distinct" to fall within the cross section requirement. As for the nature of the required distinctness, the Court in *Taylor* indicated that it is not necessary that the members of the group "act or tend to act as a class," but only that by their absence "a flavor, a distinct quality is lost." The Court has since declined "to precisely define the term 'distinctive group,'" but has declared that exclusion of a particular group was unobjectionable where it did not contravene the three pur-

---

24.   439 U.S. 357, 99 S.Ct. 664, 58 L.Ed.2d 579 (1979).

25.   Fay v. New York, 332 U.S. 261, 67 S.Ct. 1613, 91 L.Ed. 2043 (1947).

26.   Thus in Lockhart v. McCree, discussed in § 22.3 at note 38, the Court reasoned the *Taylor* cross-section requirement could not be violated by the manner in which peremptory challenges were exercised, noting the Supreme Court had "never invoked the fair cross-section principle * * * to require petit juries, as opposed to jury panels or venires, to reflect the composition of the community at large." The point was reaffirmed in Holland v. Illinois, 493 U.S. 474, 110 S.Ct. 803, 107 L.Ed.2d 905 (1990), asserting that the Sixth Amendment goal of "jury impartiality with respect to both contestants * * * would positively be obstructed by a petit jury cross-section requirement which * * * would cripple the device of peremptory challenges."

27.   Holland v. Illinois, 493 U.S. 474, 110 S.Ct. 803, 107 L.Ed.2d 905 (1990) ("the Sixth Amendment entitles every defendant to object to a venire that is not designed to represent a fair cross section of the community, whether or not the systematically excluded groups are groups to which he himself belongs").

28.   407 U.S. 493, 92 S.Ct. 2163, 33 L.Ed.2d 83 (1972).

29.   Castaneda v. Partida, 430 U.S. 482, 97 S.Ct. 1272, 51 L.Ed.2d 498 (1977) (emphasized by dissent to distinguish instant case, involving state grand jury, where defendant would have to rely upon equal protection clause and thus prove "discriminatory intent").

30.   439 U.S. 357, 99 S.Ct. 664, 58 L.Ed.2d 579 (1979).

poses of the cross-section requirement: (i) avoiding "the possibility that the composition of juries would be arbitrarily skewed in such a way as to deny criminal defendants the benefit of the common-sense judgment of the community," (ii) avoiding an "appearance of unfairness," and (iii) ensuring against deprivation of "often historically disadvantaged groups of their right as citizens to serve on juries in criminal cases."[31] Lower courts have in the main managed to avoid application of this amorphous standard by instead resolving cross section objections by finding a justification for the challenged exclusion, though decisions are now to be found holding various age and occupation groups, among others, not distinctive under *Taylor.*

This logically leads to the final point, which is that even if there is a systematic exclusion of a distinct group, this is not a constitutional violation if the exclusion is no broader than is necessary to serve a valid governmental interest. In *Taylor,* where the defective procedure was that women were not selected for jury service except when they filed a written declaration of a desire to so serve, the Court rightly concluded that this practice could not be justified on the ground than many women would find jury service unduly burdensome. Similarly, in *Duren v. Missouri,*[32] where any woman could decline jury service by so indicating on the jury-selection questionnaire, by returning the jury duty summons or simply by not showing up, the Court concluded that "exempting all women because of the preclusive domestic responsibilities of some women is insufficient justification for their disproportionate exclusion on jury venires." The Court added that "a State may have an important interest in assuring that those members of the family responsible for the care of children are available to do so," and suggested that an exemption "appro-

priately tailored to this interest would * * * survive a fair-cross-section challenge." In cases decided before and after *Taylor,* the lower courts have upheld as rationally based statutory provisions or excusal procedures resulting in exclusion or underrepresentation of young people, old people, persons not registered to vote, certain occupational groups, aliens, persons lacking proficiency in English, and convicted felons.

Despite efforts to ensure that jury selection procedures are color-blind, racial minorities continue to be underrepresented in jury pools. Underrepresentation occurs because many of the race-neutral procedures used to select jurors coincidentally exclude a disproportionate number of minorities. First, minorities are less likely to register to vote or to obtain driver's licenses and thus may be initially excluded from jury wheels. Minorities also tend to be more mobile than whites, making them more difficult to contact unless source lists are frequently updated. Finally, qualified minorities are more often excused from potential jury service because of financial hardship or difficulty in arranging transportation to the courthouse. In order to avoid fair cross-section challenges, some jurisdictions have adopted race-conscious procedures to ensure that the proportion of minorities in the jury wheel corresponds to the minority population in the community at large. The result is a list of potential jurors that consistently mirrors the racial composition of the county. These race-conscious procedures are, like other affirmative action measures, vulnerable to challenge on equal protection grounds. Supreme Court decisions in other contexts imply that the highest level of scrutiny will apply to these race-conscious methods of selecting potential jurors.[33] But courts thus far have only rarely confronted

---

31. Lockhart v. McCree, 476 U.S. 162, 106 S.Ct. 1758, 90 L.Ed.2d 137 (1986), concerning exclusion of "*Witherspoon*-excludables"; see § 22.3(c).

Members of the Court are not in agreement as to how many such groups there might be. See Holland v. Illinois, 493 U.S. 474, 110 S.Ct. 803, 107 L.Ed.2d 905 (1990) (majority says if cross-section requirement were extended to the use of peremptories "there is every reason to believe that many commonly exercised bases for peremptory challenges would be rendered unavailable," while Mar-

shall, J., dissenting, objects to the "majority's exaggerated claim that 'postmen, or lawyers, or clergymen' are distinctive groups within the meaning of our fair cross-section cases").

32. 439 U.S. 357, 99 S.Ct. 664, 58 L.Ed.2d 579 (1979).

33. E.g., City of Richmond v. J.A. Croson Company, 488 U.S. 469, 109 S.Ct. 706, 102 L.Ed.2d 854 (1989) (applying strict scrutiny to a race-conscious method of allocating municipal construction contracts).

squarely an equal protection challenge to race-conscious jury selection procedures.

(e) Vicinage. The concept of "vicinage" is frequently confused with that of "venue."[34] The former refers to the place from which the jurors must be selected, while the latter makes reference to the place at which the trial must be held. The right to have juries drawn from the vicinage is guaranteed by that part of the Sixth Amendment assuring a jury "of the State and district wherein the crime shall have been committed, which district shall have been previously ascertained by law." Vicinage provisions are also found in state constitutions, commonly declaring a right to a jury "of the county in which the offense is alleged to have been committed."

Courts have had few occasions to construe the vicinage requirement in the Sixth Amendment. As for its application in federal trials, the Supreme Court has decided that there is no constitutional right to have jurors drawn from the entire district in which the crime occurred.[35] Lower courts have extended this proposition a bit farther by holding that the Sixth Amendment confers no right to have a jury drawn in whole or in part from that portion of the district encompassing the location of the crime. This means, for example, that a trial could be had and jurors selected in a division of the district other than the division in which the crime occurred. It is noteworthy, however, that some of these decisions cautiously noted that the attitudes of jurors in the excluded area appeared to be reflected in the population of the part of the district from which the jurors were selected.

As for application of the Sixth Amendment vicinage requirement to state prosecutions, the courts have generally assumed that it is applicable for the most part. But there is not complete agreement as to what the vicinage requirement of the Sixth Amendment means in a state trial context. One view is that it merely requires that the petit jurors be drawn from

within the state and federal judicial district in which the crime was committed, so that it would be permissible for a state to draw a jury and try the defendant in a county other than that in which the crime occurred so long as the two counties were in the same federal district. *People v. Jones,*[36] on the other hand, reflects a quite different position. That court concluded that while "a jury drawn either from an entire county wherein the crime was committed or from that portion of a county wherein the crime was committed will satisfy the constitutional requirement" concerning vicinage, "a jury drawn from only a portion of a county, exclusive of the place of the commission of the crime, will not satisfy the requirement." Although the rule announced in *Jones* does not appear to depend upon demography, the court may have been influenced by the facts of the particular case. Jones resided in a precinct, where the crime occurred, which was 75% black, but he was not tried in the district containing that precinct, which was 31% black, but in another only 7% black. In any event, *Jones* was later overruled; in *Hernandez v. Municipal Court,*[37] the court held that "the boundaries of the vicinage are coterminous with the boundaries of the county" and that consequently it is sufficient that the jurors are selected from the county—they need not be from the particular judicial district where the crime occurred. It was noted that other states had declined to go as far as *Jones* and that the federal decisions (discussed above) likewise could not be squared with *Jones.*

This suggests the question of whether upon such or similar facts as in *Jones* the defendant has a valid objection based upon the cross section requirement. *Jones* rests in part on the cross section rationale, but residents of a particular county are not per se a distinct group for cross section analysis. Thus other courts have declined to invalidate trials by jurors drawn from a county other than that in which the crime was committed where there was no

34. See § 16.1(b).

35. Lewis v. United States, 279 U.S. 63, 49 S.Ct. 257, 73 L.Ed. 615 (1929); Ruthenberg v. United States, 245 U.S. 480, 38 S.Ct. 168, 62 L.Ed. 414 (1918).

36. 9 Cal.3d 546, 108 Cal.Rptr. 345, 510 P.2d 705 (1973).

37. 49 Cal.3d 713, 263 Cal.Rptr. 513, 781 P.2d 547 (1989).

significant disparity in the racial, ethnic or sexual composition of the population of the two counties.

(f) Challenge to the Array. A challenge to the array, sometimes referred to as a motion to quash the venire or panel (all jurors eligible to be called in that case), is the procedural device that is utilized to raise objections concerning the manner in which the entire panel was summoned. The objections may be constitutional in dimension, or may simply be grounded in the statutes of that jurisdiction concerning the manner in which jury panels are to be selected. As for the latter, the better view is that a defendant is entitled to relief only if there has been a "material departure" from or "substantial failure" to comply with jury selection legislation. Often the matter is put in terms of whether the particular statutory provision at issue is directory or mandatory, with the latter characterization being appropriate if its essential purpose is to insure that jurors be indifferently rather than arbitrarily selected. This does not mean that the defendant must show he has suffered prejudice because of the deviation; under the better but not unanimous view, no showing of prejudice is necessary upon a challenge to the array. This is as it should be, for in this context proof of actual harm is virtually impossible to adduce. It is typically provided that absent a showing of good cause for later filing, the challenge must be made before trial or before commencement of the voir dire examination.

§ 22.3 Voir Dire; Challenges

(a) Nature of Voir Dire. If the defendant has not waived jury trial, then it is necessary to select from the panel of prospective jurors those individuals who will actually serve as jurors in his case. The examination of prospective jurors for this purpose is commonly referred to as the voir dire, an ancient phrase literally meaning "to speak the truth." This process, by which both the defense and the prosecution try to eliminate certain prospective jurors, is a very important part of trial procedure. Prospective jurors can be chal-

lenged in two ways during voir dire: by a challenge for cause, which requires the challenging party to satisfy the judge that there is a sufficient likelihood that the prospective juror is biased in some way, or peremptory challenge, which may be exercised in specified numbers without giving any reason and without control by the court. The latter is used to eliminate those prospective jurors suspected of being biased or believed, by virtue of their backgrounds and experience, to be more likely to favor the trial opponent.

One important and legitimate function of the voir dire examination of prospective jurors is to elicit information establishing a basis for challenges for cause. A second is to facilitate the intelligent use of peremptory challenges. A third function of the voir dire, albeit one which many would not view as legitimate, is that of indoctrinating the potential jurors on the merits of the case and developing rapport. The trial judge has considerable discretion in deciding what questions may be asked of the prospective jurors. He must be free to exclude those questions that are intended solely to accomplish some improper purpose or that are not phrased in neutral, non-argumentative form, to restrict the examination of jurors within reasonable bounds so as to expedite the trial and on occasion to restrict questioning in order to give some protection to the privacy of prospective jurors.

An appellate court is unlikely to reverse a trial judge's decision not to permit certain questions unless it seems likely that as a result of the limited voir dire the jury was prejudiced. Illustrative is *Rosales–Lopez v. United States*,[1] where the four-Justice plurality opinion concluded

> it is usually best to allow the defendant to resolve this conflict by making the determination of whether or not he would prefer to have the inquiry into racial or ethnic prejudice pursued. Failure to honor his request, however, will only be reversible error where the circumstances of the case indicate that there is a reasonable possibility that racial

§ 22.3
1. 451 U.S. 182, 101 S.Ct. 1629, 68 L.Ed.2d 22 (1981).

or ethnic prejudice might have influenced the jury.

That opinion goes on to say "that federal courts must make such an inquiry when requested by a defendant accused of a violent crime and where the defendant and the victim are members of different racial or ethnic groups" because such a situation falls within the "reasonable possibility" standard. The Court then concluded no such inquiry was necessary in the instant case, where defendant, of Mexican descent, was charged with aiding members of his own ethnic group gain illegal entry into the United States.

A defendant is even less likely to prevail if he makes a constitutional challenge to the limited scope of the voir dire. Such a challenge will sometimes prevail, as is shown by *Ham v. South Carolina*.[2] That case concerned a black civil rights worker convicted of possession of marijuana. During his voir dire examination of prospective jurors, the trial judge asked general questions as to bias, prejudice or partiality,[3] but declined to ask more specific questions tendered by defense counsel which sought to elicit any possible prejudice against the defendant because of his race.[4] The Court concluded:

> Since one of the purposes of the Due Process Clause of the Fourteenth Amendment is to insure [the] "essential demands of fairness," and since a principal purpose of the adoption of the Fourteenth Amendment was to prohibit the States from invidiously discriminating on the basis of race, we think that the Fourteenth Amendment required the judge in this case to interrogate the jurors upon the subject of racial prejudice. * * * [T]he trial judge was not required to put the question in any particular form, or to ask any particular number of questions on the

subject, simply because requested to do so by petitioner. * * * In this context either of the brief, general questions urged by petitioner would appear sufficient to focus the attention of prospective jurors to any racial prejudice they might entertain.

Ham has had a rather limited impact. For one thing, the Court has as yet declined to extend the doctrine to matters other than racial prejudice. In the *Ham* case itself, the Court rejected petitioner's claim that the trial judge should have also inquired about possible prejudice against defendant because of his beard, in light of "the traditionally broad discretion accorded to the trial judge in conducting voir dire, and our inability to constitutionally distinguish possible prejudice against beards from a host of other possible similar prejudices." Similarly, the Court later held that where "the trial judge made a general inquiry into the jurors' general views concerning obscenity," *Ham* does not mean that the court in an obscenity case is required upon request "to ask questions as to whether the jurors' educational, political, and religious beliefs might affect their views on the question of obscenity."[5]

More significant is the fact that the Supreme Court and lower courts have applied *Ham* narrowly even on the question of racial prejudice. In *Ristaino v. Ross*,[6] the Court declined to find that "the need to question veniremen specifically about racial prejudice also rose to constitutional dimensions in this case," reasoning that the "mere fact that the victim of the crimes alleged[7] was a white man and the defendants were Negroes was less likely to distort the trial than were the special factors involved in *Ham*." Similarly, in *Dukes v. Waitkevitch*[8] the court held that where a black man was accused of participation in a gang rape of

---

2. 409 U.S. 524, 93 S.Ct. 848, 35 L.Ed.2d 46 (1973).

3. The three questions asked were, in substance, the following: "1. Have you formed or expressed any opinion as to the guilt or innocence of the defendant, Gene Ham? 2. Are you conscious of any bias or prejudice for or against him? 3. Can you give the State and the defendant a fair and impartial trial?"

4. They were: "1. Would you fairly try this case on the basis of the evidence and disregarding the defendant's race? 2. You have no prejudice against negroes? Against

black people? You would not be influenced by the use of the term 'black'?"

5. Hamling v. United States, 418 U.S. 87, 94 S.Ct. 2887, 41 L.Ed.2d 590 (1974).

6. 424 U.S. 589, 96 S.Ct. 1017, 47 L.Ed.2d 258 (1976).

7. Armed robbery, assault with a dangerous weapon, and assault with intent to murder.

8. 536 F.2d 469 (1st Cir.1976).

several white women, the trial court did not commit constitutional error in refusing to inquire into racial prejudice on voir dire. The incredible assumption is that a black civil rights worker charged with possession of marijuana is more likely to have prejudice distort his trial than a black defendant charged with participation in a gang rape of white women.

In *Turner v. Murray*,[9] the *Ham–Ristaino* line of authority was applied to capital cases in a special way. The Court held "that a capital defendant accused of an interracial crime is entitled to have prospective jurors informed of the race of the victim and questioned on the issue of racial bias." But only four members of the Court (not counting the Chief Justice, who concurred in the judgment without opinion) joined in the assertion that *only* the death sentence—not the guilty verdict—need be vacated. The first conclusion was attributed to "the broad discretion given the jury at the death penalty hearing, and the special seriousness of the risk of improper sentencing in a capital case"; the second to the fact that in the guilt phase of the trial "the jury had no greater discretion" than in a noncapital case, meaning that part of the case was "indistinguishable from *Ristaino*." One member of the Court found that distinction unconvincing because "the opportunity for bias to poison decision-making operates at a guilt trial in the same way as it does at a sentencing hearing." Two others attacked the distinction from the other direction, arguing that "many procedural and substantive safeguards" (e.g., the state must prove statutorily-defined aggravating factors beyond a reasonable doubt, the jury must consider any relevant mitigating evidence offered by defendant) "circumscribe the capital jury's sentencing decision," so that both the verdict and death penalty should stand.

Two other cases suggest that the trial court has less discretion over questions asked during voir dire to select a jury in a capital case than in other criminal cases. In *Lockhart v. McCree*,[10] the court observed that "the State

may challenge for cause prospective jurors whose opposition to the death penalty is so strong that it would prevent them from impartially determining a capital defendant's guilt or innocence. Ipso facto, the State must be given the opportunity to identify such prospective jurors by questioning them at voir dire about their views of the death penalty." Following this reasoning, the Court held in *Morgan v. Illinois*[11] that a trial court does not have discretion to refuse a request by the defense to ask potential jurors whether they would automatically impose a death sentence after a guilty verdict. The Court concluded: "Were voir dire not available to lay bare the foundation of petitioner's challenge for cause against those prospective jurors who would *always* impose death following conviction, his right not to be tried by such jurors would be rendered nugatory and meaningless as the State's right, in the absence of questioning, to strike those who would *never* do so."

As for the manner in which the voir dire should be conducted, in the federal system the "court may examine prospective jurors or may permit the attorneys for the parties to do so." But in the former event the court "must permit the attorneys for the parties to * * * ask further questions that the court considers proper" or "submit further questions that the court may ask if it considers them proper."[12] One study showed that over half of the federal judges questioned the jurors by themselves, about a third allowed the attorneys to ask supplemental questions, and the rest allowed the attorneys to ask all of the questions. There is also considerable variation in the permitted practice at the state level.

There is not agreement as to whether the judge or the attorney should have the predominant role in questioning prospective jurors. Proponents of attorney-conducted voir dire maintain that personal contact and selection of questions relevant to the particular trial are necessary for informed challenges, and that only the attorney knows what prejudices are

9.   476 U.S. 28, 106 S.Ct. 1683, 90 L.Ed.2d 27 (1986).

10.   476 U.S. 162, 106 S.Ct. 1758, 90 L.Ed.2d 137 (1986).

11.   504 U.S. 719, 112 S.Ct. 2222, 119 L.Ed.2d 492 (1992).

12.   Fed.R.Crim.P. 24(a).

important to explore. Proponents of judge-conducted voir dire argue that lawyer-conducted questioning takes excessive amounts of time and that lawyers abuse their privilege by asking inappropriate questions and indoctrinating the jurors. A suggested compromise of these conflicting positions is that the questioning should be conducted initially by the court, after which counsel for each side should have the opportunity, under the supervision of the court and subject to reasonable time limits, to question jurors directly.

(b) Prosecution and Defense Access to Information. Most states have adopted statutes providing for defendants in criminal cases to receive in advance of trial a list of prospective jurors. Some of these enactments confer this right upon all defendants, while some are limited to felony cases or capital cases. Even in the absence of such legislation, it has sometimes been held that the defendant upon timely motion is entitled to obtain that list in advance of trial. On the federal level, a statute declares that one "charged with treason or other capital offense shall at least three entire days before commencement of trial be furnished with * * * a list of the veniremen, * * * stating the place of abode of each venireman," which has been interpreted to mean that there is no such right in other cases.[13] However, it is provided in the Federal Jury Selection and Service Act that a defendant "shall be allowed to inspect, reproduce, and copy" those "records or papers used by the jury commission or clerk in connection with the jury selection process" at "all reasonable times during the preparation and pendency" of a motion to stay the proceedings because of noncompliance with the Act.[14]

This latter provision has been characterized by the Supreme Court as giving the defendant "essentially an unqualified right to inspect jury lists,"[15] but it is important to note that this statute is limited to instances in which a challenge to the entire panel is being made and thus is inapplicable where the list is desired only for purposes relating to conducting

the voir dire. It thus is different from the other statutes previously mentioned having as their purpose assisting the defendant in acquiring information upon which to ground challenges for cause or to exercise peremptory challenges. Some have argued that this function would be better served and time at the voir dire saved if the parties were also provided in advance of trial with additional information about each of the prospective jurors. (In limited circumstances in which there is good reason to believe the jury needs protection, the names of the jurors and their addresses and places of employment may be withheld in advance of trial and even during the jury selection. The generally-accepted rule is that a so-called anonymous jury is a permissible precaution where (1) there are strong grounds for concluding that it is necessary to enable the jury to perform its factfinding function, or to ensure juror protection; and (2) reasonable safeguards are adopted by the trial court to minimize any risk of infringement upon the fundamental rights of the accused.)

When the identity of the prospective jurors is known, the prosecution or the defense or both may undertake a pretrial investigation of them. As a general matter, the prosecution is in a better position to conduct such a pretrial investigation. Because members of the prosecution staff may have conducted earlier trials involving members of the same panel, the prosecution may be able to compile information on the voting habits of particular jurors. The prosecution will likewise have more ready access to the arrest and conviction records and other government records relating to the prospective jurors. Moreover, the prosecution may utilize the investigative services of local police or the FBI in acquiring background information. Wealthy defendants and those in so-called political cases often have pretrial investigation conducted on their behalf.

One question raised by these practices is that of whether some investigative procedures are improper. As for the mere use of law

---

13. Hamer v. United States, 259 F.2d 274 (9th Cir. 1958), construing 18 U.S.C.A. § 3432.

14. 28 U.S.C.A. § 1867(f).

15. Test v. United States, 420 U.S. 28, 95 S.Ct. 749, 42 L.Ed.2d 786 (1975).

enforcement agents to conduct investigations of prospective jurors, it has been held that it does not result in juries biased against the defendant, but merely eliminates bias against the government, and that the assertion such investigations will discourage citizens from serving as jurors is far fetched. But there are limits beyond which neither the prosecution nor defense is permitted to go; a lawyer may not "communicate with or cause another to communicate with anyone he knows to be a member of the venire from which the jury will be selected for the trial of the case,"[16] or "conduct or cause, by financial support or otherwise, another to conduct a vexatious or harassing investigation of either a venireman or a juror."[17]

Another question raised by pretrial investigation of jurors is whether the fruits of such investigations should be subject to discovery by the other party. The traditional view is that discovery of juror information by either the prosecution or defense is not allowed. Illustrative is *Hamer v. United States*,[18] where the court dismissed defendant's claim that he should have had access to the prosecutor's jury book, describing the conduct and votes of jurors in prior cases. The court asserted that otherwise the "ultimate and ridiculous conclusion" would be that "no defendant could be prosecuted by a government attorney who had more information about how jurors on that panel had voted, in other cases, than his own counsel had." However, a few courts have viewed sympathetically the proposition that the jury selection process is harmed when the parties have dramatically disparate amounts of information about the prospective jurors. It has been recognized that trial courts must have the discretion to permit a defendant, who lacks funds to investigate prospective jurors, to inspect prosecution jury records and investigations. On the notion that avenues of investigation available to the prosecution cannot be completely closed to the defense, it has been held that once a police department made its records of convictions of prospective jurors available to the prosecutor, they must be equally available to defense counsel. Defendants permitted to obtain disclosure of the prosecutor's dossier may not preserve the secrecy of their own investigative reports.

In some recent trials, social science techniques have been employed in jury selection. The first step is to survey randomly as large a sample as possible of the population from which the jury will be selected. The researchers attempt to discern attitudes relevant to the issues in the particular forthcoming trial. Data from the survey is fed into a computer with socioeconomic background characteristics (e.g., religion, age, sex, occupation) in order to identify a favorable and unfavorable juror. The questions asked on voir dire are geared to ascertaining those characteristics found to be associated with favorable or unfavorable attitudes. Instead or in addition, the jury panel may be observed in court and rated by psychologists or psychiatrists on authoritarianism scales or by kinesiologists in terms of body language. This development is certainly a cause for concern. If the outcome of a trial can be manipulated simply by impaneling jurors designated acceptable by social scientists, then trial by jury may cease to function satisfactorily. Even if these techniques are not as useful as they are made out to be, there is the matter of the public perception of the criminal justice system. The proper response to the increasing use of such juror information at voir dire is to allow its discovery by both the prosecution and the defense.

(c) Challenges for Cause. Both the defense and the prosecution may challenge an unlimited number of jurors for cause, but no juror can be removed on this ground unless the judge agrees that one of the bases for such a challenge is present. The grounds for a challenge for cause are commonly set out by statute, and are typically stated in terms of a series of specific situations: that the person lacks the legal qualifications for jury service;

16. ABA Code of Professional Responsibility, DR 7–108(A).

17. ABA Code of Professional Responsibility, DR 7–108(E).

18. 259 F.2d 274 (9th Cir.1958).

that he has previously served as a juror on some related matter, such as on the grand jury which indicted the defendant, on the petit jury which formerly tried defendant on this charge, or on a jury which tried another person charged with the same offense; that he has served or will serve as a witness regarding the subject matter of the pending trial; or that he is related in some degree to the defendant or others directly involved in this case. In addition, a more general ground for challenge is typically stated in terms such as the following:

> That the juror has a state of mind in reference to the cause or to the defendant or to the person alleged to have been injured by the offense charged, or to the person on whose complaint the prosecution was instituted, which will prevent him from acting with impartiality; but the formation of an opinion or impression regarding the guilt or innocence of the defendant shall not of itself be sufficient ground of challenge to a juror, if he declares, and the court is satisfied, that he can render an impartial verdict according to the evidence.

If the prospective juror is found to have the "state of mind" described above, then this is a case of actual bias requiring that the challenge for cause be granted. But, as the language quoted above indicates, this is not to suggest that a prospective juror must be excused merely because he knows something of the case to

be tried or has formed some opinions regarding it. It was long ago recognized that

> to say that any man who had formed an opinion on any fact conducive to the final decision of the case would therefore be considered as disqualified from serving on the jury, would exclude intelligent and observing men, whose minds were really in a situation to decide upon the whole case according to the testimony, and would perhaps be applying the letter of the rule requiring an impartial jury with a strictness which is not necessary for the preservation of the rule itself.[19]

This actual bias is not limited to specific bias, that is, a bias grounded in personal knowledge or a personal relationship. Virtually all courts authorize the questioning of jurors in areas of nonspecific bias, such as actual prejudice grounded in the prospective juror's feelings regarding the race, religion, and ethnic or other group to which the defendant belongs.

If during the voir dire a certain prospective juror actually admits to such a "state of mind," he will of course be challenged and excused.[20] But such admissions are infrequent, as a prejudiced juror is unlikely to recognize or admit his own personal prejudice. This raises the important question of whether, at least in some circumstances, bias should be implied and the prospective juror excused notwithstanding his claim of impartiality. One way in which this issue arises is when there has been

---

19. As stated by John Marshall at the trial of Aaron Burr. See United States v. Burr, 25 Fed.Cas. 49 (D.Va. 1807). The same point was made by the Supreme Court in Irvin v. Dowd, 366 U.S. 717, 81 S.Ct. 1639, 6 L.Ed.2d 751 (1961): "It is not required, however, that the jurors be totally ignorant of the facts and issues involved. In these days of swift, widespread and diverse methods of communication, an important case can be expected to arouse the interest of the public in the vicinity, and scarcely any of those best qualified to serve as jurors will not have formed some impression or opinion as to the merits of the case. This is particularly true in criminal cases. To hold that the mere existence of any preconceived notion as to the guilt or innocence of an accused, without more, is sufficient to rebut the presumption of a prospective juror's impartiality would be to establish an impossible standard. It is sufficient if the juror can lay aside his impression or opinion and render a verdict based on the evidence presented in court."

20. This is not to suggest that any single statement by a prospective juror, standing in isolation, compels granting the challenge. In Patton v. Yount, 467 U.S. 1025, 104 S.Ct. 2885, 81 L.Ed.2d 847 (1984), one juror said he had an

opinion of defendant's guilt based on pretrial publicity but that it was not "fixed" and that he would be able to change his mind "if the facts were so presented," but the Court declined to accept the habeas petitioner's claim that this juror had adopted a presumption of guilt and thus should not have been seated over his challenge for cause. The Court stated that the issue of the partiality of an individual juror was "plainly one of historical fact: did a juror swear that he could set aside any opinion he might hold and decide the case on the evidence, and should the juror's protestation of impartiality have been believed," and that consequently the state court's finding was entitled to a presumption of correctness on habeas corpus. But the Court added that "the trial court's resolution of such questions is entitled, even on direct appeal, to 'special deference,'" as "the determination is essentially one of credibility, and therefore largely one of demeanor." As for the individual expression seeming to indicate partiality, the "trial judge properly may choose to believe those statements that were the most fully articulated or that appeared to have been least influenced by leading."

extensive pretrial publicity. In *Irvin v. Dowd*,[21] for example, there had been extensive publicity announcing that defendant had confessed to six murders and 24 burglaries and that he had offered to plead guilty. On voir dire, 8 of the 12 jurors selected expressed the opinion that defendant was guilty, but all said they would render an impartial verdict. In overturning the defendant's conviction, the Supreme Court concluded that "such a statement of impartiality can be given little weight" where, as here, the voir dire reflected a "pattern of deep and bitter prejudice" in the community. But in *Murphy v. Florida*,[22] the Court rejected the contention that *Irvin* or the Court's other prior decisions[23] stood "for the proposition that juror exposure to information about a state defendant's prior convictions or to new accounts of the crime with which he is charged alone presumptively deprives the defendant of due process," so that bias should be implied in such circumstances notwithstanding the juror's claim of impartiality.

The implied bias issue has also been raised when prospective jurors are employees of the governmental unit undertaking the prosecution. But in *Dennis v. United States*,[24] the Court held that in a case where the federal government is a party, its employees are not challengeable for cause solely by reason of their employment. The Court also rejected the argument that the failure to sustain the challenge denied petitioner an "impartial jury" under the "special circumstances of this case"—a prosecution of a Communist for contempt of the House Un–American Activities Committee, where the government's interest was said to be "the vindication of a direct affront, as distinguished from its role in an ordinary prosecution," and where, because of an alleged "aura of surveillance and intimidation" said to exist because of a "Loyalty Order," government employees "would be hesitant to vote for acquittal because such action might be interpreted as 'sympathetic association' with Communism." The ruling of the Court, that a "holding of implied bias to disqualify jurors because of their relationship with the Government is no longer permissible," continues to be followed. Lower courts are not in agreement as to whether bias may be implied because the prospective juror is employed by the victim of the crime, but are generally disinclined to imply bias because of a prospective juror's membership in some special interest organization.

The implied bias issue can arise in a constitutional context and outside the voir dire, as is reflected by the Supreme Court decision in *Smith v. Phillips*.[25] The defendant, convicted in state court, sought to overturn his conviction because he later learned that during the trial one of the jurors submitted an application for employment as an investigator in the district attorney's office. On federal habeas corpus, the district court found insufficient evidence of actual bias by the juror, but nonetheless imputed bias to him because "the average man in Smith's position would believe that the verdict of the jury would directly affect the evaluation of his job application." But the Supreme Court, in concluding that defendant had not been denied due process by the juror's conduct, rejected the district court's approach. Disagreeing with the defendant's claim that because of "the human propensity for self-justification" a trial court "cannot possibly ascertain the impartiality of a juror by relying solely upon the testimony of the juror in question," the Supreme Court reaffirmed the position that "the remedy for allegations of juror partiality is a hearing in which the defendant has the opportunity to prove actual bias." *Smith* may influence lower courts, even when the issue is not cast in

---

21. 366 U.S. 717, 81 S.Ct. 1639, 6 L.Ed.2d 751 (1961).

22. 421 U.S. 794, 95 S.Ct. 2031, 44 L.Ed.2d 589 (1975). See also Patton v. Yount, 467 U.S. 1025, 104 S.Ct. 2885, 81 L.Ed.2d 847 (1984), following *Murphy*.

23. The defendant specifically relied upon Marshall v. United States, 360 U.S. 310, 79 S.Ct. 1171, 3 L.Ed.2d 1250 (1959), reversing because of "the exposure of jurors to information of a character which the trial judge ruled was

so prejudicial it could not be directly offered as evidence." The Court rejected this reliance, pointing out that the decision there rested on the Court's supervisory power over federal courts rather than on due process grounds.

24. 339 U.S. 162, 70 S.Ct. 519, 94 L.Ed. 734 (1950).

25. 455 U.S. 209, 102 S.Ct. 940, 71 L.Ed.2d 78 (1982).

constitutional terms, to be even more reluctant to resort to the implied bias theory.

Sometimes, as in *Witherspoon v. Illinois*,[26] a defendant will object that the trial court was too generous in granting challenges for cause made by the prosecution. In selecting jurors for a murder trial at which the jury would have the responsibility for deciding on the death penalty if a guilty verdict was returned, nearly half of the panel was eliminated pursuant to a statute declaring it a cause for challenge that a prospective juror states "that he has conscientious scruples against capital punishment." The Court concluded:

> If the State had excluded only those prospective jurors who stated in advance of trial that they would not even consider returning a verdict of death, it could argue that the resulting jury was simply "neutral" with respect to penalty. But when it swept from the jury all who expressed conscientious or religious scruples against capital punishment or all who opposed it in principle, the State crossed the line of neutrality. In its quest for a jury capable of imposing the death penalty, the State produced a jury uncommonly willing to condemn a man to die. * * *
>
> [W]e hold that a sentence of death cannot be carried out if the jury that imposed or recommended it was chosen by excluding veniremen for cause simply because they voiced general objections to the death penalty or expressed conscientious or religious scruples against its infliction. No defendant can constitutionally be put to death at the hands of a tribunal so selected.

More recently, the Court has held this rule equally applicable where the jury was only permitted to answer certain questions about the presence of statutorily-defined aggravated circumstances that, if present, mandate a sentence of death by the judge.[27]

Although several lower courts, relying upon language in *Witherspoon*, concluded that veniremen could be constitutionally excluded only if it was "unmistakably clear" they would "automatically" vote against the death penalty, in *Wainwright v. Witt*[28] the Court opted for a less demanding standard: "whether the juror's views would 'prevent or substantially impair the performance of his duties as a juror in accordance with his instructions and his oath.'" Requiring unmistakable clarity, the Court observed, is unrealistic, for "many veniremen simply cannot be asked enough questions to reach the point where their bias had been made 'unmistakably clear.'" And the "automatically" language was now inappropriate because it could not "be squared with the duties of present-day capital sentencing juries," who now are typically asked to respond to factual inquiries bearing on whether death is the appropriate penalty.[29]

In *Gray v. Mississippi*,[30] the Court rejected a variety of contentions made in support of the proposition that a single deviation from the *Witherspoon–Witt* standard would not inevitably nullify the sentence of death. As for the claim that the granting of an invalid *Witherspoon* motion was somehow cancelled out by the erroneous denial of an earlier valid *Witherspoon* motion, the Court reasoned that a violation of the prosecutor's statutory right to exclusion of a juror could not be equated with a violation of the defendant's Sixth Amendment rights. As for the claim that "a *Witherspoon* violation constitutes harmless error when the prosecution has an unexercised peremptory challenge that he states he would have used to excuse the juror," the Court rejected it because adoption of such an argument would

---

26. 391 U.S. 510, 88 S.Ct. 1770, 20 L.Ed.2d 776 (1968).

27. Adams v. Texas, 448 U.S. 38, 100 S.Ct. 2521, 65 L.Ed.2d 581 (1980). The Court stressed that jurors "will characteristically know that affirmative answers to the questions will result in the automatic imposition of the death penalty" and will "unavoidably exercise a range of judgment and discretion while remaining true to their instructions and their oaths."

28. 469 U.S. 412, 105 S.Ct. 844, 83 L.Ed.2d 841 (1985).

29. *Witt* also held that a trial judge's conclusion a prospective juror is disqualified for bias is to be accorded a presumption of correctness, but this was because the case arose on federal habeas corpus, and thus a state appellate court may but need not adopt that standard of review. Greene v. Georgia, 519 U.S. 145, 117 S.Ct. 578, 136 L.Ed.2d 507 (1996).

30. 481 U.S. 648, 107 S.Ct. 2045, 95 L.Ed.2d 622 (1987).

"insulate jury-selection error from meaningful appellate review," as prosecutors would routinely make such an assertion. As for the claim that the single *Witherspoon* error was harmless "because it did not have any prejudicial effect," the Court deemed this "*Chapman* harmless-error analysis"[31] inapplicable here, where the right at issue "goes to the very integrity of the legal system." The Court added that a single *Witherspoon* violation really is not "an isolated incident" when, as here, the prosecutor also used his peremptories to remove prospective jurors who expressed any degree of hesitation against the death penalty.[32]

In what is sometimes referred to as the "reverse-*Witherspoon*" situation, the defense in a capital case will wish to have prospective jurors questioned on voir dire in order to discover and challenge any of them who would automatically vote for the death penalty in every capital case. Relying upon "the requirement of impartiality in the Due Process Clause of the Fourteenth Amendment," the Court in *Morgan v. Illinois*[33] held that on a defendant's request specific inquiry into such views was constitutionally mandated. Responding to the state's claim that the trial judge's "general fairness and 'follow the law' questions" sufficed, the Court asserted that the state's "own request for questioning under *Witherspoon* * * * belies this argument." Any prospective juror found to have such views should be excused, as such a person has already formed an opinion on the merits of the case and has manifested an inability to follow jury instructions to consider mitigating circumstances. The Court warned: "If even one such juror is empaneled and the death sentence is imposed, the State is disentitled to execute the sentence."

Because the proposition was put that way, *Morgan* does not disturb the earlier decision in *Ross v. Oklahoma*,[34] where the trial judge erred in denying such a reverse-*Witherspoon* motion, but the defendant then used one of his nine peremptories to strike that juror. Four members of the Court concluded that the "defense's loss of a peremptory challenge thus resulted in a 'tribunal organized to return a verdict of death' in exactly the fashion we rejected so recently in *Gray*," but the majority disagreed. The defendant had not been denied an impartial jury, as that juror "was thereby removed from the jury as effectively as if the trial court had excused him for cause," and the loss of a peremptory was likewise no such denial because "peremptory challenges are not of constitutional dimension." As for the defendant's claim it constituted a violation of due process to deprive him, in effect, of a full complement of peremptories as provided by statute, the Court in *Ross* answered that "peremptory challenges are a creature of statute," meaning the state may "define their purpose and the manner of their exercise." Here, by state law the grant of nine peremptories in capital cases "is qualified by the requirement that the defendant must use those challenges to cure erroneous refusal by the trial court to excuse jurors for cause."[35]

Alluding to what he described as "competent scientific evidence that death-qualified jurors are partial to the prosecution on the issue of guilt or innocence," the defendant in *Witherspoon* contended that his conviction (not just the death penalty) should be set aside. But the Court found that data "too tentative and fragmentary to establish that jurors not opposed to the death penalty tend to favor the prosecution in the determination of guilt." The continued vitality of this second branch of *Witherspoon* is unclear. For one thing, there is now available more empirical support for the conclusion that a death-qualified jury is more likely to convict than a non-death-qualified one. This data might produce a different result

---

31. See § 27.6(c).

32. Powell, J., concurring, and also the four *Gray* dissenters, objected to the intimation that such use of his peremptories by the prosecutor was in any sense improper or unconstitutional.

33. 504 U.S. 719, 112 S.Ct. 2222, 119 L.Ed.2d 492 (1992).

34. 487 U.S. 81, 108 S.Ct. 2273, 101 L.Ed.2d 80 (1988).

35. The Supreme Court has refused to interpret *federal* law in this way, but the defendant nonetheless did not prevail; see *United States v. Martinez–Salazar*, discussed in note 42 infra.

unless perceived as another improper effort to obtain dismissal of prospective jurors on an implied bias theory. Secondly, it might be argued that the Douglas dissent in *Witherspoon,* concluding there is no requirement of "a showing of specific prejudice when a defendant has been deprived of his right to a jury representing a cross-section of the community," has taken on added force in light of subsequent developments concerning the constitutional right to trial by jury. There is, for example, the holding in *Taylor v. Louisiana*[36] that exclusion of women from jury panels is unconstitutional even if, in the particular case, the exclusion made not "an iota of difference." *Taylor,* of course, held only that there is a Sixth Amendment right to "the presence of a fair cross section of the community on venires, panels or lists from which petit juries are drawn." This right, the Supreme Court later concluded, is not violated by subsequent challenges to individuals on a fairly selected panel.[37]

In *Lockhart v. McCree,*[38] involving a somewhat different albeit related issue, the Court held that the Constitution does not "prohibit the removal for cause, prior to the guilt phase of a bifurcated capital trial, of prospective jurors whose opposition to the death penalty is so strong that it would prevent or substantially impair the performance of their duties as jurors at the sentencing phase of the trial." (The Court emphasized this was so even if it were shown, which the studies relied upon by the defendant did not establish, that juries so selected are "somewhat more 'conviction-prone.' ") There was no violation of the *Taylor* cross-section requirement here, the Court concluded, as it had not theretofore been invoked by the Court "to invalidate the use of either for-cause or peremptory challenges * * * or to require petit juries, as opposed to jury panels or venires, to reflect the composition of the community at large," and in any event that requirement has to do only with a "distinctive" group in the community (e.g., "blacks, women, or Mexican–Americans") and not

"groups defined solely in terms of shared attitudes that would prevent or substantially impair members of the group from performing or substantially performing one of their duties as jurors." As for defendant's claim he had been denied his constitutional right to an impartial jury, the Court responded this was not so because the exclusion complained of "serves the State's entirely proper interest in obtaining a single jury that could impartially decide all of the issues in McCree's case." The three dissenters found most unconvincing the majority's two reasons for why that interest was substantial: (i) "the possibility that, in some capital cases, the defendant might benefit at the sentencing phase of the trial from the jury's 'residual doubts' about the evidence presented at the guilt phase"; and (ii) "much of the evidence adduced at the guilt phase of the trial will also have a bearing on the penalty phase," so that two juries would require presentation of much testimony twice.

McCree was deemed controlling in *Buchanan v. Kentucky,*[39] holding defendant was not deprived of his Sixth Amendment rights when the prosecution was permitted to "death-qualify" the jury at his joint trial where the death penalty was sought against his codefendant. Defendant's reliance on the cross-section requirement was again unavailing because it "applies only to venires," and his impartial jury argument was rejected on the ground that "a balancing of jurors with different predilections" is not required. The majority stressed that joint trials are beneficial to defendants and serve to promote "the reliability and consistency of the judicial process," while the three dissenters responded that the defendant should be allowed "the option of waiving this perceived benefit" and that any interest in reliability and consistency could be served by trying the defendants jointly before a non-death-qualified jury and then having the other defendant sentenced by a death-qualified jury.

---

36. 419 U.S. 522, 95 S.Ct. 692, 42 L.Ed.2d 690 (1975).

37. Lockhart v. McCree, discussed in the text immediately following.

38. 476 U.S. 162, 106 S.Ct. 1758, 90 L.Ed.2d 137 (1986).

39. 483 U.S. 402, 107 S.Ct. 2906, 97 L.Ed.2d 336 (1987).

(d) Peremptory Challenges. "The essential nature of the peremptory challenge," the Supreme Court declared in *Swain v. Alabama*,[40] "is that it is one exercised without a reason stated, without inquiry and without being subject to the court's control." The peremptory challenge serves important functions; it (i) "teaches the litigant, and through him the community, that the jury is a good and proper mode for deciding matters and that its decision should be followed because in a real sense the jury belongs to the litigant" because "he chooses it"; (ii) "avoids trafficking in the core of truth in most common stereotypes" by making unnecessary the grounding of challenges for cause in claims of group bias, thus allowing "the covert expression of what we dare not say but know is true more often than not"; and (iii) serves "as a shield for the exercise of the challenge for cause," in that questioning to determine "the appropriateness of a cause challenge may have so alienated a potential juror that, although the lawyer has not established any basis for removal, the process itself has made it necessary to strike the juror peremptorily."[41] It is understandable, therefore, as the Court put it in *Swain*, that though " '[t]here is nothing in the Constitution of the United States which requires the Congress [or the States] to grant peremptory challenges,' * * * nonetheless the challenge is one of the most important of the rights secured to the accused."

In the federal system, for example, each side has 20 peremptories in a capital case and each has 3 in a misdemeanor case, while for a felony trial the defendant has 10 and the prosecution 6.[42] Similar provisions are found in the states, where the prosecution usually has the same number of peremptories as the defendant. There is considerable variation in the practice where more than one defendant is being tried, all the way from giving each defendant the usual number of peremptories to be exercised individually to requiring all defendants collectively to exercise the number of peremptories a single defendant would have. In some jurisdictions the parties are required to exercise their peremptories as to each juror as he is individually selected, which deprives them of the opportunity intelligently to compare several veniremen before exercising any challenges. The prevailing practice is for the prosecutor to call and examine 12 veniremen, exercise his challenges for cause and such peremptory challenges as he then wishes to use, replace those excused with others, and then tender a group of 12 to the defendant. The defendant then follows a similar procedure with this group and tenders a jury of 12 back to the prosecutor, and they continue on in this manner until both parties have exhausted their challenges or indicated their satisfaction with the jury. By contrast, under the so-called struck jury system jurors are first examined and challenged for cause by both sides, excused jurors are replaced on the panel, and the examination of replacements continues until a panel of qualified jurors is presented. The size of the panel at this time is 12 plus the number of peremptory strikes allowed all parties. The parties then proceed to exercise their peremptories in some order that will result in all exhausting their strikes at approximately the same time. This latter system, while perhaps more time consuming because in every case it

40. 380 U.S. 202, 85 S.Ct. 824, 13 L.Ed.2d 759 (1965).

41. Babcock, Voir Dire: Preserving "Its Wonderful Power," 27 Stan.L.Rev. 545, 552–55 (1975).

42. Fed.R.Crim.P. 24(b). In United States v. Martinez–Salazar, 528 U.S. 304, 120 S.Ct. 774, 145 L.Ed.2d 792 (2000), where defendant exercised all of his peremptories but used one of them to excuse a juror the trial judge erroneously refused to excuse for cause, the defendant claimed he had consequently been denied the number of peremptory challenges he was entitled to have under Fed. R.Crim.P. 24(b), so that his conviction should be reversed. The Court declined to hold "that federal law, like the Oklahoma statute considered in *Ross*, [see text at note 34 supra] should be read to require a defendant to use a peremptory challenge to strike a juror who should have been removed for cause, in order to preserve the claim that the for-cause ruling impaired the defendant's right to a fair trial," but did accept the "narrower contention" that Fed.R.Crim.P.24(b) "was not violated in this case" because it merely confers upon the defendant the choice "to stand on his objection to the erroneous denial of the challenge for cause or to use a peremptory challenge to effect an instantaneous cure of the error." The Court in *Martinez–Salazar* went on to emphasize that the case before it was not one where "the trial court deliberately misapplied the law in order to force the defendant to use a peremptory challenge to correct the court's error," and that the trial court's ruling did not "result in the seating of any juror who should have been dismissed for cause."

is necessary to examine and qualify a large group of jurors, allows more intelligent exercise of peremptories because each party, at the time he exercises each peremptory challenge, is confronted with the total number of persons from whom the final jury will be formed, and thus is always in a position to exclude the person most objectionable to him.

In *Swain v. Alabama*,[43] the defendant claimed that the prosecutor's conduct in using his peremptory challenges to remove all six blacks from the jury constituted a denial of equal protection. But the Supreme Court, after noting the credentials and purposes of peremptories and the longstanding practice of exercising peremptories on the basis of group affiliations, disagreed. The Court in *Swain* observed that to subject the prosecutor's challenges to the traditional standards of the equal protection clause would mean that the prosecutor's reasons for making a particular challenge would have to be subjected to scrutiny, which "would entail a radical change in the nature and operation of the challenge," and then concluded:

> In the light of the purpose of the peremptory system and the function it serves in a pluralistic society in connection with the institution of jury trial, we cannot hold that the Constitution requires an examination of the prosecutor's reasons for the exercise of his challenges in any given case. The presumption in any particular case must be that the prosecutor is using the State's challenges to obtain a fair and impartial jury to try the case before the court. The presumption is not overcome and the prosecutor therefore subjected to examination by allegations that in the case at hand all Negroes were removed from the jury or that they were removed because they were Negroes. Any other result, we think, would establish a rule wholly at odds with the peremptory challenge system as we know it.

The defendant in *Swain* then went on to make another claim, namely, that in the county where he was tried prosecutors consistently exercised their peremptories to prevent any blacks from serving on juries. The Court agreed "that this claim raises a different issue and it may well require a different answer." This is because if the prosecutor always challenges blacks, without regard to the nature of the crime or the defendant or the victim, then "it would appear that the purpose of the peremptory challenges is being perverted" and thus "the presumption protecting the prosecutor may well be overcome." But the Court in *Swain* then concluded that the record did not support this claim. While apparently no black had served on a jury in that county for at least 15 years, the record did not, "with any acceptable degree of clarity, show when, how often, and under what circumstances the prosecutor alone has been responsible for striking those Negroes who have appeared on petit jury panels." Although courts were inclined to say that the defendant's burden of showing such systematic exclusion by the prosecutor was not insurmountable, experience clearly indicated the virtual impossibility of doing so. A great many cases held the defendant did not meet this burden, but almost none are to be found ruling that the defendant had established such systematic exclusion by the prosecutor's use of his peremptory challenges.

In *Batson v. Kentucky*,[44] the Court finally rejected the *Swain* approach. Although the defendant presented his claim in terms of the *Taylor* fair cross-section right,[45] the Court did not decide the case on that basis, doubtless because (as the Court immediately thereafter held) that principle cannot be invoked "to invalidate the use of either for-cause or peremptory challenges to prospective jurors, or to require petit juries as opposed to jury panels or venires, to reflect the composition of the community at large."[46] Rather, *Batson* is an

---

43. 380 U.S. 202, 85 S.Ct. 824, 13 L.Ed.2d 759 (1965).

44. 476 U.S. 79, 106 S.Ct. 1712, 90 L.Ed.2d 69 (1986). *Batson* is not retroactively applicable to cases that became final before *Batson* was decided. Teague v. Lane, 489 U.S. 288, 109 S.Ct. 1060, 103 L.Ed.2d 334 (1989).

45. See § 22.2(d).

46. Lockhart v. McCree, 476 U.S. 162, 106 S.Ct. 1758, 90 L.Ed.2d 137 (1986). *Lockhart* was a challenge for cause case, but the same conclusion was later reached as to peremptory challenges in Holland v. Illinois, 493 U.S. 474, 110 S.Ct. 803, 107 L.Ed.2d 905 (1990) (asserting that the Sixth Amendment goal of "jury impartiality with respect

equal protection case and rests on the conclusions that "*Swain* has placed on defendants a crippling burden of proof" and does so unnecessarily in light of intervening decisions of the Court recognizing "that a defendant may make a prima facie showing of purposeful racial discrimination in selection of the venire by relying solely on the facts concerning its selection *in his case*." *Batson* thus holds "that a defendant may establish a prima facie case of purposeful discrimination in selection of the petit jury solely on evidence concerning the prosecutor's exercise of peremptory challenges at the defendant's trial."

Under *Batson*, the defendant upon timely objection[47] was required to show "that he is a member of a cognizable racial group" and "that the prosecutor has exercised peremptory challenges to remove from the venire members of the defendant's race." Most courts took this to mean that a white defendant could not object to the exclusion of blacks from his jury by the prosecutor's use of peremptories. But in the later case of *Powers v. Ohio*,[48] the Supreme Court rejected such a limitation. The Court first reasoned, as to the substantive guarantees of the equal protection clause, that under *Batson* the harm to be avoided is not merely trial of a defendant by a jury from which members of his own race have been eliminated, but also the harm to the community at large and to excluded jurors by excluding persons from jury service "solely by reason of

their race, a practice that forecloses a significant opportunity to participate in civic life." Moreover, the Court concluded in *Powers*, the defendant in a criminal case has standing to raise the equal protection rights of excluded jurors, who would themselves confront "considerable practical barriers" to challenging their exclusion. As for the emphasis in *Batson* on racial identity between the defendant and the excused jurors, the Court noted such racial identity simply "may provide one of the easier cases to establish both a prima facie case and a conclusive showing that wrongful discrimination has occurred."[49]

A defendant making a *Batson* challenge, who may rely on the fact that peremptory challenges provide an opportunity for discrimination, "must show that these facts and other relevant circumstances raise an inference that the prosecutor used that practice to exclude veniremen from the petit jury on account of their races," which is an "inference of purposeful discrimination." It is then for the trial court, considering "all relevant circumstances," such as a pattern of exercising strikes from the venire on the basis of race and the nature of the prosecutor's questions and statements on voir dire, to decide if the showing "creates a prima facie case of discrimination." If it does,[50] then "the burden shifts to the State to come forward with a neutral explanation[51] for challenging black jurors,"

to both contestants * * * would positively be obstructed by a petit jury cross-section requirement which * * * would cripple the device of peremptory challenges").

47. "The requirement that any *Batson* claim be raised not only before trial, but in the period between the selection of the jurors and the administration of their oaths, is a sensible rule." Ford v. Georgia, 498 U.S. 411, 111 S.Ct. 850, 112 L.Ed.2d 935 (1991) (but is no bar to federal review in this case, as it was not "firmly established and regularly followed" at time applied).

48. 499 U.S. 400, 111 S.Ct. 1364, 113 L.Ed.2d 411 (1991).

49. In the earlier case of Holland v. Illinois, 493 U.S. 474, 110 S.Ct. 803, 107 L.Ed.2d 905 (1990), foretelling *Powers*, the author of the later case, Kennedy, J., commented that "where this obvious ground for suspicion is absent," i.e., where the defendant is *not* the same race as the excluded jurors, "different methods of proof may be appropriate."

50. In Hernandez v. New York, 500 U.S. 352, 111 S.Ct. 1859, 114 L.Ed.2d 395 (1991), the prosecutor defended his peremptory strikes without a prior ruling that the defen-

dant had made out a prima facie case. The Court's plurality opinion states: "Once a prosecutor has offered a race-neutral explanation for the peremptory challenges and the trial court has ruled on the ultimate question of intentional discrimination, the preliminary issue of whether the defendant had made a prima facie showing becomes moot."

51. In Hernandez v. New York, 500 U.S. 352, 111 S.Ct. 1859, 114 L.Ed.2d 395 (1991), the plurality concluded that a "neutral explanation * * * means an explanation based on something other than the race of the juror," and that the issue is whether "a discriminatory intent" was present, not whether there resulted "a racially disproportionate impact," though if the prosecutor "articulates a basis for a peremptory challenge that results in the disproportionate exclusion of members of a certain race, the trial judge may consider that fact as evidence that the prosecutor's stated reason constitutes a pretext for racial discrimination." The Court decided the record supported the conclusion that the prosecutor's peremptory challenge in the instant case "rested neither on the intention to exclude Latino or bilingual jurors, nor on stereotypical assump-

which requires more than a denial of a discriminatory motive or the explanation "that he challenged jurors of the defendant's race on the assumption—or his intuitive judgment—that they would be partial to the defendant because of their shared race." As the Court later elaborated in *Purkett v. Elem*,[52] at this second stage it is not necessary that the prosecutor's explanation also be "at least minimally persuasive," for such a requirement would violate "the principle that the ultimate burden of persuasion regarding racial motivation rests with, and never shifts from, the opponent of the strike." But at the third stage, when the trial court must decide if that opponent did carry this burden, *Elem* emphasizes that "implausible or fantastic justifications may (and probably will) be found to be pretexts for purposeful discrimination."

Lower courts have upheld reasons having to do with the prospective juror's likely attitudes regarding the particular case, and also those which more generally indicate something about the prospective juror's fitness for service or likely attitudes regarding criminal prosecutions. A reason is more likely to pass muster if the record indicates the same reason was used in challenging white prospective jurors, and by the same token a reason is unacceptable if it appears whites were not challenged on the same basis. However, making this determination can often be difficult because a particular prospective juror is often challenged or not because of a variety of factors. A reason grounded largely in speculation rather than upon facts uncovered in the voir dire examination or otherwise is not likely to be deemed acceptable. As to the great many strikes that since *Batson* have had to be explained, the experience to date indicates it is ordinarily not difficult for prosecutors to come up with an acceptable reason; this is why some have viewed the *Batson* procedures as less an obstacle to racial discrimination than a road map to disguised discrimination, and why this experience is deemed to lend support to the view

(expressed by Justice Marshall in *Batson*) that the only effective solution is to ban peremptory challenges.

The Supreme Court declined "to formulate particular procedures to be followed" in the event of a *Batson* challenge. It would seem, however, that adversarial hearings are the appropriate method for handling most *Batson* type disputes, as defense counsel can perform two crucial functions in such a setting: pointing out to the judge where the government's stated reason may indicate bad faith; and preserving for the record and possible appeal facts bearing on the judge's decision. The Court in *Batson* declined to say whether, upon a finding of discrimination, it is better to start jury selection over with a new venire or simply to reinstate improperly challenged jurors onto the present venire. When there has been an uncorrected *Batson* violation at the trial level preserved for appeal, the Supreme Court has assumed, but never formally ruled, that the appropriate appellate remedy is automatic reversal.

In *Georgia v. McCollum*,[53] the Court held *Batson* applicable where a prosecutor sought to prevent white defendants, charged with assaulting blacks, from striking black prospective jurors because of their race. The Court reasoned that (i) "a criminal defendant's exercise of peremptory challenges in a racially discriminatory manner inflicts the harms addressed by *Batson*," denial of prospective jurors' right to serve as jurors, and loss of public confidence in the fairness of jury verdicts; (ii) such exercise of peremptories "is performing a traditional governmental function"; (iii) "the State has standing to challenge a defendant's discriminatory use of peremptory challenges," as "its own judicial process is undermined" thereby and there are significant barriers to the excluded jurors themselves obtaining relief; and (iv) the interests served by *Batson* need not "give way to the rights of a criminal defendant," as a defendant's rights to a fair trial, counsel and

tions about Latinos or bilinguals," but rather on an intent to exclude only those who "might have difficulty in accepting the translator's rendition of Spanish-language testimony."

52. 514 U.S. 765, 115 S.Ct. 1769, 131 L.Ed.2d 834 (1995).

53. 505 U.S. 42, 112 S.Ct. 2348, 120 L.Ed.2d 33 (1992).

an impartial jury do not include "the right to discriminate against a group of citizens based upon their race." If the Court's holding also applies to black defendants striking whites (as a *McCollum* concurrence assumes), then (as one of the two dissents puts it) this case may "fail to advance nondiscriminatory criminal justice," as the striking of white prospective jurors by such a defendant can produce a racially mixed jury that in turn could serve to minimize "the distorting influence of race."

While the analysis and holding in *Batson* were confined to the special problem of "racial discrimination in selection of jurors,"[54] the dissenters objected that "if conventional equal protection principles apply, then presumably defendants could object to exclusion on the basis of not only race, but also sex, age, religion or political affiliation," and a host of other characteristics. Later, in *J.E.B. v. Alabama ex rel. T.B.*,[55] the Court held "that gender, like race, is an unconstitutional proxy for jury competence and impartiality," so that *Batson* (and presumably its progeny[56]) now was extended also to cover the exercise of peremptory challenges based solely upon gender.[57] The central consideration in *J.E.B.* was that "discrimination in jury selection, whether based on race or on gender, causes harm to the litigants, the community, and the individual jurors who are wrongfully excluded from participation in the judicial process." As for the above-quoted fear of the *Batson* dissenters, *J.E.B.*'s emphasis on the fact that both race and gender classifications are subject to "heightened equal protection scrutiny" suggests *Batson*'s broadest application would be

to other classifications likewise receiving such scrutiny.[58] But *J.E.B.*'s other emphasis—on the fact that "African–Americans and women share a history of total exclusion" from jury service—might provide a basis for narrowing the ultimate scope of *Batson* even further.

(e) Alternate Jurors. The rule at common law was that if there was some reason for discharging a juror during trial, then it was necessary to discharge the entire jury and begin the trial anew. To avoid this undesirable result, statutes and court rules now provide for the selection of alternate or additional jurors during protracted trials. Two different types of statutes and rules are to be found. The most common is the alternate juror or substituted juror type, under which one or more persons specifically identified at the outset as alternates are chosen in advance of trial. If a regular juror is discharged prior to the time the jury retires (or, in a few jurisdictions, prior to the time of verdict), an alternate juror is then designated to take his place. By contrast, under the additional juror or eliminated juror system, more than 12 jurors are selected in advance of trial. If a juror must be discharged during the trial, this is done without any further action at that time. Should more than 12 jurors remain at the time the jury is to retire, the 12 who are to participate in the deliberations are selected by lot. A preference for the latter approach has sometimes been stated on the ground that it is undesirable to give a juror who might turn out to be involved in deciding the case a second-class status during some or all of the trial.

---

54. In Hernandez v. New York, 500 U.S. 352, 111 S.Ct. 1859, 114 L.Ed.2d 395 (1991), the plurality noted it had no occasion to "resolve the more difficult question of the breadth with which the concept of race should be defined for equal protection purposes. We would face a quite different case if the prosecutor had justified his peremptory challenges with the explanation that he did not want Spanish-speaking jurors. It may well be, for certain ethnic groups and in some communities, that proficiency in a particular language, like skin color, should be treated as a surrogate for race under an equal protection analysis."

55. 511 U.S. 127, 114 S.Ct. 1419, 128 L.Ed.2d 89 (1994).

56. In *J.E.B.*, it was the state that exercised the challenged peremptories. O'Connor, J., concurring, expressed

the "hope" (but not the expectation) that *J.E.B.* would not be applied to prevent "the battered wife—on trial for wounding her abusive husband—* * * from using her peremptory challenges to ensure that the jury of her peers contained as many women members as possible."

57. The Court cautioned that "strikes based on characteristics that are disproportionately associated with one gender could be appropriate, absent a showing of pretext," e.g., challenging all persons with military experience or all persons employed as nurses.

58. Thus the three dissenters in *J.E.B.* predicted extension of the *Batson* principle to peremptories based on "religious belief."

In the federal system as many as six alternates may be selected,[59] while in the states the number is typically one or two. Whether to select alternate or additional jurors pursuant to these statutes and rules and what number to select within the number authorized is generally a matter left to the discretion of the trial judge. As for the judge's decision that the circumstances are such that a juror must be excused and replaced by an alternate or additional juror, the judge has considerable discretion here as well, and the judge's action in excusing a juror will be upheld if the record shows some legitimate basis for his decision. This is because the defendant has still been tried by 12 persons selected by him.

In the federal system, it was for many years the case that alternates could replace regular jurors only "prior to the time the jury retires to consider its verdict."[60] This is no longer the case,[61] but the former federal rule is still followed in most but not all states. This position has been criticized because of the problem presented if one of the jurors in a protracted trial becomes unavailable during the deliberations. There is a growing body of authority[62] that substitution of an alternate at that time is constitutionally permissible, at least if the substituted juror had not theretofore been relieved of the obligations of a juror or otherwise become tainted and if in addition the jury was carefully instructed to begin its deliberations anew when its composition changed. But a contrary line of authority holds to the view that such substitution is unconstitutional, for if deliberations had progressed to a stage where the original eleven were in substantial agreement, they were in a position to present

a formidable obstacle to the alternate juror's attempts to persuade and convince them. Whether or not this objection has Sixth Amendment status, it casts serious doubt upon the wisdom of the substitution approach. As for sending each alternate juror into the jury room at the very beginning of deliberations with instructions not to participate until such time, should it occur, that he is substituted for some other juror, the view most often taken is that such a procedure is unsound because the alternate jurors' very presence in the jury room may inhibit certain jurors from participating freely in the deliberations.[63] Another possible solution, now authorized in federal practice,[64] simply proceeding with a jury of eleven should it become necessary to excuse one of the jurors during the course of the deliberations, would seem constitutionally permissible under *Williams v. Florida*[65] but might be opposed on the ground that the availability of any alternative to a mistrial might result in judges being too willing to excuse a juror in the minority who wished to "bail out."

§ 22.4   Challenging the Judge

(a) Right to Impartial Judge. Just as the defendant's right to jury trial is to an "impartial" jury, he also has a constitutional right to an impartial judge. As the Supreme Court held in *Tumey v. Ohio*,[1] "it certainly violates the Fourteenth Amendment and deprives a defendant in a criminal case of due process of law to subject his liberty or property to the judgment of a court, the judge of which has a direct, personal, substantial pecuniary interest in reaching a conclusion against him in his case." The Court concluded that such was the case in

---

59. Fed.R.Crim.P. 24(c).

60. Former Fed.R.Crim.P. 24(c).

61. See note 62 infra.

62. Including the 1999 revision of Fed.R.Crim.P. 24(c), which allows the trial judge to retain alternate jurors during deliberations and to replace a regular juror with an alternate when necessary, in which case "the court must instruct the jury to begin its deliberations anew."

63. Such presence "is no doubt a deviation from Rule 24(c)." United States v. Olano, 507 U.S. 725, 113 S.Ct. 1770, 123 L.Ed.2d 508 (1993). As the Court noted, "the presence of alternate jurors during jury deliberations might prejudice a defendant in two different ways: either

because the alternates actually participated in the deliberations, verbally or through 'body language'; or because the alternates' presence exerted a 'chilling' effect on the regular jurors." But the Court in *Olano* went on to hold that where the defendants "made no specific showing that the alternate jurors in this case either participated in the jury's deliberations or 'chilled' deliberations by the regular jurors," the error was not "plain error" which the defendants could raise for the first time on appeal.

64. Fed.R.Crim.P. 23(b).

65. 399 U.S. 78, 90 S.Ct. 1893, 26 L.Ed.2d 446 (1970).

§ 22.4

1. 273 U.S. 510, 47 S.Ct. 437, 71 L.Ed. 749 (1927).

Tumey, where the mayor, authorized to try certain offenses, in addition to his regular salary, received the fees and costs levied by him against violators. This was so, the Court reasoned, because the mayor's situation was one "which would offer a possible temptation to the average man as a judge to forget the burden of proof required to convict the defendant, or which might lead him not to hold the balance nice, clear, and true between the state and the accused."

In *Ward v. Monroeville,*[2] the Court held that the pecuniary interest does not necessarily have to be personal in order for *Tumey* to apply. The situation in *Ward* was that the mayor before whom defendant was compelled to stand trial for traffic offenses was responsible for village finances, and the mayor's court through fines, forfeitures, costs and fees provided a substantial portion of the village funds. The Court ruled that the "possible temptation" under the *Tumey* rule exists when "the mayor's executive responsibilities for village finances may make him partisan to maintain the high level of contribution from the mayor's court." *Dugan v. Ohio*[3] was distinguished because there the mayor had limited executive authority as one of five members of a city commission, so that his relation to the finances and financial policy of the city was too remote to warrant a presumption of bias. The Supreme Court in *Ward* also decided that a defendant "is entitled to a neutral and detached judge in the first instance," so that it made no difference that defendant had a right to trial de novo in another court.

Impartiality in the constitutional sense may also be lacking because the judge is involved in a very personal way in the matter at issue, as is reflected in the contempt cases. In *Mayberry v. Pennsylvania,*[4] for example, where a criminal defendant repeatedly insulted and vilified the trial judge during trial and at the conclusion of the trial was pronounced guilty of 11 contempts and sentenced to 11–22 years, the Court vacated the judgment of contempt. The

Court first noted that as the separate acts or outbursts occurred, the trial judge "could with propriety, have instantly acted, holding [defendant] in contempt, or excluding him from the courtroom." But when the judge waits until the end of the trial, due process requires that "another judge, not bearing the sting of these slanderous remarks, and having the impersonal authority of the law," sit in judgment on defendant's conduct. Similarly, in *Taylor v. Hayes*[5] the Court held that another judge should have been substituted for the purpose of finally disposing of contempt charges against a defense attorney where the record showed that "marked personal feelings were present on both sides" and that marks of "unseemly conduct [had] left personal stings." And in *Johnson v. Mississippi*[6] the Court ruled that an end-of-trial contempt proceeding should have been conducted by another judge because the trial judge "immediately prior to the adjudication of contempt was a defendant in one of petitioner's civil rights suits and a losing party at that."

This is not to suggest that it is objectionable that the trial judge was involved in some prior proceedings in that case and thus might be aware of facts which have no direct bearing on guilt and which could not be put in the hands of a juror trying the case. As the Supreme Court explained in *Withrow v. Larkin*[7]:

> Judges repeatedly issue arrest warrants on the basis that there is probable cause to believe that a crime has been committed and that the person named in the warrant has committed it. Judges also preside at preliminary hearings where they must decide whether the evidence is sufficient to hold a defendant for trial. Neither of these pretrial involvements has been thought to raise any constitutional barrier against the judge presiding over the criminal trial and, if the trial is without a jury, against making the necessary determination of guilt or innocence.

2.   409 U.S. 57, 93 S.Ct. 80, 34 L.Ed.2d 267 (1972).

3.   277 U.S. 61, 48 S.Ct. 439, 72 L.Ed. 784 (1928).

4.   400 U.S. 455, 91 S.Ct. 499, 27 L.Ed.2d 532 (1971).

5.   418 U.S. 488, 94 S.Ct. 2697, 41 L.Ed.2d 897 (1974).

6.   403 U.S. 212, 91 S.Ct. 1778, 29 L.Ed.2d 423 (1971).

7.   421 U.S. 35, 95 S.Ct. 1456, 43 L.Ed.2d 712 (1975).

(b) Challenge for Cause. Trial judges, like jurors, are subject to challenge for cause. Grounds for challenge usually are set forth in a statute or rule of court. These provisions sometimes include specific situations, such as where there is a family relationship between the judge and the defendant, counsel, or the victim of the crime, but in any event refer more generally to situations of bias.[8] Under some statutes it is enough that the party seeking a substitution of a judge has filed an affidavit which sufficiently states the facts and the reasons for the belief that bias or prejudice exists, while in other jurisdictions a hearing must be held on the matter and the facts showing prejudice judicially determined. Under the latter circumstances the better practice is for the matter to be heard by a judge other than the one challenged.

(c) Recusal by Judge. It is not sufficient for a judge to proceed on the assumption that he may serve in any trial except when a party has successfully alleged or proved, as may be required, that he is actually biased. As a matter of judicial ethics, the judge has a responsibility to recuse himself under certain circumstances, including whenever the judge believes his or her impartiality can reasonably be questioned. Because one concern here is with the appearance of impropriety, this ethical obligation of the judge clearly extends beyond instances of actual bias. Especially where this recusal responsibility is accepted as part of the law of the jurisdiction and is recognized as not merely a self-enforcing duty on the judge but as a matter that may be asserted also by a party to the action, the obvious result is a broader basis upon which to bring into question whether a particular judge may try a particular case. If the judge does not recuse

himself and the basis for recusal is discovered by the defendant only after conviction, a special and narrow harmless error rule applies.

(d) Peremptory Challenge. About one-third of the states have provisions allowing a party to challenge an assigned judge without alleging or proving the precise facts that lead him to believe he cannot get a fair trial. In some states, this peremptory challenge of the judge may be exercised merely by filing a notice or motion requesting transfer of the matter to another judge. Elsewhere an affidavit of prejudice, alleging that a fair trial cannot be had before the judge and that the motion is made in good faith and not for delay, will suffice. But unlike the type of provision discussed earlier, specific facts need not be alleged, and thus the provision is properly characterized as permitting a peremptory challenge. When peremptories are allowed in criminal cases, they are almost always available to both the defendant and the prosecution. Some available statistics indicate that where peremptory challenge of a judge is permitted, the right is exercised sparingly.

The arguments for a procedure of this kind are that it is a necessary means for dealing with actual but unprovable bias, and that a party will more readily accept the outcome of the trial if he perceives that the judge was fair. In opposition to allowing peremptory challenge of a judge, it is said that to allow litigants to remove judges because of their substantive views could penalize judicial independence and creativity, encourage "judge shopping," and impose burdens on judges who are not the subject of removal motions. At a minimum, these arguments justify rather strict limits on any right to peremptorily challenge a judge.[9]

---

8. In Liteky v. United States, 510 U.S. 540, 114 S.Ct. 1147, 127 L.Ed.2d 474 (1994), the Court held that *both* the federal challenge-for-cause statute, 28 U.S.C.A. § 144, and the federal recusal statute, 28 U.S.C.A. § 455, are subject to an "extrajudicial source" limitation, meaning (i) that "judicial rulings alone almost never constitute valid basis for a bias or partiality motion"; and (ii) that "opinions formed by the judge on the basis of facts introduced or events occurring in the course of the current proceedings, or of prior proceedings, do not constitute a basis for a bias or partiality motion unless they display a deep-seated favoritism or antagonism that would make fair judgment impossible."

9. ABA Standards of Judicial Administration, Standards Relating to Trial Courts § 2.32(b) (1976), states: "A party should be permitted a peremptory challenge of the judge to whom a matter has been assigned, subject to the following restrictions: (1) a party may have only one such challenge in a case; (2) the challenge must be asserted immediately upon the matter's having been assigned to the judge against whom the challenge is made and before he has made any decision regarding it; and (3) the party must be ready to proceed in the matter without delay upon its reassignment to another judge."

(e) Substitution of Judge. The provisions discussed above must be distinguished from those permitting substitution of a judge because of death, sickness or other disability of the judge before whom the trial commenced. In the federal courts, such substitution is permissible if the case is being tried by a jury and if the substituted judge "certifies familiarity with the trial record."[10] Similar provisions are to be found in some states, while some other jurisdictions allow substitution even when the case is being tried without a jury. The better view, however, is that if a judge is also the trier of facts, the same judge should hear all the witnesses, unless the parties consent to substitution. It is sometimes contended that such consent should be required even if the case is being tried by a jury, a view that may rest in part on the suggestion that the right to jury trial includes the right to have the same judge present throughout the trial.

---

10. Fed.R.Crim.P. 25(a). In addition, Fed.R.Crim.P. 25(b) allows substitution "after a verdict or finding of guilty."

Chapter 23

FAIR TRIAL AND FREE PRESS

Table of Sections

---

§ 23.1   Preventing Prejudicial Publicity

(a) The Problem of Prejudicial Publicity. News media reporting on the operation of the criminal justice process, like other types of news reporting, is protected by the First Amendment. As in the case of other reporting, criminal news reporting commonly provides many benefits that are in the public interest. The same reporting also may produce adverse consequences, including a possible adverse impact upon the fairness of the criminal trial. Much of that potential relates to the fairness of the factfinding process. One concern is that extensive media coverage will result in a jury that is not impartial and that does not base its verdict solely on evidence presented at trial. Another concern is that the process of eliminating all of the prospective jurors influenced by publicity will in itself be costly. It may leave a jury pool reflecting a highly skewed sampling of the community or force the defendant to trial in another venue. An additional concern relates to the appearance of fairness. Even if in actuality the trier of fact has not been prejudiced, the appearance of prejudice may bring the judicial process into disrepute. This chapter focuses on the criminal justice system's response to such concerns.

The possible adverse impact of news coverage on the fairness of the criminal trial can be limited in various ways. One is through procedural safeguards designed to offset the potentially pernicious influence of the coverage. Section 23.2 discusses the most prominent of those safeguards, which focus on the selection of the jury and the timing and place of the trial. Another approach is to seek to reduce or eliminate that news coverage most likely to have a prejudicial influence. The subsections that follow discuss the major procedural devices aimed at that objective.

(b) Restricting Public Statements. In *Sheppard v. Maxwell*,[1] the Supreme Court held that defendant was deprived of his due process right to a fair trial "because of the trial judge's failure to protect Sheppard sufficiently from the massive, pervasive and prejudicial publicity that attended his prosecution." In discussing the various ways in which the trial court could have exercised its "power to control the publicity about the trial," the Court asserted that "the court should have made some effort to control the release of leads, information, and gossip to the press by police officers, witnesses, and the counsel for both sides." It noted in this regard that "the trial court might well have proscribed extrajudicial statements by any lawyer, party, witness, or court official which divulged prejudicial matters, such as the refusal of Sheppard to submit to interrogation or take any lie detector tests; any statement made by Sheppard to officials; the identity of prospective witnesses or their probable testimony; any belief in guilt or innocence; or like statements concerning the merits of the case." Also, "being advised of the great public interest in the case, the mass coverage of the press, and the potential prejudicial impact of publicity, the court could * * * have requested the appropriate city and county officials to promulgate a regulation with respect to dissemination of information about the case by their employees."

Despite this strong language in *Sheppard*, there continues to be considerable uncertainty as to the extent to which it is proper as a policy and constitutional matter for the trial judge to restrict public statements of persons who are not traditionally regulated by the court in their activities relating to a case. As a result, the major focus in restricting statements has been upon the extrajudicial statements of defense counsel and prosecutors. Here, the standards of professional responsibility in every state include a provision placing

limits on the content of the attorneys' statements under specified circumstances. Those provisions operate as a general restraint, imposed in every case, and are enforced primarily through lawyer disciplinary proceedings. In addition, they provide the framework commonly incorporated by judges in the issuance of "gag orders" directed at counsel in individual cases and enforced through contempt sanctions.

The vast majority of state professional responsibility provisions, arguably as many as forty, follow verbatim or with minor variations, one of three models: (1) Disciplinary Rule 7–107 of the American Bar Association's Model Code of Professional Responsibility; (2) the original (1983) version of Model Rule 3.6 of the ABA's Model Rules of Professional Responsibility; or (3) the 1994 revision of Model Rule 3.6. These three ABA models have several common elements. First, they apply only to extrajudicial statements made in a setting where the lawyer reasonably can anticipate dissemination by the media. The cases have almost uniformly involved press conferences or interviews by reporters. Second, each imposes a general limitation on extrajudicial statements tied to the statement's likely impact upon the criminal proceedings, rather than to any specific objective of the lawyer to alter the outcome of those proceedings. Requiring proof of such an objective would undermine the effectiveness of the provision since extrajudicial statements that might have that impact almost invariably can be characterized by the defense counsel or prosecutor as aimed at other, nontrial-related functions. Moreover, even where such other objectives are in fact the lawyer's exclusive objective, the lawyer's statement may still carry a strong potential for interfering with the fair administration of justice, particularly by prejudicing prospective jurors. The three models do not deny the legitimacy of objectives other than influencing potential jurors that call for extrajudicial statements by a prosecutor or defense counsel, but conclude that those objectives must be subordinated where the statement creates a certain degree of risk to the fair

§ 23.1
1. 384 U.S. 333, 86 S.Ct. 1507, 16 L.Ed.2d 600 (1966).

administration of the criminal justice process in the individual case.

Third, the potential impact upon the criminal proceeding that brings the limitation into play is not simply the influencing of prospective jurors (although that undoubtedly is the primary concern). The standard of likely impact is not restricted to jury trials and does not create an exception for statements made after a jury has been sequestered. While the fact the trial was to the bench or that the jury had been sequestered may be important in determining whether the particular standard of likely impact is met, all three models hold open the possibility of considering other means of interfering with the due administration of justice, as by bringing pressure to bear upon the judge or potential witnesses. Finally, all three models seek to provide specifics to assist the lawyer in determining what content a statement to the media may and may not include. Disciplinary Rule 7–107 and the original version of Model Rule 3.6 seek to do both in the text of their respective provisions. The 1994 version of Model Rule 3.6 discusses only in its commentary the content of statements likely to be barred, but continues to include in the text a listing of the content that would be acceptable.

Disciplinary Rule 7–107 has the most complex structure of the three ABA proposals, and in some respects, the broadest coverage. Disciplinary Rule 7–107 announces in its first five sections (A–E), general and specific standards applicable to four different stages of the criminal proceeding—(1) the investigation, (2) from the initiation of the criminal case (i.e., the arrest or filing of the complaint) to the commencement of the trial with the start of jury selection, (3) from jury selection through to the end of the trial, and (4) from the end of the trial or disposition without trial to the imposition of sentence. Section (A) bars a lawyer connected with the investigation of a criminal matter from making other than general comments about the investigation. During the arrest/charge to trial phase of the case, section (B) prohibits prosecutors and defense attorneys from making "an extrajudicial statement that a reasonable person would expect to be

disseminated by means of public communication and that relates to" any of the following: "(1) The character, reputation, or prior criminal record (including arrests, indictments, or other charges of crime) of the accused; (2) The possibility of a plea of guilty to the offense charged or to a lesser offense; (3) The existence or contents of any confession, admission, or statement given by the accused or his refusal or failure to make a statement; (4) The performance or results of any examinations or tests or the refusal or failure of the accused to submit to examinations or tests; (5) The identity, testimony, or credibility of a prospective witness; (6) Any opinion as to the guilt or innocence of the accused, the evidence, or the merits of the case." Section (C) then adds a provision listing certain types of information that may be disseminated to the public even though its content might relate to the six areas of prohibited comment listed above. Listed here is basic factual information relating to the accused, the victim, the arrest, the investigating officers, the charge, and the court record, as well as information needed to secure public assistance in the apprehension of the accused where the accused is still at large. That information tends to be tightly circumscribed (e.g., age and residence of the accused) and therefore creates only a narrow exception to the six areas of prohibited content. Section (D) states that, during the selection of the jury or the trial, the prosecutor or defense counsel shall not make an extrajudicial statement expected to be disseminated that "relates to the trial, parties, or issues in the trial or other matters that are reasonably likely to interfere with a fair trial, except that he may quote from or refer without comment to public records of the court on the case." Finally, Section (E) states that during the sentencing phase, the prosecutors and defense attorneys shall not make an extrajudicial statement expected to be disseminated that is "reasonably likely to affect the imposition of sentence."

Although only sections (D) and (E) specifically refers to a "reasonable likelihood" of producing potential prejudice, that standard was assumed by the drafters to underlie all prohibitions. Thus, statements made during investigation that go beyond the permitted content specified in section (A) violate the rule only if they present a reasonable likelihood of interfering with an eventual fair trial. So too, although the listing in section B of statements prohibited during the pretrial stage may have been viewed by the drafters as automatic prohibitions because those statements inherently are "reasonably likely to interfere with a fair trial," courts applying the Code have insisted upon a case-by-case evaluation as to whether the particular setting met that standard of likely prejudice.

As a result of questions raised concerning both the constitutionality of Disciplinary Rule 7–107 and the validity of various distinctions drawn in that Rule, the Model Rules both modified and reshaped the limitations on extrajudicial statements in its Rule 3.6. The original (1983) version of Model Rule 3.6 was aimed at both simplifying the structure of the ethical standard and avoiding First Amendment and vagueness difficulties. The Rule was organized into three paragraphs, with paragraph (a) setting forth the general standard, paragraph (b) specifying content ordinarily in violation of paragraph (a), and paragraph (c) providing a "safe-harbor" listing of statements that will be permissible without regard to any uncertainties in the application of the general standard of paragraph (a).

The basic prohibition of paragraph (a) sets forth a single standard governing all stages of the process (in contrast to DR 7–107 which has separate provisions for various different stages). It provides:

> (a) A lawyer shall not make an extrajudicial statement that a reasonable person would expect to be disseminated by means of public communication if the lawyer knows or reasonably should know that it will have a substantial likelihood of materially prejudicing an adjudicative proceeding in the matter.

The key to this provision is the substitution of a higher standard of likely prejudice. Whereas the prohibition of DR 7–107 applies if the statement is "reasonably likely to interfere with a fair trial," Rule 3.6(a) requires a "substantial likelihood" of "materially prejudicing"

the proceeding. A "substantial likelihood" clearly would be somewhat greater than a "reasonable likelihood." Whether "materially prejudicing" requires more than "interfering with a fair trial" is less clear. Arguably, it simply restates the same type of harm in terms more appropriate to a standard that applies to all types of adjudicative proceedings and all stages of those proceedings.

Paragraph (b) of the original version of Model Rule 3.6 builds upon the six areas of prohibited comment specified in DR 7–107(B). It provides initially that "a statement referred to in paragraph (a) [i.e., an extrajudicial statement expected to be disseminated by means of a public communication] ordinarily is likely to have such an effect [i.e., to pose a substantial likelihood of material prejudice]" when the statement "relates to" any of the six areas of specified content. This provision, as described by the drafters, was designed to "transfor[m] the [six] particulars in DR 7–107 into an illustrative compilation that gives fair notice of conduct ordinarily posing unacceptable dangers to the fair administration of justice."

In its listing of the six particulars, paragraph (b) also modifies somewhat the DR 7–107(B) descriptions of their content. The six areas of suspect content are described as: (1) the character, credibility, reputation, or criminal record of a party or witness, or the identity of a witness or the expected testimony of a party or witness; (2) the possibility of a plea of guilty, or the existence or contents of any confession, admission, or statement given by the defendant or his refusal or failure to make a statement; (3) the performance or results of any examination or test or the refusal or failure of a person to submit to examination or test, or the identity or nature of physical evidence; (4) any opinion as to the guilt or innocence of the defendant; (5) information likely to be inadmissible but prejudicial; and (6) the fact defendant has been charged, unless accompanied by a statement that the charge is only an accusation and that defendant is presumed innocent.

Paragraph (c) of the original Rule 3.6 adds a "safe harbor" provision that serves the same general function as section (C) of DR 7–107, listing information that is excepted from the six areas of suspect content. Paragraph (C) provides that, "notwithstanding paragraphs (a) and (b)(1)–(5), a lawyer involved in the investigation or litigation of a matter may state without elaboration" the following: (1) "the general nature of the claim or defense"; (2) information on the public record; (3) the existence of an ongoing investigation, including its general scope and identity of persons involved (except where "prohibited by law," as in the case of grand jury investigations); (4) litigation scheduling or results; (5) a request for assistance in obtaining evidence; (6) a warning of possible danger from the person where "there is reason to believe that there exists the likelihood of substantial harm" (applicable in some instances where an accused is not apprehended); (7) information necessary to aid in the apprehension of the accused; and (8) basic factual information relating to the accused (name, residence, occupation, and family status), the arrest of the accused (fact, time, and place), and the investigating officers (identity, investigative agency, and length of investigation).

In *Gentile v. State Bar of Nevada*,[2] the Supreme Court had before it the application of a state professional responsibility rule (Nevada Rule 177) that followed largely verbatim the original version of Model Rule 3.6. The petitioner there, a defense attorney, had been disciplined for statements made at a press conference held shortly after his client's indictment (and six months before the anticipated trial). The client had been charged, following a highly publicized investigation, with the theft of cocaine and travelers' checks from a safety deposit box, rented from the client's vault company, that had been used in a police undercover operation. At the press conference, the petitioner made statements to the effect that: (1) his client was innocent and was "being used as a scapegoat"; (2) the evidence pointed to a named police undercover officer as the true thief; (3) the defense had a video tape which showed the officer in a condition described implicitly as suggesting cocaine use;

and (4) the other vault customers who alleged safety deposit thefts were not credible, as most were drug dealers or money launderers who had accused the defendant in response to police pressure when they tried to "work themselves out of something." In concluding that petitioner had violated Nevada Rule 177, the state disciplinary board found that: (1) the petitioner expected both the named police officer and the other vault customers to be prosecution witnesses; (2) the petitioner's admitted purpose for calling the press conference was to influence public sentiment and the possible venire by offsetting information that had been released by the prosecutor and police (relating, in particular, to the lack of culpability of the police officer); (3) although the subsequent trial revealed there was no actual prejudice, the content, purpose, and timing of petitioner's statements (when public interest was "at its peak") established that petitioner either knew or should have known that there was a substantial likelihood that his remarks would materially prejudice the anticipated trial; and (4) petitioner's comment went beyond the safe-harbor provision of Rule 177, which was identical to the safe-harbor provision of Model Rule 3.6(c). In particular, it did not simply "state without elaboration the general nature of the * * * client's defense."

Before the Supreme Court, the petitioner claimed that the State Bar's disciplinary sanction (a private reprimand) should be overturned because: (1) Nevada Rule 177 on its face violated the First Amendment; (2) the application of the Rule 177 prohibition to the facts of his case violated the First Amendment; and (3) Rule 177 was "void for vagueness" as interpreted by the Nevada authorities in their application of the Rule to his case. A Supreme Court majority (per Rehnquist, C.J.) rejected the first claim, and a differently composed majority (per Kennedy, J.) sustained the third claim. The Court was evenly divided (4–4) on petitioner's second claim of a First Amendment violation in the application of Rule 177. In a brief concurring opinion, Justice O'Connor joined the Rehnquist opinion on First

2. 501 U.S. 1030, 111 S.Ct. 2720, 115 L.Ed.2d 888 (1991).

Amendment facial validity and the Kennedy opinion on vagueness, but did not speak to that second claim.

Petitioner's First Amendment challenge to the facial validity of Rule 177 centered on the Rule's use of a "substantial likelihood of material prejudice" standard. Petitioner claimed that the First Amendment allowed the state to impose disciplinary sanctions only upon a showing of "a 'clear and present danger' of 'actual prejudice or imminent threat.'" Chief Justice Rehnquist's opinion for the majority on the facial validity issue flatly rejected that contention. The opinion acknowledged that the First Amendment had been held, in cases such as *Nebraska Press* (discussed in subsection (c) below), "to require a showing of clear and present danger that a malfunction in the criminal justice system will be caused before a State may prohibit media speech or publication about a particular pending trial." Accordingly, the issue presented by petitioner's claim was "whether a lawyer who represents a defendant involved with the criminal justice system may insist on the same standard before he is disciplined for public pronouncements about the case, or whether the State instead may penalize that sort of speech upon a lesser showing." Following a review of statements in earlier cases, including *Sheppard*, the opinion concluded that those cases had "rather plainly indicat[ed] that the speech of lawyers representing clients in pending cases may be regulated under a less demanding standard than that established for regulation of the press." In support of this position, Chief Justice Rehnquist noted:

> Lawyers representing clients in pending cases are key participants in the criminal justice system, and the State may demand some adherence to the precepts of that system in regulating their speech as well as their conduct. As noted by Justice Brennan in his concurring opinion in *Nebraska Press*, "[a]s officers of the court, court personnel and attorneys have a fiduciary responsibility not to engage in public debate that will redound to the detriment of the accused or that will obstruct the fair administration of justice." Because lawyers have special access

to information through discovery and client communications, their extrajudicial statements pose a threat to the fairness of a pending proceeding since lawyers' statements are likely to be received as especially authoritative.

Chief Justice Rehnquist's opinion also concluded that the Model Rule 3.6 standard on potential prejudice, incorporated in Nevada Rule 177(1), fully satisfied that "less demanding" First Amendment restriction upon state regulation of lawyer speech. The opinion stated in this regard:

> We agree with the majority of the States that the "substantial likelihood of material prejudice" standard constitutes a constitutionally permissible balance between the First Amendment rights of attorneys in pending cases and the state's interest in fair trials. * * * The "substantial likelihood" test is designed to protect the integrity and fairness of a state's judicial system, and it imposes only narrow and necessary limitations on lawyers' speech. The limitations are aimed at two principal evils: (1) comments that are likely to influence the actual outcome of the trial, and (2) comments that are likely to prejudice the jury venire, even if an untainted panel can ultimately be found. Few, if any, interests under the Constitution are more fundamental than the right to a fair trial by "impartial" jurors, and an outcome affected by extra judicial statements would violate that fundamental right. Even if a fair trial can ultimately be ensured through *voir dire*, change of venue, or some other device, these measures entail serious costs to the system. * * * The State has a substantial interest in preventing officers of the court, such as lawyers, from imposing such costs on the judicial system and on the litigants.
>
> The [Rule 3.6] restraint on speech is narrowly tailored to achieve those objectives. The regulation of attorneys' speech is limited—it applies only to speech that is substantially likely to have a materially prejudicial effect; it is neutral as to points of view, applying equally to all attorneys participating in a pending case; and it merely post-

pones the attorney's comments until after the trial. While supported by the substantial state interest in preventing prejudice to an adjudicative proceeding by those who have a duty to protect its integrity, the rule is limited on its face to preventing only speech having a substantial likelihood of materially prejudicing that proceeding.

Though a Court majority in *Gentile* sustained the facial validity of paragraph (a) of Model Rule 3.6, a differently composed majority concluded that, as applied in the case before it, the safe-harbor provision of paragraph (c) was unconstitutionally vague. Justice Kennedy's opinion for the Court on this issue looked entirely to the safe-harbor provision that allows counsel to "state without elaboration, * * * the general nature of the claim or defense." Prior to holding the press conference, the petitioner in *Gentile* had studied Rule 177 and what he considered to be the applicable case law. Relying on both constitutional cases governing the seating of jurors exposed to pretrial publicity and the safe-harbor provision, he had concluded that a limited press conference would not violate Rule 177. At his press conference, while making the statements previously described, he also told reporters that there were certain areas he could not further explore "because ethics prohibits me from doing so." Justice Kennedy pointed to both petitioner's actions and the special concerns presented by a statute that used very general terms in regulating speech. His opinion concluded that "the right to explain the 'general' nature of the defense without 'elaboration' provides insufficient guidance because 'general' and 'elaboration' are both classic terms of degree, * * * [and] have no settled usage or tradition of interpretation in law." The "fact [that petitioner] *Gentile* was found in violation of the Rules after studying them and making a conscious effort at compliance demonstrates

that [the safe-harbor provision] creates a trap for the wary as well as the unwary."

The 1994 revision of Rule 3.6 sought to respond to the *Gentile* ruling on vagueness as well as the Court's division on the protection afforded by the First Amendment as applied. In this connection, the revision made three basic changes in Rule 3.6. First, to respond to *Gentile*'s overbreadth ruling, the revision of Rule 3.6 removed the words "without elaboration" and "general" from the safe harbor provision. As a result, the revised safe-harbor permission protects a lawyer who states "the claim, offense, or defense involved," rather than just the lawyer who states "without elaboration," the "general nature of the claim or defense." A second major change, responding to Justice Kennedy's discussion of the First Amendment issue in *Gentile*, added a new safe-harbor "right of reply." Paragraph (c) of the 1994 version of Rule 3.6 provides:

> Notwithstanding paragraph (a), a lawyer may make a statement that a reasonable lawyer would believe is required to protect a client from the substantial undue prejudicial effect of recent publicity not initiated by the lawyer or the lawyer's client. A statement made pursuant to this paragraph shall be limited to such information as is necessary to mitigate the recent adverse publicity.

A third major change in the revised Rule 3.6 moved from the text of the Rule to the commentary the list of presumptively prejudicial statements. This change apparently reflects concern that a presumptive list in the text might be viewed as detracting from and raising doubt about the safe-harbors insofar as they might overlap (e.g., a right-of-reply statement that refers to a confession). It also has been described as "reflecting the ABA's recognition that a categorical approach" to disciplinary prohibitions may impose a greater "chill" on lawyer speech than a "general standard."[3]

---

3. The 1994 amendment of Rule 3.6 was accompanied by an amendment of Rule 3.8, which has not been added by most of the states adopting the revised Rule 3.6. That amendment provides: "The prosecutor in a criminal case shall ... (g) except for statements that are necessary to inform the public of the nature and extent of the prosecutor's action and that serve a legitimate law enforcement

purpose, refrain from making extrajudicial comments that have a substantial likelihood of heightening public condemnation of the accused." This change was designed to work in conjunction with Rule 3.6 by reducing the need for defense counsel to turn to the new Rule 3.6 right-of-reply. While the Rule 3.8 limitation is not tied to the "substantial likelihood of material prejudice" standard,

Notwithstanding the revisions made in light of *Gentile*, state provisions duplicating the 1994 version of Model Rule 3.6 are hardly immune from a constitutional challenge based on the reasoning of *Gentile*. Still, those revisions do make that version of Model Rule 3.6 less susceptible to a successful challenge than the original version. Professional responsibility provisions based on the Disciplinary Rule 7–107 arguably face the strongest constitutional challenge because of its use of the "reasonable likelihood" standard.[4]

Many states retain the original Rule 3.6 with its safe-harbor provision, notwithstanding the *Gentile* ruling. The revised Rule 3.6 arguably reduces the ambiguity of that provision by eliminating the restriction of the safe-harbor to a description of the "general nature" of the claim or defense, and also dropping the additional restriction that the statement describe the safe-harbor content "without elaboration." However, even a safe-harbor provision allowing a statement setting forth "the claim, offense, or defense involved" (the standard of revised Rule 3.6) is not without ambiguity. In particular, the question arises as to whether that safe-harbor includes describing the evidence that explains the offense or defense (as was done by counsel in *Gentile*), especially since the commentary to the revised Rule 3.6 continues to list comments on the character of witnesses and their anticipated testimony as "more likely than not to have a material prejudicial effect." How the old and new safe-harbor provisions fare will depend upon the reading given to the *Gentile* ruling on vagueness.

Justice Kennedy's opinion in *Gentile*, which set forth the majority's opinion on vagueness, cited several factors as contributing to the Court's vagueness ruling. The opinion noted

that Nevada had offered no prior explication of the safe-harbor provision and the terms "general nature" and "without elaboration" had no "settled usage or tradition of interpretation." Arguably, a state standard that looked to the content of some analogous descriptions of offenses or defenses (e.g., in pleadings or jury charges) would fill that void. The *Gentile* opinion also cited the efforts of counsel to stay within the safe-harbor provision, including his rejection of reporter requests for further commentary as likely to violate the Nevada Rule. Arguably, a vagueness challenge would not be available to a lawyer who made absolutely no effort to fit his statement within a possible reading of a safe-harbor provision. For example, if the attorney went into far more detail than the *Gentile* statement, providing a witness-by-witness challenge to the government's case along the lines of a closing argument at trial, a court might well conclude that here the non-elaboration limit of the original Rule 3.6 safe-harbor provision surely had not operated as a "trap for the wary." Also, of obvious importance to Justice Kennedy was the application of the safe-harbor provision in the context of a defense attorney countering adverse publicity that had been initiated by the government. Arguably, the vagueness concerns would be less pressing where the statement in question was that of a prosecutor presenting the initial public explanation of the offense charged.

Assuming that a particular jurisdiction's provision on extrajudicial statements has a constitutionally acceptable basic prohibition and is not unconstitutionally vague, there remains the potential First Amendment challenge to its application in the particular case. In *Gentile*, the Court was evenly divided on that issue. In portions of those opinions not

---

the heightening of public condemnation would seem to almost invariably carry with it a substantial potential for causing such prejudice.

4. In upholding the "substantial likelihood" standard of Model Rule 3.6, Chief Justice Rehnquist opinion for the Court in *Gentile* took note of the use of the "reasonable likelihood" standard of Disciplinary Rule 7–107, describing it as "less protective of lawyer speech." The issue remains as to whether that less protective standard is sufficient under the First Amendment. The *Gentile* majority did accept the premise under which lower courts previously

had upheld the "reasonable likelihood standard"—that the First Amendment accepts regulation of the extrajudicial speech of lawyers under a standard "less demanding" than the clear and present danger standard. However, it did not go beyond the acceptance of the "substantial likelihood" standard. The four justices joining Justice Kennedy's opinion on the First Amendment issue quite clearly found the "reasonable likelihood" standard unacceptable.

joined by Justice O'Connor, the Kennedy opinion concluded that the record "reveal[ed] no basis for the Nevada Court's conclusion that the speech presented a substantial likelihood of material prejudice," and Chief Justice Rehnquist's opinion concluded that the finding below had enough support in the record so that it could not be deemed "mistaken."

The Kennedy opinion stressed that in this First Amendment area, the Supreme Court was called upon to make its own independent review of the record. It found various factors in the record that made unsupportable a "substantial likelihood" finding, if that term was to be given "any meaningful content." The Kennedy opinion noted that: (1) the press conference was held six months before the trial; (2) the community from which the venire would eventually be drawn exceeded 600,000 in population; (3) petitioner's statement lacked "any of the more obvious bases for a finding of prejudice" (such as mention of confessions); (4) petitioner held the press conference to respond to information that had been released in the press by the police and prosecutor (including repeated press reports that the police had "complete trust" in their undercover officers and that those officers had been officially cleared after passing lie detector tests); (5) petitioner had acted with the primary motivation of merely "counter[ing] publicity already deemed prejudicial"; and (6) when the case came to trial, the jury was empaneled with no apparent difficulty, all material information disseminated at petitioner's press conference was admitted in evidence, and the jury acquitted petitioner's client.

The Rehnquist opinion agreed that "we must review the record for ourselves," but also noted that "respectful attention" should be given to the findings below because the Nevada disciplinary board and the Nevada Supreme Court were "in a far better position than we are to appreciate the likely effect of petitioner's statements * * * in a highly publicized case like this." Petitioner's strongest points were "that the statement was made well in advance of trial, and that the statements did not in fact taint the jury panel," but the Nevada Supreme Court had responded ade-

quately to both. It had noted that the timing of the statement, "when public interest * * * was at its height," and the highly inflammatory portrayal of prospective government witnesses presented a substantial likelihood of prejudicing the prospective jury, even though that did not in fact happen. The Chief Justice noted that there was evidence pro and con on this point, and he found it "persuasive" that the petitioner, by his own admission, called the press conference "for the express purpose of influencing the venire." The Chief Justice rejected in this regard the suggestion of the Kennedy opinion that this purpose was irrelevant because the attorney was seeking to combat adverse publicity on the other side. Such an approach would place upon a court the difficult test of trying to distinguish between publicity that would influence by neutralizing and that which would create an affirmative bias. But "more fundamentally, it misconceives the constitutional test for an impartial juror," for a "juror who may have been initially swayed from open mindedness by publicity favorable to the prosecution is not rendered fit for service by being bombarded by publicity favorable to the defense." The proper defense remedies for adverse publicity are voir dire, change of venue, jury instructions, and "disciplining of the prosecutor, but not self-help in the form of similarly prejudicial comments by defense counsel."

The Kennedy and Rehnquist opinions reflect a series of disagreements not only as to the interpretation of the record in *Gentile*, but as to general approach in assessing whether the substantial likelihood test is met. One issue dividing the opinions is the weight to be given to a defense attorney's objective of responding to prejudicial publicity already before the public. That issue has largely been eliminated in the 1994 revision of Model Rule 3.6, which recognizes a safe-harbor right of reply as to statements a "reasonable lawyer would believe to be needed to protect the client from the substantial undue prejudicial effect of recent publicity." Since the vast majority of jurisdictions have not adopted the 1994 revision, however, the issue remains. Lower courts have treated attorney claims that they were responding to previous prejudicial publicity as raising the question of whether the prior publicity reduces the likelihood that the attorney's comments will have a prejudicial impact. One view is that the special role of participating counsel gives special weight and a unique quality to counsel's statements, especially where the statements are inflammatory. Another is that the attorney's comments will not meet the substantial likelihood standard where "a mere drop in the ocean of publicity surrounding the trial."

Another issue dividing the Supreme Court in *Gentile* was the weight that should be given to the ease with which a jury later was selected. The scope of this division, however, is limited. There was agreement that the "standard for controlling pretrial publicity must be judged at the time a statement is made." Also, the likelihood of prejudice at that point was not to be measured by the capacity of the criminal justice system to seat an untainted jury, but by the potential for making it more difficult to obtain such a jury. The state has a "substantial interest in preventing officers of the court from imposing such costs [as "extensive voir dire" and "a change of venue"] on the judicial system and on the litigants." Thus, the subsequent selection of an unbiased jury will strongly suggest a lack of the necessary likelihood of prejudice only where such costs were not a part of that jury selection process.

The issue of timing also divided the Court in *Gentile*. Justice Kennedy stressed that the lawyer's press conference was held six months before the scheduled trial. Chief Justice Rehnquist acknowledged the relevance of the remoteness of the trial, but also noted that the lower court could give weight to the fact that the "statements were timed to have a maximum impact, when public interest in the case was at its height." Lower courts have looked to both of those factors, and have readily found sufficient likelihood of prejudice where the content was likely to have an impact and the timing was tied to an event that heightened public interest even though the trial was

still a few months away. The timing is most likely to preclude a finding of the requisite likelihood of prejudice where the statement is made after the jury has been sequestered.

Lower courts have viewed the *Gentile* rulings as also governing, at least in part, the constitutionality of trial court orders (commonly called "gag" orders) directing the prosecutor and defense counsel not to speak to the media. Where the order takes the form of simply directing counsel to abide by the limitations of the jurisdiction's professional responsibility provision on extrajudicial statements, the constitutionality of imposing contempt or other sanctions for violation of that order is tested simply by reference to the *Gentile* rulings. Where, however, the order takes the form of directing counsel not to give any statements to the media concerning the case (or not to give statements concerning specified aspects of the case), and the challenge is presented by counsel rather than the media, courts view the order as imposing a prior restraint and therefore subject to special requirements derived from *Nebraska Press Association v. Stuart*[5] as well as the *Gentile* rulings. *Nebraska Press*, discussed in subsection (c) infra, involved gag orders imposed upon the press, arguably distinct from gag orders imposed upon participating lawyers, who were viewed in *Gentile* as subject to a special responsibility to ensure that their extrajudicial statements do not threaten the fair administration of justice. Nonetheless, lower courts have viewed *Nebraska Press* as equally applicable to prior restraints imposed upon counsel except insofar as it imposed a higher standard as to likely prejudicial impact ("clear and present danger") than did *Gentile*.

Courts applying a combination of *Gentile* and *Nebraska Press* insist upon three prerequisites for the issuance of a gag order directed at counsel: (1) potential statements to the media by counsel must present a "substantial likelihood"—or a reasonable likelihood if that lesser standard is acceptable under *Gentile*—of prejudicing the criminal trial; (2) the order must be "narrowly tailored" to proscribe only

5.   See note 8 infra.

those statements that present that potential; and (3) other, less restrictive alternatives (such as voir dire, jury instructions, jury sequestration, postponement of the trial, or change of venue) must be inadequate to prevent the threatened harm. In applying the first standard, courts recognize that anticipating the impact of statements not yet made necessarily involves "some 'speculation' and the weighing of 'factors unknown and unknowable.'" For that reason, the strongest cases appear to be those in which counsel previously have made statements that were widely publicized and dealt with matters likely to sway prospective or selected jurors. Closely related to the required showing is the requirement that the order be "no broader than necessary" to preserve trial by an impartial jury. Thus, an order that bars comment "on anything to do with this case" will invariably fail. Gag orders are most likely to be sustained if they refer to highly prejudicial specifics such as the list of items designated in the original version of Model Rule 3.6 as likely to have the prohibited potential impact.

The final requirement—that the trial court consider and find insufficient less restrictive alternatives—suggests a significant departure from the approach of *Gentile*. The Court there indicated that an attorney could be disciplined for statements presenting a substantial likelihood of imposing significant administrative costs on the court in ensuring the selection of an impartial jury. The attorney was not relieved of liability because the court could manage though such procedures as extensive voir dire and change of venue to obtain an untainted jury. The prohibiting of a gag order if such procedures can respond successfully to a prejudicial impact places the total focus here on ensuring that the jury is untainted rather than avoiding the imposition of significant administrative costs. Some courts, however, have taken those other costs into consideration in evaluating the effectiveness of alternatives. Thus, in responding to defense counsel's claim that the alternative of sequestration precluded extending a gag order past the point of jury selection, one court noted that sequestration was not an acceptable alternative in what promised to be a long trial because of the "negative effects of sequestration." In general, courts appear more willing to find that alternatives are not adequate in considering gag orders imposed upon counsel than gag orders imposed upon the press.

In *United States v. Ford*,[6] the Sixth Circuit held that a gag order placed on a defendant had to be supported by a finding of likely prejudice based on the "clear and present danger" standard. The court acknowledged that "permitting an indicted defendant like Ford to defend himself publicly may result in overall publicity that is somewhat more favorable to the defendant than would occur when all participants are silenced," but concluded that insofar as that produced a disadvantage for the government, the "government must tolerate it" as an incidental cost of the defendant's First Amendment right "to repl[y] to the charges and the associated adverse publicity." Admittedly, in *Sheppard*, the Supreme Court had stated that the trial court there "might well have proscribed extrajudicial statements by any lawyer, party, witness, or court official which divulged prejudicial matter." However, "[n]o restraint on the defendant's speech was [actually] at issue in that case," and in the subsequent ruling in *Nebraska Press*, the Supreme Court had insisted upon a showing of a clear and present danger. The Sixth Circuit concluded that "no legitimate reasons [exist] for a lower threshold standard for individuals, including defendants, seeking to express themselves outside of court than for the press." As the ABA standards had noted, "'once parties and witnesses in a criminal case are outside the courtroom they have the full prerogatives of any private citizen to question, criticize, or condemn the system even though they may be swept up on its processes at the time.'" Neither defendants nor witnesses are court personnel or officers of the court. In contrast to *Ford*, the Fourth Circuit has held applicable to a gag order directed against witnesses the same standards that apply to gag orders di-

6. 830 F.2d 596 (6th Cir.1987).

rected at counsel.[7] The Fourth Circuit noted that *Nebraska Press*, in discussing alternatives to gagging the press, had quoted with added emphasis the *Sheppard* statement that "[n]either prosecutors, counsel for defense, the accused, witnesses, court staff nor enforcement officers under the jurisdiction of the court should be permitted to frustrate its function."

(c) Restricting the Media. The teaching of *Nebraska Press Association v. Stuart*[8] is that a prohibition upon the media publishing information which might be prejudicial to a criminal defendant will seldom, if ever, be a permissible means for preventing prejudicial publicity from occurring. At issue in that case were orders entered prior to the trial of a mass murder, which barred the publication of "any testimony given or evidence adduced" in court and which also barred the reporting of any confessions or incriminating statements made by the defendant to the police or to anyone else other than the press or of other facts "strongly implicative" of the defendant. The Supreme Court (per Burger, C.J.) first and unequivocally concluded that the bar on reporting what happened "at the open preliminary hearing * * * plainly violated settled principles," namely, that "once a public hearing had been held, what transpired there could not be subject to prior restraint."

As for the prohibition upon publication of information from other sources, the Chief Justice concluded that the state had not met the heavy burden imposed as a condition to securing a prior restraint. Noting a "common thread" running through the prior cases, "that prior restraints on speech and publication are the most serious and the least tolerable infringement on First Amendment rights," the Chief Justice proceeded to examine the facts of the case to determine whether the danger was great enough to justify such an invasion of free speech. "To do so," he noted, requires examination of "the evidence before the trial judge when the order was entered to determine (a) the nature and extent of pretrial news coverage; (b) whether other measures would be likely to mitigate the effects of unre-

strained pretrial publicity; (c) how effectively a restraining order would operate to prevent the threatened danger."

With respect to the first of these, it was noted that the trial judge "found only 'a clear and present danger that pretrial publicity could impinge upon the defendant's right to a fair trial,'" and that his "conclusion as to the impact of such publicity on prospective jurors was of necessity speculative, dealing as he was with factors unknown and unknowable." As to the second, the Court observed that the record did not reflect careful consideration of "the alternatives to prior restraint discussed with obvious approval in *Sheppard v. Maxwell*," that is, change of venue, continuance, voir dire, and admonitions to the jurors. These must be so ineffective that "12 [jurors] could not be found who would, under proper instructions, fulfill their sworn duty to render a just verdict exclusively on the evidence presented in open court." And as to the third point, it was noted that the trial took place in a very small community where "it is reasonable to assume" that rumors "could well be more damaging than reasonably accurate news accounts."

Although the Chief Justice declined to "rule out the possibility of showing the kind of threat to fair trial rights that would possess the requisite degree of certainty to justify" a prior restraint of the press, the other opinions in the case suggested that this possibility was a highly unlikely one. Justice White expressed "grave doubt" that a prior restraint "would ever be justifiable," while Justice Powell emphasized the "unique burden" resting on one who would justify a prior restraint. Three other justices, in an opinion by Justice Brennan, concluded that a prior restraint simply "is a constitutionally impermissible method for enforcing" the right to a fair trial. Justice Stevens agreed with that conclusion as to "information in the public domain," and indicated he might reach the same conclusion in other circumstances as well.

---

7. In re Russell, 726 F.2d 1007 (4th Cir.1984).

8. 427 U.S. 539, 96 S.Ct. 2791, 49 L.Ed.2d 683 (1976).

As for reporting that recounts public proceedings, further support for prohibiting all prior restraints is found in the Supreme Court's rejection of a prior restraint in a somewhat related context in *Oklahoma Publishing Co. v. District Court*.[9] The Court there held that the First Amendment freedom of the press was violated by a pretrial order enjoining publication of the name or picture of a minor charged with juvenile delinquency, where without objection "members of the press were in fact present at the hearing with the full knowledge of the presiding judge, the prosecutor, and the defense counsel."

Nebraska Press characterized a prior restraint as involving "an immediate and irreversible sanction," in contrast to a "criminal penalty or a judgment in a defamation case [which] is subject to the whole panoply of protections afforded by deferring the impact of the judgment until all avenues of appellate review have been exhausted." This might suggest that it would be constitutionally permissible for a state to adopt criminal statutes prohibiting certain identifiable prejudicial reporting, such as reporting a defendant's prior criminal record or his confession not yet ruled admissible. But other rulings of the Court indicate that criminal sanctions are not permissible except to "further a state interest of the highest order" which cannot be adequately protected by less stringent measures. Indeed the two key rulings holding unconstitutional criminal prosecutions involved the publication of information normally deemed confidential.

In *Smith v. Daily Mail Pub. Co.*,[10] the Court struck down a state statute making it a misdemeanor for a newspaper to publish, without written order of the juvenile court, the name of any youth charged as a juvenile offender. It reasoned that "a penal sanction for publishing lawfully obtained truthful information requires the highest form of state interest to sustain its validity," and such an interest could not be found in the state's desire to preserve the anonymity of juvenile defendants standing alone. The information published had been lawfully obtained through the newspaper's investigative efforts, so "no issue * * * [was presented] of unlawful press access to confidential judicial proceedings." The Court had previously held that the state's interest in preserving juvenile anonymity must give way to a defendant's Sixth Amendment right to confrontation (where defendant sought to impeach a critical witness by reference to a juvenile record that the defense had obtained), and the First Amendment right of the press was equally strong.

In *Landmark Communications, Inc. v. Virginia*[11] the Court held unconstitutional a state criminal statute prohibiting divulgence of information regarding proceedings before a state judicial tenure commission in the statute's application to a newspaper that lawfully acquired such information. The Court recognized that premature disclosure could endanger a judge's reputation, but noted that this legitimate interest in confidentially could otherwise be protected. Numerous other states had similar confidentiality provisions that were implemented by internal procedures and sanctions imposed upon participants who violated obligations of secrecy rather than by criminal sanction imposed upon a nonparticipant who published such information. The Court's emphasis upon the alternative of imposing sanctions upon leaking participants would appear to doom as well criminal prohibitions aimed at other interests, including avoiding the tainting of jurors, and preserving an ongoing investigation.

(d) Closed Proceedings: First Amendment Right of Access. With the Supreme Court having rejected efforts to restrain the press from reporting on an open hearing, attention naturally turned to the possibility of excluding the press and public from a hearing (or a portion of a hearing) as a means of precluding the pretrial exposure of the public to prejudicial information presented at that hearing. The constitutionality of thus closing pretrial proceedings would depend upon whether there is a press/public constitutional

9.   430 U.S. 308, 97 S.Ct. 1045, 51 L.Ed.2d 355 (1977).
10.   443 U.S. 97, 99 S.Ct. 2667, 61 L.Ed.2d 399 (1979).

11.   435 U.S. 829, 98 S.Ct. 1535, 56 L.Ed.2d 1 (1978).

right of access to such proceedings and, if so, whether a weighing of that right against the defendant's right of a fair trial would permit closure under some circumstances.

As for the contention that a constitutional right of access is to be derived from the Sixth Amendment "public trial" provision, it was rejected by the Court in *Gannett Co. v. De-Pasquale*.[12] The Court there concluded that the history of the Sixth Amendment "totally fails to demonstrate that the Framers intended to create a constitutional right in strangers to attend a pretrial proceeding * * *. In conspicuous contrast with some of the early state constitutions that provided for a public right to open civil and criminal trials, the Sixth Amendment confers the right to public trial only upon a defendant and only in a criminal case."

Although the Supreme Court in *Gannett* found it unnecessary to decide whether there existed a First Amendment right of access to criminal proceedings, that issue was addressed shortly thereafter in *Richmond Newspapers v. Virginia*,[13] a case involving the closing of a trial. Although there was no opinion of the Court in that case, seven Justices recognized that a press/public right of access is embodied in the First Amendment and is applicable to the states through the Fourteenth Amendment. As a majority later explained in *Globe Newspaper Co. v. Superior Court*,[14] the First Amendment is

> broad enough to encompass those rights that, while not unambiguously enumerated in the very terms of the Amendment, are nonetheless necessary to the enjoyment of other First Amendment rights. * * * Underlying the First Amendment right of access to criminal trials is the common understanding that "a major purpose of that Amendment was to protect the free discussion of governmental affairs" * * *. [T]o the extent that the First Amendment embraces a right of access to criminal trials, it is to ensure that

this constitutionally protected "discussion of governmental affairs" is an informed one. The Court in *Globe Newspaper* added that there were two features of the criminal justice system which "together serve to explain why a right of access to criminal trials in particular is properly afforded protection by the First Amendment": (1) such trials have historically been open to the press and public; and (2) the right of access plays a particularly significant role in the functioning of the judicial process, for public access not only enhances "the quality and safeguards the integrity of the factfinding process, with benefits to both the defendant and to society as a whole," but also "fosters an appearance of fairness, thereby heightening public respect for the judicial process."

Richmond Newspapers and *Globe Newspaper* both recognized that the First Amendment right of access was not an absolute right, but rather a "qualified" or "presumptive" right. Closure of the proceeding was possible under a sufficient showing of a compelling need. Moreover, the protection of the defendant's interest in obtaining a fair trial could be such a need, at least theoretically. Thus, the impact of recognizing a First Amendment right of access was to take away the trial court's authority to close the proceeding as a matter of discretion, and to substitute rigorous procedural and substantive prerequisites, which narrowly confined closure, as discussed in subsection(e).

While *Richmond Newspapers* and *Globe Newspaper* firmly established a First Amendment right of access to the trial itself, there remained the question of whether such a right also applied to pretrial hearings. In *Press-Enterprise I*,[15] the Court suggested that possibility in holding that the First Amendment right was applicable to the *voir dire* examination. The Court's opinion there stressed the two factors cited in *Globe*—an historical tradition of openness and the functional value of openness for the particular proceeding—rather than any characterization of the jury selection

12. 443 U.S. 368, 99 S.Ct. 2898, 61 L.Ed.2d 608 (1979).

13. 448 U.S. 555, 100 S.Ct. 2814, 65 L.Ed.2d 973 (1980).

14. 457 U.S. 596, 102 S.Ct. 2613, 73 L.Ed.2d 248 (1982).

15. Press-Enterprise v. Superior Court, 464 U.S. 501, 104 S.Ct. 819, 78 L.Ed.2d 629 (1984).

process as a part of the trial itself. In *Press–Enterprise II*,[16] the Court again relied upon those two factors, but this time held that a public right of access extended to a proceeding that clearly was not part of the trial—the preliminary hearing.

Turning to whether there existed as to preliminary hearings a "tradition of accessibility" (which would imply the "favorable judgment of experience"), the *Press–Enterprise II* Court adopted a focus quite different from that suggested in *Gannett*. In discussing the possibility of a Sixth Amendment right of the public to attend a suppression hearing, the *Gannett* majority had concluded that "there exists no persuasive evidence that at common law members of the public had any right to attend pretrial proceedings; indeed there is substantial evidence to the contrary." The *Press–Enterprise II* opinion looked more to the common practice (which was to have open preliminary hearings) than to the existence of some specifically recognized legal right of access. The Court acknowledged that the code which dominated when the preliminary hearing came into prominence in the mid–1800s (the Field Code of New York) allowed the preliminary hearing to be closed on motion of the accused, but it discounted the significance of that provision. Even in the several states that still retained the Field Code provision, the Court noted, preliminary hearings are "presumptively open to the public and are closed only for cause shown." As for the functional value of openness, its advantages in this trial-type proceeding were much the same as in the trial itself. Admittedly, the preliminary hearing, unlike a trial, cannot result in a conviction; but with so many cases being resolved without a trial, the preliminary hearing would often be the most significant stage at which the public could observe the criminal justice process.

Press–Enterprise II firmly established a two part inquiry for determining whether a particular proceeding is one to which the First Amendment right of access applies. The proceeding is to be tested by reference to "experience" and "logic." The experience prong asks "whether the place and process have historically been open to the press and the general public." The logic inquiry asks "whether public access plays a significant positive role in the functioning of the particular process in question."

The *Press–Enterprise II* experience and logic standard obviously would render constitutionally open various pretrial proceedings besides the preliminary hearing at issue there. The Court made clear, however, that one pretrial proceeding would not meet that test—the grand jury hearing. In contrasting the preliminary hearing, the Court noted that the grand jury hearing has a long history of secrecy. Also, though the dissenters in *Press–Enterprise II* argued that much of the Court's functional analysis would apply as readily to the grand jury, the traditional secrecy of grand jury proceedings has been viewed as serving the grand jury's screening and investigatory functions.[17] This distinguished the preliminary hearing, which had been closed on occasion not to serve its functional objectives, but to protect the accused's right to a fair trial.

In *El Vocero de Puerto Rico v. Puerto Rico*,[18] the Supreme Court clarified one possible ambiguity in the application of the "experience" prong of the *Press–Enterprise II* standard. The Court there held that, in assessing the historical record for a "tradition of accessibility," a court "does not look to the particular experience of any one jurisdiction, but instead 'to the experience in that type or kind of hearing throughout the United States.'" Divisions re-

---

16. Press-Enterprise Co. v. Superior Court, 478 U.S. 1, 106 S.Ct. 2735, 92 L.Ed.2d 1 (1986).

17. Lower courts have concluded that the same considerations also exempt ancillary judicial hearings on grand jury proceedings (e.g., challenges to grand jury subpoenas and grand jury witness immunity hearings). Indeed, courts have extended this "exception" to proceedings that otherwise would be open but happen to reveal information about what occurred before a grand jury. Thus, an attorney disqualification hearing has been held not to be within

the First Amendment right of access when the hearing was "permeated with information that the government had previously indicated * * * [was] grand jury information." Courts here point to a long history of conducting in camera both proceedings ancillary to the grand jury process and other pretrial proceedings that also might reveal previously undisclosed information about what has occurred or is about to occur before the grand jury.

18. 508 U.S. 147, 113 S.Ct. 2004, 124 L.Ed.2d 60 (1993).

main, however, in lower court interpretations of other aspects of the "experience" prong. In *Richmond Newspapers*, *Press–Enterprise I*, and *Press–Enterprise II*, the Court pointed to traditions of openness that were clearly established and at least a century old. Some courts view such an historical tradition, showing "clarity, generality and duration," as an absolute prerequisite for meeting the "experience" standard, at least to procedures which are not recent innovations. Other courts find no need for such a clearly established, lengthy tradition, even as to longstanding procedures, where they can point to a shift in the significance of the particular procedure. In dealing with pretrial procedures, for example, they note "the relative importance of pretrial procedure to that of trial has grown immensely in the last two hundred years" and stress that the "First Amendment must be interpreted in the context of current values and conditions." In essence, unless there is a well established tradition of exclusion of the public that remains part of the "modern trend," as in the case of the grand jury, such a court will recognize a First Amendment right of access based solely on the application of the "logic" portion of the *Press–Enterprise II* standard.

In applying the "logic" prong of *Press–Enterprise II*, lower courts look to various functional enhancements that public access would contribute to the particular procedure. Opening a judicial proceeding, it is noted, can serve one or more of the following six "societal interests": "[1] promotion of informed discussion of governmental affairs by providing the public with the more complete understanding of the judicial system; [2] promotion of the public perception of fairness which can be achieved only by permitting full public view of the proceedings; [3] providing a significant community therapeutic value as an outlet for community concern, hostility and emotion; [4] serving as a check on corrupt practices by exposing the judicial process to public scrutiny; [5] enhancement of the performance of all involved; and [6] discouragement of perjury." Virtually every procedure in the criminal justice process that impacts upon decisionmaking would be enhanced by contributing to one or

more of these societal interests. Thus, the "logic" issue becomes whether the unique function of the proceeding in question inherently creates a special need for denying public access, thereby rejecting the enhancements of openness.

Lower courts have held that the *Press–Enterprise II* standards extend the First Amendment right of access to a wide range of pretrial, mid-trial, and post-trial proceedings. These include: suppression hearings, bail hearings, entrapment hearings, change of venue hearings, competency hearings, hearings on the disqualification or withdrawal of counsel, judicial recusal hearings, plea hearings, and hearings on a motion to reduce a sentence. A post-trial hearing on allegations of juror misconduct has been placed in the same category, but a mid-trial inquiry has been held not to meet the *Press–Enterprise II* standard because it has a special function inconsistent with public access—minimizing the risk that the inquiry will "destroy the effectiveness of the [sitting] jury as a deliberative body."

Concurring in *Richmond Newspapers*, Justice Brennan noted that:

> The presumption of public trials is, of course, not at all incompatible with reasonable restrictions imposed upon courtroom behavior in the interests of decorum. * * * Thus, when engaging in interchanges at the bench, the trial judge is not required to allow public or press intrusion upon the huddle. Nor does this opinion intimate that judges are restricted in their ability to conduct conferences in chambers, inasmuch as such conferences are distinct from trial proceedings.

Relying upon that statement, lower courts consistently have held that they do not violate any right of First Amendment access when they allow presentations to be made in chambers or in sidebar conferences for appropriate administrative purposes (e.g., to ensure that the jury does not overhear the discussion), even though the press and public is thereby excluded. However, there is less certainty as to whether an administratively justified use of the sidebar or in-chambers conference renders inapplicable a First Amendment right of access in its entirety or only as to contemporaneous presence. The media representatives commonly argue that the First Amendment operates to require disclosure of the transcripts of sidebar or in-chambers conferences "contemporaneously or at the earliest practicable times," absent a judicial finding of a need to seal such transcripts under the rigorous First Amendment standards of *Press–Enterprise II*. Some courts have suggested that such a claim has merit as to "sidebar or chambers conferences in criminal cases at which evidentiary or other substantive rulings have been made." Other courts have suggested, to the contrary, that where a sidebar or in-chambers conference falls within the traditional use of such conferences, even though it produces an evidentiary ruling, that tradition negates not only a First Amendment right to presence at the conference, but also a First Amendment right of access to the transcript of the proceeding. Still others suggest that is at least the case where: (1) the conference related to a document commonly not made public (e.g., a presentence report); (2) the conference involved a matter that did not materialize as relevant to the case; or (3) the in-chambers proceeding involved a showing traditionally made ex parte, so as to avoid disclosure to the opposing party.

Numerous courts have held that the "experience and logic" test of *Press–Enterprise II* also determines whether a First Amendment right exists as to transcripts, documents, and other items relating to criminal proceedings which are within the possession or control of the court. That test most readily establishes a First Amendment right as to materials "submitted in connection with judicial proceedings that themselves implicate the right of access." Thus courts have held that a First Amendment right of access extends not only to documents introduced at trial, but to documents submitted in connection with a variety of motions and at a variety of pretrial hearings. Sometimes, however, a distinction is drawn between the right of access to the proceeding and to the document. Thus, the presentence report, although relied upon in a sentencing proceeding that is open, has a history of confidentiality and a function that refutes access to

the document itself when its contents are not revealed at the hearing. Similarly, the historic tradition of temporarily sealing the indictment of a person not yet apprehended where there was a fear of flight may operate to delay the starting point for the First Amendment right of access to indictments until the accused is apprehended.

Various courts have limited the First Amendment right of access to those documents which contributed to determinations made by the court or jury. Thus, pretrial discovery is said to involve an exchange between the parties, with no First Amendment right of access created unless the items exchanged in discovery are introduced at trial. Courts also have stated that the right of access does not extend to documents or exhibits that were never before the court because they were ruled inadmissible. Thus, where documents are submitted ex parte as part of a disclosure dispute, and the court holds that they need not be revealed at trial, the right of access does not apply because the documents are excluded from the case and public disclosure would reveal to the other side what the ex parte proceeding was designed to prevent. However, courts have divided on the status of court records relating to jurors (e.g., names and questionnaires) that were not introduced in the proceedings.

Courts also have divided over whether a First Amendment right of access applies to search warrants and search warrant affidavits when not introduced before the trial court in a suppression hearing. One view is that "a search warrant is an integral part of a criminal prosecution" and therefore is subject to a First Amendment right of access once executed. The other view is that the experience and logic standards of *Press–Enterprise II*—assuming their applicability to a proceeding that is separate from the criminal prosecution—simply do not justify a First Amendment right of access to warrants and affidavits not introduced in court. Support here is found in the historical tradition of treating search warrant issuance as an "extension of the criminal investigation itself," with the information disclosed to the magistrate "entitled to the same confidentiality accorded other aspects of the investigation" and magistrates being "highly deferential" to government requests to continue secrecy as needed by the objectives of the investigation.

In several of the cases finding no First Amendment right of access to search warrant materials, the court did find that those materials were subject to a common law right of access. A common law right of access also has been recognized as to other documents that might not be protected by a First Amendment right of access. The common law of access is based upon *Nixon v. Warner Communications, Inc.,*[19] where the Supreme Court took note of a common law right "to inspect and copy public records and documents, including judicial records and documents." The Court viewed that right as "flexible," being subject to limitation in the sound discretion of the trial court, which was to be informed by a "sensitive appreciation of the circumstances that led to [the] * * * production [of the particular document in question]." While lower courts have described this common law right as creating "a strong presumption in favor of public access to materials submitted in evidence in open court," they also have said that it does not apply to judicial documents traditionally treated as confidential and placed under seal. In addition, the courts describe the common law right as less protective of public access than the First Amendment right of access. While both require a balancing of interests, the First Amendment standard imposes a higher barrier to denying access and requires any such ruling to be more tightly tailored to the prevailing interest.

(e) Closing Proceedings and Placing Documents Under Seal: Restricting the First Amendment Right. A proceeding may be closed and a document sealed even though subject to a First Amendment right of access. As the Court declared in *Globe Newspaper Co. v. Superior Court,*[20] the right of access "is not absolute." The Court cautioned, however, that the circumstances under which the First Amendment right can be withheld "are limited"; "it must be shown that the denial is necessitated by a compelling governmental interest, and is narrowly tailored to serve that interest."

Globe Newspaper, while not involving a competing fair trial interest, illustrates the two ways in which the necessary showing—a compelling interest and a narrowly tailored restriction—can be lacking. At issue there was a statute requiring judges at rape and other sex offense trials involving an alleged victim under 18 to exclude the press and general public during the testimony of that victim. As for the state's asserted interest in encouraging minor victims of sex crimes to come forward and provide accurate information, the Court concluded there was no showing whatsoever that closure would further that interest. The state interest was not compelling because the relationship between the closure and the interest was tenuous at best. As for the interest in protecting minor victims of sex crimes from further trauma and embarrassment, the Court found it to be "a compelling one," which would allow a trial judge to "determine on a case-by-case basis whether closure is necessary to protect the welfare of a minor victim." However, that did not justify the mandatory closure necessitated by the challenged statute, which obviously was not narrowly tailored to the compelling interest.

Another illustration of the need to narrowly tailor any closure to meet an offsetting privacy interest is provided by *Press–Enterprise I.*[21] The Court there acknowledged that a prospective juror's privacy interests regarding personal matters inquired into on voir dire could outweigh public trial interests, but concluded that the court below had erred in not considering alternatives to closure and, in any event, in closing virtually all of a six week voir dire. The proper procedure, as outlined in *Press–Enterprise I*, would have been for the trial judge to inform prospective jurors of their opportunity to raise with the judge in camera

---

19. 435 U.S. 589, 98 S.Ct. 1306, 55 L.Ed.2d 570 (1978).

20. 457 U.S. 596, 102 S.Ct. 2613, 73 L.Ed.2d 248 (1982).

21. See note 15 supra.

(but on the record and with counsel present) concerns about embarrassing questions, after which the judge would decide if "there is in fact a valid basis for a belief that disclosure infringes a significant interest in privacy." If such a finding was made, then the judge could either excuse that juror or order limited closure.

"Compelling governmental interests" recognized by the Supreme Court include the juror privacy interests recognized in the Supreme Court's rulings in *Press–Enterprise I*, and the preservation of the defendant's right to a fair trial, by precluding publicity that might taint a prospective or sitting jury, recognized in *Gannett Co. v. DePasquale*[22] and *Press–Enterprise II*.[23] Lower court rulings have added several other interests that arguably could justify closure orders as to pretrial proceedings or papers filed in connection with those proceedings. These include: (1) privacy interests of both defendants and "innocent third parties," as recognized in Title III provisions authorizing sealing of wiretaps and related documents; (2) the chilling effect that disclosure of pretrial motion papers may have on the filing of such motions; (3) the privacy interests of victims, defendants or other persons (e.g., unindicted coconspirators); (4) the need to preserve the integrity of an ongoing investigation; and (5) danger to persons (e.g., informants) or property.

Where the closure is justified as protective of the accused's right to a fair trial, and is narrowly tailored to serve that interest, just how likely must it be that the publicity resulting from an open proceeding will prejudice that right? Some suggested that the Court should apply here the same clear and present danger standard held applicable to attempts to restrain reporting by the media. Others saw in *Gannett* implicit approval of the standard used by the lower court in that case: whether "an open proceeding would pose a reasonable probability of prejudice to those defendants." In *Press–Enterprise II*, the Supreme Court

adopted a standard that fell between the above alternatives. Rejecting the "reasonable likelihood" standard imposed by the lower courts there, the *Press–Enterprise II* majority set forth the following standard:

> If the interest asserted is the right of the accused to a fair trial, the preliminary hearing shall be closed only if specific findings are made that first, there is a substantial probability that the defendant's right to a fair trial will be prejudiced by publicity that closure would prevent and second, reasonable alternatives to closure cannot adequately protect the defendant's free trial rights.

Although this standard was stated in the context of the preliminary hearing, it has been viewed as the appropriate standard for "fair-trial" closures of all parts of the criminal process to which the First Amendment Right of access applies.

In determining whether the requisite substantial probability exists as to tainting a prospective jury, the trial court must consider a variety of factors, including: the particular content of the information to be disclosed and the likelihood that it would influence prospective jurors; the likelihood of media coverage; and the portion of the population within the judicial district which will be exposed to the adverse publicity. Should the court find a substantial probability that the information in question will prejudice a significant portion of the jury pool, it then must consider whether "there is a substantial probability that closure will prevent that prejudice." If the information in question is already in the public domain, the closing of the proceeding may do as much to redirect media attention to the information as opening the proceeding. Even if an open proceeding will add new prejudicial information, that information may have little impact as compared to the prejudicial information already in the public domain.

Perhaps the most critical aspect of the *Press–Enterprise II* standard is the weighing of alternatives. In *Press–Enterprise II*, the Court

---

22. See note 12 supra. *Gannett* involved a Sixth Amendment challenge, and though the Court held that the Sixth Amendment did not give the press a right of access,

it took note of defendant's interest in avoiding a tainted jury as a justification for closure.

23. See note 16 supra.

said very little about how this should be done, except to note that the lower court should have taken into account the possibility that "*voir dire*, cumbersome as it is in some circumstances," would permit a trial court to identify and exclude any prospective jurors who might have become biased upon learning of prejudicial information disclosed in an open preliminary hearing. The Court did not indicate whether it meant to impose a consideration of alternatives akin to that adopted in *Nebraska Press*,[24] where alternatives were said to prevail over a gag order unless so ineffective that they could not produce an untainted group of 12 jurors. Unlike *Nebraska Press*, there was no reference here to the change of venue alternative, with its high costs for the defendant.

Also relevant is the absence of any suggestion of a *Nebraska Press* type standard in the earlier closure case of *Richmond Newspapers v. Virginia*.[25] *Richmond Newspapers* made specific mention of "sequestration of the jurors" as an alternative, and it might have been thought that, in light of that alternative, closing the trial would never be necessary to avoid the risk of jurors learning through outside sources of something that occurred in the courtroom while they were excused. Yet *Richmond Newspapers* did not set forth any such absolute prohibition against closure, and lower courts accordingly have held that the trial judge need not inevitably opt for sequestration. Accepting this conclusion, it would follow that a judge should have even more leeway in rejecting voir dire as an alternative remedy where highly prejudicial publicity is almost certain to flow from an open pretrial hearing. Not only is the voir dire as to prospective jurors a less effective remedy than sequestration as to sitting jurors, but it may also produce a side effect of a less representative jury when the voir dire can be expected to result in the exclusion of a substantial portion of the array.

A common theme running throughout the Court's discussions of potential justifications for closure is the need for a careful consideration of the facts of the particular case. A closure order, to be upheld, must be supported by specific findings both as to the compelling interest served and the alternatives considered and found deficient to serve that interest. Findings are important not only to ensure that the trial court looked at all the relevant elements, but also to assist the appellate court which will review de novo the validity of the closure order.

The requirement that the closure order be narrowly tailored to the accused's fair trial interest typically imposes two mandates—that the closure be appropriately limited in scope and that the transcript of the closed proceeding be available to the media and public promptly after those fair trial needs have been met. In meeting the first requirement, the court must consider whether part of the proceeding can be kept open without disclosing the information that could prejudice potential jurors. Thus, in a suppression hearing, it might be possible to have an open proceeding as to the grounding for conducting the challenged wiretap without reference to the content or character of the conversations recorded. As for timing, release of the transcript of the closed proceeding after the prosecution is terminated by trial, plea, or dismissal is almost invariably required if the only compelling interest was defendant's fair trial right. In *Gannett*,[26] the trial court released the suppression hearing transcript shortly after the defendants pleaded guilty, and that action was cited as essential to meeting the trial court's First Amendment obligations. The Court noted in this regard that "public confidence cannot long be maintained where important judicial decisions are made behind closed doors and then simply announced in conclusive terms without ever revealing their factual basis to the public." Under some circumstances, release of the transcript of closed proceedings may be required even before the prosecution is terminated. Thus, when a closed suppression hearing results in a decision not to exclude the evidence in question, the compelling interest

---

24. See the text following note 8 supra.

25. See note 13 supra.

26. See note 12 supra.

for closure should be reevaluated in light of the fact that the evidence will eventually become known to jurors. In such a case, once the jury has been selected, an even stronger case can be made for disclosure of the transcript without awaiting the end of the trial.

The *Gannett* majority stressed that before the suppression hearing there had been closed, the petitioning newspaper had been given "an opportunity to be heard." The four dissenters in *Gannett* noted in this regard:

> This opportunity need not take the form of an evidentiary hearing; it need not encompass extended legal argument that results in delay; and the public need not be given prior notice that a closure order will be considered at a given time and place. But where a member of the public contemporaneously objects, the court should provide a reasonable opportunity to that person to state his objection.

Similarly, Justice Powell stated that "this opportunity extends no farther than the persons actually present at the time the motion for closure is made, for the alternative would require substantial delays in trial and pretrial proceedings while notice was given to the public."

Lower courts typically have imposed procedural requirements that go beyond *Gannett*, recognizing that the media and public have a First Amendment interest in access even though they do not happen to be present when the motion for closure is made (often the case since such motions may be made in-chambers). They have held that closure motions must be docketed sufficiently in advance of any hearing on the closure motion to afford interested members of the public an opportunity to intervene and present their views to the court. None have suggested that the court must wave a red flag and attract media attention to a previously unnoticed case by informing the local press of the possibility of closure.

§ 23.2 Overcoming Prejudicial Publicity

(a) Change of Venue on a Defense Motion. Where prejudicial publicity has already occurred, or if it seems likely that such publicity cannot be effectively prevented by the procedures discussed in § 23.1, a trial court will turn to the procedures available for ensuring that the defendant receives a fair trial, notwithstanding that publicity. One possibility is a change of venue—that is, a removal of the case to another judicial district, which hopefully is beyond the reach of the publicity. Indeed, it is constitutionally impermissible to make this remedy totally unavailable. In *Groppi v. Wisconsin*,[1] striking down a law barring changes of venue in misdemeanor cases, the Court ruled that "under the Constitution a defendant must be given an opportunity to show that a change of venue is required in his case." The statutory and rule provisions governing "fair trial" venue changes on a defense motion are discussed in § 16.3(b). This section considers the application of those provisions to cases involving significant publicity, adverse to the defendant, published prior to the selection of the jury. The "fair trial" grounding for a change of venue in such cases is that the publicity has so tainted prospective jurors that an unbiased jury may not be obtainable in the district of prosecution. Whether this grounding prevails is not determined solely by the standards prescribed in the venue-change statute or court rule. The federal constitution may also play a significant role.

The seminal Supreme Court ruling on the constitutionally required change of venue is *Rideau v. Louisiana*.[2] There, two months prior to trial, a local TV station broadcast three different times a 20–minute film of defendant admitting in detail the commission of the various offenses with which he was charged. The parish had a population of about 150,000 and the estimated audiences for these broadcasts were 24,000, 53,000 and 29,000, respectively. Defendant's change of venue motion was de-

---

§ 23.2

1. 400 U.S. 505, 91 S.Ct. 490, 27 L.Ed.2d 571 (1971). See also § 16.3(b).

2. 373 U.S. 723, 83 S.Ct. 1417, 10 L.Ed.2d 663 (1963).

nied, and he was convicted and sentenced to death. The Supreme Court held

> That it was a denial of due process of law to refuse the request for a change of venue, after the people of [the] Parish had been exposed repeatedly and in depth to the spectacle of *Rideau* personally confessing in detail to the crimes with which he was later to be charged. For anyone who has ever watched television the conclusion cannot be avoided that this spectacle, to the tens of thousands of people who saw and heard it, in a very real sense was *Rideau's* trial—at which he pleaded guilty to murder. Any subsequent court proceedings in a community so pervasively exposed to such a spectacle could be but a hollow formality.

In *Rideau*, the record indicated that three members of the jury had seen the TV broadcast, and had been seated after testifying on voir dire, that they "could lay aside any opinion, give the defendant the presumption of innocence as provided by law, base their decision solely upon the evidence, and apply the law as given by the court." But the Supreme Court declared that it did "not hesitate to hold, without pausing to examine a particularized transcript of the voir dire examination of the members of the jury, that due process of law in this case required a trial before a jury drawn from a community of people who had not seen and heard Rideau's 'interview.'" This language and that quoted above, if taken literally, would seem to mean that the defendant would likewise prevail even if all of the seated jurors had stated on voir dire that they had neither seen nor heard about the television interview. It is not entirely clear what the theoretical basis of such a decision would be. One might be that reversal is necessary as a sanction against the police for permitting one in their custody to be unnecessarily put on display before others in circumstances very likely to be prejudicial, but the Court in analogous contexts has declined to adopt similar prophylactic sanctions.[3] Also, there was no statement in the *Rideau* opinion suggesting that the Court viewed its ruling as creating a

prophylactic sanction. Another possibility is that such pervasive publicity requires a reversal because it would necessitate the excusal of so many prospective jurors as to run afoul of the cross-section requirement, but this does not square with the cross-section requirement having been treated by the Court as applying to drawing the panel from which the jury is selected and not to selecting the jury itself.[4]

The best reading of *Rideau* is that the Court there recognized that prejudicial publicity may be so inflammatory and so pervasive that the voir dire simply cannot be trusted to fully reveal the likely prejudice among prospective jurors. As a result, a change of venue will be constitutionally mandated even though the voir dire of the seated jurors does not contain sufficient signs of the jurors having been influenced to establish an "inference of actual prejudice" under the due process standards of *Irvin v. Dowd* and its progeny (discussed in subsection (f) infra). Publicity may so affect the community that individual jurors will not be able to openly acknowledge the community pressures placed upon them. Those pressures may lead them to answer with less than full candor voir dire questions concerning their familiarity with the case, but perhaps even more significantly, may impose upon them, notwithstanding their best intentions, "a sense of obligation to reach a result which will find general acceptance in the [community]." Indeed, those pressures open the possibility of reaching even that juror who truly had never previously heard of the case. Accordingly, the *Irvin v. Dowd* standard, though it does not automatically accept juror claims of impartiality, and is quite likely to identify partiality in seated jurors acknowledging awareness of the adverse publicity, is not deemed sufficient. *Rideau* establishes that certain cases are so exceptional that the risk of error under the *Irvin v. Dowd* standard is too high, and a change of venue must be granted without regard to what voir dire might reveal.

Rideau itself presented a most compelling fact situation for concluding that there was no

3. See § 2.9(e).

4. See note 26 of § 22.2(d).

need to look to the voir dire to conclude that an impartial jury almost certainly could not have been produced without a change of venue. That fact situation included the following: the information conveyed was as inflammatory and prejudicial as might be conceived—what the Court characterized as the equivalent of a guilty plea combined with a detailed description of the crimes involved; the medium of a 20–minute television program, with the defendant himself speaking in camera, was the most likely to make a lasting impression on all who saw it; there was a saturation of the community, with such a large portion of the populace viewing the film (even taking account of possible repeat viewers) that those who did not view it were almost certain to have heard about it; and the nature of the case (involving robbery, kidnapping, and murder) and the size of the community obviously made the trial an event of major importance.

Looking to the special features of the *Rideau* case, lower courts have characterized the "presumptive prejudice" standard of *Rideau* as "rarely applicable," reserved for "extreme situations," and setting a "high threshold" for the defendant to overcome. They note that it requires massive publicity and "bitter prejudice," reflecting such a pervasive and inexpressible "hostile attitude" as to render unreliable the usual safeguards for ensuring fairness in the selection and decisionmaking of jurors.[5]

In determining whether a case is appropriate for presuming prejudice, the lower courts have looked to the following factors: "(1) the nature of pretrial publicity and the particular degree to which it has circulated in the community, (2) the connection of government officials with the release of publicity, (3) the length of time between the dissemination of the publicity and the trial, (4) the severity and notoriety of the offense, (5) the area from which the jury is to be drawn, (6) other events

occurring in the community which affect or reflect the attitude of the community or individual jurors toward the defendant, and (7) any other factor likely to affect the candor or veracity of the prospective jurors on voir dire." In evaluating these factors on appellate and habeas review, state and federal courts have found only a sprinkling of cases where a refusal to grant a change of venue violated the *Rideau* standard. *Rideau* has been held not to reach even the most highly publicized cases that are covered step-by-step and scoop-by-scoop in evening newscasts and front page stories. One possible explanation for the hesitancy of state courts to extend *Rideau* much beyond it's extreme facts is the limited value of a venue change in many of the smaller states. If publicity is held to be of such a nature as to require a presumption of prejudice, a court in a small state simply may have nowhere to move the case, as the same level of publicity often is found throughout the state.

In determining whether a statutory venue-change provision requires a venue change in a pretrial publicity case, state and federal courts look to many of the same factors as are considered in applying the presumed prejudice standard of *Rideau*. However, here appellate courts commonly also view as relevant "the extent of difficulty in actually selecting an impartial jury at voir dire." Consideration is given to such indicia of difficulties as the percentage of prospective jurors dismissed for cause and whether the defense exhausted all of its peremptory challenges. In light of the relevance of such factors, trial judges are encouraged to first attempt to select a jury, although they need not do so if that seems futile.

Not surprisingly, the standard practice of trial judges on both federal and state courts is to postpone ruling on a change of venue, even where defendant claims that the presumed prejudice standard of *Rideau* is applicable, un-

---

5. In Sheppard v. Maxwell (discussed at note 1 of § 23.1), in describing judicial authority to respond to massive pretrial publicity, the Supreme Court stated that the trial court should either continue the case until the publicity abates or change venue where "there is a reasonable likelihood" that prejudicial news prior to trial will prevent a fair trial. As discussed in § 16.3(b), many state statutes and court rules require a much higher likelihood

of being unable to provide a fair jury before a change of venue is required. In light of the narrow constitutional command of *Rideau,* these standards have been viewed as not posing any significant constitutional difficulties, and *Sheppard*'s reference to a "reasonable likelihood" has been treated as merely descriptive of the authority existing in some jurisdictions.

til after an attempt to seat an impartial jury is made. Moreover, once jury selection is started, there is a tendency to pursue it through as many potential jurors as is deemed necessary to seat a jury believed to be immune from a successful constitutional challenge under the *Irvin v. Dowd* standard of actual prejudice. This may be due to the inconvenience associated with the change to another location, the concern that the citizens of the community should not be lightly treated as incapable of giving the defendant a fair trial, and the feeling that the community most directly concerned with the crime should be the place of the trial. Moreover, on an appeal following a conviction, a reviewing court is likely to be quite deferential to the trial judge's decision not to order a change of venue, provided the jury selection process passes muster under the standard of *Irvin v. Dowd*. Apart from *Rideau* claims, appellate courts review denials of a change of venue under an "abuse of discretion" standard of review, and findings of such an abuse are relatively rare.

(b) Change of Venue Without a Defense Motion. The defense will not invariably seek a change of venue in challenging prejudicial publicity. Indeed, in some instances the defense will insist upon other responses and firmly oppose a change of venue. Must the trial judge accept that position? The answer may depend on the alternative procedure sought by the defendant and the content of state venue provisions. Where, for example, the defense refuses a change of venue and insists upon a lengthy continuance as the only remedy it finds satisfactory, the trial court may appropriately question the true purpose of the demand for a continuance, particularly if the defendant is free on bail. Recognizing the societal interest in a speedy trial, the court may insist that, even where a case might conceivably fit within the "presumed prejudice" concept of *Rideau*, the trial should go forward in the district of prosecution if a jury that meets the *Irvin v. Dowd* standards can be selected. The defendant, by opposing the change of venue, has cast doubt upon the allegation of community prejudice and thereby allowed the court to focus upon whether the trial court can find the

prospective jurors to be impartial consistent with *Irvin*.

Where the defendant opposes a venue change, but insists only upon an exhaustive *voir dire* to select an impartial jury, the issue becomes more complex. The trial court should certainly attempt to respect the defendant's choice, but what if the court, after exhausting several jury panels without completing the selection process, concludes that caution and convenience require a change of venue? In that situation, courts will first seek to determine whether state provision on the transfer of venue authorizes the court to order a transfer *sua sponte* and over the objection of the defense. As discussed in § 16.3(f), transfer provisions in roughly a dozen states grant the judge such authority and several other states recognize a judge's inherent authority to grant a change of venue where a fair trial cannot be obtained in the district designated by the venue provision. In some of these jurisdictions, that authority is available only after an unsuccessful attempt has been made to select an impartial jury, and even where not required, courts often follow that route where the defense has urged staying in the venue. Assuming that a state statute or the trial court's inherent power allows the court to order a venue change sua sponte, the question then presented is whether such a change, when opposed by the defense, violates a constitutional right of the defendant. That issue also is discussed in § 16.3(f).

(c) Change of Venire. A small group of states provide by statute for a "fair trial" change of venire. Under this procedure, the trial remains in the judicial district of original venue, but the jury is selected from another judicial district. The change of venire is viewed as an alternative to the change of venue and is available under the same standard—a determination that a "fair and impartial jury cannot be impaneled" in the district of venue. In some jurisdictions, choice of this alternative requires an additional determination that it is more economical than a change of venue (a concern arising from the need to pay the travel and housing costs of the impartial jury, which is usually sequestered). Aside from that requirement, the choice between a change of venire and change of venue ordinarily lies in the discretion of the trial court. Of course, one factor to be considered is whether the local district presents a "charged atmosphere" likely to impact the fairness of trial even with a jury selected from another district.

(d) Continuance. Doubtless there are a number of cases in which the granting of a continuance is not the solution to prejudicial pretrial publicity, as where the publicity has aroused antagonism so intense that there is no reason to suppose that it would subside by any delay which would not put off the trial indefinitely. But a continuance is a useful technique when this hostility can be expected to fade within a reasonable time, as where the problem has arisen because of some event or disclosure occurring on the eve of the time set for trial. Another kind of situation is that noted by the Court in *Sheppard v. Maxwell*,[6] where the trial began two weeks before a hotly contested election at which both the judge and chief prosecutor were candidates for judgeships. The Court noted that "a short continuance would have alleviated any problem with regard to the judicial elections."

Continuances are "infrequently allowed on the grounds of prejudicial publicity, and generally only when there are extraordinary circumstances." Here, as with change of venue motions, judges are inclined to adopt a wait-and-see attitude by reserving the ruling on the continuance request until after some effort is made to select a jury. They recognize that, even if the defendant is willing to waive his right to a speedy trial, there is also a societal interest in a prompt trial. Whether the presumed prejudice doctrine of *Rideau* should be carried over to the continuance is an unresolved issue. Arguably the type of prejudicial publicity that is so inflammatory and so pervasive as to preclude reliance on voir dire is not the type that could be cured by a continuance. On postconviction review, courts stress the discretion of the trial court and focus on whether an unbiased jury was seated.

(e) Severance. In a multidefendant trial, publicity about one particular defendant might prove detrimental to other defendants joined with him for trial. By analogy to those decisions permitting a severance when the disparity in the weight of evidence against one or more defendants is such that it would tend to prejudice the defense of another defendant involved in a relatively unimportant part of the case, it would appear that the granting of a severance would be an appropriate remedy under such circumstances. However trial courts often will not grant a severance until after assessing the influence of the publicity on voir dire, and appellate courts will not grant a reversal for failure to grant a severance unless the voir dire established an "inference of actual prejudice" as to the jurors actually seated.

(f) Jury Selection. Yet another way to overcome the prejudicial impact of pretrial publicity is by a voir dire that identifies those prospective jurors influenced by the publicity and a challenge procedure that eliminates all persons in that group who actually have been biased by the publicity. The theory here is that the voir dire examination of prospective jurors will reveal which of them have actually been exposed to the pretrial publicity and what effect that exposure has had upon them. If the voir dire reveals that a prospective juror is biased, then that juror may be challenged for cause. Even if the voir dire does not establish bias to the satisfaction of the judge, the defense counsel who nonetheless believes that the pretrial publicity might have affected the prospective juror can still eliminate that juror if the defense has remaining peremptory challenges. Primary reliance is placed on the voir dire and the challenge for cause, but the peremptory challenge serves as a safety net.

As noted above, where courts refuse to adopt measures designed to avoid prejudicial publicity (e.g., closing proceedings) or to shift the venue or venire, they commonly assume that the combination of voir dire and challenges will provide an effective remedy. That assumption rests, in large part, on the assumed effectiveness of voir dire in uncovering prejudice among potential jurors, but there is reason to question whether voir dire always has that

6.   See note 5 supra.

capacity. Thus, the ABA, in its commentary to the second edition of the Criminal Justice Standards on Fair Trial and Free Press, cited three "distinct but interrelated factors" that called for "caution" in trusting voir dire to screen effectively for bias: "(1) inadequate understanding of the way pretrial publicity influences the thought process of prospective jurors; (2) the tendency among a significant number of prospective jurors to underplay the importance of exposure to prejudicial publicity and to exaggerate their ability to be impartial; and (3) persistent concern about the ability of attorneys and trial judges to discern bias, particularly at the subconscious level, even when the prospective juror is being completely candid."

The ABA Standards seek to make voir dire more effective, in part, by avoiding the risk that counsel, in questioning the prospective jurors as a group, may "contaminate" jurors previously unaware of the publicity. The Standards therefore mandate the separate examination of each prospective juror outside of the presence of the others where the case presents "a substantial possibility that individual jurors will be ineligible to serve because of exposure to potentially prejudicial material." Though that procedure has been adopted in some jurisdictions, many others give the trial judge broad discretion to insist upon group voir dire. So too, many jurisdictions give the trial court broad discretion in limiting the length and depth of the voir dire as it relates to pretrial publicity. In *Mu'Min v. Virginia*,[7] the Supreme Court considered the bearing of the Constitution on granting such discretion to the trial judge. The end result was a 5–4 decision, with the majority's ruling apparently limited to the special circumstances presented there.

In *Mu'Min*, 16 out of 26 prospective jurors (including 8 of the actual panel) answered affirmatively when asked if they had acquired any information about the case from the news media or any other source. The defense had asked that each of the prospective jurors be questioned out of the presence of the other jurors and be asked to respond to 64 proposed

questions, but the trial court concluded that it was satisfactory to question the prospective jurors in groups of four and to put to them only some of the proposed questions. The judge did ask the prospective jurors whether any information acquired from outside sources would affect their impartiality and whether they had formed an opinion in the case. None of the persons eventually seated were among those who stated that they had an opinion or were no longer impartial or who otherwise indicated possible prejudice in their answers. The defense contended that this was not constitutionally sufficient because the judge had refused to ask of those jurors who had acquired outside information additional questions concerning the content of what they had learned.

Writing for the majority in *Mu'Min*, Chief Justice Rehnquist acknowledged a content inquiry might well "be helpful in assessing whether a jury is impartial." The issue before the Court, however, was whether the failure to conduct such an inquiry "must render the defendant's trial fundamentally unfair." Traditionally, trial judges had been given "great latitude" in voir dire questioning, and while some jurisdictions had restricted that discretion by requiring content-based questions as to pretrial publicity, others had not. One difficulty posed by such questions is that they basically required the questioning of each prospective juror in isolation so that others will not be exposed to content that had not previously come to their attention. In any event, the Chief Justice noted, whether or not the judge decides to put content questions to potential jurors, the ultimate issue remains the same—whether there is a sufficient basis for the judge's assessment that the juror is credible in stating that he or she has not formed an opinion and would be impartial. In making that assessment, the judge would have to evaluate the "depth and extent of news stories that might influence a juror," and where that publicity engendered a "wave of public passion," as in *Irvin v. Dowd*,[8] it "might well * * * requir[e] more extensive examination of

7. 500 U.S. 415, 111 S.Ct. 1899, 114 L.Ed.2d 493 (1991).

8. See note 13 infra.

potential jurors than under[taken] here."
However, the publicity in this case, though
"substantial," was "not of the same kind and
extent as that found to exist in *Irvin*." In such
a case, a judge could constitutionally make a
finding of juror impartiality in light of the
responses given, without further questioning.

In her separate concurring opinion in
Mu'Min, Justice O'Connor, who supplied the
critical fifth vote for affirmance, further developed the significance of the content of the
adverse publicity and the responses of the jurors actually seated. While it was true that the
trial judge "did not know precisely what each
juror had read," he was aware "of the full
range of the information that had been reported." With this information in mind, and with
each juror having indicated that no opinion
had been formed, the trial judge could not be
said to have violated the Sixth Amendment in
accepting the jurors' assurances of impartiality. Justice O'Connor, as did Chief Justice
Rehnquist, found support for this conclusion
in *Patton v. Yount*.[9] The Court there had
drawn a distinction between two types of issues presented in prejudicial publicity cases.
One was the basically legal question as to
whether the adverse publicity had reached a
point where a presumption of prejudice required the trial court to reject assurances of
impartiality by jurors exposed to that publicity. Where that presumption was not applicable, the trial judge's determination as to credibility was basically a factual judgment, and
such credibility determinations were "entitled
to 'special deference,'" allowing for reversal
"only for 'manifest error.'" That was the kind
of determination that was presented in this
case, and while a content inquiry would have
been helpful in making such an assessment,
the judge's determination cannot be viewed as
manifest error because he decided "to evaluate
a juror's credibility instead by reference to the
full range of potentially prejudicial information that had been reported."

Post–*Mu'Min* lower court rulings suggest
that a trial court's refusal to provide an indi-

vidualized voir dire will only present a significant constitutional issue where the defense
can point to a particularized harm (e.g., a
comment by a potential juror that contaminat-
ed the entire panel) or the seating of jurors
who were familiar with the pretrial publicity
and did not readily and unequivocally state
that they could and would set it aside. Courts
have expressed greater concern that the questioning be sufficiently probing to judge the
influence of the publicity. While content questions are not a constitutional prerequisite, the
court should at least explore whether the jurors had heard about the case and whether
that exposure had influenced the juror in his
or her view of the case.

In light of the various weaknesses of voir
dire in uncovering possible juror prejudice, it
might be thought that, as a matter of caution,
the defense should be allowed to exclude automatically all jurors who have any prior information about the case. But that quite obviously is not feasible. As the Supreme Court noted
more than a century ago in *Reynolds v. United
States*:[10] "In these days of newspaper enterprise and universal education, every case of
public interest is almost, as a matter of necessity, brought to the attention of all the intelligent people in the vicinity, and scarcely any
one can be found among those best fitted for
jurors who has not read or heard of it, and
who has not some impression or some opinion
in respect to its merits." This position does
not preclude, however, distinguishing between
cases on the basis of the nature of the publicity, and finding certain types of publicity so
inherently prejudicial as to exclude any juror
familiar with that publicity. In *Marshall v.
United States*,[11] the Supreme Court appeared
to adopt such a position, but not as a constitutional standard.

The *Marshall* Court held that a federal district judge had erred in allowing the trial to
continue even though some of the sitting jurors had read newspaper articles citing defendant's two prior felony convictions and other
background information of a type that the

9. See note 16 infra.
10. 98 U.S. (8 Otto) 145, 25 L.Ed. 244 (1878).
11. 360 U.S. 310, 79 S.Ct. 1171, 3 L.Ed.2d 1250 (1959).

district judge had refused to allow in evidence because of its prejudicial character. Although the district judge had questioned the jurors and had been convinced of their credibility in assuring him that they would not be influenced by the news articles, the Court found that unsatisfactory. Relying on its supervisory power over federal court practice, the Court reversed defendant's conviction. The *per curiam* opinion accepted the proposition that "persons who have learned from news sources of a defendant's prior record are presumed to be prejudiced." However, in *Murphy v. Florida*,[12] the Court later rejected the defendant's reliance upon *Marshall* in a state case. It pointed out that a different standard applied where reversal was allowed only for a constitutional violation rather than on the Court's exercise of its supervisory authority over federal courts.

Irvin v. Dowd,[13] decided in 1961, sets forth the basic constitutional framework for determining whether the jury selection process was inadequate to combat the prejudicial impact of adverse pretrial publicity and thereby deprived the defendant of his constitutional right to an impartial tribunal. The Court noted initially that, consistent with the position taken in federal cases dating back to *Reynolds*, the quest for juror impartiality under the Constitution certainly did not require the automatic exclusion of all prospective jurors who were aware of adverse pretrial publicity. Indeed, it also did not necessarily require the exclusion of persons who had a "preconceived notion" based on that publicity, although at that point, the Constitution did require a careful examination of the totality of the circumstances. Justice Clark's opinion for a unanimous Court reasoned:

> "The theory of the law is that a juror who has formed an opinion cannot be impartial." * * * [But] to hold that the mere existence of any preconceived notion as to the guilt or innocence of an accused, without more, is sufficient to rebut the presumption of a prospective juror's impartiality would be to establish an impossible

standard. It is sufficient if the juror can lay aside his impression or opinion and render a verdict based on the evidence presented in court. * * * The adoption of such a rule, however, "cannot foreclose inquiry as to whether, in a given case, the application of that rule works a deprivation of * * * due process." [T]he test is "whether the nature and strength of the opinion formed are such as in law necessarily * * * raise the presumption of partiality."

The issue thus posed under *Irvin* is whether the adverse pretrial publicity and the circumstances surrounding its dissemination created "such a presumption of prejudice * * * that the jurors' claims that they can be impartial should not be believed." That issue, the *Irvin* Court noted, was not simply one of historical fact, but of "mixed law and fact." The answer therefore could not lie entirely in the trial judge's acceptance of the truthfulness of a juror's response that, notwithstanding the publicity and any preconceived notions, he or she could render an impartial verdict. As Chief Justice Hughes had earlier noted, "impartiality" is not a "technical conception" but a "mental attitude of appropriate indifference," and for its ascertainment, "the Constitution lays no particular tests and procedure is not chained to any ancient and artificial formula." On the other hand, the finding of impartiality by the trial judge who witnessed the jurors on *voir dire* was not to be lightly set aside; the circumstances should make "manifest" the inability of the jurors, notwithstanding their claims of impartiality, to decide the case solely upon the evidence presented at trial.

The *Irvin* Court found before it a case in which the circumstances clearly required it to impose a presumption of partiality and override the trial court's finding of jury impartiality. The media reports, described by the Court as a "barrage of newspaper headlines, articles, cartoons and pictures," had contained prejudicial and inflammatory information, including defendant's confession to six homicides, his past criminal record, and his alleged willing-

---

12. See note 15 infra.

13. 366 U.S. 717, 81 S.Ct. 1639, 6 L.Ed.2d 751 (1961).

ness to enter a guilty plea in return for a life sentence. These reports had been widely disseminated, creating a "pattern of deep and bitter prejudice" in the community. As a result, over half of the 430 venire members were excused on challenges for cause because they admitted to fixed opinions, almost 90% of those examined on the point entertained some opinion as to defendant's guilt, and eight of the twelve jurors seated had said they thought defendant was guilty. Though those jurors also said they could put aside that opinion and judge the case impartially, "where so many, so many times, admitted prejudice, such a statement of impartiality * * * [could] be given little weight." The Court concluded that "with his life at stake, it is not requiring too much that petitioner be tried in an atmosphere undisturbed by so huge a wave of public passion and by a jury other than one in which two-thirds of the members admit, before hearing any testimony, to possessing a belief in his guilt."

Irvin did not find constitutional error in the failure to grant a change of venue, but in the seating of the particular jury. Its analysis came to be described as focusing on "actual prejudice," rather than the presumed prejudice which required a change of venue in *Rideau*.[14] To succeed under an actual prejudice analysis, the defendant must "show that * * * the selection process permitted an inference of actual prejudice." That was done in *Irvin*, but not in two later cases *Murphy v. Florida* and *Patton v. Yount*. In both of these cases, the Court distinguished *Irvin* and held that the selection process did not present circumstances that would warrant presuming partiality and thereby overriding the trial judge's assessment that the seated jury was impartial.

The Court in *Murphy*[15] found insufficient the defendant's notoriety (due to previous, highly publicized criminal activities) and the fact that 20 of 78 persons questioned were excused because they indicated an opinion as to his guilt. The Court noted that the news articles about defendant's prior crimes had

appeared seven months before jury selection and were "largely factual in nature." The voir dire, moreover, evidenced no hostility towards petitioner by the jurors who were seated. There was only one "colorable claim of partiality" relating to one juror's concession that his prior impression of the defendant would "dispose him to convict." Moreover, the Court could not attach "great significance to this statement * * * in light of the leading nature of counsel's questions and the juror's other testimony indicating that he had no deep impression of petitioner at all."

Patton v. Yount[16] appeared to come closer to *Irvin* than *Murphy*. It presented, like *Irvin*, a notorious murder case tried in a small community. Here too, the reports had made reference to damaging inadmissible information, including a prior conviction for the same crime, a prior confession, and a prior plea of temporary insanity. Also, the percentage of persons in the jury panel who acknowledged having some opinion was high (77%) and eight of the fourteen seated jurors (including two alternates) admitted that at some time they had formed an opinion as to guilt. The Court noted, however, that the "extensive adverse publicity and the community sense of outrage" were "at their height" prior to defendant's first trial. The jury selection at the second trial, which was all that was before it, came four years later, at a time when "prejudicial publicity was greatly diminished and community sentiment had softened." While "a number of jurors and veniremen" had made reference to opinions earlier held, "for many, time had weakened or eliminated any conviction they had had." In the end, it could not be said that the trial judge was manifestly incorrect in concluding that the jury was impartial.

Although the Court stressed in *Murphy* and *Patton* that each case rested on the totality of its circumstances, the primary factors that appeared to distinguish *Murphy* and *Patton* from *Irvin* were: (1) the strength of the *voir dire* responses of the jurors with reference to their previously developed opinions, (2) the nature

14.   See note 1 supra.

15.   Murphy v. Florida, 421 U.S. 794, 95 S.Ct. 2031, 44 L.Ed.2d 589 (1975).

16.   467 U.S. 1025, 104 S.Ct. 2885, 81 L.Ed.2d 847 (1984).

of the pretrial publicity, and (3) the time elapsed between the height of the publicity and the trial. As for the first factor, the Court has indicated that the responses of both the jurors actually seated and all prospective jurors examined are relevant. The responses of those not seated casts light on the credibility of the seated jurors who were familiar with the same publicity. However, *Patton* strongly indicates that the responses of the total venire, even if it includes a substantial portion who must be excluded because of preconceptions they cannot readily lay aside, will not be as significant as responses of seated jurors which strongly substantiate their impartiality. *Patton* noted that 126 of 163 veniremen there "admitted they would carry an opinion into the jury box" ("a higher percentage than in *Irvin*"), but it concluded that the extensive voir dire and challenges "resulted in selecting [as jurors] those who had forgotten or would need to be persuaded again." It added that "the relevant question is not whether the community remembered the case, but whether the jurors at Yount's trial had such fixed opinions that they could not judge impartially the guilt of the defendant."

With respect to the character of the publicity, *Murphy* noted the need to "distinguish * * * largely factual publicity from that which is invidious or inflammatory" and *Patton* arguably drew a similar distinction in characterizing certain articles "as merely report[ing] events without editorial comment." As for timing, *Patton* emphasized that the publicity in *Irvin* had been intensive for a period of 6–7 months leading up to the trial, while the most extensive publicity in the case before it had ended four years earlier with the termination of the defendant's first trial.

(g) Admonishment or Sequestration of the Jury. Even if by a process of careful jury selection it has been possible to nullify the effects of prejudicial pretrial publicity, there remains the risk of prejudicial publicity during the trial. Once the trial is under way, the media may report initially or again report prejudicial information about the defendant, such as his prior record or evidence of guilt not admissible at trial, or may report prejudicial

events that occurred at trial while the jury has been excused. One way to try to deal with this is by an admonition to the jury, such as the following (proposed by the ABA standards):

During the time you serve on this jury, there may appear in the newspapers or on radio or television reports concerning this case, and you may be tempted to read, listen to, or watch them. Please do not do so. Due process of law requires that the evidence to be considered by you in reaching your verdict meet certain standards; for example, a witness may testify about events personally seen or heard but not about matters told to the witness by others. Also, witnesses must be sworn to tell the truth and must be subject to cross examination. News reports about the case are not subject to these standards, and if you read, listen to, or watch these reports, you may be exposed to information which unduly favors one side and to which the other side is unable to respond. In fairness to both sides, therefore, it is essential that you comply with this instruction.

There persists considerable difference of opinion about the effectiveness of this instruction. The concern, of course, is that such an admonition may actually whet the jurors' appetites to discover via the media information about the case which they feel is being kept from them. There is no doubt but that the instruction is not inevitably effective, as is shown by those cases in which the admonition was disregarded by some of the jurors. This being the case, it might be thought that sequestration of the jury during the trial and until a verdict is reached or the jury is discharged, so as to prevent the jurors from having access to the media during that time, is the solution.

Sequestration would appear to be an effective way of preventing the jury from being influenced by the notoriety of the case, except insofar as community sentiment is reflected in the atmosphere in the courtroom. But it is a safeguard with considerable costs, including the expense to the state, the inconvenience to the jurors, the restriction of the panel to jurors who can be separated from family responsibilities, and the possible pressure to "rush to judgment" once deliberations begin. Moreover, even if the trial judge sequestering a jury is careful not to inform the jurors which party requested the sequestration, there is the possibility that the sequestration might produce resentment by the jury which would ultimately work to the disadvantage of one of the parties in the case. Thus, while the Supreme Court in *Sheppard* cited sequestration as one remedy which must be considered by the trial judge, it is not a solution inevitably so superior to others that it must be selected by the judge. In particular, sequestration need not always be selected even over closure of a portion of the trial.

Absent a showing of actual prejudice (i.e., a juror subsequently being tainted by adverse publicity), denial of a defense motion to sequester the jury does not raise due process difficulties. State law may require sequestration in capital cases on a defense motion, but generally sequestration lies in the discretion of the trial court. Appellate reversals on an abuse of discretion standard are rare. Indeed, some courts have stated that reversal requires a showing of juror taint.

(h) Excusal of Jurors. Finally, if there is reason to believe material published during the trial might have reached the jury, the trial judge may be required to inquire of the jurors concerning their possible exposure to that material. The critical issue here is whether there is a "serious question" of possible prejudice, taking account of the "nature of the news material" and the "probability of that material having reached the jury." Where the media coverage is prominent and the jury is not sequestered, some questioning may be required even though there is no specific evidence that a juror was exposed to that coverage. With more specific evidence, as in *Marshall*, an individual voir dire may be required. Arguably, a juror who is already sitting on the jury may be more reluctant to acknowledge possible bias and thereby necessitate a mistrial. This is particularly true where the juror violated the trial judge's admonition not to read, listen to, or watch media coverage of the case.

§ 23.3　Conduct of the Trial

(a) Newsmen in the Courtroom. As we have seen, there is "embodied in the First Amendment, and applied to states through the Fourteenth Amendment," a right in the press "of access to criminal trials," and only rarely may that access be denied. But it does not follow that the trial judge lacks authority to impose restraints upon conduct of newsmen while they are in and near the courtroom. The press can serve its function without disruptive behavior. Thus, the failure of the judge to take steps to restrict such behavior may, under some circumstances, deprive the defendant of his due process right to a fair trial.

The problem is well illustrated by the case of *Sheppard v. Maxwell*,[1] involving a murder trial which was subjected to massive media coverage from the very outset. During the entire nine weeks of trial, the courtroom was crowded to capacity with representatives of the news media, and their movements in and out of the courtroom "often caused so much confusion that, despite the loud speaker system installed in the courtroom, it was difficult for the witnesses and counsel to be heard." Reporters were seated inside the bar, which "made confidential talk among Sheppard and his counsel almost impossible during the proceedings." During recesses, pictures were taken in the courtroom, and newsmen even handled and photographed trial exhibits laying on the counsel table. The corridors were crowded with photographers and TV cameramen, who took pictures of the defendant, counsel, witnesses and jurors as they entered and left the courtroom. Broadcasting facilities were set up in a room adjacent to the jury room.

Viewing the "totality of circumstances in this case," including the above recited events and exposure of the jurors to prejudicial information not admitted into evidence, the Supreme Court concluded that the defendant had been denied a fair trial. The Court emphasized that the trial judge had failed to take many

1.　384 U.S. 333, 86 S.Ct. 1507, 16 L.Ed.2d 600 (1966).

steps which could have ensured courtroom decorum. The trial court "should have adopted strict rules governing" the use of the courtroom by the newsman. Indeed, the "number of reporters in the courtroom itself could have been limited at the first sign that their presence would disrupt the trial." The failure to take such steps had produced a "carnival atmosphere."

Though many lower court cases have considered claims under *Sheppard*, "very few cases have actually presumed prejudiced due to a carnival or circus atmosphere at trial." While the activities outside the courtroom may be marked by a "Roman circus" atmosphere in many high profile cases, courts can readily control what happens in the courtroom and can take precautions to ensure that the jurors are not exposed to the commotion in the corridors and on the courthouse steps.

(b) Electronic and Photographic Coverage. A small group of states first authorized the televising of trials in the 1950s and 1960s. The number increased dramatically after the National Conference of State Chief Justices approved a resolution in 1978 to promulgate standards permitting electronic coverage in state courts. Currently, a substantial majority of the states authorize the televising of trial court proceedings. However a significant number of those states bar the televising of criminal cases where the defendant objects. Thus, only roughly half of the states authorize televising of trials even where the defendant objects, and those states all leave the final decision to the discretion of the trial judge. Ordinarily that discretion allows the trial court judge to reject televising for a variety of reasons (e.g., defendant's due process rights, scheduling, avoiding distractions), and it need not show that those reasons are "compelling" or otherwise fit within a "good cause" requirement. Courts have regularly held that the First Amendment right of access does not include a right to use cameras within the courtroom. Where camera coverage is authorized, state law requires that it be utilized

under closely controlled circumstances designed to avoid physical disruptions.

The televising of criminal trials has been before the Supreme Court on two occasions. In the first case, *Estes v. Texas*,[2] pretrial hearings were televised and were seen by some of the persons selected as jurors, and much of the trial was also televised. In a 5–4 decision, the Court reversed the conviction on the ground that the "procedure employed by the State involves such a probability that prejudice will result that deemed inherently lacking in due process." The Court added that "there are numerous situations in which it might cause actual unfairness—some so subtle as to defy detection by the accused or control by the judge," and then proceeded to enumerate some reasons why televising a trial could cause unfairness: (1) it could have an impact upon the jurors by distracting them and making the case appear a cause celebre; (2) it could have an impact upon witnesses and decrease the quality of testimony received; (3) it could have an impact upon the judge by adding to his responsibilities and by subjecting him to greater political pressure; and (4) it could have an impact upon the defendant because it would be distracting to him and might reduce the effectiveness of his attorney's representation.

It was unclear, at best, whether *Estes* announced a constitutional rule barring still photographic, radio and television coverage in all cases and under all circumstances, for the fifth vote of the majority was by Justice Harlan, who in a separate opinion concluded only that televised trials were banned "in cases like this one." The Court's subsequent references to *Estes* arguably indicated that it was not viewed as having announced a per se rule, and the Supreme Court so held in *Chandler v. Florida*.[3] *Chandler* upheld a regulated state practice that allowed electronic media and still photography coverage of public criminal proceedings over the objection of the accused. The unanimous Court emphasized that "no one has been able to present empirical data sufficient to establish that the mere presence of the broadcast media inherently has an adverse impact

---

2. 381 U.S. 532, 85 S.Ct. 1628, 14 L.Ed.2d 543 (1965).

3. 449 U.S. 560, 101 S.Ct. 802, 66 L.Ed.2d 740 (1981).

on that process," and stressed that in the instant case the televising was done pursuant to carefully crafted guidelines designed to ensure that the excesses found in the *Estes* case were avoided. Thus, the guidelines included restrictions on the type and manner of equipment used, designed to keep the recording unobtrusive, and a prohibition against the filming of the jury itself. Moreover, the guidelines "placed on [the] trial judges positive obligations to be on guard to protect the fundamental right of the accused to a fair trial." It is still open to a particular defendant, the Court added, "to show that the media's coverage of his case * * * compromised the ability of the jury to judge him fairly" or to "show that broadcast coverage of his particular case had an adverse impact on the trial participants sufficient to constitute a denial of due process." But such prejudice is not established by merely showing "juror awareness that the trial is such as to attract the attention of broadcasters."

Chapter 24

THE CRIMINAL TRIAL

Table of Sections

---

§ 24.1   The Right to a Public Trial

(a) Nature and Scope of the Right to a Public Trial. The Sixth Amendment provides that "In all criminal prosecutions, the accused shall enjoy the right to a * * * public trial." This fundamental right was one of the first sixth amendment rights held by the Supreme Court to be an essential element of due process and therefore applicable in state proceedings under the Fourteenth Amendment.[1] The sixth amendment right to a public trial belongs to the defendant rather than the public; a separate first amendment right governs the interests of the public and the press in attending a trial.[2] The sixth amendment guarantee extends to all criminal trials, including criminal contempt trials. It also extends to certain pretrial proceedings that bear a resemblance to a trial, such as suppression hearings.[3]

A defendant can benefit from a public trial in several ways. Most importantly, it is a "safeguard against any attempt to employ our courts as instruments of persecution. The knowledge that every criminal trial is subject to contemporaneous review in the forum of public opinion is an effective restraint on possible abuse of judicial power."[4] In addition, a public trial gives notice of the proceedings to potential material witnesses who might otherwise be unknown to the parties, and assures that witnesses who do testify will testify truthfully by inducing the expectation that any false testimony would be detected. In resolving issues relating to the scope of the sixth amendment right courts often look to these functions. For example, in holding the right applicable to a suppression hearing, the Court reasoned in *Waller v. Georgia* that the usual public trial interests of ensuring that the judge and prosecutor carry out their duties responsibly, encouraging witnesses to come forward, and discouraging perjury "are no less pressing in a hearing to suppress wrongfully seized evidence."

The defendant's right to a public trial is adequately protected so long as there is free public access to the trial. Although it is not

§ 24.1

1. In re Oliver, 333 U.S. 257, 68 S.Ct. 499, 92 L.Ed. 682 (1948).

2. See § 23.1(d).

3. Waller v. Georgia, 467 U.S. 39, 104 S.Ct. 2210, 81 L.Ed.2d 31 (1984) (suppression hearing). See also Press–Enter. Co. v. Superior Court of California, 478 U.S. 1, 106 S.Ct. 2735, 92 L.Ed.2d 1 (1986) (preliminary hearings).

4. *Oliver,* supra note 1.

necessary that everyone who wants to attend be accommodated, the trial must be held at a place where there are no significant inhibitions upon public attendance. The Supreme Court has stated that denial of the right to a public trial establishes grounds in itself for a new trial, the defendant need not establish that he was prejudiced in any specific way by the exclusion.[5] Predictably, the exclusion of spectators is upheld when the defendant fails to object to closure. However, the fact that the defendant can waive or forfeit his right to a public trial does not mean that he is entitled to a private trial, shielded from public scrutiny.

(b) When Closure Justified. The right to a public trial is not absolute; closure may be constitutional under limited circumstances. The defendant's interest in a public trial may be balanced against other interests which might justify closing the trial. Generally, the best course of action is for the trial judge to hold an evidentiary hearing on the issue of closure whenever it arises, though in some circumstances the judge will be able to take judicial notice of the essential facts. As the Supreme Court stated in *Waller,* "(1) the party seeking to close the hearing must advance an overriding interest that is likely to be prejudiced, (2) the closure must be no broader than necessary to protect that interest, (3) the trial court must consider reasonable alternatives to closing the proceeding, and (4) it must make findings adequate to support the closure." Thus, the task facing a trial judge in ruling upon a possible restriction of the defendant's right to a public trial is very like that facing a trial judge in considering a restriction of the public's right of access. Narrow tailoring in this context requires on-the-record consideration of alternatives to closure. The trial court's failure to make such findings led the Court in *Waller* to conclude that the trial court clearly erred in closing an entire 7–day suppression hearing to protect the privacy of persons named in tapes played for two and one-half hours.

Some lower courts have applied a test less stringent than that in *Waller* for "partial" or "trivial" closures, where, for example, some but not all members of the public are excluded. These courts require only a "substantial" or "important" rather than a "compelling" reason for limiting access in order to justify closure. The *Waller* text also has been held not to apply to a variety of mid-trial proceedings, such as bench conferences and in-chamber conferences with jurors. This effort to narrow the types of closures subject to the strict requirements of *Waller* is not surprising given the inability of appellate courts to employ harmless error analysis to avoid retrial in such cases.[6]

Trials of charges of sexual assault often prompt disputes over closure. Earlier cases took the view that in the trial of sex offenses the general public could be excluded from the courtroom to protect public morals, but today the judge would at most be allowed to exclude youthful spectators. It is not uncommon for a judge to close a portion of the trial of a sex offense for the protection of the victim, especially when the victim is a minor. Primary justification for this practice lies in protection of the personal dignity of the complaining witness. Rape constitutes an intrusion upon areas of the victim's life, both physical and psychological, to which our society attaches the deepest sense of privacy. The ordeal of describing an unwanted sexual encounter before persons with no more than a prurient interest in it aggravates the original injury. Mitigation of the ordeal is a justifiable concern of the public and of the trial court. It does not follow from this, however, that a court may automatically close trials to the public whenever even a minor victim testifies about a sexual assault. Rather, a court should "determine on a case-by-case basis whether closure is necessary" to protect the state's compelling interest in the welfare of the victim, taking into account "the

---

5. Arizona v. Fulminante, 499 U.S. 279, 111 S.Ct. 1246, 113 L.Ed.2d 302 (1991) (stating denial of right to public trial is a structural defect not subject to harmless error review).

6. See *Waller*; see also § 27.6(d).

minor victim's age, psychological maturity, and understanding, the nature of the crime, the desires of the victim, and the interests of the parents and relatives."[7] Although some states have statutes providing for the blanket exclusion of certain persons during the testimony of minor victims, statutory authorization is no substitute for the case-specific determination mandated by the Sixth Amendment.

Limited exclusion of spectators is also permissible when there is a demonstrated need to protect a witness from threatened harassment or physical harm. Exclusion has been upheld where the witness had been subjected to pretrial threats and also where actions by spectators at the trial were understandably perceived by the witness as threatening. Similarly, exclusion during the testimony of an undercover agent engaged in ongoing investigations is proper when exposure would imperil the agent and render him useless for further investigative activities. Finally, exclusion of certain spectators is also permissible when necessary to preserve order in the courtroom, just as checking the identification of spectators entering the courtroom is an appropriate means of deterring would-be trial spectators who may pose unacceptable risks to courtroom security.

§ 24.2   Presence of the Defendant

(a) Origins and Scope of the Right to be Present. The Sixth Amendment provides that "In all criminal prosecutions, the accused shall enjoy the right * * * to be confronted with the witness against him." This Confrontation Clause, which is applicable to the states via the Fourteenth Amendment,[1] encompasses the very basic right of a defendant in a criminal case to be present in the courtroom at "every stage of his trial."[2] While the right to be present is rooted to a large extent in the Confrontation Clause of the Sixth Amendment, it also has a due process component. Accordingly, it is not restricted to situations where the defendant is "actually confronting witnesses or evidence against him," but encompasses all trial-related proceedings at which defendant's presence " 'has a relation, reasonably substantial, to the fullness of his opportunity to defend against the charge.' "[3]

The right has been held to extend to jury selection[4] and to communications between the judge and jury, including the giving of jury instructions, the replaying of taped testimony in the courtroom in connection with jury deliberations, and an in-chambers conversation with a single juror that is substantive in nature. A defendant has the right to be present at the return of the verdict and at sentencing. On the other hand, the right has been held not to extend to in-chambers pretrial conferences, to hearings on post-trial motions, to brief bench conferences between judge and attorneys conducted outside the defendant's hearing, and to various other conferences characterized as relating only to the resolution of questions of law. The constitutional right to presence also does not extend to misdemeanor prosecutions.

In determining whether the right extends to a particular proceeding apart from the trial itself, the Supreme Court has looked to the function of the right as it relates to the content of the particular proceeding in the individual case. In particular, the Court has examined whether or not exclusion of the defendant interfered with the defendant's opportunity to test the evidence introduced against him, and whether or not it otherwise affected his opportunity to defend himself at trial. This approach

---

7. Globe Newspaper Co. v. Superior Court, 457 U.S. 596, 102 S.Ct. 2613, 73 L.Ed.2d 248 (1982). At issue in *Globe* was the public right of access to criminal trials embodied in the First Amendment, but lower courts have required the same case-by-case attention to the issue in determining whether there is a genuine need to encroach upon the defendant's right to a public trial.

§ 24.2

1. Pointer v. Texas, 380 U.S. 400, 85 S.Ct. 1065, 13 L.Ed.2d 923 (1965).

2. Illinois v. Allen, 397 U.S. 337, 90 S.Ct. 1057, 25 L.Ed.2d 353 (1970) (citing Lewis v. United States, 146 U.S. 370, 13 S.Ct. 136, 36 L.Ed. 1011 (1892)).

3. United States v. Gagnon, 470 U.S. 522, 105 S.Ct. 1482, 84 L.Ed.2d 486 (1985) (quoting Snyder v. Massachusetts, 291 U.S. 97, 54 S.Ct. 330, 78 L.Ed. 674 (1934)).

4. See Lewis v. United States, 146 U.S. 370, 13 S.Ct. 136, 36 L.Ed. 1011 (1892); Hopt v. Utah, 110 U.S. 574, 4 S.Ct. 202, 28 L.Ed. 262 (1884).

is illustrated by the rulings in *Kentucky v. Stincer*[5] and *United States v. Gagnon*.[6]

In *Stincer*, the defendant (but not his counsel) was excluded from an in-chambers hearing at which the trial court made a preliminary determination as to whether the two children who were the alleged victims of the charged sex offense had sufficient understanding of their obligation to tell the truth and sufficient intellectual capacity to be competent to testify. The Supreme Court initially noted that even though a particular hearing might be characterized as a "pretrial proceeding," it could still be a "stage of the trial" for confrontation clause purposes. That was true of the competency hearing since it "determines whether a key witness will testify." Under the circumstances of this case, however, the defendant's exclusion from the hearing did not interfere with his opportunity to confront the witness through cross-examination. The questions asked at the competency hearing did not relate to the crime itself (but only to each child's general capacity to recall facts and distinguish between truth and falsehood), many of the background questions asked at the hearing were repeated at trial, the children were subject to "full and complete" cross-examination at trial, and the judge's preliminary ruling at the in-chambers hearing was subject to reconsideration in light of the witnesses' trial testimony. In addition, the due process component of the defendant's right of presence was not violated as defendant's personal participation in the limited hearing would not have borne "a substantial relationship to [the] defendant's opportunity better to defend himself at trial."

In *Gagnon*, after a juror expressed concern that one of the four defendants was sketching portraits of the jurors, the judge directed the defendant to desist. At the request of defendant's counsel, the judge also announced that he would conduct a brief in camera inquiry (with defendant's counsel present) to ensure that the sketching had not prejudiced the jurors. Counsel for the defendant did not request that his client be present during this inquiry

and the attorneys representing the remaining defendants did not request that they or their clients be present. In chambers, the judge explained to the juror who had been sketched that the sketching was innocuous (the defendant simply was an artist) and received assurance from the juror that he was willing to proceed as an impartial juror. The Supreme Court concluded that due process "does not require that all the parties be present when the judge inquires into such a minor occurrence." It noted that the four defendants "could have done nothing had they been present nor would they have gained anything by attending."

Applying an analysis similar to that in *Gagnon*, some courts have held that a defendant was properly excluded from in-chambers hearings regarding the withdrawal of counsel due to defense counsel's belief that the defendant intended to commit perjury. By contrast the right is normally extended to other pretrial proceedings in which the court is required to make factual resolutions based on testimony presented at that proceeding. Statutes or court rules may well grant a right of presence that extends beyond the constitutional right.

Consistent with the objectives of the right of presence, the right is not fulfilled where the defendant is present but lacks competency or ability to understand the language of the forum. Accordingly, *Drope v. Missouri*[7] imposes a constitutional obligation upon a trial judge to "always be alert to circumstances suggesting a change that would render the accused unable to meet the standards of competence to stand trial" and to cause "further inquiry on the question" to be held whenever the circumstances indicate "a sufficient doubt" of defendant's competence. A similar obligation exists to provide an interpreter when an accused does not understand the English language.

With the development of sophisticated video conferencing equipment, prosecutors have asked courts to accept a defendant's virtual presence on screen as a substitute for his actual presence in the courtroom. Not having

---

5.   482 U.S. 730, 107 S.Ct. 2658, 96 L.Ed.2d 631 (1987).

6.   470 U.S. 522, 105 S.Ct. 1482, 84 L.Ed.2d 486 (1985).

7.   420 U.S. 162, 95 S.Ct. 896, 43 L.Ed.2d 103 (1975).

to bring an incarcerated defendant to the courthouse saves the government money, and avoids security risks associated with transporting detainees. The popularity of using off-site technology is reflected in recent amendments to the Federal Rules of Criminal Procedure to allow for alternative-site video teleconferencing for first appearances and arraignments, and in recent litigation over similar techniques at sentencing. It is hard to imagine how this sort of arrangement at the trial itself, without an express waiver by the defendant, could be consistent with the Confrontation Clause and with due process.[8] Nevertheless, the constitutionality of substituting teleconferencing for presence is an open question at pre- and post-trial stages of the prosecution, such as sentencing, where a defendant cannot claim confrontation rights.[9] Whatever the proceeding, a defendant must not be forced to settle for virtual communication with his own lawyer.

(b) Harmless Error and Waiver. Where the particular proceeding is one at which defendant had a clear right to be present (as at trial), but defendant was absent for only a brief period, that absence will not invalidate a conviction if the error is harmless beyond a reasonable doubt. If a verbatim record was made during the defendant's absence and it shows that defendant's attorney was present and that no legal error was committed in defendant's absence, then it is likely that the error will be found to be harmless.

The defendant's constitutional right to be present is one of those "basic rights that the attorney cannot waive without the fully informed and publicly acknowledged consent of the defendant."[10] Nevertheless, waiver, or rather forfeiture, of the right by the defendant is commonly found in at least three situations. First, where defendant is present in court and makes no effort to attend a bench or in-chambers examination when counsel leaves the defense table to participate, this may be taken as an intentional relinquishment of the right to be present, at least where the court in no way

suggested that defendant could not accompany counsel. Proceedings may also go forward without the defendant's presence when the defendant forfeits his right to be present by his misbehavior in the courtroom. Finally, a defendant voluntarily remains away from trial waives his right to be present. These circumstances are discussed in the two subsections that follow.

A defendant may forfeit his right to participate in the proceedings, but has no contrasting right to be absent from trial, even when his absence might assist his defense. In capital cases, for example, many jurisdictions prohibit the defense from waiving presence.

(c) The Disorderly Defendant: Forfeiture by Conduct. In *Illinois v. Allen*,[11] the Supreme Court held the right to be present could be lost by the defendant's disruptive behavior. In concluding that the trial judge acted lawfully in excluding Allen from the courtroom following his repeated outbursts, the Court declared that "there are at least three constitutionally permissible ways for a trial judge to handle an obstreperous defendant like Allen: (1) bind and gag him, thereby keeping him present; (2) cite him for contempt; (3) take him out of the courtroom until he promises to conduct himself properly." Since the first two responses were properly rejected by the trial court, the defendant could not complain when his own behavior had cost him his right to be present at his trial.

The Court in *Allen* did state there could be situations in which "binding and gagging might possibly be the fairest and most reasonable way to handle a defendant who acts as Allen did here." But it is not apparent what circumstances would justify such a conclusion. The commonly held assumption that removal is preferable to gagging or shackling the disruptive defendant, certainly finds support in language in *Allen* to the effect that "even to contemplate such a technique, must less see it, arouses a feeling that no person should be

---

8. A related issue involving video-conferencing and the Confrontation Clause is discussed at note 19.

9. See § 26.4(f).

10. Taylor v. Illinois, 484 U.S. 400, 108 S.Ct. 646, 98 L.Ed.2d 798 (1988).

11. 397 U.S. 337, 90 S.Ct. 1057, 25 L.Ed.2d 353 (1970).

tried while shackled and gagged except as a last resort." Not only is it possible that the sight of shackles and gags might have a significant effect on the jury's beliefs about the defendant, but the use of this technique is itself something of an affront to the very dignity and decorum of judicial proceedings that the judge is seeking to uphold. Moreover, one of the defendant's primary advantages of being present at the trial, his ability to communicate with his counsel, may be greatly reduced when the defendant is in a condition of total physical restraint. Since the *Allen* decision, a less-visible form of restraints has been developed—the "stun belt." Discussed more fully below, this alternative has been used in some courts to deter misbehavior by defendants who otherwise would be removed from their trials.

The Court in *Allen* also noted the limitations of the contempt alternative. A contempt citation would hardly deter a defendant who is determined to prevent any trial or who is already facing more serious sanctions than those that would follow from a contempt conviction. When restraints would unfairly prejudice the defendant, and contempt would be ineffectual, removal is likely to be the only realistic alternative.

The *Allen* ruling can best be explained as involving a "forfeiture" rather than a "waiver" of a constitutional right. Thus, whether or not the defendant actually made a "knowing and intelligent" decision to relinquish his right is not critical. However, before disorderly conduct amounts to forfeiture, two other factors, present in *Allen*, may be essential: (1) Allen was "repeatedly warned by the trial judge that he would be removed from the courtroom if he persisted in his unruly conduct"; and (2) he was "constantly informed that he could return to the trial when he would agree to conduct himself in an orderly manner." Finally, as Justice Brennan noted in his *Allen* concurrence, if a defendant is excluded "the court should make reasonable efforts to enable him to communicate with his attorney and, if possible, to keep apprised of the progress of his trial."

(d) Forfeiture by Voluntary Absence. In *Taylor v. United States*,[12] the Court held that the defendant can also lose his right to be present by absenting himself during the trial. In rejecting the defendant's contention that "his mere voluntary absence from his trial cannot be construed as an effective waiver * * * unless it is demonstrated that he knew or had been expressly warned by the trial court not only that he had a right to be present but also that the trial would continue in his absence and thereby effectively foreclose his right to testify and to confront personally the witnesses against him," the Court noted:

> It is wholly incredible to suggest that petitioner, who was at liberty on bail, had attended the opening session of his trial, and had a duty to be present at the trial, * * * entertained any doubts about his right to be present at every stage of his trial. It seems equally incredible to us * * * "that a defendant who flees from a courtroom in the midst of a trial—where judge, jury, witnesses and lawyers are present and ready to continue—would not know that as a consequence the trial could continue in his absence."

Because this analysis is also difficult to square with traditional waiver-of-rights theory, here again it would seem preferable to view the matter in terms of forfeiture of a right by misconduct.

The Court in *Taylor* relied upon the much earlier case of *Diaz v. United States*,[13] which declared that "if, after the trial has begun in his presence, [the defendant] voluntarily absents himself, this does not nullify what has been done or prevent the completion of the trial." That language "gave birth to the notion that a defendant who took flight *before* the trial commenced could not be tried in absentia." One grounding for such a distinction is that the judicial system has a greater interest in continuing what has been started than it has in proceeding with a trial that was never underway. Lower courts, however, have held that the trial of a defendant who has volun-

---

12.   414 U.S. 17, 94 S.Ct. 194, 38 L.Ed.2d 174 (1973).

13.   223 U.S. 442, 32 S.Ct. 250, 56 L.Ed. 500 (1912).

tarily stayed away may beg in without him, so long as the defendant knew when trial was to begin and there was an important interest in avoiding delay, such as when several codefendants were ready to proceed.

Even if commencing a trial without the defendant present passes constitutional muster, it may violate a local statute or court rule concerning the presence of criminal defendants. In *Crosby v. United States*,[14] for example, the Court held that the "language, history and logic" of Federal Rule 43 "support a straightforward interpretation that prohibits the trial *in absentia* of a defendant who is not present at the beginning of a trial." The Court commented, "If a clear line is to be drawn marking the point at which the costs of delay are likely to outweigh the interests of the defendant and society in having the defendant present, the commencement of trial is at least a plausible place at which to draw that line."

(e) Prejudicial Circumstances of Presence. The right to a fair trial is a fundamental liberty secured by the Fourteenth Amendment, and a "basic component" of that right is the presumption of innocence. Because that presumption is likely to be impaired if the defendant is required to stand trial in prison or jail clothing, the courts have consistently held that such a procedure is improper. The Supreme Court reached that conclusion in *Estelle v. Williams*,[15] where it was emphasized (1) "that the constant reminder of the accused's condition implicit in such distinctive, identifiable attire may affect a juror's judgment," (2) that "compelling an accused to wear jail clothing furthers no essential state policy," and (3) "that compelling the accused to stand trial in jail garb operates usually against only those who cannot post bail prior to trial." But because the record in *Estelle* was "clear that no objection was made to the trial judge concerning the jail attire either before or at any time during the trial," the Court declined to reverse the conviction, for it could not be concluded "that respondent was compelled to stand trial in jail garb or that there was sufficient reason

to excuse the failure to raise the issue before trial."

As a general rule, a defendant in a criminal case also has the right to appear before the jury free from visible shackles or other physical restraints. This right also springs from the fundamental notion that a person accused of crime is presumed innocent until his guilt has been established beyond a reasonable doubt. The defendant also has a right to have his witnesses appear without physical restraints. Though shackling witnesses does not directly affect the presumption of innocence, it nonetheless may harm his defense by detracting from the credibility of his witnesses.

Where a defense objection has been raised, a showing of extreme need is required to justify the use of visible physical restraints at trial, and this showing ordinarily must be made on the record after a hearing so that an appellate court can more readily determine whether there was an abuse of discretion. Shackles may be used on defendants or witnesses who are inmates of maximum security prisons and whose records reflect a propensity for violence or escape, but a policy of shackling all prison inmates does not meet the "extreme need" standard.

The conspicuous use of identifiable security officers at trial is treated somewhat differently. In *Holbrook v. Flynn*,[16] the Supreme Court acknowledged that the courtroom presence of a substantial number of uniformed officers could present constitutional difficulties in an extreme case, but concluded that the state generally did not have to make a specific showing of a special security need to sustain the constitutionality of deploying several such officers. Since the deployment of uniformed officers "need not be interpreted as a sign that [defendant] is particularly dangerous," but may just as readily be viewed as a measure intended to "guard against disruptions emanating from outside the court room," or as "mere elements of an impressive drama," it was not "the sort of inherently prejudicial

---

14. 506 U.S. 255, 113 S.Ct. 748, 122 L.Ed.2d 25 (1993).

15. 425 U.S. 501, 96 S.Ct. 1691, 48 L.Ed.2d 126 (1976).

16. 475 U.S. 560, 106 S.Ct. 1340, 89 L.Ed.2d 525 (1986).

practice that, like shackling, should be permitted only where justified by an essential state interest specific to each trial." The Court also concluded that, since the deployment of the security guards was "intimately related to the State's legitimate interest in maintaining custody during the proceeding," it "did not offend the Equal Protection Clause by arbitrarily discriminating against those unable to post bond or to whom bail has been denied."

Use of a "stun belt" to restrain a dangerous defendant may be less obvious to the jury, but requires the same on-the-record justification as other forms of visible restraint. This is because, as one court explained, 1) the belt "poses a far more substantial risk of interfering with a defendant's Sixth Amendment right to confer with counsel than do leg shackles," due to "the fear of receiving a painful and humiliating shock for any gesture that could be perceived as threatening," 2) a defendant wearing a belt is "likely to concentrate on doing everything he can to prevent the belt from being activated and is thus less likely to participate fully in his defense at trial" and 3) "shackles are a minor threat to the dignity of the courtroom when compared with the discharge of a stun belt, which could cause the defendant to lose control of his limbs, collapse to the floor, and defecate on himself." At least one state has prohibited the use of stun belts at criminal trials.

Questions sometimes arise concerning the location of the defendant in the courtroom during the trial. Placement of the defendant in a separate docket as a security measure may not be viewed as stigmatizing under the analysis of *Holbrook* when routine. Nevertheless, past cases indicate that it would still be unconstitutional because it places the defendant in a position where he cannot freely communicate with counsel. It is also necessary that the defendant be situated where he can see and hear the witnesses and they can see him. In *Coy v. Iowa*,[17] the Supreme Court held that the right of confrontation extends beyond cross-examination and encompasses also the right to a "face to face meeting with the witnesses

appearing before the trier of fact." *Coy* held that the defendant's confrontation right was infringed when a state trial court, seeking to protect two juvenile victims of alleged sex abuse from the emotional trauma of viewing the defendant when giving their testimony, placed between the witnesses and the defendant a screen that blocked the defendant from their sight but did allow defendant to dimly perceive them as well as hear them. In *Coy*, the trial court had acted upon a generalized legislative presumption of witness trauma without making any individualized findings.

Subsequently, in *Maryland v. Craig*,[18] the Court upheld on its face a state procedure that allowed the use of one-way closed circuit television to present the testimony of a child witness/victim in a sex abuse case. The Court in *Craig* stressed that the statute required a case-specific finding that the child would suffer from such extreme emotional trauma, due to the presence of the defendant, that he or she could not "reasonably communicate." Another factor distinguishing the case from *Coy* was the method of separation. The victim testified from another room, while the defendant, jury, and judge remained in the courtroom. This would probably have been viewed by the jury as suggesting that the witness was fearful of testifying in the courtroom setting rather than fearful of testifying while looking at the defendant. The Court majority in *Coy* had no reason to reach defendant's additional contention there that the screen was an "inherently prejudicial" method of separating the witness, although the two dissenters discounted that claim on the ground that the screen, unlike prison garb, was not the "sort of trapping that generally is associated with those who have been convicted."

The Court in 2002 declined to forward to Congress a proposed amendment to Rule 26(b) of the Federal Rules of Criminal Procedure that would have authorized the use of two-way video transmissions in criminal cases in "exceptional circumstances" with "appropriate

17. 487 U.S. 1012, 108 S.Ct. 2798, 101 L.Ed.2d 857 (1988).

18. 497 U.S. 836, 110 S.Ct. 3157, 111 L.Ed.2d 666 (1990).

safeguards," if "the witness is unavailable."[19] Justices Breyer and O'Connor dissented from the decision, and argued "it is not obvious how video testimony could abridge a defendant's Confrontation Clause rights in circumstances where an absent witness' testimony could be admitted in nonvisual form via deposition regardless." Justice Scalia filed his own statement detailing his objections to the proposed rule, including its failure to require a "case-specific finding" that admission is "necessary to further an important public policy." Compelling accusers to make their accusations in the defendant's presence is "not equivalent to making them in a room that contains a television set beaming electrons that portray the defendant's image," he argued. He distinguished the proposed video transmission from the federal rule allowing the admission of deposition testimony under some circumstances, noting that rule "accords the defendant a right to face-to-face confrontation during the deposition."

§ 24.3   The Defendant's Right of Access to Evidence

(a) Constitutional Grounding. Various statutes, common law rules, and constitutional commands combine to shape the capacity of the defense to gain access to evidence that it might use at trial. The subsections that follow describe the basic components of this defense "right of access," organized according to the type of process or protection provided. This subsection, in contrast, focuses on the diverse constitutional sources for the right of access, a subject that deserves separate consideration.

The Supreme Court has characterized various constitutional standards as combining to create "what might loosely be called the area of constitutionally guaranteed access to evidence."[1] Although the Court has not provided a comprehensive inventory of these standards, any such list would certainly include: (1) the

prosecution's duty to disclose evidence within its possession or control that is exculpatory and material; (2) the prohibition against the government's bad faith destruction of such evidence; (3) the state's duty to provide the defense with the power through subpoena to gain the production of witnesses and physical items at trial; (4) the state's duty to provide certain types of assistance or information to the defense that will allow it to use the power of subpoena to gain evidence; and (5) the prohibition against certain governmental actions that interfere with the defense use of the subpoena power. The constitutional directives listed above, each discussed in subsections that follow, have been grounded on either or both of two basic constitutional guarantees—the Fifth and Fourteenth Amendment guarantee of due process and the Sixth Amendment's command that the accused "shall have compulsory process for obtaining witnesses in his favor."

The Compulsory Process Clause naturally suggests some constitutional entitlement to trial evidence. What is surprising is how rarely the Court has relied upon that provision in its discussions of a right of access to evidence. As the Supreme Court noted in *Pennsylvania v. Ritchie*,[2] it "has had little occasion to discuss the contours of the Compulsory Process Clause." Instead, it has addressed initially under the Due Process Clause claims that the government failed to assist in identifying and locating defense witnesses, or improperly interfered with the defense's use of subpoenas. Subsequent rulings have built upon those cases while acknowledging that the Compulsory Process Clause could serve as an alternative grounding for prohibiting such interference.

The reliance upon due process to establish elements of a defense right of access has allowed the Court some flexibility in defining those elements. Fundamental fairness in an adversarial system requires that the defense be given the tools with which it can obtain

---

19. Order of April 29, 2002, re Amendments to Federal Rules of Criminal Procedure, 539 U.S. 1159 (2002).

§ 24.3

1. Arizona v. Youngblood, 488 U.S. 51, 109 S.Ct. 333, 102 L.Ed.2d 281 (1988).

2. 480 U.S. 39, 107 S.Ct. 989, 94 L.Ed.2d 40 (1987).

existing evidence that challenges the prosecution case, either by tending to establish affirmatively the defendant's innocence or by casting doubt upon the persuasiveness of the prosecution's evidence. The Court has turned to the touchstone of fundamental fairness to determine what tools are needed and what actions the state must take to either facilitate their use or to avoid interfering with their use. As discussed in Chapter 2, traditional due process methodology tends to be case-specific, focusing on the totality of the circumstances and weighing such factors as administrative justifications and burdens and the likelihood of prejudicial impact on the outcome of the particular case. The due process rulings that contribute to the "area of constitutionally-guaranteed access to evidence" have been consistent with that tradition.

As an additional source of a constitutional right of access, commentators and occasional judicial opinions have looked to the Confrontation Clause of the Sixth Amendment. The premise here is that the right of confrontation includes not only a right to cross-examine witnesses but also a right of access to material that could serve as a basis for effective cross-examination. The state's failure to provide or facilitate access to that material would be treated in the same fashion as the denial or restriction of cross-examination itself. As the following cases suggest, this theory has yet to secure a majority on the Court. Instead the Court has continued to rely upon due process rather than the Confrontation Clause when evaluating access to evidence claims.

In *United States v. Bagley*,[3] for example, the lower court had relied on a confrontation clause analysis in reversing a conviction. The defense there had requested notification of any promises made to government witnesses. The prosecution, unaware that the government's investigative agency had entered into a compensation arrangement with two key witnesses, failed to disclose that arrangement. The lower court reasoned that because the compensation agreement could have been

used to impeach the witness on cross-examination, that the failure to disclose it therefore violated the Confrontation Clause, and that reversal was required without a demonstration of prejudice. The Supreme Court rejected this line of analysis. It reasoned that failure to disclose exculpatory material, including impeachment material, traditionally had been tested by reference to the due process standards of *Brady v. Maryland*, discussed in § 24.3(b), which require a showing of a reasonable probability that the nondisclosure had altered the outcome of the case. To treat impeachment material differently from other exculpatory evidence because of its relationship to the Confrontation Clause would be both contrary to past precedent and illogical.

The case of *Pennsylvania v. Ritchie*[4] offers another example of the Court's preference for employing due process analysis rather than relying upon the Confrontation Clause when addressing the duty to disclose evidence prior to trial. The issue posed there was whether a state court violated defendant's constitutional rights in holding that, because of their confidential status, various records of a state protective service agency relating to defendant's minor daughter would not be open to defense inspection in preparing for trial. The defendant had been charged with sexually assaulting his daughter, and the state's intermediate appellate court had held that he should have been allowed to obtain from the agency that portion of its records containing verbatim recorded statements that the daughter had made to a youth counselor in reporting the alleged sexual assault. The state's high court had gone even farther, holding that the Sixth Amendment required that the entire file of the state agency be made available to defense counsel for the purpose of determining whether any other items were also relevant to the case. Relying on the Supreme Court's ruling in *Davis v. Alaska*,[5] which found a violation of the Confrontation Clause in a state court's refusal to allow the cross-examination of a key witness by reference to his juvenile record, the lower court in *Ritchie* concluded that the same

---

3.   473 U.S. 667, 105 S.Ct. 3375, 87 L.Ed.2d 481 (1985).

4.   Supra note 2, also discussed in § 24.3(f).

5.   415 U.S. 308, 94 S.Ct. 1105, 39 L.Ed.2d 347 (1974).

principle applied to the confidentiality of the records of the state protective service agency.

In the Supreme Court, a plurality concluded that defendant's constitutional claim should be judged solely under the *Brady* due process standard requiring the government "to turn over evidence in its possession that is both favorable to the accused and material to guilt or punishment." The Confrontation Clause had no bearing since the "ability to question adverse witnesses * * * does not include the power to require the pretrial disclosure of any and all information that might be useful to contradicting unfavorable testimony." The right of confrontation is a "trial right" that came into play in *Davis* because the trial judge there prohibited cross-examination with a juvenile record which was already available to the defense. *Davis* could not be read "to mean that a statutory privilege cannot be maintained when a defendant asserts a need, prior to trial, for the protected information that might be used at trial to impeach or otherwise undermine a witness' testimony," because such a reading would, in effect, "transform the Confrontation Clause into a constitutionally compelled rule of pretrial discovery." Thus, for the *Ritchie* plurality the Confrontation Clause offered no basis for pretrial access to potential impeachment material, whether that material was within the prosecutor's control, as in *Bagley*, or the control of another person. Three justices disagreed with the plurality's reading of the Confrontation Clause and two others did not reach the issue.

Applying due process standards instead, the Court in *Ritchie* required the state to disclose such information within the files of the protective service agency as was exculpatory and material. Indeed, *Ritchie* required an *in camera* review of the files by the trial judge to determine whether the state had violated this obligation. Thus, the rejection of the defendant's confrontation clause argument in *Ritchie* served only, as did a similar rejection in *Bagley*, to substitute to a due process requirement of materiality (considering both relevancy and impact on the outcome) for the re-

quirement of the Confrontation Clause that evidence be relevant to cross-examination. The next subsection examines this due process standard in more detail.

(b) Due Process Duty to Disclose Evidence Favorable to the Accused. *The origins of the Brady rule.* In *Mooney v. Holohan*,[6] decided in 1935, the Supreme Court first held that a prosecutor's use of false testimony could constitute a violation of due process. The defendant there alleged that the prosecutor had fabricated the case against him by procuring and introducing perjured testimony at trial. The Supreme Court had little difficulty in finding that defendant's claim had constitutional dimensions. A per curiam opinion noted that due process

> is a requirement that cannot be deemed to be satisfied by mere notice and hearing if a state has contrived a conviction through the pretense of a trial which in truth is but used as a means of depriving a defendant of liberty through a deliberate deception of court and jury by the presentation of testimony known to be perjured. Such a contrivance by a state to procure the conviction and imprisonment of a defendant is as inconsistent with the rudimentary demands of justice as is the obtaining of a like result by intimidation.

As discussed in § 24.3(d), a series of later rulings extended the "*Mooney* principle" to require that the prosecution not suborn perjury, not purposefully use evidence known to be false, and not allow the known false testimony of its witnesses to stand uncorrected. In *Brady v. Maryland*[7] the Supreme Court extended the *Mooney* principle to the prosecution's failure to disclose exculpatory evidence within its possession to the defense. The defendant Brady and a companion, Boblit, had been convicted of felony murder and sentenced to death. Prior to Brady's separate trial, defense counsel had asked the prosecutor to allow him to examine all of the statements that Boblit had given to the police. Counsel was shown several of Boblit's statements, but failed to receive one state-

---

6.   294 U.S. 103, 55 S.Ct. 340, 79 L.Ed. 791 (1935).

7.   373 U.S. 83, 83 S.Ct. 1194, 10 L.Ed.2d 215 (1963).

ment in which Boblit admitted that he had done the actual killing. At trial, defendant admitted his participation in the crime, but claimed that he had not himself killed the victim. Defense counsel stressed this claim in his closing argument, asking the jury to show leniency and not impose the death penalty. Following defendant's conviction, defense counsel learned of the undisclosed statement and sought a new trial based on this newly discovered evidence. The state court granted a new trial as to the issue of punishment alone. It reasoned that whether or not defendant himself killed the victim had no bearing on his liability for the homicide, and Boblit's statement therefore would not have been admissible in evidence on that issue. On the other hand, the statement could have been used to support defendant's plea for leniency as to punishment, and the prosecution's failure to disclose the statement had deprived the defendant of a fair hearing on that issue.

The Supreme Court affirmed the state court's ruling, holding that the prosecutor's nondisclosure of Boblit's statement had resulted in a denial of due process on the punishment issue. Finding that the *Mooney* principle was applicable to the "suppression of evidence favorable to the accused" as well as the presentation of false testimony, the Court reasoned that the fact finder is equally deceived when the prosecutor "withholds evidence on demand of an accused which, if made available, would tend to exculpate him or reduce the penalty." The Court also agreed with the lower court's conclusion that the prosecutor bore responsibility for such deception even though his failure to disclose "was not the result of guile." The principle of *Mooney v. Holohan,* the Court noted, "is not punishment of society for misdeeds of a prosecutor but avoidance of an unfair trial to the accused." Summarizing its ruling, the *Brady* opinion stated that "the suppression by the prosecution of evidence favorable to an accused upon request violates due process where the evidence is material

either to guilt or to punishment, irrespective of the good faith or bad faith of the prosecution."

Unfortunately, the Court's application of that rule to the facts of *Mooney* said very little about the content of the rule's critical terms. The nondisclosed evidence clearly was favorable, requested, and within the prosecution's possession. All that was left to be determined was whether the nondisclosed evidence was "material" to the issue of guilt or punishment. The use of term "material" suggested that more than favorable relevancy was required of the suppressed evidence. Materiality suggested that the evidence must also have had some significant potential for actually influencing the outcome of the case. Thus, under the *Mooney* line of cases, the false testimony to be "material" had to present some "reasonable likelihood" of affecting the jury's verdict. The *Brady* opinion, however, had no reason to carve out any specific standard of materiality for suppressed exculpatory evidence. Because the state had acknowledged that Boblit's statement was critical to the issue of punishment, the Court's discussion of materiality was limited to the relationship between the statement and the finding of guilt. The Court found that issue easy to resolved; a statement would not be viewed as material when the jury could have considered it only by disregarding a judge's instruction that it was relevant only as to another issue. Accordingly, the suppression of Boblit's statement had resulted in a due process violation as to the capital punishment determination, but not as to the conviction itself.

The Court has continued to develop the *Brady* rule in a series of subsequent cases: *United States v. Agurs,*[8] *United States v. Bagley,*[9] *Kyles v. Whitley,*[10] and *Strickler v. Greene.*[11] In *Strickler,* the Court summed up the "essential components of a *Brady* violation." Failure by the prosecution to disclose evidence to the defense, regardless of whether the defense re-

---

8.   427 U.S. 97, 96 S.Ct. 2392, 49 L.Ed.2d 342 (1976).

9.   473 U.S. 667, 105 S.Ct. 3375, 87 L.Ed.2d 481 (1985).

10.   514 U.S. 419, 115 S.Ct. 1555, 131 L.Ed.2d 490 (1995).

11.   527 U.S. 263, 119 S.Ct. 1936, 144 L.Ed.2d 286 (1999).

quested the evidence, violates due process where (1) that evidence is "favorable to the accused, either because it is exculpatory, or because it is impeaching"; (2) the evidence was "suppressed by the [government], either willfully or inadvertently;" and (3) "prejudice * * * ensued." Prejudice in this context is interchangeable with the concept of materiality, which is explored below.

Materiality—standard. In *United States v. Bagley*,[12] the Court articulated the materiality standard that it employs today. Before trial in that case, the defense requested notification of "any deals, promises, or inducements made to [government] witnesses in exchange for their testimony." The government produced signed affidavits of its two principal witnesses, private security officers, which detailed their undercover activities and concluded with the statement that the affidavits were given without any promises of reward. Following defendant's trial and conviction, it was discovered that both witnesses had signed contracts with the federal investigating agency stating that they would be paid "a sum commensurate with services and information rendered." The prosecuting attorney testified that he would have furnished the contracts if he had known of their existence, and the trial judge agreed that this should have been done. The trial judge refused to order a new trial, however, reasoning that the impeachment evidence would not have affected the outcome of defendant's bench trial. The Ninth Circuit reversed. It viewed the government's failure to disclose as impairing defendant's right of confrontation, and concluded that the violation therefore required automatic reversal. The Supreme Court rejected that conclusion and remanded for reconsideration. The eight participating Justices were in agreement that any constitutional violation here was to be judged under the due process standard of *Brady*, rather than the Confrontation Clause, and therefore automatic reversal was not appropriate. Four separate opinions were written, however, on the

standard to be applied in determining whether a new trial was required under *Brady*.

Of the two *Bagley* opinions that combined to present the majority viewpoint, that of Justice Blackmun contained the more extensive discussion of the applicable due process standard. Justice Blackmun noted initially that the false testimony cases had adopted, in effect, the traditional constitutional harmless error standard, although that standard might also be stated as a materiality test "under which the fact that testimony is perjured is considered material unless failure to disclose it would be harmless beyond a reasonable doubt." The traditional materiality phrasing—finding sufficient "any reasonable likelihood" of affecting the jury verdict—was developed prior to the establishment of the constitutional harmless error standard and merely stated the same concept. For reasons first stated in *United States v. Agurs*,[13] this standard, however expressed, did not apply to nondisclosures where there had been no specific request. Instead, the materiality that the Court standard applied in *Argus* was "stricter than the harmless-error standard but more lenient to the defense than the newly discovered evidence standard." In two post-*Agurs* decisions, the Court had "relied on and reformulated" the *Agurs* materiality standard. In determining whether the deportation of witnesses had resulted in a denial of due process, the Court had asked whether there was a "reasonable likelihood" that unavailability of their testimony "could have affected the judgment of the trier of fact."[14] And in defining the prejudice element of a claim of ineffective assistance of counsel, the Court had required that there be "a reasonable probability that, but for counsel's unprofessional errors, the result of the proceedings would have been different."[15] This reformulation, Justice Blackmun noted in *Bagley*, pointed to a single materiality standard that could be applied to all nondisclosure cases:

> We find the *Strickland* formulation of the *Agurs* test for materiality sufficiently flexi-

---

12. 473 U.S. 667, 105 S.Ct. 3375, 87 L.Ed.2d 481 (1985).

13. See note 8.

14. See § 24.3(h).

15. See § 11.10(d).

ble to cover the "no request," "general request," and "specific request" cases of prosecutorial failure to disclose evidence favorable to the accused: The evidence is material only if there is a reasonable probability that, had the evidence been disclosed to the defense, the result of the proceeding would have been different. A "reasonable probability" is a probability sufficient to undermine confidence in the outcome.

Justice White's concurring opinion in *Bagley* gave majority support to a considerable part of Justice Blackmun's opinion. Justice White agreed that nondisclosed evidence "is material only if there is a reasonable probability that, had the evidence been disclosed to the defense, the result of the proceeding would have been different." He also agreed that this standard is "sufficiently flexible" to cover all instances of prosecutorial failure to disclose evidence favorable to the accused. Taken together, the Blackmun and White opinions established a single test of materiality applicable to all nondisclosure cases, including specific request, general request, and no request cases. That test requires "a reasonable probability" that, had disclosure been made, the "result of the proceeding would have been different."

In *Kyles v. Whitley*,[16] the Court noted that "four aspects of materiality under *Bagley* bear emphasis." First, "a showing of materiality does not require demonstration by a preponderance that disclosure of the suppressed evidence would have resulted ultimately in the defendant's acquittal * * *. *Bagley's* touchstone of materiality is a 'reasonable probability' of a different result, and the adjective is important. The question is not whether the defendant would more likely than not have received a different verdict with the evidence, but whether in its absence he received a fair trial, understood as a trial resulting in a verdict worthy of confidence." Second, the "*Bagley* materiality [test] * * * is not a sufficiency of evidence test. A defendant need not demonstrate that after discounting the inculpatory evidence in light of the undisclosed evidence, there would not have been enough to convict."

Third, "once a reviewing court applying *Bagley* has found constitutional error there is no need for further harmless-error review." Fourth, "*Bagley* materiality" is to be judged by reference to the "suppressed evidence considered collectively, not item-by-item," with the focus on the "cumulative effect of suppression." While the *Kyles* ruling rested in the end on a fact-intensive analysis that has limited precedential value (especially in light of Court's close division as to that analysis), its discussion of the general character of "materiality" under *Bagley* suggested a standard that is more easily met by the defense than some lower courts had previously assumed.

Strickler v. Greene[17] is a further illustration of the Court's application of the materiality standard. In that case, notes of a police interview of an eyewitness and letters written by the witness were not disclosed, although the prosecutor followed an open file policy. These undisclosed documents cast serious doubt on significant portions of the witness's testimony. The District Court had concluded that without the witness's testimony, the jury might have been persuaded that another man, not the defendant, was the "ringleader" and would have convicted him of first degree rather than capital murder. The Supreme Court found this possibility unsupported and, more importantly, insufficient to meet the materiality standard. Reviewing the evidence in the case, and noting that the prosecutor did not rely upon the testimony at issue during the closing argument at the penalty phase, the Court concluded that the "petitioner has not convinced us that there is a reasonable probability that the jury would have returned a different verdict if [the witness's] testimony had been either severely impeached or excluded entirely."

Materiality—the significance of a specific request. Although the Court has adopted a single standard of materiality for all cases, regardless of the presence of a specific request, where a case does involve a specific request, lower courts have continued to take note of that factor. As Justice Blackmun observed in *Bag-*

16. 514 U.S. 419, 115 S.Ct. 1555, 131 L.Ed.2d 490 (1995).

17. Supra note 11.

ley, the degree of specificity and the likelihood of detrimental reliance on the prosecution's failure to respond go hand in hand. Where the request is narrow and precise, giving the prosecutor considerable direction as to what is wanted, such as a request for statements of a particular person, or a request for reports by particular experts, defense counsel is more likely to treat the prosecutor's failure to disclose as an indication that the evidence does not exist. Where the request does not have those qualities, such as a request for any material bearing on the credibility of witnesses or for any material that corroborates the defense, the defense counsel must also account for the possibility that the disclosure made was not complete because the prosecution adopted a somewhat different interpretation of what was included in the request or could not readily put together all that was encompassed by the request. Recognizing this distinction, some states require a lesser showing from defendants in specific request cases. These courts have held that in such cases once the defendant establishes that the evidence withheld was favorable to the defense, the prosecution must prove that undisclosed evidence would not have affected the verdict.

Materiality—the timing of the disclosure. Though *Brady* itself involved a request for pretrial disclosure, the *Brady* rule does not impose a general requirement that the government disclose prior to trial exculpatory evidence that is material to the issue of guilt. Due process requires only that disclosure of exculpatory evidence be made in sufficient time to permit defendant to make effective use of that evidence. This point in time has been described as "the point at which a reasonable probability will exist that the outcome would have been different if an earlier disclosure had been made." Depending upon the nature of the evidence, this standard may sometimes require pretrial disclosure. Thus, where the prosecution has the statement of a witness who could present exculpatory testimony and does not intend itself to call that witness, disclosure before trial would be necessary to ensure that the defense has an opportunity to

subpoena that witness for trial. Insofar as such disclosure exceeds what is permitted under local provisions for pretrial discovery or statutes regulating the timing of the disclosure of witness statements,[18] the constitutional obligation will prevail over those provisions.

For most exculpatory evidence, the prosecution should be able to satisfy its constitutional obligation by disclosure at trial. The burden rests with the defendant to establish that the "lateness of that disclosure so prejudiced [defendant's] preparation or presentation of his defense that he was prevented from receiving his constitutionally guaranteed fair trial." Moreover, if the defendant fails to request a continuance when disclosure is first made at trial, that failure may be viewed as negating any later claim of actual prejudice.

Although pretrial disclosure may not be required, prosecutors commonly respond to pretrial requests for specific exculpatory evidence by handing over *Brady* material prior to trial. Indeed, in many jurisdictions, pretrial "*Brady* discovery" is a regular part of discovery practice. For example, prosecutors are asked for, and commonly disclose prior to trial, routine impeachment items such as promises to witnesses. In some jurisdictions, discovery statutes or court rules contain a "*Brady* provision," which brings such disclosure within the formal discovery apparatus. In others, prosecutors simply furnish pretrial *Brady* disclosures apart from the discovery procedures and without court orders.

If the prosecutor refuses to respond to a specific pretrial request, stating that the material need not be disclosed under *Brady*, the defense may ask the trial court to examine the requested items in camera and order disclosure if it should find the items to be exculpatory and material. Courts tend to be reluctant to undertake a pretrial review of *Brady* requests. In support of this position, it is noted: (1) "the judge is ordinarily less oriented to the facts of the case and possible defenses than is the prosecuting attorney"; (2) "requiring the judge to review prosecution files for informa-

---

18. See § 24.3(c).

tion useful to the defendant casts the judge in a defense advocate's role"; and (3) in camera inspection can become a "ponderous, time-consuming task if utilized in every case merely on demand." Courts expressing such concerns ordinarily will not provide in camera inspection unless the request is limited to no more than a few items of evidence and the defendant can show some strong basis for believing that the items may be favorable to the defense. Other courts require only that the request be fairly specific (i.e., does not reflect a "fishing expedition") and the material requested is "obviously relevant, competent, and not privileged." Some prosecutors will not oppose such review, preferring to have the court order disclosure before trial rather than find a *Brady* violation following a conviction.

Courts considering pretrial review of alleged *Brady* material have at times referred to *Pennsylvania v. Ritchie*,[19] in which the Supreme Court held that the trial court may conduct a review of the specified item in camera under appropriate circumstances. In that case, involving a postconviction challenge to a trial court's refusal to order pretrial disclosure of potentially exculpatory material in the confidential records of a state protective agency, the Court initially held that the *Brady* rule set the appropriate standard for determining whether the lack of disclosure resulted in a constitutional violation. It then considered the state appellate court's decision on the appropriate procedure for making that determination in the context of confidential state records. The state court "apparently had concluded that whenever defendant alleges that protected evidence might be material, the appropriate method of assessing this claim is to grant full access to the disputed information, regardless of the state's interest in confidentiality." Rejecting that conclusion, the Supreme Court noted that it had never held—even in the absence of a confidentiality statute—that a defense counsel has a "right to conduct his own search of the state's files to argue relevance." Indeed, under "settled practice," where a defendant makes only a general

request, the prosecution decides what it must disclose under *Brady* and that decision is "final" unless the defense counsel brings to the trial court's attention the existence of particular nondisclosed exculpatory evidence. Thus, the Court continued, the trial court here could appropriately conclude, upon balancing the state's interest in the confidentiality of the record against the "benefits of an 'advocate's eye'" in aiding its materiality ruling, that its ruling should be based on an in camera review. The Court added that, within this general framework, a "trial court's discretion is not unbounded. If a defendant is aware of specific information contained in the file (e.g., the medical report [of a complainant alleged to have been sexually assaulted]), he is free to request it directly from the court, and argue in favor of materiality."

Whether a defendant is entitled to the disclosure of exculpatory evidence before entering a guilty plea is an issue that has split the lower courts. Addressing pre-guilty-plea disclosure for the first time in *United States v. Ruiz*,[20] the Court held that the Constitution does not require disclosure of impeachment information prior to a guilty plea. In *Ruiz*, the prosecutor offered the defendant a plea bargain, by which she could have obtained a reduction in sentence, but she rejected the bargain because she would not agree to the term in the agreement waiving her right to receive "impeachment information relating to any informants or other witnesses" as well as her right to receive information supporting any affirmative defense. The defendant later entered a guilty plea without any plea agreement, and then appealed when she did not obtain a reduction in sentence like that the prosecutor had included in the rejected plea agreement. She asserted that the government had an obligation to disclose impeachment evidence before a plea bargain, so that demanding a waiver of that disclosure was unlawful. The Court disagreed.

It first clarified that the issue concerned the validity of a waiver. "When a defendant pleads

---

19. 480 U.S. 39, 107 S.Ct. 989, 94 L.Ed.2d 40 (1987). See also § 24.3(a) (discussing *Ritchie*).

20. 536 U.S. 622, 122 S.Ct. 2450, 153 L.Ed.2d 586 (2002) (also discussed in § 21.3(c)).

guilty he or she, of course, forgoes not only a fair trial, but also other accompanying constitutional guarantees" such as *Brady* rights. A court may "accept a guilty plea, with its accompanying waiver of various constitutional rights, despite various forms of misapprehension under which a defendant might labor," the Court reasoned, and ignorance of impeachment information did not render the waiver invalid. The Court observed that "impeachment information is special in relation to the *fairness of a trial*, not in respect to weather a plea is voluntary ('knowing,' 'intelligent,' and 'sufficient[ly] aware'). Of course, the more information the defendant has, the more aware he is of the likely consequences of a plea, waiver, or decision, and the wiser that decision will likely be. But the Constitution does not require the prosecutor to share all useful information with the defendant." Before rejecting a due process right to the pre-plea disclosure of impeachment information, the Court also considered the "nature of the private interest at stake," "the value of the additional safeguard," and "the adverse impact of the requirement upon the Government's interest." Impeachment evidence may or may not be valuable to a defendant, depending upon how much he already knows about the Government's case, and, given Rule 11's safeguards, there was only a small risk that "in the absence of impeachment information, innocent individuals, accused of crimes, will plead guilty." An obligation to disclose impeachment information could "seriously interfere with the government's interest in obtaining guilty pleas, disrupt investigations, expose potential witnesses to serious harm, and require the government to devote substantially more resources to trial preparation prior to plea bargaining, thereby depriving the plea-bargaining process of its main resource-saving advantages," the Court concluded.

To be sure, the reasoning of the Court in *Ruiz* could support a later ruling that due process does not require the government to disclose to a defendant prior to guilty plea any of the material that *Brady* requires the government to disclose to a defendant in connection with a trial. But in *Ruiz*, the Court did not address the non-disclosure of any information other than impeachment material. Indeed, the plea agreement that was offered to Ruiz included a provision that "any [known] information establishing the factual innocence of the defendant" "has been turned over to the defendant" and that acknowledged the government's "continuing duty to provide such information."

There may be a constitutional duty on the part of the government to disclose to the defendant, prior to a guilty plea, information tending to show that the defendant is factually innocent of the offense, but this duty would be more appropriately rooted in the due process requirement that a guilty plea must be "knowing and voluntary" than in *Brady*'s trial-related protections.[21]

The character of favorable evidence. The prosecution's duty to disclose is limited by most courts to matters that would be admissible in evidence, as only such information could be relevant to the jury's decision. Other courts view admissibility as a critical end-product, but note that the duty to disclose could encompass inadmissible material where that material appears likely to lead the defense to the discovery of admissible evidence. Several decisions of the Court support restricting *Brady* violations to admissible evidence. The nondisclosed material in *Brady* was not relevant to the issue of guilt and the Court relied on that factor in holding that the element of materiality was not satisfied as to that issue. The Court in *United States v. Agurs* specifically rejected the view that the standard for judging materiality "should focus on the impact of the undisclosed evidence on the defendant's ability to prepare for trial, rather than the materiality of the evidence to the issue of guilt or innocence." That the due process duty to disclose extends only to evidence, not strategy, was reaffirmed in *Weatherford v. Bursey*.[22] The Court there rejected the contention that the government had violated *Brady* when it used

---

21. See the discussion of *Ruiz* in § 21.3(c).

22. 429 U.S. 545, 97 S.Ct. 837, 51 L.Ed.2d 30 (1977). See also § 11.8(b).

as a prosecution witness an informant who had previously assured the defendant that he would not testify against him. *Brady*, the Court noted, relates only to concealing evidence favorable to the accused, not to providing the defense with notice that will improve its preparation for meeting the government's evidence. In *Wood v. Bartholomew*,[23] the Court again emphasized the importance of admissibility, when it reasoned that because polygraph results from a test taken by a government witness could not have been introduced as evidence, the prosecutor had no *Brady* obligation to disclose those results to the defense.

Courts sometimes have been troubled by the question of whether evidence that does not point directly to the defendant's innocence nevertheless is "favorable to the accused." Most agree that evidence can be favorable even though it does no more than demonstrate that "a number of factors which could link the defendant to the crime do not." Thus, where the circumstances of the crime suggested that the offender's clothes might have been stained, and defendant's clothes were found not to have been stained, the laboratory report on the examination of his clothes were treated as "favorable" rather than "neutral" evidence. Under some circumstances, however, the rejected links may be so unlikely that the nondisclosed evidence is truly neutral. Thus, where robbers wore loose-fitting coveralls and their faces were masked, the inability of the eyewitnesses to positively identify the defendants was viewed as not really helpful to the defense and therefore not subject to *Brady*. Of course, where the question is close as to whether the evidence is "favorable" or "neutral," the nondisclosure most likely will not meet the test for materiality, discussed below, even if it is determined that the evidence is favorable.

"Suppression by the government"—Prosecution control over the evidence. In *Brady* and *Agurs*, the items not disclosed were within the prosecutor's files. The nondisclosed contracts in *Bagley* apparently were in the files of the investigative agency that had been assisted by the security guards, but the Court saw no reason to even comment on that factor in discussing the prosecution's responsibility. In *Kyles v. Whitley*,[24] the Court rejected the state's contention that a "more lenient" standard of materiality should apply where the "favorable evidence in issue * * * [was] known only to police investigators and not to the prosecutor." While "no one doubts that police investigators sometimes fail to inform a prosecutor of all they know," the Court reasoned, "neither is there any serious doubt that 'procedures and regulations can be established to carry [the prosecutor's] burden and to insure communication of all relevant information on each case to every lawyer who deals with it.'"

The prosecution's obligation under *Brady* thus extends to the files of those police agencies that were responsible for the primary investigation in the case. Information available to other members of the "prosecution team" in the particular case, including even caseworkers from social service agencies, is included in a prosecutor's obligation as well. On the other hand, the prosecution's obligation has been held not to extend to independent agencies that are not involved in the investigation of the case, such as a probation department. Some courts have suggested, however, that the prosecution, on a specific request for potentially exculpatory material not available to the defense, may have a due process obligation to attempt to obtain such material even from an independent agency such as a law enforcement agency of another jurisdiction. Among the factors a court may weigh in determining whether the prosecution has such an obligation are (1) the potential unfairness to defendant; (2) the defendant's lack of access to the evidence; (3) the burden on the prosecutor of obtaining the evidence; and (4) the degree of cooperation between the authorities, both in general and in the particular case. Other instances in which courts have interpreted due process to mandate government assistance in obtaining favorable evidence are discussed in § 24.3(g).

---

23. 516 U.S. 1, 116 S.Ct. 7, 133 L.Ed.2d 1 (1995).

24. Supra note 16.

"Suppression by the government"—Defense diligence. In *Agurs*, the Court described the *"Brady* rule" as applicable to situations "involv[ing] the discovery, after trial, of information which had been known to the prosecution but unknown to the defense." Looking to this language, courts have held that the prosecutor's constitutional obligation was not violated, notwithstanding the nondisclosure of apparently exculpatory evidence, where that evidence was known to the defense and no request for disclosure was made. Before holding the defense responsible for its lack of diligence, courts have insisted on proof that the defense was aware of the potentially exculpatory nature of the evidence as well as its existence. Defense counsel should not be expected to quiz defense witnesses about matters which counsel could not have reasonably expected a witness to have knowledge. Similar to the approach to measuring due diligence in the context of newly discovered evidence, courts tend to measure the knowledge of the defense by reference to what is known to either counsel or client. Arguably, this is inappropriate if defense counsel is deceived about the existence of particular evidence by the client. But certainly under such circumstances, when the defendant himself, and not the prosecution, is responsible for the gap in information, the case for disturbing a conviction is less compelling.

Still another troublesome issue raised by the due diligence concept is how far the defense must go to obtain the material. If the defense makes a request and the prosecutor fails to furnish the item, does the defense have the further obligation to obtain the item by subpoena (assuming that process is available), or can it proceed without the item and raise a *Brady* claim after conviction? Several decisions suggest that the defense must exhaust all efforts to obtain the item where it knows of its existence. This includes obtaining the item from an alternative source where it would be available (e.g., as to a matter of public record).

(c) Disclosure of Witness Statements— Jencks Act. Where the prosecution has within its control the prior recorded statements of its witnesses, the defense will desire to obtain those statements for use in impeaching the prosecution witnesses. Under limited circumstances, *Brady* may require that the prosecution make such statements available to the defense, but the failure to disclose impeachment material will only constitute a due process violation where the lost opportunity for impeachment is so critical that there is a reasonable probability that a different result would have been reached if the statement had been made available for that purpose.

The defense may be able to obtain the prior recorded statement under discovery rules. Some jurisdictions make prior recorded statements of witnesses automatically discoverable, but others either prohibit pretrial disclosure or allow disclosure at the discretion of the trial court. Thus, for most jurisdictions, the only avenue providing assurance that the defense will receive the prior recorded statements of prosecution witnesses is a statute, court rule, or common law ruling modeled upon the federal Jencks Act,[25] which provides for disclosure after the witness testifies at trial.

The Jencks Act was adopted by Congress in 1957 in response to the Supreme Court's ruling earlier that year in *Jencks v. United States*.[26] The Court in *Jencks* had held, in the exercise of its supervisory power, that the trial court erred in denying a defense request to inspect the prior recorded statements of two government witnesses who were F.B.I. undercover agents. The agents had acknowledged that the statements referred to the subject of their testimony, and the defense had requested the statements for use in cross-examining the witnesses. The government contended, however, that the trial court properly denied the defense request because the defense had failed to make any showing of likely inconsistency between the prior statements and the witnesses' current testimony. The Supreme Court flatly rejected that argument, noting that defendant could not be aware of any inconsistency until he viewed the reports. The Court also rejected the contention that the judge could,

---

25. 18 U.S.C.A. § 3500.

26. 353 U.S. 657, 77 S.Ct. 1007, 1 L.Ed.2d 1103 (1957).

through in camera inspection, properly determine if the statements were appropriate for use by the defense in cross-examination. The defense, the Court stated, should be given the statements so it could make its own determination as to whether they might provide a basis for cross-examination.

Controversy sparked by a vigorous dissent in *Jencks* (which accused the Court of affording defendants "a Roman holiday for rummaging through confidential information") led Congress to take immediate legislative action. The statute it produced incorporated the basic thrust of the *Jencks* decision but also introduced some procedural modification. Like the *Jencks* decision, the Jencks Act establishes a right of access that is not conditioned on showing of materiality or likely inconsistency between a witness's testimony and prior recorded statement. Following the testimony of a government witness (but not before), the trial court, on application of the defense, must direct the government to disclose any "statement" of the witness "in the possession of the United States" that "relates to the subject matter as to which the witness testified." If the government contends that the entire statement or any portion of it does not relate to the subject matter of the witness's testimony, it submits the statement to the trial court for an in camera review. The court then excises such material as it finds not to relate to the witness's testimony, orders disclosure of the remainder, and preserves the excised material so that its decision to excise can be reviewed in appeal if the case should result in a conviction. If the government elects not to make the statement available as ordered by the court, the testimony of the witness is stricken, with a mistrial declared where the court views that as appropriate.

In 1975, a new dimension was added to Jencks-type disclosure with the Supreme Court's ruling in *United States v. Nobles*.[27] In that case, as discussed in § 20.4(b), the Court upheld a trial court order that directed the *defense* to produce, for prosecution use on cross-examination, a written statement of one of the defense witnesses. Such "reverse-Jencks" disclosure was then incorporated in Federal Rule 26.2. The rule largely tracks the Jencks Act procedure, but makes it applicable to disclosure by both sides of the statement of its witnesses, excepting only the defense witness who is also the defendant. Many states have adopted provisions or procedures similar to those included in the Jencks Act. Some of these statutes have required disclosure by both sides, like the federal rule. Others have not adopted reciprocal Jencks requirements.

The issue that has caused courts the most difficulty is the classification of those "statements" that must be disclosed under the Jencks Act or similar state provision. Both the original Jencks Act and the federal rule set forth three different categories of "statements" that are within the disclosure obligation: "(1) a written statement that the witness makes and signs, or otherwise adopts or approves; (2) a substantially verbatim, contemporaneously recorded recital of the witness's oral statement that is contained in any recording or any transcription of a recording; (3) the witness' statement to a grand jury, however taken or recorded, or a transcription of such a statement."

The provision governing grand jury testimony has proven easy to apply, at least compared to the other two provisions. The definition of statement is designed to include only those recitations that represent with a high degree of precision the witness's own comments, for which the witness therefore can appropriately be held accountable. Grand jury testimony, however recorded, is likely to be put in a form that meets that requirement. Indeed, the recordings that fall within the grand jury provision would ordinarily come within the second provision as a "substantially verbatim recital," and the primary function of the grand jury provision is not so much to expand the character of acceptable recordings as to reject any suggestion that grand jury secrecy overrides the basic policy that underlies the requirement of Jencks disclosure.

---

27. 422 U.S. 225, 95 S.Ct. 2160, 45 L.Ed.2d 141 (1975).

In dealing with the other two definitions of "statements," courts have run into difficulty in part because investigators have used techniques that provide a sufficient record of the witness's interview comments to serve their purposes while at the same time not creating a document that will be subject to Jencks disclosure. In this, they have sometimes been successful and sometimes not, but their purpose of avoiding disclosure has not been viewed as itself being self-defeating. An interviewer, whether for the defense or the prosecution, has no duty to create a memorialization that constitutes a "statement" under the Jencks Act. At the same time, once such a statement has been created, the interviewer cannot destroy it on the ground that he had no obligation to create it in the first place.

The Supreme Court has noted that the Jencks Act definition of statement was drawn so as to "eliminate the danger of distortion and misrepresentation inherent in a report which merely selects portions * * * from a lengthy oral recital."[28] Rough notes will rarely themselves be sufficiently complete even if they include occasional selected quotes. On the other hand, what purports to be a substantially verbatim and full account of the witness's comments, made shortly after the interviewer took fairly detailed rough notes, could be treated as a statement of the witness where an interviewer could readily have produced a substantially verbatim record of the complete interview from the combination of his fresh memory and his notes. The requirement that the record be only "substantially verbatim" allows for some paraphrasing of the witness's statement, but it would not encompass a report written basically in the interviewer's own language.

Even if a document falls within the definition of a witness's "statement," it need not be disclosed if it does not "relate to the subject matter concerning which the witness testified." The relationship standard is measured primarily by reference to the events discussed in the witness's testimony, but also takes account of relevance for impeachment based on possible bias. However, a statement that has a bearing upon no more than an incidental subject in the witness's testimony will not have to be disclosed.

(d) The Duty to Correct False Evidence. The prosecutor's due process obligation with respect to false evidence builds upon the Supreme Court's seminal ruling in *Mooney v. Holohan.*[29] In that 1935 ruling, the Court found that the prosecutor's knowing procurement and use of perjured testimony rendered defendant's trial no more than a "pretense" in which the government utilized a "deliberate deception of judge and jury" to obtain a conviction—a result no more consistent with the "rudimentary commands of justice * * * [than] obtaining a like result by intimidation." *Mooney* involved a knowing and intentional use of perjured testimony that related directly to the defendant's commission of the offense charged, but a series of subsequent Supreme Court rulings carried the "*Mooney* principle" far beyond that fact situation. Those rulings established that *Mooney* was not limited to perjury suborned by the prosecutor, but also encompassed the prosecution's failure to correct testimony known to be perjured that the witness had advanced on his own initiative. Thus, where the witness denied that he had kissed the deceased shortly before she was killed by her husband, and claimed that they had been no more than casual friends, the prosecutor violated due process by letting that testimony stand when the prosecutor knew, from previous conversations with the witness, that the witness and the deceased had an ongoing sexual relationship.[30]

---

28. Palermo v. United States, 360 U.S. 343, 79 S.Ct. 1217, 3 L.Ed.2d 1287 (1959).

29. 294 U.S. 103, 55 S.Ct. 340, 79 L.Ed. 791 (1935), also discussed in § 24.3(b).

30. Alcorta v. Texas, 355 U.S. 28, 78 S.Ct. 103, 2 L.Ed.2d 9 (1957). The defendant claimed that he killed his wife in the heat of passion after discovering her kissing the witness. The prosecutor had told the witness not to volunteer the information that he and the wife had sexual relations on several occasions, but to answer truthfully if asked about it. The Court stresses that the witness's testimony created a "false impression" as to a material fact that could have had a bearing on the jury's rejection of defendant's provocation claim and that the prosecutor was fully aware that this was so.

Mooney was not limited to perjured statements that dealt with a substantive element of the prosecution's case. It reaches, for example, perjury related to the witness's motivation for testifying. Thus, where a key witness denied having received any promise of lenient treatment, the prosecutor's failure to correct that testimony, which he knew to be false, resulted in a denial of due process.[31] Most significantly, the knowledge element of the *Mooney* principle was held to be the collective knowledge of the prosecution, not the knowledge of the individual prosecutor. Thus, in *Giglio v. United States*,[32] where a critical prosecution witness testifies falsely that he had not received a promise that he would not be indicted, the state was not excused from correcting that statement by virtue of the trial attorney's belief that the witness was telling the truth. A promise of immunity had been made by another prosecutor who handled the case at an earlier stage, that promise was attributable "to the Government," and the due process obligation of *Mooney* was that of the prosecutor's office as a whole, for it operated as an entity in serving as "the spokesman for the Government."

Taken together, *Mooney* and its progeny establish a constitutional obligation of the prosecution as an entity not to deceive the fact finder or allow it to be deceived by the prosecution witnesses. This obligation requires that it not suborn perjury, not use evidence known to be false, and not allow known false testimony of its witnesses to stand uncorrected. Where the government fails to fulfill that obligation, it matters not whether its failure is attributable to negligence or an intent to deceive. The state in either event bears a responsibility for possibly denying the defendant a fair trial. Similarly, as lower courts have not-

ed, it matters not whether the witness giving false testimony is mistaken or intentionally lying. If the prosecution knows that the witness's statement is untrue, it has a duty to correct it.[33]

Because the *Mooney* principle is based upon the defendant's right to a fair trial, the Court has refused to go so far as to hold that the knowing failure to correct false testimony produces a due process violation without regard to whether the false testimony was likely to have had an impact upon the outcome of the trial. The false testimony must have been "material," but the standard of materiality imposed here is easier for the defendant to meet than the "reasonable probability" requirement of *Brady*. It is sufficient that the court finds a "reasonable likelihood" that a different result could have been reached if the prosecutor had revealed that the testimony was false.[34] The Court has come to look upon this standard as no more than a reformulation of the *Chapman v. California* standard for determining whether a constitutional violation constitutes harmless error.[35] As Justice Blackmun explained in his plurality opinion in *United States v. Bagley*, the materiality element of the false testimony cases was defined prior to the *Chapman* ruling. Whereas the *Mooney* line of cases spoke of requiring the reversal of a conviction if there "was any reasonable likelihood that the false testimony could have affected the judgment of the jury," *Chapman* spoke of a constitutional violation requiring the reversal of convictions unless that error was "harmless beyond a reasonable doubt." The *Chapman* Court had noted, however, that "there was little if any difference between a rule formulated as in [the *Mooney* line of cases] in terms of 'whether there is a reason-

---

31. Napue v. Illinois, 360 U.S. 264, 79 S.Ct. 1173, 3 L.Ed.2d 1217 (1959).

32. 405 U.S. 150, 92 S.Ct. 763, 31 L.Ed.2d 104 (1972).

33. Relying on *Giglio*, lower courts often speak of the *Mooney* principle as applicable when the prosecution knew or "should have known" that the testimony was false. The Supreme Court itself has used similar language. It has never suggested, however, that the government has an obligation to check a witness's statement against information that might be provided by others who have not been contacted but might be in a position to contradict the

witness. It seems likely that the phrase "should have known" was meant to encompass only the situation, as in *Giglio*, where positive information already in the possession of the prosecution established that the testimony was false. As lower courts have noted, this concept may take into consideration information known not only to the prosecution staff, but also to the police.

34. United States v. Bagley, 473 U.S. 667, 105 S.Ct. 3375, 87 L.Ed.2d 481 (1985).

35. See § 27.6(c).

able possibility that the evidence complained of might have contributed to the conviction' and a 'rule requiring the beneficiary of a constitutional error to prove beyond a reasonable doubt that the error complained of did not contribute to the verdict obtained.' " "It is therefore clear," the *Bagley* plurality concluded, that the two standards of review should be viewed as "equivalent."

(e) The Government's Obligation to Preserve Evidence. In *California v. Trombetta*,[36] the defendants, relying on "the *Brady* principle," argued that the state had a due process obligation to preserve potentially exculpatory material that came into its possession during the course of an investigation. The police there, after having the defendants submit to a Intoxilyzer (breath-analysis) test, followed their standard practice of purging the Intoxilyzer chambers with clean air, thereby destroying the breath samples. Noting that it would have been technically feasible to preserve the breath samples, and that the samples could then have been used by the defense to challenge the Intoxilyzer test results, the defendants argued that those results therefore should be suppressed. The California Court of Appeals agreed, holding that due process required the state "to establish and follow rigorous and systematic procedures to preserve the captured evidence." A unanimous Supreme Court, per Marshall, J., reversed that ruling.

Justice Marshall's *Trombetta* opinion initially noted that the question of the "government's duty to take affirmative steps to preserve evidence" was only roughly analogous to the question presented in "nondisclosure cases" such as *Brady* and *Mooney*. Special difficulties were presented "in developing rules to deal with evidence destroyed through prosecutorial neglect or oversight" he stated:

> Whenever potentially exculpatory evidence is permanently lost, courts face the treacherous task of divining the import of materials whose contents is unknown and, very often, disputed. Moreover, fashioning remedies for the illegal destruction of evidence can pose

troubling choices. In nondisclosure cases, a court can grant the defendant a new trial at which the previously suppressed evidence may be introduced. But, when evidence has been destroyed in violation of the Constitution, the court must choose between barring further prosecution or suppressing—as the California Court of Appeal did in this case— the State's most probative evidence. * * * Here * * * the police had acted in good faith, destroying material they had obtained only for the "limited purpose of providing raw data to the Intoxilyzer." There was "no allegation of official animus toward [defendants] or of a conscious effort to suppress exculpatory evidence."

Although stressing that the officers had acted "in good faith and in accord with normal practices," the *Trombetta* opinion did not rest its ruling on that factor alone. Justice Marshall also added: "Whatever duty the Constitution imposes on the States to preserve evidence, that duty must be limited to evidence that might be expected to play a significant role in the suspect's defense." Such "evidence must both possess an exculpatory value that was apparent before the evidence was destroyed, and also be of such a nature that the defendant would be unable to obtain comparable evidence by other reasonably available means." In the case before it, the Court noted, neither of these conditions were met. The established accuracy of the Intoxilyzer test indicated that "in all but a tiny fraction of cases, preserved samples would simply confirm the Intoxilyzer's results." Moreover, even if it were assumed that the test results in this case were inaccurate, that inaccuracy could be attributed only to a limited number of possible malfunctions, and all of those possibilities could be raised at trial without resort to the preserved breath samples.

In *Arizona v. Youngblood*,[37] the Court built upon the *Trombetta* reference to "good faith" in analyzing the due process implications of the loss of evidence where, unlike *Trombetta*, the defendant could not obtain "comparable

---

36. 467 U.S. 479, 104 S.Ct. 2528, 81 L.Ed.2d 413 (1984).

37. 488 U.S. 51, 109 S.Ct. 333, 102 L.Ed.2d 281 (1988).

evidence by other reasonably available means." In *Youngblood*, the defendant, convicted of the sexual molestation and kidnapping of a 10–year–old boy, had protested the state's failure to properly preserve evidence so as to permit testing for blood group identification. A hospital physician had obtained semen samples from the victim's rectum and the police had collected the victim's clothing, but due to the inadvertent failure of police criminologists to promptly perform tests on the samples and to refrigerate the clothing, it later proved impossible to perform blood group testing that could have been matched against defendant's blood. The lower court had held that because the main issue at trial was identity and the government was responsible for the destruction of evidence that could have conclusively eliminated the defendant as the perpetrator, a conviction was precluded by due process. Rejecting that reasoning, the Supreme Court majority held that "unless a criminal defendant can show bad faith on the part of the police, failure to preserve potentially useful evidence does not constitute a denial of due process of law."

The Court focused on two factors in explaining why the due process standard governing the failure to preserve evidentiary material required a showing of bad faith, though "good or bad faith" was admittedly "irrelevant" under the due process standard of *Brady*. First, as had been noted in *Trombetta*, "whenever potentially exculpatory evidence is permanently lost, courts face the treacherous task of divining the import of materials whose contents are unknown, and, very often, disputed." Second, the Court was "unwilling * * * to read the fundamental 'fairness requirement' of the Due Process Clause as imposing on the police an undifferentiated and absolute duty to retain and to preserve all material that might be of conceivable evidentiary significance in a particular prosecution." "Requiring a defendant to show bad faith on the part of the police," the Court noted, would appropriately restrict the constitutional obligation of police to preserve evidence to "that class of cases where the interests of justice most clearly require it, i.e., those cases in which the police

themselves by their conduct indicate that the evidence would form a basis for exonerating the defendant." The significance of this limitation, the Court added, was illustrated by the facts in *Youngblood*. The police there had collected the rectal swab and the clothing on the night of the crime, a full six weeks before the defendant was taken into custody. Moreover, one of the tests that the state criminologist later found he could not use (because the clothing had not been refrigerated) was a protein molecule test that the police department had only recently started to use. The suggestion of the lower court that the state had some due process obligation to employ a particular investigatory tool was mistaken: "The situation here is no different than a prosecution for drunk driving that rests on police observation alone; the defendant is free to argue to the finder of fact that a breathalyzer test might have been exculpatory, but the police do not have a constitutional duty to perform any particular tests."

Of course, *Youngblood* and *Trombetta* set forth only the minimum, constitutionally compelled obligation of the government with respect to the preservation of potential defense evidence. A greater obligation may flow from state law. Many states, for example, have rejected *Youngblood's* requirement of bad faith in interpreting their own constitutional provisions. In most jurisdictions, however, the inadvertent failure to preserve discoverable material will rarely lead to a judicial remedy, especially where the prosecution has otherwise recognized its obligation and made a good faith effort to comply (e.g., by adopting and following systematic procedures for the preservation and destruction of evidence). States have also enacted statutes requiring the preservation of biological evidence, due to the remarkable number of instances in which improved DNA analysis of biological evidence has demonstrated a defendant's innocence years after conviction. *Youngblood* himself was freed in 2000 after a new type of DNA analysis was performed on the remaining sample. The testing revealed that just as he had argued for nearly twenty years, his was indeed a case of mistaken identity. In 2002, the man whose DNA matched the sample was convicted and sentenced for the crime.

The remedies for a *Youngblood/Trombetta* violation most often sought by defendants are dismissal of the prosecution or, if the lost or destroyed evidence would have been relevant only to challenge particular evidence of the prosecution, exclusion of that evidence. In determining whether the government's failure to preserve discoverable materials requires some form of relief benefitting the defense, lower courts have tended to adopt what one court described as a "pragmatic balancing approach." The "appropriateness or extent of sanctions * * * depends upon a case-by-case assessment of the government's culpability for the loss, together with a realistic appraisal of its significance when viewed in light of its nature, its bearing upon critical issues in the case, and the strength of the government's untainted proof." If the defendant can establish that the evidence was destroyed for the very purpose of hindering the defense, such conscious impropriety may be enough to warrant relief without any further showing as to the likely impact of the destroyed evidence, as the prosecution's motivation in destroying the evidence carries with it a sufficient inference of prejudice. Of course, with the evidence not available, it will be extremely difficult to make a clear showing of exculpatory character and even where that showing can be made, the relief may be limited to informing the jury that the evidence was lost and should be assumed to have the exculpatory characteristics claimed by the defense.

(f) Defense Use of Subpoenas. All jurisdictions have statutes or court rules authorizing the defense to use the trial court's subpoena power to compel persons to appear as witnesses at trial or to produce at trial designated documents or objects. Availability of such subpoenas commonly is automatic. Where a defendant in a state case seeks to direct a subpoena to a person in another state, then the applicable Uniform Act will require the defendant (and the prosecution as well when it is using the Act) to show that the designated witness is "material and necessary."[38]

Where the defendant is financially unable to pay the witness fee, the state will bear that cost although the issuance might then require more than a mere request. For example, Federal Rule 17 requires the defendant to show both that he is unable to pay the fee and that the presence of the witness is necessary for an adequate defense. In light of the defendant's sixth amendment right to compulsory process and his fifth amendment right not to be subject to disabilities because of his financial status, necessity under the Rule has been construed to mean only "relevant, material, and useful to an adequate defense." Even under this liberal construction, however, courts have denied numerous defense requests, usually on the ground that the witness would only be cumulative or would not have personal knowledge that would allow him to give relevant testimony. Some states impose upon the indigent defendant a more substantial burden in establishing need and also make that showing a matter of public record, so that the defense request often becomes an avenue of discovery for the prosecution. Others seek to avoid the issue of need by granting to the indigent defendant the automatic authority to subpoena a certain number of witnesses at state expense (although a showing of need is required if the defense goes beyond that number).

A primary limitation on a subpoena is that it must be for "evidence," that is, information that will be admissible at trial.[39] This limitation will rarely be called into question on a subpoena directing a person to testify. The individual may be able to claim a privilege or immunity that will excuse him from testifying, but ordinarily the witness must appear and make that claim rather than seek to quash the subpoena. Still a challenge may occasionally be allowed by motion to quash when the party

---

38. Uniform Act to Secure the Attendance of Witnesses From Without A State in Criminal Proceedings, § 2, 11 U.L.A. 2 (1974).

39. United States v. Nixon, 418 U.S. 683, 94 S.Ct. 3090, 41 L.Ed.2d 1039 (1974) (holding that documents sought to subpoena under Rule 17(c) must be admissible at trial).

subpoenaed claims an absolute and clearly evident immunity from being required to testify. More frequently, the question of privilege is raised in a motion to quash directed at a subpoena duces tecum.

Whether dealing with a subpoena ad testificandum or a subpoena duces tecum, a court assessing the evidentiary character of subpoenaed testimony, documents, or other items must look beyond the local law defining witness competency, privileges, and other evidentiary limitations or immunities. For as the leading compulsory process case shows, the Constitution can override the state law and declare admissible and subject to subpoena that which would otherwise not be admissible. In that case, *Washington v. Texas*,[40] the Court held unconstitutional a local rule that made accomplices incompetent to testify for one another, although allowing them to testify for the state.[41]

A subpoena may also be challenged where the circumstances indicate that the defense's use is directed at a purpose other than a "good faith" effort to obtain evidence. Since the primary non-evidentiary use of the subpoena is discovery, this objection is presented largely in situations in which the defense seeks by subpoena duces tecum to gain production of documents or other items for inspection prior to trial (as is allowed on court order in many jurisdictions). The prosecutor or recipient of the subpoena may contend here that the defense is not seeking to examine the items in order to facilitate their later use at trial, but instead is conducting a fishing expedition in order to determine whether there is anything in the documents worth using at trial and possibly gain additional information for trial preparation. The critical factor in determining the defense's purpose here is often the scope of the subpoena. Where the subpoena seeks a specific document that clearly is relevant, courts invariably conclude that the subpoena is proper. Where the subpoena seeks a broad range of documents described generically (e.g., all documents relating to a particular transaction or a particular person), it is much more likely to be characterized as other than a good faith effort to produce evidence for use in trial. This limitation is significant even in a jurisdiction that has extremely broad pretrial discovery for the defense, as discovery obligations are limited to documents and other items within the possession or control of the prosecution, while subpoenas can be directed to third persons.

(g) Assisting the Defense in Obtaining Evidence. In some situations, the prosecution may have a duty to assist defense efforts to obtain evidence. Perhaps the most common illustration is the prosecutor's duty, imposed under discovery rules in various jurisdictions, to make its physical evidence available to the defense so that the defense may conduct its own scientific tests using that evidence.[42] Some courts, relying on *Brady*, have held that the defense has a constitutional right to such assistance where it can establish a reasonable basis for believing that the test results may be both "favorable" and "material." A contrary position argues that due process is satisfied by providing the defense with full opportunity to challenge the testimony of the prosecution's expert with respect to the physical evidence. The government may have an obligation in some jurisdictions to hold line-ups to assist the defense. While the defendant has no constitutional right to a line-up, several courts have held that due process may require the prosecution to honor a line-up request under special circumstances. Ordinarily, the defense must establish that eyewitness identification will be

---

40. 388 U.S. 14, 87 S.Ct. 1920, 18 L.Ed.2d 1019 (1967).

41. *Washington* rejected the contention that the Compulsory Process Clause dealt only with the production of the witnesses and not with the admissibility of their testimony. In *Taylor v. Illinois*, discussed in § 20.6(c), the Court reexamined this issue and reached the same conclusion. The Court there acknowledged that the position it had rejected in *Washington* was "supported by the plain language of the Clause, by the historical evidence that it was intended to provide defendants with subpoena power they lacked at common law, by some scholarly comment, and by a brief excerpt from the legislative history of the Clause." Nonetheless, the broader reading of the Clause developed in *Washington* found support in state constitutional provisions that influenced the adoption of the Sixth Amendment and the basic aim of the Amendment to promote an adversary system of adjudication.

42. See § 20.3(g).

a material issue in the case and that "there exists a reasonable likelihood of a mistaken identification which a lineup would resolve."

In some circumstances, the prosecution may have an obligation to assist the defendant in finding potential defense witnesses. In *Roviaro v. United States*,[43] the defendant, charged with (1) an illegal sale of heroin to "John Doe," and (2) illegal transportation of that heroin, sought before and during trial to ascertain Doe's identity. Those efforts were rejected on the ground that Doe was a government informer and his identity was protected by the "informer's privilege." Defendant was convicted on both counts on the basis of testimony by two police officers. One testified that, while keeping Doe under surveillance, he observed Doe drive defendant to a location where defendant first retrieved a package (later found to contain narcotics) from under a tree then transferred that package to Doe, then departed. The second officer testified that he had been hiding in the trunk of Doe's car and had heard defendant discuss with Doe the proposed transfer of the package. Before the Supreme Court, the government conceded that the nondisclosure of Doe's identity was improper as to the illegal sale charge, for as to it Doe had been an "active participant," but contended that the transportation charge was distinct and did not require disclosure. The Supreme Court disagreed. Writing for the majority, Justice Burton first sought to place in proper perspective the so-called "informer's privilege." What was at stake was "in reality the Government's privilege to withhold from disclosure the identity of persons who furnish information of violations of the law." While that privilege furthered "the public interest in effective law enforcement," it was limited in scope by "fundamental requirements of fairness." Thus, "where the disclosure of an informant's identity * * * is relevant and helpful to the defense of an accused, or is essential to a fair determination of a cause, the privilege must give way" and the government must choose between disclosing the informant's identity or dismissing its prosecution. There was, however, "no fixed

rule" as to when disclosure was required to make that choice. "The problem is one that calls for balancing" of the interests involved on a case-by-case basis, "taking into consideration the crime charged, the possible defenses, the possible significance of the informant's testimony, and other relevant factors."

On the facts of the *Roviaro* case, the Court held that the balancing process tipped in favor of requiring disclosure of the informer's identity. The defendant here was placed in the position of explaining or justifying his alleged possession of narcotics. Unless he waived his constitutional right not to take the stand on his own defense, Doe was "his one material witness." Doe's testimony "might have disclosed an entrapment" or "might have thrown doubt upon petitioner's identity or the identity of the package." He was "the only witness who might have testified to petitioner's possible lack of knowledge of the contents of the package." Doe was, in sum, "the only witness in a position to amplify or contradict the testimony of the government witnesses" and the "unfairness" of denying defendant access to Doe was "emphasized" by the government's use itself of testimony regarding an alleged conversation between defendant and Doe.

Although *Roviaro* was based on the Court's supervisory authority over the federal courts,[44] both lower courts and commentators have viewed the decision as "suggest[ing] that the decision was constitutionally compelled." Lower courts also have applied *Roviaro* in somewhat different circumstances, such as where police undercover agents were additional eyewitnesses to the alleged crime and thus were in essentially the same position vis-a-vis the offense as the informant. On the other hand, the lower courts have quite consistently held that disclosure is not required where the informant merely provided information concerning the offense, such as by telling the police of the location of contraband. However, if the informant was more than a "tipster," and arranged for the illegal transaction but was not present when it occurred, it would seem that disclo-

43. 353 U.S. 53, 77 S.Ct. 623, 1 L.Ed.2d 639 (1957).

44. McCray v. Illinois, 386 U.S. 300, 87 S.Ct. 1056, 18 L.Ed.2d 62 (1967).

sure would be called for should the defendant claim entrapment.

In order to determine more concretely the nature of an informer's potential testimony, some courts have recommended an in camera hearing. Another creative solution adopted by one judge was to order the informant to furnish written responses under oath to questions submitted by the defense.

Some authority is to be found holding that whenever *Roviaro* requires the prosecution to disclose the informer's identity, the government must also "undertake reasonable efforts" to obtain the information needed in order for defendant to find the informant. Even where the government has no responsibility for the witness, it may have an obligation to disclose information available to it that will assist the defense in finding the witness. Thus, where the prosecution knew that the defense was having trouble locating a material witness and also knew that the witness was currently incarcerated under a different name, it could not simply remain silent while the defense found itself unable to produce the witness.

(h) Government Interference with Defense Access. The teaching of *Webb v. Texas*[45] is that due process also comes into play when the court or prosecution takes steps that undermine the defense's ability to utilize the subpoena authority to gain testimony at trial. In *Webb*, the trial judge on his own initiative warned defendant's sole witness, who had an extensive criminal record and currently was serving a prison sentence, against committing perjury. The judge said if he lied he could "get into real trouble," that any lies would be "personally" brought to the attention of the grand jury by the judge, and that a perjury conviction was "probably going to mean several years," and "will be held against you * * * when you're up for parole." After hearing those remarks and the judge's comment to defense counsel that the witness could "decline to testify," the witness refused to give any testimony. Although quoting extensively

from a leading compulsory process case, the Court in *Webb* reversed defendant's conviction on due process grounds. "In the circumstances of this case," said the Court, the judge's remarks violated defendant's right to a fair trial because they had been cast in "unnecessarily strong terms" and "effectively drove that witness off the stand."

Although *Webb* involved judicial action, the same principle is applied to prosecutorial efforts to discourage prospective witnesses from testifying for the defense. Such prosecutorial action as threatening the prospective witness with prosecution (either for perjury or for some other offense) if he should testify, or isolating the prospective witness during the trial can result in a due process violation. As with the application of the *Brady* doctrine, and in contrast to *Youngblood's* standard for the failure to preserve evidence, an element of bad faith is not essential to establishing a constitutional violation. Rather, the critical questions are whether (1) the witness was important to the defense, and (2) as a result of the prosecutor's action, the defendant was denied the witness's testimony or the witness changed his testimony so as to be less favorable to the defense. As in *Webb*, due process violations have been found in cases in which the prosecution acted in the honest belief that its action was necessary to ensure against witness perjury.

Some lower courts had concluded that the *Webb* principle produced a per se due process violation when the government charged a defendant with smuggling aliens into the country and then deported many of those aliens before defendant even had an opportunity to interview them. The Supreme Court in *United States v. Valenzuela–Bernal*[46] declined to go that far. Stressing that the government was responsible both for enforcing the criminal law and faithfully executing the congressional policy favoring prompt deportation of illegal aliens, the Court concluded it was proper for the government to undertake "the prompt deportation of illegal-alien witnesses upon the

---

45.   409 U.S. 95, 93 S.Ct. 351, 34 L.Ed.2d 330 (1972).

46.   458 U.S. 858, 102 S.Ct. 3440, 73 L.Ed.2d 1193 (1982).

Executive's good-faith determination that they possess no evidence favorable to the defendant in a criminal prosecution." Accordingly, the mere act of deportation would not in itself constitute a violation of either the Due Process or Compulsory Process Clauses. To establish a violation of those constitutional guarantees, which were treated as imposing basically the same constitutional standard, the defense would have to show "that the evidence lost would be both material and favorable to the defense." But, because the prompt deportation deprived defense of an opportunity to interview the witnesses to determine precisely what favorable evidence they possessed, the defense would not be expected to render "a detailed description of their lost testimony." It would be satisfactory to make "a plausible showing that the testimony of the deported witness would have been material and favorable to the defense in ways not merely cumulative to the testimony of available witnesses." Materiality here requires a reasonable probability that the testimony could have affected the judgment of the trier of fact, although courts in making that assessment would have to "afford some leeway for the fact that the defendant necessarily proffers a description of the material evidence rather than the evidence itself."

(i) Defense Witness Immunity. *Roviaro* required the government to sacrifice a governmental interest relating to effective law enforcement in order to assist the defense in gaining access to a potentially critical witness. Commentators frequently have argued that the same principle should mandate that the government make available to the defense the testimony of witnesses who refuse to answer questions by the defense based on their fifth amendment privilege against self-incrimination. This situation is distinguishable from instances in which a witness's exercise of another privilege stymies the defense in obtaining testimony, it is argued, because here, the interest of the witness underlying the privilege can be preserved and the testimony can be

made available by a government grant of use immunity.

Lower courts have for the most part rejected these arguments and have held that the Constitution does not entitle a criminal defendant to have immunity granted to witnesses so that they can testify on the defendant's behalf. No such right has been found in the Sixth Amendment's Compulsory Process Clause, for the subpoena is made fully available by the trial court and the Compulsory Process Clause has been held not to override the exercise by witnesses of privileges as significant as the self-incrimination privilege. Finally, the due process obligation of *Brady* is held not to apply, for that deals only with the disclosure of evidence in the government's possession, not with the extraction of evidence from others.

Nevertheless, "fundamental fairness" may require a trial court to dismiss a case if the prosecution refuses to grant immunity to a defense witness under particularly egregious circumstances. For example, the Second Circuit Court of Appeals has held that a trial judge is required to order the government to grant immunity or face dismissal when the court finds (1) that the government has "engaged in discriminatory use of immunity to gain a tactical advantage"; (2) the witness's testimony is "material, exculpatory, and not cumulative;" and (3) the testimony is "unobtainable from any other source."[47]

Apart from this type of deliberate distortion of the fact-finding process, the judiciary is bound by legislation governing the granting of immunity, which typically entrusts to the executive branch the discretion as to whether to grant immunity. As one court argued, judges should not be propelled into "unchartered waters" where they are required to weigh "public interests" that are not always apparent from the record or readily measured. The prosecution's loss is not necessarily lessened because the prosecution remains free to prosecute the immunized witness based on evidence either previously or later acquired from other sources for the prosecution carries a "heavy burden"

47.　United States v. Bahadar, 954 F.2d 821 (2d Cir. 1992); United States v. Ballistrea, 101 F.3d 827 (2d Cir. 1996).

in establishing any such independent source. The government may even have to curtail its cross-examination of the witness in order to narrow the scope of the testimony that the defendant will later claim tainted his subsequent prosecution.[48] Courts have also warned that defense witness immunity could create opportunities for undermining the administration of justice by inviting cooperative perjury among law violators. Codefendants could secure use immunity for each other, and each immunized witness could exonerate his codefendant at a separate trial by falsely accepting sole responsibility for the crime, secure in the knowledge that his admission could not be used at his own trial for the substantive offense. In the end, many courts have concluded that these policy considerations may be better assessed by prosecutors than by judges.

§ 24.4   The Presentation of Evidence

(a) The Rules of Evidence and Cross Examination. The legal standards that govern the admissibility of evidence and the questioning of witnesses are the subject of separate treatises and will not be examined here. As in civil cases, those standards are derived in large part from the rules of evidence established under local law. However, in criminal cases, the implications of the defendant's constitutional rights also must be considered. The defendant's constitutional right of confrontation, for example, can prohibit the admission

of hearsay evidence offered by the prosecution that is otherwise admissible under local law.[1] The defendant's right to testify, to compulsory process, or to fundamental fairness may override privileges or rules of exclusion recognized under state law and require the admission of defense evidence that would otherwise be inadmissible.[2] Thus, assessing the admissibility of both prosecution and defense evidence requires examination of the possible bearing of constitutional guarantees as well as the rules of evidence.

In addition, rules of exclusion designed to promote other goals of criminal procedure may affect admissibility. Thus, the rule governing guilty pleas may preclude admissibility of statements made during plea negotiations, the rules on discovery may allow exclusion of evidence due to discovery violations, and rules requiring pretrial notice of intent to use evidence may be enforced through exclusion.[3] Statements made in the course of pretrial suppression hearings may be excluded at trial so that defendants are not forced to choose between giving up a valid Fourth Amendment claim or waiving the privilege against self-incrimination.[4]

The sixth amendment right of confrontation and the Due Process Clause may override state law and provide to the defendant cross-examination opportunities that would otherwise be contrary to state statute, court rule, or other rulings.[5] A witness's fifth amendment privilege

---

48. See § 8.11 discussing immunity.

§ 24.4

1. Williamson v. United States, 512 U.S. 594, 114 S.Ct. 2431, 129 L.Ed.2d 476 (1994); White v. Illinois, 502 U.S. 346, 112 S.Ct. 736, 116 L.Ed.2d 848 (1992); Idaho v. Wright, 497 U.S. 805, 110 S.Ct. 3139, 111 L.Ed.2d 638 (1990); Richardson v. Marsh, 481 U.S. 200, 107 S.Ct. 1702, 95 L.Ed.2d 176 (1987).

2. Compare Rock v. Arkansas, 483 U.S. 44, 107 S.Ct. 2704, 97 L.Ed.2d 37 (1987) (stating evidentiary rules must not be arbitrary or disproportionate to "legitimate interests" and finding that state rule prohibiting in any case the admission of hypnotically refreshed testimony was impermissible "in the absence of clear evidence * * * repudiating the validity of all posthypnosis recollections"); Green v. Georgia, 442 U.S. 95, 99 S.Ct. 2150, 60 L.Ed.2d 738 (1979) (violation of due process to exclude certain reliable evidence favorable to the defense); with Montana v. Egelhoff, 518 U.S. 37, 116 S.Ct. 2013, 135 L.Ed.2d 361 (1996) (finding state law barring the introduction of evi-

dence of intoxication by the defense does not violate due process) and United States v. Scheffer, 523 U.S. 303, 118 S.Ct. 1261, 140 L.Ed.2d 413 (1998) (rule barring introduction of polygraph evidence does not unconstitutionally abridge the right to present a defense).

3. See Michigan v. Lucas, 500 U.S. 145, 111 S.Ct. 1743, 114 L.Ed.2d 205 (1991) (upholding state rule barring defendant from introducing evidence of past sexual conduct between victim and defendant unless defendant first complies with notice and hearing requirement); Williams v. Florida, 399 U.S. 78, 90 S.Ct. 1893, 26 L.Ed.2d 446 (1970) (upholding enforcement of state rules conditioning ability to call alibi witness upon pretrial notice to the prosecution).

4. See Simmons v. United States, 390 U.S. 377, 88 S.Ct. 967, 19 L.Ed.2d 1247 (1968) discussed in § 9.2(a).

5. See Olden v. Kentucky, 488 U.S. 227, 109 S.Ct. 480, 102 L.Ed.2d 513 (1988) (holding that the trial court's refusal to permit the petitioner to cross-examine complainant about her cohabitation with her boyfriend violated the

against self-incrimination may also bar certain cross-examination questions that would otherwise be acceptable impeachment under state law (e.g., inquiring about immunized testimony or a coerced confession[6]). The assertion of the privilege against self-incrimination by the defendant is addressed in § 24.5; the problem of obtaining testimony from a defense witness who claims the privilege is addressed in § 14.3(g) and in § 24.3(i); denial of face-to-face confrontation between defendant and witness is discussed briefly in § 24.2(3); and the following subsection examines the ability of a litigant to elicit a claim of privilege from a witness.

(b) Forcing a Claim of Privilege by a Witness. Where the prosecutor or defense counsel has been informed by a witness that he or she intends to claim the privilege against self-incrimination, is it appropriate to nonetheless call the witness to the stand? To do so does not violate any rights of the witness; a witness, in contrast to a defendant, has no right not to be called to testify, but must exercise the privilege in response to each individual question. However, to force the witness to claim the privilege in open court is often to invite the jury to draw an inference unfavorable to the other side based on the witness's refusal to testify. Thus where the prosecution calls a person that the jury is likely to associate with the defendant (such as an alleged accomplice) and that person exercises the privilege, the jury might well draw the inference that the witness is guilty and, by implication, that the defendant is guilty as well (particularly where the defendant exercises his own fifth amendment right not to testify). On the other side, where the defense calls a person who has been antagonistic to the defendant and asks that person about his role in the events in question or in his assistance of the police, and that witness then claims the privilege, that

could well lend credence to a defense suggestion that the witness actually committed the crime or, at least, "framed" the defendant.

The ABA Standards provide in both the *Prosecution Functions Standards* and the *Defense Function Standards* that it is improper (indeed, "unprofessional conduct" in some instances) to "call a witness who the [prosecutor or defense counsel] knows will claim a valid privilege not to testify for the purpose of impressing upon the jury the fact of the claim of the privilege." Most lower courts also find no basis for applying a different rule to the defense and the prosecution. When a court refuses to allow a defendant to force a claim of privilege, it will often give a "neutralizing instruction" that informs the jurors that for reasons developed out of their presence, the witness is unavailable to either side, and they should draw no inference from the witness's nonappearance.

The leading Supreme Court ruling on the prosecution forcing a witness to claim the privilege on the stand is *Namet v. United States*.[7] The Court there found no improper motive on the part of the prosecutor. Although the prosecutor had been informed by the defense counsel that the witnesses in question would claim the privilege, the prosecutor was not under an obligation "to accept at face value every asserted claim of the privilege, no matter how frivolous." The prosecutor reasonably believed that the witnesses possessed nonprivileged evidence that would corroborate the government's case and was able to solicit some helpful evidence from the witnesses before they invoked the privilege. The Court did suggest, however, that reversible error could occur in two situations: (1) where the prosecutor, in calling the witness, made "a conscious and flagrant attempt to build [the prosecution's] case out of inferences arising from the use of the testimonial privilege"; and (2) where the

petitioner's sixth amendment rights); Smith v. Illinois, 390 U.S. 129, 88 S.Ct. 748, 19 L.Ed.2d 956 (1968) (holding that Sixth and Fourteenth Amendments provide the right to cross-examine an informer who was the key prosecution witness); Davis v. Alaska, 415 U.S. 308, 94 S.Ct. 1105, 39 L.Ed.2d 347 (1974) (defendant denied right of confrontation when prohibited from cross-examining a primary prosecution witness to demonstrate his probation status,

despite a state practice of protecting the anonymity of juvenile offenders); Chambers v. Mississippi, 410 U.S. 284, 93 S.Ct. 1038, 35 L.Ed.2d 297 (1973) (due process violated by application of state rule prohibiting defendant who called witness from cross-examining that witness).

6. See § 9.6(a).

7. 373 U.S. 179, 83 S.Ct. 1151, 10 L.Ed.2d 278 (1963).

facts of the particular case strongly suggest that inferences from a witness's refusal to answer did, in fact, add "critical weight to the prosecution's case" in a form not subject to cross-examination and thereby prejudiced the defense. While these two grounds were set forth as standards applicable to federal cases, at least the second appears to have gained constitutional status.

Notwithstanding *Namet's* suggestion that bad faith alone would constitute a grounding for reversal of a conviction in the federal courts, both federal and state courts have indicated that some showing of likely prejudice is also needed. Often the same circumstances on the part of the prosecution that establish bad faith will suggest likely prejudicial impact. These factors include prosecutorial misrepresentations to the court concerning the witness, the failure of the prosecutor to alert the court to the potential problem, and attempts by the prosecution to draw inferences from the witness's exercise of the privilege. In assessing prejudice courts also consider whether any inferences from the witness's assertion of privilege (1) related to central issues or collateral matters; (2) were cumulative as to a point strongly established by the prosecution's evidence; (3) were opposed by the defense through timely objection; or (4) were countered by warnings by the trial court.

(c) Sequestration of Witnesses. Witnesses on both sides of a criminal case are often sequestered in order "to lessen the danger that their testimony will be influenced by hearing what other witnesses have to say, and to increase the likelihood that they will confine themselves to truthful statements based on their own recollections."[8] From ancient times, authorities intent on discovering the truth have prevented witnesses from learning before they testify of the stories of other witnesses. This practice today is governed in large part by statute or court rule. Sequestration provisions typically will include some language as to when a sequestration order should be issued and who may be exempted from a sequestration order, but otherwise offer little guidance

about the permissible scope of sequestration or remedies for its violation.

Entitlement to sequestration and scope of sequestration. As an initial matter, the failure to sequester prosecution witnesses does not necessarily violate any right of the defendant to cross-examine those witnesses in particular or to a fair trial generally. Until recent decades, for example, judges in most courts possessed the discretion to withhold an order sequestering witnesses. Provisions such as Federal Rule of Evidence 615 now mandate sequestration upon the request of either party in many jurisdictions. Yet even where sequestration is required upon request, not all government witnesses will be sequestered. Several exceptions, discussed below, allow particular witnesses to remain present throughout the testimony of other witnesses. Although these opportunities for government witnesses to be "aided or schooled" by exposure to trial evidence pose the risk that those witnesses will slant the truth, or at least deprive the defendant of the advantage of surprise on cross-examination, similar problems are raised by some forms of witness preparation as well as by witness exposure to publicity about the case. In order for the absence of sequestration to amount to a due process violation, the defendant would, at the very least, have to demonstrate not only that the absence of sequestration likely affected the witness's testimony, but that the testimony likely affected the outcome of the case.

Disputes sometimes arise over whether a sequestration order prohibits merely the witness's presence in the courtroom during the trial testimony of other witnesses prior to the witness's own direct testimony, or whether it instead extends to control the witness's exposure to information in other ways, or at other times. Courts have not adopted a uniform practice. Some assume that a routine sequestration order inherently prohibits counsel from conferring with witnesses during breaks and recesses in the witness's testimony, or from referring, in the presence of the sequestered

---

8. Perry v. Leeke, 488 U.S. 272, 109 S.Ct. 594, 102 L.Ed.2d 624 (1989).

witness, to the testimony of other witnesses. Courts have concluded that sequestration bars witnesses from speaking to one another during the course of the trial, listening to trial reports on the radio, or participating prior to trial in group interviews with other witnesses. Other courts find that sequestration orders are not violated by these practices. Because mere exclusion from the courtroom would seem easily circumvented without further safeguards, parties who wish broader protection than the basic courtroom ban should specifically request instructions admonishing attorneys and witnesses not to engage in extra-courtroom communications.

Witnesses exempted from sequestration. Every jurisdiction provides exemptions from sequestration orders for particular witnesses. The four categories of witnesses most commonly exempted by court rule or decision are (1) parties; (2) party representatives (e.g., an investigating officer for the state); (3) victims; and (4) any witness "whose presence is * * * essential to the presentation of [a] party's cause."

Obviously the defendant must be able to attend his own trial, even if he plans to testify on his own behalf. Corporate defendants may be represented throughout the trial at the defense table although a court may require that the representative be someone who is not a witness. A representative of the state, too, may be present at trial. This person is almost always an agent who has assisted in the investigation of the case. Some states, however, have made no provision for the presence of such a representative in criminal cases, and have allowed an investigative officer to remain in the courtroom only if that officer's presence falls within the exception for persons "essential" to the presentation of the government's case. This exception may also allow expert witnesses to remain in the courtroom during the testimony of others.

In addition, a number of jurisdictions responding to victims' concerns have limited the circumstances under which judges may exclude victims or their family members from the courtroom. While some victim provisions absolutely prohibit judges from excluding victims, others include language that such a person may be sequestered if the judge concludes that person's presence would be "prejudicial." Still other jurisdictions may address the risk that a victim will alter his testimony by requiring that the victim testify first or that the jury be instructed that the victim has heard the testimony of others. In any event, the defendant's interests in a fair trial must take precedence over any statutory or state constitutional right of the victim to remain in the courtroom.

Remedies for sequestration violations. When a sequestration order is violated courts have discretion to choose from among several remedies. Mistrial is rarely ordered. Another option for significant violations is the exclusion of part or all of the witness's testimony. Alternatively, a judge may permit the witness to testify, and instruct the jury to consider the witness's exposure to trial evidence when assessing the credibility of the witness's testimony. As an additional alternative or in combination with any of these responses, a court may choose to hold the witness or those responsible for the violation in contempt.

The choice of remedy often depends on which party is offering the witness's testimony because limiting the defendant's ability to present witnesses in his defense implicates his due process right to present a defense and his sixth amendment right to compulsory process. These rights are not absolute—defense witnesses may be excluded following a sequestration violation just as they may be excluded following a discovery violation.[9] Yet to protect against undue infringement of the defendant's rights, exclusion should be avoided absent proof that the witness's testimony has actually been affected by the violation and that the testimony may affect the outcome. Some courts also require a showing that the defendant was complicit in his witness's violation before excluding or striking the testimony of a defense witness. For these reasons the favored response in many jurisdictions is allowing the

---

9.   See Taylor v. Illinois, discussed in § 20.6(c).

witness to testify, but permitting impeachment of the witness by asking the witness about the violation.

Should the government's violation be reviewed after trial, the prosecutor must prove that the defendant was not prejudiced by the trial court's failure to take appropriate remedial steps. A new trial may be necessary if the witness's testimony was "in any way tailored to the testimony he had heard" and that testimony may have affected the jury's verdict.

§ 24.5 Defendant's Rights to Remain Silent and to Testify

(a) Right Not to Take the Stand. The Self–Incrimination Clause of the Fifth Amendment, applicable to the states through the Fourteenth Amendment's Due Process Clause, states that no person "shall be compelled in any criminal case to be a witness against himself." But the constitutional privilege against compelled self-incrimination has been interpreted by the Court to be much broader than those words would suggest. As discussed earlier, assertion of the privilege is not limited to defendants, nor is it limited to criminal trials.[1] However, the Court has interpreted the privilege to have special meaning in a criminal trial as it relates to the defendant. The privilege entitles a witness not to answer specific questions posed in a criminal trial or in any other proceeding where he is under compulsion to answer if his answers would furnish a "link in the chain of evidence" needed to prosecute him for a criminal offense.[2] The privilege entitles the criminal defendant to even greater protection. The defendant need not even appear as a witness. The right of the defendant is not only to avoid being compelled to give incriminating responses to particular inquiries, but to resist being placed in a position where the inquiries can be put to him while he is under oath.[3]

There is good reason for applying the privilege so broadly in this particular context. As the Supreme Court explained in *Wilson v. United States*,[4]

> It is not every one who can safely venture on the witness stand though entirely innocent of the charge against him. Excessive timidity, nervousness when facing others and attempting to explain transactions of a suspicious character, and offences charged against him, will often confuse and embarrass him to such a degree as to increase rather than remove prejudices against him. It is not every one, however honest, who would, therefore, willingly be placed on the witness stand.

This privilege, however, cannot be invoked selectively. The Supreme Court in *Brown v. United States*[5] explained that the defendant

> has the choice, after weighing the advantage of the privilege against self-incrimination against the advantage of putting forward his version of the facts and his reliability as a witness, not to testify at all. He cannot reasonably claim that the Fifth Amendment gives him not only this choice but, if he elects to testify, an immunity from cross examination on the matters he has himself put in dispute. It would make of the Fifth Amendment not only a humane safeguard against judicially coerced self-disclosure but a positive invitation to mutilate the truth a party offers to tell.

Thus, once a defendant testifies he becomes liable to cross-examination on matters "reasonably related to the subject matter of his direct examination."[6] At a minimum, this means that he may be questioned concerning all facts relevant to the matters he has testified to on direct examination. In addition, he is subject to searching cross-examination for im-

§ 24.5

1. See §§ 6.5, 8.10, 8.11.

2. Hoffman v. United States, 341 U.S. 479, 486, 71 S.Ct. 814, 818, 95 L.Ed. 1118 (1951).

3. The right of a defendant not to testify arose only after the defendant was considered competent to testify on his own behalf. See § 24.5(d).

4. 149 U.S. 60, 13 S.Ct. 765, 37 L.Ed. 650 (1893) (discussing statutory provision authorizing a criminal defendant to testify on his own behalf).

5. 356 U.S. 148, 78 S.Ct. 622, 2 L.Ed.2d 589 (1958).

6. Jenkins v. Anderson, 447 U.S. 231, 100 S.Ct. 2124, 65 L.Ed.2d 86 (1980); Harrison v. United States, 392 U.S. 219, 88 S.Ct. 2008, 20 L.Ed.2d 1047 (1968).

peachment purposes, for by testifying he places his credibility in issue and opens the door to fair comment upon considerations affecting his veracity. A defendant does not completely waive his fifth amendment privilege at trial by testifying solely on collateral or preliminary matters, however, such as the appointment of counsel.[7]

In *Brooks v. Tennessee*,[8] the petitioner questioned the constitutionality of a statute requiring that a defendant "desiring to testify shall do so before any other testimony for the defense is heard," a rule related to the ancient practice of sequestering prospective witnesses in order to prevent them from being influenced by other testimony in the case.[9] The Court majority held that the statute "violates an accused's constitutional right to remain silent," as a defendant "cannot be absolutely certain that his witnesses will testify as expected or that they will be effective on the stand" and thus "may not know at the close of the State's case whether his own testimony will be necessary or even helpful to his cause." This statute, the Court added, "may compel even a wholly truthful defendant, who might otherwise decline to testify for legitimate reasons, to subject himself to impeachment and cross-examination at a time when the strength of his other evidence is not yet clear." The Court then went on to rule that the statute also constituted "an infringement on the defendant's right of due process," as "by requiring the accused and his lawyer to make [the choice of whether to testify] without an opportunity to evaluate the actual worth of their evidence," it deprives the accused "of the 'guiding hand of counsel' in the timing of this critical element of his defense." Chief Justice Burger, joined by Blackmun and Rehnquist, JJ., dissented. They argued that there was no violation of the right to remain silent in that the defendant was not confronted with a choice any more difficult than that approved by the Court prior cases and that there was no due process violation because counsel may "be

restricted by ordinary rules of evidence and procedure in presenting an accused's defense" even "if it might be more advantageous to present it in some other way," as illustrated by the rule forbidding counsel from asking leading questions of the defendant.

Brooks did not suggest that the state is deprived of all authority to adopt procedures, otherwise supported by the legitimate ends of procedural efficacy, where those procedures might operate to make more difficult the defendant's exercise of his choice between testifying and remaining silent. If that were the case, the state would not be allowed to force the defendant to make his choice as to whether to testify before he has a jury evaluation of the strength of the prosecution's case-in-chief. The Court will weigh, in the individual case, the nature of the state's interest and the character of the burden placed upon the defendant in making his choice, especially as it compares to burdens traditionally faced by the defense.

For example, only a year before *Brooks*, in *Crampton v. Ohio*,[10] a somewhat differently composed Court (again divided) rejected in a different procedural setting an "undue-burden" argument very much like that which won the day in *Brooks*. The defendant in *Crampton* contended that Ohio's law providing for the jury determination of the death penalty option in the proceeding in which it determined guilt created "an intolerable tension" between his constitutional right not to be compelled to be a witness against himself on the issue of guilt and his constitutional right to be heard on the issue of punishment. He argued further that the tension readily could have been avoided by the state's adoption of the bifurcated trial procedure used by other states, whereby the jury decides the issue of guilt before presentation and argument on the issue of punishment. In finding no constitutional need for a bifurcated trial, the Court concluded that "the policies of the privilege against compelled self-incrimination are not offended when a defendant in a

---

7. Simmons v. United States, 390 U.S. 377, 88 S.Ct. 967, 19 L.Ed.2d 1247 (1968), discussed in § 9.2(a).

8. 406 U.S. 605, 92 S.Ct. 1891, 32 L.Ed.2d 358 (1972), also discussed in § 20.4(d).

9. See § 24.4(d).

10. One of the cases decided in McGautha v. California, 402 U.S. 183, 91 S.Ct. 1454, 28 L.Ed.2d 711 (1971).

capital case yields to the pressure to testify on the issue of punishment at the risk of damaging his case on guilt" and that a state is not "required to provide an opportunity for [a defendant] to speak to the jury [on the issue of punishment] free from any adverse consequences on the issue of guilt." The Court acknowledged that it might well be that "bifurcated trials * * * are superior means of dealing with capital cases," but from "a constitutional standpoint," it could not "conclude that * * * the compassionate purposes of jury sentencing in capital cases are better served by having the issues of guilt and punishment determined in a single trial than by focusing the jury's attention solely on punishment after the issue of guilt has been determined." Also, a court does not offend the Constitution by denying a defendant's motion to sever multiple counts for separate trials whenever the defendant wishes to testify on one count but not the other. As discussed in § 17.1(c), before granting severance in this situation, most courts first require a showing that the testimony is significant to the defense of one charge, as well as a showing that the defendant has a strong need to remain silent on the other charge.

(b) Comment on Defendant's Silence.
Prior to *Griffin v. California*,[11] some states permitted comment by the court or the prosecutor or both regarding the defendant's failure to take the stand. In *Griffin*, the Court concluded such comments were constitutionally impermissible. The Court characterized comment on defendant's silence as "a penalty imposed by courts for exercising a constitutional privilege" in that it "cuts down on the privilege by making its assertion costly." As for the state's claim that "the inference of guilt for failure to testify as to facts peculiarly within the accused's knowledge is in any event natural and irresistible," the Court responded that this is not inevitably the case, as where a defendant declines to testify merely because his prior convictions would then be admissible for impeachment purposes.

The Court limited *Griffin* somewhat in two decisions, *Lockett v. Ohio*,[12] and *United States v. Robinson*.[13] In *Lockett*, where the prosecution repeatedly referred to the state's case as "unrefuted" and "uncontradicted," the Court concluded these comments did not "violate constitutional prohibitions [as] Lockett's own counsel had clearly focused the jury's attention on her silence, first, by outlining her contemplated defense in his opening statement and, second, by stating * * * near the close of the case, that Lockett would be the 'next witness.'" Similarly, in *Robinson*, where defense counsel had noted at several points that the government had never allowed the defendant to explain his side of the story, the Supreme Court held that *Griffin* did not bar the prosecutor's response that the defendant "could have taken the stand and explained it to you." Applying the *Lockett* principle that the prosecutorial comment must be examined in context, the Court concluded that the prosecutor's reference did not treat the defendant's silence as "substantive evidence of guilt," but was a "fair response" to a claim by defense counsel.

In *Mitchell v. United States*,[14] however, a narrow majority of the Court declined to adopt an exception to *Griffin* that would have allowed a sentencing judge to draw an adverse inference from a defendant's silence at sentencing. Justice Kennedy writing for the Court stated that the "concerns which mandate the rule of [*Griffin*] against negative inferences at a criminal trial apply with equal force at sentencing." The *Griffin* rule, he wrote, "has become an essential feature of our legal tradition" and a "vital instrument for teaching that the question in a criminal case is not whether the defendant committed the acts of which he is accused," but "whether the Government has carried its burden to prove its allegations while respecting the defendant's individual rights."

Criticizing the *Griffin* line of cases as illogical, Justice Scalia's dissenting opinion in

---

11.   380 U.S. 609, 85 S.Ct. 1229, 14 L.Ed.2d 106 (1965).

12.   438 U.S. 586, 98 S.Ct. 2954, 57 L.Ed.2d 973 (1978).

13.   485 U.S. 25, 28, 108 S.Ct. 864, 866, 99 L.Ed.2d 23 (1988).

14.   526 U.S. 314, 119 S.Ct. 1307, 143 L.Ed.2d 424 (1999), also discussed in § 26.4(c).

Mitchell argued that the reasoning of *Griffin* "runs exactly counter to normal evidentiary inferences." Moreover, the rule has no basis in the history of the Fifth Amendment, he argued, and called its adoption "a breathtaking act of sorcery." He noted that "[t]raditionally defendants were expected to speak rather extensively at both the pretrial and trial stages of a criminal proceeding," and that our "hardy forebearers, who though of compulsion in terms of the rack and oaths forced by the power of law, would not have viewed the drawing of a commonsensical inference as equivalent pressure."

The *Griffin* ruling has been heavily criticized by commentators as well. Nevertheless, it has prompted several states to enact statutes and rules barring comments on defense silence. *Griffin* has also spawned an immense body of case law addressing when a statement that does not refer directly to a defendant's failure to take stand is nonetheless an impermissible comment on that failure. Courts agree on the general standard for resolving that issue—"whether the language used was manifestly intended or was of such character that the jury would naturally and necessarily take it to be a comment on the accused's failure to testify." The variation arises in their evaluation of roughly similar remarks in roughly similar settings. Thus, a prosecutor's comment that defendant "failed to exhibit shamefulness" may be viewed by one court as a comment on defendant's failure to testify and by another as a reference to his behavior. Among the frequently challenged comments producing such a variation are those that refer to the prosecution's case as "unrefuted" or "uncontradicted." Most challenges to such comments fail, although appellate courts often avoid the need to decide whether the statement was prohibited by *Griffin* by holding that any constitutional error was harmless beyond a reasonable doubt. The defense is most likely to be successful where the comment was repeated several times, included a pointed reference to the defendant, or was made in a case in which the prosecution's evidence was such that only the defendant himself could have contradicted it.

(c) Instruction on Defendant's Silence. The Court in *Griffin* reserved decision on whether a defendant can require that the jury be instructed that his silence must be disregarded. The matter was settled in *Carter v. Kentucky:*

> A trial judge has a powerful tool at his disposal to protect the constitutional privilege—the jury instruction—and he has an affirmative constitutional obligation to use that tool when a defendant seeks its employment. No judge can prevent jurors from speculating about why a defendant stands mute in the face of a criminal accusation, but a judge can, and must, if requested to do so, use the unique power of the jury instruction to reduce that speculation to a minimum.

In *James v. Kentucky*,[15] the Court held that, notwithstanding an ambiguous distinction in state law between "admonitions" and "instructions," defense counsel's request for an admonition to the jury on defendant's right to remain silent was sufficient to invoke the protections of *Carter.* In declining to characterize counsel's action as a request for an oral rather than a written statement to the jury, the Court stated that the Constitution "does not afford the defendant the right to dictate, inconsistent with state practice, *how* the jury is to be told." Somewhat the reverse problem reached the Court in *Lakeside v. Oregon*,[16] where petitioner argued "that this protective instruction becomes constitutionally impermissible when given over the defendant's objection" because it "is like 'waving a red flag in front of the jury.'" The Court rejected that argument because it "would require indulgence in two very doubtful assumptions," namely, "that the jurors have not noticed that the defendant did not testify and will not, therefore, draw adverse inferences on their own," and "that the jurors will totally disregard the instruction, and affirmatively give

---

15. 466 U.S. 341, 104 S.Ct. 1830, 80 L.Ed.2d 346 (1984).

16. 435 U.S. 333, 98 S.Ct. 1091, 55 L.Ed.2d 319 (1978).

weight to what they have been told not to consider at all."

(d) The Defendant's Right to Testify. Although at an earlier time a criminal defendant could plead his cause in person and therefore as a practical matter—though not in theory—could furnish evidence in his own behalf, in eighteenth century England there took hold the rule that a defendant was incompetent to give testimony. This rule was based on the fear that a person so directly interested in the case was likely to testify falsely. The English rule was inherited by American jurisprudence as a part of the common law but was rejected thereafter. On the federal level, for example, the Supreme Court first abrogated the general rule of incompetency based on interest[17] and then specifically acknowledged the right of a federal defendant to testify.[18] There were similar developments at the state level so that by the end of the nineteenth century all but one state (which later changed its practice) granted criminal defendants a right to testify. As a result of the recognition of that right under local law, the Supreme Court did not find it necessary to squarely rule on the defendant's constitutional right to testify until the mid–1980s.

In *Rock v. Arkansas*,[19] the Court held that there was, indeed, a constitutional right "to testify on one's own behalf at a criminal trial." That right was said to stem from three sources: (1) the guarantee of due process (which ensures a "fair adversary process," including a "right to be heard and to offer testimony"); (2) the Sixth Amendment's Compulsory Process Clause (which "logically include[s]" defendant's "right to testify himself"); and (3) the Fifth Amendment's guarantee against compulsory self-incrimination (a "necessary corollary" of which is the defen-

dant's right to testify "in the unfettered exercise of his own will").

The defendant's right to testify is not without limitation. It may be restricted to accommodate other "legitimate interests in the criminal trial process."[20] For example, the Court has sustained sentence increases for false testimony, although those increases arguably limit the ability of a defendant to testify. The right to testify is not a license to lie.[21]

In *Portuondo v. Agard*,[22] the Court rejected the defendant's claim that his rights to be present and testify at trial were burdened impermissibly by the prosecutor's argument that his presence during the testimony of other witnesses allowed him to tailor his testimony to theirs. Writing for the Court, Justice Scalia characterized the inference the prosecutor asked the jury to draw as "natural and irresistible." The prosecutor's comments were "in accord with the longstanding rule that when a defendant takes the stand, 'his credibility may be impeached and his testimony assailed like that of any other witness.' " Allowing this argument to be made to the jury is "appropriate" and "sometimes essential—to the central function of the trial, which is to discover the truth." As the dissenting opinion noted, however, some state courts have forbidden accusations of tailoring based on presence at trial.

Rock's clear recognition of the right to testify as constitutionally grounded has, however, led to several successful challenges to restrictions placed on the exercise of the right. Restrictions, as *Rock* noted, "may not be arbitrary or disproportionate to the purposes they are designed to serve." *Rock* itself involved a ban on hypnotically refreshed testimony. The Court held that even though the state has a legitimate interest in imposing evidentiary restrictions designed to exclude unreliable evidence, that interest could not justify a per se

---

17. United States v. Murphy, 41 U.S. (16 Pet.) 203, 10 L.Ed. 937 (1842).

18. McVeigh v. United States, 78 U.S. (11 Wall.) 259, 20 L.Ed. 80 (1870).

19. 483 U.S. 44, 107 S.Ct. 2704, 97 L.Ed.2d 37 (1987).

20. See also Perry v. Leeke, 488 U.S. 272, 109 S.Ct. 594, 102 L.Ed.2d 624 (1989) (a testifying defendant, like any other witness, may be precluded from discussing his testimony with counsel during the course of giving that

testimony, including a short recess declared in the midst of his testimony).

21. See § 26.4(c) (discussing sentence enhancements for defendant's perjury); Nix v. Whiteside, 475 U.S. 157, 106 S.Ct. 988, 89 L.Ed.2d 123 (1986) (no violation of Sixth Amendment's guarantee of effective counsel for defense counsel to refuse to allow defendant to testify falsely).

22. 529 U.S. 61, 120 S.Ct. 1119, 146 L.Ed.2d 47 (2000).

exclusion of a defendant's hypnotically re-freshed testimony. Such a rule was excessive because it operated without regard either to procedural safeguards to reduce inaccuracies employed in the particular hypnosis process or to the availability of corroborating evidence and other traditional means of assessing the accuracy of the particular testimony.

The waiver of the right to testify may be subject to special requirements. In dicta, the Court in *Rock* referred to the right to testify as fundamental and referenced an ABA standard that distinguishes between decisions that are to be made by defense counsel and those to be made by the defendant, giving the choice to testify to the defendant. To insure that the defendant has made the choice himself, some courts require that the judge, outside the pres-ence of the jury, inform the defendant of his right to testify and receive a specific acknowl-edgment from the defendant that he does not wish to testify. Most jurisdictions do not re-quire an on-the-record waiver, and assume the defendant has waived his right to testify un-less he demands this right.

§ 24.6   Trial Court Evaluation of the Evidence

(a) Bench Trials. Between ten and fifteen percent of federal felony trials are bench trials. A significant portion of felony trials in state court are conducted without juries as well. For much of the nation's history, bench trials in felony cases were unusual. Courts rejected the idea that defendants could waive a jury and be tried before a judge alone. Under common law "the accused was not permitted to waive trial by jury, as generally he was not permitted to waive any right which was intended for his protection." In *Patton v. United States*,[1] the Court paved the way for felony bench trials, holding that a defendant could waive his right to a trial by jury in any criminal case. Most

states now provide for jury waiver. A number require the agreement of the prosecutor to go to trial before a judge, while a few require only the consent of the judge. Conditioning the defendant's ability to forego a jury on the consent of the court or the prosecutor denies the defendant no constitutionally protected ad-vantage, the Court explained in *Singer v. Unit-ed States*.[2] If either refuses to consent, the result is simply that the defendant is subject to trial by jury—the very thing that the Con-stitution guarantees him.

When the trial is to the bench, the judge sits as the finder of fact and makes all the judg-ments with respect to the credibility and weight of the evidence that a jury would make. However, unlike a jury, which merely renders a general verdict on each count, a judge sitting as the trier of fact often makes special find-ings. In many jurisdictions, the judge is re-quired to make such findings upon request of either party. Although the principal usefulness of findings is to facilitate appellate review where the defendant is convicted, findings may also be made in cases in which the defendant is acquitted (and perhaps later used by the defendant in advancing a claim of collateral estoppel if later prosecuted for a related of-fense).[3]

(b) Motions for Directed Acquittal. A trial court may not direct a verdict of guilty, in whole or in part, no matter how conclusive the evidence might appear. To do so would invade the defendant's constitutionally protected right to trial by jury.[4] A directed verdict of acquittal, however, is another matter, as the Supreme Court explained in *Jackson v. Virgi-nia*:[5]

[T]he traditional understanding in our sys-tem [is] that the application of the beyond-a-reasonable-doubt standard to the evidence is not irretrievably committed to jury discre-

---

§ 24.6

1. 281 U.S. 276, 50 S.Ct. 253, 74 L.Ed. 854 (1930).

2. 380 U.S. 24, 85 S.Ct. 783, 13 L.Ed.2d 630 (1965).

3. See § 17.4(a).

4. United States v. Martin Linen Supply, 430 U.S. 564, 97 S.Ct. 1349, 51 L.Ed.2d 642 (1977) (stating trial judge is prohibited from entering a judgment of conviction or di-

recting the jury to come forward with such a verdict); Connecticut v. Johnson, 460 U.S. 73, 103 S.Ct. 969, 74 L.Ed.2d 823 (1983) (conclusive presumption on issue of intent seen as functional equivalent of directed verdict on that issue and thus prohibited).

5. 443 U.S. 307, 99 S.Ct. 2781, 61 L.Ed.2d 560 (1979).

tion. To be sure, the factfinder in a criminal case has traditionally been permitted to enter an unassailable but unreasonable verdict of "not guilty." This is the logical corollary of the rule that there can be no appeal from a judgment of acquittal, even if the evidence of guilt is overwhelming. The power of the factfinder to err upon the side of mercy, however, has never been thought to include a power to enter an unreasonable verdict of guilty.

Jackson held that a defendant has a constitutional right not to be convicted "except upon evidence that is sufficient fairly to support a conclusion that every element of the crime has been established beyond a reasonable doubt." It would appear to follow that the states must provide some avenue by which the defendant can challenge the constitutional sufficiency of the evidence against him. All states do allow for such a challenge; at some stage of the trial proceedings, the trial court will have authority to review the sufficiency of the evidence and enter an acquittal if it does not meet the *Jackson* standard. When the review comes at the end of the prosecution's case-in-chief or at the close of all evidence, the trial court may order the jury to return a verdict of acquittal commonly described as a "judgment of acquittal," "directed acquittal," or "directed verdict." Trial courts also possess authority to review the sufficiency of evidence should the jury convict. This power to enter an acquittal notwithstanding a guilty verdict is known as a judgment *n.o.v.* On appeal from a conviction, the appellate court will again review the sufficiency of the evidence under the *Jackson* standard, provided that issue was properly raised at trial.

In at least one state, statute precludes the court from entering a pre-verdict judgment of acquittal even when it believes that the prosecution has completely failed to prove its case. Such a position reflects the concern that allowing trial judges to enter pre-verdict acquittals will open the door to judicial abuse and manipulation of the process, particularly since dou-

ble jeopardy would bar the prosecution from appealing the judge's decision.[6]

The vast majority of jurisdictions have not chosen to force the defendant to await review of the sufficiency of the evidence until after the jury reaches its decision. As with Federal Rule 29, they provide for a motion for judgment of acquittal that can be presented at the end of the prosecution's case, at the end of the presentation of evidence by both sides, *and* after the discharge of the jury. Typically, that motion is made at the end of the prosecution's presentation of its case-in-chief and must state specifically the deficiency in the government's proof.

(c) The Sufficiency Standard. Although the evidence before the court will differ depending on when the motion for directed acquittal is made, the basic standard for review is the same:

> [A] trial judge, in passing upon a motion for directed verdict of acquittal, must determine whether upon the evidence, giving full play to the right of the jury to determine credibility, weigh the evidence, and draw justifiable inferences of fact, a reasonable mind might fairly conclude guilt beyond a reasonable doubt. If he concludes that upon the evidence there must be such a doubt in a reasonable mind, he must grant the motion; or, to state it another way, if there is no evidence upon which a reasonable mind might fairly conclude guilt beyond a reasonable doubt, the motion must be granted. If he concludes that either of the two results, a reasonable doubt or no reasonable doubt, is fairly possible, he must let the jury decide the matter.

The formulation set forth in the above quote was characterized in *Jackson v. Virginia*[7] as "the prevailing criterion for judging motions for acquittal in federal criminal trials." *Jackson* itself did not insist on this or any other formulation, but it certainly indicated that such a standard was sufficient to fulfill the defendant's constitutional right to be convicted only where "the record evidence could rea-

---

6.   See § 25.3(c).

7.   Discussed at note 5.

sonably support a finding of guilt beyond a reasonable doubt." The Court there stressed also that "the critical inquiry on review of the sufficiency of the evidence * * * does not require a court to 'ask whether *it* believes that the evidence at the trial establishes guilt beyond a reasonable doubt,'" but "simply whether, after viewing the evidence in the light most favorable to prosecution, any trier of fact could have found the essential elements of the crime beyond a reasonable doubt."

(d) Summary and Comment on the Evidence. The common law jury trial included the privilege of the trial judge to comment to the jury about his opinion of the evidence presented, a practice thought to give to the jurors "great light and assistance."[8] While the federal courts have retained this power, in the overwhelming majority of states this function of the trial judge was removed by constitutional provision, statute or judicial decision.

In support of the federal rule reserving judicial comment, it is asserted that the judge's discussion of the evidence will serve to assist the jury and thereby to aid it in arriving at a just result. Those opposed object that the trial judge may abuse the privilege of comment and engage in "partisan advocacy." To remedy such abuse, the power to comment is subject to review in jurisdictions where it is permitted. For example, the Court reversed the conviction of a defendant whose judge had advised the jury to observe that the defendant "wiped his hands during his testimony" and added "that is almost always an indication of lying." The Court explained:

> This privilege of the judge to comment on the facts has its inherent limitations. His discretion is not arbitrary and uncontrolled, but judicial, to be exercised in conformity with the standards governing the judicial office. In commenting upon testimony he may not assume the role of a witness. He may analyze and dissect the evidence, but he

may not either distort it or add to it. His privilege of comment in order to give appropriate assistance to the jury is too important to be left without safeguarding against abuses.

§ 24.7   The Arguments of Counsel

(a) Opening Statements. Prior to the presentation of evidence, both sides may present opening statements. The prosecutor presents the initial opening statement. As for the statement by defense counsel, there is a variation in practice; in some states the defense must present its opening statement immediately following the prosecutor's statement, while elsewhere the defense may reserve its opening statement until after the close of the prosecutor's case. The timing of a defendant's opening statement raises strategic choices. Most defense attorneys prefer to provide a rebuttal to the state's story before the jury hears the evidence, in order to assist the jury in evaluating that evidence.

The Court has explained that the opening statement is "not an occasion for argument," but an opportunity to "state what evidence will be represented, to make it easier for the jurors to understand what is to follow, and to relate parts of the evidence and testimony to the whole."[1] Because the purpose of the opening statement is a narrow one, each attorney is limited to a brief statement of the issues and an outline of what counsel believes can be supported with competent and admissible evidence. Indeed, it is unprofessional conduct for the prosecutor or defense attorney "to allude to evidence to be presented unless, in a good faith there is a reasonable basis for believing that such evidence will be tendered and admitted in evidence."[2]

The prohibitions applicable to the closing argument, discussed in subsection (e) below,

---

8. Quercia v. United States, 289 U.S. 466, 53 S.Ct. 698, 77 L.Ed. 1321 (1933) (quoting Hale, History of the Common Law).

§ 24.7

1. United States v. Dinitz, 424 U.S. 600, 96 S.Ct. 1075, 47 L.Ed.2d 267 (1976).

2. ABA Standards for Criminal Justice: Discovery and Trial by Jury § 15–3.4 (3d ed. 1996).

are binding upon the opening statements as well. If anything, those prohibitions should be applied with greater strictness to opening statements, for unlike the closing arguments, these statements are not supposed to be argumentative. Yet, as is also true of misconduct during closing arguments, courts are inclined to find that an attorney's excessive remarks during opening statement are "cured" by a judge's admonition to the jury to disregard. For example, the most common appellate challenge to a prosecutor's opening statement is that it referred to evidence that subsequently was not admitted at trial. In this situation, appellate courts typically rely upon the fact that the prosecutor later disavowed the erroneous opening statement or that the jury had been given the standard instruction that it "must not regard any statements made by counsel * * * concerning the facts * * * as evidence."[3]

There are instances, however, in which the prosecutor's remarks have been so inflammatory, or the judge's response so inadequate, that an appellate court has reversed the defendant's conviction. Similarly, a trial judge's decision to grant a mistrial has been upheld when the prosecution referred in opening statement, then repeatedly during trial, to important evidence which it "should have been well aware" was inadmissible hearsay. Defense counsel's improper remarks during opening statement may also pose difficulties. Curing instructions typically are sufficient, but a judge's decision to order a mistrial over defense objection may be upheld in particularly egregious cases.[4]

(b) Closing Argument. The special significance of closing argument was recognized in *Herring v. New York*.[5] Although the trial there was to the bench rather than a jury, the Supreme Court held that there had been an unconstitutional interference with defendant's right to counsel when the trial judge an-

nounced his decision convicting the defendant without giving defense counsel the opportunity to present final argument. Justice Stewart noted that even when other aspects of fair procedure, such as compulsory process and confrontation, were in their infancy, the English criminal trial recognized the need for argument between the adversaries. The further development of those other rights, moreover, did not result in a dilution of the system's commitment to argument, but simply resulted in "shifting the primary function of argument to summation of the evidence at the close of trial, in contrast to the 'fragmented' factual argument that had been typical of the earlier common law." The result was to give such argument a central role in the adversary system:

> It can hardly be questioned that closing argument serves to sharpen and clarify the issues for resolution by the trier of fact in a criminal case. It is only after all the evidence is in that counsel for the parties are in a position to present their respective versions of the case as a whole. Only then can they argue the inferences to be drawn from all the testimony, and point out the weaknesses of their adversaries' positions. * * * The very premise of our adversary system of criminal justice is that partisan advocacy on both sides of a case will best promote the ultimate objective that the guilty be convicted and the innocent go free. In a criminal trial, which is in the end basically a factfinding process, no aspect of such advocacy could be more important than the opportunity finally to marshal the evidence for each side before submission of the case to judgment.

While recognizing the special importance of closing argument to the adversarial process, *Herring* also noted that, as with other aspects of the adversarial process, there was room as well for some degree of judicial control. The trial judge should be given "great latitude in regulating the duration and limiting the scope

---

3. Frazier v. Cupp, 394 U.S. 731, 89 S.Ct. 1420, 22 L.Ed.2d 684 (1969) (noting that a "more specific limiting instruction might have been desirable, but none was requested").

4. See Arizona v. Washington, 434 U.S. 497, 98 S.Ct. 824, 54 L.Ed.2d 717 (1978) (trial judge's decision to de-

clare a mistrial on the ground of improper and prejudicial argument is entitled to great deference). Other remedies for improper conduct by defense counsel include contempt or removal from the case, but these do not cure any effect the conduct may have had on the jury.

5. 422 U.S. 853, 95 S.Ct. 2550, 45 L.Ed.2d 593 (1975).

of closing summaries." The judge must have authority, for example, to "terminate argument when continuation would be repetitive or redundant." The judge may also "ensure that argument does not stray unduly from the mark, or otherwise impede the fair and orderly conduct of the trial." Balanced against this authority, however, is the recognition that persuasion is a matter of style as well as content, and counsel must be given considerable room to shape his or her own style in presenting argument. The closing argument traditionally has been the one place in the trial where counsel is given greatest leeway in manner of expression even as the courts strive also to bar the excesses of the overzealous advocate.

(c) Order of Closing Argument. The prevailing view with respect to the order of closing arguments is that followed in the federal system: the prosecution opens the argument, the defendant is then permitted to reply, and the prosecution then is allowed to reply in rebuttal. This structure is grounded in the notion that the fair administration of justice is best served if the defendant knows the arguments actually made by the prosecution for conviction before being faced with the decision whether to reply and what to reply.

In response to the contention that it is unfair to allow the prosecution to make both the first and the last arguments in the case, courts have observed that the prosecution and not the defendant carries the burden of proving guilt beyond a reasonable doubt. Statutes prescribing this order of argument have been upheld against due process challenges. Of course, if the prosecutor improperly interjects a new argument at the time of his rebuttal, then the trial judge might well allow defense counsel to respond to that point.

(d) The Roles of the Prosecutor and Defense Counsel. Although closing arguments are quite clearly a time for advocacy, the prosecutor is often said to be under special restraints because of his unique role in the criminal process. In the oft-quoted language of *Berger v. United States*:[6]

6. 295 U.S. 78, 55 S.Ct. 629, 79 L.Ed. 1314 (1935).

The United States Attorney is the representative not of an ordinary party to a controversy, but of a sovereignty whose obligation to govern impartially is as compelling as its obligation to govern at all; and whose interest, therefore, in a criminal prosecution is not that it shall win a case, but that justice shall be done. As such, he is in a peculiar and very definite sense the servant of the law, the twofold aim of which is that guilt shall not escape or innocence suffer. He may prosecute with earnestness and vigor—indeed, he should do so. But, while he may strike hard blows, he is not at liberty to strike foul ones. It is as much his duty to refrain from improper methods calculated to produce a wrongful conviction as it is to use every legitimate means to bring about a just one. * * * It is fair to say that the average jury, in a greater or lesser degree has confidence that these obligations, which so plainly rest upon the prosecuting attorney, will be faithfully observed. Consequently, improper suggestions, insinuations, and, especially, assertions of personal knowledge are apt to carry much weight against the accused when they should properly carry none.

Pointing to special responsibilities of the prosecutor and the special weight likely to be given to his argument, some commentators have suggested that defense counsel should be given somewhat more leeway in closing argument than the prosecution. That position is thought to follow from the need to provide every assurance that the innocent are not convicted. An acquittal based on an emotional appeal of defense counsel is said to be of far less concern, even where clearly against the weight of the evidence, than a conviction achieved through the emotional appeal of the prosecutor that is equally against the weight of the evidence. This position finds no support, however in the traditional statements of the standards of professional responsibility. They either contain a single listing, applicable to both sides, of the prohibitions governing final argument, or offer separate lists of mirror image content for the defense and the prosecution.[7] Symmetry in the restriction of prosecution and defense argument, however, is not always practiced. Appellate courts only occasionally have the opportunity to consider the propriety of defense counsel's argument. Because an acquittal cannot be challenged by prosecution appeal, the propriety of defense counsel's argument can come before the appellate court only in a case in which the defendant himself is appealing. That issue is unlikely to be presented on such an appeal, except in connection with one of three quite distinct defense objections. First, where the defense challenges the prosecution's closing argument, the propriety of the defense's closing argument may be raised by the prosecution under the "invited response" doctrine discussed below in subsection (f). Second, where the trial court viewed the defense argument as so egregious as to require a mistrial, the defendant may challenge his subsequent retrial as violating the double jeopardy prohibition. As with the invited response doctrine, the applicable standard of review here, although giving consideration to the propriety of defense counsel's argument, also requires consideration of other factors.[8] Finally, where the trial judge cut off defense argument as inappropriate, the defense may claim that such action constituted reversible error. Courts here tend to stress the broad discretion of the trial court, noting that the critical issue is not whether the appellate court agrees that counsel's argument overstepped the bounds of propriety, but whether "there has been a clear abuse of discretion resulting in some prejudice to the accused."

(e) Prohibited Argument. The traditional formulations of prohibited categories of argument are often so general that they require further definitional content through case-specific rulings if they are to provide any guidance to courts and counsel. Such rulings do provide considerable guidance, but they also have their limitations. Reported decisions discussing improper argument focus almost entirely on challenges to arguments by the prosecution since, as noted above, appellate courts rarely rule

directly on the propriety of a defense counsel's argument. Second, appellate opinions that reject challenges to alleged forensic misconduct by prosecutors are sometimes less than clear as to whether the argument of the prosecutor was (1) appropriate without regard to the argument of defense counsel, (2) appropriate only in light of defense counsel having opened the door, or (3) not prejudicial and therefore not requiring reversal even if inappropriate. Finally, appellate opinions deal with such a variety of prosecutorial comments, both upheld and rejected, that a complete description of what has been held to fall within and without a particular prohibition risks drowning the reader in a flood of endless detail. The description that follows therefore provides a far less than exhaustive review of the different categories of arguments, is limited primarily to prosecution arguments, and includes only rulings that clearly addressed the propriety of the particular comment apart from the issue of prejudice.

Going beyond the record. It is commonly stated that the prosecutor may not refer to evidence that is not within the record. To do so not only violates accepted trial norms, but also deprives the defendant of the right to cross-examine a person (the prosecutor) who is, in effect, testifying against him. The question often is presented, however, as to what is argued as evidence beyond the record, what is argued as inference from record evidence, and what is argued as common knowledge. Prosecutors are not prohibited from drawing inferences from the record, and although it is often said these factual inferences must be "reasonably" based on the record evidence, the latitude given prosecutors is very broad. The key here is that the inference be identified as such rather than represented to be a fact actually in the record. The prosecutor also is not prohibited from referring to matters of common public knowledge or basic human experience. References to common sayings about behavior, to classic illustrations, and to commonplace behavior escape the "non-record facts" prohibi-

---

7. See ABA Standards for Criminal Justice: Discovery and Trial by Jury, 15–3.4 (3d ed. 1996); ABA Model Rules of Professional Conduct, Rule 3.4.

8. See Arizona v. Washington, discussed in § 25.2(e).

tion. As with inferences, there are references that the prosecutor sees as a general illustration of human behavior the defense counsel sees as a factual reference not established in the evidence. Most often, however, references to evidence outside the record are clearly identified—as where the prosecutor refers to evidence that was suppressed, misrepresents a witness's testimony, or cites a past criminal record that never came before the jury.

Misrepresentation of the law. As with misrepresentations of the evidence, misrepresentations of the law also constitute improper argument. Counsel may anticipate jury instructions and tie the facts of the case to the elements of the law that will be set forth in those instructions. Indeed, that usually is a major component of closing argument. Because the jury is informed that the law comes from the court, and not from the attorneys, this commonly causes no significant difficulties even if an attorney should misstate somewhat the law as presented in the instruction. Occasionally, however, where the prosecutor's argument was tied in substantial part to a basic misstatement in the law (e.g., the allocation of proof), that misstatement will prove fatal. More frequently, successful challenges to prosecutorial argument have involved references (often accurate) to aspects of the law that are beyond the elements considered in the judge's charge. Indeed, those references usually are to matters on which a judge would refuse to charge a jury if requested because they detract from its responsibility to decide the issue before it. Thus, the jury would not be told that the defendant could appeal a jury's mistake in imposing the death penalty[9] or that the defendant would be released if the jury returned a certain verdict. Here, whether or not the statement of the law is correct, it deals with an aspect of the process not to be considered by the jury and therefore no more to be brought to its attention by counsel than by the court. Defense counsel, too, are limited to arguments relevant to the jury's determination, and are

often barred from commenting on the sentencing consequences of a guilty verdict, or from giving misleading explanations of legal standards.

Personal beliefs and opinions. It is improper for a prosecutor to inform the jury of his or her personal belief in the accused's guilt or in the truth or falsity of a witness's testimony. This practice is pernicious not only because the jury may view the prosecutor's opinion as "carry[ing] with it the imprimatur of the Government," but also because such comments often convey to the jury "the impression that [there exists] evidence not presented to the jury, but known to the prosecutor."[10] Of course, the prosecutor is not prohibited from explaining to the jury why it should conclude the defendant was guilty or accept or reject a particular witness's testimony. Where the prosecutor avoids a direct reference to phrases like "I think," "I believe," and "I know," it is often difficult to draw the line between a characterization based on the evidence and an expression of personal belief. Thus, one court will say that the prosecutor was vouching for the witness when he stated that the two complainants in a rape case "were good and fine girls and not the type the defendant and his witnesses alleged they were," while another will characterize as no more than advocacy the prosecutor's reference to "the 'reputable officers' and 'very sweet' complaining witness who testified for the government."

Comments on privileges and other assertions of rights. As discussed in § 24.5(b), prosecutorial comment on the defendant's failure to testify constitutes constitutional error in itself. Adverse references to the exercise of privileges by others ordinarily also are inappropriate, as will be the reference to the defense's failure to call a particular witness where that witness was known to be unavailable due to his exercise of the privilege.[11] Nor are prosecutors permitted to argue to the jury that a defendant's guilt may be inferred from his failure to consent to a search, his decision to call an attor-

---

9.   Caldwell v. Mississippi, 472 U.S. 320, 105 S.Ct. 2633, 86 L.Ed.2d 231 (1985).

10.   United States v. Young, 470 U.S. 1, 105 S.Ct. 1038, 84 L.Ed.2d 1 (1985).

11.   See § 24.4(c).

ney, or his decision to remain silent at arrest. However, should the defendant take the stand, a prosecutor may question his credibility by pointing out to the jury in closing argument that the defendant's presence allowed him to listen to the other witnesses before he testified.[12]

Appeals to emotion and prejudice. Closing arguments traditionally have included appeals to emotion. It is said to be the "time honored privilege" of counsel to "drown the stage in tears."[13] Such appeals, however, are not without bounds. The outer limit on emotional appeals is generally stated as a prohibition against "arguments calculated to inflame the passions or prejudices of the jury." Illustrative of prohibited appeals to the prejudices of the jury are references to race or religion in characterizing the qualities of the defendant or the reliability of a witness.[14] An illustration of a prohibited appeal to passion is the "Golden Rule" argument that asks the jury to step into the shoes of the victim. Still another is the dramatic and abusive characterization of the defendant (e.g., as a "cheap, slimy, scaly crook") or defense counsel (e.g., a "flat liar"). Yet, here too, distinctions will be drawn and courts will vary in their assessment of what goes "too far." The prosecutor may appropriately call the jury's attention to the plight of the victim and the seriousness of the crime, provided he does not take the "extra step" of asking the jurors to put themselves in the victim's position. So too, the prosecutor may characterize the defendant with disparagement that is reasonably deduced from the evidence in the case. Thus, while courts have held improper the characterization of a defendant as a "sexual fiend," or "Judas Iscariot," or as "hunting each other like animals," others will consider as fair comment (with some dramatic license) the description of the defendant as a "trafficker in human misery," or a "little lizard slipping through the underbrush," "a nine-headed, hydra-headed monster."

Injecting broader issues. The limitation that most frequently lends itself to the drawing of fine lines is that barring the injecting of issues "broader than the guilt or innocence of the accused." Courts ordinarily will allow the prosecutor to "dwell upon evil results of crime" and "urge fearless administration of the criminal law." They also have accepted arguments that a conviction would deter others from committing similar crimes, but this tends to come close to the impermissible. The impermissible is reached where the prosecutor asserts that a guilty verdict would relieve community fears or the threat to the jurors' families. Courts have also condemned appeals to jurors as the taxpayers who pay for the costs of the defendant's attorney, or, in death penalty cases, the costs of incarceration.

(f) The Invited Response. Arguments by the prosecution that would otherwise be improper are sometimes deemed appropriate (or at least "excusable") because the defense "opened the door" with its own improper argument and the prosecution merely "replied in kind." In *United States v. Young*,[15] the defendant challenged this "invited response" doctrine as bottomed on the false premise that "two wrongs make a right." The Supreme Court agreed that two wrongs did not make a right, but it also found justification for the doctrine where properly applied. The Court acknowledged that it was inappropriate for the prosecution to respond to the defense's improper argument with forensic misconduct of its own. The proper response, the Court stressed, is a prosecution objection, accompanied by a "request that the [trial] court give a timely warning [to defense counsel] and curative instructions to the jury." However, because a "criminal conviction is not to be lightly overturned on the basis of a prosecutor's comments alone," even though the prosecutor did not respond in the correct manner, the reviewing court cannot avoid evaluating the

---

12. Portuondo v. Agard, 529 U.S. 61, 120 S.Ct. 1119, 146 L.Ed.2d 47 (2000), discussed in § 24.5(a).

13. Dunlop v. United States, 165 U.S. 486, 498, 17 S.Ct. 375, 379, 41 L.Ed. 799 (1897).

14. McCleskey v. Kemp, 481 U.S. 279, 309 n. 30, 107 S.Ct. 1756, 95 L.Ed.2d 262 (1987) (racially based argu-

ment violates Constitution); United States v. Socony–Vacuum Oil Co., 310 U.S. 150, 60 S.Ct. 811, 84 L.Ed. 1129 (1940) (class).

15. 470 U.S. 1, 105 S.Ct. 1038, 84 L.Ed.2d 1 (1985).

prosecutor's improper, responsive comments in light of the "opening salvo" of defense counsel. Recognition of this factor, the Court noted, should not be seen as giving a "license to make otherwise improper arguments," but simply as fulfilling the task of a reviewing court, which is to determine whether the prosecutor's comments, "taken in context, unfairly prejudiced the defendant." The Court added that the invited response doctrine was limited to situations in which the prosecutor's remarks were relevant to the earlier defense comments and designed to "right the scale." This was in apparent response to Justice Brennan's complaint that too many appellate courts, "rather than apply the [invited response] doctrine as a limited corrective," treated it as "a rule of unclean hands that altogether prevents a defendant from successfully challenging * * * [even] virtually unchecked prosecutorial appeals going far beyond a fair response to defense counsel's arguments." The Court in *United States v. Robinson*,[16] relied on the invited response doctrine to uphold a prosecutor's comment on the defendant's failure to take the stand.

(g) Objections. In some localities, immediate objections to improper closing arguments are expected, while others consider it a matter of common courtesy, verging on obligation, for opposing counsel not to interrupt one another's closing arguments by objections. While appellate courts recognize that the latter custom may result in a delayed objection, they do expect an objection. Though a failure to object is not necessarily fatal to the defense's appellate challenge, it does require a more egregious error by the prosecutor and a clearer showing of prejudice to obtain a reversal. Without objection, the improper argument must reach the level required for a reversal under the plain error doctrine,[17] which was described in *Young* as demanding an error so grave as to "undermine the fundamental fairness of the trial and contribute to a miscarriage of justice."

Judicial insistence upon an objection has been challenged on the ground that objections may be counter-productive. The jury, it is argued, may resent repeated objections. Moreover, the defense attorney's objection, if sustained, may have exactly the opposite effect from that intended as the trial judge's condemnation of the argument may simply call attention to the prosecutor's improper remarks and reemphasize them in the jurors' minds. To meet the first of these concerns, appellate courts do not necessarily require that the objection be made in the presence of the jury. As for the second, the response is that the defense should at least indicate its concern and give the trial judge the opportunity to consider the appropriate remedy, whether that be a curative instruction, a mistrial, or even granting the defense an additional opportunity to argue in response.

(h) Due Process. In *Donnelly v. DeChristoforo*,[18] the Supreme Court held that improper prosecutorial argument could reach the level of a federal constitutional violation. That would occur, however, only if the argument "so infected the trial with unfairness as to make the resulting conviction a denial of due process." In finding that this standard had not been violated in *Donnelly*, the Court noted that the alleged improper remark constituted but "one moment in an extended trial," that the remark was highly ambiguous and might not have been interpreted by the jury as the defendant interpreted it (as suggesting that the defendant had been willing to plead to a lesser offense), and that the trial judge had clearly admonished the jury to disregard the remark.

In *Darden v. Wainwright*,[19] the Court considered a closing argument in a capital case that contained numerous patently improper remarks, reflecting the prosecutor's highly emotional reaction to both the defendant and the gruesome homicide with which he was charged. Nonetheless, a majority held that there had been no constitutional violation un-

---

16.   485 U.S. 25, 108 S.Ct. 864, 99 L.Ed.2d 23 (1988).

17.   See § 27.5(d).

18.   416 U.S. 637, 94 S.Ct. 1868, 40 L.Ed.2d 431 (1974).

19.   477 U.S. 168, 106 S.Ct. 2464, 91 L.Ed.2d 144 (1986).

der the appropriate standard of review—"the narrow one of due process and not the broad exercise of supervisory power." No matter how glaring the prosecutor's misconduct (the Court characterized the prosecutor's closing argument as "fully deserving the condemnation it received from every court to review it"), due process did not mandate a new trial unless that misconduct had such an impact as to deprive the defendant of a fair trial. The Court explained that various aspects of the trial, taken together, supported the lower court's conclusion that the trial " 'was not perfect— few are—but neither was it fundamentally unfair.' " These aspects included the following: the prosecutor's improper comments did not misstate or manipulate the evidence; the comments also did not implicate other specific rights of the accused; much of their objectionable content was responsive to the opening summation of the defense; the defense was able to use its final rebuttal argument (available under state rule) to portray the prosecution's argument "in a light that was more likely to engender strong disapproval than result in inflamed passions"; the trial judge instructed the jurors "several times" that their decision was to be based only on the evidence and that arguments of counsel were not evidence; and the "weight of the evidence against petitioner was heavy." Taking a quite different view of the trial as a whole, the four dissenters in *Darden* characterized the majority opinion as relying upon "an entirely unpersuasive one-page laundry list of reasons for ignoring this blatant misconduct."

(i) Standard of Review. Jurisdictions vary in their approach under local law to the prerequisites for reversing a conviction based upon improper prosecutorial argument. Some apply what is basically the due process standard of *Donnelly* and *Darden*. Others determine initially whether the prosecution's argument was improper, and if it was, then proceed to apply the same harmless error standard that is otherwise applied in the jurisdiction for nonconstitutional errors. Still others use some separate standard of potential prejudice for this particular type of error, with that stan-

dard allowing more readily for reversal than the due process standard of *Darden*. All, however, start from the premise that there must be shown some likelihood of prejudice, perhaps reflecting the view set forth by the Supreme Court in one of its earliest rulings on improper closing argument:

> There is no doubt that, in the heat of argument, counsel do occasionally make remarks that are not justified by the testimony, and which are, or may be, prejudicial to the accused. * * * If every remark made by counsel outside of the testimony were grounds for a reversal, comparatively few verdicts would stand, since in the ardor of advocacy, and in the excitement of trial, even the most experienced counsel are occasionally carried away by this temptation.[20]

In determining whether the improper remarks were likely to have had sufficient impact to require reversal, appellate courts look to a variety of factors, including the following: (1) whether the improper remarks were particularly egregious; (2) whether the improper remarks were only isolated or brief episodes in an otherwise proper argument; (3) whether the improper remarks were balanced by the comments of the defense (either themselves improper or turning the improper remarks against the prosecution); (4) whether defense counsel made a timely and strong objection to the prosecutor's improper remarks, thereby indicating fear of prejudice; (5) whether the trial judge took appropriate corrective action, such as instructing the jury to disregard the improper remarks; (6) whether the improper remarks were combined with other trial errors; and (7) whether there was overwhelming evidence of guilt. The end result will be dependent upon a consideration of all of these factors taken together; no single factor will necessarily control in itself. Thus, where the prosecutor's comments were repeated and particularly inflammatory, a reversal might be required notwithstanding the presence of other factors that would ordinarily weigh heavily in the other direction (e.g., the presence of substantial evidence of guilt).

---

20. Dunlop v. United States, 165 U.S. 486, 17 S.Ct. 375, 41 L.Ed. 799 (1897).

Appellate courts, while commonly finding a lack of prejudice flowing from improper summation by the prosecutor, have with mounting frustration expressed concern over the frequency with which such prosecutorial improprieties occur. Sometimes courts have even suggested that they might well be required to reverse convictions without a showing of prejudice in order to deter such prosecutorial misconduct, but this has been done only rarely. Critics have expressed the view that prosecutors would be effectively deterred if courts more readily reversed for misconduct in closing arguments, but others contend that this is not the case and defendants would simply receive windfall reversals, or are skeptical about the willingness of appellate courts to enforce such a remedy. Those of the latter view are more inclined to favor judicial reprimand, contempt penalties for flagrant misconduct, and disciplinary proceedings for repeated misconduct, remedies which are rarely imposed.

§ 24.8 Jury Instructions

(a) Content of Instructions. The judge provides the jury with instruction throughout the trial, from preliminary guidance about the nature of voir dire and the conduct of jurors, to instructions given during the trial qualifying the jury's use of evidence, to instruction just prior to deliberations. This latter set of instructions is the most detailed and important. The content of the charge given to the jury at the close of evidence and argument can be divided roughly into three areas: (1) the relevant principles of the substantive law of crimes; (2) the relevant principles of the law of evidence relating to proof, presumptions, and the weighing of evidence; and (3) the procedures to be followed by the jury in reaching a verdict. As to the substantive criminal law, the starting point is the offense charged and its elements. Indeed, a failure to charge each of the elements may constitute cognizable error on appeal even where the defense failed to object. As for other elements of the substantive law, such as excuses and justifications, they also must be included if there is evidence in the case that would make these principles relevant and a request for the instruction is made. The principles of the law of evidence that may be covered by a jury charge will also vary with the case. Certain basics—such as the prosecution's burden of proof beyond a reasonable doubt—will always be included.[1] The inclusion of other principles, such as permissive inferences and presumptions and recommended or required ways of weighing certain evidence (e.g., the testimony of an accomplice) will depend on their relevance to the case in light of the evidence presented. The directions relating to the jury's operations, on the other hand, tend to be fairly standardized. They cover such matters as the vote needed for a verdict, the general role of the jury as factfinder, and the process of deliberations (selection of a foreperson, requesting supplemental instructions, etc.).

The necessary content of the jury charge on these matters is left to other sources. In a growing number of jurisdictions, "pattern instructions" are available that include model charges on all of the relevant principles of evidence and jury operations as well as the substantive law for many offenses. Treatises on evidence contain lengthy discussions of errors that may be made in dealing with such matters as presumptions and the burden of proof. Treatises on the substantive law provide similar assistance as to the elements of crimes, excuses, and justifications. Matters relating to the operation of the jury, because they commonly fall outside the scope of evidence treatises, will be treated briefly in § 24.9. Instructions on defendant's silence are discussed in § 24.4 (c). The lesser-included offense doctrine is discussed below. Although that doctrine might be viewed as raising issues primarily of substantive criminal law, it deserves consideration as an aspect of criminal procedure because of its close connection to the law govern-

§ 24.8

1. Taylor v. Kentucky, 436 U.S. 478, 98 S.Ct. 1930, 56 L.Ed.2d 468 (1978); Sullivan v. Louisiana, 508 U.S. 275, 113 S.Ct. 2078, 124 L.Ed.2d 182 (1993).

ing pleadings, multiple prosecutions, and the role of the jury.

(b) Lesser–Included Offenses Generally. No area of law relating to jury instructions has created more confusion than that governing when a court may or must put before the jury for its decision a lesser-included offense, that is, an offense not specifically charged in the accusatory pleading that is both lesser in penalty and related to the offense specifically charged. Certain offenses are so closely related in content that in the course of a trial of one offense the evidence developed may support the elements of a lesser offense. When that occurs, the trial court must consider whether, on application of one of the parties or on the court's own initiative, a charge to the jury on that lesser offense is mandatory, permissive, or prohibited. The answer to that question is in most cases provided by state law, not constitutional law, and can vary considerably from one jurisdiction to another.

Application of the lesser-included offense doctrine rests on two basic inquiries. First, the court must determine whether a particular offense is a "lesser-included offense" to that charged in the accusatory pleading. If the offense is not lesser-included within the definition applied in the particular jurisdiction, then an instruction on that offense is neither required nor allowed (at least if either party objects). The various standards used in determining what constitutes a lesser-included offense for this purpose are considered below in subsection (c). Second, if state law recognizes the offense as a lesser-included offense, then the trial court must determine whether to instruct the jurors that they may consider that offense along with the higher offense. This aspect of the doctrine, which invokes differing views of the role of the jury and has certain constitutional implications, is discussed in subsection (d).

The rules regarding lesser-included offenses developed at common law to aid the prosecution in cases in which its proof may have failed as to the higher offense charged but nonetheless was sufficient to support a conviction on a

lesser offense. What was at stake for the prosecution was more than just the conservation of resources by avoiding the inconvenience of a second prosecution on the lesser offense should the jury acquit on the higher offense. The prohibition against double jeopardy barred a second prosecution for the "same offense," and for that purpose, two separate crimes could be the "same offense" if the elements of the one were totally encompassed within the elements of the other.[2] Thus, where the lesser-included offense was the "same offense" for double jeopardy purposes, which typically was the case under the definition of lesser-included offenses prevailing at common law, the prosecutor would not have had another opportunity to gain a conviction on the lesser offense. Including a jury charge on the lesser-included offense commonly presented the only opportunity the prosecution would have to gain any conviction if the higher charge were to fail.

Courts have come to recognize that a lesser-included offense instruction, under some circumstances, can also be beneficial to the defense. In some situations, the instruction prompts a "compromise verdict," allowing the defense to avoid a conviction on the higher charge that may have resulted if the jury had before it only the choice between conviction on that higher offense and outright acquittal. A jury may be convinced of guilt on the higher charge, but nevertheless use its nullification power to convict only of the lesser offense. Or, the jury may divide initially on the higher charge and rather than continue to debate that charge until reaching unanimity, choose to move to the lesser charge of which all agree that the defendant is guilty. In some jurisdictions, such a process of deliberation would be contrary to the required instruction that jury turn to the lesser-included offense only after it has unanimously found the defendant not guilty on the higher charge. Indeed, in those jurisdictions the jury may be required to return a verdict of not guilty on that higher charge along with its verdict on the lesser charge. In other jurisdictions, however, jurors

2. See § 17.4(b) discussing *Blockburger*.

are not precluded from moving to the lesser offense once it becomes clear that the jury is divided on guilt as to the higher offense. Moreover, the judge may allow the jury simply to return a verdict finding the defendant guilty of the lesser-included offense, which will be taken as an "implied acquittal" on the higher offense.[3]

(c) Defining the Lesser–Included Offense. American courts have shown considerable diversity in determining what constitutes a lesser-included offense. These standards can be organized around three distinct approaches, each of which contain some variations. The first two analyses are commonly titled the "statutory-elements" and the "cognate-pleadings" tests. The third focuses on the proof that is presented at trial, so is referred to as the "evidentiary" approach.

Statutory-elements test. The statutory-elements approach, which was the original common law position, is used today in the federal courts and in a growing number of states. Under this approach, a crime is a lesser-included offense with respect to a higher offense only if it is "necessarily included" in that higher offense, as measured by the statutory elements of the two offenses. "One offense is not 'necessarily' included in another unless the elements of the lesser are a subset of the elements of the charged offense."[4] Thus, the trial court must break down each offense by reference to its elements, without looking to how the offense may have been committed in the particular case, and ask whether it would be impossible to commit the higher offense without also committing the lesser offense. Only if that is the case can the offense be considered as the possible basis for a charge under the lesser-included offense doctrine.

To illustrate the application of the statutory-elements standard, looks to the actual crime of assault with the intent to kill. Since an assault is a necessary element of that crime, the crime of simple assault will be a lesser-included offense. An assault with intent to kill will not, however, necessarily include a touching and therefore the crime of battery will not be a lesser-included offense and instructions on such an offense would not be authorized. So too, since the use of a deadly weapon is not necessarily a part of an assault with an intent to kill, the crime of felonious assault also will not be a lesser-included crime. When the lesser offense is one defined by statute as committed in several different ways, it is a lesser-included offense if the higher offense invariably includes at least one of these alternatives. Thus, because a premeditated first-degree murder necessarily includes an intentional murder, second-degree murder will be a lesser-included offense even though second-degree murder could also be committed through depraved indifference. Where the first-degree murder statute includes both premeditated murder and felony murder, the same result ordinarily will be reached if the alternative elements will be treated as creating two separate crimes. The question will be whether premeditated murder necessarily produces a second degree intentional killing rather than whether all first-degree murders do so. Voluntary manslaughter may or may not be included as a lesser-included offense to an intentional killing depending upon how that manslaughter offense is defined. If it is viewed simply as the intentional killing minus the element of malice, then it is a lesser-included offense. If on the other hand, it is viewed as having the separate element of provocation, then the lesser offense includes an element not found in the higher and is not a lesser-included offense.

The elements test for defining lesser included offenses has the advantage of being identical to the Court's present approach for determining which offenses are the "same" under the Double Jeopardy Clause, and therefore must be tried all at once. Since the double jeopardy standard for defining the "same offense" is solely the "additional elements" test

---

3. See § 25.4(d) as to the implied acquittal doctrine; Price v. Georgia, 398 U.S. 323, 90 S.Ct. 1757, 26 L.Ed.2d 300 (1970) (noting that guilty verdict on lesser-included offense is implied acquittal of greater charge).

4. Schmuck v. United States, 489 U.S. 705, 109 S.Ct. 1443, 103 L.Ed.2d 734 (1989).

of *Blockburger*,[5] any lesser offense that would be the "same offense" under *Blockburger* would also be a lesser-included offense under the statutory-elements test. For example, the Court in *Rutledge v. United States*[6] concluded that under *Blockburger* the federal conspiracy statute, 18 U.S.C. § 846, "does not define an offense different from" the offense of conducting a continuing criminal enterprise, 18 U.S.C. § 848. The Court continued, "since the latter offense is the more serious of the two, and because only one of its elements is necessary to prove a § 846 conspiracy, it is appropriate to characterize § 846 as a lesser included offense of § 848." Other tests that create classes of lesser-included offenses narrower than the elements test "invite frequent questions concerning double jeopardy violations."

Not surprisingly, given the sustained critique of the *Blockburger* rule in the double jeopardy context, the statutory-elements method of determining which uncharged offenses are included within a charged offense has been criticized as too mechanical and inflexible. Often it excludes lesser offenses that reflect the true criminal nature of the committed conduct and that clearly are within the framework of the transaction as recognized by all of the parties. Thus, in a case in which the defendant was charged with beating his jailor, the court held that the lesser offense of resisting a peace officer was not lesser-included to the charged offense of battery upon a peace officer; the offense of resisting required that the offender know that the person resisted was a peace officer while under the battery offense the status of the victim need not be known. Of course since the alleged victim was a jailor, defendant knew very well that he was a peace officer.

In *Schmuck v. United States*,[7] the Supreme Court held that the statutory elements test was the proper approach under the Federal Rules and rejected the criticism of the test. The defendant in *Schmuck* was indicted under the mail fraud statute, with the government's proof at trial showing a scheme in which de-

fendant rolled back odometers on used cars and then sold those cars to unwitting car dealers for resale to retail customers. The lower court had divided on whether the defendant was entitled to an instruction on the lesser charge of odometer tampering. Under a statutory-elements test, odometer tampering clearly was not lesser-included because the elements of mail fraud did not require odometer tampering as such, but simply any type of fraud. The dissenters below had argued for a fact-oriented standard, known as the "inherent relationship test," which took account of how the greater offense allegedly was committed. They argued that otherwise it was "hard to imagine how any lesser included offense could ever be considered under the elements test" where the offense, as in mail fraud, was "umbrella like" in its coverage. The Supreme Court rejected this position and held that the majority below had been correct in applying the statutory-elements test. The Court relied on the language of Federal Rule 31(c) (which refers to "necessarily included" offenses) and the common law sources underlying that rule, and went on to explain:

> [T]he elements test is far more certain and predictable in its application than the inherent relationship approach. Because the elements approach involves a textual comparison of criminal statutes and does not depend on inferences that may be drawn from evidence introduced at trial, the elements approach permits both sides to know in advance what jury instructions will be available and to plan their trial strategies accordingly. The objective elements approach, moreover, promotes judicial economy by providing a clearer rule of decision and by permitting appellate courts to decide whether jury instructions were wrongly refused without reviewing the entire evidentiary record for nuances of inference.

The elements test for lesser included offenses provides yet another context in which courts have had to articulate the difference between an "element" of an offense and a sentence enhancement. This very issue arose in the

---

5. See § 17.4(b).

6. 517 U.S. 292, 116 S.Ct. 1241, 134 L.Ed.2d 419 (1996).

7. Supra note 4.

case of *Carter v. United States*,[8] where the government argued that among the elements of the property offense that defendant claimed was included in the charged offense was the requirement that the defendant take property of a value exceeding $1000. The defendant maintained that this fact was a mere sentence enhancement and not an element, and thus should not be part of the *Blockburger/Schmuck* analysis. The Court disagreed, reasoning that "the constitutional questions that would be raised by interpreting the valuation requirement to be a sentencing factor persuade us to adopt the view that the valuation requirement is an element." Shortly following the *Carter* decision, the Court held in *Apprendi v. New Jersey*,[9] that any fact, other than prior conviction, that raises the statutory maximum sentence is not a sentence enhancement, but an element. After *Apprendi*, facts that lengthen the maximum sentence beyond that otherwise allowed by statute must be factored into the *Blockburger/Schmuck* analysis as elements.

Cognate-pleadings test. The cognate-pleadings approach is distinguishable from the statutory-elements approach in two respects. First, it does not insist that the elements of the lesser offense be a subset of the higher offense. It is sufficient that the lesser offense have certain elements in common with the higher offense, which thereby makes it a "cognate" or "allied" offense even though it also has other elements not essential to the greater crime. Second, the relationship between the offenses is determined not by a comparison of statutory elements in the abstract, but by reference to the pleadings in the specific case. The key ordinarily is whether the allegations in the pleading charging the higher offense include all of the elements of the lesser offense. Thus, joyriding will be a lesser-included offense to grand larceny when the pleadings allege that the item stolen was an automobile, that it was taken knowingly without permis-sion of the owner, and that the asportation occurred by the driving away of the automobile.

The precise reach of the pleadings approach is sometimes unclear. Consider one case in which the defendant was charged with "aggravated criminal assault" of a ten-year-old, specifically, the sexual penetration by defendant of the victim. The majority concluded that the defendant was not entitled to an instruction on "aggravated criminal sexual abuse," because the lesser offense involved sexual conduct (touching or fondling for the purpose of sexual arousal), and the indictment described only sexual penetration.

The pleadings approach has also been criticized as making more difficult the task of the trial judge and counsel. Unlike the elements approach which requires only a comparison of the statutory definitions of the greater and lesser offenses, under the pleadings approach a court must examine the charging document with an eye to what offenses are hidden within its allegations and seek as well to separate those allegations.

Proponents of the pleadings approach view it as a good compromise between the statutory-elements approach and a more open-ended evidentiary approach. It avoids the mechanical aspect of the elements test that excludes those lesser offenses that are commonly presented in the actual commission of a higher offense. In jurisdictions that continue to adhere to *Grady v. Corbin*, rather than *Blockburger*,[10] the prosecutor, by alleging the basic mode of conduct, can ensure inclusion of those lesser offenses that will be treated as the "same offense" for double jeopardy purposes. At the same time, the defense is not without means to ensure that other lesser offenses are included. While the prosecutor controls the initial pleading, the wording of a charging instrument can never preclude instructions on lesser offenses completely subsumed within the charged offense. Moreover, since the pleadings are the key, both parties are given notice in advance of trial of what lesser offenses may be included.

8. 530 U.S. 255, 120 S.Ct. 2159, 147 L.Ed.2d 203 (2000).

9. *Apprendi* is discussed in § 26.4 (i).

10. See § 17.4(b).

Evidentiary approach. The evidentiary approach to defining lesser-included offenses looks to the actual proof submitted at trial, rather than to the pleadings alone, to assess the relationship between the lesser and higher offense. The lesser offense may have elements that are not part of the higher offense; all that is required is that some or all of the proof actually admitted to establish elements of the higher offense also establish the lesser offense. Courts applying this approach have imposed further requirements that limit its reach.

One common limitation is that the same basic *conduct* must provide the foundation for both the higher charge and the lesser charge. Thus, where the defendant was charged with the fraudulent use of a credit card and that alleged fraud consisted of the defendant's misrepresentation of himself as the owner of the card, the lesser offense of receiving property under false pretenses was a lesser-included offense.

Another variation on this limitation of the evidentiary approach has been described as the "inherent relationship" test. An offense is lesser included when (1) the lesser offense is "established by the evidence adduced at trial on the proof of the higher offense" and (2) there is also "an inherent relationship between the greater and lesser offenses, i.e., they must relate to the protection of the same interests, and must be so related that in the general nature of these crimes * * * proof of the lesser offense is necessarily presented as part of the showing of the commission of the greater offense." So described, the inherent relationship test would seem to apply only where the lesser offense almost always is present in the commission of the higher offense. This would include, for example, joyriding under auto theft, as the driving away of the car is as common to auto theft as unlawful entry is to burglary. It presumably would not include tampering with an odometer under mail fraud as such tampering can hardly be described as a typical ingredient of a mail fraud scheme.

Critics of the evidentiary approach claim that the evidentiary focus is so flexible as to make "nearly impossible" the necessary formulation of "general governing principles." They also see that approach as opening the door to so many potential lesser-included offenses which are often unknown at the outset of trial as to place both prosecutor and defense in an untenable position in preparing for trial. In *Schmuck*, the Supreme Court, in rejecting the inherent relationship test, added the criticism that for the defendant this guesswork may not be consistent with due process. The Court noted: "If, as mandated under the inherent-relationship approach, the determination whether the offenses are sufficiently related to permit an instruction is delayed until all the evidence is developed at trial, the defendant may not have constitutionally sufficient notice to support a lesser included offense instruction requested by the prosecutor if the elements of that lesser offense are not part of the indictment." Furthermore, now that the Court has resurrected the elements test of *Blockburger* as the standard for determining the meaning of "same offense" under the Double Jeopardy Clause,[11] the evidentiary approach is not needed in order to prevent the possibility that overlooked lesser offenses would later be barred by double jeopardy.

As for the problem of notice, supporters of the evidentiary approach maintain that with the prosecution's proof commonly known to both parties from the outset, parties can readily anticipate what the lesser-included offenses will be. Moreover, prudent courts can apply the standard only when the *defense* requests the charge and apply one of the other approaches for prosecution requests. This solution gives no unfair advantage to the defense over the prosecution. In most cases the prosecution can foresee whether the proof is likely to develop strongly favoring a verdict on a lesser included offense, in which event the indictment should so charge, which is the prosecutor's option. If the evidence is such that a jury can rationally choose —and is likely to choose—the lesser offense, then the interests of justice call for the defense to have the option of the lesser-included offense—whether

11. See § 17.4(b).

or not the prosecution chose to put it in the indictment.

Not only does a broader definition of lesser-included offense create the need for courts to protect defendants from surprise when such offenses are tendered to the jury at trial, but the broader definition also affects appellate remedies. As a remedy for failure of proof on a greater charge, an appellate court may order the entry of conviction on only those lesser offenses completely subsumed in the greater charge.

(d) Entitlements to Lesser Offense Charges. Though a lesser offense fits the jurisdiction's definition of a lesser-included offense, and though the evidence before the jury would sustain a conviction on that offense, it does not necessarily follow that the jury will be charged on that offense. Among the factors that will determine whether such a charge may or must be given are (1) the state of the evidence, (2) the presence of a request, and (3) the presence of an objection to the charge.

Courts in every jurisdiction have held that a defendant is entitled to a lesser-included offense instruction where the evidence warrants it. In some circumstances due process guarantees a criminal defendant an instruction on a lesser-included offense. In *Beck v. Alabama*,[12] the Supreme Court held that due process was violated by the operation of a state's capital punishment statute that prevented the trial court from giving the jury the option of convicting on a lesser-included, non-capital offense even though the evidence there placed in dispute that element which separated the capital offense from the non-capital offense. In elevating the rule to constitutional status, the Court noted that every state other than Alabama agreed that a defendant was entitled to a lesser-included offense instruction where the evidence warrants it, and reasoned that "the failure to give the jury the 'third option' of convicting on a lesser included offense would seem inevitably to enhance the risk of an unwarranted conviction. Such a risk cannot be

tolerated in a case in which the defendant's life is at stake." The Court explained:

> On the one hand, the unavailability of the third option on convicting on a lesser included offense may encourage the jury to convict for an impermissible reason—its belief that the defendant is guilty of some serious crime and should be punished. On the other hand, the apparently mandatory nature of the death penalty [in Alabama] may encourage it to acquit for an equally impermissible reason that, whatever his crime, the defendant does not deserve death. * * * These two extraneous factors * * * introduce a level of uncertainty and unreliability into the factfinding process that cannot be tolerated in a capital case.

In *Schad v. Arizona*,[13] the Court made it clear that *Beck* did not require the charging of all lesser-included offenses supported by the evidence in every case, but rather that a lesser-included offense charge is required only when needed "to eliminate the distortion of the factfinding process that is created when the jury is forced into an all-or-nothing choice between capital murder and innocence." Thus, in *Schad*, the Court rejected the capital defendant's argument that his jury should have been instructed on the offenses of robbery and theft in addition to premeditated murder, felony murder, and second-degree murder. The Court explained that the second-degree murder charge had provided the third option mandated in *Beck*.

As to whether or not *Beck* should apply outside the death penalty context, imposing a due process requirement in all prosecutions, it is significant that the rule is directed towards ensuring the reliability of convictions, not sentences. To that extent it would limit the judge's instructional authority in any criminal case where the defendant appears "plainly guilty of some offense," but the jury is presented with no alternatives other than a conviction of a serious offense or acquittal, posing the risk that the jury will resolve its doubts about the elements of the charged offense in

12. 447 U.S. 625, 100 S.Ct. 2382, 65 L.Ed.2d 392 (1980).

13. 501 U.S. 624, 111 S.Ct. 2491, 115 L.Ed.2d 555 (1991).

favor of conviction. Still the Court's reasoning in *Schad* suggested that *Beck* is a rule for only capital cases, as it focuses on the special importance of reliability in capital cases.

Aside from *Beck's* commands, requirements for lesser-included offense instructions vary among jurisdictions. In the federal courts and most states, judges do not charge on a lesser-included offense if there is no dispute about the additional fact or facts which, coupled with the lesser offense, produce the higher offense charged in the indictment. For the trial court to give such a charge under those circumstances is to invite the jury to exercise inappropriately a degree of mercy by finding defendant guilty of a lesser crime, when the proof truly justified conviction as charged.[14] When there is no evidentiary basis for the lesser charge, a judge is not required to charge the jury on that offense, even when the offense would provide an alternative to either an acquittal of all offenses or conviction of a capital crime.[15] In other words, that the defendant has no constitutionally protected right to present to the jury the option of nullification in the form of a lesser-included offense.

A small group of states adheres to an alternative approach which recognizes that a jury "may reject all or part of the state's evidence, whether controverted or not." In these states, upon a defense request, the lesser-included offense must be charged even where the only evidence in dispute relates equally to the lesser and higher offense. This facilitation of jury compromise is somewhat limited; the lesser-included offenses that must be charged despite the lack of evidentiary support are only those that are "necessarily included" under the statutory-elements approach. However, certain additions may also be made under this "jury function theory," sometimes by statutory command, to encompass all of the lesser degrees of the same crime. Thus, attempt offenses (which may not always be necessarily included because they sometimes require a greater mens rea) may available to the defense for any crime as to which an attempt is possible even though no dispute exists as to whether the crime, if committed, was completed.

Just as courts have divided over whether a jury must be given the option of convicting a defendant of a lesser-included offense when all evidence points to the greater offense and there is no rational basis for concluding that the defendant committed a lesser crime, courts also disagree about if and when a jury may be told that it may convict the defendant of a lesser offense when the statute of limitations on the lesser offense has expired, barring conviction. The several approaches to this problem can be grouped into two categories: those that permit waiver of the limitations bar and those that do not.

The federal position falls within the first category. In *Spaziano v. Florida*,[16] the court considered whether *Beck* required that a lesser-included offense instruction be given in a capital case when the lesser-included crime was time-barred. A majority of justices agreed that due process did not mandate instructions on a time-barred offense. The Court explained that "where no lesser included offense exists, a lesser included offense instruction detracts from, rather than enhances, the rationality of the process." Thus, in order for a defendant to secure an instruction on a time-barred lesser-included offense, the defendant must first waive the limitations defense.[17] In favor of waivability, it has been argued that the statute of limitations defense is like any other affirmative defense. A conviction of a time-barred lesser offense may stand if the defendant chooses to forgo the defense and submit the lesser offense as an option. A request for instructions on a time-barred offense may be sufficient waiver in some courts, while other courts will require that the judge inform the

---

14. See Sparf v. United States, 156 U.S. 51, 15 S.Ct. 273, 39 L.Ed. 343 (1895); Berra v. United States, 351 U.S. 131, 76 S.Ct. 685, 100 L.Ed. 1013 (1956); Sansone v. United States, 380 U.S. 343, 85 S.Ct. 1004, 13 L.Ed.2d 882 (1965).

15. Hopper v. Evans, 456 U.S. 605, 102 S.Ct. 2049, 72 L.Ed.2d 367 (1982).

16. 468 U.S. 447, 104 S.Ct. 3154, 82 L.Ed.2d 340 (1984).

17. Four Justices in *Spaziano* went on to state that the defendant ought to be entitled to waive the limitations defense, while two justices refused to join this comment.

defendant specifically about the consequences of waiving the defense. Once a defendant has waived the defense, he cannot thereafter complain if the jury convicts him of the time-barred offense.

Other states treat the statute of limitations bar as a jurisdictional prerequisite, not subject to waiver by the defense. A defendant in such a state may be equally inclined to give his jury the option of conviction on a lesser rather than a greater offense. Indeed, the evidence at trial may fit more easily the lesser offense than the greater one. State courts have demonstrated considerable imagination in their responses to this dilemma. The simplest solution, adopted by several states, is to forbid any instructions on the lesser offense. Others, reasoning that the jury's role is to determine which offense was committed, not to determine whether or not the defendant will be punished for that offense, require the judge to instruct the jury on the lesser offense as if it was not time-barred, but enter a judgment of acquittal should the jury convict the defendant of the lesser offense rather than the greater (not time-barred) offense. A third response rejects both of these options in favor of informing the jury of the consequences of its choices, allowing instructions on the time-barred lesser offense only when accompanied by an explanation to the jury that a conviction on the lesser offense is barred by the statute of limitations so that if the jurors conclude that the evidence would support a conviction of the lesser crime only, they must acquit the defendant. Finally, some states have enacted provisions that suspend the time-bar for offenses for that are included in greater offenses for which the limitations period has not run, or equalize the time limitations for a greater offense and those lesser offenses included within that offense.

Each of these responses has its drawbacks. The first alternative runs the risk of confusing jurors who suspect the defendant committed a lesser crime but are left in the dark, and the second has been criticized as "tricking the jury," since a jury that concludes that a defendant should be convicted of a lesser offense is never told that its guilty verdict will be ineffectual. While supporters might respond that withholding the limitations information is no more tricking a jury than refusing to tell a jury of the sentencing consequences of its verdict in this situation, the conviction itself, not just the punishment, is rendered illusory. The alternative of instructing the jury to acquit due to the time-bar if it finds the defendant guilty of only the time-barred lesser offense does provide the jurors with more accurate information about the lesser-included offense option and its effect, but poses the risk that jurors otherwise inclined to convict the defendant of a lesser offense will choose to convict the defendant of the greater offense just to insure that the defendant is convicted of something. The statutory solution seems to alleviate the problem most effectively, although the opportunity it presents to secure a lesser conviction otherwise time-barred by statute might lead a prosecutor to bring charges that he otherwise might not bring.

Just as a trial judge is not required by the Constitution to instruct a capital jury concerning lesser offenses barred by the statute of limitations, the Constitution does not mandate that a trial judge instruct a capital jury on offenses that, under state law, are not considered lesser offenses of the crime charged. In *Hopkins v. Reeves*,[18] the Court rejected the Nebraska defendant's claim that he was entitled to instructions on second-degree murder and manslaughter in addition to instructions on felony murder. The Court observed that Nebraska courts did not recognize any lesser-included homicide offenses for felony murder. Requiring the requested instructions under these circumstances, the Court reasoned, would not enhance the reliability of the conviction and would impose an unauthorized limit on the "state's prerogative to structure its criminal law."

Even when the evidence clearly supports a lesser-included offense which is not time-barred, in most jurisdictions a judge does not commit error in failing to charge where no request is made for a charge. This position has

18.   524 U.S. 88, 118 S.Ct. 1895, 141 L.Ed.2d 76 (1998).

been justified on the grounds that the parties should be permitted to control the course of the proceedings.

Where no request is made, a court may propose including an instruction on a lesser-included offense and then proceed if neither side objects. If the defendant should object, however, an additional complication enters the picture, even though the evidentiary posture clearly supports the charge. Theoretically, if a sufficient evidentiary basis exists for a conviction of a necessarily included lesser offense, then the court should charge on that offense without regard to the defense's position. The defense and prosecution may be willing to gamble on all-or-nothing verdicts, but the court's responsibility extends to the jury and ensuring its awareness of its authority. Assuming adequate notice of the possibility that such an instruction would be given, the defense has no more reason to complain about a properly supported instruction given by the judge sua sponte than about an instruction given on request of the prosecutor. In practice, however, judges may not give the instruction where the prosecution does not request it and the defense is opposed. They know that if they abide by the defendant's wishes, the defense will not be heard to complain about this issue on appeal. Indeed, some appellate courts have suggested that the use of the lesser-included charge should be largely controlled "by permitting counsel to decide on tactics."

§ 24.9 Jury Procedures

(a) **Sequestering the Jury.** Sequestration of the jury in a criminal case, that is, keeping the jury together and in seclusion, is a step which may be undertaken during the course of trial and deliberations because of the risk of outside influence on the decisionmaking process. At common law, such confinement of the jury (also known as the rule against juror "separation") was undertaken in all cases as a matter of course. Sequestration was intended to prevent contamination of the jury by extraneous communications and unfair publicity, but also served to coerce agreement by withholding from the jurors their accustomed comforts and conveniences, making their confine-

ment so unpleasant and irksome that they would be willing to end it as soon as possible. Eventually, as court reformers became concerned about the conditions of jury service and trials lengthened, most jurisdictions abandoned rules barring juror separation. In the federal courts and most states today, the trial judge has the discretion to permit a jury to disperse during trial as well as deliberations.

Understandably, "the ancient common law doctrine prohibiting jury separation is not generally thought to be such an integral part of the right to a jury trial that sequestration has constitutional status." Nor are the reasons for that doctrine so compelling that the old rule should be continued as a matter of local law. The notion that jurors should be coerced to agree by discomfort certainly is an anachronism today. Indeed, if "[i]ntellectual conviction, not physical endurance, should be the basis of a juror's decision," as it certainly should, then it is best to allow the trial judge the power to release the jury. Today, most agree that jurors "are more likely to perform their duty fairly and correctly when they are not subjected to extended periods of arbitrary and pointless personal confinement." And concerns about jury tampering and exposure are less pressing when judges give jurors careful and repeated admonitions to avoid publicity and other discussions of the case, and employ other steps to protect jurors from outside influence. Accordingly, sequestration typically is ordered in noncapital cases only when such steps appear inadequate to insulate the jury. When a jury sequestration order is violated, a defendant's interest in an untainted jury does not require a new trial, absent a showing that the defendant was prejudiced by the separation.

(b) **Jury Questions and Note–Taking.** Must jurors merely watch and listen as the trial unfolds? In most courtrooms that depends on the discretion of the trial judge. Juror questions to witnesses may assist in reducing juror confusion and inattention, but they also decrease the control of the parties over the case somewhat. A juror's ability to ask questions of witnesses, when recognized, is subject to the trial court's authority to screen questions and exclude those it deems inappropriate. Ordinarily, this authority is implemented by directing the jurors to write out any questions they may have after each witness has finished testifying and to submit those questions to the judge. If after providing counsel the opportunity to object to the question out of hearing of the jury, the judge finds the question to be appropriate, then the judge may ask the question of the witness. If the judge concludes that the question relates to inadmissible or irrelevant matter, the judge can simply note that the question will not be asked. If jurors were allowed to ask their questions directly without judicial screening, counsel would be placed in the delicate position of having to object to a juror's request in the presence of the juror.

Juror note-taking is much more common in criminal trials than juror questioning of witnesses. The prevailing view at one time was that judges should rarely grant permission to jurors to take notes. Note-taking was thought to be an unwise practice because (1) the best note-taker would come to dominate the jury; (2) jurors, not having an overview of the case, would include in their notes interesting sidelights and ignore important (but often boring) facts; (3) a dishonest juror might falsify notes; (4) the act of taking notes would draw the juror's attention away from the demeanor of the witness and leave the juror writing rather than watching and listening; and (5) the notes would receive undue attention during deliberations. For the most part, these problems are surmountable with appropriate instructions. Thus, jurors are warned that if they take notes, they should take care not to let note-taking distract them from hearing and observing the full testimony of the witness, they should not discuss their notes with fellow jurors until deliberations begin, they should rely on their notes as memory aids and not as a substitute for independent recollection, and a juror not taking notes should not be overly influenced by another's notes, as notes are "not entitled to any greater weight than the recollection or impression of each juror."

(c) Items Taken to the Jury Room. When the jury begins its deliberations, it ordinarily may have with it the charging instrument and written jury instructions where they are used. In most jurisdictions, the trial judge has discretion to allow the jurors to take with them other materials, such as pertinent exhibits, which have been received in evidence. Where that practice is followed, an exception ordinarily is made for depositions that have been read into the record, as they are simply another form of testimony and should not be given any greater attention than other testimony.

For some time, it was not feasible to give the jury a transcript in all but the exceptional cases where attorneys, at their own expense, were able to secure daily transcripts. Today, however, where courts use a tape recorded or computer-generated transcript, that recording presumably could be made available in every case. Nonetheless, the practice of not providing transcripts or transcript-substitutes continues. This suggests that the concern is not so much about cost, as it is about the problems of certifying the recording as accurate, ensuring there is no undue emphasis of certain testimony, and the potential of bogging down the deliberations with a rerun of the trial.

It sometimes happens that the jury after retiring will submit to the trial judge a request to review certain testimony or evidence. A number of states have statutes or court rules which appear to require the judge to honor such a request, but the courts are not in agreement as to whether these provisions are mandatory or discretionary. In other states the judge has discretion as to whether to act favorably upon the jury's request. If the judge grants the request, it is advisable that the judge instruct the jury to review other evidence relating to the same factual issue "so as not to give undue prominence to the evidence requested."

(d) The Deadlocked Jury. After the jury has been deliberating for some time, it may report to the judge that it has been unable to reach a unanimous decision.[1] Except in a few

§ 24.9

1. On jury unanimity, see §§ 22.1 (e); 24.10(c).

states where statutes limit the number of times a judge may order a jury to renew deliberations, the law allows the judge to send the jury back for further deliberations once, twice, or several times. However, the court may not require or threaten to require the jury to deliberate for an unreasonable length of time. The length of the trial, the nature or complexity of the case, the volume and nature of the evidence, the presence of multiple counts or multiple defendants, and the jurors' statements to the court concerning the probability of agreement may all be considered by the court in determining the reasonableness of the deliberation period. The judge is given considerable discretion in this regard, but there are limits. If the judge declares a mistrial without making an adequate effort to ensure that the jury is incapable of reaching a verdict, the mistrial may not be justified by "manifest necessity," and double jeopardy may bar a retrial.

The judge, when determining whether further deliberations by the jury are likely to be fruitful, should not inquire into the numerical division of the jury, that is, how it is divided (e.g., 6–6 or 11–1). Many years ago the Supreme Court criticized the practice even when the response did not reveal which votes were for and which against conviction,[2] and the Court later condemned the practice in no uncertain terms:

> We deem it essential to the fair and impartial conduct of the trial, that the inquiry itself should be regarded as ground for reversal. Such procedure serves no useful purpose that cannot be attained by questions not requiring the jury to reveal the nature or extent of its division. Its effect upon a divided jury will often depend upon circumstances which cannot properly be known to the trial judge or to the appellate courts and may vary widely in different situations, but in general its tendency is coercive. It can rarely be resorted to without bringing to bear in some degree, serious, although not

measurable, improper influence upon the jury, from whose deliberations every consideration other than that of the evidence and the law as expounded in a proper charge, should be excluded. Such a practice, which is never useful and is generally harmful, is not to be sanctioned.[3]

This decision was grounded in the Court's supervisory power over the federal courts and thus is not a constitutional rule binding upon the states. Despite arguments that such a result ought to be required as an aspect of the sixth amendment right to trial by an impartial jury, several jurisdictions have concluded that inquiry into numerical division is proper so long as the judge does not ask whether the majority is for or against conviction or so long as the inquiry is not accompanied by other coercive conduct.

Limitations on the steps the judge may take to "encourage" agreement by a deadlocked jury have also been the subject of much litigation. In *Allen v. United States*,[4] the Supreme Court held that the trial judge had not committed error in giving a deadlocked jury the following supplemental instruction:

> [A]lthough the verdict must be the verdict of each individual juror, and not a mere acquiescence in the conclusion of his fellows, yet they should examine the question submitted with candor, and with a proper regard and deference to the opinions of each other: that it was their duty to decide the case if they could conscientiously do so; that they should listen, with a disposition to be convinced, to each other's arguments: that, if much the larger number were for conviction, a dissenting juror should consider whether his doubt was a reasonable one which made no impression upon the minds of so many men, equally honest, equally intelligent with himself. If, upon the other hand, the majority were for acquittal, the minority ought to ask themselves whether they might not reason-

---

2. Burton v. United States, 196 U.S. 283, 25 S.Ct. 243, 49 L.Ed. 482 (1905).

3. Brasfield v. United States, 272 U.S. 448, 47 S.Ct. 135, 71 L.Ed. 345 (1926).

4. 164 U.S. 492, 17 S.Ct. 154, 41 L.Ed. 528 (1896).

ably doubt the correctness of a judgment which was not concurred in by the majority.

This kind of instruction, commonly referred to as the *"Allen* charge" or "dynamite charge," has been used for years in state and federal courts. But many courts are inclined to require the use of more guarded language. Though most courts in turning away from *Allen* have done so on other than constitutional grounds, arguments have been made that the *Allen* charge violates due process because (1) it defeats the unanimity rule, (2) it does violence to the beyond a reasonable doubt standard, (3) the jury does not remain impartial, and (4) the jury is instructed to consider matters extraneous to the guilt or innocence of the accused. Some lower courts have prohibited the giving of *Allen* charges altogether as an exercise of its supervisory authority.

In *Lowenfield v. Phelps*,[5] the Supreme Court upheld against constitutional challenge in a capital case a charge that did not go as far as *Allen* but arguably had more of a "coercive" quality than many lower courts would recommend. The jury in *Lowenfield* was deliberating during the penalty phase of a capital case when it requested advice from the judge, noting deadlock. After polling the jury about whether further deliberation would be helpful the judge directed the jurors to "discuss the evidence with the objective of reaching a just verdict if you can do so without violence to [your] individual judgment," but it did not include a direction to minority jurors to consider the views of majority and to ask themselves whether their position was reasonably founded in light of that taken by the majority. Rather, the charge told the jurors not to "hesitate to reexamine your own views and to change your opinion if you are convinced you are wrong," while adding a warning against "surrendering your honest belief * * * solely because of the opinion of your fellow jurors or for the mere purpose of returning a verdict." Within thirty minutes, the jury returned with a verdict of death. The court rejected the defense's claim that the charge had combined with other circumstances to create an unac-

ceptable potential for coercion and noted that the general observations in *Allen* concerning the value of jurors being open to the views of others and "securing unanimity by a comparison of views" had "continuing validity."

Lower courts determining whether particular instructions are impermissibly coercive typically consider all of the circumstances, particularly (1) the context of the supplemental instruction, (2) the length of the period of deliberations following the constructions, (3) the total time of deliberations, and (4) any other coercion or pressure on the jury.

(e) Polling the Jury. Once the jury reaches a verdict and that verdict is announced in court, the defendant, assuming the verdict is guilty, may wish to poll the jury. Polling is a procedure under which each juror is separately asked whether he or she concurs in the verdict. Its purpose is to determine whether the verdict announced actually reflects the conscience of each of the jurors. In the great majority of jurisdictions, the jury must be polled upon the request of a party, while elsewhere the matter is left to the discretion of the trial judge. The right to a poll is waived if not requested before the jury has dispersed, and the defendant need not be specifically advised of his right to poll the jury.

The poll is conducted by the judge or the clerk of court. A common practice is to ask: "Was this then and is this now your verdict?" If a juror indicates some hesitancy or ambivalence, then it is the trial judge's duty to ascertain the juror's present intent by affording the juror the opportunity to make an unambiguous reply as to his present state of mind. If the poll reveals that there are not a sufficient number of votes for a valid verdict, then under the better view the court has the discretion either to direct the jury to retire for further deliberations or to discharge the jury.

(f) Jury Misconduct. *Scope.* The term "jury misconduct" often is used to describe both action by jurors that is contrary to their responsibilities and conduct by others which contaminates the jury process with extraneous influence. Much of the jury behavior consid-

---

5. 484 U.S. 231, 108 S.Ct. 546, 98 L.Ed.2d 568 (1988).

ered to be misconduct is prohibited specifically in preliminary instructions. Jurors are told not to talk to each other about the case until deliberations begin; not to talk to anyone else about the case or about anything or anyone related to the case until the trial has ended; not to converse on any matter with the attorneys, witnesses, or defendant; not to read, view, or listen to any media reports of the case or anyone or anything related to it; and not to do any research or investigation on their own. Misconduct, then, includes various actions that are inconsistent with such admonitions— such as discussing the merits of the case with another juror prior to deliberations, co-worker, family member, or bailiff; inspecting the scene of the crime; reading a newspaper article about the defendant; conducting experiments; or using a dictionary to define a term mentioned by the judge.

Other aspects of misconduct in the jury process follow logically from the role of the jury. Efforts to intimidate, bribe, or otherwise pressure jurors are clearly inconsistent with juror independence. Presenting information to a juror outside the trial process interferes with jury's responsibility to rule on the basis of only the evidence before it. The juror who is intoxicated as he listens to testimony fails to fulfill his obligation to listen attentively to the evidence. Physically abusive behavior towards other jurors is impermissible, and racist arguments and speech by jurors, too, have been condemned. The prospective juror who lies during voir dire questioning undermines the selection process. In the end, whether motivated by good faith or bad, any action by an outsider or by a juror himself that has the potential for interfering with juror decision-making in accordance with the juror's responsibilities constitutes misconduct.

Responding to proof of misconduct. The critical element in shaping the proper response to juror misconduct is the court's assessment of its likely prejudicial impact, regardless of whether the misconduct is revealed during or after trial. The method by which that assessment must take place, however, is not settled.

Courts disagree, as a preliminary matter, when the defendant must prove, or the prosecutor must disprove, prejudice. In *Remmer v. United States*,[6] a case involving an alleged attempt to bribe a juror and a subsequent FBI investigation of that attempt, the Supreme Court described the extraneous influence upon the juror as "presumptively prejudicial." State and federal courts have since used that designation to characterize a good many instances of misconduct. When prejudice is presumed, the burden of proof required to overcome such a presumption varies. Many courts suggest that the government must eliminate all "reasonable possibility" of prejudicial impact—a standard also expressed as requiring proof beyond a reasonable doubt that the misconduct did not influence the juror. Others suggest only that the presumption must be "overcome" and that it must be "adequately demonstrated" that there was no prejudicial impact.

Other courts have concluded that the subsequent adoption of rules of evidence and later opinions of the Court have undermined any suggestion in *Remmer* that a presumption of prejudice is required. As discussed below, rules of evidence such as Federal Rule 606(b) prohibit the use of juror testimony by either party to impeach a verdict once delivered by the jury. This makes it difficult for the government to prove after trial that the alleged misconduct had no effect on the verdict, causing some courts to be reluctant to invoke the presumption. Also, in *Smith v. Phillips*,[7] the Court stated that the remedy for jury misconduct was "an opportunity" for the *defendant* "to prove actual bias." An increasing number of lower courts have, accordingly, required that the defendant demonstrate some "likelihood of prejudice" before the government will be assigned the burden of proving harmlessness, at least in cases that involve irregularities other than jury tampering.

The decision whether or not to hold a hearing at which witnesses may testify about the effect of the alleged misconduct is within the

---

6.   347 U.S. 227, 74 S.Ct. 450, 98 L.Ed. 654 (1954).

7.   455 U.S. 209, 102 S.Ct. 940, 71 L.Ed.2d 78 (1982).

trial court's discretion, unless the defendant demonstrates a prima facie case of misconduct, in which case the hearing must be held. These hearings may be conducted in camera, a procedure that comports with due process, at least when the trial judge solicits and reviews questions for jurors in advance with counsel, and reports the results promptly. The usual practice is for the judge to question jurors separately in the presence of counsel.

In two cases decided during the mid-1960s, the Supreme Court held that misconduct in the jury proceedings reached the level of a constitutional violation. *Turner v. Louisiana*[8] found that a defendant's right to an impartial jury was violated when two deputy sheriffs, who were key prosecution witnesses, were placed in charge of the jury and fraternized with the jurors throughout the proceedings. In *Parker v. Gladden*,[9] a bailiff said of defendant to a juror: "Oh, that wicked fellow, he is guilty." The Court found that the comment violated not only the defendant's right to an impartial jury, as in *Turner*, but also his right to confront witnesses against him, since the bailiff was seen as presenting evidence outside the trial process.

An inquiry somewhat different from whether the misconduct in question might have influenced the juror in his evaluation of case is appropriate when the misconduct consists of a juror's failure to respond accurately to a question posed on voir dire. The leading federal case on such misconduct is *McDonough Power Equipment v. Greenwood*.[10] Although a civil case, *McDonough* has been applied by the lower federal courts to criminal cases as well. A juror there failed to disclose that his son had been injured by an apparently defective product and the defense claimed that this falsehood had deprived it of an opportunity to intelligently exercise its peremptory challenges. The Supreme Court held, however, that a party raising such a claim "must first demonstrate that a juror failed to answer honestly a material question on voir dire, and then further show that a correct response would have provided a valid basis for a challenge for cause." Not only does this standard condition relief on the risks that a party was deprived of a challenge for cause, but it also applies only where the juror answered dishonestly. A false answer produced by a juror's misunderstanding of the question would not warrant relief, nor would an answer which the juror realized only later was mistaken.

Remedies. Where the misconduct challenge is established during trial, and the applicable prejudice standard is met, the trial court has several remedial options. If the misconduct affected only one or a very few jurors, and if alternate jurors are available, the jurors affected by the misconduct can be replaced. If, as in the federal system, courts are authorized to proceed with less than the full number of jurors, the affected juror or jurors may be discharged without declaring a mistrial provided the requisite number of jurors remain. A judge should exercise great caution in removing a juror accused of misconduct when the judge learns that the juror is also a holdout for the defense. The judge's decision, however, typically will be reviewed under an abuse of discretion standard. In some instances, the court might conclude that a strong charge to the jurors will sufficiently negate the potential for prejudice. Finally, where none of the above alternatives are feasible, the trial court may order a mistrial.

Where the misconduct challenge is established after the verdict has been returned by the jury, the only remedy is the granting of a new trial. This is true even if the misconduct affected a single juror and that juror's vote was not needed (i.e., the jurisdiction accepted less than unanimous verdicts), as the juror participated in the deliberations and may have influenced others.

(g) Limitations on Juror Testimony About Misconduct. When allegations of impropriety are raised during trial, judges are permitted, even required in some circumstances, to question jurors about misconduct. Once the jury has returned its verdict, howev-

---

8.   379 U.S. 466, 85 S.Ct. 546, 13 L.Ed.2d 424 (1965).

9.   385 U.S. 363, 87 S.Ct. 468, 17 L.Ed.2d 420 (1966).

10.   464 U.S. 548, 104 S.Ct. 845, 78 L.Ed.2d 663 (1984).

er, access to information from jurors themselves is more limited. The prevailing standard today is that set forth in Rule 606(b) of the Federal Rules of Evidence. That Rule notes initially that, upon an inquiry into the validity of a verdict, "a juror may not testify as to any matter or statement occurring during the course of the jury's deliberations or the effect of anything upon his or any other juror's mind or emotions as influencing him to assent to or dissent from the verdict or * * * concerning his mental processes in connection therewith." For example, the rule bars efforts to demonstrate through juror testimony that the jurors discussed impermissible evidence or inferences, that smoking jurors coerced nonsmoking jurors to change their votes by refusing to obey the judge's non-smoking order, or that jurors engaged in discussions about the case prior to deliberations. This is a universally accepted prohibition, although a minority of states recognize limited exceptions. For example, evidence may be received in several states to show the verdict was reached by lot on the theory that "judicial economy is a weak justification for a completely arbitrary disposition of parties' rights." A second exception has been recognized by some courts for proof of racial bias during deliberations.

These rules have been premised upon sound reasons for limiting after-the-fact inquiry into jury verdicts. As the Supreme Court explained in *McDonald v. Pless*,[11] if verdicts were subject to attack based on the testimony of those who participated in them, then

> all verdicts could be, and many would be, followed by an inquiry in the hope of discovering something which might invalidate the finding. Jurors would be harassed and beset by the defeated party in an effort to secure from them evidence of facts which might establish misconduct sufficient to set aside a verdict. If evidence thus secured could be thus used, the result would be to make what was intended to be a private deliberation the constant subject of public investigation; to the destruction of all frankness and freedom of discussion and conference.

An additional provision of the Federal Rule acknowledges certain circumstances in which impeaching testimony by a juror may be received: "a juror may testify on the question whether extraneous prejudicial information was improperly brought to the jury's attention or whether any outside influence was improperly brought to bear upon any juror." An increasing number of state courts are following essentially this approach, although not always stated in those terms. As noted in the previous subsection, the Supreme Court in *Parker v. Gladden* held that extraneous prejudicial information improperly brought to a juror's attention could violate the defendant's sixth amendment rights both to confrontation of witnesses and to an impartial jury. The *Parker* ruling has led courts to recognize a limited avenue of jury impeachment of a verdict by reference to such extraneous information, although the juror may be prohibited from testifying as to whether that information was mentioned during deliberations or actually influenced his or her vote. As one state court put it, "where the Supreme Court holds that a particular series of events, when proven, violates a defendant's constitutional rights, implicit in that determination is the right of the defendant to prove facts substantiating his claim."

It should be emphasized, however, that both *Parker* and the Federal Rule refer only to external influences. The Supreme Court noted in *Tanner v. United States*[12] that no constitutional difficulties were presented in a jurisdiction prohibiting impeaching testimony by a juror about "internal" influences. *Tanner* held that juror use of drugs and alcohol during trial was not an "external influence" within the Federal Rule 606(b) exception and therefore juror testimony about such use was barred under that Rule. Juror intoxication was to be treated no differently than mental incompetence or inattentiveness, matters that had long been viewed as "internal" influences. Rejecting the petitioners' contention that this exclusion of juror testimony infringed upon their right to a jury both "impartial and mentally competent," the Court noted that the sixth amendment right to "an unimpaired jury" was adequately protected by "several aspects of the trial process." It cited in this regard the availability of voir dire to examine the suitability of a prospective juror, the ability of counsel and the court to observe juror behavior during the trial, the ability of jurors to report misconduct to the trial judge during the trial, and the defense's ability to impeach a verdict by use of non-juror evidence of misconduct.

"The right to use juror evidence," courts have noted, "necessarily implies a method to gather that evidence," and thus the recognition of even the limited possibility of verdict impeachment through juror testimony naturally prompts the question of whether it is permissible for counsel to interview the jurors after the verdict in an effort to discover grounds for challenging the verdict. As a matter of legal ethics, there is no absolute bar to such contacts, but in many jurisdictions such contacts must be first authorized, and sometimes closely supervised, by the trial court.

§ 24.10 Jury Verdicts

(a) Special Verdicts and Special Interrogatories. The use of "special verdicts," or special interrogatories, whereby the jury is required to respond to a series of fact questions in connection with the return of its verdict, is a common practice in civil cases but not in criminal cases. The reason why this is so was explained in *United States v. Spock,*[1] where the jury was called upon to answer a series of questions called "special findings" about the defendants' conduct, if it reached a verdict of guilty on the charge that the defendants conspired to counsel, aid, and abet registrants to resist the draft. In reversing the convictions, the court expressed concern

> with the subtle, and perhaps open, direct effect that answering special questions may have upon the jury's ultimate conclusion. There is no easier way to reach, and perhaps force, a verdict of guilty than to approach it

step by step. A juror, wishing to acquit, may be formally catechized. By a progression of questions each of which seems to require an answer unfavorable to the defendant, a reluctant juror may be led to vote for a conviction which, in the large, he would have resisted. * * * It may be said that since the law should be logical and consistent, if the questions were proper in substance this would be a desirable rather than an undesirable result. [But in criminal cases there are other considerations, especially] the principle that the jury, as the conscience of the community, must be permitted to look at more than logic. * * * The constitutional guarantees of due process and trial by jury require that a criminal defendant be afforded the full protection of a jury unfettered, directly or indirectly.

Although the *Spock* decision was grounded in the court's supervisory power, the above language makes it apparent that the issue may be of constitutional dimensions. The sixth amendment right to jury trial includes the right to a jury decision independent of the judge, and may protect the power of the jury to disregard the law and acquit, exercising what is commonly known as jury nullification. The general verdict facilitates jury independence by allowing the jury to sidestep the outcome that may follow inescapably from a careful dissection of the crime for each of the factual elements dictated by law. The general verdict also creates the opportunity for jurors to agree upon the same verdict for different reasons and disguises the jury's decisionmaking process from scrutiny. By supplanting or supplementing the general verdict, special verdicts and special interrogatories can limit jury independence. As a result, courts have considered their use at least "suspect" as a matter of due process. Federal and state courts typically disallow special interrogatories in criminal cases where the defendant objects to their use.

The bar against special interrogatories has been lifted by judges in many cases, however. Verdict forms specifying the theory under which the jury found a defendant guilty have

---

§ 24.10

1. 416 F.2d 165 (1st Cir.1969).

withstood constitutional challenge. When particular information about the basis of a jury's verdict is relevant to sentencing, courts have approved of special interrogatories that require the jury to specify the needed information. The rationale advanced for the use of special interrogatories in these cases is questionable; a jury's finding concerning sentencing facts is not a prerequisite for imposing sentences linked to those facts. A judge may find that a fact exists for sentencing purposes even after a jury has rejected that fact as not proven beyond a reasonable doubt; sentencing facts need only be established by a preponderance of the evidence. As the court explained in *Edwards v. United States*,[2] regardless of the jury's actual beliefs about a fact relevant to sentencing, a sentencing judge has an independent duty to assess that fact.

Many courts also will allow special findings when a defendant requests such findings. In some circumstances, a defendant may conclude that forcing the jurors to record their determination on the specific elements of the crime will persuade a conviction-prone jury to consider acquittal. In others, the defense may conclude that any risks with respect to nullification and compromise verdicts are more than offset by the bearing that special findings will have on the use of collateral estoppel in subsequent prosecution or the ability to appeal a conviction.

Finally, many courts have upheld the use of special verdicts or interrogatories, even over the defendant's objection, when the questions asked of the jury did not "prejudice" the defendant. These recent cases reflect a more limited view of the jury's role than that protected in *Spock*. The "jury" guaranteed to the accused by the Constitution, they suggest, may not include the ability to deliver a general verdict unencumbered by special findings, but only the ability to *reach* a general verdict, *before* being asked to specify, in cases of conviction only, the basis of that verdict.

(b) Inconsistent Verdicts or Findings.

In the federal courts it is not necessary that the verdict returned by a jury be logically consistent in all respects. Inconsistency regarding separate counts against a single defendant was addressed in *Dunn v. United States*.[3] The Court declared that the "most that can be said in such cases is that the verdict shows that either in the acquittal or the conviction the jury did not speak their real conclusions, but that does not show that they were not convinced of the defendant's guilt." The point was elaborated in *United States v. Dotterweich*,[4] involving an inconsistency with respect to jointly tried defendants. The Court rejected one defendant's contention that he was entitled to relief because the jury had convicted him, the corporation president, but had not convicted the co-defendant corporation. "Whether the jury's verdict was the result of carelessness or compromise or a belief that the responsible individual should suffer the penalty instead of merely increasing, as it were, the cost of running the business of the corporation, is immaterial," the Court explained. "Juries may indulge in precisely such motives or vagaries."

Written before the Court held in *Ashe v. Swenson* that collateral estoppel is a basic element of the double jeopardy protection of the Fifth Amendment, see § 17.4(a), the *Dunn* opinion reasoned that the same inconsistent verdicts would have been allowed if the different charges had been tried separately. *Ashe* undercut this assumption, as it barred attempts to reprove facts once litigated and rejected in an earlier trial. In *United States v. Powell*,[5] however, the Court concluded that the *Dunn* rule remained supported by "a sound rationale that is independent of the theories of res judicata." The defendant in *Powell* was convicted of using the telephone to facilitate the commission of certain felonies, but acquitted on the felony counts themselves. She argued that where a jury was told that it must find the defendant guilty of the predicate felony in order to convict on the compound of-

---

2. 523 U.S. 511, 118 S.Ct. 1475, 140 L.Ed.2d 703 (1998).

3. 284 U.S. 390, 52 S.Ct. 189, 76 L.Ed. 356 (1932).

4. 320 U.S. 277, 64 S.Ct. 134, 88 L.Ed. 48 (1943).

5. 469 U.S. 57, 105 S.Ct. 471, 83 L.Ed.2d 461 (1984).

fense, but then acquits on the former and convicts on the latter, the logical explanation for the inconsistency is a jury mistake adverse to the defendant. The *Powell* Court disagreed. The *Dunn* rule rested in part on the fact that "it is unclear whose ox had been gored" by an inconsistent verdict. That uncertainty presented the distinct possibility that the inconsistency *favored* the defendant. Still, it could not positively be shown that the inconsistency was a product of an error that worked either for or against the defendant. Any attempt at an "individualized assessment of the reason for the inconsistency would be based either on pure speculation or would require inquiries into the jury's deliberations that courts generally will not undertake." Considering the government's inability to appeal the acquittal, the Court concluded that "inconsistent verdicts should not be reviewable." Defendants retain the ability to challenge the sufficiency of the evidence supporting the verdict, the Court noted. Where the evidence is sufficient to sustain the conviction on the compound offense, it can hardly be said that this conviction was a "mistake" and acquittal on the predicate offense was "the one the jury 'really meant.'" Since the defendant was "given the benefit of her acquittal on the counts on which she was acquitted, * * * it is neither irrational nor illogical to require her to accept the burden of conviction on the counts on which the jury convicted."

Although most state courts have followed the same approach, a minority have taken the position that such inconsistency is grounds for overturning a conviction. In support of the latter view, it has been argued that "an enlightened jurisprudence should not thus permit the jailing of accused persons on a record exhibiting verdicts in which a jury simultaneously says 'yes' and 'no' in answer to a single critical question." In light of the difficulty posed by inconsistent verdicts, some jurisdictions have approved of the practice of refusing to accept such verdicts when first delivered. Judges in these courts resubmit the charges to the jury, explaining the inconsistency and asking the jury to reconsider its instructions. Other courts consider this refusal

to accept an acquittal to be a violation of the defendant's rights under the Double Jeopardy Clause. This difference in approach is largely attributable to different understandings of when a jury's declaration becomes a verdict of acquittal triggering the double jeopardy bar.

What if the inconsistency appears in the findings of a judge who has tried the case without a jury? *Dunn* would seem to have little application in this context because it would not "enhance respect for law or for the courts by recognizing for a judge the same right to indulge in 'vagaries' in the disposition of criminal charges that, for historic reasons, has been granted the jury." But in *Harris v. Rivera*,[6] the Supreme Court refused to find that "an apparent inconsistency in a trial judge's verdict" requires relief as a constitutional matter. The Court noted that there were various constitutional reasons for explaining the apparent inconsistency between the finding of defendant guilty and his accomplice not guilty: (1) that the judge had "a lingering doubt" about the guilt of the accomplice which he "might not be able to articulate in a convincing manner," in which case the law should not influence him "to convict all"; (2) that the judge made an error of law concerning the acquitted defendant, which as a constitutional matter certainly need not "redound to the benefit" of the convicted defendant; and (3) that "the acquittal is the product of a lenity that judges are free to exercise at the time of sentencing but generally are forbidden to exercise when ruling on guilt or innocence," which also would not amount to a constitutional violation, for there is "nothing in the Federal Constitution that would prevent a State from empowering its judges to render verdicts of acquittal whenever they are convinced that no sentence should be imposed for reasons that are unrelated to guilt or innocence."

(c) **Multi–Theory Verdicts.** Is a defendant entitled to jury instructions that require that the jurors be in agreement on the theoretical basis of the defendant's guilt? In *Schad v.*

6. 454 U.S. 339, 102 S.Ct. 460, 70 L.Ed.2d 530 (1981).

Arizona,[7] the Supreme Court examined the constitutional aspects of this issue. The defendant there was convicted of first-degree murder, defined by state law as murder that is "wilful, deliberate or premeditated * * * or which is committed * * * in the perpetration of, or attempt to perpetrate * * * robbery." The case was submitted to the jury under instructions that did not require unanimity on either of the available theories of premeditated murder and felony murder. In an opinion joined by three other members of the Court, Justice Souter declared that the Due Process Clause places "limits on a State's capacity to define different courses of conduct, or states of mind, as merely alternative means of committing a single offense, thereby permitting a defendant's conviction without jury agreement as to which course or state actually occurred." It was, of course, well established that "an indictment need not specify which overt act, among several named, was the means by which a crime was committed" and that juries could return "general verdicts" in such cases without agreeing upon a "single means of commission." However, due process has long been held to impose a requisite degree of specificity, so that no person is punished "save upon proof of some specific illegal conduct." That requisite degree of specificity would be compromised if the state were allowed to join separate offenses without directions to the jury to return separate verdicts on each, and the same would be true if a state were allowed to obtain a conviction under a single statutory offense "so generic" in coverage as to permit any combination of separate crimes to suffice for conviction. Thus, the critical issue was to ascertain "the point at which differences between means become so important that they may not reasonably be viewed as alternatives to a common end, but must be treated as differentiating what the Constitution requires to be treated as separate offenses."

Justice Souter initially rejected two possible standards for drawing the line required by due process. One, suggested in lower court rulings, was to ask whether the different alternatives fell into "distinct conceptual groupings," but this was unsatisfactory because "conceptual groupings may be identified at various levels of generality, and we have no *a priori* standard to determine what level of generality is appropriate." Another, suggested by the *Schad* dissenters, would rest on the characterization of the alternatives as independent elements of the offense, but having the Court render its own judgment in this regard "runs afoul of the fundamental principle that we are not free to substitute our own interpretations of state statutes for those of a State's courts." In the end, no "single criterion" could control. Ultimately, the Court's "sense of appropriate specificity" must be a "distillate of the concept of due process with its demands for fundamental fairness." In translating this demand for fairness into "concrete judgments," the Court would look initially to both "history and widespread practice as guides to fundamental values." At the same time, it would proceed from a "threshold presumption of legislative competence to determine the appropriate relationship between means and ends in defining the elements of the crime."

Applying this general approach, Justice Souter found that the Arizona statute provided sufficient specificity in treating premeditation and felony murder as alternative modes of establishing the "blameworthy state of mind required to prove a single offense of first-degree murder." Here "substantial historical and contemporary echoes" supported that characterization. At common law, "the intent to kill and the intent to commit a felony were alternative aspects of the single concept of 'malice aforethought.'" American jurisdictions, though modifying the common law by legislation classifying murder by degrees, had "in most cases retained premeditated murder and some form of felony murder * * * as alternative means of satisfying the mental state that first degree murder presupposes." A series of state decisions interpreting these first degree murder statutes reflected "widespread acceptance" of the concept that they simply established alternative means of satisfying the mens rea element of a single crime and there-

---

7. 501 U.S. 624, 111 S.Ct. 2491, 115 L.Ed.2d 555 (1991).

fore required unanimity only as to that ultimate element of mens rea and not as to the means themselves. Cautioning that it cannot be said "that either history or current practice is dispositive," Justice Souter also emphasized the lack of "moral disparity" in the two alternative mental states. "Whether or not everyone would agree that the mental state that precipitates death in the course of robbery is the moral equivalent of premeditation, it is clear that such equivalence could reasonably be found, which is enough to rule out the argument that this moral disparity bars treating them as alternative means to satisfy the mental element of a single offense."

Justice Scalia, providing the fifth vote for affirmance, relied solely upon the fact that the challenged practice was "as old as the common law and still in existence in the vast majority of States." He was critical of the plurality's "moral equivalence" test, and noted that if it were not for the historical and current acceptance of a general verdict in first-degree murder cases, he "might well be with the dissenters in this case."

The four dissenters (per White, J.) argued that the statute here, "under a single heading, criminalizes several alternative patterns of conduct." The jury charge therefore violated due process, since "a State [cannot] invoke more than one statutory alternative, each with different specified elements, without requiring that the jury indicate on which of the alternatives it has based the defendant's guilt." The issue was not one of appropriate specificity, the dissent argued, but a due process requirement that the jury find proof beyond a reasonable doubt of each of the elements required for criminal liability as specified by the state.

In 1999, six justices in *Richardson v. United States*[8] interpreted the federal "continuing criminal enterprise" statute[9] to require separate, unanimous findings on each individual underlying offense making up the required "continuing series of violations," thus avoiding the question whether such an interpretation was required by the Constitution. Al

though the Court specifically declined to reach the constitutional question, the Court's discussion relied at points on the plurality opinion in *Schad*, and presented potentially relevant policy concerns. The statute in *Richardson* forbid any "person" from "engaging in a continuing criminal enterprise," defined as involving a violation of the drug statutes where "such violation is a part of a continuing series of violations." The Court began its discussion of statutory interpretation by noting that "[c]alling a particular kind of fact an 'element' carries certain legal consequences. * * * The consequence that matters for this case is that a jury in a federal criminal case cannot convict unless it unanimously finds that the Government has proved each element." Specifically, the Court asked whether the phrase "series of violations" creates several elements, in respect to which the jury must agree unanimously, or one "series" element, in respect to which the violations constitute mere means or facts.

First, interpreting the statute to require unanimity on each separate "violation" making up the series, the Court reasoned, was consistent with "a tradition of requiring juror unanimity where the issue is whether a defendant has engaged in conduct that violates the law." Second, this interpretation avoids the "dangers of unfairness" that are risked by the alternative interpretation, considering the "word 'violations' covers many different kinds of behavior of varying degrees of seriousness." This broad range "increases the likelihood that treating violations simply as alternative means, by permitting a jury to avoid discussion of the specific factual details of each violation, will cover-up wide disagreement among the jurors about just what the defendant did, or did not do." Third, because the statute invites proof of multiple offenses, failing to require agreement on each violation "significantly aggravates the risk (present at least to a small degree whenever multiple means are at issue) that jurors, unless required to focus upon specific factual detail, will fail to do so, simply concluding from testimony, say, of bad reputation, that where there is smoke there

8. 526 U.S. 813, 119 S.Ct. 1707, 143 L.Ed.2d 985 (1999).

9. 81 U.S.C.A. § 848.

must be fire." Finally, "the Constitution itself limits a State's power to define crimes in ways that would permit juries to convict while disagreeing about means, at least where that definition risks serious unfairness and lacks support in history or tradition," the Court noted, citing *Schad*. "We have no reason to believe that Congress intended to come close to, or to test, those constitutional limits when it wrote this statute." The Court rejected arguments that its reasoning would require the jury to agree on "specific sales to specific street level users," noting that it would be enough to show that a defendant supplied "a runner in his organization with large quantities of drugs on or about particular dates as alleged in an indictment." Assuming without deciding that the jury need not agree about the "brute facts that make up other statutory elements" of the offense, the Court distinguished those elements as differing "in respect to language, breadth, tradition, and the other factors we have discussed."[10]

Reaching the constitutional issue, Justice Kennedy, joined by Justices O'Connor and Ginsburg, argued that the Constitution did not forbid their interpretation of the statute as setting forth one "series" element that may be established without juror agreement as to means. "The CCE statute does not in any way implicate the suggestion in *Schad* that an irrational single crime consisting of, for instance, either robbery or failure to file a tax return would offend due process. * * * Although the continuing series may consist of different drug crimes, the mere proof of a series does not suffice to convict. The Government must also prove action in concert with five or more persons, a leadership role for the defendant with respect to those persons, and substantial income or resources derived from the continuing series. The presence of these additional elements distinguishes the CCE statute from a simple recidivism statute * * *." The dissent observed, "One could concede, arguendo, that if Congress were to pass a habitual-offender statute the sole element of which was the

existence of a series of crimes without a requirement of jury unanimity on any underlying offense, then the statute would raise serious questions as to fairness and rationality because the jury's discretion would be so unconstrained. The statute before us is not of that type, for the various elements work together to channel the jury's attention toward a certain kind of ongoing enterprise." Speaking to the "moral equivalence" aspect of the plurality's test in *Schad*, the dissent argued that since "the continuity itself is what Congress sought to prohibit with the series element," it "makes no difference if the violations in the series involve comparable amounts of drugs."

(d) Partial Verdicts. The term "partial verdict" is used here to refer to the situation in which the jury after some deliberation returns a verdict as to only some of the counts or some of the defendants prior to deciding the remaining matters before it. The return and receipt of a partial verdict as to less than all defendants or less than all counts is permitted in the federal courts, and the practice is also accepted in state procedure. A court may accept the partial verdict and then discharge the jury because of its inability to agree regarding the remaining matters, or accept the partial verdict and then require the jury to resume deliberations on matters still to be decided. Once a partial verdict has been accepted, however, it may not be reconsidered by the jury or impeached, even while the jury deliberates remaining charges.

§ 24.11 Post–Verdict Motions

(a) Judgment of Acquittal. A post-verdict motion asking the court to enter an acquittal, notwithstanding the contrary jury verdict, is universally available. Though jurisdictions vary in the titles they give to this motion, it operates basically as a motion for directed acquittal, which was discussed in § 24.6(b). The prevailing view is that, as in the federal system, the post-verdict motion can be made even if an earlier motion for directed acquittal was available and not made. The standard

---

10. The dissenters objected that this fails to provide any analysis that might explain how the elements differ, and "also ignores the point that they are all ways of ensuring that the accused directs schemes of sufficient size, duration, and effectiveness to warrant special punishment * * * ."

applied in reviewing the evidence is that applied to the earlier motion, as discussed in § 24.6(c). However, defense counsel recognizing pragmatically that the jury's verdict could influence the judge's application of that standard will rarely chance delaying until after the verdict the initial challenge to the evidence.

(b) New Trial. Motions for new trial take two forms. In many jurisdictions, the motion for new trial may challenge the verdict as against the weight of the evidence. This objection is quite distinct from a challenge to the sufficiency of the evidence. It does not contend that a rational trier of fact could not reach the conclusion that the jury reached, but instead asks the trial court to become, in effect, a "thirteenth juror." As such, the trial court has the authority to grant the defense a second opportunity where that court concludes that, despite the abstract sufficiency of the evidence, the conviction is against the weight of the evidence.[1] In making that judgment, the judge is not commanded, as he would be in ruling on a motion for directed acquittal, to leave issues of credibility to the jury. Other courts recognizing the thirteenth-juror concept would not characterize the trial judge's authority as quite so extensive. They stress that the test is not simply whether the trial court would have reached a different result if it were the finder of fact and they note that a judge should always be cautious in overturning a jury's judgment, yet they acknowledge at the same time that in this context the trial court may act on its own independent evaluation of the evidence.

The motion may also challenge the conviction for trial error or pretrial error that would justify reversal of a conviction on appeal. Ordinarily, a defendant must raise the motion within a fairly brief period after the guilty verdict is returned. Federal Rule 33, for example, requires that such a new trial motion be made within seven days, unless the trial court grants an extension within that seven day period. This short period ensures that the court can move promptly to sentencing, because ordinarily any motion for new trial will be ruled upon before sentence is entered.

In deciding motions for new trial that challenge the procedures or evidence that produced the conviction, the court is limited by the harmless error rule.[2] The court also will be bound by the raise-or-waive rule and other rules requiring that challenges be presented at a particular point in the proceeding (e.g., pretrial challenges to errors in preliminary proceedings). In some jurisdictions, the defense must present in the new trial motion objections that it intends to raise on appeal. Requiring a new trial motion as a prerequisite for appellate review is intended "to allow a trial court some opportunity to review and correct its own errors and thereby, in some instances, avoid the extra travail and expense of an appeal."

(c) Newly Discovered Evidence. All jurisdictions recognize what is often described as a delayed motion for new trial based upon newly discovered evidence. In some jurisdictions, as under Federal Rule 33, the motion must be made within a certain time period, but that time period is quite lengthy (three years under Rule 33). Other jurisdictions allow the motion to be made within 10 or 15 days. Several do not set a time limit and permit the motion to be made at any time.

In *Herrera v. Collins*[3] the Court held that due process was not violated by a state's reliance on a time limit to refuse to consider newly discovered evidence, notwithstanding the defendant's claim that the evidence would establish his "actual innocence" of an offense for which he had been sentenced to death. State law there imposed a 60–day limit on such new trial motions, and the defendant had not presented his newly discovered evidence (affidavits of persons stating that defendant's now deceased brother had admitted that he committed the crime, including one witness who claimed he had seen the brother do the

---

1. Tibbs v. Florida, 457 U.S. 31, 42, 102 S.Ct. 2211, 2218, 72 L.Ed.2d 652 (1982).

2. See § 27.6.

3. 506 U.S. 390, 113 S.Ct. 853, 122 L.Ed.2d 203 (1993). *Herrera* is also discussed in § 28.3(f).

killing) until eight years after trial. The Court stated that, in light of the common law restrictions on such new trial motions to the same term of court, "we cannot say that Texas" refusal to entertain petitioner's newly discovered evidence eight years after his conviction transgresses a principle of fundamental fairness "rooted in the traditions and conscience of our people." The Court majority also rejected defendant's claim that the Eighth Amendment would be violated by imposing the death penalty notwithstanding his alleged showing of "actual innocence." The majority noted that, "assum[ing] for the sake of argument" that a "truly persuasive demonstration of 'actual innocence' would render the execution of defendant unconstitutional, and warrant federal habeas relief if there were no state avenue open to process such a claim," the "threshold showing for such an assumed right would necessarily be extraordinarily high" and the defendant's showing fell "far short of any such threshold."

As *Herrera* illustrates, claims of newly discovered evidence, at least where raised after the brief period generally allowed for new trial motions, tend to be viewed with "great caution." Courts are naturally skeptical of claims

that a defendant, fairly convicted, with proper representation by counsel, should now be given a second opportunity because of new information that has suddenly been acquired. They also recognize that the "passage of time inevitably ripens the finality of the judgment as it increases the prosecution's difficulties of again proving a case."[4] Accordingly, rather exacting standards have been developed for the motion for new trial based on newly discovered evidence. The basic points of reference are (1) the evidence must be new to the defense, (2) the failure to learn of the evidence earlier must not be due to a lack of proper diligence, (3) and the evidence must reach a certain level of significance as measured by reference to the other evidence in the trial.

Recent exonerations by DNA testing have revealed that mistaken eyewitness identification is one of the most common reasons for wrongful convictions. These developments, together with continuing advances in DNA testing technology that allow for reliable testing of smaller and older samples, have prompted some states to enact specific provisions for granting DNA testing post-trial, with relaxed time limitations for motions raising newly discovered evidence.

4. See McCleskey v. Zant, 499 U.S. 467, 491, 111 S.Ct. 1454, 1468, 113 L.Ed.2d 517 (1991) (the " 'erosion of memory' and the 'dispersion of witnesses' that occur with

the passage of time prejudice the government and diminish the chances of a reliable criminal adjudication").

Chapter 25

DOUBLE JEOPARDY

Table of Sections

---

§ 25.1   Dimensions of the Guarantee

(a) Introduction. The Double Jeopardy Clause of the Fifth Amendment states: "Nor shall any person be subject for the same offence to be twice put in jeopardy of life or limb." Although this language might seem to limit only the retrial of a person for the same crime, its influence extends far beyond that setting. As a result, discussions of the double jeopardy limitation occur throughout this treatise.[1] The most significant and direct impact of

§ 25.1

1. See e.g., § 17.4 (joinder); § 21.5(e) (plea withdrawal); § 24.8 (lesser offense instructions); § 26.7 (sentencing); § 27.3 (prosecution appeals).

the Double Jeopardy Clause is in the area of retrials and that is the aspect of double jeopardy law considered in this chapter. Sections two, three, and four consider retrials on the same charges by the same sovereign. Section five deals with a second prosecution by a different sovereign. Combined with the discussion in § 17.4(b) of attempts by the same sovereign to punish a defendant again for violations that may be the "same offence" for double jeopardy purposes, this material presents the core of the double jeopardy prohibition.

An overview of the general features of the double jeopardy guarantee is appropriately placed here. The overview brings together those structural principles that shape the double jeopardy bar. These principles inform not only the retrial issues discussed in this chapter, but also the various double jeopardy issues discussed elsewhere.

(b) Policies and History. The most complete discussion by the Supreme Court of the policies underlying the Double Jeopardy Clause is found in *United States v. DiFrancesco*.[2] As Justice Blackmun noted, the preservation of the "finality of judgments" is commonly said to be "the," "the primary," or at least "a" purpose of the double jeopardy bar. This is not to suggest, however, that the Double Jeopardy Clause is "simply res judicata dressed in prison grey." Finality here is concerned less with avoiding the costs of redundant litigation and relieving crowded dockets and more with protecting the defendant against the oppression of prosecution. Thus, as Justice Blackmun also noted, the "general design" of the bar against double jeopardy was that set forth in an oft-quoted passage from Justice Black's opinion in *Green v. United States*:[3]

> The constitutional prohibition against "double jeopardy" was designed to protect an individual from being subjected to the hazards of trial and possible conviction more than once for an alleged offense. * * * The underlying idea, one that is deeply ingrained in at least the Anglo–American system of

jurisprudence, is that the State with all its resources and power should not be allowed to make repeated attempts to convict an individual for an alleged offense, thereby subjecting him to embarrassment, expense, and ordeal and compelling him to live in a continuing state of anxiety and insecurity, as well as enhancing the possibility that even though innocent he may be found guilty.

As *DiFrancesco* further explained, the potential for governmental oppression described by Justice Black is restrained in several ways by preserving the "finality" or "integrity" of final judgments. Initially, the protection of the innocent is served by what Justice Blackmun characterized as the "special weight" accorded to an "acquittal." The "public interest in the finality of criminal judgments" here is recognized to be "so strong that an acquitted defendant may not be retried even though 'the acquittal was based on an egregiously erroneous foundation.'" This "absolute finality" is "justified on the ground that however mistaken the individual acquittal may have been there would be an unacceptably high risk" to the innocent in allowing the government to override such a judgment and proceed anew. Where the verdict is that of the jury, there is always the possibility that the acquittal reflects the "jury's prerogative to acquit against the evidence." Moreover, to allow an acquittal to be less than final is to accept the possibility that a progression of juries could acquit, with each verdict losing its finality due to a prosecution error, until, sooner or later, some jury would finally convict. The danger of an "erroneous conviction from [such] repeated trials" is considered too great to acknowledge any exception to the absolute finality of the acquittal. Where "the innocence of the accused has been confirmed by a final judgment, the Constitution conclusively presumes [through the Double Jeopardy Clause] that a second trial would be unfair."

The threat of governmental oppression cited in *Green* poses a concern that goes beyond the threat to the innocent. There is also the un-

---

2. 449 U.S. 117, 101 S.Ct. 426, 66 L.Ed.2d 328 (1980).

3. 355 U.S. 184, 78 S.Ct. 221, 2 L.Ed.2d 199 (1957).

fairness of using the criminal prosecution to inflict additional burdens upon the individual, guilty or innocent, by subjecting him to "the embarrassment, expense, and ordeal" of repeated trials. The Double Jeopardy Clause protects against such unfairness by according finality to judgments of conviction as well as acquittal. A defendant who is convicted and wishes to end the matter there can do so by simply accepting that judgment. This also serves to avoid the "continual state of anxiety and insecurity" mentioned in *Green*, because one consequence of allowing the prosecution to reprosecute after a conviction would be to allow it to seek a higher sentence for the same conviction. Indeed, speaking to the defendant's entitlement to repose following his acceptance of his conviction, the Supreme Court has noted that "it is the punishment that would legally follow the second conviction [if retrial were permitted] which is the real danger guarded against by the Constitution."[4] Accordingly, as *DiFrancesco* noted, the guarantee against double jeopardy has been said to consist of three separate constitutional protections. "It protects against a second prosecution for the same offense after acquittal. It protects against a second prosecution for the same offense after conviction. And it protects against multiple punishments for the same offense."

One might have thought that due to its central concern for preserving the finality of judgments the Double Jeopardy Clause would apply only where a verdict had been reached. That conclusion might also follow from the grounding of the bar against double jeopardy in the common law pleas of *autrefois acquit* (formerly acquitted), *autrefois convict* (formerly convicted), and pardon.[5] However, the Supreme Court recognized at an early point that the protection of verdict finality could be subverted by actions that terminated a trial prior to verdict and thereby took away from the defendant his opportunity to gain an acquittal.

If such actions allowed the prosecution to begin over again, the finality of a likely acquittal could be avoided; the prosecution would have the opportunity to regroup and try again simply by not allowing the trial to proceed to a final verdict. Thus, the Court has recognized as an aspect of bar against double jeopardy the protection of "the defendant's 'valued right' to have his trial completed by a particular tribunal."[6] Implicit in this protection are the suggestions that not only must there be a barrier to manipulation of a trial's termination by the prosecution, but also that the termination of a trial before a verdict is returned may harm the defendant even without such manipulation. Every jury has its own character and the initial jury may be more favorably disposed to the defendant than the next jury. Apart from any difference in the trier of fact, "if the Government may reprosecute, it gains an advantage from what it learns at the first trial about the strengths of the defense case and the weakness of its own."[7] On the other hand, since the protection being afforded here was designed basically as a supplement to the core interest in preserving the integrity of judgments, the Court has concluded that these potential harms may be offset by other interests. The result is a case-by-case balancing approach, as compared to the more absolute standards imposed to protect the finality of verdicts.

The Double Jeopardy Clause has been described by commentators as both a constitutional guarantee serving multiple purposes and as a guarantee serving a single purpose— "verdict finality"—that has several strands. But function alone cannot explain double jeopardy law; it has also been shaped by history. Indeed, the Court has stated that this is an area in which it is sensible to apply Justice Holmes' aphorism that "a page of history is worth a volume of logic," as it involves a guarantee that "is rooted in history and is not an evolving concept like * * * due process."[8]

4. Ex parte Lange, 85 U.S. (18 Wall.) 163, 21 L.Ed. 872 (1873).

5. See 4 W. Blackstone, Commentaries on The Laws of England *335–36 (4th ed. 1970).

6. Wade v. Hunter, 336 U.S. 684, 69 S.Ct. 834, 93 L.Ed. 974 (1949).

7. United States v. DiFrancesco, supra note 2.

8. Richardson v. United States, 468 U.S. 317, 104 S.Ct. 3081, 82 L.Ed.2d 242 (1984); Gore v. United States, 357 U.S. 386, 78 S.Ct. 1280, 2 L.Ed.2d 1405 (1958).

The guarantee, the Court has noted, dates back to Greek and Roman times. It was well established in the common law of England before this nation's independence; it was carried into the jurisprudence of this country as part of the common law; and it was recognized in some form by every state either in its constitution or common law.[9]

Application of a truly functional approach would often take the doctrine beyond its historical content. On occasion, the Court has been willing to move in that direction. For example, *Ashe v. Swensen* held that collateral estoppel was an element of double jeopardy based on the close functional relationship between that doctrine and the traditional acquittal rule in protecting a final adjudication favorable to the defense.[10] On the other hand, although one could argue that it constitutes oppression like that described in *Green* for a prosecutor to bring four separate prosecutions against a person who allegedly robbed the same bank by the same method on four consecutive days, the Court clearly is not willing to insist that those prosecutions take place simultaneously, given the traditional understanding of the phrase "the same offence."[11] Here, as in various other areas, well-established historical distinctions have continued to override concerns about the functional validity of those distinctions.

The combination of several related but somewhat distinct values underlying the Double Jeopardy Clause and an uneven response to history has produced a body of double jeopardy doctrine that various commentators have criticized variously as inconsistent, confusing, outmoded in a modern day procedural system, unduly technical, and too readily subject to manipulation by prosecutor and judge. On occasion, the Court itself has acknowledged that at least some of these criticisms are not far off the mark. Indeed, it has described its double jeopardy decisions as "a veritable Sargasso Sea which would not fail to challenge the most

intrepid judicial navigator."[12] Thus it is not surprising that the Court has been led on more than one occasion to "rethink" and revise seemingly settled aspects of its double jeopardy jurisprudence, and it would not be surprising if that process of rethinking and revision continued into the future.

(c) Proceedings to Which Applicable. Read literally, the fifth amendment prohibition against a person being "twice put in jeopardy of life or limb" for "the same offence" would seem to be applicable only to criminal prosecutions and, indeed, only to those risking capital or corporal punishment. But the guarantee has been given a somewhat broader construction. For one thing, as the Court held in *Ex parte Lange*,[13] the Double Jeopardy Clause extends to all "crimes." The Court in *Lange* reasoned: (1) the double jeopardy bar was based on the common law pleas of *autrefois acquit* and *autrefois convict*; (2) while "almost every offense was punished with death or other punishment touching the person" when those pleas originally were recognized, the pleas subsequently were held to apply to "felonies, minor crimes, and misdemeanors alike"; and (3) the double jeopardy provision should follow the common law extension of the pleas and apply to all criminal offenses without regard to the particular form of punishment opposed.

Generally, the prohibition has no application in noncriminal cases. As the Supreme Court stated in its 1938 decision in *Helvering v. Mitchell*:[14] "Congress may impose both a criminal and a civil sanction in respect to the same act or omission; for the double jeopardy clause prohibits merely punishing twice, or attempting a second time to punish criminally, for the same offense." But merely labeling a proceeding as civil is not the end of the matter, as a legislature should not be able to bypass so easily the constitutional safeguards required in criminal proceedings. In some circumstances, a

---

9. Benton v. Maryland, 395 U.S. 784, 89 S.Ct. 2056, 23 L.Ed.2d 707 (1969) (finding double jeopardy protection fully applicable to the states).

10. See § 17.4(a).

11. See § 17.4(b).

12. Albernaz v. United States, 450 U.S. 333, 101 S.Ct. 1137, 67 L.Ed.2d 275 (1981).

13. Supra note 4.

14. 303 U.S. 391, 58 S.Ct. 630, 82 L.Ed. 917 (1938).

"civil" proceeding should, despite its legislative label, be treated as a criminal proceeding.[15]

Assessments of whether a civil action must be treated for double jeopardy purposes as a criminal proceeding require the application of a test developed by the Court in *Kennedy v. Mendoza–Martinez*,[16] and *United States v. Ward*.[17] *Kennedy* involved a challenge to a statute that divested an American of his citizenship as a penalty for draft evasion. The Court concluded that the statute was "essentially penal in character," thus requiring observance of the rights to notice, confrontation, compulsory process, trial by jury, and the assistance of counsel that are guaranteed in criminal cases by the Fifth and Sixth Amendments. The Court in *Kennedy* listed the following considerations as "relevant" to the determination of "whether an Act of Congress is penal or regulatory in character":

[1] Whether the sanction involves an affirmative disability or restraint, [2] whether it has historically been regarded as a punishment, [3] whether it comes into play only on a finding of scienter, [4] whether its operation will promote the traditional aims of punishment-retribution and deterrence, [5] whether the behavior to which it applies is already a crime, [6] whether an alternative purpose to which it may rationally be connected is assignable for it, and [7] whether it appears excessive in relation to the alternative purpose assigned.

Because forfeiture of citizenship traditionally had been considered punishment and the legislative history of the forfeiture provisions "conclusively" showed that the measure was intended to be punitive, the Court in *Kennedy* concluded that the deprivation of citizenship was a criminal sanction for evading the draft,

requiring the procedural safeguards incident to a criminal prosecution.

In *Ward*, the Court considered whether a penalty provided in the Water Pollution Control Act was a criminal sanction that would entitle a person to the protection of the Fifth Amendment's privilege against self-incrimination. The Court acknowledged that the conduct subject to penalty was also subject to criminal prosecution, but noted that this was the only factor weighing in favor of characterizing the sanction as penal. The respondent failed to offer "the 'clearest proof' that the penalty * * * is punitive in either purpose or effect."

For a brief period between 1989 and 1997, the *Kennedy–Ward* test was not the sole measure of whether defendants facing both civil and criminal penalties for the same misdeed were entitled to relief under the Double Jeopardy Clause. In a unanimous decision in *United States v. Halper*,[18] the Court interpreted the Double Jeopardy Clause as regulating the imposition of successive civil and criminal sanctions for the same offense whenever the civil sanction could be characterized as "punitive." A "punitive" civil sanction following a criminal sanction was barred by the Double Jeopardy Clause, the Court held, even though the civil sanction did not amount to a "criminal" sanction under the *Kennedy* analysis. The United States had initially prosecuted Halper for filing 65 false claims defrauding the government of a total of $585. After the defendant was convicted and sentenced for these offenses, the government sought $130,000 in "civil penalties" for the same fraudulent claims under the False Claims Act. Noting the great disparity between the monetary sanction sought and the actual loss suffered, the Court held that the civil penalties could be explained

---

15. See also Breed v. Jones, 421 U.S. 519, 95 S.Ct. 1779, 44 L.Ed.2d 346 (1975), in which the Court held that a defendant could not be tried criminally for the same offense which was the basis of a prior adjudicatory hearing in juvenile court. The Court stressed that "in terms of potential consequences, there is little to distinguish an adjudicatory hearing such as was held in this case from a traditional criminal prosecution." The Court's reference in *Breed* to comparable physical, psychological, and financial burdens could readily have been extended to place certain civil litigation or administrative hearings within the reach

of the prohibition against double jeopardy. Instead, *Breed* has been viewed as a part of the general "constitutionalization" of the juvenile court process.

16. 372 U.S. 144, 83 S.Ct. 554, 9 L.Ed.2d 644 (1963).

17. 448 U.S. 242, 100 S.Ct. 2636, 65 L.Ed.2d 742 (1980).

18. 490 U.S. 435, 109 S.Ct. 1892, 104 L.Ed.2d 487 (1989).

only as serving the "retributive or deterrent purposes" associated with "punishment." For several years, the *Halper* decision was considered to have established a middle ground between purely criminal and purely civil sanctions: civil sanctions "punitive" enough to trigger double jeopardy protections, yet still so civil in character that their imposition need not be accompanied by other constitutional safeguards provided in criminal cases

But *Halper's* three-tiered approach to double jeopardy was short-lived. In *Department of Revenue v. Kurth Ranch*,[19] a closely divided Court concluded that the Double Jeopardy Clause barred a proceeding to collect drug taxes from defendants who had already pleaded guilty to drug charges but distinguished *Halper*. The Court reasoned that because "tax statutes serve a purpose quite different from civil penalties," *Halper's* analysis, which compared the penalty to the actual cost to the government, was inappropriate for determining whether a tax was punishment. The tax was barred nevertheless by the Double Jeopardy Clause because of its "unusual" nature, "high rate" (eight times the value of the drugs), and "obvious deterrent purpose." The positions of the four dissenting justices in *Kurth Ranch* reflected disagreements over the reach and application of the *Halper* test that would eventually lead to its abandonment. Justice Rehnquist argued that the drug tax passed the *Halper* test and was not punitive, as it reflected the "nonpenal purpose of raising revenue." Justice O'Connor also viewed the drug tax as remedial, arguing that the defendant failed to show "the absence of a rational relationship between the amount of sanction and the government's nonpunitive objectives." Justice Scalia, joined by Justice Thomas, chose to reject the *Halper* approach entirely, stating that it was "time to put the *Halper* genie back in the bottle," and to acknowledge that double jeopardy "prohibits not

multiple punishments, but only multiple prosecutions."

Two years later, in *United States v. Ursery*,[20] the Court's retreat from *Halper* picked up steam. Distinguishing *Halper* once again, the Court held that the Double Jeopardy Clause did not bar the United States from first punishing a defendant for a drug offense in a criminal action and then forfeiting in a civil proceeding the assets that the defendant had used to commit that offense. The Court rejected the analysis of *Halper* as inappropriate for civil forfeiture, as it was "difficult to determine whether a particular forfeiture bears no rational relationship to the nonpunitive purposes of that forfeiture." Instead of *Halper*, the Court applied the analysis employed in *United States v. One Assortment of 89 Firearms*.[21] That case had relied upon the several factors of *Kennedy v. Mendoza–Martinez* in order to determine whether a forfeiture was "so punitive as to require application of the full panoply of constitutional protections required in a criminal trial." Under this analysis, the civil forfeiture provision in *Ursery* was nonpunitive, in both purpose and effect. Forfeiture of property used to commit drug crimes "encourages property owners to take care in managing their property," ensures that those persons "will not permit that property to be used for illegal purposes," and ensures that law violators "will not profit from their illegal acts." Given the Court's holding just three years earlier in *Austin v. United States*[22] that the very same forfeiture provision was not remedial, but instead was punitive enough to fall within the scope of the Excessive Fines Clause of the Eighth Amendment, the decision in *Ursery* meant that punishment for double jeopardy purposes would not be coextensive with punishment under the Eighth Amendment.

In *Kansas v. Hendricks*,[23] the Court once again addressed a claim that double jeopardy

19. 511 U.S. 767, 114 S.Ct. 1937, 128 L.Ed.2d 767 (1994).

20. 518 U.S. 267, 116 S.Ct. 2135, 135 L.Ed.2d 549 (1996).

21. 465 U.S. 354, 104 S.Ct. 1099, 79 L.Ed.2d 361 (1984).

22. 509 U.S. 602, 113 S.Ct. 2801, 125 L.Ed.2d 488 (1993).

23. 521 U.S. 346, 117 S.Ct. 2072, 138 L.Ed.2d 501 (1997).

barred a civil sanction, this time confinement under a state statute that authorized the civil commitment of persons who due to a "mental abnormality" or a "personality disorder" are likely to engage in "predatory acts of sexual violence." Once again the Court applied the multi-factor analysis of *Kennedy v. Mendoza–Martinez*, not *Halper*, and concluded that the defendant failed "to satisfy [the] heavy burden" of demonstrating, with "the clearest proof," that "the statutory scheme [is] so punitive either in purpose or effect as to negate [the state's] intention" to deem it "civil." Regarding the statute's purpose, the Court reasoned that the statute did "not make a criminal conviction a prerequisite for commitment," as persons acquitted or otherwise "absolved of criminal responsibility" were also eligible for confinement. Nor did the statute "affix culpability for prior criminal conduct," but instead considered such conduct as merely evidence of "mental abnormality" or "future dangerousness." Confinement under the statute did not turn on the presence of "scienter," a finding the Court stated was "evidence that confinement under the statute is not intended to be retributive." Finally, deterrence was not intended, the Court concluded, because the conditions of confinement under the statute resembled those of a mental institution, not a prison, and because persons suffering from mental abnormality or personality disorder are "unlikely to be deterred by the threat of confinement." The Court rejected defense claims that the potential of indefinite incarceration under the statute coupled with the state's failure to provide treatment rendered the statute's confinement punitive. Justice Kennedy concurred providing the fifth vote, but warned that if civil confinement "were to become a mechanism for retribution or general deterrence, or if it were shown that mental abnormality is too imprecise a category to offer a

solid basis for concluding that civil detention is justified, our precedents would not suffice to validate it."[24]

The demise of the three-tiered approach to double jeopardy in *Halper* finally came with the case of *Hudson v. United States*.[25] In *Hudson*, the justices considered whether the Double Jeopardy Clause barred the United States from pursuing criminal charges against defendants who had already been ordered to pay monetary penalties and who had been prohibited from participating in the affairs of any banking institution in a prior civil proceeding initiated by the Office of the Comptroller of the Currency. The majority admitted that "*Halper's* deviation from longstanding double jeopardy principles was ill considered." *Halper's* "test for determining whether a particular sanction is 'punitive,' and thus subject to the strictures of the Double Jeopardy Clause has proved unworkable," the Court declared. In particular, it was not possible under *Halper* "to determine whether the Double Jeopardy Clause is violated until a defendant has proceeded through a trial to judgment," and when employed to bar civil proceedings following criminal proceedings, *Halper's* approach "flies in the face of the notion that the Double Jeopardy Clause forbids the government from even 'attempting a second time to punish criminally.' "

Applying the *Kennedy–Ward* test, the *Hudson* majority concluded that the prior sanctions were not criminal penalties, and thus double jeopardy did not bar indictment. The monetary penalties had been designated by Congress as "civil," and Congress's decision to confer debarment authority upon an administrative agency was "prima facie evidence" that debarment was intended as a civil sanction. The Court concluded that there was "very little showing, to say nothing of the 'clearest proof' required by *Ward*," that these sanctions

---

24. The Court later explained in *Kansas v. Crane*, 534 U.S. 407, 122 S.Ct. 867, 151 L.Ed.2d 856 (2002), that in order to prevent civil commitment from "becom[ing] a 'mechanism for retribution or general deterrence'—functions properly those of criminal law, not civil commitment"—due process requires "proof of serious difficulty in controlling behavior" before the criminal process can be sidestepped. The "lack of ability to control behavior"

when considered with the nature of the psychiatric diagnosis, and the severity of the mental abnormality, "must be sufficient to distinguish the dangerous sexual offender whose serious mental illness, abnormality, or disorder subjects him to civil commitment from the dangerous but typical recidivist convicted in an ordinary criminal case."

25. 522 U.S. 93, 118 S.Ct. 488, 139 L.Ed.2d 450 (1997), also discussed in § 17.4(b).

were actually criminal. Debarment was " 'certainly nothing approaching the "infamous punishment" of imprisonment,' " and thus did not involve "affirmative disability or restraint." Historically, neither debarment nor the monetary sanction had been viewed as punishment, and both were imposed "without regard to the violator's state of mind." The Court acknowledged that the deterrent effect of the sanctions and the existence of criminal liability for the conduct underlying the sanctions weighed in favor of a finding that the sanctions were criminal, but these features were not sufficient, given the other factors, to preempt Congress's choice to impose these sanctions outside the criminal process. "To hold that the mere presence of a deterrent purpose renders such sanctions 'criminal' for double jeopardy purposes would severely undermine the Government's ability to engage in effective regulation of institutions such as banks."

Hudson did allow that "some of the ills at which *Halper* was directed are addressed by other constitutional provisions." Sanctions that are "downright irrational" are regulated by the Due Process and Equal Protection Clauses, the Court noted. And, hinting that the *Halper* test for punishment may retain vitality under the Eighth Amendment even as it perished as double jeopardy doctrine, the Court cited *Austin*, observing that the Eighth Amendment also protects against "excessive civil fines, including forfeitures." These protections are undoubtedly much narrower than *Halper's* double jeopardy bar, but may provide relief when civil sanctions are unusually severe or arbitrary.

Once a statute is adjudged to be civil, a defendant is powerless to prove that as actually applied to him the statute's effect is punitive. As a divided Court explained in *Seling v. Young,*[26] the punitive nature of a given statute must be determined on the face of the statute. The decision barred Young from challenging his confinement under a statute similar to that

in *Hendricks* by proving allegations that the conditions of his confinement were punitive and did not include treatment for his personality disorder. To accept such "as applied" challenges, reasoned the Court, "would never conclusively resolve whether a particular scheme is punitive and would thereby prevent a final determination of the scheme's validity under the Double Jeopardy and Ex Post Facto Clauses."[27]

(d) When Jeopardy Attaches. Termination of a proceeding before jeopardy has attached does not bar a second proceeding or otherwise entitle a defendant to relief under the Double Jeopardy Clause, while termination thereafter brings into play the various rules of double jeopardy. Thus the time at which jeopardy attaches was said in *Crist v. Bretz* to be the "linchpin for all double jeopardy jurisprudence."[28]

Jury Trials. In *Crist,* the Court held that the point at which jeopardy attaches is the moment at which the entire jury has been selected and has taken the oath required for service at trial. In that case, a mistrial was granted without sufficient reason after the jury was sworn but before the first witness was called to the stand. The lower court held that this did not prevent retrial because of a state rule that jeopardy attaches in both jury and non-jury cases only after the first witness is sworn. The state contended that the sworn-jury standard, traditionally applied in federal courts, was "no more than an arbitrarily chosen rule of convenience, similar in its lack of constitutional status to the federal requirement of a unanimous verdict of 12 jurors." Rejecting that contention, the Court stressed the historical development of the double jeopardy bar. Though the fifth amendment guarantee was once viewed as protecting only the finality of judgment and thus came into play only after entry of a judgment of conviction or acquittal, over the years the defendant's "valued right to have his trial completed before a particular

26. 531 U.S. 250, 121 S.Ct. 727, 148 L.Ed.2d 734 (2001).

27. The analysis used to determine whether or not a sanction is punitive for purposes of the Double Jeopardy

Clause is also employed to determine the applicability of the Ex Post Facto Clause. See Smith v. Doe, 538 U.S. 84, 123 S.Ct. 1140, 155 L.Ed.2d 164 (2003).

28. 437 U.S. 28, 98 S.Ct. 2156, 57 L.Ed.2d 24 (1978).

tribunal'' had become an essential element of the constitutional guarantee. This meant that the commencement of jeopardy at the time the jury is sworn had become a part of that guarantee, as it "reflects and protects the defendant's interest in retaining a chosen jury." The Court concluded, "We cannot hold that this rule, so grounded, is only at the periphery of double jeopardy concerns. Those concerns—the finality of judgments, the minimization of harassing exposure to the harrowing experience of a criminal trial, and the valued right to continue with the chosen jury—have combined to produce the federal law that in a jury trial jeopardy attached when the jury is empaneled and sworn."

The effect of this rule is illustrated by *Downum v. United States*[29] and *Serfass v. United States*.[30] In *Downum*, a mistrial was declared without sufficient reason just after the jury had been sworn but before any testimony had been taken, and thus retrial was impermissible. But in *Serfass* a dismissal by the trial judge which was arguably an acquittal did not bar a later trial because the defendant had sought a jury trial and the judge entered the dismissal before the jury was selected.

Bench Trials. In a case which is to be tried by a judge without a jury, jeopardy attaches only after the first witness has been sworn. Until evidence is actually presented, the court is free to terminate the proceedings without triggering the double jeopardy bar against a second proceeding. Thus, opening statements or other pretrial motions are not enough, but the consideration of a stipulated statement of facts is sufficient for jeopardy to attach.[31] The different rules regarding attachment in bench and jury trials have been justified as historically grounded, and tailored to the aims of safeguarding a defendant's investment in the initial proceeding and protecting him from prosecutorial manipulation.

Guilty pleas. As for those cases in which a guilty plea ends the case without trial, jeopardy attaches when the court accepts the defendant's plea unconditionally and enters the judgment of conviction. In *Ohio v. Johnson*,[32] a state trial judge, over the prosecutor's objection, accepted a plea to a lesser-included offense, and sought to treat that plea as a final conviction barring prosecution on the greater offense charged. The Court disagreed, reasoning that the defendant had no authority to subdivide the indictment, enter a plea to only one part, and then maintain that the plea ended the case. The state not having agreed and the court lacking the capacity to deny the prosecution the opportunity to prove its charge, the guilty plea could not be taken as a final judgment disposing of the higher charge. The state had not sought to present the lesser-included and higher charges in separate proceedings, and the defense could not force separate treatment and then "use the double jeopardy clause as a sword to prevent the State from completing its prosecution on the remaining charges." Like the defendants in *Serfass* and *Sanford*, discussed below, the defendant in *Johnson* can be said to have attempted to gain an acquittal without allowing the prosecution the opportunity to present its case-in-chief.

When court lacks jurisdiction. Under English common law, exceptions to the pleas of prior conviction or acquittal existed where the trial court lacked jurisdiction, the theory being that a defendant before such a court was not actually placed in jeopardy. The Supreme Court in *United States v. Ball*[33] refused to follow one application of that English rule, rejecting the government's contention that a defendant had not been placed in jeopardy because he had been tried under a defective indictment. In the later case of *Kepner v. United States*,[34] the Court's lengthy discussion of the Double Jeopardy Clause referred at several

---

29.   372 U.S. 734, 83 S.Ct. 1033, 10 L.Ed.2d 100 (1963), discussed in § 25.2(d).

30.   420 U.S. 377, 95 S.Ct. 1055, 43 L.Ed.2d 265 (1975), discussed at note 35 infra.

31.   Finch v. United States, 433 U.S. 676, 97 S.Ct. 2909, 53 L.Ed.2d 1048 (1977).

32.   467 U.S. 493, 104 S.Ct. 2536, 81 L.Ed.2d 425 (1984).

33.   163 U.S. 662, 16 S.Ct. 1192, 41 L.Ed. 300 (1896).

34.   195 U.S. 100, 24 S.Ct. 797, 49 L.Ed. 114 (1904).

points to the finality of a verdict issued by a trial court "having jurisdiction." The Court also spoke of application of the Double Jeopardy Clause where a defendant has been tried before a "tribunal properly organized and competent to try him." The limitation apparently was not to "jurisdiction" in its broadest sense, for *Ball* seemingly had rejected such a prerequisite, but to the authority of the court to render judgment.

This quite narrow concept of judicial "competency" or "jurisdiction" acting as a prerequisite for double jeopardy protection is illustrated by *Serfass v. United States*.[35] There the Court cited *Kepner* in holding that the Double Jeopardy Clause did not come into play because the judgment in question was entered by a judge who did not have "jurisdiction to try the question of the guilt or innocence of the accused." The trial court in *Serfass* made factual as well as legal determinations in granting a motion to dismiss prior to the scheduled trial date. If that ruling were viewed simply as pretrial dismissal, then jeopardy obviously had not attached. The defense argued, however, that the ruling should be viewed as the equivalent of an acquittal after a bench trial, for the judge had ruled that the evidence available to him through the disclosure of a government file established an automatic defense to the charge. That argument failed on several grounds. If the ruling were to be taken as an acquittal, then the judge clearly lacked authority to enter such an order at that point in the proceeding. No jury had been selected (nor was any evidence presented), and the presentation of the file to the judge could not be viewed as a form of bench trial, since the parties had not waived their right to a jury.

A similar lack of authority defeated an attempt to portray a dismissal as an acquittal in *United States v. Sanford*,[36] although jeopardy there clearly had attached and the issue was whether jeopardy had been terminated by a verdict on the evidence. In that case, a hung jury in the original trial resulted in the scheduling of a retrial. Four months later, prior to

the second trial, the trial judge dismissed the indictment on the basis of his view of the evidence at the first trial. Defendant claimed that the judge's ruling had been an acquittal and was therefore entitled to finality. The Supreme Court rejected that claim because the judge was not a "competent tribunal" at that point for entering an acquittal; if the judge had entered his order within seven days after the ending of the first trial, which was the period allowed for a post-trial judgment of acquittal, then that order would have been treated as an acquittal and would have precluded further proceedings.[37] As it stood, however, the ruling was no different than that in *Serfass*.

In applying the *Ball* Court's suggestion that any acquittal or conviction "before a court having no jurisdiction" is "absolutely void, and therefore no bar to subsequent indictment and trial in a court which has jurisdiction of the offense," lower courts have noted that jurisdiction in a double jeopardy context is a "jurisprudential greased pig." These rulings construe the exception for lack of jurisdiction narrowly but allow retrial in a variety of circumstances. For example, criminal proceedings are not barred by a prior juvenile court proceeding that was based on defendant's misrepresentation as to his age, nor is a trial in juvenile court foreclosed after a defendant is erroneously tried as an adult in criminal court.

Fraudulently obtained acquittals. A few courts have put aside the usual double jeopardy rules and ignored a first proceeding where the defendant has used fraud or corruption to obtain an acquittal. The circumstances in which such an exception would apply are rare indeed, as the government may have to show beyond a reasonable doubt that a defendant participated in the bribing of the decisionmaker to gain his own acquittal. The exception has at least two plausible rationales. One could argue that a defendant is never really in "jeopardy" if he has fixed his case (i.e., jeopardy never "attached"). Alternatively, a defendant

35. Supra note 30.

36. 429 U.S. 14, 97 S.Ct. 20, 50 L.Ed.2d 17 (1976).

37. See United States v. Martin Linen Supply, 430 U.S. 564, 97 S.Ct. 1349, 51 L.Ed.2d 642 (1977) (finding an order entered within the 7–day period to be an acquittal).

may be said to have forfeited his double jeopardy rights by fraud. Whatever the basis, any such exception to the otherwise nearly absolute ban on reconsideration of acquittals must be carefully confined.

(e) Termination of Jeopardy. In *Kepner v. United States*,[38] Justice Holmes, in a dissenting opinion, formulated a concept of "continuing jeopardy" which only later gained some influence. Holmes argued that once jeopardy attached, it continued on through the proceedings that flowed from that original charge. "Logically and rationally," Holmes argued, "a man cannot be said to be more than once in jeopardy on the same cause, however often he may be tried. The jeopardy is one continuing jeopardy from its beginning to the end of the cause." Under this view, there would be no prohibition against retrial on the original charge following a successful government appeal from an acquittal. Retrial would be available after erroneous acquittals as well as convictions. The majority in *Kepner* rejected that position, as it concluded that the acquittal terminated the initial jeopardy so that a second trial would place the defendant twice in jeopardy. A conviction, too, is final, unless the defendant chooses to question it, as discussed in § 25.4.

In *Justices of Boston Municipal Court v. Lydon*,[39] however, the Court relied upon the continuing jeopardy rationale in the context of a trial de novo system of appeal. After being convicted in the magistrate's court, the defendant in that case sought to raise on appeal to the general trial court the alleged insufficiency of the evidence underlying that conviction. The general trial court ruled that such a challenge was not allowed, because the only remedy available was a trial de novo. Defendant then responded that if the prosecution's case before the magistrate court was insufficient to sustain a conviction, he should have been acquitted and the trial de novo would now place him twice in jeopardy. The Supreme Court majority, in rejecting that argument, viewed the trial in the magistrate's court and the trial

de novo as a two-stage continuous proceeding rather than as two separate trials. Thus, the defendant's claim was no different than that of the defendant who has a motion for directed acquittal denied at the end of the prosecution's case-in-chief and then is forced to continue to the end of the trial. If the evidence is sufficient at the end of the trial, he may be convicted, and he cannot claim to have been twice exposed to jeopardy because he should have been acquitted at the end of the case-in-chief.

The trial that is terminated without a verdict on defendant's guilt or innocence, as when a mistrial is declared, also presents a case in which jeopardy is continuing. Thus, in *Richardson v. United States*,[40] the Court in a mistrial case reached a result that paralleled that in *Justices of Boston Municipal Court*. The defendant claimed that he should not be forced to a second trial following a jury deadlock that resulted in a mistrial since the trial judge had erred in failing to grant defendant's motion for a judgment of acquittal based on the insufficiency of the evidence at that first trial. The Court rejected that contention as improperly viewing the first and second trials as separate subjections to jeopardy. "The failure of the jury to reach a verdict," the Court reasoned, "is not an event which terminates jeopardy." Accordingly, the government remained "entitled to resolution of the case by verdict from the jury," and the situation presented was essentially that of a completed first stage in an ongoing proceeding.

Conditioning the termination of jeopardy upon the presence of a verdict relates back to the primary concern of double jeopardy law with the protection of verdict finality. However, the Court has also recognized a need to guard against subversion of that protection through governmental action that denies the defendant the opportunity to see the trial through to a verdict. It therefore has found in the Double Jeopardy Clause, as discussed in § 25.2, certain restrictions upon judicial authority to grant a mistrial. Where those re-

---

38. Supra note 34.

39. 466 U.S. 294, 104 S.Ct. 1805, 80 L.Ed.2d 311 (1984).

40. 468 U.S. 317, 104 S.Ct. 3081, 82 L.Ed.2d 242 (1984).

strictions are violated, the retrial of the defendant amounts, in effect, to a second jeopardy. Thus, while a mistrial declared consistent with double jeopardy principles does not terminate jeopardy, as recognized in *Richardson*, a mistrial that violates those principles will be viewed otherwise.

(f) The "Same Offense". Offenses for double jeopardy purposes are not necessarily defined by reference to separate titles or separate statutory sections. Two offenses may have different titles and be prohibited by different statutory sections yet constitute the "same offence" for double jeopardy purposes. As discussed in § 17.4(b), whether offenses are the same for double jeopardy purposes requires an inquiry into the elements of the two crimes. However, as discussed in § 17.4(a), even if the two offenses are not the same, an acquittal in the first prosecution may bar a second prosecution under the doctrine of collateral estoppel, which is also an aspect of the bar against double jeopardy.

Although two offenses would otherwise be the same when tested by reference to their statutory elements, separate prosecutions will not be prohibited when different sovereigns (state and federal, or different states) are involved. Under the doctrine of dual sovereignty, discussed in § 25.5, prosecutions by different sovereigns for precisely the same conduct even under identical statutes are not barred by the double jeopardy prohibition.

(g) Reprosecutions: An Overview. The balance of this chapter is concerned with the double jeopardy implications of a second prosecution that rests on much the same criminal conduct as an earlier prosecution. The overview that follows, at the risk of oversimplification, brings together the essence of the double jeopardy principles relevant to reprosecutions that are elaborated upon both in this chapter and in several others. Those principles are:

(1) Multiple initiation of a prosecution that never reached the point of bringing jeopardy into play, as where the prosecution repetitively files complaints that are subsequently rejected in judicial or grand jury screening, does not create a double jeopardy difficulty. See § 25.1(d).

(2) Multiple prosecutions that produce multiple trials are not prohibited if they are for different offenses—unless collateral estoppel applies because the first trial resulted in an acquittal based on a failure of proof as to an element also required for the offense presented in the second trial. See § 17.4(a), (b).

(3) Separate prosecutions producing separate trials on statutory offenses that are the same offense are not prohibited where the defendant, by his request or otherwise, is solely responsible for the separate trials. See § 17.4(b).

(4) Multiple trials on a single charge are not prohibited if the first trial resulted in a mistrial that was justified under the manifest necessity doctrine or was requested or consented to by the defense (absent judicial or prosecutorial overreaching that is aimed at forcing the mistrial). See § 25.2.

(5) If a prosecution is dismissed after jeopardy attached, and that dismissal is based on some preliminary error that does not permanently terminate the prosecution, but allows the prosecution to reprosecute after curing that error (as where the dismissal was based on a defective pleading), that dismissal is treated in much the same fashion as a mistrial. Where the principles governing mistrials would allow the government to cure the error and return for a retrial, the government may also seek appellate review of the dismissal and renew the prosecution if the appellate court holds that the dismissal was erroneous. See §§ 25.2(f), 27.3(d).

(6) If after jeopardy attached a prosecution is dismissed on a ground permanently terminating the prosecution (e.g., denial of a speedy trial), and the defendant moved for the dismissal, double jeopardy does not prohibit a prosecution appeal and a subsequent retrial if the dismissal is held to be erroneous. See § 25.3(a).

(7) If the jury reaches a verdict of acquittal or the judge grants a judgment of acquittal, double jeopardy bars a new trial even if it appears that the acquittal was based on an

erroneous interpretation of the law. Included in the concept of an acquittal is the implied acquittal that comes when a jury returns a verdict of guilty on a lesser-included offense and fails to indicate its disposition of the higher charge. One exception to the concept that an acquittal ends all further proceedings arises when the trial judge grants a judgment of acquittal after the jury returned a guilty verdict. Here, if the appellate court should find that the judge erred in entering the acquittal, the jury verdict of conviction can be restored. See §§ 25.3, 25.4(d), 27.3(d).

(8) If there is a jury verdict of conviction, defendant may rest on the conviction, and it will bar any reprosecution on the same offense in much the same manner as an acquittal. If the defendant appeals the conviction and it is reversed, then the defendant ordinarily may be proceeded against by reprosecution without running afoul of the double jeopardy bar. The one exception is where the appellate court sets aside the conviction on the ground that the evidence of guilt was insufficient. See § 25.4.

(9) If a second trial is allowed after an overturned conviction, the court is not barred by double jeopardy from imposing a greater sentence on reconviction for the same offense than had been imposed on the original conviction. The resentenced defendant must, however, receive credit for any time served on the first sentence. Moreover, double jeopardy will not bar government appeal of a sentence when authorized by statute. See §§ 26.7, 26.8, 27.3.

(10) Multiple prosecutions that would otherwise be barred under the principles noted above are not prohibited where the prosecutions are brought by separate sovereigns (state and federal, or different states). See § 25.5.

§ 25.2　Reprosecution Following Mistrial

(a) With Defendant's Consent. The concern in this section is exclusively with when it is constitutionally permissible to undertake another prosecution for the same offense after the trial judge has declared a mistrial. A mistrial must be distinguished from a dismissal,

which is discussed later.[1] Essentially, the difference between the two is that a dismissal is granted for an error or defect thought to present an absolute barrier to conviction on the offense charged, while a mistrial is declared merely because of circumstances that make it impossible or impracticable to continue the particular trial to conclusion.

The mistrial situation that is most straightforward in terms of the double jeopardy guarantee is that which is brought about by the request of the defendant. The leading case is *United States v. Dinitz*,[2] where the trial judge excluded defense counsel from the case for misconduct and then gave the defendant the choice of a recess while the court of appeals passed upon the exclusion, a mistrial, or continuation of the trial with the assistant defense counsel. The defendant opted for mistrial, but the court of appeals held he could not be retried because there was no manifest necessity for the mistrial and defendant's action had not constituted a valid waiver of his double jeopardy claim. The Supreme Court disagreed, noting that there is a significant distinction between a mistrial declared by the court sua sponte, where the "manifest necessity" test applies, and one granted at defendant's request, where "a motion by the defendant for mistrial is ordinarily assumed to remove any barrier to reprosecution, even if the defendant's motion is necessitated by prosecutorial or judicial error." That rule, the Court explained, is fully consistent with the purposes underlying the double jeopardy protection:

> The defendant may reasonably conclude that a continuation of the tainted proceeding would result in a conviction followed by a lengthy appeal and, if a reversal is secured, by a second prosecution. In such circumstances, a defendant's mistrial request has objectives not unlike the interests served by the Double Jeopardy Clause—the avoidance of the anxiety, expense, and delay occasioned by multiple prosecutions.

§ 25.2

1.　See § 25.3(a).

2.　424 U.S. 600, 96 S.Ct. 1075, 47 L.Ed.2d 267 (1976).

As for the contention of the court of appeals that Dinitz had not voluntarily waived his double jeopardy protection because of the "Hobson's choice" with which he was confronted, the Court responded that "traditional waiver concepts have little relevance" in this context. Rather, the "important consideration * * * is that the defendant retains primary control over the course to be followed in the event of such error." The approach of the court of appeals, the Supreme Court added, would often deprive the defendant of the type of relief which would be most desirable for him. "In the event of severely prejudicial error a defendant might well consider an immediate new trial a preferable alternative to the prospect of a probable conviction followed by an appeal, a reversal of the conviction, and a later retrial."

Although in *Dinitz* the defendant actually requested a mistrial, the "consent doctrine" of that case also applies in those instances in which the defendant did not move for a mistrial but expressed agreement with the judge's announced intention to grant one. Some courts have gone so far as to suggest that silence constitutes tacit consent even where defense counsel was not asked for his views on the mistrial. But mere silence is a far cry from consent or waiver, especially when the proceedings are fast paced, the termination of the proceedings abrupt, or the defendant's opportunity to raise a meaningful objection is otherwise impaired. Moreover, the mere fact that a codefendant has moved for a mistrial should not necessarily bind the defendant joined with him for trial.

A related problem arises when a defendant fails to bring a motion to suppress illegally obtained evidence before trial, and waits until jeopardy attaches. In this situation, some courts have construed the defendant's motion as consent to a mistrial, so as to preserve the government's statutory right to appeal what would have been, absent the defendant's delay, a pretrial ruling.

(b) The "Goaded" Mistrial Motion. As the Supreme Court recognized in *United States v. Jorn*,[3] even if a mistrial was brought about with the consent of the defendant, double jeopardy bars reprosecution when the circumstances prompting the mistrial were "attributable to prosecutorial or judicial overreaching." Exactly what it would take to constitute such overreaching remained undefined until 1982, when a sharply divided Court in *Oregon v. Kennedy*[4] held that "[o]nly where the governmental conduct in question is intended to 'goad' the defendant into moving for a mistrial may a defendant raise the bar of Double Jeopardy to a second trial after having succeeded in aborting the first on his own motion." The Court explained that in such a case, "the defendant's valued right to complete his trial before the first jury would be a hollow shell if the inevitable motion for mistrial were held to prevent a later invocation of the bar of double jeopardy in all circumstances."

The Court in *Kennedy* reasoned that an "intent" test was necessary in order to have "a manageable standard to apply" in mistrial cases. The intent standard, the Court explained, "merely calls for the [trial] court to make a finding of fact," using the "familiar process in our criminal justice system" of "[i]nferring the existence or nonexistence of intent from objective facts and circumstances." By contrast, a broader bad faith or harassment standard would be difficult to apply and would be at issue in virtually every case, as "[e]very act on the part of a rational prosecutor during a trial is designed to 'prejudice' the defendant by placing before the judge or jury evidence leading to a finding of his guilt." A second consideration was that a broader test would be counterproductive because it would influence the denial of mistrial requests: "Knowing that the granting of the defendant's motion for mistrial would all but inevitably bring with it an attempt to bar a second trial on grounds of double jeopardy, the judge presiding over the first trial might well be more loath to grant a defendant's motion for mistrial."

---

3.   400 U.S. 470, 91 S.Ct. 547, 27 L.Ed.2d 543 (1971).

4.   456 U.S. 667, 102 S.Ct. 2083, 72 L.Ed.2d 416 (1982).

Four justices dissented from the Court's standard, although joining in its judgment on the facts of the case. They maintained that it should be "sufficient that the court is persuaded that egregious prosecutorial misconduct has rendered unmeaningful the defendant's choice to continue or to abort the proceeding." Where the prosecution's intentional misconduct had forced the defense to seek a mistrial, the Double Jeopardy Clause should protect the defense from a retrial without regard to whether the prosecutor had intended to force the mistrial motion, to harass and embarrass the defendant, or to ensure a conviction. The dissenters rejected the majority's concern that such a standard would lead defense counsel to seek to turn every act of prosecutorial error into an overreaching that forced a mistrial motion and thereby barred retrial. They argued that their proposed requirement of a two-pronged ruling of (1) "deliberate misconduct" and (2) resulting prejudice "that * * * at least substantially reduced the probability of an acquittal" would limit successful overreaching claims to the "rare and compelling case." Several state courts, relying on their state constitutions, have adopted standards for overreaching similar to that advanced by the *Kennedy* minority.

The *Kennedy* dissenters also argued that it would be virtually impossible for a defendant to prevail under the Court's intent standard: "It is almost inconceivable that a defendant would prove that the prosecutor's deliberate misconduct was motivated by an intent to provoke a mistrial instead of an intent simply to prejudice the defendant." The dissenters argued that even when the prosecution's case was weak and seemed destined for jury rejection, one could just as readily assume that intentional prejudice introduced by the prosecutor was designed to turn the jury around rather than to force a mistrial. Justice Powell, who also concurred in the majority's opinion, wrote separately to underscore the majority's apparent response to this contention. While the intention of the prosecutor was the key, " 'subjective' intent often may be unknowable," and therefore a trial court would "rely primarily upon the objective facts and circumstances of the particular case" in determining intent. The strength of the evidence would seem to be one of the most telling of those circumstances, along with the timing of the misconduct, the immediate event that provoked the misconduct, and whether it came after a trial court warning that continued misconduct could lead to a mistrial. Looking to these factors, at least in the scenario posed by the minority of a last-ditch introduction of prejudice in a weak case, a trial court could quite readily conclude that the prosecutor met the intent test of the *Kennedy* majority.

(c) The "Manifest Necessity" Standard. As for when the declaration of a mistrial by the trial judge sua sponte or over the defendant's objection bars a second trial, the "fountainhead decision" is *United States v. Perez*.[5] In that case, a unanimous Court held that the failure of the jury to agree on a verdict of either acquittal or conviction did not bar retrial of the defendant. The Court reasoned:

> We think, that in all cases of this nature, the law has invested Courts of justice with the authority to discharge a jury from giving any verdict, whenever, in their opinion, taking all the circumstances into consideration, there is a manifest necessity for the act, or the ends of public justice would otherwise be defeated. They are to exercise a sound discretion on the subject; and it is impossible to define all the circumstances, which would render it proper to interfere. To be sure, the power ought to be used with the greatest of caution, under urgent circumstances * * *.

The Court in *Perez* spoke of either a "manifest necessity" or the "ends of public justice" requiring the mistrial. Later opinions collapsed these alternatives into a single standard, described as a "manifest necessity" standard that means less than what the words might suggest on their face. As the Court stated in *Arizona v. Washington*[6]: "The words 'manifest necessity' appropriately characterize the magnitude of the prosecutor's burden. * * * [But] it is manifest that the key word 'necessity'

---

5. 22 U.S. (9 Wheat) 579, 6 L.Ed. 165 (1824).

6. 434 U.S. 497, 98 S.Ct. 824, 54 L.Ed.2d 717 (1978).

cannot be interpreted literally; instead, contrary to the teaching of Webster, we assume that there are degrees of necessity and we require a 'high degree' before concluding that the mistrial is appropriate."

In the end, the manifest necessity standard requires a balancing process. On the one side, the court considers the defendant's interest in having the trial completed in a single proceeding, preserving the possibility of obtaining an acquittal before that "particular tribunal." On the other side is the strength of the justification for turning to a mistrial rather than attempting to carry the trial through to a verdict. Of course lurking in the background is the recognition that an appellate court ruling holding that the trial judge improperly balanced these factors by ordering a mistrial operates to deprive the state of any full opportunity to establish the guilt of a person who well may be guilty. On top of these considerations, the Court in *Kennedy*[7] indicated that manifest necessity will not provide the complete answer as to whether a retrial is permissible. Even if the mistrial was compelled by necessity so great as to be almost absolute, where the condition that prevented the trial from continuing was purposely created by the prosecution in order to compel a mistrial, the rationale of *Kennedy* suggests that double jeopardy would bar a retrial. A prosecution can no more be allowed to "goad" a judge into declaring a mistrial than to goad a defendant into requesting one.

The Supreme Court has emphasized that each manifest necessity ruling is grounded on its own facts. The manifest necessity standard "abjures the application of any mechanical formula by which to judge the propriety of declaring a mistrial in the varying and often unique situations arising during the course of a criminal trial."[8] At the same time, some general guidelines can be abstracted from past cases. The two subsections that follow examine the most significant of these guidelines.

(d) Manifest Necessity and Alternatives to a Mistrial. Much of the case law applying the manifest necessity doctrine depends upon the proper evaluation of alternatives to a mistrial. The Supreme Court has insisted that the trial judge give consideration to such alternatives and that the failure to do so may, in itself, lead to a finding of a lack of manifest necessity. Illustrative is *United States v. Jorn.*[9] The trial judge, upon concluding that the government's witnesses did not understand the extent to which they might incriminate themselves, ordered a mistrial so as to allow the witnesses to consult with attorneys before deciding whether to testify. In finding a lack of manifest necessity, the plurality stressed that the trial judge gave absolutely "no consideration" to the alternative of a trial continuance, and "indeed, * * * acted so abruptly in discharging the jury" that the parties were given no opportunity to suggest the alternative of a continuance or to object in advance to the jury discharge. The Court concluded that where, as here, a trial judge simply "made no effort to exercise sound discretion to assure that * * * there was a manifest necessity for the * * * sua sponte declaration of a mistrial," a "reprosecution would violate the double jeopardy provision of the Fifth Amendment." In the later case of *Arizona v. Washington*,[10] the Court rejected the contention that *Jorn* required the trial judge to make explicit findings as to the need for a mistrial in light of alternatives, but it did insist that there be apparent from the trial record a "sufficient justification" for the mistrial ruling that reflected consideration of those alternatives.

The alternatives to mistrial that must be considered may include those requiring a relinquishment of rights, or an alteration of the usual trial process. Consider, for example, the case in which a juror is disqualified, discharged, or excused because of illness, leaving less than the requisite number of jurors to complete the case. If the jurisdiction is one in which the trial may continue with eleven jurors on agreement of the judge and the parties,

---

7. Supra note 4.

8. Illinois v. Somerville, 410 U.S. 458, 93 S.Ct. 1066, 35 L.Ed.2d 425 (1973).

9. Supra note 3.

10. Supra note 6.

may a judge declare a mistrial if the defense but not the prosecution desires to continue through to verdict with a smaller jury? Because of the risk of prosecutorial manipulation, several courts have held that a mistrial is inappropriate where the state blocks the eleven-juror alternative and gives no compelling reason for insisting upon the twelve-person jury that can be obtained only through a new trial. Elsewhere it has been held that the prosecution is never obligated to waive its right to a twelve-person jury.

In some instances, the defect that has occasioned the request for a mistrial does not prevent the case from being fairly tried to a verdict, but will render any conviction inherently defective. The argument has been advanced that defense should have the right in such cases to insist that the trial continue through to verdict, especially where the defect was the fault of the prosecution. That position, however, was rejected in *Illinois v. Somerville*.[11] The trial court there had declared a mistrial, upon request of the prosecution and over the defendant's objection, when the prosecution discovered on the first day of trial that its theft indictment was fatally defective. The indictment had failed to allege the necessary *mens rea* element of an intent to permanently deprive, and under Illinois law, that defect was jurisdictional in nature, being neither waivable by the defense nor curable by amendment. Under that circumstance, the trial court considered continuation of the trial to be inconsistent with the ends of justice since any conviction the trial might produce would automatically be set aside by the defense. The Supreme Court majority held that this conclusion was allowable under the manifest necessity standard. Attesting to the continuing validity of the doctrine of *Wade v. Hunter*[12] that "a defendant's valued right to have his trial completed by a particular tribunal must in some instances be subordinated to the public's interest in fair trials designed to end in just judgments," the Court concluded that the public interest justified the mistrial in this case:

> A trial judge properly exercises his discretion to declare a mistrial if an impartial verdict cannot be reached, or if a verdict of conviction could be reached but would have to be reversed on appeal due to an obvious procedural error in the trial. If an error would make reversal on appeal a certainty, it would not serve "the ends of public justice" to require that the Government proceed with its proof, when, if it succeeded before the jury, it would automatically be stripped of that success by an appellate court.

As illustrations of other instances in which a mistrial was constitutionally permissible because the prosecution was in a similar no-win situation attributable to a fatal defect in the proceedings, the Court in *Somerville* referred to *Thompson v. United States*,[13] upholding a mistrial declared after the trial judge learned one of the jurors was disqualified because he had served on the indicting grand jury, and *Lovato v. New Mexico*,[14] where the trial judge properly directed the case moved back to the pleading stage because after jeopardy had attached it was discovered that the defendant had not pleaded to the indictment.

While such cases as *Somerville*, *Thompson*, and *Lovato* support the notion that ordinarily there is a "manifest necessity" when it develops at trial that the prosecution is in a no-win posture because of a legal defect that would provide relief from conviction, this is not inevitably so. The *Somerville* Court cautioned that "the declaration of a mistrial on the basis of a rule or a defective procedure that lent itself to prosecutorial manipulation would involve an entirely different question," but added that such a situation was not before it. Although the defect was the responsibility of the prosecutor's office, which drafted the indictment, a prosecutor was not likely to include an inherent defect in a charging instrument for the purpose of later seeking a mistrial if his case did not progress well.

---

11.   Supra note 8.

12.   336 U.S. 684, 69 S.Ct. 834, 93 L.Ed. 974 (1949).

13.   155 U.S. 271, 15 S.Ct. 73, 39 L.Ed. 146 (1894).

14.   242 U.S. 199, 37 S.Ct. 107, 61 L.Ed. 244 (1916).

The Court distinguished in this regard its ruling in *Downum v. United States*.[15] The prosecutor in *Downum* had recognized on the morning of the scheduled trial that a key witness had not been subpoenaed and had not been found. Relying on the promise of the witness's spouse to let the marshall know when she found him, and apparently assuming that he would be found before the trial began that afternoon, the prosecutor went ahead with the jury selection. When the witness failed to appear in the afternoon, the prosecution moved for mistrial on the ground that the witness was critical to obtaining a conviction on two of the six counts. That motion then was granted over the objection of the defense (which asked that the two counts be dismissed for nonprosecution and the trial continue on the other six). The Supreme Court, in holding that the mistrial was not justified by manifest necessity, did not distinguish between the two counts on which the witness's testimony was critical and the remaining four counts. While the facts in *Downum* indicated that the prosecutor there had not in fact manipulated the justification for the mistrial so as to save a case in which he misjudged the strength of the state's evidence, the mistrial was sought to save a case that appeared to be headed toward an acquittal because of an event the prosecutor could have anticipated. In *Somerville*, in contrast, the prosecution was not motivated in any sense by concern that it could not prove its case. The *Somerville* majority distinguished *Downum* in this regard, noting that the mistrial there had "operated as a post-jeopardy continuance to allow the prosecution an opportunity to strengthen its case."

The Court emphasized in *Arizona v. Washington*[16] that the "strictest scrutiny is appropriate when the basis for the mistrial is the unavailability of critical prosecution evidence." Of course, there may be situations where the prosecution can survive that scrutiny by showing that critical evidence suddenly became unavailable through circumstances beyond its control and reasonable anticipation (e.g., a witness's sudden illness). Where there clearly is no effort to avoid the consequences of an earlier miscalculation as to the strength of the prosecution's case, lower courts have distinguished *Downum* and sustained mistrials as consistent with the manifest necessity standard.

(e) Manifest Necessity and Trial Court Discretion. In various instances, a particular circumstance clearly would justify a mistrial, and the critical issue is how much deference will be given to the trial judge's judgment as to the existence of that circumstance. One common case in this category is that in which the jury is hopelessly deadlocked. As the Supreme Court noted in *Arizona v. Washington*, such a situation presents the "classic basis" for a proper mistrial as there is no sense in proceeding if a verdict cannot be reached. The deadlocked jury, the Court noted, also presents a situation in which the trial judge must be given broad discretion: "If retrial of the defendant were barred whenever an appellate court views the 'necessity' for a mistrial differently from the trial judge, there would be a danger that the latter, cognizant of the serious societal consequences of an erroneous ruling, would employ coercive means to break the apparent deadlock." Consistent with this analysis, lower court decisions have accorded great deference to trial court rulings in hung jury cases, extending even to cases where, for example, the trial judge relied on the foreperson's statement of deadlock without polling the other jurors, or where the judge failed to assure that the deadlock applied to all counts. The decisions tend to be based on an evaluation of a wide range of circumstances, and the lack of manifest necessity will be found when several different circumstances point to a trial judge's failure to take account of the defendant's interest in obtaining a verdict in his first trial. Among the factors considered in this regard are: (1) whether the defense argued that the jury not be discharged; (2) the length of the deliberations; (3) the complexity of the issues; and (4) the nature of the communications between judge and jury.

---

15.   372 U.S. 734, 83 S.Ct. 1033, 10 L.Ed.2d 100 (1963).

16.   Supra note 6.

Arizona v. Washington itself presented still another situation in which the trial judge will be given considerable leeway in evaluating the justification. The trial court there had granted a mistrial after defense counsel in opening argument made an improper and prejudicial reference to the prosecution having withheld exculpatory evidence in an earlier trial. The Supreme Court acknowledged that "some trial judges might have proceeded with the trial after giving the jury appropriate cautionary instructions." However, it added, in making certain types of mistrial determinations, trial judges must be given "broad discretion" in deciding "whether or not 'manifest necessity' justifies a discharge of the jury." The classic illustration was the trial judge's decision as to whether to discharge or require further deliberations from a hung jury. "[A]long the spectrum of trial problems which may warrant a mistrial and which vary in their amenability to appellate scrutiny, the difficulty which led to the mistrial in this case also [fell] in an area where the trial judge's determination is entitled to special respect." Two reasons supported this conclusion: (1) the trial judge had heard the argument and observed the reaction of the jury, had seen and heard the jurors during voir dire, and was most familiar with the evidence and the background of the case, and thus was "far more 'conversant with the factors relevant to the determination' than any reviewing court can possibly be"; and (2) because alternative remedies would "not necessarily remove the risk of bias," a contrary result would mean that "unscrupulous defense counsel are to be allowed an unfair advantage." Where the record revealed that the "trial court acted responsibly and deliberately, after according careful consideration to respondent's interest in having the trial concluded in a single proceeding," the judge's ruling in an area of such broad discretion should not be overturned.

Commentators have questioned whether the great deference *Washington* extended to the trial judge's evaluation of the need for a mistrial in responding to prejudicial misconduct during a trial should extend to situations in which the prejudicial impact would be borne by the defendant rather than the prosecution. They argue that the judge here should give deference to the defense, and if the defense prefers to proceed to verdict and rely on an instruction to the jury to attempt to cure the prejudice, then the manifest necessity standard should not approve the mistrial. Support for this position is found in the Supreme Court's comment in *United States v. Dinitz*[17] that the "important consideration, for purposes of the Double Jeopardy Clause, is that the defendant retains primary control over the course to be followed in the event of such error." Several lower courts have suggested, however, that trial judges must be given considerable leeway here, just as in *Washington*, because the judge may also give weight to the need to preserve the "appearance of impartiality." They conclude that this interest may justify a mistrial notwithstanding the defense's willingness to accept the risk that the jury may have been prejudiced against it.

The Supreme Court's ruling in *Gori v. United States*[18] arguably suggests that the trial judge should be given even greater deference when he acts to protect the defendant, but the continuing force of that ruling is subject to question. In that case, the trial judge "on his own motion and with neither approval nor objection by counsel," declared a mistrial during the government's direct examination of its fourth witness. The trial judge apparently had believed that the prosecutor's questioning "presaged inquiry calculated to inform the jury of other crimes by the accused" and had declared the mistrial "to forestall" that prejudice. Unlike the situation presented in the later case of *Arizona v. Washington*, the trial judge in *Gori* acted without any significant deliberation or consideration of the views of counsel. Nonetheless, a closely divided Supreme Court held that reprosecution was not barred by double jeopardy. The majority viewed the mistrial order as "neither apparently justified nor clearly erroneous" and emphasized the need for granting the trial court

---

17. Supra note 2.

18. 367 U.S. 364, 81 S.Ct. 1523, 6 L.Ed.2d 901 (1961).

leeway in the exercise of its discretion. The majority concluded: "We are unwilling, where it clearly appears that a mistrial has been granted in the sole interest of the defendant, to hold that its necessary consequence is to bar all retrial."

In *United States v. Jorn*,[19] where the Court stressed the judge's failure to consider alternatives to mistrial, the government had sought to rely on *Gori*. The judge there had directed that the prosecution's witnesses not testify until they discussed their waiver of the self-incrimination privilege with counsel, and the net effect of those discussions, if the witnesses did not testify, would be to benefit the defense. Looking to *Gori*, the government argued that even a mistrial order that constitutes an "abuse of discretion" should not preclude a retrial when the mistrial ruling "benefitted" the defendant. The Supreme Court plurality rejected that contention, noting that: (1) if "benefit" was to be measured by reference to the person whom the judge was seeking to prevent from being prejudiced, then that person was the witness rather than the defendant, and (2) if "benefit" was to turn on "a post hoc assessment as to which party would in fact have been aided" in the "hypothetical event" that the judge had ruled differently, then that concept unacceptably rested "on an exercise in pure speculation." The plurality concluded that *Jorn* therefore was clearly distinguishable from "a case of mistrial made 'in the sole interest of the defendant'" as presented in *Gori*. It added, however:

> Further, we think that a limitation on the abuse-of-discretion principle based on an appellate court's assessment of which side benefitted from the mistrial ruling does not adequately satisfy the policies underpinning the double jeopardy provision. Reprosecution after a mistrial has unnecessarily been declared by the trial court obviously subjects the defendant to the same personal strain and insecurity regardless of the motivation underlying the trial judge's action.

(f) Dismissals Equivalent to Mistrials. In some instances, as discussed in § 25.3(a), a dismissal may be imposed as a permanent ending to all prosecution, but in other instances, a dismissal is granted in apparent contemplation of the renewal of the prosecution. Such is the case, for example, if the dismissal is based on some curable error in the course of the preliminary proceedings or an error in the charging instrument. Most often, such dismissals are issued before trial, but occasionally they will occur after jeopardy has attached. The leading case on such dismissals, *Lee v. United States*,[20] indicates that they will be treated as the functional equivalents of mistrials, and governed by the same double jeopardy principles.

The Court in *Lee* was confronted with a situation in which the defendant had moved to dismiss the information after the prosecutor's opening statement in a bench trial, the trial court had tentatively denied the motion subject to further study, and then at the close of the two-hour trial the court took a brief recess and granted the motion to dismiss. In holding that the defendant could be tried again, the Court rejected the contention that he should not have had to undergo the first trial because the court was made aware of the defective information before jeopardy attached. The Court concluded that the defendant "had only himself to blame" for the events as they developed, for by "the last-minute timing of his motion to dismiss, he virtually assured the attachment of jeopardy." Justice Brennan, concurring, emphasized that "an entirely different case would be presented if the petitioner had afforded the trial judge ample opportunity to rule on his motion prior to trial, and the court, in failing to take advantage of this opportunity [had] permitted the attachment of jeopardy before ordering dismissal of the information."

The Court in *Lee* then concluded that the mistrial came within the *Dinitz* rule, as "by failing to withdraw the motion after jeopardy had attached," the defendant "virtually invited the court to interrupt the proceedings before formalizing a finding on the merits." Of

---

19. Supra note 3.

20. 432 U.S. 23, 97 S.Ct. 2141, 53 L.Ed.2d 80 (1977).

particular significance was the fact that the court's initial remarks "left little doubt that the denial was subject to further consideration at an available opportunity in the proceedings—a fact of which the court reminded counsel after the close of the prosecution's evidence," following which defense counsel "made no effort to withdraw the motion." By contrast, in cases where the defendant has moved for a mistrial but has withdrawn that motion prior to the judge's ruling, lower courts have held that the *Dinitz* rule does not apply. Of course, if the pleading defect is not waivable, the withdrawal of the motion should not be critical. Under *Somerville*, the dismissal on the judge's own motion, or on request of the prosecution, would be supported by manifest necessity.

§ 25.3   Reprosecution Following Acquittal or Dismissal

(a) Dismissals vs. Acquittals. In contrast to either a mistrial or a dismissal of the type presented in *Lee*,[1] there are dismissals that constitute a permanent bar to the prosecution of the charge. In *United States v. Jenkins*,[2] decided in 1975, the Court assumed that the Double Jeopardy Clause granted to the defendant the right to rely on such a "final judgment" in much the same manner as an acquittal or conviction where it came after jeopardy had attached. Accordingly, a government appeal from such a post-jeopardy "judgment discharging the defendant" was barred whenever "further proceedings of some sort, devoted to the resolution of factual issues going to the elements of the offense charged, would have been required upon reversal and remand." However, three years after *Jenkins*, in *United States v. Scott*,[3] the Court retreated from the *Jenkins* ruling insofar as it treated similarly all final judgments.

Scott presented the question of the permissibility of a government appeal following the trial judge's midtrial dismissal of the prosecution on the ground of prejudicial pretrial delay. In overruling *Jenkins*, which had relied upon the principle "that the State with all its resources and power should not be allowed to make repeated attempts to convict an individual for an alleged offense," the Court in *Scott* affirmed the soundness of that proposition as to an acquitted defendant, but distinguished the defendant who was the beneficiary of the defense-requested dismissal. Justice Rehnquist (who had also written for the Court in *Jenkins*) offered the following analysis:

It is quite true that the Government with all its resources and power should not be allowed to make repeated attempts to convict an individual for an alleged offense. This truth is expressed in the three common law pleas of *autrefois acquit, autrefois convict,* and pardon which lie at the core of the area protected by the Double Jeopardy Clause. As we have recognized in [numerous] cases * * * a defendant once acquitted may not be again subjected to trial without violating the Double Jeopardy Clause. * * * But that situation is obviously a far cry from the present case, where the Government was quite willing to continue with its production of evidence to show the defendant guilty before the jury first empaneled to try him, but the defendant elected to seek termination of the trial on grounds unrelated to guilt or innocence. This is scarcely a picture of an all-powerful state relentlessly pursuing a defendant who had either been found not guilty or who had at least insisted on having the issue of guilt submitted to the first trier of fact. It is instead a picture of a defendant who chooses to avoid conviction and imprisonment, not because of his assertion that the Government has failed to make out a case against him, but because of a legal claim that the Government's case against him must fail even though it might satisfy the trier of fact that he was guilty beyond a reasonable doubt. * * *

[A] defendant is acquitted only when "the ruling of the judge," whatever its label, actually represents a resolution in defendant's

1. See § 25.2(f).

2. 420 U.S. 358, 95 S.Ct. 1006, 43 L.Ed.2d 250 (1975).

3. 437 U.S. 82, 98 S.Ct. 2187, 57 L.Ed.2d 65 (1978).

favor, correct or not, of some or all of the factual elements of the offense charged. * * * We think that in a case such as this the defendant, by deliberately choosing to seek termination of the proceedings against him on a basis unrelated to factual guilt or innocence of the offense of which he is accused, suffers no injury cognizable under the Double Jeopardy Clause if the Government is permitted to appeal from such a ruling of the trial court in favor of the defendant [and to reprosecute if successful on appeal].

The Court in *Scott* added that it was not thereby adopting the view that defendant had "waived" his double jeopardy protection, but rather was only concluding that the scope of the Double Jeopardy Clause was not such as to "relieve a defendant from the consequences of his voluntary choice." Because the defendant in *Scott* had moved for dismissal, this was an accurate characterization of the situation there. But that will not always be the case. If the trial judge "was the instigator and the primary mover of the events that led to the dismissal of the indictment" and "took complete control of the proceedings and set off on a course over which the defendant had no control," then the "voluntary choice" which was an essential ingredient of *Scott* is not present. The issue then presented is whether the dismissal should be treated as a mistrial allowing retrial if the judge's action was justified by manifest necessity.

Similarly, a trial court may put off ruling on a defendant's pre-trial motion to dismiss until the evidence presented at trial furnishes it with a better basis for determining whether the defendant was prejudiced. That shift in timing would not appear to be a sufficient basis for denying the prosecution the opportunity to challenge the court's ruling unless the court, in shifting the timing of its ruling and thereby depriving the defense of the completion of the first trial, acted without a justification sufficient to meet the manifest necessity standard.

The Court in *Scott* stressed that, in distinguishing between a dismissal that does not bar

retrial and may be appealed, and a dismissal that does bar retrial because it is equivalent to an acquittal, the "trial judge's characterization of his own action cannot control the classification of the action." The critical question rather was whether or not the trial court's ruling was based on a failure of proof in establishing the "factual elements of the offense." The dissent argued that this distinction would not be easily applied. It questioned, in particular, how the majority could hold that delay in prosecution was a defense that did not produce an "acquittal" while offering as illustrations of defenses that did produce "acquittals" both insanity and entrapment. The majority responded that both of those defenses went to the basic substantive element of individual "culpability," while "the dismissal for preindictment delay represents a legal judgment that a defendant, although criminally culpable, may not be punished because of a supposed constitutional violation." Thus, a trial court's ruling that the prosecution's case-in-chief failed to establish venue, though framed as a judgment of acquittal, does not preclude retrial because venue is an element "more procedural than substantive" which does not go to culpability.

(b) The Jury Acquittal. The Supreme Court has long held that when a jury in a criminal case has returned a verdict of not guilty, the double jeopardy prohibition bars further prosecution of the defendant for the same offense. That standard was laid down in *United States v. Ball*,[4] and it has been accepted ever since as the cornerstone of double jeopardy jurisprudence. The Court has noted that this absolute bar finds support in the common law plea of *autrefois acquit* as well as the policy underlying the Double Jeopardy Clause. As to the latter, the most frequently cited policy justification is that set forth in *Scott*: "To permit a second trial after an acquittal, however mistaken the acquittal may have been, would present an unacceptably high risk that the Government with its vast superior resources, might wear down the defendant so

4. 163 U.S. 662, 16 S.Ct. 1192, 41 L.Ed. 300 (1896).

that 'even though innocent, he may be found guilty.' "

Some commentators questioned the *Scott* explanation by comparison of the risk allowed to the innocent when the trial results in a conviction influenced by trial error. In such a case, as will be seen in § 25.4, the defendant may obtain a reversal of his conviction, but he then may be retried even though it is quite possible that the jury would have acquitted him if not for the trial error that required the reversal. On the other side, the critics note, when a trial results in an acquittal, that verdict is final even though a court believes it almost certain that the jury would have convicted if not for a trial error that favored the defense. They therefore ask, if the defendant must bear the risk of being retried when the state introduced an error into the trial which now requires reversal of his conviction, why should he not likewise bear the risk of being retried when error in his favor was introduced in a trial which resulted in his acquittal. In each instance, it is argued, one cannot be certain what the jury would have done if not for the error, so there is no reason to assign to one defendant more than the other the risk of being an innocent who could be convicted on retrial.

One answer to the above line of criticism is that the fundamental policy concern here lies not so much in protection of the innocent as in granting a sense of repose to the defendant who went through a trial that produced a final decision on his guilt or innocence. The defendant who challenges a conviction is willing to put aside the finality of that verdict, but the defendant who is acquitted obviously does not desire to put aside his sense of repose. Another argument that does not depend upon characterizing the defendant's appeal as waiver is to recognize that the acquittal could be an exercise of the jury nullification. Double jeopardy in this sense would protect the beneficiaries of the jury's leniency, as well as the factually innocent. Still another answer to the critics is that, while estimating the impact of a trial error always presents uncertainties, whether the result is a conviction or an acquittal, only in the latter situation is there concrete evidence, in the form of a not guilty verdict, that the jury may have resolved factual issues in favor of the defendant's innocence. That concrete evidence entitles the defendant to the benefit of the doubt that conclusively presumes his innocence, while a conviction, even where probably influenced by trial error, offers no such starting point for assuming the jurors would have found defendant not guilty except for the error.

(c) Acquittal by the Judge. The Supreme Court has long treated as parallel the directed acquittal entered by the judge and the jury verdict of not guilty. Critics of this position have noted that the protection of the jury's right of nullification is not at stake in the judicial acquittal, and that the protection of a factual resolution favorable to the defendant also is not necessarily at stake. While some directed acquittals are based on a judicial evaluation of the persuasiveness of the evidence, others are based solely on the trial court's view of the substantive law. Where that view is erroneous, there is no basis for arguing that the acquittal must be given finality in order to protect the innocent.

A practical response to this line of argument is that eliminating the finality of directed verdicts would discourage defense requests for directed verdicts. If such a distinction were drawn, where the judge had a view of the substantive law that would render the prosecution's case clearly insufficient, the defense, instead of asking for a directed verdict, could allow the case to go to the jury under the judge's view of the law so that the jury would then acquit. It is unclear whether this practical consideration, or some other consideration, has convinced the Supreme Court to treat all directed acquittals alike, and to treat all as parallel to a jury acquittal. The Court simply has noted, without extensive explanation, that the Double Jeopardy Clause "nowhere distinguishes" between bench and jury acquittals. Thus, double jeopardy bars reprosecution following judicial termination of a trial by directed acquittal, without regard to whether the judicial determination as to the insufficiency of the evidence is based on its total lack of its persuasiveness, its failure "as a matter of law" due to the substantive content of the offense in question, or an erroneous decision to exclude essential proof.

The leading case on judicial acquittals is *Sanabria v. United States.*[5] The trial judge in that case granted a judgment of acquittal that flowed from two alleged errors. First, the trial court excluded certain evidence as being legally irrelevant under its view that the indictment had failed to set forth a particular basis for liability. Second, in reviewing the evidence that remained, the trial court applied an erroneous reading of the substantive law by limiting liability for participation in illegal enterprises to persons actually engaged in the illegal activities. The Supreme Court viewed the critical issue before it as whether the trial judge's ruling was actually an acquittal. Although the trial court had looked to the indictment in striking certain evidence, it had not dismissed the indictment for failure to plead an offense, but had taken the indictment as stating an offense under a limited theory of liability, excluded evidence not consistent with that theory, and then held the remaining evidence insufficient under that theory. The Court therefore concluded:

> [W]e believe the ruling below is properly to be characterized as an erroneous evidentiary ruling, which led to an acquittal for insufficient evidence. That judgment of acquittal, however erroneous, bars further prosecution on any aspect of the count and hence bars appellate review of the trial court's error.

As the Court noted in *Smalis v. Pennsylvania*,[6] whether a ruling constitutes an acquittal depends upon its substance, not its characterization, or label under state law.[7]

Sanabria places the trial court in a position to control the double jeopardy consequences of its rulings. In some instances, the charging instrument will fail to allege all of the elements of the crime, and the trial judge may be able to choose between a dismissal of the in-

dictment or information as in *Lee*, or an acquittal for the failure to establish all of the elements of the crime (the prosecution not having offered evidence on what it failed to plead). The presence of such discretion, in turn, raises the question as to whether the defense properly can place the trial court in a position where it lacks that discretion by failing to object to the charging instrument before trial and then, at trial, objecting only to the lack of proof rather than the deficiency of the pleading. *Sanabria* allowed a roughly similar tactic but did so in a manner that left open the possibility of a different response to the precise tactic posed above. Because the acquittal in *Sanabria* was intertwined with the trial judge's ruling that certain evidence was not admissible, a matter which the defendant could have raised before trial, the government argued that the delay by the defendant constituted a "waiver" of his subsequent double jeopardy objection. A similar consideration entered into the Court's decision to permit retrial following the midtrial dismissal in *Lee*, but the Court in *Sanabria* reasoned that double jeopardy principles applicable to mistrials "have no bearing" on acquittal cases. The Court then noted that the issue of the admissibility of evidence was unlike such issues as whether a statute is unconstitutional, in that a ruling in defendant's favor would not have barred conviction on the existing charge and a defendant could not be faulted for not having raised the issue prior to the time that jeopardy attached. This rationale seemingly holds open the possibility that a "forfeiture" or "waiver" will be found where the legal interpretation that leads to a directed acquittal could have been resolved before trial.

(d) Pre-jeopardy "Acquittals." Even when the judge's ruling unquestionably is grounded solely on a determination that there is insufficient evidence for conviction, it does not inevitably follow that the ruling will be treated as an acquittal under *Sanabria* and *Scott*. The ruling cannot be placed in that

---

5. 437 U.S. 54, 98 S.Ct. 2170, 57 L.Ed.2d 43 (1978).

6. 476 U.S. 140, 106 S.Ct. 1745, 90 L.Ed.2d 116 (1986)

7. See also Price v. Vincent, 538 U.S. 634, 123 S.Ct. 1848, 155 L.Ed.2d 877 (2003) (holding that the state

court's finding that the trial judge's comments were not sufficiently final to terminate jeopardy was a reasonable application of clearly established law).

category if it is issued in a pretrial setting, as that is before jeopardy has attached. As discussed in § 25.1(d), verdict finality will not attach where the trial court has no authority to sit as a tribunal judging the weight of the government's evidence, and it has none prior to trial. On the other hand, once the trial has started, an acquittal will be treated as such even though it was not granted in accord with proper procedures. Thus, in *Fong Foo v. United States*,[8] a judge's entry of an acquittal because he viewed the government's initial witnesses as inherently incredible constituted a bar to further proceedings even though the judge went beyond the relevant Federal Rules provision by directing the acquittal before the prosecution had completed its case-in-chief.

(e) Postconviction Judgments of Acquittal. In *United States v. Wilson*,[9] after the jury returned a verdict of guilty, the trial court reconsidered an earlier motion and dismissed the indictment on the ground that the government's preindictment delay had resulted in a denial of due process. *Wilson* was decided before *Scott* and the question was open at the time as to whether such a ruling should be treated as the equivalent of an acquittal for double jeopardy purposes. The Court had no need to consider that issue, however, as it concluded that double jeopardy would not bar an appeal from the trial court's ruling in any event. The key to double jeopardy, the Court reasoned, was exposing the defendant to multiple trials. Although "review of any ruling of law discharging a defendant obviously enhances the likelihood of conviction and subjects him to continuing expense and anxiety, a defendant has no legitimate claim to benefit from an error of law when that error could be corrected without subjecting him to a second trial before a second trier of fact." That was exactly the case here. If the trial judge's ruling was reversed, the appellate court would merely reinstate the jury's verdict and defendant would not be tried again.

Wilson did not in fact involve an acquittal, but in *United States v. Jenkins*,[10] the Court

relied upon *Wilson* in noting: "[W]here the jury returns a verdict of guilt, but the trial court thereafter enters a judgment of acquittal, an appeal is permitted." *Scott*, in turn, adhered to this aspect of the *Jenkins* opinion, as it noted that a judgment of acquittal bars an appeal only "when a second trial would be necessitated by a reversal." The Court added that this principle, as announced in *Jenkins*, had not been repudiated by "the Court's heavy emphasis on the finality of an acquittal" in more recent cases.

The end result of the position established in the above opinions, albeit without a direct ruling on point, is to give to trial judges a means for preserving the government's opportunity to appeal where the judge sides with the defense on a legal issue that will control as to the sufficiency of the evidence. Assume for example, that an issue first arises at trial concerning the admissibility of evidence, that the evidence is crucial to the prosecution's case, and that the judge believes that it is inadmissible, but considers this position debatable and most appropriately decided finally by an appellate court. In such a situation, to preserve the prosecution's right of appeal and grant the defense the acquittal that the judge believes it deserves, the judge may take the following approach: allow the evidence to go before the jury, and if the jury should convict, then grant a post-verdict judgment of acquittal on the ground that the evidence is inadmissible and that without it, the prosecution's proof is insufficient. Similarly, if there is disagreement as to whether the prosecution must prove a certain element to establish a crime, the judge can send the case to the jury on instructions that do not require the finding of that element and then, if the jury convicts, grant a post-verdict judgment of acquittal on the ground that proof of the element is wanting.

In a bench trial, the process is even easier, as the judge can make findings of facts and indicate that he would hold the defendant guilty except for his adoption of a certain legal

---

8. 369 U.S. 141, 82 S.Ct. 671, 7 L.Ed.2d 629 (1962).

9. 420 U.S. 332, 95 S.Ct. 1013, 43 L.Ed.2d 232 (1975).

10. Supra note 2.

interpretation that produces an acquittal. That ruling can then readily be viewed by the appellate court and if it disagrees as to the legal interpretation, remanded for entry of the judgment of guilt, which can be done without further fact finding. However, as *Jenkins* indicates, if the trial judge fails to make adequate findings, so that further factual determinations will be needed, that circumstance will be treated as subjecting the defendant to multiple trials even though the same judge would be finding the facts on the basis of evidence previously admitted.[11]

§ 25.4   Reprosecution Following Conviction

(a) The General Rule. In the seminal double jeopardy decision of *Ball v. United States*,[1] the Supreme Court recognized an exception to the general constitutional prohibition against reprosecuting a person for an offense of which he has already been convicted. That exception, as is now understood, is that the Double Jeopardy Clause does not bar reprosecution where the convicted defendant has managed through appeal or some other procedure to set aside his conviction on grounds other than the insufficiency of evidence. Although uncertainty existed for some time as to the doctrinal basis for this rule, the Supreme Court has stated that the "most reasonable" justification for the *Ball* rule is that advanced by Justice Harlan in *United States v. Tateo*[2]:

> While different theories have been advanced to support the permissibility of retrial, of greater importance than the conceptual abstractions employed to explain the *Ball* principle are the implications of that principle for the sound administration of justice. Corresponding to the right of an accused to be given a fair trial is the societal interest in punishing one whose guilt is clear after he has obtained such a trial. It would be a high price indeed for society to pay were every

accused granted immunity from punishment because of any defect sufficient to constitute reversible error in the proceedings leading to conviction. From the standpoint of a defendant, it is at least doubtful that appellate courts would be as zealous as they now are in protecting against the effects of improprieties at the trial or pre-trial stage if they knew that reversal of a conviction would put the accused irrevocably beyond the reach of further prosecution. In reality, therefore, the practice of retrial serves defendants' rights as well as society's interest.

This rule is in some tension with the Court's later declaration that some misconduct by the judge or prosecution resulting in mistrial may, depending upon the circumstances, bar retrial.[3] Under the *Ball* rule, however, retrial apparently will not be prohibited if the same misconduct fails to end the trial (either because defendant's mistrial motion is denied or because defendant did not move for a mistrial), a conviction results, and the conviction is reversed on appeal because of the overreaching.

Moved by this seeming incongruity, some courts have barred retrial whenever prosecutorial misconduct was sufficient for a mistrial, despite the defendant's failure to move for a mistrial. Without such a bar, these courts reason, a prosecutor apprehending an acquittal can fend off the anticipated acquittal by misconduct of which the defendant is unaware until after the verdict. Other courts have rejected claims that double jeopardy bars retrial following the reversal of a conviction due to misconduct, unless the defendant can demonstrate that in acting improperly the prosecutor acted with the goal of aborting the trial. Such a standard would never be met when the misconduct was covert and discovered only after trial, as such action shows intent to win the trial, not to end it. The Court itself has not

---

11.   See also Finch v. United States, 433 U.S. 676, 97 S.Ct. 2909, 53 L.Ed.2d 1048 (1977) (the bar against retrial after acquittal applies notwithstanding the objection of the dissent that a retrial would be based on a factual stipulation entered into by the parties and therefore would not produce the same ordeal, embarrassment, and expense as a factually contested retrial).

§ 25.4

1.   163 U.S. 662, 16 S.Ct. 1192, 41 L.Ed. 300 (1896).

2.   377 U.S. 463, 84 S.Ct. 1587, 12 L.Ed.2d 448 (1964).

3.   See § 25.2(c).

expressed any inclination to institute a misconduct exception to the *Ball* rule.

(b) The Evidence Insufficiency Exception. It was not until the case of *Burks v. United States*[4] that the Supreme Court held that the *Ball* rule did not apply where the appellate reversal was based on the insufficiency of the evidence at trial to sustain a guilty verdict. In holding that a remand in such circumstances is inconsistent with the double jeopardy prohibition, a unanimous Court emphasized that if the trial court had done what the reviewing court said should have been done "a judgment of acquittal would have been entered and, of course, petitioner could not be retried for the same offense." Under the Double Jeopardy Clause, "it should make no difference that the *reviewing* court, rather than the trial court, determined the evidence to be insufficient."

The *Burks* opinion rejected several earlier decisions that had misconstrued *Ball* as allowing a retrial in a such a case. In concluding that *Ball* was limited to the separate problem of a reversal based upon trial error, the *Burks* opinion reasoned that

> reversal for trial error, as distinguished from evidentiary insufficiency, does not constitute a decision that the government has failed to prove its case. As such, it implies nothing with respect to the guilt or innocence of the defendant. Rather, it is a determination that a defendant has been convicted through a judicial process which is defective in some fundamental respect, e.g., incorrect receipt or rejection of evidence, incorrect instructions, or prosecutorial misconduct. When this occurs, the accused has a strong interest in obtaining a fair readjudication of his guilt free from error, just as society maintains a valid concern for insuring that the guilty are punished.

The same cannot be said when a defendant's conviction has been overturned due to a failure of proof at trial, in which case the prosecution cannot complain of prejudice, for it has been given one fair opportunity to offer whatever proof it could assemble. Moreover, such an appellate reversal means that the government's case was so lacking that it should not have even been *submitted* to the jury. Since absolute finality is afforded a jury's *verdict* of acquittal—no matter how erroneous its decision—it is difficult to conceive how society has any greater interest in retrying a defendant when, on review, it is decided as a matter of law that the jury could not properly have returned a verdict of guilty.

Just as appeal is permissible from a trial court's granting of a motion for acquittal after a jury verdict of guilty, the Double Jeopardy Clause does not bar review of an appellate court's entry of an acquittal after conviction, that is, its conclusion that there was insufficient evidence to convict. Here too, if the government prevails, the defendant is not subject to a new trial, but to reinstatement of the trial court's judgment of conviction.

A finding of insufficient evidence to support a conviction by either a trial court or appellate court must be distinguished from a ruling that the conviction was against the weight of the evidence. Unlike the directed acquittal, which holds that the evidence is insufficient for any reasonable juror to find guilt, the granting of a new trial on the ground that the verdict is against the weight of the evidence recognizes that the jurors could rationally reach the result that they reached, but grants the defendant another chance because the trial court has concerns, based on that judge's own evaluation of the evidence, that an injustice may have been done. The difference is illustrated by two Supreme Court cases following *Burks*. In *Hudson v. Louisiana*,[5] the trial court had granted a new trial following conviction on the ground that there "certainly [was] not evidence beyond a reasonable doubt, to sustain the verdict," and the defendant argued that this made the trial court's ruling one on the sufficiency of the evidence and barred a new trial. Relying on *Burks*, the Supreme Court agreed. It rejected the contention that *Burks* was inapplicable because the trial court had

---

4. 437 U.S. 1, 98 S.Ct. 2141, 57 L.Ed.2d 1 (1978).

5. 450 U.S. 40, 101 S.Ct. 970, 67 L.Ed.2d 30 (1981).

found that there was some evidence of guilt. The reasoning of *Burks*, the Court concluded, was not limited to insufficiency rulings based on a total lack of evidence. In *Tibbs v. Florida*,[6] in contrast, it was clear the appellate court was acting only as a "thirteenth juror," rendering a "weight of the evidence" reversal. Here, a closely divided Supreme Court held that *Burks* did not apply. The majority stressed that such a reversal does not rest on the premise that an acquittal was the only proper verdict the jury could have reached, but simply expresses the appellate court's disagreement with the jury's resolution of the conflicting testimony. The *Tibbs* majority reasoned that just as a deadlocked jury does not result in an acquittal barring retrial, an appellate court's disagreement, as the "thirteenth juror," with the trial jurors' weighing of the evidence also does not require the special deference accorded verdicts of acquittal. Such a reversal, the Court stressed, is designed primarily to "give the defendant a second chance" in "the interests of justice." It was not true, as the dissent argued, that the appellate court in practical effect was stating that the conviction would not stand without additional evidence. Precisely the same evidence could lead to an appellate court affirmance of any ensuing conviction, for while "reversal of a first conviction based on sharply conflicting testimony may serve the interests of justice, reversal of a second conviction based on the same evidence may not." The *Burks* doctrine also will not apply when a conviction is reversed by an appellate court due to other types of deficiencies, such as a charge that does not encompass the defendant's conduct, or an error in instructing the jury.[7]

When the evidence is found on appeal to be insufficient only as to a greater offense, and the jury's actual verdict shows that it found the existence of every element of the lesser offense, the reviewing court may remand the case for entry of judgment of conviction on the lesser offense, or allow retrial of the lesser included offense. This power to modify the judgment may derive from statute, court rule, or judicial decision. In the federal system, the Court approved of the practice in *Morris v. Mathews*[8] in a somewhat different context. The defendant in *Morris* successfully appealed his conviction of aggravated murder, demonstrating that due to an earlier plea of guilty, the charge was barred by double jeopardy. The state's high court ordered that his conviction be reduced to the lesser offense of murder, a charge on which the jury had received instruction, and which was not barred by double jeopardy. The United States Supreme Court affirmed, reasoning that "where it is clear that the jury necessarily found that the defendant's conduct satisfies the elements of the lesser included offense, it would be incongruous always to order yet another trial as a means of curing a violation of the Double Jeopardy Clause."

Although most courts have applied similar reasoning to justify retrial or the entry of judgment of conviction on a lesser offense whenever a conviction for a greater offense is overturned due to insufficient evidence, some states limit the remedy to retrial of the lesser offense, a position that suggests some discomfort with entering judgments of conviction without a verdict of guilty on that particular offense. Indeed, even retrial in some states will be available only when the jury was actually instructed on the lesser offense at the first trial. Courts in these jurisdictions are less certain that any jury that convicts of the greater offense would necessarily have convicted of the lesser, and have argued that the state should not be able to "go for broke" at trial, hoping that without a lesser offense instruction the jury will convict on the higher offense, confident that if that conviction is overturned, conviction on the lesser offense can be had without submission to a jury. In response it has also been observed that such a limitation "creates the anomaly of forcing a defendant to make himself subject to retrial if he requests a lesser-included offense in those cases in which

---

6.   457 U.S. 31, 102 S.Ct. 2211, 72 L.Ed.2d 652 (1982).

7.   Montana v. Hall, 481 U.S. 400, 107 S.Ct. 1825, 95 L.Ed.2d 354 (1987).

8.   475 U.S. 237, 106 S.Ct. 1032, 89 L.Ed.2d 187 (1986).

he challenges the sufficiency of the evidence with respect to the higher offense.''

(c) The Determination of Sufficiency. When a defendant appeals a verdict of conviction and raises insufficiency of the evidence together with trial error, will the failure to review the sufficiency of evidence bar retrial? Many lower courts have found that the failure to reverse a conviction for insufficient evidence and ordering instead a retrial is violative of the Double Jeopardy Clause. Support for this position may be found in Justice Brennan's opinion in *Justices of Boston* where he stated that without assurance that insufficiency claims will be reviewed prior to retrial, "the protections established in *Burks* * * * would become illusory." Double jeopardy protection, he argued, should not depend "on the grace of the reviewing court." Other justices had also indicated that a court could not consider retrial without first determining that the evidence was sufficient for a reasonable trier of fact to find guilt beyond a reasonable doubt.

Other courts have held that double jeopardy does not prohibit retrial in cases in which convictions were reversed for trial error and insufficiency claims were left unaddressed. While the Court has recognized appellate determinations of insufficiency as having the effect of an acquittal, these courts reason that there is no comparable acquittal-like event when an appellate court remands for new trial due to trial error.

When reviewing the sufficiency of evidence for conviction, a court must determine which evidence to consider. *Lockhart v. Nelson*[9] explained that even in a case requiring remand due to the erroneous admission of evidence, all of the evidence admitted must be considered.[10] Reversals based on "such ordinary trial errors" as the "incorrect receipt or rejection of evidence" remain subject to the *Ball* rule. Where the evidentiary insufficiency exists only because of the appellate court's initial conclusion that there was error in admit-

ting prosecution evidence, the reversal, under the logic of *Burks*, should be characterized simply as one based upon a "trial error." The "basis for the *Burks* exception to the general rule is that a reversal for insufficiency of the evidence should be treated no differently than a trial court's granting a judgment of acquittal at the close of all the evidence." Since a "trial court in passing on such a motion considers all of the evidence it has admitted," to "make the analogy complete it must be the same quantum of evidence which is considered by the reviewing court" in determining whether double jeopardy bars a retrial. Thus *Burks* should bar a retrial only if all of the admitted evidence, even erroneously admitted evidence, was insufficient. Where that is not the case, allowing a retrial following reversal is consistent with giving the prosecution "one fair opportunity to offer whatever proof it could assemble." Had the trial court excluded the inadmissible evidence, the prosecution would have been given the opportunity to introduce other evidence on the same point, and allowing a retrial where the proof is deemed insufficient on appeal only because of that inadmissible evidence merely recreates the situation that would have existed if not for the trial court's error. As one court put it, the appellate court applying *Burks* is "assessing the legal sufficiency of the evidence not at the trial that will be, but at the trial that was." Nevertheless, a state may interpret its own law to provide more protection than *Lockhart*, by requiring that any review of the sufficiency of the evidence be "based only on the evidence that was properly admitted at trial."

This leaves the question of which evidence to consider if the appellate court determines that the trial judge erroneously *excluded* prosecution evidence. The Supreme Court in *Burks* noted "there is no claim in this case that the trial court committed error by excluding prosecution evidence which, if received would have

---

9. 488 U.S. 33, 109 S.Ct. 285, 102 L.Ed.2d 265 (1988).

10. *Lockhart* involved a recidivist prosecution in which the prosecution erroneously relied on a prior conviction as to which defendant had received a pardon. The Court noted that there was "no indication that the prosecutor

* * * was attempting to deceive the [trial] court" in using that conviction, and it therefore "had no occasion to consider what the result would be if the case were otherwise." On retrial, the prosecution substituted another prior conviction of the defendant.

rebutted any claim of evidentiary insufficiency." This statement has been taken as suggesting that a reprosecution would not be barred if the insufficiency of the government's evidence would have been "cured" by evidence erroneously excluded by the trial court. Such a view is arguably inconsistent, however, with the *Lockhart* premise that the appellate court should, in effect, stand in the shoes of the trial court and consider the evidence that was before it.

(d) Conviction as Implied Acquittal.

The teaching of *Green v. United States*[11] is that under some circumstances a conviction of one crime must, for double jeopardy purposes, be taken as an acquittal of another crime. In that case the defendant Green was charged with first degree murder, and the jury was informed that they could find him guilty either of that crime or the lesser-included offense of second degree murder. The jury returned a verdict of guilty on the latter charge but said nothing as to the first degree murder charge. Green's conviction was reversed on appeal for trial error, and he was then retried on the original first degree murder charge and convicted of that offense. In holding that the Double Jeopardy Clause barred conviction on that charge, the Supreme Court explained:

> Green was in direct peril of being convicted and punished for first degree murder at his first trial. He was forced to run the gauntlet once on that charge and the jury refused to convict him. When given the choice between finding him guilty of either first or second degree murder it chose the latter. In this situation the great majority of cases in this country have regarded the jury's verdict as an implicit acquittal on the charge of first degree murder. But the result in this case need not rest alone on the assumption, which we believe legitimate, that the jury for one reason or another, acquitted Green of murder in the first degree. For here, the jury was dismissed without returning any express verdict on that

charge and without Green's consent. Yet it was given a full opportunity to return a verdict and no extraordinary circumstances appeared which prevented it from doing so. Therefore it seems clear, under established principles of former jeopardy, that Green's jeopardy for first degree murder came to an end when the jury was discharged so that he could not be retried for that offense. * * * In brief, we believe this case can be treated no differently, for purposes of former jeopardy, than if the jury had returned a verdict which expressly read: "We find the defendant not guilty of murder in the first degree but guilty of murder in the second degree."

The defendant in *Green* would have prevailed even if the jury at the second trial had found him guilty of second degree murder, the same result as at the first trial, upon reprosecution for first degree murder. As the Court explained in *Price v. Georgia*,[12] "to be subjected to a second trial for first-degree murder is an ordeal not to be viewed lightly." In *Price*, the defendant, on trial for murder, was found guilty of voluntary manslaughter. After the conviction was reversed on appeal Price was retried for murder, again with the same result. The Court held the second trial violated double jeopardy, noting that it was possible that "the murder charge against the petitioner induced the jury to find him guilty of the less serious offense rather than to continue to debate his innocence."

However, as *Morris v. Mathews*[13] later noted, the appropriate remedy for the double jeopardy violation that occurs when a defendant is tried on a jeopardy-barred offense (along with a non-barred offense) is not always to order a new trial. If the jury in the second trial convicted on the jeopardy-barred count, an adequate remedy was simply to reduce that conviction to the lesser-included offense that was not jeopardy-barred. In *Price*, the Court was concerned that the jury had reached a compromise verdict (i.e., some jurors may have pre-

---

11. 355 U.S. 184, 78 S.Ct. 221, 2 L.Ed.2d 199 (1957).

12. 398 U.S. 323, 90 S.Ct. 1757, 26 L.Ed.2d 300 (1970).

13. 475 U.S. 237, 106 S.Ct. 1032, 89 L.Ed.2d 187 (1986).

ferred conviction on the jeopardy-barred higher charge, others may have preferred acquittal, and they may have compromised with a verdict of guilty on the second degree murder charge). In *Morris*, in contrast, with the jury having convicted on the higher, jeopardy-barred count, it necessarily found, without any compromise, that the defendant's conduct also satisfied the elements of the lesser-included, non-barred offense. It would be "incongruous," said the Court, to remedy the double jeopardy violation that occurred in trying the defendant again for the higher offense by "ordering yet another trial" when the jury, uninfluenced by that violation, had found defendant guilty of the lesser-included offense that was not jeopardy-barred.

An implied acquittal is not necessarily present where the jury has been told that it should look first at a single charge and then not bother with the other charges if it finds guilt on that charge. Saying nothing as to the other charges indicates only that they were not reached. Assuming that the unreached charges were not lesser-included in the sense that conviction on the higher necessarily includes conviction on the lesser, the issue then becomes whether the jury charge that, in effect, kept defendant from receiving a verdict on the other charges is justified under the standards applied to mistrials. Also, no acquittal of a greater offense is suggested by conviction of a lesser offense when the jury is unable to reach agreement on the higher offense, and this "disagreement is formally entered on the record."

When a defendant is charged with both greater and lesser offenses, an acquittal is not present where a defendant enters a guilty plea to a lesser charge over the government's objection. The acceptance of the guilty plea and even the determination that there is a factual basis for it does not constitute an inferential finding of not guilty of the higher charge.[14]

§ 25.5   Reprosecution by a Different Sovereign

(a) Federal Prosecution After State. In the case of *United States v. Lanza*[1] the Supreme Court promulgated what is customarily referred to as the "dual sovereignty" doctrine: "an act denounced as a crime by both national and state sovereignties is an offense against the peace and dignity of both and may be punished by each." That the dual sovereignty doctrine allows a federal prosecution notwithstanding a prior state prosecution for the same conduct was later affirmed in *Abbate v. United States*.[2] There, defendants who allegedly had conspired to dynamite telephone company facilities pleaded guilty to a state charge of conspiring to injure the property of another and received a three-month sentence, after which they were prosecuted in federal court for conspiring to injure those facilities that were part of a communications system "operated and controlled by the United States." The Court held that the federal conviction was not prohibited by the double jeopardy clause.

In declining to depart from the *Lanza* rule, the majority in *Abbate* reiterated the fears voiced in earlier cases that

> if the States are free to prosecute criminal acts violating their laws, and the resultant state prosecutions bar federal prosecutions based on the same acts, federal law enforcement must necessarily be hindered. For example, the petitioners in this case insist that their Illinois convictions resulting in three months' prison sentences should bar this federal prosecution which could result in a sentence of up to five years. Such a disparity will very often arise when, as in this case, the defendants' acts impinge more seriously on a federal interest than on a state interest.

Criticism of *Abbate* intensified after the Supreme Court held that the Double Jeopardy Clause of the Fifth Amendment was also applicable to the states through the Fourteenth Amendment[3] and rejected efforts to limit other constitutional rights with "dual sovereignty"

---

14. Ohio v. Johnson, 467 U.S. 493, 104 S.Ct. 2536, 81 L.Ed.2d 425 (1984).

§ 25.5

1. 260 U.S. 377, 43 S.Ct. 141, 67 L.Ed. 314 (1922).

2. 359 U.S. 187, 79 S.Ct. 666, 3 L.Ed.2d 729 (1959).

3. Benton v. Maryland, 395 U.S. 784, 89 S.Ct. 2056, 23 L.Ed.2d 707 (1969).

reasoning similar to that in *Abbate*.[4] Despite this attack, the dual sovereignty doctrine has become more firmly entrenched over time.[5]

Although not compelled to do so by the Constitution, the executive branch of the federal government has chosen to limit those cases in which it pursues criminal sanctions against defendants who have already been prosecuted by state authorities. Shortly after the *Abbate* decision, the Attorney General issued a memorandum to all United States Attorneys noting the need for cooperation "with state and local authorities to the end that the trial occur in the jurisdiction, whether it be state or federal, where the public interest is best served," and barring a federal trial "when there has already been a state prosecution for substantially the same act or acts" except with the approval of an Assistant Attorney General. This policy was noted by the Supreme Court in *Petite v. United States*[6] and has since been referred to as the *Petite* policy.[7] It has served as the basis for dismissing indictments and vacating convictions, on the government's motion, in numerous cases in which federal prosecutions were inadvertently initiated after state prosecutions. Indeed, in *Rinaldi v. United States*[8] it was held that it is an abuse of discretion for a district court to refuse to va-cate a conviction where such action was requested by the government on the ground that it had violated its *Petite* policy. But the defendant may not obtain a dismissal of an indictment, over the objection of the government, simply because the United States Attorney failed to obtain prior approval of an Assistant Attorney General as required by that policy. The policy is an internal guideline, and if the government now concludes that the separate prosecution is appropriate under the criteria it has specified, the defendant cannot complain either that those guidelines were incorrectly interpreted in his case or that the internal process requirements were not met. While the *Petite* policy has enabled the federal prosecution of defendants perceived by many to have been unjustly acquitted by local juries, some have criticized the "proliferation" of successive prosecutions in federal court after state changes.

(b) State Prosecution After Federal. The reverse of the *Abbate* situation was presented in the companion case of *Bartkus v. Illinois*,[9] where after defendant's acquittal in federal court for robbery of a federally insured bank he was convicted in state court for the same bank robbery. The Court again applied

---

4. Murphy v. Waterfront Com'n, 378 U.S. 52, 84 S.Ct. 1594, 12 L.Ed.2d 678 (1964) ("dual sovereignty" doctrine does not limit scope of privilege against self-incrimination); Elkins v. United States, 364 U.S. 206, 80 S.Ct. 1437, 4 L.Ed.2d 1669 (1960) (pre-*Mapp* case rejecting "silver platter" doctrine which allowed state police to turn over fruits of unconstitutional search for use in federal prosecution).

5. See United States v. Wheeler, 435 U.S. 313, 98 S.Ct. 1079, 55 L.Ed.2d 303 (1978) (federal prosecution of an Indian was not barred by his earlier conviction in a tribal court because Indian tribes had retained their "sovereign power to punish tribal offenders" and thus were comparable to states in that respect). *Abbate* was also cited with approval in Montana Department of Revenue v. Kurth Ranch, 511 U.S. 767, 114 S.Ct. 1937, 128 L.Ed.2d 767 (1994), discussed in § 25.1(c).

6. 361 U.S. 529, 80 S.Ct. 450, 4 L.Ed.2d 490 (1960).

7. Now set forth in the United States Attorneys' Manual § 9–2.142, these guidelines preclude "the initiation or continuation of a federal prosecution, following a prior state or federal prosecution based on substantially the same act[s] or transaction[s]" unless (1) the matter "involve[s] a substantial federal interest"; (2) "the prior prosecution must have left that interest demonstrably unvindicated"; (3) "applying the same test applicable to all federal prosecutions, the government must believe that the defendant(s)' conduct constitutes a federal offense, and that the admissible evidence probably will be sufficient to obtain and sustain a conviction by an unbiased trier of fact"; and (4) "the prosecution must be approved by the appropriate Assistant Attorney General." The Guidelines go on to state that "the Department will presume that a prior prosecution, regardless of result, has vindicated the relevant federal interest," but notes that there may be an unvindicated federal interest "[w]hen a conviction was not achieved in the prior prosecution because of * * * [1] incompetence, corruption, intimidation, or undue influence; [2] [when there was] court or jury nullification, in clear disregard of the evidence or the law; [3] the unavailability of significant evidence, * * *; [4] the failure in a prior state prosecution to prove an element of a state offense which is not an element of the contemplated federal offense; or [5] the exclusion of charges in a prior federal prosecution out of concern for fairness to other defendants or for significant resource considerations that favored separate federal prosecutions." Also, the Guidelines authorize a second prosecution when a conviction was achieved in the prior prosecution, if "the prior sentence was manifestly inadequate in light of the federal interest involved."

8. 434 U.S. 22, 98 S.Ct. 81, 54 L.Ed.2d 207 (1977).

9. 359 U.S. 121, 79 S.Ct. 676, 3 L.Ed.2d 684 (1959).

the dual sovereignty doctrine and upheld the state conviction. Once more the concern was that the action of one sovereign should not cut off the enforcement of a superior interest by the other. Citing *Screws v. United States*,[10] a federal civil rights prosecution where the permissible punishment was but a few years while at the state level defendant's conduct was a capital offense, the Court declared that were

> the federal prosecution of a comparatively minor offense to prevent state prosecution of so grave an infraction of state law, the result would be a shocking and untoward deprivation of the historic right and obligation of the States to maintain peace and order within their confines. It would be in derogation of our federal system to displace the reserved power of States over state offenses by reason of prosecution of minor federal offenses by federal authorities beyond the control of the States.

Many states have followed *Bartkus* in interpreting their state constitutional provisions on the subject of double jeopardy, although some have held that their constitutional provisions bar a state prosecution in the *Bartkus* situation. About half of the states have also adopted statutes prohibiting state prosecution for offenses that relate to a previous federal prosecution, but these statutes vary considerably as to the extent of the prohibition. Some do not allow a state prosecution based on the same offense prosecuted elsewhere, others bar subsequent prosecutions of the same conduct, or of the same "act or omission," and a few bar a state prosecution whenever based upon the "same transaction" as the prior federal prosecution. A state may also isolate a particular class of cases for protection from dual prosecutions, such as controlled substance offenses.[11]

(c) State–State and State–Municipal. Prosecution by two different states for basically the same conduct is quite unusual as state jurisdictional authority tends to be tied to a territorial principle. However, as discussed in § 16.3(c), certain criminal transactions may have a sufficient bearing on two states (usually adjoining) as to produce criminal liability in both for basically the same harm and conduct. Where such successive prosecutions are brought, as in *Heath v. Alabama*,[12] the double jeopardy bar does not apply because each state is a separate sovereign. In *Heath*, where two states prosecuted the defendant for the same murder (which occurred in Georgia in the course of a kidnaping that started in Alabama and provided the grounding for a felony-murder charge in that state), Justice Marshall argued in dissent that the fundamental fairness standard of due process was violated in light of the cooperative effort of the two states aimed at securing a death sentence in the second state after defendant had entered a guilty plea to avoid the death penalty in the first. The majority, however, did not consider that issue to be before it and ruled only on the double jeopardy claim, which failed under the dual sovereignty doctrine.

The *Heath* situation must be distinguished from one involving successive municipal and state prosecutions, as in *Waller v. Florida*.[13] Petitioner had removed a canvas mural which was affixed to a wall in city hall and had carried it through the streets until, after a scuffle with police, it was recovered in damaged condition. Following his conviction for violating two city ordinances (destruction of city property and disorderly breach of the peace), he was convicted of the felony of grand larceny in violation of state law. On the basis of the state court's assumptions that the felony charge was based on the "same acts" as the city ordinance violations and "that the ordinance violations were included offenses of the felony charge," the Supreme Court unanimously held that the second trial violated the double jeopardy prohibition. As the Court had concluded on a prior occasion,[14] cities are not

---

10.   325 U.S. 91, 65 S.Ct. 1031, 89 L.Ed. 1495 (1945).

11.   For a detailed review of each state's law, see Kurland, Successive Criminal Prosecutions: The Dual Sovereignty Exception to Double Jeopardy in State and Federal Courts (2001).

12.   474 U.S. 82, 106 S.Ct. 433, 88 L.Ed.2d 387 (1985).

13.   397 U.S. 387, 90 S.Ct. 1184, 25 L.Ed.2d 435 (1970).

14.   Reynolds v. Sims, 377 U.S. 533, 84 S.Ct. 1362, 12 L.Ed.2d 506 (1964).

sovereign entities but rather "have been traditionally regarded as subordinate governmental instrumentalities created by the State to assist in the carrying out of state governmental functions." This meant, the Court concluded in *Waller*, that "the judicial power to try petitioner * * * in municipal court springs from the same organic law that created the state court of general jurisdiction," and thus the "dual sovereignty" doctrine has no application here.

Lower courts have recognized some deserving exceptions to this rule. One is that prosecution for the state crime is not barred if that offense was not fully consummated when the ordinance prosecution was brought, as where the victim dies after an ordinance prosecution for assault. This is consistent with the standard applied to prosecutions under separate state statutes. Another exception is the "collusion exception," which would allow state prosecution when the ordinance conviction was procured by collusion between the offender and city officials for the purpose of protecting the offender against more serious state charges. The willingness of courts to lift the double jeopardy bar in this situation parallels that of some courts assessing the double jeopardy implications of fraudulently obtained acquittals discussed in § 25.1(d).

Chapter 26

SENTENCING PROCEDURES

Table of Sections

---

§ 26.1 Legislative Structuring of Sentencing: Sanctions

(a) Structure and Procedure. The primary focus of this chapter is sentencing procedure. It begins with a fairly detailed description of the structure of sentencing authority. The rules governing sentencing procedure tend to follow from the structure of sentencing authority established by the legislature, which includes: (1) the authorization of specific types of punishments and the placing of limitations on their use; (2) the allocation of responsibility for individual sentencing decisions; and (3) the provision of guidance to the primary sentencer, the trial court, in the exercise of its discretion.

Procedures often vary with the type of sanction under consideration. Concerns about procedural rights are heightened where the sentence involves incarceration rather than a fine or community release, and are most prominent when the penalty is death. Subsections (b) through (f) of this section will consider five categories of sanctions: capital punishment, incarceration, community release (probation), intermediate sanctions, and financial sanctions. Some of the procedural limitations unique to certain sanctions will also be addressed in this section.

The allocation of responsibility for determining the individual sentence also tends to shape sentencing procedure. Where that sentencing responsibility rests with the jury, sentencing procedures are most likely to resemble the rules applied at trial. Where the sentencing decision is allocated to an administrative agency (as in parole), the process is likely to be somewhat less formal than where it is allocated to a judge. Variations in the allocation of sentencing authority are discussed in § 26.2.

The degree of discretion granted to the sentencer also bears upon procedure, especially as to judicial sentencing. Where a sentence follows automatically from the establishment of a particular fact there is a tendency to look to a trial-type hearing to determine that fact. Where the range of discretion is broad and allows the judge to weigh a multitude of factors, with no single factor critical in itself, the tendency is to use a more informal process. For much of the twentieth century, the degree of discretion allocated to the judge in state sentencing systems was fairly uniform. The rehabilitative philosophy had taken hold in legislatures and courts, and by the 1970s each state followed an indeterminate sentencing scheme that offered the judge and the paroling authorities broad ranges within which to choose an appropriate sentence for individual offenders. During the past several decades that uniformity has disappeared. Concerns for treating like cases alike, insuring stiff penalties for certain crimes or criminals perceived to be particularly dangerous to society, and predicting correctional spending led many legislatures to abolish parole and impose significant constraints on judicial discretion. At the same time alternatives to incarceration have multiplied, as have the opportunities for victims to participate in the sentencing process. The fifty-two jurisdictions now follow a patchwork of approaches. Although each state is bound to comply with the Constitution's guarantees for the sentencing process, the Court has interpreted these requirements to be quite minimal, except in the context of capital sentencing. This hands-off approach to the constitutional regulation of sentencing has permitted legislatures to pursue diverse sentencing philosophies and experiment with innovative sanctions and procedures. The remainder of this section considers different types of sanctions presently used in the state and federal systems. Section 26.2 examines the roles of various government actors in selecting the appropriate punishment. Section 26.3 considers variations in the legislative approach to guiding discretionary judicial decisionmaking. Section 26.4 summarizes the Constitution's limitations on the sentencing process.

(b) Capital Punishment. Capital punishment is authorized by statute in all but twelve states. The death penalty has long been the subject of intense debate in the United States. Capital punishment was at one point in this nation's history the authorized sanction for most felonies. With criminal law reform and the establishment of the first penitentiaries in the 1790s and early 1800s, incarceration replaced the death penalty for most felony offenses. By the twentieth century, legislative reform in most states had narrowed considerably the class of felonies punishable by death.

In 1972, less than ten years after the Supreme Court held that the Eighth Amendment's prohibition against cruel and unusual punishment applied to the states,[1] litigation challenging the constitutionality of capital punishment culminated in the decision *Furman v. Georgia.*[2] There, a sharply divided Court held that the death penalty was so arbitrarily and randomly imposed that it violated the Eighth Amendment. Each of the justices in the majority wrote a separate opinion and no single analysis prevailed, but the positioning of the justices left open the possibility that capital punishment could be upheld if properly structured in its application. In several cases decided in 1976, the Court upheld the post-*Furman* death sentencing provisions of three states and struck down two others, sketching an outline of the constitutional requirements for imposing the sentence of death. These cases, particularly *Gregg v. Georgia*[3] and *Woodson v. North Carolina,*[4] have guided the

Court's regulation of capital punishment ever since.

In addition to the Court's close regulation of death sentencing procedure under the Constitution, special statutory requirements typically apply to the capital sentencing portion of the trial and to subsequent judicial review of the death sentence determination. Consequently the procedures for imposing the penalty of death are extensive and complex. We include here only a brief summary of their range. Although most of these procedural requirements are unique to death sentencing, the Court's efforts to interpret the Constitution's safeguards in this context have influenced the development of rules for regulating other types of sentencing as well.

Contemporary capital punishment statutes build upon the basic structure of the statute upheld in *Gregg.* The Georgia statute authorized the imposition of the death penalty for murder under a procedure designed to provide the sentencing decisionmaker with full information and specific guidance. Major features of the Georgia statute included: (1) capital sentencing authority rested initially with the jury, unless the defendant chose a bench trial; (2) in a bifurcated proceeding, the jury first determined guilt and then at a separate hearing, during which the jury considered additional evidence relating only to sentencing, it determined whether to recommend a death sentence; (3) the statute specified aggravating circumstances, one of which the jury had to find was established beyond a reasonable doubt before it could consider imposing the death penalty; (4) the jury was also directed to consider mitigating circumstances, but was not required to find that any existed before deciding not to impose the death penalty; and (5) the statute provided for automatic appellate review of the sentence on the whole record, in which the appellate court was required to determine whether the sentence was imposed arbitrarily, whether it lacked sufficient evidentiary support, or was "disproportionate

§ 26.1

1. Robinson v. California, 370 U.S. 660, 82 S.Ct. 1417, 8 L.Ed.2d 758 (1962).

2. 408 U.S. 238, 92 S.Ct. 2726, 33 L.Ed.2d 346 (1972).

3. 428 U.S. 153, 96 S.Ct. 2909, 49 L.Ed.2d 859 (1976).

4. 428 U.S. 280, 96 S.Ct. 2978, 49 L.Ed.2d 944 (1976).

to the penalty imposed in similar cases." The Court has upheld several variations on this pattern. Statutes that allow the judge, rather than the jury, the ultimate death-determination authority have been upheld,[5] statutes that require a sentencer to weigh aggravating circumstances against mitigating circumstances,[6] and statutes that provide for appeal without proportional review.[7]

The need for consistency is one of the two major concerns that have shaped the Court's modern death penalty jurisprudence. The Court's insistence on clear, objective standards for defining the class of offenders who are eligible for the death penalty[8] addresses that concern. In *Woodson*,[9] and later in *Lockett v. Ohio*,[10] the Court articulated a second goal. On the same day that it upheld Georgia's guided discretion approach to capital punishment in *Gregg*, the Court in *Woodson* struck down a North Carolina statute that mandated the sentence of death for first-degree murder. Several states had enacted mandatory death penalty legislation after *Furman*, in response to the Court's condemnation in that case of the arbitrary and discriminatory application of more discretionary schemes. *Woodson* rejected this

response. The Eighth Amendment, the Court declared, requires "the particularized consideration" of the offense and offender.[11] In *Lockett*, the Court held that the Eighth Amendment requires that the sentencer must "not be precluded from considering as a mitigating factor, any aspect of a defendant's character or record and any of the circumstances of the offense that the defendant proffers as a basis for a sentence less than death."[12] The tension between these two goals—one preserving discretion, the other limiting its exercise—permeates all sentencing procedure. Yet in capital cases, some justices have found the simultaneous pursuit of consistency and flexibility to be intolerable. Justice Scalia has advocated abandoning the *Woodson–Lockett* principle of individualized sentencing, while Justice Blackmun has concluded that death sentencing can never be constitutional due to the difficulty of accommodating both concerns satisfactorily.[13] At present, however, the two principles continue to find expression in the Court's death penalty decisions.

Capital sentencing hearings are subject to various trial-type restrictions designed to advance these aims. These include restrictions on

---

5. Harris v. Alabama, 513 U.S. 504, 115 S.Ct. 1031, 130 L.Ed.2d 1004 (1995); Hildwin v. Florida, 490 U.S. 638, 109 S.Ct. 2055, 104 L.Ed.2d 728 (1989); Spaziano v. Florida, 468 U.S. 447, 104 S.Ct. 3154, 82 L.Ed.2d 340 (1984); Proffitt v. Florida, 428 U.S. 242, 96 S.Ct. 2960, 49 L.Ed.2d 913 (1976) (jury verdict merely advisory to judge). The decision in King v. Arizona, discussed in § 26.4 (i) at note 60, holding that a jury must find facts increasing the statutory maximum penalty, has recently raised doubts about the constitutionality of some of these statutes.

6. Clemons v. Mississippi, 494 U.S. 738, 110 S.Ct. 1441, 108 L.Ed.2d 725 (1990) (examining death sentencing in state where jury weighs aggravating against mitigating factors and holding that appellate reweighing or harmless error analysis permitted when jury considers invalid aggravating circumstance in a weighing state); see also Jurek v. Texas, 428 U.S. 262, 96 S.Ct. 2950, 49 L.Ed.2d 929 (1976) (upholding special issue statute under which sentencer answers three questions affirmatively in order to impose the death penalty).

7. Pulley v. Harris, 465 U.S. 37, 104 S.Ct. 871, 79 L.Ed.2d 29 (1984).

8. See e.g., Tuilaepa v. California, 512 U.S. 967, 114 S.Ct. 2630, 129 L.Ed.2d 750 (1994) (aggravating circumstance must narrow the class of offenders subject to the death penalty and must not be unconstitutionally vague).

9. Supra note 4.

10. 438 U.S. 586, 98 S.Ct. 2954, 57 L.Ed.2d 973 (1978).

11. See also Sumner v. Shuman, 483 U.S. 66, 107 S.Ct. 2716, 97 L.Ed.2d 56 (1987) (Eighth Amendment bars mandatory death penalty for murder in prison by one serving life sentence); Roberts v. Louisiana, 428 U.S. 325, 96 S.Ct. 3001, 49 L.Ed.2d 974 (1976).

12. The Court has continued to refine the limits of this requirement. Eddings v. Oklahoma, 455 U.S. 104, 102 S.Ct. 869, 71 L.Ed.2d 1 (1982) (error to exclude evidence of defendant's troubled family background); Skipper v. South Carolina, 476 U.S. 1, 106 S.Ct. 1669, 90 L.Ed.2d 1 (1986) (error to exclude evidence of defendant's good behavior as pretrial detainee); Penry v. Lynaugh, 492 U.S. 302, 109 S.Ct. 2934, 106 L.Ed.2d 256 (1989) (error to prevent sentencing jury from considering defendant's mental retardation and abuse as child as mitigating factors); McKoy v. North Carolina, 494 U.S. 433, 110 S.Ct. 1227, 108 L.Ed.2d 369 (1990) (striking down statute that required jury to unanimously agree that mitigating factor existed before giving it effect); Graham v. Collins, 506 U.S. 461, 113 S.Ct. 892, 122 L.Ed.2d 260 (1993) (not error to fail to instruct jury to consider defendant's age as a mitigating factor, but only as it bears upon the defendant's "continuing threat to society").

13. See Callins v. Collins, 510 U.S. 1141, 114 S.Ct. 1127, 127 L.Ed.2d 435 (1994) (Blackmun, J., dissenting from denial of certiorari); 114 S.Ct. at 1127–28 (Scalia, J., concurring); Walton v. Arizona, 497 U.S. 639, 110 S.Ct. 3047, 111 L.Ed.2d 511 (1990) (Scalia, J., concurring).

the evidence that can be introduced to prove mitigating and aggravating factors and limitations on the judge's charge to the jury. Rules regarding the disclosure of evidence considered in capital sentencing may be more generous to the defense than in non-capital cases. Jury procedures in capital cases also differ from those at other trials. Common variations include the provision of more peremptory challenges, the careful screening during voir dire for jurors capable of exercising discretion to recommend either life or death, and the more frequent sequestration of the jury during deliberations.

In addition to regulating the procedures for death sentencing, the Court has narrowed the categories of offenders and offenses subject to capital punishment under the Eighth Amendment. The Court has held that death is a disproportionate punishment for rape[14] and for felony murder when the defendant was not himself a major participant in the killing.[15] The Eighth Amendment also bars the execution of a prisoner who is insane,[16] mentally retarded,[17] or who was only 15 years old at the time of the crime,[18] but does not prohibit the execution of a defendant who was 17 years old at the time of the crime.[19]

(c) Incarceration. The sanction of incarceration is authorized by statute for nearly all offenses except a limited class of misdemeanors. In 2000, 68% of felons convicted in state court were sentenced to prison (generally, for one year or more) or to jail. Legislation authorizing incarceration provides the range of allowable incarceration for each offense, specifies whether sentences will be indeterminate (parole eligible) or determinate (no parole available), and often prescribes alternative sentences or sentence enhancements for some offenses or offenders. This section contains a brief description of these different sentences.

Indeterminate sentences. The indeterminate sentence sets a maximum and minimum term of incarceration and leaves the task of determining the precise date at which the release will actually occur to the parole board. Introduced on a large scale in the late nineteenth century, the indeterminate sentence became the standard form of incarceration sentence for felony cases during the early twentieth century, and as of 1975 was the sentencing practice in every state. The primary rationale for the indeterminate sentence was that it permitted the actual term of imprisonment to fit the rehabilitative progress of an offender as it developed during his confinement. The indeterminate sentence presumably encouraged inmates to reform. Moreover, because a parolee continued to be subject to supervision for the remainder of his maximum term and could be returned to prison if he violated his parole conditions, indeterminate sentencing was designed to facilitate the gradual reintegration of the inmate into society.

Since the 1960s, critics of this "medical model" of sentencing have charged that prison programs fail to promote rehabilitation and have questioned the capacity of parole boards to predict future behavior. Opponents of indeterminate sentencing also condemn the sentencing disparities that flow from the broad discretion delegated to parole authorities. As a result, Congress and a significant number of state legislatures have discarded indeterminate sentences and moved to determinate sentences—fixed terms set by the court with no allowance for an early release by a parole board. Most of the states, however, have not been convinced. Connecticut found, for example, that eliminating parole caused massive prison overcrowding, and as a result reinstated parole after one year. More than half of the

---

14. Coker v. Georgia, 433 U.S. 584, 97 S.Ct. 2861, 53 L.Ed.2d 982 (1977).

15. Tison v. Arizona, 481 U.S. 137, 107 S.Ct. 1676, 95 L.Ed.2d 127 (1987) (capital punishment not disproportionate for felony-murder defendants who had not intended to kill but who had assisted killers in prison escape and had exhibited "reckless indifference to human life").

16. Ford v. Wainwright, 477 U.S. 399, 106 S.Ct. 2595, 91 L.Ed.2d 335 (1986).

17. Atkins v. Virginia, 536 U.S. 304, 122 S.Ct. 2242, 153 L.Ed.2d 335 (2002).

18. Thompson v. Oklahoma, 487 U.S. 815, 108 S.Ct. 2687, 101 L.Ed.2d 702 (1988).

19. Stanford v. Kentucky, 492 U.S. 361, 109 S.Ct. 2969, 106 L.Ed.2d 306 (1989).

states continue to use indeterminate sentences for felony cases, although some have narrowed the range of indeterminacy, or have adopted parole guidelines to reduce release disparities.

Legislation providing for indeterminate sentencing always sets an upper limit on the maximum term for each offense. In some states, the judge sets the minimum term. In other jurisdictions, the judge sets only the maximum term (at or under the legislative upper limit) and the minimum is automatically set by law as a percentage of that maximum term. In a third set of jurisdictions, the judge sets both the maximum and minimum terms, so long as the maximum is not higher than the upper limit set by the legislature. As discussed in § 26.3, indeterminate sentencing may be accompanied by regulation of the exercise of judicial discretion, particularly through sentencing guidelines. The sentencing process will vary depending upon whether the indeterminate sentencing structure includes that additional element.

Determinate sentences. The determinate sentence sets a definite term of incarceration that the offender must serve, within the statutory maximum term. Parole is not available. Determinate sentences have always been the norm for misdemeanors (one year or less) and are now being used in a significant number of states for felony offenses as well. Although there is no parole release prior to the end of the term set by the court, "good time" provisions can result in release before the full term is served in both determinate and indeterminate jurisdictions. For most felonies, jurisdictions using determinate sentences impose an automatic period of supervision after a felon serves his term that operates in much the same way as parole supervision. As explained in § 26.3, legislatures providing for determinate sentencing may use mandatory minimum terms of incarceration, presumptive sentencing, or sentencing guidelines to guide the discretion of judges in setting felony sentences.

Sentence enhancements. Extended term or "enhancement" provisions increase an offender's sentence based upon a specified circumstance. Enhancements commonly are tied to a record of past convictions or to aggravating circumstances in the commission of the offense. Most states have provisions authorizing a more severe sentence upon a finding that the defendant possessed or used a firearm or other weapon. Statutes boosting sentences for a variety of other conditions include enhancements for crimes committed in specified locations, for specified reasons, or against specified victims. Enhancements may require the addition of a certain term of years to the maximum sentence the judge would otherwise impose for the offense, or the imposition of a higher minimum sentence. Where jurisdictions provide by statute for lengthy maximum sentences, they may prefer not to use extended terms and simply take such factors into account in guiding judicial discretion in setting the sentence within those maximums. As discussed in § 26.4(i), the Constitution may require special procedures beyond those typically applied in sentencing for some enhancements. Enhancements may also be subject to more formal procedures by statutory command.

(d) Community Release. An outgrowth of the rehabilitative model of sentencing that dominated sentencing practices for the first half of the twentieth century, the supervised release of adult offenders was approved in all states by 1967. Judicial authority to grant probation is dependent upon legislative authorization. All jurisdictions have provisions authorizing the use of probation for certain offenses, but none permit it for all offenses. While commentators have argued that the liberty interest of the defendant should create a presumption against using a sentence of incarceration unless there has been a case-specific finding by the sentencing court that incarceration is the least restrictive sanction needed to achieve the purposes of punishments, this principle does not appear to be a requirement of due process.

The general probation statute in each jurisdiction will usually specify when probation is prohibited. Probation is also unavailable when statutes impose mandatory minimum sentences of incarceration. The range of offenses excluded from probation varies considerably from one jurisdiction to another. As might be expected, probation is ordinarily not available for capital offenses or for offenders sentenced under recidivist or habitual offender provisions. The majority of states also deny probation for other serious offenses such as second-degree murder, kidnapping, sexual assault, and crimes involving the use of a dangerous weapon. Statutes denying the availability of probation for various classes of offenses have withstood constitutional challenges alleging the denial of equal protection and due process, the imposition of cruel and unusual punishment, and the violation of the doctrine of separation of powers. Other states prohibit probation for violent crimes depending on the characteristics of the victim. Compulsory jail terms may preclude probation for certain low-level felonies (e.g., unlawful possession of weapon) and even certain misdemeanors (e.g., driving with a revoked license).

In some states, the relevant legislation simply identifies those offenses that are subject to probation and does not seek to provide any guidance to the court in deciding between probation and incarceration. Other jurisdictions provide some general guidance, including the criteria that should be used in selecting probation. These provisions, following the pattern of the Model Penal Code § 7.01, commonly create a presumption in favor of probation, noting that the sentencing judge shall impose a sentence of probation unless the judge is of the opinion that imprisonment is necessary because of such factors as the risk that the defendant will commit another crime, defendant's need for treatment, or concern that a sentence of probation will depreciate the seriousness of the defendant's crime. Where jurisdictions use sentencing guidelines, those guidelines commonly regulate probation as well as incarceration. When the guideline range does not include probation as an alternative, the court may in some cases justify that sentence as a departure from the guidelines. The statute authorizing probation often will set the permissible length of the term of probation, list mandatory conditions of probation, include a non-exclusive list of optional conditions, and set forth a general standard governing the judge's choice of probation conditions.

(e) Intermediate Sanctions. Until recently, imprisonment and probation have been the primary options for sentencing felony offenders in the United States. Beginning in the early 1980s, legislatures and courts began to develop various types of sanctions that are harsher than probation, but do not involve imprisonment. These innovative sentences have been adopted because of frustration with traditional methods of punishment. The continued reliance on incarceration has led to a massive increase in inmate population over the past three decades. Prison overcrowding has, in turn, raised the risk of physical violence between inmates and has required the costly construction of additional prison space, the housing of habitual offenders together with less-seasoned prisoners, and the early release of potentially dangerous felons. At the same time, the resources of probation departments have been strained as felons, including violent offenders, are frequently placed on community release. To cope, courts and legislatures in every state have looked to various non-custodial options. Every jurisdiction has adopted some form of intermediate sanction by statute, and many states have implemented a broad range of alternative sentences. The most common types of intermediate sanctions are summarized below.

Boot camp, also referred to as "shock incarceration," is a correctional program that provides military-style training and discipline to offenders who are generally young, have no prior prison experience, and who have committed non-violent crimes. Participation in boot camp generally serves as a prerequisite for probationary release. The duration, daily routine, and specific objectives of the different programs vary considerably. While most camps initially were not intended to deal with drug offenders in particular, many programs now focus on these offenders and provide drug education, counseling, and treatment. The programs generally last from three to four months. Once offenders have successfully completed the programs they are released on probation for the remainder of their sentences.

The determination of who participates in a "shock" program is in most states delegated to the sentencing judge, although a handful of states allow corrections authorities to make the placement decision.

Home confinement—requiring offenders to remain at their residence during specified periods of the day—is another method of diverting non-violent offenders from prison. Home confinement may be imposed as a special condition of a sentence of probation, or it may be ordered as a separate punitive sanction. Home confinement costs less than incarceration, and allows a court to tailor the confinement period and restrictions to meet the particular needs of the offender while minimizing the threat to public safety. Correctional officers enforce compliance with restrictions through telephone calls and unannounced visits to the offender's residence or through electronic monitoring. Electronically monitored offenders either wear transmitters to track their movements or furnish voice or electronic identification (through the use of an "encoder device") in response to random phone calls at their residences. As with probation conditions, the confinement period and other restrictions of an order of house arrest should be communicated clearly to offenders to satisfy the fair notice requirements of due process. Similarly, to avoid first amendment challenges, home confinement should provide sufficient exceptions for religious activities. In order to require offenders to pay electronic monitoring fees, courts must inquire into the ability of an offender to pay in order to protect the equal protection rights of indigent defendants. Numerous cases have arisen concerning whether courts are required to credit a period served in probationary or pre-trial home confinement as "time served" upon the subsequent imprisonment of a defendant. While a split of authority remains, most state courts deny credit for periods of house arrest.

Other novel means of providing increased surveillance or treatment for offenders during probation also deserve mention. A number of states combine probation with participation in *day reporting programs* as a means of increasing the surveillance of probationers and im-

posing upon them a more structured daily routine. Day reporting centers often focus on offenders who have not fared well under routine probation due to drug and alcohol problems or other reasons. These programs may be available to defendants convicted of relatively serious offenses. Most centers offer drug treatment and education, group counseling, job-seeking training, and job placement services, and require participants to adhere to a stringent schedule including community service, routine and random drug tests, and frequent contacts with the program authorities.

Day reporting centers are increasingly integrated with another type of intermediate sanction, *intensive supervision probation* (ISP). Undertaken in some form by every state, ISP also targets offenders deemed inappropriate for routine probation. ISP programs include numerous contacts with a probation officer, increased random drug testing, stricter enforcement of probation conditions, required community service, and some form of house arrest, usually evening curfews. Unlike an order of home confinement, which is generally imposed by a judge when a more punitive sanction seems warranted, most jurisdictions consider the decision to place offenders in intensive supervision programs to be a discretionary option of probation officials. Finally, an order to perform *community service* is a commonly imposed sanction, either combined with other types of sentences or included as a special condition of probation.

(f) Financial Sanctions. All jurisdictions provide for the use of fines in misdemeanor cases, and often allow the fine to be the only sanction for such offenses. Fines are also authorized for many felonies and are the primary sanction for corporate defendants. Despite its widespread use, the fine is not considered as serious a penalty as incarceration for individual offenders, and is usually imposed in addition to a term of incarceration in felony cases.

Where a fine is an authorized sanction, the legislature typically sets an upper limit and allows the court complete discretion to set the fine at any point up to that maximum. In most instances, the upper limit is a set dollar figure.

Alternatively, the maximum fine may be stated as a multiplier of the financial gain achieved by the offender or the financial loss to the victim, or as a per diem penalty. Some jurisdictions limit the judge's discretion to select a fine from within the prescribed range by specifying factors a judge must consider when determining if and how much to fine an offender, and by requiring judges to make findings on these factors.

Before imposing a fine, a court should make findings regarding the defendant's ability to pay monetary sanctions. The capacity of a defendant to make payments is of obvious significance in determining the amount of a fine and the method for its payment. It may also have constitutional significance. For example, in *Williams v. Illinois*,[20] the Court concluded that although indigent defendants need not necessarily *receive* the same sentences as those who are not indigent, a state may not extend the maximum duration fixed by statute for indigents unable to pay the fine by requiring the indigent defendant to serve more than the maximum term of imprisonment through a "work off" provision. The Court in *Tate v. Short*[21] again invalidated on equal protection grounds a legislative scheme under which a defendant unable to pay a fine for an offense punishable by fine only was sentenced to jail to "work off" the fine at a rate of five dollars a day. The Court noted that the state had chosen to punish the offense through fine alone.

Finally, in *Bearden v. Georgia*,[22] the Court considered the limits, if any, on the ability of a Court to imprison a defendant following unsuccessful, yet reasonable efforts to pay a fine. Although there had been no showing as to why the defendant had failed to make payments in accordance with the conditions of his probation, Justice O'Connor's opinion for the Court noted: "If the probationer could not pay despite sufficient bona fide efforts to acquire the resources to do so, the court must consider alternative measures of punishment other than imprisonment. Only if alternate measures are not adequate to meet the State's

interest in punishment and deterrence may the court imprison a probationer who has made sufficient bona fide efforts to pay." She concluded that "to do otherwise would deprive the probationer of his conditional freedom simply because through no fault of his own, he cannot pay the fine. Such a deprivation would be contrary to the fundamental fairness required by the Fourteenth Amendment." Four justices objected, noting in an opinion authored by Justice White that there is "nothing in the Constitution to prevent the trial court from revoking probation and imposing a term of imprisonment if revocation does not automatically result in the imposition of a long jail term and if the sentencing court makes a good-faith effort to impose a jail sentence that in terms of the state's sentencing objectives will be roughly equivalent to the fine and restitution that the defendant failed to pay." Since *Bearden*, lower courts have upheld sentences of incarceration, contempt, or community service following an indigent's failure to pay a monetary sanction, but only if the judge determines first that the defendant was unable to make payments despite bona fide efforts.

A variety of other financial restrictions may be included in a sentence. The most common of these is restitution. Restitution has long been imposed as a condition of probation without a specific statutory directive, but the victims' rights movement has led to additional restitution requirements. Many jurisdictions consider the general sentencing process adequate for a fair determination of those factual issues that might be resolved in ordering restitution. For other jurisdictions, the process applied may be somewhat different from that applied to sentencing generally. Restitution orders are therefore given separate consideration in § 26.6(c). A second financial directive that has gained prominence in recent years is the forfeiture order. This special sanction is also discussed separately, in § 26.6(d). Additional financial sanctions may include court costs and other costs of prosecution, probation supervi-

---

20. 399 U.S. 235, 90 S.Ct. 2018, 26 L.Ed.2d 586 (1970).
21. 401 U.S. 395, 91 S.Ct. 668, 28 L.Ed.2d 130 (1971).

22. 461 U.S. 660, 103 S.Ct. 2064, 76 L.Ed.2d 221 (1983).

sion fees, and payments for alcohol or drug treatment.

§ 26.2 Legislative Structuring of Sentencing: The Allocation of Sentencing Authority

(a) Judicial Sentencing. The legislature determines not only what sanctions will be allowed and what the parameters of those sanctions will be, but also which actor will be responsible for deciding what sentence should be imposed in the individual case. The legislature's primary choice here is the trial judge. Indeed, the judge is so commonly the sentencer that sentencing often is viewed as exclusively a judicial function. As discussed in the subsections that follow, however, such exclusivity is rarely the case. In almost every jurisdiction, the jury will have a sentencing role with respect to at least one kind of sanction and an executive agency will have a role in determining the length of terms of incarceration. Still, because the judge remains dominant in the sentencing arena, in this section we will discuss only briefly non-judicial sentencing determinations and then turn in more detail to the process of judicial sentencing.

(b) Jury Sentencing. The Supreme Court has repeatedly held that there is no sixth amendment right to jury sentencing.[1] Nevertheless jury sentencing is an established feature in the processing of at least some criminal cases in most jurisdictions. Jury sentencing is most common in capital cases where it is the norm. A small number of states leave the final determination of whether to impose the death penalty to the judge rather than the jury, but require the jury to make a recommendation to the judge based upon its evaluation of aggravating and mitigating factors. For example, Alabama law provides that upon finding at least one aggravating circumstance, the judge can

"override" the jury's recommendation of life imprisonment and impose the death penalty, a process the Court upheld in *Harris v. Alabama*.[2]

A substantial number of jurisdictions permit the jury to determine the sentence in at least some non-capital cases as well. Most of these jurisdictions use jury sentencing only for "special offender" sentencing (e.g., recidivist) or for special sanctions (e.g., criminal forfeitures) where the sentence is conditioned upon the determination of particular historical facts. A handful of states, however, provide for jury sentencing in many, if not all, felony cases. Even though a state provides for jury sentencing in felony cases, the jury is likely not to be the most frequent sentencer. The jury's authority to sentence commonly is limited to cases in which the defendant goes to trial before a jury. The jury's function in a jury sentencing system is to set the terms of a sentence of incarceration, staying within the maximum and minimum limits set by the legislature. Where probation is an allowable alternative sentence for the particular offense, the choice of that alternative will not necessarily be within the jury's authority. The jurisdiction may reserve the probation determination to the judge, and give to one judge the power to set aside the jury's sentence and substitute the alternative of probation or even a suspended sentence.

Jury sentencing may involve either a unitary or bifurcated trial of the guilt and sentencing issues. The Supreme Court upheld the constitutionality of the unitary trial in *Spencer v. Texas*[3] and *McGautha v. California*.[4] The three cases consolidated in *Spencer* each involved the jury's consideration, before conviction, of evidence relevant to sentencing but not to guilt. Each defendant had been charged

§ 26.2

1. Hildwin v. Florida, 490 U.S. 638, 109 S.Ct. 2055, 104 L.Ed.2d 728 (1989) (explaining that there is no sixth amendment right to a jury determination of a fact that is "not an element of the offense, but instead 'a sentencing factor' that comes into play only after the defendant has been found guilty"); Libretti v. United States, 516 U.S. 29, 116 S.Ct. 356, 133 L.Ed.2d 271 (1995) (holding that the Sixth Amendment does not require a jury trial on the

forfeitability of assets for criminal forfeiture, as forfeiture is a sentence, not an element of an offense).

2. 513 U.S. 504, 115 S.Ct. 1031, 130 L.Ed.2d 1004 (1995). The Court's decision in *Ring v. Arizona* has cast some doubt over some "judge override" statutes. *Ring* is discussed in § 26.4 (i) at note 60.

3. 385 U.S. 554, 87 S.Ct. 648, 17 L.Ed.2d 606 (1967).

4. 402 U.S. 183, 91 S.Ct. 1454, 28 L.Ed.2d 711 (1971).

under the Texas habitual criminal statute. One of the defendants, convicted of murder, became eligible for the death penalty because of his previous murder conviction, and was sentenced to death. The other two defendants were convicted for robbery and burglary— their prior offenses led to life sentences. In each case the trial judge had admitted documents establishing the defendant's prior convictions but instructed the jury not to consider the prior convictions in passing upon the issue of guilt or innocence. Rejecting the claims of the defendants that the admission of the prior offense evidence violated due process, the Court noted that there were various situations in which a judge could admit evidence of prior offenses on the issue of guilt under traditional rules of evidence, albeit with limiting instructions. Accordingly, "to say [that] the United States Constitution is infringed simply because this type of evidence may be prejudicial and limiting instructions inadequate to vitiate prejudicial effects, would make inroads into this entire complex code of state criminal evidentiary law, and would threaten other large areas of trial jurisprudence."[5] The Court recognized that a bifurcated procedure might eliminate the jury's exposure to prior convictions in passing on the guilt of the defendant, but noted that the single-stage procedure was of "longstanding and widespread use," and reflected a state's judgment as to the "best" procedure based upon "a wide variety of criteria." Those included the "particular jurisdiction's allocation of responsibility between court and jury" and "accommodat[ion] to the State's established trial procedures," as well as the assessment of "which method is apt to be the least prejudicial in terms of the effect of the prior-crime evidence on the ultimate issue of guilt." The Court concluded: "To say that the two-stage jury trial in the English–Connecticut style is probably the fairest, as some commentators and courts have suggested, and with which we might well agree were the matter before us in a legislative or rule-making context, is a far cry from a constitutional determination that this method of handling

the problem is compelled by the Fourteenth Amendment."

In *McGautha*, the Court addressed a different due process challenge to the unitary proceeding. There the Court rejected the claim by a capital defendant that the single-stage trial denied him the right to present evidence on the issue of sentence when he exercised his self-incrimination privilege not to testify on the issue of guilt. The unitary procedure required the defendant to choose either (1) to exercise his privilege not to testify on guilt and forego his right to testify regarding the sentence or (2) to exercise the right to testify on sentencing matters and subject himself to cross examination on issues relevant to guilt. The defendant argued that by forcing him to choose between rights, the unitary procedure unduly burdened his right to present evidence in opposition to the penalty of death, particularly since a bifurcated proceeding would eliminate the need to choose one right or the other. The Court responded, "the Constitution does not * * * always forbid requiring [the defendant] to choose" between constitutionally protected courses of action during the criminal process. "The threshold question is whether compelling the election impairs to an appreciable extent any of the policies behind the rights involved." The Court concluded that "the policies of the privilege against compelled self-incrimination are not offended when a defendant in a capital case yields to the pressure to testify on the issue of punishment at the risk of damaging his case on guilt," nor must a state allow a defendant to speak to the jury at sentencing "free from any adverse consequences on the issue of guilt."

McGautha was decided before the Court struck down death sentencing as unconstitutionally arbitrary in *Furman*. When the Court later upheld several death sentencing statutes enacted in response to the *Furman* decision, it emphasized the provision of a separate penalty phase as one of the features that reduces the risk of arbitrary application. Because all jurisdictions that authorize jury determinations of issues related to death sentencing presently

---

5. See also Estelle v. McGuire, 502 U.S. 62, 112 S.Ct. 475, 116 L.Ed.2d 385 (1991) (rejecting due process chal-

lenge to the erroneous admission of prior crimes evidence under Rule 404 of the Federal Rules of Evidence).

provide for a separate penalty phase, courts have not had the opportunity to address whether the Court's post-*Furman* decisions have undercut *McGautha* and would now prohibit the imposition of a death sentence under a similar unified proceeding. In *Marshall v. Lonberger*,[6] however, the Court upheld the murder conviction of a defendant whose jury had specifically determined during the guilt phase that he had been convicted before, an aggravating factor relevant to sentencing alone. Affirming the rule in *Spencer*, the majority rejected the argument of the four dissenters that the Constitution prohibits a "one-stage enhancement procedure." The Court concluded that the failure to completely segregate the guilt and penalty phases did not deprive a capital defendant of any constitutional right. In non-capital contexts where the jury may determine sentencing facts such as the defendant's habitual offender status, the forfeitability of assets, or the existence of a fact triggering a sentence enhancement, lower courts continue to hold that bifurcation is not constitutionally required.

(c) Administrative Agency Decisions. *Release on parole.* In jurisdictions that use indeterminate sentences of incarceration, the parole board plays an important role in determining the actual term of imprisonment. With rehabilitation as the dominant sentencing objective, some jurisdictions adopting indeterminate sentencing initially went so far as to give the parole board exclusive authority over the actual term of incarceration within the maximum term set by statute. Today, many legislatures obviously have less (if any) faith in prisons as a place of rehabilitation, and have developed a much greater interest in the retributive and general deterrence functions of punishment. As discussed in § 26.1(c) some have moved to determinate sentencing that eliminates parole and the parole board. Even where indeterminate sentences are retained, the period over which parole may be granted tends to be more restricted than under the earlier statutes. Also, certain classes of offenders (usually those sentenced to life sentences)

will be declared by statute to be ineligible for parole.

Jurisdictions vary in the guidance given to parole boards in their determination of whether to release a prisoner who has served his minimum sentence. Some provide no direction by legislation. In several jurisdictions, parole boards have fashioned comprehensive guidelines, similar to the sentencing guidelines discussed in § 26.3(e), using a point allocation system to measure such basic factors as the seriousness of the defendant's criminal behavior, the probability of his recidivism, and his institutional behavior. The risk of recidivism is measured by reference to criteria that include the offender's prior criminal record (including juvenile proceedings), the number of prior incarcerations, age at the time of first commitment, history of drug use, education, verified employment opportunity, and the existence of a family with which he might live. Prison behavior is measured largely by reference to loss of good-time credits and efforts directed toward self-improvement.

Some states have adopted legislation setting forth general criteria for release on parole. In large part, these criteria seek to ensure that dangerous offenders will not be released. They provide, for example, that the board only may release an offender who has served his minimum sentence if it "is satisfied that * * * [t]he inmate will be paroled * * * without danger to society." The criteria also may refer to other factors that a parole board is likely to consider (e.g., suitable employment), but may make those factors absolute prerequisites rather than discretionary concerns. Occasionally, a statute will be worded so that the inmate is entitled to be released if certain criteria are met. The Supreme Court dealt with such a statute in *Greenholtz v. Inmates of Nebraska Penal & Correctional Complex*,[7] and concluded the result of that statutory structure was to vest in the inmate a due process right to limited procedural protections.

The Court in *Greenholtz* had before it two issues: (1) whether the inmate's interest in

---

6.　459 U.S. 422, 103 S.Ct. 843, 74 L.Ed.2d 646 (1983).

7.　442 U.S. 1, 99 S.Ct. 2100, 60 L.Ed.2d 668 (1979).

parole release was a protectable interest under the Due Process Clause, and (2) if so, whether the procedures followed by the Nebraska parole board satisfied due process requirements. Speaking for the Court to the first issue, Chief Justice Warren Burger reasoned that the inmate's interest in parole release did not, in general, establish a protectable right. The Chief Justice noted that "there is no constitutional or inherent right of a convicted person to be released before expiration of a valid sentence." Moreover, a state's decision to establish a parole system did not in itself give the inmate "a legitimate claim of entitlement," as the state was free to give the parole board absolute control over "the sensitive choices presented by the * * * decision to grant parole release." A state could recognize "that there is no prescribed or defined combination of acts" which should "mandate release," and that "the choice involves a synthesis of record facts and personal observation, filtered through the experience of the decision-maker and leading to a predictive judgment as to what is best both for the individual inmate and for the community." The end result is then "an 'equity' type judgment" that cannot be said to give the inmate more than "a mere hope that the benefit will be obtained." Although "the presence of a parole system by itself does not give rise to a constitutionally protected liberty interest in parole release," the Nebraska did create "a protectable expectation of parole." That statute stated that the parole board "shall order [the inmate's] release unless it is of the opinion" that any of four conditions existed. While those conditions involved judgments that were necessarily "subjective in part and predictive in part," the mandatory structure of the provision nonetheless served to "bind" the parole board and thereby created an "expectancy of release * * * [requiring] some measure of constitutional protection." The Chief Justice added: "However, we emphasize that this statute has unique structure and language and thus whether any other state statute provides a protective entitlement must be decided on a case-by-case basis."

In *Board of Pardons v. Allen*,[8] the Court held that a Montana parole statute also created an expectation of parole that entitled an inmate to due process protections. Although the "shall" directive in the Montana statute was modified by a condition that designated that findings be made, the Court refused to find any significant difference in "a statute that mandates release 'unless' certain findings are made [i.e., *Greenholtz*] * * * and a statute that mandates release 'if,' 'when,' or 'subject to' such findings being made." "Any such statute," the Court noted, "creates a presumption that release will be granted."

Sandin v. Conner,[9] a 1995 decision revising the test for determining when prisoners are entitled to procedural protections for decisions affecting not parole, but good time, is in some tension with the *Greenholtz* analysis. In *Sandin*, the Court rejected the claim of a prisoner facing loss of the opportunity to earn good time. He claimed a due process right to present witnesses at his disciplinary hearing, but the Court found that the prisoner had no "protected liberty interest that would entitle him to the procedural protections set forth in *Wolff*."[10] Justice Rehnquist on behalf of the Court criticized the "methodology" used to identify such an interest that was first "foreshadowed" in *Greenholtz* and then adopted in later cases. This analysis, based on the creation of expectations, shifted the focus of the liberty interest inquiry from the "nature of the deprivation" to the "language of a particular regulation," encouraging prisoners to "comb regulations in search of mandatory language on which to base entitlements to various state conferred privileges," creating "disincentives for States to codify prison management procedures in the interest of uniform treatment," and leading to "the involvement of federal courts in the day-to-day management of prisons, often squandering judicial resources with little offsetting benefit to anyone." The

---

8.   482 U.S. 369, 107 S.Ct. 2415, 96 L.Ed.2d 303 (1987).

9.   515 U.S. 472, 115 S.Ct. 2293, 132 L.Ed.2d 418 (1995).

10.   See Wolff v. McDonnell, discussed at note 11 infra.

Court in *Sandin* offered a different test—those liberty interests that are protected by due process will be "generally limited to freedom from restraint which, while not exceeding the sentence in such an unexpected manner as to give rise to protection by the Due Process Clause of its own force * * * nonetheless imposes atypical and significant hardship on the inmate in relation to the ordinary incidents of prison life."

As for the effect of its ruling on *Greenholtz* and *Allen*, the *Sandin* Court noted that its decision did not "technically require us to overrule any holding of this Court." Yet by requiring unique hardship in order to trigger due process safeguards, *Sandin* could exclude routine parole release decisions from the sphere of decisions protected by due process. On the other hand, the Court in *Sandin* distinguished the determination at issue in that case (risking lost opportunity to earn good time) from determinations that inevitably affect the duration of [an inmate's] sentence. The Court in *Sandin* also referred favorably to *Wolff v. McDonnell*,[11] a case which had required at least minimal procedural protections in the context of proceedings affecting earned good time, even though the revocation of good-time credit is not an atypical hardship. Lower courts continue to apply *Greenholtz* and *Allen*, rather than *Sandin*, when examining the interests created by parole schemes.

Greenholtz also continues to guide lower courts on the separate issue of what procedural safeguards due process requires in parole proceedings where a protectable interest is present. In *Greenholtz*, the Court stressed that due process had long been held to have a "flexible" content that "calls for such procedural protections as the particular situation demands." Consideration had to be given to the predictive and subjective aspects of the release determination, the need to allow experimentation with a judgment "involving analysis of psychological factors combined with fact evaluation guided by * * * practical experience," the danger of creating a "continuing state of adversary relations between society and the inmate," and the concern that the imposition of procedures viewed as "burdensome and unwarranted" would lead states to "abandon or curtail parole." In light of these considerations, the Court in *Greenholtz* held the lower court had erred in holding that due process mandated a formal hearing in all cases. The Nebraska Board did not grant such a hearing where, after examining the inmate's file and holding a personal interview, it concluded that the inmate was not a good risk for release. To require that it go beyond this inquiry, and hold a formal hearing would "provide at best a negligible decrease in the risk of error," especially since the inmate was allowed to present letters and statements on his behalf at the interview.

Greenholtz also held that the court below had erred in requiring the parole board to provide to the inmate a summary of the evidence on which it relied. There had been no challenge by inmates regarding their access to their prison files, and the factual information governing the parole decision ordinarily came from the files. To require a final board summary of the evidence "would tend to convert the process into an adversary proceeding and to equate the Board's parole-release determination with a guilt determination." It was, in fact, "essentially an experienced prediction based on a host of variables," and in that context, the Constitution "does not require more" than what the state was doing. It was sufficient that the "Nebraska procedure affords an opportunity to be heard, and when parole is denied it informs the inmate in what respects he falls short of qualifying for parole."

States commonly provide to potential parolees the procedures that were held in *Greenholtz* to be adequate to meet due process demands. At one time, the practice in many states was to simply review the file, but informal hearings or "interviews" conducted by a hearing officer or a board member are now the norm. The prisoner usually will be informed of the general nature of the information in his file, or have access to that file, and will be

---

11. 418 U.S. 539, 94 S.Ct. 2963, 41 L.Ed.2d 935 (1974).

given the opportunity to offer corrections or otherwise state his case for parole. In many jurisdictions, an inmate is entitled to a more formal hearing where he may be represented by counsel (usually only if he can retain counsel on his own), present his own witnesses, and be present during the testimony of persons opposing his release (although cross-examination is ordinarily not permitted). Where release is denied, the inmate commonly is informed of the basis for that decision, although the statement of grounds may be quite general.

Parole boards also are assigned the responsibility of determining whether parole should be revoked due to a violation of a parole condition. The Supreme Court in a series of cases beginning with *Morrissey v. Brewer*,[12] has set forth a series of due process prerequisites, applicable to the revocation of parole and probation. These start with a prompt preliminary hearing following the parolee's arrest to determine whether there is probable cause to believe he has violated the parole condition (unless that is established per se by his conviction on a criminal charge). That hearing is later followed by an adversarial, trial-type hearing, with counsel appointed under some circumstances. Explaining why due process required so much more in a parole revocation proceeding, the Court in *Greenholtz* noted:

> [P]arole *release* and parole *revocation* are quite different. There is a crucial distinction between being deprived of a liberty one has, as in parole, and being denied a conditional liberty that one desires. The parolees in *Morrissey* were at liberty and as such could "be gainfully employed and [were] free to be with family and friends and to form the other enduring attachments of normal life." The inmates here, on the other hand, are confined and thus subject to all of the necessary restraints that inhere in a prison. * * * A second important difference between discretionary parole *release* from confinement and *termination* of parole lies in the nature

of the decision that must be made in each case. As we recognized in *Morrissey*, the parole-revocation determination actually requires two decisions: whether the parolee in fact acted in violation of one or more conditions of parole and whether the parolee should be recommitted either for his or society's benefit. "The first step in a revocation decision thus involves a wholly retrospective factual question." The parole-release decision, however, is more subtle and depends on an amalgam of elements, some of which are factual but many of which are purely subjective appraisals by the Board members. * * * Unlike the revocation decision, there is no set of facts which, if shown, mandate a decision favorable to the individual.[13]

Regardless of the availability of parole, executive agencies may reduce sentences through "good-time" credit. The executive department in charge of prisons usually has the responsibility for calculating the good-time credit, which involves applying a statutory formula to calculate the amount of credit, and determining whether the inmate's behavior qualifies him for such credit. Credit usually is calculated as a percentage of the time served or according to the "class" achieved by the prisoner. In many jurisdictions, that percentage increases as the prisoner serves more time or is reclassified. Prisoners in some states may eventually receive more than two days credit for each day served. In a jurisdiction with indeterminate sentences, the good-time credit may be deducted from the court-imposed maximum or minimum sentence. In some jurisdictions, good-time credit can also be gained by certain work assignments or educational achievements.

Good time is lost by a violation of prison rules. Ordinarily, any significant violation carries with it the loss of a certain amount of credit. Major misconduct can result in the loss of more than a year, the equivalent of a felony conviction in terms of impact upon actual in-

---

12. 408 U.S. 471, 92 S.Ct. 2593, 33 L.Ed.2d 484 (1972).

13. See also Young v. Harper, 520 U.S. 143, 117 S.Ct. 1148, 137 L.Ed.2d 270 (1997) (holding "preparole" pro-

gram to reduce overcrowding was equivalent to parole, so that revocation of preparole status must meet *Morrissey* standards).

carceration. *Wolff v. McDonnell*[14] held that such a sanction brought into play due process, although not the full range of procedural requirements demanded in the parole revocation setting. As discussed earlier, some aspects of the Court's later opinion in *Sandin v. Conner* undermined the Court's determination in *Wolff* that state law can create a constitutionally protected liberty interest in the retention of earned good time credit. The *Sandin* Court held that an inmate's confinement in segregation and potential loss of the opportunity to *earn* good-time credits will not trigger due process protections. The Court explained that only "restraint which * * * imposes atypical and significant hardship on the inmate" will give rise to due process protection, and good-time revocation, like the loss of an opportunity to earn good time, does not necessarily fit this definition. However, the Court in *Sandin* cited *Wolff* with approval and suggested that due process protection should be afforded if, as is the case with good-time revocation, "the state's action will inevitably affect the duration of [the inmate's] sentence." Since *Sandin*, lower courts continue to follow *Wolff* in the revocation setting.

Assuming due process protects an inmate at a disciplinary hearing, *Wolff* held that due process requires the following: (1) advance written notice of the disciplinary charges; (2) a hearing at which the inmate can call witnesses and present documentary evidence, except where those rights will jeopardize institutional safety or correctional goals; and (3) "a written statement by the factfinders as to evidence relied upon and the reasons" for taking disciplinary action. In addition, the decision must be supported by "some evidence."[15] The Court in *Edwards v. Balisok*[16] stated in dicta that due process would also forbid "the decision of a biased hearing officer who dishonestly suppresses evidence of innocence." Prison officials

are free to grant or deny inmates the opportunity to cross-examine witnesses,[17] although lower courts have insisted that due process requires that evidence offered against an accused inmate carry some indicia of reliability. Lower courts have also held that inmates must receive meaningful assistance from a prison employee in presenting a defense, at least where the inmate is hampered in the preparation of his defense by illiteracy or by the complexity of issues. In sum, the process due a defendant in this context is greater than that due an inmate applying for parole but less than what is required in order to revoke parole or probation.

In all jurisdictions an offender may also receive relief from a sentence through reprieve, remission, commutation, or pardon. Taken together, these devices are often described as "executive clemency." A reprieve merely delays the execution of a sentence. Remission relieves the offender of the responsibility of paying a fine or forfeiting property. Commutation reduces a term of imprisonment. The pardon absolves the defendant of guilt and thereby eliminates the basis for imposing any punishment. Clemency power in most states is shared between the governor and an administrative board or advisory group. A minority of states allow either the governor or the board the sole authority to make clemency decisions.

The discretion to grant or deny clemency is nearly absolute.[18] The Court in *Connecticut Board of Pardons v. Dumschat*[19] held that a prisoner has no liberty interest protected by due process in a commutation, even where seventy-five percent of the prisoners in his situation had received commutations upon application. Connecticut, like most states, had granted unfettered "discretion" to an executive agency to exercise the clemency power,

---

14. Supra note 11.

15. Superintendent, Mass. Correctional Inst. v. Hill, 472 U.S. 445, 105 S.Ct. 2768, 86 L.Ed.2d 356 (1985) (due process requires "some evidence" to support the disciplinary board's decision).

16. 520 U.S. 641, 117 S.Ct. 1584, 137 L.Ed.2d 906 (1997).

17. See *Wolff*, supra note 11 (noting concerns about the risk of reprisal against inmate informant).

18. Ex parte Grossman, 267 U.S. 87, 45 S.Ct. 332, 69 L.Ed. 527 (1925); Ex parte Garland, 71 U.S. (4 Wall.) 333, 18 L.Ed. 366 (1866) (discussing pardon power of the President).

19. 452 U.S. 458, 101 S.Ct. 2460, 69 L.Ed.2d 158 (1981).

designating no procedure nor criteria for the commutation decision. Under these circumstances, commutation or pardon is, the Court concluded, "simply a unilateral hope." As a result, the prisoner was not entitled to any particular procedural safeguards in the clemency process.

The Court rekindled the debate over due process and clemency procedures in 1993. In the course of rejecting a claim of innocence by a capital habeas petitioner, the Supreme Court noted in *Herrera v. Collins* that "the traditional remedy for claims of innocence based on new evidence, discovered too late in the day to file a new trial motion, has been executive clemency."[20] Following this apparent reliance upon clemency as a presumably meaningful source of post-conviction relief, defendants renewed their arguments that due process entitles clemency applicants to a hearing, an unbiased decisionmaker, and other procedural rights. The Court revisited the issue in *Ohio Adult Parole Authority v. Woodard*,[21] this time in the context of a claim that Ohio's clemency procedures were constitutionally inadequate. Five justices agreed that unlike non-capital prisoners seeking release, whose interest in liberty has already "been extinguished," a death row prisoner seeking commutation of his sentence faces future deprivation of "life that he still has," and that this "crucial distinction" supports "some minimal procedural safeguards." The process provided to the prisoner in *Woodard*, however, met this standard. Woodard had received notice that he was entitled to an opportunity to participate in a prehearing interview with parole board members (without counsel) three days before the interview. Participation in the clemency hearing itself by either Woodard or his counsel was permitted only at the discretion of the parole board chair. A majority of justices went on to suggest that judicial intervention might be warranted in another case, if a state made its clemency decisions by flipping a coin, for example, or "arbitrarily denied a prisoner any access to its clemency process." As for non-capital cases, the opinion of the Chief Justice,

joined by Justices Scalia, Kennedy, and Thomas, appears to extinguish any constitutional entitlement to procedural safeguards before clemency is denied. No expectation of clemency is created even by a state's decision to mandate clemency review. Instead, clemency is a "matter of grace committed to the executive authority."

Even if an inmate has no constitutional basis to claim that his application for clemency was denied unfairly, he may be entitled to the basic elements of fair procedure before clemency, once granted, is revoked. As described above, in the context of parole and probation, the Court has held that revocation proceedings require greater safeguards than initial denials. When clemency takes the form of release, it makes sense to treat clemency revocations like parole revocations as both situations carry the risk of re-imprisonment. If the Court continues to require minimal procedural protections for the revocation of earned good time, the revocation of a reprieve from a death sentence or release due to commutation would appear to demand equivalent safeguards. However, if the heightened protections in *Morrissey* and *Wolff* are premised not on what is at stake for the inmate, but on the state's insistence on proof of a factual prerequisite (the inmate's misconduct, or violation of a condition of parole or probation), then clemency decisions—which involve no similar factual predicates—may not require heightened safeguards.

§ 26.3   The Guidance of Judicial Discretion

(a) Unguided Discretion. Judicial discretion in sentencing has always been subject to some statutory limitations. As discussed in § 26.1, those limitations have varied with the sanction. In the case of fines, the primary statutory limits have been the unavailability of that sanction for certain crimes and the upper limit on the amount of the fine. As for probation, statutory limits include prohibitions against use of that sentence for certain crimes, and parameters for the length of the probation

---

20. 506 U.S. 390, 113 S.Ct. 853, 122 L.Ed.2d 203 (1993).

21. 523 U.S. 272, 118 S.Ct. 1244, 140 L.Ed.2d 387 (1998).

term and the conditions that can be imposed. The traditional statutory limitations for incarceration are the upper limit for the term, the required use of that upper limit as the maximum term in some indeterminate sentencing jurisdictions, the requirement that the minimum for an indeterminate sentence be no more than a certain fraction of the maximum, and, for certain offenses, mandatory minimum terms. The discretion of the sentencing judge to set a sentence within these limitations has, until quite recently, been granted without further legislative guidance.

Reluctance to provide additional statutory guidance for the court's exercise of sentencing discretion is often attributed to the need to individualize sentences so that the sentence best achieves the rehabilitation of each offender. The individualization of punishment, and the judicial discretion that makes that tailoring possible has also found support in the other goals of punishment. Deterrence, incapacitation, and even retribution may require that a judge draw distinctions between offenders who commit the same crime. Because the legislature can hardly take into consideration all of the factors that distinguish one particular offense and offender from another, a certain amount of individualization (and hence discretion) traditionally has been afforded to the judge.

(b) The Challenge to Unguided Discretion. It is not surprising that this tradition of unguided judicial discretion produced variations in sentences that appeared to lack any reasonable basis. Sentences differed from locality to locality, for just as the value systems of different communities within a single jurisdiction placed similar crimes and similar offenders in a different light, the value systems of different jurisdictions led to different authorized punishments for similarly defined crimes. There were variations as well among different judges in the same judicial district, as each was guided by his own sentencing philosophy and view of human nature. Studies also pointed to inconsistencies in the sentences of individual judges, apparently as a result of extraneous factors that happened to influence the judge's attitude in dealing with a particular case. For many years, such disparities were accepted as a necessary cost of individualization, although some trial courts experimented with procedures that sought through the exchange of views to produce greater consistency among judges of that court. Then, by the 1970s, a combination of factors, including concern about the potential for racial and class bias in sentencing, resulted in concerted efforts nationwide to "do something" about discretionary sentencing and the disparities it produced.

Four approaches for controlling judicial discretion, each examined below, eventually gained widespread support: (1) more frequent use of mandatory minimum sentences tied to the existence of particular facts, (2) presumptive sentencing setting out specific presumed sentence levels for each offense, (3) sentencing guidelines, and (4) appellate review to enforce these and other limits on judicial discretion in sentencing. A majority of jurisdictions have significantly curtailed sentencing discretion in one or more of these ways, a development that has had considerable influence in reshaping the sentencing process.

Limiting judicial discretion in sentencing cannot, of course, fully eliminate disparity in the penalties that offenders may receive. The executive, through law enforcement, charging, bargaining, and clemency, retains significant, often unreviewable, power to select which offenders will be subjected to legislatively authorized penalties. Jurors also retain the ability to protect an offender from the penalty designated by statute in the very small percentage of cases that go to trial before a jury. As legislatures remove from judges the discretion to differentiate between offenses and offenders, the discretion of prosecutors and juries takes on added significance. It is therefore not surprising that the adoption of these limits on judicial discretion in sentencing has coincided with renewed concern among academics, judges, and legislators, about the abuse of discretion by prosecutors and juries.

(c) Mandatory Minimum Sentences. The mandatory minimum sentence is a form of determinate sentencing designed to control the discretion of judges and parole boards. These statutes mandate minimum terms of imprisonment for any offender who commits a particular offense, or impose mandatory enhancements for offenders who commit offenses under certain conditions. The "three-strikes-and-you're-out" laws discussed in § 26.6(b) are examples, imposing lengthy mandatory terms for certain repeat offenders. Congress has enacted a number of statutes imposing mandatory minimum sentences. By 1994, all fifty states had enacted one or more mandatory sentencing laws.

This has been a "hit or miss" approach to reform. The crimes selected for mandatory minimums often have been those that happened to capture the public eye at a particular moment. In addition, prosecutors regularly circumvent mandatory minimums through initial charging and charge bargaining. The effects of the increased application of mandatory sentences have been widely criticized. Justice Breyer has noted that "My colleague, Justice Kennedy, along with most judges in the federal system, believes that mandatory minimums are 'imprudent, unwise, and often an unjust mechanism for sentencing.' "[1] Regardless of one's view of the success of mandatory minimum sentencing statutes, their proliferation has increased the significance of fact-finding at sentencing, prompting calls for procedural safeguards greater than those commonly employed in traditional discretionary sentencing.

(d) Presumptive Sentencing. In the 1970s and early 1980s, several states adopted presumptive sentencing systems (sometimes termed "statutory determinate sentencing"), under which the legislature initially sets a "presumptive" term of incarceration for each offense or class of offenses within the statutory maximum term for that offense or class of offenses. That presumptive term is stated as a range of years or as a set number of years. The judge cannot set an offender's sentence lower or higher than the specified term unless mitigating or aggravating factors justify a departure. The permissible range for departures is

also set by the legislature, and in some jurisdictions, relevant aggravating and mitigating circumstances are specified by the legislature. The presumptive sentencing structure substantially narrows judicial discretion by requiring the judge to justify departures from the presumptive sentence by reference to specific aggravating and mitigating circumstances that in large part rest on historical fact. Also, in contrast to the practice under traditional discretionary sentencing, which requires no explanation of the reasons for the sentence, the judge must set forth findings that justify any upward or downward departure.

(e) Sentencing Guidelines. A guidelines system also uses a presumptive sentence and a system of departures, but the presumptive sentence ranges are set by a legislatively created sentencing commission or by the highest court, rather than by the legislature itself. In many jurisdictions, guidelines deal with fines and community-release sentences as well as terms of incarceration. Since Minnesota first adopted presumptive sentencing guidelines in 1980, they have proved more popular than the presumptive sentence scheme described in § 26.3(d) above. Well over a dozen states and the federal government have adopted sentencing guidelines.

The presumed sentence in a guidelines system is determined through the use of a sentencing table or grid that designates the recommended sentencing range for the particular case. On one axis of the grid is a ranking of the criminal history of the offender. The other axis ranks the severity of the crime by reference to such factors as the harm caused, the range of the criminal activity, and the role of the offender. The severity scale utilizes a point system that starts with a certain number for the basic offense and then adds and subtracts points for specified factors. The presumptive sentence ranges tend to be fairly narrow. For example, if the severity scale places a crime in the middle range, the presumed sanction may be 20 to 24 months for a person with no prior

§ 26.3

1. Breyer, Federal Sentencing Guidelines Revisited, 11 Fed.Sent.Rep. 180, 184 (1999).

convictions (in the first criminal history category) and 90 to 104 months for a person in the highest criminal history category. Presumed ranges at certain low levels will include probation as an alternative. Plea-bargained reductions on charges may affect the sentence, but their impact is more limited where a jurisdiction uses a "real offense" system. The severity scale is likely to be such that the point total under a lesser offense often can come close to what it would be under the higher offense. Some state systems are designed to allow for the adjustment of recommended sentence ranges in response to changes in correctional resources. The presumed range under a sentence guidelines system is not binding upon the court; judges may depart upward or downward. The court must set forth its reasons for departure, however, and those reasons may be limited by statute. Appellate review will be available both as to departures and as to the judicial determination of the proper score under the severity range and the proper placement in the criminal history category.

The application of a sentencing guidelines system can best be illustrated by example, and for that purpose we use the Federal Sentencing Guidelines. The federal guidelines initially place each crime in one of nineteen offense category designations. This permits the grouping of various offenses of a similar character. "Offenses against the person," for example, include homicide, kidnapping, assault, and other threatening behavior. A base level is set for each offense, and added to this are points for offense characteristics. The base level for kidnapping, for example, is 24. The specific offense characteristics include a ransom demand (6 level increase), victim injury (2 to 4 level increase based on nature of injury), use of a dangerous weapon (2 level increase), the period elapsed before the release of the victim (a reduction of 1 level or an increase of level, depending upon whether the kidnapping lasted less than 24 hours or more than 30 days), sexual exploitation of victim (increase of 3 levels), and connection to another offense (4 level increase). After the level is set by reference to the offense characteristics, adjustments are made. The guidelines include five

major categories of adjustments: (1) victim-related adjustments; (2) adjustments for the defendant's role in the offense; (3) adjustments for obstructing the administration of justice; (4) adjustments for multiple count convictions; and (5) adjustments for a defendant's acceptance of responsibility. Thus, for example, the severity level will be increased if the victim was especially vulnerable due to age (2 levels) or was a public official (3 levels) or if the defendant was the leader of the criminal activity (4 levels). It will be reduced if the defendant was a "minimal participant" (4 levels) or if the defendant "clearly demonstrate[d] acceptance of responsibility for his offense" (2 levels). With these adjustments, the total offense level will be set.

The next step is determining the defendant's criminal history category. A separate new composite number is constructed much like that for the offense level. The criminal-history category is determined by the sum of the points given for each prior federal or state sentence. The number of points per sentence varies depending upon whether the sentence included imprisonment and upon the length of imprisonment. If the defendant should fall into the category of a "career offender," then the offense level itself can be affected.

Once the offense level and the criminal history category are set, the presumed sentence is determined by the Commission's sentencing table. For example, for a kidnapping defendant with an offense level of 30 and a criminal history category of II, the table produces a sentence of 108 to 135 months. If the table produces a presumed sentence of 0 to 6 months, probation would be an alternative under the presumed sentence. If it produces a sentence no higher than 6 to 12 months, a community release program involving intermittent confinement or community confinement would be within the presumed sentence.

The district court is not bound to sentence within the guidelines, but may depart (except in crimes involving sex or children) when it finds "an aggravating or mitigating circumstance * * * that was not adequately taken into consideration" by the Commission's relevant guideline. In some instances, the guidelines themselves provide specific guidance for possible departures, such as a government motion for downward departure based upon the defendant having provided substantial assistance in the investigation or prosecution of another person. Whether the departure is based upon a ground suggested by the guidelines or upon other grounds, the specific reason for departure must be set forth in the record. Indeed, even where a sentence within the presumed range is imposed, the court still must set forth "its reasons for its imposition of the particular sentence" (i.e., explain its application of the guidelines), and where the guideline range exceeds 24 months, it must give the reason for imposing a sentence at a particular point within the range. These determinations are then subject to appellate review.

Fact-finding is particularly important in guidelines sentencing. Unlike a presumptive sentencing structure that requires findings as to certain circumstances only where there is a departure from the presumed sentence, sentencing guidelines require that a series of findings be made in every case. The guidelines system accordingly requires a sentencing process that affords each side an opportunity both to submit its own information relating to the guideline factors and to challenge information before the court. The process must also provide for a fair resolution by the sentencing judge of disputes as to the presence or proper interpretation of those factors. In addition, it must provide a record sufficient for appellate review as to factual and legal determinations made both in setting the presumed sentence and in any departure from that sentence. As will be seen in § 26.4, these functions of the process have led guideline jurisdictions to alter their sentencing process from that traditionally employed in sentencing dominated by unguided judicial discretion.

Compared to the federal guidelines, state sentencing guidelines systems grant more judicial discretion and involve fewer sentencing factors. Many incorporate intermediate, nonconfinement penalties and tend to recommend less severe sentences than the federal guidelines. Indeed, the popularity of sentencing guidelines in the states is due in part to the success of guidelines in limiting prison growth and accompanying costs.

(f) Concurrent and Consecutive Sentences. When a defendant is subject to more than one sentence, judges in most jurisdictions retain the discretion to determine whether those sentences must be served consecutively (one after the other) or concurrently (simultaneously). This choice can arise when a defendant is convicted of multiple offenses at the same trial, or is convicted while subject to a sentence for a prior offense in the same or another jurisdiction. The Double Jeopardy Clause prohibits the imposition of consecutive sentences for the "same offence." As discussed in § 17.4, the Court seems to have settled on the *Blockburger* test, otherwise known as the "same elements" test, for determining when two offenses are really the "same" offense. Should a defendant be convicted of two offenses, each containing an element not found in the other, a judge may impose consecutive sentences without violating the defendant's right to be free from double jeopardy. Many state constitutions and state statutes contain more restrictive definitions of which offenses are separate. Consequently, a court may be precluded under state law from imposing consecutive sentences otherwise permissible under the United States Constitution.

These constitutional constraints leave considerable room for judges to "stack" sentences or run them simultaneously. Without additional limits, this discretion can undercut legislative efforts to regularize sentence length, by allowing grossly disparate total terms of incarceration for similarly situated offenders. To guard against this sort of disparity, statutes in every jurisdiction further limit judicial discretion by establishing a presumption of either consecutive or concurrent sentences, mandating consecutive sentences for specified offense combinations, or laying out conditions under which concurrent or consecutive sentences may be imposed. The law in most states instructs courts to presume that multiple sentences run concurrently, although some states follow the opposite approach, presuming that all sentences will be consecutive. Still other states adopt a hybrid approach, imposing a presumption in favor of concurrent sentencing under some circumstances, but establishing a presumption of consecutive sentencing in others. The statutory guidance given judges as to what circumstances would rebut a statutory presumption varies, sometimes including checklists of factors that must first be found or weighed. Certain offenses may carry mandatory consecutive sentences. For example, statutes typically require that sentences for crimes committed while incarcerated or on parole or probation, violations of habitual offender provisions, and firearm offenses must be imposed consecutively to other sentences.

(g) Appellate Review. In common law jurisdictions other than the United States, appellate review of sentences has been the principal method used to develop consistency in sentencing. The traditional position in this country, however, as stated by the Supreme Court in *Dorszynski v. United States*,[2] has been that "once it is determined that a sentence is within the limits set forth in the statute under which it is imposed, appellate review is at an end."[3] This position of no substantive review of sentences may have been a practical accommodation of the absence of any requirement that trial judges record the reasons for their sentences. It also followed from the nature of traditional indeterminate sentencing. Sentencing was not subject to established criteria, except for the statutory framework that set its outer limits, and the appellate court therefore had no standards it could invoke to determine whether a particular sentence was excessive in length or otherwise inappropriate. Of course, this analysis did not apply to the procedures used in setting the sentence. A defendant could challenge or appeal a violation of statutory or constitutional requirements in the sentencing process. So, too, an appellate challenge was available where the judge was alleged to have exceeded his sentencing "authority" as defined by statute and the Constitution. For example, in the federal courts before the Guidelines, an appellate court could reject a sentence where it constituted cruel and unusu-

al punishment, where the judge relied upon impermissible criteria such as race, or where the judge failed to fulfill his statutory obligation to exercise discretion and used a "fixed and mechanical" sentencing policy. On occasion, even in a jurisdiction professing to allow no substantive review, an appellate court might strike down a sentence within the statutory limits because it was so excessive as to "shock" the court.

Although several states retain this very limited review of sentencing, it has long been rejected in a substantial number of states. The case for reviewing at least whether there was a "clear abuse" or where the sentencing judge "was clearly mistaken" includes the following arguments: (1) unchecked discretion leads to the imposition of sentences "which may be excessively severe, excessively lenient, or excessively disparate in relation to similarly situated defendants who have committed similar crimes and which thereby create a feeling of betrayal on the part of the defendant and the public, with confidence in the criminal justice system correspondingly diminished"; (2) while the "interplay between society and crime" conceivably could justify some degree of disparity based on "different priorities of the community," it certainly did not justify "disparity in sentences which results from considerations such as the race or economic status of a defendant or the personal bias and attitude of an individual sentencing judge"; (3) the claimed increased burden on appellate courts in providing sentence review was exaggerated because "[m]any defendants now appeal their convictions simply because of their dissatisfaction with the severity of their sentences, [with their] * * * appeals based upon the subterfuge of attacking their convictions rather than directly attacking what concerns them most, the appropriateness of their sentences"; (4) such defendants sometimes win because the appellate judges agree that their sentences are inappropriate and "strain the law to reach the desired relief," and therefore "a wider scope of

---

2. 418 U.S. 424, 94 S.Ct. 3042, 41 L.Ed.2d 855 (1974).

3. See also Koon v. United States, 518 U.S. 81, 116 S.Ct. 2035, 135 L.Ed.2d 392 (1996) (citing *Dorszynski* for

the proposition that "[b]efore the Guidelines system, a federal criminal sentence within statutory limits was, for all practical purposes, not reviewable on appeal").

sentence review" should "promote honesty and clarity in criminal appeals"; and (5) even if the "number of sentences * * * which would warrant relief are few, any injustice committed is still deserving a remedy" and the failure to provide such relief undermines "public confidence in the courts."

In some states in order to facilitate appellate review, courts have been required to "articulate on the record its reasons for the sentence given." Such a requirement traditionally has not been applied to unguided discretionary sentencing, and that may explain in part why in many jurisdictions allowing for limited appellate review under an abuse of discretion standard, such review has had only a limited impact. Thus, one study of appellate review in such jurisdictions found that the rate of sentence review was moderate in about half of them, seldom in a quarter, and almost nil in the remaining quarter. The key appeared to be that meaningful review was often impossible to achieve, absent a statement of grounds by the sentencing judge and the development of standards with which the propriety of those grounds could be assessed.

With the advent of presumptive sentencing and sentencing guidelines, the landscape of appellate sentencing review in this country has been altered dramatically. Both sentencing schemes provide for appellate review as an integral part of the sentencing structure. "Without the discipline of review," it has been argued, sentencing limits "created at the system. In the case of presumptive sentencing, that review is likely to be focused on departures, because here the court will have a statement of grounds justifying the sentence." Under guideline sentencing, the criteria and the statement of reasons will exist for sentences within the guidelines as well as for departures, making review possible in all cases.

In the federal system, review extends to all errors in the application of guidelines (as well as to violations of statutory and constitutional standards). This reaches beyond the correctness of the sentencing court's interpretation of the guidelines and also includes its factual assessments. As to the latter, a "clearly erroneous standard" will apply as with other factual findings.[4] In reviewing departures from the range specified by the guidelines, the Court explained in *Koon v. United States*,[5] the court of appeals must ask whether the sentencing court abused its discretion, but this standard was later changed to de novo review by Congress in an effort to restrict downward departures.[6] State systems review departures using various standards, and there is variation even among the five states most experienced with using sentencing guidelines.

Allowing the government (as opposed to the defendant) to appeal a sentence was highly controversial when traditional sentencing was reviewed by only a limited "abuse" standard. With presumptive and guideline sentencing now presenting clear issues of legal interpretation as well as specific factual findings, and the Supreme Court having upheld the constitutionality appellate review of sentencing,[7] prosecution appeals described in are now widely accepted.

§ 26.4　Due Process: The Framework for Sentencing Procedure

(a) *Williams v. New York*. Although decided over a half-century ago, *Williams v. New York*[1] remains the leading ruling on the content of due process as it applies to procedures in traditional discretionary sentencing. Commentators have steadily predicted that the "revolution" that transformed much of constitutional criminal procedure after *Williams* will soon reach sentencing and that recent developments reducing the sentencing discretion of

---

4. The same standard is also employed when reviewing certain "fact-bound" legal decisions at sentencing. Buford v. United States, 532 U.S. 59, 121 S.Ct. 1276, 149 L.Ed.2d 197 (2001), discussed in § 27.5(e).

5. 518 U.S. 81, 116 S.Ct. 2035, 135 L.Ed.2d 392 (1996).

6. PROTECT Act, 117 Stat. 650, modifying 18 U.S.C.A. § 3742.

7. See United States v. DiFrancesco, discussed in § 26.7(b), rejecting double jeopardy challenge to government's appeal of sentence.

§ 26.4

1. 337 U.S. 241, 69 S.Ct. 1079, 93 L.Ed. 1337 (1949).

judges should render *Williams* and its reasoning obsolete. So far, such predictions have not been realized. The Supreme Court continues to cite with approval the principles expressed in Justice Black's opinion for the Court in *Williams*.[2] Compared to the Court's fundamental refashioning of constitutional requirements for other phases of the criminal process, its more conservative application of due process in sentencing appears almost frozen in time, even as sentencing itself has been transfigured by legislative reform.

Williams itself was a capital case decided at a time when the process of capital sentencing was not much different than the sentencing procedure typically followed in non-capital cases. Williams had been sentenced to death by the trial judge, notwithstanding the jury's recommendation of a life sentence. In the trial court, a presentence investigation report had been compiled by the probation department following conviction and presented to the judge, apparently without disclosure to the defense. The judge had then held a brief sentencing hearing at which first the defendant and then his counsel had been allowed to address the issue of whether the judge should follow the jury's recommendation. The judge then explained why he felt the death sentence should be imposed. He pointed both to the "shocking details of the crime as shown by the trial evidence" and to information contained in the presentence report. The judge noted that the presentence investigation "had revealed many material facts concerning the appellant's background which though relevant to the question of punishment could not properly have been brought to the attention of the jury." Referring specifically to the defendant's involvement in 30 other burglaries in the vicinity, he noted that although the defendant had not been convicted of those crimes, he "had information that [defendant] had confessed to some and had been identified as the perpetrator of others." The judge also referred to "certain activities * * * as shown by the probation report" indicating that defendant

possessed a "morbid sexuality" and was a "menace to society." Justice Black, following his description of these remarks by the judge, observed: "The accuracy of the statements made by the judge as to appellant's background and past practices were not challenged by appellant or his counsel, nor was the judge asked to disregard any of them or afford appellant a chance to refute or otherwise discredit any of them by cross-examination or otherwise."

Justice Black described the question before the Court as relating "to the rules of evidence applicable to the manner in which a judge may obtain information to guide him in the imposition of sentence." The defendant had raised a "broad constitutional challenge" to the "New York procedural policy [that] encourages [the judge] to consider information about the convicted person's past life, health, habits, conduct and mental and moral propensities." The defendant had challenged that policy as contrary to basic due process principles ensuring that an accused be given "reasonable notice" and be afforded "an opportunity to examine adverse witnesses." Rejecting this broad challenge, Justice Black referred to both the history and function of sentencing.

As to history, Justice Black noted that "both before and since the American colonies became a nation, courts in this country and in England practiced a policy under which the sentencing judge could exercise a wide discretion in the sources and types of evidence used to assist him in determining the kind and extent of punishment to be imposed within the limits fixed by law." As to function, Justice Black stressed the distinction between the roles of the factfinder at trial and the sentencing judge. The trial was concerned "solely with the issue of guilt of a particular offense" and utilized rules of evidence designed to "narrowly confine" the factfinder to material "strictly relevant" to that issue. A sentencing judge was not so confined. His task demanded the possession of "the fullest information possible concerning the defendant's life and characteris-

---

2. See e.g., United States v. Watts, 519 U.S. 148, 117 S.Ct. 633, 136 L.Ed.2d 554 (1997); Witte v. United States, 515 U.S. 389, 115 S.Ct. 2199, 132 L.Ed.2d 351 (1995).

tics." This was especially true under the "modern philosophy of penology that the punishment should fit the offender and not merely the crime."

Having established the need for a range of information far broader than that considered at trial, Justice Black then turned to the form in which such relevant information was presented:

Under the practice of individualizing punishments, investigational techniques have been given an important role. Probation workers making reports of their investigations have not been trained to prosecute but to aid offenders. Their reports have been given a high value by conscientious judges who want to sentence persons on the best available information rather than on guess-work and inadequate information. To deprive sentencing judges of this kind of information would undermine modern penological procedural policies. * * * We must recognize that most of the information now relied upon by judges to guide them in the intelligent imposition of sentences would be unavailable if information were restricted to that given in open court by witnesses subject to cross-examination. And the modern probation report draws on information concerning every aspect of a defendant's life. The type and extent of this information make totally impractical if not impossible open court testimony with cross-examination. Such a procedure could endlessly delay criminal administration in a retrial of collateral issues.

Justice Black acknowledged that "leaving a judge free to avail himself of out-of-court information does secure to him a discretionary power [that is] susceptible to abuse," but noted that the same kind of broad judgmental authority is available to the judge in evaluating such factors as the defendant's demeanor at trial. The Court could not say that "due process renders a sentence void because a judge gets additional out-of-court information" when "no constitutional objection would have been possible if the judge had sentenced appellant to death because appellant's trial manner impressed the judge that appellant had a bad risk

for society, or if the judge had sentenced him to death for no reason at all."

Williams is considered the leading ruling on at least three basic elements of due process in sentencing procedure: (1) the range of the factors that a judge may consider in imposing a sentence; (2) the right of the defendant to be informed of the factors being considered by the judge and of the evidence being advanced in support of those factors; and (3) the opportunity given to the defendant to challenge the existence and relevancy of those factors. The bearing of *Williams* upon each of these elements is considered in the subsections that follow, along with modifications or reinforcement provided by post-*Williams* rulings. The defendant's opportunity to challenge sentencing information has been broken down further into four separate aspects: (1) the right to the assistance of counsel at sentencing; (2) the right to insist that sentencing information be reliable through cross-examination, corroboration, or other means; (3) the right of the defendant to speak and to submit his own evidence at the sentencing stage; and (4) the standard of proof required for facts relevant to sentencing. The Court's due process rulings on these issues form the framework for sentencing procedure in all jurisdictions. Additional requirements are provided by statute, rule, or judicial decision.

(b) The Range of Relevant Information. *Williams* opens to the sentencing court's consideration a wide range of facts that may be relevant to the sentencing decision. In particular, *Williams* clearly upholds what is now described as "real offense" sentencing—that is, sentencing that looks beyond the statutory elements of the charged offense and considers the gravity of the defendant's actual conduct. Indeed, *Williams* obviously considers as relevant many acts of the defendant extending beyond the transaction that gave rise to the charged offense. Thus, a court does not violate due process when in setting a sentence, it considers the unrelated criminal conduct of the defendant, even if that conduct did not result in a criminal conviction (as in the case of the burglaries cited by the judge in *Williams*).

The consequences of considering the non-conviction activities of an offender are most striking under a sentencing system that assigns to that activity a particular penalty. For example, a judge who imposes a sentence under the federal guidelines must consider all "relevant conduct" when determining the offense level. The guidelines' provision on relevant conduct states that, in determining the base offense level and specific offense characteristics, the court shall consider all acts aided or abetted by the defendant, or for which the defendant would be "otherwise accountable," that occurred during the commission of the offense of conviction, in preparation for that offense, in the course of attempting to avoid detection or responsibility for that offense, or that were otherwise in furtherance of that offense. The guidelines thus look to the character of the "real offense" to determine the sentence range, even though the offender may have been acquitted of that conduct, or never charged. This practice of assigning punishment on the basis of conduct which was never proven beyond a reasonable doubt to a jury nor admitted by the defendant in a plea proceeding has been criticized vigorously by many commentators and judges as violating of various constitutional safeguards and as bad policy. Despite this assault, the practice of considering unproven offenses during sentencing continues with very little regulation from the Court.

Williams also treats as relevant aspects of the defendant's life that go beyond antisocial conduct. The Court noted the need for the sentencing judge, in evaluating the "lives and personalities of convicted offenders," to draw on information concerning "every aspect of a defendant's life." Indeed, the Court cited in this connection the federal presentence report form that directed the probation officer to gather information concerning such factors as "family history," "home and neighborhood," "education," "religion," "interests and activi-ties," "employment," and "health (physical and mental)."

In light of this sweeping description of relevant information in *Williams*, it could be argued that there is no aspect of a defendant's life that may not be weighed in assessing the appropriate sentence under a discretionary sentencing scheme. Post–*Williams* rulings, however, have held that due process does limit or even bar consideration of a small group of factors. First, the Court has limited the consideration by the sentencing judge of the defendant's exercise of procedural rights within the criminal justice process. Those rulings are discussed in a later section, § 26.4(c). Second, as discussed in the text below, the Equal Protection Clause prohibits judges from basing their sentencing decisions upon the race or gender of defendant or victim, or upon the defendant's exercise of fundamental rights.

McCleskey v. Kemp[3] indicates that the race of the defendant or victim is an element that simply may not be considered, negatively or positively, in sentencing. In *McCleskey*, the Court explained that "purposeful discrimination" in sentencing based upon the race of the victim or defendant would be unconstitutional under traditional equal protection analysis. While the sentencing jury in a capital case had the authority to "consider *any* factor relevant to the defendant's background, character, and the offense," the authority did not extend so far as to allow the more harsh treatment of a particular defendant because of his or her race or because of the race of the victim. The Court in *McCleskey* added, however, that the defendant carried the burden of "proving" the existence of such purposeful discrimination by "the decisionmakers in his case." It concluded that this burden could not be met by simply showing a statistical disparity across capital sentencing decisions throughout the state. In refusing to accept the statistical disparity as sufficient even to create a rebuttable presumption of discriminatory purpose, the Court distinguished its willingness to draw an inference of intentional discrimination from statistical proof in other settings (e.g., jury and grand

---

3. 481 U.S. 279, 107 S.Ct. 1756, 95 L.Ed.2d 262 (1987).

jury venire-selection). There, the statistics related to "fewer entities" and "fewer variables [were] relevant to the challenged decisions." Thus, while race is a factor that may not be considered in sentencing, the defense is unlikely to carry its burden of showing that race was considered absent a remark of the judge or a juror referring specifically to that factor.

Although the race of the victim or defendant (and, presumably, the gender of the victim or defendant) cannot be the basis for setting a sentence, evidence that the defendant selected his victim because of the victim's race can be relevant, and serve as the basis for an enhanced penalty, held the Court in *Wisconsin v. Mitchell*.[4] Wisconsin enacted a statute that increased the maximum sentence for an offense if the defendant "intentionally selects" the victim because of the "race, religion, color, disability, sexual orientation, national origin or ancestry of that person." The Supreme Court of Wisconsin invalidated the statute on first amendment grounds, concluding that it punished "bigoted thought" not conduct. The United States Supreme Court, relying on its decision in *Barclay v. Florida*,[5] disagreed. In *Barclay*, the Court upheld a death sentence after the sentencing judge considered evidence that the defendant was a member of the Black Liberation Army and desired to provoke a "race war." The Court held that the evidence was relevant to several aggravating factors. The Court in *Mitchell* also relied upon cases upholding federal and state antidiscrimination laws to conclude that Mitchell's first amendment rights were not violated by the application of the Wisconsin statute. Bias-inspired conduct, the Court explained, "is thought to inflict greater individual and societal harm. * * * The state's desire to redress * * * perceived harms provides an adequate explanation for its penalty-enhancement provision over and above mere disagreement with the offender's beliefs or biases."

The first amendment rights of the defendant do protect against the sentencer's consider-ation of irrelevant evidence of defendant's protected beliefs or activity. In *Dawson v. Delaware*,[6] the Court explained that "although the Constitution does not erect a per se barrier to the admission of evidence concerning one's beliefs and associations at sentencing when those beliefs and associations are protected by the First Amendment," the First and Fourteenth Amendments do prohibit the introduction in a capital sentencing proceeding of such evidence when it is "totally without relevance" to the sentencing proceeding. In *Dawson*, the prosecution had introduced evidence that the defendant was a member of the Aryan Brotherhood, had the name of the organization as well as swastikas tattooed on his hand, and had painted a swastika on his cell wall. The Court concluded that the prosecution had failed to demonstrate how this evidence of the defendant's "abstract beliefs" was relevant to prove or disprove any aggravating or mitigating circumstance. As a result, the introduction of this evidence was barred by the First Amendment. Evidence of political or religious association that is relevant to future dangerousness is presumably not barred by *Dawson*. Only the absence of any link between protected activity and sentencing issues will require resentencing. Accordingly, one court vacated a death sentence after the jury learned of the activities of a satanic cult to which defendants belonged, another ordered resentencing when the jury heard evidence that the defendant had been a victim of incest and had engaged in homosexuality.

Sentencing guidelines that set specified "prices" or sentence increases for particular facts have prompted two additional arguments for limiting the use of certain information at sentencing. The first argument arises from a situation known as sentencing entrapment—when a government agent convinces the defendant to engage in conduct carrying penalties higher than those accompanying the conduct he was predisposed to commit in order to increase the defendant's sentence. A court con-

---

4. 508 U.S. 476, 113 S.Ct. 2194, 124 L.Ed.2d 436 (1993).

5. 463 U.S. 939, 103 S.Ct. 3418, 77 L.Ed.2d 1134 (1983).

6. 503 U.S. 159, 112 S.Ct. 1093, 117 L.Ed.2d 309 (1992).

vinced that entrapment has occurred may refuse to apply the applicable sentence increase
or may depart below the recommended sentence. The second situation in which a court
might refuse to consider certain facts advanced
by the government is termed "sentence manipulation." Unlike entrapment, sentence manipulation depends only upon the conduct of the
government, not the predisposition of the defendant. Particularly outrageous conduct by
the government undertaken in order to increase a defendant's sentence has been held in
some cases to be a violation of due process.

**(c) Consideration of the Defendant's
Exercise of Procedural Rights.** The Supreme Court has held in several different contexts that a defendant is denied due process
when the sentencing court "punishes" him for
his exercise of a procedural right in the criminal justice process. Thus, in *North Carolina v.
Pearce*,[7] the Court unanimously agreed that
the sentencing judge could not impose a higher
sentence upon a defendant in retaliation for
his having successfully appealed his original
conviction. The Court acknowledged that
Williams allowed the sentencing court on reconviction to take into consideration conduct
of the defendant subsequent to his first conviction "that may throw new light upon defendant's * * * 'moral propensities,'" but that
did not authorize "punish[ing] a person because he has done what the law plainly allows
him to do" in pursuing an appeal. To allow
such "vindictiveness" to play a part in his
sentence would be to allow the sentencing
court "to put a price on an appeal" and thereby inhibit the "free and unfettered" exercise
of that right as granted under state law. In
Pearce, the Court conceded that the "existence
of a retaliatory motivation would * * * be
extremely difficult to prove in any individual
case," and concluded that further steps were
needed to free the defendant "of the apprehension" of retaliation. It therefore established a
presumption of vindictiveness under the special circumstances presented there, involving
an increased sentence imposed upon reconviction for the same offense that had lead to the

conviction overturned on appeal. However,
apart from that special situation, further discussed in § 26.8, the defendant does not have
the benefit of such a presumption. To establish
a due process violation, he must show by reference to the sentencing record that the judge in
fact sentenced vindictively, seeking to punish
defendant for his exercise of some procedural
right.

Despite its ruling in *Pearce*, the Supreme
Court has allowed the sentencing court to consider other choices that a defendant may make
regarding trial rights. Thus, as discussed in
§ 21.2, the Court has repeatedly noted in its
guilty plea cases that while the sentencing
court may not punish with an increased sentence the defendant who goes to trial, it may
accomplish the same result by rewarding with
a reduced sentence the defendant who pleads
guilty. The reward is justified because the entry of a guilty plea produces conditions that
justify leniency in accordance with the traditional functions of sentencing. The defendant
who pleads guilty proffers to the state various
administrative advantages, allows for the more
effective attainment of the objectives of punishment by hastening its imposition, and acknowledges his responsibility for the offense.
Consideration of such factors through a reduction of sentence is consistent with the objective of individualizing punishment as noted in
Williams, even though granting leniency to
the defendant who pleads guilty may have the
same practical effect of discouraging the exercise of the right to go to trial as a vindictive
sentence aimed at the exercise of that right.

In *United States v. Grayson*,[8] the Court
adopted a similar analysis in holding that the
trial judge could weigh against the defendant
his misuse of a trial right that reflected badly
upon his character. In that case, the defendant's testimony on his own behalf at trial had
been contradicted in several crucial respects by
the government's rebuttal evidence. The trial
judge explained to the defendant at sentencing
that he was taking into account "the fact that
your defense was a complete fabrication without the slightest merit whatsoever." As the

---

7. See § 26.8.

8. 438 U.S. 41, 98 S.Ct. 2610, 57 L.Ed.2d 582 (1978).

Supreme Court noted, lower courts, relying on *Williams*, had almost without exception concluded that "a defendant's truthfulness or mendacity while testifying on his own behalf * * * [is] probative of his attitudes toward society and prospects for rehabilitation and hence relevant to sentencing." The defendant did not contest the relevance of his truthfulness to his sentence. Instead, he argued that the Court, in order to preserve due process rights, "not only must prohibit the impermissible sentencing practice of incarcerating for the purpose of saving the Government the burden of bringing a separate and subsequent perjury prosecution but also must prohibit the otherwise *permissible* practice of considering a defendant's untruthfulness for the purpose of illuminating his need for rehabilitation and society's need for protection." In support of this claim, the defendant presented two interrelated reasons. First, both permissible and impermissible sentencing practices may have the same practical effect: additional time in prison. Second, he argued that it "is virtually impossible * * * to identify and establish the impermissible practice." The Supreme Court was not persuaded.

The Court cited three factors that led it to reject the due process standard urged by the defendant. First, the judge's function in a discretionary sentencing scheme, as set forth in *Williams*, "demonstrates that it is proper—indeed, even necessary for the rational exercise of discretion—to consider the defendant's whole person and personality, as manifested by his conduct at trial and his testimony under oath, for whatever light those might shed in the sentencing decision." The " 'parlous' effort to appraise 'character,' " the Court noted, "degenerates into a game of chance to the extent that a sentencing judge is deprived of relevant information." Second, the risk of improper use here was no different than that presented in *Williams*, where the Court permitted the sentencing judge to consider burglaries for which the defendant had not been convicted despite the risk that the judge might use his knowledge of those prior offenses "for an improper purpose." Third, the efficacy of the "exclusion-

ary rule" suggested by defendant was open to serious doubt, as "no rule of law, even one garbed in constitutional terms, can prevent improper use of firsthand observations of perjury." The "integrity of the [sentencing] judges" necessarily provides "the only, and in our view, adequate assurance" against improper use of such information. Finally, the Court also rejected the defendant's claim that the sentencing judge's action impermissibly "chilled" his constitutional right to testify in his own behalf, noting that this right "is narrowly the right to testify truthfully in accordance with the oath" and that there "is no protected right to commit perjury."

The Court revisited the issue in *United States v. Dunnigan*.[9] There, the defendant challenged the trial judge's decision to increase her sentence after finding that the defendant had perjured herself at trial. A unanimous Court held that the sentence increase was authorized under the federal sentencing guidelines for "willfully obstructing or impeding proceedings" and did not violate due process. Because "an accused may give inaccurate testimony due to confusion, mistake or faulty memory," or may testify truthfully regarding a defense which the jury rejects, the Court cautioned that "a district court must review the evidence and make independent findings necessary to establish" perjury. It defined perjury as "giving false testimony concerning a material matter with the willful intent to provide false testimony." The Court, as in *Grayson*, rejected the defendant's argument that allowing a perjury enhancement would impermissibly punish or chill the exercise of the right to testify. Finally, the Court admitted that unlike the earlier sentencing system considered in *Grayson*, the federal guidelines do not encompass rehabilitation as a goal of sentencing, but explained that perjury by the accused is nevertheless relevant in setting a federal sentence. The "willingness to frustrate judicial proceedings to avoid criminal liability suggests that the need for incapacitation and retribution is heightened as compared with the defendant charged with the same crime who allows judi-

---

9. 507 U.S. 87, 113 S.Ct. 1111, 122 L.Ed.2d 445 (1993).

cial proceedings to progress without resorting to perjury."

When a defendant does assert the privilege against self incrimination at sentencing regarding a factual matter, a court is prohibited from drawing an adverse inference about that factual issue from the defendant's silence, held the Court in *Mitchell v. United States*.[10] In *Mitchell*, the defendant pleaded guilty to several drug offenses, reserving the right to contest drug quantity at sentencing. At the sentencing hearing, the defendant did not contradict, through her own testimony, the assertions of government witnesses who testified that the defendant had sold over 5 kilograms of cocaine, an amount carrying a mandatory minimum sentence of ten years. In explaining to the defendant why he credited the testimony of the government's witnesses, the trial judge stated, "I held it against you that you didn't come forward today and tell me that you really only did this a couple of times * * *. I'm taking the position that you should come forward and explain your side of this issue." The Supreme Court found this inference to violate the defendant's rights under the Fifth Amendment. It concluded that the concerns underlying the rule against negative inferences from assertions of the privilege at trial, established in *Griffin v. California*,[11] also mandate a ban on adverse inferences from the assertion of the self-incrimination privilege at sentencing.

The Court in *Mitchell* declined, however, to express a view on whether the defendant's silence at sentencing "bears on the determination of lack of remorse, or upon acceptance of responsibility" for downward departure under the guidelines. By limiting its opinion to inferences about facts alone, the Court left open the possibility that a valid assertion of the privilege could be considered for some purposes (assessing the defendant's character or willingness to cooperate, for example), but not other purposes (assessing the existence of particular sentencing facts).[12]

(d) Notice. Due process also guarantees the defendant some information concerning the reasons for his sentence. The extent of that disclosure was addressed in *Williams*. The judge in *Williams* had told the defendant that he was taking into consideration both the defendant's participation in various burglaries, and certain other activities noted in the presentence report that evidenced defendant's "morbid sexuality." This explanation, however, hardly provided full notice of the basis for the sentencing judge's conclusions relating to the defendant's past behavior. As to the burglaries, the judge noted that defendant had confessed as to "some" and had been identified as the perpetrator as to "others," but did not state which of the burglaries fell in each category, how he knew that defendant had confessed (or precisely what defendant was supposed to have said), or who had identified the defendant as the perpetrator. As to the other activities, the judge did not identify the precise nature of those activities, or what the presentence report offered in support of the conclusion that he had engaged in those activities. In arguing that the sentencing court should have before it the sworn testimony of relevant witnesses, the defendant had explained that this was necessary to give him "reasonable notice." The Court, in rejecting that contention and holding that the sentencing judge could rely on "out-of-court information" suggested that the provision of such notice might well undercut the sentencing judge's ability to use such information. It noted that most of that information would be "unavailable" if the sources had to appear and

---

10. 526 U.S. 314, 119 S.Ct. 1307, 143 L.Ed.2d 424 (1999).

11. Discussed in § 24.5(b).

12. Nearly two decades earlier, in Roberts v. United States, 445 U.S. 552, 100 S.Ct. 1358, 63 L.Ed.2d 622 (1980), a case mentioned only by the dissent in *Mitchell*, the Court had declined to consider whether a sentencing judge could deny a defendant a reduced sentence for cooperation due to his refusal on self-incrimination grounds to assist in the investigation of his former associ-

ates. The *Roberts* court noted that there was insufficient indication in that case that the defendant's refusal to cooperate was actually based upon the privilege. Compare McKune v. Lile, 536 U.S. 24, 122 S.Ct. 2017, 153 L.Ed.2d 47 (2002) (privilege against self incrimination not violated by a prison clinical rehabilitation program for sex offenders that required offenders to admit to all of their past criminal sexual conduct or else be reclassified and moved into maximum security with additional cell mates and fewer prison privileges).

give testimony in open court. Indeed, the Court stated that "no federal constitutional objection would have been possible * * * if the judge had sentenced [defendant] to death giving no reason at all."

In light of these aspects of *Williams,* it is not surprising that an Advisory Committee Note accompanying Federal Rule 32 in 1966 stated: "It is not a denial of due process of law for a court in sentencing to rely on a report of a presentence investigation without disclosing such report to the defendant or giving him an opportunity to rebut it." While the Supreme Court had not had occasion to consider a constitutional challenge to a rule leaving disclosure to the discretion of the judge, it did transmit to Congress the Federal Rule that incorporated that standard. Moreover, it did so over the objection of Justice Douglas, who maintained that the "rule for the federal courts * * * ought not to be one which permits a judge to impose sentence on the basis of information of which the defendant may be unaware and to which he has not been afforded an opportunity to reply."

Whatever the correct reading of *Williams* as to notice, today that issue must be analyzed in light of the Supreme Court's ruling in *Gardner v. Florida*[13] and later cases interpreting *Gardner.* The trial judge in *Gardner* had sentenced the defendant to death without stating on the record the substance of information in the presentence report that he might have considered material to his decision. This was held to be unconstitutional, but there was no opinion for the Court as to why. Justices White and Blackmun concluded that the procedure violated the Eighth Amendment, Justice Marshall concluded that the state's cavalier approach to the death penalty required reassessment of the constitutionality of the underlying statute, and the Chief Justice concurred in the reversal without opinion. Three justices, in a plurality opinion by Justice Stevens, concluded that there had been a violation of due process, and Justice Brennan expressed general agreement with the analysis of that opinion.

The plurality opinion viewed *Williams* as distinguishable in two respects. First, in *Williams* relevant information had been disclosed but went unchallenged; in the instant case, there was no similar opportunity for petitioner's counsel to challenge the accuracy or materiality of any such information. Second, since *Williams* had been decided a majority of the Court had recognized that death sentencing requires closer scrutiny and had clarified that "the sentencing process, as well as the trial itself, must satisfy the requirements of the Due Process Clause." Decisions like *Mempa v. Rhay*[14] and *Specht v. Patterson*[15] had firmly established that "the defendant has a legitimate interest in the character of the procedure which leads to the imposition of sentence even if he may have no right to object to a particular result of the sentencing process." The plurality argued that these developments demanded application of the traditional due process balancing approach that weighed the interests in non-disclosure asserted by the state against the interests of the defendant in a procedure that ensured a rationally imposed death sentence.

The state in *Gardner* sought to justify its practice of nondisclosure by reference to several interests. It maintained that (1) an assurance of confidentiality was "essential to enable investigators to obtain relevant but sensitive disclosures from persons unwilling to comment publicly about a defendant's character"; (2) judges could be trusted to rely only on reliable information; and (3) disclosure of the presentence report would cause delay. The plurality found each of those justifications to be flawed. While assurances of secrecy were "conductive to the transmission of confidences," those confidences might "bear no closer relationship to fact than the average rumor or gossip." The "risk that some of the information accepted in confidence may be erroneous or may be misinterpreted, by the investigator or by the sentencing judge, [was] manifest." The assumption that trial judges could be relied upon to exercise their discretion in a responsible man-

13.   430 U.S. 349, 97 S.Ct. 1197, 51 L.Ed.2d 393 (1977).

14.   See § 26.4(e).

15.   See § 26.4(i).

ner, even though relying on "secret information," was contrary to the Court's eighth amendment rulings and rested on the "erroneous premise that the participation of counsel is superfluous to the process of evaluating the relevance and significance of aggravating and mitigating factors." Finally, the likelihood of significant delay clearly was "overstated" if, as the Court would presume, the "reports prepared by professional probation officers * * * are generally reliable." Moreover, if a critical point should be disputed, the "the time invested in ascertaining the truth should surely be well spent if it makes the difference between life and death." Thus, the defendant's interest in a reliable process clearly prevailed, and a defendant was denied due process "when the death sentence was imposed, at least in part, on the basis of information which he had no opportunity to deny or explain."

Twenty years after *Gardner*, in *Gray v. Netherland*,[16] the Court clarified that the scope of the notice guaranteed by *Gardner* in capital cases does not include discovery of that information *in advance* of sentencing. The petitioner in *Gray* argued that the government violated his due process rights by failing to inform him until the night before the penalty phase that it would be presenting witness testimony concerning alleged prior offenses. Previously, the prosecutor had told defense counsel that he would limit this evidence to statements of the defendant. The Court rejected the petitioner's claim to advance notice of the prosecutor's changed strategy. It likened the claim to that of the defendant in *Weatherford v. Bursey*,[17] who had argued that due process prohibited the prosecutor from presenting at trial the surprise testimony of an undercover agent. The agent, in order to preserve his cover, had told defendant and his counsel that he would not be testifying. The Court in *Weatherford* rejected the argument that due process banned such surprise testimony. Emphasizing that

"there is no general constitutional right to discovery in a criminal case," the Court in *Gray* distinguished *Gardner* as a case involving "secret" not surprise testimony, noting that "Gardner literally had no opportunity to even see the confidential information [in his presentence report], let alone contest it." No constitutional violation occurred in *Gray*, reasoned the Court, when the defendant had "the opportunity to hear the testimony of [the witnesses] in open court, and to cross-examine them." *Gray*, then, suggests that due process does not require the disclosure of sentencing information in advance of sentencing, even in capital cases. Some state courts, however, have indicated that a denial of discovery before the sentencing stage, in any case, can result in a violation of due process under state constitutional provisions.[18]

The constitutionality of failing entirely to disclose certain sentencing information to the defense in non-capital cases remains unsettled. First of all, *Gardner*, a death penalty case, may not dictate notice standards in non-capital cases. As the Court later explained in *Lankford v. Idaho*,[19] where it held that a capital defendant is entitled to adequate notice that a judge might sentence him to death, the "threatened loss" in a capital case is "so severe" that "the need for notice is even more pronounced" than in non-capital cases. Significant too is the Court's statement in *O'Dell v. Netherland*[20] that Justice White's concurring opinion in *Gardner* states the holding in that case. Justice White concurred in *Gardner* on a basis that would not in all likelihood require the same outcome in a non-capital case—that reliance upon secret information in sentencing a defendant to death violated the Eighth Amendment, not due process. On the other hand, most of the arguments that the Court rejected in *Gardner*, and most of the concerns that it expressed there regarding the subversion of reliable factfinding, apply equally to

---

16. 518 U.S. 152, 116 S.Ct. 2074, 135 L.Ed.2d 457 (1996).

17. 429 U.S. 545, 97 S.Ct. 837, 51 L.Ed.2d 30 (1977).

18. See also the discussion in § 24.3 (b) of the government's obligation under *Brady* not to suppress evidence favorable to the defense, when there is a reasonable proba-

bility that disclosure would have led to a different outcome.

19. 500 U.S. 110, 111 S.Ct. 1723, 114 L.Ed.2d 173 (1991).

20. 521 U.S. 151, 117 S.Ct. 1969, 138 L.Ed.2d 351 (1997).

nondisclosure in non-capital sentencing under modern presumptive sentencing schemes prevalent today. Just as a death sentence must be justified by reference to statutorily identified aggravating factors and subject to appellate scrutiny, similar fact-dependent inquiries and extensive review are now integral to many modern non-capital sentencing systems.

Assuming due process might require disclosure of sentencing information in non-capital cases, the appropriate analysis for assessing what due process requires has been the subject of debate. The balancing test of *Mathews v. Eldridge*,[21] a case decided by the Court a year before *Gardner*, is one favorite of judges faced with the task of determining whether a particular procedural safeguard at sentencing is required as matter of due process; and has been advanced as one analysis for determining the extent to which notice is required by due process in the context of sentencing. Under *Mathews*, the disclosure required may vary with the type of information at issue and the circumstances of the case. This approach was adopted by three justices of the Supreme Court dissenting in *Burns v. United States*.[22] In *Burns*, the defendant had received his presentence report, but was not told that the court was contemplating an upward departure from the guidelines range. The majority avoided addressing whether due process required such notice by concluding that such disclosure was required by Rule 32. The dissenters, however, concluded that Congress did not intend to mandate such disclosure, nor was disclosure required as a matter of due process. Examining the particular disclosure in its specific context of sentencing under the federal guidelines, the dissenting justices applied the balancing test of *Mathews* and decided that "the risk of error under the procedures already required and the probable value of a further notice requirement are sufficiently low" that failure to require advance notice of the court's intent to depart "passes constitutional muster."

But in *Medina v. California*,[23] a majority of justices disapproved of the use of the *Mathews* test in the criminal setting. *Mathews*, the Court declared, "does not provide the appropriate framework for assessing the validity of state procedural rules which, like the one at bar, are part of the criminal process." Raising a point also expressed recently in another case, Justice Kennedy stated for the Court, "The Bill of Rights speaks in explicit terms to many aspects of criminal procedure, and the expansion of those constitutional guarantees under the open-ended rubric of the Due Process Clause invites undue interference with both considered legislative judgments and the careful balance that the Constitution strikes between liberty and order." Instead, a state law defining procedure in criminal cases must be tested by the "less intrusive" analysis in *Patterson v. New York*,[24] which provides that such a statute is "not subject to proscription under the Due Process Clause unless it offends some principle of justice so rooted in the traditions and conscience of our people as to be ranked as fundamental." Justice O'Connor, joined by Justice Souter, defended the application of *Mathews* in her concurring opinion, arguing that the "balancing of equities that *Mathews* outlines remains a useful guide in due process cases." She went on to suggest that *Mathews* was particularly helpful in "the context of modern administrative procedures" where there is "no historical practice to consider," such as "the new administrative regime established by the federal criminal sentencing guidelines" considered in *Burns*.

Even while the contours of the constitutional right to notice of sentencing information remain less than clear, a defendant's statutory entitlement to review such information is well-established in most jurisdictions. Typically judges are required by statute or court rule to state the reasons for a sentence at sentencing. As discussed in § 26.5(c), presentence reports commonly are made available to defendants,

---

21.   424 U.S. 319, 96 S.Ct. 893, 47 L.Ed.2d 18 (1976).

22.   501 U.S. 129, 111 S.Ct. 2182, 115 L.Ed.2d 123 (1991).

23.   505 U.S. 437, 112 S.Ct. 2572, 120 L.Ed.2d 353 (1992) (refusing to employ *Mathews* to determine whether

the defendant's right to due process was violated by a state statute that placed upon him the burden of proving his mental incompetency before trial).

24.   432 U.S. 197, 97 S.Ct. 2319, 53 L.Ed.2d 281 (1977).

even in non-capital cases, providing defendants with some opportunity to review and object to factual allegations that may influence the sentence.

(e) The Right to the Assistance of Counsel. One of the most fundamental features of fair procedure in the trial setting is the right to the assistance of counsel. Prior to *Williams,* the Court had indicated that due process required that a defendant have the assistance of counsel at sentencing.[25] After the Court held in *Gideon* that the sixth amendment right to counsel applies in state proceedings, it held in *Mempa v. Rhay*[26] that the Sixth Amendment guaranteed a defendant the assistance of counsel at his combined probation revocation and sentencing hearing. The Court noted that sentencing is a "stage of a criminal proceeding where substantial rights of a criminal accused may be affected." Subsequently, the Supreme Court has reiterated that the sixth amendment right to the effective assistance of counsel extends through the sentencing phase of a criminal prosecution, at least in cases where a conviction carries imprisonment.[27]

Due process may require the provision of counsel at post-trial proceedings that fall outside the scope of the Sixth Amendment, such as parole or probation revocation proceedings.[28] Some states jurisdictions provide defendants with counsel at sentencings which do not involve imprisonment, or at all probation revocation hearings.

Proceedings prior to sentencing, too, may be protected by the sixth amendment right to counsel. In *Estelle v. Smith,*[29] the Supreme Court held that a psychiatrist's examination of the defendant for "future dangerousness," a factual prerequisite for the sentence of death in Texas, was a "critical stage" at which the right to counsel attached. The Court held that the statements elicited from the defendant in

that case could not be used in his capital sentencing hearing. Lower courts, however, have distinguished the situation in *Estelle* from other efforts to obtain sentencing information during the typical presentence interview by a probation officer, at least in non-capital cases, reasoning that the probation officer is a neutral party, and the non-adversarial interview is not a "critical stage" requiring the assistance of counsel. Although counsel is not required at these interviews, a jurisdiction may permit counsel's attendance.

(f) Ensuring the Reliability of Sentencing Information. The Court in *Williams* indicated that the exercise of sentencing discretion requires access to a wide spectrum of information, and that information need not be limited to evidence tested by trial-type standards and procedures. The Court stated flatly that due process did not require that a "sentencing judge * * * be denied an opportunity to obtain pertinent information [as] a requirement of rigid adherence to restrictive rules of evidence properly applicable to the trial." In light of this statement, courts have not questioned the constitutional validity of statutes providing that the rules of evidence, apart from those dealing with privilege, do not apply to the sentencing process. The Court has in subsequent decisions clarified that due process does require that the information on which courts rely when setting a sentence must meet some threshold of reliability. That requirement is the subject of this subsection.

In response to the defendant's claim that he was entitled to examine adverse witnesses at sentencing, the *Williams* Court explained that requiring "open court testimony with cross-examination" would be "totally impractical if not impossible" in the sentencing context. Lower courts generally rely on *Williams* to reject defense demands for evidentiary hear-

---

25. Townsend v. Burke, 334 U.S. 736, 68 S.Ct. 1252, 92 L.Ed. 1690 (1948), discussed in § 26.4(f).

26. 389 U.S. 128, 88 S.Ct. 254, 19 L.Ed.2d 336 (1967).

27. Lockhart v. Fretwell, 506 U.S. 364, 113 S.Ct. 838, 122 L.Ed.2d 180 (1993) (defendant has right to effective assistance of counsel at capital sentencing); Strickland v. Washington, 466 U.S. 668, 104 S.Ct. 2052, 80 L.Ed.2d 674 (1984) (same). See also Glover v. United States, 531 U.S.

198, 121 S.Ct. 696, 148 L.Ed.2d 604 (2001) (several months' difference in sentence constitutes "prejudice" for purposes of *Strickland* analysis).

28. See § 26.2(c).

29. 451 U.S. 454, 101 S.Ct. 1866, 68 L.Ed.2d 359 (1981).

ings with trial-type testing of sentencing information. Nevertheless, whether a defendant has a right to confrontation at sentencing has proved to be a controversial question in modern sentencing systems that, unlike the discretionary sentencing examined in *Williams,* clearly tie the severity of a sentence to particular findings of fact. For example, although the federal courts of appeals have declined to recognize a federal defendant's right to confrontation under either the Sixth Amendment or the Due Process Clause in the guidelines setting, several of these decisions have been divided, with dissenters arguing that *Williams* fails to account for the increased importance that fact-finding carries in guidelines sentencing. State courts, with some exceptions, have also continued to reject defense claims of entitlement to cross-examination at sentencing.

The Court in *Williams* did indicate that due process may require some reliability in fact-finding, short of that level ensured by trial-type procedures, when it added that "what we have said is not to be accepted as holding that sentencing procedure is immune from scrutiny under the due process clause," and cited *Townsend v. Burke.*[30] In *Townsend,* the defendant, unassisted by counsel, entered a plea of guilty, then had a brief sentencing hearing. A police officer recited the details of the crime and the judge then proceeded to ask the defendant a series of questions that focused on the defendant's prior criminal record. The judge referred to several convictions and asked about the circumstances of one. When the defendant stated that the offense was committed by his brother, and that he had been tried for the offense but was "not guilty," the court responded by moving on to ask about other offenses. In the course of that questioning, certain facetious remarks by the judge indicated that he thought the defendant had committed all of the offenses. As was later established, the charge on one of those additional offenses had been dismissed and defendant had indeed been found not guilty on the charge he attributed to his brother, as well as another charge. The Supreme Court concluded

that "this uncounseled defendant was either overreached by the prosecutor's submission of information to the court or was prejudiced by the court's own misreading of the record." It noted that "counsel, if any had been present," surely would have been "under a duty to prevent the court from proceeding on such false assumptions." With the defendant having been so disadvantaged by the lack of counsel, and the sentencing court having sentenced based on "assumptions concerning his criminal record which were materially untrue, * * * [the] result, whether caused by carelessness or design," was a lack of due process. The Court added that it did not mean to say that "mere error in resolving a question of fact on a plea of guilty by an uncounseled defendant in a non-capital case would necessarily indicate a want of due process of law." For "fair prosecutors and conscientious judges, sometimes are misinformed * * *, and even an erroneous judgment, based on scrupulous and diligent search for the truth, may be due process of law." Here, however, counsel clearly would have "taken steps to see that the sentence was not predicated on misinformation or misreading of court records."

In *United States v. Tucker*[31] the Court relied upon *Townsend* in holding that the defendant's sentence could not stand where the judge had relied upon defendant's prior felony convictions without knowledge that those convictions were constitutionally infirm because defendant had been denied his constitutional right to appointed counsel in the proceedings that had produced the convictions. Tucker, who was represented by counsel, had *not* objected when the sentencing court had noted that it was taking into consideration three prior convictions that the defendant had acknowledged while being cross-examined at trial. Nonetheless, the Court concluded that a new sentencing proceeding was necessary because the "sentence [was] founded at least in part upon misinformation of constitutional magnitude." As in *Townsend v. Burke,* "this prisoner was sentenced on the basis of as-

---

30. 334 U.S. 736, 68 S.Ct. 1252, 92 L.Ed. 1690 (1948).

31. 404 U.S. 443, 92 S.Ct. 589, 30 L.Ed.2d 592 (1972).

sumptions concerning his criminal record which were materially untrue.''

The Court has interpreted *Townsend* and *Tucker* so narrowly that they have become practically useless to defendants who seek at sentencing to challenge the judge's consideration of a prior conviction, unless the defendant can show he was denied counsel altogether on the prior charge. Upholding the use of uncounseled misdemeanor convictions in sentencing in *Nichols v. United States*,[32] the Court reasoned that the defendant could have "been sentenced more severely based simply on evidence of the underlying conduct" which the state need prove only by a preponderance of the evidence. Surely, then it must be "constitutionally permissible to consider a prior uncounseled misdemeanor conviction based on the same conduct, where that conduct had to be proven beyond a reasonable doubt." In *Custis v. United States*,[33] the Court again upheld a lower court's refusal to examine the constitutionality of the defendant's prior convictions. The prosecutor had sought a mandatory sentence enhancement under the Armed Career Criminal Act based on three prior state felony convictions. The defendant argued he had received ineffective assistance of counsel in those cases and that under *Tucker* the resulting convictions could not be used to enhance his federal sentence. The Court rejected this argument, noting that in *Tucker* the violation of *Gideon* had rendered void defendant's earlier conviction and that this defect carried over to any enhanced sentence based upon the void conviction. The defect in *Tucker*, the Court emphasized, had not even been called to the attention of the trial court that imposed the enhanced sentence, yet the defect's "jurisdictional" nature allowed it to be raised in Tucker's collateral attack challenging his enhanced

sentence. Unlike the *Gideon* violation in *Tucker*—a "unique constitutional defect" because of its jurisdictional character—challenges to prior convictions based on other types of constitutional defects could not be raised as a basis for attacking the use of those convictions in sentencing[34]. Defendant must instead seek collateral relief from the prior convictions in state court, then, if successful, "apply for reopening of any federal sentence enhanced by the state sentences.''

As to other types of information considered at sentencing, lower courts have interpreted *Townsend* and *Tucker* generally to guarantee only that a defendant not be sentenced based upon "materially untrue" assumptions and to require that sentencing information carry a "sufficient indicia of reliability" to support its probable accuracy. The latter phrase has been used by the Court to describe the threshold showing necessary to overcome a challenge under the Confrontation Clause to hearsay at trial,[35] but the due process test for reliability in sentencing is less restrictive than the Court's confrontation standard. Hearsay information of the type included in presentence reports is typically allowed over constitutional objection, and the reliability of challenged statements may be established by corroborating evidence.[36] Some courts have insisted that due process bars reliance on particular types of questionable information (e.g., the hearsay statements of an unidentified informant) unless corroborative evidence or some other factor provides a reasonable basis for assuming it is trustworthy. Many jurisdictions allow the judge to indicate that a contested matter will not be taken into account as an alternative to determining whether the fact exists.

32. 511 U.S. 738, 114 S.Ct. 1921, 128 L.Ed.2d 745 (1994).

33. 511 U.S. 485, 114 S.Ct. 1732, 128 L.Ed.2d 517 (1994).

34. The Court in Daniels v. United States, 532 U.S. 374, 121 S.Ct. 1578, 149 L.Ed.2d 590 (2001), and Lackawanna County District Attorney v. Coss, 532 U.S. 394, 121 S.Ct. 1567, 149 L.Ed.2d 608 (2001), reiterated this rationale. In each case, the Court declined to allow a collateral attack to a sentence (under 28 U.S.C.A. § 2244 by Coss, a state prisoner; under § 2255 by Daniels, a federal prison-

er). Each petitioner had challenged his sentence claiming it was enhanced because of a prior conviction that was allegedly flawed due to ineffective assistance of counsel. Daniels also alleged that his prior convictions were defective because his decision to plead guilty to those charges was not knowing or voluntary.

35. Idaho v. Wright, 497 U.S. 805, 110 S.Ct. 3139, 111 L.Ed.2d 638 (1990).

36. See § 26.5(a).

(g) The Right to be Heard: Allocution and the Right to Offer Rebuttal Evidence. While some opportunity to object to the sentencing information relied upon by the court is generally considered part of the due process guaranteed to criminal defendants under the Constitution, that opportunity, at least in non-capital cases, does not necessarily include either the right to present evidence, or the right to make a personal unsworn statement to the sentencer, otherwise known as the right of allocution.

Defense Submissions. In several capital cases the Court has indicated that the defendant must be given the opportunity to present mitigating evidence on his own behalf at sentencing, basing this entitlement in the Due Process Clause as well as the Eighth Amendment. In *Gardner v. Florida*,[37] the Court found that a capital defendant had been denied this right where his counsel was given no opportunity "to challenge the accuracy or materiality" of information relied upon by the judge. The same principle was invoked in *Mempa v. Rhay*,[38] a non-capital case, where the Court explained that "counsel was necessary to assist defendant in marshaling the facts, *introducing evidence of mitigating circumstances* and * * * present[ing] his case as to sentence * * *." In addition, the Court's recognition of a due process right to present evidence in proceedings for parole and probation revocation,[39] situations in which the defendant's liberty interests as well as the risks of error are certainly no higher than they are during the initial sentencing proceeding, would also support constitutional protection for the defen-

dant's ability to present evidence at the sentencing hearing.

Nonetheless, courts occasionally have suggested that no such right to be heard exists.[40] In *McGautha v. California*,[41] the Court sidestepped the issue. One of the petitioners had claimed that because the sentencing in his capital case was left to the jury and because the state had refused to utilize a bifurcated trial, he had lost his right to present evidence on the issue of sentence when he exercised his self-incrimination privilege not to testify at trial. Rejecting that claim, the Court noted:

> This Court has not directly determined whether or to what extent the concept of due process of law requires that a criminal defendant wishing to present evidence or argument presumably relevant to the issues involved in sentencing should be permitted to do so. Assuming, without deciding, that the Constitution does require such an opportunity, there was no denial of such a right in Crampton's case. The Ohio Constitution guarantees defendants the right to have their counsel argue in summation for mercy as well as for acquittal. * * * [Also,] the record in Crampton's case does not reveal that any evidence offered on the part of the defendant was excluded on the ground that it was relevant solely to the issue of punishment.

Notwithstanding these conflicting signals about the necessity of providing to the defendant an opportunity to submit sentencing information to the court, judges traditionally have afforded defendants this opportunity. Courts often limit such presentations. Defense submissions may be rejected when the defen-

---

37. 430 U.S. 349, 97 S.Ct. 1197, 51 L.Ed.2d 393 (1977).

38. 389 U.S. 128, 88 S.Ct. 254, 19 L.Ed.2d 336 (1967) (emphasis added).

39. See Black v. Romano, 471 U.S. 606, 614, 105 S.Ct. 2254, 2259, 85 L.Ed.2d 636 (1985).

40. One such statement is found in Specht v. Patterson, discussed in § 26.4(i), where Justice Douglas began his opinion for the Court with the comment: "We held in *Williams v. New York*, that the Due Process Clause of the Fourteenth Amendment did not require a judge to have [sentencing] hearings and to give the convicted person an opportunity to participate in those hearings when he came to determine the sentence to be imposed." Other aspects of the *Specht* opinion suggest that Justice Douglas was referring only to a trial-type hearing, and that certainly is

the more appropriate reading of *Williams*. The Court in *Williams* obviously did not have before it the question of whether the defense could be denied the opportunity to present its own evidence relevant to the sentencing function. Moreover, the reasoning of the *Williams* Court does not support the denial of a defense right to be heard. Justice Black's opinion stressed that "modern concepts have made it all the more necessary that a sentencing judge not be denied an opportunity to obtain pertinent information." A court can hardly argue that out-of-court information is relevant but only when offered by the government.

41. 402 U.S. 183, 91 S.Ct. 1454, 28 L.Ed.2d 711 (1971).

dant fails to raise a timely and specific objection to sentencing information, or absents himself from sentencing. A court may also reject a defendant's submission whenever it rules that the disputed fact will not be taken into account in sentencing.

Courts also may limit the form that a defense presentation may take. Due process does not necessarily require formal hearings at sentencing during which the parties may present evidence on disputed facts. An entitlement to an evidentiary hearing is still viewed by many courts as "compromising the flexibility of the sentencing process." Accordingly, the extent to which statutes and court rules permit defense presentations on sentencing issues varies considerably from jurisdiction to jurisdiction. Many states give judges the discretion to grant or deny evidentiary hearings. In these jurisdictions, defendant may be limited to submitting a written report rather than presenting live testimony. Often, formal hearings will be required by statute for certain types of penalties, such as restitution or forfeiture. Evidentiary hearings are common, but not required, under federal law. Federal Rule 32(i) provides for a sentencing hearing at which the court "may" permit the parties to introduce evidence on objections to the presentence report. The United States Sentencing Guidelines Manual in Guideline 6A1.3 states that the "parties shall be given an adequate opportunity to present information" as to any factor "reasonably in dispute." The commentary to this guideline adds that an "evidentiary hearing may sometimes be the only reliable way to resolve disputed issues."

Allocution. The right of a defendant to make an unsworn statement on his own behalf at sentencing, known as the right of allocution, is recognized in most jurisdictions by court rule or statute and in some states by the state constitution. The right has its origins in the common law practice of allowing a defendant to state legal reasons why his sentence should not be imposed. This tradition arose at a time when the defendant had no right to be represented by counsel or to testify on his own behalf. Today, with counsel to speak for him and the ability to testify under oath, the defendant's need to make an unsworn statement in order to get across his side of the story to the sentencer is considerably less pressing. But the opportunity to personally address the sentencer retains both symbolic and practical significance. It may increase for some defendants the perceived equity of the process. Moreover, as the Supreme Court noted in *Green v. United States*,[42] a case which held that merely affording counsel a chance to speak fails to fulfill the allocution requirement in the federal rules, there are times when a plea in mitigation can best be presented by the defendant: "The most persuasive counsel may not be able to speak for a defendant as the defendant might, with halting eloquence, speak for himself." Allocution today typically includes any reason why the defendant feels a particular sentence should not be pronounced, but may be limited by the court to comments of a reasonable duration, to comments directed to the judge not the jury, or, in some jurisdictions, to "a plea for mercy" rather than a statement of historical fact.

Despite this widespread acceptance, the Supreme Court has not yet decided whether silencing a defendant who wishes to speak at sentencing is constitutional error. In *Hill v. United States*,[43] the Court held that in a case where defendant is represented by counsel, absent "aggravating circumstances," the failure of a judge to comply with Rule 32 of the Federal Rules of Criminal Procedure and ask the defendant whether he wished to say anything before imposition of sentence "is not a fundamental defect which inherently results in a complete miscarriage of justice" necessitating that the sentence be vacated. Also relevant in this regard is the Court's decision in *McGautha v. California.*[44] There, a petitioner claimed that because the sentencing in his capital case was left to the jury and because the state had refused to utilize a bifurcated trial, he had lost his right to present evidence on the issue of sentence when he exercised his

42. 365 U.S. 301, 81 S.Ct. 653, 5 L.Ed.2d 670 (1961).

43. 368 U.S. 424, 82 S.Ct. 468, 7 L.Ed.2d 417 (1962).

44. 402 U.S. 183, 91 S.Ct. 1454, 28 L.Ed.2d 711 (1971).

self-incrimination privilege not to testify at trial. Rejecting this claim, the Court noted that even assuming a criminal defendant had a right to present evidence or argument relevant to sentencing, there was no denial of the right in that case. The Court explained that defense *counsel* was given the opportunity to argue for leniency, and that the state is not required to provide an opportunity for the defendant to speak to the jury free from any adverse consequences on the issue of guilt. Citing *McGautha*, some lower courts have upheld a judge's insistence that defendants be sworn as witnesses and be subject to cross-examination in order to speak at sentencing. The risk that the defendant's statements at sentencing may be used against him later may deter a defendant from exercising any allocution opportunity. To eliminate this "hard testimonial choice," some courts have advocated use immunity for statements made by defendants during sentencing proceedings.

(h) Burden of Proof. When a sentence depends upon particular facts, the degree of certainty by which the existence of those facts must be established during sentencing is also an important element of due process. In *McMillan v. Pennsylvania*,[45] the Court considered this issue in a case involving sentencing under a statute that mandated a minimum sentence of five years upon proof that defendant visibly possessed a weapon during the commission of his offense. The statute directed the sentencing judge to determine whether possession was established by a preponderance of the evidence introduced at the trial and sentencing hearing. The defendant challenged this scheme as constitutionally deficient. The Court initially rejected defendant's reliance upon decisions requiring proof beyond a reasonable doubt in criminal cases, as that standard had been held to be required by due process only as to the elements defining the

crime.[46] The preponderance standard was sufficient for sentencing facts, the Court explained, at least where there was no allegation that the sentencing enhancement was so significant that it became "a tail which wags the dog of the substantive offense." The Court rejected the contention that at least a clear and convincing evidence standard should be required where, as here, the sentencing factor in question had a mandatory consequence. The preponderance standard, it noted, was constitutionally acceptable at trial for proof of defenses and mitigating factors that do not negate elements of the crime. Additionally, the court observed, "sentencing courts have traditionally heard evidence and found facts without any prescribed burden at all."

In *United States v. Watts*,[47] the Court in a per curiam opinion rejected the claim that due process is compromised whenever a sentencing court increases a sentence based upon conduct for which the defendant had been previously tried and acquitted. Citing *Williams* and *McMillan*, the Court reasoned that "application of the preponderance standard at sentencing generally satisfies due process" and that "a jury's verdict of acquittal does not prevent the sentencing court from considering conduct underlying the acquitted charge, so long as that conduct has been proved by a preponderance of the evidence."

While the Court in *McMillan* and *Watts* found that the preponderance standard was sufficient in the situations presented in those cases, it has not addressed whether a different standard might be appropriate in other contexts. Capital cases may require more exacting standards, for example. Less exacting standards may also be consistent with due process in some situations. Many lower courts, for example, adopt the information set forth in the presentence report without further inqui-

45. 477 U.S. 79, 106 S.Ct. 2411, 91 L.Ed.2d 67 (1986).

46. Thus, the Court had previously held that the reasonable doubt requirement did not apply to factors relating to the level of the crime where those factors were not elements of the legislative definition of the crime. See e.g. Patterson v. New York, 432 U.S. 197, 97 S.Ct. 2319, 53 L.Ed.2d 281 (1977) (where mitigating factor of provocation did not negate the required mental element for murder and, therefore, was not an element of that offense or the

lesser offense of manslaughter, the state could shift the burden of proof as to provocation to the defense, under a preponderance standard, rather than require the prosecution to prove beyond a reasonable doubt that provocation did not exist).

47. 519 U.S. 148, 117 S.Ct. 633, 136 L.Ed.2d 554 (1997).

ry, provided it has some minimal basis, unless the defendant identifies specific factual inaccuracies or offers "rebuttal evidence." Other courts will shift the burden of rebutting sentencing information only after the government has first established the reliability of its allegations. The burden of proving facts that may prompt a more lenient sentence is often placed on the defendant. In *Walton v. Arizona*,[48] a plurality of justices reasoned that a state may require a capital defendant to prove mitigating circumstances relevant to sentencing by a preponderance, so long as the prosecution first proves the elements of the offense and the existence of aggravating circumstances. As the Court stated in *Apprendi v. New Jersey*:[49]

> If facts found by a jury support a guilty verdict of murder, the judge is authorized by that jury verdict to sentence the defendant to the maximum sentence provided by the murder statute. If the defendant can escape the statutory maximum by showing, for example, that he is a war veteran, then a judge that finds the fact of veteran status is neither exposing the defendant to a deprivation of liberty greater than that authorized by the verdict according to statute, nor is the Judge imposing upon the defendant a greater stigma than that accompanying the jury verdict alone. Core concerns animating the jury and burden-of-proof requirements are thus absent from such a scheme.[50]

(i) Heightened Protection for Exceptional Enhancements that Constitute Separate Offenses. It is clear from the preceding discussion that *Williams* remains influential in the Court's rulings upholding as consistent with due process a wide variety of sentencing procedures. There are, however, limits to a legislature's ability to characterize certain penalties as mere sentence enhancements rather than as separate offenses. In

Specht v. Patterson,[51] the Court found that the Colorado legislature had exceeded these limits. The Court held that the penalty in that case was so like a separate offense and so unlike a sentence that it required the "full panoply" of trial-type procedural safeguards.

Specht involved a constitutional challenge to the Colorado Sex Offenders Act. The Act gave the trial court the authority to impose an indeterminate sentence of one day to life upon a person convicted of any one of a group of specified sex offenses, if the trial court was "of the opinion that [the] person, if at large, constitutes a threat of bodily harm to members of the public, or is an habitual offender and mentally ill." The trial court had to order "a complete psychiatric exam" and the report of that exam, including the psychiatrist's recommendation as to disposition, was to be considered by it in deciding whether to apply the Act. The defendant in *Specht* had been sentenced to an indeterminate life sentence under the Act following his conviction for indecent liberties, an offense carrying a maximum sentence of ten years. He challenged the application of the Act as denying him due process because the court's finding was made "(1) without a hearing at which * * * [he] could confront and cross-examine adverse witnesses and present evidence of his own by use of compulsory process * * * and (2) on the basis of hearsay evidence to which * * * [he was] not allowed access." In sustaining the defendant's challenge, the Court distinguished *Williams*, calling the situation before it "radically different." The Colorado act, the *Specht* Court noted, did "not make the commission of a specified crime the basis for sentencing." Rather "it ma[de] one conviction the basis for commencing another proceeding under another Act," a proceeding that must take the form of a full judicial hearing. Turning to the par-

---

48. 497 U.S. 639, 110 S.Ct. 3047, 111 L.Ed.2d 511 (1990).

49. Discussed in § 26.4(i).

50. The Court later repudiated that portion of *Walton* that upheld as complying with the Sixth Amendment the state's law authorizing judicial rather than jury determination of aggravating facts necessary for the death sentence. See Ring v. Arizona, discussed at note 60. However, the Court in *Ring* expressly noted that Ring had made no

Sixth Amendment claim with respect to mitigating circumstances, leaving open the constitutional requirements for establishing mitigating factors in sentencing. It follows that due process would permit legislatures to place upon the defendant the burden of proving mitigating factors in non-capital cases as well.

51. 386 U.S. 605, 87 S.Ct. 1209, 18 L.Ed.2d 326 (1967).

ticular rights required for that hearing, the Court stated: "Due process requires that [defendant] be present with counsel, have an opportunity to be heard, be confronted with witnesses against him, have the right to cross-examine, and to offer evidence of his own. And there must be findings adequate to make meaningful any appeal that is allowed."

The Court in two subsequent cases refused to treat an enhancement as a separate offense. It first distinguished *Specht* in its decision in *McMillan v. Pennsylvania*.[52] The enhancement provision challenged in *McMillan* imposed a mandatory minimum term of five years upon a finding that the defendant "visibly possessed a firearm" during the commission of the offense. The issue before the Court was whether due process required proof of the enhancement factor by a standard more demanding than that of a "preponderance of the evidence." Although *Specht* had not dealt with the burden of proof issue, the defendant in *McMillan* argued that had *Specht* been decided following the Court's holding that due process required a reasonable doubt standard of proof for a criminal offense, it would have required that standard for distinct post-trial findings triggering enhanced penalties. Responding to that contention, the *McMillan* Court admitted that in certain limited circumstances, facts not identified as elements of the offense charged must be treated as such, but not in this case. "The finding of visible possession of a firearm of course 'ups the ante' for a defendant, or it would not be challenged here," the Court stated, "but it does so only in the way that we have previously mentioned, by raising the minimum sentence that may be imposed by the trial court."

In *Almendarez–Torres v. United States*,[53] the Court rejected heightened protections for recidivist enhancements. It held that a recidivist statute that increased the defendant's maximum sentence from two to *twenty* years upon a finding of a prior conviction did not constitute a separate crime, nor was the prior conviction a separate "element" that should have been charged in the indictment. It expressed no view on whether a higher burden of proof would be required for other especially dramatic sentence enhancements.

The Court next avoided the necessity of addressing this constitutional question head on when it considered in *Jones v. United States*[54] a federal statute that provided a sentence maximum 15 years for the crime of carjacking, and a sentence maximum of 25 years if "serious bodily injury * * * results." The Court concluded that as a matter of statutory interpretation, the statute defined separate offenses, one carrying a maximum sentence of 25 years, and another carrying a maximum sentence of 15 years. Serious bodily harm, the Court decided, was an element that must be proven beyond a reasonable doubt to a jury, rejecting the government's invitation to interpret the statute as designating a single offense with the finding of serious injury serving as "merely a sentencing factor." It noted that another provision in the same statute increased the penalty range to life in prison if "death results." Drawing on *McMillan*, the Court explained that the government's interpretation of the statute would raise serious constitutional questions. It would "shrink" the jury's role "from the significance usually carried by determinations of guilt to the relative importance of low-level gatekeeping: in some cases a jury finding of fact necessary for a maximum 15–year sentence would merely open the door to a judicial finding sufficient for life imprisonment." Reviewing the historical background of the right to jury trial, the *Jones* majority stated that the "diminution of the jury's significance by removing control over facts determining a statutory sentencing would resonate with the claims of earlier controversies, to raise a genuine Sixth Amendment issue not yet settled." The principle "animating" the Court's view that the government's view of the statute "may violate the Constitution," was that "under the Due Process Clause of the Fifth Amendment and

---

52. 477 U.S. 79, 106 S.Ct. 2411, 91 L.Ed.2d 67 (1986), also discussed in § 26.4(h).

53. 523 U.S. 224, 118 S.Ct. 1219, 140 L.Ed.2d 350 (1998).

54. 526 U.S. 227, 119 S.Ct. 1215, 143 L.Ed.2d 311 (1999).

the notice and jury trial guarantees of the Sixth Amendment, any fact (other than prior conviction) that increases the maximum penalty for a crime must be charged in an indictment, submitted to a jury, and proven beyond a reasonable doubt." *Almendarez–Torres*, the Court explained, did not resolve these constitutional questions, because of the "constitutional distinctiveness" of recidivism. "[U]nlike virtually any other consideration used to enlarge the possible penalty for an offense, and certainly unlike the factor before us in this case, a prior conviction must itself have been established through procedures satisfying the fair notice, reasonable doubt, and jury trial guarantees."

The very next term, in *Apprendi v. New Jersey*,[55] the Court adopted the principle announced in *Jones*. Apprendi had been charged with several weapons offenses after firing shots into the home of an African–American family. A New Jersey "hate-crime" statute provided an enhanced sentence range for any crime, once a judge determine by a preponderance that the defendant "in committing the crime acted with a purpose to intimidate an individual or group of individuals because of race, color, gender, handicap, religion, sexual orientation or ethnicity." In Apprendi's case, it meant that the potential sentence range would double, from ten years for the underlying offense of possession of a weapon for an unlawful purpose, to twenty years. As part of his plea agreement Apprendi reserved the right to challenge the enhancement, and at sentencing he contested the allegation of biased purpose, presenting his own testimony and the testimony of character witnesses to contradict the allegation by the state that he had admitted that he shot at the house because the occupants were black. The trial judge found the state's evidence more credible, and ruled that the enhancement applied. The United States Supreme Court found that Apprendi had been denied his right to a jury determination be-

yond a reasonable doubt of each offense element.

Writing for the Court, Justice Stevens stated, "Other than the fact of a prior conviction, any fact that increases the penalty for a crime beyond the prescribed statutory maximum must be submitted to a jury, and proved beyond a reasonable doubt." He defended the ruling as supported by precedent as well as the historical practice of American and English courts. Justice Thomas (joined in part by Justice Scalia) concurred, supporting an even broader rule designating as elements prior convictions, as well as all factual findings that modify the permissible sentencing range, including mandatory minimums.[56]

In separate opinions representing the four dissenting justices, Justices O'Connor and Breyer warned that the "watershed change in constitutional law" adopted by the Court may threaten laudable efforts to control judicial discretion through determinate sentencing, including the United States Sentencing Guidelines. Justice Stevens noted, however, that only those facts that increase the *maximum* penalty range must be treated as elements, so that the ruling should not disturb legislative efforts like the Guidelines that guide or limit judicial discretion *within* the stated statutory maximum punishment for the offense proven beyond a reasonable doubt.

Even this narrower rule, the dissenters argued, was objectionable as: 1) unsupported by history and prior decisions of the Court; 2) "unworkable" in light of the large number of factors that are necessarily considered in sentencing; 3) unwise, in that it may require either that courts use costly bifurcated jury proceedings or that a defendant deny committing the crime yet offer proof about how he committed it ("I did not sell drugs, but I sold no more than 500 grams"); and 4) "pure formalism," easily avoided by raising the sentence maximum for a crime so that the very same statutory sentence enhancements operate without jury consideration to control sen-

---

55. 530 U.S. 466, 120 S.Ct. 2348, 147 L.Ed.2d 435 (2000).

56. This broader rule would doom *Almendarez–Torres* and *McMillan*, but Justice Stevens' opinion for the Court

rejected the claim that it was overruling *McMillan*, and specifically declined to reconsider *Almendarez–Torres* or the issue of what is an element for purposes of indictment under the Grand Jury Clause of the Fifth Amendment.

tences within that maximum. For example, by rewriting the statute in *Jones* so that carjacking is punishable by life in prison, with a judicial finding of the absence of aggravating factors triggering lower sentence maximums, Congress could continue to assign the determination of those aggravating factors to a judge rather than a jury. Similarly, New Jersey could rewrite its offenses to authorize higher sentence maximums, but provide lower penalty limits unless a judge found biased purpose by a preponderance.

"While a State could, hypothetically, undertake to revise its entire criminal code in the manner the dissent suggests—extending all statutory maximum sentences to, for example, 50 years and giving judges guided discretion as to a few specially selected factors within that range," Justice Stevens responded, "this possibility seems remote." Citing Justice Powell's dissenting opinion in *Patterson*, he argued that "structural democratic constraints exist to discourage legislatures from enacting penal statutes that expose every defendant convicted of, for example, weapons possession, to a maximum sentence exceeding that which is in the legislature's judgment generally proportional to the crime." The rule ensures that a state must " 'make its choices concerning the substantive content of its criminal laws with full awareness of the consequence, unable to mask substantive policy choices' of exposing all who are convicted to the maximum sentence it provides." So exposed, the Court continued, " 'the political check on potentially harsh legislative action is then more likely to operate.' " Even if "such an extensive revision of the State's entire criminal code were enacted for the purpose the dissent suggests, or if New Jersey simply reversed the burden of the hate crime finding (effectively assuming a crime was performed with a purpose to intimidate and then requiring a defendant to prove that it was not) we would be required to question whether the revision was constitutional under this Court's prior decisions."

In *Harris v. United States*,[57] in a narrow 4:1:4 vote, the Court rejected the reasoning of Justice Thomas' concurring opinion in *Apprendi* and reaffirmed *McMillan*. In *Harris*, the defendant challenged his mandatory minimum sentence arguing that a jury, not a judge, should have determined the fact that triggered that higher minimum. Justice Kennedy, writing for a plurality of four justices,[58] reasoned that while "any fact extending the defendant's sentence beyond the maximum authorized by the jury's verdict would have been considered an element of an aggravated crime—and thus the domain of the jury—by those who framed the Bill of Rights[, t]he same cannot be said of a fact increasing the mandatory minimum (but not extending the sentence beyond the statutory maximum), for the jury's verdict has authorized the judge to impose the minimum with or without the finding." Courts at the founding and in the mid–19th century "were not as a general matter required to decide whether a fact giving rise to a mandatory minimum sentence within the available range was to be alleged in the indictment and proved to the jury." Judges considered sentencing facts when exercising their discretion within the statutory range, and those facts "do not become [elements] merely because legislatures require the judge to impose a minimum sentence when those facts are found—a sentence the judge could have imposed absent the finding." Justice Breyer, concurring, maintained that *Apprendi* was wrongly decided and joined the Court's opinion only "to the extent that it holds that *Apprendi* does not apply to mandatory minimums." The plurality's reliance on "historical evidence" prompted Justice Stevens, writing for the dissenters, to comment: "Whether one raises the floor or raises the ceiling it is impossible to dispute that the defendant is exposed to greater punishment than is otherwise prescribed. This is no less true because mandatory minimum sentences are a 20th century phenomena." *Harris* appears to have insulated mandatory minimum

---

57. 536 U.S. 545, 122 S.Ct. 2406, 153 L.Ed.2d 524 (2002).

58. Justice Kennedy's opinion was joined in full by Chief Justice Rehnquist and Justice Scalia. Justice O'Con-

nor concurred, joining Justice Kennedy's opinion in its entirety, but maintaining, "I dissented in *Jones* and *Apprendi* and still believe both were wrongly decided."

sentencing statutes, as well as the mandatory sentencing guidelines schemes that resemble them, from attack under *Apprendi*.

In *United States v. Cotton*,[59] the Court made clear that *Apprendi* did require the government to allege in the indictment those facts that raised the sentence maximum, but held that the failure to do so was subject to plain error review. In *Ring v. Arizona*,[60] a majority of justices admitted that the Court in *Apprendi* had interpreted Arizona death penalty law incorrectly when it had reasoned that state law authorized the death penalty upon the jury's conviction of a defendant for first degree murder. Rather, state law required an additional finding of an aggravating fact before a death sentence could be imposed. That additional fact, after *Apprendi*, must be found by a jury beyond a reasonable doubt. The Court overruled that decision. To the extent that the decision in *Walton v. Arizona*[61] had held otherwise, *Ring* threw into question hundreds of death sentences from the handful of states that had statutes like Arizona's which allowed judges to make findings of aggravating facts needed to impose capital punishment.

§ 26.5 Sentencing Information

(a) Evidentiary Standards. The traditional policy regarding the range and nature of the information that may be considered by a sentencing judge is succinctly stated in 18 U.S.C.A. § 3661:

> No limitation shall be placed on the information concerning the background, character, and conduct of a person convicted of an offense which a court * * * may receive and consider for the purpose of imposing an appropriate sentence.

This policy finds support in the Supreme Court's reasoning in *Williams v. New York*,[1] and its comment there that "modern concepts individualizing punishment have made it all the more necessary that a sentencing judge not be denied an opportunity to obtain pertinent information by a requirement of rigid adherence to restrictive rules of evidence properly applicable to the trial." The Federal Rules of Evidence incorporate this traditional position in Rule 1101(d), which provides that "the rules (other than with respect to privileges) do not apply in * * * sentencing." Similar provisions are found in the many state statutes or rules governing the rules of evidence. As discussed in § 26.4(f) affidavits may be received at sentencing even though the defendant has no opportunity to confront or cross-examine the affiant. The sentencing court can consider other types of hearsay, whether contained in the presentence report or offered by the prosecution or defense. The court may also consider testimony given at a trial, even when the defendant was not a participant in that trial.

Evidence obtained in violation of the Fourth Amendment and thus barred from trial use may be considered at sentencing as well. Statements elicited in violation of a defendant's sixth amendment right to counsel must be excluded, however, as are statements elicited in violation of the defendant's rights under the Fifth Amendment, at least from capital sentencing proceedings. As the Court explained in *Estelle v. Smith*,[2] "any effort by the State to compel respondent to testify against his will at the sentencing hearing would contravene the Fifth Amendment * * *. [T]he State's attempt to establish respondent's future dangerousness by relying on the unwarned statements he made to [a psychiatrist before trial] similarly infringes Fifth Amendment values." State-

---

59. 535 U.S. 625, 122 S.Ct. 1781, 152 L.Ed.2d 860 (2002).

60. 536 U.S. 584, 122 S.Ct. 2428, 153 L.Ed.2d 556 (2002).

61. See note 48.

§ 26.5

1. 337 U.S. 241, 69 S.Ct. 1079, 93 L.Ed. 1337 (1949). *Williams* and the scope of sentencing information is discussed in § 26.4(a) and (b).

2. 451 U.S. 454, 101 S.Ct. 1866, 68 L.Ed.2d 359 (1981) (statements taken during psychiatric exam in violation of fifth amendment privilege against self-incrimination and sixth amendment right to counsel could not be introduced at capital sentencing hearing).

ments made in presentence interviews to probation officers need not be preceded by warnings, however, so that the rule in *Estelle* has not affected their use. In sum, with the possible exception of privileged material, the basic approach, as stated in the official commentary to the U.S. Sentencing Guidelines, is that "any information may be considered, so long as it has 'sufficient indicia of reliability to support its probable accuracy.' "

Notwithstanding the above policy, courts and commentators have noted the need for caution in utilizing certain categories of evidence. For example, several courts have suggested that hearsay from an unnamed informant should not be included in a presentence report unless there is "good cause" for the nondisclosure of the informant's identity or there is sufficient corroboration. Other courts have exercised caution in considering the testimony of drug addicts.

Another troublesome area involves the treatment of various criminal justice records. Law enforcement compilations of prior criminal records require some degree of caution for several reasons. First, there is a tendency to accept such records as inherently reliable, without seeking any type of corroboration. In fact, "rap sheets" have proven to be incorrect with alarming frequency. Second, informal methods of communication sometimes utilized may result in even correct records being mistakenly reported. There is also a need to identify prior convictions that fall within *United States v. Tucker*,[3] which held that a defendant's sentencing could not stand when imposed by a judge who considered a prior uncounseled conviction. As a result, although the Court has held that due process does not bar the consideration of conduct by the defendant of which he was acquitted or not charged[4] many courts limit the use of arrest records to establish such conduct.

(b) The Presentence Report. The presentence report is a singularly important document for the sentencing and correctional processes. It often serves as the primary source of information about the defendant and the offense, supplemented by trial evidence, victims' statements, the defendant's allocution, or other submissions by defense and prosecution. The report is prepared by a probation officer and represents the product of the officer's presentence investigation. The report provides information bearing upon the choice between probation and imprisonment, upon the probation conditions that should be imposed if the former alternative is chosen, and upon the length of the prison term that should be imposed if the latter alternative is selected. In addition, the report is usually the major source of information for other significant decisions: the probation officer's determination of the appropriate level of supervision if the defendant is placed on probation; and if the defendant is incarcerated, decisions regarding the institution at which he will be held, his classification within the institution, his release on parole, and his supervision during parole.

A probation officer usually prepares a presentence report after an in-depth interview with the defendant in order to obtain his account of the offense and information about the defendant's background and circumstances. The probation officer contacts the prosecutor and law enforcement agents connected with the case in order to get their version of the offense and other information they may have about defendant's activities. The probation officer will ascertain the defendant's prior criminal record and may contact various individuals and agencies who might provide additional information about the defendant, such as members of his family, present and past employers, the victim of the crime, and medical, educational, financial, and military institutions with whom the defendant has had dealings. In its final form, the presentence report usually contains information about a defendant's prior criminal record, financial condition, and any circumstances affecting defendant's behavior that may be helpful in sentencing or correctional treatment.

---

3. 404 U.S. 443, 92 S.Ct. 589, 30 L.Ed.2d 592 (1972), discussed in § 26.4(f).

4. See United States v. Watts, 519 U.S. 148, 117 S.Ct. 633, 136 L.Ed.2d 554 (1997), discussed in § 26.4(h).

Under a presumptive sentencing system, the presentence report will respond to each of the elements identified in the statutory listing of aggravating or mitigating factors, and under a guidelines system, it will consider all of the factors contributing to the offense level and the criminal-history category.[5] The inclusion of a detailed description of the crime is especially important where the defendant pleads guilty, as the court will not have the trial evidence to look to in applying the various distinctions relevant to characterizing the offense.

In the federal system and in some states, the presentence report may be prepared prior to the defendant's guilty plea or conviction. There are several reasons for delaying preparation of the presentence report until after the determination of guilt, most importantly the danger that prior to conviction the contents of the report might come to the attention of the court, the prosecution, or the jury. The Supreme Court has intimated that disclosure of the report before conviction may prejudice the judge and constitute reversible error.[6] It may often be wise, however, for the defense to give its consent to having the judge inspect the report earlier, so that the judge will have a basis for determining whether he will concur in a plea agreement which has been reached by the parties.

Many jurisdictions make the use of the presentence report mandatory for all felony cases. Others require a report unless the judge makes a specific finding that the evidence on the record is sufficient to stand alone. Many states leave the decision to order a presentence report to the discretion of the judge, although some then require it for certain dispositions (e.g., probation).

(c) Disclosure of the Presentence Report. At one time, there was a presumption against disclosure of the presentence report to the defense due to concerns that disclosure would (1) impair the collection of vital information from persons afraid of reprisal or public notoriety, and (2) damage the defendant's rehabilitation by adversely affecting his relationships with family, friends, or the probation officer who might supervise his community release. Those arguments were found wanting in light of the experience of courts that had experimented with regular disclosure of presentence reports. At the same time, decisions such as *Gardner* cast doubt upon the constitutionality of failing to give the defense any notice of the contents of the report.[7] The end result was the gradual emergence of a consensus that disclosure should be the norm. Today the vast majority of jurisdictions have adopted, by statute, court rule, or judicial decision, mandatory disclosure of at least a portion of the presentence report. Where disclosure is authorized, the applicable standard ordinarily provides that disclosure will be made to the defendant, as well as to defense counsel and the prosecution.

Among those jurisdictions mandating disclosure, the majority have provisions authorizing the court to withhold portions of the report under certain circumstances. When exclusions are authorized, they tend to be fairly limited. Federal Rule 32(d)(3) is typical. It provides that the report must not include (1) "any diagnoses that, if disclosed, might seriously disrupt a rehabilitation program," (2) "sources of information obtained upon a promise of confidentiality," or (3) "any other information that, if disclosed, might result in physical or other harm to the defendant or others." Federal prisoners are not banned from receiving a copy of their presentence report under the Freedom of Information Act, but are not enti-

---

5. Under the federal guidelines system, for example, the probation officer is required to inform the court of: (1) the defendant's history and characteristics as well as any circumstances helpful in imposing sentence or in correctional treatment; (2) the guideline categories that the officer believes apply to the particular case; (3) the kinds of sentences and the sentencing range believed to apply; (4) any factors that may indicate that a sentence of a different type would be appropriate; (5) pertinent policy statements issued by the Sentencing Commission; (6) the financial, social, psychological, and medical impact on any

victims; (7) the nature and extent of non-prison programs available to the defendant; (8) information sufficient for the court to order restitution; (9) the results and report of any study ordered by the court; and (10) any other information required by the court.

6. Gregg v. United States, 394 U.S. 489, 89 S.Ct. 1134, 22 L.Ed.2d 442 (1969) (finding no evidence that judge saw the report before the jury verdict was returned).

7. See § 26.4 (d).

tled to "any information in the report that relates to confidential sources, diagnostic opinions, and other information that may cause harm to the defendant or to third parties."[8] Although some have criticized the federal exceptions to disclosure as unduly broad, most states recognize similar exceptions, banning disclosure of such matters as the sentencing recommendation of the probation officer or diagnostic reports.

Statute or rule also regulates the timing of disclosure. Recognizing that early disclosure is needed in order to provide the defense an opportunity to check the accuracy of the report, particularly in jurisdictions employing guidelines or other presumptive sentencing systems in which each fact may mean added prison time, many provisions require disclosure of the report well in advance of the sentencing hearing. Where there are no specific timing requirements, courts require that the report be disclosed early enough to provide the defendant and his counsel a reasonable opportunity to review the report before sentencing.

Information in the presentence report is often shared with corrections agencies and used after sentencing in connection with various correctional decisions. In the federal system, for example, personnel of the Federal Bureau of Prisons use the presentence report in making decisions affecting every aspect of an inmate's confinement, from his institutional designation and custody level to his living quarters and work assignment. In addition, paroling authorities use the report to provide information about the offense and the offender in their parole decisions. The fact that the presentence report is used at the correctional stage in these ways is often given inadequate attention by defense counsel. Such usage means, for one thing, that there is even more reason for counsel to take all available measures to ensure that the factual allegations in the report are correct. For another, it means that steps which are adequate to keep false or disputed allegations out of the sentencing process will not necessarily ensure that the defendant is not adversely affected later by those very allegations. For example, a sentencing

court may foreclose any contest as to disputed allegations by an assurance that it will completely disregard that part of the report in sentencing. Or, the judge may actually make a finding for the record that a certain allegation in the report is false, but without causing the report itself to be corrected. If either of these steps fail to be communicated to later users of the presentence report then subsequent decisions of importance to the defendant may be based upon assertions previously determined to be false or at least to be not so obviously true as to be worthy of reliance. In an effort to avoid such consequences, defense counsel at sentencing may request that a notation be appended to the presentence report regarding what allegations were found to be unsupported and what allegations were disregarded because they were disputed. Such clarification is now required in the federal system.

Access to presentence reports by third parties is strictly limited by courts. The party seeking disclosure usually must demonstrate a particularized compelling need, similar to the showing required for access to grand jury proceedings, in order to protect the privacy and safety of defendants, victims, and other sources of sentencing information.

(d) Victim Impact Statements. In recent years, the victims' rights movement has resulted in the widespread adoption of statutes or constitutional provisions that authorize or require consideration of victim impact statements during the sentencing stage. These provisions, also discussed in § 1.4(k), typically allow victims the right to make an oral statement at sentencing or provide that the victim's written statement appear in the presentence report, or both. The victim is usually defined as any individual who suffers direct or threatened physical, emotional, or financial harm as a result of the crime. The function of the victim statement is to provide information about the financial, emotional, and physical effects of the crime on the victim and the victim's family. It may also include information regarding the circumstances surrounding the crime and the manner in which it was

---

8. United States Dep't of Justice v. Julian, 486 U.S. 1, 108 S.Ct. 1606, 100 L.Ed.2d 1 (1988).

perpetrated as well as, in some states, the victim's views on the appropriate sentence. Unlike the presentence report, which would only summarize the probation officer's interview of the victim, the victim impact statement is sometimes presented in the victim's own words. Where there are numerous victims and obtaining a statement from each would not be feasible, one or more representative statements may be used. Of course, the victim is not required to make an impact statement, and some evidence suggests that victims often fail to exercise their opportunity to do so.

As discussed in § 26.4 and earlier in this section, due process typically does not require that information presented at sentencing meet evidentiary standards applied at trial, nor does it bar the use of hearsay in connection with sentencing. Nevertheless, some courts require that victim statements be made under oath to meet minimal standards of reliability, or permit a judge to exclude statements that are too prejudicial.

The use of victim statements has been particularly controversial in capital cases. Four years after holding that the Eighth Amendment barred the use of victim impact statements in capital cases as irrelevant to the sentencing decision,[9] the Court in *Payne v. Tennessee*[10] reversed itself. The Court reasoned that the use of victim impact evidence serves the legitimate purpose of illustrating the harm caused by a defendant's crime and is "surely relevant in determining [a defendant's] blameworthiness." Despite the Court's endorsement in *Payne* of the constitutionality of victim evidence, several states continue to limit its introduction in capital cases.

§ 26.6 Special Sentences

(a) Special Sentences and Special Procedures. Sentencing statutes may provide for extended or alternative terms of imprisonment or special financial sanctions. These provisions may carry with them special sentencing procedures, including advanced notice of the use of the special sentencing provision, trial-type procedures as to the proof of historical facts, and specified burdens of production and persuasion. The extent to which due process requires such safeguards is discussed generally in § 26.4. The sections that follow deal more specifically with four significant special sentences: recidivist penalties, restitution, forfeiture, and penalties for dangerous offenders.

(b) Recidivist Statutes. Most states have enacted provisions that authorize extended terms for repeat offenders, variously labeled as "recidivists," "second offenders," "persistent violators," and "habitual criminals." In recent years, a growing number of states and the federal government have adopted "three-strikes-and-you're-out" legislation that imposes a mandatory sentence on repeat offenders.[1] A handful of these statutes mandate a life sentence upon the third felony regardless of the classification of the prior felonies. Others require that the prior felonies involve violence, narcotics, or the use of a firearm. Jurisdictions also differ as to how many of the "strikes" must be of the specified nature. A small number of states have adopted two-strikes provisions for particularly serious felonies while others have adopted four-strikes provisions.

Many jurisdictions treat a defendant's prior record just like any other sentencing fact, following the theory that repeat-offender status merely enhances the sentence for the defendant's current crime and is not a separate offense. The prosecutor initiates the repeat-offender proceeding after conviction and prior to the imposition of the sentence for the principal offense. In *Almendarez–Torres v. United States*,[2] the Court confirmed that heightened protections are not constitutionally required

---

9. Booth v. Maryland, 482 U.S. 496, 107 S.Ct. 2529, 96 L.Ed.2d 440 (1987) (reasoning that "while the full range of foreseeable consequences of a defendant's actions may be relevant in other criminal and civil contexts, we cannot agree that it is relevant in the unique circumstances of a capital sentencing hearing").

10. 501 U.S. 808, 111 S.Ct. 2597, 115 L.Ed.2d 720 (1991).

§ 26.6

1. See Ewing v. California, 538 U.S. 11, 123 S.Ct. 1179, 155 L.Ed.2d 108 (2003) (rejecting eighth amendment challenge to sentence under California's three-strikes law).

2. 523 U.S. 224, 118 S.Ct. 1219, 140 L.Ed.2d 350 (1998).

for recidivist enhancements. The case involved a statutory provision extending to twenty years the maximum two-year penalty for unauthorized reentry into the United States, upon a finding that the initial decision to deport the defendant "was subsequent to a conviction for commission of an aggravated felony." The Court rejected the defendant's claim that the existence of the prior conviction was an "element" that should have been charged in the indictment. Withholding notice of intent to seek penalties under a recidivist statute until after conviction had also been upheld by the Supreme Court in *Oyler v. Boles.*[3] Earlier cases also established that due process did not require that a jury determine the existence of a prior conviction,[4] or that a prior conviction be proven beyond a reasonable doubt. Instead, a judicial determination of the prior offense by a preponderance of the evidence was sufficient.[5] Although the Court in *Almendarez–Torres* took care to express "no view on whether some heightened standard of proof might apply to sentencing determinations which bear significantly on the severity of sentence," its reasoning certainly undercut the basis for applying a more exacting burden of proof for recidivist status. Construing recidivism to carry the same protections as an element, the Court explained, "would mark an abrupt departure from a longstanding tradition of treating recidivism as go[ing] to the punishment only." In Apprendi v. New Jersey, discussed in § 26.4(i) the Court declined to disturb *Almendarez–Torres,* ruling: "Other than the fact of a prior conviction, any fact that increases the penalty for a crime beyond the prescribed statutory maximum must be submitted to a jury, and proved beyond a reasonable doubt."

In light of the effect of recidivist statutes in extending the defendant's term beyond the maximum allowed for the offense of conviction, a substantial number of jurisdictions impose more formal procedures for determining repeat-offender status, though these procedures may not be constitutionally required. Pretrial notice of intent to seek recidivist penalties is mandated by statute in many of these jurisdictions, and some require that the notice of intent to seek recidivist penalties be included in the indictment or information. In many states, a jury decides whether the defendant is a habitual offender, usually the same jury that decided the defendant's guilt. Most require that the repeat offender issue be withheld from the factfinder until guilt is determined, even though, as discussed in § 26.2(b), a bifurcated trial is not required by due process.[6] Often the prosecutor must prove the defendant's prior convictions beyond a reasonable doubt at these trial-like hearings. The rules of evidence typically apply, requiring prosecutors to prove the defendant's past conviction through public records or witnesses subject to cross-examination.

Factual disputes about whether a defendant was indeed convicted are no longer common in recidivist proceedings, as they once were in the 19th century before the development of reliable methods of identification. More common are legal disputes about whether or not particular convictions count under the particular repeat offender statute. Convictions pardoned on the ground of innocence, stale convictions, juvenile convictions, and certain convictions from other jurisdictions may be excluded by statute. Or, a statute may require that in order for the prior offense to qualify, it must have been committed in a particular manner. Many recidivist statutes have been held to require that each prior felony conviction arise from a distinct transaction, on the theory that

3. 368 U.S. 448, 82 S.Ct. 501, 7 L.Ed.2d 446 (1962).

4. Hildwin v. Florida, 490 U.S. 638, 640, 109 S.Ct. 2055, 104 L.Ed.2d 728 (1989) (upholding judicial rather than jury determination, noting that "the existence of an aggravating factor is not an element of the offense but instead is a sentencing factor that comes into play only after the defendant has been found guilty").

5. See *Oyler,* supra note 3, and Parke v. Raley, 506 U.S. 20, 113 S.Ct. 517, 121 L.Ed.2d 391 (1992) (holding

that due process does not require the state to prove a prior conviction by clear and convincing evidence).

6. See § 26.2(b), discussing Spencer v. Texas, 385 U.S. 554, 87 S.Ct. 648, 17 L.Ed.2d 606 (1967) and Marshall v. Lonberger, 459 U.S. 422, 103 S.Ct. 843, 74 L.Ed.2d 646 (1983). See also Daniels v. United States, 532 U.S. 374, 121 S.Ct. 1578, 149 L.Ed.2d 590 (2001); Lackawanna County District Attorney v. Coss, 532 U.S. 394, 121 S.Ct. 1567, 149 L.Ed.2d 608 (2001).

it is the defendant's repeated failure to reform himself after each conviction that warrants greater deterrence through a higher sentence. Other jurisdictions do not combine convictions arising from the same trial. Challenges to the legality of the prior conviction during habitual offender proceedings are sometimes allowed, but collateral attacks to the legality of prior convictions may be strictly limited by statute without violating due process.[7]

(c) Restitution. Orders directing convicted defendants to make monetary payments to their victims have received increased attention as a result of the victim's rights movement. Restitution may be ordered pursuant to the sentencing court's general authority to impose relevant conditions of probation or pursuant to a statutory authorization to direct any convicted defendant to pay restitution without regard to whether he is placed on probation. Approximately half of the states and the federal government mandate restitution for enumerated crimes. Many of these mandatory provisions, however, authorize the court to decline to impose restitution upon stating "compelling and extraordinary reasons."

Before restitution may be imposed, the court must identify the "victim" entitled to restitution. This is an easy enough task where the crime inflicted immediate harm upon a particular individual, but it becomes more complicated where the offense relates to the interests of the public in general, as do many regulatory offenses. Restitution statutes generally define the "victim" as someone who has suffered actual property or pecuniary loss as a direct result of the defendant's criminal conduct, excluding those who took part in the crime.

Once the victim is identified, the court must determine precisely what losses can be considered in measuring the amount of restitution. Restitution typically is not permitted for mental anguish and suffering. It is limited to "ascertainable" loss. Depending on the statute, a defendant may be liable for losses beyond those caused by the offense for which the

defendant is convicted. It is up to the prosecutor to prove the amount of loss.

In general, courts have held that due process is satisfied when restitution is adjudicated using the procedures ordinarily applied to other historical facts in sentencing, although a few jurisdictions insist on trial-type hearings where factual issues concerning restitution are placed in dispute. Since in most cases assessing restitution presents factual determinations no more complex, uncertain, or significant in terms of consequence than factual determinations made routinely under guideline or presumptive sentencing structures, these extra safeguards are undoubtedly not compelled by due process.

(d) Forfeiture. Criminal forfeiture is a form of punishment that authorizes the government to seize certain assets of the defendant.[8] Modern criminal forfeiture is of relatively recent origin. The Framers prohibited the English practice of "forfeiture of estate," a criminal penalty that deprived a convicted felon of the ability to transfer any of his property at death. Thereafter, criminal forfeiture disappeared almost entirely from American law until 1970 when Congress provided for the criminal forfeiture of certain specified assets as a penalty for violating RICO. Subsequently, Congress and many state legislatures have authorized criminal forfeiture as a punishment for drug offenses and various other crimes. The scope of assets subject to forfeiture is limited by statute to that property possessing a prescribed relationship with the criminal activity. Common categories of forfeitable assets include "proceeds" of the underlying criminal activity and property used to "facilitate" that activity. Some statutes permit the forfeiture of "substitute assets" of the defendant if the designated property is no longer available.

Forfeiture statutes generally mandate special procedures for determining which assets are subject to forfeiture. These procedures, including notice and jury trial, tend to be more protective of the defendant's interests than those followed in typical sentencing. Yet as the

---

7. See Custis v. United States, 511 U.S. 485, 114 S.Ct. 1732, 128 L.Ed.2d 517 (1994), discussed in § 26.4(f).

8. Criminal forfeiture must be distinguished from civil forfeiture, which is discussed briefly in § 25.1(c).

Supreme Court explained in *Libretti v. United States*,[9] the legislature's choice to provide heightened safeguards does not alter forfeiture from a punishment into a separate, substantive crime. For the purposes of constitutional analysis, criminal forfeiture following a conviction is merely another type of sentence.

Criminal forfeiture statutes sometimes authorize the issuance of pretrial restraining orders and seizures of forfeitable assets after indictment or information, and even, in some circumstances, before indictment. The Supreme Court in *United States v. James Daniel Good Real Property*,[10] addressed a due process challenge to the ex parte seizure of real property prior to civil forfeiture. Applying the *Mathews* balancing test, the Court held that in order to seize real property for civil forfeiture, the government must provide notice and an opportunity to contest the seizure in a hearing. Although the Court expressly stated that it did "not address what sort of procedures are required for preforfeiture seizures of real property in the context of criminal forfeiture," an immediate postrestraint adversary hearing is probably also required by due process when the government restrains real property under the federal criminal forfeiture provisions.

Assets intended for attorney's fees may become the subject of a restraining or forfeiture order. Neither the seizure nor the forfeiture of attorneys fees, the Court has held, violates the guarantee to effective representation of counsel under the Sixth Amendment.[11] The government gains title to the forfeited assets upon the defendant's commission of the criminal act giving rise to the forfeiture and the defendant, the Court explained, has no constitutional right "to spend another person's money for services rendered by an attorney, even if those funds are the only way that that defendant will be able to retain the attorney of his choice." Third-party claims to forfeited property may be raised in a separate civil proceeding following the criminal forfeiture conviction.

A judge may be obligated to examine the forfeiture for excessiveness under the Excessive Fines Clause of the Eighth Amendment. In *Alexander v. United States*,[12] the Court held that criminal forfeiture is a fine subject to the eighth amendment prohibition against excessive fines. Excessiveness of an order of forfeiture under the Eighth Amendment, the Court later explained in *United States v. Bajakajian*,[13] is to be measured using a "standard of gross disproportionality" established in earlier cases. Applying that standard, the Court concluded that the forfeiture of more than $357,000 in cash was "grossly disproportional to the gravity of the defendant's offense," willful failure to report the removal of the currency from the United States, bearing "no articulable correlation to any injury suffered by the Government."

(e) "Dangerous" Offenders. Some states provide for extended terms not only for defendants who are persistent offenders, but also for those who are, in the opinion of the sentencer, particularly dangerous offenders. These "dangerous offender" provisions differ from habitual offender or other enhancement provisions for aggravating circumstances in that they impose extended sentences only after a specific finding of future "dangerousness" on the part of the defendant. The prediction of dangerousness, made by the sentencing judge, is often based on a psychiatric evaluation of some kind. Reasonable notice of the government's intent to seek this sentence and the right to call and cross-examine witnesses on the issue of dangerousness are particularly important features of these statutes given the unique predictive determination the judge must make.

§ 26.7   Resentencing: Double Jeopardy

(a) Resentencing Following Reconviction and the *Bullington* Rule. Where the conviction of a defendant is overturned on

---

9. 516 U.S. 29, 116 S.Ct. 356, 133 L.Ed.2d 271 (1995).

10. 510 U.S. 43, 114 S.Ct. 492, 126 L.Ed.2d 490 (1993).

11. Caplin & Drysdale v. United States, 491 U.S. 617, 109 S.Ct. 2646, 105 L.Ed.2d 528 (1989) (forfeiture); United States v. Monsanto, 491 U.S. 600, 109 S.Ct. 2657, 105 L.Ed.2d 512 (1989) (pretrial restraint).

12. 509 U.S. 544, 113 S.Ct. 2766, 125 L.Ed.2d 441 (1993).

13. 524 U.S. 321, 118 S.Ct. 2028, 141 L.Ed.2d 314 (1998).

appeal under circumstances permitting reprosecution, and the second prosecution results in a valid conviction, the question arises what weight must be given to the original sentence under the Double Jeopardy Clause. One aspect of that question, addressed by the Supreme Court in *North Carolina v. Pearce*,[1] is "whether, in computing the new sentence, the Constitution requires that credit must be given for that part of the original sentence already served." Emphasizing that one of the protections of the Double Jeopardy Clause is "against multiple punishments for the same offense," a unanimous Court answered that question in the affirmative.

A second issue presented in *Pearce* was whether, assuming proper credit is given for time already served, the trial court may impose a longer sentence on reconviction than was imposed following the original conviction. The defendants challenged their longer sentences as violating three distinct constitutional guarantees: double jeopardy, equal protection, and due process. The Court rejected the equal protection claim, and ruled that the Due Process Clause did not in all circumstances bar a longer sentence (a point pursued at length in § 26.8, below). It then rejected the double jeopardy claim, declining to depart from the longstanding rule "that a corollary of the power to retry a defendant is the power, upon the defendant's reconviction, to impose whatever sentence may be legally authorized, whether or not it is greater than the sentence imposed after the first conviction." This was a sensible rule, the *Pearce* majority asserted, for "it rests ultimately upon the premise that the original conviction has, at the defendant's behest, been wholly nullified and the slate wiped clean."

This aspect of the *Pearce* ruling was distinguished in *Bullington v. Missouri*,[2] where a divided Court held that a state could not seek the death penalty on a retrial where the original jury had decided against imposing capital punishment following a trial-type sentencing procedure. The majority noted that under Missouri law the jury determination as to capital punishment involved application of specific factual standards, relating to the presence of aggravating and mitigating factors, following an extensive trial-type hearing in which the prosecution bore the burden of proof beyond a reasonable doubt. The original jury's determination not to impose capital punishment was therefore comparable to a trial acquittal as to the issue of the death penalty, rather than to the traditional sentencing determination.

The special character of *Bullington* was reflected in the distinctions drawn there between capital sentencing and the resentencing that had been upheld in *United States v. DiFrancesco*.[3] In *DiFrancesco*, which is discussed in subsection (b), the Court had rejected a double jeopardy challenge to a provision that allowed the prosecutor to appeal a sentencing judge's alleged error in the application of a sentencing provision for dangerous offenders, and authorized resentencing if the appellate court found that there had been error. While *DiFrancesco* also involved a special factfinding determination by the sentencer, appellate review there was "on the record of the sentencing court" and did not involve giving the government "the opportunity to convince a second fact finder of its view of the facts." Moreover, the choice initially presented to the sentencing judge in *DiFrancesco* was far broader than that given to the jury in *Bullington*, which had "only two choices, death or life imprisonment." Finally, the government's burden of proof in *DiFrancesco* as to special offender status was only by a preponderance of the evidence, rather than the reasonable doubt standard applied in Missouri capital sentencing hearings. With all of these factors distinguishing the capital sentencing process, the longstanding rule that the defendant may receive any legally authorized sentence upon retrial, even if it is greater than the sentence imposed the first time, would not be extended to "this very different situation."

---

§ 26.7

1. 395 U.S. 711, 89 S.Ct. 2072, 23 L.Ed.2d 656 (1969).

2. 451 U.S. 430, 101 S.Ct. 1852, 68 L.Ed.2d 270 (1981).

3. 449 U.S. 117, 101 S.Ct. 426, 66 L.Ed.2d 328 (1980).

Bullington was applied in *Arizona v. Rumsey*,[4] involving a capital sentencing proceeding with similar characteristics. The Court there held that the sentencing judge's imposition of a life sentence for want of proof of any aggravating circumstances, though prompted by his erroneous interpretation of the statute defining those circumstances, barred later resentencing of death in light of the Court's earlier cases holding "that an acquittal on the merits bars retrial even if based on legal error." *Poland v. Arizona*[5] reached a different result on the basis of a different initial ruling by the sentencing judge. The sentencing judge there initially imposed a death sentence on the basis of one statutorily prescribed aggravating factor, but refused to rely on another aggravating factor because of a mistaken view of its scope. After the appellate court found the evidence insufficient to support the aggravating factor relied upon by the sentencing judge, but also corrected the judge as to the scope of the second factor, the sentencing judge again imposed the death penalty, this time relying on the second factor. The Supreme Court stressed that here, unlike *Rumsey*, the sentencing judge had never held that the state "failed to prove its case" as to the death penalty; rulings on separate aggravating factors were not akin to rulings on separate offenses (as to which there may be separate acquittals) since they serve only as guidelines for the available sentencing decision. Similarly, if a sentencing jury deadlocks on sentencing, neither judge nor jury has "acquitted" the defendant and the government is free to seek the death sentence in a retrial.[6]

The analogy drawn by the *Bullington* Court between a trial acquittal and a sentencing determination made by the trier of fact under guidelines that refer to specific factors so far has been applied by the Supreme Court only to capital sentencing, and even there has been limited to situations in which there was a clear ruling that the prosecution had failed to make its case. In *Schiro v. Farley*,[7] the Court declined to read the Double Jeopardy Clause to bar a judge's finding at sentencing of intentional murder as an aggravating factor after the trial jury had convicted defendant of felony murder, not intentional murder. The Court reasoned that double jeopardy does not exempt a defendant from "relitigat[ing] in a sentencing proceeding conduct for which he was previously tried" and explained that the initial sentencing challenged in the case posed a situation "manifestly different from the successive sentencings at issue in *Bullington*". In *Monge v. California*,[8] the Court held that Double Jeopardy Clause does not preclude retrial of a prior conviction allegation in non-capital sentencing proceedings. "Even assuming," that Court reasoned, "that the proceeding on the prior conviction allegation has the 'hallmarks' of a trial that we identified in *Bullington*, a critical component of our reasoning in that case was the capital sentencing context." Noting the severity of the penalty of death and the acute need for reliability in capital sentencing proceedings, the Court refused to extend *Bullington* to non-capital sentencing.

(b) Resentencing and Sentencing Appeals. In jurisdictions that allow appellate review of sentences, two situations may produce a more severe sentence following appeal. First, where the defendant's appeal is viewed as opening the door to appellate court assessment of all aspects of the sentence, the appellate court may decide not only that the defendant's complaint is not well taken, but that the sentence is too low and should be raised. Second, where the prosecution is allowed to appeal a sentence, the appellate court may sustain the prosecution's challenge and impose a higher sentence, or remand for consideration of a higher sentence. The leading double jeopardy decision, *United States v. DiFrancesco*,[9] involved the latter situation.

The Federal Organized Crime Control Act authorized the imposition of an increased sen-

---

4.   467 U.S. 203, 104 S.Ct. 2305, 81 L.Ed.2d 164 (1984).

5.   476 U.S. 147, 106 S.Ct. 1749, 90 L.Ed.2d 123 (1986).

6.   Sattazahn v. Pennsylvania, 537 U.S. 101, 123 S.Ct. 732, 154 L.Ed.2d 588 (2003).

7.   510 U.S. 222, 114 S.Ct. 783, 127 L.Ed.2d 47 (1994).

8.   524 U.S. 721, 118 S.Ct. 2246, 141 L.Ed.2d 615 (1998).

9.   449 U.S. 117, 101 S.Ct. 426, 66 L.Ed.2d 328 (1980).

tence upon a convicted "dangerous offender" and granted the government the right, under specified conditions, to gain appellate review of that sentence. In *DiFrancesco*, the trial judge had concluded that the defendant fell within the Act's dangerous offender definition and imposed an additional sentence, but ordered that the sentence run concurrently with the sentence for the underlying offense. The government appealed, arguing that the use of a concurrent dangerous offender sentence constituted an abuse of sentencing discretion since it added only one year to the length of the defendant's incarceration. The Supreme Court upheld the constitutionality of the appellate review provision and agreed with the prosecution as to the sentencing judge's error.

The Court noted initially that its "decisions in the sentencing area clearly establish that a sentence does not have the qualities of constitutional finality that attend an acquittal." That principle was reflected in *Pearce*. For "while *Pearce* dealt with the imposition of a new sentence after retrial rather than, as here, after appeal, that difference [was] no more than a 'conceptual nicety.' " Functionally, the Court stressed, resentencing here would be quite different from a retrial on guilt:

> The basic design of the double jeopardy provision, * * * is, as a bar against repeated attempts to convict, with consequent subjection of the defendant to embarrassment, expense, anxiety, and insecurity, and the possibility that he may be found guilty even though innocent. These considerations, however, have no significant application to the prosecution's statutorily granted right to review a sentence. This limited appeal does not involve a retrial or approximate the ordeal of a trial on the basic issue of guilt or innocence. Under [the Federal Act], the appeal is to be taken promptly and is essentially on the record of the sentencing court. The defendant, of course, is charged with knowledge of the statute and its appeal provisions, and has no expectation of finality in his sentence until the appeal is concluded or the time to appeal has expired.

(c) Resentencing by the Trial Judge. Yet another group of double jeopardy issues are presented where the trial judge, in a system utilizing traditional judicial sentencing, initially imposes a particular sentence and then, learning of some deficiency in that original sentence, alters the sentence to the prejudice of the defendant. Here *Pearce* is distinguishable because there has been no reversal of the underlying conviction, and *DiFrancesco* is distinguishable because reconsideration is not part of a specifically authorized review procedure analogous to appellate review of the sentence. *Ex Parte Lange*,[10] an 1870s Supreme Court ruling, contained language so broad as to suggest that all such resentencing was constitutionally prohibited, but later cases have limited that precedent to the "specific context" there presented.

In *Lange*, the applicable penal statute authorized a sentence of a fine *or* imprisonment, but the trial court erroneously imposed a sentence consisting of both the maximum term of imprisonment (one year) and the maximum fine ($200). After having paid the fine and having served five days in prison, the defendant petitioned the trial court for relief, demanding his immediate release on the ground that the imprisonment portion of the sentence could not be imposed along with the fine. Recognizing its error in imposing both a fine and imprisonment, the trial court vacated the original sentence and imposed a new sentence limited to imprisonment for the maximum term of one year. The Supreme Court held that the new sentence violated a double jeopardy prohibition against imposing "multiple punishments" for the same offense, and the defendant therefore was entitled to his release, as he had fully satisfied one of the two allowable alternative sentences by paying the fine. The *Lange* opinion spoke at points of the "finality" of a "judgment" once it is "carried into execution," rendering the trial court powerless to substitute a new sentence. But it also stressed that the end result of the resentencing was to impose upon the defendant punishment beyond that authorized by statute. The

10. 85 U.S. (18 Wall.) 163, 21 L.Ed. 872 (1874).

fine having been paid and passed into the Treasury (where it was beyond the reach of judiciary), the defendant would have suffered both a fine *and* imprisonment, and even the imprisonment would be for five days more than the one-year maximum allowed by law. The Supreme Court eventually came to read this element of imposing "excessive" punishment, as measured by the legislatively authorized sanction for the offense, to be the key to the double jeopardy violation in the resentencing in *Lange.*

In its first major analysis of the *Lange* opinion, *United States v. Benz*,[11] the Court held that *Lange's* discussion of the "finality" of the initially imposed sentence did not mean that the trial court lacked authority to reconsider and reduce a sentence during the same term of court in which it was initially imposed. Since such resentencing was in defendant's favor, the Court's reasoning did not foreclose the possibility that the double jeopardy prohibition barred an increased sentence following the initial imposition of a sentence. Subsequently, in *Bozza v. United States*,[12] the Court upheld the action of a trial court in *increasing* a previously announced sentence to meet the mandatory minimum required by statute. In that case, however, the trial court had corrected its error within hours of the announcement of its original sentence and before the defendant was transported to the penitentiary to serve his prison term. Thus, the case could be viewed as one in which the initially announced sentence had not yet been "imposed," although the Court's opinion focused on the fact that the trial judge had modified the originally announced sentence simply to correct his error and provide the sentence required by law. "The Constitution," the Court noted, "does not require that sentencing should be a game in which a wrong move by the judge means immunity for the prisoner."

In re Bradley,[13] like *Lange* and in contrast to *Bozza*, presented a situation in which resentencing occurred after the defendant had fulfilled part of the initial sentence. Indeed, as in *Lange*, the first of two sanctions imposed under an impermissible cumulative sentence had been fully satisfied before the trial court sought to resentence the defendant. The sentencing statute applicable in *Bradley* provided for punishment of a fine *or* imprisonment, but the trial court had erroneously imposed an initial sentence of both fine and imprisonment. Two days later, after defendant had paid the fine, the trial court realized its mistake, amended its sentencing order to vacate the fine, and directed that the moneys paid be returned to the defendant. Although, with the return of the fine, the trial court's order would have produced an ultimate sentence not in excess of that allowed by statute, the Supreme Court held that *Lange* barred the resentencing and defendant therefore was entitled to his immediate release. The Court reasoned that since the defendant had fully satisfied "one valid alternative provision of the original sentence," which constituted the limit of the punishment allowed under the penal statute, the trial court had lost authority to impose any further punishment. The subsequent amendment of the sentence to return the fine, it noted, "could not avoid the satisfaction of the judgment," and *Lange* therefore controlled.

Bradley, with little discussion of the issue, had indicated that *Lange's* prohibition against multiple punishments was tied to the execution of the original sentence, and not merely the quantum of the punishment eventually imposed. However, the Supreme Court's later decision in *DiFrancesco*, and its rulings in cases involving legislatively authorized cumulative punishments imposed in a single proceeding for a course of conduct constituting a single offense,[14] suggested otherwise. Although not involving resentencing, those opinions

---

11. 282 U.S. 304, 51 S.Ct. 113, 75 L.Ed. 354 (1931).

12. 330 U.S. 160, 67 S.Ct. 645, 91 L.Ed. 818 (1947).

13. 318 U.S. 50, 63 S.Ct. 470, 87 L.Ed. 608 (1943).

14. See Missouri v. Hunter, 459 U.S. 359, 103 S.Ct. 673, 74 L.Ed.2d 535 (1983) (upholding multiple sentences imposed on a defendant convicted in the same trial of both armed robbery and armed criminal action, where the

latter mandated a separate and additional punishment for any person committing a felony with a weapon; the double jeopardy limitation on multiple punishments does not prohibit the legislature from providing for more severe punishment through dual statutory punishment of the same conduct).

characterized the multiple punishment prohibition of *Lange* as directed basically against imposing punishment beyond that authorized by the legislature. Building upon those comments, a divided Court in *Jones v. Thomas*[15] held that the multiple punishment prohibition did not bar resentencing that fell within the statutory limits where defendant received full credit for the time served under the original sentence. In *Jones*, the defendant (Thomas) had been convicted of felony murder and the underlying felony of attempted robbery, both charges being tried in the same proceeding as they presented the same offense for double jeopardy purposes. The trial court originally had sentenced defendant to consecutive terms of fifteen years for the attempted robbery and life imprisonment for the felony murder. After the initial sentence for the attempted robbery had been satisfied (due to several years' incarceration and a subsequent commutation), the state's highest court held that the felony murder statute did not authorize separate punishments for the felony murder and the underlying felony. The trial court then vacated the attempted robbery sentence, leaving only the felony murder sentence, and gave the defendant credit for the entire time of his incarceration under the vacated sentence as against the remaining life sentence for felony murder. Defendant claimed that the credit was not sufficient, that he had fully satisfied one of two sentences allowable under state law, and that imposition of further imprisonment pursuant to the trial court's modification of the sentence would constitute multiple punishment contrary to *Lange* and *Bradley*. Rejecting defendant's reliance upon *Lange*, the Supreme Court majority noted that here, unlike *Lange*, the consequence of upholding the modified sentence was not to impose punishment in excess of that authorized by statute. The multiple punishment prohibition of *Lange*, as applied in *Lange* itself and as interpreted in *DiFrancesco* and the cumulative punishment cases, therefore was not violated.

The *Jones* majority acknowledged, however, that *Bradley* provided a "closer analogy" to the resentencing before it, for just as the judge here provided credit for the time served in order to keep the sentence within that authorized by the legislature, the judge there sought to return the fine. However, *Bradley* involved alternative punishments, each intended by the legislature to be sufficient in itself for the single offense on which the defendant stood convicted. *Jones*, in contrast, presented "separate sentences imposed for what the sentencing court thought to be separately punishable offenses, one far more serious than the other." While the legislature would have viewed each of the allowable punishments as appropriate for the particular offense in a "true alternative sentences case" (such as *Bradley*), it hardly could be deemed here to have viewed a punishment for attempted robbery as sufficient for felony murder. Moreover, the alternative sentences in *Bradley* "were of a different type, fine and imprisonment," whereas the two sentences in *Jones* were of the same type (imprisonment). It "would not have been possible to 'credit' a fine against time in prison," but the crediting of time served under one sentence against the term of another "has long been an accepted practice." Moreover, where both sentences are for terms of imprisonment, the application of *Bradley*, grounded as it would be upon the completion of the shorter sentence, would produce "anomalous results" based on fortuitous circumstances. A defendant previously incarcerated for the period of the shorter sentence would be able to advance a double jeopardy claim if he had been sentenced to the shorter imprisonment term as the first of the two consecutive sentences, but a defendant sentenced to the longer term as the first consecutive sentence would have no such claim, as he would not have completed either branch of his sentence, even though incarcerated for the same length of time prior to the resentencing.

Although *Jones* held that the *Lange* prohibition against multiple sentences was limited to excessive punishment and narrowly construed *Bradley*, it acknowledged that another interest protected by the double jeopardy prohibition—a defendant's "legitimate expectation of finality" in an imposed sentence—

---

15. 491 U.S. 376, 109 S.Ct. 2522, 105 L.Ed.2d 322 (1989).

could also stand as a bar to resentencing. The *Jones* majority did not disagree with the dissent's contention that "the Double Jeopardy Clause protects not only against punishment in excess of legislative intent, but also against additions to a sentence in a subsequent proceeding that upset a legitimate expectation of finality." Neither did it disagree with the dissent's illustration of an unconstitutional resentencing, notwithstanding an ultimate sentence less than the authorized maximum—a case "where a judge imposes only a 15 year sentence under a statute that permitted 15 years to life, has second thoughts after the defendant serves the sentence, and calls him back to impose another 10 years." The majority concluded that the case before it simply did not present the concerns raised by such a case as the defendant here "plainly had no expectation of serving only an attempted robbery sentence" when the sentencing court announced its initial sentence, which included the life term as part of the cumulative sentence. In *DiFrancesco*, the Court similarly had taken note of defendant's legitimate expectation of finality, but had concluded that the sentencing procedure there gave rise to no such expectation. *DiFrancesco* reasoned that the double jeopardy protection of such an interest did not preclude the use of an appeal procedure, known to defendant at the outset, as that procedure forewarned the defendant that the final determination of his sentence would not come until after that appeal and the defendant had no constitutional right to the initial setting of a final sentence (as evidenced by the well-accepted practice of setting the imprisonment term in probation revocation cases only after probation is revoked).

Double jeopardy could bar resentencing even where the new sentence did not either impose punishment beyond the statutory maximum or override defendant's prior fulfillment of a true alternative sentence. Such a case might be presented where the modification of a sentence after its original imposition results in punishment beyond that originally announced (in contrast to *Jones*) and is not made pursuant to an initially announced procedure for review and subsequent modification (in contrast to

DiFrancesco). Exactly what time span is needed between the initial imposition of the sentence and the modification to create a protected expectation of finality is unclear. It seems likely, however, that the modification could present constitutional difficulties even though the time span is not as extreme as that in the hypothetical offered by the *Jones* dissenters (where the modification came after defendant had completed the initially announced ten year sentence). The *DiFrancesco* majority took note of the early common law rule which held that the trial court could not add to a previously announced and executed prison sentence if that addition was made after the same term of court. It also noted the more stringent "established practice in federal courts" that permitted a sentencing judge to "recall a defendant and increase his sentence" only if the defendant "had not yet begun to serve the sentence"—although the Court added that it would "venture no comment as to this limitation." Of course, a defendant may not have a "legitimate" expectation of finality in a previously imposed sentence apart from the factors that precluded such an expectation in *Jones* and *DiFrancesco*. The dissenters in *Jones* described *Bozza* as such a case, noting that "the defendant [there] could not argue that his *legitimate* expectation of finality in the original sentence had been violated, because he was charged with knowledge that the court lacked statutory authority to impose the subminimum sentence in the first instance." Lower courts have suggested that a defendant could not rely on a legitimate expectation of finality where the subsequent upward modification responded to defendant's intentional deception in the original sentencing proceeding.

(d) Sentencing Based Upon Other Criminal Conduct. The Supreme Court has long held that where a judge sentencing on a current conviction increases the sentence in light of past convictions for other offenses, the increase does not constitute a resentencing on those other offenses and therefore does not present double jeopardy concerns. For example, in a case involving a kidnapping and a murder, the Supreme Court held that double jeopardy was not violated where the trial court, in sentencing defendant to capital punishment on the kidnapping charge, took account of the murder (on which defendant had previously pled guilty and received a life sentence).[16] So too, it matters not that sentencing law attaches a specific sentencing consequence to the prior conviction on a separate offense. Thus, the Court has held that recidivist statutes, which provide for specific punishment enhancement based on prior convictions, do not violate double jeopardy as the enhancement "is not to be viewed as either a new jeopardy or additional penalty for the earlier crime, but instead as a stiffened penalty for the latest crime, which is considered to be an aggravated offense because a repetitive one."[17]

In *Witte v. United States*,[18] the Court held that these principles combined to preclude a double jeopardy objection to prosecution and punishment for an offense that had been the basis for a sentence enhancement in a prior prosecution. When the defendant in *Witte* was prosecuted for a narcotics offense, he argued that the offense had been fully considered as "relevant conduct" during the sentencing on an earlier narcotics charge, and that double jeopardy therefore precluded "further punishment" for that conduct. The Court rejected this claim, concluding that the federal sentencing guidelines directed the sentencing judge in the first case to consider "relevant conduct" only as an aid in setting the punishment for the offense of conviction "within the scope of the legislatively authorized penalty" for that offense. Considering such evidence did not amount to punishment for those related offenses.

The Court recently reaffirmed these principles in a closely divided decision in *Monge v. California*.[19] In the course of discussing why double jeopardy did not bar the state's second

attempt to establish a prior conviction for recidivist penalties, Justice O'Connor, writing for the Court, explained that sentence enhancements that follow from prior convictions have not been "construed as additional punishment for the previous offense; rather they act to increase the sentence 'because of the manner in which [the defendant] committed the crime of conviction.' " The enhanced sentence is simply " 'a stiffened penalty for the latest crime, which is considered to be an aggravated offense because a repetitive one.' "

§ 26.8 Resentencing: The Prohibition Against Vindictiveness

(a) Presumed Vindictiveness: The *Pearce* Ruling. In *North Carolina v. Pearce*,[1] the petitioners successfully overturned their original convictions in post-conviction proceedings, were retried and convicted on the same charges, and then were sentenced to imprisonment terms that were longer than those imposed on the original convictions. The petitioners claimed that the trial courts had imposed heavier sentences in order to punish them for having challenged their original convictions. The Supreme Court unanimously concluded that such a sentencing purpose violates due process. Justice Stewart's opinion for the Court noted that a court is "without right to put a price on an appeal" and that "vindictiveness against a defendant for having successfully attacked his first conviction" could "play no part" in the sentencing on retrial.

While agreeing that vindictive sentencing was constitutionally barred, the Court in *Pearce* was divided as to how it should approach the claim that the sentences before it had actually been based on such a "retaliatory motivation." On that issue, a majority concluded that it was unnecessary to determine

16. Williams v. Oklahoma, 358 U.S. 576, 79 S.Ct. 421, 3 L.Ed.2d 516 (1959). The Supreme Court emphasized that the murder and the kidnapping were separate crimes, and that the trial court could consider "all the circumstances of the crime," including the fact that the victim was murdered, in deciding the proper sentence to be imposed for the kidnapping.

17. Oyler v. Boles, 368 U.S. 448, 82 S.Ct. 501, 7 L.Ed.2d 446 (1962); Gryger v. Burke, 334 U.S. 728, 68 S.Ct. 1256, 92 L.Ed. 1683 (1948); Witte v. United States,

515 U.S. 389, 115 S.Ct. 2199, 132 L.Ed.2d 351(1995) (citing other recidivist cases).

18. 515 U.S. 389, 115 S.Ct. 2199, 132 L.Ed.2d 351 (1995).

19. 524 U.S. 721, 118 S.Ct. 2246, 141 L.Ed.2d 615 (1998). *Monge* is discussed in § 26.7(a).

§ 26.8

1. 395 U.S. 711, 89 S.Ct. 2072, 23 L.Ed.2d 656 (1969).

whether the trial judges had in fact acted vindictively. Due process also required that a "defendant be freed of apprehension of such a retaliatory motivation on the part of the sentencing judge," since that apprehension could itself "deter a defendant's exercise of the right to appeal or collaterally attack his first conviction." Accordingly, the majority reasoned, where a higher sentence was imposed following a successful defense challenge to a conviction (and subsequent reconviction and resentencing), it would presume vindictiveness and impose upon the resentencing judge the burden of rebutting that presumption. This would be done through what was later described as the "prophylactic limitation" of *Pearce*. The *Pearce* majority described that limitation as follows:

> In order to assure the absence of such a motivation, we have concluded that whenever a judge imposes a more severe sentence upon a defendant after a new trial, the reasons for his doing so must affirmatively appear. Those reasons must be based upon objective information concerning identifiable conduct on the part of the defendant occurring after the time of the original sentencing proceeding. And the factual data upon which the increased sentence is based must be made part of the record, so that the constitutional legitimacy of the increased sentence may be fully reviewed on appeal.

Justice White in a concurring opinion agreed that a presumption of vindictiveness was appropriate and that rebuttal of that presumption required that the trial court set forth legitimate reasons for the increased sentence. He disagreed, however, with the Court's limitation of those reasons. An "increased sentence on retrial" should be allowed, he noted, "on any objective, identifiable factual data not known to the trial judge at the time of the original sentencing proceeding." Justice Black objected that "nothing in the Due Process Clause grants [to] the Court" the authority "to prescribe particular devices 'in order to assure the absence of such a motivation.' " The Court, from his perspective, was engaging

in "pure legislation." Later decisions discussed in the sections that follow have retreated from the implications of *Pearce* in light of the objections raised by Justices White and Black.

(b) Rebutting the *Pearce* Presumption. The issue of what conduct would rebut the *Pearce* presumption was not reached until fifteen years later, when the Court decided *Wasman v. United States*.[2] The Court, consistent with Justice White's opinion in *Pearce*, refused to restrict the rebuttal of the *Pearce* presumption of vindictiveness to "identifiable conduct of the defendant occurring after the time of the original proceeding. The trial judge in *Wasman* had noted when imposing the original sentence that no consideration would be given to those criminal charges then pending against the defendant; it was that court's policy to consider only the prior convictions of a defendant." Following a successful appeal, retrial, and reconviction, the same judge imposed a second sentence higher than the first. The greater sentence was justified by reference to a conviction (on a previously pending charge) that had occurred during the interim between the first and second sentence. Defendant maintained that *Pearce* did not allow the higher sentence to be based on the intervening conviction since that conviction, though occurring after the time of the original sentence, was "not itself 'conduct on the part of the defendant' " that had occurred after the original sentence. A unanimous Supreme Court rejected that claim, noting that *Pearce's* prophylactic rule must be given a common sense interpretation consistent with the function of that rule. There was no suggestion of actual vindictiveness, and allowing consideration of an intervening conviction did not open the door to vindictive sentencing. Indeed, *Pearce* itself had suggested the appropriateness of giving weight to that factor. Although referring to the post-sentence conduct of the defendant, *Pearce* had also noted that a "trial judge is not constitutionally precluded * * * [from imposing a higher sentence] in light of events subsequent to the first trial that may have thrown new light upon defendant's life, health, habits, conduct, and mental and moral propensities."

2. 468 U.S. 559, 104 S.Ct. 3217, 82 L.Ed.2d 424 (1984).

As this statement suggested, there was "no logical support for [drawing] a distinction between 'events' and 'conduct' of the defendant occurring after the initial sentencing insofar as the kind of information that may be relied upon to show a nonvindictive motive is concerned."

While *Wasman* opened the *Pearce* prophylactic rule to intervening events extending beyond defendant's own conduct, the Supreme Court's next ruling, in *Texas v. McCullough*, went farther. A divided Court there basically restructured *Pearce's* prophylactic rule to allow an increased sentence to be based on any new information logically relevant to sentencing. Although initially holding that the *Pearce's* prophylactic rule did not apply to the setting of the case before it, the *McCullough* majority went on to consider whether the justifications for the higher sentence there offered by the trial judge would have been sufficient "even if the *Pearce* presumption were to apply here." Chief Justice Burger's opinion for the Court noted initially that the *Pearce* opinion had not "intended to describe exhaustively all of the possible circumstances in which a sentence increase could be justified." In particular, "restricting justifications for a sentence increase to *only* 'events that occurred subsequent to the original sentencing proceedings' could in some circumstances lead to absurd results." Such a restriction would, for example, prohibit an increased sentence where the initial sentence was based on the assumption that the defendant had no prior criminal record, but it was later learned in the second sentencing investigation that defendant had been using an alias and in fact had a long criminal record of serious offenses. Prohibiting a higher sentence in such a case was a "bizarre" result that *Pearce* obviously had not intended. Accordingly, *Pearce* should be read, as the Court had suggested in *United States v. Goodwin*,[3] as establishing "a presumption of vindictiveness, which may be overcome only by objective information * * * justifying the increased sentence." Admittedly, "a defendant

may be reluctant to appeal if there is a risk that new, probative evidence supporting a longer sentence may be revealed on retrial," but *Pearce* itself, in allowing justified higher sentences, had refused to accept such a " 'chilling effect' as sufficient reason to create a constitutional prohibition against considering relevant information" in sentencing following a retrial.

Having found that *Pearce's* prophylactic rule could be satisfied by "objective information" not considered in the initial sentencing, the *McCullough* Court had no difficulty with the "careful explanation of the trial judge" in the case before it. The trial judge had cited "the testimony of two new witnesses which she concluded 'had a direct effect upon the strength of the State's case at both the guilt and punishment phases of the trial.' " She had "also found that McCullough had been released from confinement only four months before the murder, another obviously relevant fact not before the sentencing jury in the first trial." This "new objective information also amply justified McCullough's increased sentence."

(c) Applying the *Pearce* Presumption in Other Resentencing Settings. Prior to the ruling in *McCullough*, the vindictiveness presumption of *Pearce* had been held not to apply to all settings presenting a resentencing following a reversed conviction and subsequent reconviction. Distinguished in this regard had been jury sentencing and sentences imposed by a higher court following a trial de novo. In *Colten v. Kentucky*,[4] the Supreme Court held that a Kentucky trial court, when sentencing a defendant following a trial de novo "appeal" of a misdemeanor conviction, did not have to set forth reasons justifying a sentence higher than that which had been imposed by the magistrate. A divided Court concluded that the Kentucky "two-tier system of administering criminal justice" did not contain the same potential for vindictive sentencing as was found in *Pearce*. Accordingly, there was no basis for

---

3. 457 U.S. 368, 102 S.Ct. 2485, 73 L.Ed.2d 74 (1982), discussed in § 13.5(a). *Goodwin* had held that a presumption of vindictiveness did not apply to the pretrial prosecu-

torial charging setting presented there, but had also discussed the significance of the presumption in general.

4. 407 U.S. 104, 92 S.Ct. 1953, 32 L.Ed.2d 584 (1972).

assuming that "defendants convicted in Kentucky's inferior courts would be deterred from seeking a second trial out of fear of judicial vindictiveness." Three factors, in particular, were stressed: (1) the court which conducted the trial de novo and imposed the second sentence was not the same court as had tried the case initially; unlike *Pearce*, this was not a case of a court being "asked to do over what it had thought it had already done correctly"; (2) the de novo court was not being asked to "find error in another court's work," but simply to provide the defendant with the same trial that would have been provided if his case had begun in that court; and (3) the attitude of the Kentucky courts was that the inferior courts were not "designed or equipped to conduct error-free trials," but were "courts of convenience," so there was no suggestion that a defendant "ought to be satisfied" with the informal proceeding provided by an inferior court.

Chaffin v. Stynchcombe[5] held that the prophylactic rule of *Pearce* also did not apply to jury sentencing. A closely divided Court concluded that, unlike the situation in *Pearce*, the potential for vindictive sentencing by a jury was "*de minimis* in a properly controlled retrial." Two factors were stressed. First, the jury sitting in the second trial would not know of the earlier sentence. While it probably would be aware that there had been an earlier trial, it would not know whether that trial was on the same charge or whether it resulted in a conviction or a mistrial. Second, as was true in *Colten*, "the second sentence is not meted out by the same judicial authority" that had its earlier proceeding reversed on appeal. The jury has no personal stake in the earlier proceeding, and it "is unlikely to be sensitive to the institutional interests that might occasion higher sentences by a judge desirous of discouraging what he regards as meritless appeals." Responding to the dissent, the *Chaffin* majority also rejected the contention that the application of *Pearce* to sentencing by judge, but not to sentencing by juries, placed an unconstitutional burden on the defendant's right to a jury trial. It was true that the

defendant who chose trial by jury (and thereby jury sentencing) opened the door to a more severe second sentence, a result that *Pearce* ordinarily would bar if the defendant had chosen a bench trial. But this distinction in the possible consequence of selecting a jury over a bench trial did not impose the kind of "needless burden" held invalid in other cases.[6] Here, the distinction flowed from a legitimate state policy that favored unfettered jury sentencing, with each jury allowed to make its determination based on its own assessment of the evidence before it.

One factor emphasized in both *Colten* and *Chaffin* was the presence of different sentencers at the first and second proceedings. However, this factor was generally assumed by lower courts to be irrelevant when the different sentencers were both trial judges of the same court. Although the second trial judge would have no "personal stake" in the earlier proceedings, that judge arguably would still have an "institutional interest" in discouraging appeals from the trial court's rulings. In *McCullough*, the Supreme Court strongly suggested that such an "institutional interest" was too speculative a basis for imposing the *Pearce* presumption of vindictiveness (and thereby requiring a higher sentence to be justified in accordance with *Pearce's* prophylactic rule). *McCullough* did not itself involve one trial judge imposing on a reconviction a higher sentence than another trial judge of the same court had assessed after the initial conviction. Defendant McCullough had originally been sentenced by a jury, then was resentenced by the trial judge after a successful motion for new trial based upon prosecutorial misconduct. The Supreme Court found that there was little reason to presume vindictiveness in this situation:

In contrast to *Pearce*, McCullough's second trial came about because the trial judge herself concluded that the prosecutor's misconduct required it. * * * "[U]nlike the judge who has been reversed," the trial judge here had no motivation to engage in "self-vindi-

---

5. 412 U.S. 17, 93 S.Ct. 1977, 36 L.Ed.2d 714 (1973).

6. See United States v. Jackson, 390 U.S. 570, 88 S.Ct. 1209, 20 L.Ed.2d 138 (1968).

cation." In such circumstances, there is also no justifiable concern about "institutional interests that might occasion higher sentences by a judge desirous of discouraging what he regards as meritless appeals."

The *McCullough* majority also rejected the dissent's suggestion that a judge might well grant a defense motion for a new trial yet be vindictive either because she was forced to "publicly concede" that the trial had been flawed (or face appellate reversal) or because the prosecutorial error requiring a new trial did not really cast doubt upon defendant's guilt and she therefore would be required to "sit through a trial whose result was a foregone conclusion." Such assumptions, the Court noted were far too "speculative" to support application of the *Pearce* presumption. The Court would not "adopt the view that the judicial temperament of our Nation's trial judges will suddenly change upon the filing of a successful trial motion." Indeed, its fallacy was suggested in this very case when the defendant chose to be resentenced by the judge who had granted the new trial motion rather than the jury.

Having relied upon the special circumstances of the case before it, the *McCullough* Court then went on to indicate why the presumption is inappropriate when the allegedly vindictive sentence is imposed by a different sentencer. In such circumstances, the Court reasoned, "a sentence 'increase' cannot truly be said to have taken place." Indeed, the Court explained, "it no more follows that such a sentence is a vindictive penalty for seeking a [new] trial than that the [first sentencer] imposed a lenient penalty." When "the second sentencer provides an on-the-record, wholly logical, nonvindictive reason for the sentence" *Pearce* does not require more. Relying on *McCullough*, lower courts generally hold that the presumption of vindictiveness is applicable only when there is one sentencer. Some state courts, however, have interpreted their state constitutions as providing greater protection in this context.

In *Alabama v. Smith*,[7] the Court there overturned an aspect of the *Pearce* ruling—its ap-

plication of the presumption in a companion case of *Simpson v. Rice*—that had long troubled lower courts. Unlike defendant Pearce's case, which presented differing sentences imposed after two trials, defendant Rice's case involved a vacated guilty plea and a higher sentence imposed after a subsequent trial and reconviction. *Smith* concluded that the application of the presumption to the situation presented in *Rice* could not be sustained in light of post-*Pearce* rulings such as *Colten*, *Chaffin*, and *McCullough*, which had held that the presumption of vindictiveness properly applied only in circumstances presenting "a 'reasonable likelihood' that the increase in sentence is the product of actual vindictiveness on the part of the sentencing authority." "[W]hen a greater penalty is imposed after trial than was imposed after a prior guilty plea," the *Smith* Court reasoned, the presumption should not apply, "for the increase in sentence is not more likely than not attributable to the vindictiveness on the part of the sentencing judge." Because the information considered by the judge in accepting a guilty plea "will usually be far less than that brought out in a full trial on the merits," the judge imposing a second sentence after that trial is likely to have had "a fuller appreciation of the nature and extent of the crime charged." So too, the defendant's conduct during trial may have given the judge "insights into his moral character and suitability for rehabilitation.". Still another relevant distinction is that, "after trial, the factors that may indicate leniency as consideration for the guilty plea are no longer present." The Court also noted that since the trial court had originally accepted a guilty plea and then conducted a trial after that plea was vacated, it would not be in a position of "simply 'doing over what it thought it had already done correctly.'"

Although the Court has not yet spoken directly on the issue, lower courts also apply the *Pearce* rule to resentencing to correct an invalid sentence as well as resentencing following the appeal of an invalid conviction. Some states have extended the rule in *Pearce* to bar inquiry as to the defendant's intent to appeal

---

7. 490 U.S. 794, 109 S.Ct. 2201, 104 L.Ed.2d 865 (1989).

at initial sentencing. The presumption of vindictiveness has also been applied when, after a defendant's successful appeal of his initial parole decision, a parole board imposes a longer period of time which must pass before it would next consider releasing the defendant on parole.

Chapter 27

APPEALS

Table of Sections

---

§ 27.1 Constitutional Protection of the Defendant's Right to Appeal

(a) No Federal Constitutional Right. Following dictum written over a century ago, the Supreme Court has consistently maintained that the due process guaranteed to the accused by the Constitution does not include access to appellate review of criminal convictions. In 1894, the Court in *McKane v. Durston*[1] upheld a state's denial of bail pending appeal, reasoning that the state had no consti-

§ 27.1

1. 153 U.S. 684, 14 S.Ct. 913, 38 L.Ed. 867 (1894).

tutional obligation to provide appellate review at all. It stated:

> An appeal from a judgment of conviction is not a matter of absolute right, independently of [state] constitutional or statutory provisions allowing such appeal. A review by an appellate court of the final judgment in a criminal case, however grave the offense of which the accused is convicted, was not at common-law, and is not now, a necessary element of due process of law. It is wholly within the discretion of the state to allow or not to allow such a review.

McKane was written at a time when appellate review had only recently been introduced into the federal judicial structure. Congress did not grant circuit courts the authority to review federal criminal convictions until 1879, and did not give the Supreme Court jurisdiction to entertain writs of error in federal criminal cases until 1889. While the appellate review process in the state courts developed more quickly, it remained quite limited well into the mid–1800s.[2]

Today appellate review is a much more important element of the criminal justice process than it was when *McKane* was decided. As discussed in the sections that follow, every state and the federal government provides some means of appellate review for defendants in criminal cases. In the federal system and in most states, statutes or state constitutional provisions guarantee defendants in all felony cases a right to appellate review. In misdemeanor cases, defendants commonly have a right of review in the general trial court (in some states, by trial de novo) with subsequent discretionary appellate review. Some constitutional rights can be meaningfully enforced only by appeal, such as the right to an unbiased trial judge or the effective assistance of trial counsel. The significance of appellate review for the enforcement of constitutional rights of the accused has led some commentators and judges to advocate a constitutional conclusion different from that expressed in *McKane*. The Court, however, has yet to reconsider its position in *McKane*.[3]

(b) Constitutional Protection of the Statutory Right of Appeal. Various strands of constitutional doctrine protect the defendant's access to the appellate review that is provided under state law. Perhaps the most significant cases in this regard are the equal protection decisions safeguarding indigents' access to appellate review. As noted in Chapter 11, under *Griffin v. Illinois* once a state grants a right of appeal to criminal defendants, it cannot condition that right in a manner that violates the constitutional guarantee of equal protection. The *Griffin* principle has been used primarily to ensure that the indigent defendant has equal access to the appellate process. Thus, the state is precluded from conditioning appellate review on an appellate transcript and then failing to provide a free transcript for an indigent appellant.[4] Similarly, *Douglas v. California*[5] held that to ensure the indigent defendant "meaningful access" to the appellate process, the state must provide the defendant with appointed counsel for his first appeal. *Anders v. California*[6] added to this protection by ensuring that appointed counsel could not

2. Martinez v. Court of Appeal of California, 528 U.S. 152, 120 S.Ct. 684, 145 L.Ed.2d 597 (2000) (finding no historical basis for a right to self-representation on appeal and stating, "Appeals of right in federal courts were nonexistent for the first century of our Nation, and appellate review of any sort was 'rarely allowed.' * * * The States, also, did not generally recognize an appeal as of right until Washington became the first to constitutionalize the right explicitly in 1889. There was similarly no right to appeal in criminal cases at common law, and appellate review of any sort was 'limited' and 'rarely used.' ").

3. In Jones v. Barnes, 463 U.S. 745, 103 S.Ct. 3308, 77 L.Ed.2d 987 (1983), the majority pronounced simply, "There is, of course, no constitutional right to an appeal." See also Ross v. Moffitt, 417 U.S. 600, 94 S.Ct. 2437, 41 L.Ed.2d 341 (1974); Douglas v. California, 372 U.S. 353, 83

S.Ct. 814, 9 L.Ed.2d 811 (1963), both discussed in § 11.1(d); Pennsylvania v. Finley, 481 U.S. 551, 107 S.Ct. 1990, 95 L.Ed.2d 539 (1987) (reasoning that there is no right to counsel in discretionary appeal, given that "the State need not provide any appeal at all"); Goeke v. Branch, 514 U.S. 115, 115 S.Ct. 1275, 131 L.Ed.2d 152 (1995), quoted in § 27.5(c) at note 14. See also *Martinez*, supra note 1.1, (Scalia, J., concurring) ("a State could, as far as the federal Constitution is concerned, subject its trial-court determinations to no review whatever").

4. See § 11.2(e), discussing Griffin v. Illinois, 351 U.S. 12, 76 S.Ct. 585, 100 L.Ed. 891 (1956).

5. See § 11.1(d).

6. See § 11.2(c).

withdraw from that obligation by mere assertion that the appeal would be frivolous. The constitutional guarantee of effective assistance of counsel on the first appeal granted of right under state law is not limited to appointed counsel. The Supreme Court has held that the Constitution guarantees to all defendants a right to be represented by counsel on such an appeal and to effective assistance by such counsel.[7] However, beyond that point, as on application for discretionary review, the defendant has no such guarantee.[8]

The prohibition against vindictiveness in sentencing also serves to safeguard the defendant's right of appeal under state law. In *North Carolina v. Pearce*, discussed in § 26.8, the Court established a presumption of vindictiveness for cases in which a defendant, retried and reconvicted after a successful appeal, receives a sentence from the same judge that is higher than that imposed following his original trial. The Court in *Pearce* was unanimous in holding that due process was denied where a sentencing judge sought to punish a defendant for having taken an appeal by imposing a more severe sentence following reconviction. Justice Stewart's opinion for the Court noted that "a court is 'without right to put a price on an appeal.'" As in *Griffin*, though a state had no duty to establish avenues of appellate review, it could not subject those avenues, once established, to "unreasoned distinctions" that would deter a defendant's "free and unfettered" exercise of his right to challenge his conviction.

Although the defendant has been granted some sort of right to appeal his conviction in every jurisdiction, he is not guaranteed review of each and every trial court ruling. Appellate review typically is limited to claims that challenge trial court decisions that can be characterized as "final judgments" or that fit within an exception to the final judgment rule, claims that are not moot, and claims that are not expressly waived by agreement or forfeited by the defendant's failure to comply with procedural requirements. Moreover, even meritorious claims may not produce relief on appeal if the error reviewed is considered by the reviewing court to be "harmless." These and other limits on appellate relief are examined in the sections that follow.

§ 27.2 Defense Appeals and the Final Judgment Rule

(a) The Statutory Requirement of a Final Judgment. The statutory provisions that govern defense appeals uniformly reflect the view that piecemeal appellate review of litigation is generally inappropriate and therefore appeals ordinarily should be allowed only from a final judgment. Special double jeopardy concerns guide the implementation of this policy in the context of prosecution appeals, which are discussed in § 27.3. This section considers the final judgment rule as it applies to appeals by defendants, potential defendants (e.g., grand jury targets), and third parties (e.g., witnesses).

In many jurisdictions defense appeals in criminal cases are governed by the same statutes that regulate civil appeals. The federal provision, 28 U.S.C. § 1291, is typical. It provides that the "courts of appeals * * * shall have jurisdiction of appeals from all final decisions of the district courts * * *." Counterpart state statutes often refer to appeals from "final orders." In those states with separate statutes governing defense appeals in criminal cases the statutes commonly refer to a "final judgment of conviction." Notwithstanding such references to "convictions," the prevailing view is that an appealable final judgment does not come with conviction alone, but requires the imposition of a sentence for that conviction. This is consistent with the view frequently expressed in civil cases that a judgment is final only "when it ends the litigation on the merits and leaves nothing for the court to do but execute the judgment."[1]

---

7. See Evitts v. Lucey, discussed in §§ 11.1(b), 11.7(a). See also Ohio Adult Parole Auth. v. Woodard, 523 U.S. 272, 118 S.Ct. 1244, 140 L.Ed.2d 387 (1998) (discussing basis for *Evitts*).

8. See Murray v. Giarratano, 492 U.S. 1, 109 S.Ct. 2765, 106 L.Ed.2d 1 (1989), discussed in § 11.7(a).

§ 27.2

1. Cunningham v. Hamilton County, 527 U.S. 198, 119 S.Ct. 1915, 144 L.Ed.2d 184 (1999) (order imposing sanctions on attorney under Fed.R.Civ.P. 37 was not a final decision appealable under 28 U.S.C.A. § 1291, even where attorney no longer represents a party in the case).

(b) Underlying Policies and Statutory Exceptions. The final judgment rule reflects a determination that, on balance, postponing an appeal until a final judgment is reached best protects the interests of the litigants in a fair and accessible process while conserving judicial resources. Weighing against the final judgment rule is the possibility that not allowing an interlocutory appeal from a potentially erroneous pretrial ruling may result in a final judgment that will be reversed on appeal, causing the litigants to repeat the entire trial. Retrial brings additional expense and anxiety for the defendant and trial participants. It can also produce a final determination that is considerably different from what it might have been had the error been caught before the case was first tried, since delay can result in memory lapses, strategic advantages, and less effective impeachment of witnesses.

Yet the costs of permitting interlocutory appeals are thought to be greater. Awaiting a final judgment benefits litigants as a group even if it does occasionally require a particular litigant to undergo an unnecessary trial. Permitting either or both parties to postpone a trial with interlocutory appeals is likely to result in even greater delay in final adjudication than allowing appeals only from final judgment. Interlocutory review would be especially wasteful, it is argued, because most trial court rulings are correct and even those that are incorrect are unlikely, in the end, to taint the final judgment. The end result of freely allowing interlocutory appeals would be a greater injustice to litigants overall than is occasioned by that small portion of cases in which trials must be repeated because appellate review was delayed until after final judgment was reached. That injustice would be particularly likely when the adversaries had unequal resources and interests in securing or avoiding a prompt disposition of the case. The party interested in a prompt adjudication would be at the mercy of an opponent willing and able to delay litigation by appealing adverse pretrial rulings.

The advantages of the final judgment rule in securing efficient judicial administration are even more apparent. The rule provides savings for both trial and appellate courts. A major responsibility of the trial court is self-correction, and the delay of appellate review until final judgment permits the trial court to reassess its decisions in light of later trial developments. From the perspective of the appellate court, rulings also are better judged in light of the completed proceeding when more information is available with which to assess the impact of the error upon the outcome of the trial. Even errors that require a new trial are judged more efficiently since a single appeal may consider more than one error. Most significantly, the final judgment rule avoids appeals that become unnecessary as the case develops. Thus, pretrial rulings often become moot when the party adversely affected by the erroneous ruling ultimately gains a favorable jury verdict.

While all of the above considerations have relevance to both civil and criminal cases, the delay that can accompany interlocutory appeals is especially pernicious in the criminal justice process, where a speedy trial advances a "societal interest * * * which exists separate from * * * the interests of the accused."[2] In his frequently quoted opinion in *Cobbledick v. United States*,[3] Justice Frankfurter emphasized the dangers of delay in urging strict adherence to the final judgment rule in criminal cases. He noted:

These considerations of policy are especially compelling in the administration of criminal justice. * * * An accused is entitled to scrupulous observance of constitutional safeguards. But encouragement of delay is fatal to the vindication of the criminal law. Bearing the discomfiture and cost of a prosecution for crime even by an innocent person is one of the painful obligations of citizenship. The correctness of a trial court's rejection even of a constitutional claim made by the accused in the process of prosecution must

---

2. See Barker v. Wingo, discussed in § 18.1(b). See also DiBella v. United States, 369 U.S. 121, 82 S.Ct. 654, 7 L.Ed.2d 614 (1962).

3. 309 U.S. 323, 60 S.Ct. 540, 84 L.Ed. 783 (1940).

await his conviction before its reconsideration by an appellate tribunal.

The viewpoint expressed in *Cobbledick* has dominated the federal statutory scheme for defense appeals in criminal cases. While Congress has adopted several statutory provisions allowing interlocutory appeals in civil cases, only two federal statutes authorize interlocutory appeals in criminal cases. One, 18 U.S.C. § 3731, is quite narrow and carefully limited to prosecution appeals; the other, 18 U.S.C. § 3154(c), provides both the defense and the prosecution with a right to appeal orders concerning pretrial release or detention.

A substantial number of states have much broader provisions permitting interlocutory appeals by defendants in criminal cases on a discretionary basis. Several have adopted provisions similar to 28 U.S.C. § 1291(b) that apply to criminal as well as civil cases, and require that the trial judge certify that immediate appeal is warranted. Others simply provide for interlocutory appeal by leave of the appellate court, without requiring certification by the trial judge. Such provisions often identify a series of factors to be considered by the appellate court in determining whether to grant review, such as whether immediate review will "clarify an issue of general importance in the administration of justice" or "protect the petitioner from substantial or irreparable injury." Jurisdictions with such provisions have not rejected Justice Frankfurter's conclusion that defendants may be required, as one of the "painful obligations of citizenship," to "bear the discomfiture and cost" of an unnecessary trial. Rather, they have concluded that the final judgment rule should be subject to exception where the circumstances of the individual case convince the appellate court that the protection of the defendant's substantive rights or the conservation of judicial resources would be better served by interlocutory review.

(c) Collateral Orders. The final judgment rule has been modified by judicial developments in both criminal and civil cases. One major judicially recognized "exception" to the

final judgment rule is the collateral order doctrine, established in the civil case of *Cohen v. Beneficial Industrial Loan Corp.*[4] In that case, the defendant in a stockholder's derivative suit sought to appeal a district court's pretrial ruling refusing to direct the plaintiffs to post a security bond. The Supreme Court held that the ruling was appealable under 28 U.S.C. § 1291. A final decision, the Court noted, did not necessarily have to terminate an action. Given a "practical rather than technical construction," the final judgment concept also encompassed certain orders collateral to the basic litigation. These were described as "that small class [of orders] which finally determine claims of right separable from, and collateral to, rights asserted in the action, too important to be denied review and too independent of the cause itself to require that appellate consideration be deferred until the whole case is adjudicated."

The required characteristics of decisions appealable as collateral orders were expressed in *Coopers & Lybrand v. Livesay*[5] as follows:

> To come within the "small class" of decisions excepted from the final-judgment rule by *Cohen*, the order must conclusively determine the disputed question, resolve an important issue completely separate from the merits of the action, and be effectively unreviewable on appeal from a final judgment.

The first of these three prerequisites demands that the trial court ruling not be "tentative, informal, or incomplete," but constitute a firm and final decision on the issue. If there is a reasonable prospect that the trial court might alter its rulings, immediate appellate intrusion clearly is not appropriate. As to the second prerequisite, it demands that the issue ruled upon not "affect, or * * * be affected by" any subsequent decision on the merits of the case. If the trial court ruling is not "independent of the cause" itself, determining rights "separable from and collateral to [those] rights asserted in the action," then review prior to the ultimate disposition constitutes a wasteful use of appellate resources. Depending

---

4. 337 U.S. 541, 69 S.Ct. 1221, 93 L.Ed. 1528 (1949).

5. 437 U.S. 463, 98 S.Ct. 2454, 57 L.Ed.2d 351 (1978).

upon the disposition of the case, permitting appeal will produce either an unnecessary review or a review that will only be repeated, possibly in a new light that would require the appellate court to withdraw from an earlier ruling. The second prerequisite also requires that the issue resolved by the trial court be not only independent but "important." Thus, in *Cohen* the Court noted that the trial court order there might not have been appealable if the only issue presented was one of the proper exercise of the trial court's discretion. Finally, the third prerequisite insists that interlocutory appeal be withheld if review on appeal following the final disposition would provide a satisfactory remedy. For example, in authorizing interlocutory review in *Cohen,* the Court noted that the petitioner's right to security for its costs would be lost, "probably irreparably," if review came only after the petitioner had won the case on the merits.

The Supreme Court first applied the collateral order doctrine to a criminal case in *Stack v. Boyle.*[6] The defendants there were unable to make bail and sought habeas corpus relief after the trial court denied their motion to reduce bail. The Supreme Court concluded that the use of the habeas remedy was inappropriate since the defendants had an unexhausted remedy available in a direct appeal from the trial court's order. The Court said very little about why the bail ruling met the prerequisites of *Cohen.* It noted only that, as in *Cohen,* the rejected motion "did not merely invoke the discretion of the district court," as it "challenged the bail as violating statutory and constitutional standards." In a concurring opinion, Justice Jackson, the author of *Cohen,* added a brief explanation. "An order fixing bail," he noted, "can be reviewed without halting the main trial—its issues are entirely independent of the issues to be tried—and unless it can be reviewed before sentence, it can never be reviewed at all."

Six years later, the Court in *Carroll v. United States*[7] warned against the extension of the *Cohen* rule to criminal cases and characterized those orders in criminal cases that fit within the *Cohen* exception as "very few." For a substantial period thereafter, lower court and Supreme Court rulings treated *Stack* as almost a one-of-a-kind ruling. A broad range of pretrial rulings in criminal cases were held not to fall within the collateral order doctrine including orders denying motions to suppress evidence[8] and orders denying or granting a transfer or change of venue.[9]

In *Abney v. United States,*[10] the Supreme Court added an additional ruling to the list of orders deemed collateral. The Court there held appealable the denial of a pretrial defense motion seeking dismissal of an indictment on double jeopardy grounds. Chief Justice Burger's opinion for the Court concluded that the trial court's order met all the prerequisites for fitting within " 'the small class of cases' that *Cohen* has placed beyond the confines of the final-judgment rule." Initially, there had been a "fully consummated decision" of the trial court. The denial of the motion to dismiss had constituted a "complete, formal and * * * final rejection" of the defendant's double jeopardy claim. Secondly, the double jeopardy issue was "collateral to, and separable from, the principal issue at the accused's impending criminal trial, i.e., whether or not the accused is guilty of the offense charged." The defendant's challenge did not go to the "merits of the charge against him" nor did it relate to the evidence the government might use in proving its case. Finally, "the rights conferred upon the criminal accused by the Double Jeopardy Clause would be significantly undermined if appellate review of double jeopardy claims were postponed until after conviction and sentence." The function of the Double Jeopardy Clause, the Court stressed, was not simply to insulate the defendant against being subjected to double punishment, but also to protect the

6. 342 U.S. 1, 72 S.Ct. 1, 96 L.Ed. 3 (1951).

7. 354 U.S. 394, 77 S.Ct. 1332, 1 L.Ed.2d 1442 (1957) (holding that the trial court's ruling granting the defendant's motion to suppress was not a "collateral order" and was not subject to interlocutory appeal by the government).

8. DiBella v. United States, supra note 2.

9. Parr v. United States, 351 U.S. 513, 76 S.Ct. 912, 100 L.Ed. 1377 (1956).

10. 431 U.S. 651, 97 S.Ct. 2034, 52 L.Ed.2d 651 (1977).

defendant against being forced "to endure the personal strain, public embarrassment, and expense of a criminal trial more than once for the same offense." Reversal on appeal from a conviction following a second trial was too late to afford protection against "being twice put to trial for the same offense." Admittedly, allowing review prior to trial might "encourage some defendants to engage in dilatory appeals," but that was a necessary cost of protecting the double jeopardy right. Moreover, that problem, the Court noted, could be "obviated by * * * summary procedures and calendars [designed] to weed out frivolous claims of former jeopardy."

Unlike the claim in *Stack*, which would have been moot if reviewed following conviction, the claim in *Abney* was held for other reasons not to be adequately protected by review of conviction. Arguably, various other claims could fall in the same category. In *Helstoski v. Meanor*,[11] the Court found appealable an order denying a former Congressman's claim that the indictment against him violated the Speech or Debate Clause (which provides that "for any speech or debate," a Congressperson "shall not be questioned in any Place"). But in *United States v. MacDonald*[12] and *United States v. Hollywood Motor Car Company*,[13] the Court concluded that trial court orders rejecting speedy trial and vindictive prosecution claims prior to trial did not have the special qualities needed to fall under the "collateral order exception," which was to be construed "with the utmost strictness in criminal cases."

A critical factor distinguishing *Abney* and *Helstoski* on the one hand, and *MacDonald and Hollywood Motor Car* on the other, was the Court's characterization of the nature of the claim presented by defendant's pretrial motion. *Helstoski* held that the constitutional right of a Congressperson not to "be questioned" encompassed a protection against trial itself, not just conviction, and therefore was analogous to the double jeopardy claim presented in *Abney*. The claims presented in *Hol-*

lywood Motor Car and *MacDonald* did not include the right not to be tried at all. The dissenters in *Hollywood Motor Car* argued that the constitutional prohibition against vindictive prosecution should encompass protection against the burdens of trial, but the majority viewed the scope of the right quite differently. While earlier vindictive prosecution cases had spoken of a defendant's right "not to be hailed into court" by a prosecutor who added a more serious criminal charge in order to punish the defendant for his earlier exercise of a procedural right in connection with a lesser charge,[14] those cases had also recognized that the appropriate relief was simply the dismissal of the charge added vindictively. The defendant was never thought to be free of retrial on the original charge that was not tainted by vindictiveness. Hence, the petitioner's claim could not be characterized as presenting "a right not to be tried," but only as "a right whose remedy requires the dismissal of charges." As in the case of other challenges to the validity of a charge, such as a challenge to the constitutionality of the statute on which a charge is based, dismissal on an appeal following a conviction constituted an adequate remedy. Thus, what was at stake here was not a right, "the legal and practical value of which would be destroyed if it were not vindicated before trial." In *MacDonald*, a unanimous Court similarly characterized a defendant's speedy trial claim as not encompassing a "right not to be tried." It was "the delay before trial, not the trial itself that offends the constitutional guarantee." Indeed, to present an appeal prior to trial would threaten many of the interests protected by the Speedy Trial Clause.

MacDonald also distinguished *Abney* on other grounds. The determination as to whether there had been a denial of a speedy trial was often dependent upon an assessment of the prejudice caused by the delay, which could best be considered "only after the relevant facts

---

11.   442 U.S. 500, 99 S.Ct. 2445, 61 L.Ed.2d 30 (1979).

12.   435 U.S. 850, 98 S.Ct. 1547, 56 L.Ed.2d 18 (1978).

13.   458 U.S. 263, 102 S.Ct. 3081, 73 L.Ed.2d 754 (1982).

14.   See e.g., Blackledge v. Perry, discussed in § 13.5(a).

had been developed at trial." Hence, the pre-trial denial of the defendant's motion could not be considered a "complete, formal, and final rejection" of that claim, and the prejudice element of the claim could not be viewed as separable from the trial on the merits. Also, unlike the double jeopardy claim presented in *Abney*, which required an initial showing of prior jeopardy, there was "nothing about * * * a speedy trial claim which inherently limits the availability of the claim." If a right to immediate appeal were recognized, "any defendant" could raise such a claim in anticipation of a dilatory pretrial appeal. Given this reasoning and the Court's insistence that the claim present a right "not to be tried," any door to immediate appeals left open in *Abney* would seem to have been tightly shut by *MacDonald*.

In *Sell v. United States*,[15] the Court added to the short list of collateral orders subject to appeal a trial court's decision to forcibly medicate a defendant into competency for trial. "By the time of trial," the Court reasoned, the defendant "will have undergone forced medication—the very harm that he seeks to avoid. He cannot undo that harm if he is acquitted. Indeed, if he is acquitted, there will be no appeal through which he might obtain review." This, combined with "the severity of the intrusion and corresponding importance of the constitutional issue, readily distinguish" the order authorizing forced medication from the examples given by the dissenting justices, concluded the Court. The orders that the dissenters warned would be appealable under the majority's rule included an order requiring a defendant to wear an electronic bracelet, an order prohibiting the defendant from wearing a "Black Power" t-shirt in front of the jury, or an order compelling testimony in violation of the Fifth Amendment.

Other, earlier attempts to expand the "very few" instances in which pretrial rulings come within *Cohen* have been rejected by the Court. *Flanagan v. United States*[16] presented a defen-

dant's attempt to appeal an order disqualifying defense counsel on conflict grounds under Federal Rule 44(c). In an earlier ruling involving a disqualification motion in a civil case, the Court had concluded that even if such a motion raised an "issue completely separate from the merits of the action," it still did not meet the *Cohen* test because denial of immediate review would not lead to "irreparable harm" in light of relief that could be granted (through a new trial) on review of the final disposition of the case. The petitioners in *Flanagan* argued that the situation was different in a criminal case because even though there had been improper disqualification of defense counsel, relief on appeal from a conviction would be available only upon a showing that the loss of preferred counsel resulted in some "specifically demonstrated prejudice to the defense." That would require an impossibly speculative judgment, assuming that the replacement counsel had been competent. Responding to this contention, the Supreme Court noted that providing fully effective review would present no difficulty if the asserted right to counsel of one's choice were treated like the sixth amendment right to represent oneself, with a denial of the right requiring automatic reversal. Even if a showing of prejudice were required, as petitioner contended, the second condition of *Cohen*—"that the order be truly collateral"—was not satisfied. Assuming that a constitutional violation was tied to a finding of prejudice, a disqualification order could hardly be said to be "independent of the issues to be tried." The "effect of the disqualification on the defense, and hence whether the asserted right had been violated, cannot be fairly assessed until the substance of the prosecution's and defendant's case is known." In this respect, the petitioner's claim was analogous to the speedy trial claim presented in *MacDonald*.

In *Midland Asphalt Corp. v. United States*,[17] the defendant had stronger grounds for argu-

---

15. 539 U.S. 166, 123 S.Ct. 2174, 156 L.Ed.2d 197 (2003).

16. 465 U.S. 259, 104 S.Ct. 1051, 79 L.Ed.2d 288 (1984).

17. 489 U.S. 794, 109 S.Ct. 1494, 103 L.Ed.2d 879 (1989). Related to the raise-or-waive rule is the common-sense principle that a party introducing evidence cannot complain on appeal that the evidence was erroneously

ing that his constitutional claim would be "effectively unreviewable on appeal from a conviction," but the Court held that the ruling below still fell outside the *Cohen* exception because the very quality that made it unreviewable on appeal also established that it was not truly collateral to a decision on the merits of the case. The trial court in *Midland Asphalt* had denied the defendant's motion to dismiss the indictment based on an alleged violation of Federal Rule 6(e). The Supreme Court reasoned that if, under *Mechanik v. United States*,[18] such a ruling would be considered harmless error after conviction due to the subsequent petit jury finding of guilt beyond a reasonable doubt, the trial court's denial did not "resolve an important issue completely separate from the merits of the action." Instead, the trial court's ruling would "involve considerations 'enmeshed in the merits of the dispute' * * * [that] would * * * 'be affected by' the decision on the merits."[19]

The collateral order of doctrine of *Cohen* is applied in many states, and several others apply doctrines that are similar. These jurisdictions generally reach the same results as the federal courts, and often follow closely the leading Supreme Court rulings. Another group of states, however, does not recognize even the narrow exception to the final judgment concept recognized in *Cohen*. In most of these jurisdictions, alternative routes are available to defendants for obtaining immediate review of the few orders that the federal courts would describe as collateral. Some provide review through writ or through discretionary interlocutory appeal, for example, but this does not furnish defendants with the assurance of re-

view that they would have with a right to appeal under the collateral order doctrine. Some courts have questioned whether such an arrangement, insofar as it fails to grant a right to immediate appeal from a denial of a double jeopardy claim, is constitutionally acceptable under *Abney*. But *Abney* is better interpreted as a case interpreting the federal statute governing appeals, not the scope of the constitutional prohibition against double jeopardy, so that its holding is not binding on state courts interpreting their own law.

(d) Independent Proceedings. The collateral order doctrine permits an immediate appeal from orders that clearly are a part of the ongoing litigation. Certain proceedings, though related to ongoing or contemplated litigation, may be viewed as sufficiently separate from that litigation so that an order terminating that proceeding is itself a final judgment and therefore appealable. The crucial question here, the Supreme Court has noted, is whether the proceeding is "independent * * * or merely a step in the trial of the criminal case."[20]

Perhaps the clearest illustration of an independent proceeding is the third-party challenge to an order issued in a criminal case. Consider, for example, a news organization's objection to a trial court ruling that portions of a trial will be closed to the public. If the defendant, rather than a news organization, had objected to the closure, the trial court's rejection of that objection would be part of the criminal case and its immediate appeal subject to the limitations of the *Cohen* doctrine. When a third party such as a news organization brings an action to vindicate its alleged right to be present at the proceedings, that action is

---

admitted. The Court in *Ohler v. United States*, 529 U.S. 753, 120 S.Ct. 1851, 146 L.Ed.2d 826 (2000), rejected the defendant's argument that this principle should not apply when an accused seeks to "draw the sting" of his prior convictions by admitting them during direct examination before the prosecution has a chance to use them to impeach the defendant's credibility on cross-examination. A defendant who does this, the Court concluded, forfeits his ability to appeal the trial court's denial of a previous motion in limine to exclude those prior convictions. Consequently, a federal defendant has a hard choice if he becomes faced with what he thinks is an erroneous ruling rejecting his efforts to bar the government from introducing prior convictions: preserve the right to appeal and not mention the evidence on direct, risking that the jury will

conclude that the defendant was trying to conceal the conviction and is not to be believed; forfeit the right to appeal in the hopes of deflating the prosecution's impeachment efforts; or not testify at all.

18. See § 15.6(e).

19. See also *Cunningham*, cited in § 27.2(a), where the Court held, in a civil case, that an order imposing financial sanctions on an attorney for a discovery violation was not immediately appealable, noting that immediate appeal would undermine judicial discretion to structure sanctions and give rise to piecemeal appeals and delays.

20. Cogen v. United States, 278 U.S. 221, 49 S.Ct. 118, 73 L.Ed. 275 (1929).

deemed independent and the denial of its challenge is appealable by that party as a final judgment without applying the *Cohen* standards. Similarly, while the denial of a defense motion to strike surplusage in an indictment would not be appealable by the defendant, an unindicted co-conspirator may appeal from an order rejecting his motion to strike his name from the indictment.

Where the party seeking to appeal is a defendant or a potential defendant who has sought relief that would have a direct bearing on the criminal trial, both federal and state courts are much less likely to find that the denial of such relief is subject to immediate appeal. The leading case on the application of the independent proceeding doctrine in this context is *DiBella v. United States*.[21] A unanimous Supreme Court there held nonappealable the denial of a defense motion to suppress that had been filed before the defendant was indicted but after he had been arrested. The Court, per Frankfurter, J., reasoned that the factors that led to the characterization of a post-indictment suppression ruling as an interlocutory order were equally applicable to a pre-indictment ruling. Because the disposition of the motion, whether made before or after indictment, would "necessarily determine the conduct of the [eventual] trial," the ruling was not "fairly severable from the context of a larger litigious process." Similarly, whether the suppression motion was filed before or after indictment, the same "practical reasons" existed for not granting immediate review. First, treating "such a disjointed ruling on the admissibility of a potential item of evidence as an independent proceeding, with full panoply of appeal and attendant stay, [would] entail serious disruption of the conduct of a criminal trial." Second, appellate intervention prior to trial would result in a "truncated presentation of the issue of admissibility because the legality of the search too often cannot truly be determined until the evidence at the trial has brought all circumstances to light."

Although holding that pre-indictment and post-indictment suppression motions would be treated alike for the purpose of appellate review, Justice Frankfurter held open the possibility that under some circumstances a precharge ruling on a motion challenging an illegal search could be immediately appealable. After noting that when the criminal process has reached the stage of an arrest or a filing of a complaint, a suppression motion must be viewed "as a step in the criminal case preliminary to the trial thereof," he added: "Only if the motion is solely for return of property and is in no way tied to a criminal prosecution *in esse* against the movant can the proceedings be regarded as independent."

In judging whether a defendant may appeal under *DiBella* an order denying a motion under Federal Rule 41 for the return of unlawfully seized property, lower courts have divided over exactly when a prosecution is "in esse" ("in being"). Specifically, they have disagreed about the significance of the initiation of a grand jury investigation. Noting that the *DiBella* opinion characterized a presentation before a grand jury as a "part of the federal prosecution," many courts hold that the prosecution is "in esse" whenever the movant is the target of a grand jury investigation. Others maintain that a prosecution requires more than mere investigation.

(e) Grand Jury Proceedings. Application of both the independent proceeding and collateral order doctrines has proven especially troublesome in the analysis of court orders growing out of grand jury proceedings. Even though the absence of indictment makes each grand jury proceeding "party-less," courts have refused to treat all challenges by witnesses and others to grand jury orders as independent proceedings subject to appeal prior to resolution of the criminal case. In *Cobbledick v. United States*,[22] the Supreme Court held that the denial of a witness's motion to quash a grand jury subpoena was not appealable. The Court distinguished the proceeding to enforce an administrative subpoena which is commonly regarded as an independent action for agency discovery, thereby rendering

---

21. 369 U.S. 121, 82 S.Ct. 654, 7 L.Ed.2d 614 (1962).

22. 309 U.S. 323, 60 S.Ct. 540, 84 L.Ed. 783 (1940).

orders granting or quashing an agency subpoena final and appealable. The ongoing grand jury proceeding, *Cobbledick* noted, was instead part of the ongoing prosecution:

> The proceeding before a grand jury constitutes "a judicial inquiry" * * * of the most ancient lineage. The duration of its life, frequently short, is limited by statute. It is no less important to safeguard against undue interruption the inquiry instituted by a grand jury than to protect from delay the progress of the trial after an indictment has been found. * * * That a grand jury proceeding has no defined litigants and that none may emerge from it, is irrelevant to the issue.

The Court did recognize one avenue for appeal by a grand jury witness, however. In the context of a trial, the Court had held that the rejection of a witness's objection to a subpoena was not a final order. To gain appellate review, the witness had to refuse to comply and be held in contempt, which did produce a final order. The same requirement, *Cobbledick* held, was applicable to the grand jury witness. If the witness "chooses to disobey and is held in contempt," an immediate appeal will be allowed. That appeal "may involve an interruption of * * * the investigation," but allowing it is essential to preserve the witness's rights. "[N]ot to allow this interruption," the Court reasoned, "would forever preclude review of the witness's claim, for his alternatives are to abandon the claim or languish in jail." Accordingly, once held in contempt, the "witness' situation becomes so severed from the main proceeding as to permit an appeal."

In addition, an exception to the contempt prerequisite exists when a subpoena duces tecum is directed at a person other than the appellant and that person cannot be expected to risk contempt for the purpose of protecting the appellant's interest in the property or information subpoenaed. This exception was established in *Perlman v. United States.*[23] In *Perlman,* the clerk of a federal court was directed to produce before a grand jury documents that Perlman had deposited with the clerk in connection with a patent infringement suit. Claiming a continuing right to those documents, Perlman challenged the order directed to the clerk and subsequently appealed from the denial of that challenge. As later explained in *United States v. Ryan,*[24] Perlman's appeal was allowed without the witness (the clerk) meeting the contempt prerequisite of *Cobbledick* because the witness did not share Perlman's interest in challenging the order. Without immediate review, Perlman would have been "powerless to avert the mischief of the [challenged] order." In *Ryan,* the Court stressed that *Perlman* created only a narrow exception to a sound policy that, in the interest of limiting appeals that would disrupt "expedition in the administration of the criminal law," puts the objecting witness to the inhibiting cost of standing in contempt. The lower courts have applied the exception to a variety of situations in which the interests of the party subpoenaed do not coincide with those of the person objecting to the subpoena. For example, appeals have been allowed from an order denying an appellant's motion to quash subpoenas directing her treating physician to turn over her medical records, an order upholding a subpoena to a grand jury target's supervisor, an order denying a bank depositor's motion to quash a grand jury subpoena issued to his bank, and an order denying a record custodian's motion to quash a subpoena issued to a corporation.

Where the challenge to ongoing grand jury proceedings does not relate to the appearance of a witness, the contempt alternative of *Cobbledick* may not be available. In such cases, courts focus on whether the person seeking to appeal (who is usually the target of the investigation) will have a subsequently available appellate remedy if an immediate appeal from the denial of his request for relief is not available. Thus, if the target is objecting to the alleged use of the grand jury to develop evidence for a civil case, a court is likely to hold that an immediate appeal is not permissible since a later objection (and appeal) is available

---

23. 247 U.S. 7, 38 S.Ct. 417, 62 L.Ed. 950 (1918).

24. 402 U.S. 530, 91 S.Ct. 1580, 29 L.Ed.2d 85 (1971).

if the government should seek to transfer any such evidence to a potential civil litigant or to use it in a civil proceeding. Similarly, if the target claims that the grand jury proceeding is being tainted by misconduct, a court may hold that such an objection can be advanced when (and if) an indictment is issued and an appeal can then be taken when (and if) the target is convicted. Some courts are less willing than others, however, to view such subsequent avenues of appeal as adequate. Thus, appeals have been allowed from rulings denying motions to preclude grand-jury gathering of evidence to be used in prosecuting a pending indictment, and motions requesting an evidentiary hearing into the alleged resumption of prosecutorial misconduct that had led to the dismissal of a prior indictment.

Once the grand jury investigation has ended, a petitioner seeking relief unrelated to an on-going prosecution can more readily claim that his request involves an independent proceeding. Thus, an appeal can be taken from the grant or denial of a Rule 6(e) motion for disclosure of grand jury minutes for use in an unrelated proceeding.

§ 27.3 Prosecution Appeals

(a) Constitutional Constraints. For much of the nineteenth century, most states denied the government an opportunity to appeal an acquittal through writ of error, and many states disallowed writs of error for the state in criminal cases altogether. Government appeals of acquittals were considered a violation of the defendant's freedom from double jeopardy, a right originally guaranteed to most state defendants by state constitutional provisions and to federal defendants by the Fifth Amendment. As discussed in more detail in Chapter 25, the Double Jeopardy Clause, now applicable to the States under the Due Process Clause, continues to bar the government from appealing a variety of rulings.

(b) The Need for Specific Statutory Authorization. Absent specific statutory authorization, the prosecution lacks the right to appeal an adverse ruling in a criminal case. The policy underlying that position was set forth by the Supreme Court's 1892 ruling in *United States v. Sanges*.[1] Congress had granted federal defendants the statutory right to apply for writs of error in criminal cases, but had not extended the same opportunity to the government. Consequently, the Court concluded, "the defendant, having been once put upon his trial and discharged by the court, is not to be again vexed for the same cause, unless the legislature, acting within its constitutional authority, has made express provision for a review of the judgment at the instance of the government."

After Congress adopted in 1907 a statute allowing government appeals under specified circumstances, the Supreme Court, consistent with *Sanges*, strictly limited such appeals to the letter of that provision. Government attempts to gain more expansive appellate review using the general appeals statute, 18 U.S.C. § 1291 (allowing for appeals from final decisions), were rejected by the Supreme Court in *Carroll v. United States*:[2]

> [A]ppeals by the Government in criminal cases are something unusual, exceptional, not favored. The history shows resistance of the Court to the opening of an appellate route for the Government until it was plainly provided by the Congress, and after that a close restriction of its uses to those authorized by the statute.

In *Arizona v. Manypenny*,[3] the Court reiterated this limitation and reviewed its basis, noting that the Court's "continuing refusal to assume that the United States possesses any inherent right to appeal" reflects the need "to check the Federal Government's possible misuse of its enormous prosecutorial powers." Requiring Congress "to speak with a clear voice when extending to the Executive a right to expand criminal prosecutions" through appeal places the responsibility for "such assertions

1. 144 U.S. 310, 12 S.Ct. 609, 36 L.Ed. 445 (1892).

2. 354 U.S. 394, 77 S.Ct. 1332, 1 L.Ed.2d 1442 (1957).

3. 451 U.S. 232, 101 S.Ct. 1657, 68 L.Ed.2d 58 (1981).

of authority over citizens in the democratically elected Legislature where it belongs."

This philosophy is repeated frequently in state as well as federal decisions. All of the states now have provisions allowing prosecution appeals from at least a limited class of orders in criminal cases. These provisions, like the Criminal Appeals Act governing federal criminal cases (18 U.S.C. § 3731),[4] typically list which interlocutory and final orders may be appealed by the prosecution. In many jurisdictions, these provisions restrict the government's right to appeal further than the limitations on appeal imposed by the final judgment rule and the Double Jeopardy Clause.

(c) Pretrial Rulings. Statutes regulating appeals by the prosecution commonly authorize appeals from pretrial rulings that would be considered final judgments, as well as from other interlocutory orders.

Final judgments. As to final judgments, some statutes refer broadly to appeals from all "final judgments," or, as in the federal provision, from all "dismissals of an indictment or information * * * as to one or more counts." These provisions encompass dismissals based upon such grounds as the insufficiency of the accusatory pleading, prior jeopardy, denial of a speedy trial, lack of sufficient evidence to support a bindover, prosecutorial misconduct, and the unconstitutionality of the underlying statute. Other jurisdictions restrict the category of appealable final judgments to dismissals based on a deficiency in the pleading itself. A few states have even more restrictive provisions, providing a prosecution appeal as of right only from a ruling holding unconstitutional the statute forming the basis for the charges. In addition, some states limit the final judgments that a prosecutor may appeal to dismissals of felony indictments.

Interlocutory pretrial rulings generally. The states also vary in their treatment of prosecution appeals from interlocutory pretrial rulings. As noted in § 27.2, with some exceptions,

a defendant typically cannot appeal an adverse interlocutory order, but can gain review of the adverse pretrial ruling on appeal if he is convicted. The prosecution, however, is in a quite different position. If the government is not allowed an immediate appeal from an adverse interlocutory ruling, there will be no opportunity for later appellate review should the defendant be acquitted, since the double jeopardy prohibition then bars further prosecution. This circumstance has led a few jurisdictions to provide the prosecution with the opportunity to appeal nearly any adverse pretrial interlocutory order. Most jurisdictions, however, have stopped short of conferring such broad authority, considering the interests of the defendant and society in the swift resolution of criminal cases to be worthy of greater protection. After all, interlocutory appeals may interrupt a case and delay trial for months, during which time proof may be lost and the defendant may remain incarcerated. Most jurisdictions fall between these two extremes and allow the prosecution to appeal from designated categories of pretrial interlocutory orders.

Suppression Orders. The interlocutory order most frequently included in statutes authorizing appeal by the prosecution is the suppression order. The federal government and most states have adopted legislation providing for review of suppression orders as a matter of right. An order suppressing evidence generally is held not to fall within a provision authorizing appeals from a "final judgment" or a "dismissal of an indictment" since it does not formally terminate the proceeding. Two grounds are advanced in support of allowing the prosecution to appeal from a trial court's decision to grant a defendant's motion to suppress evidence. One justification is the special need for appellate court rulings on legal issues relating to searches and seizures and interrogation. The law in this area is so uncertain, it has been argued, that law enforcement officers dissatisfied with the rulings of individual trial

---

4. 18 U.S.C.A. § 3731 provides:

In a criminal case an appeal by the United States shall lie to a court of appeals from a decision, judgment, or order of a district court dismissing an indictment or information or granting a new trial after verdict or judgment,

as to any one or more counts, or any part thereof, except that no appeal shall lie where the double jeopardy clause of the United States Constitution prohibits further prosecution.

judges will persist in a challenged practice until they obtain a favorable decision from another trial judge, and perhaps a favorable ruling on appeal after a resulting conviction. The better rule, it is argued, is to give the prosecution the opportunity to gain immediate review of those trial court rulings that it considers questionable.

Several state provisions authorizing the appeal of suppression orders by the government limit that authority to the appeal of orders relating to illegal practices by police in obtaining evidence. Other statutes, such as 18 U.S.C. § 3731, speak generally of orders "suppressing or excluding" evidence, and have been held applicable to a broad range of pretrial orders limiting the government's proof at trial. Appealable rulings have included orders quashing witness subpoenas, orders barring testimony due to defense claims of privilege and work-product protection, and orders excluding testimony as a sanction for the prosecution's failure to comply with discovery rules. The broader review extended to prosecutors under these statutes builds upon the second justification for allowing the prosecution to appeal suppression orders, namely the recognition that the practical effect of such an order is, in many cases, equivalent to dismissal. A ruling suppressing evidence often eliminates the heart of the prosecution's case. With the opportunity to appeal such rulings, even those that result from its own motions in limine, the prosecution may have the opportunity to gain appellate review of a wide range of orders that otherwise would be subsumed in an acquittal.

Consistent with this case-ending justification for review, some states condition appeal on a prosecutor's certification that the suppression order will eliminate any "reasonable possibility" of a successful prosecution. The federal statute and a number of state provisions, for example, require certification that "the appeal is not taken for the purpose of delay and that the [suppressed] evidence is a substantial proof of a fact material in the proceeding." In other jurisdictions, certification is not required, but the prosecution must otherwise establish that the trial court's ruling will have a substantial impact upon the outcome of the prosecution.

Other interlocutory orders. Many jurisdictions allowing prosecution appeals from pretrial interlocutory orders do not extend that authority beyond orders suppressing evidence. Several jurisdictions, however, authorize appeals from one or more additional categories of interlocutory rulings that the legislature considers essential to review before final judgment. For example, the Bail Reform Act allows a prosecution appeal from a district court's pretrial release order. Rather than designate particular categories of orders that a prosecutor may appeal as of right, some states limit the prosecution's ability to appeal using the standards that apply to defense requests for interlocutory review, or rely on the discretion of the court. At least one state grants a right to appeal if the interlocutory ruling will have a "reasonable likelihood of causing either serious impairment to or a termination of the prosecution."

(d) Post–Jeopardy Rulings. Statutory provisions authorizing government appeals typically include one or more provisions applicable to rulings issued after jeopardy has attached. Most allow a prosecution appeal from "an order arresting judgment." These provisions have not met significant opposition because (1) the order arresting judgment clearly constitutes a final judgment; (2) since the defendant has been found guilty prior to the issuance of the order, reversal on appeal does not require a new trial but simply requires reinstituting the original verdict; and (3) the order arresting judgment commonly must be based on grounds that are unrelated to the factual innocence of the defendant (e.g., lack of jurisdiction).

While only the second factor cited above applies to the grant of a new trial following a conviction, the federal system and a substantial number of states now allow the prosecution to appeal from a new trial order. Such an appeal permits the court to make and the prosecution to challenge underlying rulings that could not have been appealed if they had been made before or during trial. The new trial order might be based, for example, on a trial court's post-verdict determination that the trial had been marred by improper joinder or an erroneous charge to the jury. If the trial court had originally ruled in favor of the defendant on the same points, the end result would have been a mistrial (on the joinder issue) or perhaps an acquittal (depending upon the influence of the jury charge), and the prosecution would not have had the opportunity to appeal either ruling.

Statutory provisions that allow the prosecutor to appeal from the dismissal of an indictment or information may also provide a basis for a post-jeopardy appeal. Although some of these provisions refer specifically to dismissals prior to trial, most do not contain that limitation. Where the dismissal occurred after jeopardy attached, but before a verdict was reached, reprosecution will be barred by the double jeopardy prohibition if the "dismissal" was in fact an "acquittal" or constituted the equivalent of a mistrial not justified by either "manifest necessity" or a defense request.[5] Federal law and several state provisions expressly prohibit an appeal from a post-jeopardy "dismissal" where reprosecution would be barred. In other jurisdictions, statutes have been interpreted not to allow an appeal where reprosecution is prohibited by the Constitution.

Because the provisions authorizing the government to appeal from suppression orders apply only to *pretrial* suppression rulings, conceivably a defendant could cut off appellate review by delaying his motion to suppress until after jeopardy has attached. In the case of the typical suppression motion claiming the unconstitutional acquisition of evidence, however, statutes ordinarily require that such a motion be presented before trial. Nevertheless, most jurisdictions allow the trial court at least limited discretion to entertain a defense motion to suppress made during trial, and there will be cases in which the circumstances justify allowing an otherwise untimely motion (e.g., where defendant lacked a reasonable opportunity to present the motion before trial). To

enable the government to defeat deliberate manipulation of the government's statutory right to appeal by the defense, some courts treat a defendant's successful mid-trial suppression motion as implicit consent to the granting of a mistrial, consent that would overcome any subsequent double jeopardy objection to reprosecution.

Where a guilty verdict has been returned, but the judge rejects that verdict and enters an acquittal, double jeopardy again does not bar appellate review.[6] Appeal from such an order is not clearly authorized, however, by the usual provisions governing prosecution appeals. Accordingly, several states have adopted provisions specifically allowing appeals from acquittals entered by the trial court following a guilty verdict. Finally, prosecutors in most jurisdictions are allowed to appeal sentences, as well.[7]

§ 27.4 Review by Writ

(a) Extraordinary Writs Generally. Where a trial court's order is not appealable, the defense or prosecution may seek review from a higher court through an application for one of the writs commonly described as "extraordinary" writs. These include the writ of habeas corpus, described more fully in Chapter 28, the writ of mandamus, and the writ of prohibition. The writs of mandamus and prohibition (or a local law replacement for those writs) provide an avenue for both prosecution and defense to obtain review of a broad range of rulings that are not appealable. Both sides may use the writs to gain review of interlocutory pretrial orders not otherwise subject to immediate review. Since the defense has a right to appeal from all final judgments, it has no need to look to the writs to obtain review of final orders. The prosecution, however, may be forced to turn to the writs where particular final orders, though they could be appealed consistent with double jeopardy, are not within the authorization of statute specifying the decisions that may be appealed by the government.

---

5. See § 25.3(a).
6. See § 25.3(e).

7. See § 26.3(g).

(b) Prohibition and Mandamus: Traditional Limits and Modern Extensions. The writs of prohibition and mandamus traditionally were available only to control jurisdictional excesses. Prohibition was used to confine a lower court to the lawful exercise of its prescribed jurisdiction and mandamus was used to compel it to exercise that jurisdiction. When raising jurisdictional issues, the writs serve to protect the "interests of the judicial system as a whole" by correcting action or inaction contrary to the structural limits at the foundation of that. The writs have also been employed in cases that were properly before a court. A writ of mandamus requires a lower court to take action that it had no discretion to avoid (action commonly described as "ministerial" in nature), and the writ of prohibition will bar an order that the lower court lacked authority to issue under any set of circumstances. Although some states continue to adhere to these traditional limits, most have moved substantially beyond them.

Some courts maintain that use of the writs in criminal cases must be very carefully limited to jurisdictional issues. Others recognize considerable leeway in exercising the writs, at least when it is the defendant and not the government who seeks relief. Among the factors that courts consider in determining whether the writs should apply to non-jurisdictional claims, the availability of an alternative means of obtaining relief (e.g., through a subsequent appeal) is prominent. Nevertheless, the error is clear and the harm to the petitioner is unlikely to be remedied by a later appeal, if the issue presented is of great significance, or if there is a need to preclude recurring error, the appellate court may conclude that the advantages of immediate disposition outweigh the policies of finality.

Even in those jurisdictions that reach a broad range of issues under the writs, courts continue to stress that the writs should be sparingly allowed. This reluctance reflects both the apprehension that the writs could be used so frequently that their use would imperil the policies that limit the right of appeal, particularly the final judgment rule, and the concern that the writs not become a form of open-ended discretionary review for orders not appealable as of right.

(c) Defense Petitions. Certain types of defense claims will be subject to review by writ without question. Allegations that the lower court lacked jurisdiction over the proceeding are reviewable, as discussed above. Review by writ also has been available where the grand jury or prosecutor lacked authority to initiate prosecution of a particular crime, venue was improper, or the lower court otherwise lacked authority to try the particular offense. Also reviewed are claims thought to address impending harm that is either irreparable, or that goes beyond the hardship of a possibly needless or flawed trial. Such claims include the alleged violation of the statutory or constitutional right to a speedy trial, the denial of an allegedly meritorious double jeopardy claim, allegations that the trial would be conducted by the wrong decisionmaker, or allegations that compliance with an interlocutory order will force a loss of privacy or privilege which would not be remedied by a ruling excluding the evidence from trial.

In some jurisdictions, defense access to the writs is even broader, and appellate courts will consider an application by writ directed at almost any pretrial ruling, provided the legal issue presented has some general significance. Among the states adopting this generous view of the writs, California has made particularly extensive use of the writs in criminal cases. California courts have reviewed by writ pretrial orders denying defense motions to obtain broader pretrial discovery, to change venue to a community less saturated with publicity, to dismiss an indictment where the prosecutor failed to present exculpatory evidence to the grand jury, to appoint a requested attorney as defense counsel, to place defendant in a statutorily prescribed diversion program, to substitute a trial judge, and to exclude from consideration in a pending prosecution a prior conviction obtained without an effective waiver of counsel. The "common thread" woven through these cases, the California Supreme Court has noted, is "the responsiveness of appellate tribunals when initiative is required to protect a defendant's fundamental right to a fair trial," recognizing that "the burden, expense and delay involved in a trial" may often render "an appeal from an eventual judgment an inadequate remedy."

(d) Prosecution Applications. Prosecutors to use the extraordinary writs to gain appellate review of a wide variety of orders issued at various stages of the criminal process. The prosecution, for example, may seek to obtain review of significant pretrial interlocutory orders. As discussed in § 27.3, apart from suppression rulings, such orders will not be appealable in many jurisdictions. Where appeals of final judgments are limited to a particular class of orders, the prosecutor may also look to the writs to gain review of a pretrial dismissal that does not fit within the appeals statute. Finally, the writs may be used by prosecutors to gain review of unappealable rulings entered after a jury returns a guilty verdict. Thus, where the appeals statute refers only to appeals from post-conviction orders arresting a judgment or dismissing an indictment, challenges to the grant of a new trial or the entry of a judgment n.o.v. may be pursued through a writ application. In jurisdictions in which the prosecution does not have a right to appeal a sentence, the writs have been used to challenge sentences.

Some courts hold that a writ will be available to the prosecution only when the lower court "acted in excess of its jurisdiction" by issuing an order that it had no authority to issue under any circumstances, or by failing to issue an order that it had no discretion under any circumstances not to issue. Other courts have held that a writ will issue to correct a gross abuse of discretion where a significant prosecution interest is at stake. Still other courts hold that the prosecution may use the writs to gain review of any ruling that raises a legal question of general significance.

There are two concerns that may lead a court to apply more stringent standards to prosecution petitions than are applied to either civil cases or defense petitions in criminal cases. Courts frequently note the need to approach the prosecution's use of the writs with "an awareness * * * that a man is entitled to a speedy trial."[1] Courts also express concern that the writs not be used so as to undermine the limitations that the legislature has placed on the prosecution's right to appeal. The significance of each of these concerns varies with the nature of the lower court ruling challenged by the prosecutor.

For example, a prosecutor's application for a writ will not always threaten the defendant's interest in a speedy trial. Review of orders issued prior to indictment or during an investigation do delay the charging determination, but the person affected is hardly in the same position as a defendant awaiting trial. Similarly, if the government challenges an order issued after the defendant was tried and found guilty, there is delay in the final disposition, but usually not in the presentation of evidence. Delay generally causes far less judicial concern where the only consequence of the delay is, for example, a continued period of uncertainty as to what sentence will be imposed. Thus, when appellate review of a sentence is not available, the writs are regularly used by the prosecution to obtain review of sentences that are allegedly outside the trial court's sentencing authority. The most serious threat to the defendant's speedy trial interest is presented by a government petition seeking review of an interlocutory pretrial ruling. Many courts insist that the writs here be used only to challenge a ruling that the trial court clearly had no authority to issue under any circumstances. Some courts, however, are willing to make the defendant bear the burden of delay in order to benefit the system as a whole by correcting an erroneous application of a trial judge's authority, especially when the error could have a recurring impact within the jurisdiction.

Federal courts generally limit the government's access to mandamus to "rare cases" in

---

§ 27.4

1. See Will v. United States, 389 U.S. 90, 88 S.Ct. 269, 19 L.Ed.2d 305 (1967).

which the lower court's order falls outside the limits of judicial power and poses irreparable harm, but they have also recognized mandamus can be appropriate when an application presents an issue that is "novel, of great importance, and likely to recur." Thus federal courts have extended review to an order assessing fees against the government, an order not to execute an arrest warrant, an order refusing to convene a grand jury, an order denying the press access to jury lists, and even an order adopting an erroneous jury instruction.

§ 27.5   The Scope of Appellate Review

(a) Mootness. An appellate court will not review a lower court decision, in either a civil or criminal case, where events have rendered the claim moot. One such event is the death of the defendant. Should the defendant die pending discretionary or collateral review, courts typically will simply dismiss the petition or appeal and let the underlying judgment or ruling stand.[1] When a defendant dies pending direct review, however, most courts are willing to take further action. Many courts will set aside the conviction and dismiss the indictment or information. Such abatement is premised on the theory that without it, the defendant would be deprived of his statutory right to review, and that abatement prevents both recovery against the decedent's estate (if there is a fine) and the use of the conviction in civil litigation against the estate. Other courts, reasoning that "it seems unreasonable automatically to * * * pretend the defendant was never indicted, tried, and found guilty," choose instead to dismiss the appeal and vacate the conviction only if the deceased's personal representative or the state moves for the substitution of another person for the deceased party pursuant to court rule, enabling the appeal to go ahead. Heightened concern for the rights of victims has also persuaded some judges that abatement is inappropriate, as it "creates an unacceptable and ultimately painful legal fiction for the surviving victims which implies that the defendants have somehow been exonerated."

Traditionally, a criminal appeal also was viewed as moot once the sentence imposed by the trial court was fully satisfied, that is, when the defendant had paid his fine and served the full period of imprisonment or probation. While at least one jurisdiction still adheres to this view, most have departed from it by adopting one or more "exceptions" to the fully-satisfied-sentence standard.

Collateral consequences. The most significant exception is known as the collateral consequences exception. A case is not moot, under this exception, notwithstanding full satisfaction of the sentence, if the defendant is still subject to a collateral legal disability as a result of his conviction. Courts taking a narrow view of this exception require the defendant to show that a particular adverse collateral consequence is likely to be applied to him (e.g., that he is a member of a licensed profession and the conviction will result in the loss of his license). Merely pointing to the "hypothetical effects" of a conviction is insufficient.

In *Sibron v. New York*,[2] the Supreme Court adopted for the federal courts a more liberal view of the collateral consequences exception. The Supreme Court in *Sibron* construed its earlier mootness opinions as having "abandoned all inquiry into the actual existence of specific collateral consequences and in effect presumed that they existed." The "mere possibility" that there would be "adverse collateral legal consequences" was sufficient to keep a case "from ending 'ignominiously in the limbo of mootness.'" Sibron's case met that "mere possibility" standard because New York statutes would allow his conviction to be used to impeach him if he should become a defendant in a future trial, and they required that the conviction be considered in sentencing should

§ 27.5

1. See Dove v. United States, 423 U.S. 325, 96 S.Ct. 579, 46 L.Ed.2d 531 (1976) (dismissing petition for certiorari following petitioner's death); Warden v. Palermo, 431 U.S. 911, 97 S.Ct. 2166, 53 L.Ed.2d 221 (1977) (dismissing petition, citing *Dove*); Mintzes v. Buchanon, 471 U.S. 154,

105 S.Ct. 2006, 85 L.Ed.2d 120 (1985); United States v. Green, 507 U.S. 545, 113 S.Ct. 1835, 123 L.Ed.2d 260 (1993) (per curiam) (dismissing petition, citing *Buchanon*).

2. 392 U.S. 40, 88 S.Ct. 1889, 20 L.Ed.2d 917 (1968).

he be convicted of a future offense. Moreover, the fact that Sibron was already a multiple offender was not critical. Sentencing judges and trial juries might be willing to discount a certain number of prior transgressions. It was "impossible * * * to say at what point the number of convictions on a man's record renders his reputation irredeemable." Also, the Court could not "foretell what opportunities might present themselves in the future for the removal of [the] other convictions."

In holding that the mere possibility of collateral legal consequences forestalled a finding of mootness, the *Sibron* opinion stressed the broad range of legal disabilities that traditionally attach to a criminal conviction. The Court also emphasized the importance of accommodating both "the constitutional rule against entertaining moot controversies" and the need for an efficient system of adjudication. There was nothing "abstract or feigned" about the appeal before it, and neither the defendant nor the prosecution had been "wanting in diligence or fervor in the litigation." Moreover, "the question of the validity of [Sibron's] criminal conviction" could arise in "many [future] contexts," and it was "always preferable to litigate a matter when it is directly and principally in dispute, rather than in a proceeding where it is collateral to the central controversy." Reviewing the conviction on direct appeal would ensure that the dispute would be fully litigated when it was "fresh," and when additional facts could be gathered, if necessary, "without a substantial risk that witnesses will die or memories fade."

Building upon *Sibron,* most courts have taken the position that the possibility of adverse collateral consequences from a criminal conviction will be " 'presumed' as an 'obvious fact of life.' " Even where a defendant's conviction is for a low-level misdemeanor, a careful search of state law is likely to turn up some provision through which the conviction could come back to haunt him. In those misdemeanor cases in which defendants have lost their appeals to a mootness finding, they apparently sought to rely on the consequences of adverse treatment

by private parties rather than disabilities that flowed from state or federal law.

The presumption of adverse collateral consequences may be limited to challenges to convictions. In *Spencer v. Kemna*,[3] the Court refused to presume that a defendant who has served his sentence and challenges not his conviction, but rather the revocation of his parole, continues to suffer collateral consequences from the revocation sufficient to keep his habeas corpus proceeding alive after he was released from the confinement brought about by the revocation. The Court distinguished *Sibron*, first discounting the decision as one that developed prior to the tightening of the requirements for establishing standing under Article III, and second, observing that while "the presumption of significant collateral consequences is likely to comport with reality" when a defendant challenges a conviction, the same cannot be said when a defendant challenges the revocation of parole. The *Spencer* Court also drew upon reasoning in *Lane v. Williams*,[4] a case concluding that the presumption of adverse consequences will not apply when a defendant on habeas review challenges the penalty imposed for a parole violation. Just as adverse collateral consequences could not be presumed when a defendant challenged the penalty imposed for a parole or probation violation, the presumption was also inappropriate when the challenge went to the validity of the revocation itself. The appellant's predictions of harm from an unreviewed revocation proceeding were speculative, the Court in *Spencer* concluded, for the parole violation would be only one factor among many that would be considered by a parole board in any future parole decision, and even then would only become relevant if the defendant at some future date committed a crime and was returned to prison. The Court also went on to reject as speculative any apprehension that the revocation would be used to impeach the defendant, or introduced as substantive evidence, should the defendant appear in a future criminal proceeding. Moreover, the Court discounted possible employment or sentencing repercussions

---

3. 523 U.S. 1, 118 S.Ct. 978, 140 L.Ed.2d 43 (1998).

4. 455 U.S. 624, 102 S.Ct. 1322, 71 L.Ed.2d 508 (1982).

from the parole violation as "insufficient to keep the controversy alive." *Spencer* has compelled at least one lower court to question "whether the burden of establishing collateral consequences of a judgment other than a conviction can, after *Spencer*, ever be carried when * * * the only consequences of which the defendant is complaining are contingent upon his committing future crimes or future disciplinary violations."

Issues "capable of repetition, yet evading review." One other common exception exists under which courts will examine an otherwise moot claim on appeal, regardless of whether it is the death of the defendant, the completion of sentence, or some other event that has rendered the claim moot. Courts regularly decide appeals, notwithstanding mootness, where the issue presented is "capable of repetition, yet evading review." In the federal courts, this doctrine applies only where "(1) the challenged action [is] in its duration too short to be fully litigated prior to cessation or expiration, and (2) there [is] a reasonable expectation that the same complaining party [will] be subject to the same action again." In *Spencer*, for example, after holding that the defendant's challenge to his parole revocation did not qualify under the collateral consequences exception, the Court rejected review under the "capable-of-repetition" doctrine as well. The Court concluded that the defendant had not shown either "that the time between parole revocation and expiration of sentence is always so short as to evade review" or that there was "a reasonable likelihood that he [would] once again be paroled and have that parole revoked."

States do not necessarily insist on such an exacting showing, and may require only a likelihood that *other* litigants will confront the same issues, accompanied by some barrier to review. Most states, however, also require that in order for a court to reach an otherwise moot, but recurring question, the question must be important or of "broad public interest." The issues that courts have addressed under this exception are quite varied, and in-clude press access to court proceedings and documents, the meaning or constitutionality of new statutes, issues regarding release from custody prior to trial or pending appeal, and a variety of sentencing issues.

(b) The Concurrent Sentence Doctrine. Where a defendant receives concurrent sentences on each of several counts of an indictment, and the appellate court upholds the conviction on any one count carrying a sentence at least equal to a remaining challenged count, the validity of the conviction remaining on the count will not be reviewed in jurisdictions that continue to adhere to what is commonly termed the "concurrent sentence doctrine." Prior to the Supreme Court's decision in *Sibron*, this doctrine was often described as an application of traditional mootness principles. There was thought to be no "live controversy" as to the remaining counts since, once a count carrying an equal concurrent sentence was affirmed, reversal of the remaining counts would not reduce the length of the defendant's confinement. In *Benton v. Maryland*,[5] the Supreme Court held that in light of its *Sibron* ruling the concurrent sentence doctrine could no longer be justified on mootness grounds. The defendant had an obvious interest in challenging each and every count on which he was convicted because separate collateral consequences could flow from each. It was possible, for example, that petitioner might find himself in a jurisdiction in which each of the counts was treated separately under a recidivist statute. Although "this possibility might well be a remote one, it is enough," the *Benton* opinion noted, "to give this case an adversary cast and make it justiciable."

While rejecting mootness as a grounding for the concurrent sentence doctrine, the *Benton* opinion left open the possibility that the doctrine might be justified as a "rule of judicial convenience," to be applied at the discretion of the appellate court. The Court has since applied the doctrine in *Barnes v. United States*,[6] where it noted that while challenges to certain remaining counts were not moot, it would "de-

---

5. 395 U.S. 784, 89 S.Ct. 2056, 23 L.Ed.2d 707 (1969).

6. 412 U.S. 837, 93 S.Ct. 2357, 37 L.Ed.2d 380 (1973).

cline as a discretionary matter" to rule on their validity.[7] In *Ray v. United States*,[8] however, the Court emphasized the limits of the discretion a court may exercise in declining to address a defendant's challenge to a conviction for a count which carries a sentence concurrent to the sentence on another count. The Court held that because Ray was obligated to pay a $50 "special assessment" for each count of conviction, the sentences were not truly concurrent, precluding application of the doctrine.[9]

Some lower federal courts have concluded that *Ray* essentially abolished the doctrine for direct review of federal convictions, since the count-by-count assessment is mandated by statute. Several state courts and one federal court of appeals have rejected the use of the concurrent sentence doctrine entirely, even as a rule of judicial convenience, concluding that whatever convenience is achieved through application of the concurrent sentence doctrine is dwarfed by the potential injury to the defendant. Those state courts that continue to apply the concurrent sentence doctrine stress its value in preserving scarce judicial resources and in avoiding the unnecessary consideration of potentially difficult legal questions.

(c) Waiver or Forfeiture of the Right to Appeal. *Express waiver of right to appeal.* Some appeals are barred because the defendant expressly waives his right to appeal. With increasing frequency, negotiated plea bargains include an express waiver of the right to appeal by the defendant. A defendant may agree to waive the right to appeal only his sentence, to waive his right to appeal his conviction after trial in return for a favorable sentence recommendation, or to give up the right to appeal both conviction and sentence as part of a plea agreement. The validity of these waivers has been tested in most jurisdictions. A few courts have refused to enforce them on the grounds

that they violate "public policy" by allowing prosecutors to insulate their own errors from appellate scrutiny. Most courts uphold appeal waivers, so long as the waiver is made voluntarily and with an understanding of the consequences. These courts are persuaded that because other important constitutional rights of the defendant may be waived by plea agreement, there is no basis for barring waiver of the right to appeal, a right that is not even guaranteed by the Constitution, but by statute. Courts also point to the importance of plea bargaining, the value of saving appellate resources, and the advantages gained by the defendant in entering the agreement. Some courts disallow such waivers in cases carrying the sentence of death, or allow waiver, but impose more stringent requirements for ensuring that a defendant's waiver of appellate rights is informed and voluntary. Moreover, courts that otherwise honor waivers have noted that an appeal waiver cannot foreclose appellate review of allegations that the trial court relied on a constitutionally impermissible factor, such as race, in setting the defendant's sentence, or that a sentence was imposed in violation of the plea bargain. Courts that otherwise honor broad waivers of the right to appeal will also entertain claims on appeal that the defendant's waiver of appeal rights was entered into unknowingly, or without the effective assistance of counsel.

Forfeiture of the right to appeal—the fugitive disentitlement doctrine. The right to appeal may be relinquished by less deliberate means as well. As the Court explained in *Ortega–Rodriguez v. United States*,[10] "it has been settled for well over a century that an appellate court may dismiss the appeal of a defendant who is a fugitive from justice during the pendency of his appeal." This rule is aptly termed the "fugitive disentitlement doctrine." Prac-

---

7. See also Andresen v. Maryland, 427 U.S. 463, 96 S.Ct. 2737, 49 L.Ed.2d 627 (1976) (noting, but not applying, doctrine); Pinkus v. United States, 436 U.S. 293, 98 S.Ct. 1808, 56 L.Ed.2d 293 (1978) (finding doctrine inapplicable due to additional fine imposed for challenged conviction).

8. 481 U.S. 736, 107 S.Ct. 2093, 95 L.Ed.2d 693 (1987) (per curiam).

9. See also Rutledge v. United States, 517 U.S. 292, 116 S.Ct. 1241, 134 L.Ed.2d 419 (1996) (noting $50 assessment amounts to cumulative punishment).

10. 507 U.S. 234, 113 S.Ct. 1199, 122 L.Ed.2d 581 (1993).

tically speaking, any judgment reached on appeal would be unenforceable against an absent appellant. Moreover, dismissal discourages escape, encourages voluntary surrender, and advances "an interest in efficient, dignified appellate practice."[11] This integrity justification may explain the Court's decisions in *Allen v. Georgia*,[12] and *Estelle v. Dorrough*,[13] each upholding state rules providing for the dismissal of the appeals of prisoners who escape during the pendency of their appeal, but are recaptured.

In the federal courts, the of dismissal is not available, however to punish an appellant who escapes *prior* to filing his appeal, held the Court in *Ortega–Rodriguez*. Escape and recapture prior to invoking appellate jurisdiction, the Court concluded, does not interrupt proceedings in the court of appeals, and flouts not the authority of the court of appeals, but only the authority of the District Court. The District Court can tailor a response to deter such misconduct that is "more finely calibrated" than "the blunderbuss of dismissal" available to the court of appeals, the Supreme Court reasoned. Moreover, the Court feared that dismissal would be invoked inappropriately as a response to much less egregious misconduct prior to appeal. Many states agree with the Court's rationale in *Ortega–Rodriguez*, and reject automatic dismissal of appeals filed by former fugitives, reserving dismissal for cases in which the defendant's conduct significantly interferes with the appellate process. Yet because the limits imposed in *Ortega–Rodriguez* were an exercise of the Court's supervisory powers over the federal courts and were not mandated by the Constitution,[14] state courts remain free to apply much more sweeping disentitlement rules, such as a rule dismissing a defendant's appeal when his escape merely delayed sentencing for a few months.

Forfeiture of the right to appeal—issues not raised in the trial court. Perhaps no standard governing the scope of appellate review is more frequently applied than the rule that "an error not raised and preserved at trial will not be considered on appeal." Even a constitutional right "may be forfeited in criminal as well as civil cases by the failure to make timely assertion of the right."[15] The values underlying this rule were aptly summarized by the Oregon Court of Appeals:

> There are many rationales for the raise-or-waive rule: that it is a necessary corollary of our adversary system in which issues are framed by the litigants and presented to a court; that fairness to all parties requires a litigant to advance his contentions at a time when there is an opportunity to respond to them factually, if his opponent chooses to; that the rule promotes efficient trial proceedings; that reversing for error not preserved permits the losing side to second-guess its tactical decisions after they do not produce the desired result; and that there is something unseemly about telling a lower court it was wrong when it never was presented with the opportunity to be right. The principal rationale, however, is judicial economy. There are two components to judicial economy: (1) if the losing side can obtain an appellate reversal because of error not objected to, the parties and public are put to the expense of retrial that could have been avoided had an objection been made; and (2) if an issue had been raised in the trial court, it could have been resolved there, and the parties and public would be spared the expense of an appeal.[16]

There is, of course, nothing in these rationales that requires that the "raise-or-waive" rule be absolute, and all jurisdictions recognize one or more situations in which issues not raised below will be considered on appeal. The plain

---

11.   Ortega–Rodriguez v. United States, supra note 10.

12.   166 U.S. 138, 17 S.Ct. 525, 41 L.Ed. 949 (1897).

13.   420 U.S. 534, 95 S.Ct. 1173, 43 L.Ed.2d 377 (1975).

14.   See Goeke v. Branch, 514 U.S. 115, 115 S.Ct. 1275, 131 L.Ed.2d 152 (1995) (stating that *Ortega–Rodriguez* was based on the Court's supervisory powers, and quoting the dissenting opinion in that case, "There can be no

argument that the fugitive dismissal rule * * * violates the Constitution because a convicted criminal has no constitutional right to an appeal.").

15.   Yakus v. United States, 321 U.S. 414, 444, 64 S.Ct. 660, 677, 88 L.Ed. 834 (1944).

16.   State v. Applegate, 39 Or.App. 17, 591 P.2d 371 (1979). See also § 28.4(d).

error rule, discussed in the next subsection, is the most important of these "exceptions" to the raise-or-waive rule. Several other exceptions, discussed below, either do not cover as broad a range of objections, or are not as widely accepted, but they nevertheless have a fairly significant impact upon the scope of review in many jurisdictions.

It is a basic premise of the raise-or-waive rule that the defense will have ample opportunity to present its objection before the trial court in compliance with the jurisdiction's procedural rules. Where that opportunity was not present, or was not likely to be exercised for some legitimate reason, the defendant's failure to raise his objection below is likely to be excused. The clearest case for considering an issue not raised in accordance with a particular procedural requirement occurs when that requirement fails to allow the defense a reasonable time within which to raise the issue. In other situations the general timing requirements may be fair, but the defendant may be in a special situation where the failure to comply was excusable. Thus, appellate courts may also consider objections not raised at trial where an intervening ruling established the grounds for the objection and counsel's failure to raise the issue was understandable in light of the controlling precedent at the time of trial.

A lack of jurisdiction also is treated as a "venerable exception" to the raise-or-waive rule.[17] However, courts tend to utilize a definition of a jurisdictional defect for this purpose that is narrower than in other areas in which jurisdictional claims may be given separate treatment. A challenge to subject matter jurisdiction clearly may be raised for the first time on appeal, and many courts will also consider on a similar basis an allegation that the offense occurred outside the territorial jurisdiction of the state. Courts generally are reluctant, however, to include within the jurisdictional category objections to other aspects of the proceedings. While several appellate courts allow a first-time challenge to the constitutionality of the statute on which the prosecution is based, most hold that such an objection also is not jurisdictional and therefore cannot be raised unless it fits within some other exception to the raise-or-waive rule. Similarly, most jurisdictions consider a double jeopardy claim as a defect that cannot be raised for the first time on appeal. On the other hand, the failure of the information or indictment to state an offense can be raised initially on appeal in many states, due to its characterization as a jurisdictional error. In *United States v. Cotton*,[18] however, the Court held that the failure to allege an element of the offense for which the defendant was sentenced is not jurisdictional error, noting that even the failure to allege any federal offense at all does not deprive the court of jurisdiction.[19] If a federal defendant raises such an error for the first time on appeal, that error must be reviewed under Rule 52's plain error standard, described below, just as any nonjurisdictional error would be reviewed.[20]

Finally, appellate courts in numerous states have noted their discretion to consider an issue on appeal, notwithstanding the lack of objection below, when appellate review of that issue would serve the interest of judicial economy. Thus, a court may consider an issue raised for the first time on appeal where there is a strong possibility of reoccurrence or the issue is one of public policy or of broad concern. Ordinarily, failure to comply with the procedural requirements for raising claims at trial also will block collateral review of those claims, as discussed in § 28.4. One common exception to this principle is that in most jurisdictions, claims of ineffective assistance typically need not be raised at trial, or even on

17. Peretz v. United States, 501 U.S. 923, 953, 111 S.Ct. 2661, 2678, 115 L.Ed.2d 808 (1991) (Scalia, J., dissenting).

18. 535 U.S. 625, 122 S.Ct. 1781, 152 L.Ed.2d 860 (2002).

19. The Court relied upon Lamar v. United States, 240 U.S. 60, 36 S.Ct. 255, 60 L.Ed. 526 (1916) ("a district court 'has jurisdiction of all crimes cognizable under the authority of the United States ... [and] [t]he objection that the indictment does not charge a crime against the United States goes only to the merits of the case.'").

20. See also § 19.3 (discussing *Cotton*).

direct appeal, but may be raised for the first time on collateral review.

(d) Plain Error. All but a few jurisdictions recognize the authority of an appellate court to grant relief on the basis of a plain error even though that error was not properly raised and preserved at the trial level. The plain error exception is recognized in Federal Rule 52(b) and in similar provisions in most states. Others have adopted it as a common law exception to the raise-or-waive rule, based upon the appellate court's inherent authority to prevent a "miscarriage of justice." The doctrine usually extends to all types of errors.[21] In some jurisdictions, however, the doctrine is restricted to a limited class of "plain errors." Thus, one state limits review to unpreserved errors that are discoverable "by a mere inspection of the pleadings and proceedings * * * without inspection of the evidence." Another includes only errors that could not have been cured by the trial judge if an objection had been made at trial. Several apply it only to the most flagrant constitutional violations. As for those jurisdictions without such limitations, opinions have emphasized that "no talismanic method exists for determining plain error," and each case must be examined on its own facts. There are, however, certain factors which clearly have a positive influence on an appellate court's willingness to find plain error. The more closely balanced the evidence, for example, the greater the likelihood that an error otherwise not viewed as sufficiently patent or fundamental will meet the standard. Courts have also acknowledged that errors of constitutional magnitude will be noticed more freely under the plain error doctrine than violations of most statutes or common law standards.

In *United States v. Olano,*[22] and *Johnson v. United States,*[23] the Supreme Court developed a four-step analysis for determining whether an error is subject to review as "plain error" under Federal Rule 52(b). This framework has been adopted by several states in interpreting the scope of their own rules or statues. As the Court summarized in *Johnson*, an appellate court can correct an error not raised at trial only if there is (1) error, (2) that is plain, (3) that "affects substantial rights," and (4) "seriously affects the fairness, integrity, or public reputation of judicial proceedings." Applying this analysis, the Court held that neither the trial court's violation of Federal Rule 24(c) in *Olano*, allowing alternate jurors to be present during jury deliberations, nor the failure to submit the question of materiality to the jury in a perjury prosecution in *Johnson,* qualified as "plain error" subject to correction under Federal Rule 52.

Initially, the Court in *Olano* reasoned, for an error to be presented, the appellant must have "forfeited" his right to appellate review of an error by the failure to make a timely assertion of that right rather than "waived" his right to review that error. Second, the error must be "plain," which "is synonymous with 'clear,' or equivalently 'obvious.'" "At a minimum," the Court explained, the error must be "clear under current law." *Johnson* added that clear errors will also include actions that violated rules established after trial but applied retroactively on direct review. In *Johnson*, the Court concluded that even though the trial court's action was not recognized as error by the Supreme Court until after Johnson's trial, "it is enough that an error be 'plain' at the time of appellate consideration," at least in a case where "the law at the time of trial was settled and clearly contrary to the law at the time of appeal." Otherwise, defense counsel would "inevitably" make "a long and virtually useless laundry list of objections to rulings that were plainly supported by existing precedent."

The third requirement specified in *Olano* was that the error must "affec[t] substantial rights," that is, the error "must have been prejudicial" in the sense of "affect[ing] the outcome" of the lower court proceedings.

---

21. United States v. Vonn, 535 U.S. 55, 122 S.Ct. 1043, 152 L.Ed.2d 90 (2002) (express mention of harmless error but not plain error review in Rule 11 did not repeal by implication the application of Rule 52(b) to Rule 11 errors).

22. 507 U.S. 725, 113 S.Ct. 1770, 123 L.Ed.2d 508 (1993).

23. 520 U.S. 461, 117 S.Ct. 1544, 137 L.Ed.2d 718 (1997).

Here, however, in contrast to a harmless error inquiry, "the defendant rather than the Government bears the burden of persuasion with respect to prejudice." In *Olano*, the Court concluded that the erroneous presence of alternate jurors during deliberations did not meet this requirement, noting that the defendants had not shown that the error had prejudiced them and refusing to find that the error was "inherently prejudicial."

Finally, the Court in *Olano* explained, Federal Rule 52(b) is "permissive rather than mandatory," and allows rather than requires correction when an error is found to be "plain" and "affecting substantial rights." In previous cases the Court had indicated that this discretion should be employed "in those circumstances in which a miscarriage of justice would otherwise result."[24] However, in contrast to the position taken in its habeas corpus jurisprudence, this use of "miscarriage of justice" in plain-error cases was not meant to restrict plain-error review to only those errors that caused "the conviction or sentencing of an actually innocent defendant." An appellate court should, in addition, "correct a plain forfeited error affecting substantial rights if the error 'seriously affects the fairness, integrity, or public reputation of judicial proceedings.'" This determination, the Court later explained in *Johnson*, was to be made on an analysis of the facts of the individual case. In *Johnson*, the record showed that the error in question—failure to submit the element of materiality to the jury—did not seriously affect either the outcome, or the "fairness, integrity, or public reputation of judicial proceedings" because the evidence supporting materiality was "overwhelming." "Indeed," the Court ventured, "it would be the reversal of a conviction such as this which would have that effect."

Despite the Court's representations in *Johnson*, it is not clear what showing other than innocence would warrant relief under Rule 52(b). The Court's unanimous decision in *United States v. Cotton*,[25] in which defendants objected on appeal to the government's failure to allege an element of the greater drug offense for which they were sentenced, illustrates how difficult this fourth step is to overcome if proof of guilt is strong. The *Cotton* Court refused to grant relief, noting the "overwhelming and uncontroverted evidence" that the defendants were guilty of the greater offense.

The Court has furnished one example of a rare case where unraised error requires relief despite no showing of prejudice. The Court in *Nguyen v. United States*[26] sidestepped the *Olano* analysis, preferring instead to vacate, under the Court's supervisory powers, an appellate order upholding the convictions of two drug defendants, because the appellate panel included a non-Article III judge. The majority reasoned that neither the failure to object nor an express stipulation of the parties could have created authority that Congress carefully withheld. Rejecting in a footnote the dissenters' argument that under *Olano* no relief was required, the majority noted that allowing the judgment to stand would "call into serious question the integrity as well as the public reputation of judicial proceedings * * * for *no one* other than a properly constituted panel of Article III judges was empowered to exercise appellate jurisdiction in these cases."

(e) Standard of Review. Assuming that review is not precluded by the doctrines examined in the preceding sections, a reviewing court must decide how much deference to accord the trial court's decision in order to determine whether or not that decision was erroneous. As in civil cases, different standards of review are used by appellate courts to examine different types of trial court decisions. The Supreme Court has summed up the law on this topic succinctly: "For purposes of standard of review, decisions by judges are traditionally divided into three categories, denominated questions of law (reviewable de novo), questions of fact (reviewable for clear error)

---

24. See United States v. Frady, 456 U.S. 152, 102 S.Ct. 1584, 71 L.Ed.2d 816 (1982); United States v. Young, 470 U.S. 1, 105 S.Ct. 1038, 84 L.Ed.2d 1 (1985) (holding prosecutor's remarks did not constitute "plain error").

25. 535 U.S. 625, 122 S.Ct. 1781, 152 L.Ed.2d 860 (2002).

26. 539 U.S. 69, 123 S.Ct. 2130, 156 L.Ed.2d 64 (2003).

and matters of discretion (reviewable for 'abuse of discretion').''[27]

For some issues, the standard of review will be dictated by statute. When not specified by statute, courts will choose the standard to apply. In general, concerns of efficiency and accuracy will determine the standard applied. Deferential standards of review are used when the trial judge is likely to have more information or expertise than reviewing judges, or when uniform rules to guide trial courts are not essential. Although states are free to adopt standards of direct review for federal constitutional issues that are more exacting than those adopted by federal courts,[28] because the standard of review (like the applicability of harmless error) is part and parcel of the federal right itself, a state court may be prohibited from adopting standards of review that are more deferential than the standards adopted by federal courts.

Abuse of discretion review. Some trial court decisions are considered erroneous only if the reviewing court determines that the trial court "abused its discretion." Abuse of discretion has been defined variously as "exceeding the bounds of reason or disregard of the rules or principles of law or practice," a decision "no reasonable person" could reach, or one that leaves the appellate court with a "definite and firm conviction that the district court committed a clear error of judgment." This most lenient oversight is applied to decisions to admit or exclude evidence,[29] to rulings on motions for recusal, substitution of counsel, continuance, severance, discovery,[30] jury instructions, specific performance of plea agreements, as well as motions for mistrial or new trial.

Sentencing decisions in some jurisdictions remain subject to review for abuse of discre-

tion. Other jurisdictions apply a more stringent standard of review for findings of fact, statutory interpretations, or decisions weighing aggravating and mitigating factors in capital cases.[31]

Decisions reviewed for abuse of discretion share one or more common characteristics. They often depend upon the trial judge's firsthand observations of the litigants and the evidence, observations that cannot be replicated by reviewing judges who have access only to the written record. Second, they often involve the judge's ability to control the trial proceedings. Third, decisions reviewed for abuse of discretion often address issues about which the trial judge has a greater understanding than an appellate judge. Finally discretionary decisions tend to be context specific and resistant to general rules.

Clearly erroneous review. Factual findings by trial judges may form the basis for relief on appeal if found to be "clearly erroneous." Judge Learned Hand once concluded that "it is idle to try and unpack the meaning of the phrase, 'clearly erroneous.' ''[32] Nevertheless, other judges have tried, explaining that a finding of fact is clearly erroneous when "a court is left with a firm and definite conviction that a mistake has been committed."[33] The differences between this standard and the abuse of discretion standard are somewhat elusive, to say the least. This type of review is common for decisions concerning the presence or absence of discriminatory intent, the competency of a defendant, the breach of a plea agreement, the intelligence and voluntariness of a waiver, and factual decisions underlying rulings on motions to suppress.

Appeals of guilty verdicts by juries and guilty findings by judges based on insufficiency of evidence are evaluated by asking, "whether,

---

27. Pierce v. Underwood, 487 U.S. 552, 108 S.Ct. 2541, 101 L.Ed.2d 490 (1988).

28. See e.g., Greene v. Georgia, 519 U.S. 145, 117 S.Ct. 578, 136 L.Ed.2d 507 (1996) (per curiam).

29. See Old Chief v. United States, 519 U.S. 172, 117 S.Ct. 644, 136 L.Ed.2d 574 (1997); United States v. Abel, 469 U.S. 45, 105 S.Ct. 465, 83 L.Ed.2d 450 (1984).

30. See Bracy v. Gramley, 520 U.S. 899, 117 S.Ct. 1793, 138 L.Ed.2d 97 (1997).

31. See Clemons v. Mississippi, 494 U.S. 738, 110 S.Ct. 1441, 108 L.Ed.2d 725 (1990) (review of weighing of aggravating and mitigating factors de novo).

32. United States v. Aluminum Co. of America, 148 F.2d 416 (2d Cir.1945).

33. United States v. United States Gypsum Co., 333 U.S. 364, 68 S.Ct. 525, 92 L.Ed. 746 (1948).

after viewing the evidence in the light most favorable to the prosecution, any rational trier of fact could have found the essential elements beyond a reasonable doubt."[34]

De novo review. The trial judge's better vantage point for making factual assessments warrants greater deference to the factual findings of a trial judge,[35] but appellate judges are equally well situated to decide legal questions. Appellate judges also benefit from deliberation as a panel, which can reduce the risk of error. Consequently, determinations of law by the trial court are reviewed de novo on direct appeal and no weight is given to the legal conclusions of the trial judge. De novo review also promotes uniformity and predictability.[36] Questions reviewed in this manner include questions of statutory or constitutional interpretation, and questions concerning the scope of the attorney client privilege.

Mixed questions of law and fact requiring the application of legal principles to historical fact usually receive do novo review.[37] For example, whether or not there was probable cause to justify a warrantless search, whether a defendant had received the notice required by due process, was denied the effective assistance of counsel, or whether a statute as applied to a defendant violates the First Amendment are all questions reviewed de novo on appeal. On the other hand, the Court in *Buford v. United States*,[38] rejected de novo review for certain "fact-bound" legal decisions at sentencing. Instead, the court held that these decisions deserve the deference of clearly erroneous review because the trial court's greater experience with trials, sentencing, and the particular finding in issue "will help that judge draw the proper inferences" and because the finding "depend[ed] heavily upon an understanding of the significance of case-specific details." The Court also pointed out that uniform precedent had little value for the question at issue, which was whether the defendant's convictions were consolidated, hence "related," for purposes of sentencing.

§ 27.6 Harmless Error

(a) Origins of Harmless Error Review. The practice of applying the concept of harmless error to the review of criminal cases had its roots in English jurisprudence. During the mid–1800s English courts adopted a rule of appellate review that became known as the Exchequer Rule. Under that rule, a trial error as to the admission of evidence was presumed to have caused prejudice and therefore required a new trial. The presumption of prejudice was designed to ensure that the appellate court did not encroach upon the jury's fact-finding function by discounting the improperly admitted evidence and sustaining the verdict on its belief that the remaining evidence established guilt. Early American courts adopted and applied this rule to a wide range of trial errors. Retrials for seemingly insignificant errors mounted, and appellate courts were criticized as "impregnable citadels of technicality." Reformers urged adoption of harmless error legislation. Their efforts began to bear fruit during the early 1900s when a substantial number of states adopted such legislation. By the 1960s all 50 states had harmless error statutes or rules. The federal statute, adopted in 1919, provided the model for much of the state legislation. It required a federal appellate court to "give judgment after an examination of the entire record before the court, without regard to technical errors, defects, or exceptions which do not affect the substantial rights of the parties."

(b) Harmless Error Review of Nonconstitutional Errors. American appellate courts initially applied harmless error legislation to nonconstitutional error alone. Some state courts reviewing nonconstitutional errors today continue to use two modes of analysis when applying harmless error statutes. For

---

34. Jackson v. Virginia, 443 U.S. 307, 99 S.Ct. 2781, 61 L.Ed.2d 560 (1979).

35. See Anderson v. Bessemer City, 470 U.S. 564, 105 S.Ct. 1504, 84 L.Ed.2d 518 (1985).

36. See Ornelas v. United States, 517 U.S. 690, 116 S.Ct. 1657, 134 L.Ed.2d 911 (1996).

37. See Thompson v. Keohane, 516 U.S. 99, 116 S.Ct. 457, 133 L.Ed.2d 383 (1995).

38. 532 U.S. 59, 121 S.Ct. 1276, 149 L.Ed.2d 197 (2001).

rights that might loosely be described as concerned with the structure of the proceeding, courts have looked to whether the error was merely a technical violation or took from the defendant the substantive protection of the right. A violation of the substance of such a right automatically requires a new trial, so that the strength of the evidence supporting the conviction is irrelevant. Examples of this automatic-reversal analysis include decisions reviewing errors in jury selection and changes of venue. A second analysis, which considers the likely impact of the error on case outcome, is applied to trial errors that determine what evidence is presented to the jury, such as rulings on admissibility and joinder. It also is applied to erroneous pretrial rulings that have an impact upon the presentation of evidence, such as rulings on discovery, and to actions of the judge and prosecutor that may have influenced the jury in its evaluation of the evidence, such as erroneous jury instructions or trial misconduct by the prosecutor. Finally, this impact-on-outcome analysis is applied to violations of rules regulating plea bargaining and plea taking, and to errors in sentencing.

In the federal courts the harmless error standard of Federal Rule 52(a) governs the direct appeal of federal cases. Rule 52(a) appears to require impact-on-outcome analysis for all categories of nonconstitutional error. In *United States v. Lane*,[1] the Court stated that "Rule 52(a) admits of no broad exceptions to its applicability," rejecting "bright-line per se rules whether to conduct harmless error analysis." The Court in *Lane* applied harmless error analysis to a misjoinder of parties in violation of Federal Rule 8(b). In dissent, Justice Stevens argued that such an error should not be subject to harmless error analysis for two reasons. First, Rule 8(b) implicates an "independent value besides reliability of outcome," namely "our deep abhorrence of the motion of

'guilt by association.' " Second, the impact of the error upon the outcome "cannot be measured with precision." The majority, holding the traditional harmless error standard to be applicable, characterized Rule 8(b) as ensuring reliability by setting the scope of relevancy in the admission of evidence and saw the impact of its violation as no more difficult to measure than other evidentiary errors.

In *United States v. Mechanik*,[2] the Court rejected defendant's claim that certain grand jury errors should be exempt from harmless error review under Rule 52(a). According to the Court, most grand jury error is *necessarily* harmless beyond a reasonable doubt if followed by an otherwise valid conviction. The Court explained that a subsequent guilty verdict renders harmless any error in failing to dismiss an indictment due to a violation of Federal Rule 6(d). However, if the error during the grand jury process is raised in a motion to dismiss and considered by the trial court prior to trial, relief may be available, but only if the traditional standard for harmless error was satisfied. In explaining this pretrial application of harmless error review to grand jury error, the Court in *Bank of Nova Scotia v. United States*[3] emphasized that "a federal court may not invoke supervisory power to circumvent the harmless-error inquiry prescribed by" Rule 52(a). The Court explained, "federal courts have no more discretion to disregard the Rule's mandate than they do to disregard constitutional or statutory provisions."[4] Indeed, in interpreting a different subsection of Rule 52—the plain error provision in 52(b)— the Court in *Johnson v. United States*[5] rejected the petitioner's claim that the "error she complains of [failure to submit an essential element to the jury] is 'structural' " and thus not subject to the restrictions in the Rule. The Court explained that Rule 52 "by its terms governs direct appeals from judgments of con-

§ 27.6

1. 474 U.S. 438, 106 S.Ct. 725, 88 L.Ed.2d 814 (1986).

2. 475 U.S. 66, 106 S.Ct. 938, 89 L.Ed.2d 50 (1986).

3. 487 U.S. 250, 108 S.Ct. 2369, 101 L.Ed.2d 228 (1988).

4. See also Peguero v. United States, 526 U.S. 23, 119 S.Ct. 961, 143 L.Ed.2d 18 (1999) (noting, in the course of a

decision requiring a showing of prejudice before granting habeas relief for the failure to inform a defendant of his right to appeal, that "Rule 52(a) * * * prohibits federal courts from granting relief based on errors that 'do not affect substantial rights' ").

5. 520 U.S. 461, 117 S.Ct. 1544, 137 L.Ed.2d 718 (1997), also discussed in § 27.5(d).

viction in the federal system," and that creating an exception to it, even for the serious *constitutional* violation reviewed in *Johnson*, would be inappropriate and unauthorized. The same arguments certainly would support application of subsection (a) of Rule 52 to all nonconstitutional errors raised in federal cases on direct appeal.

Once an appellate court concludes that an error is subject to harmless error review, the court must identify the proper standard for measuring the impact of the error on the outcome of the proceeding. One test, described as the "correct result" test of harmless error, asks whether, in light of all of the admissible evidence (including any defense evidence improperly excluded), the jury's finding of guilt is clearly correct. Critics of this formula contend that it converts the appellate court into the trier of fact and fails to recognize that the defendant has a right to a fair trial even when he is clearly guilty. The Supreme Court looked to both of those factors in rejecting a "correct result" standard under Rule 52 in *Kotteakos v. United States*.[6] In the course of an extensive discussion of the harmless error guidelines to be applied by federal courts, Justice Rutledge noted:

Some aids to right judgment may be stated more safely in negative than in affirmative form. Thus, it is not the appellate court's function to determine guilt or innocence. Nor is it to speculate upon probable reconviction and decide according to how the speculation comes out. Appellate judges cannot escape such impressions. But they may not make them sole criteria for reversal or affirmance. Those judgments are exclusively for the jury * * *. But this does not mean that the appellate court can escape altogether taking account of the outcome. To weigh the error's effect against the entire setting of the record without relation to the verdict or judgment would be almost to work in a vacuum. In criminal causes that outcome is conviction. This is different, or may be, from guilt in fact. It is guilt in law, established by the judgment of laymen. And the question

is, not were they right in their judgment, regardless of the error or its effect upon the verdict. It is rather what effect the error had or reasonably may be taken to have had upon the jury's decision. The crucial thing is the impact of the thing done wrong in the minds of other men, not on one's own, in the total setting.

The Court in *Kotteakos* offered the following standard:

If, when all is said and done, the conviction is sure that the error did not influence the jury, or had but very slight effect, the verdict and the judgment should stand, except perhaps where the departure is from a constitutional norm or a specific command of Congress. But if one cannot say, with fair assurance, after pondering all that happened without stripping the erroneous action from the whole, that the judgment was not substantially swayed by the error, it is impossible to conclude that substantial rights were not affected.

Some commentators and state courts have favored still another standard, one that resembles the analysis the Supreme Court has required for the review of constitutional errors. Adopted in a leading case by the Pennsylvania Supreme Court, this approach requires that the appellate court must be convinced "beyond a reasonable doubt" that there is no "reasonable possibility" that the error contributed to the verdict.[7] This standard is viewed as more stringent than *Kotteakos*, and it is supported as providing greater protection against a "lenient" application of the harmless error rule that would effectively undercut the force of procedural requirements. Several reasons have been advanced for preferring this test over the *Kotteakos* standard. First, a nonconstitutional evidentiary or procedural error can cause just as much prejudice to the defendant as constitutional error, and the prejudice that it causes can be just as hard to assess. Second, the reasonable-doubt standard is already in "wide use," and applying it to all errors obviates "an

---

6. 328 U.S. 750, 66 S.Ct. 1239, 90 L.Ed. 1557 (1946).

7. Commonwealth v. Story, 476 Pa. 391, 383 A.2d 155 (1978).

unnecessary inquiry into whether the error is constitutionally based." Some argue in addition that any lesser standard would be inconsistent with the constitutional requirement that guilt be determined under a reasonable-doubt standard. Most state courts, however, view the trial-proof standard as a false analogy, no more applicable in testing the harmlessness of an error than in making the initial assessment as to whether the error occurred.

As various courts have acknowledged, the principle that the error should be judged by its likely impact on the jury's judgment, whatever the standard as to requisite probability of impact, is only the first step of the harmless error inquiry. Courts have also sought, with varying success, to identify the *process* for determining whether a particular error is so unlikely to have influenced the jury's judgment that it meets the applicable probability standard. Considerable attention has been given, for example, to the allocation of the burden of showing potential prejudice. In *Kotteakos*, the Supreme Court rejected the idea of uniformly placing the burden on either party. Any presumption of prejudice, shifting the burden to one side or the other, should "aris[e] from the nature of the error and its 'natural effect' for or against prejudice in the particular setting."

Another significant issue is what weight should be assigned to overwhelming evidence of guilt in determining the impact of a trial error. Once it is agreed that the impact of an error must be measured in light of all of the evidence before the jury, it does not follow that an overwhelming prosecution case will inevitably render the error harmless. In *O'Neal v. McAninch*,[8] a case concerning the application of the *Kotteakos* standard on collateral review, the Court described the appropriate inquiry as whether the error "had substantial and injurious effect or influence in determining the jury's verdict," not whether, despite the error, the jury reached the right result. One method of measuring that impact, and ensuring that the weight of the state's evidence does not become determinative, is to match the poten-

tial element of prejudice against the state's evidence. For example, to render harmless the erroneous admission of potentially prejudicial evidence, it would have to be shown that the government had properly introduced other, more persuasive evidence on the same point. Most courts, however, view a requirement that the prosecution's evidence independently establish the same fact as the inadmissible evidence as unduly restrictive. Even without a "perfect match," strong prosecution evidence may indicate that a particular error was most unlikely to have contributed to the jury's verdict. For example, erroneously admitted evidence may have been the only evidence casting doubt upon defendant's reputation for honesty, but it may nevertheless have been inconsequential in light of strong eyewitness testimony clearly establishing that the defendant had committed the crime.

Many courts apply what may be described as a comparative analysis of the likely impact of the error and the overwhelming evidence. The question to be answered, they note, is "whether the properly admitted evidence of guilt is so overwhelming and the prejudicial effect of the error is so insignificant by comparison" that the court can say, with the requisite degree of certainty, that the error could not have contributed to the verdict. As for some types of error, such as the erroneous admission or exclusion of evidence, overwhelming evidence of guilt will ordinarily lead to the conclusion that the error was harmless. It would take evidence of an extraordinary quality to conclude that its erroneous admission or exclusion may have contributed to the verdict where the government had before the jury other evidence that would clearly and positively establish guilt.

(c) Application to Constitutional Violations. Prior to the 1960s, it was assumed that constitutional violations could never be regarded as harmless error. Aside from one ambiguous ruling at the turn of the century, a Supreme Court finding of constitutional error had always resulted in a reversal of the defendant's conviction. Since the Court's opinions had never sought to analyze those reversals

---

8. 513 U.S. 432, 115 S.Ct. 992, 130 L.Ed.2d 947 (1995).

under a harmless error rule, both commentators and lower courts concluded that the rule simply did not apply to constitutional violations.

This assumption was called into question by the due process revolution of the 1900s and its dramatic expansion of federal constitutional regulation of state procedures. In the 1963 case of *Fahy v. Connecticut*,[9] the Court was faced with the possible application of the harmless error rule to a violation of one of the leading "expansionist" decisions of the 1960s. The state court there had held harmless a violation of the requirement of *Mapp v. Ohio* that evidence obtained through an unconstitutional search not be admitted into evidence at trial. The Supreme Court majority found it unnecessary to decide whether the harmless error rule applied to *Mapp* violations. If it was assumed arguendo that the rule applied, the state court had still erred in its analysis of the alleged harmlessness of the *Mapp* violation in this particular case. The four dissenters in *Fahy* did reach the issue reserved by the majority. They could "see no reason" why the harmless error rule should not apply, as there was "no necessary connection between the fact that evidence was unconstitutionally seized and the degree of harm caused by its admission."

Four years later, in *Chapman v. California*,[10] the Court majority resolved the issue left open in *Fahy*. *Chapman* involved a clear violation of the Court's recent decision in *Griffin v. California* prohibiting comment on the defendant's failure to testify at trial.[11] The California Supreme Court, stressing the overwhelming evidence of guilt, had held the *Griffin* violation harmless. Before the Supreme Court, the defendant contended that no constitutional error could be harmless, while the prosecution claimed that the state court could appropriately apply to a constitutional violation the same harmless error standard it applied to nonconstitutional errors. The Court majority rejected both arguments.

The *Chapman* majority held initially that federal rather than state law determined whether the harmless error rule applied to constitutional violations, and if so, whether a particular constitutional violation was harmless. "Whether a conviction for a crime should stand when a state had failed to accord federally constitutionally guaranteed rights" was as much a matter of constitutional law as the definition of the constitutional right itself. The Court then turned to the question of whether the Constitution required automatic reversal as to all constitutional errors. It was true, the Court noted, that a rule of automatic reversal had been applied to certain constitutional errors in the past, but that did not mean constitutional errors could never be treated as harmless. A proper harmless error standard could appropriately be applied to some constitutional violations, including a violation of the *Griffin* ruling. That standard required the appellate court to be convinced "beyond a reasonable doubt that the error complained of did not contribute to the verdict obtained."

The *Chapman* opinion presented a two-step analysis for an appellate court dealing with a constitutional error. First, the court must determine if the error falls in that category of violations subject to the harmless error rule or instead falls in that category of errors requiring automatic reversal. Second, if the harmless error rule is applicable, the court must determine the impact of the error in the case before it under the federal standard laid down in *Chapman*. These two determinations are examined in the subsections that follow.

(d) Harmless Error or Automatic Reversal. The *Chapman* opinion focused primarily on responding to the contention that the harmless error rule should never apply to constitutional error. Its reasoning in this regard was very much like that offered by the dissenters in *Fahy*. The Court found no basis in theory or past precedent for granting constitutional errors a blanket exemption from this rule of appellate review. It noted that the harmless error statutes, including the federal

9. 375 U.S. 85, 84 S.Ct. 229, 11 L.Ed.2d 171 (1963).

10. 386 U.S. 18, 87 S.Ct. 824, 17 L.Ed.2d 705 (1967).

11. See § 24.4(b).

provision, did not on their face distinguish between federal constitutional errors and non-constitutional errors. These statutes, the Court noted, served "a very useful purpose insofar as they block setting aside convictions for small errors or defects that have little, if any, likelihood of having changed the result of the trial." The Court was not prepared to conclude that there could not be "some constitutional errors which in the setting of a particular case are so unimportant and insignificant that they may, consistent with the Federal Constitution, be deemed harmless."

The *Chapman* opinion acknowledged that prior cases had indicated "that there are some constitutional rights so basic to a fair trial that their infraction can never be treated as harmless error." A footnote to this statement cited and described three illustrative cases: "*Payne v. Arkansas* (coerced confessions)[12]; *Gideon v. Wainwright* (right to counsel)[13]; [and] *Tumey v. Ohio* (impartial judge).[14]" The Court made no attempt to identify the characteristics that distinguished these constitutional errors from the *Griffin* violation before it. An improper comment on defendant's silence was the type of "trial error" as to which a harmless error analysis traditionally had been applied, and the Court apparently concluded that once it was decided that "some constitutional errors" could be deemed harmless, the *Griffin* violation clearly fell within that group.[15]

The *Chapman* opinion was criticized for providing "little guidance on the matter of determining when an error automatically requires reversal and when it does not." It was obvious that the Court's citation to three constitutional errors requiring automatic reversal was only by example and did not serve to exhaust the list of constitutional violations to be so treated. As Justice Stewart noted, past precedent had clearly indicated that certain other violations would also be placed in the automatic-

reversal category. The *Chapman* opinion said only that "some constitutional errors," including a *Griffin* violation, could be deemed harmless. It did not clearly indicate whether "some" would be "most," "many," or only a "few." That determination awaited further development, but the logic of *Chapman* did exclude from the outset two very different types of constitutional violations.

The very nature of the harmless error inquiry made harmless error analysis irrelevant to one major group of constitutional violations. Where the constitutional error is one that requires the remedy of barring reprosecution, reversal is automatic upon concluding that there was such a violation. That is the case, for example, where defendant establishes a violation of his right to a speedy trial or the bar against double jeopardy.

An additional group of violations were destined not to be subject to the *Chapman's* harmless error test because they were harmful by definition, inherently incapable of meeting the rigorous *Chapman* prerequisite for finding an error to be harmless. *Chapman* insisted upon a judicial finding of lack of prejudicial impact "beyond a reasonable doubt." As a result, it would be wasted effort to look to *Chapman* where the constitutional violation is one of those that already requires—as an element of the violation—a finding of likely prejudicial impact. Typically, those violations do not exist unless the challenged behavior presented a "reasonable probability" of having affected the outcome of the proceeding. Examples include a finding that counsel's representation was ineffective under the *Strickland* standard, or that nondisclosed exculpatory evidence was material under the *Bagley* standard. As the Court explained in *Kyles v. Whitley*,[16] "once a reviewing court applying *Bagley* has found constitutional error there is no need for further harmless error review." Indeed, one

---

12. 356 U.S. 560, 78 S.Ct. 844, 2 L.Ed.2d 975 (1958). See § 6.2.

13. 372 U.S. 335, 83 S.Ct. 792, 9 L.Ed.2d 799 (1963).

14. 273 U.S. 510, 47 S.Ct. 437, 71 L.Ed. 749 (1927). See § 21.4(a).

15. Only Justice Stewart disagreed with that conclusion. He suggested that recognition of a harmless constitu-

tional error should be limited narrowly to constitutional requirements, like the exclusionary rule, that involved a balancing of a deterrence objective against the exclusion of "relevant and reliable evidence."

16. 514 U.S. 419, 115 S.Ct. 1555, 131 L.Ed.2d 490 (1995).

issue that has repeatedly divided the Court in the years since *Chapman* is whether particular conduct should be viewed as a constitutional violation in itself, with that violation then to be subject to the *Chapman* standard, or whether instead it should be viewed as error only if the defendant can first establish a reasonable probability of that conduct having a prejudicial impact upon the outcome of the proceeding.

Leaving aside those constitutional violations that bar reprosecution and those that already require a finding of probable impact upon outcome, the *Chapman* harmless error analysis still offered the potential of applying to a broad range of constitutional errors. In the years after *Chapman,* that potential was fully realized. *Chapman's* harmless error standard has now been held by the Supreme Court to apply to each of the following constitutional violations: improper comment on the defendant's failure to testify;[17] admission of evidence obtained in violation of the Fourth Amendment;[18] admission of evidence obtained in violation of an accused's right to counsel;[19] admission at trial of an out-of-court statement of a non-testifying codefendant in violation of the Sixth Amendment's Confrontation Clause;[20] admission of evidence at the sentencing stage of a capital case in violation of the right to counsel;[21] erroneous use during trial of defendant's silence following *Miranda* warnings;[22] a restriction on a defendant's right to cross-examine in violation of the Sixth Amendment's Confrontation Clause;[23] denial of the right to present exculpatory evidence,[24] denial of the right to be present during a trial proceeding;[25] denial of an indigent's right to appointed counsel at a preliminary hearing;[26] a jury instruction containing an unconstitutional rebuttable presumption;[27] a jury instruction containing an unconstitutional conclusive presumption;[28] an unconstitutionally overbroad jury instruction in a capital case;[29] the submission of an invalid aggravating factor to the jury in a capital sentencing proceeding,[30] and even a the omission of an element of the offense in the instructions to the jury.[31] In its

---

17. See e.g., *Chapman*; Anderson v. Nelson, 390 U.S. 523, 88 S.Ct. 1133, 20 L.Ed.2d 81 (1968).

18. Chambers v. Maroney, 399 U.S. 42, 90 S.Ct. 1975, 26 L.Ed.2d 419 (1970); Bumper v. North Carolina, 391 U.S. 543, 88 S.Ct. 1788, 20 L.Ed.2d 797 (1968).

19. United States v. Wade, 388 U.S. 218, 87 S.Ct. 1926, 18 L.Ed.2d 1149 (1967) (lineups); Milton v. Wainwright, 407 U.S. 371, 92 S.Ct. 2174, 33 L.Ed.2d 1 (1972) (statements). See also Moore v. Illinois, 434 U.S. 220, 98 S.Ct. 458, 54 L.Ed.2d 424 (1977) (remanding for harmless error review of error in introduction of evidence of pretrial identification made in violation of right to counsel).

20. See e.g., Schneble v. Florida, 405 U.S. 427, 92 S.Ct. 1056, 31 L.Ed.2d 340 (1972); Harrington v. California, 395 U.S. 250, 89 S.Ct. 1726, 23 L.Ed.2d 284 (1969).

21. Satterwhite v. Texas, 486 U.S. 249, 108 S.Ct. 1792, 100 L.Ed.2d 284 (1988).

22. Brecht v. Abrahamson, 507 U.S. 619, 113 S.Ct. 1710, 123 L.Ed.2d 353 (1993), also discussed in § 28.3(g).

23. Lee v. Illinois, 476 U.S. 530, 106 S.Ct. 2056, 90 L.Ed.2d 514 (1986); Delaware v. Van Arsdall, supra note 74. See also Coy v. Iowa, 487 U.S. 1012, 108 S.Ct. 2798, 101 L.Ed.2d 857 (1988) (denial of face-to-face confrontation).

24. Crane v. Kentucky, 476 U.S. 683, 106 S.Ct. 2142, 90 L.Ed.2d 636 (1986).

25. Rushen v. Spain, 464 U.S. 114, 104 S.Ct. 453, 78 L.Ed.2d 267 (1983).

26. Coleman v. Alabama, 399 U.S. 1, 90 S.Ct. 1999, 26 L.Ed.2d 387 (1970), discussed in § 14.4.

27. Rose v. Clark, 478 U.S. 570, 106 S.Ct. 3101, 92 L.Ed.2d 460 (1986) (harmless error applies to an unconstitutional shift in the burden of proof as to the element of malice even where the defendant contests intent; "[i]n many cases, the predicate facts conclusively establish intent, so that no rational jury could find that the defendant committed the relevant criminal act but did not intend to cause injury," thereby rendering the erroneous instruction "simply superfluous").

28. Carella v. California, 491 U.S. 263, 109 S.Ct. 2419, 105 L.Ed.2d 218 (1989). See also Yates v. Evatt, 500 U.S. 391, 111 S.Ct. 1884, 114 L.Ed.2d 432 (1991).

29. Pope v. Illinois, 481 U.S. 497, 107 S.Ct. 1918, 95 L.Ed.2d 439 (1987) (where state court in an obscenity prosecution unconstitutionally charged the jury to apply community standards in determining whether the distributed magazines lacked literary or artistic value, rather than to judge the "value factor" on an objective basis, the error would be harmless if the reviewing court could conclude that "no rational juror, if properly instructed, could find value in the magazines").

30. Stringer v. Black, 503 U.S. 222, 112 S.Ct. 1130, 117 L.Ed.2d 367 (1992).

31. See Neder v. United States, discussed infra at note 57. See also California v. Roy, 519 U.S. 2, 117 S.Ct. 337, 136 L.Ed.2d 266 (1996) (holding that an error in the instruction that defines the crime—a failure to inform the jury that it had to find that defendant, convicted of aiding another's murder, had the "knowledge [and] intent or purpose of committing, encouraging, or facilitating" the confederate's crime—was "trial error," not the "structural" sort that defies analysis by harmless error standards).

1991 decision in *Arizona v. Fulminante*,[32] the Court overruled one of *Chapman's* three illustrations of errors requiring automatic reversal, and held that harmless error analysis is applicable to the admission of a coerced confession.

The Court has said that "[W]hile there are some errors to which *Chapman* does not apply, they are the exception and not the rule."[33] These "exceptions," in which harmless error is not applied, extend beyond the Court's classic examples of the denial of an impartial adjudicator or the denial of counsel. Following *Chapman*, the rule of automatic reversal has been held by the Court to apply to the denial of defendant's constitutional right to self-representation;[34] race or gender discrimination in the selection of the petit jury;[35] the improper exclusion of a juror because of his views on capital punishment;[36] race or gender discrimination in the selection of the grand jury;[37] the violation of the *Anders* standards governing the withdrawal of appointed appellate counsel;[38] the denial of the right of a defendant to consult with his counsel during an overnight trial recess;[39] the denial of a defendant's right to a public trial;[40] an erroneous reasonable doubt instruction to the jury,[41] representation by counsel acting under an actual conflict of interest that adversely affects his performance;[42] and the failure of the trial court to make an appropriate inquiry into a possible conflict of interest under those special circumstances that constitutionally mandate such an inquiry.[43]

In *Arizona v. Fulminante*, the majority characterized those errors placed within the automatic-reversal category as involving "structural defect[s] affecting the framework within which the trial proceeds, rather than simply an error in the trial process itself." Their nature was quite distinct, the Court noted, from those errors held subject to the *Chapman* harmless error standard. The latter group of violations were tied together by the "common thread" of "involv[ing] 'trial error'—error which occurred during the presentation of the case to the jury and which may therefore be quantitatively assessed in the context of other

32. 499 U.S. 279, 111 S.Ct. 1246, 113 L.Ed.2d 302 (1991).

33. Rose v. Clark, 478 U.S. 570, 106 S.Ct. 3101, 92 L.Ed.2d 460 (1986).

34. McKaskle v. Wiggins, 465 U.S. 168, 104 S.Ct. 944, 79 L.Ed.2d 122 (1984), discussed in § 11.5(f).

35. Batson v. Kentucky, 476 U.S. 79, 106 S.Ct. 1712, 90 L.Ed.2d 69 (1986) ("If the trial court decides that the facts establish, prima facie, purposeful discrimination and the prosecutor does not come forward with a neutral explanation for his action, our precedents require that petitioner's conviction be reversed."); J.E.B. v. Alabama ex rel. T.B., 511 U.S. 127, 114 S.Ct. 1419, 128 L.Ed.2d 89 (1994).

36. See Gray v. Mississippi, 481 U.S. 648, 107 S.Ct. 2045, 95 L.Ed.2d 622 (1987), discussed in § 22.3(c).

37. Rose v. Mitchell, 443 U.S. 545, 99 S.Ct. 2993, 61 L.Ed.2d 739 (1979); Vasquez v. Hillery, 474 U.S. 254, 106 S.Ct. 617, 88 L.Ed.2d 598 (1986). See also Ballard v. United States, 329 U.S. 187, 67 S.Ct. 261, 91 L.Ed. 181 (1946), characterized later by the Court as a case like *Vasquez*, in which "[t]he nature of the violation," the exclusion of women from the grand jury, "allowed a presumption that the defendant was prejudiced, and any inquiry into harmless error would have required unguarded speculation." Bank of Nova Scotia v. United States, 487 U.S. 250, 108 S.Ct. 2369, 101 L.Ed.2d 228 (1988).

38. Penson v. Ohio, 488 U.S. 75, 109 S.Ct. 346, 102 L.Ed.2d 300 (1988).

39. Geders v. United States, 425 U.S. 80, 96 S.Ct. 1330, 47 L.Ed.2d 592 (1976), discussed in § 11.8(a).

40. Waller v. Georgia, 467 U.S. 39, 104 S.Ct. 2210, 81 L.Ed.2d 31 (1984).

41. Sullivan v. Louisiana, 508 U.S. 275, 113 S.Ct. 2078, 124 L.Ed.2d 182 (1993), discussed infra.

42. Cuyler v. Sullivan, 446 U.S. 335, 100 S.Ct. 1708, 64 L.Ed.2d 333 (1980); Burger v. Kemp, 483 U.S. 776, 107 S.Ct. 3114, 97 L.Ed.2d 638 (1987), discussed in § 11.9(d).

43. Holloway v. Arkansas, 435 U.S. 475, 98 S.Ct. 1173, 55 L.Ed.2d 426 (1978), discussed in § 11.9(b). The Court has also reversed convictions without inquiry into harmlessness in order to remedy the constructive amendment of an indictment, see § 19.3 but this particular category of structural error is threatened by subsequent precedent. In United States v. Cotton, 535 U.S. 625, 122 S.Ct. 1781, 152 L.Ed.2d 860 (2002), the Court refused to exempt this sort of error from plain error review and instead relied on uncontroverted evidence of guilt to uphold the conviction and sentence despite the absence of an essential element from the indictment. See § 27.5(d) at n. 20.01. Although the Court in *Cotton* distinguished the case before it from the earlier cases in which defendants had objected in the trial court to indictment errors and received relief without regard to harmlessness, those earlier cases have been undermined by *Chapman's* subsequent application of harmless error review to constitutional error generally, the application of harmless error review to missing elements in jury instructions, and a number of decisions minimizing the significance of the grand jury's screening function. See United States v. Williams, 504 U.S. 36, 112 S.Ct. 1735, 118 L.Ed.2d 352 (1992); United States v. Mechanik, 475 U.S. 66, 106 S.Ct. 938, 89 L.Ed.2d 50 (1986), discussed in § 15.6.

evidence presented in order to determine whether its admission was harmless beyond a reasonable doubt." Although the Court has later discounted the idea of a "rigid dichotomy," preferring to refer to the difference as a "spectrum of constitutional errors,"[44] it has also continued to cite to *Fulminante's* classification scheme as authoritative.[45]

In some instances, constitutional violations have fallen in the automatic-reversal category because the right violated is not primarily concerned with ensuring reliable verdicts, but serves an entirely different function. The refusal to apply *Chapman* to a denial of defendant's right to proceed pro se was so explained in *McKaskle v. Wiggins*.[46] That right, the Court noted, is designed to permit the defendant to control his own destiny, even though its exercise "usually increases the likelihood of a trial outcome unfavorable to the defendant"; accordingly, "its denial is not amenable to 'harmless error' analysis." The broader function of the right violated may also explain, in part, the Court's refusal to apply a harmless-error analysis in the jury selection cases. The Court has required automatic reversal even where a single juror was excluded unconstitutionally and there was no suggestion of bias on the part of the jurors actually selected.[47] This position may follow from those functions of the jury trial guarantees (e.g., community participation) that extend beyond simply providing the defendant with a factfinding process that is reliable. Indeed, the Court in its post-*Batson* decisions has characterized jury discrimination as impairing not the rights of defendants, but the rights of potential jurors.[48]

Of course, the recognition that a constitutional right serves a function other than promoting the reliability of verdicts does not in itself place that error beyond the reach of *Chapman*. The self-incrimination privilege serves a variety of functions beyond the protection of the innocent,[49] yet *Chapman* itself applied the harmless error standard to an infringement of that right. Admittedly, those additional functions might be thought less significant in the context of the *Griffin* prohibition against adverse prosecutorial comment, but they certainly are at the core of prohibition against the admission of coerced confessions, which has also been held subject to the *Chapman* rule. The key may be that unlike some of the other rights which, when violated warrant a rule of automatic reversal, the self-incrimination privilege operates solely as a prohibition against the use of evidence. So too, while the Fourth Amendment serves privacy interests unrelated to factfinding reliability, in applying *Chapman* to *Mapp* violations the Court was concerned only with a bar against evidentiary use that serves basically a prophylactic function and does not itself preclude a violation of privacy. Not surprisingly in light of the other limitations imposed upon the *Mapp* exclusionary rule,[50] the Court concluded that a requirement of automatic reversal was not needed to satisfy that prophylactic function.

Closely linked to the idea that some errors require reversal in order to vindicate an interest other than verdict reliability are the Court's references to the need to protect the integrity of the judicial process. This "judicial integrity" rationale has been cited as an explanation for the requirements of automatic-reversal in both the jury selection cases and in *Tumey*, the paradigmatic example of a biased judge. Finally the need for deterrence of error may play a role in the decision to require relief regardless of harm, particularly when other rationales for requiring reversal are wanting. Thus, the Court has noted "that racial discrimination in the selection of grand jurors is so pernicious, and other remedies so impractical, that the remedy of automatic reversal was

---

44. Brecht v. Abrahamson, 507 U.S. 619, 113 S.Ct. 1710, 123 L.Ed.2d 353 (1993).

45. See Johnson v. United States, 520 U.S. 461, 117 S.Ct. 1544, 137 L.Ed.2d 718 (1997). The dual approach also resembles the traditional distinction that in the past has been used to divide nonconstitutional violations into errors that might be harmless and those that will always require reversal. See § 27.6(b).

46. Supra note 34.

47. Supra note 35.

48. See § 22.3(d).

49. See §§ 1.4(h), 8.12.

50. See §§ 3.1, 9.1, 9.3, 9.4.

necessary as a prophylactic means of deterring grand jury discrimination in the future."[51]

Another critical factor in determining the applicability of harmless error analysis is the impact of allowing harmless error review upon the function that the right is designed to achieve. Consider, for example, the withdrawal of appellate counsel without the procedures specified by *Anders*.[52] Here, a subsequent analysis could determine that the appeal truly was frivolous and that defendant was not hurt since counsel would have been allowed to withdraw after filing an *Anders* brief. But as the court noted in *Penson v. Ohio*,[53] applying *Chapman* to an *Anders* violation would leave the defendant without the very protection that *Anders* sought to provide when it barred withdrawal on counsel's bare assertion that the appeal was frivolous. In applying a harmless error analysis, *Penson* noted, the appellate court would be required to assess the potential merits of the defendant's appeal, finding the error harmless or not harmless according to its view as to whether a reversal on the merits would be required. To allow such an analysis would thereby "render * * * meaningless the protections afforded * * * by *Anders*."[54]

Undoubtedly one characteristic of violations requiring automatic reversal that is frequently mentioned by the Supreme Court is the "inherently indeterminate" impact of the violation upon the outcome of the trial. Unlike most errors at trial, such errors do not relate to the introduction or evaluation of particular items of evidence. Thus, in *Sullivan v. Louisiana*,[55] the Court deemed "structural" and requiring automatic reversal a constitutional error in charging the jury on the reasonable doubt standard. The *Sullivan* Court initially identified the resulting constitutional violation

as extending beyond the due process requirement that the state establish guilt beyond a reasonable doubt, and including also the "interrelated" sixth amendment right to a "jury verdict of guilty beyond a reasonable doubt." Because of the constitutionally deficient instruction, there simply had not been such a verdict, and therefore application of *Chapman* would be contrary to the basic logic of *Chapman's* harmless error analysis. *Chapman* directs a reviewing court to determine the basis on which the jury rested its verdict, and to ask whether that verdict "was surely unattributable to the error." Here since there never was a jury verdict of guilty beyond a reasonable doubt, the "most an appellate court could conclude is that a jury surely would have found petitioner guilty beyond a reasonable doubt"— an inquiry *Chapman* prohibits. The Court distinguished cases involving unconstitutional jury instructions relating to presumptions, reasoning that a court reviewing such error is able to assess the bearing of the presumption upon the jury's verdict by reference to the various findings the jury did make. "But the essential connection to a 'beyond a reasonable doubt' factual finding cannot be made where the instructional error consists of a misdescription of the burden of proof which vitiates all the jury's findings."

Sullivan's reasoning appeared to prohibit harmless error review of a judge's complete failure to submit an element to the jury, or at least limit harmless error review to cases in which the actual verdict delivered by the jury necessarily included a finding of guilt beyond a reasonable doubt on that element. In *Neder v. United States*,[56] the Court interpreted *Sullivan* differently. Neder had been convicted of sever-

---

51. United States v. Mechanik, 475 U.S. 66, 106 S.Ct. 938, 89 L.Ed.2d 50 (1986) (describing jury selection cases). See also § 11.8.

52. See § 11.2(c).

53. Supra note 38.

54. A similar consideration may form the basis for the Court's decision in Holloway v. Arkansas, supra note 43, holding not subject to harmless error analysis a trial court's failure to inquire into a possible conflict of interest when the circumstances strongly suggest such a conflict exists. It might be possible in a postconviction hearing to determine that, notwithstanding those circumstances,

there was in fact no actual conflict and thus the lack of a hearing was not prejudicial. But the very premise of the constitutionally mandated inquiry was that postconviction review was not adequate protection where such special circumstances existed. Though allowing a postconviction harmless error inquiry would not go so far as to "render meaningless" *Holloway's* inquiry requirement, it would certainly undermine a basic premise of that requirement.

55. 508 U.S. 275, 113 S.Ct. 2078, 124 L.Ed.2d 182 (1993).

56. 527 U.S. 1, 119 S.Ct. 1827, 144 L.Ed.2d 35 (1999).

al charges of fraud as well as filing a false tax return. The trial judge, in accordance with the Court of Appeals precedent at the time and over the objection of the defendant, did not include materiality as an element of these crimes in its charge to the jury. Subsequent Supreme Court precedent refuted the trial judge's assumption that materiality was a question for the court, not the jury, raising in Neder's case the question whether the failure to instruct the jury on this element could be considered harmless. The Supreme Court in *Neder* admitted that it would not be "illogical to extend the reasoning of *Sullivan*" to this case, but concluded that "[w]e do not think the Sixth Amendment requires us to veer away from settled precedent to reach such a result." Assessments of the harmlessness of an omitted instruction, the Court reasoned, do not differ from assessments the harmlessness of instructions that erroneously describe an element[57] or that involve an unconstitutional presumption[58]—all foreclose independent jury consideration of whether the facts proved establish beyond a reasonable doubt the element in question. By contrast, the Court continued, the error in *Sullivan* "vitiate[d] *all* of the jury's findings."

With this limited view of *Sullivan's* reach, the majority rejected the reading of *Sullivan* advanced by the dissent that harmless error review may be applied "only when the jury *actually renders* a verdict—that is when it has found the defendant guilty of all the elements of the crime." The dissenters argued that misdescribing or omitting an element "*can* be harmless, if the elements of guilt that the jury *did* find necessarily embraced the one omitted or misdescribed."[59] The majority rejected this rule as inconsistent with prior precedent. Moreover, the Court maintained, it would mandate a case-by-case approach to the determination whether an error is structural, which it claimed would be inconsistent with prior cases. "Under our cases, a constitutional error is either structural or it is not." A case-by-case approach would require a reviewing court in each case of misdescription "to determine just how serious a 'misdescription' it was," posing difficult issues of interpretation particularly when reviewing state convictions. The dissenters rejected the Court's claim that the structural/trial error determination had avoided case-by-case analysis, noting its use in grand jury discrimination and biased judge cases. Even if the Court were right about the novelty of the burden such a test would impose on reviewing courts, the dissenters argued, "it would seem a small price to pay for keeping the appellate function consistent with the Sixth Amendment."

The *Neder* Court also dismissed the dissenters' prediction that the decision undercut the prohibition against directed verdicts of guilt in criminal cases, stating only, "Happily, our course of constitutional adjudication has not been characterized by this 'in for a penny, in for a pound' approach." Particularly considering that trial judges by omitting an element from the jury's instruction can, under the Court's decision in *Neder*, obtain the equivalent of a directed verdict of guilt on that element, the Court's failure to offer a substantive response to the dissenters' point left much to the lower courts to resolve. The Court also did not address whether its reasoning would allow for harmless error review when more than one element was omitted or misdescribed, or when a different kind of element, say mens rea, was omitted from the jury's instructions.

(e) Applying the Reasonable Doubt Standard for Constitutional Errors. When the Court in *Chapman* sought to fashion a federal harmless error standard for constitutional errors, it looked to the analysis it had adopted earlier in *Fahy v. Connecticut*.[60] In a passage that is generally viewed as the key to *Chapman* ruling, the *Chapman* Court reasoned:

---

57. See Pope v. Illinois, 481 U.S. 497, 107 S.Ct. 1918, 95 L.Ed.2d 439 (1987); California v. Roy, 519 U.S. 2, 117 S.Ct. 337, 136 L.Ed.2d 266 (1996).

58. See Yates v. Evatt, 500 U.S. 391, 111 S.Ct. 1884, 114 L.Ed.2d 432 (1991); Carella v. California, 491 U.S. 263, 109 S.Ct. 2419, 105 L.Ed.2d 218 (1989).

59. Justice Stevens concurred in *Neder* on this basis, finding that the verdict "necessarily included a finding" on the issue of materiality.

60. Supra note 9.

"The question is whether there is a reasonable possibility that the evidence complained of might have contributed to the conviction." * * * An error in admitting plainly relevant evidence which possibly influenced the jury adversely to a litigant cannot, under *Fahy*, be conceived of as harmless. Certainly error, constitutional error, in illegally admitting highly prejudicial evidence or comments, casts on someone other than the person prejudiced by it a burden to show that it was harmless. It is for that reason that the original common-law harmless error rule put the burden on the beneficiary of the error either to prove that there was no injury or to suffer a reversal of his erroneously obtained judgment. There is little, if any, difference between our statement in *Fahy* about "whether there is a reasonable possibility that the evidence complained of might have contributed to the conviction" and requiring the beneficiary of a constitutional error to prove beyond a reasonable doubt that the error complained of did not contribute to the verdict obtained. We, therefore, do no more than adhere to the meaning of our *Fahy* case when we hold, as we now do, that before a federal constitutional error can be held harmless, the court must be able to declare a belief that it was harmless beyond a reasonable doubt.

The *Chapman* standard clearly rejected a "correct result" test, especially if the correct result was to be measured simply by sufficient evidence to sustain a conviction. The standard looked not to whether the jury could have convicted without regard to the error, or whether the appellate court itself would have convicted without the error, but to whether the error had influenced the jury in reaching its verdict. It required that the appellate court be convinced "beyond a reasonable doubt"

that there was no "reasonable possibility" that the error contributed to the jury's verdict. The *Chapman* opinion did not clearly indicate, however, precisely what weight was to be given to the presence of overwhelming untainted evidence in making that judgment.

The Court has appeared to move back and forth between relying heavily upon the presence of proof of guilt in its harmless error analysis, and considering that proof as less central to the inquiry. In *Harrington v. California*,[61] a case evaluating the introduction of the confessions of two codefendants who did not take the stand,[62] Justice Douglas noted in his opinion for the court that the untainted evidence against the defendant was "so overwhelming" that if this *Bruton* violation were not deemed harmless, the Court would, in effect, be placing *Bruton* violations in the category of errors subject to the automatic-reversal rule. Subsequent decisions in *Milton v. Wainwright*,[63] and *Schneble v. Florida*,[64] relied heavily on the presence of "overwhelming evidence of guilt."

In *Fulminante v. Arizona*,[65] five justices appeared to return to an analysis that looked primarily to the influence on the conviction, rather than relying entirely on the weight of the evidence of guilt. In finding the admission of defendant's coerced confession was not harmless, Justice White wrote for the majority,[66] "[I]t must be determined whether the State has met its burden of demonstrating that the admission of the confession * * * did not contribute to Fulminante's conviction."[67] Read broadly, the Court's opinion in *Sullivan* also undercut attempts to gauge the harmlessness or error simply by assessing the weight of the evidence of guilt. The appropriate analysis, the Court explained, was not to ask whether a

61. 395 U.S. 250, 89 S.Ct. 1726, 23 L.Ed.2d 284 (1969).

62. See § 17.2(b).

63. 407 U.S. 371, 92 S.Ct. 2174, 33 L.Ed.2d 1 (1972).

64. 405 U.S. 427, 92 S.Ct. 1056, 31 L.Ed.2d 340 (1972).

65. Supra note 32.

66. *Fulminante* included separate majorities on three separate issues—the presence of a constitutional violation, the applicability of harmless error analysis to that violation, and the harmlessness of the error. Justice White's

opinion concluding that the error was not harmless was joined by Justices Marshall, Blackmun, Stevens, and Kennedy.

67. *Fulminante*, opinion of White, J., writing for five Justices on the separate issue of whether the error was harmless. See also Justice Kennedy's concurring opinion, in which he argued that the court must "appreciate the indelible impact a full confession may have on the trier of fact."

hypothetical jury would surely have convicted. "The Sixth Amendment," Justice Scalia wrote for the Court, "requires more than appellate speculation about a hypothetical jury's action, or else directed verdicts for the State would be sustainable on appeal; it requires an actual jury finding of guilty."

More recently, the Court in *Neder* applied an analysis more like that used in *Harrington*. The Court stated that "where a reviewing court concludes beyond a reasonable doubt that the omitted element was uncontested and supported by overwhelming evidence, such that the jury verdict would have been the same absent the error, the erroneous instruc-tion is properly found to be harmless." The Court concluded that the evidence in *Neder* "incontrovertibly establishe[d]" the omitted element of materiality. Indeed, "the evidence supporting materiality was so overwhelming * * * that Neder did not argue to the jury—and does not argue here—that" his statements could be found immaterial. The Court added, "If," after "a thorough examination of the record," the reviewing court "cannot conclude beyond a reasonable doubt that the jury ver-dict would have been the same absent the error—for example, where the defendant con-tested the omitted element and raised evidence sufficient to support a contrary finding—it should not find the error harmless."

Chapter 28

POST CONVICTION REVIEW: COLLATERAL REMEDIES

Table of Sections

---

§ 28.1   Current Collateral Remedies and Historical Antecedents

(a) The Nature of Collateral Remedies. What avenues, if any, are available to a convicted defendant for challenging his conviction after all opportunities for appellate review have been exhausted? The answer to that question is the subject of several extensive treatises.[1] Every jurisdiction has one or more procedures through which defendants can present post-appeal challenges to their convictions on at least limited grounds. In addition, through the federal writ of habeas corpus, a state defendant may challenge his state conviction on federal constitutional grounds in the federal courts.

The various state and federal procedures for presenting post-appeal challenges are commonly described as "collateral remedies." That description is not limited to separately filed suits challenging some aspect of a judgment in a criminal case, but means simply that the remedy "provide[s] an avenue for upsetting judgments [of conviction] that have become otherwise final."[2] Most common collateral remedies today are derived from the common law writs of habeas corpus and coram nobis. The common law habeas proceeding was a separate civil action in which a petitioner challenged his continued detention by attacking the conviction on which his detention was based. Because the petitioner sought release from custody, the petition was filed in the court having jurisdiction over the official who held the petitioner in custody (e.g., the prison warden), rather than the court that had entered judgment of conviction. The writ of coram nobis directly attacked the conviction and was pursued in the court of conviction, but it

also was commonly viewed as an independent civil action. While some of today's post-conviction proceedings are viewed as independent civil actions, many are considered part of the original criminal case, similar to a post-appeal motion for a new trial.

This chapter focuses on the contemporary federal writ of habeas corpus. Federal habeas is the one collateral remedy available to all state prisoners. It also provides the doctrinal framework for the primary post-conviction remedy for federal prisoners challenging their convictions: the motion to vacate a sentence under 28 U.S.C. § 2255. In addition, many states have modeled their own collateral remedies after the federal writ.

(b) The Common Law Writ of Habeas Corpus. The common law writ of habeas corpus, simply defined, is a judicial order directing a person to have the body of another brought before a tribunal at a certain time and place. The writ apparently takes its name from its directive, originally stated in Latin, that the court would "have the body." As initially developed sometime before the thirteenth century, the writ was a process by which courts compelled the attendance of parties whose presence would facilitate their proceedings. It was not until the mid-fourteenth century that it came to be used as an independent proceeding designed to challenge illegal detention. The subsequent sixteenth-century characterization of habeas corpus as the Great Writ of Liberty—the alleged procedural underpinning of the guarantees of the Magna Carta—stemmed primarily from battles fought in establishing its effectiveness against imprisonment by the Crown without judicial authorization.

The use of the writ to enforce the Magna Carta's guarantee of adherence to the "law of

---

§ 28.1

1. See J. Leibman & R. Hertz, Federal Habeas Corpus Practice and Procedure (3d ed. 1998); L. Yackle, Postconviction Remedies (1981 & Supp. 1997); I. Robbins, The Law and Processes of Postconviction Remedies (1982).

2. Mackey v. United States, 401 U.S. 667, 91 S.Ct. 1160, 28 L.Ed.2d 404 (1971).

the land" (later described as "due process") was forcefully advocated in 1627 by leading counsel in *Darnel's Case*,[3] where the writ was sought to gain release of five knights imprisoned for refusing to comply with the King's "forced loan" program. The King's Bench apparently accepted counsels' contention that the writ could be used to enforce the Magna Carta's guarantee, but responded that it could not look beyond the Crown's return, which stated on its face that the detention was lawfully authorized. Dissatisfaction with this ruling eventually led to the 1641 Act that removed the power of the Crown to arrest without probable cause and granted to any arrested person immediate access by writ of habeas corpus to a judicial determination of the legality of his detention. When procedural difficulties undermined the effectiveness of that Act, the Parliament responded with the celebrated Habeas Corpus Act of 1679. The 1679 Act reinforced judicial authority to use the writ to release persons illegally detained by the Crown, but specifically excluded from its coverage persons confined as a result of criminal conviction.

Although it could be argued that the exclusion in the 1679 Act eliminated the authority of English courts to issue the writ on behalf of convicted persons, it seems unlikely that Parliament intended to bar use of the writ in such cases, at least where the court of conviction lacked jurisdiction. In *Bushell's Case*,[4] decided in 1670, the writ had been used to order the release of a juror who had been held in contempt for refusing to return a guilty verdict as directed by the trial court. Justice Brennan concluded in *Fay v. Noia*[5] that *Bushell's Case* established that the writ was available at common law to challenge imprisonment based on a conviction obtained in violation of due process. However, Justice Powell later suggested that Justice Brennan's reading of *Bushell's Case* was far too broad.[6] In any event, as a remedy

for persons detained upon a conviction, the writ historically had very limited utility and was rarely successful.

English habeas corpus jurisprudence was transplanted into post-colonial America, and the Judiciary Act of 1789 granted federal courts limited habeas review. During Reconstruction, Congress passed the Habeas Corpus Act of 1867, which broadened significantly federal power to review the judgments of state court. For the first time federal courts were given the power to grant writs of habeas corpus when any person was held "in violation of the Constitution." Despite the significant changes in the statute that have occurred since that era, the history of the writ and its use in federal courts during the nineteenth century continue to inform the Court's application of the contemporary commands of Congress.

§ 28.2 The Statutory Structure and Habeas Policy

(a) Constitutional Right or Legislative Grace? In a clause commonly known as the Suspension Clause, Article I of the United States Constitution states: "[T]he Privilege of the Writ of Habeas Corpus shall not be suspended, unless when in Cases of Rebellion or Invasion the Public Safety may require it."[1] On its face, this provision suggests that federal courts have the inherent authority to issue the writ in the absence of a valid suspension. Such a reading would establish, in effect, a constitutional right to habeas relief, at least to the extent such relief was available at common law, for persons held in custody. Although the Court occasionally had suggested that the 1867 provision making the federal writ available to state prisoners might have constitutional roots, the Court did not find it necessary to consider whether the Suspension Clause guarantees that authority until Congress cut back significantly the availability of the writ in

3. 3 How.St.Tr. 1 (1627) (also known as the *Case of the Five Knights*).

4. 124 Eng.Rep. 1006 (C.P.1670); 6 State Trials 999 (1670).

5. 372 U.S. 391, 83 S.Ct. 822, 9 L.Ed.2d 837 (1963), also discussed in § 28.3(c).

6. Schneckloth v. Bustamonte, 412 U.S. 218, 93 S.Ct. 2041, 36 L.Ed.2d 854 (1973), discussed in § 28.3(c).

§ 28.2

1. U.S. Const. Art. I, § 9. cl.2.

1996. The Court in *Felker v. Turpin*[2] unanimously rejected the contention that the Clause was violated by those provisions of the Antiterrorism and Effective Death Penalty Act of 1996 that sharply limit habeas relief for petitioners filing successive petitions. Chief Justice Rehnquist's opinion for the Court initially noted that "the writ of habeas corpus known to the Framers was quite different from that which exists today" as the writ at that time was available "only to prisoners confined under the authority of the United States, not under state authority" and "[t]he class of judicial actions reviewable by the writ was more restricted as well." It "was not until 1867 that Congress made the writ generally available * * * [to state prisoners,] [a]nd it was not until well into this century that this Court interpreted that provision to allow a final judgment of conviction in a state court to be collaterally attacked." The *Felker* Court assumed, however, for purposes of its decision, "that the Suspension Clause of the Constitution refers to the writ as it exists today, rather than as it existed in 1789." The Court had long recognized that "judgments about the proper scope of the writ are 'normally for Congress to make.'" In enacting new restrictions on successive petitions in 1996, Congress dealt with an area of habeas law which the Court had previously described as the product of "a complex and evolving body of equitable principles informed and controlled by historical usage, statutory developments and judicial decisions." The new limitations were "well within the compass of this evolutionary process." Noting that the 1996 Act did not repeal the authority of the Supreme Court to entertain original habeas petitions filed under 28 U.S.C. § 2241, the Court concluded that the limitations on successive petitions did "not amount to a suspension of the writ contrary to Article I, § 9."

In INS v. St. Cyr,[3] the Court invoked the principle of constitutional doubt to interpret the 1996 amendments to two statutes in a way that did not prohibit habeas review of a question of law, specifically whether certain discre-

tionary relief was available for aliens whose convictions were obtained through plea agreements and who would have been eligible for that discretionary relief at the time of their plea. It reasoned that "even assuming that the Suspension Clause protects only the writ as it existed in 1789," for the Court to interpret the 1996 statutes to have withdrawn the power of federal judges to resolve a pure question of law affecting the detention of aliens would present "a serious Suspension Clause issue," considering the statute "provided no adequate substitute * * *." The Court noted that historically it is in the context of reviewing the legality of executive detention that the writ's protections have been strongest. In dissent, three justices reached the Suspension Clause issue and argued that the Clause prohibits Congress only from temporarily eliminating access to the writ for certain areas or classes of claimants, and does not prohibit permanent alteration of its content.

(b) Statutory Structure: From the 1867 Act to the 1996 Act. For over a century, the Habeas Corpus Act of 1867 provided the basic statutory framework for federal habeas relief on behalf of state prisoners. Although several key provisions have now been superseded by provisions of the 1996 Antiterrorism and Effective Death Penalty Act, an understanding of the earlier statute is an essential backdrop to litigation under the new provisions.

The 1867 Act provided habeas relief for any person "restrained of his or her liberty," including state prisoners, who had been excluded under the 1789 Act. Relief could be granted from only those restraints imposed in violation of federal law—the Constitution, treaties, and statutes of the United States. A federal court applying the writ to a person held in state custody was not to examine the legality of the detention under state law. The 1867 Act also changed habeas procedure by providing that petitioners could "deny any of the material facts set forth in the return" or allege additional facts.

---

2. 518 U.S. 651, 116 S.Ct. 2333, 135 L.Ed.2d 827 (1996).

3. 533 U.S. 289, 121 S.Ct. 2271, 150 L.Ed.2d 347 (2001).

The objectives of the Thirty-ninth Congress in adopting the Habeas Corpus Act of 1867 have been debated for years. Of the several views advanced, two in particular attracted attention. A narrow reading assumed that the Act incorporated the "historical meaning and scope"[4] of the writ, including earlier cases that had limited habeas review to a determination of whether the convicting court had jurisdiction over the person and the subject matter. Commentators adhering to this position have contended that this reading fully satisfies the major concern of Congress in adopting the 1867 Act, which was that the states not be allowed to keep the newly freed slaves from exercising their rights by applying to them broadly phrased state laws that were contrary to the recently enacted Thirteenth Amendment and Civil Rights Act. The Civil Rights Act of 1866 provided citizens "of every race or color" should be "subject to like punishment, pains and penalties and to none other." Detention pursuant to a state statute in violation of the Constitution could be challenged under the writ, consistent with the earlier habeas rulings, because the unconstitutionality of the statute deprived the state court of its jurisdiction.

The competing, broader view of the 1867 Act would have extended the writ beyond jurisdictional defects. Proponents of this view also looked to the Reconstruction-era context in which the habeas statute was adopted. They argued that Congress expected that the courts of the Southern states would be totally unreceptive to Reconstruction legislation and wanted to give the federal courts superintending control to ensure that there would be full recognition of the federal rights in the 1866 Civil Rights Act and the Fourteenth Amendment.

In the 1960s the Court adopted this broader interpretation of the Act's purpose in several expansive decisions, noting that the writ was capable of growth to meet "changed conceptions of the kind of criminal proceedings so fundamentally defective as to make imprisonment pursuant to them constitutionally intol-

erable."[5] But by the mid–1970s the tide had turned, and the Court's interpretations of the habeas statute narrowed. Still, the Court continued to apply the writ substantially beyond the review of jurisdictional defects. Meanwhile, Congress offered little further direction, adding various provisions to the habeas statute over the years, none of which modified the core statutory authorization set forth in the 1867 Act. In 1976 habeas cases became subject to the "Rules Governing 2254 Cases in the United States District Courts," supplementing the statutory provisions.

(c) The Current Statute. In 1996, Congress enacted the Antiterrorism and Effective Death Penalty Act (AEDPA), substantially changing and narrowing the basic provisions of the 1867 Act. The current statutory provisions governing the writ are found in 28 U.S.C. §§ 2241–2266. What follows is a very brief outline of the most important provisions governing the writ for persons in state custody, provisions that will be examined in more detail in later sections of this chapter.

Section 2241, unchanged by the 1996 amendments, contains the basic authorization of the federal courts to issue the writ, with subsection (c) setting forth the conditions under which the writ may "extend to a prisoner." Subsection (c)(3), with only a slight alteration of the language of the 1867 Act, provides that the writ may issue when the prisoner "is in custody in violation of the Constitution or laws or treaties of the United States." Section 2254, dealing specifically with applications "on behalf of a person in custody pursuant to the judgment of a state court," repeats that language. Section 2241 also provides authority for the Supreme Court to grant a petition filed originally with the High Court, although Rule 20.4(a) of the Supreme Court Rules limits such relief to "exceptional circumstances."

Section 2243, also unchanged, deals primarily with matters of procedure (e.g., the use of show cause orders and the timing of the hearings), but ends by noting that the habeas

---

4. Bator, Finality in Criminal Law and Federal Habeas Corpus for State Prisoners, 76 Harv.L.Rev. 441 (1963).

5. Fay v. Noia, 372 U.S. 391, 83 S.Ct. 822, 9 L.Ed.2d 837 (1963).

court, after concluding its hearing, shall "dispose of the matter as law and justice require." This provision has been cited by the Court as evidencing the "equitable nature" of the habeas remedy.

Section 2244, completely revised in 1996, deals with second or successive petitions. It sets forth circumstances under which a judge may refuse to consider a petition on the basis of the disposition of an earlier petition and includes a one-year limitations period during which a petitioner may apply for a writ of habeas corpus.

Under § 2253 a state prisoner has no absolute entitlement to appeal a district court's denial of his petition, but must first seek and obtain a "certificate of appealability" from a circuit justice or judge, by demonstrating a "substantial showing of the denial of a constitutional right."[6]

Sections 2254(b) and (c) contain the requirement that a state prisoner exhaust state remedies before federal relief may be granted. New § 2254(d), perhaps the most important section added by the 1996 Act, defines the circumstances under which a writ may be granted when the petitioner's claim was adjudicated on the merits in state court. New § 2254(e) governs factfinding and evidentiary hearings, and includes a presumption concerning state factfinding.

New §§ 2261 through 2266 impose special restrictive standards for considering habeas petitions by state prisoners sentenced to death in states which have adopted certain "mechanism for the appointment, compensation, and payment of reasonable litigation expenses of competent counsel in State postconviction proceedings brought by indigent prisoners whose capital sentences have been upheld on direct review." Section 2263 imposes a 180–day time period in which to file such a petition, with an extension for extraordinary circumstances. Under § 2266, the district court ordinarily must render a final ruling on the petition within 180 days of filing, and if that ruling is appealed, the Court of Appeals has 120 days

after the final brief is filed to resolve the appeal. Under § 2264, the federal habeas court may consider only "claims that have been raised and decided on the merits" in state courts, except when the failure to raise the claim was the result of (1) state action violating the Constitution, (2) a factual predicate that could not have been discovered through due diligence in time to present the claim in state proceedings, and (3) the Supreme Court's subsequent recognition of a new federal right that is made "retroactively applicable."

(d) Balancing Within the Statutory Framework. Except where the language of the statute is quite specific, the Court generally has considered its task in interpreting the habeas statute as one of achieving the appropriate balance between the value of expansive habeas review and the costs of providing such review. Although the 1996 Act has restricted the circumstances under which the Court is free to balance such interests, and has tipped that balance distinctly in the direction of narrowing relief, plenty of room for judicial policy analysis remains under the revised statute.

The benefits of expansive collateral review for both state and federal prisoners have been advocated most forcefully in the opinions of Justice Brennan. Plenary review of constitutional claims on collateral attack, Justice Brennan maintained, is essential to fulfilling the historic function of habeas corpus—providing relief against the detention of persons in violation of their fundamental liberties. An open-ended mechanism, he stated, is needed, in particular, to consider claims that were not presented in the original proceeding that led to conviction, often through no fault of the defendant himself. "Conventional notions of finality of litigation," including concepts of res judicata, should "have no place where life or liberty is at stake and infringement of constitutional rights is alleged."[7]

While critics of Justice Brennan's viewpoint tend to focus on the costs of providing a broad, "continuing mechanism for relief," they also question whether a second review by a habeas

---

6. Miller–El v. Cockrell, 537 U.S. 322, 123 S.Ct. 1029, 154 L.Ed.2d 931 (2003).

7. Sanders v. United States, 373 U.S. 1, 83 S.Ct. 1068, 10 L.Ed.2d 148 (1963).

court will be more accurate than the first review in state court.[8] In response, supporters of broad habeas review maintain that constitutional rights are sufficiently important that disagreement between the habeas court and the state court should be a sufficient reason to grant relief.

Expansive habeas review is supported by the institutional and political premises underlying the Fourteenth Amendment, as well as the 1867 Habeas Act, which are said to give "federal courts the 'last say' with respect to questions of federal law."[9] Federal habeas corpus rests, it is said, on "the proposition that persons convicted of crimes in state courts are entitled to at least one opportunity to litigate their federal claims in a federal forum."[10] Since the Supreme Court obviously lacks the resources necessary to review more than a few of the state cases in which direct review is sought, the lower federal courts must serve as its functional surrogate in providing federal habeas review. This role of the federal habeas courts, it is argued, also provides greater uniformity in constitutional interpretation.

The demand for a federal forum, Justice Brennan noted, is not based on any doubts as to the personal integrity of state judges, but rather on the recognition of the institutional limitations under which state judges operate. As he explained in his dissent in *Stone v Powell*:[11]

State judges popularly elected may have difficulty resisting popular pressures not experienced by federal judges given lifetime tenure designed to immunize them from such influences, and the federal habeas statutes reflect the congressional judgment that such

detached federal review is a salutary safeguard * * *.

Other Supreme Court justices, however, have questioned the assumption that institutional factors render state judges less receptive to federal constitutional claims than federal judges. Justice O'Connor has noted, for example, that many states utilize merit selection systems that give state judges security against "majoritarian pressures" comparable to that provided by the life tenure afforded federal judges.[12] Critics of Brennan's position argue that the Court should not downgrade, on the basis of largely speculative impressions, the obligation of state judges to uphold federal law. Without substantial evidence of concerted failure by state courts to abide by their obligations, it should not be assumed that federal habeas courts must review federal claims notwithstanding entirely adequate state procedures for considering those claims. The appropriate assumption, it is argued, is that adopted by the Supreme Court in *Stone v. Powell*.[13] The Court there noted:

Despite differences in institutional environment and the unsympathetic attitude to federal constitutional claims of some state judges in years past, we are unwilling to assume that there now exists a general lack of appropriate sensitivity to constitutional rights in the trial and appellate courts of the several States. * * * [T]here is "no intrinsic reason why the fact that a man is a federal judge should make him more competent, or conscientious, or learned with respect to the [consideration of Fourth Amendment claims] than his neighbor in the state courthouse."

---

8. Justice Jackson expressed such skepticism with reference even to review by the Supreme Court itself. He noted: "[R]eversal by a higher court is not proof that justice is thereby better done. There is no doubt that if there were a super-Supreme Court, a substantial proportion of our reversals of state courts would be reversed. We are not final because we are infallible, but we are infallible only because we are final." Brown v. Allen, 344 U.S. 443, 73 S.Ct. 397, 97 L.Ed. 469 (1953) (Jackson, J., concurring).

9. Kaufman v. United States, 394 U.S. 217, 89 S.Ct. 1068, 22 L.Ed.2d 227 (1969). See also Rose v. Mitchell, 443 U.S. 545, 99 S.Ct. 2993, 61 L.Ed.2d 739 (1979).

10. *Kaufman*, supra note 9.

11. 428 U.S. 465, 96 S.Ct. 3037, 49 L.Ed.2d 1067 (1976). Also discussed in § 28.3(c).

12. O'Connor, Trends in the Relationship Between the Federal and State Courts From the Perspective of a State Court Judge, 22 Wm. & Mary L.Rev. 801, 812–15 (1981) (written prior to her appointment to the Supreme Court, but reflecting a viewpoint reiterated in her opinions, see e.g., Engle v. Isaac, 456 U.S. 107, 102 S.Ct. 1558, 71 L.Ed.2d 783 (1982)).

13. Supra note 11.

The costs of expansive federal habeas review, especially as to state cases, have been discussed at length in the opinions of various justices, but most of these discussions build on arguments advanced initially by Justice Powell. He stressed primarily three costs. First, broad habeas review is said to result in an unwise expenditure of scarce judicial resources. Second, systematic habeas review of state decisions is said to be inconsistent with the "constitutional balance upon which the doctrine of federalism is founded."[14] Finally, plenary habeas review is said to work against the important objective of achieving a rational point of finality in the criminal justice process.

On the first issue, the federal courts in 2000, for example, ruled upon roughly 21,345 habeas petitions filed by state prisoners. Of the state habeas petitions filed in 1995, relief was granted in only a tiny proportion, less than 2%, of those petitions.[15] Prisoner petitions under § 2254 and § 2255 (federal prisoners) make up well over 10% of the total docket of the courts of appeals. As prison populations continue to expand, that share of the caseload may increase. Justice Powell argued that it would be wiser to devote such a significant expenditure of the finite resources of the federal judiciary to other portions of the federal docket, civil actions "which affect intimately the lives of greater numbers of people" and criminal trials and appeals. The failure to restrict the scope of habeas may work against even that small class of state prisoners for whom habeas review may be necessary to ensure a full and fair opportunity for litigation of their constitutional claim. Thus, Justice Jackson, commenting upon a "progressive trivialization of the writ" that could "inundate the dockets of the lower courts" warned that "he who must search a haystack for a needle is likely to end up with the attitude that the needle is not worth the search."[16] Proponents of broad review argue that the burden imposed upon the federal courts is exaggerated. Evidentiary hearings are held in only a tiny fraction of the petitions filed, for example. Moreover, they argue, the burden imposed is justified by the importance of the quest. Thus, Justice Schaefer of Illinois, responding to Justice Jackson's comment, noted: "It is not a needle we are looking for in these stacks of papers, but the rights of a human being."[17]

Justice Powell further characterized expansive federal habeas review as "tend[ing] to undermine the values inherent in our federal system of government." State appellate courts may so resent the review of their decisions by federal district judges, he warned, that they will "simply abdicate in favor of the federal jurisdiction." Yet, with only a small percentage of all state defendants likely to seek federal habeas corpus review, the primary protection of constitutional rights must come from a state judiciary that has a strong sense of responsibility for performing that function. Proponents of broad habeas review argue that these "federalism costs" of habeas review have largely dissipated. State courts have become accustomed to such review, they argue, and any remaining state court resentment is due to a failure to understand that reversal of state court decisions occurs only rarely and usually only after review by a federal court of appeals. Indeed, some have argued that federal habeas review has had a positive impact on federal-state relations, having encouraged a useful dialogue between federal and state courts. Fi-

---

14. Schneckloth v. Bustamonte, 412 U.S. 218, 93 S.Ct. 2041, 36 L.Ed.2d 854 (1973) (concurring opinion).

15. The percentage of petitions granted has been somewhat higher in capital cases. Of state habeas petitions filed by death row inmates in 1995, 3.9% were successful in obtaining at least partial relief for the petitioner. A study of the 5,760 death sentences imposed in the U.S. between 1973 and 1995 revealed that *two of every five* death sentences reviewed in federal habeas court were overturned. Of every 100 death sentences imposed, 41 were turned back at the state direct appeal phase because of "serious error," another 6 were rejected at the state post conviction stage, and another 21 were thrown out by

federal courts as a result of habeas proceedings. The study defined "serious error" as "error that substantially undermines the reliability of the guilt finding or death sentence imposed at trial," the most common being "egregiously incompetent defense lawyering," and "prosecutorial suppression of evidence that the defendant is innocent or does not deserve the death penalty." J. Liebman, J. Fagan & V. West, A Broken System: Error Rates in Capital Cases, 1973–95 (2000).

16. Brown v. Allen, supra note 8.

17. Schaefer, Federalism and State Criminal Procedure, 70 Harv.L.Rev. 1, 25 (1956).

nally, the proponents note that even if friction is inevitable, an unjustly incarcerated prisoner should not have his liberty sacrificed on the altar of improving federal-state relations.

Justice Powell also cited as a third cost of broad habeas review its detrimental impact upon those interests underlying the achievement in the criminal justice process of a definite point of finality. Deterrence depends upon the expectation that one violating the law will swiftly and certainly be subject to punishment, but the reopening of convictions through habeas corpus is said to cast doubt upon the judicial system's ability to achieve that objective. Society can rightfully question, it is argued, whether broad habeas review does not invite defendants to postpone presentation of their claims to that point at which a successful petition cannot feasibly be followed by reprosecution. Justice Powell noted further that broad habeas review undercuts the need "at some point [for] the law * * * to convey to those in custody that a wrong has been committed, that consequent punishment has been imposed, that one should no longer look back with the view to resurrecting every imaginable basis for further litigation but rather should look forward to rehabilitation and to becoming a constructive citizen." Expansive habeas review is also said to undercut society's need to reach a point of repose, where it can say that the system has gone far enough and one can now safely assume that "justice has been done."

(e) Competing Models of Habeas Review. Over the years, the opinions of the justices have offered a variety of alternative approaches to balancing the cost and benefits of habeas review. The basic contours of those distinct but not necessarily conflicting theories are set forth below.

Ensuring responsible state court adjudication of constitutional rights: the "one fair chance" model. One of the narrowest models of habeas review is that which views the primary function of the writ as ensuring that the state judicial systems fulfill their obligation to apply in a responsible manner the prevailing constitutional doctrine. Such a model, supplemented by the traditional review of jurisdictional defects, furnished the foundation for the standards that governed habeas review for a good part of the first half of the twentieth century. Utilizing what was later described as a "due process" approach to habeas review, those standards looked to whether the state process had afforded the habeas petitioner an adequate opportunity to gain a fair determination of his constitutional claim. One of the primary champions of this approach was Professor Paul Bator, who argued that, as a general principle, federal court review was no more likely than state court review to guarantee a result "correct in an ultimate sense," and that adding federal review on top of state review therefore was simply a wasteful and unnecessary interference with the state criminal justice process, provided the defendant had available a meaningful review from the state system.[18] Contemporary advocates of this view have included Justices Scalia and Thomas.[19]

Two developments in federal habeas doctrine prior to the 1996 Act followed this model. *Stone v. Powell* barred habeas relitigation of a fourth amendment claim provided the state procedure granted the defendant a "full and fair opportunity" for litigating that claim. More significantly *Teague v. Lane*[20] restricted habeas review by reference to the function of ensuring that state courts make a conscientious effort to fulfill their obligation to enforce federal constitutional guarantees. In order to deter state courts from disregarding federal constitutional precedent, *Teague* held that, as to most constitutional claims, the federal habeas court need only apply constitutional doctrine as it stood when the state courts applied it. This meant that the habeas court, in examining the constitutional law as it then stood, had to accept any reasonable state court interpretation of that law even though the habeas

---

18. Bator, supra note 4.

19. See e.g., Withrow v. Williams, 507 U.S. 680, 113 S.Ct. 1745, 123 L.Ed.2d 407 (1993) (Scalia, J., concurring in part and dissenting in part); California v. Roy, 519 U.S.

2, 117 S.Ct. 337, 136 L.Ed.2d 266 (1996) (Scalia, J., concurring).

20. 489 U.S. 288, 318, 109 S.Ct. 1060, 1079, 103 L.Ed.2d 334 (1989), discussed in § 28.6.

court believed that a more expansive interpretation is the better one. Amended § 2254(d) now codifies this general approach, barring relief for claims litigated on their merits in state court unless the state court decision was contrary to or involved an "unreasonable" application of "clearly established Federal law."[21]

Vindicating federal constitutional rights in a federal forum. The broadest model of habeas review was that espoused by Justice Brennan. In his view, a defendant could be denied habeas relief because he (or in some instances, his counsel) abused either the state process or the habeas process, yet the habeas court also had discretion to grant relief notwithstanding such abuse. Comity generally required that the state be given an opportunity to rule on a constitutional claim before it was taken to federal courts, but only if it could provide that ruling expeditiously. Today, the model advocated by Justice Brennan has been rejected. Perhaps the only aspect remaining is the broad definition of "custody" advanced in the 1960s. Well before the 1996 amendments, the Court had already narrowed relief for defaulted claims and held that fourth amendment violations were not cognizable on habeas review. The 1996 amendments further limited access to federal evidentiary hearings, narrowed relief for claims raised in second petitions, barred late petitions, and required federal courts to defer to "reasonable" state court interpretations and applications of established federal law.

Surrogate supreme courts. Another model of federal habeas review considers the federal habeas courts as primarily quasi-appellate courts, serving as a replacement for a Supreme Court that can review only a small fraction of all petitions for certiorari presented to it. The initial focus of this "surrogate" model was the importance of development and interpretation of federal constitutional guarantees by federal, not state, courts. This model found its strongest support in decisions of the 1950s, but was weakened by the Court's decision in *Teague v. Lane*, which forbid habeas courts from expanding the rights of criminal defendants. *Teague* barred the announcement of new rules in habeas cases, except in a few narrow circumstances. The 1996 amendments narrowed those circumstances further still. So circumscribed, habeas litigation is now a poor vehicle for developing federal law. Still, to the limited extent that habeas courts supplement Supreme Court review in correcting bias in state courts, the surrogate model retains vitality.

The "fundamental fairness" model. Justice Stevens, in a series of opinions in the 1980s, advanced a "fundamental fairness" model of habeas review. Justice Stevens's position was that "constitutional errors are not fungible," at least with respect to remedies.[22] Just as there are some errors that call for automatic reversal and some that call for reversal on appeal only if deemed not to have been harmless, there are some errors "important enough" to require reversal on direct appeal but not important enough to require the overturning of a conviction on collateral review, and some errors so significant that they should be recognized on habeas review under almost any circumstance. In this latter category, Justice Stevens placed "errors so fundamental that they infect the validity of the underlying judgment itself, or the integrity by which that judgment was obtained," such as a trial dominated by mob violence, the prosecutor's knowing use of perjured testimony, or the admission of a confession "extorted from the defendant by brutal methods." While Justice Stevens agreed courts must be cautious when considering claims that were not raised at trial (in part on the premise that the tardiness in their presentation suggests in itself their likely irrelevance), he was willing to push aside even weighty state interests in procedural regularity when a clear denial of fundamental fairness was presented. Although neither the Court majority nor Congress accepted Justice Stevens's fundamental fairness doctrine, both adopted the basic premise that

---

21. 28 U.S.C.A. § 2254(d), discussed in § 28.6(g).

22. See Rose v. Lundy, 455 U.S. 509, 538, 102 S.Ct. 1198, 1213, 71 L.Ed.2d 379 (1982) (Stevens, J., dissenting).

certain claims should prevail over limits that would otherwise bar habeas review.[23]

Protection of the "innocent." In 1969 Justice Black, in a brief dissent from a majority ruling granting collateral relief based on a fourth amendment violation, noted: "I would always require that the convicted defendant raise the kind of constitutional claim that casts some shadow of a doubt on his guilt."[24] This comment was expanded upon in a highly influential article by Judge Henry Friendly, with the provocative title "Is Innocence Irrelevant?"[25] Judge Friendly argued that "with a few important exceptions," "convictions should be subject to collateral attack only when the prisoner supplements his constitutional plea with a colorable claim of innocence." There were important distinctions in the manner in which Judge Friendly and Justice Black would have used habeas review as a safety net for the innocent. Justice Black focused on the general nature of the constitutional claim, asking whether its basic function is to protect the innocent by safeguarding the reliability of the guilt determining process. Judge Friendly, on the other hand, focused on actual factual innocence on a case-by-case basis. The defendant would have to show factual innocence that may have gone unrecognized due to a constitutional violation that affected the determination of guilt.

Both versions of habeas review as a safety net for the innocent have been incorporated into various aspects of habeas law. Innocence has not, however, become the exclusive theme of habeas review. With one exception, see § 28.3(f), habeas review remains focused on the question of whether a constitutional right was violated, not whether a petitioner is in fact innocent. On the other hand, whether or not a claim affects the reliability of a guilty verdict may be critical in determining whether review will be available notwithstanding a failure by the petitioner or his counsel to raise the claim in a timely manner, a failure that would otherwise bar review. The Court's holding in

Stone v. Powell that claims of fourth amendment error ordinarily are not cognizable on habeas review is based in part on the recognition that such error does not jeopardize the reliability of a conviction.

The mixing of models. Current law, as the above discussion indicates, does not exclusively follow any one model of habeas review. Rather, the new statute and the doctrinal landscape against which it must be interpreted contain elements, sometimes inconsistent, of several different models. In part, this is a product of stare decisis, and the failure of any single model to capture the full support of a majority of the Court, or Congress. Because the Court's interpretation of the writ has so frequently shifted with changes in the Court's composition, and because the Court has so often returned to concepts that appeared to have been rejected in an earlier period and used them as at least a springboard for reshaping habeas doctrine, attention will be given in the sections that follow to where the law has been as well as to where it now stands.

§ 28.3   Cognizable Claims

(a) Cognizable Claimants: The Custody Requirement. The federal habeas corpus statutes, from the 1789 Act to the AEDPA, have all provided that the writ extend to a person "in custody." Presently, §§ 2241 and 2254 provide that the writ is limited to persons "in custody in violation of the Constitution or laws or treaties of the United States." Not surprisingly, as the Court expanded the scope of the writ in its treatment of such matters as the range of cognizable claims during the 1960s, it also broadened the element of custody. Subsequent decisions have continued to interpret generously the meaning of custody under the statute, despite markedly restrictive readings of other requirements for habeas relief. Still today, "custody" may exist not only when a petitioner is incarcerated, but also

---

23. See e.g., Teague v. Lane, supra note 20 (Stevens, J., concurring); § 28.5(b) and (d).

24. Kaufman v. United States, supra note 9 (Black, J., dissenting).

25. Friendly, Is Innocence Irrelevant? Collateral Attack on Criminal Judgments, 38 U.Chi.L.Rev. 142 (1970).

when a petitioner suffers certain significant "present restraints."

The 1963 decision of *Jones v. Cunningham*[1] was the critical ruling extending the concept of "custody" beyond actual incarceration. The Court there held, in an opinion by Justice Black, that a petitioner subject to typical conditions of parole was "in custody" for the purposes of § 2254. Justice Black concluded "there are other restraints on a man's liberty, restraints not shared by the public generally, which have been thought sufficient in the English-speaking world to support the issuance of habeas corpus." For example, he noted, the writ had been made available to an alien seeking entry into the United States, or to a person contesting the legality of induction into the military service.

Turning to the restraints that had been imposed upon the petitioner in *Jones*, Justice Black concluded that they clearly were of a degree sufficient to justify use of the writ. Four aspects of petitioner's parole were cited. He was restricted in his lawful physical movement, unable to leave his community or change residence without special permission. He was subject to special regulations which restricted other aspects of his liberty, including the requirements that he obtain special permission before operating an automobile and that he report regularly to his parole officer. He was threatened with reincarceration for the duration of his original sentence for even the most insignificant violation of the parole regulations. Moreover, he could be ordered back to prison for violation of parole without a judicial hearing. The particular significance of each of these elements of restraint was not clear, but taken together they were "enough to invoke the help of The Great Writ."

In *Hensley v. Municipal Court*,[2] *Jones* was held applicable to a habeas petitioner who was at large on his own recognizance pending execution of the sentence on his misdemeanor conviction. Due to an unusual combination of stays, the petitioner had been able to pursue his appeals within the state system and present his habeas application before starting to serve his one-year sentence. Petitioner continued to be bound by the conditions imposed during his pretrial release. He had agreed to "appear at all times and places" as ordered by the court, to waive extradition if he failed to appear and was apprehended outside the state, and to be subject to a court order at any time that could revoke his release. The state contended that these conditions were less restrictive than those imposed on the petitioner in *Jones*. The Court did not disagree. It held that, nevertheless, the petitioner was "in custody" within the meaning of the habeas statute. Justice Brennan's opinion for the Court concluded that Hensley was subject to "restraints not shared by the public generally" which placed his freedom of movement "in the hands of judicial officers who may demand his presence at any time." In *Justices of Boston Municipal Court v. Lydon*,[3] the Court held that a person released on his own recognizance pending a trial *de novo* was in custody, at least where the terms of the recognizance imposed restraints roughly similar to those found in *Hensley*, such that the petitioner was subject to restraints "not shared by the public generally." Even narrowly construed, *Lydon, Hensley*, and *Jones* support the lower court rulings that the restraints attending probation are sufficient to establish custody. Similar treatment is due the suspended sentence that poses a threat of future imprisonment if the petitioner fails to comply with a condition that does not restrict his freedom of movement.

Many disadvantages flowing from conviction do not constitute custody for purposes of habeas review, however. In *Maleng v. Cook*,[4] for example, the Court rejected the petitioner's contention that he remained in custody at the time he had filed his petition, notwithstanding the prior expiration of his sentence, because of the "possibility" that the conviction "will be used to enhance the sentences imposed for any subsequent crimes of which he is convicted."

§ 28.3
1. 371 U.S. 236, 83 S.Ct. 373, 9 L.Ed.2d 285 (1963).
2. 411 U.S. 345, 93 S.Ct. 1571, 36 L.Ed.2d 294 (1973).

3. 466 U.S. 294, 104 S.Ct. 1805, 80 L.Ed.2d 311 (1984).
4. 490 U.S. 488, 109 S.Ct. 1923, 104 L.Ed.2d 540 (1989).

The Court responded that since almost all states have habitual offender statutes, acceptance of such a contention "would read the 'in custody' requirement out of the statute." Such a reading would also "be contrary to clear implication of the opinion in *Carafas v. La-Vallee*," a case, discussed below, in which the Court assumed that such collateral consequences are not sufficient alone to establish custody. In addition to the mere possibility of a future enhanced sentence, other consequences deemed insufficient to establish custody include the payment of a fine (despite the possibility of physical restraint as a penalty for nonpayment), the revocation of professional licenses, the suspension of drivers licenses, the prohibition against possessing firearms, and the inability to hold public office.

In *Carafas v. LaVallee*[5] the petitioner filed his habeas application while still in prison, but he was unconditionally discharged (upon completion of his sentence) while the habeas court's denial of relief was on appeal. The state contended that appellate review of the denial was barred because the case was moot. Rejecting this claim, the Supreme Court noted that petitioner remained subject to various disabilities as a result of his conviction. He could not, for example, engage in certain businesses, hold public office, or serve as a juror. Under the collateral consequences doctrine of *Sibron v. New York*,[6] the case clearly was not moot.[7] The unconditional release did present, however, a "substantial issue" as to whether the custody requirement of the federal habeas statutes was met. The *Carafas* Court noted that there was no suggestion in the habeas statute itself that jurisdiction once gained was subsequently lost because the petitioner was no longer in custody. So long as the applicant

was in custody when the writ was filed, the habeas court has jurisdiction, which it retains pending a final disposition of the case. A contrary view, the Court noted, would "only aggravate the hardships that may result from the 'intolerable delays in affording justice.'" A habeas petitioner "should not be thwarted * * * simply because the path of litigation has been so long * * * that he served his sentence." Thus, if custody exists at the time of the filing of the petition, the litigation can proceed so long as the case does not become moot.

In 1968 the Court in *Peyton v. Rowe*[8] extended the concept of custody to a prisoner serving the first of two consecutive sentences who attacks in his habeas petition the second conviction or sentence. Neither the text nor history of the statute indicated that the writ was available only to secure immediate release, the Court reasoned. "[P]ractically speaking," the prisoner was in custody "under the aggregate of the consecutive sentences imposed on [him]," and postponing the habeas challenge to the conviction underlying the second sentence could result in dimmed memories, the death of witnesses, and other impediments to the accurate assessment of a petitioner's claim and a state's chances of convicting the prisoner at retrial. In *Braden v. 30th Judicial Circuit Court*,[9] the Court faced a challenge by a prisoner in one jurisdiction to a pending prosecution in another. There, an Alabama prisoner was subject to a detainer filed with his Alabama warden by Kentucky officials pursuing a pending felony charge in Kentucky. The petitioner contended that the Kentucky charge was barred by that state's failure to afford him a speedy trial. In earlier cases the Court had noted that a detainer could have a significant

---

5.   391 U.S. 234, 88 S.Ct. 1556, 20 L.Ed.2d 554 (1968).

6.   392 U.S. 40, 88 S.Ct. 1889, 20 L.Ed.2d 917 (1968) discussed in § 27.5(a).

7.   The Court's decision in Lane v. Williams, 455 U.S. 624, 102 S.Ct. 1322, 71 L.Ed.2d 508 (1982), signaled a stricter standard for assessing the mootness of habeas claims. In *Lane*, the Court reasoned that speculative adverse consequences, such as the influence on future discretionary decisions, are insufficient to save a claim from mootness. *Lane* held moot a challenge to a parole term following the unconditional release of the prisoner who had been incarcerated for violating that term. The Court

found the collateral consequences that followed from the parole violation were insufficient to defeat a finding of mootness, stating, "[c]ollateral review of a final judgment is not an endeavor to be taken lightly." Such review, the Court noted, is "not warranted absent a showing that the complainant suffers actual harm from the judgment that he seeks to avoid." Mootness is discussed generally in § 27.5(a).

8.   391 U.S. 54, 88 S.Ct. 1549, 20 L.Ed.2d 426 (1968).

9.   410 U.S. 484, 93 S.Ct. 1123, 35 L.Ed.2d 443 (1973).

impact upon conditions of current custody as well as affect the prisoner's chances of parole. In light of these rulings, it required only a footnote for the majority in *Braden* to dispose of the contention that the petitioner was not "in custody" as to the Kentucky charge. Justice Brennan's opinion for the Court explained that "the considerations which were held in *Peyton* to warrant a prompt resolution of the claim also apply with full force in this context." It made no difference that the "future custody" under attack would be imposed by a separate sovereign, since the Alabama warden acted "as the agent of the Commonwealth of Kentucky in holding the petitioner pursuant to the Kentucky detainer." *Garlotte v. Fordice*[10] extended the rationale of *Peyton* to allow a petitioner to challenge a conviction underlying a sentence already served, when that petitioner is incarcerated under consecutive sentences. The Court stated, "consecutive sentences should be treated as a continuous series," and explained that a prisoner "remains 'in custody' under all of his sentences until all are served."

(b) Constitutional–Jurisdictional Defects. Petitioners "in custody" who seek habeas relief must also demonstrate that they are in custody in violation of federal law. For over a century, first under the 1789 Act and later under the 1867 Act, Supreme Court rulings limited federal habeas review for convicted prisoners to those claims that challenged the jurisdiction of the court of conviction.[11] While federal habeas review is no longer so limited, the Court's development of the concept of a constitutional-jurisdictional defect during that period remains important. In some states, courts may look to the early Supreme Court decisions in determining the scope of their state collateral remedies. The inclusion of ju-

risdictional defects also remains the common starting point for interpretations of the scope of the current federal writ. For although the justices have disagreed as to what constitutional claims beyond the jurisdictional category should be cognizable under federal writ, they have agreed that the writ should reach at least those constitutional objections that were said historically to have deprived the trial court of its jurisdiction.

That the earliest Supreme Court rulings looked only to jurisdictional defects is not surprising in light of the history of the common law writ, and the long-accepted principle that a judgment did not become "final" when it was "void" due to the trial court's lack of jurisdiction over either the subject matter or the person. Consistent with this principle, the Supreme Court initially took a narrow view of what constituted a jurisdictional defect. In *Ex parte Watkins*,[12] the Court refused to review a federal prisoner's claim that his conviction was obtained on an indictment that failed to state a crime. Chief Justice Marshall's opinion for the Court noted: "A judgment * * * concludes the subject on which it is rendered" and "puts an end to inquiry" unless "that judgment be an absolute nullity," but "it is not a nullity if the [trial] court has general jurisdiction of the subject, although it should be erroneous." Professor Bator succinctly described the Court's analysis in *Watkins* and other early cases: "[S]ubstantive error on the part of a court of competent jurisdiction does not render detention 'illegal' for purposes of habeas corpus, because, to use Chief Justice Marshall's striking phrase, 'the law trusts that court with the whole subject.'"[13]

In 1873, in *Ex parte Lange*,[14] the Court initiated what has been described as "a long pro-

---

10. 515 U.S. 39, 115 S.Ct. 1948, 132 L.Ed.2d 36 (1995).

11. But consider INS v. St. Cyr, 533 U.S. 289, 121 S.Ct. 2271, 150 L.Ed.2d 347 (2001), where five Justices declared that, "In England prior to 1789, in the Colonies, and in this Nation during the formative years of our Government, the writ of habeas corpus was available to nonenemy aliens as well as to citizens," to challenge detention in civil and criminal cases, and "was not limited to challenges to the jurisdiction of the custodian, but encompassed detentions based on errors of law, including the erroneous application or interpretation of statutes. It was used to command the discharge of seamen who had a

statutory exemption from impressment into the British Navy, to emancipate slaves, and to obtain the freedom of apprentices and asylum inmates.... [T]hose early cases contain no suggestion that habeas relief in cases involving executive detention was available only for constitutional error."

12. 28 U.S. (3 Pet.) 193, 7 L.Ed. 650 (1830).

13. Bator, cited in § 28.2 at note 4, at 466.

14. 85 U.S. (18 Wall.) 163, 21 L.Ed. 872 (1873).

cess of expansion of the concept of a lack of jurisdiction." Lange contended that he had been twice sentenced for the same offense, in violation of the Fifth Amendment's Double Jeopardy Clause, when he had been resentenced to a term of imprisonment after having paid the fine originally imposed. Carefully disclaiming the use of habeas as a writ of error, the Supreme Court ordered Lange released from imprisonment because the lower court's jurisdiction terminated upon the satisfaction of the original sentence. The *Lange* ruling was extended in *Ex parte Wilson*[15] to a defendant who challenged his sentence on the ground that it imposed punishment for an "infamous" crime even though he had not been indicted by a grand jury as the Fifth Amendment required. Both *Lange* and *Wilson* stressed the trial court's lack of power to impose a sentence beyond its jurisdictional authority, rather than the constitutional character of the petitioners' claims. Accordingly, during the same period, when a federal prisoner sought habeas relief on the ground that he had been retried in violation of the Double Jeopardy Clause, the Court held that his claim was not cognizable as a habeas challenge since the trial court obviously had jurisdiction to determine whether a retrial was permissible.[16]

Ex parte Siebold,[17] decided in 1879, produced another doctrinal expansion of the concept of a jurisdictional defect. The Court held there that a prisoner could properly raise in a petition for habeas corpus the claim that the statute under which he was convicted violated the United States Constitution. If the petitioner was correct in his claim, the Court noted, then "the foundation of the whole proceeding" would be affected. Since "an unconstitutional law is void and is as no law," a "conviction obtained under it is not merely erroneous, but is illegal and void." The trial court's authority to try the petitioners "arose solely upon these laws," so if the "laws were unconstitutional and void," the trial court "acquired no jurisdiction of the causes." The Court did not explain why

a trial court had jurisdiction when double jeopardy barred a retrial or an indictment failed to state an offense, but lacked jurisdiction when it erroneously concluded that the statute underlying the indictment was constitutional. The unconstitutional statute was, of course, an incurable defect in the proceeding, but the same was true of the double jeopardy bar to a retrial. The unconstitutional statute could more readily be seen, perhaps, as affecting the foundation of the proceeding under the legal analysis of the times.

Frank v. Mangum[18] and *Moore v. Dempsey*,[19] decided in 1915 and 1923, have been viewed as cases that departed from the jurisdictional limitation, but they also can be read as having simply extended the analysis of *Siebold*. Both cases involved claims of a mob-dominated trial, and the majority opinions in both suggested that such a claim went to the "jurisdiction" of the trial court. The Court in *Frank* noted that the writ would only lie "where the judgment under which the prisoner is detained is shown to be absolutely void for want of jurisdiction in the court that pronounced it, either because such jurisdiction was absent at the beginning or because it was lost in the course of the proceedings." It also accepted, however, petitioner's contention that his claim would fall within the loss-of-jurisdiction category since mob domination "in effect wrought a dissolution of the [trial] court, so that the proceedings were *coram non judice.*" In *Moore*, the Court similarly noted that where the "proceeding is a mask," the Court noted, with the "counsel, jury, and judge * * * swept to the fatal end by an irresistible wave of public passion," the trial becomes "absolutely void."

In *Johnson v. Zerbst*,[20] Justice Black's opinion for the Court expanded upon the "loss-of-jurisdiction" analysis of *Frank* and *Moore*. The petitioner in *Johnson*, a federal prisoner, claimed that his conviction had been obtained in violation of the Sixth Amendment because the trial judge had failed to provide him with

---

15.   114 U.S. 417, 5 S.Ct. 935, 29 L.Ed. 89 (1885).

16.   In re Bigelow, 113 U.S. 328, 5 S.Ct. 542, 28 L.Ed. 1005 (1885).

17.   100 U.S. (10 Otto.) 371, 25 L.Ed. 717 (1879).

18.   237 U.S. 309, 35 S.Ct. 582, 59 L.Ed. 969 (1915).

19.   261 U.S. 86, 43 S.Ct. 265, 67 L.Ed. 543 (1923).

20.   304 U.S. 458, 58 S.Ct. 1019, 82 L.Ed. 1461 (1938).

appointed counsel. Justice Black concluded that such a defect was cognizable on habeas review. He reasoned:

> Since the Sixth Amendment constitutionally entitles one charged with crime to the assistance of counsel, compliance with this constitutional mandate is an essential jurisdictional prerequisite to a federal court's authority to deprive an accused of his life or liberty. * * * A court's jurisdiction at the beginning of trial may be lost "in the course of the proceedings" [quoting *Frank*] due to failure to complete the court—as the Sixth Amendment requires—by providing counsel for an accused. * * * If this requirement of the Sixth Amendment is not complied with, the court no longer has jurisdiction to proceed. The judgment of conviction pronounced by a court without jurisdiction if void, and one imprisoned thereunder may obtain release by habeas corpus.

Four years after *Johnson v. Zerbst*, the Court faced on habeas review a constitutional claim that it could not so readily characterize as undermining the structure of the proceeding and therefore causing the trial court to "lose jurisdiction." In *Waley v. Johnston*,[21] the petitioner claimed that his guilty plea had been coerced by an F.B.I. agent. In a per curiam opinion, the Court concluded that petitioner's claim was subject to habeas review:

> The facts relied on are dehors the record and their effect on the judgment was not open to consideration and review on appeal. In such circumstances the use of the writ in the federal courts to test the constitutional validity of a conviction for crime is not restricted to those cases where the judgment of conviction is void for want of jurisdiction of the trial court to render it. It extends also to those exceptional cases where the conviction has been in disregard of the constitutional rights of the accused, and where the writ is the only effective means of preserving his rights.

As various commentators have noted, *Waley* "finally dispensed with the fiction of 'jurisdiction,'" a concept that had been expanded beyond definable bounds in cases such as *Frank, Moore,* and *Johnson*.

Although subsequent cases dealing with the scope of habeas review typically have not looked to whether the claimed defect deprived the trial court of its authority to proceed, the classification of error as jurisdictional or nonjurisdictional lives on in other contexts. In a series of cases determining what claims may be raised on habeas following a valid plea of guilty, the Court has invoked the jurisdictional-defect distinction.[22] Cognizable claims in this context have been limited to "incurable" defects that deprived the trial court of its authority to proceed notwithstanding the valid guilty plea (such as a double jeopardy violation that barred the prosecution under which the plea was taken). In addition, the Court in *Custis v. United States*[23] used the concept of "jurisdictional" defect to distinguish between claims that can be raised to challenge a prior conviction used to enhance a federal sentence and claims that cannot be raised in that setting.

(c) Other Constitutional Claims: From *Brown v. Allen* to *Stone v. Powell*. While *Waley* put to rest the jurisdictional-defect limitation on habeas relief, it did not go so far as to hold that all constitutional claims were subject to habeas review. The Court had stressed that petitioner's claim rested on facts outside the record. It was not the type of claim that petitioner could readily have raised in the original proceeding that produced his conviction or on appeal. Accordingly, if the claim was ever to be reviewed by a federal court, that review would have to come on collateral attack. The same was true of the claim presented in *Mooney v. Holohan*,[24] where the petitioner contended that his conviction had been based on the prosecution's knowing use of perjured testimony. Thus, it was still possible to argue after *Waley* that, "for purposes of habeas corpus, a

21. 316 U.S. 101, 62 S.Ct. 964, 86 L.Ed. 1302 (1942).

22. See § 21.6(a).

23. 511 U.S. 485, 114 S.Ct. 1732, 128 L.Ed.2d 517 (1994), discussed in § 26.4(f).

24. 294 U.S. 103, 55 S.Ct. 340, 79 L.Ed. 791 (1935).

detention was not to be deemed 'unlawful' if based upon the judgment of a competent state court which had afforded full corrective process for the litigation of questions touching on federal rights." It was not until 1953, in *Brown v. Allen*,[25] that the Court flatly rejected that position.

At issue in *Brown* was whether a federal habeas court could review the petitioner's claims of grand jury and trial jury discrimination and the admission of a coerced confession. The claims had been fully litigated and decided against the petitioner in the state courts. A majority agreed that the habeas court should consider and render its own independent judgment on the merits of petitioner's claims, notwithstanding the state adjudication. While the state court rulings were entitled to the same respect ordinarily given to opinions of a court of another jurisdiction, they did not preclude federal review of those claims on a habeas application. The habeas court could rely on the state court's findings of fact (unless there was a vital flaw in the latter's factfinding procedures), but it was required to "exercise its own independent judgment" as to the legal consequences of those facts. This mandate, Justice Frankfurter argued in one of the lead opinions, followed the purposes of the 1867 Act. Simply put, that Act gave to federal courts the "final say" on federal claims. The habeas writ guaranteed federal review of the petitioner's federal claim, not simply a fair state consideration of the claim, for such consideration "may have misconceived a federal constitutional right."

In *Fay v. Noia*,[26] the Supreme Court reaffirmed and defended its *Brown* decision. Responding to criticism that *Brown* had departed unjustifiably from past precedent, Justice Brennan's majority opinion traced the history of the writ from the common law through earlier Supreme Court decisions. He concluded that the writ had always been available "to remedy any kind of governmental restraint contrary to fundamental law" (as evidenced, in particular, by *Bushell's Case*[27]), and that this objective logically encompassed detention imposed pursuant to a conviction that had been obtained in violation of the defendant's constitutional rights. *Brown* accordingly had been consistent with the "historic office of The Great Writ," as well as the language of the federal habeas provisions, in holding that all constitutional claims were cognizable under the writ, without regard to their relationship to the trial court's jurisdiction or the full litigation of the claim in the state proceedings.

In *Schneckloth v. Bustamonte*,[28] a decade after *Noia*, Justice Powell, joined by three other justices, expressed agreement with a position voiced in an earlier opinion by Justice Black,[29] in which Justice Black had argued that the writ should not be available for any "constitutional flaw, regardless of its nature, regardless of his guilt or innocence, and regardless of the circumstances of the case." The "great historic role of the writ," he maintained, "has been to ensure that reliability of the guilt-determining process," so it was appropriate to give weight to the relationship of the constitutional error to "the element of probable or possible innocence." In *Schneckloth*, Justice Powell argued that a "nonguilt-related claim," such as the admission at trial of unconstitutionally seized evidence, should not be considered on collateral attack, provided "the petitioner was provided a fair opportunity to raise and have adjudicated the question in state courts." Justice Powell contended that this conclusion was supported by the underlying function of the fourth amendment exclusionary rule, recognition of the traditionally narrow scope of the writ as applied to persons detained pursuant to a conviction, and an appropriate balancing of the benefits and costs of habeas review.

Shortly thereafter, in *Stone v. Powell*,[30] Justice Powell had his majority. By a 6–3 vote, with Justice Powell writing for the Court,

---

25. 344 U.S. 443, 73 S.Ct. 397, 97 L.Ed. 469 (1953).

26. 372 U.S. 391, 83 S.Ct. 822, 9 L.Ed.2d 837 (1963).

27. See § 28.1, at note 4.

28. 412 U.S. 218, 93 S.Ct. 2041, 36 L.Ed.2d 854 (1973).

29. Kaufman v. United States, 394 U.S. 217, 89 S.Ct. 1068, 22 L.Ed.2d 227 (1969) (Black, J., dissenting).

30. 428 U.S. 465, 96 S.Ct. 3037, 49 L.Ed.2d 1067 (1976).

Stone held that "where the State has provided an opportunity for full and fair litigation of a Fourth Amendment claim, the Constitution does not require that a state prisoner be granted federal habeas corpus relief on the ground that the evidence obtained in an unconstitutional search and seizure was introduced at his trial." Justice Powell's opinion in *Stone* emphasized the function of the exclusionary rule rather than the general role of federal habeas review. The exclusionary rule, Justice Powell noted, was not a "personal constitutional right," but a "judicially created means of effectuating rights secured by the Fourth Amendment," which had a "primary function" of deterring police illegality. Accordingly, it "has never been interpreted to proscribe the introduction of illegally seized evidence in all proceedings against all persons." Thus, the Court had previously concluded, through the application of a "balancing process," that the exclusionary rule would not "prevent the use of illegally seized evidence in grand jury proceedings" or "exclude such evidence from use for impeachment of a defendant." Applying the same "balancing process," the majority concluded, it was clear that "the additional contribution, if any, of the consideration of search-and-seizure claims of state prisoners in collateral review is small in relation to the costs."

In reaching this conclusion, Justice Powell proceeded from the premise that the deterrent function of the exclusionary rule was served effectively by enforcement at trial and on direct appeal. There was no reason to assume that "any specific disincentive already created by the risk of exclusion * * * [in those proceedings] would be enhanced if there were the further risk that a conviction obtained in a state court and affirmed on direct review might be overturned in collateral proceedings often occurring years after the incarceration of the defendant." Petitioners argued that habeas review was essential because state courts might not enforce the Fourth Amendment as rigorously as federal courts, and the effectiveness of the exclusionary remedy as a deterrent

therefore depended upon police awareness that "federal habeas might reveal flaws in a search or seizure that went undetected" in the state proceedings. The Court in *Stone* refused to accept such "a basic mistrust of state courts as fair and competent forums for adjudication of constitutional rights."

Turning to the other side of its cost/benefit ledger, the *Stone* majority first noted that the exclusionary rule necessarily "deflects the truthfinding application of the process and often frees the guilty." While these costs were justified by the deterrence gained from applying the rule in the original proceedings, they could not be sustained by the marginal increase in deterrence that might be provided by the rule's application in a collateral proceeding. Moreover, "resort to habeas corpus, especially for purposes other than to assure that no innocent person suffers an unconstitutional loss of liberties," entailed additional costs, including the consumption of scarce federal judicial resources, the delayed finality of criminal proceedings, and the frustration of good-faith state court efforts to honor federal constitutional rights.

(d) Post–*Stone* Rulings and the 1996 Amendments. The Court has considered, and rejected, the possible extension of *Stone* to claims other than fourth amendment violations on four separate occasions. In *Jackson v. Virginia*[31] the Court examined whether a federal habeas court, considering a due process challenge to the sufficiency of the evidence before the state trier of fact, had to look to the *In re Winship*[32] standard of proof beyond a reasonable doubt, or to a lesser standard, taken from a pre-*Winship* ruling, that would hold due process violated only when the record was "wholly devoid of any relevant evidence of a crucial element of the offense charged." Since the *Winship*-derived standard was clearly related to the reliability of the guilt-determining process, it might have been thought that there would be no doubt as to its application on habeas review. However, three dissenting justices, in an opinion by Justice Stevens, argued against its application. Justice Stevens con-

---

31. 443 U.S. 307, 99 S.Ct. 2781, 61 L.Ed.2d 560 (1979).

32. 397 U.S. 358, 90 S.Ct. 1068, 25 L.Ed.2d 368 (1970).

tended that the *Winship* standard would have an especially pernicious impact if applied on federal habeas review. The state argued that *Winship* review was unwarranted on habeas once the petitioner had received a "full and fair hearing" on his insufficient evidence claim in the state's appellate court. Responding to these contentions, the majority, per Stewart, J., noted the constitutional issue presented here was "far different" from that presented in *Stone*: "The question whether a defendant has been convicted upon inadequate evidence is central to the basic question of guilt or innocence."

In *Rose v. Mitchell*[33] the Court again refused to extend *Stone*, this time to a constitutional claim that the justices agreed had no bearing on the reliability of the truth-finding process at trial. The habeas petitioner in *Mitchell* claimed that the foreman of the indicting grand jury had been selected on the basis of racial discrimination in violation of the Equal Protection Clause of the Fourteenth Amendment. Relying largely on the analysis advanced in his concurring opinion in *Schneckloth*, Justice Powell, joined by Justice Rehnquist, argued in his dissent that this claim should not be cognizable on habeas review. The defendant had been found guilty by a fairly drawn petit jury, following a fair trial, so the claim clearly did not involve the "protect[ion] of the innocent from incarceration." The historical function of the writ, Justice Powell contended, did not justify its use solely for the purpose of "furthering the general societal goal of grand jury integrity." A five-justice majority, however, disagreed.

Justice Blackmun's opinion for the *Mitchell* majority offered several reasons for not extending *Stone* to bar habeas review of grand jury discrimination claims. Initially, the Court noted that while *Stone* assumed that state courts were as capable as federal courts in dealing with fourth amendment claims, the same could not be said of grand jury discrimination claims. Such a claim required the state bench to review its own procedures rather than the actions of police. In most cases, the

trial court that initially rules on the claim will be the same court that has responsibility for the grand jury selection process. These differences, the Court noted, led it "to doubt that claims of [grand jury discrimination] in general will receive the type of full and fair hearings deemed essential to the holding of *Stone*." For similar reasons, it could not be said here, as it was said in *Stone*, that federal habeas review would have no significant "educative and deterrent effect." There was "strong reason to believe that federal review would indeed reveal flaws not appreciated by state judges perhaps too close to the day-to-day operation of the system." While *Stone* doubted that habeas rulings would have a substantial additional deterrent or educative impact with respect to the police, the responsible state officials here, the courts and their employees, were very likely to take note of the federal decisions and respond accordingly.

Justice Blackmun also stressed the differences in the nature of the rights involved. *Stone* had characterized the exclusionary rule as a "judicially created remedy" rather than a "personal constitutional right." The same could not be said regarding grand jury discrimination. Indeed, unlike the exclusionary rule, the prohibition against racial discrimination in the criminal justice process had been applied to the states "for nearly a century." Moreover, the "costs associated with quashing an indictment returned by an improperly constituted grand jury" were "significantly less than those associated with suppressing evidence." A prisoner who "is guilty in fact" is "less likely to go free" since the prosecution, after reindictment, can retry the defendant on the same evidence. Finally, the "constitutional interests" that are vindicated in rectifying grand jury discrimination were characterized as "substantially more compelling than those at issue in *Stone*." Racial discrimination "strikes at the core concerns of the Fourteenth Amendment and at fundamental values of our society and our legal system." The "harm is not only to the accused," but "to society as a whole."

33.   443 U.S. 545, 99 S.Ct. 2993, 61 L.Ed.2d 739 (1979).

In *Kimmelman v. Morrison*,[34] the state contended that the reasoning of *Stone* barred habeas review of the petitioner's claim of ineffective assistance of counsel where counsel's incompetency lay solely in failing at trial to properly present an objection to the introduction of damaging evidence that had been seized in violation of the Fourth Amendment. Rejecting that argument, the Court held that a claim of ineffective assistance is based on a separate constitutional right and therefore is cognizable even though the alleged incompetency consisted of counsel's mishandling of a fourth amendment objection. Habeas review of such a claim, the Court reasoned, was entirely consistent with *Stone*. Such review served to vindicate the defendant's right to a fair trial within the structure of an adversary system, not merely the exclusionary rule. The Court added, however, that such review imposed upon the petitioner more demanding elements of proof that would habeas review of the fourth amendment claim itself. Although a "meritorious Fourth Amendment claim [would] be necessary to the success of the Sixth Amendment claim," habeas petitioners also must establish under the standard of *Strickland v. Washington* that "they have been denied a fair trial by the gross incompetence of their attorneys." In other words, a claimant would still have to establish "prejudice" from counsel's failure to pursue a meritorious motion to suppress key, but reliable evidence.

Taken together, *Jackson*, *Kimmelman*, and *Mitchell* suggested that if *Stone* was to be extended to any other constitutional claim, the most likely candidate would be a prophylactic rule of comparatively recent vintage, aimed at controlling police behavior, and resulting in the exclusion of reliable evidence. However, in *Withrow v. Williams*,[35] a closely divided Court refused to extend *Stone* to the one claim that seemingly had the best chance of being placed in this category—a violation of *Miranda*. Several features of *Miranda* violations, the majority reasoned, distinguished those violations from the *Mapp* violations considered in *Stone*.

First, *Miranda*, "prophylactic though it may be, in protecting a defendant's fifth amendment privilege, * * * safeguards a fundamental trial right [of the individual]." Second, unlike *Mapp*'s exclusionary rule, *Miranda* did not serve only "some value necessarily divorced from the correct ascertainment of guilt." Rather, by "bracing against the possibility of unreliable statements in every instance of in-custody interrogation, *Miranda* serves to guard against the use of unreliable statements at trial." Finally, "eliminating [habeas] review of *Miranda* claims would not significantly benefit the federal courts in their exercise of habeas jurisdiction or advance the cause of federalism in any substantial way, * * * as it would not prevent a state prisoner from simply converting his barred *Miranda* claim into a due process [voluntariness] claim" that would still be cognizable on habeas review.

The analysis of the *Withrow* majority appears to effectively confine *Stone* to the unique qualities of the *Mapp* violation. Just as *Miranda* was distinguished from *Mapp* by tying it to the underlying self-incrimination privilege and the bar against involuntary confessions, other prophylactic rules can be distinguished by tying them to underlying constitutional rights deemed fundamental personal guarantees. The relation of *Miranda* to the "correct ascertainment of guilt" is no closer than that of other standards excluding seemingly reliable evidence and once thought to be prime candidates for extensions of *Stone* (e.g., *Massiah* violations).

The AEDPA does not appear to modify this line of decisions. In particular, new § 2254(d), the section governing which claims litigated on the merits in state court may serve as grounds for relief, does not limit relief to claims related to reliability, nor does it otherwise allude to the rule in *Stone*. Instead, § 2254(d) permits relief based on claims adjudicated in state court only when the state decision involved an unreasonable interpretation or application of clearly established federal law. Arguably, it is

34. 477 U.S. 365, 106 S.Ct. 2574, 91 L.Ed.2d 305 (1986).

35. 507 U.S. 680, 113 S.Ct. 1745, 123 L.Ed.2d 407 (1993).

possible to read the language of § 2254(d) as displacing *Stone,* so that claims for relief based on a state court's unreasonable interpretation of fourth amendment law would be cognizable under the new statute. But such a reading seems so contrary to the thrust of the amendments in narrowing habeas relief that it seems improbable that Congress intended this result, absent a more explicit legislative rejection of the two-decade-old rule in *Stone.*

(e) The Opportunity for Full and Fair Litigation. Consistent with its assumption that state courts would conscientiously enforce fourth amendment rights, the *Stone* Court held that federal habeas review would be available if the state had not provided the petitioner an "opportunity for full and fair litigation." This "exception" arguably is broader than what would be needed simply to serve *Stone's* view of the deterrent function of the exclusionary rule. Certainly, if a state regularly fails to provide an adequate litigation opportunity, its enforcement of the exclusionary rule would not provide a substantial deterrent and habeas review would then provide more than a marginal increment in deterrence. The *Stone* exception, however, focuses on the individual case. Thus, the *Stone* majority apparently concluded that even though the exclusionary rule is a "judicially created" remedy rather than a "personal constitutional right," the defendant is entitled to at least one opportunity for a "full and fair consideration" of his claim.

The *Stone* opinion offered little by way of definition of its full and fair opportunity standard. The Court referred at different points to "a fair and full opportunity to raise and have adjudicated the question," an opportunity for "full and fair consideration" of the claim, and an opportunity for "full and fair litigation * * * at trial and on direct review." Some courts viewed as the most significant guideline the Court's citation to *Townsend v. Sain*[36] which was preceded by the signal "Cf." The *Townsend* opinion specified those circumstances under which a federal habeas court was required to hold evidentiary hearings. Several of the six situations cited there were in no

way attributable to defective state court procedures (e.g., where new evidence was found), but two described defective state proceedings in language similar to that found in *Stone*— where the state factfinding procedure "was not adequate to afford a full and fair hearing," and where, for any other reason, it appears that "the state trier of fact did not afford the habeas applicant a full and fair hearing." In discussing these two situations, the *Townsend* opinion referred to "serious procedural errors * * * in such things as the burden of proof" that render the process "seriously inadequate for the ascertainment of the truth" even though not so defective "as to violate the Constitution."

Lower courts assessing the adequacy of state procedures often apply a two-step inquiry asking (1) whether the state procedural mechanism is satisfactory in the abstract, and (2) whether there was a failure of the mechanism in the individual case. A finding of inadequacy is most likely to come under the second inquiry. Thus, it was held that a petitioner did not receive a full and fair opportunity when his counsel was appointed one day before the expiration of the time period for presenting a suppression motion and when in denying counsel's oral request for an extension the trial court applied an unwritten local rule mandating a written application. Similarly, a petitioner was denied an adequate opportunity to present his claim where the state appellate court rejected the claim based on a recent decision which had not been raised by the state.

An erroneous application of the Fourth Amendment, without more, does not constitute a denial of an opportunity for full and fair litigation. It is said to be "of no consequence whether the state courts employed an incorrect legal standard, misapplied the correct standard, or erred in finding the underlying facts." Support for this position is found in the fact that the state appellate court in one of the cases before the Court in *Stone* apparently applied an incorrect legal standard. Lower courts have also noted that if the *Stone* excep-

---

36. 372 U.S. 293, 83 S.Ct. 745, 9 L.Ed.2d 770 (1963), discussed in § 28.7(a).

tion could be based on the misapplication of fourth amendment standards, "*Stone's* bar would become a nullity, since petitioners would routinely allege the necessary error."

(f) "Bare Innocence" Claims—*Herrera v. Collins.* The Court has long insisted that habeas relief was limited to petitioners who could demonstrate some flaw in the process by which they were convicted or that the punishment was otherwise imposed in violation of federal law. A showing of innocence alone was not a basis for relief, as the writ was designed to ensure that state court processes comply with the Constitution, not to enlist federal courts to duplicate guilt-innocence determinations. Indeed, nothing would seem to upset more the interests in finality and comity than the prospect of allowing a defendant, fairly convicted in state court upon constitutionally sufficient evidence, to reopen his conviction with "new" evidence of innocence discovered years after trial, especially when the state itself carefully confines its own review of such claims. As the Court narrowed access to the writ in the 1970s and '80s, a showing of possible or probable innocence became a common ingredient of habeas relief, but only as a gateway to habeas review of a separate constitutional claim. For example, a petitioner who could persuade a federal court that he may be innocent could overcome a procedural default for which he could not show "cause and prejudice," or pursue in a second petition a claim he had failed to raise in his first petition.

In 1993, in *Herrera v. Collins*,[37] the Court considered whether habeas relief was available for claims of "bare innocence," and if so, when such claims required relief. Herrera had been convicted of murder and sentenced to death, but claimed that several new affidavits demonstrated that his brother had committed the crime. State law required defendants to bring motions for new trial based on newly discovered evidence within thirty days of trial; *Herrera* had missed this deadline, so a state challenge to his conviction and sentence was unavail-

able. He argued in federal court that the execution of an innocent man would violate the Eighth and Fourteenth Amendments, although he alleged no constitutional violation during the state prosecution. Despite considerable ambiguity in their opinions, most of the justices seemed to agree that in extremely unusual circumstances, a claim of innocence, even one unaccompanied by a separate constitutional claim, could compel relief. Justice Rehnquist wrote: "We may assume, for the sake of argument in deciding this case, that in a capital case a truly persuasive demonstration of 'actual innocence' made after trial would render the execution of a defendant unconstitutional, and warrants federal habeas relief if there were no state avenue open to process such a claim." The showing required "would necessarily be extraordinarily high." While the Court's recognition of such a bare-innocence claim was only dictum, the Court has made the same assumption in a later case,[38] and many lower courts since *Herrera* have held that such claims are at least theoretically cognizable.

The chances that such a claim will succeed are extremely small, and the questions such a claim raises are numerous and daunting. First, exactly what type of showing of innocence is required? Because most lower courts have found claims of innocence unconvincing, they have avoided answering this question with more specificity than that offered by the justices in *Herrera*, who stated only that the showing of innocence must be "truly persuasive." The tenor of the opinions in *Herrera* suggests that the Court had in mind a demonstration more stringent than one that would leave a factfinder to believe the petitioner is "probably" innocent, perhaps requiring proof of innocence "beyond a reasonable doubt."

Second, the meaning of the Court's requirement that there be "no state avenue open to process such a claim" is unclear. If the state's provision of even the most limited, rarely exer-

---

37. 506 U.S. 390, 113 S.Ct. 853, 122 L.Ed.2d 203 (1993).

38. See Schlup v. Delo, 513 U.S. 298, 115 S.Ct. 851, 130 L.Ed.2d 808 (1995) (stating that "If there were no

question about the fairness of the criminal trial, a *Herrera*-type claim would have to fail unless the federal habeas court is itself convinced that those facts unquestionably establish [the defendant's] innocence.").

cised clemency relief is sufficient to preclude a claim of bare innocence in habeas court, then bare innocence claims are truly hypothetical.

Third, who is eligible to raise a *Herrera* claim? The Court's opinion spoke of a showing of innocence that would make an *execution* unconstitutional, suggesting that the claim is open only to defendants sentenced to death. Yet, if punishment of the factually innocent is what the Constitution forbids, limiting relief to capital defendants is difficult to justify. Also, with innocence of the offense as the focus, the petitioner who concedes he committed the crime but disputes the factual allegations that make him eligible for the death penalty may also be barred from raising a *Herrera* claim.

Finally, the effect of the 1996 amendments on the viability of bare-innocence claims is unknown. New § 2254(d)(2) precludes relief for claims adjudicated on the merits in state court unless the adjudication of the claim "resulted in a decision that was based on an unreasonable determination of the facts in light of the *evidence presented in the State court proceeding*" (emphasis added). If a claim of innocence under *Herrera* is equivalent to the claim of not guilty raised at every state criminal trial, then this section would seem to preclude relief entirely.

(g) Harmless Error on Habeas Review. In *Brecht v. Abrahamson*,[39] the Court held the *Chapman* harmless error standard was too stringent to apply on habeas review.[40] It reasoned: "Overturning final and presumptively correct convictions on collateral review because the State cannot prove that an error is harmless under *Chapman* undermines the States' interest in finality and infringes upon their sovereignty over criminal matters. Moreover, granting habeas relief merely because there is a 'reasonable possibility' that trial error contributed to the verdict [the *Chapman* standard] is at odds with the historic meaning of habeas corpus—to afford relief to those whom society has 'grievously wronged.'" Con-

cluding that the "imbalance of the costs and benefits of applying the *Chapman* harmless-error standard on collateral review counsels in favor of applying a less onerous standard on habeas review," the *Brecht* majority opted for application of the *Kotteakos* standard, which federal appellate courts have traditionally applied on direct review to non-constitutional errors. "Under this standard," the majority noted, habeas petitioners "are not entitled to habeas relief based on trial error unless they can establish that it resulted in 'actual prejudice.'" As the Court explained later in *Calderon v. Coleman*,[41] the standard "protects the State's sovereign interest in punishing offenders and its good-faith attempts to honor constitutional rights." Noting the "significant" social costs of retrial or resentencing, the Court has decided that the states should not be forced to bear those costs "based on mere speculation that the defendant was prejudiced by trial error; the court must find that the defendant was actually prejudiced by the error."

In *O'Neal v. McAninch*,[42] the Court majority rejected the government's contention that the habeas petitioner bore the "burden of establishing" that a constitutional error was "prejudicial" under the *Brecht–Kotteakos* harmless-error standard. The Court noted initially that characterizing the harmless error inquiry as one controlled by a "burden of proof" was misleading, for harmless-error analysis "does not involve a judge who shifts a 'burden' to help control the presentation of evidence at trial, but rather involves judges who apply a legal standard (harmlessness) to a record that the presentation of evidence is no longer likely to affect." According to the Court, a judge better puts the question as whether "I, the judge, think that the error substantially influenced the jury's decision"? Imposing a burden on the petitioner could produce a misapplication of this standard "where the record is so evenly balanced that a conscientious judge is

39. 507 U.S. 619, 113 S.Ct. 1710, 123 L.Ed.2d 353 (1993).

40. The *Chapman* standard is discussed in § 27.6(c).

41. 525 U.S. 141, 119 S.Ct. 500, 142 L.Ed.2d 521 (1998).

42. 513 U.S. 432, 115 S.Ct. 992, 130 L.Ed.2d 947 (1995).

in grave doubt as to harmlessness of an error." If the judge is left with a "grave doubt" that the error may have had a "substantial influence," then the "conviction cannot stand."

There are at least two situations in which a habeas court need not apply the *Brecht* standard. First, in *Kyles v. Whitley*,[43] the Court explained that this standard is met whenever a petitioner establishes certain constitutional violations that already require a showing of prejudice. Thus, for example, no harmlessness analysis is required once a court determines that a petitioner has established a due process violation under *Brady*. Second, *Brecht* spoke only to "trial type" errors, to which *Chapman* would otherwise apply. It did not reach the proper treatment of "structural errors" that would not be subject to harmless error analysis on direct review. Lower courts have assumed that structural errors, once proven, require relief on habeas review without a showing of harm or prejudice, just as they do on direct appeal.

§ 28.4 Claims Foreclosed by State Procedural Defaults

(a) Claims "Defaulted" in State Court—The Policy Debate. When a petitioner has failed to present his claim in the state proceedings in accordance with state procedural requirements, and the state courts have held that this lapse bars consideration of the claim on the merits, the issue presented to the habeas court is under what conditions, if any, should that state procedural default also bar federal habeas review of the claim. Although the 1996 amendments specify the consequences of state procedural default in a particular class of capital cases, the consequence of default in other cases is not addressed by the amendments, nor was procedural default addressed by the statute prior to the 1996 amendments. In the absence of controlling language from Congress, federal courts have applied the rules for reviewing defaulted claims that were developed under the pre–1996 provisions in a long line of decisions of the Supreme Court.

These decisions reflect deep differences of opinion over the significance of two sets of competing interests. On the one hand, the petitioner has an obvious interest in obtaining review of a federal constitutional claim at least once. The nation, too, has an interest in ensuring that constitutional commands are followed in state proceedings. On the other hand, the state has a stake in the finality of the judgments of its courts, and in the effective enforcement of its procedural rules. Also weighing against habeas review of a claim forfeited in state court for failure to comply with a procedural rule is the risk that federal review will require initial factfinding long after the critical event has passed. Depending on the type of claim raised by the petitioner, delay may result in the loss of the opportunity to punish admitted offenders when the erosion of memory and dispersion of witnesses render retrial difficult or impossible.

The Supreme Court has also expressed concern that habeas review not reward what has been described as "sandbagging" tactics by defense counsel. If habeas review is available for claims not addressed in state court, there are arguably some situations in which counsel may prefer not to raise an issue at trial, holding it in reserve as a means of obtaining a new trial through the writ if the trial should result in a conviction. Consider, for example, an objection to grand jury discrimination in a case in which the grand jury would almost certainly have indicted even if fairly composed. Raising the issue before trial will "only delay the inevitable prosecution," but holding the issue in reserve opens up the possibility of gaining, years later after memories have faded, a second trial through habeas review if the first results in a conviction.

When the defaulted claim is one that if raised successfully would have absolutely barred prosecution (as in the case of a double jeopardy or speedy trial claim), there is no incentive to sandbag and any forfeiture would almost certainly be the result of inadvertence or negligence. When a forfeiture is attributable to the ignorance or negligence of counsel, Jus-

---

43. 514 U.S. 419, 115 S.Ct. 1555, 131 L.Ed.2d 490 (1995).

tice Brennan has argued that "closing the federal courthouse doors" is an "unnecessary and misdirected sanction."[1] Not only is "the potential loss of all valuable state remedies" a sufficient sanction under this view, the defendant is not the person responsible for the default. In response, it has been argued that this objection is adequately met by allowing review in those cases in which the defendant can show that counsel's negligence in forfeiting a claim by failing to comply with procedure amounted to a violation of the Sixth Amendment under the standards of *Strickland*.[2]

Another concern repeatedly noted by the Court in its decisions that address habeas review of claims defaulted in state court is that federal review after a state court's efforts to enforce its own procedural rules demonstrates a lack of respect for the state justice system. "Comity," it is argued, may require deference to such state decisions, in order to maintain the appropriate federal balance and prevent strained federal-state relations.

(b) Which Defaults Count: The "Adequate State Ground" Standard. The present standards for determining which defaulted claims are reviewable in habeas proceedings and which are not are discussed in § 28.4(c)–(g). The different issue addressed in this subsection is when a federal court will recognize that there has been a default in state court, so that such standards will be applicable.

Prior to the 1963 decision of *Fay v. Noia*,[3] federal courts applied to state procedural defaults the same standard that would have been applied if the case had come to the Supreme Court on direct review from the state courts. The Court had long held that on direct review it would not reach the merits of an appellant's constitutional claim if the court below had relied upon an "adequate state ground." If the state court ruling had been based on a state ground, independent of the federal constitutional claim, then that ground would necessar-

ily control the outcome of the case. Even if the Court were to find that there had been a constitutional violation, it lacked authority to review the question of state law and the state court's ruling would therefore have to be affirmed. Although this analysis was developed initially in connection with state rulings based on substantive grounds, it soon was held applicable to rulings involving procedural grounds as well. Application of the same principle on habeas review was viewed as consistent with the role of the habeas court as a functional surrogate of the Supreme Court in providing a federal forum for federal claims. If a procedural default constituted an independent and adequate state ground, thereby barring direct review by the Supreme Court, it would also bar federal habeas review. Thus, a defendant whose default was not excused by the state court could obtain review of his claim in federal court only if the state procedural ruling did not constitute an adequate state ground.

Daniels v. Allen,[4] a companion case to *Brown v. Allen*,[5] offers a dramatic example of the effect of this adequate state ground standard on habeas review. Like the defendants in *Brown*, Daniels had raised at trial constitutional challenges to the composition of the jury and to the use of an allegedly coerced confession. Daniels' counsel, however, had failed to file a timely appeal. The trial court had granted the defense 60 days in which to prepare and serve its statement of the case on appeal, but that statement was not delivered until the 61st day. The state appellate court refused to hear the appeal even though, if the papers had been mailed on the 60th day, as permitted under court rules, they would not have arrived any earlier. A divided Supreme Court held that the procedural default barred federal habeas review of the petitioner's claims. In dissent, Justice Black characterized the majority's ruling as having adopted a philosophy which, when combined with *Brown*, "prompts this Court to

---

1. Brennan, J., dissenting in Wainwright v. Sykes, 433 U.S. 72, 97 S.Ct. 2497, 53 L.Ed.2d 594 (1977).

2. Engle v. Isaac, infra note 18. Review of claims defaulted due to the ineffective assistance of counsel is discussed in § 28.4(d).

3. Discussed in §§ 28.3(c) and 28.4(c).

4. 344 U.S. 443, 73 S.Ct. 437, 97 L.Ed. 469 (1953).

5. See § 28.3(c), discussing *Brown*.

grant a second review where the state has granted one but to deny any review at all where the state has granted none."

As the following sections explain, the Court eventually abandoned the adequate state ground analysis as the sole measure of the propriety of federal review of a claim defaulted in state court. Under present standards, described in §§ 28.4(c)–(g), habeas review may be available despite an adequate and independent state procedural ground for default. Nevertheless, the adequacy of the state's application of its procedural rule remains a threshold issue in any case in which procedural default is raised as a defense by the state. As the Court explained in *Dugger v. Adams*,[6] a procedural default will not bar habeas review if *either* (1) the state procedural rule had been applied so unevenly as not to constitute an adequate state ground *or* (2) the default was excused under the cause-and-prejudice standard, described below in § 28.4(c).

The present standard for assessing when a state ground is adequate looks to whether it serves a "legitimate state interest,"[7] and to the evenhandedness of its application by state courts. A state may not manipulate its rules to evade federal rights, or exercise its procedural discretion to discriminate against the presentation of such rights. For example, a state procedural rule that was not firmly established at the time of a defendant's trial cannot be applied retroactively as a basis for deeming untimely his objection to jury selection. Such a rule is "inadequate to serve as an independent state ground."[8] State procedural rulings are also inadequate to bar federal review when applied in such an arbitrary manner as to "force resort to arid ritual of meaningless form."[9] A rule must be "regularly" and "consistently" applied by state courts to be considered an adequate ground for barring habeas

review. A federal court may also review a petitioner's constitutional claim if the petitioner substantially complied with the essential requirements of the state's procedural rule, and "nothing would [have] be[en] gained by requiring" more exacting adherence to the rule.[10]

In order for a state to rely on the defense of procedural default in a habeas action, not only must it show that the state court's reason for rejecting the petitioner's claim was "adequate," the state must also show that the court's reason was "independent," that is, based on *state*, not federal law. A state court's decision is not "independent" if either 1) the " 'resolution of [a] state procedural law question depends on a federal constitutional ruling,' " or 2) the state court decision actually rested on such a ruling.[11]

(c) The Development of the "Cause-and-Prejudice" Standard. For more than a decade before it settled on the current "cause-and-prejudice" test for reviewing defaulted claims, the Court applied an approach more favorable to petitioners known as the "deliberate bypass" standard. Established in *Fay v. Noia*,[12] the "deliberate bypass" standard allowed federal review of claims defaulted in state court unless the failure to comply with state law was a product of a "deliberate bypassing" of "the orderly procedure of the state courts."

The petitioner in *Noia* and two codefendants had been convicted primarily on the basis of signed confessions, which they maintained at trial were coerced. Noia's two codefendants took unsuccessful appeals, but subsequent legal proceedings resulted in their release on findings that the confessions had been obtained in violation of the Fourteenth Amendment. Noia had failed to appeal following his conviction, but responding to the release of his

---

6. 489 U.S. 401, 109 S.Ct. 1211, 103 L.Ed.2d 435 (1989).

7. See Henry v. Mississippi, 379 U.S. 443, 85 S.Ct. 564, 13 L.Ed.2d 408 (1965).

8. Ford v. Georgia, 498 U.S. 411, 111 S.Ct. 850, 112 L.Ed.2d 935 (1991).

9. Staub v. City of Baxley, 355 U.S. 313, 78 S.Ct. 277, 2 L.Ed.2d 302 (1958).

10. Lee v. Kemna, 534 U.S. 362, 122 S.Ct. 877, 151 L.Ed.2d 820 (2002).

11. Stewart v. Smith, 536 U.S. 856, 122 S.Ct. 2578, 153 L.Ed.2d 762 (2002) (quoting Ake v. Oklahoma, 470 U.S. 68, 105 S.Ct. 1087, 84 L.Ed.2d 53 (1985)).

12. 372 U.S. 391, 83 S.Ct. 822, 9 L.Ed.2d 837 (1963).

codefendants, sought to utilize the state remedy of coram nobis. That relief was denied on the ground that his failure to appeal precluded collateral inquiry into the voluntariness of his confession. The Supreme Court, in an opinion by Justice Brennan, held that federal court review of Noia's claim was not foreclosed by the default in state court. Noting that the Court had long held that state procedural rulings would be rejected when they "made burdensome the vindication of federal rights," Justice Brennan concluded that sufficient deference to a state's "substantial interest in exacting compliance with their procedural rules," was provided by denial of direct review, which placed a burden upon the noncomplying defendant to seek habeas review. The discretion of the federal courts to refuse to review a claim defaulted in state court was appropriately limited to situations in which "the suitor's conduct in relation to the matter at hand may disentitle him to relief." If an applicant who "understandingly and knowingly forewent the privilege of seeking to vindicate his federal claims in the State courts, whether for strategic, tactical, or any other reasons that can fairly be described as the deliberate bypassing of state procedures, then it is open to the federal court on habeas to deny him all relief if the state courts refused to entertain his federal claims on the merits."

Although *Fay v. Noia* was widely recognized as one of the landmark decisions of the Warren Court, its protections were soon eroded. In *Henry v. Mississippi*[13] the Court indicated that the defendant's personal participation in the decision that led to the default was not required, at least as to those constitutional objections that could be controlled by counsel alone. *Murch v. Mottram*[14] added that a deliberate bypass by counsel did not require knowledge that the tactical maneuver would result in a procedural default under state law, provided counsel had "reasonable warning" that he ran that risk. Just ten years after *Noia*, the deliberate bypass standard was rejected for use during the collateral review of constitutional

claims by federal prisoners. In *Davis v. United States*,[15] the Court considered a claim of racial discrimination in the selection of a grand jury, raised by a federal defendant in a collateral attack on his conviction under 28 U.S.C. § 2255 filed three years after his trial. The Supreme Court rejected Davis's argument that his failure to raise that claim at trial should be judged under the deliberate bypass standard. The Court noted that if Davis's case had come before it on direct review, it would have been decided under Federal Rule 12(b). That Rule provided that the failure to raise before trial a defect such as grand jury discrimination would "constitute a waiver, but the court for cause shown may grant relief from the waiver." The Court found it "inconceivable" that Congress, having foreclosed such a claim from review in the initial proceeding, meant to allow it nonetheless to be presented on collateral attack. Accordingly, the Rule 12(b) standard was held to apply under § 2255 as well as in the original proceeding. This meant that the petitioner could have his claim considered only if his failure to object was justified by "cause shown" and accompanied by a showing of "actual prejudice."

Francis v. Henderson[16] extended the cause-and-prejudice test of *Davis* to a state prisoner seeking federal habeas review of grand jury discrimination. A state statute required objections to the grand jury's composition to be raised before trial and the petitioner had failed to object, resulting in a procedural default. Without mentioning the deliberate bypass standard, the Court held that the standard announced in was applicable. The state requirement of a pretrial objection, the Court noted, served many of the same salutary purposes as Federal Rule 12(b). "Surely," the Court concluded, "considerations of comity and federalism require that * * * [habeas courts] give no less effect to the same clear interests when asked to overturn state convictions."

---

13.   379 U.S. 443, 85 S.Ct. 564, 13 L.Ed.2d 408 (1965). See also § 11.6(a).

14.   409 U.S. 41, 93 S.Ct. 71, 34 L.Ed.2d 194 (1972).

15.   411 U.S. 233, 93 S.Ct. 1577, 36 L.Ed.2d 216 (1973).

16.   425 U.S. 536, 96 S.Ct. 1708, 48 L.Ed.2d 149 (1976).

Conceivably, the Court could have limited the "cause-and-prejudice" test to the context of grand jury discrimination claims, which, by their nature, provide counsel some incentive to "sandbag." In *Wainwright v. Sykes*,[17] however, the Court chose instead to expand the test to trial errors as well. The petitioner Sykes had sought habeas relief on the ground that his conviction had been based on a confession obtained without his full understanding of the *Miranda* warnings. Although the state's rules required at least a contemporaneous objection to the admission of illegally obtained evidence, there had been no objection before or during the trial. Justice Rehnquist's opinion for the Court explained that the issue before the Court was "whether the rule of *Francis v. Henderson,* barring federal habeas review absent a showing of 'cause' and 'prejudice' attendant to a state procedural waiver [should] be applied to a waived objection to the admission of a confession at trial." For reasons discussed below, the Court answered that question in the affirmative.

The *Sykes* opinion offered three reasons for preferring the *Francis* test over *Noia's* deliberate bypass standard. First, the "contemporaneous-objection" rule applied in the state court deserved "greater respect" than the deliberate bypass standard would give it, because "it is employed by a coordinate jurisdiction within the federal system" and because of the many valid interests it served, including ensuring the development of a factual record when "the recollections of witnesses are freshest," allowing the judge "who observed the demeanor of the witnesses [at trial] to make the factual determinations," offering the opportunity for exclusion at a point where doing so will make "a major contribution to finality in a criminal litigation," and forcing the prosecution at a propitious time "to take a hard look" which might lead it to decide not to take the challenged action.

Second, the Court expressed the view that the "rule of *Fay v. Noia,* broadly stated, may encourage 'sandbagging' on the part of defense lawyers, who may take their chances on a verdict of not guilty in a state trial court with the intent to raise their constitutional claims in a federal habeas court if their initial gamble does not pay off." Justice Brennan, in dissent, argued that the deliberate bypass standard barred exactly that tactical maneuver, but the majority apparently concluded that the potential looseness of that standard in application (and perhaps *Noia's* recognition of district court discretion to ignore a bypass) offered a continuing incentive to sandbag.

Finally the *Sykes* majority criticized the deliberate bypass rule for detracting from the appropriate role of the trial. The "failure of the federal habeas courts generally to require compliance with a contemporaneous-objection rule [would] tend to detract from the perception of the trial in a criminal case * * * as a decisive and portentous event." The "adoption of the *Francis* rule," on the other hand, would have "the salutary effect of making the trial on the merits the 'main event,' so to speak, rather than a 'tryout on the road' for what will later be the determinative federal habeas hearing." Responding to the dissenters, the majority also stressed that the cause and prejudice test would still serve the basic function of habeas review, and "not prevent a federal habeas court from adjudicating for the first time the federal constitutional claim of a defendant who in the absence of such an adjudication will be the victim of a miscarriage of justice." This miscarriage-of-justice is discussed in subsection 28.4(f), below.

In *Engle v. Isaac*[18] and *United States v. Frady,*[19] the Court soon extended the cause-and-prejudice test to claims of faulty jury instructions, errors that unlike the *Miranda* violation alleged in *Sykes* clearly related to the reliability of the trial process. *Issac* was a case in which the state prisoner claimed that he had been denied due process by a jury charge that required the defense to carry the burden of proving self-defense by a preponderance of the evidence. *Frady* presented a challenge by a

17. 433 U.S. 72, 97 S.Ct. 2497, 53 L.Ed.2d 594 (1977).

18. 456 U.S. 107, 102 S.Ct. 1558, 71 L.Ed.2d 783 (1982).

19. 456 U.S. 152, 102 S.Ct. 1584, 71 L.Ed.2d 816 (1982).

federal prisoner to a jury charge that allegedly required the jury to presume malice and thereby relieved the government of its obligation to prove a major element of the offense. Neither defendant had objected at trial, an oversight each argued was excused because the invalidity of the instruction was not apparent under the then prevailing precedent. Writing for the majority in both cases, Justice O'Connor declared that each default was subject to the cause-and-prejudice standard and concluded that under that standard, neither claim was subject to review. The costs of the "liberal allowance" of habeas review—the degradation of the "prominence of the trial," the difficulties of retrials long after the event, and the impact upon the interests of the state—were escalated "when a trial default has barred a prisoner from obtaining adjudication of his constitutional claim in the state courts," she explained in *Isaac*. These considerations "do not depend upon the type of claim raised by the prisoner."

In *Murray v. Carrier*,[20] the Court found "unpersuasive" the contention that the concerns underlying *Sykes* have less force as to a default on appeal and therefore such a default should be governed by a separate standard, or at least a more lenient view of "cause." The cause-and-prejudice standard was still needed to ensure proper respect for the significant state interests served by requiring appellate resolution of claims "shortly after trial, while evidence is still available both to assess the defendant's claim and to retry the defendant effectively if he prevails." Eventually, in *Coleman v. Thompson*,[21] Justice O'Connor finally put *Noia* to rest, stating: "We now make it explicit: In all cases in which a state prisoner has defaulted his federal claims in state court pursuant to an independent and adequate state procedural rule, federal habeas review of the claim is barred unless the prisoner can demonstrate cause for the default and actual prejudice as a result of the alleged violation of federal law, or demonstrates that failure to consider the claims will result in a fundamental miscarriage of justice."

(d) The Meaning of Cause. *Ineffective Assistance of Counsel as Cause.* The Court has made clear that the defendant must bear the cost of his counsel's error in failing to raise a claim properly in state court, provided that the error does not amount to a violation of the right of effective assistance of counsel under the Sixth Amendment. As Justice O'Connor explained in *Coleman*:

> Attorney error that constitutes ineffective assistance of counsel is cause * * * not because * * * the error is so bad that "the lawyer ceases to be an agent of the petitioner." Rather, * * * "if the procedural default is the result of ineffective assistance of counsel, the Sixth Amendment itself requires that responsibility for the default be imputed to the State." In other words, it is not the gravity of the attorney's error that matters, but that it constitutes a violation of petitioner's right to counsel, so that the error must be seen as an external factor, i.e., "imputed to the State." * * * Where a petitioner defaults a claim as a result of the denial of the right to effective assistance of counsel, the State, which is responsible for the denial as a constitutional matter, must bear the cost of any resulting default and the harm to state interests that federal habeas review entails.

The Court has considered a variety of failings on the part of counsel under this standard. For example, where the defendant has a constitutional right to counsel and counsel, without first obtaining defendant's acquiescence, makes a decision that relinquishes a right over which the defendant has personal control, such action traditionally has been viewed as constitutionally ineffective assistance of counsel. On the other hand, in *Isaac* the Court concluded "the futility of presenting an objection to state courts cannot alone constitute cause for a failure to object at trial." A defendant who "perceives a constitutional claim and believes it may find favor in the federal courts" cannot "bypass the state courts simply because he thinks they will be

20.   477 U.S. 478, 106 S.Ct. 2639, 91 L.Ed.2d 397 (1986).

21.   501 U.S. 722, 111 S.Ct. 2546, 115 L.Ed.2d 640 (1991).

unsympathetic to the claim." Also, as the Court explained in *Murray v. Carrier*,[22] the "mere fact that counsel failed to recognize the factual or legal basis for a claim, or failed to raise the claim despite recognizing it, does not constitute cause for a procedural default." "So long as defendant is represented by counsel whose performance is not constitutionally ineffective," the Court concluded, "we discern no inequity in requiring him to bear the risk of attorney error that results in a procedural default."

Even attorney incompetence equivalent to that required under *Strickland* will not be sufficient to establish cause if counsel's failure takes place in a phase of the criminal process during which the defendant has no sixth amendment right to the effective assistance of counsel. In *Coleman*, defense counsel had failed to file a timely notice of appeal from a denial of a state habeas corpus petition. The Court concluded that because the defendant had no constitutional right to the assistance of counsel in such a collateral proceeding, the incompetency of his attorney could not give rise to a constitutional claim of ineffective assistance. Such incompetency, not amounting to a constitutional violation in itself, did not constitute cause. "[I]n those circumstances where the State has no responsibility to ensure that the petitioner was represented by competent counsel," Justice O'Connor explained, "it is the petitioner" not the state "who must bear the burden of a failure to follow state procedural rules."

Rather than pursue the underlying constitutional claim forfeited by his attorney's failings, a petitioner may choose to seek relief on the basis of the sixth amendment violation itself. Competency of counsel for sixth amendment purposes generally looks to the overall performance of counsel. This will work to defendant's advantage where counsel's failures extend beyond the default on the cognizable constitutional claim. Even where counsel's only error related to the default, as the Court

noted in *Carrier*, "the right to effective assistance of counsel * * * may in a particular case be violated by even an isolated error of counsel if that error is sufficiently egregious and prejudicial." Indeed, if the defaulted claim involves a violation of rights under the Fourth Amendment, a petitioner will not receive review unless he casts his claim as a denial of the sixth amendment right to the effective assistance of counsel.[23] About 1 in 4 habeas petitions, according to one study, include a claim of ineffective assistance of counsel.

In *Edwards v. Carpenter*,[24] however, the Court emphasized that an ineffective-assistance-of counsel claim asserted as cause for the procedural default of another claim may itself be procedurally defaulted. After completing one round through state appellate and post-conviction procedure, Carpenter had tried to reopen his state appeal and claim that his appellate counsel had been ineffective in failing to challenge the sufficiency of the evidence against him, but he was rebuffed by the state courts, who said that it was too late to challenge the effectiveness of his appellate counsel. In order to get beyond this default in federal court, the Court explained, Carpenter would have to show cause for failing to raise his ineffective assistance claim on time under state law. This complex system of rules prompted Justice Breyer to question why a prisoner, who may well be acting pro se, must lose his constitutional claim because he "runs afoul of state procedural rules governing the presentation to state courts of the 'cause' for his not having followed state procedural rules for the presentation of his basic federal claim."

In most states a claim of ineffective assistance of counsel need not be raised until after a prisoner's direct appeal, in a state post-conviction proceeding. The Court explained the rationale for this departure from the usual rules requiring claims to be raised in the trial court, prior to appeal, in *Massaro v. United*

---

22. 477 U.S. 478, 106 S.Ct. 2639, 91 L.Ed.2d 397 (1986).

23. See Kimmelman v. Morrison, 477 U.S. 365, 106 S.Ct. 2574, 91 L.Ed.2d 305 (1986), discussed in § 28.3(b).

24. 529 U.S. 446, 120 S.Ct. 1587, 146 L.Ed.2d 518 (2000).

States.[25] Were defendants required to raise ineffectiveness claims on appeal, the Court explained, "trial counsel [would] be unwilling to help appellate counsel familiarize himself with a record for the purpose of understanding how it reflects trial counsel's own incompetence," and "[a]ppellate courts would waste time and resources attempting to address some claims that were meritless and other claims that, though colorable, would be handled more efficiently if addressed in the first instance" on collateral review by the trial court. The trial court considering a post-conviction challenge is "the forum best suited to developing the facts necessary to determining the adequacy of representation during an entire trial. The court may take testimony from witnesses from witnesses * * * and from the counsel alleged to have rendered the deficient performance." When presented in the trial court, rather than on appeal, a claim of ineffective assistance "often will be ruled upon by the same * * * judge who presided at trial, [who] should have an advantageous perspective for determining the effectiveness of counsel's conduct and whether any deficiencies were prejudicial."

Novelty of Claim As Cause. For a short time, the novelty of a constitutional claim was one basis for excusing the failure to raise that claim in state court. A divided Court held in *Reed v. Ross*[26] that the failure to raise a claim "so novel that its legal basis [was] not reasonably available" did not "seriously implicate any of the concerns that might otherwise require deference to a state's procedural bar" and therefore should not preclude habeas review. Justice Brennan's opinion for the Court reasoned that neither courts nor attorneys are likely to appreciate truly novel claims, and that "encouraging defense counsel to include any and all remotely plausible constitutional claims that could, some day, gain recognition" could be disruptive to orderly proceedings in state court. Subsequently, in *Teague v. Lane*,[27]

the Court limited habeas review to claims based on the law as it stood when the defendant's conviction became final, except in rare circumstances described in § 28.6(e). The 1996 amendments also bar relief unless the state court decision was "contrary to, or involved an unreasonable application of, clearly established Federal law, as determined by the Supreme Court of the United States."[28] The practical impact of *Reed* following these changes is slim indeed. A petitioner cannot successfully argue both that "clearly established Federal law, as determined by the Supreme Court" supported his claim, and that his claim was "so novel that its legal basis [was] not reasonably available" to counsel in state proceedings.

State Interference as Cause. Yet another circumstance that constitutes "cause" was noted in *Murray v. Carrier*.[29] The Court there explained that absent ineffective assistance of counsel, the "existence of cause for a procedural default must ordinarily turn on whether the prisoner can show [that] some objective factor external to the defense impeded counsel's efforts to comply with the state's procedural rule." A showing of " 'some interference by officials' " that made compliance impracticable" would constitute cause, stated the Court, citing *Brown v. Allen's* reference to a case in which a warden had suppressed the prisoner's timely appeal papers. Later, in *Amadeo v. Zant*,[30] the Court held that the state's concealment of a prosecutor's request to jury commissioners to underrepresent African Americans and women would suffice as cause for defense counsel's failure to object to the composition of the jury at trial. *Strickler v. Greene*[31] provided another example of governmental interference with a defendant's ability to raise a claim. In *Strickler*, the petitioner had failed to raise his *Brady* claim in state court. The Court found that he had established cause for this failure "because (a) the prosecution withheld exculpatory evidence; (b) petitioner reasonably relied

25.   538 U.S. 500, 123 S.Ct. 1690, 155 L.Ed.2d 714 (2003).

26.   468 U.S. 1, 104 S.Ct. 2901, 82 L.Ed.2d 1 (1984).

27.   489 U.S. 288, 109 S.Ct. 1060, 103 L.Ed.2d 334 (1989), discussed in § 28.6(b)–(e).

28.   See 28 U.S.C.A. § 2254(d), discussed in § 28.6(f).

29.   Supra note 20.

30.   486 U.S. 214, 108 S.Ct. 1771, 100 L.Ed.2d 249 (1988).

31.   527 U.S. 263, 119 S.Ct. 1936, 144 L.Ed.2d 286 (1999).

on the prosecution's open file policy as fulfilling the prosecution's duty to disclose such evidence; and (c) the Commonwealth confirmed petitioner's reliance on the open file policy by asserting during state habeas proceedings that the petitioner had already received 'everything known to the government.' " Although the Court declined to decide whether any one or two of these factors would be sufficient to constitute cause, lower courts have subsequently held that the government's concealment of exculpatory evidence from the defense, rendering the factual basis for a *Brady* claim unavailable to the defense, will constitute cause excusing the failure to raise that *Brady* claim on time in state court.

In order to amount to cause the state's interference must actually have impeded the defendant's efforts to comply with procedural rules. In *McCleskey v Zant*,[32] for example, the Court held that the prosecution's failure to disclose a recorded statement of an informant prior to a second habeas petition did not constitute "cause" and therefore did not relieve the petitioner of the forfeiture that occurred when counsel failed to include in the first petition a sixth amendment challenge to the use of the informant's statement at trial. The Court concluded that the recorded statement was not "critical" to the substance of petitioner's sixth amendment challenge (which had been raised in an earlier state habeas proceeding), and that petitioner had sufficient information to raise the claim in his first petition in any event. The Court described the question before it as "whether petitioner possessed, or by reasonable means could have obtained, a sufficient basis to allege a claim in the first petition and pursue the matter through the habeas process." It noted further that a petitioner's inability to obtain relevant evidence "fails to establish cause if other known or discoverable evidence could have supported the claim," and that the failure to assert the claim "will not be excused merely because evidence discovered later might also have supported or

strengthened the claim." The state's delay in providing a defendant with a transcript of trial proceedings also will not constitute cause for failing to raise a claim unless the petitioner was prevented from making the claim by that delay. This will not be the case when the factual and legal basis for the claim was apparent at the time of trial, or was known to the defendant prior to receiving the transcript.

(e) The Meaning of Prejudice. Assuming that cause is established, what type of showing will establish "actual prejudice"? In *Kyles v. Whitley*[33] and *Strickler v. Greene*,[34] the Court clarified that in order to establish prejudice under *Sykes*, a petitioner must demonstrate that there is a "reasonable probability that the result of the trial would have been different." A "reasonable probability" is described as a probability sufficient to "undermine confidence in the verdict." This produces consistency in cases where the defendant seeks to convert the procedural default into a sixth amendment claim of ineffective assistance of counsel, because the reasonable probability standard is also used to measure the prejudice prong of such sixth amendment claims.

(f) The "Miscarriage of Justice" Exception. Justice O'Connor's opinion in *Engle v. Isaac* stressed that "cause" and "prejudice" were not rigid concepts, but were based upon general principles of "comity and finality." "In appropriate cases," Justice O'Connor noted, "those principles must yield to the imperative of fundamentally unjust incarceration." An exception to the cause-and-prejudice requirement was also noted in *Sykes* when the Court stated that the standard developed there would not bar habeas relief for a victim of a "miscarriage of justice." The initial discussions of the scope of this exception to the cause-and-prejudice requirement came in *Murray v. Carrier*[35] and *Smith v. Murray*.[36] The Court in *Carrier* explained that "in an extraordinary case, where a constitutional violation

---

32. 499 U.S. 467, 111 S.Ct. 1454, 113 L.Ed.2d 517 (1991).

33. 514 U.S. 419, 115 S.Ct. 1555, 131 L.Ed.2d 490 (1995).

34. Supra note 31.

35. Supra note 20.

36. 477 U.S. 527, 106 S.Ct. 2661, 91 L.Ed.2d 434 (1986).

has probably resulted in the conviction of one who is actually innocent, a federal habeas court may grant the writ even in the absence of a showing of cause for the procedural default." With this exception, the cause-and-prejudice test established a "sound and workable means of channeling the discretion of federal habeas courts" in treating procedural defaults at the state level.

Speaking further to the "unjust incarceration" exception in *Smith*, the Court noted that the exception's focus was on "actual" as distinct from "legal innocence." The petitioner there claimed that the state court had violated his self-incrimination privilege when it allowed into evidence at his capital sentencing hearing a psychiatrist's testimony recounting a damaging statement defendant had made during a psychiatric examination without being warned as to its possible use against him. Unlike the dissenters, the Court majority did not ask whether the erroneous introduction of that evidence might have had a bearing on the jury's recommendation that petitioner be sentenced to death. Such an impact-upon-outcome inquiry would have been appropriate in applying the "actual prejudice" prong of the test, but that prong was not relevant since the Court had earlier determined that the procedural default was not justified by "cause." For the purpose of determining whether there was a miscarriage-of-justice, the key was whether admission of the defendant's statement to the psychiatrist had "pervert[ed] the jury's deliberations concerning the ultimate question whether *in fact* petitioner constituted a continuing threat to society." Since there was no suggestion that his statement was "false or in any way misleading," it had not adversely influenced the factual correctness of the jurors' verdict even though that verdict might have been otherwise if the statement had been excluded as constitutionally inadmissible. *Sawyer v. Whitley*[37] confirmed that the actual innocence concept applied not only to the habeas petitioner claiming to be innocent of the crime for which he was convicted, but also to the petitioner sentenced to death who claims that

a procedurally defaulted constitutional error in capital sentencing resulted in a death sentence for one "actually innocent of the death penalty." In order to succeed, the Court stated, a petitioner making such a sentencing claim must "show by clear and convincing evidence that but for a constitutional error no reasonable juror would find the petitioner eligible for the death penalty."

Schlup v. Delo[38] clarified that the burden of establishing "actual innocence" sufficient to overcome the absence of cause and prejudice was not quite as demanding where the procedurally defaulted constitutional claim related to the determination of the petitioner's guilt, not sentence. Thus, where the alleged constitutional violation resulted in the failure of the factfinder to have before it evidence that was both reliable and exculpatory, the habeas petitioner has to show only that "it is more likely than not that no reasonable juror would have convicted him in light of the new evidence." The Court noted that a standard less demanding than the clear-and-convincing-evidence standard of *Sawyer* was appropriate because the "individual interest in avoiding injustice is most compelling" in claims of actual innocence as to the commission of the crime itself ("the quintessential miscarriage of justice [being] * * * the execution of a person who is entirely innocent"). The *Schlup* Court concluded that in such a case, this standard struck an appropriate balance—"ensur[ing] that petitioner's case is truly 'extraordinary,' while still providing a meaningful avenue by which to avoid a manifest injustice."

Interpreting the "miscarriage of justice" exception to provide an opportunity for reviewing only those claims of error that implicate actual innocence may prevent habeas review of defaulted claims of error that would not affect the accuracy of a jury's verdict of guilt or eligibility for the death sentence. Such claims include grand jury error preceding an otherwise valid conviction, violations of the prohibition against double jeopardy, and denials of speedy or public trials. Also excluded are

37. 505 U.S. 333, 112 S.Ct. 2514, 120 L.Ed.2d 269 (1992).

38. 513 U.S. 298, 115 S.Ct. 851, 130 L.Ed.2d 808 (1995).

claims based on the introduction of reliable evidence obtained in violation of a defendant's right to counsel or privilege against self-incrimination, claims that a petitioner's jury venire was selected in violation of the Sixth or Fourteenth Amendments, as well as claims of selective prosecution. In other words, once defaulted in state court, claims unrelated to factual innocence do not receive the same oversight in federal court as do claims that are related to the conviction or punishment of a factually innocent individual. The Court's willingness to restrict collateral review of such claims suggests that it has concluded that sufficient incentive to comply with these particular constitutional requirements is provided by litigation on behalf of those defendants who, while still in state court, manage to learn of and effectively raise such claims. As *Schlup* explained, "Explicitly tying the miscarriage of justice exception to innocence thus accommodates both the systemic interests in finality, comity, and conservation of judicial resources, and the overriding individual interest in doing justice in the 'extraordinary case.' "

It is doubtful, however, that construing the "miscarriage of justice" exception of the crime of conviction to apply only to petitioners who can demonstrate factual innocence adequately accommodates "the overriding individual interest in doing justice" in at least one hypothetical situation. Should the Court choose to apply retroactively under its *Teague* analysis[39] a constitutional rule of criminal procedure unrelated to factual innocence, the petitioner's

procedural default of a claim under that rule arguably should be excused, even if he is unable to demonstrate factual innocence as defined in *Schlup* or *Sawyer*.[40]

For a petitioner who is seeking relief from a conviction following a plea of guilty, actual innocence means "factual innocence," based on "any admissible evidence of petitioner's guilt even if that evidence was not presented during petitioner's plea colloquy," declared the Court in *Bousley v. United States*.[41] Furthermore, the Court added, in cases when there is "record evidence" that "the government has foregone more serious charges in the course of plea bargaining, petitioner's showing of actual innocence must also extend to those charges." As Justice Scalia observed in his dissent in *Bousley*, the majority's approach raises a number of difficulties for application. First, by limiting the innocence inquiry to the consideration of "admissible" evidence, the Court departed from earlier decisions authorizing the consideration of illegally admitted, albeit reliable, evidence when assessing actual innocence.[42] Second, the factual record to support a plea-based conviction is bound to be considerably less developed than a trial transcript, consisting in many cases of only the prosecutor's proffer of factual basis for the charge. Third, the factual basis for bargained-away charges may not appear in the record at all. Finally, as some lower courts have noted, the logic of *Bousley*, which prevents a petitioner from raising a defaulted challenge to a sentence he bargained for, while escaping punish-

---

39. As discussed in § 28.6(b)–(e), *Teague v. Lane* held that a habeas court could apply only those constitutional rules existing at the time the state judgment became final, unless the "new" rule relied upon by the petitioner either 1) protects a class of conduct from criminal punishment or a class of persons from capital punishment or 2) relates to the accuracy of the conviction and constitutes a watershed ruling that alters the bedrock procedural elements essential to the fairness of the proceeding.

40. This result is also supported by an analysis of the new statute. New § 2244(b)(2)(A) allows a petitioner to raise a new claim in a successive petition based on a retroactively applied rule, with no extra showing of innocence, even though the petitioner failed to include the claim in the earlier petition. In addition, § 2244(d)(1)(C) allows a petitioner to file a petition beyond the one-year limitations period if his claim is based on such a rule, without any added showing of innocence, and § 2264(a)(2) allows specifically for consideration of a defaulted claim

based on new federal right to be applied retroactively, again without an additional showing of actual innocence. If the review of claims invoking rules that would be applied retroactively under *Teague* is acceptable in these contexts, it was probably intended to extend to first petitions as well, despite the petitioner's failure to raise the claim properly in state court. Admittedly, new § 2254(e)(2) may cut against this interpretation. It insists on a showing of innocence in addition to retroactive application in order to secure a hearing if a petitioner fails to develop the factual basis for his claim in state court. For a discussion of this added requirement for evidentiary hearings, see § 28.7(b).

41. 523 U.S. 614, 118 S.Ct. 1604, 140 L.Ed.2d 828 (1998).

42. See e.g., Calderon v. Thompson, 523 U.S. 538, 118 S.Ct. 1489, 140 L.Ed.2d 728 (1998).

ment for dismissed counts that he actually committed, should require a defendant to establish factual innocence of dropped charges that were as serious as the challenged offense, not simply those that were "more serious."

The discussion of the fundamental miscarriage of justice exception in pre-*Schlup* opinions appeared to be based on the premise that a habeas petitioner who made the requisite showing of actual innocence and established a non-harmless constitutional error would be *entitled* to relief notwithstanding the procedural default. Justice Scalia, dissenting in *Schlup*, argued that the miscarriage of justice exception should be a discretionary remedy. Justice O'Connor, the critical fifth vote for a 5–4 majority, responded that the "Court does not, and need not decide" that issue. Thus, it remains open.

(g) Procedural Default After the 1996 Amendments in *Certain Capital Cases.* Section 2264(a), governing claims by petitioners under sentences of death from states that have met the requirements of § 2261,[43] is the only provision added by the Antiterrorism and Effective Death Penalty Act that speaks directly to the consequence of procedural default in state court. It directs the habeas court to consider only "claims that have been raised and decided on the merits in the state courts" unless the "failure to raise the claim properly is: (1) the result of State action in violation of the Constitution or laws of the United States; (2) the result of the Supreme Court's recognition of a new Federal right that is made retroactively applicable; or (3) based on a factual predicate that could not have been discovered through the exercise of due diligence in time to present the claim for State or Federal post-conviction review." For those capital cases covered by this provision, it operates as the legislative replacement of the *Sykes* cause-and-prejudice standard and its "fundamental miscarriage of justice" exception.

§ 28.5　Claims Foreclosed Due to Premature, Successive, or Delayed Applications

(a) Exhaustion of State Remedies. *Overview and origins.* The "exhaustion doctrine" denies federal habeas relief to a state prisoner who has failed to give the state courts an adequate opportunity to rule on his claim, provided the state procedure for gaining review is still open to him. The doctrine, presently codified in § 2254, requires the petitioner to "exhaust" his available state remedies before seeking federal relief. It is " 'principally designed to protect the state courts' role in the enforcement of federal law and prevent the disruption of state judicial proceedings.' "[1] Over half of all of habeas petitions dismissed are dismissed for failure to exhaust state remedies.

Both the "equitable nature" of the doctrine and the considerations underlying its exercise were set in place by the Court's seminal opinion in *Ex parte Royall*.[2] Decided in 1886, *Royall* was one of the first cases under the 1867 Habeas Act to reach the Supreme Court. The petitioner there, while awaiting trial in his state case, sought federal habeas relief on the ground that the pending state prosecution was based on an unconstitutional statute. Sustaining the lower court's denial of the writ, the Supreme Court noted:

> The [statute's] injunction to hear the case summarily, and thereupon "to dispose of the party as law and justice require" does not deprive the court of discretion as to the time and mode in which it will exert the powers conferred upon it. That discretion should be exercised in the light of the relations existing, under our system of government, between the judicial tribunals of the Union and of the States, and in recognition of the fact that the public good requires that those relations be not disturbed by unnecessary conflict between courts equally bound to

---

43.　See § 28.2(c).

1.　Duncan v. Walker, 533 U.S. 167, 121 S.Ct. 2120, 150 L.Ed.2d 251 (2001).

2.　117 U.S. 241, 6 S.Ct. 734, 29 L.Ed. 868 (1886).

guard and protect rights secured by the Constitution.

After presenting the various considerations of comity that favored respecting the state's opportunity to exercise its processes, the Court repeated its conclusion that the circuit court had "discretion whether it will discharge [petitioner] * * * in advance of his trial," but added that such discretion was "to be subordinated to any special circumstances requiring immediate action."

Soon the Court extended the "principles settled in *Royall's Case*" to the petition of a convicted state defendant who had not yet utilized "his writ of error from the highest court in the state." Initially, various cases were viewed as presenting exceptional circumstances under which exhaustion was not required, but after the turn of the century, exhaustion "developed into a much more rigid requirement." By 1944, the Court was able to announce as settled law that "ordinarily an application for habeas corpus by one detained under a state court judgment of conviction will be entertained * * * only after all state remedies available, including all appellate remedies in the state courts and in this Court by appeal or writ of certiorari have been exhausted."[3]

In its 1948 revision of the habeas statutes, Congress added two provisions incorporating the exhaustion requirement. The first provision is carried forward today in § 2254(b)(1), which sets forth the general requirement of exhaustion: "An application for a writ of habeas corpus on behalf of a person in custody pursuant to the judgment of a State court shall not be granted unless it appears that (A) the applicant has exhausted the remedies available in the courts of the State, or (B)(i) there is either an absence of available State corrective process or (ii) circumstances exist that render such process ineffective to protect the rights of the applicant." Section 2254(c) today also provides that an applicant may not be deemed to have exhausted his remedies "if he has a right under the law of the State to

raise, by any available procedure, the question presented."

In *Brown v. Allen*[4] the Supreme Court examined the meaning of the 1948 provision and held that a petitioner who had fully pursued his claim on direct appeal from his conviction was not thereafter required to repeat the process through state collateral remedies. Stating the proposition more broadly in a separate opinion also receiving majority support, Justice Frankfurter noted: "Section 2254 does not * * * require repeated attempts to invoke the same remedy nor more than one attempt where there are alternative remedies." Since *Brown*, the Supreme Court has assumed substantial leeway in determining the precise content of the exhaustion requirement. The Court's approach has depended to a considerable extent on its view of the policies underlying the exhaustion requirement. These policies are close cousins to those that the Court has stressed in giving deference to state procedural defaults. Justice O'Connor explained the objectives of the exhaustion rule in *Rose v. Lundy*:[5]

The exhaustion doctrine is principally designed to protect the state courts' role in the enforcement of federal law and prevent disruption of state judicial proceedings. * * * Because "it would be unseemly in our dual system of government for a federal district court to upset a state court conviction without an opportunity to the state courts to correct a constitutional violation," federal courts apply the doctrine of comity, which "teaches that one court should defer action on causes properly within its jurisdiction until the courts of another sovereignty with concurrent powers, and already cognizant of the litigation, have had an opportunity to pass upon the matter." * * * A rigorously enforced total exhaustion rule will encourage state prisoners to seek full relief first from the state courts, thus giving those courts the first opportunity to review all claims of constitutional error. As the number of prisoners who exhaust all of their federal claims increases, state courts may

---

3. Ex parte Hawk, 321 U.S. 114, 64 S.Ct. 448, 88 L.Ed. 572 (1944).

4. 344 U.S. 443, 73 S.Ct. 397, 97 L.Ed. 469 (1953).

5. Discussed infra at note 13.

become increasingly familiar with and hospitable toward federal constitutional issues. * * * Equally as important, federal claims that have been fully exhausted in state courts will more often be accompanied by a complete factual record to aid the federal courts in their review.

Not surprisingly, the Court has applied the exhaustion requirement quite strictly. In *Duckworth v. Serrano*,[6] for example, the lower court had granted habeas relief without requiring exhaustion in "view of the clear violation" of the petitioner's rights and "in the interest of judicial economy." The Court reversed in a per curiam opinion, noting: "An exception is made [to the § 2254 requirement] only if there is no opportunity to obtain redress in state court or if the corrective process is so clearly deficient as to render futile any effort to obtain relief."

Some situations may require a petitioner to present the same claim more than once to the state's highest court. The Supreme Court has suggested that an intervening Supreme Court decision which casts petitioner's claim in a new light requires him to reapply for state relief if still available.[7] On the other hand, when the highest state court changes its own view of preexisting Supreme Court precedent, the petitioner need not return to the state courts, since the state's opportunity to reach the correct result when it first heard petitioner's case had not been altered.[8] Nor must a petitioner return to the state courts after later state decisions have invalidated the statute under which he was prosecuted.[9] Many lower courts have held, however, that a change in state procedural law, allowing consideration of a constitutional claim previously rejected on procedural grounds, will require the petitioner to return to the state courts. It might be

argued that the state had ample opportunity to alter its procedure when the petitioner was first before it. Yet the procedural change would not ordinarily be attributable to any preexisting requirements of federal law.

Exceptions to exhaustion. The delay inherent in applying an exhaustion requirement has been characterized as "an unnecessary price to exact from a person, in the name of comity or judicial economy, where state procedures offer no practical hope of swift vindication of his federal claim." Section 2254(b) recognizes this position in noting that further state review is not required where there is either "an absence of available state corrective process" or "circumstances * * * render such process ineffective to protect the rights of the applicant."

The petitioner will be deemed to have exhausted any state remedy that is no longer available to him because of a procedural bar. For example, if a defendant fails to take advantage of a state remedy within the time specified by state law, the remedy will be considered unavailable to him. In this situation the petitioner will have to establish cause for his default in order to get beyond the procedural bar. As one court put it, "Having avoided the Scylla of exhaustion, [the petitioner] must also steer by the Charybdis of procedural default before his petition can be heard on the merits."

Futile or uncertain remedies constitute "ineffective" avenues under the statute and need not be exhausted.[10] As Justice Rutledge once noted, the exhaustion requirement does not require that the habeas court accept a state "merry-go-round of habeas corpus, coram nobis, and writ of error."[11] A theoretical system of relief need not be pursued. As the Court

---

6. 454 U.S. 1, 102 S.Ct. 18, 70 L.Ed.2d 1 (1981).

7. Picard v. Connor, note 14 infra. In discussing whether the state had been given a fair opportunity to consider petitioner's claim, the Court put aside what it apparently viewed as easier cases of nonexhaustion. Cited among such examples was "a case in which an intervening change in federal law cast the legal issue in a fundamentally different light." The Court then added citations to two lower court cases that required the petitioner to return to the state courts in such a case.

8. Roberts v. LaVallee, 389 U.S. 40, 88 S.Ct. 194, 19 L.Ed.2d 41 (1967).

9. Francisco v. Gathright, 419 U.S. 59, 95 S.Ct. 257, 42 L.Ed.2d 226 (1974).

10. Duckworth v. Serrano, supra note 6; Blackledge v. Perry, 417 U.S. 21, 94 S.Ct. 2098, 40 L.Ed.2d 628 (1974).

11. Marino v. Ragen, 332 U.S. 561, 68 S.Ct. 240, 92 L.Ed. 170 (1947) (concurring opinion).

noted in *Bartone v. United States*,[12] where "procedural snarls or obstacles preclude an effective state remedy * * *, federal courts have no other choice but to grant relief in collateral proceedings." A state remedy can also be rendered "ineffective" if there has been inordinate delay in the administration of that remedy. Of course, the fault for the delay must rest with the state rather than the petitioner.

Finally, the 1996 amendments added § 2254(b)(2), which provides: "An application for a writ of habeas corpus may be denied on the merits, notwithstanding the failure of the applicant to exhaust the remedies available in the courts of the State." This provision gives to habeas courts no greater authority to *grant* relief for unexhausted claims, but expressly authorizes them to *deny* relief by skipping the exhaustion analysis and rejecting a petitioner's claim on the merits.

Mixed petitions. Rose v. Lundy[13] presented the question of whether a federal habeas court had to dismiss a petition containing both exhausted and unexhausted claims or whether it could instead simply rule on those claims that were unexhausted. That issue, Justice O'Connor noted in her opinion for the Court, was to be resolved in light of the "policies underlying the statutory provision." Those policies, she concluded, required that the habeas court dismiss a mixed petition. This would leave the petitioner with the alternatives of either (1) returning to the state courts and exhausting all of his claims so they could then be presented together in a single petition or (2) dropping his unexhausted claims and filing a new petition containing only the exhausted claims. Justice Stevens in dissent argued that habeas court should adopt a more flexible rule that avoided delay, but the majority placed greater emphasis upon fulfilling what it viewed as the salutary objectives of the exhaustion doctrine.

Providing a "fair opportunity"—presenting the claim to the state courts. In order to provide the state with a fair opportunity to decide his claim, a petitioner must (1) present to the state courts a claim substantially equivalent to the claim he raises in his federal petition and (2) allow the state courts to complete their review of that claim.

As the Supreme Court noted in *Picard v. Connor*,[14] the exhaustion requirement "would serve no purpose if it could be satisfied by raising one claim in the state courts and another in the federal courts." A petitioner must present to the state court "the substance" of his claim in a manner sufficient to give that court "a fair opportunity" to rule upon it.[15] *Picard* itself illustrates a situation in which there was so much variation between the theories advanced before the state and federal courts that the state court never had "a fair opportunity" to rule on the contention raised in the federal courts. That case involved a state practice under which the grand jury originally indicted a named individual and a fictitious "John Doe," with the true name of the alleged accomplice then added by amendment following his arrest. Before the state courts, petitioner argued that amendment of the indictment to substitute his name for John Doe violated his right to be prosecuted only upon an indictment actually issued by the grand jury. On habeas review, the federal court held for petitioner but relied on a different theory. The amendment of the indictment did not violate due process since the state had no constitutional obligation to proceed by indictment; but once having granted the protection of a grand jury indictment to defendants generally, the state had denied petitioner equal protection by utilizing the John Doe indictment. The Supreme Court held that while the same facts were before both state and federal courts, the state court could not be expected to consider the equal protection claim sua sponte,

---

12. 375 U.S. 52, 84 S.Ct. 21, 11 L.Ed.2d 11 (1963).

13. 455 U.S. 509, 102 S.Ct. 1198, 71 L.Ed.2d 379 (1982).

14. 404 U.S. 270, 92 S.Ct. 509, 30 L.Ed.2d 438 (1971).

15. See also Keeney v. Tamayo–Reyes, 504 U.S. 1, 112 S.Ct. 1715, 118 L.Ed.2d 318 (1992), stating, "Comity con-

cerns dictate that the requirement of exhaustion is not satisfied by the mere statement of a federal claim in state court. Just as the State must afford the petitioner a full and fair hearing on his federal claim, so must the petitioner afford the State a full and fair opportunity to address and resolve the claim on the merits."

and it had not been raised in any fashion before the state courts. While a claim could be presented without citing "book and verse in the federal constitution," it could not be said that the original challenge in the state courts was the "substantial equivalent" of the unconstitutional discrimination claim.

In *Anderson v. Harless*,[16] *Duncan v. Henry*,[17] and *Gray v. Netherland*,[18] the Court reached similar conclusions. When the petitioner in *Anderson* challenged in the state courts a jury charge on "malice," he characterized the challenge as simply "erroneous" and cited a state case that referred only to a due process requirement that the jury instructions "properly explain" the law. This was not sufficient indication of the theory advanced in the federal courts that the charge created a mandatory presumption contrary to the prosecution's constitutional obligation to prove guilt beyond a reasonable doubt. In *Duncan*, the Court concluded that arguing a claim raised under state law does not satisfy the exhaustion requirement because the claim must be clearly identified as one made under federal law and the "mere similarity of claims is insufficient to exhaust." So too, in *Gray*, the petitioner did not fairly present to the state courts his claim that the state misled him about evidence it intended to introduce, when he had referred in the state courts to a broad federal due process right and cited cases that forbid the use of secret testimony. The cases cited by petitioner in state court and those he later cited in federal court, the Court explained, "arise in widely differing contexts."

Just as different legal claims or claims originating in state law will not suffice as a fair presentation to the state court, neither will factual claims significantly different than those advanced in federal court. Where a petitioner presents newly discovered evidence "such as to place the case in a significantly different and stronger evidentiary posture than it was when the state courts considered it," that the petitioner must first give the

state courts an opportunity to consider the evidence.

Speaking to the second element of the state's fair opportunity to review a claim—allowing a state to complete its review—the Court held in *Brown v. Allen* that a petitioner need only give the state system a single opportunity to rule on his claim, and that a petitioner need not pursue collateral remedies in state court in addition to direct appeal. Ordinarily that opportunity must be extended to the highest reaches of the state judiciary, usually the state supreme court. In *O'Sullivan v. Boerckel*,[19] the Court held that a petitioner is required to invoke "one full round of the State's established appellate review process," but need not invoke "extraordinary remedies when those remedies are alternatives to the standard review process and where the state courts have not provided relief through those remedies in the past." When the state's appellate process includes discretionary review by the state supreme court, a petitioner must pursue this remedy before seeking relief in federal court.

(b) Time Limits for Filing Petitions. Although a petition with unexhausted claims is filed too early, a petition may also be filed too late. Prior to the enactment of the Antiterrorism and Effective Death Penalty Act in 1996, the only time limitation imposed on the filing of a habeas corpus petition was that flowing from the application of the doctrine of laches contained in Rule 9 of the Rules Governing Section 2254 Cases. Rule 9(a) provided that a petition may be dismissed if "the state has been prejudiced in its ability to respond to the petition by delay in filing unless the petitioner shows that it is based on grounds of which he could not have had knowledge by the exercise of reasonable diligence before the circumstances prejudicial to the state occurred." If the petition was not filed until many years after conviction, that was of no consequence, provided the state was unable to show that delay prejudiced its ability to respond to the

16. 459 U.S. 4, 103 S.Ct. 276, 74 L.Ed.2d 3 (1982).

17. 513 U.S. 364, 115 S.Ct. 887, 130 L.Ed.2d 865 (1995) (per curiam).

18. 518 U.S. 152, 116 S.Ct. 2074, 135 L.Ed.2d 457 (1996).

19. 526 U.S. 838, 119 S.Ct. 1728, 144 L.Ed.2d 1 (1999).

petition. Indeed, in *Lonchar v. Thomas*,[20] the Court held that a district court could not rely on general equitable principles—independent of those embodied in Rule 9(a)—to dismiss a death row inmate's first habeas petition on the ground that the inmate purposely delayed filing it.

The 1996 legislation included, for the first time, a specific time limitation for the filing of federal habeas petitions. New § 2244(d) now provides a one-year period for filing a habeas petition, running from the date on which the judgment challenged "became final by the conclusion of direct review or the expiration of the time for seeking such review," and excluding any period during which a properly filed collateral attack was pending before the state courts.[21] A later starting point is provided where: (1) state action in violation of the Constitution or other federal law impeded the timely filing of the habeas petition; (2) the petition relies on a constitutional right that was initially recognized by the Supreme Court after the date of finality and that also was held to be retroactive in application; or (3) the petition relies on a constitutional claim as to which the factual predicate could not have been discovered at the date of finality by the exercise of due diligence. These exceptions resemble other provisions added elsewhere to the habeas statute by the AEDPA.[22] Rule 9(a)'s discretionary authority has essentially been replaced by the more rigid limitations period adopted as part of the AEDPA.

The harsh effects of the new time limit have been tempered somewhat by lower court rulings. Due to the pro se petitioner's lack of control over the filing of documents, the petition will be deemed filed at the moment petitioner delivers it to prison officials for mailing to the district court. Lower courts have also interpreted the statute to allow for "equitable tolling" of the limitations period in extraordinary circumstances, despite the lack of any reference to such an exception in the statute itself.[23] As for the time at which the limitation period begins to run, the provision refers only to the "conclusion" of direct review. This language has been construed by lower courts as the date on which direct review is concluded in the Supreme Court or the expiration of time for seeking such review.[24]

(c) Claims Advanced in a Prior Petition. Under the current statute, as explained more fully below, a habeas petitioner may raise any given claim only once. This limitation is a significant departure from the common law rule that the doctrine of res judicata

---

20. 517 U.S. 314, 116 S.Ct. 1293, 134 L.Ed.2d 440 (1996).

21. See Carey v. Saffold, 536 U.S. 214, 122 S.Ct. 2134, 153 L.Ed.2d 260 (2002) (finding that so long as the state petition was filed in the state court within the time specified by state law, the federal limitations period did not run, noting that if a state would prefer that federal courts reach its prisoners' claims sooner, it need only change its own law); Duncan v. Walker, 533 U.S. 167, 121 S.Ct. 2120, 150 L.Ed.2d 251 (2001) (interpreting § 2244(d) to allowing tolling only for properly filed collateral attacks in state court, holding that an application for federal habeas review does not toll the limitations period, reasoning that this interpretation of the provision provides a powerful incentive to exhaust state remedies before turning to federal court, while at the same time limiting the harm to the interest in finality); Artuz v. Bennett, 531 U.S. 4, 121 S.Ct. 361, 148 L.Ed.2d 213 (2000) (limitations period is tolled so long as an application for state post conviction relief has been "delivered to, and accepted by the appropriate court officer for placement into the official record" and when "its delivery and acceptance are in compliance with the applicable laws and rules governing filings," such as "time limits" for delivery and filing fees).

22. See §§ 2244(b), discussed in § 28.5(c) and (d); 2254(e)(2), discussed in § 28.7(b). In Tyler v. Cain, 533 U.S. 656, 121 S.Ct. 2478, 150 L.Ed.2d 632 (2001), discussed in §§ 28.5(d), four justices in dissent noted that in order to avoid unfairness, § 2244(d)(1)(C) should be interpreted to permit the one-year period to run "from the time that the Court has 'made' the new rule retroactive, not from the time it initially recognized that new right." The majority did not address this issue.

23. In Duncan v. Walker, supra note 21, Justices Souter and Stevens expressed approval of the lower court's use of their equitable powers to toll the limitations period. Justice Souter suggested equitable tolling "could present a serious issue on facts different from those before us." Justice Stevens argued that nothing "in the text of legislative history of AEDPA, precludes a federal court from deeming the limitations period tolled for [a federal habeas] petition as a matter of equity." He reasoned that "federal courts may well conclude that Congress simply overlooked the class of petitioners whose timely filed habeas petitions remain pending in district court past the limitations period, only to be dismissed after the court belatedly realizes that one or more claims have not been exhausted."

24. See also Clay v. United States, 537 U.S. 522, 123 S.Ct. 1072, 155 L.Ed.2d 88 (2003) (construing when time limitations period begins for filing § 2255 application, and discussing similar issue for § 2254 petitioners).

did not apply to the rulings of the habeas court. Denied relief by one judge, a prisoner could simply turn to another, seeking the same relief on the same grounds. Although numerous explanations are plausible, the refusal of the common law to limit habeas applications through the doctrine of res judicata is most frequently attributed to the traditional absence of direct appellate review of writ denials. Accordingly, in *Salinger v. Loisel*,[25] a 1924 ruling, the Supreme Court concluded that, with appellate review long available in the federal system, a habeas court could give the rejection of a previous application such weight as it deemed appropriate in light of factors such as the "fullness of the consideration" given to the prior application.

The demise of this flexible approach was gradual. When the habeas statutes were revised in 1948, § 2244 provided that no federal habeas court was "required to entertain an application" by a federal or state prisoner if "the legality of the [the applicant's] detention has been determined * * * on a prior application for a writ of habeas corpus and the petition presents no new ground not theretofore presented and determined, and the judge * * * is satisfied that the ends of justice will not be served by such inquiry." The benchmark ruling on the application of this early statute is *Sanders v. United States*.[26] The Court in *Sanders* considered the two-pronged question: What weight, if any, should be given to a prior disposition where the habeas petition presents (1) the same ground advanced in the prior application or (2) a ground not previously advanced? The Court's answer to the second prong of this question is discussed in the next subsection. As to the first, the Court set forth the following standard:

> Controlling weight may be given to denial of a prior application for federal habeas corpus or § 2255 relief only if (1) the same ground

presented in the subsequent application was determined adversely to the applicant on the prior application, (2) the prior determination was on the merits, and (3) the ends of justice would not be served by reaching the merits of the subsequent application.

In 1966, Congress enacted former § 2244(b), essentially codifying the first two *Sanders* guidelines. It provided that a successive application "need not be entertained" unless the application alleges a "factual or other ground not adjudicated in the hearing of the earlier application." In *Kuhlmann v. Wilson*,[27] seven justices agreed that under this provision, the "ends of justice" standard could still serve as an appropriate point of reference for determining when that discretion should be exercised to consider a claim previously decided on its merits, but as to the content of that standard, the justices disagreed. Three justices argued for a standard like that adopted in *Sanders*, while a plurality of four justices construed an "ends of justice" more narrowly. They argued that the exception should be limited to circumstances in which the prisoner's interest in relitigation outweighed the "countervailing interests served by * * * finality," and to those situations in which the prisoner retains the most "powerful and legitimate interest in obtaining release from custody." This is present, the plurality reasoned, "only where the petitioner supplements his constitutional claim with a colorable showing of factual innocence."

The Antiterrorism and Effective Death Penalty Act of 1996 replaced the provision interpreted in *Kuhlmann* with a new § 2244(b)(1), which simply states: "A claim presented in second or successive habeas corpus application under section 2254 that was presented in a prior application shall be dismissed."[28] The new provision appears to impose an absolute bar to federal court review of previously raised claims. In particular, the statute removes the

---

25. 265 U.S. 224, 44 S.Ct. 519, 68 L.Ed. 989 (1924).

26. 373 U.S. 1, 83 S.Ct. 1068, 10 L.Ed.2d 148 (1963).

27. 477 U.S. 436, 106 S.Ct. 2616, 91 L.Ed.2d 364 (1986).

28. A return trip to federal court with the same claim following a dismissal for failure to exhaust is not "successive" under § 2244(b). Stewart v. Martinez–Villareal, 523

U.S. 637, 118 S.Ct. 1618, 140 L.Ed.2d 849 (1998). See also Slack v. McDaniel, 529 U.S. 473, 120 S.Ct. 1595, 146 L.Ed.2d 542 (2000) ("A petition filed after a mixed petition has been dismissed under *Rose v. Lundy*[, discussed in § 28.5(a), at note 13] before the district court adjudicated any claims is to be treated as 'any other first petition' and is not a second or successive petition.").

prior authority of federal courts to consider again a claim by a petitioner who could supplement his previously presented constitutional claim with a newly discovered evidence of "actual innocence."

Theoretically, if a claim in a successive petition was based on a Supreme Court decision that established a new rule of constitutional law falling within one of two exceptions recognized for retroactive application, it to might be considered a different "claim" subject to review under (b)(2), even when a similar claim (made prior to the declaration of the new rule) was raised in the earlier petition. Section 2244(b)(2), discussed below, allows a habeas court to consider a claim raised for the first time in a second or successive petition when that claim "relies on a new rule of constitutional law, made retroactive to cases on collateral review by the Supreme Court, that was previously unavailable."

(d) New Claims in Second or Successive Petitions. A new claim in a successive petition was treated prior to the 1996 amendments much like a claim that the petitioner failed to raise properly in state court. Even before the enactment of former § 2244 in 1966, the "abuse-of-the-writ doctrine" recognized that "the prisoner who on prior motion * * * has deliberately withheld a ground for relief need not be heard if he asserts that ground on a successive motion; his action is inequitable—an abuse of the remedy—and the court may in its discretion deny him a hearing."[29] In *Sanders*,[30] the Court furnished two illustrations of defense tactics that would constitute an abuse of writ. The first was the prisoner who "withholds one of two grounds for federal collateral relief at the time of filing his first application in the hope of being granted two hearings rather than one." The second was the situation in which "the prisoner deliberately abandons one of his grounds at the first hearing." *Sanders* noted, however, that the federal habeas court always had "the

duty" to "reach the merits" when the "ends of justice" so demand.

When Congress reframed the successive application provision in 1966, former § 2244 provided that the federal habeas court "need not entertain" a successive petition "unless the application alleges and is predicted on a factual or other ground not adjudicated on the hearing of the earlier application * * * and unless the court * * * is satisfied that the applicant has in the earlier application deliberately withheld the newly asserted ground or otherwise abused the writ." Rule 9(b) of the § 2254 Rules added that the habeas court may dismiss the application if it finds "the failure of the petitioner to assert those [new and different] grounds in a prior petition constituted an abuse of writ." These provisions were interpreted by the Court in *McCleskey v. Zant*.[31] The Court rejected the earlier requirement that state show the petitioner deliberately withheld a claim. Instead, it adopted the less generous cause-and-prejudice test, concluding that a "determination of inexcusable neglect in the abuse of writ context" would be assessed by reference to the "same standard used to determine whether to excuse procedural defaults." That standard was appropriate, the Court reasoned, because "[t]he doctrines of procedural default and abuse of writ implicate nearly identical concerns flowing from the significant costs of federal habeas review." Accordingly, a new claim would be barred unless the failure of the petitioner to have raised the claim in an earlier petition was justified under the cause-and-prejudice standard that excuses the failure to have raised a claim in the original state proceedings in accordance with state procedures. In addition, *McClesky* held that a new claim would be considered, notwithstanding the absence of excuse under the cause-and-prejudice standard, where necessary to "correct a miscarriage of justice." This would require a "colorable showing of factual innocence," as set forth in *Kuhlmann*[32] and in procedural default cases such as *Murray v.*

---

29. See Wong Doo v. United States, 265 U.S. 239, 44 S.Ct. 524, 68 L.Ed. 999 (1924); Price v. Johnston, 334 U.S. 266, 68 S.Ct. 1049, 92 L.Ed. 1356 (1948).

30. Supra note 26.

31. 499 U.S. 467, 111 S.Ct. 1454, 113 L.Ed.2d 517 (1991).

32. Supra note 27.

Carrier,[33] and thereby would provide " 'an additional safeguard against compelling an innocent man to suffer an unconstitutional loss of liberty.' "

The 1996 Antiterrorism and Effective Death Penalty Act replaced the § 2244(b) provision interpreted in *McCleskey* with a quite different provision on new claims. The new § 2244(b)(2) directs that a second or successive application[34] advancing a "claim" not presented in a prior application "shall be dismissed" unless one of two specified exceptions is found applicable.

The first exception, contained in § 2244(b)(2)(A), allows for review if the claim relies on a new rule of constitutional law, previously unavailable, that the Supreme Court has made retroactively applicable on collateral review. This standard would appear to take its content from *Teague v. Lane*, discussed in § 28.6(c)–(e), which bars federal courts from granting relief to state prisoners based on rules of law that were not already dictated by precedent at the time the state judgment became final, unless the new rule is one that either (1) protects a class of conduct from criminal punishment or a class of persons from capital punishment or (2) relates to the accuracy of the conviction and constitutes a watershed ruling that alters the bedrock procedural elements essential to the fairness of the proceeding. Notably, unlike *Teague*, which allowed lower courts to determine for themselves when a new rule must be applied retroactively pending consideration of retroactivity by the Supreme Court, the changes to the habeas statute adopted in 1996 limit the consideration of claims in successive petitions to new rules rendered retroactive "by the Supreme Court." In *Tyler v. Cain*,[35] the Court interpreted this provision to require a petitioner who brings a second or successive petition to identify a decision from the Court itself that holds that the new rule on which the petitioner relies is retroactively applicable to cases on collateral review. This avenue around the ban on successive petitions is available only to those petitioners who can point to a Supreme

Court holding that "necessarily dictate[s] retroactivity of the new rule." It is not sufficient to point to a decision that either 1) "establishes principles of retroactivity and leaves the application of those principles to lower courts," or 2) suggests in dictum that the new rule is retroactively applicable, the Court explained. The Court rejected Tyler's claim that this interpretation would have the effect of blocking relief entirely for petitioners seeking to raise a valid claim in a second petition, noting, "we do not have license to question" the decision of Congress to establish stringent procedural requirements for retroactive application of new rules.

The second exception, recognized in § 2244(b)(2)(B), allows for the review of certain successive claims based on newly discovered evidence. This exception has two requirements. The factual predicate for the new claim must be one that could not have been discovered previously through "due diligence." Second, the "facts underlying the claim, if proven and viewed in light of the evidence as a whole" must be "sufficient to establish by clear and convincing evidence that but for the constitutional error, no reasonable factfinder would have found the applicant guilty of the underlying offense." Section 2244(b)(2), then, is much narrower than the *Sykes/McClesky* formula that it superseded. *McClesky* allowed for review of a new claim with a showing of cause and prejudice or actual innocence. Under the new provision, only one type of situation other than a retroactively applied rule, discussed earlier, counts as cause. Only where the petitioner can demonstrate that he was unable with due diligence to discover the factual predicate for the new claim will his claim be considered. This may encompass many cases of state interference that would have qualified as "cause" under the former standards (*Brady* violations and the like). But many petitioners who would have been able to establish "cause" under the old standard can no longer demonstrate under the new standard that the factual

---

33. Discussed in § 28.4.

34. On the meaning of second or successive application, see note 28.

35. 533 U.S. 656, 121 S.Ct. 2478, 150 L.Ed.2d 632 (2001).

predicate for their claims was previously undiscoverable. For example, the incompetence of trial or appellate counsel in failing to discover, or to recognize the significance of, certain facts, even if amounting to a denial of the right to the effective assistance of counsel, falls short of proof that the facts could not have been discovered by a duly diligent attorney and client.

Limiting the scope of the § 2244(b)(2) exception for claims in successive petitions even further is the requirement that a petitioner must also show that "the facts underlying the claim, if proven and viewed in light of the evidence as a whole, would be sufficient to establish by clear and convincing evidence that, but for constitutional error, no reasonable factfinder would have found the applicant guilty of the underlying offense." Several features of this innocence standard are notable. First, the showing of innocence required is more demanding than the showing mandated by the standard in *Schlup v. Delo*.[36] Section 2244(b)(2) imposes a clear and convincing evidence standard like that urged by the *Schlup* dissenters. Second, unlike the application of the fundamental miscarriage concept in *Sawyer v. Whitley*,[37] where the Court dealt with "actual innocence of the death penalty," the new provision permits relief only for petitioners who can show that no reasonable factfinder would have found the petitioner guilty of "the underlying offense," conceivably prohibiting successive claims challenging only a sentence.

The innocence test in § 2244(b)(2) also restricts the types of errors that may be reviewed under the exception to those that would affect a jury's assessment of guilt. Review of newly discovered errors that do not affect the factfinder's assessment of guilt, such as the introduction of evidence obtained in violation of the defendant's right to counsel, would presumably be barred. A claim based on newly discovered evidence that the petitioner's

jury venire was selected in violation of the Sixth or Fourteenth Amendments, or that the defendant was singled out for prosecution because of his race or gender, also would not qualify. Because a similar showing of effect on guilt—either "prejudice" or "actual innocence"—is required in order to obtain federal review of such a claim even in a first petition should the defendant fail to raise it in state court, a state could completely escape scrutiny of such errors by successfully secreting the facts that would prove the violation until after the petitioner's first habeas petition is filed. As mentioned earlier in the discussion of the actual innocence exception to the cause and prejudice analysis for claims defaulted in state court,[38] this scheme seems to assume that sufficient incentive to comply with these innocence-neutral constitutional requirements would be provided by scrutiny of the claims of defendants who manage to discover and effectively raise such claims while still in state court.

(e) The New "Gatekeeping" Provision. Another innovation of § 2244(b) is its subdivision (3) making the court of appeals the "gatekeeper" in applying the standards described above for second or successive petitions. Before filing a second or successive petition, the petitioner must seek from the court of appeals an order authorizing the district court to consider the second or successive petition. The new statute states that a three-judge panel must rule on whether the "application makes a prima facie showing" that it will satisfy the standard for filing a second or successive petition, and make that ruling within 30 days. Some courts of appeals have construed the 30-day limit to be "hortatory or advisory rather than mandatory," citing separation of powers concerns and the absence of any enforcement provision. While courts of appeals are understandably reluctant to bind themselves to demanding (or even unrealistic) deadlines, an

36. See § 28.4(g), discussing *Schlup*.

37. See § 28.4(g), discussing *Sawyer*.

38. See § 28.4(g). The Court has yet to decide which of the restrictions on successive petitions in § 2244 apply as well to petitions filed originally in the Supreme Court

under § 2241. See Felker v. Turpin, 518 U.S. 651, 116 S.Ct. 2333, 135 L.Ed.2d 827 (1996) (noting "whether or not we are bound by these restrictions they certainly inform our consideration of original habeas corpus petitions").

overly relaxed approach to the 30–day period may undercut Congressional efforts to streamline habeas proceedings.

Under the new statute, the panel's decision granting or denying the application is "not appealable" and "shall not be the subject of a petition for rehearing or for a writ of certiorari."[39] Thus, at this point, if the application is denied, the petitioner cannot seek further judicial action, apart from the extraordinary procedure recognized in *Felker v. Turpin*,[40] an original petition to the Supreme Court.

§ 28.6 Constitutional Interpretation on Habeas Review

(a) The Changing Role of Federal Habeas Courts. Both of the separate opinions for the Court in the 1953 decision *Brown v. Allen*[1] flatly rejected the contention that a state court's interpretation of the Constitution should be binding on the federal habeas court. *Brown* directed federal habeas courts to "independently apply the correct constitutional standards" to a petitioner's claim "no matter how fair and completely the claim had been litigated in state courts." The function of the 1867 Habeas Act, characterized by Justice Frankfurter, was to give to federal courts the "final say" on the merits of a state prisoner's federal constitutional claim. In exercising de novo review of constitutional questions, the federal habeas court was to give the state court's adjudication no more "weight" than what "federal practice [commonly] gives to the conclusion of a court of last resort of another jurisdiction on federal constitutional issues." Almost forty years after *Brown*, *Teague v. Lane*[2] substantially altered the nature of that "final say" given to the federal habeas courts. Following *Teague*, which barred retroactive application of new rules of constitutional law to habeas petitions, the task of the federal habeas court is not to ask how the Constitution should be interpreted now, but to ask

whether the state court's interpretation was a reasonable reading of the Supreme Court precedent prevailing when the opportunity for direct review of the prisoner's conviction ended.

The passage of the 1996 Act altered habeas review of state court decisions further still, as § 2254(d) now bars relief unless "the adjudication of the claim by the State court * * * resulted in a decision that was contrary to, or involved an unreasonable application of, clearly established Federal Law as determined by the Supreme Court of the United States * * *." This new standard for reviewing state court decisions appears to incorporate several aspects of the *Teague* inquiry, but it did not displace *Teague*. As the Court explained in *Horn v. Banks*,[3] "[T]he AEDPA and *Teague* inquiries are distinct * * *. [I]n addition to performing any analysis required by the AEDPA, a federal court considering a habeas petition must conduct a threshold *Teague* analysis when the issue is properly raised by the state." The meaning of § 2254(d) is discussed in subsection (g), following an analysis of *Teague* and its progeny.

(b) *Teague* and the Application of New Rules to State Convictions. The habeas petitioner in *Teague* raised a constitutional objection to the prosecutor's use of peremptory challenges to exclude African Americans from his jury. While his habeas petition was working its way through the federal appellate process, the Supreme Court decided *Batson v. Kentucky*,[4] which established an equal protection safeguard against racial discrimination in the use of peremptory challenges. The petitioner in *Teague* argued that *Batson* sustained his constitutional claim. He further argued that even if *Batson* decision had come too late for him to take advantage of the *Batson* ruling itself, a similar prohibition should be incorporated into the sixth amendment right to a jury venire selected from a fair cross-section of the

---

39. 28 U.S.C.A. § 2244(b)(3)(E).

40. Discussed in § 28.2(a).

§ 28.6

1. 344 U.S. 443, 73 S.Ct. 397, 97 L.Ed. 469 (1953).

2. 489 U.S. 288, 109 S.Ct. 1060, 103 L.Ed.2d 334 (1989).

3. 536 U.S. 266, 122 S.Ct. 2147, 153 L.Ed.2d 301 (2002).

4. See § 22.3.

community, a right that had been recognized several years prior to his conviction.

The issue addressed by the Court was whether a habeas petitioner could gain the benefit of a Supreme Court ruling that had come after the exhaustion of the direct appellate review of his conviction and had clearly expanded constitutional protection beyond what previous precedent had required. A majority agreed that, subject to certain exceptions, a habeas petitioner's conviction should be reviewed by reference to the "law prevailing at the time [his] conviction became final."

Justice O'Connor's plurality opinion derived this "law-at-the-time" principle from what was described as the "deterrence function" of the habeas writ. A central function of federal habeas review, it was argued, is ensuring that the state courts faithfully apply the prevailing "constitutional principles" as announced by the Supreme Court. Because the Supreme Court's docket limitations preclude its review of all but a small number of state court departures from prevailing constitutional principles, habeas review in the lower federal courts was needed to deter state courts from taking advantage of the likelihood that their departures from prevailing precedents would escape Supreme Court review. Federal habeas review was to "serve as a necessary incentive for trial and appellate judges * * * to conduct their proceedings in a manner consistent with established constitutional principles." Such a "deterrence function" requires only that the conviction be reviewed by reference to the law prevailing at the time of its final review in the state system. The state courts can hardly be required to have applied constitutional principles that did not yet exist. Hence, a federal habeas court, as a general principle, should not invalidate a conviction based upon a "new ruling" of constitutional law issued after state review had ended. The *Teague* plurality opinion recognized two exceptions to the "law-at-the-time" principle, which are discussed in subsection (e).

Unless the exceptions apply, a habeas petitioner could not obtain the benefit of either 1) a "new" Supreme Court ruling decided after his conviction became final, or 2) a "new" expansion of the protection established by preexisting precedent (i.e., the Supreme Court rulings prevailing at the time the conviction became final). As the Court stated later in *Stringer v. Black*,[5] "the interests in finality, predictability and comity underlying our new rule jurisprudence may be undermined [either] * * * by the invocation of a rule that was not dictated by precedent * * * [or by] the application of an old rule in a manner that was not dictated by precedent." Thus, the *Teague* Court, concluded that a habeas court could neither apply retroactively the *Batson* decision, which came after the defendant's conviction had become final, nor itself establish a new ruling by reading a similar prohibition into a series of sixth amendment cases that had been decided before the defendant's conviction became final.

Having subsequently applied *Teague* in a dozen different cases, the Court has distilled the "*Teague* inquiry" into "three steps."[6] Each of those steps will be explored in the following subsections. First, the habeas court must determine the date on which the petitioner's conviction became final. Second, the habeas court must consider "whether 'a state court considering [the petitioner's] claim at the time his conviction became final would have felt compelled by existing precedent to conclude that the rule [he] seeks was required by the Constitution.'"[7] If not, then the rule is new, and as a third step the "court must determine whether the rule nonetheless falls within one of the two narrow exceptions to the *Teague* doctrine." The Supreme Court also applies the *Teague* analysis as a "threshold matter" before reaching the merits of a petitioner's claim. However, because "the *Teague* inquiry requires a detailed analysis of federal constitutional law," and "[c]onstitutional is-

---

5. 503 U.S. 222, 112 S.Ct. 1130, 117 L.Ed.2d 367 (1992).

6. O'Dell v. Netherland, 521 U.S. 151, 117 S.Ct. 1969, 138 L.Ed.2d 351 (1997).

7. Id. (quoting Lambrix v. Singletary, 520 U.S. 518, 117 S.Ct. 1517, 137 L.Ed.2d 771 (1997)).

sues are generally to be avoided," the Court has suggested that normally a habeas court should first consider other prerequisites for habeas review, such as whether the petitioner is "in custody" or whether the state judgment was based on an independent and adequate state ground, before turning to the *Teague* analysis.[8]

(c) Determining When a State Conviction Becomes Final. A petitioner's state conviction is final only after the time for filing a petition for certiorari from the state judgment affirming the conviction has expired, or after the Court has denied certiorari.[9] This point in time is arguably inconsistent with the deterrence rationale of *Teague*, since the opportunity of the state courts to evade federal law normally ends prior to the time defendant seeks certiorari review in the United States Supreme Court. The assumption may be that if certiorari were sought, the Court could remand the case to the state court for reconsideration in light of its new rule, so that the state appellate court would have an opportunity to apply any new ruling handed down between the time of its decision and the Supreme Court's disposal of a petition for certiorari. Even where the defense fails to seek certiorari the defendant is likely to have had a chance to petition the state court for a rehearing prior to the exhaustion of the time period for filing for certiorari.

(d) The "New Rule" Concept. The second step in applying *Teague* is the determination of whether the rule on which the petitioner relies is a "new" rule of criminal procedure, given precedent at the time the conviction became final.[10] Speaking for a plurality in *Teague*, Justice O'Connor advanced a broad definition of a new ruling that was later extended to include applications of prior prece-

dent that would not have been classified as new rulings under the Supreme Court's previous retroactivity decisions. She acknowledged that it was "often difficult to determine when a case announces a new rule," and declined to "attempt to define the spectrum of what may or may not constitute a new rule" for retroactivity purposes. She added, however, that

> in general * * * a case announces a new rule when it breaks new ground or imposes a new obligation on the States or the Federal Government. See e.g., *Rock v. Arkansas*,[11] (per se rule excluding all hypnotically refreshed testimony infringes impermissibly on a criminal defendant's right to testify on his behalf); *Ford v. Wainwright*,[12] (Eighth Amendment prohibits the execution of prisoners who are insane). To put it differently, a case announces a new rule if the result was not dictated by precedent existing at the time the defendant's conviction became final.

Because *Rock* and *Ford* were quite expansive interpretations of past precedents, as was the ruling petitioner sought to gain in *Teague*, it was far from clear as to how literally lower courts should read Justice O'Connor's reference to a result "not dictated" by precedent. In *Penry v. Lynaugh*[13] the Court suggested that what was "dictated" should not be read too narrowly, and that it would include the application of the logic of the earlier precedent to an analogous situation. The case involved a petitioner's challenge that the Texas capital sentencing scheme unconstitutionally limited the jury's consideration of mitigating evidence. Justice O'Connor, speaking for the *Penry* majority, concluded that upholding petitioner's challenge did not demand a new rule as it "merely asked the State to fulfill the assur-

---

8. Lambrix v. Singletary, supra note 7.

9. See Sawyer v. Smith, 497 U.S. 227, 232, 110 S.Ct. 2822, 2826, 111 L.Ed.2d 193 (1990); Saffle v. Parks, 494 U.S. 484, 110 S.Ct. 1257, 108 L.Ed.2d 415 (1990).

10. The Court in Bousley v. United States, discussed in § 21.4(c), and in § 28.4(g), explained that *Teague* bars only application of new rules of *procedure*, not interpretations of substantive law. "[D]ecisions of this Court holding that a substantive federal criminal statute does not reach certain conduct * * * necessarily carry a significant risk that a defendant stands convicted of 'an act that the law

does not make criminal.' * * * Accordingly, it would be inconsistent with the doctrinal underpinnings of habeas review to preclude petitioner from relying" on such a decision in a proceeding under § 2255.

11. See § 24.5(d), discussing *Rock*.

12. 477 U.S. 399, 106 S.Ct. 2595, 91 L.Ed.2d 335 (1986).

13. 492 U.S. 302, 109 S.Ct. 2934, 106 L.Ed.2d 256 (1989).

ances upon which [the Court's prior precedent] was based" by applying a general prohibition that was "clear" under earlier rulings. In *Stringer v. Black*[14] the Court held that the rule of *Clemons v. Mississippi*,[15] which applied a rule concerning invalid aggravating factors in death sentencing to "weighing" states, also was not "new" under *Teague*. The majority noted: "The purpose of the new rule doctrine is to validate reasonable interpretations of existing precedents. Reasonableness in this, as in many other contexts, is an objective standard, and the ultimate decision * * * [must be] based on an objective reading of the relevant cases."

More frequently, however, the Court has found that the rule advanced by a petitioner is new, precluding habeas relief. In *Butler v. McKellar*,[16] for example, the Court rejected the petitioner's claim that the rule upon which he relied fell within the "logical compass" of an earlier precedent and as a result was not a new rule. There had been a significant difference among the lower courts as to whether the rule advanced by the petitioner followed from that precedent, and that division of authority in itself provided proof that the state court in rejecting the rule had adopted a position "susceptible to debate among reasonable minds."

Two closely divided decisions by the Court in 1997 illustrate that the "new rule" concept of *Teague* continues to create difficult questions of application. In Lambrix v. Singletary[17] the majority characterized *Teague*'s holding this way: It was not enough that the rule sought to be applied by the habeas petitioner was "a reasonable interpretation of prior law—perhaps even the most reasonable one"; *Teague* asks "whether no other interpretation was reasonable." Applying this standard, the majority detailed three "reasonable" approaches that would have suggested a rule other than the one the petitioner advanced,

given the precedent at the time that his conviction became final. Four justices disagreed.

Similarly, in *O'Dell v. Netherland*,[18] the Court held that its decision in *Simmons v. South Carolina*,[19] which provided that a capital defendant should be permitted to inform his sentencing jury that he may be ineligible for parole, was a new rule for *Teague* purposes. The majority first reviewed the "complex" "legal landscape" present at the time the petitioner's conviction became final. One line of cases had protected the right of a capital defendant to introduce certain mitigating evidence at his sentencing hearing, specifically, evidence that he had behaved himself in prison and would not pose a danger if incarcerated. The majority found it significant that one of the cases relied upon by the petitioner "produced seven opinions, none for a majority of the Court," and noted that the holding of that case was that expressed by the justice who concurred on the narrowest grounds. The majority also disavowed the statement by the Court in the *Simmons* case itself that its decision was "compelled" by another earlier case, noting that this characterization failed to demonstrate that *Simmons* was not new under *Teague*. A competing line of cases, the majority argued, established the "general proposition that the States retained the prerogative to determine how much (if at all) juries would be informed about the postsentencing legal regime." Thus, "a reasonable jurist * * * would not have felt compelled to adopt the rule later set out in *Simmons*" and could have "drawn a distinction between information about a defendant" and information concerning "postsentencing legal eventualities." The majority explained, "*Teague* asks state court judges to judge reasonably, not presciently." The four dissenters protested that "our decision in *Simmons* applied a fundamental principle that is as old as the adversary system itself, and that

14. 503 U.S. 222, 112 S.Ct. 1130, 117 L.Ed.2d 367 (1992).

15. 494 U.S. 738, 110 S.Ct. 1441, 108 L.Ed.2d 725 (1990).

16. 494 U.S. 407, 110 S.Ct. 1212, 108 L.Ed.2d 347 (1990).

17. Supra note 7.

18. Supra note 6.

19. 512 U.S. 154, 114 S.Ct. 2187, 129 L.Ed.2d 133 (1994).

had been quite clearly articulated by the Court in two earlier opinions."

A habeas court's application of *Teague* necessarily lacks the precedential effect of other federal court pronouncements of constitutional law. Such a decision declares only whether a decision interpreting the Constitution, handed down months or years earlier by a state court, was "reasonable" at the time it was decided. The habeas court under *Teague* does not measure the state decision against either the current or the best interpretation of federal law. Nevertheless, a number of critics have accused the Supreme Court of using the *Teague* analysis as an indirect method of expressing its views on the merits of a constitutional question advanced in a habeas petition. A conclusion that a rule is "new" is sometimes interpreted by lower courts as tantamount to a decision by the Court that the Constitution does not include the rule, while a conclusion that a rule is not new signals the Court's approval of that interpretation of the Constitution on the merits.

(e) The *Teague* Exceptions. Two exceptions to the prohibition against applying new rules on habeas review were recognized in *Teague*. The justices relied upon arguments made by Justice Harlan in an earlier case that retroactive application should be permissible only as to two types of new rulings.

Rules establishing constitutionally protected conduct. In *Teague*, Justice O'Connor's plurality opinion and Justice Stevens's concurring opinion expressly approved of an exception for rulings that "place certain kinds of primary, private individual conduct beyond the power of the criminal law-making authority."[20] A prior example of such a rule was a holding that a statute creating an offense violated the self-incrimination privilege; all defendants previously convicted of that offense were entitled to the benefit of that new ruling.[21] Since *Teague*,

the Court has reserved this exception for rules that either "decriminalize a class of conduct" or "prohibit the imposition of capital punishment on a particular class of persons."[22] As a result, few rules have qualified.[23]

Rules of fundamental fairness protecting accuracy. The *Teague* plurality also argued that new rulings that implicate "fundamental fairness" by mandating procedures "central to an accurate determination of innocence or guilt" should be applied retroactively. This was consistent with a basic function of the habeas writ: "to assure that no man has been incarcerated under a procedure which creates an impermissibly large risk that the innocent will be convicted." Speaking for the plurality, Justice O'Connor stated in *Teague* that procedures "central to an accurate determination of innocence or guilt" were best illustrated by what Justice Stevens had once described as the "classic" grounds for habeas review—the mob-dominated trial, the knowing use of perjured testimony, and conviction based on a confession "extorted from defendant by brutal methods." The plurality opinion added that it seemed "unlikely that many such components of basic due process have yet to emerge."

Justices Stevens and Blackmun stated in *Teague* that they would retain this exception as described somewhat differently by Justice Harlan. Justice Harlan had described a second exception for decisions that establish a "watershed rule of criminal procedure," "implicit in the concept of ordered liberty." His formula did not necessarily include an innocence component, and referred to the basic "fundamental fairness" standard applied to define due process prior to the adoption of the selective incorporation doctrine.

Under either formula, the second *Teague* exception is quite restrictive. Holding out the Court's decision in *Gideon* as the "paradig-

---

20. Mackey v. United States, 401 U.S. 667, 91 S.Ct. 1160, 28 L.Ed.2d 404 (1971) (Harlan, J.).

21. See United States v. United States Coin and Currency, 401 U.S. 715, 91 S.Ct. 1041, 28 L.Ed.2d 434 (1971) (retroactive application of ruling that invalidated, on fifth amendment grounds, a forfeiture proceeding for money possessed by one who failed to comply with the wagering tax law).

22. Graham v. Collins, 506 U.S. 461, 477, 113 S.Ct. 892, 902, 122 L.Ed.2d 260 (1993).

23. See Penry v. Lynaugh, 492 U.S. 302, 109 S.Ct. 2934, 106 L.Ed.2d 256 (1989) (discussing rule barring execution of mentally ill defendant).

matic example of a watershed rule of criminal procedure," the Court has examined at least seven new rules of law against the second exception and found that none of them fits its narrow confines. Some rulings fail the requirement that they affect the accuracy of a criminal judgment. Consider, for example, the new ruling advanced by the petitioner in *Teague*— an innovative reading of the Sixth Amendment's cross-section requirement that would have provided a *Batson*-like prohibition against racially discriminatory use of peremptory challenges. Though a *Batson*-type rule might promote accuracy in a systemic sense, it did not necessarily affect accuracy in any particular case, and it therefore fell outside of *Teague*'s second exception.

Other new rules fail the exception because they are not sufficiently fundamental. In *Sawyer v. Smith*[24] the "new rule" in question was one prohibiting a prosecutorial closing argument which suggested that the ultimate responsibility for determining the appropriateness of the death penalty rested on the appellate court and thereby reduced the jury's sense of responsibility. This rule certainly was "aimed at improving the accuracy of the trial." It was not, however, a "watershed ruling" in this regard; it did not "alter our understanding of the *bedrock procedural elements* essential to the fairness of the proceeding." Rather it was a per se prohibition of a particular type of argument that served basically to supplement the traditional due process prohibition against closing arguments that "so infected the trial with unfairness" as to violate due process. Other rules rejected by the Court as insufficiently fundamental include: a rule providing to capital defendants jury instructions concerning "mitigating evidence of youth, family background, and positive character traits";[25] a rule barring jury instructions that do not warn the jury that it

could not find the defendant guilty of murder without even considering voluntary manslaughter;[26] a double jeopardy bar limiting successive noncapital sentencing proceedings;[27] and a rule that would have required notice of evidence to be used at sentencing.[28] None of these rules satisfied the two-pronged test requiring that the rule both "relate to the accuracy of the conviction" and "alter our understanding of the 'bedrock procedural elements' essential to the fundamental fairness of a proceeding."

In *Tyler v. Cain*,[29] the justices discussed at length the meaning of *Teague*'s second exception, without actually applying it. The case resolved the meaning of the words "made retroactive * * * by the Supreme Court" in the provision governing successive petitions. In the course of deciding that this language required the Court itself to "hold" that the new rule is retroactive, the Court explained that a decision holding that a rule falls within the second *Teague* exception is not the same as a decision holding that a rule is "structural error," not subject to harmless-error analysis. Specifically, the Court did not "ma[k]e" the rule in *Cage v. Louisiana*,[30] retroactive when it held in *Sullivan v. Louisiana*,[31] that *Cage* error is structural. "The standard for determining whether an error is structural * * * is not coextensive with the second *Teague* exception," the Court explained, noting that "[c]lassifying an error as structural does not necessarily alter our understanding of [the] bedrock procedural elements" essential to the fairness of the proceeding. "On the contrary, the second *Teague* exception is reserved only for truly 'watershed' rules" and "[a]s we have recognized, it is unlikely that any of these watershed rules 'ha[s] yet to emerge.'" Writing for four justices in dissent, Justice Breyer would not have decoupled "structural error" analysis from the test for the second exception under

---

24. Supra note 9.

25. Graham v. Collins, supra note 22.

26. Gilmore v. Taylor, 508 U.S. 333, 113 S.Ct. 2112, 124 L.Ed.2d 306 (1993).

27. Caspari v. Bohlen, 510 U.S. 383, 114 S.Ct. 948, 127 L.Ed.2d 236 (1994).

28. Gray v. Netherland, 518 U.S. 152, 116 S.Ct. 2074, 135 L.Ed.2d 457 (1996).

29. 533 U.S. 656, 121 S.Ct. 2478, 150 L.Ed.2d 632 (2001).

30. 498 U.S. 39, 111 S.Ct. 328, 112 L.Ed.2d 339 (1990).

31. 508 U.S. 275, 113 S.Ct. 2078, 124 L.Ed.2d 182 (1993).

Teague. He recognized that unlike rules identifying "structural error," rules that fit within the second exception must involve error that "undermines the accuracy" of the outcome, but argued that the Court in *Sullivan* had already emphasized that *Cage* error does just that. To be retroactively applicable, a new rule must also "alter our understanding" of the fundamental procedural elements essential to a fair trial, another requirement not necessary for structural error, Justice Breyer noted, but he observed that there was no dispute that *Cage's* rule was "new." The only way to "make" *Cage* retroactive, the dissenters protested, "is to repeat [the] *Sullivan* reasoning in a case triggered by a prisoner's filing a first habeas petition or in some other case that presents the issue in a posture that allows such language to have the status of a holding," a process they found "unnecessarily complex and wasteful."

Lower courts also have rejected arguments to bring within the second exception many additional procedural rules, including that established by *Ake v. Oklahoma*[32] regarding an indigent capital defendant's due process right to the assistance of a psychiatric expert in cases of insanity. Among those very few new rulings that lower courts have held do qualify for the second exception are the requirement of a proper instruction on reasonable doubt, the prohibition against requiring unanimity for findings of mitigating circumstances in death cases, and the duty to advise a defendant of the risks of proceeding without counsel.

(f) Review of State Court Decisions After the 1996 Amendments. Section 2254(d) now provides:

An application for a writ of habeas corpus on behalf of a person in custody pursuant to the judgment of a State court shall not be granted with respect to any claim that was adjudicated on the merits in State court proceedings unless the adjudication of the claim

(1) resulted in a decision that was contrary to, or involved an unreasonable application of, clearly established Federal law, as determined by the Supreme Court of the United States; or

(2) resulted in a decision that was based on an unreasonable determination of the facts in light of the evidence presented in the State court proceeding.

New § 2254(d)(2), governing the review of state determinations of fact, will be discussed in § 28.7(b) and (c). New § 2254(d)(1), governing the review of state determination and applications of law, is discussed below. Both provisions govern petitions which were filed after the effective date of the Act—April 24, 1996.[33] The inquiry under § 2254(d) did not displace *Teague*; relief will only be available for those petitioners who are able to meet the requirements of both § 2254(d) and *Teague*.[34]

Standards for reviewing state court determinations and applications of law. Section 2254(d)(1) states that federal courts may grant habeas relief only when the state decision is "contrary to, or involved an unreasonable application of, clearly established Federal law as determined by the Supreme Court of the United States." Interpreting this provision in *(Terry) Williams v. Taylor*,[35] the Court held that under "the 'contrary to' clause, a federal habe-

---

32. See § 11.2(e).

33. See Lindh v. Murphy, 521 U.S. 320, 117 S.Ct. 2059, 138 L.Ed.2d 481 (1997) (holding that the 1996 amendments apply only to petitions filed after the effective date of the Act).

34. Horn v. Banks, 536 U.S. 266, 122 S.Ct. 2147, 153 L.Ed.2d 301 (2002). See also Stewart v. LaGrand, 526 U.S. 115, 119 S.Ct. 1018, 143 L.Ed.2d 196 (1999), where the Court rejected the petitioner's claim that execution by lethal gas was cruel and unusual. The Court's reference to *Teague*, in its entirety, read: "To hold otherwise, and to hold that the Eighth Amendment protections cannot be waived in the capital context, would create and apply a new procedural rule in violation of *Teague v. Lane*.* * * ."

In Breard v. Greene, 523 U.S. 371, 118 S.Ct. 1352, 140 L.Ed.2d 529 (1998), the Court considered the petition of a foreign national who argued that his conviction was in violation of the Vienna Convention on Consular Relations. In holding that the claim had been procedurally defaulted, the Court noted that even assuming that petitioner could qualify for an evidentiary hearing under § 2254(a) and (e)(2) due to the novelty of his claims under the Vienna Convention, "such novel claims would be barred on habeas review under *Teague v. Lane*."

35. 529 U.S. 362, 120 S.Ct. 1495, 146 L.Ed.2d 389 (2000).

as court may grant the writ if the state court arrives at a conclusion opposite to that reached by this Court on a question of law or if the state court decides a case differently than this Court has on a set of materially indistinguishable facts." The "unreasonable application" clause limits relief to cases in which "the state court identifies the correct governing legal principle from this court's decision but unreasonably applies that principle to the facts of the prisoner's case." The inquiry into reasonableness is objective, and does not turn on whether "one of the Nation's jurists has applied the relevant federal law in the same manner the state court did in the habeas petitioner's case." Furthermore, stated the Court, drawing upon the discussion in *Wright v. West*,[36] "an unreasonable application of federal law is different from an incorrect application of federal law." It is not enough that a state court decision applying federal law was erroneous, "that application must also be unreasonable." Later, in *Bell v. Cone*,[37] the Court emphasized that for a defendant to succeed in challenging a state court's rejection of his ineffectiveness of counsel claim, "he must do more than show that he would have satisfied *Strickland*'s test if his claim were being analyzed in the first instance, * * * [r]ather he must show that the [state court] applied *Strickland* to the facts of his case in an objectively unreasonable manner."[38]

Six justices in *Williams* agreed that the state court decision in that case was "both contrary to and involved an unreasonable application of this Court's clearly established precedent." First, the Virginia Supreme Court misinterpreted the Court's decision in *Strickland*,[39] erroneously assuming that a later decision of the

Court had modified the test for prejudice to require more than "mere outcome determination." Second, because it failed to "consider the totality of the omitted mitigation evidence," the state court unreasonably applied *Strickland* to Williams' case when it found that the grossly deficient performance did not prejudice Williams.[40]

The Court applied this analysis to two separate state-court rulings the next term in *Penry v. Johnson (Penry II)*.[41] First, the Court found objectively reasonable (as well as harmless, even if error) a Texas court's decision that *Estelle v. Smith*,[42] barring the government from introducing in a capital sentencing proceeding a psychiatrist's opinion regarding future dangerousness, did not prohibit admission into Penry's sentencing hearing of a psychiatric evaluation prepared for a competency hearing in an unrelated case prior to the charged offense. The Court noted many grounds on which the state court acted reasonably in distinguishing *Estelle*: Penry, unlike the defendant in *Estelle*, had placed his mental condition in issue; Penry's own counsel, albeit his former counsel, had requested the examination and psychiatrist, whereas the examination in *Estelle* had ordered the examination and picked the doctor; the evidence was introduced during cross examination of Penry's expert witness, unlike in *Estelle* where the government introduced the predictions of dangerousness as part of its affirmative case for a death sentence; and finally, "in *Estelle,* the defendant was charged with a capital crime at the time of his competency exam, and it was thus clear that his future dangerousness would be a specific issue at sentencing," while Penry "had not yet murdered" the victim at the time of

---

36. 505 U.S. 277, 112 S.Ct. 2482, 120 L.Ed.2d 225 (1992).

37. 535 U.S. 685, 122 S.Ct. 1843, 152 L.Ed.2d 914 (2002).

38. See also § 11.10(d), discussing *Cone*.

39. Discussed in § 11.7(c).

40. See also Wiggins v. Smith, 539 510, 123 S.Ct. 2527, 156 L.Ed.2d 471 (2003) (state court's decision upholding death sentence was an unreasonable application of *Strickland*); Price v. Vincent, 538 U.S. 634, 123 S.Ct. 1848, 155 L.Ed.2d 877 (2003) (concluding, "Even if we agreed * * * that the Double Jeopardy Clause should be read to prevent continued prosecution of a defendant" under the circum-

stances in this case," it was at least reasonable for the state court to conclude otherwise."); Lockyer v. Andrade, 538 U.S. 63, 123 S.Ct. 1166, 155 L.Ed.2d 144 (2003) (finding, 5:4, that the state court's decision to reject an offender's eighth amendment challenge to his sentence of two consecutive 25–to–life terms for petty theft was an objectively reasonable application of clearly established law).

41. 532 U.S. 782, 121 S.Ct. 1910, 150 L.Ed.2d 9 (2001).

42. 451 U.S. 454, 101 S.Ct. 1866, 68 L.Ed.2d 359 (1981).

his interview. Second, a majority of justices in *Penry II* went on to find objectively *un*reasonable the state court's decision to uphold the death sentence despite a faulty instruction on mitigating evidence. The majority concluded that the state courts had not complied with the Court's earlier ruling in the same case, twelve years earlier, in *Penry I*, when it had vacated Penry's death sentence due to the same faulty instructions.

*"Clearly established * * * by the Supreme Court."* The language "clearly established Federal law, as determined by the Supreme Court of the United States," was interpreted in *Williams* as restricting "the source of clearly established law to this Court's jurisprudence." The provision refers to "the holdings, as opposed to the dicta, of this Court's decisions as of the time of the relevant state-court decision." Except for this one change, under the new statute "whatever would qualify as an old rule under our *Teague* jurisprudence will constitute 'clearly established Federal law, as determined by the Supreme Court of the United States.' "[43]

§ 28.7 Factfinding and Evidentiary Hearings

(a) The Special Status of State Factfinding. According to the Court in *Brown v. Allen*,[1] a federal habeas court could, in most circumstances, rely upon state court findings of historical fact rather than conduct its own independent factfinding. Nevertheless, as Justice Reed noted, the habeas court had the power to retry the facts. "Where there is material conflict of fact in the [state] transcripts of evidence as to deprivation of constitutional rights, the [habeas court] may properly depend upon the state's resolution" in the absence of "unusual circumstances calling for a hearing." Similarly, Justice Frankfurter stated that the habeas court could rely upon the state court's determination of adjudicated factual issues "unless a vital flaw be found in the [state's] process of ascertaining such facts."

The justices did not explain why federal courts were permitted to accept the state court's determination of fact but not its determination of the legal consequences of those facts. The statute at the time suggested no distinction between factual and legal determinations, and one might have argued that the protection of a federal claim in a federal forum required independent assessment of the facts as well as the law. However, the distinction has been justified on several grounds. It has been argued that there is less need for independent federal factfinding because judicial loyalty to state institutional interests is more likely to influence a state judge's application of constitutional standards than it is to impair the accuracy of that judge's fact-finding process. Also, any value that federal procedures and federal judges would bring to the accuracy of the factfinding process is, arguably, more than offset by the advantage the state court has in hearing testimony soon after the events in question occurred. Finally, independent federal factfinding exacerbates many of the costs of habeas review, substantially extending the call on scarce federal judicial resources and increasing the friction between state and federal courts.

Today, the distinction between the habeas court's review of the state court's factual and legal determinations is not as stark as it was in *Brown*. As discussed in § 28.6(g), § 2254(d) as amended in 1996 requires a certain amount of deference to the legal as well as factual determinations of state courts. Still, differences in reviewing the two types of decisions persist.

The present rules regarding federal review of state court fact-finding and the provision of evidentiary hearings in federal habeas proceedings have evolved from a 1963 decision, *Townsend v. Sain*.[2] In *Townsend*, the Court addressed the question when a petitioner was entitled to an evidentiary hearing and concluded that a habeas court must hold an evidentia-

---

43. See § 28.6 (b)–(e).

§ 28.7

1. 344 U.S. 443, 73 S.Ct. 397, 97 L.Ed. 469 (1953).

2. 372 U.S. 293, 83 S.Ct. 745, 9 L.Ed.2d 770 (1963).

ry hearing if the habeas applicant did not receive a "full and fair" evidentiary hearing in a state court, either at the time of trial or in a collateral proceeding. Specifically, the Court explained, a hearing was required if:

(1) the merits of the factual dispute were not resolved in the state hearing; (2) the state factual determination is not fairly supported by the record as a whole; (3) the fact-finding procedure employed by the state court was not adequate to afford a full and fair hearing; (4) there is a substantial allegation of newly discovered evidence; (5) the material facts were not adequately developed at the state court hearing; or (6) for any reason it appears that the state trier of fact did not afford the habeas applicant a full and fair hearing.

Former § 2254(d), enacted in 1966 to regulate fact-finding in habeas proceedings, appeared to track much of *Townsend*. The 1996 Act, however, substantially altered the treatment of state fact-finding in habeas proceedings. Because at least some of the prior doctrine that was developed under *Townsend* and former § 2254(d) may inform the meaning of the new provisions and continue to apply in proceedings under § 2255, that doctrine will be examined in the sections that follow.

(b) Factual Default: When the Relevant Facts Were Not Developed in State Court. Under former § 2254(d), a petitioner's failure to develop facts in state court would require a federal hearing only in limited circumstances, explained the Court in *Keeney v. Tamayo–Reyes*.[3] In *Keeney,* the Court applied to a petitioner's failure to develop facts the standards it had adopted for a petitioner's failure raise a claim in accordance with state procedure. Absent a showing of actual innocence, only those petitioners who could show "cause" for and "prejudice" from their failure to develop facts adequately in state court were entitled to an opportunity to develop those facts in federal court.

The AEDPA narrowed even further a petitioner's access to evidentiary hearings in fed-eral court when facts had not been developed in state court. As amended, § 2254(e)(2) states that the federal habeas court shall not hold an evidentiary hearing on a claim as to which there was "a failure to develop the factual basis" in state court proceedings, unless that claim rests on either (1) an intervening new rule held to apply retroactively, *or* (2) a factual predicate not previously discoverable with due diligence, *and* the facts underlying the claim would be sufficient to "establish by clear and convincing evidence that but for the constitutional error, no reasonable factfinder would have found the applicant guilty of the underlying offense."

In *(Michael) Williams v. Taylor,*[4] the Court construed this provision to govern only cases in which the failure to develop in state court the factual basis of a claim was due to some fault of the petitioner or his counsel. The opening clause of this provision—"failure to develop"—the Court concluded, requires "lack of diligence or some greater fault, attributable to the prisoner or to the prisoner's counsel." If a claim had been "pursued with diligence but remained undeveloped in state court because, for instance, the prosecution concealed the facts, a prisoner lacking clear and convincing evidence of innocence could be barred from a hearing on the claim even if he could satisfy § 2254(d) * * * [The clause] does not bear this harsh reading." "Diligence for purpose of the opening clause depends upon whether the prisoner made a reasonable attempt, in light of the information available at the time, to investigate and pursue claims in state court; it does not depend * * * upon whether those efforts could have been successful." Diligence, the Court continued, "will require in the usual case that the prisoner, at a minimum, seek an evidentiary hearing in state court in the manner prescribed by state law." If petitioner shows that he had been diligent, an evidentiary hearing is not barred by § 2254(e).

Applying this provision in *Williams,* the Court found that Williams was diligent in his efforts to develop the facts supporting his juror

---

3.   504 U.S. 1, 112 S.Ct. 1715, 118 L.Ed.2d 318 (1992).

4.   529 U.S. 420, 120 S.Ct. 1479, 146 L.Ed.2d 435 (2000).

bias and prosecutorial misconduct claims in state court. The facts supporting juror bias were not revealed during state proceedings because the allegedly biased juror's answers to questions posed to her by the court and counsel during voir dire were misleading, and because the prosecutor had "completely forgotten" his earlier legal representation of the juror in her divorce from the state's witness. "Defense counsel had no reason to believe" that the juror had been married to the state's witness or been represented by the prosecutor. The "standards of trial practice" did not require "counsel to check public records containing personal information pertaining to each and every juror."

Williams had not been diligent, ruled the Court, in developing the basis for his *Brady* claim in state court. Petitioner's state habeas counsel had notice of the existence and materiality of the psychiatric report in question, but made no effort to find the report other than a making a general request for all psychological tests. "Given knowledge of the report's existence and potential importance, a diligent attorney would have done more." Because he was not diligent in developing the factual basis for this claim, an evidentiary hearing on the claim was unavailable unless the stringent requirements of § 2254(e) were met.

Under these requirements, a petitioner must first show that "the legal or factual basis of the claims did not exist at the time of the state court proceedings," a demonstration he could make either by showing that his claim was based on a "new rule of constitutional law" not available at the time of the earlier proceedings (§ 2254(e)(2)(A)(i)) or by showing that had he exercised due diligence, "the factual predicate could not have been discovered" (§ 2254(e)(2)(A)(ii)).

Second, § 2254(e)(2)(B) requires a petitioner seeking to develop facts undeveloped in state court to show prejudice—that the new facts, if proven, "would be sufficient to establish be clear and convincing evidence" that "no reasonable factfinder would have found the [petitioner] guilty of the underlying offense" if the

constitutional error had not occurred. This provision specifically codifies the Supreme Court's definition of actual innocence announced in *Sawyer v. Whitley*,[5] and the later limitation placed on that definition in the dissent in *Schlup v. Delo*.[6]

The term "offense" in the passage "but for the constitutional error, no reasonable factfinder would have found the applicant guilty of the underlying offense" has troubled courts interpreting § 2254(e)(2)(B) in the same way that it has divided courts interpreting the same phrase in § 2244. If offense is interpreted to refer only to the crime and not to the penalty, then the statute would seem to bar evidentiary hearings in cases of factual default in state court when a petitioner can show only "innocence of the death penalty," and not innocence of the underlying crime. In *Williams*, the petitioner conceded he could not show "by clear and convincing evidence, that no reasonable factfinder would have found [him] guilty of capital murder but for" the *Brady* error.

(c) Presuming the Correctness of State Court Determinations of Fact. Former § 2254(d) provided that "a determination after a hearing on the merits of a factual dispute made by a state court of competent jurisdiction * * * evidenced by * * * reliable and adequate written indicia * * * shall be presumed to be correct," unless the habeas court finds that one of eight conditions are present. Those conditions were:

(1) that the merits of the factual dispute were not resolved in the State court hearing; (2) that the factfinding procedure employed by the State court was not adequate to afford a full and fair hearing; (3) that the material facts were not adequately developed at the State court hearing; (4) that the State court lacked jurisdiction of the subject matter or over the person of the applicant in the State court proceeding; (5) that the applicant was an indigent and the State court, in deprivation of his constitutional right, failed to appoint counsel to represent him in

---

5. Discussed in § 28.4(g).

6. Discussed in § 28.4(g).

the State court proceeding; (6) that the applicant did not receive a full, fair, and adequate hearing in the State court proceeding; or (7) that the applicant was otherwise denied due process of law in the State court proceeding; (8) or unless that part of the record of the State court proceeding in which the determination of such factual issue was made, pertinent to a determination of the sufficiency of the evidence to support such factual determination, is produced as provided for hereinafter, and the Federal court on a consideration of such part of the record as a whole concludes that such factual determination is not fairly supported by the record.

According to the former statute, upon "due proof" of a state finding of fact not exempted by any of these conditions, the "burden shall rest upon the applicant to establish by convincing evidence that the factual determination by the State court was erroneous." Following the enactment of this language, the Supreme Court applied it repeatedly[7] finding that the presumption of correctness applies to factual determinations by state appellate courts as well as trial courts, and that the presumption does not allow a federal court to substitute its own judgments as to the credibility of witnesses.

The Antiterrorism and Effective Death Penalty Act carried forward the presumption that state court findings of fact are correct, but replaced former § 2254(d) with two provisions: § 2254(d)(2) and § 2254(e)(1). New § 2254(e)(1) provides that "a determination of a factual issue by a State court shall be presumed to be correct," with the petitioner having the "burden of rebutting the presumption of correctness by clear and convincing evidence." New § 2254(d)(2) provides that relief shall not be granted for any claim adjudicated on the merits in state court unless the state decision "was based on an unreasonable deter-

mination of the facts in light of the evidence presented in the state court proceeding."

Neither provision references the eight procedural deficiencies cited in the former statute that rendered the presumption inapplicable. This could mean that the presumption of correctness now applies without regard to the presence or absence of these conditions. Alternatively, the statute may be read as replacing the explicit procedural requirements of former § 2254(d) with the reasonableness requirement in new § 2254(d)(2). If so, a federal court must still examine the state court's factual determinations for procedural regularity.

Although the relationship of the two sections is not clear, one can read § 2254(e)(1) as providing the standard by which a petitioner must demonstrate that any state finding of fact is unreasonable under § 2254(d)(2). In other words, a state finding can be deemed unreasonable under § 2254(d)(2) only if the petitioner manages to show clear and convincing evidence that the state court acted unreasonably.

(d) Distinguishing Mixed Determinations of Law and Fact from FactFinding. The rules governing state court findings of fact in the former § 2254(d) applied only to a state court's determination of "historic fact" as opposed to "a mixed determination of law and fact that requires the application of legal principles to the historical facts."[8] The 1996 amendments appear to maintain this distinction, using essentially the same language: "determination of a factual issue" compared to "determination of the facts" under prior law. Thus, the reach of the presumption of correctness contained in new § 2254(e)(1), like the presumption under its predecessor, former § 2254(d), seems to be limited to pure questions of historical fact.

The Court has not always found the distinction between a "factual" and a "mixed" determination easy to apply. Its rulings in the *Sumner v. Mata*[9] litigation are illustrative. In *Mata*,

7. LaVallee v. Delle Rose, 410 U.S. 690, 93 S.Ct. 1203, 35 L.Ed.2d 637 (1973);Maggio v. Fulford, 462 U.S. 111, 103 S.Ct. 2261, 76 L.Ed.2d 794 (1983); Marshall v. Lonberger, 459 U.S. 422, 103 S.Ct. 843, 74 L.Ed.2d 646 (1983); Sumner v. Mata, 449 U.S. 539, 101 S.Ct. 764, 66 L.Ed.2d 722 (1981).

8. Cuyler v. Sullivan, 446 U.S. 335, 100 S.Ct. 1708, 64 L.Ed.2d 333 (1980).

9. Supra note 7.

the Court divided sharply over whether state court findings concerning the admission of a pretrial photo-identification were limited to historic fact. The state court had held there was no showing that the witnesses had been "influenced" by the investigating officer, that the witnesses had an "adequate opportunity" to view the crime, and that their initial descriptions of the assailant were "accurate." The habeas court, holding that the photo-identification was impermissibly suggestive, concluded that the circumstances surrounding the witnesses's observation of the crime were suspect, that the witnesses had failed to give sufficiently detailed initial descriptions, and that "considerable pressure" had been brought to bear on them. After the Supreme Court first remanded the case to the habeas court for an explanation as to why it had not applied former § 2254(d), the habeas court responded that the section did not apply since its rulings dealt with mixed questions of fact and law. Reviewing the case again, the Supreme Court held in *Mata II*[10] that the lower court had erred. The Court agreed that "the ultimate question as to the constitutionality of the pretrial identification procedures used in this case is a mixed question of law and fact that is not governed by § 2254." But, the Court went on, "the questions of fact that underlie this ultimate conclusion," including whether the witnesses "had an opportunity to observe the crime or were too distracted; whether the witnesses gave a detailed, accurate description; and whether the witnesses were under pressure" were "questions of fact as to which the statutory presumption applies."

A series of Supreme Court rulings after *Mata*, each considering the appropriate treatment of state trial court rulings relating to juror prejudice, also applied the distinction between mixed findings and purely factual findings. In *Patton v. Yount*,[11] the presumption of correctness did not apply to a state court's finding as to whether prejudicial publicity had made a fair trial impossible, but it did apply to the finding, based on a juror's responses on voir dire, that the individual juror was not biased. Similarly, *Rushen v. Spain*[12] held that former § 2254(d) was applicable to a finding that a juror's ex parte communication with the judge had no bearing on the juror's impartiality, and in *Wainwright v. Witt*[13] the Court applied former § 2254(d) to a finding that a prospective juror's opposition to capital punishment would substantially impair her ability to comply with the trial court's instructions.

Recognizing the sharp division within the Court, Justice O'Connor in *Miller v. Fenton*[14] sought to explain why the "appropriate methodology for distinguishing questions of fact from questions of law has been, to say the least, elusive." She noted there that the Court's "difficulty" may stem "from the practical truth that the decision to label an issue a 'question of law,' a 'question of fact' or a 'mixed question of law and fact' is sometimes as much a matter of allocation as it is of analysis. * * * At least in those instances in which Congress has not spoken and in which the issue falls somewhere between a pristine legal standard and a simple historical fact, the fact/law distinction at times has turned on a determination that, as a matter of the sound administration of justice, one judicial actor is better positioned than another to decide the issue in question." Justice O'Connor cited earlier cases that had held the "voluntariness" of a confession to be "a legal question requiring independent federal determination," and noted that "on rare occasions in years past the Court has justified independent federal or appellate review as a means of compensating for 'perceived shortcomings of the trier of fact by way of bias or some other factor.'" As an example of a setting in which these considerations led to the opposite conclusion, Justice O'Connor cited the prejudiced juror cases. Where, as in those cases, "the issue involves the credibility of witnesses and therefore turns

10. Sumner v. Mata, 455 U.S. 591, 102 S.Ct. 1303, 71 L.Ed.2d 480 (1982).

11. 467 U.S. 1025, 104 S.Ct. 2885, 81 L.Ed.2d 847 (1984).

12. 464 U.S. 114, 104 S.Ct. 453, 78 L.Ed.2d 267 (1983).

13. 469 U.S. 412, 105 S.Ct. 844, 83 L.Ed.2d 841 (1985).

14. 474 U.S. 104, 106 S.Ct. 445, 88 L.Ed.2d 405 (1985).

largely on an evaluation of demeanor," the process of "applying law to fact" was appropriately left to the trial court "according its determinations presumptive weight."

The ruling in *Miller v. Fenton* itself reflected the broad range of factors that may enter into the characterization of a particular issue as one within or without the presumption of correctness. The Court there held that the voluntariness of a confession was a "legal inquiry requiring plenary federal review." "Subsidiary factual questions," such as whether a drug had certain properties or whether the police used certain interrogation tactics, are considered questions of fact alone, but not the "ultimate question whether, under the totality of the circumstances, the challenged confession was obtained in a manner compatible with the requirements of the Constitution." Voluntariness was held in *Miller* to be an issue beyond the presumption of correctness due to the combined influence of *stare decisis*, congressional intent, the "uniquely legal dimension" of the voluntariness determination, and "practical considerations" that favored "independent federal review" as necessary to "protec[t] the rights at stake."

Admitting that it has found the characterization of a question as one of law or fact "sometimes slippery" the Court in *Thompson v. Keohane*[15] reviewed its earlier decisions in the area and held that a state court determination of whether or not a defendant was "in custody" for *Miranda* purposes is a mixed question of law and fact that is not subject to the presumption of correctness under former § 2254(d). The question of custody turns on whether there was a "formal arrest or restraint on freedom of movement, of the degree associated with a formal arrest." As in *Miller*, the Court reasoned that assessments of credibility were not crucial to the proper assessment of this issue.

(e) Discovery. Discovery in habeas proceedings is more limited than discovery in other civil proceedings in federal court. Rule 6 of the Rules Governing § 2254 Cases allows discovery under the Federal Rules of Civil Procedure "if, and to the extent that, the judge in the exercise of his discretion and for good cause shown grants leave to do so." Generalized statements about the possible existence of material do not constitute "good cause," nor is good cause established unless discovery would assist the court to resolve a factual dispute that, if resolved in petitioner's favor, would entitle him to relief.

In *Bracy v. Gramley*[16] the Court considered Rule 6 in the context of a case in which the petitioner had been sentenced to death by a judge who was later convicted of taking bribes from other defendants to fix their cases. The petitioner argued that the judge had convicted him and sentenced him to death in order to "cover up" for this illegal activity. The Court held that this was "good cause" for discovery since the allegations provided "reason to believe that the petitioner may, if the facts are fully developed, be able to demonstrate that he is * * * entitled to relief," and that it was "an abuse of discretion not to permit any discovery."

---

15. 516 U.S. 99, 116 S.Ct. 457, 133 L.Ed.2d 383 (1995).

16. 520 U.S. 899, 117 S.Ct. 1793, 138 L.Ed.2d 97 (1997).

Appendix

RESEARCHING CRIMINAL PROCEDURE LAW

Analysis

Section 1. Introduction

Criminal Procedure provides a strong base for analyzing even the most complex problem involving issues related to the law of criminal procedure. Whether your research requires examination of case law, statutes, expert commentary, or other materials, West books and Westlaw are excellent sources of information.

To keep you informed of current developments, Westlaw provides frequently updated databases. With Westlaw, you have unparalleled legal research resources at your fingertips.

Additional Resources

If you have not previously used Westlaw or if you have questions not covered in this appendix, call the West Reference Attorneys at 1–800–REF–ATTY (1–800–733–2889). The West Reference Attorneys are trained, licensed attorneys, available 24 hours a day to assist you with your Westlaw search questions. To subscribe to Westlaw, call 1–800–344–5008 or visit westlaw.com at **www.westlaw.com**.

Section 2. Westlaw Databases

Each database on Westlaw is assigned an abbreviation called an *identifier*, which you can use to access the database. You can find identifiers for Westlaw databases in the online Westlaw Directory and in the printed *Westlaw Database Directory*. When you need to know more detailed information about a database, use Scope. Scope contains coverage information, lists of related databases, and valuable search tips.

The following chart lists selected Westlaw databases that contain information pertaining to criminal procedure. For a complete list of criminal procedure databases, see the online Westlaw Directory or the printed *Westlaw Database Directory*. Because new information is continually being added to Westlaw, you should also check the tabbed Westlaw page and the online Westlaw Directory for new database information.

Selected Criminal Procedure Databases on Westlaw

Database	Identifier	Coverage
Federal and State Case Law Combined		
Federal and State Case Law	ALLCASES	Begins with 1945
Federal and State Case Law–Before 1945	ALLCASES–OLD	1789–1944
Death Penalty–Federal and State Cases	DP–CS–ALL	Varies by court
State Case Law		
Multistate Criminal Justice Cases	MCJ–CS	Varies by state
Individual State Criminal Justice Cases	XXCJ–CS (where XX is a state's two-letter postal abbreviation)	Varies by state
Death Penalty–Multistate Cases	MDP–CS	Varies by state
Federal Case Law		
Federal Criminal Justice–Cases	FCJ–CS	Begins with 1798
Federal Criminal Justice–Supreme Court Cases	FCJ–SCT	Begins with 1790
Federal Criminal Justice–Courts of Appeals Cases	FCJ–CTA	Begins with 1891
Federal Criminal Justice–District Courts Cases	FCJ–DCT	Begins with 1789
Death Penalty–Federal Cases	FDP–CS	Begins with 1789
Federal Rules Decisions® Cases	FRD–CS	Begins with 1938
Homeland Security and Antiterrorism–Cases	HOMELAND–CS	Varies by source

Database	Identifier	Coverage
Briefs, Pleadings, and Other Court Documents		
Federal Criminal Justice Briefs	FCJ–BRIEF	Begins with 1870
Notable Trials Transcripts and Documents	TRIALS–ALL	Varies
Texas Court of Criminal Appeals Briefs	TX–COCA–BRIEF	Begins with 1990
Texas Court of Criminal Appeals Petitions	TX–COCA–PETITION	Begins with 1990
Trial Motions	MOTIONS	Begins with 2000
Trial Pleadings	PLEADINGS	Begins with 2000
White–Collar Crime Reporter Court Documents	ANWCCR–DOC	Begins with 2000
State Statutes, Rules, and Regulations		
Criminal Justice–Individual State Statutes	XXCJ–ST (where XX is a state's two-letter postal abbreviation)	Current data
Death Penalty–Multistate Statutes	MDP–ST	Current data
Criminal Justice–Individual State Court Rules	XXCJ–RULES (where XX is a state's two-letter postal abbreviation)	Current data
State Administrative Code Multibase	ADC–ALL	Current data
Individual State Administrative Code	XX–ADC (where XX is a state's two-letter postal abbreviation)	Current data
Federal Statutes, Rules, and Regulations		
Death Penalty–Federal Statutes	FDP–USCA	Current data
Federal Criminal Justice–U.S. Code Annotated	FCJ–USCA	Current data
Federal Criminal Justice–Rules	FCJ–RULES	Current data
Federal Criminal Justice–Code of Federal Regulations	FCJ–CFR	Current data
Federal Criminal Justice–Federal Register	FCJ–FR	Begins with July 1980
Homeland Security and Antiterrorism–Codes and Administrative Materials	HOMELAND–CODREG	Varies by source
Arnold & Porter Legislative History: USA Patriot Act of 2001	PATRIOT–LH	Full history
Administrative Materials		
Bureau of Alcohol, Tobacco, and Firearms	ATF	Begins with 1973
Department of Justice News Releases	DOJ–NR	Begins with January 1995
Foreign Corrupt Practices Act	DOJ–FCPA	Begins with 1980
United States Attorneys Manual	USAM	Current data

Database	Identifier	Coverage
Jury Instructions		
Federal Jury Practice and Instructions–Criminal	FED–JICRIM	Current data
California Jury Instructions–Criminal	CA–CALJIC	Current data
Colorado Jury Instructions–Criminal	CO–JICRIM	Current data
Connecticut Practice Series: Jury Instructions–Criminal	CT–JICRIM	Current data
Florida Standard Jury Instructions–Criminal	FL–JICRIM	Current data
Georgia Suggested Pattern Jury Instructions: Volume II: Criminal Cases	GA–JICRIM	Current data
Hawaii Criminal Jury Instructions	HICRIM–JI	Current data
Illinois Non–Pattern Jury Instructions–Criminal	IL–NPJICRM	Current data
Illinois Pattern Jury Instructions–Criminal	IL–IPICRIM	Current data
Louisiana Civil Law Treatise–Criminal Jury Instructions	LA–JICRIM	Current data
Maryland Jury Instructions–Criminal	MD–JICRIM	Current data
Massachusetts Criminal Jury Instructions	MA–JICRIM	Current data
Michigan Non–Standard Jury Instructions–Criminal	MI–NSJICR	Current data
Minnesota Practice Series: Jury Instruction Guides–Criminal	MN–JICRIM	Current data
Mississippi Model Jury Instructions–Criminal	MSPRACJICR	Current data
Nebraska Jury Instructions–Criminal 2d	NE–JICRIM	Current data
New Jersey Criminal Jury Instructions	NJ–JICRIM	Current data
New Mexico Criminal Jury Instructions	NMCRIM–JI	Current data
Ohio Jury Instructions–Criminal	OH–JICRIM	Current data
Tennessee Practice Series: Tennessee Pattern Jury Instructions–Criminal	TNPRACJICR	Current data
Texas Criminal Jury Charges	TX–JICRIM	Current data
Vernon's® Oklahoma Forms 2d, Oklahoma Uniform Jury Instructions–Criminal	OK–JICRIM	Current data
Virginia Practice Series: Virginia Jury Instructions	VA–JI	Current data
Washington Pattern Jury Instructions–Criminal	WA–WPIC	Current data

Database	Identifier	Coverage
Sentencing Guidelines		
Federal Sentencing Guidelines	FCJ–FSG	Current data
Federal Sentencing Guidelines–Old	FCJ–FSG–OLD	1987–2003
Federal Sentencing Reporter	FCJ–FSR	Begins with June 1988
Federal Sentencing Law and Practice	FSLP	2004 edition
Legal Texts, Periodicals, and Practice Materials		
ABA Standards for Criminal Justice	ABA–SCJ	Second and third editions
American Journal of Criminal Law	AMJCRL	Selected coverage begins with 1985 (vol. 13); full coverage begins with 1994 (vol. 21, no. 2)
Buffalo Criminal Law Review	BFCRIMLR	Full coverage begins with 1997 (vol. 1)
Capital Defense Journal	CAPDEFJ	Full coverage begins with 1999 (vol. 12)
Champion	CHAMP	Full coverage begins with 1996 (vol. 20–Nov)
CJER Mandatory Criminal Jury Instructions Handbook	CJER–MCJIH	12th edition
Colorado Practice Series: Criminal Practice and Procedure	COPRAC–CPP	Current data
Complete Manual of Criminal Forms	CMCRF	Current data
Constitutional Rights of the Accused	CONRTACC	Third edition
Crime and Justice	CRIMEJ	Full coverage begins with 1993 (vol. 18)
Criminal Justice	CRIMJUST	Selected coverage begins with 1986 (vol. 1)
Criminal Justice–Law Reviews, Texts, and Bar Journals	CJ–TP	Varies by publication
Criminal Law Defenses	CRLDEF	Current data
Criminal Law Forum	CRIMLF	Selected coverage begins with 1990 (vol. 2); full coverage begins with 1993 (vol. 4, no. 2)
Criminal Practice Manual	CRPMAN	Current data
Criminal Procedure	CRIMPROC	Current data
Criminal Procedure Checklists, Fifth Amendment and Sixth Amendment	CPLIST	Current data
Criminal Trial Techniques	CRTRTECH	Current data
Death Penalty–Texts and Periodicals	DP–TP	Varies by publication
Everytrial Criminal Defense Resource Book	CRDEFRB	Current data

Database	Identifier	Coverage
Eyewitness Identification: Legal and Practical Problems	EYEWITN	Current data
Federal Bail and Detention Handbook	PLIREF–BAIL	Current data
Federal Criminal Rules Handbook	FEDCRIMRHB	Current data
Federal Grand Jury: A Guide to Law and Practice	FEDGRJURY	Current data
Federal Habeas Practitioner Guide	FEDHABPRAC	Current data
Federal Judicial Center Publications	FJC	Begins with 1978
Federal Practice and Procedure (Wright and Miller)–Criminal	FPP–CRIM	Current data
Federal Probation	FEDPROB	Full coverage begins with 1994 (vol. 58–Jun)
Federal Rules Decisions Articles	FRD–ART	Begins with 1938
Grand Jury Law and Practice	GRJURLAW	Current data
Homeland Security and Antiterrorism–Texts and Periodicals	HOMELAND–TP	Varies by publication
Immigration Law and Crimes	IMLC	Current data
Journal of Criminal Law and Criminology	JCRLC	Selected coverage begins with 1983 (vol. 74); full coverage begins with 1993 (vol. 84, no. 3)
Journal of Forensic Document Examination	JFDE	Full coverage begins with 1993 (vol. 6)
Lentz School Security	SCHOOLSEC	2004 edition
Military Criminal Law Evidence	MCLE	July 15, 1987
New England Journal on Criminal and Civil Confinement	NENGJCCC	Selected coverage begins with 1989 (vol. 15)
PLI Criminal Law Materials from Both Course Handbooks and Reference Books	PLICRIM–ALL	Current data
Police Misconduct: Law and Litigation	POLICEMISC	2003 edition
Postconviction Remedies	PCREM	Current data
Prosecutor	PROSC	Full coverage begins with 1994 (vol. 28)
Prosecutorial Misconduct	PROSMIS	Current data
Search and Seizure: A Treatise on the Fourth Amendment	SEARCHSZR	Current data
Search and Seizure Checklists	SSLIST	Current data
Searches and Seizures, Arrests and Confessions 2d	SSAC	Current data
Search Warrant Law Deskbook	SRCHWARLAW	Current data
Substantive Criminal Law	SUBCRL	Current data

Database	Identifier	Coverage
West's–R®–R McKinney's–R®–R Forms–Criminal Procedure Law	MCF–CPL	Current data
Wharton's Criminal Evidence	CRIMEVID	Current data
Wharton's Criminal Law	CRIMLAW	15th edition
White Collar Crime	WCCR	Second edition
News and Information		
Business Crimes Bulletin	BUSCRIMB	Begins with March 1995
Criminal Law News	CRIMLWNEWS	Begins with October 2003
Criminal Law Newsletter	CRIMLNWS	Begins with November 2002
Criminal Practice Guides	CRPGUIDE	Begins with January 2000
Criminal Practice Report	CRPREPORT	Begins with January 2001
Cybercrime Law Report	CYBERCRLR	Begins with June 2001
Homeland Security–News	HOMELAND–NEWS	Begins with September 2001
International Enforcement Law Reporter	INTLELREP	Begins with January 2000
Law Officers' Bulletin	LAWOFFBULL	Begins with January 2001
New York Criminal Law News	NYCLN	Begins with 1995
Westlaw Topical Highlights–Criminal Justice	WTH–CJ	Current data
White-Collar Crime Reporter	ANWCCR	Begins with November 1996
Directories		
West Legal Directory–R®–R–Criminal	WLD–CJ	Current data

Section 3. Retrieving a Document with a Citation: Find and Hypertext Links

3.1   Find

Find is a Westlaw service that allows you to retrieve a document by entering its citation. Find allows you to retrieve documents from any page in westlaw.com without accessing or changing databases. Find is available for many documents, including case law (state and federal), the *United States Code Annotated*®, state statutes, administrative materials, and texts and periodicals.

To use Find, simply type the citation in the *Find this document by citation* text box at the tabbed Westlaw page and click **GO**. The following list provides some examples:

To find this document:	Access Find and type:
Miranda v. Arizona 86 S. Ct. 1602 (1966)	**86 sct 1602**
Miller-El v. Johnson 261 F.3d 445 (5th Cir. 2001)	**261 f3d 445**
18 U.S.C.A. § 3109	**18 usca 3109**
Fed. R. Crim. Proc. 17	**frcrp 17**
Cal. Penal Code § 1036	**ca penal s 1036**

To find this document:	Access Find and type:
Fla. Stat. Ann. § 924.056	**fl st s 924.056**

For a complete list of publications that can be retrieved with Find and their abbreviations, click **Find** on the toolbar and then click **Publications List**.

3.2 Hypertext Links

Use hypertext links to move from one location to another on Westlaw. For example, use hypertext links to go directly from the statute, case, or law review article you are viewing to a cited statute, case, or article; from a headnote to the corresponding text in the opinion; or from an entry in a statutes index database to the full text of the statute.

Section 4. Searching with Natural Language

Overview: With Natural Language, you can retrieve documents by simply describing your issue in plain English. If you are a relatively new Westlaw user, Natural Language searching can make it easier for you to retrieve cases that are on point. If you are an experienced Westlaw user, Natural Language gives you a valuable alternative search method to the Terms and Connectors search method described in Section 5.

When you enter a Natural Language description, Westlaw automatically identifies legal phrases, removes common words, and generates variations of terms in your description. Westlaw then searches for the concepts in your description. Concepts may include significant terms, phrases, legal citations, or topic and key numbers. Westlaw retrieves the documents that most closely match the concepts in your description, beginning with the document most likely to match.

4.1 Natural Language Search

Access a database, such as the Federal Criminal Justice–Cases database (FCJ–CS). Click **Natural Language** and type the following description in the text box:

expectation of privacy of passenger in car (automobile)

4.2 Browsing Search Results

Best Mode: To display the best portion (the portion that most closely matches your description) of each document in a Natural Language search result, click the **Best** arrows at the bottom of the right frame.

Term Mode: Click the **Term** arrows at the bottom of the right frame to display portions of the document that contain your search terms.

Previous/Next Document: Click the left or right **Doc** arrow at the bottom of the right frame to view the previous or the next document in the search result.

Section 5. Searching with Terms and Connectors

Overview: With Terms and Connectors searching, you enter a query consisting of key terms from your issue and connectors specifying the relationship between these terms.

Terms and Connectors searching is useful when you want to retrieve a document for which you know specific details, such as the title or the fact situation. Terms and Connectors searching is also useful when you want to retrieve all documents containing specific terms.

5.1 Terms

Plurals and Possessives: Plurals are automatically retrieved when you enter the singular form of a term. This is true for both regular and irregular plurals (e.g., **child** retrieves *children*). If you enter the plural form of a term, you will not retrieve the singular form.

If you enter the nonpossessive form of a term, Westlaw automatically retrieves the possessive form as well. However, if you enter the possessive form, only the possessive form is retrieved.

Compound Words and Abbreviations: When a compound word is one of your search terms, use a hyphen to retrieve all forms of the word. For example, the term **non-judicial** retrieves *non-judicial*, *nonjudicial*, and *non judicial*.

When using an abbreviation as a search term, place a period after each of the letters to retrieve any of its forms. For example, the term **a.c.l.u.** retrieves *ACLU*, *A.C.L.U.*, *A C L U*, and *A. C. L. U.* Note: The abbreviation does not retrieve the phrase *American Civil Liberties Union*, so remember to add additional alternative terms such as **"american civil liberties union"** to your query.

The Root Expander and the Universal Character: When you use the Terms and Connectors search method, placing the root expander (!) at the end of a root term generates all other terms with that root. For example, adding the ! to the root *suppress* in the query

suppress! /s confession

instructs Westlaw to retrieve such terms as *suppress*, *suppressed*, *suppressing*, and *suppression*.

The universal character (*) stands for one character and can be inserted in the middle or at the end of a term. For example, the term

withdr*w

will retrieve *withdraw* and *withdrew*. Adding two asterisks to the root *jur*

jur*

instructs Westlaw to retrieve all forms of the root with up to two additional characters. Terms such as *juror* or *jury* are retrieved by this query. However, terms with more than two letters following the root, such as *jurisdiction,* are not retrieved. Plurals are always retrieved, even if the plural form of the term has more than two letters following the root.

Phrase Searching: To search for an exact phrase, place it within quotation marks. For example, to search for references to *probable cause*, type **"probable cause"**. When you are using the Terms and Connectors search method, you should use phrase searching only if you are certain that the terms in the phrase will not appear in any other order.

5.2 Alternative Terms

After selecting the terms for your query, consider which alternative terms are necessary. For example, if you are searching for the term *constitutional*, you might also want to search for the term *unconstitutional*. You should consider both synonyms and antonyms as alternative terms. You can also use the Westlaw thesaurus to add alternative terms to your query.

5.3 Connectors

After selecting terms and alternative terms for your query, use connectors to specify the relationship that must exist between search terms in your retrieved documents. The connectors are described below:

Type:	To retrieve documents with:	Example:
& (and)	both terms	**interrogat! & custodial**
a space (or)	either term or both terms	**wire-tap! electronic**

Type:	To retrieve documents with:	Example:
/p	search terms in the same paragraph	**pre-trial /p discovery**
/s	search terms in the same sentence	**right /s counsel**
+s	the first search term preceding the second within the same sentence	**burden +s proof prov!**
/n	search terms within *n* terms of each other (where *n* is a number from 1 to 255)	**search! /5 seiz!**
+n	the first search term preceding the second by *n* terms (where *n* is a number from 1 to 255)	**speedy +5 trial**
" "	search terms appearing in the same order as in the quotation marks	**"voir dire"**

Type:	To exclude documents with:	Example:
% (but not)	search terms following the % symbol	**r.i.c.o. % "puerto rico"**

5.4 Field Restrictions

Overview: Documents in each Westlaw database consist of several segments, or *fields*. One field may contain the citation, another the title, another the synopsis, and so forth. Not all databases contain the same fields. Also depending on the database, fields with the same name may contain different types of information.

To view a list of fields and their contents for a specific database, see Scope for that database. Note that in some databases not every field is available for every document.

To retrieve only those documents containing your search terms in a specific field, restrict your search to that field. To restrict your search to a specific field, type the field name or abbreviation followed by your search terms enclosed in parentheses. For example, to retrieve a U.S. Supreme Court case titled *Groh v. Ramirez*, access the Federal Criminal Justice–Supreme Court Cases database (FCJ–SCT) and search for your terms in the title field (ti):

ti(groh & ramirez)

The fields discussed below are available in Westlaw case law databases you might use for researching issues related to criminal procedure.

Digest and Synopsis Fields: The digest (di) and synopsis (sy) fields summarize the main points of a case. The synopsis field contains a brief description of a case. The digest field contains the topic and headnote fields and includes the complete hierarchy of concepts used by West's editors to classify the headnotes to specific West digest topic and key numbers. Restricting your search to the synopsis and digest fields limits your result to cases in which your terms are related to a major issue in the case.

Consider restricting your search to one or both of these fields if

- you are searching for common terms or terms with more than one meaning, and you need to narrow your search; or
- you cannot narrow your search by using a smaller database.

For example, to retrieve U.S. Supreme Court cases that discuss the effective assistance of counsel, access the FCJ–SCT database and type the following query:

sy,di(effective ineffective /s counsel)

Headnote Field: The headnote field (he) is part of the digest field but does not contain the topic names or numbers, hierarchical classification information, or key numbers. The headnote field contains a one-sentence summary for each point of law in a case and any supporting citations given by the author of the opinion. A headnote field restriction is useful when you are searching for specific statutory sections or rule numbers. For example, to retrieve headnotes from federal courts of appeals cases that cite 18 U.S.C.A. § 3109, access the Federal Criminal Justice–Courts of Appeals Cases database (FCJ–CTA) and type the following query:

he(18 +s 3109)

Topic Field: The topic field (to) is also part of the digest field. It contains the hierarchical classification information, including the West digest topic names and numbers and the key numbers. You should restrict search terms to the topic field in a case law database if

- a digest field search retrieves too many documents; or
- you want to retrieve cases with digest paragraphs classified under more than one topic.

For example, the topic Searches and Seizures has the topic number 349. To retrieve federal district court cases that discuss searches of luggage at airports, access the Federal Criminal Justice–District Courts Cases database (FCJ–DCT) and type a query like the following:

to(349) /p airport /p luggage baggage suit-case

To retrieve cases classified under more than one topic and key number, search for your terms in the topic field. For example, to retrieve recent California criminal cases discussing the granting of a new trial, which may be classified to such topics as Appeal and Error (30), Criminal Law (110), Double Jeopardy (135h), and New Trial (275), access the California Criminal Justice Cases database (CACJ–CS) and type a query like the following:

to("new trial") & da(aft 2002)

For a complete list of West digest topics and their corresponding topic numbers, access the Custom Digest by choosing **Key Numbers and Digest** from the *More* drop-down list on the toolbar.

> *Note*: Slip opinions and cases from topical services do not contain the West digest, headnote and topic fields.

Prelim and Caption Fields: When searching in a database containing statutes, rules, or regulations, restrict your search to the prelim (pr) and caption (ca) fields to retrieve documents in which your terms are important enough to appear in a section name or heading. For example, to retrieve federal statutes regarding the use of pen registers, access the Federal Criminal Justice–U.S. Code Annotated database (FCJ–USCA) and type the following:

pr,ca(pen /s register)

5.5 Date Restrictions

You can use Westlaw to retrieve documents *decided* or *issued* before, after, or on a specified date, as well as within a range of dates. The following sample queries contain date restrictions:

da(2003) & plea +3 bargain
da(aft 1998) & "poisonous tree"
da(6/14/1995) & search /s warrant

You can also search for documents *added to a database* on or after a specified date, as well as within a range of dates, which is useful for updating your research. The following sample queries contain added-date restrictions:

ad(aft 2002) & burden +s prov! proof

ad(aft 11/9/2001 & bef 6/23/2002) & "habeas corpus"

Section 6. Searching with Topic and Key Numbers

To retrieve cases that address a specific point of law, use topic and key numbers as your search terms. If you have an on-point case, run a search using the topic and key number from the relevant headnote in an appropriate database to find other cases containing headnotes classified to that topic and key number. For example, to search for federal cases containing headnotes classified under topic 135h (Double Jeopardy) and key number 98 (Failure of Jurors to Agree), access the FCJ–CS database and enter the following query:

135hk98

For a complete list of West digest topics and their corresponding topic numbers, access the Custom Digest by choosing **Key Numbers and Digest** from the *More* drop-down list on the toolbar.

> *Note*: Slip opinions and cases from topical services do not contain the West topic and key numbers.

6.1 Custom Digest

The Custom Digest contains the complete topic and key number outline used by West attorney-editors to classify headnotes. You can use the Custom Digest to obtain a single document containing all case law headnotes from a specific jurisdiction that are classified under a particular topic and key number.

Access the Custom Digest by choosing **Key Numbers and Digest** from the *More* drop-down list on the toolbar. Select up to 10 topics and key numbers from the easy-to-browse outline and click **Search selected**. Then follow the displayed instructions.

For example, to research issues involving sentencing, scroll down the Custom Digest page until topic 350h, *Sentencing and Punishment*, is displayed. Click the plus symbols (+) to display key number information. Select the check box next to each key number you want to include in your search, then click **Search selected**. Select the jurisdiction from which you want to retrieve headnotes and, if desired, type additional search terms and select a date restriction. Click **Search**.

6.2 KeySearch

KeySearch is a research tool that helps you find cases and secondary sources in a specific area of the law. KeySearch guides you through the selection of terms from a classification system based on the West Key Number System® and then uses the key numbers and their underlying concepts to automatically formulate a query for you.

To access KeySearch, click **KeySearch** on the toolbar. Then browse the list of topics and subtopics and select a topic or subtopic to search by clicking the hypertext links. For example, to search for cases that discuss continuance of a criminal trial because of an unavailable witness, click **Criminal Justice** at the first KeySearch page. Then click **Continuance** and **Absence of**

Witness at the next two pages. Select the source from which you want to retrieve documents and, if desired, type additional search terms. Click **Search**.

Section 7. Verifying Your Research with Citation Research Services

Overview: A citation research service, such as KeyCite, is a tool that helps you ensure that your cases, statutes, regulations, and administrative decisions are good law; retrieve cases, legislation, articles, or other documents that cite them; and verify the spelling and format of your citations.

7.1   KeyCite for Cases

KeyCite for cases covers case law on Westlaw, including unpublished opinions. KeyCite for cases provides the following:

- direct appellate history of a case, including related references, which are opinions involving the same parties and facts but resolving different issues
- negative indirect history of a case, which consists of cases outside the direct appellate line that may have a negative impact on its precedential value
- the title, parallel citations, court of decision, docket number, and filing date of a case
- citations to cases, administrative decisions, secondary sources, and briefs on Westlaw that have cited a case
- complete integration with the West Key Number System so you can track legal issues discussed in a case

7.2   KeyCite for Statutes and Regulations

KeyCite for statutes and regulations covers the *United States Code Annotated* (USCA®), the *Code of Federal Regulations* (CFR), statutes from all 50 states, and regulations from selected states. KeyCite for statutes and regulations provides

- links to session laws or rules amending or repealing a statute or regulation
- statutory credits and historical notes
- citations to pending legislation affecting a federal statute or a statute from selected states
- citations to cases, administrative decisions, secondary sources, and briefs that have cited a statute or regulation

7.3   KeyCite for Administrative Materials

KeyCite for administrative materials includes the following:

- National Labor Relations Board decisions beginning with 1935
- Board of Contract Appeals decisions (varies by agency)
- Board of Immigration Appeals decisions beginning with 1940
- Comptroller General decisions beginning with 1921
- Environmental Protection Agency decisions beginning with 1974
- Federal Communications Commission decisions beginning with 1960
- Federal Energy Regulatory Commission (Federal Power Commission) decisions beginning with 1931
- Internal Revenue Service revenue rulings beginning with 1954
- Internal Revenue Service revenue procedures beginning with 1954
- Internal Revenue Service private letter rulings beginning with 1954

- Internal Revenue Service technical advice memoranda beginning with 1954
- *Public Utilities Reports* beginning with 1974
- U.S. Merit Systems Protection Board decisions beginning with 1979
- U.S. Patent and Trademark Office decisions beginning with 1984
- U.S. Tax Court (Board of Tax Appeals) decisions beginning with 1924
- U.S. patents beginning with 1976

7.4 KeyCite Alert

KeyCite Alert monitors the status of your cases, statutes, regulations, and administrative decisions and automatically sends you updates at the frequency you specify when their KeyCite information changes.

Section 8. Researching with Westlaw: Examples

8.1 Retrieving Law Review Articles

Recent law review articles are often a good place to begin researching a legal issue because law review articles serve as an excellent introduction to a new topic or review for an old one, providing terminology to help you formulate a query; as a finding tool for pertinent primary authority, such as cases, statutes, and rules; and in some instances, as persuasive secondary authority.

Suppose you need to gain background information on the right to counsel.

Solution

- To retrieve law review articles relevant to your issue, access the Criminal Justice–Law Reviews, Texts, and Bar Journals database (CJ–TP). Using the Natural Language search method, enter a description like the following:

right to counsel

- If you have a citation to an article in a specific publication, use Find to retrieve it. For more information on Find, see Section 3.1 of this appendix. For example, to retrieve the article found at 16 S. Ill. U. L.J. 101, access Find and type

16 s ill u lj 101

- If you know the title of an article but not the journal in which it was published, access the CJ–TP database and search for key terms in the title field. For example, to retrieve the article "Distinguishing Fifth and Sixth Amendment Rights to Counsel During Police Questioning," type the following Terms and Connectors query:

ti(distinguishing & counsel & questioning)

8.2 Retrieving Case Law

Suppose you need to retrieve Texas cases dealing with the burden of proof needed to establish a plea of insanity in a murder case.

Solution

- Access the Texas Criminal Justice Cases database (TXCJ–CS). Type a Terms and Connectors query such as the following:

burden /5 proof prov! /p insan! /p murder

- When you know the citation for a specific case, use Find to retrieve it. For more information on Find, see Section 3.1 of this appendix. For example, to retrieve *Martinez v. State*, 867 S.W.2d 30 (Tex. Crim. App. 1993), access Find and type

867 sw2d 30

- If you find a topic and key number that is on point, run a search using that topic and key number to retrieve additional cases discussing that point of law. For example, to retrieve Texas state cases containing headnotes classified under topic 110 (Criminal Law) and key number 331 (Insanity), access the TXCJ–CS database and type the following query:

110k331

- To retrieve cases written by a particular judge, add a judge field (ju) restriction to your query. For example, to retrieve Texas state cases written by Judge Cochran that contain headnotes classified under topic 203 (Homicide), access the TXCJ–CS database and type the following query:

ju(cochran) & to(203)

- You can also use KeySearch and the Custom Digest to retrieve cases and headnotes that discuss the issue you are researching.

8.3 Retrieving Statutes and Regulations

Suppose you need to retrieve federal statutes and regulations addressing the use of warrants in searches and seizures.

Solution

- Access the FCJ–USCA database. Search for your terms in the prelim and caption fields using the Terms and Connectors search method:

pr,ca(search! & seiz! & warrant)

- When you know the citation for a specific statute or regulation, use Find to retrieve it. For example, to retrieve 18 U.S.C.A. § 2236, access Find and type

18 usca 2236

- To look at surrounding sections, use the Table of Contents service. Click **Table of Contents** on the Links tab in the left frame. To display a section listed in the Table of Contents, click its hypertext link. You can also use Documents in Sequence to retrieve the sections following 18 U.S.C.A. § 2236 even if the subsequent sections were not retrieved with your search or Find request. Choose **Documents in Sequence** from the Tools menu at the bottom of the right frame.

8.4 Using KeyCite

Suppose one of the cases you retrieve in your case law research is *Ake v. Oklahoma*, 105 S. Ct. 1087 (1985).

Solution

- Use KeyCite to retrieve direct and negative indirect history for *Ake*. Access KeyCite and type **105 sct 1087**.

- Use KeyCite to display citing references for *Ake*. Click **Citing References** on the Links tab in the left frame.

8.5 Following Recent Developments

If you are researching issues related to criminal procedure, it is important to keep up with recent developments. How can you do this efficiently?

Solution

One of the easiest ways to follow recent developments in criminal law and procedure is to access the Westlaw Topical Highlights–Criminal Justice database (WTH–CJ). The WTH–CJ database contains summaries of recent legal developments, including court decisions, legislation, and materials released by administrative agencies. When you access the WTH–CJ database, you automatically retrieve a list of documents added to the database in the last two weeks.

You can also use the WestClip® clipping service to stay informed of recent developments of interest to you. WestClip will run your Terms and Connectors queries on a regular basis and deliver the results to you automatically. You can run WestClip queries in legal and news and information databases.

Table of Cases

A

C

G

H

I

J

K

L

N

O

*

Index

References are to Sections

†

0–314–15211–3

90000

9 780314 152114